College Edition

HARPER COLLINS
SPANISH
DICTIONARY

College Edition

HARPER COLLINS
SPANISH
DICTIONARY

SPANISH · ENGLISH   ENGLISH · SPANISH

HarperCollins*Publishers*

contributors/colaboradores
Jeremy Butterfield, Mike Gonzalez, Gerry Breslin,
Alicia Harland, Val McNulty,
M.ª Ángeles Recio Corral, M.ª José Sánchez Blanco

American language consultants/inglés norteamericano
Professor Halvor Clegg, Professor Willis Fails

editorial staff/redacción
John Forry, Jane Horwood, Irene Lakhani

ISBN 0-06-275507-2
ISBN 0-06-276509-4 (pbk)

94 95 96 97 98 RRD/HOR 19 18 17 16 15 14 13 12 11 10 09 08 07 06

ÍNDICE DE MATERIAS

CONTENTS

INTRODUCCIÓN

Para comprender el inglés

Este diccionario, nuevo y completamente puesto al día, pone a disposición del usuario de la lengua una cobertura amplia y a la vez práctica de los usos lingüísticos más corrientes del inglés de hoy, e incluye la terminología necesaria en el dominio empresarial y de la microinformática, así como una numerosa selección de las abreviaturas, siglas y topónimos que suelen aparecer en la prensa. A fin de facilitar la labor del lector, se mencionan también las formas irregulares de los verbos ingleses, con indicaciones que hacen referencia a las formas básicas, donde se encuentra la traducción.

Para expresarse en inglés

A fin de ayudar al lector a expresarse correcta e idiomáticamente en inglés, el diccionario contiene frecuentes indicaciones – a manera de glosas de orientación – que pueden servirle para encontrar la traducción más apropiada en un contexto dado. Todas las palabras de uso más corriente en la lengua reciben tratamiento detallado, en el que se mencionan muchas ilustraciones de sus usos característicos.

Para acompañarle en su trabajo

Nos hemos esmerado en hacer de este nuevo diccionario de Collins una compilación fiable y fácil de utilizar que responda a sus necesidades laborales y de estudio. Nuestra esperanza es que le sirva mucho tiempo como fiel compañero de trabajo en todo lo que le haga falta mientras maneja el inglés como lengua extranjera.

INTRODUCTION

Understanding Spanish

This new and thoroughly up-to-date dictionary provides the user with wide-ranging, practical coverage of current usage, including terminology relevant to business and office automation, and a comprehensive selection of abbreviations, acronyms and geographical names commonly found in the press. You will also find, for ease of consultation, irregular forms of Spanish verbs and nouns with a cross-reference to the basic form where a translation is given.

Self-expression in Spanish

To help you express yourself correctly and idiomatically in Spanish, numerous indications – think of them as signposts – guide you to the most appropriate translation for your context. All the most commonly used words are given detailed treatment, with many examples of typical usage.

A working companion

Much care has been taken to make this new Collins dictionary thoroughly reliable, easy to use and relevant to your work and study. We hope it will become a long-serving companion for all your foreign language needs.

ABREVIATURAS

ABBREVIATIONS

adjetivo, locución adjetiva	**a**	adjective, adjectival phrase
abreviatura	**ab(b)r**	abbreviation
adverbio, locución adverbial	**ad**	adverb, adverbial phrase
administración, lengua administrativa	**ADMIN**	administration
agricultura	**AGR**	agriculture
América Latina	**AM**	Latin America
anatomía	**ANAT**	anatomy
arquitectura	**ARQ, ARCH**	architecture
astrología, astronomía	**ASTRO**	astrology, astronomy
el automóvil	**AUT(O)**	automobiles
aviación, viajes aéreos	**AVIAT**	flying, air travel
biología	**BIO(L)**	biology
botánica, flores	**BOT**	botany
inglés británico	**Brit**	British English
química	**CHEM**	chemistry
lengua familiar (! vulgar)	**col (!)**	colloquial usage (! particularly offensive)
comercio, finanzas, banca	**COM(M)**	commerce, finance, banking
informática	**COMPUT**	computing
conjunción	**conj**	conjunction
construcción	**CONSTR**	building
compuesto	**cpd**	compound element
cocina	**CULIN**	cookery
economía	**ECON**	economics
electricidad, electrónica	**ELEC**	electricity, electronics
enseñanza, sistema escolar	**ESCOL**	education, schools
España	**Esp**	Spain
especialmente	**esp**	especially
exclamación, interjección	**excl**	exclamation, interjection
femenino	**f**	feminine
lengua familiar (! vulgar)	**fam (!)**	colloquial usage (! particularly offensive)
ferrocarril	**FERRO**	railroad
uso figurado	**fig**	figurative use
fotografía	**FOTO**	photography
(verbo inglés) del cual la partícula es inseparable	**fus**	(phrasal verb) where the particle is inseparable
generalmente	**gen**	generally
geografía, geología	**GEO**	geography, geology
geometría	**GEOM**	geometry
informática	**INFORM**	computing
invariable	**inv**	invariable
irregular	**irg**	irregular
lo jurídico	**JUR**	law
América Latina	**LAm**	Latin America
gramática, lingüística	**LING**	grammar, linguistics
literatura	**LIT**	literature
masculino	**m**	masculine
matemáticas	**MAT(H)**	mathematics
medicina	**MED**	medical term, medicine
masculino/femenino	**m/f**	masculine/feminine
lo militar, ejército	**MIL**	military matters
música	**MUS**	music

sustantivo, nombre	**n**	noun
navegación, náutica	**NAUT**	sailing, navigation
sustantivo numérico	**num**	numeral noun
complemento	**obj**	(grammatical) object
	o.s.	oneself
peyorativo	**pey, pej**	derogatory, pejorative
fotografía	**PHOT**	photography
fisiología	**PHYSIOL**	physiology
plural	**pl**	plural
política	**POL**	politics
participio de pasado	**pp**	past participle
prefijo	**pref**	prefix
preposición	**prep**	preposition
pronombre	**pron**	pronoun
psicología, psiquiatría	**PSICO, PSYCH**	psychology, psychiatry
tiempo pasado	**pt**	past tense
sustantivo no empleado en el plural	**q**	collective (uncountable) noun, not used in plural
ferrocarril	**RAIL**	railroad
religión, lo eclesiástico	**REL**	religion, church service
	sb	somebody
enseñanza, sistema escolar	**SCOL**	education, schools
singular	**sg**	singular
España	**Sp**	Spain
	sth	something
subjuntivo	**subjun**	subjunctive
sujeto	**su(b)j**	(grammatical) subject
sufijo	**suff**	suffix
tauromaquia	**TAUR**	bullfighting
también	**tb**	also
técnica, tecnología	**TEC(H)**	technical term, technology
telecomunicaciones	**TELEC, TEL**	telecommunications
televisión	**TV**	television
imprenta, tipografía	**TIP, TYP**	typography, printing
sistema universitario	**UNIV**	universities
inglés norteamericano	**US**	American English
verbo	**vb**	verb
verbo intransitivo	**vi**	intransitive verb
verbo pronominal	**vr**	reflexive verb
verbo transitivo	**vt**	transitive verb
zoología, animales	**ZOOL**	zoology
marca registrada	**®**	registered trademark
indica un equivalente cultural	**≈**	introduces a cultural equivalent

SPANISH PRONUNCIATION

CONSONANTS

b	[b, ʙ]	*b*oda *b*om*b*a la*b*or	see notes on *v* below
c	[k]	*c*aja	*c* before *a*, *o* or *u* is pronounced as in *c*at
ce, ci	[se, sē]	*c*ero *c*ielo	*c* before *e* or *i* is pronounced as in *s*in
ch	[ch]	*ch*iste	*ch* is pronounced as *ch* in *ch*air
d	[d, ʈħ]	*d*anés ciu*d*ad	at the beginning of a phrase or after *l* or *n*, *d* is pronounced as in English. In any other position it is pronounced like *th* in *th*e
g	[g, ǥ]	*g*afas pa*g*a	*g* before *a*, *o* or *u* is pronounced as in *g*ap, if at the beginning of a phrase or after *n*. In other positions the sound is softened
ge, gi	[he, hē]	*g*ente *g*irar	*g* before *e* or *i* is pronounced similar to *ch* in Scottish lo*ch* or German o*ch*
h		*h*aber	*h* is always silent in Spanish
j	[h]	*j*ugar	*j* is pronounced similar to *ch* in Scottish lo*ch* or German o*ch*
ll	[y]	ta*ll*e	*ll* is pronounced like the *lli* in mi*lli*on
ñ	[ny]	ni*ñ*o	*ñ* is pronounced like the *ni* in o*ni*on
q	[k]	*q*ue	*q* is pronounced as *k* in *k*ing
r, rr	[r, rr]	quita*r* ga*rr*a	*r* is always pronounced in Spanish; *rr* is trilled
s	[s]	qui*z*ás i*s*la	*s* is usually pronounced as in pa*ss*, but before *b*, *d*, *g*, *l*, *m* or *n* it is pronounced as in ro*s*e
v	[b, ʙ]	*v*ía en*v*iar di*v*idir	*v* is pronounced something like *b*. At the beginning of a phrase or after *m* or *n* it is pronounced as *b* in *b*oy. In any other position it is pronounced with the lips in position to pronounce *b* of *b*oy, but not meeting
w	[b, ʙ, w]	*w*áter *w*hisky	pronounced either like Spanish *b*, or like English *w*
z	[s]	tena*z*	*z* is pronounced as in *s*in

f, k, l, m, n, p, t and x are pronounced as in English.

VOWELS

a	[à]	p*a*ta	not as long as *a* in p*a*lm. When followed by a consonant in the same syllable (i.e. in a closed syllable), as in am*a*nte, the *a* is short, as in *a*dd
e	[e]	m*e*	like *e* in *e*nd. In a closed syllable, as in g*e*nte, the *e* is short as in p*e*t
i	[ē]	p*i*no	as in m*e*an or mach*i*ne
o	[o]	l*o*	as in s*o*. In a closed syllable, as in c*o*ntrol, the *o* is short as in p*o*t
u	[o͞o]	l*u*nes	as in p*oo*l. It is silent after *q*, and in *gue, gui*, unless marked *güe, güi* e.g. antig*ü*edad, when it is pronounced like *w* in *w*in

SEMIVOWELS

i, y	[y]	b*i*en h*i*elo *y*unta	pronounced like *y* in *y*et
u	[w]	h*u*evo f*u*ente antig*ü*edad	unstressed *u* between consonant and vowel is pronounced like *w* in *w*in. See also notes on *u* above

DIPHTHONGS

ai, ay	[àē]	b*ai*le	as *i* in r*i*de
au	[ào͞o]	*au*to	as *ou* in sh*ou*t
ei, ey	[eē]	bu*ey*	as *ay* in b*ay*
eu	[eo͞o]	d*eu*da	both elements pronounced independently [e] and [o͞o]
oi, oy	[oē]	h*oy*	as *oy* in t*oy*

STRESS

The rules of stress in Spanish are as follows:

(a) when a word ends in a vowel or in *n* or *s*, the second last syllable is stressed: pat*a*ta, pat*a*tas, c*o*me, c*o*men
(b) when a word ends in a consonant other than *n* or *s*, the stress falls on the last syllable: par*e*d, habl*a*r
(c) when the rules set out in a and b are not applied, an acute accent appears over the stressed vowel: com*ú*n, geograf*í*a, ingl*é*s

In the phonetic transcription, the symbol ['] follows the syllable on which the stress falls.

The symbol [·] shows where two consonants should be pronounced separately.

PRONUNCIACIÓN INGLESA

VOCALES Y DIPTONGOS

	Ejemplo inglés	Ejemplo español/explicación
[a]	add, map	Se mantienen los labios en la posición de e en pena y luego se pronuncia el sonido a
[ā]	ace, rate	e cerrada seguida por una i débil
[är]	care, air	Una e abierta, parecida a la de perro. La r se pronuncia.
[â]	palm, father, odd	Entre a de padre y o de noche
[e]	end, pet	Como en perro
[ē]	even, tree	Como en fino
[ə]	above, darken	Sonido indistinto parecido a una e u o casi mudas
[i]	it, give	Más breve que en si
[ī]	ice, write	Como en fraile
[ō]	open, so	Como en solo
[ô]	law, dog, order	Como en torre
[oi]	oil, boy	Como en voy
[ou]	out, now	Como en pausa
[o͞o]	pool, food	Sonido largo, como en cura
[o͝o]	took, full	Sonido breve, parecido a la u de burro
[u]	up, done	a muy breve
[ûr]	urn, term	Entre e y o. La r se pronuncia.
[yo͞o]	use, few	Como en ciudad

CONSONANTES

	Ejemplo inglés	*Ejemplo español/explicación*
[b]	*b*at, ru*b*	Como en *b*omba, tum*b*a
[ch]	*ch*eck, cat*ch*	Como en *ch*ocolate
[d]	*d*og, ro*d*	Como en con*d*e, an*d*ar
[g]	*g*o, lo*g*	Como en *g*rande, *g*ol
[h]	*h*ope, *h*ate	Como la jota hispanoamericana
[j]	*j*oy, le*dge*	Como en la *ll* andaluza y en *G*eneralitat (catalán)
[k]	*c*ool, ta*k*e	Como en *c*aña, Es*c*ocia
[ng]	ri*ng*, so*ng*	Como en ví*n*culo
[r]	*r*un, poo*r*	Se pronuncia con la punta de la lengua hacia atrás y sin hacerla vibrar
[s]	*s*ee, pa*ss*	Como en ca*s*a, *s*esión
[sh]	*s*ure, ru*sh*	Como en *ch*ambre (francés), ro*x*o (portugués)
[th]	*th*in, bo*th*	Como en re*c*eta, *z*apato
[th̬]	*th*is, ba*th*e	Como en la *d* de habla*d*o, verda*d*
[v]	*v*ain, e*v*e	Con los labios en la posición de la *f* de *f*ondo, pero es sonoro
[w]	*w*in, a*w*ay	Como en la *u* de h*u*evo, p*u*ede
[y]	*y*et, *y*earn	Como en *y*a
[z]	*z*est, mu*s*e	Como en de*s*de, mi*s*mo
[zh]	vi*s*ion, plea*s*ure	Como en *j*ournal (francés)

p, f, m, n, l, t iguales que en español
El signo ['] indica la sílaba acentuada. El símbolo [·] indica que las dos consonantes a ambos lados del símbolo deben pronunciarse separadamente.

SPANISH VERB FORMS

1 Gerund. *2* Imperative. *3* Present. *4* Preterite. *5* Future. *6* Present subjunctive. *7* Imperfect subjunctive. *8* Past participle. *9* Imperfect.
Etc indicates that the irregular root is used for all persons of the tense, e.g. **oír**: *6* oiga, oigas, oigamos, oigáis, oigan.

acertar *2* acierta *3* acierto, aciertas, acierta, aciertan *6* acierte, aciertes, acierte, acierten

acordar *2* acuerda *3* acuerdo, acuerdas, acuerda, acuerdan *6* acuerde, acuerdes, acuerde, acuerden

advertir *1* advirtiendo *2* advierte *3* advierto, adviertes, advierte, advierten *4* advirtió, advirtieron *6* advierta, adviertas, advierta, advirtamos, advirtáis, adviertan *7* advirtiera *etc*

agradecer *3* agradezco *6* agradezca *etc*

aparecer *3* aparezco *6* aparezca *etc*

aprobar *2* aprueba *3* apruebo, apruebas, aprueba, aprueban *6* apruebe, apruebes, apruebe, aprueben

atravesar *2* atraviesa *3* atravieso, atraviesas, atraviesa, atraviesan *6* atraviese, atravieses, atraviese, atraviesen

caber *3* quepo *4* cupe, cupiste, cupo, cupimos, cupisteis, cupieron *5* cabré *etc* *6* quepa *etc* *7* cupiera *etc*

caer *1* cayendo *3* caigo *4* cayó, cayeron *6* caiga *etc* *7* cayera *etc*

calentar *2* calienta *3* caliento, calientas, calienta, calientan *6* caliente, calientes, caliente, calienten

cerrar *2* cierra *3* cierro, cierras, cierra, cierran *6* cierre, cierres, cierre, cierren

COMER *1* comiendo *2* come, comed *3* como, comes, come, comemos, coméis, comen *4* comí, comiste, comió, comimos, comisteis, comieron *5* comeré, comerás, comerá, comeremos, comeréis, comerán *6* coma, comas, coma, comamos, comáis, coman *7* comiera, comieras, comiera, comiéramos, comierais, comieran *8* comido *9* comía, comías, comía, comíamos, comíais, comían

conocer *3* conozco *6* conozca *etc*

contar *2* cuenta *3* cuento, cuentas, cuenta, cuentan *6* cuente, cuentes, cuente, cuenten

costar *2* cuesta *3* cuesto, cuestas, cuesta, cuestan *6* cueste, cuestes, cueste, cuesten

dar *3* doy *4* di, diste, dio, dimos, disteis, dieron *7* diera *etc*

decir *2* di *3* digo *4* dije, dijiste, dijo, dijimos, dijisteis, dijeron *5* diré *etc* *6* diga *etc* *7* dijera *etc* *8* dicho

despertar *2* despierta *3* despierto, despiertas, despierta, despiertan *6* despierte, despiertes, despierte, despierten

divertir *1* divirtiendo *2* divierte *3* divierto, diviertes, divierte, divierten *4* divirtió, divirtieron *6* divierta, diviertas, divierta, divirtamos, divirtáis, diviertan *7* divirtiera *etc*

dormir *1* durmiendo *2* duerme *3* duermo, duermes, duerme, duermen *4* durmió, durmieron *6* duerma, duermas, duerma, durmamos, durmáis, duerman *7* durmiera *etc*

empezar *2* empieza *3* empiezo, empiezas, empieza, empiezan *4* empecé *6* empiece, empieces, empiece, empecemos, empecéis, empiecen

entender *2* entiende *3* entiendo, entiendes, entiende, entienden *6* entienda, entiendas, entienda, entiendan

ESTAR *2* está *3* estoy, estás, está, están *4* estuve, estuviste, estuvo, estuvimos, estuvisteis, estuvieron *6* esté, estés, esté, estén *7* estuviera *etc*

HABER *3* he, has, ha, hemos, han *4* hube, hubiste, hubo, hubimos, hubisteis, hubieron *5* habré *etc* *6* haya *etc* *7* hubiera *etc*

HABLAR *1* hablando *2* habla, hablad *3* hablo, hablas, habla, hablamos, habláis, hablan *4* hablé, hablaste, habló, hablamos, hablasteis, hablaron *5* hablaré, hablarás, hablará, hablaremos, hablaréis, hablarán *6* hable, hables, hable, hablemos, habléis, hablen *7* hablara, hablaras, hablara, habláramos, hablarais, hablaran *8* hablado *9* hablaba, hablabas, hablaba, hablábamos, hablabais, hablaban

hacer *2* haz *3* hago *4* hice, hiciste, hizo, hicimos, hicisteis, hicieron *5* haré *etc* *6* haga *etc* *7* hiciera *etc* *8* hecho

instruir *1* instruyendo *2* instruye *3* instruyo, instruyes, instruye, instruyen *4* instruyó, instruyeron *6* instruya *etc* *7* instruyera *etc*

ir *1* yendo *2* ve *3* voy, vas, va, vamos, vais, van *4* fui, fuiste, fue, fuimos, fuisteis, fueron *6* vaya, vayas, vaya, vayamos, vayáis, vayan *7* fuera *etc* *8* iba, ibas, iba, íbamos, ibais, iban

jugar *2* juega *3* juego, juegas, juega, juegan *4* jugué *6* juegue *etc*

leer *1* leyendo *4* leyó, leyeron *7* leyera *etc*

morir *1* muriendo *2* muere *3* muero, mueres, muere, mueren *4* murió, murieron *6* muera, mueras, muera, muramos, muráis, mueran *7* muriera *etc* *8* muerto

mostrar *2* muestra *3* muestro, muestras, muestra, muestran *6* muestre, muestres, muestre, muestren

mover *2* mueve *3* muevo, mueves, mueve, mueven *6* mueva, muevas, mueva, muevan

negar *2* niega *3* niego, niegas, niega, niegan *4* negué *6* niegue, niegues, niegue, neguemos, neguéis, nieguen

ofrecer *3* ofrezco *6* ofrezca *etc*

oír *1* oyendo *2* oye *3* oigo, oyes, oye, oyen *4* oyó, oyeron *6* oiga *etc* *7* oyera *etc*

oler *2* huele *3* huelo, hueles, huele, huelen *6* huela, huelas, huela, huelan

parecer *3* parezco *6* parezca *etc*

pedir *1* pidiendo *2* pide *3* pido, pides, pide, piden *4* pidió, pidieron *6* pida *etc* *7* pidiera *etc*

pensar *2* piensa *3* pienso, piensas, piensa, piensan *6* piense, pienses, piense, piensen

perder *2* pierde *3* pierdo, pierdes, pierde, pierden *6* pierda, pierdas, pierda, pierdan

poder *1* pudiendo *2* puede *3* puedo, puedes, puede, pueden *4* pude, pudiste, pudo, pudimos, pudisteis, pudieron *5* podré *etc* *6* pueda, puedas, pueda, puedan *7* pudiera *etc*

poner *2* pon *3* pongo *4* puse, pusiste, puso, pusimos, pusisteis, pusieron *5* pondré *etc* *6* ponga *etc* *7* pusiera *etc* *8* puesto

preferir *1* prefiriendo *2* prefiere *3* prefiero, prefieres, prefiere, prefieren *4* prefirió, prefirieron *6* prefiera, prefieras, prefiera, prefiramos, prefiráis, prefieran *7* prefiriera *etc*

querer *2* quiere *3* quiero, quieres, quiere, quieren *4* quise, quisiste, quiso, quisimos, quisisteis, quisieron *5* querré *etc* *6* quiera, quieras, quiera, quieran *7* quisiera *etc*

reír *2* ríe *3* río, ríes, ríe, ríen *4* rio, rieron *6* ría, rías, ría, riamos, riáis, rían *7* riera *etc*

repetir *1* repitiendo *2* repite *3* repito, repites, repite, repiten *4* repitió, repitieron *6* repita *etc* *7* repitiera *etc*

rogar *2* ruega *3* ruego, ruegas, ruega, ruegan *4* rogué *6* ruegue, ruegues, ruegue, roguemos, roguéis, rueguen

saber *3* sé *4* supe, supiste, supo, supimos, supisteis, supieron *5* sabré *etc* *6* sepa *etc* *7* supiera *etc*

salir *2* sal *3* salgo *5* saldré *etc* *6* salga *etc*

seguir *1* siguiendo *2* sigue *3* sigo, sigues, sigue, siguen *4* siguió, siguieron *6* siga *etc* *7* siguiera *etc*

sentar *2* sienta *3* siento, sientas, sienta, sientan *6* siente, sientes, siente, sienten

sentir *1* sintiendo *2* siente *3* siento, sientes, siente, sienten *4* sintió, sintieron *6* sienta, sientas, sienta, sintamos, sintáis, sientan *7* sintiera *etc*

SER *2* sé *3* soy, eres, es, somos, sois, son *4* fui, fuiste, fue, fuimos, fuisteis, fueron *6* sea *etc* *7* fuera *etc* *9* era, eras, era, éramos, erais, eran

servir *1* sirviendo *2* sirve *3* sirvo, sirves, sirve, sirven *4* sirvió, sirvieron *6* sirva *etc* *7* sirviera *etc*

soñar *2* sueña *3* sueño, sueñas, sueña, sueñan *6* sueñe, sueñes, sueñe, sueñen

tener *2* ten *3* tengo, tienes, tiene, tienen *4* tuve, tuviste, tuvo, tuvimos, tuvisteis, tuvieron *5* tendré *etc* *6* tenga *etc* *7* tuviera *etc*

traer *1* trayendo *3* traigo *4* traje, trajiste, trajo, trajimos, trajisteis, trajeron *6* traiga *etc* *7* trajera *etc*

valer *2* val *3* valgo *5* valdré *etc* *6* valga *etc*

venir *2* ven *3* vengo, vienes, viene, vienen *4* vine, viniste, vino, vinimos, vinisteis, vinieron *5* vendré *etc* *6* venga *etc* *7* viniera *etc*

ver *3* veo *6* vea *etc* *8* visto *9* veía *etc*

vestir *1* vistiendo *2* viste *3* visto, vistes, viste, visten *4* vistió, vistieron *6* vista *etc* *7* vistiera *etc*

VIVIR *1* viviendo *2* vive, vivid *3* vivo, vives, vive, vivimos, vivís, viven *4* viví, viviste, vivió, vivimos, vivisteis, vivieron *5* viviré, vivirás, vivirá, viviremos, viviréis, vivirán *6* viva, vivas, viva, vivamos, viváis, vivan *7* viviera, vivieras, viviera, viviéramos, vivierais, vivieran *8* vivido *9* vivía, vivías, vivía, vivíamos, vivíais, vivían

volver *2* vuelve *3* vuelvo, vuelves, vuelve, vuelven *6* vuelva, vuelvas, vuelva, vuelvan *8* vuelto

VERBOS IRREGULARES EN INGLÉS

present	pt	pp	present	pt	pp
arise (arising)	arose	arisen	eat	ate	eaten
			fall	fell	fallen
awake (awaking)	awoke	awaked	feed	fed	fed
			feel	felt	felt
be (am, is, are, being)	was, were	been	fight	fought	fought
			find	found	found
bear	bore	born(e)	flee	fled	fled
beat	beat	beaten	fling	flung	flung
become (becoming)	became	become	fly (flies)	flew	flown
			forbid (forbidding)	forbade	forbidden
befall	befell	befallen			
begin (beginning)	began	begun	forecast	forecast	forecast
			forego	forewent	foregone
behold	beheld	beheld	foresee	foresaw	foreseen
bend	bent	bent	foretell	foretold	foretold
beseech	besought	besought	forget (forgetting)	forgot	forgotten
beset (besetting)	beset	beset			
			forgive (forgiving)	forgave	forgiven
bet (betting)	bet (also betted)	bet (also betted)	forsake (forsaking)	forsook	forsaken
bid (bidding)	bid (also bade)	bid (also bidden)	freeze (freezing)	froze	frozen
bind	bound	bound	get (getting)	got	got, (US) gotten
bite (biting)	bit	bitten			
bleed	bled	bled	give (giving)	gave	given
blow	blew	blown	go (goes)	went	gone
break	broke	broken	grind	ground	ground
breed	bred	bred	grow	grew	grown
bring	brought	brought	hang	hung (also hanged)	hung (also hanged)
build	built	built			
burn	burned (also burnt)	burned (also burnt)	have (has; having)	had	had
burst	burst	burst	hear	heard	heard
buy	bought	bought	hide (hiding)	hid	hidden
can	could	(been able)	hit (hitting)	hit	hit
cast	cast	cast	hold	held	held
catch	caught	caught	hurt	hurt	hurt
choose (choosing)	chose	chosen	keep	kept	kept
cling	clung	clung	kneel	knelt (also kneeled)	knelt (also kneeled)
come (coming)	came	come			
			know	knew	known
cost	cost	cost	lay	laid	laid
creep	crept	crept	lead	led	led
cut (cutting)	cut	cut	lean	leaned (also leant)	leaned (also leant)
deal	dealt	dealt			
dig (digging)	dug	dug	leap	leaped (also leapt)	leaped (also leapt)
do (3rd person: he/ she/it/does)	did	done	learn	learned (also learnt)	learned (also learnt)
draw	drew	drawn	leave (leaving)	left	left
dream	dreamed (also dreamt)	dreamed also dreamt)	lend	lent	lent
			let (letting)	let	let
drink	drank	drunk	lie (lying)	lay	lain
drive (driving)	drove	driven	light	lighted (also lit)	lighted (also lit)
dwell	dwelt	dwelt	lose (losing)	lost	lost

present	pt	pp	present	pt	pp
make (**making**)	made	made	**spell**	spelled (*also* spelt)	spelled (*also* spelt)
may	might	—	**spend**	spent	spent
mean	meant	meant	**spill**	spilled (*also* spilt)	spilled (*also* spilt)
meet	met	met	**spin** (**spinning**)	spun	spun
mistake (**mistaking**)	mistook	mistaken	**spit** (**spitting**)	spat	spat
mow	mowed	mowed (*also* mown)	**split** (**splitting**)	split	split
must	(had to)	(had to)	**spoil**	spoiled (*also* spoilt)	spoiled (*also* spoilt)
pay	paid	paid	**spread**	spread	spread
put (**putting**)	put	put	**spring**	sprang	sprung
quit (**quitting**)	quit (*also* quitted)	quit (*also* quitted)	**stand**	stood	stood
read	read	read	**steal**	stole	stolen
rend	rent	rent	**stick**	stuck	stuck
rid (**ridding**)	rid	rid	**sting**	stung	stung
ride (**riding**)	rode	ridden	**stink**	stank	stunk
ring	rang	rung	**stride** (**striding**)	strode	stridden
rise (**rising**)	rose	risen	**strike** (**striking**)	struck	struck (*also* stricken)
run (**running**)	ran	run	**strive** (**striving**)	strove	striven
saw	sawed	sawn	**swear**	swore	sworn
say	said	said	**sweep**	swept	swept
see	saw	seen	**swell**	swelled	swelled (*also* swollen)
seek	sought	sought	**swim** (**swimming**)	swam	swum
sell	sold	sold			
send	sent	sent	**swing**	swung	swung
set (**setting**)	set	set	**take** (**taking**)	took	taken
shake (**shaking**)	shook	shaken	**teach**	taught	taught
shall	should	—	**tear**	tore	torn
shear	sheared	sheared (*also* shorn)	**tell**	told	told
			think	thought	thought
shed (**shedding**)	shed	shed	**throw**	threw	thrown
shine (**shining**)	shone	shone	**thrust**	thrust	thrust
			tread	trod	trodden
shoot	shot	shot	**wake** (**waking**)	woke (*also* waked)	waked (*also* woken)
show	showed	shown			
shrink	shrank	shrunk	**waylay**	waylaid	waylaid
shut (**shutting**)	shut	shut	**wear**	wore	worn
sing	sang	sung	**weave** (**weaving**)	wove (*also* weaved)	woven (*also* weaved)
sink	sank	sunk			
sit (**sitting**)	sat	sat	**wed** (**wedding**)	wedded	wedded (*also* wed)
slay	slew	slain			
sleep	slept	slept	**weep**	wept	wept
slide (**sliding**)	slid	slid	**win** (**winning**)	won	won
sling	slung	slung	**wind**	wound	wound
slit (**slitting**)	slit	slit	**withdraw**	withdrew	withdrawn
smell	smelled (*Brit* smelt)	smelled (*Brit* smelt)	**withhold**	withheld	withheld
			withstand	withstood	withstood
sow	sowed	sown (*also* sowed)	**wring**	wrung	wrung
speak	spoke	spoken	**write** (**writing**)	wrote	written
speed	sped (*also* speeded)	sped (*also* speeded)			

NÚMEROS

NUMBERS

uno (un, una)★	1	one
dos	2	two
tres	3	three
cuatro	4	four
cinco	5	five
seis	6	six
siete	7	seven
ocho	8	eight
nueve	9	nine
diez	10	ten
once	11	eleven
doce	12	twelve
trece	13	thirteen
catorce	14	fourteen
quince	15	fifteen
dieciséis	16	sixteen
diecisiete	17	seventeen
dieciocho	18	eighteen
diecinueve	19	nineteen
veinte	20	twenty
veintiuno(-un, -una)★	21	twenty-one
veintidós	22	twenty-two
treinta	30	thirty
treinta y uno(un, una)★	31	thirty-one
treinta y dos	32	thirty-two
cuarenta	40	forty
cincuenta	50	fifty
sesenta	60	sixty
setenta	70	seventy
ochenta	80	eighty
noventa	90	ninety
cien(ciento)★★	100	a hundred, one hundred
ciento uno(un, una)★	101	a hundred and one
ciento dos	102	a hundred and two
ciento cincuenta y seis	156	a hundred and fifty-six
doscientos(as)	200	two hundred
trescientos(as)	300	three hundred
quinientos(as)	500	five hundred
mil	1,000	a thousand
mil tres	1,003	a thousand and three
dos mil	2,000	two thousand
un millón	1,000,000	a million

★ 'uno' (+ 'veintiuno' etc) agrees in gender (but not number) with its noun: treinta y una personas; the masculine form is shortened to 'un' unless it stands alone: veintiún caballos, veintiuno.

★★ 'ciento' is used in compound numbers, except when it multiplies: ciento diez, but cien mil. 'Cien' is used before nouns: cien hombres, cien casas.

NÚMEROS

NUMBERS

primero(primer, primera), 1º, 1ᵉʳ/1ª, 1ᵉʳᵃ	first, 1st
segundo(a), 2º/2ª	second, 2nd
tercero(tercer, tercera), 3º, 3ᵉʳ/3ª, 3ᵉʳᵃ	third, 3rd
cuarto(a), 4º/4ª	fourth, 4th
quinto(a)	fifth, 5th
sexto(a)	sixth, 6th
séptimo(a)	seventh
octavo(a)	eighth
noveno(a); nono(a)	ninth
décimo(a)	tenth
undécimo(a)	eleventh
duodécimo(a)	twelfth
decimotercio(a)	thirteenth
decimocuarto(a)	fourteenth
decimoquinto(a)	fifteenth
decimosexto(a)	sixteenth
decimoséptimo(a)	seventeenth
decimoctavo(a)	eighteenth
decimonono(a)	nineteenth
vigésimo(a)	twentieth
vigésimo primero(a)	twenty-first
vigésimo segundo(a)	twenty-second
trigésimo(a)	thirtieth
trigésimo primero(a)	thirty-first
trigésimo segundo(a)	thirty-second
cuadragésimo(a)	fortieth
quincuagésimo(a)	fiftieth
sexagésimo(a)	sixtieth
septuagésimo(a)	seventieth
octogésimo(a)	eightieth
nonagésimo(a)	ninetieth
centésimo(a)	hundredth
centésimo primero(a)	hundred-and-first
milésimo(a)	thousandth

A

A, a [à] *nf* (*letra*) A, a; **A de Antonio** A for Able.

a [à] *prep* (*a + el = al*) (*lugar*) at; (*dirección*) to; (*destino*) to, towards; (*tiempo*) at; (*complemento de objeto*): **quiero ~ mis padres** I love my parents; (*manera*): **hacerlo ~ la fuerza** to do it by force; (*con verbo*): **empezó ~ llover** it started raining; **~ la derecha/izquierda** on the right/left; **al lado de** beside, at the side of; **subir ~ un avión/tren** to board a plane/train; **está ~ 7 km de aquí** it is 7 km (away) from here; **hablar ~ larga distancia** to speak long distance; **~ las cuatro** at four o'clock; **~ eso de las cuatro** at about four o'clock; **¿~ qué hora?** (at) what time?; **~ los 30 años** at 30 years of age; **al día siguiente** the next day; **al poco tiempo** a short time later; **al verlo yo** when I saw it; **ir ~ caballo/pie** to go on horseback/foot; **poco ~ poco** little by little; **de dos ~ tres** from two to three; **ocho horas al día** eight hours a *o* per day; **al año/~ la semana** a year/week later; **50 ptas el kilo** 50 pesetas a kilo; **enseñar ~ leer** to teach to read; **voy ~ llevarlo** I am going to carry it; **cercano ~** near (to); **por miedo ~** out of fear of; **¡~ comer!** let's eat!; **¡~ que llueve!** I bet it's going to rain!; **¿~ qué viene eso?** what's the meaning of this?; **~ ver** let's see.

A. *abr* (*ESCOL*: = *aprobado*) pass.

AA *nfpl abr* = *Aerolíneas Argentinas*.

ab. *abr* (= *abril*) Apr.

abad, esa [àbàth', the'sà] *nm/f* abbot/abbess.

abadía [àbàthe'à] *nf* abbey.

abajo [àbà'ho] *ad* (*situación*) (down) below, underneath; (*en edificio*) downstairs; (*dirección*) down, downwards; **~ de** *prep* below, under; **el piso de ~** the downstairs apartment; **la parte de ~** the lower part; **¡~ el gobierno!** down with the government!; **cuesta/río ~** downhill/downstream; **de arriba ~** from top to bottom; **el firmante** the undersigned; **más ~** lower *o* further down.

abalance [àbàlàn'se] *etc vb* V **abalanzarse**.

abalanzarse [àbàlànsàr'se] *vr*: **~ sobre** *o* **contra** to throw o.s. at.

abalorios [àbàlo'ryos] *nmpl* (*chucherías*) trinkets.

abanderado [àbànderà'tho] *nm* standard bearer.

abandonado, a [àbàndonà'tho, à] *a* derelict; (*desatendido*) abandoned; (*desierto*) deserted; (*descuidado*) neglected.

abandonar [àbàndonàr'] *vt* to leave; (*persona*) to abandon, desert; (*cosa*) to abandon, leave behind; (*descuidar*) to neglect; (*renunciar a*) to give up; (*INFORM*) to quit; **~se** *vr*: **~se a** to abandon o.s. to; **~se al alcohol** to take to drink.

abandono [àbàndo'no] *nm* (*acto*) desertion, abandonment; (*estado*) abandon, neglect; (*renuncia*) withdrawal, retirement; **ganar por ~** to win by default.

abanicar [àbànkàr'] *vt* to fan.

abanico [àbàne'ko] *nm* fan; (*NAUT*) derrick; **en ~** fan-shaped.

abanique [àbàne'ke] *etc vb* V **abanicar**.

abaratar [àbàràtàr'] *vt* to lower the price of ♦ *vi,* **~se** *vr* to go *o* come down in price.

abarcar [àbàrkàr'] *vt* to include, embrace; (*contener*) to comprise; (*AM*) to monopolize; **quien mucho abarca poco aprieta** don't bite off more than you can chew.

abarque [àbàr'ke] *etc vb* V **abarcar**.

abarrotado, a [àbàrrotà'tho, à] *a* packed; **~ de** packed *o* bursting with.

abarrote [àbàrro'te] *nm* packing; **~s** *nmpl* (*AM*) groceries, provisions.

abarrotero, a [àbàrrote'ro, à] *nm/f* (*AM*) grocer.

abastecedor, a [àbàsteseħor', à] *a* supplying ♦ *nm/f* supplier.

abastecer [àbàsteser'] *vt* to supply (*de* with).

abastecimiento [àbàstesemyen'to] *nm* supply.

abastezca [àbàstes'kà] *etc vb* V **abastecer**.

abasto [àbà'sto] *nm* supply; (*abundancia*) abundance; **no dar ~ a algo** not to be able to cope with sth.

abatible [àbàte'ble] *a*: **asiento ~** tip-up seat.

abatido, a [àbàte'tho, à] *a* dejected, downcast; **estar muy ~** to be very depressed.

abatimiento [àbàtemyen'to] *nm* (*depresión*) dejection, depression.

abatir [àbàter'] *vt* (*muro*) to demolish; (*pájaro*) to shoot *o* bring down; (*fig*) to depress; **~se** *vr* to get depressed; **~se sobre**

to swoop o pounce on.
abdicación [àbdhēkásyon'] *nf* abdication.
abdicar [àbdhēkár'] *vi* to abdicate; ~ **en uno** to abdicate in favor of sb.
abdique [àbdhē'ke] *etc vb* V **abdicar.**
abdomen [àbdho'men] *nm* abdomen.
abecedario [àbesedhá'ryo] *nm* alphabet.
abedul [àbedhōōl'] *nm* birch.
abeja [àbe'há] *nf* bee; (*fig: hormiguita*) hard worker.
abejorro [àbeho'rro] *nm* bumblebee.
aberración [àberrásyon'] *nf* aberration.
aberrante [àberrán'te] *a* (*disparatado*) ridiculous.
abertura [àbertōō'rá] *nf* = **apertura.**
abeto [àbe'to] *nm* fir.
abierto, a [àbyer'to, á] *pp de* **abrir** ♦ *a* open; (*AM*) generous; (*fig: carácter*) frank.
abigarrado, a [àbēgárrá'dho, á] *a* multicolored; (*fig*) motley.
abismal [àbēsmál'] *a* (*fig*) vast, enormous.
abismar [àbēsmár'] *vt* to humble, cast down; ~**se** *vr* to sink; (*AM*) to be amazed; ~**se en** (*fig*) to be plunged into.
abismo [àbēs'mo] *nm* abyss; **de sus ideas a las mías hay un** ~ our views are worlds apart.
abjurar [àbhōōrár'] *vt* to abjure, forswear ♦ *vi*: ~ **de** to abjure, forswear.
ablandar [àblándár'] *vt* to soften up; (*conmover*) to touch; (*CULIN*) to tenderize ♦ *vi*, ~**se** *vr* to get softer.
abnegación [àbnegásyon'] *nf* self-denial.
abnegado, a [àbnegá'dho, á] *a* self-sacrificing.
abobado, a [àbobá'dho, á] *a* silly.
abobamiento [àbobámyen'to] *nm* (*asombro*) bewilderment.
abocado, a [àboká'dho, á] *a*: **verse** ~ **al desastre** to be heading for disaster.
abochornar [àbotchornár'] *vt* to embarrass; ~**se** *vr* to get flustered; (*BOT*) to wilt; ~**se de** to get embarrassed about.
abofetear [àbofeteár'] *vt* to slap (in the face).
abogacía [àbogásē'á] *nf* legal profession; (*ejercicio*) practice of the law.
abogado, a [àbogá'dho, á] *nm/f* lawyer; (*notario*) ≈ notary; (*asesor*) counsel; (*en tribunal*) attorney (*US*), barrister (*Brit*); ~ **defensor** defense attorney; ~ **del diablo** devil's advocate.
abogar [àbogár'] *vi*: ~ **por** to plead for; (*fig*) to advocate.
abogue [àbo'ge] *etc vb* V **abogar.**
abolengo [àbolen'go] *nm* ancestry, lineage.
abolición [àbolēsyon'] *nf* abolition.
abolir [àbolēr'] *vt* to abolish; (*cancelar*) to cancel.
abolladura [àboyádhōō'rá] *nf* dent.
abollar [àboyár'] *vt* to dent.

abominable [àbomēná'ble] *a* abominable.
abominación [àbomēnásyon'] *nf* abomination.
abonado, a [àboná'dho, á] *a* (*deuda*) paid (-up) ♦ *nm/f* subscriber.
abonar [àbonár'] *vt* to pay; (*deuda*) to settle; (*terreno*) to fertilize; (*idea*) to endorse; ~**se** *vr* to subscribe; ~ **dinero en una cuenta** to pay money into an account, credit money to an account.
abono [àbo'no] *nm* payment; fertilizer; subscription.
abordable [àbordhá'ble] *a* (*persona*) approachable.
abordar [àbordhár'] *vt* (*barco*) to board; (*asunto*) to broach; (*individuo*) to approach.
aborigen [àborē'hen] *nm/f* aborigine.
aborrecer [àborreser'] *vt* to hate, loathe.
aborrezca [àborres'ká] *etc vb* V **aborrecer.**
abortar [àbortár'] *vi* (*malparir*) to have a miscarriage; (*deliberadamente*) to have an abortion.
aborto [àbor'to] *nm* miscarriage; abortion.
abotagado, a [àbotagá'dho, á] *a* swollen.
abotonar [àbotonár'] *vt* to button (up), do up.
abovedado, a [àbobedhá'dho, á] *a* vaulted, domed.
abr. *abr* (= *abril*) Apr.
abrace [àbrá'se] *etc vb* V **abrazar.**
abrasar [àbrásár'] *vt* to burn (up); (*AGR*) to dry up, parch.
abrazadera [àbrásádhe'rá] *nf* bracket.
abrazar [àbrásár'] *vt* to embrace, hug; ~**se** *vr* to embrace, hug each other.
abrazo [àbrá'so] *nm* embrace, hug; **un** ~ (*en carta*) with best wishes.
abrebotellas [àbrebote'yás] *nm inv* bottle opener.
abrecartas [àbrekár'tás] *nm inv* letter opener.
abrelatas [àbrelá'tás] *nm inv* can (*US*) o tin (*Brit*) opener.
abrevadero [àbrebádhe'ro] *nm* watering place.
abreviar [àbrebyár'] *vt* to abbreviate; (*texto*) to abridge; (*plazo*) to reduce ♦ *vi*: **bueno, para** ~ well, to cut a long story short.
abreviatura [àbrebyátōō'rá] *nf* abbreviation.
abridor [àbrēdhor'] *nm* (*de botellas*) bottle opener; (*de latas*) can (*US*) o tin (*Brit*) opener.
abrigar [àbrēgár'] *vt* (*proteger*) to shelter; (*suj: ropa*) to keep warm; (*fig*) to cherish; ~**se** *vr* to take shelter, protect o.s (*de* from); (*con ropa*) to cover (o.s.) up; **¡abrígate bien!** wrap up well!
abrigo [àbrē'go] *nm* (*prenda*) coat, overcoat; (*lugar protegido*) shelter; **al** ~ **de** in

the shelter of.

abrigue |àhrē'gc| *etc vb* V **abrigar**.

abril |àhrēl'| *nn* April.

abrillantar |àhrēyàntàr'| *vt* (*pulir*) to polish; (*fig*) to enhance.

abrir |àhrēr'| *vt* to open (up); (*camino etc*) to open up; (*apetito*) to whet; (*lista*) to head ♦ *vi* to open; ~se *vr* to open (up); (*extenderse*) to open out; (*cielo*) to clear; ~ **un negocio** to start up a business; **en un** ~ **y cerrar de ojos** in the twinkling of an eye; ~se **paso** to find *o* force a way through.

abrochar |àhrotchàr'| *vt* (*con botones*) to button (up); (*AM*) to staple; (*zapato, con broche*) to do up; ~se *vr:* ~se **los zapatos** to tie one's shoelaces.

abrogación |àhrogàsyon'| *nf* repeal.

abrogar |àhrogàr'| *vt* to repeal.

abrumador, a |àhrōōmàthor', à| *a* (*mayoría*) overwhelming.

abrumar |àhrōōmàr'| *vt* to overwhelm; (*sobrecargar*) to weigh down.

abrupto, a |àhrōōp'to, à| *a* abrupt; (*empinado*) steep.

absceso |àhsc'so| *nn* abscess.

absentismo |àhscntēs'mo| *nn* (*de obreros*) absenteeism.

absolución |àhsolōōsyon'| *nf* (*REL*) absolution; (*JUR*) acquittal.

absoluto, a |àhsolōō'to, à| *a* absolute; (*total*) utter, complete; **en** ~ *ad* not at all.

absolver |àhsolhcr'| *vt* to absolve; (*JUR*) to pardon; (: *acusado*) to acquit.

absorbente |àhsorhen'tc| *a* absorbent; (*interesante*) absorbing, interesting; (*exigente*) demanding.

absorber |àhsorhcr'| *vt* to absorb; (*embeber*) to soak up; ~se *vr* to become absorbed.

absorción |àhsorsyon'| *nf* absorption; (*COM*) takeover.

absorto, a |àhsor'to, à| *pp de* **absorber** ♦ *a* absorbed, engrossed.

abstemio, a |àhstc'myo, à| *a* teetotal.

abstención |àhstcnsyon'| *nf* abstention.

abstendré |àhstcndrc'| *etc vb* V **abstenerse**.

abstenerse |àhstcncr'sc| *vr:* ~ **(de)** to abstain *o* refrain (from).

abstenga |àhstcn'gà| *etc vb* V **abstenerse**.

abstinencia |àhstēncn'syà| *nf* abstinence; (*ayuno*) fasting.

abstracción |àhstràksyon'| *nf* abstraction.

abstracto, a |àhstràk'to, à| *a* abstract; **en** ~ in the abstract.

abstraer |àhstràcr'| *vt* to abstract; ~se *vr* to be *o* become abstracted.

abstraído, a |àhstràc'tho, à| *a* absentminded.

abstraiga |àhstrà'cgà| *etc*, **abstraje** |àhstrà'hc| *etc*, **abstrayendo** |àhstràycn'do|

etc vb V **abstraer**.

abstuve |àhstōō'hc| *etc vb* V **abstenerse**.

absuelto |àhswcl'to| *pp de* **absolver**.

absurdo, a |àhsōōr'tho, à| *a* absurd; **lo** ~ **es que** ... the ridiculous thing is that ... ♦ *nn* absurdity.

abuchear |àhōōtchcàr'| *vt* to boo.

abucheo |àhōōtchc'o| *nn* booing; **ganarse un** ~ (*TEATRO*) to be booed.

abuela |àhwc'là| *nf* grandmother; **¡cuéntaselo a tu** ~**!** (*fam!*) do you think I was born yesterday? (*fam*); **no tener/necesitar** ~ (*fam*) to be full of o.s./blow one's own horn (*US*) *o* trumpet (*Brit*).

abuelita |àhwclē'tà| *nf* grandma.

abuelo |àhwc'lo| *nn* grandfather; (*antepasado*) ancestor; ~s *nmpl* grandparents.

abulense |àhōōlcn'sc| *a* of Ávila ♦ *nm/f* native *o* inhabitant of Ávila.

abulia |àhōō'lyà| *nf* lethargy.

abultado, a |àhōōltà'tho, à| *a* bulky.

abultar |àhōōltàr'| *vt* to enlarge; (*aumentar*) to increase; (*fig*) to exaggerate ♦ *vi* to be bulky.

abundancia |àhōōndàn'syà| *nf:* **una** ~ **de** plenty of; **en** ~ in abundance.

abundante |àhōōndàn'tc| *a* abundant, plentiful.

abundar |àhōōndàr'| *vi* to abound, be plentiful; ~ **en una opinión** to share an opinion.

aburguesarse |àhōōrgcsàr'sc| *vr* to become middle-class.

aburrido, a |àhōōrrē'tho, à| *a* (*hastiado*) bored; (*que aburre*) boring.

aburrimiento |àhōōrrēmycn'to| *nn* boredom, tedium.

aburrir |àhōōrrēr'| *vt* to bore; ~se *vr* to be bored, get bored; ~se **como una almeja** *u* **ostra** to be bored stiff.

abusar |àhōōsàr'| *vi* to go too far; ~ **de** to abuse.

abusivo, a |àhōōsē'ho, à| *a* (*precio*) exorbitant.

abuso |àhōō'so| *nn* abuse; ~ **de confianza** betrayal of trust.

abyecto, a |àhyck'to, à| *a* wretched, abject.

A.C. *abr* (= *Año de Cristo*) A.D.

a/c *abr* (= *al cuidado de*) c/o; (= *a cuenta*) on account.

acá |àkà'| *ad* (*lugar*) here; **pasearse de** ~ **para allá** to walk up and down; **¡vente para** ~**!** come over here!; **¿de cuándo** ~**?** since when?

acabado, a |àkàhà'tho, à| *a* finished, complete; (*perfecto*) perfect; (*agotado*) worn out; (*fig*) masterly ♦ *nn* finish.

acabar |àkàhàr'| *vt* (*llevar a su fin*) to finish, complete; (*consumir*) to use up; (*rematar*) to finish off ♦ *vi* to finish, end; (*morir*) to die; ~se *vr* to finish, stop; (*terminarse*) to be over; (*agotarse*) to run out; ~ **con** to put an end to; ~ **mal** (*historia*) to turn out badly; **esto acabará conmigo** this will be the end of me; ~ **de llegar** to have just arrived; **acababa de hacerlo** I had just done it; ~ **haciendo** o **por hacer algo** to end up (by) doing sth; **¡se acabó!** (*¡basta!*) that's enough!; (*se terminó*) it's all over!; **se me acabó el tabaco** I ran out of cigarettes.

acabóse |ákáḅo'se| *nm*: **esto es el** ~ this is the limit.

academia |ákáḍe'myá| *nf* academy.

académico, a |ákáḍe'mēko, á| *a* academic.

acaecer |ákáeser'| *vi* to happen, occur.

acaezca |ákács'ká| *etc vb V* **acaecer**.

acalorado, a |ákálorá'ḍo, á| *a* (*discusión*) heated.

acalorarse |ákálorár'se| *vr* (*fig*) to get heated.

acallar |ákáyár'| *vt* (*silenciar*) to silence; (*calmar*) to pacify.

acampar |ákámpár'| *vi* to camp.

acanalado, a |ákánálá'ḍo, á| *a* (*hierro*) corrugated.

acanalar |ákánálár'| *vt* to groove; (*ondular*) to corrugate.

acantilado |ákántēlá'ḍo| *nm* cliff.

acaparador, a |ákápárá'ḍor', á| *nm/f* monopolizer.

acaparar |ákápárár'| *vt* to monopolize; (*acumular*) to hoard.

acaramelado, a |ákárámelá'ḍo, á| *a* (*CULIN*) toffee-coated; (*fig*) sugary.

acariciar |ákáriṡyár'| *vt* to caress; (*esperanza*) to cherish.

acarrear |ákárreár'| *vt* to transport; (*fig*) to cause, result in; **le acarreó muchos disgustos** it brought him lots of problems.

acaso |áká'so| *ad* perhaps, maybe ♦ *nm* chance; **(por) si** ~ (just) in case.

acatamiento |ákátámyen'to| *nm* respect; (*de la ley*) observance.

acatar |ákátár'| *vt* to respect; (*ley*) to obey, observe.

acatarrarse |ákátárrár'se| *vr* to catch a cold.

acaudalado, a |ákáoo̅ḍálá'ḍo, á| *a* well-off.

acaudillar |ákáoo̅ḍēyár'| *vt* to lead, command.

acceder |ákseḍer'| *vi* to accede, agree; ~ **a** (*INFORM*) to access.

accesar |áksesár'| *vt* to access.

accesible |áksesē'ḅle| *a* accessible; ~ **a** open to.

accésit, *pl* **accésits** |ákse'sēt, akse'sēts| *nm* consolation prize.

acceso |ákse'so| *nm* access, entry; (*camino*) access road; (*MED*) attack, fit; (*de cólera*) fit; (*POL*) accession; (*INFORM*) access; ~ **aleatorio/directo/secuencial** o **en serie** (*IN-*

FORM) random/direct/sequential o serial access; **de** ~ **múltiple** multi-access.

accesorio, a |ákseso'ryo, á| *a* accessory ♦ *nm* accessory; ~**s** *nmpl* (*AUTO*) accessories, extras; (*TEATRO*) props.

accidentado, a |áksēḍentá'ḍo, á| *a* uneven; (*montañoso*) hilly; (*azaroso*) eventful ♦ *nm/f* accident victim.

accidental |áksēḍentál'| *a* accidental; (*empleo*) temporary.

accidentarse |áksēḍentár'se| *vr* to have an accident.

accidente |áksēḍen'te| *nm* accident; **por** ~ by chance; ~**s** *nmpl* unevenness *sg*, roughness *sg*.

acción |áksyon'| *nf* action; (*acto*) action, act; (*TEATRO*) plot; (*COM*) share; (*JUR*) action, lawsuit; **capital en acciones** share capital; ~ **liberada/ordinaria/preferente** fully-paid/ordinary/preference share.

accionamiento |áksyonámyen'to| *nm* (*de máquina*) operation.

accionar |áksyonár'| *vt* to work, operate; (*INFORM*) to drive.

accionista |áksyonē'stá| *nm/f* shareholder.

acebo |áse'ḅo| *nm* holly; (*árbol*) holly tree.

acechanza |ásetchán'sá| *nf* = **acecho**.

acechar |ásetchár'| *vt* to spy on; (*aguardar*) to lie in wait for.

acecho |áse'tcho| *nm*: **estar al** ~ **(de)** to lie in wait (for).

acedera |áseḍe'rá| *nf* sorrel.

aceitar |ásētár'| *vt* to oil, lubricate.

aceite |ásē'te| *nm* oil; (*de oliva*) olive oil; ~ **de hígado de bacalao** cod-liver oil.

aceitera |ásēte'rá| *nf* oilcan.

aceitoso, a |ásēto'so, á| *a* oily.

aceituna |ásētoo̅'ná| *nf* olive.

aceitunado, a |ásētoo̅ná'ḍo, á| *a* olive *cpd*; **de tez aceitunada** olive-skinned.

acelerador |áselerá'ḍor'| *nm* gas pedal (*US*), accelerator (*Brit*).

acelerar |áselerár'| *vt* to accelerate; ~**se** *vr* to hurry.

acelga |ásel'gá| *nf* chard, beet.

acendrado, a |ásendrá'ḍo, á| *a*: **de** ~ **carácter español** typically Spanish.

acendrar |ásendrár'| *vt* to purify.

acento |ásen'to| *nm* accent; (*acentuación*) stress; ~ **cerrado** strong o thick accent.

acentuar |ásentwár'| *vt* to accent; to stress; (*fig*) to accentuate; (*INFORM*) to highlight.

acepción |ásepsyon'| *nf* meaning.

aceptación |áseptásyon'| *nf* acceptance; (*aprobación*) approval.

aceptar |áseptár'| *vt* to accept; to approve.

acequia |áse'kyá| *nf* irrigation ditch.

acera |áse'rá| *nf* sidewalk (*US*), pavement (*Brit*).

acerado, a |áserá'ḍo, á| *a* steel; (*afilado*) sharp; (*fig*: *duro*) steely; (*: mordaz*) biting.

acerbo, a |àser'ko, à| *a* bitter; *(fig)* harsh.

acerca |àser'kà| *ad* about, concerning.

acercar |àserkàr'| *vt* to bring *o* move nearer; **~se** *vr* to approach, come near.

acerico |àserē'ko| *nm* pincushion.

acero |àse'ro| *nm* steel; **~ inoxidable** stainless steel.

acerque |àser'ke| *etc vb* V **acercar**.

acérrimo, a |àse'rrēmo, à| *a* *(partidario)* staunch; *(enemigo)* bitter.

acertado, a |àsertà'đo, à| *a* correct; *(apropiado)* apt; *(sensato)* sensible.

acertar |àsertàr'| *vt* *(blanco)* to hit; *(solución)* to get right; *(adivinar)* to guess ♦ *vi* to get it right, be right; **~ a** to manage to; **~ con** to happen *o* hit on.

acertijo |àsertē'ho| *nm* riddle, puzzle.

acervo |àser'ko| *nm* heap; **~ común** undivided estate.

aciago, a |àsyà'go, à| *a* ill-fated, fateful.

acicalar |àsēkàlàr'| *vt* to polish; *(adornar)* to adorn; **~se** *vr* to get dressed up.

acicate |àsēkà'te| *nm* spur; *(fig)* incentive.

acidez |àsēđes'| *nf* acidity.

ácido, a |à'sēđo, à| *a* sour, acid ♦ *nm* acid; *(fam: droga)* LSD.

acierto |àsyer'to| *etc vb* V **acertar** ♦ *nm* success; *(buen paso)* wise move; *(solución)* solution; *(habilidad)* skill, ability; *(al adivinar)* good guess; **fue un ~ suyo** it was a sensible choice on his part.

aclamación |àklàmàsyon'| *nf* acclamation; *(aplausos)* applause.

aclamar |àklàmàr'| *vt* to acclaim; to applaud.

aclaración |àklàràsyon'| *nf* clarification, explanation.

aclarar |àklàràr'| *vt* to clarify, explain; *(ropa)* to rinse ♦ *vi* to clear up; **~se** *vr* *(suj: persona: explicarse)* to understand; *(fig: asunto)* to become clear; **~se la garganta** to clear one's throat.

aclaratorio, a |àklàràto'ryo, à| *a* explanatory.

aclimatación |àklēmàtàsyon'| *nf* acclimation *(US)*, acclimatization *(Brit)*.

aclimatar |àklēmàtàr'| *vt* to acclimate *(US)*, acclimatize *(Brit)*; **~se** *vr* to become *o* get acclimated; **~se a algo** to get used to sth.

acné |àkne'| *nm* acne.

acobardar |àkoßàrđàr'| *vt* to daunt, intimidate; **~se** *vr* *(atemorizarse)* to be intimidated; *(echarse atrás)*: **~se (ante)** to shrink back (from).

acodarse |àkođàr'se| *vr*: **~ en** to lean on.

acogedor, a |àkoheđor', à| *a* welcoming; *(hospitalario)* hospitable.

acoger |àkoher'| *vt* to welcome; *(abrigar)* to shelter; **~se** *vr* to take refuge; **~se a** *(pretexto)* to take refuge in; *(ley)* to resort to.

acogida |àkohē'đà| *nf* reception; refuge.

acogollar |àkogoyàr'| *vt* *(AGR)* to cover up ♦ *vi* to sprout.

acoja |àko'hà| *etc vb* V **acoger**.

acojonante |àkohonàn'te| *a* *(Esp fam)* tremendous.

acolchar |àkoltchàr'| *vt* to pad; *(fig)* to cushion.

acólito |àko'lēto| *nm* *(REL)* acolyte; *(fig)* minion.

acometer |àkometer'| *vt* to attack; *(emprender)* to undertake.

acometida |àkometē'đà| *nf* attack, assault.

acomodado, a |àkomođà'đo, à| *a* *(persona)* well-to-do.

acomodador, a |àkomođàđor', à| *nm/f* usher(ette).

acomodar |àkomođàr'| *vt* to adjust; *(alojar)* to accommodate; **~se** *vr* to conform; *(instalarse)* to install o.s.; *(adaptarse)* to adapt o.s.; **¡acomódese a su gusto!** make yourself comfortable!

acomodaticio, a |àkomođàtē'syo, à| *a* *(pey)* accommodating, obliging; *(manejable)* pliable.

acompañamiento |àkompànyàmyen'to| *nm* *(MUS)* accompaniment.

acompañante, a |àkompànyàn'te, à| *nm/f* companion.

acompañar |àkompànyàr'| *vt* to accompany, go with; *(documentos)* to enclose; **¿quieres que te acompañe?** do you want me to come with you?; **~ a uno a la puerta** to see sb to the door *o* out; **le acompaño en el sentimiento** please accept my condolences.

acompasar |àkompàsàr'| *vt* *(MUS)* to mark the rhythm of.

acomplejado, a |àkomplehà'đo, à| *a* neurotic.

acomplejar |àkomplehàr'| *vt* to give a complex to; **~se** *vr*: **~se (con)** to get a complex (about).

acondicionado, a |àkondēsyonà'đo, à| *a* *(TEC)* in good condition.

acondicionador |àkondēsyonàđor'| *nm* conditioner.

acondicionar |àkondēsyonàr'| *vt* to get ready, prepare; *(pelo)* to condition.

acongojar |àkongohàr'| *vt* to distress, grieve.

aconsejable |àkonsehà'ßle| *a* advisable.

aconsejar |àkonsehàr'| *vt* to advise, counsel; **~se** *vr*: **~se con** *o* **de** to consult.

acontecer |àkonteser'| *vi* to happen, occur.

acontecimiento |àkontesēmyen'to| *nm* event.

acontezca |àkontes'kà| *etc vb* V **acontecer**.

acopiar |àkopyàr'| *vt* *(recoger)* to gather; *(COM)* to buy up.

acopio [åko'pyo] *nm* store, stock.
acoplador [åkoplåthor'] *nm*: ~ **acústico** (*INFORM*) acoustic coupler.
acoplamiento [åkoplåmyen'to] *nm* coupling, joint.
acoplar [åkoplår'] *vt* to fit; (*ELEC*) to connect; (*vagones*) to couple.
acoquinar [åkokēnår'] *vt* to scare; ~**se** *vr* to get scared.
acorazado, a [åkoråså'tho, å] *a* armorplated (*US*), armour-plated (*Brit*), armored (*US*), armoured (*Brit*) ♦ *nm* battleship.
acordar [åkorthår'] *vt* (*resolver*) to agree, resolve; (*recordar*) to remind; ~**se** *vr* to agree; ~**se (de algo)** to remember (sth).
acorde [åkor'the] *a* (*MUS*) harmonious; ~ **con** (*medidas etc*) in keeping with ♦ *nm* chord.
acordeón [åkortheon'] *nm* accordion.
acordonado, a [åkorthoná'tho, å] *a* (*calle*) cordoned-off.
acorralar [åkorrålår'] *vt* to round up, corral; (*fig*) to intimidate.
acortar [åkortår'] *vt* to shorten; (*duración*) to cut short; (*cantidad*) to reduce; ~**se** *vr* to become shorter.
acosar [åkosår'] *vt* to pursue relentlessly; (*fig*) to hound, pester; ~ **a uno a preguntas** to pester sb with questions.
acostar [åkostår'] *vt* (*en cama*) to put to bed; (*en suelo*) to lay down; (*barco*) to bring alongside; ~**se** *vr* to go to bed; to lie down.
acostumbrar [åkostōōmbrår'] *vt*: ~ **a uno a algo** to get sb used to sth ♦ *vi*: ~ **(a hacer algo)** to be in the habit (of doing sth); ~**se** *vr*: ~**se a** to get used to.
acotación [åkotåsyon'] *nf* (*apunte*) marginal note; (*GEO*) elevation mark; (*de límite*) boundary mark; (*TEATRO*) stage direction.
acotar [åkotår'] *vt* (*terreno*) to mark out; (*fig*) to limit; (*caza*) to protect.
ácrata [å'kråtå] *a*, *nm/f* anarchist.
acre [å'kre] *a* (*sabor*) sharp, bitter; (*olor*) acrid; (*fig*) biting ♦ *nm* acre.
acrecentar [åkresentår'] *vt* to increase, augment.
acreciente [åkresyen'te] *etc vb* V **acrecentar**.
acreditado, a [åkrethētá'tho, å] *a* (*POL*) accredited; (*COM*): **una casa acreditada** a reputable firm.
acreditar [åkrethētår'] *vt* (*garantizar*) to vouch for, guarantee; (*autorizar*) to authorize; (*dar prueba de*) to prove; (*COM: abonar*) to credit; (*embajador*) to accredit; ~**se** *vr* to become famous; (*demostrar valía*) to prove one's worth; ~**se de** to get a reputation for.
acreedor, a [åkreethor', å] *a*: ~ **a** worthy of ♦ *nm/f* creditor; ~ **común/diferido/con ga-**

rantía (*COM*) unsecured/deferred/secured creditor.
acribillar [åkrēhēyår'] *vt*: ~ **a balazos** to riddle with bullets.
acrimonia [åkrēmo'nyå], **acritud** [åkrētōōth'] *nf* acrimony.
acrobacia [åkrohå'syå] *nf* acrobatics; ~ **aérea** aerobatics.
acróbata [åkro'håtå] *nm/f* acrobat.
acta [åk'tå] *nf* certificate; (*de comisión*) minutes *pl*, record; ~ **de nacimiento/de matrimonio** birth/marriage certificate; ~ **notarial** affidavit; **levantar** ~ (*JUR*) to make a formal statement o deposition.
actitud [åktētōōth'] *nf* attitude; (*postura*) posture; **adoptar una** ~ **firme** to take a firm stand.
activar [åktēhár'] *vt* to activate; (*acelerar*) to speed up.
actividad [åktēhēthåth'] *nf* activity; **estar en plena** ~ to be in full swing.
activo, a [åktē'ho, å] *a* active; (*vivo*) lively ♦ *nm* (*COM*) assets *pl*; ~ **y pasivo** assets and liabilities; ~ **circulante/fijo/inmaterial/invisible** (*COM*) current/fixed/intangible/invisible assets; ~ **realizable** liquid assets; ~**s congelados** o **bloqueados** frozen assets; **estar en** ~ (*MIL*) to be on active service.
acto [åk'to] *nm* act, action; (*ceremonia*) ceremony; (*TEATRO*) act; **en el** ~ immediately; **hacer** ~ **de presencia** (*asistir*) to attend (formally).
actor [åktor'] *nm* actor; (*JUR*) plaintiff.
actora [åkto'rå] *a*: **parte** ~ prosecution; (*demandante*) plaintiff.
actriz [åktrēs'] *nf* actress.
actuación [åktwåsyon'] *nf* action; (*comportamiento*) conduct, behavior; (*JUR*) proceedings *pl*; (*desempeño*) performance.
actual [åktwål'] *a* present(-day), current; **el 6 del** ~ the 6th of this month.
actualice [åktwålē'se] *etc vb* V **actualizar**.
actualidad [åktwålēthåth'] *nf* present; ~**es** *nfpl* news *sg*; **en la** ~ nowadays, at present; **ser de gran** ~ to be current.
actualización [åktwålēsåsyon'] *nf* updating, modernization.
actualizar [åktwålēsår'] *vt* to update, modernize.
actualmente [åktwålmen'te] *ad* at present; (*hoy día*) nowadays.
actuar [åktwår'] *vi* (*obrar*) to work, operate; (*actor*) to act, perform ♦ *vt* to work, operate; ~ **de** to act as.
actuario, a [åktwå'ryo, å] *nm/f* clerk; (*COM*) actuary.
acuarela [åkwåre'lå] *nf* watercolor (*US*), watercolour (*Brit*).
acuario [åkwå'ryo] *nm* aquarium; **A~** (*ASTRO*) Aquarius.

acuartelar |ákwàrtclár'| *vt* (*MIL*: *alojar*) to quarter.

acuático, a |ákwá'tčko, á| *a* aquatic.

acuciar |ákōōsyár'| *vt* to urge on.

acuclillarse |ákōōklčyár'sc| *vr* to crouch down.

acuchillar |ákōōtchčyàr'| *vt* (*TEC*) to plane (down), smooth.

ACUDE |ákōō'thc| *nf abr* = *Asociación de Consumidores y Usuarios de España*.

acudir |ákōōthčr'| *vi* to attend, turn up; ~ **a** to turn to; ~ **en ayuda de** to go to the aid of; ~ **a una cita** to keep an appointment; ~ **a una llamada** to answer a call; **no te- ner a quién** ~ to have nobody to turn to.

acuerdo |ákwcr'tho| *etc vb* V **acordar** ♦ *nm* agreement; (*POL*) resolution; ~ **de pago respectivo** (*COM*) no-fault (*US*) *o* knock-for-knock (*Brit*) agreement; **A~ general sobre aranceles aduaneros y comercio** (*COM*) General Agreement on Tariffs and Trade; **tomar un** ~ to pass a resolution; **¡de** ~! agreed!; **de** ~ **con** (*persona*) in agreement with; (*acción, documento*) in accordance with; **de común** ~ by common consent; **estar de** ~ (*persona*) to agree; **llegar a un** ~ to come to an understanding.

acueste |ákwc'stc| *etc vb* V **acostar**.

acullá |ákōōyá'| *ad* over there.

acumular |ákōōmōōlár'| *vt* to accumulate, collect.

acunar |ákōōnár'| *vt* to rock (to sleep).

acuñar |ákōōnyár'| *vt* (*moneda*) to mint; (*frase*) to coin.

acuoso, a |ákwo'so, á| *a* watery.

acupuntura |ákōōpōōntōō'rá| *nf* acupuncture.

acurrucarse |ákōōrrōōkár'sc| *vr* to crouch; (*ovillarse*) to curl up.

acurruque |ákōōrrōō'kc| *etc vb* V **acurrucarse**.

acusación |ákōōsásyon'| *nf* accusation.

acusado, a |ákōōsá'tho, á| *a* (*JUR*) accused; (*marcado*) marked; (*acento*) strong.

acusar |ákōōsár'| *vt* to accuse; (*revelar*) to reveal; (*denunciar*) to denounce; (*emoción*) to show; ~ **recibo** to acknowledge receipt; **su rostro acusó extrañeza** his face registered surprise; **~se** *vr* to confess (*de* to).

acuse |ákōō'sc| *nm*: ~ **de recibo** acknowledgement of receipt.

acusete |ákōōsc'tc| *nm/f*, **acusón, ona** |ákōōson', oná| *nm/f* telltale, sneak.

acústico, a |ákōō'stčko, á| *a* acoustic ♦ *nf* (*de una sala etc*) acoustics *pl*; (*ciencia*) acoustics *sg*.

achacar |átchákár'| *vt* to attribute.

achacoso, a |átcháko'so, á| *a* sickly.

achantar |átchántár'| *vt* (*fam*) to scare, frighten; **~se** *vr* to back down.

achaque |átchá'kc| *etc vb* V **achacar** ♦ *nm*

ailment.

achatar |átchátár'| *vt* to flatten.

achicar |átchčkár'| *vt* to reduce; (*humillar*) to humiliate; (*NAUT*) to bale out; **~se** (*ropa*) to shrink; (*fig*) to humble o.s.

achicoria |átchčko'ryá| *nf* chicory.

achicharrar |átchčtchárrár'| *vt* to scorch, burn.

achinado, a |átchčná'tho, á| *a* (*ojos*) slanting.

achique |átchč'kc| *etc vb* V **achicar**.

achuchar |átchōōtchár'| *vt* to crush.

achuchón |átchōōtchon'| *nm* shove; **tener un** ~ (*MED*) to be poorly.

ADA |á'thá| *nf abr* (*Esp*: = *Ayuda del Auto-movilista*) ≈ AAA (*US*), AA, RAC (*Brit*).

adagio |áthá'hyo| *nm* adage; (*MUS*) adagio.

adalid |áthálčth'| *nm* leader, champion.

adaptación |átháptásyon'| *nf* adaptation.

adaptador |átháptáthor'| *nm* (*ELEC*) adapter.

adaptar |áthàptár'| *vt* to adapt; (*acomodar*) to fit; (*convertir*): ~ (**para**) to convert (to).

adecentar |áthcscntár'| *vt* to tidy up.

adecuado, a |áthckwá'tho, á| *a* (*apto*) suitable; (*oportuno*) appropriate; **el hombre ~ para el puesto** the right man for the job.

adecuar |áthckwár'| *vt* (*adaptar*) to adapt; (*hacer apto*) to make suitable.

adefesio |áthcfc'syo| *nm* (*fam*): **estaba he-cha un** ~ she looked a sight.

a. de J.C. *abr* (= *antes de Jesucristo*) B.C.

adelantado, a |áthclántá'tho, á| *a* advanced; (*reloj*) fast; **pagar por** ~ to pay in advance.

adelantamiento |áthclántámycn'to| *nm* advance, advancement; (*AUTO*) passing (*US*), overtaking (*Brit*).

adelantar |áthclántár'| *vt* to move forward; (*avanzar*) to advance; (*acelerar*) to speed up; (*AUTO*) to pass (*US*), overtake (*Brit*) ♦ *vi* (*ir delante*) to go ahead; (*progresar*) to improve; (*tb*: **~se** *vr*: *tomar la delantera*) to go forward, advance; **~se a uno** to get ahead of sb; **~se a los deseos de uno** to anticipate sb's wishes.

adelante |áthclán'tc| *ad* forward(s), on-ward(s), ahead ♦ *excl* come in!; **de hoy en** ~ from now on; **más** ~ later on; (*más allá*) further on.

adelanto |áthclán'to| *nm* advance; (*mejora*) improvement; (*progreso*) progress; (*di-nero*) advance; **los ~s de la ciencia** the advances of science.

adelgace |áthclgá'sc| *etc vb* V **adelgazar**.

adelgazar |áthclgàsár'| *vt* to thin (down); (*afilar*) to taper ♦ *vi* to get thin; (*con régi-men*) to slim down, lose weight.

ademán |áthcmán'| *nm* gesture; **ademanes** *nmpl* manners; **en** ~ **de** as if to.

además |áthcmás'| *ad* besides; (*por otra*

parte) moreover; (*también*) also; ~ **de** besides, in addition to.

adentrarse [àḋentrár'se] *vr*: ~ **en** to go into, get inside; (*penetrar*) to penetrate (into).

adentro [àḋen'tro] *ad* inside, in; **mar** ~ out to sea; **tierra** ~ inland ♦ *nmpl*: **dijo para sus** ~**s** he said to himself.

adepto, a [àḋep'to, á] *nm/f* supporter.

aderece [àḋere'se] *etc vb V* **aderezar**.

aderezar [àḋeresár'] *vt* (*ensalada*) to dress; (*comida*) to season.

aderezo [àḋere'so] *nm* dressing; seasoning.

adeudar [àḋeōoḋár'] *vt* to owe; ~**se** *vr* to get into debt; ~ **una suma en una cuenta** to debit an account with a sum.

a.D.g. *abr* (= *a Diós gracias*) D.G. (thanks be to God).

adherirse [àḋerēr'se] *vr*: ~ **a** to adhere to; (*fig*) to follow.

adhesión [àḋesyon'] *nf* adhesion; (*fig*) adherence.

adhesivo, a [àḋesē'ḣo, á] *a* adhesive ♦ *nm* sticker.

adhiera [àḋye'rá] *etc*, **adhiriendo** [àḋēryen'do] *etc vb V* **adherirse**.

adición [àḋēsyon'] *nf* addition.

adicional [àḋēsyonál'] *a* additional; (*INFORM*) add-on.

adicionar [àḋēsyonár'] *vt* to add.

adicto, a [àḋēk'to, á] *a*: ~ **a** (*droga etc*) addicted to; (*dedicado*) devoted to ♦ *nm/f* supporter, follower; (*toxicómano etc*) addict.

adiestrar [àḋyestrár'] *vt* to train, teach; (*conducir*) to guide, lead; ~**se** *vr* to practice (*US*), practise (*Brit*); (*enseñarse*) to train o.s.

adinerado, a [àḋēnerá'ḋo, á] *a* wealthy.

adiós [àḋyos'] *excl* (*para despedirse*) goodbye!; (*al pasar*) hello!

aditivo [àḋētē'ḣo] *nm* additive.

adivinanza [àḋēḣēnán'sá] *nf* riddle.

adivinar [àḋēḣēnár'] *vt* (*profetizar*) to prophesy; (*conjeturar*) to guess.

adivino, a [àḋēḣē'no, á] *nm/f* fortune-teller.

adj *abr* (= *adjunto*) encl.

adjetivo [àḋḣetē'ḣo] *nm* adjective.

adjudicación [àḋḣōōḋēkásyon'] *nf* award; (*COM*) adjudication.

adjudicar [àḋḣōōḋēkár'] *vt* to award; ~**se** *vr*: ~**se algo** to appropriate sth.

adjudique [àḋḣōōḋē'ke] *etc vb V* **adjudicar.**

adjuntar [àḋḣōōntár'] *vt* to attach, enclose.

adjunto, a [àḋḣōōn'to, á] *a* attached, enclosed ♦ *nm/f* assistant.

adminículo [àḋmēnē'kōōlo] *nm* gadget.

administración [àḋmēnēstrásyon'] *nf* administration; (*dirección*) management; ~ **pública** civil service; **A**~ **de Correos**

General Post Office.

administrador, a [àḋmēnēstrà'ḋor', á] *nm/f* administrator; manager(ess).

administrar [àḋmēnēstrár'] *vt* to administer.

administrativo, a [àḋmēnēstrátē'ḣo, á] *a* administrative.

admirable [àḋmērá'ḅle] *a* admirable.

admiración [àḋmērásyon'] *nf* admiration; (*asombro*) wonder; (*LING*) exclamation mark.

admirar [àḋmērár'] *vt* to admire; (*extrañar*) to surprise; ~**se** *vr* to be surprised; **se admiró de saberlo** he was amazed to hear it; **no es de** ~ **que** ... it's not surprising that ...

admisible [àḋmēsē'ḅle] *a* admissible.

admisión [àḋmēsyon'] *nf* admission; (*reconocimiento*) acceptance.

admitir [àḋmētēr'] *vt* to admit; (*aceptar*) to accept; (*dudas*) to leave room for; **esto no admite demora** this must be dealt with immediately.

admón. *abr* (= *administración*) admin.

admonición [àḋmonēsyon'] *nf* warning.

adobar [àḋoḅár'] *vt* (*preparar*) to prepare; (*cocinar*) to season.

adobe [àḋo'ḅe] *nm* adobe, sun-dried brick.

adocenado, a [àḋosená'ḋo, á] *a* (*fam*) mediocre.

adoctrinar [àḋoktrēnár'] *vt* to indoctrinate.

adolecer [àḋoleser'] *vi*: ~ **de** to suffer from.

adolescente [àḋolesen'te] *nm/f* adolescent, teenager ♦ *a* adolescent, teenage.

adolezca [àḋoles'ká] *etc vb V* **adolecer.**

adonde [àḋon'ḋe] *conj* (to) where.

adónde [àḋon'ḋe] *ad* = **dónde.**

adondequiera [àḋonḋekye'rá] *adv* wherever.

adopción [àḋopsyon'] *nf* adoption.

adoptar [àḋoptár'] *vt* to adopt.

adoptivo, a [àḋoptē'ḣo, á] *a* (*padres*) adoptive; (*hijo*) adopted.

adoquín [àḋokēn'] *nm* paving stone.

adorar [àḋorár'] *vt* to adore.

adormecer [àḋormeser'] *vt* to put to sleep; ~**se** *vr* to become sleepy; (*dormirse*) to fall asleep.

adormezca [àḋormes'ká] *etc vb V* **adormecer.**

adormilarse [àḋormēlár'se] *vr* to doze.

adornar [àḋornár'] *vt* to adorn.

adorno [àḋor'no] *nm* adornment; (*decoración*) decoration.

adosado, a [àḋosá'ḋo, á] *a*: **una casa adosada** a semi-detached house.

adquiera [àḋkye'rá] *etc vb V* **adquirir.**

adquirir [àḋkērēr'] *vt* to acquire, obtain.

adquisición [àḋkēsēsyon'] *nf* acquisition; (*compra*) purchase.

adrede [àd̥re'd̥e] *ad* on purpose.
Adriático [àd̥ryá'tēko] *nm*: **el (Mar)** ~ the Adriatic (Sea).
adscribir [àd̥skrēb̥ēr'] *vt* to appoint; **estuvo adscrito al servicio de** ... he was attached to ...
adscrito [àd̥skrē'to] *pp de* **adscribir**.
aduana [àd̥wá'ná] *nf* customs *pl*; *(impuesto)* (customs) duty.
aduanero, a [àd̥wáne'ro, à] *a* customs *cpd* ♦ *nm/f* customs officer.
aducir [àd̥ōōsēr'] *vt* to adduce; *(dar como prueba)* to offer as proof.
adueñarse [àd̥wenyàr'se] *vr*: ~ **de** to take possession of.
adulación [àd̥ōōlásyon'] *nf* flattery.
adular [àd̥ōōlár'] *vt* to flatter.
adulterar [àd̥ōōlterár'] *vt* to adulterate ♦ *vi* to commit adultery.
adulterio [àd̥ōōlte'ryo] *nm* adultery.
adúltero, a [àd̥ōōl'tero, à] *a* adulterous ♦ *nm/f* adulterer/adulteress.
adulto, a [àd̥ōōl'to, à] *a, nm/f* adult.
adusto, a [àd̥ōōs'to, à] *a* stern; *(austero)* austere.
aduzca [àd̥ōōs'ká] *etc vb* V **aducir**.
advenedizo, a [àd̥b̥ened̥ē'so, à] *nm/f* upstart.
advenimiento [àd̥b̥enēmyen'to] *nm* arrival; *(al trono)* accession.
adverbio [àd̥b̥er'b̥yo] *nm* adverb.
adversario, a [àd̥b̥ersà'ryo, à] *nm/f* adversary.
adversidad [àd̥b̥ersēd̥àd̥'] *nf* adversity; *(contratiempo)* setback.
adverso, a [àd̥b̥er'so, à] *a* adverse; *(suerte)* bad.
advertencia [àd̥b̥erten'syá] *nf* warning; *(prefacio)* preface, foreword.
advertir [àd̥b̥ertēr'] *vt (observar)* to notice; *(avisar)*: ~ **a uno de** to warn sb about *o* of.
Adviento [àd̥b̥yen'to] *nm* Advent.
advierta [àd̥b̥yer'tá] *etc*, **advirtiendo** [àd̥b̥ērtyen'd̥o] *etc vb* V **advertir**.
adyacente [àd̥yásen'te] *a* adjacent.
AECE [àe'se] *nf abr* = *Asociación Española de Cooperación Europea*.
aéreo, a [àe'reo, à] *a* aerial; *(tráfico)* air *cpd*.
aerobic [àero'b̥ēk] *nm* aerobics *sg*.
aerodeslizador [àerod̥eslēsàd̥or'], **aerodeslizante** [àerod̥eslēsán'te] *nm* hovercraft.
aeródromo [àero'd̥romo] *nm* airdrome *(US)*, aerodrome *(Brit)*.
aerograma [àerogrà'má] *nm* airmail letter.
aeromozo, a [àeromo'so, à] *nm/f (AM)* air steward(ess).
aeronáutica [àeronà'ōōtēká] *nf* aeronautics *sg*.
aeronave [àeronà'b̥e] *nm* spaceship.

aeroplano [àeroplà'no] *nm* airplane *(US)*, aeroplane *(Brit)*.
aeropuerto [àeropwer'to] *nm* airport.
aerosol [àerosol'] *nm* aerosol, spray.
AES *nm abr* = *Acuerdo Económico y Social*.
a/f *abr* (= *a favor*) in favor.
afabilidad [àfàb̥ēlēd̥àd̥'] *nf* affability, pleasantness.
afable [àfá'b̥le] *a* affable, pleasant.
afamado, a [àfámá'd̥o, à] *a* famous.
afán [àfán'] *nm* hard work; *(deseo)* desire; **con** ~ keenly.
afanar [àfánár'] *vt* to harass; *(fam)* to swipe; ~**se** *vr*: ~**se por** to strive to.
afanoso, a [àfáno'so, à] *a (trabajo)* hard; *(trabajador)* industrious.
AFE [à'fe] *nf abr* (= *Asociación de Futbolistas Españoles*) ≈ F.A.
afear [àfeár'] *vt* to disfigure.
afección [àfeksyon'] *nf* affection; *(MED)* disease.
afectación [àfektásyon'] *nf* affectation.
afectado, a [àfektá'd̥o, à] *a* affected.
afectar [àfektár'] *vt* to affect, have an effect on; *(AM: dañar)* to hurt; **por lo que afecta a esto** as far as this is concerned.
afectísimo, a [àfektē'sēmo, à] *a* affectionate; ~ **suyo** yours truly.
afectivo, a [àfektē'b̥o, à] *a* affective.
afecto, a [àfek'to, à] *a*: ~ **a** fond of; *(JUR)* subject to ♦ *nm* affection; **tenerle** ~ **a uno** to be fond of sb.
afectuoso, a [àfektwo'so, à] *a* affectionate.
afeitar [àfeētár'] *vt* to shave; ~**se** *vr* to shave.
afeminado, a [àfemēná'd̥o, à] *a* effeminate.
aferrado, a [àferrà'd̥o, à] *a* stubborn.
aferrar [àferrár'] *vt* to moor; *(fig)* to grasp ♦ *vi* to moor; ~**se** *vr (agarrarse)* to cling on; ~**se a un principio** to stick to a principle; ~**se a una esperanza** to cling to a hope.
affmo., a. *abr* (= *afectísimo, a*) Yours.
Afganistán [àfgánēstán'] *nm* Afghanistan.
afgano, a [àfgá'no, à] *a, nm/f* Afghan.
afiance [àfyàn'se] *etc vb* V **afianzar**.
afianzamiento [àfyànsámyen'to] *nm* strengthening; security.
afianzar [àfyànsár'] *vt* to strengthen, secure; ~**se** *vr* to steady o.s.; *(establecerse)* to become established.
afición [àfēsyon'] *nf*: ~ **a** fondness *o* liking for; **la** ~ the fans *pl*; **pinto por** ~ I paint as a hobby.
aficionado, a [àfēsyoná'd̥o, à] *a* keen, enthusiastic; *(no profesional)* amateur ♦ *nm/f* enthusiast, fan; amateur.
aficionar [àfēsyonár'] *vt*: ~ **a uno a algo** to make sb like sth; ~**se** *vr*: ~**se a algo** to grow fond of sth.
afiche [àfē'tche] *nm (AM)* poster.

afierre |àfyc'rrc| *etc vb V* **aferrar.**

afilado, a |àfēlá'tho, à| *a* sharp.

afilador |àfēlàthor'| *nm* (*persona*) knife grinder.

afilalápices |àfēlàlá'pēscs| *nm inv* pencil sharpener.

afilar |àfēlár'| *vt* to sharpen; ~se *vr* (*cara*) to grow thin.

afiliación |àfēlyásyon'| *nf* (*de sindicatos*) membership.

afiliado, a |àfēlyà'tho, à| *a* subsidiary ♦ *nm/f* affiliate.

afiliarse |àfēlyàr'sc| *vr* to affiliate.

afín |àfēn'| *a* (*parecido*) similar; (*conexo*) related.

afinar |àfēnár'| *vt* (*TEC*) to refine; (*MUS*) to tune ♦ *vi* to play/sing in tune.

afincarse |àfēnkàr'sc| *vr* to settle.

afinidad |àfēnēthàth'| *nf* affinity; (*parentesco*) relationship; **por** ~ by marriage.

afirmación |àfērmásyon'| *nf* affirmation.

afirmar |àfērmár'| *vt* to affirm, state; (*sostener*) to strengthen; ~se *vr* (*recuperar el equilibrio*) to steady o.s.; ~se **en lo dicho** to stand by what one has said.

afirmativo, a |àfērmátē'ho, à| *a* affirmative.

aflicción |àflēksyon'| *nf* affliction; (*dolor*) grief.

afligir |àflēhēr'| *vt* to afflict; (*apenar*) to distress; ~se *vr*: ~se (**por** *o* **con** *o* **de**) to grieve (about *o* at); **no te aflijas tanto** you must not let it affect you like this.

aflija |àflē'hà| *etc vb V* **afligir.**

aflojar |àflohár'| *vt* to slacken; (*desatar*) to loosen, undo; (*relajar*) to relax ♦ *vi* (*amainar*) to drop; (*bajar*) to go down; ~se *vr* to relax.

aflorar |àflorár'| *vi* (*GEO, fig*) to come to the surface, emerge.

afluencia |àflōōen'syà| *nf* flow.

afluente |àflōōen'tc| *a* flowing ♦ *nm* (*GEO*) tributary.

afluir |àflōōēr'| *vi* to flow.

afluya |àflōō'yà| *etc*, **afluyendo** |àflōōycn'do| *etc vb V* **afluir.**

afmo., a. *abr* (= *afectísimo, a suyo, a*) Yours.

afónico, a |àfo'nēko, à| *a*: **estar** ~ to have a sore throat; to have lost one's voice.

aforar |àforár'| *vt* (*TEC*) to gauge; (*fig*) to value.

aforo |àfo'ro| *nm* (*TEC*) gauging; (*de teatro etc*) capacity; **el teatro tiene un** ~ **de 2,000** the theater can seat 2,000.

afortunado, a |àfortōōná'tho, à| *a* fortunate, lucky.

afrancesado, a |àfrànsesá'tho, à| *a* francophile.

afrenta |àfren'tà| *nf* affront, insult; (*deshonra*) dishonor (*US*), dishonour (*Brit*), shame.

afrentoso, a |àfrcnto'so, à| *a* insulting; shameful.

África |à'frēkà| *nf* Africa; ~ **del Sur** South Africa.

africano, a |àfrēkà'no, à| *a, nm/f* African.

afrontar |àfrontár'| *vt* to confront; (*poner cara a cara*) to bring face to face.

afuera |àfwc'rà| *ad* out, outside; **por** ~ on the outside; ~s *nfpl* outskirts.

ag., ag.º *abr* (= *agosto*) Aug.

agachar |àgàtchár'| *vt* to bend, bow; ~se *vr* to stoop, bend.

agalla |àgà'yà| *nf* (*ZOOL*) gill; ~s *nfpl* (*MED*) tonsillitis *sg*; (*ANAT*) tonsils; **tener** ~s (*fam*) to have guts.

agarradera |àgàrráthc'rà| *nf* (*AM*), **agarradero** |àgàrráthc'ro| *nm* handle; ~s *npl* pull *sg*, influence *sg*.

agarrado, a |àgàrrá'tho, à| *a* mean, stingy.

agarrar |àgàrrár'| *vt* to grasp, grab; (*AM*) to take, catch ♦ *vi* (*planta*) to take root; ~se *vr* to hold on (tightly); (*meterse uno con otro*) to grapple (with each other); **agarrársela con uno** (*AM*) to pick on sb.

agarrotar |àgàrrotár'| *vt* (*lío*) to tie tightly; (*persona*) to squeeze tightly; (*reo*) to garrotte; ~se *vr* (*motor*) to seize up; (*MED*) to stiffen.

agasajar |àgàsàhár'| *vt* to treat well, fête.

agazapar |àgàsàpár'| *vt* (*coger*) to grab hold of; ~se *vr* (*agacharse*) to crouch down.

agencia |àhen'syà| *nf* agency; ~ **de créditos/publicidad/viajes** credit/advertising/travel agency; ~ **inmobiliaria** real estate office (*US*), estate agent's (office) (*Brit*); ~ **de matrimonios** ≈ dating service (*US*), marriage bureau (*Brit*).

agenciar |àhcnsyàr'| *vt* to bring about; ~se *vr* to look after o.s.; ~se **algo** to get hold of sth.

agenda |àhcn'dà| *nf* diary; ~ **telefónica** telephone directory.

agente |àhen'tc| *nm* agent; (*de policía*) policeman; ~ **femenino** policewoman; ~ **acreditado** (*COM*) accredited agent; ~ **de bolsa** stockbroker; ~ **inmobiliario** realtor (*US*), estate agent (*Brit*); ~ **de negocios** (*COM*) business agent; ~ **de seguros** insurance broker; ~ **de viajes** travel agent.

ágil |à'hēl| *a* agile, nimble.

agilidad |àhēlēthàth'| *nf* agility, nimbleness.

agitación |àhētàsyon'| *nf* (*de mano etc*) shaking, waving; (*de líquido etc*) stirring; agitation.

agitar |àhētár'| *vt* to wave, shake; (*líquido*) to stir; (*fig*) to stir up, excite; ~se *vr* to get excited; (*inquietarse*) to get worried *o* upset.

aglomeración |àglomerásyon'| *nf*: ~ **de tráfico/gente** traffic jam/mass of people.

aglomerar |àglomerár'| *vt*, ~se *vr* to crowd

together.

agnóstico, a [àgno'stĕko, à] *a, nm/f* agnostic.

agobiante [àgobyán'te] *a (calor)* oppressive.

agobiar [àgobyár'] *vt* to weigh down; *(oprimir)* to oppress; *(cargar)* to burden; **sentirse agobiado por** to be overwhelmed by.

agobio [àgo'byo] *nm (peso)* burden; *(fig)* oppressiveness.

agolpamiento [àgolpámyen'to] *nm* crowd.

agolparse [àgolpàr'se] *vr* to crowd together.

agonía [àgonē'á] *nf* death throes *pl*; *(fig)* agony, anguish.

agonice [àgonē'se] *etc vb* V **agonizar**.

agonizante [àgonēsàn'te] *a* dying.

agonizar [àgonēsàr'] *vi (tb: estar agonizando)* to be dying.

agorero, a [àgore'ro, à] *a* ominous ♦ *nm/f* soothsayer; **ave agorera** bird of ill omen.

agostar [àgostár'] *vt (quemar)* to parch; *(fig)* to wither.

agosto [àgo'sto] *nm* August; *(fig)* harvest; **hacer su ~** to make one's fortune.

agotado, a [àgotá'tho, à] *a (persona)* exhausted; *(acabado)* finished; *(COM)* sold out; (: *libros)* out of print; *(pila)* dead.

agotador, a [àgotáthor', à] *a* exhausting.

agotamiento [àgotámyen'to] *nm* exhaustion.

agotar [àgotár'] *vt* to exhaust; *(consumir)* to drain; *(recursos)* to use up, deplete; **~se** *vr* to be exhausted; *(acabarse)* to run out; *(libro)* to go out of print.

agraciado, a [àgràsyá'tho, à] *a (atractivo)* attractive; *(en sorteo etc)* lucky.

agraciar [àgràsyár'] *vt (JUR)* to pardon; *(con premio)* to reward; *(hacer más atractivo)* to make more attractive.

agradable [àgràthá'ble] *a* pleasant, nice.

agradar [àgràthár'] *vt, vi* to please; **~se** *vr* to like each other.

agradecer [àgràtheser'] *vt* to thank; *(favor etc)* to be grateful for; **le agradecería me enviara ...** I would be grateful if you would send me ...; **~se** *vr*: **¡se agradece!** much obliged!

agradecido, a [àgràthesē'tho, à] *a* grateful; **¡muy ~!** thanks a lot!

agradecimiento [àgràthesēmyen'to] *nm* thanks *pl*; gratitude.

agradezca [àgràthes'kà] *etc vb* V **agradecer**.

agrado [àgrá'tho] *nm*: **ser de tu** *etc* **~** to be to your *etc* liking.

agrandar [àgràndár'] *vt* to enlarge; *(fig)* to exaggerate; **~se** *vr* to get bigger.

agrario, a [àgrá'ryo, à] *a* agrarian, land *cpd*; *(política)* agricultural, farming.

agravante [àgràbàn'te] *a* aggravating ♦ *nf*

complication; **con la ~ de que ...** with the further difficulty that ...

agravar [àgràbàr'] *vt (pesar sobre)* to make heavier; *(irritar)* to aggravate; **~se** *vr* to worsen, get worse.

agraviar [àgràbyár'] *vt* to offend; *(ser injusto con)* to wrong; **~se** *vr* to take offense.

agravio [àgrá'byo] *nm* offense *(US)*, offence *(Brit)*; wrong; *(JUR)* grievance.

agraz [àgràs'] *nm (uva)* sour grape; **en ~** *(fig)* immature.

agredir [àgrethēr'] *vt* to attack.

agregado [àgregá'tho] *nm* aggregate; *(persona)* attaché; *(profesor)* assistant professor.

agregar [àgregár'] *vt* to gather; *(añadir)* to add; *(persona)* to appoint.

agregue [àgre'ge] *etc vb* V **agregar**.

agresión [àgresyon'] *nf* aggression; *(ataque)* attack.

agresivo, a [àgresē'bo, à] *a* aggressive.

agreste [àgre'ste] *a (rural)* rural; *(fig)* rough.

agriar [àgryár'] *vt (fig)* to (turn) sour; **~se** *vr* to turn sour.

agrícola [àgrē'kolà] *a* farming *cpd*, agricultural.

agricultor, a [àgrēkōōltor', à] *nm/f* farmer.

agricultura [àgrēkōōltōō'rà] *nf* agriculture, farming.

agridulce [àgrēthōōl'se] *a* bittersweet; *(CULIN)* sweet and sour.

agrietarse [àgryetár'se] *vr* to crack; *(la piel)* to chap.

agrimensor, a [àgrēmensor', à] *nm/f* surveyor.

agrio, a [àg'ryo, à] *a* bitter.

agro [á'gro] *nm* farming, agriculture.

agronomía [àgronomē'á] *nf* agronomy, agriculture.

agrónomo, a [àgro'nomo, à] *nm/f* agronomist, agricultural expert.

agropecuario, a [àgropekwá'ryo, à] *a* farming *cpd*, agricultural.

agrupación [àgrōōpàsyon'] *nf* group; *(acto)* grouping.

agrupar [àgrōōpár'] *vt* to group; *(INFORM)* to block; **~se** *vr (POL)* to form a group; *(juntarse)* to gather.

agua [á'gwà] *nf* water; *(NAUT)* wake; *(ARQ)* slope of a roof; **~s** *nfpl (de joya)* water *sg*, sparkle *sg*; *(MED)* water *sg*, urine *sg*; *(NAUT)* waters; **~s abajo/arriba** downstream/upstream; **~ bendita/destilada/potable** holy/distilled/drinking water; **~ caliente** hot water; **~ corriente** running water; **~ de colonia** eau de cologne; **~ mineral (con/sin gas)** carbonated/non-carbonated mineral water; **~s jurisdiccionales** territorial waters; **~s mayores**

excrement *sg*; ~ **pasada no mueve molino** it's no use crying over spilt milk; **estar con el** ~ **al cuello** to be up to one's neck; **venir como** ~ **de mayo** to be a godsend.

aguacate |ȧgwȧkȧ'tc| *nm* avocado.

aguacero |ȧgwȧsc'ro| *nm* (heavy) shower, downpour.

aguachirle |ȧgwȧtchēr'lc| *nm* (*bebida*) dishwater.

aguado, a |ȧgwȧ'ƚ̣ho, ȧ| *a* watery, watered down ♦ *nf* (*AGR*) watering place; (*NAUT*) water supply; (*ARTE*) watercolor (*US*), watercolour (*Brit*).

aguafiestas |ȧgwȧfyc'stȧs| *nm/f inv* spoilsport.

aguafuerte |ȧgwȧfwcr'tc| *nf* etching.

aguamar |ȧgwȧmȧr'| *nm* jellyfish.

aguanieve |ȧgwȧnyc'ƕc| *nf* sleet.

aguantable |ȧgwȧntȧ'ƕlc| *a* bearable, tolerable.

aguantar |ȧgwȧntȧr'| *vt* to bear, put up with; (*sostener*) to hold up ♦ *vi* to last; ~**se** *vr* to restrain o.s.; **no sé cómo aguanta** I don't know how he can take it.

aguante |ȧgwȧn'tc| *nm* (*paciencia*) patience; (*resistencia*) endurance; (*DEPORTE*) stamina.

aguar |ȧgwȧr'| *vt* to water down; (*fig*): ~ **la fiesta a uno** to spoil sb's fun.

aguardar |ȧgwȧrƚ̣hȧr'| *vt* to wait for.

aguardentoso, a |ȧgwȧrƚ̣hcnto'so, ȧ| *a* (*pey: voz*) husky, gruff.

aguardiente |ȧgwȧrƚ̣hycn'tc| *nm* brandy, liquor.

aguarrás |ȧgwȧrrȧs'| *nm* turpentine.

aguce |ȧgōō'sc| *etc vb V* **aguzar**.

agudeza |ȧgōōƚ̣hc'sȧ| *nf* sharpness; (*ingenio*) wit.

agudice |ȧgōōƚ̣hc'sc| *etc vb V* **agudizar**.

agudizar |ȧgōōƚ̣hcsȧr'| *vt* to sharpen; (*crisis*) to make worse; ~**se** *vr* to worsen, deteriorate.

agudo, a |ȧgōō'ƚ̣ho, ȧ| *a* sharp; (*voz*) highpitched, piercing; (*dolor, enfermedad*) acute.

agüe |ȧ'gwc| *etc vb V* **aguar**.

agüero |ȧgwc'ro| *nm*: **buen/mal** ~ good/bad omen; **ser de buen** ~ to augur well; **pájaro de mal** ~ bird of ill omen.

aguerrido, a |ȧgcrrē'ƚ̣ho, ȧ| hardened; (*fig*) experienced.

aguijar |ȧgēhȧr'| *vt* to goad; (*incitar*) to urge on ♦ *vi* to hurry along.

aguijón |ȧgēhon'| *nm* (*ZOOL*) stinger (*US*), sting (*Brit*); (*fig*) spur.

aguijonear |ȧgēhoncȧr'| *vt* = **aguijar**.

águila |ȧ'gēlȧ| *nf* eagle; (*fig*) genius.

aguileño, a |ȧgēlc'nyo, ȧ| *a* (*nariz*) aquiline; (*rostro*) sharp-featured.

aguinaldo |ȧgēnȧl'do| *nm* Christmas box.

aguja |ȧgōō'hȧ| *nf* needle; (*de reloj*) hand;

(*ARQ*) spire; (*TEC*) firing-pin; ~**s** *nfpl* (*ZOOL*) ribs; (*FERRO*) points.

agujerear |ȧgōōhcrcȧr'| *vt* to make holes in; (*penetrar*) to pierce.

agujero |ȧgōōhc'ro| *nm* hole.

agujetas |ȧgōōhc'tȧs| *nfpl* stitch *sg*; (*rigidez*) stiffness *sg*.

aguzar |ȧgōōsȧr'| *vt* to sharpen; (*fig*) to incite; ~ **el oido** to prick up one's ears.

aherrumbrarse |ȧcrrōōmbrȧr'sc| *vr* to get rusty.

ahí |ȧē'| *ad* there; (*allá*) over there; **de** ~ **que** so that, with the result that; ~ **llega** here he comes; **por** ~ (*dirección*) that way; **¡hasta** ~ **hemos llegado!** so it has come to this!; **¡**~ **va!** (*objeto*) here it comes!; (*individuo*) there he goes!; ~ **donde le ve** as sure as he's standing there.

ahijado, a |ȧēhȧ'ƚ̣ho, ȧ| *nm/f* godson/ daughter.

ahijar |ȧēhȧr'| *vt*: ~ **algo a uno** (*fig*) to attribute sth to sb.

ahínco |ȧēn'ko| *nm* earnestness; **con** ~ eagerly.

ahíto, a |ȧē'to, ȧ| *a*: **estoy** ~ I'm full up.

ahogado, a |ȧogȧ'ƚ̣ho, ȧ| *a* (*en agua*) drowned; (*emoción*) pent-up; (*grito*) muffled.

ahogar |ȧogȧr'| *vt* (*en agua*) to drown; (*asfixiar*) to suffocate, smother; (*fuego*) to put out; ~**se** *vr* (*en agua*) to drown; (*por asfixia*) to suffocate.

ahogo |ȧo'go| *nm* (*MED*) breathlessness; (*fig*) distress; (*problema económico*) financial difficulty.

ahogue |ȧo'gc| *etc vb V* **ahogar**.

ahondar |ȧondȧr'| *vt* to deepen, make deeper; (*fig*) to go deeply into ♦ *vi*: ~ **en** to go deeply into.

ahora |ȧo'rȧ| *ad* now; (*hace poco*) a moment ago, just now; (*dentro de poco*) in a moment; ~ **voy** I'm coming; ~ **mismo** right now; ~ **bien** now then; **por** ~ for the present.

ahorcado, a |ȧorkȧ'ƚ̣ho, ȧ| *nm/f* hanged person.

ahorcar |ȧorkȧr'| *vt* to hang; ~**se** *vr* to hang o.s.

ahorita |ȧorē'tȧ| *ad* (*fam*) right now.

ahorque |ȧor'kc| *etc vb V* **ahorcar**.

ahorrar |ȧorrȧr'| *vt* (*dinero*) to save; (*esfuerzos*) to save, avoid; ~**se** *vr*: ~**se molestias** to save o.s. trouble.

ahorrativo, a |ȧorrȧtē'ƕo, ȧ| *a* thrifty.

ahorro |ȧo'rro| *nm* (*acto*) saving; (*frugalidad*) thrift; ~**s** *nmpl* savings.

ahuecar |ȧwckȧr'| *vt* to hollow (out); (*voz*) to deepen ♦ *vi*: **¡ahueca!** (*fam*) beat it! (*fam*); ~**se** *vr* to give o.s. airs.

ahueque |ȧwc'kc| *etc vb V* **ahuecar**.

ahumar |ȧōōmȧr'| *vt* to smoke, cure; (*lle-*

nar de humo) to fill with smoke ♦ *vi* to smoke; ~**se** *vr* to fill with smoke.

ahuyentar [àōoyentár'] *vt* to drive off, frighten off; (*fig*) to dispel.

AI *nf abr* (= *Amnistía Internacional*) Amnesty International.

AINS *nf abr* (*Esp*) = *Administración Institucional Nacional de Sanidad*.

airado, a [àērá'tho, á] *a* angry.

airar [àērár'] *vt* to anger; ~**se** *vr* to get angry.

aire [á'ēre] *nm* air; (*viento*) wind; (*corriente*) draft (*US*), draught (*Brit*); (*MUS*) tune; ~**s** *nmpl*: **darse** ~**s** to give o.s. airs; **al** ~ **libre** in the open air; ~ **acondicionado** air conditioning; **tener** ~ **de** to look like; **estar de buen/mal** ~ to be in a good/bad mood; **estar en el** ~ (*RADIO*) to be on the air; (*fig*) to be up in the air.

airear [àērèár'] *vt* to ventilate; (*fig: asunto*) to air; ~**se** *vr* to take the air.

airoso, a [àēro'so, á] *a* windy; drafty (*US*), draughty (*Brit*); (*fig*) graceful.

aislado, a [àēslá'tho, á] *a* (*remoto*) isolated; (*incomunicado*) cut off; (*ELEC*) insulated.

aislante [àēslán'te] *nm* (*ELEC*) insulator.

aislar [àēslár'] *vt* to isolate; (*ELEC*) to insulate; ~**se** *vr* to cut o.s. off.

ajar [àhár'] *vt* to spoil; (*fig*) to abuse; ~**se** *vr* to get crumpled; (*fig: piel*) to get wrinkled.

ajardinado, a [àhárthēná'tho, á] *a* landscaped.

ajedrez [àhethres'] *nm* chess.

ajenjo [àhen'ho] *nm* (*bebida*) absinth(e).

ajeno, a [àhe'no, á] *a* (*que pertenece a otro*) somebody else's; ~ **a** foreign to; ~ **de** free from, devoid of; **por razones ajenas a nuestra voluntad** for reasons beyond our control.

ajetreado, a [àhetreá'tho, á] *a* busy.

ajetrearse [àhetreár'se] *vr* (*atarearse*) to bustle about; (*fatigarse*) to tire o.s. out.

ajetreo [àhetre'o] *nm* bustle.

ají [àhē'] *nm* chili, red pepper; (*salsa*) chili sauce.

ajilimoje [àhēlēmo'he] *nm* sauce of garlic and pepper; ~**s** *nmpl* (*fam*) odds and ends.

ajo [á'ho] *nm* garlic; ~ **porro** o **puerro** leek; (**tieso**) **como un** ~ (*fam*) snobbish; **estar en el** ~ to be mixed up in it.

ajorca [àhor'ká] *nf* bracelet.

ajuar [àhwár'] *nm* household furnishings *pl*; (*de novia*) trousseau; (*de niño*) layette.

ajustado, a [àhōostá'tho, á] *a* (*tornillo*) tight; (*cálculo*) right; (*ropa*) tight(-fitting); (*DEPORTE: resultado*) close.

ajustar [àhōostár'] *vt* (*adaptar*) to adjust; (*encajar*) to fit; (*TEC*) to engage; (*TIP*) to make up; (*apretar*) to tighten; (*concertar*) to agree (on); (*reconciliar*) to reconcile;

(*cuenta*) to settle ♦ *vi* to fit.

ajuste [àhōō'ste] *nm* adjustment; (*COSTURA*) fitting; (*acuerdo*) compromise; (*de cuenta*) settlement; (*INFORM*) patch.

al [àl] = **a** + **el**; *V* **a**.

ala [á'lá] *nf* wing; (*de sombrero*) brim; (*futbolista*) wing; **andar con el** ~ **caída** to be downcast; **cortar las** ~**s a uno** to clip sb's wings; **dar** ~ **a uno** to encourage sb.

alabanza [àlàhán'sà] *nf* praise.

alabar [àlàhár'] *vt* to praise.

alacena [àlàse'ná] *nf* closet (*US*), cupboard (*Brit*).

alacrán [àlákrán'] *nm* scorpion.

ALADI [àlá'thē] *nf abr* = *Asociación Latinoamericana de Integración*.

alado, a [àlá'tho, á] *a* winged.

alambicado, a [àlàmbēká'tho, á] *a* distilled; (*fig*) affected.

alambicar [àlàmbēkár'] *vt* to distil.

alambique [àlàmbē'ke] *etc vb V* **alambicar** ♦ *nm* still.

alambrada [àlàmbrá'thá] *nf*, **alambrado** [àlàmbrá'tho] *nm* wire fence; (*red*) wire netting.

alambre [àlám'bre] *nm* wire; ~ **de púas** barbed wire.

alambrista [àlàmbrē'stá] *nm/f* tightrope walker.

alameda [àlàme'thá] *nf* (*plantío*) poplar grove; (*lugar de paseo*) avenue, boulevard.

álamo [á'lámo] *nm* poplar; ~ **temblón** aspen.

alano [álá'no] *nm* mastiff.

alarde [àlár'the] *nm* show, display; **hacer** ~ **de** to boast of.

alardear [àlártheár'] *vi* to boast.

alargar [àlárgár'] *vt* to lengthen, extend; (*paso*) to hasten; (*brazo*) to stretch out; (*cuerda*) to pay out; (*conversación*) to prolong; ~**se** *vr* to get longer.

alargue [àlár'ge] *etc vb V* **alargar**.

alarido [àlárē'tho] *nm* shriek.

alarma [àlár'má] *nf* alarm; **voz de** ~ warning note; **dar la** ~ to raise the alarm.

alarmante [àlàrmán'te] *a* alarming.

alavés, esa [àlàhes', e'sá] *a* of Álava ♦ *nm/f* native o inhabitant of Álava.

alazán [àlásán'] *nm* sorrel.

alba [àl'há] *nf* dawn.

albacea [àlháse'á] *nm/f* executor/executrix.

albaceteño, a [àlhásete'nyo, á] *a* of Albacete ♦ *nm/f* native o inhabitant of Albacete.

albahaca [àlhá'ká] *nf* (*BOT*) basil.

Albania [àlhá'nyá] *nf* Albania.

albañal [àlhányál'] *nm* drain, sewer.

albañil [àlhányēl'] *nm* bricklayer; (*cantero*) mason.

albarán [àlhárán'] *nm* (*COM*) invoice.

albarda [àlhár'thá] *nf* packsaddle.

albaricoque [àlhárēko'ke] *nm* apricot.

albedrío [ålheťhrē'o] *nm*: **libre** ~ free will.

alberca [ålber'ká] *nf* reservoir; (*AM*) swimming pool.

albergar [ålhergár'] *vt* to shelter; (*esperanza*) to cherish; **~se** *vr* (*refugiarse*) to shelter; (*alojarse*) to lodge.

albergue [ålher'ge] *etc vb* V **albergar** ♦ *nm* shelter, refuge; ~ **de juventud** youth hostel.

albis [ål'hēs] *adv*: **quedarse en** ~ not to have a clue.

albóndiga [ålhon'dēgá] *nf* meatball.

albor [ålhor'] *nm* whiteness; (*amanecer*) dawn.

alborada [ålhorá'ťhá] *nf* dawn; (*diana*) reveille.

alborear [ålhoreár'] *vi* to dawn.

albornoz [ålhornos'] *nm* (*para el baño*) bathrobe.

alborotadizo, a [ålhorotáťhē'so, á] *a* excitable.

alborotar [ålhorotár'] *vi* to make a racket ♦ *vt* to agitate, stir up; **~se** *vr* to get excited; (*mar*) to get rough.

alboroto [ålhoro'to] *nm* row, uproar.

alboroce [ålhoro'se] *etc vb* V **alborozar**.

alborozar [ålhorosár'] *vt* to gladden; **~se** *vr* to rejoice, be overjoyed.

alborozo [ålhoro'so] *nm* joy.

albricias [ålhrē'syás] *nfpl*; ¡~! good news!

álbum, *pl* **álbums** o **álbumes** [ål'hōōm] *nm* album.

albumen [ålhōō'men] *nm* egg white, albumen.

alcachofa [ålkátcho'fá] *nf* (globe) artichoke; (*TIP*) (typewriter) element; (*de ducha*) shower head.

alcahueta [ålkáwe'tá] *nf* procuress.

alcahuete [ålkáwe'te] *nm* pimp.

alcalde, esa [ålkál'de, ålkálde'sá] *nm/f* mayor(ess).

alcaldía [ålkáldē'á] *nf* mayoralty; (*lugar*) mayor's office.

álcali [ål'kálē] *nm* (*QUÍMICA*) alkali.

alcance [ålkán'se] *etc vb* V **alcanzar** ♦ *nm* (*MIL, RADIO*) range; (*fig*) scope; (*COM*) adverse balance, deficit; **estar al/fuera del** ~ **de uno** to be within/beyond one's reach; (*fig*) to be within one's powers/over one's head; **de gran** ~ (*MIL*) long-range; (*fig*) far-reaching.

alcancía [ålkánsē'á] *nf* money box.

alcanfor [ålkánfor'] *nm* camphor.

alcantarilla [ålkántárē'yá] *nf* (*de aguas cloacales*) sewer; (*en la calle*) gutter.

alcanzar [ålkánsár'] *vt* (*algo: con la mano, el pie*) to reach; (*alguien: en el camino etc*) to catch up (with); (*autobús*) to catch; (*suj: bala*) to hit, strike ♦ *vi* (*ser suficiente*) to be enough; ~ **a hacer** to manage to do.

alcaparra [ålkápá'rrá] *nf* (*BOT*) caper.

alcatraz [ålkátrás'] *nm* pelican.

alcázar [ålká'sár] *nm* fortress; (*NAUT*) quarter-deck.

alce [ål'se] *etc vb* V **alzar**.

alcista [ålsē'stá] *a* (*COM, ECON*): **mercado** ~ bull market; **la tendencia** ~ the upward trend ♦ *nm* speculator.

alcoba [ålko'há] *nf* bedroom.

alcohol [ålkol'] *nm* alcohol; **no bebe** ~ he doesn't drink (alcohol).

alcoholice [ålkolē'se] *etc vb* V **alcoholizarse**.

alcohólico, a [ålko'lēko, á] *a, nm/f* alcoholic.

alcoholímetro [ålkolē'metro] *nm* Breathalyzer ®.

alcoholismo [ålkolēs'mo] *nm* alcoholism.

alcoholizarse [ålkolēsár'se] *vr* to become an alcoholic.

alcornoque [ålkorno'ke] *nm* cork tree; (*fam*) idiot.

alcotana [ålkotá'ná] *nf* pickaxe; (*DEPORTE*) ice-axe.

alcurnia [ålkōōr'nyá] *nf* lineage.

alcuzas [ålkōō'sás] *nfpl* (*AM*) cruet *sg*.

aldaba [åldá'há] *nf* (door) knocker.

aldea [ålde'á] *nf* village.

aldeano, a [åldeá'no, á] *a* village *cpd* ♦ *nm/f* villager.

ale [á'le] *excl* come on!, let's go!

aleación [åleásyon'] *nf* alloy.

aleatorio, a [åleáto'ryo, á] *a* random, contingent; **acceso** ~ (*INFORM*) random access.

aleccionador, a [åleksyonáťhor', á] *a* instructive.

aleccionar [åleksyonár'] *vt* to instruct; (*adiestrar*) to train.

aledaño, a [åleťhá'nyo, á] *a*: ~ **a** bordering on ♦ *nmpl*: **~s** outskirts.

alegación [ålegásyon'] *nf* allegation.

alegar [ålegár'] *vt* (*dificultad etc*) to plead; (*JUR*) to allege ♦ *vi* (*AM*) to argue; ~ **que** ... to give as an excuse that ...

alegato [ålegá'to] *nm* (*JUR*) allegation; (*escrito*) indictment; (*declaración*) statement; (*AM*) argument.

alegoría [ålegorē'á] *nf* allegory.

alegrar [ålegrár'] *vt* (*causar alegría*) to cheer (up); (*fuego*) to poke; (*fiesta*) to liven up; **~se** *vr* (*fam*) to get merry o tight; **~se de** to be glad about.

alegre [ålc'gre] *a* happy, cheerful; (*fam*) merry, tipsy; (*licencioso*) risqué, blue.

alegría [ålegrē'á] *nf* happiness; merriment; ~ **vital** joie de vivre.

alegrón [ålegron'] *nm* (*fig*) sudden joy.

alegue [ålc'ge] *etc vb* V **alegar**.

alejamiento [ålchámyen'to] *nm* removal; (*distancia*) remoteness.

alejar |àlchàr'| *vt* to move away, remove; (*fig*) to estrange; ~**se** *vr* to move away.

alelado, a |àlclà'tɦo. à| *a* (*bobo*) foolish.

alelar |àlclàr'| *vt* to bewilder.

aleluya |àlcloo'yà| *nm* (*canto*) hallelujah.

alemán, ana |àlcmàn'. à'nà| *a*, *nm/f* German ♦ *nm* (*lengua*) German.

Alemania |àlcmà'nyà| *nf* Germany; ~ **Occidental/Oriental** West/East Germany.

alentador, a |àlcntàɦor'. à| *a* encouraging.

alentar |àlcntàr'| *vt* to encourage.

alergia |àlcr'hyà| *nf* allergy.

alero |àlc'ro| *nm* (*de tejado*) eaves *pl*; (*de foca*, DEPORTE) flipper; (AUTO) mudguard, fender (*US*).

alerta |àlcr'tà| *a inv*, *nm* alert.

aleta |àlc'tà| *nf* (*de pez*) fin; (*de ave*) wing; (*de coche*) mudguard.

aletargar |àlctàrgàr'| *vt* to make drowsy; (*entumecer*) to make numb; ~**se** *vr* to grow drowsy; to become numb.

aletargue |àlctàr'ge| *etc vb* V **aletargar**.

aletear |àlctcàr'| *vi* to flutter; (*ave*) to flap its wings; (*individuo*) to wave one's arms.

alevín |àlcɦèn'| *nm*, **alevino** |àlcɦè'no| *nm* fry, young fish.

alevosía |àlcɦosè'à| *nf* treachery.

alfabetización |àlfàɦctèsàsyon'| *nf*: **campaña de** ~ literacy campaign.

alfabeto |àlfàɦc'to| *nm* alphabet.

alfajor |àlfàɦor'| *nm* (*Esp: polvorón*) cookie eaten at Christmas time.

alfalfa |àlfàl'fà| *nf* alfalfa, lucerne.

alfaque |àlfà'kc| *nm* (NAUT) bar, sandbank.

alfar |àlfàr'| *nm* (*taller*) potter's workshop; (*arcilla*) clay.

alfarería |àlfàrcrè'à| *nf* pottery; (*tienda*) pottery shop.

alfarero |àlfàrc'ro| *nm* potter.

alféizar |àlfc'èsàr| *nm* window-sill.

alférez |àlfc'rcs| *nm* (MIL) second lieutenant; (NAUT) ensign.

alfil |àlfèl'| *nm* (AJEDREZ) bishop.

alfiler |àlfèlcr'| *nm* pin; (*broche*) clip; (*pinza*) clothespin (*US*), clothes peg (*Brit*); **prendido con** ~**es** shaky.

alfiletero |àlfèlctc'ro| *nm* needle case.

alfombra |àlfom'bràl| *nf* carpet; (*más pequeña*) rug.

alfombrar |àlfombràr'| *vt* to carpet.

alfombrilla |àlfombrè'yà| *nf* rug, mat.

alforja |àlfor'hà| *nf* saddlebag.

alforza |àlfor'sà| *nf* pleat.

algarabía |àlgàràɦè'à| *nf* (*fam*) gibberish; (*griterío*) hullabaloo.

algarada |àlgàrà'ɦà| *nf* outcry; **hacer** *o* **levantar una** ~ to kick up a tremendous fuss.

Algarbe |àlgàr'ɦc| *nm*: **el** ~ the Algarve.

algarrobo |àlgàrro'ɦo| *nm* carob tree.

algas |àl'gàs| *nfpl* seaweed *sg*.

algazara |àlgàsà'rà| *nf* din, uproar.

álgebra |àl'hcɦrà| *nf* algebra.

álgido, a |àl'hèɦo. à| *a* icy; (*momento etc*) crucial, decisive.

algo |àl'go| *pron* something; (*en frases interrogativas*) anything ♦ *ad* somewhat, rather; **por** ~ **será** there must be some reason for it; **es** ~ **difícil** it's a bit awkward.

algodón |àlgoɦon'| *nm* cotton; (*planta*) cotton plant; ~ **de azúcar** cotton candy (*US*), candy floss (*Brit*); ~ **hidrófilo** absorbent cotton (*US*), cotton wool (*Brit*).

algodonero, a |àlgoɦonc'ro. à| *a* cotton *cpd* ♦ *nm/f* cotton grower ♦ *nm* cotton plant.

algoritmo |àlgorèt'mo| *nm* algorithm.

alguacil |àlgwàsèl'| *nm* constable (*US*), bailiff (*Brit*); (TAUR) mounted official.

alguien |àl'gycn| *pron* someone, somebody; (*en frases interrogativas*) anybody.

alguno, a |àlgoo'no. à| *a* (*delante de nm*: **algún**) some; (*después de n*): **no tiene talento alguno** he has no talent, he hasn't any talent ♦ *pron* (*alguien*) someone, somebody; **algún que otro libro** some book or other; **algún día iré** I'll go one *o* some day; **sin interés alguno** without the slightest interest; **alguno que otro** an occasional one; **algunos piensan** some (people) think; **alguno de ellos** one of them.

alhaja |àlà'hà| *nf* jewel; (*tesoro*) precious object, treasure.

alhelí |àlclè'| *nm* wallflower, stock.

aliado, a |àlyà'ɦo. à| *a* allied.

aliancista |àlyànsè'stà| (*Esp POL*) *a* of Alianza Popular ♦ *nm/f* member/supporter of Alianza Popular.

alianza |àlyàn'sà| *nf* (POL *etc*) alliance; (*anillo*) wedding ring.

aliar |àlyàr'| *vt* to ally; ~**se** *vr* to form an alliance.

alias |à'lyàs| *ad* alias.

alicaído, a |àlèkàè'ɦo. à| *a* (MED) weak; (*fig*) depressed.

alicantino, a |àlèkàntè'no. à| *a* of Alicante ♦ *nm/f* native *o* inhabitant of Alicante.

alicate(s) |àlèkà'tc(s)| *nm(pl)* pliers *pl*; ~ **de uñas** nail clippers.

aliciente |àlèsycn'tc| *nm* incentive; (*atracción*) attraction.

alienación |àlycnàsyon'| *nf* alienation.

aliento |àlycn'to| *etc vb* V **alentar** ♦ *nm* breath; (*respiración*) breathing; **sin** ~ breathless; **de un** ~ in one breath; (*fig*) in one shot.

aligerar |àlèhcràr'| *vt* to lighten; (*reducir*) to shorten; (*aliviar*) to alleviate; (*mitigar*) to ease.

alijo |àlè'ho| *nm* (NAUT) unloading; (*contrabando*) smuggled goods.

alimaña |àlèmà'nyà| *nf* pest.

alimentación [álēmentásyon'] *nf* (*comida*) food; (*acción*) feeding; (*tienda*) grocery; ~ **continua** (*en fotocopiadora etc*) continuous feed.

alimentador [álēmentátħor'] *nm*: ~ **de papel** sheet-feeder.

alimentar [álēmentár'] *vt* to feed; (*nutrir*) to nourish; ~**se** *vr*: ~**se** (**de**) to feed (on).

alimenticio, a [álēmentē'syo, á] *a* food *cpd*; (*nutritivo*) nourishing, nutritious.

alimento [álēmen'to] *nm* food; (*nutrición*) nourishment; ~**s** *nmpl* (*JUR*) alimony *sg*.

alimón [álēmon'|: **al** ~ *ad* jointly, together.

alineación [álēneásyon'] *nf* alignment; (*DEPORTE*) line-up.

alineado, a [álēneá'ħo, á] *a* (*TIP*): (**no**) ~ (un)justified; ~ **a la izquierda/derecha** left/right justified.

alinear [álēneár'] *vt* to align; (*TIP*) to justify; ~**se** *vr* to line up; ~**se en** to fall in with.

aliñar [álēnyár'] *vt* (*CULIN*) to dress.

aliño [álē'nyo] *nm* (*CULIN*) dressing.

alisar [álēsár'] *vt* to smooth.

aliso [álē'so] *nm* alder.

alistamiento [álēstámyen'to] *nm* recruitment.

alistar [álēstár'] *vt* to recruit; ~**se** *vr* to enlist; (*inscribirse*) to enroll (*US*), enrol (*Brit*).

aliviar [álēbyár'] *vt* (*carga*) to lighten; (*persona*) to relieve; (*dolor*) to relieve, alleviate.

alivio [álē'byo] *nm* alleviation, relief; ~ **de luto** half-mourning.

aljibe [álħē'ħe] *nm* cistern.

alma [ál'má] *nf* soul; (*persona*) person; (*TEC*) core; **se le cayó el** ~ **a los pies** he became very disheartened; **entregar el** ~ to pass away; **estar con el** ~ **en la boca** to be scared to death; **lo siento en el** ~ I am truly sorry; **tener el** ~ **en un hilo** to have one's heart in one's throat (*US*) *o* mouth (*Brit*); **estar como** ~ **en pena** to suffer; **ir como** ~ **que lleva el diablo** to go at breakneck speed.

almacén [álmásen'] *nm* (*depósito*) warehouse, store; (*MIL*) magazine; (*AM*) shop; (**grandes**) **almacenes** *nmpl* department store *sg*; ~ **depositario** (*COM*) depository.

almacenaje [álmásená'he] *nm* storage; ~ **secundario** (*INFORM*) backup storage.

almacenamiento [álmásenámyen'to] *nm* (*INFORM*) storage; ~ **temporal en disco** disk spooling.

almacenar [álmásenár'] *vt* to store, put in storage; (*INFORM*) to store; (*proveerse*) to stock up with.

almacenero [álmásene'ro] *nm* warehouseman; (*AM*) shopkeeper.

almanaque [álmáná'ke] *nm* almanac.

almeja [álme'há] *nf* clam.

almenas [álmc'nás] *nfpl* battlements.

almendra [álmen'drá] *nf* almond.

almendro [álmen'dro] *nm* almond tree.

almeriense [álmeryen'se] *a* of Almería ♦ *nm/f* native *o* inhabitant of Almería.

almiar [álmyár'] *nm* haystack.

almíbar [álmē'ħár] *nm* syrup.

almidón [álmēħon'] *nm* starch.

almidonado, a [álmēħoná'ħo, á] *a* starched.

almidonar [álmēħonár'] *vt* to starch.

almirantazgo [álmērántás'ǥo] *nm* admiralty.

almirante [álmērán'te] *nm* admiral.

almirez [álmērcs'] *nm* mortar.

almizcle [álmēs'kle] *nm* musk.

almizclero [álmēskle'ro] *nm* musk deer.

almohada [álmoá'ħá] *nf* pillow; (*funda*) pillowcase.

almohadilla [álmoáħē'yá] *nf* cushion; (*TEC*) pad; (*AM*) pincushion.

almohadillado, a [álmoáħēyá'ħo, á] *a* (*acolchado*) padded.

almohadón [álmoáħon'] *nm* large pillow.

almorcé [álmorse'], **almorcemos** [álmorse'mos] *etc vb V* **almorzar**.

almorranas [álmorrá'nás] *nfpl* piles, hemorrhoids (*US*), haemorrhoids (*Brit*).

almorzar [álmorsár'] *vt*: ~ **una tortilla** to have an omelette for lunch ♦ *vi* to (have) lunch.

almuerce [álmwer'se] *etc vb V* **almorzar**.

almuerzo [álmwer'so] *etc vb V* **almorzar** ♦ *nm* lunch.

alocado, a [áloká'ħo, á] *a* crazy.

alojamiento [álohámyen'to] *nf* lodging(s) (*pl*); (*viviendas*) housing.

alojar [álohár'] *vt* to lodge; ~**se** *vr*: ~**se en** to stay at; (*bala*) to lodge in.

alondra [álon'drá] *nf* lark, skylark.

alpargata [álpárgá'tá] *nf* rope-soled canvas shoe.

Alpes [ál'pes] *nmpl*: **los** ~ the Alps.

alpinismo [álpēnēs'mo] *nm* mountaineering, climbing.

alpinista [álpēnē'stá] *nm/f* mountaineer, climber.

alpiste [álpē'ste] *nm* (*semillas*) birdseed; (*AM fam*: *dinero*) dough; (*fam*: *alcohol*) booze.

alquería [álkerē'á] *nf* farmhouse.

alquilar [álkēlár'] *vt* (*suj*: *propietario*: *inmuebles, coche*) to rent; (: *TV*) to rent (out); (*suj*: *alquilador*: *inmuebles, TV*) to rent; (: *coche*) to rent, hire (*Brit*); "**se alquila casa**" "house to rent (*US*) *o* to let (*Brit*)".

alquiler [álkēler'] *nm* renting, letting; hiring; (*arriendo*) rent; hire charge; **de** ~ for hire; ~ **de automóviles** car hire.

alquimia [álkē'myá] *nf* alchemy.

alquitrán [álkētrán'] *nm* tar.

alrededor [álrcthethor'] *ad* around, about; **~es** *nmpl* surroundings; **~ de** *prep* around, about; **mirar a su ~** to look around one.

Alsacia [álsá'syá] *nf* Alsace.

alta [ál'tá] *nf* (certificate of) discharge; **dar a uno de ~** to discharge sb; **darse de ~** (*MIL*) to join, enrol; (*DEPORTE*) to declare o.s. fit.

altanería [áltáncrē'á] *nf* haughtiness, arrogance.

altanero, a [áltánc'ro, á] *a* haughty, arrogant.

altar [áltár'] *nm* altar.

altavoz [áltáhos'] *nm* loudspeaker; (*amplificador*) amplifier.

alteración [álterásyon'] *nf* alteration; (*alboroto*) disturbance; **~ del orden público** breach of the peace.

alterar [álterár'] *vt* to alter; to disturb; **~se** *vr* (*persona*) to get upset.

altercado [álterká'tho] *nm* argument.

alternar [álternár'] *vt* to alternate ♦ *vi*, **~se** *vr* to alternate; (*turnar*) to take turns; **~ con** to mix with.

alternativo, a [álternátē'ho, á] *a* alternative; (*alterno*) alternating ♦ *nf* alternative; (*elección*) choice; **alternativas** *nfpl* ups and downs; **tomar la alternativa** (*TAUR*) to become a fully-qualified bullfighter.

alterno, a [álter'no, á] *a* (*BOT. MAT*) alternate; (*ELEC*) alternating.

alteza [áltc'sá] *nf* (*tratamiento*) highness.

altibajos [áltēhá'hos] *nmpl* ups and downs.

altillo [áltē'yo] *nm* (*GEO*) small hill; (*AM*) attic.

altiplanicie [áltēplánē'syc] *nf*, **altiplano** [áltēplá'no] *nm* high plateau.

altisonante [áltēsonán'tc] *a* high-flown, high-sounding.

altitud [áltētōōth'] *nf* altitude, height; **a una ~ de** at a height of.

altivez [áltēhcs'] *nf* haughtiness, arrogance.

altivo, a [áltē'ho, á] *a* haughty, arrogant.

alto, a [ál'to, á] *a* high; (*persona*) tall; (*sonido*) high, sharp; (*noble*) high, lofty; (*GEO, clase*) upper ♦ *nm* halt; (*MUS*) alto; (*GEO*) hill; (*AM*) pile ♦ *ad* (*estar*) high; (*hablar*) loud, loudly ♦ *excl* halt!; **la pared tiene 2 metros de ~** the wall is 2 meters high; **en alta mar** on the high seas; **en voz alta** in a loud voice; **las altas horas de la noche** the wee (*US*) o small (*Brit*) hours; **en lo ~ de** at the top of; **pasar por ~** to overlook; **~s y bajos** ups and downs; **poner la radio más ~** to turn the radio up; **¡más ~, por favor!** louder, please!

altoparlante [áltopárlán'tc] *nm* (*AM*) loudspeaker.

altramuz [áltrámōōs'] *nm* lupin.

altura [áltōō'rá] *nf* height; (*NAUT*) depth;

(*GEO*) latitude; **la pared tiene 1.80 de ~** the wall is 1 meter 80cm high; **a esta ~ del año** at this time of the year; **estar a la ~ de las circunstancias** to rise to the occasion; **ha sido un partido de gran ~** it has been a terrific match.

alubia [álōō'hyá] *nf* French bean, kidney bean.

alucinación [álōōsēnásyon'] *nf* hallucination.

alucinante [álōōsēnán'tc] *a* (*fam: estupendo*) great, super.

alucinar [álōōsēnár'] *vi* to hallucinate ♦ *vt* to deceive; (*fascinar*) to fascinate.

alud [álōōth'] *nm* avalanche; (*fig*) flood.

aludir [álōōthēr'] *vi*: **~ a** to allude to; **darse por aludido** to take the hint; **no te des por aludido** don't take it personally.

alumbrado [álōōmbrá'tho] *nm* lighting.

alumbramiento [álōōmbrámycn'to] *nm* lighting; (*MED*) childbirth, delivery.

alumbrar [álōōmbrár'] *vt* to light (up) ♦ *vi* (*iluminar*) to give light; (*MED*) to give birth.

aluminio [álōōmē'nyo] *nm* aluminum (*US*), aluminium (*Brit*).

alumnado [álōōmná'tho] *nm* (*UNIV*) student body; (*ESCOL*) pupils.

alumno, a [álōōm'no, á] *nm/f* pupil, student.

alunice [álōōnē'sc] *etc vb V* **alunizar**.

alunizar [álōōnēsár'] *vi* to land on the moon.

alusión [álōōsyon'] *nf* allusion.

alusivo, a [álōōsē'ho, á] *a* allusive.

aluvión [álōōhyon'] *nm* (*GEO*) alluvium; (*fig*) flood; **~ de improperios** torrent of abuse.

alvéolo [álhc'olo] *nm* (*ANAT*) alveolus; (*fig*) network.

alza [ál'sá] *nf* rise; (*MIL*) sight; **~s fijas/graduables** fixed/adjustable sights; **al o en ~** (*precio*) rising; **jugar al ~** to speculate on a rising o bull market; **cotizarse o estar en ~** to be rising.

alzado, a [álsá'tho, á] *a* (*gen*) raised; (*COM: precio*) fixed; (: *quiebra*) fraudulent; **por un tanto ~** for a lump sum ♦ *nf* (*de caballos*) height; (*JUR*) appeal.

alzamiento [álsámycn'to] *nm* (*aumento*) rise, increase; (*acción*) lifting, raising; (*mejor postura*) higher bid; (*rebelión*) rising; (*COM*) fraudulent bankruptcy.

alzar [álsár'] *vt* to lift (up); (*precio, muro*) to raise; (*cuello de abrigo*) to turn up; (*AGR*) to gather in; (*TIP*) to gather; **~se** *vr* to get up, rise; (*rebelarse*) to revolt; (*COM*) to go fraudulently bankrupt; (*JUR*) to appeal; **~se con el premio** to carry off the prize.

allá [áyá'] *ad* (*lugar*) there; (*por ahí*) over there; (*tiempo*) then; **~ abajo** down there; **más ~** further on; **más ~ de** beyond; **¡~**

tú! that's your problem!

allanamiento [àyànámyen'to] *nm*: ~ **de morada** housebreaking.

allanar [àyànàr'] *vt* to flatten, level (out); (*igualar*) to smooth (out); (*fig*) to subdue; (*JUR*) to burgle, break into; ~**se** *vr* to fall down; ~**se a** to submit to, accept.

allegado, a [àyeǥà'tho, à] *a* near, close ♦ *nm/f* relation.

allende [àyen'de] *ad* on the other side ♦ *prep*: ~ **los mares** beyond the seas.

allí [àyē'] *ad* there; ~ **mismo** right there; **por** ~ over there; (*por ese camino*) that way.

a.m. *abr* (*AM*: = *ante meridiem*) a.m.

ama [à'mà] *nf* lady of the house; (*dueña*) owner; (*institutriz*) governess; (*madre adoptiva*) foster mother; ~ **de casa** housewife; ~ **de cría** *o* **de leche** wet-nurse; ~ **de llaves** housekeeper.

amabilidad [àmàhēlēthàth'] *nf* kindness; (*simpatía*) niceness.

amabilísimo, a [àmàhēlē'sēmo, à] *a* superlativo de **amable**.

amable [àmá'hle] *a* kind; nice.

amaestrado, a [àmàestrà'tho, à] *a* (*animal*) trained; (: *en circo etc*) performing.

amaestrar [àmàestràr'] *vt* to train.

amagar [àmàǥàr'] *vt*, *vi* to threaten.

amago [àmà'ǥo] *nm* threat; (*gesto*) threatening gesture; (*MED*) symptom.

amague [àmà'ǥe] *etc vb V* **amagar**.

amainar [àmàēnàr'] *vt* (*NAUT*) to lower, take in; (*fig*) to calm ♦ *vi*, ~**se** *vr* to drop, die down; **el viento amaina** the wind is dropping.

amalgama [àmàlǥà'mà] *nf* amalgam.

amalgamar [àmàlǥàmàr'] *vt* to amalgamate; (*combinar*) to combine, mix.

amamantar [àmàmàntàr'] *vt* to suckle, nurse.

amancebarse [àmànsehàr'se] *vr* (*pareja*) to live together.

amanecer [àmàneser'] *vi* to dawn; (*fig*) to appear, begin to show ♦ *nm* dawn; **el niño amaneció afiebrado** the child woke up with a fever.

amanerado, a [àmànerà'tho, à] *a* affected.

amanezca [àmànes'kà] *etc vb V* **amanecer**.

amansar [àmànsàr'] *vt* to tame; (*persona*) to subdue; ~**se** *vr* (*persona*) to calm down.

amante [àmàn'te] *a*: ~ **de** fond of ♦ *nm/f* lover.

amanuense [àmànwen'se] *nm* (*escribiente*) scribe; (*copista*) copyist; (*POL*) secretary.

amañar [àmànyàr'] *vt* (*gen*) to do skilfully; (*pey: resultado*) to alter.

amaño [àmà'nyo] *nm* (*habilidad*) skill; ~**s** *nmpl* (*TEC*) tools; (*fig*) tricks.

amapola [àmàpo'là] *nf* poppy.

amar [àmàr'] *vt* to love.

amarar [àmàràr'] *vi* (*AVIAT*) to land (on the sea).

amargado, a [àmárǥà'tho, à] *a* bitter; embittered.

amargar [àmàrǥàr'] *vt* to make bitter; (*fig*) to embitter; ~**se** *vr* to become embittered.

amargo, a [àmàr'ǥo, à] *a* bitter.

amargor [àmàrǥor'] *nm* (*sabor*) bitterness; (*fig*) grief.

amargue [àmàr'ǥe] *etc vb V* **amargar**.

amargura [àmàrǥōō'rà] *nf*=**amargor**.

amarillento, a [àmàrēyen'to, à] *a* yellowish; (*tez*) sallow.

amarillismo [àmàrēyēs'mo] *nm* (*de prensa*) sensationalist journalism.

amarillo, a [àmàrē'yo, à] *a*, *nm* yellow.

amarra [àmà'rrà] *nf* (*NAUT*) mooring line; ~**s** *nfpl* (*fig*) protection *sg*; **tener buenas** ~**s** to have good connections; **soltar** ~**s** to set off.

amarrar [àmàrràr'] *vt* to moor; (*sujetar*) to tie up.

amartillar [àmàrtēyàr'] *vt* (*fusil*) to cock.

amasar [àmàsàr'] *vt* to knead; (*mezclar*) to mix, prepare; (*confeccionar*) to concoct.

amasijo [àmàsē'ho] *nm* kneading; mixing; (*fig*) hodgepodge.

amateur [à'màtōor] *nm/f* amateur.

amatista [àmàtē'stà] *nf* amethyst.

amazacotado, a [àmàsàkotà'tho, à] *a* (*terreno, arroz etc*) lumpy.

amazona [àmàso'nà] *nf* horsewoman.

Amazonas [àmàso'nàs] *nm*: **el (Río)** ~ the Amazon.

ambages [àmbà'hes] *nmpl*: **sin** ~ in plain language.

ámbar [àm'bàr] *nm* amber.

Amberes [àmbe'res] *nm* Antwerp.

ambición [àmbēsyon'] *nf* ambition.

ambicionar [àmbēsyonàr'] *vt* to aspire to.

ambicioso, a [àmbēsyo'so, à] *a* ambitious.

ambidextro, a [àmbētheks'tro, à] *a* ambidextrous.

ambientación [àmbyentàsyon'] *nf* (*CINE, LIT etc*) setting; (*RADIO etc*) sound effects.

ambientar [àmbyentàr'] *vt* (*gen*) to give an atmosphere to; (*LIT etc*) to set.

ambiente [àmbyen'te] *nm* (*tb fig*) atmosphere; (*medio*) environment.

ambigüedad [àmbēǥwethàth'] *nf* ambiguity.

ambigüo, a [àmbē'ǥwo, à] *a* ambiguous.

ámbito [àm'bēto] *nm* (*campo*) field; (*fig*) scope.

ambos, as [àm'bos, às] *apl*, *pron pl* both.

ambulancia [àmbōōlàn'syà] *nf* ambulance.

ambulante [àmbōōlàn'te] *a* travelling, itinerant; (*biblioteca*) mobile.

ambulatorio [àmbōōlàto'rēo] *nm* state health-service clinic.

ameba [àme'hà] *nf* amoeba.

amedrentar [àmethrentàr'] *vt* to scare.

amén |ȧmen'| *excl* amen; ~ **de** *prép* besides, in addition to; **en un decir** ~ in the twinkling of an eye; **decir** ~ **a todo** to have no mind of one's own.

amenace |ȧmenȧ'se| *etc vb V* **amenazar.**

amenaza |ȧmenȧ'sȧ| *nf* threat.

amenazar |ȧmenȧsȧr'| *vt* to threaten ♦ *vi*: ~ **con hacer** to threaten to do.

amenguar |ȧmengwȧr'| *vt* to diminish; (*fig*) to dishonor (*US*), dishonour (*Brit*).

amengüe |ȧmen'gwe| *etc vb V* **amenguar.**

amenidad |ȧmeneċhȧċh'| *nf* pleasantness.

ameno, a |ȧme'no, ȧ| *a* pleasant.

América |ȧme'rēkȧ| *nf* America; Latin America; ~ **del Norte/del Sur** North/South America; ~ **Central/Latina** Central/Latin America.

americano, a |ȧmerēkȧ'no, ȧ| *a, nm/f* American ♦ *nf* coat, jacket.

americe |ȧmerē'se| *etc vb V* **amerizar.**

amerizaje |ȧmerēsȧ'he| *nm* (*AVIAT*) landing (on the sea).

amerizar |ȧmerēsȧr'| *vi* (*AVIAT*) to land (on the sea).

ametralladora |ȧmetrȧyȧċho'rȧ| *nf* machine gun.

amianto |ȧmyȧn'to| *nm* asbestos.

amigable |ȧmēgȧ'ble| *a* friendly.

amígdala |ȧmēg'ċhȧlȧ| *nf* tonsil.

amigdalitis |ȧmēgċhȧlē'tēs| *nf* tonsillitis.

amigo, a |ȧmē'go, ȧ| *a* friendly ♦ *nm/f* friend; (*amante*) lover; ~ **de lo ajeno** thief; ~ **corresponsal** penfriend; **hacerse** ~**s** to become friends; **ser** ~ **de** to like, be fond of; **ser muy** ~**s** to be close friends.

amigote |ȧmēgo'te| *nm* pal.

amilanar |ȧmēlȧnȧr'| *vt* to scare; ~**se** *vr* to get scared.

aminorar |ȧmēnorȧr'| *vt* to diminish; (*reducir*) to reduce; ~ **la marcha** to slow down.

amistad |ȧmēstȧċh'| *nf* friendship; ~**es** *nfpl* friends.

amistoso, a |ȧmēsto'so, ȧ| *a* friendly.

amnesia |ȧmne'syȧ| *nf* amnesia.

amnistía |ȧmnēstē'ȧ| *nf* amnesty.

amnistiar |ȧmnēstyȧr'| *vt* to amnesty, grant an amnesty to.

amo |ȧ'mo| *nm* owner; (*jefe*) boss.

amodorrarse |ȧmoċhorrȧr'se| *vr* to get sleepy.

amolar |ȧmolȧr'| *vt* to annoy.

amoldar |ȧmoldȧr'| *vt* to mold (*US*), mould (*Brit*); (*adaptar*) to adapt.

amonestación |ȧmonestȧsyon'| *nf* warning; **amonestaciones** *nfpl* wedding announcement.

amonestar |ȧmonestȧr'| *vt* to warn; to announce the wedding of.

amontonar |ȧmontonȧr'| *vt* to collect, pile up; ~**se** *vr* (*gente*) to crowd together; (*acumularse*) to pile up; (*datos*) to accu-

mulate; (*desastres*) to come one on top of another.

amor |ȧmor'| *nm* love; (*amante*) lover; **hacer el** ~ to make love; ~ **propio** self-respect; **por (el)** ~ **de Dios** for God's sake; **estar al** ~ **de la lumbre** to be close to the fire.

amoratado, a |ȧmorȧtȧ'ċho, ȧ| *a* purple, blue with cold; (*con cardenales*) bruised.

amordace |ȧmorċhȧ'se| *etc vb V* **amordazar.**

amordazar |ȧmorċhȧsȧr'| *vt* to muzzle; (*fig*) to gag.

amorfo, a |ȧmor'fo, ȧ| *a* amorphous, shapeless.

amorío |ȧmorē'o| *nm* (*fam*) love affair.

amoroso, a |ȧmoro'so, ȧ| *a* affectionate, loving.

amortajar |ȧmortȧhȧr'| *vt* (*fig*) to shroud.

amortice |ȧmortē'se| *etc vb V* **amortizar.**

amortiguador |ȧmortēgwȧċhor'| *nm* shock absorber; (*parachoques*) bumper; (*silenciador*) silencer; ~**es** *nmpl* (*AUTO*) suspension *sg*.

amortiguar |ȧmortēgwȧr'| *vt* to deaden; (*ruido*) to muffle; (*color*) to soften.

amortigüe |ȧmortē'gwe| *etc vb V* **amortiguar.**

amortización |ȧmortēsȧsyon'| *nf* redemption; repayment; (*COM*) capital allowance.

amortizar |ȧmortēsȧr'| *vt* (*ECON: bono*) to redeem; (: *capital*) to write off; (: *préstamo*) to pay off.

amoscarse |ȧmoskȧr'se| *vr* to get cross.

amosque |ȧmos'ke| *etc vb V* **amoscarse.**

amotinar |ȧmotēnȧr'| *vt* to stir up, incite (to riot); ~**se** *vr* to mutiny.

amparar |ȧmpȧrȧr'| *vt* to protect; ~**se** *vr* to seek protection; (*de la lluvia etc*) to shelter.

amparo |ȧmpȧ'ro| *nm* help, protection; **al** ~ **de** under the protection of.

amperímetro *nm* ammeter.

amperio |ȧmpe'ryo| *nm* ampère, amp.

ampliable |ȧmplyȧ'ble| *a* (*INFORM*) expandable.

ampliación |ȧmplyȧsyon'| *nf* enlargement; (*extensión*) extension.

ampliar |ȧmplyȧr'| *vt* to enlarge; to extend.

amplificación |ȧmplēfēkȧsyon'| *nf* enlargement.

amplificador |ȧmplēfēkȧċhor'| *nm* amplifier.

amplificar |ȧmplēfēkȧr'| *vt* to amplify.

amplifique |ȧmplēfē'ke| *etc vb V* **amplificar.**

amplio, a |ȧmplyo, ȧ| *a* spacious; (*falda etc*) full; (*extenso*) extensive; (*ancho*) wide.

amplitud |ȧmplētooċh'| *nf* spaciousness; extent; (*fig*) amplitude; ~ **de miras** broadmindedness; **de gran** ~ far-reaching.

ampolla [ámpo'yá] *nf* blister; (*MED*) ampoule.

ampuloso, a [ámpōōlo'so, á] *a* bombastic, pompous.

amputar [ámpōōtár'] *vt* to cut off, amputate.

amueblar [ámweblár'] *vt* to furnish.

amurallar [ámōōráyár'] *vt* to wall up *o* in.

amusgar [ámōōsgár'] *vt* (*orejas*) to lay back; (*ojos*) to screw up.

amusgue [ámōōs'ge] *etc vb* V **amusgar**.

anacarado, a [ánákárá'tho, á] *a* mother-of-pearl *cpd*.

anacardo [ánákár'tho] *nm* cashew (nut).

anacronismo [ánákronēs'mo] *nm* anachronism.

ánade [á'nàthe] *nm* duck.

anadear [ánàtheár'] *vi* to waddle.

anales [áná'les] *nmpl* annals.

analfabetismo [ánálfábetēs'mo] *nm* illiteracy.

analfabeto, a [ánálfábe'to, á] *a, nm/f* illiterate.

analgésico [ánálhe'sēko] *nm* painkiller, analgesic.

analice [ánálē'se] *etc vb* V **analizar**.

análisis [áná'lēsēs] *nm inv* analysis; ~ **de costos-beneficios** cost-benefit analysis; ~ **de mercados** market research; ~ **de sangre** blood test.

analista [ánálē'stá] *nm/f* (*gen*) analyst; (*POL, HISTORIA*) chronicler; ~ **de sistemas** (*INFORM*) systems analyst.

analizar [ánálēsár'] *vt* to analyze.

analogía [ánálohē'á] *nf* analogy; **por** ~ **con** by analogy with.

análogo, a [áná'logo, á] *a* analogous, similar.

ananá(s) [ániná'(s)] *nm* pineapple.

anaquel [ánákel'] *nm* shelf.

anaranjado, a [ánáránhá'tho, á] *a* orange (-colored).

anarquía [ánárkē'á] *nf* anarchy.

anarquismo [ánárkēs'mo] *nm* anarchism.

anarquista [ánárkē'stá] *nm/f* anarchist.

anatematizar [ánátemátēsár'] *vt* (*REL*) to anathematize; (*fig*) to curse.

anatemice [ánáteme'se] *etc vb* V **anatemizar**.

anatomía [ánátomē'á] *nf* anatomy.

anca [án'ká] *nf* rump, haunch; ~**s** *nfpl* (*fam*) behind *sg*; **llevar a uno en** ~**s** to carry sb behind one.

anciano, a [ánsyá'no, á] *a* old, aged ♦ *nm/f* old man/woman ♦ *nm* elder.

ancla [án'klá] *nf* anchor; **levar** ~**s** to weigh anchor.

ancladero [ánklàthe'ro] *nm* anchorage.

anclar [ánklár'] *vi* to (drop) anchor.

ancho, a [ántch'o, á] *a* wide; (*falda*) full;

(*fig*) liberal ♦ *nm* width; (*FERRO*) gauge; **le viene muy** ~ **el cargo** (*fig*) the job is too much for him; **ponerse** ~ to get conceited; **quedarse tan** ~ to go on as if nothing had happened; **estar a sus anchas** to be at one's ease.

anchoa [ántcho'á] *nf* anchovy.

anchura [ántchōō'rá] *nf* width; (*extensión*) wideness.

anchuroso, a [ántchōōro'so, á] *a* wide.

andadas [ándá'thás] *nfpl* (*aventuras*) adventures; **volver a las** ~ to backslide.

andaderas [ándáthe'rás] *nfpl* baby-walker *sg*.

andadura [ándáthōō'rá] *nf* gait; (*de caballo*) pace.

Andalucía [ándálōōsē'á] *nf* Andalusia.

andaluz, a [ándálōōs', á] *a, nm/f* Andalusian.

andamiaje [ándámjá'hc] *nm*, **andamio** [ándá'myo] *nm* scaffold(ing).

andanada [ándáná'thá] *nf* (*fig*) reprimand; **soltarle a uno una** ~ to give sb a piece of one's mind.

andante [ándán'te] *a*: **caballero** ~ knight-errant.

andar [ándár'] *vt* to go, cover, travel ♦ *vi* to go, walk, travel; (*funcionar*) to go, work; (*estar*) to be ♦ *nm* walk, gait, pace; ~**se** *vr* (*irse*) to go away *o* off; ~ **a pie/a caballo/en bicicleta** to go on foot/on horseback/by bicycle; **¡anda!** (*sorpresa*) go on!; **anda en** *o* **por los 40** he's about 40; **¿en qué andas?** what are you up to?; **andamos mal de dinero/tiempo** we're badly off for money/we're short of time; ~**se por las ramas** to beat about the bush; **no** ~**se con rodeos** to call a spade a spade (*fam*); **todo se andará** all in good time; **anda por aquí** it's around here somewhere; ~ **haciendo algo** to be doing sth.

andariego, a [ándárye'go, á] *a* fond of travelling.

andas [án'dás] *nfpl* stretcher *sg*.

andén [ánden'] *nm* (*FERRO*) platform; (*NAUT*) quayside; (*AM: de la calle*) sidewalk (*US*), pavement (*Brit*).

Andes [án'des] *nmpl*: **los** ~ the Andes.

andino, a [ándē'no, á] *a* Andean, of the Andes.

andorga [ándor'gá] *nf* belly.

Andorra [ándo'rrá] *nf* Andorra.

andrajo [ándrá'ho] *nm* rag.

andrajoso, a [ándráho'so, á] *a* ragged.

andurriales [ándōōrryá'les] *nmpl* out-of-the-way place *sg*, the sticks; **en esos** ~ in that godforsaken spot.

anduve [ándōō'he], **anduviera** [ándōōhye'rá] *etc vb* V **andar**.

anécdota [ánek'thotá] *nf* anecdote, story.

anegar [ánegár'] *vt* to flood; (*ahogar*) to

drown; ~**se** *vr* to drown; (*hundirse*) to sink.

anegue [ànè'ge] *etc vb V* **anegar.**

anejo, a [àne'ho, à] *a* attached ♦ *nm* (*ARQ*) annexe.

anemia [àne'myà] *nf* anemia (*US*), anaemia (*Brit*).

anestésico [àneste'sēko] *nm* anesthetic (*US*), anaesthetic (*Brit*).

anexar [àneksàr'] *vt* to annex; (*documento*) to attach; (*INFORM*) to append.

anexión [àneksyon'] *nf,* **anexionamiento** [àneksyonàmyen'to] *nm* annexation.

anexo, a [ànek'so, à] *a* attached ♦ *nm* annexe.

anfibio, a [ànfē'hyo, à] *a* amphibious ♦ *nm* amphibian.

anfiteatro [ànfētcà'tro] *nm* amphitheater; (*TEATRO*) dress circle.

anfitrión, ona [ànfētryon', onà] *nm/f* host(ess).

ángel [àn'hel] *nm* angel; ~ **de la guarda** guardian angel; **tener** ~ to have charm.

Ángeles [àn'heles] *nmpl:* **los** ~ Los Angeles.

angelical [ànhelēkàl'], **angélico, a** [ànhe'lēko, à] *a* angelic(al).

angina [ànhē'nà] *nf* (*MED*): ~ **de pecho** angina; **tener** ~**s** to have a sore throat *o* throat infection.

anglicano, a [ànglēkà'no, à] *a, nm/f* Anglican.

Angola [àngo'là] *nf* Angola.

angoleño, a [àngole'nyo, à] *a, nm/f* Angolan.

angosto, a [àngo'sto, à] *a* narrow.

anguila [àngē'là] *nf* eel; ~**s** slipway *sg*.

angula [àngōō'là] *nf* elver, baby eel.

ángulo [àn'gōōlo] *nm* angle; (*esquina*) corner; (*curva*) bend.

angustia [àngōōs'tyà] *nf* anguish.

angustiar [àngōōstyàr'] *vt* to distress, grieve; ~**se** *vr* to be distressed (*por* at, on account of).

anhelante [ànelàn'te] *a* eager; (*deseoso*) longing.

anhelar [ànelàr'] *vt* to be eager for; to long for, desire ♦ *vi* to pant, gasp.

anhelo [àne'lo] *nm* eagerness; desire.

anidar [ànēthàr'] *vt* (*acoger*) to take in, shelter ♦ *vi* to nest; (*fig*) to make one's home.

anilina [ànēlē'nà] *nf* aniline.

anillo [ànē'yo] *nm* ring; ~ **de boda** wedding ring; ~ **de compromiso** engagement ring; **venir como** ~ **al dedo** to suit to a tee.

ánima [à'nēmà] *nf* soul; **las** ~**s** the Angelus (bell) *sg*.

animación [ànēmàsyon'] *nf* liveliness; (*vitalidad*) life; (*actividad*) bustle.

animado, a [ànēmà'tho, à] *a* (*vivo*) lively;

(*vivaz*) animated; (*concurrido*) bustling; (*alegre*) in high spirits; **dibujos** ~**s** cartoon *sg*.

animador, a [ànēmàthor', à] *nm/f* (*TV*) host(ess) ♦ *nf* (*DEPORTE*) cheerleader.

animadversión [ànēmàthersyon'] *nf* ill-will, antagonism.

animal [ànēmàl'] *a* animal; (*fig*) stupid ♦ *nm* animal; (*fig*) fool; (*bestia*) brute.

animalada [ànēmàlà'thà] *nf* (*gen*) silly thing (to do *o* say); (*ultraje*) disgrace.

animar [ànēmàr'] *vt* (*BIO*) to animate, give life to; (*fig*) to liven up, brighten up, cheer up; (*estimular*) to stimulate; ~**se** *vr* to cheer up, feel encouraged; (*decidirse*) to make up one's mind.

ánimo [à'nēmo] *nm* soul, mind; (*valentía*) courage ♦ *excl* cheer up!; **cobrar** ~ to take heart; **dar** ~(**s**) **a** to encourage.

animoso, a [ànēmo'so, à] *a* brave; (*vivo*) lively.

aniñado, a [ànēnyà'tho, à] *a* (*facción*) child-like; (*carácter*) childish.

aniquilar [ànēkēlàr'] *vt* to annihilate, destroy.

anís [ànēs'] *nm* (*grano*) aniseed; (*licor*) anisette.

aniversario [ànēhersà'ryo] *nm* anniversary.

Ankara [ànkà'rà] *nf* Ankara.

ano [à'no] *nm* anus.

anoche [ànotch'e] *ad* last night; **antes de** ~ the night before last.

anochecer [ànotcheser'] *vi* to get dark ♦ *nm* nightfall, dark; **al** ~ at nightfall.

anochezca [ànotches'kà] *etc vb V* **anochecer.**

anomalía [ànomàlē'à] *nf* anomaly.

anodino, a [ànothē'no, à] *a* dull, anodyne.

anonimato [ànonēmà'to] *nm* anonimity.

anónimo, a [àno'nēmo, à] *a* anonymous; (*COM*) limited ♦ *nm* (*carta*) anonymous letter; (: *maliciosa*) poison-pen letter.

anormal [ànormàl'] *a* abnormal.

anotación [ànotàsyon'] *nf* note; annotation.

anotar [ànotàr'] *vt* to note down; (*comentar*) to annotate.

anquilosado, a [ànkēlosà'tho, à] *a* (*fig*) stale, out of date.

anquilosamiento [ànkēlosàmyen'to] *nm* (*fig*) paralysis, stagnation.

ansia [àn'syà] *nf* anxiety; (*añoranza*) yearning.

ansiar [ànsyàr'] *vt* to long for.

ansiedad [ànsyethàth'] *nf* anxiety.

ansioso, a [ànsyo'so, à] *a* anxious; (*anhelante*) eager; ~ **de** *o* **por algo** greedy for sth.

antagónico, a [àntàgo'nēko, à] *a* antagonistic; (*opuesto*) contrasting.

antagonista [àntàgonē'stà] *nm/f* antagonist.

antaño [àntà'nyo] *ad* long ago.

Antártico [àntàr'tēko] *nm*: **el** ~ the Antarctic.

Antártida [àntàr'tēt̪há] *nf* Antarctica.

ante [àn'te] *prep* before, in the presence of; (*encarado con*) faced with ♦ *nm* suede; ~ **todo** above all.

anteanoche [ànteànotch'e] *ad* the night before last.

anteayer [àntèàyer'] *ad* the day before yesterday.

antebrazo [àntebrà'so] *nm* forearm.

antecámara [àntekà'màrà] *nf* (ARQ) anteroom; (*antesala*) waiting room; (POL) lobby.

antecedente [àntescèhen'te] *a* previous ♦ *nm*: ~**s** *nmpl* (*profesionales*) background *sg*; ~**s penales** criminal record; **no tener** ~**s** to have a clean record; **estar en** ~**s** to be well-informed; **poner a uno en** ~**s** to put sb in the picture.

anteceder [àntesèher'] *vt* to precede, go before.

antecesor, a [àntesesor', à] *nm/f* predecessor.

antedicho, a [àntet̪hetch'o, à] *a* aforementioned.

antelación [àntelàsyon'] *nf*: **con** ~ in advance.

antemano [àntemà'no]: **de** ~ *ad* beforehand, in advance.

antena [ànte'nà] *nf* antenna; (*de televisión etc*) aerial.

anteojeras [ànteohe'rás] *nfpl* blinders (US), blinkers (*Brit*).

anteojo [ànteo'ho] *nm* eyeglass; ~**s** *nmpl* (*esp AM*) glasses, spectacles.

antepasados [àntepàsà'thos] *nmpl* ancestors.

antepecho [àntepetch'o] *nm* guardrail, parapet; (*repisa*) ledge, sill.

antepondré [àntepondre'] *etc vb* V **anteponer**.

anteponer [ànteponer'] *vt* to place in front; (*fig*) to prefer.

anteponga [àntepon'gà] *etc vb* V **anteponer**.

anteproyecto [ànteproyek'to] *nm* preliminary sketch; (*fig*) blueprint; (POL): ~ **de ley** draft bill.

antepuesto, a [àntepwe'sto, à] *pp de* **anteponer**.

antepuse [àntepōō'se] *etc vb* V **anteponer**.

anterior [ànteryor'] *a* preceding, previous.

anterioridad [ànteryorèt̪hàt̪h'] *nf*: **con** ~ **a** prior to, before.

anteriormente [ànteryormen'te] *ad* previously, before.

antes [àn'tes] *ad* sooner; (*primero*) first; (*con prioridad*) before; (*hace tiempo*) previously, once; (*más bien*) rather ♦ *prep*: ~ **de** before ♦ *conj*: ~ **(de) que** before; ~

bien (but) rather; **dos días** ~ two days before *o* previously; **mucho/poco** ~ long/ shortly before; ~ **muerto que esclavo** better dead than enslaved; **tomo el avión** ~ **que el barco** I take the plane rather than the boat; **cuanto** ~, **lo** ~ **posible** as soon as possible; **cuanto** ~ **mejor** the sooner the better.

antesala [àntesà'là] *nf* anteroom.

antiadherente [àntèàt̪heren'te] *a* non-stick.

antiaéreo, a [àntèàe'reo, à] *a* anti-aircraft.

antialcohólico, a [àntèàlko'lēko, à] *a*: **centro** ~ (MED) detoxification unit.

antibalas [àntēbà'làs] *a inv*: **chaleco** ~ bullet-proof jacket.

antibiótico [àntēbyo'teko] *nm* antibiotic.

anticiclón [àntēsēklon'] *nm* (METEOROLOGÍA) anti-cyclone.

anticipación [àntēsēpàsyon'] *nf* anticipation; **con 10 minutos de** ~ 10 minutes early.

anticipado, a [àntēsēpà't̪ho, à] *a* (in) advance; **por** ~ in advance.

anticipar [àntēsēpàr'] *vt* to anticipate; (*adelantar*) to bring forward; (COM) to advance; ~**se** *vr*: ~**se a su época** to be ahead of one's time.

anticipo [àntēsē'po] *nm* (COM) advance; V *tb* **anticipación**.

anticonceptivo, a [àntēkonseptē'ho, à] *a*, *nm* contraceptive; **métodos** ~**s** contraceptive devices.

anticongelante [àntēkonhelàn'te] *nm* antifreeze.

anticonstitucional [àntēkonstētōōsyonàl'] *a* unconstitutional.

anticuado, a [àntēkwà't̪ho, à] *a* out-of-date, old-fashioned; (*desusado*) obsolete.

anticuario [àntēkwà'ryo] *nm* antique dealer.

anticuerpo [àntēkwer'po] *nm* (MED) antibody.

antidemocrático, a [àntēt̪hemokrà'tēko, à] *a* undemocratic.

antideportivo, a [àntēt̪heportē'ho, à] *a* unsporting.

antideslumbrante [àntēt̪heslōōmbràn'te] *a* (INFORM) anti-dazzle.

antídoto [àntē't̪hoto] *nm* antidote.

antidroga [àntēt̪hro'gà] *a inv* anti-drug; **brigada** ~ drug squad.

antiestético, a [àntēeste'tēko, à] *a* unsightly.

antifaz [àntēfàs'] *nm* mask; (*velo*) veil.

antigás [àntēgàs'] *a inv*: **careta** ~ gasmask.

antigualla [àntēgwà'yà] *nf* antique; (*reliquia*) relic; ~**s** *nfpl* old things.

antiguamente [àntēgwàmen'te] *ad* formerly; (*hace mucho tiempo*) long ago.

antigüedad [àntēgwet̪hàt̪h'] *nf* antiquity; (*artículo*) antique; (*rango*) seniority.

antiguo, a [àntē'gwo, à] *a* old, ancient; (*que*

fue) former; **a la antigua** in the old-fashioned way.

antihigiénico, a [àntēhye'nēko, à] *a* unhygienic.

antihistamínico, a [àntēstàmē'nēko, à] *a*, *nm* antihistamine.

antiinflacionista [àntēnflàsyonē'stà] *a* anti-inflationary, counter-inflationary.

antílope [àntē'lope] *nm* antelope.

antillano, a [àntēyà'no, à] *a, nm/f* West Indian.

Antillas [àntē'yàs] *nfpl*: **las** ~ the West Indies, the Antilles; **el mar de las** ~ the Caribbean Sea.

antimonopolios [àntēmonopo'lyos] *a inv*: **ley** ~ anti-trust law.

antinatural [àntēnàtŏŏrál'] *a* unnatural.

antiparras [àntēpà'rràs] *nfpl* (*fam*) specs.

antipatía [àntēpàtē'à] *nf* antipathy, dislike.

antipático, a [àntēpà'tēko, à] *a* disagreeable, unpleasant.

Antípodas [àntē'poᵗhàs] *nfpl*: **las** ~ the antipodes.

antiquísimo, a [àntēkē'sēmo, à] *a* ancient.

antirreglamentario, a [àntērreǥlàmentà'ryo, à] *a* (*gen*) unlawful; (*POL etc*) unconstitutional.

antirrobo [àntērro'ᵇo] *a inv*: **(dispositivo)** ~ (*para casas etc*) burglar alarm; (*para coches*) car alarm.

antisemita [àntēsemē'tà] *a* anti-Semitic ♦ *nm/f* anti-Semite.

antiséptico, a [àntēsep'tēko, à] *a, nm* antiseptic.

antítesis [àntē'tesēs] *nf inv* antithesis.

antiterrorista [àntēterrorē'stà] *a* antiterrorist; **la lucha** ~ the fight against terrorism.

antojadizo, a [àntohàᵗhē'so, à] *a* capricious.

antojarse [àntohàr'se] *vr* (*desear*): **se me antoja comprarlo** I have a mind to buy it; (*pensar*): **se me antoja que** I have a feeling that.

antojo [ànto'ho] *nm* caprice, whim; (*rosa*) birthmark; (*lunar*) mole; **hacer a su** ~ to do as one pleases.

antología [àntolohē'à] *nf* anthology.

antonomasia [àntonomá'syà] *nf*: **por** ~ par excellence.

antorcha [àntortch'à] *nf* torch.

antro [àn'tro] *nm* cavern; ~ **de corrupción** (*fig*) den of iniquity.

antropófago, a [àntropo'fàǥo, à] *a, nm/f* cannibal.

antropología [àntropolohē'à] *nf* anthropology.

anual [ànwàl'] *a* annual.

anualidad [ànwàlēᵗhàᵗh'] *nf* annuity, annual payment; ~ **vitalicia** life annuity.

anuario [ànwà'ryo] *nm* yearbook.

anudar [ànŏŏhàr'] *vt* to knot, tie; (*unir*) to join; ~**se** *vr* to get tied up; **se me anudó**

la voz I got a lump in my throat.

anulación [ànŏŏlàsyon'] *nf* annulment; cancellation; repeal.

anular [ànŏŏlàr'] *vt* to annul, cancel; (*suscripción*) to cancel; (*ley*) to repeal ♦ *nm* ring finger.

anunciación [ànŏŏnsyàsyon'] *nf* announcement; **A~** (*REL*) Annunciation.

anunciante [ànŏŏnsyàn'te] *nm/f* (*COM*) advertiser.

anunciar [ànŏŏnsyàr'] *vt* to announce; (*proclamar*) to proclaim; (*COM*) to advertise.

anuncio [ànŏŏn'syo] *nm* announcement; (*señal*) sign; (*COM*) advertisement; (*cartel*) poster; (*TEATRO*) bill; ~**s por palabras** classified ads.

anverso [àmber'so] *nm* obverse.

anzuelo [ànswe'lo] *nm* hook; (*para pescar*) fish hook; **tragar el** ~ to swallow the bait.

añadidura [ànyàᵗhēᵗhŏŏ'rà] *nf* addition, extra; **por** ~ besides, in addition.

añadir [ànyàᵗhēr'] *vt* to add.

añejo, a [ànye'ho, à] *a* old; (*vino*) vintage; (*jamón*) well-cured.

añicos [ànyē'kos] *nmpl*: **hacer** ~ to smash, shatter; **hacerse** ~ to smash, shatter.

añil [ànyēl'] *nm* (*BOT, color*) indigo.

año [à'nyo] *nm* year; **¡Feliz A~ Nuevo!** Happy New Year!; **tener 15** ~**s** to be 15 (years old); **los** ~**s 80** the eighties; ~ **bisiesto/escolar** leap/school year; ~ **fiscal** fiscal *o* tax year; **estar de buen** ~ to be in good shape; **en el** ~ **de la nana** in the year one (*US*) *o* dot (*Brit*); **el** ~ **que viene** next year.

añoranza [ànyorán'sà] *nf* nostalgia; (*anhelo*) longing.

añoso, a [ànyo'so, à] *a* ancient, old.

aojar [àohàr'] *vt* to put the evil eye on.

aovado, a [àohà'ᵗho, à] *a* oval.

aovar [àohàr'] *vi* to lay eggs.

apabullar [àpàbŏŏyàr'] *vt* (*lit, fig*) to crush.

apacentar [àpàsentàr'] *vt* to pasture, graze.

apacible [àpàsē'ble] *a* gentle, mild.

apaciente [àpàsyen'te] *etc vb V* **apacentar.**

apaciguar [àpàsēǥwàr'] *vt* to pacify, calm (down).

apacigüe [àpàsē'ǥwe] *etc vb V* **apaciguar.**

apadrinar [àpàᵗhrēnàr'] *vt* to sponsor, support; (*REL*) to act as godfather to.

apagado, a [àpàǥà'ᵗho, à] *a* (*volcán*) extinct; (*color*) dull; (*voz*) quiet; (*sonido*) muted, muffled; (*persona: apático*) listless; **estar** ~ (*fuego, luz*) to be out; (*radio, TV etc*) to be off.

apagar [àpàǥàr'] *vt* to put out; (*color*) to tone down; (*sonido*) to silence, muffle; (*sed*) to quench; (*INFORM*) to toggle off; ~**se** *vr* (*luz, fuego*) to go out; (*sonido*) to die away; (*pasión*) to wither; ~ **el sistema** ♦ (*INFORM*) to close *o* shut down.

apagón |ápágon'| *nm* blackout.

apague |ápá'ġe| *etc vb* V **apagar.**

apalabrar |ápáláḥrár'| *vt* to agree to; *(obrero)* to engage.

Apalaches |ápálátch'es| *nmpl*: **(Montes)** ~ Appalachians.

apalear |ápálcár'| *vt* to beat, thrash; *(AGR)* to winnow.

apañar |ápányár'| *vt* to pick up; *(asir)* to take hold of, grasp; *(reparar)* to mend, patch up; ~**se** *vr* to manage, get along; **apañárselas por su cuenta** to look after number one *(fam)*.

apaño |ápá'nyo| *nm* *(COSTURA)* patch; *(maña)* skill; **esto no tiene** ~ there's no answer to this one.

aparador |ápáráḥor'| *nm* sideboard; *(escaparate)* shop window.

aparato |ápárá'to| *nm* apparatus; *(máquina)* machine; *(doméstico)* appliance; *(boato)* ostentation; *(INFORM)* device; ~ **de facsímil** facsimile (machine), fax; ~ **respiratorio** respiratory system; ~**s de mando** *(AVIAT etc)* controls.

aparatoso, a |ápáráto'so, á| *a* showy, ostentatious.

aparcamiento |ápárkámyen'to| *nm* parking lot *(US)*, car park *(Brit)*.

aparcar |ápárkár'| *vt, vi* to park.

aparear |ápárcár'| *vt* *(objetos)* to pair, match; *(animales)* to mate; ~**se** *vr* to form a pair; to mate.

aparecer |ápárcscr'| *vi*, ~**se** *vr* to appear; **apareció borracho** he turned up drunk.

aparejado, a |ápárchá'ḥo, á| *a* fit, suitable; **ir** ~ **con** to go hand in hand with; **llevar** *o* **traer** ~ to involve.

aparejar |ápárchár'| *vt* to prepare; *(caballo)* to saddle, harness; *(NAUT)* to fit out, rig out.

aparejo |ápárc'ho| *nm* preparation; *(de caballo)* harness; *(NAUT)* rigging; *(de poleas)* block and tackle.

aparentar |ápárcntár'| *vt* *(edad)* to look; *(fingir)*: ~ **tristeza** to pretend to be sad.

aparente |ápárcn'tc| *a* apparent; *(adecuado)* suitable.

aparezca |ápárcs'ká| *etc vb* V **aparecer.**

aparición |ápárcsyon'| *nf* appearance; *(de libro)* publication; *(fantasma)* specter.

apariencia |ápáryen'syá| *nf* (outward) appearance; **en** ~ outwardly, seemingly.

aparque |ápár'kc| *etc vb* V **aparcar.**

apartado, a |ápártá'ḥo, á| *a* separate; *(lejano)* remote ♦ *nm* *(tipográfico)* paragraph; ~ **(de correos)** post office box.

apartamento |ápártámen'to| *nm* apartment, flat *(Brit)*.

apartamiento |ápártámyen'to| *nm* separation; *(aislamiento)* remoteness; *(AM)* apartment, flat *(Brit)*.

apartar |ápártár'| *vt* to separate; *(quitar)* to remove; *(MINERALOGÍA)* to extract; ~**se** *vr* *(separarse)* to separate, part; *(irse)* to move away; *(mantenerse aparte)* to keep away.

aparte |ápár'tc| *ad* *(separadamente)* separately; *(además)* besides ♦ *prep*: ~ **de** apart from ♦ *nm* *(TEATRO)* aside; *(tipográfico)* new paragraph; "**punto y** ~" "new paragraph".

apasionado, a |ápásyoná'ḥo, á| *a* passionate; *(pey)* biassed, prejudiced ♦ *nm/f* admirer.

apasionar |ápásyonár'| *vt* to arouse passion in; ~**se** *vr* to get excited; **le apasiona el fútbol** she's crazy about football.

apatía |ápátc'á| *nf* apathy.

apático, a |ápá'tčko, á| *a* apathetic.

apátrida |ápá'trčḥá| *a* stateless.

Apdo. *nm abr* (= *Apartado (de Correos)*) P.O. Box.

apeadero |ápcáḥc'ro| *nm* stop, stopping place.

apearse |ápcár'sc| *vr* *(jinete)* to dismount; *(bajarse)* to get down *o* out; *(de coche)* to get out, alight; **no** ~ **del burro** to refuse to back down.

apechugar |ápctchōōġár'| *vi*: ~ **con algo** to face up to sth.

apechugue |ápctchōō'ġc| *etc vb* V **apechugar.**

apedrear |ápcḥrcár'| *vt* to stone.

apegarse |ápcġár'sc| *vr*: ~ **a** to become attached to.

apego |ápc'ġo| *nm* attachment, devotion.

apegue |ápc'ġc| *etc vb* V **apegarse.**

apelación |ápclásyon'| *nf* appeal.

apelar |ápclár'| *vi* to appeal; ~ **a** *(fig)* to resort to.

apelativo |ápclátč'ḥo| *nm* *(LING)* common noun; *(AM)* surname.

apelmazado, a |ápclmásá'ḥo, á| *a* compact, solid.

apelotonar |ápclotonár'| *vt* to roll into a ball; ~**se** *vr* *(gente)* to crowd together.

apellidar |ápcyčḥár'| *vt* to call, name; ~**se** *vr*: **se apellida Pérez** her (sur)name's Pérez.

apellido |ápcyč'ḥo| *nm* surname.

apenar |ápcnár'| *vt* to grieve, trouble; ~**se** *vr* to grieve.

apenas |ápc'nás| *ad* scarcely, hardly ♦ *conj* as soon as, no sooner.

apéndice |ápcn'dčsc| *nm* appendix.

apendicitis |ápcndčsč'tčs| *nf* appendicitis.

Apeninos |ápcnč'nos| *nmpl* Apennines.

apercibimiento |ápcrsčḥčmyen'to| *nm* *(aviso)* warning.

apercibir |ápcrsčḥčr'| *vt* to prepare; *(avisar)* to warn; *(JUR)* to summon; *(AM)* to notice, see; ~**se** *vr* to get ready; ~**se de** to notice.

aperitivo |àpcrētē'ħo| *nm* (*bebida*) aperitif; (*comida*) appetizer.

apero |àpc'ro| *nm* (*AGR*) implement; **~s** *nmpl* farm equipment *sg*.

aperrear |àpcrrcár'| *vt* to set the dogs on; (*fig*) to plague.

apertura |àpcrtōō'rá| *nf* (*gen*) opening; (*POL*) openness, liberalization; (*TEATRO etc*) beginning; **~ de un juicio hipotecario** (*COM*) foreclosure.

aperturismo |àpcrtōōrēs'mo| *nm* (*POL*) (policy of) liberalization.

apesadumbrar |àpcsáħōōmbrár'| *vt* to grieve, sadden; **~se** *vr* to distress o.s.

apestar |àpcstár'| *vt* to infect ♦ *vi*: **~(a)** to stink (of).

apestoso, a |àpcsto'so, à| *a* (*hediondo*) stinking; (*asqueroso*) sickening.

apetecer |àpctcscr'| *vt*: **¿te apetece una tortilla?** does an omelet appeal to you?

apetecible |àpctcsē'ħlc| *a* desirable; (*comida*) tempting.

apetezca |àpctcs'ká| *etc vb V* **apetecer**.

apetito |àpctē'to| *nm* appetite.

apetitoso, a |àpctēto'so, à| *a* (*gustoso*) appetizing; (*fig*) tempting.

apiadarse |àpyáħár'sc| *vr*: **~ de** to take pity on.

ápice |à'pēsc| *nm* apex; (*fig*) whit, iota; **ni un ~** not a whit; **no ceder un ~** not to budge an inch.

apicultor, a |àpēkōōltor', à| *nm/f* beekeeper, apiarist.

apicultura |àpēkōōltōō'rá| *nf* beekeeping.

apiladora |àpēláħo'rá| *nf* (*para máquina impresora*) stacker.

apilar |àpēlár'| *vt* to pile o heap up; **~se** *vr* to pile up.

apiñado, a |àpēnyá'ħo, à| *a* (*apretado*) packed.

apiñar |àpēnyár'| *vt* to crowd; **~se** *vr* to crowd o press together.

apio |à'pyo| *nm* celery.

apisonadora |àpēsonáħo'rá| *nf* (*máquina*) steamroller.

aplacar |àplákár'| *vt* to placate; **~se** *vr* to calm down.

aplace |àplà'sc| *etc vb V* **aplazar**.

aplanamiento |àplánámycn'to| *nm* smoothing, levelling.

aplanar |àplánár'| *vt* to smooth, level; (*allanar*) to roll flat, flatten; **~se** *vr* (*edificio*) to collapse; (*persona*) to get discouraged.

aplaque |àplà'kc| *etc vb V* **aplacar**.

aplastar |àplàstár'| *vt* to squash (flat); (*fig*) to crush.

aplatanarse |àplátánár'sc| *vr* to get lethargic.

aplaudir |àpláōōħēr'| *vt* to applaud.

aplauso |àplà'ōōso| *nm* applause; (*fig*)

approval, acclaim.

aplazamiento |àplásámycn'to| *nm* postponement.

aplazar |àplásár'| *vt* to postpone, defer.

aplicación |àplēkásyon'| *nf* application; (*esfuerzo*) effort; **aplicaciones de gestión** business applications.

aplicado, a |àplēká'ħo, à| *a* diligent, hardworking.

aplicar |àplēkár'| *vt* (*gen*) to apply; (*poner en vigor*) to put into effect; (*esfuerzos*) to devote; **~se** *vr* to apply o.s.

aplique |àplē'kc| *etc vb V* **aplicar** ♦ *nm* wall light o lamp.

aplomo |àplo'mo| *nm* aplomb, self-assurance.

apocado, a |àpoká'ħo, à| *a* timid.

apocamiento |àpokámycn'to| *nm* timidity; (*depresión*) depression.

apocarse |àpokár'sc| *vr* to feel small o humiliated.

apocopar |àpokopár'| *vt* (*LING*) to shorten.

apodar |àpoħár'| *vt* to nickname.

apoderado |àpoħcrá'ħo| *nm* agent, representative.

apoderar |àpoħcrár'| *vt* to authorize, empower; (*JUR*) to grant (a) power of attorney to; **~se** *vr*: **~se de** to take possession of.

apodo |àpo'ħo| *nm* nickname.

apogeo |àpohc'o| *nm* peak, summit.

apolillado, a |àpolēyá'ħo, à| *a* moth-eaten.

apolillarse |àpolēyár'sc| *vr* to get moth-eaten.

apología |àpolohē'á| *nf* eulogy; (*defensa*) defense (*US*), defence (*Brit*).

apoltronarse |àpoltronár'sc| *vr* to get lazy.

apoplejía |àpoplchē'á| *nf* apoplexy, stroke.

apoque |àpo'kc| *etc vb V* **apocar**.

apoquinar |àpokēnár'| *vt* (*fam*) to cough up.

aporrear |àporrcár'| *vt* to beat (up).

aportación |àportásyon'| *nf* contribution.

aportar |àportár'| *vt* to contribute ♦ *vi* to reach port; **~se** *vr* (*AM*) to arrive, come.

aposentar |àposcntár'| *vt* to lodge, put up.

aposento |àposcn'to| *nm* lodging; (*habitación*) room.

apósito |àpo'sēto| *nm* (*MED*) dressing.

apostar |àpostár'| *vt* to bet, stake; (*tropas etc*) to station, post ♦ *vi* to bet.

aposta(s) |àpo'stá(s)| *ad* on purpose.

apostatar |àpostátár'| *vi* (*REL*) to apostatize; (*fig*) to change sides.

apostilla |àpostē'yá| *nf* note, comment.

apóstol |àpo'stol| *nm* apostle.

apóstrofo |àpos'trofo| *nm* apostrophe.

apostura |àpostōō'rá| *nf* neatness, elegance.

apoteósico, a |àpotco'sēko, à| *a* tremendous.

apoyar |àpoyár'| *vt* to lean, rest; (*fig*) to

support, back; ~**se** *vr*: ~**se en** to lean on.

apoyo [ápo'yo] *nm* support, backing.

apreciable [ápresyá'ɣle] *a* considerable; (*fig*) esteemed.

apreciación [ápresyásyon'] *nf* appreciation; (*COM*) appraisal (*US*), valuation (*Brit*).

apreciar [ápresyár'] *vt* to evaluate, assess; (*COM*) to appreciate, appraise (*US*), value (*Brit*) ♦ *vi* (*ECON*) to appreciate.

aprecio [ápre'syo] *nm* appraisal (*US*), valuation (*Brit*), estimate; (*fig*) appreciation.

aprehender [áprender'] *vt* to apprehend, detain; (*ver*) to see, observe.

aprehensión [ápreensyon'] *nf* detention, capture.

apremiante [ápremyán'te] *a* urgent, pressing.

apremiar [ápremyár'] *vt* to compel, force ♦ *vi* to be urgent, press.

apremio [ápre'myo] *nm* urgency; ~ **de pago** demand note.

aprender [áprender'] *vt*, *vi* to learn; ~ **a conducir** to learn to drive; ~**se** *vr*: ~**se algo** to learn sth (off) by heart.

aprendiz, a [áprendēs', á] *nm/f* apprentice; (*principiante*) learner, trainee; ~ **de comercio** business trainee.

aprendizaje [áprendēsá'he] *nm* apprenticeship.

aprensión [áprensyon'] *nm* apprehension, fear.

aprensivo, a [áprensē'ɣo, á] *a* apprehensive.

apresar [ápresár'] *vt* to seize; (*capturar*) to capture.

aprestar [áprestár'] *vt* to prepare, get ready; (*TEC*) to prime, size; ~**se** *vr* to get ready.

apresto [ápre'sto] *nm* (*gen*) preparation; (*sustancia*) size.

apresurado, a [ápresōōrá'ɣo, á] *a* hurried, hasty.

apresuramiento [ápresōōrámyen'to] *nm* hurry, haste.

apresurar [ápresōōrár'] *vt* to hurry, accelerate; ~**se** *vr* to hurry, make haste; **me apresuré a sugerir que** ... I hastily suggested that ...

apretado, a [ápretá'ɣo, á] *a* tight; (*escritura*) cramped.

apretar [ápretár'] *vt* to squeeze, press; (*mano*) to clasp; (*dientes*) to grit; (*TEC*) to tighten; (*presionar*) to press together, pack ♦ *vi* to be too tight; ~**se** *vr* to crowd together; ~ **la mano a uno** to shake sb's hand; ~ **el paso** to quicken one's step.

apretón [ápreton'] *nm* squeeze; ~ **de manos** handshake.

aprieto [áprye'to] *etc vb* V **apretar** ♦ *nm* squeeze; (*dificultad*) difficulty, jam; **estar en un** ~ to be in a jam; **ayudar a uno a**

salir de un ~ to help sb out of trouble.

aprisa [áprē'sá] *ad* quickly, hurriedly.

aprisionar [áprēsyonár'] *vt* to imprison.

aprobación [áproɣásyon'] *nf* approval.

aprobado [áproɣá'ɖo] *nm* (*nota*) passing grade (*US*), pass mark (*Brit*).

aprobar [áproɣár'] *vt* to approve (of); (*examen, materia*) to pass ♦ *vi* to pass.

apropiación [ápropyásyon'] *nf* appropriation.

apropiado, a [ápropyá'ɖo, á] *a* appropriate.

apropiarse [ápropyár'se] *vr*: ~ **de** to appropriate.

aprovechado, a [áproɣetchá'ɖo, á] *a* industrious, hardworking; (*económico*) thrifty; (*pey*) unscrupulous.

aprovechamiento [áproɣetchámyen'to] *nm* use, exploitation.

aprovechar [áproɣetchár'] *vt* to use; (*explotar*) to exploit; (*experiencia*) to profit from; (*oferta, oportunidad*) to take advantage of ♦ *vi* to progress, improve; ~**se** *vr*: ~**se de** to make use of; (*pey*) to take advantage of; ¡**que aproveche!** enjoy your meal!

aprovisionar [áproɣēsyonár'] *vt* to supply.

aproximación [áproksēmásyon'] *nf* approximation; (*de lotería*) consolation prize.

aproximadamente [áproksēmáṭhámen'te] *ad* approximately.

aproximado, a [áproksēmá'ɖo, á] *a* approximate.

aproximar [áproksēmár'] *vt* to bring nearer; ~**se** *vr* to come near, approach.

apruebe [áprwe'ɦe] *etc vb* V **aprobar**.

aptitud [áptētōōṭh'] *nf* aptitude; (*capacidad*) ability; ~ **para los negocios** business sense.

apto, a [áp'to, á] *a* (*apropiado*) fit, suitable (*para* for, to); (*hábil*) capable; ~**/no** ~ **para menores** (*CINE*) suitable/unsuitable for children.

apuesto, a [ápwe'sto, á] *etc vb* V **apostar** ♦ *a* neat, elegant ♦ *nf* bet, wager.

apuntador [ápōōntáɖor'] *nm* prompter.

apuntalar [ápōōntálár'] *vt* to prop up.

apuntar [ápōōntár'] *vt* (*con arma*) to aim at; (*con dedo*) to point at *o* to; (*anotar*) to write (down); (*datos*) to record; (*TEATRO*) to prompt; ~**se** *vr* (*DEPORTE*: *tanto, victoria*) to score; (*ESCOL*) to enroll (*US*), enrol (*Brit*); ~ **una cantidad en la cuenta de uno** to charge a sum to sb's account; ~**se en un curso** to enroll in a course; ¡**yo me apunto!** count me in!

apunte [ápōōn'te] *nm* note; (*TEATRO*: *voz*) prompt; (: *texto*) prompt book.

apuñalar [ápōōnyálár'] *vt* to stab.

apurado, a [ápōōrá'ɖo, á] *a* needy; (*difícil*) difficult; (*peligroso*) dangerous; (*AM*) hurried, rushed; **estar en una situación apurada** to be in a tight spot; **estar ~ to be** in a hurry.

apurar [àpōōrár'] *vt* (*agotar*) to drain; (*recursos*) to use up; (*molestar*) to annoy; **~se** *vr* (*preocuparse*) to worry; (*darse prisa*) to hurry.

apuro [àpōō'ro] *nm* (*aprieto*) fix, jam; (*escasez*) want, hardship; (*vergüenza*) embarrassment; (*AM*) haste, urgency.

aquejado, a [àkehá'tho, à] *a:* ~ **de** (*MED*) afflicted by.

aquejar [àkehár'] *vt* (*afligir*) to distress; **le aqueja una grave enfermedad** he suffers from a serious disease.

aquel, aquella, aquellos, as [àkel', àke'yá, àke'yos, ás] *a* that; (*pl*) those.

aquél, aquélla, aquéllos, as [àkel', àke'yá, àke'yos, ás] *pron* that (one); (*pl*) those (ones).

aquello [àke'yo] *pron* that, that business.

aquí [àkē'] *ad* (*lugar*) here; (*tiempo*) now; ~ **arriba** up here; ~ **mismo** right here; ~ **yace** here lies; **de ~ a ocho días** a week from now.

aquietar [àkyetár'] *vt* to calm (down).

Aquisgrán [àkēsgrán'] *nm* Aachen, Aix-la-Chapelle.

A.R. *abr* (= *Alteza Real*) R.H.

ara [à'rá] *nf* (*altar*) altar; **en ~s de** for the sake of.

árabe [à'ràhe] *a* Arab, Arabian, Arabic ♦ *nm/f* Arab ♦ *nm* (*LING*) Arabic.

Arabia [àrá'hyá] *nf* Arabia; ~ **Saudí** *o* **Saudita** Saudi Arabia.

arábigo, a [àrá'hēgo, à] *a* Arab, Arabian, Arabic.

arácnido [àràk'nētho] *nm* arachnid.

arado [àrá'tho] *nm* plow (*US*), plough (*Brit*).

aragonés, esa [àràgones', e'sá] *a, nm/f* Aragonese ♦ *nm* (*LING*) Aragonese

arancel [àránsel'] *nm* tariff, duty; ~ **de aduanas** (customs) duty.

arandela [àrànde'lá] *nf* (*TEC*) washer; (*chorrera*) frill.

araña [àrá'nyá] *nf* (*ZOOL*) spider; (*lámpara*) chandelier.

arañar [àrà/nyàr'] *vt* to scratch.

arañazo [àrànyá'so] *nm* scratch.

arar [àrár'] *vt* to plow (*US*), plough (*Brit*), till.

araucano, a [àráōōká'no, à] *a, nm/f* Araucanian.

arbitraje [àrhētrà'he] *nm* arbitration.

arbitrar [àrhētrár'] *vt* to arbitrate in; (*recursos*) to bring together; (*DEPORTE*) to referee ♦ *vi* to arbitrate.

arbitrariedad [àrhētràryethàth'] *nf* arbitrariness; (*acto*) arbitrary act.

arbitrario, a [àrhētrà'ryo] *a* arbitrary.

arbitrio [àrhē'tryo] *nm* free will; (*JUR*)

adjudication, decision; **dejar al ~ de uno** to leave to sb's discretion.

árbitro [àr'hētro] *nm* arbitrator; (*DEPORTE*) referee; (*TENIS*) umpire.

árbol [àr'hol] *nm* (*BOT*) tree; (*NAUT*) mast; (*TEC*) axle, shaft.

arbolado, a [àrholá'tho, à] *a* wooded; (*camino*) tree-lined ♦ *nm* woodland.

arboladura [àrholàthōō'rá] *nf* rigging.

arbolar [àrholár'] *vt* to hoist, raise.

arboleda [àrhole'thá] *nf* grove, plantation.

arbusto [àrhōō'sto] *nm* bush, shrub.

arca [àr'ká] *nf* chest, box; **A~ de la Alianza** Ark of the Covenant; **A~ de Noé** Noah's Ark.

arcada [àrkà'thá] *nf* arcade; (*de puente*) arch, span; **~s** *nfpl* retching *sg*.

arcaico, a [àrká'ēko, à] *a* archaic.

arce [àr'se] *nm* maple tree.

arcén [àrsen'] *nm* (*de autopista*) hard shoulder; (*de carretera*) shoulder.

arcilla [àrsē'yá] *nf* clay.

arco [àr'ko] *nm* arch; (*MAT*) arc; (*MIL, MUS*) bow; ~ **iris** rainbow.

arcón [àrkon'] *nm* large chest.

archiconocido, a [àrtchēkonosē'tho, à] *a* extremely well-known.

archipiélago [àrtchēpye'làgo] *nm* archipelago.

archisabido, a [àrtchēsáhē'tho, à] *a* extremely well-known.

archivador [àrtchēhàthor'] *nm* filing cabinet; ~ **colgante** suspension file.

archivar [àrtchēhár'] *vt* to file (away); (*INFORM*) to archive.

archivo [àrtchē'ho] *nm* archive(s) (*pl*); (*INFORM*) file, archive; **A~ Nacional** Public Record Office; **~s policíacos** police files; **nombre de ~** (*INFORM*) filename; ~ **maestro** (*INFORM*) master file; ~ **de transacciones** (*INFORM*) transactions file.

arder [àrther'] *vt* to burn; ~ **sin llama** to smolder (*US*), smoulder (*Brit*); **estar que arde** (*persona*) to fume.

ardid [àrthēth'] *nm* ruse.

ardiente [àrthyen'te] *a* ardent.

ardilla [àrthē'yá] *nf* squirrel.

ardor [àrthor'] *nm* (*calor*) heat, warmth; (*fig*) ardor (*US*), ardour (*Brit*); ~ **de estómago** heartburn.

arduo, a [àr'thwo, à] *a* arduous.

área [à'reá] *nf* area; (*DEPORTE*) penalty area; ~ **de excedentes** (*INFORM*) overflow area.

ARENA [àre'ná] *nf abr* (*El Salvador: POL*) = *Alianza Republicana Nacionalista*.

arena [àre'ná] *nf* sand; (*de una lucha*) arena.

arenal [àrenál'] *nm* (*arena movediza*) quicksand.

arenga [àren'gá] *nf* (*fam*) sermon.

arengar |árengár'| *vt* to harangue.
arengue |áren'ge| *etc vb V* **arengar**.
arenillas |árenē'yás| *nfpl* (*MED*) stones.
arenisca |árenēs'ko, á| *nf* sandstone; (*cascajo*) grit.
arenoso, a |áreno'so, á| *a* sandy.
arenque |áren'ke| *nm* herring.
arete |áre'te| *nm* earring.
argamasa |árgámá'sá| *nf* mortar, plaster.
Argel |árhel'| *n* Algiers.
Argelia |árhe'lyá| *nf* Algeria.
argelino, a |árhelē'no, á| *a, nm/f* Algerian.
Argentina |árhentē'ná| *nf*: (**la**) ~ the Argentine, Argentina.
argentino, a |árhentē'no, á| *a* Argentinian; (*de plata*) silvery ♦ *nm/f* Argentinian.
argolla |árgo'yá| *nf* (large) ring.
argot |árgo'| *nm, pl* **argots** |árgo', árgos'| slang.
argucia |árgōō'syá| *nf* subtlety, sophistry.
argüir |árgwēr'| *vt* to deduce; (*discutir*) to argue; (*indicar*) to indicate, imply; (*censurar*) to reproach ♦ *vi* to argue.
argumentación |árgōōmentásyon'| *nf* (line of) argument.
argumentar |árgōōmentár'| *vt, vi* to argue.
argumento |árgōōmen'to| *nm* argument; (*razonamiento*) reasoning; (*de novela etc*) plot; (*CINE, TV*) storyline.
arguyendo |árgōōyen'do| *etc vb V* **argüir**.
aria |á'ryá| *nf* aria.
aridez |árēthes'| *nf* aridity, dryness.
árido, a |á'rētho, á| *a* arid, dry; ~**s** *nmpl* dry goods.
Aries |á'ryes| *nm* Aries.
ariete |árye'te| *nm* battering ram.
ario, a |á'ryo, á| *a* Aryan.
arisco, a |árēs'ko, á| *a* surly; (*insociable*) unsociable.
aristocracia |árēstokrá'syá| *nf* aristocracy.
aristócrata |árēsto'krátá| *nm/f* aristocrat.
aristocrático, a |árēstokrá'tēko, á| *a* aristocratic.
aritmética |árētme'tēká| *nf* arithmetic.
aritmético, a |árētme'tēko, á| *a* arithmetic(al) ♦ *nm/f* arithmetician.
arma |ár'má| *nf* arm; ~**s** *nfpl* arms; ~ **blanca** blade, knife; (*espada*) sword; ~ **de fuego** firearm; ~**s cortas** small arms; **rendir las** ~**s** to lay down one's arms; **ser de** ~**s tomar** to be somebody to be reckoned with.
armada |ármá'thá| *nf* armada; (*flota*) fleet; *V tb* **armado**.
armadillo |ármáthē'yo| *nm* armadillo.
armado, a |ármá'tho, á| *a* armed; (*TEC*) reinforced.
armador |ármáthor'| *nm* (*NAUT*) shipowner.
armadura |ármáthōō'rá| *nf* (*MIL*) armor (*US*), armour (*Brit*); (*TEC*) framework; (*ZOOL*) skeleton; (*FÍSICA*) armature.

armamentista |ármámentē'stá| **armamentístico, a** |ármámentē'stēko, á| *a* arms *cpd*.
armamento |ármámen'to| *nm* armament; (*NAUT*) fitting-out.
armar |ármár'| *vt* (*soldado*) to arm; (*máquina*) to assemble; (*navío*) to fit out; ~**la**, ~ **un lío** to start a row; ~**se** *vr*: ~**se de valor** to summon up one's courage.
armario |ármá'ryo| *nm* wardrobe.
armatoste |ármáto'ste| *nm* (*mueble*) monstrosity; (*máquina*) contraption.
armazón |ármáson'| *nf o m* body, chassis; (*de mueble etc*) frame; (*ARQ*) skeleton.
armería |ármerē'á| *nf* (*museo*) military museum; (*tienda*) gunsmith's.
armiño |ármē'nyo| *nm* stoat; (*piel*) ermine.
armisticio |ármēstē'syo| *nm* armistice.
armonía |ármonē'á| *nf* harmony.
armónica |ármo'nēká| *nf* harmonica; *V tb* **armónico**.
armonice |ármonē'se| *etc vb V* **armonizar**.
armónico, a |ármo'nēko, á| *a* harmonic.
armonioso, a |ármonyo'so, á| *a* harmonious.
armonizar |ármonēsár'| *vt* to harmonize; (*diferencias*) to reconcile ♦ *vi* to harmonize; ~ **con** (*fig*) to be in keeping with; (*colores*) to blend in with.
arnés |árnes'| *nm* armor (*US*), armour (*Brit*); **arneses** *nmpl* harness *sg*.
aro |á'ro| *nm* ring; (*tejo*) quoit; (*AM*: *pendiente*) earring; **entrar por el** ~ to give in.
aroma |áro'má| *nm* aroma.
aromático, a |áromá'tēko, á| *a* aromatic.
arpa |ár'pá| *nf* harp.
arpegio |árpe'hyo| *nm* (*MUS*) arpeggio.
arpía |árpē'á| *nf* (*fig*) shrew.
arpillera |árpēye'rá| *nf* sacking, sackcloth.
arpón |árpon'| *nm* harpoon.
arquear |árkeár'| *vt* to arch, bend; ~**se** *vr* to arch, bend.
arqueo |árke'o| *nm* (*gen*) arching; (*NAUT*) tonnage.
arqueología |árkeolohē'á| *nf* archeology.
arqueológico, a |árkeolo'hēko, á| *a* archeological.
arqueólogo, a |árkeo'logo, á| *nm/f* archeologist.
arquero |árke'ro| *nm* archer, bowman.
arquetipo |árketē'po| *nm* archetype.
arquitecto, a |árkētek'to, á| *nm/f* architect; ~ **paisajista** *o* **de jardines** landscape gardener.
arquitectónico, a |árkētekto'nēko, á| *a* architectural.
arquitectura |árkētektōō'rá| *nf* architecture.
arrabal |árrabál'| *nm* suburb; (*AM*) slum; ~**es** *nmpl* outskirts.

arrabalero, a |àrràbálc'ro. à| *a* (*fig*) common, coarse.

arracimarse |àrràscmár'sc| *vr* to cluster together.

arraigado, a |àrràĉgá'tho. à| *a* deep-rooted; (*fig*) established.

arraigar |àrràĉgár'| *vt* to establish ♦ *vi*, ~se *vr* to take root; (*persona*) to settle.

arraigo |àrrà'ĉgo| *nm* (*raíces*) roots *pl*; (*bienes*) property; (*influencia*) hold; **hombre de** ~ man of property.

arraigue |àrrà'ĉgc| *etc vb V* **arraigar.**

arrancada |àrrànká'thá| *nf* (*arranque*) sudden start; (*AM: fuga*) sudden dash.

arrancar |àrrànkár'| *vt* (*sacar*) to extract, pull out; (*arrebatar*) to snatch (away); (*pedazo*) to tear off; (*página*) to rip out; (*suspiro*) to heave; (*AUTO*) to start; (*INFORM*) to boot; (*fig*) to extract; ~ **información a uno** to extract information from sb ♦ *vi* (*AUTO, máquina*) to start; (*ponerse en marcha*) to get going; ~ **de** to stem from.

arranque |àrràn'kc| *etc vb V* **arrancar** ♦ *nm* sudden start; (*AUTO*) start; (*fig*) fit, outburst.

arras |à'rràs| *nfpl* pledge *sg*, security *sg*.

arrasar |àrràsàr'| *vt* (*aplanar*) to level, flatten; (*destruir*) to demolish.

arrastrado, a |àrràstrá'tho. à| *a* poor, wretched; (*AM*) servile.

arrastrador |àrràstràthor'| *nm* (*en máquina impresora*) tractor.

arrastrar |àrràstrár'| *vt* to drag (along); (*fig*) to drag down, degrade; (*suj: agua, viento*) to carry away ♦ *vi* to drag; ~se *vr* to crawl; (*fig*) to grovel; **llevar algo arrastrado** to drag sth along.

arrastre |àrràs'trc| *nm* drag, dragging; (*DEPORTE*) crawl; **estar para el** ~ (*fig*) to have had it; ~ **de papel por fricción/por tracción** (*en máquina impresora*) friction/tractor feed.

array |àrrà'ĉ| *nm* (*INFORM*) array; ~ **empaquetado** (*INFORM*) packed array.

arrayán |àrràyàn'| *nm* myrtle.

arre |à'rrc| *excl* gee up!

arrear |àrreár'| *vt* to drive on, urge on ♦ *vi* to hurry along.

arrebañaduras |àrrebànyàthōō'ràs| *nfpl* leftovers *pl*.

arrebañar |àrrebànyár'| *vt* (*juntar*) to scrape together.

arrebatado, a |àrrebàtá'tho. à| *a* rash, impetuous; (*repentino*) sudden, hasty.

arrebatar |àrrebàtár'| *vt* to snatch (away), seize; (*fig*) to captivate; ~se *vr* to get carried away, get excited.

arrebato |àrrebà'to| *nm* fit of rage, fury; (*éxtasis*) rapture; **en un** ~ **de cólera** in an outburst of anger.

arrebol |àrrebol'| *nm* (*colorete*) rouge; ~es

nmpl red clouds.

arrebolar |àrrebolár'| *vt* to redden; ~se *vr* (*enrojecer*) to blush.

arrebujar |àrrebōōhár'| *vt* (*objetos*) to jumble together; ~se *vr* to wrap o.s. up.

arreciar |àrresyár'| *vi* to get worse; (*viento*) to get stronger.

arrecife |àrrcsĉ'fc| *nm* reef.

arrechucho |àrrctchōōtch'o| *nm* (*MED*) turn.

arredrar |àrrethrár'| *vt* (*hacer retirarse*) to drive back; ~se *vr* (*apartarse*) to draw back; ~se **ante algo** to shrink away from sth.

arreglado, a |àrreglá'tho. à| *a* (*ordenado*) neat, orderly; (*moderado*) moderate, reasonable.

arreglar |àrreglár'| *vt* (*poner orden*) to tidy up; (*algo roto*) to fix, repair; (*problema*) to solve; ~se *vr* to reach an understanding; **arreglárselas** (*fam*) to get by, manage.

arreglo |àrrc'glo| *nm* settlement; (*orden*) order; (*acuerdo*) agreement; (*MUS*) arrangement, setting; (*INFORM*) array; **con** ~ **a** in accordance with; **llegar a un** ~ to reach a compromise.

arrellanarse |àrrcyànàr'sc| *vr* to sprawl; ~ **en el asiento** to lie back in one's chair.

arremangar |àrrcmángár'| *vt* to roll up, turn up; ~se *vr* to roll up one's sleeves.

arremangue |àrrcmàn'gc| *etc vb V* **arremangar.**

arremeter |àrremetcr'| *vt* to attack, assault; ~ **contra uno** to attack sb.

arremetida |àrrcmctĉ'thá| *nf* assault.

arremolinarse |àrrcmolĉnàr'sc| *vr* to crowd around, mill around; (*corriente*) to swirl, eddy.

arrendador, a |àrrcndáthor'. à| *nm/f* landlord/lady.

arrendamiento |àrrcndàmycn'to| *nm* letting; (*el alquilar*) renting; (*contrato*) lease; (*alquiler*) rent.

arrendar |àrrcndár'| *vt* to let; to hire; to lease; to rent.

arrendatario, a |àrrcndàtá'ryo. à| *nm/f* tenant.

arreo |àrrc'o| *nm* adornment; ~s *nmpl* harness *sg*, trappings.

arrepentimiento |àrrcpcntĉmycn'to| *nm* regret, repentance.

arrepentirse |àrrcpcntĉr'sc| *vr* to repent; ~ **de (haber hecho) algo** to regret (doing) sth.

arrepienta |àrrcpycn'tá| *etc*, **arrepintiendo** |àrrcpĉntycn'do| *etc vb V* **arrepentirse.**

arrestar |àrrcstár'| *vt* to arrest; (*encarcelar*) to imprison.

arresto |àrrc'sto| *nm* arrest; (*MIL*) detention; (*audacia*) boldness, daring; ~ **domiciliario** house arrest.

arriar |árryàr'| *vt* (*velas*) to haul down; (*bandera*) to lower, strike; (*un cable*) to pay out.

arriate |árryà'tc| *nm* (*BOT*) bed; (*camino*) road.

arriba |árrē'ḥá| *ad* (*posición*) above, overhead, on top; (*en casa*) upstairs; (*dirección*) up, upwards; ~ **de** above, higher (up) than; ~ **del todo** at the very top; **el piso de** ~ the apartment upstairs; **de** ~ **abajo** from top to bottom; (*persona*) from head to foot; **calle** ~ up the street; **lo** ~ **mencionado** the aforementioned; ~ **de 20 pesetas** more than 20 pesetas; **de 10 dólares para** ~ from 10 dollars upwards; ¡~ **España!** long live Spain!; ¡~ **las manos!** hands up!

arribar |árrēḥár'| *vi* to put into port; (*llegar*) to arrive.

arribista |árrēḥē'stá| *nm/f* parvenu(e), upstart.

arriendo |árryen'do| *etc vb V* **arrendar** ♦ *nm* = **arrendamiento**.

arriero |árryc'ro| *nm* muleteer.

arriesgado, a |árrycsgá'tḥo, á| *a* (*peligroso*) risky; (*audaz*) bold, daring.

arriesgar |árrycsgár'| *vt* to risk; (*poner en peligro*) to endanger; ~**se** *vr* to take a risk.

arriesgue |árrycs'gc| *etc vb V* **arriesgar**.

arrimar |árrēmár'| *vt* (*acercar*) to bring close; (*poner de lado*) to set aside; ~**se** *vr* to come close *o* closer; ~**se a** to lean on; (*fig*) to keep company with; (*buscar ayuda*) to seek the protection of; **arrímate a mí** cuddle up to me.

arrinconado, a |árrēnkoná'tḥo, á| *a* forgotten, neglected.

arrinconar |árrēnkonár'| *vt* to put in a corner; (*fig*) to put to one side; (*abandonar*) to push aside.

arriscado, a |árrēská'tḥo, á| *a* (*GEO*) craggy; (*fig*) bold, resolute.

arroba |árro'ḥá| *nf* (*peso*) 25 pounds; **tiene talento por** ~**s** he has loads of talent.

arrobado, a |árroḥá'tḥo, á| *a* entranced, enchanted.

arrobamiento |árroḥámyen'to| *nm* ecstasy.

arrobar |árroḥár'| *vt* to enchant; ~**se** *vr* to be enraptured; (*místico*) to go into a trance.

arrodillarse |árrotḥēyár'sc| *vr* to kneel (down).

arrogancia |árrogán'syá| *nf* arrogance.

arrogante |árrogán'tc| *a* arrogant.

arrojar |árrohár'| *vt* to throw, hurl; (*humo*) to emit, give out; (*COM*) to yield, produce; ~**se** *vr* to throw *o* hurl o.s.

arrojo |árro'ho| *nm* daring.

arrollador, a |árroyátḥor', á| *a* crushing, overwhelming.

arrollar |árroyár'| *vt* (*enrollar*) to roll up;

(*suj: inundación*) to wash away; (*AUTO*) to run over; (*DEPORTE*) to crush.

arropar |árropár'| *vt* to cover (up), wrap up; ~**se** *vr* to wrap o.s. up.

arrostrar |árrostrár'| *vt* to face (up to); ~**se** *vr*: ~**se con uno** to face up to sb.

arroyo |árro'yo| *nm* stream; (*de la calle*) gutter; **poner a uno en el** ~ to turn sb onto the streets.

arroz |árros'| *nm* rice; ~ **con leche** rice pudding.

arruga |árrōō'gá| *nf* fold; (*de cara*) wrinkle; (*de vestido*) crease.

arrugar |árrōōgár'| *vt* to fold; to wrinkle; to crease; ~**se** *vr* to get wrinkled; to get creased.

arrugue |árrōō'gc| *etc vb V* **arrugar**.

arruinar |árrwēnár'| *vt* to ruin, wreck; ~**se** *vr* to be ruined.

arrullar |árrōōyár'| *vi* to coo ♦ *vt* to lull to sleep.

arrumaco |árrōōmá'ko| *nm* (*caricia*) caress; (*halago*) piece of flattery.

arrumbar |árrōōmbár'| *vt* (*objeto*) to discard; (*individuo*) to silence.

arsenal |árscnál'| *nm* naval dockyard; (*MIL*) arsenal.

arsénico |ársc'nēko| *nm* arsenic.

arte |ár'tc| *nm* (*gen m en sg y siempre f en pl*) art; (*maña*) skill, guile; **por** ~ **de magia** (as if) by magic; **no tener** ~ **ni parte en algo** to have nothing whatsoever to do with sth; ~**s** *nfpl* arts; **Bellas A**~**s** Fine Art *sg*; ~**s y oficios** arts and crafts.

artefacto |ártcfák'to| *nm* appliance; (*ARQUEOLOGÍA*) artifact (*US*), artefact (*Brit*).

arteria |ártc'ryá| *nf* artery.

artesa |ártc'sá| *nf* trough.

artesanía |ártcsánē'á| *nf* craftsmanship; (*artículos*) handicrafts *pl*.

artesano, a |ártcsá'no, á| *nm/f* artisan, craftsman/woman.

ártico, a |ár'tēko, á| *a* Arctic ♦ *nm*: **el Á**~ the Arctic.

articulación |ártēkōōlásyon'| *nf* articulation; (*MED, TEC*) joint.

articulado, a |ártēkōōlá'tḥo, á| *a* articulated; jointed.

articular |ártēkōōlár'| *vt* to articulate; to join together.

articulista |ártēkōōlē'stá| *nm/f* columnist, contributor (to a newspaper).

artículo |ártē'kōōlo| *nm* article; (*cosa*) thing, article; (*TV*) feature, report; ~ **de fondo** leader, editorial; ~**s** *nmpl* goods; ~**s de marca** (*COM*) proprietary goods.

artífice |ártē'fēsc| *nm* artist, craftsman; (*fig*) architect.

artificial |ártēfēsyàl'| *a* artificial.

artificio |ártēfē'syo| *nm* art, skill; (*artesa-*

nia) craftsmanship; (*astucia*) cunning.
artilugio [àrtēlōō'hyo] *nm* gadget.
artillería [àrtēyerē'à] *nf* artillery.
artillero [àrtēye'ro] *nm* artilleryman, gunner.
artimaña [àrtēmá'nyà] *nf* trap, snare; (*astucia*) cunning.
artista [àrtē'stà] *nm/f* (*pintor*) artist, painter; (*TEATRO*) artist, artiste.
artístico, a [àrtē'stēko, à] *a* artistic.
artritis [àrtrē'tēs] *nf* arthritis.
arveja [àrᵇe'hà] *nf* (*AM*) pea.
Arz. *abr* (= *Arzobispo*) Abp.
arzobispo [àrsobēs'po] *nm* archbishop.
as [às] *nm* ace; ~ **del fútbol** star football player.
asa [à'sà] *nf* handle; (*fig*) lever.
asado [àsà'tho] *nm* roast (meat).
asador [àsàthor'] *nm* (*varilla*) spit; (*aparato*) spit roaster.
asadura(s) [àsàthōō'rà(s)] *nf(pl)* entrails *pl*, offal *sg*; (*CULIN*) chitterlings *pl*.
asaetar [àsàetàr'] *vt* (*fig*) to bother.
asalariado, a [àsàlàryà'tho, à] *a* paid, wage-earning, salaried ♦ *nm/f* wage earner.
asaltador, a [àsàltàthor', à], **asaltante** [àsàltà'nte] *nm/f* assailant.
asaltar [àsàltàr'] *vt* to attack, assault; (*fig*) to assail.
asalto [àsàl'to] *nm* attack, assault; (*DEPORTE*) round.
asamblea [àsàmble'à] *nf* assembly; (*reunión*) meeting.
asar [àsàr'] *vt* to roast; ~ **al horno/a la parrilla** to bake/grill; ~**se** *vr* (*fig*): **me aso de calor** I'm roasting; **aquí se asa uno vivo** it's boiling hot here.
asbesto [àsᵇe'sto] *nm* asbestos.
ascendencia [àsᵈenden'syà] *nf* ancestry; (*AM*) ascendancy; **de** ~ **francesa** of French origin.
ascender [àsender'] *vi* (*subir*) to ascend, rise; (*ser promovido*) to gain promotion ♦ *vt* to promote; ~ **a** to amount to.
ascendiente [àsendyen'te] *nm* influence ♦ *nm/f* ancestor.
ascensión [àsensyon'] *nf* ascent; **la A**~ the Ascension.
ascenso [àsen'so] *nm* ascent; (*promoción*) promotion.
ascensor [àsensor'] *nm* elevator (*US*), lift (*Brit*).
ascético, a [àse'tēko, à] *a* ascetic.
ascienda [àsyen'dà] *etc vb* V **ascender**.
asco [às'ko] *nm*: **el ajo me da** ~ I hate *o* loathe garlic; **hacer** ~**s de algo** to turn up one's nose at sth; **estar hecho un** ~ to be filthy; **poner a uno de** ~ to call sb all sorts of names *o* every name under the sun; **¡qué** ~! how revolting *o* disgusting!
ascua [às'kwà] *nf* ember; **arrimar el** ~ **a su**

sardina to look after number one; **estar en** ~**s** to be on tenterhooks.
aseado, a [àseà'tho, à] *a* clean; (*arreglado*) tidy; (*pulcro*) smart.
asear [àseàr'] *vt* (*lavar*) to wash; (*ordenar*) to tidy (up).
asechanza [àsetchàn'sà] *nf* trap, snare.
asechar [àsetchàr'] *vt* to set a trap for.
asediar [àsethyàr'] *vt* (*MIL*) to besiege, lay siege to; (*fig*) to chase, pester.
asedio [àse'thyo] *nm* siege; (*COM*) run.
asegurado, a [àsegōōrà'tho, à] *a* insured.
asegurador, a [àsegōōràthor', à] *nm/f* insurer.
asegurar [àsegōōràr'] *vt* (*consolidar*) to secure, fasten; (*dar garantía de*) to guarantee; (*preservar*) to safeguard; (*afirmar, dar por cierto*) to assure, affirm; (*tranquilizar*) to reassure; (*tomar un seguro*) to insure; ~**se** *vr* to assure o.s., make sure.
asemejarse [àsemehàr'se] *vr* to be alike; ~ **a** to be like, resemble.
asentado, a [àsentà'tho, à] *a* established, settled.
asentar [àsentàr'] *vt* (*sentar*) to seat, sit down; (*poner*) to place, establish; (*alisar*) to level, smooth down *o* out; (*anotar*) to note down ♦ *vi* to be suitable, suit.
asentimiento [àsentēmyen'to] *nm* assent, agreement.
asentir [àsentēr'] *vi* to assent, agree.
aseo [àse'o] *nm* cleanliness; ~**s** *nmpl* restroom *sg* (*US*), toilet *sg* (*Brit*), cloakroom *sg*.
aséptico, a [àsep'tēko, à] *a* germ-free, free from infection.
asequible [àsekē'ᵇle] *a* (*precio*) reasonable; (*meta*) attainable; (*persona*) approachable.
aserradero [àserràᵈe'ro] *nm* sawmill.
aserrar [àserràr'] *vt* to saw.
aserrín [àserrēn'] *nm* sawdust.
asesinar [àsesēnàr'] *vt* to murder; (*POL*) to assassinate.
asesinato [àsesēnà'to] *nm* murder; assassination.
asesino, a [àsesē'no, à] *nm/f* murderer, killer; (*POL*) assassin.
asesor, a [àsesor', à] *nm/f* adviser, consultant; (*COM*) assessor, consultant; ~ **administrativo** management consultant.
asesorar [àsesoràr'] *vt* (*JUR*) to advise, give legal advice to; (*COM*) to act as consultant to; ~**se** *vr*: ~**se con** *o* **de** to take advice from, consult.
asesoría [àsesorē'à] *nf* (*cargo*) consultancy; (*oficina*) consultant's office.
asestar [àsestàr'] *vt* (*golpe*) to deal; (*arma*) to aim; (*tiro*) to fire.
aseverar [àseᵛeràr'] *vt* to assert.
asfaltado, a [àsfàltà'tho, à] *a* asphalted ♦ *nm* (*pavimento*) asphalt.

asfalto [àsfál'to] *nm* asphalt.

asfixia [àsfēk'syà] *nf* asphyxia, suffocation.

asfixiar [àsfēksyár'] *vt* to asphyxiate, suffocate.

asga [às'gà] *etc vb* V **asir.**

así [àsē'] *ad* (*de esta manera*) in this way, like this, thus; (*aunque*) although; (*tan pronto como*) as soon as; ~ **que** so; ~ **como** as well as; ~ **y todo** even so; *¿no es* ~? isn't it?, didn't you? *etc*; ~ **de grande** this big; *¡~* **sea!** so be it!; ~ **es la vida** such is life, that's life.

Asia [à'syà] *nf* Asia.

asiático, a [àsyá'tēko, à] *a, nm/f* Asian, Asiatic.

asidero [àsēthe'ro] *nm* handle.

asiduidad [àsēthwēthàth'] *nf* assiduousness.

asiduo, a [àsē'thwo, à] *a* assiduous; (*frecuente*) frequent ♦ *nm/f* regular (customer).

asiento [àsyen'to] *etc vb* V **asentar, asentir** ♦ *nm* (*mueble*) seat, chair; (*de coche, en tribunal etc*) seat; (*localidad*) seat, place; (*fundamento*) site; ~ **delantero/trasero** front/back seat.

asierre [àsye'rre] *etc vb* V **aserrar.**

asignación [àsēgnàsyon'] *nf* (*atribución*) assignment; (*reparto*) allocation; (*COM*) allowance; ~ **(semanal)** pocket money; ~ **de presupuesto** budget appropriation.

asignar [àsēgnár'] *vt* to assign, allocate.

asignatura [àsēgnátōō'rà] *nf* subject; (*curso*) course.

asilado, a [àsēlà'tho, à] *nm/f* refugee.

asilo [àsē'lo] *nm* (*refugio*) asylum, refuge; (*establecimiento*) home, institution; ~ **político** political asylum.

asimilación [àsēmēlàsyon'] *nf* assimilation.

asimilar [àsēmēlár'] *vt* to assimilate.

asimismo [àsēmēs'mo] *ad* in the same way, likewise.

asintiendo [àsēntyen'do] *etc vb* V **asentir.**

asir [àsēr'] *vt* to seize, grasp; ~**se** *vr* to take hold; ~**se** **a** o **de** to seize.

asistencia [àsēsten'syà] *nf* presence; (*TEATRO*) audience; (*MED*) attendance; (*ayuda*) assistance; ~ **social** social o welfare work.

asistente, a [àsēsten'te, à] *nm/f* assistant ♦ *nm* (*MIL*) orderly ♦ *nf* daily help; **los** ~**s** those present; ~ **social** social worker.

asistido, a [àsēstē'tho, à] *a* (*AUTO:* *dirección*) power-assisted; ~ **por ordenador** computer-assisted.

asistir [àsēstēr'] *vt* to assist, help ♦ *vi*: ~ **a** to attend, be present at.

asma [às'mà] *nf* asthma.

asno [às'no] *nm* donkey; (*fig*) ass.

asociación [àsosyàsyon'] *nf* association; (*COM*) partnership.

asociado, a [àsosyà'tho, à] *a* associate ♦ *nm/f* associate; (*COM*) partner.

asociar [àsosyár'] *vt* to associate; ~**se** *vr* to become partners.

asolar [àsolár'] *vt* to destroy.

asolear [àsoleár'] *vt* to put in the sun; ~**se** *vr* to sunbathe.

asomar [àsomár'] *vt* to show, stick out ♦ *vi* to appear; ~**se** *vr* to appear, show up; ~ **la cabeza por la ventana** to put one's head out of the window.

asombrar [àsombrár'] *vt* to amaze, astonish; ~**se** *vr*: ~**se (de)** (*sorprenderse*) to be amazed (at); (*asustarse*) to be frightened (at).

asombro [àsom'bro] *nm* amazement, astonishment.

asombroso, a [àsombro'so, à] *a* amazing, astonishing.

asomo [àso'mo] *nm* hint, sign; **ni por** ~ by no means.

asonancia [àsonán'syà] *nf* (*LIT*) assonance; (*fig*) connection; **no tener** ~ **con** to bear no relation to.

aspa [às'pà] *nf* (*cruz*) cross; (*de molino*) sail; **en** ~ X-shaped.

aspaviento [àspàvyen'to] *nm* exaggerated display of feeling; (*fam*) fuss.

aspecto [àspek'to] *nm* (*apariencia*) look, appearance; (*fig*) aspect; **bajo ese** ~ from that point of view.

aspereza [àspere'sà] *nf* roughness; (*agrura*) sourness; (*de carácter*) surliness.

áspero, a [às'pero, à] *a* rough; sour; harsh.

aspersión [àspersyon'] *nf* sprinkling; (*AGR*) spraying.

aspiración [àspēràsyon'] *nf* breath, inhalation; (*MUS*) short pause; **aspiraciones** *nfpl* aspirations.

aspiradora [àspēràtho'rà] *nf* vacuum cleaner.

aspirante [àspēràn'te] *nm/f* (*candidato*) candidate; (*DEPORTE*) contender.

aspirar [àspērár'] *vt* to breathe in ♦ *vi*: ~ **a** to aspire to.

aspirina [àspērē'nà] *nf* aspirin.

asquear [àskeár'] *vt* to sicken ♦ *vi* to be sickening; ~**se** *vr* to feel disgusted.

asquerosidad [àskerosēthàth'] *nf* (*suciedad*) filth; (*dicho*) obscenity; (*truco*) dirty trick.

asqueroso, a [àskero'so, à] *a* disgusting, sickening.

asta [à'stà] *nf* lance; (*arpón*) spear; (*mango*) shaft, handle; (*ZOOL*) horn; **a media** ~ at half mast.

astado, a [àstà'tho, à] *a* horned ♦ *nm* bull.

asterisco [àsterēs'ko] *nm* asterisk.

astilla [àstē'yà] *nf* splinter; (*pedacito*) chip; ~**s** *nfpl* firewood *sg.*

astillarse [àstēyár'se] *vr* to splinter; (*fig*) to shatter.

astillero [àstēye'ro] *nm* shipyard.

astringente [àstrĕnhen'te] *a, nm* astringent.

astro [às'tro] *nm* star.

astrología [àstrolohĕ'à] *nf* astrology.

astrólogo, a [àstro'logo, à] *nm/f* astrologer.

astronauta [àstroná'ōōtá] *nm/f* astronaut.

astronave [àstroná'ḫe] *nm* spaceship.

astronomía [àstronomĕ'à] *nf* astronomy.

astrónomo, a [àstro'nomo, à] *nm/f* astronomer.

astroso, a [àstro'so, à] *a* (*desaliñado*) untidy; (*vil*) contemptible.

astucia [àstōō'syà] *nf* astuteness; (*destreza*) clever trick.

asturiano, a [àstōōryà'no, à] *a, nm/f* Asturian.

Asturias [àstōō'ryàs] *nfpl* Asturias; **Príncipe de** ~ crown prince.

astuto, a [àstōō'to, à] *a* astute; (*taimado*) cunning.

asueto [àswe'to] *nm* holiday; (*tiempo libre*) time off; **día de** ~ day off; **tarde de** ~ (*trabajo*) afternoon off; (*ESCOL*) halfholiday.

asumir [àsōōmĕr'] *vt* to assume.

asunción [àsōōnsyon'] *nf* assumption.

asunto [àsōōn'to] *nm* (*tema*) matter, subject; (*negocio*) business; **¡eso es** ~ **mío!** that's my business!; **~s exteriores** foreign affairs; **~s a tratar** agenda *sg*.

asustadizo, a [àsōōstàthĕ'so, à] *a* easily frightened.

asustar [àsōōstàr'] *vt* to frighten; **~se** *vr* to be/become frightened.

atacante [àtákán'te] *nm/f* attacker.

atacar [àtákár'] *vt* to attack.

atadura [àtàthōō'rà] *nf* bond, tie.

atajar [àtàhár'] *vt* (*gen*) to stop; (*ruta de fuga*) to cut off; (*discurso*) to interrupt ♦ *vi* to take a short cut.

atajo [àtá'ho] *nm* short cut; (*DEPORTE*) tackle.

atalaya [àtàlà'yà] *nf* watchtower.

atañer [àtànyer'] *vi*: ~ **a** to concern; **en lo que atañe a eso** with regard to that.

ataque [àtá'ke] *etc vb V* **atacar** ♦ *nm* attack; ~ **cardíaco** heart attack.

atar [àtár'] *vt* to tie, tie up; ~ **la lengua a uno** (*fig*) to silence sb.

atardecer [àtàrthĕser'] *vi* to get dark ♦ *nm* evening; (*crepúsculo*) dusk.

atardezca [àtàrthes'kà] *etc vb V* **atardecer**.

atareado, a [àtàreá'tho, à] *a* busy.

atascar [àtáskár'] *vt* to clog up; (*obstruir*) to jam; (*fig*) to hinder; **~se** *vr* to stall; (*cañería*) to get blocked up; (*fig*) to get bogged down; (*en discurso*) to dry up.

atasco [àtás'ko] *nm* obstruction; (*AUTO*) traffic jam.

atasque [àtás'ke] *etc vb V* **atascar**.

ataúd [àtàōōth'] *nm* coffin.

ataviar [àtàbyàr'] *vt* to deck, array; **~se** *vr* to dress up.

atavío [àtàbĕ'o] *nm* attire, dress; **~s** *nmpl* finery *sg*.

ateísmo [àteĕs'mo] *nm* atheism.

atemorice [àtemorĕ'se] *etc vb V* **atemorizar**.

atemorizar [àtemorĕsár'] *vt* to frighten, scare; **~se** *vr* to get frightened *o* scared.

Atenas [àtĕ'nàs] *nf* Athens.

atención [àtensyon'] *nf* attention; (*bondad*) kindness ♦ *excl* (be) careful!, look out!; **en** ~ **a esto** in view of this.

atender [àtender'] *vt* to attend to, look after; (*TEC*) to service; (*enfermo*) to care for; (*ruego*) to comply with ♦ *vi* to pay attention; ~ **a** to attend to; (*detalles*) to take care of.

atendré [àtendre'] *etc vb V* **atenerse**.

atenerse [àtener'se] *vr*: ~ **a** to abide by, adhere to.

atenga [àten'gà] *etc vb V* **atenerse**.

ateniense [àtenyen'se] *a, nm/f* Athenian.

atentado [àtentà'tho] *nm* crime, illegal act; (*asalto*) assault; (*terrorista*) attack; ~ **contra la vida de uno** attempt on sb's life; ~ **golpista** (*POL*) attempted coup.

atentamente [àtentàmen'te] *ad*: **le saluda** ~ Yours truly (*US*) *o* faithfully (*Brit*).

atentar [àtentár'] *vi*: ~ **a** *o* **contra** to commit an outrage against.

atento, a [àten'to, à] *a* attentive, observant; (*cortés*) polite, thoughtful; **su atenta (carta)** (*COM*) your letter.

atenuante [àtenwàn'te] *a*: **circunstancias ~s** extenuating *o* mitigating circumstances ♦ *nfpl*: **~s** extenuating *o* mitigating circumstances.

atenuar [àtenwàr'] *vt* to attenuate; (*disminuir*) to lessen, minimize.

ateo, a [àte'o, à] *a* atheistic ♦ *nm/f* atheist.

aterciopelado, a [àtersyopelà'tho, à] *a* velvety.

aterido, a [àterĕ'tho, à] *a*: ~ **de frío** frozen stiff.

aterrador, a [àterràthor', à] *a* frightening.

aterrar [àterrár'] *vt* to frighten; (*aterrorizar*) to terrify; **~se** *vr* to be frightened; to be terrified.

aterrice [àterrĕ'se] *etc vb V* **aterrizar**.

aterrizar [àterrĕsár'] *vi* to land.

aterrorice [àterrorĕ'se] *etc vb V* **aterrorizar**.

aterrorizar [àterrorĕsár'] *vt* to terrify.

atesorar [àtesorár'] *vt* to hoard, store up.

atestado, a [àtestá'tho, à] *a* packed ♦ *nm* (*JUR*) affidavit.

atestar [àtestár'] *vt* to pack, stuff; (*JUR*) to attest, testify to.

atestiguar [àtestĕgwàr'] *vt* to testify to, bear witness to.

atestigüe [àtestĕ'gwe] *etc vb V* **atestiguar**.

atiborrar [àtĕborràr'] *vt* to fill, stuff; **~se** *vr* to stuff o.s.

atice |átē'se| *etc vb* V **atizar.**

ático |á'tēko| *nm* attic; ~ **de lujo** penthouse apartment.

atienda |átyen'dá| *etc vb* V **atender.**

atildar |átēldár'| *vt* to criticize; (*TIP*) to put a tilde over; ~**se** *vr* to spruce o.s. up.

atinado, a |átēná'tho, á| *a* correct; (*sensato*) sensible.

atinar |átēnár'| *vi* (*acertar*) to be right; ~ **con** *o* **en** (*solución*) to hit upon; ~ **a hacer** to manage to do.

atiplado, a |átēplá'tho, á| *a* (*voz*) high-pitched.

atisbar |átēsbár'| *vt* to spy on; (*echar ojeada*) to peep at.

atizar |átēsár'| *vt* to poke; (*horno etc*) to stoke; (*fig*) to stir up, rouse.

atlántico, a |átlàn'tēko, á| *a* Atlantic ♦ *nm*: **el (Océano) A**~ the Atlantic (Ocean).

atlas |át'làs| *nm* atlas.

atleta |átle'tá| *nm/f* athlete.

atlético, a |átle'tēko, á| *a* athletic.

atletismo |átletēs'mo| *nm* athletics *sg*.

atmósfera |átmos'ferá| *nf* atmosphere.

atolondramiento |átolondrámyen'to| *nm* bewilderment; (*insensatez*) silliness.

atolladero |átoyáthe'ro| *nm*: **estar en un** ~ to be in a jam.

atollar |átoyár'| *vi*, ~**se** *vr* to get stuck; (*fig*) to get into a jam.

atómico, a |áto'mēko, á| *a* atomic.

atomizador |átomēsáthor'| *nm* atomizer.

átomo |á'tomo| *nm* atom.

atónito, a |áto'nēto, á| *a* astonished, amazed.

atontado, a |átontá'tho, á| *a* stunned; (*bobo*) silly, daft.

atontar |átontár'| *vt* to stun; ~**se** *vr* to become confused.

atorar |átorár'| *vt* to obstruct; ~**se** *vr* (*atragantarse*) to choke.

atormentar |átormentár'| *vt* to torture; (*molestar*) to torment; (*acosar*) to plague, harass.

atornillar |átornēyár'| *vt* to screw on *o* down.

atosigar |átosēgár'| *vt* to harass.

atosigue |átosē'ge| *etc vb* V **atosigar.**

atrabiliario, a |átráhēlyá'ryo, á| *a* bad-tempered.

atracadero |átrákáthe'ro| *nm* pier.

atracador, a |átrákáthor', á| *nm/f* robber.

atracar |átrákár'| *vt* (*NAUT*) to moor; (*robar*) to hold up, rob ♦ *vi* to moor; ~**se** *vr* (*hartarse*) to stuff o.s.

atracción |átráksyon'| *nf* attraction.

atraco |átrá'ko| *nm* holdup, robbery.

atractivo, a |átráktē'ho, á| *a* attractive ♦ *nm* attraction; (*belleza*) attractiveness.

atraer |átráér'| *vt* to attract; **dejarse** ~ **por**

to be tempted by.

atragantarse |átrágántár'se| *vr*: ~ **(con algo)** to choke (on sth); **se me ha atragantado el chico ese/el inglés** I can't take that kid/English.

atraiga |átrá'ēgá| *etc*, **atraje** |átrà'he| *etc vb* V **atraer.**

atrancar |átránkár'| *vt* (*con tranca, barra*) to bar, bolt.

atranque |átrán'ke| *etc vb* V **atrancar.**

atrapar |átrápár'| *vt* to trap; (*resfriado etc*) to catch.

atraque |átrá'ke| *etc vb* V **atracar.**

atrás |átrás'| *ad* (*movimiento*) back(wards); (*lugar*) behind; (*tiempo*) previously; **ir hacia** ~ to go back(wards); to go to the rear; **estar** ~ to be behind *o* at the back.

atrasado, a |átrásá'tho, á| *a* slow; (*pago*) overdue, late; (*país*) backward.

atrasar |átrásár'| *vi* to be slow; ~**se** *vr* to remain behind; (*llegar tarde*) to arrive late.

atraso |átrá'so| *nm* slowness; lateness, delay; (*de país*) backwardness; ~**s** *nmpl* arrears.

atravesar |átráhesár'| *vt* (*cruzar*) to cross (over); (*traspasar*) to pierce; (*período*) to go through; (*poner al través*) to lay *o* put across; ~**se** *vr* to come in between; (*intervenir*) to interfere.

atraviese |átráhye'se| *etc vb* V **atravesar.**

atrayendo |átráyen'do| *vb* V **atraer.**

atrayente |átráyen'te| *a* attractive.

atreverse |átreher'se| *vr* to dare; (*insolentarse*) to be insolent.

atrevido, a |átrehē'tho, á| *a* daring; insolent.

atrevimiento |átrehēmyen'to| *nm* daring; insolence.

atribución |átrēhōōsyon'| *nf* (*LIT*) attribution; **atribuciones** *nfpl* (*POL*) functions; (*ADMIN*) responsibilities.

atribuir |átrēhōōēr'| *vt* to attribute; (*funciones*) to confer.

atribular |átrēhōōlár'| *vt* to afflict, distress.

atributo |átrēhōō'to| *nm* attribute.

atribuya |átrēhōō'yá| *etc*, **atribuyendo** |átrēhōōyen'do| *etc vb* V **atribuir.**

atril |átrēl'| *nm* lectern; (*MUS*) music stand.

atrio |á'tryo| *nm* (*REL*) porch.

atrocidad |átrosētháth'| *nf* atrocity, outrage.

atronador, a |átronáthor', á| *a* deafening.

atropellar |átropeyár'| *vt* (*derribar*) to knock over *o* down; (*empujar*) to push (aside); (*AUTO*) to run over *o* down; (*agraviar*) to insult; ~**se** *vr* to act hastily.

atropello |átrope'yo| *nm* (*AUTO*) accident; (*empujón*) push; (*agravio*) wrong; (*atrocidad*) outrage.

atroz |átros'| *a* atrocious, awful.

atto., a. *abr* (= *atento, a*) Yours truly (*US*)

o faithfully (*Brit*).

attrezzo [àtrɛ'so] *nm* props *pl*.

atuendo [àtwen'do] *nm* attire.

atufar [àtōōfár'] *vt* (*suj*: *olor*) to overcome; (*molestar*) to irritate; **~se** *vr* (*fig*) to get cross.

atún [àtōōn'] *nm* tuna, tunny.

aturdir [àtōōrthɛr'] *vt* to stun; (*suj*: *ruido*) to deafen; (*fig*) to dumbfound, bewilder.

atur(r)ullar [àtōōr(r)ōōyár'] *vt* to bewilder.

atusar [àtōōsár'] *vt* (*cortar*) to trim; (*alisar*) to smooth (down).

atuve [àtōō'bɛ] *etc vb* V **atenerse**.

audacia [àōōthá'syà] *nf* boldness, audacity.

audaz [àōōthás'] *a* bold, audacious.

audible [àōōthɛ'blɛ] *a* audible.

audición [àōōthēsyon'] *nf* hearing; (*TEATRO*) audition; **~ radiofónica** radio concert.

audiencia [àōōthyɛn'syà] *nf* audience; (*JUR*) high court; (*POL*): **~ pública** public inquiry.

audífono [àōōthē'fono] *nm* hearing aid.

auditor [àōōthɛtor'] *nm* (*JUR*) judge-advocate; (*COM*) auditor.

auditorio [àōōthēto'ryo] *nm* audience; (*sala*) auditorium.

auge [à'ōōhɛ] *nm* boom; (*clímax*) climax; (*ECON*) expansion; **estar en ~** to thrive.

augurar [àōōgōōrár'] *vt* to predict; (*presagiar*) to portend.

augurio [àōōgōō'ryo] *nm* omen.

aula [à'ōōlà] *nf* classroom.

aullar [àōōyàr'] *vi* to howl, yell.

aullido [àōōyē'tho] *nm* howl, yell.

aumentar [àōōmɛntár'] *vt* to increase; (*precios*) to raise; (*producción*) to step up; (*con microscopio, anteojos*) to magnify ♦ *vi*, **~se** *vr* to increase, be on the increase.

aumento [àōōmɛn'to] *nm* increase; rise.

aun [àōōn'] *ad* even.

aún [àōōn'] *ad* still, yet.

aunque [àōōn'kɛ] *conj* though, although, even though.

aúpa [àōō'pá] *excl* up!, come on! (*fam*): **una función de ~** a slap-up do; **una paliza de ~** a good beating.

aupar [àōōpár'] *vt* (*levantar*) to help up; (*fig*) to praise.

aura [à'ōōrà] *nf* (*atmósfera*) aura.

aureola [àōōrɛo'là] *nf* halo.

auricular [àōōrēkōōlár'] *nm* earpiece, receiver; **~es** *nmpl* headphones.

aurora [àōōro'rà] *nf* dawn; **~ boreal(is)** northern lights *pl*.

auscultar [àōōskōōltár'] *vt* (*MED*: *pecho*) to listen to, sound.

ausencia [àōōsɛn'syà] *nf* absence.

ausentarse [àōōsɛntár'sɛ] *vr* to go away; (*por poco tiempo*) to go out.

ausente [àōōsɛn'tɛ] *a* absent ♦ *nm/f* (*ESCOL*) absentee; (*JUR*) missing person.

auspicios [àōōspē'syos] *nmpl* auspices; (*protección*) protection *sg*.

austeridad [àōōstɛrēthàth'] *nf* austerity.

austero, a [àōōstɛ'ro, à] *a* austere.

austral [àōōstrál'] *a* southern ♦ *nm* monetary unit of Argentina.

Australia [àōōstrá'lyà] *nf* Australia.

australiano, a [àōōstràlyà'no, à] *a*, *nm/f* Australian.

Austria [à'ōōstryà] *nf* Austria.

austriaco, a [àōōstryà'ko, à] **austríaco, a** [àōōstrē'àko, à] *a*, *nm/f* Austrian.

autenticar [àōōtɛntēkár'] *vt* to authenticate.

auténtico, a [àōōtɛn'tēko, à] *a* authentic.

autentique [àōōtɛntē'kɛ] *etc vb* V **autenticar**.

auto [à'ōōto] *nm* (*coche*) car; (*JUR*) edict, decree; (: *orden*) writ; **~s** *nmpl* (*JUR*) proceedings; (: *acta*) court record *sg*; **~ de comparecencia** summons, subpoena; **~ de ejecución** writ of execution.

autoadhesivo, a [àōōtoàthɛsē'ho, à] *a* self-adhesive; (*sobre*) self-sealing.

autoalimentación [àōōtoàlēmɛntàsyon'] *nf* (*INFORM*): **~ de hojas** automatic paper feed.

autobiografía [àōōtoḥyográfē'à] *nf* autobiography.

autobús [àōōtoḥōōs'] *nm* bus.

autocar [àōōtokár'] *nm* coach; **~ de línea** inter-city coach.

autocomprobación [àōōtokomproḥàsyon'] *nf* (*INFORM*) self-test.

autóctono, a [àōōtok'tono, à] *a* native, indigenous.

autodefensa [àōōtothɛfɛn'sà] *nf* self-defense (*US*), self-defence (*Brit*).

autodeterminación [àōōtothɛtɛrmēnàsyon'] *nf* self-determination.

autodidacto, a [àōōtothēthák'to, à] *a* self-taught.

autoescuela [àōōtoɛskwɛ'là] *nf* driving school.

autofinanciado, a [àōōtofēnànsyà'tho, à] *a* self-financing.

autógrafo [àōōto'gràfo] *nm* autograph.

automación [àōōtomàsyon'] *nf* = **automatización**.

autómata [àōōto'mátà] *nm* automaton.

automatice [àōōtomátē'sɛ] *etc vb* V **automatizar**.

automático, a [àōōtomá'tēko, à] *a* automatic ♦ *nm* snap fastener.

automatización [àōōtomátēsàsyon'] *nf*: **~ de fábricas** factory automation; **~ de oficinas** office automation.

automatizar [àōōtomátēsár'] *vt* to automate.

automotor, triz [àōōtomotor', trē'z] *a* self-propelled ♦ *nm* diesel train.

automóvil [àōōtomo'ḥēl] *nm* (motor) automobile (US), car (Brit).

automovilismo [àōōtomoḥēlēs'mo] nm (DEPORTE) (sports) car racing.

automovilista [àōōtomoḥēlē'stá] nm/f motorist, driver.

automovilístico, a [àōōtomoḥēlē'stēko, à] a (industria) car cpd.

autonomía [àōōtonomē'á] nf autonomy; **Estatuto de A~** (Esp) Devolution Statute.

autonómico, a [àōōtono'mēko, à] a (Esp POL) relating to autonomy, autonomous; **gobierno ~** autonomous government.

autónomo, a [àōōto'nomo, à] a autonomous; (INFORM) stand-alone, offline.

autopista [àōōtopē'stá] nf freeway (US), motorway (Brit).

autopsia [àōōtop'syá] nf autopsy.

autor, a [àōōtor', à] nm/f author; **los ~es del atentado** those responsible for the attack.

autorice [àōōtorē'se] etc vb V **autorizar**.

autoridad [àōōtorēthàth'] nf authority; **~ local** local authority.

autoritario, a [àōōtorētá'ryo, à] a authoritarian.

autorización [àōōtorēsásyon'] nf authorization.

autorizado, a [àōōtorēsá'tho, à] a authorized; (aprobado) approved.

autorizar [àōōtorēsár'] vt to authorize; to approve.

autorretrato [àōōtorretrá'to] nm self-portrait.

autoservicio [àōōtoserḥē'syo] nm self-service shop o store; (restaurante) self-service restaurant.

autostop [àōōtostop'] nm hitch-hiking; **hacer ~** to hitch-hike.

autostopista [àōōtostopē'stá] nm/f hitch-hiker.

autosuficiencia [àōōtosōōfēsyen'syá] nf self-sufficiency.

autovía [àōōtoḥē'á] nf ≈ state highway (US), A road (Brit).

auxiliar [àōōksēlyár'] vt to help ♦ nm/f assistant.

auxilio [àōōksē'lyo] nm assistance, help; **primeros ~s** first aid sg.

Av abr (= Avenida) Av(e).

a/v abr (COM: = a vista) on receipt.

aval [àḥál'] nm guarantee; (persona) guarantor.

avalancha [àḥálántch'á] nf avalanche.

avalar [àḥálár'] vt (COM etc) to underwrite; (fig) to endorse.

avalista [àḥálē'stá] nm (COM) endorser.

avance [àḥán'se] etc vb V **avanzar** ♦ nm advance; (pago) advance payment; (CINE) preview.

avanzado, a [àḥánsá'tho, à] a advanced; **de edad avanzada, ~ de edad** elderly.

avanzar [àḥánsár'] vt, vi to advance.

avaricia [àḥárē'syá] nf avarice, greed.

avaricioso, a [àḥárēsyo'so, à] a avaricious, greedy.

avaro, a [àḥá'ro, à] a miserly, mean ♦ nm/f miser.

avasallar [àḥásáyár'] vt to subdue, subjugate.

avatar [àḥátár'] nm change; **~es** nmpl ups and downs.

Avda abr (= Avenida) Av(e).

ave [à'ḥe] nf bird; **~ de rapiña** bird of prey.

avecinarse [àḥesēnár'se] vr (tormenta, fig) to approach, be on the way.

avejentar [àḥehentár'] vt, vi, **~se** vr to age.

avellana [àḥeyá'ná] nf hazelnut.

avellano [àḥeyá'no] nm hazel tree.

avemaría [àḥemárē'á] nm Hail Mary, Ave Maria.

avena [àḥe'ná] nf oats pl.

avendré [àḥendre'] etc, **avenga** [àḥen'gá] etc vb V **avenir**.

avenida [àḥenē'thá] nf (calle) avenue.

avenir [àḥenēr'] vt to reconcile; **~se** vr to come to an agreement, reach a compromise.

aventajado, a [àḥentáhá'tho, à] a outstanding.

aventajar [àḥentáhár'] vt (sobrepasar) to surpass, outstrip.

aventar [àḥentár'] vt to fan, blow; (grano) to winnow.

aventón [àḥenton'] nm (AM) push; **pedir ~** to hitch a ride (US) o lift (Brit).

aventura [àḥentōō'rá] nf adventure; **~ sentimental** love affair.

aventurado, a [àḥentōōrá'tho, à] a risky.

aventurar [àḥentōōrár'] vt to risk; **~se** vr to dare; **~se a hacer algo** to venture to do sth.

aventurero, a [àḥentōōre'ro, à] a adventurous.

avergoncé [àḥergonse'], **avergoncemos** [àḥergonse'mos] etc vb V **avergonzar**.

avergonzar [àḥergonsár'] vt to shame; (desconcertar) to embarrass; **~se** vr to be ashamed; to be embarrassed.

avergüence [àḥergwen'se] etc vb V **avergonzar**.

avería [àḥerē'á] nf (TEC) breakdown, fault.

averiado, a [àḥeryá'tho, à] a broken-down.

averiguación [àḥerēgwásyon'] nf investigation; (determinación) ascertainment.

averiguar [àḥerēgwár'] vt to investigate; (descubrir) to find out, ascertain.

averigüe [àḥerē'gwe] etc vb V **averiguar**.

aversión [àḥersyon'] nf aversion, dislike; **cobrar ~ a** to take a strong dislike to.

avestruz [àḥestrōōs'] nm ostrich.

aviación [àḥyásyon'] nf aviation; (fuerzas aéreas) air force.

aviado, a [àhyá'tho, á] *a*: **estar ~ to be in a mess.**

aviador, a [àhyáthor', á] *nm/f* aviator, airman/woman.

aviar [àhyár'] *vt* to prepare, get ready.

avicultura [àhèkōōltōō'rá] *nf* poultry farming.

avidez [àhèthes'] *nf* avidity, eagerness.

ávido, a [á'hètho, á] *a* avid, eager.

aviente [àhyen'te] *etc vb V* **aventar.**

avieso, a [àhye'so, á] *a* (*torcido*) distorted; (*perverso*) wicked.

avinagrado, a [àhènàgrá'tho, á] *a* sour, acid.

avinagrarse [àhènàgrár'se] *vr* to turn sour.

avine [àhè'ne] *etc vb V* **avenir.**

Aviñón [àhènyon'] *nm* Avignon.

avío [àhè'o] *nm* preparation; **~s** *nmpl* gear *sg*, kit *sg*.

avión [àhyon'] *nm* airplane (*US*), aeroplane (*Brit*); (*ave*) martin; **~ de reacción** jet (plane); **por ~** (*CORREOS*) by air mail.

avioneta [àhyone'tá] *nf* light aircraft.

avisar [àhèsár'] *vt* (*advertir*) to warn, notify; (*informar*) to tell; (*aconsejar*) to advise, counsel.

aviso [àhè'so] *nm* warning; (*noticia*) notice; (*COM*) demand note; (*INFORM*) prompt; **~ escrito** notice in writing; **sin previo ~** without warning; **estar sobre ~** to be on the look-out.

avispa [àhès'pá] *nf* wasp.

avispado, a [àhèspá'tho, á] *a* sharp, clever.

avispero [àhèspe'ro] *nm* wasp's nest.

avispón [àhèspon'] *nm* hornet.

avistar [àhèstár'] *vt* to sight, spot.

avitaminosis [àhètámēno'sēs] *nf inv* vitamin deficiency.

avituallar [àhètwáyár'] *vt* to supply with food.

avivar [àhèhár'] *vt* to strengthen, intensify; **~se** *vr* to revive, acquire new life.

avizor [àhèsor'] *a*: **estar ojo ~** to be on the alert.

avizorar [àhèsorár'] *vt* to spy on.

axila [àksè'lá] *nf* armpit.

axioma [àksyo'má] *nm* axiom.

ay [áè] *excl* (*dolor*) ow!, ouch!; (*aflicción*) oh!, oh dear!; **¡~ de mí!** poor me!

aya [á'yá] *nf* governess; (*niñera*) nanny.

ayer [àyer'] *ad, nm* yesterday; **antes de ~** the day before yesterday; **~ por la tarde** yesterday afternoon/evening.

ayo [á'yo] *nm* tutor.

ayote [àyo'te] *nm* (*AM*) pumpkin.

Ayto. *abr* = **Ayuntamiento.**

ayuda [àyōō'thá] *nf* help, assistance; (*MED*) enema; (*AM*) laxative ♦ *nm* page.

ayudante, a [àyōōthàn'te, á] *nm/f* assistant, helper; (*ESCOL*) assistant; (*MIL*) adjutant.

ayudar [àyōōthàr'] *vt* to help, assist.

ayunar [àyōōnár'] *vi* to fast.

ayunas [àyōō'nàs] *nfpl*: **estar en ~** (*no haber comido*) to be fasting; (*ignorar*) to be in the dark.

ayuno [àyōō'no] *nm* fasting.

ayuntamiento [àyōōntámyen'to] *nm* (*consejo*) town/city council; (*edificio*) town/city hall; (*cópula*) sexual intercourse.

azabache [ásáhàtch'e] *nm* jet.

azada [ásá'thá] *nf* hoe.

azafata [ásáfà'tá] *nf* flight attendant.

azafrán [ásáfrán'] *nm* saffron.

azahar [ásáár'] *nm* orange/lemon blossom.

azar [ásár'] *nm* (*casualidad*) chance, fate; (*desgracia*) misfortune, accident; **por ~** by chance; **al ~** at random.

azaroso, a [ásáro'so, á] *a* (*arriesgado*) risky; (*vida*) eventful.

azogue [áso'ge] *nm* mercury.

azor [ásor'] *nm* goshawk.

azoramiento [ásorámyen'to] *nm* alarm; (*confusión*) confusion.

azorar [ásorár'] *vt* to alarm; **~se** *vr* to get alarmed.

Azores [áso'res] *nfpl*: **las (Islas) ~** the Azores.

azotar [ásotár'] *vt* to whip, beat; (*pegar*) to spank.

azotaina [ásotá'ēná] *nf* beating.

azote [áso'te] *nm* (*látigo*) whip; (*latigazo*) lash, stroke; (*en las nalgas*) spank; (*calamidad*) calamity.

azotea [ásote'á] *nf* (flat) roof.

azteca [áste'ká] *a, nm/f* Aztec.

azúcar [ásōō'kár] *nm* sugar.

azucarado, a [ásōōkárá'tho, á] *a* sugary, sweet.

azucarero, a [ásōōkáre'ro, á] *a* sugar *cpd* ♦ *nm* sugar bowl.

azuce [ásōō'se] *etc vb V* **azuzar.**

azucena [ásōōse'ná] *nf* white lily.

azufre [ásōō'fre] *nm* sulfur (*US*), sulphur (*Brit*).

azul [ásōōl'] *a, nm* blue; **~ celeste/marino** sky/navy blue.

azulejo [ásōōle'ho] *nm* tile.

azulgrana [ásōōlgrá'ná] *a inv* of Barcelona Football Club ♦ *nm*: **los A~** the Barcelona F.C. players *o* team.

azuzar [ásōōsár'] *vt* to incite, egg on.

B

B, b [be] *nf* (*letra*) B, b; **B de Barcelona** B

for Baker.

B.A. *abr* = **Buenos Aires.**

baba [bá'ħá] *nf* spittle, saliva; **se le caía la** ~ (*fig*) he was thrilled to pieces (*US*) *o* bits (*Brit*).

babear [báħeár'] *vi* (*echar saliva*) to slobber; (*niño*) to dribble; (*fig*) to drool, slaver.

babel [báħel'] *nm o f* bedlam.

babero [báħe'ro] *nm* bib.

Babia [bá'ħyá] *nf*: **estar en** ~ to be day-dreaming.

bable [bá'ħle] *nm* Asturian (dialect).

babor [báħor'] *nm* port (side); **a** ~ to port.

babosa, a [báħo'so, á] *a* slobbering; (*ZOOL*) slimy; (*AM*) silly.

babucha [báħōōtch'á] *nf* slipper.

baca [bá'ká] *nf* (*AUTO*) luggage *o* roof rack.

bacalao [bákálá'o] *nm* cod (fish).

bacanal [bákánál'] *nf* orgy.

bacilo [báse'lo] *nm* bacillus, germ.

bacinica [básēnē'ká] *nf*, **bacinilla** [básnē'yá] *nf* chamber pot.

bacteria [bákte'ryá] *nf* bacterium, germ.

báculo [bá'kōōlo] *nm* stick, staff; (*fig*) support.

bache [bátch'e] *nm* pothole, rut; (*fig*) bad patch.

bachillerato [bátchēyerá'to] *nm* (*ESCOL*) ≈ High School diploma.

badajo [báħá'ho] *nm* clapper (*of a bell*).

bagaje [bá̤á'he] *nm* baggage; (*fig*) background.

bagatela [bá̤áte'lá] *nf* trinket, trifle.

Bahama [báá'má]: **las (Islas)** ~, **las** ~**s** *nfpl* the Bahamas.

bahía [báē'á] *nf* bay.

bailar [báēlár'] *vt*, *vi* to dance.

bailarín, ina [báēlárēn', ēná] *nm/f* dancer; (*de ballet*) ballet dancer.

baile [bá'ēle] *nm* dance; (*formal*) ball.

baja [bá'há] *nf* drop, fall; (*ECON*) slump; (*MIL*) casualty; (*paro*) redundancy; **dar de** ~ (*soldado*) to discharge; (*empleado*) to dismiss, fire; **darse de** ~ (*retirarse*) to drop out; (*MED*) to be ill; (*dimitir*) to resign; **estar de** ~ (*enfermo*) to be off sick; (*BOLSA*) to be dropping *o* falling; **jugar a la** ~ (*ECON*) to speculate on a fall in prices; *V tb* **bajo.**

bajada [báhá'ħá] *nf* descent; (*camino*) slope; (*de aguas*) ebb.

bajamar [báhámár'] *nf* low tide.

bajar [báhár'] *vi* to go *o* come down; (*temperatura, precios*) to drop, fall ♦ *vt* (*cabeza*) to bow; (*escalera*) to go *o* come down; (*radio etc*) to turn down; (*precio, voz*) to lower; (*llevar abajo*) to take down; ~**se** *vr* (*de vehículo*) to get out; (*de autobús*) to get off; ~ **de** (*coche*) to get out of; (*autobús*) to get off; ~**le los humos a uno** (*fig*) to

cut sb down to size.

bajeza [báhe'sá] *nf* baseness; (*una* ~) vile deed.

bajío [báhē'o] *nm* shoal, sandbank; (*AM*) lowlands *pl*.

bajista [báhē'stá] *nm/f* (*MUS*) bassist ♦ *a* (*BOLSA*) bear *cpd*.

bajo, a [bá'ho, á] *a* (*terreno*) low(-lying); (*mueble, número, precio*) low; (*piso*) ground; (*de estatura*) small, short; (*color*) pale; (*sonido*) faint, soft, low; (*voz, tono*) deep; (*metal*) base ♦ *ad* (*hablar*) softly, quietly; (*volar*) low ♦ *prep* under, below, underneath ♦ *nm* (*MUS*) bass; **hablar en voz baja** to whisper; ~ **la lluvia** in the rain.

bajón [báhon'] *nm* fall, drop.

bajura [báhōō'rá] *nf*: **pesca de** ~ coastal fishing.

bala [bá'lá] *nf* bullet.

balacera [bálase'rá] *nf* (*AM*) shoot-out.

balada [bálá'ħá] *nf* ballad.

baladí [bálá'ħē'] *a* trivial.

baladrón, ona [bálá'ħron', o'ná] *a* boastful.

baladronada [bálá'ħroná'ħá] *nf* (*dicho*) boast, brag; (*hecho*) piece of bravado.

balance [bálán'se] *nm* (*COM*) balance; (: *libro*) balance sheet; (: *cuenta general*) inventory (*US*), stocktaking (*Brit*); ~ **de comprobación** trial balance; ~ **consolidado** consolidated balance sheet; **hacer** ~ to make an inventory (*US*) *o* take stock (*Brit*).

balancear [bálánseár'] *vt* to balance ♦ *vi*, ~**se** *vr* to swing (to and fro); (*vacilar*) to hesitate.

balanceo [bálánse'o] *nm* swinging.

balanza [bálán'sá] *nf* scales *pl*, balance; ~ **comercial** balance of trade; ~ **de pagos/de poder(es)** balance of payments/of power; (*ASTRO*): **B**~ Libra.

balar [bálár'] *vi* to bleat.

balaustrada [bálá'ōōstrá'ħá] *nf* balustrade; (*pasamanos*) banister.

balazo [bálá'so] *nm* (*tiro*) shot; (*herida*) bullet wound.

balboa [bálħo'á] *nf* Panamanian currency unit.

balbucear [bálħōōseár'] *vi*, *vt* to stammer, stutter.

balbuceo [bálħōōse'o] *nm* stammering, stuttering.

balbucir [bálħōōsēr'] *vi*, *vt* to stammer, stutter.

balbuzca [bálħōōs'ká] *etc vb V* **balbucir.**

Balcanes [bálká'nes] *nmpl*: **los (Montes)** ~ the Balkans, the Balkan Mountains; **la Península de los** ~ the Balkan Peninsula.

balcón [bálkon'] *nm* balcony.

balda [bál'dá] *nf* (*estante*) shelf.

baldar [báldár'] *vt* to cripple; (*agotar*) to

exhaust.

balde |bál'de| *nm* bucket, pail; **de ~** *ad* (for) free, for nothing; **en ~** *ad* in vain.

baldío, a |báldē'o, á| *a* uncultivated; (*terreno*) waste; (*inútil*) vain ♦ *nm* wasteland.

baldosa |báldo'sá| *nf* (*azulejo*) floor tile; (*grande*) flagstone.

balear |bálcár'| *a* Balearic, of the Balearic Islands ♦ *nm/f* native *o* inhabitant of the Balearic Islands.

Baleares |bálcá'rcs| *nfpl*: **las (Islas) ~** the Balearics, the Balearic Islands.

balido |bálē'tho| *nm* bleat, bleating.

balín |bálēn'| *nm* pellet; **balines** *nmpl* buckshot *sg*.

balística |bálē'stēká| *nf* ballistics *pl*.

baliza |bálē'sá| *nf* (*AVIAT*) beacon; (*NAUT*) buoy.

balneario, a |bálneá'ryo, á| *a*: **estación balnearia** (bathing) resort ♦ *nm* spa, health resort.

balompié |bálompye'| *nm* football.

balón |bálon'| *nm* ball.

baloncesto |bálonse'sto| *nm* basketball.

balonmano |bálonmá'no| *nm* handball.

balonvolea |bálombole'á| *nm* volleyball.

balsa |bál'sá| *nf* raft; (*BOT*) balsa wood.

bálsamo |bál'sámo| *nm* balsam, balm.

balsón |bálson'| *nm* (*AM*) swamp, bog.

báltico, a |bál'tēko, á| *a* Baltic; **el (Mar) B~** the Baltic (Sea).

baluarte |bálwár'tc| *nm* bastion, bulwark.

ballena |báye'ná| *nf* whale.

ballenero, a |báyene'ro, á| *a*: **industria ballenera** whaling industry ♦ *nm* (*pescador*) whaler; (*barco*) whaling ship.

ballesta |báye'stá| *nf* crossbow; (*AUTO*) spring.

ballet, *pl* **ballets** |bále', báles'| *nm* ballet.

bambolear |bámboleár'| *vi*, **~se** *vr* to swing, sway; (*silla*) to wobble.

bamboleo |bámbole'o| *nm* swinging, swaying; wobbling.

bambú |bámbōō'| *nm* bamboo.

banal |bánál'| *a* banal, trivial.

banana |báná'ná| *nf* (*AM*) banana.

bananal |bánánál'| *nm* (*AM*) banana plantation.

banano |báná'no| *nm* (*AM*) banana tree.

banasta |báná'stá| *nf* large basket, hamper.

banca |bán'ká| *nf* (*asiento*) bench; (*COM*) banking.

bancario, a |bánká'ryo, á| *a* banking *cpd*, bank *cpd*; **giro ~** bank draft.

bancarrota |bánkárro'tá| *nf* bankruptcy; **declararse en** *o* **hacer ~** to go bankrupt.

banco |bán'ko| *nm* bench; (*ESCOL*) desk; (*COM*) bank; (*GEO*) stratum; **~ comercial** *o* **mercantil** commercial bank; **~ por acciones** joint-stock bank; **~ de crédito/de ahorros** credit/savings bank; **~ de arena** sand-

bank; **~ de datos** (*INFORM*) data bank; **~ de hielo** iceberg.

banda |bán'dá| *nf* band; (*cinta*) ribbon; (*pandilla*) gang; (*MUS*) brass band; (*NAUT*) side, edge; **la B~ Oriental** Uruguay; **~ sonora** soundtrack; **~ transportadora** conveyor belt.

bandada |bándá'thá| *nf* (*de pájaros*) flock; (*de peces*) shoal.

bandeja |bánde'há| *nf* tray; **~ de entrada/salida** in-tray/out-tray.

bandera |bánde'rá| *nf* (*de tela*) flag; (*estandarte*) banner; (*INFORM*) marker, flag; **izar la ~** to hoist the flag.

banderilla |bánderē'yá| *nf* banderilla; (*tapa*) savory appetizer (*served on a cocktail stick*).

banderín |bánderēn'| *nm* pennant, small flag.

banderola |bándero'lá| *nf* (*MIL*) pennant.

bandido |bándē'tho| *nm* bandit.

bando |bán'do| *nm* (*edicto*) edict, proclamation; (*facción*) faction; **pasar al otro ~** to change sides; **los ~s** (*REL*) wedding announcement.

bandolera |bándole'rá| *nf*: **bolsa de ~** shoulder bag.

bandolero |bándole'ro| *nm* bandit.

bandoneón |bándoneon'| *nm* (*AM*) large accordion.

BANESTO |báne'sto| *nm abr* = *Banco Español de Crédito*.

banquero |bánke'ro| *nm* banker.

banqueta |bánke'tá| *nf* stool; (*AM: en la calle*) sidewalk (*US*), pavement (*Brit*).

banquete |bánke'te| *nm* banquet; (*para convidados*) formal dinner; **~ de boda** wedding breakfast.

banquillo |bánkē'yo| *nm* (*JUR*) dock, prisoner's bench; (*banco*) bench; (*para los pies*) footstool.

bañador |bányáthor'| *nm* bathing suit (*US*), swimming costume (*Brit*).

bañar |bányár'| *vt* (*niño*) to bath, bathe; (*objeto*) to dip; (*de barniz*) to coat; **~se** *vr* (*en el mar*) to bathe, swim; (*en la bañera*) to have a bath.

bañero, a |bánye'ro, á| *nm* lifeguard ♦ *nf* bath (tub).

bañista |bánye'stá| *nm/f* bather.

baño |bá'nyo| *nm* (*en bañera*) bath; (*en río, mar*) dip, swim; (*cuarto*) bathroom; (*bañera*) bath (tub); (*capa*) coating; **ir a tomar los ~s** to bathe at a spa (*US*) *o* take the waters (*Brit*).

baptista |báptē'stá| *nm/f* Baptist.

baqueta |báke'tá| *nf* (*MUS*) drumstick.

bar |bár| *nm* bar.

barahúnda |báráōōn'dá| *nf* uproar, hubbub.

baraja |bárá'há| *nf* pack (of cards).

barajar |báráhár'| *vt* (*naipes*) to shuffle;

(fig) to mix up.
baranda |bárán'dá|, **barandilla** |bárántʰc'yá|
nf (pasamanos) handrail.
baratija |bárátc'há| *nf* trinket; *(fig)* trifle;
~**s** *nfpl (COM)* cheap goods.
baratillo |bárátc'yo| *nm (tienda)* junkshop;
(subasta) bargain sale; *(conjunto de cosas)*
second-hand goods *pl.*
barato, a |bárá'to, á| *a* cheap ♦ *ad* cheap,
cheaply.
baratura |báratōō'rá| *nf* cheapness.
baraúnda |báráōōn'dá| *nf* = **barahúnda.**
barba |bár'há| *nf (mentón)* chin; *(pelo)*
beard; **tener ~** to be unshaven; **hacer algo
en las ~s de uno** to do sth under sb's very
nose; **reírse en las ~s de uno** to laugh in
sb's face.
barbacoa |bárháko'á| *nf (parrilla)* barbe-
cue; *(carne)* barbecued meat.
barbaridad |bárhárcʰáth'| *nf* barbarity;
(acto) barbarism; *(atrocidad)* outrage; **una
~ de** *(fam)* loads of; **¡qué ~!** *(fam)* how
awful!; **cuesta una ~** *(fam)* it costs a fortune.
barbarie |bárhá'ryc| *nf,* **barbarismo**
|bárhárc'smo| *nm* barbarism; *(crueldad)*
barbarity.
bárbaro, a |bár'háro, á| *a* barbarous, cruel;
(grosero) rough, uncouth ♦ *nm/f* barbarian
♦ *ad:* **lo pasamos ~** *(fam)* we had a great
time; **¡qué ~!** *(fam)* how marvelous!; **un
éxito ~** *(fam)* a terrific success; **es un
tipo ~** *(fam)* he's a great bloke.
barbecho |bárhetch'o| *nm* fallow land.
barbero |bárhc'ro| *nm* barber, hairdresser.
barbilampiño |bárhclámpc'nyo| *a* smooth-
faced; *(fig)* inexperienced.
barbilla |bárhc'yá| *nf* chin, tip of the chin.
barbo |bár'ho| *nm:* ~ **de mar** red mullet.
barbotar |bárhotár'|, **barbotear** |bárhotcár'|
vt, vi to mutter, mumble.
barbudo, a |bárhōō'tho, á| *a* bearded.
barbullar |bárhōōyár'| *vi* to jabber away.
barca |bár'ká| *nf (small) boat; ~ **pesquera**
fishing boat; ~ **de pasaje** ferry.
barcaza |bárká'sá| *nf* barge; ~ **de des-
embarco** landing craft.
Barcelona |bárselo'ná| *nf* Barcelona.
barcelonés, esa |bárselones', c'sá| *a* of *o*
from Barcelona ♦ *nm/f* native *o* inhabitant
of Barcelona.
barco |bár'ko| *nm* boat; *(buque)* ship; *(COM
etc)* vessel; ~ **de carga** cargo boat; ~ **de
guerra** warship; ~ **de vela** sailing ship; **ir
en** ~ to go by boat.
baremo |bárc'mo| *nm* scale; *(tabla de
cuentas)* ready reckoner.
barítono |bárc'tono| *nm* baritone.
barman |bár'mán| *nm* bartender.
Barna. *abr* = **Barcelona.**
barnice |bárnc'se| *etc vb V* **barnizar.**

barniz |bárnc's'| *nm* varnish; *(en la loza)*
glaze; *(fig)* veneer.
barnizar |bárncsár'| *vt* to varnish; *(loza)* to
glaze.
barómetro |báro'mctro| *nm* barometer.
barquero |bárkc'ro| *nm* boatman.
barquilla |bárkc'yá| *nf (NAUT)* log.
barquillo |bárkc'yo| *nm* cone.
barra |bá'rrá| *nf* bar, rod; *(JUR)* rail;
(: *banquillo)* dock; *(de un bar, café)* bar;
(de pan) French loaf; *(palanca)* lever; ~
de carmín *o* **de labios** lipstick; ~ **de espaciado** *(INFORM)* space bar; ~ **inversa**
backslash; **no pararse en** ~**s** to stick *o*
stop at nothing.
barrabasada |bárráhásá'thá| *nf* (piece of)
mischief.
barraca |bárrá'ká| *nf* hut, cabin; *(en Va-
lencia)* thatched farmhouse; *(en feria)*
booth.
barracón |bárrákon'| *nm (caseta)* big hut.
barragana |bárrágá'ná| *nf* concubine.
barranca |bárrán'ká| *nf* ravine, gully.
barranco |bárrán'ko| *nm* ravine; *(fig)*
difficulty.
barrena |bárrc'ná| *nf* drill.
barrenar |bárrenár'| *vt* to drill (through),
bore.
barrendero, a |bárrcnde'ro, á| *nm/f* street-
sweeper.
barreno |bárrc'no| *nm* large drill.
barreño |bárrc'nyo| *nm* wash basin.
barrer |bárrcr'| *vt* to sweep; *(quitar)* to
sweep away; *(MIL, NAUT)* to sweep, rake
(with gunfire) ♦ *vi* to sweep up.
barrera |bárrc'rá| *nf* barrier; *(MIL)* barri-
cade; *(FERRO)* crossing gate; **poner ~s a**
to hinder; ~ **arancelaria** *(COM)* tariff
barrier; ~ **comercial** *(COM)* trade barrier.
barriada |bárryá'thá| *nf* quarter, district.
barricada |bárréká'thá| *nf* barricade.
barrida |bárrc'thá| *nf,* **barrido** |bárrc'tho| *nm*
sweep, sweeping.
barriga |bárrc'gá| *nf* belly; *(panza)* paunch;
(vientre) guts *pl;* **echar** ~ to get middle-
age spread.
barrigón, ona |bárrcgon', o'ná|, **barrigudo,
a** |bárrcgōō'tho, á| *a* potbellied.
barril |bárrcl'| *nm* barrel, cask; **cerveza de
~** draught beer.
barrio |bá'rryo| *nm (vecindad)* neighborhood
(US), neighbourhood *(Brit)*; *(en las
afueras)* suburb; ~**s bajos** poor quarter *sg;*
~ **chino** red-light district.
barriobajero, a |bárryobáhe'ro, á| *a
(vulgar)* common.
barro |bá'rro| *nm (lodo)* mud; *(objetos)*
earthenware; *(MED)* pimple.
barroco, a |bárro'ko, á| *a* Baroque; *(fig)*
elaborate ♦ *nm* Baroque.
barrote |bárro'te| *nm (de ventana etc)* bar.

barruntar [bárrōōntár'] *vt* (*conjeturar*) to guess; (*presentir*) to suspect.

barrunto [bárrōōn'to] *nm* guess; suspicion.

bartola [bárto'lá]: **a la ~** *ad*: **tirarse a la ~** to take it easy, be lazy.

bártulos [bár'tōōlos] *nmpl* things, belongings.

barullo [bárōō'yo] *nm* row, uproar.

basa [bá'sá] *nf* (*ARQ*) base.

basamento [básámen'to] *nm* base, plinth.

basar [básár'] *vt* to base; **~se** *vr*: **~se en** to be based on.

basca [bás'ká] *nf* nausea.

báscula [bás'kōōlá] *nf* (platform) scales *pl*; **~ biestable** (*INFORM*) flip-flop, toggle.

bascular [báskōōlár'] *vt* (*INFORM*) to toggle.

base [bá'se] *nf* base; **a ~ de** on the basis of, based on; (*mediante*) by means of; **a ~ de bien** in abundance; **~ de conocimiento** knowledge base; **~ de datos** database.

básico, a [bá'sēko, á] *a* basic.

Basilea [básēle'á] *nf* Basle.

basílica [básē'lēká] *nf* basilica.

basilisco [básēlēs'co] *nm* (*AM*) iguana; **estar hecho un ~** to be hopping mad.

bastante [bástán'te] *a* (*suficiente*) enough, sufficient; (*no poco(s)*) quite a lot of ♦ *ad* (*suficientemente*) enough, sufficiently; (*muy*) quite, rather; **es ~ alto** (*como*) **para alcanzarlo** he's tall enough to reach it.

bastar [bástár'] *vi* to be enough *o* sufficient; **~se** *vr* to be self-sufficient; **~ para** to be enough to; **¡basta!** (that's) enough!

bastardilla [bástárthē'yá] *nf* italics *pl*.

bastardo, a [bástár'tho, á] *a*, *nm/f* bastard.

bastidor [bástēthor'] *nm* frame; (*de coche*) chassis; (*ARTE*) stretcher; (*TEATRO*) wing; **entre ~es** behind the scenes.

basto, a [bá'sto, á] *a* coarse, rough ♦ *nmpl*: **~s** (*NAIPES*) clubs.

bastón [báston'] *nm* stick, staff; (*para pasear*) walking stick; **~ de mando** baton.

bastonazo [bástoná'so] *nm* blow with a stick.

basura [básōō'rá] *nf* rubbish, garbage (*US*), refuse (*Brit*).

basurero [básōōre'ro] *nm* (*hombre*) garbage man (*US*), dustman (*Brit*); (*lugar*) garbage (*US*) *o* rubbish (*Brit*) dump; (*cubo*) trash can (*US*), (rubbish) bin (*Brit*).

bata [bá'tá] *nf* (*gen*) housecoat; (*cubretodo*) smock, overall (*Brit*); (*MED, TEC etc*) lab(oratory) coat.

batacazo [bátáká'so] *nm* bump.

batalla [bátá'yá] *nf* battle; **de ~** for everyday use.

batallar [bátáyár'] *vi* to fight.

batallón [bátáyon'] *nm* battalion.

batata [bátá'tá] *nf* (*AM: CULIN*) sweet potato.

bate [bá'te] *nm* (*DEPORTE*) bat.

bateador [báteáthor'] *nm* batter, batsman.

batería [báterē'á] *nf* battery; (*MUS*) drums *pl*; (*TEATRO*) footlights *pl*; **~ de cocina** kitchen utensils *pl*.

batiburrillo [bátēbōōrrē'yo] *nm* hotchpotch.

batido, a [bátē'tho, á] *a* (*camino*) beaten, well-trodden ♦ *nm* (*CULIN*) batter; **~ (de leche)** milk shake ♦ *nf* (*AM*) (police) raid.

batidora [bátētho'rá] *nf* beater, mixer; **~ eléctrica** food mixer, blender.

batir [bátēr'] *vt* to beat, strike; (*vencer*) to beat, defeat; (*revolver*) to beat, mix; (*pelo*) to back-comb; **~se** *vr* to fight; **~ palmas** to clap, applaud.

batuta [bátōō'tá] *nf* baton; **llevar la ~** (*fig*) to be the boss.

baudio [bá'ōōthyo] *nm* (*INFORM*) baud.

baúl [báōōl'] *nm* trunk; (*AUTO*) trunk (*US*), boot (*Brit*).

bautice [báōōtē'se] *etc vb* V **bautizar**.

bautismo [báōōtēs'mo] *nm* baptism, christening.

bautista [báōōtēs'tá] *a*, *nm/f* Baptist.

bautizar [báōōtēsár'] *vt* to baptize, christen; (*fam: diluir*) to water down; (*dar apodo*) to dub.

bautizo [báōōtē'so] *nm* baptism, christening.

bávaro, a [bá'háro, á] *a*, *nm/f* Bavarian.

Baviera [báhye'rá] *nf* Bavaria.

baya [bá'yá] *nf* berry; *V tb* **bayo**.

bayeta [báye'tá] *nf* (*trapo*) floorcloth; (*AM: pañal*) diaper (*US*), nappy (*Brit*).

bayo, a [bá'yo, á] *a* bay.

bayoneta [báyone'tá] *nf* bayonet.

baza [bá'sá] *nf* trick; **meter ~** to butt in.

bazar [básár'] *nm* bazaar.

bazofia [báso'fyá] *nf* hogwash (*US*), pigswill (*Brit*); (*libro etc*) trash.

beato, a [beá'to, á] *a* blessed; (*piadoso*) pious.

bebé, pl bebés [bebe', bebes'] *nm* baby.

bebedero, a [bebethe'ro, á] *nm* (*para animales*) drinking trough.

bebedizo, a [bebethē'so, á] *a* drinkable ♦ *nm* potion.

bebedor, a [bebethor', á] *a* hard-drinking.

beber [beber'] *vt*, *vi* to drink; **~ a sorbos/tragos** to sip/gulp; **se lo bebió todo** he drank it all up.

bebido, a [bebē'tho, á] *a* drunk ♦ *nf* drink.

beca [be'ká] *nf* grant, scholarship.

becado, a [beká'tho, á] *nm/f*, **becario, a** [beká'ryo, á] *nm/f* scholarship holder.

becerro [bese'rro] *nm* yearling calf.

becuadro [bekwá'thro] *nm* (*MUS*) natural sign.

bedel [bethel'] *nm* porter, janitor.

befarse [befár'se] *vr*: **~ de algo** to scoff at sth.

béisbol [be'ēshol] *nm* baseball.

beldad |beldàth'| *nf* beauty.
Belén |belen'| *nm* Bethlehem; **b~** (*de Navidad*) nativity scene, crib.
belga |bel'ɣà| *a, nm/f* Belgian.
Bélgica |bel'hēkà| *nf* Belgium.
Belgrado |belɣrá'tho| *nm* Belgrade.
Belice |belē'se| *nm* Belize.
bélico, a |be'lēko, á| *a* (*actitud*) warlike.
belicoso, a |belēko'so, á| *a* (*guerrero*) warlike; (*agresivo*) aggressive, bellicose.
beligerante |belēheràn'te| *a* belligerent.
bellaco, a |beyá'ko, á| *a* sly, cunning ♦ *nm* villain, rogue.
belladona |beyàtho'nà| *nf* deadly nightshade.
bellaquería |beyàkerē'á| *nf* (*acción*) dirty trick; (*calidad*) wickedness.
belleza |beye'sà| *nf* beauty.
bello, a |be'yo, á| *a* beautiful, lovely; **Bellas Artes** Fine Art *sg*.
bellota |beyo'tá| *nf* acorn.
bemol |bemol'| *nm* (*MUS*) flat; **esto tiene ~es** (*fam*) this is a tough one.
bencina |bēnsē'nà| *nf* (*AM*) gas (*US*), petrol (*Brit*).
bendecir |bendesēr'| *vt* to bless; **~ la mesa** to say grace.
bendición |bendēsyon'| *nf* blessing.
bendiga |bendē'ɣà| *etc,* **bendije** |bendē'he| *etc,* **bendiré** |bendēre'| *etc vb V* **bendecir.**
bendito, a |bendē'to, á| *pp de* **bendecir** ♦ *a* (*santo*) blessed; (*agua*) holy; (*afortunado*) lucky; (*feliz*) happy; (*sencillo*) simple ♦ *nm/f* simple soul; **¡~ sea Dios!** thank goodness!; **es un ~** he's sweet; **dormir como un ~** to sleep like a log.
benedictino, a |benethēktē'no, á| *a, nm* Benedictine.
benefactor, a |benefáktor', à| *nm/f* benefactor/benefactress.
beneficencia |benefēsen'syá| *nf* charity.
beneficiar |benefēsyár'| *vt* to benefit, be of benefit to; **~se** *vr* to benefit, profit.
beneficiario, a |benefēsyá'ryo, á| *nm/f* beneficiary; (*de cheque*) payee.
beneficio |benefē'syo| *nm* (*bien*) benefit, advantage; (*COM*) profit, gain; **a ~ de** for the benefit of; **en ~ propio** to one's own advantage; **~ bruto/neto** gross/net profit; **~ por acción** earnings *pl* per share.
beneficioso, a |benefēsyo'so, á| *a* beneficial.
benéfico, a |bene'fēko, á| *a* charitable; **sociedad benéfica** charity (organization).
benemérito, a |beneme'rēto, á| *a* meritorious ♦ *nf:* **la Benemérita** (*Esp*) the Civil Guard.
beneplácito |beneplá'sēto| *nm* approval, consent.
benevolencia |benecholen'syá| *nf* benevolence, kindness.

benévolo, a |bene'holo, á| *a* benevolent, kind.
Bengala |benɡá'lá| *nf* Bengal; **el Golfo de ~** the Bay of Bengal.
bengala |benɡá'lá| *nf* (*MIL*) flare; (*fuego*) Bengal light; (*materia*) rattan.
bengalí |benɡálē'| *a, nm/f* Bengali.
benignidad |benēɡnēthàth'| *nf* (*afabilidad*) kindness; (*suavidad*) mildness.
benigno, a |benēɡ'no, á| *a* kind; (*suave*) mild; (*MED: tumor*) benign, non-malignant.
benjamín |benhámēn'| *nm* youngest child.
beodo, a |beo'tho, á| *a* drunk ♦ *nm/f* drunkard.
berberecho |berḫeretch'o| *nm* cockle.
berenjena |berenhe'ná| *nf* eggplant, aubergine.
berenjenal |berenhenàl'| *nm* (*AGR*) eggplant *o* aubergine bed; (*fig*) mess; **en buen ~ nos hemos metido** we've got ourselves into a fine mess.
bergantín |berɣántēn'| *nm* brig(antine).
Berlín |berlēn'| *nm* Berlin.
berlinés, esa |berlēnes', esá| *a* of *o* from Berlin ♦ *nm/f* Berliner.
bermejo, a |berme'ho, á| *a* red.
bermellón |bermeyon'| *nm* vermilion.
berrear |berreár'| *vi* to bellow, low.
berrido |berrē'tho| *nm* bellow(ing).
berrinche |berrēntch'e| *nm* (*fam*) temper, tantrum.
berro |be'rro| *nm* watercress.
berza |ber'sá| *nf* cabbage; **~ lombarda** red cabbage.
besamel |besámel'|, **besamela** |besáme'lá| *nf* (*CULIN*) white sauce, bechamel sauce.
besar |besár'| *vt* to kiss; (*fig: tocar*) to graze; **~se** *vr* to kiss (one another).
beso |be'so| *nm* kiss.
bestia |bes'tyá| *nf* beast, animal; (*fig*) idiot; **~ de carga** beast of burden; **¡~!** you idiot!; **¡no seas ~!** (*bruto*) don't be such a brute!; (*idiota*) don't be such an idiot!
bestial |bestyál'| *a* bestial; (*fam*) terrific.
bestialidad |bestyálēthàth'| *nf* bestiality; (*fam*) stupidity.
besugo |besoo'ɡo| *nm* sea bream; (*fam*) idiot.
besuguera |besooɡe'rá| *nf* (*CULIN*) fish pan.
besuquear |besookeár'| *vt* to cover with kisses; **~se** *vr* to kiss and cuddle.
bético, a |be'tēko, á| *a* Andalusian.
betún |betoon'| *nm* shoe polish; (*QUÌMICA*) bitumen, asphalt.
Bib. *abr* = **Biblioteca.**
biberón |bēḫeron'| *nm* bottle.
Biblia |bēḫ'lyá| *nf* Bible.
bíblico, a |bē'hlēko, á| *a* biblical.
bibliografía |bēḫlyoɡráfē'á| *nf* bibliography.
biblioteca |bēḫlyote'ká| *nf* library; (*estantes*) bookcase, bookshelves *pl*; **~ de**

consulta reference library.
bibliotecario, a [bēblyotekáʼryo, á] *nm/f* librarian.
B.I.C. [bēk] *nf abr* (= *Brigada de Investigación Criminal*) ≈ FBI (*US*), CID (*Brit*).
bicarbonato [bēkárbonáʼto] *nm* bicarbonate.
bici [bēʼsē] *nf* (*fam*) bike.
bicicleta [bēsēkleʼtá] *nf* bicycle, cycle.
bicoca [bēkoʼká] *nf* (*Esp fam*) cushy job; (*AM: bofetada*) slap.
bicho [bētchʼo] *nm* (*animal*) small animal; (*sabandija*) bug, insect; (*TAUR*) bull; ~ **raro** (*fam*) strange bird.
bidé [bēʼthe'] *nm* bidet.
bidireccional [bēdēreksyonálʼ] *a* bidirectional.
bidón [bēthon'] *nm* (*grande*) drum; (*pequeño*) can.
bien [byen] *nm* good; (*interés*) advantage, benefit; **hombre de** ~ honest man; **el** ~ **público** the common *o* public good; **~es de capital** (*COM*) capital goods; **~es inmuebles/muebles** real estate *sg*/personal property *sg*; **~es de consumo** consumer goods; **~es de producción** industrial goods; **~es raíces** real estate *sg* ♦ *a*: **de casa** ~ well brought up ♦ *ad* well; (*correctamente*) properly, right; (*oler*) nice; (*muy*) very; **más** ~ rather; **hablas** ~ **(el español)** you speak good Spanish; **estar** ~ **de salud/dinero** to be well/well off; **estar a** ~ **con uno** to be on good terms with sb ♦ *excl*: **¡(muy)** ~! well done! ♦ *conj*: **no** ~ **llovió, bajó la temperatura** no sooner had it rained than the temperature dropped; ~ **que** although.
bienal [byenálʼ] *a* biennial.
bienaventurado, a [byenábentōōráʼtho, á] *a* (*feliz*) happy; (*afortunado*) fortunate; (*REL*) blessed.
bienestar [byenestárʼ] *nm* well-being; **estado de** ~ welfare state.
bienhechor, a [byenetchorʼ, á] *a* beneficent ♦ *nm/f* benefactor/benefactress.
bienio [byeʼnyo] *nm* two-year period.
bienvenido, a [byembenēʼtho, á] *a* welcome ♦ *excl* welcome! ♦ *nf* welcome; **dar la bienvenida a uno** to welcome sb.
bifásico, a [bēfáʼsēko, á] *a* (*ELEC*) two-phase.
bife [bēʼfe] *nm* (*AM*) steak.
bifurcación [bēfōōrkásyon'] *nf* fork; (*FERRO, INFORM*) branch.
bigamia [bēgáʼmyá] *nf* bigamy.
bígamo, a [bēʼgámo, á] *a* bigamous ♦ *nm/f* bigamist.
bígaro [bēʼgáro] *nm* winkle.
bigote [bēgoʼte] *nm* (*tb*: ~**s**) mustache (*US*), moustache (*Brit*).
bigotudo, a [bēgotōōʼtho, á] *a* with a big

mustache.
bigudí [bēgōōthē'] *nm* (hair-)curler.
bikini [bēkēʼnē] *nm* bikini; (*CULIN*) toasted cheese and ham sandwich.
bilbaíno, a [bēlháēʼno, á] *a* of *o* from Bilbao ♦ *nm/f* native *o* inhabitant of Bilbao.
bilingüe [bēlēn'gwe] *a* bilingual.
bilis [bēʼlēs] *nf inv* bile.
billar [bēyárʼ] *nm* billiards *sg*; (*lugar*) billiard hall; (*galería de atracciones*) amusement arcade; ~ **americano** pool.
billete [bēyeʼte] *nm* ticket; (*de banco*) bill (*US*), banknote (*Brit*); (*carta*) note; ~ **sencillo**, ~ **de ida solamente/**~ **de ida y vuelta** one-way (*US*) *o* single (*Brit*) ticket/round-trip (*US*) *o* return (*Brit*) ticket; **sacar (un)** ~ to get a ticket; **un** ~ **de 5 dólares** a five-dollar bill.
billetera [bēyeteʼrá] *nf*, **billetero** [bēyeteʼro] *nm* wallet.
billón [bēyon'] *nm* billion.
bimensual [bēmenswálʼ] *a* twice monthly.
bimestral [bēmestrálʼ] *a* bimonthly.
bimestre [bēmesʼtre] *nm* two-month period.
bimotor [bēmotorʼ] *a* twin-engined ♦ *nm* twin-engined plane.
binario, a [bēnáʼryo, á] *a* (*INFORM*) binary.
binóculo [bēnoʼkōōlo] *nm* pince-nez.
biografía [byográfēʼá] *nf* biography.
biógrafo, a [bēoʼgráfo, á] *nm/f* biographer.
biología [bēolohēʼá] *nf* biology.
biológico, a [bēoloʼhēko, á] *a* biological; **guerra biológica** biological warfare.
biólogo, a [bēoʼlogo, á] *nm/f* biologist.
biombo [byomʼbo] *nm* (folding) screen.
biopsia [bēopʼsyá] *nf* biopsy.
bioquímico, a [bēokēʼmēko, á] *a* biochemical ♦ *nm/f* biochemist ♦ *nf* biochemistry.
bióxido [bēokʼsētho] *nm* dioxide.
bipartidismo [bēpártēthēsʼmo] *nm* (*POL*) two-party system.
birlar [bērlárʼ] *vt* (*fam*) to pinch.
birlibirloque [bērlēbērloʼke] *nm*: **por arte de** ~ (as if) by magic.
Birmania [bērmáʼnyá] *nf* Burma.
birmano, a [bērmáʼno, á] *a nm/f* Burmese.
birrete [bērreʼte] *nm* (*JUR*) judge's cap.
bis [bēs] *excl* encore! ♦ *ad* (*dos veces*) twice; **viven en el 27** ~ they live at 27a.
bisabuelo, a [bēsábweʼlo, á] *nm/f* great-grandfather/mother; **~s** *nmpl* great-grandparents.
bisagra [bēsáʼgrá] *nf* hinge.
bisbisar [bēsbēsárʼ], **bisbisear** [bēsbēseárʼ] *vt* to mutter, mumble.
bisbiseo [bēsbēseʼo] *nm* muttering.
biselar [bēselárʼ] *vt* to bevel.
bisexual [bēsekswálʼ] *a* bisexual.
bisiesto [bēsyeʼsto] *a*: **año** ~ leap year.
bisnieto, a [bēsnyeʼto, á] *nm/f* great-grandson/daughter; **~s** *nmpl* great-

grandchildren.

bisonte [bēson'te] *nm* bison.

bisoñé [bēsonye'] *nm* toupée.

bisoño, a [bēso'nyo, á] *a* green, inexperienced.

bistec [bēstek'], **bisté** [bēste'] *nm* steak.

bisturí [bēstōōrē'] *nm* scalpel.

bisutería [bēsōōterē'á] *nf* imitation *o* costume jewellery.

bit [bēt] *nm* (*INFORM*) bit; ~ **de parada** stop bit; ~ **de paridad** parity bit.

bitio [bē'tyo] *nm* (*INFORM*) bit.

bizantino, a [bēsántē'no, á] *a* Byzantine; (*fig*) pointless.

bizarría [bēsárrē'á] *nf* (*valor*) bravery; (*generosidad*) generosity.

bizarro, a [bēsá'rro, á] *a* brave; generous.

bizcar [bēskár'] *vi* to squint.

bizco, a [bēs'ko, á] *a* cross-eyed.

bizcocho [bēskotch'o] *nm* (*CULIN*) sponge cake.

bizque [bēs'ke] *etc vb V* **bizcar**.

bizquear [bēskeár'] *vi* to squint.

blanco, a [blán'ko, á] *a* white ♦ *nm/f* white man/woman, white ♦ *nm* (*color*) white; (*en texto*) blank; (*MIL, fig*) target ♦ *nf* (*MUS*) half note (*US*), minim (*Brit*); **en ~** blank; **cheque en ~** blank check; **votar en ~** to not mark one's ballot paper; **quedarse en ~** to be disappointed; **noche en ~** sleepless night; **estar sin ~** to be broke; **ser el ~ de las burlas** to be the butt of jokes.

blancura [blánkōō'rá] *nf* whiteness.

blandengue [blánden'ge] *a* (*fam*) soft, weak.

blandir [blándēr'] *vt* to brandish.

blando, a [blán'do, á] *a* soft; (*tierno*) tender, gentle; (*carácter*) mild; (*fam*) cowardly ♦ *nm/f* (*POL etc*) soft-liner.

blandura [blándōō'rá] *nf* softness; tenderness; mildness.

blanquear [blánkeár'] *vt* to whiten; (*fachada*) to whitewash; (*paño*) to bleach ♦ *vi* to turn white.

blanquecino, a [blánkesē'no, á] *a* whitish.

blasfemar [blásfemár'] *vi* to blaspheme; (*fig*) to curse.

blasfemia [blásfe'myá] *nf* blasphemy.

blasfemo, a [blásfe'mo, á] *a* blasphemous ♦ *nm/f* blasphemer.

blasón [bláson'] *nm* coat of arms; (*fig*) honor or (*US*), honour (*Brit*).

blasonar [blásonár'] *vt* to emblazon ♦ *vi* to boast, brag.

bledo [ble'tho] *nm*: **(no) me importa un ~** I couldn't care less.

blindado, a [blēndá'tho, á] *a* (*MIL*) armorplated (*US*), armour-plated (*Brit*); (*antibalas*) bulletproof; **coche** *o* (*AM*) **carro ~** armored car; **puertas blindadas** security doors.

blindaje [blēndá'he] *nm* armor (*US*), armour (*Brit*), armor-plating.

bloc [blok] *pl* **blocs** [blok, blos] *nm* writing pad; (*ESCOL*) notebook; ~ **de dibujos** sketch pad.

bloque [blo'ke] *nm* (*tb INFORM*) block; (*POL*) bloc; ~ **de cilindros** cylinder block.

bloquear [blokeár'] *vt* (*NAUT etc*) to blockade; (*aislar*) to cut off; (*COM, ECON*) to freeze; **fondos bloqueados** frozen assets.

bloqueo [bloke'o] *nm* blockade; (*COM*) freezing, blocking.

blusa [blōō'sá] *nf* blouse.

B.º *abr* (*FINANZAS*: = *banco*) bank; (*COM*: = *beneficiario*) beneficiary.

boato [boá'to] *nm* show, ostentation.

bobada [bohá'thá] *nf* foolish action (*o* statement); **decir ~s** to talk nonsense.

bobalicón, ona [bohálēkon', oná] *a* utterly stupid.

bobería [bohcrē'á] *nf* = **bobada**.

bobina [bohē'ná] *nf* (*TEC*) bobbin; (*FOTO*) spool; (*ELEC*) coil, winding.

bobo, a [bo'ho, á] *a* (*tonto*) daft, silly; (*cándido*) naïve ♦ *nm/f* fool, idiot ♦ *nm* (*TEATRO*) clown, funny man.

boca [bo'ká] *nf* mouth; (*de crustáceo*) pincer; (*de cañón*) muzzle; (*entrada*) mouth, entrance; (*INFORM*) slot; **~s** *nfpl* (*de río*) mouth *sg*; ~ **abajo/arriba** face down/up; **a ~ jarro** point-blank; **se me hace la ~ agua** my mouth is watering; **todo salió a pedir de ~** it all turned out perfectly; **en ~ de** (*AM*) according to; **la cosa anda de ~ en ~** the story is going the rounds; **¡cállate la ~!** (*fam*) shut up!; **quedarse con la ~ abierta** to be dumbfounded; **no abrir la ~** to keep quiet; ~ **del estómago** pit of the stomach; ~ **de metro** subway (*US*) *o* tube (*Brit*) entrance.

bocacalle [bokáká'ye] *nf* (entrance to a) street; **la primera ~** the first turning *o* street.

bocadillo [bokáthē'yo] *nm* sandwich.

bocado [boká'tho] *nm* mouthful, bite; (*de caballo*) bridle; ~ **de Adán** Adam's apple.

bocajarro [bokáhá'rro]: **a ~** *ad* (*MIL*) at point-blank range; **decir algo a ~** to say sth bluntly.

bocanada [bokáná'thá] *nf* (*de vino*) mouthful, swallow; (*de aire*) gust, puff.

bocazas [boká'sás] *nm/f inv* (*fam*) bigmouth.

boceto [bose'to] *nm* sketch, outline.

bocina [bosē'ná] *nf* (*MUS*) trumpet; (*AUTO*) horn; (*para hablar*) megaphone; **tocar la ~** (*AUTO*) to sound one's horn.

bocinazo [bosēná'so] *nm* (*AUTO*) toot.

bocio [bo'syo] *nm* (*MED*) goiter (*US*), goitre (*Brit*).

bocha [botch'á] *nf* bowl; **~s** *nfpl* bowls *sg*.

bochinche [botchēntch'e] *nm* (*fam*) uproar.

bochorno |botchor'no| *nm* (*vergüenza*) embarrassment; (*calor*): **hace** ~ it's very muggy.

bochornoso, a |botchorno'so, á| *a* muggy; embarrassing.

boda |bo'ðá| *nf* (*tb:* ~**s**) wedding, marriage; (*fiesta*) wedding reception; ~**s de plata/de oro** silver/golden wedding *sg.*

bodega |boðhc'gá| *nf* (*de vino*) (wine) cellar; (*bar*) bar; (*restaurante*) restaurant; (*depósito*) storeroom; (*de barco*) hold.

bodegón |boðhcgon'| *nm* (*ARTE*) still life.

bodrio |boðhrē'o| *nm:* **el libro es un** ~ the book is awful *o* rubbish.

B.O.E. |bo'c| *nm abr* (= *Boletín Oficial del Estado*) ≈ The Congressional Record (*US*), Hansard (*Brit*).

bofe |bo'fc| *nm* (*tb:* ~**s**: *de res*) lungs *pl*; **echar los** ~**s** to slave (away).

bofetada |bofctá'ðá| *nf* slap (in the face); **dar de** ~**s a uno** to punch sb.

bofetón |bofcton'| *nm* = **bofetada**.

boga |bo'gá| *nf*: **en** ~ in vogue.

bogar |bogár'| *vi* (*remar*) to row; (*navegar*) to sail.

bogavante |bogáhán'tc| *nm* (*NAUT*) stroke, first rower; (*ZOOL*) lobster.

Bogotá |bogotá'| *n* Bogota.

bogotano, a |bogotá'no, á| *a* of *o* from Bogota ♦ *nm/f* native *o* inhabitant of Bogota.

bogue |bo'gc| *etc vb V* **bogar**.

bohemio, a |boc'myo, á| *a, nm/f* Bohemian.

boicot, *pl* **boicots** |bočko'(t)| *nm* boycott.

boicotear |bočkotcár'| *vt* to boycott.

boicoteo |bočkotc'o| *nm* boycott.

boina |bo'ēná| *nf* beret.

bola |bo'lá| *nf* ball; (*canica*) marble; (*NAIPES*) (grand) slam; (*betún*) shoe polish; (*mentira*) tale, story; ~**s** *nfpl* (*AM*) bolas; ~ **de billar** billiard ball; ~ **de nieve** snowball.

bolado |bolá'ðo| *nm* (*AM*) deal.

bolchevique |boltchckē'kc| *a, nm/f* Bolshevik.

boleadoras |bolcáðho'rás| *nfpl* (*AM*) bolas *sg.*

bolera |bolc'rá| *nf* skittle *o* bowling alley.

boleta |bolc'tá| *nf* (*AM*: *billete*) ticket; (: *permiso*) pass, permit.

boletería |bolctcrē'á| *nf* (*AM*) ticket office.

boletín |bolctēn'| *nm* bulletin; (*periódico*) journal, review; ~ **escolar** (*Esp*) school report; ~ **de noticias** news bulletin; ~ **de pedido** application form; ~ **de precios** price list; ~ **de prensa** press release.

boleto |bolc'to| *nm* ticket; ~ **de apuestas** betting slip.

boli |bo'lē| *nm* ballpoint.

boliche |bolētch'c| *nm* (*bola*) jack; (*juego*) bowls *sg*; (*lugar*) bowling alley; (*AM*: *tienda*) small grocery store.

bólido |bo'lēðho| *nm* meteorite; (*AUTO*) racing car.

bolígrafo |bolē'gráfo| *nm* ball-point pen.

bolillo |bolē'yo| *nm* (*COSTURA*) bobbin (for lacemaking).

bolívar |bolē'hár| *nm* monetary unit of Venezuela.

Bolivia |bolē'hyá| *nf* Bolivia.

boliviano, a |bolēhyá'no, á| *a, nm/f* Bolivian.

bolo |bo'lo| *nm* ninepin (*US*), skittle (*Brit*); (*píldora*) (large) pill; **(juego de)** ~**s** ninepines *sg* (*US*), skittles *sg* (*Brit*).

Bolonia |bolo'nyá| *nf* Bologna.

bolsa |bol'sá| *nf* (*cartera*) purse; (*saco*) bag; (*AM*) pocket; (*ANAT*) cavity, sac; (*COM*) stock exchange; (*MINERÍA*) pocket; ~ **de agua caliente** hot water bottle; ~ **de aire** air pocket; ~ **de papel** paper bag; ~ **de plástico** plastic bag; ~ **de trabajo** employment bureau; **jugar a la** ~ to play the market.

bolsillo |bolsē'yo| *nm* pocket; (*cartera*) purse; **de** ~ pocket *cpd*; **meterse a uno en el** ~ to get sb eating out of one's hand.

bolsista |bolsē'stá| *nm/f* stockbroker.

bolso |bol'so| *nm* (*bolsa*) bag; (*de mujer*) handbag.

bollo |bo'yo| *nm* (*pan*) roll; (*dulce*) scone; (*bulto*) bump, lump; (*abolladura*) dent; ~**s** *nmpl* (*AM*) troubles.

bomba |bom'bá| *nf* (*MIL*) bomb; (*TEC*) pump; (*AM*: *globo*) balloon; (: *borrachera*) drunkenness ♦ *a* (*fam*): **noticia** ~ bombshell ♦ *ad* (*fam*): **pasarlo** ~ to have a great time; ~ **atómica/de humo/de retardo** atomic/smoke/time bomb; ~ **de gasolina** gasoline (*US*) *o* petrol (*Brit*) pump; ~ **de incendios** fire engine.

bombacho, a |bombátch'o, á| *a* (*AM*) baggy.

bombardear |bombárðhcár'| *vt* to bombard; (*MIL*) to bomb.

bombardeo |bombárðhc'o| *nm* bombardment; bombing.

bombardero |bombárðhc'ro| *nm* bomber.

bombear |bombcár'| *vt* (*agua*) to pump (out *o* up); (*MIL*) to bomb; (*FÚTBOL*) to lob; ~**se** *vr* to warp.

bombero |bombc'ro| *nm* fireman; **(cuerpo de)** ~**s** fire brigade.

bombilla |bombē'yá| *nf* (*Esp*) (light) bulb.

bombín |bombēn'| *nm* derby (*US*), bowler hat (*Brit*).

bombo |bom'bo| *nm* (*MUS*) bass drum; (*TEC*) drum; (*fam*) exaggerated praise; **hacer algo a** ~ **y platillo** to make a great song and dance about sth; **tengo la cabeza hecha un** ~ I've got a splitting headache.

bombón |bombon'| *nm* chocolate; (*belleza*) beauty.

bombona [bombo'ná] *nf*: ~ **de butano** gas cylinder.

bombonería [bomboncrẽ'á] *nf* candy store (*US*), sweetshop (*Brit*).

bonaerense [bonácrcn'sc] *a* of o from Buenos Aires ♦ *nm/f* native o inhabitant of Buenos Aires.

bonancible [bonánsẽ'ɦle] *a* (*tiempo*) fair, calm.

bonanza [bonán'sá] *nf* (*NAUT*) fair weather; (*fig*) bonanza; (*MINERÍA*) rich pocket o vein.

bondad [bondáɖ'] *nf* goodness, kindness; **tenga la** ~ **de** (please) be good enough to.

bondadoso, a [bondáɖho'so, á] *a* good, kind.

boniato [bonyá'to] *nm* sweet potato, yam.

bonificación [bonẽfẽkásyon'] *nf* (*COM*) allowance, discount; (*pago*) bonus; (*DEPORTE*) extra points *pl*.

bonito, a [bonẽ'to, á] *a* (*lindo*) pretty; (*agradable*) nice ♦ *ad* (*AM fam*) well ♦ *nm* (*atún*) tuna (fish).

bono [bo'no] *nm* voucher; (*FIN*) bond; ~ **de billetes de metro** booklet of metro tickets; ~ **del Tesoro** treasury bill.

bonobús [bonoɦōōs'] *nm* (*Esp*) bus pass.

boquear [bokeár'] *vi* to gasp.

boquerón [bokeron'] *nm* (*pez*) (kind of) anchovy; (*agujero*) large hole.

boquete [boke'tc] *nm* gap, hole.

boquiabierto, a [bokẽáɦyer'to, á] *a* open-mouthed (in astonishment); **quedar** ~ to be left aghast.

boquilla [bokẽ'yá] *nf* (*para riego*) nozzle; (*para cigarro*) cigarette holder; (*MUS*) mouthpiece.

borbollar [borɦoyár'], **borbollear** [borɦo-yeár'] *vi* to bubble.

borbollón [borɦoyon'] *nm* bubbling; **hablar a borbollones** to jabber; **salir a borbollo-nes** (*agua*) to gush out.

borbotar [borɦotár'] *vi* = **borbollar**.

borbotón [borɦoton'] *nm*: **salir a borboto-nes** to gush out.

borda [bor'ɖá] *nf* (*NAUT*) gunwale; **echar** o **tirar algo por la** ~ to throw sth overboard.

bordado [borɖá'ɖho] *nm* embroidery.

bordar [borɖár'] *vt* to embroider.

borde [bor'ɖe] *nm* edge, border; (*de camino etc*) side; (*en la costura*) hem; **al** ~ **de** (*fig*) on the verge o brink of; **ser** ~ (*Esp fam*) to be a pain in the neck.

bordear [borɖeár'] *vt* to border.

bordillo [borɖẽ'yo] *nm* curb (*US*), kerb (*Brit*).

bordo [bor'ɖho] *nm* (*NAUT*) side; **a** ~ on board.

Borgoña [borɡo'nyá] *nf* Burgundy.

borgoña [borɡo'nyá] *nm* burgundy.

borinqueño, a [borẽnke'nyo, á] *a*, *nm/f* Puerto Rican.

borla [bor'lá] *nf* (*gen*) tassel; (*de gorro*) pompon.

borra [bo'rrá] *nf* (*pelusa*) fluff; (*sedimento*) sediment.

borrachera [borrátchc'rá] *nf* (*ebriedad*) drunkenness; (*orgía*) spree, binge.

borracho, a [borrá'tcho, á] *a* drunk ♦ *nm/f* (*que bebe mucho*) drunkard, drunk; (*temporalmente*) drunk, drunk man/woman ♦ *nm* (*CULIN*) cake soaked in liqueur or spirit.

borrador [borráɖhor'] *nm* (*escritura*) first draft, rough sketch; (*cuaderno*) scribbling pad; (*goma*) eraser, rubber (*Brit*); (*COM*) daybook; (*para pizarra*) eraser (*US*), duster (*Brit*); **hacer un nuevo** ~ **de** (*COM*) to redraft.

borrajear [borráhcár'] *vt*, *vi* to scribble.

borrar [borrár'] *vt* to erase, rub out; (*tachar*) to delete; (*cinta*) to wipe out; (*INFORM: archivo*) to delete, erase; (*POL etc: eliminar*) to wipe out.

borrasca [borrás'ká] *nf* (*METEOROLOGÍA*) storm.

borrascoso, a [borrásko'so, á] *a* stormy.

borrego, a [borrc'ɡo, á] *nm/f* lamb; (*oveja*) sheep; (*fig*) simpleton.

borricada [borrẽká'ɖhá] *nf* foolish action/statement.

borrico, a [borrẽ'ko, á] *nm* donkey; (*fig*) stupid man ♦ *nf* she-donkey; (*fig*) stupid woman.

borrón [borron'] *nm* (*mancha*) stain; ~ **y cuenta nueva** let bygones be bygones.

borroso, a [borro'so, á] *a* vague, unclear; (*escritura*) illegible; (*escrito*) smudgy; (*FOTO*) blurred.

Bósforo [bos'foro] *nm*: **el (Estrecho del)** ~ the Bosp(h)orus.

bosque [bos'ke] *nm* wood; (*grande*) forest.

bosquejar [boskehár'] *vt* to sketch.

bosquejo [boske'ho] *nm* sketch.

bosta [bos'tá] *nf* dung, manure.

bostece [boste'sc] *etc vb* V **bostezar**.

bostezar [bostesár'] *vi* to yawn.

bostezo [boste'so] *nm* yawn.

bota [bo'tá] *nf* (*calzado*) boot; (*saco*) leather wine bottle; **ponerse las** ~**s** (*fam*) to strike it rich.

botadura [botáɖhōō'rá] *nf* launching.

botánico, a [botá'nẽko, á] *a* botanical ♦ *nm/f* botanist ♦ *nf* botany.

botar [botár'] *vt* to throw, hurl; (*NAUT*) to launch; (*fam*) to throw out ♦ *vi* to bounce.

botarate [botárá'te] *nm* (*imbécil*) idiot.

bote [bo'te] *nm* (*salto*) bounce; (*golpe*) thrust; (*vasija*) tin, can; (*embarcación*) boat; **de** ~ **en** ~ packed, jammed full; ~ **salvavidas** lifeboat; **dar un** ~ to jump; **dar** ~**s** (*AUTO etc*) to bump; ~ **de la basura**

(*AM*) trashcan (*US*), dustbin (*Brit*).

botella [bote'yá] *nf* bottle; ~ **de vino** (*contenido*) bottle of wine; (*recipiente*) wine bottle.

botellero [botçye'ro] *nm* wine rack.

botica [botē'ká] *nf* pharmacy, chemist's (shop) (*Brit*).

boticario, a [botēká'ryo, á] *nm/f* pharmacist, chemist (*Brit*).

botijo [botē'ho] *nm* (earthenware) jug; (*tren*) excursion train.

botín [botēn'] *nm* (*calzado*) half boot; (*polaina*) spat; (*MIL*) booty; (*de ladrón*) loot.

botiquín [botēkēn'] *nm* (*armario*) medicine chest; (*portátil*) first-aid kit.

botón [boton'] *nm* button; (*BOT*) bud; (*de florete*) tip; ~ **de arranque** (*AUTO etc*) starter; ~ **de oro** buttercup; **pulsar el** ~ **to** press the button.

botones [boto'nes] *nm inv* bellhop (*US*), bellboy (*Brit*).

botulismo [botōōlēs'mo] *nm* botulism, food poisoning.

bóveda [bo'νetħá] *nf* (*ARQ*) vault.

bovino, a [boħē'no, á] *a* bovine; (*AGR*): **ganado** ~ cattle.

boxeador [bokseátħor'] *nm* boxer.

boxear [bokseár'] *vi* to box.

boxeo [bokse'o] *nm* boxing.

boya [bo'yá] *nf* (*NAUT*) buoy; (*flotador*) float.

boyante [boyán'te] *a* (*NAUT*) buoyant; (*feliz*) buoyant; (*próspero*) prosperous.

bozal [bosál'] *nm* (*de caballo*) halter; (*de perro*) muzzle.

bozo [bo'so] *nm* (*pelusa*) fuzz; (*boca*) mouth.

bracear [bráseár'] *vi* (*agitar los brazos*) to wave one's arms.

bracero [bráse'ro] *nm* laborer (*US*), labourer (*Brit*); (*en el campo*) farmhand.

bracete [bráse'te]: **de** ~ *ad* arm in arm.

braga [brá'ġá] *nf* (*cuerda*) sling, rope; (*de bebé*) diaper (*US*), nappy (*Brit*); ~**s** *nfpl* (*de mujer*) panties.

braguero [bráġe'ro] *nm* (*MED*) truss.

bragueta [bráġe'tá] *nf* fly, zipper (*US*).

braguetazo [bráġetá'so] *nm* (*AM*) marriage of convenience.

braille [brecl] *nm* braille.

bramante [brámán'te] *nm* twine, string.

bramar [brámár'] *vi* to bellow, roar.

bramido [brámē'tħo] *nm* bellow, roar.

branquias [brán'kyás] *nfpl* gills.

brasa [brá'sá] *nf* live *o* hot coal; **carne a la** ~ grilled meat.

brasero [bráse'ro] *nm* brazier; (*AM: chimenea*) fireplace.

Brasil [brásēl'] *nm*: (**el**) ~ Brazil.

brasileño, a [brásēle'nyo, á] *a, nm/f* Brazilian.

brava [brá'ħá]: **a la** ~ *ad* by force.

bravata [bráħá'tá] *nf* boast.

braveza [bráħe'sá] *nf* (*valor*) bravery; (*ferocidad*) ferocity.

bravío, a [bráħē'o, á] *a* wild; (*feroz*) fierce.

bravo, a [brá'ħo, á] *a* (*valiente*) brave; (*bueno*) fine, splendid; (*feroz*) ferocious; (*salvaje*) wild; (*mar etc*) rough, stormy; (*CULIN*) hot, spicy ♦ *excl* bravo!

bravucón, ona [bráħōōkon', o'ná] *a* swaggering ♦ *nm/f* braggart.

bravura [bráħōō'rá] *nf* bravery; ferocity; (*pey*) boast.

braza [brá'sá] *nf* fathom; **nadar a la** ~ to swim; (*the*) breast-stroke.

brazada [brásá'tħá] *nf* stroke.

brazado [brásá'tħo] *nm* armful.

brazalete [brásále'te] *nm* (*pulsera*) bracelet; (*banda*) armband.

brazo [brá'so] *nm* arm; (*ZOOL*) foreleg; (*BOT*) limb, branch; ~**s** *nmpl* (*braceros*) hands, workers; ~ **derecho** (*fig*) right-hand man; **a** ~ **partido** hand-to-hand; **cogidos** *etc* **del** ~ arm in arm; **no dar su** ~ **a torcer** not to give way easily; **huelga de** ~**s caídos** sit-down strike.

brea [bre'á] *nf* pitch, tar.

brebaje [breħá'he] *nm* potion.

brécol [bre'kol] *nm* broccoli.

brecha [bretch'á] *nf* breach; (*hoyo vacío*) gap, opening.

brega [bre'ġá] *nf* (*lucha*) struggle; (*trabajo*) hard work.

bregar [breġár'] *vi* (*luchar*) to struggle; (*trabajar mucho*) to slog away.

bregue [bre'ġe] *etc vb* **V bregar**.

breña [bre'nyá] *nf* rough ground.

Bretaña [bretá'nyá] *nf* Brittany.

brete [bre'te] *nm* (*cepo*) shackles *pl*; (*fig*) predicament; **estar en un** ~ to be in a jam.

bretón, ona [breton', o'ná] *a, nm/f* Breton.

breva [bre'ħá] *nf* (*BOT*) early fig; (*puro*) flat cigar; **¡no caerá esa** ~! no such luck!

breve [bre'ħe] *a* short, brief; **en** ~ (*pronto*) shortly; (*en pocas palabras*) in short ♦ *nf* (*MUS*) breve.

brevedad [breħetħátħ'] *nf* brevity, shortness.

breviario [breħyá'ryo] *nm* (*REL*) breviary.

brezal [bresál'] *nm* moor(land), heath.

brezo [bre'so] *nm* heather.

bribón, ona [breħon', o'ná] *a* idle, lazy ♦ *nm/f* (*vagabundo*) vagabond; (*pícaro*) rascal, rogue.

bricolaje [brēkolá'he] *nm* do-it-yourself.

brida [brē'tħá] *nf* bridle, rein; (*TEC*) clamp; **a toda** ~ at top speed.

bridge [bretch] *nm* (*NAIPES*) bridge.

brigada [breġá'tħá] *nf* (*unidad*) brigade; (*trabajadores*) squad, gang ♦ *nm* warrant

officer.

brigadier [brĕgáthycr'] *nm* brigadier(-general).

brigantino, a [brĕgántē'no, á] *a* of *o* from Corunna ♦ *nm/f* native *o* inhabitant of Corunna.

brillante [brĕyàn'tc] *a* brilliant; (*color*) bright; (*joya*) sparkling ♦ *nm* diamond.

brillantez [brĕyántcs'] *nf* (*color etc*) brightness; (*fig*) brilliance.

brillar [brĕyàr'] *vi* (*tb fig*) to shine; (*joyas*) to sparkle; ~ **por su ausencia** to be conspicuous by one's absence.

brillo [brē'yo] *nm* shine; (*brillantez*) brilliance; (*fig*) splendor (*US*), splendour (*Brit*); **sacar** ~ **a** to polish.

brincar [brĕnkár'] *vi* to skip about, hop about, jump about; **está que brinca** he's hopping mad.

brinco [brēn'ko] *nm* jump, leap; **a** ~s by fits and starts; **de un** ~ at one leap.

brindar [brĕndár'] *vi*: ~ **a** *o* **por** to drink (a toast) to ♦ *vt* to offer, present; **le brinda la ocasión de** it offers *o* affords him the opportunity to; ~**se** *vr*: ~**se a hacer algo** to offer to do sth.

brindis [brēn'dēs] *nm inv* toast; (*TAUR*) (ceremony of) dedication.

brinque [brēn'ke] *etc vb* V **brincar.**

brío [brē'o] *nm* spirit, verve.

brioso, a [brēo'so, á] *a* spirited.

brisa [brē'sá] *nf* breeze.

británico, a [brĕtá'nēko, á] *a* British ♦ *nm/f* Briton, British person; **los** ~**s** the British.

brizna [brēs'ná] *nf* (*hebra*) strand, thread; (*de hierba*) blade; (*trozo*) piece; (*AM*) drizzle.

broca [bro'ká] *nf* (*COSTURA*) bobbin; (*TEC*) drill bit; (*clavo*) tack.

brocado [broká'tho] *nm* brocade.

brocal [brokál'] *nm* rim.

brocha [brotch'á] *nf* (large) paintbrush; ~ **de afeitar** shaving brush; **pintor de** ~ **gorda** painter and decorator; (*fig*) poor painter.

brochazo [brotchá'so] *nm* brush-stroke; **a grandes** ~**s** (*fig*) in general terms.

broche [brotch'e] *nm* brooch.

broma [bro'má] *nf* joke; (*inocentada*) practical joke; **en** ~ in fun, as a joke; **gastar una** ~ **a uno** to play a joke on sb; **tomar algo a** ~ to take sth as a joke.

bromear [bromeár'] *vi* to joke.

bromista [bromē'stá] *a* fond of joking ♦ *nm/f* joker, wag.

bromuro [bromōō'ro] *nm* bromide.

bronca [bron'ká] *nf* row; (*regañada*) scolding; **armar una** ~ to kick up a fuss; **echar una** ~ **a uno** to tell sb off.

bronce [bron'se] *nm* bronze; (*latón*) brass.

bronceado, a [bronseá'tho, á] *a* bronze

cpd; (*por el sol*) tanned ♦ *nm* (sun)tan; (*TEC*) bronzing.

bronceador [bronseátho'r'] *nm* suntan lotion.

broncearse [bronseár'se] *vr* to get a suntan.

bronco, a [bron'ko, á] *a* (*manera*) rude, surly; (*voz*) harsh.

bronquios [bron'kyos] *nmpl* bronchial tubes.

bronquitis [bronkē'tēs] *nf inv* bronchitis.

brotar [brotár'] *vt* (*tierra*) to produce ♦ *vi* (*BOT*) to sprout; (*aguas*) to gush (forth); (*lágrimas*) to well up; (*MED*) to break out.

brote [bro'te] *nm* (*BOT*) shoot; (*MED, fig*) outbreak.

broza [bro'sá] *nf* (*BOT*) dead leaves *pl*; (*fig*) rubbish.

bruces [broo'ses]: **de** ~ *ad*: **caer** *o* **dar de** ~ to fall headlong, fall flat.

bruja [broo'há] *nf* witch.

Brujas [broo'hás] *nf* Bruges.

brujería [broohere'á] *nf* witchcraft.

brujo [broo'ho] *nm* wizard, magician.

brújula [broo'hoolá] *nf* compass.

bruma [broo'má] *nf* mist.

brumoso, a [broomo'so, á] *a* misty.

bruñendo [broonyen'do] *etc vb* V **bruñir.**

bruñido [broonyē'tho] *nm* polish.

bruñir [broonyēr'] *vt* to polish.

brusco, a [broos'ko, á] *a* (*súbito*) sudden; (*áspero*) brusque.

Bruselas [broose'lás] *nf* Brussels.

brusquedad [brooskethath'] *nf* suddenness; brusqueness.

brutal [brootál'] *a* brutal.

brutalidad [brootáléthath'] *nf* brutality.

bruto, a [broo'to, á] *a* (*idiota*) stupid; (*bestial*) brutish; (*peso*) gross ♦ *nm* brute; **a la bruta, a lo** ~ roughly; **en** ~ raw, unworked.

Bs.As. *abr* = **Buenos Aires.**

buba [boo'há] *nf* tumor (*US*), tumour (*Brit*).

bucal [bookál'] *a* oral; **por vía** ~ orally.

bucanero [bookáne'ro] *nm* buccaneer.

bucear [booseár'] *vi* to dive ♦ *vt* to explore.

buceo [boose'o] *nm* diving; (*fig*) investigation.

bucle [boo'kle] *nm* curl; (*INFORM*) loop.

buche [boo'tche] *nm* (*de ave*) crop; (*ZOOL*) maw; (*fam*) belly.

budín [boothēn'] *nm* pudding.

budismo [boothēs'mo] *nm* Buddhism.

buen [bwen] *a* V **bueno.**

buenamente [bwenámen'tc] *ad* (*fácilmente*) easily; (*voluntariamente*) willingly.

buenaventura [bwenáhentoo'rá] *nf* (*suerte*) good luck; (*adivinación*) fortune; **decir** *o* **echar la** ~ **a uno** to tell sb's fortune.

bueno, a [bwe'no, á], **buen** [bwen] *a* (*amable*) kind; (*MED*) well ♦ *excl* right!, all right!; **¡buenas!** afternoon! (fam); **¡buen día!, ¡buenos días!** good morning!; good afternoon!; hello!; **¡buenas tardes!** good afternoon!; good evening!; **¡buenas noches!** good evening!; good night!; **los buenos** (CINE) the goodies; **¡buen sinvergüenza resultó!** a fine rascal he turned out to be; **el bueno de Manolo** good old Manolo; **fue muy bueno conmigo** he was very good to me; **de buenas a primeras** all of a sudden; **por las buenas o por las malas** by hook or by crook; **bueno, ¿y qué?** well, so what?

Buenos Aires [bwenosá'ēres] nm Buenos Aires.

buey [bweē] nm ox.

búfalo [bōō'fálo] nm buffalo.

bufanda [bōōfán'dá] nf scarf.

bufar [bōōfár'] vi to snort.

bufete [bōōfe'te] nm (despacho de abogado) lawyer's office; **establecer su ~** to set up in legal practice.

buffer [bōō'fer] nm (INFORM) buffer.

bufón [bōōfon'] nm clown.

bufonada [bōōfoná'ðá] nf (dicho) jest; (hecho) piece of buffoonery; (TEATRO) farce.

buhardilla [bōōárðe'yá] nf attic.

búho [bōō'o] nm owl; (fig) hermit, recluse.

buhonero [bōōone'ro] nm pedler (US), pedlar (Brit).

buitre [bwē'tre] nm vulture.

bujía [bōōhē'á] nf (vela) candle; (ELEC) candle (power); (AUTO) spark plug.

bula [bōō'lá] nf (papal) bull.

bulbo [bōōl'ḅo] nm (BOT) bulb.

bulevar [bōōleḅár'] nm boulevard.

Bulgaria [bōōlǧá'ryá] nf Bulgaria.

búlgaro, a [bōōl'ǧáro, á] a, nm/f Bulgarian.

bulo [bōō'lo] nm false rumour.

bulto [bōōl'to] nm (paquete) package; (fardo) bundle; (tamaño) size, bulkiness; (MED) swelling, lump; (silueta) vague shape; (estatua) bust, statue; **hacer ~** to take up space; **escurrir el ~** to make o.s. scarce; (fig) to dodge the issue.

bulla [bōō'yá] nf (ruido) uproar; (de gente) crowd; **armar o meter ~** to kick up a row.

bullendo [bōōyen'do] etc vb V **bullir.**

bullicio [bōōyē'syo] nm (ruido) uproar; (movimiento) bustle.

bullicioso, a [bōōyēsyo'so, á] a (ruidoso) noisy, (calle etc) busy; (situación) turbulent.

bullir [bōōyēr'] vi (hervir) to boil; (burbujear) to bubble; (mover) to move, stir; (insectos) to swarm; **~ de** (fig) to teem o seethe with.

buñuelo [bōōnywe'lo] nm ≈ doughnut, donut (US).

BUP [bōōp] nm abr (Esp ESCOL:= Bachillerato Unificado y Polivalente) secondary education and leaving diploma for 14-17 age group.

buque [bōō'ke] nm ship, vessel; **~ de guerra** warship; **~ mercante** merchant ship; **~ de vela** sailing ship.

burbuja [bōōrḅōō'há] nf bubble; **hacer ~s** to bubble; (gaseosa) to fizz.

burbujear [bōōrḅōōheár'] vi to bubble.

burdel [bōōrðel'] nm brothel.

Burdeos [bōōrðe'os] nm Bordeaux.

burdo, a [bōōr'ðo, á] a coarse, rough.

burgalés, esa [bōōrǧáles', e'sá] a of o from Burgos ♦ nm/f native o inhabitant of Burgos.

burgués, esa [bōōrǧes', e'sá] a middle-class, bourgeois; **pequeño ~** lower middle-class; (POL, pey) petty bourgeois.

burguesía [bōōrǧesē'á] nf middle class, bourgeoisie.

burla [bōōr'lá] nf (mofa) gibe; (broma) joke; (engaño) trick; **hacer ~ de** to make fun of.

burladero [bōōrláðe'ro] nm (bullfighter's) refuge.

burlador, a [bōōrláðor', á] a mocking ♦ nm/f mocker; (bromista) joker ♦ nm (libertino) seducer.

burlar [bōōrlár'] vt (engañar) to deceive; (seducir) to seduce ♦ vi, **~se** vr to joke; **~se de** to make fun of.

burlesco, a [bōōrles'ko, á] a burlesque.

burlón, ona [bōōrlon', o'ná] a mocking.

buró [bōōro'] nm bureau.

burocracia [bōōrokrá'syá] nf bureaucracy.

burócrata [bōōro'krátá] nm/f bureaucrat.

buromática [bōōromá'tēká] nf office automation.

burrada [bōōrrá'ðá] nf stupid act; **decir ~s** to talk nonsense.

burro, a [bōō'rro, á] nm/f (ZOOL) donkey; (fig) ass, idiot ♦ a stupid; **caerse del ~** to realize one's mistake; **no ver tres en un ~** to be as blind as a bat.

bursátil [bōōrsá'tēl] a stock-exchange cpd.

bus [bōōs] nm bus.

busca [bōōs'ká] nf search, hunt; **en ~ de** in search of.

buscador, a [bōōskáðor', á] nm/f searcher.

buscapiés [bōōskápyes'] nm inv firecracker (US), jumping jack (Brit).

buscapleitos [bōōskáple'ētos] nm/f inv troublemaker.

buscar [bōōskár'] vt to look for; (beneficio) to seek; (enemigo) to seek out; (traer) to bring, fetch; (provocar) to provoke; (INFORM) to search ♦ vi to look, search, seek; **ven a ~me a la oficina** come and pick me up at the office; **~le 3 o 4 pies al gato** to split hairs; "**~ y reemplazar**" (INFORM) "search and replace"; **se busca secretaria**

secretary wanted; **se la buscó** he asked for it.

buscavidas [bōoskåhē'thás] *nm/f inv* snooper; (*persona ambiciosa*) go-getter.

buscón, ona [bōoskon', o'ná] *a* thieving ♦ *nm* petty thief ♦ *nf* whore.

busilis [bōosē'lēs] *nm inv* (*fam*) snag.

busque [bōos'kc] *etc vb V* **buscar.**

búsqueda [bōos'kethá] *nf* = **busca.**

busto [bōo'sto] *nm* (*ANAT, ARTE*) bust.

butaca [bōotá'ká] *nf* armchair; (*de cine, teatro*) seat.

butano [bōotá'no] *nm* butane (gas); **bombona de** ~ gas cylinder.

butifarra [bōotēfá'rrá] *nf* Catalan sausage.

buzo [bōo'so] *nm* diver.

buzón [bōoson'] *nm* (*gen*) mailbox (*US*), letter box (*Brit*); (*en la calle*) pillar box (*Brit*); (*TELEC*) mailbox; **echar al** ~ to post.

byte [bäēt] *nm* (*INFORM*) byte.

C

C, c [sc] *nf* (*letra*) C, c; **C de Carmen** C for Charlie.

C. *abr* (= *centígrado*) C.; (= *compañía*) Co.

c. *abr* (= *capítulo*) ch.

C/ *abr* (= *calle*) St, Rd.

c/ *abr* (*COM*: = *cuenta*) a/c.

ca [ká] *excl* not a bit of it!

c.a. *abr* (= *corriente alterna*) A.C.

cabal [kábál'] *a* (*exacto*) exact; (*correcto*) right, proper; (*acabado*) finished, complete; ~**es** *nmpl*: **estar en sus** ~**es** to be in one's right mind.

cábala [ká'bálá] *nf* (*REL*) cab(b)ala; (*fig*) cabal, intrigue; ~**s** *nfpl* guess *sg*, supposition *sg*.

cabalgadura [kábálgáthōo'rá] *nf* mount, horse.

cabalgar [kábálgàr'] *vt, vi* to ride.

cabalgata [kábálgá'tá] *nf* procession.

cabalgue [kábál'gc] *etc vb V* **cabalgar.**

cabalístico, a [kábálē'stēko, á] *a* (*fig*) mysterious.

caballa [kábá'yá] *nf* mackerel.

caballeresco, a [kábáyeres'ko, á] *a* noble, chivalrous.

caballería [kábáyerē'á] *nf* mount; (*MIL*) cavalry.

caballeriza [kábáyerē'sá] *nf* stable.

caballerizo [kábáyerē'so] *nm* groom, stableman.

caballero [kábáyc'ro] *nm* gentleman; (*de la orden de caballería*) knight; (*trato directo*) sir; "**C**~**s**" "Gentlemen".

caballerosidad [kábáycrosētháth'] *nf* chivalry.

caballete [kábáyc'tc] *nm* (*AGR*) ridge; (*ARTE*) easel.

caballito [kábáyē'to] *nm* (*caballo pequeño*) small horse, pony; (*juguete*) rocking horse; ~**s** *nmpl* merry-go-round *sg*; ~ **de mar** seahorse; ~ **del diablo** dragonfly.

caballo [kábá'yo] *nm* horse; (*AJEDREZ*) knight; (*NAIPES*) queen; ~ **de vapor** *o* **de fuerza** horsepower; **es su** ~ **de batalla** it's his hobby-horse; ~ **blanco** (*COM*) backer.

cabaña [kábá'nyá] *nf* (*casita*) hut, cabin.

cabaré, cabaret, *pl* **cabarets** [kábárc', kábárcs'] *nm* cabaret.

cabecear [kábcscár'] *vi* to nod.

cabecera [kábcsc'rá] *nf* (*gen*) head; (*de distrito*) chief town; (*de cama*) headboard; (*IMPRENTA*) headline.

cabecilla [kábcsē'yá] *nm* ringleader.

cabellera [kábeyc'rá] *nf* (head of) hair; (*de cometa*) tail.

cabello [kábc'yo] *nm* (*tb*: ~**s**) hair *sg*.

caber [kábcr'] *vi* (*entrar*) to fit, go; **caben 3 más** there's room for 3 more; **cabe preguntar si...** one might ask whether...; **cabe que venga más tarde** he may come later.

cabestrillo [kábcstrē'yo] *nm* sling.

cabestro [kábcs'tro] *nm* halter.

cabeza [kábc'sá] *nf* head; (*POL*) chief, leader; **caer de** ~ to fall head first; **sentar la** ~ to settle down; ~ **de lectura/escritura** read/write head; ~ **impresora** *o* **de impresión** printhead.

cabezada [kábcsá'thá] *nf* (*golpe*) butt; **dar una** ~ to nod off.

cabezal [kábcsál'] *nm*: ~ **impresor** print head.

cabezón, ona [kábeson', o'ná] *a* with a big head; (*vino*) heady; (*obstinado*) obstinate, stubborn.

cabezota [kábcso'tá] *a inv* obstinate, stubborn.

cabezudo, a [kábcsōo'tho, á] *a* with a big head; (*obstinado*) obstinate, stubborn.

cabida [kábē'thá] *nf* space; **dar** ~ **a** to make room for; **tener** ~ **para** to have room for.

cabildo [kábēl'do] *nm* (*de iglesia*) chapter; (*POL*) town council.

cabina [kábē'ná] *nf* (*de camión*) cabin; ~ **telefónica** (tele)phone booth.

cabizbajo, a [kábēsbá'ho, á] *a* crestfallen, dejected.

cable [ká'ble] *nm* cable; (*de aparato*) lead; ~ **aéreo** (*ELEC*) overhead cable; **conectar con** ~ (*INFORM*) to hardwire.

cabo [ká'bo] *nm* (*de objeto*) end, extremity; (*MIL*) corporal; (*NAUT*) rope, cable; (*GEO*) cape; (*TEC*) thread; **al ~ de 3 días** after 3 days; **de ~ a rabo** *o* ~ from beginning to end; (*libro: leer*) from cover to cover; **llevar a ~** to carry out; **atar ~s** to tie up the loose ends; **C~ de Buena Esperanza** Cape of Good Hope; **C~ de Hornos** Cape Horn; **las Islas de C~ Verde** the Cape Verde Islands.

cabra [ká'bra] *nf* goat; **estar como una ~** (*fam*) to be nuts.

cabré [kábre'] *etc vb V* **caber**.

cabrear [kábreár'] *vt* to annoy; **~se** *vr* to fly off the handle.

cabrío, a [kábre'o, á] *a* goatish; **macho ~** (he-)goat, billy goat.

cabriola [kábryo'lá] *nf* caper.

cabritilla [kábrēté'yá] *nf* kid, kidskin.

cabrito [kábre'to] *nm* kid.

cabrón [kábron'] *nm* (*fig: fam!*) bastard (*!*).

caca [ká'ká] *nf* (*palabra de niños*) pooh ♦ *excl*: **no toques, ¡~!** don't touch, it's dirty!

cacahuete [kákáwe'te] *nm* (*Esp*) peanut.

cacao [ká'ká'o] *nm* cocoa; (*BOT*) cacao.

cacarear [kákáreár'] *vi* (*persona*) to boast; (*gallina*) to cackle.

cacatúa [kákátōō'á] *nf* cockatoo.

cacereño, a [kásere'nyo, á] *a* of *o* from Cáceres ♦ *nm/f* native *o* inhabitant of Cáceres.

cacería [kásere'á] *nf* hunt.

cacerola [kásero'lá] *nf* pan, saucepan.

cacique [kásē'ke] *nm* chief, local ruler; (*POL*) local party boss; (*fig*) despot.

caciquismo [kásēkēs'mo] *nm* system of dominance by the local boss.

caco [ká'ko] *nm* pickpocket.

cacofonía [kákofonē'á] *nf* cacophony.

cacto [kák'to] *nm*, **cactus** [kák'tōōs] *nm inv* cactus.

cacha [kátch'á] *nf* (*mango*) handle; (*nalga*) buttock.

cacharro [kátchá'rro] *nm* (*vasija*) (earthenware) pot; (*cerámica*) piece of pottery; (*AM fam*) useless object; **~s** *nmpl* pots and pans.

cachear [kátcheár'] *vt* to search, frisk.

cachemir [kátchemēr'] *nm* cashmere.

cacheo [kátche'o] *nm* searching, frisking.

cachete [kátche'te] *nm* (*ANAT*) cheek; (*bofetada*) slap (in the face).

cachimba [kátchēm'bá] *nf* pipe.

cachiporra [kátchēpo'rrá] *nf* (billy) club (*US*), truncheon (*Brit*).

cachivache [kátchēbátch'e] *nm* piece of junk; **~s** *nmpl* trash *sg*, junk *sg*.

cacho, a [kátch'o, á] *nm* (small) bit; (*AM: cuerno*) horn.

cachondearse [kátchondeár'se] *vr*: **~ de uno** to tease sb.

cachondeo [kátchonde'o] *nm* (*fam*) farce, joke; (*guasa*) laugh.

cachondo, a [kátchon'do, á] *a* (*ZOOL*) in heat; (*persona*) horny; (*gracioso*) funny.

cachorro, a [kátcho'rro, á] *nm/f* (*perro*) pup, puppy; (*león*) cub.

cada [ká'thá] *a inv* each; (*antes de número*) every; **~ día** each day, every day; **~ dos días** every other day; **~ uno/a** each one, every one; **~ vez más** more and more; **uno de ~ diez** one out of every ten; **¿~ cuánto?** how often?

cadalso [káthál'so] *nm* scaffold.

cadáver [káthá'ber] *nm* (dead) body, corpse.

cadavérico, a [káthá'bé'rēko, á] *a* cadaverous; (*pálido*) deathly pale.

cadena [káthe'ná] *nf* chain; (*TV*) channel; **reacción en ~** chain reaction; **trabajo en ~** assembly line work; **~ perpetua** (*JUR*) life imprisonment; **~ de caracteres** (*INFORM*) character string.

cadencia [káthen'syá] *nf* cadence, rhythm.

cadera [káthe'rá] *nf* hip.

cadete [káthe'te] *nm* cadet.

Cádiz [ká'thēs] *nm* Cadiz.

caducar [káthōōkár'] *vi* to expire.

caducidad [káthōōsētháth'] *nf*: **fecha de ~** expiration (*US*) *o* expiry (*Brit*) date; (*de comida*) sell-by date.

caduco, a [káthōō'ko, á] *a* (*idea etc*) outdated, outmoded; **de hoja caduca** deciduous.

caduque [káthōō'ke] *etc vb V* **caducar**.

C.A.E. *abr* (= *cóbrese al entregar*) COD.

caer [káer'] *vi*, **~se** *vr* to fall (down); (*noche, fecha*) to fall; (*pago*) to fall due; (*AM*) to drop in; **dejar ~** to drop; **estar por ~** to be due to happen; **me cae bien/mal** I get on well with him/I can't stand him; **~ en la cuenta** to catch on; **su cumpleaños cae en viernes** her birthday falls on a Friday.

café, pl cafés [káfe', káfes'] *nm* (*bebida, planta*) coffee; (*lugar*) café ♦ *a* (*color*) brown; **~ con leche** coffee with cream (*US*), white coffee (*Brit*); **~ solo, ~ negro** (*AM*) (small) black coffee.

cafeína [káfeē'ná] *nf* caffein(e).

cafetal [káfetál'] *nm* coffee plantation.

cafetera [káfete'rá] *nf V* **cafetero**.

cafetería [káfeterē'á] *nf* cafe.

cafetero, a [káfete'ro, á] *a* coffee *cpd* ♦ *nf* coffee pot; **ser muy ~** to be a coffee addict.

cafre [ká'fre] *nm/f*: **como ~s** (*fig*) like savages.

cagar [kágár'] (*fam!*) *vt* to shit (*!*); (*fig*) to bungle, mess up ♦ *vi* to take (*US*) *o* have (*Brit*) a shit (*!*); **~se** *vr*: **¡me cago en diez** (*etc*)! shit! (*!*).

cague [ká'ge] *etc vb V* **cagar**.

caído, a [káē'tho, á] *a* fallen; (*INFORM*)

down ♦ *nf* fall; (*declive*) slope; (*disminución*) fall, drop; ~ **del cielo** out of the blue; **a la caída del sol** at sunset; **sufrir una caída** to have a fall.

caiga [ká'ĕҳá] *etc vb V* **caer.**

caimán [káĕmán'] *nm* alligator.

Cairo [ká'ĕro] *nm:* **el** ~ Cairo.

caja [ká'há] *nf* box; (*ataúd*) casket (*US*); coffin; (*para reloj*) case; (*de ascensor*) shaft; (*COM*) cashbox; (*ECON*) fund; (*donde se hacen los pagos*) checkout; (*en supermercado*) checkout, till; (*TIP*) case; ~ **de ahorros** savings bank; ~ **de cambios** gearbox; ~ **fuerte**, ~ **de caudales** safe, strongbox; **ingresar en** ~ to be paid in.

cajero, a [káhe'ro, á] *nm/f* cashier; (*en banco*) (bank) teller ♦ *nm:* ~ **automático** cash dispenser, A.T.M.

cajetilla [káhetĕ'yá] *nf* (*de cigarrillos*) pack (*US*), packet (*Brit*).

cajista [káhĕ'stá] *nm/f* typesetter.

cajón [káhon'] *nm* big box; (*de mueble*) drawer.

cal [kál] *nf* lime; **cerrar algo a** ~ **y canto** to shut sth firmly.

cala [ká'lá] *nf* (*GEO*) cove, inlet; (*de barco*) hold.

calabacín [kálábásĕn'] *nm*, **calabacita** [kálábásĕ'tá] *nf* (*AM*) (*BOT*) zucchini (*US*), courgette (*Brit*).

calabaza [kálábá'sá] *nf* (*BOT*) pumpkin; **dar** ~**s a** (*candidato*) to fail.

calabozo [káláђo'so] *nm* (*cárcel*) prison; (*celda*) cell.

calado, a [kálá'ђo, á] *a* (*prenda*) lace *cpd* ♦ *nm* (*TEC*) fretwork; (*NAUT*) draft (*US*), draught (*Brit*) ♦ *nf* (*de cigarrillo*) puff; **estar** ~ **(hasta los huesos)** to be soaked (to the skin).

calamar [kálámár'] *nm* squid.

calambre [kálám'bre] *nm* (*tb:* ~**s**) cramp.

calamidad [kálámĕ'ђáђ'] *nf* calamity, disaster; (*persona*): **es una** ~ he's a dead loss.

calamina [kálámĕ'ná] *nf* calamine.

cálamo [ká'lámo] *nm* (*BOT*) stem; (*MUS*) reed.

calaña [kálá'nyá] *nf* model, pattern; (*fig*) nature, stamp.

calar [kálár'] *vt* to soak, drench; (*penetrar*) to pierce, penetrate; (*comprender*) to see through; (*vela, red*) to lower; ~**se** *vr* (*AUTO*) to stall; ~**se las gafas** to put one's glasses on.

calavera [kálá͟ђe'rá] *nf* skull.

calcañal [kálkányál'], **calcañar** [kálkányár'], **calcaño** [kálká'nyo] *nm* heel.

calcar [kálkár'] *vt* (*reproducir*) to trace; (*imitar*) to copy.

calce [kál'se] *etc vb V* **calzar.**

calceta [kálse'tá] *nf* (knee-length) stocking; **hacer** ~ to knit.

calcetín [kálsetĕn'] *nm* sock.

calcinar [kálsĕnár'] *vt* to burn, blacken.

calcio [kál'syo] *nm* calcium.

calco [kál'ko] *nm* tracing.

calcomanía [kálkománĕ'á] *nf* transfer.

calculadora [kálkōōlàђo'rá] *nf* calculator.

calcular [kálkōōlár'] *vt* (*MAT*) to calculate, compute; ~ **que** ... to reckon that ....

cálculo [kál'kōōlo] *nm* calculation; (*MED*) (gall)stone; (*MAT*) calculus; ~ **de costo** pricing (*US*), costing (*Brit*); ~ **diferencial** differential calculus; **obrar con mucho** ~ to act cautiously.

caldear [káldeár'] *vt* to warm (up), heat (up); (*metales*) to weld.

caldera [kálde'rá] *nf* boiler.

calderero [káldere'ro] *nm* boilermaker.

calderilla [kálderĕ'yá] *nf* (*moneda*) small change.

caldero [kálde'ro] *nm* small boiler.

caldo [kál'do] *nm* stock; (*consomé*) consommé; ~ **de cultivo** (*BIO*) culture medium; **poner a** ~ **a uno** to give sb a dressing-down; **los** ~**s jerezanos** sherries.

calé [ká'le] *a* gipsy *cpd*.

calefacción [kálefáksyon'] *nf* heating; ~ **central** central heating.

calendario [kálendá'ryo] *nm* calendar.

calentador [kálentáђor'] *nm* heater.

calentar [kálentár'] *vt* to heat (up); (*fam: excitar*) to turn on; (*AM: enfurecer*) to anger; ~**se** *vr* to heat up, warm up; (*fig: discusión etc*) to get heated.

calentura [kálentōō'rá] *nf* (*MED*) fever, (high) temperature; (*de boca*) mouth sore.

calero, a [kále'ro, á] *a* lime *cpd*.

calibrar [kálĕђrár'] *vt* to gauge, measure.

calibre [kálĕ'ђre] *nm* (*de cañón*) calibre, bore; (*diámetro*) diameter; (*fig*) calibre.

calidad [kálĕђáђ'] *nf* quality; **de** ~ quality *cpd*; ~ **de borrador** (*INFORM*) draft quality; ~ **de carta** *o* **de correspondencia** (*INFORM*) letter quality; ~ **texto** (*INFORM*) text quality; **en** ~ **de** in the capacity of.

cálido, a [ká'lĕђo, á] *a* hot; (*fig*) warm.

caliente [kályen'te] *etc vb V* **calentar** ♦ *a* hot; (*fig*) fiery; (*disputa*) heated; (*fam: cachondo*) horny.

calificación [kálĕfĕkásyon'] *nf* qualification; (*de alumno*) grade, mark; ~ **de sobresaliente** first-class mark.

calificar [kálĕfĕkár'] *vt* to qualify; (*alumno*) to grade, mark; ~ **de** to describe as.

calificativo, a [kálĕfĕkátĕ'ђo] *a* qualifying ♦ *nm* qualifier, epithet.

califique [kálĕfĕ'ke] *etc vb V* **calificar.**

californiano, a [kálĕfornyá'no, á] *a, nm/f* Californian.

calina [kálĕ'ná] *nf* haze.

cáliz [ká'lĕs] *nm* (*BOT*) calyx; (*REL*) chalice.

calma [kál'má] *nf* calm; (*pachorra*) slow-

ness; (*COM, ECON*) calm, lull; ~ **chicha**
dead calm; ¡~!, ¡**con** ~! take it easy!

calmante [kálmàn'te] *a* soothing ♦ *nm* sedative, tranquillizer.

calmar [kálmár'] *vt* to calm, calm down;
(*dolor*) to relieve ♦ *vi*, ~**se** *vr* (*tempestad*)
to abate; (*mente etc*) to become calm.

calmoso, a [kálmo'so, á] *a* calm, quiet.

caló [kálo'] *nm* (*de gitanos*) gipsy language,
Romany; (*argot*) slang.

calor [kálor'] *nm* heat; (~ *agradable*)
warmth; **entrar en** ~ to get warm; **tener**
~ to be *o* feel hot.

caloría [kálorē'á] *nf* calorie.

calorífero, a [kálorē'fero, á] *a* heatproducing, heat-giving ♦ *nm* heating
system.

calque [kál'ke] *etc vb* V **calcar**.

calumnia [káloōm'nyá] *nf* slander; (*por
escrito*) libel.

calumniar [káloōmnyár'] *vt* to slander; to libel.

calumnioso, a [káloōmnyo'so, á] *a* slanderous; libellous.

caluroso, a [káloōro'so, á] *a* hot; (*sin exceso*) warm; (*fig*) enthusiastic.

calva [kál'há] *nf* bald patch; (*en bosque*)
clearing.

calvario [kálhá'ryo] *nm* stations *pl* of the
cross; (*fig*) cross, heavy burden.

calvicie [kálhē'sye] *nf* baldness.

calvo, a [kál'ho, á] *a* bald; (*terreno*) bare,
barren; (*tejido*) threadbare ♦ *nm* bald
man.

calza [kál'sá] *nf* wedge, chock.

calzado, a [kálsá'tho, á] *a* shod ♦ *nm* footwear ♦ *nf* roadway, highway.

calzador [kálsáthor'] *nm* shoehorn.

calzar [kálsár'] *vt* (*zapatos etc*) to wear; (*un
mueble*) to put a wedge under; (*TEC: rueda
etc*) to scotch; ~**se** *vr*: ~**se los zapatos** to
put on one's shoes; ¿**qué (número) calza?**
what size do you take?

calzón [kálson'] *nm* (*tb:* **calzones**) shorts
pl; (*AM: de hombre*) pants; (*: de mujer*)
panties.

calzonazos [kálsoná'sos] *nm inv* henpecked
husband.

calzoncillos [kálsonsē'yos] *nmpl* underpants.

callado, a [káyá'tho, á] *a* quiet, silent.

callar [káyár'] *vt* (*asunto delicado*) to keep
quiet about, say nothing about; (*omitir*) to
pass over in silence; (*persona, oposición*) to
silence ♦ *vi*, ~**se** *vr* to keep quiet, be silent; (*dejar de hablar*) to stop talking;
¡**calla!**, be quiet!; ¡**cállate!**, ¡**cállese!** shut
up!; ¡**cállate la boca!** shut your mouth!

calle [ká'ye] *nf* street; (*DEPORTE*) lane; ~
arriba/abajo up/down the street; ~ **de
sentido único** one-way street; **poner a uno**

(**de patitas**) **en la** ~ to kick sb out.

calleja [káye'há] *nf* alley, narrow street.

callejear [káyeheár'] *vi* to wander (about)
the streets.

callejero, a [káyehe'ro, á] *a* street *cpd* ♦ *nm*
street map.

callejón [káyehon'] *nm* alley, passage;
(*GEO*) narrow pass; ~ **sin salida** cul-desac; (*fig*) blind alley.

callejuela [káyehwe'lá] *nf* side-street, alley.

callista [káyē'stá] *nm/f* chiropodist.

callo [ká'yo] *nm* callus; (*en el pie*) corn; ~**s**
nmpl (*CULIN*) tripe *sg*.

calloso, a [káyo'so, á] *a* callous (*US*),
calloused (*Brit*).

cama [ká'má] *nf* bed; (*GEO*) stratum; ~
individual/de matrimonio single/double
bed; **guardar** ~ to be ill in bed.

camada [kámá'thá] *nf* litter; (*de personas*)
gang, band.

camafeo [kámáfe'o] *nm* cameo.

cámara [ká'márá] *nf* (*POL etc*) chamber;
(*habitación*) room; (*sala*) hall; (*CINE*)
movie camera; (*fotográfica*) camera; ~ **de
aire** inner tube; ~ **alta/baja** upper/lower
house; ~ **de comercio** chamber of
commerce; ~ **de gas** gas chamber; **a** ~
lenta in slow motion.

camarada [kámárá'thá] *nm* comrade,
companion.

camaradería [kámárátherē'á] *nf* comradeship.

camarero, a [kámáre'ro, á] *nm* waiter ♦ *nf*
(*en restaurante*) waitress; (*en casa, hotel*)
maid.

camarilla [kámárē'yá] *nf* (*clan*) clique;
(*POL*) lobby.

camarín [kámárēn'] *nm* (*TEATRO*) dressing
room.

camarón [kámáron'] *nm* shrimp.

camarote [kámáro'te] *nm* (*NAUT*) cabin.

cambiable [kámbyá'hle] *a* (*variable*)
changeable, variable; (*intercambiable*)
interchangeable.

cambiante [kámbyán'te] *a* variable.

cambiar [kámbyár'] *vt* to change; (*trocar*)
to exchange ♦ *vi* to change; ~**se** *vr* (*mudarse*) to move; (*de ropa*) to change; ~(**se**)
de ... to change one's ...; ~ **de idea/de
ropa** to change one's mind/clothes.

cambiazo [kámbyá'so] *nm*: **dar el** ~ **a uno**
to swindle sb.

cambio [kám'byo] *nm* change; (*trueque*)
exchange; (*COM*) rate of exchange; (*oficina*) foreign exchange office (*US*), bureau de
change (*Brit*); (*dinero menudo*) small
change; **en** ~ on the other hand; (*en lugar
de eso*) instead; ~ **de divisas** (*COM*)
foreign exchange; ~ **de línea** (*INFORM*)
line feed; ~ **de página** (*INFORM*) form
feed; ~ **a término** (*COM*) future (*US*) *o*

forward (*Brit*) exchange; ~ **de velocidades** gearshift; ~ **de vía** switch (*US*), points *pl* (*Brit*).

cambista [kàmbē'stá] *nm* (*COM*) exchange broker.

Camboya [kàmbo'yà] *nf* Cambodia, Kampuchea.

camboyano, a [kàmboyá'no, à] *a, nm/f* Cambodian, Kampuchean.

camelar [kàmelàr'] *vt* (*con mujer*) to flirt with; (*persuadir*) to cajole.

camelo [kàme'lo] *nm*: **me huele a** ~ it smells fishy.

camello [kàme'yo] *nm* camel; (*fam*: *traficante*) pusher.

camerino [kàmerē'no] *nm* (*TEATRO*) dressing room.

camilla [kàmē'yà] *nf* (*MED*) stretcher.

caminante [kàmēnàn'te] *nm/f* traveller.

caminar [kàmēnàr'] *vi* (*marchar*) to walk, go; (*viajar*) to travel, journey ♦ *vt* (*recorrer*) to cover, travel.

caminata [kàmēnà'tà] *nf* long walk.

camino [kàmē'no] *nm* way, road; (*sendero*) track; **a medio** ~ halfway (there); **en el** ~ on the way, en route; ~ **de** on the way to; ~ **particular** private road; ~ **vecinal** country road; **C~s, Canales y Puertos** (*UNIV*) Civil Engineering; **ir por buen** ~ (*fig*) to be on the right track.

camión [kàmyon'] *nm* truck (*US*), lorry (*Brit*); ~ **de bomberos** fire engine.

camionero [kàmyone'ro] *nm* truck (*US*) o lorry (*Brit*) driver, trucker (*esp US*).

camioneta [kàmyone'tà] *nf* van, light truck; (*AM*: *carro*) station wagon.

camisa [kàmē'sá] *nf* shirt; (*BOT*) skin; ~ **de dormir** nightdress; ~ **de fuerza** straitjacket.

camisería [kàmēserē'à] *nf* outfitter's (shop).

camiseta [kàmēse'tà] *nf* tee-shirt; (*ropa interior*) vest; (*de deportista*) top.

camisón [kàmēson'] *nm* nightie, nightgown.

camomila [kàmomē'là] *nf* camomile.

camorra [kàmo'rrà] *nf*: **armar** ~ to kick up a row; **buscar** ~ to look for trouble.

campamento [kàmpàmen'to] *nm* camp.

campana [kàmpà'nà] *nf* bell.

campanada [kàmpànà'thà] *nf* peal.

campanario [kàmpànà'ryo] *nm* belfry.

campanilla [kàmpànē'yà] *nf* (*campana*) small bell.

campante [kàmpàn'te] *a*: **siguió tan** ~ he went on as if nothing had happened.

campaña [kàmpà'nyà] *nf* (*MIL, POL*) campaign; **hacer** ~ (**en pro de/contra**) to campaign (for/against); ~ **de venta** sales campaign.

campechano, a [kàmpetchà'no, à] *a* open.

campeón, ona [kàmpeon', o'nà] *nm/f* champion.

campeonato [kàmpeoná'to] *nm* championship.

campesino, a [kàmpesē'no, à] *a* country *cpd*, rural; (*gente*) peasant *cpd* ♦ *nm/f* countryman/woman; (*agricultor*) farmer.

campestre [kàmpes'tre] *a* country *cpd*, rural.

camping [kàm'pēn] *nm* camping; (*lugar*) campsite; **ir de** o **hacer** ~ to go camping.

campiña [kàmpē'nyà] *nf* countryside.

campista [kàmpē'stà] *nm/f* camper.

campo [kàm'po] *nm* (*fuera de la ciudad*) country, countryside; (*AGR, ELEC, INFORM*) field; (*de fútbol*) field (*US*), pitch (*Brit*); (*de golf*) course; (*MIL*) camp; ~ **de batalla** battlefield; ~ **de minas** minefield; ~ **petrolífero** oilfield; ~ **visual** field of vision; ~ **de concentración/de internación/de trabajo** concentration/internment/labor camp.

camposanto [kàmposán'to] *nm* cemetery.

CAMPSA [kàmp'sà] *nf abr* (*Esp COM*) = *Compañía Arrendataria del Monopolio de Petróleos, S.A.*

campus [kàm'pōōs] *nm inv* (*UNIV*) campus.

camuflaje [kàmōōflà'he] *nm* camouflage.

can [kàn] *nm* dog, mutt (*fam*).

cana [kà'nà] *nf V* **cano**.

Canadá [kànàthá'] *nm* Canada.

canadiense [kànàthyen'se] *a, nm/f* Canadian ♦ *nf* fur-lined jacket.

canal [kànál'] *nm* canal; (*GEO*) channel, strait; (*de televisión*) channel; (*de tejado*) gutter; **C~ de la Mancha** English Channel; **C~ de Panamá** Panama Canal.

canalice [kànálē'se] *etc vb V* **canalizar**.

canalizar [kànálēsàr'] *vt* to channel.

canalón [kànálon'] *nm* (*conducto vertical*) drainpipe; (*del tejado*) gutter; **canalones** *nmpl* (*CULIN*) cannelloni.

canalla [kànà'yà] *nf* rabble, mob ♦ *nm* swine.

canallada [kànàyà'thà] *nf* (*hecho*) dirty trick.

canapé, *pl* canapés [kànàpc', kànàpes'] *nm* sofa, settee; (*CULIN*) canapé.

Canarias [kànà'ryàs] *nfpl*: **las (Islas)** ~ the Canaries, the Canary Isles.

canario, a [kànà'ryo, à] *a* of o from the Canary Isles ♦ *nm/f* native o inhabitant of the Canary Isles ♦ *nm* (*ZOOL*) canary.

canasta [kànà'stà] *nf* (round) basket.

canastilla [kànàstē'yà] *nf* small basket; (*de niño*) layette.

canasto [kànà'sto] *nm* large basket.

cancela [kànse'là] *nf* (wrought-iron) gate.

cancelación [kànselàsyon'] *nf* cancellation.

cancelar [kànselàr'] *vt* to cancel; (*una deuda*) to write off.

cáncer [kàn'ser] *nm* (*MED*) cancer; **C~** (*ASTRO*) Cancer.

canciller [kànsēyer'] *nm* chancellor.

canción [kánsyon'] *nf* song; ~ **de cuna** lullaby.

cancionero [kánsyonc'ro] *nm* song book.

cancha [kántch'á] *nf* (de *baloncesto, tenis etc*) court; (*AM: de fútbol*) field (*US*), pitch (*Brit*).

candado [kándá'ño] *nm* padlock.

candela [kánde'lá] *nf* candle.

candelabro [kándelá'ñro] *nm* candelabra.

candelero [kándelc'ro] *nm* (*para vela*) candlestick; (*de aceite*) oil lamp.

candente [kánden'te] *a* red-hot; (*tema*) burning.

candidato, a [kándếña'to, á] *nm/f* candidate; (*para puesto*) applicant.

candidatura [kándếñátoō'rá] *nf* candidature.

candidez [kándếñes'] *nf* (*sencillez*) simplicity; (*simpleza*) naiveté.

cándido, a [kán'dếño, á] *a* simple; naive.

candil [kándếl'] *nm* oil lamp.

candilejas [kánñếlc'hás] *nfpl* (*TEATRO*) footlights.

candor [kándor'] *nm* (*sinceridad*) frankness; (*inocencia*) innocence.

canela [káne'lá] *nf* cinnamon.

canelo [káne'lo] *nm*: **hacer el** ~ to act the fool.

cangrejo [kángrc'ho] *nm* crab.

canguro [kángoō'ro] *nm* (*ZOOL*) kangaroo; (*de niños*) baby-sitter; **hacer de** ~ to baby-sit.

caníbal [kánế'ñál] *a, nm/f* cannibal.

canica [kánế'ká] *nf* marble.

canícula [kánế'koōlá] *nf* midsummer heat.

caniche [kánếtch'c] *nm* poodle.

canijo, a [kánế'ho, á] *a* frail, sickly.

canilla [kánế'yá] *nf* (*TEC*) bobbin.

canino, a [kánế'no, á] *a* canine ♦ *nm* canine (tooth).

canje [kánhc'] *nm* exchange; (*trueque*) swap.

canjear [kánhcár'] *vt* to exchange; (*trocar*) to swap.

cano, a [ká'no, á] *a* gray- o grey-haired, white-haired ♦ *nf* (*tb*: **canas**) white o gray hair; **tener canas** to be going gray.

canoa [káno'á] *nf* canoe.

canon [ká'non] *nm* canon; (*pensión*) rent; (*COM*) tax.

canonice [kánonế'sc] *etc vb V* **canonizar**.

canónico, a [káno'nếko, á] *a*: **derecho** ~ canon law.

canónigo [káno'nếgo] *nm* canon.

canonizar [kánonếsár'] *vt* to canonize.

canoro, a [káno'ro, á] *a* melodious.

cansado, a [kánsá'ño, á] *a* tired, weary; (*tedioso*) tedious, boring; **estoy** ~ **de hacerlo** I'm sick of doing it.

cansancio [kánsán'syo] *nm* tiredness, fatigue.

cansar [kánsár'] *vt* (*fatigar*) to tire, tire out; (*aburrir*) to bore; (*fastidiar*) to bother; ~**se** *vr* to tire, get tired; (*aburrirse*) to get bored.

cantabro, a [kántá'ñro, á] *a, nm/f* Cantabrian.

cantábrico, a [kántá'ñrếko, á] *a* Cantabrian; **Mar C**~ Bay of Biscay; **(Montes) C**~**s, Cordillera Cantábrica** Cantabrian Mountains.

cantante [kántán'te] *a* singing ♦ *nm/f* singer.

cantaor, a [kántáor', á] *nm/f* Flamenco singer.

cantar [kántár'] *vt* to sing ♦ *vi* to sing; (*insecto*) to chirp; (*rechinar*) to squeak; (*fam: criminal*) to squeal ♦ *nm* (*acción*) singing; (*canción*) song; (*poema*) poem; ~ **a uno las cuarenta** to give sb a piece of one's mind; ~ **a dos voces** to sing a duet.

cántara [kán'tárá] *nf* large pitcher.

cántaro [kán'táro] *nm* pitcher, jug.

cante [kán'te] *nm*: ~ **jondo** flamenco singing.

cantera [kántc'rá] *nf* quarry.

cántico [kán'tếko] *nm* (*REL*) canticle; (*fig*) song.

cantidad [kántếñáñ'] *nf* quantity, amount; (*ECON*) sum ♦ *ad* (*fam*) a lot; ~ **alzada** lump sum; ~ **de** lots of.

cantilena [kántếlc'ná] *nf* = **cantinela**.

cantimplora [kántếmplo'rá] *nf* (*frasco*) water bottle, canteen.

cantina [kántế'ná] *nf* cafeteria (*US*), canteen (*Brit*); (*de estación*) buffet.

cantinela [kántếnc'lá] *nf* ballad, song.

canto [kán'to] *nm* singing; (*canción*) song; (*borde*) edge, rim; (*de un cuchillo*) back; ~ **rodado** boulder.

cantón [kánton'] *nm* canton.

cantor, a [kántor', á] *nm/f* singer.

canturrear [kántoōrrcár'] *vi* to sing softly.

canuto [kánoō'to] *nm* (*tubo*) small tube; (*fam: droga*) joint.

caña [ká'nyá] *nf* (*BOT: tallo*) stem, stalk; (*carrizo*) reed; (*vaso*) tumbler; (*de cerveza*) glass of beer; (*ANAT*) shinbone; ~ **de azúcar** sugar cane; ~ **de pescar** fishing rod.

cañada [kányá'ñá] *nf* (*entre dos montañas*) gully, ravine; (*camino*) cattle track.

cáñamo [ká'nyámo] *nm* (*BOT*) hemp.

cañaveral [kányáñcrál'] *nm* (*BOT*) reedbed; (*AGR*) sugar-cane field.

caño [ká'nyo] *nm* (*tubo*) tube, pipe; (*de aguas servidas*) sewer; (*MUS*) pipe; (*NAUT*) navigation channel; (*de fuente*) jet.

cañón [kányon'] *nm* (*MIL*) cannon; (*de fusil*) barrel; (*GEO*) canyon, gorge.

cañonazo [kányoná'so] *nm* (*MIL*) gunshot.

cañonera [kányonc'rá] *nf* (*tb*: **lancha** ~)

gunboat.

caoba [káo'bá] nf mahogany.

caos [ká'os] nm chaos.

caótico, a [káo'tēko, á] a chaotic.

cap. abr (= capítulo) ch.

capa [ká'pá] nf cloak, cape; (CULIN) coating; (GEO) layer, stratum; (de pintura) coat; **de ~ y espada** cloak-and-dagger; **so ~ de** under the pretext of; **~s sociales** social groups.

capacidad [kápásēt̨hát̨h'] nf (medida) capacity; (aptitud) capacity, ability; **una sala con ~ para 900** a hall seating 900; **~ adquisitiva** purchasing power.

capacitación [kápásētásyon'] nf training.

capacitar [kápásētár'] vt: **~ a uno para algo** to qualify sb for sth; (TEC) to train sb for sth.

capacho [kápátch'o] nm wicker basket.

capar [kápár'] vt to castrate, geld.

caparazón [kápáráson'] nm (ZOOL) shell.

capataz [kápátás'] nm foreman.

capaz [kápás'] a able, capable; (amplio) capacious, roomy.

capcioso, a [kápsyo'so, á] a wily, deceitful; **pregunta capciosa** trick question.

capellán [kápeyàn'] nm chaplain; (sacerdote) priest.

caperuza [káperōō'sá] nf hood; (de bolígrafo) cap.

capicúa [kápēkōō'á] nf reversible number, e.g. 1441.

capilar [kápēlár'] a hair cpd.

capilla [kápē'yá] nf chapel.

capital [kápētál'] a capital ♦ nm (COM) capital ♦ nf (ciudad) capital (city); **~ activo/ en acciones** working/share o equity capital; **~ arriesgado** venture capital; **~ autorizado** o **social** authorized capital; **~ emitido** issued capital; **~ improductivo** idle money; **~ invertido** o **utilizado** invested capital; **~ pagado** paid-up capital **~ de riesgo** risk capital; **~ social** equity o share capital; **inversión de ~es** capital investment.

capitalice [kápētálē'se] etc vb V **capitalizar.**

capitalismo [kápētálēs'mo] nm capitalism.

capitalista [kápētálē'stá] a, nm/f capitalist.

capitalizar [kápētálēsár'] vt to capitalize.

capitán [kápētán'] nm captain; (fig) leader.

capitana [kápētá'ná] nf flagship.

capitanear [kápētáneár'] vt to captain.

capitanía [kápētánē'á] nf captaincy.

capitel [kápētel'] nm (ARQ) capital.

capitolio [kápēto'lyo] nm capitol.

capitulación [kápētōōlásyon'] nf (rendición) capitulation, surrender; (acuerdo) agreement, pact; **capitulaciones matrimoniales** marriage contract sg.

capitular [kápētōōlár'] vi to come to terms, make an agreement; (MIL) to surrender.

capítulo [kápē'tōōlo] nm chapter.

capó [kápo'] nm (AUTO) hood (US), bonnet (Brit).

capón [kápon'] nm capon.

caporal [káporál'] nm chief, leader.

capota [kápo'tá] nf (de mujer) bonnet; (AUTO) top (US), hood (Brit).

capote [kápo'te] nm (abrigo: de militar) greatcoat; (de torero) cloak.

Capricornio [káprēkor'nyo] nm Capricorn.

capricho [káprētch'o] nm whim, caprice.

caprichoso, a [káprētcho'so, á] a capricious.

cápsula [káp'sōōlá] nf capsule; **~ espacial** space capsule.

captar [káptár'] vt (comprender) to understand; (RADIO) to pick up; (atención, apoyo) to attract.

captura [káptōō'rá] nf capture; (JUR) arrest.

capturar [káptōōrár'] vt to capture; (JUR) to arrest; (datos) to input.

capucha [kápōōtch'á] nf hood, cowl.

capullo [kápōō'yo] nm (ZOOL) cocoon; (BOT) bud; (fam) idiot.

caqui [ká'kē] nm khaki.

cara [ká'rá] nf (ANAT, de moneda) face; (aspecto) appearance; (de disco) side; (fig) boldness; (descara) nerve ♦ prep: **~ a** facing; **de ~ a** opposite, facing; **dar la ~** to face the consequences; **echar algo en ~ a uno** to reproach sb for sth; **¿~ o cruz?** heads or tails?; **¡ qué ~ más dura!** what a nerve!; **de una ~** (disquete) single-sided.

carabina [kárábē'ná] nf carbine, rifle; (persona) chaperone.

carabinero [kárábēne'ro] nm (de aduana) customs officer; (AM) gendarme.

Caracas [kárá'kás] nm Caracas.

caracol [kárákol'] nm (ZOOL) snail; (concha) (sea)shell; **escalera de ~** spiral staircase.

caracolear [kárákoleár'] vi (caballo) to prance about.

carácter, pl **caracteres** [kárák'ter, kárákte'res] nm character; **~ de cambio de página** (INFORM) form feed character; **caracteres de imprenta** (TIP) type(face) sg; **~ libre** (INFORM) wildcard character; **tener buen/mal ~** to be good-natured/bad tempered.

caracterice [kárákterē'se] etc vb V **caracterizar.**

característico, a [kárákterē'stēko, á] a characteristic ♦ nf characteristic.

caracterizar [kárákterēsár'] vt (distinguir) to characterize, typify; (honrar) to confer (a) distinction on.

caradura [kárát̨hōō'rá] nm/f sassy (US) o cheeky person; **es un ~** he's got a nerve.

carajo |kàrá'ho| *nm* (*fam!*): ¡~! shit!(*!*); ¡qué ~ ! what the hell!; **me importa un ~** I don't give a damn.

caramba |kàrám'bá| *excl* well!, good gracious!

carámbano |kàràm'bàno| *nm* icicle.

carambola |kàràmbo'là| *nf*: **por** ~ by a fluke.

caramelo |kàrámc'lo| *nm* (*dulce*) candy (*US*), sweet (*Brit*); (*azúcar fundido*) caramel.

carapacho |kàràpátch'o| *nm* shell, carapace.

caraqueño, a |kàrákc'nyo, à| *a* of *o* from Caracas ♦ *nm/f* native *o* inhabitant of Caracas.

carátula |kàrá'tōōlà| *nf* (*máscara*) mask; (*TEATRO*): **la** ~ the stage.

caravana |kàràhá'nà| *nf* caravan; (*fig*) group; (*de autos*) line of traffic (*US*), tailback (*Brit*).

carbón |kàrḅon'| *nm* coal; ~ **de leña** charcoal; **papel** ~ carbon paper.

carbonatado, a |kàrḅonotá'ḍo, à| *a* carbonated.

carbonato |kàrḅona'to| *nm* carbonate; ~ **sódico** sodium carbonate.

carboncillo |kàrḅonsē'yo| *nm* (*ARTE*) charcoal.

carbonice |kàrḅonē'se| *etc vb V* **carbonizar.**

carbonilla |kàrḅonē'yà| *nf* coal dust.

carbonizar |kàrḅonēsàr'| *vt* to carbonize; (*quemar*) to char; **quedar carbonizado** (*ELEC*) to be electrocuted.

carbono |kàrḅo'no| *nm* carbon.

carburador |kàrḅōōràḍhor'| *nm* carburetor (*US*), carburettor (*Brit*).

carburante |kàrḅōōràn'tc| *nm* fuel.

carca |kàr'kà| *a, nm/f inv* reactionary.

carcajada |kàrkàhá'ḍà| *nf* (loud) laugh, guffaw.

cárcel |kàr'sel| *nf* prison, jail; (*TEC*) clamp.

carcelero, a |kàrselc'ro, à| *a* prison *cpd* ♦ *nm/f* guard (*US*), warder (*Brit*).

carcomer |kàrkomer'| *vt* to bore into, eat into; (*fig*) to undermine; ~**se** *vr* to become worm-eaten; (*fig*) to decay.

carcomido, a |kàrkomē'ḍo, à| *a* worm-eaten; (*fig*) rotten.

cardar |kàrḍàr'| *vt* (*TEC*) to card, comb.

cardenal |kàrḍhenál'| *nm* (*REL*) cardinal; (*MED*) bruise.

cárdeno, a |kàr'ḍheno, à| *a* purple; (*lívido*) livid.

cardíaco, a |kàrḍhē'áko, à| *a* cardiac, heart *cpd*

cardinal |kàrḍhenál'| *a* cardinal.

cardiólogo, a |kàrḍhyo'logo, à| *nm/f* cardiologist.

cardo |kàr'ḍho| *nm* thistle.

carear |kàreàr'| *vt* to bring face to face; (*comparar*) to compare; ~**se** *vr* to come face to face, meet.

carecer |kàreser'| *vi*: ~ **de** to lack, be in need of.

carencia |kàren'syà| *nf* lack; (*escasez*) shortage; (*MED*) deficiency.

carente |kàren'tc| *a*: ~ **de** lacking in, devoid of.

carestía |kàrcstē'à| *nf* (*escasez*) scarcity, shortage; (*COM*) high cost; **época de** ~ period of shortage.

careta |kàrc'tà| *nf* mask.

carey |kàrc'ē| *nm* tortoiseshell.

carezca |kàres'kà| *etc vb V* **carecer.**

carga |kàr'gà| *nf* (*peso, ELEC*) load; (*de barco*) cargo, freight; (*FINANZAS*) tax, duty; (*MIL*) charge; (*INFORM*) loading; (*obligación, responsabilidad*) duty, obligation; ~ **aérea** (*COM*) air cargo; ~ **útil** (*COM*) payload; **la** ~ **fiscal** the tax burden.

cargadero |kàrgàḍhe'ro| *nm* loading bay.

cargado, a |kàrgá'ḍho, à| *a* loaded; (*ELEC*) live; (*café, té*) strong; (*cielo*) overcast.

cargador, a |kàrgàḍhor', à| *nm/f* loader; (*NAUT*) stevedore ♦ *nm* (*INFORM*): ~ **de discos** disk pack.

cargamento |kàrgámen'to| *nm* (*acción*) loading; (*mercancías*) load, cargo.

cargante |kàrgán'tc| *a* (*persona*) trying.

cargar |kàrgár'| *vt* (*barco, arma*) to load; (*ELEC*) to charge; (*impuesto*) to impose; (*COM: algo en cuenta*) to charge, debit; (*MIL: enemigo*) to charge ♦ *vi* (*AUTO*) to load (up); (*inclinarse*) to lean; (*INFORM*) to load, feed in; ~ **con** to pick up, carry away; ~**se** *vr* (*fam: estropear*) to break; (: *matar*) to bump off; (*ELEC*) to become charged.

cargo |kàr'go| *nm* (*COM etc*) charge, debit; (*puesto*) post, office; (*responsabilidad*) duty, obligation; (*fig*) weight, burden; (*JUR*) charge; **altos** ~**s** high-ranking officials; **una cantidad en** ~ **a uno** a sum chargeable to sb; **hacerse** ~ **de** to take charge *o* responsibility for.

cargue |kàr'ge| *etc vb V* **cargar.**

carguero |kàrge'ro| *nm* freighter, cargo boat; (*avión*) freight plane.

Caribe |kàrē'ḅe| *nm*: **el** ~ the Caribbean.

caribeño, a |kàrēḅe'nyo, à| *a* Caribbean.

caricatura |kàrēkátōō'rà| *nf* caricature.

caricia |kàrē'syà| *nf* caress; (*a animal*) pat, stroke.

caridad |kàrēḍhàḍh'| *nf* charity.

caries |kà'ryes| *nf inv* (*MED*) tooth decay.

carilla |kàrē'yà| *nf* (*TIP*) page.

cariño |kàrē'nyo| *nm* affection, love; (*caricia*) caress; (*en carta*) love ... .

cariñoso, a |kàrēnyo'so, à| *a* affectionate.

carioca |kàryo'kà| *a* (*AM*) of *o* from Rio de Janeiro ♦ *nm/f* native *o* inhabitant of Rio de

Janeiro.

carisma [kárēs'má] *nm* charisma.

caritativo, a [kárētátē'ho, á] *a* charitable.

cariz [kárēs'] *nm*: **tener** *o* **tomar buen/mal** ~ to look good/bad.

carmesí [kármesē'] *a, nm* crimson.

carmín [kármēn'] *nm* (*color*) carmine; ~ **(de labios)** lipstick.

carnal [kárnál'] *a* carnal; **primo** ~ first cousin.

carnaval [kárnábál'] *nm* carnival.

carne [kár'ne] *nf* flesh; (*CULIN*) meat; ~ **de cañón** cannon fodder; ~ **de cerdo/de cordero/de ternera/de vaca** pork/lamb/veal/beef; ~ **picada** ground meat (*US*), mince (*Brit*); ~ **de gallina** (*fig*) gooseflesh.

carné [kárne'] *nm* = **carnet**.

carnero [kárne'ro] *nm* sheep, ram; (*carne*) mutton.

carnet, *pl* **carnets** [kárne', kárnes'] *nm*: ~ **de conducir** driver's license; ~ **de identidad** identity card.

carnicería [kárnēserē'á] *nf* butcher's (shop); (*fig*: *matanza*) carnage, slaughter.

carnicero, a [kárnēse'ro, á] *a* carnivorous ♦ *nm/f* (*tb fig*) butcher ♦ *nm* carnivore.

carnívoro, a [kárnē'horo, á] *a* carnivorous ♦ *nm* carnivore.

carnoso, a [kárno'so, á] *a* beefy, fat.

caro, a [ká'ro, á] *a* dear; (*COM*) expensive ♦ *ad* dearly; **vender** ~ to sell at a high price.

carpa [kár'pá] *nf* (*pez*) carp; (*de circo*) big top; (*AM*: *de camping*) tent.

carpeta [kárpe'tá] *nf* folder, file.

carpetazo [kárpetá'so] *nm*: **dar** ~ **a** to shelve.

carpintería [kárpēnterē'á] *nf* carpentry.

carpintero [kárpēnte'ro] *nm* carpenter; **pájaro** ~ woodpecker.

carraca [kárrá'ká] *nf* (*DEPORTE*) rattle.

carraspear [kárráspeár'] *vi* (*aclararse*) to clear one's throat.

carraspera [kárráspe'rá] *nf* hoarseness.

carrera [kárre'rá] *nf* (*acción*) run(ning); (*espacio recorrido*) run; (*certamen*) race; (*trayecto*) course; (*profesión*) career; (*ESCOL. UNIV*) course; (*de taxi*) ride; (*en medias*) ladder; **a la** ~ at (full) speed; **caballo de** ~(s) racehorse; ~ **de armamentos** arms race.

carrerilla [kárrerē'yá] *nf*: **decir algo de** ~ to reel sth off; **tomar** ~ to get up speed.

carreta [kárre'tá] *nf* wagon, cart.

carrete [kárre'te] *nm* reel, spool; (*TEC*) coil.

carretera [kárrete'rá] *nf* (main) road, highway; ~ **nacional** ≈ state highway (*US*), A road (*Brit*); ~ **de circunvalación** beltway (*US*), ring road (*Brit*).

carretilla [kárretē'yá] *nf* trolley; (*AGR*) (wheel)barrow.

carril [kárrēl'] *nm* furrow; (*de autopista*) lane; (*FERRO*) rail.

carrillo [kárrē'yo] *nm* (*ANAT*) cheek; (*TEC*) pulley.

carrizo [kárrē'so] *nm* reed.

carro [ká'rro] *nm* cart, wagon; (*MIL*) tank; (*AM*: *coche*) car; (*TIP*) carriage; ~ **blindado** armored car.

carrocería [kárroserē'á] *nf* body, bodywork *q* (*Brit*).

carroña [kárro'nyá] *nf* carrion *q*.

carroza [kárro'sá] *nf* (*vehículo*) coach ♦ *nm/ f* (*fam*) old fogey.

carrusel [kárrōōsel'] *nm* merry-go-round.

carta [kár'tá] *nf* letter; (*CULIN*) menu; (*naipe*) card; (*mapa*) map; (*JUR*) document; ~ **aérea** aerogramme; ~ **de crédito** credit card; ~ **de crédito documentaria** (*COM*) documentary letter of credit; ~ **de crédito irrevocable** (*COM*) irrevocable letter of credit; ~ **certificada/urgente** registered/special delivery letter; ~ **marítima** chart; ~ **de pedido** (*COM*) order; ~ **verde** (*AUTO*) *international insurance certificate*; ~ **de vinos** wine list; **echar una** ~ **al correo** to mail a letter; **echar las** ~**s a uno** to tell sb's fortune.

cartabón [kártáhon'] *nm* triangle (*US*), set square (*Brit*).

cartel [kártel'] *nm* (*anuncio*) poster, placard; (*ESCOL*) wall chart; (*COM*) cartel.

cartelera [kártele'rá] *nf* billboard; (*en periódico etc*) listings *pl*, entertainments guide; **"en** ~**"** "showing".

cartera [kárte'rá] *nf* (*de bolsillo*) wallet; (*de colegial, cobrador*) satchel; (*de señora*) handbag; (*para documentos*) briefcase; **ministro sin** ~ (*POL*) minister without portfolio; **ocupa la** ~ **de Agricultura** he is Minister of Agriculture; ~ **de pedidos** (*COM*) order book; **efectos en** ~ (*ECON*) holdings.

carterista [kárterē'stá] *nm/f* pickpocket.

cartero [kárte'ro] *nm* mailman (*US*), postman (*Brit*).

cartílago [kártē'láyo] *nm* cartilage.

cartilla [kártē'yá] *nf* (*ESCOL*) primer, first reading book; ~ **de ahorros** bank book.

cartón [kárton'] *nm* cardboard.

cartucho [kártōōtch'o] *nm* (*MIL*) cartridge; (*bolsita*) paper cone; ~ **de datos** (*INFORM*) data cartridge.

cartulina [kártōōlē'ná] *nf* fine cardboard, card.

CASA [ká'sá] *nf abr* (*Esp AVIAT*) = *Construcciones Aeronáuticas S.A.*

casa [ká'sá] *nf* house; (*hogar*) home; (*edificio*) building; (*COM*) firm, company; ~ **consistorial** town hall; ~ **de huéspedes** boarding house; ~ **de socorro** first aid station (*US*) *o* post (*Brit*); ~ **de citas** (*fam*) brothel; **ir a** ~ to go home; **salir de** ~ to

go out; (*para siempre*) to leave home;
echar la ~ por la ventana (*gastar*) to
spare no expense.

casadero, a [kàsà'ĥe'ro, à] *a* marriageable.

casado, a [kàsá'ĥo, á] *a* married ♦ *nm/f*
married man/woman.

casamiento [kàsámyen'to] *nm* marriage,
wedding.

casar [kàsàr'] *vt* to marry; (*JUR*) to quash,
annul; **~se** *vr* to marry, get married; **~se**
por lo civil to have a civil wedding, get
married in a registry office (*Brit*) .

cascabel [kàskàĥel'] *nm* (small) bell;
(*ZOOL*) rattlesnake.

cascada [kàskà'ĥá] *nf* waterfall.

cascajo [kàskà'ho] *nm* gravel, stone chippings *pl*.

cascanueces [kàskánwe'ses] *nm inv*: **un ~**
a pair of nutcrackers.

cascar [kàskàr'] *vt* to split; (*nuez*) to crack
♦ *vi* to chatter; **~se** *vr* to crack, split,
break (open).

cáscara [kàs'kàrá] *nf* (*de huevo, fruta seca*)
shell; (*de fruta*) skin; (*de limón*) peel.

cascarón [kàskàron'] *nm* (broken) eggshell.

cascarrabias [kàskàrrá'ĥyàs] *nm/f inv* (*fam*)
hothead.

casco [kàs'ko] *nm* (*de bombero, soldado*)
helmet; (*cráneo*) skull; (*NAUT: de barco*)
hull; (*ZOOL: de caballo*) hoof; (*botella*)
empty bottle; (*de ciudad*): **el ~ antiguo**
the old part; **el ~ urbano** the town center.

caserío [kàserē'o] *nm* hamlet, group of
houses; (*casa*) country house.

casero, a [kàse'ro, à] *a*: **ser muy ~** (*persona*) to be homeloving; **"comida casera"**
"home cooking" ♦ *nm/f* (*propietario*)
landlord/lady; (*COM*) property manager
(*US*), house agent (*Brit*).

caserón [kàseron'] *nm* large (ramshackle)
house.

caseta [kàse'tà] *nf* hut; (*para bañista*) cubicle; (*de feria*) stall.

casete [kàse'te] *nm o f* cassette.

casi [kà'sē] *ad* almost; **~ nunca** hardly ever,
almost never; **~ nada** next to nothing; **~
te caes** you almost *o* nearly fell.

casilla [kàsē'yá] *nf* (*casita*) hut, cabin; (*TEA-
TRO*) box office; (*para cartas*) box; (*AJE-
DREZ*) square; **sacar a uno de sus ~ s** to
make sb lose his temper.

casillero [kàsēye'ro] *nm* (mail)boxes.

casino [kàsē'no] *nm* club; (*de juego*) casino.

caso [kà'so] *nm* case; (*suceso*) event; **en ~
de ...** in case of ...; **el ~ es que** the fact is
that; **en el mejor de los ~s** at best; **en
ese ~** in that case; **en todo ~** in any case;
en último ~ as a last resort; **hacer ~ a** to
pay attention to; **hacer ~ omiso de** to fail
to mention, pass over; **hacer *o* venir al ~**
to be relevant.

caspa [kàs'pà] *nf* dandruff.

Caspio [kàs'pyo] *a*: **Mar ~** Caspian Sea.

casque [kàs'ke] *etc vb* V **cascar**.

cassette [kàset'] *nf o m* cassette.

casta [kà'stà] *nf* caste; (*raza*) breed; (*linaje*) lineage.

castaña [kàstà'nyá] *nf* V **castaño**.

castañetear [kàstànyeteàr'] *vi* (*dientes*) to
chatter.

castaño, a [kàstà'nyo, à] *a* chestnut
(-colored), brown ♦ *nm* chestnut tree ♦ *nf*
chestnut; (*fam: golpe*) punch; **~ de Indias**
horse chestnut tree.

castañuelas [kàstànywe'làs] *nfpl* castanets.

castellano, a [kàsteyà'no, à] *a* Castilian;
(*fam*) Spanish ♦ *nm/f* Castilian; (*fam*)
Spaniard ♦ *nm* (*LING*) Castilian, Spanish.

castellonense [kàsteyonen'se] *a* of *o* from
Castellón de la Plana ♦ *nm/f* native *o* inhabitant of Castellón de la Plana.

castidad [kàstēĥàĥ'] *nf* chastity, purity.

castigar [kàstēgàr'] *vt* to punish; (*DEPORTE*)
to penalize; (*afligir*) to afflict.

castigo [kàstē'go] *nm* punishment; (*DE-
PORTE*) penalty.

castigue [kàstē'ge] *etc vb* V **castigar**.

Castilla [kàstē'yà] *nf* Castile.

castillo [kàstē'yo] *nm* castle.

castizo, a [kàstē'so, à] *a* (*LING*) pure; (*de
buena casta*) purebred, pedigree; (*auténtico*) genuine.

casto, a [kà'sto, à] *a* chaste, pure.

castor [kàstor'] *nm* beaver.

castrar [kàstràr'] *vt* to castrate; (*gato*) to
neuter; (*BOT*) to prune.

castrense [kàstren'se] *a* army *cpd*, military.

casual [kàswàl'] *a* chance, accidental.

casualidad [kàswàlēĥàĥ'] *nf* chance, accident; (*combinación de circunstancias*)
coincidence; **¡qué ~!** what a coincidence!

casualmente [kàswàlmen'te] *ad* by chance.

cataclismo [kàtàklēs'mo] *nm* cataclysm.

catador [kàtàĥor'] *nm* taster.

catadura [kàtàĥōō'rà] *nf* (*aspecto*) looks *pl*.

catalán, ana [kàtàlán', á'ná] *a*, *nm/f* Catalan
♦ *nm* (*LING*) Catalan.

catalizador [kàtàlēsàĥor'] *nm* catalyst.

catalogar [kàtàlogàr'] *vt* to catalog (*US*),
catalogue; **~ (de)** (*fig*) to classify (as).

catálogo [kàtà'logo] *nm* catalog (*US*), catalogue.

catalogue [kàtàlo'ge] *etc vb* V **catalogar**.

Cataluña [kàtàlōō'nyá] *nf* Catalonia.

catar [kàtàr'] *vt* to taste, sample.

catarata [kàtàrà'tà] *nf* (*GEO*) (water)fall;
(*MED*) cataract.

catarro [kàtà'rro] *nm* catarrh; (*constipado*)
cold.

catástrofe [kàtàs'trofe] *nf* catastrophe.

catecismo [kàtesēs'mo] *nm* catechism.

cátedra [kà'teĥrá] *nf* (*UNIV*) chair, professorship; (*ESCOL*) senior teacher's post; **sentar ~ sobre un argumento** to take one's stand on an argument.

catedral [kåtcᴛ̣ʜɾál'] *nf* cathedral.

catedrático, a [kåtcᴛ̣ʜɾá'tē̆ko, á] *nm/f* professor; (*ESCOL*) senior teacher.

categoría [kåtcᴛ̣oɾē̆'á] *nf* category; (*rango*) rank, standing; (*calidad*) quality; **de ~** (*hotel*) top-class; **de baja ~** (*oficial*) low-ranking; **de segunda ~** second-rate; **no tiene ~** he has no standing.

categórico, a [kåtcᴛ̣o'ɾē̆ko, á] *a* categorical.

caterva [kåter'ʜᴀ̤] *nf* throng, crowd.

cateto, a [kåtc'to, á] *nm/f* yokel.

cátodo [ká'toᴛ̣ʜo] *nm* cathode.

catolicismo [kåtolē̆sḗs'mo] *nm* Catholicism.

católico, a [ká̤to'lḗko, á] *a, nm/f* Catholic.

catorce [kátor'se] *num* fourteen.

Cáucaso [ká'ōōkáso] *nm* Caucasus.

cauce [ká'ōōse] *nm* (*de río*) riverbed; (*fig*) channel.

caución [ká̤ōōsyon'] *nf* bail.

caucionar [ká̤ōōsyonár'] *vt* (*JUR*) to bail (out), go bail for.

caucho [ká'ōōtcho] *nm* rubber; (*AM*: *llanta*) tire (*US*), tyre (*Brit*).

caudal [ká̤ōōᴛ̣ʜál'] *nm* (*de río*) volume, flow; (*fortuna*) wealth; (*abundancia*) abundance.

caudaloso, a [ká̤ōōᴛ̣ʜálo'so, á] *a* (*río*) large; (*persona*) wealthy, rich.

caudillo [ká̤ōōᴛ̣ʜē̆'yo] *nm* leader, chief.

caudillaje [ká̤ōōᴛ̣ʜēyá'ʜe] *nm* leadership.

causa [ká'ōōsá] *nf* cause; (*razón*) reason; (*JUR*) lawsuit, case; **a o por ~ de** because of, on account of.

causar [ká̤ōōsár'] *vt* to cause.

cáustico, a [ká'ōōstē̆ko, á] *a* caustic.

cautela [ká̤ōōte'lá] *nf* caution, cautiousness.

cauteloso, a [ká̤ōōtelo'so, á] *a* cautious, wary.

cautivar [ká̤ōōtē̆ár'] *vt* to capture; (*fig*) to captivate.

cautiverio [ká̤ōōtē̆e'ryo] *nm,* **cautividad** [ká̤ōōtē̆ē̆ʜᴀ̤ᴛ̣ʜ'] *nf* captivity.

cautivo, a [ká̤ōōtē̆'ᴋo, á] *a, nm/f* captive.

cauto, a [ká'ōōto, á] *a* cautious, careful.

cava [ká'ʜᴀ̤] *nf* (*bodega*) (wine) cellar ♦ *nm* (*vino*) champagne-type wine.

cavar [kábár'] *vt* to dig; (*AGR*) to till.

caverna [káber'ná] *nf* cave, cavern.

cavernoso, a [ká̤ber'no'so, á] *a* cavernous; (*voz*) resounding.

cavidad [ká̤ʜēᴛ̣ʜ'] *nf* cavity.

cavilación [ká̤bēlásyon'] *nf* deep thought.

cavilar [ká̤bēlár'] *vt* to ponder.

cayado [ká̤yá'ᴛ̣ʜo] *nm* (*de pastor*) crook; (*de obispo*) crozier.

cayendo [ká̤yen'do] *etc vb* V **caer.**

caza [ká'sá] *nf* (*acción: gen*) hunting; (: *con fusil*) shooting; (*una ~*) hunt, chase; (*animales*) game; **coto de ~** hunting estate ♦

nm (*AVIAT*)- fighter.

cazador, a [kå̤sáᴛ̣ʜor', á] *nm/f* hunter/ huntress ♦ *nf* jacket.

cazaejecutivos [kå̤sáchekōōtē̆'ᴋos] *nm inv* (*COM*) headhunter.

cazar [kásár'] *vt* to hunt; (*perseguir*) to chase; (*prender*) to catch; **~las al vuelo** to be pretty sharp.

cazasubmarinos [kå̤sásōōᴋmárē̆'nos] *nm inv* (*NAUT*) destroyer; (*AVIAT*) anti-submarine craft.

cazo [ká'so] *nm* saucepan.

cazuela [káswc'lá] *nf* (*vasija*) pan; (*guisado*) casserole.

cazurro, a [kásōō'rro, á] *a* surly.

CC *nm abr* (*POL*: = *Comité Central*) Central Committee.

c/c. *abr* (*COM*: = *cuenta corriente*) checking (*US*) o current (*Brit*) account.

CCI *nf abr* (*COM*: = *Cámara de Comercio Internacional*) ICC.

CC.OO. *nfpl abr* = **Comisiones Obreras.**

c/d *abr* (= *en casa de*) c/o; (= *con descuento*) with discount.

CDN *nm abr* = *Centro Dramático Nacional.*

CE *nm abr* (= *Consejo de Europa*) Council of Europe ♦ *nf abr* (= *Comunidad Europea*) EC.

cebada [scʜá'ʜᴀ̤] *nf* barley.

cebar [scʜár'] *vt* (*animal*) to fatten (up); (*anzuelo*) to bait; (*MIL, TEC*) to prime; **~se** *vr:* **~se en** to vent one's fury on, take it out on.

cebo [sc'ʜo] *nm* (*para animales*) feed, food; (*para peces, fig*) bait; (*de arma*) charge.

cebolla [scʜo'yá] *nf* onion.

cebollín [scʜoyē̆n'] *nm* green onion (*US*), spring onion (*Brit*).

cebón, ona [scʜon', oná] *a* fat, fattened.

cebra [sc'ʜrá] *nf* zebra; **paso de ~** zebra crossing.

CECA [se'ká] *nf abr* (= *Comunidad Europea del Carbón y del Acero*) ECSC.

ceca [se'ká] *nf:* **andar** *o* **ir de la ~ a la Meca** to chase about all over the place.

cecear [seseár'] *vi* to lisp.

ceceo [sese'o] *nm* lisp.

cecina [sesē̆'ná] *nf* cured *o* smoked meat.

cedazo [seᴛ̣ʜá'so] *nm* sieve.

ceder [seᴛ̣ʜer'] *vt* (*entregar*) to hand over; (*renunciar a*) to give up, part with ♦ *vi* (*renunciar*) to give in, yield; (*disminuir*) to diminish, decline; (*romperse*) to give way; (*viento*) to die down; (*fiebre etc*) to abate; **"ceda el paso"** (*AUTO*) "yield" (*US*), "give way" (*Brit*).

cedro [se'ᴛ̣ʜro] *nm* cedar.

cédula [se'ᴛ̣ʜōōlá] *nf* certificate, document; **~ en blanco** blank check.

CEE *nf abr* (= *Comunidad Económica Europea*) EEC.

cegar [seɡár'] vt to blind; (tubería etc) to blóck up, stop up ♦ vi to go blind; ~se vr to be blinded (de by).

cegué [seɡe'] etc vb V **cegar**.

ceguemos [seɡe'mos] etc vb V **cegar**.

ceguera [seɡe'rá] nf blindness.

Ceilán [seēlán'] nm Ceylon, Sri Lanka.

ceja [se'há] nf eyebrow; ~s **pobladas** bushy eyebrows; **arquear las** ~s to raise one's eyebrows; **fruncir las** ~s to frown.

cejar [sehár'] vi (fig) to back down; **no** ~ to keep it up, stick to it.

cejijunto, a [schēhōōn'to, á] a with bushy eyebrows; (fig) scowling.

celada [selá'thá] nf ambush, trap.

celador, a [selàthor', á] nm/f (de edificio) watchman; (de museo etc) attendant; (de cárcel) guard (US), warder (Brit).

celda [sel'dá] nf cell.

celebérrimo, a [selebe'rrēmo, á] a superlativo de **célebre**.

celebración [selebrásyon'] nf celebration.

celebrar [selebrár'] vt to celebrate; (alabar) to praise ♦ vi to be glad; ~se vr to occur, take place.

célebre [se'lebre] a celebrated, renowned.

celebridad [selebrethá th'] nf fame; (persona) celebrity.

celeridad [selerēthá th'] nf: **con** ~ promptly.

celeste [sele'ste] a sky-blue; (cuerpo etc) heavenly ♦ nm sky blue.

celestial [selestyál'] a celestial, heavenly.

celibato [selebá'to] nm celibacy.

célibe [se'lēbe] a, nm/f celibate.

celo [se'lo] nm zeal; (REL) fervor; (pey) envy; ~s nmpl jealousy sg; **dar** ~s **a uno** to make sb jealous; **tener** ~s **de uno** to be jealous of sb; **en** ~ (animales) in heat.

celofán [selofán'] nm cellophane.

celosía [selosē'á] nf lattice (window).

celoso, a [selo'so, á] a (envidioso) jealous; (trabajador) zealous; (desconfiado) suspicious.

celta [sel'tá] a Celtic ♦ nm/f Celt.

célula [se'lōōlá] nf cell.

celular [selōōlár'] a: **tejido** ~ cell tissue.

celuloide [selōōlo'ēthe] nm celluloid.

celulosa [selōōlo'sá] nf cellulose.

cementerio [semente'ryo] nm cemetery, graveyard; ~ **de coches** junkyard (US), used-car dump (Brit).

cemento [semen'to] nm cement; (hormigón) concrete; (AM: cola) glue.

CEN nm abr (Esp) = Consejo de Economía Nacional.

cena [se'ná] nf evening meal, dinner.

cenagal [senáɡál'] nm bog, quagmire.

cenar [senár'] vt to have for dinner, dine on ♦ vi to have dinner, dine.

cencerro [sense'rro] nm cowbell; **estar como un** ~ (fam) to be crazy.

cenicero [senēse'ro] nm ashtray.

cenit [senēt'] nm zenith.

ceniciento, a [senēsyen'to, á] a ash-colored, ashen.

ceniza [senē'sá] nf ash, ashes pl.

censar [sensár'] vt to take a census of.

censo [sen'so] nm census; ~ **electoral** list of registered voters (US), electoral roll (Brit).

censor [sensor'] nm censor; ~ **de cuentas** (COM) auditor; ~ **jurado de cuentas** certified public accountant (US), chartered accountant (Brit).

censura [sensōō'rá] nf (POL) censorship; (moral) censure, criticism.

censurable [sensōōrá'ble] a reprehensible.

censurar [sensōōrár'] vt (idea) to censure; (cortar: película) to censor.

centella [sente'yá] nf spark.

centellear [senteyeár'] vi (metal) to gleam; (estrella) to twinkle; (fig) to sparkle.

centelleo [senteye'o] nm gleam(ing); twinkling; sparkling.

centenar [sentenár'] nm hundred.

centenario, a [sentená'ryo, á] a one hundred years old ♦ nm centennial (US), centenary (Brit).

centeno [sente'no] nm rye.

centésimo, a [sente'sēmo, á] a, nm hundredth.

centígrado [sentē'ɡrátho] a centigrade.

centigramo [sentēɡrá'mo] nm centigram (US), centigramme (Brit).

centilitro [sentēlē'tro] nm centiliter (US), centilitre (Brit).

centímetro [sentē'metro] nm centimeter (US), centimetre (Brit).

céntimo, a [sen'tēmo, á] a hundredth ♦ nm cent.

centinela [sentēne'lá] nm sentry, guard.

centollo, a [sento'yo, á] nm/f large (o spider) crab.

central [sentrál'] a central ♦ nf head office; (TEC) plant; (TELEC) exchange; ~ **nuclear** nuclear power station.

centralice [sentrálē'se] etc vb V **centralizar**.

centralita [sentrálē'tá] nf (TELEC) switchboard.

centralización [sentrálēsàsyon'] nf centralization.

centralizar [sentrálēsár'] vt to centralize.

centrar [sentrár'] vt to center (US), centre (Brit).

céntrico, a [sen'trēko, á] a central.

centrifugar [sentrēfōōɡár'] vt (ropa) to spin-dry.

centrifugue [sentrēfōō'ɡe] etc vb V **centrifugar**.

centrista [sentrē'stá] a center (US), centre (Brit) cpd.

centro [sen'tro] nm center (US), centre (Brit); ~ **de beneficios** (COM) profit center; ~ **comercial** shopping center; ~ **de computatión** computer center; ~ **(de determinación) de costos** (*COM*) cost center; ~ **delantero** (*DEPORTE*) center forward; ~ **docente** teaching institution; ~ **juvenil** youth club; ~ **social** community center; **ser del** ~ (*POL*) to be a moderate.

centroafricano, a [sentroáfrēká'no, á] *a*: **la República Centroafricana** the Central African Republic.

centroamericano, a [sentroåmerēká'no, á] *a, nm/f* Central American.

centrocampista [sentrokámpē'stá] *nm/f* (*DEPORTE*) halfback.

cent(s). *abr* (= *céntimo(s)*) c.

ceñir [senyēr'] *vt* (*rodear*) to encircle, surround; (*ajustar*) to fit (tightly); (*apretar*) to tighten; ~**se** *vr*: ~**se algo** to put sth on; ~**se al asunto** to stick to the matter in hand.

ceño [se'nyo] *nm* frown, scowl; **fruncir el** ~ to frown, knit one's brow.

CEOE *nf abr* = *Confederación Española de Organizaciones Empresariales*.

cepa [se'pá] *nf* (*de vid, fig*) stock; (*BIO*) strain.

CEPAL [sepál'] *nf abr* (= *Comisión Económica de las Naciones Unidas para la América Latina*) Economic Commission for Latin America.

cepillar [sepēyár'] *vt* to brush; (*madera*) to plane (down).

cepillo [sepē'yo] *nm* brush; (*para madera*) plane; (*REL*) poorbox, alms box.

cepo [se'po] *nm* (*caza*) trap.

CEPSA [sep'sá] *nf abr* (*COM*) = *Compañía Española de Petróleos, S.A.*

cera [se'rá] *nf* wax; ~ **de abejas** beeswax.

cerámica [será'mēká] *nf* pottery; (*arte*) ceramics *sg*.

ceramista [serámē'stá] *nm/f* potter.

cerbatana [serbátá'ná] *nf* blowgun.

cerca [ser'ká] *nf* fence ♦ *ad* near, nearby, close; **por aquí** ~ nearby ♦ *prep*: ~ **de** (*cantidad*) nearly, about; (*distancia*) near, close to ♦ *nmpl*: ~**s** foreground *sg*.

cercado [serká'ðo] *nm* enclosure.

cercanía [serkánē'á] *nf* nearness, closeness; ~**s** *nfpl* outskirts, suburbs; **tren de** ~**s** commuter *o* local train.

cercano, a [serká'no, á] *a* close, near; (*pueblo etc*) nearby; **C~ Oriente** Near East.

cercar [serkár'] *vt* to fence in; (*rodear*) to surround.

cerciorar [sersyorár'] *vt* (*asegurar*) to assure; ~**se** *vr* (*descubrir*) to find out (*de* about); (*asegurarse*) to make sure (*de* of).

cerco [ser'ko] *nm* (*AGR*) enclosure; (*AM*) fence; (*MIL*) siege.

Cerdeña [serðe'nyá] *nf* Sardinia.

cerdo [ser'ðo] *nm* pig; **carne de** ~ pork.

cereal [sereál'] *nm* cereal; ~**es** *nmpl* cereals, grain *sg*.

cerebro [sere'bro] *nm* brain; (*fig*) brains *pl*; **ser un** ~ (*fig*) to be brilliant.

ceremonia [seremo'nyá] *nf* ceremony; **reunión de** ~ formal meeting; **hablar sin** ~ to speak plainly.

ceremonial [seremonyál'] *a, nm* ceremonial.

ceremonioso, a [seremonyo'so, á] *a* ceremonious; (*cumplido*) formal.

cereza [sere'sá] *nf* cherry.

cerezo [sere'so] *nm* cherry tree.

cerilla [serē'yá] *nf* (*fósforo*) match.

cerner [serner'] *vt* to sift, sieve; ~**se** *vr* to hover.

cernidor [sernēðor'] *nm* sieve.

cero [se'ro] *nm* nothing, zero; (*DEPORTE*) zip (*US*), nil (*Brit*); **8 grados bajo** ~ 8 degrees below zero; **a partir de** ~ from scratch.

cerque [ser'ke] *etc vb* V **cercar**.

cerrado, a [serrá'ðo, á] *a* closed, shut; (*con llave*) locked; (*tiempo*) cloudy, overcast; (*curva*) sharp; (*acento*) thick, broad; **a puerta cerrada** (*JUR*) in camera.

cerradura [serráðōo'rá] *nf* (*acción*) closing; (*mecanismo*) lock.

cerrajería [serráherē'á] *nf* locksmith's craft; (*tienda*) locksmith's (shop).

cerrajero, a [serráhe'ro, á] *nm/f* locksmith.

cerrar [serrár'] *vt* to close, shut; (*paso, carretera*) to close; (*grifo*) to turn off; (*trato, cuenta, negocio*) to close; ~ **con llave** to lock; ~ **el sistema** (*INFORM*) to close *o* shut down the system; ~ **un trato** to strike a bargain ♦ *vi* to close, shut; (*la noche*) to fall; ~**se** *vr* to close, shut; (*herida*) to heal.

cerro [se'rro] *nm* hill; **andar por las** ~**s de Úbeda** to wander from the point, digress.

cerrojo [serro'ho] *nm* (*herramienta*) bolt; (*de puerta*) latch.

certamen [sertá'men] *nm* competition, contest.

certero, a [serte'ro, á] *a* (*gen*) accurate.

certeza [serte'sá], **certidumbre** [sertēðōom'-bre] *nf* certainty.

certificación [sertēfēkásyon'] *nf* certification; (*JUR*) affidavit.

certificado, a [sertēfēká'ðo, á] *a* certified; (*CORREOS*) registered ♦ *nm* certificate.

certificar [sertēfēkár'] *vt* (*asegurar, atestar*) to certify.

certifique [sertēfē'ke] *etc vb* V **certificar**.

cervatillo [serbátē'yo] *nm* fawn.

cervecería [serbeserē'á] *nf* (*fábrica*) brewery; (*taberna*) beer hall (*US*), public house (*Brit*).

cerveza [serbe'sá] *nf* beer.

cervical [serbēkál'] *a* cervical.

cerviz [serβes'] *nf* nape of the neck.
cesación [sesásyon'] *nf* cessation, suspension.
cesante [sesán'te] *a* laid off.
cesantía [sesántē'á] *nf* (*AM*) unemployment.
cesar [sesár'] *vi* to cease, stop ♦ *vt* (*en el trabajo*) to lay off; (*funcionario*) to remove from office.
cese [se'se] *nm* (*de trabajo*) dismissal; (*de pago*) suspension.
cesión [sesyon'] *nf*: ~ **de bienes** surrender of property.
césped [ses'peθ] *nm* grass, lawn.
cesta [se'stá] *nf* basket.
cesto [se'sto] *nm* (large) basket, hamper.
cetrería [setrerē'á] *nf* falconry.
cetrino, a [setrē'no, á] *a* (*tez*) sallow.
cetro [se'tro] *nm* scepter.
Ceuta [seōō'tá] *nf* Ceuta.
ceutí [seōōtē'] *a* of o from Ceuta ♦ *nm/f* native o inhabitant of Ceuta.
C.F. *nm abr* (= *Club de Fútbol*) F.C.
cfr. *abr* (= *confróntese, compárese*) cf.
cg. *abr* (= *centígramo*) cg.
CGS *nf abr* (*Guatemala, El Salvador*) = *Confederación General de Sindicatos*.
CGT *nf abr* (*Colombia, México, Nicaragua*) = *Confederación General de Trabajadores*; (*Argentina*) = *Confederación General del Trabajo*.
ch... *V bajo la letra* CH, *después de* C.
C.I. *nm abr* (= *coeficiente intelectual o de inteligencia*) I.Q.
Cía *abr* (= *compañía*) Co.
cianuro [syánōō'ro] *nm* cyanide.
ciática [syá'tēká] *nf* sciatica.
cicatrice [sēkátrē'se] *etc vb V* **cicatrizar**.
cicatriz [sēkátrēs'] *nf* scar.
cicatrizar [sēkátrēsár'] *vt* to heal; ~**se** *vr* to heal (up), form a scar.
cíclico, a [sē'klēko, á] *a* cyclical.
ciclismo [sēklēs'mo] *nm* cycling.
ciclista [sēklē'stá] *nm/f* cyclist.
ciclo [sē'klo] *nm* cycle.
ciclón [sēklon'] *nm* cyclone.
cicuta [sēkōō'tá] *nf* hemlock.
C.I.D. *nm abr* = *Centro Internacional para el Desarrollo* (*Ginebra*).
ciego, a [sye'ġo, á] *etc vb V* **cegar** ♦ *a* blind ♦ *nm/f* blind man/woman; **a ciegas** blindly.
ciegue [sye'ġe] *etc vb V* **cegar**.
cielo [sye'lo] *nm* sky; (*REL*) heaven; (*ARQ: tb:* ~ **raso**) ceiling; ¡~**s!** good heavens!; **ver el** ~ **abierto** to see one's chance.
ciempiés [syempyes'] *nm inv* centipede.
cien [syen] *num V* **ciento**.
ciénaga [sye'náġá] *nf* marsh, swamp.
ciencia [syen'syá] *nf* science; ~**s** *nfpl* science *sg*; **saber algo a** ~ **cierta** to know sth for certain.
ciencia-ficción [syen'syáfēksyon'] *nf* science fiction.

cieno [sye'no] *nm* mud, mire.
científico, a [syentē'fēko, á] *a* scientific ♦ *nm/f* scientist.
ciento [syen'to], **cien** *num* hundred; **pagar al 10 por ciento** to pay at 10 percent.
cierne [syer'ne] *etc vb V* **cerner** ♦ *nm*: **en** ~ in blossom; **en** ~**(s)** (*fig*) in its infancy.
cierre [sye'rre] *etc vb V* **cerrar** ♦ *nm* closing, shutting; (*con llave*) locking; (*RADIO, TV*) sign-off; ~ **de cremallera** zip (fastener); **precios de** ~ (*BOLSA*) closing prices; ~ **del sistema** (*INFORM*) system shutdown.
cierto, a [syer'to, á] *a* sure, certain; (*un tal*) a certain; (*correcto*) right, correct; ~ **hombre** a certain man; **ciertas personas** certain o some people; **sí, es** ~ yes, that's correct; **por** ~ by the way; **lo** ~ **es que** ... the fact is that ...; **estar en lo** ~ to be right.
ciervo [syer'βo] *nm* (*ZOOL*) deer; (: *macho*) stag.
cierzo [syer'so] *nm* north wind.
CIES *nm abr* = *Consejo Interamericano Económico y Social*.
cifra [sē'frá] *nf* number, figure; (*cantidad*) number, quantity; (*secreta*) code; ~ **global** lump sum; ~ **de negocios** (*COM*) turnover; **en** ~**s redondas** in round figures; ~ **de referencia** (*COM*) bench mark; ~ **de ventas** (*COM*) sales figures.
cifrado, a [sēfrá'ðo, á] *a* in code.
cifrar [sēfrár'] *vt* to code, write in code; (*resumir*) to abridge; (*calcular*) to calculate.
cigala [sēġá'lá] *nf* Norway lobster.
cigarra [sēġá'rrá] *nf* cicada.
cigarrera [sēġárre'rá] *nf* cigar case.
cigarrillo [sēġárre'yo] *nm* cigarette.
cigarro [sēġá'rro] *nm* cigarette; (*puro*) cigar.
cigüeña [sēġwe'nyá] *nf* stork.
CIJ *nf abr* (= *Corte Internacional de Justicia*) International Court of Justice.
cilíndrico, a [sēlēn'drēko, á] *a* cylindrical.
cilindro [sēlēn'dro] *nm* cylinder.
cima [sē'má] *nf* (*de montaña*) top, peak; (*de árbol*) top; (*fig*) height.
címbalo [sēm'bálo] *nm* cymbal.
cimbrar [sēmbrár'], **cimbrear** [sēmbreár'] *vt* to brandish; ~**se** *vr* to sway.
cimentar [sēmentár'] *vt* to lay the foundations of; (*fig: reforzar*) to strengthen; (: *fundar*) to found.
cimiento [sēmyen'to] *etc vb V* **cimentar** ♦ *nm* foundation.
cinc [sēnk] *nm* zinc.
cincel [sēnsel'] *nm* chisel.
cincelar [sēnselár'] *vt* to chisel.
cinco [sēn'ko] *num* five; (*fecha*) fifth; **las** ~ five o'clock; **no estar en sus** ~ (*fam*) to be off one's rocker.

cincuenta [sĕnkwen'tà] *num* fifty.

cincuentón, ona [sĕnkwenton', o'nà] *a*, *nm/f* fifty-year old.

cincha [sĕntch'à] *nf* girth, saddle strap.

cincho [sĕntch'o] *nm* sash, belt.

cine [sē'ne] *nm* movies *pl*; **el ~ mudo** silent films *pl*; **hacer ~** to make films.

cineasta [sĕneá'stà] *nm/f* (*director de cine*) film-maker *o* director.

cine-club [sē'neklōōb'] *nm* film club.

cinéfilo, a [sĕne'fēlo, à] *nm/f* film buff.

cinematográfico, a [sĕnemátogrà'fēko, à] *a* film *cpd*.

cínico, a [sē'nēko, à] *a* cynical; (*descarado*) shameless ♦ *nm/f* cynic.

cinismo [sēnēs'mo] *nm* cynicism.

cinta [sēn'tà] *nf* band, strip; (*de tela*) ribbon; (*película*) reel; (*de máquina de escribir*) ribbon; (*métrica*) tape measure; (*magnetofónica*) tape; **~ adhesiva** adhesive tape; **~ aislante** insulating tape; **~ de carbón** carbon ribbon; **~ magnética** (*INFORM*) magnetic tape; **~ métrica** tape measure; **~ de múltiples impactos** (*en impresora*) multistrike ribbon; **~ de tela** (*para máquina de escribir*) fabric ribbon; **~ transportadora** conveyor belt.

cinto [sēn'to] *nm* belt, girdle.

cintura [sēntōō'rà] *nf* waist; (*medida*) waistline.

cinturón [sēntōōron'] *nm* belt; (*fig*) belt, zone; **~ salvavidas** lifebelt; **~ de seguridad** safety belt.

ciña [sē'nyà] *etc*, **ciñendo** [sēnyen'tþo] *etc vb V* **ceñir.**

CIP [sēp] *nm abr* = *Club Internacional de Prensa* (*Madrid*).

ciprés [sēpres'] *nm* cypress (tree).

circo [sēr'ko] *nm* circus.

circuito [sērkwē'to] *nm* circuit; (*DEPORTE*) lap; **TV por ~ cerrado** closed-circuit TV; **~ experimental** (*INFORM*) breadboard; **~ impreso** printed circuit; **~ lógico** (*INFORM*) logical circuit.

circulación [sērkōōlásyon'] *nf* circulation; (*AUTO*) traffic; ''**cerrado a la ~ rodada**'' ''closed to vehicles''.

circular [sērkōōlár'] *a*, *nf* circular ♦ *vt* to circulate ♦ *vi* to circulate; (*dinero*) to be in circulation; (*AUTO*) to drive; (*autobús*) to run.

círculo [sēr'kōōlo] *nm* circle; (*centro*) clubhouse; (*POL*) political group.

circuncidar [sērkōōnsēdàr'] *vt* to circumcise.

circunciso, a [sērkōōnsē'so, à] *pp de* **circuncidar.**

circundante [sērkōōndán'te] *a* surrounding.

circundar [sērkōōndàr'] *vt* to surround.

circunferencia [sērkōōnferen'syà] *nf* circumference.

circunloquio [sērkōōnlo'kyo] *nm* circumlocution.

circunscribir [sērkōōnskrēēr'] *vt* to circumscribe; **~se** *vr* to be limited.

circunscripción [sērkōōnskrēpsyon'] *nf* division; (*POL*) constituency.

circunscrito [sērkōōnskrē'to] *pp de* **circunscribir.**

circunspección [sērkōōnspeksyon'] *nf* circumspection, caution.

circunspecto, a [sērkōōnspek'to, à] *a* circumspect, cautious.

circunstancia [sērkōōnstán'syà] *nf* circumstance; **~s agravantes/extenuantes** aggravating/extenuating circumstances; **estar a la altura de las ~s** to rise to the occasion.

circunstante [sērkōōnstán'te] *nm/f* onlooker, bystander.

circunvalación [sērkōōmbálásyon'] *nf*: **carretera de ~** beltway (*US*), ring road (*Brit*).

cirio [sē'ryo] *nm* (wax) candle.

ciruela [sērwe'là] *nf* plum; **~ pasa** prune.

ciruelo [sērwe'lo] *nm* plum tree.

cirugía [sērōōhē'á] *nf* surgery; **~ estética** *o* **plástica** plastic surgery.

cirujano [sērōōhá'no] *nm* surgeon.

cisco [sēs'ko] *nm*: **armar un ~** to kick up a row; **estar hecho ~** to be a wreck.

cisma [sēs'mà] *nm* schism; (*POL etc*) split.

cisne [sēs'ne] *nm* swan; **canto de ~** swan song.

cisterna [sēster'nà] *nf* cistern, tank.

cistitis [sēstē'tēs] *nf* cystitis.

cita [sē'tà] *nf* appointment, meeting; (*de novios*) date; (*referencia*) quotation; **acudir/faltar a una ~** to turn up for/miss an appointment.

citación [sētásyon'] *nf* (*JUR*) summons *sg*.

citar [sētár'] *vt* to make an appointment with, arrange to meet; (*JUR*) to summons; (*un autor, texto*) to quote; **~se** *vr*: **~se con uno** to arrange to meet sb; **se citaron en el cine** they arranged to meet at the cinema.

cítara [sē'tárà] *nf* zither.

cítrico, a [sē'trēko, à] *a* citric ♦ *nm*: **~s** citrus fruits.

CiU *nm abr* (*POL*) = *Convergència i Unió*.

ciudad [syōōtþàþ'] *nf* town; (*capital de país etc*) city; **~ universitaria** university campus; **C~ del Cabo** Cape Town; **la C~ Condal** Barcelona.

ciudadanía [syōōtþàþánē'à] *nf* citizenship.

ciudadano, a [syōōtþàþá'no, à] *a* civic ♦ *nm/f* citizen.

ciudadrealeño, a [syōōtþàþrcálc'nyo, à] *a* of *o* from Ciudad Real ♦ *nm/f* native *o* inhabitant of Ciudad Real.

cívico, a [sē'hēko, à] *a* civic; (*fig*) public-spirited.

civil |sēhēl'| *a* civil ♦ *nm* (*guardia*) policeman.

civilice |sēhēlē'sc| *etc vb V* **civilizar**.

civilización |sēhēlēsásyon'| *nf* civilization.

civilizar |sēhēlēsár'| *vt* to civilize.

civismo |sēhēs'mo| *nm* public spirit.

cizaña |sēsá'nyá| *nf* (*fig*) discord; **sembrar** ~ to sow discord.

cl. *abr* (= *centilitro*) cl.

clamar |klámár'| *vt* to clamor (*US*) *o* clamour (*Brit*) for, clamor (*US*), clamour (*Brit*) ♦ *vi* to cry out, clamor (*US*), clamour (*Brit*).

clamor |klámor'| *nm* (*grito*) cry, shout; (*fig*) clamor (*US*), clamour (*Brit*), protest.

clamoroso, a |klámoro'so, á| *a* (*éxito etc*) resounding.

clandestinidad |klándcstēnētháth'| *nf* secrecy.

clandestino, a |klándcstē'no, á| *a* clandestine; (*POL*) underground.

clara |klá'rá| *nf* (*de huevo*) eggwhite.

claraboya |klárábo'yá| *nf* skylight.

clarear |klárcár'| *vi* (*el día*) to dawn; (*el cielo*) to clear up, brighten up; ~**se** *vr* to be transparent.

clarete |klárc'tc| *nm* rosé (wine).

claridad |klárētháth'| *nf* (*del día*) brightness; (*de estilo*) clarity.

clarificar |klárēfēkár'| *vt* to clarify.

clarifique |klárēfē'kc| *etc vb V* **clarificar**.

clarín |klárēn'| *nm* bugle.

clarinete |klárēnc'tc| *nm* clarinet.

clarividencia |klárēvēthcn'syá| *nf* clairvoyance; (*fig*) far-sightedness.

claro, a |klá'ro, á| *a* clear; (*luminoso*) bright; (*color*) light; (*evidente*) clear, evident; (*poco espeso*) thin ♦ *nm* (*en bosque*) clearing ♦ *ad* clearly ♦ *excl* of course!; **hablar** ~ (*fig*) to speak plainly; **a las claras** openly; **no sacamos nada en** ~ we couldn't get anything definite.

clase |klá'sc| *nf* class; (*tipo*) kind, sort; (*ESCOL etc*) class; (: *aula*) classroom; ~ **alta/media/obrera** upper/middle/working class; **dar** ~**s** to teach.

clásico, a |klá'sēko, á| *a* classical; (*fig*) classic.

clasificable |klásēfēká'hlc| *a* classifiable.

clasificación |klásēfēkásyon'| *nf* classification; (*DEPORTE*) league; (*COM*) ratings *pl*.

clasificador |klásēfēkáthor'| *nm* filing cabinet.

clasificar |klásēfēkár'| *vt* to classify; (*INFORM*) to sort; ~**se** *vr* (*DEPORTE*: *torneo*) to qualify.

clasifique |klásēfē'kc| *etc vb V* **clasificar**.

clasista |klásē'stá| *a* (*fam*: *actitud*) snobbish.

claudia |klá'oōthyá| *nf* greengage.

claudicar |kláoōthēkár'| *vi* (*fig*) to back down.

claudique |kláoōthē'kc| *etc vb V* **claudicar**.

claustro |klá'oōstro| *nm* cloister; (*UNIV*) staff; (*junta*) senate.

cláusula |klá'oōsoōlá| *nf* clause; ~ **de exclusión** (*COM*) exclusion clause.

clausura |kláoōsoō'rá| *nf* closing, closure.

clausurar |kláoōsoōrár'| *vt* (*congreso etc*) to close, bring to a close; (*POL etc*) to adjourn; (*cerrar*) to close (down).

clavado, a *a* nailed ♦ *excl* exactly!, precisely!

clavar |klávár'| *vt* (*tablas etc*) to nail (together); (*con alfiler*) to pin; (*clavo*) to hammer in; (*cuchillo*) to stick, thrust; (*mirada*) to fix; (*fam*: *estafar*) to cheat.

clave |klá'hc| *nf* key; (*MUS*) clef; ~ **de búsqueda** (*INFORM*) search key; ~ **de clasificación** (*INFORM*) sort key.

clavel |kláhcl'| *nm* carnation.

claveteado |kláhctcá'thο| *nm* studding.

clavicémbalo |kláhēscm'bálo| *nm* harpsichord.

clavicordio |kláhēkor'thyo| *nm* clavicord.

clavícula |kláhē'koōlá| *nf* collar bone.

clavija |kláhē'há| *nf* peg, pin; (*MUS*) peg; (*ELEC*) plug.

clavo |klá'ho| *nm* (*de metal*) nail; (*BOT*) clove; **dar en el** ~ (*fig*) to hit the nail on the head.

claxon |klák'son|, *pl* **claxons** *nm* horn; **tocar el** ~ to sound one's horn.

clemencia |klcmcn'syá| *nf* mercy, clemency.

clemente |klcmcn'tc| *a* merciful, clement.

cleptómano, a |klcpto'máno, á| *nm/f* kleptomaniac.

clerical |klcrēkál'| *a* clerical.

clérigo |klc'rēgo| *nm* priest, clergyman.

clero |klc'ro| *nm* clergy.

cliché |klētchc'| *nm* cliché; (*TIP*) stencil; (*FOTO*) negative.

cliente, a |klycn'tc, á| *nm/f* client, customer.

clientela |klycntc'lá| *nf* clientele, customers *pl*; (*COM*) goodwill; (*MED*) patients *pl*.

clima |klē'má| *nm* climate.

climatizado, a |klēmátcsá'thο, á| *a* air-conditioned.

clínico, a |klē'nēko, á| *a* clinical ♦ *nf* clinic; (*particular*) private hospital.

clip *nm*, *pl* **clips** |klcp, klēs| paper clip.

cloaca |kloá'ká| *nf* sewer, drain.

clorhídrico, a |klorē'drēko, á| *a* hydrochloric.

cloro |klo'ro| *nm* chlorine.

cloroformo |klorofor'mo| *nm* chloroform.

cloruro |kloroō'ro| *nm* chloride; ~ **sódico** sodium chloride.

club, *pl* **clubs** *o* **clubes** |kloōb, kloōs, klu'hcs| *nm* club; ~ **de jóvenes** youth club.

cm *abr* (= *centímetro*) cm.

CN *nf abr* (= *Carretera Nacional*) ≈ A road.

C.N.T. *nf abr* (*Esp*) = *Confederación Nacional de Trabajo;* (*AM*) = *Confederación Nacional de Trabajadores.*

coacción [koáksyon'] *nf* coercion, compulsion.

coaccionar [koáksyonár'] *vt* to coerce, compel.

coagular [koágōōlár'] *vt,* ~**se** *vr* (*sangre*) to clot; (*leche*) to curdle.

coágulo [koá'gōōlo] *nm* clot.

coalición [koálēsyon'] *nf* coalition.

coartada [koártá'tḥá] *nf* alibi.

coartar [koártár'] *vt* to limit, restrict.

coba [ko'ḥá] *nf*: **dar** ~ **a uno** to soft-soap sb.

cobarde [koḥár'tḥe] *a* cowardly ♦ *nm/f* coward.

cobardía [koḥártḥē'á] *nf* cowardice.

cobaya [koḥá'yá] *nf*, **cobayo** [koḥá'yo] *nm* guinea pig.

cobertizo [koḥertē'so] *nm* shelter.

cobertor [koḥertor'] *nm* bedspread.

cobertura [koḥertōō'rá] *nf* cover; (*COM*) collateral (*US*) coverage (*Brit*); ~ **de dividendo** (*COM*) dividend cover.

cobija [koḥē'há] *nf* (*AM*) blanket.

cobijar [koḥehár'] *vt* (*cubrir*) to cover; (*abrigar*) to shelter; ~**se** *vr* to take shelter.

cobijo [koḥē'ho] *nm* shelter.

cobra [ko'ḥrá] *nf* cobra.

cobrador, a [koḥrátḥor', á] *nm/f* (*de autobús*) conductor/conductress; (*de impuestos, gas*) collector.

cobrar [koḥrár'] *vt* (*cheque*) to cash; (*sueldo*) to collect, draw; (*objeto*) to recover; (*precio*) to charge; (*deuda*) to collect ♦ *vi* to draw one's pay; ~**se** *vr* to recover, get on well; **cóbrese al entregar** cash on delivery (COD); **a** ~ (*COM*) receivable; **cantidades por** ~ sums due.

cobre [ko'ḥre] *nm* copper; ~**s** *nmpl* brass instruments.

cobrizo, a [koḥrē'so, á] *a* coppery.

cobro [ko'ḥro] *nm* (*de cheque*) cashing; (*pago*) payment; **presentar al** ~ to cash; *V tb* **llamada.**

coca [ko'ká] *nf* coca.

Coca-Cola ® [ko'káko'lá] *nf* Coca-Cola ®.

cocaína [kokáē'ná] *nf* cocaine.

cocainómano, a [kokáēno'máno, á] *nm/f* cocaine addict.

cocción [koksyon'] *nf* (*CULIN*) cooking; (*el hervir*) boiling.

cocear [koseár'] *vi* to kick.

cocer [koser'] *vt, vi* to cook; (*en agua*) to boil; (*en horno*) to bake.

cocido, a [kosē'tḥo, á] *a* boiled ♦ *nm* stew.

cocina [kosē'ná] *nf* kitchen; (*aparato*) cooker; (*acto*) cookery; ~ **casera** home cooking; ~ **eléctrica** electric stove; ~ **francesa** French cuisine; ~ **de gas** gas stove.

cocinar [kosēnár'] *vt, vi* to cook.

cocinero, a [kosēne'ro, á] *nm/f* cook.

coco [ko'ko] *nm* coconut; (*fantasma*) bogeyman; (*fam: cabeza*) nut; **comer el** ~ **a uno** (*fam*) to brainwash sb.

cocodrilo [kokotḥrē'lo] *nm* crocodile.

cocotero [kokote'ro] *nm* coconut palm.

cóctel [kok'tel] *nm* (*bebida*) cocktail; (*reunión*) cocktail party.

coctelera [koktele'rá] *nf* cocktail shaker.

coche [kotch'e] *nm* (*AUTO*) automobile (*US*), car; (*de tren, de caballos*) coach, carriage; (*para niños*) baby carriage (*US*); pram (*Brit*); ~ **de bomberos** fire engine; ~ **celular** paddy wagon; ~ (**comedor**) (*FERRO*) (dining) car; ~ **fúnebre** hearse.

coche-cama [kotch'ek'á'má], *pl* **coches-cama** *nm* (*FERRO*) sleeping car, sleeper (*Brit*).

cochera [kotche'rá] *nf* garage; (*de autobuses, trenes*) depot.

coche-restaurante, *pl* **coches-restaurante** [kotch'erestáōōrán'te] *nm* (*FERRO*) dining-car, diner.

cochinada [kotchēná'tḥá] *nf* dirty trick.

cochinillo [kotchēnē'yo] *nm* piglet, suckling pig.

cochino, a [kotchē'no, á] *a* filthy, dirty ♦ *nm/f* pig.

cod. *abr* (= *código*) code.

codazo [kotḥá'so] *nm*: **dar un** ~ **a uno** to nudge sb.

codear [kotḥeár'] *vi* to elbow, jostle; ~**se** *vr*: ~**se con** to rub shoulders with.

códice [ko'tḥēse] *nm* manuscript, codex.

codicia [kotḥē'syá] *nf* greed; (*fig*) lust.

codiciar [kotḥēsyár'] *vt* to covet.

codicioso, a [kotḥēsyo'so, á] *a* covetous.

codificador [kotḥēfēkátḥor'] *nm* (*INFORM*) encoder; ~ **digital** digitizer.

código [ko'tḥēgo] *nm* code; ~ **de barras** (*COM*) bar code; ~ **binario** binary code; ~ **de caracteres** (*INFORM*) character code; ~ **de (la) circulación** highway code; ~ **civil** common law; ~ **de control** (*INFORM*) control code; ~ **máquina** (*INFORM*) machine code; ~ **militar** military law; ~ **de operación** (*INFORM*) operational *o* machine code; ~ **penal** penal code; ~ **de práctica** code of practice.

codillo [kotḥē'yo] *nm* (*ZOOL*) knee; (*TEC*) elbow (joint).

codo [ko'tḥo] *nm* (*ANAT, de tubo*) elbow; (*ZOOL*) knee; **hablar por los** ~**s** to talk a blue streak (*US*) *o* 19 to the dozen (*Brit*).

codorniz [kotḥornēs'] *nf* quail.

coeficiente [koefēsyen'te] *nm* (*MAT*) coefficient; (*ECON etc*) rate; ~ **intelectual** *o* **de inteligencia** intelligence quotient.

coerción [koersyon'] *nf* coercion.

coercitivo, a [koersētē'ḥo, á] *a* coercive.

coetáneo, a [koetá'neo, á] *nm/f:* ~s contemporaries.

coexistencia [koeksēsten'syá] *nf* coexistence.

coexistir [koeksēstēr'] *vi* to coexist.

cofia [ko'fyá] *nf* (*de enfermera*) (white) cap.

cofradía [kofráthē'á] *nf* brotherhood, fraternity.

cogedor [kohethor'] *nm* dustpan.

coger [koher'] *vt* (*Esp*) to take (hold of); (*objeto caído*) to pick up; (*frutas*) to pick, harvest; (*resfriado, ladrón, pelota*) to catch; (*AM fam!*) to lay (*!*); ~ **a uno desprevenido** to take sb unawares ♦ *vi:* ~ **por el buen camino** to take the right road; ~**se** *vr* (*el dedo*) to catch; ~**se a algo** to get hold of sth.

cogida [kohē'thá] *nf* gathering, harvesting; (*de peces*) catch; (*TAUR*) goring.

cogollo [kogo'yo] *nm* (*de lechuga*) heart; (*fig*) core, nucleus.

cogote [kogo'te] *nm* back o nape of the neck.

cohabitar [koáhētár'] *vi* to live together, cohabit.

cohecho [koetch'o] *nm* (*acción*) bribery; (*soborno*) bribe.

coherencia [koeren'syá] *nf* coherence.

coherente [koeren'te] *a* coherent.

cohesión [koesyon'] *nm* cohesion.

cohete [koe'te] *nm* rocket.

cohibido, a [koēhē'tho, á] *a* (*PSICO*) inhibited; (*tímido*) shy; **sentirse** ~ to feel embarrassed.

cohibir [koēhēr'] *vt* to restrain, restrict; ~**se** *vr* to feel inhibited.

COI *nm abr* (= *Comité Olímpico Internacional*) IOC.

coima [ko'ēmá] *nf* (*fam*) bribe.

coincidencia [koēnsēthen'syá] *nf* coincidence.

coincidir [koēnsēthēr'] *vi* (*en idea*) to coincide, agree; (*en lugar*) to coincide.

coito [ko'ēto] *nm* intercourse, coitus.

cojear [koheár'] *vi* (*persona*) to limp, hobble; (*mueble*) to wobble, rock.

cojera [kohe'rá] *nf* lameness; (*andar cojo*) limp.

cojín [kohēn'] *nm* cushion.

cojinete [kohēne'te] *nm* small cushion, pad; (*TEC*) (ball) bearing.

cojo, a [ko'ho, á] *etc vb V* **coger** ♦ *a* (*que no puede andar*) lame, crippled; (*mueble*) wobbly ♦ *nm/f* lame person, cripple.

cojón [kohon'] *nm* (*fam!*) ball (*!*), testicle; **¡cojones!** shit! (*!*).

cojonudo, a [kohonōō'tho, á] *a* (*Esp fam*) great, fantastic.

col [kol] *nf* cabbage; ~**es de Bruselas** Brussels sprouts.

col., col.ª *abr* (= *columna*) col.

cola [ko'lá] *nf* tail; (*de gente*) line (*US*), queue (*Brit*); (*lugar*) end, last place; (*para pegar*) glue, gum; (*de vestido*) train; **hacer** ~ to line (*US*), queue (up) (*Brit*).

colaboración [koláhorásyon'] *nf* (*gen*) collaboration; (*en periódico*) contribution.

colaborador, a [koláhoráthor', á] *nm/f* collaborator; contributor.

colaborar [koláhorár'] *vi* to collaborate.

colación [kolásyon'] *nf:* **sacar a** ~ to bring up.

colado, a [kolá'tho, á] *a* (*metal*) cast ♦ *nf:* **hacer la colada** to do the washing.

colador [koláthor'] *nm* (*de té*) strainer; (*para verduras etc*) colander.

colapso [koláp'so] *nm* collapse; ~ **nervioso** nervous breakdown.

colar [kolár'] *vt* (*líquido*) to strain off; (*metal*) to cast ♦ *vi* to ooze, seep (through); ~**se** *vr* to cut in line (*US*) *o* jump the queue (*Brit*); (*en mitin*) to sneak in; (*equivocarse*) to slip up; ~**se en** to get into without paying; (*en una fiesta*) to gatecrash.

colateral [koláterál'] *nm* collateral.

colcha [koltch'á] *nf* bedspread.

colchón [koltchon'] *nm* mattress; ~ **inflable** inflatable mattress.

colchoneta [coltchone'tá] *nf* (*en gimnasio*) mat.

colear [koleár'] *vi* (*perro*) to wag its tail.

colección [koleksyon'] *nf* collection.

coleccionar [koleksyonár'] *vt* to collect.

coleccionista [koleksyonē'stá] *nm/f* collector.

colecta [kolek'tá] *nf* collection.

colectivo, a [kolektē'ho, á] *a* collective, joint ♦ *nm* (*AM*) (small) bus.

colector [kolektor'] *nm* collector; (*sumidero*) sewer.

colega [kole'gá] *nm/f* colleague.

colegial, a [kolehyál', á] *a* (*ESCOL etc*) school *cpd*, college *cpd* ♦ *nm/f* schoolboy/girl.

colegio [kole'hyo] *nm* college; (*escuela*) school; (*de abogados etc*) association; ~ **de internos** boarding school; **ir al** ~ to go to school.

colegir [kolehēr'] *vt* (*juntar*) to collect, gather; (*deducir*) to infer, conclude.

cólera [ko'lerá] *nf* (*ira*) anger; **montar en** ~ to get angry ♦ *nm* (*MED*) cholera.

colérico, a [kole'rēko, á] *a* angry, furious.

colesterol [kolesterol'] *nm* cholesterol.

coleta [kole'tá] *nf* pigtail.

coletazo [koletá'so] *nm:* **dar un** ~ (*animal*) to flap its tail; **los últimos** ~s death throes.

colgado, a [kolgá'tho, á] *pp de* **colgar** ♦ *a* hanging; (*ahorcado*) hanged; **dejar** ~ **a uno** to let sb down.

colgajo [kolgá'ho] *nm* tatter.

colgante [kolgán'te] *a* hanging; *V* **puente** ♦

nm (joya) pendant.

colgar [kolgár'] *vt* to hang (up); *(tender: ropa)* to hang out ♦ *vi* to hang; *(teléfono)* to hang up.

colgué [kolge'], **colguemos** [kolge'mos] *etc vb V* **colgar.**

colibrí [kolēbrē'] *nm* hummingbird.

coliflor [kolēflor'] *nf* cauliflower.

coligiendo [kolēhyen'do] *etc vb V* **colegir.**

colija [kolē'há] *etc vb V* **colegir.**

colilla [kolē'yá] *nf* cigarette end.

colina [kolē'ná] *nf* hill.

colindante [kolēndán'te] *a* adjacent, neighboring.

colindar [kolēndár'] *vi* to adjoin, be adjacent.

colisión [kolēsyon'] *nf* collision; **~ de frente** head-on crash.

colitis [kolē'tēs] *nf inv*: **tener ~** to have diarrhea *(US)*, diarrhoea *(Brit)*.

colmado, a [kolmá'tho, á] *a* full ♦ *nm* grocer's shop.

colmar [kolmár'] *vt* to fill to the brim; *(fig)* to fulfil, realize.

colmena [kolme'ná] *nf* beehive.

colmillo [kolmē'yo] *nm (diente)* eye tooth; *(de elefante)* tusk; *(de perro)* fang.

colmo [kol'mo] *nm* height, summit; **para ~ de desgracias** to cap it all; **¡eso es ya el ~!** that's the last straw!

colocación [kolokásyon'] *nf (acto)* placing; *(empleo)* job, position; *(situación)* place, position; *(COM)* placement.

colocar [kolokár'] *vt* to place, put, position; *(poner en empleo)* to find a job for; **~ dinero** to invest money; **~se** *vr* to place o.s.; *(conseguir trabajo)* to find a job.

colofón [kolofon'] *nm*: **como ~ de las conversaciones** as a sequel to o following the talks.

Colombia [kolom'byá] *nf* Colombia.

colombiano, a [kolombyá'no, á] *a, nm/f* Colombian.

colon [ko'lon] *nm* colon.

Colonia [kolo'nyá] *nf* Cologne.

colonia [kolo'nyá] *nf* colony; *(de casas)* housing development *(US)* o estate *(Brit)*; *(agua de ~)* cologne; **~ escolar** summer camp (for schoolchildren).

colonice [kolonē'se] *etc vb V* **colonizar.**

colonización [kolonēsásyon'] *nf* colonization.

colonizador, a [kolonēsáthor', á] *a* colonizing ♦ *nm/f* colonist, settler.

colonizar [kolonēsár'] *vt* to colonize.

colono [kolo'no] *nm (POL)* colonist, settler; *(AGR)* tenant farmer.

coloque [kolo'ke] *etc vb V* **colocar.**

coloquio [kolo'kyo] *nm* conversation; *(congreso)* conference; *(INFORM)* handshake.

color [kolor'] *nm* color *(US)*, colour *(Brit)*;

a todo ~ in full color; **verlo todo ~ de rosa** to see everything through rose-colored spectacles; **le salieron los ~es** she blushed.

colorado, a [kolorá'tho, á] *a (rojo)* red; *(AM: chiste)* dirty; **ponerse ~** to blush.

colorante [kolorán'te] *nm* coloring *(US)*, colouring *(Brit)*.

colorar [kolorár'] *vt* to color *(US)*, colour *(Brit)*; *(teñir)* to dye.

colorear [koloreár'] *vt* to color *(US)*, colour *(Brit)*.

colorete [kolore'te] *nm* blusher.

colorido [kolorē'tho] *nm* color(ing) *(US)*, colour(ing) *(Brit)*.

columbrar [koloōmbrár'] *vt* to glimpse, spy.

columna [koloōm'ná] *nf* column; *(pilar)* pillar; *(apoyo)* support; **~ blindada** *(MIL)* armored column; **~ vertebral** spine, spinal column.

columpiar [koloōmpyár'] *vt*, **~se** *vr* to swing.

columpio [koloōm'pyo] *nm* swing.

collar [koyár'] *nm* necklace; *(de perro)* collar.

coma [ko'má] *nf* comma ♦ *nm (MED)* coma.

comadre [komá'thre] *nf (madrina)* godmother; *(vecina)* neighbor *(US)*, neighbour *(Brit)*; *(chismosa)* gossip.

comadrear [komáthreár'] *vi* to gossip.

comadreja [komáthre'há] *nf* weasel.

comadrona [komáthro'ná] *nf* midwife.

comandancia [komándán'syá] *nf* command.

comandante [komándán'te] *nm* commandant; *(grado)* major.

comandar [komándár'] *vt* to command.

comando [komán'do] *nm (MIL: mando)* command; (: *grupo)* commando unit; *(INFORM)* command; **~ de búsqueda** search command.

comarca [komár'ká] *nf* region.

comarcal [komárkál'] *a* local.

comba [kom'bá] *nf (curva)* curve; *(en viga)* warp; *(cuerda)* skipping rope; **saltar a la ~** to skip.

combar [kombár'] *vt* to bend, curve.

combate [kombá'te] *nm* fight; *(fig)* battle; **fuera de ~** out of action.

combatiente [kombátyen'te] *nm* combatant.

combatir [kombátēr'] *vt* to fight, combat.

combatividad [kombátēvēthath'] *nf (actitud)* fighting spirit; *(agresividad)* aggressiveness.

combativo, a [kombátē'vo, á] *a* full of fight.

combinación [kombēnásyon'] *nf* combination; *(QUÍMICA)* compound; *(bebida)* cocktail; *(plan)* scheme, setup; *(prenda)* slip.

combinado, a [kombēná'tho, á] *a*: **plato ~** main course served with vegetables.

combinar |kombēnár'| *vt* to combine; (*colores*) to match.

combustible |kombōōstē'ble| *nm* fuel.

combustión |kombōōstyon'| *nf* combustion.

comedia |kome'ᵭyá| *nf* comedy; (*TEATRO*) play, drama; (*fig*) farce.

comediante |komeᵭyán'te| *nm/f* (comic) actor/actress.

comedido, a |komeᵭē'ᵭo, á| *a* moderate.

comedirse |komeᵭēr'se| *vr* to behave moderately; (*ser cortés*) to be courteous.

comedor, a |komeᵭor', á| *nm/f* (*persona*) glutton ♦ *nm* (*habitación*) dining room; (*restaurante*) restaurant; (*cantina*) cafeteria (*US*), canteen (*Brit*).

comencé |komense'|, **comencemos** |komense'mos| *etc vb* V **comenzar**.

comensal |komensál'| *nm/f* fellow guest/diner.

comentar |komentár'| *vt* to comment on; (*fam*) to discuss; **comentó que**... he made the comment that....

comentario |komentá'ryo| *nm* comment, remark; (*LIT*) commentary; **~s** *nmpl* gossip *sg*; **dar lugar a ~s** to cause gossip.

comentarista |komentárē'stá| *nm/f* commentator.

comenzar |komensár'| *vt, vi* to begin, start, commence; **~ a hacer algo** to begin *o* start doing *o* to do sth.

comer |komer'| *vt* to eat; (*DAMAS, AJEDREZ*) to take, capture; (*párrafo etc*) to skip ♦ *vi* to eat; (*almorzar*) to have lunch; **~se** *vr* to eat up; **~ el coco a** (*fam*) to brainwash; **¡a ~!** food's ready!

comerciable |komersyá'ble| *a* marketable, saleable.

comercial |komersyál'| *a* commercial; (*relativo al negocio*) business *cpd*.

comerciante |komersyán'te| *nm/f* trader, merchant; (*tendero*) shopkeeper; **~ exclusivo** (*COM*) sole trader.

comerciar |komersyár'| *vi* to trade, do business.

comercio |komer'syo| *nm* commerce, trade; (*negocio*) business; (*grandes empresas*) big business; (*fig*) dealings *pl*; **~ autorizado** (*COM*) licensed trade; **~ exterior** foreign trade.

comestible |komestē'ble| *a* eatable, edible ♦ *nmpl*: **~s** food *sg*, foodstuffs; (*COM*) groceries.

cometa |kome'tá| *nm* comet ♦ *nf* kite.

cometer |kometer'| *vt* to commit.

cometido |kometē'ᵭo| *nm* (*misión*) task, assignment; (*deber*) commitment.

comezón |komeson'| *nf* itch, itching.

comicios |komē'syos| *nmpl* elections; (*voto*) voting *sg*.

cómico, a |ko'mēko, á| *a* comic(al) ♦ *nm/f* comedian; (*de teatro*) (comic) actor/actress.

comida |komē'ᵭá| *etc vb* V **comedirse** ♦ *nf* (*alimento*) food; (*almuerzo, cena*) meal; (*de mediodía*) lunch.

comidilla |komēᵭē'yá| *nf*: **ser la ~ de la ciudad** to be the talk of the town.

comience |komyen'se| *etc vb* V **comenzar**.

comienzo |komyen'so| *etc vb* V **comenzar** ♦ *nm* beginning, start; **dar ~ a un acto** to begin a ceremony; **~ del archivo** (*INFORM*) top-of-file.

comilón, ona |komēlon', o'ná| *a* greedy ♦ *nf* (*fam*) blow-out.

comillas |komē'yás| *nfpl* quotation marks.

comino |komē'no| *nm* cumin (seed); **no me importa un ~** I don't give a damn.

comisaría |komēsárē'á| *nf* precinct (*US*), police station; (*MIL*) commissariat.

comisario |komēsá'ryo| *nm* (*MIL etc*) commissary; (*POL*) commissar.

comisión |komēsyon'| *nf* (*COM*: *pago*) commission, rake-off (*fam*); (: *junta*) board; (*encargo*) assignment; **~ mixta/permanente** joint/standing committee; **Comisiones Obreras** (*Esp*) Workers' Unions.

comisura |komēsōō'rá| *nf*: **~ de los labios** corner of the mouth.

comité, *pl* **comités** *nm* |komēte', komētes'| committee; work council.

comitiva |komētē'bá| *nf* suite, retinue.

como |ko'mo| *ad* as; (*tal ~*) like; (*aproximadamente*) about, approximately ♦ *conj* (*ya que, puesto que*) as, since; (*en seguida que*) as soon as; (*si:* ~*+subjun*) if; **¡~ no!** of course!; **~ no lo haga hoy** unless he does it today; **~ si** as if; **es tan alto ~ ancho** it is as high as it is wide.

cómo |ko'mo| *ad* how?, why? ♦ *excl* what?, I beg your pardon? ♦ *nm*: **el ~ y el porqué** the whys and wherefores; **¿~ está Ud?** how are you?; **¿~ no?** why not?; **¿~ son?** what are they like?

cómoda |ko'moᵭá| *nf* chest of drawers.

comodidad |komoᵭēᵭáᵭ'| *nf* comfort; **venga a su ~** come at your convenience.

comodín |komoᵭēn'| *nm* joker; (*INFORM*) wild card; **símbolo ~** wildcard character.

cómodo, a |ko'moᵭo, á| *a* comfortable; (*práctico, de fácil uso*) convenient.

comoquiera |komokye'rá| *conj*: **~ que** (+ *subjun*) in whatever way; **~ que sea eso** however that may be.

comp. *abr* (= *compárese*) cp.

compacto, a |kompák'to, á| *a* compact.

compadecer |kompáᵭeser'| *vt* to pity, be sorry for; **~se** *vr*: **~se de** to pity, be sorry for.

compadezca |kompáᵭes'ká| *etc vb* V **compadecer**.

compadre |kompá'ᵭre| *nm* (*padrino*)

godfather; (*amigo*) friend, pal.

compaginar [kompáhēnár'] *vt*: ~ **A con B** to bring A into line with B; ~**se** *vr*: ~**se con** to tally with, square with.

compañerismo [kompányerēs'mo] *nm* friendship (*US*), comradeship (*Brit*).

compañero, a [kompánye'ro, á] *nm/f* companion; (*novio*) boyfriend/girlfriend; ~ **de clase** classmate.

compañía [kompányē'á] *nf* company; ~ **afiliada** associated company; ~ **concesionadora** franchiser; ~ **(no) cotizable** (un)listed company; ~ **inversionista** investment trust; **hacer ~ a uno** to keep sb company.

comparación [kompárásyon'] *nf* comparison; **en ~ con** in comparison with.

comparar [kompárár'] *vt* to compare.

comparativo, a [kompárátē'ḥo, á] *a* comparative.

comparecencia [kompáresen'syá] *nf* (*JUR*) appearance (in court); **orden de ~** summons *sg*.

comparecer [kompáreser'] *vi* to appear (in court).

comparezca [kompáres'ká] *etc vb V* **comparecer**.

comparsa [kompár'sá] *nm/f* extra.

compartimiento [kompártēmyen'to] *nm* (*FERRO*) compartment.

compartir [kompártēr'] *vt* to divide (up), share (out).

compás [kompás'] *nm* (*MUS*) beat, rhythm; (*MAT*, *NAUT etc*) compass; **al ~** in time.

compasión [kompásyon'] *nf* compassion, pity.

compasivo, a [kompásē'ḥo, á] *a* compassionate.

compatibilidad [kompátēḥēlēḥáḥ'] *nf* (*tb INFORM*) compatibility.

compatible [kompátē'ḥle] *a* compatible.

compatriota [kompátryo'tá] *nm/f* compatriot, fellow countryman/woman.

compendiar [kompendyár'] *vt* to summarize; (*libro*) to abridge.

compendio [kompen'dyo] *nm* summary; abridgement.

compenetración [kompenetrásyon'] *nf* (*fig*) mutual understanding.

compenetrarse [kompenetrár'se] *vr* (*fig*): ~ **(muy) bien** to get on (very) well together.

compensación [kompensásyon'] *nf* compensation; (*JUR*) damages *pl*; (*COM*) clearing.

compensar [kompensár'] *vt* to compensate; (*pérdida*) to make up for.

competencia [kompeten'syá] *nf* (*incumbencia*) domain, field; (*COM*) receipt; (*JUR*, *habilidad*) competence; (*rivalidad*) competition.

competente [kompeten'te] *a* (*JUR*, *persona*) competent; (*conveniente*) suitable.

competer [kompeter'] *vi*: ~ **a** to be the responsibility of, fall to.

competición [kompetēsyon'] *nf* competition.

competidor, a [kompetēᶜt͟hor', á] *nm/f* competitor.

competir [kompetēr'] *vi* to compete.

compilación [kompēlásyon'] *nf* compilation; **tiempo de ~** (*INFORM*) compile time.

compilador [kompēlát͟hor'] *nm* compiler.

compilar [kompēlár'] *vt* to compile.

compita [kompē'tá] *etc vb V* **competir**.

complacencia [komplásen'syá] *nf* (*placer*) pleasure; (*satisfacción*) satisfaction; (*buena voluntad*) willingness.

complacer [kompláser'] *vt* to please; ~**se** *vr* to be pleased.

complaciente [komplásyen'te] *a* kind, obliging, helpful.

complazca [komplás'ká] *etc vb V* **complacer**.

complejo, a [komple'ho, á] *a*, *nm* complex.

complementario, a [komplementá'ryo, á] *a* complementary.

completar [kompletár'] *vt* to complete.

completo, a [komple'to, á] *a* complete; (*perfecto*) perfect; (*lleno*) full ♦ *nm* full complement.

complicado, a [komplēká'ᵗ͟ho, á] *a* complicated; **estar ~ en** to be involved in.

complicar [komplēkár'] *vt* to complicate.

cómplice [kom'plēse] *nm/f* accomplice.

complique [komplē'ke] *etc vb V* **complicar**.

complot, *pl* **complots** [komplo'(t), komplos'] *nm* plot; (*conspiración*) conspiracy.

compondré [kompondre'] *etc vb V* **componer**.

componenda [komponen'dá] *nf* compromise; (*pey*) shady deal.

componer [komponer'] *vt* to make up, put together; (*MUS*, *LIT*, *IMPRENTA*) to compose; (*algo roto*) to mend, repair; (*adornar*) to adorn; (*arreglar*) to arrange; (*reconciliar*) to reconcile; ~**se** *vr*: ~**se de** to consist of; **componérselas para hacer algo** to manage to do sth.

componga [kompon'gá] *etc vb V* **componer**.

comportamiento [komportámyen'to] *nm* behavior (*US*), behaviour (*Brit*), conduct.

comportarse [komportár'se] *vr* to behave.

composición [komposēsyon'] *nf* composition.

compositor, a [komposētor', á] *nm/f* composer.

compostelano, a [kompostelá'no, á] *a* of o from Santiago de Compostela ♦ *nm/f* native o inhabitant of Santiago de Compostela.

compostura [kompostōō'rá] *nf* (*repara-*

ción) mending, repair; (_composición_) composition; (_acuerdo_) agreement; (_actitud_) composure.

compota [kompo'tá] _nf_ compote, preserve.

compra [kom'prá] _nf_ purchase; ~s _nfpl_ purchases, shopping _sg_; **hacer la ~/ir de** ~s to do the/go shopping; ~ **a granel** (_COM_) bulk buying; ~ **proteccionista** (_COM_) support buying.

comprador, a [komprá‌‌θor', á] _nm/f_ buyer, purchaser.

comprar [komprár'] _vt_ to buy, purchase; ~ **deudas** (_COM_) to factor.

compraventa [komprá‌βen'tá] _nf_ (_JUR_) contract of sale.

comprender [komprender'] _vt_ to understand; (_incluir_) to comprise, include.

comprensible [komprensē'ble] _a_ understandable.

comprensión [komprensyon'] _nf_ understanding; (_totalidad_) comprehensiveness.

comprensivo, a [komprensē'‌ho, á] _a_ comprehensive; (_actitud_) understanding.

compresa [kompre'sá] _nf_ compress; ~ **higiénica** sanitary napkin (_US_) o towel (_Brit_).

compresión [kompresyon'] _nf_ compression.

comprimido, a [kompremē'‌ho] _a_ compressed ♦ _nm_ (_MED_) pill, tablet; **en caracteres ~s** (_TIP_) condensed.

comprimir [kompremēr'] _vt_ to compress; (_fig_) to control; (_INFORM_) to pack.

comprobación [komproba‌syon'] _nf_: ~ **general de cuentas** (_COM_) general audit.

comprobante [komprobán'te] _nm_ proof; (_COM_) voucher; ~ **(de pago)** receipt.

comprobar [komprobár'] _vt_ to check; (_probar_) to prove; (_TEC_) to check, test.

comprometedor, a [komprometeθor', á] _a_ compromising.

comprometido, a [kompromete'‌ho, á] _a_ (_situación_) awkward; (_escritor etc_) committed.

comprometer [komprometer'] _vt_ to compromise; (_exponer_) to endanger; ~**se** _vr_ to compromise o.s.; (_involucrarse_) to get involved.

compromiso [krompromē'so] _nm_ (_obligación_) obligation; (_cita_) engagement, date; (_cometido_) commitment; (_convenio_) agreement; (_dificultad_) awkward situation; **libre de** ~ (_COM_) without obligation.

comprueba [komprwe'bá] _etc vb V_ **comprobar**.

compuerta [kompwer'tá] _nf_ (_en canal_) sluice, floodgate; (_INFORM_) gate.

compuesto, a [kompwe'sto, á] _pp de_ **componer** ♦ _a_: ~ **de** composed of, made up of ♦ _nm_ compound; (_MED_) preparation.

compulsar [kompōōlsár'] _vt_ (_cotejar_) to collate, compare; (_JUR_) to make an

attested copy of.

compulsivo, a [kompōōlsē'‌ho, á] _a_ compulsive.

compuse [compōō'se] _etc vb V_ **componer**.

computador [kompōōtá‌θor'] _nm_, **computadora** [kompōōtá‌θo'rá] _nf_ computer; ~ **central** mainframe computer; **computador especializado** dedicated computer; ~ **personal** personal computer.

computar [kompōōtár'] _vt_ to calculate, compute.

cómputo [kom'pōōto] _nm_ calculation, computation.

comulgar [komōōlgár'] _vi_ to receive communion.

comulgue [komōōl'ge] _etc vb V_ **comulgar**.

común [komōōn'] _a_ (_gen_) common; (_corriente_) ordinary; **por lo** ~ generally ♦ _nm_: **el** ~ the community.

comuna [komōō'ná] _nf_ commune; (_AM_) district.

comunicación [komōōnēkásyon'] _nf_ communication; (_informe_) report.

comunicado [komōōnēká'‌ho] _nm_ announcement; ~ **de prensa** press release.

comunicar [komōōnēkár'] _vt_ to communicate; (_ARQ_) to connect ♦ _vi_ to communicate; to send a report; ~**se** _vr_ to communicate; **está comunicando** (_TELEC_) the line's busy.

comunicativo, a [komōōnēkátē'‌ho, á] _a_ communicative.

comunidad [komōōnē‌θá‌θ'] _nf_ community; ~ **de vecinos** residents' association; **C~ Económica Europea (CEE)** European Economic Community (EEC).

comunión [komōōnyon'] _nf_ communion.

comunique [komōōnē'ke] _etc vb V_ **comunicar**.

comunismo [komōōnēs'mo] _nm_ communism.

comunista [komōōnē'stá] _a, nm/f_ communist.

con [kon] _prep_ with; (_a pesar de_) in spite of; (_hacia: tb_: **para** ~) towards; ~ **arreglo a** in accordance with; ~ **que** so, and so; ~ **tal que** so long as; ~ **apretar el botón** by pressing the button; ~ **todo, él la quiere mucho** in spite of it all, he loves her dearly.

conato [koná'to] _nm_ attempt; ~ **de robo** attempted robbery.

cóncavo, a [kon'ká‌ho, á] _a_ concave.

concebir [konsebēr'] _vt_ to conceive; (_imaginar_) to imagine ♦ _vi_ to conceive.

conceder [konseθer'] _vt_ to concede.

concejal, a [konsehál', á] _nm/f_ town councilman (_US_) o councillor (_Brit_).

concejo [konse'ho] _nm_ council.

concentración [konsentrásyon'] _nf_ concentration.

concentrar [konsentràr'] *vt*, ~**se** *vr* to concentrate.

concepción [konsepsyon'] *nf* conception.

concepto [konsep'to] *nm* concept; **por ~ de** as, by way of; **tener buen ~ de uno** to think highly of sb; **bajo ningún ~** under no circumstances.

conceptuar [konseptwàr'] *vt* to judge.

concernir [konsernēr'] *vi*: **en lo que concierne a** concerning.

concertar [konsertàr'] *vt* (MUS) to harmonize; (*acordar: precio*) to agree; (: *tratado*) to conclude; (*trato*) to arrange, fix up; (*combinar: esfuerzos*) to coordinate; (*reconciliar: personas*) to reconcile ♦ *vi* to harmonize, be in tune.

concesión [konsesyon'] *nf* concession; (COM: *fabricación*) license (US), licence (*Brit*).

concesionario, a [konsesyonà'ryo, à] *nm/f* (COM) (licensed) dealer, agent, concessionaire; (: *de venta*) franchisee; (: *de transportes etc*) contractor.

conciencia [konsyen'syà] *nf* (*moral*) conscience; (*conocimiento*) awareness; **libertad de ~** freedom of worship; **tener/tomar ~ de** to be/become aware of; **tener la ~ limpia** *o* **tranquila** to have a clear conscience; **tener plena ~ de** to be fully aware of.

concienciar [konsyensyàr'] *vt* to make aware; ~**se** *vr* to become aware.

concienzudo, a [konsyensōō'tho, à] *a* conscientious.

concierne [konsyer'ne] *etc vb V* **concernir**.

concierto [konsyer'to] *etc vb V* **concertar** ♦ *nm* concert; (*obra*) concerto.

conciliación [konsēlyàsyon'] *nf* conciliation.

conciliar [konsēlyàr'] *vt* to reconcile ♦ *a* (REL) of a council; ~ **el sueño** to get to sleep.

concilio [konsē'lyo] *nm* council.

concisión [konsēsyon'] *nf* conciseness.

conciso, a [konsē'so, à] *a* concise.

conciudadano, a [konsyōōthàthà'no, à] *nm/f* fellow citizen.

concluir [konklōōēr'] *vt* (*acabar*) to conclude; (*inferir*) to infer, deduce ♦ *vi*, ~**se** *vr* to conclude; **todo ha concluido** it's all over.

conclusión [konklōōsyon'] *nf* conclusion; **llegar a la ~ de que** ... to come to the conclusion that ....

concluya [konklōō'yà] *etc vb V* **concluir**.

concluyente [konklōōyen'te] *a* (*prueba, información*) conclusive.

concordancia [konkorthàn'syà] *nf* agreement.

concordar [konkorthàr'] *vt* to reconcile ♦ *vi* to agree, tally.

concordia [konkor'thyà] *nf* harmony.

concretamente [konkretàmen'te] *ad* specifically, to be exact.

concretar [konkretàr'] *vt* to make concrete, make more specific; (*problema*) to pinpoint; ~**se** *vr* to become more definite.

concreto, a [konkre'to, à] *a*, *nm* (AM) concrete; **en ~** (*en resumen*) to sum up; (*específicamente*) specifically; **no hay nada en ~** there's nothing definite.

concubina [konkōōbē'nà] *nf* concubine.

concuerde [konkwer'the] *etc vb V* **concordar**.

concupiscencia [konkōōpēsen'syà] *nf* (*avancia*) greed; (*lujuria*) lustfulness.

concurrencia [konkōōrren'syà] *nf* turnout.

concurrido, a [konkōōrrē'tho, à] *a* (*calle*) busy; (*local, reunión*) crowded.

concurrir [konkōōrrēr'] *vi* (*juntarse: ríos*) to meet, come together; (: *personas*) to gather, meet.

concursante [konkōōrsàn'te] *nm* competitor.

concursar [konkōōrsàr'] *vi* to compete.

concurso [konkōōr'so] *nm* (*de público*) crowd; (ESCOL, DEPORTE, *competencia*) competition; (COM) invitation to tender; (*examen*) open competition; (*TV etc*) quiz; (*ayuda*) help, cooperation.

concha [kontch'à] *nf* shell.

condado [kondà'tho] *nm* county.

condal [kondàl'] *a*: **la ciudad ~** Barcelona.

conde [kon'de] *nm* count.

condecoración [kondekoràsyon'] *nf* (MIL) medal, decoration.

condecorar [kondekoràr'] *vt* to decorate.

condena [konde'nà] *nf* sentence; **cumplir una ~** to serve a sentence.

condenación [kondenàsyon'] *nf* condemnation; (REL) damnation.

condenado, a [kondenà'tho, à] *a* (JUR) condemned; (*fam: maldito*) damned ♦ *nm/f* (JUR) convicted person.

condenar [kondenàr'] *vt* to condemn; (JUR) to convict; ~**se** *vr* (JUR) to confess (one's guilt); (REL) to be damned.

condensar [kondensàr'] *vt* to condense.

condesa [konde'sà] *nf* countess.

condescendencia [kondesenden'syà] *nf* condescension; **aceptar algo por ~** to accept sth so as not to hurt feelings.

condescender [kondesender'] *vi* to acquiesce, comply.

condescienda [kondesyen'dà] *etc vb V* **condescender**.

condición [kondēsyon'] *nf* (*gen*) condition; (*rango*) social class; **condiciones** *nfpl* (*cualidades*) qualities; (*estado*) condition; **a ~ de que** ... on condition that ...; **las condiciones del contrato** the terms of the contract; **condiciones de trabajo** working conditions; **condiciones de venta** conditions of sale.

condicionamiento [kondēsyonamyen'to] *nm* conditioning.

condicional [kondēsyonál'] *a* conditional.

condicionar [kondēsyonár'] *vt* (*acondicionar*) to condition; ~ **algo a algo** to make sth conditional *o* dependent on sth.

condimento [kondēmen'to] *nm* seasoning.

condiscípulo, a [kondēsē'pōolo, á] *nm/f* fellow student.

condolerse [kondoler'se] *vr* to sympathize.

condominio [kondomē'nyo] *nm* (*COM*) joint ownership.

condón [kondon'] *nm* condom.

condonar [kondonár'] *vt* (*JUR: reo*) to reprieve; (*COM: deuda*) to cancel.

conducente [kondōōsen'te] *a:* ~ **a** conducive to, leading to.

conducir [kondōōsēr'] *vt* to take, convey; (*ELEC etc*) to carry; (*AUTO*) to drive; (*negocio*) to manage ♦ *vi* to drive; (*fig*) to lead; ~**se** *vr* to behave.

conducta [kondōōk'tá] *nf* conduct, behavior (*US*), behaviour (*Brit*).

conducto [kondōōk'to] *nm* pipe, tube; (*fig*) channel; (*ELEC*) lead; **por** ~ **de** through.

conductor, a [kondōōktor', á] *a* leading, guiding ♦ *nm* (*FISICA*) conductor; (*de vehículo*) driver.

conduela [kondwe'lá] *etc vb V* **condolerse**.

conduje [kondōō'he] *etc vb V* **conducir**.

conduzca [kondōōs'ká] *etc vb V* **conducir**.

conectado, a [konektá'ðo, á] *a* (*ELEC*) connected, plugged in; (*INFORM*) on-line.

conectar [konektár'] *vt* to connect (up), plug in; (*INFORM*) to toggle on; ~**se** *vr* (*INFORM*) to log in (on).

conejillo [konehē'yo] *nm:* ~ **de Indias** guinea pig.

conejo [kone'ho] *nm* rabbit.

conexión [koneksyon'] *nf* connection; (*INFORM*) logging in (on).

confabularse [konfáßōōlár'se] *vr:* ~ **(para hacer algo)** to plot, conspire (to do sth).

confección [konfeksyon'] *nf* (*preparación*) preparation, making-up; (*industria*) clothing industry; (*producto*) article; **de** ~ (*ropa*) off-the-rack (*US*) *o* peg (*Brit*).

confeccionar [konfe(k)syonár'] *vt* to make (up).

confederación [konfeðeyrásyon'] *nf* confederation.

conferencia [konferen'syá] *nf* conference; (*lección*) lecture; (*TELEC*) call; ~ **de cobro revertido** (*TELEC*) collect (*US*) *o* reversed-charge (*Brit*) call; ~ **cumbre** summit (conference).

conferenciante [konferensyán'te] *nm/f* lecturer.

conferir [konferēr'] *vt* to award.

confesar [konfesár'] *vt* (*admitir*) to confess,

admit; (*error*) to acknowledge; (*crimen*) to own up to.

confesión [konfesyon'] *nf* confession.

confesionario [konfesyoná'ryo] *nm* confessional.

confeso, a [konfe'so, á] *a* (*JUR etc*) self-confessed.

confeti [konfe'tē] *nm* confetti.

confiado, a [konfyá'ðo, á] *a* (*crédulo*) trusting; (*seguro*) confident; (*presumido*) conceited, vain.

confianza [konfyán'sá] *nf* trust; (*aliento, confidencia*) confidence; (*familiaridad*) intimacy, familiarity; (*pey*) vanity, conceit; **margen de** ~ credibility gap; **tener** ~ **con uno** to be on close terms with sb.

confiar [konfyár'] *vt* to entrust ♦ *vi* (*fiarse*) to trust; (*contar con*) to rely; ~**se** *vr* to put one's trust.

confidencia [konfēðen'syá] *nf* confidence.

confidencial [konfēðensyál'] *a* confidential.

confidente [konfēðen'te] *nm/f* confidant/e; (*policial*) informer.

confiera [konfye'rá] *etc vb V* **conferir**.

confiese [konfye'se] *etc vb V* **confesar**.

configuración [konfēgōōrásyon'] *nf* (*tb INFORM*) configuration; **la** ~ **del terreno** the lie of the land; ~ **de bits** (*INFORM*) bit pattern.

configurar [konfēgōōrár'] *vt* to shape, form.

confín [konfēn'] *nm* limit; **confines** *nmpl* confines, limits.

confinar [konfēnár'] *vi* to confine; (*desterrar*) to banish.

confiriendo [konfēryen'do] *etc vb V* **conferir**.

confirmar [konfērmár'] *vt* to confirm; (*JUR etc*) to corroborate; **la excepción confirma la regla** the exception proves the rule.

confiscar [konfēskár'] *vt* to confiscate.

confisque [konfēs'ke] *etc vb V* **confiscar**.

confitado, a [konfētá'ðo, á] *a:* **fruta confitada** candied (*US*) *o* crystallised (*Brit*) fruit.

confite [konfē'te] *nm* candy (*US*), sweet (*Brit*).

confitería [konfētere'á] *nf* confectionery; (*tienda*) candy store (*US*), confectioner's (shop) (*Brit*).

confitura [konfētōō'rá] *nf* jam.

conflagración [konfláγrásyon'] *nf* conflagration.

conflictivo, a [konflēktē'ßo, á] *a* (*asunto, propuesta*) controversial; (*país, situación*) troubled.

conflicto [konflēk'to] *nm* conflict; (*fig*) clash; (: *dificultad*): **estar en un** ~ to be in a jam; ~ **laboral** labor dispute.

confluir [konflōōēr'] *vi* (*ríos etc*) to meet; (*gente*) to gather.

confluya [konflōō'yá] *etc vb V* **confluir**.

conformar [konformár'] *vt* to shape, fashion ♦ *vi* to agree; **~se** *vr* to conform; (*resignarse*) to resign o.s.
conforme [konfor'me] *a* alike, similar; (*de acuerdo*) agreed, in agreement; (*satisfecho*) satisfied ♦ *ad* as ♦ *excl* agreed! ♦ *nm* agreement ♦ *prep*: ~ **a** in accordance with.
conformidad [konformēt̬hát̬h'] *nf* (*semejanza*) similarity; (*acuerdo*) agreement; (*resignación*) resignation; **de/en** ~ **con** in accordance with; **dar su** ~ to consent.
conformismo [konformēs'mo] *nm* conformism.
conformista [konformē'stá] *nm/f* conformist.
confortable [konfortá'ble] *a* comfortable.
confortar [konfortár'] *vt* to comfort.
confraternidad [konfráternēt̬hát̬h'] *nf* brotherhood; **espíritu de** ~ feeling of unity.
confrontación [konfrontásyon'] *nf* confrontation.
confrontar [konfrontár'] *vt* to confront; (*dos personas*) to bring face to face; (*cotejar*) to compare ♦ *vi* to border.
confundir [konfōōndēr'] *vt* (*borrar*) to blur; (*equivocar*) to mistake, confuse; (*mezclar*) to mix; (*turbar*) to confuse; **~se** *vr* (*hacerse borroso*) to become blurred; (*turbarse*) to get confused; (*equivocarse*) to make a mistake; (*mezclarse*) to mix.
confusión [konfōōsyon'] *nf* confusion.
confusionismo [konfōōsyonēs'mo] *nm* confusion, uncertainty.
confuso, a [konfōō'so, á] *a* (*gen*) confused; (*recuerdo*) hazy; (*estilo*) obscure.
congelación [konhelásyon'] *nf* freezing; ~ **de créditos** credit freeze.
congelado, a [konhelá't̬ho, á] *a* frozen ♦ *nmpl*: **~s** frozen food(s) (*sg*).
congelador [konhelát̬hor'], **congeladora** [konhelát̬ho'rá] *nf* (*aparato*) freezer, deep freeze.
congelar [konhelár'] *vt* to freeze; **~se** *vr* (*sangre, grasa*) to congeal.
congeniar [konhenyár'] *vi* to get along (well).
congénito, a [konhe'neto, á] *a* congenital.
congestión [konhestyon'] *nf* congestion.
congestionado, a [konhestyoná't̬ho, á] *a* congested.
congestionar [konhestyonár'] *vt* to congest; **~se** *vr* to become congested; **se le congestionó la cara** his face became flushed.
conglomeración [konglomerásyon'] *nf* conglomeration.
conglomerado [konglomerá't̬ho] *nm* conglomerate.
Congo [kon'go] *nm*: **el** ~ the Congo.
congoja [kongo'há] *nf* distress, grief.

congraciarse [kongrásyár'se] *vr* to ingratiate o.s.
congratular [kongrátōōlár'] *vt* to congratulate.
congregación [kongreg̬ásyon'] *nf* congregation.
congregar [kongreg̬ár'] *vt*, **~se** *vr* to gather together.
congregue [kongre'g̬e] *etc vb* V **congregar**.
congresista [kongresē'stá] *nm/f* delegate, congressman/woman.
congreso [kongre'so] *nm* congress; **C~ de los Diputados** (*Esp POL*) ≈ House of Representatives (*US*), House of Commons (*Brit*).
congrio [kong'ryo] *nm* conger (eel).
congruente [kongrwen'te], **congruo, a** [kong'rwo, á] *a* congruent, congruous.
conjetura [konhetōō'rá] *nf* guess; (*COM*) guesstimate.
conjeturar [konhetōōrár'] *vt* to guess.
conjugar [konhōōg̬ár'] *vt* to combine, fit together; (*LING*) to conjugate.
conjugue [konhōō'g̬e] *etc vb* V **conjugar**.
conjunción [konhōōnsyon'] *nf* conjunction.
conjunto, a [konhōōn'to, á] *a* joint, united ♦ *nm* whole; (*MUS*) band; (*vestido*) ensemble; (*INFORM*) set; **en** ~ as a whole; ~ **integrado de programas** (*INFORM*) integrated software package.
conjura [konhōō'rá] *nf* plot, conspiracy.
conjurar [konhōōrár'] *vt* (*REL*) to exorcise; (*peligro*) to ward off ♦ *vi* to plot.
conjuro [konhōō'ro] *nm* spell.
conllevar [konyehár'] *vt* to bear; (*implicar*) to imply, involve.
conmemoración [konmemorásyon'] *nf* commemoration.
conmemorar [konmemorár'] *vt* to commemorate.
conmigo [konmē'g̬o] *pron* with me.
conminar [konmēnár'] *vt* to threaten.
conmiseración [konmēsérásyon'] *nf* pity, commiseration.
conmoción [konmosyon'] *nf* shock; (*POL*) disturbance; (*fig*) upheaval; ~ **cerebral** (*MED*) concussion.
conmovedor, a [konmohet̬hor', á] *a* touching, moving; (*emocionante*) exciting.
conmover [konmoher'] *vt* to shake, disturb; (*fig*) to move; **~se** *vr* (*fig*) to be moved.
conmueva [konmwe'há] *etc vb* V **conmover**.
conmutación [konmōōtásyon'] *nf* (*INFORM*) switching; ~ **de mensajes** message switching; ~ **por paquetes** packet switching.
conmutador [konmōōtát̬hor'] *nm* switch; (*AM TELEC*) switchboard.
conmutar [konmōōtár'] *vt* (*JUR*) to commute.
connivencia [konnēhen'syá] *nf*: **estar en** ~

con to be in collusion with.
cono [ko'no] *nm* cone.
conocedor, a [konoseθor', ə] *a* expert, knowledgeable ♦ *nm/f* expert, connoisseur.
conocer [konoser'] *vt* to know; (*por primera vez*) to meet, get to know; (*entender*) to know about; (*reconocer*) to recognize; ~**se** *vr* (*una persona*) to know o.s.; (*dos personas*) to (get to) know each other; **darse a ~** (*presentarse*) to make o.s. known; **se conoce que ...** (*parece*) apparently ....
conocido, a [konoθe'iθo, ə] *a* (well-)known ♦ *nm/f* acquaintance.
conocimiento [konoseθmyen'to] *nm* knowledge; (*MED*) consciousness; (*NAUT*: *tb*: ~ **de embarque**) bill of lading; ~**s** *nmpl* (*personas*) acquaintances; (*saber*) knowledge *sg*; **hablar con ~ de causa** to speak from experience; ~ **(de embarque) aéreo** (*COM*) air waybill.
conotación [konotàsyon'] *nf* connotation.
conozca [konos'kà] *etc vb* V **conocer**.
conque [kon'ke] *conj* and so, so then.
conquense [konken'se] *a* of *o* from Cuenca ♦ *nm/f* native *o* inhabitant of Cuenca.
conquista [konke'stà] *nf* conquest.
conquistador, a [konkestàθor', ə] *a* conquering ♦ *nm* conqueror.
conquistar [konkestàr'] *vt* (*MIL*) to conquer; (*puesto, simpatía*) to win; (*enamorar*) to win the heart of.
consabido, a [konsàɓe'iθo, ə] *a* (*frase etc*) old; (*pey*): **las consabidas excusas** the same old excuses.
consagrado, a [konsàgrà'iθo, ə] *a* (*REL*) consecrated; (*actor*) established.
consagrar [konsàgràr'] *vt* (*REL*) to consecrate; (*fig*) to devote.
consciente [konsyen'te] *a* conscious; **ser** *o* **estar ~ de** to be aware of.
consecución [konsekoōsyon'] *nf* acquisition; (*de fin*) attainment.
consecuencia [konsekwen'syà] *nf* consequence, outcome; (*firmeza*) consistency; **de ~ of** importance.
consecuente [konsekwen'te] *a* consistent.
consecutivo, a [konsekoōte'ho, ə] *a* consecutive.
conseguir [konsegēr'] *vt* to get, obtain; (*sus fines*) to attain.
consejero, a [konseche'ro, ə] *nm/f* adviser, consultant; (*POL*) councilor (*US*), councillor (*Brit*); (*COM*) director; (*en comisión*) member.
consejo [konse'ho] *nm* advice; (*POL*) council; (*COM*) board; **un ~ a** piece of advice; **~ de administración** board of directors; **~ de guerra** court-martial; **C~ de Europa** Council of Europe.
consenso [konsen'so] *nm* consensus.
consentido, a [konsente'iθo, ə] *a* (*mimado*)

spoiled.
consentimiento [konsentēmyen'to] *nm* consent.
consentir [konsentēr'] *vt* (*permitir, tolerar*) to consent to; (*mimar*) to pamper, spoil ♦ *vi* to agree, consent; ~ **que uno haga algo** to allow sb to do sth.
conserje [konser'he] *nm* caretaker; (*portero*) porter.
conservación [konserɓàsyon'] *nf* conservation; (*de alimentos, vida*) preservation.
conservador, a [konserɓàθor', ə] *a* (*POL*) conservative ♦ *nm/f* conservative.
conservadurismo [konserɓàθoōres'mo] *nm* (*POL etc*) conservatism.
conservante [konserɓàn'te] *nm* preservative.
conservar [konserɓàr'] *vt* (*gen*) to preserve; (*recursos*) to conserve, keep; (*alimentos, vida*) to preserve; ~**se** *vr* to survive.
conservas [konserɓàs] *nfpl*: ~ **(alimenticias)** canned (*US*) *o* tinned (*Brit*) goods.
conservatorio [konserɓàto'ryo] *nm* (*MUS*) conservatory; (*AM*) greenhouse.
considerable [konseθerà'ɓle] *a* considerable.
consideración [konseθeràsyon'] *nf* consideration; (*estimación*) respect; **de ~** important; **tomar en ~** to take into account.
considerado, a [konseθerà'iθo, ə] *a* (*atento*) considerate; (*respetado*) respected.
considerar [konseθeràr'] *vt* (*gen*) to consider; (*meditar*) to think about; (*tener en cuenta*) to take into account.
consienta [konsyen'tà] *etc vb* V **consentir**.
consigna [konse'g'nà] *nf* (*orden*) order, instruction; (*para equipajes*) luggage checkroom (*US*), left-luggage office (*Brit*).
consignación [konseg'nàsyon'] *nf* consignment; ~ **de créditos** allocation of credits.
consignador [konseg'nàθor'] *nm* (*COM*) consignor.
consignar [konseg'nàr'] *vt* (*COM*) to send; (*créditos*) to allocate.
consignatario, a [konseg'nàtà'ryo, ə] *nm/f* (*COM*) consignee.
consigo [konse'go] *etc vb* V **conseguir** ♦ *pron* (*m*) with him; (*f*) with her; (*usted*) with you; (*reflexivo*) with o.s.
consiguiendo [konseg'yen'do] *etc vb* V **conseguir**.
consiguiente [konseg'yen'te] *a* consequent; **por ~** and so, therefore, consequently.
consintiendo [konsentyen'do] *etc vb* V **consentir**.
consistente [konsesten'te] *a* consistent; (*sólido*) solid, firm; (*válido*) sound; ~ **en** consisting of.
consistir [konsestēr'] *vi*: ~ **en** (*componerse*

de) to consist of; (*ser resultado de*) to be due to.

consola [konso'lá] *nf* console, control panel; (*mueble*) console table; ~ **de mando** (*INFORM*) control console; ~ **de visualización** visual display console.

consolación [konsolásyon'] *nf* consolation.

consolar [konsolár'] *vt* to console.

consolidar [konsolēthár'] *vt* to consolidate.

consomé, *pl* **consomés** *nm* [konsome', konsomes'] consommé, clear soup.

consonancia [konsonán'syá] *nf* harmony; **en** ~ **con** in accordance with.

consonante [konsonán'te] *a* consonant, harmonious ♦ *nf* consonant.

consorcio [konsor'syo] *nm* (*COM*) consortium, syndicate.

consorte [konsor'te] *nm/f* consort.

conspicuo, a [konspē'kwo, á] *a* conspicuous.

conspiración [konspērásyon'] *nf* conspiracy.

conspirador, a [konspēráthor', á] *nm/f* conspirator.

conspirar [konspērár'] *vi* to conspire.

constancia [konstán'syá] *nf* (*gen*) constancy; (*certeza*) certainly; **dejar** ~ **de algo** to put sth on record.

constante [konstán'te] *a, nf* constant.

constar [konstár'] *vi* (*evidenciarse*) to be clear *o* evident; ~ **(en)** to appear (in); ~ **de** to consist of; **hacer** ~ to put on record; **me consta que** ... I have evidence that ...; **que conste que lo hice por ti** believe me, I did it for your own good.

constatar [konstátár'] *vt* (*controlar*) to check; (*observar*) to note.

constelación [konstelásyon'] *nf* constellation.

consternación [konsternásyon'] *nf* consternation.

constipado, a [konstēpá'tho, á] *a*: **estar** ~ to have a cold ♦ *nm* cold.

constitución [konstētōōsyon'] *nf* constitution.

constitucional [konstētōōsyonál'] *a* constitutional.

constituir [konstētōōēr'] *vt* (*formar, componer*) to constitute, make up; (*fundar, erigir, ordenar*) to constitute, establish; (*ser*) to be; ~**se** *vr* (*POL etc*: *cuerpo*) to be composed; (: *fundarse*) to be established.

constitutivo, a [konstētōōtē'ho, á] *a* constitutive, constituent.

constituya [konstētōō'yá] *etc vb V* **constituir.**

constituyente [konstētōōyen'te] *a* constituent.

constreñir [konstrenyēr'] *vt* (*obligar*) to compel, oblige; (*restringir*) to restrict.

constriño [konstrē'nyo] *etc*, **constriñendo**

[konstrēnyen'do] *etc vb V* **constreñir.**

construcción [konstrōōksyon'] *nf* construction, building.

constructor, a [konstrōōktor', á] *nm/f* builder.

construir [konstrōōēr'] *vt* to build, construct.

construyendo [konstrōōyen'do] *etc vb V* **construir.**

consuelo [konswe'lo] *etc vb V* **consolar** ♦ *nm* consolation, solace.

consuetudinario, a [konswetōōthēná'ryo, á] *a* customary; **derecho** ~ common law.

cónsul [kon'sōōl] *nm* consul.

consulado [konsōōlá'tho] *nm* (*sede*) consulate; (*cargo*) consulship.

consulta [konsōōl'tá] *nf* consultation; (*MED*: *consultorio*) consulting room; (*INFORM*) enquiry; **horas de** ~ office (*US*) *o* surgery (*Brit*) hours; **obra de** ~ reference book.

consultar [konsōōltár'] *vt* to consult; ~ **un archivo** (*INFORM*) to search a file.

consultor, a [konsōōltor', á] *nm*: ~ **en dirección de empresas** management consultant.

consultorio [konsōōlto'ryo] *nm* (*MED*) doctor's office (*US*), surgery (*Brit*).

consumado, a [konsōōmá'tho, á] *a* perfect; (*bribón*) out-and-out.

consumar [konsōōmár'] *vt* to complete, carry out; (*crimen*) to commit; (*sentencia*) to carry out.

consumición [konsōōmēsyon'] *nf* consumption; (*bebida*) drink; (*comida*) food; ~ **mínima** cover charge.

consumido, a [konsōōmē'tho, á] *a* (*flaco*) skinny.

consumidor, a [konsōōmēthor', á] *nm/f* consumer.

consumir [konsōōmēr'] *vt* to consume; ~**se** *vr* to be consumed; (*persona*) to waste away.

consumismo [konsōōmēs'mo] *nm* (*COM*) consumerism.

consumo [konsōō'mo] *nm* consumption; **bienes de** ~ consumer goods.

contabilice [kontáthēlē'se] *etc vb V* **contabilizar.**

contabilidad [kontáthēlētháth'] *nf* accounting, book-keeping; (*profesión*) accountancy; (*COM*): ~ **analítica** variable pricing (*US*) *o* costing (*Brit*); ~ **de costos** cost accounting; ~ **de doble partida** double-entry book-keeping; ~ **de gestión** management accounting; ~ **por partida simple** single-entry book-keeping.

contabilizar [kontáthēlē'sár] *vt* to enter in the accounts.

contable [kontá'hle] *nm/f* bookkeeper; (*licenciado*) accountant; ~ **de costos** (*COM*) cost accountant.

contacto [konták'to] *nm* contact; **lentes de** ~ contact lenses; **estar en** ~ **con** to be in touch with.

contado, a [kontá'ðo, á] *a*: ~**s** (*escasos*) numbered, scarce, few ♦ *nm*: **al** ~ for cash; **pagar al** ~ to pay (in) cash; **precio al** ~ cash price.

contador [kontaðor'] *nm* (*aparato*) meter; (*AM*: *contable*) accountant.

contaduría [kontaðoorē'á] *nf* accountant's office.

contagiar [kontahyár'] *vt* (*enfermedad*) to pass on, transmit; (*persona*) to infect; ~**se** *vr* to become infected.

contagio [kontá'hyo] *nm* infection.

contagioso, a [kontáhyo'so, á] *a* infectious; (*fig*) catching.

contaminación [kontámēnásyon'] *nf* (*gen*) contamination; (*del ambiente etc*) pollution.

contaminar [kontámēnár'] *vt* (*gen*) to contaminate; (*aire, agua*) to pollute; (*fig*) to taint.

contante [kontán'te] *a*: **dinero** ~ (**y sonante**) hard cash.

contar [kontár'] *vt* (*páginas, dinero*) to count; (*anécdota etc*) to tell ♦ *vi* to count; ~**se** *vr* to be counted, figure; ~ **con** to rely on, count on; **sin** ~ not to mention; **le cuento entre mis amigos** I count him among my friends.

contemplación [kontemplásyon'] *nf* contemplation; **no andarse con contemplaciones** not to stand on ceremony.

contemplar [kontemplár'] *vt* to contemplate; (*mirar*) to look at.

contemporáneo, a [kontemporá'neo, á] *a, nm/f* contemporary.

contemporizar [kontemporēsár'] *vi*: ~ **con** to keep in with.

contención [kontensyon'] *nf* (*JUR*) suit; **muro de** ~ retaining wall.

contencioso, a [kontensyo'so, á] *a* (*JUR etc*) contentious ♦ *nm* (*POL*) conflict, dispute.

contender [kontender'] *vi* to contend; (*en un concurso*) to compete.

contendiente [kontendyen'te] *nm/f* contestant.

contendrá [kontendrá'] *etc vb* V **contener**.

contenedor [konteneðor'] *nm* container.

contenedorización [konteneðoresásyon'] *nf* (*COM*) containerization.

contener [kontener'] *vt* to contain, hold; (*risa etc*) to hold back, contain; ~**se** *vr* to control o restrain o.s.

contenga [konten'gá] *etc vb* V **contener**.

contenido, a [kontenē'ðo, á] *a* (*moderado*) restrained; (*risa etc*) suppressed ♦ *nm* contents *pl*, content.

contentar [kontentár'] *vt* (*satisfacer*) to sat-

isfy; (*complacer*) to please; (*COM*) to endorse; ~**se** *vr* to be satisfied.

contento, a [konten'to, á] *a* contented, content; (*alegre*) pleased; (*feliz*) happy.

contestación [kontestásyon'] *nf* answer, reply; ~ **a la demanda** (*JUR*) defense plea.

contestador [kontestáðor'] *nm*: ~ **automático** answering machine.

contestar [kontestár'] *vt* to answer (back), reply; (*JUR*) to corroborate, confirm.

contexto [kontek'sto] *nm* context.

contienda [kontyen'dá] *nf* contest, struggle.

contiene [kontye'ne] *etc vb* V **contener**.

contigo [kontē'go] *pron* with you.

contiguo, a [kontē'gwo, á] *a* (*de al lado*) next; (*vecino*) adjacent, adjoining.

continente [kontēnen'te] *a, nm* continent.

contingencia [kontēnhen'syá] *nf* contingency; (*riesgo*) risk; (*posibilidad*) eventuality.

contingente [kontēnhen'te] *a* contingent ♦ *nm* contingent; (*COM*) quota.

continuación [kontēnwásyon'] *nf* continuation; **a** ~ then, next.

continuar [kontēnwár'] *vt* to continue, go on with; (*reanudar*) to resume ♦ *vi* to continue, go on; ~ **hablando** to continue talking o to talk.

continuidad [kontēnwēðáð'] *nf* continuity.

continuo, a [kontē'nwo, á] *a* (*sin interrupción*) continuous; (*acción perseverante*) continual.

contonearse [kontoneár'se] *vr* (*hombre*) to swagger; (*mujer*) to swing her hips.

contorno [kontor'no] *nm* outline; (*GEO*) contour; ~**s** *nmpl* neighborhood *sg*, surrounding area *sg*.

contorsión [kontorsyon'] *nf* contortion.

contra [kon'trá] *prep* against; (*COM: giro*) on ♦ *ad* against ♦ *a, nm/f* (*POL fam*) counter-revolutionary ♦ *nm con* ♦ *nf*: **la C**~ (**nicaragüense**) the Contras *pl*.

contraalmirante [kontráálmērán'te] *nm* rear admiral.

contraataque [kontráátá'ke] *nm* counterattack.

contrabajo [kontrábá'ho] *nm* double bass.

contrabandista [kontrábánde'stá] *nm/f* smuggler.

contrabando [kontrábán'do] *nm* (*acción*) smuggling; (*mercancías*) contraband; ~ **de armas** gun-running.

contracción [kontráksyon'] *nf* contraction.

contracorriente [kontrákorryen'te] *nf* cross-current.

contrachapado [kontrátchápá'ðo] *nm* plywood.

contradecir [kontráðesēr'] *vt* to contradict.

contradicción [kontráðēksyon'] *nf* contradiction; **espíritu de** ~ contrariness.

contradiciendo [kontráðēsyen'do] *etc vb*

V **contradecir.**

contradictorio, a [kontráthēkto'ryo, à] *a* contradictory.

contradicho [kontráthētch'o] *pp de* **contradecir.**

contradiga [kontráthē'gà] *etc,* **contradije** [kontráthē'he], **contradirá** [kontráthērà'] *etc vb V* **contradecir.**

contraer [kontráer'] *vt* to contract; (*hábito*) to acquire; (*limitar*) to restrict; **~se** *vr* to contract; (*limitarse*) to limit o.s.

contragolpe [kontrágol'pe] *nm* backlash.

contrahaga [kontráà'gà] *etc,* **contraharé** [kontráàre'] *etc vb V* **contrahacer.**

contrahecho, a [kontráetch'o, à] *pp de* **contrahacer** ♦ *a* fake; (*ANAT*) hunchbacked.

contrahice [kontráē'se] *etc vb V* **contrahacer.**

contraiga [kontrá'ēgà] *etc vb V* **contraer.**

contraindicaciones [kontráēndēkàsyo'nes] *nfpl* (*MED*) contraindications.

contraje [kontrá'he] *etc vb V* **contraer.**

contraluz [kontrálōōs'] *nf* (*FOTO etc*) back lighting; **a ~** against the light.

contramaestre [kontrámáes'tre] *nm* foreman.

contraorden [kontráor'then] *nf* counterorder, countermand.

contrápartida [kontrápártē'thá] *nf* (*COM*) balancing entry; **como ~ (de)** in return (for), as *o* in compensation (for).

contrapelo [kontrápe'lo]: **a ~** *ad* the wrong way.

contrapesar [kontrápesàr'] *vt* to counterbalance; (*fig*) to offset.

contrapeso [kontrápe'so] *nm* counterweight; (*fig*) counterbalance; (*COM*) makeweight.

contrapondré [kontrápondre'] *etc vb V* **contraponer.**

contraponer [kontráponer'] *vt* (*cotejar*) to compare; (*oponer*) to oppose.

contraponga [kontrápon'gà] *etc vb V* **contraponer.**

contraproducente [kontráprothōōsen'te] *a* counterproductive.

contrapuesto [kontrápwe'sto] *pp de* **contraponer.**

contrapunto [kontrápōōn'to] *nm* counterpoint.

contrapuse [kontrápōō'se] *etc vb V* **contraponer.**

contrariar [kontráryàr'] *vt* (*oponerse*) to oppose; (*poner obstáculo*) to impede; (*enfadar*) to annoy.

contrariedad [kontráryethàth'] *nf* (*oposición*) opposition; (*obstáculo*) obstacle, setback; (*disgusto*) vexation, annoyance.

contrario, a [kontrá'ryo, à] *a* contrary; (*persona*) opposed; (*sentido, lado*) opposite

♦ *nm/f* enemy, adversary; (*DEPORTE*) opponent; **al ~, por el ~** on the contrary; **de lo ~** otherwise.

Contrarreforma [kontrárrefor'má] *nf* Counter-Reformation.

contrarrestar [kontrárrestár'] *vt* to counteract.

contrarrevolución [kontrárreholōōsyon'] *nf* counter-revolution.

contrasentido [kontrásentē'tho] *nm* contradiction; **es un ~ que él ...** it doesn't make sense for him to ... .

contraseña [kontráse'nyá] *nf* countersign; (*frase*) password.

contrastar [kontrástár'] *vt* to resist ♦ *vi* to contrast.

contraste [kontrá'ste] *nm* contrast.

contrata [kontrá'tá] *nf* (*JUR*) written contract; (*empleo*) hiring.

contratar [kontrátár'] *vt* (*firmar un acuerdo para*) to contract for; (*empleados, obreros*) to hire; (*DEPORTE*) to sign up; **~se** *vr* to sign on.

contratiempo [kontrátyem'po] *nm* (*revés*) setback; (*accidente*) mishap; **a ~** (*MUS*) off-beat.

contratista [kontrátē'stà] *nm/f* contractor.

contrato [kontrá'to] *nm* contract; **~ de compraventa** contract of sale; **~ a precio fijo** fixed-price contract; **~ a término** future (*US*) *o* forward (*Brit*) contract; **~ de trabajo** contract of employment *o* service.

contravalor [kontráhálor'] *nm* exchange value.

contravención [kontráhensyon'] *nf* contravention, violation.

contravendré [kontráhendre'] *etc,* **contravenga** [kontráhen'gà] *etc vb V* **contravenir.**

contravenir [kontráhenēr'] *vi*: **~ a** to contravene, violate.

contraventana [kontráhentá'ná] *nf* shutter.

contraviene [kontráhye'ne] *etc,* **contraviniendo** [kontráhēnyen'do] *etc vb V* **contravenir.**

contrayendo [kontráyen'do] *vb V* **contraer.**

contribución [kontrēhōōsyon'] *nf* (*municipal etc*) tax; (*ayuda*) contribution; **exento de contribuciones** tax-free.

contribuir [kontrēhōōēr'] *vt, vi* to contribute; (*COM*) to pay (in taxes).

contribuyendo [kontrēhōōyen'do] *etc vb V* **contribuir.**

contribuyente [kontrēhōōyen'te] *nm/f* (*COM*) taxpayer; (*que ayuda*) contributor.

contrincante [kontrēnkán'te] *nm* opponent, rival.

control [kontrol'] *nm* control; (*inspección*) inspection, check; (*COM*): **~ de calidad** quality control; **~ de cambios** exchange control; **~ de costos** cost control; **~ de créditos** credit control; **~ de existencias**

stock control; ~ **de precios** price control.
controlador, a |kontrolàthor', á| *nm/f* controller; ~ **aéreo** air-traffic controller.
controlar *vt* to control; to inspect, check; (*COM*) to audit.
controversia |kontroher'syá| *nf* controversy.
contubernio |kontōōher'nyo| *nm* ring, conspiracy.
contumaz |kontōōmás'| *a* obstinate, stubbornly disobedient.
contundente |kontōōnden'te| *a* (*prueba*) conclusive; (*fig: argumento*) convincing; **instrumento** ~ blunt instrument.
contusión |kontōōsyon'| *nf* bruise.
contuve |kontōō'he| *etc vb V* **contener.**
convalecencia |kombálesen'syá| *nf* convalescence.
convalecer |kombáleser'| *vi* to convalesce, get better.
convaleciente |kombálesyen'te| *a, nm/f* convalescent.
convalezca |kombáles'ká| *etc vb V* **convalecer.**
convalidar |kombálethár'| *vt* (*título*) to recognize.
convencer |kombenser'| *vt* to convince; (*persuadir*) to persuade.
convencimiento |kombensēmyen'to| *nm* (*acción*) convincing; (*persuasión*) persuasion; (*certidumbre*) conviction; **tener el ~ de que** ... to be convinced that ... .
convención |kombensyon'| *nf* convention.
convendré |kombendre'| *etc,* **convenga** |komben'gá| *etc vb V* **convenir.**
conveniencia |kombenyen'syá| *nf* suitability; (*conformidad*) agreement; (*utilidad, provecho*) usefulness; ~**s** *nfpl* conventions; (*COM*) property *sg*; **ser de la ~ de uno** to suit sb.
conveniente |kombenyen'te| *a* suitable; (*útil*) useful; (*correcto*) fit, proper; (*aconsejable*) advisable.
convenio |kombe'nyo| *nm* agreement, treaty; ~ **de nivel crítico** threshold agreement.
convenir |kombenēr'| *vi* (*estar de acuerdo*) to agree; (*ser conveniente*) to suit, be suitable; **"sueldo a ~"** "salary to be agreed"; **conviene recordar que...** it should be remembered that... .
convento |komben'to| *nm* monastery; (*de monjas*) convent.
convenza |komben'sá| *etc vb V* **convencer.**
convergencia |komberhen'syá| *nf* convergence.
converger |komberher'|, **convergir** |komber'hēr'| *vi* to converge; **sus esfuerzos convergen a un fin común** their efforts are directed towards the same objective.
converja |komber'há| *etc vb V* **converger, convergir.**

conversación |kombersásyon'| *nf* conversation.
conversar |kombersár'| *vi* to talk, converse.
conversión |kombersyon'| *nf* conversion.
converso, a |komber'so, á| *nm/f* convert.
convertir |kombertēr'| *vt* to convert; (*transformar*) to transform, turn; (*COM*) to (ex)change; ~**se** *vr* (*REL*) to convert.
convicción |kombēksyon'| *nf* conviction.
convicto, a |kombēk'to, á| *a* convicted; (*condenado*) condemned.
convidado, a |kombēthá'tho, á| *nm/f* guest.
convidar |kombēthár'| *vt* to invite.
conviene |kombye'ne| *etc vb V* **convenir.**
convierta |kombyer'tá| *etc vb V* **convertir.**
convincente |kombēnsen'te| *a* convincing.
conviniendo |kombēnyen'do| *etc vb V* **convenir.**
convirtiendo |kombērtyen'do| *etc vb V* **convertir.**
convite |kombē'te| *nm* invitation; (*banquete*) banquet.
convivencia |kombēhen'syá| *nf* coexistence, living together.
convivir |kombēhēr'| *vi* to live together; (*POL*) to coexist.
convocar |kombokár'| *vt* to summon, call (together).
convocatoria |kombokáto'ryá| *nf* summons *sg*; (*anuncio*) notice of meeting; (*ESCOL*) examination session.
convoque |kombo'ke| *etc vb V* **convocar.**
convoy |komboy'| *nm* (*FERRO*) train.
convulsión |kombōōlsyon'| *nf* convulsion; (*POL etc*) upheaval.
conyugal |konyōōgál'| *a* conjugal; **vida ~** màrried life.
cónyuge |kon'yōōhe| *nm/f* spouse, partner.
coña |ko'nyá| *nf:* **tomar algo a ~** (*fam!*) to take sth as a joke.
coñac *pl* **coñacs** |ko'nyá(k), ko'nyás| *nm* cognac, brandy.
coñazo |konyá'so| *nm* (*fam*) pain; **dar el ~** to be a real pain.
coño |ko'nyo| (*fam!*) *nm* cunt(*!*) ♦ *excl* (*enfado*) shit(*!*); (*sorpresa*) damn it to hell(*!*) (*US*), bloody hell(*!*) (*Brit*); **¡qué ~!** what a pain in the ass (*US*) o arse(*!*) (*Brit*).
cooperación |kooperásyon'| *nf* cooperation.
cooperar |kooperár'| *vi* to cooperate.
cooperativo, a |kooperátē'ho, á| *a* cooperative ♦ *nf* cooperative.
coordenada |koorthená'dá| *nf* (*MAT*) coordinate; (*fig*): ~**s** *nfpl* guidelines, framework *sg*.
coordinación |koorthēnásyon'| *nf* coordination.
coordinador, a |koorthēnáthor', á| *nm/f* coordinator ♦ *nf* coordinating committee.
coordinar |koorthēnár'| *vt* to coordinate.
copa |ko'pá| *nf* (*tb DEPORTE*) cup; (*vaso*)

glass; (de árbol) top; (de sombrero) crown; **~s** nfpl (NAIPES) ≈ hearts; **(tomar una)** ~ (to have a) drink; **ir de ~s** to go out for a drink.

coparticipación [kopártēscṕásyon'] nf (COM) co-ownership.

Copenhague [kopcná'gc] Copenhagen.

copete [kopc'tc] nm tuft (of hair); **de alto ~** aristocratic, upper-crust (fam).

copia [ko'pyà] nf copy; (ARTE) replica; (COM etc) duplicate; (INFORM): **~ impresa** hard copy; **~ de respaldo** o **de seguridad** backup copy; **hacer ~ de seguridad** to back up; **~ de trabajo** working copy; **~ vaciada** dump.

copiadora [kopyàtho'rà] nf photocopier; **~ al alcohol** spirit duplicator.

copiar [kopyár'] vt to copy; **~ al pie de la letra** to copy word for word.

copioso, a [kopyo'so, à] a copious, plentiful.

copita [kopc'tà] nf (small) glass; (GOLF) tee.

copla [ko'plà] nf verse; (canción) (popular) song.

copo [ko'po] nm: **~s de maíz** cornflakes; **~ de nieve** snowflake.

coprocesador [koproscsàthor'] nm (INFORM) co-processor.

coproducción [koprothōōksyon'] nf (CINE etc) joint production.

copropietarios [kopropyctà'ryos] nmpl (COM) joint owners.

cópula [ko'pōōlà] nf copulation.

copular [kopōōlár'] vi to copulate.

coqueta [kokc'tà] a flirtatious, coquettish ♦ nf (mujer) flirt.

coquetear [kokctcár'] vi to flirt.

coraje [korà'hc] nm courage; (ánimo) spirit; (ira) anger.

coral [korál'] a choral ♦ nf choir ♦ nm (ZOOL) coral.

Corán [korán'] nm: **el ~** the Koran.

coraza [korà'sà] nf (armadura) armor (US), armour (Brit); (blindaje) armor-plating.

corazón [koráson'] nm heart; (BOT) core; **corazones** nmpl (NAIPES) hearts; **de buen ~** kind-hearted; **de todo ~** wholeheartedly; **estar mal del ~** to have heart trouble.

corazonada [korásoná'thà] nf impulse; (presentimiento) presentiment, hunch.

corbata [korbà'tà] nf necktie (US), tie (Brit).

corbeta [korbc'tà] nf corvette.

Córcega [kor'scgà] nf Corsica.

corcel [korscl'] nm steed.

corcovado, a [korkohà'tho, à] a hunchbacked ♦ nm/f hunchback.

corchete [kortchc'tc] nm catch, clasp; **~s** nmpl (TIP) square brackets.

corcho [kor'tcho] nm cork; (PESCA) float.

cordel [kortħcl'] nm cord, line.

cordero [kortħc'ro] nm lamb; (piel) lambskin.

cordial [kortħyàl'] a cordial ♦ nm cordial, tonic.

cordialidad [kortħyálēthàtħ'] nf warmth, cordiality.

cordillera [kortħcyc'rà] nf range (of mountains).

Córdoba [kor'tħohà] nf Cordova.

cordobés, esa [kortħohcs', c'sà] a, nm/f Cordovan.

cordón [kortħon'] nm (cuerda) cord, string; (de zapatos) lace; (ELEC) cord (US), flex (Brit); (MIL etc) cordon.

cordura [kortħōō'rà] nf (MED) sanity; (fig) good sense.

Corea [korc'à] nf Korea; **~ del Norte/Sur** North/South Korea.

coreano, a [korcà'no, à] a, nm/f Korean.

corear [korcár'] vt to chorus.

coreografía [korcográfc'à] nf choreography.

corista [korc'stà] nf (TEATRO etc) chorus girl.

cornada [korná'thà] nf (TAUR etc) butt, goring.

corneta [kornc'tà] nf bugle.

cornisa [kornc'sà] nf cornice.

Cornualles [kornwà'ycs] nm Cornwall.

cornudo, a [kornōō'tħo, à] a (ZOOL) horned; (marido) cuckolded.

coro [ko'ro] nm chorus; (conjunto de cantores) choir.

corolario [korolá'ryo] nm corollary.

corona [koro'nà] nf crown; (de flores) garland.

coronación [koronásyon'] nf coronation.

coronar [koronár'] vt to crown.

coronel [koroncl'] nm colonel.

coronilla [koronc'yà] nf (ANAT) crown (of the head); **estar hasta la ~ (de)** to be utterly fed up (with).

corporación [korporásyon'] nf corporation.

corporal [korporál'] a corporal, bodily.

corpulento, a [korpōōlcn'to à] a (persona) well-built.

corral [korrál'] nm (patio) farmyard; (AGR: de aves) poultry yard; (redil) pen.

correa [korrc'à] nf strap; (cinturón) belt; (de perro) lead, leash; **~ transportadora** conveyor belt.

correaje [korrcà'hc] nm (AGR) harness.

corrección [korrcksyon'] nf correction; (reprensión) rebuke; (cortesía) good manners; (INFORM): **~ por líneas** line editing; **~ en pantalla** screen editing; **~ (de pruebas)** (TIP) proofreading.

correccional [korrcksyonàl'] nm reformatory.

correcto, a [korrck'to, à] a correct; (persona) well-mannered.

corredera [korreħe'rá] *nf*: **puerta de** ~ sliding door.

corredizo, a [korreħe'so, á] *a* (*puerta etc*) sliding; (*nudo*) running.

corredor, a [korreħor', á] *a* running; (*rápido*) fast ♦ *nm/f* (*DEPORTE*) runner ♦ *nm* (*pasillo*) corridor; (*balcón corrido*) gallery; (*COM*) agent, broker; (*pasillo*) corridor, passage; ~ **de bienes raíces** real-estate broker; ~ **de bolsa** stockbroker; ~ **de seguros** insurance broker.

corregir [korreħer'] *vt* (*error*) to correct; (*amonestar, reprender*) to rebuke, reprimand; ~**se** *vr* to reform.

correo [korre'o] *nm* mail (*US*), post (*Brit*); (*persona*) courier; **C~s** *nmpl* Post Office *sg*; ~ **aéreo** airmail; ~ **certificado** registered mail; ~ **electrónico** electronic mail; ~ **urgente** special delivery; **a vuelta de** ~ by return mail.

correr [korrer'] *vt* to run; (*viajar*) to cover, travel; (*riesgo*) to run; (*aventura*) to have; (*cortinas*) to draw; (*cerrojo*) to shoot ♦ *vi* to run; (*líquido*) to run, flow; (*rumor*) to go round; ~**se** *vr* to slide, move; (*colores*) to run; (*fam: tener orgasmo*) to come; **echar a** ~ to break into a run; ~ **con los gastos** to pay the expenses; **eso corre de mi cuenta** I'll take care of that.

correspondencia [korresponden'syá] *nf* correspondence; (*FERRO*) connection; (*reciprocidad*) return; ~ **directa** (*COM*) direct mail.

corresponder [korresponder'] *vi* to correspond; (*convenir*) to be suitable; (*pertenecer*) to belong; (*tocar*) to concern; (*favor*) to repay; ~**se** *vr* (*por escrito*) to correspond; (*amarse*) to love one another; **"a quien corresponda"** "to whom it may concern".

correspondiente [korrespondyen'te] *a* corresponding; (*respectivo*) respective.

corresponsal [korresponsál'] *nm/f* (*newspaper*) correspondent; (*COM*) agent.

corretaje [korretá'he] *nm* (*COM*) brokerage.

corretear [korreteár'] *vi* to loiter.

corrido, a [korre'ħo, á] *a* (*avergonzado*) abashed; (*fluido*) fluent ♦ *nf* run, dash; (*de toros*) bullfight; **de** ~ fluently; **3 noches corridas** 3 nights running; **un kilo** ~ a good kilo.

corriente [korryen'te] *a* (*agua*) running; (*fig*) flowing; (*dinero, cuenta etc*) current; (*común*) ordinary, normal ♦ *nf* current; (*fig: tendencia*) course ♦ *nm* current month; ~ **f de aire** draft (*US*), draught (*Brit*); ~ **eléctrica** electric current; **las ~s modernas del arte** modern trends in art; **estar al** ~ **de** to be informed about.

corrigiendo [korreħyen'do] *etc vb* V **corregir**.

corrija [korre'há] *etc vb* V **corregir**.

corrillo [korre'yo] *nm* ring, circle (of people); (*fig*) clique.

corro [ko'rro] *nm* ring, circle (of people); **la gente hizo** ~ the people formed a ring.

corroborar [korroborár'] *vt* to corroborate.

corroer [korroer'] *vt* (*tb fig*) to corrode, eat away; (*GEO*) to erode.

corroyendo [korroyen'do] *etc vb* V **corroer**.

corromper [korromper'] *vt* (*madera*) to rot; (*fig*) to corrupt.

corrompido, a [korrompe'ħo, á] *a* corrupt.

corrosivo, a [korrose'ħo, á] *a* corrosive.

corrupción [korroopsyon'] *nf* rot, decay; (*fig*) corruption.

corsario [korsá'ryo] *nm* privateer, corsair.

corsé [korse'] *nm* corset.

corso, a [kor'so, á] *a, nm/f* Corsican.

cortacésped [kortáses'peħ] *nm* lawn mower.

cortado, a [kortá'ħo, á] *a* (*con cuchillo*) cut; (*leche*) sour; (*confuso*) confused; (*desconcertado*) embarrassed; (*tímido*) shy ♦ *nm* coffee with cream (*US*), white coffee (with a little milk) (*Brit*).

cortadora [kortá'ħo'rá] *nf* cutter, slicer.

cortadura [kortá'ħoo'rá] *nf* cut.

cortante [kortán'te] *a* (*viento*) biting; (*frío*) bitter.

cortapisa [kortápe'sá] *nf* (*restricción*) restriction; (*traba*) snag.

cortar [kortár'] *vt* to cut; (*suministro*) to cut off; (*un pasaje*) to cut out; (*comunicación*) to cut off ♦ *vi* to cut; ~**se** *vr* (*turbarse*) to become embarrassed; (*leche*) to turn, curdle; ~ **por lo sano** to settle things once and for all; ~**se el pelo** to have one's hair cut.

cortauñas [kortáoo'nyás] *nm inv* nail clippers *pl*.

corte [kor'te] *nm* cut, cutting; (*filo*) edge; (*de tela*) piece, length; (*COSTURA*) tailoring ♦ *nf* (*real*) (royal) court; ~ **y confección** dressmaking; ~ **de corriente** *o* **luz** power cut; **me da** ~ **pedírselo** I'm embarrassed to ask him for it; **¡qué** ~ **le di!** I left him with no comeback!; **C~ Internacional de Justicia** International Court of Justice; **las C~s** the Spanish Parliament *sg*; **hacer la** ~ **a** to woo, court.

cortedad [korteħáħ'] *nf* shortness; (*fig*) bashfulness, timidity.

cortejar [korteħár'] *vt* to court.

cortejo [korte'ho] *nm* entourage; ~ **fúnebre** funeral procession, cortège.

cortés [kortes'] *a* courteous, polite.

cortesano, a [kortesá'no, á] *a* courtly.

cortesía [kortese'á] *nf* courtesy.

corteza [korte'sá] *nf* (*de árbol*) bark; (*de pan*) crust; (*de fruta*) peel, skin; (*de queso*) rind.

cortijo [kortē'ho] *nm* farmhouse.

cortina [kortē'ná] *nf* curtain; ~ **de humo** smoke screen.

corto, a [kor'to, á] *a* (*breve*) short; (*tímido*) bashful; ~ **de luces** not very bright; ~ **de oído** hard of hearing; ~ **de vista** short-sighted; **estar** ~ **de fondos** to be short of funds.

cortocircuito [kortosērkwē'to] *nm* short-circuit,

cortometraje [kortometrá'he] *nm* (*CINE*) short.

Coruña [korōō'nyá] *nf:* **La** ~ Corunna.

coruñés, esa [korōōnyes', e'sá] *a* of *o* from Corunna ♦ *nm/f* native *o* inhabitant of Corunna.

corvo, a [kor'ko, á] *a* curved; (*nariz*) hooked ♦ *nf* back of knee.

cosa [ko'sá] *nf* thing; (*asunto*) affair; ~ **de** about; **eso es** ~ **mía** that's my business; **es poca** ~ it's not important; **¡qué** ~ **más rara!** how strange; **en** ~ **de 10 minutos** in about 10 minutes.

cosaco, a [kosá'ko, á] *a, nm/f* Cossack.

coscorrón [koskorron'] *nm* bump on the head.

cosecha [kose'tchá] *nf* (*AGR*) harvest; (*acto*) harvesting; (*de vino*) vintage; (*producción*) yield.

cosechadora [kosetchádho'rá] *nf* combine (*US*), combine harvester (*Brit*).

cosechar [kosetchár'] *vt* to harvest, gather (in).

coser [koser'] *vt* to sew; (*MED*) to stitch (up).

cosido [kosē'tho] *nm* sewing.

cosmético, a [kosme'tēko, á] *a, nm* cosmetic.

cosmopolita [kosmopolē'tá] *a* cosmopolitan.

coso [ko'so] *nm* bullring.

cosquillas [koskē'yás] *nfpl:* **hacer** ~ to tickle; **tener** ~ to be ticklish.

cosquilleo [koskēye'o] *nm* tickling (sensation).

cosquilloso, a [koskēyo'so, á] *a* ticklish.

costa [ko'stá] *nf* (*GEO*) coast; **C~ Brava** Costa Brava; **C~ Cantábrica** Cantabrian Coast; **C~ de Marfil** Ivory Coast; **C~ del Sol** Costa del Sol; **a** ~ (*COM*) at cost; **a** ~ **de** at the expense of; **a toda** ~ at any price.

costado [kostá'tho] *nm* side; **de** ~ (*dormir*) on one's side; **español por los 4** ~**s** Spanish through and through.

costal [kostál'] *nm* sack.

costalada [kostálá'thá] *nf* bad fall.

costar [kostár'] *vt* (*valer*) to cost; **me cuesta hablarle** I find it hard to talk to him; **¿cuánto cuesta?** how much does it cost?

Costa Rica [kostárē'ká] *nf* Costa Rica.

costarricense [kostárrēsen'se], **costarriqueño, a** [kostárrēke'nyo, á] *a, nm/f* Costa Rican.

coste [ko'ste] *nm* (*COM*): ~ **promedio** average cost; ~**s fijos** fixed costs; *V tb* **costo.**

costear [kosteár'] *vt* to pay for; (*COM etc*) to finance; (*NAUT*) to sail along the coast of; ~**se** *vr* (*negocio*) to pay for itself, cover its costs.

costeño, a [koste'nyo, á] *a* coastal.

costilla [kostē'yá] *nf* rib; (*CULIN*) cutlet.

costo [ko'sto] *nm* cost, price; ~ **directo** direct cost; ~ **de expedición** shipping charges; ~ **de sustitución** replacement cost; ~ **unitario** unit cost; ~ **de la vida** cost of living.

costoso, a [kosto'so, á] *a* costly, expensive.

costra [kos'trá] *nf* (*corteza*) crust; (*MED*) scab.

costumbre [kostōōm'bre] *nf* custom, habit; **como de** ~ as usual.

costura [kostōō'rá] *nf* sewing, needlework; (*confección*) dressmaking; (*zurcido*) seam.

costurera [kostōōre'rá] *nf* dressmaker.

costurero [kostōōre'ro] *nm* sewing box *o* case.

cotejar [kotehár'] *vt* to compare.

cotejo [kote'ho] *nm* comparison.

cotice [kotē'se] *etc vb V* **cotizar.**

cotidiano, a [kotēthyá'no, á] *a* daily, day to day.

cotilla [kotē'yá] *nf* busybody, gossip.

cotillear [kotēyeár'] *vi* to gossip.

cotización [kotēsásyon'] *nf* (*COM*) quotation, price; (*de club*) dues *pl*.

cotizado, a [kotēsá'tho, á] *a* (*fig*) highly-prized.

cotizar [kotēsár'] *vt* (*COM*) to quote, price; ~**se** *vr* (*fig*) to be highly prized; ~**se a** to sell at; (*BOLSA*) to stand at, be quoted at.

coto [ko'to] *nm* (*terreno cercado*) enclosure; (*de caza*) reserve; (*COM*) price-fixing agreement; **poner** ~ **a** to put a stop to.

cotorra [koto'rrá] *nf* (*ZOOL:* *loro*) parrot; (*fam: persona*) windbag.

COU [koōō] *nm abr* (*Esp = Curso de Orientación Universitario*) one year course leading to high school diploma and university entrance examinations.

coyote [koyo'te] *nm* coyote, prairie wolf.

coyuntura [koyōōntōō'rá] *nf* (*ANAT*) joint; (*fig*) juncture, occasion; **esperar una** ~ **favorable** to await a favorable moment.

coz [kos] *nf* kick.

CP *nm abr* (= *computador personal*) PC.

C.P. *abr* (*Esp*) = *Caja Postal*.

C.P.A. *nf abr* (= *Caja Postal de Ahorros*) Post Office Savings Bank.

CP/M *nm abr* (= *Programa de control para microprocesadores*) CP/M.

CPN *nm abr* (*Esp*) = *Cuerpo de la Policía*

Nacional.

cps *abr* (= *caracteres por segundo*) c.p.s.

crac [krák] *nm* (*ECON*) crash.

cráneo [krá'neo] *nm* skull, cranium.

crápula [krá'pōōlá] *nf* drunkenness.

cráter [krá'ter] *nm* crater.

creación [kreásyon'] *nf* creation.

creador, a [kreáthor', á] *a* creative ♦ *nm/f* creator.

crear [kreár'] *vt* to create, make; (*originar*) to originate; (*INFORM*: *archivo*) to create; ~**se** *vr* (*comité etc*) to be set up.

crecer [kreser'] *vi* to grow; (*precio*) to rise; ~**se** *vr* (*engreírse*) to get cocky.

creces [kre'ses]: **con** ~ *ad* amply, fully.

crecido, a [kresē'tho, á] *a* (*persona, planta*) full-grown; (*cantidad*) large ♦ *nf* (*de río*) flood.

creciente [kresyen'te] *a* growing; (*cantidad*) increasing; (*luna*) crescent ♦ *nm* crescent.

crecimiento [kresēmyen'to] *nm* growth; (*aumento*) increase; (*COM*) rise.

credenciales [krethensyá'les] *nfpl* credentials.

crédito [kre'thēto] *nm* credit; **a** ~ on credit; **dar** ~ **a** to believe (in); ~ **al consumidor** consumer credit; ~ **rotativo** *o* **renovable** revolving credit.

credo [kre'tho] *nm* creed.

crédulo, a [kre'thōōlo, á] *a* credulous.

creencia [kreen'syá] *nf* belief.

creer [kreer'] *vt, vi* to think, believe; (*considerar*) to think, consider; ~**se** *vr* to believe o.s. (to be); ~ **en** to believe in; **¡ya lo creo!** I should think so!

creíble [kreē'hle] *a* credible, believable.

creído, a [kreē'tho, á] *a* (*engreído*) conceited.

crema [kre'má] *a inv* cream (colored) ♦ *nf* cream; (*natillas*) custard; **la** ~ **de la sociedad** the cream of society.

cremallera [kremáye'rá] *nf* zipper (*US*), zip (fastener) (*Brit*).

cremoso, a [kremo'so, á] *a* creamy.

crepitar [krepētár'] *vi* (*fuego*) to crackle.

crepúsculo [krepōōs'kōōlo] *nm* twilight, dusk.

crespo, a [kres'po, á] *a* (*pelo*) curly.

crespón [krespon'] *nm* crêpe.

cresta [kres'tá] *nf* (*GEO, ZOOL*) crest.

Creta [kre'tá] *nf* Crete.

creyendo [kreyen'do] *etc vb V* **creer**.

creyente [kreyen'te] *nm/f* believer.

crezca [kres'ká] *etc vb V* **crecer**.

cría [krē'á] *etc vb V* **criar** ♦ *nf V* **crío, a**.

criada [krēá'thá] *nf V* **criado, a**.

criadero [krēáthe'ro] *nm* nursery; (*ZOOL*) breeding place.

criadillas *nfpl* [kryáthē'yás] *nfpl* (*CULIN*) bull's (*o* sheep's) testicles.

criado, a [krēá'tho, á] *nm* servant ♦ *nf* servant, maid.

criador [krēáthor'] *nm* breeder.

crianza [krēán'sá] *nf* rearing, breeding; (*fig*) breeding; (*MED*) lactation.

criar [krēár'] *vt* (*amamantar*) to suckle, feed; (*educar*) to bring up; (*producir*) to grow, produce; (*animales*) to breed; ~**se** *vr* to grow (up); **Dios los cría y ellos se juntan** birds of a feather flock together.

criatura [krēátōō'rá] *nf* creature; (*niño*) baby, (small) child.

criba [krē'há] *nf* sieve.

cribar [krēhár'] *vt* to sieve.

crimen [krē'men] *nm* crime; ~ **pasional** crime of passion.

criminal [krēmēnál'] *a, nm/f* criminal.

crin [krēn] *nf* (*tb*: ~**es**) mane.

crío, a [krē'o, á] *nm/f* (*fam*: *chico*) kid ♦ *nf* (*de animales*) rearing, breeding; (*animal*) young.

criollo, a [krēo'yo, á] *a* (*gen*) Creole; (*AM*) native (to America), national ♦ *nm/f* (*gen*) Creole; (*AM*) native American.

crisis [krē'sēs] *nf inv* crisis; ~ **nerviosa** nervous breakdown.

crisol [krēsol'] *nm* (*TEC*) crucible; (*fig*) melting pot.

crispar [krēspár'] *vt* (*músculo*) to cause to contract; (*nervios*) to set on edge.

cristal [krēstál'] *nm* crystal; (*de ventana*) glass, pane; (*lente*) lens; **de** ~ glass *cpd*; ~ **ahumado/tallado** smoked/cut glass.

cristalería [krēstálerē'á] *nf* (*tienda*) glassware shop; (*objetos*) glassware.

cristalice [krēstálē'se] *etc vb V* **cristalizar**.

cristalino, a [krēstálē'no, á] *a* crystalline; (*fig*) clear ♦ *nm* lens of the eye.

cristalizar [krēstálēsár'] *vt, vi* to crystallize.

cristiandad [krēstyándáth'] *nf*, **cristianismo** [krēstyánēs'mo] *nm* Christianity.

cristiano, a [krēstyá'no, á] *a, nm/f* Christian; **hablar en** ~ to speak proper Spanish; (*fig*) to speak clearly.

Cristo [krē'sto] *nm* (*dios*) Christ; (*crucifijo*) crucifix.

Cristóbal [krēsto'hál] *nm*: ~ **Colón** Christopher Columbus.

criterio [krēte'ryo] *nm* criterion; (*juicio*) judgement; (*enfoque*) attitude, approach; (*punto de vista*) view, opinion; ~ **de clasificación** (*INFORM*) sort criterion.

criticar [krētēkár'] *vt* to criticize.

crítico, a [krē'tēko, á] *a* critical ♦ *nm* critic ♦ *nf* criticism; (*TEATRO etc*) review, notice; **la crítica** the critics *pl*.

critique [krētē'ke] *etc vb V* **criticar**.

croar [kroár'] *vi* to croak.

croata [kroá'tá] *a, nm/f* Croat(ian).

cromado [kromá'tho] *nm* chromium plating, chrome.

cromo [kro'mo] *nm* chrome; (*TIP*) colored

(*US*) *o* coloured print (*Brit*).

crónico, a [kro'něko, á] *a* chronic ♦ *nf* chronicle, account; (*de periódico*) feature, article.

cronometraje [kronometrá'he] *nm* timing.

cronómetro [krono'metro] *nm* (*DEPORTE*) stopwatch; (*TEC etc*) chronometer.

croqueta [kroke'tá] *nf* croquette, rissole.

croquis [kro'kěs] *nm inv* sketch.

cruce [krōō'se] *etc vb V* **cruzar** ♦ *nm* crossing; (*de carreteras*) crossroads; (*AUTO etc*) junction, intersection; (*BIO: proceso*) crossbreeding; **luces de** ~ low-beam (*US*) *o* dipped (*Brit*) headlights.

crucero [krōōse'ro] *nm* (*NAUT: barco*) cruise ship; (: *viaje*) cruise.

crucificar [krōōsěfěkár'] *vt* to crucify; (*fig*) to torment.

crucifijo [krōōsěfě'ho] *nm* crucifix.

crucifique [krōōsěfě'ke] *etc vb V* **crucificar**.

crucigrama [krōōsěgrá'má] *nm* crossword (puzzle).

crudeza [krōōthe'sá] *nf* (*rigor*) harshness; (*aspereza*) crudeness.

crudo, a [krōō'tho, á] *a* raw; (*no maduro*) unripe; (*petróleo*) crude; (*rudo, cruel*) cruel; (*agua*) hard; (*clima etc*) harsh ♦ *nm* crude (oil).

cruel [krwel] *a* cruel.

crueldad [krweldáth'] *nf* cruelty.

cruento, a [krwen'to, á] *a* bloody.

crujido [krōōhě'tho] *nm* (*de madera etc*) creak.

crujiente [krōōhyen'te] *a* (*galleta etc*) crunchy.

crujir [krōōhěr'] *vi* (*madera etc*) to creak; (*dedos*) to crack; (*dientes*) to grind; (*nieve, arena*) to crunch.

cruz [krōōs] *nf* cross; (*de moneda*) tails *sg*; (*fig*) burden; ~ **gamada** swastika; **C~ Roja** Red Cross.

cruzado, a [krōōsá'tho, á] *a* crossed ♦ *nm* crusader ♦ *nf* crusade.

cruzar [krōōsár'] *vt* to cross; (*palabras*) to exchange; ~**se** *vr* (*líneas etc*) to cross, intersect; (*personas*) to pass each other; ~**se de brazos** to fold one's arms; (*fig*) not to lift a finger to help; ~**se con uno en la calle** to pass sb in the street.

c.s.f. *abr* (= *costo, seguro y flete*) c.a.f. (*US*), c.i.f. (*Brit*).

CSIC [sesěk'] *nm abr* (*Esp ESCOL*) = *Consejo Superior de Investigaciones Científicas*.

cta, c.ta *abr* (= *cuenta*) a/c.

cta. cto. *abr* (= *carta de crédito*) L.C.

cte. *abr* (= *corriente, de los corrientes*) inst.

CTNE *nf abr* (*TELEC*) = *Compañía Telefónica Nacional de España*.

c/u *abr* (= *cada uno*) ea.

cuaderno [kwáther'no] *nm* notebook; (*de escuela*) workbook (*US*), exercise book

(*Brit*); (*NAUT*) logbook.

cuadra [kwá'thrá] *nf* (*caballeriza*) stable; (*AM*) (city) block.

cuadrado, a [kwáthrá'tho, á] *a* square ♦ *nm* (*MAT*) square.

cuadragésimo, a [kwáthráhe'sěmo, á] *num* fortieth.

cuadrángulo [kwáthrán'gōōlo, á] *nm* quadrangle.

cuadrante [kwáthrán'te] *nm* quadrant.

cuadrar [kwáthrár'] *vt* to square; (*TIP*) to justify ♦ *vi*: ~ **con** (*cuenta*) to square with, tally with; ~**se** *vr* (*soldado*) to stand to attention; ~ **por la derecha/izquierda** to right-/left-justify.

cuadrícula [kwáthrě'kōōlá] *nf* (*TIP etc*) grid, ruled squares.

cuadriculado, a [kwáthrěkōōlá'tho, á] *a*: **papel** ~ squared *o* graph paper.

cuadrilátero [kwáthrělá'tero] *nm* (*DEPORTE*) boxing ring; (*GEOM*) quadrilateral.

cuadrilla [kwáthrě'yá] *nf* (*amigos*) party, group; (*pandilla*) gang; (*obreros*) team.

cuadro [kwá'thro] *nm* square; (*PINTURA*) painting; (*TEATRO*) scene; (*diagrama: tb*: ~ **sinóptico**) chart, table, diagram; (*DEPORTE, MED*) team; (*POL*) executive; ~ **de mandos** control panel; **a** ~**s** checkered (*US*), check *cpd* (*Brit*).

cuadruplicarse [kwáthrōōplěkár'se] *vr* to quadruple.

cuádruplo, a [kwá'thrōōplo, á], **cuádruple** [kwá'thrōōple] *a* quadruple.

cuajado, a [kwáhá'do, á] *a*: ~ **de** (*fig*) full of ♦ *nf* (*de leche*) curd.

cuajar [kwáhár'] *vt* to thicken; (*leche*) to curdle; (*sangre*) to congeal; (*adornar*) to adorn; (*CULIN*) to set ♦ *vi* (*nieve*) to lie; (*fig*) to become set, become established; (*idea*) to be received, be acceptable; ~**se** *vr* to curdle; to congeal; (*llenarse*) to fill up.

cuajo [kwá'ho] *nm*: **arrancar algo de** ~ to tear sth out by its roots.

cual [kwál] *ad* like, as ♦ *pron*: **el** ~ *etc* which; (*persona: sujeto*) who; (: *objeto*) whom; **lo** ~ (*relativo*) which; **allá cada** ~ every man to his own taste; **son a** ~ **más gandul** each is as idle as the other; **cada** ~ each one ♦ *a* such as; **tal** ~ just as it is.

cuál [kwál] *pron interrogativo* which (one), what.

cualesquier(a) [kwálěskyer'(á)] *pl de* **cualquier(a)**.

cualidad [kwálětháth'] *nf* quality.

cualificado, a [kwálěfěká'tho, á] *a* (*obrero*) skilled, qualified.

cualquiera [kwálkyc'rá], **cualquier** [kwál-kyer'], *pl* **cualesquier(a)** *a* any ♦ *pron* anybody, anyone; (*quienquiera*) whoever; **en cualquier momento** any time; **en cualquier**

parte anywhere; **cualquiera que sea** whichever it is; (*persona*) whoever it is.

cuán |kwán| *adv* how.

cuando |kwàn'do| *ad* when; (*aún si*) if, even if ♦ *conj* (*puesto que*) since ♦ *prep*: **yo, ~ niño** ... when I was a child ..., as a child I ...; **~ no sea así** even if it is not so; **~ más** at (the) most; **~ menos** at least; **~ no** if not, otherwise; **de ~ en ~** from time to time; **ven ~ quieras** come when(ever) you like.

cuándo |kwán'do| *ad* when; **¿desde ~?, ¿de ~ acá?** since when?

cuantía |kwàntē'á| *nf* (*alcance*) extent; (*importancia*) importance.

cuantioso, a |kwántyo'so, á| *a* substantial.

cuanto, a |kwàn'to, á| *a, pron*: **llévate todo ~ quieras** take as much as you like; **en ~** (*en seguida que*) as soon as; (*ya que*) since, inasmuch as; **en ~ a** as for; **~ más difícil sea** the more difficult it is; **~ más hace (tanto) menos avanza** the more he does, the less he progresses; **~s más invitados vengan tantas más comidas habrá que preparar** the more guests come, the more meals will have to be cooked; **~ antes** as soon as possible; **unos ~s libros** a few books.

cuánto, a |kwàn'to, á| *a* (*exclamación*) what a lot of; (*interrogativo: sg*) how much?; (: *pl*) how many? ♦ *pron, ad* how; (*interrogativo: sg*) how much?; (: *pl*) how many? ♦ *excl*: **¡~ me alegro!** I'm so glad!; **¡cuánta gente!** what a lot of people!; **¿~ tiempo?** how long?; **¿~ cuesta?** how much does it cost?; **¿a ~s estamos?** what's the date?; **¿~ hay de aquí a Bilbao?** how far is it from here to Bilbao?; **Señor no sé ~s** Mr. So-and-So.

cuarenta |kwàrcn'tà| *num* forty.

cuarentena |kwàrcntc'ná| *nf* (*MED etc*) quarantine; (*conjunto*) forty(-odd).

cuarentón, ona |kwàrcnton', o'ná| *a* forty-year-old, fortyish ♦ *nm/f* person of about forty.

cuaresma |kwàrcs'má| *nf* Lent.

cuarta |kwár'tà| *nf* V **cuarto**.

cuartear |kwàrtcár'| *vt* to quarter; (*dividir*) to divide up; **~se** *vr* to crack, split.

cuartel |kwàrtcl'| *nm* (*de ciudad*) quarter, district; (*MIL*) barracks *pl*; **~ general** headquarters *pl*.

cuartelazo |kwàrtclá'so| *nm* coup, military uprising.

cuarteto |kwàrtc'to| *nm* quartet.

cuartilla |kwàrtē'yá| *nf* (*hoja*) sheet (of paper); **~s** *nfpl* (*TIP*) copy *sg*.

cuarto, a |kwár'to, á| *a* fourth ♦ *nm* (*MAT*) quarter, fourth; (*habitación*) room ♦ *nf* (*MAT*) quarter, fourth; (*palmo*) span; **~ de baño** bathroom; **~ de estar** living room; **~**

de hora quarter (of an) hour; **~ de kilo** quarter kilo; **no tener un ~** to be broke (*fam*).

cuarzo |kwàr'so| *nm* quartz.

cuatrero |kwátrc'ro| *nm* (*AM*) rustler, stock thief.

cuatro |kwá'tro| *num* four; **las ~** four o'clock; **el ~ de octubre** (on) the fourth of October; *V tb* **seis**.

cuatrocientos, as |kwátrosycn'tos, ás| *num* four hundred; *V tb* **seiscientos**.

Cuba |kōō'há| *nf* Cuba.

cuba |kōō'há| *nf* cask, barrel; **estar como una ~** (*fam*) to be soused (*US*) o sloshed (*Brit*).

cubalibre |kōōhálē'hrc| *nm* (white) rum and coke ®.

cubano, a |kōōhá'no, á| *a, nm/f* Cuban.

cubata |kōōhá'tá| *nm* = **cubalibre**.

cubertería |kōōhcrtcrē'á| *nf* knives and forks.

cúbico, a |kōō'hēko, á| *a* cubic.

cubierto, a |kōōhycr'to, á| *pp de* **cubrir** ♦ *a* covered; (*cielo*) overcast ♦ *nm* cover; (*en la mesa*) place setting ♦ *nf* cover, covering; (*neumático*) tire (*US*), tyre (*Brit*); (*NAUT*) deck; **~s** *nmpl* utensils (*US*), cutlery *sg* (*Brit*); **a ~ de** covered with o in; **precio del ~** cover charge.

cubil |kōōhēl'| *nm* den.

cubilete |kōōhēlc'tc| *nm* (*en juegos*) cup.

cubito |kōōhē'to| *nm*: **~ de hielo** ice cube.

cubo |kōō'ho| *nm* cube; (*balde*) bucket, tub; (*TEC*) drum; **~ de la basura** garbage can (*US*), dustbin (*Brit*).

cubrecama |kōōhrcká'má| *nm* (*AM*) bedspread.

cubrir |kōōhrēr'| *vt* to cover; (*vacante*) to fill; (*BIO*) to mate with; (*gastos*) to meet; **~se** *vr* (*cielo*) to become overcast; (*COM: gastos*) to be met o paid; (: *deuda*) to be covered; **~ las formas** to keep up appearances; **lo cubrieron las aguas** the waters closed over it; **el agua casi me cubría** I was almost out of my depth.

cucaracha |kōōkárátch'á| *nf* cockroach.

cuclillas |kōōklē'yás| *nfpl*: **en ~** squatting.

cuco, a |kōō'ko, á| *a* pretty; (*astuto*) sharp ♦ *nm* cuckoo.

cucurucho |kōōkōōrōōtch'o| *nm* paper cone, cornet.

cuchara |kōōtchá'rá| *nf* spoon; (*TEC*) scoop.

cucharada |kōōtchàrá'thá| *nf* spoonful; **~ colmada** heaped spoonful.

cucharadita |kōōtchàráthē'tà| *nf* teaspoonful.

cucharita |kōōtchárē'tà| *nf* teaspoon.

cucharón |kōōtcháron'| *nm* ladle.

cuchichear |kōōtchētchcár'| *vi* to whisper.

cuchicheo |kōōtchētchc'o| *nm* whispering.

cuchilla |kōōtchē'yá| *nf* (large) knife; (*de*

arma blanca) blade; ~ **de afeitar** razor blade; **pasar a** ~ to put to the sword.

cuchillo [kōōtchē'yo] *nm* knife.

cuchitril [kōōtchētrēl'] *nm* hovel; (*habitación etc*) pigsty.

cuece [kwe'se] *etc vb V* **cocer.**

cuele [kwe'le] *etc vb V* **colar.**

cuelgue [kwel'ge] *etc vb V* **colgar.**

cuello [kwe'yo] *nm* (ANAT) neck; (*de vestido, camisa*) collar.

cuenca [kwen'ká] *nf* (ANAT) eye socket; (GEO: *valle*) bowl, deep valley; (: *fluvial*) basin.

cuenco [kwen'ko] *nm* (earthenware) bowl.

cuenta [kwen'tá] *etc vb V* **contar** ♦ *nf* (*cálculo*) count, counting; (*en café, restaurante*) check (US), bill (Brit); (COM) account; (*de collar*) bead; (*fig*) account; **a fin de** ~**s** in the end; **en resumidas** ~**s** in short; **caer en la** ~ to catch on; **dar** ~ **a uno de sus actos** to account to sb for one's actions; **darse** ~ **de** to realize; **tener en** ~ to bear in mind; **echar** ~**s** to take stock; ~ **de atrás** countdown; ~ **corriente/de ahorros/a plazo (fijo)** checking (US) *o* current (Brit)/savings/deposit account; ~ **de asignación** appropriation account; ~ **de caja** cash account; ~ **de capital** capital account; ~ **por cobrar** account receivable; ~ **de crédito** credit *o* loan account; ~ **de gastos e ingresos** income and expenditure account; ~ **por pagar** account payable; **abonar una cantidad en** ~ **a uno** to credit a sum to sb's account; **ajustar** *o* **liquidar una** ~ to settle an account; **pasar la** ~ to send the bill.

cuentagotas [kwentàgo'tás] *nm inv* (MED) dropper; **a** *o* **con** ~ (*fam, fig*) drop by drop, bit by bit.

cuentakilómetros [kwentàkēlo'metros] *nm inv* (*de distancias*) ≈ odometer (US), milometer (Brit); (*velocímetro*) speedometer.

cuentista [kwentē'stá] *nm/f* gossip; (LIT) short-story writer.

cuento [kwen'to] *etc vb V* **contar** ♦ *nm* story; (LIT) short story; ~ **de hadas** fairy tale; **es el** ~ **de nunca acabar** it's an endless business; **eso no viene a** ~ that's irrelevant.

cuerda [kwer'tá] *nf* rope; (*hilo*) string; (*de reloj*) spring; (MUS: *de violín etc*) string; (MAT) chord; (ANAT) cord; ~ **floja** tightrope; ~**s vocales** vocal cords; **dar** ~ **a un reloj** to wind up a clock.

cuerdo, a [kwer'tho, á] *a* sane; (*prudente*) wise, sensible.

cuerno [kwer'no] *nm* (ZOOL: *gen*) horn; (: *de ciervo*) antler; **poner los** ~**s a** (*fam*) to cuckold; **saber a** ~ **quemado** to leave a nasty taste.

cuero [kwe'ro] *nm* (ZOOL) skin, hide; (TEC) leather; **en** ~**s** stark naked; ~ **cabelludo** scalp.

cuerpo [kwer'po] *nm* body; (*cadáver*) corpse; (*fig*) main part; ~ **de bomberos** fire department (US) *o* brigade (Brit); ~ **diplomático** diplomatic corps; **luchar** ~ **a** ~ to fight hand-to-hand; **tomar** ~ (*plan etc*) to take shape.

cuervo [kwer'ho] *nm* (ZOOL) raven, crow.

cuesta [kwe'stá] *etc vb V* **costar** ♦ *nf* slope; (*en camino etc*) hill; ~ **arriba/abajo** uphill/downhill; **a** ~**s** on one's back.

cuestión [kwestyon'] *nf* matter, question, issue; (*riña*) quarrel, dispute; **eso es otra** ~ that's another matter.

cuestionar [kwestyonár'] *vt* to question.

cueva [kwe'há] *nf* cave.

cueza [kwe'sá] *etc vb V* **cocer.**

cuidado [kwēthá'tho] *nm* care, carefulness; (*preocupación*) care, worry ♦ *excl* careful!, look out!; **eso me tiene sin** ~ I'm not worried about that.

cuidadoso, a [kwēthàtho'so, á] *a* careful; (*preocupado*) anxious.

cuidar [kwēthár'] *vt* (MED) to care for; (*ocuparse de*) to take care of, look after; (*detalles*) to pay attention to ♦ *vi*: ~ **de** to take care of, look after; ~**se** *vr* to look after o.s.; ~**se de hacer algo** to take care to do something.

cuita [kwē'tá] *nf* (*preocupación*) worry, trouble; (*pena*) grief.

culata [kōōlá'tá] *nf* (*de fusil*) butt.

culatazo [kōōlátá'so] *nm* kick, recoil.

culebra [kōōle'hrá] *nf* snake; ~ **de cascabel** rattlesnake.

culebrear [kōōlehreár'] *vi* to wriggle along; (*río*) to meander.

culinario, a [kōōlēná'ryo, á] *a* culinary, cooking *cpd*.

culminación [kōōlmēnásyon'] *nf* culmination.

culminante [kōōlmēnán'te] *a*: **momento** ~ climax, highlight, highspot.

culminar [kōōlmēnár'] *vi* to culminate.

culo [kōō'lo] *nm* (*fam: asentaderas*) bottom, backside, bum (Brit); (: *ano*) ass(hole) (US!), arse(hole) (Brit!); (*de vaso*) bottom.

culpa [kōōl'pá] *nf* fault; (JUR) guilt; ~**s** *nfpl* sins; **por** ~ **de** through, because of; **tener la** ~ **(de)** to be to blame (for).

culpabilidad [kōōlpáhēlētháth'] *nf* guilt.

culpable [kōōlpá'hle] *a* guilty ♦ *nm/f* culprit; **confesarse** ~ to plead guilty; **declarar** ~ **a uno** to find sb guilty.

culpar [kōōlpár'] *vt* to blame; (*acusar*) to accuse.

cultivadora [kōōltēhátho'rá] *nf* cultivator.

cultivar [kōōltēhár'] *vt* to cultivate; (*co-*

secha) to raise; (*talento*) to develop.

cultivo [kōōltē'ħo] *nm* (*acto*) cultivation; (*plantas*) crop; (*BIO*) culture.

culto, a [kōōl'to, á] *a* (*cultivado*) cultivated; (*que tiene cultura*) cultured, educated ♦ *nm* (*homenaje*) worship; (*religión*) cult; (*POL etc*) cult.

cultura [kōōltōō'rá] *nf* culture.

culturismo [kōōltōōrēs'mo] *nm* body building.

cumbre [kōōm'bre] *nf* summit, top; (*fig*) top, height; **conferencia (en la)** ~ summit (conference).

cumpleaños [kōōmpleá'nyos] *nm inv* birthday.

cumplido, a [kōōmplē'ħo, á] *a* complete, perfect; (*abundante*) plentiful; (*cortés*) courteous ♦ *nm* compliment; **visita de** ~ courtesy call.

cumplidor, a [kōōmplēħor', á] *a* reliable.

cumplimentar [kōōmplēmentár'] *vt* to congratulate; (*órdenes*) to carry out.

cumplimiento [kōōmplēmyen'to] *nm* (*de un deber*) fulfilment, execution, performance; (*acabamiento*) completion; (*COM*) expiration (*US*), expiry (*Brit*).

cumplir [kōōmplēr'] *vt* (*orden*) to carry out, obey; (*promesa*) to carry out, fulfil; (*condena*) to serve; (*años*) to reach, attain ♦ *vi* (*pago*) to fall due; (*plazo*) to expire; ~**se** *vr* (*plazo*) to expire; (*plan etc*) to be fulfilled; (*vaticinio*) to come true; **hoy cumple dieciocho años** he is eighteen today; ~ **con** (*deberes*) to carry out, fulfil.

cúmulo [kōō'mōōlo] *nm* (*montón*) heap; (*nube*) cumulus.

cuna [kōō'ná] *nf* cradle, cot; **canción de** ~ lullaby.

cundir [kōōndēr'] *vi* (*noticia*, *rumor*, *pánico*) to spread; (*rendir*) to go a long way.

cuneta [kōōne'tá] *nf* ditch.

cuña [kōō'nyá] *nf* (*TEC*) wedge; (*COM*) advertising spot; (*MED*) bedpan; **tener** ~**s** to have influence.

cuñado, a [kōōnyà'ħo, á] *nm/f* brother/ sister-in-law.

cuño [kōō'nyo] *nm* (*TEC*) die-stamp; (*fig*) stamp.

cuota [kwo'tá] *nf* (*parte proporcional*) share; (*cotización*) fee, dues *pl*; ~ **inicial** (*COM*) down payment.

cupo [kōō'po] *etc vb* V **caber** ♦ *nm* quota, share; (*COM*): ~ **de importación** import quota; ~ **de ventas** sales quota.

cupón [kōōpon'] *nm* coupon.

cúpula [kōō'pōōlá] *nf* (*ARQ*) dome.

cura [kōō'rá] *nf* (*curación*) cure; (*método curativo*) treatment ♦ *nm* priest; ~ **de emergencia** emergency treatment.

curación [kōōrásyon'] *nf* cure; (*acción*) curing.

curado, a [kōōrá'ħo, á] *a* (*CULIN*) cured; (*pieles*) tanned.

curar [kōōrár'] *vt* (*MED: herida*) to treat, dress; (: *enfermo*) to cure; (*CULIN*) to cure, salt; (*cuero*) to tan ♦ *vi*, ~**se** *vr* to get well, recover.

curda [kōōr'ħá] (*fam*) *nm* drunk ♦ *nf*: **agarrar una/estar** ~ to get/be soused (*US*) *o* sloshed (*Brit*).

curiosear [kōōryoseár'] *vt* to glance at, look over ♦ *vi* to look round, wander round; (*explorar*) to poke about.

curiosidad [kōōryosēħáħ'] *nf* curiosity.

curioso, a [kōōryo'so, á] *a* curious; (*aseado*) neat ♦ *nm/f* bystander, onlooker; ¡**qué** ~! how odd!

curita [kōōrē'tá] *nf* (*AM*) bandaid (*US*), sticking plaster (*Brit*).

currante [kōōrrán'te] *nm/f* (*fam*) worker.

currar [kōōrrár'] *vi* (*fam*), **currelar** [kōōrrelár'] *vi* (*fam*) to work.

currículo [kōōrrē'kōōlo] *nm*, **currículum** [kōōrrē'kōōlōōm] *nm* curriculum vitae.

curro [kōō'rro] *nm* (*fam*) work, job.

cursar [kōōrsár'] *vt* (*ESCOL*) to study.

cursi [kōōr'sē] *a* (*fam*) pretentious; (: *amanerado*) affected.

cursilería [kōōrsēlerē'á] *nf* (*vulgaridad*) bad taste; (*amaneramiento*) affectation.

cursillo [kōōrsē'yo] *nm* short course.

cursiva [kōōrsē'ħá] *nf* italics *pl*.

curso [kōōr'so] *nm* (*dirección*) course; (*fig*) progress; (*ESCOL*) school year; (*UNIV*) academic year; **en** ~ (*año*) current; (*proceso*) going on, under way; **moneda de** ~ **legal** legal tender.

cursor [kōōrsor'] *nm* (*INFORM*) cursor; (*TEC*) slide.

curtido, a [kōōrtē'ħo, á] *a* (*cara etc*) weather-beaten; (*fig: persona*) experienced.

curtir [kōōrtēr'] *vt* (*piel*) to tan; (*fig*) to harden.

curvo, a [kōōr'ħo, á] *a* (*gen*) curved; (*torcido*) bent ♦ *nf* (*gen*) curve, bend; **curva de rentabilidad** (*COM*) break-even chart.

cúspide [kōōs'pēħe] *nf* (*GEO*) summit, peak; (*fig*) top, pinnacle.

custodia [kōōsto'ħyá] *nf* (*cuidado*) safekeeping; (*JUR*) custody.

custodiar [kōōstoħyár'] *vt* (*conservar*) to keep, take care of; (*vigilar*) to guard.

custodio [kōōsto'ħyo] *nm* guardian, keeper.

cutícula [kōōtē'kōōlá] *nf* cuticle.

cutis [kōō'tēs] *nm inv* skin, complexion.

cutre [kōō'tre] *a* (*fam: lugar*) nasty; (: *persona*) inferior.

cuyo, a [kōō'yo, á] *pron* (*de quien*) whose; (*de que*) whose, of which; **la señora en cuya casa me hospedé** the lady in whose house I stayed; **el asunto cuyos detalles**

conoces the affair the details of which you know; **por ~ motivo** for which reason.
C.V. *abr* (= *caballos de vapor*) H.P.
C y F *abr* (= *costo y flete*) C & F.

CH

Ch, ch [tche] *nf* (*letra*) Ch, ch.
chabacano, a [tchàħàkà'no, à] *a* vulgar, coarse.
chabola [tchàħo'là] *nf* shack; **~s** *nfpl* shanty town *sg*.
chabolismo [tchàħolēs'mo] *nm*: **el problema del ~** the problem of substandard housing, the shanty town problem.
chacal [tchàkàl'] *nm* jackal.
chacarero [tchàkàre'ro] *nm* (*AM*) small farmer.
chacra [tchá'krà] *nf* (*AM*) small farm.
chacha [tchàtch'à] *nf* (*fam*) maid.
cháchara [tchàtch'àrà] *nf* chatter; **estar de ~** to chatter away.
chafar [tchàfár'] *vt* (*aplastar*) to crush, flatten; (*arruinar*) to ruin.
chaflán [tchàflàn'] *nm* (*TEC*) bevel.
chal [tchàl] *nm* shawl.
chalado, a [tchàlà'ħo, à] *a* (*fam*) crazy.
chalé, pl chalés [tchàle', tchàles'] *nm* villa, ≈ detached house.
chaleco [tchàle'ko] *nm* vest (*US*), waistcoat (*Brit*); **~ antibala** bulletproof vest; **~ salvavidas** life jacket.
chalet, pl chalets [tchà'le, tchà'les] *nm* = **chalé**.
chalupa [tchàlōō'pá] *nf* launch, boat.
chamaco, a [tchàmà'ko, à] *nm/f* boy/girl.
chamarra [tchàmà'rrà] *nf* sheepskin jacket; (*AM*: *poncho*) blanket.
champán [tchàmpán'] *nm*, **champaña** [tchàmpá'nyà] *nm* champagne.
champiñón [tchàmpēnyon'] *nm* mushroom.
champú [tchàmpōō'] (*pl* **champúes, champús**) *nm* shampoo.
chamuscar [tchàmōōskár'] *vt* to scorch, sear, singe.
chamusque [tchàmōōs'ke] *etc vb* V **chamuscar**.
chamusquina [tchàmōōskē'nà] *nf* singeing.
chancla [tchàn'klà] *nf* (*AM*: *zapato viejo*) old shoe.
chancleta [tchànkle'tà] *nf* sandal, slipper.
chancho, a [tchántch'o, à] *nm/f* (*AM*) pig.
chanchullo [tchàntchōō'yo] *nm* (*fam*) swindle, wangle.

chandal [tchàndàl'] *nm* tracksuit.
chantaje [tchàntà'he] *nm* blackmail; **hacer ~ a uno** to blackmail sb.
chanza [tchàn'sà] *nf* joke.
chao [tchào] *excl* (*fam*) see ya (*US*), bye.
chapa [tchà'pá] *nf* (*de metal*) plate, sheet; (*de madera*) board, panel; (*de botella*) bottle top; (*insignia*) (lapel) badge; (*AM*: *AUTO*) license (*US*) o number (*Brit*) plate; **de 3 ~s** (*madera*) 3-ply.
chapado, a [tchàpá'ħo, à] *a* (*metal*) plated; (*muebles etc*) finished.
chaparrón [tchàpárron'] *nm* downpour, cloudburst.
chapotear [tchàpoteár'] *vt* to sponge down ♦ *vi* (*fam*) to splash about.
chapucero, a [tchàpōōse'ro, à] *a* rough, crude ♦ *nm/f* bungler.
chapurr(e)ar [tchàpōōrr(e)àr'] *vt* (*idioma*) to speak badly.
chapuza [tchàpōō'sà] *nf* botched job; (*AM*: *estafa*) trick, swindle.
chapuzón [tchàpōōson'] *nm*: **darse un ~** to go for a dip.
chaqueta [tchàke'tà] *nf* jacket; **cambiar la ~** (*fig*) to change sides.
charca [tchár'kà] *nf* pond, pool.
charco [tchár'ko] *nm* pool, puddle.
charcutería [tchárkōōterē'à] *nf* (*tienda*) shop selling chiefly pork meat products; (*productos*) cooked pork meats *pl*.
charla [tchár'là] *nf* talk, chat; (*conferencia*) lecture.
charlar [tchàrlàr'] *vi* to talk, chat.
charlatán, ana [tchàrlàtàn', à'nà] *nm/f* chatterbox; (*estafador*) trickster.
charol [tchàrol'] *nm* varnish; (*cuero*) patent leather.
charro, a [tchà'rro, à] *a* Salamancan; (*AM*) Mexican; (*ropa*) loud, gaudy; (*AM*: *costumbres*) traditional ♦ *nm/f* Salamancan; Mexican.
chárter [tchár'ter] *a inv*: **vuelo ~** charter flight.
chascarrillo [tchàskárrē'yo] *nm* (*fam*) funny story.
chasco [tchàs'ko] *nm* (*broma*) trick, joke; (*desengaño*) disappointment.
chasis [tchà'sēs] *nm inv* (*AUTO*) chassis; (*FOTO*) plateholder.
chasquear [tchàskeár'] *vt* (*látigo*) to crack; (*lengua*) to click.
chasquido [tchàskē'ħo] *nm* (*de lengua*) click; (*de látigo*) crack.
chatarra [tchàtá'rrà] *nf* scrap (metal).
chato, a [tchà'to, à] *a* flat; (*nariz*) snub ♦ *nm* wine tumbler; **beber unos ~s** to have a few drinks.
chauvinismo [tchoħēnēs'mo] *nm* chauvinism.
chauvinista [tchoħēnē'stà] *a, nm/f* chauvin-

ist.

chaval, a [tchàhàl', à] *nm/f* kid (*fam*), boy/
girl.

chavo [tchá'ho] *nm* (*AM: fam*) boy, kid.

checo, a *a, nm/f* Czech ♦ *nm* (*LING*) Czech.

checo(e)slovaco, a [tcheko(e)slohà'ko, à]
a, nm/f Czech, Czechoslovak.

Checo(e)slovaquia [tcheko(e)slohà'kyà] *nf*
Czechoslovakia.

chepa [tche'pà] *nf* hump.

cheque [tche'ke] *nm* check (*US*), cheque
(*Brit*); ~ **abierto** check payable to bearer
(*US*), open cheque (*Brit*); ~ **en blanco**
blank check; ~ **cruzado** check marked for
deposit only (*US*), crossed cheque (*Brit*); ~
al portador check payable to bearer; ~ **ca-
ducado** stale check; ~ **de viajero** traveler's check.

chequeo [tcheke'o] *nm* (*MED*) check-up;
(*AUTO*) service.

chequera [tcheke'rà] *nf* (*AM*) checkbook
(*US*), chequebook (*Brit*).

chévere [tche'here] *a* (*AM*) great, fabulous
(*fam*).

chico, a [tche'ko, à] *a* small, little ♦ *nm/f*
child; (*muchacho*) boy; (*muchacha*) girl.

chicano, a [tchekà'no, à] *a* chicano,
Mexican-American.

chicle [tche'kle] *nm* chewing gum.

chicha [tchètch'à] *nf* (*AM*) maize liquor.

chícharo [tchètch'àro] *nm* (*AM*) pea.

chicharra [tchètchá'rrà] *nf* harvest bug, cicada.

chicharrón [tchètchárron'] *nm* (pork) crackling.

chichón [tchètchon'] *nm* bump, lump.

chiflado, a [tcheflà'tho, à] *a* (*fam*) crazy,
round the bend ♦ *nm/f* nutcase.

chiflar [tcheflár'] *vt* to hiss, boo.

Chile [tche'le] *nm* Chile.

chile [tche'le] *nm* chilli, pepper.

chileno, a [tchele'no, à] *a, nm/f* Chilean.

chillar [tcheyár'] *vi* (*persona*) to yell,
scream; (*animal salvaje*) to howl; (*cerdo*)
to squeal; (*puerta*) to creak.

chillido [tcheyè'tho] *nm* (*de persona*) yell,
scream; (*de animal*) howl; (*de frenos*)
screech(ing).

chillón, ona [tcheyon', o'nà] *a* (*niño*) noisy;
(*color*) loud, gaudy.

chimenea [tchemene'à] *nf* chimney; (*hogar*) fireplace.

chimpancé, pl chimpancés [tchèmpànse',
tchèmpànses'] *nm* chimpanzee.

China [tche'nà] *nf*: (**la**) ~ China.

china [tche'nà] *nf* pebble.

chinchar [tchentchár'] (*fam*) *vt* to pester,
annoy; ~**se** *vr* to get cross; ¡**chínchate!**
tough!

chinche [tchentch'e] *nf* bug; (*TEC*)
thumbtack (*US*), drawing pin (*Brit*) ♦ *nm/f*

nuisance, pest.

chincheta [tchentche'tà] *nf* thumbtack (*US*),
drawing pin (*Brit*).

chingar [tchengár'] *vt* (*AM: fam!*) to fuck
(up)(!) ♦ *vi* (*AM: bromear*) to joke; (: *fracasar*) to fail, fall through.

chingue [tchen'ge] *etc vb* V **chingar**.

chino, a [tche'no, à] *a, nm/f* Chinese ♦ *nm*
(*LING*) Chinese.

chip [tchep] *nm* (*INFORM*) chip.

chipirón [tchepèron'] *nm* squid.

Chipre [tche'pre] *nf* Cyprus.

chipriota [tchepryo'tà], **chipriote** [tchepryo'-
te] *a* Cypriot, Cyprian ♦ *nm/f* Cypriot.

chiquillada [tchekèyà'dà] *nf* childish prank.

chiquillo, a [tchekè'yo, à] *nm/f* kid (*fam*),
youngster, child.

chiquito, a [tchekè'to, à] *a* a very small, tiny
♦ *nm/f* kid (*fam*).

chirigota [tcherègo'tà] *nf* joke.

chirimbolo [tcherèmbo'lo] *nm* thingamajig
(*fam*).

chirimoya [tcherèmo'yà] *nf* cherimoya
(*US*), custard apple (*Brit*).

chiringuito [tcherènge'to] *nm* refreshment
stall o stand.

chiripa [tcherè'pà] *nf* fluke; **por** ~ by
chance.

chirona [tchero'nà], (*AM*) **chirola** [tchero'là]
nf (*fam*) clink, jail.

chirriar [tcherryár'] *vi* (*goznes*) to creak,
squeak; (*pájaros*) to chirp, sing.

chirrido [tcherrè'tho] *nm* creak(ing),
squeak(ing); (*de pájaro*) chirp(ing).

chis [tchès] *excl* sh!

chisme [tchès'me] *nm* (*habladurías*) piece of
gossip; (*fam: objeto*) thingamajig.

chismoso, a [tchèsmo'so, à] *a* gossiping ♦
nm/f gossip.

chispa [tchès'pà] *nf* spark; (*fig*) sparkle;
(*ingenio*) wit; (*fam*) drunkenness.

chispeante [tchèspeàn'te] *a* (*tb fig*) sparkling.

chispear [tchèspeàr'] *vi* to spark; (*lloviznar*)
to drizzle.

chisporrotear [tchèsporroteàr'] *vi* (*fuego*)
to throw out sparks; (*leña*) to crackle;
(*aceite*) to hiss, splutter.

chistar [tchèstár'] *vi*: **no** ~ not to say a
word.

chiste [tche'ste] *nm* joke, funny story; ~
verde dirty joke.

chistoso, a [tchèsto'so, à] *a* (*gracioso*)
funny, amusing; (*bromista*) witty.

chistu [tche'stōō] *nm* = **txistu**.

chivarse [tchèhàr'se] *vr* (*fam*) to squeal.

chivatazo [tchèhàtà'so] *nm* (*fam*) tip-off;
dar ~ to inform.

chivo, a [tche'ho, à] *nm/f* (billy/nanny-)goat;
~ **expiatorio** scapegoat.

chocante [tchokàn'te] *a* startling; (*extraño*)

odd; (*ofensivo*) shocking.

chocar |tchokår'| *vi* (*coches etc*) to collide, crash; (*MIL.*, *fig*) to clash ♦ *vt* to shock; (*sorprender*) to startle; ~ **con** to collide with; (*fig*) to run into, run up against; **¡chócala!** (*fam*) put it there!

chocolate |tchokolá'tc| *a* chocolate ♦ *nm* chocolate; (*fam*) dope, marijuana.

chocolatería |tchokolátcrē'á| *nf* chocolate factory (*o* shop).

chochear |tchotchcår'| *vi* to dodder, be senile.

chocho, a |tchotch'o, á| *a* doddering, senile; (*fig*) soft, doting.

chófer |tcho'fer|, **chofer** |tchofcr'| *nm* driver.

chollo |tcho'yo| *nm* (*fam*) bargain.

chopo |tcho'po| *nm* black poplar.

choque |tcho'kc| *etc vb* V **chocar** ♦ *nm* (*impacto*) impact; (*golpe*) jolt; (*AUTO*) crash; (*fig*) conflict.

chorizo |tchorē'so| *nm* hard pork *sausage*, (*type of*) salami; (*ladrón*) crook.

chorra |tcho'rrá| *nf* luck.

chorradas |tchorrá'thás| *nfpl* (*objetos*) rubbish *sg*, junk *sg*; **decir** ~ to talk rubbish *o* nonsense.

chorrear |tchorrcár'| *vt* to pour ♦ *vi* to gush (out), spout (out); (*gotear*) to drip, trickle.

chorreras |tchorrc'rás| *nfpl* (*COSTURA*) frill *sg*.

chorro |tcho'rro| *nm* jet; (*caudalito*) dribble, trickle; (*fig*) stream; **salir a** ~**s** to gush forth; **con propulsión a** ~ jet-propelled.

chotearse |tchotcár'sc| *vr* to joke.

choteo |tchotc'o| *nm* kidding.

choto |tcho'to| *nm* (*cabrito*) kid.

chovinismo |tchohĕnē̄s'mo| *nm* = **chauvinismo**.

chovinista |tchohĕnē̄'stá| *a*, *nm/f* = **chauvinista**.

choza |tcho'sá| *nf* hut, shack.

chubasco |tchōō̄hás'ko| *nm* squall.

chubasquero |tchōō̄háskc'ro| *nm* foul-weather gear (*US*), oilskins *pl* (*Brit*).

chuchería |tchōō̄tchcrē'á| *nf* trinket.

chucho |tchōō̄tch'o| *nm* (*ZOOL*) mongrel.

chufa |tchōō̄'fá| *nf* chufa, earth almond, tiger nut; **horchata de** ~**s** *drink made from chufas*.

chuleta |tchōō̄le'tá| *nf* chop, cutlet; (*ESCOL etc: fam*) crib.

chulo, a |tchōō̄'lo, á| *a* (*encantador*) charming; (*aire*) proud; (*pey*) fresh; (*fam: estupendo*) great, fantastic ♦ *nm* (*pícaro*) rascal; (*madrileño*) working-class Madrilenian; (*rufián: tb:* ~ **de putas**) pimp.

chumbera |tchōō̄mbe'rá| *nf* prickly pear.

chungo, a |tchōō̄n'go, á| (*fam*) *a* lousy ♦ *nf*: **estar de chunga** to be in a merry mood.

chupado, a |tchōō̄pá'tho, á| *a* (*delgado*)

skinny, gaunt; **está** ~ (*fam*) it's simple, it's dead easy.

chupar |tchōō̄pár'| *vt* to suck; (*absorber*) to absorb; ~**se** *vr* to grow thin; **para** ~**se los dedos** mouthwatering.

chupatintas |tchōō̄pátēn'tás| *nm inv* penpusher.

chupete |tchōō̄pc'tc| *nm* pacifier (*US*), dummy (*Brit*).

churrasco |tchōō̄rrás'ko| *nm* (*AM*) barbecue, barbecued meat.

churrería |tchōō̄rrcrē'á| *nf* fritter stall *o* shop.

churrete |tchōō̄rrc'tc| *nm* grease spot.

churrigueresco, a |tchōō̄rrēgcrcs'ko, á| *a* (*ARQ*) baroque; (*fig*) excessively ornate.

churro, a |tchōō̄'rro, á| *a* coarse ♦ *nm* (*CULIN*) (type of) fritter; (*chapuza*) botch, mess.

churruscar |tchōō̄rrōō̄skár'| *vt* to fry crisp.

churrusque |tchōō̄rrōō̄s'kc| *etc vb* V **churruscar**.

churumbel |tchōō̄rōō̄ombcl'| *nm* (*fam*) kid.

chus |tchōō̄s| *excl*: **no decir ni** ~ **ni mus** not to say a word.

chusco, a |tchōō̄s'ko, á| *a* funny.

chusma |tchōō̄s'má| *nf* rabble, mob.

chutar |tchōō̄tár'| *vi* (*DEPORTE*) to shoot (at goal); **esto va que chuta** it's going fine.

chuzo |tchōō̄'so| *nm*: **llueve a** ~**s, llueven** ~**s de punta** it's raining cats and dogs.

D

D, d |dc| *nf* (*letra*) D, d; **D de Dolores** D for Dog.

D. *abr* = **Don**.

Da., D.ª *abr* = **Doña**.

dactilar |dáktclár'| *a*: **huellas** ~**es** fingerprints.

dactilógrafo, a |dáktēlo'gráfo, á| *nm/f* typist.

dádiva |dá'thĕhá| *nf* (*donación*) donation; (*regalo*) gift.

dadivoso, a |dáthĕho'so, á| *a* generous.

dado, a |dá'tho, á| *pp de* **dar** ♦ *nm* die; ~**s** *nmpl* dice ♦ *a*: **en un momento** ~ at a certain point; **ser** ~ **a** (**hacer algo**) to be very fond of (doing sth); ~ **que** *conj* given that.

daga |dá'gá| *nf* dagger.

daltónico, a |dálto'nĕko, á| *a* color-blind (*US*), colour-blind (*Brit*).

daltonismo |dáltonēs'mo| *nm* color (*US*) *o*

colour (*Brit*) blindness.

dama [dà'mà] *nf* (*gen*) lady; (*AJEDREZ*)
queen; ~**s** *nfpl* checkers (*US*), draughts
(*Brit*); **primera** ~ (*TEATRO*) leading lady;
(*POL*) first lady (*US*), president's wife; ~
de honor (*de reina*) lady-in-waiting; (*de
novia*) bridesmaid.

damasco [dàmàs'ko] *nm* (*tela*) damask.

damnificado, a [dàmnēfēkà'tho, à] *nm/f*:
los ~**s** the victims.

damnificar [dàmnēfēkár'] *vt* to harm;
(*persona*) to injure.

damnifique [dàmnēfē'ke] *etc vb* V
damnificar.

dance [dàn'se] *etc vb* V **danzar**.

danés, esa [dànes', e'sá] *a* Danish ♦ *nm/f*
Dane ♦ *nm* (*LING*) Danish.

Danubio [dànoo'hyo] *nm* Danube.

danza [dàn'sá] *nf* (*gen*) dancing; (*una* ~)
dance.

danzar [dànsár'] *vt, vi* to dance.

danzarín, ina [dànsárēn', ē'ná] *nm/f* dancer.

dañar [dànyár'] *vt* (*objeto*) to damage;
(*persona*) to hurt; (*estropear*) to spoil; ~**se**
vr (*objeto*) to get damaged.

dañino, a [dànyē'no, à] *a* harmful.

daño [dà'nyo] *nm* (*a un objeto*) damage; (*a
una persona*) harm, injury; ~**s y perjuicios**
(*JUR*) damages; **hacer** ~ **a** to damage;
(*persona*) to hurt, injure; **hacerse** ~ to
hurt o.s.

dar [dár] *vt* to give; (*entregar: objeto*) to
hand; (*grito*) to let out; (*noticias*) to tell;
(*olor*) to give off; (*lección*) to teach; (*TEA-
TRO*) to perform, put on; (*película*) to
show; (*COM*) to yield; (*naipes*) to deal; (*la
hora*): ~ **las 3** to strike 3 ♦ *vi*: ~ **a** to
look out on(to), overlook; ~ **como** *o* **por** to
consider, regard as; ~ **con** (*persona etc*) to
meet, run into; (*idea*) to hit on; ~ **contra**
to knock against, bang into; ~ **en** to strike,
hit; ~ **de sí** to give, stretch; ~ **para** to be
enough for; ~ **que hablar** to set people
talking; ~**se** *vr* (*suceso*) to happen; (*presentarse*) to occur; (*AGR*) to grow; ~**se a**
to be given to; ~**se por** to consider o.s.;
dárselas de to pose as; **se me dan muy
bien/mal los idiomas** I am very good/bad
at languages; ~ **de comer/beber a uno** to
give sb sth to eat/drink; **¡dale!** go on!; ~**le
a uno por hacer algo** to take it into one's
head to do sth; **lo mismo da** it makes no
difference; **da lo mismo** *o* **qué más da** it's
all the same; **me da igual** I don't care; ~
en el blanco to hit the mark; **me da asco/
miedo** it sickens/frightens me; **me da pena**
it makes me sad; ~**se prisa** to hurry (up).

dardo [dár'tho] *nm* dart.

dársena [dár'senà] *nf* (*NAUT*) dock.

datar [dàtár'] *vi*: ~ **de** to date from.

dátil [dà'tēl] *nm* date.

dativo [dàtē'ho] *nm* (*LING*) dative.

dato [dà'to] *nm* fact, piece of information;
(*MAT*) datum; ~**s** *nmpl* (*INFORM*) data; ~**s
de entrada/salida** input/output data; ~**s
personales** personal particulars.

dcha. *abr* (= *derecha*) r.h.

d. de J. C. *abr* (= *después de Jesucristo*)
A.D.

de [de] *prep* (*posesión*) of; (*origen, distancia*) from; **la ciudad** ~ **Madrid** the city
of Madrid; **el coche de mi amigo/mis amigos** my friend's car/my friends' car; **el
más caro del negocio/mundo** the most
expensive in the shop/world; **un libro** ~
Unamuno a book by Unamuno; **un chico** ~
15 años a 15-year-old boy; **un viaje** ~ **2
días** a two-day journey; **un libro grato** ~
leer a nice book to read; **libro** ~ **cocina**
cookbook; **el hombre** ~ **largos cabellos** the
man with long hair; **guantes** ~ **cuero**
leather gloves; **vuelo 507** ~ **Londres** flight
507 from London; **es** ~ **Sevilla** she's from
Seville; **estar loco** ~ **alegría** to be overjoyed; ~ **un salto** with one bound; ~ **niño**
as a child; **fue a Londres** ~ **profesor** he
went to London as a teacher; **una** ~ **dos**
one or the other; **3** ~ **cada 4** three out of
every four; ~ **día/noche** by day/night; ~
mañana in the morning; **vestido** ~ **negro**
dressed in black; **más/menos** ~ **3** more/
less than 3; ~ **cara a** facing; ~ **ser posible**
if possible.

dé [de] *vb* V **dar**.

deambular [deàmboolár'] *vi* to stroll,
wander.

debajo [dehà'ho] *ad* underneath; ~ **de** below, under; **por** ~ **de** beneath.

debate [dehà'te] *nm* debate.

debatir [dehàtēr'] *vt* to debate; ~**se** *vr* to
struggle.

debe [de'he] *nm* (*en cuenta*) debit side; ~ **y
haber** debit and credit.

deber [deher'] *nm* duty ♦ *vt* to owe ♦ *vi*:
debe (de) it must, it should; **debo hacerlo**
I must do it; **debe de ir** he should go; ~**se
vr**: ~**se a** to be owing *o* due to; **¿qué** *o*
cuánto le debo? how much is it?; ~**es**
nmpl (*ESCOL*) homework *sg*.

debidamente [dehēthàmen'te] *ad* properly;
(*rellenar: documento, solicitud*) duly.

debido, a [dehē'tho, à] *a* proper, due; ~ **a**
due to, because of; **en debida forma** duly.

débil [de'hēl] *a* weak; (*persona: física-
mente*) feeble; (*salud*) poor; (*voz, ruido*)
faint; (*luz*) dim.

debilidad [dehēlēthàth'] *nf* weakness;
feebleness; dimness; **tener** ~ **por uno** to
have a soft spot for sb.

debilitar [dehēlētár'] *vt* to weaken; ~**se** *vr*
to grow weak.

débito [de'hēto] *nm* debit; (*deuda*) debt.

debutante [deḇōōtán'te] *nm/f* beginner.
debutar [deḇōōtár'] *vi* to make one's debut.
década [de'káṭ̇á] *nf* decade.
decadencia [dekáṭ̇en'syá] *nf* (*estado*) decadence; (*proceso*) decline, decay.
decadente [dekáṭ̇en'te] *a* decadent.
decaer [dekáer'] *vi* (*declinar*) to decline; (*debilitarse*) to weaken; (*salud*) to fail; (*negocio*) to fall off.
decaído, a [dekáé'ṭ̇o, á] *a*: **estar ~** (*persona*) to be down.
decaiga [dekáʾēg̣á] *etc vb* V **decaer**.
decaimiento [dekáēmyen'to] *nm* (*declinación*) decline; (*desaliento*) discouragement; (*MED: depresión*) depression.
decanato [dekáná'to] *nm* (*cargo*) deanship; (*despacho*) dean's office.
decano, a [dekáʾno, á] *nm/f* (*UNIV etc*) dean; (*de grupo*) senior member.
decantar [dekántár'] *vt* (*vino*) to decant.
decapitar [dekápētár'] *vt* to behead.
decayendo [dekáyen'do] *etc vb* V **decaer**.
decena [desc'ná] *nf*: **una ~** ten (or so).
decencia [desen'syá] *nf* (*modestia*) modesty; (*honestidad*) respectability.
decenio [desc'nyo] *nm* decade.
decente [desen'te] *a* (*correcto*) proper; (*honesto*) respectable.
decepción [desepsyon'] *nf* disappointment.
decepcionante [desepsyonán'te] *a* disappointing.
decepcionar [desepsyonár'] *vt* to disappoint.
decibel [desēḇel'], **decibelio** [desēḇe'lyo] *nm* decibel.
decidido, a [desēṭ̇ē'ṭ̇o, á] *a* decided; (*resuelto*) resolute.
decidir [desēṭ̇ēr'] *vt* (*persuadir*) to convince, persuade; (*resolver*) to decide ♦ *vi* to decide; **~se** *vr*: **~se a** to make up one's mind to; **~se por** to decide o settle on, choose.
décimo, a [de'sēmo, á] *num* tenth ♦ *nf* (*esp en lotería*) tenth part.
decimoctavo, a [desēmoktá'ḇo, á] *num* eighteenth; *V tb* **sexto**.
decimoséptimo, a [desēmosep'tēmo, á] *num* seventeenth; *V tb* **sexto**.
decimosexto, a [desēmosek'sto, á] *num* sixteenth; *V tb* **sexto**.
decimotercero, a [desēmoterse'ro, á], **decimotercio, a** [desēmoter'syo, á] *num* thirteenth; *V tb* **sexto**.
decir [desēr'] *vt* (*expresar*) to say; (*contar*) to tell; (*hablar*) to speak; (*indicar*) to show; (*revelar*) to reveal; (*fam: nombrar*) to call ♦ *nm* saying; **~se** *vr*: **se dice** it is said, they say; (*se cuenta*) the story goes; **¿cómo se dice en inglés "cursi"?** what's the English for "cursi"?; **~ para/entre sí** to say to o.s.; **~ por ~** to talk for talking's

sake; **dar que ~ (a la gente)** to make people talk; **querer ~** to mean; **es ~** that is to say, namely; **ni que ~ tiene que...** it goes without saying that...; **como quien dice** so to speak; **¡quién lo diría!** would you believe it!; **el qué dirán** gossip; **¡diga!, ¡dígame!** (*en tienda etc*) can I help you?; (*TELEC*) hello?; **le dije que fuera más tarde** I told her to go later; **es un ~** it's just a phrase.
decisión [desēsyon'] *nf* decision; (*firmeza*) decisiveness; (*voluntad*) determination.
decisivo, a [desēsē'ḇo, á] *a* decisive.
declamar [deklámár'] *vt, vi* to declaim; (*versos etc*) to recite.
declaración [deklárásyon'] *nf* (*manifestación*) statement; (*explicación*) explanation; (*JUR: testimonio*) evidence; **~ de derechos** (*POL*) bill of rights; **~ de impuestos** (*COM*) tax return; **~ de ingresos** *o* **de renta** *o* **fiscal** (*AM*) income tax return; **~ jurada** affidavit; **falsa ~** (*JUR*) misrepresentation.
declarar [deklárár'] *vt* to declare ♦ *vi* to declare; (*JUR*) to testify; **~se** *vr* (*opinión*) to make one's opinion known; (*a una chica*) to propose; (*guerra, incendio*) to break out; **~ culpable/inocente a uno** to find sb guilty/not guilty; **~se culpable/inocente** to plead guilty/not guilty.
declinación [deklēnásyon'] *nf* (*decaimiento*) decline; (*LING*) declension.
declinar [deklēnár'] *vt* (*gen, LING*) to decline; (*JUR*) to reject ♦ *vi* (*el día*) to draw to a close.
declive [deklē'ḇe] *nm* (*cuesta*) slope; (*inclinación*) incline; (*fig*) decline; (*COM: tb: ~ económico*) slump.
decodificador [dekoṭ̇ēfēkáṭ̇or'] *nm* (*INFORM*) decoder.
decolorarse [dekolorár'se] *vr* to become discolored (*US*) o discoloured (*Brit*).
decomisar [dekomēsár'] *vt* to seize, confiscate.
decoración [dekorásyon'] *nf* decoration; (*TEATRO*) scenery, set; **~ de escaparates** window dressing.
decorado [dekorá'ṭ̇o] *nm* (*CINE, TEATRO*) scenery, set.
decorador, a [dekoráṭ̇or', á] *nm/f* (*de interiores*) (interior) decorator; (*TEATRO*) stage o set designer.
decorar [dekorár'] *vt* to decorate.
decorativo, a [dekorátē'ḇo, á] *a* ornamental, decorative.
decoro [deko'ro] *nm* (*respeto*) respect; (*dignidad*) decency; (*recato*) propriety.
decoroso, a [dekoro'so, á] *a* (*decente*) decent; (*modesto*) modest; (*digno*) proper.
decrecer [dekreser'] *vi* to decrease, diminish; (*nivel de agua*) to go down; (*días*) to

draw in.

decrépito, a [dekrc'pĕto, á] a decrepit.

decretar [dekretár'] vt to decree.

decreto [dekre'to] nm decree; (POL) act.

decreto-ley [dekretoleĕ'], pl **decretos-leyes** nm decree.

decrezca [dekres'ká] etc vb V **decrecer**.

decúbito [dekōō'bĕto] nm (MED): ~ **prono/supino** prone/supine position.

dedal [dethál'] nm thimble.

dedalera [dethále'rá] nf foxglove.

dédalo [de'thálo] nm (laberinto) labyrinth; (fig) tangle, mess.

dedicación [dethĕkásyon'] nf dedication; **con ~ exclusiva** o **plena** full-time.

dedicar [dethĕkár'] vt (libro) to dedicate; (tiempo, dinero) to devote; **~se** vr: **~se a** to devote o.s. to (hacer algo doing sth); (carrera, estudio) to go in for, take up; **¿a qué se dedica usted?** what do you do (for a living)?

dedicatoria [dethĕkáto'ryá] nf (de libro) dedication.

dedillo [dethĕ'yo] nm: **saber algo al ~** to have sth at one's fingertips.

dedique [dethĕ'ke] etc vb V **dedicar**.

dedo [de'tho] nm finger; (de vino etc) drop; **~ (del pie)** toe; **~ pulgar** thumb; **~ índice** index finger; **~ mayor** o **cordial** middle finger; **~ anular** ring finger; **~ meñique** little finger; **contar con los ~s** to count on one's fingers; **comerse los ~s** to get very impatient; **entrar a ~** to get a job by pulling strings; **hacer ~** (fam) to hitch (a ride (US) o lift (Brit)); **poner el ~ en la llaga** to put one's finger on it; **no tiene dos ~s de frente** he's pretty dense.

deducción [dethōōksyon'] nf deduction.

deducir [dethōōsĕr'] vt (concluir) to deduce, infer; (COM) to deduct.

deduje [dethōō'he] etc, **dedujera** [dethōōhe'-rá] etc, **deduzca** [dethōō'ská] etc vb V **deducir**.

defección [defeksyon'] nf defection, desertion.

defecto [defek'to] nm defect, flaw; (de cara) imperfection; **~ de pronunciación** speech defect; **por ~** (INFORM) default; **~ latente** (COM) latent defect.

defectuoso, a [defektwo'so, á] a defective, faulty.

defender [defender'] vt to defend; (ideas) to uphold; (causa) to champion; (amigos) to stand up for; **~se** vr to defend o.s.; **~se bien** to give a good account of o.s.; **me defiendo en inglés** (fig) I can get by in English.

defendible [defendĕ'ble] a defensible.

defensa [defen'sá] nf defense (US), defence (Brit); (NAUT) fender, bumper pad (US) ♦ nm (DEPORTE) defense (US), back; **en ~**

propia in self-defense.

defensivo, a [defensĕ'ho, á] a defensive ♦ nf: **a la defensiva** on the defensive.

defensor, a [defensor', á] a defending ♦ nm/f (abogado ~) defense (US) o defending (Brit) counsel; (protector) protector; **~ del pueblo** (Esp) ≈ ombudsman.

deferir [deferĕr'] vt (JUR) to refer, delegate ♦ vi: **~ a** to defer to.

deficiencia [defĕsyen'syá] nf deficiency.

deficiente [defĕsyen'te] a (defectuoso) defective; **~ en** lacking o deficient in ♦ nm/f: **ser un ~ mental** to be mentally handicapped.

déficit, ~s [de'fĕsĕt] nm (COM) deficit; (fig) lack, shortage; **~ presupuestario** budget deficit.

defienda [defyen'dá] etc vb V **defender**.

defiera [defye'rá] etc vb V **deferir**.

definición [defĕnĕsyon'] nf definition; (IN-FORM: de pantalla) resolution.

definido, a [defĕnĕ'tho, á] a (tb LING) definite; **bien ~** well o clearly defined; **~ por el usuario** (INFORM) user-defined.

definir [defĕnĕr'] vt (determinar) to determine, establish; (decidir, INFORM) to define; (aclarar) to clarify.

definitivo, a [defĕnĕtĕ'ho, á] a (edición, texto) definitive; (fecha) definite; **en definitiva** definitively; (en conclusión) finally; (en resumen) in short.

defiriendo [defĕryen'do] etc vb V **deferir**.

deflacionario, a [deflásyoná'ryo, á], **deflacionista** [deflásyonĕ'stá] a deflationary.

deflector [deflektor'] nm (TEC) baffle.

deformación [deformásyon'] nf (alteración) deformation; (RADIO etc) distortion.

deformar [deformár'] vt (gen) to deform; **~se** vr to become deformed.

deforme [defor'me] a (informe) deformed; (feo) ugly; (mal hecho) misshapen.

deformidad [deformĕtháth'] nf (forma anormal) deformity; (fig: defecto) (moral) shortcoming.

defraudar [defráōōthár'] vt (decepcionar) to disappoint; (estafar) to cheat; to defraud; **~ impuestos** to evade tax.

defunción [defōōnsyon'] nf decease, demise.

degeneración [dehenerásyon'] nf (de las células) degeneration; (moral) degeneracy.

degenerar [dehenerár'] vi to degenerate; (empeorar) to get worse.

deglutir [deglootĕr'] vt, vi to swallow.

degolladero [degoyáthe'ro] nm (ANAT) throat; (cadalso) scaffold; (matadero) slaughterhouse.

degollar [degoyár'] vt to slaughter.

degradar [degráthár'] vt to debase, degrade; (INFORM: datos) to corrupt; **~se** vr to demean o.s.

degüelle [deǥwe'ye] *etc vb* V **degollar.**
degustación [deǥoōstásyon'] *nf* sampling, tasting.
deificar [deĉfĕkár'] *vt* (*persona*) to deify.
deifique [deĉfĕ'ke] *etc vb* V **deificar.**
dejadez [dehắɦes'] *nf* (*negligencia*) neglect; (*descuido*) untidiness, carelessness.
dejado, a [dehá'ho, á] *a* (*desaliñado*) slovenly; (*negligente*) careless; (*indolente*) lazy.
dejar [dehár'] *vt* (*gen*) to leave; (*permitir*) to allow, let; (*abandonar*) to abandon, forsake; (*actividad, empleo*) to give up; (*beneficios*) to produce, yield ♦ *vi*: ~ **de** (*parar*) to stop; ~**se** *vr* (*abandonarse*) to let o.s. go; **no puedo ~ de fumar** I can't give up smoking; **no dejes de visitarles** don't fail to visit them; **no dejes de comprar un billete** make sure you buy a ticket; ~ **a un lado** to leave *o* set aside; ~ **caer** to drop; ~ **entrar/salir** to let in/out; ~ **pasar** to let through; **¡déjalo!** (*no te preocupes*) don't worry about it; **te dejo en tu casa** I'll drop you off at your place; **deja mucho que desear** it leaves a lot to be desired; ~**se persuadir** to allow o.s. to *o* let o.s. be persuaded; **¡déjate de tonterías!** stop messing around!
deje [de'he] *nm* (trace of) accent.
dejo [de'ho] *nm* (*LING*) accent.
del [del] = **de + el,** *ver* **de.**
del. *abr* (*ADMIN*: = *Delegación*) district office.
delantal [delántál'] *nm* apron.
delante [delán'te] *ad* in front; (*enfrente*) opposite; (*adelante*) ahead ♦ *prep*: ~ **de** in front of, before; **la parte de** ~ the front part; **estando otros** ~ with others present.
delantero, a [delánte'ro, á] *a* front; (*patas de animal*) fore ♦ *nm* (*DEPORTE*) forward ♦ *nf* (*de vestido, casa etc*) front part; (*TEATRO*) front row; (*DEPORTE*) forward line; **llevar la delantera (a uno)** to be ahead (of sb).
delatar [delátár'] *vt* to inform on *o* against, betray; **los delató a la policía** he reported them to the police.
delator, a [delátor', á] *nm/f* informer.
delegación [deleǥásyon'] *nf* (*acción, delegados*) delegation; (*COM: oficina*) district office, branch; ~ **de poderes** (*POL*) devolution; ~ **de policía** police station.
delegado, a [deleǥá'ho, á] *nm/f* delegate; (*COM*) agent.
delegar [deleǥár'] *vt* to delegate.
delegue [dele'ǥe] *etc vb* V **delegar.**
deleitar [deleĉtár'] *vt* to delight; ~**se** *vr*: ~**se con** *o* **en** to delight in, take pleasure in.
deleite [delc'ĕte] *nm* delight, pleasure.

deletrear [deletreár'] *vt* (*tb fig*) to spell (out).
deletreo [deletre'o] *nm* spelling; (*fig*) interpretation, decipherment.
deleznable [delesná'hle] *a* (*frágil*) fragile; (*fig: malo*) poor; (*excusa*) feeble.
delfín [delfēn'] *nm* dolphin.
delgadez [delǥáɦes'] *nf* thinness, slimness.
delgado, a [delǥá'ho, á] *a* thin; (*persona*) slim, thin; (*tierra*) poor; (*tela etc*) light, delicate ♦ *ad*: **hilar (muy)** ~ (*fig*) to split hairs.
deliberación [delĉħerásyon'] *nf* deliberation.
deliberar [delĉħerár'] *vt* to debate, discuss ♦ *vi* to deliberate.
delicadeza [delĉkáɦe'sá] *nf* delicacy; (*refinamiento, sutileza*) refinement.
delicado, a [delĉká'ho, á] *a* delicate; (*sensible*) sensitive; (*rasgos*) dainty; (*gusto*) refined; (*situación: difícil*) tricky; (: *violento*) embarrassing; (*punto, tema*) sore; (*persona: difícil de contentar*) hard to please; (: *sensible*) touchy, hypersensitive; (: *atento*) considerate.
delicia [delĉ'syá] *nf* delight.
delicioso, a [delĉsyo'so, á] *a* (*gracioso*) delightful; (*exquisito*) delicious.
delictivo, a [delĉktĕ'ho, á] *a* criminal *cpd*.
delimitar [delĉmĕtár'] *vt* to delimit.
delincuencia [delēnkwen'syá] *nf*: ~ **juvenil** juvenile delinquency; **cifras de la** ~ crime rate.
delincuente [delēnkwen'te] *nm/f* delinquent; (*criminal*) criminal; ~ **sin antecedentes** first offender; ~ **habitual** hardened criminal.
delineante [delēneán'te] *nm/f* draftsman (*US*), draughtsman (*Brit*).
delinear [delēneár'] *vt* to delineate; (*dibujo*) to draw; (*contornos, fig*) to outline; ~ **un proyecto** to outline a project.
delinquir [delēnkēr'] *vi* to commit an offense.
delirante [delērán'te] *a* delirious.
delirar [delērár'] *vi* to be delirious, rave; (*fig: desatinar*) to talk nonsense.
delirio [delē'ryo] *nm* (*MED*) delirium; (*palabras insensatas*) ravings *pl*; ~ **de grandeza** megalomania; ~ **de persecución** persecution mania; **con** ~ (*fam*) madly; **¡fue el** ~**!** (*fam*) it was great!
delito [delē'to] *nm* (*gen*) crime; (*infracción*) offense (*US*), offence (*Brit*).
demacrado, a [demákrá'ho, á] *a* emaciated.
demagogo [demáǥo'ǥo] *nm* demagogue.
demanda [demán'dá] *nf* (*pedido, COM*) demand; (*petición*) request; (*pregunta*) inquiry; (*reivindicación*) claim; (*JUR*) action, lawsuit; (*TEATRO*) call; (*ELEC*) load; ~ **de**

pago demand for payment; **escribir en ~ de ayuda** to write asking for help; **entablar ~** (*JUR*) to sue; **presentar ~ de divorcio** to sue for divorce; **~ final** final demand; **~ indirecta** derived demand; **~ de mercado** market demand.

demandado, a [demándá'θo, á] *nm/f* defendant; (*en divorcio*) respondent.

demandante [demándán'te] *nm/f* claimant; (*JUR*) plaintiff.

demandar [demándár'] *vt* (*gen*) to demand; (*JUR*) to sue, file a lawsuit against, start proceedings against; **~ a uno por calumnia/daños y perjuicios** to sue sb for libel/damages.

demarcación [demárkásyon'] *nf* (*de terreno*) demarcation.

demás [demás'] *a:* **los ~ niños** the other children, the remaining children ♦ *pron:* **los/las ~** the others, the rest (of them); **lo ~** the rest (of it); **por ~** moreover; (*en vano*) in vain; **y ~** etcetera.

demasía [demásē'á] *nf* (*exceso*) excess, surplus; **comer en ~** to eat to excess.

demasiado, a [demásyá'θo, á] *a:* **~ vino** too much wine; **~s libros** too many books ♦ *ad* (*antes de a, ad*) too; **¡es ~!** it's too much!; **es ~ pesado para levantar** it is too heavy to lift; **~ lo sé** I know it only too well; **hace ~ calor** it's too hot.

demencia [demen'syá] *nf* (*locura*) madness.

demencial [demensyál'] *a* crazy.

demente [demen'te] *a* mad, insane ♦ *nm/f* lunatic.

demérito [deme'rēto] *nm* (*falta*) fault; (*AM: depreciación*) depreciation.

democracia [demokrá'syá] *nf* democracy.

demócrata [demo'krátá] *nm/f* democrat.

democratacristiano, a [demokrátákrēstyá'no, á] *a, nm/f* Christian Democrat.

democrático, a [demokrá'tēko, á] *a* democratic.

democristiano, a [demokrēstyá'no, á] *a, nm/f* Christian Democrat.

demográfico, a [demográ'fēko, á] *a* demographic, population *cpd*; **la explosión demográfica** the population explosion.

demoledor, a [demoleθor', á] *a* (*fig: argumento*) overwhelming; (: *ataque*) shattering.

demoler [demoler'] *vt* to demolish; (*edificio*) to tear down.

demolición [demolēsyon'] *nf* demolition.

demonio [demo'nyo] *nm* devil, demon; **¡~s!** hell!; **¿cómo ~s?** how the hell?; **¿qué ~s será?** what the devil can it be?; **¿dónde ~ lo habré dejado?** where the hell can I have left it?; **tener el ~ en el cuerpo** (*no parar*) to be always on the go.

demora [demo'rá] *nf* delay.

demorar [demorár'] *vt* (*retardar*) to delay,

hold back; (*dilatar*) to hold up ♦ *vi* to linger, stay on; **~se** *vr* to linger, stay on; (*retrasarse*) to take a long time.

demos [de'mos] *vb* V **dar**.

demostración [demostrásyon'] *nf* (*gen*, *MAT*) demonstration; (*de cariño, fuerza*) show; (*de teorema*) proof; (*de amistad*) gesture; (*de cólera, gimnasia*) display; **~ comercial** commercial exhibition.

demostrar [demostrár'] *vt* (*probar*) to prove; (*mostrar*) to show; (*manifestar*) to demonstrate.

demostrativo, a [demostrátē'βo, á] *a* demonstrative.

demudado, a [demōōθá'θo, á] *a* (*rostro*) pale; (*fig*) upset; **tener el rostro ~** to look pale.

demudar [demōōθár'] *vt* to change, alter; **~se** *vr* (*expresión*) to alter; (*perder color*) to change color (*US*) o colour (*Brit*).

demuela [demwe'lá] *etc vb* V **demoler**.

demuestre [demwes'tre] *etc vb* V **demostrar**.

den [den] *vb* V **dar**.

denegación [denegásyon'] *nf* refusal, denial.

denegar [denegár'] *vt* (*rechazar*) to refuse; (*negar*) to deny; (*JUR*) to reject.

denegué [denege'], **deneguemos** [denege'mos] *etc*, **deniego** [denye'go] *etc*, **deniegue** [denye'ge] *etc vb* V **denegar**.

denigrante [denēgrán'te] *a* (*injurioso*) insulting; (*deshonroso*) degrading.

denigrar [denēgrár'] *vt* (*desacreditar*) to denigrate; (*injuriar*) to insult.

denodado, a [denoθá'θo, á] *a* bold, brave.

denominación [denomēnásyon'] *nf* (*acto*) naming; (*clase*) denomination; **~ de origen** (*vino*) guarantee of vintage, ≈ appellation contrôlée.

denostar [denostár'] *vt* to insult.

denotar [denotár'] *vt* (*indicar*) to indicate, denote.

densidad [densēθáθ'] *nf* (*FÍSICA*) density; (*fig*) thickness; **~ de caracteres** (*INFORM*) pitch.

denso, a [den'so, á] *a* (*apretado*) solid; (*espeso, pastoso*) thick; (*fig*) heavy.

dentado, a [dentá'θo, á] *a* (*rueda*) cogged; (*filo*) jagged; (*sello*) perforated; (*BOT*) dentate.

dentadura [dentáθōō'rá] *nf* (set of) teeth *pl;* **~ postiza** dentures *pl.*

dentellada [dentcyá'θá] *nf* (*mordisco*) bite, nip; (*señal*) tooth mark; **partir algo a ~s** to sever sth with one's teeth.

dentera [dente'rá] *nf* (*sensación desagradable*) the shivers *pl.*

dentición [dentēsyon'] *nf* (*acto*) teething; (*ANAT*) dentition; **estar con la ~** to be teething.

dentífrico, a [dentē'frēko, á] a dental, tooth cpd ♦ nm toothpaste; **pasta dentífrica** toothpaste.

dentista [dentē'stá] nm/f dentist.

dentro [den'tro] ad inside ♦ prep: ~ **de** in, inside, within; **allí** ~ in there; **mirar por** ~ to look inside; ~ **de lo posible** as far as possible; ~ **de todo** all in all; ~ **de tres meses** within three months.

denuedo [denwe'ðo] nm boldness, daring.

denuesto [denwe'sto] nm insult.

denuncia [denōōn'syá] nf (delación) de-nunciation; (acusación) accusation; (de accidente) report; **hacer o poner una** ~ to report an incident to the police.

denunciable [denōōnsyá'ßle] a indictable, punishable.

denunciador, a [denōōnsyáðor', á], **de-nunciante** [denōōnsyán'te] nm/f accuser; (delator) informer.

denunciar [denōōnsyár'] vt to report; (dela-tar) to inform on o against.

Dep. abr (= Departamento) Dept.; (= Depó-sito) dep.

deparar [depárár'] vt (brindar) to provide o furnish with; (suj: futuro, destino) to have in store for; **los placeres que el viaje nos deparó** the pleasures which the trip afforded us.

departamento [departámen'to] nm (sección administrativa) department, sec-tion; (AM: piso) apartment (US), flat (Brit); (distrito) department, province; ~ **de envíos** (COM) shipping department; ~ **de máquinas** (NAUT) engine room.

departir [depártēr'] vi to talk, converse.

dependencia [dependen'syá] nf de-pendence; (POL) dependency; (COM) office, section; (sucursal) branch office; (ARQ: cuarto) room; ~**s** nfpl outbuildings.

depender [depender'] vi: ~ **de** to depend on; (contar con) to rely on; (de autoridad) to be under, be answerable to; **depende it** (all) depends; **no depende de mí** it's not up to me.

dependienta [dependyen'tá] nf sales-woman, sales assistant.

dependiente [dependyen'te] a dependent ♦ nm salesman, sales assistant.

depilación [depēlásyon'] nf hair removal.

depilar [depēlár'] vt (con cera: piernas) to remove hair from; (cejas) to pluck.

depilatorio, a [depēláto'ryo, á] a depilatory ♦ nm hair remover.

deplorable [deplorá'ßle] a deplorable.

deplorar [deplorár'] vt to deplore.

depondré [depondre'] etc vb V **deponer**.

deponer [deponer'] vt (armas) to lay down; (rey) to depose; (gobernante) to oust; (ministro) to remove from office ♦ vi (JUR) to give evidence; (declarar) to make a statement.

deponga [depon'gá] etc vb V **deponer**.

deportación [deportásyon'] nf deportation.

deportar [deportár'] vt to deport.

deporte [depor'te] nm sport.

deportista [deportē'stá] a sports cpd ♦ nm/f sportsman/woman.

deportivo, a [deportē'ßo, á] a (club, perió-dico) sports cpd ♦ nm sports car.

deposición [deposēsyon'] nf (de funcionario etc) removal from office; (JUR: testimonio) evidence.

depositante [deposētán'te], **depositador, a** [deposētáðor', á] nm/f depositor.

depositar [deposētár'] vt (dinero) to depos-it; (mercaderías) to put away, store; ~**se** vr to settle; ~ **la confianza en uno** to place one's trust in sb.

depositario, a [deposētá'ryo, á] nm/f trustee; ~ **judicial** official receiver.

depósito [depo'sēto] nm (gen) deposit; (de mercaderías) warehouse, store; (de ani-males, coches) pound; (de agua, gasolina etc) tank; (en retrete) tank; ~ **afianzado** bonded warehouse; ~ **bancario** bank depos-it; ~ **de cadáveres** mortuary; ~ **de made-ras** lumber (US) o timber (Brit) yard; ~ **de suministro** feeder bin.

depravar [deprávár'] vt to deprave, corrupt; ~**se** vr to become depraved.

depreciación [depresyásyon'] nf deprecia-tion.

depreciar [depresyár'] vt to depreciate, re-duce the value of; ~**se** vr to depreciate, lose value.

depredador, a [depreðáðor', á] (ZOOL) a predatory ♦ nm predator.

depredar [depreðár'] vt to pillage.

depresión [depresyon'] nf (gen, MED) de-pression; (hueco) hollow; (en horizonte, ca-mino) dip; (merma) drop; (ECON) slump, recession; ~ **nerviosa** nervous breakdown.

deprimente [deprimen'te] a depressing.

deprimido, a [deprimē'ðo, á] a depressed.

deprimir [deprimēr'] vt to depress; ~**se** vr (persona) to become depressed.

deprisa [deprē'sá] ad V **prisa**.

depuesto [depwe'sto] pp de **deponer**.

depuración [depōōrásyon'] nf purification; (POL) purge; (INFORM) debugging.

depurador [depōōráðor'] nm purifier.

depurar [depōōrár'] vt to purify; (purgar) to purge; (INFORM) to debug.

depuse [depōō'se] etc vb V **deponer**.

der., der.º abr (= derecho) r.

derecha [deretch'á] nf V **derecho**.

derechazo [deretchá'so] nm (BOXEO) right; (TENIS) forehand drive; (TAUR) a pass with the cape.

derechista [deretchē'stá] (POL) a right-wing ♦ nm/f right-winger.

derecho, a [deretch'o, á] *a* right, right-hand ♦ *nm* (*privilegio*) right; (*título*) claim, title; (*lado*) right(-hand) side; (*leyes*) law ♦ *nf* right(-hand) side ♦ *ad* straight, directly; ~**s** *nmpl* dues; (*profesionales*) fees; (*impuestos*) taxes; (*de autor*) royalties; **la(s) derecha(s)** (*pl*) (*POL*) the Right; ~**s civiles** civil rights; ~**s de muelle** (*COM*) docking fees (*US*), dock dues (*Brit*); ~**s de patente** patent rights; ~**s portuarios** (*COM*) harbor fees (*US*), harbour dues (*Brit*); ~ **de propiedad literaria** copyright; ~ **de retención** (*COM*) lien; ~ **de timbre** (*COM*) stamp duty; ~ **de votar** right to vote; ~ **a voto** voting right; **Facultad de D**~ Law School (*US*), Faculty of Law (*Brit*); **a derechas** rightly, correctly; **de derechas** (*POL*) right-wing; "**reservados todos los** ~**s**" "all rights reserved"; **¡no hay** ~**!** it's not fair!; **tener** ~ **a** to have a right to; **a la derecha** on the right; (*dirección*) to the right.

deriva [derē'bá] *nf*: **ir** *o* **estar a la** ~ to drift, be adrift.

derivación [derebásyon'] *nf* derivation.

derivado, a [derēbá'tho, á] *a* a derived ♦ *nm* (*LING*) derivative; (*INDUSTRIA, QUÍMICA*) by-product.

derivar [derebár'] *vt* to derive; (*desviar*) to direct ♦ *vi*, ~**se** *vr* to derive, be derived; ~**(se) de** (*consecuencia*) to spring from.

dermatólogo, a [dermáto'logo, á] *nm/f* dermatologist.

dérmico, a [der'mēko, á] *a* skin *cpd*.

derogación [derogásyon'] *nf* repeal.

derogar [derogár'] *vt* (*ley*) to repeal; (*contrato*) to revoke.

derogue [dero'ge] *etc vb V* **derogar**.

derramamiento [derrámámyen'to] *nm* (*dispersión*) spilling; (*fig*) squandering; ~ **de sangre** bloodshed.

derramar [derrámár'] *vt* to spill; (*verter*) to pour out; (*esparcir*) to scatter; ~**se** *vr* to pour out; ~ **lágrimas** to weep.

derrame [derrá'me] *nm* (*de líquido*) spilling; (*de sangre*) shedding; (*de tubo etc*) overflow; (*perdida*) leakage; (*MED*) discharge; (*declive*) slope; ~ **cerebral** brain hemorrhage (*US*) *o* haemorrhage (*Brit*); ~ **sinovial** water on the knee.

derredor [derrethor'] *ad*: **al** *o* **en** ~ **de** around, about.

derrengado, a [derrenga'tho, á] *a* (*torcido*) bent; (*cojo*) crippled; **estar** ~ (*fig*) to ache all over; **dejar** ~ **a uno** (*fig*) to wear sb out.

derretido, a [derretē'tho, á] *a* melted; (*metal*) molten; **estar** ~ **por uno** (*fig*) to be crazy about sb.

derretir [derretēr'] *vt* (*gen*) to melt; (*nieve*) to thaw; (*fig*) to squander; ~**se** *vr* to melt.

derribar [derrēbár'] *vt* to knock down; (*construcción*) to demolish; (*persona, gobierno, político*) to bring down.

derribo [derrē'bo] *nm* (*de edificio*) demolition; (*LUCHA*) take-down (*US*), throw (*Brit*); (*AVIAT*) shooting down; (*POL*) overthrow; ~**s** *nmpl* rubble *sg*, debris *sg*.

derrita [derrē'tá] *etc vb V* **derretir**.

derrocar [derrokár'] *vt* (*gobierno*) to bring down, overthrow; (*ministro*) to oust.

derrochador, a [derrotchá'thor', á] *a, nm/f* spendthrift.

derrochar [derrotchár'] *vt* (*dinero, recursos*) to squander; (*energía, salud*) to be bursting with *o* full of.

derroche [derrotch'e] *nm* (*despilfarro*) waste, squandering; (*exceso*) extravagance; **con un** ~ **de buen gusto** with a fine display of good taste.

derroque [derro'ke] *etc vb V* **derrocar**.

derrota [derro'tá] *nf* (*NAUT*) course; (*MIL*) defeat, rout; **sufrir una grave** ~ (*fig*) to suffer a grave setback.

derrotar [derrotár'] *vt* (*gen*) to defeat.

derrotero [derrote'ro] *nm* (*rumbo*) course; **tomar otro** ~ (*fig*) to adopt a different course.

derrotista [derrotē'stá] *a, nm/f* defeatist.

derruir [derrōōēr'] *vt* to demolish, tear down.

derrumbamiento [derrōōmbámyen'to] *nm* (*caída*) plunge; (*demolición*) demolition; (*desplome*) collapse; ~ **de tierra** landslide.

derrumbar [derrōōmbár'] *vt* to throw down; (*despeñar*) to fling *o* hurl down; (*volcar*) to upset; ~**se** *vr* (*hundirse*) to collapse; (: *techo*) to fall in, cave in; (*fig: esperanzas*) to collapse.

derrumbe [derrōōm'be] *nm* = **derrumbamiento**.

derruyendo [derrōōyen'do] *etc vb V* **derruir**.

des [des] *vb V* **dar**.

desabastecido, a [desábástesē'tho, á] *a*: **estar** ~ **de algo** to be short of *o* out of sth.

desabotonar [desábotonár'] *vt* to unbutton, undo ♦ *vi* (*flores*) to blossom; ~**se** *vr* to come undone.

desabrido, a [desábrē'tho, á] *a* (*comida*) insipid, tasteless; (*persona: soso*) dull; (: *antipático*) rude, surly; (*respuesta*) sharp; (*tiempo*) unpleasant.

desabrigado, a [desábrega'tho, á] *a* (*sin abrigo*) not sufficiently protected; (*fig*) exposed.

desabrigar [desábregár'] *vt* (*quitar ropa a*) to remove the clothing of; (*descubrir*) to uncover; (*fig*) to deprive of protection; ~**se** *vr*: **me desabrigué en la cama** the bedclothes came off.

desabrigue [desábrē'ge] *etc vb V* **desabri-**

gar.

desabrochar [desábrotchár'] vt (botones, broches) to undo, unfasten; ~se vr (ropa etc) to come undone.

desacatar [desákátár'] vt (ley) to disobey.

desacato [desáká'to] nm (falta de respeto) disrespect; (JUR) contempt.

desacertado, a [desásertá'tho, á] a (equivocado) mistaken; (inoportuno) unwise.

desacierto [desásyer'to] nm (error) mistake, error; (dicho) unfortunate remark.

desaconsejable [desákonsehá'ble] a inadvisable.

desaconsejado, a [desákonsehá'tho, á] a ill-advised.

desaconsejar [desákonsehár'] vt: ~ algo a uno to advise sb against sth.

desacoplar [desákoplár'] vt (ELEC) to disconnect; (TEC) to take apart.

desacorde [desákor'the] a (MUS) discordant; (fig: opiniones) conflicting; estar ~ con algo to disagree with sth.

desacreditar [desákrethetár'] vt (desprestigiar) to discredit, bring into disrepute; (denigrar) to run down.

desactivar [desáktehár'] vt to deactivate; (bomba) to defuse.

desacuerdo [desákwer'tho] nm (conflicto) disagreement, discord; (error) error, blunder; en ~ con not in agreement with.

desafiador, a [desáfyáthor', á], **desafiante** [desáfyán'te] a (insolente) defiant; (retador) challenging ♦ nm/f challenger.

desafiar [desáfyár'] vt (retar) to challenge; (enfrentarse a) to defy.

desafilado, a [desáfēlá'tho, á] a blunt.

desafinado, a [desáfēná'tho, á] a: estar ~ to be out of tune.

desafinarse [desáfēnár'se] vr to go out of tune.

desafío [desáfē'o] nm (reto) challenge; (combate) duel; (resistencia) defiance.

desaforadamente [desáforáthámen'te] ad: gritar ~ to shout one's head off.

desaforado, a [desáforá'tho, á] a (grito) ear-splitting; (comportamiento) outrageous.

desafortunadamente [desáfortōōnáthámen'te] ad unfortunately.

desafortunado, a [desáfortōōná'tho, á] a (desgraciado) unfortunate, unlucky.

desagradable [deságráthá'ble] a (fastidioso, enojoso) unpleasant; (irritante) disagreeable; ser ~ con uno to be rude to sb.

desagradar [deságráthár'] vi (disgustar) to displease; (molestar) to bother.

desagradecido, a [deságráthesé'tho, á] a ungrateful.

desagrado [deságrá'tho] nm (disgusto) displeasure; (contrariedad) dissatisfaction; con ~ unwillingly.

desagraviar [deságrátyár'] vt to make amends to.

desagravio [deságrá'hyo] nm (satisfacción) amends; (compensación) compensation.

desagregarse [deságregár'se] vr to disintegrate.

desagregue [deságre'ge] etc vb V **desagregarse.**

desaguadero [deságwáthe'ro] nm drain.

desagüe [desá'gwe] nm (de un líquido) drainage; (cañería: tb: tubo de ~) drainpipe; (salida) outlet, drain.

desaguisado, a [deságēsá'tho, á] a illegal ♦ nm outrage.

desahogado, a [desáogá'tho, á] a (holgado) comfortable; (espacioso) roomy.

desahogar [desáogár'] vt (aliviar) to ease, relieve; (ira) to vent; ~se vr (distenderse) to relax; (desfogarse) to let off steam (fam); (confesarse) to confess, get sth off one's chest (fam).

desahogo [desáo'go] nm (alivio) relief; (comodidad) comfort, ease; vivir con ~ to be comfortably off.

desahogue [desáo'ge] etc vb V **desahogar.**

desahuciado, a [desáōōsyá'tho, á] a hopeless.

desahuciar [desáōōsyár'] vt (enfermo) to give up hope for; (inquilino) to evict.

desahucio [desáōō'syo] nm eviction.

desairado, a [desáērá'tho, á] a (menospreciado) disregarded; (desgarbado) shabby; (sin éxito) unsuccessful; quedar ~ to come off badly.

desairar [desáērár'] vt (menospreciar) to slight, snub; (cosa) to disregard; (COM) to default on.

desaire [desá'ēre] nm (menosprecio) slight; (falta de garbo) unattractiveness; dar o hacer un ~ a uno to offend sb; ¿me va usted a hacer ese ~? I won't take no for an answer!

desajustar [desáhōōstár'] vt (desarreglar) to disarrange; (desconcertar) to throw off balance; (fig: planes) to upset; ~se vr to get out of order; (aflojarse) to loosen.

desajuste [desáhōō'ste] nm (de máquina) disorder; (avería) breakdown; (situación) imbalance; (desacuerdo) disagreement.

desalentador, a [desálentáthor', á] a discouraging.

desalentar [desálentár'] vt (desanimar) to discourage; ~se vr to get discouraged.

desaliento [desályen'to] etc vb V **desalentar** ♦ nm discouragement; (abatimiento) depression.

desalineación [desálēneásyon'] nf misalignment.

desaliñado, a [desálēnyá'tho, á] a (descuidado) slovenly; (raído) shabby; (desordenado) untidy; (negligente) careless.

desaliño [desálē'nyo] nm (descuido) slovenliness; (*negligencia*) carelessness.

desalmado, a |dɛsálmá'tɦo, á| *a* (*cruel*) cruel, heartless.

desalojar [dɛsálohár'] *vt* (*gen*) to remove, expel; (*expulsar, echar*) to eject; (*abandonar*) to move out of ♦ *vi* to move out; **la policía desalojó el local** the police cleared people out of the place.

desalquilar [dɛsálkɛlár'] *vt* to vacate, move out; ~**se** *vr* to become vacant.

desamarrar [dɛsámárrár'] *vt* to untie; (*NAUT*) to cast off.

desamor [dɛsámor'] *nm* (*frialdad*) indifference; (*odio*) dislike.

desamparado, a [dɛsámpárá'tɦo, á| *a* (*persona*) helpless; (*lugar: expuesto*) exposed; (: *desierto*) deserted.

desamparar [dɛsámpárár'] *vt* (*abandonar*) to desert, abandon; (*JUR*) to leave defenseless (*US*) o defenceless (*Brit*); (*barco*) to abandon.

desamparo [dɛsámpá'ro] *nm* (*acto*) desertion; (*estado*) helplessness.

desamueblado, a [dɛsámweɦlá'tɦo, á| *a* unfurnished.

desandar [dɛsándár'] *vt*: ~ **lo andado** o **el camino** to retrace one's steps.

desanduve [dɛsándo͞o'ɦe] *etc*, **desanduviera** [dɛsándo͞oɦyc'rá] *etc vb V* **desandar**.

desangelado, a [dɛsánhelá'tɦo, á| *a* (*habitación, edificio*) lifeless.

desangrar [dɛsángrár'] *vt* to bleed; (*fig: persona*) to bleed dry; (*lago*) to drain; ~**se** *vr* to lose a lot of blood; (*morir*) to bleed to death.

desanimado, a [dɛsánɛmá'tɦo, á| *a* (*persona*) downhearted; (*espectáculo, fiesta*) dull.

desanimar [dɛsánɛmár'] *vt* (*desalentar*) to discourage; (*deprimir*) to depress; ~**se** *vr* to lose heart.

desánimo [dɛsá'nɛmo] *nm* despondency; (*abatimiento*) dejection; (*falta de animación*) dullness.

desanudar [dɛsáno͞otɦár'] *vt* to untie; (*fig*) to clear up.

desapacible [dɛsápásɛ'ɦle] *a* unpleasant.

desaparecer [dɛsápáreser'] *vi* to disappear; (*el sol, la luz*) to vanish; (~ *de vista*) to drop out of sight; (*efectos, señales*) to wear off.

desaparecido, a [dɛsápáresɛ'tɦo, á| *a* missing; (*especie*) extinct ♦ *nm*: ~**s** (*en accidente etc*) people missing.

desaparezca [dɛsápáres'ká| *etc vb V* **desaparecer.**

desaparición [dɛsápárɛsyon'] *nf* disappearance; (*de especie etc*) extinction.

desapasionado, a [dɛsápásyoná'tɦo, á| *a* dispassionate, impartial.

desapego [dɛsápe'ɡo] *nm* (*frialdad*) coolness; (*distancia*) detachment.

desapercibido, a |dɛsápersɛ̄ɦɛ̄'tɦo, á| *a* unnoticed; (*desprevenido*) unprepared; **pasar** ~ to go unnoticed.

desaplicado, a |dɛsáplɛká'do, á| *a* lazy.

desaprender [dɛsáprender'] *vt* to forget; (*lo aprendido*) to unlearn.

desaprensivo, a |dɛsáprensɛ̄'ɦo, á| *a* unscrupulous.

desaprobar [dɛsáproɦár'] *vt* (*reprobar*) to disapprove of; (*condenar*) to condemn; (*no consentir*) to reject.

desaprovechado, a |dɛsáproɦetchá'tɦo, á| *a* (*oportunidad, tiempo*) wasted; (*estudiante*) lazy.

desaprovechar [dɛsáproɦetchár'] *vt* to waste; (*talento*) not to use to the full ♦ *vi* (*perder terreno*) to lose ground.

desapruebe [dɛsáprwc'ɦe] *etc vb V* **desaprobar.**

desarmar [dɛsármár'] *vt* (*MIL, fig*) to disarm; (*TEC*) to take apart, dismantle.

desarme [dɛsár'me] *nm* disarmament.

desarraigado, a |dɛsárráẽɡá'tɦo, á| *a* (*persona*) without roots, rootless.

desarraigar [dɛsárráẽɡár'] *vt* to uproot; (*fig: costumbre*) to root out; (: *persona*) to banish.

desarraigo [dɛsárrá'ẽɡo] *nm* uprooting.

desarraigue [dɛsárrá'ẽɡe] *etc vb V* **desarraigar.**

desarreglado, a |dɛsárreɡlá'tɦo, á| *a* (*desordenado*) disorderly, untidy; (*hábitos*) irregular.

desarreglar [dɛsárreɡlár'] *vt* to mess up; (*desordenar*) to disarrange; (*trastocar*) to upset, disturb.

desarreglo [dɛsárre'ɡlo] *nm* (*de casa, persona*) untidiness; (*desorden*) disorder; (*TEC*) trouble; (*MED*) upset; **viven en el mayor** ~ they live in complete chaos.

desarrollado, a |dɛsárroyá'tɦo, á| *a* developed.

desarrollar [dɛsárroyár'] *vt* (*gen*) to develop; (*extender*) to unfold; (*teoría*) to explain; ~**se** *vr* to develop; (*extenderse*) to open (out); (*film*) to develop; (*fig*) to grow; (*tener lugar*) to take place; **aquí desarrollan un trabajo muy importante** they carry on o out very important work here; **la acción se desarrolla en Roma** (*CINE etc*) the scene is set in Rome.

desarrollo [dɛsárro'yo] *nm* development; (*de acontecimientos*) unfolding; (*de industria, mercado*) expansion, growth; **país en vías de** ~ developing country; **la industria está en pleno** ~ industry is expanding steadily.

desarrugar [dɛsárro͞oɡár'] *vt* (*alisar*) to smooth (out); (*ropa*) to remove the wrinkles (*US*) o creases (*Brit*) from.

desarrugue [dɛsárro͞o'ɡe] *etc vb V* **desarru-**

gar.

desarticulado, a [desártĕkōōlä'd̦o, á] a disjointed.

desarticular [desártĕkōōlár'] vt (huesos) to dislocate, put out of joint; (objeto) to take apart; (grupo terrorista etc) to break up.

desaseado, a [desáscá'd̦o, á] a (sucio) dirty; (desaliñado) untidy.

desaseo [desáse'o] nm (suciedad) dirtiness; (desarreglo) untidiness.

desasga [desás'gá] etc vb V **desasir**.

desasir [desásĕr'] vt to loosen; ~**se** vr to extricate o.s.; ~**se de** to let go, give up.

desasosegar [desásosegár'] vt (inquietar) to disturb, make uneasy; ~**se** vr to become uneasy.

desasosegué [desásosege'], **desasoseguemos** [desásosege'mos] etc vb V **desasosegar**.

desasosiego [desásosyc'go] etc vb V **desasosegar ♦** nm (intranquilidad) uneasiness, restlessness; (ansiedad) anxiety; (POL etc) unrest.

desasosiegue [desásosyc'ge] etc vb V **desasosegar**.

desastrado, a [desástrá'd̦o, á] a (desaliñado) shabby; (sucio) dirty.

desastre [desás'tre] nm disaster; ¡un ~! how awful!; **la función fue un** ~ the show was a shambles.

desastroso, a [desástro'so, á] a disastrous.

desatado, a [desátá'd̦o, á] a (desligado) untied; (violento) violent, wild.

desatar [desátár'] vt (nudo) to untie; (paquete) to undo; (perro, odio) to unleash; (misterio) to solve; (separar) to detach; ~**se** vr (zapatos) to come untied; (tormenta) to break; (perder control de sí) to lose self-control; ~**se en injurias** to pour out a stream of insults.

desatascar [desatáskár'] vt (cañería) to unblock, clear; (carro) to pull out of the mud; ~ **a uno** (fig) to get sb out of a jam.

desatasque [desatás'ke] etc vb V **desatascar**.

desatención [desátensyon'] nf (descuido) inattention; (distracción) absent-mindedness.

desatender [desátender'] vt (no prestar atención a) to disregard; (abandonar) to neglect.

desatento, a [desáten'to, á] a (distraído) inattentive; (descortés) discourteous.

desatienda [desátyen'dá] etc vb V **desatender**.

desatinado, a [desátēná'd̦o, á] a foolish, silly.

desatino [desátē'no] nm (idiotez) foolishness, folly; (error) blunder; ~**s** nmpl nonsense sg; ¡qué ~! how silly!, what rubbish!

desatornillar [desátornĕyár'] vt to unscrew.

desatrancar [desátránkár'] vt (puerta) to unbolt; (cañería) to unblock.

desatranque [desátrán'ke] etc vb V **desatrancar**.

desautorice [desáōōtorē'se] etc vb V **desautorizar**.

desautorizado, a [desáōōtorēsá'd̦o, á] a unauthorized.

desautorizar [desáōōtorēsár'] vt (oficial) to deprive of authority; (informe) to deny.

desavendré [desáhendre'] etc vb V **desavenir**.

desavenencia [desáhenen'syá] nf (desacuerdo) disagreement; (discrepancia) quarrel.

desavenga [desáhen'gá] etc vb V **desavenir**.

desavenido, a [desáhenē'd̦o, á] a (opuesto) contrary; (reñidos) in disagreement; **ellos están** ~**s** they are at odds.

desavenir [desáhener'] vt (enemistar) to make trouble between; ~**se** vr to have a falling out (US), fall out (Brit).

desaventajado, a [desáhentáhá'd̦o, á] a (inferior) inferior; (poco ventajoso) disadvantageous.

desaviene [desáhyc'ne] etc, **desaviniendo** [desáhényen'do] etc vb V **desavenir**.

desayunar [desáyōōnár'] vi, ~**se** vr to have breakfast ♦ vt to have for breakfast; ~ **con café** to have coffee for breakfast; ~ **con algo** (fig) to get the first news of sth.

desayuno [desáyōō'no] nm breakfast.

desazón [desáson'] nf (angustia) anxiety; (MED) discomfort; (fig) annoyance.

desazonar [desásonár'] vt (fig) to annoy, upset; ~**se** vr (enojarse) to be annoyed; (preocuparse) to worry, be anxious.

desbancar [desbánkár'] vt (quitar el puesto a) to oust; (suplantar) to supplant (in sb's affections).

desbandada [desbándá'd̦á] nf rush; ~ **general** mass exodus; **a la** ~ in disorder.

desbandarse [desbándár'se] vr (MIL) to disband; (fig) to flee in disorder.

desbanque [desbán'ke] etc vb V **desbancar**.

desbarajuste [desbáráhōō'ste] nm confusion, disorder; ¡qué ~! what a mess!

desbaratar [desbárátár'] vt (gen) to mess up; (plan) to spoil; (deshacer, destruir) to ruin ♦ vi to talk nonsense; ~**se** vr (máquina) to break down; (persona: irritarse) to fly off the handle (fam).

desbarrar [desbárrár'] vi to talk nonsense.

desbloquear [desblokeár'] vt (negociaciones, tráfico) to get going again; (COM: cuenta) to unfreeze.

desbocado, a [desbokȧ'd̦o, á] a (caballo) runaway; (herramienta) worn.

desbocar [desbokár'] vt (vasija) to break

the rim of; ~**se** *vr* (*caballo*) to bolt; (*persona*: *soltar injurias*) to let out a stream of insults.

desboque [desbo'ke] *etc vb V* **desbocar**.

desbordamiento [desbordhamyen'to] *nm* (*de río*) overflowing; (*INFORM*) overflow; (*de cólera*) outburst; (*de entusiasmo*) upsurge.

desbordar [desbordhár'] *vt* (*sobrepasar*) to go beyond; (*exceder*) to exceed ♦ *vi*, ~**se** *vr* (*líquido, río*) to overflow; (*entusiasmo*) to erupt; (*persona*: *exaltarse*) to get carried away.

desbravar [desbrahár'] *vt* (*caballo*) to break in; (*animal*) to tame.

descabalgar [deskáhálgár'] *vi* to dismount.

descabalgue [deskáhál'ge] *etc vb V* **descabalgar**.

descabellado, a [deskáheyá'tho, á] *a* (*disparatado*) wild, crazy; (*insensato*) preposterous.

descabellar [deskáheyár'] *vt* to ruffle; (*TAUR*: *toro*) to give the coup de grace to.

descabezado, a [deskáhesá'tho, á] *a* (*sin cabeza*) headless; (*insensato*) wild.

descafeinado, a [deskáfeéná'tho, á] *a* decaffeinated ♦ *nm* decaffeinated coffee.

descalabrar [deskáláhrár'] *vt* to smash; (*persona*) to hit; (: *en la cabeza*) to hit on the head; (*NAUT*) to cripple; (*dañar*) to harm, damage; ~**se** *vr* to hurt one's head.

descalabro [deskálá'hro] *nm* blow; (*desgracia*) misfortune.

descalce [deskál'se] *etc vb V* **descalzar**.

descalificar [deskáléfékár'] *vt* to disqualify; (*desacreditar*) to discredit.

descalifique [deskáléfé'ke] *etc vb V* **descalificar**.

descalzar [deskálsár'] *vt* (*zapato*) to take off.

descalzo, a [deskál'so, á] *a* barefoot(ed); (*fig*) destitute; **estar (con los pies) ~(s)** to be barefooted.

descambiar [deskámbyár'] *vt* to exchange.

descaminado, a [deskáméná'tho, á] *a* (*equivocado*) on the wrong road; (*fig*) misguided; **en eso no anda usted muy ~** you're not far wrong there.

descamisado, a [deskámésá'tho, á] *a* barechested.

descampado [deskámpá'tho] *nm* open space, piece of empty ground; **comer al ~** to eat in the open air.

descansado, a [deskánsá'tho, á] *a* (*gen*) rested; (*que tranquiliza*) restful.

descansar [deskánsár'] *vt* (*gen*) to rest; (*apoyar*): ~ **(sobre)** to lean (on) ♦ *vi* to rest, have a rest; (*echarse*) to lie down; (*cadáver, restos*) to lie; **¡que usted descanse!** sleep well!; ~ **en** (*argumento*) to be based on.

descansillo [deskánsé'yo] *nm* (*de escalera*) landing.

descanso [deskán'so] *nm* (*reposo*) rest; (*alivio*) relief; (*pausa*) break; (*DEPORTE*) interval, half time; **día de ~** day off; ~ **de enfermedad/maternidad** sick/maternity leave; **tomarse unos días de ~** to take a few days' leave *o* rest.

descapitalizado, a [deskápétálésá'tho, á] *a* undercapitalized.

descapotable [deskápotá'hle] *nm* (*tb:* **coche ~**) convertible.

descarado, a [deskárá'tho, á] *a* (*sin vergüenza*) shameless; (*insolente*) sassy (*US*), cheeky (*Brit*).

descarga [deskár'gá] *nf* (*ARQ, ELEC, MIL*) discharge; (*NAUT*) unloading.

descargador [deskárgá'thor'] *nm* (*de barcos*) stevedore.

descargar [deskárgár'] *vt* to unload; (*golpe*) to let fly; (*arma*) to fire; (*ELEC*) to discharge; (*pila*) to run down; (*conciencia*) to relieve; (*COM*) to pay off; (*persona*: *de una obligación*) to release; (: *de una deuda*) to free; (*JUR*) to clear ♦ *vi* (*río*): ~ **(en)** to flow (into); ~**se** *vr* to unburden o.s.; ~**se de algo** to get rid of sth.

descargo [deskár'go] *nm* (*de obligación*) release; (*COM*: *recibo*) receipt; (: *de deuda*) discharge; (*JUR*) evidence; ~ **de una acusación** acquittal on a charge.

descargue [deskár'ge] *etc vb V* **descargar**.

descarnado, a [deskárná'tho, á] *a* scrawny; (*fig*) bare; (*estilo*) straightforward.

descaro [deskáro] *nm* nerve.

descarriar [deskárryár'] *vt* (*descaminar*) to misdirect; (*fig*) to lead astray; ~**se** *vr* (*perderse*) to lose one's way; (*separarse*) to stray; (*pervertirse*) to err, go astray.

descarrilamiento [deskárrēlámyen'to] *nm* (*de tren*) derailment.

descarrilar [deskárrēlár'] *vi* to be derailed.

descartable [deskártá'hle] *a* (*INFORM*) temporary.

descartar [deskártár'] *vt* (*rechazar*) to reject; (*eliminar*) to rule out; ~**se** *vr* (*NAIPES*) to discard; ~**se de** to shirk.

descascarar [deskáskárár'] *vt* (*naranja, limón*) to peel; (*nueces, huevo duro*) to shell; ~**se** *vr* to peel (off).

descascarillado, a [deskáskárēyá'tho, á] *a* (*paredes*) peeling.

descendencia [desenden'syá] *nf* (*origen*) origin, descent; (*hijos*) offspring; **morir sin dejar ~** to die without issue.

descendente [desenden'te] *a* (*cantidad*) diminishing; (*INFORM*) top-down.

descender [desender'] *vt* (*bajar*: *escalera*) to go down; ♦ *vi* to descend; (*temperatura, nivel*) to fall, drop; (*líquido*) to run; (*cortina etc*) to fall (*US*), hang (*Brit*); (*fuerzas,* *persona*) to fail, get weak; ~ **de** to be descended from.

descendiente [desendyen'te] *nm/f* descendant.

descenso [desen'so] *nm* descent; (*de temperatura*) drop; (*de producción*) downturn; (*de calidad*) decline; (*MINERÍA*) collapse; (*bajada*) slope; (*fig: decadencia*) decline; (*de empleado etc*) demotion.

descentrado, a [desentrá'tho, á] *a* (*pieza de una máquina*) off-center (*US*), off-centre (*Brit*); (*rueda*) out of balance; (*persona*) bewildered; (*desequilibrado*) unbalanced; (*problema*) out of focus; **todavía está algo** ~ he is still somewhat out of touch.

descentralice [desentrálē'se] *etc vb V* **descentralizar.**

descentralizar [desentrálēsár'] *vt* to decentralize.

descerrajar [deserrahár'] *vt* (*puerta*) to break open.

descienda [desyen'dá] *etc vb V* **descender.**

descifrable [desēfrá'ble] *a* (*gen*) decipherable; (*letra*) legible.

descifrar [desēfrár'] *vt* (*escritura*) to decipher; (*mensaje*) to decode; (*problema*) to solve; (*misterio*) to solve.

descocado, a [deskoká'tho, á] *a* (*descarado*) sassy (*US*), cheeky (*Brit*); (*desvergonzado*) brazen.

descoco [desko'ko] *nm* (*descaro*) sassy (*US*), cheek (*Brit*); (*atrevimiento*) brazenness.

descolgar [deskolgár'] *vt* (*bajar*) to take down; (*desde una posición alta*) to lower; (*de una pared etc*) to unhook; (*teléfono*) to pick up; ~**se** *vr* to let o.s. down; ~**se por** (*bajar escurriéndose*) to slip down; (*pared*) to climb down; **dejó el teléfono descolgado** he left the phone off the hook.

descolgué [deskolge'], **descolguemos** [deskolge'mos] *etc vb V* **descolgar.**

descolocado, a [deskoloká'tho, á] *a*: **estar** ~ (*cosa*) to be out of place; (*criada*) to be unemployed.

descolorido, a [deskolorē'tho, á] *a* (*color, tela*) faded; (*pálido*) pale; (*fig: estilo*) colorless (*US*), colourless (*Brit*).

descollar [deskoyár'] *vi* (*sobresalir*) to stand out; (*montaña etc*) to rise; **la obra que más descuella de las suyas** his most outstanding work.

descompaginar [deskompáhēnár'] *vt* (*desordenar*) to disarrange, mess up.

descompasado, a [deskompásá'tho, á] *a* (*sin proporción*) out of all proportion; (*excesivo*) excessive; (*hora*) unearthly.

descompondré [deskompondre'] *etc vb V* **descomponer.**

descompensar [deskompensár'] *vt* to unbalance.

descomponer [deskomponer'] *vt* (*gen, LING, MAT*) to break down; (*desordenar*) to disarrange, disturb; (*materia orgánica*) to rot, decompose; (*TEC*) to put out of order; (*facciones*) to distort; (*estómago etc*) to upset; (*planes*) to mess up; (*persona: molestar*) to upset; (: *irritar*) to annoy; ~**se** *vr* (*corromperse*) to rot, decompose; (*estómago*) to get upset; (*el tiempo*) to change (for the worse); (*TEC*) to break down.

descomponga [deskompon'gá] *etc vb V* **descomponer.**

descomposición [deskomposēsyon'] *nf* (*gen*) breakdown; (*de fruta etc*) decomposition; (*putrefacción*) rotting; (*de cara*) distortion; ~ **de vientre** (*MED*) stomach upset, diarrhea (*US*), diarrhoea (*Brit*).

descompostura [deskompostōō'rá] *nf* (*TEC*) breakdown; (*desorganización*) disorganization; (*desorden*) untidiness.

descompuesto, a [deskompwe'sto, á] *pp de* **descomponer** ♦ *a* (*corrompido*) decomposed; (*roto*) broken.

descompuse [deskompōō'se] *etc vb V* **descomponer.**

descomunal [deskomōōnál'] *a* (*enorme*) huge; (*fam: excelente*) fantastic.

desconcertado, a [deskonsertá'tho, á] *a* disconcerted, bewildered.

desconcertar [deskonsertár'] *vt* (*confundir*) to baffle; (*incomodar*) to upset; (*orden*) to disturb; ~**se** *vr* (*turbarse*) to be upset; (*confundirse*) to be bewildered.

desconcierto [deskonsyer'to] *etc vb V* **desconcertar** ♦ *nm* (*gen*) disorder; (*desorientación*) uncertainty; (*inquietud*) uneasiness; (*confusión*) bewilderment.

desconchado, a [deskontchá'tho, á] *a* (*pintura*) peeling.

desconchar [deskontchár'] *vt* (*pared*) to strip off; (*loza*) to chip off.

desconectado, a [deskonektá'tho, á] *a* (*ELEC*) disconnected, switched off; (*INFORM*) offline; **estar** ~ **de** (*fig*) to have no contact with.

desconectar [deskonektár'] *vt* to disconnect; (*desenchufar*) to unplug; (*radio, televisión*) to switch off; (*INFORM*) to toggle off.

desconfiado, a [deskonfyá'tho, á] *a* suspicious.

desconfianza [deskonfyán'sá] *nf* distrust.

desconfiar [deskonfyár'] *vi* to be distrustful; ~ **de** (*sospechar*) to mistrust, suspect; (*no tener confianza en*) to have no faith o confidence in; **desconfío de ello** I doubt it; **desconfíe de las imitaciones** (*COM*) beware of imitations.

desconforme [deskonfor'me] *a* = **disconforme.**

descongelar [deskonhelár'] *vt* (*nevera*) to

defrost; (*comida*) to thaw; (*AUTO*) to de-ice; (*COM, POL*) to unfreeze.

descongestionar [desconhestyonár'] *vt* (*cabeza, tráfico*) to clear; (*calle, ciudad*) to relieve congestion in; (*fig: despejar*) to clear.

desconocer [deskonoser'] *vt* (*ignorar*) not to know, be ignorant of; (*no aceptar*) to deny; (*repudiar*) to disown.

desconocido, a [deskonosē'tho, á] *a* un-known; (*que no se conoce*) unfamiliar; (*no reconocido*) unrecognized ♦ *nm/f* stranger; (*recién llegado*) newcomer; **está ~** he is hardly recognizable.

desconocimiento [deskonosēmyen'to] *nm* (*falta de conocimientos*) ignorance; (*repudio*) disregard.

desconozca [deskonos'ká] *etc vb* V **desconocer**.

desconsiderado, a [deskonsētherá'tho, á] *a* inconsiderate; (*insensible*) thoughtless.

desconsolado, a [deskonsolá'tho, á] *a* (*afligido*) disconsolate; (*cara*) sad; (*desanimado*) dejected.

desconsolar [deskonsolár'] *vt* to distress; **~se** *vr* to despair.

desconsuelo [deskonswe'lo] *etc vb* V **desconsolar** ♦ *nm* (*tristeza*) distress; (*desesperación*) despair.

descontado, a [deskontá'tho, á] *a:* **por ~** of course; **dar por ~ (que)** to take it for granted (that).

descontar [deskontár'] *vt* (*deducir*) to take away, deduct; (*rebajar*) to discount.

descontento, a [deskonten'to, á] *a* dissatisfied ♦ *nm* dissatisfaction, discontent.

descontrolado, a [deskontrolá'tho, á] *a* (*AM*) uncontrolled.

desconvendré [deskombendre'] *etc*, **desconvenga** [deskomben'gá] *etc vb* V **desconvenir**.

desconvenir [deskombenēr'] *vi* (*personas*) to disagree; (*no corresponder*) not to fit; (*no convenir*) to be inconvenient.

desconviene [deskombye'ne] *etc*, **desconviniendo** [deskombēnyen'do] *etc vb* V **desconvenir**.

descorazonar [deskorásonár'] *vt* to discourage, dishearten; **~se** *vr* to get discouraged, lose heart.

descorchador [deskortchá'thor'] *nm* corkscrew.

descorchar [deskortchár'] *vt* to uncork, open.

descorrer [deskorrer'] *vt* (*cortina, cerrojo*) to draw back; (*velo*) to remove.

descortés [deskortes'] *a* (*mal educado*) discourteous; (*grosero*) rude.

descortesía [deskortesē'á] *nf* discourtesy; (*grosería*) rudeness.

descoser [deskoser'] *vt* to unstitch; **~se** *vr*

to come apart (at the seams); (*fam: descubrir un secreto*) to blurt out a secret; **~se de risa** to split one's sides laughing.

descosido, a [deskosē'tho, á] *a* (*costura*) unstitched; (*desordenado*) disjointed ♦ *nm:* **como un ~** (*obrar*) wildly; (*beber, comer*) to excess; (*estudiar*) like mad.

descoyuntar [deskoyōōntár'] *vt* (*ANAT*) to dislocate; (*hechos*) to twist; **~se** *vr:* **~se un hueso** (*ANAT*) to put a bone out of joint; **~se de risa** (*fam*) to split one's sides laughing.

descrédito [deskre'thēto] *nm* discredit; **caer en ~** to fall into disrepute; **ir en ~ de** to be to the discredit of.

descreído, a [deskreē'tho, á] *a* (*incrédulo*) incredulous; (*falto de fe*) unbelieving.

descremado, a [deskremá'tho, á] *a* skimmed.

descremar [deskremár'] *vt* (*leche*) to skim.

describir [deskrēbēr'] *vt* to describe.

descripción [deskrēpsyon'] *nf* description.

descrito [deskrē'to] *pp de* **describir**.

descuajar [deskwáhár'] *vt* (*disolver*) to melt; (*planta*) to pull out by the roots; (*extirpar*) to eradicate, wipe out; (*desanimar*) to dishearten.

descuajaringarse [deskwáháréngár'se] *vr* to fall apart.

descuajaringue [deskwáháren'ge] *etc vb* V **descuajaringarse**.

descuartice [deskwárte'se] *etc vb* V **descuartizar**.

descuartizar [deskwártēsár'] *vt* (*animal*) to carve up, cut up; (*fig: hacer pedazos*) to tear apart.

descubierto, a [deskōōhyer'to, á] *pp de* **descubrir** ♦ *a* uncovered, bare; (*persona*) bare-headed; (*cielo*) clear; (*coche*) open; (*campo*) treeless ♦ *nm* (*lugar*) open space; (*COM: en el presupuesto*) shortage; (: *bancario*) overdraft; **al ~** in the open; **poner al ~** to lay bare; **quedar al ~** to be exposed; **estar en ~** to be overdrawn.

descubridor, a [deskōōhre'thor', á] *nm/f* discoverer.

descubrimiento [deskōōhrēmyen'to] *nm* (*hallazgo*) discovery; (*de criminal, fraude*) detection; (*revelación*) revelation; (*de secreto etc*) disclosure; (*de estatua etc*) unveiling.

descubrir [deskōōhrēr'] *vt* to discover, find; (*petróleo*) to strike; (*inaugurar*) to unveil; (*vislumbrar*) to detect; (*sacar a luz: crimen*) to bring to light; (*revelar*) to reveal, show; (*poner al descubierto*) to expose to view; (*naipes*) to lay down; (*quitar la tapa de*) to uncover; (*cacerola*) to take the lid off; (*enterarse de: causa, solución*) to find out; (*divisar*) to see, make out; (*delatar*) to give away, betray; **~se** *vr* to reveal o.s.;

(*quitarse sombrero*) to take off one's hat; (*confesar*) to confess; (*fig: salir a luz*) to come out o to light.

descuelga [deskwel'ɡa] *etc*, **descuelgue** [deskwel'ɡe] *etc vb* **V descolgar**.

descuelle [deskwe'ye] *etc vb* **V descollar**.

descuento [deskwen'to] *etc vb* **V descontar** ♦ *nm* discount; ~ **del 3%** 3% off; **con** ~ at a discount; ~ **por pago al contado** (*COM*) cash discount; ~ **por volumen de compras** (*COM*) volume discount.

descuidado, a [deskwēthá'tho, a] *a* (*sin cuidado*) careless; (*desordenado*) untidy; (*olvidadizo*) forgetful; (*dejado*) neglected; (*desprevenido*) unprepared.

descuidar [deskwēthár'] *vt* (*dejar*) to neglect; (*olvidar*) to overlook ♦ *vi*, ~**se** *vr* (*distraerse*) to be careless; (*estar desaliñado*) to let o.s. go; (*desprevenirse*) to drop one's guard; **¡descuida!** don't worry!

descuidero, a [deskwēthe'ro, a] *nm/f* sneak thief.

descuido [deskwē'tho] *nm* (*dejadez*) carelessness; (*olvido*) negligence; (*un* ~) oversight; **al** ~ casually; (*sin cuidado*) carelessly; **al menor** ~ if my *etc* attention wanders for a minute; **con** ~ thoughtlessly; **por** ~ by an oversight.

desde [des'the] *prep* from; ~ **entonces** since then; **¿**~ **cuándo es esto así?** how long has it been like this?; ~ **lejos** from afar; ~ **ahora en adelante** from now on(wards); ~ **hace 3 días** for 3 days; ~ **luego** of course ♦ *conj*: ~ **que** since; ~ **que puedo recordar** for as long as I can remember.

desdecir [desthesēr'] *vi*: ~ **de** (*no merecer*) to be unworthy of; (*no corresponder*) to clash with; ~**se** *vr*: ~**se de** to go back on.

desdén [desthen'] *nm* scorn.

desdentado, a [desthentá'tho, a] *a* toothless.

desdeñable [desthenyá'hle] *a* contemptible; **nada** ~ far from negligible, considerable.

desdeñar [desthenyár'] *vt* (*despreciar*) to scorn.

desdeñoso, a [desthenyo'so, a] *a* scornful.

desdibujar [desthēhōōhár'] *vt* to blur (the outlines of); ~**se** *vr* to get blurred, fade (away); **el recuerdo se ha desdibujado** the memory has become blurred.

desdiciendo [desthēsyen'do] *etc vb* **V desdecir**.

desdichado, a [desthētchá'tho, a] *a* (*sin suerte*) unlucky; (*infeliz*) unhappy; (*día*) ill-fated ♦ *nm/f* (*pobre desgraciado*) poor devil.

desdicho, a [desthētch'o, a] *pp de* **desdecir** ♦ *nf* (*desgracia*) misfortune; (*infelicidad*) unhappiness.

desdiga [desthē'ɡa] *etc*, **desdije** [desdē'he]

etc vb **V desdecir**.

desdoblado, a [desthohlá'tho, a] *a* (*personalidad*) split.

desdoblar [desthohlár'] *vt* (*extender*) to spread out; (*desplegar*) to unfold.

deseable [deseá'hle] *a* desirable.

desear [deseár'] *vt* to want, desire, wish for; **¿qué desea la señora?** (*tienda etc*) what can I do for you, madam?; **estoy deseando que esto termine** I'm longing for this to finish.

desecar [desekár'] *vt*, **desecarse** *vr* to dry up.

desechable [desetchá'hle] *a* (*envase etc*) disposable.

desechar [desetchár'] *vt* (*basura*) to throw out o away; (*ideas*) to reject, discard; (*miedo*) to cast aside; (*plan*) to drop.

desecho [desetch'o] *nm* (*desprecio*) contempt; (*lo peor*) dregs *pl*; ~**s** *nmpl* rubbish *sg*, waste *sg*; **de** ~ (*hierro*) scrap; (*producto*) waste; (*ropa*) cast-off.

desembalar [desembalár'] *vt* to unpack.

desembarace [desembará'se] *etc vb* **V desembarazar**.

desembarazado, a [desembárásá'tho, a] *a* (*libre*) clear, free; (*desenvuelto*) free and easy.

desembarazar [desembárásár'] *vt* (*desocupar*) to clear; (*desenredar*) to free; ~**se** *vr*: ~**se de** to free o.s. of, get rid of.

desembarazo [desembárá'so] *nm* (*acto*) clearing; (*AM: parto*) birth; (*desenfado*) ease.

desembarcadero [desembárkáthe'ro] *nm* wharf.

desembarcar [desembárkár'] *vt* (*personas*) to land; (*mercancías etc*) to unload ♦ *vi*, ~**se** *vr* (*de barco, avión*) to disembark; (*esp AM: de tren, autobús*) to alight.

desembarco [desembár'ko] *nm* landing.

desembargar [desembárɡár'] *vt* (*gen*) to free; (*JUR*) to remove the embargo on.

desembargue [desembár'ɡe] *etc vb* **V desembargar**.

desembarque [desembár'ke] *etc vb* **V desembarcar** ♦ *nm* disembarkation; (*de pasajeros*) landing; (*de mercancías*) unloading.

desembocadura [desembokáthōō'rá] *nf* (*de río*) mouth; (*de calle*) opening.

desembocar [desembokár'] *vi*: ~ **en** to flow into; (*fig*) to result in.

desemboce [desembo'se] *etc vb* **V desembozar**.

desembolsar [desembolsár'] *vt* (*pagar*) to pay out; (*gastar*) to lay out.

desembolso [desembol'so] *nm* payment.

desemboque [desembo'ke] *etc vb* **V desembocar**.

desembozar [desembosár'] *vt* to unmask.

desembragar [desembráɡár'] *vt* (*TEC*) to

disengage; (embrague) to release ♦ vi (AUTO) to release the clutch.

desembrague [desembrá'ge] etc vb V **desembragar**.

desembrollar [desembroyár'] vt (madeja) to unravel; (asunto, malentendido) to sort out.

desembuchar [desembōōtchár'] vt to disgorge; (fig) to come out with ♦ vi (confesar) to spill the beans (fam); **¡desembucha!** out with it!

desemejante [desemehán'te] a dissimilar; ~ **de** different from, unlike.

desemejanza [desemehán'sá] nf dissimilarity.

desempacar [desempákár'] vt to unpack.

desempañar [desempányár'] vt (cristal) to clean; (AUTO) to defog (US), demist (Brit).

desempaque [desempá'ke] etc vb V **desempacar**.

desempaquetar [desempáketár'] vt to unpack, unwrap.

desempatar [desempátár'] vi to break a tie; **volvieron a jugar para** ~ they held a play-off.

desempate [desempá'te] nm (FÚTBOL) play-off; (TENIS) tie-break(er).

desempeñar [desempenyár'] vt (cargo) to hold; (papel) to play; (deber, función) to perform, carry out; (lo empeñado) to redeem; ~**se** vr to get out of debt; ~ **un papel** (fig) to play (a role).

desempeño [desempe'nyo] nm occupation; (de lo empeñado) redeeming; **de mucho** ~ very capable.

desempleado, a [desempleá'tho, á] a unemployed, out of work ♦ nm/f unemployed person.

desempleo [desemple'o] nm unemployment.

desempolvar [desempolhár'] vt (muebles etc) to dust; (lo olvidado) to revive.

desencadenar [desenkáthenár'] vt to unchain; (ira) to unleash; (provocar) to cause, set off; ~**se** vr to break loose; (tormenta) to burst; (guerra) to break out; **se desencadenó una lucha violenta** a violent struggle ensued.

desencajar [desenkáhár'] vt (hueso) to put out of joint; (mandíbula) to dislocate; (mecanismo, pieza) to disconnect, disengage.

desencantar [desenkántár'] vt to disillusion, disenchant.

desencanto [desenkán'to] nm disillusionment, disenchantment.

desencoger [desenkoher'] vt (extender) to spread out; (desdoblar) to smooth out; ~**se** vr to lose one's timidity.

desencoja [desenko'há] etc vb V **desencoger**.

desenchufar [desentchōōfár'] vt to unplug,

disconnect.

desenfadado, a [desenfáthá'tho, á] a (desenvuelto) uninhibited; (descarado) forward; (en el vestir) casual.

desenfado [desenfá'tho] nm (libertad) freedom; (comportamiento) free and easy manner; (descaro) forwardness; (desenvoltura) self-confidence.

desenfocado, a [desenfoká'tho, á] a (FOTO) out of focus.

desenfrenado, a [desenfrená'tho, á] a (descontrolado) uncontrolled; (inmoderado) unbridled.

desenfrenarse [desenfrenár'se] vr (persona: desmandarse) to lose all self-control; (multitud) to run riot; (tempestad) to burst; (viento) to rage.

desenfreno [desenfre'no] nm (vicio) wildness; (falta de control) lack of self-control; (de pasiones) unleashing.

desenganchar [desengántchár'] vt (gen) to unhook; (FERRO) to uncouple; (TEC) to disengage.

desengañar [desengányár'] vt to disillusion; (abrir los ojos a) to open the eyes of; ~**se** vr to become disillusioned; **¡desengáñate!** don't you believe it!

desengaño [desengá'nyo] nm disillusionment; (decepción) disappointment; **sufrir un** ~ **amoroso** to be disappointed in love.

desengrasar [desengrásár'] vt to degrease.

desenlace [desenlá'se] etc vb V **desenlazar** ♦ nm outcome; (LIT) ending.

desenlazar [desenlásár'] vt (desatar) to untie; (problema) to solve; (aclarar: asunto) to unravel; ~**se** vr (desatarse) to come undone; (LIT) to end.

desenmarañar [desenmárányár'] vt (fig) to unravel.

desenmascarar [desenmáskárár'] vt to unmask, expose.

desenredar [desenrethár'] vt to resolve.

desenrollar [desenroyár'] vt to unroll, unwind.

desenroscar [desenroskár'] vt (tornillo etc) to unscrew.

desenrosque [desenros'ke] etc vb V **desenroscar**.

desentenderse [desentender'se] vr: ~ **de** to pretend not to know about; (apartarse) to have nothing to do with.

desentendido, a [desentendē'tho, á] a: **hacerse el** ~ to pretend not to notice; **se hizo el** ~ he didn't take the hint.

desenterrar [desenterrár'] vt to exhume; (tesoro, fig) to unearth, dig up.

desentierre [desentye'rre] etc vb V **desenterrar**.

desentonar [desentonár'] vi (MUS) to sing (o play) out of tune; (no encajar) to be out of place; (color) to clash.

desentorpecer [desentorpeser'] vt (miembro) to stretch; (fam: persona) to smarten up.

desentorpezca [desentorpes'ká] etc vb V desentorpecer.

desentrañar [desentrányár'] vt (misterio) to unravel.

desentrenado, a [desentrena'dho, á] a out of training.

desentumecer [desentōōmeser'] vt (pierna etc) to stretch; (DEPORTE) to loosen up.

desentumezca [desentōōmes'ká] etc vb V desentumecer.

desenvainar [desembáēnár'] vt (espada) to draw, unsheathe.

desenvoltura [desemboltōō'rá] nf (libertad, gracia) ease; (descaro) free and easy manner; (al hablar) fluency.

desenvolver [desembolber'] vt (paquete) to unwrap; (fig) to develop; ~se vr (desarrollarse) to unfold, develop; (suceder) to go off; (prosperar) to prosper; (arreglárselas) to cope.

desenvolvimiento [desembolhēmyen'to] nm (desarrollo) development; (de idea) exposition.

desenvuelto, a [desembwel'to, á] pp de desenvolver ♦ a (suelto) easy; (desenfadado) confident; (al hablar) fluent; (pey) forward.

desenvuelva [desembw'elhá] etc vb V desenvolver.

deseo [dese'o] nm desire, wish; ~ de saber thirst for knowledge; **buen** ~ good intentions pl; **arder en** ~s **de algo** to yearn for sth.

deseoso, a [deseo'so, á] a: **estar** ~ **de hacer** to be anxious to do.

deseque [dese'ke] etc vb V desecar.

desequilibrado, a [desekēlēhrá'dho, á] a unbalanced ♦ nm/f unbalanced person; ~ **mental** mentally disturbed person.

desequilibrar [desekēlēhrár'] vt (mente) to unbalance; (objeto) to throw out of balance; (persona) to throw off balance.

desequilibrio [desekēlē'hrēo] nm (de mente) unbalance; (entre cantidades) imbalance; (MED) unbalanced mental condition.

desertar [desertár'] vt (JUR: derecho de apelación) to forfeit ♦ vi to desert; ~ **de sus deberes** to neglect one's duties.

desértico, a [deser'tēko, á] a desert cpd; (vacío) deserted.

desesperación [desesperásyon'] nf desperation, despair; (irritación) fury; **es una** ~ it's maddening; **es una** ~ **tener que** ... it's infuriating to have to ... .

desesperado, a [desesperá'dho, á] a (persona: sin esperanza) desperate; (caso, situación) hopeless; (esfuerzo) furious ♦ nm:

como un ~ like mad ♦ nf: **hacer algo a la desesperada** to do sth as a last resort o in desperation.

desesperance [desesperàn'se] etc vb V desesperanzar.

desesperante [desesperàn'te] a (exasperante) infuriating; (persona) hopeless.

desesperanzar [desesperánsár'] vt to drive to despair; ~se vr to lose hope, despair.

desesperar [desesperár'] vt to drive to despair; (exasperar) to drive to distraction ♦ vi: ~ **de** to despair of; ~se vr to despair, lose hope.

desestabilice [desestáhēlē'se] etc vb V desestabilizar.

desestabilizar [desestáhēlēsár'] vt to destabilize.

desestimar [desestēmár'] vt (menospreciar) to have a low opinion of; (rechazar) to reject.

desfachatez [desfàtchàtes'] nf (insolencia) impudence; (descaro) rudeness.

desfalco [desfál'ko] nm embezzlement.

desfallecer [desfáyeser'] vi (perder las fuerzas) to become weak; (desvanecerse) to faint.

desfallecido, a [desfáyesē'dho, á] a (débil) weak.

desfallezca [desfáyes'ká] etc vb V desfallecer.

desfasado, a [desfásá'dho, á] a (anticuado) old-fashioned; (TEC) out of phase.

desfasar [desfásár'] vt to phase out.

desfase [desfá'se] nm (diferencia) gap.

desfavorable [desfáhorá'hle] a unfavorable (US), unfavourable (Brit).

desfavorecer [desfáhoreser'] vt (sentar mal) not to suit.

desfavorezca [desfáhores'ká] etc vb V desfavorecer.

desfiguración [desfēgōōrásyon'] nf, **desfiguramiento** [desfēgōōrámyen'to] nm (de persona) disfigurement; (de monumento) defacement; (FOTO) blurring.

desfigurar [desfēgōōrár'] vt (cara) to disfigure; (cuerpo) to deform; (cuadro, monumento) to deface; (FOTO) to blur; (sentido) to twist; (suceso) to misrepresent.

desfiladero [desfēláthe'ro] nm gorge, defile.

desfilar [desfēlár'] vi to parade; **desfilaron ante el general** they marched past the general.

desfile [desfē'le] nm procession; (MIL) parade; ~ **de modelos** fashion show.

desflorar [desflorár'] vt (mujer) to deflower; (arruinar) to tarnish; (asunto) to touch on.

desfogar [desfogár'] vt (fig) to vent ♦ vi (NAUT: tormenta) to burst; ~se vr (fig) to let off steam.

desfogue [desfo'ge] etc vb V desfogar.

desgajar [desgáhár'] vt (arrancar) to tear

off; (*romper*) to break off; (*naranja*) to split into segments; ~**se** *vr* to come off.

desgana [desga'na] *nf* (*falta de apetito*) loss of appetite; (*renuencia*) unwillingness; **hacer algo a** ~ to do sth unwillingly.

desganado, a [desgana'ðo, a] *a*: **estar** ~ (*sin apetito*) to have no appetite; (*sin entusiasmo*) to have lost interest.

desgañitarse [desgaɲi̯etár'se] *vr* to shout o.s. hoarse.

desgarbado, a [desgarβa'ðo, a] *a* (*sin gracia*) clumsy, ungainly.

desgarrador, a [desgárráθor', a] *a* heart-rending.

desgarrar [desgárrár'] *vt* to tear (up); (*fig*) to shatter.

desgarro [desga'rro] *nm* (*en tela*) tear; (*aflicción*) grief; (*descaro*) impudence.

desgastar [desgastár'] *vt* (*deteriorar*) to wear away *o* down; (*estropear*) to spoil; ~**se** *vr* to get worn out.

desgaste [desga'ste] *nm* wear (and tear); (*de roca*) erosion; (*de cuerda*) fraying; (*de metal*) corrosion; ~ **económico** drain on one's resources.

desglosar [desglosár'] *vt* to detach.

desgobernar [desgoβernár'] *vt* (*POL*) to misgovern; (*asunto*) to handle badly; (*ANAT*) to dislocate.

desgobierno [desgoβyer'no] *etc vb V* **desgobernar** ♦ *nm* (*POL*) misgovernment, misrule.

desgracia [desgra'sya] *nf* misfortune; (*accidente*) accident; (*vergüenza*) disgrace; (*contratiempo*) setback; **por** ~ unfortunately; **en el accidente no hay que lamentar** ~**s personales** there were no casualties in the accident; **caer en** ~ to fall from grace; **tener la** ~ **de** to be unlucky enough to.

desgraciadamente [desgrasyaðamen'te] *ad* unfortunately.

desgraciado, a [desgrasya'ðo, a] *a* (*sin suerte*) unlucky, unfortunate; (*miserable*) wretched; (*infeliz*) miserable ♦ *nm/f* (*malo*) swine; (*infeliz*) poor creature.

desgraciar [desgrasyár'] *vt* (*estropear*) to spoil; (*ofender*) to displease.

desgranar [desgranár'] *vt* (*trigo*) to thresh; (*guisantes*) to shell; ~ **un racimo** to pick the grapes from a bunch; ~ **mentiras** to come out with a string of lies.

desgravación [desgraβasyon'] *nf* (*COM*): ~ **de impuestos** tax relief; ~ **personal** personal allowance.

desgravar [desgraβár'] *vt* (*producto*) to reduce the tax *o* duty on.

desgreñado, a [desgreɲa'ðo, a] *a* dishevelled.

deshabitado, a [desaβeta'ðo, a] *a* uninhabited.

deshabitar [desaβetár'] *vt* (*casa*) to leave empty; (*despoblar*) to depopulate.

deshacer [desasér'] *vt* (*lo hecho*) to undo, unmake; (*proyectos*: *arruinar*) to spoil; (*casa*) to break up; (*TEC*) to take apart; (*enemigo*) to defeat; (*diluir*) to melt; (*contrato*) to break; (*intriga*) to solve; (*cama*) to strip; (*maleta*) to unpack; (*paquete*) to unwrap; (*nudo*) to untie; (*costura*) to unpick; ~**se** *vr* (*desatarse*) to come undone; (*estropearse*) to be spoiled; (*descomponerse*) to fall to pieces; (*disolverse*) to melt; (*despedazarse*) to come apart *o* undone; ~**se de** to get rid of; (*COM*) to dump, unload; ~**se en** (*cumplidos, elogios*) to be lavish with; ~**se en lágrimas** to burst into tears; ~**se por algo** to be crazy about sth.

deshaga [desa'ga] *etc*, **desharé** [desáre'] *etc vb V* **deshacer**.

des(h)arrapado, a [desárrápa'ðo, a] *a* ragged; (**de aspecto**) ~ shabby.

deshecho, a [desetch'o, a] *pp de* **deshacer** ♦ *a* (*lazo, nudo*) undone; (*roto*) smashed; (*despedazado*) in pieces; (*cama*) unmade; (*MED*: *persona*) weak, emaciated; (: *salud*) broken; **estoy** ~ I'm shattered.

deshelar [deselár'] *vt* (*cañería*) to thaw; (*heladera*) to defrost.

desheredar [desereðár'] *vt* to disinherit.

deshice [dese'se] *etc vb V* **deshacer**.

deshidratación [desiðratasyon'] *nf* dehydration.

deshidratar [desiðratár'] *vt* to dehydrate.

deshielo [desye'lo] *etc vb V* **deshelar** ♦ *nm* thaw.

deshilachar [desilátchár'] *vt*, **deshilacharse** *vr* to fray.

deshilar [desilár'] *vt* (*tela*) to unravel.

deshilvanado, a [desilβana'ðo, a] *a* (*fig*) disjointed, incoherent.

deshinchar [desintchár'] *vt* (*neumático*) to let down; (*herida etc*) to reduce (the swelling of); ~**se** *vr* (*neumático*) to go flat; (*hinchazón*) to go down.

deshojar [desohár'] *vt* (*árbol*) to strip the leaves off; (*flor*) to pull the petals off; ~**se** *vr* to lose its leaves *etc*.

deshollinar [desoyenár'] *vt* (*chimenea*) to sweep.

deshonesto, a [desone'sto, a] *a* (*no honrado*) dishonest; (*indecente*) indecent.

deshonor [desonor'] *nm* dishonor (*US*), dishonour (*Brit*), disgrace; (*un* ~) insult, affront.

deshonra [deson'ra] *nf* (*deshonor*) dishonor (*US*), dishonour (*Brit*); (*vergüenza*) shame.

deshonrar [desonrár'] *vt* to dishonor (*US*), dishonour (*Brit*).

deshonroso, a [desonro'so, a] *a* dishonorable (*US*), dishonourable (*Brit*), disgraceful.

deshora [deso'rà] **a** ~ *ad* at the wrong time; (*llegar*) unexpectedly; (*acostarse*) at some unearthly hour.

deshuesar [deswesár'] *vt* (*carne*) to bone; (*fruta*) to stone.

desidia [desē'thyá] *nf* (*pereza*) idleness.

desierto, a [desyer'to, á] *a* (*casa, calle, negocio*) deserted; (*paisaje*) bleak ♦ *nm* desert.

designación [desēgnásyon'] *nf* (*para un cargo*) appointment; (*nombre*) designation.

designar [desēgnár'] *vt* (*nombrar*) to designate; (*indicar*) to fix.

designio [desēg'nyo] *nm* plan; **con el** ~ **de** with the intention of.

desigual [desēgwàl'] *a* (*lucha*) unequal; (*diferente*) different; (*terreno*) uneven; (*tratamiento*) unfair; (*cambiadizo: tiempo*) changeable; (: *carácter*) unpredictable.

desigualdad [desēgwáldàth'] *nf* (ECÓN, POL) inequality; (*de carácter, tiempo*) unpredictability; (*de escritura*) unevenness; (*de terreno*) roughness.

desilusión [desēlōōsyon'] *nf* disillusionment; (*decepción*) disappointment.

desilusionar [desēlōōsyonár'] *vt* to disillusion; (*decepcionar*) to disappoint; ~**se** *vr* to become disillusioned.

desinencia [desēnen'syá] *nf* (LING) ending.

desinfectar [desēnfektár'] *vt* to disinfect.

desinfestar [desēnfestár'] *vt* to decontaminate.

desinflación [desēnflásyon'] *nf* (COM) disinflation.

desinflar [desēnflár'] *vt* to deflate; ~**se** *vr* (*neumático*) to go down *o* flat.

desintegración [desēntegrásyon'] *nf* disintegration; ~ **nuclear** nuclear fission.

desintegrar [desēntegrár'] *vt* (*gen*) to disintegrate; (*átomo*) to split; (*grupo*) to break up; ~**se** *vr* to disintegrate; to split; to break up.

desinterés [desēnteres'] *nm* (*objetividad*) disinterestedness; (*altruismo*) unselfishness.

desinteresado, a [desēnteresá'tho, á] *a* (*imparcial*) disinterested; (*altruista*) unselfish.

desintoxicar [desēntoksēkár'] *vt* to detoxify; ~**se** *vr*: ~**se de** (*rutina, trabajo*) to get away from.

desintoxique [desēntoksē'ke] *etc vb* V **desintoxicar.**

desistir [desēstēr'] *vi* (*renunciar*) to stop, desist; ~ **de** (*empresa*) to give up; (*derecho*) to waive.

deslavazado, a [deslàbàsá'tho, á] *a* (*lacio*) limp; (*desteñido*) faded; (*insípido*) colorless (US), colourless (Brit); (*incoherente*) disjointed.

desleal [desleál'] *a* (*infiel*) disloyal; (COM: *competencia*) unfair.

deslealtad [desleàltàth'] *nf* disloyalty.

desleído, a [deslcē'tho, á] *a* weak.

desleír [deslcēr'] *vt* (*líquido*) to dilute; (*sólido*) to dissolve.

deslenguado, a [deslengwà'tho, á] *a* (*grosero*) foul-mouthed.

deslía [deslē'á] *etc vb* V **desleír.**

desliar [deslyár'] *vt* (*desatar*) to untie; (*paquete*) to open; ~**se** *vr* to come undone.

deslice [deslē'se] *etc vb* V **deslizar.**

desliendo [deslēen'do] *etc vb* V **desleír.**

desligar [deslēgár'] *vt* (*desatar*) to untie, undo; (*separar*) to separate; ~**se** *vr* (*de un compromiso*) to extricate o.s.

desligue [deslē'ge] *etc vb* V **desligar.**

deslindar [deslēndár'] *vt* (*señalar las lindes de*) to mark out, fix the boundaries of; (*fig*) to define.

desliz [deslēs'] *nm* (*fig*) lapse; ~ **de lengua** slip of the tongue; **cometer un** ~ to slip up.

deslizar [deslēsár'] *vt* to slip, slide; ~**se** *vr* (*escurrirse: persona*) to slip, slide; (: *coche*) to skid; (*aguas mansas*) to flow gently; (*error*) to creep in; (*tiempo*) to pass; (*persona: irse*) to slip away; ~**se en un cuarto** to slip into a room.

deslomar [deslomár'] *vt* (*romper el lomo de*) to break the back of; (*fig*) to wear out; ~**se** *vr* (*fig fam*) to work one's guts out.

deslucido, a [deslōōsē'tho, á] *a* dull; (*torpe*) awkward, graceless; (*deslustrado*) tarnished; (*fracasado*) unsuccessful; **quedar** ~ to make a poor impression.

deslucir [deslōōsēr'] *vt* (*deslustrar*) to tarnish; (*estropear*) to spoil, ruin; (*persona*) to discredit; **la lluvia deslució el acto** the rain ruined the ceremony.

deslumbrar [deslōōmbrár'] *vt* (*con la luz*) to dazzle; (*cegar*) to blind; (*impresionar*) to dazzle; (*dejar perplejo a*) to puzzle, confuse.

deslustrar [deslōōstrár'] *vt* (*vidrio*) to frost; (*quitar lustre a*) to dull; (*reputación*) to sully.

desluzca [deslōōs'ká] *etc vb* V **deslucir.**

desmadrarse [desmáthrár'se] *vr* (*fam*) to run wild.

desmán [desmán'] *nm* (*exceso*) outrage; (*abuso de poder*) abuse.

desmandarse [desmándár'se] *vr* (*portarse mal*) to behave badly; (*excederse*) to get out of hand; (*caballo*) to bolt.

desmantelar [desmántelár'] *vt* (*deshacer*) to dismantle; (*casa*) to strip; (*organización*) to disband; (MIL) to raze; (*andamio*) to take down; (NAUT) to unrig.

desmaña [desmá'nyá] *nf* clumsiness.

desmaquillador [desmákēyàthor'] *nm* make-up remover.

desmayado, a |desmàyá'tho. á| *a* (*sin senti-do*) unconscious; (*carácter*) dull; (*débil*) faint, weak; (*color*) pale.

desmayar |desmàyár'| *vi* to lose heart; ~**se** *vr* (*MED*) to faint.

desmayo |desmà'yo| *nm* (*MED*: *acto*) faint; (*estado*) unconsciousness; (*depresión*) dejection; (*de voz*) faltering; **sufrir un** ~ to have a fainting fit.

desmedido, a |desmethè'tho, á| *a* excessive; (*ambición*) boundless.

desmedrado, a |desmethrà'tho, á| *a* (*estro-peado*) impaired; (*MED*) run down.

desmejorado, a |desmehorà'tho, á| *a*: **está muy desmejorada** (*MED*) she's not looking too well.

desmejorar |desmehorár'| *vt* (*dañar*) to impair, spoil; (*MED*) to weaken.

desmembración |desmembrásyon'| *nf* dismemberment; (*fig*) break-up.

desmembrar |desmembrár'| *vt* (*MED*) to dismember; (*fig*) to separate.

desmemoriado, a |desmemoryà'tho, á| *a* forgetful, absent-minded.

desmentir |desmentēr'| *vt* (*contradecir*) to contradict; (*refutar*) to deny; (*rumor*) to squelch (*US*), scotch (*Brit*) ♦ *vi*: ~ **de** to refute; ~**se** *vr* to contradict o.s.

desmenuce |desmenōō'se| *etc vb* V **desme-nuzar**.

desmenuzar |desmenōōsár'| *vt* (*deshacer*) to crumble; (*carne*) to chop; (*examinar*) to examine closely.

desmerecer |desmereser'| *vt* to be unworthy of ♦ *vi* (*deteriorarse*) to deteriorate.

desmerezca |desmeres'ká| *etc vb* V **desme-recer**.

desmesurado, a |desmesōōrà'tho, á| *a* (*desmedido*) disproportionate; (*enorme*) enormous; (*ambición*) boundless; (*descara-do*) insolent.

desmiembre |desmyem'bre| *etc vb* V **desmembrar**.

desmienta |desmyen'tá| *etc vb* V **desmentir**.

desmigajar |desmēgáhár'|, **desmigar** |des-mēgár'| *vt* to crumble.

desmigue |desmē'ge| *etc vb* V **desmigar**.

desmilitarice |desmēlētárē'se| *etc vb* V **desmilitarizar**.

desmilitarizar |desmēlētárēsár'| *vt* to demilitarize.

desmintiendo |desmēntyen'do| *etc vb* V **desmentir**.

desmochar |desmotchár'| *vt* (*árbol*) to lop; (*texto*) to cut, hack about.

desmontable |desmontà'ble| *a* (*que se qui-ta*) detachable; (*en compartimientos*) sectional; (*que se puede plegar etc*) collapsible.

desmontar |desmontár'| *vt* (*deshacer*) to

dismantle; (*motor*) to strip down; (*máqui-na*) to take apart; (*escopeta*) to uncock; (*tienda de campaña*) to take down; (*tierra*) to level; (*quitar los árboles a*) to clear; (*ji-nete*) to throw ♦ *vi* to dismount.

desmonte |desmon'te| *nm* (*de tierra*) levelling; (*de árboles*) clearing; (*terreno*) levelled ground; (*FERRO*) cutting.

desmoralice |desmorálē'se| *etc vb* V **desmoralizar**.

desmoralizador, a |desmorálēsáthor', á| *a* demoralizing.

desmoralizar |desmorálēsár'| *vt* to demoralize.

desmoronado, a |desmoronà'tho, á| *a* (*casa, edificio*) dilapidated.

desmoronamiento |desmoronámyen'to| *nm* (*tb fig*) crumbling.

desmoronar |desmoronár'| *vt* to wear away, erode; ~**se** *vr* (*edificio, dique*) to fall into disrepair; (*economía*) to decline.

desmovilice |desmohēlē'se| *etc vb* V **desmovilizar**.

desmovilizar |desmohēlēsár'| *vt* to demobilize.

desnacionalización |desnásyonálēsásyon'| *nf* denationalization.

desnacionalizado, a |desnásyonálēsá'tho, á| *a* (*industria*) denationalized; (*persona*) stateless.

desnatado, a |desnátá'tho, á| *a* skimmed.

desnatar |desnátár'| *vt* (*leche*) to skim; **le-che sin** ~ whole milk.

desnaturalice |desnátōōrálē'se| *etc vb* V **desnaturalizar**.

desnaturalizado, a |desnátōōrálēsá'tho, á| *a* (*persona*) unnatural; **alcohol** ~ methylated spirits.

desnaturalizar |desnátōōrálēsár'| *vt* (*QUÍ-MICA*) to denature; (*corromper*) to pervert; (*sentido de algo*) to distort; ~**se** *vr* (*perder la nacionalidad*) to give up one's nationality.

desnivel |desnēhel'| *nm* (*de terreno*) unevenness; (*POL*) inequality; (*diferencia*) difference.

desnivelar |desnēhelár'| *vt* (*terreno*) to make uneven; (*fig*: *desequilibrar*) to unbalance; (*balanza*) to tip.

desnuclearizado, a |desnōōkleárēsá'tho, á| *a*: **región desnuclearizada** nuclear-free zone.

desnudar |desnōōthár'| *vt* (*desvestir*) to undress; (*despojar*) to strip; ~**se** *vr* (*desvestirse*) to get undressed.

desnudez |desnōōthes'| *nf* (*de persona*) nudity; (*fig*) bareness.

desnudo, a |desnōō'tho, á| *a* (*cuerpo*) naked; (*árbol, brazo*) bare; (*paisaje*) flat; (*estilo*) unadorned; (*verdad*) plain ♦ *nm/f* nude; ~ **de** devoid *o* bereft of; **la retrató al**

~ he painted her in the nude; **poner al** ~ to lay bare.

desnutrición |dɛsnōōtrɛ̄syon'| *nf* malnutrition.

desnutrido, a |dɛsnōōtrɛ̄'ð̣o, á| *a* undernourished.

desobedecer |dɛsoḅɛ̄ḥɛscr'| *vt, vi* to disobey.

desobedezca |dɛsoḅɛ̄ḥɛs'ká| *etc vb V* **desobedecer.**

desobediencia |dɛsoḅɛ̄ḥyɛn'syä| *nf* disobedience.

desocupado, a |dɛsocōōpá'ð̣o, á| *a* at leisure; (*desempleado*) unemployed; (*deshabitado*) empty, vacant.

desocupar |dɛsocōōpár'| *vt* to vacate; ~**se** *vr* (*quedar libre*) to be free; **se ha desocupado aquella mesa** that table's free now.

desodorante |dɛsoð̣orán'tɛ| *nm* deodorant.

desoiga |dɛso'ɛ̄ɡá| *etc vb V* **desoír.**

desoír |dɛsoɛ̄r'| *vt* to ignore, disregard.

desolación |dɛsolàsyon'| *nf* (*de lugar*) desolation; (*fig*) grief.

desolar |dɛsolár'| *vt* to ruin, lay waste.

desolladero |dɛsoyáð̣ɛ'ro| *nm* slaughterhouse.

desollar |dɛsoyár'| *vt* (*quitar la piel a*) to skin; (*criticar*): ~ **vivo a** to criticize unmercifully.

desorbitado, a |dɛsorḅɛ̄tá'ð̣o, á| *a* (*excesivo*) excessive; (*precio*) exorbitant; **con los ojos** ~**s** pop-eyed.

desorbitar |dɛsorḅɛ̄tár'| *vt* (*exagerar*) to exaggerate; (*interpretar mal*) to misinterpret; ~**se** *vr* (*persona*) to lose one's sense of proportion; (*asunto*) to get out of hand.

desorden |dɛsor'ð̣ɛn| *nm* confusion; (*de casa, cuarto*) mess; (*político*) disorder; **desórdenes** *nmpl* (*alborotos*) disturbances; (*excesos*) excesses; **en** ~ (*gente*) in confusion.

desordenado, a |dɛsorð̣ɛná'ð̣o, á| *a* (*habitación, persona*) untidy; (*objetos: revueltos*) in a mess, jumbled; (*conducta*) disorderly.

desordenar |dɛsorð̣ɛnár'| *vt* (*gen*) to disarrange; (*pelo*) to mess up; (*cuarto*) to make a mess in; (*causar confusión a*) to throw into confusion.

desorganice |dɛsorɡánɛ̄'sɛ| *etc vb V* **desorganizar.**

desorganizar |dɛsorɡánɛ̄sàr'| *vt* to disorganize.

desorientar |dɛsoryɛntár'| *vt* (*extraviar*) to mislead; (*confundir, desconcertar*) to confuse; ~**se** *vr* (*perderse*) to lose one's way.

desovar |dɛsovár'| *vi* (*peces*) to spawn; (*insectos*) to lay eggs.

desoyendo |dɛsoyɛn'ḍo| *etc vb V* **desoír.**

despabilado, a |dɛspáḅɛ̄lá'ð̣o, á| *a* (*despierto*) wide-awake; (*fig*) alert, sharp.

despabilar |dɛspáḅɛ̄lár'| *vt* (*despertar*) to wake up; (*fig: persona*) to liven up; (*trabajo*) to get through quickly ♦ *vi*, ~**se** *vr* to wake up; (*fig*) to get a move on.

despacio |dɛspá'syo| *ad* (*lentamente*) slowly; (*en voz baja*) softly; **¡~!** take it easy!

despacito |dɛspásɛ̄'to| *ad* (*fam*) slowly; (*suavemente*) softly.

despachar |dɛspátchár'| *vt* (*negocio*) to do, complete; (*resolver: problema*) to settle; (*correspondencia*) to deal with; (*fam: comida*) to polish off; (: *bebida*) to gulp down (*US*), knock back (*Brit*); (*enviar*) to send, dispatch; (*vender*) to sell, deal in; (*COM: cliente*) to attend to; (*billete*) to issue; (*mandar ir*) to send away ♦ *vi* (*decidirse*) to get things settled; (*apresurarse*) to hurry up; ~**se** *vr* to finish off; (*apresurarse*) to hurry up; ~**se de algo** to get rid of sth; ~**se a su gusto con uno** to give sb a piece of one's mind; **¿quién despacha?** is anybody serving?

despacho |dɛspátch'o| *nm* (*oficina*) office; (: *en una casa*) study; (*de paquetes*) dispatch; (*COM: venta*) sale (of goods); (*comunicación*) message; ~ **de billetes** *o* **boletos** (*AM*) booking office; ~ **de localidades** box office; **géneros sin** ~ unsaleable goods; **tener buen** ~ to find a ready sale.

despachurrar |dɛspátchōōrrár'| *vt* (*aplastar*) to crush; (*persona*) to flatten.

despampanante |dɛspámpánán'tɛ| *a* (*fam: chica*) stunning.

desparejado, a |dɛspárchá'ð̣o, á|, **desparejo, a** |dɛspárɛ'ho, á| *a* odd.

desparpajo |dɛspárpá'ho| *nm* (*desenvoltura*) self-confidence; (*pey*) nerve.

desparramar |dɛspárrámár'| *vt* (*esparcir*) to scatter; (*líquido*) to spill.

despatarrar |dɛspátárrár'| *vt* (*asombrar*) to amaze; ~**se** *vr* (*abrir las piernas*) to open one's legs wide; (*caerse*) to tumble; (*fig*) to be flabbergasted.

despavorido, a |dɛspáḅorɛ̄'ð̣o, á| *a* terrified.

despectivo, a |dɛspɛktɛ̄'ḥo, á| *a* (*despreciativo*) derogatory; (*LING*) pejorative.

despechar |dɛspɛtchár'| *vt* (*provocar ira a*) to enrage; (*fam: destetar*) to wean.

despecho |dɛspɛtch'o| *nm* spite; **a** ~ **de** in spite of; **por** ~ out of (sheer) spite.

despedace |dɛspɛð̣á'sɛ| *etc vb V* **despedazar.**

despedazar |dɛspɛð̣ásár'| *vt* to tear to pieces.

despedida |dɛspɛð̣ɛ̄'ð̣á| *nf* (*adiós*) goodbye, farewell; (*antes de viaje*) send-off; (*en carta*) closing formula; (*de obrero*) dismissal; (*INFORM*) log off (*US*), logout (*Brit*); **cena/función de** ~ farewell dinner/

performance; **regalo de** ~ parting gift; ~ **de soltero/soltera** stag/shower party.

despedir [despeðér'] *vt* (*visita*) to see off, show out; (*empleado*) to dismiss; (*inquilino*) to evict; (*objeto*) to hurl; (*olor etc*) to give out *o* off; ~**se** *vr* (*dejar un empleo*) to give up one's job; (*INFORM*) to log out *o* off; ~**se de** to say goodbye to; **se despidieron** they said goodbye to each other.

despegado, a [despegá'ðo, á] *a* (*separado*) detached; (*persona: poco afectuoso*) cold, indifferent ♦ *nm/f*: **es un** ~ he has cut himself off from his family.

despegar [despegár'] *vt* to unstick; (*sobre*) to open ♦ *vi* (*avión*) to take off; (*cohete*) to blast off; ~**se** *vr* to come loose, come unstuck; **sin** ~ **los labios** without uttering a word.

despego [despe'go] *nm* detachment.

despegue [despe'ge] *etc vb* V **despegar** ♦ *nm* takeoff; (*de cohete*) blastoff.

despeinado, a [despeiná'ðo, á] *a* dishevelled, unkempt.

despeinar [despeinár'] *vt* (*pelo*) to ruffle; **¡me has despeinado todo!** you've completely ruined my hairdo!

despejado, a [despehá'ðo, á] *a* (*lugar*) clear, free; (*cielo*) clear; (*persona*) wide-awake, bright.

despejar [despehár'] *vt* (*gen*) to clear; (*misterio*) to clarify, clear up; (*MAT: incógnita*) to find ♦ *vi* (*el tiempo*) to clear; ~**se** *vr* (*tiempo, cielo*) to clear (up); (*misterio*) to become clearer; (*cabeza*) to clear; **¡despejen!** (*moverse*) move along!; (*salirse*) everybody out!

despeje [despe'he] *nm* (*DEPORTE*) clearance.

despelotarse [despelotár'se] *vr* (*fam*) to strip off; (*fig*) to let one's hair down.

despeluce [despeloo'se] *etc vb* V **despeluzar.**

despeluzar [despeloosár'] *vt* (*pelo*) to tousle; ~ **a uno** (*fig*) to horrify sb.

despellejar [despeyehár'] *vt* (*animal*) to skin; (*criticar*) to criticize unmercifully; (*fam: arruinar*) to fleece.

despensa [despen'sá] *nf* (*armario*) pantry; (*NAUT*) storeroom; (*provisión de comestibles*) stock of food.

despeñadero [despenyáðe'ro] *nm* (*GEO*) cliff, precipice.

despeñar [despenyár'] *vt* (*arrojar*) to fling down; ~**se** *vr* to fling o.s. down; (*caer*) to fall headlong.

desperdiciar [desperðioiár'] *vt* (*comida, tiempo*) to waste; (*oportunidad*) to throw away.

desperdicio [desperðioi'syo] *nm* (*despilfarro*) squandering; (*residuo*) waste; ~**s** *nmpl* (*basura*) rubbish *sg*, refuse *sg*, garb-

age *sg* (*US*); (*residuos*) waste *sg*; ~**s de cocina** kitchen scraps; **el libro no tiene** ~ the book is excellent from beginning to end.

desperdigar [desperðigár'] *vt* (*esparcir*) to scatter; (*energía*) to dissipate; ~**se** *vr* to scatter.

desperdigue [desperðige'ge] *etc vb* V **desperdigar.**

desperece [despere'se] *etc vb* V **desperezarse.**

desperezarse [desperesár'se] *vr* to stretch.

desperfecto [desperfek'to] *nm* (*deterioro*) slight damage; (*defecto*) flaw, imperfection.

despertador [despertaðor'] *nm* alarm clock; ~ **de viaje** travelling clock.

despertar [despertár'] *vt* (*persona*) to wake up; (*recuerdos*) to revive; (*esperanzas*) to raise; (*sentimiento*) to arouse ♦ *vi*, ~**se** *vr* to awaken, wake up; ~**se a la realidad** to wake up to reality ♦ *nm* awakening.

despiadado, a [despyaðá'ðo, á] *a* (*ataque*) merciless; (*persona*) heartless.

despido [despē'ðo] *etc vb* V **despedir** ♦ *nm* dismissal; ~ **improcedente** *o* **injustificado** wrongful dismissal; ~ **injusto** unfair dismissal; ~ **voluntario** voluntary dismissal (*US*) *o* redundancy (*Brit*).

despierto, a [despyer'to, á] *etc vb* V **despertar** ♦ *a* awake; (*fig*) sharp, alert.

despilfarrado, a [despilfárrá'ðo, á] *a* (*malgastador*) wasteful; (*con dinero*) spendthrift ♦ *nm/f* spendthrift.

despilfarrar [despilfárrár'] *vt* (*gen*) to waste; (*dinero*) to squander.

despilfarro [despilfá'rro] *nm* (*derroche*) squandering; (*lujo desmedido*) extravagance.

despintar [despintár'] *vt* (*quitar pintura a*) to take the paint off; (*hechos*) to distort ♦ *vi*: **A no despinta a B** A is in no way inferior to B; ~**se** *vr* (*desteñir*) to fade.

despiojar [despyohár'] *vt* to delouse.

despistado, a [despistá'ðo, á] *a* (*distraído*) vague, absent-minded; (*poco práctico*) impractical; (*confuso*) confused; (*desorientado*) off the track ♦ *nm/f* (*tipo: distraído*) scatterbrain, absent-minded person.

despistar [despistár'] *vt* to throw off the track *o* scent; (*fig*) to mislead, confuse; ~**se** *vr* to take the wrong road; (*fig*) to become confused.

despiste [despis'te] *nm* (*AUTO etc*) swerve; (*error*) slip; (*distracción*) absent-mindedness; **tiene un terrible** ~ he's terribly absent-minded.

desplace [desplá'se] *etc vb* V **desplazar.**

desplante [desplán'te] *nm*: **hacer un** ~ **a uno** to be rude to sb.

desplazado, a [desplásá'ðo, á] *a* (*pieza*) wrongly placed ♦ *nm/f* (*inadaptado*) misfit;

sentirse un poco ~ to feel rather out of place.

desplazamiento [desplásámyen'to] nm displacement; (viaje) journey; (de opinión, votos) shift, swing; (INFORM) scrolling; ~ hacia arriba/abajo (INFORM) scroll up/down.

desplazar [desplasár'] vt (gen) to move; (FÍSICA, NAUT, TEC) to displace; (tropas) to transfer; (suplantar) to take the place of; (INFORM) to scroll; ~se vr (persona, vehículo) to travel, go; (objeto) to move, shift; (votos, opinión) to shift, swing.

desplegar [desplegár'] vt (tela, papel) to unfold, open out; (bandera) to unfurl; (alas) to spread; (MIL) to deploy; (manifestar) to display.

desplegué [desplege'], **despleguemos** [desplege'mos] etc vb V **desplegar**.

despliegue [desplye'ge] etc vb V **desplegar** ♦ nm unfolding, opening; deployment, display.

desplomarse [desplomár'se] vr (edificio, gobierno, persona) to collapse; (derrumbarse) to topple over; (precios) to slump; **se ha desplomado el techo** the ceiling has fallen in.

desplumar [desploomár'] vt (ave) to pluck; (fam: estafar) to fleece.

despoblado, a [despohlá'tho, á] a (sin habitantes) uninhabited; (con pocos habitantes) depopulated; (con insuficientes habitantes) underpopulated ♦ nm deserted spot.

despojar [despohár'] vt (alguien: de sus bienes) to divest of, deprive of; (casa) to strip, leave bare; (de su cargo) to strip of; ~se vr (desnudarse) to undress; ~se de (ropa, hojas) to shed; (poderes) to relinquish.

despojo [despo'ho] nm (acto) plundering; (objetos) plunder, loot; ~s nmpl (de ave, res) offal sg.

desposado, a [desposá'tho, á] a, nm/f newly-wed.

desposar [desposár'] vt (suj: sacerdote: pareja) to marry; ~se vr (casarse) to marry, get married.

desposeer [desposeer'] vt (despojar) to dispossess; ~ a uno de su autoridad to strip sb of his authority.

desposeído, a [deposeé'tho, á] nm/f: los ~s the have-nots.

desposeyendo [desposeyen'do] etc vb V **desposeer**.

desposorios [desposo'ryos] nmpl (esponsales) betrothal sg; (boda) marriage ceremony sg.

déspota [des'potá] nm/f despot.

despotricar [despotrekár'] vi: ~ contra to moan o complain about.

despotrique [despotré'ke] etc vb V **despo-**

tricar.

despreciable [despresyá'hle] a (moralmente) despicable; (objeto) worthless; (cantidad) negligible.

despreciar [despresyár'] vt (desdeñar) to despise, scorn; (afrentar) to slight.

despreciativo, a [despresyáté'ho, á] a (observación, tono) scornful, contemptuous; (comentario) derogatory.

desprecio [despre'syo] nm scorn, contempt; slight.

desprender [desprender'] vt (soltar) to loosen; (separar) to separate; (desatar) to unfasten; (olor) to give off; ~se vr (botón: caerse) to fall off; (: abrirse) to unfasten; (olor, perfume) to be given off; ~se de to follow from; ~se de algo (ceder) to give sth up; (desembarazarse) to get rid of sth; **se desprende que** it transpires that.

desprendido, a [desprendé'do, á] a (pieza) loose; (sin abrochar) unfastened; (desinteresado) disinterested; (generoso) generous.

desprendimiento [desprendémyen'to] nm (gen) loosening; (generosidad) disinterestedness; (indiferencia) detachment; (de gas) leak; (de tierra, rocas) landslide.

despreocupado, a [despreokoopá'tho, á] a (sin preocupación) unworried, unconcerned; (tranquilo) nonchalant; (en el vestir) casual; (negligente) careless.

despreocuparse [despreokoopár'se] vr to be carefree; (dejar de inquietarse) to stop worrying; (ser indiferente) to be unconcerned; ~ de to have no interest in.

desprestigiar [desprestéhyár'] vt (criticar) to run down, disparage; (desacreditar) to discredit.

desprestigio [despresté'hyo] nm (denigración) disparagement; (impopularidad) unpopularity.

desprevenido, a [despreheneé'tho, á] a (no preparado) unprepared, unready; **coger** (Esp) o **agarrar** (AM) **a uno** ~ to catch sb unawares.

desproporción [desproporsyon'] nf disproportion, lack of proportion.

desproporcionado, a [desproporsyoná'tho, á] a disproportionate, out of proportion.

despropósito [despropo'séto] nm (salida de tono) irrelevant remark; (disparate) piece of nonsense.

desprovisto, a [desprohé'sto, á] a: ~ de devoid of; **estar** ~ **de** to lack.

después [despwes'] ad afterwards, later; (desde entonces) since (then); (próximo paso) next; **poco** ~ soon after; **un año** ~ a year later; ~ **se debatió el tema** next the matter was discussed ♦ prep: ~ **de** (tiempo) after, since; (orden) next (to); ~ **de comer** after lunch; ~ **de corregido el texto** after the text had been corrected; ~

de esa fecha (*pasado*) since that date; (*futuro*) from o after that date; ~ **de todo** after all; ~ **de verlo** after seeing it, after I *etc* saw it; **mi nombre está** ~ **del tuyo** my name comes next to yours ♦ *conj*: ~ **(de) que** after; ~ **(de) que lo escribí** after o since I wrote it, after writing it.

despuntar [despōōntár'] *vt* (*lápiz*) to blunt ♦ *vi* (*BOT*: *plantas*) to sprout; (: *flores*) to bud; (*alba*) to break; (*día*) to dawn; (*persona*: *descollar*) to stand out.

desquiciar [deskēsyár'] *vt* (*puerta*) to take off its hinges; (*descomponer*) to upset; (*persona*: *turbar*) to disturb; (: *volver loco a*) to unhinge.

desquitarse [deskētár'se] *vr* to obtain satisfaction; (*COM*) to recover a debt; (*fig*: *vengarse de*) to get one's own back; ~ **de una pérdida** to make up for a loss.

desquite [deskē'te] *nm* (*satisfacción*) satisfaction; (*venganza*) revenge.

Dest. *abr* = **destinatario.**

destacado, a [destáká'tho, á] *a* outstanding.

destacamento [destákámen'to] *nm* (*MIL*) detachment.

destacar [destákár'] *vt* (*ARTE*: *hacer resaltar*) to make stand out; (*subrayar*) to emphasize, point up; (*MIL*) to detach, detail; (*INFORM*) to highlight ♦ *vi*, ~**se** *vr* (*resaltarse*) to stand out; (*persona*) to be outstanding o exceptional; **quiero** ~ **que...** I wish to emphasize that...; ~**(se) contra** o **en** o **sobre** to stand out o be outlined against.

destajo [destá'ho] *nm*: **a** ~ (*por pieza*) by the job; (*con afán*) eagerly; **trabajar a** ~ to do piecework; (*fig*) to work one's fingers to the bone.

destapar [destápár'] *vt* (*botella*) to open; (*cacerola*) to take the lid off; (*descubrir*) to uncover; ~**se** *vr* (*descubrirse*) to get uncovered; (*revelarse*) to reveal one's true character.

destape [destá'pe] *nm* nudity; (*fig*) permissiveness; **el** ~ **español** the *process of liberalization in Spain after Franco's death.*

destaque [destá'ke] *etc vb V* **destacar.**

destartalado, a [destártálá'tho, á] *a* (*desordenado*) untidy; (*casa etc*: *grande*) rambling; (: *ruinoso*) tumbledown.

destellar [desteyár'] *vi* (*diamante*) to sparkle; (*metal*) to glint; (*estrella*) to twinkle.

destello [deste'yo] *nm* (*de diamante*) sparkle; (*de metal*) glint; (*de estrella*) twinkle; (*de faro*) signal light; **no tiene un** ~ **de verdad** there's not a grain of truth in it.

destemplado, a [destemplá'tho, á] *a* (*MUS*) out of tune; (*voz*) harsh; (*MED*) out of

sorts; (*METEOROLOGÍA*) unpleasant, nasty.

destemplar [destemplár'] *vt* (*MUS*) to put out of tune; (*alterar*) to upset; ~**se** *vr* (*MUS*) to lose its pitch; (*descomponerse*) to get out of order; (*persona*: *irritarse*) to get upset; (*MED*) to get out of sorts.

desteñir [destenyēr'] *vt* to fade ♦ *vi*, ~**se** *vr* to fade; **esta tela no destiñe** this fabric will not run.

desternillarse [desternēyár'se] *vr*: ~ **de risa** to split one's sides laughing.

desterrado, a [desterrá'tho, á] *nm/f* (*exiliado*) exile.

desterrar [desterrár'] *vt* (*exilar*) to exile; (*fig*) to banish, dismiss.

destetar [destetár'] *vt* to wean.

destiempo [destyem'po]: **a** ~ *ad* at the wrong time.

destierro [destye'rro] *etc vb V* **desterrar** ♦ *nm* exile; **vivir en el** ~ to live in exile.

destilar [destēlár'] *vt* to distil; (*pus, sangre*) to ooze; (*fig*: *rebosar*) to exude; (: *revelar*) to reveal ♦ *vi* (*gotear*) to drip.

destilería [destēlerē'á] *nf* distillery; ~ **de petróleo** oil refinery.

destinar [destēnár'] *vt* (*funcionario*) to appoint, assign; (*fondos*) to set aside; **es un libro destinado a los niños** it is a book (intended o meant) for children; **una carta que viene destinada a usted** a letter for you, a letter addressed to you.

destinatario, a [destēnátá'ryo, á] *nm/f* addressee; (*COM*) payee.

destino [destē'no] *nm* (*suerte*) destiny; (*de viajero*) destination; (*función*) use; (*puesto*) post, placement; ~ **público** public appointment; **salir con** ~ **a** to leave for; **con** ~ **a Londres** (*avión, barco*) (bound) for London; (*carta*) to London.

destiña [destē'nyá] *etc*, **destiñendo** [destēnyen'do] *etc vb V* **desteñir.**

destitución [destētōōsyon'] *nf* dismissal, removal.

destituir [destētōōēr'] *vt* (*despedir*) to dismiss; (: *ministro, funcionario*) to remove from office.

destituyendo [destētōōyen'do] *etc vb V* **destituir.**

destornillador [destornēyáthor'] *nm* screwdriver.

destornillar [destornēyár'] *vt*, ~**se** *vr* (*tornillo*) to unscrew.

destrabar [destrábár'] *vt* to untie, unfetter.

destreza [destre'sá] *nf* (*habilidad*) skill; (*maña*) dexterity.

destripar [destrēpár'] *vt* (*animal*) to gut; (*reventar*) to mangle.

destronar [destronár'] *vt* (*rey*) to dethrone; (*fig*) to overthrow.

destroncar [destronkár'] *vt* (*árbol*) to chop off, lop; (*proyectos*) to ruin; (*discurso*) to interrupt.

destronque [destron'ke] *etc vb* V **destroncar**.

destroce [destro'se] *etc vb* V **destrozar**.

destrozar [destrosár'] *vt* (*romper*) to smash, break (up); (*estropear*) to ruin; (*nervios*) to shatter; ~ **a uno en una discusión** to crush sb in an argument.

destrozo [destro'so] *nm* (*acción*) destruction; (*desastre*) smashing; ~**s** *nmpl* (*pedazos*) pieces; (*daños*) havoc *sg*.

destrucción [destrŏŏksyon'] *nf* destruction.

destructor, a [destrŏŏktor', à] *a* destructive ♦ *nm* (NAUT) destroyer.

destruir [destrŏŏér'] *vt* to destroy; (*casa*) to demolish; (*equilibrio*) to upset; (*proyecto*) to spoil; (*esperanzas*) to dash; (*argumento*) to demolish.

destruyendo [destrŏŏyen'do] *etc vb* V **destruir**.

desuelle [deswe'ye] *etc vb* V **desollar**.

desueve [deswe'he] *etc vb* V **desovar**.

desunión [desŏŏnyon'] *nf* (*separación*) separation; (*discordia*) disunity.

desunir [desŏŏnér'] *vt* to separate; (TEC) to disconnect; (*fig*) to cause a quarrel *o* rift between.

desuso [desŏŏ'so] *nm* disuse; **caer en** ~ to fall into disuse, become obsolete; **una expresión caída en** ~ an obsolete expression.

desvaído, a [desbáē'tho, à] *a* (*color*) pale; (*contorno*) blurred.

desvalido, a [desbálē'tho, à] *a* (*desprotegido*) destitute; (*sin fuerzas*) helpless; **niños** ~**s** waifs and strays.

desvalijar [desbálēhár'] *vt* (*persona*) to rob; (*casa, tienda*) to burgle; (*coche*) to break into.

desvalorice [desbálorē'se] *etc vb* V **desvalorizar**.

desvalorizar [desbálorēsár'] *vt* to devalue.

desván [desbàn'] *nm* attic.

desvanecer [desbáneser'] *vt* (*disipar*) to dispel; (*recuerdo, temor*) to banish; (*borrar*) to blur; ~**se** *vr* (*humo etc*) to vanish, disappear; (*duda*) to be dispelled; (*color*) to fade; (*recuerdo, sonido*) to fade away; (MED) to pass out.

desvanecido, a [desbánesē'tho, à] *a* (MED) faint; **caer** ~ to fall in a faint.

desvanecimiento [desbánesēmyen'to] *nm* (*desaparición*) disappearance; (*de dudas*) dispelling; (*de colores*) fading; (*evaporación*) evaporation; (MED) fainting spell (US) *o* fit (Brit).

desvanezca [desbánes'kà] *etc vb* V **desvanecer**.

desvariar [desbáryàr'] *vi* (*enfermo*) to be delirious; (*delirar*) to talk nonsense.

desvarío [desbárē'o] *nm* delirium; (*desatino*) absurdity; ~**s** *nmpl* ravings.

desvelar [desbelár'] *vt* to keep awake; ~**se** *vr* (*no poder dormir*) to stay awake; (*vigilar*) to be vigilant *o* watchful; ~**se por algo** (*inquietarse*) to be anxious about sth; (*poner gran cuidado*) to take great care over sth.

desvelo [desbe'lo] *nm* lack of sleep; (*insomnio*) sleeplessness; (*fig*) vigilance; ~**s** *nmpl* (*preocupación*) anxiety *sg*, effort *sg*.

desvencijado, a [desbensēhà'tho, à] *a* (*silla*) rickety; (*máquina*) broken-down.

desvencijar [desbensēhár'] *vt* (*romper*) to break; (*soltar*) to loosen; (*persona: agotar*) to exhaust; ~**se** *vr* to come apart.

desventaja [desbentà'hà] *nf* disadvantage; (*inconveniente*) drawback.

desventajoso, a [desbentàho'so, à] *a* disadvantageous, unfavorable (US), unfavourable (Brit).

desventura [desbentŏŏ'rà] *nf* misfortune.

desventurado, a [desbentŏŏrà'tho, à] *a* (*desgraciado*) unfortunate; (*de poca suerte*) ill-fated.

desvergonzado, a [desbergonsà'tho, à] *a* (*sin vergüenza*) shameless; (*descarado*) insolent ♦ *nm/f* shameless person.

desvergüenza [desbergwen'sà] *nf* (*descaro*) shamelessness; (*insolencia*) impudence; (*mala conducta*) effrontery; **esto es una** ~ this is disgraceful; **¡qué** ~! what a nerve!

desvestir [desbestēr'] *vt*, **desvestirse** *vr* to undress.

desviación [desbyàsyon'] *nf* deviation; (AUTO: *rodeo*) diversion, detour; (: *carretera de circunvalación*) beltway (US), ring road (Brit); ~ **de la circulación** traffic diversion; **es una** ~ **de sus principios** it is a departure from his usual principles.

desviar [desbyàr'] *vt* to turn aside; (*balón, flecha, golpe*) to deflect; (*pregunta*) to parry; (*ojos*) to avert, turn away; (*río*) to alter the course of; (*navío*) to divert, reroute; (*conversación*) to sidetrack; ~**se** *vr* (*apartarse del camino*) to turn aside; (: *barco*) to go off course; (AUTO: *dar un rodeo*) to make a detour; ~**se de un tema** to get away from the point.

desvincular [desbēnkŏŏlár'] *vt* to free, release; ~**se** *vr* (*aislarse*) to be cut off; (*alejarse*) to cut o.s. off.

desvío [desbē'o] *etc vb* V **desviar** ♦ *nm* (*desviación*) detour, diversion; (*fig*) indifference.

desvirtuar [desbērtwár'] *vt* (*estropear*) to spoil; (*argumento, razonamiento*) to detract from; (*efecto*) to counteract; (*sentido*) to distort; ~**se** *vr* to spoil.

desvistiendo [desbēstyen'do] *etc vb* V **desvestir**.

desvivirse [desbēbēr'se] *vr*: ~ **por** to long for, crave for; ~ **por los amigos** to do anything for one's friends.

detalladamente [dctáyáṭhȧmen'tc] *ad* (*con detalles*) in detail; (*extensamente*) at great length.

detallar [dctȧyár'] *vt* to detail; (*asunto por asunto*) to itemize.

detalle [dctá'yc] *nm* detail; (*fig*) gesture, token; **al ~** in detail; (*COM*) retail *cpd*; **comercio al ~** retail trade; **vender al ~** to sell retail; **no pierde ~** he doesn't miss a trick; **me observaba sin perder ~** he watched my every move; **tiene muchos ~s** she is very considerate.

detallista [dctáyē'stȧ] *nm/f* retailer ♦ *a* (*meticuloso*) meticulous; **comercio ~** retail trade.

detectar [dctcktár'] *vt* to detect.

detector [dctcktor'] *nm* (*NAUT, TEC* etc) detector; **~ de mentiras/de minas** lie/mine detector.

detención [dctcnsyon'] *nf* (*acción*) stopping; (*estancamiento*) stoppage; (*retraso*) holdup, delay; (*JUR: arresto*) arrest; (*cuidado*) care; **~ de juego** (*DEPORTE*) stoppage of play; **~ ilegal** unlawful detention.

detendré [dctendrc'] *etc vb V* **detener**.

detener [dctcncr'] *vt* (*gen*) to stop; (*JUR: arrestar*) to arrest; (: *encarcelar*) to detain; (*objeto*) to keep; (*retrasar*) to hold up, delay; (*aliento*) to hold; **~se** *vr* to stop; **~se en** (*demorarse*) to delay over, linger over.

detenga [dctcn'gȧ] *etc vb V* **detener**.

detenidamente [dctcnēṭhȧmen'tc] *ad* (*minuciosamente*) carefully; (*extensamente*) at great length.

detenido, a [dctcnē'ṭho, ȧ] *a* (*arrestado*) under arrest; (*minucioso*) detailed; (*examen*) thorough; (*tímido*) timid ♦ *nm/f* person under arrest, prisoner.

detenimiento [dctcnēmycn'to] *nm* care; **con ~** thoroughly.

detentar [dctcntár'] *vt* to hold; (*sin derecho: título*) to hold unlawfully; (: *puesto*) to occupy unlawfully.

detergente [dctcrhcn'tc] *a, nm* detergent.

deteriorado, a [dctcryorá'ṭho, ȧ] *a* (*estropeado*) damaged; (*desgastado*) worn.

deteriorar [dctcryorár'] *vt* to spoil, damage; **~se** *vr* to deteriorate.

deterioro [dctcryo'ro] *nm* deterioration.

determinación [dctcrmēnȧsyon'] *nf* (*empeño*) determination; (*decisión*) decision; (*de fecha, precio*) settling, fixing.

determinado, a [dctcrmēnȧ'ṭho, ȧ] *a* (*preciso*) fixed, set; (*LING: artículo*) definite; (*persona: resuelto*) determined; **un día ~** on a certain day; **no hay ningún tema ~** there is no particular theme.

determinar [dctcrmēnár'] *vt* (*plazo*) to fix;

(*precio*) to settle; (*daños, impuestos*) to assess; (*pleito*) to decide; (*causar*) to cause; **~se** *vr* to decide; **el reglamento determina que...** the rule states that...; **aquello determinó la caída del gobierno** that brought about the fall of the government; **esto le determinó** this made him decide.

detestable [dctcstá'ḫlc] *a* (*persona*) hateful; (*acto*) detestable.

detestar [dctcstár'] *vt* to detest.

detonar [dctonár'] *vi* to detonate.

detracción [dctráksyon'] *nf* (*denigración*) disparagement.

detractor, a [dctráktor', ȧ] *a* disparaging ♦ *nm/f* detractor.

detrás [dctrás'] *ad* behind; (*atrás*) at the back ♦ *prep*: **~ de** behind; **por ~ de uno** (*fig*) behind sb's back; **salir de ~** to come out from behind; **por ~** behind.

detrimento [dctrēmen'to] *nm*: **en ~ de** to the detriment of.

detuve [dctoō'ḫc] *etc vb V* **detener**.

deuda [dcoō'ṭhȧ] *nf* (*condición*) indebtedness, debt; (*cantidad*) debt; **~ a largo plazo** long-term debt; **~ exterior/pública** foreign/national debt; **~ incobrable** *o* **morosa** bad debt; **~s activas/pasivas** assets/liabilities; **contraer ~s** to get into debt.

deudor, a [dcoō'ṭhor', ȧ] *nm/f* debtor; **~ hipotecario** mortgager; **~ moroso** defaulter.

devaluación [dchȧlwȧsyon'] *nf* devaluation.

devaluar [dchȧloōȧr'] *vt* to devalue.

devanador [dchȧnȧṭhor'] *nm* (*carrete*) spool, bobbin.

devanar [dchȧnár'] *vt* (*hilo*) to wind; **~se** *vr*: **~se los sesos** to rack one's brains.

devaneo [dchȧnc'o] *nm* (*MED*) delirium; (*desatino*) nonsense; (*fruslería*) idle pursuit; (*amorío*) flirtation.

devastar [dchȧstár'] *vt* (*destruir*) to devastate.

devendré [dchendrc'] *etc*, **devenga** [dchen'gȧ] *etc vb V* **devenir**.

devengar [dchengár'] *vt* (*salario: ganar*) to earn; (: *tener que cobrar*) to be due; (*intereses*) to bring in, accrue, earn.

devengue [dchen'gc] *etc vb V* **devengar**.

devenir [dchcncr'] *vi*: **~ en** to become, turn into ♦ *nm* (*movimiento progresivo*) process of development; (*transformación*) transformation.

deviene [dchyc'nc] *etc*, **deviniendo** [dchēnycn'do] *etc vb V* **devenir**.

devoción [dchosyon'] *nf* devotion; (*afición*) strong attachment.

devolución [dcholoōsyon'] *nf* (*reenvío*) return, sending back; (*reembolso*) repayment; (*JUR*) devolution.

devolver [dcholḫcr'] *vt* (*lo extraviado, prestado*) to give back; (*a su sitio*) to put back; (*carta al correo*) to send back;

(*COM*) to repay, refund; (*visita, la pala-bra*) to return; (*salud, vista*) to restore; (*fam: vomitar*) to throw up ♦ *vi* (*fam*) to be sick; ~ **mal por bien** to return ill for good; ~ **la pelota a uno** to give sb tit for tat.

devorar [deḅorár'] *vt* to devour; (*comer ávi-damente*) to gobble up; (*fig: fortuna*) to run through; **todo lo devoró el fuego** the fire consumed everything; **le devoran los celos** he is consumed with jealousy.

devoto, a [deḅo'to, á] *a.* (*REL: persona*) devout; (: *obra*) devotional; (*amigo*): ~ **(de uno)** devoted (to sb) ♦ *nm/f* admirer; **los ~s** (*REL*) the faithful; **su muy ~** your devoted servant.

devuelto [deḅwel'to], **devuelva** [deḅwel'ḅá] *etc vb V* **devolver.**

D.F. *abr* (*México*) = *Distrito Federal.*

dg. *abr* (= *decigramo*) dg.

D.G. *abr* = *Dirección General*; (= *Director General*) D.G.

DGS *nf abr* = *Dirección General de Seguri-dad*; = *Dirección General de Sanidad.*

DGT *nf abr* = *Dirección General de Tráfico*; = *Dirección General de Turismo.*

di [dē] *vb V* **dar; decir.**

día [dē'á] *nm* day; ~ **de asueto** day off; ~ **festivo** holiday; ~ **hábil/inhábil** working/ non-working day; ~ **de inocentes** (*28 De-cember*) ≈ All Fools' Day; ~ **lectivo** teach-ing day; ~ **libre** day off; **D~ de Reyes** Epiphany (*6 January*); **¿qué ~ es?** what's the date?; **estar/poner al ~** to be/keep up to date; **el ~ de hoy/de mañana** today/ tomorrow; **el ~ menos pensado** when you least expect it; **al ~ siguiente** on the following day; **todos los ~s** every day; **un ~ sí y otro no** every other day; **vivir al ~** to live from hand to mouth; **de ~** by day, in daylight; **del ~** (*estilos*) fashionable; (*menú*) today's; **de un ~ para otro** any day now; **en pleno ~** in full daylight; **en su ~** in due time; **¡hasta otro ~!** so long!

diablo [dyá'ḅlo] *nm* (*tb fig*) devil; **pobre ~** poor devil; **hace un frío de todos los ~s** it's hellishly cold.

diablura [dyàḅloō'rá] *nf* prank; (*travesura*) mischief.

diabólico, a [dyáḅo'lēko, á] *a* diabolical.

diáfano, a [dyá'fáno, á] *a* (*tela*) diaphanous; (*agua*) crystal-clear.

diafragma [dyáfráġ'má] *nm* diaphragm.

diagnosis [dyáġno'sēs] *nf inv*, **diagnóstico** [dēáġno'stēko] *nm* diagnosis.

diagrama [dyáġrá'má] *nm* diagram; ~ **de barras** (*COM*) bar chart; ~ **de dispersión** (*COM*) scatter diagram; ~ **de flujo** (*IN-FORM*) flowchart.

dialecto [dyálek'to] *nm* dialect.

dialogar [dyáloġàr'] *vt* to write in dialogue

form ♦ *vi* (*conversar*) to have a conversa-tion; ~ **con** (*POL*) to hold talks with.

diálogo [dyá'loġo] *nm* dialogue.

dialogue [dyàlo'ġe] *etc vb V* **dialogar.**

diamante [dyámàn'te] *nm* diamond.

diametralmente [dyámetrálmen'te] *ad* dia-metrically; ~ **opuesto a** diametrically opposed to.

diámetro [dēá'metro] *nm* diameter; ~ **de giro** (*AUTO*) turning circle; **faros de gran ~** wide-angle headlights.

diana [dyá'ná] *nf* (*MIL*) reveille; (*de blanco*) center (*US*), centre (*Brit*), bull's-eye.

diantre [dyàn'tre] *nm*: **¡~!** (*fam*) oh hell!

diapasón [dyá'pàson'] *nm* (*instrumento*) tuning fork; (*de violín etc*) fingerboard; (*de voz*) tone.

diapositiva [dyáposētē'ḅá] *nf* (*FOTO*) slide, transparency.

diario, a [dyá'ryo, á] *a* daily ♦ *nm* newspa-per; (*libro diario*) diary; (: *COM*) daybook; (*COM: gastos*) daily expenses; ~ **de nave-gación** (*NAUT*) logbook; ~ **hablado** (*RADIO*) news (bulletin); ~ **de sesiones** parliamentary report; **a ~** daily; **de** *o* **para ~** everyday.

diarrea [dyàrre'á] *nf* diarrhea (*US*), diar-rhoea (*Brit*).

diatriba [dyátrē'ḅá] *nf* diatribe, tirade.

dibujante [deḅooḥàn'te] *nm/f* (*de bosque-jos*) artist; (*de dibujos animados*) cartoon-ist; (*de moda*) designer; ~ **de publicidad** commercial artist.

dibujar [deḅooḥàr'] *vt* to draw, sketch; **~se** *vr* (*emoción*) to show; **~se contra** to be outlined against.

dibujo [deḅoō'ho] *nm* drawing; (*TEC*) de-sign; (*en papel, tela*) pattern; (*en perió-dico*) cartoon; (*fig*) description; **~s anima-dos** cartoons; ~ **del natural** drawing from life.

dic., dic.ᵉ *abr* (= *diciembre*) Dec.

diccionario [dēksyoná'ryo] *nm* dictionary.

diciembre [dēsyem'bre] *nm* December.

diciendo [dēsyen'do] *etc vb V* **decir.**

dictado [dēktá'ḍo] *nm* dictation; **escribir al ~** to take dictation; **los ~s de la conciencia** (*fig*) the dictates of conscience.

dictador [dēktàḍor'] *nm* dictator.

dictadura [dēktàḍoō'rá] *nf* dictatorship.

dictáfono ® [dēktá'fono] *nm* Dictaphone ®.

dictamen [dēktá'men] *nm* (*opinión*) opin-ion; (*informe*) report; ~ **contable** auditor's report; ~ **facultativo** (*MED*) medical re-port.

dictar [dēktár'] *vt* (*carta*) to dictate; (*JUR*: *sentencia*) to pass; (*decreto*) to issue; (*AM*: *clase*) to give; (: *conferencia*) to de-liver.

dicharachero, a [dētcháràtche'ro, á] *a* talkative ♦ *nm/f* (*ingenioso*) wit;

(*parlanchín*) chatterbox.

dicho, a [dētch'o, á] *pp de* **decir** ♦ *a* (*susodicho*) aforementioned ♦ *nm* saying; (*proverbio*) proverb; (*ocurrencia*) bright remark ♦ *nf* (*buena suerte*) good luck; **mejor** ~ rather; ~ **y hecho** no sooner said than done.

dichoso, a [dētcho'so, á] *a* (*feliz*) happy; (*afortunado*) lucky; ¡**aquel ~ coche!** (*fam*) that blessed car!

diecinueve [dyesēnwe'he] *num* nineteen; (*fecha*) nineteenth; *V tb* **seis.**

dieciochesco, a [dyesēotches'ko, á] *a* eighteenth-century.

dieciocho [dyesēotch'o] *num* eighteen; (*fecha*) eighteenth; *V tb* **seis.**

dieciséis [dyesēse'ēs] *num* sixteen; (*fecha*) sixteenth; *V tb* **seis.**

diecisiete [dyesēsye'te] *num* seventeen; (*fecha*) seventeenth; *V tb* **seis.**

diente [dyen'te] *nm* (*ANAT, TEC*) tooth; (*ZOOL*) fang; (: *de elefante*) tusk; (*de ajo*) clove; ~ **de león** dandelion; ~**s postizos** false teeth; **enseñar los** ~**s** (*fig*) to show one's teeth; **hablar entre** ~**s** to mutter, mumble; **hincar el** ~ **en** (*comida*) to bite into.

diera [dye'rá] *etc vb V* **dar.**

diéresis [dēe'resēs] *nf* dieresis.

dieron [dye'ron] *vb V* **dar.**

diesel [dē'sel] *a*: **motor** ~ diesel engine.

diestro, a [dyes'tro, á] *a* (*derecho*) right; (*hábil*) skillful; (: *con las manos*) handy ♦ *nm* (*TAUR*) matador ♦ *nf* right hand; **a** ~ **y siniestro** (*sin método*) wildly.

dieta [dye'tá] *nf* diet; ~**s** *nfpl* expenses; **estar a** ~ to be on a diet.

dietético, a [dyete'tēko, á] *a* dietetic ♦ *nm/f* dietician.

diez [dyes] *num* ten; (*fecha*) tenth; **hacer las** ~ **de últimas** (*NAIPES*) to sweep the board; *V tb* **seis.**

difamación [dēfámásyon'] *nf* slander; libel.

difamar [dēfámár'] *vt* (*JUR: hablando*) to slander; (: *por escrito*) to libel.

difamatorio, a [dēfámáto'ryo, á] *a* slanderous; libellous.

diferencia [dēferen'syá] *nf* difference; **a** ~ **de** unlike; **hacer** ~ **entre** to make a distinction between; ~ **salarial** (*COM*) wage differential.

diferencial [dēferensyál'] *nm* (*AUTO*) differential.

diferenciar [dēferensyár'] *vt* to differentiate between ♦ *vi* to differ; ~**se** *vr* to differ, be different; (*distinguirse*) to distinguish o.s.

diferente [dēferen'te] *a* different.

diferido [dēferē'tho] *nm*: **en** ~ (*TV etc*) recorded.

diferir [dēferēr'] *vt* to defer.

difícil [dēfē'sēl] *a* difficult; (*tiempos, vida*)

hard; (*situación*) delicate; **es un hombre** ~ he's a difficult man to get along with.

difícilmente [dēfē'sēlmente] *ad* (*con dificultad*) with difficulty; (*apenas*) hardly.

dificultad [dēfēkōōltáth'] *nf* difficulty; (*problema*) trouble; (*objeción*) objection.

dificultar [dēfēkōōltár'] *vt* (*complicar*) to complicate, make difficult; (*estorbar*) to obstruct; **las restricciones dificultan el comercio** the restrictions hinder trade.

dificultoso, a [dēfēkōōlto'so, á] *a* (*difícil*) difficult, hard; (*fam: cara*) odd, ugly; (*persona: exigente*) fussy.

difiera [dēfye'rá] *etc*, **difiriendo** [dēfēryen'do] *etc vb V* **diferir.**

difuminar [dēfōōmēnár'] *vt* to blur.

difundir [dēfōōndēr'] *vt* (*calor, luz*) to diffuse; (*RADIO*) to broadcast; ~**se** *vr* to spread (out); ~ **una noticia** to spread a piece of news.

difunto, a [dēfōōn'to, á] *a* dead, deceased ♦ *nm/f*: **el** ~ the deceased.

difusión [dēfōōsyon'] *nf* (*de calor, luz*) diffusion; (*de noticia, teoría*) dissemination; (*de programa*) broadcasting; (*programa*) broadcast.

difuso, a [dēfōō'so, á] *a* (*luz*) diffused; (*conocimientos*) widespread; (*estilo, explicación*) wordy.

diga [dē'gá] *etc vb V* **decir.**

digerir [dēherēr'] *vt* to digest; (*fig*) to absorb; (*reflexionar sobre*) to think over.

digiera [dēhye'rá] *etc*, **digiriendo** [dēhēryen'do] *etc vb V* **digerir.**

digital [dēhētál'] *a* (*INFORM*) digital; (*dactilar*) finger *cpd* ♦ *nf* (*BOT*) foxglove; (*droga*) digitalis.

digitalizador [dēhētálēsáthor'] *nm* (*INFORM*) digitizer.

dignarse [dēgnár'se] *vr* to deign to.

dignidad [dēgnētháth'] *nf* dignity; (*honra*) honor (*US*), honour (*Brit*); (*rango*) rank; (*persona*) dignitary; **herir la** ~ **de uno** to hurt sb's pride.

dignificar [dēgnēfēkár'] *vt* to dignify.

dignifique [dēgnēfē'ke] *etc vb V* **dignificar.**

digno, a [dēg'no, á] *a* worthy; (*persona: honesto*) honorable (*US*), honourable (*Brit*); ~ **de elogio** praiseworthy; ~ **de mención** worth mentioning; **es** ~ **de verse** it is worth seeing; **poco** ~ unworthy.

digresión [dēgresyon'] *nf* digression.

dije [dē'he] *etc*, **dijera** [dēhe'rá] *etc vb V* **decir.**

dilación [dēlásyon'] *nf* delay; **sin** ~ without delay, immediately.

dilapidar [dēlápēthár'] *vt* to squander, waste.

dilatación [dēlátásyon'] *nf* (*expansión*) dilation.

dilatado, a [dēlátá'tho, á] *a* dilated;

(*período*) long drawn-out; (*extenso*) extensive.

dilatar [dēlátár'] *vt* (*gen*) to dilate; (*prolongar*) to prolong; (*aplazar*) to delay; **~se** *vr* (*pupila etc*) to dilate; (*agua*) to expand.

dilema [dēle'má] *nm* dilemma.

diligencia [dēlēhen'syá] *nf* diligence; (*rapidez*) speed; (*ocupación*) errand, job; (*carruaje*) stagecoach; **~s** *nfpl* (*JUR*) formalities; **~s judiciales** judicial proceedings; **~s previas** inquest *sg*.

diligente [dēlēhen'te] *a* diligent; **poco ~** lazy.

dilucidar [dēlōōsēt̄ár'] *vt* (*aclarar*) to elucidate, clarify; (*misterio*) to clear up.

diluir [dēlōōēr'] *vt* to dilute; (*aguar*, *fig*) to water down.

diluviar [dēlōōt̄yár'] *vi* to pour with rain.

diluvio [dēlōō't̄yo] *nm* deluge, flood; **un ~ de cartas** (*fig*) a flood of letters.

diluyendo [dēlōōyen'do] *etc vb* V **diluir**.

dimanar [dēmánár'] *vi*: **~ de** to arise *o* spring from.

dimensión [dēmensyon'] *nf* dimension; **dimensiones** *nfpl* size *sg*; **tomar las dimensiones de** to take the measurements of.

dimes [dē'mes] *nmpl*: **andar en ~ y diretes con uno** to bicker *o* squabble with sb.

diminuto, a [dēmēnōō'to, á] *a* tiny, diminutive.

dimisión [dēmēsyon'] *nf* resignation.

dimitir [dēmētēr'] *vt* (*cargo*) to give up; (*despedir*) to sack ♦ *vi* to resign.

dimos [dē'mos] *vb* V **dar**.

Dinamarca [dēnámár'ká] *nf* Denmark.

dinamarqués, esa [dēnámárkes', e'sá] *a* Danish ♦ *nm/f* Dane ♦ *nm* (*LING*) Danish.

dinámico, a [dēná'mēko, á] *a* dynamic ♦ *nf* dynamics *sg*.

dinamita [dēnámē'tá] *nf* dynamite.

dinamitar [dēnámētár'] *vt* to dynamite.

dínamo [dē'námo] *nf* dynamo.

dinastía [dēnástē'á] *nf* dynasty.

dinerada [dēnērá't̄á] *nf*, **dineral** [dēnērál'] *nm* fortune.

dinero [dēne'ro] *nm* money; (**~ en circulación**) currency; **~ caro** (*COM*) expensive (*US*) *o* dear (*Brit*) money; **~ contante (y sonante)** hard cash; **~ de curso legal** legal tender; **~ efectivo** cash, ready cash; **es hombre de ~** he is a man of means; **andar mal de ~** to be short of money; **ganar ~ a espuertas** to make money hand over fist.

dintel [dēntel'] *nm* lintel; (*umbral*) threshold.

diñar [dēnyár'] *vt* (*fam*) to give; **~la** to kick the bucket.

dio [dyo] *vb* V **dar**.

Dios [dyos] *nm* God; **~ mediante** God willing; **a ~ gracias** thank heaven; **a la buena de ~** any old how; **una de ~ es Cristo** an almighty row; **~ los cría y ellos se juntan** birds of a feather flock together; **como ~ manda** as is proper; **¡~ mío!** (oh,) my God!; **¡por ~!** for God's sake!; **¡válgame ~!** bless my soul!

dios [dyos] *nm* god.

diosa [dyo'sá] *nf* goddess.

Dip. *abr* (= *Diputación*) ≈ CC.

diploma [dēplo'má] *nm* diploma.

diplomacia [dēplomá'syá] *nf* diplomacy; (*fig*) tact.

diplomado, a [dēplomá't̄o, á] *a* qualified ♦ *nm/f* holder of a diploma; (*UNIV*) graduate.

diplomático, a [dēplomá'tēko, á] *a* (*cuerpo*) diplomatic; (*que tiene tacto*) tactful ♦ *nm/f* diplomat.

diptongo [dēpton'go] *nm* diphthong.

diputación [dēpōōtásyon'] *nf* delegation; **~ permanente** (*POL*) standing committee; **~ provincial** ≈ county commission (*US*) *o* council (*Brit*).

diputado, a [dēpōōtá't̄o, á] *nm/f* delegate; (*POL*) ≈ representative (*US*), ≈ member of parliament (*Brit*).

dique [dē'ke] *nm* dike (*US*), dyke (*Brit*); (*rompeolas*) breakwater; **~ de contención** dam.

Dir. *abr* = **dirección**; (= *director*) dir.

diré [dēre'] *etc vb* V **decir**.

dirección [dēreksyon'] *nf* direction; (*fig*: *tendencia*) trend; (*señas*, *tb INFORM*) address; (*AUTO*) steering; (*gerencia*) management; (*de periódico*) editorship; (*en escuela*) principalship (*US*), headship (*Brit*); (*POL*) leadership; (*junta*) board of directors; (*despacho*) director's/manager's/headmaster's/editor's office; **~ absoluta** (*INFORM*) absolute address; **~ administrativa** office management; **~ asistida** power-assisted steering; **D~ General de Seguridad/Turismo** State Security/Tourist Office; **~ relativa** (*INFORM*) relative address; **~ única** *o* **prohibida** one-way; **tomar la ~ de una empresa** to take over the running of a company.

direccionamiento [dēreksyonámyen'to] *nm* (*INFORM*) addressing.

directivo, a [dērectē't̄o, á] *a* (*junta*) managing; (*función*) administrative ♦ *nm* (*COM*) manager.

directo, a [dērek'to, á] *a* direct; (*línea*) straight; (*inmediato*) immediate; (*tren*) through; (*TV*) live; **en ~** (*INFORM*) on line; **transmitir en ~** to broadcast live.

director, a [dērektor', á] *a* leading ♦ *nm/f* director; (*ESCOL*) principal (*US*), head (teacher) (*Brit*); (*gerente*) manager(ess); (*de compañía*) president; (*jefe*) head; (*PRENSA*) editor; (*de prisión*) warden (*US*), governor (*Brit*); (*MUS*) conductor; **~ adjunto** assistant manager; **~ de cine** film director; ~ **comercial** marketing manager; ~ **ejecutivo** executive director; ~ **de empresa** company president (US) o director (Brit); ~ **general** general manager; ~ **gerente** managing director; ~ **de sucursal** branch manager.

directorial [dērektoryàl'] a (COM) managing, executive; **clase** ~ management.

directorio [dērekto'ryo] nm (INFORM) directory.

directrices [dērektrē'ses] nfpl guidelines.

dirigencia [dērēhen'syà] nf (POL) leadership.

dirigente [dērēhen'te] a leading ♦ nm/f (POL) leader; **los ~s del partido** the party leaders.

dirigible [dērēhē'ble] a (AVIAT, NAUT) steerable ♦ nm blimp (US), airship (Brit).

dirigir [dērēhēr'] vt to direct; (acusación) to level; (carta) to address; (obra de teatro, film) to produce, direct; (MUS) to conduct; (comercio) to manage; (expedición) to lead; (sublevación) to head; (periódico) to edit; (guiar) to guide; **~se** vr: **~se a** to go towards, make one's way towards; (hablar con) to speak to; **~se a uno solicitando algo** to apply to sb for sth; **"diríjase a ..."** "apply to ...".

dirigismo [dērēhēs'mo] nm management, control; ~ **estatal** state control.

dirija [dērē'hà] etc vb V **dirigir**.

dirimir [dērēmēr'] vt (contrato, matrimonio) to dissolve.

discado [dēskà'tho] nm: ~ **automático** autodial.

discernir [dēsernēr'] vt to discern ♦ vi to distinguish.

discierna [dēsyer'nà] etc vb V **discernir**.

disciplina [dēsēplē'nà] nf discipline.

disciplinar [dēsēplēnàr'] vt to discipline; (enseñar) to school; (MIL) to drill; (azotar) to whip.

discípulo, a [dēsē'pōōlo, à] nm/f disciple; (seguidor) follower; (ESCOL) pupil.

disco [dēs'ko] nm disk (US), disc (Brit); (DEPORTE) discus; (TELEC) dial; (AUTO: semáforo) light; (MUS) record; (INFORM) disk; ~ **de arranque** boot disk; ~ **compacto** compact disc; ~ **de densidad sencilla/doble** single/double density disk; ~ **de larga duración** long-playing record (L.P.); ~ **flexible** o **floppy** floppy disk; ~ **de freno** brake disc; ~ **maestro** master disk; ~ **de reserva** backup disk; ~ **rígido** hard disk; ~ **de una cara/dos caras** single-/double-sided disk; ~ **virtual** ramdisk.

discóbolo [dēsko'bolo] nm discus thrower.

discográfico, a [dēskogrà'fēko, à] a record cpd; **casa discográfica** record company; **sello** ~ label.

díscolo, a [dēs'kolo, à] a (rebelde) unruly.

disconforme [dēskonfor'me] a differing; **estar ~ (con)** to be in disagreement (with).

discordar [dēskorthàr'] vi (MUS) to be out of tune; (estar en desacuerdo) to disagree; (colores, opiniones) to clash.

discorde [dēskor'the] a (sonido) discordant; (opiniones) clashing.

discordia [dēskor'thyà] nf discord.

discoteca [dēskotē'kà] nf disco(theque).

discreción [dēskresyon'] nf discretion; (reserva) prudence; **¡a ~!** (MIL) at ease!; **añadir azúcar a ~** (CULIN) add sugar to taste; **comer a ~** to eat as much as one wishes.

discrecional [dēskresyonàl'] a (facultativo) discretionary; **parada ~** flag stop (US), request stop (Brit).

discrepancia [dēskrepàn'syà] nf (diferencia) discrepancy; (desacuerdo) disagreement.

discrepante [dēskrepàn'te] a divergent; **hubo varias voces ~s** there were some dissenting voices.

discreto, a [dēskre'to, à] a (diplomático) discreet; (sensato) sensible; (reservado) quiet; (sobrio) sober; (mediano) fair, fairly good; **le daremos un plazo ~** we'll allow him a reasonable time.

discriminación [dēskrēmēnàsyon'] nf discrimination.

discuerde [dēskwer'the] etc vb V **discordar**.

disculpa [dēskōōl'pà] nf excuse; (pedir perdón) apology; **pedir ~s a/por** to apologize to/for.

disculpar [dēskōōlpàr'] vt to excuse, pardon; **~se** vr to excuse o.s.; to apologize.

discurrir [dēskōōrrēr'] vt to contrive, think up ♦ vi (pensar, reflexionar) to think, meditate; (recorrer) to roam, wander; (río) to flow; (el tiempo) to pass, flow by.

discurso [dēskōōr'so] nm speech; ~ **de clausura** closing speech; **pronunciar un ~** to make a speech; **en el ~ del tiempo** with the passage of time.

discusión [dēskōōsyon'] nf (diálogo) discussion; (riña) argument; **tener una ~** to have an argument.

discutible [dēskōōtē'ble] a debatable; **de mérito ~** of dubious worth.

discutido, a [dēskōōtē'tho, à] a controversial.

discutir [dēskōōtēr'] vt (debatir) to discuss; (pelear) to argue about; (contradecir) to argue against ♦ vi to discuss; (disputar) to argue; ~ **de política** to argue about politics; **¡no discutas!** don't argue!

disecar [dēsekàr'] vt (para conservar: animal) to stuff; (: planta) to dry.

diseminar [dēsemēnàr'] vt to disseminate, spread.

disentir |dĕsɛntēr'| *vi* to dissent, disagree.

diseño |dĕsɛ'nyo| *nm* (*TEC*) design; (*ARTE*) drawing; (*COSTURA*) pattern; **de ~ italiano** Italian-designed; **~ asistido por ordenador** computer-assisted design, CAD.

diseque |dĕsɛ'kɛ| *etc vb* V **disecar**.

disertar |dĕsɛrtár'| *vi* to speak.

disfrace |dĕsfrá'sɛ| *etc vb* V **disfrazar**.

disfraz |dĕsfrás'| *nm* (*máscara*) disguise; (*traje*) fancy dress; (*excusa*) pretext; **bajo el ~ de** under the cloak of.

disfrazado, a |dĕsfrásá'tho, á| *a* disguised; **ir ~ de** to masquerade as.

disfrazar |dĕsfrásár'| *vt* to disguise; **~se** *vr* to dress (o.s.) up; **~se de** to disguise o.s. as.

disfrutar |dĕsfrōōtár'| *vt* to enjoy ♦ *vi* to enjoy o.s.; **¡que disfrutes!** have a good time; **~ de** to enjoy, possess; **~ de buena salud** to enjoy good health.

disfrute |dĕsfrōō'tɛ| *nm* (*goce*) enjoyment; (*aprovechamiento*) use.

disgregar |dĕsgrɛgár'| *vt* (*desintegrar*) to disintegrate; (*manifestantes*) to disperse; **~se** *vr* to disintegrate, break up.

disgregue |dĕsgrɛ'gɛ| *etc vb* V **disgregar**.

disgustar |dĕsgōōstár'| *vt* (*no gustar*) to displease; (*contrariar*, *enojar*) to annoy; to upset; **~se** *vr* to be annoyed; (*dos personas*) to fall out; **estaba muy disgustado con el asunto** he was very upset about the affair.

disgusto |dĕsgōō'sto| *nm* (*repugnancia*) disgust; (*contrariedad*) annoyance; (*desagrado*) displeasure; (*tristeza*) grief; (*riña*) quarrel; (*avería*) misfortune; **hacer algo a ~** to do sth unwillingly; **matar a uno a ~s** to drive sb to distraction.

disidente |dĕsɛ́then'tɛ| *nm* dissident.

disienta |dĕsyɛn'tá| *etc vb* V **disentir**.

disimulado, a |dĕsɛ̄mōōlá'tho, á| *a* (*solapado*) furtive, underhand; (*oculto*) covert; **hacerse al ~** to pretend not to notice.

disimular |dĕsɛ̄mōōlár'| *vt* (*ocultar*) to hide, conceal ♦ *vi* to dissemble.

disimulo |dĕsɛ̄mōō'lo| *nm* (*fingimiento*) dissimulation; **con ~** cunningly.

disipar |dĕsɛpár'| *vt* (*duda*, *temor*) to dispel; (*esperanza*) to destroy; (*fortuna*) to squander; **~se** *vr* (*nubes*) to vanish; (*dudas*) to be dispelled; (*indisciplinarse*) to dissipate.

diskette |dĕskɛt'| *nm* (*INFORM*) diskette, floppy disk.

dislate |dĕslá'tɛ| *nm* (*absurdo*) absurdity; **~s** *nmpl* nonsense *sg*.

dislocar |dĕslokár'| *vt* (*gen*) to dislocate; (*tobillo*) to sprain.

disloque |dĕslo'kɛ| *etc vb* V **dislocar** ♦ *nm*: **es el ~** (*fam*) it's the last straw.

disminución |dĕsmɛ̄nōōsyon'| *nf* diminu-

tion.

disminuir |dĕsmɛ̄nōōēr'| *vt* to decrease, diminish; (*estrechar*) to lessen; (*temperatura*) to lower; (*gastos*, *raciones*) to cut down; (*dolor*) to relieve; (*autoridad*, *prestigio*) to weaken; (*entusiasmo*) to dampen ♦ *vi* (*días*) to grow shorter; (*precios*, *temperatura*) to drop, fall; (*velocidad*) to reduce; (*población*, *beneficios*, *número*) to decrease; (*memoria*, *vista*) to fail.

disminuyendo |dĕsmɛ̄nōōyɛn'do| *etc vb* V **disminuir**.

disociar |dĕsosyár'| *vt* to disassociate; **~se** *vr* to disassociate o.s.

disoluble |dĕsolōō'blɛ| *a* soluble.

disolución |dĕsolōōsyon'| *nf* (*acto*) dissolution; (*QUÍMICA*) solution; (*COM*) liquidation; (*moral*) dissoluteness.

disoluto, a |dĕsolōō'to, á| *a* dissolute.

disolver |dĕsolbɛr'| *vt* (*gen*) to dissolve; (*manifestación*) to break up; **~se** *vr* to dissolve; (*COM*) to go into liquidation.

disonar |dĕsonár'| *vi* (*MUS*) to be out of tune; **~ con** (*fig*) to be out of keeping with.

dispar |dĕspár'| *a* (*distinto*) different; (*irregular*) uneven.

disparado, a |dĕspárá'tho, á| *a*: **entrar ~** to shoot in; **salir ~** to shoot out; **ir ~** to go like mad.

disparador |dĕspárátho̱r'| *nm* (*de arma*) trigger; (*FOTO*, *TEC*) release; **~ atómico** aerosol; **~ de bombas** bomb release.

disparar |dĕspárár'| *vt*, *vi* to shoot, fire; **~se** *vr* (*arma de fuego*) to go off; (*persona*: *marcharse*) to rush off; (*caballo*) to bolt; (*enojarse*) to lose control.

disparatado, a |dĕspárátá'tho, á| *a* crazy.

disparatar |dĕspárátár'| *vi* (*decir disparates*) to talk nonsense; (*hacer disparates*) to blunder.

disparate |dĕspárá'tɛ| *nm* (*tontería*) foolish remark; (*error*) blunder; **decir ~s** to talk nonsense; **¡qué ~!** how absurd!; **costar un ~** to cost a hell of a lot.

disparo |dĕspá'ro| *nm* shot; (*acto*) firing; **~s** *nmpl* shooting *sg*, (exchange of) shots (*sg*); **~ inicial** (*de cohete*) blastoff.

dispendio |dĕspen'dyo| *nm* waste.

dispensar |dĕspensár'| *vt* to dispense; (*ayuda*) to give; (*honores*) to grant; (*disculpar*) to excuse; **¡usted dispense!** I beg your pardon!; **~ a uno de hacer algo** to excuse sb from doing sth.

dispensario |dĕspensá'ryo| *nm* (*clínica*) community clinic; (*de hospital*) outpatients' department.

dispersar |dĕspersár'| *vt* to disperse; (*manifestación*) to break up; **~se** *vr* to scatter.

disperso, a |dĕsper'so, á| *a* scattered.

displicencia |dĕsplɛ̄sen'syá| *nf* (*mal humor*) peevishness; (*desgana*) lack of enthusiasm.

displicente [dēssēplēsen'te] *a* (*malhumorado*) peevish; (*poco entusiasta*) unenthusiastic.

dispondré [dēspondre'] *etc vb* V **disponer**.

disponer [dēsponer'] *vt* (*arreglar*) to arrange; (*ordenar*) to put in order; (*preparar*) to prepare, get ready ♦ *vi*: ~ **de** to have, own; ~**se** *vr*: ~**se para** to prepare to, prepare for; **la ley dispone que...** the law provides that...; **no puede** ~ **de esos bienes** she cannot dispose of those properties.

disponga [dēspon'gá] *etc vb* V **disponer**.

disponibilidad [dēsponēbēlēdáth'] *nf* availability; ~**es** *nfpl* (*COM*) resources, financial assets.

disponible [dēsponē'ble] *a* available; (*tiempo*) spare; (*dinero*) on hand.

disposición [dēsposēsyon'] *nf* arrangement, disposition; (*de casa*, *INFORM*) layout; (*ley*) order; (*cláusula*) provision; (*aptitud*) aptitude; ~ **de ánimo** attitude of mind; **última** ~ last will and testament; **a la** ~ **de** at the disposal of; **a su** ~ at your service.

dispositivo [dēsposētē'ho] *nm* device, mechanism; ~ **de alimentación** hopper; ~ **de almacenaje** storage device; ~ **periférico** peripheral (device); ~ **de seguridad** safety catch; (*fig*) security measure.

dispuesto, a [dēspwe'sto, á] *pp de* **disponer** ♦ *a* (*arreglado*) arranged; (*preparado*) disposed; (*persona: dinámico*) bright; **estar** ~/**poco** ~ **a hacer algo** to be inclined/reluctant to do sth.

dispuse [dēspoo'se] *etc vb* V **disponer**.

disputa [dēspoo'tá] *nf* (*discusión*) dispute, argument; (*controversia*) controversy.

disputar [dēspootár'] *vt* (*discutir*) to dispute, question; (*contender*) to contend for ♦ *vi* to argue.

disquete [dēske'te] *nm* (*INFORM*) diskette, floppy disk.

Dist. *abr* (= *distancia*, *Distrito*) dist.

distancia [dēstán'syá] *nf* distance; (*de tiempo*) interval; ~ **de parada** braking distance; ~ **del suelo** (*AUTO etc*) height off the ground; **a gran** o **a larga** ~ long-distance; **mantenerse a** ~ to keep one's distance; (*fig*) to remain aloof; **guardar las** ~**s** to keep one's distance.

distanciado, a [dēstánsyá'tho, á] *a* (*remoto*) remote; (*fig: alejado*) far apart; **estamos** ~**s en ideas** our ideas are poles apart.

distanciamiento [dēstánsyámyen'to] *nm* (*acto*) spacing out; (*estado*) remoteness; (*fig*) distance.

distanciar [dēstánsyár'] *vt* to space out; ~**se** *vr* to become estranged.

distante [dēstán'te] *a* distant.

distar [dēstár'] *vi*: **dista 5 kms de aquí** it is 5 kms from here; **¿dista mucho?** is it far?; **dista mucho de la verdad** it's very far from the truth.

diste [dē'ste], **disteis** [dē'stēs] *vb* V **dar**.

distensión [dēstensyon'] *nf* distension; (*POL*) détente; ~ **muscular** (*MED*) muscular strain.

distinción [dēstēnsyon'] *nf* distinction; (*elegancia*) elegance; (*honor*) honor (*US*), honour (*Brit*); **a** ~ **de** unlike; **sin** ~ indiscriminately; **sin** ~ **de edades** irrespective of age.

distinga [dēstēn'gá] *etc vb* V **distinguir**.

distinguido, a [dēstēngē'tho, á] *a* distinguished; (*famoso*) prominent, well-known; (*elegante*) elegant.

distinguir [dēstēngēr'] *vt* to distinguish; (*divisar*) to make out; (*escoger*) to single out; (*caracterizar*) to mark out; ~**se** *vr* to be distinguished; (*destacarse*) to distinguish o.s.; **a lo lejos no se distingue** it's not visible from a distance.

distintivo, a [dēstēntē'ho, á] *a* distinctive; (*signo*) distinguishing ♦ *nm* (*de policía etc*) badge; (*fig*) characteristic.

distinto, a [dēstēn'to, á] *a* different; (*claro*) clear; ~**s** several, various.

distorsión [dēstorsyon'] *nf* (*ANAT*) twisting; (*RADIO etc*) distortion.

distracción [dēstráksyon'] *nf* distraction; (*pasatiempo*) hobby, pastime; (*olvido*) absent-mindedness, distraction.

distraer [dēstráer'] *vt* (*atención*) to distract; (*divertir*) to amuse; (*fondos*) to embezzle ♦ *vi* to be relaxing; ~**se** *vr* (*entretenerse*) to amuse o.s.; (*perder la concentración*) to allow one's attention to wander; ~ **a uno de su pensamiento** to divert sb from his train of thought; **el pescar distrae** fishing is a relaxation.

distraído, a [dēstráē'tho, á] *a* (*gen*) absent-minded; (*desatento*) inattentive; (*entretenido*) amusing ♦ *nm*: **hacerse el** ~ to pretend not to notice; **con aire** ~ idly; **me miró distraída** she gave me a casual glance.

distraiga [dēstrá'egá] *etc*, **distraje** [dēstrá'he] *etc*, **distrajera** [dēstráhe'rá] *etc*, **distrayendo** [dēstráyen'do] *vb* V **distraer**.

distribución [dēstrēboosyon'] *nf* distribution; (*entrega*) delivery; (*en estadística*) distribution, incidence; (*ARQ*) layout; ~ **de premios** prize giving; **la** ~ **de los impuestos** the incidence of taxes.

distribuidor, a [dēstrēbooēthor', á] *nm/f* (*persona: gen*) distributor; (: *CORREOS*) sorter; (: *COM*) dealer; **su** ~ **habitual** your regular dealer.

distribuir [dēstrēbooēr'] *vt* to distribute; (*prospectos*) to hand out; (*cartas*) to deliver; (*trabajo*) to allocate; (*premios*) to award; (*dividendos*) to pay; (*peso*) to distribute; (ARQ) to plan.

distribuyendo [dĕstrĕhōōyen'do] etc vb V **distribuir.**

distrito [dĕstrē'to] nm (sector, territorio) region; (barrio) district; ~ **electoral** constituency; ~ **postal** postal district.

disturbio [dĕstōōr'byo] nm disturbance; (desorden) riot; **los ~s** the troubles.

disuadir [dĕswàḥēr'] vt to dissuade.

disuasión [dĕswàsyon'] nf dissuasion; (MIL) deterrent; ~ **nuclear** nuclear deterrent.

disuasivo, a [dĕswàsē'ḥo, á] a dissuasive; **arma disuasiva** deterrent.

disuelto [dĕswel'to] pp de **disolver.**

disuelva [dĕswel'ḥá] etc vb V **disolver.**

disuene [dĕswe'ne] etc vb V **disonar.**

disyuntiva [dĕsyōōntē'ḥá] nf (dilema) dilemma.

DIU [dē'ōō] nm abr (= dispositivo intrauterino) I.U.D.

diurno, a [dyōōr'no, á] a day cpd, diurnal.

diva [dē'ḥá] nf prima donna.

divagar [dĕḥàgàr'] vi (desviarse) to digress.

divague [dĕḥà'ge] etc vb V **divagar.**

diván [dĕḥán'] nm divan.

divergencia [dĕḥerhen'syá] nf divergence.

divergir [dĕḥerḥēr'] vi (líneas) to diverge; (opiniones) to differ; (personas) to disagree.

diverja [dĕḥer'há] etc vb V **divergir.**

diversidad [dĕḥersēḥàḥ'] nf diversity, variety.

diversificación [dĕḥersēfēkàsyon'] nf (COM) diversification.

diversificar [dĕḥersēfēkàr'] vt to diversify.

diversifique [dĕḥersēfē'ke] etc vb V **diversificar.**

diversión [dĕḥersyon'] nf (gen) entertainment; (actividad) hobby, pastime.

diverso, a [dĕḥer'so, á] a diverse; (diferente) different ♦ nm: **~s** (COM) sundries; **~s libros** several books.

divertido, a [dĕḥertē'ḥo, á] a (chiste) amusing, funny; (fiesta etc) enjoyable; (película, libro) entertaining; **está ~** (irónico) this is going to be fun.

divertir [dĕḥertēr'] vt (entretener, recrear) to amuse, entertain; **~se** vr (pasarlo bien) to have a good time; (distraerse) to amuse o.s.

dividendo [dĕḥēḥen'do] nm (COM): **~s** nmpl dividends; **~s por acción** earnings per share; ~ **definitivo** final dividend.

dividir [dĕḥēḥēr'] vt (gen) to divide; (separar) to separate; (distribuir) to distribute, share out.

divierta [dĕḥyer'tá] etc vb V **divertir.**

divinidad [dĕḥēnēḥàḥ'] nf (esencia divina) divinity; **la D~** God.

divino, a [dĕḥē'no, á] a divine; (fig) lovely.

divirtiendo [dĕḥērtyen'do] etc vb V **divertir.**

divisa [dĕḥē'sá] nf (emblema, moneda) emblem, badge; **~s** nfpl currency sg; (COM) foreign exchange sg; **control de ~s** exchange control; ~ **de reserva** reserve currency.

divisar [dĕḥēsàr'] vt to make out, distinguish.

división [dĕḥēsyon'] nf division; (de partido) split; (de país) partition.

divisorio, a [dĕḥēso'ryo, á] a (línea) dividing; **línea divisoria de las aguas** watershed.

divorciado, a [dĕḥorsyà'ḥo, á] a divorced; (opinion) split ♦ nm/f divorcé(e).

divorciar [dĕḥorsyàr'] vt to divorce; **~se** vr to get divorced.

divorcio [dĕḥor'syo] nm divorce; (fig) split.

divulgación [dĕḥōōlgàsyon'] nf (difusión) spreading; (popularización) popularization.

divulgar [dĕḥōōlgàr'] vt (desparramar) to spread; (popularizar) to popularize; (hacer circular) to divulge, circulate; **~se** vr (secreto) to leak out; (rumor) to spread.

divulgue [dĕḥōōl'ge] etc vb V **divulgar.**

DM abr = **decimal.**

dm. abr (= decímetro) dm.

Dña. abr = **Doña.**

DNI nm abr Esp: = **Documento Nacional de Identidad.**

dobladillo [doḥlàḥē'yo] nm (de vestido) hem; (de pantalón: vuelta) turn-up (Brit), cuff (US).

doblaje [doḥlà'he] nm (CINE) dubbing.

doblar [doḥlàr'] vt to double; (papel) to fold; (caño) to bend; (la esquina) to turn, go round; (film) to dub ♦ vi to turn; (campana) to toll; **~se** vr (plegarse) to fold (up), crease; (encorvarse) to bend.

doble [do'ḥle] a (gen) double; (de dos aspectos) dual; (cuerda) thick; (fig) two-faced ♦ nm double ♦ nm/f (TEATRO) double, stand-in; **~s** nmpl (DEPORTE) doubles sg; ~ **o nada** double or nothing; ~ **página** double-page spread; **con ~ sentido** with a double meaning; **el ~** twice the quantity o as much; **su sueldo es el ~ del mío** his salary is twice (as much as) mine; (INFORM): ~ **cara** double-sided; ~ **densidad** double density; ~ **espacio** double spacing.

doblegar [doḥlegàr'] vt to fold, crease; **~se** vr to yield.

doblegue [doḥle'ge] etc vb V **doblegar.**

doblez [doḥles'] nm (pliegue) fold, hem ♦ nf (falsedad) duplicity.

doc. abr (= docena) doz.; (= documento) doc.

doce [do'se] num twelve; (fecha) twelfth; **las ~** twelve o'clock; V tb **seis.**

docena [dose'ná] nf dozen; **por ~s** by the dozen.

docente [dosen'te] a: **centro/personal ~**

teaching institution/staff.

dócil [do'sēl] *a* (*pasivo*) docile; (*manso*) gentle; (*obediente*) obedient.

docto, a [dok'to, à] *a* learned, erudite ♦ *nm/f* scholar.

doctor, a [doktor', à] *nm/f* doctor; ~ **en filosofía** Doctor of Philosophy.

doctorado [doktorà'ᵭo] *nm* doctorate.

doctorarse [doktoràr'se] *vr* to get a doctorate.

doctrina [doktrē'ná] *nf* doctrine, teaching.

documentación [dokōōmentàsyon'] *nf* documentation; (*de identidad etc*) papers *pl*.

documental [dokōōmentál'] *a, nm* documentary.

documentar [dokōōmentár'] *vt* to document; ~**se** *vr* to gather information.

documento [dokōōmen'to] *nm* (*certificado*) document; (*JUR*) exhibit; ~**s** *nmpl* papers; ~ **justificativo** voucher; ~ **nacional de identidad** national identity card.

dogo [do'go] *nm* bulldog.

dólar [do'lár] *nm* dollar.

dolencia [dolen'syá] *nf* (*achaque*) ailment; (*dolor*) ache.

doler [doler'] *vt, vi* to hurt; (*fig*) to grieve; ~**se** *vr* (*de su situación*) to grieve, feel sorry; (*de las desgracias ajenas*) to sympathize; (*quejarse*) to complain; **me duele el brazo** my arm hurts; **no me duele el dinero** I don't mind about the money; **¡ahí le duele!** you've put your finger on it!

doliente [dolyen'te] *a* (*enfermo*) sick; (*dolorido*) aching; (*triste*) sorrowful; **la familia** ~ the bereaved family.

dolor [dolor'] *nm* pain; (*fig*) grief, sorrow; ~ **de cabeza** headache; ~ **de estómago** stomach ache; ~ **de oídos** earache; ~ **sordo** dull ache.

dolorido, a [dolorē'ᵭo, à] *a* (*MED*) sore; **la parte dolorida** the part which hurts.

doloroso, a [doloro'so, à] *a* (*MED*) painful; (*fig*) distressing.

domar [domár'] *vt* to tame.

domesticado, a [domestēká'ᵭo, à] *a* (*amansado*) tame.

domesticar [domestēkár'] *vt* to tame.

doméstico, a [dome'stēko, à] *a* domestic ♦ *nm/f* servant; **economía doméstica** home economy; **gastos** ~**s** household expenses.

domestique [domestē'ke] *etc vb V* **domesticar.**

domiciliación [domēsēlyásyon'] *nf:* ~ **de pagos** (*COM*) standing order, direct debit.

domiciliar [domēsēlyár'] *vt* to domicile; ~**se** *vr* to take up (one's) residence.

domiciliario, a [domēsēlyá'ryo, à] *a:* **arresto** ~ house arrest.

domicilio [domēsē'lyo] *nm* home; ~ **particular** private residence; ~ **social** (*COM*) head office, registered office; **servicio a** ~

delivery service; **sin** ~ **fijo** of no fixed abode.

dominante [domēnán'te] *a* dominant; (*person*) domineering.

dominar [domēnár'] *vt* (*gen*) to dominate; (*países*) to rule over; (*adversario*) to overpower; (*caballo, nervios, emoción*) to control; (*incendio, epidemia*) to bring under control; (*idiomas*) to be fluent in ♦ *vi* to dominate, prevail; ~**se** *vr* to control o.s.

domingo [domēn'go] *nm* Sunday; **D**~ **de Ramos** Palm Sunday; **D**~ **de Resurrección** Easter Sunday; *V tb* **sábado.**

dominguero, a [domēnge'ro, à] *a* Sunday *cpd.*

dominical [domēnēkál'] *a* Sunday *cpd*; **periódico** ~ Sunday newspaper.

dominio [domē'nyo] *nm* (*tierras*) domain; (*POL*) dominion; (*autoridad*) power, authority; (*supremacía*) supremacy; (*de las pasiones*) grip, hold; (*de idioma*) command; **ser del** ~ **público** to be widely known.

dominó [domēno'] *nm* (*pieza*) domino; (*juego*) dominoes.

dom.º *abr* (= *domingo*) Sun.

don [don] *nm* (*talento*) gift; **D**~ **Juan Gómez** Mr Juan Gomez o Juan Gomez Esq.; **tener** ~ **de gentes** to known how to handle people; ~ **de lenguas** gift for languages; ~ **de mando** (qualities of) leadership; ~ **de palabra** gift of gab (*US*) o the gab (*Brit*).

donaire [donà'ēre] *nm* charm.

donante [donàn'te] *nm/f* donor; ~ **de sangre** blood donor.

donar [donàr'] *vt* to donate.

donativo [donàtē'ᵭo] *nm* donation.

doncella [donse'yá] *nf* (*criada*) maid.

donde [don'de] *ad* where ♦ *prep:* **el coche está allí** ~ **el farol** the car is over there by the lamppost o where the lamppost is; **por** ~ through which; **a** ~ to where, to which; **en** ~ where, in which; **es a** ~ **vamos nosotros** that's where we're going.

dónde [don'de] *ad interrogativo* where?; **¿a** ~ **vas?** where are you going (to)?; **¿de** ~ **vienes?** where have you come from?; **¿en** ~**?** where?; **¿por** ~**?** where?, whereabouts?; **¿por** ~ **se va al estadio?** how do you get to the stadium?

dondequiera [dondekye'rà] *ad* anywhere ♦ *conj:* ~ **que** wherever; **por** ~ everywhere, all over the place.

donostiarra [donostyá'rrà] *a* of o from San Sebastián ♦ *nm/f* native o inhabitant of San Sebastián.

doña [do'nyá] *nf título de mujer que no se traduce.*

dopar [dopár'] *vt* to dope, drug.

doquier [dokyer'] *ad:* **por** ~ all over, everywhere.

dorado, a [dorá'tʃo, á] *a* (*color*) golden; (*TEC*) gilt.

dorar [dorár'] *vt* (*TEC*) to gild; (*CULIN*) to brown, cook lightly; ~ **la píldora** to sweeten the pill.

dormilón, ona [dormēlon', o'ná] *a* fond of sleeping ♦ *nm/f* sleepyhead.

dormir [dormēr'] *vt*: ~ **la siesta por la tarde** to have an afternoon nap ♦ *vi* to sleep; ~**se** *vr* (*persona, brazo, pierna*) to fall asleep; ~**la** (*fam*) to sleep it off; ~ **la mona** (*fam*) to sleep off a hangover; ~ **como un lirón** *o* **tronco** to sleep like a log; ~ **a pierna suelta** to sleep soundly.

dormitar [dormētár'] *vi* to doze.

dormitorio [dormēto'ryo] *nm* bedroom; ~ **común** dormitory.

dorsal [dorsál'] *a* dorsal ♦ *nm* (*DEPORTE*) number.

dorso [dor'so] *nm* back; **escribir algo al ~** to write sth on the back; **"vease al ~"** "see other side", "please turn over".

DOS *nm abr* (= *sistema operativo de disco*) DOS.

dos [dos] *num* two; (*fecha*) second; **los ~** the two of them, both of them; **cada ~ por tres** every 5 minutes; **de ~ en ~** in twos; **estamos a ~** (*TENIS*) the score is deuce; *V tb* **seis.**

doscientos, as [dosyen'tos, ás] *num* two hundred; *V tb* **seiscientos.**

dosel [dosel'] *nm* canopy.

dosificar [dosēfēkár'] *vt* (*CULIN, MED, QUÍMICA*) to measure out; (*no derrochar*) to be sparing with.

dosifique [dosēfē'ke] *etc vb V* **dosificar.**

dosis [do'sēs] *nf inv* dose, dosage.

dossier [dosyer'] *nm* dossier, file.

dotación [dotásyon'] *nf* (*acto, dinero*) endowment; (*plantilla*) staff; (*NAUT*) crew; **la ~ es insuficiente** we are under-staffed.

dotado, a [dotá'tʃo, á] *a* gifted; ~ **de** (*persona*) endowed with; (*máquina*) equipped with.

dotar [dotár'] *vt* to endow; (*TEC*) to fit; (*barco*) to man; (*oficina*) to staff.

dote [do'te] *nf* (*de novia*) dowry; ~**s** *nfpl* (*talentos*) gifts.

doy [doy] *vb V* **dar.**

Dpto. *abr* (= *Departamento*) dept.

Dr(a). *abr* (= *Doctor, Doctora*) Dr.

draga [drá'gá] *nf* dredge.

dragado [drágá'tʃo] *nm* dredging.

dragar [drágár'] *vt* to dredge; (*minas*) to sweep.

drague [drá'ge] *etc vb V* **dragar.**

drama [drá'má] *nm* drama; (*obra*) play.

dramático, a [drámá'tēko, á] *a* dramatic ♦ *nm/f* dramatist; (*actor*) actor; **obra dramática** play.

dramaturgo, a [drámátōōr'go, á] *nm/f*

dramatist, playwright.

dramón [drámon'] *nm* (*TEATRO*) melodrama; **¡qué ~!** what a scene!

drenaje [drená'he] *nm* drainage.

drenar [drenár'] *vt* to drain.

droga [dro'gá] *nf* drug; (*DEPORTE*) dope; **el problema de la ~** the drug problem.

drogadicto, a [drogátʃēk'to, á] *nm/f* drug addict.

drogar [drogár'] *vt* to drug; (*DEPORTE*) to dope; ~**se** *vr* to take drugs.

drogue [dro'ge] *etc vb V* **drogar.**

droguería [drogerē'á] *nf* pharmacy.

Dto., D.ᵗᵒ *abr* = **descuento.**

Dtor(a). *abr* (= *Director, Directora*) Dir.

ducado [dōōká'tʃo] *nm* duchy, dukedom.

ducentésimo, a [dōōsente'sēmo, á] *a* two hundredth; *V tb* **sexto, a.**

dúctil [dōōk'tēl] *a* (*metal*) ductile; (*persona*) easily influenced.

ducha [dōōtch'á] *nf* (*baño*) shower; (*MED*) douche.

ducharse [dōōtchár'se] *vr* to take a shower.

ducho, a [dōōtch'o, á] *a*: ~ **en** (*experimentado*) experienced in; (*hábil*) skilled at.

duda [dōō'tʃá] *nf* doubt; **sin ~** no doubt, doubtless; **¡sin ~!** of course!; **no cabe ~** there is no doubt about it; **no le quepa ~** make no mistake about it; **no quiero poner en ~ su conducta** I don't want to call his behavior into question; **sacar a uno de la ~** to settle sb's doubts; **tengo una ~** I have a question.

dudar [dōōtʃár'] *vt* to doubt ♦ *vi* to doubt, have doubts; ~ **acerca de algo** to be uncertain about sth; **dudó en comprarlo** he hesitated to buy it; **dudan que sea verdad** they doubt whether *o* if it's true.

dudoso, a [dōōtʃo'so, á] *a* (*incierto*) hesitant; (*sospechoso*) doubtful; (*conducta*) dubious.

duelo [dwe'lo] *etc vb V* **doler** ♦ *nm* (*combate*) duel; (*luto*) mourning; **batirse en ~** to fight a duel.

duende [dwen'de] *nm* imp, goblin; **tiene ~** there's something magic about him.

dueño, a [dwe'nyo, á] *nm/f* (*propietario*) owner; (*de pensión, taberna*) landlord/lady; (*de casa, perro*) master/mistress; (*empresario*) employer; **ser ~ de sí mismo** to have self-control; (*libre*) to be one's own boss; **eres ~ de hacer como te parezca** you're free to do as you think fit; **hacerse ~ de una situación** to take command of a situation.

duerma [dwer'má] *etc vb V* **dormir.**

duermevela [dwermebe'lá] *nf* (*fam*) nap, snooze.

Duero [dwe'ro] *nm* Douro.

dulce [dōōl'se] *a* sweet; (*carácter, clima*) gentle, mild ♦ *ad* gently, softly ♦ *nm* sweet.

dulcificar |dŏōlsc̄fc̄kár'| *vt* (*fig*) to soften.
dulcifique |dŏōlsc̄fc̄'kc̄| *etc vb* V **dulcificar**.
dulzura |dŏōlsŏō'rä| *nf* sweetness; (*ternura*) gentleness.
Dunquerque |dŏōnkcr'kc̄| *nm* Dunkirk.
dúo |dŏō'o| *nm* duet, duo.
duodécimo, a |dŏōot̄hc'sc̄mo, ä| *a* twelfth; V *tb* **sexto, a**.
dup., dup.do *abr* (= *duplicado*) duplicated.
dúplex |dŏō'plcks| *nm inv* (*piso*) flat on two floors; (*TELEC*) link-up; (*INFORM*): ~ **integral** full duplex.
duplicar |dŏōplc̄kár'| *vt* (*hacer el doble de*) to duplicate; (*cantidad*) to double; ~**se** *vr* to double.
duplique |dŏōplc̄'kc̄| *etc vb* V **duplicar**.
duque |dŏō'kc̄| *nm* duke.
duquesa |dŏōkc̄'sä| *nf* duchess.
duración |dŏōräsyon'| *nf* duration, length; (*de máquina*) life; ~ **media de la vida** average life expectancy; **de larga** ~ (*enfermedad*) lengthy; (*pila*) long-life; (*disco*) long-playing; **de poca** ~ short.
duradero, a |dŏōrät̄hc'ro, ä| *a* (*tela*) hard-wearing; (*fe, paz*) lasting.
durante |dŏōrán'tc̄| *ad* during; ~ **toda la noche** all night long; **habló** ~ **una hora** he spoke for an hour.
durar |dŏōrár'| *vi* (*permanecer*) to last; (*recuerdo*) to remain; (*ropa*) to wear (well).
durazno |dŏōrás'no| *nm* (*AM: fruta*) peach; (: *árbol*) peach tree.
durex |dŏō'rcks| *nm* (*AM: tira adhesiva*) Scotch tape ® (*US*), Sellotape ® (*Brit*).
dureza |dŏōrc̄'sä| *nf* (*cualidad*) hardness; (*de carácter*) toughness.
durmiendo |dŏōrmycn'do| *etc vb* V **dormir**.
durmiente |dŏōrmycn'tc̄| *a* sleeping ♦ *nm/f* sleeper.
duro, a |dŏō'ro, ä| *a* hard; (*carácter*) tough; (*pan*) stale; (*cuello, puerta*) stiff; (*clima, luz*) harsh ♦ *ad* hard ♦ *nm* (*moneda*) five peseta cóin; **el sector** ~ **del partido** the hardliners *pl* in the party; **ser** ~ **con uno** to be tough with o hard on sb; ~ **de mollera** (*torpe*) dense; **de oído** hard of hearing; **trabajar** ~ to work hard; **estar sin un** ~ to be broke.

E

E, e |c| *nf* (*letra*) E, e; **E de Enrique** E for Easy.
E *abr* (= *este*) E.

e |c| *conj* (*delante de* i- e hi-, *pero no* hie-) and; V *tb* **y**.
e/ *abr* (*COM:* = *envio*) shpt.
ebanista |c̄hänc'stä| *nm/f* cabinetmaker.
ébano |c̄'häno| *nm* ebony.
ebrio, a |c̄h'ryo, ä| *a* drunk.
Ebro |c̄'hro| *nm* Ebro.
ebullición |c̄hŏōyc̄syon'| *nf* boiling; **punto de** ~ boiling point.
eccema |cksc̄'mä| *nm* (*MED*) eczema.
eclesiástico, a |cklcsyä'stc̄ko, ä| *a* ecclesiastical; (*autoridades etc*) church *cpd* ♦ *nm* clergyman.
eclipse |cklc̄p'sc̄| *nm* eclipse.
eco |c'ko| *nm* echo; **encontrar un** ~ **en** to produce a response from; **hacerse** ~ **de una opinión** to echo an opinion; **tener** ~ to catch on.
ecología |ckolohc̄'ä| *nf* ecology.
ecológico, a |ckolo'hc̄ko, ä| *a* ecological.
economato |ckonomä'to| *nm* cooperative store.
economía |ckonomc̄'ä| *nf* (*sistema*) economy; (*cualidad*) thrift; ~ **dirigida** planned economy; ~ **doméstica** housekeeping; ~ **mixta** mixed economy; ~ **sumergida** black economy; **hacer** ~**s** to economize; ~**s de escala** economies of scale.
economice |ckonomc̄'sc̄| *etc vb* V **economizar**.
económico, a |ckono'mc̄ko, ä| *a* (*barato*) cheap, economical; (*persona*) thrifty; (*COM: año etc*) financial; (: *situación*) economic.
economista |ckonomc̄'stä| *nm/f* economist.
economizar |ckonomc̄sär'| *vt* to economize on ♦ *vi* (*ahorrar*) to save up; (*pey*) to be miserly.
ecuador |ckwät̄hor'| *nm* equator; **(el) E~** Ecuador.
ecuánime |ckwä'nc̄mc̄| *a* (*carácter*) level-headed; (*estado*) calm.
ecuatorial |ckwätoryäl'| *a* equatorial.
ecuatoriano, a |ckwätoryä'no, ä| *a, nm/f* Ecuador(i)an.
ecuestre |ckwcs'trc̄| *a* equestrian.
echar |ctchár'| *vt* to throw; (*agua, vino*) to pour (out); (*CULIN*) to put in, add; (*dientes*) to cut; (*discurso*) to give; (*empleado: despedir*) to fire; (*hojas*) to sprout; (*cartas*) to mail (*US*), post (*Brit*); (*humo*) to emit, give out; (*reprimenda*) to deal out; (*cuenta*) to make up; (*freno*) to put on ♦ *vi*: ~ **a correr/llorar** to break into a run/burst into tears; ~ **a reir** to burst out laughing; ~**se** *vr* to lie down; ~ **abajo** (*gobierno*) to overthrow; (*edificio*) to demolish; ~ **la buenaventura a uno** to tell sb's fortune; ~ **la culpa a** to lay the blame on; ~ **de menos** to miss; ~**se atrás** to move back(wards); (*fig*) to go back on what one

has said; ~**se una novia** to get o.s. a girlfriend; ~**se una siestecita** to have a nap.

echarpe [etchár'pe] *nm* (woman's) stole.

ed. *abr* (= *edición*) ed.

edad [etháth'] *nf* age; **¿qué ~ tienes?** how old are you?; **tiene ocho años de ~** he is eight (years old); **de ~ corta** young; **ser de ~ mediana/avanzada** to be middle-aged/getting on in years; **ser mayor de ~** to be of age; **llegar a mayor ~** to come of age; **ser menor de ~** to be under age; **la E~ Media** the Middle Ages.

Edén [ethen'] *nm* Eden.

edición [ethēsyon'] *nf* (*acto*) publication; (*ejemplar*) edition; **"al cerrar la ~"** (*TIP*) "stop press".

edicto [ethēk'to] *nm* edict, proclamation.

edificante [ethēfēkán'te] *a* edifying.

edificar [edēfēkár'] *vt* (*ARQ*) to build.

edificio [ethēfē'syo] *nm* building; (*fig*) edifice, structure.

edifique [ethēfē'ke] *etc vb* V **edificar**.

Edimburgo [ethēmbōōr'go] *nm* Edinburgh.

editar [ethētár'] *vt* (*publicar*) to publish; (*preparar textos, tb INFORM*) to edit.

editor, a [ethētor', á] *nm/f* (*que publica*) publisher; (*redactor*) editor ♦ *a:* **casa ~a** publishing company.

editorial [ethētoryál'] *a* editorial ♦ *nm* leading article, editorial ♦ *nf* (*tb:* **casa ~**) publishers.

editorialista [ethētoryálē'stá] *nm/f* editor.

edredón [ethrethon'] *nm* eiderdown, quilt.

educación [ethōōkásyon'] *nf* education; (*crianza*) upbringing; (*modales*) (good) manners *pl*; (*formación*) training; **sin ~** ill-mannered; **¡qué falta de ~!** how rude!

educado, a [ethōōká'tho, á] *a* well-mannered; **mal ~** ill-mannered.

educar [ethōōkár'] *vt* to educate; (*criar*) to bring up; (*voz*) to train.

eduque [ethōō'ke] *etc vb* V **educar**.

EE.UU. *nmpl abr* (= *Estados Unidos*) USA.

efectista [efektē'stá] *a* sensationalist.

efectivamente [efektēhámen'te] *ad* (*como respuesta*) exactly, precisely; (*verdaderamente*) really; (*de hecho*) in fact.

efectivo, a [efektē'ho, á] *a* effective; (*real*) actual, real ♦ *nm:* **pagar en ~** to pay (in) cash; **hacer ~ un cheque** to cash a check.

efecto [efek'to] *nm* effect, result; (*objetivo*) purpose, end; **~s** *nmpl* (*personales*) effects; (*bienes*) goods; (*COM*) assets; (*ECON*) bills, securities; **~s de consumo** consumer goods; **~s a cobrar** bills receivable; **~s personales** personal effects; **~ secundarios** (*COM*) spin-off effects; **~s sonoros** sound effects; **hacer o surtir ~** to have the desired effect; **hacer ~** (*impresionar*) to make an impression; **llevar algo a ~** to carry sth out; **en ~** in fact; (*res-*

puesta) exactly, indeed.

efectuar [efektwár'] *vt* to carry out; (*viaje*) to make.

efervescente [eferhesen'te] *a* (*bebida*) fizzy, bubbly.

eficacia [efēká'syá] *nf* (*de persona*) efficiency; (*de medicamento etc*) effectiveness.

eficaz [efēkás'] *a* (*persona*) efficient; (*acción*) effective.

eficiencia [efēsyen'syá] *nf* efficiency.

eficiente [efēsyen'te] *a* efficient.

efigie [efē'hye] *nf* effigy.

efímero, a [efē'mero, á] *a* ephemeral.

efusión [efōōsyon'] *nf* outpouring; (*en el trato*) warmth; **con ~** effusively.

efusivo, a [efōōsē'ho, á] *a* effusive; **mis más efusivas gracias** my warmest thanks.

EGB *nf abr* (*Esp ESCOL*)=*Educación General Básica.*

Egeo [che'o] *nm:* **(Mar) ~** Aegean (Sea).

egipcio, a [chēp'syo, á] *a, nm/f* Egyptian.

Egipto [chēp'to] *nm* Egypt.

egocéntrico, a [egosen'trēko, á] *a* self-centered (*US*), self-centred (*Brit*).

egoísmo [egoēs'mo] *nm* egoism.

egoísta [egoē'stá] *a* egoistical, selfish ♦ *nm/f* egotist, egoist.

egolatra [egolá'trá] *a* big-headed.

egregio, a [egre'hyo, á] *a* eminent, distinguished.

eh [e] *excl* hey!, hi!

Eire [e'ēre] *nm* Eire.

ej. *abr* (= *ejemplo*) ex.

eje [e'he] *nm* (*GEO, MAT*) axis; (*POL, fig*) axis, main line; (*de rueda*) axle; (*de máquina*) shaft, spindle.

ejecución [chekōōsyon'] *nf* execution; (*cumplimiento*) fulfilment; (*actuación*) performance; (*JUR: embargo de deudor*) attachment.

ejecutar [chekōōtár'] *vt* to execute, carry out; (*matar*) to execute; (*cumplir*) to fulfil; (*MUS*) to perform; (*JUR: embargar*) to attach, distrain; (*deseos*) to fulfill (*US*), fulfil (*Brit*); (*INFORM*) to run.

ejecutivo, a [chekōōtē'ho, á] *a, nm/f* executive; **el (poder) ~** the Executive (Power).

ejecutor [chekōōtor'] *nm* (*tb:* ~ **testamentario**) executor.

ejecutoria [chekōōto'ryá] *nf* (*JUR*) final judgment.

ejemplar [chemplár'] *a* exemplary ♦ *nm* example; (*ZOOL*) specimen; (*de libro*) copy; (*de periódico*) number, issue; **~ de regalo** complimentary copy; **sin ~** unprecedented.

ejemplificar [chemplēfēkár'] *vt* to exemplify, illustrate.

ejemplifique [chemplēfē'ke] *etc vb* V **ejemplificar**.

ejemplo [ehem'plo] *nm* example; (*caso*) instance; **por** ~ for example; **dar** ~ to set an example.

ejercer [eherser'] *vt* to exercise; (*funciones*) to perform; (*negocio*) to manage; (*influencia*) to exert; (*un oficio*) to practice (*US*), practise (*Brit*); (*poder*) to wield ♦ *vi*: ~ **de** to practice as.

ejercicio [ehersē'syo] *nm* exercise; (*MIL*) drill; (*COM*) fiscal *o* financial year; (*período*) tenure; ~ **acrobático** (*AVIAT*) stunt; ~ **comercial** business year; ~**s espirituales** (*REL*) retreat *sg*; **hacer** ~ to take exercise.

ejercitar [ehersētár'] *vt* to exercise; (*MIL*) to drill.

ejército [eher'sēto] *nm* army; ~ **de ocupación** army of occupation; ~ **permanente** standing army; **entrar en el** ~ to join the army, join up.

ejerza [eher'sá] *etc vb V* **ejercer**.

ejote [eho'te] *nm* (*AM*) green bean.

el [el], *pl* **los** *artículo definido msg* the; **me gusta** ~ **fútbol** I like football; ~ **General Prim** General Prim ♦ *pron demostrativo*: **mi libro y** ~ **de usted** my book and yours; ~ **de Pepe es mejor** Pepe's is better ♦ *pron relativo*: ~ **que** he *etc* who, whoever, the one(s) that; ~ **que compramos no vale** the one we bought is no good.

él [el] *pron* (*persona*) he; (*cosa*) it; (*después de prep: persona*) him; (: *cosa*) it; **mis libros y los de** ~ my books and his.

elaboración [elàḅoràsyon'] *nf* (*producción*) manufacture; ~ **de presupuestos** (*COM*) budgeting.

elaborar [elàḅorár'] *vt* (*producto*) to make, manufacture; (*preparar*) to prepare; (*madera, metal etc*) to work; (*proyecto etc*) to work on *o* out.

elasticidad [elàstēsēḍàth'] *nf* elasticity.

elástico, a [elá'stēko, à] *a* elastic; (*flexible*) flexible ♦ *nm* elastic; (*gomita*) elastic band.

elección [eleksyon'] *nf* election; (*selección*) choice, selection; **elecciones parciales** off-year election *sg* (*US*), by-election *sg* (*Brit*); **elecciones generales** general election *sg*.

electo, a [elek'to, à] *a* elect; **el presidente** ~ the president-elect.

electorado [elektorà'tho] *nm* electorate, voters *pl*.

electrice [elektrē'se] *etc vb V* **electrizar**.

electricidad [elektrēsēḍàth'] *nf* electricity.

electricista [elektrēsē'stá] *nm/f* electrician.

eléctrico, a [elek'trēko, à] *a* electric.

electrizar [elektrēsár'] *vt* (*FERRO, fig*) to electrify.

electro... [elek'tro] *pref* electro....

electrocución [elektrokōōsyon'] *nf* electrocution.

electrocutar [elektrokōōtár'] *vt* to electro-

cute.

electrodo [elektro'tho] *nm* electrode.

electrodomésticos [elektrothome'stēkos] *nmpl* (electrical) household appliances; (*COM*) major appliances (*US*), white goods (*Brit*).

electroimán [electroēmán'] *nm* electromagnet.

electromagnético, a [elektromágne'tēko, à] *a* electromagnetic.

electrónico, a [elektro'nēko, à] *a* electronic ♦ *nf* electronics *sg*; **proceso** ~ **de datos** (*INFORM*) electronic data processing.

electrotecnia [elektrotek'nyà] *nf* electrical engineering.

electrotécnico, a [elektrotek'nēko, à] *nm/f* electrical engineer.

electrotermo [elektroter'mo] *nm* immersible (*US*) *o* immersion (*Brit*) heater.

elefante [elefán'te] *nm* elephant.

elegancia [elegán'syà] *nf* elegance, grace; (*estilo*) stylishness.

elegante [elegán'te] *a* elegant, graceful; (*traje etc*) smart, fashionable; (*decoración*) tasteful.

elegía [elehē'á] *nf* elegy.

elegir [elehēr'] *vt* (*escoger*) to choose, select; (*optar*) to opt for; (*presidente*) to elect.

elemental [elementál'] *a* (*claro, obvio*) elementary; (*fundamental*) elemental, fundamental.

elemento [elemen'to] *nm* element; (*fig*) ingredient; (*AM*) person, individual; (*tipo raro*) odd person; (*de pila*) cell; ~**s** *nmpl* elements, rudiments; **estar en su** ~ to be in one's element; **vino a verle un** ~ someone came to see you.

elenco [elen'ko] *nm* catalog(ue), list; (*TEATRO*) cast.

elevación [elebàsyon'] *nf* elevation; (*acto*) raising, lifting; (*de precios*) rise; (*GEO etc*) height, altitude.

elevar [elebár'] *vt* to raise, lift (up); (*precio*) to put up; (*producción*) to step up; (*informe etc*) to present; ~**se** *vr* (*edificio*) to rise; (*precios*) to go up; (*transportarse, enajenarse*) to get carried away; **la cantidad se eleva a ...** the total amounts to ... .

eligiendo [elēhyen'tho] *etc*, **elija** [elē'há] *etc vb V* **elegir**.

eliminar [elēmēnár'] *vt* to eliminate, remove; (*olor, persona*) to get rid of; (*DEPORTE*) to eliminate, knock out.

eliminatoria [elēmēnàto'ryà] *nf* heat, preliminary (round).

elite [elē'te] *nf* elite.

elocuencia [elokwen'syà] *nf* eloquence.

elocuente [elokwen'te] *a* eloquent; (*fig*) significant; **un dato** ~ a fact which speaks for itself.

elogiar [elohyár'] *vt* to praise, eulogize.

elogio [elo'hyo] *nm* praise; **queda por encima de todo** ~ it's beyond praise; **hacer** ~ **de** to sing the praises of.

elote [elo'te] *nm* (*AM*) corn on the cob.

El Salvador *nm* El Salvador.

eludir [eloōθēr'] *vt* (*evitar*) to avoid, evade; (*escapar*) to escape, elude.

ella [e'yá] *pron* (*persona*) she; (*cosa*) it; (*después de prep: persona*) her; (: *cosa*) it; **de** ~ hers.

ellas [e'yàs] *pron V* **ellos**.

ello [e'yo] *pron neutro* it; **es por** ~ **que ...** that's why ... .

ellos, as [e'yos, às] *pron personal pl* they; (*después de prep*) them; **de** ~ theirs.

E.M. *abr* (*MIL*:=*Estado Mayor*) G.S.

Em.ª *abr* = **Eminencia**.

emanar [emánár'] *vi*: ~ **de** to emanate from, come from; (*derivar de*) to originate in.

emancipar [emánsēpár'] *vt* to emancipate; ~**se** *vr* to become emancipated, free o.s.

embadurnar [embáθōōrnár'] *vt* to smear.

embajada [embáhá'θá] *nf* embassy.

embajador, a [embáhàθor', à] *nm/f* ambassador/ambassadress.

embaladura [embálàθōō'rá] *nf* (*AM*), **embalaje** [embálá'he] *nm* packing.

embalar [embálár'] *vt* (*envolver*) to package, wrap (up); (*envasar*) to package ♦ *vi* to sprint.

embalsamar [embálsámár'] *vt* to embalm.

embalsar [embálsár'] *vt* (*río*) to dam (up); (*agua*) to retain.

embalse [embál'se] *nm* (*presa*) dam; (*lago*) reservoir.

embarace [embárá'se] *etc vb V* **embarazar**.

embarazada [embárásá'θá] *af* pregnant ♦ *nf* pregnant woman.

embarazar [embárásár'] *vt* to obstruct, hamper; ~**se** *vr* (*aturdirse*) to become embarrassed; (*confundirse*) to get into a mess.

embarazo [embárá'so] *nm* (*de mujer*) pregnancy; (*impedimento*) obstacle, obstruction; (*timidez*) embarrassment.

embarazoso, a [embáráso'so, à] *a* (*molesto*) awkward; (*violento*) embarrassing.

embarcación [embárkásyon'] *nf* (*barco*) boat, craft; (*acto*) embarkation; ~ **de arrastre** trawler; ~ **de cabotaje** coastal vessel.

embarcadero [embárkàθe'ro] *nm* pier, wharf.

embarcar [embárkár'] *vt* (*cargamento*) to ship, stow; (*persona*) to embark, put on board; (*fig*): ~ **a uno en una empresa** to involve sb in an undertaking; ~**se** *vr* to embark, go on board; (*marinero*) to sign on.

embargar [embárgár'] *vt* (*frenar*) to restrain; (*sentidos*) to overpower; (*JUR*) to seize, impound.

embargo [embár'go] *nm* (*JUR*) seizure; (*COM etc*) embargo; **sin** ~ still, however, nonetheless.

embargue [embár'ge] *etc vb V* **embargar**.

embarque [embár'ke] *etc vb V* **embarcar** ♦ *nm* shipment, loading.

embarrancar [embárránkár'] *vt, vi* (*NAUT*) to run aground; (*AUTO etc*) to run into a ditch.

embarranque [embárrán'ke] *etc vb V* **embarrancar**.

embarullar [embárōōyár'] *vt* to make a mess of.

embate [embá'te] *nm* (*de mar, viento*) beating, violence.

embaucador, a [embáōōkàθor', à] *nm/f* (*estafador*) trickster; (*impostor*) impostor.

embaucar [embáōōkár'] *vt* to trick, fool.

embauque [embá'ōōke] *etc vb V* **embaucar**.

embebecido, a [embeþesē'θo, à] *a* fascinated.

embeber [embeþer'] *vt* (*absorber*) to absorb, soak up; (*empapar*) to saturate ♦ *vi* to shrink; ~**se** *vr*: ~**se en un libro** to be engrossed o absorbed in a book.

embelesado, a [embelesá'θo, à] *a* spellbound.

embelesar [embelesár'] *vt* to enchant; ~**se** *vr*: ~**se (con)** to be enchanted (by).

embellecer [embeyeser'] *vt* to embellish, beautify.

embellezca [embeyes'ká] *etc vb V* **embellecer**.

embestida [embestē'θá] *nf* attack, onslaught; (*carga*) charge.

embestir [embestēr'] *vt* to attack, assault; to charge, attack ♦ *vi* to attack.

embistiendo [embēstyen'do] *etc vb V* **embestir**.

emblandecer [emblándeser'] *vt* to soften; (*fig*) to mollify; ~**se** *vr* to relent.

emblandezca [emblándes'ká] *etc vb V* **emblandecer**.

emblanquecer [emblánkeser'] *vt* to whiten, bleach; ~**se** *vr* to turn white.

emblanquezca [emblánkes'ká] *etc vb V* **emblanquecer**.

emblema [emble'má] *nm* emblem.

embobado, a [emboþá'θo, à] *a* (*atontado*) stunned, bewildered.

embobar [emboþár'] *vt* (*asombrar*) to amaze; (*fascinar*) to fascinate; ~**se** *vr*: ~**se con** o **de** o **en** to be amazed at; to be fascinated by.

embocadura [embokàθōō'rá] *nf* narrow entrance; (*de río*) mouth; (*MUS*) mouthpiece.

embolado [embolá'ŏo] *nm* (*TEATRO*) bit part, minor role; (*fam*) trick.

embolia [embo'lyá] *nf* (*MED*) embolism; ~ **cerebral** clot on the brain.

émbolo [em'bolo] *nm* (*AUTO*) piston.

embolsar [embolsár'] *vt* to pocket, put in one's pocket.

emboquillado, a [embokēyá'ŏo, á] *a* (*cigarrillo*) tipped, filter *cpd*.

emborrachar [emborrátchár'] *vt* to make drunk; ~**se** *vr* to get drunk.

emboscada [emboská'ŏá] *nf* (*celada*) ambush.

embotar [embotár'] *vt* to blunt, dull; ~**se** *vr* (*adormecerse*) to go numb.

embotellamiento [emboteyámyen'to] *nm* (*AUTO*) traffic jam.

embotellar [emboteyár'] *vt* to bottle; ~**se** *vr* (*circulación*) to get into a jam.

embozo [embo'so] *nm* muffler, mask.

embragar [embrágár'] *vt* (*AUTO, TEC*) to engage; (*partes*) to connect ♦ *vi* to let in the clutch.

embrague [embrá'ge] *etc vb* V **embragar** ♦ *nm* (*tb*: **pedal de** ~) clutch.

embravecer [embráheser'] *vt* to enrage, infuriate; ~**se** *vr* to become furious; (*mar*) to get rough; (*tormenta*) to rage.

embravecido, a [embráhesē'ŏo, á] *a* (*mar*) rough; (*persona*) furious.

embriagador, a [embryágáthor', á] *a* intoxicating.

embriagar [embryágár'] *vt* (*emborrachar*) to make drunk; (*alegrar*) to delight; ~**se** *vr* (*emborracharse*) to get drunk.

embriague [embryá'ge] *etc vb* V **embriagar.**

embriaguez [embryáges'] *nf* (*borrachera*) drunkenness.

embrión [embryon'] *nm* embryo.

embrionario, a [embryoná'ryo, á] *a* embryonic.

embrollar [embroyár'] *vt* (*asunto*) to confuse, complicate; (*persona*) to involve, embroil; ~**se** *vr* (*confundirse*) to get into a mess.

embrollo [embro'yo] *nm* (*enredo*) confusion; (*aprieto*) fix, jam.

embromar [embromár'] *vt* (*burlarse de*) to tease, make fun of.

embrujado, a [embrōohá'ŏo, á] *a* (*persona*) bewitched; **casa embrujada** haunted house.

embrutecer [embrōoteser'] *vt* (*atontar*) to stupefy; ~**se** *vr* to be stupefied.

embrutezca [embrōotes'ká] *etc vb* V **embrutecer.**

embudo [embōo'ŏo] *nm* funnel.

embuste [embōo'ste] *nm* trick; (*mentira*) lie; (*hum*) fib.

embustero, a [embōoste'ro, á] *a* lying, deceitful ♦ *nm/f* (*tramposo*) cheat; (*mentiroso*) liar; (*hum*) fibber.

embutido [embōotē'ŏo] *nm* (*CULIN*) sausage; (*TEC*) inlay.

embutir [embōotēr'] *vt* to insert; (*TEC*) to inlay; (*llenar*) to pack tight, cram.

emergencia [emerhen'syá] *nf* emergency; (*surgimiento*) emergence.

emergente [emerhen'te] *a* resultant, consequent; (*nación*) emergent.

emerger [emerher'] *vi* to emerge, appear.

emeritense [emerēten'se] *a* of *o* from Mérida ♦ *nm/f* native *o* inhabitant of Mérida.

emerja [emer'há] *etc vb* V **emerger.**

emigración [emēgrásyon'] *nf* emigration; (*de pájaros*) migration.

emigrado, a [emēgrá'ŏo, á] *nm/f* emigrant; (*POL etc*) émigré(e).

emigrante [emēgrán'te] *a, nm/f* emigrant.

emigrar [emēgrár'] *vi* (*personas*) to emigrate; (*pájaros*) to migrate.

eminencia [emēnen'syá] *nf* eminence; (*en títulos*): **Su E~** His Eminence; **Vuestra E~** Your Eminence.

eminente [emēnen'te] *a* eminent, distinguished; (*elevado*) high.

emisario [emēsá'ryo] *nm* emissary.

emisión [emēsyon'] *nf* (*acto*) emission; (*COM etc*) issue; (*RADIO, TV*: *acto*) broadcasting; (: *programa*) broadcast, program (*US*), programme (*Brit*); ~ **de acciones** (*COM*) share issue; ~ **gratuita de acciones** (*COM*) rights issue; ~ **de valores** (*COM*) flotation.

emisor, a [emēsor', á] *nm* transmitter ♦ *nf* radio *o* broadcasting station.

emitir [emētēr'] *vt* (*olor etc*) to emit, give off; (*moneda etc*) to issue; (*opinión*) to express; (*voto*) to cast; (*señal*) to send out; (*RADIO*) to broadcast; ~ **una señal sonora** to beep.

emoción [emosyon'] *nf* emotion; (*excitación*) excitement; (*sentimiento*) feeling; **¡qué ~!** how exciting!; (*irónico*) what a thrill!

emocionado, a [emosyoná'ŏo, á] *a* deeply moved, stirred.

emocionante [emosyonán'te] *a* (*excitante*) exciting, thrilling.

emocionar [emosyonár'] *vt* (*excitar*) to excite, thrill; (*conmover*) to move, touch; (*impresionar*) to impress; ~**se** *vr* to get excited.

emotivo, a [emotē'ŏo, á] *a* emotional.

empacar [empákár'] *vt* (*gen*) to pack; (*en caja*) to bale, crate.

empacharse [empátchár'se] *vr* (*MED*) to get indigestion.

empacho [empátch'o] *nm* (*MED*) indigestion; (*fig*) embarrassment.

empadronamiento [empáŏronámyen'to]

nm census; *(de electores)* list of registered voters *(US)*, electoral register *(Brit)*.

empadronarse [cmpáthronár'sc] *vr* (*POL*: *como elector*) to register.

empalagar [cmpálágár'] *vt* (*suj: comida*) to cloy ♦ *vi* to pall.

empalagoso, a [cmpálágo'so, á] *a* cloying; *(fig)* tiresome.

empalague [cmpálá'gc] *etc vb V* **empalagar**.

empalizada [cmpálēsá'thá] *nf* fence; *(MIL)* palisade.

empalmar [cmpálmár'] *vt* to join, connect ♦ *vi* (*dos caminos*) to meet, join.

empalme [cmpál'mc] *nm* joint, connection; *(de vías)* junction; *(de trenes)* connection.

empanada [cmpáná'thá] *nf* pie.

empanar [cmpánár'] *vt* (*CULIN*) to cook *o* roll in breadcrumbs *o* pastry.

empantanarse [cmpántánár'sc] *vr* to get swamped; *(fig)* to get bogged down.

empañarse [cmpányár'sc] *vr* (*nublarse*) to get misty, steam up.

empapar [cmpápár'] *vt* (*mojar*) to soak, saturate; *(absorber)* to soak up, absorb; ~**se** *vr*: ~**se de** to soak up.

empapelar [cmpápclár'] *vt* (*paredes*) to paper.

empaque [cmpá'kc] *etc vb V* **empacar**.

empaquetar [cmpákctár'] *vt* to pack, package up; *(COM)* to package.

emparedado [cmpárcthá'tho] *nm* sandwich.

emparejar [cmpárchár'] *vt* to pair ♦ *vi* to catch up.

emparentar [cmpárcntár'] *vi*: ~ **con** to marry into.

empariente [cmpáryen'tc] *etc vb V* **emparentar**.

empastar [cmpástár'] *vt* (*embadurnar*) to paste; *(diente)* to fill.

empaste [cmpá'stc] *nm* (*de diente*) filling.

empatar [cmpátár'] *vi* to draw, tie.

empate [cmpá'tc] *nm* draw, tie; **un** ~ **a cero** a no-score draw.

empecé [cmpesc'], **empecemos** [cmpc- sc'mos] *etc vb V* **empezar**.

empecinado, a [cmpcsēná'tho, á] *a* (*AM*) stubborn.

empedernido, a [cmpcthcrnē'tho, á] *a* hard, heartless; *(fijado)* hardened, inveterate; **un fumador** ~ a heavy smoker.

empedrado, a [cmpcthrá'tho, á] *a* paved ♦ *nm* paving.

empedrar [cmpcthrár'] *vt* to pave.

empeine [cmpc'ēnc] *nm* (*de pie, zapato*) instep.

empellón [cmpcyon'] *nm* push, shove; **abrirse paso a empellones** to push *o* shove one's way past *o* through.

empeñado, a [cmpcnyá'tho, á] *a* (*persona*) determined; *(objeto)* pawned.

empeñar [cmpcnyár'] *vt* (*objeto*) to pawn, pledge; *(persona)* to compel; ~**se** *vr* (*obligarse*) to bind o.s., pledge o.s.; *(endeudarse)* to get into debt; ~**se en hacer** to be set on doing, be determined to do.

empeño [cmpc'nyo] *nm* (*determinación*) determination; *(cosa prendada)* pledge; **casa de** ~**s** pawnshop; **con** ~ insistently; *(con celo)* eagerly; **tener** ~ **en hacer algo** to be bent on doing sth.

empeoramiento [cmpcorámycn'to] *nm* worsening.

empeorar [cmpcorár'] *vt* to make worse, worsen ♦ *vi* to get worse, deteriorate.

empequeñecer [cmpckcnycscr'] *vt* to dwarf; *(fig)* to belittle.

empequeñezca [cmpckcnycs'ká] *etc vb V* **empequeñecer**.

emperador [cmpcráthor'] *nm* emperor.

emperatriz [cmpcrátrēs'] *nf* empress.

emperrarse [cmpcrrár'sc] *vr* to get stubborn; ~ **en algo** to persist in sth.

empezar [cmpcsár'] *vt, vi* to begin, start; **empezó a llover** it started to rain; **bueno, para** ~ well, to start with.

empiece [cmpyc'sc] *etc vb V* **empezar**.

empiedre [cmpyc'thrc] *etc vb V* **empedrar**.

empiezo [cmpyc'so] *etc vb V* **empezar**.

empinado, a [cmpēná'tho, á] *a* steep.

empinar [cmpēnár'] *vt* to raise; *(botella)* to tip up; ~**se** *vr* (*persona*) to stand on tiptoe; *(animal)* to rear up; *(camino)* to climb steeply; ~ **el codo** to booze *(fam)*.

empingorotado, a [cmpēngorotá'tho, á] *a* *(fam)* stuck-up.

empírico, a [cmpē'rēko, á] *a* empirical.

emplace [cmplá'sc] *etc vb V* **emplazar**.

emplaste [cmplá'stc], **emplasto** [cmplá'sto] *nm* (*MED*) plaster.

emplazamiento [cmplásámyén'to] *nm* site, location; *(JUR)* summons *sg*.

emplazar [cmplásár'] *vt* (*ubicar*) to site, place, locate; *(JUR)* to summons; *(convocar)* to summon.

empleado, a [cmpleá'tho, á] *nm/f* (*gen*) employee; *(de banco etc)* clerk; ~ **público** civil servant.

emplear [cmpleár'] *vt* (*usar*) to use, employ; *(dar trabajo a)* to employ; ~**se** *vr* (*conseguir trabajo*) to be employed; *(ocuparse)* to occupy o.s.; ~ **mal el tiempo** to waste time; **¡te está bien empleado!** it serves you right!

empleo [cmple'o] *nm* (*puesto*) job; *(puestos: colectivamente)* employment; *(uso)* use, employment; **"modo de** ~**"** "instructions for use".

emplumar [cmploomár'] *vt* (*estafar*) to swindle.

empobrecer [cmpobrcscr'] *vt* to impoverish; ~**se** *vr* to become poor *o* impoverished.

empobrecimiento [empobresēmyen'to] *nm* impoverishment.

empobrezca [empobres'ká] *etc vb* V **empobrecer.**

empolvar [empolßár'] *vt (cara)* to powder; ~**se** *vr* to powder one's face; *(superficie)* to get dusty.

empollar [empoyár'] *vt* to incubate; *(ESCOL fam)* to swot (up) ♦ *vi (gallina)* to brood; *(ESCOL fam)* to bone up.

empollón, ona [empoyon', oná] *nm/f (ESCOL fam)* swot.

emponzoñar [emponsonyár'] *vt (esp fig)* to poison.

emporio [empo'ryo] *nm* emporium, trading center; *(AM: gran almacén)* department store.

empotrado, a [empotrá'ðo, á] *a (armario etc)* built-in.

empotrar [empotrár'] *vt* to embed; *(armario etc)* to build in.

emprender [emprender'] *vt* to undertake; *(empezar)* to begin, embark on; *(acometer)* to tackle, take on; ~ **marcha a** to set out for.

empreñar [emprenyár'] *vt* to make pregnant; ~**se** *vr* to become pregnant.

empresa [empre'sá] *nf* enterprise; *(COM: sociedad)* firm, company; *(: negocio)* business; *(esp TEATRO)* management; ~ **filial** *(COM)* subsidiary company; ~ **matriz** *(COM)* parent company.

empresario, a [empresá'ryo, á] *nm/f (COM)* businessman/woman, entrepreneur; *(TEC)* manager; *(MUS: de ópera etc)* impresario; ~ **de pompas fúnebres** mortician *(US)*, undertaker *(Brit)*.

empréstito [empre'stēto] *nm* (public) loan; *(COM)* loan capital.

empujar [empōōhár'] *vt* to push, shove.

empuje [empōō'he] *nm* thrust; *(presión)* pressure; *(fig)* vigor *(US)*, vigour *(Brit)*, drive.

empujón [empōōhon'] *nm* push, shove; **abrirse paso a empujones** to shove one's way through.

empuñadura [empōōnyáðōō'rá] *nf (de espada)* hilt; *(de herramienta etc)* handle.

empuñar [empōōnyár'] *vt (asir)* to grasp, take (firm) hold of; ~ **las armas** *(fig)* to take up arms.

emulación [emōōlásyon'] *nf* emulation.

emular [emōōlár'] *vt* to emulate; *(rivalizar)* to rival.

émulo, a [e'mōōlo, á] *nm/f* rival, competitor.

en [en] *prep (gen)* in; *(sobre)* on, upon; *(tiempo)* in, on; *(tipo)* by; **meter** ~ **el bolsillo** to put in *o* into one's pocket; **vivir** ~ **Toledo** to live in Toledo; ~ **casa** at

home; **lo terminó** ~ **6 días** he finished it in 6 days; ~ **(el mes de) enero** in (the month of) January; ~ **aquel momento/aquella época** at that moment/that time; ~ **aquel día/aquella ocasión** on that day/that occasion; **ha aumentado** ~ **un 20 por ciento** it has increased by 20%; ~ **serio** seriously; ~ **fin** well, well then; **ir de puerta** ~ **puerta** to go from door to door; **(viajar)** ~ **tren** (to travel) by train.

enajenación [enáhenásyon'] *nf*, **enajenamiento** [enáhenámyen'to] *nm* alienation; *(fig: distracción)* absent-mindedness; *(: embelesamiento)* rapture, trance; ~ **mental** mental derangement.

enajenar [enáhenár'] *vt* to alienate; *(fig)* to carry away.

enamorado, a [enámorá'ðo, á] *a* in love ♦ *nm/f* lover; **estar** ~ **(de)** to be in love (with).

enamorar [enámorár'] *vt* to win the love of; ~**se** *vr:* ~**se (de)** to fall in love (with).

enano, a [ená'no, á] *a* tiny, dwarf ♦ *nm/f* dwarf; *(pey)* runt.

enarbolar [enárßolár'] *vt (bandera etc)* to hoist; *(espada etc)* to brandish.

enardecer [enárðeser'] *vt (pasiones)* to fire, inflame; *(persona)* to fill with enthusiasm; ~**se** *vr* to get excited; ~**se por** to get enthusiastic about.

enardezca [enárdes'ká] *etc vb* V **enardecer.**

encabece [enkáße'se] *etc vb* V **encabezar.**

encabezado [enkáßesá'ðo] *nm (COM)* header.

encabezamiento [enkáßesámyen'to] *nm (de carta)* heading; *(COM)* billhead, letterhead; *(de periódico)* headline; *(preámbulo)* foreword, preface; ~ **normal** *(TIP etc)* running head.

encabezar [enkáßesár'] *vt (movimiento, revolución)* to lead, head; *(lista)* to head; *(carta)* to put a heading to; *(libro)* to entitle.

encadenar [enkáðenár'] *vt* to chain (together); *(poner grilletes a)* to shackle.

encajar [enkáhár'] *vt (ajustar):* ~ **en** to fit (into); *(meter a la fuerza)* to push in; *(máquina etc)* to house; *(partes)* to join; *(fam: golpe)* to give, deal; *(entrometer)* to insert ♦ *vi* to fit (well); *(fig: corresponder a)* to match; ~**se** *vr:* ~**se en un sillón** to squeeze into a chair.

encaje [enká'he] *nm (labor)* lace.

encajonar [enkáhonár'] *vt* to box (up), put in a box.

encalar [enkálár'] *vt (pared)* to whitewash.

encallar [enkáyár'] *vi (NAUT)* to run aground.

encaminado, a [enkámēná'ðo, á] *a:* **medidas encaminadas a ...** measures designed to *o* aimed at ...

encaminar [enkámēnár'] *vt* to direct, send; ~**se** *vr*: ~**se a** to set out for; ~ **por** (*expedición etc*) to route via.

encandilar [enkándēlár'] *vt* to dazzle; (*persona*) to daze, bewilder.

encanecer [enkáneser'] *vi*, **encanecerse** *vr* (*pelo*) to go grey.

encanezca [enkánes'ká] *etc vb V* **encanecer**.

encantado, a [enkántá'ǒo, á] *a* delighted; ¡~! how do you do!, pleased to meet you.

encantador, a [enkántáǒor', á] *a* charming, lovely ♦ *nm/f* magician, enchanter/enchantress.

encantar [enkántár'] *vt* to charm, delight; (*cautivar*) to fascinate; (*hechizar*) to bewitch, cast a spell on.

encanto [enkán'to] *nm* (*magia*) spell, charm; (*fig*) charm, delight; (*expresión de ternura*) sweetheart; **como por** ~ as if by magic.

encapotado, a [enkápotá'ǒo, á] *a* (*cielo*) overcast.

encapricharse [enkáprētchár'se] *vr*: **se ha encaprichado con ir** ... he's taken it into his head to go ...; **se ha encaprichado** he's digging his heels in.

encaramar [enkárámár'] *vt* (*subir*) to raise, lift up; ~**se** *vr* (*subir*) to perch; ~**se a** (*árbol etc*) to climb.

encararse [enkárár'se] *vr*: ~ **a** *o* **con** to confront, come face to face with.

encarcelar [enkárselár'] *vt* to imprison, jail.

encarecer [enkáreser'] *vt* to raise the price of ♦ *vi*, ~**se** *vr* to get more expensive.

encarecidamente [enkáresēǒámen'te] *ad* earnestly.

encarecimiento [enkáresēmyen'to] *nm* price increase.

encarezca [enkáres'ká] *etc vb V* **encarecer**.

encargado, a [enkárgá'ǒo, á] *a* in charge ♦ *nm/f* agent, representative; (*responsable*) person in charge.

encargar [enkárgár'] *vt* to entrust; (*COM*) to order; (*recomendar*) to urge, recommend; ~**se** *vr*: ~**se de** to look after, take charge of; ~ **algo a uno** to put sb in charge of sth.

encargo [enkár'ɣo] *nm* (*pedido*) assignment, job; (*responsabilidad*) responsibility; (*recomendación*) recommendation; (*COM*) order.

encargue [enkár'ɣe] *etc vb V* **encargar**.

encariñarse [enkáreñyár'se] *vr*: ~ **con** to grow fond of, get attached to.

encarnación [enkárnásyon'] *nf* incarnation, embodiment.

encarnado, a [enkárná'ǒo, á] *a* (*color*) red; **ponerse** ~ to blush.

encarnar [enkárnár'] *vt* to personify; (*TEATRO: papel*) to play ♦ *vi* (*REL etc*) to become incarnate.

encarnizado, a [enkárnēsá'ǒo, á] *a* (*lucha*) bloody, fierce.

encarrilar [enkárrēlár'] *vt* (*tren*) to put back on the rails; (*fig*) to correct, put on the right track.

encasillar [enkáseyár'] *vt* (*TEATRO*) to typecast; (*clasificar: pey*) to pigeonhole.

encauce [enká'ōōse] *etc vb V* **encauzar**.

encausar [enkáōōsár'] *vt* to prosecute, sue.

encauzar [enkáōōsár'] *vt* to channel; (*fig*) to direct.

encendedor [ensendeǒor'] *nm* lighter.

encender [ensender'] *vt* (*con fuego*) to light; (*incendiar*) to set fire to; (*luz, radio*) to put on, switch on; (*INFORM*) to toggle on, switch on; (*avivar: pasiones etc*) to inflame; (*despertar: entusiasmo*) to arouse; (: *odio*) to awaken; ~**se** *vr* to catch fire; (*excitarse*) to get excited; (*de cólera*) to flare up; (*el rostro*) to blush.

encendidamente [ensendēǒámen'te] *ad* passionately.

encendido, a [ensendē'ǒo, á] *a* alight; (*aparato*) (switched) on; (*mejillas*) glowing; (*cara: por el vino etc*) flushed; (*mirada*) passionate ♦ *nm* (*AUTO*) ignition; (*de faroles*) lighting.

encerado, a [enserá'ǒo, á] *a* (*suelo*) waxed, polished ♦ *nm* (*ESCOL*) blackboard; (*hule*) oilcloth.

encerar [enserár'] *vt* (*suelo*) to wax, polish.

encerrar [enserrár'] *vt* (*confinar*) to shut in *o* up; (*con llave*) to lock in *o* up; (*comprender, incluir*) to include, contain; ~**se** *vr* to shut *o* lock o.s. up *o* in.

encerrona [enserro'ná] *nf* trap.

encía [ensē'á] *nf* (*ANAT*) gum.

enciclopedia [ensēklope'ǒyá] *nf* encyclopedia.

encienda [ensyen'dá] *etc vb V* **encender**.

encierro [ensye'rro] *etc vb V* **encerrar** ♦ *nm* shutting in *o* up; (*calabozo*) prison; (*AGR*) pen; (*TAUR*) penning.

encima [ensē'má] *ad* (*sobre*) above, over; (*además*) besides; ~ **de** (*en*) on, on top of; (*sobre*) above, over; (*además de*) besides, on top of; **por** ~ **de** over; ¿**llevas dinero** ~**?** have you (got) any money on you?; **se me vino** ~ it took me by surprise.

encina [ensē'ná] *nf* (holm) oak.

encinta [ensēn'tá] *af* pregnant.

enclenque [enklen'ke] *a* weak, sickly.

encoger [enkoher'] *vt* (*gen*) to shrink, contract; (*fig: asustar*) to scare; (: *desanimar*) to discourage; ~**se** *vr* to shrink, contract; (*fig*) to cringe; ~**se de hombros** to shrug one's shoulders.

encoja [enko'há] *etc vb V* **encoger**.

encojar [enkohár'] *vt* to lame; (*tullir*) to cripple; ~**se** *vr* to go lame; to become crippled.

encolar [enkolár'] vt (engomar) to glue, paste; (pegar) to stick down.

encolerice [enkolerē'se], etc vb V **encolerizar.**

encolerizar [enkolerēsár'] vt to anger, provoke; ~**se** vr to get angry.

encomendar [enkomendár'] vt to entrust, commend; ~**se** vr: ~**se a** to put one's trust in.

encomiar [enkomyár'] vt to praise, pay tribute to.

encomienda [enkomyen'dá] etc vb V **encomendar ♦** nf (encargo) charge, commission; (elogio) tribute; ~ **postal** (AM) parcel post.

encomio [enko'myo] nm praise, tribute.

encono [enko'no] nm (rencor) rancor (US), rancour (Brit), spite.

encontrado, a [enkontrá'ho, á] a (contrario) contrary, conflicting; (hostil) hostile.

encontrar [enkontrár'] vt (hallar) to find; (inesperadamente) to meet, run into; ~**se** vr to meet (each other); (situarse) to be (situated); (persona) to find o.s., be; (entrar en conflicto) to crash, collide; ~**se con** to meet; ~**se bien (de salud)** to feel well; **no se encuentra aquí en este momento** he's not in at the moment.

encontronazo [enkontroná'so] nm collision, crash.

encorvar [enkorhár'] vt to curve; (inclinar) to bend (down); ~**se** vr to bend down, bend over.

encrespado, a [enkrespá'ho, á] a (pelo) curly; (mar) rough.

encrespar [enkrespár'] vt (cabellos) to curl; (fig) to anger, irritate; ~**se** vr (el mar) to get rough; (fig) to get cross o irritated.

encrucijada [enkrōōsēhá'há] nf crossroads sg; (empalme) junction.

encuadernación [enkwáhernásyon'] nf binding; (taller) bindery.

encuadernador, a [enkwáhernáhor', á] nm/f bookbinder.

encuadrar [enkwáhrár'] vt (retrato) to frame; (ajustar) to fit, insert; (encerrar) to contain.

encubierto [enkōōhyer'to] pp de **encubrir.**

encubrir [enkōōhrēr'] vt (ocultar) to hide, conceal; (criminal) to harbor (US), harbour (Brit), shelter; (ayudar) to be an accomplice in.

encuentro [enkwen'tro] etc vb V **encontrar ♦** nm (de personas) meeting; (AUTO etc) collision, crash; (DEPORTE) match, game; (MIL) encounter.

encuesta [enkwe'stá] nf inquiry, investigation; (sondeo) public opinion poll; ~ **judicial** post mortem.

encumbrado, a [enkōōmbrá'ho, á] a eminent, distinguished.

encumbrar [enkōōmbrár'] vt (persona) to exalt; ~**se** vr (fig) to become conceited.

encharcar [entchárkár'] vt to swamp, flood; ~**se** vr to become flooded.

encharque [entchár'ke] etc vb V **encharcar.**

enchufar [entchōōfár'] vt (ELEC) to plug in; (TEC) to connect, fit together; (COM) to merge.

enchufe [entchōō'fe] nm (ELEC: clavija) plug; (: toma) socket; (de dos tubos) joint, connection; (fam: influencia) contact, connection; (: puesto) cushy job; ~ **de clavija** jack plug; **tiene un ~ en el ministerio** he can pull strings at the ministry.

endeble [ende'hle] a (argumento, excusa, persona) weak.

endemoniado, a [endemonyá'ho, á] a possessed (of the devil); (travieso) devilish.

enderece [endere'se] etc vb V **enderezar.**

enderezar [endéresár'] vt (poner derecho) to straighten (out); (: verticalmente) to set upright; (fig) to straighten o sort out; (dirigir) to direct; ~**se** vr (persona sentada) to sit up straight.

endeudarse [endeōōhár'se] vr to get into debt.

endiablado, a [endyáhlá'ho, á] a devilish, diabolical; (hum) mischievous.

endilgar [endēlgár'] vt (fam): ~ **algo a uno** to saddle sb with sth; ~ **un sermón a uno** to give sb a lecture.

endilgue [endēl'ge] etc vb V **endilgar.**

endomingarse [endomēngár'se] vr to dress up, put on one's best clothes.

endomingue [endomēn'ge] etc vb V **endomingarse.**

endosante [endosán'te] nm/f endorser.

endosar [endosár'] vt (cheque etc) to endorse.

endulce [endōōl'se] etc vb V **endulzar.**

endulzar [endōōlsár'] vt to sweeten; (suavizar) to soften.

endurecer [endōōreser'] vt to harden; ~**se** vr to harden, grow hard.

endurecido, a [endōōresē'ho, á] a (duro) hard; (fig) hardy, tough; **estar ~ a algo** to be hardened o used to sth.

endurezca [endōōres'ká] etc vb V **endurecer.**

ene. abr (= enero) Jan.

enemigo, a [enemē'go, á] a enemy, hostile ♦ nm/f enemy ♦ nf enmity, hostility; **ser ~ de** (persona) to dislike; (suj: tendencia) to be inimical to.

enemistad [enemēstáh'] nf enmity.

enemistar [enemēstár'] vt to make enemies of, cause a rift between; ~**se** vr to become enemies; (amigos) to have a falling out (US), fall out (Brit).

energético, a [enerhe'tēko, á] a: **política**

energética energy policy.
energía [enerhē'á] *nf* (*vigor*) energy, drive; (*TEC*, *ELEC*) energy, power.
enérgico, a [ener'hēko, á] *a* (*gen*) energetic; (*ataque*) vigorous; (*ejercicio*) strenuous; (*medida*) bold; (*voz, modales*) forceful.
energúmeno, a [energōō'meno, á] *nm/f* madman/woman; **ponerse como un ~ con uno** to get furious with sb.
enero [ene'ro] *nm* January.
enervar [enerhár'] *vt* (*poner nervioso a*) to get on sb's nerves.
enésimo, a [ene'sēmo, á] *a* (*MAT*) nth; **por enésima vez** (*fig*) for the umpteenth time.
enfadado, a [enfáthá'tho, á] *a* angry, annoyed.
enfadar [enfáthár'] *vt* to anger, annoy; **~se** *vr* to get angry o annoyed.
enfado [enfá'tho] *nm* (*enojo*) anger, annoyance; (*disgusto*) trouble, bother.
énfasis [en'fásēs] *nm* emphasis, stress; **poner ~ en** to stress.
enfático, a [enfá'tēko, á] *a* emphatic.
enfatizado, a [enfátēsá'tho, á] *a*: **en caracteres ~s** (*INFORM*) emphasized.
enfermar [enfermár'] *vt* to make ill ♦ *vi* to fall ill, be taken ill; **su actitud me enferma** his attitude makes me sick; **~ del corazón** to develop heart trouble.
enfermedad [enfermetháth'] *nf* illness; **~ venérea** venereal disease.
enfermera [enferme'rá] *nf* V **enfermero**.
enfermería [enfermerē'á] *nf* infirmary; (*de colegio etc*) sick bay.
enfermero, a [enferme'ro, á] *nm* (male) nurse ♦ *nf* nurse; **enfermera jefa** head nurse (*US*), matron (*Brit*).
enfermizo, a [enfermē'so, á] *a* (*persona*) sickly, unhealthy; (*fig*) unhealthy.
enfermo, a [enfer'mo, á] *a* ill, sick ♦ *nm/f* invalid, sick person; (*en hospital*) patient.
enfilar [enfēlár'] *vt* (*aguja*) to thread; (*calle*) to go down.
enflaquecer [enflákeser'] *vt* (*adelgazar*) to make thin; (*debilitar*) to weaken.
enflaquezca [enflákes'ká] *etc vb* V **enflaquecer**.
enfocar [enfokár'] *vt* (*foto etc*) to focus; (*problema etc*) to consider, look at.
enfoque [enfo'ke] *etc vb* V **enfocar** ♦ *nm* focus; (*acto*) focusing; (*óptica*) approach.
enfrascado, a [enfráská'tho, á] *a*: **estar ~ en algo** (*fig*) to be wrapped up in sth.
enfrascar [enfráskár'] *vt* to bottle; **~se** *vr*: **~se en un libro** to bury o.s. in a book.
enfrasque [enfrás'ke] *etc vb* V **enfrascar**.
enfrentamiento [enfrentámyen'to] *nm* confrontation.
enfrentar [enfrentár'] *vt* (*peligro*) to face (up to), confront; (*oponer*) to bring face to

face; **~se** *vr* (*dos personas*) to face o confront each other; (*DEPORTE: dos equipos*) to meet; **~se a o con** to face up to, confront.
enfrente [enfren'te] *ad* opposite; **~ de** *prep* opposite, facing; **la casa de ~** the house opposite, the house across the street.
enfriamiento [enfrēámyen'to] *nm* chilling, refrigeration; (*MED*) cold, chill.
enfriar [enfrēár'] *vt* (*alimentos*) to cool, chill; (*algo caliente*) to cool down; (*habitación*) to air, freshen; (*entusiasmo*) to dampen; **~se** *vr* to cool down; (*MED*) to get chilled (*US*), catch a chill (*Brit*); (*amistad*) to cool.
enfurecer [enfōōreser'] *vt* to enrage, madden; **~se** *vr* to become furious, fly into a rage; (*mar*) to get rough.
enfurezca [enfōōres'ká] *etc vb* V **enfurecer**.
engalanar [engálánár'] *vt* (*adornar*) to adorn; (*ciudad*) to decorate; **~se** *vr* to get dressed up.
enganchar [engántchár'] *vt* to hook; (*ropa*) to hang up; (*dos vagones*) to hitch up; (*TEC*) to couple, connect; (*MIL*) to recruit; (*fam: atraer: persona*) to rope into; **~se** *vr* (*MIL*) to enlist, join up; **~se (a)** (*drogas*) to get hooked (on).
enganche [engántch'e] *nm* hook; (*TEC*) coupling, connection; (*acto*) hooking (up); (*MIL*) recruitment, enlistment; (*AM: depósito*) deposit.
engañar [engányár'] *vt* to deceive; (*estafar*) to cheat, swindle ♦ *vi*: **las apariencias engañan** appearances are deceptive; **~se** *vr* (*equivocarse*) to be wrong; (*asimismo*) to deceive o kid o.s.; **engaña a su mujer** he's unfaithful to o cheats on his wife.
engaño [engá'nyo] *nm* deceit; (*estafa*) trick, swindle; (*error*) mistake, misunderstanding; (*ilusión*) delusion.
engañoso, a [engányo'so, á] *a* (*tramposo*) crooked; (*mentiroso*) dishonest, deceitful; (*aspecto*) deceptive; (*consejo*) misleading.
engarce [engár'se] *etc vb* V **engarzar**.
engarzar [engársár'] *vt* (*joya*) to set, mount; (*fig*) to link, connect.
engatusar [engátōōsár'] *vt* (*fam*) to coax.
engendrar [enhendrár'] *vt* to breed; (*procrear*) to beget; (*fig*) to cause, produce.
engendro [enhen'dro] *nm* (*BIO*) fetus; (*fig*) monstrosity; (*idea*) brainchild.
englobar [englohár'] *vt* (*comprender*) to include, comprise; (*incluir*) to lump together.
engomar [engomár'] *vt* to glue, stick.
engordar [engorthár'] *vt* to fatten ♦ *vi* to get fat, put on weight.
engorro [engo'rro] *nm* bother, nuisance.
engorroso, a [engorro'so, á] *a* bothersome, trying.
engranaje [engráná'he] *nm* (*AUTO*) gear;

(*juego*) gears *pl*.

engrandecer |engrándeser'| *vt* to enlarge, magnify; (*alabar*) to praise, speak highly of; (*exagerar*) to exaggerate.

engrandezca |engrándes'ká| *etc vb* V **engrandecer.**

engrasar |engrásár'| *vt* (*TEC*: *poner grasa*) to grease; (: *lubricar*) to lubricate, oil; (*manchar*) to make greasy.

engrase |engrá'se| *nm* greasing, lubrication.

engreído, a |engreē'tho, á| *a* vain, conceited.

engrosar |engrosár'| *vt* (*ensanchar*) to enlarge; (*aumentar*) to increase; (*hinchar*) to swell.

engrudo |engroō'tho| *nm* paste.

engruese |engrwe'se| *etc vb* V **engrosar.**

engullir |engoōyēr'| *vt* to gobble, gulp (down).

enhebrar |enehrár'| *vt* to thread.

enhiesto, a |enye'sto, á| *a* (*derecho*) erect; (*bandera*) raised; (*edificio*) lofty.

enhorabuena |enoráhwe'ná| *excl* congratulations.

enigma |enēg'má| *nm* enigma; (*problema*) puzzle; (*misterio*) mystery.

enigmático, a |enēgmá'tēko, á| *a* enigmatic.

enjabonar |enháhonár'| *vt* to soap; (*barba*) to lather; (*fam*: *adular*) to soft-soap; (: *regañar*) to tick off.

enjalbegar |enhálhegár'| *vt* (*pared*) to whitewash.

enjalbegue |enhálhe'ge| *etc vb* V **enjalbegar.**

enjambre |enhám'hre| *nm* swarm.

enjaular |enháoōlár'| *vt* to (put in a) cage; (*fam*) to jail, lock up.

enjuagadientes |enhwágádyen'tes| *nm inv* mouthwash.

enjuagar |enhwágár'| *vt* (*ropa*) to rinse (out).

enjuague |enhwá'ge| *etc vb* V **enjuagar** ♦ *nm* (*MED*) mouthwash; (*de ropa*) rinse, rinsing.

enjugar |enhoōgár'| *vt* to wipe (off); (*lágrimas*) to dry; (*déficit*) to wipe out.

enjugue |enhoō'ge| *etc vb* V **enjugar.**

enjuiciar |enhwēsyár'| *vt* (*JUR*: *procesar*) to prosecute, try; (*fig*) to judge.

enjuto, a |enhoō'to, á| *a* dry, dried up; (*fig*) lean, skinny.

enlace |enlá'se| *etc vb* V **enlazar** ♦ *nm* link, connection; (*relación*) relationship; (*tb*: ~ **matrimonial**) marriage; (*de trenes*) connection; ~ **de datos** data link; ~ **sindical** shop steward; ~ **telefónico** telephone link-up.

enlazar |enlásár'| *vt* (*unir con lazos*) to bind together; (*atar*) to tie; (*conectar*) to link, connect; (*AM*) to lasso.

enlodar |enlothár'| *vt* to cover in mud; (*fig*: *manchar*) to stain; (: *rebajar*) to debase.

enloquecer |enlokeser'| *vt* to drive mad ♦ *vi*, ~**se** *vr* to go mad.

enloquezca |enlokes'ká| *etc vb* V **enloquecer.**

enlutado, a |enloōtá'tho, á| *a* (*persona*) in mourning.

enlutar |enloōtár'| *vt* to dress in mourning; ~**se** *vr* to go into mourning.

enmarañar |enmárányár'| *vt* (*enredar*) to tangle up, entangle; (*complicar*) to complicate; (*confundir*) to confuse; ~**se** *vr* (*enredarse*) to become entangled; (*confundirse*) to get confused.

enmarcar |enmárkár'| *vt* (*cuadro*) to frame; (*fig*) to provide a setting for.

enmarque |enmár'ke| *etc vb* V **enmarcar.**

enmascarar |enmáskárár'| *vt* to mask; (*intenciones*) to disguise; ~**se** *vr* to put on a mask.

enmendar |enmendár'| *vt* to emend, correct; (*constitución etc*) to amend; (*comportamiento*) to reform; ~**se** *vr* to reform, mend one's ways.

enmienda |enmyen'dá| *etc vb* V **enmendar** ♦ *nf* correction; amendment; reform.

enmohecerse |enmoeser'se| *vr* (*metal*) to rust, go rusty; (*muro*, *plantas*) to go moldy.

enmohezca |enmoes'ká| *etc vb* V **enmohecerse.**

enmudecer |enmoōtheser'| *vt* to silence ♦ *vi*, ~**se** *vr* (*perder el habla*) to fall silent; (*guardar silencio*) to remain silent; (*por miedo*) to be struck dumb.

enmudezca |enmoōthes'ká| *etc vb* V **enmudecer.**

ennegrecer |ennegreser'| *vt* (*poner negro*) to blacken; (*oscurecer*) to darken; ~**se** *vr* to turn black; (*oscurecerse*) to get dark, darken.

ennegrezca |ennegres'ká| *etc vb* V **ennegrecer.**

ennoblecer |ennohleser'| *vt* to ennoble.

ennoblezca |ennohles'ká| *etc vb* V **ennoblecer.**

en.º *abr* (= *enero*) Jan.

enojadizo, a |enoháthē'so, á| *a* irritable, short-tempered.

enojar |enohár'| *vt* (*encolerizar*) to anger; (*disgustar*) to annoy, upset; ~**se** *vr* to get angry; to get annoyed.

enojo |eno'ho| *nm* (*cólera*) anger; (*irritación*) annoyance; ~**s** *nmpl* trials, problems.

enojoso, a |enoho'so, á| *a* annoying.

enorgullecerse |enorgoōyeser'se| *vr* to be proud; ~ **de** to pride o.s. on, be proud of.

enorgullezca |enorgoōyes'ká| *etc vb* V **enorgullecerse.**

enorme |enor'me| *a* enormous, huge; (*fig*)

monstrous.

enormidad [enormɛ̃tháth'] *nf* hugeness, immensity.

enraice [enráè'se] *etc vb* V **enraizar**.

enraizar [enráèsár'] *vi* to take root.

enrarecido, a [enráresē'tho, á] *a* rarefied.

enredadera [enretháthe'rá] *nf* (BOT) creeper, climbing plant.

enredar [enrethár'] *vt* (cables, hilos etc) to tangle (up), entangle; (situación) to complicate, confuse; (meter cizaña) to sow discord among o between; (implicar) to embroil, implicate; ~se *vr* to get entangled, get tangled (up); (situación) to get complicated; (persona) to get embroiled; (AM: fam) to meddle.

enredo [enre'tho] *nm* (maraña) tangle; (confusión) mix-up, confusion; (intriga) intrigue; (apuro) jam; (amorío) love affair.

enrejado [enrehá'tho] *nm* grating; (de ventana) lattice; (en jardín) trellis.

enrevesado, a [enrebesá'tho, á] *a* (asunto) complicated, involved.

enriquecer [enrēkeser'] *vt* to make rich; (fig) to enrich; ~se *vr* to get rich.

enriquezca [enrēkes'ká] *etc vb* V **enriquecer**.

enrojecer [enroheser'] *vt* to redden ♦ *vi*, ~se *vr* (persona) to blush.

enrojezca [enrohes'ká] *etc vb* V **enrojecer**.

enrolar [enrolár'] *vt* (MIL) to enlist; (reclutar) to recruit; ~se *vr* (MIL) to join up; (afiliarse) to enrol, sign on.

enrollar [enroyár'] *vt* to roll (up), wind (up); ~se *vr*: ~se con uno to get involved with sb.

enroque [enro'ke] *nm* (AJEDREZ) castling.

enroscar [enroskár'] *vt* (torcer, doblar) to twist; (arrollar) to coil (round), wind; (tornillo, rosca) to screw in; ~se *vr* to coil, wind.

enrosque [enros'ke] *etc vb* V **enroscar**.

ensalada [ensálá'thá] *nf* salad; (lío) mix-up.

ensaladilla [ensáláthe'yá] *nf* (tb: ~ rusa) ≈ Russian salad.

ensalce [ensál'se] *etc vb* V **ensalzar**.

ensalzar [ensálsár'] *vt* (alabar) to praise, extol; (exaltar) to exalt.

ensamblador [ensámblàthor'] *nm* (INFORM) assembler.

ensambladura [ensámblàthōō'rá] *nf*, **ensamblaje** [ensámblá'he] *nm* assembly; (TEC) joint.

ensamblar [ensámblár'] *vt* (montar) to assemble; (madera etc) to join.

ensanchar [ensántchár'] *vt* (hacer más ancho) to widen; (agrandar) to enlarge, expand; (COSTURA) to let out; ~se *vr* to get wider, expand; (pey) to put on airs.

ensanche [ensántch'e] *nm* (de calle) widening; (de negocio) expansion.

ensangrentado, a [ensángrentá'tho, á] *a* bloodstained, covered with blood.

ensangrentar [ensángrentár'] *vt* to stain with blood.

ensangriente [ensángryen'te] *etc vb* V **ensangrentar**.

ensañar [ensáñár'] *vt* to enrage; ~se *vr*: ~se con to treat brutally.

ensartar [ensártár'] *vt* (gen) to string (together); (carne) to spit, skewer.

ensayar [ensáyár'] *vt* to test, try (out); (TEATRO) to rehearse.

ensayista [ensáyē'stá] *nm/f* essayist.

ensayo [ensá'yo] *nm* test, trial; (QUÍMICA) experiment; (TEATRO) rehearsal; (DEPORTE) try; (ESCOL, LITERATURA) essay; pedido de ~ (COM) trial order; ~ general (TEATRO) dress rehearsal; (MUS) full rehearsal.

ensenada [ensená'thá] *nf* inlet, cove.

enseña [ense'nyá] *nf* ensign, standard.

enseñante [ensenyán'te] *nm/f* teacher.

enseñanza [ensenyán'sá] *nf* (educación) education; (acción) teaching; (doctrina) teaching, doctrine; ~ primaria/ secundaria/superior primary/secondary/ higher education.

enseñar [ensenyár'] *vt* (educar) to teach; (instruir) to teach, instruct; (mostrar, señalar) to show.

enseres [ense'res] *nmpl* belongings.

ENSIDESA [ensēthe'sá] *abr* (Esp COM) = Empresa Nacional Siderúrgica, S. A.

ensillar [ensēyár'] *vt* to saddle (up).

ensimismarse [ensēmēsmár'se] *vr* (abstraerse) to become lost in thought; (estar absorto) to be lost in thought; (AM) to become conceited.

ensordecer [ensortheser'] *vt* to deafen ♦ *vi* to go deaf.

ensordezca [ensorthes'ká] *etc vb* V **ensordecer**.

ensortijado, a [ensortēhá'tho, á] *a* (pelo) curly.

ensuciar [ensōōsyár'] *vt* (manchar) to dirty, soil; (fig) to defile; ~se *vr* (mancharse) to get dirty; (niño) to dirty (o wet) o.s.

ensueño [enswe'nyo] *nm* (sueño) dream, fantasy; (ilusión) illusion; (soñando despierto) daydream; de ~ dream-like.

entablado [entáblá'tho] *nm* (piso) floorboards *pl*; (armazón) boarding.

entablar [entáblár'] *vt* (recubrir) to board (up); (AJEDREZ, DAMAS) to set up; (conversación) to strike up; (JUR) to file ♦ *vi* to draw.

entablillar [entáblēyár'] *vt* (MED) to (put in a) splint.

entallar [entáyár'] *vt* (traje) to tailor ♦ *vi*: el traje entalla bien the suit fits well.

ente [en'te] *nm* (organización) body, organization; (*compañía*) company; (*fam: perso-na*) odd character; (*ser*) being; ~ **público** (*Esp*) state(-owned) body.

entender [entender'] *vt* (*comprender*) to understand; (*darse cuenta*) to realize; (*querer decir*) to mean ♦ *vi* to understand; (*creer*) to think, believe ♦ *nm*: **a mi** ~ in my opinion; ~ **de** to know all about; ~ **algo de** to know a little about; ~ **en** to deal with, have to do with; ~**se** *vr* (*comprenderse*) to be understood; (*2 personas*) to get on together; (*ponerse de acuerdo*) to agree, reach an agreement; **dar a** ~ **que** ... to lead to believe that ...; ~**se mal** not to get along; **¿entiendes?** (do you) understand?

entendido, a [entendē'ᵗђo, á] *a* (*comprendido*) understood; (*hábil*) skilled; (*inteligente*) knowledgeable ♦ *nm/f* (*experto*) expert ♦ *excl* agreed!

entendimiento [entendēmyen'to] *nm* (*comprensión*) understanding; (*inteligencia*) mind, intellect; (*juicio*) judgement.

enterado, a [enterá'ᵗђo, á] *a* well-informed; **estar** ~ **de** to know about, be aware of; **no darse por** ~ to pretend not to understand.

enteramente [enterámen'te] *ad* entirely, completely.

enterar [enterár'] *vt* (*informar*) to inform, tell; ~**se** *vr*: ~**se de** to find out about.

entereza [entere'sá] *nf* (*totalidad*) entirety; (*fig: carácter*) strength of mind; (*honradez*) integrity.

enternecedor, a [enternesēᵗђor', á] *a* touching.

enternecer [enterneser'] *vt* (*ablandar*) to soften; (*apiadar*) to touch, move; ~**se** *vr* to be touched, be moved.

enternezca [enternes'ká] *etc vb* V **enternecer.**

entero, a [ente'ro, á] *a* (*total*) whole, entire; (*fig: recto*) honest; (: *firme*) firm, resolute ♦ *nm* (*MAT*) integer; (*COM: punto*) point; (*AM: pago*) payment; **las acciones han subido dos** ~**s** the shares have gone up two points.

enterrador [enterráᵗђor'] *nm* gravedigger.

enterrar [enterrár'] *vt* to bury; (*fig*) to forget.

entibiar [entēᵗђyár'] *vt* (*enfriar*) to cool; (*calentar*) to warm; ~**se** *vr* (*fig*) to cool.

entidad [entēᵗђáᵗђ'] *nf* (*empresa*) firm, company; (*organismo*) body; (*sociedad*) society; (*FILOSOFÍA*) entity.

entienda [entyen'dá] *etc vb* V **entender.**

entierro [entye'rro] *etc vb* V **enterrar** ♦ *nm* (*acción*) burial; (*funeral*) funeral.

entomología [entomolohē'á] *nf* entomology.

entomólogo, a [entomo'logo, á] *nm/f* entomologist.

entonación [entonàsyon'] *nf* (*LING*) intonation; (*fig*) conceit.

entonar [entonár'] *vt* (*canción*) to intone; (*colores*) to tone; (*MED*) to tone up ♦ *vi* to be in tune; ~**se** *vr* (*engreírse*) to put on airs.

entonces [enton'ses] *ad* then, at that time; **desde** ~ since then; **en aquel** ~ at that time; (**pues**) ~ and so; **el** ~ **embajador de España** the then Spanish ambassador.

entornar [entornár'] *vt* (*puerta, ventana*) to half close, leave ajar; (*los ojos*) to half-close.

entorno [entor'no] *nm* setting, environment; ~ **de redes** (*INFORM*) network environment.

entorpecer [entorpeser'] *vt* (*entendimiento*) to dull; (*impedir*) to obstruct, hinder; (: *tránsito*) to slow down, delay.

entorpezca [entorpes'ká] *etc vb* V **entorpecer.**

entrado, a [entrá'ᵗђo, á] *a*: ~ **en años** elderly; (**una vez**) ~ **el verano** in the summer(time), when summer comes ♦ *nf* (*acción*) entry, access; (*sitio*) entrance, way in; (*principio*) beginning; (*COM*) receipts *pl*, takings *pl*; (*CULIN*) entrée; (*DEPORTE*) innings *sg*; (*TEATRO*) house, audience; (*para el cine etc*) ticket; (*INFORM*) input; (*ECON*): **entradas** *nfpl* income *sg*; **entradas brutas** gross receipts; **entradas y salidas** (*COM*) income and expenditure; **entrada de aire** (*TEC*) air intake *o* inlet; **de entrada** right away; "**entrada gratis**" "admission free"; **entrada de datos vocal** (*INFORM*) voice input; **tiene entradas** he's losing his hair.

entrante [entrán'te] *a* next, coming; (*POL*) incoming ♦ *nm* inlet; (*CULIN*) starter; **mes/año** ~ next month/year.

entraña [entrá'nyá] *nf* (*fig: centro*) heart, core; (*raíz*) root; ~**s** *nfpl* (*ANAT*) entrails; (*fig*) heart *sg*.

entrañable [entrànyá'ᵇle] *a* close, intimate.

entrañar [entrànyár'] *vt* to entail.

entrar [entrár'] *vt* (*introducir*) to bring in; (*persona*) to show in; (*INFORM*) to input ♦ *vi* (*meterse*) to go *o* come in, enter; (*comenzar*): ~ **diciendo** to begin by saying; **le entraron ganas de reír** he felt a sudden urge to laugh; **no me entra** I can't get the hang of it.

entre [en'tre] *prep* (*dos*) between; (*en medio de*) among(st); (*por*): **se abrieron paso** ~ **la multitud** they forced their way through the crowd; ~ **una cosa y otra** what with one thing and another.

entreabierto [entreá^ᵇyer'to] *pp de* **entreabrir.**

entreabrir [entreá^ᵇrēr'] *vt* to half-open, open halfway.

entreacto [entreák'to] *nm* interval.

entrecano, a [entreká'no, á] *a* graying (*US*), greying (*Brit*); **ser** ~ (*persona*) to be going gray.

entrecejo [entrese'ho] *nm*: **fruncir el** ~ to frown.

entrecomillado, a [entrekoméyá'tʰo, á] *a* in quotation marks.

entrecortado, a [entrekortá'tʰo, á] *a* (*respiración*) labored (*US*), laboured (*Brit*), difficult; (*habla*) faltering.

entrecot [entreko'(t)] *nm* (*CULIN*) sirloin steak.

entrecruce [entrekrōō'se] *etc vb* V **entrecruzarse**.

entrecruzarse [entrekrōōsár'se] *vr* (*BIO*) to interbreed.

entrechocar [entretchokár'] *vi* (*dientes*) to chatter.

entrechoque [entretcho'ke] *etc vb* V **entrechocar**.

entredicho [entretʰḗtch'o] *nm* (*JUR*) injunction; **poner en** ~ to cast doubt on; **estar en** ~ to be in doubt.

entrega [entre'gá] *nf* (*de mercancías*) delivery; (*de premios*) presentation; (*de novela etc*) installment (*US*), instalment (*Brit*); "~ **a domicilio**" "home delivery service".

entregar [entregár'] *vt* (*dar*) to hand (over), deliver; (*ejercicios*) to hand in; ~**se** *vr* (*rendirse*) to surrender, give in, submit; ~**se a** (*dedicarse*) to devote o.s. to; **a** ~ (*COM*) to be supplied.

entregue [entre'ge] *etc vb* V **entregar**.

entrelace [entrelá'se] *etc vb* V **entrelazar**.

entrelazar [entrelásár'] *vt* to entwine.

entremedias [entreme'tʰyás] *ad* (*en medio*) in between, halfway.

entremeses [entreme'ses] *nmpl* hors d'œuvres.

entremeter [entremeter'] *vt* to insert, put in; ~**se** *vr* to meddle, interfere.

entremetido, a [entremetḗ'tʰo, á] *a* meddling, interfering.

entremezclar [entremesklár'] *vt*, ~**se** *vr* to intermingle.

entrenador, a [entrenátʰor', á] *nm/f* trainer, coach.

entrenamiento [entrenámyen'to] *nm* training.

entrenar [entrenár'] *vt* (*DEPORTE*) to train; (*caballo*) to exercise; ~**se** *vr* to train.

entrepierna [entrepyer'ná] *nf* (*tb*: ~**s**) crotch.

entresacar [entresákár'] *vt* to pick out, select.

entresaque [entresá'ke] *etc vb* V **entresacar**.

entresuelo [entreswe'lo] *nm* mezzanine, entresol; (*TEATRO*) dress *o* first circle.

entretanto [entretán'to] *ad* meanwhile, meantime.

entretejer [entreteher'] *vt* to interweave.

entretela [entrete'lá] *nf* (*de ropa*) interlining; ~**s** *nfpl* heart-strings.

entretendré [entretendre'] *etc vb* V **entretener**.

entretener [entretener'] *vt* (*divertir*) to entertain, amuse; (*detener*) to hold up, delay; (*mantener*) to maintain; ~**se** *vr* (*divertirse*) to amuse o.s.; (*retrasarse*) to delay, linger; **no le entretengo más** I won't keep you any longer.

entretenga [entreten'gá] *etc vb* V **entretener**.

entretenido, a [entretenḗ'tʰo, á] *a* entertaining, amusing.

entretenimiento [entretenḗmyen'to] *nm* entertainment, amusement; (*mantenimiento*) upkeep, maintenance.

entretiene [entretye'ne] *etc*, **entretuve** [entretōō'ke] *etc vb* V **entretener**.

entreveía [entrebeḗ'á] *etc vb* V **entrever**.

entrever [entreher'] *vt* to glimpse, catch a glimpse of.

entrevista [entrebḗ'stá] *nf* interview.

entrevistar [entrebḗstár'] *vt* to interview; ~**se** *vr*: ~**se con** to have an interview with, see; **el ministro se entrevistó con el Rey ayer** the minister had an audience with the King yesterday.

entrevisto [entrebḗ'sto] *pp de* **entrever**.

entristecer [entrḗsteser'] *vt* to sadden, grieve; ~**se** *vr* to grow sad.

entristezca [entrḗstes'ká] *etc vb* V **entristecer**.

entrometerse [entrometer'se] *vr*: ~ (**en**) to interfere (in *o* with).

entrometido, a [entrometḗ'tʰo, á] *a* interfering, meddlesome.

entroncar [entronkár'] *vi* to be connected *o* related.

entronque [entron'ke] *etc vb* V **entroncar**.

entuerto [entwer'to] *nm* wrong, injustice; ~**s** *nmpl* (*MED*) afterpains.

entumecer [entōōmeser'] *vt* to numb, benumb; ~**se** *vr* (*por el frío*) to go *o* become numb.

entumecido, a [entōōmesḗ'tʰo, á] *a* numb, stiff.

entumezca [entōōmes'ká] *etc vb* V **entumecer**.

enturbiar [entōōrhyár'] *vt* (*el agua*) to make cloudy; (*fig*) to confuse; ~**se** *vr* (*oscurecerse*) to become cloudy; (*fig*) to get confused, become obscure.

entusiasmar [entōōsyásmár'] *vt* to excite, fill with enthusiasm; (*gustar mucho*) to delight; ~**se** *vr*: ~**se con** *o* **por** to get enthusiastic *o* excited about.

entusiasmo [entōōsyás'mo] *nm* enthusiasm; (*excitación*) excitement.

entusiasta [entōōsyá'stá] *a* enthusiastic ♦

nm/f enthusiast.

enumerar [enōōmerár'] *vt* to enumerate.

enunciación [enōōnsyásyon'] *nf*, **enunciado** [enōōnsyà'tho] *nm* enunciation; (*declaración*) declaration, statement.

enunciar [enōōnsyár'] *vt* to enunciate; to declare, state.

envainar [embáēnár'] *vt* to sheathe.

envalentonar [embálentonár'] *vt* to give courage to; ~**se** *vr* (*pey*: *jactarse*) to boast, brag.

envanecer [embáneser'] *vt* to make conceited; ~**se** *vr* to grow conceited.

envanezca [embánes'ká] *etc vb* V **envanecer**.

envasar [embásár'] *vt* (*empaquetar*) to pack, wrap; (*enfrascar*) to bottle; (*enlatar*) to can; (*embolsar*) to pocket.

envase [embá'se] *nm* packing, wrapping; bottling; canning; pocketing; (*recipiente*) container; (*paquete*) package; (*botella*) bottle; (*lata*) can, tin (*Brit*).

envejecido, a [embehesē'tho, á] *a* old, aged; (*de aspecto*) old-looking.

envejecer [embeheser'] *vt* to make old, age ♦ *vi*, ~**se** *vr* (*volverse viejo*) to grow old; (*parecer viejo*) to age.

envejezca [embehes'ká] *etc vb* V **envejecer**.

envenenar [embenenár'] *vt* to poison; (*fig*) to embitter.

envergadura [embergáthōō'rá] *nf* (*expansión*) expanse; (*NAUT*) breadth; (*fig*) scope; **un programa de gran** ~ a wide-ranging program.

envés [embes'] *nm* (*de tela*) back, wrong side.

enviado, a [embyá'tho, á] *nm/f* (*POL*) envoy; ~ **especial** (*de periódico*, *TV*) special correspondent.

enviar [embyár'] *vt* to send.

enviciar [embēsyár'] *vt* to corrupt ♦ *vi* (*trabajo etc*) to be addictive; ~**se** *vr*: ~**se (con** *o* **en)** to get addicted (to).

envidia [embē'thyá] *nf* envy; **tener** ~ **a** to envy, be jealous of.

envidiar [embēthyár'] *vt* (*desear*) to envy; (*tener celos de*) to be jealous of.

envidioso, a [embēthyo'so, á] *a* envious, jealous.

envío [embē'o] *nm* (*acción*) sending; (*de mercancías*) consignment; (*de dinero*) remittance; (*en barco*) shipment; **gastos de** ~ postage and handling (*US*) *o* packing (*Brit*); ~ **contra reembolso** COD shipment.

enviudar [embyōōthár'] *vi* to be widowed.

envoltura [emboltōō'rá] *nf* (*cobertura*) cover; (*embalaje*) wrapper, wrapping.

envolver [embolher'] *vt* to wrap (up); (*cubrir*) to cover; (*enemigo*) to surround; (*implicar*) to involve, implicate.

envuelto [embwel'to], **envuelva** [embwel'há] *etc vb* V **envolver**.

enyesar [enyesár'] *vt* (*pared*) to plaster; (*MED*) to cast (*US*), put in plaster (*Brit*).

enzarzarse [ensársár'se] *vr*: ~ **en algo** to get mixed up in sth.

E.P.D. *abr* (= *en paz descanse*) R.I.P.

épico, a [e'pēko, á] *a* epic ♦ *nf* epic (poetry).

epidemia [epēthe'myá] *nf* epidemic.

epidémico, a [epēthe'mēko, á] *a* epidemic.

epifanía [epēfánē'á] *nf* Epiphany.

epilepsia [epēlep'syá] *nf* epilepsy.

epílogo [epē'logo] *nm* epilogue.

episcopado [epēscopá'tho] *nm* (*cargo*) bishopric; (*obispos*) bishops *pl* (*collectively*).

episodio [epēso'thyo] *nm* episode; (*suceso*) incident.

epístola [epē'stolá] *nf* epistle.

epitafio [epētá'fyo] *nm* epitaph.

época [e'poká] *nf* period, time; (*temporada*) season; (*HISTORIA*) age, epoch; **hacer** ~ to be epoch-making.

equidad [ekētháth'] *nf* equity, fairness.

equilibrar [ekēlēhrár'] *vt* to balance.

equilibrio [ekēlēh'ryo] *nm* balance, equilibrium; ~ **político** balance of power.

equilibrista [ekēlēhrē'stá] *nm/f* (*funámbulo*) tightrope walker; (*acróbata*) acrobat.

equinoccio [ekēnok'syo] *nm* equinox.

equipaje [ekēpá'he] *nm* baggage (*US*), luggage (*Brit*); (*avíos*) equipment, kit; ~ **de mano** hand luggage; **hacer el** ~ to pack.

equipar [ekēpár'] *vt* (*proveer*) to equip.

equiparar [ekēpárár'] *vt* (*igualar*) to put on the same level; (*comparar*) to compare (*con* with); ~**se** *vr*: ~**se con** to be on a level with.

equipo [ekē'po] *nm* (*conjunto de cosas*) equipment; (*DEPORTE*, *grupo*) team; (*de obreros*) shift; (*de máquinas*) plant; (*turbinas etc*) set; ~ **de caza** hunting gear; ~ **físico** (*INFORM*) hardware; ~ **médico** medical team.

equis [e'kēs] *nf* (the letter) X.

equitación [ekētásyon'] *nf* (*acto*) riding; (*arte*) horsemanship.

equitativo, a [ekētátē'ho, á] *a* equitable, fair.

equivaldré [ekēháldre'] *etc vb* V **equivaler**.

equivalencia [ekēhálen'syá] *nf* equivalence.

equivalente [ekēhálen'te] *a*, *nm* equivalent.

equivaler [ekēháler'] *vi*: ~ **a** to be equivalent *o* equal to; (*en rango*) to rank as.

equivalga [ekēhál'gá] *etc vb* V **equivaler**.

equivocación [ekēhokásyon'] *nf* mistake, error; (*malentendido*) misunderstanding.

equivocado, a [ekēhoká'tho, á] *a* wrong, mistaken.

equivocarse |ckčʰokár'sc| *vr* to be wrong, make a mistake; ~ **de camino** to take the wrong road.

equívoco, a |ckē'ʰoko, á| *a* (*dudoso*) suspect; (*ambiguo*) ambiguous ♦ *nm* ambiguity; (*malentendido*) misunderstanding.

equivoque |ckēʰo'kc| *etc vb* V **equivocar.**

era |c'rá| *vb* V **ser** ♦ *nf* erá, age; (*AGR*) threshing floor.

erais |c'rács|, **éramos** |c'rámos|, **eran** |c'rán| *vb* V **ser.**

erario |crá'ryo| *nm* exchequer, treasury.

eras |c'rás|, **eres** |c'rcs| *vb* V **ser.**

ergonomía |crgonomē'á| *nf* ergonomics *sg*, human engineering.

erguir |crgēr'| *vt* to raise, lift; (*poner dere-cho*) to straighten; ~**se** *vr* to straighten up.

erice |crē'sc| *etc vb* V **erizarse.**

erigir |crēhēr'| *vt* to erect, build; ~**se** *vr*: ~**se en** to set o.s. up as.

erija |crē'há| *etc vb* V **erigir.**

erizado, a |crēsá'tʰo, á| *a* bristly.

erizarse |crēsár'sc| *vr* (*pelo: de perro*) to bristle; (: *de persona*) to stand on end.

erizo |crē'so| *nm* hedgehog; ~ **de mar** sea urchin.

ermita |crmē'tá| *nf* hermitage.

ermitaño, a |crmētá'nyo, á| *nm/f* hermit.

erosionar |crosyonár'| *vt* to erode.

erótico, a |cro'tēko, á| *a* erotic.

erotismo |crotēs'mo| *nm* eroticism.

erradicar |crrátʰēkár'| *vt* to eradicate.

erradique |crrátʰē'kc| *etc vb* V **erradicar.**

errado, a |crrá'tʰo, á| *a* mistaken, wrong.

errante |crrán'tc| *a* wandering, errant.

errar |crrár'| *vi* (*vagar*) to wander, roam; (*equivocarse*) to be mistaken ♦ *vt*: ~ **el camino** to take the wrong road; ~ **el tiro** to miss.

errata |crrá'tá| *nf* misprint.

erre |c'rrc| *nf* (the letter) R; ~ **que** ~ stubbornly.

erróneo, a |crro'nco, á| *a* (*equivocado*) wrong, mistaken; (*falso*) false, untrue.

error |crror'| *nm* error, mistake; (*INFORM*) bug; ~ **de imprenta** misprint; ~ **de lectura/escritura** (*INFORM*) read/write error; ~ **sintáctico** syntax error; ~ **judicial** miscarriage of justice.

eructar |crōōktár'| *vt* to belch, burp.

erudición |crōōtʰēsyon'| *nf* erudition, learning.

erudito, a |crōōtʰē'to, á| *a* erudite, learned ♦ *nm/f* scholar; **los** ~**s en esta materia** the experts in this field.

erupción |crōōpsyon'| *nf* eruption; (*MED*) rash; (*de violencia*) outbreak; (*de ira*) outburst.

es |cs| *vb* V **ser.**

E/S *abr* (*INFORM*: entrada/salida) I/O.

esa |c'sá|, **esas** |c'sás| *a demostrativo* V **ese.**

ésa |c'sá|, **ésas** |c'sás| *pron* V **ése.**

esbelto, a |csbcl'to, á| *a* slim, slender.

esbirro |csbē'rro| *nm* henchman.

esbozar |csbosár'| *vt* to sketch, outline.

esbozo |csbo'so| *nm* sketch, outline.

escabeche |cskábctch'c| *nm* brine; (*de aceitunas etc*) pickle; **en** ~ pickled.

escabechina |cskábctchē'ná| *nf* (*batalla*) massacre; **hacer una** ~ (*ESCOL*) to fail a lot of students.

escabroso, a |cskábro'so, á| *a* (*accidentado*) rough, uneven; (*fig*) tough, difficult; (: *atrevido*) risqué.

escabullirse |cskábōōyēr'sc| *vr* to slip away; (*largarse*) to clear out.

escafandra |cskáfán'drá| *nf* (*buzo*) diving suit; (~ *espacial*) spacesuit.

escala |cská'lá| *nf* (*proporción, MUS*) scale; (*de mano*) ladder; (*AVIAT*) stopover; (*de colores etc*) range; ~ **de tiempo** time scale; ~ **de sueldos** salary scale; **una investigación a** ~ **nacional** a nationwide inquiry; **reproducir según** ~ to reproduce to scale; **hacer** ~ **en** to stop off *o* over at.

escalada |cskálá'tʰá| *nf* (*de montaña*) climb; (*de pared*) scaling.

escalafón |cskáláfon'| *nm* (*escala de salarios*) salary scale, wage scale.

escalar |cskálár'| *vt* to climb, scale ♦ *vi* (*MIL, POL*) to escalate.

escaldar |cskáldár'| *vt* (*quemar*) to scald; (*escarmentar*) to teach a lesson.

escalera |cskálc'rá| *nf* stairs *pl*, staircase; (*escala*) ladder; (*NAIPES*) run; (*de camión*) tailgate; ~ **mecánica** escalator; ~ **de caracol** spiral staircase; ~ **de incendios** fire escape.

escalfar |cskálfár'| *vt* (*huevos*) to poach.

escalinata |cskálēná'tá| *nf* staircase.

escalofriante |cskálofryán'tc| *a* chilling.

escalofrío |cskálofrē'o| *nm* (*MED*) chill; ~**s** *nmpl* (*fig*) shivers.

escalón |cskálon'| *nm* step, stair; (*de escalera*) rung; (*fig: paso*) step; (*al éxito*) ladder.

escalonar |cskálonár'| *vt* to spread out; (*tierra*) to terrace; (*horas de trabajo*) to stagger.

escalope |cskálo'pc| *nm* (*CULIN*) cutlet (*US*), escalope (*Brit*).

escama |cská'má| *nf* (*de pez, serpiente*) scale; (*de jabón*) flake; (*fig*) resentment.

escamar |cskámár'| *vt* (*pez*) to scale; (*producir recelo*) to make wary.

escamotear |cskámotcár'| *vt* (*fam: robar*) to lift, swipe; (*hacer desaparecer*) to make disappear.

escampar |cskámpár'| *vb impersonal* to stop raining.

escanciar |cskánsyár'| *vt* (*vino*) to pour (out).

escandalice [eskándálē'se] *etc vb* V **escandalizar**.

escandalizar [eskándálēsár'] *vt* to scandalize, shock; ~**se** *vr* to be shocked; (*ofenderse*) to be offended.

escándalo [eskán'dálo] *nm* scandal; (*alboroto*, *tumulto*) row, uproar; **armar un** ~ to make a scene; **¡es un ~!** it's outrageous!

escandaloso, a [eskándálo'so, á] *a* scandalous, shocking; (*risa*) hearty; (*niño*) noisy.

Escandinavia [eskándēná'ñyá] *nf* Scandinavia.

escandinavo, a [eskándēná'ño, á] *a*, *nm/f* Scandinavian.

escaño [eská'nyo] *nm* bench; (*POL*) seat.

escapada [eskápá'ñá] *nf* (*huida*) escape, flight; (*deportes*) breakaway; (*viaje*) quick trip.

escapar [eskápár'] *vi* (*gen*) to escape, run away; (*DEPORTE*) to break away; ~**se** *vr* to escape, get away; (*agua*, *gas*, *noticias*) to leak (out); **se me escapa su nombre** his name escapes me.

escaparate [eskápárá'te] *nm* shop window; (*COM*) showcase.

escapatoria [eskápáto'ryá] *nf*: **no tener** ~ (*fig*) to have no way out.

escape [eská'pe] *nm* (*huida*) escape; (*de agua*, *gas*) leak; (*de motor*) exhaust; **salir a** ~ to rush out.

escapismo [eskápēs'mo] *nm* escapism.

escarabajo [eskáráñá'ho] *nm* beetle.

escaramuza [eskárámōō'sá] *nf* skirmish; (*fig*) brush.

escarbar [eskárñár'] *vt* (*gallina*) to scratch; (*fig*) to inquire into, investigate.

escarcha [eskártch'á] *nf* frost.

escarlata [eskárlá'tá] *a inv* scarlet.

escarlatina [eskárlátē'ná] *nf* scarlet fever.

escarmentar [eskármentár'] *vt* to punish severely ♦ *vi* to learn one's lesson; **¡para que escarmientes!** that'll teach you!

escarmiento [eskármyen'to] *etc vb* V **escarmentar** ♦ *nm* (*ejemplo*) lesson; (*castigo*) punishment.

escarnio [eskár'nyo] *nm* mockery; (*injuria*) insult.

escarola [eskáro'lá] *nf* (*BOT*) endive.

escarpado, a [eskárpá'ño, á] *a* (*pendiente*) sheer, steep; (*rocas*) craggy.

escasamente [eskásámen'te] *ad* (*insuficientemente*) scantily; (*apenas*) scarcely.

escasear [eskáseár'] *vi* to be scarce.

escasez [eskáses'] *nf* (*falta*) shortage, scarcity; (*pobreza*) poverty; **vivir con** ~ to live on next to nothing.

escaso, a [eská'so, á] *a* (*poco*) scarce; (*raro*) rare; (*ralo*) thin, sparse; (*limitado*) limited; (*recursos*) scanty; (*público*) sparse; (*posibilidad*) slim; (*visibilidad*) poor.

escatimar [eskátēmár'] *vt* (*limitar*) to skimp (on), be sparing with; **no** ~ **esfuerzos (para)** to spare no effort (to).

escayola [eskáyo'lá] *nf* cast (*US*), plaster (*Brit*).

escayolar [eskáyolár'] *vt* to cast (*US*), put in plaster (*Brit*).

escena [ese'ná] *nf* scene; (*decorado*) scenery; (*escenario*) stage; **poner en** ~ to put on.

escenario [esená'ryo] *nm* (*TEATRO*) stage; (*CINE*) set; (*fig*) scene; **el** ~ **del crimen** the scene of the crime; **el** ~ **político** the political scene.

escenografía [esenográfē'á] *nf* set *o* stage design.

escepticismo [eseptēsēs'mo] *nm* scepticism.

escéptico, a [esep'tēko, á] *a* sceptical ♦ *nm/f* sceptic.

escindir [esēndēr'] *vt* to split; ~**se** *vr* (*facción*) to split off; ~**se en** to split into.

escisión [esēsyon'] *nf* (*MED*) excision; (*fig*, *POL*) split; ~ **nuclear** nuclear fission.

esclarecer [esklárecer'] *vt* (*iluminar*) to light up, illuminate; (*misterio*, *problema*) to shed light on.

esclarezca [eskláres'ká] *etc vb* V **esclarecer**.

esclavice [eskláñē'se] *etc vb* V **esclavizar**.

esclavitud [eskláñētōōñ'] *nf* slavery.

esclavizar [eskláñēsár'] *vt* to enslave.

esclavo, a [esklá'ño, á] *nm/f* slave.

esclusa [esklōō'sá] *nf* (*de canal*) lock; (*compuerta*) floodgate.

escoba [esko'ñá] *nf* broom; **pasar la** ~ to sweep up.

escobazo [eskoñá'so] *nm* (*golpe*) blow with a broom; **echar a uno a** ~**s** to kick sb out.

escocer [eskoser'] *vi* to burn, sting; ~**se** *vr* to chafe, get chafed.

escocés, esa [eskoses', esá] *a* Scottish; (*whisky*) Scotch ♦ *nm/f* Scotsman/woman, Scot; (*whisky*) Scotch ♦ *nm* (*LING*) Scots *sg*; **tela escocesa** tartan.

Escocia [esko'syá] *nf* Scotland.

escoger [eskoher'] *vt* to choose, pick, select.

escogido, a [eskohē'ño, á] *a* chosen, selected; (*calidad*) choice, select; (*persona*): **ser muy** ~ to be very fussy.

escoja [esko'há] *etc vb* V **escoger**.

escolar [eskolár'] *a* school *cpd* ♦ *nm/f* schoolboy/girl, pupil.

escolaridad [eskoláreñáñ'] *nf* schooling; **libro de** ~ school record.

escolarización [eskolárēsásyon'] *nf*: ~ **obligatoria** compulsory education.

escolarizado, a [eskolárēsá'ño, á] *a*, *nm/f*: **los** ~**s** those in *o* attending school.

escolta [eskol'tá] *nf* escort.

escoltar [eskoltár'] *vt* to escort; (*proteger*)

to guard.

escollo [esko'yo] *nm* (*arrecife*) reef, rock; (*fig*) pitfall.

escombros [eskom'bros] *nmpl* (*basura*) rubbish *sg*; (*restos*) debris *sg*.

esconder [eskonder'] *vt* to hide, conceal; ~**se** *vr* to hide.

escondidas [eskondē'thàs] *nfpl* (*AM*) hide-and-seek *sg*; **a** ~ secretly; **hacer algo a** ~ **de uno** to do sth behind sb's back.

escondite [eskondē'te] *nm* hiding place; (*juego*) hide-and-seek.

escondrijo [eskondrē'ho] *nm* hiding-place, hideout.

escopeta [eskope'tà] *nf* shotgun; ~ **de aire comprimido** air gun.

escoria [esko'ryà] *nf* (*desecho mineral*) slag; (*fig*) scum, dregs *pl*.

Escorpio [eskor'pyo] *nm* (*ASTRO*) Scorpio.

escorpión [eskorpyon'] *nm* scorpion.

escotado, a [eskotá'tho, à] *a* a low-cut.

escotar [eskotár'] *vt* (*vestido: ajustar*) to cut to fit; (*cuello*) to cut low.

escote [esko'te] *nm* (*de vestido*) low neck; **pagar a** ~ to share the expenses.

escotilla [eskotē'yà] *nf* (*NAUT*) hatchway.

escotillón [eskotēyon'] *nm* trapdoor.

escozor [eskosor'] *nm* (*dolor*) sting(ing).

escribano, a [eskrēhá'no, à], **escribiente** [eskrēhyen'te] *nm/f* clerk; (*secretario judicial*) court *o* lawyer's clerk.

escribir [eskrēhēr'] *vt*, *vi* to write; ~ **a máquina** to type; **¿cómo se escribe?** how do you spell it?

escrito, a [eskrē'to, à] *pp de* **escribir** ♦ *a* written, in writing; (*examen*) written ♦ *nm* (*documento*) document; (*manuscrito*) text, manuscript; **por** ~ in writing.

escritor, a [eskrētor', à] *nm/f* writer.

escritorio [eskrēto'ryo] *nm* desk; (*oficina*) office.

escritura [eskrētōo'rà] *nf* (*acción*) writing; (*caligrafía*) (hand)writing; (*JUR: documento*) deed; (*COM*) indenture; ~ **de propiedad** title deed; **Sagrada E~** (Holy) Scripture; ~ **social** articles *pl* of association.

escroto [eskro'to] *nm* scrotum.

escrúpulo [eskrōo'pōolo] *nm* scruple; (*minuciosidad*) scrupulousness.

escrupuloso, a [eskrōopōolo'so, à] *a* scrupulous.

escrutar [eskrōotár'] *vt* to scrutinize, examine; (*votos*) to count.

escrutinio [eskrōotē'nyo] *nm* (*examen atento*) scrutiny; (*POL: recuento de votos*) count(ing).

escuadra [eskwà'thrà] *nf* (*TEC*) square; (*MIL etc*) squad; (*NAUT*) squadron; (*de coches etc*) fleet.

escuadrilla [eskwàthrē'yà] *nf* (*de aviones*)

squadron; (*AM: de obreros*) gang.

escuadrón [eskwàthron'] *nm* squadron.

escuálido, a [eskwà'lētho, à] *a* skinny, scraggy; (*sucio*) squalid.

escucha [eskōotch'à] *nf* (*acción*) listening ♦ *nm* (*TELEC: sistema*) monitor; (*oyente*) listener; **estar a la** ~ to listen in; **estar de** ~ to spy; ~**s teléfonicas** (*telephone*) tapping *sg*.

escuchar [eskōotchár'] *vt* to listen to; (*consejo*) to heed ♦ *vi* to listen; ~**se** *vr*: **se escucha muy mal** (*AM TELEC*) it's a very bad connection (*US*) *o* line (*Brit*).

escudarse [eskōothár'se] *vr*: ~ **en** (*fig*) to hide behind.

escudería [eskōotherē'à] *nf*: **la** ~ **Ferrari** the Ferrari team.

escudero [eskōothe'ro] *nm* squire.

escudilla [eskōothē'yà] *nf* bowl, basin.

escudo [eskōo'tho] *nm* shield; ~ **de armas** coat of arms.

escudriñar [eskōothrēnyár'] *vt* (*examinar*) to investigate, scrutinize; (*mirar de lejos*) to scan.

escuece [eskwe'se] *etc vb* **V escocer**.

escuela [eskwe'là] *nf* (*tb fig*) school; ~ **normal** teacher training college; ~ **de párvulos** kindergarten.

escueto, a [eskwe'to, à] *a* plain, (*estilo*) simple; (*explicación*) concise.

escueza [eskwe'sà] *etc vb* **V escocer**.

escuincle [eskwēn'kle] *nm* (*AM fam*) kid.

esculpir [eskōolpēr'] *vt* to sculpt; (*grabar*) to engrave; (*tallar*) to carve.

escultor, a [eskōoltor', à] *nm/f* sculptor.

escultura [eskōoltōo'rà] *nf* sculpture.

escupidera [eskōopēthe'rà] *nf* spittoon.

escupir [eskōopēr'] *vt* to spit (out) ♦ *vi* to spit.

escurreplatos [eskōorreplá'tos] *nm inv* plate rack.

escurridizo, a [eskōorrēthē'so, à] *a* slippery.

escurrir [eskōorrēr'] *vt* (*ropa*) to wring out; (*verduras, platos*) to drain ♦ *vi* (*los líquidos*) to drip; ~**se** *vr* (*secarse*) to drain; (*resbalarse*) to slip, slide; (*escaparse*) to slip away.

ese [e'se] *nf* (the letter) S; **hacer** ~**s** (*carretera*) to zigzag; (*borracho*) to reel about.

ese [e'se], **esa** [e'sà], **esos** [e'sos], **esas** [e'sàs] *a demostrativo* (*sg*) that; (*pl*) those.

ése [e'se], **ésa** [e'sà], **ésos** [e'sos], **ésas** [e'sàs] *pron* (*sg*) that (one); (*pl*) those (ones); **ése** ... **éste** ... the former ... the latter ...; **¡no me vengas con ésas!** don't give me any more of that nonsense!

esencia [esen'syà] *nf* essence.

esencial [esensyál'] *a* essential; (*principal*) chief; **lo** ~ the main thing.

esfera [esfe'rà] *nf* sphere; (*de reloj*) face; ~

de acción scope; ~ **terrestre** globe.
esférico, a [esfe'rēko, à] *a* spherical.
esfinge [esfēn'he] *nf* sphinx.
esforcé [esforse'], **esforcemos** [esforse'mos] *etc vb V* **esforzar.**
esforzado, a [esforsà'tho, à] *a* (*enérgico*) energetic, vigorous.
esforzarse [esforsàr'se] *vr* to exert o.s., make an effort.
esfuerce [esfwer'se] *etc vb V* **esforzar.**
esfuerzo [esfwer'so] *etc vb V* **esforzar** ♦ *nm* effort; **sin** ~ effortlessly.
esfumarse [esfŏŏmár'se] *vr* (*apoyo, esperanzas*) to fade away; (*persona*) to vanish.
esgrima [esgrē'má] *nf* fencing.
esgrimidor [esgrēmēthor'] *nm* fencer.
esgrimir [esgrēmēr'] *vt* (*arma*) to brandish; (*argumento*) to use ♦ *vi* to fence.
esguince [esgēn'se] *nm* (*MED*) sprain.
eslabón [eslàbon'] *nm* link; ~ **perdido** (*BIO, fig*) missing link.
eslabonar [eslàbonár'] *vt* to link, connect.
eslavo, a [eslà'bo, à] *a* Slav, Slavonic ♦ *nm/f* Slav ♦ *nm* (*LING*) Slavonic.
eslogan [eslo'gàn] *nm, pl* **eslogans** = **slogan.**
eslora [eslo'rá] *nf* (*NAUT*) length.
esmaltar [esmáltár'] *vt* to enamel.
esmalte [esmál'te] *nm* enamel; ~ **de uñas** nail polish.
esmerado, a [esmerá'tho, à] *a* careful, neat.
esmeralda [esmerál'dà] *nf* emerald.
esmerarse [esmerár'se] *vr* (*aplicarse*) to take great pains, exercise great care; (*afanarse*) to work hard; (*hacer lo mejor*) to do one's best.
esmero [esme'ro] *nm* (great) care.
esmirriado, a [esmērryà'tho, à] *a* puny.
esmoquin [esmo'kēn] *nm* tuxedo (*US*), dinner jacket (*Brit*).
esnob [esnob'] *a inv* (*persona*) snobbish; (*coche etc*) posh ♦ *nm/f* snob.
esnobismo [esnŏbēs'mo] *nm* snobbery.
eso [e'so] *pron* that, that thing *o* matter; ~ **de su coche** that business about his car; ~ **de ir al cine** all that about going to the movies; **a** ~ **de las cinco** at about five o'clock; **en** ~ thereupon, at that point; **por** ~ therefore; ~ **es** that's it; **nada de** ~ far from it; **¡**~ **sí que es vida!** now this is really living!; **por** ~ **te lo dije** that's why I told you; **y** ~ **que llovía** in spite of the fact it was raining.
esófago [eso'fàgo] *nm* (*ANAT*) esophagus (*US*), oesophagus (*Brit*).
esos [e'sos] *a demostrativo V* **ese.**
ésos [e'sos] *pron V* **ése.**
esp. *abr* (= *español*) Sp., Span.
espabilar [espàbēlàr'] *vt*, **espabilarse** *vr* = **despabilar(se).**

espaciado [espàsyá'tho] *nm* (*INFORM*) spacing.
espacial [espàsyál'] *a* (*del espacio*) space *cpd.*
espaciar [espàsyàr'] *vt* to space (out).
espacio [espà'syo] *nm* space; (*MUS*) interval; (*RADIO, TV*) program (*US*), programme (*Brit*); **el** ~ space; **ocupar mucho** ~ to take up a lot of room; **a dos** ~**s, a doble** ~ (*TIP*) double-spaced; **por** ~ **de** during, for.
espacioso, a [espàsyo'so, à] *a* spacious, roomy.
espada [espà'thá] *nf* sword; ~**s** *nfpl* (*NAIPES*) spades; **estar entre la** ~ **y la pared** to be between the devil and the deep blue sea ♦ *nm* swordsman; (*TAUR*) matador.
espadachín [espàthátchēn'] *nm* (*esgrimidor*) skilled swordsman.
espaguetis [espàge'tēs] *nmpl* spaghetti *sg.*
espalda [espál'dà] *nf* (*gen*) back; (*NATACIÓN*) backstroke; ~**s** *nfpl* (*hombros*) shoulders; **a** ~**s de uno** behind sb's back; **estar de** ~**s** to have one's back turned; **tenderse de** ~**s** to lie (down) on one's back; **volver la** ~ **a uno** to give sb the cold-shoulder.
espaldarazo [espáldàrà'so] *nm* (*tb fig*) slap on the back.
espaldilla [espálthē'yà] *nf* shoulder blade.
espantadizo, a [espántàthē'so, à] *a* timid, easily frightened.
espantajo [espántà'ho] *nm*, **espantapájaros** [espántàpá'hàros] *nm inv* scarecrow.
espantar [espántàr'] *vt* (*asustar*) to frighten, scare; (*ahuyentar*) to frighten off; (*asombrar*) to horrify, appal; ~**se** *vr* to get frightened *o* scared; to be appalled.
espanto [espán'to] *nm* (*susto*) fright; (*terror*) terror; (*asombro*) astonishment; **¡qué** ~**!** how awful!
espantoso, a [espánto'so, à] *a* frightening, terrifying; (*ruido*) dreadful.
España [espà'nyà] *nf* Spain; **la** ~ **de pandereta** touristy Spain.
español, a [espànyol', à] *a* Spanish ♦ *nm/f* Spaniard ♦ *nm* (*LING*) Spanish.
españolice [espànyolē'se] *etc vb V* **españolizar.**
españolizar [espànyolēsàr'] *vt* to make Spanish, Hispanicize; ~**se** *vr* to adopt Spanish ways.
esparadrapo [espàràthrà'po] *nm* bandaid (*US*), (sticking) plaster.
esparcido, a [espàrsē'tho, à] *a* scattered.
esparcimiento [espàrsēmyen'to] *nm* (*dispersión*) spreading; (*derramamiento*) scattering; (*fig*) cheerfulness.
esparcir [espàrsēr'] *vt* to spread; (*derramar*) to scatter; ~**se** *vr* to spread (out); to

scatter; (*divertirse*) to enjoy o.s.

espárrago [espá'rràgo] *nm* (*tb*: ~**s**) asparagus; **estar hecho un** ~ to be as thin as a rake; **¡vete a freír ~s!** (*fam*) go to hell!

espasmo [espás'mo] *nm* spasm.

esparto [espár'to] *nm* esparto (grass).

esparza [espár'sá] *etc vb* V **esparcir.**

espátula [espá'tōōlá] *nf* (*MED*) spatula; (*ARTE*) palette knife; (*CULIN*) fish slice.

especia [espe'syá] *nf* spice.

especial [espesyál'] *a* special.

especialidad [espesyálētháth'] *nf* specialty (*US*), speciality (*Brit*); (*ESCOL*: *ramo*) specialization.

especialista [espesyálē'stá] *nm/f* specialist; (*CINE*) stuntman/woman.

especializado, a [espesyálēsá'tho, á] *a* specialized; (*obrero*) skilled.

especie [espe'syc] *nf* (*BIO*) species; (*clase*) kind, sort; **pagar en** ~ to pay in kind.

especificar [espesēfēkár'] *vt* to specify.

específico, a [espesē'fēko, á] *a* specific.

especifique [espesēfē'ke] *etc vb* V **especificar.**

espécimen [espe'sēmen], *pl* **especímenes** *nm* specimen.

espectáculo [espektá'kōōlo] *nm* (*gen*) spectacle; (*TEATRO etc*) show; (*función*) performance; **dar un** ~ to make a scene.

espectador, a [espektáthor', á] *nm/f* spectator; (*de incidente*) onlooker; **los ~es** (*TEATRO*) the audience *sg*.

espectro [espek'tro] *nm* ghost; (*fig*) specter (*US*), spectre (*Brit*).

especulación [espekōōlásyon'] *nf* speculation; ~ **bursátil** speculation on the Stock Market.

especular [espekōōlár'] *vt, vi* to speculate.

especulativo, a [espekōōlátē'ho, á] *a* speculative.

espejismo [espehēs'mo] *nm* mirage.

espejo [espe'ho] *nm* mirror; (*fig*) model; ~ **retrovisor** rear-view mirror; **mirarse al** ~ to look (at o.s.) in the mirror.

espeluznante [espelōōsnán'te] *a* horrifying, hair-raising.

espera [espe'rá] *nf* (*pausa, intervalo*) wait; (*JUR*: *plazo*) respite; **en** ~ **de** waiting for; (*con expectativa*) expecting; **en** ~ **de su contestación** awaiting your reply.

esperance [esperán'se] *etc vb* V **esperanzar.**

esperanza [esperán'sá] *nf* (*confianza*) hope; (*expectativa*) expectation; **hay pocas ~s de que venga** there is little prospect of his coming.

esperanzador, a [esperánsáthor', á] *a* hopeful, encouraging.

esperanzar [esperánsár'] *vt* to give hope to.

esperar [esperár'] *vt* (*aguardar*) to wait for; (*tener expectativa de*) to expect; (*desear*) to hope for ♦ *vi* to wait; to expect; to hope; ~**se** *vr*: **como podía ~se** as was to be expected; **hacer** ~ **a uno** to keep sb waiting; **ir a** ~ **a uno** to go and meet sb; ~ **un bebé** to be expecting.

esperma [esper'má] *nf* sperm.

esperpento [esperpen'to] *nm* (*persona*) sight (*fam*); (*disparate*) (piece of) nonsense.

espesar [espesár'] *vt* to thicken; ~**se** *vr* to thicken, get thicker.

espeso, a [espe'so, á] *a* thick; (*bosque*) dense; (*nieve*) deep; (*sucio*) dirty.

espesor [espesor'] *nm* thickness; (*de nieve*) depth.

espesura [espesōō'rá] *nf* (*bosque*) thicket.

espetar [espetár'] *vt* (*reto, sermón*) to give.

espía [espē'á] *nm/f* spy.

espiar [espēár'] *vt* (*observar*) to spy on ♦ *vi*: ~ **para** to spy for.

espiga [espē'gá] *nf* (*BOT*: *de trigo etc*) ear; (: *de flores*) spike.

espigado, a [espēgá'tho, á] *a* (*BOT*) ripe; (*fig*) tall, slender.

espigón [espēgon'] *nm* (*BOT*) ear; (*NAUT*) breakwater.

espina [espē'ná] *nf* thorn; (*de pez*) bone; ~ **dorsal** (*ANAT*) spine; **me da mala** ~ I don't like the look of it.

espinaca [espēná'ká] *nf* (*tb*: ~**s**) spinach.

espinar [espēnár'] *nm* (*matorral*) thicket.

espinazo [espēná'so] *nm* spine, backbone.

espinilla [espēnē'yá] *nf* (*ANAT*: *tibia*) shin(bone); (: *en la piel*) blackhead.

espino [espē'no] *nm* hawthorn.

espinoso, a [espēno'so, á] *a* (*planta*) thorny, prickly; (*fig*) bony; (*problema*) knotty.

espionaje [espyoná'he] *nm* spying, espionage.

espiral [espērál'] *a, nf* spiral; **la** ~ **inflacionista** the inflationary spiral.

espirar [espērár'] *vt, vi* to breathe out, exhale.

espiritista [espērētē'stá] *a, nm/f* spiritualist.

espíritu [espē'rētōō] *nm* spirit; (*mente*) mind; (*inteligencia*) intelligence; (*REL*) spirit, soul; **E~ Santo** Holy Ghost; **con** ~ **amplio** with an open mind.

espiritual [espērētwál'] *a* spiritual.

espita [espē'tá] *nf* faucet (*US*), tap (*Brit*).

esplendidez [esplendēthes'] *nf* (*abundancia*) lavishness; (*magnificencia*) splendor (*US*), splendour (*Brit*).

espléndido, a [esplen'dētho, á] *a* (*magnífico*) magnificent, splendid; (*generoso*) generous, lavish.

esplendor [esplendor'] *nm* splendor (*US*), splendour (*Brit*).

espliego [esplye'go] *nm* lavender.

espolear [espoleár'] *vt* to spur on.

espoleta |espolc'tá| *nf* (*de bomba*) fuse.

espolvorear |espolhorcár'| *vt* to dust, sprinkle.

esponja |espon'há| *nf* sponge; (*fig*) sponger.

esponjoso, a |esponho'so, á| *a* spongy.

esponsales |esponsá'les| *nmpl* betrothal *sg*.

espontaneidad |espontánccthath'| *nf* spontaneity.

espontáneo, a |espontá'nco, á| *a* spontaneous; (*improvisado*) impromptu; (*persona*) natural.

espora |espo'rá| *nf* spore.

esporádico, a |esporá'thcko, á| *a* sporadic.

esposa |espo'sá| *nf* V **esposo**.

esposar |esposár'| *vt* to handcuff.

esposo, a |espo'so, á| *nm* husband ♦ *nf* wife; **esposas** *nfpl* handcuffs.

espuela |espwc'lá| *nf* spur; (*fam: trago*) one for the road.

espuerta |espwcr'tá| *nf* basket, pannier.

espuma |espōō'má| *nf* foam; (*de cerveza*) froth, head; (*de jabón*) lather; (*de olas*) surf.

espumarajo |espōōmárá'ho| *nm* froth, foam; **echar ~s (de rabia)** to splutter with rage.

espumoso, a |espōōmo'so, á| *a* frothy, foamy; (*vino*) sparkling.

esputo |espōō'to| *nm* (*saliva*) spit; (*MED*) sputum.

esqueje |eskc'hc| *nm* (*BOT*) cutting.

esquela |eskc'lá| *nf:* **~ mortuoria** announcement of death.

esqueleto |eskclc'to| *nm* skeleton; (*lo esencial*) bare bones (of a matter); **en ~** unfinished.

esquema |eskc'má| *nm* (*diagrama*) diagram; (*dibujo*) plan; (*plan*) scheme; (*FILOSOFIA*) schema.

esquí |eskč'|, *pl* **esquís** *nm* (*objeto*) ski; (*deporte*) skiing; **~ acuático** water-skiing; **hacer ~** to go skiing.

esquiador, a |eskyáthor', á| *nm/f* skier.

esquiar |eskyár'| *vi* to ski.

esquila |eskč'lá| *nf* (*campanilla*) small bell; (*encerro*) cowbell.

esquilar |eskclár'| *vt* to shear.

esquimal |eskčmál'| *a, nm/f* Eskimo.

esquina |eskč'ná| *nf* corner; **doblar la ~** to turn the corner.

esquinar |eskčnár'| *vi* (*hacer esquina*) to form a corner ♦ *vt* (*madera*) to square (off); **~se** *vr* (*pelearse*) to quarrel.

esquinazo |eskčná'so| *nm:* **dar ~ a uno** to give sb the slip.

esquirla |eskčr'lá| *nf* splinter.

esquirol |eskčrol'| *nm* scab.

esquivar |eskčhár'| *vt* to avoid; (*evadir*) to dodge, elude.

esquivo, a |eskč'ho, á| *a* (*altanero*) aloof; (*desdeñoso*) scornful, disdainful.

esquizofrenia |eskčsofrc'nyá| *nf* schizophrenia.

esta |c'stá| *a demostrativo* V **este**.

ésta |c'stá| *pron* V **éste**.

está |cstá'| *vb* V **estar**.

estabilice |cstáhčlč'sc| *etc vb* V **estabilizar**.

estabilidad |cstáhčlčthath'| *nf* stability.

estabilización |cstáhčlčsásyon'| *nf* (*COM*) stabilization.

estabilizar |cstáhčlčsár'| *vt* to stabilize; (*fijar*) to make steady; (*precios*) to peg; **~se** *vr* to become stable.

estable |cstá'hlc| *a* stable.

establecer |cstáhlcscr'| *vt* to establish; (*fundar*) to set up; (*colonos*) to settle; (*récord*) to set (up); **~se** *vr* to establish o.s.; (*echar raíces*) to settle (down); (*COM*) to start up.

establecimiento |cstáhlcccmycn'to| *nm* establishment; (*fundación*) institution; (*de negocio*) start-up; (*de colonias*) settlement; (*local*) establishment; **~ comercial** business house.

establezca |cstáhlcs'ká| *etc vb* V **establecer**.

establo |cstá'hlo| *nm* (*AGR*) stall; (: *esp AM*) barn.

estaca |cstá'ká| *nf* stake, post; (*de tienda de campaña*) peg.

estacada |cstáká'thá| *nf* (*cerca*) fence, fencing; (*palenque*) stockade; **dejar a uno en la ~** to leave sb in the lurch.

estación |cstásyon'| *nf* station; (*del año*) season; **~ de autobuses/ferrocarril** bus/railway station; **~ balnearia (de turistas)** seaside resort; **~ de servicio** service station; **~ terminal** terminus; **~ de trabajo** (*COM*) work station; **~ transmisora** transmitter; **~ de visualización** display unit.

estacionamiento |cstásyonámycn'to| *nm* (*AUTO*) parking; (*MIL*) stationing.

estacionar |cstásyonár'| *vt* (*AUTO*) to park; (*MIL*) to station.

estacionario, a |cstásyoná'ryo, á| *a* stationary; (*COM: mercado*) slack.

estadio |cstá'thyo| *nm* (*fase*) stage, phase; (*DEPORTE*) stadium.

estadista |cstáthč'stá| *nm* (*POL*) statesman; (*ESTADÍSTICA*) statistician.

estadística |cstáthč'stčká| *nf* (*una ~*) figure, statistic; (*ciencia*) statistics *sg*.

estado |cstá'tho| *nm* (*POL: condición*) state; **~ civil** marital status; **~ de cuenta(s)** bank statement, statement of accounts; **~ de excepción** (*POL*) state of emergency; **~ financiero** (*COM*) financial statement; **~ mayor** (*MIL*) staff; **~ de pérdidas y ganancias** (*COM*) profit and loss statement, operating statement; **E~s Unidos (EE.UU.)** United States (of America)

(USA); **estar en ~ (de buena esperanza)** to be pregnant.

estadounidense [estáᴛhoōōnēᴛhen'se] *a* United States *cpd*, American ♦ *nm/f* United States citizen, American.

estafa [está'fá] *nf* swindle, trick; (*com etc*) racket.

estafar [estáfár'] *vt* to swindle, defraud.

estafeta [estáfe'tá] *nf* (*oficina de correos*) post office; **~ diplomática** diplomatic bag.

estalactita [estáláktē'tá] *nf* stalactite.

estalagmita [estálágmē'tá] *nf* stalagmite.

estallar [estáyár'] *vi* to burst; (*bomba*) to explode, go off; (*volcán*) to erupt; (*vidrio*) to shatter; (*látigo*) to crack; (*epidemia, guerra, rebelión*) to break out; **~ en llanto** to burst into tears.

estallido [estáyē'ᴛho] *nm* explosion; (*de látigo, trueno*) crack; (*fig*) outbreak.

estambre [estám'bre] *nm* (*tela*) worsted; (*bot*) stamen.

Estambul [estámbōōl'] *nm* Istanbul.

estamento [estámen'to] *nm* (social) class.

estampa [estám'pá] *nf* (*impresión, imprenta*) print, engraving; (*imagen, figura: de persona*) appearance.

estampado, a [estámpá'ᴛho, á] *a* printed ♦ *nm* (*impresión: acción*) printing; (: *efecto*) print; (*marca*) stamping.

estampar [estámpár'] *vt* (*imprimir*) to print; (*marcar*) to stamp; (*metal*) to engrave; (*poner sello en*) to stamp; (*fig*) to stamp, imprint.

estampida [estámpē'ᴛhá] *nf* stampede.

estampido [estámpē'ᴛho] *nm* bang, report.

estampilla [estámpē'yá] *nf* (*sello de goma*) (rubber) stamp; (*am*) stamp.

están [están'] *vb* V **estar.**

estancado, a [estánká'ᴛho, á] *a* (*agua*) stagnant.

estancamiento [estánkámyen'to] *nm* stagnation.

estancar [estánkár'] *vt* (*aguas*) to hold up, hold back; (*com*) to monopolize; (*fig*) to block, hold up; **~se** *vr* to stagnate.

estancia [están'syá] *nf* (*permanencia*) stay; (*sala*) room; (*am*) farm, ranch.

estanciero [estánsye'ro] *nm* (*am*) farmer, rancher.

estanco, a [están'ko, á] *a* watertight ♦ *nm* cigar store (*us*), tobacconist's (shop) (*Brit*).

estándar [están'dár] *a, nm* standard.

estandarice [estándárē'se] *etc vb* V **estandarizar.**

estandarizar [estándárēsár'] *vt* to standardize.

estandarte [estándár'te] *nm* banner, standard.

estanque [están'ke] *etc vb* V **estancar** ♦ *nm* (*lago*) pool, pond; (*agr*) reservoir.

estanquero, a [estánke'ro, á] *nm/f* tobacconist.

estante [están'te] *nm* (*armario*) rack, stand; (*biblioteca*) bookcase; (*anaquel*) shelf; (*am*) pier.

estantería [estánterē'á] *nf* shelving, shelves *pl*.

estaño [está'nyo] *nm* tin.

estar [estár'] *vi* (*gen*) to be; (*en casa*) to be in; (*ubicarse*) to be found; (*presente*) to be present; **~se** *vr*: **¡estate quieto!** keep still!; **se está bien aquí** it's nice here; **estamos a 2 de mayo** it is the 2nd of May; **¿cómo está usted?** how are you?; **~ enfermo** *o* **mal** to be ill; **~ viejo/joven** (*parecerse*) to seem old/young; **¿a cuánto estamos de Madrid?** (*seguido de una preposición*) how far are we from Madrid?; **~ de fiesta** *o* **vacaciones** to be on vacation; **las uvas están a 5 pesetas** grapes are at 5 pesetas; **María no está** Maria isn't in; **está fuera** (*de casa*) she's out; (*de ciudad*) she's away; **está de camarero** he's working as a waiter; **estaba de uniforme** he was (dressed) in uniform; **el problema está en que ...** the problem lies in the fact that ...; **no estoy para bromas** I'm not in the mood for jokes *o* joking; **~ por** (*moción*) to be in favor of; (*persona*) to support, back; **está por hacer** it remains to be done; **¿estamos?** are we agreed?; **¡ya está!** that's it!, there you are!; **¡ya está bien!** that's enough!

estarcir [estársēr'] *vt* to stencil.

estarza [estár'sá] *etc vb* V **estarcir.**

estas [e'stás] *a demostrativo* V **este.**

éstas [e'stás] *pron* V **éste.**

estás [estás'] *vb* V **estar.**

estatal [estátál'] *a* state *cpd*.

estático, a [está'tēko, á] *a* static.

estatua [está'twá] *nf* statue.

estatura [estátōō'rá] *nf* stature, height.

estatutario, a [estátōōtá'ryo, á] *a* statutory.

estatuto [estátōō'to] *nm* (*jur*) statute; (*de ciudad*) bye-law; (*de comité*) rule; **~s sociales** (*com*) articles of association.

este [es'te] *a* (*lado*) east; (*dirección*) easterly ♦ *nm* east; **en la parte del ~** in the eastern part.

este [e'ste], **esta** [e'stá], **estos** [e'stos], **estas** [e'stás] *a demostrativo* (*sg*) this; (*pl*) these.

éste [e'ste], **ésta** [e'stá], **éstos** [e'stos], **éstas** [e'stás] *pron* (*sg*) this (one); (*pl*) these (ones); **ése ... éste ...** the former ... the latter ....

esté [este'] *vb* V **estar.**

estela [este'lá] *nf* wake, wash; (*fig*) trail.

estelar [estelár'] *a* (*astro*) stellar; (*teatro*) star *cpd*.

estén [esten'] *vb* V **estar.**

estenografía [estenográfē'á] *nf* shorthand.

estentóreo, a [estento'reo, á] *a* (*sonido*) strident; (*voz*) booming.

estepa [este'pá] *nf* (*GEO*) steppe.

estera [este'rà] *nf* (*alfombra*) mat; (*tejido*) matting.

estercolero [esterkole'ro] *nm* manure heap, dunghill.

estéreo [este'reo] *a inv, nm* stereo.

estereofónico, a [estereofo'nēko, á] *a* stereophonic.

estereotipar [estereotēpár'] *vt* to stereotype.

estereotipo [estereotē'po] *nm* stereotype.

estéril [este'rēl] *a* sterile, barren; (*fig*) vain, futile.

esterilice [esterēlē'se] *etc vb V* **esterilizar.**

esterilizar [esterēlēsár'] *vt* to sterilize.

esterilla [esterē'yá] *nf* (*alfombrilla*) small mat.

esterlina [esterlē'ná] *a*: **libra ~** pound sterling.

esternón [esternon'] *nm* breastbone.

estertor [estertor'] *nm* death rattle.

estés [estes'] *vb V* **estar.**

esteta [este'tá] *nm/f* esthete (*US*), aesthete (*Brit*).

esteticienne [estetēsyen'] *nf* beautician.

estético, a [este'tēko, á] *a* esthetic (*US*), aesthetic (*Brit*) ♦ *nf* (a)esthetics *sg.*

estetoscopio [estetosko'pyo] *nm* stethoscope.

estibador [estēbàthor'] *nm* stevedore.

estibar [estēbàr'] *vt* (*NAUT*) to stow.

estiércol [estyer'kol] *nm* dung, manure.

estigma [estēg'má] *nm* stigma.

estigmatice [estēgmátē'se] *etc vb V* **estigmatizar.**

estigmatizar [estēgmátēsár'] *vt* to stigmatize.

estilar [estēlàr'] *vi*, **~se** *vr* (*estar de moda*) to be in fashion; (*usarse*) to be used.

estilice [estēlē'se] *etc vb V* **estilizar.**

estilizar [estēlēsár'] *vt* to stylize; (*TEC*) to design.

estilo [estē'lo] *nm* style; (*TEC*) stylus; (*NATACIÓN*) stroke; **~ de vida** lifestyle; **al ~ de** in the style of; **algo por el ~** something along those lines.

estilográfica [estēlogrà'fēká] *nf* fountain pen.

estima [estē'má] *nf* esteem, respect.

estimación [estēmásyon'] *nf* (*evaluación*) estimation; (*aprecio, afecto*) esteem, regard.

estimado, a [estēmá'tho, á] *a* esteemed; **"E~ Señor"** "Dear Sir".

estimador [estēmàthor'] *nm* (*COM*) estimator.

estimar [estēmár'] *vt* (*evaluar*) to estimate; (*valorar*) to appraise (*US*), value (*Brit*); (*apreciar*) to esteem, respect; (*pensar, considerar*) to think, reckon.

estimulante [estēmōōlàn'te] *a* stimulating ♦ *nm* stimulant.

estimular [estēmōōlàr'] *vt* to stimulate; (*excitar*) to excite; (*animar*) to encourage.

estímulo [estē'mōōlo] *nm* stimulus; (*ánimo*) encouragement; (*INFORM*) prompt.

estío [estē'o] *nm* summer.

estipendio [estēpen'dyo] *nm* salary; (*COM*) stipend.

estipulación [estēpōōlásyon'] *nf* stipulation, condition.

estipular [estēpōōlàr'] *vt* to stipulate.

estirado, a [estērá'tho, á] *a* (*tenso*) (stretched *o* drawn) tight; (*fig: persona*) stiff, pompous; (*engreído*) stuck-up.

estirar [estērár'] *vt* to stretch; (*dinero, suma etc*) to stretch out; (*cuello*) to crane; (*dinero*) to eke out; (*discurso*) to stretch out; **~ la pata** (*fam*) to kick the bucket; **~se** *vr* to stretch.

estirón [estēron'] *nm* pull, tug; (*crecimiento*) spurt, sudden growth; **dar un ~** (*niño*) to shoot up.

estirpe [estēr'pe] *nf* stock, lineage.

estival [estēbál'] *a* summer *cpd.*

esto [e'sto] *pron* this, this thing *o* matter; **~ de la boda** this business about the wedding; **en ~** at this *o* that point; **por ~** for this reason.

estocada [estoká'thá] *nf* (*acción*) stab; (*TAUR*) death blow.

Estocolmo [estokol'mo] *nm* Stockholm.

estofa [esto'fá] *nf*: **de baja ~** poor-quality.

estofado [estofá'tho] *nm* stew.

estofar [estofár'] *vt* (*bordar*) to quilt; (*CULIN*) to stew.

estoico, a [esto'eko, á] *a* (*FILOSOFÍA*) stoic(al); (*fig*) cold, indifferent.

estomacal [estomàkál'] *a* stomach *cpd*; **trastorno ~** stomach upset.

estómago [esto'màgo] *nm* stomach; **tener ~** to be thick-skinned.

estoque [esto'ke] *nm* rapier, sword.

estorbar [estorbàr'] *vt* to hinder, obstruct; (*fig*) to bother, disturb ♦ *vi* to be in the way.

estorbo [estor'ho] *nm* (*molestia*) bother, nuisance; (*obstáculo*) hindrance, obstacle.

estornino [estornē'no] *nm* starling.

estornudar [estornōōthár'] *vi* to sneeze.

estornudo [estornōō'tho] *nm* sneeze.

estos [e'stos] *a demostrativo V* **este.**

éstos [e'stos] *pron V* **éste.**

estoy [esto'e] *vb V* **estar.**

estrabismo [estrábēs'mo] *nm* squint.

estrado [estrá'tho] *nm* (*tarima*) platform; (*MUS*) bandstand; **~s** *nmpl* law courts.

estrafalario, a [estráfàlà'ryo, á] *a* odd, eccentric; (*desarreglado*) slovenly, sloppy.

estrago [estrá'go] *nm* ruin, destruction; **ha-**

cer ~s en to wreak havoc among.

estragón [estrá̱gon'] *nm* (*CULIN*) tarragon.

estrambólico, a [estrámbo'lĕko, á] *a* (*AM*), **estrambótico, a** [estrámbo'tĕko, á] *a* odd, eccentric.

estrangulación [estrángōōlásyon'] *nf* strangulation.

estrangulador, a [estrángōōlát̡or', á] *nm/f* strangler ♦ *nm* (*TEC*) throttle; (*AUTO*) choke.

estrangulamiento [estrángōōlámyen'to] *nm* (*AUTO*) bottleneck.

estrangular [estrángōōlár'] *vt* (*persona*) to strangle; (*MED*) to strangulate.

estraperlista [estráperlĕ'stá] *nm/f* black marketeer.

estraperlo [estráper'lo] *nm* black market.

estratagema [estrátáhe'má] *nf* (*MIL*) stratagem; (*astucia*) cunning.

estratega [estráte'g̱á] *nm/f* strategist.

estrategia [estráte'hyá] *nf* strategy.

estratégico, a [estráte'hĕko, á] *a* strategic.

estratificar [estrátĕfĕkár'] *vt* to stratify.

estratifique [estrátĕfĕ'ke] *etc vb* V **estratificar.**

estrato [estrá'to] *nm* stratum, layer.

estratosfera [estrátosfe'rá] *nf* stratosphere.

estrechar [estretchár'] *vt* (*reducir*) to narrow; (*vestido*) to take in; (*persona*) to hug, embrace; ~**se** *vr* (*reducirse*) to narrow, grow narrow; (*2 personas*) to embrace; ~ **la mano** to shake hands.

estrechez [estretches'] *nf* narrowness; (*de ropa*) tightness; (*intimidad*) intimacy; (*COM*) want o shortage of money; **estrecheces** *nfpl* financial difficulties.

estrecho, a [estretch'o, á] *a* narrow; (*apretado*) tight; (*íntimo*) close, intimate; (*miserable*) miserly ♦ *nm* strait; ~ **de miras** narrow-minded; **E~ de Gibraltar** Strait of Gibraltar.

estrella [estre'yá] *nf* star; ~ **fugaz** shooting star; ~ **de mar** starfish; **tener (buena)/ mala** ~ to be lucky/unlucky.

estrellado, a [estreyá't̡o, á] *a* (*forma*) star-shaped; (*cielo*) starry; (*huevos*) fried.

estrellar [estreyár'] *vt* (*hacer añicos*) to smash (to pieces); (*huevos*) to fry; ~**se** *vr* to smash; (*chocarse*) to crash; (*fracasar*) to fail.

estrellato [estreyá'to] *nm* stardom.

estremecer [estremeser'] *vt* to shake; ~**se** *vr* to shake, tremble; ~ **de** (*horror*) to shudder with; (*frío*) to shiver with.

estremecimiento [estremesĕmyen'to] *nm* (*temblor*) trembling, shaking.

estremezca [estremes'ká] *etc vb* V **estremecer.**

estrenar [estrenár'] *vt* (*vestido*) to wear for the first time; (*casa*) to move into; (*película, obra de teatro*) to present for the first

time; ~**se** *vr* (*persona*) to make one's début; (*película*) to have its premiere; (*TEATRO*) to open.

estreno [estre'no] *nm* (*primer uso*) first use; (*CINE etc*) premiere.

estreñido, a [estrenyĕ't̡o, á] *a* constipated.

estreñimiento [estrenyĕmyen'to] *nm* constipation.

estrépito [estre'pĕto] *nm* noise, racket; (*fig*) fuss.

estrepitoso, a [estrepĕto'so, á] *a* noisy; (*fiesta*) rowdy.

estrés [estres'] *nm* stress.

estresante [estresán'te] *a* stressful.

estría [estrĕ'á] *nf* groove; ~**s (en el cutis)** stretchmarks.

estribación [estrĕbásyon'] *nf* (*GEO*) spur; **estribaciones** *nfpl* foothills.

estribar [estrĕbár'] *vi*: ~ **en** to rest on, be supported by; **la dificultad estriba en el texto** the difficulty lies in the text.

estribillo [estrĕbĕ'yo] *nm* (*LITERATURA*) refrain; (*MUS*) chorus.

estribo [estrĕ'bo] *nm* (*de jinete*) stirrup; (*de coche, tren*) step; (*de puente*) support; (*GEO*) spur; **perder los** ~**s** to fly off the handle.

estribor [estrĕbor'] *nm* (*NAUT*) starboard.

estricnina [estrĕknĕ'ná] *nf* strychnine.

estricto, a [estrĕk'to, á] *a* (*riguroso*) strict; (*severo*) severe.

estridente [estrĕt̡en'te] *a* (*color*) loud; (*voz*) raucous.

estro [es'tro] *nm* inspiration.

estrofa [estro'fá] *nf* verse.

estropajo [estropá'ho] *nm* scourer.

estropear [estropeár'] *vt* (*arruinar*) to spoil; (*dañar*) to damage ♦ *vi* (*coche*) to break down; ~**se** *vr* (*objeto*) to get damaged; (*la piel etc*) to be ruined.

estropicio [estropĕ'syo] *nm* (*rotura*) breakage; (*efectos*) harmful effects *pl.*

estructura [estrōōktōō'rá] *nf* structure.

estruendo [estrwen'do] *nm* (*ruido*) racket, din; (*fig: alboroto*) uproar, turmoil.

estrujar [estrōōhár'] *vt* (*apretar*) to squeeze; (*aplastar*) to crush; (*fig*) to drain, bleed.

estuario [estwá'ryo] *nm* estuary.

estuche [estōōtch'e] *nm* box, case.

estudiante [estōōt̡yán'te] *nm/f* student.

estudiantil [estōōt̡yántĕl'] *a inv* student *cpd.*

estudiantina [estōōt̡yántĕ'ná] *nf* student music group.

estudiar [estōōt̡yár'] *vt* to study; (*propuesta*) to think about o over; ~ **para abogado** to study to become a lawyer.

estudio [estōō't̡yo] *nm* study; (*encuesta*) research; (*proyecto*) plan; (*piso*) studio apartment; (*CINE, ARTE, RADIO*) studio;

~s *nmpl* studies; (*erudición*) learning *sg*; **cursar** *o* **hacer** ~s to study; ~ **de casos prácticos** case study; ~ **de desplazamientos y tiempos** (*COM*) time and motion study; ~s **de motivación** motivational research *sg*; ~ **del trabajo** (*COM*) work study; ~ **de viabilidad** (*COM*) feasibility study.

estudioso, a [estōōᵗʰyo'so, á] *a* studious.

estufa [estōō'fá] *nf* heater, fire.

estulticia [estōōltē'syá] *nf* foolishness.

estupefaciente [estōōpefásyen'te] *a, nm* narcotic.

estupefacto, a [estōōpefák'to, á] *a* speechless, thunderstruck.

estupendamente [estōōpendámen'te] *ad* (*fam*): **estoy** ~ I feel great; **le salió** ~ he did it very well.

estupendo, a [estōōpen'do, á] *a* wonderful, terrific; (*fam*) great; ¡~! that's great!, fantastic!

estupidez [estōōpēᵗʰes'] *nf* (*torpeza*) stupidity; (*acto*) stupid thing (to do); **fue una** ~ **mía** that was a silly thing for me to do *o* say.

estúpido, a [estōō'pēᵗʰo, á] *a* stupid, silly.

estupor [estōōpor'] *nm* stupor; (*fig*) astonishment, amazement.

estupro [estōō'pro] *nm* rape.

estuve [estōō'he] *etc*, **estuviera** [estōōhye'rá] *etc vb* V **estar**.

esvástica [eshá'stēká] *nf* swastika.

ETA [e'tá] *nf abr* (*POL*:=*Euskadi Ta Askatasuna*) ETA, *Basque separatist movement.*

etapa [etá'pá] *nf* (*de viaje*) stage; (*DEPORTE*) leg; (*parada*) stopping place; (*fig*) stage, phase; **por** ~s gradually *o* in stages.

etarra [etá'rrá] *a* ETA *cpd* ♦ *nm/f* member of ETA.

etc. *abr* (= *etcétera*) etc.

etcétera [etse'terá] *ad* etcetera.

etéreo, a [cte'reo, á] *a* ethereal.

eternice [eternē'se] *etc vb* V **eternizar**.

eternidad [eternēᵗʰáᵗʰ'] *nf* eternity.

eternizarse [eternēsár'se] *vr*: ~ **en hacer algo** to take ages to do sth.

eterno, a [eter'no, á] *a* eternal, everlasting; (*despectivo*) never-ending.

ético, a [e'tēko, á] *a* ethical ♦ *nf* ethics.

etimología [etēmolohē'á] *nf* etymology.

etiqueta [etēke'tá] *nf* (*modales*) etiquette; (*rótulo*) label, tag; **de** ~ formal.

étnico, a [et'nēko, á] *a* ethnic.

eucalipto [eōōkálēp'to] *nm* eucalyptus.

Eucaristía [eōōkárēstē'á] *nf* Eucharist.

eufemismo [eōōfemēs'mo] *nm* euphemism.

euforia [eōōfo'ryá] *nf* euphoria.

eufórico, a [eōōfo'rēko, á] *a* euphoric.

eunuco [eōōnōō'ko] *nm* eunuch.

Europa [eōōro'pá] *nf* Europe.

europeice [eōōrope'ēse] *etc vb* V **europei-**

zar.

europeizar [eōōropeēsár'] *vt* to Europeanize; ~**se** *vr* to become Europeanized.

europeo, a [eōōrope'o, á] *a, nm/f* European.

éuscaro, a [e'ōōskáro, á] *a, nm/f* Basque.

Euskadi [eōōská'ᵗʰē] *nm* the Basque Provinces *pl*.

euskera, eusquera [eōōske'rá] *nm* (*LING*) Basque.

eutanasia [eōōtáná'syá] *nf* euthanasia.

evacuación [ehákwásyon'] *nf* evacuation.

evacuar [ehákwár'] *vt* to evacuate.

evadir [eháᵗʰēr'] *vt* to evade, avoid; ~**se** *vr* to escape.

evaluación [ehálwásyon'] *nf* evaluation, assessment.

evaluar [ehálwár'] *vt* to evaluate, assess.

evangélico, a [ehánhe'lēko, á] *a* evangelical.

evangelio [ehánhe'lyo] *nm* gospel.

evaporación [eháporásyon'] *nf* evaporation.

evaporar [eháporár'] *vt* to evaporate; ~**se** *vr* to vanish.

evasión [ehásyon'] *nf* escape, flight; (*fig*) evasion; ~ **fiscal** *o* **tributaria** tax evasion.

evasivo, a [ehásē'ho, á] *a* evasive, noncommittal ♦ *nf* (*pretexto*) excuse; **contestar con evasivas** to avoid giving a straight answer.

evento [ehen'to] *nm* event; (*eventualidad*) eventuality.

eventual [ehentwál'] *a* possible, conditional (upon circumstances); (*trabajador*) casual, temporary.

Everest [eherest'] *nm*: **el (Monte)** ~ (Mount) Everest.

evidencia [ehēᵗʰen'syá] *nf* evidence, proof; **poner en** ~ to make clear; **ponerse en** ~ (*persona*) to show o.s. up.

evidenciar [ehēᵗʰensyár'] *vt* (*hacer patente*) to make evident; (*probar*) to prove, show; ~**se** *vr* to be evident.

evidente [ehēᵗʰen'te] *a* obvious, clear, evident.

evitar [ehētár'] *vt* (*evadir*) to avoid; (*impedir*) to prevent; (*peligro*) to escape; (*molestia*) to save; (*tentación*) to shun; **si puedo** ~**lo** if I can help it.

evocador, a [ehokáᵗʰor', á] *a* (*sugestivo*) evocative.

evocar [ehokár'] *vt* to evoke, call forth.

evolución [eholōōsyon'] *nf* (*desarrollo*) evolution, development; (*cambio*) change; (*MIL*) maneuver (*US*), manoeuvre (*Brit*).

evolucionar [eholōōsyonár'] *vi* to evolve; (*MIL, AVIAT*) to maneuver (*US*), manoeuvre (*Brit*).

evoque [eho'ke] *etc vb* V **evocar**.

ex [eks] *a* ex-; **el** ~ **ministro** the former minister, the ex-minister.

exabrupto [eksáhrōōp'to] *nm* interjection.

exacción [cksáksyon'] *nf* (*acto*) exaction; (*de impuestos*) demand.

exacerbar [cksáscrhár'] *vt* to irritate, annoy.

exactamente [cksáktámen'tc] *ad* exactly.

exactitud [cksáktētōōth'] *nf* exactness; (*precisión*) accuracy; (*puntualidad*) punctuality.

exacto, a [cksák'to, á] *a* exact; accurate; punctual; ¡~! exactly!; **eso no es del todo** ~ that's not quite right; **para ser** ~ to be precise.

exageración [cksáhcrásyon'] *nf* exaggeration.

exagerado, a [cksáhcrä'tho, á] *a* (*relato*) exaggerated; (*precio*) excessive; (*persona*) over-demonstrative; (*gesto*) theatrical.

exagerar [cksáhcrár'] *vt* to exaggerate; (*exceder*) to overdo.

exaltado, a [cksáltä'tho, á] *a* (*apasionado*) over-excited, worked up; (*exagerado*) extreme; (*fanático*) hot-headed; (*discurso*) impassioned ♦ *nm/f* (*fanático*) hothead; (*POL*) extremist.

exaltar [cksáltár'] *vt* to exalt, glorify; ~**se** *vr* (*excitarse*) to get excited *o* worked up.

examen [cksá'men] *nm* examination; (*de problema*) consideration; ~ **de** (*encuesta*) inquiry into; ~ **de ingreso** entrance examination; ~ **de conducir** driving test; ~ **eliminatorio** qualifying examination.

examinar [cksámēnár'] *vt* to examine; (*poner a prueba*) to test; (*inspeccionar*) to inspect; ~**se** *vr* to be examined, take an examination.

exánime [cksá'nēmc] *a* lifeless; (*fig*) exhausted.

exasperar [cksáspcrár'] *vt* to exasperate; ~**se** *vr* to get exasperated, lose patience.

Exc.ª *abr* = **Excelencia.**

excarceler [ckskárcclár'] *vt* to release (from prison).

excavador, a [ckskáhàthor', á] *nm/f* (*persona*) excavator ♦ *nf* (*TEC*) digger.

excavar [ckskáhár'] *vt* to excavate, dig (out).

excedencia [cksethen'syá] *nf* (*MIL*) leave; (*ESCOL*) sabbatical.

excedente [cksethen'tc] *a, nm* excess, surplus.

exceder [cksether'] *vt* to exceed, surpass; ~**se** *vr* (*extralimitarse*) to go too far; (*sobrepasarse*) to excel o.s.

excelencia [cksclen'syá] *nf* excellence; **E**~ Excellency; **por** ~ par excellence.

excelente [cksclen'tc] *a* excellent.

excelso, a [cksel'so, á] *a* lofty, sublime.

excentricidad [cksentrēsēthàth'] *nf* eccentricity.

excéntrico, a [cksen'trēko, á] *a, nm/f* eccentric.

excepción [cksepsyon'] *nf* exception; **la** ~ **confirma la regla** the exception proves the rule.

excepcional [cksepsyonál'] *a* exceptional.

excepto [cksep'to] *ad* excepting, except (for).

exceptuar [ckseptwár'] *vt* to except, exclude.

excesivo, a [cksesē'ho, á] *a* excessive.

exceso [ckse'so] *nm* excess; (*COM*) surplus; ~ **de equipaje/peso** excess luggage/weight; ~ **de velocidad** speeding; **en** *o* **por** ~ excessively.

excitación [cksētásyon'] *nf* (*sensación*) excitement; (*acción*) excitation.

excitado, a [cksētá'tho, á] *a* excited; (*emociones*) aroused.

excitante [cksētán'tc] *a* exciting; (*MED*) stimulating ♦ *nm* stimulant.

excitar [cksētár'] *vt* to excite; (*incitar*) to urge; (*emoción*) to stir up; (*esperanzas*) to raise; (*pasión*) to arouse; ~**se** *vr* to get excited.

exclamación [cksklámásyon'] *nf* exclamation.

exclamar [cksklámár'] *vi* to exclaim; ~**se** *vr*: ~**se** (**contra**) to complain (about).

excluir [cksklōōēr'] *vt* to exclude; (*dejar fuera*) to shut out; (*solución*) to reject; (*posibilidad*) to rule out.

exclusión [cksklōōsyon'] *nf* exclusion.

exclusiva [cksklōōsē'hà] *nf* V **exclusivo.**

exclusive [cksklōōsē'hc] *prep* exclusive of, not counting.

exclusivo, a [cksklōōsē'ho, á] *a* exclusive ♦ *nf* (*PRENSA*) exclusive, scoop; (*COM*) sole right *o* agency; **derecho** ~ sole *o* exclusive right.

excluyendo [cksklōōyen'do] *etc vb* V **excluir.**

Excma., Excmo. *abr* (= *Excelentísima, Excelentísimo*) courtesy title.

excombatiente [ckskombátyen'tc] *nm* war veteran, ex-serviceman (*Brit*).

excomulgar [ckskomōōlgár'] *vt* (*REL*) to excommunicate.

excomulgue [ckskomōōl'gc] *etc vb* V **excomulgar.**

excomunión [ckskomōōnyon'] *nf* excommunication.

excoriar [ckskoryár'] *vt* to flay, skin.

excremento [ckskremen'to] *nm* excrement.

exculpar [ckskōōlpár'] *vt* to exonerate; (*JUR*) to acquit; ~**se** *vr* to exonerate o.s.

excursión [ckskōōrsyon'] *nf* excursion, outing; **ir de** ~ to go (off) on a trip.

excursionista [ckskōōrsyonē'stá] *nm/f* (*turista*) sightseer.

excusa [ckskōō'sá] *nf* excuse; (*disculpa*) apology; **presentar sus** ~**s** to excuse o.s.

excusado, a [ckskōōsá'tho, á] *a* unnecessary; (*disculpado*) excused, forgiven.

excusar [ekskōōsár'] *vt* to excuse; (*evitar*) to avoid, prevent; **~se** *vr* (*disculparse*) to apologize.

execrable [eksekrà'ble] *a* appalling.

exención [eksensyon'] *nf* exemption.

exento, a [eksen'to, à] *pp de* **eximir ♦** *a* exempt.

exequias [ekse'kyàs] *nfpl* funeral rites.

exhalación [eksálásyon'] *nf* (*del aire*) exhalation; (*vapor*) fumes *pl*, vapor (*US*), vapour (*Brit*); (*rayo*) shooting star; **salir como una ~** to shoot out.

exhalar [eksálár'] *vt* to exhale, breathe out; (*olor etc*) to give off; (*suspiro*) to breathe, heave.

exhaustivo, a [eksáōōstē'ho, à] *a* exhaustive.

exhausto, a [eksá'ōōsto, à] *a* exhausted, worn-out.

exhibición [eksēhēsyon'] *nf* exhibition; (*demostración*) display, show; (*de película*) showing; (*de equipo*) performance.

exhibicionista [eksēhēsyonē'stá] *a, nm/f* exhibitionist.

exhibir [eksēhēr'] *vt* to exhibit; to display, show; (*cuadros*) to exhibit; (*artículos*) to display; (*pasaporte*) to show; (*película*) to screen; (*mostrar con orgullo*) to show off; **~se** *vr* (*mostrarse en público*) to show o.s. off; (*fam: indecentemente*) to expose o.s.

exhortación [eksortásyon'] *nf* exhortation.

exhortar [eksortár'] *vt:* **~ a** to exhort to.

exhumar [eksōōmár'] *vt* to exhume.

exigencia [eksēhen'syá] *nf* demand, requirement.

exigente [eksēhen'te] *a* demanding; (*profesor*) strict; **ser ~ con uno** to be hard on sb.

exigir [eksēhēr'] *vt* (*gen*) to demand, require; (*impuestos*) to exact, levy; **~ el pago** to demand payment.

exiguo, a [eksē'gwo, à] *a* (*cantidad*) meager (*US*), meagre (*Brit*); (*objeto*) tiny.

exija [eksē'há] *etc vb V* **exigir.**

exiliado, a [eksēlyá'ho, à] *a* exiled, in exile ♦ *nm/f* exile.

exiliar [eksēlyár'] *vt* to exile; **~se** *vr* to go into exile.

exilio [eksē'lyo] *nm* exile.

eximio, a [eksē'myo, à] *a* (*eminente*) distinguished, eminent.

eximir [eksēmēr'] *vt* to exempt.

existencia [eksēsten'syá] *nf* existence; **~s** *nfpl* stock *sg*; **~ de mercancías** (*COM*) stock-in-trade; **tener en ~** to have in stock; **amargar la ~ a uno** to make sb's life miserable.

existir [eksēstēr'] *vi* to exist, be.

éxito [ek'sēto] *nm* (*resultado*) result, outcome; (*triunfo*) success; (*MUS, TEATRO*)

hit; **~ editorial** bestseller; **~ rotundo** smash hit; **tener ~** to be successful.

exitoso, a [eksēto'so, à] *a* successful.

éxodo [ek'sotho] *nm* exodus; **el ~ rural** urban flight.

ex oficio [eksofē'syo] *a, ad* ex officio.

exonerar [eksonerár'] *vt* to exonerate; **~ de una obligación** to free from an obligation.

exorcice [eksorsē'se] *etc vb V* **exorcizar.**

exorcismo [eksorsēs'mo] *nm* exorcism.

exorcizar [eksorsēsár'] *vt* to exorcize.

exótico, a [ekso'tēko, à] *a* exotic.

expandido, a [ekspándē'tho, à] *a:* **en caracteres ~s** (*INFORM*) double width.

expandir [ekspándēr'] *vt* to expand; (*COM*) to expand, enlarge; **~se** *vr* to expand, spread.

expansión [ekspánsyon'] *nf* expansion; (*recreo*) relaxation; **la ~ económica** economic growth; **economía en ~** expanding economy.

expansionar [ekspánsyonár'] *vt* to expand; **~se** *vr* (*dilatarse*) to expand; (*recrearse*) to relax.

expansivo, a [ekspánsē'ho, à] *a* expansive; (*efusivo*) communicative.

expatriado, a [ekspátryá'tho, à] *nm/f* (*emigrado*) expatriate; (*exiliado*) exile.

expatriarse [ekspátryàr'se] *vr* to emigrate; (*POL*) to go into exile.

expectación [ekspektásyon'] *nf* (*esperanza*) expectation; (*ilusión*) excitement.

expectativa [ekspektátē'há] *nf* (*espera*) expectation; (*perspectiva*) prospect; **~ de vida** life expectancy; **estar a la ~** to wait and see (what will happen).

expedición [ekspethēsyon'] *nf* (*excursión*) expedition; **gastos de ~** shipping charges.

expedientar [ekspethyentár'] *vt* to open a file on; (*funcionario*) to discipline, start disciplinary proceedings against.

expediente [ekspethyen'te] *nm* expedient; (*JUR: procedimento*) action, proceedings *pl*; (*: papeles*) dossier, file, record; **~ judicial** court proceedings *pl*; **~ académico** (student's) record.

expedir [ekspethēr'] *vt* (*despachar*) to send, forward; (*pasaporte*) to issue; (*cheque*) to make out.

expedito, a [ekspethē'to, à] *a* (*libre*) clear, free.

expeler [ekspeler'] *vt* to expel, eject.

expendedor, a [ekspendethor', à] *nm/f* (*vendedor*) dealer; (*TEATRO*) ticket agent ♦ *nm* (*aparato*) (vending) machine; **~ de cigarrillos** cigarette machine.

expendeduría [ekspendedōōrē'á] *nf* (*estanco*) cigar store (*US*), tobacconist's (shop) (*Brit*).

expensas [ekspen'sás] *nfpl* (*JUR*) costs; **a ~ de** at the expense of.

experiencia [eksperyen'syá] *nf* experience.
experimentado, a [eksperĕmentá'tʰo, á] *a* experienced.
experimentar [eksperĕmentár'] *vt* (*en laboratorio*) to experiment with; (*probar*) to test, try out; (*notar, observar*) to experience; (*deterioro, pérdida*) to suffer; (*aumento*) to show; (*sensación*) to feel.
experimento [eksperĕmen'to] *nm* experiment.
experto, a [eksper'to, á] *a* expert ♦ *nm/f* expert.
expiar [ekspĕár'] *vt* to atone for.
expida [ekspĕ'tʰá] *etc vb* V **expedir**.
expirar [ekspĕrár'] *vi* to expire.
explanada [eksplaná'tʰá] *nf* (*paseo*) esplanade; (*a orillas del mar*) promenade.
explayarse [ekspláyár'se] *vr* (*en discurso*) to speak at length; ~ **con uno** to confide in sb.
explicación [eksplĕkásyon'] *nf* explanation.
explicar [eksplĕkár'] *vt* to explain; (*teoría*) to expound; (*UNIV*) to lecture in; ~**se** *vr* to explain (o.s.); **no me lo explico** I can't understand it.
explícito, a [eksplĕ'sĕto, á] *a* explicit.
explique [eksplĕ'ke] *etc vb* V **explicar**.
exploración [eksplorásyon'] *nf* exploration; (*MIL*) reconnaissance.
explorador, a [eksploráthor', á] *nm/f* (*pionero*) explorer; (*MIL*) scout ♦ *nm* (*MED*) probe; (*radar*) (radar) scanner.
explorar [eksplorár'] *vt* to explore; (*MED*) to probe; (*radar*) to scan.
explosión [eksplosyon'] *nf* explosion.
explosivo, a [eksplosĕ'ʰo, á] *a* explosive.
explotación [eksplotásyon'] *nf* exploitation; (*de planta etc*) running; (*de mina*) working; (*de recurso*) development; ~ **minera** mine; **gastos de** ~ operating costs.
explotar [eksplotár'] *vt* to exploit; (*planta*) to run, operate; (*mina*) to work ♦ *vi* (*bomba etc*) to explode, go off.
expondré [ekspondre'] *etc vb* V **exponer**.
exponer [eksponer'] *vt* to expose; (*cuadro*) to display; (*vida*) to risk; (*idea*) to explain; (*teoría*) to expound; (*hechos*) to set out; ~**se** *vr*: ~**se a (hacer) algo** to run the risk of (doing) sth.
exponga [ekspon'gá] *etc vb* V **exponer**.
exportación [eksportásyon'] *nf* (*acción*) export; (*mercancías*) exports *pl*.
exportador, a [eksportáthor', á] *a* (*país*) exporting ♦ *nm/f* exporter.
exportar [eksportár'] *vt* to export.
exposición [eksposĕsyon'] *nf* (*gen*) exposure; (*de arte*) show, exhibition; (*COM*) display; (*feria*) show, fair; (*explicación*) explanation; (*de teoría*) exposition; (*narración*) account, statement.
exprés [ekspres'] *a inv* (*café*) espresso ♦ *nm*

(*AM*) express (train).
expresado, a [ekspresá'tʰo, á] *a* abovementioned.
expresamente [ekspresámen'te] *ad* (*concretamente*) expressly; (*a propósito*) on purpose.
expresar [ekspresár'] *vt* to express; (*redactar*) to phrase, put; (*emoción*) to show; ~**se** *vr* to express o.s.; (*dato*) to be stated; **como abajo se expresa** as stated below.
expresión [ekspresyon'] *nf* expression; ~ **familiar** colloquialism.
expresivo, a [ekspresĕ'ʰo, á] *a* expressive; (*cariñoso*) affectionate.
expreso, a [ekspre'so, á] *a* (*explícito*) express; (*claro*) specific, clear; (*tren*) fast ♦ *nm* (*FERRO*) fast train ♦ *ad*: **mandar** ~ to send by express (delivery).
exprimidor [eksprĕmĕtʰor'] *nm* (lemon) squeezer.
exprimir [eksprĕmĕr'] *vt* (*fruta*) to squeeze; (*zumo*) to squeeze out.
ex profeso [eksprofe'so] *ad* (*ADMIN, JUR*) on purpose.
expropiar [ekspropyár'] *vt* to expropriate.
expuesto, a [ekspwe'sto, á] *pp de* **exponer** ♦ *a* exposed; (*cuadro etc*) on show, on display; **según lo** ~ **arriba** according to what has been stated above.
expulsar [ekspŏ̄olsár'] *vt* (*echar*) to eject, throw out; (*alumno*) to expel; (*despedir*) to fire; (*DEPORTE*) to eject (*US*), send off (*Brit*).
expulsión [ekspŏ̄olsyon'] *nf* expulsion; (*DEPORTE*) ejection (*US*), sending-off (*Brit*).
expuse [ekspŏ̄o'se] *etc vb* V **exponer**.
expurgar [ekspŏ̄orgár'] *vt* to expurgate.
exquisito, a [ekskĕsĕ'to, á] *a* exquisite; (*comida*) delicious; (*afectado*) affected.
Ext. *abr* (= *Exterior*) ext.; (= *Extensión*) ext.
éxtasis [ek'stásĕs] *nm* ecstasy.
extemporáneo, a [ekstemporá'neo, á] *a* unseasonal.
extender [ekstender'] *vt* to extend; (*los brazos*) to stretch out, hold out; (*mapa, tela*) to spread (out), open (out); (*mantequilla*) to spread; (*certificado*) to issue; (*cheque, recibo*) to make out; (*documento*) to draw up; ~**se** *vr* to extend; (*terreno*) to stretch o spread (out); (*persona: en el suelo*) to stretch out; (*en el tiempo*) to extend, last; (*costumbre, epidemia*) to spread; (*guerra*) to escalate; ~**se sobre un tema** to enlarge on a subject.
extendido, a [ekstendĕ'tʰo, á] *a* (*abierto*) spread out, open; (*brazos*) outstretched; (*costumbre etc*) widespread.
extensible [ekstensĕ'ʰle] *a* extending.
extensión [ekstensyon'] *nf* (*de terreno, mar*) expanse, stretch; (*MUS*) range; (*de*

conocimientos) extent; (de programa) scope; (de tiempo) length, duration; (TELEC) extension; ~ de plazo (COM) extension; en toda la ~ de la palabra in every sense of the word; de ~ (INFORM) add-on.

extenso, a [eksten'so, á] a extensive.

extenuar [ekstenwár'] vt (debilitar) to weaken.

exterior [eksteryor'] a (de fuera) external; (afuera) outside, exterior; (apariencia) outward; (deuda, relaciones) foreign ♦ nm exterior, outside; (aspecto) outward appearance; (DEPORTE) forward (US), wing(er) (Brit); (países extranjeros) abroad; asuntos ~es foreign affairs; al ~ outwardly, on the outside; en el ~ abroad; noticias del ~ foreign o overseas news.

exteriorice [eksteryorē'se] etc vb V **exteriorizar**.

exteriorizar [eksteryorēsár'] vt (emociones) to show, reveal.

exteriormente [eksteryormen'te] ad outwardly.

exterminar [ekstermēnár'] vt to exterminate.

exterminio [ekstermē'nyo] nm extermination.

externo, a [ekster'no, á] a (exterior) external, outside; (superficial) outward ♦ nm/f day pupil.

extienda [ekstyen'dá] etc vb V **extender**.

extinción [ekstēnsyon'] nf extinction.

extinga [ekstēn'gá] etc vb V **extinguir**.

extinguido, a [ekstēngē'tho, á] a (animal, volcán) extinct; (fuego) out, extinguished.

extinguir [ekstēngēr'] vt (fuego) to extinguish, put out; (raza, población) to wipe out; ~se vr (fuego) to go out; (BIO) to die out, become extinct.

extinto, a [ekstēn'to, á] a extinct.

extintor [ekstēntor'] nm (fire) extinguisher.

extirpar [ekstērpár'] vt (vicios) to eradicate, stamp out; (MED) to remove (surgically).

extorsión [ekstorsyon'] nf blackmail.

extra [eks'trá] a inv (tiempo) extra; (vino) vintage; (chocolate) good-quality; (gasolina) high-octane ♦ nm/f extra ♦ nm (bono) bonus; (periódico) special edition.

extracción [ekstráksyon'] nf extraction; (en lotería) draw; (de carbón) mining.

extracto [ekstrák'to] nm extract.

extradición [ekstráthēsyon'] nf extradition.

extradicionar [ekstráthēsyonár'], **extraditar** [ekstráthētár'] vt to extradite.

extraer [ekstráer'] vt to extract, take out.

extrafino, a [ekstráfē'no, á] a extra-fine; **azúcar ~** caster sugar.

extraiga [ekstrá'ēgá] etc, **extraje** [ekstrá'he] etc, **extrajera** [ekstráhe'rá] etc vb V **extraer**.

extralimitarse [ekstrálēmētár'se] vr to go

too far.

extranjerismo [ekstránherēs'mo] nm foreign word o phrase etc.

extranjero, a [ekstránhe'ro, á] a foreign ♦ nm/f foreigner ♦ nm foreign lands pl; en el ~ abroad.

extrañamiento [ekstrányámyen'to] nm estrangement.

extrañar [ekstrányár'] vt (sorprender) to find strange o odd; (echar de menos) to miss; ~se vr (sorprenderse) to be amazed, be surprised; (distanciarse) to become estranged, grow apart; me extraña I'm surprised.

extrañeza [ekstránye'sá] nf (rareza) strangeness, oddness; (asombro) amazement, surprise.

extraño, a [ekstrá'nyo, á] a (extranjero) foreign; (raro, sorprendente) strange, odd.

extraoficial [ekstráofēsyál'] a unofficial, informal.

extraordinario, a [ekstráorthēnár'ryo, á] a extraordinary; (edición, número) special ♦ nm (de periódico) special edition; **horas extraordinaras** overtime sg.

extrarradio [ekstrárrá'thyo] nm suburbs pl.

extrasensorial [ekstrásensoryál'] a: **percepción ~** extrasensory perception.

extraterrestre [ekstráterres'tre] a of o from outer space ♦ nm/f creature from outer space.

extravagancia [ekstráhágán'syá] nf oddness; outlandishness; (rareza) peculiarity; ~s nfpl (tonterías) nonsense sg.

extravagante [ekstráhágán'te] a (excéntrico) eccentric; (estrafalario) outlandish.

extraviado, a [ekstráhyá'tho, á] a lost, missing.

extraviar [ekstráhyár'] vt to mislead, misdirect; (perder) to lose, misplace; ~se vr to lose one's way, get lost; (objeto) to go missing, be mislaid.

extravío [ekstráhē'o] nm loss; (fig) misconduct.

extrayendo [ekstráyen'do] vb V **extraer**.

extremado, a [ekstremá'tho, á] a extreme, excessive.

Extremadura [ekstremáthōō'rá] nf Estremadura.

extremar [ekstremár'] vt to carry to extremes; ~se vr to do one's utmost, make every effort.

extremaunción [ekstremáōōnsyon'] nf extreme unction, last rites pl.

extremidad [ekstremē'tháth'] nf (punta) extremity; (fila) edge; ~es nfpl (ANAT) extremities.

extremo, a [ekstre'mo, á] a extreme; (más alejado) furthest; (último) last ♦ nm end; (situación) extreme; **E~ Oriente** Far East; **en último ~** as a last resort; **pasar de un**

~ **a otro** (*fig*) to go from one extreme to the other; **con** ~ in the extreme; **la extrema derecha** (*POL*) the far right; ~ **derecho/izquierdo** (*DEPORTE*) outside right/ left.

extrínseco, a [ekstrēn'seko, á] *a* extrinsic.

extrovertido, a [ekstrohertē'tho, á] *a* extrovert, outgoing ♦ *nm/f* extrovert.

exuberancia [eksōōherán'syá] *nf* exuberance.

exuberante [eksōōherán'te] *a* exuberant; (*fig*) luxuriant, lush.

exudar [eksōōthár'] *vt, vi* to exude.

exultar [eksōōltár'] *vi:* ~ **(en)** to exult (in); (*pey*) to gloat (over).

exvoto [eksho'to] *nm* votive offering.

eyacular [eyákōōlár'] *vt, vi* to ejaculate.

F

F,f [e'fe] *nf* (*letra*) F, f; **F de Francia** F for Fox.

f.ª *abr* (*COM*: = *factura*) Inv.

f.a.b. *abr* (= *franco a bordo*) f.o.b.

fabada [fábá'thá] *nf bean and sausage stew.*

fábrica [fá'hrēká] *nf* factory; ~ **de moneda** mint; **marca de** ~ trademark; **precio de** ~ factory price.

fabricación [fábrēkásyon'] *nf* (*manufactura*) manufacture; (*producción*) production; **de** ~ **casera** home-made; **de** ~ **nacional** domestically produced; ~ **en serie** mass production.

fabricante [fábrēkán'te] *nm/f* manufacturer.

fabricar [fábrēkár'] *vt* (*manufacturar*) to manufacture, make; (*construir*) to build; (*cuento*) to fabricate, devise; ~ **en serie** to mass-produce.

fabrique [fábrē'ke] *etc vb V* **fabricar.**

fabril [fábrēl'] *a:* **industria** ~ manufacturing industry.

fábula [fá'hōōlá] *nf* (*cuento*) fable; (*chisme*) rumor (*US*), rumour (*Brit*); (*mentira*) fib.

FACA [fá'ká] *nm abr* (*Esp AVIAT*)=*Futuro Avión de Combate y Ataque.*

facción [fáksyon'] *nf* (*POL*) faction; **facciones** *nfpl* (*del rostro*) features.

faceta [fáse'tá] *nf* facet.

fácil [fá'sēl] *a* (*simple*) easy; (*sencillo*) simple, straightforward; (*probable*) likely; (*respuesta*) facile; ~ **de usar** (*INFORM*) user-friendly.

facilidad [fásēlētháth'] *nf* (*capacidad*) ease; (*sencillez*) simplicity; (*de palabra*) fluency;

~**es** *nfpl* facilities; "~**es de pago**" (*COM*) "credit facilities","payment terms".

facilitar [fásēlētár'] *vt* (*hacer fácil*) to make easy; (*proporcionar*) to provide; (*documento*) to issue; **le agradecería me facilitara** ... I would be grateful if you could let me have ....

fácilmente [fá'sēlmente] *ad* easily.

facsímil [fáksē'mēl] *nm* (*documento*) facsimile; **enviar por** ~ to fax.

factible [fáktē'hle] *a* feasible.

factor [fáktor'] *nm* factor; (*COM*) agent; (*FERRO*) freight clerk.

factoría [fáktorē'á] *nf* (*COM*: *agencia*) agency; (: *fábrica*) factory.

factura [fáktōō'rá] *nf* (*cuenta*) bill; (*nota de pago*) invoice; (*hechura*) manufacture; **presentar** ~ **a** to invoice.

facturación [fáktōōrásyon'] *nf* (*COM*) invoicing; (: *ventas*) turnover; ~ **de equipajes** luggage check-in.

facturar [fáktōōrár'] *vt* (*COM*) to invoice, charge for; (*AVIAT*) to check in; (*equipaje*) to check (*US*), register (*Brit*).

facultad [fákōōltáth'] *nf* (*aptitud, ESCOL etc*) faculty; (*poder*) power.

facultativo, a [fákōōltátē'ho, á] *a* optional; (*de un oficio*) professional; **prescripción facultativa** medical prescription.

facha [fátch'á] (*fam*) *nm/f* fascist, right-wing extremist ♦ *nf* (*aspecto*) look; (*cara*) face; **¡qué** ~ **tienes!** you look a sight!

fachada [fátchá'thá] *nf* (*ARQ*) façade, front; (*TIP*) title page; (*fig*) façade, outward show.

FAD *nm abr* (*Esp*)=*Fondo de Ayuda y Desarrollo.*

faena [fáe'ná] *nf* (*trabajo*) work; (*quehacer*) task, job; ~**s domésticas** housework *sg.*

faenar [fáenár'] *vi* to fish.

fagot [fáĝot'] *nm* (*MUS*) bassoon.

faisán [fáēsán'] *nm* pheasant.

faja [fá'há] *nf* (*para la cintura*) sash; (*de mujer*) corset; (*de tierra*) strip.

fajo [fá'ho] *nm* (*de papeles*) bundle; (*de billetes*) role, wad.

falange [fálán'he] *nf:* **la F~** (*POL*) the Falange.

falda [fál'dá] *nf* (*prenda de vestir*) skirt; (*GEO*) foothill; ~ **escocesa** kilt.

fálico, a [fá'lēko, á] *a* phallic.

falo [fá'lo] *nm* phallus.

falsear [fálseár'] *vt* to falsify; (*firma etc*) to forge ♦ *vi* (*MUS*) to be out of tune.

falsedad [fálsetháth'] *nf* falseness; (*hipocresía*) hypocrisy; (*mentira*) falsehood.

falsificación [fálsēfēkásyon'] *nf* (*acto*) falsification; (*objeto*) forgery.

falsificar [fálsēfēkár'] *vt* (*firma etc*) to forge; (*voto etc*) to rig; (*moneda*) to counterfeit.

falsifique |fálsēfē'kc| *etc vb* V **falsificar**.

falso, a |fál'so, á| *a* false; (*erróneo*) wrong, mistaken; (*firma, documento*) forged; (*documento, moneda etc*) fake; **en ~** falsely; **dar un paso en ~** to trip; (*fig*) to take a false step.

falta |fál'tá| *nf* (*defecto*) fault, flaw; (*privación*) lack, want; (*ausencia*) absence; (*carencia*) shortage; (*equivocación*) mistake; (*JUR*) default; (*DEPORTE*) foul; (*TENIS*) fault; **~ de ortografía** spelling mistake; **~ de respeto** disrespect; **echar en ~** to miss; **hacer ~ hacer algo** to be necessary to do sth; **me hace ~ una pluma** I need a pen; **sin ~** without fail; **por ~ de** through *o* for lack of.

faltar |fáltár'| *vi* (*escasear*) to be lacking, be wanting; (*ausentarse*) to be absent, be missing; **¿falta algo?** is anything missing?; **falta mucho todavía** there's plenty of time yet; **¿falta mucho?** is there long to go?; **faltan 2 horas para llegar** there are 2 hours to go till arrival; **~ (al respeto) a uno** to be disrespectful to sb; **~ a una cita** to miss an appointment; **~ a la verdad** to lie; **¡no faltaba más!** that's the last straw!

falto, a |fál'to, á| *a* (*desposeído*) deficient, lacking; (*necesitado*) poor, wretched; **estar ~ de** to be short of.

falla |fá'yá| *nf* (*defecto*) fault, flaw.

fallar |fáyár'| *vt* (*JUR*) to pronounce sentence on; (*NAIPES*) to trump ♦ *vi* (*memoria*) to fail; (*plan*) to go wrong; (*motor*) to miss; **~ a uno** to let sb down.

fallecer |fáyescr'| *vi* to pass away, die.

fallecido, a |fáycsē'tho, á| *a* late ♦ *nm/f* deceased.

fallecimiento |fáycsēmycn'to| *nm* decease, demise.

fallezca |fáycs'ká| *etc vb* V **fallecer**.

fallido, a |fáyē'tho, á| *a* vain; (*intento*) frustrated, unsuccessful; (*esperanza*) disappointed.

fallo |fá'yo| *nm* (*JUR*) verdict, ruling; (*decisión*) decision; (*de jurado*) findings; (*fracaso*) failure; (*DEPORTE*) miss; (*INFORM*) bug.

fama |fá'má| *nf* (*renombre*) fame; (*reputación*) reputation.

famélico, a |fámc'lēko, á| *a* starving.

familia |fámē'lyá| *nf* family; **~ política** in-laws *pl*.

familiar |fámēlyár'| *a* (*relativo a la familia*) family *cpd*; (*conocido, informal*) familiar; (*estilo*) informal; (*LING*) colloquial ♦ *nm/f* relative, relation.

familiarice |fámēlyárē'sc| *etc vb* V **familiarizarse**.

familiaridad |fámēlyárēthath'| *nf* familiarity; (*informalidad*) homeliness.

familiarizarse |fámēlyárēsár'sc| *vr*: **~ con** to familiarize o.s. with.

famoso, a |fámo'so, á| *a* (*renombrado*) famous.

fanático, a |fáná'tēko, á| *a* fanatical ♦ *nm/f* fanatic; (*CINE, DEPORTE etc*) fan.

fanatismo |fánátēs'mo| *nm* fanaticism.

fanfarrón, ona |fánfárron', oná| *a* boastful; (*pey*) showy.

fango |fán'go| *nm* mud.

fangoso, a |fángo'so, á| *a* muddy.

fantasear |fántáscár'| *vi* to fantasize; **~ con una idea** to toy with an idea.

fantasía |fántásē'á| *nf* fantasy, imagination; (*MUS*) fantasia; (*capricho*) whim; **joyas de ~** imitation jewellery *sg*.

fantasma |fántás'má| *nm* (*espectro*) ghost, apparition; (*presumido*) show-off.

fantástico, a |fántá'stēko, á| *a* (*irreal, fam*) fantastic.

FAO |fá'o| *nf abr* (= *Organización de las Naciones Unidas para la Agricultura y la Alimentación*) FAO.

fardar |fárthár'| *vi* to show off; **~ de** to boast about.

fardo |fár'tho| *nm* bundle; (*fig*) burden.

farmacéutico, a |fármásc'ōōtēko, á| *a* pharmaceutical ♦ *nm/f* pharmacist, chemist (*Brit*).

farmacia |fármá'syá| *nf* (*ciencia*) pharmacy; (*tienda*) drugstore (*US*), chemist's (shop) (*Brit*), pharmacy; **~ de turno** pharmacy on call (*US*), duty chemist (*Brit*).

fármaco |fár'máko| *nm* medicine, drug.

faro |fá'ro| *nm* (*NAUT: torre*) lighthouse; (*señal*) beacon; (*AUTO*) headlamp; **~s antiniebla** fog lamps; **~s delanteros/traseros** headlights/rear lights.

farol |fárol'| *nm* (*luz*) lantern, lamp; (*FERRO*) headlamp; (*poste*) lamppost; **echarse un ~** (*fam*) to show off.

farola |fáro'lá| *nf* street light, lamppost.

farruco, a |fárrōō'ko, á| *a* (*fam*): **estar** *o* **ponerse ~** to get aggressive.

farsa |fár'sá| *nf* (*gen*) farce.

farsante |fársán'tc| *nm/f* fraud, fake.

FASA |fá'sá| *nf abr* (*Esp AUTO*) = *Fábrica de Automóviles, S.A.*

fascículo |fásē'kōōlo| *nm* (*gen*) part, installment (*US*), instalment (*Brit*).

fascinante |fásēnán'tc| *a* fascinating.

fascinar |fásēnár'| *vt* to fascinate; (*encantar*) to captivate.

fascismo |fásēs'mo| *nm* fascism.

fascista |fásēs'tá| *a, nm/f* fascist.

fase |fá'sc| *nf* phase.

fastidiar |fástēthyár'| *vt* (*disgustar*) to annoy, bother; (*estropear*) to spoil; **~se** *vr* (*disgustarse*) to get annoyed *o* cross; **¡no fastidies!** you're joking!; **¡que se fastidie!** (*fam*) he'll just have to put up with it!

fastidio [fàstē'thyo] *nm* (*disgusto*) annoyance.

fastidioso, a [fàstēthyo'so, à] *a* (*molesto*) annoying.

fastuoso, a [fàstwo'so, à] *a* (*espléndido*) magnificent; (*banquete etc*) lavish.

fatal [fátál'] *a* (*gen*) fatal; (*desgraciado*) ill-fated; (*fam: malo, pésimo*) awful ♦ *ad* terribly; **lo pasó ~** he had a terrible time (of it).

fatalidad [fàtálēthàth'] *nf* (*destino*) fate; (*mala suerte*) misfortune.

fatídico, a [fátē'thēko, à] *a* fateful.

fatiga [fàtē'gà] *nf* (*cansancio*) fatigue, weariness; **~s** *nfpl* hardships.

fatigar [fàtēgàr'] *vt* to tire, weary; **~se** *vr* to get tired.

fatigoso, a [fàtēgo'so, à] *a* (*cansador*) tiring.

fatigue [fàtē'ge] *etc vb* V **fatigar**.

fatuo, a [fá'two, à] *a* (*vano*) fatuous; (*presuntuoso*) conceited.

fauces [fà'ōōses] *nfpl* (*ANAT*) gullet *sg*; (*fam*) jaws.

fauna [fà'ōōnà] *nf* fauna.

favor [fàbor'] *nm* favor (*US*), favour (*Brit*); **haga el ~ de ...** would you be so good as to ..., kindly ...; **por ~** please; **a ~ in** favo(u)r; **a ~ de** to be in favo(u)r of; (*COM*) to the order of.

favorable [fàborá'ble] *a* favorable (*US*), favourable (*Brit*); (*condiciones etc*) advantageous.

favorecer [fàboreser'] *vt* to favor (*US*), favour (*Brit*); (*amparar*) to help; (*vestido etc*) to become, flatter; **este peinado le favorece** this hairstyle suits him.

favorezca [fàbores'kà] *etc vb* V **favorecer**.

favorito, a [fàborē'to, à] *a, nm/f* favorite (*US*), favourite (*Brit*).

faz [fás] *nf* face; **la ~ de la tierra** the face of the earth.

F.C., f.c. *abr* = **ferrocarril**.

FE *nf abr* = *Falange Española*.

fe [fe] *nf* (*REL*) faith; (*confianza*) belief; (*documento*) certificate; **de buena ~** (*JUR*) bona fide; **prestar ~ a** to believe, credit; **actuar con buena/mala ~** to act in good/bad faith; **dar ~ de** to bear witness to; **~ de erratas** errata.

fealdad [feáldàth'] *nf* ugliness.

feb., feb.º *abr* (= *febrero*) Feb.

febrero [febre'ro] *nm* February.

febril [febrēl'] *a* feverish; (*movido*) hectic.

fécula [fe'kōōlà] *nf* starch.

fecundación [fekōōndásyon'] *nf* fertilization; **~ in vitro** in vitro fertilization, I.V.F.

fecundar [fekōōndàr'] *vt* (*generar*) to fertilize, make fertile.

fecundidad [fekōōndēthàth'] *nf* fertility; (*fig*) productiveness.

fecundo, a [fekōōn'do, à] *a* (*fértil*) fertile; (*fig*) prolific; (*productivo*) productive.

fecha [fetch'à] *nf* date; **~ límite** *o* **tope** closing *o* last date; **~ límite de venta** (*de alimentos*) sell-by date; **~ de caducidad** (*de alimentos*) sell-by date; (*de contrato*) expiration (*US*) *o* expiry (*Brit*) date; **en ~ próxima** soon; **hasta la ~** to date, so far; **~ de vencimiento** (*COM*) due date; **~ de vigencia** (*COM*) effective date.

fechar [fetchàr'] *vt* to date.

federación [fetheràsyon'] *nf* federation.

federal [fetherál'] *a* federal.

federalismo [fetherálēs'mo] *nm* federalism.

FEF *nf abr* = *Federación Española de Fútbol*.

felicidad [felēsēthàth'] *nf* (*satisfacción, contento*) happiness; **~es** *nfpl* best wishes, congratulations.

felicitaciones [felēsētàsyo'nes] *nfpl* congratulations.

felicitar [felēsētàr'] *vt* to congratulate.

feligrés, esa [felēgres', esà] *nm/f* parishioner.

feliz [felēs'] *a* (*contento*) happy; (*afortunado*) lucky.

felonía [felonē'à] *nf* felony, crime.

felpa [fel'pà] *nf* (*terciopelo*) plush; (*toalla*) towelling.

felpudo [felpōō'tho] *nm* doormat.

femenino, a [femenē'no, à] *a* feminine; (*ZOOL etc*) female ♦ *nm* (*LING*) feminine.

feminismo [femēnēs'mo] *nm* feminism.

feminista [femēnē'stà] *a, nm/f* feminist.

fenomenal [fenomenál'] *a* phenomenal; (*fam*) great, terrific.

fenómeno [feno'meno] *nm* phenomenon; (*fig*) freak, accident ♦ *ad*: **lo pasamos ~** we had a great time ♦ *excl* great!, marvelous! (*US*), marvellous! (*Brit*).

feo, a [fe'o, à] *a* (*gen*) ugly; (*desagradable*) bad, nasty ♦ *nm* insult; **hacer un ~ a uno** to offend sb; **más ~ que Picio** as ugly as sin.

féretro [fe'retro] *nm* (*ataúd*) coffin; (*sarcófago*) bier.

feria [fe'ryà] *nf* (*gen*) fair; (*AM: mercado*) market; (*descanso*) holiday, day off; (*AM: cambio*) small change; **~ comercial** trade fair; **~ de muestras** trade show.

feriado, a [feryà'tho, à] *a* (*AM*) *a*: **día ~** (public) holiday ♦ *nm* (public) holiday.

fermentar [fermentàr'] *vi* to ferment.

fermento [fermen'to] *nm* leaven, leavening.

ferocidad [ferosēthàth'] *nf* fierceness, ferocity.

ferocísimo, a [ferosē'sēmo, à] *a superlativo de* **feroz**.

feroz [feros'] *a* (*cruel*) cruel; (*salvaje*) fierce.

férreo, a [fe'rreo, à] *a* iron *cpd*; (*TEC*)

ferrous; (fig) (of) iron.

ferretería [fɛrrɛtɛrɛ̄'á] nf (tienda) hardware store, ironmonger's (shop) (Brit).

ferrocarril [fɛrrokárrēl'] nm railroad, railway (Brit); ~ **de vía estrecha/única** narrow-gauge/single-track railway o line.

ferroviario, a [fɛrrovyáryo', á] a rail cpd, railroad cpd (US), railway cpd (Brit) ♦ nm: ~s railroad (US) o railway (Brit) workers.

fértil [fɛr'tēl] a (productivo) fertile; (rico) rich.

fertilice [fɛrtēlē'se] etc vb V **fertilizar.**

fertilidad [fɛrtēlēthá̄th'] nf (gen) fertility; (productividad) fruitfulness.

fertilizar [fɛrtēlēsár'] vt to fertilize.

fervor [fɛrβor'] nm fervor (US), fervour (Brit).

fervoroso, a [fɛrβoro'so, á] a fervent.

festejar [festehár'] vt (agasajar) to wine and dine, fête; (galantear) to court; (celebrar) to celebrate.

festejo [feste'ho] nm (diversión) entertainment; (galanteo) courtship; (fiesta) celebration.

festín [festēn'] nm feast, banquet.

festival [festēβál'] nm festival.

festividad [festēβēthá̄th'] nf festivity.

festivo, a [festē'βo, á] a (de fiesta) festive; (fig) witty; (CINE, LIT) humorous; **día ~** holiday.

fetiche [fetētch'e] nm fetish.

fetichista [fetētchē'stá] a fetishistic ♦ nm/f fetishist.

fétido, a [fe'tētho, á] a (hediondo) foul-smelling.

feto [fe'to] nm fetus; (fam) monster.

FF.AA. nfpl abr (MIL) = **Fuerzas Armadas.**

FF.CC. nmpl abr = **Ferrocarriles.**

fiable [fēá'hle] a (persona) trustworthy; (máquina) reliable.

fiado [fēá'tho] nm: **comprar al ~** to buy on credit; **en ~** on bail.

fiador, a [fēáthor', á] nm/f (JUR) surety, guarantor; (COM) backer; **salir ~ por uno** to post (US) o stand (Brit) bail for sb.

fiambre [fyám'bre] a (CULIN) (served) cold ♦ nm (CULIN) cold cut; (fam) corpse, stiff.

fiambrera [fyámbre'rá] nf ≈ dinner pail (US), lunch box.

fianza [fyán'sá] nf surety; (JUR): **libertad bajo ~** release on bail.

fiar [fēár'] vt (salir garante de) to guarantee; (JUR) to post (US) o stand (Brit) bail for; (vender a crédito) to sell on credit; (secreto) to confide ♦ vi: ~ **(de)** to trust (in); **ser de ~** to be trustworthy; ~**se** vr: ~ **de** to trust (in), rely on.

fiasco [fyás'ko] nm fiasco.

fibra [fē'hrá] nf fiber (US), fibre (Brit); (fig) vigor (US), vigour (Brit); ~ **óptica** (IN-

FORM) optical fiber.

ficción [fēksyon'] nf fiction.

ficticio, a [fēktē'syo, á] a (imaginario) fictitious; (falso) fabricated.

ficus [fē'kōōs] nm inv (BOT) rubber plant.

ficha [fētch'á] nf (TELEC) token; (en juegos) counter, marker; (en casino) chip; (COM, ECON) check (US), tally; (INFORM) file; (tarjeta) (index) card; (ELEC) plug; (en hotel) registration form; ~ **policíaca** police dossier.

fichaje [fētchá'he] nm signing(-up).

fichar [fētchár'] vt (archivar) to file, index; (DEPORTE) to sign (up) ♦ vi (deportista) to sign (up); (obrero) to clock in o on; **estar fichado** to have a record.

fichero [fētche'ro] nm card index; (archivo) filing cabinet; (COM) box file; (INFORM) file, archive; (de policía) criminal records; ~ **activo** (INFORM) active file; ~ **archivado** (INFORM) archived file; ~ **indexado** (INFORM) index file; ~ **de reserva** (INFORM) backup file; ~ **de tarjetas** card index; **nombre de ~** filename.

fidedigno, a [fēthethēg'no, á] a reliable.

fideicomiso [fēthēēkomē'so] nm (COM) trust.

fidelidad [fēthēlēthá̄th'] nf (lealtad) fidelity, loyalty; (exactitud: de dato etc) accuracy; **alta ~** high fidelity, hi-fi.

fidelísimo, a [fēthēlē'sēmo, á] a superlativo de **fiel.**

fideos [fēthe'os] nmpl noodles.

fiduciario, a [fēthōōsyá'ryo, á] nm/f fiduciary.

fiebre [fye'hre] nf (MED) fever; (fig) fever, excitement; ~ **amarilla/del heno** yellow/hay fever; ~ **palúdica** malaria; **tener ~** to have a temperature.

fiel [fyel] a (leal) faithful, loyal; (fiable) reliable; (exacto) accurate ♦ nm (aguja) needle, pointer; **los ~es** the faithful.

fieltro [fyel'tro] nm felt.

fiera [fye'rá] nf V **fiero.**

fiereza [fyere'sá] nf (ZOOL) wildness; (bravura) fierceness.

fiero, a [fye'ro, á] a (cruel) cruel; (feroz) fierce; (duro) harsh ♦ nm/f (fig) fiend ♦ nf (animal feroz) wild animal o beast; (fig) dragon.

fiesta [fye'stá] nf party; (de pueblo) festival; (vacaciones: tb: ~s) holiday; ~ **nacional** national (US) o bank (Brit) holiday; **mañana es ~** it's a holiday tomorrow; ~ **de guardar** (REL) day of obligation.

figura [fēgōō'rá] nf (gen) figure; (forma, imagen) shape, form; (NAIPES) face card.

figurado, a [fēgōōrá'tho, á] a figurative.

figurar [fēgōōrár'] vt (representar) to represent; (fingir) to feign ♦ vi to figure; ~**se** vr (imaginarse) to imagine; (suponer) to suppose; **ya me lo figuraba** I thought as much.

fijador [fēhádʰor'] *nm* (*FOTO etc*) fixative; (*de pelo*) cream (*US*), gel (*Brit*).

fijar [fēhár'] *vt* (*gen*) to fix; (*cartel*) to post, put up; (*estampilla*) to affix, stick (on); (*pelo*) to set; (*fig*) to settle (on), decide; **~se** *vr*: **~se en** to notice; **¡fíjate!** just imagine!; **¿te fijas?** see what I mean?

fijo, a [fē'ho, á] *a* (*gen*) fixed; (*firme*) firm; (*permanente*) permanent; (*trabajo*) steady; (*color*) fast ♦ *ad*: **mirar ~** to stare.

fila [fē'lá] *nf* row; (*MIL*) rank; (*cadena*) line; (*MIL*) rank; (*en marcha*) file; **~ india** single file; **ponerse en ~** to line up, get into line; **primera ~** front row.

filántropo, a [fēlán'tropo, á] *nm/f* philanthropist.

filarmónico, a [fēlármo'nēko, á] *a*, *nf* philharmonic.

filatelia [fēláte'lyá] *nf* philately, stamp collecting.

filatelista [fēlátelē'stá] *nm/f* philatelist, stamp collector.

filete [fēle'te] *nm* (*carne*) fillet steak; (*de cerdo*) tenderloin; (*pescado*) fillet; (*MEC: rosca*) thread.

filiación [fēlyásyon'] *nf* (*POL etc*) affiliation; (*señas*) particulars *pl*; (*MIL, POLICÍA*) records *pl*.

filial [fēlyál'] *a* filial ♦ *nf* subsidiary; (*sucursal*) branch.

filibustero [fēlēbōōste'ro] *nm* pirate.

Filipinas [fēlēpē'nás] *nfpl*: **las (Islas) ~** the Philippines.

filipino, a [fēlēpē'no, á] *a*, *nm/f* Philippine.

film [fēlm], *pl* **films** *nm* movie.

filmación [fēlmásyon'] *nf* filming, shooting.

filmar [fēlmár'] *vt* to film, shoot.

filmoteca [fēlmote'ká] *nf* film library.

filo [fē'lo] *nm* (*gen*) edge; **sacar ~ a** to sharpen; **al ~ del medio día** at about midday; **de doble ~** double-edged.

filología [fēlolohē'á] *nf* philology.

filólogo, a [fēlo'logo, á] *nm/f* philologist.

filón [fēlon'] *nm* (*MINERÍA*) vein, lode; (*fig*) gold mine.

filosofía [fēlosofē'á] *nf* philosophy.

filosófico, a [fēloso'fēko, á] *a* philosophic(al).

filósofo, a [fēlo'sofo, á] *nm/f* philosopher.

filtración [fēltrásyon'] *nf* (*TEC*) filtration; (*INFORM*) sorting; (*fig: de fondos*) misappropriation; (*de datos*) leak.

filtrar [fēltrár'] *vt*, *vi* to filter, strain; (*información*) to leak; **~se** *vr* to filter; (*fig: dinero*) to dwindle.

filtro [fēl'tro] *nm* (*TEC, utensilio*) filter.

fin [fēn] *nm* end; (*objetivo*) aim, purpose; **a ~ de cuentas** in the end; **al ~ y al cabo** when all's said and done; **a ~ de** in order

to; **por ~** finally; **en ~** in short; **~ de archivo** (*INFORM*) end-of-file; **~ de semana** weekend; **sin ~** endless(ly).

final [fēnál'] *a* final ♦ *nm* end, conclusion ♦ *nf* (*DEPORTE*) championship (*US*), final (*Brit*).

finalice [fēnálē'se] *etc vb V* **finalizar**.

finalidad [fēnálēdʰád'] *nf* finality; (*propósito*) purpose, aim.

finalista [fēnálē'stá] *nm/f* finalist.

finalizar [fēnálēsár'] *vt* to end, finish ♦ *vi* to end, come to an end; **~ la sesión** (*INFORM*) to log off *o* out (*Brit*).

financiación [fēnánsyásyon'] *nf* financing.

financiar [fēnánsyár'] *vt* to finance.

financiero, a [fēnánsye'ro, á] *a* financial ♦ *nm/f* financier.

finanzas [fēnán'sás] *nfpl* finances.

finca [fēn'ká] *nf* country estate.

fineza [fēne'sá] *nf* (*cualidad*) fineness; (*modales*) refinement.

fingir [fēnhēr'] *vt* (*simular*) to simulate, feign; (*pretextar*) to fake ♦ *vi* (*aparentar*) to pretend; **~se** *vr*: **~se dormido** to pretend to be asleep.

finiquitar [fēnēkētár'] *vt* (*ECON: cuenta*) to settle and close.

Finisterre [fēnēste'rre] *nm*: **el cabo de ~** Cape Finisterre.

finja [fēn'há] *etc vb V* **fingir**.

finlandés, esa [fēnlándes', esá] *a* Finnish ♦ *nm/f* Finn ♦ *nm* (*LING*) Finnish.

Finlandia [fēnlán'dyá] *nf* Finland.

fino, a [fē'no, á] *a* fine; (*delgado*) slender; (*de buenas maneras*) polite, refined; (*inteligente*) shrewd; (*punta*) sharp; (*gusto*) discriminating; (*oído*) sharp; (*jerez*) fino, dry ♦ *nm* (*jerez*) dry sherry.

finura [fēnōō'rá] *nf* (*calidad*) fineness; (*cortesía*) politeness; (*elegancia*) elegance; (*agudeza*) shrewdness.

FIP [fēp] *nf abr* (*Esp*)=*Formación Intensiva Profesional*.

firma [fēr'má] *nf* signature; (*COM*) firm, company.

firmante [fērmán'te] *a*, *nm/f* signatory; **los abajo ~s** the undersigned.

firmar [fērmár'] *vt* to sign; **~ un contrato** (*COM: colocarse*) to sign on; **firmado y sellado** signed and sealed.

firme [fēr'me] *a* firm; (*estable*) stable; (*sólido*) solid; (*constante*) steady; (*decidido*) resolute; (*duro*) hard; **¡~s!** (*MIL*) attention!; **oferta en ~** (*COM*) firm offer ♦ *nm* road (surface).

firmemente [fērmemen'te] *ad* firmly.

firmeza [fērme'sá] *nf* firmness; (*constancia*) steadiness; (*solidez*) solidity.

fiscal [fēskál'] *a* fiscal ♦ *nm* (*JUR*) ≈ district attorney.

fiscalice [fēskálē'se] *etc vb V* **fiscalizar**.

fiscalizar [fēskálēsár'] *vt* (*controlar*) to control; (*registrar*) to inspect (officially); (*fig*) to criticize.

fisco [fēs'ko] *nm* (*hacienda*) treasury, exchequer (*Brit*); **declarar algo al** ~ to declare sth for tax purposes.

fisgar [fēsg̱ár'] *vt* to pry into.

fisgue [fēs'g̱e] *etc vb* V **fisgar**.

físico, a [fē'sēko, á] *a* physical ♦ *nm* physique; (*aspecto*) appearance, looks ♦ *nm/f* physicist ♦ *nf* physics *sg*.

fisonomía [fēsonomē'á] *nf* physiognomy, features *pl*.

fisonomista [fēsonomē'stá] *nm/f*: **ser buen** ~ to have a good memory for faces.

flac(c)idez [flá(k)sēt̄es'] *nf* softness, flabbiness.

flác(c)ido, a [flá'(k)sēt̄o, á] *a* flabby.

flaco, a [flá'ko, á] *a* (*muy delgado*) skinny, thin; (*débil*) weak, feeble.

flagrante [flág̱rán'te] *a* flagrant.

flamante [flámán'te] *a* (*fam*) brilliant; (: *nuevo*) brand-new.

flamear [flámeár'] *vt* (*CULIN*) to flambé.

flamenco, a [flámen'ko, á] *a* (*de Flandes*) Flemish; (*baile, música*) gipsy ♦ *nm/f* Fleming; **los** ~**s** the Flemish ♦ *nm* (*LING*) Flemish; (*baile, música*) flamenco.

flan [flán] *nm* custard (*US*), creme caramel (*Brit*).

flanco [flán'ko] *nm* side; (*MIL*) flank.

Flandes [flán'des] *nm* Flanders.

flanquear [flánkeár'] *vt* to flank; (*MIL*) to outflank.

flaquear [flákeár'] *vi* (*debilitarse*) to weaken; (*persona*) to slack.

flaqueza [fláke'sá] *nf* (*delgadez*) thinness, leanness; (*fig*) weakness.

flaquísimo, a [flákē'sēmo, á] *a superlativo de* **flaco**.

flash [flás], *pl* **flashes** [flás] *nm* (*FOTO*) flash.

flato [flá'to] *nm*: **el** (*o* **un**) ~ the (*o* a) stitch.

flauta [flá'ō͞otá] (*MUS*) *nf* flute ♦ *nm/f* flautist, flute player.

fleco [fle'ko] *nm* fringe.

flecha [fletch'á] *nf* arrow.

flechazo [fletchá'so] *nm* (*acción*) bowshot; (*fam*): **fue un** ~ it was love at first sight.

flema [fle'má] *nm* phlegm.

flemático, a [flemá'tēko, á] *a* phlegmatic; (*tono etc*) matter-of-fact.

flemón [flemon'] *nm* (*MED*) gumboil.

flequillo [flekē'yo] *nm* (*pelo*) bangs *pl* (*US*), fringe (*Brit*).

fletar [fletár'] *vt* (*COM*) to charter; (*embarcar*) to load; (*AUTO*) to lease (purchase).

flete [fle'te] *nm* (*carga*) freight; (*alquiler*) charter; (*precio*) freightage.

flexible [fleksē'ble] *a* flexible; (*individuo*) compliant.

flipper [flē'per] *nm* pinball machine.

flirtear [flērteár'] *vi* to flirt.

FLN *nm abr* (*POL*: *Esp, Perú, Venezuela*) = *Frente de Liberación Nacional*.

flojera [flohe'rá] *nf* (*AM*) laziness; **me da** ~ I can't be bothered.

flojo, a [flo'ho, á] *a* (*gen*) loose; (*sin fuerzas*) limp; (*débil*) weak; (*viento*) light; (*bebida*) weak; (*trabajo*) poor; (*actitud*) lazy; (*precio*) low; (*COM*: *mercado*) dull.

flor [flor] *nf* flower; (*piropo*) compliment; **la** ~ **y nata de la sociedad** (*fig*) the cream of society; **en la** ~ **de la vida** in the prime of life; **a** ~ **de** on the surface of.

florecer [floreser'] *vi* (*BOT*) to flower, bloom; (*fig*) to flourish.

floreciente [floresyen'te] *a* (*BOT*) in flower, flowering; (*fig*) thriving.

Florencia [floren'syá] *nf* Florence.

florero [flore'ro] *nm* vase.

florezca [flores'ká] *etc vb* V **florecer**.

florista [florē'stá] *nm/f* florist.

flota [flo'tá] *nf* fleet.

flotación [flotásyon'] *nf* (*COM*) flotation.

flotador [flotát̄or'] *nm* (*gen*) float; (*para nadar*) life preserver (*US*), rubber ring (*Brit*); (*de cisterna*) ballcock.

flotante [flotán'te] *a* floating; (*INFORM*): **de coma** ~ floating-point.

flotar [flotár'] *vi* to float.

flote [flo'te] *nm*: **a** ~ afloat; **ponerse a** ~ (*fig*) to get back on one's feet.

FLS *nm abr* (*POL*: *Nicaragua*)=*Frente de Liberación Sandinista*.

fluctuación [flōō͞oktwásyon'] *nf* fluctuation.

fluctuante [flōō͞oktwán'te] *a* fluctuating.

fluctuar [flōō͞oktwár'] *vi* (*oscilar*) to fluctuate.

fluidez [flōō͞et̄es'] *nf* fluidity; (*fig*) fluency.

flúido, a [flōō͞o'ēt̄o, á] *a* fluid; (*lenguaje*) fluent; (*estilo*) smooth ♦ *nm* (*líquido*) fluid.

fluir [flōō͞er'] *vi* to flow.

flujo [flōō͞o'ho] *nm* flow; (*POL*) swing; (*NAUT*) rising tide; ~ **y reflujo** ebb and flow; ~ **de sangre** (*MED*) hemorrhage (*US*), haemorrhage (*Brit*); ~ **positivo/negativo de efectivo** (*COM*) positive/negative cash flow.

flujograma [flōō͞ohog̱rá'má] *nm* flowchart.

fluoruro [flworō͞o'ro] *nm* fluoride.

fluvial [flōō͞obēál'] *a* fluvial, river *cpd*.

fluyendo [flōō͞oyen'do] *etc vb* V **fluir**.

F.M. *nf abr* (= *Frecuencia Modulada*) F.M.

FMI *nm abr* (= *Fondo Monetario Internacional*) I.M.F.

F.N. *nf abr* (*Esp POL*)=*Fuerza Nueva* ♦ *nm* = *Frente Nacional*.

FNPT *nm abr* (*Esp*)=*Fondo Nacional de Protección del Trabajo*.

f.º *abr* (= *folio*) fo., fol.

foca [fo'ká] *nf* seal.

foco [fo'ko] *nm* focus; (*centro*) focal point;

fofo, a |fo'fo, à| *a* (*esponjoso*) soft, spongy; (*músculo*) flabby.

fogata |foɣá'tá| *nf* (*hoguera*) bonfire.

fogón |foɣon'| *nm* (*de cocina*) ring.

fogoso, a |foɣo'so, à| *a* spirited.

fol. *abr* (= *folio*) fo., fol.

folio |fo'lyo| *nm* folio; (*hoja*) leaf.

follaje |foɣá'hc| *nm* foliage.

follar |foɣár'| *vt, vi* (*fam!*) to fuck(*!*).

folletinesco, a |foyctēncs'ko, à| *a* melodramatic.

folleto |foyc'to| *nm* pamphlet; (*COM*) brochure; (*prospecto*) leaflet; (*ESCOL etc*) handout.

follón |foyon'| *nm* (*fam: lío*) mess; (: *conmoción*) fuss, rumpus; **armar un ~** to kick up a fuss; **se armó un ~** there was a hell of a row.

fomentar |fomentár'| *vt* (*MED*) to foment; (*fig: promover*) to promote, foster; (*odio etc*) to stir up.

fomento |fomen'to| *nm* (*fig: ayuda*) fostering; (*promoción*) promotion.

fonda |fon'dá| *nf* inn.

fondear |fondcár'| *vt* (*NAUT: sondear*) to sound; (*barco*) to search.

fondo |fon'do| *nm* (*de caja etc*) bottom; (*medida*) depth; (*de coche, sala*) back; (*ARTE etc*) background; (*reserva*) fund; (*fig: carácter*) nature; **~s** *nmpl* (*COM*) funds, resources; **~ de amortización** (*COM*) sinking fund; **F~ Monetario Internacional** International Monetary Fund; **~ del mar** sea bed *o* floor; **una investigación a ~** a thorough investigation; **en el ~** deep down; **tener buen ~** to be good-natured.

fonética |fonc'tēkà| *nf* phonetics *sg*.

fonógrafo |fono'ɡráfo| *nm* (*AM*) phonograph, gramophone.

fonología |fonolohē'á| *nf* phonology.

fontanería |fontáncrē'á| *nf* plumbing.

fontanero |fontánc'ro| *nm* plumber.

footing |foō'tēn| *nm* jogging; **hacer ~** to jog.

F.O.P. |fop| *nfpl abr* (*Esp*) = **Fuerzas del Orden Público**.

forajido |foráhē'ðo| *nm* outlaw.

foráneo, a |forá'nco, à| *a* foreign ♦ *nm/f* outsider.

forastero, a |foráste'ro, à| *nm/f* stranger.

forcé |forse'| *vb V* **forzar**.

forcejear |forsehcár'| *vi* (*luchar*) to struggle.

forcemos |forse'mos| *etc vb V* **forzar**.

forense |foren'sc| *a* forensic ♦ *nm/f* pathologist.

forestal |forestál'| *a* forest *cpd*.

forjar |forhár'| *vt* to forge; (*formar*) to form.

forma |for'má| *nf* (*figura*) form, shape; (*molde*) mold (*US*), mould (*Brit*), pattern; (*MED*) fitness; (*método*) way, means; **estar en ~** to be fit; **~ de pago** (*COM*) method of payment; **las ~s** the conventions; **de ~ que** ... so that ...; **de todas ~s** in any case.

formación |formásyon'| *nf* (*gen*) formation; (*enseñanza*) training; **~ profesional** vocational training; **~ fuera del trabajo** off-the-job training; **~ en el trabajo** *o* **sobre la práctica** on-the-job training.

formal |formál'| *a* (*gen*) formal; (*fig: persona*) serious; (: *de fiar*) reliable; (*conducta*) steady.

formalice |formálē'sc| *etc vb V* **formalizar**.

formalidad |formálēðaħ'| *nf* formality; seriousness; reliability; steadiness.

formalizar |formálēsár'| *vt* (*JUR*) to formalize; (*plan*) to draw up; (*situación*) to put in order, regularize; **~se** *vr* (*situación*) to be put in order, be regularized.

formar |formár'| *vt* (*componer*) to form, shape; (*constituir*) to make up, constitute; (*ESCOL*) to train, educate ♦ *vi* (*MIL*) to fall in; (*DEPORTE*) to line up; **~se** *vr* (*ESCOL*) to be trained (*o* educated); (*cobrar forma*) to form, take form; (*desarrollarse*) to develop.

formatear |formátcár'| *vt* (*INFORM*) to format.

formateo |formátc'o| *nm* (*INFORM*) formatting.

formato |formá'to| *nm* (*INFORM*): **sin ~** (*disco, texto*) unformatted; **~ de registro** record format.

formidable |formēðá'hlc| *a* (*temible*) formidable; (*asombroso*) tremendous.

fórmula |for'mōōlà| *nf* formula.

formulario |formōōlá'ryo| *nm* form; **~ de solicitud/de pedido** (*COM*) application/order form; **llenar un ~** to fill in a form; **~ contínuo desplegable** (*INFORM*) fanfold paper.

fornicar |fornēkár'| *vi* to fornicate.

fornido, a |fornē'ðo, à| *a* well-built.

fornique |fornē'kc| *etc vb V* **fornicar**.

foro |fo'ro| *nm* (*gen*) forum; (*JUR*) court.

forofo, a |foro'fo, à| *nm/f* fan.

FORPPA |for'pà| *nm abr* (*Esp*) = *Fondo de Ordenación y Regulación de Productos y Precios Agrarios*.

forrado, a |forrá'ðo, à| *a* (*ropa*) lined; (*fam*) well-heeled.

forrar |forrár'| *vt* (*abrigo*) to line; (*libro*) to cover; (*coche*) to upholster; **~se** *vr* (*fam*) to line one's pockets.

forro |fo'rro| *nm* (*de cuaderno*) cover; (*costura*) lining; (*de sillón*) upholstery.

fortalecer |fortáleser'| *vt* to strengthen; **~se** *vr* to fortify o.s.; (*opinión etc*) to become stronger.

fortaleza [fortále'sá] *nf* (*MIL*) fortress, stronghold; (*fuerza*) strength; (*determinación*) resolution.

fortalezca [fortáles'ká] *etc vb* V **fortalecer**.

fortificar [fortéfékár'] *vt* to fortify; (*fig*) to strengthen.

fortifique [fortéfé'ke] *etc vb* V **fortificar**.

fortísimo, a [fortés'imo, á] *a superlativo de* **fuerte**.

fortuito, a [fortwé'to, á] *a* accidental, chance *cpd*.

fortuna [fortoo'ná] *nf* (*suerte*) fortune; (good) luck; (*riqueza*) fortune, wealth.

forzar [forsár'] *vt* (*puerta*) to force (open); (*compeler*) to compel; (*violar*) to rape; (*ojos etc*) to strain.

forzoso, a [forso'so, á] *a* necessary; (*inevitable*) inescapable; (*obligatorio*) compulsory.

forzudo, a [forsoo'tho, á] *a* burly.

fosa [fo'sá] *nf* (*sepultura*) grave; (*en tierra*) pit; (*MED*) cavity; **~s nasales** nostrils.

fosfato [fosfá'to] *nm* phosphate.

fósforo [fos'foro] *nm* (*QUÍMICA*) phosphorus; (*cerilla*) match.

fósil [fo'sél] *a* fossil, fossilized ♦ *nm* fossil.

foso [fo'so] *nm* ditch; (*TEATRO*) pit; (*AUTO*): **~ de reconocimiento** inspection pit.

foto [fo'to] *nf* photo, snap(shot); **sacar una ~** to take a photo *o* picture.

fotocopia [fotoko'pyá] *nf* photocopy.

fotocopiadora [fotokopyátho'rá] *nf* photocopier.

fotocopiar [fotokopyár'] *vt* to photocopy.

fotoestilo [fotoesté'lo] *nm* (*INFORM*) light pen.

fotografía [fotográfé'á] *nf* (*arte*) photography; (*una ~*) photograph.

fotografiar [fotográfyár'] *vt* to photograph.

fotógrafo, a [foto'gráfo, á] *nm/f* photographer.

fotómetro [foto'metro] *nm* (*FOTO*) light meter.

foulard [foolár'] *nm* head(scarf).

FP *nf abr* (*Esp*: *ESCOL, COM*) = *Formación Profesional* ♦ *nm abr* (*POL*) = *Frente Popular*.

FPLP *nm abr* (*POL*: = *Frente Popular para la Liberación de Palestina*) PFLP.

Fr. *abr* (= *Fray*) Fr.; (= *franco*) Fr.

frac [frák], *pl* **fracus** *o* **fraques** [frá'kes] *nm* dress coat, tails.

fracasar [frákásár'] *vi* (*gen*) to fail; (*plan etc*) to fall through.

fracaso [fráká'so] *nm* (*desgracia, revés*) failure; (*de negociaciones etc*) collapse, breakdown.

fracción [fráksyon'] *nf* fraction; (*POL*) faction, splinter group.

fraccionamiento [fráksyonámyen'to] *nm* (*AM*) housing development (*US*) *o* estate (*Brit*).

fractura [fráktoo'rá] *nf* fracture, break.

fragancia [frágán'syá] *nf* (*olor*) fragrance, perfume.

fragante [frágán'te] *a* fragrant, scented.

fraganti [frágán'té]: **in ~** *ad*: **coger a uno in ~** to catch sb red-handed.

frágil [frá'hél] *a* (*débil*) fragile; (*COM*) breakable; (*fig*) frail, delicate.

fragilidad [fráhélétháth'] *nf* fragility; (*de persona*) frailty.

fragmento [frágmen'to] *nm* fragment; (*pedazo*) piece; (*de discurso*) excerpt; (*de canción*) snatch.

fragor [frágor'] *nm* (*ruido intenso*) din.

fragua [frá'gwá] *nf* forge.

fraguar [frágwár'] *vt* to forge; (*fig*) to concoct ♦ *vi* to harden.

fragüe [frá'gwe] *etc vb* V **fraguar**.

fraile [frá'éle] *nm* (*REL*) friar; (: *monje*) monk.

frambuesa [frámbwe'sá] *nf* raspberry.

francés, esa [fránses', esá] *a* French ♦ *nm/f* Frenchman/woman ♦ *nm* (*LING*) French.

Francia [frán'syá] *nf* France.

franco, a [frán'ko, á] *a* (*cándido*) frank, open; (*COM*: *exento*) free ♦ *nm* (*moneda*) franc; **~ de derechos** duty-free; **~ al costado del buque** (*COM*) free alongside ship; **~ puesto sobre vagón** (*COM*) free on rail; **~ a bordo** free on board.

francotirador, a [fránkotéráthor', á] *nm/f* sniper.

franela [fráne'lá] *nf* flannel.

franja [frán'há] *nf* fringe; (*de uniforme*) stripe; (*de tierra etc*) strip.

franquear [fránkeár'] *vt* (*camino*) to clear; (*carta, paquete postal*) to frank, stamp; (*obstáculo*) to overcome; (*COM etc*) to free, exempt.

franqueo [fránke'o] *nm* postage.

franqueza [fránke'sá] *nf* (*candor*) frankness.

franquicia [fránké'syá] *nf* exemption; **~ aduanera** exemption from customs duties.

franquísimo, a [fránké'sémo, á] *a superlativo de* **franco**.

franquista [fránké'stá] *a* pro-Franco ♦ *nm/f* supporter of Franco.

frasco [frás'ko] *nm* bottle, flask; **~ al vacío** (vacuum) flask.

frase [frá'se] *nf* sentence; (*locución*) phrase, expression; **~ hecha** set phrase; (*despectivo*) cliché.

fraude [frá'oothe] *nm* (*cualidad*) dishonesty; (*acto*) fraud, swindle.

fraudulento, a [frá'oothoolen'to, á] *a* fraudulent.

frazada [frásá'thá] *nf* (*AM*) blanket.

frecuencia [frekwen'syå] *nf* frequency; **con**
~ frequently, often; ~ **de red** (*INFORM*)
mains frequency; ~ **del reloj** (*INFORM*)
clock speed; ~ **telefónica** voice frequency.

frecuente [frekwen'te] *a* frequent;
(*costumbre*) common; (*vicio*) rife.

fregadero [freɣáđe'ro] *nm* (kitchen) sink.

fregador, a [freɣáđor', å] *nm/f* (*tb*: ~ **de
platos**) dishwasher.

fregar [freɣár'] *vt* (*frotar*) to scrub; (*platos*)
to wash (up); (*AM*) to annoy.

fregona [freɣo'nå] *nf* (*utensilio*) mop; (*pey*:
sirvienta) maid.

fregué [freɣe'], **freguemos** [freɣe'mos] *etc vb*
V **fregar**.

freír [freēr'] *vt* to fry.

fréjol [fre'hol] *nm* = **fríjol**.

frenar [frenár'] *vt* to brake; (*fig*) to check.

frenazo [frenå'so] *nm*: **dar un** ~ to brake
sharply.

frenesí [frenese'] *nm* frenzy.

frenético, a [frene'teko, å] *a* frantic; **ponerse** ~ to lose one's head.

freno [fre'no] *nm* (*TEC, AUTO*) brake; (*de
cabalgadura*) bit; (*fig*) check.

frente [fren'te] *nm* (*ARQ, MIL, POL*) front;
(*de objeto*) front part ♦ *nf* forehead, brow;
~ **de batalla** battle front; **hacer** ~ **común
con uno** to make common cause with sb;
~ **a** in front of; (*en situación opuesta de*)
opposite; **chocar de** ~ to crash head-on;
hacer ~ **a** to face up to.

fresa [fre'så] *nf* (*Esp*: *fruta*) strawberry; (*de
dentista*) drill.

fresco, a [fres'ko, å] *a* (*nuevo*) fresh; (*huevo*) newly-laid; (*frío*) cool; (*descarado*)
sassy (*US*), cheeky (*Brit*) ♦ *nm* (*aire*) fresh
air; (*ARTE*) fresco ♦ *nm/f* (*fam*) shameless
person; (*persona insolente*) impudent
person; **tomar el** ~ to get some fresh air;
¡qué ~! what a mouth (*US*) o cheek (*Brit*)!

frescor [freskor'] *nm* freshness.

frescura [freskoo'rå] *nf* freshness; (*descaro*)
nerve; (*calma*) calmness.

fresno [fres'no] *nm* ash (tree).

fresón [freson'] *nm* strawberry.

frialdad [fryáldáth'] *nf* (*gen*) coldness; (*indiferencia*) indifference.

fricción [freksyon'] *nf* (*gen*) friction; (*acto*)
rub(bing); (*MED*) massage; (*POL, fig etc*)
friction, trouble.

friega [frye'ɡå] *etc*, **friegue** [frye'ɡe] *etc vb V*
fregar.

friendo [frēen'do] *etc vb V* **freír**.

frigidez [frēhíđes'] *nf* frigidity.

frígido, a [frē'hēđo, å] *a* frigid.

frigorífico, a [frēɡorē'fēko, å] *a* refrigera-
ting; **instalación frigorífica** cold-storage
plant ♦ *nm* refrigerator; (*camión*) freezer
truck (*US*) o lorry (*Brit*).

frijol [frēhol'], **fríjol** [frē'hol] *nm* kidney bean.

frió [frēo'] *vb V* **freír**.

frío, a [frē'o, å] *etc vb V* **freír** ♦ *a* cold; (*fig*:
indiferente) unmoved, indifferent; (*poco entusiasta*) chilly ♦ *nm* cold(ness); indifference; **¡qué** ~! how cold it is!

friolero, a [fryole'ro, å] *a* sensitive to cold.

frito, a [frē'to, å] *pp de* **freír** ♦ *a* fried ♦ *nm*
fry; **me trae** ~ **ese hombre** I'm sick and
tired of that man; ~**s variados** mixed grill.

frívolo, a [frē'ḃolo, å] *a* frivolous.

frondoso, a [frondo'so, å] *a* leafy.

frontera [fronte'rå] *nf* frontier; (*línea divisoria*) border; (*zona*) frontier area.

fronterizo, a [fronterē'so, å] *a* frontier *cpd*;
(*contiguo*) bordering.

frontal [frontál'] *nm*: **choque** ~ head-on
collision.

frontón [fronton'] *nm* (*DEPORTE*: *cancha*)
jai alai court; (: *juego*) jai alai.

frotar [frotár'] *vt* to rub; (*fósforo*) to strike;
~**se** *vr*: ~**se las manos** to rub one's hands.

frs. *abr* (= *francos*) fr.

fructífero, a [frookte'fero, å] *a* productive,
fruitful.

frugal [frooɡál'] *a* frugal.

fruncir [froonsēr'] *vt* (*COSTURA*) to gather;
(*ceño*) to frown; (*labios*) to purse.

frunza [froon'så] *etc vb V* **fruncir**.

frustrar [froostrár'] *vt* to frustrate; ~**se** *vr*
to be frustrated; (*plan etc*) to fail.

fruta [froo'tå] *nf* fruit.

frutal [frootál'] *a* fruit-bearing, fruit *cpd* ♦
nm: (*árbol*) ~ fruit tree.

frutería [frooterē'å] *nf* fruit shop.

frutero, a [froote'ro, å] *a* fruit *cpd* ♦ *nm/f*
fruit vendor ♦ *nm* fruit dish o bowl.

frutilla [froote'yå] *nf* (*AM*) strawberry.

fruto [froo'to] *nm* (*BOT*) fruit; (*fig*: *resultado*) result, outcome; ~**s secos** ≈ nuts and
raisins.

FSLN *nm abr* (*POL*: *Nicaragua*)=*Frente
Sandinista de Liberación Nacional*.

fue [fwe] *vb V* **ser, ir**.

fuego [fwe'ɡo] *nm* (*gen*) fire; (*CULIN*: *gas*)
ring; (*MIL*) fire; (*fig*: *pasión*) fire, passion;
~**s artificiales** o **de artificio** fireworks;
prender ~ **a** to set fire to; **a** ~ **lento** on a
low heat; **¡alto el** ~! cease fire!; **estar entre dos** ~**s** to be in the crossfire; **¿tienes**
~? have you (got) a light?

fuel-oil [fooelo'él] *nm* kerosene (*US*),
paraffin (*Brit*).

fuelle [fwe'ye] *nm* bellows *pl*.

fuente [fwen'te] *nf* fountain; (*manantial,
fig*) spring; (*origen*) source; (*plato*) large
dish; ~ **de alimentación** (*INFORM*) power
supply; **de** ~ **desconocida/fidedigna** from
an unknown/reliable source.

fuera [fwe'rå] *etc vb* **ser, ir** ♦ *ad* out(side);
(*en otra parte*) away; (*excepto, salvo*)
except, save ♦ *prep*: ~ **de** outside; (*fig*) be-

sides; ~ **de alcance** out of reach; ~ **de combate** out of action; (*boxeo*) knocked out; ~ **de sí** beside o.s.; **por** ~ (on the) outside; **los de** ~ strangers, newcomers; **estar** ~ (*en el extranjero*) to be abroad.

fuera-borda [fwerá↕or'ṭá] *nm inv* outboard engine *o* motor.

fuerce [fwer'se] *etc vb V* **forzar.**

fuero [fwe'ro] *nm* (*carta municipal*) municipal charter; (*leyes locales*) local *o* regional law code; (*privilegio*) privilege; (*autoridad*) jurisdiction; (*fig*): **en mi** *etc* ~ **interno** in my *etc* heart of hearts ..., deep down ....

fuerte [fwer'te] *a* strong; (*golpe*) hard; (*ruido*) loud; (*comida*) rich; (*lluvia*) heavy; (*dolor*) intense ♦ *ad* strongly; hard; loud(ly) ♦ *nm* (*MIL*) fort, strongpoint; (*fig*): **el canto no es mi** ~ singing is not my strong point.

fuerza [fwer'sá] *etc vb V* **forzar** ♦ *nf* (*fortaleza*) strength; (*TEC, ELEC*) power; (*coacción*) force; (*violencia*) violence; (*MIL*: *tb*: ~**s**) forces *pl*; ~ **de arrastre** (*TEC*) pulling power; ~ **de brazos** manpower; ~ **mayor** force majeure; ~ **bruta** brute force; ~**s armadas (FF.AA.)** armed forces; ~ **de Orden Público (F.O.P.)** police (forces); ~ **vital** vitality; **a** ~ **de** by (means of); **cobrar** ~**s** to recover one's strength; **tener** ~**s para** to have the strength to; **a la** ~ forcibly, by force; **con** ~ **legal** (*COM*) legally binding; **por** ~ of necessity; ~ **de voluntad** willpower.

fuga [foo'gá] *nf* (*huida*) flight, escape; (*de enamorados*) elopement; (*de gas etc*) leak; ~ **de cerebros** (*fig*) brain drain.

fugarse [foogár'se] *vr* to flee, escape.

fugaz [foogás'] *a* fleeting.

fugitivo, a [foohētē'ṭo, á] *a* fugitive, fleeing ♦ *nm/f* fugitive.

fugue [foo'ge] *etc vb V* **fugarse.**

fui [fwē] *etc vb V* **ser, ir.**

fulano, a [foolá'no, á] *nm/f* so-and-so, what's-his-name.

fulgor [foolġor'] *nm* brilliance.

fulminante [foolmēnán'te] *a* (*pólvora*) fulminating; (*fig*: *mirada*) withering; (*MED*) fulminant; (*fam*) terrific, tremendous.

fumador, a [foomáṭhor', á] *nm/f* smoker; **no** ~ non-smoker.

fumar [foomár'] *vt, vi* to smoke; ~**se** *vr* (*disipar*) to squander; ~ **en pipa** to smoke a pipe.

funámbulo, a [foonám'boolo, á], **funambulista** [foonámboolē'stá] *nm/f* tightrope walker.

función [foonsyon'] *nf* function; (*de puesto*) duties *pl*; (*TEATRO etc*) show; **entrar en funciones** to take up one's duties; ~ **de**

tarde/de noche matinée/evening performance.

funcionamiento [foonsyonámyen'to] *nm* functioning; (*TEC*) working; **en** ~ (*COM*) on line; **entrar en** ~ to come into operation.

funcionar [foonsyonár'] *vi* (*gen*) to function; (*máquina*) to work; "**no funciona**" "out of order".

funcionario, a [foonsyoná'ryo, á] *nm/f* official; (*público*) civil servant.

funda [foon'dá] *nf* (*gen*) cover; (*de almohada*) pillowcase; ~ **protectora del disco** (*INFORM*) disk-jacket.

fundación [foondásyon'] *nf* foundation.

fundado, a [foondá'ṭho, á] *a* (*justificado*) well-founded.

fundamental [foondámentál'] *a* fundamental, basic.

fundamentar [foondámentár'] *vt* (*poner base*) to lay the foundations of; (*establecer*) to found; (*fig*) to base.

fundamento [foondámen'to] *nm* (*base*) foundation; (*razón*) grounds; **eso carece de** ~ that is groundless.

fundar [foondár'] *vt* to found; (*crear*) to set up; (*fig*: *basar*): ~ (**en**) to base *o* found (on); ~**se** *vr*: ~**se en** to be founded on.

fundición [foondēsyon'] *nf* (*acción*) smelting; (*fábrica*) foundry; (*TIP*) font.

fundir [foondēr'] *vt* (*gen*) to fuse; (*metal*) to smelt, melt down; (*COM*) to merge; (*estatua*) to cast; ~**se** *vr* (*colores etc*) to merge, blend; (*unirse*) to fuse together; (*ELEC*: *fusible, lámpara etc*) to blow; (*nieve etc*) to melt.

fúnebre [foo'neḅre] *a* funeral *cpd*, funereal.

funeral [foonerál'] *nm* funeral.

funeraria [foonerá'ryá] *nf* mortician's (*US*), undertaker's (*Brit*).

funesto, a [foone'sto, á] *a* ill-fated; (*desastroso*) fatal.

furgón [foorgon'] *nm* wagon.

furgoneta [foorgone'tá] *nf* (*AUTO, COM*) pickup (truck).

furia [foo'ryá] *nf* (*ira*) fury; (*violencia*) violence.

furibundo, a [foorēḅoon'do, á] *a* furious.

furioso, a [fooryo'so, á] *a* (*iracundo*) furious; (*violento*) violent.

furor [fooror'] *nm* (*cólera*) rage; (*pasión*) frenzy, passion; **hacer** ~ to be a sensation.

furtivo, a [foortē'ṭo, á] *a* furtive ♦ *nm* poacher.

furúnculo [fooroon'koolo] *nm* (*MED*) boil.

fuselaje [foosela'he] *nm* fuselage.

fusible [foosē'ḅle] *nm* fuse.

fusil [foosēl'] *nm* rifle.

fusilamiento [foosēlámyen'to] *nm* (*JUR*) execution by firing squad.

fusilar [foosēlár'] *vt* to shoot.

fusión [fōōsyon'] *nf* (*gen*) melting; (*unión*) fusion; (*COM*) merger, amalgamation.

fusionar [fōōsyonár'] *vt* to fuse (together); (*COM*) to merge; **~se** *vr* (*COM*) to merge, amalgamate.

fusta [fōō'stá] *nf* (*látigo*) riding crop.

fútbol [fōō'hol] *nm* football.

futbolín [fōōthōlēn'] *nm* table football.

futbolista [fōōthōlē'stá] *nm/f* football player.

fútil [fōō'tēl] *a* trifling.

futilidad [fōōtēlēthàth'], **futileza** [fōōtēle'sà] *nf* triviality.

futuro, a [fōōtōō'ro, à] *a* future ♦ *nm* future; (*LING*) future tense; **~s** *nmpl* (*COM*) futures.

G

G, g [he] *nf* (*letra*) G, g; **G de Gerona** G for George.

g/ *abr* = **giro**.

gabán [gàbàn'] *nm* overcoat.

gabardina [gàbàrthē'ná] *nf* (*tela*) gabardine; (*prenda*) raincoat.

gabinete [gàbēnc'te] *nm* (*POL*) cabinet; (*estudio*) study; (*de abogados etc*) office; **~ de consulta/de lectura** consulting/reading room.

gacel [gàsel'] *nm*, **gacela** [gàsc'lá] *nf* gazelle.

gaceta [gàsc'tà] *nf* gazette.

gacetilla [gàsctē'yà] *nf* (*en periódico*) news in brief; (*de personalidades*) gossip column.

gacha [gàtch'á] *nf* mush; **~s** *nfpl* porridge *sg*.

gacho, a [gàtch'o, à] *a* (*encorvado*) bent down; (*orejas*) drooping.

gaditano, a [gàthētà'no, à] *a* of *o* from Cadiz ♦ *nm/f* native *o* inhabitant of Cadiz.

GAE *nm abr* (*Esp MIL*)=*Grupo Aéreo Embarcado*.

gaélico, a [gàc'lēko, à] *a* Gaelic ♦ *nm/f* Gael ♦ *nm* (*LING*) Gaelic.

gafar [gàfàr'] *vt* (*fam: traer mala suerte*) to put a jinx on.

gafas [gà'fàs] *nfpl* glasses; **~ oscuras** dark glasses; **~ de sol** sunglasses.

gafe [gà'fe] *a*: **ser ~** to be jinxed ♦ *nm* (*fam*) jinx.

gaita [gà'ētà] *nf* flute; (**~ gallega**) bagpipes *pl*; (*dificultad*) bother; (*cosa engorrosa*) tough job.

gajes [gà'hes] *nmpl* (*salario*) pay *sg*; **los ~**

del oficio occupational hazards; **~ y emolumentos** perquisites.

gajo [gà'ho] *nm* (*gen*) bunch; (*de árbol*) bough; (*de naranja*) segment.

gala [gà'là] *nf* full dress; (*fig: lo mejor*) cream, flower; **~s** *nfpl* finery *sg*; **estar de ~** to be in one's best clothes; **hacer ~ de** to display, show off; **tener algo a ~** to be proud of sth.

galaico, a [gàlá'ēko, à] *a* Galician.

galán [gàlàn'] *nm* lover, gallant; (*hombre atractivo*) ladies' man; (*TEATRO*): **primer ~** leading man.

galano, a [gàlá'no, à] *a* (*elegante*) elegant; (*bien vestido*) smart.

galante [gàlàn'te] *a* gallant; (*atento*) charming; (*cortés*) polite.

galantear [gàlàntcàr'] *vt* (*hacer la corte a*) to court, woo.

galanteo [gàlàntc'o] *nm* (*coqueteo*) flirting; (*de pretendiente*) wooing.

galantería [gàlàntcrē'à] *nf* (*caballerosidad*) gallantry; (*cumplido*) politeness; (*piropo*) compliment.

galápago [gàlá'pàgo] *nm* (*ZOOL*) turtle.

galardonar [gàlàrthonár'] *vt* (*premiar*) to reward; (*una obra*) to award a prize for.

galaxia [gàlàk'syà] *nf* galaxy.

galbana [gàlbà'nà] *nf* (*pereza*) sloth, laziness.

galeote [gàlco'tc] *nm* galley slave.

galera [gàlc'rá] *nf* (*nave*) galley; (*carro*) wagon; (*MED*) hospital ward; (*TIP*) galley.

galería [gàlcrē'á] *nf* (*gen*) gallery; (*balcón*) veranda(h); (*de casa*) corridor; (*fam: público*) audience; **~ secreta** secret passage.

Gales [gà'lcs] *nm*: **(el País de) ~** Wales.

galés, esa [gàlcs', csà] *a* Welsh ♦ *nm/f* Welshman/woman ♦ *nm* (*LING*) Welsh.

galgo, a [gàl'go, à] *nm/f* greyhound.

Galia [gà'lyà] *nf* Gaul.

Galicia [gàlē'syà] *nf* Galicia.

galicismo [gàlēsēs'mo] *nm* gallicism.

Galilea [gàlēlc'à] *nf* Galilee.

galimatías [gàlēmátē'às] *nm inv* (*asunto*) rigmarole; (*lenguaje*) gibberish, nonsense.

galo, a [gà'lo, à] *a* Gallic; (= *francés*) French ♦ *nm/f* Gaul.

galón [gàlon'] *nm* (*COSTURA*) braid; (*MIL*) stripe; (*medida*) gallon.

galopar [gàlopár'] *vi* to gallop.

galope [gàlo'pe] *nm* gallop; **al ~** (*fig*) in great haste; **a ~ tendido** at full gallop.

galvanice [gàlhànē'sc] *etc vb V* **galvanizar**.

galvanizar [gàlhànēsàr'] *vt* to galvanize.

gallardía [gàyàrthē'à] *nf* (*gracia*) gracefulness; (*valor*) bravery; (*elegancia*) elegance; (*nobleza*) nobleness.

gallego, a [gàyc'go, à] *a* Galician; (*AM pey*) Spanish ♦ *nm/f* Galician; (*AM pey*) Spaniard ♦ *nm* (*LING*) Galician.

galleta [gàye'tà] *nf* cookie (*US*), biscuit (*Brit*); (*fam: bofetada*) whack, slap.

gallina [gàyē'nà] *nf* hen ♦ *nm* (*fam*) coward; ~ **ciega** blind man's buff; ~ **llueca** brooding (*US*) o broody (*Brit*) hen.

gallinero [gàyēne'ro] *nm* (*criadero*) henhouse; (*TEATRO*) gods *sg*, top gallery; (*voces*) hubbub.

gallo [gà'yo] *nm* cock, rooster; (*MUS*) false o wrong note; (*cambio de voz*) break in the voice; **en menos que canta un** ~ in an instant.

gama [gà'mà] *nf* (*MUS*) scale; (*fig*) range; (*ZOOL*) doe.

gamba [gàm'bà] *nf* prawn.

gamberrada [gàmberrà'tħà] *nf* act of hooliganism.

gamberro, a [gàmbe'rro, à] *nm/f* hooligan, 'lout.

gamo [gà'mo] *nm* (*ZOOL*) buck.

gamuza [gàmōō'sà] *nf* chamois; (*bayeta*) duster; (*AM: piel*) suede.

gana [gà'nà] *nf* (*deseo*) desire, wish; (*apetito*) appetite; (*voluntad*) will; (*añoranza*) longing; **de buena** ~ willingly; **de mala** ~ reluctantly; **me dan** ~s **de** I feel like, I want to; **tener** ~s **de** to feel like; **no me da la (real)** ~ I don't (damned well) want to; **son** ~s **de molestar** they're just trying to make trouble.

ganadería [gànàħerē'à] *nf* (*ganado*) livestock; (*ganado vacuno*) cattle *pl*; (*cría, comercio*) cattle raising.

ganadero, a [gànàħe'ro, à] *a* stock *cpd* ♦ *nm* stockman.

ganado [gànà'tħo] *nm* livestock; ~ **caballar/cabrío** horses *pl*/ goats *pl*; ~ **lanar** u **ovejuno** sheep *pl*; ~ **porcino/vacuno** pigs *pl*/cattle *pl*.

ganador, a [gànàtħor', à] *a* winning ♦ *nm/f* winner; (*ECON*) earner.

ganancia [gànàn'syà] *nf* (*lo ganado*) gain; (*aumento*) increase; (*beneficio*) profit; ~s *nfpl* (*ingresos*) earnings; (*beneficios*) profit *sg*, winnings; ~s **y pérdidas** profit and loss; ~ **bruta/líquida** gross/net profit; ~s **de capital** capital gains; **sacar** ~ **de** to draw profit from.

ganapán [gànàpán'] *nm* (*obrero casual*) odd-job man; (*individuo tosco*) lout.

ganar [gànàr'] *vt* (*obtener*) to get, obtain; (*sacar ventaja*) to gain; (*COM*) to earn; (*DEPORTE, premio*) to win; (*derrotar*) to beat; (*alcanzar*) to reach; (*MIL: objetivo*) to take; (*apoyo*) to gain, win ♦ *vi* (*DEPORTE*) to win; ~**se** *vr*: ~**se la vida** to earn one's living; **se lo ha ganado** he deserves it; ~ **tiempo** to gain time.

ganchillo [gàntchē'yo] *nm* (*para croché*) crochet hook; (*arte*) crochet work.

gancho [gàntch'o] *nm* (*gen*) hook; (*colga-*

dor) hanger; (*pey: revendedor*) tout; (*fam: atractivo*) sex appeal; (*BOXEO: golpe*) hook.

gandul, a [gàndōōl', à] *a*, *nm/f* good-for-nothing.

ganga [gàn'gà] *nf* (*cosa*) bargain; (*buena situación*) cushy job.

Ganges [gàn'hes] *nm*: **el (Río)** ~ the Ganges.

ganglio [gàn'glyo] *nm* (*ANAT*) ganglion; (*MED*) swelling.

gangrena [gàngre'nà] *nf* gangrene.

gansada [gànsà'tħà] *nf* (*fam*) stupid thing (to do).

ganso, a [gàn'so, à] *nm/f* (*ZOOL*) gander/ goose; (*fam*) idiot.

Gante [gàn'te] *nm* Ghent.

ganzúa [gànsōō'à] *nf* skeleton key ♦ *nm/f* burglar.

gañán [gànyán'] *nm* farmhand.

garabatear [gàràħàteár'] *vt* to scribble, scrawl.

garabato [gàràħà'to] *nm* (*gancho*) hook; (*garfio*) grappling iron; (*escritura*) scrawl, scribble; (*fam*) sex appeal.

garaje [gàrà'he] *nm* garage.

garante [gàràn'te] *a* responsible ♦ *nm/f* guarantor.

garantía [gàràntē'à] *nf* guarantee; (*seguridad*) pledge; (*compromiso*) undertaking; (*JUR: caución*) warranty; **de máxima** ~ absolutely guaranteed; ~ **de trabajo** job security.

garantice [gàràntē'se] *etc vb V* **garantizar**.

garantir [gàràntēr'], **garantizar** [gàràntēsár'] *vt* (*hacerse responsable de*) to vouch for; (*asegurar*) to guarantee.

garbanzo [gàrħàn'so] *nm* chickpea.

garbeo [gàrħe'o] *nm*: **darse un** ~ to go for a walk.

garbo [gàr'ħo] *nm* grace, elegance; (*aire*) jauntiness; (*de mujer*) glamor; **andar con** ~ to walk gracefully.

garboso, a [gàrħo'so, à] *a* graceful, elegant.

garfa [gàr'fà] *nf* claw.

garfio [gàr'fyo] *nm* grappling iron; (*gancho*) hook; (*ALPINISMO*) climbing iron.

gargajo [gàrgà'ho] *nm* phlegm, sputum.

garganta [gàrgàn'tà] *nf* (*interna*) throat; (*externa, de botella*) neck; (*GEO: barranco*) ravine; (*desfiladero*) narrow pass.

gargantilla [gàrgàntē'yà] *nf* necklace.

gárgara [gàr'gàrà] *nf* gargle, gargling; **hacer** ~s to gargle; **¡vete a hacer** ~s! (*fam*) go to blazes!

gárgola [gàr'golà] *nf* gargoyle.

garita [gàrē'tà] *nf* cabin, hut; (*MIL*) sentry box; (*puesto de vigilancia*) lookout post.

garito [gàrē'to] *nm* (*lugar*) gaming house o den.

Garona [gàro'nà] *nm*: **el (Río)** ~ the Ga-
ronne.

garra [gà'rrà] *nf* (*de gato*, *TEC*) claw; (*de
ave*) talon; (*fam*) hand, paw; (*fig*: *de
canción etc*) bite; **caer en las** ~**s de uno** to
fall into sb's clutches.

garrafa [gàrrà'fà] *nf* carafe, decanter.

garrafal [gàrràfál'] *a* enormous, terrific;
(*error*) terrible.

garrapata [gàrràpà'tà] *nf* (*ZOOL*) tick.

garrido, a [gàrrē'tho, à] *a* handsome.

garrotazo [gàrrotà'so] *nm* blow with a stick
o club.

garrote [gàrro'te] *nm* (*palo*) stick; (*porra*)
club, cudgel; (*suplicio*) garrotte.

garza [gàr'sà] *nf* heron.

garzo, a [gàr'so, à] *a* blue.

gas [gàs] *nm* gas; (*vapores*) fumes *pl*; ~**es
de escape** exhaust (fumes).

gasa [gà'sà] *nf* gauze; (*de pañal*) diaper
(*US*) *o* nappy (*Brit*) liner.

gaseoso, a [gàseo'so, à] *a* carbonated ♦ *nf*
lemonade, pop (*fam*).

gasoducto [gàsothōok'to] *nm* gas pipeline.

gasoil [gàso'ēl], **gasóleo** [gàso'leo] *nm* diesel
(oil).

gasolina [gàsolē'nà] *nf* gas(oline) (*US*),
petrol (*Brit*).

gasolinera [gàsolēne'rà] *nf* gas (*US*) *o* petrol (*Brit*) station.

gastado, a [gàstà'tho, à] *a* (*ropa*) worn out;
(*usado*: *frase etc*) trite.

gastar [gàstàr'] *vt* (*dinero*, *tiempo*) to spend;
(*consumir*) to use (up), consume; (*desperdiciar*) to waste; (*llevar*) to wear; ~**se**
vr to wear out; (*terminarse*) to run out;
(*estropearse*) to waste; ~ **bromas** to crack
jokes; **¿qué número gastas?** what size
(shoe) do you take?

gasto [gà'sto] *nm* (*desembolso*) expenditure,
spending; (*cantidad gastada*) outlay,
expense; (*consumo*, *uso*) use; (*desgaste*)
waste; ~**s** *nmpl* (*desembolsos*) expenses;
(*cargos*) charges, costs; ~ **corriente** (*COM*)
revenue expenditure; ~ **fijo** (*COM*) fixed
charge; ~**s bancarios** bank charges; ~**s
corrientes** running expenses; ~**s de distribución** (*COM*) distribution costs; ~**s generales** overhead (*US*), overheads (*Brit*); ~**s
de mantenimiento** maintenance expenses;
~**s operacionales** operating costs; ~**s de
tramitación** (*COM*) handling charge *sg*; ~**s
vencidos** (*COM*) accrued charges; **cubrir**
~**s** to cover expenses; **meterse en** ~**s** to
incur expense.

gastronomía [gàstronomē'à] *nf* gas-
tronomy.

gata [gà'tà] *nf* (*ZOOL*) she-cat; **andar a** ~**s**
to go on all fours.

gatear [gàteàr'] *vi* to go on all fours.

gatillo [gàtē'yo] *nm* (*de arma de fuego*)

trigger; (*de dentista*) forceps.

gato [gà'to] *nm* (*ZOOL*) cat; (*TEC*) jack; ~
de Angora Angora cat; ~ **montés** wildcat;
dar a uno ~ **por liebre** to take sb in; **aquí
hay** ~ **encerrado** there's something fishy
here.

gatuno, a [gàtōō'no, à] *a* feline.

gaucho, a [gà'ōōtcho, à] *a*, *nm/f* gaucho.

gaveta [gàbe'tà] *nf* drawer.

gavilán [gàbēlàn'] *nm* sparrowhawk.

gavilla [gàbē'yà] *nf* sheaf.

gaviota [gàbyo'tà] *nf* seagull.

gay [ge] *a*, *nm* gay, homosexual.

gazapo [gàsà'po] *nm* young rabbit.

gaznate [gàsnà'te] *nm* (*pescuezo*) gullet;
(*garganta*) windpipe.

gazpacho [gàspàtch'o] *nm* gazpacho.

gelatina [hèlàtē'nà] *nf* jello (*US*), jelly
(*Brit*); (*polvos etc*) gelatine.

gema [he'mà] *nf* gem.

gemelo, a [heme'lo, à] *a*, *nm/f* twin; ~**s**
nmpl (*de camisa*) cufflinks; ~**s de campo**
field glasses, binoculars; ~**s de teatro**
opera glasses.

gemido [hemē'tho] *nm* (*quejido*) moan,
groan; (*lamento*) wail, howl.

Géminis [hc'mēnēs] *nm* (*ASTRO*) Gemini.

gemir [hemēr'] *vi* (*quejarse*) to moan,
groan; (*animal*) to whine; (*viento*) to howl.

gen. *abr* (*LING*) = **género; genitivo.**

gendarme [hendàr'mc] *nm* (*AM*) policeman.

genealogía [heneàlohē'à] *nf* genealogy.

generación [henerásyon'] *nf* generation;
primera/segunda/tercera/cuarta ~ (*IN-
FORM*) first/second/third/fourth generation.

generado, a [henerà'tho, à] *a* (*INFORM*): ~
por ordenador computer generated.

generador [heneràthor'] *nm* generator; ~
de programas (*INFORM*) program generator.

general [henerál'] *a* general; (*común*)
common; (*pey*: *corriente*) rife; (*frecuente*)
usual ♦ *nm* general; ~ **de brigada/de división** brigadier-/major-general; **por lo** *o* **en**
~ in general.

generalice [heneràlē'se] *etc vb V* **generalizar.**

generalidad [heneràlēthàth'] *nf* generality.

Generalitat [heneràlētàt'] *nf* Catalan parliament.

generalización [henerálēsàsyon'] *nf* gen-
eralization.

generalizar [henerálēsàr'] *vt* to generalize;
~**se** *vr* to become generalized, spread; (*difundirse*) to become widely known.

generalmente [henerálmen'te] *ad* generally.

generar [henerár'] *vt* to generate.

genérico, a [hene'rēko, à] *a* generic.

género [he'nero] *nm* (*clase*) kind, sort;

(*tipo*) type; (*BIO*) genus; (*LING*) gender; (*COM*) material; ~**s** *nmpl* (*productos*) goods; ~ **humano** human race; ~ **chico** (*zarzuela*) Spanish operetta; ~**s de punto** knitwear *sg*.

generosidad [heneroseθàíh'] *nf* generosity.

generoso, a [henero'so, à] *a* generous.

genial [henyàl'] *a* inspired; (*idea*) brilliant; (*afable*) genial.

genialidad [henyàleθàíh'] *nf* (*singularidad*) genius; (*acto genial*) stroke of genius; **es una ~ suya** it's one of his brilliant ideas.

genio [he'nyo] *nm* (*carácter*) nature, disposition; (*humor*) temper; (*facultad creadora*) genius; **mal ~** bad temper; ~ **vivo** quick *o* hot temper; **de mal ~** bad-tempered.

genital [henētál'] *a* genital ♦ *nm*: ~**es** genitals, genital organs.

genocidio [henoseíhyo] *nm* genocide.

Génova [he'nohà] *nf* Genoa.

genovés, esa [henohes', esà] *a*, *nm/f* Genoese.

gente [hen'te] *nf* (*personas*) people *pl*; (*raza*) race; (*nación*) nation; (*parientes*) relatives *pl*; ~ **bien/baja** upper-class/lower-class people *pl*; ~ **menuda** (*niños*) children *pl*; **es buena ~** (*fam*: *esp AM*) he's a good sort.

gentil [hentēl'] *a* (*elegante*) graceful; (*encantador*) charming; (*REL*) gentile.

gentileza [hentēle'sà] *nf* grace; charm; (*cortesía*) courtesy; **por ~ de** by courtesy of.

gentilicio, a [hentēlē'syo, à] *a* (*familiar*) family *cpd*.

gentío [hentē'o] *nm* crowd, throng.

gentuza [hentōō'sà] *nf* (*pey*: *plebe*) rabble; (: *chusma*) riffraff.

genuflexión [henōōfleksyon'] *nf* genuflexion.

genuino, a [henwē'no, à] *a* genuine.

GEO [he'o] *nmpl abr* (*Esp*:= *Grupos Especiales de Operaciones*) Special Police Units *used in anti-terrorist operations etc.*

geografía [heoɣràfē'à] *nf* geography.

geográfico, a [heoɣrà'fēko, à] *a* geographic(al).

geología [heolohē'à] *nf* geology.

geólogo, a [heo'loɣo, à] *nm/f* geologist.

geometría [heometrē'à] *nf* geometry.

geométrico, a [heome'trēko, à] *a* geometric(al).

geranio [herà'nyo] *nm* (*BOT*) geranium.

gerencia [heren'syà] *nf* management; (*cargo*) post of manager; (*oficina*) manager's office.

gerente [heren'te] *nm/f* (*supervisor*) manager; (*jefe*) director.

geriatría [heryàtrē'à] *nf* (*MED*) geriatrics *sg*.

germano, a [hermà'no, à] *a* German,

Germanic ♦ *nm/f* German.

germen [her'men] *nm* germ.

germinar [hermēnàr'] *vi* to germinate; (*brotar*) to sprout.

gerundense [herōōnden'se] *a* of *o* from Gerona ♦ *nm/f* native *o* inhabitant of Gerona.

gerundio [herōōn'dyo] *nm* (*LING*) gerund.

gesticulación [hestēkōōlásyon'] *nf* (*ademán*) gesticulation; (*mueca*) grimace.

gestión [hestyon'] *nf* management; (*diligencia, acción*) negotiation; **hacer las gestiones preliminares** to do the groundwork; ~ **de cartera** (*COM*) portfolio management; ~ **financiera** (*COM*) financial management; ~ **interna** (*INFORM*) housekeeping; ~ **de personal** personnel management; ~ **de riesgos** (*COM*) risk management.

gestionar [hestyonàr'] *vt* (*lograr*) to try to arrange; (*llevar*) to manage.

gesto [he'sto] *nm* (*mueca*) grimace; (*ademán*) gesture; **hacer ~s** to make faces.

gestor, a [hestor', à] *a* managing ♦ *nm/f* manager; (*promotor*) promoter; (*agente*) business agent.

gestoría [hestorē'à] *nf agency undertaking business with government departments, insurance companies etc.*

Gibraltar [hēɣràltár'] *nm* Gibraltar.

gibraltareño, a [hēɣràltàre'nyo, à] *a* of *o* from Gibraltar ♦ *nm/f* native *o* inhabitant of Gibraltar.

gigante [hēɣàn'te] *a*, *nm/f* giant.

gijonés [hēhones', esà] *a* of *o* from Gijón ♦ *nm/f* native *o* inhabitant of Gijón.

gilipollas [hēlēpo'yàs] (*fam*) *a inv* daft ♦ *nm/f* idiot.

gima [hē'mà] *etc vb V* **gemir**.

gimnasia [hēmnà'syà] *nf* gymnastics *pl*; **confundir la ~ con la magnesia** to get things mixed up.

gimnasio [hēmnà'syo] *nm* gymnasium, gym.

gimnasta [hēmnà'stà] *nm/f* gymnast.

gimotear [hēmoteàr'] *vi* to whine, whimper; (*lloriquear*) to snivel.

Ginebra [hēne'ɣrà] *n* Geneva.

ginebra [hēne'ɣrà] *nf* gin.

ginecológico, a [hēnekolo'hēko, à] *a* gyn(a)ecological.

ginecólogo, a [hēneko'loɣo, à] *nm/f* gyn(a)ecologist.

gira [hē'rà] *nf* tour, trip.

girado, a [hērà'tho, à] *nm/f* (*COM*) drawee.

girar [hēràr'] *vt* (*dar la vuelta*) to turn (around); (: *rápidamente*) to spin; (*COM*: *giro postal*) to draw; (*comerciar: letra de cambio*) to issue ♦ *vi* to turn (round); (*dar vueltas*) to rotate; (*rápido*) to spin; **la conversación giraba en torno a las elecciones** the conversation centered on the election; ~ **en descubierto** to overdraw.

girasol [hĕrásol'] *nm* sunflower.

giratorio, a [hĕráto'ryo, á] *a* (*gen*) revolving; (*puente*) swing *cpd*; (*silla*) swivel *cpd*.

giro [hĕ'ro] *nm* (*movimiento*) turn, revolution; (*LING*) expression; (*COM*) draft; (*de sucesos*) trend, course; ~ **bancario** money order; ~ **de existencias** (*COM*) stock turnover; ~ **postal** money order; ~ **a la vista** (*COM*) sight draft.

gis [hĕs] *nm* (*AM*) chalk.

gitano, a [hĕtá'no, á] *a*, *nm/f* gypsy.

glacial [glásyál'] *a* icy, freezing.

glaciar [glásyár'] *nm* glacier.

glándula [glán'dŏŏlá] *nf* (*ANAT, BOT*) gland.

glicerina [glĕserĕ'ná] *nf* (*TEC*) glycerin(e).

global [globál'] *a* (*en conjunto*) global; (*completo*) total; (*investigación*) full; (*suma*) lump *cpd*.

globo [glo'bo] *nm* (*esfera*) globe, sphere; (*aeróstato, juguete*) balloon.

glóbulo [glo'bŏŏlo] *nm* globule; (*ANAT*) corpuscle; ~ **blanco/rojo** white/red corpuscle.

gloria [glo'ryá] *nf* glory; (*fig*) delight; (*delicia*) bliss.

glorieta [glorye'tá] *nf* (*de jardín*) arbor (*US*), arbour (*Brit*); (*AUTO*) traffic circle (*US*), roundabout (*Brit*); (*plaza redonda*) circus; (*cruce*) junction.

glorificar [glorĕfĕkár'] *vt* (*enaltecer*) to glorify, praise.

glorifique [glorĕfĕ'ke] *etc vb V* **glorificar**.

glorioso, a [gloryo'so, á] *a* glorious.

glosa [glo'sá] *nf* comment; (*explicación*) gloss.

glosar [glosár'] *vt* (*comentar*) to comment on.

glosario [glosá'ryo] *nm* glossary.

glotón, ona [gloton', oná] *a* gluttonous, greedy ♦ *nm/f* glutton.

glotonería [glotonerĕ'á] *nf* gluttony, greed.

glúteo [glŏŏ'teo] *nm* (*fam: nalga*) buttock.

gnomo [no'mo] *nm* gnome.

gobernación [gobernásyon'] *nf* government, governing; (*POL*) Provincial Governor's office.

gobernador, a [gobernàdhor', á] *a* governing ♦ *nm/f* governor.

gobernanta [gobernán'tá] *nf* (*AM: niñera*) governess.

gobernante [gobernán'te] *a* governing ♦ *nm* ruler, governor ♦ *nf* (*en hotel etc*) maid (*US*), housekeeper (*Brit*).

gobernar [gobernár'] *vt* (*dirigir*) to guide, direct; (*POL*) to rule, govern ♦ *vi* to govern; (*NAUT*) to steer; ~ **mal** to misgovern.

gobierno [gobyer'no] *etc vb V* **gobernar** ♦ *nm* (*POL*) government; (*gestión*) management; (*dirección*) guidance, direction; (*NAUT*) steering; (*puesto*) governorship.

goce [go'se] *etc vb V* **gozar** ♦ *nm* enjoyment.

godo, a [go'dho, á] *nm/f* Goth; (*AM pey*) Spaniard.

gol [gol] *nm* goal.

gola [go'lá] *nf* gullet; (*garganta*) throat.

golear [goleár'] *vt* (*marcar*) to score a goal against.

golf [golf] *nm* golf.

golfo, a [gol'fo, á] *nm/f* (*pilluelo*) street urchin; (*vago*) tramp; (*gorrón*) loafer; (*gamberro*) lout ♦ *nm* (*GEO*) gulf ♦ *nf* (*fam: prostituta*) hooker.

golondrina [golondrĕ'ná] *nf* swallow.

golosina [golosĕ'ná] *nf* tidbit (*US*), titbit (*Brit*); (*dulce*) candy (*US*), sweet (*Brit*).

goloso, a [golo'so, á] *a* sweet-toothed; (*fam: glotón*) greedy.

golpe [gol'pe] *nm* blow; (*de puño*) punch; (*de mano*) smack; (*de remo*) stroke; (*FÚTBOL*) kick; (*TENIS etc*) hit, shot; (*mala suerte*) misfortune; (*fam: atraco*) heist (*US*), job; (*fig: choque*) clash; **no dar** ~ to be bone idle; **de un** ~ with one blow; **de** ~ suddenly; ~ **(de estado)** coup (d'état); ~ **de gracia** coup de grâce (*tb fig*); ~ **de fortuna/maestro** stroke of luck/ genius; **cerrar una puerta de** ~ to slam a door.

golpear [golpeár'] *vt*, *vi* to strike, knock; (*asestar*) to beat; (*de puño*) to punch; (*golpetear*) to tap; (*mesa*) to bang.

goma [go'má] *nf* (*caucho*) rubber; (*elástico*) elastic; (*tira*) rubber *o* elastic (*Brit*) band; (*fam: preservativo*) condom; (*droga*) hashish; (*explosivo*) plastic explosive; ~ **(de borrar)** eraser, rubber (*Brit*); ~ **de mascar** chewing gum; ~ **de pegar** gum, glue.

goma-espuma [gomáespŏŏ'má] *nf* foam rubber.

gomina [gomĕ'ná] *nf* (*AM*) hair cream.

gomita [gomĕ'tá] *nf* rubber *o* elastic (*Brit*) band.

góndola [gon'dolá] *nf* (*barco*) gondola; (*de tren*) freight car (*US*), goods wagon (*Brit*).

gordo, a [gor'dho, á] *a* (*gen*) fat; (*persona*) plump; (*agua*) hard; (*fam*) enormous ♦ *nm/f* fat man *o* woman; **el (premio)** ~ (*en lotería*) first prize; ¡~! (*fam*) fatty!

gordura [gordhŏŏ'rá] *nf* fat; (*corpulencia*) fatness, stoutness.

gorgojo [gorgo'ho] *nm* (*insecto*) grub.

gorgorito [gorgorĕ'to] *nm* (*gorjeo*) trill, warble.

gorila [gorĕ'lá] *nm* gorilla; (*fam*) tough, thug; (*guardaespaldas*) bodyguard.

gorjear [gorheár'] *vi* to twitter, chirp.

gorjeo [gorhe'o] *nm* twittering, chirping.

gorra [go'rrá] *nf* (*gen*) cap; (*de niño*) bonnet; (*militar*) bearskin; ~ **de montar/ de paño/de punto/de visera** riding/cloth/

knitted/peaked cap; **andar** o **ir** o **vivir de** ~ to sponge, scrounge; **entrar de** ~ *fam*) to gatecrash.

gorrión [gorryon'] *nm* sparrow.

gorro [go'rro] *nm* cap; (*de niño, mujer*) bonnet; **estoy hasta el** ~ I am fed up.

gorrón, ona [gorron', oná] *nm* pebble; (*TEC*) pivot ♦ *nm/f* scrounger.

gorronear [gorroneár'] *vi* (*fam*) to sponge, scrounge.

gota [go'tá] *nf* (*gen*) drop; (*de pintura*) blob; (*de sudor*) bead; (*MED*) gout; ~ **a** ~ drop by drop; **caer a** ~**s** to drip.

gotear [goteár'] *vi* to drip; (*escurrir*) to trickle; (*salirse*) to leak; (*cirio*) to gutter; (*lloviznar*) to drizzle.

gotera [gote'rá] *nf* leak.

gótico, a [go'tēko, á] *a* Gothic.

gozar [gosár'] *vi* to enjoy o.s.; ~ **de** (*disfrutar*) to enjoy; (*poseer*) to possess; ~ **de buena salud** to enjoy good health.

gozne [gos'ne] *nm* hinge.

gozo [go'so] *nm* (*alegría*) joy; (*placer*) pleasure; ¡mi ~ **en el pozo!** just my luck!

g.p. *nm abr* (= *giro postal*) m.o.

GPI *nm abr* (*Esp POL*)=*Grupo Parlamentario Independiente*.

gr. *abr* (= *gramo(s)*) g.

grabación [grábásyon'] *nf* recording.

grabado, a [gráβá'ðo, á] *a* (*MUS*) recorded; (*en cinta*) taped, on tape ♦ *nm* print, engraving; ~ **al agua fuerte** etching; ~ **al aguatinta** aquatint; ~ **en cobre** copperplate; ~ **en madera** woodcut; ~ **rupestre** rock carving.

grabador, a [gráβáðor', á] *nm/f* engraver ♦ *nf* tape-recorder; ~**a de cassettes** cassette recorder.

grabar [gráβár'] *vt* to engrave; (*discos, cintas*) to record; (*impresionar*) to impress.

gracejo [gráse'ho] *nm* (*humor*) wit, humor (*US*), humour (*Brit*); (*elegancia*) grace.

gracia [grá'syá] *nf* (*encanto*) grace, gracefulness; (*REL*) grace; (*chiste*) joke; (*humor*) humor (*US*), humour (*Brit*), wit; ¡muchas ~**s!** thanks very much!; ~**s a** thanks to; **tener** ~ (*chiste etc*) to be funny; ¡qué ~! how funny!; (*irónico*) what a nerve!; **no me hace** ~ I'm not keen on it; **con** ~**s anticipadas/repetidas** thanking you in advance/again; **dar las** ~**s a uno por algo** to thank sb for sth.

grácil [grá'sēl] *a* (*sutil*) graceful; (*delgado*) slender; (*delicado*) delicate.

gracioso, a [grásyo'so, á] *a* (*garboso*) graceful; (*chistoso*) funny; (*cómico*) comical; (*agudo*) witty; (*título*) gracious ♦ *nm/f* (*TEATRO*) comic character, fool; **su graciosa Majestad** His/Her Gracious Majesty.

grada [grá'ðá] *nf* (*de escalera*) step; (*de anfiteatro*) tier, row; ~**s** *nfpl* (*de estadio*) stands (*US*), terraces (*Brit*).

gradación [gráðásyon'] *nf* gradation; (*serie*) graded series.

gradería [gráðerē'á] *nf* (*gradas*) (flight of) steps *pl*; (*de anfiteatro*) tiers *pl*, rows *pl*; ~ **cubierta** covered stand.

grado [grá'ðo] *nm* degree; (*etapa*) stage, step; (*nivel*) rate; (*de parentesco*) degree; (*de aceite, vino*) grade; (*grada*) step; (*ESCOL*) grade (*US*), class, year; (*UNIV*) degree; (*LING*) degree of comparison; (*MIL*) rank; **de buen** ~ willingly; **en sumo** ~, **en** ~ **superlativo** in the highest degree.

graduación [gráðwásyon'] *nf* (*acto*) gradation; (*clasificación*) rating; (*del alcohol*) proof, strength; (*ESCOL*) graduation; (*MIL*) rank; **de alta** ~ high-ranking.

gradual [gráðwál'] *a* gradual.

graduar [gráðwár'] *vt* (*gen*) to graduate; (*medir*) to gauge; (*TEC*) to calibrate; (*UNIV*) to confer a degree on; (*MIL*) to commission; ~**se** *vr* to graduate; ~**se la vista** to have one's eyes tested.

grafía [gráfē'á] *nf* (*escritura*) writing; (*ortografía*) spelling.

gráfico, a [grá'fēko, á] *a* graphic; (*fig: vívido*) vivid, lively ♦ *nm* diagram ♦ *nf* graph; ~ **de barras** (*COM*) bar chart; ~ **de sectores** o **de tarta** (*COM*) pie chart; ~**s** *nmpl* (*tb INFORM*) graphics; ~**s empresariales** (*COM*) business graphics.

grafito [gráfē'to] *nm* (*TEC*) graphite, black lead.

grafología [gráfolohē'á] *nf* graphology.

gragea [gráhe'á] *nf* (*MED*) pill; (*caramelo*) dragée.

grajo [grá'ho] *nm* rook.

Gral. *abr* (*MIL*: = *General*) Gen.

gramático, a [grámá'tēko, á] *nm/f* (*persona*) grammarian ♦ *nf* grammar.

gramo [grá'mo] *nm* gram (*US*), gramme (*Brit*).

gran [grán] *a V* **grande**.

grana [grá'ná] *nf* (*BOT*) seedling; (*color*) scarlet; **ponerse como la** ~ to go as red as a beet.

granada [gráná'ðá] *nf* pomegranate; (*MIL*) grenade; ~ **de mano** hand grenade; ~ **de metralla** shrapnel shell.

granadino, a [gránáðē'no, á] *a* of o from Granada ♦ *nm/f* native o inhabitant of Granada ♦ *nf* grenadine.

granar [gránár'] *vi* to seed.

granate [gráná'te] *nm* garnet.

Gran Bretaña [grámbretá'nyá] *nf* Great Britain.

Gran Canaria [gránkáná'ryá] *nf* Grand Canary.

grancanario, a [gránkáná'ryo, á] *a* of o from Grand Canary ♦ *nm/f* native o inhabitant of Grand Canary.

grande |gràn'dc|, **gran** *a* (*de tamaño*) big, large; (*alto*) tall; (*distinguido*) great; (*impresionante*) grand ♦ *nm* grandee; **¿cómo es de ~?** how big is it?, what size is it?; **pasarlo en ~** to have a tremendous time.

grandeza |gràndc'sà| *nf* greatness; (*tamaño*) bigness; (*esplendidez*) grandness; (*nobleza*) nobility.

grandioso, a |gràndyo'so, à| *a* magnificent, grand.

grandullón, ona |gránthōōyon', onà| *a* oversized.

granel |gràncl'| *nm* (*montón*) heap; **a ~** (*COM*) in bulk.

granero |gràne'ro| *nm* granary, barn.

granice |grànē'sc| *etc vb V* **granizar.**

granito |grànē'to| *nm* (*AGR*) small grain; (*roca*) granite.

granizada |gràncsà'thà| *nf* hailstorm; (*fig*) hail; **una ~ de balas** a hail of bullets.

granizado |gràncsà'tho| *nm* iced drink; **~ de café** iced coffee.

granizar |gràncsàr'| *vi* to hail.

granizo |grànē'so| *nm* hail.

granja |gràn'hà| *nf* (*gen*) farm; **~ avícola** chicken *o* poultry farm.

granjear |grànhcàr'| *vt* (*cobrar*) to earn; (*ganar*) to win; (*avanzar*) to gain; **~se** *vr* (*amistad etc*) to gain for o.s.

granjero, a |g;rànhe'ro, à| *nm/f* farmer.

grano |grà'no| *nm* grain; (*semilla*) seed; (*baya*) berry; (*MED*) pimple, spot; (*partícula*) particle; (*punto*) speck; **~s** *nmpl* cereals; **~ de café** coffee bean; **ir al ~** to get to the point.

granuja |gránōō'hà| *nm* rogue; (*golfillo*) urchin.

grapa |grà'pà| *nf* staple; (*TEC*) clamp; (*sujetador*) clip, fastener; (*ARQ*) cramp.

GRAPO |grà'po| *nm abr* (*Esp POL*)=Grupo de Resistencia Antifascista Primero de Octubre.

grasa |grà'sà| *nf V* **graso.**

grasiento, a |grásyen'to, à| *a* greasy; (*de aceite*) oily; (*mugriento*) filthy.

graso, a |grà'so, à| *a* fatty; (*aceitoso*) greasy, oily ♦ *nf* (*gen*) grease; (*de cocina*) fat, lard; (*sebo*) suet; (*mugre*) filth; (*AUTO*) oil; (*lubricante*) grease; **~ de ballena** blubber; **~ de pescado** fish oil.

gratificación |grátēfēkàsyon'| *nf* (*propina*) tip; (*aguinaldo*) gratuity; (*bono*) bonus; (*recompensa*) reward.

gratificar |grátēfēkàr'| *vt* (*dar propina*) to tip; (*premiar*) to reward; **"se gratificará"** "a reward is offered".

gratifique |grátēfē'ke| *etc vb V* **gratificar.**

gratis |grà'tēs| *ad* free, for nothing.

gratitud |grátētōōth'| *nf* gratitude.

grato, a |grà'to, à| *a* (*agradable*) pleasant,

agreeable; (*bienvenido*) welcome; **nos es ~ informarle que ...** we are pleased to inform you that ....

gratuito, a |gràtwē'to, à| *a* (*gratis*) free; (*sin razón*) gratuitous; (*acusación*) unfounded.

grava |grà'hà| *nf* (*guijos*) gravel; (*piedra molida*) crushed stone; (*en carreteras*) gravel.

gravamen |gràhà'mcn| *nm* (*carga*) burden; (*impuesto*) tax; **libre de ~** (*ECON*) free from encumbrances.

gravar |gràhàr'| *vt* to burden; (*COM*) to tax; (*ECON*) to assess for tax; **~ con impuestos** to burden with taxes.

grave |grà'he| *a* heavy; (*fig, MED*) grave, serious; (*importante*) important; (*herida*) severe; (*MUS*) low, deep; (*LING*: *acento*) grave; **estar ~** to be seriously ill.

gravedad |gràhethàth'| *nf* gravity; (*fig*) seriousness; (*grandeza*) importance; (*dignidad*) dignity; (*MUS*) depth.

grávido, a |grà'hētho, à| *a* (*preñada*) pregnant.

gravilla |gràhē'yá| *nf* gravel.

gravitación |gràhētàsyon'| *nf* gravitation.

gravitar |gràhētàr'| *vi* to gravitate; **~ sobre** to rest on.

gravoso, a |gràho'so, à| *a* (*pesado*) burdensome; (*costoso*) costly.

graznar |gràsnàr'| *vi* (*cuervo*) to squawk; (*pato*) to quack; (*hablar ronco*) to croak.

graznido |gràsnē'tho| *nm* squawk; croak.

Grecia |gre'syà| *nf* Greece.

gregario, a |gregà'ryo, à| *a* gregarious; **instinto ~** herd instinct.

gremio |gre'myo| *nm* (*asociación*) professional association, guild.

greña |gre'nyà| *nf* (*cabellos*) shock of hair; (*maraña*) tangle; **andar a la ~** to bicker, squabble.

greñudo, a |grenyōō'tho, à| *a* (*persona*) dishevelled; (*hair*) tangled.

gresca |gres'kà| *nf* uproar; (*trifulca*) row.

griego, a |grye'go, à| *a* Greek, Grecian ♦ *nm/f* Greek ♦ *nm* (*LING*) Greek.

grieta |grye'tà| *nf* crack; (*hendidura*) chink; (*quiebra*) crevice; (*MED*) chap; (*POL*) rift.

grifa |grē'fà| *nf* (*fam*: *droga*) marijuana.

grifo |grē'fo| *nm* faucet (*US*), tap (*Brit*); (*AM*) gas (*US*) *o* petrol (*Brit*) station.

grilletes |grēye'tes| *nmpl* fetters, shackles.

grillo |grē'yo| *nm* (*ZOOL*) cricket; (*BOT*) shoot; **~s** *nmpl* shackles, irons.

grima |grē'mà| *nf* (*horror*) loathing; (*desagrado*) reluctance; (*desazón*) uneasiness; **me da ~** it makes me sick.

gringo, a |grēn'go, à| *a* (*AM*) *a* (*pey*: *extranjero*) foreign; (: *norteamericano*) Yankee; (*idioma*) foreign ♦ *nm/f* foreigner; Yankee.

gripe |grē'pe| *nf* flu, influenza.

gris [grēs] *a* gray (*US*), grey (*Brit*).

grisáceo, a [grēsă'seo, à] *a* grayish (*US*), greyish (*Brit*).

gritar [grētár'] *vt, vi* to shout, yell; **¡no gritès!** stop shouting!

grito [grē'to] *nm* shout, yell; (*de horror*) scream; **a ~ pelado** at the top of one's voice; **poner el ~ en el cielo** to scream bloody murder; **es el último ~** (*de moda*) it's the latest thing.

groenlandés, esa [groenlándes', esà] *a* Greenland *cpd* ♦ *nm/f* Greenlander.

Groenlandia [groenlán'dyà] *nf* Greenland.

grosella [grose'yà] *nf* (red)currant; **~ negra** blackcurrant.

grosería [groserē'à] *nf* (*actitud*) rudeness; (*comentario*) vulgar comment; (*palabrota*) swearword.

grosero, a [grose'ro, à] *a* (*poco cortés*) rude, bad-mannered; (*ordinario*) vulgar, crude.

grosor [grosor'] *nm* thickness.

grotesco, a [grotes'ko, à] *a* grotesque; (*absurdo*) bizarre.

grúa [grōō'à] *nf* (*TEC*) crane; (*de petróleo*) derrick; **~ corrediza** *o* **móvil/de pescante/puente/de torre** mobile/jib/overhead/tower crane.

grueso, a [grwe'so, à] *a* thick; (*persona*) stout; (*calidad*) coarse ♦ *nm* bulk; (*espesor*) thickness; (*densidad*) density; (*de gente*) main body, mass; **el ~ de** the bulk of.

grulla [grōō'yà] *nf* (*ZOOL*) crane.

grumete [grōōme'te] *nm* (*NAUT*) cabin boy.

grumo [grōō'mo] *nm* (*coágulo*) clot, lump; (*masa*) dollop.

gruñido [grōōnyē'tho] *nm* grunt, growl; (*fig*) grumble.

gruñir [grōōnyēr'] *vi* (*animal*) to grunt, growl; (*fam*) to grumble.

gruñón, ona [grōōnyon', onà] *a* grumpy ♦ *nm/f* grumbler.

grupa [grōō'pà] *nf* (*ZOOL*) rump.

grupo [grōō'po] *nm* group; (*TEC*) unit, set; (*de árboles*) cluster; **~ sanguíneo** blood group.

gruta [grōō'tà] *nf* grotto.

Gta. *abr* (*AUTO*) = **Glorieta.**

guadalajareño, a [gwàthàlàhàrc'nyo, à] *a* of *o* from Guadalajara ♦ *nm/f* native *o* inhabitant of Guadalajara.

Guadalquivir [gwàthàlkēhēr'] *nm*: **el (Río) ~ the** Guadalquivir.

guadaña [gwàthà'nyà] *nf* scythe.

guadañar [gwàthànyàr'] *vt* to scythe, mow.

Guadiana [gwàthyà'nà] *nm*: **el (Río) ~ the** Guadiana.

guagua [gwà'gwà] *nf* (*AM, Canarias*) bus; (*AM: criatura*) baby.

guajolote [gwàholo'te] *nm* (*AM*) turkey.

guano [gwà'no] *nm* guano.

guantada [gwàntà'thà] *nf*, **guantazo** [gwàntà'so] *nm* slap.

guante [gwàn'te] *nm* glove; **se ajusta como un ~** it fits like a glove; **echar el ~ a uno** to catch hold of sb; (*fig: policía*) to catch sb.

guapo, a [gwà'po, à] *a* good-looking; (*mujer*) pretty, attractive; (*hombre*) handsome; (*elegante*) smart ♦ *nm* lover, gallant.

guarda [gwàr'thà] *nm/f* (*persona*) warden, keeper ♦ *nf* (*acto*) guarding; (*custodia*) custody; (*TIP*) flyleaf, endpaper; **~ forestal** game warden.

guarda(a)gujas [gwàrdàgōō'hàs] *nm inv* (*FERRO*) switchman.

guardabarros [gwàrthàhà'rros] *nm inv* fender (*US*), mudguard (*Brit*).

guardabosques [gwàrdàhos'kes] *nm inv* game warden.

guardacostas [gwàrdàko'stàs] *nm inv* coastguard vessel.

guardacoches [gwàrthàkotch'es] *nm/f inv* (*celador*) parking attendant.

guardador, a [gwàrthàthor', à] *a* protective; (*tacaño*) mean, stingy ♦ *nm/f* guardian, protector.

guardaespaldas [gwàrdàespàl'dàs] *nm/f inv* bodyguard.

guardameta [gwàrthàme'tà] *nm* goalkeeper.

guardapolvo [gwàrdàpol'ho] *nm* dust cover; (*prenda de vestir*) overalls *pl*.

guardar [gwàrthàr'] *vt* (*gen*) to keep; (*vigilar*) to guard, watch over; (*conservar*) to put away; (*dinero: ahorrar*) to save; (*promesa etc*) to keep; (*ley*) to observe; (*rencor*) to bear; (*INFORM: archivo*) to save; **~se** *vr* (*preservarse*) to protect o.s.; **~se de algo** (*evitar*) to avoid sth; (*abstenerse*) to refrain from sth; **~se de hacer algo** to be careful not to do sth; **guardársela a uno** to have it in for sb.

guardarropa [gwàrthàrro'pà] *nm* (*armario*) wardrobe; (*en establecimiento público*) cloakroom.

guardería [gwàrthcrē'à] *nf* nursery.

guardia [gwàr'thyà] *nf* (*MIL*) guard; (*cuidado*) care, custody; **estar de ~** to be on guard; **montar ~** to mount guard; **la G~ Civil** the Civil Guard; **~ municipal** *o* **urbana** municipal police ♦ *nm/f* guard; (*policía*) policeman/woman; **un ~ civil** a Civil Guard(sman); **un(a) ~ nacional** a policeman/woman; **~ urbano** traffic policeman.

guardián, ana [gwàrthyán', ànà] *nm/f* (*gen*) guardian, keeper.

guarecer [gwàreser'] *vt* (*proteger*) to protect; (*abrigar*) to shelter; **~se** *vr* to take refuge.

guarezca [gwàres'kà] *etc vb* V **guarecer.**

guarida [gwárē'thá] *nf* (*de animal*) den, lair; (*de persona*) haunt, hideout; (*refugio*) refuge.

guarnecer [gwárneser'] *vt* (*equipar*) to provide; (*adornar*) to adorn; (*TEC*) to reinforce.

guarnezca [gwárnes'ká] *etc vb* V **guarnecer.**

guarnición [gwárnēsyon'] *nf* (*de vestimenta*) trimming; (*de piedra*) mount; (*CULIN*) garnish; (*arneses*) harness; (*MIL*) garrison.

guarro, a [gwá'rro, á] *nm/f* pig; (*fig*) dirty o slovenly person.

guasa [gwá'sá] *nf* joke; **con** *o* **de** ~ jokingly, in fun.

guasón, ona [gwáson', oná] *a* witty; (*bromista*) joking ♦ *nm/f* wit; joker.

Guatemala [gwátemá'lá] *nf* Guatemala.

guatemalteco, a [gwátemálte'ko, á] *a, nm/f* Guatemalan.

guateque [gwáte'ke] *nm* (*fiesta*) party, binge.

guayaba [gwáyá'há] *nf* (*BOT*) guava.

Guayana [gwáyá'ná] *nf* Guyana, Guaiana.

guyanés, esa [gwáyánes', esá] *a, nm/f* Guyanese.

gubernamental [gōōhernámentál'], **gubernativo, a** [gōōhernátē'ho, á] *a* governmental.

guedeja [gethe'há] *nf* long hair.

guerra [ge'rrá] *nf* war; (*arte*) warfare; (*pelea*) struggle; ~ **atómica/bacteriológica/ nuclear/de guerrillas** atomic/germ/nuclear/ guerrilla warfare; **Primera/Segunda G~ Mundial** First/Second World War; ~ **de precios** (*COM*) price war; ~ **civil/fría** civil/ cold war; ~ **a muerte** fight to the death; **de** ~ military, war *cpd*; **estar en** ~ to be at war; **dar** ~ to be annoying.

guerrear [gerreár'] *vi* to wage war.

guerrero, a [gerre'ro, á] *a* fighting; (*carácter*) warlike ♦ *nm/f* warrior.

guerrilla [gerrē'yá] *nf* guerrilla warfare; (*tropas*) guerrilla band o group.

guerrillero, a [gerrēye'ro, á] *nm/f* guerrilla (fighter); (*contra invasor*) partisan.

guía [gē'á] *etc vb* V **guiar** ♦ *nm/f* (*persona*) guide ♦ *nf* (*libro*) guidebook; (*manual*) handbook; (*INFORM*) prompt; ~ **de ferrocarriles** railway timetable; ~ **telefónica** telephone directory; ~ **del turista/del viajero** tourist/traveller's guide.

guiar [geár'] *vt* to guide, direct; (*dirigir*) to lead; (*orientar*) to advise; (*AUTO*) to steer; ~**se** *vr*: ~**se por** to be guided by.

guijarro [gēhá'rro] *nm* pebble.

guillotina [gēyotē'ná] *nf* guillotine.

guinda [gēn'dá] *nf* sour (*US*) o morello (*Brit*) cherry; (*licor*) cherry liqueur.

guindar [gēndár'] *vt* to hoist; (*fam: robar*) to rip off.

guindilla [gēndē'yá] *nf* chilli pepper.

Guinea [gēnc'á] *nf* Guinea.

guineo, a [gēnc'o, á] *a* Guinea *cpd*, Guinean ♦ *nm/f* Guinean.

guiñapo [gēnyá'po] *nm* (*harapo*) rag; (*persona*) rogue.

guiñar [gēnyár'] *vi* to wink.

guiño [gē'nyo] *nm* (*parpadeo*) wink; (*muecas*) grimace; **hacer** ~**s a** (*enamorados*) to make eyes at.

guiñol [gēnyol'] *nm* (*TEATRO*) puppet theater.

guión [gēon'] *nm* (*LING*) hyphen, dash; (*esquema*) summary, outline; (*CINE*) script.

guionista [gyonē'stá] *nm/f* scriptwriter.

guipuzcoano, a [gēpōōskoá'no, á] *a* of o from Guipúzcoa ♦ *nm/f* native o inhabitant of Guipúzcoa.

guirigay [gērēgá'ē] *nm* (*griterío*) uproar; (*confusión*) chaos.

guirnalda [gērnál'dá] *nf* garland.

guisa [gē'sá] *nf*: **a** ~ **de** as, like.

guisado [gēsá'tho] *nm* stew.

guisante [gēsán'te] *nm* pea.

guisar [gēsár'] *vt, vi* to cook; (*fig*) to arrange.

guiso [gē'so] *nm* cooked dish.

guita [gē'tá] *nf* twine; (*fam: dinero*) dough.

guitarra [gētá'rrá] *nf* guitar.

guitarrista [gētárrē'stá] *nm/f* guitarist.

gula [gōō'lá] *nf* gluttony, greed.

gusano [gōōsá'no] *nm* maggot, worm; (*de mariposa, polilla*) caterpillar; (*fig*) worm; (*ser despreciable*) creep; ~ **de seda** silkworm.

gustar [gōōstár'] *vt* to taste, sample ♦ *vi* to please, be pleasing; ~ **de algo** to like o enjoy sth; **me gustan las uvas** I like grapes; **le gusta nadar** she likes o enjoys swimming; **¿gusta Ud?** would you like some?; **como Ud guste** as you wish.

gusto [gōō'sto] *nm* (*sentido, sabor*) taste; (*agrado*) liking; (*placer*) pleasure; **tiene un** ~ **amargo** it has a bitter taste; **tener buen** ~ to have good taste; **sobre** ~**s no hay nada escrito** there's no accounting for tastes; **de buen/mal** ~ in good/bad taste; **sentirse a** ~ to feel at ease; **¡mucho** *o* **tanto** ~ **(en conocerle)!** how do you do?, pleased to meet you; **el** ~ **es mío** the pleasure is mine; **tomar** ~ **a** to take a liking to; **con** ~ willingly, gladly.

gustoso, a [gōōsto'so, á] *a* (*sabroso*) tasty; (*agradable*) pleasant; (*con voluntad*) willing, glad; **lo hizo** ~ he did it gladly.

gutural [gōōtōōrál'] *a* guttural.

H

H, h [átch'e] *nf* (*letra*) H, h; **H de Historia** H for How.

h. *abr* (= *hora(s)*) h., hr(s).; (= *hacia*) c. ♦ *nmpl abr* (= *habitantes*) pop.

H. *abr* (*QUÍMICA*: = *Hidrógeno*) H; (= *Hectárea(s)*) ha.; (*COM*: = *Haber*) cr.

ha [á] *vb* V **haber.**

Ha. *abr* (= *Hectárea(s)*) ha.

haba [á'há] *nf* bean; **son ~s contadas** it goes without saying; **en todas partes cuecen ~s** it's the same (story) the whole world over.

Habana [ahá'ná] *nf*: **la ~** Havana.

habanero, a [ahane'ro, á] *a* of *o* from Havana ♦ *nm/f* native *o* inhabitant of Havana ♦ *nf* (*MUS*) habanera.

habano [ahá'no] *nm* Havana cigar.

habeas corpus [ahe'áskor'pōōs] *nm* (*LAW*) habeas corpus.

haber [aher'] *vt* (*LAW etc*): **todos los inventos habidos y por ~** all inventions present and future; **en el encuentro habido ayer** in the fight which occurred yesterday ♦ *vb auxiliar* (*en tiempos compuestos*) to have; **de ~lo sabido** if I had known (it); **lo hubiéramos hecho** we would have done it; **antes de ~lo visto** before seeing him; **~ de** to have to ♦ *vb impersonal*: **hay** there is/are; **hay un hombre/2 hombres en la calle** there is one man/there are two men in the street; **ha habido problemas** there have been problems; **hay sol** it is sunny; **hay que** it is necessary to, one must; **hay que hacerlo** it has to be done; **¿habrá tiempo?** will there be time?; **tomará lo que haya** he'll take whatever there is; **lo que hay es que ...** it's like this, ...; **¿cuánto hay de aquí a Cuzco?** how far is it from here to Cuzco?; **¿qué hay?** how's it going?; **no hay de qué** don't mention it; **~se** *vr*: **habérselas con uno** (*tener delante*) to be up against sb ♦ *nm* (*ingreso*) income; (*COM*: *crédito*) credit; (*balance*) credit side; (: *tb*: **~es**) assets *pl*.

habichuela [ahetchwe'lá] *nf* kidney bean.

hábil [á'hěl] *a* (*listo*) clever, smart; (*capaz*) fit, capable; (*experto*) expert; **día ~** working day.

habilidad [ahělětháth'] *nf* (*gen*) skill, ability; (*inteligencia*) cleverness; (*destreza*) expertness, expertise; (*JUR*) competence.

~ (para) fitness (for); **tener ~ manual** to be good with one's hands.

habilitación [ahělětásyon'] *nf* qualification; (*colocación de muebles*) furnishing; (*financiamiento*) financing; (*oficina*) payroll (*US*) *o* paymaster's (*Brit*) office.

habilitado [ahělětá'tho] *nm* paymaster.

habilitar [ahělětár'] *vt* to qualify; (*autorizar*) to authorize; (*capacitar*) to enable; (*dar instrumentos*) to equip; (*financiar*) to finance.

hábilmente [ahělmen'te] *ad* skilfully, expertly.

habitable [ahetá'hle] *a* inhabitable.

habitación [ahetásyon'] *nf* (*cuarto*) room; (*casa*) dwelling, abode; (*BIO*: *morada*) habitat; **~ sencilla** *o* **individual** single room; **~ doble** *o* **de matrimonio** double room.

habitante [ahetán'te] *nm/f* inhabitant.

habitar [ahetár'] *vt* (*residir en*) to inhabit; (*ocupar*) to occupy ♦ *vi* to live.

hábito [á'heto] *nm* habit; **tener el ~ de hacer algo** to be in the habit of doing sth.

habitual [ahetwál'] *a* habitual.

habituar [ahetwár'] *vt* to accustom; **~se** *vr*: **~se a** to get used to.

habla [á'hlá] *nf* (*capacidad de hablar*) speech; (*idioma*) language; (*dialecto*) dialect; **perder el ~** to become speechless; **de ~ francesa** French-speaking; **estar al ~** to be in contact; (*TELEC*) to be on the line; **¡González al ~!** (*TELEC*) Gonzalez speaking!

hablador, a [ahláthor', á] *a* talkative ♦ *nm/f* chatterbox.

habladuría [ahláthōōrē'á] *nf* rumor (*US*), rumour (*Brit*); **~s** *nfpl* gossip *sg*.

hablante [ahlán'te] *a* speaking ♦ *nm/f* speaker.

hablar [ahlár'] *vt* to speak, talk ♦ *vi* to speak; **~se** *vr* to speak to each other; **~ con** to speak to; **¡hable!, ¡puede ~!** (*TELEC*) go ahead (*US*), you're through! (*Brit*); **de eso ni ~** no way; **~ alto/bajo/claro** to speak loudly/quietly/plainly *o* bluntly; **~ de** to speak of *o* about; **"se habla inglés"** "English spoken here"; **no se hablan** they are not on speaking terms.

habré [ahre'] *etc vb* V **haber.**

hacedor, a [ásethor', á] *nm/f* maker.

hacendado, a [ásendá'tho, á] *a* property-owning ♦ *nm* (*terrateniente*) large landowner.

hacendoso, a [ásendo'so, á] *a* industrious, hard-working.

hacer [áser'] *vt* (*gen*) to make; (*crear*) to create; (*TEC*) to manufacture; (*preparar*) to prepare; (*ejecutar*) to do, execute; (*obligar*) to force, compel; (*dinero*) to earn; (*volver*) to make, turn ♦ *vi* (*comportarse*) to act, behave; (*disimular*) to pretend; (*convenir, ser apto*) to be suitable; ~**se** *vr* (*fabricarse*) to be made, be done; (*volverse*) to become; (*acostumbrarse a*) to get used to; ~ **bien/mal** to act rightly/ wrongly; **hace frío/calor** it's cold/hot; **hace un momento/dos años** a moment/two years ago; **hace poco** a little while ago; **te hacíamos en el Perú** we assumed you were in Peru; **hágale entrar** show him in; ~ **polvo algo** to smash sth to pieces; ~ **polvo a uno** to exhaust sb; ~ **un papel** (*TEATRO*) to play a role *o* part; **¿qué le vamos a ~?** what can we do about it?; **¿qué haces ahí?** what are you up to?; ~ **como que** *o* **como si** to act as though *o* as if; **dar que** ~ to cause trouble; ~ **de** to act as; **¿hace?** will it do?; **me hice un traje** I had a suit made; ~**se el sordo** to turn a deaf ear; ~**se el tonto** *o* **el sueco** to act dumb, play the innocent; ~**se a** (~) **algo** to get used to (doing) sth; ~**se viejo** to grow old; ~**se con algo** to get hold of sth; ~**se a un lado** to stand aside; **se hace tarde** it's getting late; **se me hace imposible trabajar** I'm finding it impossible to work; **no le hace** it doesn't matter.

hacia [à'syà] *prep* (*en dirección de, actitud*) towards; (*cerca de*) near; ~ **arriba/abajo** up(wards)/down(wards); ~ **mediodía** about noon.

hacienda [àsyen'dà] *nf* (*propiedad*) property; (*finca*) farm; (*AM*) ranch; ~ **pública** public finance; (**Ministerio de**) **H**~ Treasury Department (*US*), Exchequer (*Brit*).

hacina [àsē'nà] *nf* pile, stack.

hacinar [àsēnàr'] *vt* to pile (up); (*AGR*) to stack; (*fig*) to overcrowd.

hacha [àtch'à] *nf* axe; (*antorcha*) torch.

hache [àtch'e] *nf* (the letter) H; **llámele usted** ~ call it what you will.

hachís [àtchēs'] *nm* hashish.

hada [à'thà] *nf* fairy; ~ **madrina** fairy godmother.

hado [à'tho] *nm* fate, destiny.

haga [à'gà] *etc vb V* **hacer**.

Haití [àētē'] *nm* Haiti.

haitiano, a [àētyà'no, à] *a, nm/f* Haitian.

hala [à'là] *excl* (*vamos*) come on!; (*anda*) get on with it!

halagar [àlàgàr'] *vt* (*lisonjear*) to flatter.

halago [àlà'go] *nm* (*adulación*) flattery.

halague [àlà'ge] *etc vb V* **halagar**.

halagüeño, a [àlàgwe'nyo, à] *a* flattering.

halcón [àlkon'] *nm* falcòn, hawk.

hálito [à'lēto] *nm* breath.

halitosis [àlēto'sēs] *nf* halitosis, bad breath.

halo [à'lo] *nm* halo.

halterofilia [àlterofē'lyà] *nf* weightlifting.

hallar [àyàr'] *vt* (*gen*) to find; (*descubrir*) to

discover; (*toparse con*) to run into; ~**se** *vr* to be (situated); (*encontrarse*) to find o.s.; **se halla fuera** he is away; **no se halla** he feels out of place.

hallazgo [àyàs'go] *nm* discovery; (*cosa*) find.

hamaca [àmá'kà] *nf* hammock.

hambre [àm'bre] *nf* hunger; (*carencia*) famine; (*inanición*) starvation; (*fig*) longing; **tener** ~ to be hungry.

hambriento, a [àmbryen'to, à] *a* hungry, starving ♦ *nm/f* starving person; **los** ~**s** the hungry; ~ **de** hungry *o* longing for.

Hamburgo [àmbōōr'go] *nm* Hamburg.

hamburguesa [àmbōōrge'sà] *nf* hamburger.

hampa [àm'pà] *nf* underworld.

hampón [àmpon'] *nm* thug.

han [àn] *vb V* **haber**.

haragán, ana [àràgàn', ànà] *a, nm/f* good-for-nothing.

haraganear [àràgàncàr'] *vi* to idle, loaf about.

harapiento, a [àràpyen'to, à] *a* tattered, in rags.

harapo [àrà'po] *nm* rag.

hardware [hàr'dwer] *nm* (*INFORM*) hardware.

haré [àre'] *etc vb V* **hacer**.

harén [àren'] *nm* harem.

harina [àrē'nà] *nf* flour; **eso es** ~ **de otro costal** that's a horse of a different color.

harinero, a [àrēne'ro, à] *nm/f* flour merchant.

harinoso, a [àrēno'so, à] *a* floury.

hartar [àrtàr'] *vt* to satiate, glut; (*fig*) to tire, sicken; ~**se** *vr* (*de comida*) to fill o.s., gorge o.s.; (*cansarse*) to get fed up (*de* with).

hartazgo [àrtàs'go] *nm* surfeit, glut.

harto, a [àr'to, à] *a* (*lleno*) full; (*cansado*) fed up ♦ *ad* (*bastante*) enough; (*muy*) very; **estar** ~ **de** to be fed up with; **¡estoy** ~ **de decírtelo!** I'm sick and tired of telling you (so)!

hartura [àrtōō'rà] *nf* (*exceso*) surfeit; (*abundancia*) abundance; (*satisfacción*) satisfaction.

has [às] *vb V* **haber**.

Has. *abr* (= *Hectáreas*) ha.

hasta [à'stà] *ad* even ♦ *prep* (*alcanzando a*) as far as, up/down to; (*de tiempo: a tal hora*) till, until; (: *antes de*) before ♦ *conj*: ~ **que** until; ~ **luego** *o* **ahora** (*fam*)/**el sábado** see you soon/on Saturday; ~ **la fecha** (up) to date; ~ **nueva orden** until further notice; ~ **en Valencia hiela a veces** even in Valencia it freezes sometimes.

hastiar [àstyàr'] *vt* (*gen*) to weary; (*aburrir*) to bore; ~**se** *vr*: ~**se de** to get fed up with.

hastío |ástē'o| *nm* weariness; boredom.

hatajo |átá'ho| *nm*: **un ~ de gamberros** a bunch of hooligans.

hatillo |átē'yo| *nm* belongings *pl*, kit; (*montón*) bundle, heap.

Hawai |áwá'ē| *nm* (*tb*: **las Islas ~**) Hawaii.

hawaiano, a |áwáyá'no, á| *a, nm/f* Hawaian.

hay |áē| *vb V* **haber.**

Haya |á'yá| *nf*: **la ~** The Hague.

haya |á'yá| *etc vb V* **haber ♦** *nf* beech tree.

hayal |áyál'| *nm* beech grove.

haz |ás| *vb V* **hacer ♦** *nm* bundle, bunch; (*rayo: de luz*) beam **♦** *nf*: **~ de la tierra** face of the earth.

hazaña |ásá'nyá| *nf* feat, exploit; **sería una ~** it would be a great achievement.

hazmerreír |ásmcrrcē'r'| *nm inv* laughing stock.

HB *abr* (= *Herri Batasuna*) *Basque political party.*

he |c| *vb V* **haber ♦** *ad*: **~ aquí** here is, here are; **~ aquí por qué** ... that is why ....

hebilla |chē'yá| *nf* buckle, clasp.

hebra |c'hrá| *nf* thread; (*BOT*: *fibra*) fiber (*US*), fibre (*Brit*), grain.

hebreo, a |chrc'o, á| *a, nm/f* Hebrew **♦** *nm* (*LING*) Hebrew.

Hébridas |c'hrēthás| *nfpl*: **las ~** the Hebrides.

hectárea |cktá'rcá| *nf* hectare.

hechice |ctchē'sc| *etc vb V* **hechizar.**

hechicera |ctchēsc'rá| *nf* witch.

hechizar |ctchēsá'r| *vt* to cast a spell on, bewitch.

hechizo |ctchē'so| *nm* witchcraft, magic; (*acto de magia*) spell, charm.

hecho, a |ctch'o, á| *pp de* **hacer ♦** *a* complete; (*maduro*) mature; (*COSTURA*) ready-to-wear **♦** *nm* deed, act; (*dato*) fact; (*cuestión*) matter; (*suceso*) event **♦** *excl* agreed!, done!; **¡bien ~!** well done!; **de ~** in fact, as a matter of fact; (*POL etc*: *a, ad*) **de** facto; **de ~ y de derecho** de facto and de jure; **~ a la medida** made-to-measure; **a lo ~, pecho** it's no use crying over spilt milk.

hechura |ctchōō'rá| *nf* making, creation; (*producto*) product; (*forma*) form, shape; (*de persona*) build; (*TEC*) craftsmanship.

heder |cthcr'| *vi* to stink, smell; (*fig*) to be unbearable.

hediondez |cthyondcs'| *nf* stench, stink; (*cosa*) stinking thing.

hediondo, a |cthyon'do, á| *a* stinking.

hedor |cthor'| *nm* stench.

helada |clá'thá| *nf* frost.

heladera |clàthc'rá| *nf* (*AM*: *refrigerador*) refrigerator.

heladería |clàthcrē'á| *nf* ice-cream parlor (*US*) *o* parlour (*Brit*).

helado, a |clá'tho, á| *a* frozen; (*glacial*) icy; (*fig*) chilly, cold **♦** *nm* ice-cream; **dejar ~ a uno** to dumbfound sb.

helador, a |clàthor', á| *a* (*viento etc*) icy, freezing.

helar |clár'| *vt* to freeze, ice (up); (*dejar atónito*) to amaze; (*desalentar*) to discourage **♦** *vi*, **~se** *vr* to freeze; (*AVIAT, FERRO etc*) to ice (up), freeze up; (*líquido*) to set.

helecho |clctch'o| *nm* bracken, fern.

helénico, a |clc'nēko, á| *a* Hellenic, Greek.

heleno |clc'no, á| *nm/f* Hellene, Greek.

hélice |c'lēsc| *nf* spiral; (*TEC*) propeller; (*MAT*) helix.

helicóptero |clēkop'tcro| *nm* helicopter.

helmántico, a |clmán'tēko, á| *a of o* from Salamanca.

helvético, a |clhc'tēko, á| *a, nm/f* Swiss.

hembra |cm'brá| *nf* (*BOT, ZOOL*) female; (*mujer*) woman; (*TEC*) nut; **un elefante ~** a female elephant.

hemeroteca |cmcrotc'ká| *nf* newspaper library.

hemofilia |cmofē'lyá| *nf* hemophilia (*US*), haemophilia (*Brit*).

hemorragia |cmorrá'hyá| *nf* hemorrhage (*US*), haemorrhage (*Brit*).

hemorroides |cmorro'ēthcs| *nfpl* hemorrhoids (*US*), haemorrhoids (*Brit*).

hemos |c'mos| *vb V* **haber.**

henar |cnár'| *nm* meadow, hayfield.

henchir |cntchē'r| *vt* to fill, stuff; **~se** *vr* (*llenarse de comida*) to stuff o.s. (with food); (*inflarse*) to swell (up).

Hendaya |cndá'yá| *nf* Hendaye.

hender |cndcr'| *vt* to cleave, split.

hendidura |cndēthōō'rá| *nf* crack, split; (*GEO*) fissure.

heno |c'no| *nm* hay.

herbario, a |crhá'ryo, á| *a* herbal **♦** *nm* (*colección*) herbarium; (*especialista*) herbalist; (*botánico*) botanist.

herbicida |crhēsē'thá| *nm* weedkiller.

heredad |crctháth'| *nf* landed property; (*granja*) farm.

heredar |crcthár'| *vt* to inherit.

heredero, a |crcthc'ro, á| *nm/f* heir(ess); **~ del trono** heir to the throne.

hereditario, a |crcthētá'ryo, á| *a* hereditary.

hereje |crc'hc| *nm/f* heretic.

herejía |crchē'á| *nf* heresy.

herencia |crcn'syá| *nf* inheritance; (*fig*) heritage; (*BIO*) heredity.

herético, a |crc'tēko, á| *a* heretical.

herido, a |crē'tho, á| *a* injured, wounded; (*fig*) offended **♦** *nm/f* casualty **♦** *nf* wound, injury.

herir |crēr'| *vt* to wound, injure; (*fig*) to offend; (*conmover*) to touch, move.

hermana |crmá'ná| *nf V* **hermano.**

hermanar [ermánár'] *vt* to match; (*unir*) to join; (*ciudades*) to make sister cities (*US*), twin (*Brit*).

hermanastro, a [ermánás'tro, á] *nm/f* stepbrother/sister.

hermandad [ermándáth'] *nf* brotherhood; (*de mujeres*) sisterhood; (*sindicato etc*) association.

hermano, a [ermá'no, á] *a* similar ♦ *nm* brother ♦ *nf* sister; ~ **gemelo** twin brother; ~ **político** brother-in-law; ~ **primo** first cousin; **mis** ~**s** my brothers, my brothers and sisters; **hermana política** sister-in-law.

hermético, a [erme'tēko, á] *a* hermetic; (*fig*) watertight.

hermoso, a [ermo'so, á] *a* beautiful, lovely; (*estupendo*) splendid; (*guapo*) handsome.

hermosura [ermosōō'rá] *nf* beauty; (*de hombre*) handsomeness.

héroe [e'roe] *nm* hero.

heroicidad [eroēsētháth'] *nf* heroism; (*una* ~) heroic deed.

heroico, a [ero'ēko, á] *a* heroic.

heroína [eroē'ná] *nf* (*mujer*) heroine; (*droga*) heroin.

heroísmo [eroēs'mo] *nm* heroism.

herpes [er'pes] *nmpl o nfpl* (*MED: gen*) herpes *sg*; (: *de la piel*) shingles *sg*.

herradura [erráthōō'rá] *nf* horseshoe.

herraje [errá'he] *nm* (*trabajos*) ironwork.

herramienta [errámyen'tá] *nf* tool.

herrería [errerē'á] *nf* blacksmith's workshop (*US*), smithy (*Brit*); (*TEC*) forge.

herrero [erre'ro] *nm* blacksmith.

herrumbre [errōōm'bre] *nf* rust.

herrumbroso, a [errōōmbro'so, á] *a* rusty.

hervidero [erbēthe'ro] *nm* (*fig*) swarm; (*POL etc*) hotbed.

hervir [erbēr'] *vi* to boil; (*burbujear*) to bubble; (*fig*); ~ **de** to teem with; ~ **a fuego lento** to simmer.

hervor [erbor'] *nm* boiling; (*fig*) ardor (*US*), ardour (*Brit*), fervor (*US*), fervour (*Brit*).

heterogéneo, a [eterohe'neo, á] *a* heterogeneous.

heterosexual [eterosekswál'] *a*, *nm/f* heterosexual.

hez [es] *nf* (*tb*: **heces** *pl*) dregs.

hibernar [ēbernár'] *vi* to hibernate.

hice [ē'se] *etc vb V* **hacer**.

hidalgo, a [ēthál'go, á] *a* noble; (*honrado*) honorable (*US*), honourable (*Brit*) ♦ *nm/f* noble(man/woman).

hidratante [ēthrátán'te] *a*: **crema** ~ moisturizing cream, moisturizer.

hidratar [ēthrátár'] *vt* to moisturize.

hidrato [ēthrá'to] *nm* hydrate; ~ **de carbono** carbohydrate.

hidráulico, a [ēthrá'ōōlēko, á] *a* hydraulic ♦ *nf* hydraulics *sg*.

hidro... [ēthro] *pref* hydro..., water-....

hidroavión [ēthroáhyon'] *nm* seaplane.

hidroeléctrico, a [ēthroelek'trēko, á] *a* hydroelectric.

hidrófilo, a [ēthro'fēlo, á] *a* absorbent; **algodón** ~ absorbent cotton (*US*), cotton wool (*Brit*).

hidrofobia [ēthrofo'hyá] *nf* hydrophobia, rabies.

hidrófugo, a [ēthro'fōōgo, á] *a* waterproof.

hidrógeno [ēthro'heno] *nm* hydrogen.

hieda [ye'thá] *etc vb V* **heder**.

hiedra [ye'thrá] *nf* ivy.

hiel [yel] *nf* gall, bile; (*fig*) bitterness.

hielo [ye'lo] *etc vb V* **helar** ♦ *nm* (*gen*) ice; (*escarcha*) frost; (*fig*) coldness, reserve; **romper el** ~ (*fig*) to break the ice.

hiena [ye'ná] *nf* (*ZOOL*) hyena.

hiera [ye'rá] *etc vb V* **herir**.

hierba [yer'há] *nf* (*pasto*) grass; (*CULIN, MED: planta*) herb; **mala** ~ weed; (*fig*) evil influence.

hierbabuena [yerháhwe'ná] *nf* mint.

hierro [ye'rro] *nm* (*metal*) iron; (*objeto*) iron object; ~ **acanalado** corrugated iron; ~ **colado** *o* **fundido** cast iron; **de** ~ iron *cpd*.

hierva [yer'há] *etc vb V* **hervir**.

hígado [ē'gátho] *nm* liver; ~**s** *nmpl* (*fig*) guts; **echar los** ~**s** to wear o.s. out.

higiene [ēhye'ne] *nf* hygiene.

higiénico, a [ēhye'nēko, á] *a* hygienic.

higo [ē'go] *nm* fig; ~ **seco** dried fig; ~ **chumbo** prickly pear; **de** ~**s a brevas** once in a blue moon.

higuera [ēge'rá] *nf* fig tree.

hijastro, a [ēhás'tro, á] *nm/f* stepson/daughter.

hijo, a [ē'ho, á] *nm/f* son/daughter, child; (*uso vocativo*) dear; ~**s** *nmpl* children, sons and daughters; **sin** ~**s** childless; ~**/hija político/a** son-/daughter-in-law; ~ **pródigo** prodigal son; ~ **de papá/mamá** daddy's/mama's boy; ~ **de puta** (*fam!*) bastard(!), son of a bitch(!); **cada** ~ **de vecino** any Tom, Dick or Harry.

hilacha [ēlátch'á] *nf* ravelled thread; ~ **de acero** steel wool.

hilado, a [ēlá'tho, á] *a* spun.

hilandero, a [ēlánde'ro, á] *nm/f* spinner.

hilar [ēlár'] *vt* to spin; (*fig*) to reason, infer; ~ **delgado** to split hairs.

hilera [ēle'rá] *nf* row, file.

hilo [ē'lo] *nm* thread; (*BOT*) fiber (*US*), fibre (*Brit*); (*tela*) linen; (*metal*) wire; (*de agua*) trickle, thin stream; (*de luz*) beam, ray; (*de conversación*) thread, theme; (*de pensamientos*) train; **colgar de un** ~ (*fig*) to hang by a thread; **traje de** ~ linen suit.

hilvanar [ēlhánár'] *vt* (*COSTURA*) to baste (*US*), tack (*Brit*); (*fig*) to do hurriedly.

Himalaya [ēmálá'yá] *nm*: **el ~, los Montes ~** the Himalayas.

himno [ēm'no] *nm* hymn; **~ nacional** national anthem.

hincapié [ēnkápyc'] *nm*: **hacer ~ en** to emphasize, stress.

hincar [ēnkár'] *vt* to drive (in), thrust (in); (*diente*) to sink; **~se** *vr*: **~se de rodillas** to kneel down.

hincha [ēntch'á] *nm/f* (*fam: DEPORTE*) fan.

hinchado, a [ēntchá'tho, á] *a* (*gen*) swollen; (*persona*) pompous.

hinchar [ēntchár'] *vt* (*gen*) to swell; (*inflar*) to blow up, inflate; (*fig*) to exaggerate; **~se** *vr* (*inflarse*) to swell up; (*fam: llenarse*) to stuff o.s.; (*fig*) to get conceited; **~se de reír** to have a good laugh.

hinchazón [ēntcháson'] *nf* (*MED*) swelling; (*protuberancia*) bump, lump; (*altivez*) arrogance.

hindú [ēndōō'] *a, nm/f* Hindu.

hinojo [ēno'ho] *nm* fennel.

hinque [ēn'ke] *etc vb V* **hincar**.

hipar [ēpár'] *vi* to hiccup.

hiper... [ēper] *pref* hyper....

hiperactivo, a [ēperáktē'ho, á] *a* hyperactive.

hipermercado [ēpermerká'tho] *nm* hypermarket, superstore (*Brit*).

hipersensible [ēpersensē'hle] *a* hypersensitive.

hípico, a [ē'pēko, á] *a* horse *cpd*, equine; **club ~** riding club.

hipnotice [ēpnotē'se] *etc vb V* **hipnotizar**.

hipnotismo [ēpnotēs'mo] *nm* hypnotism.

hipnotizar [ēpnotēsár'] *vt* to hypnotize.

hipo [ē'po] *nm* hiccups *pl*; **quitar el ~ a uno** to cure sb's hiccups.

hipocondría [ēpokondrē'á] *nf* hypochondria.

hipocondríaco, a [ēpokondry'áko, á] *a, nm/f* hypochondriac.

hipocresía [ēpokresē'á] *nf* hypocrisy.

hipócrita [ēpo'krētá] *a* hypocritical ♦ *nm/f* hypocrite.

hipodérmico, a [ēpother'mēko, á] *a*: **aguja hipodérmica** hypodermic needle.

hipódromo [ēpo'thromo] *nm* racetrack.

hipopótamo [ēpopo'támo] *nm* hippopotamus.

hipoteca [ēpote'ká] *nf* mortgage; **redimir una ~** to pay off a mortgage.

hipotecario, a [ēpoteká'ryo, á] *a* mortgage *cpd*.

hipótesis [ēpo'tesēs] *nf inv* hypothesis; **es una ~ (nada más)** that's just a theory.

hipotético, a [ēpote'tēko, á] *a* hypothetic(al).

hiriendo [ēryen'do] *etc vb V* **herir**.

hiriente [ēryen'te] *a* offensive, wounding.

hirsuto, a [ērsōō'to, á] *a* hairy.

hirviendo [ērhyen'do] *etc vb V* **hervir**.

hisopo [ēso'po] *nm* (*REL*) sprinkler; (*BOT*) hyssop; (*de algodón*) swab.

hispánico, a [ēspá'nēko, á] *a* Hispanic, Spanish.

hispanidad [ēspánētháth'] *nf* (*cualidad*) Spanishness; (*POL*) Spanish o Hispanic world.

hispanista [ēspánē'stá] *nm/f* (*UNIV etc*) Hispan(ic)ist.

hispano, a [ēspá'no, á] *a* Hispanic, Spanish, Hispano- ♦ *nm/f* Spaniard.

Hispanoamérica [ēspánoáme'rēká] *nf* Spanish o Latin America.

hispanoamericano, a [ēspánoámerēká'no, á] *a, nm/f* Spanish o Latin American.

hispanohablante [ēspánoáhlán'te], **hispanoparlante** [ēspánopárlán'te] *a* Spanish-speaking.

histeria [ēste'ryá] *nf* hysteria.

histérico, a [ēste'rēko, á] *a* hysterical.

histerismo [ēsterēs'mo] *nm* (*MED*) hysteria; (*fig*) hysterics.

histograma [ēstográ'má] *nm* histogram.

historia [ēsto'ryá] *nf* history; (*cuento*) story, tale; **~s** *nfpl* (*chismes*) gossip *sg*; **dejarse de ~s** to come to the point; **pasar a la ~** to go down in history.

historiador, a [ēstoryáthor', á] *nm/f* historian.

historial [ēstoryál'] *nm* record; (*profesional*) résumé (*US*), curriculum vitae, c.v.; (*MED*) case history.

historiar [ēstoryár'] *vt* to chronicle, write the history of.

histórico, a [ēsto'rēko, á] *a* historical; (*fig*) historic.

historieta [ēstorye'tá] *nf* tale, anecdote; (*dibujos*) comic strip.

histrionismo [ēstryonēs'mo] *nm* (*TEATRO*) acting; (*fig*) histrionics *pl*.

hito [ē'to] *nm* (*fig*) landmark; (*objetivo*) goal, target; (*fig*) milestone.

hizo [ē'so] *vb V* **hacer**.

Hna(s). *abr* (= *Hermana(s)*) Sr(s).

Hno(s). *abr* (= *Hermano(s)*) Bro(s).

hocico [osē'ko] *nm* snout; (*fig*) grimace.

hockey [ho'kē] *nm* hockey; **~ sobre hielo** ice hockey.

hogar [ogár'] *nm* fireplace, hearth; (*casa*) home; (*vida familiar*) home life.

hogareño, a [ogáre'nyo, á] *a* home *cpd*; (*persona*) home-loving.

hogaza [ogá'sá] *nf* (*pan*) large loaf.

hoguera [oge'rá] *nf* (*gen*) bonfire; (*para herejes*) stake.

hoja [o'há] *nf* (*gen*) leaf; (*de flor*) petal; (*de hierba*) blade; (*de papel*) sheet; (*página*) page; (*formulario*) form; (*de puerta*) leaf; **~ de afeitar** razor blade; **~ de cálculo electrónico** spreadsheet; **~ de trabajo** (*IN-*

FORM) worksheet; **de ~ ancha** broad-leaved; **de ~ caduca/perenne** deciduous/evergreen.

hojalata [ohálá'tá] *nf* tin(plate).

hojaldre [ohál'dre] *nm* (*CULIN*) puff pastry.

hojarasca [ohárás'ká] *nf* (*hojas*) dead *o* fallen leaves *pl*; (*fig*) rubbish.

hojear [oheár'] *vt* to leaf through, turn the pages of.

hola [o'lá] *excl* hello!

Holanda [olán'dá] *nf* Holland.

holandés, esa [olándes', esá] *a* Dutch ♦ *nm/f* Dutchman/woman; **los holandeses** the Dutch ♦ *nm* (*LING*) Dutch.

holgado, a [olǥá'ðo, á] *a* loose, baggy; (*rico*) well-to-do.

holganza [olǥán'sá] *nf* (*ocio*) leisure; (*diversión*) amusement.

holgar [olǥár'] *vi* (*descansar*) to rest; (*sobrar*) to be superfluous; **huelga decir que** it goes without saying that.

holgazán, ana [olǥásán', áná] *a* idle, lazy ♦ *nm/f* loafer.

holgazanear [olǥásáneár'] *vi* to laze *o* loaf around.

holgué [olǥe'], **holguemos** [olǥe'mos] *etc vb* V **holgar**.

holgura [olǥōō'rá] *nf* looseness, bagginess; (*TEC*) play, free movement; (*vida*) comfortable living, luxury.

hollar [oyár'] *vt* to tread (on), trample.

hollín [oyēn'] *nm* soot.

hombre [om'bre] *nm* man; (*raza humana*): **el ~** man(kind) ♦ *excl*: **¡sí ~!** (*claro*) of course!; (*para énfasis*) man; **~ de negocios** businessman; **~-rana** frogman; **~ de bien** *o* **pro** honest man; **~ de confianza** right-hand man; **~ de estado** statesman; **el ~ medio** the average man.

hombrera [ombre'rá] *nf* shoulder strap.

hombro [om'bro] *nm* shoulder; **arrimar el ~** to lend a hand; **encogerse de ~s** to shrug one's shoulders.

hombruno, a [ombrōō'no, á] *a* mannish.

homenaje [omená'he] *nm* (*gen*) homage; (*tributo*) tribute; **un partido ~** a benefit match.

homicida [omēsē'ðá] *a* homicidal ♦ *nm/f* murderer.

homicidio [omēsē'ðyo] *nm* murder, homicide; (*involuntario*) manslaughter.

homologación [omoloǥásyon'] *nf* (*de sueldo, condiciones*) parity.

homólogo, a [omo'loǥo, á] *nm/f* counterpart, opposite number.

homónimo [omo'nēmo] *nm* (*tocayo*) namesake.

homosexual [omosekswál'] *a, nm/f* homosexual.

hondo, a [on'do, á] *a* deep; **lo ~** the depth(s) (*pl*), the bottom; **con ~ pesar**

with deep regret.

hondonada [ondoná'ðá] *nf* hollow, depression; (*cañón*) ravine; (*GEO*) lowland.

hondura [ondōō'rá] *nf* depth, profundity.

Honduras [ondōō'rás] *nf* Honduras.

hondureño, a [ondōōre'nyo, á] *a, nm/f* Honduran.

honestidad [onestēðáð'] *nf* purity, chastity; (*decencia*) decency.

honesto, a [one'sto, á] *a* chaste; decent; honest; (*justo*) just.

hongo [on'go] *nm* (*BOT*: *gen*) fungus; (: *comestible*) mushroom; (: *venenoso*) toadstool; (*sombrero*) derby (*US*), bowler (hat) (*Brit*); **~s del pie** athlete's foot *sg*.

honor [onor'] *nm* (*gen*) honor (*US*), honour (*Brit*); (*gloria*) glory; **~ profesional** professional etiquette; **en ~ a la verdad** to be fair.

honorable [onorá'ƀle] *a* honorable (*US*), honourable (*Brit*).

honorario, a [onorá'ryo, á] *a* honorary ♦ *nm*: **~s** fees.

honorífico, a [onorē'fēko, á] *a* honorable (*US*), honourable (*Brit*); **mención honorífica** honorable mention.

honra [on'rá] *nf* (*gen*) honor (*US*), honour (*Brit*); (*renombre*) good name; **~s fúnebres** funeral rites; **tener algo a mucha ~** to be proud of sth.

honradez [onráðes'] *nf* honesty; (*de persona*) integrity.

honrado, a [onrá'ðo, á] *a* honest, upright.

honrar [onrár'] *vt* to honor (*US*), honour (*Brit*); **~se** *vr*: **~se con algo/de hacer algo** to be honored by sth/to do sth.

honroso, a [onro'so, á] *a* (*honrado*) honorable (*US*), honourable (*Brit*); (*respetado*) respectable.

hora [o'rá] *nf* hour; (*tiempo*) time; **¿qué ~ es?** what time is it?; **¿a qué ~?** at what time?; **media ~** half an hour; **a la ~ de comer/de recreo** at lunchtime/at playtime; **a primera ~** first thing (in the morning); **a última ~** at the last moment; **noticias de última ~** last-minute news; **a altas ~s** in the wee small hours; **a la ~ en punto** on the dot; **¡a buena ~!** about time, too!; **en mala ~** unluckily; **dar la ~** to strike the hour; **poner el reloj en ~** to set one's watch; **~s de oficina/de trabajo** office/working hours; **~s de visita** visiting times; **~s extra** *o* **extraordinarias** overtime *sg*; **~s punta** rush hours; **no ver la ~ de** to look forward to; **¡ya era ~!** and about time too!

horadar [oráðár'] *vt* to drill, bore.

horario, a [orá'ryo, á] *a* hourly, hour *cpd* ♦ *nm* timetable; **~ comercial** business hours.

horca [or'ká] *nf* gallows *sg*; (*AGR*) pitchfork.

horcajadas |orkáhá'ɖás|: **a** ~ *ad* astride.
horchata |ortchá'tá| *nf* *cold drink made from almonds and water*, almond milk.
horda |or'ɖá| *nf* horde.
horizontal |orēsontál'| *a* horizontal.
horizonte |orēson'te| *nm* horizon.
horma |or'má| *nf* mold (*US*), mould (*Brit*); ~ **(de calzado)** last; ~ **de sombrero** hat block.
hormiga |ormē'gá| *nf* ant; ~**s** *nfpl* (*MED*) pins and needles.
hormigón |ormēgon'| *nm* concrete; ~ **armado/pretensado** reinforced/prestressed concrete.
hormigueo |ormēge'o| *nm* (*comezón*) itch; (*fig*) uneasiness.
hormona |ormo'ná| *nf* hormone.
hornada |orná'ɖá| *nf* batch of loaves (*etc*).
hornillo |ornē'yo| *nm* (*cocina*) portable stove.
horno |or'no| *nm* (*CULIN*) oven; (*TEC*) furnace; (*para cerámica*) kiln; ~ **microondas** microwave (oven); **alto** ~ blast furnace; ~ **crematorio** crematorium.
horóscopo |oros'kopo| *nm* horoscope.
horquilla |orkē'yá| *nf* hairpin; (*AGR*) pitchfork.
horrendo, a |orren'do, á| *a* horrendous, frightful.
horrible |orrē'ɦle| *a* horrible, dreadful.
horripilante |orrēpēlán'te| *a* hair-raising, horrifying.
horripilar |orrēpēlár'| *vt*: ~ **a uno** to horrify sb; ~**se** *vr* to be horrified.
horror |orror'| *nm* horror, dread; (*atrocidad*) atrocity; **¡qué** ~! (*fam*) oh, my God!; **estudia horrores** he studies a hell of a lot.
horrorice |orrorē'se| *etc vb* V **horrorizar.**
horrorizar |orrorēsár'| *vt* to horrify, frighten; ~**se** *vr* to be horrified.
horroroso, a |orroro'so, á| *a* horrifying, ghastly.
hortaliza |ortálē'sá| *nf* vegetable.
hortelano, a |ortelá'no, á| *nm/f* (market) gardener.
hortera |orte'rá| *a* (*fam*) vulgar.
hortícola |ortē'kolá| *a* horticultural.
horticultura |ortēkōoltōo'rá| *nf* horticulture.
hosco, a |os'ko, á| *a* dark; (*persona*) sullen, gloomy.
hospedaje |ospeɖá'he| *nm* (cost of) board and lodging.
hospedar |ospeɖár'| *vt* to put up; ~**se** *vr*: ~**se (con/en)** to stay o lodge (with/at).
hospedería |ospeɖherē'á| *nf* (*edificio*) inn; (*habitación*) guest room.
hospicio |ospē'syo| *nm* (*para niños*) orphanage.
hospital |ospētál'| *nm* hospital.
hospitalario, a |ospētálá'ryo, á| *a* (*acoge-*

dor) hospitable.
hospitalice |ospētálē'se| *etc vb* V **hospitalizar.**
hospitalidad |ospētálēɖháɖ'| *nf* hospitality.
hospitalizar |ospētálēsár'| *vt* to send o take to hospital, hospitalize.
hosquedad |oskeɖháɖ'| *nf* sullenness.
hostal |ostál'| *nm* small hotel.
hostelería |ostelerē'á| *nf* hotel business o trade.
hostelero, a |ostele'ro, á| *nm/f* innkeeper, landlord/lady.
hostia |os'tyá| *nf* (*REL*) host, consecrated wafer; (*fam: golpe*) whack, punch ♦ *excl*: **¡~(s)!** (*fam!*) damn!
hostigar |ostēgár'| *vt* to whip; (*fig*) to harass, pester.
hostigue |ostē'ge| *etc vb* V **hostigar.**
hostil |ostēl'| *a* hostile.
hostilidad |ostēlēɖháɖ'| *nf* hostility.
hotel |otel'| *nm* hotel.
hotelero, a |otele'ro, á| *a* hotel *cpd* ♦ *nm/f* hotelier.
hoy |oē| *ad* (*este día*) today; (*en la actualidad*) now(adays) ♦ *nm* present time; ~ **(en) día** now(adays); **el día de** ~, ~ **día** (*AM*) this very day; ~ **por** ~ right now; **de** ~ **en ocho días** a week from today; **de** ~ **en adelante** from now on.
hoya |o'yá| *nf* pit; (*sepulcro*) grave; (*GEO*) valley.
hoyo |o'yo| *nm* hole, pit; (*tumba*) grave; (*GOLF*) hole; (*MED*) pockmark.
hoyuelo |oywe'lo| *nm* dimple.
hoz |os| *nf* sickle.
hube |ōō'ɦe| *etc vb* V **haber.**
hucha |ōōtch'á| *nf* money box.
hueco, a |we'ko, á| *a* (*vacío*) hollow, empty; (*resonante*) booming; (*sonido*) resonant; (*persona*) conceited; (*estilo*) pompous ♦ *nm* hollow, cavity; (*agujero*) hole; (*de escalera*) well; (*de ascensor*) shaft; (*vacante*) vacancy; ~ **de la mano** hollow of the hand.
huela |we'lá| *etc vb* V **oler.**
huelga |wel'gá| *etc vb* V **holgar** ♦ *nf* strike; **declararse en** ~ to go on strike; ~ **general** general strike; ~ **de hambre** hunger strike; ~ **oficial** official strike.
huelgue |wel'ge| *etc vb* V **holgar.**
huelguista |welgē'stá| *nm/f* striker.
huella |we'yá| *nf* (*acto de pisar, pisada*) tread(ing); (*marca del paso*) footprint, footstep; (: *de animal, máquina*) track; ~ **digital** fingerprint; **sin dejar** ~ without leaving a trace.
huérfano, a |wer'fáno, á| *a* orphan(ed); (*fig*) unprotected ♦ *nm/f* orphan.
huerta |wer'tá| *nf* truck farm (*US*), market garden (*Brit*); (*Murcia, Valencia*) irrigated region.

huerto |wer'to| *nm* kitchen garden; (*de árboles frutales*) orchard.

hueso |wc'so| *nm* (ANAT) bone; (*de fruta*) pit (*US*), stone; **sin ~** (*carne*) boned; **estar en los ~s** to be nothing but skin and bones; **ser un ~** (*profesor*) to be terribly strict; **un ~ duro de roer** a hard nut to crack.

huésped, a |wcs'pcth, á| *nm/f* (*invitado*) guest; (*habitante*) resident; (*anfitrión*) host(ess).

huesudo, a |wcs͞oo'tho, á| *a* bony, big-boned.

huevera |wchc'rá| *nf* eggcup.

huevo |wc'ho| *nm* egg; (*fam!*) ball(!), testicle; **~ duro/escalfado/estrellado** *o* **frito/pasado por agua** hard-boiled/poached/fried/soft-boiled egg; **~s revueltos** scrambled eggs; **me costó un ~** (*fam!*) it was hard work; **tener ~s** (*fam!*) to have guts.

huida |͞oo͞c'thá| *nf* escape, flight; **~ de capitales** (COM) flight of capital.

huidizo, a |͞oo͞cthc'so, á| *a* (*tímido*) shy; (*pasajero*) fleeting.

huir |͞oo͞cr'| *vt* (*escapar*) to flee, escape; (*evadir*) to avoid ♦ *vi* to flee, run away; **~se** *vr* (*escaparse*) to escape.

hule |͞oo'lc| *nm* (*encerado*) oilskin.

hulla |͞oo'yá| *nf* bituminous coal.

humanice |͞oo͞mánc'sc| *etc vb* V **humanizar**.

humanidad |͞oo͞mánctháth'| *nf* (*género humano*) man(kind); (*cualidad*) humanity; (*fam: gordura*) corpulence.

humanitario, a |͞oo͞mánctá'ryo, á| *a* humanitarian; (*benévolo*) humane.

humanizar |͞oo͞máncsár'| *vt* to humanize; **~se** *vr* to become more human.

humano, a |͞oo͞má'no, á| *a* (*gen*) human; (*humanitario*) humane ♦ *nm* human; **ser ~** human being.

humareda |͞oo͞márc'thá| *nf* cloud of smoke.

humeante |͞oo͞mcán'tc| *a* smoking, smoky.

humedad |͞oo͞mctháth'| *nf* (*del clima*) humidity; (*de pared etc*) dampness; **a prueba de ~** waterproof.

humedecer |͞oo͞mcthcscr'| *vt* to moisten, wet; **~se** *vr* to get wet.

humedezca |͞oo͞mcthcs'ká| *etc vb* V **humedecer**.

húmedo, a |͞oo'mctho, á| *a* (*mojado*) damp, wet; (*tiempo etc*) humid.

humildad |͞oo͞mēldáth'| *nf* humility, humbleness.

humilde |͞oo͞mēl'dc| *a* humble, modest; (*clase etc*) low, modest.

humillación |͞oo͞mēyásyon'| *nf* humiliation.

humillante |͞oo͞mēyán'tc| *a* humiliating.

humillar |͞oo͞mēyár'| *vt* to humiliate; **~se** *vr* to humble o.s., grovel.

humo |͞oo'mo| *nm* (*de fuego*) smoke; (*gas nocivo*) fumes *pl*; (*vapor*) steam; **~s** *nmpl*

(*fig*) conceit *sg*; **irse todo en ~** (*fig*) to vanish without trace; **bajar los ~s a uno** to take sb down a peg or two.

humor |͞oo͞mor'| *nm* (*disposición*) mood, temper; (*lo que divierte*) humor (*US*), humour (*Brit*); **de buen/mal ~** in a good/bad mood.

humorado, a |͞oo͞morá'tho, á| *a*: **bien ~** good-humored (*US*), good-humoured (*Brit*); **mal ~** bad-tempered, cross ♦ *nf* witticism.

humorismo |͞oo͞morēs'mo| *nm* humor (*US*), humour (*Brit*).

humorista |͞oo͞morē'stá| *nm/f* comic.

humorístico, a |͞oo͞morē'stĕko, á| *a* funny, humorous.

hundimiento |͞oo͞ndēmycn'to| *nm* (*gen*) sinking; (*colapso*) collapse.

hundir |͞oo͞ndēr'| *vt* to sink; (*edificio, plan*) to ruin, destroy; **~se** *vr* to sink, collapse; (*fig: arruinarse*) to be ruined; (*desaparecer*) to disappear; **se hundió la economía** the economy collapsed; **se hundieron los precios** prices slumped.

húngaro, a |͞oo͞n'gáro, á| *a*, *nm/f* Hungarian ♦ *nm* (LING) Hungarian, Magyar.

Hungría |͞oo͞ngrē'á| *nf* Hungary.

huracán |͞oo͞rákán'| *nm* hurricane.

huraño, a |͞oo͞rá'nyo, á| *a* (*antisocial*) unsociable.

hurgar |͞oo͞rgár'| *vt* to poke, jab; (*remover*) to stir (up); **~se** *vr*: **~se (las narices)** to pick one's nose.

hurgonear |͞oo͞rgoncár'| *vt* to poke.

hurgue |͞oo͞r'gc| *etc vb* V **hurgar**.

hurón |͞oo͞ron'| *nm* (ZOOL) ferret.

huronera |͞oo͞ronc'rá| *nf* (*fig*) den.

hurra |͞oo'rrá| *excl* hurray!, hurrah!

hurtadillas |͞oo͞rtáthc'yás|: **a ~** *ad* stealthily, on the sly.

hurtar |͞oo͞rtár'| *vt* to steal; **~se** *vr* to hide, keep out of the way.

hurto |͞oo͞r'to| *nm* theft, stealing; (*lo robado*) (piece of) stolen property, loot.

husmear |͞oo͞smcár'| *vt* (*oler*) to sniff out, scent; (*fam*) to pry into ♦ *vi* to smell bad.

huso |͞oo'so| *nm* (TEC) spindle; (*de torno*) drum.

huy |͞oo'ē| *excl* (*dolor*) ow!, ouch!; (*sorpresa*) well!; (*alivio*) phew!

huyendo |͞oo͞ycn'do| *etc vb* V **huir**.

I, i |ē| *nf* (*letra*) I, i; **I de Inés** I for Item.

I.A. *abr* = **inteligencia artificial.**

iba [ē'ḥá] *etc vb V* **ir.**

Iberia [ēḥe'ryá] *nf* Iberia.

ibérico, a [ēḥe'rēko, á] *a* Iberian; **la Península ibérica** the Iberian Peninsula.

ibero, a [ēḥe'ro, á], **íbero, a** [ē'ḥero, á] *a*, *nm/f* Iberian.

iberoamericano, a [ēḥeroámerēká'no, á] *a*, *nm/f* Latin American.

íbice [iḥ'ise] *nm* ibex.

ibicenco, a [ēḥēsen'ko, á] *a* of *o* from Ibiza ♦ *nm/f* native *o* inhabitant of Ibiza.

Ibiza [ēḥē'sá] *nf* Ibiza.

ice [ē'se] *etc vb V* **izar.**

iceberg [ēseber'] *nm* iceberg.

ICONA [ēko'ná] *nm abr* (*Esp*)=*Instituto Nacional para la Conservacion de la Naturaleza.*

ícono [ē'kono] *nm* (*tb INFORM*) icon.

iconoclasta [ēkonoklá'stá] *a* iconoclastic ♦ *nm/f* iconoclast.

ictericia [ēktcrē'syá] *nf* jaundice.

íd. *abr* = **ídem.**

ida [ē'ḥá] *nf* going, departure; ~ **y vuelta** round trip, return; ~**s y venidas** comings and goings.

IDE [ēḥe] *nf abr* (= *Iniciativa de Defensa Estratégica*) SDI.

idea [ēḥe'á] *nf* idea; (*impresión*) opinion; (*propósito*) intention; ~ **genial** brilliant idea; **a mala** ~ out of spite; **no tengo la menor** ~ I haven't a clue.

ideal [ēḥeál'] *a*, *nm* ideal.

idealice [ēḥcálē'se] *etc vb V* **idealizar.**

idealista [ēḥcálē'stá] *a* idealistic ♦ *nm/f* idealist.

idealizar [ēḥcálēsár'] *vt* to idealize.

idear [ēḥeár'] *vt* to think up; (*aparato*) to invent; (*viaje*) to plan.

ídem [ē'ḥem] *pron* ditto.

idéntico, a [ēḥen'tēko, á] *a* identical.

identidad [ēḥentēḥáḥ'] *nf* identity; ~ **corporativa** corporate identity *o* image.

identificación [ēḥentēfēkásyon'] *nf* identification.

identificar [ēḥentēfēkár'] *vt* to identify; ~**se** *vr:* ~**se con** to identify with.

identifique [ēḥentēfē'ke] *etc vb V* **identificar.**

ideología [ēḥcolohē'á] *nf* ideology.

ideológico, a [ēḥcolo'hēko, á] *a* ideological.

idílico, a [ēḥē'lēko, á] *a* idyllic.

idioma [ēḥyo'má] *nm* language.

idiomático, a [ēḥyomá'tēko, á] *a* idiomatic.

idiota [ēḥyo'tá] *a* idiotic ♦ *nm/f* idiot.

idiotez [ēḥyotes'] *nf* idiocy.

ídolo [ē'ḥolo] *nm* (*tb fig*) idol.

idoneidad [ēḥoncēḥáḥ'] *nf* suitability; (*capacidad*) aptitude.

idóneo, a [ēḥo'neo, á] *a* suitable.

iglesia [ēḡle'syá] *nf* church; ~ **parroquial** parish church; **¡con la** ~ **hemos topado!** now we're really up against it!

ignición [ēḡnēsyon'] *nf* ignition.

ignominia [ēḡnomē'nyá] *nf* ignominy.

ignominioso, a [ēḡnomēnyo'so, á] *a* ignominious.

ignorado, a [ēḡnorá'ḥo, á] *a* unknown; (*dato*) obscure.

ignorancia [ēḡnorán'syá] *nf* ignorance; **por** ~ through ignorance.

ignorante [ēḡnorán'te] *a* ignorant, uninformed ♦ *nm/f* ignoramus.

ignorar [ēḡnorár'] *vt* not to know, be ignorant of; (*no hacer caso a*) to ignore; **ignoramos su paradero** we don't know his whereabouts.

ignoto, a [ēḡno'to, á] *a* unknown.

igual [ēḡwál'] *a* equal; (*similar*) like, similar; (*mismo*) (the) same; (*constante*) constant; (*temperatura*) even ♦ *nm/f* equal; **al** ~ **que** *prep, conj* like, just like; ~ **que** the same as; **sin** ~ peerless; **me da** *o* **es** ~ I don't care, it makes no difference; **no tener** ~ to be unrivalled; **son** ~**es** they're the same.

iguala [ēḡwá'lá] *nf* equalization; (*COM*) agreement.

igualada [ēḡwálá'ḥá] *nf* equalizer.

igualar [ēḡwálár'] *vt* (*gen*) to equalize, make equal; (*terreno*) to make even; (*COM*) to agree upon; ~**se** *vr* (*platos de balanza*) to balance out; ~**se (a)** (*equivaler*) to be equal (to).

igualdad [ēḡwáldáḥ'] *nf* equality; (*similaridad*) sameness; (*uniformidad*) uniformity; **en** ~ **de condiciones** on an equal basis.

igualmente [ēḡwálmen'te] *ad* equally; (*también*) also, likewise ♦ *excl* the same to you!

ikurriña [ēkōōrrē'nyá] *nf* Basque flag.

ilegal [ēleḡál'] *a* illegal.

ilegitimidad [ēlchētēmēḥáḥ'] *nf* illegitimacy.

ilegítimo, a [ēlchē'tēmo, á] *a* illegitimate.

ileso, a [ēle'so, á] *a* unhurt, unharmed.

ilícito, a [ēlē'sēto, á] *a* illicit.

ilimitado, a [ēlēmētá'ḥo, á] *a* unlimited.

Ilma., Ilmo. *abr* (= *Ilustrísima, Ilustrísimo*) courtesy title.

ilógico, a [ēlo'hēko, á] *a* illogical.

iluminación [ēlōōmēnásyon'] *nf* illumination; (*alumbrado*) lighting; (*fig*) enlightenment.

iluminar [ēlōōmēnár'] *vt* to illuminate, light (up); (*fig*) to enlighten.

ilusión [ēlōōsyon'] *nf* illusion; (*quimera*) delusion; (*esperanza*) hope; (*emoción*) excitement, thrill; **hacerse ilusiones** to build up one's hopes; **no te hagas ilusiones** don't build up your hopes *o* get too excited.

ilusionado, a [ēlōōsyoná'tho, á] *a* excited.

ilusionista [ēlōōsyonē'stá] *nm/f* illusionist (*US*), conjurer (*Brit*).

iluso, a [ēlōō'so, á] *a* gullible, easily deceived ♦ *nm/f* dreamer, visionary.

ilusorio, a [ēlōōso'ryo, á] *a* (*de ilusión*) illusory, deceptive; (*esperanza*) vain.

ilustración [ēlōōstrásyon'] *nf* illustration; (*saber*) learning, erudition; **la l~** the Enlightenment.

ilustrado, a [ēlōōstrá'tho, á] *a* illustrated; learned.

ilustrar [ēlōōstrár'] *vt* to illustrate; (*instruir*) to instruct; (*explicar*) to explain, make clear; **~se** *vr* to acquire knowledge.

ilustre [ēlōōs'tre] *a* famous, illustrious.

imagen [ēmá'hen] *nf* (*gen*) image; (*dibujo*, *TV*) picture; (*REL*) statue; **ser la viva ~ de** to be the spitting *o* living image of; **a su ~** in one's own image.

imaginación [ēmáhēnásyon'] *nf* imagination; (*fig*) fancy; **ni por ~** on no account; **no se me pasó por la ~ que...** it never even occurred to me that ... .

imaginar [ēmáhēnár'] *vt* (*gen*) to imagine; (*idear*) to think up; (*suponer*) to suppose; **~se** *vr* to imagine; **¡imagínate!** just imagine!, just fancy!; **imagínese que... suppose that ...; me imagino que sí** I should think so.

imaginario, a [ēmáhēná'ryo, á] *a* imaginary.

imaginativo, a [ēmáhēnátē'tho, á] *a* imaginative ♦ *nf* imagination.

imán [ēmán'] *nm* magnet.

iman(t)ar [ēmán(t)ár'] *vt* to magnetize.

imbécil [ēmbe'sēl] *nm/f* imbecile, idiot.

imbecilidad [ēmbesēlēthàth'] *nf* imbecility, stupidity.

imberbe [ēmber'he] *a* beardless.

imborrable [ēmborrá'hle] *a* indelible; (*inolvidable*) unforgettable.

imbuir [ēmbōōēr'] *vi* to imbue.

imbuyendo [ēmbōōyen'do] *etc vb* V **imbuir.**

imitación [ēmētásyon'] *nf* imitation; (*parodia*) mimicry; **a ~ de** in imitation of; **desconfíe de las imitaciones** (*COM*) beware of copies *o* imitations.

imitador, a [ēmētáthor', á] *a* imitative ♦ *nm/f* imitator; (*TEATRO*) mimic.

imitar [ēmētár'] *vt* to imitate; (*parodiar*, *remedar*) to mimic, ape; (*copiar*) to follow.

impaciencia [ēmpásyen'syá] *nf* impatience.

impacientar [ēmpásyentár'] *vt* to make impatient; (*enfadar*) to irritate; **~se** *vr* to get impatient; (*inquietarse*) to fret.

impaciente [ēmpásyen'te] *a* impatient; (*nervioso*) anxious.

impacto [ēmpàk'to] *nm* impact.

impagado, a [ēmpàgá'tho, á] *a* unpaid, still to be paid.

impar [ēmpár'] *a* odd ♦ *nm* odd number.

imparable [ēmpárá'hle] *a* unstoppable.

imparcial [ēmpársyál'] *a* impartial, fair.

imparcialidad [ēmpársyálēthàth'] *nf* impartiality, fairness.

impartir [ēmpártēr'] *vt* to impart, give.

impasible [ēmpásē'hle] *a* impassive.

impavidez [ēmpáhēthes'] *nf* fearlessness, intrepidness.

impávido, a [ēmpá'hētho, á] *a* fearless, intrepid.

IMPE [ēm'pe] *nm abr* (*Esp COM*)=*Instituto de la Mediana y Pequeña Empresa.*

impecable [ēmpeká'hle] *a* impeccable.

impedido, a [ēmpethē'tho, á] *a*: **estar ~** to be an invalid ♦ *nm/f*: **ser un ~ físico** to be an invalid.

impedimento [ēmpethēmen'to] *nm* impediment, obstacle.

impedir [ēmpethēr'] *vt* (*obstruir*) to impede, obstruct; (*estorbar*) to prevent; **~ el tráfico** to block the traffic.

impeler [ēmpeler'] *vt* to drive, propel; (*fig*) to impel.

impenetrabilidad [ēmpenetráhēlēthàth'] *nf* impenetrability.

impenetrable [ēmpenetrá'hle] *a* impenetrable; (*fig*) incomprehensible.

impensable [ēmpensá'hle] *a* unthinkable.

impepinable [ēmpepēná'hle] *a* (*fam*) certain, inevitable.

imperante [ēmperàn'te] *a* prevailing.

imperar [ēmperár'] *vi* (*reinar*) to rule, reign; (*fig*) to prevail, reign; (*precio*) to be current.

imperativo, a [ēmperátē'tho, á] *a* (*persona*) imperious; (*urgente*, *LING*) imperative.

imperceptible [ēmperseptē'hle] *a* imperceptible.

imperdible [ēmperthē'hle] *nm* safety pin.

imperdonable [ēmperthoná'hle] *a* unforgivable, inexcusable.

imperecedero, a [ēmperesethe'ro, á] *a* undying.

imperfección [ēmperfeksyon'] *nf* imperfection; (*falla*) flaw, fault.

imperfecto, a [ēmperfek'to, á] *a* faulty, imperfect ♦ *nm* (*LING*) imperfect tense.

imperial [ēmperyál'] *a* imperial.

imperialismo [ēmperyálē'mo] *nm* imperialism.

imperialista [ēmperyálē'stá] *a* imperialist(ic) ♦ *nm/f* imperialist.

impericia [ēmperē'syá] *nf* (*torpeza*) unskilfulness; (*inexperiencia*) inexperience.

imperio [ēmpe'ryo] *nm* empire; (*autoridad*) rule, authority; (*fig*) pride, haughtiness; **vale un ~** (*fig*) it's worth a fortune.

imperioso, a [ēmperyo'so, á] *a* imperious; (*urgente*) urgent; (*imperativo*) imperative.

impermeable [ēmpermeá'hle] *a* (*a prueba*

de agua) waterproof ♦ *nm* raincoat, mac (*Brit*).

impersonal [ēmpersonál'] *a* impersonal.

impertérrito, a [ēmperte'rrēto, á] *a* undaunted.

impertinencia [ēmpertēnen'syá] *nf* impertinence.

impertinente [ēmpertēnen'te] *a* impertinent.

imperturbable [ēmpertōōrḫá'ḫle] *a* imperturbable; (*sereno*) unruffled; (*impasible*) impassive.

ímpetu [im'petōō] *nm* (*impulso*) impetus, impulse; (*impetuosidad*) impetuosity; (*violencia*) violence.

impetuosidad [ēmpetwosēṭḫáṭḫ'] *nf* impetuousness; (*violencia*) violence.

impetuoso, a [ēmpetwo'so, á] *a* impetuous; (*río*) rushing; (*acto*) hasty.

impida [ēmpē'ṭḫá] *etc vb* V **impedir**.

impío, a [ēmpē'o, á] *a* impious, ungodly; (*cruel*) cruel, pitiless.

implacable [ēmplákǎ'ḫle] *a* implacable, relentless.

implantación [ēmplántásyon'] *nf* implantation; (*introducción*) introduction.

implicar [ēmplēkár'] *vt* to involve; (*entrañar*) to imply; **esto no implica que ...** this does not mean that ....

implícito, a [ēmplē'sēto, á] *a* (*tácito*) implicit; (*sobreentendido*) implied.

implique [ēmplē'ke] *etc vb* V **implicar**.

implorar [ēmplorár'] *vt* to beg, implore.

impoluto, a [ēmpolōō'to, á] *a* unpolluted, pure.

impondré [ēmpondre'] *etc vb* V **imponer**.

imponente [ēmponen'te] *a* (*impresionante*) impressive, imposing; (*solemne*) grand ♦ *nm/f* (*COM*) depositor.

imponer [ēmponer'] *vt* (*gen*) to impose; (*tarea*) to assign; (*exigir*) to exact; (*miedo*) to inspire; (*COM*) to deposit; ~**se** *vr* to assert o.s.; (*prevalecer*) to prevail; (*costumbre*) to develop; ~**se un deber** to assume a duty.

imponga [ēmpon'gá] *etc vb* V **imponer**.

imponible [ēmponē'ḫle] *a* (*COM*) taxable, subject to tax; (*importación*) dutiable, subject to duty; **no** ~ tax-exempt, tax-free.

impopular [ēmpopōōlár'] *a* unpopular.

importación [ēmportásyon'] *nf* (*acto*) importing; (*mercancías*) imports *pl*.

importancia [ēmportán'syá] *nf* importance; (*valor*) value, significance; (*extensión*) size, magnitude; **no dar** ~ **a** to consider unimportant; (*fig*) to make light of; **no tiene** ~ it's nothing.

importante [ēmportán'te] *a* important; valuable, significant.

importar [ēmportár'] *vt* (*del extranjero*) to import; (*costar*) to amount to; (*implicar*)

to involve ♦ *vi* to be important, matter; **me importa un bledo** I don't give a damn; **¿le importa que fume?** do you mind if I smoke?; **¿te importa prestármelo?** would you mind lending it to me?; **¿qué importa?** what difference does it make?; **no importa** it doesn't matter; **no le importa** he doesn't care, it doesn't bother him; **"no importa precio"** "cost no object".

importe [ēmpor'te] *nm* (*total*) amount; (*valor*) value.

importunar [ēmportōōnár'] *vt* to bother, pester.

importuno, a [ēmportōō'no, á] *a* (*inoportuno, molesto*) inopportune; (*indiscreto*) troublesome.

imposibilidad [ēmposēḫēlēṭḫáṭḫ'] *nf* impossibility; **mi** ~ **para hacerlo** my inability to do it.

imposibilitado, a [ēmposēḫēlētá'ṭḫo, á] *a*: **verse** ~ **para hacer algo** to be unable to do sth.

imposibilitar [ēmposēḫēlētár'] *vt* to make impossible, prevent.

imposible [ēmposē'ḫle] *a* impossible; (*insoportable*) unbearable, intolerable; **es** ~ it's out of the question; **es** ~ **de predecir** it's impossible to forecast o predict.

imposición [ēmposēsyon'] *nf* imposition; (*COM*) tax; (*inversión*) deposit; **efectuar una** ~ to make a deposit.

impostor, a [ēmpostor', á] *nm/f* impostor.

impostura [ēmpostōō'rá] *nf* fraud, imposture.

impotencia [ēmpoten'syá] *nf* impotence.

impotente [ēmpoten'te] *a* impotent.

impracticable [ēmpráktēká'ḫle] *a* (*irrealizable*) impracticable; (*intransitable*) impassable.

imprecar [ēmprekár'] *vi* to curse.

imprecisión [ēmpresēsyon'] *nf* lack of precision, vagueness.

impreciso, a [ēmpresē'so, á] *a* imprecise, vague.

impredecible [ēmpreṭḫesē'ḫle], **impredictible** [ēmpreṭḫēktē'ḫle] *a* unpredictable.

impregnar [ēmpregnár'] *vt* to impregnate; (*fig*) to pervade; ~**se** *vr* to become impregnated.

imprenta [ēmpren'tá] *nf* (*acto*) printing; (*aparato*) press; (*casa*) printer's; (*letra*) print.

impreque [ēmpre'ke] *etc vb* V **imprecar**.

imprescindible [ēmpresēndē'ḫle] *a* essential, vital.

impresión [ēmpresyon'] *nf* impression; (*IMPRENTA*) printing; (*edición*) edition; (*FOTO*) print; (*marca*) imprint; ~ **digital** fingerprint.

impresionable [ēmpresyoná'ḫle] *a* (*sensible*) impressionable.

impresionado, a [ĕmpresyoná'tho, á] a impressed; (FOTO) exposed.

impresionante [ĕmpresyonán'te] a impressive; (tremendo) tremendous; (maravilloso) great, marvelous (US), marvellous (Brit).

impresionar [ĕmpresyonár'] vt (connover) to move; (afectar) to impress, strike; (película fotográfica) to expose; ~se vr to be impressed; (connoverse) to be moved.

impresionista [ĕmpresyonē'stá] a impressionist(ic); (ARTE) impressionist ♦ nm/f impressionist.

impreso, a [ĕmpre'so, á] pp de **imprimir** ♦ a printed ♦ nm printed paper/book etc; ~s nmpl printed matter sg; ~ **de solicitud** application form.

impresora [ĕmpreso'rá] nf (INFORM) printer; ~ **de chorro de tinta** ink-jet printer; ~ **(por) láser** laser printer; ~ **de línea** line printer; ~ **de matriz (de agujas)** dot-matrix printer; ~ **de rueda** o **de margarita** daisy-wheel printer.

imprevisible [ĕmprehēsē'hle] a unforeseeable; (individuo) unpredictable.

imprevisión [ĕmprehēsyon'] nf shortsightedness; (irreflexión) thoughtlessness.

imprevisto, a [ĕmprehē'sto, á] a unforeseen; (inesperado) unexpected ♦ nm: ~s (dinero) incidentals, unforeseen expenses.

imprimir [ĕmprēmēr'] vt to stamp; (textos) to print; (INFORM) to output, print out.

improbabilidad [ĕmprohāhēlēthath'] nf improbability, unlikelihood.

improbable [ĕmprohā'hle] a improbable; (inverosímil) unlikely.

improcedente [ĕmprosethen'te] a inappropriate; (JUR) inadmissible.

improductivo, a [ĕmprothōōktē'ho, á] a unproductive.

impronunciable [ĕmpronōōnsyá'hle] a unpronounceable.

improperio [ĕmprope'ryo] nm insult; ~s nmpl abuse sg.

impropiedad [ĕmpropyethath'] nf impropriety (of language).

impropio, a [ĕmpro'pyo, á] a improper; (inadecuado) inappropriate.

improvisación [ĕmprohēsásyon'] nf improvisation.

improvisado, a [ĕmprohēsá'tho, á] a improvised, impromptu.

improvisar [ĕmprohēsár'] vt to improvise; (comida) to rustle up ♦ vi to improvise; (MUS) to extemporize; (TEATRO etc) to ad-lib.

improviso [ĕmprohē'so]: ad **de** ~ unexpectedly, suddenly; (MUS etc) impromptu.

imprudencia [ĕmprōōthen'syá] nf imprudence; (indiscreción) indiscretion; (descuido) carelessness.

imprudente [ĕmprōōthen'te] a imprudent; indiscreet.

Impte. abr (= Importe) amt.

impúdico, a [ĕmpōō'thēko, á] a shameless; (lujurioso) lecherous.

impudor [ĕmpōōthor'] nm shamelessness; (lujuria) lechery.

impuesto, a [ĕmpwe'sto, á] pp de **imponer** ♦ a imposed ♦ nm tax; (derecho) duty; **anterior al** ~ pre-tax; **sujeto a** ~ taxable; ~ **de lujo** luxury tax; ~ **de plusvalía** capital gains tax; ~ **sobre la propiedad** property tax; ~ **sobre la renta** income tax; ~ **sobre la renta de las personas físicas (IRPF)** personal income tax; ~ **sobre la riqueza** wealth tax; ~ **de transferencia de capital** capital transfer tax; ~ **de venta** sales tax; ~ **sobre el valor añadido (IVA)** value added tax (VAT).

impugnar [ĕmpōōgnár'] vt to oppose, contest; (refutar) to refute, impugn.

impulsar [ĕmpōōlsár'] vt = **impeler**.

impulso [ĕmpōōl'so] nm impulse; (fuerza, empuje) thrust, drive; (fig: sentimiento) urge, impulse; **a** ~**s del miedo** driven on by fear.

impune [ĕmpōō'ne] a unpunished.

impunemente [ĕmpōōnemen'te] ad with impunity.

impureza [ĕmpōōre'sá] nf impurity; (fig) lewdness.

impuro, a [ĕmpōō'ro, á] a impure; lewd.

impuse [ĕmpōō'se] etc vb V **imponer**.

imputación [ĕmpōōtásyon'] nf imputation.

imputar [ĕmpōōtár'] vt: ~ **a** to attribute to, to impute to.

inabordable [ĕnáhorthá'hle] a unapproachable.

inacabable [ĕnákáhá'hle] a (infinito) endless; (interminable) interminable.

inaccesible [ĕnáksesē'hle] a inaccessible; (fig: precio) beyond one's reach, prohibitive; (individuo) aloof.

inacción [ĕnáksyon'] nf inactivity.

inaceptable [ĕnáseptá'hle] a unacceptable.

inactividad [ĕnáktēhēthath'] nf inactivity; (COM) dullness.

inactivo, a [ĕnáktē'ho, á] a inactive; (COM) dull; (población) non-working.

inadaptación [ĕnátháptásyon'] nf maladjustment.

inadaptado, a [ĕnátháptá'tho, á] a maladjusted ♦ nm/f misfit.

inadecuado, a [ĕnáthekwá'tho, á] a (insuficiente) inadequate; (inapto) unsuitable.

inadmisible [ĕnáthmēsē'hle] a inadmissible.

inadvertido, a [ĕnáthhertē'tho, á] a (no visto) unnoticed.

inagotable [ĕnágotá'hle] a inexhaustible.

inaguantable [ĕnágwántá'hle] a unbearable.

inalcanzable |ĭnálkánsá'ђlc| a unattainable.
inalterable |ĭnáltčrá'ђlc| a immutable, unchangeable.
inamovible |ĭnámoђč'ђlc| a fixed, immovable; (TEC) undetachable.
inanición |ĭnánčsyon'| nf starvation.
inanimado, a |ĭnánčmá'íђo, á| a inanimate.
inánime |ĭná'nčmc| a lifeless.
inapelable |ĭnápclá'ђlc| a (JUR) unappealable; (fig) irremediable.
inapetencia |ĭnápctcn'syá| nf lack of appetite.
inaplicable |ĭnáplčká'ђlc| a not applicable.
inapreciable |ĭnáprcsyá'ђlc| a invaluable.
inapto, a |ĭnáp'to| a unsuited.
inarrugable |ĭnárrōōgá'ђlc| a permanent press.
inasequible |ĭnásckč'ђlc| a unattainable.
inaudito, a |ĭnáōōþč'to, á| a unheard-of.
inauguración |ĭnáōōgōōrásyon'| nf inauguration; (de exposición) opening.
inaugurar |ĭnáōōgōōrár'| vt to inaugurate; to open.
I.N.B. abr (= Instituto Nacional de Bachillerato) ≈ high school.
inca |ĭn'ká| nm/f Inca.
INCAE |ĭnká'c| nm abr = Instituto Centroamericano de Administración de Empresas.
incaico, a |ĭnká'čko, á| a Inca.
incalculable |ĭnkálkōōlá'ђlc| a incalculable.
incandescente |ĭnkándcsscn'tc| a incandescent.
incansable |ĭnkánsá'ђlc| a tireless, untiring.
incapacidad |ĭnkápásčíђáíђ'| nf incapacity; (incompetencia) incompetence; ~ **física/mental** physical/mental disability.
incapacitar |ĭnkápásčtár'| vt (inhabilitar) to incapacitate, handicap; (descalificar) to disqualify.
incapaz |ĭnkápás'| a incapable; ~ **de hacer algo** unable to do sth.
incautación |ĭnkáōōtásyon'| nf seizure, confiscation.
incautarse |ĭnkáōōtár'sc| vr: ~ **de** to seize, confiscate.
incauto, a |ĭnká'ōōto, á| a (imprudente) incautious, unwary.
incendiar |ĭnscndyár'| vt to set fire to; (fig) to inflame; ~**se** vr to catch fire.
incendiario, a |ĭnscndyá'ryo, á| a incendiary ♦ nm/f arsonist.
incendio |ĭnscn'dyo| nm fire; ~ **intencionado** arson.
incentivo |ĭnscntč'ђo| nm incentive.
incertidumbre |ĭnscrtčíђōōm'brc| nf (inseguridad) uncertainty; (duda) doubt.
incesante |ĭnscsán'tc| a incessant.
incesto |ĭnsc'sto| nm incest.
incidencia |ĭnsčíђcn'syá| nf (MAT) incidence; (fig) effect.

incidente |ĭnsčíђcn'tc| nm incident.
incidir |ĭnsčíђčr'| vi: ~ **en** (influir) to influence; (afectar) to affect; ~ **en un error** to be mistaken.
incienso |ĭnsycn'so| nm incense.
incierto, a |ĭnsycr'to, á| a uncertain.
incineración |ĭnsčncrásyon'| nf incineration; (de cadáveres) cremation.
incinerar |ĭnsčncrár'| vt to burn; to cremate.
incipiente |ĭnsčpycn'tc| a incipient.
incisión |ĭnsčsyon'| nf incision.
incisivo, a |ĭnsčsč'ђo, á| a sharp, cutting; (fig) incisive.
inciso |ĭnsč'so| nm (LING) clause, sentence; (coma) comma; (JUR) subsection.
incitante |ĭnsčtán'tc| a (estimulante) exciting; (provocativo) provocative.
incitar |ĭnsčtár'| vt to incite, rouse.
incivil |ĭnsčččl'| a rude, uncivil.
inclemencia |ĭnklcmcn'syá| nf (severidad) harshness, severity; (del tiempo) inclemency.
inclemente |ĭnklcmcn'tc| a harsh, severe; inclement.
inclinación |ĭnklčnásyon'| nf (gen) inclination; (de tierras) slope, incline; (de cabeza) nod, bow; (fig) leaning, bent.
inclinar |ĭnklčnár'| vt to incline; (cabeza) to nod, bow ♦ vi to lean, slope; ~**se** vr to bow; (encorvarse) to stoop; ~**se a** (parecerse) to take after, resemble; ~**se ante** to bow down to; **me inclino a pensar que ...** I'm inclined to think that ... .
incluir |ĭnklōōčr'| vt to include; (incorporar) to incorporate; (meter) to enclose; **todo incluido** (COM) inclusive.
inclusive |ĭnklōōsč'ђc| ad inclusive ♦ prep including.
incluso, a |ĭnklōō'so, á| a included ♦ ad inclusively; (hasta) even.
incluyendo |ĭnklōōycn'do| etc vb V **incluir**.
incobrable |ĭnkoђrá'ђlc| a irrecoverable; (deuda) bad.
incógnita |ĭnkog'nčtá| nf (fig) mystery.
incógnito |ĭnkog'nčto|: **de** ~ ad incognito.
incoherencia |ĭnkocrcn'syá| nf incoherence; (falta de conexión) disconnectedness.
incoherente |ĭnkocrcn'tc| a incoherent.
incoloro, a |ĭnkolo'ro, á| a colorless (US), colourless (Brit).
incólume |ĭnko'lōōmc| a safe; (indemne) unhurt, unharmed.
incombustible |ĭnkombōōstč'ђlc| a (gen) fire-resistant; (telas) fireproof.
incomestible |ĭnkomcstč'ђlc| a inedible.
incomodar |ĭnkomoíђár'| vt to inconvenience; (molestar) to bother, trouble; (fastidiar) to annoy; ~**se** vr to put o.s. out; (fastidiarse) to get annoyed; **no se incomode** don't bother.

incomodidad [ēnkomoθ̱ēθ̱áθ̱'] *nf* inconvenience; (*fastidio, enojo*) annoyance; (*de vivienda*) discomfort.

incómodo, a [ēnko'moθ̱o, á] *a* (*inconfortable*) uncomfortable; (*molesto*) annoying; (*inconveniente*) inconvenient; **sentirse ~** to feel ill at ease.

incomparable [ēnkompárá'blc] *a* incomparable.

incomparecimiento [ēnkompárccēmyen'to] *nm* (*JUR etc*) failure to appear.

incompatible [ēnkompátē'blc] *a* incompatible.

incompetencia [ēnkompeten'syá] *nf* incompetence.

incompetente [ēnkompeten'tc] *a* incompetent.

incompleto, a [ēnkomple'to, á] *a* incomplete, unfinished.

incomprensible [ēnkomprcnsē'blc] *a* incomprehensible.

incomunicado, a [ēnkomōōnēká'θ̱o, á] *a* (*aislado*) cut off, isolated; (*confinado*) in solitary confinement.

incomunicar [ēnkomōōnēkár'] *vt* (*gen*) to cut off; (*preso*) to put into solitary confinement; **~se** *vr* (*fam*) to go into one's shell.

incomunique [ēnkomōōnē'kc] *etc vb* V **incomunicar**.

inconcebible [ēnkonsehē'blc] *a* inconceivable.

inconcluso, a [ēnkonklōō'so, á] *a* (*inacabado*) unfinished.

inconcuso, a [ēnkonkōō'so, á] *a* indisputable, undeniable.

incondicional [ēnkondēsyonál'] *a* unconditional; (*apoyo*) wholehearted; (*partidario*) staunch.

inconexo, a [ēnkonck'so, á] *a* unconnected; (*desunido*) disconnected; (*incoherente*) incoherent.

inconfeso, a [ēnkonfe'so, á] *a* unconfessed; **un homosexual ~** a closet homosexual.

inconfundible [ēnkonfōōndē'blc] *a* unmistakable.

incongruente [ēnkongrwen'te] *a* incongruous.

inconmensurable [ēnkonmensōōrá'blc] *a* immeasurable, vast.

inconsciencia [ēnkonsyen'syá] *nf* unconsciousness; (*fig*) thoughtlessness.

inconsciente [ēnkonsyen'te] *a* unconscious; thoughtless; (*ignorante*) unaware; (*involuntario*) unwitting.

inconsecuencia [ēnkonsekwen'syá] *nf* inconsistency.

inconsecuente [ēnkonsekwen'te] *a* inconsistent.

inconsiderado, a [ēnkonsēθ̱erá'θ̱o, á] *a* inconsiderate.

inconsistente [ēnkonsēsten'te] *a* in-

consistent; (*CULIN*) lumpy; (*endeble*) weak; (*tela*) flimsy.

inconstancia [ēnkonstán'syá] *nf* inconstancy; (*de tiempo*) changeability; (*capricho*) fickleness.

inconstante [ēnkonstán'tc] *a* inconstant; changeable; fickle.

incontable [ēnkontá'blc] *a* countless, innumerable.

incontestable [ēnkontestá'blc] *a* unanswerable; (*innegable*) undeniable.

incontinencia [ēnkontēnen'syá] *nf* incontinence.

incontrolado, a [ēnkontrolá'θ̱o, á] *a* uncontrolled.

incontrovertible [ēnkontrohertē'blc] *a* undeniable, incontrovertible.

inconveniencia [ēnkombenyen'syá] *nf* unsuitability, inappropriateness; (*descortesía*) impoliteness.

inconveniente [ēnkombenyen'te] *a* unsuitable; impolite ♦ *nm* obstacle; (*desventaja*) disadvantage; **el ~ es que ...** the trouble is that ...; **no hay ~ en** *o* **para hacer eso** there is no objection to doing that; **no tengo ~** I don't mind.

incorporación [ēnkorporásyon'] *nf* incorporation; (*fig*) inclusion.

incorporado, a [ēnkorporá'θ̱o, á] *a* (*TEC*) built-in.

incorporar [ēnkorporár'] *vt* to incorporate; (*abarcar*) to embody; (*CULIN*) to mix; **~se** *vr* to sit up; **~se a** to join.

incorrección [ēnkorreksyon'] *nf* incorrectness, inaccuracy; (*descortesía*) bad-mannered behavior (*US*) *o* behaviour (*Brit*).

incorrecto, a [ēnkorrek'to, á] *a* incorrect, wrong; (*comportamiento*) bad-mannered.

incorregible [ēnkorrehē'blc] *a* incorrigible.

incorruptible [ēnkorrōōptē'blc] *a* incorruptible.

incorrupto, a [ēnkorrōōp'to, á] *a* uncorrupted; (*fig*) pure.

incredulidad [ēnkreθ̱ōōlēθ̱áθ̱'] *nf* incredulity; (*escepticismo*) scepticism.

incrédulo, a [ēnkre'tḇōōlo, á] *a* incredulous, unbelieving; sceptical.

increíble [ēnkrcē'blc] *a* incredible.

incrementar [ēnkrementár'] *vt* (*aumentar*) to increase; (*alzar*) to raise; **~se** *vr* to increase.

incremento [ēnkremen'to] *nm* increment; (*aumento*) rise, increase; **~ de precio** rise in price.

increpar [ēnkrepár'] *vt* to reprimand.

incriminar [ēnkrēmēnár'] *vt* (*JUR*) to incriminate.

incruento, a [ēnkrwen'to, á] *a* bloodless.

incrustar [ēnkrōōstár'] *vt* to incrust; (*piedras: en joya*) to inlay; (*fig*) to graft;

(*TEC*) to set.

incubar [ēnkōōkár'] *vt* to incubate; (*fig*) to hatch.

incuestionable [ēnkwestyoná'ɧle] *a* unchallengeable.

inculcar [ēnkōōlkár'] *vt* to inculcate.

inculpar [ēnkōōlpár'] *vt*: ~ **de** (*acusar*) to accuse of; (*achacar, atribuir*) to charge with, blame for.

inculque [ēnkōōl'ke] *etc vb V* **inculcar**.

inculto, a [ēnkōōl'to, á] *a* (*persona*) uneducated, uncultured; (*fig: grosero*) uncouth ♦ *nm/f* ignoramus.

incumbencia [ēnkōōmben'syá] *nf* obligation; **no es de mi ~** it is not my field.

incumbir [ēnkōōmbēr'] *vi*: ~ **a** to be incumbent upon; **no me incumbe a mí** it is no concern of mine.

incumplimiento [ēnkōōmplēmyen'to] *nm* non-fulfilment; (*COM*) repudiation; ~ **de contrato** breach of contract; **por** ~ by default.

incurrir [ēnkōōrrēr'] *vi*: ~ **en** to incur; (*crimen*) to commit; ~ **en un error** to make a mistake.

indagación [ēndágásyon'] *nf* investigation; (*búsqueda*) search; (*JUR*) inquest.

indagar [ēndágár'] *vt* to investigate; to search; (*averiguar*) to ascertain.

indague [ēndá'ge] *etc vb V* **indagar**.

indebido, a [ēndebē'ṭho, á] *a* undue; (*dicho*) improper.

indecente [ēndesen'te] *a* indecent, improper; (*lascivo*) obscene.

indecible [ēndesē'ɧle] *a* unspeakable; (*indescriptible*) indescribable.

indeciso, a [ēndesē'so, á] *a* (*por decidir*) undecided; (*vacilante*) hesitant.

indefenso, a [ēndefen'so, á] *a* defenceless.

indefinido, a [ēndefēnē'ṭho, á] *a* indefinite; (*vago*) vague, undefined.

indeleble [ēndele'ɧle] *a* indelible.

indemne [ēndem'ne] *a* (*objeto*) undamaged; (*persona*) unharmed, unhurt.

indemnice [ēndemnē'se] *etc vb V* **indemnizar**.

indemnización [ēndemnēsásyon'] *nf* (*acto*) indemnification; (*suma*) indemnity; ~ **de cese**, ~ **de despido** severance pay; **doble** ~ double indemnity.

indemnizar [ēndemnēsár'] *vt* to indemnify; (*compensar*) to compensate.

independencia [ēndependen'syá] *nf* independence.

independice [ēndependē'se] *etc vb V* **independizar**.

independiente [ēndependyen'te] *a* (*libre*) independent; (*autónomo*) self-sufficient; (*INFORM*) stand-alone.

independizar [ēndependēsár'] *vt* to make independent; ~**se** *vr* to become inde-

pendent.

indescifrable [ēndesēfrá'ɧle] *a* (*MIL: código*) indecipherable; (*fig: misterio*) impenetrable.

indeterminado, a [ēndetermēná'ṭho, á] *a* (*tb LING*) indefinite; (*desconocido*) indeterminate.

India [ēn'dyá] *nf*: **la** ~ India.

indiano, a [ēndyá'no, á] *a* (Spanish-) American ♦ *nm* Spaniard who has made good in America.

indicación [ēndēkásyon'] *nf* indication; (*dato*) piece of information; (*señal*) sign; (*sugerencia*) suggestion, hint; **indicaciones** *nfpl* (*COM*) instructions.

indicado, a [ēndēká'ṭho, á] *a* (*apto*) right, appropriate.

indicador [ēndēká'ṭhor'] *nm* indicator; (*TEC*) gauge, meter; (*aguja*) hand, pointer; (*de carretera*) roadsign; ~ **de encendido** (*INFORM*) power-on indicator.

indicar [ēndēkár'] *vt* (*mostrar*) to indicate, show; (*suj: termómetro etc*) to read, register; (*señalar*) to point to.

indicativo, a [ēndēkátē'ṭho, á] *a* indicative ♦ *nm* (*RADIO*) call letters (*US*) *o* sign (*Brit*); ~ **de nacionalidad** (*AUTO*) national identification plate.

índice [ēn'dēse] *nm* index; (*catalogo*) catalog(ue); (*ANAT*) index finger, forefinger; ~ **del coste de (la) vida** cost-of-living index; ~ **de crédito** credit rating; ~ **de materias** table of contents; ~ **de natalidad** birth rate; ~ **de precios al por menor (IPM)** (*COM*) retail price index (RPI).

indicio [ēndē'syo] *nm* indication, sign; (*en pesquisa etc*) clue; (*INFORM*) marker, mark.

indiferencia [ēndēferen'syá] *nf* indifference; (*apatía*) apathy.

indiferente [ēndēferen'te] *a* indifferent; **me es** ~ it makes no difference to me.

indígena [ēndē'hen
á] *a* indigenous, native ♦ *nm/f* native.

indigencia [ēndēhen'syá] *nf* poverty, need.

indigenista [ēndēhenē'stá] (*AM*) *a* pro-Indian ♦ *nm/f* (*estudiante*) student of Indian cultures; (*POL etc*) promoter of Indian cultures.

indigestar [ēndēhestár'] *vt* to cause indigestion to; ~**se** *vr* to get indigestion.

indigestión [ēndēhestyon'] *nf* indigestion.

indigesto, a [ēndēhe'sto, á] *a* undigested; (*indigestible*) indigestible; (*fig*) turgid.

indignación [ēndēgnásyon'] *nf* indignation.

indignante [ēndēgnán'te] *a* outrageous, infuriating.

indignar [ēndēgnár'] *vt* to anger, make indignant; ~**se** *vr*: ~**se por** to get indignant about.

indigno, a [ēndēg'no, á] *a* (*despreciable*)

low, contemptible; (*inmerecido*) unworthy.

indio, a [ēn'dyo, á] *a*, *nm/f* Indian.

indique [ēndē'ke] *etc vb* V **indicar**.

indirecto, a [ēndērek'to, á] *a* indirect ♦ *nf* insinuation, innuendo; (*sugerencia*) hint.

indisciplina [ēndēsēplē'ná] *nf* (*gen*) lack of discipline; (*MIL*) insubordination.

indiscreción [ēndēskresyon'] *nf* (*imprudencia*) indiscretion; (*irreflexión*) tactlessness; (*acto*) gaffe, faux pas; ..., **si no es ~** ..., if I may say so.

indiscreto, a [ēndēskre'to, á] *a* indiscreet.

indisculpable [ēndēskōolpá'ble] *a* inexcusable, unforgivable.

indiscutible [ēndēskōotē'ble] *a* indisputable, unquestionable.

indispensable [ēndēspensá'ble] *a* indispensable.

indispondré [ēndēspondre'] *etc vb* V **indisponer**.

indisponer [ēndēsponer'] *vt* to spoil, upset; (*salud*) to make ill; **~se** *vr* to fall ill; **~se con uno** to fall out with sb.

indisponga [ēndēspon'gá] *etc vb* V **indisponer**.

indisposición [ēndēsposēsyon'] *nf* indisposition; (*desgana*) unwillingness.

indispuesto, a [ēndēspwe'sto, á] *pp de* **indisponer** ♦ *a* indisposed; **sentirse ~** to feel unwell.

indispuse [ēndēspōo'se] *etc vb* V **indisponer**.

indistinto, a [ēndēstēn'to, á] *a* indistinct; (*vago*) vague.

individual [ēndēhē'thwál'] *a* individual; (*habitación*) single ♦ *nm* (*DEPORTE*) singles *sg*.

individuo, a [ēndēhē'thwo, á] *a* individual ♦ *nm* individual.

indocumentado, a [ēndokōomentá'tho, á] *a* without identity papers.

Indochina [ēndotchē'ná] *nf* Indochina.

indoeuropeo, a [ēndoeōorope'o, á] *a*, *nm/f* Indo-European.

índole [ēn'dole] *nf* (*naturaleza*) nature; (*clase*) sort, kind.

indolencia [ēndolen'syá] *nf* indolence, laziness.

indoloro, a [ēndolo'ro, á] *a* painless.

indómito, a [ēndo'mēto, á] *a* indomitable.

Indonesia [ēndone'syá] *nf* Indonesia.

indonesio, a [ēndone'syo, á] *a*, *nm/f* Indonesian.

inducción [ēndōoksyon'] *nf* (*FILOSOFÍA*, *ELEC*) induction; **por ~** by induction.

inducir [ēndōosēr'] *vt* to induce; (*inferir*) to infer; (*persuadir*) to persuade; **~ a uno en el error** to mislead sb.

indudable [ēndōothá'ble] *a* undoubted; (*incuestionable*) unquestionable; **es ~ que** ... there is no doubt that ... .

indulgencia [ēndōolhen'syá] *nf* indulgence; (*JUR etc*) leniency; **proceder sin ~ contra** to proceed ruthlessly against.

indultar [ēndōoltár'] *vt* (*perdonar*) to pardon, reprieve; (*librar de pago*) to exempt.

indulto [ēndōol'to] *nm* pardon; exemption.

indumentaria [ēndōomentá'ryá] *nf* (*ropa*) clothing, dress.

industria [ēndōos'tryá] *nf* industry; (*habilidad*) skill; **~ agropecuaria** farming and fishing; **~ pesada** heavy industry; **~ petrolífera** oil industry.

industrial [ēndōostryál'] *a* industrial ♦ *nm* industrialist.

INE [ē'ne] *nm abr* (*Esp*)=*Instituto Nacional de Estadística*.

inédito, a [ēne'thēto, á] *a* (*libro*) unpublished; (*nuevo*) unheard-of.

inefable [ēnefá'ble] *a* ineffable, indescribable.

ineficacia [ēnefēká'syá] *nf* (*de medida*) ineffectiveness; (*de proceso*) inefficiency.

ineficaz [ēnefēkás'] *a* (*inútil*) ineffective; (*ineficiente*) inefficient.

ineludible [ēnelōothē'ble] *a* inescapable, unavoidable.

INEN [ē'nen] *nm abr* (*México*)=*Instituto Nacional de Energía Nuclear*.

inenarrable [ēnenárrá'ble] *a* inexpressible.

ineptitud [ēneptētōoth'] *nf* ineptitude, incompetence.

inepto, a [ēnep'to, á] *a* inept, incompetent.

inequívoco, a [ēnekē'boko, á] *a* unequivocal; (*inconfundible*) unmistakable.

inercia [ēner'syá] *nf* inertia; (*pasividad*) passivity.

inerme [ēner'me] *a* (*sin armas*) unarmed; (*indefenso*) defenseless (*US*), defenceless (*Brit*).

inerte [ēner'te] *a* inert; (*inmóvil*) motionless.

inesperado, a [ēnesperá'tho, á] *a* unexpected, unforeseen.

inestable [ēnestá'ble] *a* unstable.

inevitable [ēnebētá'ble] *a* inevitable.

inexactitud [ēneksáktētōoth'] *nf* inaccuracy.

inexacto, a [ēneksák'to, á] *a* inaccurate; (*falso*) untrue.

inexistente [ēneksēsten'te] *a* non-existent.

inexperiencia [ēneksperyen'syá] *nf* inexperience, lack of experience.

inexperto, a [ēneksper'to, á] *a* (*novato*) inexperienced.

inexplicable [ēneksplēká'ble] *a* inexplicable.

inexpresable [ēnekspresá'ble] *a* inexpressible.

inexpresivo, a [ēnekspresē'bo, á] *a* inexpressive; (*ojos*) dull.

inexpugnable [ēnekspōogná'ble] *a* (*MIL*) impregnable; (*fig*) firm.

infalible [ĕnfálē'ble] a infallible; (indefectible) certain, sure; (plan) foolproof.

infame [ĕnfá'me] a infamous.

infamia [ĕnfá'myä] nf infamy; (deshonra) disgrace.

infancia [ĕnfán'syä] nf infancy, childhood; **jardín de la ~** nursery school.

infanta [ĕnfán'tä] nf (hija del rey) infanta princess.

infante [ĕnfán'te] nm (hijo del rey) infante, prince.

infantería [ĕnfánterē'ä] nf infantry.

infantil [ĕnfántēl'] a child's, children's; (pueril, aniñado) infantile; (cándido) childlike.

infarto [ĕnfár'to] nm (tb: **~ de miocardio**) heart attack.

infatigable [ĕnfátēgá'ble] a tireless, untiring.

infección [ĕnfeksyon'] nf infection.

infeccioso, a [ĕnfeksyo'so, ä] a infectious.

infectar [ĕnfektár'] vt to infect; **~se** vr: **~se (de)** (tb fig) to become infected (with).

infecundidad [ĕnfekōōndēthäth'] nf (de tierra) infertility, barrenness; (de mujer) sterility.

infecundo, a [ĕnfekōōn'do, ä] a infertile, barren; sterile.

infeliz [ĕnfelēs'] a (desgraciado) unhappy, wretched; (inocente) gullible ♦ nm/f (desgraciado) wretch; (inocentón) simpleton.

inferior [ĕnferyor'] a inferior; (situación, MAT) lower ♦ nm/f inferior, subordinate; **cualquier número ~ a 9** any number less than o under o below 9; **una cantidad ~** a lesser quantity.

inferir [ĕnferēr'] vt (deducir) to infer, deduce; (causar) to cause.

infértil [ĕnfer'tēl] a infertile.

infestar [ĕnfestár'] vt to infest.

infidelidad [ĕnfēthelēthäth'] nf (gen) infidelity, unfaithfulness.

infiel [ĕnfyel'] a unfaithful, disloyal; (falso) inaccurate ♦ nm/f infidel, unbeliever.

infiera [ĕnfye'rä] etc vb V **inferir**.

infierno [ĕnfyer'no] nm hell; **¡vete al ~!** go to hell; **está en el quinto ~** it's in the middle of nowhere.

infiltrar [ĕnfēltrár'] vt to infiltrate; **~se** vr to infiltrate, filter; (líquidos) to percolate.

ínfimo, a [ēn'fēmo] a (vil) vile, mean; (más bajo) lowest; (peor) worst; (miserable) wretched.

infinidad [ĕnfēnēthäth'] nf infinity; (abundancia) great quantity; **~ de** vast numbers of; **~ de veces** countless times.

infinito, a [ĕnfēnē'to, ä] a infinite; (fig) boundless ♦ ad infinitely ♦ nm infinite; (MAT) infinity; **hasta lo ~** ad infinitum.

infiriendo [ĕnfēryen'do] etc vb V **inferir**.

inflación [ĕnflásyon'] nf (hinchazón) swelling; (monetaria) inflation; (fig) conceit.

inflacionario, a [ĕnflásyoná'ryo, ä] a inflationary.

inflacionismo [ĕnflásyonēs'mo] nm (ECON) inflation.

inflacionista [ĕnflásyonē'stä] a inflationary.

inflamar [ĕnflámár'] vt to set on fire; (MED, fig) to inflame; **~se** vr to catch fire; to become inflamed.

inflar [ĕnflár'] vt (hinchar) to inflate, blow up; (fig) to exaggerate; **~se** vr to swell (up); (fig) to get conceited.

inflexible [ĕnfleksē'ble] a inflexible; (fig) unbending.

infligir [ĕnflēhēr'] vt to inflict.

inflija [ĕnflē'hä] etc vb V **infligir**.

influencia [ĕnflwen'syä] nf influence.

influenciar [ĕnflwensyár'] vt to influence.

influir [ĕnflōōēr'] vt to influence ♦ vi to have influence, carry weight; **~ en** o **sobre** to influence, affect; (contribuir a) to have a hand in.

influjo [ĕnflōō'ho] nm influence; **~ de capitales** (ECON etc) capital influx.

influyendo [ĕnflōōyen'do] etc vb V **influir**.

influyente [ĕnflōōyen'te] a influential.

información [ĕnformásyon'] nf information; (noticias) news sg; (informe) report; (INFORM: datos) data; (JUR) inquiry; **I~** (oficina) Information; (TELEC) Directory Assistance (US), Directory Enquiries (Brit); (mostrador) Information Desk; **una ~** a piece of information; **abrir una ~** (JUR) to begin proceedings; **~ deportiva** (en periódico) sports section.

informal [ĕnformál'] a (gen) informal.

informante [ĕnformán'te] nm/f informant.

informar [ĕnformár'] vt (gen) to inform; (revelar) to reveal, make known ♦ vi (JUR) to plead; (denunciar) to inform; (dar cuenta de) to report on; **~se** vr to find out; **~se de** to inquire into.

informática [ĕnformá'tēkä] nf V **informático**.

informatice [ĕnformátē'se] etc vb V **informatizar**.

informático, a [ĕnformá'tēko, ä] a computer cpd ♦ nf (TEC) information technology; computing; (ESCOL) computer science o studies; **~ de gestión** commercial computing.

informatización [ĕnformátēsásyon'] nf computerization.

informatizar [ĕnformátēsár'] vt to computerize.

informe [ĕnfor'me] a shapeless ♦ nm report; (dictamen) statement; (MIL) briefing; (JUR) plea; **~s** nmpl information sg; (datos) data; **~ anual** annual report; **~ del juez** summation (US), summing-up (Brit).

infortunio [ĕnfortōō'nyo] nm misfortune.

infracción [ĕnfráksyon'] *nf* infraction, infringement; (*AUTO*) violation (*US*), offence (*Brit*).

infraestructura [ĕnfrácstrŏŏktŏŏ'rá] *nf* infrastructure.

in fraganti [ĕnfrágán'tĕ] *ad*: **pillar a uno ~** to catch sb red-handed.

infranqueable [ĕnfránkcá'hlc] *a* impassable; (*fig*) insurmountable.

infrarrojo, a [ĕnfrárro'ho, á] *a* infrared.

infringir [ĕnfrĕnhĕr'] *vt* to infringe, contravene.

infrinja [ĕnfrĕn'há] *etc vb V* **infringir**.

infructuoso, a [ĕnfrŏŏktwo'so, á] *a* fruitless, unsuccessful.

infundado, a [ĕnfŏŏndá'tho, á] *a* groundless, unfounded.

infundir [ĕnfŏŏndĕr'] *vt* to infuse, instil; **~ ánimo a uno** to encourage sb; **~ miedo a uno** to intimidate sb.

infusión [ĕnfŏŏsyon'] *nf* infusion; **~ de manzanilla** camomile tea.

Ing. *abr* = **Ingeniero**.

ingeniar [ĕnhcnyár'] *vt* to think up, devise; **~se** *vr* to manage; **~se para** to manage to.

ingeniería [ĕnhcnycrĕ'á] *nf* engineering; **~ de sistemas** (*INFORM*) systems engineering.

ingeniero, a [ĕnhcnyc'ro, á] *nm/f* engineer; **~ de sonido** sound engineer; **~ de caminos** civil engineer.

ingenio [ĕnhc'nyo] *nm* (*talento*) talent; (*agudeza*) wit; (*habilidad*) ingenuity, inventiveness; (*TEC*): **~ azucarero** sugar refinery.

ingenioso, a [ĕnhcnyo'so, á] *a* ingenious, clever; (*divertido*) witty.

ingente [ĕnhcn'tc] *a* huge, enormous.

ingenuidad [ĕnhcnwĕthàth'] *nf* ingenuousness; (*sencillez*) simplicity.

ingenuo, a [ĕnhc'nwo, á] *a* ingenuous.

ingerir [ĕnhcrĕr'] *vt* to ingest; (*tragar*) to swallow; (*consumir*) to consume.

ingiera [ĕnhyc'rá] *etc*, **ingiriendo** [ĕnhĕryen'tho] *etc vb V* **ingerir**.

Inglaterra [ĕngláte'rrá] *nf* England.

ingle [ĕn'glc] *nf* groin.

inglés, esa [ĕnglcs', csá] *a* English ♦ *nm/f* Englishman/woman ♦ *nm* (*LING*) English; **los ingleses** the English.

ingratitud [ĕngrátĕtŏŏth'] *nf* ingratitude.

ingrato, a [ĕngrá'to, á] *a* ungrateful; (*tarea*) thankless.

ingravidez [ĕngrá́hĕthcs'] *nf* weightlessness.

ingrediente [ĕngrethyen'tc] *nm* ingredient.

ingresar [ĕngrcsár'] *vt* (*dinero*) to deposit ♦ *vi* to come o go in; **~ en** (*club*) to join; (*MIL, ESCOL*) to enroll (*US*) o enrol (*Brit*) in; **~ en el hospital** to go into hospital.

ingreso [ĕngrc'so] *nm* (*entrada*) entry; (: *en hospital etc*) admission; (*MIL, ESCOL*)

enrolment; **~s** *nmpl* (*dinero*) income *sg*; (: *COM*) receipts *pl*; **~ gravable** taxable income *sg*; **~s accesorios** fringe benefits; **~s brutos** gross receipts; **~s devengados** earned income *sg*; **~s exentos de impuestos** non-taxable income *sg*; **~s personales disponibles** disposable personal income *sg*.

inhábil [ĕná'hĕl] *a* unskilful, clumsy.

inhabitable [ĕnáhĕtá'hlc] *a* uninhabitable.

inhabituado, a [ĕnáhĕtwá'tho, á] *a* unaccustomed.

inhalador [ĕnáláthor'] *nm* (*MED*) inhaler.

inhalar [ĕnálár'] *vt* to inhale.

inherente [ĕncrcn'tc] *a* inherent.

inhibición [ĕnhĕbĕsyon'] *nf* inhibition.

inhibir [ĕnhĕr'] *vt* to inhibit; (*REL*) to restrain; **~se** *vr* to keep out.

inhospitalario, a [ĕnospĕtálá'ryo, á], **inhóspito, a** [ĕnos'pĕto, á] *a* inhospitable.

inhumación [ĕnŏŏmásyon'] *nf* burial, interment.

inhumano, a [ĕnŏŏmà'no, á] *a* inhuman.

INI [ĕ'nĕ] *nm abr* = **Instituto Nacional de Industria**.

inicial [ĕnĕsyál'] *a, nf* initial.

inicialice [ĕnĕsyálĕ'sc] *etc vb V* **inicializar**.

inicializar [ĕnĕsyálĕsàr'] *vt* (*INFORM*) to initialize.

iniciar [ĕnĕsyár'] *vt* (*persona*) to initiate; (*empezar*) to begin, commence; (*conversación*) to start up; **~ a uno en un secreto** to let sb into a secret; **~ la sesión** (*INFORM*) to log on *o* in (*Brit*).

iniciativa [ĕnĕsyátĕ'há] *nf* initiative; (*liderazgo*) leadership; **la ~ privada** private enterprise.

inicuo, a [ĕnĕ'kwo, á] *a* iniquitous.

inigualado, a [ĕnĕgwálá'tho, á] *a* unequalled.

ininteligible [ĕnĕntelchĕ'hlc] *a* unintelligible.

ininterrumpido, a [ĕnĕnterrŏŏmpĕ'tho, á] *a* uninterrupted; (*proceso*) continuous; (*progreso*) steady.

injerencia [ĕnhcrcn'syá] *nf* interference.

injertar [ĕnhcrtár'] *vt* to graft.

injerto [ĕnhcr'to] *nm* graft; **~ de piel** skin graft.

injuria [ĕnhŏŏ'ryá] *nf* (*agravio, ofensa*) offense (*US*), offence (*Brit*); (*insulto*) insult; **~s** *nfpl* abuse *sg*.

injuriar [ĕnhŏŏryár'] *vt* to insult.

injurioso, a [ĕnhŏŏryo'so, á] *a* offensive; insulting.

injusticia [ĕnhŏŏstĕ'syá] *nf* injustice, unfairness; **con ~** unjustly.

injusto [ĕnhŏŏ'sto, á] *a* unjust, unfair.

inmaculado, a [ĕnmákŏŏlá'tho, á] *a* immaculate, spotless.

inmadurez [ĕnmáthŏŏres'] *nf* immaturity.

inmaduro, a [ĕnmáthŏŏ'ro, á] *a* immature;

(*fruta*) unripe.

inmediaciones [ēnmethyásyo'nes] *nfpl* environs.

inmediatez [ēnmethyátes'] *nf* immediacy.

inmediato, a [ēnmethyá'to, á] *a* immediate; (*contiguo*) adjoining; (*rápido*) prompt; (*próximo*) neighboring (*US*), neighbouring (*Brit*), next; **de ~** immediately.

inmejorable [ēnmehorá'hle] *a* unsurpassable; (*precio*) unbeatable.

inmemorable [ēnmemorá'hle], **inmemorial** [ēnmemoryál'] *a* immemorial.

inmenso, a [ēnmen'so, á] *a* immense, huge.

inmerecido, a [ēnmeresē'tho, á] *a* undeserved.

inmergir [ēnmerhēr'] *vt* to immerse.

inmersión [ēnmersyon'] *nf* immersion; (*buzo*) dive.

inmigración [ēnmēgrásyon'] *nf* immigration.

inmigrante [ēnmēgrán'te] *a, nm/f* immigrant.

inmiscuirse [ēnmēskōōēr'se] *vr* to interfere, meddle.

inmiscuyendo [ēnmēskōōyen'do] *etc vb* V **inmiscuirse**.

inmobiliario, a [ēnmobēlyá'ryo, á] *a* real-estate *cpd*, property *cpd* ♦ *nf* real estate agency (*US*), estate agency (*Brit*).

inmolar [ēnmolár'] *vt* to immolate, sacrifice.

inmoral [ēnmorál'] *a* immoral.

inmortal [ēnmortál'] *a* immortal.

inmortalice [ēnmortálē'se] *etc vb* V **inmortalizar**.

inmortalizar [ēnmortálēsár'] *vt* to immortalize.

inmotivado, a [ēnmotēhá'tho, á] *a* motiveless; (*sospecha*) groundless.

inmóvil [ēnmo'hēl] *a* immobile.

inmueble [ēnmwe'hle] *a*: **bienes ~s** real estate *sg*, real (*US*) o landed (*Brit*) property *sg* ♦ *nm* property.

inmundicia [ēnmōōndē'syá] *nf* filth.

inmundo, a [ēnmōōn'do, á] *a* filthy.

inmunidad [ēnmōōnēthath'] *nf* immunity; (*fisco*) exemption; **~ diplomática/parlamentaria** diplomatic/parliamentary immunity.

inmutarse [ēnmōōtár'se] *vr*: **siguió sin ~** he carried on unperturbed.

innato, a [ēnná'to, á] *a* innate.

innecesario, a [ēnnesesá'ryo, á] *a* unnecessary.

innegable [ēnnegá'hle] *a* undeniable.

innoble [ēnno'hle] *a* ignoble.

innocuo, a [ēnno'kwo, á] *a* innocuous, harmless.

innovación [ēnnohasyon'] *nf* innovation.

innovador, a [ēnnoháthor', á] *a* innovatory, innovative ♦ *nm/f* innovator.

innovar [ēnnohár'] *vt* to introduce.

innumerable [ēnnōōmerá'hle], **innúmero, a** [ēnnōō'mero, á] *a* countless.

inocencia [ēnosen'syá] *nf* innocence.

inocentada [ēnosentá'thá] *nf* practical joke.

inocente [ēnosen'te] *a* (*ingenuo*) naive, innocent; (*inculpable*) innocent; (*sin malicia*) harmless ♦ *nm/f* simpleton; **día de los (Santos) I~s** ≈ April Fool's Day.

inocuidad [ēnokwēthath'] *nf* harmlessness.

inocular [ēnokōōlár'] *vt* to inoculate.

inocuo, a [ēno'kwo, á] *a* (*sustancia*) harmless.

inodoro, a [ēnotho'ro, á] *a* odorless (*US*), odourless (*Brit*) ♦ *nm* washroom (*US*), lavatory (*Brit*).

inofensivo, a [ēnofensē'ho, á] *a* inoffensive.

inolvidable [ēnolhēthá'hle] *a* unforgettable.

inoperante [ēnoperán'te] *a* ineffective.

inopinado, a [ēnopēná'tho, á] *a* unexpected.

inoportuno, a [ēnoportōō'no, á] *a* untimely; (*molesto*) inconvenient; (*inapropiado*) inappropriate.

inoxidable [ēnoksēthá'hle] *a* stainless; **acero ~** stainless steel.

inquebrantable [ēnkehrántá'hle] *a* unbreakable; (*fig*) unshakeable.

inquiera [ēnkye'rá] *etc vb* V **inquirir**.

inquietante [ēnkyetán'te] *a* worrying.

inquietar [ēnkyetár'] *vt* to worry, trouble; **~se** *vr* to worry, get upset.

inquieto, a [ēnkye'to, á] *a* anxious, worried; **estar ~ por** to be worried about.

inquietud [ēnkyetōōth'] *nf* anxiety, worry.

inquilino, a [ēnkēlē'no, á] *nm/f* tenant; (*COM*) lessee.

inquina [ēnkē'ná] *nf* (*aversión*) dislike; (*rencor*) ill will; **tener ~ a uno** to have a grudge against sb.

inquiriendo [ēnkēryen'do] *etc vb* V **inquirir**.

inquirir [ēnkērēr'] *vt* to enquire into, investigate.

insaciable [ēnsásyá'hle] *a* insatiable.

insalubre [ēnsálōō'hre] *a* unhealthy; (*condiciones*) unsanitary.

INSALUD [ēnsálōōth'] *nm abr* (*Esp*) = *Instituto Nacional de la Salud*.

insano, a [ēnsá'no, á] *a* (*loco*) insane; (*malsano*) unhealthy.

insatisfacción [ēnsátēsfáksyon'] *nf* dissatisfaction.

insatisfecho, a [ēnsátēsfetch'o, á] *a* (*condición*) unsatisfied; (*estado de ánimo*) dissatisfied.

inscribir [ēnskrēhēr'] *vt* to inscribe; (*en lista*) to put; (*en censo*) to register; **~se** *vr* to register; (*ESCOL etc*) to enroll (*US*), enrol (*Brit*).

inscripción [ēnskrēpsyon'] *nf* inscription; (*ESCOL etc*) enrollment (*US*), enrolment (*Brit*); (*en censo*) registration.

inscrito [ēnskrē'to] *pp de* **inscribir**.

insecticida [ĕnsektēsē'ŧhá] *nm* insecticide.
insecto [ĕnsek'to] *nm* insect.
inseguridad [ĕnsegōōrēŧháŧh'] *nf* insecurity.
inseguro, a [ĕnsegōō'ro, á] *a* insecure; (*inconstante*) unsteady; (*incierto*) uncertain.
inseminación [ĕnsemēnásyon'] *nf*: ~ **artificial** artificial insemination (A.I.).
inseminar [ĕnsemēnár'] *vt* to inseminate, fertilize.
insensato, a [ĕnsensá'to, á] *a* foolish, stupid.
insensibilice [ĕnsensēhēlē'se] *etc vb* V **insensibilizar.**
insensibilidad [ĕnsensēhēlēŧháŧh'] *nf* (*gen*) insensitivity; (*dureza de corazón*) callousness.
insensibilizar [ĕnsensēhēlēsár'] *vt* to desensitize; (*MED*) to anesthetize (*US*), anaesthetize (*Brit*); (*eufemismo*) to knock out *o* unconscious.
insensible [ĕnsensē'hle] *a* (*gen*) insensitive; (*movimiento*) imperceptible; (*sin sentido*) numb.
insertar [ĕnsertár'] *vt* to insert.
inservible [ĕnserhē'hle] *a* useless.
insidioso, a [ĕnsēŧhyo'so, á] *a* insidious.
insigne [ĕnsēg'ne] *a* distinguished; (*famoso*) notable.
insignia [ĕnsēg'nyá] *nf* (*señal distintiva*) badge; (*estandarte*) flag.
insignificante [ĕnsēgnēfēkán'te] *a* insignificant.
insinuar [ĕnsēnwár'] *vt* to insinuate, imply; ~**se** *vr*: ~**se con uno** to ingratiate o.s. with sb.
insípido, a [ĕnsē'pēŧho, á] *a* insipid.
insistencia [ĕnsēsten'syá] *nf* insistence.
insistir [ĕnsēstēr'] *vi* to insist; ~ **en algo** to insist on sth; (*enfatizar*) to stress sth.
insobornable [ĕnsohornáhle] *a* incorruptible.
insolación [ĕnsolásyon'] *nf* (*MED*) sunstroke.
insolencia [ĕnsolen'syá] *nf* insolence.
insolente [ĕnsolen'te] *a* insolent.
insólito, a [ĕnso'lēto, á] *a* unusual.
insoluble [ĕnsolōō'hle] *a* insoluble.
insolvencia [ĕnsolhen'syá] *nf* insolvency.
insomne [ĕnsom'ne] *a* sleepless ♦ *nm/f* insomniac.
insomnio [ĕnsom'nyo] *nm* insomnia.
insondable [ĕnsondá'hle] *a* bottomless.
insonorización [ĕnsonorēsásyon'] *nf* soundproofing.
insonorizado, a [ĕnsonorēsá'ŧho, á] *a* (*cuarto etc*) soundproof.
insoportable [ĕnsoportá'hle] *a* unbearable.
insoslayable [ĕnsoslayá'hle] *a* unavoidable.
insospechado, a [ĕnsospetchá'ŧho, á] *a* (*inesperado*) unexpected.
insostenible [ĕnsostenē'hle] *a* untenable.

inspección [ĕnspeksyon'] *nf* inspection, check; **l**~ inspectorate.
inspeccionar [ĕnspeksyonár'] *vt* (*examinar*) to inspect, examine; (*controlar*) to check; (*INFORM*) to peek.
inspector, a [ĕnspektor', á] *nm/f* inspector.
inspectorado [ĕnspektorá'ŧho] *nm* inspectorate.
inspiración [ĕnspērásyon'] *nf* inspiration.
inspirador, a [ĕnspēráŧhor', á] *a* inspiring.
inspirar [ĕnspērár'] *vt* to inspire; (*MED*) to inhale; ~**se** *vr*: ~**se en** to be inspired by.
instalación [ĕnstálásyon'] *nf* (*equipo*) fittings *pl*, equipment; ~ **eléctrica** wiring.
instalar [ĕnstálár'] *vt* (*establecer*) to install (*US*), instal (*Brit*); (*erguir*) to set up, erect; ~**se** *vr* to establish o.s.; (*en una vivienda*) to move into.
instancia [ĕnstán'syá] *nf* (*solicitud*) application; (*ruego*) request; (*JUR*) petition; **a** ~ **de** at the request of; **en última** ~ in the last resort.
instantáneo, a [ĕnstántá'neo, á] *a* instantaneous ♦ *nf* snap(shot); **café** ~ instant coffee.
instante [ĕnstán'te] *nm* instant, moment; **en un** ~ in a flash.
instar [ĕnstár'] *vt* to press, urge.
instaurar [ĕnstáōōrár'] *vt* (*establecer*) to establish, set up.
instigador, a [ĕnstēgáŧhor', á] *nm/f* instigator; ~ **de un delito** (*JUR*) accessory before the fact.
instigar [ĕnstēgár'] *vt* to instigate.
instigue [ĕnstē'ge] *etc vb* V **instigar.**
instintivo, a [ĕnstēntē'ho, á] *a* instinctive.
instinto [ĕnstēn'to] *nm* instinct; **por** ~ instinctively.
institución [ĕnstētōōsyon'] *nf* institution, establishment; ~ **benéfica** charitable foundation.
instituir [ĕnstētōōēr'] *vt* to establish; (*fundar*) to found.
instituto [ĕnstētōō'to] *nm* (*gen*) institute; **l**~ **Nacional de Enseñanza** (*Esp*) ≈ high (*US*) *o* comprehensive (*Brit*) school; **l**~ **Nacional de Industria (INI)** (*Esp COM*) *government agency to encourage industrial development.*
institutriz [ĕnstētōōtrēs'] *nf* governess.
instituyendo [ĕnstētōōyen'do] *etc vb* V **instituir.**
instrucción [ĕnstrōōksyon'] *nf* instruction; (*enseñanza*) education, teaching; (*JUR*) proceedings *pl*; (*MIL*) training; (*DEPORTE*) coaching; (*conocimientos*) knowledge; (*INFORM*) statement; **instrucciones para el uso** directions for use; **instrucciones de funcionamiento** operating instructions.
instructivo, a [ĕnstrōōktē'ho, á] *a* instructive.

instruir [ēnstrōōēr'] *vt* (*gen*) to instruct; (*enseñar*) to teach, educate; (*JUR: proceso*) to prepare, draw up; **~se** *vr* to learn, teach o.s.

instrumento [ēnstrōōmen'to] *nm* (*gen*, *MUS*) instrument; (*herramienta*) tool, implement; (*COM*) indenture; legal document; **~ de percusión/cuerda/viento** percussion/string(ed)/wind instrument.

instruyendo [ēnstrōōyen'do] *etc vb V* **instruir.**

insubordinarse [ēnsōōhorthēnár'se] *vr* to rebel.

insuficiencia [ēnsōōfēsyen'syá] *nf* (*carencia*) lack; (*inadecuación*) inadequacy; **~ cardíaca/renal** heart/kidney failure.

insuficiente [ēnsōōfēsyen'te] *a* (*gen*) insufficient; (*ESCOL: nota*) unsatisfactory.

insufrible [ēnsōōfrē'ble] *a* insufferable.

insular [ēnsōōlár'] *a* insular.

insulso, a [ēnsōōl'so] *a* insipid; (*fig*) dull.

insultar [ēnsōōltár'] *vt* to insult.

insulto [ēnsōōl'to] *nm* insult.

insumiso, a [ēnsōōmē'so, á] *a* (*rebelde*) rebellious.

insuperable [ēnsōōperá'ble] *a* (*excelente*) unsurpassable; (*problema etc*) insurmountable.

insurgente [ēnsōōrhen'te] *a, nm/f* insurgent.

insurrección [ēnsōōrreksyon'] *nf* insurrection, rebellion.

insustituible [ēnsōōstētwē'ble] *a* irreplaceable.

intacto, a [ēnták'to, á] *a* (*sin tocar*) untouched; (*entero*) intact.

intachable [ēntátchá'ble] *a* irreproachable.

integrado, a [ēntegrá'tho, á] *a* (*INFORM*): **circuito ~** integrated circuit.

integral [ēntegrál'] *a* integral; (*completo*) complete; (*TEC*) built-in; **pan ~** wholewheat bread.

integrante [ēntegrán'te] *a* integral ♦ *nm/f* member.

integrar [ēntegrár'] *vt* to make up, compose; (*MAT, fig*) to integrate.

integridad [ēntegrētháth'] *nf* wholeness; (*carácter, tb INFORM*) integrity; **en su ~** completely.

íntegro, a [ēn'tegro] *a* whole, entire; (*texto*) uncut, unabridged; (*honrado*) honest.

intelectual [ēntelektwál'] *a, nm/f* intellectual.

intelectualidad [ēntelektwálētháth'] *nf* intelligentsia, intellectuals *pl.*

inteligencia [ēntelēhen'syá] *nf* intelligence; (*ingenio*) ability; **~ artificial** artificial intelligence.

inteligente [ēntelēhen'te] *a* intelligent.

inteligible [ēntelēhē'ble] *a* intelligible.

intemperancia [ēntemperán'syá] *nf* excess, intemperance.

intemperie [ēntempe'rye] *nf*: **a la ~** outdoors, in the open air.

intempestivo, a [ēntempestē'ho, á] *a* untimely.

intención [ēntensyon'] *nf* (*gen*) intention, purpose; **con segundas intenciones** maliciously; **con ~** deliberately.

intencionado, a [ēntensyoná'tho, á] *a* deliberate; **bien/mal ~** well-meaning/ill-disposed, hostile.

intendencia [ēntenden'syá] *nf* management, administration; (*MIL: tb:* **cuerpo de ~**) ≈ quarter-master corps.

intensidad [ēntensētháth'] *nf* (*gen*) intensity; (*ELEC, TEC*) strength; (*de recuerdo*) vividness; **llover con ~** to rain hard.

intensificar [ēntensēfēkár'] *vt*, **intensificarse** *vr* to intensify.

intensifique [ēntensēfē'ke] *etc vb V* **intensificar.**

intensivo, a [ēntensē'ho, á] *a* intensive; **curso ~** crash course.

intenso, a [ēnten'so, á] *a* intense; (*impresión*) vivid; (*sentimiento*) profound, deep.

intentar [ēntentár'] *vt* (*tratar*) to try, attempt.

intento [ēnten'to] *nm* (*intención*) intention, purpose; (*tentativa*) attempt.

intentona [ēntento'ná] *nf* (*POL*) attempted coup.

interaccionar [ēnteráksyonár'] *vi* (*INFORM*) to interact.

interactivo, a [ēnteráktē'ho, á] *a* (*INFORM*): **computación interactiva** interactive computing.

intercalación [ēnterkálásyon'] *nf* (*INFORM*) merging.

intercalar [ēnterkálár'] *vt* to insert; (*INFORM: archivos, texto*) to merge.

intercambiable [ēnterkámbyá'ble] *a* interchangeable.

intercambio [ēnterkám'byo] *nm* (*canje*) exchange; (*trueque*) swap.

interceder [ēntersethēr'] *vi* to intercede.

interceptar [ēnterseptár'] *vt* to intercept, cut off; (*AUTO*) to hold up.

interceptor [ēnterseptor'] *nm* interceptor; (*TEC*) trap.

intercesión [ēntersesyon'] *nf* intercession.

interés [ēnteres'] *nm* (*gen, COM*) interest; (*importancia*) concern; (*parte*) share, part; (*pey*) self-interest; **~ compuesto** compound interest; **~ simple** simple interest; **con un ~ de 9 por ciento** at an interest of 9%; **dar a ~** to lend at interest; **tener ~ en** (*COM*) to hold a share in; **intereses acumulados** accrued interest *sg*; **intereses por cobrar** interest receivable *sg*; **intereses creados** vested interests; **intereses por pagar** interest payable *sg*.

interesado, a [ēnteresá'ŧho. á] *a* interested; (*prejuiciado*) prejudiced; (*pey*) mercenary, self-seeking ♦ *nm/f* person concerned; (*firmante*) the undersigned.

interesante [ēnteresán'te] *a* interesting.

interesar [ēnteresár'] *vt* to interest, be of interest to ♦ *vi* to interest, be of interest; (*importar*) to be important; ~**se** *vr*: ~**se en** *o* **por** to take an interest in; **no me interesan los toros** bullfighting does not appeal to me.

interestatal [ēnterestátál'] *a* inter-state.

interface, interfase [ēnterfá'se] *nm* (*INFORM*) interface; ~ **hombre/máquina/por menús** man/machine/menu interface.

interferir [ēnterferēr'] *vt* to interfere with; (*TELEC*) to jam ♦ *vi* to interfere.

interfiera [ēnterfye'rá] *etc*, **interfiriendo** [ēnterfēryen'do] *etc vb V* **interferir**.

interfono [ēnterfo'no] *nm* intercom.

ínterin [ēn'terēn] *ad* meanwhile ♦ *nm* interim; **en el ~** in the meantime.

interino, a [ēnterē'no, á] *a* temporary; (*empleado etc*) provisional ♦ *nm/f* temporary worker; (*MED*) on-call doctor (*US*), locum (*Brit*); (*ESCOL*) substitute teacher (*US*), supply teacher (*Brit*); (*TEATRO*) stand-in.

interior [ēnteryor'] *a* inner, inside; (*COM*) domestic, internal ♦ *nm* interior, inside; (*fig*) soul, mind; (*DEPORTE*) inside-forward; **Ministerio del I~** ≈ Ministry of the Interior; **dije para mi ~** I said to myself.

interjección [ēnterheksyon'] *nf* interjection.

interlínea [ēnterlē'neá] *nf* (*INFORM*) line feed.

interlocutor, a [ēnterlokōōtor', á] *nm/f* speaker; (*al teléfono*) person at the other end (of the line); **mi ~** the person I was speaking to.

intermediario, a [ēntermeŧhyá'ryo, á] *a* (*mediador*) mediating ♦ *nm/f* intermediary, go-between; (*mediador*) mediator.

intermedio, a [ēnterme'ŧhyo, á] *a* intermediate; (*tiempo*) intervening ♦ *nm* interval; (*POL*) recess.

interminable [ēntermēná'ḅle] *a* endless, interminable.

intermitente [ēntermēten'te] *a* intermittent ♦ *nm* (*AUTO*) indicator.

internacional [ēnternásyonál'] *a* international.

internado [ēnterná'ŧho] *nm* boarding school.

internamiento [ēnternámyen'to] *nm* internment.

internar [ēnternár'] *vt* to intern; (*en un manicomio*) to commit; ~**se** *vr* (*penetrar*) to penetrate; ~**se en** to go into *o* right inside; ~**se en un estudio** to study a subject in depth.

interno, a [ēnter'no, á] *a* internal, interior;

(*POL etc*) domestic ♦ *nm/f* (*alumno*) boarder.

interpelación [ēnterpelásyon'] *nf* appeal, plea.

interpelar [ēnterpelár'] *vt* (*rogar*) to implore; (*hablar*) to speak to; (*POL*) to ask for explanations, question formally.

interpondré [ēnterpondre'] *etc vb V* **interponer**.

interponer [ēnterponer'] *vt* to interpose, put in; ~**se** *vr* to intervene.

interponga [ēnterpon'gá] *etc vb V* **interponer**.

interposición [ēnterposēsyon'] *nf* insertion.

interpretación [ēnterpretásyon'] *nf* interpretation; (*MUS, TEATRO*) performance; **mala ~** misinterpretation.

interpretar [ēnterpretár'] *vt* to interpret.

intérprete [ēnter'prete] *nm/f* (*LING*) interpreter, translator; (*MUS, TEATRO*) performer, artist(e).

interpuesto, interpuse [ēnterpwe'sto], [ēnterpōō'se] *etc vb V* **interponer**.

interrogación [ēnterrogásyon'] *nf* interrogation; (*LING*: *tb*: **signo de ~**) question mark; (*TELEC*) polling.

interrogante [ēnterrogán'te] *a* questioning ♦ *nm* question mark; (*fig*) question mark, query.

interrogar [ēnterrogár'] *vt* to interrogate, question.

interrogatorio [ēnterrogáto'ryo] *nm* interrogation; (*MIL*) debriefing; (*JUR*) examination.

interrogue [ēnterro'ge] *etc vb V* **interrogar**.

interrumpir [ēnterrōōmpēr'] *vt* to interrupt; (*vacaciones*) to cut short; (*servicio*) to cut off; (*tráfico*) to block.

interrupción [ēnterrōōpsyon'] *nf* interruption.

interruptor [ēnterrōōptor'] *nm* (*ELEC*) switch.

intersección [ēnterseksyon'] *nf* intersection; (*AUTO*) junction.

interurbano, a [ēnterōōrḅá'no, á] *a* intercity; (*TELEC*) long-distance.

intervalo [ēnterḅá'lo] *nm* interval; (*descanso*) break; **a ~s** at intervals, every now and then.

intervención [ēnterḅensyon'] *nf* supervision; (*COM*) audit(ing); (*MED*) operation; (*TELEC*) tapping; (*participación*) intervention; ~ **quirúrgica** surgical operation; **la política de no ~** the policy of non-intervention.

intervencionista [ēnterḅensyonē'stá] *a*: **no ~** (*COM*) laissez-faire.

intervendré [ēnterḅendre'] *etc*, **intervenga** [ēnterḅen'gá] *etc vb V* **intervenir**.

intervenir [ēnterḅenēr'] *vt* (*controlar*) to control, supervise; (*COM*) to audit; (*MED*) to operate on ♦ *vi* (*participar*) to take part, participate; (*mediar*) to intervene.

interventor, a |ĕntĕrhĕntor', ă| *nm/f* inspector; (*COM*) auditor.

interviniendo |ĕntĕrhĕnyen'do| *etc vb* V **intervenir**.

interviú |ĕntĕrhyōō'| *nf* interview.

intestino |ĕntĕstĕ'no| *nm* intestine.

inti |ĕn'tĕ| *nm monetary unit of Peru*.

intimar |ĕntĕmár'| *vt* to intimate, announce; (*mandar*) to order ♦ *vi*, ~**se** *vr* to become friendly.

intimidad |ĕntĕmĕ'thăth'| *nf* intimacy; (*familiaridad*) familiarity; (*vida privada*) private life; (*JUR*) privacy.

intimidar |ĕntĕmĕ'thăr'| *vt* to intimidate, scare.

íntimo, a |ĕn'tĕmo| *a* intimate; (*pensamientos*) innermost; (*vida*) personal, private; **una boda íntima** a quiet wedding.

intolerable |ĕntolĕrá'hlĕ| *a* intolerable, unbearable.

intoxicación |ĕntoksĕkásyon'| *nf* poisoning; ~ **alimenticia** food poisoning.

intraducible |ĕntráthōōsĕ'hlĕ| *a* untranslatable.

intranquilice |ĕntránkĕlĕ'se| *etc vb* V **intranquilizarse**.

intranquilizarse |ĕntránkĕlĕsár'se| *vr* to get worried o anxious.

intranquilo, a |ĕntránkĕ'lo, ă| *a* worried.

intranscendente |ĕntránscenden'tĕ| *a* unimportant.

intransferible |ĕntránsferĕ'hlĕ| *a* not transferable.

intransigente |ĕntránsĕhen'tĕ| *a* intransigent.

intransitable |ĕntránsĕtá'hlĕ| *a* impassable.

intratable |ĕntrátá'hlĕ| *a* (*problema*) intractable; (*dificultad*) awkward; (*individuo*) unsociable.

intrepidez |ĕntrepĕ'thes'| *nf* courage, bravery.

intrépido, a |ĕntrĕ'pĕtho, ă| *a* intrepid, fearless.

intriga |ĕntrĕ'gă| *nf* intrigue; (*plan*) plot.

intrigar |ĕntrĕgár'| *vt, vi* to intrigue.

intrigue |ĕntrĕ'ge| *etc vb* V **intrigar**.

intrincado, a |ĕntrĕnká'tho, ă| *a* intricate.

intrínseco, a |ĕntrĕn'scko, ă| *a* intrinsic.

introducción |ĕntrothōōksyon'| *nf* introduction; (*de libro*) foreword; (*INFORM*) input.

introducir |ĕntrothōōsĕr'| *vt* (*gen*) to introduce; (*moneda*) to insert; (*INFORM*) to input, enter.

introduje |ĕntrothōō'he| *etc*, **introduzca** |ĕntrothōōs'kă| *etc vb* V **introducir**.

intromisión |ĕntromĕsyon'| *nf* interference, meddling.

introvertido, a |ĕntrohertĕ'tho, ă| *a*, *nm/f* introvert.

intruso, a |ĕntrōō'so, ă| *a* intrusive ♦ *nm/f* intruder.

intuición |ĕntwĕsyon'| *nf* intuition.

intuir |ĕntōōĕr'| *vt* to know by intuition, intuit.

intuyendo |ĕntōōyen'do| *etc vb* V **intuir**.

inundación |ĕnōōndásyon'| *nf* flood(ing).

inundar |ĕnōōndár'| *vt* to flood; (*fig*) to swamp, inundate.

inusitado, a |ĕnōōsĕtá'tho, ă| *a* unusual.

inútil |ĕnōō'tĕl| *a* useless; (*esfuerzo*) vain, fruitless.

inutilice |ĕnōōtĕlĕ'se| *etc vb* V **inutilizar**.

inutilidad |ĕnōōtĕlĕthăth'| *nf* uselessness.

inutilizar |ĕnōōtĕlĕsár'| *vt* to make unusable, put out of action; (*incapacitar*) to disable; ~**se** *vr* to become useless.

invadir |ĕmbáthĕr'| *vt* to invade.

invalidez |ĕmbálĕthes'| *nf* (*MED*) disablement; (*JUR*) invalidity.

inválido, a |ĕmbá'lĕtho, ă| *a* invalid; (*JUR*) null and void ♦ *nm/f* invalid.

invariable |ĕmbáryá'hlĕ| *a* invariable.

invasión |ĕmbásyon'| *nf* invasion.

invasor, a |ĕmbásor', ă| *a* invading ♦ *nm/f* invader.

invención |ĕmbensyon'| *nf* invention.

inventar |ĕmbentár'| *vt* to invent.

inventario |ĕmbentá'ryo| *nm* inventory; (*COM*) taking inventory (*US*), stocktaking (*Brit*).

inventiva |ĕmbentĕ'hă| *nf* inventiveness.

inventor, a |ĕmbentor', ă| *nm/f* inventor.

invernadero |ĕmbernáthe'ro| *nm* greenhouse.

invernal |ĕmbernál'| *a* wintry, winter *cpd*.

inverosímil |ĕmberosĕ'mĕl| *a* implausible.

inversión |ĕmbersyon'| *nf* (*COM*) investment; ~ **de capitales** capital investment; **inversiones extranjeras** foreign investment *sg*.

inverso, a |ĕmber'so, ă| *a* inverse, opposite; **en el orden** ~ in reverse order; **a la inversa** inversely, the other way round.

inversor, a |ĕmbersor', ă| *nm/f* (*COM*) investor.

invertido, a |ĕmbertĕ'tho, ă| *a* inverted; (*al revés*) reversed; (*homosexual*) homosexual ♦ *nm/f* homosexual.

invertir |ĕmbertĕr'| *vt* (*COM*) to invest; (*volcar*) to turn upside down; (*tiempo etc*) to spend.

investigación |ĕmbestĕgăsyon'| *nf* investigation; (*indagación*) inquiry; (*UNIV*) research; ~ **y desarrollo** (*COM*) research and development (R and D); ~ **de los medios de publicidad** media research; ~ **del mercado** market research.

investigador, a |ĕmbestĕgăthor', ă| *nm/f* investigator; (*UNIVERSIDAD*) research fellow.

investigar |ĕmbestĕgár'| *vt* to investigate;

(*estudiar*) to do research into.
investigue [ĕmbestē'ᵍe] *etc vb* V **investigar**.
invicto, a [ĕmbĕk'to, á] *a* unconquered.
invidente [ĕmbĕᵗhen'te] *a* sightless ♦ *nm/f* blind person; **los ~s** the sightless.
invierno [ĕmbyer'no] *nm* winter.
invierta [ĕmbyer'tá] *etc vb* V **invertir**.
inviolabilidad [ĕmbyoláhēlēthátĥ'] *nf* inviolability; **~ parlamentaria** parliamentary immunity.
invirtiendo [ĕmbĕrtyen'do] *etc vb* V **invertir**.
invisible [ĕmbēsē'ble] *a* invisible; **exportaciones/importaciones ~s** invisible exports/imports.
invitado, a [ĕmbētá'tho, á] *nm/f* guest.
invitar [ĕmbētár'] *vt* to invite; (*incitar*) to entice; **~ a uno a hacer algo** to invite sb to do sth; **~ a algo** to pay for sth; **nos invitó a cenar fuera** she took us out for dinner; **invito yo** it's on me.
invocar [ĕmbokár'] *vt* to invoke, call on; (*INFORM*) to call.
involucrar [ĕmbolōōkrár'] *vt*: **~ algo en un discurso** to bring something irrelevant into a discussion; **~ a uno en algo** to involve sb in sth; **~se** *vr* (*interesarse*) to get involved.
involuntario, a [ĕmbolōōntá'ryo, á] *a* involuntary; (*ofensa etc*) unintentional.
invoque [ĕmbo'ke] *etc vb* V **invocar**.
inyección [ĕnyeksyon'] *nf* injection.
inyectar [ĕnyektár'] *vt* to inject.
IPC *nm abr* (*Esp*: = *índice de precios al consumo*) CPI.
IPM *nm abr* (= *índice de precios al por menor*) RPI.
ir [ēr] *vi* to go; (*viajar*) to travel; (*ropa*) to suit; **~se** *vr* to go away, leave; (*mano etc*) to slip; **¡vete!** go away!; **¡vámonos!** let's go!; **~ caminando** to walk; **~ en coche/bicicleta/caballo/a pie** to drive/cycle/ride/walk; **~ de mal en peor** to go from bad to worse; **¡voy!** I'm coming!; **~ de viaje** to travel, go away; **voy para viejo** I'm getting on in years; **~ por/a por algo** to go for/go and get sth; **¡qué va!** (*no diga*) you don't say!; **(¡no!)** no way!; **esto va de veras** this is serious; **¿me va bien esto?** (*ropa*) does this suit me?; **eso no va por usted** I wasn't referring to you; **va mucho de A a B** there's a lot of difference between A and B; **¡vamos!** come on!; **vaya susto que me has dado** what a fright you gave me; **vaya donde vaya, encontrará ...** wherever you go, you will find ... .
ira [ē'rá] *nf* anger, rage.
iracundo, a [ērákōōn'do, á] *a* irascible.
Irak [ērák'] *nm* = **Iraq**.
Irán [ērán'] *nm* Iran.

iraní [ēránē'] *a, nm/f* Iranian.
Iraq [ērák'] *nm* Iraq.
iraquí [ērákē'] *a, nm/f* Iraqui.
irguiendo [ērgyen'do] *etc vb* V **erguir**.
iris [ē'rēs] *nm inv* (*arco ~*) rainbow; (*ANAT*) iris.
Irlanda [ērlán'dá] *nf* Ireland; **~ del Norte** Northern Ireland, Ulster.
irlandés, esa [ērlándes', csá] *a* Irish ♦ *nm/f* Irishman/woman ♦ *nm* (*LING*) Gaelic, Irish; **los irlandeses** *npl* the Irish.
ironía [ēronē'á] *nf* irony.
irónico, a [ēro'nēko, á] *a* ironic(al).
IRPF *nm abr* (*Esp*) =*impuesto sobre la renta de las personas físicas*.
irrazonable [ērrásoná'ble] *a* unreasonable.
irreal [ērreál'] *a* unreal.
irrealizable [ērreálēsá'ble] *a* (*gen*) unrealizable; (*meta*) unrealistic.
irrebatible [ērrebátē'ble] *a* irrefutable.
irreconocible [ērrekonosē'ble] *a* unrecognizable.
irrecuperable [ērrekōōperá'ble] *a* irrecoverable, irretrievable.
irreembolsable [ērreembolsá'ble] *a* (*COM*) non-returnable.
irreflexión [ērrefleksyon'] *nf* thoughtlessness; (*ímpetu*) rashness.
irregular [ērregōōlár'] *a* irregular; (*situación*) abnormal, anomalous; **margen izquierdo/derecho ~** (*texto*) ragged left/right (margin).
irremediable [ērremethyá'ble] *a* irremediable; (*vicio*) incurable.
irresoluto, a [ērresolōō'to, á] *a* irresolute, hesitant; (*sin resolver*) unresolved.
irrespetuoso, a [ērrespetwo'so, á] *a* disrespectful.
irresponsable [ērresponsá'ble] *a* irresponsible.
irreverente [ērreberen'te] *a* disrespectful.
irrigar [ērrēgár'] *vt* to irrigate.
irrigue [ērrē'ge] *etc vb* V **irrigar**.
irrisible [ērrēsē'ble] *a* laughable; (*precio*) absurdly low.
irrisorio, a [ērrēso'ryo, á] *a* derisory, ridiculous; (*precio*) bargain *cpd*.
irritar [ērrētár'] *vt* to irritate, annoy; **~se** *vr* to get angry, lose one's temper.
irrompible [ērrompē'ble] *a* unbreakable.
irrumpir [ērrōōmpēr'] *vi*: **~ en** to burst o rush into.
irrupción [ērrōōpsyon'] *nf* irruption; (*invasión*) invasion.
IRTP *nm abr* (*Esp*)=*impuesto sobre el rendimiento del trabajo personal*) ≈ PAYE.
isla [ēs'lá] *nf* (*GEO*) island; **I~s Británicas** British Isles; **I~s Filipinas/Malvinas/Canarias** Philippines/Falklands/Canaries.
Islam [ēslám'] *nm* Islam.
islámico, a [ēslá'mēko, á] *a* Islamic.

islandés, esa [ēslándes', esá] *a* Icelandic ♦ *nm/f* Icelander ♦ *nm* (*LING*) Icelandic.
Islandia [ēslán'dyá] *nf* Iceland.
isleño, a [ēslc'nyo. á] *a* island *cpd* ♦ *nm/f* islander.
islote [ēslo'te] *nm* small island.
isótopo [ēso'topo] *nm* isotope.
Israel [ēsráel'] *nm* Israel.
israelí [ēsráelē'] *a, nm/f* Israeli.
istmo [ēst'mo] *nm* isthmus; **el l~ de Panamá** the Isthmus of Panama.
Italia [ētá'lyá] *nf* Italy.
italiano, a [ētályá'no, á] *a, nm/f* Italian ♦ *nm* (*LING*) Italian.
itálica [ētá'lēká] *nf* (*INFORM*): **en ~** in italics.
itinerante [ētēnerán'te] *a* travel(l)ing; (*embajador*) roving.
itinerario [ētēnerá'ryo] *nm* itinerary, route.
IVA [ē'há] *nm abr* (*Esp COM*: = *Impuesto sobre el Valor Añadido*) VAT.
IVP *nm abr* = *Instituto Venezolano de Petroquímica.*
izar [ēsár'] *vt* to hoist.
izda, izq. *abr* = **izquierda.**
izdo, izq, izq. *abr* = **izquierdo.**
izquierda [ēskyer'há] *nf V* **izquierdo.**
izquierdista [ēskyerhē'stá] *a* leftist, leftwing ♦ *nm/f* left-winger, leftist.
izquierdo, a [ēskyer'ho, á] *a* left ♦ *nf* left; (*POL*) left (wing); **a la izquierda** on the left; **es un cero a la izquierda** (*fam*) he is a nonentity; **conducción por la izquierda** left-hand drive.

J

J, j [ho'tá] *nf* (*letra*) J, j; **J de José** J for Jig.
jabalí [háhálē'] *nm* wild boar.
jabalina [háhálē'ná] *nf* javelin.
jabato, a [háhá'to, á] *a* brave, bold ♦ *nm* young wild boar.
jabón [háhon'] *nm* soap; (*fam*: *adulación*) flattery; **~ de afeitar** shaving soap; **~ de tocador** toilet soap; **dar ~ a uno** to softsoap sb.
jabonar [háhonár'] *vt* to soap.
jaca [há'ká] *nf* pony.
jacinto [hásēn'to] *nm* hyacinth.
jactancia [háktán'syá] *nf* boasting, boastfulness.
jactarse [háktár'se] *vr*: **~ (de)** to boast o brag (about o of).

jadear [háheár'] *vi* to pant, gasp for breath.
jadeo [háhe'o] *nm* panting, gasping.
jaguar [hágwár'] *nm* jaguar.
jalar [hálár'] *vt* (*AM*) to pull.
jalbegue [hálhe'ge] *nm* (*pintura*) whitewash.
jalea [hále'á] *nf* jelly.
jaleo [hále'o] *nm* racket, uproar; **armar un ~** to make a racket.
jalón [hálon'] *nm* (*AM*) tug.
jalonar [hálonár'] *vt* to stake out; (*fig*) to mark.
Jamaica [hámá'ēká] *nf* Jamaica.
jamaicano, a [hámáēká'no, á] *a, nm/f* Jamaican.
jamás [hámás'] *ad* never, not ... ever; (*interrogativo*) ever; **¿~ se vio tal cosa?** did you ever see such a thing?
jamón [hámon'] *nm* ham; **~ dulce/serrano** boiled/cured ham.
Japón [hápon'] *nm*: **el ~** Japan.
japonés, esa [hápones', esá] *a, nm/f* Japanese ♦ *nm* (*LING*) Japanese.
jaque [há'ke] *nm*: **~ mate** checkmate.
jaqueca [háke'ká] *nf* (very bad) headache, migraine.
jarabe [hárá'he] *nm* syrup; **~ para la tos** cough syrup o mixture.
jarana [hárá'ná] *nf* (*juerga*) spree (*fam*); **andar/ir de ~** to be/go on a spree.
jarcia [hár'syá] *nf* (*NAUT*) ropes *pl*, rigging.
jardín [hárhēn'] *nm* garden; **~ botánico** botanical garden; **~ de (la) infancia** (*Esp*) o **de niños** (*AM*) o **infantil** (*AM*) kindergarten, nursery school.
jardinería [hárhēnerē'á] *nf* gardening.
jardinero, a [hárhēne'ro, á] *nm/f* gardener.
jarra [há'rrá] *nf* jar; (*jarro*) jug; (*de leche*) churn; (*de cerveza*) mug; **de o en ~s** with arms akimbo.
jarro [há'rro] *nm* jug.
jarrón [hárron'] *nm* vase; (*ARQUEOLOGÍA*) urn.
jaspeado, a [háspeá'do, á] *a* mottled, speckled.
jaula [há'oolá] *nf* cage; (*embalaje*) crate.
jauría [háoorē'á] *nf* pack of hounds.
jazmín [hásmēn'] *nm* jasmine.
J. C. *abr* = **Jesucristo.**
JD *nf abr* (*Esp COM*) = *Junta Democrática.*
jefa [he'fá] *nf ver* **jefe.**
jefatura [hefátoo'rá] *nf* (*liderato*) leadership; (*sede*) central office; **J~ de la aviación civil** ≈ Federal Aviation Administration (*US*), ≈ Civil Aviation Authority (*Brit*); **~ de policía** police headquarters *sg*.
jefazo [hefá'so] *nm* bigwig.
jefe, a [he'fe, á] *nm/f* (*gen*) chief, head; (*patrón*) boss; (*POL*) leader; (*COM*) manager(ess); **~ de camareros** head wait-

er; ~ **de cocina** chef; ~ **ejecutivo** (*COM*) chief executive; ~ **de estación** stationmaster; ~ **de estado** head of state; ~ **de oficina** (*COM*) office manager; ~ **de producción** (*COM*) production manager; ~ **supremo** commander-in-chief; **ser el** ~ (*fig*) to be the boss.

JEN [hen] *nf abr* (*Esp*:=*Junta de Energía Nuclear*) ≈ NRC.

jengibre [henhē'bre] *nm* ginger.

jeque [he'ke] *nm* sheik(h).

jerarquía [herárkē'á] *nf* (*orden*) hierarchy; (*rango*) rank.

jerárquico, a [herár'kēko, á] *a* hierarchic(al).

jerez [heres'] *nm* sherry; **J~ de la Frontera** Jerez.

jerezano, a [heresá'no, á] *a* of *o* from Jerez ♦ *nm/f* native *o* inhabitant of Jerez.

jerga [her'gá] *nf* (*tela*) coarse cloth; (*lenguaje*) jargon; ~ **informática** computer jargon.

jerigonza [herēgon'sá] *nf* (*jerga*) jargon, slang; (*galimatías*) nonsense, gibberish.

jeringa [herēn'gá] *nf* syringe; (*AM*) annoyance, bother; ~ **de engrase** grease gun.

jeringar [herēngár'] *vt* (*AM*) to annoy, bother.

jeringue [herēn'ge] *etc vb* V **jeringar.**

jeringuilla [herēng'ēyá] *nf* hypodermic (syringe).

jeroglífico [herog[ē'fēko] *nm* hieroglyphic.

jersé [herse'], *pl* **jersés, jersey** [herse'ē], *pl* **jerseys** *nm* jersey, pullover.

Jerusalén [herōōsálen'] *n* Jerusalem.

Jesucristo [hesōōkrē'sto] *nm* Jesus Christ.

jesuita [heswē'tá] *a, nm* Jesuit.

Jesús [hesōōs'] *nm* Jesus; **¡~!** good heavens!; (*al estornudar*) bless you!

jeta [he'tá] *nf* (*ZOOL*) snout; (*fam: cara*) mug; **¡que ~ tienes!** (*fam: insolencia*) you've got a nerve!

jícara [hē'kárá] *nf* small cup.

jiennense [hyennen'se] *a* of *o* from Jaén ♦ *nm/f* native *o* inhabitant of Jaén.

jilguero [hēlge'ro] *nm* goldfinch.

jinete, a [hēne'te, á] *nm/f* horseman/woman.

jipijapa [hēpēhá'pá] *nm* (*AM*) straw hat.

jira [hē'rá] *nf* (*de tela*) strip; (*excursión*) picnic.

jirafa [hērá'fá] *nf* giraffe.

jirón [hēron'] *nm* rag, shred.

JJ.OO. *nmpl abr* = **Juegos Olímpicos.**

jocosidad [hokosētháth'] *nf* humor (*US*), humour (*Brit*); (*chiste*) joke.

jocoso, a [hoko'so, á] *a* humorous, jocular.

joder [hother'] (*fam!*) *vt* to fuck (*!*), screw (*!*); ~**se** *vr* (*fracasar*) to fail; **¡~!** damn it!; **se jodió todo** everything was ruined.

jodido, a [hothē'tho, á] *a* (*fam!*: difícil)

awkward; **me han ~** I've been screwed(*!*).

jofaina [hofáē'ná] *nf* washbasin.

jolgorio [holgo'ryo] *nm* (*juerga*) fun, revelry.

Jordania [horthá'nyá] *nf* Jordan.

jornada [hornà'thá] *nf* (*viaje de un día*) day's journey; (*camino o viaje entero*) journey; (*día de trabajo*) working day; ~ **de 8 horas** 8-hour day; (**trabajar a**) ~ **partida** (to work a) split shift.

jornal [hornál'] *nm* (day's) wage.

jornalero [hornále'ro] *nm* (day) laborer (*US*), labourer (*Brit*).

joroba [horo'há] *nf* hump.

jorobado, a [horohá'tho, á] *a* hunchbacked ♦ *nm/f* hunchback.

jorobar [horohár'] *vt* to annoy, pester, bother; ~**se** *vr* to get cross; **¡hay que ~se!** to hell with it!; **esto me joroba** I'm fed up with this!

jota [ho'tá] *nf* letter J; (*danza*) *Aragonese dance*; (*fam*) jot, iota; **no saber ~** to have no idea.

joven [ho'ben] *a* young ♦ *nm* young man, youth ♦ *nf* young woman, girl.

jovencito, a [hohensē'to, á] *nm/f* youngster.

jovial [hohyál'] *a* cheerful, jolly.

jovialidad [hohyálētháth'] *nf* cheerfulness, jolliness.

joya [ho'yá] *nf* jewel, gem; (*fig: persona*) gem; ~**s de fantasía** imitation jewellery *sg*.

joyería [hoyerē'á] *nf* (*joyas*) jewelry (*US*), jewellery (*Brit*); (*tienda*) jewel(l)er's (shop).

joyero [hoye'ro] *nm* (*persona*) jewel(l)er; (*caja*) jewel case.

JSP *nf abr* (*COM*)=*Junta Superior de Precios.*

juanete [hwáne'te] *nm* (*del pie*) bunion.

jubilación [hōōbēlásyon'] *nf* (*retiro*) retirement.

jubilado, a [hōōbēlá'do, á] *a* retired ♦ *nm/f* retired person, senior citizen.

jubilar [hōōbēlár'] *vt* to pension off, retire; (*fam*) to discard; ~**se** *vr* to retire.

jubileo [hōōbēle'o] *nm* jubilee.

júbilo [hōō'bēlo] *nm* joy, rejoicing.

jubiloso, a [hōōbēlo'so, á] *a* jubilant.

judaísmo [hōōtháēs'mo] *nm* Judaism.

judicatura [hōōthēkátōō'rá] *nf* (*cargo de juez*) office of judge; (*cuerpo de jueces*) judiciary.

judicial [hōōthēsyál'] *a* judicial.

judío, a [hōōthē'o, á] *a* Jewish ♦ *nm* Jew ♦ *nf* Jewess, Jewish woman; (*CULIN*) bean; **judía blanca** haricot bean; **judía verde** French *o* string bean.

juego [hwe'go] *etc vb* V **jugar** ♦ *nm* (*gen*) play; (*pasatiempo, partido*) game; (*en ca-*

sino) gambling; (*deporte*) sport; (*conjunto*)
set; (*herramientas*) kit; ~ **de azar** game of
chance; ~ **de café** coffee set; ~ **de caracteres** (*INFORM*) font; ~ **limpio/sucio**
fair/foul *o* dirty play; **J~s Olímpicos**
Olympic Games; ~ **de programas** (*IN-
FORM*) integrated software; **fuera de ~**
(*DEPORTE: persona*) offside; (: *pelota*) out
of play; **por ~** in fun, for fun.
juegue [hwe'ᶃe] *etc vb* V **jugar.**
juerga [hwer'ᶃá] *nf* binge; (*fiesta*) party; **ir
de ~** to go out on a binge.
juerguista [hwerᶃe'stá] *nm/f* reveler.
jueves [hwe'ᵬes] *nm inv* Thursday.
juez [hwes] *nm/f* (*f tb:* **jueza**) judge; (*TENIS*)
umpire; ~ **de línea** linesman; ~ **de paz**
justice of the peace; ~ **de salida** starter.
jugada [hooᶃá'ðá] *nf* play; **buena ~** good
move (*o* shot *o* stroke) *etc.*
jugador, a [hooᶃáðor', á] *nm/f* player; (*en
casino*) gambler.
jugar [hooᶃár'] *vt* to play; (*en casino*) to
gamble; (*apostar*) to bet ♦ *vi* to play; to
gamble; (*COM*) to speculate; ~**se** *vr* to
gamble (away); ~**se el todo por el todo**
to stake one's all, go for broke; **¿quién juega?** whose move is it?; **¡me la han jugado!**
(*fam*) I've been had!
jugarreta [hooᶃárre'tá] *nf* (*mala jugada*)
bad move; (*trampa*) dirty trick; **hacer una
~ a uno** to play a dirty trick on sb.
juglar [hooᶃlár'] *nm* minstrel.
jugo [hoo'ᶃo] *nm* (*BOT, de fruta*) juice; (*fig*)
essence, substance; ~ **de naranja** (*esp
AM*) orange juice.
jugoso, a [hooᶃo'so, á] *a* juicy; (*fig*) substantial, important.
jugué [hooᶃe'], **juguemos** [hooᶃe'mos] *etc vb*
V **jugar.**
juguete [hooᶃe'te] *nm* toy.
juguetear [hooᶃeteár'] *vi* to play.
juguetería [hooᶃetere'á] *nf* toyshop.
juguetón, ona [hooᶃeton', oná] *a* playful.
juicio [hwe'syo] *nm* judgement; (*sana razón*)
sanity, reason; (*opinión*) opinion; (*JUR:
proceso*) trial; **estar fuera de ~** to be out
of one's mind; **a mi ~** in my opinion.
juicioso, a [hwesyo'so, á] *a* wise, sensible.
JUJEM [hoohem'] *nf abr* (*Esp MIL:=Junta
de Jefes del Estado Mayor*) joint Chiefs of
Staff.
jul. *abr* (= *julio*) Jul.
julio [hoo'lyo] *nm* July.
jumento, a [hoomen'to, á] *nm/f* donkey.
jun. *abr* (= *junio*) Jun.
junco [hoon'ko] *nm* rush, reed.
jungla [hoon'glá] *nf* jungle.
junio [hoo'nyo] *nm* June.
junta [hoon'tá] *nf* V **junto.**
juntar [hoontár'] *vt* to join, unite; (*maquinaria*) to assemble, put together; (*dinero*) to

collect; ~**se** *vr* to join, meet; (*reunirse:
personas*) to meet, assemble; (*arrimarse*)
to approach, draw closer; ~**se con uno** to
join sb.
junto, a [hoon'to, á] *a* joined; (*unido*)
united; (*anexo*) near, close; (*contiguo,
próximo*) next, adjacent ♦ *nf* (*asamblea*)
meeting, assembly; (*comité, consejo*)
board, council, committee; (*MIL, POL*)
junta; (*articulación*) joint ♦ *ad:* **todo ~** all
at once ♦ *prep:* ~ **a** near (to), next to; ~**s**
together; **junta constitutiva** (*COM*) statutory meeting; **junta directiva** (*COM*) board
of directors; **junta general extraordinaria**
(*COM*) special meeting (*US*), extraordinary
general meeting (*Brit*).
juntura [hoontoo'rá] *nf* (*punto de unión*)
join, junction; (*articulación*) joint.
jura [hoo'rá] *nf* oath, pledge; ~ **de bandera**
(ceremony of taking the) pledge of alle-
giance.
jurado [hoorá'ðo] *nm* (*JUR: individuo*) juror; (: *grupo*) jury; (*de concurso: grupo*)
panel (of judges); (: *individuo*) member of
a panel.
juramentar [hooramentár'] *vt* to swear in,
administer the oath to; ~**se** *vr* to be sworn
in, take the oath.
juramento [hooramen'to] *nm* oath; (*maldición*) oath, curse; **bajo ~** on oath; **prestar
~** to take the oath; **tomar ~ a** to swear in,
administer the oath to.
jurar [hoorár'] *vt, vi* to swear; ~ **en falso** to
commit perjury; **jurárselas a uno** to have
it in for sb.
jurídico, a [hoore'ðeko, á] *a* legal, juridical.
jurisdicción [hoorésðéksyon'] *nf* (*poder,
autoridad*) jurisdiction; (*territorio*) district.
jurisprudencia [hoorésprooðen'syá] *nf*
jurisprudence.
jurista [hoore'stá] *nm/f* jurist.
justamente [hoostámen'te] *ad* justly, fairly; (*precisamente*) just, exactly.
justicia [hooste'syá] *nf* justice; (*equidad*)
fairness, justice; **de ~** deservedly.
justiciero, a [hoostesye'ro, á] *a* just, right-
eous.
justificable [hoostéféká'ᵬle] *a* justifiable.
justificación [hoostéfékásyon'] *nf* justification; ~ **automática** (*INFORM*) automatic
justification.
justificado, a [hoostéféká'ðo, á] *a* (*TIP*):
(no) (un)justified.
justificante [hoostéfékán'te] *nm* voucher.
justificar [hoostéfékár'] *vt* (*tb TIP*) to justify; (*probar*) to verify.
justifique [hoostéfé'ke] *etc vb* V **justificar.**
justo, a [hoo'sto, á] *a* (*equitativo*) just, fair,
right; (*preciso*) exact, correct; (*ajustado*)
tight ♦ *ad* (*precisamente*) exactly, precisely; (*apenas a tiempo*) just in time; **¡~!**

that's it!, correct!; **llegaste muy** ~ you just made it; **vivir muy** ~ to be hard up.

juvenil |hōōħenčl'| *a* youthful.

juventud |hōōħentōōth'| *nf* (*adolescencia*) youth; (*jóvenes*) young people *pl*.

juzgado |hōōsħà'tho| *nm* tribunal; (*JUR*) court.

juzgar |hōōsħàr'| *vt* to judge; **a** ~ **por** ... to judge by ..., judging by ...; ~ **mal** to misjudge; **júzguelo usted mismo** see for yourself.

juzgue |hōōs'ħe| *etv vb* V **juzgar**.

K

K, k |kà| *nf* (*letra*) K, k; **K de Kilo** K for King.

K *abr* (= *1.000*) K; (*INFORM*:=*1.024*) K.

Kampuchea |kàmpōōtche'à| *nf* Kampuchea.

karate |kàrà'te| *nm* karate.

k/c. *abr* (= *kilociclos*) kc.

Kenia |ke'nyà| *nf* Kenya.

keniata |kenyà'tà| *a, nm/f* Kenyan.

kg. *abr* (= *kilogramo(s)*) kg.

kilate |kēlà'te| *nm* = **quilate.**

kilo |kē'lo| *nm* kilo.

kilobyte |kē'loħàēt| *nm* (*INFORM*) kilobyte.

kilogramo |kēlogrà'mo| *nm* kilogram (*US*), kilogramme (*Brit*).

kilolitro |kēlolē'tro| *nm* kiloliter (*US*), kilolitre (*Brit*).

kilometraje |kēlometrà'he| *nm* distance in kilometres, ≈ mileage.

kilométrico, a |kēlome'trēcko, à| *a* kilometric; (*fam*) very long; (**billete**) ~ (*FERRO*) mileage ticket.

kilómetro |kēlo'metro| *nm* kilometer (*US*), kilometre (*Brit*).

kiloocteto |kēlookte'to| *nm* (*INFORM*) kilobyte.

kilovatio |kēloħà'tyo| *nm* kilowatt.

kiosco |kyos'ko| *nm* = **quiosco.**

km *abr* (= *kilómetro(s)*) km.

km/h *abr* (= *kilómetros por hora*) km/h.

knock-out |no'kàōō|, **K.O.** |kà'o| *nm* knockout; (*golpe*) knockout blow; **dejar** *o* **poner a uno** ~ to knock sb out.

k.p.h. *abr* (= *kilómetros por hora*) km/h.

k.p.l. *abr* (= *kilómetros por litro*) ≈ m.p.g.

kv *abr* (= *kilovatio*) kw.

kv/h *abr* (= *kilovatios-hora*) kw-h.

L

L, l |c'lc| *nf* (*letra*) L, l; **L de Lorenzo** L for Love.

l. *abr* (= *litro(s)*) l.; (*JUR*) = **ley**; (*LITERATURA*: = *libro*) bk.

L/ *abr* (*COM*) = **letra.**

la |là| *artículo definido fsg* the ♦ *pron* her; (*usted*) you; (*cosa*) it ♦ *nm* (*MUS*) la; **está en** ~ **cárcel** he's in jail; ~ **del sombrero rojo** the woman/girl/one in the red hat.

laberinto |làħerēn'to| *nm* labyrinth.

labia |là'ħyà| *nf* fluency; (*pey*) glibness; **tener mucha** ~ to have the gift of gab (*US*) *o* the gab (*Brit*).

labial |làħyàl'| *a* labial.

labio |là'ħyo| *nm* lip; (*de vasija etc*) edge, rim; ~ **inferior/superior** lower/upper lip.

labor |làħor'| *nf* labor (*US*), labour (*Brit*); (*AGR*) farm work; (*tarea*) job, task; (*COSTURA*) needlework, sewing; (*punto*) knitting; ~ **de equipo** teamwork; ~ **de ganchillo** crochet.

laborable |làħorà'ħle| *a* (*AGR*) workable; **día** ~ working day.

laborar |làħoràr'| *vi* to work.

laboratorio |làħoràto'ryo| *nm* laboratory.

laborioso, a |làħoryo'so, à| *a* (*persona*) hard-working; (*trabajo*) tough.

laborista |làħorē'stà| (*Brit POL*) *a*: **Partido L**~ Labour Party ♦ *nm/f* Labour Party member *o* supporter.

labrado, a |làħrà'tho, à| *a* worked; (*madera*) carved; (*metal*) wrought ♦ *nm* (*AGR*) cultivated field.

Labrador |làħràdhor'| *nm* Labrador.

labrador, a |làħràdhor', à| *nm/f* farmer.

labranza |làħràn'sà| *nf* (*AGR*) cultivation.

labrar |làħràr'| *vt* (*gen*) to work; (*madera etc*) to carve; (*fig*) to cause, bring about.

labriego, a |làħrye'go, à| *nm/f* peasant.

laca |là'kà| *nf* lacquer; (*de pelo*) hairspray; ~ **de uñas** nail polish.

lacayo |làkà'yo| *nm* lackey.

lacerar |làseràr'| *vt* to lacerate.

lacio, a |là'syo, à| *a* (*pelo*) lank, straight.

lacón |làkon'| *nm* shoulder of pork.

lacónico, a |làko'nēko, à| *a* laconic.

lacrar |làkràr'| *vt* (*cerrar*) to seal (with sealing wax).

lacre |là'kre| *nm* sealing wax.

lacrimógeno, a |làkrēmo'heno, à| *a* (*fig*) sentimental; **gas** ~ tear gas.

lacrimoso, a [làkrēmo'so, á] *a* tearful.
lactar [làktár'] *vt, vi* to suckle, breas.-feed.
lácteo, a [làk'teo, á] *a*: **productos ~s** dairy products.
ladear [làtheár'] *vt* to tip, tilt ♦ *vi* to tilt; **~se** *vr* to lean; (*DEPORTE*) to swerve; (*AVIAT*) to bank, turn.
ladera [làthe'rá] *nf* slope.
ladino, a [làthē'no, á] *a* cunning.
lado [là'tho] *nm* (*gen*) side; (*fig*) protection; (*MIL*) flank; **~ izquierdo** left(-hand) side; **~ a ~** side by side; **al ~ de** beside; **hacerse a un ~** to stand aside; **poner de ~** to put on its side; **poner a un ~** to put aside; **me da de ~** I don't care; **por un ~ ..., por otro ~ ...** on the one hand ..., on the other (hand), ...; **por todos ~s** on all sides, all round (*Brit*).
ladrar [làthrár'] *vi* to bark.
ladrido [làthrē'tho] *nm* bark, barking.
ladrillo [làthrē'yo] *nm* (*gen*) brick; (*azulejo*) tile.
ladrón, ona [làthron', oná] *nm/f* thief.
lagar [làgár'] *nm* (wine/oil) press.
lagartija [làgártē'há] *nf* (small) lizard, wall lizard.
lagarto [làgár'to] *nm* (*ZOOL*) lizard.
lago [là'go] *nm* lake.
Lagos [là'gos] *nm* Lagos.
lágrima [là'grēmá] *nf* tear.
lagrimear [làgrēmeár'] *vi* to weep; (*ojos*) to water.
laguna [làgōō'ná] *nf* (*lago*) lagoon; (*en escrito, conocimientos*) gap.
laico, a [là'ēko, á] *a* lay ♦ *nm/f* layman/woman.
lameculos [làmekōō'los] *nm/f inv* (*fam*) crawler.
lamentable [làmentà'ble] *a* lamentable, regrettable; (*miserable*) pitiful.
lamentación [làmentàsyon'] *nf* lamentation; **ahora no sirven lamentaciones** it's no good crying over spilt milk.
lamentar [làmentár'] *vt* (*sentir*) to regret; (*deplorar*) to lament; **~se** *vr* to lament; **lo lamento mucho** I'm very sorry.
lamento [làmen'to] *nm* lament.
lamer [làmer'] *vt* to lick.
lámina [là'mēná] *nf* (*plancha delgada*) sheet; (*para estampar, estampa*) plate; (*grabado*) engraving.
laminar [làmēnár'] *vt* (*en libro*) to laminate; (*TEC*) to roll.
lámpara [làm'párá] *nf* lamp; **~ de alcohol/gas** alcohol (*US*) *o* spirit (*Brit*)/gas lamp; **~ de pie** floor (*US*) *o* standard (*Brit*) lamp.
lamparilla [làmpárē'yá] *nf* nightlight.
lamparón [làmpáron'] *nm* (*MED*) scrofula; (*mancha*) (large) grease spot.
lampiño, a [làmpē'nyo, á] *a* (*sin pelo*) hairless.

lana [là'ná] *nf* wool; (*tela*) woolen (*US*) *o* woollen (*Brit*) cloth; **(hecho) de ~** wool *cpd*.
lance [làn'se] *etc vb V* **lanzar** ♦ *nm* (*golpe*) stroke; (*suceso*) event, incident.
lancha [làntch'á] *nf* launch; **~ motora** motorboat; **~ de pesca** fishing boat; **~ salvavidas/torpedera** lifeboat/torpedo boat; **~ neumática** rubber raft (*US*) *o* dinghy (*Brit*).
Landas [làn'dás] *nfpl*: **las ~** Landes *sg*.
lanero, a [làne'ro, á] *a* wool *cpd*.
langosta [làngo'stá] *nf* (*insecto*) locust; (*crustáceo*) lobster (: *de río*) crayfish.
langostino [làngostē'no] *nm* prawn; (*de agua dulce*) crayfish.
languidecer [làngētheser'] *vi* to languish.
languidez [làngēthes'] *nf* languor.
languidezca [làngēthes'ká] *etc vb V* **languidecer**.
lánguido, a [làn'gētho, á] *a* (*gen*) languid; (*sin energía*) listless.
lanilla [lànē'yá] *nf* nap; (*tela*) thin flannel cloth.
lanolina [lànolē'ná] *nf* lanolin(e).
lanudo, a [lànōō'tho, á] *a* wooly (*US*), woolly (*Brit*), fleecy.
lanza [làn'sá] *nf* (*arma*) lance, spear; **medir ~s** to cross swords.
lanzabombas [lànsáhom'bás] *nm inv* (*AVIAT*) bomb release; (*MIL*) mortar.
lanzacohetes [lànsákoc'tes] *nm inv* rocket launcher.
lanzadera [lànsáthe'rá] *nf* shuttle.
lanzallamas [lànsáyá'más] *nm inv* flamethrower.
lanzamiento [lànsámyen'to] *nm* (*gen*) throwing; (*NAUT, COM*) launch, launching; **~ de pesos** putting the shot.
lanzar [lànsár'] *vt* (*gen*) to throw; (*con violencia*) to fling; (*DEPORTE: pelota*) to bowl; (: *US*) to pitch; (*NAUT, COM*) to launch; (*JUR*) to evict; (*grito*) to give, utter; **~se** *vr* to throw o.s.; (*fig*) to take the plunge; **~se a** (*fig*) to embark upon.
Lanzarote [lànsáro'te] *nm* Lanzarote.
lanzatorpedos [lànsátorpe'thos] *nm inv* torpedo tube.
lapa [là'pá] *nf* limpet.
La Paz *nf* La Paz.
lapicero [làpēse'ro] *nm* mechanical (*US*) *o* propelling (*Brit*) pencil; (*AM: bolígrafo*) ballpoint pen.
lápida [là'pēthá] *nf* stone; **~ conmemorativa** memorial stone; **~ mortuoria** headstone.
lapidar [làpēthár'] *vt* to stone; (*TEC*) to polish, lap.
lapidario, a [làpēthá'ryo, á] *a, nm* lapidary.
lápiz [là'pēs] *nm* pencil; **~ de color** colored pencil; **~ de labios** lipstick; **~ óptico** *o* **luminoso** light pen.

lapón, ona |làpon', onà| a Lapp ♦ nm/f Laplander, Lapp ♦ nm (LING) Lapp.

Laponia |làpo'nyà| nf Lapland.

lapso |làp'so| nm lapse; (error) error; ~ **de tiempo** interval of time.

lapsus |làp'sōōs| nm inv error, mistake.

LAR |làr| nf abr (Esp JUR) = Ley de Arrendamientos Rústicos.

largamente |làrgàmen'te| ad for a long time; (relatar) at length.

largar |làrgàr'| vt (soltar) to release; (aflojar) to loosen; (lanzar) to launch; (fam) to let fly; (velas) to unfurl; (AM) to throw; ~**se** vr (fam) to beat it; ~**se a** (AM) to start to.

largo, a |làr'go, à| a (longitud) long; (tiempo) lengthy; (persona: alta) tall; (: fig) generous ♦ nm length; (MUS) largo; **dos años** ~**s** two long years; **a** ~ **plazo** in the long term; **tiene 9 metros de** ~ it is 9 meters long; **a lo** ~ (posición) lengthways; **a lo** ~ **de** along; (tiempo) all through, throughout; **a la larga** in the long run; **me dio largas con una promesa** she put me off with a promise; **¡**~ **de aquí!** (fam) beat it!

largometraje |làrgometrà'he| nm full-length o feature film.

largue |làr'ge| etc vb V **largar**.

larguero |làrge'ro| nm (ARQ) main beam, chief support; (de puerta) jamb; (DEPORTE) crossbar; (en cama) bolster.

largueza |làrge'sà| nf generosity.

larguirucho, a |làrgerōōtch'o, à| a lanky, gangling.

larguísimo, a |làrge'sēmo, à| a superlativo de **largo**.

largura |làrgōō'rà| nf length.

laringe |làren'he| nf larynx.

laringitis |làrenhē'tēs| nf laryngitis.

larva |làr'hà| nf larva.

las |làs| artículo definido fpl the ♦ pron them; ~ **que cantan** the ones/women/girls who sing.

lasca |làs'kà| nf chip of stone.

lascivia |làsē'hyà| nf lewdness; (lujuria) lust; (fig) playfulness.

lascivo, a |làsē'ho, à| a lewd.

láser |là'ser| nm laser.

Las Palmas nf Las Palmas.

lástima |là'stēmà| nf (pena) pity; **dar** ~ to be pitiful; **es una** ~ **que** it's a pity that; **¡qué** ~**!** what a pity!; **estar hecho una** ~ to be a sorry sight.

lastimar |làstēmàr'| vt (herir) to wound; (ofender) to offend; ~**se** vr to hurt o.s.

lastimero, a |làstēme'ro, à| a pitiful, pathetic.

lastre |làs'tre| nm (TEC, NAUT) ballast; (fig) dead weight.

lata |là'tà| nf (metal) tin; (envase) can; (fam) nuisance; **en** ~ canned; **dar (la)** ~ to be a nuisance.

latente |làten'te| a latent.

lateral |làteràl'| a side, lateral ♦ nm (TEATRO) wings pl.

latido |làtē'tho| nm (del corazón) beat; (de herida) throb(bing).

latifundio |làtēfōōn'dyo| nm large estate.

latifundista |làtēfōōndē'stà| nm/f owner of a large estate.

latigazo |làtēgà'so| nm (golpe) lash; (sonido) crack; (fig: regaño) dressing-down.

látigo |là'tēgo| nm whip.

latiguillo |làtēgē'yo| nm (TEATRO) hamming.

latín |làten'| nm Latin; **saber (mucho)** ~ (fam) to be pretty sharp.

latinajo |làtēnà'ho| nm bad Latin; **echar** ~**s** to come out with Latin words.

latino, a |làtē'no, à| a Latin.

Latinoamérica |làtēnoàme'rēkà| nf Latin America.

latinoamericano, a |làtēnoàmerēkà'no, à| a, nm/f Latin American.

latir |làter'| vi (corazón, pulso) to beat.

latitud |làtētōōth'| nf (GEO) latitude; (fig) breadth, extent.

lato, a |là'to, à| a broad.

latón |làton'| nm brass.

latoso, a |làto'so, à| a (molesto) annoying; (aburrido) boring.

latrocinio |làtrosē'nyo| nm robbery.

LAU nf abr (Esp JUR)=Ley de Arrendamientos Urbanos.

laúd |làōōth'| nm lute.

laudatorio, a |làōōthàto'ryo, à| a laudatory.

laudo |là'ōōtho| nm (JUR) decision, finding.

laurear |làōōreàr'| vt to honor (US), honour (Brit), reward.

laurel |làōōrel'| nm (BOT) laurel; (CULIN) bay.

Lausana |làōōsà'nà| nf Lausanne.

lava |là'hà| nf lava.

lavable |làhà'hle| a washable.

lavabo |làhà'ho| nm (jofaina) washbasin; (retrete) washroom (US), lavatory (Brit).

lavadero |làhàthe'ro| nm laundry.

lavado |làhà'tho| nm washing; (de ropa) wash, laundry; (ARTE) wash; ~ **de cerebro** brainwashing.

lavadora |làhàtho'rà| nf washing machine.

lavamanos |làhàmà'nos| nm inv washbasin.

lavanda |làhàn'dà| nf lavender.

lavandería |làhànderē'à| nf laundry; ~ **automática** laundromat (US), launderette (Brit).

lavaparabrisas |làhàpàràhrē'sàs| nm inv windshield (US) o windscreen (Brit) washer.

lavaplatos |làhàplà'tos| nm inv dishwasher.

lavar |làhàr'| vt to wash; (borrar) to wipe away; ~**se** vr to wash o.s.; ~**se las manos**

to wash one's hands; (*fig*) to wash one's hands of it; ~ **y marcar** (*pelo*) to ⸱hampoo and set; ~ **en seco** to dry-clean.

lavativa [làḫàtē'ḫá] *nf* (*MED*) enema.

lavavajillas [làḫàḫáḫē'yàs] *nm inv* dishwasher.

laxante [láksán'te] *nm* laxative.

laxitud [láksētōōtḫ'] *nf* laxity, slackness.

lazada [làsà'tḫá] *nf* bow.

lazarillo [làsárē'yo] *nm*: **perro de** ~ guide dog.

lazo [là'so] *nm* knot; (*lazada*) bow; (*para animales*) lasso; (*trampa*) snare; (*vínculo*) tie; ~ **corredizo** slipknot.

LBE *nf abr* (*Esp JUR*)=*Ley Básica de Empleo.*

lb(s) *abr* = **libra(s).**

L/C *abr* (= *Letra de Crédito*) B/E.

Lda., Ldo. *abr* = **Licenciado, a.**

le [le] *pron* (*directo*) him (*o* her); (: *usted*) you; (*indirecto*) to him (*o* her *o* it); (: *usted*) to you.

leal [leál'] *a* loyal.

lealtad [leáltátḫ'] *nf* loyalty.

lebrel [lebrel'] *nm* greyhound.

lección [leksyon'] *nf* lesson; ~ **práctica** object lesson; **dar lecciones** to teach, give lessons; **dar una** ~ **a uno** (*fig*) to teach sb a lesson.

lector, a [lektor', á] *nm/f* reader; (*ESCOL, UNIV*) (conversation) assistant ♦ *nm*: ~ **óptico de caracteres** (*INFORM*) optical character reader ♦ *nf*: **~a de fichas** (*INFORM*) card reader.

lectura [lektōō'rá] *nf* reading; ~ **de marcas sensibles** (*INFORM*) mark sensing.

leche [letch'e] *nf* milk; (*fam!*) semen, spunk(*!*); **dar una** ~ **a uno** (*fam*) to belt sb; **estar de mala** ~ (*fam*) to be in a foul mood; **tener mala** ~ (*fam*) to be spiteful; ~ **condensada/en polvo** condensed/powdered milk; ~ **desnatada** skimmed milk; ~ **de magnesia** milk of magnesia; ¡~! hell!

lechera [letche'rá] *nf V* **lechero.**

lechería [letcherē'á] *nf* dairy.

lecherita [letcherē'tá] *nf* milk jug.

lechero, a [letche'ro, á] *a* milk *cpd* ♦ *nm* milkman ♦ *nf* (*vendedora*) milkmaid; (*recipiente*) milk pan; (*para servir*) milk churn; (*AM*) cow.

lecho [letch'o] *nm* (*cama, de río*) bed; (*GEO*) layer; ~ **mortuorio** deathbed.

lechón [letchon'] *nm* suckling (*US*) *o* sucking (*Brit*) pig.

lechoso, a [letcho'so, á] *a* milky.

lechuga [letchōō'gá] *nf* lettuce.

lechuza [letchōō'sá] *nf* (barn) owl.

leer [leer'] *vt* to read; ~ **entre líneas** to read between the lines.

legación [legásyon'] *nf* legation.

legado [legà'tḫo] *nm* (*don*) bequest; (*herencia*) legacy; (*enviado*) legate.

legajo [legà'ho] *nm* file, bundle (of papers).

legal [legál'] *a* legal, lawful; (*persona*) trustworthy.

legalice [legálē'se] *etc vb V* **legalizar.**

legalidad [legálētḫátḫ'] *nf* legality.

legalizar [legálēsár'] *vt* to legalize; (*documento*) to authenticate.

legaña [legà'nyá] *nf* sleep (*in eyes*).

legar [legár'] *vt* to bequeath, leave.

legatario, a [legátá'ryo, á] *nm/f* legatee.

legendario, a [lehendá'ryo, á] *a* legendary.

legible [lehē'ḫle] *a* legible; ~ **por máquina** (*INFORM*) machine-readable.

legión [lehyon'] *nf* legion.

legionario, a [lehyoná'ryo, á] *a* legionary ♦ *nm* legionnaire.

legislación [lehēslásyon'] *nf* legislation; (*leyes*) laws *pl*; ~ **antimonopolio** (*COM*) anti-trust legislation.

legislar [lehēslár'] *vt* to legislate.

legislativo, a [lehēslátē'ḫo, á] *a*: (**elecciones**) **legislativas** ≈ general elections.

legitimar [lehētēmár'] *vt* to legitimize.

legítimo, a [lehē'tēmo, á] *a* (*genuino*) authentic; (*legal*) legitimate, rightful.

lego, a [le'go, á] *a* (*REL*) secular; (*ignorante*) ignorant ♦ *nm* layman.

legua [le'gwá] *nf* league; **se ve** (*o* **nota**) **a la** ~ you can tell (it) a mile off.

legue [le'ge] *etc vb V* **legar.**

leguleyo [legōōle'yo] *nm* (*pey*) shyster (*US*) *o* petty (*Brit*) lawyer.

legumbres [legōōm'bres] *nfpl* vegetables.

leído [leē'tḫo, á] *a* well-read.

lejanía [lehánē'á] *nf* distance.

lejano, a [lehá'no, á] *a* far-off; (*en el tiempo*) distant; (*fig*) remote; **L~ Oriente** Far East.

lejía [lehē'á] *nf* bleach.

lejísimos [lehē'sēmos] *ad* a long, long way.

lejos [le'hos] *ad* far, far away; **a lo** ~ in the distance; **de** *o* **desde** ~ from afar; **está muy** ~ it's a long way (away); ¿**está** ~? is it far?; ~ **de** *prep* far from.

lelo, a [le'lo, á] *a* silly ♦ *nm/f* idiot.

lema [le'má] *nm* motto; (*POL*) slogan.

lencería [lenserē'á] *nf* (*telas*) linen, drapery; (*ropa interior*) lingerie.

lendakari [lendáká'rē] *nm* head of the Basque Autonomous Government.

lengua [len'gwá] *nf* tongue; ~ **materna** mother tongue; ~ **de tierra** (*GEO*) spit *o* tongue of land; **dar a la** ~ to chatter; **morderse la** ~ to hold one's tongue; **sacar la** ~ **a uno** to stick one's tongue out at sb.

lenguado [lengwá'tḫo] *nm* sole.

lenguaje [lengwá'he] *nm* language; (*forma de hablar*) (mode of) speech; ~ **comercial** business language; ~ **ensamblador/de alto**

nivel (*INFORM*) assembly/high-level language; ~ **máquina** (*INFORM*) machine language; ~ **original** source language; ~ **periodístico** journalese; ~ **de programación** (*INFORM*) programming language; **en** ~ **llano** ≈ in plain English.

lenguaraz [lengwáràs'] *a* talkative; (*pey*) foul-mouthed.

lengüeta [lengwe'tá] *nf* (*ANAT*) epiglottis; (*de zapatos*) tongue; (*MUS*) reed.

lenidad [lenẽthàth'] *nf* lenience.

Leningrado [lenẽngrá'tho] *nm* Leningrad.

lente [len'te] *nm o nf* lens; (*lupa*) magnifying glass; ~**s** *pl* glasses; ~**s de contacto** contact lenses.

lenteja [lente'há] *nf* lentil.

lentejuela [lentehwe'lá] *nf* sequin.

lentilla [lentẽ'yá] *nf* contact lens.

lentitud [lentẽtōōth'] *nf* slowness; **con** ~ slowly.

lento, a [len'to, á] *a* slow.

leña [le'nyá] *nf* firewood; **dar** ~ **a** to thrash; **echar** ~ **al fuego** to add fuel to the flames.

leñador, a [lenyàthor', á] *nm/f* woodcutter.

leño [le'nyo] *nm* (*trozo de árbol*) log; (*madera*) timber; (*fig*) blockhead.

Leo [le'o] *nm* (*ASTRO*) Leo.

león [leon'] *nm* lion; ~ **marino** sea lion.

leonera [leone'rá] *nf* (*jaula*) lion's cage; **parece una** ~ it's shockingly dirty.

leonés, esa [leones', esá] *a*, *nm/f* Leonese ♦ *nm* (*LING*) Leonese.

leonino, a [leonẽ'no, á] *a* leonine.

leontina [leontẽ'ná] *nf* watch chain.

leopardo [leopár'tho] *nm* leopard.

leotardos [leotár'thos] *nmpl* tights.

lepra [le'prá] *nf* leprosy.

leproso, a [lepro'so, á] *nm/f* leper.

lerdo, a [ler'tho, á] *a* (*lento*) slow; (*patoso*) clumsy.

leridano, a [lerẽthà'no, á] *a of o from* Lérida ♦ *nm/f* native *o* inhabitant of Lérida.

les [les] *pron* (*directo*) them; (: *ustedes*) you; (*indirecto*) to them; (: *ustedes*) to you.

lesbiana [lesbyà'ná] *nf* lesbian.

lesión [lesyon'] *nf* wound, lesion; (*DEPORTE*) injury.

lesionado, a [lesyoná'tho, á] *a* injured ♦ *nm/f* injured person.

lesionar [lesyonár'] *vt* (*dañar*) to hurt; (*herir*) to wound; ~**se** *vr* to get hurt.

letal [letál'] *a* lethal.

letanía [letánẽ'á] *nf* litany; (*retahíla*) long list.

letárgico, a [letár'hẽko, á] *a* lethargic.

letargo [letár'go] *nm* lethargy.

Letonia [leto'nyá] *nf* Latvia.

letra [le'trá] *nf* letter; (*escritura*) handwriting; (*COM*) letter, bill, draft; (*MUS*) lyrics *pl*; ~**s** *nfpl* (*UNIV*) arts; ~ **bastardilla/negrilla** italics *pl*/bold type; ~ **de cambio** bill of exchange; ~ **de imprenta** print; ~ **inicial/mayúscula/minúscula** initial/capital/small letter; **lo tomó al pie de la** ~ he took it literally; ~ **bancaria** (*COM*) bank draft; ~ **de patente** (*COM*) letters patent *pl*; **escribir 4** ~**s a uno** to drop a line to sb.

letrado, a [letrá'tho, á] *a* learned; (*fam*) pedantic ♦ *nm/f* lawyer.

letrero [letre'ro] *nm* (*cartel*) sign; (*etiqueta*) label.

letrina [letrẽ'ná] *nf* latrine.

leucemia [leōōse'myá] *nf* leukemia (*US*), leukaemia (*Brit*).

leva [le'há] *nf* (*NAUT*) weighing anchor; (*MIL*) recruiting; (*TEC*) lever.

levadizo, a [leháthẽ'so, á] *a*: **puente** ~ drawbridge.

levadura [leháthōō'rá] *nf* yeast, leaven; ~ **de cerveza** brewer's yeast.

levantamiento [lehántámyen'to] *nm* raising, lifting; (*rebelión*) revolt, uprising; (*GEO*) survey; ~ **de pesos** weightlifting.

levantar [lehántár'] *vt* (*gen*) to raise; (*del suelo*) to pick up; (*hacia arriba*) to lift (up); (*plan*) to make, draw up; (*mesa*) to clear; (*campamento*) to strike; (*fig*) to cheer up, hearten; ~**se** *vr* to get up; (*enderezarse*) to straighten up; (*rebelarse*) to rebel; (*sesión*) to be adjourned; (*niebla*) to lift; (*viento*) to rise; ~**se (de la cama)** to get up, get out of bed; ~ **el ánimo** to cheer up.

levante [lehàn'te] *nm* east; (*viento*) east wind; **el L**~ *region of Spain extending from Castellón to Murcia.*

levantino, a [lehántẽ'no, á] *a of o* from the *Levante* ♦ *nm/f*: **los** ~**s** the people of the *Levante*.

levar [lehár'] *vi* to weigh anchor.

leve [le'he] *a* light; (*fig*) trivial; (*mínimo*) slight.

levedad [lehethàth'] *nf* lightness; (*fig*) levity.

levita [lehẽ'tá] *nf* frock coat.

léxico, a [lek'sẽko, á] *a* lexical ♦ *nm* (*vocabulario*) vocabulary; (*LING*) lexicon.

ley [leẽ] *nf* (*gen*) law; (*metal*) standard; **decreto-**~ decree law; **de buena** ~ (*fig*) genuine; **según la** ~ in accordance with the law, by law, in law.

leyenda [leyen'dá] *nf* legend; (*TIP*) inscription.

leyendo [leyen'do] *etc vb* V **leer**.

liar [lẽár'] *vt* to tie (up); (*unir*) to bind; (*envolver*) to wrap (up); (*enredar*) to confuse; (*cigarrillo*) to roll; ~**se** *vr* (*fam*) to get involved; (*confundirse*) to get mixed up; ~**se a palos** to get involved in a fight.

lib. *abr* (= *libro*) bk.

libanés, esa |lĕḥánes', csä| *a, nm/f* Lebanese.

Líbano |lĕ'ḥáno| *nm*: **el** ~ the Lebanon.

libar |lĕḥár'| *vt* to suck.

libelo |lĕḥe'lo| *nm* satire, lampoon; (*JUR*) petition.

libélula |lĕḥe'loōlá| *nf* dragonfly.

liberación |lĕḥerásyon'| *nf* liberation; (*de la cárcel*) release.

liberado, a |lĕḥerá'ḥo, á| *a* liberated; (*COM*) paid-up.

liberal |lĕḥerál'| *a, nm/f* liberal.

liberalidad |lĕḥerálĕ'ḥáḥ'| *nf* liberality, generosity.

liberar |lĕḥerár'| *vt* to liberate.

libertad |lĕḥertáḥ'| *nf* liberty, freedom; ~ **de asociación/de culto/de prensa/de comercio/de palabra** freedom of association/of worship/of the press/of trade/of speech; ~ **condicional** probation; ~ **bajo palabra** parole; ~ **bajo fianza** bail; **estar en** ~ to be free; **poner a uno en** ~ to set sb free.

libertador, a |lĕḥertáḥor', á| *a* liberating ♦ *nm/f* liberator.

libertar |lĕḥertár'| *vt* (*preso*) to set free; (*de una obligación*) to release; (*eximir*) to exempt.

libertino, a |lĕḥertē'no, á| *a* permissive ♦ *nm/f* permissive person.

Libia |lĕ'ḥyá| *nf* Libya.

libio, a |lĕ'ḥyo, á| *a, nm/f* Libyan.

libra |lĕ'ḥrá| *nf* pound; **L**~ (*ASTRO*) Libra; ~ **esterlina** pound sterling.

librador, a |lĕḥráḥor', á| *nm/f* drawer.

libramiento |lĕḥrámyen'to| *nm* rescue; (*COM*) delivery.

libranza |lĕḥrán'sá| *nf* (*COM*) draft; (*letra de cambio*) bill of exchange.

librar |lĕḥrár'| *vt* (*de peligro*) to save; (*batalla*) to wage, fight; (*de impuestos*) to exempt; (*cheque*) to make out; (*JUR*) to exempt; ~**se** *vr*: ~**se de** to escape from, free o.s. from; **de buena nos hemos librado** we're well out of that.

libre |lĕ'ḥre| *a* (*gen*) free; (*lugar*) unoccupied; (*tiempo*) spare; (*asiento*) vacant; (*COM*): ~ **a bordo** free on board; ~ **de franqueo** postage-free; ~ **de impuestos** free of tax; **tiro** ~ free kick; **los 100 metros** ~ the 100 meters free-style (race); **al aire** ~ in the open air; **¿estás** ~**?** are you free?

librecambio |lĕḥrekàm'byo| *nm* free trade.

librecambista |lĕḥrekámbē'stá| *a* free-trade *cpd* ♦ *nm* free-trader.

librería |lĕḥrerē'á| *nf* (*tienda*) bookstore (*US*), bookshop (*Brit*); (*estante*) bookcase; ~ **de ocasión** secondhand bookshop.

librero, a |lĕḥre'ro, á| *nm/f* bookseller.

libreta |lĕḥre'tá| *nf* notebook; (*pan*) one-pound loaf; ~ **de ahorros** savings book.

libro |lĕ'ḥro| *nm* book; ~ **de actas** minute book; ~ **de bolsillo** paperback; ~ **de cabecera** bedside book; ~ **de caja** (*COM*) cashbook; ~ **de caja auxiliar** (*COM*) petty cash book; ~ **de cocina** cookbook; ~ **de consulta** reference book; ~ **de cuentas** account book; ~ **de cuentos** storybook; ~ **de cheques** check (*US*) o cheque (*Brit*) book; ~ **diario** journal; ~ **de entradas y salidas** (*COM*) daybook; ~ **de honor** visitors' book; ~ **mayor** (*COM*) general ledger; ~ **de reclamaciones** complaints book; ~ **de texto** textbook.

Lic. *abr* = **Licenciado, a**.

licencia |lĕscn'syá| *nf* (*gen*) license (*US*), licence (*Brit*); (*permiso*) permission; ~ **por enfermedad/con goce de sueldo** sick/paid leave; ~ **de armas/de caza** gun/game license; ~ **de exportación** (*COM*) export license; ~ **poética** poetic license.

licenciado, a |lĕscnsyá'ḥo, á| *a* licensed ♦ *nm/f* graduate; **L**~ **en Filosofía y Letras** Bachelor of Arts.

licenciar |lĕscnsyár'| *vt* (*empleado*) to dismiss; (*permitir*) to permit, allow; (*soldado*) to discharge; (*estudiante*) to confer a degree upon; ~**se** *vr*: ~**se en letras** to get an arts degree.

licenciatura |lĕscnsyátoō'rá| *nf* (*título*) degree; (*estudios*) course of study (*US*), degree course (*Brit*).

licencioso, a |lĕscnsyo'so, á| *a* licentious.

liceo |lĕsc'o| *nm* (high) school.

licitación |lĕsctásyon'| *nf* bidding; (*oferta*) tender, offer.

licitador |lĕsctáḥor'| *nm* bidder; (*AM*) auctioneer.

licitante |lĕsctán'tc| *nm* bidder.

licitar |lĕsctár'| *vt* to bid for; (*AM*) to sell by auction ♦ *vi* to bid.

lícito, a |lĕ'scto, á| *a* (*legal*) lawful; (*justo*) fair, just; (*permisible*) permissible.

licor |lĕkor'| *nm* liquor (*US*), spirits *pl* (*Brit*); (*con hierbas etc*) liqueur.

licuadora |lĕkwáḥo'rá| *nf* blender.

licuar |lĕkwár'| *vt* to liquidize.

lid |lĕḥ| *nf* combat; (*fig*) controversy.

líder |lĕ'ḥer| *nm/f* leader.

liderato |lĕḥerá'to| *nm* leadership.

lidia |lĕ'ḥyá| *nf* bullfighting; (*una* ~) bullfight; **toros de** ~ fighting bulls.

lidiar |lĕḥyár'| *vt, vi* to fight.

liebre |lyc'ḥrc| *nf* hare; **dar gato por** ~ to con.

Lieja |lyc'há| *nf* Liège.

lienzo |lyen'so| *nm* linen; (*ARTE*) canvas; (*ARQ*) wall.

lifting |lĕf'tēn| *nm* facelift.

liga |lĕ'gá| *nf* (*de medias*) garter, suspender; (*confederación*) league; (*AM*: *gomita*)

rubber band.
ligadura [lēgáthōō'rá] *nf* bond, tie; (*MED, MUS*) ligature.
ligamento [lēgámen'to] *nm* (*ANAT*) ligament; (*atadura*) tie; (*unión*) bond.
ligar [lēgár'] *vt* (*atar*) to tie; (*unir*) to join; (*MED*) to bind up; (*MUS*) to slur; (*fam*) to get off with, pick up ♦ *vi* to mix, blend; (*fam*) to get off with sb; (*2 personas*) to get off with one another; **~se** *vr* (*fig*) to commit o.s.; **~ con** (*fam*) to get off with, pick up; **~se a uno** to get off with o pick up sb.
ligereza [lēhere'sá] *nf* lightness; (*rapidez*) swiftness; (*agilidad*) agility; (*superficialidad*) flippancy.
ligero, a [lēhe'ro, á] *a* (*de peso*) light; (*tela*) thin; (*rápido*) swift, quick; (*ágil*) agile, nimble; (*de importancia*) slight; (*de carácter*) flippant, superficial ♦ *ad* quickly, swiftly; **a la ligera** superficially; **juzgar a la ligera** to jump to conclusions.
ligón [lēgon'] *nm* (*fam*) Romeo.
ligue [lē'ge] *etc vb* V **ligar** ♦ *nm/f* boyfriend/girlfriend ♦ *nm* (*persona*) pick-up.
liguero [lēge'ro] *nm* garter (*US*) o suspender (*Brit*) belt.
lija [lē'há] *nf* (*ZOOL*) dogfish; (**papel de**) **~** sandpaper.
Lila [lē'lá] *nf* Lille.
lila [lē'lá] *a inv, nf* lilac ♦ *nm* (*fam*) twit.
lima [lē'má] *nf* file; (*BOT*) lime; **~ de uñas** nail file; **comer como una ~** to eat like a horse.
limar [lēmár'] *vt* to file; (*alisar*) to smooth over; (*fig*) to polish up.
limitación [lēmētásyon'] *nf* limitation, limit; **~ de velocidad** speed limit.
limitado, a [lēmētá'tho, á] *a* limited; **sociedad limitada** (*COM*) corporation (*US*), limited company (*Brit*).
limitar [lēmētár'] *vt* to limit; (*reducir*) to reduce, cut down ♦ *vi*: **~ con** to border on; **~se** *vr*: **~se a** to limit o confine o.s. to.
límite [lē'mēte] *nm* (*gen*) limit; (*fin*) end; (*frontera*) border; **como ~** at (the) most; (*fecha*) at the latest; **no tener ~s** to know no bounds; **~ de crédito** (*COM*) credit limit; **~ de página** (*INFORM*) page break; **~ de velocidad** speed limit.
limítrofe [lēmē'trofe] *a* neighboring (*US*), neighbouring (*Brit*).
limón [lēmon'] *nm* lemon ♦ *a*: **amarillo ~** lemon-yellow.
limonada [lēmoná'thá] *nf* lemonade.
limonero [lēmone'ro] *nm* lemon tree.
limosna [lēmos'ná] *nf* alms *pl*; **pedir ~** to beg; **vivir de ~** to live on charity.
limpiabotas [lēmpyáḅo'tás] *nm/f inv* shoeshine boy/girl.
limpiacristales [lēmpyákrēstá'les] *nm inv*

(*detergente*) window cleaner.
limpiador, a [lēmpyáthor', á] *a* cleaning, cleansing ♦ *nm/f* cleaner.
limpiaparabrisas [lēmpyápáráḅrē'sás] *nm inv* windshield (*US*) o windscreen (*Brit*) wiper.
limpiar [lēmpyár'] *vt* to clean; (*con trapo*) to wipe; (*quitar*) to wipe away; (*zapatos*) to shine, polish; (*casa*) to tidy up; (*fig*) to clean up; (: *purificar*) to cleanse, purify; (*MIL*) to mop up; **~ en seco** to dry-clean.
limpieza [lēmpye'sá] *nf* (*estado*) cleanliness; (*acto*) cleaning; (: *de las calles*) cleansing; (: *de zapatos*) polishing; (*habilidad*) skill; (*fig: POLICÍA*) clean-up; (*pureza*) purity; (*MIL*): **operación de ~** mopping-up operation; **~ en seco** dry cleaning.
limpio, a [lēm'pyo, á] *a* clean; (*moralmente*) pure; (*ordenado*) tidy; (*despejado*) clear; (*COM*) clear, net; (*fam*) honest ♦ *ad*: **jugar ~** to play fair; **pasar a** (*Esp*) o **en** (*AM*) **~** to make a clean (*US*) o fair (*Brit*) copy; **sacar algo en ~** to get benefit from sth; **~ de** free from.
linaje [lēná'he] *nm* lineage, family.
linajudo, a [lēnáhōō'tho, á] *a* highborn, noble.
linaza [lēná'sá] *nf* linseed; **aceite de ~** linseed oil.
lince [lēn'se] *nm* lynx; **ser un ~** (*fig: observador*) to be very observant; (: *astuto*) to be shrewd.
linchar [lēntchár'] *vt* to lynch.
lindante [lēndán'te] *a* adjoining; **~ con** bordering on.
lindar [lēndár'] *vi* to adjoin; **~ con** to border on; (*ARQ*) to abut on.
linde [lēn'de] *nm* o *nf* boundary.
lindero, a [lēnde'ro, á] *a* adjoining ♦ *nm* boundary.
lindo, a [lēn'do, á] *a* pretty, lovely ♦ *ad*: **nos divertimos de lo ~** we had a wonderful time; **canta muy ~** (*AM*) he sings beautifully.
línea [lē'neá] *nf* (*gen, moral, POL etc*) line; (*talle*) figure; (*INFORM*): **en ~** on-line; **fuera de ~** off line; **~ de estado** status line; **~ de formato** format line; **~ aérea** airline; **~ de alto el fuego** ceasefire line; **~ de fuego** firing line; **~ de meta** goal line; (*de carrera*) finishing line; **~ de montaje** assembly line; **~ dura** (*POL*) hard line; **~ recta** straight line; **la ~ de 1989** (*moda*) the 1989 look.
lineal [lēneál'] *a* linear; (*INFORM*) on-line.
lingote [lēngo'te] *nm* ingot.
lingüista [lēngwē'stá] *nm/f* linguist.
lingüística [lēngwē'stēká] *nf* linguistics *sg*.
linimento [lēnēmen'to] *nm* liniment.
lino [lē'no] *nm* linen; (*BOT*) flax.

linóleo [lēno'leo] *nm* linoleum.

linterna [lēnter'ná] *nf* lantern, lamp; ~ **eléctrica** *o* **a pilas** flashlight (*US*), torch (*Brit*).

lío [lē'o] *nm* bundle; (*desorden*) muddle, mess; (*fam: follón*) fuss; (: *relación amorosa*) affair; **armar un** ~ to make a fuss; **meterse en un** ~ to get into a jam; **tener un** ~ **con uno** to be having an affair with sb.

liquen [lē'ken] *nm* lichen.

liquidación [lēkēthásyon'] *nf* liquidation; (*cuenta*) settlement; **venta de** ~ clearance sale.

liquidar [lēkēthár'] *vt* (*QUÍMICA*) to liquefy; (*COM*) to liquidate; (*deudas*) to pay off; (*empresa*) to sell off; ~ **a uno** to bump sb off, rub sb out (*fam*).

líquido, a [lē'kētho, á] *a* liquid; (*ganancia*) net ♦ *nm* liquid; (*COM: efectivo*) ready cash *o* money; (: *ganancia*) net amount *o* profit; ~ **imponible** net taxable income.

lira [lē'rá] *nf* (*MUS*) lyre; (*moneda*) lira.

lírico, a [lē'rēko, á] *a* lyrical.

lirio [lē'ryo] *nm* (*BOT*) iris.

lirismo [lērēs'mo] *nm* lyricism; (*sentimentalismo*) sentimentality.

lirón [lēron'] *nm* (*ZOOL*) dormouse; (*fig*) sleepyhead.

Lisboa [lēsbo'á] *nf* Lisbon.

lisboeta [lēsboe'tá] *a* of *o* from Lisbon ♦ *nm/f* native *o* inhabitant of Lisbon.

lisiado, a [lēsyá'tho, á] *a* injured ♦ *nm/f* cripple.

lisiar [lēsyár'] *vt* to maim; ~**se** *vr* to injure o.s.

liso, a [lē'so, á] *a* (*terreno*) flat; (*cabello*) straight; (*superficie*) even; (*tela*) plain; **lisa y llanamente** in plain language, plainly.

lisonja [lēson'há] *nf* flattery.

lisonjear [lēsonheár'] *vt* to flatter; (*fig*) to please.

lisonjero, a [lēsonhe'ro, á] *a* flattering; (*agradable*) gratifying, pleasing ♦ *nm/f* flatterer.

lista [lē'stá] *nf* list; (*de alumnos*) school list (*US*) *o* register (*Brit*); (*de libros*) catalog(ue); (*de correos*) poste restante; (*de platos*) menu; (*de precios*) price list; **pasar** ~ to call the roll; (*ESCOL*) to call roll (*US*) *o* the register (*Brit*); ~ **de correos** general delivery (*US*), poste restante (*Brit*); ~ **de direcciones** mailing list; ~ **electoral** list of voters (*US*), electoral roll (*Brit*); ~ **de espera** waiting list; **tela a** ~**s** striped material.

listado, a [lēstá'tho, á] *a* striped ♦ *nm* (*COM, INFORM*) listing; ~ **paginado** (*INFORM*) paged listing.

listar [lēstár'] *vt* (*INFORM*) to list.

listo, a [lē'sto, á] *a* (*perspicaz*) smart, clever; (*preparado*) ready; ~ **para usar** ready-to-use; **¿estás** ~**?** are you ready?; **pasarse de** ~ to be too smart for one's britches.

listón [lēston'] *nm* (*tela*) ribbon; (*de madera, metal*) strip.

litera [lēte'rá] *nf* (*en barco, tren*) berth; (*en dormitorio*) bunk, bunk bed.

literal [lēterál'] *a* literal.

literario, a [lēterá'ryo, á] *a* literary.

literato, a [lēterá'to, á] *nm/f* writer.

literatura [lēterátōō'rá] *nf* literature.

litigante [lētēgán'te] *nm/f* litigant, claimant.

litigar [lētēgár'] *vt* to fight ♦ *vi* (*JUR*) to go to court; (*fig*) to dispute, argue.

litigio [lētē'hyo] *nm* (*JUR*) lawsuit; (*fig*): **en** ~ **con** in dispute with.

litigue [lētē'ge] *etc vb* V **litigar**.

litografía [lētografē'á] *nf* lithography; (*una* ~) lithograph.

litoral [lētorál'] *a* coastal ♦ *nm* coast, seaboard.

litro [lē'tro] *nm* liter (*US*), litre (*Brit*).

Lituania [lētwá'nyá] *nf* Lithuania.

liturgia [lētōōr'hyá] *nf* liturgy.

liviano, a [lēvyá'no, á] *a* (*persona*) fickle; (*cosa, objeto*) trivial.

lívido, a [lē'vētho, á] *a* livid.

líving [lē'vēn], *pl* **livings** *nm* living room.

ll... V bajo la letra LL, después de L.

lo [lo] *artículo definido neutro*: ~ **bueno** the good; ~ **mío** what is mine; ~ **difícil es que** ... the difficult thing about it is that ...; **no saben** ~ **aburrido que es** they don't know how boring it is; **viste a** ~ **americano** he dresses in the American style ♦ *pron* (*persona*) him; (*cosa*) it; ~ **de** that matter of; ~ **que** what, that which; **toma** ~ **que quieras** take what(ever) you want; ~ **que sea** whatever; **¡toma** ~ **que he dicho!** I stand by what I said!

loa [lo'á] *nf* praise.

loable [loá'ble] *a* praiseworthy.

LOAPA [loá'pá] *nf abr* (*Esp JUR*) = *Ley Orgánica de Armonización del Proceso Autónomo.*

loar [loár'] *vt* to praise.

lobato [lobá'to] *nm* (*ZOOL*) wolf cub.

lobo [lo'bo] *nm* wolf; ~ **de mar** (*fig*) salty old sailor; ~ **marino** seal.

lóbrego, a [lo'brego, á] *a* dark; (*fig*) gloomy.

lóbulo [lo'bōōlo] *nm* lobe.

LOC *nm abr* (= *lector óptico de caracteres*) OCR.

locación [locásyon'] *nf* lease.

local [lokál'] *a* local ♦ *nm* place, site; (*oficinas*) premises *pl*.

localice [lokálē'se] *etc vb* V **localizar**.

localidad [lokálētháth'] *nf* (*barrio*) locality; (*lugar*) location; (*TEATRO*) seat, ticket.

localizar [lokálēsár'] *vt* (*ubicar*) to locate, find; (*encontrar*) to find, track down; (*restringir*) to localize; (*situar*) to place.

loción [losyon'] *nf* lotion, wash.

loco, a [lo'ko, á] *a* mad; (*fig*) wild, mad ♦ *nm/f* lunatic, madman/woman; ~ **de atar**, (*AM*) ~ **rematado** raving mad; **a lo** ~ without rhyme or reason; **ando** ~ **con el examen** the exam is driving me crazy; **estar** ~ **de alegría** to be overjoyed *o* over the moon.

locomoción [lokomosyon'] *nf* locomotion.

locomotora [lokomoto'rá] *nf* engine, locomotive.

locuaz [lokwás'] *a* loquacious, talkative.

locución [lokōōsyon'] *nf* expression.

locura [lokōō'rá] *nf* madness; (*acto*) crazy act.

locutor, a [lokōōtor', á] *nm/f* (*RADIO*) announcer; (*comentarista*) commentator; (*TV*) newscaster.

locutorio [lokōōto'ryo] *nm* (*TELEC*) telephone booth.

lodo [lo'do] *nm* mud.

logia [lo'hyá] *nf* (*MIL, de masones*) lodge; (*ARQ*) loggia.

lógico, a [lo'hēko, á] *a* logical; (*correcto*) natural; (*razonable*) reasonable ♦ *nm* logician ♦ *nf* logic; **es** ~ **que** ... it stands to reason that ...; **ser de una lógica aplastante** to be as clear as day.

logística [lohē'stēká] *nf* logistics *pl*.

lograr [lográr'] *vt* (*obtener*) to get, obtain; (*conseguir*) to achieve, attain; ~ **hacer** to manage to do; ~ **que uno venga** to manage to get sb to come; ~ **acceso a** (*INFORM*) to access.

logro [lo'gro] *nm* achievement, success; (*COM*) profit.

logroñés, esa [logronyes', esá] *a* of *o* from Logroño ♦ *nm/f* native *o* inhabitant of Logroño.

Loira [lo'ērá] *nm* Loire.

loma [lo'má] *nf* hillock, low ridge.

Lombardía [lombárthē'á] *nf* Lombardy.

lombriz [lombrēs'] *nf* (earth)worm.

lomo [lo'mo] *nm* (*de animal*) back; (*CULIN*: *de cerdo*) pork loin; (: *de vaca*) rib steak; (*de libro*) spine.

lona [lo'ná] *nf* canvas.

loncha [lontch'á] *nf* = **lonja**.

lonche [lontch'e] *nm* (*AM*) lunch.

lonchería [lontcherē'á] *nf* (*AM*) diner (*US*), snack bar.

londinense [londēnen'se] *a* London *cpd*, of *o* from London ♦ *nm/f* Londoner.

Londres [lon'dres] *nm* London.

longaniza [longánē'sá] *nf* pork sausage.

longitud [lonhētōōth'] *nf* length; (*GEO*) longitude; **tener 3 metros de** ~ to be 3 meters long; ~ **de onda** wavelength; **salto**

de ~ long jump.

lonja [lon'há] *nf* slice; (*de tocino*) rasher; (*COM*) market, exchange; ~ **de pescado** fish market.

lontananza [lontánán'sá] *nf* background; **en** ~ far away, in the distance.

loor [loor'] *nm* praise.

Lorena [lore'ná] *nf* Lorraine.

loro [lo'ro] *nm* parrot.

los [los] *artículo definido mpl* the ♦ *pron* them; (*ustedes*) you; **mis libros y** ~ **de usted** my books and yours.

losa [lo'sá] *nf* stone; ~ **sepulcral** gravestone.

lote [lo'te] *nm* portion, share; (*COM*) lot; (*INFORM*) batch.

lotería [loterē'á] *nf* lottery; (*juego*) lotto; **le tocó la** ~ he won a big prize in the lottery; (*fig*) he got lucky; ~ **nacional** national lottery; ~ **primitiva** (*Esp*) *type of state-run lottery*.

lotero, a [lote'ro, á] *nm/f* seller of lottery tickets.

Lovaina [lohá'ēná] *nf* Louvain.

loza [lo'sá] *nf* crockery; ~ **fina** china.

lozanía [losánē'á] *nf* (*lujo*) luxuriance.

lozano, a [losá'no, á] *a* luxuriant; (*animado*) lively.

lubina [lōōbē'ná] *nf* (*ZOOL*) sea bass.

lubricante [lōōbrēkán'te] *a, nm* lubricant.

lubricar [lōōbrēkár'], **lubrificar** [lōōbrēfēkár'] *vt* to lubricate.

lubrifique [lōōbrēfē'ke] *etc vb V* **lubrificar**.

lubrique [lōōbrē'ke] *etc vb V* **lubricar**.

lucense [lōōsen'se] *a* of *o* from Lugo ♦ *nm/f* native *o* inhabitant of Lugo.

Lucerna [lōōser'ná] *nf* Lucerne.

lucero [lōōse'ro] *nm* (*ASTRO*) bright star; (*fig*) brilliance; ~ **del alba/de la tarde** morning/evening star.

luces [lōō'ses] *nfpl de* **luz**.

lucidez [lōōsēthes'] *nf* lucidity.

lucido, a [lōōsē'tho, á] *a* (*espléndido*) splendid, brilliant; (*elegante*) elegant; (*exitoso*) successful.

lúcido, a [lōō'sētho, á] *a* lucid.

luciérnaga [lōōsyer'nágá] *nf* glow-worm.

lucimiento [lōōsēmyen'to] *nm* (*brillo*) brilliance; (*éxito*) success.

lucio [lōō'syo] *nm* (*ZOOL*) pike.

lucir [lōōsēr'] *vt* to illuminate, light (up); (*ostentar*) to show off ♦ *vi* (*brillar*) to shine; ~**se** *vr* (*irónico*) to make a fool of o.s.; (*ostentarse*) to show off.

lucrativo, a [lōōkrátē'ho, á] *a* lucrative, profitable; **institución no lucrativa** non profit-making institution.

lucro [lōō'kro] *nm* profit, gain; ~**s y daños** (*COM*) profit and loss *sg*.

luctuoso, a [lōōktwo'so, á] *a* mournful.

lucha [lōōtch'á] *nf* fight, struggle; ~ **de clases** class struggle; ~ **libre** wrestling.

luchar [lōōtchàr'] *vi* to fight.

luego [lwe'g̣o] *ad* (*después*) next; (*más tarde*) later, afterwards; **desde ~** of course; **¡hasta ~!** see you later!, so long!; **¿y ~?** what next?

lugar [lōōg̣àr'] *nm* place; (*sitio*) spot; (*pueblo*) village, town; **en ~ de** instead of; **en primer ~** in the first place, firstly; **dar ~ a** to give rise to; **hacer ~** to make room; **fuera de ~** out of place; **tener ~** to take place; **~ común** commonplace; **yo en su ~** if I were him; **no hay ~ para preocupaciones** there is no cause for concern.

lugareño, a [lōōg̣àre'nyo, à] *a* village *cpd* ♦ *nm/f* villager.

lugarteniente [lōōg̣àrtenyen'te] *nm* deputy.

lúgubre [lōō'g̣ōōbre] *a* mournful.

lujo [lōō'ho] *nm* luxury; (*fig*) profusion, abundance; **de ~** luxury *cpd*, de luxe.

lujoso, a [lōōho'so, à] *a* luxurious.

lujuria [lōōhōō'ryà] *nf* lust.

lumbre [lōōm'bre] *nf* (*luz*) light; (*fuego*) fire; **cerca de la ~** near the fire, at the fireside; **¿tienes ~?** (*para cigarro*) have you got a light?

lumbrera [lōōmbre'rà] *nf* luminary; (*fig*) leading light.

luminoso, a [lōōmēno'so, à] *a* luminous, shining; (*idea*) bright, brilliant.

luna [lōō'nà] *nf* moon; (*vidrio: escaparate*) plate glass; (*: de un espejo*) glass; (*: de gafas*) lens; (*fig*) crescent; **~ creciente/llena/menguante/nueva** crescent/full/waning/new moon; **~ de miel** honeymoon; **estar en la ~** to have one's head in the clouds.

lunar [lōōnàr'] *a* lunar ♦ *nm* (*ANAT*) mole; **tela a ~es** spotted material.

lunes [lōō'nes] *nm inv* Monday.

luneta [lōōne'tà] *nf* lens.

lupa [lōō'pà] *nf* magnifying glass.

lusitano, a [lōōsētà'no, à], **luso, a** [lōō'so, à] *a, nm/f* Portuguese.

lustrar [lōōstràr'] *vt* (*mueble*) to polish; (*zapatos*) to shine.

lustre [lōōs'tre] *nm* polish; (*fig*) luster (*US*), lustre (*Brit*); **dar ~ a** to polish.

lustro [lōōs'tro] *nm* period of five years.

lustroso, a [lōōstro'so, à] *a* shining.

luterano, a [lōōterà'no, à] *a* Lutheran.

luto [lōō'to] *nm* mourning; (*congoja*) grief, sorrow; **llevar el** *o* **vestirse de ~** to be in mourning.

luxación [lōōksàsyon'] *nf* (*MED*) dislocation; **tener una ~ de tobillo** to have a dislocated ankle.

Luxemburgo [lōōksembōōr'g̣o] *nm* Luxembourg.

luz [lōōs], *pl* **luces** *nf* (*tb fig*) light; (*fam*) electricity; **dar a ~ un niño** to give birth to a child; **sacar a la ~** to bring to light;

dar la ~ to switch on the light; **encender** (*Esp*) *o* **prender** (*AM*)**/apagar la ~** to switch the light on/off; **les cortaron la ~** their (electricity) supply was cut off; **a la ~ de** in the light of; **a todas luces** by any reckoning; **hacer la ~ sobre** to shed light on; **tener pocas luces** to be dim *o* stupid; **~ de la luna/del sol** *o* **solar** moonlight/sunlight; **~ eléctrica** electric light; **~ roja/verde** red/green light; **~ de cruce** (*AUTO*) low-beam (*US*) *o* dipped (*Brit*) headlight; **~ de freno** brake light; **~ intermitente/trasera** flashing/rear light; **luces de tráfico** traffic lights; **el Siglo de las Luces** the Age of Enlightenment; **traje de luces** bullfighter's costume.

luzca [lōōs'kà] *etc vb V* **lucir**.

LL

Ll, ll [e'ye] *nf* (*letra*) Ll, ll.

llaga [yà'g̣à] *nf* wound.

llagar [yàg̣àr'] *vt* to make sore; (*herir*) to wound.

llague [yà'g̣e] *etc vb V* **llagar**.

llama [yà'mà] *nf* flame; (*fig*) passion; (*ZOOL*) llama; **en ~s** burning, ablaze.

llamada [yàmà'ṭhà] *nf* call; (*a la puerta*) knock; (*: timbre*) ring; **~ a cobro revertido** collect (*US*) *o* reverse-charge (*Brit*) call; **~ al orden** call to order; **~ a pie de página** reference note; **~ a procedimiento** (*INFORM*) procedure call; **~ interurbana** long-distance call.

llamamiento [yàmàmyen'to] *nm* call; **hacer un ~ a uno para que haga algo** to appeal to sb to do sth.

llamar [yàmàr'] *vt* to call; (*convocar*) to summon; (*invocar*) to invoke; (*atraer con gesto*) to beckon; (*atención*) to attract; (*TELEC: tb: ~ por teléfono*) to call, telephone; (*MIL*) to call ♦ *vi* (*por teléfono*) to telephone; (*a la puerta*) to knock; (*por señas*) to beckon; **~se** *vr* to be called, be named; **¿cómo se llama usted?** what's your name?; **¿quién llama?** (*TELEC*) who's calling?, who's that?; **no me llama la atención** (*fam*) it doesn't appeal to me.

llamarada [yàmàrà'ṭhà] *nf* (*llamas*) blaze; (*rubor*) flush; (*fig*) flare-up.

llamativo, a [yàmàtē'ṿo, à] *a* showy; (*color*) loud.

llamear [yàmeàr'] *vi* to blaze.

llanamente [yànàmen'te] *ad* (*lisamente*)

smoothly; (*sin ostentaciones*) plainly; (*sinceramente*) frankly; *V tb* **liso**.

llaneza [yànc'sá] *nf* (*gen*) simplicity; (*honestidad*) straightforwardness, frankness.

llano, a [yá'no, á] *a* (*superficie*) flat; (*persona*) straightforward; (*estilo*) clear ♦ *nm* plain, flat ground.

llanta [yàn'tá] *nf* (wheel) rim; (*AM: tb*: ~ **de goma**) tire (*US*), tyre (*Brit*); (: *cámara*) inner (tube).

llanto [yàn'to] *nm* weeping; (*fig*) lamentation; (*canción*) dirge, lament.

llanura [yànōō'rá] *nf* (*lisura*) flatness, smoothness; (*GEO*) plain.

llave [yà'hc] *nf* key; (*de gas, agua*) faucet (*US*), tap (*Brit*); (*MECÁNICA*) wrench; (*de la luz*) switch; (*MUS*) key; ~ **inglesa** monkey wrench; ~ **maestra** master key; ~ **de contacto** (*AUTO*) ignition key; ~ **de paso** stopcock; **echar** ~ **a** to lock up.

llavero [yàhc'ro] *nm* keyring.

llavín [yàhĕn'] *nm* latchkey.

llegada [ycgá'thá] *nf* arrival.

llegar [ycgár'] *vt* to bring up, bring over ♦ *vi* to arrive; (*bastar*) to be enough; ~**se** *vr*: ~**se a** to approach; ~ **a** (*alcanzar*) to reach; to manage to, succeed in; ~ **a saber** to find out; ~ **a ser famoso/el jefe** to become famous/the boss; ~ **a las manos** to come to blows; ~ **a las manos de** to come into the hands of; **no llegues tarde** don't be late; **esta cuerda no llega** this rope isn't long enough.

llegue [yc'gc] *etc vb V* **llegar**.

llenar [ycnár'] *vt* to fill; (*superficie*) to cover; (*espacio, tiempo*) to fill, take up; (*formulario*) to fill in *o* out; (*deber*) to fulfil; (*fig*) to heap; ~**se** *vr* to fill (up); ~**se de** (*fam*) to stuff o.s. with.

lleno, a [yc'no, á] *a* full, filled; (*repleto*) full up ♦ *nm* (*abundancia*) abundance; (*TEATRO*) full house; **dar de** ~ **contra un muro** to hit a wall head-on.

llevadero, a [ycàthc'ro, á] *a* bearable, tolerable.

llevar [ycbár'] *vt* to take; (*ropa*) to wear; (*cargar*) to carry; (*quitar*) to take away; (*en coche*) to drive; (*transportar*) to transport; (*ruta*) to follow, keep to; (*traer: dinero*) to carry; (*suj: camino etc*): ~ **a** to lead to; (*MAT*) to carry; (*aguantar*) to bear; (*negocio*) to conduct, direct; to manage; ~**se** *vr* to carry off, take away; **llevamos dos días aquí** we have been here for two days; **él me lleva 2 años** he's 2 years older than me; ~ **adelante** (*fig*) to carry forward; ~ **por delante a uno** (*en coche etc*) to run sb over; (*fig*) to ride roughshod over sb; ~ **la ventaja** to be winning *o* in the lead; ~ **los libros** (*COM*)

to keep the books; **llevo las de perder** I'm likely to lose; **no las lleva todas consigo** he's not all there; **nos llevó a cenar fuera** she took us out for a meal; ~**se a uno por delante** (*atropellar*) to run sb over; ~**se bien** to get on well (together).

llorar [yorár'] *vt* to cry, weep ♦ *vi* to cry, weep; (*ojos*) to water; ~ **a moco tendido** to sob one's heart out; ~ **de risa** to cry with laughter.

lloriquear [yorĕkcár'] *vi* to snivel, whimper.

lloro [yo'ro] *nm* crying, weeping.

llorón, ona [yoron', oná] *a* tearful ♦ *nm/f* cry-baby.

lloroso, a [yoro'so, á] *a* (*gen*) weeping, tearful; (*triste*) sad, sorrowful.

llover [yohĕr'] *vi* to rain; ~ **a cántaros** *o* **a cubos** *o* **a mares** to rain cats and dogs, pour (down); **ser una cosa llovida del cielo** to be a godsend; **llueve sobre mojado** it never rains but it pours.

llovizna [yohĕs'ná] *nf* drizzle.

lloviznar [yohĕsnár'] *vi* to drizzle.

llueve [ywc'hc] *etc vb V* **llover**.

lluvia [yōō'hyá] *nf* rain; (*cantidad*) rainfall; (*fig: balas etc*) hail, shower; ~ **radioactiva** radioactive fallout; **día de** ~ rainy day; **una** ~ **de regalos** a shower of gifts.

lluvioso, a [yōōhyo'so, á] *a* rainy.

M

M, m [c'mc] *nf* (*letra*) M, m; **M de Madrid** M for Mike.

M. *abr* (*FERRO*) = **Metro**.

m. *abr* (= *metro(s)*) m; (= *minuto(s)*) min., m; (= *masculino*) m., masc.

M.ª *abr* = **María**.

macabro, a [màká'hro, á] *a* macabre.

macaco [màká'ko] *nm* (*ZOOL*) rhesus monkey; (*fam*) runt, squirt.

macana [màká'ná] *nf* (*AM: porra*) club; (: *mentira*) lie, fib; (: *tontería*) piece of nonsense.

macanudo, a [màkánōō'tho, á] *a* (*AM fam*) great.

macarra [màká'rrá] *nm* (*fam*) thug.

macarrones [màkàrro'nes] *nmpl* macaroni *sg*.

macedonia [màsĕho'nyá] *nf*: ~ **de frutas** fruit salad.

macerar [màsĕrár'] *vt* (*CULIN*) to soak, macerate; ~**se** *vr* to soak, soften.

maceta [màsc'tá] *nf* (*de flores*) pot of flowers; (*para plantas*) flowerpot.

macetero [másete'ro] *nm* flowerpot stand *o* holder.

macilento, a [másēlen'to, á] *a* (*pálido*) pale; (*ojeroso*) haggard.

macizo, a [másē'so, á] *a* (*grande*) massive; (*fuerte, sólido*) solid ♦ *nm* mass, chunk; (*GEO*) massif.

macrobiótico, a [mákrobyo'tēko, á] *a* macrobiotic.

macro-comando [mákrokomán'do] *nm* (*INFORM*) macro (command).

macroeconomía [mákroekonomē'á] *nf* (*COM*) macroeconomics *sg*.

mácula [má'kōōlá] *nf* stain, blemish.

macuto [mákōō'to] *nm* (*MIL*) knapsack.

machacar [mátchákár'] *vt* to crush, pound; (*moler*) to grind (up); (*aplastar*) to mash ♦ *vi* (*insistir*) to go on, keep on.

machacón, ona [mátchakon', oná] *a* (*pesado*) tiresome; (*insistente*) insistent; (*monótono*) monotonous.

machamartillo [mátchámártē'yo]: **a ~** *ad*: **creer a ~** (*firmemente*) to believe firmly.

machaque [mátchá'ke] *etc vb* V **machacar**.

machete [mátche'te] *nm* (*AM*) machete, (large) knife.

machismo [mátchēs'mo] *nm* sexism; male chauvinism.

machista [mátchē'stá] *a, nm* sexist; male chauvinist.

macho [mátch'o] *a* male; (*fig*) virile ♦ *nm* male; (*fig*) he-man, tough guy (*US*); (*TEC*: *perno*) pin, peg; (*ELEC*) pin, plug; (*COSTURA*) hook.

machucar [mátchōōkár'] *vt* to pound.

machuque [mátchōō'ke] *etc vb* V **machucar**.

Madagascar [mátþágáskár'] *nm* Madagascar.

madeja [mátþe'há] *nf* (*de lana*) skein, hank.

madera [mátþe'rá] *nf* wood; (*fig*) nature, character; (: *aptitud*) aptitude; **una ~** a piece of wood; **~ contrachapada** *o* **laminada** plywood; **tiene buena ~** he's made of solid stuff; **tiene ~ de futbolista** he's got the makings of a football player.

maderaje [mátþerá'he], **maderamen** [mátþerá'men] *nm* timber; (*trabajo*) woodwork, timbering.

maderero [mátþere'ro] *nm* timber merchant.

madero [mátþe'ro] *nm* beam; (*fig*) ship.

madrastra [mátþrás'trá] *nf* stepmother.

madre [má'þre] *a* mother *cpd*; (*AM*) tremendous ♦ *nf* mother; (*de vino etc*) dregs *pl*; **~ adoptiva/política/soltera** foster mother/mother-in-law/unmarried mother; **sin ~** motherless; **¡~ mía!** oh dear!; **¡tu ~!** (*fam!*) fuck off! (*!*); **salirse de ~** (*río*) to burst its banks; (*persona*) to lose all

self-control.

madreperla [mátþreper'lá] *nf* mother-of-pearl.

madreselva [mátþresel'há] *nf* honeysuckle.

Madrid [mátþrēþ'] *n* Madrid.

madriguera [mátþrēge'rá] *nf* burrow.

madrileño, a [mátþrēle'nyo, á] *a* of *o* from Madrid ♦ *nm/f* native *o* inhabitant of Madrid.

Madriles [mátþrē'les] *nmpl*: **Los ~** (*fam*) Madrid *sg*.

madrina [mátþrē'ná] *nf* godmother; (*ARQ*) prop, shore; (*TEC*) brace; **~ de boda** bridesmaid.

madroño [mátþro'nyo] *nm* (*BOT*) strawberry tree, arbutus.

madrugada [mátþrōōgá'þá] *nf* early morning, wee small hours; (*alba*) dawn, daybreak; **a las 4 de la ~** at 4 o'clock in the morning.

madrugador, a [mátþrōōgáþor', á] *a* early-rising.

madrugar [mátþrōōgár'] *vi* to get up early; (*fig*) to get a head start.

madrugue [mátþrōō'ge] *etc vb* V **madrugar**.

madurar [mátþōōrár'] *vt, vi* (*fruta*) to ripen; (*fig*) to mature.

madurez [mátþōōres'] *nf* ripeness; (*fig*) maturity.

maduro, a [mátþōō'ro, á] *a* ripe; (*fig*) mature; **poco ~** unripe.

MAE *nm abr* (*Esp POL*)=*Ministerio de Asuntos Exteriores*.

maestra [máes'trá] *nf* V **maestro**.

maestría [máestrē'á] *nf* mastery; (*habilidad*) skill, expertise.

maestro, a [máes'tro, á] *a* masterly; (*perito*) skilled, expert; (*principal*) main; (*educado*) trained ♦ *nm/f* master/mistress; (*profesor*) teacher ♦ *nm* (*autoridad*) authority; (*MUS*) maestro; (*AM*) skilled workman; **~ albañil** master mason; **~ de obras** foreman.

mafioso [máfyo'so] *nm* (*AM*) gangster.

Magallanes [mágáyá'nes] *nm*: **Estrecho de ~** Strait of Magellan.

magia [má'hyá] *nf* magic.

mágico, a [má'hēko, á] *a* magic(al) ♦ *nm/f* magician.

magisterio [máhēste'ryo] *nm* (*enseñanza*) teaching; (*profesión*) teaching profession; (*maestros*) teachers *pl*.

magistrado [máhēstrá'þo] *nm* magistrate.

magistral [máhēstrál'] *a* magisterial; (*fig*) masterly.

magistratura [máhēstrátōō'rá] *nf* magistracy; **M~ del Trabajo** (*Esp*) ≈ Industrial Tribunal.

magnánimo, a [mágná'nēmo, á] *a* magnanimous.

magnate [mágná'te] *nm* magnate, tycoon;

~ **de la prensa** press baron.
magnesio [mågne'syo] *nm* (*QUÍMICA*) magnesium.
magnetice [mågnetē'se] *etc vb V* **magnetizar**.
magnético, a [mågne'tēko, á] *a* magnetic.
magnetizar [mågnetēsár'] *vt* to magnetize.
magnetofón [mågnetofon'], **magnetófono** [mågneto'fono] *nm* tape recorder.
magnetofónico, a [mågnetofo'nēco, á] *a*: **cinta magnetofónica** recording tape.
magnicidio [mågnēsē'thyo] *nm* assassination (*of an important person*).
magnífico, a [mågnē'fēko, á] *a* splendid, magnificent.
magnitud [mågnētōōth'] *nf* magnitude.
mago, a [má'go, á] *nm/f* magician, wizard; **los Reyes M~s** the Magi, the Three Wise Men.
magrear [mågreår'] *vt* (*fam*) to feel up.
magrez [mågres'] *nf* leanness.
magro, a [má'gro, á] *a* (*persona*) thin, lean; (*carne*) lean.
maguey [måge'ē] *nm* (*AM BOT*) agave.
magulladura [mågōōyáthōō'rá] *nf* bruise.
magullar [mågōōyár'] *vt* (*amoratar*) to bruise; (*dañar*) to damage; (*fam*: *golpear*) to bash, beat.
Maguncia [mågōōn'syá] *nf* Mainz.
mahometano, a [måometá'no, á] *a* Mohammedan.
mahonesa [måone'sá] *nf* = **mayonesa**.
maicena [måēsc'ná] *nf* cornflour, corn starch (*US*).
maillot [måyot'] *nm* bathing suit (*US*), swimming costume (*Brit*); (*DEPORTE*) vest.
maitre [mc'tre] *nm* head waiter.
maíz [måēs'] *nm* corn (*US*), maize (*Brit*); sweet corn.
majadero, a [måháthe'ro, á] *a* silly, stupid.
majar [måhár'] *vt* to crush, grind.
majareta [måhåre'tá] *a* (*fam*) cracked, nuts.
majestad [måhestáth'] *nf* majesty; **Su M~** His/Her Majesty; (**Vuestra**) **M~** Your Majesty.
majestuoso, a [måhestwo'so, á] *a* majestic.
majo, a [má'ho, á] *a* nice; (*guapo*) attractive, good-looking; (*elegante*) smart.
mal [mål] *ad* badly; (*equivocadamente*) wrongly; (*con dificultad*) with difficulty ♦ *a* = **malo, a** ♦ *nm* evil; (*desgracia*) misfortune; (*daño*) harm, damage; (*MED*) illness ♦ *conj*: ~ **que le pese** whether he likes it or not; **me entendió** ~ he misunderstood me; **hablar** ~ **de uno** to speak ill of sb; **huele** ~ it smells bad; **ir de** ~ **en peor** to go from bad to worse; **oigo/veo** ~ I can't hear/see very well; **si** ~ **no recuerdo** if my memory serves me right; **¡menos** ~! just as well!; ~ **que bien** right-

ly or wrongly; **no hay** ~ **que por bien no venga** every cloud has a silver lining; ~ **de ojo** evil eye.
mala [má'lá] *nf V* **malo**.
malabarismo [målábárēs'mo] *nm* juggling.
malabarista [målábárē'stá] *nm/f* juggler.
malaconsejado, a [målákonsehá'tho, á] *a* ill-advised.
malacostumbrado, a [målákostōōmbrá'tho, á] *a* (*consentido*) spoiled.
malacostumbrar [målákostōōmbrár'] *vt*: ~ **a uno** to get sb into bad habits.
malagueño, a [målåge'nyo, á] *a* of *o* from Málaga ♦ native *o* inhabitant of Málaga.
malaria [målá'ryá] *nf* malaria.
Malasia [målá'syá] *nf* Malaysia.
malavenido, a [målábenē'tho, á] *a* incompatible.
malayo, a [målá'yo, á] *a* Malay(an) ♦ *nm/f* Malay ♦ *nm* (*LING*) Malay ♦ *excl*: **¡malaya!** (*AM*) damn!
malcarado, a [målkárá'tho, á] *a* ugly, grim-faced.
malcriado, a [målkryá'tho, á] *a* (*consentido*) spoiled.
malcriar [målkryár'] *vt* to spoil, pamper.
maldad [måldáth'] *nf* evil, wickedness.
maldecir [måldesēr'] *vt* to curse ♦ *vi*: ~ **de** to speak ill of.
maldiciendo [måldēsyen'do] *etc vb V* **maldecir**.
maldición [måldēsyon'] *nf* curse; **¡~!** curse it!, damn!
maldiga [måldē'gå] *etc*, **maldije** [måldē'he] *etc*, **maldiré** [måldēre'] *etc vb V* **maldecir**.
maldito, a [måldē'to, á] *a* (*condenado*) damned; (*perverso*) wicked ♦ *nm*: **el** ~ **the** devil; **¡~ sea!** damn it!; **no le hace** ~ (**el**) **caso** he doesn't take a damned bit of notice.
maleable [måleá'ble] *a* malleable.
maleante [måleán'te] *a* wicked ♦ *nm/f* criminal, crook.
malecón [målekon'] *nm* pier, jetty.
maledicencia [måledēthesen'syá] *nf* slander, scandal.
maleducado, a [måledōōká'tho, á] *a* bad-mannered, rude.
maleficio [målefē'syo] *nm* curse, spell.
malentendido [målentendē'tho] *nm* misunderstanding.
malestar [målestár'] *nm* (*gen*) discomfort; (*enfermedad*) indisposition; (*fig*: *inquietud*) uneasiness; (*POL*) unrest; **siento un** ~ **en el estómago** my stomach is upset.
maleta [måle'tá] *nf* case, suitcase; (*AUTO*) trunk (*US*), boot (*Brit*); **hacer la** ~ to pack.
maletera [målete'rá] *nf* (*AM AUTO*) trunk (*US*), boot (*Brit*).
maletero [målete'ro] *nm* (*AUTO*) trunk

(US), boot (Brit); (persona) porter.

maletín [máletēn'] nm small case, bag; (portafolio) briefcase.

malevolencia [málebolen'syá] nf malice, spite.

malévolo, a [mále'holo, á] a malicious, spiteful.

maleza [mále'sá] nf (hierbas malas) weeds pl; (arbustos) thicket.

malgache [málgátch'e] a of o from Madagascar ♦ nm/f native o inhabitant of Madagascar.

malgastar [málgástár'] vt (tiempo, dinero) to waste; (recursos) to squander; (salud) to ruin.

malhechor, a [máletchor', á] nm/f delinquent; (criminal) criminal.

malhumorado, a [málōōmorá'tho, á] a bad-tempered.

malicia [mále'syá] nf (maldad) wickedness; (astucia) slyness, guile; (mala intención) malice, spite; (carácter travieso) mischievousness.

malicioso, a [málēsyo'so, á] a wicked, evil; sly, crafty; malicious, spiteful; mischievous.

malignidad [málēgnētháth'] nf (MED) malignancy; (malicia) malice.

maligno, a [málēg'no, á] a evil; (dañino) pernicious, harmful; (malévolo) malicious; (MED) malignant ♦ nm: el ~ the devil.

malintencionado, a [málēntensyoná'tho, á] a (comentario) hostile; (persona) malicious.

malnutrido, a [málnōōtrē'tho, á] a undernourished.

malo, a [má'lo, á] a (mal before nmsg) bad; (calidad) poor; (falso) false; (espantoso) dreadful; (niño) naughty ♦ nm/f villain ♦ nm (CINE fam) bad guy ♦ nf spell of bad luck; **estar** ~ to be ill; **andar a malas con uno** to be on bad terms with sb; **estar de malas** (mal humor) to be in a bad mood; **lo** ~ **es que** ... the trouble is that ....

malograr [málográr'] vt to spoil; (plan) to upset; (ocasión) to waste; ~**se** vr (plan etc) to fail, come to grief; (persona) to die before one's time.

maloliente [málolyen'te] a stinking, smelly.

malparado, a [málpárá'tho, á] a: **salir** ~ to come off badly.

malparir [málpárēr'] vi to have a miscarriage.

malpensado, a [málpensá'tho, á] a evil-minded.

malquerencia [málkeren'syá] nf dislike.

malquistar [málkēstár'] vt: ~ **a dos personas** to cause a rift between two people; ~**se** vr to fall out.

malsano, a [málsá'no, á] a unhealthy.

malsonante [málsonán'te] a (palabra)

nasty, rude.

Malta [mál'tá] nf Malta.

malteada [málteá'thá] nf (AM) milk shake.

maltés, esa [máltes', esá] a, nm/f Maltese.

maltraer [máltráer'] vt (abusar) to insult, abuse; (maltratar) to ill-treat.

maltratar [máltrátár'] vt to ill-treat, mistreat.

maltrecho, a [máltretch'o, á] a battered, damaged.

malva [mál'há] nf mallow; ~ **loca** hollyhock; (**de color de**) ~ mauve.

malvado, a [málhá'tho, á] a evil, villainous.

malvavisco [málháhēs'ko] nm marshmallow.

malvender [málhender'] vt to sell off cheap o at a loss.

malversación [málhersásyon'] nf embezzlement, misappropriation.

malversar [málhersár'] vt to embezzle, misappropriate.

Malvinas [málhē'nás] nfpl: **Islas** ~ Falkland Islands.

malla [má'yá] nf (de una red) mesh; (red) network; (de baño) swimsuit; (de ballet, gimnasia) leotard; ~**s** nfpl tights; ~ **de alambre** wire mesh.

Mallorca [máyor'ká] nf Majorca.

mallorquín, ina [máyorkēn', ēná] a, nm/f Majorcan ♦ nm (LING) Majorcan.

mama [má'má] nf (de animal) teat; (de mujer) breast.

mamá [mámá'] nf (fam) mom(my) (US), mum(my) (Brit).

mamar [mámár'] vt (pecho) to suck; (fig) to absorb, assimilate ♦ vi to suck; **dar de** ~ to (breast-)feed; (animal) to suckle.

mamarracho [mámárrátch'o] nm sight, mess.

mamífero, a [mámē'fero, á] a mammalian, mammal cpd ♦ nm mammal.

mamón, ona [mámon', oná] a small, baby cpd ♦ nm/f small baby; (fam) idiot.

mamotreto [mámotre'to] nm hefty volume; (fam) whopping great thing.

mampara [mámpá'rá] nf (entre habitaciones) partition; (biombo) screen.

mamporro [mámpo'rro] nm (fam): **dar un** ~ **a** to clout.

mampostería [mámposterē'á] nf masonry.

mamut [mámōōt'] nm mammoth.

maná [máná'] nm manna.

manada [máná'thá] nf (ZOOL) herd; (: de leones) pride; (: de lobos) pack; **llegaron en** ~**s** (fam) they came in droves.

Managua [máná'gwá] n Managua.

manantial [mánántyál'] nm spring; (fuente) fountain; (fig) source.

manar [mánár'] vt to run with, flow with ♦ vi to run, flow; (abundar) to abound.

manaza [máná'sá] nf big hand ♦ a, nm/f

inv: ~**s**: **ser un** ~**s** to be clumsy.
mancebo [mánse'ho] *nm* (*joven*) young man.
mancilla [mánsē'yà] *nf* stain, blemish.
mancillar [mánsēyár'] *vt* to stain, sully.
manco, a [mán'ko, à] *a* one-armed; one-handed; (*fig*) defective, faulty; **no ser** ~ to be useful *o* active.
mancomunar [mánkomōōnár'] *vt* to unite, bring together; (*recursos*) to pool; (*JUR*) to make jointly responsible.
mancomunidad [mánkomōōnēthàth'] *nf* union, association; (*comunidad*) community; (*JUR*) joint responsibility.
mancha [mántch'á] *nf* stain, mark; (*de tinta*) blot; (*de vegetación*) patch; (*imperfección*) stain, blemish, blot; (*boceto*) sketch, outline; **la M**~ La Mancha.
manchado, a [mántchá'tho, à] *a* (*sucio*) dirty; (*animal*) spotted; (*ave*) speckled; (*tinta*) smudged.
manchar [mántchár'] *vt* to stain, mark; (*ZOOL*) to patch; (*ensuciar*) to soil, dirty; ~**se** *vr* to get dirty; (*fig*) to dirty one's hands.
manchego, a [mántche'go, à] *a* of *o* from La Mancha ♦ *nm/f* native *o* inhabitant of La Mancha.
mandadero [mándáthe'ro] *nm* messenger.
mandado [mándá'tho] *nm* (*orden*) order; (*recado*) commission, errand.
mandamás [mándámás'] *a nm/f inv* boss; **ser un** ~ to be very bossy.
mandamiento [mándámyen'to] *nm* (*orden*) order, command; (*REL*) commandment; ~ **judicial** warrant.
mandar [mándár'] *vt* (*ordenar*) to order; (*dirigir*) to lead, command; (*país*) to rule over; (*enviar*) to send; (*pedir*) to order, ask for ♦ *vi* to be in charge; (*pey*) to be bossy; **¿mande?** pardon?; **¿manda usted algo más?** is there anything else?; ~ **a uno a paseo** *o* **a la porra** to tell sb to go to hell; **se lo mandaremos por correo** we'll mail (*US*) *o* post (*Brit*) it to you; ~ **hacer un traje** to have a suit made.
mandarín [mándárēn'] *nm* petty bureaucrat.
mandarina [mándárē'ná] *nf* (*fruta*) tangerine, mandarin (orange).
mandatario, a [mándátá'ryo, à] *nm/f* (*representante*) agent; **primer** ~ head of state.
mandato [mándá'to] *nm* (*orden*) order; (*POL*: *período*) term of office; (: *territorio*) mandate; (*INFORM*) command; ~ **judicial** (search) warrant.
mandíbula [mándē'bōōlá] *nf* jaw.
mandil [mándēl'] *nm* (*delantal*) apron.
mando [mán'do] *nm* (*MIL*) command; (*de país*) rule; (*el primer lugar*) lead; (*POL*) term of office; (*TEC*) control; ~ **a la**

izquierda left-hand drive; **los altos** ~**s** the high command *sg*; ~ **por botón** push-button control; **al** ~ **de** in charge of; **tomar el** ~ to take the lead.
mandolina [mándolē'ná] *nf* mandolin(e).
mandón, ona [mándon', oná] *a* bossy, domineering.
manecilla [mánesē'yà] *nf* (*TEC*) pointer; (*de reloj*) hand.
manejable [mánehà'hle] *a* manageable; (*fácil de usar*) handy.
manejar [mánehár'] *vt* to manage; (*máquina*) to work, operate; (*caballo etc*) to handle; (*casa*) to run, manage; (*AM AUTO*) to drive; **"~ con cuidado"** "handle with care" ♦ *vi* (*AM AUTO*) to drive; ~**se** *vr* (*comportarse*) to act, behave; (*arreglárselas*) to manage.
manejo [máne'ho] *nm* management; handling; running; driving; (*facilidad de trato*) ease, confidence; (*de idioma*) command; ~**s** *nmpl* intrigues; **tengo** ~ **del francés** I have a good command of French.
manera [máne'rá] *nf* way, manner, fashion; (*ARTE, LITERATURA etc*: *estilo*) manner, style; ~**s** *nfpl* (*modales*) manners; **su** ~ **de ser** the way he is; (*aire*) his manner; **de mala** ~ (*fam*) badly, unwillingly; **de ninguna** ~ no way, by no means; **de otra** ~ otherwise; **de todas** ~**s** at any rate; **en gran** ~ to a large extent; **sobre** ~ exceedingly; **a mi** ~ **de ver** in my view; **no hay** ~ **de persuadirle** there's no way of convincing him.
manga [mán'gà] *nf* (*de camisa*) sleeve; (*de riego*) hose; **de** ~ **corta/larga** short-/long-sleeved; **andar** ~ **por hombro** (*desorden*) to be topsy-turvy; **tener** ~ **ancha** to be easy-going.
mangante [mángán'te] *a* (*descarado*) brazen ♦ *nm* (*mendigo*) beggar.
mangar [mángár'] *vt* (*unir*) to plug in; (*fam*: *birlar*) to pinch, nick, swipe; (*mendigar*) to beg.
mango [mán'go] *nm* handle; (*BOT*) mango; ~ **de escoba** broomstick.
mangonear [mángoneár'] *vt* to boss about ♦ *vi* to be bossy.
mangue [mán'ge] *etc vb* V **mangar**.
manguera [mánge'rà] *nf* (*de riego*) hose; (*tubo*) pipe; ~ **de incendios** fire hose.
maní(s) [mánē'] *nm, pl* **maníes** *o* **manises** (*AM*: *cacahuete*) peanut; (: *planta*) groundnut plant.
manía [mánē'á] *nf* (*MED*) mania; (*fig*: *moda*) rage, craze; (*disgusto*) dislike; (*malicia*) spite; **tiene** ~**s** she's a bit fussy; **tener** ~ **a uno** to dislike sb.
maníaco, a [mánē'áko, à] *a* maniac(al) ♦ *nm/f* maniac.
maniatar [mányátár'] *vt* to tie the hands of.

maniático, a |mànyà'tēko, à| *a* maniac(al); (*loco*) crazy; (*tiquismiquis*) fussy ♦ *nm/f* maniac.

manicomio |mánēko'myo| *nm* insane asylum (*US*), mental hospital (*Brit*).

manicuro, a |mánēkōō'ro, à| *nm/f* manicurist ♦ *nf* manicure.

manido, a |mánē'tho, à| *a* (*tema etc*) trite, stale.

manifestación |mánēfcstásyon'| *nf* (*declaración*) statement, declaration; (*demostración*) show, display; (*POL*) demonstration.

manifestante |mánēfcstán'tc| *nm/f* demonstrator.

manifestar |mànēfcstár'| *vt* to show, manifest; (*declarar*) to state, declare; **~se** *vr* to show, become apparent; (*POL*: *desfilar*) to demonstrate; (: *reunirse*) to hold a mass meeting.

manifiesto, a |mánēfyc'sto, à| *etc vb V* **manifestar** ♦ *a* clear, manifest ♦ *nm* manifesto; **poner algo de ~** (*aclarar*) to make sth clear; (*revelar*) to reveal sth; **quedar ~** to be plain *o* clear.

manija |mánē'há| *nf* handle.

manilla |mánē'yá| *nf* (*de reloj*) hand; **~s (de hierro)** *nfpl* handcuffs.

manillar |mánēyár'| *nm* handlebars *pl*.

maniobra |mányo'hrá| *nf* maneuvering (*US*), manoeuvring (*Brit*); (*maneja*) handling; (*fig*: *movimiento*) maneuver (*US*), manoeuvre (*Brit*), move; (: *estratagema*) trick, stratagem; **~s** *nfpl* maneuvers (*US*), manoeuvres (*Brit*).

maniobrar |mánēohrár'| *vt* to maneuver (*US*), manoeuvre (*Brit*); (*manejar*) to handle ♦ *vi* to maneuver (*US*), manoeuvre (*Brit*).

manipulación |mánēpōōlásyon'| *nf* manipulation; (*COM*) handling.

manipular |mánēpōōlár'| *vt* to manipulate; (*manejar*) to handle.

maniquí |mánēkē'| *nm/f* model ♦ *nm* dummy.

manirroto, a |mánērro'to, à| *a* lavish, extravagant ♦ *nm/f* spendthrift.

manita |mánē'tá| *nf* little hand; **~s de plata** artistic hands.

manitas |mánē'tás| *a inv* good with one's hands ♦ *nm/f inv*: **ser un ~** to be very good with one's hands.

manito |mánē'to| *nm* (*AM*: *en conversación*) pal.

manivela |mánēhc'lá| *nf* crank.

manjar |mánhár'| *nm* (tasty) dish.

mano |má'no| *nf* hand; (*ZOOL*) foot, paw; (*de pintura*) coat; (*serie*) lot, series; **a ~** by hand; **a ~ derecha/izquierda** on (*o* to) the right(-hand side)/left(-hand side); **he-**cho a **~** handmade; **a ~s llenas** lavishly, generously; **de primera ~** (at) first hand; **de segunda ~** (at) second hand; **robo a ~ armada** armed robbery; **Pedro es mi ~ derecha** Pedro is my right-hand man; **~ de obra** manpower; **~ de santo** sure remedy; **darse la(s) ~(s)** to shake hands; **echar una ~ a** to lend a hand; **echar una ~ a** to lay hands on; **echar ~ de** to make use of; **estrechar la ~ a uno** to shake sb's hand; **traer o llevar algo entre ~s** to deal *o* be busy with sth; **está en tus ~s** it's up to you; **se le fue la ~** his hand slipped; (*fig*) he went too far; **¡~s a la obra!** to work!

manojo |máno'ho| *nm* handful, bunch; **~ de llaves** bunch of keys.

manómetro |máno'mctro| *nm* (pressure) gauge.

manopla |máno'plá| *nf* (*paño*) wash cloth; **~s** *nfpl* mittens.

manoseado, a |mánoscá'tho, à| *a* wellworn.

manosear |mánoscár'| *vt* (*tocar*) to handle, touch; (*desordenar*) to mess up, rumple; (*insistir en*) to overwork; (*acariciar*) to caress, fondle; (*pey*: *persona*) to feel up.

manotazo |mánotá'so| *nm* slap, smack.

mansalva |mánsál'há|: **a ~** *ad* indiscriminately.

mansedumbre |mánscthōōm'brc| *nf* gentleness, meekness; (*de animal*) tameness.

mansión |mánsyon'| *nf* mansion.

manso, a |mán'so, à| *a* gentle, mild; (*animal*) tame.

manta |mán'tá| *nf* blanket; (*AM*) poncho.

manteca |mántc'ká| *nf* fat; (*AM*) butter; **~ de cacahuete/cacao** peanut/cocoa butter; **~ de cerdo** lard.

mantecado |mántcká'tho| *nm* (*AM*) ice cream.

mantecoso, a |mántcko'so, à| *a* fat, greasy; **queso ~** soft cheese.

mantel |mántcl'| *nm* tablecloth.

mantelería |mántclcrē'á| *nf* table linen.

mantendré |mántcndrc'| *etc vb V* **mantener.**

mantener |mántcncr'| *vt* to support, maintain; (*alimentar*) to sustain; (*conservar*) to keep; (*TEC*) to maintain, service; **~se** *vr* (*seguir de pie*) to be still standing; (*no ceder*) to hold one's ground; (*subsistir*) to sustain o.s., keep going; **~ algo en equilibrio** to keep sth balanced; **~se a distancia** to keep one's distance; **~se firme** to hold one's ground.

mantenga |mántcn'gá| *etc vb V* **mantener.**

mantenimiento |mántcnēmycn'to| *nm* maintenance; sustenance; (*sustento*) support.

mantequería |mántckcrē'á| *nf* (*ultramarinos*) grocer's (shop).

mantequilla [mántekē'yá] *nf* butter.

mantilla [mántē'yá] *nf* mantilla; **estar en ~s** (*persona*) to be terribly innocent; (*proyecto*) to be in its infancy.

manto [mán'to] *nm* (*capa*) cloak; (*de ceremonia*) robe, gown.

mantón [mánton'] *nm* shawl.

mantuve [mántōō'he] *etc vb V* **mantener**.

manual [mánwál'] *a* manual ♦ *nm* manual, handbook; **habilidad ~** manual skill.

manufactura [mánōōfáktōō'rá] *nf* manufacture; (*fábrica*) factory.

manuscrito, a [mánōōskrē'to, á] *a* handwritten ♦ *nm* manuscript.

manutención [mánōōtensyon'] *nf* maintenance; (*sustento*) support.

manzana [mánsá'ná] *nf* apple; (*ARQ*) block; **~ de la discordia** (*fig*) bone of contention.

manzanal [mánsánál'] *nm* apple orchard.

manzanilla [mánsánē'yá] *nf* (*planta*) camomile; (*infusión*) camomile tea; (*vino*) manzanilla.

manzano [mánsá'no] *nm* apple tree.

maña [má'nyá] *nf* (*gen*) skill, dexterity; (*pey*) guile; (*costumbre*) habit; (*una ~*) trick, knack; **con ~** craftily.

mañana [mányá'ná] *ad* tomorrow ♦ *nm* future ♦ *nf* morning; **de o por la ~** in the morning; **¡hasta ~!** see you tomorrow!; **pasado ~** the day after tomorrow; **~ por la ~** tomorrow morning.

mañanero, a [mányáne'ro, á] *a* early-rising.

mañoso, a [mányo'so, á] *a* (*hábil*) skilful; (*astuto*) smart, clever.

mapa [má'pá] *nm* map.

maqueta [máke'tá] *nf* (scale) model.

maquiavélico, a [mákyáhe'lēko, á] *a* Machiavellian.

maquillador, a [mákēyáthor', á] *nm/f* (*TEATRO etc*) make-up artist.

maquillaje [mákēyá'he] *nm* make-up; (*acto*) making up.

maquillar [mákēyár'] *vt* to make up; **~se** *vr* to put on (some) make-up.

máquina [má'kēná] *nf* machine; (*de tren*) locomotive, engine; (*FOTO*) camera; (*AM: coche*) car; (*fig*) machinery; (*: proyecto*) plan, project; **a toda ~** at full speed; **escrito a ~** typewritten; **~ de escribir** typewriter; **~ de coser/lavar** sewing/washing machine; **~ de facsímil** facsimile (machine), fax; **~ de franqueo** franking machine; **~ tragaperras** slot machine.

maquinación [mákēnásyon'] *nf* machination, plot.

maquinal [mákēnál'] *a* (*fig*) mechanical, automatic.

maquinar [mákēnár'] *vt, vi* to plot.

maquinaria [mákēná'ryá] *nf* (*máquinas*) machinery; (*mecanismo*) mechanism, works *pl*.

maquinilla [mákēnē'yá] *nf* small machine; (*torno*) winch; **~ de afeitar** razor; **~ eléctrica** electric razor.

maquinista [mákēnē'stá] *nm* (*FERRO*) engineer (*US*), engine driver (*Brit*); (*TEC*) operator; (*NAUT*) engineer.

mar [már] *nm* sea; **~ de fondo** groundswell; **~ llena** high tide; **~ adentro o afuera** out at sea; **en alta ~** on the high seas; **por ~** by sea *o* boat; **hacerse a la ~** to put to sea; **a ~es** in abundance; **un ~ de** lots of; **es la ~ de guapa** she is ever so pretty; **el M~ Negro/Báltico** the Black/Baltic Sea; **el M~ Muerto/Rojo** the Dead/Red Sea; **el M~ del Norte** the North Sea.

mar. *abr* (= *marzo*) Mar.

maraña [márá'nyá] *nf* (*maleza*) thicket; (*confusión*) tangle.

maravilla [máráhē'yá] *nf* marvel, wonder; (*BOT*) marigold; **hacer ~s** to work wonders; **a (las mil) ~s** wonderfully well.

maravillar [máráhēyár'] *vt* to astonish, amaze; **~se** *vr* to be astonished, be amazed.

maravilloso, a [máráhēyo'so, á] *a* wonderful, marvelous (*US*), marvellous (*Brit*).

marbellí [márheyē'] *a* of *o* from Marbella ♦ *nm/f* native *o* inhabitant of Marbella.

marca [már'ká] *nf* mark; (*sello*) stamp; (*COM*) make, brand; (*de ganado*) brand; (: *acto*) branding; (*NAUT*) seamark; (: *boya*) marker; (*DEPORTE*) record; **de ~** excellent, outstanding; **~ de fábrica** trademark; **~ propia** own brand; **~ registrada** registered trademark.

marcación [márkásyon'] *nf* (*TELEC*): **~ automática** autodial.

marcado, a [márká'tho, á] *a* marked, strong.

marcador [márkáthor'] *nm* marker; (*rotulador*) marker (pen); (*de libro*) bookmark; (*DEPORTE*) scoreboard; (: *persona*) scorer.

marcar [márkár'] *vt* to mark; (*número de teléfono*) to dial; (*gol*) to score; (*números*) to record, keep a tally of; (*el pelo*) to set; (*suj: termómetro*) to register; (*tarea*) to assign; (*COM*) to put a price on ♦ *vi* (*DEPORTE*) to score; (*TELEC*) to dial; **mi reloj marca las 2** it's 2 o'clock by my watch; **~ el compás** (*MUS*) to keep time.

marcial [mársyál'] *a* martial, military.

marciano, a [mársyá'no, á] *a* Martian, of *o* from Mars.

marco [már'ko] *nm* frame; (*DEPORTE*) goal-posts *pl*; (*moneda*) mark; (*fig*) setting; (*contexto*) framework; **~ de chimenea** mantelpiece.

marcha [mártch'á] *nf* march; (*DEPORTE*) walk; (*TEC*) running, working; (*AUTO*) gear; (*velocidad*) speed; (*fig*) progress; (*dirección*) course; **dar ~ atrás** to reverse, put into reverse; **estar en** ~ to be under way, be in motion; **hacer algo sobre la** ~ to do sth as you *etc* go along; **poner en** ~ to put into gear; **ponerse en** ~ to start, get going; **a** ~**s forzadas** (*fig*) with all speed; **¡en** ~**!** (*MIL*) forward march!; (*fig*) let's go!; **"**~ **moderada"** (*AUTO*) "drive slowly"; **que tiene** *o* **de mucha** ~ (*fam*) very lively.

marchante, a [mártchán'te, à] *nm/f* dealer, merchant.

marchar [mártchár'] *vi* (*ir*) to go; (*funcionar*) to work, go; (*fig*) to go, proceed; ~**se** *vr* to go (away), leave; **todo marcha bien** everything is going well.

marchitar [mártchētár'] *vt* to wither, dry up; ~**se** *vr* (*BOT*) to wither; (*fig*) to fade away.

marchito, a [mártchē'to, à] *a* withered, faded; (*fig*) in decline.

marchoso, a [mártcho'so, à] *a* (*fam: animado*) lively; (: *moderno*) modern.

marea [màre'à] *nf* tide; (*llovizna*) drizzle; ~ **alta/baja** high/low tide; ~ **negra** oil slick.

mareado, a [màreà'tho, à] *a*: **estar** ~ (*con náuseas*) to feel nauseated; (*aturdido*) to feel dizzy.

marear [màreár'] *vt* (*fig: irritar*) to annoy, upset; (*MED*): ~ **a uno** to make sb feel sick; ~**se** *vr* (*tener náuseas*) to feel sick; (*desvanecerse*) to feel faint; (*aturdirse*) to feel dizzy; (*fam: emborracharse*) to get tipsy.

marejada [màrehà'thà] *nf* (*NAUT*) swell, heavy sea.

maremágnum [màremág'nōōm], **maremagno** [màremàg'no] *nm* (*fig*) ocean, abundance.

maremoto [màremo'to] *nm* tidal wave.

mareo [màre'o] *nm* (*náusea*) sick feeling; (*aturdimiento*) dizziness; (*fam: lata*) nuisance.

marfil [màrfēl'] *nm* ivory.

margarina [màrgàrē'nà] *nf* margarine.

margarita [màrgàrē'tà] *nf* (*BOT*) daisy; (**rueda**) ~ (*en máquina impresora*) daisy wheel.

margen [már'hen] *nm* (*borde*) edge, border; (*fig*) margin, space; ~ **de beneficio** *o* **de ganancia** profit margin; ~ **comercial** mark-up; ~ **de confianza** credibility gap ♦ *nf* (*de río etc*) bank; **dar** ~ **para** to give an opportunity for; **dejar a uno al** ~ to leave sb out (in the cold); **mantenerse al** ~ to keep out (of things); **al** ~ **de lo que digas** despite what you say.

marginado, a [màrhēnà'tho, à] *nm/f* outcast.

marginar [màrhēnár'] *vt* to exclude.

marica [màrē'kà] *nm* (*fam*) sissy; (*homosexual*) queer.

Maricastaña [màrēkàstà'nyà] *nf*: **en los días** *o* **en tiempos de** ~ way back, in the good old days.

maricón [màrēkon'] *nm* (*fam*) queer.

marido [màrē'tho] *nm* husband.

mariguana [màrēgwà'nà], **marijuana** [màrēhwà'nà] *nf* marijuana, cannabis.

marimacho [màrēmátch'o] *nf* (*fam*) mannish woman.

marimorena [màrēmore'nà] *nf* fuss, row; **armar una** ~ to kick up a fuss.

marina [màrē'nà] *nf* navy; ~ **mercante** merchant marine (*US*), merchant navy (*Brit*).

marinero, a [màrēnc'ro, à] *a* sea *cpd*; (*barco*) seaworthy ♦ *nm* sailor, seaman.

marino, a [màrē'no, à] *a* sea *cpd*, marine ♦ *nm* sailor; ~ **de agua dulce/de cubierta/ de primera** landlubber/deckhand/able seaman.

marioneta [màryonc'tà] *nf* puppet.

mariposa [màrēpo'sà] *nf* butterfly.

mariposear [màrēposeár'] *vi* (*revolotear*) to flutter about; (*ser inconstante*) to be fickle; (*coquetear*) to flirt.

mariquita [màrēkē'tà] *nm* (*fam*) sissy; (*homosexual*) queer ♦ *nf* (*ZOOL*) ladybug (*US*), ladybird (*Brit*).

mariscos [màrēs'kos] *nmpl* shellfish *sg*, seafood *sg*.

marisma [màrēs'mà] *nf* marsh, swamp.

marisquería [màrēskerē'à] *nf* shellfish bar, seafood restaurant.

marítimo, a [màrē'tēmo, à] *a* sea *cpd*, maritime.

marmita [màrmē'tà] *nf* pot.

mármol [már'mol] *nm* marble.

marmóreo, a [màrmo'reo, à] *a* marble.

marmota [màrmo'tà] *nf* (*ZOOL*) marmot; (*fig*) sleepyhead.

maroma [màro'mà] *nf* rope.

marque [már'ke] *etc vb* V **marcar**.

marqués, esa [màrkes', esà] *nm/f* marquis/ marchioness.

marquesina [màrkesē'nà] *nf* (*de parada*) bus-shelter.

marquetería [màrketerē'à] *nf* marquetry, inlaid work.

marrano, a [màrrà'no, à] *a* filthy, dirty ♦ *nm* (*ZOOL*) pig; (*malo*) swine; (*sucio*) dirty pig.

marrar [màrrár'] *vi* to miss; (*fig*) to miss the mark.

marras [mà'rràs]: **de** ~ *ad*: **es el problema de** ~ it's the same old problem.

marrón [màrron'] *a* brown.

marroquí [màrrokē'] *a*, *nm/f* Moroccan ♦ *nm* Morocco (leather).

Marruecos [màrrwe'kos] *nm* Morocco.

marta [már'tà] *nf* (*animal*) (pine) marten; (*piel*) sable.

Martes [már'tes] *nm inv* Mars.

martes [már'tes] *nm inv* Tuesday; ~ **de carnaval** Shrove Tuesday.

martillar [mártēyár'], **martillear** [mártēyeár'] *vt* to hammer.

martilleo [mártēye'o] *nm* hammering.

martillo [mártē'yo] *nm* hammer; (*de presidente de asamblea, comité*) gavel; ~ **neumático** jackhammer (*US*), pneumatic drill (*Brit*).

Martinica [mártēnē'ká] *nf* Martinique.

mártir [már'tēr] *nm/f* martyr.

martirice [mártērē'se] *etc vb V* **martirizar**.

martirio [mártē'ryo] *nm* martyrdom; (*fig*) torture, torment.

martirizar [mártērēsár'] *vt* (*REL*) to martyr; (*fig*) to torture, torment.

marxismo [márksēs'mo] *nm* Marxism.

marxista [márksē'stá] *a nm/f* Marxist.

marzo [már'so] *nm* March.

mas [más] *conj* but.

más [más] *a, ad* (*comparativo*) more; (*superlativo*) most; (*otro*) another, more ♦ *conj* and, plus; **A es ~ difícil que B** A is more difficult *o* harder than B; **cada vez ~ difícil** more and more difficult, harder and harder; **es ~ de medianoche** it's after midnight; **el libro ~ leído del año** the most widely-read book of the year; **un kilómetro ~** one more kilometer; **él es el ~ inteligente** he is the most intelligent (one); **¡qué perro ~ feo!** what an ugly dog!; ~ **de 6** more than 6; ~ **que/~ de lo que pensaba** more than he thought; ~ **bien** rather; **así no ~** (*AM*) just like that; **es ~** furthermore; **de ~** extra; **estar de ~** to be unnecessary; **¡qué ~ da!** what does it matter?; ~ **o menos** more or less; **a las 8 a ~ tardar** at 8 o'clock at the latest; **vale tarde que nunca** better late than never; **no ~ se fue se acordó** (*AM*) no sooner had she left than she remembered.

masa [má'sá] *nf* (*mezcla*) dough; (*volumen*) volume, mass; (*FÍSICA*) mass; **en ~ en masse; las ~s** (*POL*) the masses.

masacrar [másákrár'] *vt* to massacre.

masacre [másá'kre] *nf* massacre.

masaje [másá'he] *nm* massage; **dar ~ a** to massage.

masajista [másáhē'stá] *nm/f* masseur/masseuse.

mascar [máskár'] *vt, vi* to chew; (*fig*) to mumble, mutter.

máscara [más'kárá] *nf* (*tb INFORM*) mask ♦ *nm/f* masked person; ~ **antigás** gas mask.

mascarada [máskárá'thá] *nf* masquerade.

mascarilla [máskárē'yá] *nf* mask; (*vaciado*) deathmask; (*maquillaje*) face pack.

mascarón [máskáron'] *nm* large mask; ~ **de proa** figurehead.

masculino, a [máskōōlē'no, á] *a* masculine; (*BIO*) male ♦ *nm* (*LING*) masculine.

mascullar [máskōōyár'] *vt* to mumble, mutter.

masilla [másē'yá] *nf* putty.

masivo, a [másē'bo, á] *a* (*en masa*) mass.

masón [máson'] *nm* (free)mason.

masonería [másonerē'á] *nf* (free)masonry.

masoquista [másokē'stá] *a* masochistic ♦ *nm/f* masochist.

masque [más'ke] *etc vb V* **mascar**.

masticar [mástēkár'] *vt* to chew; (*fig*) to ponder over.

mástil [má'stēl] *nm* (*de navío*) mast; (*de guitarra*) neck.

mastín [mástēn'] *nm* mastiff.

mastique [mástē'ke] *etc vb V* **masticar**.

masturbación [mástōōrbásyon'] *nf* masturbation.

masturbarse [mástōōrbár'se] *vr* to masturbate.

Mat. *abr* = **Matemáticas**.

mata [má'tá] *nf* (*arbusto*) bush, shrub; (*de hierbas*) tuft; (*campo*) field; (*manojo*) tuft, blade; ~**s** *nfpl* scrub *sg*; ~ **de pelo** mop of hair; ~ **a salto de** ~ (*día a día*) from day to day; (*al azar*) haphazardly.

matadero [mátáthe'ro] *nm* slaughterhouse.

matador, a [mátáthor', á] *a* killing ♦ *nm/f* killer ♦ *nm* (*TAUR*) matador, bullfighter.

matamoscas [mátámos'kás] *nm inv* (*palo*) fly swatter.

matanza [mátán'sá] *nf* slaughter.

matar [mátár'] *vt* to kill; (*tiempo, pelota*) to kill ♦ *vi* to kill; ~**se** *vr* (*suicidarse*) to kill o.s., commit suicide; (*morir*) to be *o* get killed; (*gastarse*) to wear o.s. out; ~ **el hambre** to stave off hunger; ~ **a uno a disgustos** to make sb's life miserable; ~**las callando** to go about things quietly; ~**se trabajando** to kill o.s. with work; ~**se por hacer algo** to struggle to do sth.

matarife [mátárē'fe] *nm* slaughterman.

matasellos [mátáse'yos] *nm inv* postmark.

matasanos [mátásá'nos] *nm inv* quack.

mate [má'te] *a* (*sin brillo: color*) dull, matt ♦ *nm* (*en ajedrez*) (check)mate; (*AM: hierba*) maté; (: *vasija*) gourd.

matemático, a [mátemá'tēko, á] *a* mathematical ♦ *nm/f* mathematician ♦ **matemáticas** *nfpl* mathematics *sg*.

materia [máte'ryá] *nf* (*gen*) matter; (*TEC*) material; (*ESCOL*) subject; **en ~ de** on the subject of; (*en cuanto a*) as regards; ~ **prima** raw material; **entrar en ~** to get down to business.

material [máteryál'] *a* material; (*dolor*) physical; (*real*) real; (*literal*) literal ♦ *nm* material; (*TEC*) equipment; ~ **de construcción** building material; ~**es de derribo** rubble *sg*.

materialismo [máteryálēs'mo] *nm* materialism.

materialista [máteryále'stá] *a* material-ist(ic).

materialmente [máteryálmen'te] *ad* materially; (*fig*) absolutely.

maternal [máternál'] *a* motherly, maternal.

maternidad [máternéɩ̃háɩ̃'] *nf* motherhood, maternity.

materno, a [máter'no, á] *a* maternal; (*lengua*) mother *cpd*.

matice [máté'se] *etc vb V* **matizar.**

matinal [mátēnál'] *a* morning *cpd*.

matiz [mátés'] *nm* shade; (*de sentido*) shade, nuance; (*ironía etc*) touch.

matizar [mátēsár'] *vt* (*variar*) to vary; (*ARTE*) to blend; ~ **de** to tinge with.

matón [máton'] *nm* bully.

matorral [mátorrál'] *nm* thicket.

matraca [mátrá'ká] *nf* rattle; (*fam*) nuisance.

matraz [mátrás'] *nm* (*QUÍMICA*) flask.

matriarcado [mátryárká'ɩ̃ho] *nm* matriarchy.

matrícula [mátré'kōōlá] *nf* (*registro*) registration (*US*), register (*Brit*); (*ESCOL*: *inscripción*) registration; (*AUTO*) registration number; (: *placa*) license plate (*US*), number plate (*Brit*).

matricular [mátrēkōōlár'] *vt* to register.

matrimonial [mátrēmonyál'] *a* matrimonial.

matrimonio [mátrēmo'nyo] *nm* (*pareja*) (married) couple; (*acto*) marriage; ~ **civil/clandestino** civil/secret marriage; **contraer ~** (**con**) to marry.

matriz [mátrēs'] *nf* (*ANAT*) womb; (*TEC*) mold (*US*), mould (*Brit*); (*MAT*) matrix; **casa ~** (*COM*) head office.

matrona [mátro'ná] *nf* (*persona de edad*) matron.

matutino, a [mátōōtē'no, á] *a* morning *cpd*.

maula [má'ōōlá] *a* (*persona*) good-for-nothing ♦ *nm/f* (*vago*) idler, slacker ♦ *nf* (*persona*) dead loss (*fam*).

maullar [máōōyár'] *vi* to mew, miaow.

maullido [máōōyē'ɩ̃ho] *nm* mew(ing), miaow(ing).

Mauricio [máōōrē'syo] *nm* Mauritius.

Mauritania [máōōrētá'nyá] *nf* Mauritania.

mausoleo [máōōsole'o] *nm* mausoleum.

maxilar [máksēlár'] *nm* jaw(bone).

máxima [mák'sēmá] *nf V* **máximo.**

máxime [mák'sēme] *ad* especially.

máximo, a [mák'sēmo, á] *a* maximum; (*más alto*) highest; (*más grande*) greatest ♦ *nm* maximum ♦ *nf* maxim; **como ~** at most; **al ~** to the utmost.

mayo [má'yo] *nm* May.

mayonesa [máyone'sá] *nf* mayonnaise.

mayor [máyor'] *a* main, chief; (*adulto*) grown-up, adult; (*JUR*) of age; (*de edad avanzada*) elderly; (*MUS*) major;

(*comparativo*: *de tamaño*) bigger; (: *de edad*) older; (*superlativo*: *de tamaño*) biggest; (*tb*: *fig*) greatest; (: *de edad*) oldest ♦ *nm* chief, boss; (*adulto*) adult; **al por ~** wholesale; ~ **de edad** adult; *V tb* **mayores.**

mayores [máyo'res] *nmpl* grown-ups; **llegar a ~es** to get out of hand.

mayoral [máyorál'] *nm* foreman.

mayordomo [máyorɩ̃ho'mo] *nm* butler.

mayoría [máyorē'á] *nf* majority, greater part; **en la ~ de los casos** in most cases; **en su ~** on the whole.

mayorista [máyorē'stá] *nm/f* wholesaler.

mayoritario, a [máyorētá'ryo, á] *a* majority *cpd*; **gobierno ~** majority government.

mayúsculo, a [máyōōs'kōōlo, á] *a* (*fig*) big, tremendous ♦ *nf* capital (letter); **mayúsculas** *nfpl* capitals; (*TIP*) upper case *sg*.

maza [má'sá] *nf* (*arma*) mace; (*DEPORTE*) bat; (*POLO*) stick.

mazacote [másáko'te] *nm* hard mass; (*CULIN*) dry doughy food; (*ARTE, LITERATURA etc*) mess, hodgepodge.

mazapán [másápán'] *nm* marzipan.

mazmorra [másmo'rrá] *nf* dungeon.

mazo [má'so] *nm* (*martillo*) mallet; (*de mortero*) pestle; (*de flores*) bunch; (*DEPORTE*) bat.

mazorca [másor'ká] *nf* (*BOT*) spike; (*de maíz*) cob, ear.

MCAC *nm abr* = **Mercado Común de la América Central.**

MCI *nm abr* = **Mercado Común Iberoamericano.**

me [me] *pron* (*directo*) me; (*indirecto*) (to) me; (*reflexivo*) (to) myself; **¡dámelo!** give it to me!; ~ **lo compró** (*de mí*) he bought it from me; (*para mí*) he bought it for me.

mear [meár'] (*fam*) *vt* to piss on (!) ♦ *vi* to pee, piss (!), take (*US*) o have (*Brit*) a piss (!); ~**se** *vr* to wet o.s.

Meca [me'ká] *nf*: **La ~** Mecca.

mecánica [meká'nēká] *nf V* **mecánico.**

mecanice [mekáné'se] *etc vb V* **mecanizar.**

mecánico, a [meká'nēko, á] *a* mechanical; (*repetitivo*) repetitive ♦ *nm/f* mechanic ♦ *nf* (*estudio*) mechanics *sg*; (*mecanismo*) mechanism.

mecanismo [mekánēs'mo] *nm* mechanism; (*engranaje*) gear.

mecanizar [mekánēsár'] *vt* to mechanize.

mecanografía [mekánoɡráfē'á] *nf* typewriting.

mecanografiado, a [mekánoɡráfyá'ɩ̃ho, á] *a* typewritten ♦ *nm* typescript.

mecanógrafo, a [mekáno'ɡráfo, á] *nm/f* (*copy*) typist.

mecate [meká'te] *nm* (*AM*) rope.

mecedora [meseɩ̃ho'rá] *nf* rocking chair.

mecenas [mese'nás] *nm inv* patron.

mecenazgo |mesenás'go| *nm* patronage.

mecer |meser'| *vt* (*cuna*) to rock; ~**se** *vr* to rock; (*rama*) to sway.

mecha |metch'á| *nf* (*de vela*) wick; (*de bomba*) fuse; **a toda** ~ at full speed; **ponerse** ~**s** to streak one's hair.

mechero |metchc'ro| *nm* (cigarette) lighter.

mechón |metchon'| *nm* (*gen*) tuft; (*manojo*) bundle; (*de pelo*) lock.

medalla |metha'yá| *nf* medal.

media |me'thyá| *nf* V **medio**.

mediado, a |methyá'tho, a| *a* half-full; (*trabajo*) half-completed; **a** ~**s de** in the middle of, halfway through.

medianamente |methyánámen'te| *ad* (*moderadamente*) moderately, fairly; (*regularmente*) moderately well.

mediano, a |methyá'no, á| *a* (*regular*) medium, average; (*mediocre*) mediocre; (**de tamaño**) ~ medium-sized.

medianoche |methyánotch'e| *nf* midnight.

mediante |methyán'te| *ad* by (means of), through.

mediar |methyár'| *vi* (*tiempo*) to elapse; (*interceder*) to mediate, intervene; (*existir*) to exist; **media el hecho de que ...** there is the fact that ....

medicación |methēkásyon'| *nf* medication, treatment.

medicamento |methēkámen'to| *nm* medicine, drug.

medicina |methēsē'ná| *nf* medicine.

medición |methēsyon'| *nf* measurement.

médico, a |me'thēko, á| *a* medical ♦ *nm/f* doctor; ~ **de cabecera** family doctor; ~ **pediatra** pediatrician (*US*), paediatrician (*Brit*); ~ **residente** intern (*US*), house physician.

medida |methē'thá| *nf* measure; (*medición*) measurement; (*de camisa, zapato etc*) size, fitting; (*prudencia*) moderation, prudence; **en cierta/gran** ~ up to a point/to a great extent; **un traje a la** ~ tailor-made suit; ~ **de cuello** collar size; **a** ~ **de** in proportion to; (*de acuerdo con*) in keeping with; **con** ~ with restraint; **sin** ~ immoderately; **a** ~ **que ...** (at the same time) as ...; **tomar** ~**s** to take steps.

medio, a |me'thyo, á| *a* half (a); (*punto*) mid, middle; (*promedio*) average ♦ *ad* half ♦ *nm* (*centro*) middle; (*promedio*) average; (*método*) means, way; (*ambiente*) environment ♦ *nf* ~**s panti** pantyhose (*US*), tights (*Brit*); (*prenda de vestir*) stocking, (*AM*) sock; (*promedio*) average; **a** ~**s** barely; **pagar a** ~**s** to share the cost; **media hora** half an hour; ~ **litro** half a liter; **las tres y media** half after three; **M**~ **Oriente** Middle East; **a** ~ **camino** halfway (there); ~ **dormido** half asleep; **a** ~ **terminar** half finished; **en** ~ in the middle;

(*entre*) in between; **por** ~ **de** by (means of), through; **en los** ~**s financieros** in financial circles; **encontrarse en su** ~ to be in one's element; ~ **circulante** (*COM*) money supply; V *tb* **medios**.

mediocre |methyo'kre| *a* middling, average; (*pey*) mediocre.

mediocridad |methyokrētháth'| *nf* middling quality; (*pey*) mediocrity.

mediodía |methyothē'á| *nm* midday, noon.

mediopensionista |methyopensyonē'stá| *nm/f* day boy/girl.

medios |me'thyos| *nmpl* means, resources.

medir |methēr'| *vt* (*gen*) to measure ♦ *vi* to measure; ~**se** *vr* (*moderarse*) to be moderate, act with restraint; **¿cuánto mides?** — **mido 1.50 m** how tall are you? — I am 1.50 m tall.

meditar |methētár'| *vt* to ponder, think over, meditate on; (*planear*) to think out ♦ *vi* to ponder, think, meditate.

mediterráneo, a |methētcrrá'neo, á| *a* Mediterranean ♦ *nm*: **el** (**mar**) **M**~ the Mediterranean (Sea).

medrar |methrár'| *vi* to increase, grow; (*mejorar*) to improve; (*prosperar*) to prosper, thrive; (*animal, planta etc*) to grow.

medroso, a |methro'so, á| *a* fearful, timid.

médula |me'thōōlá| *nf* (*ANAT*) marrow; (*BOT*) pith; ~ **espinal** spinal cord; **hasta la** ~ (*fig*) to the core.

medusa |methōō'sá| *nf* (*Esp*) jellyfish.

megabyte |me'gáháčt| *nm* (*INFORM*) megabyte.

megáfono |megá'fono| *nm* megaphone.

megalomanía |megálománē'á| *nf* megalomania.

megalómano, a |megálo'máno, á| *nm/f* megalomaniac.

megaocteto |megáokte'to| *nm* (*INFORM*) megabyte.

mejicano, a |mehēká'no, á| *a, nm/f* Mexican.

Méjico |me'hēko| *nm* Mexico.

mejilla |mehē'yá| *nf* cheek.

mejillón |mehēyon'| *nm* mussel.

mejor |mehor'| *a, ad* (*comparativo*) better; (*superlativo*) best; **lo** ~ the best thing; **lo** ~ **de la vida** the prime of life; **a lo** ~ probably; (*quizá*) maybe; ~ **dicho** rather; **tanto** ~ so much the better; **es el** ~ **de todos** he's the best of all.

mejora |meho'rá| *nf*, **mejoramiento** |mehorámyen'to| *nm* improvement.

mejorar |mehorár'| *vt* to improve, make better ♦ *vi*, ~**se** *vr* to improve, get better; (*COM*) to do well, prosper; ~ **a** to be better than; **los negocios mejoran** business is picking up.

mejoría |mehorē'á| *nf* improvement; (*restablecimiento*) recovery.

melancólico, a [melánko'lēko, à] a (triste) sad, melancholy; (soñador) dreamy.

melena [mele'nà] nf (de persona) long hair; (ZOOL) mane.

melillense [melēyen'se] a of o from Melilla. ♦ nm/f native o inhabitant of Melilla.

melocotón [melokoton'] nm (Esp) peach.

melodía [meloṱē'à] nf melody; (aire) tune.

melodrama [meloṱḥrà'má] nm melodrama.

melodramático, a [meloṱḥràmá'tēko, à] a melodramatic.

melón [melon'] nm melon.

melopea [melope'à] nf (fam): **tener una ~** to be soused (US) o sloshed (Brit).

meloso, a [melo'so, à] a honeyed, sweet; (empalagoso) sickly, cloying; (voz) sweet; (zalamero) smooth.

mella [me'yà] nf (rotura) notch, nick; **hacer ~** (fig) to make an impression.

mellizo, a [meyē'so, à] a, nm/f twin ♦ nm (AM): **~s** cufflinks.

membrete [membre'te] nm letterhead.

membrillo [membrē'yo] nm quince; **carne de ~** quince jelly.

memo, a [me'mo, à] a silly, stupid ♦ nm/f idiot.

memorable [memorà'ḥle] a memorable.

memorándum [memorán'dōōm] nm (libro) notebook; (comunicación) memorandum.

memoria [memo'ryà] nf (gen) memory; (artículo) (learned) paper; **~s** nfpl (de autor) memoirs; **~ anual** annual report; **aprender algo de ~** to learn sth by heart; **si tengo buena ~** if my memory serves me right; **venir a la ~** to come to mind; (INFORM): **~ de acceso aleatorio** random access memory, RAM; **~ auxiliar** backing storage; **~ fija** read-only memory, ROM; **~ fija programable** programmable memory; **~ del teclado** keyboard memory.

memorice [memorē'se] etc vb V **memorizar.**

memorizar [memorēsàr'] vt to memorize.

menaje [menà'he] nm (muebles) furniture; (utensilios domésticos) household equipment; **~ de cocina** kitchenware.

mencionar [mensyonàr'] vt to mention; (nombrar) to name; **sin ~ ...** let alone ....

mendicidad [mendēsēḥàṱh'] nf begging.

mendigar [mendēgàr'] vt to beg (for).

mendigo, a [mendē'go, à] nm/f beggar.

mendigue [mendē'ge] etc vb V **mendigar.**

mendrugo [mendrōō'go] nm crust.

menear [meneàr'] vt to move; (cola) to wag; (cadera) to swing; (fig) to handle; **~se** vr to shake; (balancearse) to sway; (moverse) to move; (fig) to get a move on.

menester [menester'] nm (necesidad) necessity; **~es** nmpl (deberes) duties; **es ~ hacer algo** it is necessary to do sth, sth must be done.

menestra [menes'trà] nf: **~ de verduras** vegetable stew.

mengano, a [mengà'no, à] nm/f Mr (o Mrs o Miss) So-and-so.

mengua [men'gwà] nf (disminución) decrease; (falta) lack; (pobreza) poverty; (fig) discredit; **en ~ de** to the detriment of.

menguante [mengwàn'te] a decreasing, diminishing; (luna) waning; (marea) ebb cpd.

menguar [mengwàr'] vt to lessen, diminish; (fig) to discredit ♦ vi to diminish, decrease; (fig) to decline.

mengüe [men'gwe] etc vb V **menguar.**

menopausia [menopá'ōōsyà] nf menopause.

menor [menor'] a (más pequeño: comparativo) smaller; (número) less, lesser; (: superlativo) smallest; (número) least; (más joven: comparativo) younger; (: superlativo) youngest; (MUS) minor ♦ nm/f (joven) young person, juvenile; **Juanito es ~ que Pepe** Juanito is younger than Pepe; **ella es la ~ de todas** she is the youngest of all; **no tengo la ~ idea** I haven't the faintest idea; **al por ~** retail; **~ de edad** under age.

Menorca [menor'kà] nf Minorca.

menoría [menorē'à] n (AM COM): **a ~** retail.

menorquín, ina [menorkēn', ēnà] a, nm/f Minorcan.

menos [me'nos] a (comparativo: sg) less; (: pl) fewer; (superlativo: sg) least; (: pl) fewest ♦ ad (comparativo) less; (superlativo) least ♦ conj, prep except ♦ nm (MAT) minus; **~ de lo que piensas** less than you think; **es el ~ inteligente de los 4** he is the least intelligent of the 4; **eso es lo de ~** that's the least of it; **es lo ~ que puedo hacer** it's the least I can do; **lo ~ posible** as little as possible; **a ~ que** unless; **~ de 5** less than 5; **hay 7 de ~** we're 7 short; **no es rico, ni mucho ~** he's far from being rich; **ir o venir a ~** to come down in the world; **al o por lo ~** at least; **¡~ mal!** just as well!; **¡todo ~ eso!** anything but that!; **¿qué ~?** (fam) what else did you expect?; **las 7 ~ 20** (hora) 20 to 7.

menoscabar [menoskàḥàr'] vt (estropear) to damage, harm; (fig) to discredit.

menospreciar [menospresyàr'] vt to underrate, undervalue; (despreciar) to scorn, despise.

menosprecio [menospre'syo] nm underrating, undervaluation; scorn, contempt.

mensaje [mensà'he] nm message; **~ de error** (INFORM) error message.

mensajero, a [mensàhe'ro, à] nm/f messenger.

menstruación [menstrwàsyon'] nf menstruation.

menstruar |menstrwár'| *vi* to menstruate.

mensual |menswál'| *a* monthly; **100 ptas** ~**es** 100 ptas. a month.

mensualidad |menswäléthàth'| *nf* (*salario*) monthly salary; (*COM*) monthly payment o installment.

menta |men'tà| *nf* mint.

mentado, a |mentá'tho, à| *a* (*mencionado*) aforementioned; (*famoso*) well-known.

mental |mentál'| *a* mental.

mentalidad |mentáléthàth'| *nf* mentality, way of thinking.

mentar |mentár'| *vt* to mention, name.

mente |men'te| *nf* mind; (*inteligencia*) intelligence; **no tengo en ~ hacer eso** it is not my intention to do that.

mentecato, a |menteká'to, à| *a* silly, stupid ♦ *nm/f* fool, idiot.

mentir |mentér'| *vi* to lie; **¡miento!** sorry, I'm wrong!

mentira |mentē'rà| *nf* (*una ~*) lie; (*acto*) lying; (*invención*) fiction; ~ **piadosa** white lie; **una ~ como una casa** a whopping great lie (*fam*); **parece ~ que** ... it seems incredible that ..., I can't believe that ....

mentiroso, a |mentēro'so, à| *a* lying; (*falso*) deceptive ♦ *nm/f* liar.

mentís |mentēs'| *nm inv* denial; **dar el ~ a** to deny.

mentón |menton'| *nm* chin.

menú |menōō'| *nm* (*tb INFORM*) menu; (*en restaurante*) set meal; **guiado por ~** (*INFORM*) menu-driven.

menudear |menōōtheár'| *vt* (*repetir*) to repeat frequently ♦ *vi* (*ser frecuente*) to be frequent; (*detallar*) to go into great detail.

menudencia |menōōthen'syà| *nf* (*bagatela*) trifle; ~**s** *nfpl* odds and ends.

menudillos |menōōthē'yos| *nmpl* giblets.

menudo, a |menōō'tho, à| *a* (*pequeño*) small, tiny; (*sin importancia*) petty, insignificant; **¡~ negocio!** (*fam*) some deal!; **a ~** often, frequently.

meñique |menyē'ke| *nm* little finger.

meollo |meo'yo| *nm* (*fig*) essence, core.

mequetrefe |meketre'fe| *nm* good-for-nothing, whippersnapper.

mercader |merkáther'| *nm* merchant.

mercadería |merkátherē'á| *nf* commodity; ~**s** *nfpl* goods, merchandise *sg*.

mercado |merká'tho| *nm* market; ~ **en baja** falling market; **M~ Común** Common Market; ~ **de demanda/de oferta** seller's/ buyer's market; ~ **laboral** labor market; ~ **objetivo** target market; ~ **de productos básicos** commodity market; ~ **de valores** stock market; ~ **exterior/interior** o **nacional/libre** overseas/domestic/free market.

mercancía |merkánsē'á| *nf* commodity; ~**s** *nfpl* goods, merchandise *sg*; ~**s en deposi-**

to bonded goods; ~**s perecederas** perishable goods.

mercancías |merkánsē'às| *nm inv* freight train (*US*), goods train.

mercantil |merkántēl'| *a* mercantile, commercial.

mercenario, a |mersená'ryo, à| *a, nm* mercenary.

mercería |merserē'á| *nf* (*artículos*) notions *pl* (*US*), haberdashery (*Brit*); (*tienda*) notions store (*US*), haberdasher's shop (*Brit*), drapery (*Brit*).

mercurio |merkōō'ryo| *nm* mercury.

merecedor, a |meresethor', à| *a* deserving; ~ **de confianza** trustworthy.

merecer |mereser'| *vt* to deserve, merit ♦ *vi* to be deserving, be worthy; **merece la pena** it's worthwhile.

merecido, a |meresē'tho, à| *a* (well-) deserved; **llevarse su ~** to get one's deserts.

merendar |merendár'| *vt* to have for lunch (*US*) o tea (*Brit*) ♦ *vi* to have lunch (*US*) o tea (*Brit*); (*en el campo*) to have a picnic.

merendero |merende'ro| *nm* (*café*) tearoom; (*en el campo*) picnic spot.

merengue |meren'ge| *nm* meringue.

merezca |meres'kà| *etc vb V* **merecer**.

meridiano |merēthyá'no| *nm* (*ASTRO, GEO*) meridian; **la explicación es de una claridad meridiana** the explanation is as clear as day.

meridional |merēthyonál'| *a* Southern ♦ *nm/f* Southerner.

merienda |meryen'dà| *etc vb V* **merendar** ♦ *nf* (light) tea, afternoon snack; (*de campo*) picnic; ~ **de negros** free-for-all.

mérito |me'rēto| *nm* merit; (*valor*) worth, value; **hacer ~s** to make a good impression; **restar ~ a** to detract from.

meritorio, a |merēto'ryo, à| *a* deserving.

merluza |merlōō'sà| *nf* hake; **coger una ~** (*fam*) to get soused (*US*) o sozzled (*Brit*).

merma |mer'mà| *nf* decrease; (*pérdida*) wastage.

mermar |mermár'| *vt* to reduce, lessen ♦ *vi* to decrease, dwindle.

mermelada |mermelá'thà| *nf* jam; ~ **de naranja** marmalade.

mero, a |me'ro, à| *a* mere, simple; (*AM fam*) very ♦ *nm* (*ZOOL*) grouper.

merodear |merotheár'| *vi* (*MIL*) to maraud; (*de noche*) to prowl (about); (*curiosear*) to snoop around.

mes |mes| *nm* month; (*salario*) month's pay; **el ~ corriente** this o the current month.

mesa |me'sà| *nf* table; (*de trabajo*) desk; (*COM*) counter; (*en mitin*) platform; (*GEO*) plateau; (*ARQ*) landing; ~ **de noche/de tijera/de operaciones** u **operatoria** bedside/folding/operating table; ~ **redonda**

(*reunión*) round table; ~ **digitalizadora** (*IN-FORM*) graph pad; ~ **directiva** board; ~ **y cama** room and board; **poner/quitar la** ~ to set/clear the table.

mesarse [mesár'se] *vr*: ~ **el pelo** *o* **los cabellos** to tear one's hair out.

mesera [mese'rá] *nf* (*AM*) waitress.

mesero [mese'ro] *nm* (*AM*) waiter.

meseta [mese'tá] *nf* (*GEO*) meseta, tableland; (*ARQ*) landing.

mesilla [mesē'yá], **mesita** [mesē'tá] *nf*: ~ **de noche** bedside table.

mesón [meson'] *nm* inn.

mestizo, a [mestē'so, á] *a* half-breed, of mixed race; (*ZOOL*) crossbred ♦ *nm/f* half-breed.

mesura [mesōōrá] *nf* (*calma*) calm; (*moderación*) moderation, restraint; (*cortesía*) courtesy.

mesurar [mesōōrár'] *vt* (*contener*) to restrain; ~**se** *vr* to restrain o.s.

meta [me'tá] *nf* goal; (*de carrera*) finish; (*fig*) goal, aim, objective.

metafísico, a [metáfē'sēko, á] *a* metaphysical ♦ *nf* metaphysics *sg*.

metafórico, a [metáfo'rēko, á] *a* metaphorical.

metáfora [metá'forá] *nf* metaphor.

metal [metál'] *nm* (*materia*) metal; (*MUS*) brass.

metálico, a [metá'lēko, á] *a* metallic; (*de metal*) metal ♦ *nm* (*dinero contante*) cash.

metalurgia [metálōōr'hyá] *nf* metallurgy.

metalúrgico, a [metálōōr'hēko, á] *a* metallurgic(al); **industria** ~**a** steel industry.

metamorfosear [metámorfoseár'] *vt*: ~ **(en)** to metamorphose *o* transform (into).

metamorfosis [metámorfo'sēs] *nf inv* metamorphosis, transformation.

metedura [metetħōō'rá] *nf*: ~ **de pata** (*fam*) blunder.

meteoro [meteo'ro] *nm* meteor.

meteorólogo, a [meteoro'logo, á] *nm/f* meteorologist; (*RADIO, TV*) weatherman.

meter [meter'] *vt* (*colocar*) to put, place; (*introducir*) to put in, insert; (*involucrar*) to involve; (*causar*) to make, cause; ~**se** *vr*: ~**se en** to go into, enter; (*fig*) to interfere in, meddle in; ~**se a** to start; ~**se a escritor** to become a writer; ~**se con uno** to provoke sb, pick a quarrel with sb; ~ **prisa a uno** to hurry sb up.

meticuloso, a [metēkōō'lo'so, á] *a* meticulous, thorough.

metido, a [metē'tħo, á] *a*: **estar muy** ~ **en un asunto** to be deeply involved in a matter; ~ **en años** elderly; ~ **en carne** plump.

metódico, a [meto'tħēko, á] *a* methodical.

metodismo [metotħēs'mo] *nm* Methodism.

método [me'totħo] *nm* method.

metomentodo [metomento'tħo] *nm inv* meddler, busybody.

metraje [metrá'he] *nm* (*CINE*) length; **cinta de largo/corto** ~ full-length film/short.

metralleta [metráye'tá] *nf* sub-machine-gun.

métrico, a [me'trēko, á] *a* metric; **cinta métrica** tape measure.

metro [me'tro] *nm* meter (*US*), metre (*Brit*); (*tren*: *tb*: **metropolitano**) subway (*US*), underground (*Brit*); (*instrumento*) ruler; ~ **cuadrado/cúbico** square/cubic meter.

mexicano, a [mehēká'no, á] *a, nm/f* (*AM*) Mexican.

México [me'hēko] *nm* (*AM*) Mexico; **Ciudad de** ~ Mexico City.

meza [me'sá] *etc vb* V **mecer.**

mezcla [mes'klá] *nf* mixture; (*fig*) blend.

mezclar [mesklár'] *vt* to mix (up); (*armonizar*) to blend; (*combinar*) to merge; ~**se** *vr* to mix, mingle; ~ **en** to get mixed up in, get involved in.

mezcolanza [meskolán'sá] *nf* hodgepodge, jumble.

mezquindad [meskēndátħ'] *nf* (*cicatería*) meanness; (*miras estrechas*) pettiness; (*acto*) mean action.

mezquino, a [meskē'no, á] *a* (*cicatero*) mean ♦ *nm/f* (*avaro*) miser; (*miserable*) petty individual.

mezquita [meskē'tá] *nf* mosque.

MF *abr* (= *Modulación de Frecuencia*) FM.

mg. *abr* (= *miligramo(s)*) mg.

mi [mē] *a posesivo* my ♦ *nm* (*MUS*) E.

mí [mē] *pron* me, myself; **¿y a** ~ **qué?** so what?

miaja [myá'há] *nf* crumb; **ni una** ~ (*fig*) not the least little bit.

micro [mē'kro] *nm* (*RADIO*) mike, microphone; (*AM*) minibus.

microbio [mēkro'ħyo] *nm* microbe.

microbús [mēkroħōōs'] *nm* minibus.

microcomputador [mēkrokompōōtátħor'] *nm*, **microcomputadora** [mēkrokompōōtátħo'rá] *nf* micro(computer).

microchip [mēkrotchēp'] *nm* microchip.

microeconomía [mēkroekonomē'á] *nf* microeconomics *sg*.

microficha [mēkrofētch'á] *nf* microfiche.

micrófono [mēkro'fono] *nm* microphone.

microinformática [mēkroēnformá'tēká] *nf* microcomputing.

micrómetro [mēkro'metro] *nm* micrometer.

microonda [mēkroon'dá] *nf* microwave; **horno** ~**s** microwave oven.

microordenador [mēkroordenátħor'] *nm* microcomputer.

micropastilla [mēkropástē'yá], **microplaqueta** [mēkroplákē'tá] *nf* (*INFORM*) chip, wafer.

microplaquita [mēkroplákē'tá] *nf*: ~ **de si-**

licio silicon chip.

microprocesador [mēkroprosesáth̥or'] *nm* microprocessor.

microprograma [mēkroprogrà'mâ] *nm* (*INFORM*) firmware.

microscopio [mēkrosko'pyo] *nm* microscope.

midiendo [mēth̥yen'do] *etc vb V* **medir.**

MIE *nm abr* (*Esp*)=*Ministerio de Industria y Energía.*

miedo [mye'th̥o] *nm* fear; (*nerviosismo*) apprehension, nervousness; **meter** ~ **a** to scare, frighten; **tener** ~ to be afraid; **de** ~ wonderful, marvelous; **¡qué ~!** (*fam*) how awful!; **me da** ~ it scares me; **hace un frío de** ~ (*fam*) it's terribly cold.

miedoso, a [myeth̥o'so, â] *a* fearful, timid.

miel [myel] *nf* honey; **no hay** ~ **sin hiel** there's no rose without a thorn.

miembro [myem'bro] *nm* limb; (*socio*) member; (*de institución*) fellow; ~ **viril** penis.

mientes [myen'tes] *etc vb V* **mentar; mentir ♦** *nfpl:* **no parar** ~ **en** to pay no attention to; **traer a las** ~ to recall.

mientras [myen'trâs] *conj* while; (*duración*) as long as **♦** *ad* meanwhile; ~ **(que)** whereas; ~ **tanto** meanwhile; ~ **más tiene, más quiere** the more he has, the more he wants.

miérc. *abr* (= *miércoles*) Wed.

miércoles [myer'koles] *nm inv* Wednesday; ~ **de ceniza** Ash Wednesday.

mierda [myer'th̥â] *nf* (*fam!*) shit (*!*), crap (*!*); (*fig*) filth, dirt; **¡vete a la ~!** go to hell!

mies [myes] *nf* (ripe) corn, wheat, grain.

miga [mē'g̥â] *nf* crumb; (*fig: meollo*) essence; **hacer buenas ~s** (*fam*) to get on well; **esto tiene su** ~ there's more to this than meets the eye.

migración [mēg̥rásyon'] *nf* migration.

mil [mēl] *num* thousand; **dos ~ dólares** two thousand dollars.

milagro [mēlà'g̥ro] *nm* miracle; **hacer ~s** (*fig*) to work wonders.

milagroso, a [mēlàg̥ro'so, â] *a* miraculous.

Milán [mēlàn'] *nm* Milan.

milenario, a [mēlenà'ryo, â] *a* millennial; (*fig*) very ancient.

milenio [mēle'nyo] *nm* millennium.

milésimo, a [mēle'sēmo, â] *num* thousandth.

mili [mē'lē] *nf:* **hacer la** ~ (*fam*) to do one's military service.

milicia [mēlē'syâ] *nf* (*MIL*) militia; (*servicio militar*) military service.

milímetro [mēlē'metro] *nm* millimeter (*US*), millimetre (*Brit*).

militante [mēlētân'te] *a* militant.

militar [mēlētàr'] *a* military **♦** *nm/f* soldier **♦** *vi* to serve in the army; (*fig*) to militate,

fight.

milla [mē'yâ] *nf* mile; ~ **marina** nautical mile.

millar [mēyàr'] *num* thousand; **a ~es** in thousands.

millón [mēyon'] *num* million.

millonario, a [mēyonà'ryo, â] *nm/f* millionaire.

millonésimo, a [mēyone'sēmo, â] *num* millionth.

mimado, a [mēmá'th̥o, â] *a* spoiled.

mimar [mēmár'] *vt* to spoil, pamper.

mimbre [mēm'bre] *nm* wicker; **de** ~ wicker *cpd*, wickerwork.

mímica [mē'mēkâ] *nf* (*para comunicarse*) sign language; (*imitación*) mimicry.

mimetismo [mēmetēs'mo] *nm* mimicry.

mimo [mē'mo] *nm* (*caricia*) caress; (*de niño*) spoiling; (*TEATRO*) mime; (: *actor*) mime artist.

mina [mē'nâ] *nf* mine; (*pozo*) shaft; (*de lápiz*) lead refill; **hullera** *o* ~ **de carbón** coalmine.

minar [mēnàr'] *vt* to mine; (*fig*) to undermine.

mineral [mēnerál'] *a* mineral **♦** *nm* (*GEO*) mineral; (*mena*) ore.

minería [mēnerē'â] *nf* mining.

minero, a [mēne'ro, â] *a* mining *cpd* **♦** *nm/f* miner.

miniatura [mēnyàtōō'râ] *a inv, nf* miniature.

minicomputador [mēnēkompōōtáth̥or'] *nm* minicomputer.

minidisco [mēnēth̥ēs'ko] *nm* diskette.

minifalda [mēnēfál'dâ] *nf* miniskirt.

minifundio [mēnēfōōn'dyo] *nm* smallholding, small farm.

mínimo, a [mē'nēmo, â] *a* minimum; (*insignificante*) minimal **♦** *nm* minimum; **precio/salario** ~ minimum price/wage; **lo** ~ **que pueden hacer** the least they can do.

minino [mēnē'no, â] *nm/f* (*fam*) kitty.

ministerio [mēnēste'ryo] *nm* department (*US*), ministry (*Brit*); **M~ de Asuntos Exteriores** State Department (*US*), Foreign Office (*Brit*); **M~ del Comercio e Industria** Department of Trade and Industry; **M~ de (la) Gobernación** *o* **del Interior** Ministry of the Interior; **M~ de Hacienda** Treasury Department (*US*), Treasury (*Brit*).

ministro, a [mēnēs'tro, â] *nm/f* secretary, (*esp US*) minister; **M~ de Hacienda** Secretary of the Treasury (*US*), Chancellor of the Exchequer (*Brit*); **M~ de (la) Gobernación** *o* **del Interior** ≈ Secretary of the Interior (*US*), Home Secretary (*Brit*).

minoría [mēnorē'â] *nf* minority.

mintiendo [mēntyen'do] *etc vb V* **mentir.**

minucia [mēnōō'syâ] *nf* (*detalle insignificante*) trifle; (*bagatela*) mere nothing.

minuciosidad |mēnōōsyosēthâth'| *nf* (*meticulosidad*) thoroughness, meticulousness.

minucioso, a |mēnōōsyo'so, à| *a* thorough, meticulous; (*prolijo*) very detailed.

minúsculo, a |mēnōōs'kōōlo, à| *a* tiny, minute ♦ *nf* small letter; **minúsculas** *nfpl* (*TIP*) lower case *sg.*

minusvalía |mēnōōsḥálē'à| *nf* physical handicap; (*COM*) depreciation, capital loss.

minusválido, a |mēnōōsḥá'lētḥo, à| *a* (physically) handicapped *o* disabled ♦ *nm/f* disabled person.

minuta |mēnōō'tà| *nf* (*de comida*) menu; (*de abogado etc*) fee.

minutero |mēnōōtē'ro| *nm* minute hand.

minuto |mēnōō'to| *nm* minute.

Miño |mē'nyo| *nm:* **el (río)** ~ the Miño.

mío, a |mē'o, à| *a, pron:* **el** ~ mine; **un amigo** ~ a friend of mine; **lo** ~ what is mine; **los** ~**s** my people, my relations.

miope |myo'pē| *a* nearsighted.

miopía |myopē'à| *nf* nearsightedness.

MIR |mēr| *nm abr* (*POL*)=*Movimiento de Izquierda Revolucionaria;* (*Esp MED*) *Médico Interno y Residente.*

mira |mē'rà| *nf* (*de arma*) sight(s) (*pl*); (*fig*) aim, intention; **de amplias/estrechas** ~**s** broad-/narrow-minded.

mirada |mērà'thà| *nf* look, glance; (*expresión*) look, expression; ~ **de soslayo** sidelong glance; ~ **fija** stare, gaze; ~ **perdida** distant look; **echar una** ~ **a** to glance at; **levantar/bajar la** ~ to look up/down; **resistir la** ~ **de uno** to stare sb out.

mirado, a |mērà'tho, à| *a* (*sensato*) sensible; (*considerado*) considerate; **bien/mal** ~ well/not well thought of.

mirador |mēràthor'| *nm* viewpoint, vantage point.

miramiento |mēràmyen'to| *nm* (*consideración*) considerateness; **tratar sin** ~ **a uno** to ride roughshod over sb.

mirar |mērár'| *vt* to look at; (*observar*) to watch; (*considerar*) to consider, think over; (*vigilar, cuidar*) to watch, look after ♦ *vi* to look; (*ARQ*) to face; ~**se** *vr* (*dos personas*) to look at each other; ~ **algo/a uno de reojo** *o* **de través** to look askance at sth/sb; ~ **algo/a uno por encima del hombro** to look down on sth/sb; ~ **bien/mal** to think highly of/have a poor opinion of; ~ **fijamente** to stare *o* gaze at; ~ **por** (*fig*) to look after; ~ **por la ventana** to look out of the window; ~**se al espejo** to look at o.s. in the mirror; ~**se a los ojos** to look into each other's eyes.

mirilla |mērē'yà| *nf* (*agujero*) spyhole, peephole.

mirlo |mēr'lo| *nm* blackbird.

misa |mē'sà| *nf* mass; ~ **del gallo** midnight mass (*on Christmas Eve*); ~ **de difuntos** requiem mass; **como en** ~ in dead silence; **estos datos van a** ~ (*fig*) these facts are utterly trustworthy.

misántropo |mēsàn'tropo| *nm* misanthrope, misanthropist.

miscelánea |mēscelá'neà| *nf* miscellany.

miserable |mēscrà'ḥle| *a* (*avaro*) stingy; (*nimio*) miserable, paltry; (*lugar*) squalid; (*fam*) vile, despicable ♦ *nm/f* (*malvado*) rogue.

miseria |mēsc'ryà| *nf* misery; (*pobreza*) poverty; (*tacañería*) stinginess; (*condiciones*) squalor; **una** ~ a pittance.

misericordia |mēscrēkor'thyà| *nf* (*compasión*) compassion, pity; (*perdón*) forgiveness, mercy.

misil |mēscl'| *nm* missile.

misión |mēsyon'| *nf* mission; (*tarea*) job, duty; (*POL*) assignment; **misiones** *nfpl* (*REL*) overseas missions.

misionero, a |mēsyonc'ro, à| *nm/f* missionary.

mismamente |mēsmàmen'tc| *ad* (*fam: sólo*) only, just.

mismísimo, a |mēsmē'scmo, à| *a superlativo* selfsame, very (same).

mismo, a |mēs'mo, à| *a* (*semejante*) same; (*después de pronombre*) -self; (*para énfasis*) very ♦ *ad:* **aquí/ayer/hoy** ~ right here/only yesterday/this very day; **ahora** ~ right now ♦ *conj:* **lo** ~ **que** just like, just as; **por lo** ~ for the same reason; **el** ~ **traje** the same suit; **en ese** ~ **momento** at that very moment; **vino el** ~ **Ministro** the Minister himself came; **yo** ~ **lo vi** I saw it myself; **lo hizo por sí** ~ he did it by himself; **lo** ~ the same (thing); **da lo** ~ it's all the same; **quedamos en las mismas** we're no further forward.

misógino |mēso'hēno| *nm* misogynist.

miss |mēs| *nf* beauty queen.

misterio |mēstc'ryo| *nm* mystery; (*lo secreto*) secrecy.

misterioso, a |mēstcryo'so, à| *a* mysterious; (*inexplicable*) puzzling.

misticismo |mēstēscs'mo| *nm* mysticism.

místico, a |mē'stēko, à| *a* mystic(al) ♦ *nm/f* mystic ♦ *nf* mysticism.

mitad |mētàth'| *nf* (*medio*) half; (*centro*) middle; ~ **(y)** ~ half-and-half; (*fig*) yes and no; **a** ~ **de precio** (at) half-price; **en** *o* **a** ~ **del camino** halfway along the road; **cortar por la** ~ to cut through the middle.

mítico, a |mē'tēko, à| *a* mythical.

mitigar |mētēgár'| *vt* to mitigate; (*dolor*) to relieve; (*sed*) to quench; (*ira*) to appease; (*preocupación*) to allay; (*soledad*) to alleviate.

mitigue |mētē'gc| *etc vb V* **mitigar**.

mitin |mē'tēn| *nm* (*esp POL*) meeting.

mito [mē'to] *nm* myth.
mitología [mētolohē'á] *nf* mythology.
mitológico, a [mētolo'hēko, á] *a* mythological.
mixto, a [mēk'sto, á] *a* mixed; (*comité*) joint.
ml. *abr* (= *mililitro*) ml.
MLN *nm abr* (*POL*)=*Movimiento de Liberación Nacional.*
mm. *abr* (= *milímetro*) mm.
m/n *abr* (*ECON*) = *moneda nacional.*
M.º *abr* (*POL*: = *Ministerio*) Min.
m/o *abr* (*COM*) = *mi orden.*
mobiliario [mohēlyá'ryo] *nm* furniture.
mocedad [mosetháth'] *nf* youth.
moción [mosyon'] *nf* motion; ~ **compuesta** (*POL*) composite motion.
moco [mo'ko] *nm* mucus; **limpiarse los ~s** to blow one's nose; **no es ~ de pavo** it's no trifle.
mocoso, a [moko'so, á] *a* snivelling; (*fig*) ill-bred ♦ *nm/f* (*fam*) brat.
mochila [motchē'lá] *nf* backpack.
moda [mo'thá] *nf* fashion; (*estilo*) style; **de o a la ~** in fashion, fashionable; **pasado de ~** out of fashion; **vestido a la última ~** trendily dressed.
modal [mothál'] *a* modal ♦ *nm*: ~**es** *nmpl* manners.
modalidad [mothálētháth'] *nf* (*clase*) kind, variety; (*manera*) way; (*INFORM*) mode; ~ **de texto** (*INFORM*) text mode.
modelar [mothelár'] *vt* to model.
modelo [mothe'lo] *a inv* model ♦ *nm/f* model ♦ *nm* (*patrón*) pattern; (*norma*) standard.
módem [mo'them] *nm* (*INFORM*) modem.
moderado, a [motherá'tho, á] *a* moderate.
moderar [motherár'] *vt* to moderate; (*violencia*) to restrain, control; (*velocidad*) to reduce; ~**se** *vr* to restrain o.s., control o.s.
modernice [mothernē'se] *etc vb* V **modernizar.**
modernizar [mothernēsár'] *vt* to modernize; (*INFORM*) to upgrade.
moderno, a [mother'no, á] *a* modern; (*actual*) present-day; (*equipo etc*) up-to-date.
modestia [mothes'tyá] *nf* modesty.
modesto, a [mothe'sto, á] *a* modest.
módico, a [mo'thēko, á] *a* moderate, reasonable.
modificar [mothēfēkár'] *vt* to modify.
modifique [mothēfē'ke] *etc vb* V **modificar.**
modismo [mothēs'mo] *nm* idiom.
modisto, a [mothē'sto, á] *nm/f* dressmaker.
modo [mo'tho] *nm* (*manera, forma*) way, manner; (*INFORM. MUS*) mode; (*LING*) mood; ~**s** *nmpl* manners; (*INFORM*) "instructions for use"; ~ **de gobierno** form of government; **a ~ de** like; **de este ~** in this way; **de ningún ~** in no way; **de**

todos ~s at any rate; **de un ~ u otro** (in) one way or another.
modorra [motho'rrá] *nf* drowsiness.
modoso, a [motho'so, á] *a* (*educado*) quiet, well-mannered.
modulación [mothōōlásyon'] *nf* modulation; ~ **de frecuencia** (*RADIO*) frequency modulation, FM.
mofarse [mofár'se] *vr*: ~ **de** to mock, scoff at.
moflete [mofle'te] *nm* fat cheek, chubby cheek.
mogollón [mogoyon'] (*fam*) *nm*: ~ **de discos** *etc* loads of records *etc* ♦ *ad*: **un ~** a hell of a lot.
mohín [moēn'] *nm* (*mueca*) (wry) face; (*pucheros*) pout.
mohino, a [moē'no, á] *a* (*triste*) gloomy, depressed; (*enojado*) sulky.
moho [mo'o] *nm* (*BOT*) mold (*US*), mould (*Brit*); mildew; (*en metal*) rust.
mohoso, a [moo'so, á] *a* moldy (*US*), mouldy (*Brit*); rusty.
mojado, a [mohá'tho, á] *a* wet; (*húmedo*) damp; (*empapado*) drenched.
mojar [mohár'] *vt* to wet; (*humedecer*) to damp(en), moisten; (*calar*) to soak; ~**se** *vr* to get wet; ~ **el pan en el café** to dip o dunk one's bread in one's coffee.
mojigato, a [mohēgá'to, á] *a* (*hipócrita*) hypocritical; (*santurrón*) sanctimonious; (*gazmoño*) prudish ♦ *nm/f* hypocrite; sanctimonious person; prude.
mojón [mohon'] *nm* (*hito*) landmark; (*en un camino*) signpost; (~ *kilométrico*) milestone.
mol. *abr* (= *molécula*) mol.
molar [molár'] *nm* molar ♦ *vt* (*fam*): **lo que más me mola es ...** what I'm really into is ...; **¿te mola un pitillo?** would you like a smoke?
molde [mol'de] *nm* mold (*US*), mould (*Brit*); (*vaciado*) cast; (*de costura*) pattern; (*fig*) model.
moldear [moldeár'] *vt* to mold (*US*), mould (*Brit*); (*en yeso etc*) to cast.
mole [mo'le] *nf* mass, bulk; (*edificio*) pile.
moler [moler'] *vt* to grind, crush; (*pulverizar*) to pound; (*trigo etc*) to mill; (*cansar*) to tire out, exhaust; ~ **a uno a palos** to give sb a beating.
molestar [molestár'] *vt* to bother; (*fastidiar*) to annoy; (*incomodar*) to inconvenience, put out; (*perturbar*) to trouble, upset ♦ *vi* to be a nuisance; ~**se** *vr* to bother; (*incomodarse*) to go to a lot of trouble; (*ofenderse*) to take offense; **¿le molesta el ruido?** do you mind the noise?; **siento ~le** I'm sorry to trouble you.
molestia [moles'tyá] *nf* bother, trouble; (*incomodidad*) inconvenience; (*MED*) dis-

comfort; **no es ninguna** ~ it's no trouble at all.

molesto, a |mole'sto. á| a (que fastidia) annoying; (incómodo) inconvenient; (inquieto) uncomfortable, ill at ease; (enfadado) annoyed; **estar** ~ (MED) to be in some discomfort; **estar** ~ **con uno** (fig) to be cross with sb; **me sentí** ~ I felt embarrassed.

molido, a |mole'tho, á| a (machacado) ground; (pulverizado) powdered; **estar** ~ (fig) to be exhausted o dead beat.

molinero |moléne'ro| nm miller.

molinillo |moléné'yo| nm hand mill; ~ **de carne/café** meat grinder (US) o mincer (Brit)/coffee grinder.

molino |mole'no| nm (edificio) mill; (máquina) grinder.

Molucas |moloo'kás| nfpl: **las (Islas)** ~ the Moluccas, the Molucca Islands.

molusco |moloos'ko| nm mollusc.

mollera |moye'rá| nf (ANAT) crown of the head; (fam: seso) brains pl; **duro de** ~ (estúpido) thick.

momentáneo, a |momentá'neo, á| a momentary.

momento |momen'to| nm (gen) moment; (TEC) momentum; **de** ~ at the moment, for the moment; **por el** ~ for the time being.

momia |mo'myá| nf mummy.

mona |mo'ná| nf V **mono.**

Mónaco |mo'náko| nm Monaco.

monada |moná'thá| nf (de niño) charming habit; (cosa primorosa) lovely thing; (chica) pretty girl; **¡qué** ~! isn't it cute?

monaguillo |monáge'yo| nm altar boy.

monarca |monár'ká| nm/f monarch, ruler.

monarquía |monárké'á| nf monarchy.

monárquico, a |monár'kéko, á| nm/f royalist, monarchist.

monasterio |monáste'ryo| nm monastery.

monda |mon'dá| nf (poda) pruning; (: de árbol) lopping; (: de fruta) peeling; (cáscara) skin; **¡es la** ~! (fam: fantástico) it's great!; (: el colmo) it's the limit!; (: persona: gracioso) he's a knockout!

mondadientes |mondá'thyen'tes| nm inv toothpick.

mondar |mondár'| vt (limpiar) to clean; (pelar) to peel; ~**se** vr: ~**se de risa** (fam) to split one's sides laughing.

moneda |mone'thá| nf (tipo de dinero) currency, money; (pieza) coin; **una** ~ **de 5 pesetas** a 5 peseta coin; ~ **de curso** legal tender; ~ **extranjera** foreign exchange; **es** ~ **corriente** (fig) it's common knowledge.

monedero |monethe'ro| nm purse.

monegasco, a |monegás'ko, á| a o of o from Monaco, Monegasque ♦ nm/f Monegasque.

monetario, a |monetá'ryo, á| a monetary,

financial.

monetarista |monetáré'stá| a, nm/f monetarist.

monitor |monétor'| nm (INFORM) monitor; ~ **en color** color monitor; ~ **fósfor verde** green screen.

monja |mon'há| nf nun.

monje |mon'he| nm monk.

mono, a |mo'no, á| a (bonito) lovely, pretty; (gracioso) nice, charming ♦ nm/f monkey, ape ♦ nm dungarees pl; (overol) overalls pl; **una chica muy mona** a very pretty girl; **dormir la** ~ to sleep it off.

monolingüe |monolén'gwe| a monolingual.

monólogo |mono'logo| nm monologue.

monopatín |monopáten'| nm skateboard.

monopolice |monopolé'se| etc vb V **monopolizar.**

monopolio |monopo'lyo| nm monopoly; ~ **total** absolute monopoly.

monopolista |monopolé'stá| a, nm/f monopolist.

monopolizar |monopolésár'| vt to monopolize.

monosílabo, a |monosé'láho, á| a monosyllabic ♦ nm monosyllable.

monotonía |monotoné'á| nf (sonido) monotone; (fig) monotony.

monótono, a |mono'tono, á| a monotonous.

mono-usuario, a |monooóswá'ryo, á| a (INFORM) single-user.

monóxido |monok'sétho| nm monoxide; ~ **de carbono** carbon monoxide.

Mons. abr (REL) = **Monseñor.**

monseñor |monsenyor'| nm monsignor.

monserga |monser'gá| nf (lenguaje confuso) gibberish; (tonterías) drivel.

monstruo |monst'rwo| nm monster ♦ a inv fantastic.

monstruoso, a |monstrwo'so, á| a monstrous.

monta |mon'tá| nf total, sum; **de poca** ~ unimportant, of little account.

montacargas |montákár'gás| nm inv freight elevator (US), service lift (Brit).

montador |montádor'| nm (para montar) mounting block; (profesión) fitter; (CINE) film editor.

montaje |montá'he| nm assembly; (organización) fitting up; (TEATRO) décor; (CINE) montage.

montante |montán'te| nm (poste) upright; (soporte) stanchion; (ARQ: de puerta) transom; (: de ventana) mullion; (suma) amount, total.

montaña |montá'nyá| nf (monte) mountain; (sierra) mountains pl, mountainous area; (AM: selva) forest; ~ **rusa** roller coaster.

montañero, a |montánye'ro, á| a mountain cpd ♦ nm/f mountaineer, climber.

montañés, esa |montányes', ésá| a

mountain cpd; (de Santander) of o from the Santander region ♦ nm/f highlander; native o inhabitant of the Santander region.

montañismo [montáɲēs'mo] nn mountaineering, climbing.

montañoso, a [montáɲyo'so, à] a mountainous.

montar [montár'] vt (subir a) to mount, get on; (caballo etc) to ride; (TEC) to assemble, put together; (negocio) to set up; (colocar) to lift on to; (CINE: película) to edit; (TEATRO: obra) to stage, put on; (CULIN: batir) to whip, beat ♦ vi to mount, get on; (sobresalir) to overlap; ~ en cólera to get angry; ~ un número o numerito to make a scene; tanto monta it's all the same.

montaraz [montàrás'] a mountain cpd, highland cpd; (pey) uncivilized.

monte [mon'te] nm (montaña) mountain; (bosque) woodland; (área sin cultivar) wild area, wild country; ~ de piedad pawnshop; ~ alto forest; ~ bajo scrub(land).

montera [monte'rà] nf (sombrero) cloth cap; (de torero) bullfighter's hat.

monto [mon'to] nm total, amount.

montón [monton'] nm heap, pile; un ~ de (fig) heaps of, lots of; a montones by the score, galore.

montura [montōō'rà] nf (cabalgadura) mount; (silla) saddle; (arreos) harness; (de joya) mounting; (de gafas) frame.

monumento [monōōmen'to] nm monument; (de conmemoración) memorial.

monzón [monson'] nm monsoon.

moña [mo'nyà] nf hair ribbon.

moño [mo'nyo] nm (de pelo) bun; estar hasta el ~ (fam) to be fed up.

MOPU [mo'pōō] nm abr (Esp)=Ministerio de Obras Públicas y Urbanismo.

moqueta [moke'tà] nf fitted carpet.

moquillo [mokē'yo] nm (enfermedad) distemper.

mora [mo'rà] nf (BOT) mulberry; (: zarzamora) blackberry; (COM): en ~ in arrears.

morado, a [morà'tho, à] a purple, violet ♦ nm bruise ♦ nf (casa) dwelling, abode; pasarlas moradas to have a tough time of it.

moral [moràl'] a moral ♦ nf (ética) ethics pl; (moralidad) morals pl, morality; (ánimo) morale; tener baja la ~ to be in low spirits.

moraleja [moràle'hà] nf moral.

moralice [moràlē'se] etc vb V moralizar.

moralidad [moràlēthàth'] nf morals pl, morality.

moralizar [moràlēsàr'] vt to moralize.

morar [moràr'] vi to live, dwell.

moratoria [moràto'ryà] nf moratorium.

morbosidad [morbosēthàth'] nf morbidity.

morboso, a [morbo'so, à] a morbid.

morcilla [morsē'yà] nf blood sausage.

mordaz [mordhás'] a (crítica) biting, scathing.

mordaza [mordhà'sà] nf (para la boca) gag; (TEC) clamp.

morder [morder'] vt to bite; (mordisquear) to nibble; (fig: consumir) to eat away, eat into ♦ vi, ~se to bite; está que muerde he's hopping mad; ~se la lengua to hold one's tongue.

mordiscar [mordhēskár'] vt to nibble at; (con fuerza) to gnaw at; (pinchar) to nip.

mordisco [mordhēs'ko] nm bite.

mordisque [mordhēs'ke] etc vb V mordiscar.

mordisquear [mordhēskeàr'] vt=mordiscar.

moreno, a [more'no, à] a (color) (dark) brown; (de tez) dark; (de pelo ~) dark-haired; (negro) black ♦ nm/f (de tez) dark-skinned man/woman; (de pelo) dark-haired man/woman.

moretón [moreton'] nm (fam) bruise.

morfina [morfē'nà] nf morphine.

morfinómano, a [morfēno'màno, à] a addicted to hard drugs ♦ nm/f drug addict.

moribundo, a [morēbōōn'do, à] a dying ♦ nm/f dying person.

morir [morēr'] vi to die; (fuego) to die down; (luz) to go out; ~se vr to die; (fig) to be dying; (FERRO etc: vías) to end; (calle) to come out; fue muerto a tiros/en un accidente he was shot (dead)/was killed in an accident; ~ de frío/hambre to die of cold/starve to death; ¡me muero de hambre! (fig) I'm starving!; ~se por algo to be dying for sth; ~se por uno to be crazy about sb.

moro, a [mo'ro, à] a Moorish ♦ nm/f Moor; ¡hay ~s en la costa! watch out!

moroso, a [moro'so, à] a (lento) slow ♦ nm (COM) bad debtor, defaulter; deudor ~ (COM) slow payer.

morral [morràl'] nm knapsack.

morro [mo'rro] nm (ZOOL) snout, nose; (AUTO, AVIAT) nose; (fam: labio) (thick) lip; beber a ~ to drink from the bottle; caer de ~ to nosedive; estar de ~s (con uno) to be in a bad mood (with sb); tener ~ to have a nerve.

morrocotudo, a [morrokotōō'tho, à] a (fam) (fantástico) wonderful; (riña, golpe) tremendous; (fuerte) strong; (pesado) heavy; (difícil) awkward.

morsa [mor'sà] nf walrus.

mortaja [mortà'hà] nf shroud; (TEC) mortise; (AM) cigarette paper.

mortal [mortàl'] a mortal; (golpe) deadly.

mortalidad [mortàlēthàth'], **mortandad** [mortàndàth'] nf mortality.

mortecino, a [mortesē'no, à] a (débil)

weak; (*luz*) dim; (*color*) dull.

mortero |morte'ro| *nm* mortar.

mortífero, a |mortē'fero, á| *a* deadly, lethal.

mortificar |mortēfēkár'| *vt* to mortify; (*atormentar*) to torment.

mortifique |mortēfē'ke| *etc vb V* **mortificar**.

mortuorio, a |mortwo'ryo, á| *a* mortuary, death *cpd*.

Mosa |mo'sá| *nm*: **el (Río)** ~ the Meuse.

mosca |mos'ká| *nf* fly; **por si las** ~s just in case; **estar** ~ (*desconfiar*) to smell a rat; **tener la** ~ **en** *o* **detrás de la oreja** to be wary.

moscovita |moskohē'tá| *a* Muscovite, Moscow *cpd* ♦ *nm/f* Muscovite.

Moscú |moskōō'| *nm* Moscow.

mosquearse |moskeár'se| *vr* (*fam: enfadarse*) to get cross; (: *ofenderse*) to take offense (*US*) *o* offence (*Brit*).

mosquitero |moskēte'ro| *nm* mosquito net.

mosquito |moskē'to| *nm* mosquito.

mostaza |mostá'sá| *nf* mustard.

mosto |mo'sto| *nm* unfermented grape juice.

mostrador |mostráthor'| *nm* (*de tienda*) counter; (*de café*) bar.

mostrar |mostrár'| *vt* to show; (*exhibir*) to display, exhibit; (*explicar*) to explain; ~**se** *vr*: ~**se amable** to be kind; to prove to be kind; **no se muestra muy inteligente** he doesn't seem (to be) very intelligent; ~ **en pantalla** (*INFORM*) to display.

mota |mo'tá| *nf* speck, tiny piece; (*en diseño*) dot.

mote |mo'te| *nm* (*apodo*) nickname.

motín |motēn'| *nm* (*del pueblo*) revolt, uprising; (*del ejército*) mutiny.

motivar |motēbár'| *vt* (*causar*) to cause, motivate; (*explicar*) to explain, justify.

motivo |motē'bo| *nm* motive, reason; (*ARTE, MUS*) motif; **con** ~ **de** (*debido a*) because of; (*en ocasión de*) on the occasion of; (*con el fin de*) in order to; **sin** ~ for no reason at all.

moto |mo'to|, **motocicleta** |motosēkle'tá| *nf* motorcycle.

motor, a |motor', á| *a* (*TEC*) motor (*US*), motive (*Brit*); (*ANAT*) motor ♦ *nm* motor, engine; ~ **a chorro** *o* **de reacción/de explosión** jet engine/internal combustion engine ♦ *nf* motorboat.

motorismo |motorēs'mo| *nm* motorcycling.

motorizado, a |motorēsá'tho, á| *a* motorized.

motosierra |motosye'rrá| *nf* mechanical saw.

movedizo, a |mobethē'so, á| *a* (*inseguro*) unsteady; (*fig*) unsettled, changeable; (*persona*) fickle.

mover |mober'| *vt* to move; (*cambiar de lugar*) to shift; (*cabeza: para negar*) to

shake; (: *para asentir*) to nod; (*accionar*) to drive; (*fig*) to cause, provoke; ~**se** *vr* to move; (*mar*) to get rough; (*viento*) to rise; (*fig: apurarse*) to get a move on; (: *transformarse*) to be on the move.

movible |mobē'ble| *a* (*no fijo*) movable; (*móvil*) mobile; (*cambiadizo*) changeable.

movido, a |mobē'tho, á| *a* (*FOTO*) blurred; (*persona*) *activo*) active; (*mar*) rough; (*día*) hectic ♦ *nf* move; **la movida madrileña** the Madrid scene.

móvil |mo'bēl| *a* mobile; (*pieza de máquina*) moving; (*mueble*) movable ♦ *nm* motive.

movilice |mobēlē'se| *etc vb V* **movilizar**.

movilidad |mobēlēthath'| *nf* mobility.

movilizar |mobēlēsár'| *vt* to mobilize.

movimiento |mobēmyen'to| *nm* (*gen*, *LITERATURA, POL*) movement; (*TEC*) motion; (*actividad*) activity; (*MUS*) tempo; **el M**~ the Falangist Movement; ~ **de bloques** (*INFORM*) block move; ~ **de mercancías** (*COM*) turnover, volume of business; ~ **obrero/sindical** workers'/trade union movement; ~ **sísmico** earth tremor.

Mozambique |mosámbē'ke| *nm* Mozambique.

mozambiqueño, a |mosámbēke'nyo, á| *a*, *nm/f* Mozambican.

mozo, a |mo'so, á| *a* (*joven*) young; (*soltero*) single, unmarried ♦ *nm/f* (*joven*) youth, young man/girl; (*camarero*) waiter; (*camarera*) waitress; ~ **de estación** porter.

MPAIAC |emepáyák'| *nm abr* (*Esp POL*) = *Movimiento para la Autodeterminación y la Independencia del Archipiélago Canario.*

mucama |mōōká'má| *nf* (*AM*) maid.

muchacho, a |mōōtchátch'o, á| *nm/f* (*niño*) boy/girl; (*criado*) servant/servant *o* maid.

muchedumbre |mōōtchethōōm'bre| *nf* crowd.

muchísimo, a |mōōtchē'sēmo, á| *a* (*superlativo de* **mucho**) lots and lots of, ever so much ♦ *ad* ever so much.

mucho, a |mōōtch'o, á| *a* (*sg*) a lot of; (*gen en frase negativa o interrogativa*) much; (*pl*) many, a lot of, lots of ♦ *ad* (*en cantidad*) a lot, a great deal, much; (*del tiempo*) long; (*muy*) very ♦ *pron*: **tengo** ~ **que hacer** I have a lot to do; ~**s dicen que** a lot of people say that; **como** ~ at (the) most; **ni con** ~ not nearly; **ni** ~ **menos** far from it; **por** ~ **que** however much; **me alegro/lo siento** ~ I'm very glad/sorry.

muda |mōō'thá| *nf* (*de ropa*) change of clothing; (*ZOOL*) moult; (*de serpiente*) slough.

mudanza |mōōthán'sá| *nf* (*cambio*) change; (*de casa*) move; **estar de** ~ to be moving.

mudar |mōōthár'| *vt* to change; (*ZOOL*) to

shed ♦ *vi* to change; ~**se** *vr* (*la ropa*) to change; ~**se de casa** to move.

mudo, a |mōō'tho, á| *a* dumb; (*callado, película*) silent; (*LING: letra*) mute; (: *consonante*) voiceless; **quedarse** ~ (**de**) (*fig*) to be dumb with; **quedarse** ~ **de asombro** to be speechless.

mueble |mwc'hlc| *nm* piece of furniture; ~**s** *nmpl* furniture *sg*.

mueble-bar |mwchlchár'| *nm* cocktail cabinet.

mueca |mwc'kà| *nf* face, grimace; **hacer** ~**s a** to make faces at.

muela |mwc'là| *etc vb* V **moler** ♦ *nf* (*diente*) tooth; (: *de atrás*) molar; (*de molino*) millstone; (*de afilar*) grindstone; ~ **del juicio** wisdom tooth.

muelle |mwc'yc| *a* (*blando*) soft; (*fig*) soft, easy ♦ *nm* spring; (*NAUT*) wharf; (*malecón*) jetty.

muera |mwc'rà| *etc vb* V **morir.**

muerda |mwcr'thà| *etc vb* V **morder.**

muermo |mwcr'mo| *nm* (*fam*) wimp.

muerte |mwcr'tc| *nf* death; (*homicidio*) murder; **dar** ~ **a** to kill; **de mala** ~ (*fam*) lousy, rotten; **es la** ~ (*fam*) it's deadly boring.

muerto, a |mwcr'to, á| *pp de* **morir** ♦ *a* dead; (*color*) dull ♦ *nm/f* dead man/woman; (*difunto*) deceased; (*cadáver*) corpse; **cargar con el** ~ (*fam*) to take the rap; **echar el** ~ **a uno** to pass the buck; **hacer el** ~ (*nadando*) to float; **estar** ~ **de cansancio** to be dead tired.

muestra |mwcs'trà| *etc vb* V **mostrar** ♦ *nf* (*señal*) indication, sign; (*demostración*) demonstration; (*prueba*) proof; (*estadística*) sample; (*modelo*) model, pattern; (*testimonio*) token; **dar** ~**s de** to show signs of; ~ **al azar** (*COM*) random sample.

muestrario |mwcstrà'ryo| *nm* collection of samples; (*exposición*) showcase.

muestreo |mwcstrc'o| *nm* sample, sampling.

mueva |mwc'hà| *etc vb* V **mover.**

mugir |mōōhēr'| *vi* (*vaca*) to moo.

mugre |mōō'grc| *nf* dirt, filth, muck.

mugriento, a |mōōgryen'to, á| *a* dirty, filthy mucky.

muja |mōō'hà| *etc vb* V **mugir.**

mujer |mōōhcr'| *nf* woman; (*esposa*) wife.

mujeriego |mōōheryc'go| *nm* womanizer.

mula |mōō'là| *nf* mule.

muladar |mōōláthár'| *nm* dungheap, dunghill.

mulato, a |mōōlá'to, á| *a, nm/f* mulatto.

muleta |mōōlc'tà| *nf* (*para andar*) crutch; (*TAUR*) stick with red cape attached.

muletilla |mōōletē'yà| *nf* (*palabra*) pet word, tag; (*de cómico*) catch phrase.

multa |mōōl'tà| *nf* fine; **echar** *o* **poner una** ~ **a** to fine.

multar |mōōltàr'| *vt* to fine; (*DEPORTE*) to penalize.

multiacceso |mōōltyàksc'so| *a* (*INFORM*) multi-access.

multicopista |mōōltēkopē'stà| *nm* duplicator.

multinacional |mōōltēnásyonàl'| *a, nf* multinational.

múltiple |mōōl'tēplc| *a* multiple; (*pl*) many, numerous; **de tarea** ~ (*INFORM*) multitasking; **de usuario** ~ (*INFORM*) multiuser.

multiplicar |mōōltēplēkàr'| *vt* (*MAT*) to multiply; (*fig*) to increase; ~**se** *vr* (*BIO*) to multiply; (*fig*) to be everywhere at once.

multiplique |mōōltēplē'kc| *etc vb* V **multiplicar.**

multitud |mōōltētōōth'| *nf* (*muchedumbre*) crowd; ~ **de** lots of.

multitudinario, a |mōōltētōōthēná'ryo, á| *a* (*numeroso*) multitudinous; (*de masa*) mass *cpd*.

mullido, a |mōōyē'tho, á| *a* (*cama*) soft; (*hierba*) soft, springy.

mundanal |mōōndánàl'| *a* worldly; **lejos del** ~ **ruido** far from the madding crowd.

mundano, a |mōōndá'no, á| *a* worldly; (*de moda*) fashionable.

mundial |mōōndyál'| *a* world-wide, universal; (*guerra, récord*) world *cpd*.

mundialmente |mōōndyálmcn'tc| *ad* world-wide; ~ **famoso** world-famous.

mundo |mōōn'do| *nm* world; (*ámbito*) world, circle; **el otro** ~ the next world; **el** ~ **del espectáculo** show business; **todo el** ~ everybody; **tener** ~ to be experienced, know one's way around; **el** ~ **es un pañuelo** it's a small world; **no es nada del otro** ~ it's nothing special; **se le cayó el** ~ (**encima**) his world fell apart.

munición |mōōnēsyon'| *nf* (*MIL: provisiones*) stores *pl*, supplies *pl*; (: *de armas*) ammunition.

municipal |mōōnēsēpàl'| *a* (*elección*) municipal; (*concejo*) town *cpd*, local; (*piscina etc*) public ♦ *nm* (*guardia*) policeman.

municipio |mōōnēsē'pyo| *nm* (*ayuntamiento*) town council, corporation; (*territorio administrativo*) town, municipality.

Munich |mōō'nētch| *nm* Munich.

muniqués, esa |mōōnēkes', esà| *a* of *o* from Munich ♦ *nm/f* native *o* inhabitant of Munich.

muñeca |mōōnye'kà| *nf* (*ANAT*) wrist; (*juguete*) doll.

muñeco |mōōnye'ko| *nm* (*figura*) figure; (*marioneta*) puppet; (*fig*) puppet, pawn; (*niño*) pretty little boy; ~ **de nieve** snowman.

muñón |mōōnyon'| *nm* (*ANAT*) stump.

mural [mo͞orál'] a mural, wall cpd ♦ nm mural.

muralla [mo͞orá'yá] nf (city) wall(s) (pl).

murciano, a [mo͞orsyá'no, á] a of o from Murcia ♦ nm/f native o inhabitant of Murcia.

murciélago [mo͞orsye'lágo] nm bat.

murga [mo͞or'gá] nf (banda) band of street musicians; **dar la** ~ to be a nuisance.

murmullo [mo͞ormo͞o'yo] nm murmur(ing); (cuchicheo) whispering; (de arroyo) murmur, rippling; (de hojas, viento) rustle, rustling; (ruido confuso) hum(ming).

murmuración [mo͞ormo͞orásyon'] nf gossip; (críticas) backbiting.

murmurador, a [mo͞ormo͞orádhor', á] a gossiping; (criticón) backbiting ♦ nm/f gossip; backbiter.

murmurar [mo͞ormo͞orár'] vi to murmur, whisper; (criticar) to criticize; (cotillear) to gossip.

muro [mo͞o'ro] nm wall; ~ **de contención** retaining wall.

musaraña [mo͞osárá'nyá] nf (ZOOL) shrew; (insecto) creepy-crawly; **pensar en las** ~s to daydream.

muscular [mo͞osko͞olár'] a muscular.

músculo [mo͞os'ko͞olo] nm muscle.

museo [mo͞ose'o] nm museum; ~ **de arte** o **de pintura** art gallery; ~ **de cera** waxworks.

musgo [mo͞os'go] nm moss.

músico, a [mo͞o'sěko, á] a musical ♦ nm/f musician ♦ nf music; **irse con la música a otra parte** to clear out.

musitar [mo͞osětár'] vt, vi to mutter, mumble.

muslo [mo͞os'lo] nm thigh; (de pollo) leg, drumstick.

mustio, a [mo͞os'tyo, á] a (persona) depressed, gloomy; (planta) faded, withered.

musulmán, ana [mo͞oso͞olmán', áná] nm/f Moslem, Muslim.

mutación [mo͞otásyon'] nf (BIO) mutation; (: cambio) (sudden) change.

mutilar [mo͞otělár'] vt to mutilate; (a una persona) to maim.

mutis [mo͞o'těs] nm inv (TEATRO) exit; **hacer** ~ (TEATRO: retirarse) to exit, go off; (fig) to say nothing.

mutualidad [mo͞otwálědhádh'] nf (reciprocidad) mutual character; (asociación) benefit (US) o friendly (Brit) society.

mutuamente [mo͞otwámen'te] ad mutually.

mutuo, a [mo͞o'two, á] a mutual.

muy [mwě] ad very; (demasiado) too; **M~ Señor mío** Dear Sir; ~ **bien** (de acuerdo) all right; ~ **de noche** very late at night; **eso es** ~ **de él** that's just like him; **eso es** ~ **español** that's typically Spanish.

N

N, n [e'ne] nf (letra) N, n; **N de Navarra** N for Nan.

N abr (= norte) N.

N. abr (= noviembre) Nov.

n. abr (LING: = nombre) n; (= nacido) b.

n/ abr = **nuestro, a.**

nabo [ná'ho] nm turnip.

nácar [ná'kár] nm mother-of-pearl.

nacer [náser'] vi to be born; (huevo) to hatch; (vegetal) to sprout; (río) to rise; (fig) to begin, originate, have its origins; **nació para poeta** he was born to be a poet; **nadie nace enseñado** we all have to learn; **nació una sospecha en su mente** a suspicion formed in her mind.

nacido, a [náse͏̈'tho, á] a born; **recién** ~ newborn.

naciente [násyen'te] a new, emerging; (sol) rising.

nacimiento [násěmyen'to] nm birth; (fig) birth, origin; (de Navidad) Nativity; (linaje) descent, family; (de río) source; **ciego de** ~ blind from birth.

nación [násyon'] nf nation; (pueblo) people; **Naciones Unidas** United Nations.

nacional [násyonál'] a national; (COM, ECON) domestic.

nacionalice [násyonále͏̈'se] etc vb V **nacionalizar.**

nacionalismo [násyonále͏̈s'mo] nm nationalism.

nacionalista [násyonále͏̈'stá] a, nm/f nationalist.

nacionalizar [násyonálěsár'] vt to nationalize; ~**se** vr (persona) to become naturalized.

nada [ná'thá] pron nothing ♦ ad not at all, in no way ♦ nf nothingness; **no decir** ~ to say nothing, not to say anything; **de** ~ don't mention it; ~ **de eso** nothing of the kind; **antes de** ~ right away; **como si** ~ as if it didn't matter; **no ha sido** ~ it's nothing; **la** ~ the void.

nadador, a [náthádhor', á] nm/f swimmer.

nadar [náthár'] vi to swim; ~ **en la abundancia** (fig) to be rolling in money.

nadie [ná'thye] pron nobody, no-one; ~ **habló** nobody spoke; **no había** ~ there was nobody there, there wasn't anybody there; **es un don** ~ he's a nobody o nonentity.

nado [ná'tho]: **a** ~ ad: **pasar a** ~ to swim

across.

nafta [náf'tá] *nf (AM)* gas(oline) *(US)*, petrol *(Brit)*.

naftalina [náftálē'ná] *nf*: **bolas de** ~ mothballs.

naipe [ná'ēpe] *nm* (playing) card; ~**s** *nmpl* cards.

nal. *abr* (= *nacional*) nat.

nalgas [nál'gás] *nfpl* buttocks.

Namibia [námē'ḫyá] *nf* Namibia.

nana [ná'ná] *nf* lullaby.

Nápoles [ná'poles] *nf* Naples.

napolitano, a [nápolētá'no, á] *a* of *o* from Naples, Neapolitan ♦ *nm/f* Neapolitan.

naranja [nárán'há] *a inv, nf* orange; **media** ~ *(fam)* better half; ¡~**s de la China!** nonsense!

naranjada [náránhá'ḍá] *nf* orangeade.

naranjo [nárán'ho] *nm* orange tree.

Narbona [nárḫo'ná] *nf* Narbonne.

narciso [nársē'so] *nm* narcissus.

narcotice [nárkotē'se] *etc vb* V **narcotizar.**

narcótico, a [nárkō'tēko, á] *a, nm* narcotic.

narcotizar [nárkotēsár'] *vt* to drug.

narcotraficante [nárkotráfēkán'te] *nm/f* narcotics *o* drug trafficker.

narcotráfico [nárkotrá'fēko] *nm* narcotics *o* drug trafficking.

nardo [nár'ḍo] *nm* lily.

narices [nárē'ses] *nfpl* V **nariz.**

narigón, ona [nárēgon', o'ná], **narigudo, a** [nárēgōo'ḍo, á] *a* big-nosed.

nariz [nárēs'] *nf* nose; **narices** *nfpl* nostrils; ¡**narices!** *(fam)* rubbish!; **delante de las narices de uno** under one's (very) nose; **estar hasta las narices** to be completely fed up; **meter las narices en algo** to poke one's nose into sth.

narración [nárrásyon'] *nf* narration.

narrador, a [nárráḍor', á] *nm/f* narrator.

narrar [nárrár'] *vt* to narrate, recount.

narrativo, a [nárrátē'ḫo, á] *a* narrative ♦ *nf* narrative, story.

nasal [násál'] *a* nasal.

N.ª S.ªa *abr* = *Nuestra Señora*.

nata [ná'tá] *nf* cream *(tb fig)*; *(en leche cocida etc)* skin; ~ **batida** whipped cream.

natación [nátásyon'] *nf* swimming.

natal [nátál'] *a* natal; *(país)* native; **ciudad** ~ home town.

natalicio [nátálē'syo] *nm* birthday.

natalidad [nátálēḍáḍ'] *nf* birth rate.

natillas [nátē'yás] *nfpl* (egg) custard *sg.*

natividad [nátēḍēḍáḍ'] *nf* nativity.

nativo, a [nátē'ḫo, á] *a, nm/f* native.

nato, a [ná'to, á] *a* born; **un músico** ~ a born musician.

natural [nátōōrál'] *a* natural; *(fruta etc)* fresh ♦ *nm/f* native ♦ *nm* disposition, temperament; **buen** ~ good nature; **fruta al** ~ fruit in its own juice.

naturaleza [nátōōrále'sá] *nf* nature; *(género)* nature, kind; ~ **muerta** still life.

naturalice [nátōōrále'se] *etc vb* V **naturalizarse.**

naturalidad [nátōōrálēḍáḍ'] *nf* naturalness.

naturalización [nátōōrálēsásyon'] *nf* naturalization.

naturalizarse [nátōōrálēsár'se] *vr* to become naturalized; *(aclimatarse)* to become acclimated *(US)* o acclimatized *(Brit)*.

naturalmente [nátōōrálmen'te] *ad* naturally; ¡~! of course!

naufragar [náōōfrágár'] *vi (barco)* to sink; *(gente)* to be shipwrecked; *(fig)* to fail.

naufragio [náōōfrá'hyo] *nm* shipwreck.

náufrago, a [ná'ōōfrágo, á] *nm/f* castaway, shipwrecked person.

naufrague [náōōfrá'ge] *etc vb* V **naufragar.**

náusea [ná'ōōseá] *nf* nausea; **me da** ~**s** it makes me feel sick.

nauseabundo, a [náōōseáḫōōn'do, á] *a* nauseating, sickening.

náutico, a [ná'ōōtēko, á] *a* nautical; **club** ~ sailing *o* yacht club ♦ *nf* navigation, seamanship.

navaja [náḫá'há] *nf (cortaplumas)* pocketknife; ~ **(de afeitar)** razor.

Navarra [náḫá'rrá] *nf* Navarre.

navarro, a [náḫá'rro, á] *a* of *o* from Navarre, Navarrese ♦ *nm/f* Navarrese ♦ *nm (LING)* Navarrese.

nave [ná'ḫe] *nf (barco)* ship, vessel; *(ARQ)* nave; ~ **espacial** spaceship; **quemar las** ~**s** to burn one's boats.

navegación [náḫegásyon'] *nf* navigation; *(viaje)* sea journey; ~ **aérea** air traffic; ~ **costera** coastal shipping; ~ **fluvial** river navigation.

navegante [náḫegán'te] *nm/f* navigator.

navegar [náḫegár'] *vi (barco)* to sail; *(avión)* to fly ♦ *vt* to sail; to fly; *(dirigir el rumbo de)* to navigate.

navegue [náḫe'ge] *etc vb* V **navegar.**

navidad [náḫēḍáḍ'] *nf* Christmas; ~**es** *nfpl* Christmas time *sg*; **día de** ~ Christmas Day; **por** ~**es** at Christmas (time); ¡**felices** ~**es!** Merry Christmas.

navideño, a [náḫēḍe'nyo, á] *a* Christmas *cpd.*

navío [náḫē'o] *nm* ship.

nazi [ná'sē] *a, nm/f* Nazi.

n/cta *abr (COM)* = *nuestra cuenta.*

N. de la R. *abr* (= *nota de la redacción*) editor's note.

N. de la T./del T. *abr* (= *nota de la traductora/del traductor*) translator's note.

NE *abr* (= *nor(d)este*) NE.

neblina [neḫlē'ná] *nf* mist.

nebuloso, a [neḫōōlo'so, á] *a* foggy; *(calinoso)* misty; *(indefinido)* nebulous, vague ♦

nf nebula.

necedad [nesetháth'] *nf* foolishness; (*una* ~) foolish act.

necesario, a [nesesá'ryo, á] *a* necessary; **si fuera** *o* **fuese** ~ if need(s) be.

neceser [neseser'] *nm* vanity case; (*bolsa grande*) traveling case (*US*), holdall (*Brit*).

necesidad [neseséthath'] *nf* need; (*lo inevitable*) necessity; (*miseria*) poverty, need; **en caso de** ~ in case of need *o* emergency; **hacer sus** ~**es** to relieve o.s.

necesitado, a [nesesétá'tho, á] *a* needy, poor; ~ **de** in need of.

necesitar [nesesétár'] *vt* to need, require ♦ *vi*: ~ **de** to have need of; ~**se** *vr* to be needed; (*anuncios*) **"necesítase coche"** "car wanted".

necio, a [ne'syo, á] *a* foolish ♦ *nm/f* fool.

necrología [nekrolohē'á] *nf* obituary.

necrópolis [nekro'polēs] *nf inv* cemetery.

nectarina [nektárē'ná] *nf* nectarine.

neerlandés, esa [neerlándes', esá] *a* Dutch ♦ *nm/f* Dutchman/woman ♦ *nm* (*LING*) Dutch; **los neerlandeses** the Dutch.

nefando, a [nefán'do, á] *a* unspeakable.

nefasto, a [nefá'sto, á] *a* ill-fated, unlucky.

negación [negásyon'] *nf* negation; (*LING*) negative; (*rechazo*) refusal, denial.

negado, a [negá'tho, á] *a*: ~ **para** inept at, unfitted for.

negar [negár'] *vt* (*renegar, rechazar*) to refuse; (*prohibir*) to refuse, deny; (*desmentir*) to deny; ~**se** *vr*: ~**se a hacer algo** to refuse to do sth.

negativo, a [negátē'ho, á] *a* negative ♦ *nm* (*FOTO*) negative; (*MAT*) minus ♦ *nf* (*gen*) negative; (*rechazo*) refusal, denial; **negativa rotunda** flat refusal.

negligencia [neglēhen'syá] *nf* negligence.

negligente [neglēhen'te] *a* negligent.

negociable [negosyá'ble] *a* (*COM*) negotiable.

negociado [negosyá'tho] *nm* department, section.

negociante [negosyán'te] *nm/f* businessman/woman.

negociar [negosyár'] *vt, vi* to negotiate; ~ **en** to deal in, trade in.

negocio [nego'syo] *nm* (*COM*) business; (*asunto*) affair, business; (*operación comercial*) deal, transaction; (*AM*) firm; (*lugar*) place of business; **los** ~**s** business *sg*; **hacer** ~ to do business; **el** ~ **del libro** the book trade; ~ **autorizado** licensed trade; **hombre de** ~**s** businessman; ~ **sucio** shady deal; **hacer un buen** ~ to pull off a profitable deal; **¡mal** ~**!** it looks bad!

negra [ne'grá] *nf V* **negro**.

negrita [negrē'tá] *nf* (*TIP*) bold face; **en** ~ in bold (type).

negro, a [ne'gro, á] *a* black; (*suerte*) awful,

atrocious; (*humor etc*) sad; (*lúgubre*) gloomy ♦ *nm* (*color*) black ♦ *nm/f* Negro/Negress, black ♦ *nf* (*MUS*) quarter note (*US*), crotchet (*Brit*); ~ **como la boca del lobo** pitch-black; **estoy** ~ **con esto** I'm getting desperate about it; **ponerse** ~ (*fam*) to get cross.

negrura [negrōō'rá] *nf* blackness.

negué [nege'], **neguemos** [nege'mos] *etc vb V* **negar**.

nene, a [ne'ne, á] *nm/f* baby, small child.

nenúfar [nenōō'fár] *nm* water lily.

neologismo [neolohēs'mo] *nm* neologism.

neoyorquino, a [neoyorkē'no, á] *a* New York *cpd* ♦ *nm/f* New Yorker.

neozelandés, esa [neoselándes', esá] *a* New Zealand *cpd* ♦ *nm/f* New Zealander.

nepotismo [nepotēs'mo] *nm* nepotism.

nervio [ner'byo] *nm* (*ANAT*) nerve; (: *tendón*) tendon; (*fig*) vigor (*US*), vigour (*Brit*); (*TEC*) rib; **crispar los** ~**s a uno**, **poner los** ~**s de punta a uno** to get on sb's nerves.

nerviosismo [nerbyosēs'mo] *nm* nervousness, nerves *pl*.

nervioso, a [nerbyo'so, á] *a* nervous; (*sensible*) nervy, highly-strung; (*impaciente*) restless; **¡no te pongas** ~**!** take it easy!

nervudo, a [nerbōō'tho, á] *a* tough; (*mano*) sinewy.

neto, a [ne'to, á] *a* clear; (*limpio*) clean; (*COM*) net.

neumático, a [neōōmá'tēko, á] *a* pneumatic ♦ *nm* (*Esp*) tire (*US*), tyre (*Brit*); ~ **de recambio** spare tire (*US*) *o* tyre (*Brit*).

neumonía [neōōmonē'á] *nf* pneumonia.

neuralgia [neōōrál'hyá] *nf* neuralgia.

neurastenia [neōōráste'nyá] *nf* neurasthenia; (*fig*) excitability.

neurasténico, a [neōōráste'nēko, á] *a* neurasthenic; excitable.

neurólogo, a [neōōro'logo, á] *nm/f* neurologist.

neurosis [neōōro'sēs] *nf inv* neurosis.

neurótico, a [neōōro'tēko, á] *a, nm/f* neurotic.

neutral [neōōtrál'] *a* neutral.

neutralice [neōōtrálē'se] *etc vb V* **neutralizar**.

neutralizar [neōōtrálēsár'] *vt* to neutralize; (*contrarrestar*) to counteract.

neutro, a [ne'ōōtro, á] *a* (*BIO, LING*) neuter.

neutrón [neōōtron'] *nm* neutron.

nevado, a [nebá'tho, á] *a* snow-covered; (*montaña*) snow-capped; (*fig*) snowy, snow-white ♦ *nf* snowstorm; (*caída de nieve*) snowfall.

nevar [nebár'] *vi* to snow ♦ *vt* (*fig*) to whiten.

nevera [nebe'rá] *nf* (*Esp*) refrigerator.

nevería [neberē'á] *nf* (*AM*) ice-cream parlor

(*US*) *o* parlour (*Brit*).

nevisca |nɛβēs'ká| *nf* flurry of snow.

nexo |nɛk'so| *nm* link, connection.

n/f *abr* (*COM*) = *nuestro favor*.

ni |nē| *conj* nor, neither; (*tb*: ~ **siquiera**) not even; ~ **que** not even if; ~ **blanco** ~ **negro** neither white nor black; ~ **el uno** ~ **el otro** neither one nor the other.

Nicaragua |nēkárà'gwá| *nf* Nicaragua.

nicaragüense |nēkáràgwen'sɛ| *a*, *nm/f* Nicaraguan.

nicotina |nēkotē'ná| *nf* nicotine.

nicho |nētch'o| *nm* niche.

nido |nē'ɗo| *nm* nest; (*fig*) hiding place; ~ **de ladrones** den of thieves.

niebla |nyɛ'blá| *nf* fog; (*neblina*) mist; **hay** ~ it is foggy.

niego |nyɛ'go| *etc*, **niegue** |nyɛ'gɛ| *etc vb* V **negar**.

nieto, a |nyɛ'to, á| *nm/f* grandson/daughter; ~**s** *nmpl* grandchildren.

nieve |nyɛ'βɛ| *etc vb* V **nevar ♦** *nf* snow; (*AM*) ice cream; **copo de** ~ snowflake.

Nigeria |nēĵē'ryá| *nf* Nigeria.

nigeriano, a |nēĵeryá'no, á| *a*, *nm/f* Nigerian.

nigromancia |nēgromán'syá| *nf* necromancy, black magic.

nihilista |nēēlē'stá| *a* nihilistic **♦** *nm* nihilist.

Nilo |nē'lo| *nm*: **el (Río)** ~ the Nile.

nimbo |nēm'bo| *nm* (*aureola*) halo; (*nube*) nimbus.

nimiedad |nēmyeɗáɗ'| *nf* smallmindedness; (*trivialidad*) triviality; (*una* ~) trifle, tiny detail.

nimio, a |nē'myo, á| *a* trivial, insignificant.

ninfa |nēn'fá| *nf* nymph.

ninfómana |nēnfo'máná| *nf* nymphomaniac.

ninguno, a |nēngōo'no, á| *a* (**ningún** *delante de nmsg*) no **♦** *pron* (*nadie*) nobody; (*ni uno*) none, not one; (*ni uno ni otro*) neither; **de ninguna manera** by no means, not at all; **no voy a ninguna parte** I'm not going anywhere.

niña |nē'nyá| *nf* V **niño**.

niñera |nēnye'rá| *nf* nursemaid, nanny.

niñería |nēnyerē'á| *nf* childish act.

niñez |nēnyes'| *nf* childhood; (*infancia*) infancy.

niño, a |nē'nyo, á| *a* (*joven*) young; (*inmaduro*) immature **♦** *nm* (*chico*) boy, child **♦** *nf* girl, child; (*ANAT*) pupil; **los** ~**s** the children; ~ **bien** rich kid; ~ **expósito** foundling; ~ **de pecho** babe-in-arms; ~ **prodigio** child prodigy; **de** ~ as a child; **ser el** ~ **mimado de uno** to be sb's pet; **ser la niña de los ojos de uno** to be the apple of sb's eye.

nipón, ona |nēpon', oná| *a*, *nm/f* Japanese; **los nipones** the Japanese.

níquel |nē'kel| *nm* nickel.

niquelar |nēkelár'| *vt* (*TEC*) to nickel-plate.

níspero |nēs'pero| *nm* medlar.

nitidez |nētēɛ̄es'| *nf* (*claridad*) clarity; (: *de atmósfera*) brightness; (: *de imagen*) sharpness.

nítido, a |nē'tēɗo, á| *a* bright; (*fig*) pure; (*imagen*) clear, sharp.

nitrato |nētrá'to| *nm* nitrate.

nitrógeno |nētro'heno| *nm* nitrogen.

nitroglicerina |nētroglēserē'ná| *nf* nitroglycerine.

nivel |nēβel'| *nm* (*GEO*) level; (*norma*) level, standard; (*altura*) height; ~ **de aceite** oil level; ~ **de aire** spirit level; ~ **de vida** standard of living; **al** ~ **de** on a level with, at the same height as; (*fig*) on a par with; **a 900m sobre el** ~ **del mar** at 900m above sea level.

nivelado, a |nēβelá'ɗo, á| *a* level, flat; (*TEC*) flush.

nivelar |nēβelár'| *vt* to level out; (*fig*) to even up; (*COM*) to balance.

Niza |nē'sá| *nf* Nice.

n/l. *abr* (*COM*) = *nuestra letra*.

NNE *abr* (= *nornordeste*) NNE.

NNO *abr* (= *nornoroeste*) NNW.

NN. UU. *nfpl abr* (= *Naciones Unidas*) UN *sg*.

NO *abr* (= *noroeste*) NW.

no |no| *ad* no; (*con verbo*) not **♦** *excl* no!; ~ **tengo nada** I don't have anything, I have nothing; ~ **es el mío** it's not mine; **ahora** ~ not now; **¿**~ **lo sabes?** don't you know?; ~ **mucho** not much; ~ **bien termine, lo entregaré** as soon as I finish I'll hand it over; **¡a que** ~ **lo sabes!** I bet you don't know!; **¡cómo** ~**!** of course!; **pacto de** ~ **agresión** non-aggression pact; **los países** ~ **alineados** the non-aligned countries; **el** ~ **va más** the ultimate; **la** ~ **intervención** non-intervention.

N.º *abr* (= *número*) No.

n/o *abr* (*COM*) = *nuestra orden*.

noble |no'blɛ| *a*, *nm/f* noble; **los** ~**s** the nobility *sg*.

nobleza |no'blɛ'sá| *nf* nobility.

noción |nosyon'| *nf* notion; **nociones** *nfpl* elements, rudiments.

nocivo, a |nosē'βo, á| *a* harmful.

noctambulismo |noktàmbōōlēs'mo| *nm* sleepwalking.

noctámbulo, a |noktàm'bōōlo, á| *nm/f* sleepwalker.

nocturno, a |noktōōr'no, á| *a* (*de la noche*) nocturnal, night *cpd*; (*de la tarde*) evening *cpd* **♦** *nm* nocturne.

noche |notch'ɛ| *nf* night, night-time; (*la tarde*) evening; (*fig*) darkness; **de** ~, **por la** ~ at night; **ayer por la** ~ last night; **esta** ~ tonight; **(en) toda la** ~ all night; **hacer** ~ **en un sitio** to spend the night in a place; **se hace de** ~ it's getting dark.

Nochebuena |notchehwe'ná| *nf* Christmas Eve.

Nochevieja |notchehye'há| *nf* New Year's Eve.

nodriza |nothrē'sá| *nf* wet nurse; **buque** *o* **nave** ~ supply ship.

Noé |noc'| *nm* Noah.

nogal |nogál'| *nm* walnut tree; (*madera*) walnut.

nómada |no'máthá| *a* nomadic ♦ *nm/f* nomad.

nomás |nomás'| *ad*: (*AM*: *gen*) just; (: *tan sólo*) only.

nombramiento |nombrámyen'to| *nm* naming; (*a un empleo*) appointment; (*POL etc*) nomination; (*MIL*) commission.

nombrar |nombrár'| *vt* (*gen*) to name; (*mencionar*) to mention; (*designar*) to appoint, nominate; (*MIL*) to commission.

nombre |nom'brc| *nm* name; (*sustantivo*) noun; (*fama*) renown; ~ **y apellidos** name in full; ~ **común/propio** common/proper noun; ~ **de pila/de soltera** Christian/ maiden name; ~ **de fichero** (*INFORM*) file name; **en** ~ **de** in the name of, on behalf of; **sin** ~ nameless; **su conducta no tiene** ~ his behavior is utterly despicable.

nomenclatura |nomenklátōō'rá| *nf* nomenclature.

nomeolvides |nomeolhē'thes| *nm inv* forget-me-not.

nómina |no'mēná| *nf* (*lista*) list; (*COM*: *tb*: ~**s**) payroll.

nominal |nomēnál'| *a* nominal; (*valor*) face *cpd*; (*LING*) noun *cpd*, substantival.

nominar |nomēnár'| *vt* to nominate.

nominativo, a |nomēnátē'ho, á| *a* (*LING*) nominative; (*COM*): **un cheque** ~ **a X** a check made out to X.

non |non| *a* odd, uneven ♦ *nm* odd number; **pares y** ~**es** odds and evens.

nonagésimo, a |nonáhc'sēmo, á| *num* ninetieth.

nono, a |no'no, á| *num* ninth.

nordeste |northc'stc| *a* north-east, north-eastern, north-easterly ♦ *nm* north-east; (*viento*) north-east wind, north-easterly.

nórdico, a |nor'thēko, á| *a* (*del norte*) northern, northerly; (*escandinavo*) Nordic, Norse ♦ *nm/f* northerner; (*escandinavo*) Norseman/woman ♦ *nm* (*LING*) Norse.

noreste |norc'stc| *a*, *nm* = **nordeste**.

noria |no'ryá| *nf* (*AGR*) waterwheel; (*de carnaval*) Ferris (*US*) o big (*Brit*) wheel.

norma |nor'má| *nf* standard, norm, rule; (*patrón*) pattern; (*método*) method.

normal |normál'| *a* (*corriente*) normal; (*habitual*) usual, natural; (*TEC*) standard; **Escuela N**~ teacher training college; (**gasolina**) ~ regular (*US*), two-star petrol

(*Brit*).

normalice |normálē'sc| *etc vb* V **normalizar**.

normalidad |normálētháth'| *nf* normality; **restablecer la** ~ to restore order.

normalización |normálēsásyon'| *nf* (*COM*) standardization.

normalizar |normálēsár'| *vt* (*reglamentar*) to normalize; (*COM, TEC*) to standardize; ~**se** *vr* to return to normal.

Normandía |normándē'á| *nf* Normandy.

normando, a |normàn'do, á| *a*, *nm/f* Norman.

normativo, a |normátē'ho, á| *a*: **es** ~ **en todos los coches nuevos** it is standard in all new cars.

noroeste |noroc'ste| *a* north-west, north-western, north-westerly ♦ *nm* north-west; (*viento*) north-west wind, north-westerly.

norte |nor'tc| *a* north, northern, northerly ♦ *nm* north; (*fig*) guide.

Norteamérica |nortcáme'rēká| *nf* North America.

norteamericano, a |nortcámerēká'no, á| *a*, *nm/f* (North) American.

norteño, a |norte'nyo, á| *a* northern ♦ *nm/f* northerner.

Noruega |norwe'gá| *nf* Norway.

noruego, a |norwe'go, á| *a*, *nm/f* Norwegian ♦ *nm* (*LING*) Norwegian.

nos |nos| *pron* (*directo*) us; (*indirecto*) (to) us; (*reflexivo*) (to) ourselves; (*recíproco*) (to) each other; ~ **levantamos a las 7** we get up at 7.

nosotros, as |noso'tros, ás| *pron* (*sujeto*) we; (*después de prep*) us; ~ (**mismos**) ourselves.

nostalgia |nostál'hyá| *nf* nostalgia, homesickness.

nostálgico, a |nostál'hēko, á| *a* nostalgic, homesick.

nota |no'tá| *nf* note; (*ESCOL*) grade (*US*), mark (*Brit*); (*de fin de año*) final grade (*US*), report (*Brit*); (*COM etc*) footnote; (*COM*) account; ~ **de aviso** advice slip (*US*), advice note (*Brit*); ~ **de crédito/ débito** credit/debit note; ~ **de gastos** expenses claim; ~ **de sociedad** gossip column; **tomar** ~**s** to take notes.

notable |notá'hlc| *a* noteworthy, notable; (*ESCOL etc*) outstanding ♦ *nm/f* notable.

notar |notár'| *vt* to notice, note; (*percibir*) to feel; (*ver*) to see; ~**se** *vr* to be obvious; **se nota que** ... one observes that ....

notaría |notárē'á| *nf* (*profesión*) profession of notary; (*despacho*) notary's office.

notarial |notáryál'| *a* (*estilo*) legal; **acta** ~ affidavit.

notario |notá'ryo| *nm* notary; (*abogado*) lawyer.

noticia |notē'syá| *nf* (*información*) piece of

news; (*TV etc*) news item; **las ~s** the news
sg; **según nuestras ~s** according to our information; **tener ~s de uno** to hear from
sb.

noticiar [notēsyár'] *vt* to notify.

noticiario [notēsyá'ryo] *nm* (*CINE*) newsreel; (*TV*) news bulletin.

noticiero [notēsye'ro] *nm* newspaper, gazette; (*AM*: *also:* ~ **telediario**) news bulletin.

notificación [notēfēkásyon'] *nf* notification.

notificar [notēfēkár'] *vt* to notify, inform.

notifique [notēfē'ke] *etc vb* V **notificar**.

notoriedad [notoryetháth'] *nf* fame, renown.

notorio, a [noto'ryo, á] *a* (*público*) wellknown; (*evidente*) obvious.

nov. *abr* (= *noviembre*) Nov.

novatada [nohátá'thá] *nf* (*burla*) teasing,
hazing (*US*); **pagar la ~** to learn the hard
way.

novato, a [nohá'to, á] *a* inexperienced ♦
nm/f beginner, novice.

novecientos, as [nohesyen'tos, ás] *num*
nine hundred.

novedad [nohetháth'] *nf* (*calidad de nuevo*)
newness, novelty; (*noticia*) piece of news;
(*cambio*) change, (new) development; (*sorpresa*) surprise; **~es** *nfpl* (*noticia*) latest
(news) *sg*.

novedoso, a [nohetho'so, á] *a* novel.

novel [nohel'] *a* new; (*inexperto*) inexperienced ♦ *nm/f* beginner.

novela [nohe'lá] *nf* novel; ~ **policíaca** detective story.

novelero, a [nohele'ro, á] *a* highly imaginative.

novelesco, a [noheles'ko, á] *a* fictional; (*romántico*) romantic; (*fantástico*) fantastic.

novelista [nohelē'stá] *nm/f* novelist.

novelística [nohelē'stēká] *nf*: **la ~** fiction,
the novel.

noveno, a [nohe'no, á] *num* ninth.

noventa [nohen'tá] *num* ninety.

novia [no'hyá] *nf* V **novio**.

noviazgo [nohyás'go] *nm* engagement.

novicio, a [nohē'syo, á] *nm/f* novice.

noviembre [nohyem'bre] *nm* November.

novilla [nohē'yá] *nf* heifer.

novillada [nohēyá'thá] *nf* (*TAUR*) bullfight
with young bulls.

novillero [nohēye'ro] *nm* novice bullfighter.

novillo [nohē'yo] *nm* young bull, bullock;
hacer ~s (*fam*) to play hooky (*US*) *o*
truant (*Brit*).

novio, a [no'hyo, á] *nm/f* boyfriend/
girlfriend; (*prometido*) fiancé/fiancée; (*recién casado*) bridegroom/bride; **los ~s** the
newly-weds.

novísimo, a [nohē'sēmo, á] *a superlativo de*
nuevo, a.

NPI *nm abr* (*INFORM*: = *número personal
de identificación*) PIN.

N. S. *abr* = *Nuestro Señor*.

ntra., ntro. *abr* = **nuestra, nuestro**.

NU *nfpl abr* (= *Naciones Unidas*) UN.

nubarrón [nōōhárron'] *nm* storm cloud.

nube [nōō'he] *nf* cloud; (*MED*: *ocular*)
cloud, film; (*fig*) mass; **una ~ de críticas** a
storm of criticism; **los precios están por
las ~s** prices are sky-high; **estar en las ~s**
to be daydreaming.

nublado, a [nōōhlá'tho, á] *a* cloudy ♦ *nm*
storm cloud.

nublar [nōōhlár'] *vt* (*oscurecer*) to darken;
(*confundir*) to cloud; **~se** *vr* to cloud over.

nuca [nōō'ká] *nf* nape of the neck.

nuclear [nōōkleár'] *a* nuclear.

nuclearizado, a [nōōkleárēsá'tho, á] *a*: **países ~s** countries possessing nuclear
weapons.

núcleo [nōō'kleo] *nm* (*centro*) core; (*FÍSI
CA*) nucleus.

nudillo [nōōthē'yo] *nm* knuckle.

nudo [nōō'tho] *nm* knot; (*unión*) bond; (*de
problema*) crux; (*FERRO*) junction; (*fig*)
lump; ~ **corredizo** slipknot; **con un ~ en
la garganta** with a lump in one's throat.

nudoso, a [nōōtho'so, á] *a* knotty; (*tronco*)
gnarled; (*bastón*) knobby (*US*), knobbly
(*Brit*).

nueces [nwe'ses] *nfpl de* **nuez**.

nuera [nwe'rá] *nf* daughter-in-law.

nuestro, a [nwes'tro, á] *a posesivo* our ♦
pron ours; ~ **padre** our father; **un amigo
~** a friend of ours; **es el ~** it's ours; **los
~s** our people; (*DEPORTE*) our *o* the local
team *o* side.

nueva [nwe'há] *nf* V **nuevo**.

Nueva Escocia *nf* Nova Scotia.

nuevamente [nwehámen'te] *ad* (*otra vez*)
again; (*de nuevo*) anew.

Nueva York [-york'] *nf* New York.

Nueva Zeland(i)a [-seländ'(y)á] *nf* New
Zealand.

nueve [nwe'he] *num* nine.

nuevo, a [nwe'ho, á] *a* (*gen*) new ♦ *nf* piece
of news; **¿qué hay de ~?** (*fam*) what's
new?; **de ~** again.

Nuevo Méjico *nm* New Mexico.

nuez [nwes], *pl* **nueces** *nf* (*del nogal*) walnut; (*fruto*) nut; ~ **de Adán** Adam's apple;
~ **moscada** nutmeg.

nulidad [nōōlētháth'] *nf* (*incapacidad*) incompetence; (*abolición*) nullity; (*individuo*)
nonentity; **es una ~** he's a dead loss.

nulo, a [nōō'lo, á] *a* (*inepto, torpe*) useless;
(*inválido*) (null and) void; (*DEPORTE*)
drawn, tied.

núm. *abr* (= *número*) no.

numen [nōō'men] *nm* inspiration.

numeración [nōōmerásyon'] *nf* (*cifras*)

numbers *pl*; (*arábiga, romana etc*) numerals *pl*; ~ **de línea** (*INFORM*) line numbering.

numeral [nōōmerál'] *nm* numeral.

numerar [nōōmerár'] *vt* to number; ~**se** *vr* (*MIL etc*) to number off.

numerario, a [nōōmerá'ryo, á] *a* numerary; **profesor** ~ permanent *o* tenured member of teaching staff ♦ *nm* hard cash.

numérico, a [nōōme'rēko, á] *a* numerical.

número [nōō'mero] *nm* (*gen*) number; (*tamaño: de zapato*) size; (*ejemplar: de diario*) number, issue; (*TEATRO etc*) turn, act, number; **sin** ~ numberless, unnumbered; ~ **binario** (*INFORM*) binary number; ~ **de matrícula/de teléfono** registration/telephone number; ~ **personal de identificación** (*INFORM etc*) personal identification number; ~ **de serie** (*COM*) serial number; ~ **atrasado** back issue.

numeroso, a [nōōmero'so, á] *a* numerous; **familia numerosa** large family.

nunca [nōōn'ká] *ad* (*jamás*) never; (*con verbo negativo*) ever; ~ **lo pensé** I never thought it; **no viene** ~ he never comes; ~ **más** never again.

nuncio [nōōn'syo] *nm* (*REL*) nuncio.

nupcias [nōōp'syás] *nfpl* wedding *sg*, nuptials.

nutria [nōō'tryá] *nf* otter.

nutrición [nōōtrēsyon'] *nf* nutrition.

nutrido, a [nōōtrē'tho, á] *a* (*alimentado*) nourished; (*fig: grande*) large; (*abundante*) abundant; **mal** ~ undernourished; ~ **de** full of.

nutrir [nōōtrēr'] *vt* to feed, nourish; (*fig*) to feed, strengthen.

nutritivo, a [nōōtrētē'tho, á] *a* nourishing, nutritious.

nylon [nēlon'] *nm* nylon.

Ñ

Ñ, ñ [e'nye] *nf* (*letra*) Ñ, ñ.

ñato, a [nyá'to, á] *a* (*AM*) snub-nosed.

ñoñería [nyonyerē'á], **ñoñez** [nyonyes'] *nf* insipidness.

ñoño, a [nyo'nyo, á] *a* (*AM: tonto*) silly, stupid; (*soso*) insipid; (*persona: débil*) spineless.

ñoquis [ɲyo'kēs] *nmpl* (*CULIN*) gnocchi.

O

O, o [o] *nf* (*letra*) O, o; **O de Oviedo** O for Oboe.

O *abr* (= *oeste*) W.

o [o] *conj* or; ~ ... ~ either ... or; ~ **sea** that is.

o/ *nm* (*COM*: = *orden*) o.

OACI *nf abr* (= *Organización de la Aviación Civil Internacional*) ICAO.

oasis [oá'sēs] *nm inv* oasis.

obcecado, a [obseká'tho, á] *a* blind; (*terco*) stubborn.

obcecarse [obsekár'se] *vr* to be obstinate; ~ **en hacer** to insist on doing.

obceque [obse'ke] *etc vb V* obcecarse.

obedecer [obetheser'] *vt* to obey; ~ **a** (*MED etc*) to yield to; (*fig*) ~ **a ...**, ~ **al hecho de que ...** to be due to ..., arise from ....

obedezca [obethes'ká] *etc vb V* obedecer.

obediencia [obethyen'syá] *nf* obedience.

obediente [obethyen'te] *a* obedient.

obertura [obertōō'rá] *nf* overture.

obesidad [obesēthàth'] *nf* obesity.

obeso, a [obe'so, á] *a* obese.

óbice [o'bēse] *nm* obstacle, impediment.

obispado [obēspá'tho] *nm* bishopric.

obispo [obēs'po] *nm* bishop.

óbito [o'bēto] *nm* demise.

objeción [obhesyon'] *nf* objection; **hacer una** ~, **poner objeciones** to raise objections, object.

objetante [obhetán'te] *nm/f* objector; (*POL*) heckler.

objetar [obhetár'] *vt, vi* to object.

objetivo, a [obhetē'ho, á] *a* objective ♦ *nm* objective; (*fig*) aim; (*FOTO*) lens.

objeto [obhe'to] *nm* (*cosa*) object; (*fin*) aim.

objetor, a [obhetor', á] *nm/f* objector; ~ **de conciencia** conscientious objector.

oblea [oble'á] *nf* (*REL, fig*) wafer; (*INFORM*) chip, wafer.

oblicuo, a [oblē'kwo, á] *a* oblique; (*mirada*) sidelong.

obligación [oblēgásyon'] *nf* obligation; (*COM*) bond, debenture.

obligar [oblēgár'] *vt* to force; ~**se** *vr*: ~ **a** to commit o.s. to.

obligatorio, a [oblēgáto'ryo, á] *a* compulsory, obligatory.

obligue [oblē'ge] *etc vb V* obligar.

oboe [obo'e] *nm* oboe; (*músico*) oboist.

Ob.ᵖᵒ *abr* (= *Obispo*) Bp.

obra [o'βrå] *nf* work; (*hechura*) piece of work; (*ARQ*) construction, building; (*libro*) book; (*MUS*) opus; (*TEATRO*) play; ~ **de arte** work of art; ~ **maestra** masterpiece; ~ **de consulta** reference book; ~**s completas** complete works; ~ **benéfica** charity; "~**s**" (*en carretera*) "men at work"; ~**s públicas** public works; **por** ~ **de** thanks to (the efforts of); ~**s son amores y no buenas razones** actions speak louder than words.

obrar [o'βrår'] *vt* to work; (*tener efecto*) to have an effect on ♦ *vi* to act, behave; (*tener efecto*) to have an effect; **la carta obra en su poder** the letter is in his/her possession.

obr. cit. *abr* (= *obra citada*) op. cit.

obrero, a [o'βre'ro, å] *a* working; (*movimiento*) labor *cpd* (*US*), labour *cpd* (*Brit*); **clase obrera** working class ♦ *nm/f* (*gen*) worker; (*sin oficio*) laborer (*US*), labourer (*Brit*).

obscenidad [obsenēθåθ'] *nf* obscenity.

obsceno, a [obse'no, å] *a* obscene.

obscu... = **oscu...**

obsequiar [obsekyår'] *vt* (*ofrecer*) to present; (*agasajar*) to make a fuss of, lavish attention on.

obsequio [obse'kyo] *nm* (*regalo*) gift; (*cortesía*) courtesy, attention.

obsequioso, a [obsekyo'so, å] *a* attentive.

observación [obserβåsyon'] *nf* observation; (*reflexión*) remark; (*objeción*) objection.

observador, a [obserβåθor', å] *a* observant ♦ *nm/f* observer.

observancia [obserβån'syå] *nf* observance.

observar [obserβår'] *vt* to observe; (*notar*) to notice; (*leyes*) to observe, respect; (*reglas*) to abide by.

observatorio [obserβåto'ryo] *nm* observatory; ~ **del tiempo** weather station.

obsesión [obsesyon'] *nf* obsession.

obsesionar [obsesyonår'] *vt* to obsess.

obsolescencia [obsolesen'syå] *nf*: ~ **incorporada** (*COM*) built-in obsolescence.

obstaculice [obståkōōlē'se] *etc vb V* **obstaculizar.**

obstaculizar [obståkōōlēsår'] *vt* (*dificultar*) to hinder, hamper.

obstáculo [obstá'kōōlo] *nm* (*gen*) obstacle; (*impedimento*) hindrance, drawback.

obstante [obstán'te]: **no** ~ *ad* nevertheless; (*de todos modos*) all the same ♦ *prep* in spite of.

obstetricia [obstetrē'syå] *nf* obstetrics *sg*.

obstétrico, a [obste'trēko, å] *a* obstetric ♦ *nm/f* obstetrician.

obstinado, a [obstēnå'ðo, å] *a* (*gen*) obstinate; (*terco*) stubborn.

obstinarse [obstēnår'se] *vr* to dig one's heels in; ~ **en** to persist in.

obstrucción [obstrōōksyon'] *nf* obstruction.

obstruir [obstrōōēr'] *vt* to obstruct; (*bloquear*) to block; (*estorbar*) to hinder.

obstruyendo [obstrōōyen'do] *etc vb V* **obstruir.**

obtención [obtensyon'] *nf* (*COM*) procurement.

obtendré [obtendre'] *etc vb V* **obtener.**

obtener [obtener'] *vt* (*conseguir*) to obtain; (*ganar*) to gain.

obtenga [obten'gå] *etc vb V* **obtener.**

obturación [obtōōråsyon'] *nf* plugging, stopping; (*FOTO*): **velocidad de** ~ shutter speed.

obturador [obtōōråθor'] *nm* (*FOTO*) shutter.

obtuve [obtōō'βe] *etc vb V* **obtener.**

obús [oβōōs'] *nm* (*MIL*) shell.

obviar [obβyår'] *vt* to obviate, remove.

obvio, a [oβ'βyo, å] *a* obvious.

ocasión [okåsyon'] *nf* (*oportunidad*) opportunity, chance; (*momento*) occasion, time; (*causa*) cause; **de** ~ secondhand; **con** ~ **de** on the occasion of; **en algunas ocasiones** sometimes; **aprovechar la** ~ to seize one's opportunity.

ocasionar [okåsyonår'] *vt* to cause.

ocaso [okå'so] *nm* sunset; (*fig*) decline.

occidental [oksēðentál'] *a* western ♦ *nm/f* westerner ♦ *nm* west.

occidente [oksēðen'te] *nm* west; **el O~** the West.

occiso, a [oksē'so, å] *nm/f*: **el** ~ (*AM*) the deceased; (*de asesinato*) the victim.

océano [ose'åno] *nm* ocean; **el** ~ **Índico** Indian Ocean.

O.C.D.E. *nf abr* (= *Organización de Cooperación y Desarrollo Económicos*) OECD.

OCI [o'sē] *nf abr* (*POL*: *Venezuela, Perú*) = *Oficina Central de Información.*

ocio [o'syo] *nm* (*tiempo*) leisure; (*pey*) idleness; "**guía del** ~" entertainment guide.

ociosidad [osyosēðåθ'] *nf* idleness.

ocioso, a [osyo'so, å] *a* (*inactivo*) idle; (*inútil*) useless.

oct. *abr* (= *octubre*) Oct.

octanaje [oktånå'he] *nm*: **de alto** ~ high octane.

octano [oktå'no] *nm* octane.

octavilla [oktåβē'yå] *nm* leaflet, pamphlet.

octavo, a [oktá'βo, å] *num* eighth.

octeto [okte'to] *nm* (*INFORM*) byte.

octogenario, a [oktohenå'ryo, å] *a*, *nm/f* octogenarian.

octubre [oktoo'βre] *nm* October.

OCU [o'kōō] *nf abr* (*Esp*:=*Organización de Consumidores y Usuarios*) ≈ Consumers' Association.

ocular [okōōlár'] *a* ocular, eye *cpd*; **testigo** ~ eyewitness.
oculista [okōōlē'stá] *nm/f* oculist.
ocultar [okōōltár'] *vt* (*esconder*) to hide; (*callar*) to conceal; (*disfrazar*) to screen; ~**se** *vr* to hide (o.s.); ~**se a la vista** to keep out of sight.
oculto, a [okōōl'to, á] *a* hidden; (*fig*) secret.
ocupación [okōōpásyon'] *nf* occupation; (*tenencia*) occupancy.
ocupado, a [okōōpá'tho, á] *a* (*persona*) busy; (*plaza*) occupied, taken; (*teléfono*) busy; **¿está ocupada la silla?** is that seat taken?
ocupar [okōōpár'] *vt* (*gen*) to occupy; (*puesto*) to hold, fill; (*individuo*) to engage; (*obreros*) to employ; (*confiscar*) to seize; ~**se** *vr*: ~**se de** *o* **en** to concern o.s. with; (*cuidar*) to look after; ~**se de lo suyo** to mind one's own business.
ocurrencia [okōōrren'syá] *nf* (*ocasión*) occurrence; (*agudeza*) witticism.
ocurrir [okōōrrēr'] *vi* to happen; ~**se** *vr*: **se me ocurrió que ...** it occurred to me that ...; **¿se te ocurre algo?** can you think of *o* come up with anything? **¿qué ocurre?** what's going on?
ochenta [otchen'tá] *num* eighty.
ocho [otch'o] *num* eight; (*fecha*) eighth; ~ **días** a week.
oda [o'thá] *nf* ode.
ODECA [othe'ká] *nf abr*=*Organización de Estados Centroamericanos.*
odiar [othyár'] *vt* to hate.
odio [o'thyo] *nm* (*gen*) hate, hatred; (*disgusto*) dislike.
odioso, a [othyo'so, á] *a* (*gen*) hateful; (*malo*) nasty.
odontología [othontolohē'á] *nf* dentistry, dental surgery.
odontólogo, a [othonto'logo, á] *nm/f* dentist, dental surgeon.
odre [o'thre] *nm* wineskin.
O.E.A. *nf abr* (= *Organización de Estados Americanos*) O.A.S.
OECE *nf abr* (= *Organización Europea de Cooperación Económica*) OEEC.
OELA [oc'lá] *nf abr* = *Organización de Estados Latinoamericanos.*
oeste [oc'ste] *nm* west; **una película del** ~ a western.
ofender [ofender'] *vt* (*agraviar*) to offend; (*insultar*) to insult; ~**se** *vr* to take offense.
ofensa [ofen'sá] *nf* offense (*US*), offence (*Brit*); (*insulto*) slight.
ofensivo, a [ofensē'bo, á] *a* (*insultante*) insulting; (*MIL*) offensive ♦ *nf* offensive.
ofensor, a [ofensor', á] *a* offending ♦ *nm/f* offender.
oferta [ofer'tá] *nf* offer; (*propuesta*) proposal; (*para contrato*) bid, tender; **la** ~ **y la**

demanda supply and demand; **artículos en** ~ goods for sale; ~ **excedentaria** (*COM*) excess supply; ~ **monetaria** money supply; ~ **pública de compra** (*COM*) takeover bid; ~**s de trabajo** (*en periódicos*) job openings (*US*) *o* situations vacant (*Brit*) column.
oficial [ofēsyál'] *a* official ♦ *nm* official; (*MIL*) officer.
oficialista [ofēsyálē'stá] *a* (*AM*) (pro-) government; **el candidato** ~ the governing party's candidate.
oficiar [ofēsyár'] *vt* to inform officially ♦ *vi* (*REL*) to officiate.
oficina [ofēsē'ná] *nf* office; ~ **de colocación** employment agency; ~ **de información** information bureau; ~ **de objetos perdidos** lost-and-found department (*US*), lost property office (*Brit*); ~ **de turismo** tourist office.
oficinista [ofēsēnē'stá] *nm/f* clerk; **los** ~**s** white-collar workers.
oficio [ofē'syo] *nm* (*profesión*) profession; (*puesto*) position; (*REL*) service; (*función*) function; (*comunicado*) official letter; **ser del** ~ to be an old hand; **tener mucho** ~ to have a lot of experience; ~ **de difuntos** funeral service; **de** ~ officially.
oficioso, a [ofēsyo'so, á] *a* (*pey*) officious; (*no oficial*) unofficial, informal.
ofimática [ofēmá'tēká] *nf* office automation.
ofrecer [ofreser'] *vt* (*dar*) to offer; (*proponer*) to propose; ~**se** *vr* (*persona*) to offer o.s., volunteer; (*situación*) to present itself; **¿qué se le ofrece?, ¿se le ofrece algo?** what can I do for you?, can I get you anything?
ofrecimiento [ofresēmyen'to] *nm* offer, offering.
ofrendar [ofrendár'] *vt* to offer, contribute.
ofrezca [ofres'ká] *etc vb* V **ofrecer.**
oftalmología [oftálmolohē'á] *nf* ophthalmology.
oftalmólogo, a [oftálmo'logo, á] *nm/f* ophthalmologist.
ofuscación [ofōōskásyon'] *nf*, **ofuscamiento** [ofōōskámyen'to] *nm* (*fig*) bewilderment.
ofuscar [ofōōskár'] *vt* (*confundir*) to bewilder; (*enceguecer*) to dazzle, blind.
ofusque [ofōōs'ke] *etc vb* V **ofuscar.**
ogro [o'gro] *nm* ogre.
OIC *nf abr*=*Organización Interamericana del Café*; (*COM*)=*Organización Internacional del Comercio.*
oída [oē'thá] *nf*: **de** ~**s** by hearsay.
oído [oē'tho] *nm* (*ANAT, MUS*) ear; (*sentido*) hearing; ~ **interno** inner ear; **de** ~ by ear; **apenas pude dar crédito a mis** ~**s** I could scarcely believe my ears; **hacer** ~**s sordos a** to turn a deaf ear to.
OIEA *nm abr* (= *Organismo Internacional de Energía Atómica*) IAEA.

oiga |o'ēg̣á| *etc vb V* **oír.**

OIR |oēr'| *nf abr* (= *Organización Internacional para los Refugiados*) IRO.

oír |oēr'| *vt* (*gen*) to hear; (*atender a*) to listen to; ¡**oye!** (*sorpresa*) I say!, say! (*US*); ¡**oiga!** (*TELEC*) hello?; ~ **misa** to attend mass; **como quien oye llover** without paying (the slightest) attention.

O.I.T. *nf abr* (= *Organización Internacional del Trabajo*) ILO.

ojal |ohál'| *nm* buttonhole.

ojalá |ohálá'| *excl* if only (it were so)!, some hope! ◆ *conj* if only...!, would that...!; ~ **que venga hoy** I hope he comes today; ¡~ **pudiera!** I wish I could!

ojeada |ohcá'ṭḥá| *nf* glance; **echar una ~ a** to take a quick look at.

ojera |ohc'rá| *nf*: **tener ~s** to have bags under one's eyes.

ojeriza |oherē'sá| *nf* ill-will; **tener ~ a** to have a grudge against, have it in for.

ojeroso, a |ohero'so, á| *a* haggard.

ojete |ohc'tc| *nm* eye(let).

ojo |o'ho| *nm* eye; (*de puente*) span; (*de cerradura*) keyhole ◆ *excl* careful!; **tener ~ para** to have an eye for; **~s saltones** bulging o goggle eyes; **~ de buey** porthole; **~ por ~** an eye for an eye; **en un abrir y cerrar de ~s** in the twinkling of an eye; **a ~s vistas** openly; (*crecer etc*) before one's (very) eyes; **a ~ (de buen cubero)** roughly; **~s que no ven, corazón que no siente** out of sight, out of mind; **ser el ~ derecho de uno** (*fig*) to be the apple of sb's eye.

ola |o'lá| *nf* wave; **~ de calor/frío** heatwave/cold spell; **la nueva ~** the latest fashion; (*CINE, MUS*) (the) new wave.

OLADE |olá'ṭḥe| *nf abr* = *Organización Latinoamericana de Energía.*

olé |ole'| *excl* bravo!, olé!

oleada |olcá'ṭḥá| *nf* big wave, swell; (*fig*) wave.

oleaje |olcá'he| *nm* swell.

óleo |o'lco| *nm* oil.

oleoducto |olcoṭ͞o͞ok'to| *nm* (oil) pipeline.

oler |oler'| *vt* (*gen*) to smell; (*inquirir*) to pry into; (*fig: sospechar*) to sniff out ◆ *vi* to smell; **~ a** to smell of; **huele mal** it smells bad, it stinks.

olfatear |olfáteár'| *vt* to smell; (*fig: sospechar*) to sniff out; (*inquirir*) to pry into.

olfato |olfá'to| *nm* sense of smell.

oligarquía |olēg̣árkē'á| *nf* oligarchy.

olimpíada |olēmpē'áṭḥá| *nf*: **las O~s** the Olympics.

olímpico, a |olēm'pēko, á| *a* Olympian; (*deportes*) Olympic.

oliva |olē'ḥá| *nf* (*aceituna*) olive; **aceite de ~** olive oil.

olivar |olēḥár'| *nm* olive grove o plantation.

olivo |olē'ḥo| *nm* olive tree.

olmo |ol'mo| *nm* elm (tree).

olor |olor'| *nm* smell.

oloroso, a |oloro'so, á| *a* scented.

OLP *nf abr* (= *Organización para la Liberación de Palestina*) PLO.

olvidadizo, a |olḥēṭḥáṭḥē'so, á| *a* (*desmemoriado*) forgetful; (*distraído*) absent-minded.

olvidar |olḥēṭḥár'| *vt* to forget; (*omitir*) to omit; (*abandonar*) to leave behind; **~se** *vr* (*fig*) to forget o.s.; **se me olvidó** I forgot.

olvido |olḥē'ṭḥo| *nm* oblivion; (*acto*) oversight; (*descuido*) slip; **caer en el ~** to fall into oblivion.

olla |o'yá| *nf* pan; (*para hervir agua*) kettle; (*comida*) stew; **~ a presión** pressure cooker.

O.M. *abr* (*POL*) = *Orden Ministerial.*

ombligo |omblē'g̣o| *nm* navel.

OMI *nf abr* (= *Organización Marítima Internacional*) IMO.

ominoso, a |omēno'so, á| *a* ominous.

omisión |omēsyon'| *nf* (*abstención*) omission; (*descuido*) neglect.

omiso, a |omē'so, á| *a*: **hacer caso ~ de** to ignore, pass over.

omitir |omētēr'| *vt* to leave o miss out, omit.

omnipotente |omnēpoten'tc| *a* omnipotent.

omnipresente |omnēpresen'tc| *a* omnipresent.

omnívoro, a |omnē'ḥoro, á| *a* omnivorous.

omóplato |omo'pláto| *nm* shoulder blade.

OMS *nf abr* (= *Organización Mundial de la Salud*) WHO.

ONCE |on'sc| *nf abr* (= *Organización Nacional de Ciegos Españoles*) charity for the blind.

once |on'sc| *num* eleven ◆ *nf* (*AM*): **~s** snack *sg.*

onda |on'dá| *nf* wave; **~ corta/larga/media** short/long/medium wave; **~s acústicas/ hertzianas** acoustic/Hertzian waves; **~ sonora** sound wave.

ondear |ondeár'| *vi* to wave; (*tener ondas*) to be wavy; (*agua*) to ripple; **~se** *vr* to swing, sway.

ondulación |ond͞o͞olásyon'| *nf* undulation.

ondulado, a |ond͞o͞olá'ṭḥo, á| *a* wavy ◆ *nm* wave.

ondulante |ond͞o͞olán'tc| *a* undulating.

ondular |ond͞o͞olár'| *vt* (*el pelo*) to wave ◆ *vi*, **~se** *vr* to undulate.

oneroso, a |onero'so, á| *a* onerous.

onomástico, a |onomá'stēko, á| *a*: **fiesta onomástica** saint's day ◆ *nm* saint's day.

ONU |o'n͞o͞o| *nf abr V* **Organización de las Naciones Unidas.**

onubense |on͞o͞oḥen'sc| *a* of o from Huelva. ◆ *nm/f* native o inhabitant of Huelva.

ONUDI |on͞o͞o'ṭḥē| *nf abr* (= *Organización de las Naciones Unidas para el Desarrollo*

Industrial) UNIDO (*United Nations Industrial Development Organization*).

onza [on'sá] *nf* ounce.

O.P. *nfpl abr* = **obras públicas**; (*COM*) = *Oficina Principal*.

opaco, a [opá'ko, á] *a* opaque; (*fig*) dull.

ópalo [o'pálo] *nm* opal.

opción [opsyon'] *nf* (*gen*) option; (*derecho*) right, option; **no hay** ~ there is no alternative.

O.P.E.P. [opep'] *nf abr* (= *Organización de Países Exportadores de Petróleo*) OPEC.

ópera [o'perá] *nf* opera; ~ **bufa** *o* **cómica** comic opera.

operación [operásyon'] *nf* (*gen*) operation; (*COM*) transaction, deal; ~ **"llave en manos"** (*INFORM*) turnkey operation; ~ **a plazo** (*COM*) future (*US*) *o* forward (*Brit*) transaction; **operaciones accesorias** (*INFORM*) housekeeping; **operaciones a término** (*COM*) futures.

operador, a [operáthor', á] *nm/f* operator; (*CINE*: *proyección*) projectionist; (: *rodaje*) cameraman.

operante [operán'te] *a* operating.

operar [operár'] *vt* (*producir*) to produce, bring about; (*MED*) to operate on ♦ *vi* (*COM*) to operate, deal; ~**se** *vr* to occur; (*MED*) to have an operation; **se han operado grandes cambios** great changes have been made *o* have taken place.

operario, a [operá'ryo, á] *nm/f* operative.

opereta [opere'tá] *nf* operetta.

opinar [opinár'] *vt* (*estimar*) to think ♦ *vi* (*enjuiciar*) to give one's opinion; ~ **bien de** to think well of, have a good opinion of.

opinión [opēnyon'] *nf* (*creencia*) belief; (*criterio*) opinion; **la** ~ **pública** public opinion.

opio [o'pyo] *nm* opium.

opíparo, a [opē'páro, á] *a* sumptuous.

opondré [opondre'] *etc vb V* **oponer**.

oponente [oponen'te] *nm/f* opponent.

oponer [oponer'] *vt* (*resistencia*) to put up, offer; (*negativa*) to raise; ~**se** *vr* (*objetar*) to object; (*estar frente a frente*) to be opposed; (*dos personas*) to oppose each other; ~ **A a B** to set A against B; **me opongo a pensar que ...** I refuse to believe *o* think that ....

oponga [opon'gá] *etc vb V* **oponer**.

Oporto [opor'to] *nm* Oporto.

oportunidad [oportoōnēthàth'] *nf* (*ocasión*) opportunity; (*posibilidad*) chance.

oportunismo [oportoōnēs'mo] *nm* opportunism.

oportunista [oportoōnē'stá] *nm/f* opportunist; (*infección*) opportunistic.

oportuno, a [oportoō'no, á] *a* (*en su tiempo*) opportune, timely; (*respuesta*) suitable; **en el momento** ~ at the right moment.

oposición [oposēsyon'] *nf* opposition; **oposiciones** *nfpl* public examinations; **ganar un puesto por oposiciones** to win a post by public competitive examination; **hacer oposiciones a, presentarse a unas oposiciones a** to take a competitive examination for.

opositor, a [oposētor', á] *nm/f* (*adversario*) opponent; (*concurrente*) competitor.

opresión [opresyon'] *nf* oppression.

opresivo, a [opresē'ho, á] *a* oppressive.

opresor, a [opresor', á] *nm/f* oppressor.

oprimir [oprēmēr'] *vt* to squeeze; (*asir*) to grasp; (*pulsar*) to press; (*fig*) to oppress.

oprobio [opro'hyo] *nm* (*infamia*) ignominy; (*descrédito*) shame.

optar [optár'] *vi* (*elegir*) to choose; ~ **a** *o* **por** to opt for.

optativo, a [optátē'ho, á] *a* optional.

óptico, a [op'tēko, á] *a* optic(al) ♦ *nm/f* optician ♦ *nf* optics *sg*; (*fig*) viewpoint.

optimismo [optēmēs'mo] *nm* optimism.

optimista [optēmē'stá] *nm/f* optimist.

óptimo, a [op'tēmo, á] *a* (*el mejor*) very best.

opuesto, a [opwe'sto, á] *pp de* **oponer** ♦ *a* (*contrario*) opposite; (*antagónico*) opposing.

opulencia [opoōlen'syá] *nf* opulence.

opulento, a [opoōlen'to, á] *a* opulent.

opuse [opoō'se] *etc vb V* **oponer**.

ORA [o'rá] *abr* (*Esp*: = *Ordenación de la Regulación del Aparcamiento*) parking regulations.

ora [o'rá] *ad*: ~ **tú** ~ **yo** now you, now me.

oración [orásyon'] *nf* (*discurso*) speech; (*REL*) prayer; (*LING*) sentence.

oráculo [orá'koōlo] *nm* oracle.

orador, a [oráthor', á] *nm/f* orator; (*conferenciante*) speaker.

oral [orál'] *a* oral; **por vía** ~ (*MED*) orally.

orangután [orángoōtán'] *nm* orang-utan.

orar [orár'] *vi* (*REL*) to pray.

oratoria [oráto'ryá] *nf* oratory.

orbe [or'he] *nm* orb, sphere; (*fig*) world; **en todo el** ~ all over the globe.

órbita [or'hētá] *nf* orbit; (*ANAT*: *ocular*) (eye-)socket.

orden [or'then] *nm* (*gen*) order; (*INFORM*) command; ~ **público** public order, law and order; (*números*) **del** ~ **de** about; **de primer** ~ first-rate; **en** ~ **de prioridad** in order of priority ♦ *nf* (*gen*) order; ~ **bancaria** banker's order; ~ **de compra** (*COM*) purchase order; ~ **del día** agenda; **eso ahora está a la** ~ **del día** that is now the order of the day; **a la** ~ **de usted** at your service; **dar la** ~ **de hacer algo** to give the order to do sth.

ordenación [orthenásyon'] *nf* (*estado*)

order; (*acto*) ordering; (*REL*) ordination.

ordenado, a |orðenáˈðo, ạ| *a* (*metódico*) methodical; (*arreglado*) orderly.

ordenador |orðenaðor'| *nm* computer; ~ **central** mainframe computer; ~ **de gestión** business computer; ~ **de sobremesa** desktop computer.

ordenanza |orðenánˈsá| *nf* ordinance; ~**s municipales** by-laws ♦ *nm* (*COM etc*) messenger; (*MIL*) orderly; (*bedel*) porter.

ordenar |orðenár'| *vt* (*mandar*) to order; (*poner orden*) to put in order, arrange; ~**se** *vr* (*REL*) to be ordained.

ordeñadora |orðenyáðoˈrá| *nf* milking machine.

ordeñar |orðenyár'| *vt* to milk.

ordinariez |orðenáryes'| *nf* (*cualidad*) coarseness, vulgarity; (*una* ~) coarse remark *o* joke *etc*.

ordinario, a |orðenáˈryo, á| *a* (*común*) ordinary, usual; (*vulgar*) vulgar, common.

ordinograma |orðenográˈmá| *nm* flowchart.

orear |oreár'| *vt* to air; ~**se** *vr* (*ropa*) to air.

orégano |oreˈgáno| *nm* oregano.

oreja |oreˈhá| *nf* ear; (*MECÁNICA*) lug, flange.

orensano, a |orensáˈno, á| *a* of *o* from Orense ♦ *nm/f* native *o* inhabitant of Orense.

orfanato |orfanáˈto|, **orfanatorio** |orfanáto'ryo| *nm* orphanage.

orfandad |orfándáˈð'| *nf* orphanhood.

orfebre |orfeˈbre| *nm* gold-/silversmith.

orfebrería |orfebreréˈá| *nf* gold/silver work.

orfelinato |orfelináˈto| *nm* orphanage.

orfeón |orfeon'| *nm* (*MUS*) choral society.

organice |orgánˈseˈse| *etc vb V* **organizar**.

orgánico, a |orgáˈnˈeko, á| *a* organic.

organigrama |orgánˈegráˈmá| *nm* flow chart; (*de organización*) organization chart.

organillo |orgánˈeˈyo| *nm* barrel organ.

organismo |orgánˈesˈmo| *nm* (*BIO*) organism; (*POL*) organization; **O~ Internacional de Energía Atómica** International Atomic Energy Agency.

organista |orgánˈesˈtá| *nm/f* organist.

organización |orgánˈesásyon'| *nf* organization; **O~ de las Naciones Unidas (ONU)** United Nations Organization **O~ del Tratado del Atlántico Norte (OTAN)** North Atlantic Treaty Organization (NATO).

organizador, a |orgánˈesáˈðor', á| *a* organizing; **el comité** ~ the organizing committee ♦ *nm/f* organizer.

organizar |orgánˈesár'| *vt* to organize.

órgano |or'gáno| *nm* organ.

orgasmo |orgásˈmo| *nm* orgasm.

orgía |orˈhéˈá| *nf* orgy.

orgullo |orgōoˈyo| *nm* (*altanería*) pride; (*autorespeto*) self-respect.

orgulloso, a |orgōoyoˈso, ạ| *a* (*gen*) proud; (*altanero*) haughty.

orientación |oryentásyon'| *nf* (*posición*) position; (*dirección*) direction; ~ **profesional** occupational guidance.

oriental |oryentál'| *a* oriental; (*región etc*) eastern ♦ *nm/f* oriental.

orientar |oryentár'| *vt* (*situar*) to orientate; (*señalar*) to point; (*dirigir*) to direct; (*guiar*) to guide; ~**se** *vr* to get one's bearings; (*decidirse*) to decide on a course of action.

oriente |oryen'te| *nm* east; **el O~** the East, the Orient; **Cercano/Medio/Lejano O~** Near/ Middle/Far East.

orificio |oréfˈsyo| *nm* orifice.

origen |oréˈhen| *nm* origin; (*nacimiento*) lineage, birth; **dar** ~ **a** to cause, give rise to.

original |orðénál'| *a* (*nuevo*) original; (*extraño*) odd, strange ♦ *nm* original; (*TIP*) manuscript; (*TEC*) master (copy).

originalidad |orðénáléˈðáˈð'| *nf* originality.

originar |orðénár'| *vt* to originate; ~**se** *vr* to originate.

originario, a |orðénáˈryo, á| *a* (*nativo*) native; (*primordial*) original; **ser** ~ **de** to originate from; **país** ~ country of origin.

orilla |oréˈyá| *nf* (*borde*) border; (*de río*) bank; (*de bosque, tela*) edge; (*de mar*) shore; **a** ~**s de** on the banks of.

orillar |oréyár'| *vt* (*bordear*) to skirt, go around; (*COSTURA*) to edge; (*resolver*) to wind up; (*tocar: asunto*) to touch briefly on; (*dificultad*) to avoid.

orín |orén'| *nm* rust.

orina |oréˈná| *nf* urine.

orinal |orénál'| *nm* (chamber) pot.

orinar |orénár'| *vi* to urinate; ~**se** *vr* to wet o.s.

orines |oré'nes| *nmpl* urine *sg*.

oriundo, a |oryōon'do, á| *a*: ~ **de** native of.

orla |or'lá| *nf* edge, border; (*ESCOL*) graduation photograph.

ornamentar |ornámentár'| *vt* (*adornar, ataviar*) to adorn; (*revestir*) to bedeck.

ornamento |ornámen'to| *nm* ornament.

ornar |ornár'| *vt* to adorn.

ornitología |ornétolohéˈá| *nf* ornithology, bird watching.

ornitólogo, a |ornéto'logo, á| *nm/f* ornithologist.

oro |o'ro| *nm* gold; ~ **en barras** gold ingots; **de** ~ gold, golden; **no es** ~ **todo lo que reluce** all that glitters is not gold; **hacerse de** ~ to make a fortune; *V tb* **oros**.

orondo, a |oron'do, á| *a* (*vasija*) rounded; (*individuo*) smug, self-satisfied.

oropel |oropel'| *nm* tinsel.

oros |o'ros| *nmpl* (*NAIPES*) hearts.

orquesta |orkeˈstá| *nf* orchestra; ~ **de**

cámara/sinfónica chamber/symphony orchestra; ~ **de jazz** jazz band.

orquídea |orkē'ŧheá| *nf* orchid.

ortiga |ortē'ġá| *nf* nettle.

ortodoxo, a |ortoŧhok'so, á| *a* orthodox.

ortografía |ortoġráfē'á| *nf* spelling.

ortopedia |ortope'ŧhyá| *nf* orthopedics *sg* (*US*), orthopaedics *sg* (*Brit*).

oruga |oroō'ġá| *nf* caterpillar.

orujo |oroō'ho| *nm* *type of strong grape liqueur made from grape pressings*.

orzuelo |orswe'lo| *nm* (*MED*) stye.

os |os| *pron* (*gen*) you; (*a vosotros*) (to) you; (*reflexivo*) (to) yourselves; (*mutuo*) (to) each other; **vosotros ~ laváis** you wash yourselves; **¡callar~!** (*fam*) shut up!

osa |o'sá| *nf* (she-)bear; **O~ Mayor/Menor** Ursa Major/Minor.

osadía |osáŧhē'á| *nf* daring; (*descaro*) impudence.

osamenta |osámen'tá| *nf* skeleton.

osar |osár'| *vi* to dare.

oscense |oscen'se| *a* of *o* from Huesca ♦ *nm/f* native *o* inhabitant of Huesca.

oscilación |osēlásyon'| *nf* (*movimiento*) oscillation; (*fluctuación*) fluctuation; (*vacilación*) hesitation; (*columpio*) swinging, movement to and fro.

oscilar |osēlár'| *vi* to oscillate: to fluctuate: to hesitate.

ósculo |os'kōōlo| *nm* kiss.

oscurecer |oskōōreser'| *vt* to darken ♦ *vi* to grow dark; **~se** *vr* to grow *o* get dark.

oscurezca |oskōōres'ká| *etc vb V* **oscurecer**.

oscuridad |oskōōrēŧháŧh'| *nf* obscurity; (*tinieblas*) darkness.

oscuro, a |oskōō'ro, á| *a* dark; (*fig*) obscure; (*indefinido*) confused; (*cielo*) overcast, cloudy; (*futuro etc*) uncertain; **a oscuras** in the dark.

óseo, a |o'seo, á| *a* bony; (*MED etc*) bone *cpd*.

oso |o'so| *nm* bear; **~ blanco/gris/pardo** polar/grizzly/brown bear; **~ de peluche** teddy bear; **~ hormiguero** anteater; **hacer el ~** to play the fool.

Ostende |osten'de| *nm* Ostend.

ostensible |ostensē'hle| *a* obvious.

ostensiblemente |ostensēhlemen'te| *ad* perceptibly, visibly.

ostentación |ostentásyon'| *nf* (*gen*) ostentation; (*acto*) display.

ostentar |ostentár'| *vt* (*gen*) to show; (*pey*) to flaunt, show off; (*poseer*) to have, possess.

ostentoso, a |ostento'so, á| *a* ostentatious, showy.

osteópata |osteo'pátá| *nm/f* osteopath.

ostra |os'trá| *nf* oyster ♦ *excl*: **¡~s!** (*fam*) sugar!

ostracismo |ostrásēs'mo| *nm* ostracism.

OTAN |o'tán| *nf abr V* **Organización del Tratado del Atlántico Norte**.

OTASE |otá'se| *nf abr* (= *Organización del Tratado del Sudeste Asiático*) SEATO.

otear |oteár'| *vt* to observe; (*fig*) to look into.

otero |ote'ro| *nm* low hill, hillock.

otitis |otē'tēs| *nf* earache.

otoñal |otonyál'| *a* autumnal.

otoño |oto'nyo| *nm* fall (*US*), autumn.

otorgamiento |otorġámyen'to| *nm* conferring, granting; (*JUR*) execution.

otorgar |otorġár'| *vt* (*conceder*) to concede; (*dar*) to grant; (*poderes*) to confer; (*premio*) to award.

otorgue |otor'ġe| *etc vb V* **otorgar**.

otorrinolaringólogo, a |otorrēnolárēngo'loġo, á| *nm/f* (*MED: tb*: **otorrino**) ear, nose and throat specialist.

otro, a |o'tro, á| *a* (*sg*) another; (*pl*) other ♦ *pron* another one; **~s** others; **otra cosa** something else; **de otra manera** otherwise; **en ~ tiempo** formerly, once; **¡otra!** (*TEATRO*) encore!; **otra parte** elsewhere; **otra vez** again; **ni uno ni ~** neither one nor the other; **~ tanto** the same again; **~ dijo que ...** somebody else said that ...

otrora |otro'rá| *ad* formerly; **el ~ señor del país** the one-time ruler of the country.

OUA *nf abr* (= *Organización de la Unidad Africana*) OAU.

ovación |ohásyon'| *nf* ovation.

ovacionar |ohásyonár'| *vt* to cheer.

oval |ohál'|, **ovalado, a** |ohálá'ŧho, á| *a* oval.

óvalo |o'hálo| *nm* oval.

oveja |ohe'há| *nf* sheep; **~ negra** (*fig*) black sheep (of the family).

overol |oherol'| *nm* (*AM*) overalls *pl*.

ovetense |oheten'se| *a* of *o* from Oviedo ♦ *nm/f* native *o* inhabitant of Oviedo.

ovillo |ohē'yo| *nm* (*de lana*) ball; (*fig*) tangle; **hacerse un ~** to curl up (into a ball).

OVNI |oh'nē| *nm abr* (= *objeto volante no identificado*) UFO.

ovulación |ohōōlásyon'| *nf* ovulation.

óvulo |o'hōōlo| *nm* ovum.

oxidación |oksēŧhásyon'| *nf* rusting.

oxidar |oksēŧhár'| *vt* to rust; **~se** *vr* to go rusty; (*TEC*) to oxidize.

óxido |ok'sēŧho| *nm* oxide.

oxigenado, a |oksēhená'ŧho, á| *a* (*QUÍMICA*) oxygenated; (*pelo*) bleached.

oxigenar |oksēhenár'| *vt* to oxygenate; **~se** *vr* to become oxygenated; (*fam*) to get some fresh air.

oxígeno |oksē'heno| *nm* oxygen.

oyendo |oyen'do| *etc vb V* **oír**.

oyente |oyen'te| *nm/f* listener, hearer; (*ESCOL*) auditor (*US*), unregistered *o* occasional student (*Brit*).

ozono [oso'no] *nm* ozone.

P

P, p [pe] *nf* (*letra*) P, p; **P de París** P for Peter.
P *abr* (*REL*: = *padre*) Fr.; = **papa**.
p. *abr* (= *página*) p.
p.a. *abr* = **por autorización**.
pabellón [páẹeyon'] *nm* bell tent; (*ARQ*) pavilion; (*de hospital etc*) block, section; (*bandera*) flag; ~ **de conveniencia** (*COM*) flag of convenience; ~ **de la oreja** outer ear.
pábilo [pá'ḅēlo] *nm* wick.
pábulo [pá'ḅōolo] *nm* food; **dar** ~ **a** to feed, encourage.
PAC *nf abr* (= *Política Agrícola Común*) CAP.
pacense [pásen'se] *a* of o from Badajoz ♦ *nm/f* native o inhabitant of Badajoz.
paceño, a [páce'nyo, á] *a* of o from La Paz ♦ *nm/f* native o inhabitant of La Paz.
pacer [páser'] *vi* to graze ♦ *vt* to graze on.
paciencia [pásyen'syá] *nf* patience; ¡~! be patient!; ¡~ **y barajar!** don't give up!; **perder la** ~ to lose one's temper.
paciente [pásyen'te] *a, nm/f* patient.
pacificación [pásēfēkásyon'] *nf* pacification.
pacificar [pásēfēkár'] *vt* to pacify; (*tranquilizar*) to calm.
pacífico, a [pásē'fēko, á] *a* peaceful; (*persona*) peace-loving; (*existencia*) pacific; **el (Océano) P**~ the Pacific (Ocean).
pacifique [pásēfē'ke] *etc vb V* **pacificar**.
pacifismo [pásēfēs'mo] *nm* pacifism.
pacifista [pásēfē'stá] *nm/f* pacifist.
pacotilla [pákotē'yá] *nf* trash; **de** ~ shoddy.
pactar [páktár'] *vt* to agree to, agree on ♦ *vi* to come to an agreement.
pacto [pák'to] *nm* (*tratado*) pact; (*acuerdo*) agreement.
pachá [pátchá'] *nm*: **vivir como un** ~ to live like a king.
pachorra [pátcho'rrá] *nf* (*indolencia*) slowness; (*tranquilidad*) calmness.
pachucho, a [pátchōotch'o, á] *a* (*fruta*) overripe; (*persona*) sickly (*US*), off-colour (*Brit*).
padecer [páḍeser'] *vt* (*sufrir*) to suffer; (*soportar*) to endure, put up with; (*ser víctima de*) to be a victim of ♦ *vi*: ~ **de** to suffer from.
padecimiento [páḍesēmyen'to] *nm* suffering.

padezca [páḍes'ká] *etc vb V* **padecer**.
padrastro [páḍrás'tro] *nm* stepfather.
padre [pá'ḍre] *nm* father ♦ *a* (*fam*): **un éxito** ~ a tremendous success; ~**s** *nmpl* parents; ~ **espiritual** confessor; **P**~ **Nuestro** Lord's Prayer; ~ **político** father-in-law; **García** ~ García senior; **¡tu** ~! (*fam!*) up yours! (*!*).
padrino [páḍrē'no] *nm* godfather; (*fig*) sponsor, patron; ~**s** *nmpl* godparents; ~ **de boda** best man.
padrón [páḍron'] *nm* (*censo*) census, roll; (*de socios*) register.
paella [páe'yá] *nf* paella, *dish of rice with meat, shellfish etc*.
paga [pá'ǥá] *nf* (*dinero pagado*) payment; (*sueldo*) pay, wages *pl*.
pagadero, a [páǥáḍe'ro, á] *a* payable; ~ **a la entrega/a plazos** payable on delivery/in instalments.
pagano, a [páǥá'no, á] *a, nm/f* pagan, heathen.
pagar [páǥár'] *vt* (*gen*) to pay; (*las compras, crimen*) to pay for; (*deuda*) to pay (off); (*fig: favor*) to repay ♦ *vi* to pay; ~**se** *vr*: ~**se con algo** to be content with sth; **¡me las pagarás!** I'll get you for this!
pagaré [páǥáre'] *nm* I.O.U.
página [pá'hēná] *nf* page.
paginación [páhēnásyon'] *nf* (*INFORM. TIP*) pagination.
paginar [páhēnár'] *vt* (*INFORM. TIP*) to paginate.
pág(s). *abr* (= *página(s)*) p(p).
pago [pá'ǥo] *nm* (*dinero*) payment; (*fig*) return; ~ **anticipado/a cuenta/a la entrega/en especie/inicial** advance payment/ payment on account/cash on delivery/ payment in kind/down payment; ~ **a título gracioso** ex gratia payment; **en** ~ **de** in return for.
pague [pá'ǥe] *etc vb V* **pagar**.
país [páēs'] *nm* (*gen*) country; (*región*) land; **los P**~**es Bajos** the Low Countries; **el P**~ **Vasco** the Basque Country.
paisaje [páēsá'he] *nm* countryside, landscape; (*vista*) scenery.
paisano, a [páēsá'no, á] *a* of the same country ♦ *nm/f* (*compatriota*) fellow countryman/woman; **vestir de** ~ (*soldado*) to be in civilian clothes; (*guardia*) to be in plain clothes.
paja [pá'há] *nf* straw; (*fig*) trash, rubbish; (*en libro, ensayo*) padding; **riñeron por un quítame allá esas** ~**s** they quarrelled over a trifle.
pajarita [páhárē'tá] *nf* bow tie.
pájaro [pá'háro] *nm* bird; (*fam: astuto*) clever fellow; **tener la cabeza a** ~**s** to be featherbrained.

pajita |páhē'tá| *nf* (drinking) straw.
pajizo, a |páhē'so, á| *a* (*de paja*) straw *cpd*; (*techo*) thatched; (*color*) straw-colored (*US*), straw-coloured (*Brit*).
pakistaní |pákēstánē'| *a*, *nm/f* Pakistani.
pala |pá'lá| *nf* (*de mango largo*) spade; (*de mango corto*) shovel; (*raqueta etc*) bat; (: *de tenis*) racquet; (*CULIN*) slice; ~ **matamoscas** fly swatter.
palabra |pálá'hrá| *nf* (*gen, promesa*) word; (*facultad*) (power of) speech; (*derecho de hablar*) right to speak; **faltar a su** ~ to go back on one's word; **quedarse con la** ~ **en la boca** to stop short; (*en reunión, comité etc*) **tomar la** ~ to speak, take the floor; **pedir la** ~ to ask to be allowed to speak; **tener la** ~ to have the floor; **no encuentro** ~**s para expresarme** words fail me.
palabrota |pálàhro'tá| *nf* swearword.
palacio |pálá'syo| *nm* palace; (*mansión*) mansion, large house; ~ **de justicia** courthouse; ~ **municipal** town/city hall.
palada |pálá'tùá| *nf* shovelful, spadeful; (*de remo*) stroke.
paladar |pálàtùár'| *nm* palate.
paladear |pàlàtùcár'| *vt* to taste.
palanca |pálán'ká| *nf* lever; (*fig*) pull, influence; ~ **de cambio** (*AUTO*) gearshift (*US*), gear lever (*Brit*); ~ **de freno** (*AUTO*) brake lever; ~ **de gobierno** *o* **de control** (*INFORM*) joystick.
palangana |pálángá'ná| *nf* washbasin.
palco |pál'ko| *nm* box.
palenque |pálcn'kc| *nm* (*cerca*) stockade, fence; (*área*) arena, enclosure; (*de gallos*) pit.
palentino, a |pálcntē'no, á| *a* of *o* from Palencia ♦ *nm/f* native *o* inhabitant of Palencia.
paleolítico, a |pálcolē'tēko, á| *a* paleolithic.
paleontología |pálcontolohē'á| *nf* paleontology.
Palestina |pálcstē'ná| *nf* Palestine.
palestino, a |pálcstē'no, á| *a*, *nm/f* Palestinian.
paletización |pálctēsásyon'| *nf* palletization.
paleto, a |pálc'to, á| *nm/f* hick (*US*), yokel ♦ *nf* (*pala*) small shovel; (*ARTE*) palette; (*ANAT*) shoulder blade; (*AM*) Popsicle ® (*US*), ice lolly (*Brit*).
paliar |pályár'| *vt* (*mitigar*) to mitigate; (*disfrazar*) to conceal.
paliativo |pályàtē'ho| *nm* palliative.
palidecer |pálcthcscr'| *vi* to turn pale.
palidez |pálcthcs'| *nf* paleness.
palidezca |pálcthcs'ká| *etc vb V* **palidecer**.
pálido, a |pá'lētho, á| *a* pale.
palillo |pálē'yo| *nm* small stick; (*para dientes*) toothpick; ~**s (chinos)** chopsticks; **estar hecho un** ~ to be as thin as a rake.
palique |pálē'kc| *nm*: **estar de** ~ (*fam*) to

have a chat.
paliza |pálē'sá| *nf* beating, thrashing; **dar** *o* **propinar** (*fam*) **una** ~ **a uno** to give sb a thrashing.
palma |pál'má| *nf* (*ANAT*) palm; (*árbol*) palm tree; **batir** *o* **dar** ~**s** to clap, applaud; **llevarse la** ~ to triumph, win.
palmada |pálmá'tùá| *nf* slap; ~**s** *nfpl* clapping *sg*, applause *sg*.
Palma de Mallorca *nf* Palma.
palmar |pálmár'| *vi* (*tb*: ~**la**) to die, kick the bucket.
palmear |pálmcár'| *vi* to clap.
palmero, a |pálmc'ro, á| *a* of the island of Palma ♦ *nm/f* native *o* inhabitant of the island of Palma ♦ *nm* (*AM*), *nf* palm tree.
palmo |pál'mo| *nm* (*medida*) span; (*fig*) small amount; ~ **a** ~ inch by inch.
palmotear |pálmotcár'| *vi* to clap, applaud.
palmoteo |pálmotc'o| *nm* clapping, applause.
palo |pá'lo| *nm* stick; (*poste*) post, pole; (*mango*) handle, shaft; (*golpe*) blow, hit; (*de golf*) club; (*de béisbol*) bat; (*NAUT*) mast; (*NAIPES*) suit; **vermut a** ~ **seco** straight vermouth; **de tal** ~ **tal astilla** like father like son.
paloma |pálo'má| *nf* dove, pigeon; ~ **mensajera** carrier *o* homing pigeon.
palomilla |pálomē'yá| *nf* moth; (*TEC*: *tuerca*) wing nut; (*soporte*) bracket.
palomitas |pálomē'tás| *nfpl* popcorn *sg*.
palpable |pálpá'hlc| *a* palpable; (*fig*) tangible.
palpar |pálpár'| *vt* to touch, feel.
palpitación |pálpētàsyon'| *nf* palpitation.
palpitante |pálpētàn'tc| *a* palpitating; (*fig*) burning.
palpitar |pálpētár'| *vi* to palpitate; (*latir*) to beat.
palta |pál'tá| *nf* (*AM*) avocado.
palúdico, a |pálōō'thēko, á| *a* marshy.
paludismo |pálōōthēs'mo| *nm* malaria.
palurdo, a |pálōōr'tho, á| *a* coarse, uncouth ♦ *nm/f* hick (*US*), yokel.
pampa |pám'pá| *nf* (*AM*) pampa(s), prairie.
pamplinas |pámplē'nás| *nfpl* nonsense *sg*.
pamplonés, esa |pámploncs', csá|, **pamplonica** |pámplonē'ká| *a* of *o* from Pamplona ♦ *nm/f* native *o* inhabitant of Pamplona.
pan |pán| *nm* bread; (*una barra*) loaf; ~ **de molde** sliced loaf; ~ **integral** wholemeal bread; ~ **rallado** breadcrumbs *pl*; **eso es** ~ **comido** it's a cinch; **llamar al** ~ ~ **y al vino vino** to call a spade a spade.
pana |pá'ná| *nf* corduroy.
panadería |pánáthcrē'á| *nf* baker's (shop).
panadero, a |pánáthc'ro, á| *nm/f* baker.
panal |pánál'| *nm* honeycomb.
Panamá |pánámá'| *nm* Panama.
panameño, a |pánámc'nyo, á| *a* Panama-

nian.

pancarta |pånkår'tá| *nf* placard, banner.

pancho, a |pàntch'o, á| *a*: **estar tan ~ to** remain perfectly calm.

panda |pån'dá| *nm* panda ♦ *nf* gang.

pandereta |pånderc'tá| *nf* tambourine.

pandilla |påndē'yå| *nf* set, group; *(de crimi-nales)* gang; *(pey)* clique.

pando, a |pán'do, á| *a* sagging.

panel |påncl'| *nm* panel; **~ acústico** acoustic screen.

panera |pånc'rá| *nf* bread basket.

panfleto |pånflc'to| *nm (POL etc)* pamphlet; *(AM)* lampoon.

pánico |på'nēko| *nm* panic.

panorama |pånorå'má| *nm* panorama; *(vista)* view.

pantalón |påntålon'| *nm*, **pantalones** |påntálo'nes| *nmpl* pants *pl (US)*, trousers *pl*; **pantalones vaqueros** jeans *pl*.

pantalla |påntá'yå| *nf (de cine)* screen; *(cubre-luz)* lampshade; *(INFORM)* screen, display; **servir de ~ a** to be a blind for; **~ de cristal líquido** liquid crystal display; **~ táctil** touch-sensitive screen; **~ de ayuda** help screen; **~ plana** flat screen.

pantano |påntá'no| *nm (ciénaga)* marsh, swamp; *(depósito: de agua)* reservoir; *(fig)* jam, fix, difficulty.

pantera |pånte'rá| *nf* panther.

pantomima |påntomē'má| *nf* pantomime.

pantorrilla |påntorrē'yå| *nf* calf (of the leg).

pantufla |påntōō'flå| *nf* slipper.

panza |pån'sá| *nf* belly, paunch.

panzón, ona |pånson', oná|, **panzudo, a** |pånsōō'tho, á| *a* fat, potbellied.

pañal |pányál'| *nm* diaper *(US)*, nappy *(Brit)*; **estar todavía en ~es** to be still wet behind the ears.

pañería |pányerē'á| *nf (artículos)* drapery; *(tienda)* dry-goods store *(US)*, draper's *(shop) (Brit)*.

pañero, a |pånye'ro, á| *nm/f* fabric dealer *(US)*, draper *(Brit)*.

paño |på'nyo| *nm (tela)* cloth; *(pedazo de tela)* (piece of) cloth; *(trapo)* duster, rag; **~ de cocina** dishcloth; **~ higiénico** sanitary napkin *(US)* o towel *(Brit)*; **~s menores** underclothes; **~s calientes** *(fig)* half-measures; **no andarse con ~s calientes** to pull no punches.

pañuelo |pånywe'lo| *nm* handkerchief, hanky *(fam)*; *(para la cabeza)* (head)scarf.

papa |på'på| *nf (AM)* potato ♦ *nm*: **el P~** the Pope.

papá |påpá'| *nm, pl* **papás** *(fam)* pop *(US)*, dad, daddy; **~s** *nmpl* parents; **hijo de ~** rich kid.

papagayo |påpágå'yo| *nm* parrot.

papanatas |påpåná'tás| *nm inv (fam)* sucker, simpleton.

paparrucha |påpårrōōtch'á| *nf (tontería)* piece of nonsense.

papaya |påpá'yå| *nf* papaya.

papel |påpcl'| *nm (gen)* paper; *(hoja de papel)* sheet of paper; *(TEATRO)* part, role; **~es** *nmpl* identification papers; **~ de calco/carbón/de cartas** tracing paper/carbon paper/stationery; **~ continuo** *(INFORM)* continuous feed paper; **~ de envolver/de empapelar** brown paper, wrapping paper/wallpaper; **~ de aluminio/higiénico** tinfoil/toilet paper; **~ del** o **de pagos al Estado** government bonds *pl*; **~ de lija** sandpaper; **~ moneda** paper money; **~ plegado (en abanico** o **en acordeón)** fanfold paper; **~ secante** blotting paper; **~ térmico** thermal paper.

papeleo |påpclc'o| *nm* red tape.

papelera |påpclc'rá| *nf (cesto)* wastepaper basket; *(escritorio)* desk.

papelería |påpelerē'á| *nf (tienda)* stationer's *(shop) (Brit)*.

papeleta |påpclc'tá| *nf (pedazo de papel)* slip o bit of paper; *(POL)* ballot paper; *(ESCOL)* report; **¡vaya ~!** this is a tough one!

paperas |påpe'rás| *nfpl* mumps *sg*.

papilla |påpē'yå| *nf (de bebé)* baby food; *(pey)* mush; **estar hecho ~** to be dog-tired.

paquete |påkc'te| *nm (caja)* packet; *(bulto)* parcel; *(AM fam)* nuisance, bore; *(INFORM)* package *(of software)*; *(vacaciones)* package tour; **~ de aplicaciones** *(INFORM)* applications package; **~ integrado** *(INFORM)* integrated package; **~ de gestión integrado** integrated management software; **~s postales** parcel post *sg*.

paquistaní |påkēstánē'| *a, nm/f* = **pakistaní**.

par |pår| *a (igual)* like, equal; *(MAT)* even ♦ *nm* equal; *(de guantes)* pair; *(de veces)* couple; *(dignidad)* peer; *(GOLF, COM)* par ♦ *nf par*; **~es o nones** odds or evens; **abrir de ~ en ~** to open wide; **a la ~** par; **sobre/bajo la ~** above/below par.

para |på'rá| *prep (gen)* for; **no es ~ comer** it's not for eating; **decir ~ sí** to say to o.s.; **¿~ qué lo quieres?** what do you want it for?; **se casaron ~ separarse otra vez** they married only to separate again; **~ entonces** by then o that time; **lo tendré ~ mañana** I'll have it for tomorrow; **ir ~ casa** to go home, head for home; **~ profesor es muy estúpido** he's very stupid for a teacher; **¿quién es usted ~ gritar así?** who are you to shout like that?; **tengo bastante ~ vivir** I have enough to live on.

parabellum |pårábelōōm'| *nm* (automatic) pistol.

parabién |pårábyen'| *nm* congratulations *pl*.

parábola |pårá'holá| *nf* parable; *(MAT)* parabola.

parabrisas [párábrē'sàs] *nm inv* windshield (*US*), windscreen (*Brit*).

paracaídas [párákáē'thás] *nm inv* parachute.

paracaidista [párákáēthē'stá] *nm/f* parachutist; (*MIL*) paratrooper.

parachoques [párátcho'kes] *nm inv* fender (*US*), bumper (*Brit*); shock absorber.

parada [párá'thá] *nf* V **parado**.

paradero [párá'the'ro] *nm* stopping-place; (*situación*) whereabouts.

parado, a [párá'tho, á] *a* (*persona*) motionless, standing still; (*fábrica*) closed, at a standstill; (*coche*) stopped; (*de pie*) standing (up); (*sin empleo*) unemployed, idle; (*confuso*) confused ♦ *nf* (*gen*) stop; (*acto*) stopping; (*de industria*) shutdown, stoppage; (*lugar*) stopping-place; **salir bien** ~ to come off well; **parada de autobús** bus stop; **parada discrecional** flag (*US*) o request (*Brit*) stop; **parada en seco** sudden stop; **parada de taxis** taxi stand (*US*) o rank (*Brit*).

paradoja [párátho'há] *nf* paradox.

paradójico, a [párátho'hēko, á] *a* paradoxical.

parador [páráthor'] *nm* (luxury) hotel.

parafrasear [páráfráseár'] *vt* to paraphrase.

paráfrasis [párá'frásēs] *nf inv* paraphrase.

paraguas [párá'gwàs] *nm inv* umbrella.

Paraguay [párágwá'ē] *nm*: **el** ~ Paraguay.

paraguayo, a [párágwá'yo, á] *a, nm/f* Paraguayan.

paraíso [páráē'so] *nm* paradise, heaven; ~ **fiscal** (*COM*) tax haven.

paraje [párá'he] *nm* place, spot.

paralelo, a [párále'lo, á] *a, nm* parallel; **en** ~ (*ELEC, INFORM*) (in) parallel.

paralice [párálē'se] *etc vb V* **paralizar**.

parálisis [párá'lēsēs] *nf inv* paralysis; ~ **cerebral** cerebral palsy; ~ **progresiva** creeping paralysis.

paralítico, a [párálē'tēko, á] *a, nm/f* paralytic.

paralizar [párálēsár'] *vt* to paralyze (*US*) o paralyse (*Brit*); ~**se** *vr* to become paralyzed; (*fig*) to come to a standstill.

parámetro [párá'metro] *nm* parameter.

paramilitar [párámēlētár'] *a* paramilitary.

páramo [pá'rámo] *nm* bleak plateau.

parangón [párángon'] *nm*: **sin** ~ incomparable.

paraninfo [páránēn'fo] *nm* (*ESCOL*) auditorium.

paranoico, a [páráno'ēko, á] *a, nm/f* paranoid.

parapetarse [párápetár'se] *vr* to shelter.

parapléjico, a [páráple'hēko, á] *a, nm/f* paraplegic.

parar [párár'] *vt* to stop; (*progreso etc*) to check, halt; (*golpe*) to ward off ♦ *vi* to

stop; (*hospedarse*) to stay, put up; ~**se** *vr* to stop; (*AM*) to stand up; **no** ~ **de hacer algo** to keep on doing sth; **ha parado de llover** it has stopped raining; **van a** ~ **en la comisaría** they're going to end up in the police station; **no sabemos en qué va a** ~ **todo esto** we don't know where all this is going to end; ~**se a hacer algo** to stop to do sth; ~**se en** to pay attention to.

pararrayos [párárrá'yos] *nm inv* lightning rod (*US*) o conductor (*Brit*).

parásito, a [párá'sēto, á] *nm/f* parasite.

parasol [párásol'] *nm* parasol, sunshade.

parcela [párse'lá] *nf* plot, piece of ground.

parcial [pársyál'] *a* (*pago*) part-; (*eclipse*) partial; (*juez*) prejudiced, biased.

parcialidad [pársyálēthálh'] *nf* (*prejuicio*) prejudice, bias.

parco, a [pár'ko, á] *a* (*frugal*) sparing; (*moderado*) moderate.

parche [pártch'e] *nm* patch.

pardo, a [pár'tho, á] *a* (*color*) brown; (*cielo*) overcast; (*voz*) flat, dull.

parear [páreár'] *vt* (*juntar, hacer par*) to match, put together; (*calcetines*) to put into pairs; (*BIO*) to mate.

parecer [páreser'] *nm* (*opinión*) opinion, view; (*aspecto*) looks *pl* ♦ *vi* (*tener apariencia*) to seem, look; (*asemejarse*) to look like, seem like; (*aparecer, llegar*) to appear; ~**se** *vr* to look alike, resemble each other; ~**se a** to look like, resemble; **al** ~ apparently; **me parece que** I think (that), it seems to me that.

parecido, a [páresē'tho, á] *a* similar ♦ *nm* similarity, likeness, resemblance; ~ **a** like, similar to; **bien** ~ good-looking, nice-looking.

pared [páreth'] *nf* wall; ~ **divisoria/medianera** dividing/party wall; **subirse por las** ~**es** (*fam*) to go up the wall.

paredón [párethon'] *nm*: **llevar a uno al** ~ to put sb up against a wall, shoot sb.

parejo, a [páre'ho, á] *a* (*igual*) equal; (*liso*) smooth, even ♦ *nf* (*dos*) pair; (: *de personas*) couple; (*el otro: de un par*) other one (of a pair); (: *persona*) partner; (*Guardias*) Civil Guard patrol.

parentela [párente'lá] *nf* relations *pl*.

parentesco [párentes'ko] *nm* relationship.

paréntesis [páren'tesēs] *nm inv* parenthesis; (*digresión*) digression; (*en escrito*) bracket.

parezca [páres'ká] *etc vb V* **parecer**.

parida [párē'thá] *nf*: ~ **mental** (*fam*) dumb idea.

pariente, a [páryen'te, á] *nm/f* relative, relation.

parihuela [párēwe'lá] *nf* stretcher.

paripé [párēpe'] *nm*: **hacer el** ~ to put on an act.

parir |pàrēr'| *vt* to give birth to ♦ *vi* (*mujer*) to give birth, have a baby; (*yegua*) to foal; (*vaca*) to calve.

París |pàrēs'| *nm* Paris.

parisiense |pàrēsyen'se|, **parisiano, a** |pàrēsyà'no, à| *a, nm/f* Parisian.

parking |pàr'kēn| *nm* parking lot (*US*), car park (*Brit*).

parlamentar |pàrlàmentàr'| *vi* (*negociar*) to parley.

parlamentario, a |pàrlàmentà'ryo, à| *a* parliamentary ♦ *nm/f* member of parliament.

parlamento |pàrlàmen'to| *nm* (*POL*) parliament; (*JUR*) speech.

parlanchín, ina |pàrlàntchēn'. ēnà| *a* loose-tongued, indiscreet ♦ *nm/f* chatterbox.

parlotear |pàrloteàr'| *vi* to chatter, prattle.

parloteo |pàrlote'o| *nm* chatter, prattle.

parné |pàrne'| *nm* (*fam: dinero*) dough.

paro |pà'ro| *nm* (*huelga*) stoppage (of work), strike; (*desempleo*) unemployment; **subsidio de ~** unemployment benefit; **hay ~ en la industria** work in the industry is at a standstill; **~ del sistema** (*INFORM*) system shutdown.

parodia |pàro'thyà| *nf* parody.

parodiar |pàrothyàr'| *vt* to parody.

parpadear |pàrpàthceàr'| *vi* (*los ojos*) to blink; (*luz*) to flicker.

parpadeo |pàrpàthce'o| *nm* (*de ojos*) blinking, winking; (*de luz*) flickering.

párpado |pàr'pàtho| *nm* eyelid.

parque |pàr'ke| *nm* (*lugar verde*) park; **~ de atracciones/de bomberos/zoológico** fairground/fire station/zoo.

parquímetro |pàrke'metro| *nm* parking meter.

párrafo |pà'rràfo| *nm* paragraph; **echar un ~** (*fam*) to have a chat.

parranda |pàrràn'dà| *nf* (*fam*) spree, binge.

parrilla |pàrre'yà| *nf* (*CULIN*) grill; (*de coche*) grille; (**carne de**) **~** barbecue.

parrillada |pàrrēyà'thà| *nf* barbecue.

párroco |pà'rroko| *nm* parish priest.

parroquia |pàrro'kyà| *nf* parish; (*iglesia*) parish church; (*COM*) clientele, customers *pl*.

parroquiano, a |pàrrokyà'no, à| *nm/f* parishioner; client, customer.

parsimonia |pàrsēmo'nyà| *nf* (*frugalidad*) sparingness; (*calma*) deliberateness; **con ~** calmly.

parte |pàr'te| *nm* message; (*informe*) report; **~ meteorológico** weather forecast ♦ *nf* part; (*lado, cara*) side; (*de reparto*) share; (*JUR*) party; **en alguna ~ de Europa** somewhere in Europe; **en cualquier ~** anywhere; **por ahí no se va a ninguna ~** that leads nowhere; (*fig*) this is getting us nowhere; **en gran ~** to a large extent; **la**

mayor ~ de los españoles most Spaniards; **de algún tiempo a esta ~** for some time past; **de ~ de uno** on sb's behalf; **¿de ~ de quién?** (*TELEC*) who is speaking?; **por ~ de** on the part of; **yo por mi ~** I for my part; **por una ~ ... por otra ~** on the one hand, ... on the other (hand); **dar ~ a uno** to report to sb; **tomar ~** to take part.

partera |pàrte'rà| *nf* midwife.

parterre |pàrte'rre| *nm* (*de flores*) (flower) bed.

partición |pàrtēsyon'| *nf* division, sharing-out; (*POL*) partition.

participación |pàrtēsēpàsyon'| *nf* (*acto*) participation, taking part; (*parte*) share; (*COM*) stock; (*de lotería*) shared prize; (*aviso*) notice, notification; **~ en los beneficios** profit-sharing; **~ minoritaria** minority interest.

participante |pàrtēsēpàn'te| *nm/f* participant.

participar |pàrtēsēpàr'| *vt* to notify, inform ♦ *vi* to take part, participate; **~ en una empresa** (*COM*) to invest in an enterprise; **le participo que ...** I have to tell you that ....

partícipe |pàrtē'sēpe| *nm/f* participant; **hacer ~ a uno de algo** to inform sb of sth.

participio |pàrtēsē'pyo| *nm* participle; **~ de pasado/presente** past/present participle.

partícula |pàrtē'koolà| *nf* particle.

particular |pàrtēkoolàr'| *a* (*especial*) particular, special; (*individual, personal*) private, personal ♦ *nm* (*punto, asunto*) particular, point; (*individuo*) individual; **tiene coche ~** he has a car of his own; **no dijo mucho sobre el ~** he didn't say much about the matter.

particularice |pàrtēkoolàrē'se| *etc vb V* **particularizar**.

particularidad |pàrtēkoolàrēthàth'| *nf* peculiarity; **tiene la ~ de que ...** one of its special features is (that) ....

particularizar |pàrtēkoolàrēsàr'| *vt* to distinguish; (*especificar*) to specify; (*detallar*) to give details about.

partida |pàrtē'thà| *nf* (*salida*) departure; (*COM*) entry, item; (*juego*) game; (*grupo, bando*) band, group; **mala ~** dirty trick; **~ de nacimiento/matrimonio/defunción** birth/ marriage/death certificate; **echar una ~** to have a game.

partidario, a |pàrtēthà'ryo, à| *a* partisan ♦ *nm/f* (*DEPORTE*) supporter; (*POL*) partisan.

partidismo |pàrtēthēs'mo| *nm* (*JUR*) partisanship, bias; (*POL*) party politics.

partido |pàrtē'tho| *nm* (*POL*) party; (*encuentro*) game, match; (*apoyo*) support; (*equipo*) team; **~ amistoso** (*DEPORTE*) friendly (game); **~ de fútbol** soccer game; **sacar ~ de** to profit from, benefit from; **to-**

mar ~ to take sides.

partir [pártēr'] *vt* (*dividir*) to split, divide; (*compartir, distribuir*) to share (out), distribute; (*romper*) to break open, split open; (*rebanada*) to cut (off) ♦ *vi* (*tomar camino*) to set off, set out; (*comenzar*) to start (off *o* out); ~**se** *vr* to crack *o* split *o* break (in two *etc*); **a** ~ **de** (starting) from; ~**se de risa** to split one's sides (laughing).

parto [pár'to] *nm* birth, delivery; (*fig*) product, creation; **estar de** ~ to be in labor.

parvulario [párkōōlá'ryo] *nm* nursery school, kindergarten.

párvulo, a [pár'kōōlo, á] *nm/f* infant.

pasa [pá'sá] *nf V* **paso**.

pasada [pásá'thá] *nf V* **pasado**.

pasadizo [pásáthē'so] *nm* (*pasillo*) passage, corridor; (*callejuela*) alley.

pasado, a [pásá'tho, á] *a* past; (*malo: comida, fruta*) bad; (*muy cocido*) overdone; (*anticuado*) out of date ♦ *nm* past; (*LING*) past (tense) ♦ *nf* passing, passage; (*acción de pulir*) rub, polish; ~ **mañana** the day after tomorrow; **el mes** ~ last month; ~**s dos días** after two days; **lo** ~, ~ let bygones be bygones; ~ **de moda** old-fashioned; ~ **por agua** (*huevo*) boiled; **de pasada** in passing, incidentally; **una mala pasada** a dirty trick.

pasador [pásáthor'] *nm* (*gen*) bolt; (*de pelo*) pin.

pasaje [pásá'he] *nm* (*gen*) passage; (*pago de viaje*) fare; (*los pasajeros*) passengers *pl*; (*pasillo*) passageway.

pasajero, a [pásáhe'ro, á] *a* passing; (*ave*) migratory ♦ *nm/f* passenger; (*viajero*) traveler (*US*), traveller (*Brit*).

pasamanos [pásámá'nos] *nm inv* rail, handrail; (*de escalera*) banister.

pasamontañas [pásámontá'nyás] *nm inv* ski mask.

pasaporte [pásápor'te] *nm* passport.

pasar [pásár'] *vt* (*gen*) to pass; (*tiempo*) to spend; (*durezas*) to suffer, endure; (*noticia*) to give, pass on; (*película*) to show; (*persona*) to take, conduct; (*río*) to cross; (*barrera*) to pass through; (*falta*) to overlook, tolerate; (*contrincante*) to surpass, do better than; (*coche*) to pass, overtake; (*contrabando*) to smuggle (in/out); (*enfermedad*) to give, infect with ♦ *vi* (*gen*) to pass, go; (*terminarse*) to be over; (*ocurrir*) to happen; ~**se** *vr* (*efectos*) to pass, be over; (*flores*) to fade; (*comida*) to go bad; (*fig*) to overdo it, go too far *o* over the top; ~ **de** to go beyond, exceed; **¡pase!** come in!; **nos hicieron** ~ they showed us in; ~ **por** to get; ~ **por alto** to skip; ~ **por una crisis** to go through a crisis; **se hace** ~ **por médico** he passes himself off as a doctor; ~**lo bien/bomba** *o* **de maravilla** to have a

good/great time; ~**se al enemigo** to go over to the enemy; ~**se de la raya** to go too far; **¡no te pases!** don't try me!; **se me pasó** I forgot; **se me pasó el turno** I missed my turn; **no se le pasa nada** nothing escapes him, he misses nothing; **ya se te pasará** you'll get over it; **¿qué pasa?** what's happening?, what's going on?, what's up?; **¡cómo pasa el tiempo!** time just flies!; **pase lo que pase** come what may; **el autobús pasa por nuestra casa** the bus goes past our house.

pasarela [pásáre'lá] *nf* footbridge; (*en barco*) gangway.

pasatiempo [pásátyem'po] *nm* pastime, hobby; (*distracción*) amusement.

Pascua, pascua [pás'kwá] *nf*: ~ (**de Resurrección**) Easter; ~ **de Navidad** Christmas; ~**s** *nfpl* Christmas time; **¡felices** ~**s!** Merry Christmas; **de** ~**s a Ramos** once in a blue moon; **hacer la** ~ *a* (*fam*) to annoy, bug.

pase [pá'se] *nm* pass; (*CINE*) performance, showing; (*COM*) permit; (*JUR*) license (*US*), licence (*Brit*).

pasear [páseár'] *vt* to take for a walk; (*exhibir*) to parade, show off ♦ *vi*, ~**se** *vr* to walk, go for a walk; ~ **en coche** to go for a drive.

paseo [páse'o] *nm* (*avenida*) avenue; (*distancia corta*) short walk; ~ **marítimo** promenade; **dar un** ~ to go for a walk; **mandar a uno a** ~ to tell sb to go to blazes; **¡vete a** ~! get lost!

pasillo [pásē'yo] *nm* passage, corridor.

pasión [pásyon'] *nf* passion.

pasional [pásyonál'] *a* passionate; **crimen** ~ crime of passion.

pasivo, a [pásē'ho, á] *a* passive; (*inactivo*) inactive ♦ *nm* (*COM*) liabilities *pl*, debts *pl*; (*de cuenta*) debit side; ~ **circulante** current liabilities.

pasma [pás'má] *nm* (*fam*) cop.

pasmado, a [pásmá'tho, á] *a* (*asombrado*) astonished; (*atontado*) bewildered.

pasmar [pásmár'] *vt* (*asombrar*) to amaze, astonish; ~**se** *vr* to be amazed *o* astonished.

pasmo [pás'mo] *nm* amazement, astonishment; (*fig*) wonder, marvel.

pasmoso, a [pásmo'so, á] *a* amazing, astonishing.

paso, a [pá'so, á] *a* dried ♦ *nm* (*gen, de baile*) step; (*modo de andar*) walk; (*huella*) footprint; (*rapidez*) speed, pace, rate; (*camino accesible*) way through, passage; (*cruce*) crossing; (*pasaje*) passing, passage; (*GEO*) pass; (*estrecho*) strait; (*fig*) step, measure; (*apuro*) difficulty ♦ *nf* raisin; **pasa de Corinto/de Esmirna** currant/sultana; ~ **a** ~ step by step; **a ese** ~ (*fig*) at that rate; **salir al** ~ **de** *o* **a** to waylay; **salir del** ~ to get out of trouble; **dar un** ~ **en falso** to trip; (*fig*) to take a false step; **estar de** ~ to be passing through; ~ **atrás** step backwards; (*fig*) backward step; ~ **elevado/subterráneo** overpass/underpass; **prohibido el** ~ no entry; **ceda el** ~ give way.

pasota |pàso'tá| *a, nm/f* (*fam*)≈ dropout; **ser un (tipo)** ~ to be a bit of a dropout; (*ser indiferente*) not to care about anything.

pasotismo |pàsotēs'mo| *nm* underground *o* alternative culture.

pasta |pá'stá| *nf* (*gen*) paste; (*CULIN*: *masa*) dough; (: *de bizcochos etc*) pastry; (*fam*) money, dough; (*encuadernación*) hardback; ~**s** *nfpl* (*bizcochos*) pastries, small cakes; (*fideos, espaguetis etc*) noodles, spaghetti *sg etc*; ~ **de dientes** *o* **dentífrica** toothpaste; ~ **de madera** wood pulp.

pastar |pástár| *vt, vi* to graze.

pastel |pástél| *nm* (*dulce*) cake; (*de carne*) pie; (*ARTE*) pastel; (*fig*) plot; ~**es** *nmpl* pastry *sg*, confectionery *sg*.

pastelería |pástclerē'á| *nf* cake shop, pastry shop.

pasteurizado, a |pástcōōrēsá'ðho, á| *a* pasteurized.

pastilla |pástē'yá| *nf* (*de jabón, chocolate*) cake, bar; (*píldora*) tablet, pill.

pastizal |pástēsál'| *nm* pasture.

pasto |pá'sto| *nm* (*hierba*) grass; (*lugar*) pasture, field; (*fig*) food, nourishment.

pastor, a |pástor', á| *nm/f* shepherd(ess) ♦ *nm* clergyman, pastor; (*ZOOL*) sheepdog; ~ **alemán** Alsatian.

pastoso, a |pá'sto'so, á| *a* (*material*) doughy, pasty; (*lengua*) furry; (*voz*) mellow.

pat. *abr* (= *patente*) pat.

pata |pá'tá| *nf* (*pierna*) leg; (*pie*) foot; (*de muebles*) leg; ~**s arriba** upside down; **a cuatro** ~**s** on all fours; **meter la** ~ to put one's foot in it; ~ **de cabra** (*TEC*) crowbar; ~**s de gallo** crow's feet; **tener buena/mala** ~ to be lucky/unlucky.

patada |pátá'ðhá| *nf* stamp; (*puntapié*) kick; **a** ~**s** in abundance; (*trato*) roughly; **echar a uno a** ~**s** to kick sb out.

patalear |pátálcár'| *vi* to stamp one's feet.

pataleo |pátálc'o| *nm* stamping.

patán |pátán'| *nm* rustic, yokel.

patata |pátá'tá| *nf* potato; ~**s fritas** *o* **a la española** chips, French fries; ~**s a la inglesa** potato chips (*US*), crisps (*Brit*); **ni** ~ (*fam*) nothing at all; **no entendió ni** ~ he didn't understand a single word.

patear |pátcár'| *vt* (*pisar*) to stamp on, trample (on); (*pegar con el pie*) to kick ♦ *vi* to stamp (with rage), stamp one's foot.

patentar |pátcntár'| *vt* to patent.

patente |pátcn'tc| *a* obvious, evident; (*COM*) patent ♦ *nf* patent.

paternal |pátcrnál'| *a* fatherly, paternal.

paternalista |pátcrnálē'stá| *a* (*tono, actitud etc*) patronizing.

paternidad |pátcrnēthátĥ'| *nf* fatherhood, parenthood; (*JUR*) paternity.

paterno, a |pátcr'no, á| *a* paternal.

patético, a |pátc'tēko, á| *a* pathetic, moving.

patíbulo |pátē'hōōlo| *nm* scaffold, gallows.

patillas |pátē'yás| *nfpl* sideburns.

patín |pátēn'| *nm* skate; (*de tobogán*) runner; ~ **de hielo** ice skate; ~ **de ruedas** roller skate.

patinaje |pátēná'hc| *nm* skating.

patinar |pátēnár'| *vi* to skate; (*resbalarse*) to skid, slip; (*fam*) to slip up, blunder.

patinazo |pátēná'so| *nm* (*AUTO*) skid; **dar un** ~ (*fam*) to blunder.

patio |pá'tyo| *nm* (*de casa*) patio, courtyard; ~ **de recreo** playground.

pato |pá'to| *nm* duck; **pagar el** ~ (*fam*) to take the blame.

patológico, a |pátolo'hēko, á| *a* pathological.

patoso, a |páto'so, á| *a* awkward, clumsy.

patraña |pátrá'nyá| *nf* story, fib.

patria |pá'tryá| *nf* native land, mother country; ~ **chica** home town.

patrimonio |pátrēmo'nyo| *nm* inheritance; (*fig*) heritage; (*COM*) net worth.

patriota |pátryo'tá| *nm/f* patriot.

patriotero, a |pátryotc'ro, á| *a* chauvinistic.

patriótico, a |pátryo'tēko, á| *a* patriotic.

patriotismo |pátryotēs'mo| *nm* patriotism.

patrocinar |pátrosēnár'| *vt* to sponsor; (*apoyar*) to back, support.

patrocinio |pátrosē'nyo| *nm* sponsorship; backing, support.

patrón, ona |pátron', oná| *nm/f* (*jefe*) boss, chief, master/mistress; (*propietario*) landlord/lady; (*REL*) patron saint ♦ *nm* (*COSTURA*) pattern; (*TEC*) standard; ~ **oro** gold standard.

patronal |pátronál'| *a*: **la clase** ~ management; **cierre** ~ lockout.

patronato |pátroná'to| *nm* sponsorship; (*acto*) patronage; (*COM*) employers' association; (*fundación*) trust; **el** ~ **de turismo** the tourist board.

patrulla |pátrōō'yá| *nf* patrol.

patrullar |pátrōōyár'| *vi* to patrol.

paulatino, a |páōōláté'no, á| *a* gradual, slow.

paupérrimo, a |páōōpc'rrēmo, á| *a* very poor, poverty-stricken.

pausa |pá'ōōsá| *nf* pause; (*intervalo*) break; (*interrupción*) interruption; (*TEC*: *en video-*

grabadora) pause; **con** ~ slowly.
pausado, a [páōōsá'tħo, á] *a* slow, deliberate.
pauta [pá'ōōtá] *nf* line, guide line.
pavimento [páħēmen'to] *nm* (ARQ) flooring.
pavo [pá'ħo] *nm* turkey; *(necio)* silly thing, idiot; ~ **real** peacock; **¡no seas** ~! don't be silly!
pavonearse [páħoneár'se] *vr* to swagger, show off.
pavor [páħor'] *nm* dread, terror.
payasada [páyásá'tħá] *nf* ridiculous thing (to do); ~**s** *nfpl* clowning *sg*.
payaso, a [páyá'so, á] *nm/f* clown.
payo, a [pá'yo, á] *a, nm/f* non-gipsy.
paz [pás] *nf* peace; *(tranquilidad)* peacefulness, tranquillity; **dejar a uno en** ~ to leave sb alone *o* in peace; **hacer las paces** to make peace; *(fig)* to make up; **¡haya** ~! stop it!
pazca [pás'ká] *etc vb* V **pacer**.
PC *nm abr* (POL: = *Partido Comunista)* CP.
P.C.E. *nm abr* = *Partido Comunista Español.*
PCL *nf abr* (= *pantalla de cristal líquido)* LCD.
PCUS [pekōōs'] *nm abr* (= *Partido Comunista de la Unión Soviética)* Soviet Communist Party.
P.D. *abr* (= *posdata)* P.S.
PDC *nm abr* (POL) = *Partido Demócrata Cristiano.*
pdo. *abr* (= *pasado)* ult.
peaje [peá'hc] *nm* toll; **autopista de** ~ turnpike *(US)*, toll motorway *(Brit)*.
peatón [peáton'] *nm* pedestrian; **paso de peatones** crosswalk *(US)*, pedestrian crossing *(Brit)*.
peca [pe'ká] *nf* freckle.
pecado [pcká'tħo] *nm* sin.
pecador, a [pckátħor', á] *a* sinful ♦ *nm/f* sinner.
pecaminoso, a [pckámēno'so, á] *a* sinful.
pecar [pckár'] *vi* (REL) to sin; *(fig)*: ~ **de generoso** to be too generous.
peculiar [pckōōlyár'] *a* special, peculiar; *(característico)* typical, characteristic.
peculiaridad [pckōōlyárētħatħ'] *nf* peculiarity; special feature, characteristic.
pecho [petch'o] *nm* (ANAT) chest; *(de mujer)* breast(s) *(pl)*, bosom; *(corazón)* heart, breast; *(valor)* courage, spirit; **dar el** ~ **a** to breast-feed; **tomar algo a** ~ to take sth to heart; **no le cabía en el** ~ he was bursting with happiness.
pechuga [pctchōō'gá] *nf* breast (of chicken *etc)*.
pedagogo [petħáğo'ğo] *nm* pedagogue, teacher.
pedal [petħál'] *nm* pedal; ~ **de embrague**

clutch (pedal); ~ **de freno** footbrake.
pedalear [petħáleár'] *vi* to pedal.
pedante [petħán'tc] *a* pedantic ♦ *nm/f* pedant.
pedantería [petħántcrē'á] *nf* pedantry.
pedazo [petħá'so] *nm* piece, bit; **hacerse** ~**s** to fall to pieces; *(romperse)* to smash, shatter; **un** ~ **de pan** a scrap of bread; *(fig)* a terribly nice person.
pedernal [petħernál'] *nm* flint.
pedestre [petħes'trc] *a* pedestrian; **carrera** ~ foot race.
pediatra [petħyá'trá] *nm/f* pediatrician *(US)*, paediatrician *(Brit)*.
pediatría [petħyátrē'á] *nf* pediatrics *sg (US)*, paediatrics *sg (Brit)*.
pedicuro, a [petħēkōō'ro, á] *nm/f* podiatrist *(US)*, chiropodist *(Brit)*.
pedido [petħē'tħo] *nm* (COM: *mandado)* order; *(petición)* request; ~**s en cartera** *(COM)* backlog.
pedir [petħēr'] *vt* to ask for, request; *(comida,* COM: *mandar)* to order; *(exigir: precio)* to ask; *(necesitar)* to need, demand, require ♦ *vi* to ask; ~ **prestado** to borrow; ~ **disculpas** to apologize; **me pidió que cerrara la puerta** he asked me to shut the door; **¿cuánto piden por el coche?** how much are they asking for the car?
pedo [pe'tħo] *(fam) a inv*: **estar** ~ to be soused ♦ *nm* fart *(!)*.
pedrea [petħrc'á] *nf (granizada)* hailstorm; *(de lotería)* minor prizes.
pedrisco [petħrēs'ko] *nm (granizo)* hail; *(granizada)* hailstorm.
Pedro [pe'tħro] *nm* Peter; **entrar como** ~ **por su casa** to come in as if one owned the place.
pega [pe'gá] *nf (dificultad)* snag; **de** ~ false, dud; **poner** ~**s** to raise objections.
pegadizo, a [pegátħē'so, á] *a (canción etc)* catchy.
pegajoso, a [pegáho'so, á] *a* sticky, adhesive.
pegamento [pegámen'to] *nm* gum.
pegar [pegár'] *vt (papel, sellos)* to stick (on); *(con cola)* to glue; *(cartel)* to post, stick up; *(coser)* to sew (on); *(unir: partes)* to join, fix together; *(MED)* to give, infect with; *(dar: golpe)* to give, deal ♦ *vi (adherirse)* to stick, adhere; *(ir juntos: colores)* to match, go together; *(golpear)* to hit; *(quemar: el sol)* to strike hot, burn *(fig)*; ~**se** *vr (gen)* to stick; *(dos personas)* to hit each other, fight; ~**le a algo** to be a great one for sth; ~ **un grito** to let out a yell; ~ **un salto** to jump (with fright); ~ **fuego** to catch fire; ~ **en** to touch; ~**se un tiro** to shoot o.s.; **no pega** that doesn't seem right; **ese sombrero no pega con el abrigo** that hat doesn't go with the coat.

pegatina [peɣáté'ná] *nf* (*POL etc*) sticker.
pegote [peɣo'te] *nm* (*fig*) patch, ugly mend; **tirarse** ~**s** (*fam*) to come on strong.
pegue [pe'ɣe] *etc vb* V **pegar**.
peinado [peɛ̃ná'ðo] *nm* (*en peluquería*) hairdo; (*estilo*) hair style.
peinar [peɛ̃nár'] *vt* to comb sb's hair; (*hacer estilo*) to style; ~**se** *vr* to comb one's hair.
peine [pe'ɛ̃ne] *nm* comb.
peineta [peɛ̃ne'tá] *nf* ornamental comb.
p.ej. *abr* (= *por ejemplo*) e.g.
Pekín [pekén'] *n* Peking.
pela [pe'lá] *nf* (*Esp fam*) peseta; V *tb* **pelas**.
pelado, a [pelá'ðo, á] *a* (*cabeza*) shorn; (*fruta*) peeled; (*campo, fig*) bare; (*AM fam: sin dinero*) broke.
pelaje [pelá'he] *nm* (*ZOOL*) fur, coat; (*fig*) appearance.
pelambre [pelám'bre] *nm* long hair, mop.
pelar [pelár'] *vt* (*fruta, patatas*) to peel; (*cortar el pelo a*) to cut the hair of; (*quitar la piel: animal*) to skin; (*ave*) to pluck; (*habas etc*) to shell; ~**se** *vr* (*la piel*) to peel off; **corre que se las pela** (*fam*) he runs like nobody's business.
pelas [pe'lás] *nfpl* (*Esp fam*) dough.
peldaño [peldá'nyo] *nm* step; (*de escalera portátil*) rung.
pelea [pele'á] *nf* (*lucha*) fight; (*discusión*) quarrel, row.
peleado, a [pelea'ðo, á] *a*: **estar** ~ (**con uno**) to have fallen out (with sb).
pelear [peleár'] *vi* to fight; ~**se** *vr* to fight; (*reñirse*) to fall out, quarrel.
pelele [pele'le] *nm* (*figura*) guy, dummy; (*fig*) puppet.
peletería [peleterě'á] *nf* furrier's, fur shop.
pelícano [pelě'káno] *nm* pelican.
pelicorto, a [pelěkor'to, á] *a* short-haired.
película [pelě'koolá] *nf* (*CINE*) movie; (*cobertura ligera*) film, thin covering; (*FOTO: rollo*) roll *o* reel of film; ~ **de dibujos (animados)** cartoon film; ~ **muda** silent film; **de** ~ (*fam*) astonishing, out of this world.
peligro [pelě'ɣro] *nm* danger; (*riesgo*) risk; "~ **de muerte**" "danger"; **correr** ~ **de** to be in danger of; **con** ~ **de la vida** at the risk of one's life.
peligrosidad [pelěɣrosěðàð'] *nf* danger, riskiness.
peligroso, a [pelěɣro'so, á] *a* dangerous; risky.
pelirrojo, a [pelěrro'ho, á] *a* red-haired, red-headed.
pelma [pel'má] *nm/f*, **pelmazo** [pelmá'so] *nm* (*fam*) pest.
pelo [pe'lo] *nm* (*cabellos*) hair; (*de barba, bigote*) whisker; (*de animal: pellejo*) fur, coat; (*de perro etc*) hair, coat; (*de ave*) down; (*de tejido*) nap; (*TEC*) fiber (*US*),

fibre (*Brit*); **a** ~ bareheaded; (*desnudo*) naked; **al** ~ just right; **venir al** ~ to be exactly what one needs; **por los** ~**s** by the skin of one's teeth; **escaparse por un** ~ to have a close shave; **se me pusieron los** ~**s de punta** my hair stood on end; **no tener** ~**s en la lengua** to be outspoken, not mince words; **tomar el** ~ **a uno** to pull sb's leg.
pelón, ona [pelon', oná] *a* hairless, bald.
pelota [pelo'tá] *nf* ball; (*fam: cabeza*) nut (*fam*); **en** ~(**s**) stark naked; ~ **vasca** jai alai; **devolver la** ~ **a uno** (*fig*) to turn the tables on sb; **hacer la** ~ to brown nose.
pelotón [peloton'] *nm* (*MIL*) squad, detachment.
peluca [peloo'ká] *nf* wig.
peluche [peloo'tch'e] *nm*: **muñeco de** ~ stuffed (*US*) *o* soft (*Brit*) toy.
peludo, a [peloo'ðo, á] *a* hairy, shaggy.
peluquería [pelookerě'á] *nf* hairdresser's; (*para hombres*) barber's (shop).
peluquero, a [pelooke'ro, á] *nm/f* hairdresser; barber.
peluquín [pelookén'] *nm* toupée.
pelusa [peloo'sá] *nf* (*BOT*) down; (*COSTURA*) fluff.
pellejo [peye'ho] *nm* (*de animal*) skin, hide; **salvar el** ~ to save one's skin.
pellizcar [peyěskár'] *vt* to pinch, nip.
pellizco [peyěs'ko] *nm* (*gen*) pinch.
pellizque [peyěs'ke] *etc vb* V **pellizcar**.
PEMEX [pemeks'] *nm abr* = *Petróleos Mejicanos*.
PEN [pen] *nm abr* (*Esp*) = *Plan Energético Nacional*.
pena [pe'ná] *nf* (*congoja*) grief, sadness; (*remordimiento*) regret; (*dificultad*) trouble; (*dolor*) pain; (*JUR*) sentence; (*DEPORTE*) penalty; **merecer** *o* **valer la** ~ to be worthwhile; **a duras** ~**s** with great difficulty; **so** ~ **de** on pain of; ~ **capital** capital punishment; ~ **de muerte** death penalty; ~ **pecuniaria** fine; **¡qué** ~**!** what a shame *o* pity!
penal [penál'] *a* penal ♦ *nm* (*cárcel*) prison.
penalidad [penáléðàð'] *nf* (*problema, dificultad*) trouble, hardship; (*JUR*) penalty, punishment.
penalty [penál'té] *nm* (*DEPORTE*) penalty.
penar [penár'] *vt* to penalize; (*castigar*) to punish ♦ *vi* to suffer.
pender [pender'] *vi* (*colgar*) to hang; (*JUR*) to be pending.
pendiente [pendyen'te] *a* pending, unsettled ♦ *nm* earring ♦ *nf* hill, slope; **tener una asignatura** ~ to have to retake a subject.
pendón [pendon'] *nm* banner, standard.
pene [pe'ne] *nm* penis.
penene [pene'ne] *nm/f* = **PNN**.
penetración [penetrásyon'] *nf* (*acto*) penetration; (*agudeza*) sharpness, insight.

penetrante |penetrán'te| *a* (*herida*) deep; (*persona, arma*) sharp; (*sonido*) penetrating, piercing; (*mirada*) searching; (*viento, ironía*) biting.

penetrar |penetrár'| *vt* to penetrate, pierce; (*entender*) to grasp ♦ *vi* to penetrate, go in; (*líquido*) to soak in; (*emoción*) to pierce.

penicilina |penēsēlē'nā| *nf* penicillin.

península |penēn'sōōlā| *nf* peninsula; **P~ Ibérica** Iberian Peninsula.

peninsular |penēnsōōlár'| *a* peninsular.

penique |penē'ke| *nm* penny; **~s** *nmpl* pence.

penitencia |penēten'syá| *nf* (*remordimiento*) penitence; (*castigo*) penance; **en ~** as a penance.

penitencial |penētensyál'| *a* penitential.

penitenciaría |penētensyárē'á| *nf* prison, penitentiary.

penitenciario, a |penētensyá'ryo, á| *a* prison *cpd*.

penoso, a |peno'so, á| *a* laborious, difficult.

pensado, a |pensá'tho, á| *a*: **bien/mal ~** well intentioned/cynical; **en el momento menos ~** when least expected.

pensador, a |pensáthor', á| *nm/f* thinker.

pensamiento |pensámyen'to| *nm* (*gen*) thought; (*mente*) mind; (*idea*) idea; (*BOT*) pansy; **no le pasó por el ~** it never occurred to him.

pensar |pensár'| *vt* to think; (*considerar*) to think over, think out; (*proponerse*) to intend, plan, propose; (*imaginarse*) to think up, invent ♦ *vi* to think; **~ en** to think of *o* about; (*anhelar*) to aim at, aspire to; **dar que ~ a uno** to give sb food for thought.

pensativo, a |pensátē'ho, á| *a* thoughtful, pensive.

pensión |pensyon'| *nf* (*casa*) boarding house, guest house; (*dinero*) pension; (*cama y comida*) room and board; **~ de jubilación** retirement pension; **~ escalada** graduated pension; **~ completa** full board.

pensionista |pensyonē'stá| *nm/f* (*jubilado*) (old-age) pensioner; (*quien vive en pensión*) lodger; (*ESCOL*) boarder.

pentágono |pentá'gono| *nm* pentagon: **el P~** (*US*) the Pentagon.

pentagrama |pentágrá'má| *nm* (*MUS*) stave, staff.

penúltimo, a |penōōl'tēmo, á| *a* penultimate, second to last.

penumbra |penōōm'brá| *nf* half-light, semi-darkness.

penuria |penōō'ryá| *nf* shortage, want.

peña |pe'nyá| *nf* (*roca*) rock; (*cuesta*) cliff, crag; (*grupo*) group, circle; (*DEPORTE*) supporters' club; (*AM*: *club*) folk club.

peñasco |penyás'ko| *nm* large rock, boulder.

peñón |penyon'| *nm* crag; **el P~** the Rock (of Gibraltar).

peón |peon'| *nm* laborer (*US*), labourer (*Brit*); (*AM*) farmhand; (*TEC*) spindle, shaft; (*AJEDREZ*) pawn.

peor |peor'| *a* (*comparativo*) worse; (*superlativo*) worst ♦ *ad* worse; worst; **de mal en ~** from bad to worse; **tanto ~** so much the worse; **A es ~ que B** A is worse than B; **Z es el ~ de todos** Z is the worst of all.

pepinillo |pepēnē'yo| *nm* gherkin.

pepino |pepē'no| *nm* cucumber; **(no) me importa un ~** I don't care two hoots.

pepita |pepē'tá| *nf* (*BOT*) pip; (*MINERÍA*) nugget.

pepito |pepē'to| *nm* meat sandwich.

peque |pe'ke| *etc vb* V **pecar.**

pequeñez |pekenyes'| *nf* smallness, littleness; (*trivialidad*) trifle, triviality.

pequeño, a |peke'nyo, á| *a* small, little; (*cifra*) small, low; (*bajo*) short; **~ burgués** lower middle-class.

pequinés, esa |pekēnes', esá| *a*, *nm/f* Pekinese.

pera |pe'rá| *a inv* classy; **niño ~** spoiled upper-class brat ♦ *nf* pear; **eso es pedir ~s al olmo** that's asking the impossible.

peral |perál'| *nm* pear tree.

percance |perkán'se| *nm* setback, misfortune.

percatarse |perkátár'se| *vr*: **~ de** to notice, take note of.

percebe |perse'he| *nm* (*ZOOL*) barnacle; (*fam*) idiot.

percepción |persepsyon'| *nf* (*vista*) perception; (*idea*) notion, idea; (*COM*) collection.

perceptible |perseptē'hle| *a* perceptible, noticeable; (*COM*) payable, receivable.

percibir |persēhēr'| *vt* to perceive, notice; (*ver*) to see; (*peligro etc*) to sense; (*COM*) to earn, receive, get.

percusión |perkōōsyon'| *nf* percussion.

percusor |perkōōsor'|, **percutor** |perkōōtor'| *nm* (*TEC*) hammer; (*de arma*) firing pin.

percha |pertch'á| *nf* (*poste*) pole, support; (*gancho*) peg; (*de abrigos*) coat stand; (*colgador*) coat hanger; (*de ave*) perch.

perchero |pertche'ro| *nm* clothes rack.

perdedor, a |perthethor', á| *a* losing ♦ *nm/f* loser.

perder |perther'| *vt* to lose; (*tiempo, palabras*) to waste; (*oportunidad*) to lose, miss; (*tren*) to miss ♦ *vi* to lose; **~se** *vr* (*extraviarse*) to get lost; (*desaparecer*) to disappear, be lost to view; (*arruinarse*) to be ruined; **echar a ~** (*comida*) to spoil, ruin; (*oportunidad*) to waste; **tener buen ~** to be a good loser; **¡no te lo pierdas!** don't miss it!; **he perdido la costumbre** I have got out of the habit.

perdición |perthēsyon'| *nf* perdition; (*fig*) ruin.

pérdida |per'θeθá| *nf* loss; *(de tiempo)* waste; *(COM)* net loss; ~**s** *nfpl* *(COM)* losses; **¡no tiene ~!** you can't go wrong!; ~ **contable** *(COM)* book loss.

perdido, a |perθe'θo, á| *a* lost; **estar ~ por** to be crazy about; **es un caso ~** he is a hopeless case.

perdiz |perθes'| *nf* partridge.

perdón |perθon'| *nm* *(disculpa)* pardon, forgiveness; *(clemencia)* mercy; **¡~!** sorry!, I beg your pardon!; **con ~** if I may, if you don't mind.

perdonar |perθonár'| *vt* to pardon, forgive; *(la vida)* to spare; *(excusar)* to exempt, excuse ♦ *vi* to pardon, forgive; **¡perdone (usted)!** sorry!, I beg your pardon!; **perdone, pero me parece que ...** excuse me, but I think ...

perdurable |perθoorá'hle| *a* lasting; *(eterno)* everlasting.

perdurar |perθoorár'| *vi* *(resistir)* to last, endure; *(seguir existiendo)* to stand, still exist.

perecer |pereser'| *vi* to perish, die.

peregrinación |peregrēnásyon'| *nf* *(REL)* pilgrimage.

peregrino, a |peregrē'no| *a* *(extraño)* strange; *(singular)* rare ♦ *nm/f* pilgrim.

perejil |perehēl'| *nm* parsley.

perenne |peren'ne| *a* everlasting, perennial.

perentorio, a |perento'ryo, á| *a* *(urgente)* urgent; *(terminante)* peremptory; *(fijo)* set, fixed.

pereza |pere'sá| *nf* *(flojera)* laziness; *(lentitud)* sloth, slowness.

perezca |peres'ká| *etc vb* V **perecer**.

perezoso, a |pereso'so, á| *a* lazy; slow, sluggish.

perfección |perfeksyon'| *nf* perfection; **a la ~** to perfection.

perfeccionar |perfeksyonár'| *vt* to perfect; *(acabar)* to complete, finish.

perfecto, a |perfek'to, á| *a* perfect ♦ *nm* *(LING)* perfect (tense).

perfidia |perfe'θyá| *nf* perfidy, treachery.

pérfido, a |per'feθo, á| *a* perfidious, treacherous.

perfil |perfēl'| *nm* *(parte lateral)* profile; *(silueta)* silhouette, outline; *(TEC)* (cross) section; ~**es** *nmpl* features; *(fig)* social graces; ~ **del cliente** *(COM)* customer profile; **en ~** from the side, in profile.

perfilado, a |perfēlá'θo, á| *a* *(bien formado)* well-shaped; *(largo: cara)* long.

perfilar |perfēlár'| *vt* *(trazar)* to outline; *(dar carácter a)* to shape, give character to; ~**se** *vr* to be silhouetted *(en* against); **el proyecto se va perfilando** the project is taking shape.

perforación |perforásyon'| *nf* perforation; *(con taladro)* drilling.

perforadora |perforáθo'rá| *nf* drill; ~ **de fichas** card-punch.

perforar |perforár'| *vt* to perforate; *(agujero)* to drill, bore; *(papel)* to punch a hole in ♦ *vi* to drill, bore.

perfumado, a |perfoomá'θo, á| *a* scented, perfumed.

perfumar |perfoomár'| *vt* to scent, perfume.

perfume |perfoo'me| *nm* perfume, scent.

pergamino |pergáme'no| *nm* parchment.

pericia |pere'syá| *nf* skill, expertise.

periferia |perēfe'ryá| *nf* periphery; *(de ciudad)* outskirts *pl*.

periférico, a |perēfe'rēko, á| *a* peripheral ♦ *nm* *(INFORM)* peripheral; *(AUTO)* beltway *(US)*, ring road *(Brit)*; **barrio ~** outlying district.

perímetro |perē'metro| *nm* perimeter.

periódico, a |peryo'θēko, á| *a* periodic(al) ♦ *nm* (news)paper; ~ **dominical** Sunday (news)paper.

periodismo |peryoθēs'mo| *nm* journalism.

periodista |peryoθe'stá| *nm/f* journalist.

periodístico, a |peryoθē'stēko, á| *a* journalistic.

periodo |peryo'θo|, **período** |perē'oθo| *nm* period; ~ **contable** *(COM)* accounting period.

peripuesto, a |perēpwe'sto, á| *a* dressed up; **tan ~** all dressed up.

perito, a |perē'to, á| *a* *(experto)* expert; *(diestro)* skilled, skilful ♦ *nm/f* expert; skilled worker; *(técnico)* technician.

perjudicar |perhooθēkár'| *vt* *(gen)* to damage, harm; *(fig)* to prejudice.

perjudicial |perhooθēsyál'| *a* damaging, harmful; *(en detrimento)* detrimental.

perjudique |perhooθē'ke| *etc vb* V **perjudicar**.

perjuicio |perhwē'syo| *nm* damage, harm; **en/sin ~ de** to the detriment of/without prejudice to.

perjurar |perhoorár'| *vi* to commit perjury.

perla |per'lá| *nf* pearl; **me viene de ~s** it suits me fine.

permanecer |permáneser'| *vi* *(quedarse)* to stay, remain; *(seguir)* to continue to be.

permanencia |permánen'syá| *nf* *(duración)* permanence; *(estancia)* stay.

permanente |permánen'te| *a* *(que queda)* permanent; *(constante)* constant; *(comisión etc)* standing ♦ *nf* perm; **hacerse una ~** to have one's hair permed.

permanezca |permánes'ká| *etc vb* V **permanecer**.

permisible |permēsē'hle| *a* permissible, allowable.

permiso |permē'so| *nm* permission; *(licencia)* permit, license *(US)*, licence *(Brit)*; **con ~** excuse me; **estar de ~** *(MIL)* to be on leave; ~ **de conducir** *o*

conductor driver's license (US), driving licence (Brit); ~ **de exportación/importación** export/import license.

permitir |permētēr'| vt to permit, allow; ~**se** vr: ~**se algo** to allow o.s. sth; **no me puedo** ~ **ese lujo** I can't afford that; **¿me permite?** may I?; **si lo permite el tiempo** weather permitting.

permuta |permōō'tá| nf exchange.

permutar |permōōtár'| vt to switch, exchange; ~ **destinos con uno** to swap o exchange jobs with sb.

pernicioso, a |pernēsyo'so, á| a (maligno, MED) pernicious; (persona) wicked.

perno |per'no| nm bolt.

pernoctar |pernoktár'| vi to stay for the night.

pero |pe'ro| conj but; (aún) yet ♦ nm (defecto) flaw, defect; (reparo) objection; **¡no hay** ~ **que valga!** there are no buts about it.

perogrullada |perogrōōyá'thá| nf platitude, truism.

perol |perol'| nm, **perola** |pero'lá| nf pan.

peronista |peronē'stá| a, nm/f Peronist.

perorar |perorár'| vi to make a speech.

perorata |perorá'tá| nf long-winded speech.

perpendicular |perpendēkōōlár'| a perpendicular; **el camino es** ~ **al río** the road is at right angles to the river.

perpetrar |perpetrár'| vt to perpetrate.

perpetuamente |perpetwámen'te| ad perpetually.

perpetuar |perpetwár'| vt to perpetuate.

perpetuo, a |perpe'two, á| a perpetual; (JUR etc: condena) life cpd.

Perpiñán |perpēnyán'| nm Perpignan.

perplejo, a |perple'ho, á| a perplexed, bewildered.

perra |pe'rrá| nf bitch; (fam: dinero) money; (: manía) mania, crazy idea; (: rabieta) tantrum; **estar sin una** ~ to be flat broke.

perrera |perre'rá| nf kennel.

perro |pe'rro| nm dog; ~ **caliente** hot dog; "~ **peligroso"** "beware of the dog"; **ser** ~ **viejo** to be an old hand; **tiempo de** ~**s** filthy weather; ~ **que ladra no muerde** his bark is worse than his bite.

persa |per'sá| a, nm/f Persian ♦ nm (LING) Persian.

persecución |persekōōsyon'| nf pursuit, hunt, chase; (REL, POL) persecution.

perseguir |persegēr'| vt to pursue, hunt; (cortejar) to chase after; (molestar) to pester, annoy; (REL, POL) to persecute; (JUR) to prosecute.

perseverante |persebherán'te| a persevering, persistent.

perseverar |perseverár'| vi to persevere, persist; ~ **en** to persevere in, persist with.

persiana |persyá'ná| nf (Venetian) blind.

persiga |persē'gá| etc vb V **perseguir.**

persignarse |persēgnár'se| vr to cross o.s.

persiguiendo |persēgyen'tho| etc vb V **perseguir.**

persistente |persēsten'te| a persistent.

persistir |persēstēr'| vi to persist.

persona |perso'ná| nf person; **10** ~**s** 10 people; **tercera** ~ third party; (LING) third person; **en** ~ in person o the flesh; **por** ~ a head; **es buena** ~ he's a good sort.

personaje |personá'he| nm important person, celebrity; (TEATRO) character.

personal |personál'| a (particular) personal; (para una persona) single, for one person ♦ nm (plantilla) personnel, staff; (NAUT) crew; (fam: gente) people.

personalidad |personálētháth'| nf personality; (JUR) status.

personarse |personár'se| vr to appear in person; ~ **en** to present o.s. at, report to.

personificar |personēfēkár'| vt to personify.

personifique |personēfē'ke| etc vb V **personificar.**

perspectiva |perspektē'bhá| nf perspective; (vista, panorama) view, panorama; (posibilidad futura) outlook, prospect; **tener algo en** ~ to have sth in view.

perspicacia |perspēká'syá| nf discernment, perspicacity.

perspicaz |perspēkás'| a shrewd.

persuadir |perswáthēr'| vt (gen) to persuade; (convencer) to convince; ~**se** vr to become convinced.

persuasión |perswásyon'| nf (acto) persuasion; (convicción) conviction.

persuasivo, a |perwásē'ho, á| a persuasive; convincing.

pertenecer |pertenesēr'| vi: ~ **a** to belong to; (fig) to concern.

perteneciente |pertenesyen'te| a: ~ **a** belonging to.

pertenencia |pertenen'syá| nf ownership; ~**s** nfpl possessions, property sg.

pertenezca |pertenes'ká| etc vb V **pertenecer.**

pértiga |per'tēgá| nf pole; **salto de** ~ pole vault.

pertinaz |pertēnás'| a (persistente) persistent; (terco) obstinate.

pertinente |pertēnen'te| a relevant, pertinent; (apropiado) appropriate; ~ **a** concerning, relevant to.

pertrechar |pertretchár'| vt (gen) to supply; (MIL) to supply with ammunition and stores; ~**se** vr: ~**se de algo** to provide o.s. with sth.

pertrechos |pertretch'os| nmpl (gen) implements; (MIL) supplies and stores.

perturbación |pertōōrbhásyon'| nf (POL) disturbance; (MED) upset, disturbance; ~ **del**

orden público breach of the peace.

perturbador, a |pertŏŏrháthor'. á| *a (que perturba)* perturbing, disturbing; *(subversivo)* subversive.

perturbar |pertŏŏrhár'| *vt (el orden)* to disturb; *(MED)* to upset, disturb; *(mentalmente)* to perturb.

Perú |perŏŏ'| *nm:* **el ~** Peru.

peruano, a |perwá'no. á| *a, nm/f* Peruvian.

perversión |perhersyon'| *nf* perversion.

perverso, a |perher'so. á| *a* perverse; *(depravado)* depraved.

pervertido, a |perhertē'tho. á| *a* perverted ♦ *nm/f* pervert.

pervertir |perhertēr'| *vt* to pervert, corrupt.

pervierta |perhyer'tá| *etc,* **pervirtiendo** |perhērtyen'do| *etc vb V* **pervertir.**

pesa |pe'sá| *nf* weight; *(DEPORTE)* shot.

pesadez |pesáthes'| *nf (calidad de pesado)* heaviness; *(lentitud)* slowness; *(aburrimiento)* tediousness; **es una ~ tener que ...** it's a bind having to ...

pesadilla |pesáthē'yá| *nf* nightmare, bad dream; *(fig)* worry, obsession.

pesado, a |pesá'tho. á| *a (gen)* heavy; *(lento)* slow; *(difícil, duro)* tough, hard; *(aburrido)* tedious, boring; *(bochornoso)* sultry ♦ *nm/f* bore; **tener el estómago ~** to feel bloated; **¡no seas ~!** come off it!

pesadumbre |pesáthŏŏm'bre| *nf* grief, sorrow.

pésame |pe'sáme| *nm* expression of condolence, message of sympathy; **dar el ~** to express one's condolences.

pesar |pesár'| *vt* to weigh; *(fig)* to weigh heavily on; *(afligir)* to grieve ♦ *vi* to weigh; *(ser pesado)* to weigh a lot, be heavy; *(fig: opinión)* to carry weight ♦ *nm (sentimiento)* regret; *(pena)* sorrow; **a ~ de (que)** in spite of, despite; **no me pesa haberlo hecho** I'm not sorry I did it.

pesca |pes'ká| *nf (acto)* fishing; *(cantidad de pescado)* catch; **~ de altura/en bajura** deep sea/coastal fishing; **ir de ~** to go fishing.

pescadería |peskáthere'á| *nf* fish market *(US)*, fish shop *(Brit)*.

pescadilla |peskáthē'yá| *nf* whiting.

pescado |peská'tho| *nm* fish.

pescador, a |peskáthor'. á| *nm/f* fisherman/ woman.

pescar |peskár'| *vt (coger)* to catch; *(tratar de coger)* to fish for; *(fam: lograr)* to get hold of, land; *(conseguir: trabajo)* to manage to get; *(sorprender)* to catch unawares ♦ *vi* to fish, go fishing.

pescuezo |peskwe'so| *nm* neck.

pese |pe'se| *prep:* **~ a** despite, in spite of.

pesebre |pese'hre| *nm* manger.

peseta |pese'tá| *nf* peseta.

pesetero, a |pesete'ro, á| *a* money-grubbing.

pesimista |pesēmē'stá| *a* pessimistic ♦ *nm/f* pessimist.

pésimo, a |pe'sēmo, á| *a* abominable, vile.

peso |pe'so| *nm* weight; *(balanza)* scales *pl*; *(AM COM)* monetary unit; *(moneda)* peso; *(DEPORTE)* shot; **~ bruto/neto** gross/net weight; **de poco ~** light(weight); **levantamiento de ~s** weightlifting; **vender a ~** to sell by weight; **argumento de ~** weighty argument; **eso cae de su ~** that goes without saying.

pesque |pes'ke| *etc vb V* **pescar.**

pesquero, a |peske'ro. á| *a* fishing *cpd*.

pesquisa |peskē'sá| *nf* inquiry, investigation.

pestaña |pestá'nyá| *nf (ANAT)* eyelash; *(borde)* rim.

pestañear |pestányeár'| *vi* to blink.

peste |pe'ste| *nf* plague; *(fig)* nuisance; *(mal olor)* stink, stench; **~ negra** Black Death; **echar ~s** to swear, fume.

pesticida |pestēsē'thá| *nm* pesticide.

pestilencia |pestēlen'syá| *nf (mal olor)* stink, stench.

pestillo |pestē'yo| *nm* bolt, latch; *(cerrojo)* catch; *(picaporte)* (door) handle.

petaca |petá'ká| *nf (de cigarrillos)* cigarette case; *(de pipa)* tobacco pouch; *(AM: maleta)* suitcase.

pétalo |pe'tálo| *nm* petal.

petardo |petár'tho| *nm* firework, firecracker.

petición |petēsyon'| *nf (pedido)* request, plea; *(memorial)* petition; *(JUR)* plea; **a ~ de** at the request of; **~ de aumento de salarios** wage demand *o* claim.

petirrojo |petērro'ho| *nm* robin.

peto |pe'to| *nm (corpiño)* bodice; *(TAUR)* horse's padding.

pétreo, a |pe'treo, á| *a* stony, rocky.

petrificar |petrēfēkár'| *vt* to petrify.

petrifique |petrēfē'ke| *etc vb V* **petrificar.**

petrodólar |petrotho'lár| *nm* petrodollar.

petróleo |petro'leo| *nm* oil, petroleum.

petrolero, a |petrole'ro, á| *a* petroleum *cpd* ♦ *nm (COM)* oil man; *(buque)* (oil) tanker.

petulancia |petŏŏlán'syá| *nf (insolencia)* vanity, opinionated nature.

peyorativo, a |peyorátē'ho, á| *a* pejorative.

pez |pes| *nm* fish; **~ de colores** goldfish; **~ espada** swordfish; **estar como el ~ en el agua** to feel completely at home.

pezón |peson'| *nm* teat, nipple.

pezuña |pesŏŏ'nyá| *nf* hoof.

piadoso, a |pyátho'so. á| *a (devoto)* pious, devout; *(misericordioso)* kind, merciful.

Piamonte |pyámon'te| *nm* Piedmont.

pianista |pyánē'stá| *nm/f* pianist.

piano |pyá'no| *nm* piano; **~ de cola** grand piano.

piar |pyár| *vi* to cheep.

piara |pyá'rá| *nf (manada)* herd, drove.

PIB *nm abr (Esp COM:=Producto Interno Bruto)* GDP.

pibe, a |pē'ɦe, á| *nm/f (AM)* boy/girl, kid, child.

pica |pē'ká| *nf (MIL)* pike; *(TAUR)* goad; **poner una ~ en Flandes** to bring off something difficult.

picadero |pēkáɦe'ro| *nm* riding school.

picadillo |pēkáɦē'yo| *nm* mince.

picado, a |pēká'ɦo, á| *a* pricked, punctured; *(mar)* choppy; *(diente)* bad; *(tabaco)* cut; *(enfadado)* cross.

picador |pēkáɦor'| *nm (TAUR)* picador; *(minero)* faceworker.

picadura |pēkáɦōō'rá| *nf (pinchazo)* puncture; *(de abeja)* sting; *(de mosquito)* bite; *(tabaco picado)* cut tobacco.

picante |pēkán'te| *a (comida, sabor)* hot; *(comentario)* racy, spicy.

picaporte |pēkápor'te| *nm (tirador)* handle; *(pestillo)* latch.

picar |pēkár'| *vt (agujerear, perforar)* to prick, puncture; *(billete)* to punch, clip; *(abeja)* to sting; *(mosquito, serpiente)* to bite; *(persona)* to ˈnibble (at); *(incitar)* to incite, goad; *(dañar, irritar)* to annoy, bother; *(quemar: lengua)* to burn, sting ♦ *vi (pez)* to bite; take the bait; *(el sol)* to burn, scorch; *(abeja, MED)* to sting; *(mosquito)* to bite; **~se** *vr (agriarse)* to turn sour; *(mar)* to get choppy; *(ofenderse)* to take offense *(US)* o offence *(Brit)*; **me pican los ojos** my eyes sting; **me pica el brazo** my arm itches.

picardía |pēkárɦē'á| *nf* villainy; *(astucia)* slyness, craftiness; *(una ~)* dirty trick; *(palabra)* rude/bad word o expression.

picaresco, a |pēkáres'ko, á| *a (travieso)* roguish, rascally; *(LIT)* picaresque.

pícaro, a |pē'káro, á| *a (malicioso)* villainous; *(travieso)* mischievous ♦ *nm (astuto)* sly sort; *(sinvergüenza)* rascal, scoundrel.

picazón |pēkáson'| *nf (comezón)* itch; *(ardor)* sting(ing feeling); *(remordimiento)* pang of conscience.

pico |pē'ko| *nm (de ave)* beak; *(punto agudo)* peak, sharp point; *(TEC)* pick, pickax *(US)*, pickaxe *(Brit)*; *(GEO)* peak, summit; *(labia)* talkativeness; **no abrir el ~** to keep quiet; **~ parásito** *(ELEC)* spike; **y ~** and a bit; **son las 3 y ~** it's just after 3; **tiene 50 libros y ~** he has 50-odd books; **me costó un ~** it cost me quite a bit.

picor |pēkor'| *nm* itch; *(ardor)* sting(ing feeling).

picota |pēko'tá| *nf* pillory; **poner a uno en la ~** *(fig)* to ridicule sb.

picotada |pēkotá'ɦá| *nf*, **picotazo** |pēkotá'so| *nm (de pájaro)* peck; *(de in-*

secto) sting, bite.

picotear |pēkoteár'| *vt* to peck ♦ *vi* to nibble, pick.

pictórico, a |pēkto'rēko, á| *a* pictorial; **tiene dotes pictóricas** she has a talent for painting.

picudo, a |pēkōō'ɦo, á| *a* pointed, with a point.

pichón, ona |pētchon'. oná| *nm/f (paloma)* young pigeon; *(apelativo)* darling, dearest.

pidiendo |pēɦyen'do| *etc vb V* **pedir.**

pie |pye| *(pl ~s) nm (gen, MAT)* foot; *(de cama, página, escalera)* foot, bottom; *(TEATRO)* cue; *(fig: motivo)* motive, basis; *(: fundamento)* foothold; **~s planos** flat feet; **ir a ~** to go on foot, walk; **estar de ~** to be standing (up); **ponerse de ~** to stand up; **al ~ de la letra** *(citar)* literally, verbatim; *(copiar)* exactly, word for word; **de ~s a cabeza** from head to foot; **en ~ de guerra** on a war footing; **sin ~s ni cabeza** pointless, absurd; **dar ~ a** to give cause for; **no dar ~ con bola** to be no good at anything; **saber de qué ~ cojea uno** to know sb's weak spots.

piedad |pyeɦáɦ'| *nf (lástima)* pity, compassion; *(clemencia)* mercy; *(devoción)* piety, devotion; **tener ~ de** to take pity on.

piedra |pye'ɦrá| *nf* stone; *(roca)* rock; *(de mechero)* flint; *(METEOROLOGÍA)* hailstone; **primera ~** foundation stone; **~ de afilar** grindstone; **~ arenisca/caliza** sand-/limestone.

piel |pyel| *nf (ANAT)* skin; *(ZOOL)* skin, hide; *(de oso)* fur; *(cuero)* leather; *(BOT)* skin, peel ♦ *nm/f:* **~ roja** redskin.

pienso |pyen'so| *etc vb V* **pensar** ♦ *nm (AGR)* feed.

pierda |pyer'ɦá| *etc vb V* **perder.**

pierna |pyer'ná| *nf* leg; **en ~s** bare-legged.

pieza |pye'sá| *nf* piece; *(habitación)* room; *(MUS)* piece, composition; *(TEATRO)* work, play; **~ de recambio** o **repuesto** extra *(US)*, spare (part); **~ de ropa** article of clothing; **quedarse de una ~** to be dumbfounded.

pigmeo, a |pēgme'o, á| *a, nm/f* pigmy.

pija |pē'ɦá| *nf V* **pijo, a.**

pijama |pēɦá'má| *nm* pijama *(US)*, pyjamas *pl (Brit)*.

pijo, a |pē'ɦo, á| *nm/f (fam)* upper-class twit.

pijotada |pēɦotá'ɦá| *nf* nuisance.

pila |pē'lá| *nf (ELEC)* battery; *(montón)* heap, pile; *(fuente)* sink; *(REL: tb: ~ bautismal)* font; **nombre de ~** Christian o first name; **tengo una ~ de cosas que hacer** *(fam)* I have heaps o stacks of things to do; **~ de discos** *(INFORM)* disk pack.

pilar |pēlár'| *nm* pillar; *(de puente)* pier;

(*fig*) prop, mainstay.

píldora [pēl'dorá] *nf* pill; **la ~ (anti-conceptiva)** the pill; **tragarse la ~** to be taken in.

pileta [pēle'tà] *nf* basin, bowl; (*AM*) swimming pool.

pilón [pēlon'] *nm* pillar, post; (*ELEC*) pylon; (*bebedero*) drinking trough; (*de fuente*) basin.

piloto [pēlo'to] *nm* pilot; (*AUTO*) rear light, tail light; (*conductor*) driver ♦ *a inv*: **planta ~** pilot plant; **luz ~** side light.

piltrafa [pēltrà'fà] *nf* (*carne*) poor quality meat; (*fig*) worthless object; (: *individuo*) wretch.

pillaje [pēyà'he] *nm* pillage, plunder.

pillar [pēyàr'] *vt* (*fam*: *coger*) to catch; (: *agarrar*) to grasp, seize; (: *entender*) to grasp, catch on to; (*suj*: *coche etc*) to run over; **~ un resfriado** (*fam*) to catch a cold.

pillo, a [pē'yo, à] *a* villainous; (*astuto*) sly, crafty ♦ *nm/f* rascal, rogue, scoundrel.

pimentón [pēmenton'] *nm* (*polvo*) paprika.

pimienta [pēmyen'tà] *nf* pepper.

pimiento [pēmyen'to] *nm* pepper, pimiento.

pimpante [pēmpàn'te] *a* (*encantador*) charming; (*tb*: **tan ~**) smug, self-satisfied.

PIN *nm abr* (*Esp COM*: = *Producto Interior Neto*) net domestic product.

pinacoteca [pēnàkote'kà] *nf* art gallery.

pinar [pēnàr'] *nm* pinewood.

pincel [pēnsel'] *nm* paintbrush.

pincelada [pēnselà'thà] *nf* brushstroke; **última ~** (*fig*) finishing touch.

pinchar [pēntchàr'] *vt* (*perforar*) to prick, pierce; (*neumático*) to puncture; (*incitar*) to prod; **~se** *vr* (*con droga*) to inject o.s.; (*neumático*) to burst, puncture; **no ~ ni cortar** (*fam*) to cut no ice; **tener un neumático pinchado** to have a puncture *o* a flat tire (*US*) *o* tyre (*Brit*).

pinchazo [pēntchà'so] *nm* (*perforación*) prick; (*de llanta*) flat (*US*), puncture (*Brit*).

pinche [pēntch'e] *nm* (*de cocina*) kitchen boy, scullion.

pinchito [pēntchē'to] *nm* shish kebab.

pincho [pēntch'o] *nm* point; (*aguijón*) spike; (*CULIN*) savory (*US*) *o* savoury (*Brit*) (snack); **~ moruno** shish kebab; **~ de tortilla** small slice of omelette.

pingüe [pēn'gwe] *a* (*grasoso*) greasy; (*cosecha*) bumper *cpd*; (*negocio*) lucrative.

pingüino [pēngwē'no] *nm* penguin.

pino [pē'no] *nm* pine (tree); **vivir en el quinto ~** to live in the middle of nowhere.

pinta [pēn'tà] *nf* spot; (*gota*) spot, drop; (*aspecto*) appearance; **look(s)** (*pl*); (*medida*) pint; **tener buena ~** to look good, look well; **por la ~** by the look of it.

pintadas [pēntà'thàs] *nfpl* political graffiti.

pintado, a [pēntà'tho. à] *a* spotted; (*de muchos colores*) colorful (*US*), colourful (*Brit*); **me sienta que ni ~**, **viene que ni ~** it suits me to a tee.

pintar [pēntàr'] *vt* to paint ♦ *vi* to paint; (*fam*) to count, be important; **~se** *vr* to put on make-up; **pintárselas solo para hacer algo** to manage to do sth by o.s.; **no pinta nada** (*fam*) he has no say.

pintor, a [pēntor'. à] *nm/f* painter; **~ de brocha gorda** house painter; (*fig*) bad painter.

pintoresco, a [pēntores'ko. à] *a* picturesque.

pintura [pēntōō'rà] *nf* painting; **~ a la acuarela** watercolor; **~ al óleo** oil painting; **~ rupestre** cave painting.

pinza [pēn'sà] *nf* (*ZOOL*) claw; (*para colgar ropa*) clothespin (*US*), clothes peg (*Brit*); (*TEC*) pincers *pl*; **~s** *nfpl* (*para depilar*) tweezers.

piña [pē'nyà] *nf* (*fruto del pino*) pine cone; (*fruta*) pineapple; (*fig*) group.

piñón [pēnyon'] *nm* (*BOT*) pine nut; (*TEC*) pinion.

PIO *nm abr* (*Esp*: = *Patronato de Igualdad de Oportunidades*) ≈ Office of Economic Opportunity.

pío, a [pē'o. à] *a* (*devoto*) pious, devout; (*misericordioso*) merciful ♦ *nm*: **no decir ni ~** not to breathe a word.

piojo [pyo'ho] *nm* louse.

piojoso, a [pyoho'so. à] *a* lousy; (*sucio*) dirty.

piolet [pyole'], *pl* **~s** [-s] *nm* ice ax (*US*) *o* axe (*Brit*).

pionero, a [pyone'ro. à] *a* pioneering ♦ *nm/f* pioneer.

pipa [pē'pà] *nf* pipe; (*BOT*) seed, pip.

pipí [pēpē'] *nm* (*fam*): **hacer ~** to go wee-wee.

pipiolo [pēpyo'lo] *nm* youngster; (*novato*) novice, greenhorn.

pique [pē'ke] *etc vb V* **picar** ♦ *nm* (*resentimiento*) pique, resentment; (*rivalidad*) rivalry, competition; **irse a ~** to sink; (*familia*) to be ruined; **tener un ~ con uno** to have a grudge against sb.

piqueta [pēke'tà] *nf* pick, pickax (*US*), pickaxe (*Brit*).

piquete [pēke'te] *nm* (*agujerito*) small hole; (*MIL*) squad, party; (*de obreros*) picket; **~ secundario** secondary picket.

pirado, a [pērà'tho. à] *a* (*fam*) round the bend.

piragua [pērà'gwà] *nf* canoe.

piragüismo [pēràgwēs'mo] *nm* (*DEPORTE*) canoeing.

pirámide [pērà'mēthe] *nf* pyramid.

pirarse [pēràr'se] *vr*: **~(las)** (*largarse*) to beat it (*fam*); (*ESCOL*) to cut class.

pirata |pĕrá'tá| a: **edición/disco** ~ pirate edition/bootleg record ♦ nm pirate; (INFORM) hacker.

pirenaico, a |pĕrená'čko, á| a Pyrenean.

Pirineo(s) |pĕrĕne'o(s)| nm(pl) Pyrenees pl.

piropo |pĕro'po| nm compliment, (piece of) flattery; **echar ~s a** to make flirtatious remarks to.

pirulí |pĕrōōlĕ'| nm carameled (US) o toffee (Brit) apple; lollipop.

pisada |pĕsá'thá| nf (paso) footstep; (huella) footprint.

pisar |pĕsár'| vt (caminar sobre) to walk on, tread on; (apretar con el pie) to press; (fig) to trample on, walk all over ♦ vi to tread, step, walk; ~ **el acelerador** to step on the accelerator; ~ **fuerte** (fig) to act determinedly.

piscina |pĕsĕ'ná| nf swimming pool.

Piscis |pĕ'sĕs| nm (ASTRO) Pisces.

piso |pĕ'so| nm (suelo, de edificio) floor; (apartamento) apartment; **primer** ~ second (US) o first (Brit) floor.

pisotear |pĕsoteár'| vt to trample (on o underfoot); (fig: humillar) to trample on.

pisotón |pĕsoton'| nm (con el pie) stamp.

pista |pĕ'stá| nf track, trail; (indicio) clew (US), clue (Brit); (INFORM) track; ~ **de auditoría** (COM) audit trail; ~ **de aterrizaje** runway; ~ **de baile** dance floor; ~ **de tenis** tennis court; ~ **de hielo** ice rink; **estar sobre la** ~ **de uno** to be on sb's trail.

pistola |pĕsto'lá| nf pistol; (TEC) spray-gun.

pistolero, a |pĕstole'ro, á| nm/f gunman, gangster ♦ nf holster.

pistón |pĕston'| nm (TEC) piston; (MUS) valve.

pitar |pĕtár'| vt (hacer sonar) to blow; (partido) to referee; (rechiflar) to whistle at, boo; (actor, obra) to hiss ♦ vi to whistle; (AUTO) to toot one's horn; (AM) to smoke; **salir pitando** to beat it.

pitido |pĕtĕ'tho| nm whistle.

pitillo |pĕtĕ'yo| nm cigarette.

pito |pĕ'to| nm whistle; (de coche) horn; (cigarrillo) cigarette; (fam: de marijuana) joint; (fam!) prick (!); **me importa un** ~ I don't care two hoots.

pitón |pĕton'| nm (ZOOL) python.

pitonisa |pĕtonĕ'sá| nf fortune-teller.

pitorrearse |pĕtorreár'se| vr: ~ **de** to scoff at, make fun of.

pitorreo |pĕtorre'o| nm joke, laugh; **estar de** ~ to be in a joking mood.

píxel |pĕk'sel| nm (INFORM) pixel.

pizarra |pĕsá'rrá| nf (piedra) slate; (encerado) blackboard.

pizca |pĕs'ká| nf pinch, (fig) speck, trace; **ni** ~ not a bit.

placa |plá'ká| nf plate; (MED) dental plate; (distintivo) badge; ~ **de matrícula** license

(US) o number (Brit) plate; ~ **madre** (IN-FORM) mother board.

placentero, a |pláscnte'ro, á| a pleasant, agreeable.

placer |pláscr'| nm pleasure; **a** ~ at one's pleasure.

plácido, a |plá'sĕtho, á| a placid.

plaga |plá'gá| nf pest; (MED) plague; (fig) swarm.

plagar |plágár'| vt to infest, plague; (llenar) to fill; **plagado de** riddled with; **han plagado la ciudad de carteles** they have plastered the town with posters.

plagio |plá'hyo| nm plagiarism.

plague |plá'ge| etc vb V **plagar**.

plan |plán| nm (esquema, proyecto) plan; (idea, intento) idea, intention; (de curso) program (US), programme (Brit); ~ **cotizable de jubilación** contributory pension plan; ~ **de estudios** curriculum; ~ **de incentivos** (COM) incentive plan; **tener** ~ (fam) to have a date; **tener un** ~ (fam) to have an affair; **en** ~ **cachondeo** for a laugh; **en** ~ **económico** (fam) on the cheap; **vamos en** ~ **de turismo** we're going as tourists; **si te pones en ese** ~ ... if that's your attitude ...

plana |plá'ná| nf V **plano**.

plancha |plántch'á| nf (para planchar) iron; (rótulo) plate, sheet; (NAUT) gangway; (CULIN) grill; **pescado a la** ~ grilled fish.

planchado, a |plántchá'tho, á| a (ropa) ironed; (traje) pressed ♦ nm ironing.

planchar |plántchár'| vt to iron ♦ vi to do the ironing.

planeador |pláneáthor'| nm glider.

planear |pláneár'| vt to plan ♦ vi to glide.

planeta |pláne'tá| nm planet.

planetario, a |plánctá'ryo, á| a planetary ♦ nm planetarium.

planicie |plánĕ'sye| nf plain.

planificación |plánĕfĕkásyon'| nf planning; ~ **corporativa** (COM) corporate planning; ~ **familiar** family planning; **diagrama de** ~ (COM) planner.

plano, a |plá'no, á| a flat, level, even; (liso) smooth ♦ nm (MAT, TEC, AVIAT) plane; (FOTO) shot; (ARQ) plan; (GEO) map; (de ciudad) map, street plan ♦ nf sheet of paper, page; (TEC) trowel **primer** ~ close-up; **caer de** ~ to fall flat; **rechazar algo de** ~ to turn sth down flat; **le daba el sol de** ~ (fig) the sun shone directly on it; **en primera plana** on the front page; **plana mayor** staff.

planta |plán'tá| nf (BOT, TEC) plant; (ANAT) sole of the foot, foot; (AM: personal) permanent staff; ~ **baja** ground floor.

plantación |plántásyon'| nf (AGR) plantation; (acto) planting.

plantar |plántár'| vt (BOT) to plant;

(puesto) to put in; *(levantar)* to erect, set up; **~se** *vr* to stand firm; **~ a uno en la calle** to chuck sb out; **dejar plantado a uno** *(fam)* to stand sb up; **~se en** to reach, get to.

plantear |plàntcàr'| *vt (problema)* to pose; *(dificultad)* to raise; **se lo plantearé** I'll put it to him.

plantel |plàntcl'| *nm (fig)* group, set.

plantilla |plàntč'yà| *nf (de zapato)* insole; *(personal)* personnel; **ser de ~** to be on the staff.

plantío |plàntč'o| *nm (acto)* planting; *(lugar)* plot, bed, patch.

plantón |plànton'| *nm (MIL)* guard, sentry; *(fam)* long wait; **dar (un) ~ a uno** to stand sb up.

plañir |plànyčr'| *vi* to mourn.

plasmar |plàsmár'| *vt (dar forma)* to mold *(US)*, mould *(Brit)*, shape; *(representar)* to represent ♦ *vi:* **~ en** to take the form of.

plasta |plà'stà| *nf* soft mass, lump; *(desastre)* botch, mess.

plasticidad |plàstčsčihàt̪h'| *nf (fig)* expressiveness.

plasticina |plàstčsč'nà|, *(AM)* **plastilina** |plàstčlč'nà| *nf* modeling clay *(US)*, Plasticine ® *(Brit)*.

plástico, a |plà'stčko, à| *a* plastic ♦ *nf (art of)* sculpture, modeling *(US)*, modelling *(Brit)* ♦ *nm* plastic.

plastificar |plàstčfčkár'| *vt (documento)* to laminate.

plastifique |plàstčfč'kc| *etc vb V* **plastificar**.

plata |plà'tà| *nf (metal)* silver; *(cosas hechas de plata)* silverware; *(AM)* cash, dough *(fam)*; **hablar en ~** to speak bluntly *o* frankly.

plataforma |plàtàfor'mà| *nf* platform; **~ de lanzamiento/perforación** launch(ing) pad/ drilling rig.

plátano |plà'tàno| *nm (fruta)* banana; *(árbol)* plane tree; *(bananero)* banana tree.

platea |plàtc'à| *nf (TEATRO)* pit.

plateado, a |plàtcà'tho, à| *a* silver; *(TEC)* silver-plated.

platense |plàtcn'sc| *(fam)* = **rioplatense**.

plática |plà'tčkà| *nf* talk, chat; *(REL)* sermon.

platicar |plàtčkár'| *vi* to talk, chat.

platillo |plàtč'yo| *nm* saucer; *(de limosnas)* collection plate; **~s** *nmpl* cymbals; **~ volador** *o* **volante** flying saucer; **pasar el ~** to pass the hat.

platino |plàtč'no| *nm* platinum; **~s** *nmpl* *(AUTO)* (contact) points.

platique |plàtč'kc| *etc vb V* **platicar**.

plato |plà'to| *nm* plate, dish; *(parte de comida)* course; *(guiso)* dish; **~ frutero/ sopero** fruit/soup dish; **pagar los ~s rotos** *(fam)* to take the rap.

playa |plà'yà| *nf* beach; *(costa)* seaside; **~ de estacionamiento** *(AM)* car park.

playera |plàyc'rà| *nf (AM: camiseta)* T-shirt; **~s** *nfpl* canvas shoes; *(TENIS)* tennis shoes.

plaza |plà'sà| *nf* square; *(mercado)* market(place); *(sitio)* room, space; *(en vehículo)* seat, place; *(colocación)* post, job; **~ de abastos** food market; **~ mayor** main square; **~ de toros** bullring; **hacer la ~** to do the daily shopping; **reservar una ~** to reserve a seat; **el hotel tiene 100 ~s** the hotel has 100 beds.

plazca |plàs'kà| *etc vb V* **placer**.

plazo |plà'so| *nm (lapso de tiempo)* time, period, term; *(fecha de vencimiento)* expiration *(US)* o expiry *(Brit)* date; *(pago parcial)* installment *(US)*, instalment *(Brit)*; **a corto/largo ~** short-/long-term; **comprar a ~s** to buy on time *(US)* o hire purchase *(Brit)*, pay for in installments; **nos dan un ~ de 8 días** they allow us a week.

plazoleta |plàsolc'tà|, **plazuela** |plàswc'là| *nf* small square.

pleamar |plcàmár'| *nf* high tide.

plebe |plc'hc| *nf:* **la ~** the common people *pl*, the masses *pl*; *(pey)* the plebes *pl (US)*, plebs *pl (Brit)*.

plebeyo, a |plchc'yo, à| *a* plebeian; *(pey)* coarse, common.

plebiscito |plchčsč'to| *nm* plebiscite.

pleca |plc'kà| *nf (INFORM)* backslash.

plegable |plcgà'hlc| *a* pliable; *(silla)* folding.

plegar |plcgàr'| *vt (doblar)* to fold, bend; *(COSTURA)* to pleat; **~se** *vr* to yield, submit.

plegaria |plcgà'ryà| *nf (oración)* prayer.

plegué, |plcgc'|, **pleguemos** |plcgc'mos| *etc vb V* **plegar**.

pleitear |plcčtcàr'| *vi (JUR)* to plead, conduct a lawsuit; *(litigar)* to go to court.

pleito |plc'čto| *nm (JUR)* lawsuit, case; *(fig)* dispute, feud; **~s** *nmpl* litigation *sg*; **entablar ~** to bring an action *o* a lawsuit; **poner ~** to sue.

plenario, a |plcnà'ryo, à| *a* plenary, full.

plenilunio |plcnčlōō'nyo| *nm* full moon.

plenitud |plcnčtōōt̪h'| *nf* plenitude, fullness; *(abundancia)* abundance.

pleno, a |plc'no, à| *a* full; *(completo)* complete ♦ *nm* plenum; **en ~** as a whole; *(por unanimidad)* unanimously; **en ~ día** in broad daylight; **en ~ verano** at the height of summer; **en plena cara** right in the face.

pleuresía |plcōōrcsč'à| *nf* pleurisy.

plexiglás |plcksčglàs'| ® *nm* acrylic glass, Plexiglas *(US)* ®.

plica |plč'kà| *nf* sealed envelope *o* document; *(en un concurso)* sealed entry.

pliego [plye'ɡo] etc vb V **plegar** ♦ nm (hoja) sheet (of paper); (carta) sealed letter/document; ~ **de condiciones** details pl, specifications pl.

pliegue [plye'ɡe] etc vb V **plegar** ♦ nm fold, crease; (de vestido) pleat.

plisado [plēsá'tho] nm pleating.

plomero [plome'ro] nm plumber.

plomizo, a [plome'so, á] a leaden, lead-colored (US), lead-coloured (Brit).

plomo [plo'mo] nm (metal) lead; (ELEC) fuse; **caer a** ~ to fall heavily o flat.

pluma [plōō'má] nf (ZOOL) feather; ~ **estilográfica**, ~ **fuente** (AM) fountain pen.

plumazo [plōōmá'so] nm (lit, fig) stroke of the pen.

plumero [plōōme'ro] nm (quitapolvos) feather duster; **ya te veo el** ~ I know what you're up to.

plumón [plōōmon'] nm (AM: fino) felt-tip pen; (: ancho) marker.

plural [plōōrál'] a plural ♦ nm: **en** ~ in the plural.

pluralidad [plōōrálēthátʰ'] nf plurality; **una** ~ **de votos** a majority of votes.

pluriempleo [plōōrēemple'o] nm moonlighting.

plus [plōōs] nm bonus.

plusmarquista [plōōsmárkē'stá] nm/f (DEPORTE) record holder.

plusvalía [plōōsválē'á] nf (mayor valor) appreciation, added value; (COM) goodwill.

plutocracia [plōōtokrá'syá] nf plutocracy.

PM nf abr (MIL: = Policía Militar) MP.

p.m. abr (= post meridiem) p.m.; (= por minuto) per minute.

PMA nm abr (= Programa Mundial de Alimentos) World Food Program.

pmo. abr (= próximo) prox.

PN nf abr (MIL: = Policía Naval) Naval Police.

PNB nm abr (Esp COM: = producto nacional bruto) GNP.

P.N.D. nm abr (ESCOL: = personal no docente) non-teaching staff.

PNN nm/f abr (= profesor no numerario) untenured teacher; (Esp COM: = producto nacional neto) net national product.

PNUD nm abr (= Programa de las Naciones Unidas para el Desarrollo) United Nations Development Programme.

PNV nm abr (Esp POL)=Partido Nacional Vasco.

P.º abr (= Paseo) Av(e).

p.o. abr = por orden.

población [poblásyon'] nf population; (pueblo, ciudad) town, city; ~ **activa** working population.

poblado, a [poblá'tho, á] a inhabited; (barba) thick; (cejas) bushy ♦ nm (aldea) village; (pueblo) (small) town; ~ **de** (lle-no) filled with; **densamente** ~ densely populated.

poblador, a [poblátʰor', á] nm/f settler, colonist.

poblar [poblár'] vt (colonizar) to colonize; (fundar) to found; (habitar) to inhabit; ~**se** vr: ~**se de** to fill up with; (irse cubriendo) to become covered with.

pobre [po'bre] a poor ♦ nm/f poor person; (mendigo) beggar; **los** ~**s** the poor; ¡~! poor thing!; ~ **diablo** (fig) poor wretch o devil.

pobreza [pobre'sá] nf poverty.

pocilga [posēl'ɡá] nf pigsty.

pócima [po'sēmá], **poción** [posyon'] nf potion; (brebaje) concoction, nasty drink.

pocito [posē'to] nf (AM) coffee cup.

poco, a [po'ko, á] a little; (escaso) slight, scanty; ~**s** few ♦ ad (no mucho) little, not much ♦ nm: **un** ~ a little, a bit; **tener a uno en** ~ to think little o not think much of sb; **por** ~ almost, nearly; ~ **a** ~ little by little, gradually; **a** ~ **de hacer** shortly after doing; **dentro de** ~ (+ presente o futuro) shortly; (+ pasado) soon after; **hace** ~ a short time ago, not long ago; ~ **más o menos** more or less.

pocho, a [potch'o, á] a (flor, color) faded, discolored; (persona) pale; (fruta) over-ripe; (deprimido) depressed.

poda [po'thá] nf (acto) pruning; (temporada) pruning season.

podar [pothár'] vt to prune.

podenco [pothen'ko] nm hound.

poder [pother'] vi (sujeto: persona) to be able to, can; (permiso) can, may; (posibilidad, hipótesis) may ♦ nm (gen, JUR, POL) power; (autoridad) authority; ¡**puede!** who knows!, maybe!; **puede que sea así** it may be, maybe; ¿**se puede?** may I come in?; ¿**puedes con eso?** can you manage that?; **el dinero puede mucho** money talks; **A le puede a B** (fam) A is more than a match for B; **a más no** ~ to the utmost; **no** ~ **menos de hacer algo** not to be able to help doing sth; **no** ~ **más** to have had enough; ~ **adquisitivo** purchasing power; ~ **ejecutivo/legislativo** executive/legislative power; **estar en el** ~, **ocupar el** ~ to be in power; **por** ~(**es**) by proxy.

poderío [potherē'o] nm power; (autoridad) authority.

poderoso, a [pothero'so, á] a powerful.

podré [po'dre'] etc vb V **poder**.

podrido, a [pothrē'tho, á] a rotten, bad; (fig) rotten, corrupt.

podrir [pothrēr'] = **pudrir**.

poema [poe'má] nm poem.

poesía [poesē'á] nf poetry.

poeta [poe'tá] nm poet.

poético, a [poe'tēko, á] a poetic(al).

poetisa [poetē'sà] nf (woman) poet.

póker [po'ker] nm poker.

polaco, a [polá'ko, á] a Polish ♦ nm/f Pole ♦ nm (LING) Polish.

polar [polár'] a polar.

polarice [polárē'se] etc vb V **polarizar.**

polaridad [polárēṭhàṭh'] nf polarity.

polarizar [polárēsár'] vt to polarize.

polea [pole'á] nf pulley.

polémica [pole'mēkà] nf polemics sg; (una ~) controversy.

polemice [poleme'se] etc vb V **polemizar.**

polémico, a [pole'mēko, á] a polemic(al).

polemizar [polemēsár'] vi to indulge in a polemic, argue.

polen [po'len] nm pollen.

poli [po'lē] nm (fam) cop (fam) ♦ nf: **la ~** the cops pl (fam).

policía [polēsē'á] nm/f policeman/woman ♦ nf police.

policíaco, a [polēsē'áko, á] a police cpd; **novela policíaca** detective story.

polietileno [polēetēle'no] nm polyethylene (US), polythene (Brit).

polifacético, a [polēfáse'tēko, á] a (persona, talento) many-sided, versatile.

poligamia [polēg̃á'myà] nf polygamy.

polígamo, a [polē'g̃ámo, á] a polygamous ♦ nm polygamist.

polígono [polē'g̃ono] nm (MAT) polygon; (solar) building lot; (zona) area; (unidad vecina) housing estate; **~ industrial** industrial estate.

polilla [polē'yá] nf moth.

Polinesia [polēne'syá] nf Polynesia.

polinesio, a [polēne'syo, á] a, nm/f Polynesian.

polio [po'lyo] nf polio.

Polisario [polēsá'ryo] nm abr (POL: tb: **Frente ~**)=Frente Político de Liberación del Sáhara y Río de Oro.

politécnico [polētek'nēko] nm polytechnic.

político, a [polē'tēko, á] a political; (discreto) tactful; (pariente) in-law ♦ nm/f politician ♦ nf politics sg; (económica, agraria) policy; **padre ~** father-in-law; **política exterior/de ingresos y precios** foreign/ prices and incomes policy.

politicastro [polētēkás'tro] nm (pey) politician, politico.

póliza [po'lēsá] nf certificate, voucher; (impuesto) tax o fiscal stamp; **~ de seguro(s)** insurance policy.

polizón [polēson'] nm (AVIAT, NAUT) stowaway.

polo [po'lo] nm (GEO, ELEC) pole; (helado) Popsicle ® (US), ice lolly (Brit); (DEPORTE) polo; (suéter) turtle-neck; **P~ Norte/Sur** North/South Pole; **esto es el ~ opuesto de lo que dijo antes** this is the exact opposite of what he said before.

Polonia [polo'nyá] nf Poland.

poltrona [poltro'ná] nf reclining chair, easy chair.

polución [polōōsyon'] nf pollution; **~ ambiental** environmental pollution.

polvera [polh̄e'rá] nf powder compact.

polvo [pol'h̄o] nm dust; (QUÍMICA, CULIN, MED) powder; (fam!) screw(!); **en ~** powdered; **~ de talco** talcum powder; **estar hecho ~** to be worn out o exhausted; **hacer algo ~** to smash sth; **hacer ~ a uno** to shatter sb; V tb **polvos.**

pólvora [pol'h̄orá] nf gunpowder; (fuegos artificiales) fireworks pl; **propagarse como la ~** (noticia) to spread like wildfire.

polvorosa [polh̄oro'sá] a (fam): **poner pies en ~** to beat it.

polvoriento, a [polh̄oryen'to, á] a (superficie) dusty; (sustancia) powdery.

polvos [pol'h̄os] nmpl powder sg.

pollera [poye'rá] nf (criadero) hencoop; (AM) skirt, overskirt.

pollería [poyerē'á] nf poultry shop (US), poulterer's (shop) (Brit).

pollo [po'yo] nm chicken; (joven) young man; (señorito) playboy; **~ asado** roast chicken.

pomada [pomá'ḍhá] nf pomade.

pomelo [pome'lo] nm grapefruit.

pómez [po'mes] nf: **piedra ~** pumice stone.

pompa [pom'pá] nf (burbuja) bubble; (bomba) pump; (esplendor) pomp, splendor (US), splendour (Brit); **~s funebres** funeral sg.

pomposo, a [pompo'so, á] a splendid, magnificent; (pey) pompous.

pómulo [po'mōōlo] nm cheekbone.

ponche [pontch'e] nm punch.

poncho [pontch'o] nm (AM) poncho, cape.

ponderar [ponderár'] vt (considerar) to weigh, consider; (elogiar) to praise highly, speak in praise of.

pondré [pondre'] etc vb V **poner.**

ponencia [ponen'syá] nf (exposición) (learned) paper, communication; (informe) report.

poner [poner'] vt (gen) to put; (colocar) to place, set; (ropa) to put on; (problema, la mesa) to set; (telegrama) to send; (TELEC) to connect; (RADIO, TV) to switch on, turn on; (tienda) to open, set up; (nombre) to give; (añadir) to add; (TEATRO, CINE) to put on; (+ adjetivo) to make, turn; (suponer) to suppose ♦ vi (ave) to lay (eggs); **~se** vr to put o place o.s.; (ropa) to put on; (+ adjetivo) to turn, get, become; (el sol) to set; **~ al tanto** to keep informed; **~ algo en duda** to cast doubt on sth; **~ de relieve** (INFORM) to highlight; **póngame con el Señor X** get me Mr X, put me through to Mr X; **¡no te**

pongas así! don't be like that!; ~**se cómodo** to make o.s. comfortable; ~**se delante** (*estorbar*) to get in the way; ~**se a bien con uno** to get on good terms with sb; ~**se rojo** to blush; ~**se a** to begin to; ~**se en** (*lugar*) to get to, arrive at.

ponga [pon'gá] *etc vb V* **poner.**

poniente [ponyen'te] *nm* west.

p.º n.º *abr* (= *peso neto*) nt. wt.

pontevedrés, esa [pontehetḥres', esá] *a* of *o* from Pontevedra ♦ *nm/f* native *o* inhabitant of Pontevedra.

pontificado [pontēfēká'tḥo] *nm* papacy, pontificate.

pontífice [pontē'fēse] *nm* pope, pontiff; **el Sumo P**~ His Holiness the Pope.

pontón [ponton'] *nm* pontoon.

ponzoña [ponso'nyá] *nf* poison, venom.

ponzoñoso, a [ponsonyo'so, á] *a* poisonous, venomous.

popa [po'pá] *nf* stern; **a** ~ astern, abaft; **de** ~ **a proa** fore and aft.

popular [popōōlár'] *a* popular; (*del pueblo*) of the people.

popularice [popōōláré'se] *etc vb V* **popularizarse.**

popularidad [popōōlárethaḥ'] *nf* popularity.

popularizarse [popōōlárēsár'se] *vr* to become popular.

poquísimo, a [pokē'sēmo, á] *a* (*superlativo de* **poco**) very little; (*pl*) very few; (*casi nada*) hardly any.

poquito [pokē'to] *nm*: **un** ~ a little bit ♦ *ad* a little, a bit; **a** ~**s** bit by bit.

por [por] *prep* (+ *infin*: *para*) so as to; (*a favor de, hacia*) for; (*a causa de*) out of, because of, from; (*según*) according to; (*por agencia de*) by; (*a cambio de*) for, in exchange for; (*en lugar de*) instead of, in place of; (*durante*) for; **10** ~ **10 son 100** 10 times 10 is 100; **será** ~ **poco tiempo** it won't be for long; ~ **correo/avión** by mail/plane; ~ **centenares** by the hundred; (**el**) **10** ~ **ciento** 10 percent; **en orden** in order; **ir a Bilbao** ~ **Santander** to go to Bilbao via Santander; **pasar** ~ **Madrid** to pass through Madrid; **camina** ~ **la izquierda** walk on the left; ~ **todo el país** throughout the country; **entra** ~ **delante/detrás** come/go in by the front/back (door); ~ **la calle** along the street; ~ **la mañana** in the morning; ~ **la noche** at night; **$2** ~ **hora** $2 an hour; ~ **allí** over there; **está** ~ **el norte** it's somewhere in the north; ~ **mucho que quisiera, no puedo** much as I would like to, I can't; **te doy éste** ~ **aquél** I'll swap you this one for that one; **¿**~ **qué?** why?; ~ **(lo) tanto** so, therefore; ~ **cierto** (*seguro*) certainly; (*a propósito*) by the way; ~ **ejemplo** for example; ~ **favor** please; ~

fuera/dentro outside/inside; ~ **mí ... so far as I'm concerned ...; **hazlo** ~ **mí** do it for my sake; ~ **si** (**acaso**) just in case; ~ **sí mismo** *o* **sólo** by o.s.

porcelana [porselá'ná] *nf* porcelain; (*china*) china.

porcentaje [porsentá'he] *nm* percentage; ~ **de actividad** (*INFORM*) hit rate.

porción [porsyon'] *nf* (*parte*) portion, share; (*cantidad*) quantity, amount.

porche [portch'e] *nm* (*de una plaza*) arcade; (*de casa*) porch.

pordiosear [portḥyoseár'] *vi* to beg.

pordiosero, a [portḥyose'ro, á] *nm/f* beggar.

porfía [porfē'á] *nf* persistence; (*terquedad*) obstinacy.

porfiado, a [porfyá'tḥo, á] *a* persistent; obstinate.

porfiar [porfyár'] *vi* to persist, insist; (*disputar*) to argue stubbornly.

pormenor [pormenor'] *nm* detail, particular.

pormenorice [pormenorē'se] *etc vb V* **pormenorizar.**

pormenorizar [pormenorēsár'] *vt* to (set out in) detail ♦ *vi* to go into detail.

pornografía [pornográfē'á] *nf* pornography.

poro [po'ro] *nm* pore.

poroso, a [poro'so, á] *a* porous.

poroto [poro'to] *nm* (*AM*) bean.

porque [por'ke] *conj* (*a causa de*) because; (*ya que*) since; ~ **sí** because I feel like it.

porqué [porke'] *nm* reason, cause.

porquería [porkerē'á] *nf* (*suciedad*) filth, muck, dirt; (*acción*) dirty trick; (*objeto*) small thing, trifle; (*fig*) rubbish.

porqueriza [porkerē'sá] *nf* pigsty.

porra [po'rrá] *nf* (*arma*) stick, club; (*cachiporra*) billyclub (*US*), truncheon (*Brit*); **¡**~**s!** bother!; **¡vete a la** ~**!** go to hell!

porrazo [porrá'so] *nm* (*golpe*) blow; (*caída*) bump; **de un** ~ in one fell swoop.

porrón [porron'] *nm* glass wine jar with a long spout.

port [por'(t)] *nm* (*INFORM*) port.

portada [portá'tḥá] *nf* (*TIP*) title page; (: *de revista*) cover.

portador, a [portátḥor', á] *nm/f* carrier, bearer; (*COM*) bearer, payee.

portaequipajes [portáekēpá'hes] *nm inv* trunk (*US*), boot (*Brit*); (*baca*) luggage rack.

portafolio [portáfo'lyo] *nm*: ~ **de inversiones** (*COM*) investment portfolio.

portal [portál'] *nm* (*entrada*) vestibule, hall; (*pórtico*) porch, doorway; (*puerta de entrada*) main door; (*DEPORTE*) goal; ~**es** *nmpl* arcade *sg*.

portaligas [portálē'gás] *nm inv* garter (*US*) *o* suspender (*Brit*) belt.

portamaletas |portámále'tàs| *nm inv* roof rack.

portamonedas |portámone'tħás| *nm inv* purse.

portar |portár'| *vt* to carry, bear; ~**se** *vr* to behave, conduct o.s.; ~**se mal** to misbehave; **se portó muy bien conmigo** he treated me very well.

portátil |portá'tēl| *a* portable.

portaviones |portáħyo'nes| *nm inv* aircraft carrier.

portavoz |portáħos'| *nm/f* spokesman/woman.

portazo |portá'so| *nm*: **dar un** ~ to slam the door.

porte |por'te| *nm (COM)* transport; *(precio)* freight charges *pl*; *(CORREOS)* postage; ~ **debido** *(COM)* freight C.O.D.; ~ **pagado** *(COM)* post-paid.

portento |porten'to| *nm* marvel, wonder.

portentoso, a |portento'so, á| *a* marvellous, extraordinary.

porteño, a |porte'nyo, á| *a* of *o* from Buenos Aires ♦ *nm/f* native *o* inhabitant of Buenos Aires.

portería |porterē'á| *nf (oficina)* porter's office; *(gol)* goal.

portero, a |porte'ro, á| *nm/f* porter; *(conserje)* caretaker; *(DEPORTE)* goalkeeper.

pórtico |por'tēko| *nm (porche)* portico, porch; *(fig)* gateway; *(arcada)* arcade.

portilla |portē'yá| *nf*, **portillo** |portē'yo| *nm* gate.

portorriqueño, a |portorrēke'nyo, á| *a*, *nm/f* Puerto Rican.

portuario, a |portwá'ryo| *a (del puerto)* port *cpd*; *(del muelle)* dock *cpd*; **trabajador** ~ stevedore.

Portugal |portōōgál'| *nm* Portugal.

portugués, esa |portōōges', esá| *a*, *nm/f* Portuguese ♦ *nm (LING)* Portuguese.

porvenir |porħenēr'| *nm* future.

pos |pos| **en** ~ **de**: *prep* after, in pursuit of.

posada |posá'ħá| *nf (refugio)* shelter, lodging; *(mesón)* guest house; **dar** ~ **a** to give shelter to, take in.

posaderas |posáħe'rás| *nfpl* backside *sg*, buttocks.

posar |posár| *vt (en el suelo)* to lay down, put down; *(la mano)* to place, put gently ♦ *vi* to sit, pose; ~**se** *vr* to settle; *(pájaro)* to perch; *(avión)* to land, come down.

posdata |posħá'tá| *nf* postscript.

pose |po'se| *nf (ARTE, afectación)* pose.

poseedor, a |poseēħor', á| *nm/f* owner, possessor; *(de récord, puesto)* holder.

poseer |poseer'| *vt* to have, possess, own; *(ventaja)* to enjoy; *(récord, puesto)* to hold.

poseído, a |poseē'ħo, á| *a* possessed; **estar muy** ~ **de** to be very vain about.

posesión |posesyon'| *nf* possession; **tomar**

~ **(de)** to take over.

posesionarse |posesyonár'se| *vr*: ~ **de** to take possession of, take over.

posesivo, a |posesē'ħo, á| *a* possessive.

poseyendo |poseyen'do| *etc vb V* **poseer**.

posibilidad |posēħēlēħáħ'| *nf* possibility; *(oportunidad)* chance.

posibilitar |posēħēlētár'| *vt* to make possible, permit; *(hacer factible)* to make feasible.

posible |posē'ħle| *a* possible; *(factible)* feasible ♦ *nm*: ~**s** means; *(bienes)* funds, assets; **de ser** ~ if possible; **en** *o* **dentro de lo** ~ as far as possible; **lo antes** ~ as quickly as possible.

posición |posēsyon'| *nf (gen)* position; *(rango social)* status.

positivo, a |posētē'ħo, á| *a* positive ♦ *nf (FOTO)* print.

poso |po'so| *nm* sediment.

posponer |posponer'| *vt* to put behind *o* below; *(aplazar)* to postpone.

posponga |despon'gá| *etc*, **pospuesto** |pospwe'sto|, **pospuse** |pospōō'se| *etc vb V* **posponer**.

posta |po'stá| *nf (de caballos)* relay, team; **a** ~ on purpose, deliberately.

postal |postál'| *a* postal ♦ *nf* postcard.

poste |po'ste| *nm (de telégrafos)* post, pole; *(columna)* pillar.

postergar |postergár'| *vt (esp AM)* to put off, postpone, delay.

postergue |poster'ge| *etc vb V* **postergar**.

posteridad |posterēħáħ'| *nf* posterity.

posterior |posteryor'| *a* back, rear; *(siguiente)* following, subsequent; *(más tarde)* later; **ser** ~ **a** to be later than.

posterioridad |posteryorēħáħ'| *nf*: **con** ~ later, subsequently.

postgraduado, a |postgráħwá'ħo, á| *a*, *nm/f* postgraduate.

pos(t)guerra |pos(t)ge'rrá| *nf* postwar period; **en la** ~ after the war.

postigo |postē'go| *nm (portillo)* postern; *(contraventana)* shutter.

postín |postēn'| *nm (fam)* elegance; **de** ~ posh; **darse** ~ to show off.

postizo, a |postē'so, á| *a* false, artificial; *(sonrisa)* false, phoney ♦ *nm* hairpiece.

postor, a |postor', á| *nm/f* bidder; **mejor** ~ highest bidder.

postrado, a |postrá'ħo, á| *a* prostrate.

postrar |postrár'| *vt (derribar)* to cast down, overthrow; *(humillar)* to humble; *(MED)* to weaken, exhaust.

postre |pos'tre| *nm* sweet, dessert ♦ *nf*: **a la** ~ in the end, when all is said and done; **para** ~ *(fam)* to top it off; **llegar a los** ~**s** *(fig)* to come too late.

postrero, a |postre'ro, á| *a (delante de nmsg*: **postrer**: *último)* last; (: *que viene* *detrás*) rear.

postrimerías [postrēmerē'ás] *nf,,l* final stages.

postulado [postoōlá'tho] *nm* postulate.

postulante [postoōlán'te] *nm/f* petitioner; (*REL*) postulant.

póstumo, a [po'stōōmo, á] *a* posthumous.

postura [postoō'rá] *nf* (*del cuerpo*) posture, position; (*fig*) attitude, position.

post-venta [poshen'tá] *a* (*COM*) after-sales.

potable [potá'hle] *a* drinkable.

potaje [potá'he] *nm* thick vegetable soup.

pote [po'te] *nm* pot, jar.

potencia [poten'syá] *nf* power; (*capacidad*) capacity; ~ (**en caballos**) horsepower; **en** ~ potential, in the making; **las grandes** ~**s** the great powers.

potencial [potensyál'] *a, nm* potential.

potenciar [potensyár'] *vt* (*promover*) to promote; (*fortalecer*) to boost.

potente [poten'te] *a* powerful.

potestad [potestáth'] *nf* authority; **patria** ~ paternal authority.

potosí [potosē'] *nm* fortune; **cuesta un** ~ it costs the earth.

potra [po'trá] *nf* (*ZOOL*) filly; **tener** ~ to be lucky.

potro [po'tro] *nm* (*ZOOL*) colt; (*DEPORTE*) vaulting horse.

pozo [po'so] *nm* well; (*de río*) deep pool; (*de mina*) shaft; ~ **negro** cesspool; **ser un** ~ **de ciencia** (*fig*) to be deeply learned.

PP *abr* (= *por poderes*) pp; (= *porte pagado*) postage paid.

p.p.m. *abr* (= *palabras por minuto*) wpm.

práctica [prák'tēká] *nf V* **práctico.**

practicable [práktēká'hle] *a* practicable; (*camino*) passable, usable.

practicante [práktēkán'te] *nm/f* (*MED*: *ayudante de doctor*) medical assistant; (: *enfermero*) nurse; (*quien practica algo*) practitioner ♦ *a* practicing (*US*), practising (*Brit*).

practicar [práktēkár'] *vt* to practice (*US*), practise (*Brit*); (*deporte*) to go in for, play; (*ejecutar*) to carry out, perform.

práctico, a [prák'tēko, á] *a* (*gen*) practical; (*conveniente*) handy; (*instruído*: *persona*) skilled, expert ♦ *nf* practice; (*método*) method; (*arte, capacidad*) skill; **en la práctica** in practice.

practique [práktē'ke] *etc vb V* **practicar.**

pradera [práthe'rá] *nf* meadow; (*en EE.UU.*) prairie.

prado [prá'tho] *nm* (*campo*) meadow, field; (*pastizal*) pasture.

Praga [prá'gá] *nf* Prague.

pragmático, a [prágmá'tēko, á] *a* pragmatic.

preámbulo [preám'boōlo] *nm* preamble, introduction; **decir algo sin** ~**s** to say

sth without beating about the bush.

precalentar [prekálentár'] *vt* to preheat.

precaliente [prekályen'te] *etc vb V* **precalentar.**

precario, a [preká'ryo, á] *a* precarious.

precaución [prekáōōsyon'] *nf* (*medida preventiva*) preventive measure, precaution; (*prudencia*) caution, wariness.

precaver [prekáher'] *vt* to guard against; (*impedir*) to forestall; ~**se** *vr*: ~**se de** *o* **contra algo** to (be on one's) guard against sth.

precavido, a [prekáhē'tho, á] *a* cautious, wary.

precedencia [presethen'syá] *nf* precedence; (*prioridad*) priority; (*superioridad*) greater importance, superiority.

precedente [presethen'te] *a* preceding; (*anterior*) former ♦ *nm* precedent; **sin** ~(**s**) unprecedented; **establecer** *o* **sentar un** ~ to establish *o* set a precedent.

preceder [presether'] *vt, vi* to precede, go/come before.

precepto [presep'to] *nm* precept.

preceptor [preseptor'] *nm* (*maestro*) teacher; (: *particular*) tutor.

preciado, a [presyá'tho, á] *a* (*estimado*) esteemed, valuable.

preciar [presyár'] *vt* to esteem, value; ~**se** *vr* to boast; ~**se de** to pride o.s. on.

precinto [presēn'to] *nm* (*COM*: *tb*: ~ **de garantía**) seal.

precio [pre'syo] *nm* (*de mercado*) price; (*costo*) cost; (*valor*) value, worth; (*de viaje*) fare; ~ **de coste** *o* **de cobertura** cost price; ~ **al contado** cash price; ~ **al detalle** *o* **al por menor** retail price; ~ **al detallista** wholesale price; ~ **de entrega inmediata** spot price; ~ **de oferta** offer price; ~ **de oportunidad** bargain price; ~ **de salida** minimum price; ~ **tope** top price; ~ **unitario** unit price; **no tener** ~ (*fig*) to be priceless; **"no importa** ~**"** "cost no object".

preciosidad [presyosētháth'] *nf* (*valor*) (high) value, (great) worth; (*encanto*) charm; (*cosa bonita*) beautiful thing; **es una** ~ it's lovely, it's really beautiful.

precioso, a [presyo'so, á] *a* precious; (*de mucho valor*) valuable; (*fam*) lovely, beautiful.

precipicio [presēpē'syo] *nm* cliff, precipice; (*fig*) abyss.

precipitación [presēpētásyon'] *nf* (*prisa*) haste; (*lluvia*) rainfall; (*QUÍMICA*) precipitation.

precipitado, a [presēpētá'tho, á] *a* hasty, rash; (*salida*) hasty, sudden ♦ *nm* (*QUÍMICA*) precipitate.

precipitar [presēpētár'] *vt* (*arrojar*) to hurl, throw; (*apresurar*) to hasten; (*acelerar*) to speed up, accelerate; (*QUÍMICA*) to precipitate; ~se *vr* to throw o.s.; (*apresurarse*) to rush; (*actuar sin pensar*) to act rashly; ~se hacia to rush towards.

precisado, a [presēsá'tho, á] *a*: **verse ~ a hacer algo** to be obliged to do sth.

precisamente [presēsámen'te] *ad* precisely; (*justo*) precisely, exactly, just; ~ **por eso** for that very reason; ~ **fue él quien lo dijo** as a matter of fact he said it; **no es eso** ~ it's not really that.

precisar [presēsár'] *vt* (*necesitar*) to need, require; (*fijar*) to determine exactly, fix; (*especificar*) to specify; (*señalar*) to pinpoint.

precisión [presēsyon'] *nf* (*exactitud*) precision.

preciso, a [presē'so, á] *a* (*exacto*) precise; (*necesario*) necessary, essential; (*estilo, lenguaje*) concise; **es ~ que lo hagas** you must do it.

precocidad [prekosētháth'] *nf* precociousness, precocity.

preconcebido, a [prekonsehē'tho, á] *a* preconceived.

preconice [prekonē'se] *etc vb V* **preconizar.**

preconizar [prekonēsár'] *vt* (*aconsejar*) to advise; (*prever*) to foresee.

precoz [prekos'] *a* (*persona*) precocious; (*calvicie*) premature.

precursor, a [prekōōrsor', á] *nm/f* precursor.

predecir [prethesēr'] *vt* to predict, foretell, forecast.

predestinado, a [prethestēná'tho, á] *a* predestined.

predeterminar [prethetermēnár'] *vt* to predetermine.

prédica [pre'thēká] *nf* sermon.

predicador, a [prethēkáthor', á] *nm/f* preacher.

predicar [prethēkár'] *vt, vi* to preach.

predicción [prethēksyon'] *nf* prediction; (*pronóstico*) forecast; ~ **del tiempo** weather forecast(ing).

predicho [prethētch'o], **prediga** [prethē'gá] *etc*, **predije** [prethē'he] *etc vb V* **predecir.**

predilecto, a [prethēlek'to, á] *a* favorite (*US*), favourite (*Brit*).

predio [pre'thyo] *nm* property, estate.

predique [prethē'ke] *etc vb V* **predicar.**

prediré [prethēre'] *etc vb V* **predecir.**

predispondré [prethēspondre'] *etc vb V* **predisponer.**

predisponer [prethēsponer'] *vt* to predispose; (*pey*) to prejudice.

predisponga [prethēspon'gá] *etc vb V* **predisponer.**

predisposición [prethēsposēsyon'] *nf* predisposition, inclination; prejudice, bias; (*MED*) tendency.

predispuesto [prethēspwe'sto], **predispuse** [prethēspōō'se] *etc vb V* **predisponer.**

predominante [prethomēnán'te] *a* predominant; (*preponderante*) prevailing; (*interés*) controlling.

predominar [prethomēnár'] *vt* to dominate ♦ *vi* to predominate; (*prevalecer*) to prevail.

predominio [prethomē'nyo] *nm* predominance; prevalence.

preescolar [preeskolár'] *a* preschool.

preestreno [preestre'no] *nm* preview, press view.

prefabricado, a [prefábrēká'tho, á] *a* prefabricated.

prefacio [prefá'syo] *nm* preface.

preferencia [preferen'syá] *nf* preference; **de ~** preferably; **localidad de ~** reserved seat.

preferible [preferē'ble] *a* preferable.

preferir [preferēr'] *vt* to prefer.

prefiera [prefye'rá] *etc vb V* **preferir.**

prefijo [prefē'ho] *nm* prefix.

prefiriendo [prefēryen'do] *etc vb V* **preferir.**

pregón [pregon'] *nm* proclamation, announcement.

pregonar [pregonár'] *vt* to proclaim, announce; (*mercancía*) to hawk.

pregonero [pregone'ro] *nm* town crier.

pregunta [pregōōn'tá] *nf* question; ~ **capciosa** catch question; **hacer una ~** to ask a question.

preguntar [pregōōntár'] *vt* to ask; (*cuestionar*) to question ♦ *vi* to ask; ~se *vr* to wonder; ~ **por uno** to ask for sb; ~ **por la salud de uno** to ask after sb's health.

preguntón, ona [pregōōnton', oná] *a* inquisitive.

prehistórico, a [preēsto'rēko, á] *a* prehistoric.

prejuicio [prehwē'syo] *nm* prejudgement; (*preconcepción*) preconception; (*pey*) prejudice, bias.

prejuzgar [prehōōsgár'] *vt* (*predisponer*) to prejudge.

prejuzgue [prehōōs'ge] *etc vb V* **prejuzgar.**

preliminar [prelēmēnár'] *a, nm* preliminary.

preludio [prelōō'thyo] *nm* (*MUS, fig*) prelude.

prematuro, a [prematōō'ro, á] *a* premature.

premeditación [premethētásyon'] *nf* premeditation.

premeditado, a [premethētá'tho, á] *a* premeditated, deliberate; (*intencionado*) wilful.

premeditar [premethētár'] *vt* to premeditate.

premiar [premyár'] *vt* to reward; (*en un concurso*) to give a prize to.

premio [pre'myo] *nm* reward; prize; (*COM*) premium; ~ **gordo** first prize.

premonición [premonēsyon'] *nf* premonition.

premura [premōō'rá] *nf* (*prisa*) haste, urgency.

prenatal [prenátál'] *a* antenatal, prenatal.

prenda [pren'dá] *nf* (*ropa*) garment, article of clothing; (*garantía*) pledge; (*fam*) darling!; ~s *nfpl* talents, gifts; **dejar algo en** ~ to pawn sth; **no soltar** ~ to give nothing away; (*fig*) not to say a word.

prendar [prendár'] *vt* to captivate, enchant; ~**se de algo** to fall in love with sth.

prendedor [prendeṭhor'] *nm* broach (*US*), brooch (*Brit*).

prender [prender'] *vt* (*captar*) to catch, capture; (*detener*) to arrest; (*coser*) to pin, attach; (*sujetar*) to fasten ♦ *vi* to catch; (*arraigar*) to take root; ~**se** *vr* (*encenderse*) to catch fire.

prendido, a [prendē'ḍho, á] *a* (*AM: luz etc*) on.

prensa [pren'sá] *nf* press; **la P**~ the press; **tener mala** ~ to have *o* get a bad press; **la** ~ **nacional** the national press.

prensar [prensár'] *vt* to press.

preñado, a [prenyá'ḍho, á] *a* (*mujer*) pregnant; ~ **de** pregnant with, full of.

preñez [prenyes'] *nf* pregnancy.

preocupación [preokōōpásyon'] *nf* worry, concern; (*ansiedad*) anxiety.

preocupado, a [preokōōpá'ḍho, á] *a* worried, concerned; anxious.

preocupar [preokōōpár'] *vt* to worry; ~**se** *vr* to worry; ~**se de algo** (*hacerse cargo*) to take care of sth; ~**se por algo** to worry about sth.

preparación [prepárásyon'] *nf* (*acto*) preparation; (*estado*) preparedness, readiness; (*entrenamiento*) training.

preparado, a [prepárá'ḍho, á] *a* (*dispuesto*) prepared; (*CULIN*) ready (to serve) ♦ *nm* (*MED*) preparation; ¡~**s, listos, ya!** ready, set (*US*) *o* steady (*Brit*), go!

preparar [preparár'] *vt* (*disponer*) to prepare, get ready; (*TEC: tratar*) to prepare, process, treat; (*entrenar*) to teach, train; ~**se** *vr*: ~**se a** *o* **para hacer algo** to prepare *o* get ready to do sth.

preparativo, a [preparátē'ḥo] *a* preparatory, preliminary ♦ *nm*: ~**s** preparations.

preparatoria [preparáto'ryá] *n* (*AM*) senior high school (*US*), sixth form college (*Brit*).

prerrogativa [prerrogátē'ḥá] *nf* prerogative, privilege.

presa [pre'sá] *nf* (*cosa apresada*) catch; (*víctima*) victim; (*de animal*) prey; (*de agua*) dam; **hacer** ~ **en** to clutch (on to), seize; **ser** ~ **de** (*fig*) to be a prey to.

presagiar [presáhyár'] *vt* to threaten.

presagio [presá'hyo] *nm* omen.

presbítero [presḥē'tero] *nm* priest.

prescindir [presēnder'] *vi*: ~ **de** (*privarse de*) to do without, go without; (*descartar*) to dispense with; **no podemos** ~ **de él** we can't manage without him.

prescribir [preskrēḥēr'] *vt* to prescribe.

prescripción [preskrēpsyon'] *nf* prescription; ~ **facultativa** medical prescription.

prescrito [preskrē'to] *pp de* **prescribir**.

preseleccionar [preseleksyonár'] *vt* (*DEPORTE*) to seed.

presencia [presen'syá] *nf* presence; **en** ~ **de** in the presence of.

presencial [presensyál'] *a*: **testigo** ~ eyewitness.

presenciar [presensyár'] *vt* to be present at; (*asistir a*) to attend; (*ver*) to see, witness.

presentación [presentásyon'] *nf* presentation; (*introducción*) introduction.

presentador, a [presēntáḥor', á] *nm/f* master of ceremonies (*US*), compère (*Brit*).

presentar [presentár'] *vt* to present; (*ofrecer*) to offer; (*mostrar*) to show, display; (*renuncia*) to tender; (*moción*) to propose; (*a una persona*) to introduce; ~**se** *vr* (*llegar inesperadamente*) to appear, turn up; (*ofrecerse: como candidato*) to run, stand; (*aparecer*) to show, appear; (*solicitar empleo*) to apply; ~ **al cobro** (*COM*) to present for payment; ~**se a la policía** to report to the police.

presente [presen'te] *a* present ♦ *nm* present; (*LING*) present (tense); (*regalo*) gift; **los** ~**s** those present; **hacer** ~ to state, declare; **tener** ~ to remember, bear in mind; **la carta** ~, **la** ~ this letter.

presentimiento [presentēmyen'to] *nm* premonition, presentiment.

presentir [presentēr'] *vt* to have a premonition of.

preservación [preserḥásyon'] *nf* protection, preservation.

preservar [preserḥár'] *vt* to protect, preserve.

preservativo [preserḥátē'ḥo] *nm* condom.

presidencia [presēḥen'syá] *nf* presidency; (*de comité*) chairmanship; **ocupar la** ~ to preside, be in *o* take the chair.

presidente [presēḥen'te] *nm/f* president; chairman/woman; (*en parlamento*) speaker; (*JUR*) presiding magistrate.

presidiario [presēḥyá'ryo] *nm* convict.

presidio [presē'ḥyo] *nm* prison, penitentiary.

presidir [presēḥēr'] *vt* (*dirigir*) to preside at, preside over; (: *comité*) to take the chair at; (*dominar*) to dominate, rule ♦ *vi* to preside; to take the chair.

presienta [presyen'tá] *etc*, **presintiendo** [presēntyen'do] *etc vb V* **presentir**.

presión [presyon'] *nf* pressure; ~ **arterial** *o*

sanguínea blood pressure; **a** ~ under pressure.

presionar [presyonár'] *vt* to press; (*botón*) to push, press; (*fig*) to press, put pressure on ♦ *vi*: ~ **para** *o* **por** to press for.

preso, a [pre'so, á] *a*: **estar** ~ **de terror** *o* **pánico** to be panic-stricken ♦ *nm/f* prisoner; **tomar** *o* **llevar** ~ **a uno** to arrest sb, take sb prisoner.

prestación [prestásyon'] *nf* (*aportación*) lending; (*INFORM*) capability; ~ **de juramento** oath-taking; ~ **personal** obligatory service.

prestado, a [prestá'tho, á] *a* on loan; **dar algo** ~ to lend sth; **pedir** ~ to borrow.

prestamista [prestáme'stá] *nm/f* moneylender.

préstamo [pre'stámo] *nm* loan; ~ **con garantía** loan against collateral; ~ **hipotecario** mortgage.

prestar [prestár'] *vt* to lend, loan; (*atención*) to pay; (*ayuda*) to give; (*servicio*) to do, render; (*juramento*) to take, swear; ~**se** *vr* (*ofrecerse*) to offer *o* volunteer.

prestatario, a [prestátá'ryo, á] *nm/f* borrower.

presteza [preste'sá] *nf* speed, promptness.

prestidigitador [prestēthēhētáthor'] *nm* magician.

prestigio [prestē'hyo] *nm* prestige; (*reputación*) face; (*renombre*) good name.

prestigioso, a [prestēhyo'so, á] *a* (*honorable*) prestigious; (*famoso, renombrado*) renowned, famous.

presto, a [pre'sto, á] *a* (*rápido*) quick, prompt; (*dispuesto*) ready ♦ *ad* at once, right away.

presumido, a [presōōmē'tho, á] *a* conceited.

presumir [presōōmēr'] *vt* to presume ♦ *vi* (*tener aires*) to be conceited; **según cabe** ~ as may be presumed, presumably; ~ **de listo** to think o.s. very smart.

presunción [presōōnsyon'] *nf* presumption; (*sospecha*) suspicion; (*vanidad*) conceit.

presunto, a [presōōn'to, á] *a* (*supuesto*) supposed, presumed; (*así llamado*) so-called.

presuntuoso, a [presōōntwo'so, á] *a* conceited, presumptuous.

presupondré [presōōpondre'] *etc vb* V **presuponer.**

presuponer [presōōponer'] *vt* to presuppose.

presuponga [presōōpon'gá] *etc vb* V **presuponer.**

presupuestar [presōōpwestár'] *vi* to budget ♦ *vt*: ~ **algo** to budget for sth.

presupuestario, a [presōōpwestá'ryo, á] *a* (*FINANZAS*) budgetary, budget *cpd*.

presupuesto [presōōpwe'sto] *pp de* **presu-**

poner ♦ *nm* (*FINANZAS*) budget; (*estimación: de costo*) estimate; **asignación de** ~ (*COM*) budget appropriation.

presupuse [presōōpōō'se] *etc vb* V **presuponer.**

presuroso, a [presōō'ro'so, á] *a* (*rápido*) quick, speedy; (*que tiene prisa*) hasty.

pretencioso, a [pretensyo'so, á] *a* pretentious.

pretender [pretender'] *vt* (*intentar*) to try to, seek to; (*reivindicar*) to claim; (*buscar*) to seek, try for; (*cortejar*) to woo, court; ~ **que** to expect that; **¿qué pretende usted?** what are you after?

pretendiente [pretendyen'te] *nm/f* (*candidato*) candidate, applicant; (*amante*) suitor.

pretensión [pretensyon'] *nf* (*aspiración*) aspiration; (*reivindicación*) claim; (*orgullo*) pretension.

pretérito, a [prete'rēto, á] *a* (*LING*) past; (*fig*) past, former.

pretextar [pretekstár'] *vt* to plead, use as an excuse.

pretexto [pretek'sto] *nm* pretext; (*excusa*) excuse; **so** ~ **de** under pretext of.

pretil [pretēl'] *nm* (*valla*) parapet; (*baranda*) handrail.

prevalecer [prebáleser'] *vi* to prevail.

prevaleciente [prebálesyen'te] *a* prevailing, prevalent.

prevalezca [prebáles'ká] *etc vb* V **prevalecer.**

prevención [prebensyon'] *nf* (*preparación*) preparation; (*estado*) preparedness, readiness; (*medida*) prevention; (*previsión*) foresight, forethought; (*precaución*) precaution.

prevendré [prebendre'] *etc*, **prevenga** [preben'gá] *etc vb* V **prevenir.**

prevenido, a [prebenē'tho, á] *a* prepared, ready; (*cauteloso*) cautious; **estar** ~ (*preparado*) to be ready; **ser** ~ (*cuidadoso*) to be cautious; **hombre** ~ **vale por dos** forewarned is forearmed.

prevenir [prebenēr'] *vt* (*impedir*) to prevent; (*prever*) to foresee, anticipate; (*predisponer*) to prejudice, bias; (*avisar*) to warn; (*preparar*) to prepare, get ready; ~**se** *vr* to get ready, prepare; ~**se contra** to take precautions against.

preventivo, a [prebentē'ho, á] *a* preventive, precautionary.

prever [preber'] *vt* to foresee; (*anticipar*) to anticipate.

previniendo [prebēnyen'do] *etc vb* V **prevenir.**

previo, a [pre'hyo, á] *a* (*anterior*) previous, prior ♦ *prep*: ~ **acuerdo de los otros** subject to the agreement of the others; ~ **pago de los derechos** on payment of the fees.

previsible |prɔbēsē'hle| a foreseeable.

previsión |prɔbēsyon'| nf (perspicacia) foresight; (predicción) forecast; (prudencia) caution; ~ **de ventas** (COM) sales forecast.

previsor, a |prɔbēsor', á| a (precavido) farsighted; (prudente) thoughtful.

previsto |prɔbē'sto| pp de **prever**.

prieto, a |prye'to, á| a (oscuro) dark; (fig) stingy; (comprimido) tight, compressed.

prima |prē'má| nf V **primo**.

primacía |prēmásē'á| nf primacy.

primar |prēmár'| vi (tener primacía) to occupy first place; ~ **sobre** to have priority over.

primario, a |prēmá'ryo, á| a primary.

primavera |prēmáhe'rá| nf (temporada) spring; (período) springtime.

primaveral |prēmáherál'| a spring cpd, springlike.

primero, a |prēme'ro, á| a (delante de nmsg: **primer**) first; (fig) prime; (anterior) former; (básico) fundamental ♦ ad first; (más bien) sooner, rather ♦ nf (AUTO) first gear; (FERRO) first class; **de primera** (fam) first-class, first-rate; **de buenas a primeras** suddenly; **primera dama** (TEATRO) leading lady.

primicias |prēmē'syàs| nfpl first fruits (tb fig).

primitivo, a |prēmētē'ho, á| a primitive; (original) original; (COM: acción) ordinary.

primo, a |prē'mo, á| a (MAT) prime ♦ nm/f cousin; (fam) fool, dupe ♦ nf (COM) bonus; (seguro) premium; (a la exportación) subsidy; ~ **hermano** first cousin; **materias primas** raw materials; **hacer el** ~ to be taken for a ride.

primogénito, a |prēmohe'nēto, á| a firstborn.

primordial |prēmorthyál'| a basic, fundamental.

primoroso, a |prēmoro'so, á| a exquisite, fine.

princesa |prēnse'sà| nf princess.

principado |prēnsēpá'tho| nm principality.

principal |prēnsēpál'| a principal, main; (más destacado) foremost; (piso) second (US), first (Brit); (INFORM) foreground ♦ nm (jefe) chief, principal.

príncipe |prēn'sēpe| nm prince; ~ **heredero** crown prince; ~ **de gales** (tela) check.

principiante |prēnsēpyán'te| nm/f beginner; (novato) novice.

principiar |prēnsēpyár'| vt to begin.

principio |prēnsē'pyo| nm (comienzo) beginning, start; (origen) origin; (base) rudiment, basic idea; (moral) principle; **a ~s de** at the beginning of; **desde el** ~ from the first; **en un** ~ at first.

pringar |prēngár'| vt (CULIN: pan) to dip; (ensuciar) to dirty; ~**se** vr to get splashed o soiled; ~ **a uno en un asunto** (fam) to involve sb in a matter.

pringoso, a |prēngo'so, á| a greasy; (pegajoso) sticky.

pringue |prēn'ge| etc vb V **pringar** ♦ nm (grasa) grease, fat, dripping.

prioridad |prēorētháth'| nf priority; (AUTO) right of way.

prioritario, a |prēorētá'ryo, á| a (INFORM) foreground.

prisa |prē'sá| nf (apresuramiento) hurry, haste; (rapidez) speed; (urgencia) (sense of) urgency; **correr** ~ to be urgent; **darse** ~ to hurry up; **estar de** o **tener** ~ to be in a hurry.

prisión |prēsyon'| nf (cárcel) prison; (período de cárcel) imprisonment.

prisionero, a |prēsyone'ro, á| nm/f prisoner.

prismáticos |prēsmá'tēkos| nmpl binoculars.

privación |prēbásyon'| nf deprivation; (falta) want, privation; **privaciones** nfpl hardships, privations.

privado, a |prēbá'tho, á| a (particular) private; (POL: favorito) favorite (US), favourite (Brit); **en** ~ privately, in private; "~ **y confidencial**" "private and confidential".

privar |prēbár'| vt to deprive; ~**se** vr: ~**se de** (abstenerse) to deprive o.s. of; (renunciar) to give up.

privativo, a |prēbátē'ho, á| a exclusive.

privilegiado, a |prēbēlchyá'tho, á| a privileged; (memoria) very good ♦ nm/f (afortunado) privileged person.

privilegiar |prēbēlchyár'| vt to grant a privilege to; (favorecer) to favor (US), favour (Brit).

privilegio |prēbēle'hyo| nm privilege; (concesión) concession.

pro |pro| nm o nf profit, advantage ♦ prep: **asociación** ~ **ciegos** association for the blind ♦ pref: ~ **soviético/americano** pro-Soviet/-American; **en** ~ **de** on behalf of, for; **los** ~**s y los contras** the pros and cons.

proa |pro'á| nf (NAUT) bow, prow.

probabilidad |probáhēlētháth'| nf probability, likelihood; (oportunidad, posibilidad) chance, prospect.

probable |probá'hle| a probable, likely; **es** ~ **que** + subjun it is probable o likely that; **es** ~ **que no venga** he probably won't come.

probador |probáthor'| nm (persona) taster (of wine etc); (en una tienda) fitting room.

probar |probár'| vt (demostrar) to prove; (someter a prueba) to test, try out; (ropa) to try on; (comida) to taste ♦ vi to try; ~**se** vr: ~**se un traje** to try on a suit.

probeta [proḥe'tá] *nf* test tube.
problema [proḥle'má] *nm* problem.
procaz [prokás'] *a* insolent, impudent.
procedencia [proseḥen'syá] *nf* (*principio*) source, origin; (*lugar de salida*) point of departure.
procedente [proseḥen'te] *a* (*razonable*) reasonable; (*conforme a derecho*) proper, fitting; ~ **de** coming from, originating in.
proceder [proseḥer'] *vi* (*avanzar*) to proceed; (*actuar*) to act; (*ser correcto*) to be right (and proper), be fitting ♦ *nm* (*comportamiento*) behavior, conduct; **no procede obrar así** it is not right to act like that; ~ **de** to come from, originate in.
procedimiento [proseḥemyen'to] *nm* procedure; (*proceso*) process; (*método*) means, method; (*trámite*) proceedings.
prócer [pro'ser] *nm* (*persona eminente*) worthy; (*líder*) great man, leader.
procesado, a [prosesá'ḥo, á] *nm/f* accused (person).
procesador [prosesáḥor'] *nm*: ~ **de textos** (*INFORM*) word processor.
procesamiento [prosesámyen'to] *nm* (*INFORM*) processing; ~ **de datos** data processing; ~ **por lotes** batch processing; ~ **solapado** multiprogramming; ~ **de textos** word processing.
procesar [prosesár'] *vt* to try, put on trial; (*INFORM*) to process.
procesión [prosesyon'] *nf* procession; **la ~ va por dentro** he keeps his troubles to himself.
proceso [prose'so] *nm* process; (*JUR*) trial; (*lapso*) course (of time); (*INFORM*): ~ **(automático) de datos** (automatic) data processing; ~ **no prioritario** background process; ~ **por pasadas** batch processing; ~ **en tiempo real** real-time programming.
proclama [proklá'má] *nf* (*acto*) proclamation; (*cartel*) poster.
proclamar [proklámár'] *vt* to proclaim.
proclive [proklē'ḥe] *a*: ~ **(a)** inclined *o* prone (to).
procreación [prokreasyon'] *nf* procreation.
procrear [prokreár'] *vt, vi* to procreate.
procurador, a [prokŏŏráḥor', á] *nm/f* attorney.
procurar [prokŏŏrár'] *vt* (*intentar*) to try, endeavour; (*conseguir*) to get, obtain; (*asegurar*) to secure; (*producir*) to produce.
prodigio [proḥe'hyo] *nm* prodigy; (*milagro*) wonder, marvel.
prodigioso, a [proḥehyo'so, á] *a* prodigious, marvellous.
pródigo, a [pro'ḥego, á] *a* (*rico*) rich, productive; **hijo ~** prodigal son.
producción [proḥŏŏksyon'] *nf* production; (*suma de productos*) output; (*producto*) product; ~ **en serie** mass production.

producir [proḥŏŏser'] *vt* to produce; (*generar*) to cause, bring about; (*impresión*) to give; (*COM: interés*) to bear; ~**se** *vr* (*gen*) to come about, happen; (*hacerse*) to be produced, be made; (*estallar*) to break out; (*accidente*) to take place.
productividad [proḥŏŏktcheḥáth'] *nf* productivity.
productivo, a [proḥŏŏktc'ho, á] *a* productive; (*provechoso*) profitable.
producto [proḥŏŏk'to] *nm* (*resultado*) product; (*producción*) production; ~ **alimenticio** foodstuff; ~ **(nacional) bruto** gross (national) product; ~ **interno bruto** gross domestic product.
productor, a [proḥŏŏktor', á] *a* productive, producing ♦ *nm/f* producer.
produje [proḥŏŏ'he], **produjera** [proḥŏŏhe'rá], **produzca** [proḥŏŏs'ká] *etc vb* V **producir**.
proeza [proe'sá] *nf* exploit, feat.
profanar [profánár'] *vt* to desecrate, profane.
profano, a [profá'no, á] *a* profane ♦ *nm/f* (*inexperto*) layman/woman; **soy ~ en música** I don't know anything about music.
profecía [profesē'á] *nf* prophecy.
proferir [proferēr'] *vt* (*palabra, sonido*) to utter; (*injuria*) to hurl, let fly.
profesar [profesár'] *vt* (*declarar*) to profess; (*practicar*) to practise.
profesiograma [profesyoḡrá'má] *nm* job specification.
profesión [profesyon'] *nf* profession; (*confesión*) avowal; **abogado de ~, de ~ abogado** a lawyer by profession.
profesional [profesyonál'] *a* professional.
profesor, a [profesor', á] *nm/f* teacher; (*instructor*) instructor; (~ *de universidad*) professor (*US*), lecturer (*Brit*); ~ **adjunto** associate professor (*US*), assistant lecturer (*Brit*).
profesorado [profesorá'ḥo] *nm* (*profesión*) teaching profession; (*cuerpo*) faculty; (*cargo*) professorship.
profeta [profe'tá] *nm/f* prophet.
profetice [profetē'se] *etc vb* V **profetizar**.
profetizar [profetēsár'] *vt, vi* to prophesy.
profiera [profye'rá] *etc*, **profiriendo** [proferyen'do] *etc vb* V **proferir**.
profilaxis [profēlák'sēs] *nf inv* prevention.
prófugo, a [pro'fŏŏgo, á] *nm/f* fugitive; (*desertor*) deserter.
profundice [profŏŏndē'se] *etc vb* V **profundizar**.
profundidad [profŏŏndeḥáth'] *nf* depth; **tener una ~ de 30 cm** to be 30 cm deep.
profundizar [profŏŏndēsár'] *vt* (*fig*) to go deeply into, study in depth.
profundo, a [profŏŏn'do, á] *a* deep; (*misterio, pensador*) profound; **poco ~** shallow.

profusión [profōōsyon'] *nf* (*abundancia*) profusion; (*prodigalidad*) wealth.
progenie [prohe'nye] *nf* offspring.
progenitor [prohenētor'] *nm* ancestor; ~es *nmpl* (*fam*) parents.
programa [prográ'má] *nm* program (*US*), programme (*Brit*); (*INFORM*) program; ~ de estudios curriculum; ~ verificador de ortografía (*INFORM*) spelling checker.
programación [programásyon'] *nf* (*IN-FORM*) programming; ~ estructurada structured programming.
programador, a [prográmáthor', á] *nm/f* (computer) programmer; ~ de aplicaciones applications programmer.
programar [prográmár'] *vt* (*INFORM*) to program (*US*), programme (*Brit*).
programería [prográmerē'á] *nf* (*INFORM*): ~ fija firmware.
progresar [progresár'] *vi* to progress, make progress.
progresista [progresē'stá] *a, nm/f* progressive.
progresivo, a [progresē'ho, á] *a* progressive; (*gradual*) gradual; (*continuo*) continuous.
progreso [progre'so] *nm* (*tb*: ~s) progress; hacer ~s to progress, advance.
prohibición [proēhēsyon'] *nf* prohibition, ban; levantar la ~ de to remove the ban on.
prohibir [proēhēr'] *vt* to prohibit, ban, forbid; se prohíbe fumar no smoking.
prohibitivo, a [proēhētē'ho, á] *a* prohibitive.
prójimo, a [pro'hēmo, á] *nm* fellow man ♦ *nm/f* (*vecino*) neighbor (*US*), neighbour (*Brit*).
prole [pro'le] *nf* (*descendencia*) offspring.
proletariado [proletáryá'tho] *nm* proletariat.
proletario, a [proletá'ryo, á] *a, nm/f* proletarian.
proliferación [prolēferásyon'] *nf* proliferation; ~ de armas nucleares spread of nuclear arms.
proliferar [prolēferár'] *vi* to proliferate.
prolífico, a [prolē'fēko, á] *a* prolific.
prolijo, a [prolē'ho, á] *a* long-winded, tedious.
prólogo [pro'logo] *nm* prolog(ue); (*preámbulo*) preface, introduction.
prolongación [prolongásyon'] *nf* extension.
prolongado, a [prolongá'tho, á] *a* (*largo*) long; (*alargado*) lengthy.
prolongar [prolongár'] *vt* (*gen*) to extend; (*en el tiempo*) to prolong; (*calle, tubo*) to make longer, extend; ~se *vr* (*alargarse*) to extend, go on.
prolongue [prolon'ge] *etc vb* V **prolongar**.
prom. *abr* (= *promedio*) av.

promedio [prome'thyo] *nm* average; (*de distancia*) middle, mid-point.
promesa [prome'sá] *nf* promise ♦ *a:* jugador ~ promising player; faltar a una ~ to break a promise.
prometer [prometer'] *vt* to promise ♦ *vi* to show promise; ~se *vr* (*dos personas*) to get engaged.
prometido, a [prometē'tho, á] *a* promised; engaged ♦ *nm/f* fiancé/fiancée.
prominente [promēnen'te] *a* prominent.
promiscuidad [promēskwēthath'] *nf* promiscuity.
promiscuo, a [promēs'kwo, á] *a* promiscuous.
promoción [promosyon'] *nf* promotion; (*año*) class, year; ~ por correspondencia directa (*COM*) direct mail advertising (*US*) o mailshot (*Brit*); ~ de ventas sales promotion o drive.
promocionar [promosyonár'] *vt* (*COM*: *dar publicidad*) to promote.
promotor [promotor'] *nm* promoter; (*instigador*) instigator.
promover [promoher'] *vt* to promote; (*causar*) to cause; (*juicio*) to bring; (*motín*) to instigate, stir up.
promueva [promwe'há] *etc vb* V **promover**.
promulgar [promōōlgár'] *vt* to promulgate; (*fig*) to proclaim.
promulgue [promōōl'ge] *etc vb* V **promulgar**.
pronombre [pronom'bre] *nm* pronoun.
pronosticar [pronostēkár'] *vt* to predict, foretell, forecast.
pronóstico [prono'stēko] *nm* prediction, forecast; (*profecía*) omen; (*MED*: *diagnóstico*) prognosis; de ~ leve slight, not serious; ~ del tiempo weather forecast.
pronostique [pronostē'ke] *etc vb* V **pronosticar**.
prontitud [prontētōōth'] *nf* speed, quickness.
pronto, a [pron'to, á] *a* (*rápido*) prompt, quick; (*preparado*) ready ♦ *ad* quickly, promptly; (*en seguida*) at once, right away; (*dentro de poco*) soon; (*temprano*) early ♦ *nm* urge, sudden feeling; tener ~s de enojo to be quick-tempered; al ~ at first; de ~ suddenly; ¡hasta ~! see you soon!; lo más ~ posible as soon as possible; por lo ~ meanwhile, for the present; tan ~ como as soon as.
pronunciación [pronōōnsyásyon'] *nf* pronunciation.
pronunciado, a [pronōōnsyá'tho, á] *a* (*marcado*) pronounced; (*curva etc*) sharp; (*facciones*) marked.
pronunciamiento [pronōōnsyámyen'to] *nm* (*rebelión*) insurrection.
pronunciar [pronōōnsyár'] *vt* to pronounce;

(*discurso*) to make, deliver; (*JUR*: *sentencia*) to pass, pronounce; ~**se** *vr* to revolt, rise, rebel; (*declararse*) to declare o.s.; ~**se sobre** to pronounce on.

propagación |propăgăsyon'| *nf* propagation; (*difusión*) spread(ing).

propaganda |propăgăn'dă| *nf* (*política*) propaganda; (*comercial*) advertising; **hacer** ~ **de** (*COM*) to advertise.

propagar |propăgăr'| *vt* to propagate; (*difundir*) to spread, disseminate; ~**se** *vr* (*BIO*) to propagate; (*fig*) to spread.

propague |propá'ge| *etc vb* V **propagar**.

propalar |propălăr'| *vt* (*divulgar*) to divulge; (*publicar*) to publish an account of.

propasarse |propăsăr'se| *vr* (*excederse*) to go too far; (*sexualmente*) to take liberties.

propensión |propensyon'| *nf* inclination, propensity.

propenso, a |propen'so, ă| *a*: ~ **a** prone *o* inclined to; **ser** ~ **a hacer algo** to be inclined *o* have a tendency to do sth.

propiamente |propyămen'te| *ad* properly; (*realmente*) really, exactly; ~ **dicho** real, true.

propicio, a |propē'syo, ă| *a* favourable, propitious.

propiedad |propyeħáħ'| *nf* property; (*posesión*) possession, ownership; (*conveniencia*) suitability; (*exactitud*) accuracy; ~ **particular** private property; ~ **pública** (*COM*) public ownership; **ceder algo a uno en** ~ to transfer to sb the full rights over sth.

propietario, a |propyetá'ryo, ă| *nm/f* owner, proprietor.

propina |propē'nă| *nf* tip; **dar algo de** ~ to give something extra.

propinar |propenăr'| *vt* (*golpe*) to strike; (*azotes*) to give.

propio, a |pro'pyo, ă| *a* own, of one's own; (*característico*) characteristic, typical; (*conveniente*) proper; (*mismo*) selfsame, very; **el** ~ **ministro** the minister himself; **¿tienes casa propia?** have you a house of your own?; **eso es muy** ~ **de él** that's just like him; **tiene un olor muy** ~ it has a smell of its own.

propondré |propondre'| *etc vb* V **proponer**.

proponente |proponen'te| *nm* proposer, mover.

proponer |proponer'| *vt* to propose, put forward; (*candidato*) to propose, nominate; (*problema*) to pose; ~**se** *vr* to propose, plan, intend.

proponga |propon'gă| *etc vb* V **proponer**.

proporción |proporsyon'| *nf* proportion; (*MAT*) ratio; (*razón, porcentaje*) rate; **proporciones** *nfpl* dimensions; (*fig*) size *sg*; **en** ~ **con** in proportion to.

proporcionado, a |proporsyonă'ħo, ă| *a*

proportionate; (*regular*) medium, middling; (*justo*) just right; **bien** ~ well-proportioned.

proporcionar |proporsyonăr'| *vt* (*dar*) to give, supply, provide; **esto le proporciona una renta anual de** ... this brings him in a yearly income of ...

proposición |proposēsyon'| *nf* proposition; (*propuesta*) proposal.

propósito |propo'sēto| *nm* (*intención*) purpose; (*intento*) aim, intention ♦ *ad*: **a** ~ by the way, incidentally; **a** ~ **de** about, with regard to.

propuesto, a |propwe'sto, ă| *pp de* **proponer** ♦ *nf* proposal.

propulsar |propoolsăr'| *vt* to drive, propel; (*fig*) to promote, encourage.

propulsión |propoolsyon'| *nf* propulsion; ~ **a chorro** *o* **por reacción** jet propulsion.

propuse |propoo'se| *etc vb* V **proponer**.

prorrata |prorrá'tă| *nf* (*porción*) share, quota ♦ *ad* (*COM*) pro rata.

prorratear |prorrăteăr'| *vt* (*dividir*) to share out.

prórroga |pro'rrogă| *nf* (*gen*) extension; (*JUR*) stay; (*COM*) deferment.

prorrogable |prorrogá'ble| *a* which can be extended.

prorrogar |prorrogăr'| *vt* (*período*) to extend; (*decisión*) to defer, postpone.

prorrogue |prorro'ge| *etc vb* V **prorrogar**.

prorrumpir |prorroompēr'| *vi* to burst forth, break out; ~ **en gritos** to start shouting; ~ **en lágrimas** to burst into tears.

prosa |pro'să| *nf* prose.

proscribir |proskrēbēr'| *vt* to prohibit, ban; (*desterrar*) to exile, banish; (*partido*) to proscribe.

proscripción |proskrēpsyon'| *nf* prohibition, ban; banishment; proscription.

proscrito, a |proskrē'to, ă| *pp de* **proscribir** ♦ *a* (*prohibido*) banned; (*desterrado*) outlawed ♦ *nm/f* (*exilado*) exile; (*bandido*) outlaw.

prosecución |prosekoosyon'| *nf* continuation; (*persecución*) pursuit.

proseguir |prosegēr'| *vt* to continue, carry on, proceed with; (*investigación, estudio*) to pursue ♦ *vi* to continue, go on.

prosiga |prosē'gă| *etc*, **prosiguiendo** |prosēgyen'ħo| *etc vb* V **proseguir**.

prosista |prosē'stá| *nm/f* (*escritor*) prose writer.

prospección |prospeksyon'| *nf* exploration; (*del petróleo, del oro*) prospecting.

prospecto |prospek'to| *nm* prospectus; (*folleto*) leaflet, sheet of instructions.

prosperar |prosperăr'| *vi* to prosper, thrive, flourish.

prosperidad |prosperēħáħ'| *nf* prosperity; (*éxito*) success.

próspero, a [pros'pero, á] *a* prosperous, thriving, flourishing; (*que tiene éxito*) successful.

prostíbulo [prostě'ħoōlo] *nm* brothel.

prostitución [prostětoōsyon'] *nf* prostitution.

prostituir [prostětwēr'] *vt* to prostitute; ~**se** *vr* to prostitute o.s., become a prostitute.

prostituta [prostětoō'tá] *nf* prostitute.

prostituyendo [prostětoōyen'do] *etc vb V* **prostituir**.

protagonice [protáʒonē'se] *etc vb V* **protagonizar**.

protagonista [protáʒonē'stá] *nm/f* protagonist; (*LIT*: *personaje*) main character, hero(ine).

protagonizar [protáʒonēsár'] *vt* to head, take the chief role in.

protección [proteksyon'] *nf* protection.

proteccionismo [proteksyonēs'mo] *nm* (*COM*) protectionism.

protector, a [protektor'. á] *a* protective, protecting; (*tono*) patronizing ♦ *nm/f* protector; (*bienhechor*) patron; (*de la tradición*) guardian.

proteger [proteħer'] *vt* to protect; ~ **contra grabación** *o* **contra escritura** (*INFORM*) to write-protect.

protegido, a [proteħe'ħo, á] *nm/f* protégé/protégée.

proteína [protēē'ná] *nf* protein.

proteja [prote'há] *etc vb V* **proteger**.

protesta [prote'stá] *nf* protest; (*declaración*) protestation.

protestante [protestán'te] *a* Protestant.

protestar [protestár'] *vt* to protest, declare; (*fe*) to protest ♦ *vi* to protest; (*objetar*) to object; **cheque protestado por falta de fondos** insufficient funds check (*US*), cheque referred to drawer (*Brit*).

protocolo [protoko'lo] *nm* protocol; **sin ~s** (*formalismo*) informal(ly), without formalities.

prototipo [protatě'po] *nm* prototype; (*ideal*) model.

prov. *abr* (= *provincia*) prov.

provecho [proħetch'o] *nm* advantage, benefit; (*FINANZAS*) profit; **¡buen ~!** bon appétit!; **en ~ de** to the benefit of; **sacar ~ de** to benefit from, profit by.

provechoso, a [proħetcho'so, á] *a* (*ventajoso*) advantageous; (*beneficioso*) beneficial, useful; (*FINANZAS*: *lucrativo*) profitable.

proveedor, a [proħeeħor', á] *nm/f* (*abastecedor*) supplier; (*distribuidor*) dealer.

proveer [proħeer'] *vt* to provide, supply; (*preparar*) to provide, get ready; (*vacante*) to fill; (*negocio*) to transact, dispatch ♦ *vi*: ~ **a** to provide for; ~**se** *vr*: ~**se de** to provide o.s. with.

provendré [proħendre'] *etc*, **provenga**

[proħen'gá] *etc vb V* **provenir**.

provenir [proħenēr'] *vi*: ~ **de** to come from, stem from.

Provenza [proħen'sá] *nf* Provence.

proverbial [proħerħyál'] *a* proverbial; (*fig*) notorious.

proverbio [proħer'ħyo] *nm* proverb.

proveyendo [proħeyen'do] *etc vb V* **proveer**.

providencia [proħeħen'syá] *nf* providence; (*previsión*) foresight; ~**s** *nfpl* measures, steps.

provincia [proħen'syá] *nf* province; **un pueblo de ~(s)** a country town.

provinciano, a [proħēnsyá'no, á] *a* provincial; (*del campo*) country *cpd*.

proviniendo [proħēnyen'do] *etc vb V* **provenir**.

provisión [proħēsyon'] *nf* provision; (*abastecimiento*) provision, supply; (*medida*) measure, step.

provisional [proħēsyonál'] *a* provisional.

provisto, a [proħē'sto, á] *a*: ~ **de** provided *o* supplied with; (*que tiene*) having, possessing.

provocación [proħokásyon'] *nf* provocation.

provocador, a [proħokáħor', á] *a* provocative, provoking.

provocar [proħokár'] *vt* to provoke; (*alentar*) to tempt, invite; (*causar*) to bring about, lead to; (*promover*) to promote; (*estimular*) to rouse, stir, stimulate; (*protesta, explosión*) to cause, spark off; (*AM*): **¿te provoca un café?** would you like a coffee?

provocativo, a [proħokátē'ħo, á] *a* provocative.

provoque [proħo'ke] *etc vb V* **provocar**.

proxeneta [proksene'tá] *nm/f* go-between; (*de prostitutas*) pimp/procuress.

próximamente [proksēmámen'te] *ad* shortly, soon.

proximidad [proksēmēħáħ'] *nf* closeness, proximity.

próximo, a [prok'sēmo, á] *a* near, close; (*vecino*) neighbouring; (*el que viene*) next; **en fecha próxima** at an early date; **el mes ~** next month.

proyección [proyeksyon'] *nf* projection; (*CINE*) showing; (*diapositiva*) slide, transparency; (*influencia*) influence; **el tiempo de ~ es de 35 minutos** the film runs for 35 minutes.

proyectar [proyektár'] *vt* (*objeto*) to hurl, throw; (*luz*) to cast, shed; (*CINE*) to screen, show; (*planear*) to plan.

proyectil [proyektēl'] *nm* projectile, missile; ~ **(tele)dirigido** guided missile.

proyecto [proyek'to] *nm* plan; (*idea*) project; (*estimación de costo*) detailed estimate; **tener algo en ~** to be planning sth;

~ **de ley** (*POL*) bill.

proyector [proyek'tor'] *nm* (*CINE*) projector.

prudencia [proōth̲en'syà] *nf* (*sabiduría*) wisdom, prudence; (*cautela*) care.

prudente [proōth̲en'te] *a* sensible, wise, prudent; (*cauteloso*) careful.

prueba [prwe'ßà] *etc vb V* **probar** ♦ *nf* proof; (*ensayo*) test, trial; (*cantidad*) taste, sample; (*saboreo*) testing, sampling; (*de ropa*) fitting; (*DEPORTE*) event; **a** ~ **on** trial; (*COM*) on approval; **a** ~ **de** proof against; **a** ~ **de agua/fuego** waterproof/fireproof; ~ **de capacitación** (*COM*) proficiency test; ~ **de fuego** (*fig*) acid test; ~ **de vallas** hurdles; **someter a** ~ to put to the test; **¿tiene usted** ~ **de ello?** can you prove it?, do you have proof?

prurito [proōrē'to] *nm* itch; (*de bebé*) diaper (*US*) *o* nappy (*Brit*) rash; (*anhelo*) urge.

PS *nm abr* (*POL*) = *Partido Socialista*.

psico... [sēko] *pref* psycho...

psicoanálisis [sēkoànà'lēsēs] *nm* psychoanalysis.

psicoanalista [sēkoànàlē'stà] *nm/f* psychoanalyst.

psicología [sēkolohē'à] *nf* psychology.

psicológico, a [sēkolo'hēko, à] *a* psychological.

psicólogo, a [sēko'logo, à] *nm/f* psychologist.

psicópata [sēko'pàtà] *nm/f* psychopath.

psicosis [sēko'sēs] *nf inv* psychosis.

psicoterapia [sēkoterà'pyà] *nf* psychotherapy.

psiquiatra [sēkyà'trà] *nm/f* psychiatrist.

psiquiátrico, a [sēkyà'trēko, à] *a* psychiatric.

psíquico, a [sē'kēko, à] *a* psychic(al).

PSOE [peso'e] *nm abr* = *Partido Socialista Obrero Español*.

Pta. *abr* (*GEO*: = *Punta*) Pt.

pta(s). *abr* = **peseta(s).**

ptmo. *abr* (*COM*) = **préstamo.**

pts. *abr* = **pesetas.**

púa [poō'à] *nf* sharp point; (*para guitarra*) plectrum; **alambre de** ~**s** barbed wire.

púber, a [poō'ßer, à] *a, nm/f* adolescent.

pubertad [poōßertàth̲'] *nf* puberty.

publicación [poōßlēkàsyon'] *nf* publication.

publicar [poōßlēkàr'] *vt* (*editar*) to publish; (*hacer público*) to publicize; (*divulgar*) to make public, divulge.

publicidad [poōßlēsēth̲àth̲'] *nf* publicity; (*COM*) advertising; **dar** ~ **a** to publicize, give publicity to; ~ **gráfica** display advertising; ~ **en el punto de venta** point-of-sale advertising.

publicitar [poōßlēsētàr'] *vt* to publicize.

publicitario, a [poōßlēsētà'ryo, à] *a* publicity *cpd*; advertising *cpd*.

público, a [poō'ßlēko, à] *a* public ♦ *nm* public; (*TEATRO etc*) audience; (*DEPORTE*) spectators *pl*, crowd; (*restaurantes etc*) clients *pl*; **el gran** ~ the general public; **hacer** ~ to publish; (*difundir*) to disclose; ~ **objetivo** (*COM*) target audience.

publique [poōßlē'ke] *etc vb V* **publicar.**

pucherazo [poōtcherà'so] *nm* (*fraude*) electoral fiddle; **dar** ~ to rig an election.

puchero [poōtche'ro] *nm* (*CULIN*: *olla*) cooking pot; (: *guiso*) stew; **hacer** ~**s** to pout.

pudibundo, a [poōth̲ēßoōn'do, à] *a* bashful.

púdico, a [poō'th̲ēko, à] *a* modest; (*pudibundo*) bashful.

pudiendo [poōth̲yen'do] *etc vb V* **poder.**

pudiente [poōth̲yen'te] *a* (*opulento*) wealthy; (*poderoso*) powerful.

pudín [poōth̲ēn'] *nm* pudding.

pudor [poōth̲or'] *nm* modesty; (*vergüenza*) (sense of) shame.

pudoroso, a [poōth̲oro'so, à] *a* (*modesto*) modest; (*casto*) chaste.

pudrir [poōth̲rēr'] *vt* to rot; (*fam*) to upset, annoy; ~**se** *vr* to rot, decay; (*fig*) to rot, languish.

pueblerino, a [pweßlerē'no, à] *a* (*lugareño*) small-town *cpd*; (*persona*) rustic, provincial ♦ *nm/f* (*aldeano*) country person.

pueblo [pwe'ßlo] *etc vb V* **poblar** ♦ *nm* people; (*nación*) nation; (*aldea*) village; (*plebe*) common people; (*población pequeña*) small town, country town.

pueda [pwe'th̲à] *etc vb V* **poder.**

puente [pwen'te] *nm* (*gen*) bridge; (*NAUT*: *tb*: ~ **de mando**) bridge; (: *cubierta*) deck; ~ **aéreo** airlift; ~ **colgante** suspension bridge; ~ **levadizo** drawbridge; **hacer (el)** ~ (*fam*) to take a long weekend.

puerco, a [pwer'ko, à] *a* (*sucio*) dirty, filthy; (*obsceno*) disgusting ♦ *nm/f* pig/sow.

pueril [pwerēl'] *a* childish.

puerro [pwe'rro] *nm* leek.

puerta [pwer'tà] *nf* door; (*de jardín*) gate; (*portal*) doorway; (*fig*) gateway; (*gol*) goal; (*INFORM*) port; **a** ~ **cerrada** behind closed doors; ~ **corredera/giratoria** sliding/revolving door; ~ **principal/trasera** *o* **de servicio** front/back door; ~ **(de transmisión en) paralelo/serie** (*INFORM*) parallel/serial port; **tomar la** ~ (*fam*) to leave.

puerto [pwer'to] *nm* (*tb INFORM*) port; (*de mar*) seaport; (*paso*) pass; (*fig*) haven, refuge; **llegar a** ~ (*fig*) to get over a difficulty.

Puerto Rico [pwertorē'ko] *nm* Puerto Rico.

puertorriqueño, a [pwertorrēke'nyo, à] *a, nm/f* Puerto Rican.

pues [pwes] *ad* (*entonces*) then; (*¡entonces!*) well, well then; (*así que*) so ♦ *conj* (*porque*) since; ~ ... **no sé** well ... I don't know.

puesto, a |pwc'sto. á| *pp de* **poner** ♦ *a* dressed ♦ *nm* (*lugar, posición*) place; (*trabajo*) post, job; (*MIL*) post; (*COM*) stall; (*quiosco*) kiosk ♦ *conj:* ~ **que** since, as ♦ *nf* (*apuesta*) bet, stake; ~ **de mercado** market stall; ~ **de policía** police station; ~ **de socorro** first aid post; **puesta en escena** staging; **puesta en marcha** starting; **puesta del sol** sunset; **puesta a cero** (*INFORM*) reset.

pugna |pōōg'ná| *nf* battle, conflict.

pugnar |pōōgnár'| *vi* (*luchar*) to struggle, fight; (*pelear*) to fight.

puja |pōō'há| *nf* (*esfuerzo*) attempt; (*en una subasta*) bid.

pujante |pōōhán'tc| *a* strong, vigorous.

pujar |pōōhár'| *vt* (*precio*) to raise, push up ♦ *vi* (*en licitación*) to bid, bid up; (*fig: esforzarse*) to struggle, strain.

pulcro, a |pōōl'kro, á| *a* neat, tidy.

pulga |pōōl'gá| *nf* flea; **tener malas** ~s to be short-tempered.

pulgada |pōōlgá'thá| *nf* inch.

pulgar |pōōlgár'| *nm* thumb.

pulgón |pōōlgon'| *nm* plant louse, greenfly.

pulir |pōōlēr'| *vt* to polish; (*alisar*) to smooth; (*fig*) to polish up, touch up.

pulmón |pōōlmon'| *nm* lung; **a pleno** ~ (*respirar*) deeply; (*gritar*) at the top of one's voice; ~ **de acero** iron lung.

pulmonía |pōōlmonē'á| *nf* pneumonia.

pulpa |pōōl'pá| *nf* pulp; (*de fruta*) flesh, soft part.

pulpería |pōōlpcrē'á| *nf* (*AM*) small grocery store.

púlpito |pōōl'pēto| *nm* pulpit.

pulpo |pōōl'po| *nm* octopus.

pulsación |pōōlsásyon'| *nf* beat, pulsation; (*ANAT*) throb(bing); (*en máquina de escribir*) keystroke; (*de pianista, mecanógrafo*) touch; ~ **(de una tecla)** (*INFORM*) keystroke; ~ **doble** (*INFORM*) strikeover.

pulsador |pōōlsáthor'| *nm* button, push button.

pulsar |pōōlsár'| *vt* (*tecla*) to touch, tap; (*MUS*) to play; (*botón*) to press, push ♦ *vi* to pulsate; (*latir*) to beat, throb.

pulsera |pōōlsc'rá| *nf* bracelet; **reloj de** ~ wristwatch.

pulso |pōōl'so| *nm* (*MED*) pulse; **hacer algo a** ~ to do sth unaided *o* by one's own efforts.

pulular |pōōlōōlár'| *vi* (*estar plagado*): ~ **(de)** to swarm (with).

pulverice |pōōlhcrē'sc| *etc vb V* **pulverizar**.

pulverizador |pōōlhcrēsáthor'| *nm* spray, spray gun.

pulverizar |pōōlhcrēsár'| *vt* to pulverize; (*líquido*) to spray.

pulla |pōō'yá| *nf* cutting remark.

puna |pōō'ná| *nf* (*AM MED*) mountain sickness.

punce |pōōn'sc| *etc vb V* **punzar**.

punción |pōōnsyon'| *nf* (*MED*) puncture.

pundonor |pōōndonor'| *nm* (*dignidad*) self-respect.

punición |pōōnēsyon'| *nf* punishment.

punitivo, a |pōōnētē'vo, á| *a* punitive.

punta |pōōn'tá| *nf* point, tip; (*extremidad*) end; (*promontorio*) promontory; (*COSTURA*) corner; (*TEC*) small nail; (*fig*) touch, trace; **horas** ~s peak hours, rush hours; **sacar** ~ **a** to sharpen; **de** ~ on end; **de** ~ **a** from one end to the other; **estar de** ~ to be edgy; **ir de** ~ **en blanco** to be all dressed up; **tener algo en la** ~ **de la lengua** to have sth on the tip of one's tongue; **se le pusieron los pelos de** ~ her hair stood on end.

puntada |pōōntá'thá| *nf* (*COSTURA*) stitch.

puntal |pōōntál'| *nm* prop, support.

puntapié |pōōntápyc'|, *pl* **puntapiés** *nm* kick; **echar a uno a** ~s to kick sb out.

punteado, a |pōōntcá'tho, á| *a* (*moteado*) dotted; (*diseño*) of dots ♦ *nm* (*MUS*) twang.

puntear |pōōntcár'| *vt* to tick, mark; (*MUS*) to pluck.

puntería |pōōntcrē'á| *nf* (*de arma*) aim, aiming; (*destreza*) marksmanship.

puntero, a |pōōntc'ro, á| *a* leading ♦ *nm* (*señal, INFORM*) pointer; (*dirigente*) leader.

puntiagudo, a |pōōntyágōō'tho, á| *a* sharp, pointed.

puntilla |pōōntē'yá| *nf* (*TEC*) tack, braid; (*COSTURA*) lace edging; **(andar) de** ~s (to walk) on tiptoe.

puntilloso, a |pōōntēyo'so, á| *a* (*pundonoroso*) punctilious; (*susceptible*) touchy.

punto |pōōn'to| *nm* (*gen*) point; (*señal diminuta*) spot, dot; (*lugar*) spot, place; (*momento*) point, moment; (*en un examen*) grade; (*tema*) item; (*COSTURA*) stitch; (*INFORM: impresora*) pitch; (*: pantalla*) pixel; **a** ~ ready; **estar a** ~ **de** to be on the point of *o* about to; **llegar a** ~ to come just at the right moment; **al** ~ at once; **en** ~ on the dot; **estar en su** ~ (*CULIN*) to be done to perfection; **hasta cierto** ~ to some extent; **hacer** ~ to knit; **poner un motor en** ~ to tune an engine; · ~ **de partida/de congelación/de fusión** starting/freezing/melting point; ~ **de vista** point of view, viewpoint; ~ **muerto** dead center; (*AUTO*) neutral (gear); ~s **a tratar** matters to be discussed, agenda *sg*; ~ **final** period (*US*), full stop (*Brit*); **dos** ~s colon; ~ **y coma** semicolon; ~ **de interrogación** question mark; ~s **suspensivos** suspension points; ~ **de equilibrio/de pedido** (*COM*) breakeven/reorder point; ~ **inicial** *o* **de**

partida (*INFORM*) home; ~ **de referencia/ de venta** (*COM*) benchmark point/point-of-sale.

puntuación |pōōntwásyon'| *nf* punctuation; (*puntos: en examen*) grade; (: *DEPORTE*) score.

puntual |pōōntwál'| *a* (*a tiempo*) punctual; (*cálculo*) exact, accurate; (*informe*) reliable.

puntualice |pōōntwálē'se| *etc vb V* **puntualizar.**

puntualidad |pōōntwálēthàth'| *nf* punctuality; exactness, accuracy; reliability.

puntualizar |pōōntwálēsàr'| *vt* to fix, specify.

puntuar |pōōntwàr'| *vt* (*LING*, *TIP*) to punctuate; (*examen*) to grade ♦ *vi* (*DEPORTE*) to score, count.

punzada |pōōnsá'thà| *nf* (*puntura*) prick; (*MED*) stitch; (*dolor*) twinge (of pain).

punzante |pōōnsán'te| *a* (*dolor*) shooting, sharp; (*herramienta*) sharp; (*comentario*) biting.

punzar |pōōnsàr'| *vt* to prick, pierce ♦ *vi* to shoot, stab.

punzón |pōōnson'| *nm* (*TEC*) punch.

puñado |pōōnyá'tho| *nm* handful (*tb fig*); a ~s by handfuls.

puñal |pōōnyàl'| *nm* dagger.

puñalada |pōōnyálá'thà| *nf* stab.

puñeta |pōōnye'tà| *nf*: ¡~!, ¡**qué ~(s)!** (*fam!*) hell!; **mandar a uno a hacer ~s** (*fam*) to tell sb to go to hell.

puñetazo |pōōnyetá'so| *nm* punch.

puño |pōō'nyo| *nm* (*ANAT*) fist; (*cantidad*) fistful, handful; (*COSTURA*) cuff; (*de herramienta*) handle; **como un ~** (*verdad*) obvious; (*palpable*) tangible, visible; **de ~ y letra del poeta** in the poet's own handwriting.

pupila |pōōpē'là| *nf* (*ANAT*) pupil.

pupitre |pōōpē'tre| *nm* desk.

puré |pōōre'| *pl* **purés** *nm* puree; (*sopa*) (thick) soup; ~ **de patatas** mashed potatoes; **estar hecho ~** (*fig*) to be worn out.

pureza |pōōre'sà| *nf* purity.

purga |pōōr'gà| *nf* purge.

purgante |pōōrgán'te| *a, nm* purgative.

purgar |pōōrgàr'| *vt* to purge; (*POL: depurar*) to purge, liquidate; ~**se** *vr* (*MED*) to take a purge.

purgatorio |pōōrgáto'ryo| *nm* purgatory.

purgue |pōōr'ge| *etc vb V* **purgar.**

purificar |pōōrēfēkàr'| *vt* to purify; (*refinar*) to refine.

purifique |pōōrēfē'ke| *etc vb V* **purificar.**

puritano, a |pōōrētá'no, à| *a* (*actitud*) puritanical; (*iglesia, tradición*) puritan ♦ *nm/f* puritan.

puro, a |pōō'ro, à| *a* pure; (*depurado*) unadulterated; (*oro*) solid; (*cielo*) clear;

(*verdad*) simple, plain ♦ *ad*: **de ~ cansado** out of sheer tiredness ♦ *nm* cigar; **por pura casualidad** by sheer chance.

púrpura |pōōr'pōōrà| *nf* purple.

purpúreo, a |pōōrpōō'reo, à| *a* purple.

pus |pōōs| *nm* pus.

puse |pōō'se| *etc vb V* **poner.**

pústula |pōō'stōōlà| *nf* pimple, sore.

puta |pōō'tà| *nf* whore, prostitute.

putañear |pōōtànyeàr'|, **putear** |pōōteàr'| *vi* to go whoring.

putería |pōōtere'à| *nf* (*prostitución*) prostitution; (*prostíbulo*) brothel.

putrefacción |pōōtrefàksyon'| *nf* rotting, putrefaction.

pútrido, a |pōō'trētho, à| *a* rotten.

PVP *abr* (*Esp*) = *Precio Venta al Público.*

Q

Q, q |kōō| *nf* (*letra*) Q, q; **Q de Querido** Q for Queen.

q.e.g.e. *abr* (= *que en gloria esté*) R.I.P.

q.e.p.d. *abr* (= *que en paz descanse*) R.I.P.

q.e.s.m. *abr* (= *que estrecha su mano*) courtesy formula.

qm. *abr* = **quintal(es) métrico(s).**

qts. *abr* = **quilates.**

que |ke| *pron* (*sujeto: individuo*) who, that; (: *cosa*) whom, that; (*complemento: individuo*) whom, that; (: *cosa*) which, that ♦ *conj* that; **el momento en ~ llegó** the moment he arrived; **lo ~ digo** what I say; **dar ~ hablar** to give cause to talk, cause talk; **¡~ entre!** send him in!; **le ruego ~ se calle** I'm asking you to keep quiet; **¡~ sí!** yes!; **te digo ~ sí** I'm telling you, I assure you; **el ~ + *subjun*** the fact that ...; **ya** *o* **por ~** for, since, because; **yo ~ tú** if I were you; **siguió toca ~ toca** he kept on playing.

qué |ke| *a* what?, which? ♦ *pron* what?; **¡~ divertido/asco!** how funny/revolting!; **¡~ día más espléndido!** what a glorious day!; **¿~ edad tienes?** how old are you?; **¿de ~ me hablas?** what are you saying to me?; **¿~ tal?** how are you?, how are things?; **¿~ hay (de nuevo)?** what's new?; **¿~ más?** anything else?

quebrada |kebrá'thà| *nf V* **quebrado.**

quebradero |kebráthe'ro| *nm*: ~ **de cabeza** headache, worry.

quebradizo, a |kebráthē'so, à| *a* fragile; (*persona*) frail.

quebrado, a [keʰrá'tʰo, á] *a* (*roto*) broken; (*terreno*) rough, uneven ♦ *nm/f* bankrupt ♦ *nm* (*MAT*) fraction ♦ *nf* ravine; ~ **rehabilitado** discharged bankrupt.

quebradura [keʰráthoo'rá] *nf* (*fisura*) fissure; (*MED*) rupture.

quebrantadura [keʰrántáthoo'rá] *nf*, **quebrantamiento** [keʰrántámyen'to] *nm* (*acto*) breaking; (*de ley*) violation; (*estado*) exhaustion.

quebrantar [keʰrántár'] *vt* (*infringir*) to violate, transgress; ~**se** *vr* (*persona*) to fail in health.

quebranto [keʰrán'to] *nm* damage, harm; (*decaimiento*) exhaustion; (*dolor*) grief, pain.

quebrar [keʰrár'] *vt* to break, smash ♦ *vi* to go bankrupt; ~**se** *vr* to break, get broken; (*MED*) to be ruptured.

queda [ke'tʰá] *nf*: (**toque de**) ~ curfew.

quedar [ketʰár'] *vi* to stay, remain; (*encontrarse*) to be; (*restar*) to remain, be left; ~**se** *vr* to remain, stay (behind); ~ **en** (*acordar*) to agree on/to; (*acabar siendo*) to end up as; ~ **por hacer** to be still to be done; ~ **ciego/mudo** to be left blind/dumb; **no te queda bien ese vestido** that dress doesn't suit you; **quedamos a las seis** we agreed to meet at six; **eso queda muy lejos** that's a long way (away); **nos quedan 12 kms para llegar al pueblo** there are still 12 kms before we get to the village; **no queda otra** there's no alternative; ~**se** (**con**) **algo** to keep sth; ~**se con uno** (*fam*) to swindle sb; ~**se en nada** to come to nothing *o* nought; ~**se sin** to run out of.

quedo, a [ke'tʰo, á] *a* still ♦ *ad* softly, gently.

quehacer [keáser'] *nm* task, job; ~**es** (**domésticos**) household chores.

queja [ke'há] *nf* complaint.

quejarse [kehár'se] *vr* (*enfermo*) to moan, groan; (*protestar*) to complain; ~ **de que** ... to complain (about the fact) that ...

quejica [kehē'ká] *a* grumpy, complaining ♦ *nm/f* grumbler, whinger.

quejido [kehē'tʰo] *nm* moan.

quejoso, a [keho'so, á] *a* complaining.

quema [ke'má] *nf* fire; (*combustión*) burning.

quemado, a [kemá'tʰo, á] *a* burned; (*irritado*) annoyed.

quemadura [kemáthoo'rá] *nf* burn, scald; (*de sol*) sunburn; (*de fusible*) blow-out.

quemar [kemár'] *vt* to burn; (*fig: malgastar*) to burn up, squander; (*COM: precios*) to slash, cut; (*fastidiar*) to annoy, bug ♦ *vi* to be burning hot; ~**se** *vr* (*consumirse*) to burn (up); (*del sol*) to get sunburned.

quemarropa [kemárro'pá]: **a** ~ *ad* point-blank.

quemazón [kemáson'] *nf* burn; (*calor*) intense heat; (*sensación*) itch.

quena [ke'ná] *nf* (*AM*) Indian flute.

quepo [ke'po] *etc vb* V **caber.**

querella [kere'yá] *nf* (*JUR*) charge; (*disputa*) dispute.

querencia [keren'syá] *nf* (*ZOOL*) homing instinct; (*fig*) homesickness.

querer [kerer'] *vt, vi* (*desear*) to want, wish; (*amar*) to love; ~ **hacer algo** to want to do sth; **como quien no quiere la cosa** offhandedly; **sin** ~ unintentionally; **¿quiere abrir la ventana?** would you mind opening the window?; **no quiso** he refused; ~ **bien a uno** to be fond of sb.

querido, a [kerē'tʰo, á] *a* dear ♦ *nm/f* darling; (*amante*) lover; **nuestra querida patria** our beloved country.

querré [kerre'] *etc vb* V **querer.**

quesería [keserē'á] *nf* dairy; (*fábrica*) cheese factory.

quesero, a [kese'ro, á] *a*: **la industria quesera** the cheese industry ♦ *nm/f* cheesemaker ♦ *nf* cheese dish.

queso [ke'so] *nm* cheese; ~ **rallado** grated cheese; ~ **crema** cream cheese; **dárselas con** ~ **a uno** (*fam*) to put sth over on sb.

quetzal [ketsál'] *nm monetary unit of Guatemala.*

quicio [kē'syo] *nm* hinge; **estar fuera de** ~ to be beside o.s.; **sacar a uno de** ~ to drive sb up the wall.

quid [kētʰ] *nm* gist, crux; **dar en el** ~ to hit the nail on the head.

quiebra [kye'rá] *nf* break, split; (*COM*) bankruptcy; (*ECON*) slump.

quiebro [kye'ʰro] *etc vb* V **quebrar** ♦ *nm* (*del cuerpo*) swerve.

quien [kyen] *pron relativo* (*suj*) who; (*complemento*) whom; (*indefinido*): ~ **dice eso es tonto** whoever says that is a fool; **hay** ~ **piensa que** there are those who think that; **no hay** ~ **lo haga** no-one will do it; ~ **más,** ~ **menos tiene sus problemas** everybody has problems.

quién [kyen] *pron interrogativo* who; (*complemento*) whom; **¿**~ **es?** who is it?, who's there?; (*TELEC*) who's calling?

quienquiera [kyenkye'rá] (*pl* **quienesquiera**) *pron* whoever.

quiera [kye'rá] *etc vb* V **querer.**

quieto, a [kye'to, á] *a* still; (*carácter*) placid; **¡estáte** ~**!** keep still!

quietud [kyetootʰ'] *nf* stillness.

quijada [kēhá'tʰá] *nf* jaw, jawbone.

quijote [kēho'te] *nm* dreamer; **Don Q**~ Don Quixote.

quil. *abr* = **quilates.**

quilate [kēlá'te] *nm* carat.

quilo... [kē'lo] = **kilo...**

quilla [kē'yá] *nf* keel.

quimera [kēmc'rá] *nf* (*sueño*) pipe dream.

quimérico, a [kēmc'rēko, á] *a* fantastic.

químico, a [kē'mēko, á] *a* chemical ♦ *nm/f* chemist ♦ *nf* chemistry.

quincallería [kēnkáycrē'á] *nf* hardware store (*US*), ironmonger's (shop) (*Brit*).

quince [kēn'sc] *num* fifteen; ~ **días** two weeks.

quinceañero, a [kēnscányc'ro, á] *a* fifteen-year-old; (*adolescente*) teenage ♦ *nm/f* fifteen-year-old; (*adolescente*) teenager.

quincena [kēnsc'ná] *nf* two weeks; (*pago*) two weeks' pay.

quincenal [kēnscnál'] *a* biweekly.

quincuagésimo, a [kēnkwáhc'sēmo, á] *num* fiftieth.

quiniela [kēnyc'lá] *nf* football pools *pl*; ~**s** *nfpl* pools coupon *sg*.

quinientos, as [kēnycn'tos, ás] *num* five hundred.

quinina [kēnē'ná] *nf* quinine.

quinqué [kēnkc'] *nm* oil lamp.

quinquenal [kēnkcnál'] *a* five-year *cpd*.

quinqui [kēn'kē] *nm* delinquent.

quinta [kēn'tá] *nf* V **quinto**.

quintaesencia [kēntáescn'syá] *nf* quintessence.

quintal [kēntál'] *nm* (*Castilla: peso*) = 46kg; ~ **métrico** = 100kg.

quinto, a [kēn'to, á] *a* fifth ♦ *nm* (*MIL*) conscript, draftee ♦ *nf* country house; (*MIL*) call-up, draft.

quintuplo, a [kēntōō'plo, á] *a* quintuple, five-fold.

quiosco [kyos'ko] *nm* (*de música*) bandstand; (*de periódicos*) news stand.

quirófano [kēro'fáno] *nm* operating room (*US*) o theatre (*Brit*).

quiromancia [kēromán'syá] *nf* palmistry.

quirúrgico, a [kēroōr'hēko, á] *a* surgical.

quise [kē'sc] *etc vb* V **querer**.

quisque [kēs'kc] *pron fam*: **cada** o **todo** ~ (*absolutamente*) everyone.

quisquilloso, a [kēskēyo'so, á] *a* (*susceptible*) touchy; (*meticuloso*) fussy.

quiste [kē'stc] *nm* cyst.

quitaesmalte [kētáesmál'tc] *nm* nail polish remover.

quitamanchas [kētámántch'ás] *nm inv* stain remover.

quitanieves [kētányc'ħcs] *nm inv* snowplow (*US*), snowplough (*Brit*).

quitar [kētár'] *vt* to remove, take away; (*ropa*) to take off; (*dolor*) to relieve; (*vida*) to take; (*valor*) to reduce; (*hurtar*) to remove, steal ♦ *vi*: **¡quita de ahí!** get away!; ~**se** *vr* to withdraw; (*mancha*) to come off o out; (*ropa*) to take off; **me quita mucho tiempo** it takes up a lot of my time; **el café me quita el sueño** coffee

keeps me from sleeping; ~ **de en medio a uno** to get rid of sb; ~**se algo de encima** to get rid of sth; ~**se del tabaco** to give up smoking; **se quitó el sombrero** he took off his hat.

quitasol [kētásol'] *nm* parasol.

quite [kē'tc] *nm* (*esgrima*) parry; (*evasión*) dodge; **estar al** ~ to be ready to go to sb's aid.

Quito [kē'to] *n* Quito.

quizá(s) [kēsá'(s)] *ad* perhaps, maybe.

quórum [kwo'rōōm] *nm*, *pl* **quórums** [kwo'rōōm] quorum.

R

R, r [e'rre] *nf* (*letra*) R, r; **R de Ramón** R for Roger.

R. *abr* = **Remite, Remitente**.

rábano [rá'ħáno] *nm* radish; **me importa un** ~ I don't give a damn.

rabia [rá'ħyá] *nf* (*MED*) rabies *sg*; (*fig: ira*) fury, rage; **¡qué** ~**!** isn't it infuriating!; **me da** ~ it maddens me; **tener** ~ **a uno** to have a grudge against sb.

rabiar [ráħyár'] *vi* to have rabies; to rage, be furious; ~ **por algo** to long for sth.

rabieta [ráħyc'tá] *nf* tantrum, fit of temper.

rabino [ráħē'no] *nm* rabbi.

rabioso, a [ráħyo'so, á] *a* rabid; (*fig*) furious.

rabo [rá'ħo] *nm* tail.

racanear [rákáneár'] *vi* (*fam*) to loaf.

rácano [rá'káno] *nm* (*fam*) slacker.

racial [rásyál'] *a* racial, race *cpd*.

racimo [rásē'mo] *nm* bunch.

raciocinio [rásyosē'nyo] *nm* reason; (*razonamiento*) reasoning.

ración [rásyon'] *nf* portion; **raciones** *nfpl* rations.

racional [rásyonál'] *a* (*razonable*) reasonable; (*lógico*) rational.

racionalice [rásyonálē'sc] *etc vb* V **racionalizar**.

racionalizar [rásyonálēsár'] *vt* to rationalize; (*COM*) to streamline.

racionamiento [rásyonámyen'to] *nm* (*COM*) rationing.

racionar [rásyonár'] *vt* to ration (out).

racismo [rásēs'mo] *nm* racialism, racism.

racista [rásē'stá] *a, nm/f* racist.

racha [rátch'á] *nf* gust of wind; (*serie*) string, series; **buena/mala** ~ spell of good/bad luck.

radar [ràt̪ȟár'] *nm* radar.
radiación [ràt̪ȟyásyon'] *nf* radiation; (*TELEC*) broadcasting.
radiactividad [ràt̪ȟyáktēt̪ȟét̪ȟát̪ȟ'] *nf* radio-activity.
radiactivo, a [ràt̪ȟyoáktē'ḥo, à] *a* radio-active.
radiado, a [ràt̪ȟyà't̪ȟo, à] *a* radio *cpd*, broadcast.
radiador [ràt̪ȟyàt̪ȟor'] *nm* radiator.
radiante [ràt̪ȟyàn'te] *a* radiant.
radiar [ràt̪ȟyàr'] *vt* to radiate; (*TELEC*) to broadcast; (*MED*) to give radiotherapy to.
radical [ràt̪ȟēkál'] *a, nm/f* radical ♦ *nm* (*LING*) root; (*MAT*) square-root sign.
radicar [ràt̪ȟēkàr'] *vi* to take root; ~ **en** to lie in; ~**se** *vr* to establish o.s., put down (one's) roots.
radio [ra'ṭ̣ȟyo] *nf* radio; (*aparato*) radio (set) ♦ *nm* (*MAT*) radius; (*QUÍMICA*) radium; ~ **de acción** extent of one's authority, sphere of influence.
radiodifusión [ràt̪ȟyodēfōōsyon'] *nf* broadcasting.
radioemisora [ràt̪ȟyoemēso'rà] *nf* transmitter, radio station.
radiofónico, a [ràt̪ȟyofo'nēko, à] *a* radio *cpd*.
radiografía [ràt̪ȟyogràfē'à] *nf* X-ray.
radiólogo, a [ràt̪ȟyo'logo, à] *nm/f* radiologist.
radioterapia [ràt̪ȟyoterà'pyà] *nf* radiotherapy.
radioyente [ràt̪ȟyoyen'te] *nm/f* listener.
radique [ràt̪ȟē'ke] *etc vb V* **radicar.**
RAE *nf abr = Real Academia Española.*
ráfaga [rà'fàgà] *nf* gust; (*de luz*) flash; (*de tiros*) burst.
raído, a [rà̄ē't̪ȟo, à] *a* (*ropa*) threadbare; (*persona*) shabby.
raigambre [rà̄ēgàm'bre] *nf* (*BOT*) roots *pl*; (*fig*) tradition.
raíz [rà̄ēs'] (*pl* **raíces**) *nf* root; ~ **cuadrada** square root; **a** ~ **de** as a result of; (*después de*) immediately after.
raja [rà'hà] *nf* (*de melón etc*) slice; (*hendedura*) slit, split; (*grieta*) crack.
rajar [ràhàr'] *vt* to split; (*fam*) to slash; ~**se** *vr* to split, crack; ~**se de** to back out of.
rajatabla [ràhàtà'ḥlà]: **a** ~ *ad* (*estrictamente*) strictly, to the letter.
ralea [ràle'à] *nf* (*pey*) kind, sort.
ralenti [ràlen'tē] *nm* (*TV etc*) slow motion; (*AUTO*) neutral; **al** ~ in slow motion; (*AUTO*) idling.
ralo, a [rà'lo, à] *a* thin, sparse.
rallador [ràyàt̪ȟor'] *nm* grater.
rallar [ràyàr'] *vt* to grate.
RAM [ràm] *nf abr* (= *random access memory*) RAM.
rama [rà'mà] *nf* bough, branch; **andarse por**

las ~**s** (*fig, fam*) to beat about the bush.
ramaje [ràmà'ye] *nm* branches *pl*, foliage.
ramal [ràmàl'] *nm* (*de cuerda*) strand; (*FERRO*) branch line; (*AUTO*) branch (road).
rambla [ràm'blà] *nf* (*avenida*) avenue.
ramera [ràme'rà] *nf* whore, hooker.
ramificación [ràmēfēkàsyon'] *nf* ramification.
ramificarse [ràmēfēkàr'se] *vr* to branch out.
ramifique [ràmēfē'ke] *etc vb V* **ramificarse.**
ramillete [ràmēye'te] *nm* bouquet; (*fig*) select group.
ramo [rà'mo] *nm* branch, twig; (*sección*) department, section; (*sector*) field, sector.
rampa [ràm'pà] *nf* ramp.
ramplón, ona [ràmplon', onà] *a* uncouth, coarse.
rana [rà'nà] *nf* frog; **salto de** ~ leapfrog; **cuando las** ~**s críen pelos** when pigs fly.
rancio, a [ràn'syo, à] *a* (*comestibles*) stale, rancid; (*vino*) aged, mellow; (*fig*) ancient.
ranchero [ràntche'ro] *nm* (*AM*) rancher; (*pequeño propietario*) small farmer.
rancho [ràntch'o] *nm* grub (*fam*); (*AM*): *grande*) ranch; (: *pequeño*) small farm.
rango [ràn'go] *nm* rank; (*prestigio*) standing.
ranura [rànōō'rà] *nf* groove; (*de teléfono etc*) slot; ~ **de expansión** (*INFORM*) expansion slot.
rapacidad [ràpàsēt̪ȟát̪ȟ'] *nf* rapacity.
rapapolvo [ràpàpol'ḥo] *nm*: **echar un** ~ **a uno** to bawl sb out.
rapar [ràpàr'] *vt* to shave; (*los cabellos*) to crop.
rapaz [ràpàs'] *a* (*ZOOL*) predatory ♦ *nm/f* (*f*: **rapaza**) young boy/girl.
rape [rà'pe] *nm* quick shave; (*pez*) angler (fish); **al** ~ cropped.
rapé [ràpe'] *nm* snuff.
rapidez [ràpēt̪ȟes'] *nf* speed, rapidity.
rápido, a [rà'pēt̪ȟo, à] *a* fast, quick ♦ *ad* quickly ♦ *nm* (*FERRO*) express; ~**s** *nmpl* rapids.
rapiña [ràpē'nyà] *nm* robbery; **ave de** ~ bird of prey.
raptar [ràptàr'] *vt* to kidnap.
rapto [ràp'to] *nm* kidnapping; (*impulso*) sudden impulse; (*éxtasis*) ecstasy, rapture.
raqueta [ràke'tà] *nf* racquet.
raquítico, a [ràkē'tēko, à] *a* stunted; (*fig*) poor, inadequate.
raquitismo [ràkētēs'mo] *nm* rickets *sg*.
rareza [ràre'sà] *nf* rarity; (*fig*) eccentricity.
raro, a [rà'ro, à] *a* (*poco común*) rare; (*extraño*) odd, strange; (*excepcional*) remarkable; **¡qué** ~! how (very) odd!; **¡(qué) cosa más rara!** how strange!
ras [ràs] *nm*: **a** ~ **de** level with; **a** ~ **de tierra** at ground level.

rasar |rásár'| *vt* to level.

rascacielos |ráskásyc'los| *nm inv* skyscraper.

rascar |ráskár'| *vt* (*con las uñas etc*) to scratch; (*raspar*) to scrape; ~**se** *vr* to scratch (o.s.).

rasgar |rásgàr'| *vt* to tear, rip (up).

rasgo |rás'go| *nm* (*con pluma*) stroke; ~**s** *nmpl* features, characteristics; **a grandes** ~**s** in outline, broadly.

rasguear |rásgcár'| *vt* (*MUS*) to strum.

rasgue |rás'gc| *etc vb* V **rasgar**.

rasguñar |rásgōonyár'| *vt* to scratch; (*bosquejar*) to sketch.

rasguño |rásgōo'nyo| *nm* scratch.

raso, a |rá'so, á| *a* (*liso*) flat, level; (*a baja altura*) very low ♦ *nm* satin; (*campo llano*) flat country; **cielo** ~ clear sky; **al** ~ in the open.

raspador |ráspáthor'| *nm* scraper.

raspadura |ráspáthōo'rá| *nf* (*acto*) scrape, scraping; (*marca*) scratch; ~**s** *nfpl* scrapings.

raspar |ráspár'| *vt* to scrape; (*arañar*) to scratch; (*limar*) to file ♦ *vi* (*manos*) to be rough; (*vino*) to be sharp, have a rough taste.

rasque |rás'kc| *etc vb* V **rascar**.

rastra |rás'trá| *nf*: **a** ~**s** by dragging; (*fig*) unwillingly.

rastreador |rástrcáthor'| *nm* tracker; ~ **de minas** minesweeper.

rastrear |rástrcár'| *vt* (*seguir*) to track; (*minas*) to sweep.

rastrero, a |rástrc'ro, á| *a* (*BOT, ZOOL*) creeping; (*fig*) despicable, mean.

rastrillar |rástrcyár'| *vt* to rake.

rastrillo |rástrc'yo| *nm* rake.

rastro |rás'tro| *nm* (*AGR*) rake; (*pista*) track, trail; (*vestigio*) trace; **el R**~ *the Madrid fleamarket*; **perder el** ~ to lose the scent; **desaparecer sin** ~ to vanish without trace.

rastrojo |rástro'ho| *nm* stubble.

rasurador |rásōoráthor'| *nm*, (*AM*) **rasuradora** |rásōoràtho'rá| *nf* electric shaver *o* razor.

rasurarse |rásōorár'sc| *vr* to shave.

rata |rá'tá| *nf* rat.

ratear |rátcár'| *vt* (*robar*) to steal.

ratero, a |rátc'ro, á| *a* light-fingered ♦ *nm/f* pickpocket; (*AM: de casas*) burglar.

ratificar |rátcfckár'| *vt* to ratify.

ratifique |rátcfc'kc| *etc vb* V **ratificar**.

rato |rá'to| *nm* while, short time; **a** ~**s** from time to time; **al poco** ~ shortly after, soon afterwards; ~**s libres** *o* **de ocio** leisure *sg*, spare *o* free time *sg*; **hay para** ~ there's still a long way to go; **pasar el** ~ to kill time; **pasar un buen/mal** ~ to have a good/rough time.

ratón |ráton'| *nm* (*tb INFORM*) mouse.

ratonera |rátonc'rá| *nf* mousetrap.

RAU *nf abr* (= *República Árabe Unida*) UAR.

raudal |ráōoṭhál'| *nm* torrent; **a** ~**es** in abundance; **entrar a** ~**es** to pour in.

raudo, a |rá'ōoṭho, á| *a* (*rápido*) swift; (*precipitado*) rushing.

raya |rá'yá| *nf* line; (*marca*) scratch; (*en tela*) stripe; (*TIP*) dash; (*de pelo*) parting; (*límite*) boundary; (*pez*) ray; **a** ~**s** striped; **pasarse de la** ~ to overstep the mark, go too far; **tener a** ~ to keep in check.

rayado, a |ráyá'ṭho, á| *a* (*papel*) ruled; (*tela, diseño*) striped.

rayar |ráyár'| *vt* to line; to scratch; (*subrayar*) to underline ♦ *vi*: ~ **en** *o* **con** to border on; **al** ~ **el alba** at first light.

rayo |rá'yo| *nm* (*del sol*) ray, beam; (*de luz*) shaft; (*en una tormenta*) (flash of) lightning; ~ **solar** *o* **de sol** sunbeam; ~**s infrarrojos** infrared rays; ~**s X** X-rays; **como un** ~ like a shot; **la noticia cayó como un** ~ the news was a bombshell; **pasar como un** ~ to flash past.

raza |rá'sá| *nf* race; (*de animal*) breed; ~ **humana** human race; **de pura** ~ (*caballo*) thoroughbred; (*perro etc*) pedigree.

razón |ráson'| *nf* reason; (*justicia*) right, justice; (*razonamiento*) reasoning; (*motivo*) reason, motive; (*proporción*) rate; (*MAT*) ratio; **a** ~ **de 10 cada día** at the rate of 10 a day; "~: ..." "inquiries to ..."; **en** ~ **de** with regard to; **perder la** ~ to go out of one's mind; **dar** ~ **a uno** to agree that sb is right; **dar** ~ **de** to give an account of, report on; **tener/no tener** ~ to be right/wrong; ~ **directa/inversa** direct/inverse proportion; ~ **de ser** raison d'être.

razonable |rásoná'hlc| *a* reasonable; (*justo, moderado*) fair.

razonado, a |rásoná'ṭho, á| *a* (*COM: cuenta etc*) itemized.

razonamiento |rásonámyen'to| *nm* (*juicio*) judgement; (*argumento*) reasoning.

razonar |rásonár'| *vt, vi* to reason, argue.

RDA *nf* = *República Democrática Alemana*.

Rdo. *abr* (*REL*: = *Reverendo*) Rev.

reabierto |reáhyer'to| *pp de* **reabrir**.

reabrir |reáhrír'| *vt*, ~**se** *vr* to reopen.

reacción |reáksyon'| *nf* reaction; **avión a** ~ jet plane; ~ **en cadena** chain reaction.

reaccionar |reáksyonár'| *vi* to react.

reaccionario, a |reáksyoná'ryo, á| *a* reactionary.

reacio, a |reá'syo, á| *a* stubborn; **ser** *o* **estar** ~ **a** to be opposed to.

reactor |reáktor'| *nm* reactor; (*avión*) jet plane; ~ **nuclear** nuclear reactor.

readaptación |reàṭháptásyon'| *nf*: ~ **profe-**

sional industrial retraining.
reafirmar [reáfērmár'] *vt* to reaffirm.
reagrupar [reágrōōpár'] *vt* to regroup.
reajustar [reáhōōstár'] *vt* (*INFORM*) to reset.
reajuste [reáhōō'ste] *nm* readjustment; ~ **salarial** wage increase; ~ **de plantilla** modernization.
real [reál'] *a* real; (*del rey, fig*) royal; (*espléndido*) grand ♦ *nm* (*de feria*) fairground.
realce [reál'se] *etc vb* V **realzar** ♦ *nm* (*TEC*) embossing; (*lustre, fig*) splendor (*US*), splendour (*Brit*); (*ARTE*) highlight; **poner de** ~ to emphasize.
realeza [reále'sá] *nf* royalty.
realice [reálē'se] *etc vb* V **realizar**.
realidad [reálēthath'] *nf* reality; (*verdad*) truth; **en** ~ in fact.
realista [reálē'stá] *nm/f* realist.
realización [reálēsásyon'] *nf* fulfilment, realization; (*COM*) liquidation; ~ **de plusvalías** profit-taking.
realizador, a [reálēsáthor', á] *nm/f* (*TV etc*) producer.
realizar [reálēsár'] *vt* (*objetivo*) to achieve; (*plan*) to carry out; (*viaje*) to make, undertake; (*COM*) to realize; ~**se** *vr* to come about, come true; ~**se como persona** to fulfil one's aims in life.
realmente [reálmen'te] *ad* really.
realquilar [reálkēlár'] *vt* (*subarrendar*) to sublet; (*alquilar de nuevo*) to rent again.
realzar [reálsár'] *vt* (*TEC*) to raise; (*embellecer*) to enhance; (*acentuar*) to highlight.
reanimar [reánēmár'] *vt* to revive; (*alentar*) to encourage; ~**se** *vr* to revive.
reanudar [reánōōthár'] *vt* (*renovar*) to renew; (*historia, viaje*) to resume.
reaparición [reápárēsyon'] *nf* reappearance; (*vuelta*) return.
reapertura [reápertōō'rá] *nf* reopening.
rearme [reár'me] *nm* rearmament.
rebaja [rehá'há] *nf* reduction, lowering; (*COM*) discount; "**grandes ~s**" "big reductions", "sale".
rebajar [reháhár'] *vt* (*bajar*) to lower; (*reducir*) to reduce; (*precio*) to cut; (*disminuir*) to lessen; (*humillar*) to humble; ~**se** *vr*: ~**se a hacer algo** to stoop to doing sth.
rebanada [rehána'thá] *nf* slice.
rebaño [rehá'nyo] *nm* herd; (*de ovejas*) flock.
rebasar [rehásár'] *vt* (*tb*: ~ **de**) to exceed; (*AUTO*) to pass.
rebatir [rehátēr'] *vt* to refute; (*rebajar*) to reduce; (*ataque*) to repel.
rebato [rehá'to] *nm* alarm; (*ataque*) surprise attack; **llamar** *o* **tocar a** ~ (*fig*) to sound the alarm.
rebeca [rehe'ká] *nf* cardigan.
rebelarse [rehelár'se] *vr* to rebel, revolt.
rebelde [rehel'de] *a* rebellious; (*niño*) un-

ruly ♦ *nm/f* rebel; **ser** ~ **a** to be in revolt against, rebel against.
rebeldía [rehelde'á] *nf* rebelliousness; (*desobediencia*) disobedience; (*JUR*) default.
rebelión [rehelyon'] *nf* rebellion.
reblandecer [reblándeser'] *vt* to soften.
reblandezca [reblándes'ká] *etc vb* V **reblandecer.**
reboce [reho'se] *etc vb* V **rebozar.**
rebosante [rehosán'te] *a*: ~ **de** (*fig*) brimming *o* overflowing with.
rebosar [rehosár'] *vi* to overflow; (*abundar*) to abound, be plentiful; ~ **de salud** to be bursting *o* brimming with health.
rebotar [rehotár'] *vt* to bounce; (*rechazar*) to repel.
rebote [reho'te] *nm* rebound; **de** ~ on the rebound.
rebozado, a [rehosá'tho, á] *a* (*CULIN*) fried in batter *o* breadcrumbs *o* flour.
rebozar [rehosár'] *vt* to wrap up; (*CULIN*) to fry in batter *etc*.
rebuscado, a [rehōōská'tho, á] *a* affected.
rebuznar [rehōōsnár'] *vi* to bray.
recabar [rekáhár'] *vt* (*obtener*) to manage to get; ~ **fondos** to collect money.
recadero [rekáthe'ro] *nm* messenger.
recado [rekáthe'ro] *nm* message; **dejar/tomar un** ~ (*TELEC*) to leave/take a message.
recaer [rekáer'] *vi* to relapse; ~ **en** to fall to *o* on; (*criminal etc*) to fall back into, relapse into; (*premio*) to go to.
recaída [rekáē'thá] *nf* relapse.
recaiga [rekáē'gá] *etc vb* V **recaer.**
recalcar [rekálkár'] *vt* (*fig*) to stress, emphasize.
recalcitrante [rekálsētrán'te] *a* recalcitrant.
recalentar [rekálentár'] *vt* (*comida*) to warm up, reheat; (*demasiado*) to overheat; ~**se** *vr* to overheat, get too hot.
recaliente [rekályen'te] *etc vb* V **recalentar.**
recalque [rekál'ke] *etc vb* V **recalcar.**
recámara [reká'márá] *nf* (*vestidor*) dressing room; (*AM*) bedroom.
recambio [rekám'byo] *nm* spare; (*de pluma*) refill; **piezas de** ~ spares.
recapacitar [rekápásētár'] *vi* to reflect.
recargado, a [rekárgá'tho, á] *a* overloaded; (*exagerado*) over-elaborate.
recargar [rekárgár'] *vt* to overload; (*batería*) to recharge.
recargo [rekár'go] *nm* surcharge; (*aumento*) increase.
recargue [rekár'ge] *etc vb* V **recargar.**
recatado, a [rekátá'tho, á] *a* (*modesto*) modest, demure; (*prudente*) cautious.
recato [reká'to] *nm* (*modestia*) modesty, demureness; (*cautela*) caution.
recaudación [rekáōōthásyon'] *nf* (*acción*) collection; (*cantidad*) takings *pl*; (*en deporte*) gate; (*oficina*) tax office.

recaudador, a |rekáꝏthátḩor', à| *nm/f* tax collector.

recaudar |rekáꝏthár'| *vt* to collect.

recaudo |reká'ꝏtho| *nm* (*impuestos*) collection; (*JUR*) surety; **estar a buen ~** to be in safekeeping; **poner algo a buen ~** to put sth in a safe place.

recayendo |rekáyen'do| *etc vb* V **recaer.**

rece |re'se| *etc vb* V **rezar.**

recelar |reselár'| *vt*: **~ que** (*sospechar*) to suspect that; (*temer*) to fear that ♦ *vi*: **~(se) de** to distrust.

recelo |rese'lo| *nm* distrust, suspicion.

receloso, a |reselo'so, à| *a* distrustful, suspicious.

recepción |resepsyon'| *nf* reception; (*acto de recibir*) receipt.

recepcionista |resepsyoné'stá| *nm/f* receptionist.

receptáculo |reseptá'kꝏlo| *nm* receptacle.

receptivo, a |reseptē'ḩo, à| *a* receptive.

receptor, a |reseptor', à| *nm/f* recipient ♦ *nm* (*TELEC*) receiver; **descolgar el ~** to pick up the receiver.

recesión |resesyon'| *nf* (*COM*) recession.

receta |rese'tà| *nf* (*CULIN*) recipe; (*MED*) prescription.

recetar |resetár'| *vt* to prescribe.

recibidor |reseḩēthor'| *nm* entrance hall.

recibimiento |reseḩēmyen'to| *nm* reception, welcome.

recibir |reseḩēr'| *vt* to receive; (*dar la bienvenida*) to welcome; (*salir al encuentro de*) to go and meet ♦ *vi* to entertain; **~se** *vr*: **~se de** to qualify as.

recibo |rese'ḩo| *nm* receipt; **acusar ~ de** to acknowledge receipt of.

recién |resyen'| *ad* recently, newly; (*AM*) just, recently; **~ casado** newly-wed; **el ~ llegado** the newcomer; **el ~ nacido** the newborn child.

reciente |resyen'te| *a* recent; (*fresco*) fresh.

recientemente |resyentemen'te| *ad* recently.

recinto |resen'to| *nm* enclosure; (*área*) area, place.

recio, a |re'syo, à| *a* strong, tough; (*voz*) loud ♦ *ad* hard; loud(ly).

recipiente |resepyen'te| *nm* (*objeto*) container, receptacle; (*persona*) recipient.

reciprocidad |reseproseḩáḩ'| *nf* reciprocity.

recíproco, a |rese'proco, à| *a* reciprocal.

recital |resetál'| *nm* (*MUS*) recital; (*LIT*) reading.

recitar |resetár'| *vt* to recite.

reclamación |reklámásyon'| *nf* claim, demand; (*queja*) complaint; **~ salarial** pay claim.

reclamar |reklámár'| *vt* to claim, demand ♦ *vi*: **~ contra** to complain about; **~ a uno**

en justicia to take sb to court.

reclamo |reklá'mo| *nm* (*anuncio*) advertisement; (*tentación*) attraction.

reclinar |reklēnár'| *vt* to recline, lean; **~se** *vr* to lean back.

recluir |reklꝏēr'| *vt* to intern, confine.

reclusión |reklꝏsyon'| *nf* (*prisión*) prison; (*refugio*) seclusion; **~ perpetua** life imprisonment.

recluso, a |reklꝏ'so, à| *a* imprisoned; **población reclusa** prison population ♦ *nm/f* (*solitario*) recluse; (*JUR*) prisoner.

recluta |reklꝏ'tà| *nm/f* recruit ♦ *nf* recruitment.

reclutamiento |reklꝏtámyen'to| *nm* recruitment.

recluyendo |reklꝏyen'do| *etc vb* V **recluir.**

recobrar |rekoḩrár'| *vt* (*recuperar*) to recover; (*rescatar*) to get back; (*ciudad*) to recapture; (*tiempo*) to make up (for); **~se** *vr* to recover.

recodo |reko'ḩo| *nm* (*de río, camino*) bend.

recogedor, a |rekoḩeṭhor', à| *nm/f* picker, harvester.

recoger |rekoher'| *vt* to collect; (*AGR*) to harvest; (*fruta*) to pick; (*levantar*) to pick up; (*juntar*) to gather; (*pasar a buscar*) to come for, get; (*dar asilo*) to give shelter to; (*faldas*) to gather up; (*mangas*) to roll up; (*pelo*) to put up; **~se** *vr* (*retirarse*) to retire; **me recogieron en la estación** they picked me up at the station.

recogido, a |rekohē'ḩo, à| *a* (*lugar*) quiet, secluded; (*pequeño*) small ♦ *nf* (*CORREOS*) collection; (*AGR*) harvest; **recogida de datos** (*INFORM*) data capture.

recogimiento |rekohēmyen'to| *nm* collection; (*AGR*) harvesting.

recoja |reko'hà| *etc vb* V **recoger.**

recolección |rekoleksyon'| *nf* (*AGR*) harvesting; (*colecta*) collection.

recomendable |rekomendá'ḥle| *a* recommendable; **poco ~** inadvisable.

recomendación |rekomendàsyon'| *nf* (*sugerencia*) suggestion, recommendation; (*referencia*) reference; **carta de ~ para** letter of introduction to.

recomendar |rekomendár'| *vt* to suggest, recommend; (*confiar*) to entrust.

recomencé |rekomense'|, **recomencemos** |rekomense'mos| *etc vb* V **recomenzar.**

recomenzar |rekomensár'| *vt, vi* to begin again, recommence.

recomience |rekomyen'se| *etc vb* V **recomenzar.**

recomiende |rekomyen'de| *etc vb* V **recomendar.**

recomienzo |rekomyen'so| *etc vb* V **recomenzar.**

recompensa |rekompen'sà| *nf* reward, recompense; (*compensación*): **~ (de una**

pérdida) compensation (for a loss); **como** o **en** ~ **por** in return for.

recompensar [rekompensár'] vt to reward, recompense.

recompondré [rekompondre'] etc vb V **recomponer.**

recomponer [rekompóner'] vt to mend; (INFORM: texto) to reformat.

recomponga [rekompón'gà] etc, **recompuesto** [rekompwe'sto], **recompuse** [rekompōō'se] etc vb V **recomponer.**

reconciliación [rekonsēlyàsyon'] nf reconciliation.

reconciliar [rekonsēlyár'] vt to reconcile; ~**se** vr to become reconciled.

recóndito, a [rekon'dēto, à] a (lugar) hidden, secret.

reconfortar [rekonfortár'] vt to comfort.

reconocer [rekonoser'] vt to recognize; ~ **los hechos** to face the facts.

reconocido, a [rekonosē'tho, à] a recognized; (agradecido) grateful.

reconocimiento [rekonosēmyen'to] nm recognition; (registro) search; (inspección) examination; (gratitud) gratitude; (confesión) admission; ~ **óptico de caracteres** (INFORM) optical character recognition; ~ **de la voz** (INFORM) speech recognition.

reconozca [rekonos'kà] etc vb V **reconocer.**

reconquista [rekonkē'stà] nf reconquest.

reconquistar [rekonkēstár'] vt (MIL) to reconquer; (fig) to recover, win back.

reconstituyente [rekonstētōōyen'te] nm tonic.

reconstruir [rekonstrōōēr'] vt to reconstruct.

reconstruyendo [rekonstrōōyen'do] etc vb V **reconstruir.**

reconversión [recombersyon'] nf restructuring, reorganization; (tb: ~ **industrial**) modernization.

recopilación [rekopēlásyon'] nf (resumen) summary; (compilación) compilation.

recopilar [rekopēlár'] vt to compile.

récord [re'korth] a inv record; **cifras** ~ record figures ♦ nm, pl **records, récords** [re'korth] record; **batir el** ~ to break the record.

recordar [rekorthár'] vt (acordarse de) to remember; (traer a la memoria) to recall; (acordar a otro) to remind ♦ vi to remember; **recuérdale que me debe 5 dólares** remind him that he owes me 5 dollars; **que yo recuerde** as far as I can remember; **creo** ~, **si mal no recuerdo** if my memory serves me right.

recorrer [rekorrer'] vt (país) to cross, travel through; (distancia) to cover; (registrar) to search; (repasar) to look over.

recorrido [rekorre'tho] nm run, journey; **tren de largo** ~ main-line train.

pérdida) compensation (for a loss); **como** o **en** ~ **por** in return for.

recortado, a [rekortà'tho, à] a uneven, irregular.

recortar [rekortár'] vt (papel) to cut out; (el pelo) to trim; (dibujar) to draw in outline; ~**se** vr to stand out, be silhouetted.

recorte [rekor'te] nm (acción, de prensa) cutting; (de telas, chapas) trimming.

recostado, a [rekostà'tho, à] a leaning; **estar** ~ to be lying down.

recostar [rekostár'] vt to lean; ~**se** vr to lie down.

recoveco [rekobe'ko] nm (de camino, río etc) bend; (en casa) cubbyhole.

recreación [rekreàsyon'] nf recreation.

recrear [rekreár'] vt (entretener) to entertain; (volver a crear) to re-create.

recreativo, a [rekreàtē'tho, à] a recreational.

recreo [rekre'o] nm recreation; (ESCOL) recess (US), break (Brit).

recriminar [rekrēmēnár'] vt to reproach ♦ vi to recriminate; ~**se** vr to reproach each other.

recrudecer [rekrōōthéser'] vt, vi, **recrudecerse** vr to worsen.

recrudecimiento [rekrōōthesēmyen'to] nm upsurge.

recrudezca [rekrōōthes'kà] etc vb V **recrudecer.**

recta [rek'tà] nf V **recto.**

rectángulo, a [rektán'gōōlo, à] a rectangular ♦ nm rectangle.

rectificable [rektēfēká'ble] a rectifiable; **fácilmente** ~ easily rectified.

rectificación [rektēfēkàsyon'] nf correction.

rectificar [rektēfēkár'] vt to rectify; (volverse recto) to straighten ♦ vi to correct o.s.

rectifique [rektēfē'ke] etc vb V **rectificar.**

rectitud [rektētōōth'] nf straightness; (fig) rectitude.

recto, a [rek'to, à] a straight; (persona) honest, upright; (estricto) strict; (juez) fair; (juicio) sound ♦ nm rectum; (ATLETISMO) straight ♦ nf straight line; **en el sentido** ~ **de la palabra** in the proper sense of the word; **recta final** o **de llegada** home straight.

rector, a [rektor', à] a governing ♦ nm/f head, chief; (ESCOL) president (US), rector (Brit).

rectorado [rektorà'tho] nm (cargo) presidency (US), rectorship (Brit); (oficina) rector's office.

recuadro [rekwá'thro] nm box; (TIP) inset.

recuento [rekwen'to] nm inventory; **hacer el** ~ **de** to count o reckon up.

recuerdo [rekwer'tho] etc vb V **recordar** ♦ nm souvenir; ~**s** nmpl memories; ¡~**s a tu madre!** give my regards to your mother!; **"R~ de Mallorca"** "a present from Majorca"; **contar los** ~**s** to reminisce.

recueste |rckwe'ste| *etc vb* V **recostar.**
recular |rckōōlár'| *vi* to back down.
recuperable |rckōōperá'hlc| *a* recoverable.
recuperación |rckōōperásyon'| *nf* recovery; ~ **de datos** (*INFORM*) data retrieval.
recuperar |rckōōperár'| *vt* to recover; (*tiempo*) to make up; (*INFORM*) to retrieve; ~**se** *vr* to recuperate.
recurrir |rckōōrrēr'| *vi* (*JUR*) to appeal; ~ **a** to resort to; (*persona*) to turn to.
recurso |rckōōr'so| *nm* resort; (*medio*) means *pl,* resource; (*JUR*) appeal; **como último** ~ as a last resort; ~**s económicos** economic resources; ~**s naturales** natural resources.
recusar |rckōōsár'| *vt* to reject, refuse.
rechace |rctchá'se| *etc vb* V **rechazar.**
rechazar |rctchásár'| *vt* to repel, drive back; (*idea*) to reject; (*oferta*) to turn down.
rechazo |rctchá'so| *nm* (*de fusil*) recoil; (*rebote*) rebound; (*negación*) rebuff.
rechifla |rctchē'flá| *nf* hissing, booing; (*fig*) derision.
rechinar |rctchēnár'| *vi* to creak; (*dientes*) to grind; (*máquina*) to clank, clatter; (*metal seco*) to grate; (*motor*) to hum.
rechistar |rctchēstár'| *vi*: **sin** ~ without complaint.
rechoncho, a |rctchontch'o, á| *a* (*fam*) stocky, heavy-set.
red |rchh| *nf* net, mesh; (*FERRO, INFORM*) network; (*ELEC, de agua*) main (*US*), mains (*Brit*), supply system; (*de tiendas*) chain; (*trampa*) trap; **estar conectado con la** ~ to be connected to the main; ~ **local** (*INFORM*) local area network; ~ **de transmisión** (*INFORM*) data network.
redacción |rchháksyon'| *nf* (*acción*) writing; (*ESCOL*) essay, composition; (*limpieza de texto*) editing; (*personal*) editorial staff.
redactar |rchháktár'| *vt* to draw up, draft; (*periódico, INFORM*) to edit.
redactor, a |rchháktor', á| *nm/f* writer; (*en periódico*) editor.
redada |rchhá'thá| *nf* (*PESCA*) cast, throw; (*fig*) catch; ~ **policial** police raid, round-up.
redención |rchhensyon'| *nf* redemption.
redentor, a |rchhentor', á| *a* redeeming ♦ *nm/f* (*COM*) redeemer.
redescubierto |rchheskōōhycr'to| *pp de* **redescubrir.**
redescubrir |rchheskōōhrēr'| *vt* to rediscover.
redesignar |rchhesēgnár'| *vt* (*INFORM*) to rename.
redicho, a |rchhētch'o, á| *a* affected.
redil |rchhēl'| *nm* sheep pen.
redimir |rchhēmēr'| *vt* to redeem; (*rehén*) to ransom.
redistribución |rchhēstrchōōsyon'| *nf* (*COM*) redeployment.

rédito |rc'thēto| *nm* interest, yield.
redoblar |rchhohlár'| *vt* to redouble ♦ *vi* (*tambor*) to play a roll on the drums.
redoble |rchho'hlc| *nm* (*MUS*) drumroll, drumbeat; (*de trueno*) roll.
redomado, a |rchhomá'tho, á| *a* (*astuto*) sly, crafty; (*perfecto*) utter.
redonda |rchhon'dá| *nf* V **redondo.**
redondear |rchhondcár'| *vt* to round, round off; (*cifra*) to round up.
redondel |rchhondcl'| *nm* (*círculo*) circle; (*TAUR*) bullring, arena; (*AUTO*) (traffic) circle (*US*), roundabout (*Brit*).
redondo, a |rchhon'do, á| *a* (*circular*) round; (*completo*) complete ♦ *nf*: **a la redonda** around, round about; **en muchas millas a la redonda** for many miles around; **rehusar en** ~ to give a flat refusal.
reducción |rchhōōksyon'| *nf* reduction; ~ **del activo** (*COM*) divestment; ~ **de precios** (*COM*) price-cutting.
reducido, a |rchhōōsē'tho, á| *a* reduced; (*limitado*) limited; (*pequeño*) small; **quedar** ~ **a** to be reduced to.
reducir |rchhōōsēr'| *vt* to reduce, limit; (*someter*) to bring under control; ~**se** *vr* to diminish; (*MAT*): ~ **(a)** to reduce (to), convert (into); ~ **las millas a kilómetros** to convert miles into kilometers; ~**se a** (*fig*) to come *o* boil down to.
reduje |rchhō'hc| *etc vb* V **reducir.**
redundancia |rchhōōndán'syá| *nf* redundancy.
reduzca |rchhōōs'ká| *etc vb* V **reducir.**
reembolsable |rc(c)mbolsá'hlc| *a* (*COM*) redeemable, refundable.
reembolsar |rc(c)mbolsár'| *vt* (*persona*) to reimburse; (*dinero*) to repay, pay back; (*depósito*) to refund.
reembolso |rc(c)mbol'so| *nm* reimbursement; refund; **enviar algo contra** ~ to send sth cash on delivery; **contra** ~ **del flete** freight C.O.D.; ~ **fiscal** tax rebate.
reemplace |rc(c)mplá'sc| *etc vb* V **reemplazar.**
reemplazar |rc(c)mplásár'| *vt* to replace.
reemplazo |rc(c)mplá'so| *nm* replacement; **de** ~ (*MIL*) reserve.
reexportación |rc(c)ksportásyon'| *nf* (*COM*) re-export.
reexportar |rc(c)ksportár'| *vt* (*COM*) to re-export.
REF *nm abr* (*Esp ECON*) = *Régimen Económico Fiscal.*
Ref.ª *abr* (= *referencia*) ref.
referencia |rcfcrcn'syá| *nf* reference; **con** ~ **a** with reference to; **hacer** ~ **a** to refer *o* allude to; ~ **comercial** (*COM*) trade reference.
referéndum |rcfcrcn'dōōm|, *pl* **referéndums** *nm* referendum.

referente |refcren'te| *a*: ~ a concerning, relating to.

referir |refcrēr'| *vt* (*contar*) to tell, recount; (*relacionar*) to refer, relate; ~**se** *vr*: ~**se a** to refer to; ~ **al lector a un apéndice** to refer the reader to an appendix; ~ **a** (*COM*) to convert into; **por lo que se refiere a eso** as for that, as regards that.

refiera |refyc'rá| *etc vb* V **referir**.

refilón |refēlon'|: **de** ~ *ad* obliquely; **mirar a uno de** ~ to look out of the corner of one's eye at sb.

refinado, a |refēná'tho, á| *a* refined.

refinamiento |refēnámycn'to| *nm* refinement; ~ **por pasos** (*INFORM*) step by step debugging.

refinar |refēnár'| *vt* to refine.

refinería |refēncrē'á| *nf* refinery.

refiriendo |refēryen'do| *etc vb* V **referir**.

reflector |reflektor'| *nm* reflector; (*ELEC*) spotlight; (*AVIAT*, *MIL*) searchlight.

reflejar |reflchár'| *vt* to reflect; ~**se** *vr* to be reflected.

reflejo, a |refle'ho, á| *a* reflected; (*movimiento*) reflex ♦ *nm* reflection; (*ANAT*) reflex; (*en el pelo*): ~**s** *nmpl* highlights; **tiene el pelo castaño con** ~**s rubios** she has chestnut hair with blond streaks.

reflexión |reflcksyon'| *nf* reflection.

reflexionar |reflcksyonár'| *vt* to reflect on ♦ *vi* to reflect; (*detenerse*) to pause (to think); **¡reflexione!** you think it over!

reflexivo, a |reflcksē'ho, á| *a* thoughtful; (*LING*) reflexive.

refluir |reflōōēr'| *vi* to flow back.

reflujo |reflōō'ho| *nm* ebb.

refluyendo |reflōōycn'do| *etc vb* V **refluir**.

reforcé |reforse'|, **reforcemos** |reforse'mos| *etc vb* V **reforzar**.

reforma |refor'má| *nf* reform; (*ARQ etc*) repair; ~ **agraria** agrarian reform.

reformar |reformár'| *vt* to reform; (*modificar*) to change, alter; (*texto*) to revise; (*ARQ*) to repair; ~**se** *vr* to mend one's ways.

reformatear |reformátcár'| *vt* (*INFORM*: *disco*) to reformat.

reformatorio |reformàto'ryo| *nm* reformatory; ~ **de menores** reform school (*US*), remand home (*Brit*).

reforzamiento |reforsámycn'to| *nm* reinforcement.

reforzar |reforsár'| *vt* to strengthen; (*ARQ*) to reinforce; (*fig*) to encourage.

refractario, a |refráktá'ryo, á| *a* (*TEC*) heat-resistant; **ser** ~ **a una reforma** to resist *o* be opposed to a reform.

refrán |refrán'| *nm* proverb, saying.

refregar |refregár'| *vt* to scrub.

refregué |refrege'|, **refreguemos** |refrege'mos| *etc vb* V **refregar**.

refrenar |refrenár'| *vt* to check, restrain.

refrendar |refrendár'| *vt* (*firma*) to endorse, countersign; (*ley*) to approve.

refrescante |refreskán'te| *a* refreshing, cooling.

refrescar |refreskár'| *vt* to refresh ♦ *vi* to cool down; ~**se** *vr* to get cooler; (*tomar aire fresco*) to go out for a breath of fresh air; (*beber*) to have a drink.

refresco |refres'ko| *nm* soft drink, cool drink; "~**s**" "refreshments".

refresque |refres'ke| *etc vb* V **refrescar**.

refriega |refryc'gá| *etc vb* V **refregar** ♦ *nf* scuffle, brawl.

refriegue |refryc'ge| *etc vb* V **refregar**.

refrigeración |refrēhcrásyon'| *nf* refrigeration; (*de casa*) air-conditioning.

refrigerado, a |refrēhcrá'tho, á| *a* cooled; (*sala*) air-conditioned.

refrigerador |refrēhcráthor'| *nm*, (*AM*) **refrigeradora** |refrēhcrátho'rá| *nf* refrigerator.

refrigerar |refrēhcrár'| *vt* to refrigerate; (*sala*) to air-condition.

refuerce |refwcr'se| *etc vb* V **reforzar**.

refuerzo |refwcr'so| *etc vb* V **reforzar** ♦ *nm* reinforcement; (*TEC*) support.

refugiado, a |refōōhyá'tho, á| *nm/f* refugee.

refugiarse |refōōhyár'se| *vr* to take refuge, shelter.

refugio |refōō'hyo| *nm* refuge; (*protección*) shelter; (*AUTO*) street *o* traffic island; ~ **alpino** *o* **de montaña** mountain hut; ~ **subterráneo** (*MIL*) underground shelter.

refulgencia |refōōlhen'syá| *nf* brilliance.

refulgir |refōōlhēr'| *vi* to shine, be dazzling.

refulja |refōōl'há| *etc vb* V **refulgir**.

refundir |refōōndēr'| *vt* to recast; (*escrito etc*) to adapt, rewrite.

refunfuñar |refōōnfōōnyár'| *vi* to grunt, growl; (*quejarse*) to grumble.

refunfuñón, ona |refōōnfōōnyon', oná| (*fam*) *a* grumpy ♦ *nm/f* grouch.

refutación |refōōtásyon'| *nf* refutation.

refutar |refōōtár'| *vt* to refute.

regadera |regáthc'rá| *nf* watering can; **estar como una** ~ (*fam*) to be as mad as a hatter.

regadío |regáthē'o| *nm* irrigated land.

regalado, a |regálá'tho, á| *a* comfortable, luxurious; (*gratis*) free, for nothing; **lo tuvo** ~ it was handed to him on a plate.

regalar |regálár'| *vt* (*dar*) to give (as a present); (*entregar*) to give away; (*mimar*) to pamper, make a fuss of; ~**se** *vr* to treat o.s. to.

regalía |regálē'á| *nf* privilege, prerogative; (*COM*) bonus; (*de autor*) royalty.

regaliz |regálēs'| *nm* licorice.

regalo |regá'lo| *nm* (*obsequio*) gift, present; (*gusto*) pleasure; (*comodidad*) comfort.

regalón, ona |regálon', oná| *a* spoiled,

pampered.

regañadientes |rcgányáthycn'tcs|: **a** ~ *ad* reluctantly.

regañar |rcgányár'| *vt* to scold ♦ *vi* to grumble; (*dos personas*) to fall out, quarrel.

regaño |rcgá'nyo| *nm* scolding, telling-off; (*queja*) grumble.

regañón, ona |rcgányon', oná| *a* nagging.

regar |rcgár'| *vt* to water, irrigate; (*fig*) to scatter, sprinkle.

regata |rcgá'tá| *nf* (*NAUT*) race.

regatear |rcgáteár'| *vt* (*COM*) to bargain over; (*escatimar*) to be mean with ♦ *vi* to bargain, haggle; (*DEPORTE*) to dribble; **no** ~ **esfuerzo** to spare no effort.

regateo |rcgáte'o| *nm* bargaining; (*DEPORTE*) dribbling;. (*del cuerpo*) swerve, dodge.

regazo |rcgá'so| *nm* lap.

regeneración |rehencrásyon'| *nf* regeneration.

regenerar |rehencrár'| *vt* to regenerate.

regentar |rehentár'| *vt* to direct, manage; (*puesto*) to hold in an acting capacity; (*negocio*) to be in charge of.

regente, a |rchen'tc, á| *a* (*príncipe*) regent; (*director*) managing ♦ *nm* (*COM*) manager; (*POL*) regent.

régimen |rc'hēmen|, *pl* **regímenes** |rchē'menes| *nm* regime; (*reinado*) rule; (*MED*) diet; (*reglas*) (set of) rules; (*manera de vivir*) lifestyle; **estar a** ~ to be on a diet.

regimiento |rehēmyen'to| *nm* regiment.

regio, a |re'hyo, á| *a* royal, regal; (*fig: suntuoso*) splendid; (*AM fam*) great, terrific.

región |rehyon'| *nf* region; (*área*) area.

regional |rehyonál'| *a* regional.

regir |rehēr'| *vt* to govern, rule; (*dirigir*) to manage, run; (*ECON. JUR. LING*) to govern ♦ *vi* to apply, be in force.

registrador |rchēstráthor'| *nm* registrar, recorder.

registrar |rchēstrár'| *vt* (*buscar*) to search; (*en cajón*) to look through; (*inspeccionar*) to inspect; (*anotar*) to register, record; (*INFORM, MUS*) to record; ~**se** *vr* to register; (*ocurrir*) to happen.

registro |rehēs'tro| *nm* (*acto*) registration; (*MUS, libro*) register; (*lista*) list, record; (*INFORM*) record; (*inspección*) inspection, search; ~ **civil** ≈ county clerk's office (*US*), registry office (*Brit*); ~ **electoral** list of registered voters; ~ **de la propiedad** ≈ county recorder's office (*US*), land registry (office) (*Brit*).

regla |re'glá| *nf* (*ley*) rule, regulation; (*de medir*) ruler, rule; (*MED: período*) period; (~ *científica*) law, principle; **no hay** ~ **sin excepción** every rule has its exception.

reglamentación |rcglámentásyon'| *nf* (*acto*) regulation; (*lista*) rules *pl*.

reglamentar |rcglámentár'| *vt* to regulate.

reglamentario, a |rcglámentá'ryo, á| *a* statutory; **en la forma reglamentaria** in the properly established way.

reglamento |rcglámen'to| *nm* rules *pl*, regulations *pl*; ~ **del tráfico** highway code.

reglar |rcglár'| *vt* (*acciones*) to regulate; ~**se** *vr*: ~**se por** to be guided by.

regocijarse |rcgoschár'sc| *vr*: ~ **de** *o* **por** to rejoice at, be glad about.

regocijo |rcgosē'ho| *nm* joy, happiness.

regodearse |rcgothcár'sc| *vr* to be glad, be delighted; (*pey*): ~ **con** *o* **en** to gloat over.

regodeo |rcgothe'o| *nm* delight; (*pey*) perverse pleasure.

regresar |rcgresár'| *vi* to come/go back, return.

regresivo, a |rcgresē'ho, á| *a* backward; (*fig*) regressive.

regreso |rcgre'so| *nm* return; **estar de** ~ to be back, be home.

regué |rcgē'|, **reguemos** |rcgē'mos| *etc vb* V **regar**.

reguero |rcgē'ro| *nm* (*de sangre*) trickle; (*de humo*) trail.

regulación |rcgōōlásyon'| *nf* regulation; (*TEC*) adjustment; (*control*) control; ~ **del tráfico** traffic control.

regulador |rcgōōláthor'| *nm* (*TEC*) regulator; (*de radio etc*) knob.

regular |rcgōōlár'| *a* regular; (*normal*) normal, usual; (*común*) ordinary; (*organizado*) regular, orderly; (*mediano*) average; (*fam*) not bad, so-so ♦ *ad*: **estar** ~ to be so-so *o* alright ♦ *vt* (*controlar*) to control, regulate; (*TEC*) to adjust; **por lo** ~ as a rule.

regularice |rcgōōlárē'sc| *etc vb* V **regularizar**.

regularidad |rcgōōlárētháth'| *nf* regularity; **con** ~ regularly.

regularizar |rcgōōlárēsár'| *vt* to regularize.

regusto |rcgōō'sto| *nm* aftertaste.

rehabilitación |reáhēlētásyon'| *nf* rehabilitation; (*ARQ*) restoration.

rehabilitar |reáhēlētár'| *vt* to rehabilitate; (*ARQ*) to restore; (*reintegrar*) to reinstate.

rehacer |reáser'| *vt* (*reparar*) to mend, repair; (*volver a hacer*) to redo, repeat; ~**se** *vr* (*MED*) to recover.

rehaga |reá'gá| *etc*, **reharé** |reárc'| *etc*, **rehaz** |reás'|, **rehecho** |reetch'o| *vb* V **rehacer**.

rehén |reen'| *nm* hostage.

rehice |rē'se| *etc*, **rehizo** |rē'so| *vb* V **rehacer**.

rehuir |reōōēr'| *vt* to avoid, shun.

rehusar |reōōsár'| *vt*, *vi* to refuse.

rehuyendo |reōōyen'do| *etc vb* V **rehuir**.

reina |re'ēná| *nf* queen.

reinado |rēēná'tho| *nm* reign.

reinante |rēēnán'te| *a* (*fig*) prevailing.

reinar |rēēnár'| *vi* to reign; (*fig: prevalecer*) to prevail, be general.

reincidir |rēēnsēthēr'| *vi* to relapse; (*criminal*) to repeat an offence.

reincorporarse |rēēnkorporár'se| *vr*: ~ **a** to rejoin.

reinicializar |rēēnēsyálēsár'| *vt* (*INFORM*) to reset.

reino |rē'ēno| *nm* kingdom; **el R~ Unido** the United Kingdom.

reintegración |rēēntegrásyon'| *nf* (*COM*) reinstatement.

reintegrar |rēēntegrár'| *vt* (*reconstituir*) to reconstruct; (*persona*) to reinstate; (*dinero*) to refund, pay back; **~se** *vr*: **~se a** to return to.

reintegro |rēēnte'gro| *nm* refund, reimbursement; (*en banco*) withdrawal.

reír |rēēr'| *vi*, **reírse** *vr* to laugh; **~se de** to laugh at.

reiterar |rēētērár'| *vt* to reiterate; (*repetir*) to repeat.

reivindicación |rēēbēndēkásyon'| *nf* (*demanda*) claim, demand; (*justificación*) vindication.

reivindicar |rēēbēndēkár'| *vt* to claim.

reivindique |rēēbēndē'ke| *etc vb V* **reivindicar.**

reja |rē'há| *nf* (*de ventana*) grille, bars *pl*; (*en la calle*) grating.

rejamos |rēhá'mos| *etc vb V* **regir.**

rejilla |rēhē'yá| *nf* grating, grille; (*muebles*) wickerwork; (*de ventilación*) vent; (*de coche etc*) luggage rack.

rejuvenecer |rēhŏŏhēneser'| *vt*, *vi* to rejuvenate.

rejuvenezca |rēhŏŏhēnes'ká| *etc vb V* **rejuvenecer.**

relación |rēlásyon'| *nf* relation, relationship; (*MAT*) ratio; (*lista*) list; (*narración*) report; **~ costo-efectivo** *o* **costo-rendimiento** (*COM*) cost-effectiveness; **relaciones** *nfpl* (*enchufes*) influential friends, connections; **relaciones carnales** sexual relations; **relaciones comerciales** business connections; **relaciones empresariales/humanas** industrial/human relations; **relaciones laborales/públicas** labor/public relations; **con ~ a, en ~ con** in relation to; **estar en** *o* **tener buenas relaciones con** to be on good terms with.

relacionar |rēlásyonár'| *vt* to relate, connect; **~se** *vr* to be connected *o* linked.

relajación |rēláhásyon'| *nf* relaxation.

relajado, a |rēláhá'tho, á| *a* (*disoluto*) loose; (*cómodo*) relaxed; (*MED*) ruptured.

relajante |rēláhán'te| *a* relaxing; (*MED*) sedative.

relajar |rēláhár'| *vt*, **relajarse** *vr* to relax.

relamerse |rēlámer'se| *vr* to lick one's lips.

relamido, a |rēlámē'tho, á| *a* (*pulcro*) overdressed; (*afectado*) affected.

relámpago |rēlám'págo| *nm* flash of lightning ♦ *a* lightning *cpd*; **como un ~** as quick as lightning, in a flash; **visita/huelga ~** lightning visit/strike.

relampaguear |rēlámpágeár'| *vi* to flash.

relatar |rēlátár'| *vt* to tell, relate.

relativo, a |rēlátē'tho, á| *a* relative; **en lo ~** **a** concerning.

relato |rēlá'to| *nm* (*narración*) story, tale.

relegar |rēlegár'| *vt* to relegate; **~ algo al olvido** to banish sth from one's mind.

relegue |rēle'ge| *etc vb V* **relegar.**

relevante |rēlebán'te| *a* eminent, outstanding.

relevar |rēlebár'| *vt* (*sustituir*) to relieve; **~se** *vr* to relay; **~ a uno de un cargo** to relieve sb of his post.

relevo |rēle'bo| *nm* relief; **carrera de ~s** relay race; **~ con cinta** (*INFORM*) tape relay; **coger** *o* **tomar el ~** to take over, stand in.

relieve |rēlye'be| *nm* (*ARTE, TEC*) relief; (*fig*) prominence, importance; **bajo ~** basrelief; **un personaje de ~** an important man; **dar ~ a** to highlight.

religión |rēlēhyon'| *nf* religion.

religioso, a |rēlēhyo'so, á| *a* religious ♦ *nm*/ *f* monk/nun.

relinchar |rēlēntchár'| *vi* to neigh.

relincho |rēlēntch'o| *nm* neigh; (*acto*) neighing.

reliquia |rēlē'kyá| *nf* relic; **~ de familia** heirloom.

reloj |rēlo'(h)| *nm* clock; **~ de pie** grandfather clock; **~ (de pulsera)** wristwatch; **~ de sol** sundial; **~ despertador** alarm (clock); **como un ~** like clockwork; **contra (el) ~** against the clock.

relojería |rēlohere'á| *nf* (*tienda*) watchmaker's (shop); **aparato de ~** clockwork; **bomba de ~** time bomb.

relojero, a |rēlohe'ro, á| *nm*/*f* clockmaker; watchmaker.

reluciente |rēlŏŏsyen'te| *a* brilliant, shining.

relucir |rēlŏŏsēr'| *vi* to shine; (*fig*) to excel; **sacar algo a ~** to show sth off.

relumbrante |rēlŏŏmbrán'te| *a* dazzling.

relumbrar |rēlŏŏmbrár'| *vi* to dazzle, shine brilliantly.

reluzca |rēlŏŏs'ká| *etc vb V* **relucir.**

rellano |rēyá'no| *nm* (*ARQ*) landing.

rellenar |rēyenár'| *vt* (*llenar*) to fill up; (*CULIN*) to stuff; (*COSTURA*) to pad; (*formulario etc*) to fill in *o* out.

relleno, a |rēye'no, á| *a* full up; (*CULIN*) stuffed ♦ *nm* stuffing; (*de tapicería*) padding.

remachar |rēmátchár'| *vt* to rivet; (*fig*) to

hammer home, drive home.'
remache |remátch'e| *nm* rivet.
remanente |remánen'te| *nm* remainder; (*COM*), balance; (*de producto*) surplus.
remanso |remán'so| *nm* pool.
remar |remár'| *vi* to row.
rematado, a |remáta'tho, á| *a* complete, utter; **es un loco** ~ he's a raving lunatic.
rematar |remátár'| *vt* to finish off; (*animal*) to put out of its misery; (*COM*) to sell off cheap ♦ *vi* to end, finish off; (*DEPORTE*) to shoot.
remate |remá'te| *nm* end, finish; (*punta*) tip; (*DEPORTE*) shot; (*ARQ*) top; (*COM*) auction sale; **de o para** ~ to top it all off.
remediable |remethyá'ble| *a*: **fácilmente** ~ easily remedied.
remediar |remethyár'| *vt* (*gen*) to remedy; (*subsanar*) to make good, repair; (*evitar*) to avoid; **sin poder** ~**lo** without being able to prevent it.
remedio |reme'thyo| *nm* remedy; (*JUR*) recourse, remedy; **poner** ~ **a** to correct, stop; **no tener más** ~ to have no alternative; **¡qué** ~**!** there's no other way; **como último** ~ as a last resort; **sin** ~ inevitable; (*MED*) hopeless.
remedo |reme'tho| *nm* imitation; (*pey*) parody.
remendar |remendár'| *vt* to repair; (*con parche*) to patch; (*fig*) to correct.
remesa |reme'sá| *nf* remittance; (*COM*) shipment.
remiendo |remyen'do| *etc vb V* **remendar** ♦ *nm* mend; (*con parche*) patch; (*cosido*) darn; (*fig*) correction.
remilgado, a |remélgá'tho, á| *a* prim; (*afectado*) affected.
remilgo |remél'go| *nm* primness; (*afectación*) affectation.
reminiscencia |remēnēsen'syá| *nf* reminiscence.
remirar |remirár'| *vt* (*volver a mirar*) to look at again; (*examinar*) to look hard at.
remisión |remēsyon'| *nf* (*acto*) sending, shipment; (*REL*) forgiveness, remission; **sin** ~ hopelessly.
remiso, a |remē'so, á| *a* remiss.
remite |remē'te| *nm* (*en sobre*) name and address of sender.
remitente |remēten'te| *nm/f* (*CORREOS*) sender.
remitir |remētēr'| *vt* to remit, send ♦ *vi* to slacken.
remo |re'mo| *nm* (*de barco*) oar; (*DEPORTE*) rowing; **cruzar un río a** ~ to row across a river.
remoce |remo'se| *etc vb V* **remozar**.
remodelación |remodelásyon'| *nf* (*POL*): ~ **del gobierno** cabinet reshuffle.
remojar |remohár'| *vt* to steep, soak; (*galle-*

ta etc) to dip, dunk; (*fam*) to celebrate with a drink.
remojo |remo'ho| *nm* steeping, soaking; (*por la lluvia*) drenching, soaking; **dejar la ropa en** ~ to leave clothes to soak.
remojón |remohon'| *nm* soaking; **darse un** ~ (*fam*) to go (in) for a dip.
remolacha |remolátch'á| *nf* beet, beetroot (*Brit*).
remolcador |remolkáthor'| *nm* (*NAUT*) tug; (*AUTO*) tow truck (*US*), breakdown lorry (*Brit*).
remolcar |remolkár'| *vt* to tow.
remolino |remolē'no| *nm* eddy; (*de agua*) whirlpool; (*de viento*) whirlwind; (*de gente*) crowd.
remolón, ona |remolon', oná| *a* lazy ♦ *nm/f* slacker, shirker.
remolque |remol'ke| *etc vb V* **remolcar** ♦ *nm* tow, towing; (*cuerda*) towrope; **llevar a** ~ to tow.
remontar |remontár'| *vt* to mend; (*obstáculo*) to overcome; ~**se** *vr* to soar; ~**se a** (*COM*) to amount to; (*en tiempo*) to go back to, date from; ~ **el vuelo** to soar.
rémora |re'morá| *nf* hindrance.
remorder |remorther'| *vt* to distress, disturb.
remordimiento |remorthemyen'to| *nm* remorse.
remotamente |remotámen'te| *ad* vaguely.
remoto, a |remo'to, á| *a* remote.
remover |remoher'| *vt* to stir; (*tierra*) to turn over; (*objetos*) to move round.
remozar |remosár'| *vt* (*ARQ*) to refurbish; (*fig*) to brighten *o* polish up.
remuerda |remwer'thá| *etc vb V* **remorder**.
remueva |remwe'há| *etc vb V* **remover**.
remuneración |remōōnerásyon'| *nf* remuneration.
remunerado, a |remōōnerá'tho, á| *a*: **trabajo bien/mal** ~ well-/badly-paid job.
remunerar |remōōnerár'| *vt* to remunerate; (*premiar*) to reward.
renacer |renáser'| *vi* to be reborn; (*fig*) to revive.
renacimiento |renásēmyen'to| *nm* rebirth; **el R**~ the Renaissance.
renacuajo |renákwá'ho| *nm* (*ZOOL*) tadpole.
renal |renál'| *a* renal, kidney *cpd*.
Renania |renán'yá| *nf* Rhineland.
renazca |renás'ká| *etc vb V* **renacer**.
rencilla |rensē'yá| *nf* quarrel; ~**s** *nfpl* bickering *sg*.
rencor |renkor'| *nm* rancor (*US*), rancour (*Brit*), bitterness; (*resentimiento*) ill feeling, resentment; **guardar** ~ **a** to hold a grudge against.
rencoroso, a |renkoro'so, á| *a* spiteful.
rendición |rendēsyon'| *nf* surrender.

rendido, a |rendē'ťɦo, á| *a (sumiso)* submissive; *(agotado)* worn-out, exhausted; *(enamorado)* devoted.

rendija |rendē'há| *nf (hendedura)* crack; *(abertura)* aperture; *(fig)* rift, split; *(JUR)* loophole.

rendimiento |rendēmyen'to| *nm (producción)* output; *(COM)* yield, profit(s) *(pl)*; *(TEC, COM)* efficiency; ~ **de capital** *(COM)* return on capital.

rendir |rendēr'| *vt (vencer)* to defeat; *(producir)* to produce; *(dar beneficio)* to yield; *(agotar)* to exhaust ♦ *vi* to pay; *(COM)* to yield, produce; ~**se** *vr (someterse)* to surrender; *(ceder)* to yield; *(cansarse)* to wear o.s. out; ~ **homenaje** *o* **culto a** to pay homage to; **el negocio no rinde** the business doesn't pay.

renegado, a |renega'ťɦo, á| *a, nm/f* renegade.

renegar |renegár'| *vt (negar)* to deny vigorously ♦ *vi (blasfemar)* to blaspheme; ~ **de** *(renunciar)* to renounce; *(quejarse)* to complain about.

renegué |renege'|, **reneguemos** |renege'mos| *etc vb V* **renegar**.

RENFE |ren'fe| *nf abr Esp:=Red Nacional de Ferrocarriles Españoles.*

renglón |renglon'| *nm (línea)* line; *(COM)* item, article; **a** ~ **seguido** immediately after.

reniego |renye'go| *etc*, **reniegue** |renye'ge| *etc vb V* **renegar**.

reno |re'no| *nm* reindeer.

renombrado, a |renombrá'ťɦo, á| *a* renowned.

renombre |renom'bre| *nm* renown.

renovación |renoɦásyon'| *nf (de contrato)* renewal; *(ARQ)* renovation.

renovar |renoɦár'| *vt* to renew; *(ARQ)* to renovate; *(sala)* to redecorate.

renquear |renkeár'| *vi* to limp; *(fam)* to get along, scrape by.

renta |ren'tá| *nf (ingresos)* income; *(beneficio)* profit; *(alquiler)* rent; **política de** ~**s income** *(US)* o **incomes** *(Brit)* policy; ~ **gravable** *o* **imponible** taxable income; ~ **nacional (bruta)** (gross) national income; ~ **no salarial** unearned income; ~ **sobre el terreno** *(COM)* paid to owner of land; **vivir de sus** ~**s** to live on one's private income; ~ **vitalicia** annuity.

rentable |rentá'ɦle| *a* profitable; **no** ~ unprofitable.

rentar |rentár'| *vt* to produce, yield.

rentista |rentē'stá| *nm/f (accionista)* stockholder.

renuencia |renwen'syá| *nf* reluctance.

renuente |renwen'te| *a* reluctant.

renueve |renwe'ɦe| *etc vb V* **renovar**.

renuncia |renōōn'syá| *nf* resignation.

renunciar |renōōnsyár'| *vt* to renounce, give up ♦ *vi* to resign; ~ **a hacer algo** to give up doing sth.

reñido, a |renyē'ťɦo, á| *a (batalla)* bitter, hard-fought; **estar** ~ **con uno** to be on bad terms with sb; **está** ~ **con su familia** he has fallen out with his family.

reñir |renyēr'| *vt (regañar)* to scold ♦ *vi (estar peleado)* to quarrel, fall out; *(combatir)* to fight.

reo |re'o| *nm/f* culprit, offender; *(JUR)* accused.

reojo |reo'ho|: **de** ~ *ad* out of the corner of one's eye.

reorganice |reorgánē'se| *etc vb V* **reorganizar.**

reorganizar |reorgánēsár'| *vt* to reorganize.

Rep *abr* = **República.**

reparación |repárásyon'| *nf (acto)* mending, repairing; *(TEC)* repair; *(fig)* amends, reparation; **"reparaciones en el acto"** "repairs while you wait".

reparar |repárár'| *vt* to repair; *(fig)* to make amends for; *(suerte)* to retrieve; *(observar)* to observe ♦ *vi:* ~ **en** *(darse cuenta de)* to notice; *(poner atención en)* to pay attention to; **sin** ~ **en los gastos** regardless of the cost.

reparo |repá'ro| *nm (advertencia)* observation; *(duda)* doubt; *(dificultad)* difficulty; *(escrúpulo)* scruple, qualm; **poner** ~**s (a)** to raise objections (to); *(criticar)* to criticize; **no tuvo** ~ **en hacerlo** he did not hesitate to do it.

repartición |repártēsyon'| *nf* distribution; *(división)* division.

repartidor, a |repártēťɦor', á| *nm/f* distributor; ~ **de leche** milkman.

repartir |repártēr'| *vt* to distribute, share out; *(COM, CORREOS)* to deliver; *(MIL)* to partition; *(libros)* to give out; *(comida)* to serve out; *(naipes)* to deal.

reparto |repár'to| *nm* distribution; *(COM, CORREOS)* delivery; *(TEATRO, CINE)* cast; *(AM: urbanización)* housing development *(US)*, housing estate *(Brit)*; **"** ~ **a domicilio"** "home delivery service".

repasar |repásár'| *vt (ESCOL)* to revise; *(MECÁNICA)* to check, overhaul; *(COSTURA)* to mend.

repaso |repá'so| *nm* revision; *(MECÁNICA)* overhaul, checkup; *(COSTURA)* mending; ~ **general** servicing, general overhaul; **curso de** ~ refresher course.

repatriar |repátryár'| *vt* to repatriate; ~**se** *vr* to return home.

repelente |repelen'te| *a* repellent, repulsive.

repeler |repeler'| *vt* to repel; *(idea, oferta)* to reject.

repensar |repensár'| *vt* to reconsider.

repente |repen'te| *nm* sudden movement;

(fig) impulse; **de** ~ suddenly; ~ **de ira** fit of anger.

repentice |rɛpɛntēˈsɛ| *etc vb V* **repentizar.**

repentino, a |rɛpɛntēˈno, á| *a* sudden; *(imprevisto)* unexpected.

repentizar |rɛpɛntēsár'| *vi* (MUS) to sight-read.

repercusión |rɛpɛrkōōsyon'| *nf* repercussion; **de amplia** *o* **ancha** ~ far-reaching.

repercutir |rɛpɛrkōōtēr'| *vi* *(objeto)* to rebound; *(sonido)* to echo; ~ **en** *(fig)* to have repercussions *o* effects on.

repertorio |rɛpɛrtoˈryo| *nm* list; *(TEATRO)* repertoire.

repetición |rɛpɛtēsyon'| *nf* repetition.

repetido, a |rɛpɛtēˈtho, á| *a* repeated; **repetidas veces** repeatedly.

repetir |rɛpɛtēr'| *vt* to repeat; *(plato)* to have a second helping of; *(TEATRO)* to give as an encore, sing *etc* again ♦ *vi* to repeat; ~**se** *vr* to repeat o.s.; *(suceso)* to recur.

repetitivo, a |rɛpɛtētēˈho, á| *a* repetitive, repetitious.

repicar |rɛpēkár'| *vi* *(campanas)* to ring (out).

repiense |rɛpyɛnˈsɛ| *etc vb V* **repensar.**

repique |rɛpēˈkɛ| *etc vb V* **repicar** ♦ *nm* pealing, ringing.

repiqueteo |rɛpēkɛtɛˈo| *nm* pealing; *(de tambor)* drumming.

repisa |rɛpēˈsá| *nf* ledge, shelf; ~ **de chimenea** mantelpiece; ~ **de ventana** windowsill.

repitiendo |rɛpētyɛnˈdo| *etc vb V* **repetir.**

replegarse |rɛplɛgárˈsɛ| *vr* to fall back, retreat.

replegué |rɛplɛgɛˈ|, **repleguemos** |rɛplɛgɛˈmos| *etc vb V* **replegarse.**

repleto, a |rɛplɛˈto, á| *a* replete, full up; ~ **de** filled *o* crammed with.

réplica |rɛˈplēká| *nf* answer; *(ARTE)* replica; **derecho de** ~ right of *o* to reply.

replicar |rɛplēkár'| *vi* to answer; *(objetar)* to argue, answer back.

repliego |rɛplyɛˈgo| *etc vb V* **replegarse.**

repliegue |rɛplyɛˈgɛ| *etc vb V* **replegarse** ♦ *nm* (MIL) withdrawal.

replique |rɛplēˈkɛ| *etc vb V* **replicar.**

repoblación |rɛpoblásyon'| *nf* repopulation; *(de río)* restocking; ~ **forestal** reforestation.

repoblar |rɛpoblár'| *vt* to repopulate; to restock.

repollo |rɛpoˈyo| *nm* cabbage.

repondré |rɛpondrɛ'| *etc vb V* **reponer.**

reponer |rɛponɛr'| *vt* to replace, put back; *(máquina)* to re-set; *(TEATRO)* to revive; ~**se** *vr* to recover; ~ **que** to reply that.

reponga |rɛponˈgá| *etc vb V* **reponer.**

reportaje |rɛportáˈhɛ| *nm* report, article; ~ **gráfico** illustrated report.

reportar |rɛportár'| *vt* *(traer)* to bring,

carry; *(conseguir)* to obtain; *(fig)* to check; ~**se** *vr* *(contenerse)* to control o.s.; *(calmarse)* to calm down; **la cosa no le reportó sino disgustos** the affair brought him nothing but trouble.

reportero, a |rɛportɛˈro, á| *nm/f* reporter; ~ **gráfico/a** news photographer.

reposacabezas |rɛposákáhɛˈsás| *nm inv* headrest.

reposado, a |rɛposáˈtho, á| *a* *(descansado)* restful; *(tranquilo)* calm.

reposar |rɛposár'| *vi* to rest, repose; *(muerto)* to lie, rest.

reposición |rɛposēsyon'| *nf* replacement; *(CINE)* second showing; *(TEATRO)* revival.

reposo |rɛpoˈso| *nm* rest.

repostar |rɛpostár'| *vt* to replenish; *(AUTO)* to fill up (with gasoline).

repostería |rɛpostɛrēˈá| *nf* *(arte)* confectionery, pastry-making; *(tienda)* confectioner's (shop).

repostero, a |rɛpostɛˈro, á| *nm/f* confectioner.

reprender |rɛprɛndɛr'| *vt* to reprimand; *(niño)* to scold.

reprensión |rɛprɛnsyon'| *nf* rebuke, reprimand; *(de niño)* telling-off, scolding.

represa |rɛprɛˈsá| *nf* dam; *(lago artificial)* lake, pool.

represalia |rɛprɛsáˈlyá| *nf* reprisal; **tomar** ~**s** to take reprisals, retaliate.

representación |rɛprɛsɛntásyon'| *nf* representation; *(TEATRO)* performance; **en** ~ **de** representing; **por** ~ by proxy; ~ **visual** *(INFORM)* display.

representante |rɛprɛsɛntánˈtɛ| *nm/f* (POL, COM) representative; *(TEATRO)* performer.

representar |rɛprɛsɛntár'| *vt* to represent; *(significar)* to mean; *(TEATRO)* to perform; *(edad)* to look; ~**se** *vr* to imagine; **tal acto representaría la guerra** such an act would mean war.

representativo, a |rɛprɛsɛntátēˈho, á| *a* representative.

represión |rɛprɛsyon'| *nf* repression.

reprimenda |rɛprēmɛnˈdá| *nf* reprimand, rebuke.

reprimir |rɛprēmēr'| *vt* to repress; ~**se** *vr*: ~**se de hacer algo** to stop o.s. from doing sth.

reprobación |rɛprobásyon'| *nf* reproval; *(culpa)* blame.

reprobar |rɛprobár'| *vt* to censure, reprove.

réprobo, a |rɛˈproho, á| *nm/f* reprobate.

reprochar |rɛprotchár'| *vt* to reproach; *(censurar)* to condemn, censure.

reproche |rɛprotchˈɛ| *nm* reproach.

reproducción |rɛprothōōksyon'| *nf* reproduction.

reproducir |rɛprothōōsēr'| *vt* to reproduce; ~**se** *vr* to breed; *(situación)* to recur.

reproductor, a [reproħōōktor', à] *a* repro-
ductive.

reproduje [reproħōō'he], **reprodujera** [re-
proħōōhe'rà] *etc*, **reproduzca** [reprodōōs'ká]
etc vb V **reproducir**.

repruebe [reprwe'he] *etc vb V* **reprobar**.

reptar [reptár'] *vi* to creep, crawl.

reptil [reptēl'] *nm* reptile.

república [repōō'hlēká] *nf* republic; **R~ Dominicana** Dominican Republic; **R~ Democrática Alemana (RDA)** German Democratic Republic; **R~ Federal Alemana
(RFA)** Federal Republic of Germany; **R~
Árabe Unida** United Arab Republic.

republicano, a [repōōhlēká'no, à] *a*, *nm/f*
republican.

repudiar [repōōħyàr'] *vt* to repudiate; (*fe*)
to renounce.

repudio [repōō'ħyo] *nm* repudiation.

repueble [repwe'hle] *etc vb V* **repoblar**.

repuesto [repwe'sto] *pp de* **reponer** ♦ *nm*
(*pieza de recambio*) spare (part); (*abastecimiento*) supply; **rueda de ~** spare wheel;
y llevamos otro de ~ and we have another
as a spare *o* in reserve.

repugnancia [repōōgnàn'syà] *nf* re-
pugnance.

repugnante [repōōgnàn'te] *a* repugnant, repulsive.

repugnar [repōōgnár'] *vt* to disgust ♦ *vi*,
~se *vr* (*contradecirse*) to contradict each
other; (*dar asco*) to be disgusting.

repulsa [repōōl'sà] *nf* rebuff.

repulsión [repōōlsyon'] *nf* repulsion, aversion.

repulsivo, a [repōōlsē'ħo, à] *a* repulsive.

repuse [repōō'se] *etc vb V* **reponer**.

reputación [repōōtàsyon'] *nf* reputation.

reputar [repōōtár'] *vt* to consider, deem.

requemado, a [rekemá'ħo, à] *a* (*quemado*)
scorched; (*bronceado*) tanned.

requemar [rekemár'] *vt* (*quemar*) to
scorch; (*secar*) to parch; (*CULIN*) to overdo, burn; (*la lengua*) to burn, sting.

requerimiento [rekerēmyen'to] *nm* request; (*demanda*) demand; (*JUR*)
summons.

requerir [rekerēr'] *vt* (*pedir*) to ask, request; (*exigir*) to require; (*ordenar*) to call
for; (*llamar*) to send for, summon.

requesón [rekeson'] *nm* cottage cheese.

requete... [rekete] *pref* extremely.

requiebro [rekyc'hro] *nm* (*piropo*) compliment, flirtatious remark.

réquiem [re'kyem] *nm* requiem.

requiera [rekyc'rà] *etc*, **requiriendo** [re-
kēryen'do] *etc vb V* **requerir**.

requisa [rekē'sà] *nf* (*inspección*) survey, inspection; (*MIL*) requisition.

requisar [rekēsàr'] *vt* (*MIL*) to requisition;
(*confiscar*) to seize, confiscate.

requisito [rekēsē'to] *nm* requirement, requi-
site; **~ previo** prerequisite; **tener los ~s
para un cargo** to have the essential
qualifications for a job.

res [res] *nf* beast, animal.

resabio [resá'hyo] *nm* (*maña*) vice, bad
habit; (*dejo*) (unpleasant) aftertaste.

resaca [resá'ká] *nf* (*en el mar*) undertow,
undercurrent; (*fig*) backlash; (*fam*) hangover.

resaltar [resàltàr'] *vi* to project, stick out;
(*fig*) to stand out.

resarcir [resàrsēr'] *vt* to compensate; (*pagar*) to repay; **~se** *vr* to make up for; **~ a
uno de una pérdida** to compensate sb for a
loss; **~ a uno de una cantidad** to repay sb
a sum.

resarza [resár'sà] *etc vb V* **resarcir**.

resbaladizo, a [reshàlàthē'so, à] *a* slippery.

resbalar [reshàlár'] *vi*, **resbalarse** *vr* to slip,
slide; (*fig*) to slip (up); **le resbalaban las
lágrimas por las mejillas** tears were trick-
ling down his cheeks.

resbalón [reshàlon'] *nm* (*acción*) slip;
(*deslizamiento*) slide; (*fig*) slip.

rescatar [reskàtàr'] *vt* (*salvar*) to save,
rescue; (*objeto*) to get back, recover; (*cau-
tivos*) to ransom.

rescate [reskà'te] *nm* rescue; (*objeto*) recovery; **pagar un ~** to pay a ransom.

rescindir [resēndēr'] *vt* (*contrato*) to annul,
rescind.

rescisión [resēsyon'] *nf* cancellation.

rescoldo [reskol'do] *nm* embers *pl*.

resecar [resekár'] *vt* to dry off, dry thoroughly; (*MED*) to cut out, remove; **~se** *vr*
to dry up.

reseco, a [rese'ko, à] *a* very dry; (*fig*)
skinny.

resentido, a [resentē'ħo, à] *a* resentful; **es
un ~** he's bitter.

resentimiento [resentēmyen'to] *nm* resentment, bitterness.

resentirse [resentēr'se] *vr* (*debilitarse*:
persona) to suffer; **~ con** to resent; **~ de**
(*consecuencias*) to feel the effects of.

reseña [rese'nyà] *nf* (*cuenta*) account; (*informe*) report; (*LIT*) review.

reseñar [resenyàr'] *vt* to describe; (*LIT*) to
review.

reseque [rese'ke] *etc vb V* **resecar**.

reserva [reser'hà] *nf* reserve; (*reservación*)
reservation; **a ~ de que ... unless ...; con
toda ~** in strictest confidence; **de ~** spare;
tener algo de ~ to have sth in reserve; **~
de indios** Indian reservation; (*COM*): **~
para amortización** depreciation allowance;
~ de caja *o* **en efectivo** cash reserves; **~s
del Estado** government stock; **~s en oro**
gold reserves.

reservado, a [reserhà'ħo, à] *a* reserved;

(*retraído*) cold, distant ♦ *nm* private room; (*FERRO*) reserved compartment.

reservar [reserⱨár'] *vt* (*guardar*) to keep; (*FERRO, TEATRO etc*) to reserve, book; ~**se** *vr* to save o.s.; (*callar*) to keep to o.s.; ~ **con exceso** to overbook.

resfriado [resfrēă'ⱨo] *nm* cold.

resfriarse [resfrēăr'se] *vr* to cool off; (*MED*) to catch (a) cold.

resguardar [resⱨwárⱨár'] *vt* to protect, shield; ~**se** *vr*: ~**se de** to guard against.

resguardo [resⱨwár'ⱨo] *nm* defense (*US*), defence (*Brit*); (*vale*) voucher; (*recibo*) receipt, slip.

residencia [resēⱨen'syá] *nf* residence; (*UNIV*) hall of residence; ~ **para ancianos** *o* **jubilados** rest home.

residencial [resēⱨensyál'] *a* residential ♦ *nf* (*urbanización*) housing development (*US*), housing estate (*Brit*).

residente [resēⱨen'te] *a*, *nm/f* resident.

residir [resēⱨēr'] *vi* to reside, live; ~ **en** to reside *o* lie in; (*consistir en*) to consist of.

residual [resēⱨwál'] *a* residual; **aguas** ~**es** sewage.

residuo [resē'ⱨwo] *nm* residue; ~**s atmosféricos** *o* **radiactivos** fallout *sg*.

resienta [resyen'tá] *etc vb* V **resentir**.

resignación [resēgnásyon'] *nf* resignation.

resignarse [resēgnár'se] *vr*: ~ **a** *o* **con** to resign o.s. to, be resigned to.

resina [resē'ná] *nf* resin.

resintiendo [resēntyen'do] *etc vb* V **resentir**.

resistencia [resēsten'syá] *nf* (*dureza*) endurance, strength; (*oposición, ELEC*) resistance; **la R**~ (*MIL*) the Resistance.

resistente [resēsten'te] *a* strong, hardy; (*TEC*) resistant; ~ **al calor** heat-resistant.

resistir [resēstēr'] *vt* (*soportar*) to bear; (*oponerse a*) to resist, oppose; (*aguantar*) to put up with ♦ *vi* to resist; (*aguantar*) to last, endure; ~**se** *vr*: ~**se a** to refuse to, resist; **no puedo** ~ **este frío** I can't bear *o* stand this cold; **me resisto a creerlo** I refuse to believe it; **se le resiste la química** chemistry escapes her.

resol [resol'] *nm* glare of the sun.

resolución [resolōōsyon'] *nf* resolution; (*decisión*) decision; (*moción*) motion; ~ **judicial** legal ruling; **tomar una** ~ to take a decision.

resoluto, a [resolōō'to, á] *a* resolute.

resolver [resolⱨer'] *vt* to resolve; (*solucionar*) to solve, resolve; (*decidir*) to decide, settle; ~**se** *vr* to make up one's mind.

resollar [resoyár'] *vi* to breathe noisily, wheeze.

resonancia [resonán'syá] *nf* (*del sonido*) resonance; (*repercusión*) repercussion; (*fig*) wide effect, impact.

resonante [resonán'te] *a* resonant, resounding; (*fig*) tremendous.

resonar [resonár'] *vi* to ring, echo.

resoplar [resoplár'] *vi* to snort; (*por cansancio*) to puff.

resoplido [resoplē'ⱨo] *nm* heavy breathing.

resorte [resor'te] *nm* spring; (*fig*) lever.

respaldar [respáldár'] *vt* to back (up), support; (*INFORM*) to back up; ~**se** *vr* to lean back; ~**se con** *o* **en** (*fig*) to take one's stand on.

respaldo [respál'do] *nm* (*de sillón*) back; (*fig*) support, backing.

respectivo, a [respektē'ⱨo, á] *a* respective; **en lo** ~ **a** with regard to.

respecto [respek'to] *nm*: **al** ~ on this matter; **con** ~ **a**, ~ **de** with regard to, in relation to.

respetable [respetà'ⱨle] *a* respectable.

respetar [respetàr'] *vt* to respect.

respeto [respe'to] *nm* respect; (*acatamiento*) deference; ~**s** *nmpl* respects; **por** ~ **a** out of consideration for; **presentar sus** ~**s a** to pay one's respects to.

respetuoso, a [respetwo'so, á] *a* respectful.

respingar [respēngàr'] *vi* to shy.

respingo [respēn'go] *nm* start, jump.

respingue [respēn'ge] *etc vb* V **respingar**.

respiración [respērásyon'] *nf* breathing; (*MED*) respiration; (*ventilación*) ventilation.

respirar [respērár'] *vt*, *vi* to breathe; **no dejar** ~ **a uno** to hassle sb; **estuvo escuchándole sin** ~ he listened to him in complete silence.

respiratorio, a [respēràto'ryo, á] *a* respiratory.

respiro [respē'ro] *nm* breathing; (*fig: descanso*) respite, rest; (*COM*) period of grace.

resplandecer [resplándeser'] *vi* to shine.

resplandeciente [resplándesyen'te] *a* resplendent, shining.

resplandezca [resplándes'ká] *etc vb* V **resplandecer**.

resplandor [resplándor'] *nm* brilliance, brightness; (*del fuego*) blaze.

responder [responder'] *vt* to answer ♦ *vi* to answer; (*fig*) to respond; (*pey*) to answer back; (*corresponder*) to correspond; ~ **a** (*situación etc*) to respond to; ~ **a una pregunta** to answer a question; ~ **a una descripción** to fit a description; ~ **de** *o* **por** to answer for.

respondón, ona [respondon', oná] *a* mouthy (*US*), cheeky (*Brit*).

responsabilice [responsáⱨelē'se] *etc vb* V **responsabilizarse**.

responsabilidad [responsáⱨelēⱨàⱨ'] *nf* responsibility; **bajo mi** ~ on my authority; ~ **ilimitada** (*COM*) unlimited liability.

responsabilizarse [responsáβēlēsár'se] *vr* to make o.s. responsible, take charge.

responsable [responsá'ble] *a* responsible; **la persona** ~ the person in charge; **hacerse** ~ **de algo** to assume responsibility for sth.

respuesta [respwe'stá] *nf* answer, reply; (*reacción*) response.

resquebrajar [reskeβrahár'] *vt*, **resquebrajarse** *vr* to crack, split.

resquemor [reskemor'] *nm* resentment.

resquicio [reskē'syo] *nm* chink; (*hendedura*) crack.

resta [re'stá] *nf* (*MAT*) remainder.

restablecer [restáβleser'] *vt* to re-establish, restore; ~**se** *vr* to recover.

restablecimiento [restáβlesēmyen'to] *nm* re-establishment; (*restauración*) restoration; (*MED*) recovery.

restablezca [restáβles'ká] *etc vb* V **restablecer.**

restallar [restáyár'] *vi* to crack.

restante [restán'te] *a* remaining; **lo** ~ the remainder; **los** ~**s** the rest, those left (over).

restar [restár'] *vt* (*MAT*) to subtract; (*descontar*) to deduct; (*fig*) to take away ♦ *vi* to remain, be left.

restauración [restáōōrásyon'] *nf* restoration.

restaurador, a [restáōōráłłor', á] *nm/f* (*persona*) restorer.

restaurante [restáōōrán'te] *nm* restaurant.

restaurar [restáōōrár'] *vt* to restore.

restitución [restētōōsyon'] *nf* return, restitution.

restituir [restētōōēr'] *vt* (*devolver*) to return, give back; (*rehabilitar*) to restore.

restituyendo [restētōōyen'do] *etc vb* V **restituir.**

resto [re'sto] *nm* (*residuo*) rest, remainder; (*apuesta*) stake; ~**s** *nmpl* remains; (*CULIN*) leftovers, scraps; ~**s mortales** mortal remains.

restregar [restregár'] *vt* to scrub, rub.

restregué [restregé'], **restreguemos** [restrege'mos] *etc vb* V **restregar.**

restricción [restrēksyon'] *nf* restriction; **sin** ~ **de** without restrictions on *o* as to; **hablar sin restricciones** to talk freely.

restrictivo, a [restrēktē'βo, á] *a* restrictive.

restriego [restrye'ɡo] *etc*, **restriegue** [restrye'ɡe] *etc vb* V **restregar.**

restringir [restrēnhēr'] *vt* to restrict, limit.

restrinja [restrēn'há] *etc vb* V **restringir.**

resucitar [resōōsētár'] *vt*, *vi* to resuscitate, revive.

resuelto, a [reswel'to, á] *pp de* **resolver** ♦ *a* resolute, determined; **estar** ~ **a algo** to be set on sth; **estar** ~ **a hacer algo** to be determined to do sth.

resuelva [reswel'βá] *etc vb* V **resolver.**

resuello [reswe'yo] *etc vb* V **resollar** ♦ *nm* (*aliento*) breath.

resuene [reswe'ne] *etc vb* V **resonar.**

resulta [resōōl'tá] *nf* result; **de** ~**s de** as a result of.

resultado [resōōltá'ðo] *nm* result; (*conclusión*) outcome; ~**s** *nmpl* (*INFORM*) output *sg*; **dar** ~ to produce results.

resultante [resōōltán'te] *a* resulting, resultant.

resultar [resōōltár'] *vi* (*ser*) to be; (*llegar a ser*) to turn out to be; (*salir bien*) to turn out well; (*seguir*) to ensue; ~ **a** (*COM*) to amount to; ~ **de** to stem from; ~ **en** to result in, produce; **resulta que ...** (*por consecuencia*) it follows that ...; (*parece que*) it seems that ...; **el conductor resultó muerto** the driver was killed; **no resultó** it didn't work *o* come off; **me resulta difícil hacerlo** it's difficult for me to do it.

resumen [resōō'men] *nm* summary, résumé; **en** ~ in short.

resumir [resōōmēr'] *vt* to sum up; (*condensar*) to summarize; (*cortar*) to abridge, cut down; (*condensar*) to summarize; ~**se** *vr*: **la situación se resume en pocas palabras** the situation can be summed up in a few words.

resurgir [resōōrhēr'] *vi* (*reaparecer*) to reappear.

resurrección [resōōrreksyon'] *nf* resurrection.

retablo [retá'βlo] *nm* altarpiece.

retaguardia [retáɡwár'ðyá] *nf* rearguard.

retahíla [retáč'lá] *nf* series, string; (*de injurias*) volley, stream.

retal [retál'] *nm* remnant.

retar [retár'] *vt* (*gen*) to challenge; (*desafiar*) to defy, dare.

retardar [retárłhár'] *vt* (*demorar*) to delay; (*hacer más lento*) to slow down; (*retener*) to hold back.

retardo [retár'ðo] *nm* delay.

retazo [retá'so] *nm* fragment, snippet.

RETD *nf abr* (*Esp TELEC*)=*Red Especial de Transmisión de Datos.*

rete... [re'te] *pref* very, extremely.

retención [retensyon'] *nf* retention; (*de pago*) deduction; ~ **de llamadas** (*TELEC*) hold facility.

retendré [retendre'] *etc vb* V **retener.**

retener [retener'] *vt* (*guardar*) to retain, keep; (*intereses*) to withhold.

retenga [reten'gá] *etc vb* V **retener.**

reticencia [retēsen'syá] *nf* (*sugerencia*) insinuation, (malevolent) suggestion; (*engaño*) half-truth.

reticente [retēsen'te] *a* (*insinuador*) insinuating; (*engañoso*) deceptive.

retiene [retye'ne] *etc vb* V **retener.**

retina |rctē'ná| *nf* retina.

retintín |rctēntēn'| *nm* jangle, jingle; **decir algo con ~** to say sth sarcastically.

retirado, a |rctēra'ᵗᵗo, á| *a* (*lugar*) remote; (*vida*) quiet; (*jubilado*) retired ♦ *nf* (*MIL*) retreat; (*de dinero*) withdrawal; (*de embajador*) recall; (*refugio*) safe place; **batirse en retirada** to retreat.

retirante |rctērán'tc| *a*: **ser ~ a hacer algo** to be reluctant to do sth.

retirar |rctērár'| *vt* to withdraw; (*la mano*) to draw back; (*quitar*) to remove; (*dinero*) to take out, withdraw; (*jubilar*) to retire; **~se** *vr* to retreat, withdraw; (*jubilarse*) to retire; (*acostarse*) to retire, go to bed.

retiro |rctē'ro| *nm* retreat; (*jubilación*, *tb* *DEPORTE*) retirement; (*pago*) pension; (*lugar*) quiet place.

reto |re'to| *nm* dare, challenge.

retocar |rctokár'| *vt* to touch up, retouch.

retoce |reto'se| *etc vb* V **retozar**.

retoño |reto'nyo| *nm* sprout, shoot; (*fig*) offspring, child.

retoque |reto'ke| *etc vb* V **retocar** ♦ *nm* retouching.

retorcer |retorser'| *vt* to twist; (*argumento*) to turn, twist; (*manos, lavado*) to wring; **~se** *vr* to become twisted; (*persona*) to writhe; **~se de dolor** to writhe in *o* squirm with pain.

retorcimiento |rctorsēmyen'to| *nm* twist, twisting; (*fig*) deviousness.

retórico, a |reto'rēko, á| *a* rhetorical; (*pey*) affected, windy ♦ *nf* rhetoric; (*pey*) affectedness.

retornar |retornár'| *vt* to return, give back ♦ *vi* to return, go/come back.

retorno |retor'no| *nm* return; **~ del carro** (*INFORM*, *TIP*) carriage return; **~ del carro automático** (*INFORM*) wordwrap.

retortero |retorte'ro| *nm*: **andar al ~** to bustle about, have heaps of things to do; **andar al ~ por uno** to be madly in love with sb.

retortijón |retortēhon'| *nm* twist, twisting; **~ de tripas** stomach cramp.

retorzamos |retorsá'mos| *etc vb* V **retorcer**.

retozar |retosár'| *vi* (*juguetear*) to frolic, romp; (*saltar*) to gambol.

retozón, ona |retoson', oná| *a* playful.

retracción |retráksyon'| *nf* retraction.

retractarse |retráktár'se| *vr* to retract; **me retracto** I take that back.

retraerse |retráer'se| *vr* to retreat, withdraw.

retraído, a |retráē'ᵗᵗo, á| *a* shy, retiring.

retraiga |retrá'ēgá| *etc vb* V **retraerse**.

retraimiento |retráēmyen'to| *nm* retirement; (*timidez*) shyness.

retraje |retrá'he| *etc*, **retrajera** |retráhe'rá| *etc vb* V **retraerse**.

retransmisión |retránsmēsyon'| *nf* repeat (broadcast).

retransmitir |retránsmētēr'| *vt* (*mensaje*) to relay; (*TV etc*) to repeat, retransmit; (: *en vivo*) to broadcast live.

retrasado, a |retrásá'ᵗᵗo, á| *a* late; (*MED*) mentally retarded; (*país etc*) backward, underdeveloped; **estar ~** (*reloj*) to be slow; (*persona, industria*) to be *o* lag behind.

retrasar |retrásár'| *vt* (*demorar*) to postpone, put off; (*retardar*) to slow down ♦ *vi*, **~se** *vr* (*atrasarse*) to be late; (*reloj*) to be slow; (*producción*) to fall (off); (*quedarse atrás*) to lag behind.

retraso |retrá'so| *nm* (*demora*) delay; (*lentitud*) slowness; (*tardanza*) lateness; (*atraso*) backwardness; **~s** *nmpl* (*COM*) arrears; (*deudas*) deficit *sg*, debts; **llegar con ~** to be late; **llegar con 25 minutos de ~** to be 25 minutes late; **llevo un ~ de 6 semanas** I'm 6 weeks behind (with my work *etc*); **~ mental** mental deficiency.

retratar |retrátár'| *vt* (*ARTE*) to paint the portrait of; (*fotografiar*) to photograph; (*fig*) to depict, describe; **~se** *vr* to have one's portrait painted; to have one's photograph taken.

retratista |retrátē'stá| *nm/f* (*pintura*) (portrait) painter; (*FOTO*) photographer.

retrato |retrá'to| *nm* portrait; (*FOTO*) photograph; (*descripción*) portrayal, depiction; (*fig*) likeness; **ser el vivo ~ de** to be the spitting image of.

retrato-robot |retrá'toroᵇo'(t)|, *pl* **retratos-robot** *nm* identikit picture.

retrayendo |retráyen'do| *etc vb* V **retraerse**.

retreta |retre'tá| *nf* retreat.

retrete |retre'te| *nm* toilet.

retribución |retrēᵇoōsyon'| *nf* (*recompensa*) reward; (*pago*) pay, payment.

retribuir |retrēᵇoōēr'| *vt* (*recompensar*) to reward; (*pagar*) to pay.

retribuyendo |retrēᵇoōyen'do| *etc vb* V **retribuir**.

retro... |retro| *pref* retro....

retroactivo, a |retroáktē'ᵇo, á| *a* retroactive, retrospective; **dar efecto ~ a un pago** to backdate a payment.

retroalimentación |retroálēmentásyon'| *nf* (*INFORM*) feedback.

retroceder |retroseᵗor'| *vi* (*echarse atrás*) to move back(wards); (*fig*) to back down; **no ~** to stand firm; **la policía hizo ~ a la multitud** the police forced the crowd back.

retroceso |retrose'so| *nm* backward movement; (*MED*) relapse; (*COM*) recession, depression; (*fig*) backing down.

retrógrado, a |retro'gráᵗᵗo, á| *a* retrograde, retrogressive; (*POL*) reactionary.

retropropulsión |retropropoōlsyon'| *nf* jet

propulsion.

retrospectivo, a |rctrospcktē'ho, á| *a* retrospective; **mirada retrospectiva** backward glance.

retrovisor |rctroħĕsor'| *nm* rear-view mirror.

retuerce |rctwcr'sc| *etc*, **retuerza** |rctwcr'sá| *etc vb* V **retorcer.**

retumbante |rctōōmbán'tc| *a* resounding.

retumbar |rctōōmbár'| *vi* to echo, resound; (*continuamente*) to reverberate.

retuve |rctōō'ħc| *etc vb* V **retener.**

reuma |rc'ōōmá| *nm* rheumatism.

reumático, a |rcōōmá'tēko, á| *a* rheumatic.

reumatismo |rcōōmátēs'mo| *nm* rheumatism.

reunificar |rcōōnēfēkár'| *vt* to reunify.

reunifique |rcōōnēfē'kc| *etc vb* V **reunificar.**

reunión |rcōōnyon'| *nf* (*asamblea*) meeting; (*fiesta*) party; **~ en la cumbre** summit meeting; **~ de ventas** (*COM*) sales meeting.

reunir |rcōōnēr'| *vt* (*juntar*) to reunite, join (together); (*recoger*) to gather (together); (*personas*) to bring o get together; (*cualidades*) to combine; **~se** *vr* (*personas: en asamblea*) to meet, gather; **reunió a sus amigos para discutirlo** he got his friends together to talk it over.

reválida |rcħá'lēħá| *nf* (*ESCOL*) final examination.

revalidar |rcħálēħár'| *vt* (*ratificar*) to confirm, ratify.

revalorar |rcħálorár'| *vt* to revalue, reassess.

revalor(iz)ación |rcħálor(ēs)àsyon'| *nf* revaluation; (*ECON*) reassessment.

revancha |rcħántch'á| *nf* revenge; (*DEPORTE*) return match; (*BOXEO*) return fight.

revelación |rcħclásyon'| *nf* revelation.

revelado |rcħclá'ħo| *nm* developing.

revelador, a |rcħcláħor', á| *a* revealing.

revelar |rcħclár'| *vt* to reveal; (*secreto*) to disclose; (*mostrar*) to show; (*FOTO*) to develop.

revendedor, a |rcħcndcħor', á| *nm/f* retailer; (*pey*) scalper (*US*), ticket tout (*Brit*).

revendré |rcħcndrc'| *etc*, **revenga** |rcħcn'gá| *etc vb* V **revenirse.**

revenirse |rcħcnēr'sc| *vr* to shrink; (*comida*) to go bad; (*vino*) to sour; (*CULIN*) to get tough.

reventa |rcħcn'tá| *nf* resale; (*especulación*) speculation; (*de entradas*) scalping (*US*), touting (*Brit*).

reventar |rcħcntár'| *vt* to burst, explode; (*molestar*) to annoy, rile ♦ *vi*, **~se** *vr* (*estallar*) to burst, explode; **me revienta tener que ponérmelo** I hate having to wear it; **~ de** (*fig*) to be bursting with; **~ por** to

be bursting to.

reventón |rcħcnton'| *nm* (*AUTO*) blow-out (*Brit*), flat (*US*).

reverberación |rcħcrħcrásyon'| *nf* reverberation.

reverberar |rcħcrħcrár'| *vi* (*luz*) to play, be reflected; (*superficie*) to shimmer; (*nieve*) to glare; (*sonido*) to reverberate.

reverbero |rcħcrħc'ro| *nm* play; shimmer, shine; glare; reverberation.

reverencia |rcħcrcn'syä| *nf* reverence; (*inclinación*) bow.

reverenciar |rcħcrcnsyär'| *vt* to revere.

reverendo, a |rcħcrcn'do, á| *a* reverend; (*fam*) big, awful; **un ~ imbécil** an awful idiot.

reverente |rcħcrcn'tc| *a* reverent.

reverso |rcħcr'so| *nm* back, other side; (*de moneda*) reverse.

revertir |rcħcrtēr'| *vi* to revert; **~ en beneficio de** to be to the advantage of; **~ en perjuicio de** to be to the detriment of.

revés |rcħcs'| *nm* back, wrong side; (*fig*) reverse, setback; (*DEPORTE*) backhand; **al ~** the wrong way around; (*de arriba abajo*) upside down; (*ropa*) inside out; **y al ~** and vice versa; **volver algo al ~** to turn sth around; (*ropa*) to turn sth inside out; **los reveses de la fortuna** life's setbacks.

revestir |rcħcstēr'| *vt* (*poner*) to put on; (*cubrir*) to cover, coat; (*cualidad*) to have, possess; **~se** *vr* (*REL*) to put on one's vestments; (*ponerse*) to put on; **~ con** *o* **de** to arm o.s. with; **el acto revestía gran solemnidad** the ceremony had great dignity.

reviejo, a |rcħyc'ho, á| *a* very old, ancient.

reviene |rcħyc'nc| *etc vb* V **revenirse.**

reviente |rcħycn'tc| *etc vb* V **reventar.**

revierta |rcħycr'tá| *etc vb* V **revertir.**

reviniendo |rcħēnycn'do| *etc vb* V **revenirse.**

revirtiendo |rcħērtycn'do| *etc vb* V **revertir.**

revisar |rcħēsár'| *vt* (*examinar*) to check; (*texto etc*) to revise; (*JUR*) to review.

revisión |rcħēsyon'| *nf* revision; **~ aduanera** customs inspection; **~ de cuentas** audit.

revisor, a |rcħēsor', á| *nm/f* inspector; (*FERRO*) conductor; **~ de cuentas** auditor.

revista |rcħē'stá| *etc vb* V **revestir** ♦ *nf* magazine, review; (*sección*) section, page; (*TEATRO*) revue; (*inspección*) inspection; **~ literaria** literary review; **~ de libros** book reviews (page); **pasar ~ a** to review, inspect.

revivir |rcħēħēr'| *vt* (*recordar*) to revive memories of ♦ *vi* to revive.

revocación |rcħokásyon'| *nf* repeal.

revocar |rcħokár'| *vt* (*decisión*) to revoke; (*ARQ*) to plaster.

revolcar |rcħolkár'| *vt* to knock down, send flying; **~se** *vr* to roll around.

revolcón |reḥolkon'| *nm* tumble.
revolotear |reḥoloteár'| *vi* to flutter.
revoloteo |reḥolote'o| *nm* fluttering.
revolqué |reḥolke'|, **revolquemos**
|reḥolke'mos| *etc vb* V **revolcar.**
revoltijo |reḥoltē'ho| *nm* mess, jumble.
revoltoso, a |reḥolto'so, á| *a* (*travieso*)
naughty, unruly.
revolución |reḥoloōsyon'| *nf* revolution.
revolucionar |reḥoloōsyonár'| *vt* to revolu-
tionize.
revolucionario, a |reḥoloōsyoná'ryo, á| *a*,
nm/f revolutionary.
revolver |reḥolḥer'| *vt* (*desordenar*) to dis-
turb, mess up; (*agitar*) to shake; (*líquido*)
to stir; (*mover*) to move about; (*POL*) to
stir up ♦ *vi*: ~ **en** to go through, rummage
(about) in; ~**se** *vr* (*en cama*) to toss and
turn; (*METEOROLOGÍA*) to break, turn
stormy; ~**se contra** to turn on *o* against;
han revuelto toda la casa they've turned
the whole house upside down.
revólver |reḥol'ḥer| *nm* revolver.
revoque |reḥo'ke| *etc vb* V **revocar.**
revuelco |reḥwel'ko| *etc vb* V **revolcar.**
revuelo |reḥwe'lo| *nm* fluttering; (*fig*)
commotion; **armar** *o* **levantar un gran** ~ to
cause a great stir.
revuelque |reḥwel'ke| *etc vb* V **revolcar.**
revuelto, a |reḥwel'to, á| *pp de* **revolver** ♦ *a*
(*mezclado*) mixed-up, in disorder; (*mar*)
rough; (*tiempo*) unsettled ♦ *nf* (*motín*) revolt; (*agitación*) commotion; **todo estaba**
~ everything was in disorder *o* was topsy-
turvy.
revuelva |reḥwel'ḥá| *etc vb* V **revolver.**
rey |reē| *nm* king; **los R~es** the King and
Queen.
reyerta |reyer'tá| *nf* quarrel, brawl.
rezagado, a |reságá'tho, á| *a*: **quedar** ~ to
be left behind; (*estar retrasado*) to be late,
be behind ♦ *nm/f* straggler.
rezagar |reságár'| *vt* (*dejar atrás*) to leave
behind; (*retrasar*) to delay, postpone; ~**se**
vr (*atrasarse*) to fall behind.
rezague |resá'ge| *etc vb* V **rezagar.**
rezar |resár'| *vi* to pray; ~ **con** (*fam*) to
concern, have to do with.
rezo |re'so| *nm* prayer.
rezongar |resongár'| *vi* to grumble;
(*murmurar*) to mutter; (*refunfuñar*) to
growl.
rezongue |reson'ge| *etc vb* V **rezongar.**
rezumar |resoōmár'| *vt* to ooze ♦ *vi* to leak;
~**se** *vr* to leak out.
RFA *nf abr* = **República Federal Alemana.**
ría |rē'á| *nf* estuary.
riada |reá'thá| *nf* flood.
ribera |reḥe'rá| *nf* (*de río*) bank; (: *área*)
riverside.
ribete |reḥe'te| *nm* (*de vestido*) border; (*fig*)

addition.
ribetear |reḥeteár'| *vt* to edge, border.
rice |rē'se| *etc vb* V **rizar.**
ricino |rēsē'no| *nm*: **aceite de** ~ castor oil.
rico, a |rē'ko, á| *a* (*adinerado*) rich,
wealthy; (*lujoso*) luxurious; (*comida*) delicious; (*niño*) lovely, cute ♦ *nm/f* rich
person; **nuevo** ~ nouveau riche.
rictus |rēk'toōs| *nm* (*mueca*) sneer, grin; ~
de amargura bitter smile.
ridiculez |rēthēkoōles'| *nf* absurdity.
ridiculice |rēthēkoōlē'se| *etc vb* V **ridiculi-
zar.**
ridiculizar |rēthēkoōlēsár'| *vt* to ridicule.
ridículo, a |rēthē'koōlo, á| *a* ridiculous; **ha-
cer el** ~ to make a fool of o.s.; **poner a
uno en** ~ to make a fool of sb; **ponerse en**
~ to make a fool *o* laughing-stock of o.s.
riego |rye'go| *etc vb* V **regar** ♦ *nm* (*asper-
sión*) watering; (*irrigación*) irrigation.
riegue |rye'ge| *etc vb* V **regar.**
riel |ryel| *nm* rail.
rienda |ryen'dá| *nf* rein; (*fig*) restraint,
moderating influence; **dar** ~ **suelta a** to
give free rein to; **llevar las** ~**s** to be in
charge.
riendo |ryen'do| *vb* V **reír.**
riesgo |ryes'go| *nm* risk; **seguro a** *o* **contra
todo** ~ comprehensive insurance; ~ **para
la salud** health hazard; **correr el** ~ **de** to
run the risk of.
Rif |rēf| *nm* Rif(f).
rifa |rē'fá| *nf* (*lotería*) raffle.
rifar |rēfár'| *vt* to raffle.
rifeño, a |rēfe'nyo, á| *a* of the Rif(f),
Rif(f)ian ♦ *nm/f* Rif(f)ian, Rif(f).
rifle |rē'fle| *nm* rifle.
rigidez |rēhēthes'| *nf* rigidity, stiffness; (*fig*)
strictness.
rígido, a |rē'hētho, á| *a* rigid, stiff; (*moral-
mente*) strict, inflexible; (*cara*) expression-
less.
rigiendo |rēhyen'do| *etc vb* V **regir.**
rigor |rēgor'| *nm* strictness; (*dureza*) tough-
ness; (*inclemencia*) harshness; (*meticulosi-
dad*) accuracy; **el** ~ **del verano** the hottest
part of the summer; **con todo** ~ **científico**
with scientific precision; **de** ~ essential;
después de los saludos de ~ after the inevitable greetings.
riguroso, a |rēgoōro'so, á| *a* rigorous; (*ME-
TEOROLOGÍA*) harsh; (*severo*) severe.
rija |rē'há| *etc vb* V **regir** ♦ *nf* quarrel.
rima |rē'má| *nf* rhyme; ~**s** *nfpl* verse *sg*; ~
imperfecta assonance; ~ **rimando** (*fam*)
merrily.
rimar |rēmár'| *vi* to rhyme.
rimbombante |rēmbombán'te| *a* (*fig*)
pompous.
rímel, rímmel |rē'mel| *nm* mascara.
rimero |rēme'ro| *nm* stack, pile.

Rin |rēn| *nm* Rhine.

rincón |rēnkon| *nm* corner (*inside*).

rindiendo |rēndyen'do| *etc vb* V **rendir**.

rinoceronte |rēnoseron'te| *nm* rhinoceros.

riña |rē'nyá| *nf* (*disputa*) argument; (*pelea*) brawl.

riñendo |rēnyen'do| *etc vb* V **reñir**.

riñón |rēnyon'| *nm* kidney; **me costó un ~** (*fam*) it cost me an arm and a leg; **tener riñones** to have guts.

rió |rēo'| *vb* V **reír**.

río |rē'o| *etc vb* V **reír** ♦ *nm* river; (*fig*) torrent, stream; **~ abajo/arriba** downstream/upstream; **cuando el ~ suena, agua lleva** there's no smoke without fire.

Río de Janeiro |rē'otheháne'ēro| *nm* Rio de Janeiro.

Río de la Plata |rē'othelápláta| *nm* Rio de la Plata, River Plate.

Rioja |rēo'há| *nf*: **La ~** La Rioja ♦ *nm*: **r~** rioja wine.

riojano, a |ryohá'no, á| *a, nm/f* Riojan.

rioplatense |rēopláten'se| *a* of o from the River Plate region ♦ *nm/f* native o inhabitant of the River Plate region.

riqueza |rēke'sá| *nf* wealth, riches *pl*; (*cualidad*) richness.

risa |rē'sá| *nf* laughter; (*una ~*) laugh; **¡qué ~!** what a laugh!; **caerse** o **morirse de ~** to split one's sides laughing, die laughing; **tomar algo a ~** to laugh sth off.

risco |rēs'ko| *nm* crag, cliff.

risible |rēsē'ble| *a* ludicrous, laughable.

risotada |rēsotá'thá| *nf* guffaw, loud laugh.

ristra |rēs'trá| *nf* string.

ristre |rēs'tre| *nm*: **en ~** at the ready.

risueño, a |rēswe'nyo, á| *a* (*sonriente*) smiling; (*contento*) cheerful.

ritmo |rēt'mo| *nm* rhythm; **a ~ lento** slowly; **trabajar a ~ lento** to go slow.

rito |rē'to| *nm* rite.

ritual |rētwál'| *a, nm* ritual.

rival |rēbál'| *a, nm/f* rival.

rivalice |rēbálē'se| *etc vb* V **rivalizar**.

rivalidad |rēbálēsáth'| *nf* rivalry, competition.

rivalizar |rēbálēsár'| *vi*: **~ con** to rival, compete with.

rizado, a |rēsá'tho, á| *a* (*pelo*) curly; (*superficie*) ridged; (*terreno*) undulating; (*mar*) choppy ♦ *nm* curls *pl*.

rizar |rēsár'| *vt* to curl; **~se** *vr* (*el pelo*) to curl; (*agua*) to ripple; (*el mar*) to become choppy.

rizo |rē'so| *nm* curl; (*agua*) ripple.

Rma. *abr* (= *Reverendísima*) courtesy title.

Rmo. *abr* (= *Reverendísimo*) Rt. Rev.

RNE *nf abr* = *Radio Nacional de España*.

R. O. *abr* (= *Real Orden*) royal order.

robar |rohár'| *vt* to rob; (*objeto*) to steal; (*casa etc*) to break into; (*NAIPES*) to draw;

(*atención*) to steal, capture; (*paciencia*) to exhaust.

roble |ro'ble| *nm* oak.

robledal |rohlethál'|, **robledo** |roble'tho| *nm* oakwood.

robo |ro'ho| *nm* robbery, theft; (*objeto robado*) stolen article o goods *pl*; **¡esto es un ~!** this is highway robbery!

robot |roho'(t)|, *pl* **robots** *a*, *nm* robot.

robótica |roho'tēká| *nf* robotics *sg*.

robustecer |rohōōsteser'| *vt* to strengthen.

robustezca |rohōōstes'ká| *etc vb* V **robustecer**.

robusto, a |rohōō'sto, á| *a* robust, strong.

ROC *abr* (*INFORM*: = *reconocimiento óptico de caracteres*) OCR.

roca |ro'ká| *nf* rock; **la R~** the Rock (of Gibraltar).

roce |ro'se| *etc vb* V **rozar** ♦ *nm* rub, rubbing; (*caricia*) brush; (*TEC*) friction; (*en la piel*) graze; **tener ~ con** to have a brush with.

rociar |rosyár'| *vt* to sprinkle, spray.

rocín |rosēn'| *nm* nag, hack.

rocío |rosē'o| *nm* dew.

rocoso, a |roko'so, á| *a* rocky.

rodado, a |rothá'tho, á| *a* (*con ruedas*) wheeled ♦ *nf* rut.

rodaja |rothá'há| *nf* (*raja*) slice.

rodaje |rothá'he| *nm* (*CINE*) shooting, filming; (*AUTO*): **en ~** breaking in (*US*), running in (*Brit*).

Ródano |ro'tháno| *nm* Rhône.

rodar |rothár'| *vt* (*vehículo*) to wheel (along); (*escalera*) to roll down; (*viajar por*) to travel (through) ♦ *vi* to roll; (*coche*) to go, run; (*CINE*) to shoot, film; (*persona*) to move about (from place to place), drift; **echarlo todo a ~** (*fig*) to mess it all up.

Rodas |ro'thás| *nf* Rhodes.

rodear |rotheár'| *vt* to surround ♦ *vi* to go around; **~se** *vr*: **~se de amigos** to surround o.s. with friends.

rodeo |rothe'o| *nm* (*ruta indirecta*) long way around, roundabout way; (*desvío*) detour; (*evasión*) evasion; (*AM*) rodeo; **dejarse de ~s** to talk straight; **hablar sin ~s** to come to the point, speak plainly.

rodilla |rothē'yá| *nf* knee; **de ~s** kneeling.

rodillo |rothē'yo| *nm* roller; (*CULIN*) rolling-pin; (*en máquina de escribir, impresora*) platen.

rododendro |rothothen'dro| *nm* rhododendron.

roedor, a |roethor', á| *a* gnawing ♦ *nm* rodent.

roer |roer'| *vt* (*masticar*) to gnaw; (*corroer, fig*) to corrode.

rogar |rogár'| *vt* (*pedir*) to beg, ask for ♦ *vi* (*suplicar*) to beg, plead; **~se** *vr*: **se ruega**

no fumar please do not smoke; ~ **que** + *subjun* to ask to ...; **ruegue a este señor que nos deje en paz** please ask this gentleman to leave us alone; **no se hace de** ~ he doesn't have to be asked twice.

rogué [roǥe'], **roguemos** [roǥe'mos] etc vb V **rogar**.

rojizo, a [rohē'so, á] a reddish.

rojo, a [ro'ho, á] a red ♦ nm red (color); (*POL*) red; **ponerse** ~ to turn red, blush; **al** ~ **vivo** red-hot.

rol [rol] nm list, roll; (*AM*: *papel*) role.

rollizo, a [royē'so, á] a (*objeto*) cylindrical; (*persona*) plump.

rollo, a [ro'yo, á] a (*fam*) boring, tedious ♦ nm roll; (*de cuerda*) coil; (*madera*) log; (*fam*) bore; (*discurso*) boring speech; ¡qué ~! what a mess!; **la conferencia fue un** ~ the lecture was a big drag.

ROM [rom] nf abr (= *memoria de sólo lectura*) ROM.

Roma [ro'má] nf Rome; **por todas partes se va a** ~ all roads lead to Rome.

romance [román'se] nm (*LING*) Romance language; (*LIT*) ballad; **hablar en** ~ to speak plainly.

romano, a [romá'no, á] a Roman, of Rome ♦ nm/f Roman.

romanticismo [romántēsēs'mo] nm romanticism.

romántico, a [román'tēko, á] a romantic.

romería [romerē'á] nf (*REL*) pilgrimage; (*excursión*) trip, outing.

romero, a [rome'ro, á] nm/f pilgrim ♦ nm rosemary.

romo, a [ro'mo, á] a blunt; (*fig*) dull.

rompecabezas [rompekáhe'sás] nm inv riddle, puzzle; (*juego*) jigsaw (puzzle).

rompehuelgas [rompewel'ǥás] nm inv strikebreaker.

rompeolas [rompeo'lás] nm inv breakwater.

romper [romper'] vt to break; (*hacer pedazos*) to smash; (*papel, tela etc*) to tear, rip; (*relaciones*) to break off ♦ vi (*olas*) to break; (*sol, diente*) to break through; ~ **un contrato** to break a contract; ~ **a** to start (suddenly) to; ~ **a llorar** to burst into tears; ~ **con uno** to fall out with sb; **ha roto con su novio** she has broken up with her fiancé.

rompimiento [rompēmyen'to] nm (*acto*) breaking; (*fig*) break; (*quiebra*) crack; ~ **de relaciones** breaking off of relations.

ron [ron] nm rum.

roncar [ronkár'] vi (*al dormir*) to snore; (*animal*) to roar.

ronco, a [ron'ko, á] a (*afónico*) hoarse; (*áspero*) raucous.

ronda [ron'dá] nf (*de bebidas etc*) round; (*patrulla*) patrol; (*de naipes*) hand, game;

ir de ~ to do one's round.

rondar [rondár'] vt to patrol; (*a una persona*) to hang round; (*molestar*) to harass; (*a una chica*) to court ♦ vi to patrol; (*fig*) to prowl round; (*MUS*) to go serenading.

rondeño, a [ronde'nyo, á] a of o from Ronda ♦ nm/f native o inhabitant of Ronda.

ronque [ron'ke] etc vb V **roncar**.

ronquera [ronke'rá] nf hoarseness.

ronquido [ronkē'ðo] nm snore, snoring.

ronronear [ronroneár'] vi to purr.

ronroneo [ronrone'o] nm purr.

roña [ro'nyá] nf (*veterinaria*) mange; (*mugre*) dirt, grime; (*óxido*) rust.

roñoso, a [ronyo'so, á] a (*mugriento*) filthy; (*tacaño*) stingy.

ropa [ro'pá] nf clothes pl, clothing; ~ **blanca** linen; ~ **de cama** bed linen; ~ **interior** underwear; ~ **lavada** o **para lavar** washing; ~ **planchada** ironing; ~ **sucia** dirty clothes pl, washing; ~ **usada** secondhand clothes.

ropaje [ropá'he] nm gown, robes pl.

ropavejero, a [ropáhehe'ro, á] nm/f secondhand clothes dealer.

ropero [rope'ro] nm linen cupboard; (*guardarropa*) wardrobe.

roque [ro'ke] nm (*AJEDREZ*) rook, castle; **estar** ~ to be fast asleep.

rosa [ro'sá] a inv pink ♦ nf rose; (*ANAT*) red birthmark; ~ **de los vientos** the compass; **estar como una** ~ to feel as fresh as a daisy; (**color**) **de** ~ pink.

rosado, a [rosá'ðo, á] a pink ♦ nm rosé.

rosal [rosál'] nm rosebush.

rosaleda [rosále'ðá] nf rose bed o garden.

rosario [rosá'ryo] nm (*REL*) rosary; (*fig*: *serie*) string; **rezar el** ~ to say the rosary.

rosbif [rosḇēf'] nm roast beef.

rosca [ros'ká] nf (*de tornillo*) thread; (*de humo*) coil, spiral; (*pan, postre*) ring-shaped roll/pastry; **hacer la** ~ **a uno** (*fam*) to kiss (*US*) o suck (*Brit*) up to sb; **pasarse de** ~ (*fig*) to go too far.

Rosellón [roseyon'] nm Roussillon.

rosetón [roseton'] nm rosette; (*ARQ*) rose window.

rosquilla [roskē'yá] nf small ring-shaped cake; (*de humo*) ring.

rostro [ros'tro] nm (*cara*) face; (*fig*) cheek.

rotación [rotásyon'] nf rotation; ~ **de cultivos** crop rotation.

rotativo, a [rotátē'ðo, á] a rotary ♦ nm newspaper.

roto, a [ro'to, á] pp de **romper** ♦ a broken; (*en pedazos*) smashed; (*tela, papel*) torn; (*vida*) shattered ♦ nm (*en vestido*) hole, tear.

rótula [ro'tōolá] nf kneecap; (*TEC*) ball-and-socket joint.

rotulador [rotōoláðhor'] nm felt-tip pen.

rotular [rotōōlár'] vt (carta, documento) to head, entitle; (objeto) to label.

rótulo [ro'tōōlo] nm (título) heading, title; (etiqueta) label; (letrero) sign.

rotundo, a [rotōōn'do, á] a round; (enfático) emphatic.

rotura [rotōō'rá] nf (rompimiento) breaking; (MED) fracture.

roturar [rotōōrár'] vt to plough.

rozado, a [rosá'ṭo, á] a worn.

rozadura [rosáṭōō'rá] nf abrasion, graze.

rozar [rosár'] vt (frotar) to rub; (ensuciar) to dirty; (MED) to graze; (tocar ligeramente) to shave, skim; (fig) to touch o border on; ~**se** vr to rub (together); ~ **con** (fam) to rub shoulders with.

Rte. abr = **remite, remitente.**

RTVE nf abr (TV) = Radiotelevisión Española.

Ruán [rōōán'] nm Rouen.

rubéola [rōōḥe'olá] nf German measles, rubella.

rubí [rōōḥē'] nm ruby; (de reloj) jewel.

rubio, a [rōō'ḥyo, á] a fair-haired, blond(e) ♦ nm/f blond/blonde; **tabaco** ~ Virginia tobacco; (cerveza) **rubia** lager.

rubor [rōōḥor'] nm (sonrojo) blush; (timidez) bashfulness.

ruborice [rōōḥorē'se] etc vb V **ruborizarse.**

ruborizarse [rōōḥorēsár'se] vr to blush.

ruboroso, a [rōōḥoro'so, á] a blushing.

rúbrica [rōō'ḥriká] nf (título) title, heading; (de la firma) flourish; **bajo la** ~ **de** under the heading of.

rubricar [rōōḥrēkár'] vt (firmar) to sign with a flourish; (concluir) to sign and seal.

rubrique [rōōḥrē'ke] etc vb V **rubricar.**

rudeza [rōōḥe'sá] nf (tosquedad) coarseness; (sencillez) simplicity.

rudimentario, a [rōōḥēmentá'ryo, á] a rudimentary, basic.

rudo, a [rōō'ḏo, á] a (sin pulir) unpolished; (grosero) coarse; (violento) violent; (sencillo) simple.

rueda [rwe'ḏá] nf wheel; (círculo) ring, circle; (rodaja) slice, round; (en impresora etc) sprocket; ~ **delantera/trasera/de repuesto** front/back/spare wheel; ~ **impresora** (INFORM) print wheel; ~ **de prensa** press conference.

ruedo [rwe'ḏo] etc vb V **rodar** ♦ nm (contorno) edge, border; (de vestido) hem; (círculo) circle; (TAUR) arena, bullring; (esterilla) (round) mat.

ruego [rwe'ğo] etc vb V **rogar** ♦ nm request; **a** ~ **de** at the request of; "~**s y preguntas**" "question and answer session".

ruegue [rwe'ğe] etc vb V **rogar.**

rufián [rōōfyán'] nm scoundrel.

rugby [rōōğ'ḥē] nm rugby.

rugido [rōōḥē'ḏo] nm roar.

rugir [rōōḥēr'] vi to roar; (toro) to bellow; (estómago) to rumble.

rugoso, a [rōōğo'so, á] a (arrugado) wrinkled; (áspero) rough; (desigual) ridged.

ruibarbo [rwēḥár'ḥo] nm rhubarb.

ruido [rwē'ṭo] nm noise; (sonido) sound; (alboroto) racket, row; (escándalo) commotion, rumpus; ~ **de fondo** background noise; **hacer** o **meter** ~ to cause a stir.

ruidoso, a [rwēḥo'so, á] a noisy, loud; (fig) sensational.

ruin [rwēn] a (avaro) stingy.

ruina [rwē'ná] nf ruin; (colapso) collapse; (de persona) ruin, downfall; **estar hecho una** ~ to be a wreck; **la empresa le llevó a la** ~ the venture ruined him (financially).

ruindad [rwēndáṭ'] nf lowness, meanness; (acto) low o mean act.

ruinoso, a [rwēno'so, á] a ruinous; (destartalado) dilapidated, tumbledown; (COM) disastrous.

ruiseñor [rwēsenyor'] nm nightingale.

ruja [rōō'há] etc vb V **rugir.**

rula [rōō'lá], **ruleta** [rōōle'tá] nf roulette.

rulo [rōō'lo] nm (para el pelo) curler.

rulota [rōōlo'tá] nf trailer (US), caravan (Brit).

Rumania [rōōmá'nyá] nf Rumania.

rumano, a [rōōmá'no, á] a, nm/f Rumanian.

rumba [rōōm'bá] nf rumba.

rumbo [rōōm'bo] nm (ruta) route, direction; (ángulo de dirección) course, bearing; (fig) course of events; **con** ~ **a** in the direction of; **ir con** ~ **a** to be heading for; (NAUT) to be bound for.

rumboso, a [rōōmbo'so, á] a (generoso) generous.

rumiante [rōōmyán'te] nm ruminant.

rumiar [rōōmyár'] vt to chew; (fig) to ruminate over ♦ vi to chew the cud.

rumor [rōōmor'] nm (ruido sordo) low sound; (murmuración) murmur, buzz.

rumorearse [rōōmoreár'se] vr: **se rumorea que** it is rumoured that.

rumoroso, a [rōōmoro'so, á] a full of sounds; (arroyo) murmuring.

runrún [rōōnrōōn'] nm (voces) murmur, sound of voices; (fig) rumor (US), rumour (Brit); (de una máquina) whirr.

rupestre [rōōpes'tre] a rock cpd; **pintura** ~ cave painting.

ruptura [rōōptōō'rá] nf (gen) rupture; (disputa) split; (de contrato) breach; (de relaciones) breaking-off.

rural [rōōrál'] a rural.

Rusia [rōō'syá] nf Russia.

ruso, a [rōō'so, á] a, nm/f Russián ♦ nm (LING) Russian.

rústico, a [rōō'stēko, á] a rustic; (ordinario)

coarse, uncouth ♦ *nm/f* yokel ♦ *nf*: **libro en rústica** paperback (book).

ruta [rōō'tá] *nf* route.

rutina [rōōtē'nà] *nf* routine; ~ **diaria** daily routine; **por** ~ as a matter of course.

rutinario, a [rōōtēná'ryo, à] *a* routine.

S

S, s [e'se] *nf* S, s; **S de Sábado** S for Sugar.
S *abr* (= *san, santo, a*) St.; (= *sur*) S.
s. *abr* (= *siglo*) c.; (= *siguiente*) foll.
s/ *abr* (*COM*) = **su(s)**.
S.ª *abr* (= *Sierra*) Mts.
S.A. *abr* (= *Sociedad Anónima*) Ltd., Inc. (*US*); (= *Su Alteza*) His/Her Highness.
sáb. *abr* (= *sábado*) Sat.
sábado [sá'hàtho] *nm* Saturday; (*de los judíos*) Sabbath; **del** ~ **en ocho días** a week from Saturday; **un** ~ **sí y otro no, cada dos** ~**s** every other Saturday.
sabana [sàhá'nà] *nf* savannah.
sábana [sá'hànà] *nf* sheet; **se le pegan las** ~**s** he can't get up in the morning.
sabandija [sàhàndē'há] *nf* (*bicho*) bug; (*fig*) louse.
sabañón [sàhànyon'] *nm* chilblain.
sabático, a [sàhá'tēko, à] *a* (*REL, UNIV*) sabbatical.
sabelotodo [sàheloto'tho] *nm/f inv* know-all.
saber [sáher'] *vt* to know; (*llegar a conocer*) to find out, learn; (*tener capacidad de*) to know how to ♦ *vi*: ~ **a** to taste of, taste like ♦ *nm* knowledge, learning; ~**se** *vr*: **se sabe que** ... it is known that ...; **no se sabe** nobody knows; **a** ~ namely; **¿sabes conducir/nadar?** can you drive/swim?; **¿sabes francés?** do you *o* can you speak French?; ~ **de memoria** to know by heart; **lo sé** I know; **hacer** ~ to inform, let know; **que yo sepa** as far as I know; **vete** *o* **anda a** ~ your guess is as good as mine; **¿sabe?** (*fam*) you know (what I mean)?; **le sabe mal que otro la saque a bailar** it upsets him that anybody else should ask her to dance.
sabido, a [sáhē'tho, à] *a* (*consabido*) well-known; **como es** ~ as we all know.
sabiduría [sàhēthōōrē'á] *nf* (*conocimientos*) wisdom; (*instrucción*) learning; ~ **popular** folklore.
sabiendas [sáhyen'dàs]: **a** ~ *ad* knowingly; **a** ~ **de que** ... knowing full well that ....

sabihondo, a [sáhyon'do, à] *a, nm/f* know-it-all (*US*), know-all (*Brit*).
sabio, a [sá'hyo,à] *a* (*docto*) learned; (*prudente*) wise, sensible.
sablazo [sàhlá'so] *nm* (*herida*) sword wound; (*fam*) sponging; **dar un** ~ **a uno** to tap sb for money.
sabor [sáhor'] *nm* taste; (*fig*) flavor (*US*), flavour (*Brit*); **sin** ~ flavorless.
saborear [sàhoreár'] *vt* to taste; (*fig*) to relish.
sabotaje [sàhotá'he] *nm* sabotage.
saboteador, a [sàhoteáthor', à] *nm/f* saboteur.
sabotear [sàhoteár'] *vt* to sabotage.
Saboya [sàho'yà] *nf* Savoy.
sabré [sáhre'] *etc vb V* **saber**.
sabroso, a [sàhro'so, à] *a* tasty; (*fig fam*) racy.
saca [sá'kà] *nf* big sack; ~ **de correo(s)** mailbag; (*COM*) withdrawal.
sacacorchos [sàkàkortch'os] *nm inv* corkscrew.
sacapuntas [sàkàpōōn'tàs] *nm inv* pencil sharpener.
sacar [sákár'] *vt* to take out; (*fig: extraer*) to get (out); (*quitar*) to remove, get out; (*hacer salir*) to bring out; (*fondos: de cuenta*) to draw out, withdraw; (*obtener: legado etc*) to get; (*demostrar*) to show; (*conclusión*) to draw; (*novela etc*) to publish, bring out; (*ropa*) to take off; (*obra*) to make; (*premio*) to receive; (*entradas*) to get; (*TENIS*) to serve; (*FÚTBOL*) to put into play; ~ **adelante** (*niño*) to bring up; ~ **a uno a bailar** to dance with sb; ~ **a uno de sí** to infuriate sb; ~ **una foto** to take a photo; ~ **la lengua** to stick out one's tongue; ~ **buenas/malas notas** to get good/bad marks.
sacarina [sàkàrē'ná] *nf* saccharin(e).
sacerdote [sàsertho'te] *nm* priest.
saciar [sásyár'] *vt* (*hartar*) to satiate; (*fig*) to satisfy; ~**se** *vr* (*fig*) to be satisfied.
saciedad [sàsyethàth'] *nf* satiety; **hasta la** ~ (*comer*) one's fill; (*repetir*) ad nauseam.
saco [sá'ko] *nm* bag; (*grande*) sack; (*su contenido*) bagful; (*AM: chaqueta*) jacket; ~ **de dormir** sleeping bag.
sacramento [sàkràmen'to] *nm* sacrament.
sacrificar [sàkrēfēkár'] *vt* to sacrifice; (*animal*) to slaughter; (*perro etc*) to put to sleep; ~**se** *vr* to sacrifice o.s.
sacrificio [sàkrēfē'syo] *nm* sacrifice.
sacrifique [sàkrēfē'ke] *etc vb V* **sacrificar**.
sacrilegio [sàkrēle'hyo] *nm* sacrilege.
sacrílego, a [sàkrē'lego, à] *a* sacrilegious.
sacristán [sàkrēstán'] *nm* sexton.
sacristía [sàkrēstē'á] *nf* sacristy.
sacro, a [sá'kro, à] *a* sacred.
sacudida [sàkōōthē'thá] *nf* (*agitación*)

shake, shaking; (*sacudimiento*) jolt, bump; (*fig*) violent change; (*POL etc*) upheaval; ~ **eléctrica** electric shock.

sacudir |sàkōōᵗʰēr'| *vt* to shake; (*golpear*) to hit; (*ala*) to flap; (*alfombra*) to beat; ~ **a uno** (*fam*) to belt sb.

sádico, a |sà'ᵗʰēko, à| *a* sadistic ♦ *nm/f* sadist.

sadismo |sàᵗʰēs'mo| *nm* sadism.

saeta |sàe'tà| *nf* (*flecha*) arrow; (*MUS*) sacred song in flamenco style.

sagacidad |sàgàsēᵗʰàᵗʰ'| *nf* shrewdness, cleverness.

sagaz |sàgás'| *a* shrewd, clever.

sagitario |sàhētà'ryo| *nm* (*ASTRO*) Sagittarius.

sagrado, a |sàgrà'ᵗʰo, à| *a* sacred, holy.

Sáhara |sà'àrà| *nm*: **el** ~ the Sahara (desert).

saharaui |sàhàrà'wē| *a* Saharan ♦ *nm/f* native *o* inhabitant of the Sahara.

sajón, ona |sàhon', ho'nà| *a, nm/f* Saxon.

Sajonia |sàho'nyà| *nf* Saxony.

sal |sàl| *vb ver* **salir** ♦ *nf* salt; (*gracia*) wit; (*encanto*) charm; ~**es de baño** bath salts; ~ **gorda** *o* **de cocina** kitchen *o* cooking salt.

sala |sà'là| *nf* (*cuarto grande*) large room; (~ *de estar*) living room; (*TEATRO*) house, auditorium; (*de hospital*) ward; ~ **de apelación** court; ~ **de conferencias** lecture hall; ~ **de embarque** departure lounge; ~ **de estar** living room; ~ **de fiestas** ballroom; ~ **de juntas** (*COM*) boardroom.

salado, a |sà'là'ᵗʰo, à| *a* salty; (*fig*) witty, amusing; **agua salada** salt water.

salar |sàlàr'| *vt* to salt, add salt to.

salarial |sàlàryàl'| *a* (*aumento*, *revisión*) wage *cpd*, salary *cpd*, pay *cpd*.

salario |sàlà'ryo| *nm* wage, pay.

salchicha |sàltchētch'à| *nf* (pork) sausage.

salchichón |sàltchētchon'| *nm* (salami-type) sausage.

saldar |sàldàr'| *vt* to pay; (*vender*) to sell off; (*fig*) to settle, resolve.

saldo |sàl'do| *nm* (*pago*) settlement; (*de una cuenta*) balance; (*lo restante*) remnant(s) (*pl*), remainder; (*liquidación*) sale; (*COM*): ~ **anterior** balance brought forward; ~ **acreedor/deudor** *o* **pasivo** credit/debit balance; ~ **final** final balance.

saldré |sàldrē'| *etc vb V* **salir**.

salero |sàlc'ro| *nm* salt shaker (*US*), salt cellar (*Brit*); (*ingenio*) wit; (*encanto*) charm.

salga |sàl'gà| *etc vb V* **salir**.

salida |sàlē'ᵗʰà| *nf* (*puerta etc*) exit, way out; (*acto*) leaving, going out; (*de tren*, *AVIAT*) departure; (*COM*, *TEC*) output, production; (*fig*) way out; (*resultado*) out-

come; (*COM*: *oportunidad*) opening; (*GEO*, *válvula*) outlet; (*de gas*) leak; (*ocurrencia*) witticism; **calle sin** ~ cul-de-sac; **a la** ~ **del teatro** after the theater; **dar la** ~ (*DEPORTE*) to give the starting signal; ~ **de incendios** fire escape; ~ **impresa** (*INFORM*) hard copy; **no hay** ~ there's no way out of it; **no tenemos otra** ~ we have no option; **tener** ~**s** to be witty.

saliente |sàlycn'tc| *a* (*ARQ*) projecting; (*sol*) rising; (*fig*) outstanding.

salina |sàlē'nà| *nf* salt mine; ~**s** *nfpl* saltworks *sg*.

salir |sàlēr'| *vi* to come/go out; (*resultar*) to turn out; (*partir*) to leave, depart; (*aparecer*) to appear; (*sobresalir*) to project, jut out; (*mancha*) to come out *o* off; (*disco*) to be released; (*número de lotería*, *planta*) to come up; (*pelo*) to grow; (*diente*) to come through; (*INFORM*) to quit, exit; ~**se** *vr* (*vasija*) to leak; (*animal*) to escape, get out; ~ **con** to go out with; ~ **a la superficie** to come to the surface; ~ **bien/mal** to turn out well/badly; ~ **caro/barato** to work out expensive/cheap; ~ **ganando** to come out on top; ~ **perdiendo** to lose out; **sale a su padre** he takes after his father; ~**se de la carretera** to leave the road; ~**se de la vía** to jump the rails; ~**se con la suya** to get one's own way.

saliva |sàlē'hà| *nf* saliva.

salmantino, a |sàlmàntē'no, à| *a* of *o* from Salamanca ♦ *nm/f* native *o* inhabitant of Salamanca.

salmo |sàl'mo| *nm* psalm.

salmón |sàlmon'| *nm* salmon.

salmonete |sàlmonc'tc| *nm* red mullet.

salmuera |sàlmwc'rà| *nf* pickle, brine.

salón |sàlon'| *nm* (*de casa*) living-room, lounge; (*muebles*) lounge suite; ~ **de belleza** beauty parlour; ~ **de baile** dance hall; ~ **de sesiones** assembly hall.

salpicadero |sàlpēkàᵗʰc'ro| *nm* (*AUTO*) dashboard.

salpicar |sàlpēkàr'| *vt* (*de barro*, *pintura*) to splash; (*rociar*) to sprinkle, spatter; (*esparcir*) to scatter.

salpicón |sàlpēkon'| *nm* (*acto*) splashing; (*CULIN*) meat *o* fish salad.

salpimentar |sàlpēmcntàr'| *vt* (*CULIN*) to season.

salpique |sàlpē'kc| *etc vb V* **salpicar**.

salsa |sàl'sà| *nf* sauce; (*con carne asada*) gravy; (*fig*) spice; ~ **mayonesa** mayonnaise; **estar en su** ~ (*fam*) to be in one's element.

saltado, a |sàltà'ᵗʰo, à| *a* (*desprendido*) missing; (*ojos*) bulging.

saltamontes |sàltàmon'tcs| *nm inv* grasshopper.

saltar |sàltàr'| *vt* to jump (over), leap

(over); (*dejar de lado*) to skip, miss out ♦
vi to jump, leap; (*pelota*) to bounce; (*al
aire*) to fly up; (*quebrarse*) to break; (*al
agua*) to dive; (*fig*) to explode, blow up;
(*botón*) to come off; (*corcho*) to pop out;
~**se** *vr* (*omitir*) to skip, miss; **salta a la
vista** it's obvious; ~**se todas las reglas** to
break all the rules.

salteado, a [sålteå'ðo, å] *a* (*CULIN*) sau-
té(ed).

salteador [sålteåðor'] *nm* (*tb*: ~ **de caminos**) highwayman.

saltear [sålteår'] *vt* (*robar*) to rob (in a hold-
up); (*asaltar*) to assault, attack; (*CULIN*)
to sauté.

saltimbanqui [såltēmbån'kē] *nm/f* acrobat.

salto [sål'to] *nm* jump, leap; (*al agua*) dive;
a ~**s** by jumping; ~ **de agua** waterfall; ~
de altura high jump; ~ **de cama** negligee;
~ **mortal** somersault; (*INFORM*): ~ **de línea** line feed; ~ **de línea automático**
wordwrap; ~ **de página** formfeed.

saltón, ona [sålton', onå] *a* (*ojos*) bulging,
popping; (*dientes*) protruding.

salubre [såloo'bre] *a* healthy, salubrious.

salud [sålooð'] *nf* health; **estar bien/mal de
~** to be in good/poor health; **¡(a su) ~!**
cheers!, good health!; **beber a la ~ de** to
drink (to) the health of.

saludable [sålooðå'ble] *a* (*de buena salud*)
healthy; (*provechoso*) good, beneficial.

saludar [sålooðår'] *vt* to greet; (*MIL*) to salute; **ir a ~ a uno** to drop in to see sb; **sa-
lude de mi parte a X** give my regards to
X; **le saluda atentamente** (*en carta*) yours
faithfully.

saludo [såloo'ðo] *nm* greeting; ~**s** (*en
carta*) best wishes, regards; **un ~ afectuoso** *o* **cordial** yours truly (*US*) *o* sincerely
(*Brit*).

salva [sål'ßå] *nf* (*MIL*) salvo; **una ~ de
aplausos** thunderous applause.

salvación [sålßåsyon'] *nf* salvation; (*rescate*) rescue.

salvado [sålßå'ðo] *nm* bran.

salvador [sålßåðor'] *nm* rescuer; **el S~** the
Savior (*US*) *o* Saviour (*Brit*); **El S~** El Salvador; **San S~** San Salvador.

salvadoreño, a [sålßåðore'nyo, å] *a, nm/f*
Salvadoran, Salvadorian.

salvaguardar [sålßågwårðår'] *vt* to safeguard; (*INFORM*) to back up, make a backup copy of.

salvajada [sålßåhå'ðå] *nf* savage deed,
atrocity.

salvaje [sålßå'he] *a* wild; (*tribu*) savage.

salvajismo [sålßåhēs'mo] *nm* savagery.

salvamento [sålßåmen'to] *nm* (*acción*)
rescue; (*de naufragio*) salvage; ~ **y soco-
rrismo** life-saving.

salvar [sålßår'] *vt* (*rescatar*) to save,

rescue; (*resolver*) to overcome, resolve;
(*cubrir distancias*) to cover, travel; (*hacer
excepción*) to except, exclude; (*un barco*)
to salvage; ~**se** *vr* to save o.s., escape;
¡sálvese el que pueda! every man for
himself!

salvavidas [sålßåßē'ðås] *a inv*: **bote/
chaleco/cinturón** ~ lifeboat/lifejacket/life-
belt.

salvedad [sålßeðåð'] *nf* reservation, qualification; **con la ~ de que ...** with the proviso that ....

salvia [sål'ßyå] *nf* sage.

salvo, a [sål'ßo, å] *a* safe ♦ *prep* except
(for), save; ~ **error u omisión** (*COM*)
errors and omissions excepted; **a ~** out of
danger; ~ **que** unless.

salvoconducto [sålßokonðook'to] *nm* safe-
conduct.

san [sån] *nm* (*apócope de* **santo**) saint; ~
Juan St. John.

sanar [sånår'] *vt* (*herida*) to heal; (*persona*)
to cure ♦ *vi* (*persona*) to get well, recover;
(*herida*) to heal.

sanatorio [sånåto'ryo] *nm* sanatorium.

sanción [sånsyon'] *nf* sanction.

sancionar [sånsyonår'] *vt* to sanction.

sandalia [såndå'lyå] *nf* sandal.

sándalo [sån'dålo] *nm* sandal (wood).

sandez [såndes'] *nf* (*cualidad*) foolishness;
(*acción*) stupid thing; **decir sandeces** to
talk nonsense.

sandía [såndē'å] *nf* watermelon.

sandwich [sån'dwētch], *pl* **sandwichs** *o*
sandwiches *nm* sandwich.

saneamiento [såneåmyen'to] *nm* sanitation.

sanear [såneår'] *vt* to drain; (*indemnizar*) to
compensate; (*ECON*) to reorganize.

sangrante [sångrån'te] *a* (*herida*) bleeding;
(*fig*) flagrant.

sangrar [sångrår'] *vt, vi* to bleed; (*texto*) to
indent.

sangre [sån'gre] *nf* blood; ~ **fría** sangfroid;
a ~ fría in cold blood.

sangría [sångrē'å] *nf* (*MED*) bleeding; (*CU-
LIN*) sangria, *sweetened drink of red wine
with fruit*, ≈ fruit cup.

sangriento, a [sångryen'to, å] *a* bloody.

sanguijuela [sångēhwe'lå] *nf* (*ZOOL, fig*)
leech.

sanguinario, a [sångēnå'ryo, å] *a* bloodthirsty.

sanguíneo, a [sångē'neo, å] *a* blood *cpd*.

sanguinolento, a [sångēnolen'to, å] *a* (*que
echa sangre*) bleeding; (*manchado*) bloodstained; (*ojos*) bloodshot.

sanidad [sånēðåð'] *nf* sanitation; (*calidad
de sano*) health, healthiness; ~ **pública**
public health (department).

sanitario, a [sånētå'ryo, å] *a* sanitary; (*de

la salud) health *cpd* ♦ *nm*: ~**s** restroom *sg*
(*US*), toilets (*Brit*).

San Marino [sánmåre'no] *nm*: (**La República de**) ~ San Marino.

sano, a [så'no, å] *a* healthy; (*sin daños*)
sound; (*comida*) wholesome; (*entero*)
whole, intact; ~ **y salvo** safe and sound.

santanderino, a [sántánderē'no, å] *a* of *o*
from Santander ♦ *nm/f* native *o* inhabitant
of Santander.

Santiago [sántyå'ᶃo] *nm*: ~ (**de Chile**)
Santiago.

santiamén [sántyámen'] *nm*: **en un** ~ in no
time at all.

santidad [sántēᵗħåᵗħ'] *nf* holiness, sanctity.

santificar [sántēfēkår'] *vt* to sanctify, make
holy.

santifique [sántēfē'ke] *etc vb* V **santificar**.

santiguarse [sántēᶃwår'se] *vr* to make the
sign of the cross.

santigüe [sántē'ᶃwe] *etc vb* V **santiguarse**.

santo, a [sán'to, å] *a* holy; (*fig*) wonderful,
miraculous ♦ *nm/f* saint ♦ *nm* saint's day;
hacer su santa voluntad to do as one damn
well pleases; **¿a ~ de qué ...?** why on earth
...?; **se le fue el ~ al cielo** he forgot what
he was about to say; ~ **y seña** password.

santuario [sántwå'ryo] *nm* sanctuary,
shrine.

saña [så'nyå] *nf* rage, fury.

sapo [så'po] *nm* toad.

saque [så'ke] *etc vb* V **sacar** ♦ *nm* 'ᵀᴱ*NIS*)
service, serve; (*FÚTBOL*) throw-in; ~ **inicial** kick-off; ~ **de esquina** corner (kick);
tener buen ~ to eat heartily.

saquear [såkeår'] *vt* (*MIL*) to sack; (*robar*)
to loot, plunder; (*fig*) to ransack.

saqueo [såke'o] *nm* sacking; looting,
plundering; ransacking.

sarampión [sårámpyon'] *nm* measles *sg*.

sarape [sårå'pe] *nm* (*AM*) blanket.

sarcasmo [sårkås'mo] *nm* sarcasm.

sarcástico, a [sårkå'stēko, å] *a* sarcastic.

sardina [sårᵗħē'nå] *nf* sardine.

sardo, a [sår'ᵗħo, å] *a, nm/f* Sardinian.

sardónico, a [sårᵗħo'nēko, å] *a* sardonic;
(*irónico*) ironical, sarcastic.

sargento [sårhen'to] *nm* sergeant.

SARL *abr* (= *Sociedad Anónima de
Responsabilidad Limitada*) Corp. (*US*), Ltd.
(*Brit*), plc (*Brit*).

sarna [sår'nå] *nf* itch; (*MED*) scabies.

sarpullido [sårpōō̄yē'ᵗħo] *nm* (*MED*) rash.

sarro [så'rro] *nm* deposit; (*en dientes*)
tartar.

sarta [sår'tå] *nf*, **sartal** [sårtål'] *nm* (*fig*): **una
~ de mentiras** a pack of lies.

sartén [sårten'] *nf* frying pan; **tener la ~
por el mango** to rule the roost.

sastre [sås'tre] *nm* tailor.

sastrería [såstrerē'å] *nf* (*arte*) tailoring;

(*tienda*) tailor's (shop).

Satanás [såtånás'] *nm* Satan.

satélite [såte'lēte] *nm* satellite.

satinado, a [såtēná'ᵗħo, å] *a* glossy ♦ *nm*
gloss, shine.

sátira [så'tērå] *nf* satire.

satírico, a [såtē'rēko, å] *a* satiric(al).

sátiro [så'tēro] *nm* (*MITOLOGÍA*) satyr; (*fig*)
sex maniac.

satisfacción [såtēsfåksyon'] *nf* satisfaction.

satisfacer [såtēsfáser'] *vt* to satisfy;
(*gastos*) to meet; (*deuda*) to pay; (*COM*:
letra de cambio) to honour (*US*), honour
(*Brit*); (*pérdida*) to make good; **~se** *vr* to
satisfy o.s., be satisfied; (*vengarse*) to take
revenge.

satisfaga [såtēsfå'ᶃå] *etc*, **satisfaré**
[såtēsfáre'] *etc vb* V **satisfacer**.

satisfecho, a [såtēsfetch'o, å] *pp de* **satisfacer** ♦ *a* satisfied; (*contento*) content(ed),
happy; (*tb*: ~ **de sí mismo**) self-satisfied,
smug.

satisfice [såtēsfē'se] *etc vb* V **satisfacer**.

saturar [såtōōrår'] *vt* to saturate.

sauce [så'ōōse] *nm* willow; ~ **llorón** weeping willow.

saúco [såōō'ko] *nm* (*BOT*) elder.

sauna [så'ōōnå] *nf* sauna.

savia [så'ᵛyå] *nf* sap.

saxofón [såksofon'] *nm* saxophone.

saya [så'yå] *nf* (*falda*) skirt; (*enagua*) petti-
coat.

sayo [så'yo] *nm* smock.

sazón [såson'] *nf* (*de fruta*) ripeness; **a la ~**
then, at that time.

sazonado, a [såsoná'ᵗħo, å] *a* (*fruta*) ripe;
(*CULIN*) seasoned.

sazonar [såsonår'] *vt* to ripen; (*CULIN*) to
season.

s/c *abr* (*COM*:=*su casa*) your firm; (:=*su
cuenta*) your account.

Scotch [eskotch'] *nm* (*AM*) adhesive tape.

Sdo. *abr* (*COM*:=*Saldo*) bal.

SE *abr* (= *sudeste*) SE.

se [se] *pron reflexivo* oneself; (*sg*: *m*)
himself; (: *f*) herself; (: *de una cosa*)
itself; (: *de usted*) yourself; (*pl*)
themselves; (: *de ustedes*) yourselves; (*recíproco*) each other, one another; ~ **mira
en el espejo** he looks at himself in the
mirror; **¡siénte~!** sit down; ~ **ayudan** they
help each other; ~ **miraron** (**el uno al
otro**) they looked at one another; ~ **compró hace 3 años** it was bought 3 years ago;
en esa parte ~ **habla francés** in that area
French is spoken *o* people speak French;
"~ vende coche" "car for sale"; ~ **lo daré** I'll give it to him/her/you; **él** ~ **ha com-
prado un sombrero** he has bought himself
a hat.

sé [se] *vb* V **saber, ser**.

sea [se'á] *etc vb* V **ser.**

SEAT [se'át] *nf abr=Sociedad Española de Automóviles de Turismo.*

sebo [se'ħo] *nm* fat, grease.

Sec. *abr* (= *Secretario*) Sec.

seca [se'ká] *nf* V **seco.**

secado [seká'tħo] *nm* drying; ~ **a mano** blow-dry.

secador [sekátħor'] *nm*: ~ **para el pelo** hair-dryer.

secadora [sekátħo'rá] *nf* tumble dryer; ~ **centrífuga** spin-dryer.

secano [seká'no] *nm* (*AGR*: *tb*: **tierra de** ~) dry land *o* region; **cultivo de** ~ dry farming.

secante [sekán'te] *a* (*viento*) drying ♦ *nm* blotting paper.

secar [sekár'] *vt* to dry; (*superficie*) to wipe dry; (*frente, suelo*) to mop; (*líquido*) to mop up; (*tinta*) to blot; ~**se** *vr* to dry (off); (*río, planta*) to dry up.

sección [seksyon'] *nf* section; (*COM*) department; ~ **deportiva** (*en periódico*) sports page(s).

seco, a [se'ko, á] *a* dry; (*fruta*) dried; (*persona*: *magro*) thin, skinny; (*carácter*) cold; (*antipático*) disagreeable; (*respuesta*) sharp, curt ♦ *nf* dry season; **habrá pan a secas** there will be just bread; **decir algo a secas** to say sth curtly; **parar en** ~ to stop dead.

secreción [sekresyon'] *nf* secretion.

secretaría [sekretáre'á] *nf* secretariat; (*oficina*) secretary's office.

secretariado [sekretáryá'tħo] *nm* (*oficina*) secretariat; (*cargo*) secretaryship; (*curso*) secretarial course.

secretario, a [sekretá'ryo, á] *nm/f* secretary; ~ **adjunto** (*COM*) assistant secretary.

secreto, a [sekre'to, á] *a* secret; (*información*) confidential; (*persona*) secretive ♦ *nm* secret; (*calidad*) secrecy.

secta [sek'tá] *nf* sect.

sectario, a [sektá'ryo, á] *a* sectarian.

sector [sektor'] *nm* sector (*tb INFORM*); (*de opinión*) section; (*fig*: *campo*) area, field; ~ **privado/público** (*COM, ECON*) private/public sector.

secuela [sekwe'lá] *nf* consequence.

secuencia [sekwen'syá] *nf* sequence.

secuestrar [sekwestrár'] *vt* to kidnap; (*avión*) to hijack; (*bienes*) to seize, confiscate.

secuestro [sekwes'tro] *nm* kidnapping; hijack; seizure, confiscation.

secular [sekoolár'] *a* secular.

secundar [sekoondár'] *vt* to second, support.

secundario, a [sekoondá'ryo, á] *a* secondary; (*carretera*) side *cpd*; (*INFORM*) background *cpd*.

sed [setħ] *nf* thirst; (*fig*) thirst, craving; **te-**

ner ~ to be thirsty.

seda [se'tħá] *nf* silk.

sedal [setħál'] *nm* fishing line.

sedante [setħán'te] *nm* sedative.

sede [se'tħe] *nf* (*de gobierno*) seat; (*de compañía*) headquarters *pl*, head office; **Santa S**~ Holy See.

SEDIC [setħēk'] *nf abr=Sociedad Española de Documentación e Información Científica.*

sedición [setħēsyon'] *nf* sedition.

sediento, a [setħyen'to, á] *a* thirsty.

sedimentar [setħēmentár'] *vt* to deposit; ~**se** *vr* to settle.

sedimento [setħēmen'to] *nm* sediment.

sedoso, a [setħo'so, á] *a* silky, silken.

seducción [setħōōksyon'] *nf* seduction.

seducir [setħōōsēr'] *vt* to seduce; (*sobornar*) to bribe; (*cautivar*) to charm, fascinate; (*atraer*) to attract.

seductor, a [setħōōktor', á] *a* seductive; charming, fascinating; attractive; (*engañoso*) deceptive, misleading ♦ *nm/f* seducer.

seduje [setħōō'he] *etc*, **seduzca** [setħōōs'ká] *etc vb* V **seducir.**

sefardí [sefártħē'], **sefardita** [sefártħē'tá] *a* Sephardi(c) ♦ *nm/f* Sephardi.

segador, a [segátħor', á] *nm/f* (*persona*) harvester ♦ *nf* (*TEC*) mower, reaper.

segadora-trilladora [segátħo'rátrēyátħo'rá] *nf* combine harvester.

segar [segár'] *vt* (*mies*) to reap, cut; (*hierba*) to mow, cut; (*esperanzas*) to ruin.

seglar [seglár'] *a* secular, lay.

segoviano, a [segoħyá'no, á] *a* of *o* from Segovia ♦ *nm/f* native *o* inhabitant of Segovia.

segregación [segregásyon'] *nf* segregation; ~ **racial** racial segregation.

segregar [segregár'] *vt* to segregate, separate.

segregue [segre'ge] *etc vb* V **segregar.**

seguidamente [segetħámen'te] *ad* (*sin parar*) without a break; (*inmediatamente después*) immediately after.

seguido, a [segē'tħo, á] *a* (*continuo*) continuous, unbroken; (*recto*) straight ♦ *ad* (*directo*) straight (on); (*después*) after; (*AM*: *a menudo*) often ♦ *nf*: **en seguida** at once, right away; **5 días** ~**s** 5 days running, 5 days in a row; **en seguida termino** I'll be done in a minute.

segué [sege'], **seguemos** [sege'mos] *etc vb* V **segar.**

seguimiento [segēmyen'to] *nm* chase, pursuit; (*continuación*) continuation.

seguir [segēr'] *vt* to follow; (*venir después*) to follow, come after; (*proseguir*) to continue; (*perseguir*) to chase, pursue; (*indicio*) to follow up; (*mujer*) to court ♦ *vi* (*gen*) to follow; (*continuar*) to continue, carry *o* go on; ~**se** *vr* to follow; **a** ~ to be continued; **sigo sin comprender** I still don't understand; **sigue lloviendo** it's still raining; **sigue** (en carta) over; (en libro, TV) continued; **"hágase ~"** "please forward".

según |seg̅o̅o̅n'| prep according to ♦ ad: ~ **(y conforme)** it all depends ♦ conj as; ~ **esté el tiempo** depending on the weather; ~ **me consta** as far as I know; **está ~ lo dejaste** it is just as you left it.

segundo, a |seg̅o̅o̅n'do, à| a second; (en discurso) secondly ♦ nm (gen, medida de tiempo) second; (piso) second floor ♦ nf (sentido) second meaning; ~ **(de a bordo)** (NAUT) first mate; **segunda (clase)** (FERRO) second class; **segunda (marcha)** (AUTO) second (gear); **de segunda mano** second hand.

seguramente |seg̅o̅o̅rámen'tc| ad surely; (con certeza) for sure, with certainty; (probablemente) probably; **¿lo va a comprar?** — ~ is he going to buy it? — I should think so.

seguridad |seg̅o̅o̅réthàth'| nf safety; (del estado, de casa etc) security; (certidumbre) certainty; (confianza) confidence; (estabilidad) stability; ~ **social** social security; ~ **contra incendios** fire precautions; ~ **en sí mismo** (self-)confidence.

seguro, a |seg̅o̅o̅'ro, à| a (cierto) sure, certain; (fiel) trustworthy; (libre de peligro) safe; (bien defendido, firme) secure; (datos etc) reliable; (fecha) firm ♦ ad for sure, certainly ♦ nm (dispositivo) safety device; (de cerradura) tumbler; (de arma) safety catch; (COM) insurance; ~ **contra accidentes/incendios** fire/accident insurance; ~ **contra terceros/a todo riesgo** third party/comprehensive insurance; ~ **dotal con beneficios** interest-bearing endowment insurance (US), with-profits endowment assurance (Brit); **S~ de Enfermedad** ≈ health insurance (US), ≈ National Insurance (Brit); ~ **marítimo** marine insurance; ~ **mixto** endowment insurance (US) o assurance (Brit); ~ **temporal** term insurance; ~ **de vida** life insurance.

seis |se̅c̅s| num six; ~ **mil** six thousand; **tiene ~ años** she is six (years old); **unos ~** about six; **hoy es el ~** today is the sixth.

seiscientos, as |se̅c̅ssyen'tos, às| num six hundred.

seísmo |se̅c̅s'mo| nm tremor, earthquake.

selección |scleksyon'| nf selection; ~ **múltiple** multiple choice; ~ **nacional** (DEPORTE) national team.

seleccionador, a |scleksyonàthor', à| nm/f (DEPORTE) selector.

seleccionar |scleksyonàr'| vt to pick, choose, select.

selectividad |sclektc̅he̅thàth'| nf (UNIV) entrance examination.

selecto, a |sclck'to, à| a select, choice; (escogido) selected.

selva |scl'hà| nf (bosque) forest, woods pl; (jungla) jungle; **la S~ Negra** the Black Forest.

selvático, a |sclhà'tc̅ko, à| a woodland cpd; (BOT) wild.

sellado, a |scyà'tho, à| a (documento oficial) sealed; (pasaporte) stamped.

sellar |scyàr'| vt (documento oficial) to seal; (pasaporte, visado) to stamp; (marcar) to brand; (pacto, labios) to seal.

sello |sc'yo| nm stamp; (precinto) seal; (fig: tb: ~ **distintivo**) hallmark; ~ **fiscal** revenue stamp; ~**s de prima** (COM) trading stamps.

semáforo |scmà'foro| nm (AUTO) traffic lights pl; (FERRO) signal.

semana |scmà'nà| nf week; ~ **inglesa** 5-day (work (US) o working (Brit)) week; ~ **laboral** work (US) o working (Brit) week; **S~ Santa** Holy Week; **entre ~** during the week.

semanal |scmànàl'| a weekly.

semanario |scmànà'ryo| nm weekly (magazine).

semántica |scmàn'tc̅kà| nf semantics sg.

semblante |scmblàn'tc| nm face; (fig) look.

semblanza |scmblàn'sà| nf biographical sketch, profile.

sembrar |scmbràr'| vt to sow; (objetos) to sprinkle, scatter about; (noticias etc) to spread.

semejante |scmchàn'tc| a (parecido) similar; (tal) such a, alike, similar ♦ nm fellow man, fellow creature; **son muy ~s** they are very much alike; **nunca hizo cosa ~** he never did such a o any such thing.

semejanza |scmchàn'sà| nf similarity, resemblance; **a ~ de** like, as.

semejar |scmchàr'| vi to seem like, resemble; ~**se** vr to look alike, be similar.

semen |sc'mcn| nm semen.

semental |scmcntàl'| nm (macho) stud.

sementera |scmcntc'rà| nf (acto) sowing; (temporada) planting season; (tierra) planted land.

semestral |scmcstràl'| a half-yearly, biannual.

semestre |scmcs'trc| nm period of six months; (US UNIV) semester; (COM) half-yearly payment.

semicírculo |scmc̅sc̅r'ko̅o̅lo| nm semicircle.

semiconductor |scmc̅kondo̅o̅ktor'| nm semiconductor.

semiconsciente |scmc̅konssycn'tc| a semiconscious.

semifinal |scmc̅fc̅nàl'| nf semifinal.

semilla |scmc̅'yà| nf seed.

semillero |scmc̅yc'ro| nm (AGR etc)

seedbed; (*fig*) hotbed.
seminario |seminá'ryo| *nm* (*REL*) seminary; (*ESCOL*) seminar.
semiseco |semese'ko| *nm* medium-dry.
semita |seme'tá| *a* Semitic ♦ *nm/f* Semite.
sémola |se'molá| *nf* semolina.
sempiterno, a |sempeter'no, á| *a* everlasting.
Sena |se'ná| *nm*: **el** ~ the (river) Seine.
senado |sená'ðo| *nm* senate.
senador, a |senáðor', á| *nm/f* senator.
sencillez |senseyes'| *nf* simplicity; (*de persona*) naturalness.
sencillo, a |sense'yo, á| *a* simple; (*carácter*) natural, unaffected; (*billete*) single.
senda |sen'dá| *nf*, **sendero** |sende'ro| *nm* path, track.
sendos, as |sen'dos, ás| *apl*: **les dio** ~ **golpes** he hit both of them.
senil |senel'| *a* senile.
seno |se'no| *nm* (*ANAT*) bosom, bust; (*fig*) bosom; ~**s** *nmpl* breasts; ~ **materno** womb.
sensación |sensásyon'| *nf* sensation; (*sentido*) sense; (*sentimiento*) feeling; **causar** *o* **hacer** ~ to cause a sensation.
sensacional |sensásyonál'| *a* sensational.
sensato, a |sensá'to, á| *a* sensible.
sensible |sense'ble| *a* sensitive; (*apreciable*) perceptible, appreciable; (*pérdida*) considerable.
sensiblero, a |senseßle'ro, á| *a* sentimental.
sensitivo, a |sensete'ßo, á|, **sensorial** |sensoryál'| *a* sense *cpd*.
sensor |sensor'| *nm*: ~ **de fin de papel** paper out sensor.
sensual |senswál'| *a* sensual.
sentado, a |sentá'ðo, á| *a* (*establecido*) settled; (*carácter*) sensible ♦ *nf* sitting; (*protesta*) sit-down, sit-in; **dar por** ~ to take for granted, assume; **dejar algo** ~ to establish sth firmly; **estar** ~ to sit, be sitting (down).
sentar |sentár'| *vt* to sit, seat; (*fig*) to establish ♦ *vi* (*vestido*) to suit; (*alimento*): ~ **bien/mal a** to agree/disagree with; ~**se** *vr* (*persona*) to sit, sit down; (*el tiempo*) to settle (down); (*los depósitos*) to settle; **¡siéntese!** (*do*) sit down, take a seat.
sentencia |senten'syá| *nf* (*máxima*) maxim, saying; (*JUR*) sentence; (*INFORM*) statement; ~ **de muerte** death sentence.
sentenciar |sentensyár'| *vt* to sentence.
sentido, a |sente'ðo, á| *a* (*pérdida*) regrettable; (*carácter*) sensitive ♦ *nm* sense; (*sentimiento*) feeling; (*significado*) sense, meaning; (*dirección*) direction; **mi más** ~ **pésame** my deepest sympathy; ~ **del humor** sense of humor; ~ **común** common sense; **en el buen** ~ **de la palabra** in the best sense of the word; **sin** ~ meaningless;

tener ~ to make sense; ~ **único** one-way (street).
sentimental |sentementál'| *a* sentimental; **vida** ~ love life.
sentimiento |sentemyen'to| *nm* (*emoción*) feeling, emotion; (*sentido*) sense; (*pesar*) regret, sorrow.
sentir |senter'| *vt* to feel; (*percibir*) to perceive, sense; (*lamentar*) to regret, be sorry for; (*música etc*) to have a feeling for ♦ *vi* to feel; (*lamentarse*) to feel sorry ♦ *nm* opinion, judgement; ~**se** *vr* to feel; **lo siento** I'm sorry; ~**se bien/mal** to feel well/ill; ~**se como en su casa** to feel at home.
seña |se'nyá| *nf* sign; (*MIL*) password; ~**s** *nfpl* address *sg*; ~**s personales** personal description *sg*; **por más** ~**s** moreover; **dar** ~**s de** to show signs of.
señal |senyál'| *nf* sign; (*síntoma*) symptom; (*indicio*) indication; (*FERRO, TELEC*) signal; (*marca*) mark; (*COM*) deposit; (*INFORM*) marker, mark; **en** ~ **de** as a token of, as a sign of; **dar** ~**es de** to show signs of; ~ **de auxilio/de peligro** distress/danger signal; ~ **de llamada** ring (*US*) *o* ringing (*Brit*) tone; ~ **para marcar** dial (*US*) *o* dialling (*Brit*) tone.
señalado, a |senyálá'ðo, á| *a* (*persona*) distinguished; (*pey*) notorious.
señalar |senyálár'| *vt* to mark; (*indicar*) to point out, indicate; (*significar*) to denote; (*referirse a*) to allude to; (*fijar*) to fix, settle; (*pey*) to criticize.
señalice |senyále'se| *etc vb* V **señalizar**.
señalización |senyálésasyon'| *nf* signing (*US*), signposting (*Brit*); signals *pl*.
señalizar |senyálésar'| *vt* (*AUT*) to put up road signs on; (*FERRO*) to put signals on; (*AUT: ruta*): **está bien señalizada** it's well signed.
señas |se'nyás| *nfpl* V **seña**.
señor, a |senyor', á| *a* (*fam*) lordly ♦ *nm* (*hombre*) man; (*caballero*) gentleman; (*dueño*) owner, master; (*trato: antes de nombre propio*) Mr.; (: *hablando directamente*) sir ♦ *nf* (*dama*) lady; (*trato: antes de nombre propio*) Mrs.; (: *hablando directamente*) madam; (*esposa*) wife; **los** ~**es González** Mr. and Mrs. González; **S**~ **Don Jacinto Benavente** (*en sobre*) Mr. J. Benavente, J. Benavente Esq. (*Brit*); **S**~ **Director ...** (*de periódico*) Dear Sir ...; ~ **juez** your honor; ~ **Presidente** Mr. Chairman *o* President; **Muy** ~ **mío** Dear Sir; **Muy** ~**es nuestros** Dear Sirs; **Nuestro S**~ (*REL*) Our Lord; **¿está la señora?** is the lady of the house in?; **la señora de Smith** Mrs. Smith; **Nuestra Señora** (*REL*) Our Lady.
señoría |senyore'á| *nf* rule; **su** *o* **vuestra S**~

your *o* his/her lordship/ladyship.
señorío [senyorē'o] *nm* manor; (*fig*) rule.
señorita [senyorē'tá] *nf* (*gen*) Miss; (*mujer joven*) young lady; (*maestra*) school-teacher.
señorito [senyorē'to] *nm* young gentleman; (*lenguaje de criados*) master; (*pey*) dandy.
señuelo [senywe'lo] *nm* decoy.
Sep. *abr* (= *septiembre*) Sept.
sepa [se'pá] *etc vb V* **saber.**
separable [separá'hle] *a* separable; (*TEC*) detachable.
separación [separásyon'] *nf* separation; (*división*) division; (*distancia*) gap, distance; ~ **de bienes** division of property.
separado, a [separá'tho, á] *a* separate; (*TEC*) detached; **vive ~ de su mujer** he is separated from his wife; **por ~** separately.
separador [separáthor'] *nm* (*INFORM*) delimiter.
separadora [separátho'rá] *nf*: ~ **de hojas** burster.
separar [separár'] *vt* to separate; (*silla de la mesa*) to move away; (*TEC: pieza*) to detach; (*persona: de un cargo*) to remove, dismiss; (*dividir*) to divide; **~se** *vr* (*parte*) to come away; (*partes*) to come apart; (*persona*) to leave, go away; (*matrimonio*) to separate.
separatismo [separátēs'mo] *nm* (*POL*) separatism.
sepelio [sepe'lyo] *nm* burial, interment.
sepia [se'pyá] *nf* cuttlefish.
Sept. *abr* (= *septiembre*) Sept.
septentrional [septentryonál'] *a* north *cpd*, northern.
septiembre [septyem'bre] *nm* September.
séptimo, a [sep'tēmo, á] *a, nm* seventh.
septuagésimo, a [septwáhe'sēmo, á] *a* seventieth.
sepulcral [sepōōlkrál'] *a* sepulchral; (*fig*) gloomy, dismal.
sepulcro [sepōōl'kro] *nm* tomb, grave, sepulcher (*US*), sepulchre (*Brit*).
sepultar [sepōōltár'] *vt* to bury; (*en accidente*) to trap; **quedaban sepultados en la caverna** they were trapped in the cave.
sepultura [sepōōltōō'rá] *nf* (*acto*) burial; (*tumba*) grave, tomb; **dar ~ a** to bury; **recibir ~** to be buried.
sepulturero, a [sepōōltōōre'ro, á] *nm/f* gravedigger.
seque [se'ke] *etc vb V* **secar.**
sequedad [seketháth'] *nf* dryness; (*fig*) brusqueness, curtness.
sequía [sekē'á] *nf* drought.
séquito [se'kēto] *nm* (*de rey etc*) retinue; (*POL*) followers *pl*.
ser [ser] *vi* (*gen*) to be; (*devenir*) to become ♦ *nm* being; ~ **de** (*origen*) to be from, come from; (*hecho de*) to be (made) of;

(*pertenecer a*) to belong to; **¿qué será de mí?** what will become of me?; **soy ingeniero** I'm an engineer; **soy yo** it's me; **es la una** it is one o'clock; **es de esperar que** it is to be hoped that; **era de ver** you should have seen it; **a no ~ que** unless; **de no ~ así** if it were not so, were it not so; **o sea** that is to say; **sea como sea** be that as it may; ~ **vivo** living creature.
serenarse [serenár'se] *vr* to calm down; (*mar*) to grow calm; (*tiempo*) to clear up.
sereno, a [sere'no, á] *a* (*persona*) calm, unruffled; (*el tiempo*) fine, settled; (*ambiente*) calm, peaceful ♦ *nm* night watchman.
serial [seryál'] *nm* serial.
serie [se'rye] *nf* series; (*cadena*) sequence, succession; (*TV etc*) series; (*de inyecciones*) course; **fuera de ~** out of order; (*fig*) special, out of the ordinary; **fabricación en ~** mass production; (*INFORM*): **interface/impresora en ~** serial interface/printer.
seriedad [seryetháth'] *nf* seriousness; (*formalidad*) reliability; (*de crisis*) gravity, seriousness.
serio, a [se'ryo, á] *a* serious; reliable, dependable; grave, serious; **poco ~** (*actitud*) undignified; (*carácter*) unreliable; **en ~** seriously.
sermón [sermon'] *nm* (*REL*) sermon.
sermonear [sermoneár'] *vt* (*fam*) to lecture ♦ *vi* to sermonize.
serpentear [serpenteár'] *vi* to wriggle; (*camino, río*) to wind, snake.
serpentina [serpentē'ná] *nf* streamer.
serpiente [serpyen'te] *nf* snake; ~ **boa** boa constrictor; ~ **de cascabel** rattlesnake.
serranía [serránē'á] *nf* mountainous area.
serrano, a [serrá'no, á] *a* highland *cpd*, hill *cpd* ♦ *nm/f* highlander.
serrar [serrár'] *vt* to saw.
serrín [serrēn'] *nm* sawdust.
serrucho [serrōōtch'o] *nm* handsaw.
Servia [ser'hyá] *nf* Serbia.
servicial [serhēsyál'] *a* helpful, obliging.
servicio [serhē'syo] *nm* service; (*CULIN etc*) set; **~s** *nmpl* restroom *sg* (*US*), toilet(s) (*pl*); **estar de ~** to be on duty; ~ **aduanero** *o* **de aduana** customs service; ~ **a domicilio** home delivery service; ~ **incluido** (*en hotel etc*) service charge included; ~ **militar** military service; ~ **público** (*COM*) public utility.
servidor, a [serhēthor', á] *nm/f* servant; **su seguro ~ (s.s.s.)** yours truly (*US*) *o* faithfully (*Brit*); **un ~** (*el que habla o escribe*) your humble servant.
servidumbre [serhēthōōm'bre] *nf* (*sujeción*) servitude; (*criados*) servants *pl*, staff.
servil [serhēl'] *a* servile.
servilleta [serhēye'tá] *nf* napkin.

servilletero [serbĕyete'ro] *nm* napkin ring.

servir [serbĕr'] *vt* to serve; (*comida*) to serve out *o* up; (*TENIS etc*) to serve ♦ *vi* to serve; (*camarero*) to serve, wait; (*tener utilidad*) to be of use, be useful; ~**se** *vr* to serve *o* help o.s.; ¿**en qué puedo** ~**le?** how can I help you?; ~ **vino a uno** to pour wine for sb; ~ **de guía** to act *o* serve as a guide; **no sirve para nada** it's useless; ~**se de algo** to make use of sth, use sth; **sírvase pasar** please come in.

sesenta [sesen'tá] *num* sixty.

sesentón, ona [sesenton', onà] *a*, *nm/f* sixty-year-old.

sesgado, a [sesgá'tho, à] *a* slanted, slanting.

sesgo [ses'go] *nm* slant; (*fig*) slant, twist.

sesión [sesyon'] *nf* (*POL*) session, sitting; (*CINE*) showing; (*TEATRO*) performance; **abrir/levantar la** ~ to open/close *o* adjourn the meeting; **la segunda** ~ the second showing.

seso [se'so] *nm* brain; (*fig*) intelligence; ~**s** *nmpl* (*CULIN*) brains; **devanarse los** ~**s** to rack one's brains.

sesudo, a [sesōō'tho, à] *a* sensible, wise.

Set. *abr* (= *setiembre*) Sept.

seta [se'tá] *nf* mushroom; ~ **venenosa** toadstool.

setecientos, as [setesyen'tos, ás] *num* seven hundred.

setenta [seten'tá] *num* seventy.

setiembre [setyem'bre] *nm* = **septiembre**.

seto [se'to] *nm* fence; ~ **vivo** hedge.

seudo... [seōōtho] *pref* pseudo....

seudónimo [seōōtho'nēmo] *nm* pseudonym.

Seúl [seōōl'] *nm* Seoul.

s.e.u.o. *abr* (= *salvo error u omisión*) errors and omissions excepted.

severidad [seberĕthàth'] *nf* severity.

severo, a [sebe'ro, à] *a* severe; (*disciplina*) strict; (*frío*) bitter.

Sevilla [sebĕ'yá] *nf* Seville.

sevillano, a [sebĕyá'no, à] *a* of *o* from Seville ♦ *nm/f* native *o* inhabitant of Seville.

sexagenario, a [seksáhená'ryo, à] *a* sixty-year-old ♦ *nm/f* person in his/her sixties.

sexagésimo, a [seksáhe'sēmo, à] *num* sixtieth.

sexo [sek'so] *nm* sex; **el** ~ **femenino/masculino** the female/male sex.

sexto, a [seks'to, à] *num* sixth; **Juan S**~ John the Sixth.

sexual [sekswál'] *a* sexual; **vida** ~ sex life.

s.f. *abr* (= *sin fecha*) no date.

s/f *abr* (*COM*: = *su favor*) your favor.

sgte(s). *abr* (= *siguiente(s)*) foll.

si [sē] *conj* if; (*en pregunta indirecta*) if, whether; ~ ... ~ ... whether ... or ...; **me pregunto** ~ ... I wonder if *o* whether ...; ~ **no** if not, otherwise; ¡~ **fuera verdad!** if only it were true!

sí [sē] *ad* yes ♦ *nm* consent ♦ *pron* (*uso impersonal*) oneself; (*sg: m*) himself; (: *f*) herself; (: *de cosa*) itself; (: *de usted*) yourself; (*pl*) themselves; (: *de ustedes*) yourselves; (: *recíproco*) each other; **él no quiere pero yo** ~ he doesn't want to but I do; **ella** ~ **vendrá** she will certainly come, she is sure to come; **claro que** ~ of course; **creo que** ~ I think so; **porque** ~ because that's the way it is; (*porque lo digo yo*) because I say so; ¡~ **que lo es!** I'll say it is!; ¡**eso** ~ **que no!** never; **se ríe de** ~ **misma** she laughs at herself; **cambiaron una mirada entre** ~ they gave each other a look; **de por** ~ by itself.

siamés, esa [syámes', esá] *a*, *nm/f* Siamese.

Sicilia [sēsē'lyá] *nf* Sicily.

siciliano, a [sēsēlyá'no, à] *a*, *nm/f* Sicilian ♦ *nm* (*LING*) Sicilian.

SIDA [sē'thá] *nm abr* (= *síndrome de inmunodeficiencia adquirida*) AIDS.

siderurgia [sēthĕrōōr'hyá] *nf* iron and steel industry.

siderúrgico, a [sēthĕrōōr'hēco, à] *a* iron and steel *cpd*.

sidra [sē'thrá] *nf* cider.

siega [sye'gá] *etc vb V* **segar** ♦ *nf* (*cosechar*) reaping; (*segar*) mowing; (*época*) harvest (time).

siegue [sye'ge] *etc vb V* **segar**.

siembra [syem'brá] *etc vb V* **sembrar** ♦ *nf* sowing.

siempre [syem'pre] *ad* always; (*todo el tiempo*) all the time ♦ *conj*: ~ **que** ... (: (+ *indic*) whenever ...; (+ *subjun*) provided that ...; **es lo de** ~ it's the same old story; **como** ~ as usual; **para** ~ forever.

sien [syen] *nf* (*ANAT*) temple.

siento [syen'to] *etc vb V* **sentar**, **sentir**.

sierra [sye'rrá] *etc vb V* **serrar** ♦ *nf* (*TEC*) saw; (*GEO*) mountain range; **S**~ **Leona** Sierra Leone.

siervo, a [syer'bo, à] *nm/f* slave.

siesta [sye'stá] *nf* siesta, nap; **dormir la** *o* **echarse una** *o* **tomar una** ~ to have an afternoon nap.

siete [sye'te] *num* seven.

sífilis [sē'fēlēs] *nf* syphilis.

sifón [sēfon'] *nm* syphon; **whisky con** ~ whisky and soda.

siga [sē'gá] *etc vb V* **seguir**.

sigilo [sēhē'lo] *nm* secrecy; (*discreción*) discretion.

sigla [sē'glà] *nf* initial, abbreviation.

siglo [sē'glo] *nm* century; (*fig*) age; **S**~ **de las Luces** Age of Enlightenment; **S**~ **de Oro** Golden Age.

significación [sēgnēfēkásyon'] *nf* significance.

significado [sēgnēfēká'tho] *nm* significance; (*de palabra etc*) meaning.

significar [sĕgnĕfĕkár'] *vt* to mean, signify; (*notificar*) to make known, express.

significativo, a [sĕgnĕfĕkàtē'ho, á] *a* significant.

signifique [sĕgnĕfē'kc] *etc vb* V **significar**.

signo [sēg'no] *nm* sign; ~ **de admiración** *o* **exclamación** exclamation mark; ~ **igual** equals sign; ~ **de interrogación** question mark; ~ **de más/de menos** plus/minus sign; ~**s de puntuación** punctuation marks.

siguiendo [sēgyen'do] *etc vb* V **seguir**.

siguiente [sēgyen'te] *a* following; (*próximo*) next.

sílaba [sē'làbà] *nf* syllable.

silbar [sēlbár'] *vt*, *vi* to whistle; (*silbato*) to blow; (*TEATRO etc*) to hiss.

silbato [sēlbà'to] *nm* (*instrumento*) whistle.

silbido [sēlbē'ḏo], **silbo** [sēl'bo] *nm* whistle, whistling; (*abucheo*) hiss.

silenciador [sēlensyàḏhor'] *nm* silencer.

silenciar [sēlensyár'] *vt* (*persona*) to silence; (*escándalo*) to hush up.

silencio [sēlen'syo] *nm* silence, quiet; **en el** ~ **más absoluto** in dead silence; **guardar** ~ to keep silent.

silencioso, a [sēlensyo'so, á] *a* silent, quiet.

sílfide [sēl'fēḏhe] *nf* sylph.

silicio [sēlē'syo] *nm* silicon.

silueta [sēlwe'tá] *nf* silhouette; (*de edificio*) outline; (*figura*) figure.

silvestre [sēlbes'tre] *a* (*BOT*) wild; (*fig*) rustic, rural.

silla [sē'yà] *nf* (*asiento*) chair; (*tb*: ~ **de montar**) saddle; ~ **de ruedas** wheelchair.

sillería [sēyerē'á] *nf* (*asientos*) chairs *pl*, set of chairs; (*REL*) choir stalls *pl*; (*taller*) chairmaker's workshop.

sillón [sēyon'] *nm* armchair, easy chair.

sima [sē'mà] *nf* abyss, chasm.

simbolice [sēmbolē'se] *etc vb* V **simbolizar**.

simbólico, a [sēmbo'lēko, á] *a* symbolic(al).

simbolizar [sēmbolēsàr'] *vt* to symbolize.

símbolo [sēm'bolo] *nm* symbol; ~ **gráfico** (*INFORM*) icon.

simetría [sēmetrē'á] *nf* symmetry.

simiente [sēmyen'te] *nf* seed.

similar [sēmēlár'] *a* similar.

similitud [sēmēlētōōth'] *nf* similarity, resemblance.

simio [sē'myo] *nm* ape.

simpatía [sēmpátē'á] *nf* liking; (*afecto*) affection; (*amabilidad*) kindness; (*de ambiente*) friendliness; (*de persona, lugar*) charm, attractiveness; (*solidaridad*) mutual support, solidarity; **tener** ~ **a** to like; **la famosa** ~ **andaluza** that well-known Andalusian charm.

simpatice [sēmpátē'se] *etc vb* V **simpatizar**.

simpático, a [sēmpá'tēko, á] *a* nice, pleasant; (*bondadoso*) kind; **no le hemos caído**

muy ~**s** she didn't like us very much.

simpatiquísimo, a [sēmpátĕkē'sĕmo, á] *a* (*superl de* **simpático**) ever so nice; ever so kind.

simpatizante [sēmpàtĕsán'te] *nm/f* sympathizer.

simpatizar [sēmpátĕsár'] *vi*: ~ **con** to get along with.

simple [sēm'ple] *a* simple; (*elemental*) simple, easy; (*mero*) mere; (*puro*) pure, sheer ♦ *nm/f* simpleton; **un** ~ **soldado** an ordinary soldier.

simpleza [sēmple'sà] *nf* simpleness; (*necedad*) silly thing.

simplicidad [sēmplēsĕḏhàth'] *nf* simplicity.

simplificar [sēmplēfēkár'] *vt* to simplify.

simplifique [sēmplēfē'ke] *etc vb* V **simplificar**.

simplón, ona [sēmplon', onà] *a* simple, gullible ♦ *nm/f* simple soul.

simposio [sēmpo'syo] *nm* symposium.

simulacro [sēmōōlá'kro] *nm* (*apariencia*) semblance; (*fingimiento*) sham.

simular [sēmōōlár'] *vt* to simulate; (*fingir*) to feign, sham.

simultanear [sēmōōltáncár'] *vt*: ~ **dos cosas** to do two things simultaneously.

simultáneo, a [sēmōōltá'neo, á] *a* simultaneous.

sin [sēn] *prep* without; (*a no ser por*) but for ♦ *conj*: ~ **que** (+ *subjun*) without; ~ **decir nada** without a word; ~ **verlo yo** without my seeing it; **platos** ~ **lavar** unwashed *o* dirty dishes; **la ropa está** ~ **lavar** the clothes are unwashed; ~ **que lo sepa él** without his knowing; ~ **embargo** however.

sinagoga [sēnágo'gà] *nf* synagogue.

Sinaí [sēnáē'] *nm*: **El** ~ Sinai, the Sinai Peninsula; **el Monte** ~ Mount Sinai.

sinceridad [sēnserēḏhàth'] *nf* sincerity.

sincero, a [sēnse'ro, á] *a* sincere; (*persona*) genuine; (*opinión*) frank; (*felicitaciones*) heartfelt.

síncope [sēn'kope] *nm* (*desmayo*) blackout; ~ **cardíaco** (*MED*) heart failure.

sincronice [sēnkronē'se] *etc vb* V **sincronizar**.

sincronizar [sēnkronēsár'] *vt* to synchronize.

sindical [sēndēkál'] *a* union *cpd*, trade-union *cpd*.

sindicalista [sēndēkálē'stá] *a* trade-union *cpd* ♦ *nm/f* trade unionist.

sindicar [sēndēkár'] *vt* (*obreros*) to organize, unionize; ~**se** *vr* (*obrero*) to join a union.

sindicato [sēndēká'to] *nm* (*de trabajadores*) trade(s) *o* labor (*US*) union; (*de negociantes*) syndicate.

sindique [sēndē'ke] *etc vb* V **sindicar**.

sinfín [sēnfēn'] *nm*: **un** ~ **de** a great many,

no end of.

sinfonía [sɛnfonc̃'á] *nf* symphony.

Singapur [sɛngápōōr'] *nm* Singapore.

singular [sɛngōōlár'] *a* singular; *(fig)* outstanding, exceptional; *(pey)* peculiar, odd ♦ *nm* (*LING*) singular; **en ~** in the singular.

singularice [sɛngōōlárc̃'sc] *etc vb* V **singularizar.**

singularidad [sɛngōōlárc̃ḥáḥ'] *nf* singularity, peculiarity.

singularizar [sɛngōōlárc̃sár'] *vt* to single out; **~se** *vr* to distinguish o.s., stand out.

siniestro, a [sɛnycs'tro, á] *a* left; *(fig)* sinister ♦ *nm* (*accidente*) accident; (*desastre*) natural disaster.

sinnúmero [sɛnnōō'mcro] *nm* = **sinfín.**

sino [sɛ̄'no] *nm* fate, destiny ♦ *conj* (*pero*) but; (*salvo*) except, save; **no son 8 ~ 9** there are not 8 but 9; **todos ~ él** all except him.

sinónimo, a [sɛno'nc̃mo, á] *a* synonymous ♦ *nm* synonym.

sinrazón [sɛnráson'] *nf* wrong, injustice.

sinsabor [sɛnsáḥor'] *nm* (*molestia*) trouble; (*dolor*) sorrow; (*preocupación*) uneasiness.

síntesis [sɛn'tcsɛs] *nf inv* synthesis.

sintetice [sɛntctc̃'sc] *etc vb* V **sintetizar.**

sintético, a [sɛntc̃'tc̃ko, á] *a* synthetic.

sintetizador [sɛntctc̃sáḥor'] *nm* synthesizer.

sintetizar [sɛntctc̃sár'] *vt* to synthesize.

sintiendo [sɛntycn'do] *etc vb* V **sentir.**

síntoma [sɛn'tomá] *nm* symptom.

sintonía [sɛntonc̃'á] *nf* (*RADIO*) tuning; (*melodía*) signature tune.

sintonice [sɛntonc̃'sc] *etc vb* V **sintonizar.**

sintonizador [sɛntonc̃sáḥor'] *nm* (*RADIO*) tuner.

sintonizar [sɛntonc̃sár'] *vt* (*RADIO*) to tune (in) to, pick up.

sinuoso, a [sɛnwo'so, á] *a* (*camino*) winding; (*rumbo*) devious.

sinvergüenza [sɛmbcrgwcn'sá] *nm/f* rogue, scoundrel.

sionismo [syonɛs'mo] *nm* Zionism.

siquiera [sɛkyc'rá] *conj* even if, even though ♦ *ad* at least; **ni ~** not even.

sirena [sɛrc̃'ná] *nf* siren, mermaid; (*bocina*) siren.

Siria [sɛ̄'ryá] *nf* Syria.

sirio, a [sɛ̄'ryo, á] *a, nm/f* Syrian.

sirviendo [sɛrḥycn'do] *etc vb* V **servir.**

sirviente, a [sɛrḥycn'tc, á] *nm/f* servant.

sisa [sɛ̄'sá] *nf* petty theft; (*COSTURA*) dart; (*sobaquera*) armhole.

sisar [sɛsár'] *vt* (*robar*) to thieve; (*COSTURA*) to take in.

sisear [sɛscár'] *vt, vi* to hiss.

sismógrafo [sɛsmo'gráfo] *nm* seismograph.

sistema [sɛstc̃'má] *nm* system; (*método*) method; **~ impositivo** *o* **tributario** taxa-

tion, tax system; **~ pedagógico** educational system; **~ de alerta inmediata** early-warning system; **~ binario** (*INFORM*) binary system; **~ experto** expert system; **~ de facturación** (*COM*) invoicing system; **~ de fondo fijo** (*COM*) imprest system; **~ de lógica compartida** (*INFORM*) shared logic system; **~ métrico** metric system; **~ operativo (en disco)** (*INFORM*) (disk-based) operating system.

sistemático, a [sɛstcmá'tc̃ko, á] *a* systematic.

sitiar [sɛtyár'] *vt* to besiege, lay siege to.

sitio [sɛ̄'tyo] *nm* (*lugar*) place; (*espacio*) room, space; (*MIL*) siege; **¿hay ~?** is there any room?; **hay ~ de sobra** there's plenty of room.

situación [sɛtwásyon'] *nf* situation, position; (*estatus*) position, standing.

situado, a [sɛtwá'ḥo, á] *a* situated, placed; **estar ~** (*COM*) to be financially secure.

situar [sɛtwár'] *vt* to place, put; (*edificio*) to locate, situate.

S.L. *abr* (*COM*:=*Sociedad Limitada*) ≈ Corp. (*US*), Ltd. (*Brit*).

slip [cslḗp'], *pl* **slips** *nm* pants *pl*, briefs *pl*.

slot [cslot'], *pl* **slots** *nm*: **~ de expansión** expansion slot.

S.M. *abr* (= *Su Majestad*) HM.

smoking [(c)smo'kɛ̄n] (*pl* **~s**) *nm* tuxedo (*US*), dinner jacket (*Brit*).

s/n *abr* (= *sin número*) no number.

snob [csnob'] =**esnob.**

SO *abr* (= *suroeste*) SW.

so [so] *excl* whoa!; **¡~ burro!** you idiot! ♦ *prep* under.

s/o *abr* (*COM*:=*su orden*) your order.

sobaco [soḥá'ko] *nm* armpit.

sobado, a [soḥá'ḥo, á] *a* (*ropa*) worn; (*arrugado*) crumpled; (*libro*) well-worn; (*CULIN*: *masa*) crumbly (*US*), short (*Brit*).

sobar [soḥár'] *vt* (*tela*) to finger; (*ropa*) to rumple, mess up; (*músculos*) to rub, massage.

soberanía [soḥcránc̃'á] *nf* sovereignty.

soberano, a [soḥcrá'no, á] *a* sovereign; (*fig*) supreme ♦ *nm/f* sovereign; **los ~s** the king and queen.

soberbio, a [soḥcr'ḥyo, á] *a* (*orgulloso*) proud; (*altivo*) haughty, arrogant; (*fig*) magnificent, superb ♦ *nf* pride; haughtiness, arrogance; magnificence.

sobornar [soḥornár'] *vt* to bribe.

soborno [soḥor'no] *nm* (*un ~*) bribe; (*el ~*) bribery.

sobra [so'ḥrá] *nf* excess, surplus; **~s** *nfpl* left-overs, scraps; **de ~** surplus, extra; **lo sé de ~** I'm only too aware of it; **tengo de ~** I've more than enough.

sobradamente [soḥráḥámen'tc] *ad* amply; (*saber*) only too well.

sobrado, a [soβrá'ðo, à] *a (más que suficiente)* more than enough; *(superfluo)* excessive ♦ *ad* too, exceedingly; **sobradas veces** repeatedly.

sobrante [soβrán'te] *a* remaining, extra ♦ *nm* surplus, remainder.

sobrar [soβrár'] *vt* to exceed, surpass ♦ *vi (tener de más)* to be more than enough; *(quedar)* to remain, be left (over).

sobrasada [soβrásá'ðà] *nf* ≈ sausage spread.

sobre [so'βre] *prep (gen)* on; *(encima)* on (top of); *(por encima de, arriba de)* over, above; *(más que)* more than; *(además)* in addition to, besides; *(alrededor de)* about; *(porcentaje)* in, out of; *(tema)* about, on ♦ *nm* envelope; ~ **todo** above all; **3 ~ 100** 3 in a 100, 3 out of every 100; **un libro ~ Tirso** a book about Tirso; ~ **de ventanilla** window envelope.

sobrecama [soβreká'mà] *nf* bedspread.

sobrecapitalice [soβrekápētálē'se] *etc vb V* **sobrecapitalizar**.

sobrecapitalizar [soβrekápētálēsár'] *vi* to overcapitalize.

sobrecargar [soβrekárgár'] *vt (camión)* to overload; *(COM)* to surcharge.

sobrecargue [soβrekár'ge] *etc vb V* **sobrecargar**.

sobrecoger [soβrekoher'] *vt (sobresaltar)* to startle; *(asustar)* to scare; ~**se** *vr (sobresaltarse)* to be startled; *(asustarse)* to get scared; *(quedar impresionado):* ~**se (de)** to be overawed (by).

sobrecoja [soβreko'hà] *etc vb V* **sobrecoger**.

sobredosis [soβreðo'sēs] *nf inv* overdose.

sobre(e)ntender [soβre(e)ntender'] *vt* to understand; *(adivinar)* to deduce, infer; ~**se** *vr:* **se sobre(e)ntiende que ...** it is implied that ....

sobreescribir [soβreeskrēβēr'] *vt (INFORM)* to overwrite.

sobre(e)stimar [soβre(e)stēmár'] *vt* to overestimate.

sobregiro [soβregē'ro] *nm (COM)* overdraft.

sobrehumano, a [soβreōōmà'no, à] *a* superhuman.

sobreimprimir [soβreēmprēmēr'] *vt (COM)* to merge.

sobrellevar [soβreyeβár'] *vt (fig)* to bear, endure.

sobremesa [soβreme'sá] *nf (después de comer)* after-dinner conversation; *(INFORM)* desktop; **conversación de ~** table talk.

sobremodo [soβremo'ðo] *ad* very much, enormously.

sobrenatural [soβrenátōōrál'] *a* supernatural.

sobrenombre [soβrenom'bre] *nm* nickname.

sobrepasar [soβrepásár'] *vt* to exceed, surpass.

sobrepondré [soβrepondre'] *etc vb V* **sobreponer**.

sobreponer [soβreponer'] *vt (poner encima)* to put on top; *(añadir)* to add; ~**se a** to overcome.

sobreponga [soβrepon'gà] *etc vb V* **sobreponer**.

sobreprima [soβreprē'mà] *nf (COM)* extra premium.

sobreproducción [soβreproðōōksyon'] *nf* overproduction.

sobrepuesto [soβrepwe'sto], **sobrepuse** [soβrepōō'se] *etc vb V* **sobreponer**.

sobresaldré [soβresáldre'] *etc,* **sobresalga** [soβresál'gà] *etc vb V* **sobresalir**.

sobresaliente [soβresályen'te] *a* projecting; *(fig)* outstanding, excellent; *(UNIV etc)* first class ♦ *nm (UNIV etc)* distinction.

sobresalir [soβresálēr'] *vi* to project, jut out; *(fig)* to stand out, excel.

sobresaltar [soβresáltár'] *vt (asustar)* to scare, frighten; *(sobrecoger)* to startle.

sobresalto [soβresál'to] *nm (movimiento)* start; *(susto)* scare; *(turbación)* sudden shock.

sobreseer [soβreseer'] *vt:* ~ **una causa** *(JUR)* to stop a case.

sobrestadía [soβrestàðe'à] *nf (COM)* demurrage.

sobretensión [soβretensyon'] *nf (ELEC):* ~ **transitoria** surge.

sobretodo [soβreto'ðo] *nm* overcoat.

sobrevendré [soβreβendre'] *etc,* **sobrevenga** [soβreβen'gà] *etc vb V* **sobrevenir**.

sobrevenir [soβreβenēr'] *vi (ocurrir)* to happen (unexpectedly); *(resultar)* to follow, ensue.

sobreviene [soβreβye'ne] *etc,* **sobrevine** [soβreβē'ne] *etc vb V* **sobrevenir**.

sobreviviente [soβreβēβyen'te] *a* surviving ♦ *nm/f* survivor.

sobrevivir [soβreβēβēr'] *vi* to survive; *(persona)* to outlive; *(objeto etc)* to outlast.

sobrevolar [soβreβolár'] *vt* to fly over.

sobrevuele [soβreβwe'le] *etc vb V* **sobrevolar**.

sobriedad [soβryeðáð'] *nf* sobriety, soberness; *(moderación)* moderation, restraint.

sobrino, a [soβrē'no, à] *nm/f* nephew/niece.

sobrio, a [soβ'ryo, à] *a (moderado)* moderate, restrained.

socarrón, ona [sokárron', onà] *a (sarcástico)* sarcastic, ironic(al).

socavar [sokáβár'] *vt* to undermine; *(excavar)* to dig underneath *o* below.

socavón [sokáβon'] *nm (en mina)* gallery; *(hueco)* hollow; *(en la calle)* hole.

sociable [sosyá'βle] *a (persona)* sociable, friendly; *(animal)* social.

social [sosyál'] *a* social; (*COM*) company *cpd*.

socialdemócrata [sosyáldemo'krátá] *nm/f* social democrat.

socialdemocrático, a [sosyáldemokrá'tēko, á] *a* social-democratic.

socialice [sosyálē'se] *etc vb* V **socializar**.

socialista [sosyálē'stá] *a, nm/f* socialist.

socializar [sosyálēsár'] *vt* to socialize.

sociedad [sosyetháth'] *nf* society; (*COM*) company; ~ **de ahorro y préstamo** savings and loan society; ~ **anónima (S.A.)** incorporated company (Inc.) (*US*), limited company (Ltd.) (*Brit*); ~ **de beneficiencia** benefit association (*US*), friendly society (*Brit*); ~ **de cartera** investment trust; ~ **comanditaria** (*COM*) co-ownership; ~ **conjunta** (*COM*) joint venture; ~ **inmobiliaria** savings and loan (society) (*US*), building society (*Brit*); ~ **de responsabilidad limitada** (*COM*) corporation (*US*), private limited company (*Brit*).

socio, a [so'syo, á] *nm/f* (*miembro*) member; (*COM*) partner; ~ **activo** active partner; ~ **capitalista** *o* **comanditario** silent partner.

socioeconómico, a [sosyoekono'mēko, á] *a* socio-economic.

sociología [sosyolohē'á] *nf* sociology.

sociólogo, a [sosyo'logo, á] *nm/f* sociologist.

socorrer [sokorrer'] *vt* to help.

socorrido, a [sokorrē'tho, á] *a* (*tienda*) well-stocked; (*útil*) handy; (*persona*) helpful.

socorrista [sokorrē'stá] *nm/f* first aider; (*en piscina, playa*) lifeguard.

socorro [soko'rro] *nm* (*ayuda*) help, aid; (*MIL*) relief; ¡~! help!

soda [so'thá] *nf* (*sosa*) soda; (*bebida*) soda (water).

soez [soes'] *a* dirty, obscene.

sofá [sofá'] *nm* sofa, settee.

sofá-cama [sofá'kámá] *nm* studio couch, sofa bed.

Sofia [so'fyá] *nf* Sofia.

sofisticación [sofēstēkásyon'] *nf* sophistication.

sofocado, a [sofoká'tho, á] *a*: **estar** ~ (*fig*) to be out of breath; (*ahogarse*) to feel stifled.

sofocar [sofokár'] *vt* to suffocate; (*apagar*) to smother, put out; ~**se** *vr* to suffocate; (*fig*) to blush, feel embarrassed.

sofoco [sofo'ko] *nm* suffocation; (*azoro*) embarrassment.

sofocón [sofokon'] *nm*: **llevarse** *o* **pasar un** ~ to have a sudden shock.

sofreír [sofreēr'] *vt* to fry lightly.

sofría [sofrē'á] *etc*, **sofriendo** [sofryen'do] *etc*, **sofrito** [sofrē'to] *vb* V **sofreír**.

soft(ware) [sof'(wer)] *nm* (*INFORM*) software.

soga [so'gá] *nf* rope.

sois [soēs] *vb* V **ser**.

soja [so'há] *nf* soy.

sojuzgar [sohōōsgár'] *vt* to subdue, rule despotically.

sojuzgue [sohōōs'ge] *etc vb* V **sojuzgar**.

sol [sol] *nm* sun; (*luz*) sunshine, sunlight; ~ **naciente/poniente** rising/setting sun; **tomar el** ~ to sunbathe; **hace** ~ it is sunny.

solace [solá'se] *etc vb* V **solazar**.

solamente [solámen'te] *ad* only, just.

solapa [solá'pá] *nf* (*de chaqueta*) lapel; (*de libro*) jacket.

solapado, a [solápá'tho, á] *a* sly, underhand.

solar [solár'] *a* solar, sun *cpd* ♦ *nm* (*terreno*) plot (of ground); (*local*) undeveloped site.

solaz [solás'] *nm* recreation, relaxation.

solazar [solásár'] *vt* (*divertir*) to amuse; ~**se** *vr* to enjoy o.s., relax.

soldada [soldá'thá] *nf* pay.

soldado [soldá'tho] *nm* soldier; ~ **raso** private.

soldador [soldáthor'] *nm* soldering iron; (*persona*) welder.

soldar [soldár'] *vt* to solder, weld; (*unir*) to join, unite.

soleado, a [soleá'tho, á] *a* sunny.

soledad [soletháth'] *nf* solitude; (*estado infeliz*) loneliness.

solemne [solem'ne] *a* solemn; (*tontería*) utter; (*error*) complete.

solemnidad [solemnētháth'] *nf* solemnity.

soler [soler'] *vi* to be in the habit of, be accustomed to; **suele salir a las ocho** she usually goes out at 8 o'clock; **solíamos ir todos los años** we used to go every year.

solera [sole'rá] *nf* (*tradición*) tradition; **vino de** ~ vintage wine.

solicitar [solēsētár'] *vt* (*permiso*) to ask for, seek; (*puesto*) to apply for; (*votos*) to canvass for; (*atención*) to attract; (*persona*) to pursue, chase after.

solícito, a [solē'sēto, á] *a* (*diligente*) diligent; (*cuidadoso*) careful.

solicitud [solēsētōōth'] *nf* (*calidad*) great care; (*petición*) request; (*a un puesto*) application.

solidaridad [solēthárētháth'] *nf* solidarity; **por** ~ **con** (*POL etc*) out of *o* in solidarity with.

solidario, a [solēthá'ryo, á] *a* (*participación*) joint, common; (*compromiso*) mutually binding; **hacerse** ~ **de** to declare one's solidarity with.

solidez [solēthes'] *nf* solidity.

sólido, a [so'lētho, á] *a* solid; (*TEC*) solidly made; (*bien construido*) well-built.

soliloquio [solēlo'kyo] *nm* soliloquy.

solista [solē'stá] *nm/f* soloist.

solitario, a [solětá'ryo, á] *a* (*persona*) lonely, solitary; (*lugar*) lonely, desolate ♦ *nm/f* (*reclusa*) recluse; (*en la sociedad*) loner ♦ *nm* solitaire ♦ *nf* tapeworm.

soliviantar [soléḥyántár'] *vt* to stir up, rouse (to revolt); (*enojar*) to anger; (*sacar de quicio*) to exasperate.

solo, a [so'lo, á] *a* (*único*) single, sole; (*sin compañía*) alone; (*MUS*) solo; (*solitario*) lonely; **hay una sola dificultad** there is just one difficulty; **a solas** alone, by o.s.

sólo [so'lo] *ad* only, just; (*exclusivamente*) solely; **tan ~** only just.

solomillo [solomě'yo] *nm* sirloin.

soltar [soltár'] *vt* (*dejar ir*) to let go of; (*desprender*) to unfasten, loosen; (*librar*) to release, set free; (*amarras*) to cast off; (*AUTO*: *freno etc*) to release; (*suspiro*) to heave; (*risa etc*) to let out; **~se** *vr* (*desanudarse*) to come undone; (*desprenderse*) to come off; (*adquirir destreza*) to become expert; (*en idioma*) to become fluent.

soltero, a [solte'ro, á] *a* single, unmarried ♦ *nm* bachelor ♦ *nf* single woman, spinster.

solterón [solteron'] *nm* confirmed bachelor.

solterona [soltero'ná] *nf* spinster, maiden lady; (*pey*) old maid.

soltura [soltōō'rá] *nf* looseness, slackness; (*de los miembros*) agility, ease of movement; (*en el hablar*) fluency, ease.

soluble [solōō'ḥle] *a* (*QUÍMICA*) soluble; (*problema*) solvable; **~ en agua** soluble in water.

solución [solōōsyon'] *nf* solution; **~ de continuidad** break in continuity.

solucionar [solōōsyonár'] *vt* (*problema*) to solve; (*asunto*) to settle, resolve.

solvencia [solḥen'syá] *nf* (*COM*: *estado*) solvency; (: *acción*) settlement, payment.

solventar [solḥentár'] *vt* (*pagar*) to settle, pay; (*resolver*) to resolve.

solvente [solḥen'te] *a* solvent, free of debt.

solloce [soyo'se] *etc vb V* **sollozar**.

sollozar [soyosár'] *vi* to sob.

sollozo [soyo'so] *nm* sob.

Somalia [somá'lyá] *nf* Somalia.

sombra [som'brá] *nf* shadow; (*como protección*) shade; **~s** *nfpl* darkness *sg*, shadows; **sin ~ de duda** without a shadow of doubt; **tener buena/mala ~** (*suerte*) to be lucky/ unlucky; (*carácter*) to be likeable/ disagreeable.

sombrero [sombre'ro] *nm* hat; **~ hongo** derby (*US*), bowler (hat) (*Brit*); **~ de copa** *o* **de pelo** (*AM*) top hat.

sombrilla [sombrě'yá] *nf* parasol.

sombrío, a [sombrě'o, á] *a* (*oscuro*) shady; (*fig*) sad; (*persona*) gloomy.

somero, a [some'ro, á] *a* superficial.

someter [someter'] *vt* (*país*) to conquer; (*persona*) to subject to one's will; (*in-*

forme) to present, submit; **~se** *vr* to give in, yield, submit; **~se a** to submit to; **~se a una operación** to undergo an operation.

sometimiento [sometěmyen'to] *nm* (*estado*) submission; (*acción*) presentation.

somier [somyer'], *pl* **somiers** *nm* spring mattress.

somnífero [somně'fero] *nm* sleeping pill *o* tablet.

somnolencia [somnolen'syá] *nf* sleepiness, drowsiness.

somos [so'mos] *vb V* **ser**.

son [son] *vb V* **ser** ♦ *nm* sound; **en ~ de broma** as a joke.

sonado, a [soná'ḥo, á] *a* (*comentado*) talked-of; (*famoso*) famous; (*COM*: *pey*) hyped(-up).

sonajero [sonáhe'ro] *nm* (baby's) rattle.

sonambulismo [sonámbōōlěs'mo] *nm* sleepwalking.

sonámbulo, a [sonám'bōōlo, á] *nm/f* sleepwalker.

sonar [sonár'] *vt* (*campana*) to ring; (*trompeta, sirena*) to blow ♦ *vi* to sound; (*hacer ruido*) to make a noise; (*LING*) to be sounded, be pronounced; (*ser conocido*) to sound familiar; (*campana*) to ring; (*reloj*) to strike, chime; **~se** *vr*: **~se (la nariz)** to blow one's nose; **es un nombre que suena** it's a name that's in the news; **me suena ese nombre** that name rings a bell.

sonda [son'dá] *nf* (*NAUT*) sounding; (*TEC*) bore, drill; (*MED*) probe.

sondear [sondeár'] *vt* to sound; to bore (into), drill; to probe, sound; (*fig*) to sound out.

sondeo [sonde'o] *nm* sounding; boring, drilling; (*encuesta*) poll, enquiry; **~ de la opinión pública** public opinion poll.

sónico, a [so'něko, á] *a* sonic, sound *cpd*.

sonido [soně'ḥo] *nm* sound.

sonoro, a [sono'ro, á] *a* sonorous; (*resonante*) loud, resonant; (*LING*) voiced; **efectos ~s** sound effects.

sonreír [sonreěr'] *vi*, **sonreírse** *vr* to smile.

sonría [sonrě'á] *etc*, **sonriendo** [sonryen'do] *etc vb V* **sonreír**.

sonriente [sonryen'te] *a* smiling.

sonrisa [sonrě'sá] *nf* smile.

sonrojar [sonrohár'] *vt*: **~ a uno** to make sb blush; **~se** *vr*: **~se (de)** to blush (at).

sonrojo [sonro'ho] *nm* blush.

sonsacar [sonsákár'] *vt* to wheedle, coax; **~ a uno** to pump sb for information.

sonsaque [sonsá'ke] *etc vb V* **sonsacar**.

sonsonete [sonsone'te] *nm* (*golpecitos*) tap(ping); (*voz monótona*) monotonous delivery, singsong (voice).

soñador, a [sonyáḥor', á] *nm/f* dreamer.

soñar [sonyár'] *vt*, *vi* to dream; **~ con** to dream about *o* of; **soñé contigo anoche** I dreamed about you last night.

soñoliento, a [sonyolyen'to. á] *a* sleepy, drowsy.

sopa [so'pá] *nf* soup; ~ **de fideos** noodle soup.

sopero, a [sope'ro, á] *a* (*plato, cuchara*) soup *cpd* ♦ *nm* soup plate ♦ *nf* soup tureen.

sopesar [sopesár'] *vt* (*fig*) to weigh.

sopetón [sopeton'] *nm*: **de** ~ suddenly, unexpectedly.

soplar [soplár'] *vt* (*polvo*) to blow away, blow off; (*inflar*) to blow up; (*vela*) to blow out; (*ayudar a recordar*) to prompt; (*birlar*) to rip off; (*delatar*) to squeal on ♦ *vi* to blow; (*delatar*) to squeal; (*beber*) to booze, bend the elbow.

soplete [sople'te] *nm* · blowtorch (*US*), blowlamp (*Brit*); ~ **soldador** welding torch.

soplo [so'plo] *nm* blow, puff; (*de viento*) puff, gust.

soplón, ona [soplon', oná] *nm/f* (*fam*: *chismoso*) telltale; (: *de policía*) informer, grass.

soponcio [sopon'syo] *nm* dizzy spell.

sopor [sopor'] *nm* drowsiness.

soporífero, a [soporē'fero, á] *a* sleep-inducing; (*fig*) soporific ♦ *nm* sleeping pill.

soportable [soportá'ble] *a* bearable.

soportar [soportár'] *vt* to bear, carry; (*fig*) to bear, put up with.

soporte [sopor'te] *nm* support; (*fig*) pillar, support; (*INFORM*) medium; ~ **de entrada/salida** input/output medium.

soprano [soprá'no] *nf* soprano.

sor [sor] *nf*: **S**~ **Maria** Sister Mary.

sorber [sorber'] *vt* (*chupar*) to sip; (*inhalar*) to sniff, inhale; (*absorber*) to soak up, absorb.

sorbete [sorbe'te] *nm* sherbet.

sorbo [sor'bo] *nm* (*trago*) gulp, swallow; (*chupada*) sip; **beber a** ~**s** to sip.

sordera [sorde'rá] *nf* deafness.

sórdido, a [sor'thētho, á] *a* dirty, squalid.

sordo, a [sor'tho, á] *a* (*persona*) deaf; (*ruido*) dull; (*LING*) voiceless ♦ *nm/f* deaf person; **quedarse** ~ to go deaf.

sordomudo, a [sorthomōō'tho, á] *a* deaf and dumb ♦ *nm/f* deaf-mute.

soriano, a [soryá'no, á] *a* of *o* from Soria ♦ *nm/f* native *o* inhabitant of Soria.

sorna [sor'ná] *nf* (*malicia*) slyness; (*tono burlón*) sarcastic tone.

soroche [sorotch'e] *nm* (*AM MED*) mountain sickness.

sorprendente [sorprenden'te] *a* surprising.

sorprender [sorprender'] *vt* to surprise; (*asombrar*) to amaze; (*sobresaltar*) to startle; (*coger desprevenido*) to catch unawares; ~**se** *vr*: ~**se** (**de**) to be surprised *o* amazed (at).

sorpresa [sorpre'sá] *nf* surprise.

sorpresivo, a [sorpresē'vo, á] *a* (*AM*) surprising; (*imprevisto*) sudden.

sortear [sorteár'] *vt* to draw lots for; (*rifar*) to raffle; (*dificultad*) to dodge, avoid.

sorteo [sorte'o] *nm* (*en lotería*) draw; (*rifa*) raffle.

sortija [sortē'há] *nf* ring; (*rizo*) ringlet, curl.

sortilegio [sortēle'hyo] *nm* (*hechicería*) sorcery; (*hechizo*) spell.

sosegado, a [sosegá'tho, á] *a* quiet, calm.

sosegar [sosegár'] *vt* to quieten, calm; (*el ánimo*) to reassure ♦ *vi* to rest.

sosegué [sosege'], **soseguemos** [sosege'mos] *etc vb V* **sosegar**.

sosiego [sosye'go] *etc vb V* **sosegar** ♦ *nm* quiet(ness), calm(ness).

sosiegue [sosye'ge] *etc vb V* **sosegar**.

soslayo [soslá'yo]: **de** ~ *ad* obliquely, sideways; **mirar de** ~ to look out of the corner of one's eye (at).

soso, a [so'so, á] *a* (*CULIN*) tasteless; (*fig*) dull, uninteresting.

sospecha [sospetch'á] *nf* suspicion.

sospechar [sospetchár'] *vt* to suspect ♦ *vi*: ~ **de** to be suspicious of.

sospechoso, a [sospetcho'so, á] *a* suspicious; (*testimonio, opinión*) suspect ♦ *nm/f* suspect.

sostén [sosten'] *nm* (*apoyo*) support; (*sujetador*) bra; (*alimentación*) sustenance, food.

sostendré [sostendre'] *etc vb V* **sostener**.

sostener [sostener'] *vt* to support; (*mantener*) to keep up, maintain; (*alimentar*) to sustain, keep going; ~**se** *vr* to support o.s.; (*seguir*) to continue, remain.

sostenga [sosten'gá] *etc vb V* **sostener**.

sostenido, a [sostenē'tho, á] *a* continuous, sustained; (*prolongado*) prolonged; (*MUS*) sharp ♦ *nm* (*MUS*) sharp.

sostuve [sostōō'be] *etc vb V* **sostener**.

sotana [sotá'ná] *nf* (*REL*) cassock.

sótano [so'táno] *nm* basement.

sotavento [sotáben'to] *nm* (*NAUT*) lee, leeward.

soterrar [soterrár'] *vt* to bury; (*esconder*) to hide away.

sotierre [sotye'rre] *etc vb V* **soterrar**.

soviético, a [sohye'tēko, á] *a, nm/f* Soviet; **los** ~**s** the Soviets, the Russians.

soy [soē] *vb V* **ser**.

spooling [espōō'lēn] *nm* (*INFORM*) spooling.

sport [espor'(t)] *nm* sport.

spot [espot'], *pl* **spot** *nm* (*publicitario*) ad.

Sr. *abr* (= *Señor*) Mr.

Sra. *abr* (= *Señora*) Mrs.

S.R.C. *abr* (= *se ruega contestación*) R.S.V.P.

Sres., Srs. *abr* (= *Señores*) Messrs.

Sri Lanka [srēlán'ká] *nm* Sri Lanka.

Srta. *abr* = **Señorita.**

SS *abr* (= *Santos, Santas*) SS.

S.S. *abr* (*REL*: = *Su Santidad*) H.H.

ss. *abr* (= *siguientes*) foll.

Sta. *abr* (= *Santa*) St; (= *Señorita*) Miss.

stárter [está'ter] *nm* (*AUTO*) starter.

status [stá'tōōs, está'tōōs] *nm inv* status.

Sto. *abr* (= *Santo*) St.

su [sōō] *pron* (*de él*) his; (*de ella*) her; (*de una cosa*) its; (*de ellos, ellas*) their; (*de usted, ustedes*) your.

suave [swá'be] *a* gentle; (*superficie*) smooth; (*trabajo*) easy; (*música, voz*) soft, sweet; (*clima, sabor*) mild.

suavice [swábē'se] *etc vb V* **suavizar.**

suavidad [swábēthath'] *nf* gentleness; (*de superficie*) smoothness; (*de música*) softness, sweetness.

suavizar [swábēsár'] *vt* to soften; (*quitar la aspereza*) to smooth (out); (*pendiente*) to ease; (*colores*) to tone down; (*carácter*) to mellow; (*dureza*) to temper.

subalimentado, a [sōōbálēmentá'tho, á] *a* undernourished.

subalterno, a [sōōbálter'no, á] *a* (*importancia*) secondary; (*personal*) minor, auxiliary ♦ *nm* subordinate.

subarrendar [sōōbárrendár'] *vt* to sublet.

subarriendo [sōōbárryen'do] *nm* (*COM*) sublease (*US*), leaseback (*Brit*).

subasta [sōōbás'stá] *nf* auction; **poner en** *o* **sacar a pública** ~ to put up for public auction; ~ **a la rebaja** Dutch auction.

subastador, a [sōōbástáthor', á] *nm/f* auctioneer.

subastar [sōōbástár'] *vt* to auction (off).

subcampeón, ona [sōōbkámpeon', oná] *nm/f* runner-up.

subconsciente [sōōbkonssyen'te] *a* subconscious.

subcontratar [sōōbkontrátár'] *vt* (*COM*) to subcontract.

subcontrato [sōōbkontrá'to] *nm* (*COM*) subcontract.

subdesarrollado, a [sōōbthesárroyá'tho, á] *a* underdeveloped.

subdesarrollo [sōōbthesárro'yo] *nm* underdevelopment.

subdirector, a [sōōbthērektor', á] *nm/f* assistant manager.

subdirectorio [sōōbthērekto'ryo] *nm* (*INFORM*) subdirectory.

súbdito, a [sōōb'thēto, á] *nm/f* subject.

subdividir [sōōbthēthēthēr'] *vt* to subdivide.

subempleo [sōōbemple'o] *nm* underemployment.

subestimar [sōōbestēmár'] *vt* to underestimate, underrate.

subido, a [sōōbē'tho, á] *a* (*color*) bright, strong; (*precio*) high ♦ *nf* (*de montaña etc*) ascent, climb; (*de precio*) rise, increase;

(*pendiente*) slope, hill.

subíndice [sōōbēn'dēse] *nm* (*INFORM, TIP*) subscript.

subir [sōōbēr'] *vt* (*objeto*) to raise, lift up; (*cuesta, calle*) to go up; (*colina, montaña*) to climb; (*precio*) to raise; (*empleado etc*) to promote ♦ *vi* to go/come up; (*a un coche*) to get in; (*a un autobús, tren*) to get on; (*precio*) to rise, go up; (*en el empleo*) to be promoted; (*río, marea*) to rise; ~**se** *vr* to get up, climb; ~**se a un coche** to get in(to) a car.

súbito, a [sōō'bēto, á] *a* (*repentino*) sudden; (*imprevisto*) unexpected.

subjetivo, a [sōōbhetē'bo, á] *a* subjective.

subjuntivo [sōōbhōōntē'bo] *nm* subjunctive (mood).

sublevación [sōōblebásyon'] *nf* revolt, uprising.

sublevar [sōōblebár'] *vt* to rouse to revolt; ~**se** *vr* to revolt, rise up.

sublimar [sōōblēmár'] *vt* (*persona*) to exalt; (*deseos etc*) to sublimate.

sublime [sōōblē'me] *a* sublime.

submarino, a [sōōbmárē'no, á] *a* underwater ♦ *nm* submarine.

subnormal [sōōbnormál'] *a* subnormal ♦ *nm/f* subnormal person.

suboficial [sōōbofēsyál'] *nm* non-commissioned officer.

subordinado, a [sōōbordēná'tho, á] *a, nm/f* subordinate.

subproducto [sōōbprothōōk'to] *nm* byproduct.

subrayado [sōōbráyá'tho] *nm* underlining.

subrayar [sōōbráyár'] *vt* to underline; (*recalcar*) to underline, emphasize.

subrepticio, a [sōōbreptē'syo, á] *a* surreptitious.

subrutina [sōōbrōōtē'ná] *nf* (*INFORM*) subroutine.

subsanar [sōōbsánár'] *vt* (*reparar*) to make good; (*perdonar*) to excuse; (*sobreponerse a*) to overcome.

subscribir [sōōbskrēbēr'] *vt* = **suscribir.**

subscrito [sōōbskrē'to] *pp de* **subscribir.**

subsecretario, a [sōōbsekretá'ryo, á] *nm/f* undersecretary, assistant secretary.

subsidiario, a [sōōbsēthyá'ryo, á] *a* subsidiary.

subsidio [sōōbsē'thyo] *nm* (*ayuda*) aid, financial help; (*subvención*) subsidy, grant; (*de enfermedad, paro etc*) benefit, allowance.

subsistencia [sōōbsēsten'syá] *nf* subsistence.

subsistir [sōōbsēstēr'] *vi* to subsist; (*vivir*) to live; (*sobrevivir*) to survive, endure.

subsuelo [sōōbswe'lo] *nm* subsoil.

subterfugio [sōōbterfōō'hyo] *nm* subterfuge.

subterráneo, a [sōōħterrá'neo, à] *a* underground, subterranean ♦ *nm* underpass, underground passage; (*AM*) subway (*US*), underground railway (*Brit*).
subtítulo [sōōħtē'tōōlo] *nm* subtitle, subheading.
suburbano, a [sōōħōōrħá'no, à] *a* suburban.
suburbio [sōōħōōr'ħyo] *nm* (*barrio*) slum quarter; (*afueras*) suburbs *pl*.
subvención [sōōħħensyon'] *nf* subsidy, subvention, grant; ~ **estatal** state subsidy *o* support; ~ **para la inversión** (*COM*) investment grant.
subvencionar [sōōħħensyonàr'] *vt* to subsidize.
subversión [sōōħħersyon'] *nf* subversion.
subversivo, a [sōōħħersē'ħo, à] *a* subversive.
subyacente [sōōħyásen'te] *a* underlying.
subyugar [sōōħyōōgár'] *vt* (*país*) to subjugate, subdue; (*enemigo*) to overpower; (*voluntad*) to dominate.
subyugue [sōōħyōō'ge] *etc vb V* **subyugar**.
succión [sōōksyon'] *nf* suction.
succionar [sōōksyonàr'] *vt* (*sorber*) to suck; (*TEC*) to absorb, soak up.
sucedáneo, a [sōōseħá'neo, à] *a* substitute ♦ *nm* substitute (food).
suceder [sōōseħer'] *vi* to happen; ~ **a** (*seguir*) to succeed, follow; **lo que sucede es que** ... the fact is that ...; ~ **al trono** to succeed to the throne.
sucesión [sōōsesyon'] *nf* succession; (*serie*) sequence, series; (*hijos*) issue, offspring.
sucesivamente [sōōsesēħámen'te] *ad*: **y así** ~ and so on.
sucesivo, a [sōōsesē'ħo, à] *a* successive, following; **en lo** ~ in future, from now on.
suceso [sōōse'so] *nm* (*hecho*) event, happening; (*incidente*) incident.
sucesor, a [sōōsesor', à] *nm/f* successor; (*heredero*) heir/heiress.
suciedad [sōōsyeħáħ'] *nf* (*estado*) dirtiness; (*mugre*) dirt, filth.
sucinto, a [sōōsēn'to, à] *a* (*conciso*) succinct, concise.
sucio, a [sōō'syo, à] *a* dirty; (*mugriento*) grimy; (*manchado*) grubby; (*borroso*) smudged; (*conciencia*) bad; (*conducta*) vile; (*táctica*) dirty, unfair.
Sucre [sōō'kre] *n* Sucre.
suculento, a [sōōkōōlen'to, à] *a* (*sabroso*) tasty; (*jugoso*) succulent.
sucumbir [sōōkōōmbēr'] *vi* to succumb.
sucursal [sōōkōōrsál'] *nf* branch (office); (*filial*) subsidiary.
Sudáfrica [sōōħá'frēkà] *nf* South Africa.
sudafricano, a [sōōħáfrēkà'no, à] *a*, *nm/f* South African.
Sudamérica [sōōħáme'rēkà] *nf* South America.

sudamericano, a [sōōħámerēkà'no, à] *a*, *nm/f* South American.
sudanés, esa [sōōħánes', esà] *a*, *nm/f* Sudanese.
sudar [sōōħár'] *vt*, *vi* to sweat; (*BOT*) to ooze, give off.
sudeste [sōōħe'ste] *a* south-east(ern); (*rumbo, viento*) south-easterly ♦ *nm* south-east; (*viento*) south-east wind.
sudoeste [sōōħoe'ste] *a* south-west(ern); (*rumbo, viento*) south-westerly ♦ *nm* south-west; (*viento*) south-west wind.
sudor [sōōħor'] *nm* sweat.
sudoroso, a [sōōħoro'so, à] *a* sweaty, sweating.
Suecia [swe'syà] *nf* Sweden.
sueco, a [swe'ko, à] *a* Swedish ♦ *nm/f* Swede ♦ *nm* (*LING*) Swedish; **hacerse el** ~ to pretend not to hear *o* understand.
suegro, a [swe'gro, à] *nm/f* father-/mother-in-law; **los** ~**s** one's in-laws.
suela [swe'lá] *nf* (*de zapato, tb pescado*) sole.
sueldo [swel'do] *etc vb V* **soldar** ♦ *nm* pay, wage(s) (*pl*).
suelo [swe'lo] *etc vb V* **soler** ♦ *nm* (*tierra*) ground; (*de casa*) floor.
suelto, a [swel'to, à] *etc vb V* **soltar** ♦ *a* loose; (*libre*) free; (*separado*) detached; (*ágil*) quick, agile; (*corriente*) fluent, flowing ♦ *nm* (loose) change, small change; **está muy** ~ **en inglés** he is very good at *o* fluent in English.
suene [swe'ne] *etc vb V* **sonar**.
sueño [swe'nyo] *etc vb ver* **soñar** ♦ *nm* sleep; (*somnolencia*) sleepiness, drowsiness; (*lo soñado, fig*) dream; ~ **pesado** *o* **profundo** deep *o* heavy sleep; **tener** ~ to be sleepy.
suero [swe'ro] *nm* (*MED*) serum; (*de leche*) whey.
suerte [swer'te] *nf* (*fortuna*) luck; (*azar*) chance; (*destino*) fate, destiny; (*condición*) lot; (*género*) sort, kind; **lo echaron a** ~**s** they drew lots; **tener** ~ to be lucky; **de otra** ~ otherwise, if not; **de** ~ **que** so that, in such a way that.
suéter [swe'ter], *pl* **suéters** *nm* sweater.
suficiencia [sōōfēsyen'syà] *nf* (*cabida*) sufficiency; (*idoneidad*) suitability; (*aptitud*) adequacy.
suficiente [sōōfēsyen'te] *a* enough, sufficient.
sufijo [sōōfē'ho] *nm* suffix.
sufragar [sōōfrágár'] *vt* (*ayudar*) to help; (*gastos*) to meet; (*proyecto*) to pay for.
sufragio [sōōfrá'hyo] *nm* (*voto*) vote; (*derecho de voto*) suffrage.
sufrague [sōōfrá'ge] *etc vb V* **sufragar**.
sufrido, a [sōōfrē'ħo, à] *a* (*de carácter fuerte*) tough; (*paciente*) long-suffering;

(*tela*) hard-wearing; (*color*) that does not show the dirt.

sufrimiento [sōōfrēmyen'to] *nm* suffering.

sufrir [sōōfrēr'] *vt* (*padecer*) to suffer; (*soportar*) to bear, stand, put up with; (*apoyar*) to hold up, support ♦ *vi* to suffer.

sugerencia [sōōheren'syá] *nf* suggestion.

sugerir [sōōherēr'] *vt* to suggest; (*sutilmente*) to hint; (*idea: incitar*) to prompt.

sugestión [sōōhestyon'] *nf* suggestion; (*sutil*) hint; (*poder*) hypnotic power.

sugestionar [sōōhestyonár'] *vt* to influence.

sugestivo, a [sōōhestē'ko, á] *a* stimulating; (*atractivo*) attractive; (*fascinante*) fascinating.

sugiera [sōōhye'rá] *etc*, **sugiriendo** [sōōhēryen'do] *etc vb* V **sugerir**.

suicida [sōōēsē'khá] *a* suicidal ♦ *nm/f* suicidal person; (*muerto*) suicide, person who has committed suicide.

suicidarse [sōōēsēthár'se] *vr* to commit suicide, kill o.s.

suicidio [sōōēsē'thyo] *nm* suicide.

Suiza [swē'sá] *nf* Switzerland.

suizo, a [swē'so, á] *a*, *nm/f* Swiss ♦ *nm* sugared bun.

sujeción [sōōhesyon'] *nf* subjection.

sujetador [sōōhetáthor'] *nm* fastener, clip; (*prenda femenina*) bra, brassiere.

sujetapapeles [sōōhetápápe'les] *nm inv* paper clip.

sujetar [sōōhetàr'] *vt* (*fijar*) to fasten; (*detener*) to hold down; (*fig*) to subject, subjugate; (*pelo etc*) to keep o hold in place; (*papeles*) to fasten together; **~se** *vr* to subject o.s.

sujeto, a [sōōhe'to, á] *a* fastened, secure ♦ *nm* subject; (*individuo*) individual; (*fam: tipo*) fellow, guy; **~ a** subject to.

sulfurar [sōōlfōōrár'] *vt* (*TEC*) to sulphurate; (*sacar de quicio*) to annoy; **~se** *vr* (*enojarse*) to get riled, see red, blow up.

sulfuro [sōōlfōō'ro] *nm* sulphide.

suma [sōō'má] *nf* (*cantidad*) total, sum; (*de dinero*) sum; (*acto*) adding (up), addition; **en ~** in short; **~ y sigue** (*COM*) carry forward.

sumador [sōōmáthor'] *nm* (*INFORM*) adder.

sumamente [sōōmámen'te] *ad* extremely, exceedingly.

sumar [sōōmár'] *vt* to add (up); (*reunir*) to collect, gather ♦ *vi* to add up.

sumario, a [sōōmá'ryo, á] *a* brief, concise ♦ *nm* summary.

sumergir [sōōmerhēr'] *vt* to submerge; (*hundir*) to sink; (*bañar*) to immerse, dip; **~se** *vr* (*hundirse*) to sink beneath the surface.

sumerja [sōōmer'há] *etc vb* V **sumergir**.

sumidero [sōōmēthe'ro] *nm* drain, sewer; (*TEC*) sump.

suministrador, a [sōōmēnēstráthor', á] *nm/f* supplier.

suministrar [sōōmēnēstrár'] *vt* to supply, provide.

suministro [sōōmēnēs'tro] *nm* supply; (*acto*) supplying, providing.

sumir [sōōmēr'] *vt* to sink, submerge; (*fig*) to plunge; **~se** *vr* (*objeto*) to sink; **~se en el estudio** to become absorbed in one's studies.

sumisión [sōōmēsyon'] *nf* (*acto*) submission; (*calidad*) submissiveness, docility.

sumiso, a [sōōmē'so, á] *a* submissive, docile.

súmmum [sōō'mōōm] *nm inv* (*fig*) height.

sumo, a [sōō'mo, á] *a* great, extreme; (*mayor*) highest, supreme; **a lo ~** at most.

suntuoso, a [sōōntwo'so, á] *a* sumptuous, magnificent; (*lujoso*) lavish.

sup. *abr* (= *superior*) sup.

supe [sōō'pe] *etc vb* V **saber**.

supeditar [sōōpethētár'] *vt* to subordinate; (*sojuzgar*) to subdue; (*oprimir*) to oppress; **~se** *vr*: **~se a** to subject o.s. to.

super... [sōōper] *pref* super..., over....

súper [sōō'per] *a* (*fam*) super, great.

superable [sōōperá'ble] *a* (*dificultad*) surmountable; (*tarea*) that can be performed.

superar [sōōperár'] *vt* (*sobreponerse a*) to overcome; (*rebasar*) to surpass, do better than; (*pasar*) to go beyond; (*marca, récord*) to break; (*etapa: dejar atrás*) to get past; **~se** *vr* to excel o.s.

superávit [sōōperá'hēt], *pl* **superávits** *nm* surplus.

superchería [sōōpertcherē'á] *nf* fraud, trick, swindle.

superficial [sōōperfēsyál'] *a* superficial; (*medida*) surface *cpd*.

superficie [sōōperfē'sye] *nf* surface; (*área*) area.

superfluo, a [sōōperf'lwo, á] *a* superfluous.

superíndice [sōōperēn'dēse] *nm* (*INFORM, TIP*) superscript.

superintendente [sōōperēntenden'te] *nm/f* supervisor, superintendent.

superior [sōōperyor'] *a* (*piso, clase*) upper; (*temperatura, número, nivel*) higher; (*mejor: calidad, producto*) superior, better ♦ *nm/f* superior.

superiora [sōōperyo'rá] *nf* (*REL*) mother superior.

superioridad [sōōperyorētháth'] *nf* superiority.

supermercado [sōōpermerká'tho] *nm* supermarket.

superpoblación [sōōperpoblásyon'] *nf* overpopulation; (*congestionamiento*) overcrowding.

superponer [sōōperponer'] *vt* (*INFORM*) to

overstrike.
superposición [sōōperposēsyon'] *nf* (*en impresora*) overstrike.
superpotencia [sōōperpoten'syá] *nf* superpower, great power.
superproducción [sōōperproϑōōksyon'] *nf* overproduction.
supersónico, a [sōōperso'nēko, á] *a* supersonic.
superstición [sōōperstēsyon'] *nf* superstition.
supersticioso, a [sōōperstēsyo'so, á] *a* superstitious.
supervisar [sōōperϧēsár'] *vt* to supervise; (*COM*) to superintend.
supervisor, a [sōōperϧēsor', á] *nm/f* supervisor.
supervivencia [sōōperϧēϧen'syá] *nf* survival.
suplantar [sōōplántár'] *vt* (*persona*) to supplant; (*hacerse pasar por otro*) to take the place of.
suplementario, a [sōōplementá'ryo, á] *a* supplementary.
suplemento [sōōplemen'to] *nm* supplement.
suplencia [sōōplen'syá] *nf* substitution, replacement; (*etapa*) period during which one deputizes *etc*.
suplente [sōōplen'te] *a* substitute; (*disponible*) reserve ♦ *nm/f* substitute.
supletorio, a [sōōpleto'ryo, á] *a* supplementary; (*adicional*) extra ♦ *nm* supplement; **mesa supletoria** spare table.
súplica [sōō'plēká] *nf* request; (*REL*) supplication; (*JUR*: *instancia*) petition; ~**s** *nfpl* entreaties.
suplicar [sōōplēkár'] *vt* (*cosa*) to beg (for), plead for; (*persona*) to beg, plead with; (*JUR*) to appeal to, petition.
suplicio [sōōplē'syo] *nm* torture; (*tormento*) torment; (*emoción*) anguish; (*experiencia penosa*) ordeal.
suplique [sōōplē'ke] *etc vb V* **suplicar.**
suplir [sōōplēr'] *vt* (*compensar*) to make good, make up for; (*reemplazar*) to replace, substitute ♦ *vi*: ~ **a** to take the place of, substitute for.
supo [sōō'po] *etc vb V* **saber.**
supondré [sōōpondre'] *etc vb V* **suponer.**
suponer [sōōponer'] *vt* to suppose; (*significar*) to mean; (*acarrear*) to involve ♦ *vi* to count, have authority; **era de** ~ **que** ... it was to be expected that ....
suponga [sōōpon'gá] *etc vb V* **suponer.**
suposición [sōōposēsyon'] *nf* supposition.
supremacía [sōōpremàsē'á] *nf* supremacy.
supremo, a [sōōpre'mo, á] *a* supreme.
supresión [sōōpresyon'] *nf* suppression; (*de derecho*) abolition; (*de dificultad*) removal; (*de palabra etc*) deletion; (*de restricción*)

cancellation, lifting.
suprimir [sōōprēmēr'] *vt* to suppress; (*derecho, costumbre*) to abolish; (*dificultad*) to remove; (*palabra etc, INFORM*) to delete; (*restricción*) to cancel, lift.
supuestamente [sōōpwestámen'te] *ad* supposedly.
supuesto, a [sōōpwe'sto, á] *pp de* **suponer** ♦ *a* (*hipotético*) supposed; (*falso*) false ♦ *nm* assumption, hypothesis ♦ *conj*: ~ **que** since; **dar por** ~ **algo** to take sth for granted; **por** ~ of course.
supuse [sōōpōō'se] *etc vb V* **suponer.**
sur [sōōr] *a* southern; (*rumbo*) southerly ♦ *nm* south; (*viento*) south wind.
Suráfrica [sōōrá'frēká] *etc* = **Sudáfrica** *etc*.
Suramérica [sōōràme'rēká] *etc* = **Sudamérica** *etc*.
surcar [sōōrkár'] *vt* to plow (*US*), plough (*Brit*); (*superficie*) to cut, score.
surco [sōōr'ko] *nm* (*en metal, disco*) groove; (*AGR*) furrow.
surcoreano, a [sōōrkoreá'no, á] *a, nm/f* South Korean.
sureño, a [sōōre'nyo, á] *a* southern ♦ *nm/f* southerner.
sureste [sōōre'ste] = **sudeste.**
surgir [sōōrhēr'] *vi* to arise, emerge; (*dificultad*) to come up, crop up.
surja [sōōr'há] *etc vb V* **surgir.**
suroeste [sōōroe'ste] = **sudoeste.**
surque [sōōr'ke] *etc vb V* **surcar.**
surrealismo [sōōrreálēs'mo] *nm* surrealism.
surrealista [sōōrreálē'stá] *a, nm/f* surrealist.
surtido, a [sōōrtē'ϑo, á] *a* mixed, assorted ♦ *nm* (*selección*) selection, assortment; (*abastecimiento*) supply, stock.
surtidor [sōōrtēϑor'] *nm* (*chorro*) jet, spout; (*fuente*) fountain; ~ **de gasolina** gas (*US*) o petrol (*Brit*) pump.
surtir [sōōrtēr'] *vt* to supply, provide; (*efecto*) to have, produce ♦ *vi* to spout, spurt; ~**se** *vr*: ~**se de** to provide o.s. with.
susceptible [sōōseptē'ɧle] *a* susceptible; (*sensible*) sensitive; ~ **de** capable of.
suscitar [sōōsētár'] *vt* to cause, provoke; (*discusión*) to start; (*duda, problema*) to raise; (*interés, sospechas*) to arouse.
suscribir [sōōskrēϧēr'] *vt* (*firmar*) to sign; (*respaldar*) to subscribe to, endorse; (*COM*: *acciones*) to take out an option on; ~**se** *vr* to subscribe; ~ **a uno a una revista** to take out a subscription to a magazine for sb.
suscripción [sōōskrēpsyon'] *nf* subscription.
suscrito, a [sōōskrē'to, á] *pp de* **suscribir** ♦ *a*: ~ **en exceso** oversubscribed.
susodicho, a [sōōsodētch'o, á] *a* above-mentioned.
suspender [sōōspender'] *vt* (*objeto*) to hang (up), suspend; (*trabajo*) to stop, suspend;

(*ESCOL*) to fail.

suspensión [sōōspensyon'] *nf* suspension; (*fig*) stoppage, suspension; (*JUR*) stay; ~ **de fuego** *o* **de hostilidades** ceasefire, cessation of hostilities; ~ **de pagos** suspension of payments.

suspensivo, a [sōōspensē'ḥo, á] *a*: **puntos** ~**s** suspension points.

suspenso, a [sōōspen'so, á] *a* hanging, suspended; (*ESCOL*) failed ♦ *nm* (*ESCOL*) fail(ure); **quedar** *o* **estar en** ~ to be pending.

suspicacia [sōōspēká'syá] *nf* suspicion, mistrust.

suspicaz [sōōspēkás'] *a* suspicious, distrustful.

suspirar [sōōspērár'] *vi* to sigh.

suspiro [sōōspē'ro] *nm* sigh.

sustancia [sōōstán'syá] *nf* substance; ~ **gris** (*ANAT*) grey matter; **sin** ~ lacking in substance, shallow.

sustantivo, a [sōōstántē'ḥo, á] *a* substantive; (*LING*) substantival, noun *cpd* ♦ *nm* noun, substantive.

sustentar [sōōstentár'] *vt* (*alimentar*) to sustain, nourish; (*objeto*) to hold up, support; (*idea, teoría*) to maintain, uphold; (*fig*) to sustain, keep going.

sustento [sōōsten'to] *nm* support; (*alimento*) sustenance, food.

sustituir [sōōstētōōēr'] *vt* to substitute, replace.

sustituto, a [sōōstētōō'to, á] *nm/f* substitute, replacement.

sustituyendo [sōōstētōōyen'do] *etc vb V* **sustituir.**

susto [sōō'sto] *nm* fright, scare; **dar un** ~ **a uno** to give sb a fright; **darse** *o* **pegarse un** ~ (*fam*) to get scared (*US*) *o* a fright (*Brit*).

sustraer [sōōstráer'] *vt* to remove, take away; (*MAT*) to subtract.

sustraiga [sōōstrá'ēgá] *etc*, **sustraje** [sōōstrá'he] *etc*, **sustrajera** [sōōstrá'herá] *etc vb V* **sustraer.**

sustrato [sōōstrá'to] *nm* substratum.

sustrayendo [sōōstráyen'do] *etc vb V* **sustraer.**

susurrar [sōōsōōrrár'] *vi* to whisper.

susurro [sōōsōō'rro] *nm* whisper.

sutil [sōōtēl'] *a* (*aroma*) subtle; (*tenue*) thin; (*hilo, hebra*) fine; (*olor*) delicate; (*brisa*) gentle; (*diferencia*) fine, subtle; (*inteligencia*) sharp, keen.

sutileza [sōōtēle'sá] *nf* subtlety; (*delgadez*) thinness; (*delicadeza*) delicacy; (*agudeza*) keenness.

sutura [sōōtōō'rá] *nf* suture.

suturar [sōōtōōrár'] *vt* to suture; (*juntar con puntos*) to stitch.

suyo, a [sōō'yo, á] *a* (*con artículo o después*

del verbo ser: *de él*) his; (: *de ella*) hers; (: *de ellos, ellas*) theirs; (: *de usted, ustedes*) yours; (*después de un nombre*: *de él*) of his; (: *de ella*) of hers; (: *de ellos, ellas*) of theirs; (: *de usted, ustedes*) of yours; **lo** ~ (what is) his; (*su parte*) his share, what he deserves; **los** ~**s** (*familia*) one's family *o* relations; (*partidarios*) one's own people *o* supporters; ~ **afectísimo** (*en carta*) yours truly (*US*) *o* faithfully (*Brit*); **de** ~ in itself; **eso es muy** ~ that's just like him; **hacer de las suyas** to be up to one's old tricks; **ir a la suya, ir a lo** ~ to go one's own way; **salirse con la suya** to get one's way.

T

T, t [te] *nf* (*letra*) T, t; **T de Tarragona** T for Tommy.

t *abr* = **tonelada**.

T. *abr* (= *Telefón, Telégrafo*) tel.; (*COM*) = **Tarifa; Tasa.**

t. *abr* (= *tomo(s)*) vol(s).

Tabacalera [tábákálc'rá] *nf Spanish state tobacco monopoly.*

tabaco [tábá'ko] *nm* tobacco; (*fam*) cigarettes *pl.*

tabaquería [tábákerē'á] *nf* cigar store (*US*), tobacconist's (*Brit*).

tabarra [tábá'rrá] *nf* (*fam*) nuisance; **dar la** ~ to be a pain in the neck.

taberna [táber'ná] *nf* bar.

tabernero, a [táberne'ro, á] *nm/f* (*encargado*) publican; (*camarero*) barman/barmaid.

tabique [tábē'ke] *nm* (*pared*) thin wall; (*para dividir*) partition.

tabla [tá'ḥlá] *nf* (*de madera*) plank; (*estante*) shelf; (*de anuncios*) board; (*lista, catálogo*) list; (*mostrador*) counter; (*de vestido*) pleat; (*ARTE*) panel; ~**s** *nfpl* (*TAUR, TEATRO*) boards; **hacer** ~**s** to draw; ~ **de consulta** (*INFORM*) lookup table.

tablado [táḥlá'ḥo] *nm* (*plataforma*) platform; (*suelo*) plank floor; (*TEATRO*) stage.

tablero [táḥle'ro] *nm* (*de madera*) plank, board; (*pizarra*) blackboard; (*de ajedrez, damas*) board; (*AUTO*) dashboard; ~ **de gráficos** (*INFORM*) graphics pad.

tableta [táḥle'tá] *nf* (*MED*) tablet; (*de chocolate*) bar.

tablilla [táḥlē'yá] *nf* small board; (*MED*) splint.

tablón [táḥlon'] *nm* (*de suelo*) plank; (*de techo*) beam; (*de anuncios*) bulletin board.

tabú [táḥōō'] *nm* taboo.

tabulación [táḥōōlásyon'] *nf* (*INFORM*) tab(bing).

tabulador [táḥōōláḥor'] *nm* (*INFORM. TIP*) tab.

tabuladora [táḥōōláḥo'rá] *nf*: ~ **eléctrica** electric accounting machine.

tabular [táḥōōlár'] *vt* to tabulate; (*INFORM*) to tab.

taburete [táḥōōre'te] *nm* stool.

tacaño, a [táká'nyo, á] *a* (*avaro*) stingy; (*astuto*) crafty.

tácito, a [tá'sēto, á] *a* tacit; (*acuerdo*) unspoken; (*LING*) understood; (*ley*) unwritten.

taciturno, a [tásētōōr'no, á] *a* (*callado*) silent; (*malhumorado*) sullen.

taco [tá'ko] *nm* (*BILLAR*) cue; (*libro de billetes*) book; (*manojo de billetes*) wad; (*AM*) heel; (*tarugo*) peg; (*fam: bocado*) snack; (: *palabrota*) swear word; (: *trago de vino*) swig; (*Méjico*) filled tortilla; **armarse** *o* **hacerse un** ~ to get into a mess.

tacógrafo [táko'gráfo] *nm* (*COM*) tachograph.

tacón [tákon'] *nm* heel; **de** ~ **alto** high-heeled.

taconear [tákoneár'] *vi* (*dar golpecitos*) to tap with one's heels; (*MIL etc*) to click one's heels.

taconeo [tákone'o] *nm* (heel) tapping *o* clicking.

táctico, a [ták'tēko, á] *a* tactical ♦ *nf* tactics *pl*.

tacto [ták'to] *nm* touch; (*acción*) touching; (*fig*) tact.

tacha [tátch'á] *nf* (*defecto*) flaw, defect; (*TEC*) stud; **poner** ~ **a** to find fault with; **sin** ~ flawless.

tachar [tátchár'] *vt* (*borrar*) to cross out; (*corregir*) to correct; (*criticar*) to criticize; ~ **de** to accuse of.

tachón [tátchon'] *nm* erasure; (*tachadura*) crossing-out; (*TEC*) ornamental stud; (*COSTURA*) trimming.

tachuela [tátchwe'lá] *nf* (*clavo*) tack.

tafetán [táfetán'] *nm* taffeta; **tafetanes** *nmpl* (*fam*) frills; ~ **adhesivo** *o* **inglés** bandaid (*US*), sticking plaster (*Brit*).

tafilete [táfēle'te] *nm* morocco leather.

tahona [táo'ná] *nf* (*panadería*) bakery; (*molino*) flourmill.

tahur [táōōr'] *nm* gambler; (*pey*) cheat.

tailandés, esa [táčlándes', esá] *a, nm/f* Thai ♦ *nm* (*LING*) Thai.

Tailandia [táčlán'dyá] *nf* Thailand.

taimado, a [táēmá'ḥo, á] *a* (*astuto*) sly; (*resentido*) sullen.

taita [tá'ētá] *nm* dad, daddy.

taja [tá'há] *nf* (*corte*) cut; (*repartición*) division.

tajada [táhá'ḥá] *nf* slice; (*fam*) rake-off; **sacar** ~ to get one's share.

tajadera [táháḥe'rá] *nf* (*instrumento*) chopper; (*madera*) chopping block.

tajante [táhán'te] *a* sharp; (*negativa*) emphatic; **es una persona** ~ he's an emphatic person.

tajar [táhár'] *vt* to cut, slice.

Tajo [tá'ho] *nm* Tagus.

tajo [tá'ho] *nm* (*corte*) cut; (*filo*) cutting edge; (*GEO*) cleft.

tal [tál] *a* such; **un** ~ **García** a man called García; ~ **vez** perhaps ♦ *pron* (*persona*) someone, such a one; (*cosa*) something, such a thing; ~ **como** such as; ~ **para cual** tit for tat; (*dos iguales*) two of a kind; **hablábamos de que si** ~ **si cual** we were talking about this, that and the other ♦ *ad*: ~ **como** (*igual*) just as; ~ **cual** (*como es*) just as it is; ~ **el padre, cual el hijo** like father, like son; **¿qué** ~**?** how are things?; **¿qué** ~ **te gusta?** how do you like it? ♦ *conj*: **con** ~ **(de) que** provided that.

tala [tá'lá] *nf* (*de árboles*) tree felling.

taladradora [táláḥráḥo'rá] *nf* drill; ~ **neumática** jackhammer (*US*), pneumatic drill (*Brit*).

taladrar [táláḥrár'] *vt* to drill; (*fig: suj: ruido*) to pierce.

taladro [tálá'ḥro] *nm* (*gen*) drill; (*hoyo*) drill hole; ~ **neumático** jackhammer (*US*), pneumatic drill (*Brit*).

talante [tálán'te] *nm* (*humor*) mood; (*voluntad*) will, willingness.

talar [tálár'] *vt* to fell, cut down; (*fig*) to devastate.

talco [tál'ko] *nm* (*polvos*) talcum powder; (*MINERALOGÍA*) talc.

talega [tále'gá] *nf* sack.

talego [tále'go] *nm* sack; **tener** ~ (*fam*) to have money.

talento [tálen'to] *nm* talent; (*capacidad*) ability; (*don*) gift.

TALGO, Talgo [tál'go] *nm abr* (*FERRO=tren articulado ligero Goicoechea-Oriol*) high-speed train.

talidomida [tálēḥome'ḥá] *nm* thalidomide.

talismán [tálēsmán'] *nm* talisman.

talmente [tálmen'te] *ad* (*de esta forma*) in such a way; (*hasta tal punto*) to such an extent; (*exactamente*) exactly.

talón [tálon'] *nm* (*gen*) heel; (*de cheque*) stub; (*TEC*) rim.

talonario [táloná'ryo] *nm* (*de cheques*) check (*US*) *o* cheque (*Brit*) book; (*de billetes*) book of tickets; (*de recibos*) receipt book.

talla [tá'yá] *nf* (*estatura, fig, MED*) height,

stature; (*de ropa*) size, fitting; (*palo*) measuring rod; (*ARTE*: *de madera*)) carving; (*de piedra*) sculpture.

tallado, a [tåyá'tho, å] *a* carved ♦ *nm* (*de madera*) carving; (*de piedra*) sculpture.

tallar [tåyár'] *vt* (*trabajar*) to work, carve; (*grabar*) to engrave; (*medir*) to measure; (*repartir*) to deal ♦ *vi* to deal.

tallarín [tåyárēn'] *nm* noodle.

talle [tá'ye] *nm* (*ANAT*) waist; (*medida*) size; (*física*) build; (: *de mujer*) figure; (*fig*) appearance; **de ~ esbelto** with a slim figure.

taller [tåyer'] *nm* (*TEC*) workshop; (*fábrica*) factory; (*AUTO*) garage; (*de artista*) studio.

tallo [tá'yo] *nm* (*de planta*) stem; (*de hierba*) blade; (*brote*) shoot; (*col*) cabbage; (*CULIN*) candied peel.

tamaño, a [tåmá'nyo, å] *a* (*tan grande*) such a big; (*tan pequeño*) such a small ♦ *nm* size; **de ~ natural** full-size; **¿de qué ~ es?** what size is it?

tamarindo [tåmårēn'do] *nm* tamarind.

tambaleante [tåmbålåán'te] *a* (*persona*) staggering; (*mueble*) wobbly; (*vehículo*) swaying.

tambalearse [tåmbåleár'se] *vr* (*persona*) to stagger; (*mueble*) to wobble; (*vehículo*) to sway.

también [tåmbyen'] *ad* (*igualmente*) also, too, as well; (*además*) besides; **estoy cansado — yo ~** I'm tired — so am I *o* me too.

tambor [tåmbor'] *nm* drum; (*ANAT*) eardrum; **~ del freno** brake drum; **~ magnético** (*INFORM*) magnetic drum.

tamboril [tåmborēl'] *nm* small drum.

tamborilear [tåmborēleár'] *vi* (*MUS*) to drum; (*con los dedos*) to drum with one's fingers.

tamborilero [tåmborēle'ro] *nm* drummer.

Támesis [tá'mesēs] *nm* Thames.

tamice [tåmē'se] *etc vb V* **tamizar**.

tamiz [tåmēs'] *nm* sieve.

tamizar [tåmēsár'] *vt* to sieve.

tampoco [tåmpo'ko] *ad* nor, neither; **yo ~ lo compré** I didn't buy it either.

tampón [tåmpon'] *nm* plug; (*MED*) tampon.

tan [tån] *ad* so; **~ es así que** so much so that; **¡qué cosa ~ rara!** how strange!; **no es una idea ~ buena** it is not such a good idea.

tanda [tån'då] *nf* (*gen*) series; (*de inyecciones*) course; (*juego*) set; (*turno*) shift; (*grupo*) gang.

tándem [tán'dem] *nm* tandem; (*POL*) duo.

tangente [tånhen'te] *nf* tangent; **salirse por la ~** to go off at a tangent.

Tánger [tán'her] *n* Tangier.

tangerino, a [tånhere'no, å] *a* of *o* from

Tangier ♦ *nm/f* native *o* inhabitant of Tangier.

tangible [tånhē'ble] *a* tangible.

tanino [tånē'no] *nm* tannin.

tanque [tån'ke] *nm* (*gen*) tank; (*AUTO*, *NAUT*) tanker.

tantear [tånteár'] *vt* (*calcular*) to reckon (up); (*medir*) to take the measure of; (*probar*) to test, try out; (*tomar la medida*: *persona*) to take the measurements of; (*considerar*) to weigh ♦ *vi* (*DEPORTE*) to score.

tanteo [tånte'o] *nm* (*cálculo*) (rough) calculation; (*prueba*) test, trial; (*DEPORTE*) scoring; (*adivinanzas*) guesswork; **al ~** by trial and error.

tantísimo, a [tåntē'sēmo, å] *a* so much; **~s** so many.

tanto, a [tån'to, å] *a* (*cantidad*) so much, as much; **~s** so many, as many; **20 y ~s** 20-odd ♦ *ad* (*cantidad*) so much, as much; (*tiempo*) so long, as long; **~ tú como yo** both you and I; **~ como eso** it's not as bad as that; **~ más ... cuanto que** it's all the more ... because; **~ mejor/peor** so much the better/the worse; **~ si viene como si va** whether he comes or whether he goes; **~ es así que** so much so that; **por ~, por lo ~** therefore; **me he vuelto ronco de** *o* **con ~ hablar** I have become hoarse with so much talking ♦ *conj*: **con ~ que** provided (that); **en ~ que** while; **hasta ~ (que)** until such time as ♦ *nm* (*suma*) certain amount; (*proporción*) so much; (*punto*) point; (*gol*) goal; **por ~ alzado** agreed price; **~ por ciento** percentage; **al ~** up to date; **estar al ~ de los acontecimientos** to be fully abreast of events; **un ~ perezoso** somewhat lazy; **al ~ de que** because of the fact that ♦ *pron*: **cada uno paga ~** each one pays so much; **uno de ~s** one of many; **a ~s de agosto** on such and such a day in August; **entre ~** meanwhile.

tañer [tånyer'] *vt* (*MUS*) to play; (*campana*) to ring.

T/año *abr*=*toneladas por año*.

tapa [tá'på] *nf* (*de caja, olla*) lid; (*de botella*) top; (*de libro*) cover; (*comida*) snack.

tapacubos [tåpåkōō'bos] *nm inv* hub cap.

tapadera [tåpáthe'rå] *nf* lid, cover.

tapado [tåpá'tho] *nm* (*AM: abrigo*) coat.

tapar [tåpár'] *vt* (*cubrir*) to cover; (*envolver*) to wrap *o* cover up; (*la vista*) to obstruct; (*persona, falta*) to conceal; (*AM*) to fill; **~se** *vr* to wrap o.s. up.

tapete [tåpe'te] *nm* table cover; **estar sobre el ~** (*fig*) to be under discussion.

tapia [tá'pyå] *nf* (garden) wall.

tapiar [tåpyár'] *vt* to wall in.

tapice [tåpē'se] *etc vb V* **tapizar**.

tapicería [tápēserē'á] *nf* tapestry; *(para muebles)* upholstery; *(tienda)* upholstery *(US)*, upholsterer's *(Brit)*.

tapicero, a [tápēse'ro, á] *nm/f (de muebles)* upholsterer.

tapiz [tápēs'] *nm (alfombra)* carpet; *(tela tejida)* tapestry.

tapizar [tápēsár'] *vt (pared)* to wallpaper; *(suelo)* to carpet; *(muebles)* to upholster.

tapón [tápon'] *nm (corcho)* stopper; *(TEC)* plug; *(MED)* tampon; ~ **de rosca** *o* **de tuerca** screw-top.

taponar [táponár'] *vt (botella)* to cork; *(tubería)* to block.

taponazo [táponá'so] *nm (de tapón)* pop.

tapujo [tápō̄'ho] *nm (embozo)* muffler; *(engaño)* deceit; **sin ~s** honestly.

taquigrafía [tákēgráfē'á] *nf* shorthand.

taquígrafo, a [tákē'gráfo, á] *nm/f* shorthand writer.

taquilla [tákē'yá] *nf (de estación etc)* ticket office; *(de teatro)* box office; *(suma recogida)* take *(US)*, takings *pl (Brit)*; *(archivador)* filing cabinet.

taquillero, a [tákēye'ro, á] *a:* **función taquillera** box office success ♦ *nm/f* ticket agent.

taquímetro [tákē'metro] *nm* speedometer.

tara [tá'rá] *nf (defecto)* defect; *(COM)* tare.

tarado, a [tárá'tho, á] *a (COM)* defective, imperfect; *(idiota)* stupid; *(loco)* crazy, nuts ♦ *nm/f* idiot, cretin.

tarántula [tárán'tō̄lá] *nf* tarantula.

tararear [táráreár'] *vi* to hum.

tardanza [tárthán'sá] *nf (demora)* delay; *(lentitud)* slowness.

tardar [tárthár'] *vi (tomar tiempo)* to take a long time; *(llegar tarde)* to be late; *(demorar)* to delay; **¿tarda mucho el tren?** does the train take long?; **a más ~** at the (very) latest; ~ **en hacer algo** to be slow *o* take a long time to do sth; **no tardes en venir** come soon, come before long.

tarde [tár'the] *ad (hora)* late; *(fuera de tiempo)* too late ♦ *nf (de día)* afternoon; *(de noche)* evening; ~ **o temprano** sooner or later; **de ~ en ~** from time to time; **¡buenas ~s!** *(de día)* good afternoon!; *(de noche)* good evening!; **a** *o* **por la ~** in the afternoon; in the evening.

tardío, a [tárthē'o, á] *a (retrasado)* late; *(lento)* slow (to arrive).

tardo, a [tár'tho, á] *a (lento)* slow; *(torpe)* dull; ~ **de oído** hard of hearing.

tarea [táre'á] *nf* task; ~**s** *nfpl (ESCOL)* homework *sg*; ~ **de ocasión** chore.

tarifa [tárē'fá] *nf (lista de precios)* price list; *(COM)* tariff; ~ **básica** basic rate; ~ **completa** total cost; ~ **a destajo** piece rate; ~ **doble** double time.

tarima [tárē'má] *nf (plataforma)* platform; *(taburete)* stool; *(litera)* bunk.

tarjeta [tárhe'tá] *nf* card; ~ **postal/de crédito/de Navidad** postcard/credit card/Christmas card; ~ **de circuitos** *(INFORM)* circuit board; ~ **comercial** *(COM)* calling card; ~ **dinero** cash card; ~ **gráficos** *(INFORM)* graphics card; ~ **de multifunción** *(INFORM)* multiplication card.

tarraconense [tárrákonen'se] *a* of *o* from Tarragona ♦ *nm/f* native *o* inhabitant of Tarragona.

tarro [tá'rro] *nm* jar, pot.

tarta [tár'tá] *nf (pastel)* cake; *(torta)* tart.

tartajear [tártáheár'] *vi* to stammer.

tartamudear [tártámō̄theár'] *vi* to stutter, stammer.

tartamudo, a [tártámō̄'tho, á] *a* stuttering, stammering ♦ *nm/f* stutterer, stammerer.

tartárico, a [tártá'rēko, á] *a:* **ácido ~** tartaric acid.

tártaro, a [tár'táro] *a, nm* Tartar ♦ *nm (QUIMICA)* tartar.

tarugo, a [tárō̄'go, á] *a* stupid ♦ *nm (de madera)* lump.

tarumba [tárō̄m'bá] *a (confuso)* confused.

tasa [tá'sá] *nf (precio)* (fixed) price, rate; *(valoración)* appraisal *(US)*, valuation *(Brit)*; *(medida, norma)* measure, standard; ~ **básica** *(COM)* basic rate; ~ **de cambio** exchange rate; **de ~ cero** *(COM)* zero-rated; ~ **de crecimiento** growth rate; ~ **de interés/de nacimiento** rate of interest/birth rate; ~ **de rendimiento** *(COM)* rate of return.

tasación [tásásyon'] *nf* assessment; *(fig)* appraisal.

tasador, a [tásáthor', á] *nm/f* appraiser *(US)*, valuer *(Brit)*; *(COM: de impuestos)* assessor.

tasajo [tásá'ho] *nm* dried beef.

tasar [tásár'] *vt (arreglar el precio)* to fix a price for; *(valorar)* to assess; *(limitar)* to limit.

tasca [tás'ká] *nf (fam)* pub.

tata [tá'tá] *nm (fam)* dad(dy) ♦ *nf (niñera)* nanny, maid.

tatarabuelo, a [tátárábwe'lo, á] *nm/f* great-great-grandfather/mother; **los ~s** one's great-great-grandparents.

tatuaje [tátwá'he] *nm (dibujo)* tattoo; *(acto)* tattooing.

tatuar [tátwár'] *vt* to tattoo.

taumaturgo [táō̄mátō̄r'go] *nm* miracle-worker.

taurino, a [táō̄rē'no, á] *a* bullfighting *cpd*.

Tauro [táō̄ro] *nm* Taurus.

tauromaquia [táō̄romá'kyá] *nf* (art of) bullfighting.

tautología [táō̄tolohē'á] *nf* tautology.

taxativo, a [táksátē'ho, á] *a (restringido)* limited; *(sentido)* specific.

taxi [ták'sē] *nm* taxi.

taxidermia [táksĕ'ther'myá] *nf* taxidermy.
taxímetro [táksē'metro] *nm* taximeter.
taxista [táksē'stá] *nm/f* taxi driver.
taza [tá'sá] *nf* cup; *(de retrete)* bowl; ~ **para café** coffee cup.
tazón [táson'] *nm* mug, large cup; *(escu-dilla)* basin.
TCI *nf abr* (= *tarjeta de circuito impreso*) PCB.
te [te] *pron (complemento de objeto)* you; *(complemento indirecto)* (to) you; *(reflexivo)* (to) yourself; *¿~* **duele mucho el bra- zo?** does your arm hurt a lot?; ~ **equivo- cas** you're wrong; ¡**cálma~**! calm yourself!
té [te], *pl* **tés** *nm* tea; *(reunión)* tea party.
tea [te'á] *nf (antorcha)* torch.
teatral [teátrál'] *a* theater *cpd (US)*, theatre *cpd (Brit)*; *(fig)* theatrical.
teatro [teá'tro] *nm* theater *(US)*, theatre *(Brit)*; *(LITERATURA)* plays *pl*, drama; **el** ~ *(carrera)* the theater, acting; ~ **de aficionados/de variedades** amateur/ vaudeville theater; **hacer** ~ *(fig)* to make a fuss.
tebeo [tehe'o] *nm* comic book *(US)*, comic *(Brit)*.
tecla [te'klá] *nf (INFORM, MUS, TIP)* key; *(IN- FORM)*: ~ **de anulación/de borrar** cancel/ delete key; ~ **de control/de edición** control/edit key; ~ **con flecha** arrow key; ~ **programable** user-defined key; ~ **de retorno/de tabulación** return/tab key; ~ **del cursor** cursor key; ~**s de c ntrol di- reccional del cursor** cursor control keys.
teclado [teklá'tho] *nm* keyboard *(tb IN- FORM)*; ~ **numérico** *(INFORM)* numeric keypad.
teclear [tekleár'] *vi* to strum; *(fam)* to drum ♦ *vt (INFORM)* to key (in), type in, key- board.
tecleo [tekle'o] *nm (MUS: sonido)* strum- ming; (: *forma de tocar)* fingering; *(fam)* drumming.
tecnicismo [teknēsēs'mo] *nm (carácter técnico)* technical nature; *(LING)* technical term.
técnico, a [tek'nēko, á] *a* technical ♦ *nm* technician; *(experto)* expert ♦ *nf (procedi- mientos)* technique; *(arte, oficio)* craft.
tecnócrata [tekno'krátá] *nm/f* technocrat.
tecnología [teknolohē'á] *nf* technology; ~ **de estado sólido** *(INFORM)* solid-state technology; ~ **de la información** informa- tion technology.
tecnológico, a [teknolo'hēko, á] *a* techno- logical.
tecnólogo, a [tekno'logo, á] *nm/f* techno- logist.
techado [tetchá'tho] *nm (techo)* roof; **bajo** ~ under cover.
techo [tetch'o] *nm (externo)* roof; *(interno)* ceiling.
techumbre [tetchōōm'bre] *nf* roof.
tedio [te'thyo] *nm (aburrimiento)* boredom; *(apatía)* apathy; *(fastidio)* depression.
tedioso, a [tethyo'so, á] *a* boring; *(cansado)* wearisome, tedious.
Teherán [teerán'] *nm* Teheran.
teja [te'há] *nf (azulejo)* tile; *(BOT)* lime (tree).
tejado [tehá'tho] *nm* (tiled) roof.
tejano, a [tehá'no, á] *a, nm/f* Texan ♦ *nmpl*: ~**s** *(vaqueros)* jeans.
Tejas [te'hás] *nm* Texas.
tejemaneje [tehemáne'he] *nm (actividad)* bustle; *(lío)* fuss, to-do; *(intriga)* intrigue.
tejer [teher'] *vt* to weave; *(tela de araña)* to spin; *(AM)* to knit; *(fig)* to fabricate ♦ *vi*: ~ **y destejer** to do and undo *(US)*, chop and change *(Brit)*.
tejido [tehē'tho] *nm* fabric; *(estofa, tela)* (knitted) material; *(ANAT)* tissue; *(textura)* texture.
tejo [te'ho] *nm (BOT)* yew (tree).
tel. *abr* (= *teléfono*) tel.
tela [te'lá] *nf (material)* material; *(de fruta, en líquido)* skin; *(del ojo)* film; **hay** ~ **para rato** there's lots to talk about; **poner en** ~ **de juicio** to (call into) question; ~ **de ara- ña** cobweb, spider's web.
telar [telár'] *nm (máquina)* loom; *(de tea- tro)* gridiron; ~**es** *nmpl* textile mill *sg*.
telaraña [telárá'nyá] *nf* cobweb, spider's web.
tele [te'le] *nf (fam)* TV.
tele... [tele] *pref* tele...
telecargar [telekárgár'] *vt (INFORM)* to download.
telecompras [telekom'prás] *nfpl* teleshop- ping *sg*.
telecomunicación [telekomōōnēkásyon'] *nf* telecommunication.
telecontrol [telekontrol'] *nm* remote con- trol.
telecopiadora [telekopyátho'rá] *nf*: ~ **fac- símil** fax copier.
telediario [telethyá'ryo] *nm* television news.
teledifusión [telethēfōōsyon'] *nf* (television) broadcast.
teledirigido, a [telethērēhē'tho, á] *a* remote-controlled.
teléf. *abr* (= *teléfono*) tel.
teleférico [telefe'rēko] *nm (tren)* aerial tramway *(US)*, cable-railway *(Brit)*; *(de esquí)* ski-lift.
telefilm [telefēlm'], **telefilme** [telefēl'me] *nm* TV film.
telefonazo [telefoná'so] *nm (fam)* tele- phone call; **te daré un** ~ I'll give you a call.
telefonear [telefoneár'] *vi* to telephone.
telefónicamente [telefo'nēkámente] *ad* by

(tele)phone.

telefónico, a [telefo'nĕko, á] *a* telephone *cpd* ♦ *nf*: **Telefónica** (*Esp*) *Spanish national telephone company*.

telefonista [telefonē'stá] *nm/f* telephone operator.

teléfono [tele'fono] *nm* telephone; **está hablando por** ~ he's on the phone.

telefoto [telefo'to] *nf* telephoto.

telegrafía [telegráfē'á] *nf* telegraphy.

telégrafo [tele'gráfo] *nm* telegraph; (*fam:* *persona*) telegraph boy.

telegrama [telegrá'má] *nm* telegram.

teleimpresor [teleēmpresor'] *nm* teleprinter.

telemática [telemá'tēká] *nf* telematics *sg*.

telémetro [tele'metro] *nm* rangefinder.

telenovela [telenobe'lá] *nf* soap (opera).

teleobjetivo [teleobhetē'ho] *nm* telephoto lens.

telepático, a [telepá'tēko, á] *a* telepathic.

teleproceso [teleprose'so] *nm* teleprocessing.

telescópico, a [telesko'pēko, á] *a* telescopic.

telescopio [telesko'pyo] *nm* telescope.

telesilla [telesē'yá] *nm* chairlift.

telespectador, a [telespektá'hor', á] *nm/f* viewer.

telesquí [teleskē'] *nm* ski-lift.

teletex(to) [teleteks'(to)] *nm* teletext.

teletipista [teletēpē'stá] *nm/f* teletypist.

teletipo [teletē'po] *nm* teletype(writer).

teletratamiento [teletrátámyen'to] *nm* teleprocessing.

televidente [telebē'hen'te] *nm/f* viewer.

televisar [telebēsár'] *vt* to televise.

televisión [telebēsyon'] *nf* television; ~ **en color** color (*US*) *o* colour (*Brit*) television.

televisivo, a [telebēsē'ho, á] *a* a television *cpd*.

televisor [telebēsor'] *nm* television set.

télex [te'leks] *nm* telex; **máquina** ~ telex (machine); **enviar por** ~ to telex.

telón [telon'] *nm* curtain; ~ **de boca/ seguridad** front/safety curtain; ~ **de acero** (*POL*) iron curtain; ~ **de fondo** backdrop, background.

tema [te'má] *nm* (*asunto*) subject, topic; (*MUS*) theme; ~**s de actualidad** current affairs ♦ *nf* (*obsesión*) obsession; (*manía*) ill-will; **tener** ~ **a uno** to have a grudge against sb.

temario [temá'ryo] *nm* (*ESCOL*) set of topics; (*de una conferencia*) agenda.

temático, a [temá'tēko, á] *a* thematic.

tembladera [temblá'he'rá] *nf* shaking; (*AM*) quagmire.

temblar [temblár'] *vi* to shake, tremble; (*de frío*) to shiver.

tembleque [temble'ke] *a* shaking ♦ *nm*

shaking.

temblón, ona [temblon', oná] *a* shaking.

temblor [temblor'] *nm* trembling; (*AM*: *de tierra*) earthquake.

tembloroso, a [tembloro'so, á] *a* trembling.

temer [temer'] *vt* to fear ♦ *vi* to be afraid; **temo que Juan llegue tarde** I am afraid Juan may be late.

temerario, a [temerá'ryo, á] *a* (*imprudente*) rash; (*descuidado*) reckless; (*arbitrario*) hasty.

temeridad [temerē'háh'] *nf* (*imprudencia*) rashness; (*audacia*) boldness.

temeroso, a [temero'so, á] *a* (*miedoso*) fearful; (*que inspira temor*) frightful.

temible [temē'ble] *a* fearsome.

temor [temor'] *nm* (*miedo*) fear; (*duda*) suspicion.

tímpano [tem'páno] *nm* (*MUS*) kettledrum; ~ **de hielo** ice floe.

temperamento [temperámen'to] *nm* temperament; **tener** ~ to be temperamental.

temperar [temperár'] *vt* to temper, moderate.

temperatura [temperátōō'rá] *nf* temperature.

tempestad [tempestáh'] *nf* storm; ~ **en un vaso de agua** (*fig*) tempest in a teapot (*US*), storm in a teacup (*Brit*).

tempestuoso, a [tempestwo'so, á] *a* stormy.

templado, a [templá'ho, á] *a* (*moderado*) moderate; (: *en el comer*) frugal; (: *en el beber*) abstemious; (*agua*) lukewarm; (*clima*) mild; (*MUS*) in tune, well-tuned.

templanza [templán'sá] *nf* moderation; (*en el beber*) abstemiousness; (*del clima*) mildness.

templar [templár'] *vt* (*moderar*) to moderate; (*furia*) to restrain; (*calor*) to reduce; (*solución*) to dilute; (*afinar*) to tune (up); (*acero*) to temper ♦ *vi* to moderate; ~**se** *vr* to be restrained.

temple [tem'ple] *nm* (*humor*) mood; (*coraje*) courage; (*ajuste*) tempering; (*afinación*) tuning; (*pintura*) tempera.

templo [tem'plo] *nm* (*iglesia*) church; (*pagano etc*) temple; ~ **metodista** Methodist chapel.

temporada [temporá'há] *nf* time, period; (*estación, social, DEPORTE*) season; **en plena** ~ at the height of the season.

temporal [temporál'] *a* (*no permanente*) temporary; (*REL*) temporal ♦ *nm* storm.

tempranero, a [tempránc'ro, á] *a* (*BOT*) early; (*persona*) early-rising.

temprano, a [temprá'no, á] *a* early ♦ *ad* early; (*demasiado pronto*) too soon, too early; **lo más** ~ **posible** as soon as possible.

ten [ten] *vb V* **tener.**

tenacidad [tenåsēͭħåͭħ'] *nf* (*gen*) tenacity; (*dureza*) toughness; (*terquedad*) stubbornness.

tenacillas [tenåsē'yås] *nfpl* (*gen*) iron; (*para el pelo*) curling iron (*US*) *o* tongs (*Brit*); (*MED*) forceps.

tenaz [tenås'] *a* (*material*) tough; (*persona*) tenacious; (*pegajoso*) sticky; (*terco*) stubborn.

tenaza(s) [tenå'så(s)] *nf* (*pl*) (*MED*) forceps; (*TEC*) pliers; (*ZOOL*) pincers.

tendal [tendål'] *nm* awning.

tendedero [tendeͭħe'ro] *nm* (*para ropa*) drying-place; (*cuerda*) clothes line.

tendencia [tenden'syå] *nf* tendency; (*proceso*) trend; ~ **imperante** prevailing tendency; ~ **del mercado** run of the market; **tener** ~ **a** to tend *o* have a tendency to.

tendenciosidad [tendensyosēͭħåͭħ'] *nf* tendentiousness.

tendencioso, a [tendensyo'so, å] *a* tendentious.

tender [tender'] *vt* (*extender*) to spread out; (*ropa*) to hang out; (*vía férrea, cable*) to lay; (*cuerda*) to stretch; (*trampa*) to set ♦ *vi* to tend; ~**se** *vr* to lie down; (*fig: dejarse llevar*) to let o.s. go; (: *dejar ir*) to let things go; ~ **la cama/la mesa** (*AM*) to make the bed/set the table.

ténder [ten'der] *nm* (*FERRO*) tender.

tenderete [tendere'te] *nm* (*puesto*) stall; (*carretilla*) barrow; (*exposición*) display of goods.

tendero, a [tende'ro, å] *nm/f* shopkeeper.

tendido, a [tendē'ͭħo, å] *a* (*acostado*) lying down, flat; (*colgado*) hanging ♦ *nm* (*ropa*) washing; (*TAUR*) front rows *pl* of seats; (*colocación*) laying; (*ARQ: enyesado*) coat of plaster; **a galope** ~ flat out.

tendón [tendon'] *nm* tendon.

tendré [tendre'] *etc vb V* **tener.**

tenducho [tendōōtch'o] *nm* small dirty shop.

tenebroso, a [teneͭħro'so, å] *a* (*oscuro*) dark; (*fig*) gloomy; (*siniestro*) sinister.

tenedor [teneͭħor'] *nm* (*CULIN*) fork; (*poseedor*) holder; ~ **de libros** bookkeeper; ~ **de acciones** shareholder; ~ **de póliza** policyholder.

teneduría [teneͭħōōrē'å] *nf* keeping; ~ **de libros** bookkeeping.

tenencia [tenen'syå] *nf* (*de casa*) tenancy; (*de oficio*) tenure; (*de propiedad*) possession; ~ **asegurada** security of tenure; ~ **ilícita de armas** illegal possession of weapons.

tener [tener'] *vt* (*poseer*) to have; (*en la mano*) to hold; (*suj: recipiente*) to hold, contain; (*considerar*) to consider; ~**se** *vr*

(*erguirse*) to stand; (*fig*) to control o.s.; ~ **suerte** to be lucky; ~ **permiso** to have permission; **tiene 10 años** he is 10 years old; **¿cuántos años tienes?** how old are you?; ~ **sed/hambre/frío/calor** to be thirsty/hungry/cold/hot; ~ **ganas de** to want to; ~ **celos** to be jealous; ~ **cuidado** to be careful; ~ **razón** to be right; ~ **un metro de ancho/de largo** to be one meter wide/long; ~ **a bien** to see fit to; ~ **en cuenta** to bear in mind, take into account; ~ **a menos** to consider it beneath o.s.; ~ **a uno en más (estima)** to think all the more of sb; ~ **a uno por...** to think sb...; ~ **por seguro que** to be sure that; ~ **presente** to remember, bear in mind; ~ **que** (*obligación*) to have to; **tiene que ser así** it has to be this way; **nos tiene preparada una sorpresa** he has prepared a surprise for us; **¿qué tiene?** what's the matter with him?; **¿ésas tenemos?** what's all this?; **tiene un mes de muerto** he has been dead for a month; ~**se por** (*considerarse*) to consider o.s.

tenería [tenerē'å] *nf* tannery.

tenga [ten'gå] *etc vb V* **tener.**

tenia [te'nyå] *nf* tapeworm.

teniente [tenyen'te] *nm* lieutenant; ~ **coronel** lieutenant colonel.

tenis [te'nēs] *nm* tennis; ~ **de mesa** table tennis.

tenista [tenē'stå] *nm/f* tennis player.

tenor [tenor'] *nm* (*tono*) tone; (*sentido*) meaning; (*MUS*) tenor; **a** ~ **de** on the lines of.

tenorio [teno'ryo] *nm* (*fam*) ladykiller, Don Juan.

tensar [tensår'] *vt* to tighten; (*arco*) to draw.

tensión [tensyon'] *nf* tension; (*TEC*) stress; (*MED*): ~ **arterial** blood pressure; ~ **nerviosa** nervous strain; **tener la** ~ **alta** to have high blood pressure.

tenso, a [ten'so, å] *a* tense; (*relaciones*) strained.

tentación [tentåsyon'] *nf* temptation.

tentáculo [tentå'kōōlo] *nm* tentacle.

tentador, a [tentåͭħor', å] *a* tempting ♦ *nm/f* tempter/temptress.

tentar [tentår'] *vt* (*tocar*) to touch, feel; (*seducir*) to tempt; (*atraer*) to attract; (*probar*) to try (out); (*MED*) to probe; ~ **hacer algo** to try to do sth.

tentativa [tentåtē'ͭħå] *nf* attempt; ~ **de asesinato** attempted murder.

tentempié [tentempye'] *nm* (*fam*) snack.

tenue [te'nwe] *a* (*delgado*) thin, slender; (*alambre*) fine; (*insustancial*) tenuous; (*sonido*) faint; (*neblina*) light; (*lazo, vínculo*) slight.

tenuidad [tenwēͭħåͭħ'] *nf* thinness; (*de*

tela) fineness; (*de relaciones*) tenuousness; (*ligereza*) lightness; (*sencillez*) simplicity.

teñir [tenyĕr'] *vt* to dye; (*fig*) to tinge; ~**se el pelo** to dye one's hair.

teología [teolohĕ'á] *nf* theology.

teólogo, a [teo'logo, á] *nm/f* theologist, theologian.

teorema [teore'má] *nm* theorem.

teoría [teorĕ'á] *nf* theory; **en** ~ in theory.

teóricamente [teo'rĕkámente] *ad* theoretically.

teorice [teorĕ'se] *etc vb V* **teorizar**.

teórico, a [teo'rĕko, á] *a* theoretic(al) ♦ *nm/f* theoretician, theorist.

teorizar [teorĕsár'] *vi* to theorize.

TER [ter] *nm abr* (*FERRO*)=*tren español rápido.*

terapeuta [terápe'ōōtá] *nm/f* therapist.

terapéutico, a [terápe'ōōtĕko, á] *a* therapeutic(al) ♦ *nf* therapeutics *sg.*

terapia [terá'pyá] *nf* therapy; ~ **laboral** occupational therapy.

tercer [terser'] *a V* **tercero**.

tercería [terserĕ'á] *nf* (*mediación*) mediation; (*arbitraje*) arbitration.

tercermundista [tersermōōndĕ'stá] *a* Third World *cpd.*

tercero, a [terse'ro, á] *a* third (*delante de nmsg:* **tercer**) ♦ *nm* (*árbitro*) mediator; (*JUR*) third party.

terceto [terse'to] *nm* trio.

terciado, a [tersyá'ĥo, á] *a* slanting; **azúcar** ~ brown sugar.

terciar [tersyár'] *vt* (*MAT*) to divide into three; (*inclinarse*) to slope; (*llevar*) to wear across one's chest ♦ *vi* (*participar*) to take part; (*hacer de árbitro*) to mediate; ~**se** *vr* to arise.

terciario, a [tersyá'ryo, á] *a* tertiary.

tercio [ter'syo] *nm* third.

terciopelo [tersyope'lo] *nm* velvet.

terco, a [ter'ko, á] *a* obstinate, stubborn; (*material*) tough.

tergiversación [terhĕĥersásyon'] *nf* (*deformación*) distortion; (*evasivas*) prevarication.

tergiversar [terhĕĥersár'] *vt* to distort ♦ *vi* to prevaricate.

termal [termál'] *a* thermal.

termas [ter'más] *nfpl* hot springs.

térmico, a [ter'mĕko, á] *a* thermic, thermal, heat *cpd.*

terminación [termĕnásyon'] *nf* (*final*) end; (*conclusión*) conclusion, ending.

terminal [termĕnál'] *a* terminal ♦ *nm* (*ELEC, INFORM*) terminal; ~ **conversacional** interactive terminal; ~ **de pantalla** visual display unit ♦ *nf* (*AVIAT, FERRO*) terminal.

terminante [termĕnán'te] *a* (*final*) final, definitive; (*tajante*) categorical.

terminar [termĕnár'] *vt* (*completar*) to complete, finish; (*concluir*) to end ♦ *vi* (*llegar a su fin*) to end; (*parar*) to stop; (*acabar*) to finish; ~**se** *vr* to come to an end; ~ **por hacer algo** to end up (by) doing sth.

término [ter'mĕno] *nm* end, conclusion; (*parada*) terminus; (*límite*) boundary; (*en discusión*) point; (*LING, COM*) term; ~ **medio** average; (*fig*) middle way; **en otros** ~**s** in other words; **en último** ~ (*a fin de cuentas*) in the last analysis; (*como último recurso*) as a last resort; **en** ~**s de** in terms of; **según los** ~**s del contrato** according to the terms of the contract.

terminología [termĕnolohĕ'á] *nf* terminology.

termodinámico, a [termoĥĕná'mĕko, á] *a* thermodynamic ♦ *nf* thermodynamics *sg.*

termoimpresora [termoĕmpreso'rá] *nf* thermal printer.

termómetro [termo'metro] *nm* thermometer.

termonuclear [termonōōkleár'] *a* thermonuclear.

Termo(s) ® [ter'mo(s)] *nm* Thermos ®.

termostato [termostá'to] *nm* thermostat.

ternero, a [terne'ro, á] *nm/f* (*animal*) calf ♦ *nf* (*carne*) veal.

terneza [terne'sá] *nf* tenderness.

ternilla [ternĕ'yá] *nf* gristle; (*cartílago*) cartilage.

terno [ter'no] *nm* (*traje*) three-piece suit; (*conjunto*) set of three.

ternura [ternōō'rá] *nf* (*trato*) tenderness; (*palabra*) endearment; (*cariño*) fondness.

terquedad [terkeĥáĥ'] *nf* obstinacy; (*dureza*) harshness.

terrado [terrá'ĥo] *nm* terrace.

Terranova [terráno'ĥá] *nf* Newfoundland.

terraplén [terráplen'] *nm* (*AGR*) terrace; (*FERRO*) embankment; (*MIL*) rampart; (*cuesta*) slope.

terrateniente [terrátenyen'te] *nm* landowner.

terraza [terrá'sá] *nf* (*balcón*) balcony; (*techo*) flat roof; (*AGR*) terrace.

terremoto [terremo'to] *nm* earthquake.

terrenal [terrenál'] *a* earthly.

terreno, a [terre'no, á] *a* (*de la tierra*) earthly, worldly ♦ *nm* (*tierra*) land; (*parcela*) plot; (*suelo*) soil; (*fig*) field; **un** ~ a piece of land; **sobre el** ~ on the spot; **ceder/perder** ~ to give/lose ground; **preparar el** ~ (**a**) (*fig*) to pave the way (for).

terrero, a [terre'ro, á] *a* (*de la tierra*) earthy; (*vuelo*) low; (*fig*) humble.

terrestre [terres'tre] *a* terrestrial; (*ruta*) land *cpd.*

terrible [terrĕ'ĥle] *a* (*espantoso*) terrible; (*aterrador*) dreadful; (*tremendo*) awful.

territorio [terrĕto'ryo] *nm* territory; ~ **bajo**

mandato mandated territory.

terrón [terron'] *nm* (*de azúcar*) lump; (*de tierra*) clod, lump; **terrones** *nmpl* land *sg*.

terror [terror'] *nm* terror.

terrorífico, a [terrorē'fēko, á] *a* terrifying.

terrorismo [terrorēs'mo] *nm* terrorism.

terrorista [terrorē'stá] *a, nm/f* terrorist.

terroso, a [terro'so, á] *a* earthy.

terruño [terrōō'nyo] *nm* (*pedazo*) clod; (*parcela*) plot; (*fig*) native soil; **apego al** ~ attachment to one's native soil.

terso, a [ter'so, á] *a* (*liso*) smooth; (*pulido*) polished; (*fig: estilo*) flowing.

tersura [tersōō'rá] *nf* smoothness; (*brillo*) shine.

tertulia [tertōō'lyá] *nf* (*reunión informal*) social gathering; (*grupo*) group, circle; (*sala*) clubroom; ~ **literaria** literary circle.

tesar [tesár'] *vt* to tighten up.

tesina [tesē'ná] *nf* dissertation.

tesis [te'sēs] *nf inv* thesis.

tesón [teson'] *nm* (*firmeza*) firmness; (*tenacidad*) tenacity.

tesorería [tesorerē'á] *nf* treasurership.

tesorero, a [tesore'ro, á] *nm/f* treasurer.

tesoro [teso'ro] *nm* treasure; **T~ público** (*POL*) Treasury.

testaferro [testáfe'rro] *nm* figurehead.

testamentaría [testámentárē'á] *nf* execution of a will.

testamentario, a [testámentá'ryo, á] *a* testamentary ♦ *nm/f* executor/executrix.

testamento [testámen'to] *nm* will.

testar [testár'] *vi* to make a will.

testarada [testárá'tʰá] *nf*, **testarazo** [testárá'so] *nm*: **darse un(a)** ~ (*fam*) to bump one's head.

testarudo, a [testárōō'tʰo, á] *a* stubborn.

testero, a [teste'ro, á] *nm/f* (*gen*) front ♦ *nm* (*ARQ*) front wall.

testes [te'stes] *nmpl* testes.

testículo [testē'kōōlo] *nm* testicle.

testificar [testēfēkár'] *vt* to testify; (*fig*) to attest ♦ *vi* to give evidence.

testifique [testēfē'ke] *etc vb V* **testificar**.

testigo [testē'ġo] *nm/f* witness; ~ **de cargo/descargo** witness for the prosecution/defense; ~ **ocular** eye witness; **poner a uno por** ~ to cite sb as a witness.

testimoniar [testēmonyár'] *vt* to testify to; (*fig*) to show.

testimonio [testēmo'nyo] *nm* testimony; **en** ~ **de** as a token *o* mark of; **falso** ~ perjured evidence, false witness.

teta [te'tá] *nf* (*de biberón*) nipple (*US*), teat (*Brit*); (*ANAT*) nipple; (*fam*) breast; (*fam!*) tit (*!*).

tétanos [te'tános] *nm* tetanus.

tetera [tete'rá] *nf* teapot; ~ **eléctrica** (electric) kettle.

tetilla [tetē'yá] *nf* (*ANAT*) nipple; (*de bibe-*

rón) nipple (*US*), teat (*Brit*).

tétrico, a [te'trēko, á] *a* gloomy, dismal.

textil [tekstēl'] *a* textile; ~**es** *nmpl* textiles.

texto [tek'sto] *nm* text.

textual [tekstwál'] *a* textual; **palabras** ~**es** exact words.

textura [tekstōō'rá] *nf* (*de tejido*) texture; (*de mineral*) structure.

tez [tes] *nf* (*cutis*) complexion; (*color*) coloring (*US*), colouring (*Brit*).

tfno. *abr* (= *teléfono*) tel.

ti [tē] *pron* you; (*reflexivo*) yourself.

tía [tē'á] *nf* (*pariente*) aunt; (*mujer cualquiera*) girl; (*fam: pej: vieja*) old bag; (: *prostituta*) whore.

Tibet [tēḥet'] *nm*: **El** ~ Tibet.

tibetano, a [tēḥetá'no, á] *a, nm/f* Tibetan ♦ *nm* (*LING*) Tibetan.

tibia [tē'ḥyá] *nf* tibia.

tibieza [tēḥye'sá] *nf* (*temperatura*) tepidness; (*fig*) coolness.

tibio, a [tē'ḥyo, á] *a* lukewarm, tepid.

tiburón [tēḥōōron'] *nm* shark.

tic [tēk] *nm* (*ruido*) click; (*de reloj*) tick; ~ **nervioso** (*MED*) nervous tic.

tico, a [tē'ko, á] *a, nm/f* (*AM fam*) Costa Rican.

tictac [tēkták'] *nm* (*de reloj*) tick tock.

tiemble [tyem'ble] *etc vb V* **temblar**.

tiempo [tyem'po] *nm* (*gen*) time; (*época, período*) age, period; (*METEOROLOGÍA*) weather; (*LING*) tense; (*edad*) age; (*de juego*) half; **a** ~ in time; **a un** *o* **al mismo** ~ at the same time; **al poco** ~ very soon (after); **andando el** ~ in due course; **cada cierto** ~ every so often; **con** ~ in time; **con el** ~ eventually; **de** ~ **en** ~ from time to time; **en mis** ~**s** in my time; **en los buenos** ~**s** in the good old days; **hace buen/mal** ~ the weather is fine/bad; **estar a** ~ to be in time; **hace** ~ some time ago; **hacer** ~ to kill time; **¿qué** ~ **tiene?** how old is he?; **motor de 2** ~**s** two-stroke engine; ~ **compartido** (*INFORM*) time sharing; ~ **de ejecución** (*INFORM*) run time; ~ **inactivo** (*COM*) downtime; ~ **libre** spare time; ~ **de paro** (*COM*) idle time; **a** ~ **partido** (*trabajar*) part-time; ~ **preferencial** (*COM*) prime time; **en** ~ **real** (*INFORM*) real time.

tienda [tyen'dá] *etc vb V* **tender** ♦ *nf* shop; (*más grande*) store; (*NAUT*) awning; ~ **de campaña** tent.

tiene [tye'ne] *etc vb V* **tener**.

tienta [!tyen'tá] *nf* (*MED*) probe; (*fig*) tact; **andar a** ~**s** to grope one's way along.

tiento [tyen'to] *etc vb V* **tentar** ♦ *nm* (*tacto*) touch; (*precaución*) wariness; (*pulso*) steady hand; (*ZOOL*) feeler, tentacle.

tierno, a [tyer'no, á] *a* (*blando, dulce*) tender; (*fresco*) fresh.

tierra [tye'rrá] *nf* earth; (*suelo*) soil; (*mundo*) world; (*país*) country, land; (*ELEC*) ground (*US*), earth (*Brit*); ~ **adentro** inland; ~ **natal** native land; **echar ~ a un asunto** to hush an affair up; **no es de estas ~s** he's not from these parts; **la T~ Santa** the Holy Land.

tieso, a [tye'so, á] *etc vb V* **tesar** ♦ *a* (*rígido*) rigid; (*duro*) stiff; (*fig: testarudo*) stubborn; (*fam: orgulloso*) conceited ♦ *ad* strongly.

tiesto [tye'sto] *nm* flowerpot; (*pedazo*) piece of pottery.

tiesura [tyesōō'rá] *nf* rigidity; (*fig*) stubbornness; (*fam*) conceit.

tifo [tē'fo] *nm* typhus; ~ **de América** yellow fever; ~ **asiático** cholera.

tifoidea [tēfoēthe'á] *nf* typhoid.

tifón [tēfon'] *nm* (*huracán*) typhoon; (*de mar*) tidal wave.

tifus [tē'fōōs] *nm* typhus; ~ **icteroides** yellow fever.

tigre [tē'gre] *nm* tiger; (*AM*) jaguar.

tijera [tēhe'rá] *nf* (*AM*) (*una ~*) (pair of) scissors; (*ZOOL*) claw; (*persona*) gossip; **de ~** folding; **~s** *nfpl* scissors; (*para plantas*) shears; **unas ~s** a pair of scissors.

tijeretear [tēhereteár'] *vt* to snip ♦ *vi* (*fig*) to meddle.

tila [tē'lá] *nf* (*BOT*) lime tree; (*CULIN*) lime flower tea.

tildar [tēldár'] *vt*: ~ **de** to brand as.

tilde [tēl'de] *nf* (*defecto*) defect; (*trivialidad*) triviality; (*TIP*) tilde.

tilín [tēlēn'] *nm* tinkle.

tilo [tē'lo] *nm* lime tree.

timador, a [tēmáthor', á] *nm/f* swindler.

timar [tēmár'] *vt* (*robar*) to steal; (*estafar*) to swindle; (*persona*) to con; **~se** *vr* (*fam*) to make eyes (*con uno* at sb).

timbal [tēmbál'] *nm* small drum.

timbrar [tēmbrár'] *vt* to stamp; (*sellar*) to seal; (*carta*) to postmark.

timbrazo [tēmbrá'so] *nm* ring; **dar un ~** to ring the bell.

timbre [tēm'bre] *nm* (*sello*) stamp; (*campanilla*) bell; (*tono*) timbre; (*COM*) revenue stamp (*US*), stamp duty (*Brit*).

timidez [tēmēthes'] *nf* shyness.

tímido, a [tē'mētho, á] *a* shy, timid.

timo [tē'mo] *nm* swindle; **dar un ~ a uno** to swindle sb.

timón [tēmon'] *nm* helm, rudder; **coger el ~** (*fig*) to take charge.

timonel [tēmonel'] *nm* helmsman.

timorato, a [tēmorá'to, á] *a* God-fearing; (*mojigato*) sanctimonious.

tímpano [tēm'páno] *nm* (*ANAT*) eardrum; (*MUS*) small drum.

tina [tē'ná] *nf* tub; (*baño*) bath(tub).

tinaja [tēná'há] *nf* large earthern jar.

tinerfeño, a [tēnerfe'nyo, á] *a* of *o* from Tenerife ♦ *nm/f* native *o* inhabitant of Tenerife.

tinglado [tēnglá'tho] *nm* (*cobertizo*) shed; (*fig: truco*) trick; (*intriga*) intrigue; **armar un ~** to lay a plot.

tinieblas [tēnye'blás] *nfpl* darkness *sg*; (*sombras*) shadows; **estamos en ~ sobre sus proyectos** (*fig*) we are in the dark about his plans.

tino [tē'no] *nm* (*habilidad*) skill; (*MIL*) marksmanship; (*juicio*) insight; (*moderación*) moderation; **sin ~** immoderately; **coger el ~** to get the feel *o* hang of it.

tinta [tēn'tá] *nf* ink; (*TEC*) dye; (*ARTE*) color (*US*), colour (*Brit*); ~ **china** India (*US*) *o* Indian (*Brit*) ink; **~s** *nfpl* (*fig*) shades; **medias ~s** (*fig*) half measures; **saber algo de buena ~** to have sth on good authority.

tinte [tēn'te] *nm* (*acto*) dyeing; (*fig*) tinge; (*barniz*) veneer.

tinterillo [tēnterē'yo] *nm* penpusher.

tintero [tēnte'ro] *nm* inkwell; **se le quedó en el ~** he totally forgot about it.

tintinear [tēntēneár'] *vt* to tinkle.

tinto, a [tēn'to, á] *a* (*teñido*) dyed; (*manchado*) stained ♦ *nm* red wine.

tintorera [tēntore'rá] *nf* shark.

tintorería [tēntorerē'á] *nf* dry cleaner's.

tintorero [tēntore'ro] *nm* dry cleaner('s).

tintura [tēntōō'rá] *nf* (*acto*) dyeing; (*QUÍMICA*) dye; (*farmacéutico*) tincture.

tiña [tē'nyá] *etc vb V* **teñir** ♦ *nf* (*MED*) ringworm.

tío [tē'o] *nm* (*pariente*) uncle; (*fam: viejo*) old fellow; (: *individuo*) guy.

tiovivo [tēohē'ho] *nm* merry-go-round.

típico, a [tē'pēko, á] *a* typical; (*pintoresco*) picturesque.

tiple [tē'ple] *nm* soprano (voice) ♦ *nf* soprano.

tipo [tē'po] *nm* (*clase*) type, kind; (*norma*) norm; (*patrón*) pattern; (*fam: hombre*) guy; (*ANAT*) build; (: *de mujer*) figure; (*IMPRENTA*) type; ~ **bancario/de descuento** bank/discount rate; ~ **de interés** interest rate; ~ **de interés vigente** (*COM*) current rate; ~ **de cambio** exchange rate; ~ **base** (*COM*) base rate; ~ **a término** (*COM*) future (*US*) *o* forward (*Brit*) rate; **dos ~s sospechosos** two suspicious characters; ~ **de letra** (*INFORM, TIP*) typeface; ~ **de datos** (*INFORM*) data type.

tipografía [tēpográfē'á] *nf* (*tipo*) printing; (*lugar*) printing press.

tipográfico, a [tēpográ'fēko, á] *a* printing.

tipógrafo, a [tēpo'gráfo, á] *nm/f* printer.

tíque(t) [tē'ke], *pl* **~s** [tē'kes] *nm* ticket; (*en tienda*) receipt.

tiquismiquis [tēkēsmē'kēs] *nm* fussy person ♦ *nmpl* (*querellas*) squabbling *sg*; (*escrúpulos*) silly scruples.

tira [tē'rá] *nf* strip; (*fig*) abundance ♦ *nm*: ~ **y afloja** give and take; (*cautela*) caution; **la ~ de ...** (*fam*) lots of ....

tirabuzón [tēráḫōōson'] *nm* corkscrew; (*rizo*) curl.

tiradero [tēráṭ̣he'ro] *nm* (*AM*) rubbish dump.

tirado, a [tērá'ṭḫo, á] *a* (*barato*) dirt-cheap; (*fam*: *fácil*) very easy ♦ *nf* (*acto*) cast, throw; (*distancia*) distance; (*serie*) series; (*TIP*) printing, edition; **de una tirada** in one fell swoop; **está ~** (*fam*) it's a cinch.

tirador, a [tēráṭḫor', á] *nm/f* (*persona*) shooter ♦ *nm* (*mango*) handle; (*ELEC*) cord (*US*), flex (*Brit*); ~ **certero** sniper.

tiranía [tēránē'á] *nf* tyranny.

tirano, a [tērá'no, á] *a* tyrannical ♦ *nm/f* tyrant.

tirante [tēràn'te] *a* (*cuerda*) tight, taut; (*relaciones*) strained ♦ *nm* (*ARQ*) brace; (*TEC*) stay; (*correa*) shoulder strap; ~**s** *nmpl* suspenders (*US*), braces (*Brit*).

tirantez [tērántes'] *nf* tightness; (*fig*) tension.

tirar [tērár'] *vt* to throw; (*volcar*) to upset; (*derribar*) to knock down o over; (*tiro*) to fire; (*cohete*) to launch; (*bomba*) to drop; (*edificio*) to pull down; (*desechar*) to throw out o away; (*disipar*) to squander; (*imprimir*) to print; (*dar*: *golpe*) to deal ♦ *vi* (*disparar*) to shoot; (*jalar*) to pull; (*fig*) to draw; (*interesar*) to appeal; (*fam*: *andar*) to go; (*tender a, buscar realizar*) to tend to; (*DEPORTE*) to shoot; ~**se** *vr* to throw o.s.; (*fig*) to demean o.s.; (*fam*!) to screw (!); ~ **abajo** to bring down, destroy; **tira más a su padre** he takes more after his father; ~ **de algo** to pull o tug (on) sth; **ir tirando** to manage; ~ **a la derecha** to turn o go right; **a todo** ~ at the most.

tirita [tērē'tá] *nf* bandaid (*US*), (sticking) plaster.

tiritar [tērētár'] *vi* to shiver.

tiritona [tērēto'ná] *nf* shivering (fit).

tiro [tē'ro] *nm* (*lanzamiento*) throw; (*disparo*) shot; (*tiroteo*) shooting; (*DEPORTE*) shot; (*TENIS, GOLF*) drive; (*alcance*) range; (*de escalera*) flight (of stairs); (*golpe*) blow; (*engaño*) hoax; ~ **al blanco** target practice; **caballo de** ~ draught horse; **andar de** ~**s largos** to be all dressed up; **al** ~ (*AM*) at once; **se pegó un** ~ he shot himself; **le salió el** ~ **por la culata** it backfired on him.

Tirol [tērol'] *nm*: **El** ~ the Tyrol.

tirolés, esa [tēroles', esá] *a, nm/f* Tyrolean.

tirón [tēron'] *nm* (*sacudida*) pull, tug; **de un** ~ in one fell swoop; **dar un** ~ **a** to pull at,

tug at.

tirotear [tērotcár'] *vt* to shoot at; ~**se** *vr* to exchange shots.

tiroteo [tērotc'o] *nm* exchange of shots, shooting; (*escaramuza*) skirmish.

tirria [tē'rryá] *nf*: **tener una** ~ **a uno** to have a grudge against sb.

tísico, a [tē'sēko, á] *a, nm/f* consumptive.

tisis [tē'sēs] *nf* consumption, tuberculosis.

tít. *abr*=**título**.

títere [tē'tere] *nm* puppet; **no dejar** ~ **con cabeza** to turn everything upside-down.

titilar [tētēlár'] *vi* (*luz, estrella*) to twinkle; (*parpado*) to flutter.

titiritero, a [tētērēte'ro, á] *nm/f* (*acróbata*) acrobat; (*malabarista*) juggler.

titubeante [tētōōḫeán'te] *a* (*inestable*) shaky, tottering; (*farfullante*) stammering; (*dudoso*) hesitant.

titubear [tētōōḫeár'] *vi* to stagger; (*tartamudear*) to stammer; (*vacilar*) to hesitate.

titubeo [tētōōḫe'o] *nm* staggering; stammering; hesitation.

titulado, a [tētōōlá'ṭḫo, á] *a* (*libro*) entitled; (*persona*) titled.

titular [tētōōlár'] *a* titular ♦ *nm/f* (*de oficina*) occupant; (*de pasaporte*) holder ♦ *nm* headline ♦ *vt* to title; ~**se** *vr* to be entitled.

título [tē'tōōlo] *nm* (*gen*) title; (*de diario*) headline; (*certificado*) professional qualification; (*universitario*) university degree; (*COM*) bond; (*fig*) right; ~**s** *nmpl* qualifications; **a** ~ **de** by way of; (*en calidad de*) in the capacity of; **a** ~ **de curiosidad** as a matter of interest; ~ **de propiedad** title deed; ~**s convertibles de interés fijo** (*COM*) convertible loan stock *sg*.

tiza [tē'sá] *nf* chalk; **una** ~ a piece of chalk.

tizna [tēs'ná] *nf* grime.

tiznar [tēsnár'] *vt* to blacken; (*manchar*) to smudge, stain; (*fig*) to tarnish.

tizón [tēson'], **tizo** [tē'so] *nm* brand; (*fig*) stain.

Tm. *abr*=**tonelada(s) métrica(s)**.

toalla [toá'yá] *nf* towel.

tobillo [tobē'yo] *nm* ankle.

tobogán [toḫogán'] *nm* toboggan; (*montaña rusa*) switchback; (*resbaladilla*) chute, slide.

toca [to'ká] *nf* headdress.

tocadiscos [tokáṭḫēs'kos] *nm inv* record player.

tocado, a [toká'ṭḫo, á] *a* (*fruta etc*) rotten; ♦ *nm* headdress; **estar** ~ **de la cabeza** (*fam*) to be weak in the head.

tocador [tokáṭḫor'] *nm* (*mueble*) dressing table; (*cuarto*) boudoir; (*neceser*) make-up case; (*fam*) ladies' room.

tocante [tokán'te]: ~ **a** *prep* with regard to; **en lo** ~ **a** as for, so far as concerns.

tocar [tokár'] *vt* to touch; (*sentir*) to feel;

(con la mano) to handle; (MUS) to play; (campana) to ring; (tambor) to beat; (trompeta) to blow; (topar con) to run into, strike; (referirse a) to allude to; (ser emparentado con) to be related to ♦ vi (a la puerta) to knock (on o at the door); (ser de turno) to fall to, be the turn of; (ser hora) to be due; (atañer) to concern; ~se vr (cubrirse la cabeza) to cover one's head; (tener contacto) to touch (each other); ~le a uno hacer algo to be sb's turn to do sth; ~ en (NAUT) to call at; por lo que a mí me toca as far as I am concerned; esto toca en la locura this verges on madness.

tocayo, a [toká'yo, á] nm/f namesake.

tocino [tosē'no] nm (bacon) fat; ~ de panceta bacon.

todavía [totháhē'á] ad (aun) even; (aún) still, yet; ~ más yet o still more; ~ no not yet; ~ en 1970 as late as 1970; está lloviendo ~ it's still raining.

todo, a [to'tho, á] a all; (cada) every; (entero) whole; (sentido negativo): en ~ el día lo he visto I haven't seen him all day; todas las semanas/~s los martes every week/Tuesday ♦ ad all, completely ♦ nm everything ♦ pron: ~s/todas everyone; a toda velocidad at full speed; estaba ~ ojos he was all eyes; puede ser ~ lo honesto que quiera he can be as honest as he likes; en un ~ as a whole; corriendo y ~, no llegaron a tiempo even though they ran, they still didn't arrive in time; ante ~ above all; a pesar de ~ even so, in spite of everything; con ~ still, even so; del ~ completely; después de ~ after all; sobre ~ (especialmente) after all; (en primer lugar) above all.

todopoderoso, a [tothopothero'so, á] a all powerful; (REL) almighty.

toga [to'gá] nf toga; (ESCOL) gown.

Tokio [to'kyo] n Tokyo.

toldo [tol'do] nm (para el sol) awning; (tienda) marquee; (fig) pride.

tole [to'le] nm (fam) commotion.

toledano, a [toletha'no, á] a of o from Toledo ♦ nm/f native o inhabitant of Toledo.

tolerable [tolerá'hle] a tolerable.

tolerancia [toleràn'syá] nf tolerance.

tolerante [toleràn'te] a tolerant; (fig) openminded.

tolerar [tolerár'] vt to tolerate; (resistir) to endure.

Tolón [tolon'] nm Toulon.

tolvanera [tolhàne'rá] nf dust cloud.

toma [to'má] nf (gen) taking; (MED) dose; (ELEC: tb: ~ de corriente) socket; (MEC) inlet; ~ de posesión (por presidente) inauguration; ~ de tierra (AVIAT) landing.

tomadura [tomáthōō'rá] nf: ~ de pelo hoax.

tomar [tomár'] vt (gen, CINE. FOTO. TV) to take; (actitud) to adopt; (aspecto) to take on; (notas) to take down; (beber) to drink ♦ vi to take; (AM) to drink; ~se vr to take; ~se por to consider o.s. to be; ¡toma! here you are!; ~ asiento to sit down; ~ a uno por loco to think sb mad; ~ a bien/a mal to take well/badly; ~ en serio to take seriously; ~ el pelo a uno to pull sb's leg; ~la con uno to pick a quarrel with sb; ~ por escrito to write down; toma y daca give and take.

tomate [tomá'te] nm tomato.

tomatera [tomáte'rá] nf tomato plant.

tomavistas [tomáhē'stás] nm inv movie camera.

tomillo [tomē'yo] nm thyme.

tomo [to'mo] nm (libro) volume; (fig) importance.

ton [ton] abr = tonelada ♦ nm: sin ~ ni son without rhyme or reason.

tonada [toná'thá] nf tune.

tonalidad [tonálēthàth'] nf tone.

tonel [tonel'] nm barrel.

tonelada [tonelá'thá] nf ton; ~ métrica metric ton.

tonelaje [tonelá'he] nm tonnage.

tonelero [tonele'ro] nm cooper.

tónico, a [to'nēko, á] a tonic ♦ nm (MED) tonic ♦ nf (MUS) tonic; (fig) keynote.

tonificador, a [tonēfēkáthor', á], **tonificante** [tonēfēkán'te] a invigorating, stimulating.

tonificar [tonēfēkár'] vt to tone up.

tonifique [tonēfē'ke] etc vb V **tonificar**.

tonillo [tonē'yo] nm monotonous voice.

tono [to'no] nm (MUS) tone; (altura) pitch; (color) shade; fuera de ~ inappropriate; ~ de marcar (TELEC) dial (US) o dialling (Brit) tone; darse ~ to put on airs.

tontear [tonteár'] vi (fam) to fool around; (enamorados) to flirt.

tontería [tonterē'á] nf (estupidez) foolishness; (una ~) silly thing; ~s nfpl rubbish sg, nonsense sg.

tonto, a [ton'to, á] a stupid; (ridículo) silly ♦ nm/f fool; (payaso) clown; a tontas y a locas anyhow; hacer(se) el ~ to act the fool.

topacio [topá'syo] nm topaz.

topar [topár'] vt (tropezar) to bump into; (encontrar) to find, come across; (cabra etc) to butt ♦ vi: ~ contra o en to run into; ~ con to run up against; el problema topa en eso that's where the problem lies.

tope [to'pe] a maximum ♦ nm (fin) end; (límite) limit; (riña) quarrel; (FERRO) buffer; (AUTO) bumper; al ~ end to end; fecha ~ closing date; precio ~ top price; sueldo ~ maximum salary; ~ de tabulación tab stop.

tópico, a [to'pĕko, á] *a* topical; (*MED*) local
♦ *nm* platitude, cliché; **de uso** ~ for
external application.

topo [to'po] *nm* (*ZOOL*) mole; (*fig*) blunder-
er.

topografía [topoɣráfē'á] *nf* topography.

topógrafo, a [topo'ɣráfo, á] *nm/f* topog-
rapher; (*agrimensor*) surveyor.

toponimia [toponē'myá] *nf* place names *pl*;
(*estudio*) study of place names.

toque [to'ke] *etc vb V* **tocar** ♦ *nm* touch;
(*MUS*) beat; (*de campana*) ring, chime;
(*MIL*) bugle call; (*fig*) crux; **dar un** ~ **a** to
test; **dar el último** ~ **a** to put the final
touch to; ~ **de queda** curfew.

toquetear [toketeár'] *vt* to handle; (*fam!*)
to touch up.

toquilla [tokē'yá] *nf* (*chal*) shawl.

torbellino [torbeyē'no] *nm* whirlwind; (*fig*)
whirl.

torcedura [torsetʰōō'rá] *nf* twist; (*MED*)
sprain.

torcer [torser'] *vt* to twist; (*la esquina*) to
turn; (*MED*) to sprain; (*cuerda*) to braid
(*US*), plait (*Brit*); (*ropa, manos*) to wring;
(*persona*) to corrupt; (*sentido*) to distort ♦
vi (*cambiar de dirección*) to turn; ~**se** *vr*
to twist; (*doblar*) to bend; (*desviarse*) to
go astray; (*fracasar*) to go wrong; ~ **el
gesto** to scowl; ~**se un pie** to twist one's
foot; **el coche torció a la derecha** the car
turned right.

torcido, a [torsē'tʰo, á] *a* twisted; (*fig*)
crooked ♦ *nm* curl.

tordo, a [tor'tʰo, á] *a* dappled ♦ *nm* thrush.

torear [toreár'] *vt* (*fig: evadir*) to dodge;
(*toro*) to fight ♦ *vi* to fight bulls.

toreo [tore'o] *nm* bullfighting.

torero, a [tore'ro, á] *nm/f* bullfighter.

toril [torēl'] *nm* bullpen.

tormenta [tormen'tá] *nf* storm; (*fig: confusión*) turmoil.

tormento [tormen'to] *nm* torture; (*fig*)
anguish.

tormentoso, a [tormento'so, á] *a* stormy.

tornar [tornár'] *vt* (*devolver*) to return, give
back; (*transformar*) to transform ♦ *vi* to go
back; ~**se** *vr* (*ponerse*) to become;
(*volver*) to return.

tornasol [tornasol'] *nm* (*BOT*) sunflower;
papel de ~ litmus paper.

tornasolado, a [tornásolá'tʰo, á] *a*
(*brillante*) iridescent; (*reluciente*) shimmering.

torneo [torne'o] *nm* tournament.

tornero, a [torne'ro, á] *nm/f* machinist.

tornillo [tornē'yo] *nm* screw; **apretar los** ~**s
a uno** to apply pressure on sb; **le falta un**
~ (*fam*) he's got a screw loose.

torniquete [tornēke'te] *nm* (*puerta*) turn-
stile; (*MED*) tourniquet.

torno [tor'no] *nm* (*TEC*: *grúa*) winch; (: *de
carpintero*) lathe; (*tambor*) drum; ~ **de
banco** vise (*US*), vice (*Brit*); **en** ~ **(a)**
round, about.

toro [to'ro] *nm* bull; (*fam*) he-man; **los** ~**s**
bullfighting *sg*.

toronja [toron'há] *nf* (*AM*) grapefruit.

torpe [tor'pe] *a* (*poco hábil*) clumsy,
awkward; (*movimiento*) sluggish; (*necio*)
dim; (*lento*) slow; (*indecente*) crude; (*no
honrado*) dishonest.

torpedo [torpe'tʰo] *nm* torpedo.

torpemente [torpemen'te] *ad* (*sin destreza*)
clumsily; (*lentamente*) slowly.

torpeza [torpe'sá] *nf* (*falta de agilidad*)
clumsiness; (*lentitud*) slowness; (*rigidez*)
stiffness; (*error*) mistake; (*crudeza*) obscenity.

torre [to'rre] *nf* tower; (*de petróleo*)
derrick; (*de electricidad*) pylon; (*AJE-
DREZ*) rook; (*AVIAT, MIL, NAUT*) turret.

torrencial [torrensyál'] *a* torrential.

torrente [torren'te] *nm* torrent.

tórrido, a [to'rrētʰo, á] *a* torrid.

torrija [torrē'há] *nf* fried bread; ~**s** French
toast *sg*.

torsión [torsyon'] *nf* twisting.

torso [tor'so] *nm* torso.

torta [tor'tá] *nf* cake; (*fam*) slap; **no
entendió ni** ~ he didn't understand a word
of it.

tortazo [tortá'so] *nm* (*bofetada*) slap; (*de
coche*) crash.

tortícolis [tortē'kolēs] *nm inv* stiff neck.

tortilla [tortē'yá] *nf* omelet(te); (*AM*)
tortilla, maize pancake; ~ **francesa/
española** plain/potato omelet; **cambiar** *o*
volver la ~ **a uno** to turn the tables on sb.

tortillera [tortēye'rá] *nf* (*fam!*) lesbian.

tórtola [tor'tolá] *nf* turtledove.

tortuga [tortōō'gá] *nf* tortoise; ~ **marina**
turtle.

tortuoso, a [tortwo'so, á] *a* winding.

tortura [tortōō'rá] *nf* torture.

torturar [tortōōrár'] *vt* to torture.

torvo, a [tor'ĸo, á] *a* grim, fierce.

torzamos [torsá'mos] *etc vb V* **torcer**.

tos [tos] *nf inv* cough; ~ **ferina** whooping
cough.

Toscana [toská'ná] *nf*: **La** ~ Tuscany.

tosco, a [tos'ko, á] *a* coarse.

toser [toser'] *vi* to cough; **no hay quien le
tosa** he's in a class by himself.

tostado, a [tostá'tʰo, á] *a* toasted; (*por el
sol*) dark brown; (*piel*) tanned ♦ *nf* tan;
(*pan*) piece of toast; **tostadas** *nfpl* toast *sg*.

tostador [tostátʰor'] *nm* toaster.

tostar [tostár'] *vt* to toast; (*café*) to roast;
(*al sol*) to tan; ~**se** *vr* to get brown.

total [totál'] *a* total ♦ *ad* in short; (*al fin y al
cabo*) when all is said and done ♦ *nm* total;

en ~ in all; ~ **que** to cut a long story short; ~ **de comprobación** (*INFORM*) hash total; ~ **debe/haber** (*COM*) debit/assets total.

totalidad [totáléṭháṭḥ'] *nf* whole.

totalitario, a [totálēṭá'ryo, á] *a* totalitarian.

tóxico, a [tok'sēko, á] *a* toxic ♦ *nm* poison.

toxicómano, a [toksēko'máno, á] *a* addicted to drugs ♦ *nm/f* drug addict.

tozudo, a [tosōō'ṭḥo, á] *a* obstinate.

traba [trá'ḥá] *nf* bond, tie; (*cadena*) fetter; **poner** ~**s a** to restrain.

trabajador, a [tráḥáḥáṭḥor', á] *nm/f* worker ♦ *a* hard-working.

trabajar [tráḥáḥár'] *vt* to work; (*arar*) to till; (*empeñarse en*) to work at; (*empujar: persona*) to push; (*convencer*) to persuade ♦ *vi* to work; (*esforzarse*) to strive; ¡a ~! let's get to work!; ~ **por hacer algo** to strive to do sth.

trabajo [tráḥá'ho] *nm* work; (*tarea*) task; (*POL*) labor (*US*), labour (*Brit*); (*fig*) effort; **tomarse el** ~ **de** to take the trouble to; ~ **por turno/a destajo** shift work/piecework; ~ **en proceso** (*COM*) work-in-progress.

trabajoso, a [tráḥáho'so, á] *a* hard; (*MED*) pale.

trabalenguas [tráḥálen'gwás] *nm inv* tongue twister.

trabar [tráḥár'] *vt* (*juntar*) to join, unite; (*atar*) to tie down, fetter; (*agarrar*) to seize; (*amistad*) to strike up; ~**se** *vr* to become entangled; (*reñir*) to squabble; **se le traba la lengua** he gets tongue-tied.

trabazón [tráḥáson'] *nf* (*TEC*) joining, assembly; (*fig*) bond, link.

trabucar [tráḥōōkár'] *vt* (*confundir*) to confuse, mix up; (*palabras*) to misplace.

trabuque [tráḥōō'ke] *etc vb V* **trabucar**.

tracción [tráksyon'] *nf* traction; ~ **delantera/trasera** front-wheel/rear-wheel drive.

trace [trá'se] *etc vb V* **trazar**.

tractor [tráktor'] *nm* tractor.

trad. *abr* (= *traducido*) trans.

tradición [tráṭḥēsyon'] *nf* tradition.

tradicional [tráṭḥēsyonál'] *a* traditional.

traducción [tráṭḥōōksyon'] *nf* translation; ~ **asistida por ordenador** computer-assisted translation.

traducible [tráṭḥōōsē'ḥle] *a* translatable.

traducir [tráṭḥōōsēr'] *vt* to translate; ~**se** *vr*: ~**se en** (*fig*) to entail, result in.

traductor, a [tráṭḥōōktor', á] *nm/f* translator.

traduzca [tráṭḥōōs'ká] *etc vb V* **traducir**.

traer [trácr'] *vt* to bring; (*llevar*) to carry; (*ropa*) to wear; (*incluir*) to carry; (*fig*) to cause; ~**se** *vr*: ~**se algo** to be up to sth; ~**se bien/mal** to dress well/badly; **traérselas** to be annoying; ~ **consigo** to involve,

entail; **es un problema que se las trae** it's a difficult problem.

traficante [tráfēkán'te] *nm/f* trader, dealer.

traficar [tráfēkár'] *vi* to trade; ~ **con** (*pey*) to deal illegally in.

tráfico [trá'fēko] *nm* (*COM*) trade; (*AUTO*) traffic.

trafique [tráfē'ke] *etc vb V* **traficar**.

tragaderas [tráḥáḥe'rás] *nfpl* (*garganta*) throat *sg*, gullet *sg*; (*credulidad*) gullibility *sg*.

tragaluz [tráḥálōōs'] *nm* skylight.

tragamonedas [tráḥámone'ṭḥás] *nm inv*, **tragaperras** [tráḥápe'rrás] *nm inv* slot machine.

tragar [tráḥár'] *vt* to swallow; (*devorar*) to devour, bolt down; ~**se** *vr* to swallow; (*tierra*) to absorb, soak up; **no le puedo** ~ (*persona*) I can't stand him.

tragedia [tráḥe'ṭḥyá] *nf* tragedy.

trágico, a [trá'hēko, á] *a* tragic.

trago [trá'ḡo] *nm* (*líquido*) drink; (*comido de golpe*) gulp; (*fam: de bebida*) swig; (*desgracia*) blow; ~ **amargo** (*fig*) hard time.

trague [trá'ḡe] *etc vb V* **tragar**.

traición [tráēsyon'] *nf* treachery; (*JUR*) treason; (*una* ~) act of treachery.

traicionar [tráēsyonár'] *vt* to betray.

traicionero, a [tráēsyone'ro, á] *a* = **traidor, a**.

traída [tráē'ṭḥá] *nf* carrying; ~ **de aguas** water supply.

traidor, a [tráēṭḥor', á] *a* treacherous ♦ *nm/f* traitor.

traiga [trá'ēḡá] *etc vb V* **traer**.

traje [trá'he] *etc vb V* **traer** ♦ *nm* (*gen*) dress; (*de hombre*) suit; (~ *típico*) costume; (*fig*) garb; ~ **de baño** swimsuit; ~ **de luces** bullfighter's costume; ~ **hecho a la medida** tailor-made suit.

trajera [tráhe'rá] *etc vb V* **traer**.

trajín [tráhēn'] *nm* transportation; (*fam: movimiento*) bustle; **trajines** *nmpl* goings-on.

trajinar [tráhēnár'] *vt* (*llevar*) to carry, transport ♦ *vi* (*moverse*) to bustle; (*viajar*) to travel around.

trama [trá'má] *nf* (*fig*) link; (: *intriga*) plot; (*de tejido*) weft.

tramar [trámár'] *vt* to plot; (*TEC*) to weave; ~**se** *vr* (*fig*): **algo se está tramando** there's something going on.

tramitar [trámētár'] *vt* (*asunto*) to transact; (*negociar*) to negotiate; (*manejar*) to handle.

trámite [trá'mēte] *nm* (*paso*) step; (*JUR*) transaction; ~**s** *nmpl* (*burocracia*) paperwork *sg*, procedures; (*JUR*) proceedings.

tramo [trá'mo] *nm* (*de tierra*) plot; (*de escalera*) flight; (*de vía*) section.

tramoya [trámo'yá] *nf* (*TEATRO*) piece of

stage machinery; (fig) trick.
tramoyista [trámoyē'stá] nm/f scene shifter; (fig) trickster.
trampa [trám'pá] nf trap; (en el suelo) trapdoor; (prestidigitación) magic trick; (engaño) trick; (fam) fiddle; (de pantalón) fly; **caer en la** ~ to fall into the trap; **hacer ~s** (hacer juegos de manos) to juggle, conjure; (trampear) to cheat.
trampear [trámpeár'] vt, vi to cheat.
trampilla [trámpē'yá] nf trap, hatchway.
trampista [trámpē'stá] nm/f = **tramposo.**
trampolín [trámpolēn'] nm trampoline; (de piscina etc) diving board.
tramposo, a [trámpo'so, á] a crooked, cheating ♦ nm/f crook, cheat.
tranca [trán'ká] nf (palo) stick; (viga) beam; (de puerta, ventana) bar; (borrachera) binge; **a ~s y barrancas** with great difficulty.
trancar [tránkár'] vt to bar ♦ vi to stride along.
trancazo [tránká'so] nm (golpe) blow.
trance [trán'se] nm (momento difícil) difficult moment; (situación crítica) critical situation; (estado hipnotizado) trance; **estar en ~ de muerte** to be at death's door.
tranco [trán'ko] nm stride.
tranque [trán'ke] etc vb V **trancar.**
tranquilice [tránkēlē'se] etc vb V **tranquilizar.**
tranquilidad [tránkēlēᵗháᵗh'] nf 'calma) calmness, stillness; (paz) peacefulness.
tranquilizador, a [tránkēlēsáᵗhor', á] a (música) soothing; (hecho) reassuring.
tranquilizar [tránkēlēsár'] vt (calmar) to calm (down); (asegurar) to reassure.
tranquilo, a [tránkē'lo, á] a (calmado) calm; (apacible) peaceful; (mar) calm; (mente) untroubled.
Trans. abr (COM) = **transferencia.**
transacción [tránsáksyon'] nf transaction.
transar [tránsár'] vi = **transigir.**
transbordador [tránsᵇorᵗháᵗhor'] nm ferry.
transbordar [tránsᵇorᵗhár'] vt to transfer; **~se** vr to change.
transbordo [tránsᵇor'ᵗho] nm transfer; **hacer ~** to change (trains).
transcurrir [tránskōōrrēr'] vi (tiempo) to pass; (hecho) to turn out.
transcurso [tránskōōr'so] nm passing, lapse; **en el ~ de 8 días** in the course of a week.
transeúnte [tránseōōn'te] a transient ♦ nm/f passer-by.
transferencia [tránsferen'syá] nf transference; (COM) transfer; **~ bancaria** banker's order; **~ de crédito** (COM) credit transfer; **~ electrónica de fondos** (COM) electronic funds transfer.

transferir [tránsferēr'] vt to transfer; (aplazar) to postpone.
transfiera [tránsfye'rá] etc vb V **transferir.**
transfigurar [tránsfēḡōōrár'] vt to transfigure.
transfiriendo [tránsfēryen'do] etc vb V **transferir.**
transformador [tránsformáᵗhor'] nm transformer.
transformar [tránsformár'] vt to transform; (convertir) to convert.
tránsfuga [tráns'fōōḡá] nm/f (MIL) deserter; (POL) turncoat.
transgresión [tránsɡresyon'] nf transgression.
transición [tránsēsyon'] nf transition; **período de ~** transitional period.
transido, a [tránsē'ᵗho, á] a overcome; **~ de angustia** overcome with anxiety; **~ de dolor** racked with pain.
transigir [tránsēḡēr'] vi to compromise; (ceder) to make concessions.
transija [tránsē'há] etc vb V **transigir.**
Transilvania [tránsēlᵇá'nyá] nf Transylvania.
transistor [tránsēstor'] nm transistor.
transitable [tránsētá'ᵇle] a (camino) passable.
transitar [tránsētár'] vi to go (from place to place).
tránsito [trán'sēto] nm transit; (AUTO) traffic; (parada) stop; **horas de máximo ~** rush hours; **"se prohíbe el ~"** "no thoroughfare."
transitorio, a [tránsēto'ryo, á] a transitory.
transmisión [tránsmēsyon'] nf (RADIO, TV) transmission, broadcast(ing); (transferencia) transfer; **~ en circuito** hookup; **~ en directo/exterior** live/outside broadcast; **~ de datos (en paralelo/en serie)** (INFORM) (parallel/serial) data transfer o transmission; **plena/media ~ bidireccional** (INFORM) full/half duplex.
transmitir [tránsmētēr'] vt to transmit; (RADIO, TV) to broadcast; (enfermedad) to give, pass on.
transparencia [tránspáren'syá] nf transparency; (claridad) clearness, clarity; (foto) slide.
transparentar [tránspárentár'] vt to reveal ♦ vi to be transparent.
transparente [tránspáren'te] a transparent; (aire) clear; (ligero) diaphanous ♦ nm curtain.
transpirar [tránspērár'] vi to perspire; (fig) to transpire.
transpondré [tránspondre'] etc vb V **transponer.**
transponer [tránsponer'] vt to transpose; (cambiar de sitio) to move about ♦ vi (desaparecer) to disappear; (ir más allá) to

go beyond; ~**se** *vr* to change places; (*ocultarse*) to hide; (*sol*) to go down.

transponga [tránspon'gá] *etc vb V* **transponer.**

transportación [tránsportásyon'] *nf* transportation.

transportador [tránsportátʰor'] *nm* (*MECÁNICA*): ~ **de correa** belt conveyor.

transportar [tránsportár'] *vt* to transport; (*llevar*) to carry.

transporte [tránspor'te] *nm* transport; (*COM*) transportation, haulage; **Ministerio de T~s** ≈ Department of Transportation (*US*), ≈ Ministry of Transport (*Brit*).

transpuesto [tránspwe'sto], **transpuse** [tránspōō'se] *etc vb V* **transponer.**

transversal [tránshersál'] *a* transverse, cross ♦ *nf* (*tb*: **calle** ~) cross street.

transversalmente [tránshersálmen'te] *ad* obliquely.

tranvía [tránbē'á] *nm* streetcar (*US*), tram (*Brit*).

trapecio [trápe'syo] *nm* trapeze.

trapecista [trápesē'stá] *nm/f* trapeze artist.

trapero, a [trápe'ro, á] *nm/f* ragman.

trapicheos [trápētche'os] *nmpl* (*fam*) schemes.

trapisonda [trápēson'dá] *nf* (*jaleo*) row; (*estafa*) swindle.

trapo [trá'po] *nm* (*tela*) rag; (*de cocina*) cloth; ~**s** *nmpl* (*fam: de mujer*) clothes, dresses; **a todo** ~ under full sail; **soltar el** ~ (*llorar*) to burst into tears.

tráquea [trá'keá] *nf* trachea, windpipe.

traqueteo [trákete'o] *nm* (*crujido*) crack; (*golpeteo*) rattling.

tras [trás] *prep* (*detrás*) behind; (*después*) after; ~ **de** besides; **día** ~ **día** day after day; **uno** ~ **otro** one after the other.

trascendencia [trásenden'syá] *nf* (*importancia*) importance; (*filosofía*) transcendence.

trascendental [trásendentál'] *a* important; transcendental.

trascender [trásender'] *vi* (*oler*) to smell; (*noticias*) to come out, leak out; (*eventos, sentimientos*) to spread, have a wide effect; ~ **a** (*afectar*) to reach, have an effect on; (*oler a*) to smack of; **en su novela todo trasciende a romanticismo** everything in his novel smacks of romanticism.

trascienda [trásyen'dá] *etc vb V* **trascender.**

trasegar [trásegár'] *vt* (*mover*) to move about; (*vino*) to decant.

trasegué [tráseg̃e'], **traseguemos** [tráseg̃e'mos] *etc vb V* **trasegar.**

trasero, a [tráse'ro, á] *a* back, rear ♦ *nm* (*ANAT*) bottom; ~**s** *nmpl* ancestors.

trasfondo [trásfon'do] *nm* background.

trasgo [trás'go] *nm* (*duende*) goblin.

trasgredir [trásgretʰēr'] *vt* to contravene.

trashumante [trásōōmán'te] *a* migrating.

trasiego [trásye'go] *etc vb V* **trasegar** ♦ *nm* (*cambiar de sitio*) move, switch; (*de vino*) decanting; (*trastorno*) upset.

trasiegue [trásye'g̃e] *etc vb V* **trasegar.**

trasladar [tráslátʰár'] *vt* to move; (*persona*) to transfer; (*postergar*) to postpone; (*copiar*) to copy; (*interpretar*) to interpret; ~**se** *vr* (*irse*) to go; (*mudarse*) to move; ~**se a otro puesto** to move to a new job.

traslado [tráslá'tʰo] *nm* move; (*mudanza*) move, removal; (*de persona*) transfer; (*copia*) copy; ~ **de bloque** (*INFORM*) block move, cut-and-paste.

traslucir [tráslōōsēr'] *vt* to show; ~**se** *vr* to be translucent; (*fig*) to be revealed.

trasluz [tráslōōs'] *nm* reflected light; **al** ~ against *o* up to the light.

trasluzca [tráslōōs'ká] *etc vb V* **traslucir.**

trasmano [trásmá'no]: **a** ~ *ad* (*fuera de alcance*) out of reach; (*apartado*) out of the way.

trasnochador, a [trásnotchátʰor'. á] *a* given to staying up late ♦ *nm/f* (*fig*) night bird.

trasnochar [trásnotchár'] *vi* (*acostarse tarde*) to stay up late; (*no dormir*) to have a sleepless night; (*pasar la noche*) to stay the night.

traspasar [tráspásár'] *vt* (*bala*) to pierce, go through; (*propiedad*) to sell, transfer; (*calle*) to cross over; (*límites*) to go beyond; (*ley*) to break; **"traspaso negocio"** "business for sale".

traspaso [tráspá'so] *nm* transfer; (*fig*) anguish.

traspié [tráspye'], *pl* **traspiés** *nm* (*caída*) stumble; (*tropezón*) trip; (*fig*) blunder.

trasplantar [trásplántár'] *vt* to transplant.

traste [trá'ste] *nm* (*MUS*) fret; **dar al** ~ **con algo** to ruin sth; **ir al** ~ to fall through.

trastero [tráste'ro] *nm* storage (*US*) *o* lumber (*Brit*) room.

trastienda [trástyen'dá] *nf* back room (*US*), backshop (*Brit*); **obtener algo por la** ~ to get sth by underhanded means.

trasto [trá'sto] *nm* (*mueble*) piece of furniture; (*tarro viejo*) old pot; (*pey: cosa*) piece of junk; (: *persona*) dead loss; ~**s** *nmpl* (*TEATRO*) scenery *sg*; **tirar los** ~**s a la cabeza** to have a blazing row.

trastornado, a [trástorná'tʰo. á] *a* (*loco*) mad; (*agitado*) crazy.

trastornar [trástornár'] *vt* to overturn, upset; (*fig: ideas*) to confuse; (: *nervios*) to shatter; (: *persona*) to drive crazy; ~**se** *vr* (*plan*) to fall through.

trastorno [trástor'no] *nm* (*acto*) overturning; (*confusión*) confusion; (*POL*) disturbance, upheaval; (*MED*) upset; ~ **estomacal** stomach upset; ~ **mental** mental

disorder, breakdown.
trasunto [trásōōn'to] *nm* copy.
tratable [trátá'ɦlɛ] *a* friendly.
tratado [trátá'ɬo] *nm* (*POL*) treaty; (*COM*) agreement; (*LITERATURA*) treatise.
tratamiento [trátámyɛn'to] *nm* treatment; (*TEC*) processing; (*de problema*) handling; ~ **de datos** (*INFORM*) data processing; ~ **de gráficos** (*INFORM*) graphics; ~ **de márgenes** margin settings; ~ **de textos** (*INFORM*) word processing; ~ **por lotes** (*INFORM*) batch processing; ~ **de tú** familiar address.
tratante [trátán'tɛ] *nm/f* dealer, merchandizer.
tratar [trátár'] *vt* (*ocuparse de*) to treat; (*manejar*, *TEC*) to handle; (*INFORM*) to process; (*MED*) to treat; (*dirigirse a: persona*) to address ♦ *vi*: ~ **de** (*hablar sobre*) to deal with, be about; (*intentar*) to try to; ~ **con** (*COM*) to trade in; (*negociar*) to negotiate with; (*tener contactos*) to have dealings with; ~**se** *vr* to treat each other; **se trata de la nueva piscina** it's about the new pool; **¿de qué se trata?** what's it about?
trato [trá'to] *nm* dealings *pl*; (*relaciones*) relationship; (*comportamiento*) manner; (*COM, JUR*) agreement, contract; (*título*) (form of) address; **de ~ agradable** pleasant; **de fácil ~** easy to get on with; ~ **equitativo** fair deal; **¡~ hecho!** it's a deal!; **malos ~s** ill-treatment *sg*.
trauma [trá'ōōmá] *nm* trauma.
traumático, a [tráōōmá'tēko, á] *a* traumatic.
través [tráɓɛs'] *nm* (*contratiempo*) reverse; **al ~** across, crossways; **a ~ de** across; (*sobre*) over; (*por*) through; **de ~** across; (*de lado*) sideways.
travesaño [tráɓɛsá'nyo] *nm* (*ARQ*) crossbeam; (*DEPORTE*) crossbar.
travesía [tráɓɛsē'á] *nf* (*calle*) cross-street; (*NAUT*) crossing.
travesura [tráɓɛsōō'rá] *nf* (*broma*) prank; (*ingenio*) wit.
travieso, a [tráɓyɛ'so, á] *a* (*niño*) naughty; (*adulto*) restless; (*ingenioso*) witty ♦ *nf* crossing; (*ARQ*) crossbeam.
trayecto [tráyɛk'to] *nm* (*ruta*) road, way; (*viaje*) journey; (*tramo*) stretch; (*curso*) course; **final del ~** end of the line.
trayectoria [tráyɛkto'ryá] *nf* trajectory; (*desarrollo*) development, path; **la ~ actual del partido** the party's present line.
trayendo [tráyɛn'do] *etc vb V* **traer.**
traza [trá'sá] *nf* (*ARQ*) plan, design; (*aspecto*) looks *pl*; (*señal*) sign; (*engaño*) trick; (*habilidad*) skill; (*INFORM*) trace.
trazado, a [trásá'ɬo, á] *a*: **bien ~** shapely, well-formed ♦ *nm* (*ARQ*) plan, design; (*fig*)

outline; (*de carretera etc*) line, route.
trazador [trásáɬor'] *nm* plotter; ~ **plano** flatbed plotter.
trazar [trásár'] *vt* (*ARQ*) to plan; (*ARTE*) to sketch; (*fig*) to trace; (*itinerario: hacer*) to plot; (*plan*) to follow.
trazo [trá'so] *nm* (*línea*) line; (*bosquejo*) sketch; ~**s** *nmpl* (*de cara*) lines, features.
TRB *abr* = **toneladas de registro bruto.**
trébol [trɛ'ɦol] *nm* (*BOT*) clover; ~**es** *nmpl* (*NAIPES*) clubs.
trece [trɛ'sɛ] *num* thirteen; **estar en sus ~** to stand firm.
trecho [trɛtch'o] *nm* (*distancia*) distance; (*de tiempo*) while; (*fam*) piece; **de ~ en ~** at intervals.
tregua [trɛ'gwá] *nf* (*MIL*) truce; (*fig*) lull; **sin ~** without respite.
treinta [trɛ'ēntá] *num* thirty.
treintena [trɛɛntɛ'ná] *nf* (about) thirty.
tremendo, a [trɛmɛn'do, á] *a* (*terrible*) terrible; (*imponente: cosa*) imposing; (*fam: fabuloso*) tremendous; (*divertido*) entertaining.
trémulo, a [trɛ'mōōlo, á] *a* quivering; (*luz*) flickering.
tren [trɛn] *nm* (*FERRO*) train; ~ **de aterrizaje** landing gear; ~ **directo/expreso/(de) mercancías/de pasajeros/suplementario** through/fast/freight/passenger/relief train; ~ **de vida** way of life.
trence [trɛn'sɛ] *etc vb V* **trenzar.**
trenza [trɛn'sá] *nf* (*de pelo*) braid (*US*), plait (*Brit*).
trenzar [trɛnsár'] *vt* (*el pelo*) to braid (*US*), plait (*Brit*) ♦ *vi* (*en baile*) to weave in and out; ~**se** *vr* (*AM*) to become involved.
trepa [trɛ'pá] *nf* (*subida*) climb; (*ardid*) trick.
trepador(a) [trɛpáɬor', á] *nm/f* (*fam*): **ser un(a) ~** to be on the make ♦ *nf* (*BOT*) climber.
trepar [trɛpár'] *vt, vi* to climb; (*TEC*) to drill.
trepidación [trɛpɛɬásyon'] *nf* shaking, vibration.
trepidar [trɛpɛɬár'] *vi* to shake, vibrate.
tres [trɛs] *num* three; (*fecha*) third; **las ~** three o'clock.
trescientos, as [trɛsyɛn'tos, ás] *num* three hundred.
tresillo [trɛsē'yo] *nm* three-piece suite; (*MUS*) triplet.
treta [trɛ'tá] *nf* (*COM etc*) gimmick; (*fig*) trick.
tri... [trɛ] *pref* tri..., three-....
tríada [trɛ'áɬá] *nf* triad.
triángulo [trɛán'gōōlo] *nm* triangle.
tribu [trɛ'ɦōō] *nf* tribe.
tribuna [trɛɦōō'ná] *nf* (*plataforma*) platform; (*DEPORTE*) stand; (*fig*) public speak-

ing; ~ **de la prensa** press box; ~ **del acusado** (*JUR*) dock; ~ **del jurado** jury box.

tribunal [trĕhōōnál'] *nm* (*juicio*) court; (*comisión*, *fig*) tribunal; (*ESCOL*: *examinadores*) board of examiners; **T~ Supremo** Supreme Court (*US*), High Court (*Brit*); **T~ de Justicia de las Comunidades Europeas** European Court of Justice.

tributar [trĕhōōtár'] *vt* to pay; (*las gracias*) to give; (*cariño*) to show.

tributario, a [trĕhōōtá'ryo, á] *a* (*GEO. POL*) tributary *cpd*; (*ECON*) tax *cpd*, taxation *cpd* ♦ *nm* (*GEO*) tributary ♦ *nm/f* (*COM*) taxpayer; **sistema** ~ tax system.

tributo [trĕhōō'to] *nm* (*COM*) tax.

trice [trĕ'se] *etc vb* V **trizar**.

tricornio [trĕkor'nyo] *nm* three-cornered hat.

tricotar [trĕkotár'] *vi* to knit.

tridimensional [trĕthĕmensyonál'] *a* three-dimensional.

trienal [tryenál'] *a* three-year.

trigal [trĕgál'] *nm* wheat field.

trigésimo, a [trĕhĕ'sĕmo, á] *num* thirtieth.

trigo [trĕ'go] *nm* wheat; ~**s** *nmpl* wheat field(s) (*pl*).

trigueño, a [trĕgĕ'nyo, á] *a* (*pelo*) corn-colored; (*piel*) olive-skinned.

trilogía [trĕlohĕ'á] *nf* triology.

trillado, a [trĕyá'tho, á] *a* threshed; (*fig*) trite, hackneyed.

trilladora [trĕyátho'rá] *nf* threshing machine.

trillar [trĕyár'] *vt* (*AGR*) to thresh; (*fig*) to frequent.

trillizos, as [trĕyē'sos, ás] *nmpl/nfpl* triplets.

trimestral [trĕmestrál'] *a* quarterly; (*ESCOL*) termly.

trimestre [trĕmes'tre] *nm* (*ESCOL*) term; (*COM*) quarter, financial period; (: *pago*) quarterly payment.

trinar [trĕnár'] *vi* (*MUS*) to trill; (*ave*) to sing, warble; **está que trina** he's hopping mad.

trincar [trĕnkár'] *vt* (*atar*) to tie up; (*NAUT*) to lash; (*agarrar*) to pinion.

trinchante [trĕntchán'te] *nm* (*para cortar carne*) carving knife; (*tenedor*) meat fork.

trinchar [trĕntchár'] *vt* to carve.

trinchera [trĕntche'rá] *nf* (*fosa*) trench; (*para vía*) cutting; (*impermeable*) trench-coat.

trineo [trĕne'o] *nm* sled (*US*), sledge (*Brit*).

trinidad [trĕnĕtháth'] *nf* trio; (*REL*): **la T~** the Trinity.

trino [trĕ'no] *nm* trill.

trinque [trĕn'ke] *etc vb* V **trincar**.

trinquete [trĕnke'te] *nm* (*TEC*) pawl; (*NAUT*) foremast.

tripa [trĕ'pá] *nf* (*ANAT*) intestine; (*fig, fam*) belly; ~**s** *nfpl* (*ANAT*) insides; (*CULIN*)

---

tripe *sg*; **tener mucha** ~ to be fat; **me duelen las** ~**s** I have a stomach ache.

tripartito, a [trĕpárte'to, á] *a* tripartite.

triple [trĕ'ple] *a* triple; (*tres veces*) three-fold.

triplicado, a [trĕplĕká'tho, á] *a*: **por** ~ in triplicate.

Trípoli [trĕ'pole] *nm* Tripoli.

tríptico [trĕp'tĕko] *nm* (*ARTE*) triptych; (*documento*) three-part document.

tripulación [trĕpōōlásyon'] *nf* crew.

tripulante [trĕpōōlán'te] *nm/f* crewman/woman.

tripular [trĕpōōlár'] *vt* (*barco*) to man; (*AUTO*) to drive.

triquiñuela [trĕkĕnywe'lá] *nf* trick.

tris [trĕs] *nm* crack; **en un** ~ in an instant; **estar en un** ~ **de hacer algo** to be within an inch of doing sth.

triste [trĕ'ste] *a* (*afligido*) sad; (*sombrío*) melancholy, gloomy; (*desolado*) desolate; (*lamentable*) sorry, miserable; (*viejo*) old; (*único*) single; **no queda sino un** ~ **penique** there's just one miserable penny left.

tristeza [trĕste'sá] *nf* (*aflicción*) sadness; (*melancolía*) melancholy; (*de lugar*) desolation; (*pena*) misery.

tristón, ona [trĕston', oná] *a* sad, down-hearted.

trituradora [trĕtōōrátho'rá] *nf* shredder.

triturar [trĕtōōrár'] *vt* (*moler*) to grind; (*mascar*) to chew; (*documentos*) to shred.

triunfador, a [trĕōōnfátho'r, á] *a* triumphant; (*ganador*) winning ♦ *nm/f* winner.

triunfante [trĕōōnfán'te] *a* triumphant; (*ganador*) winning.

triunfar [trĕōōnfár'] *vi* (*tener éxito*) to triumph; (*ganar*) to win; (*NAIPES*) to be trumps; **triunfan corazones** hearts are trumps; ~ **en la vida** to succeed in life.

triunfo [trĕōōn'fo] *nm* triumph; (*NAIPES*) trump.

trivial [trĕhyál'] *a* trivial.

trivialice [trĕhyálĕ'se] *etc vb* V **trivializar**.

trivializar [trĕhyálĕsár'] *vt* to minimize, play down.

triza [trĕ'sá] *nf* bit, piece; **hacer algo** ~**s** to smash sth to bits; (*papel*) to tear sth to shreds.

trizar [trĕsár'] *vt* to smash to bits.

trocar [trokár'] *vt* (*COM*) to exchange; (*dinero, de lugar*) to change; (*palabras*) to exchange; (*confundir*) to confuse; (*vomitar*) to vomit; ~**se** *vr* (*confundirse*) to get mixed up; (*transformarse*): ~**se (en)** to change (into).

trocha [trotch'á] *nf* (*sendero*) by-path; (*atajo*) short cut.

troche [trotch'e] *nm*: **a** ~ **y moche** *ad* helter-skelter, pell-mell.

trofeo [trofe'o] *nm* (*premio*) trophy; (*éxito*) success.
tromba [trom'bá] *nf* whirlwind; ~ **de agua** cloudburst.
trombón [trombon'] *nm* trombone.
trombosis [trombo'sēs] *nf inv* thrombosis.
trompa [trom'pá] *nf* (*MUS*) horn; (*de elefante*) trunk; (*trompo*) humming top; (*hocico*) snout; (*ANAT*) tube, duct ♦ *nm* (*MUS*) horn player; ~ **de Falopio** Fallopian tube; **cogerse una** ~ (*fam*) to get plastered.
trompada [trompá'ĥá] *nf*, **trompazo** [trompá'so] *nm* (*choque*) bump, bang; (*puñetazo*) punch.
trompeta [trompe'tá] *nf* trumpet; (*clarín*) bugle ♦ *nm* trumpeter.
trompo [trom'po] *nm* spinning top.
trompón [trompon'] *nm* bump.
tronado, a [troná'ĥo, á] *a* broken-down.
tronar [tronár'] *vt* (*AM*) to shoot ♦ *vi* to thunder; (*fig*) to rage; (*fam*) to go broke.
tronco [tron'ko] *nm* (*de árbol, ANAT*) trunk; (*de planta*) stem; **estar hecho un** ~ to be sound asleep.
tronchar [trontchár'] *vt* (*árbol*) to chop down; (*fig: vida*) to cut short; (*esperanza*) to shatter; (*persona*) to tire out; ~**se** *vr* to fall down; ~**se de risa** to split one's sides with laughter.
tronera [trone'rá] *nf* (*MIL*) loophole; (*ARQ*) small window.
trono [tro'no] *nm* throne.
tropa [tro'pá] *nf* (*MIL*) troop; (*soldados*) soldiers *pl*; (*soldados rasos*) ranks *pl*; (*gentío*) mob.
tropecé [tropese'], **tropecemos** [tropese'mos] *etc vb V* **tropezar**.
tropel [tropel'] *nm* (*muchedumbre*) crowd; (*prisa*) rush; (*montón*) throng; **acudir** *etc* **en** ~ to come *etc* in a mad rush.
tropelía [tropelē'á] *nm* outrage.
tropezar [tropesár'] *vi* to trip, stumble; (*fig*) to slip up; ~**se** *vr* (*dos personas*) to run into each other; ~ **con** (*encontrar*) to run into; (*topar con*) to bump into.
tropezón [tropeson'] *nm* trip; (*fig*) blunder; (*traspié*): **dar un** ~ to trip.
tropical [tropēkál'] *a* tropical.
trópico [tro'pēko] *nm* tropic.
tropiece [tropye'se] *etc vb V* **tropezar**.
tropiezo [tropye'so] *etc vb V* **tropezar** ♦ *nm* (*error*) slip, blunder; (*desgracia*) misfortune; (*revés*) setback; (*obstáculo*) snag; (*discusión*) quarrel.
troqué [troke'], **troquemos** [troke'mos] *etc vb V* **trocar**.
trotamundos [trotámōōn'dos] *nm inv* globetrotter.
trotar [trotár'] *vi* to trot; (*viajar*) to travel about.
trote [tro'te] *nm* trot; (*fam*) travel(l)ing; **de**

mucho ~ durable.
Troya [tro'yá] *nf* Troy; **aquí fue** ~ now there's nothing but ruins.
trozo [tro'so] *nm* bit, piece; (*LITERATURA, MUS*) passage; **a** ~**s** in bits.
truco [trōō'ko] *nm* (*habilidad*) knack; (*engaño*) trick; (*CINE*) trick effect *o* photography; ~**s** *nmpl* billiards *sg*; ~ **publicitario** advertising gimmick.
trucha [trōōtch'á] *nf* (*pez*) trout; (*TEC*) crane.
trueco [trwe'ko] *etc vb V* **trocar**.
trueno [trwe'no] *etc vb V* **tronar** ♦ *nm* (*gen*) thunder; (*estampido*) boom; (*de arma*) bang.
trueque [trwe'ke] *etc vb V* **trocar** ♦ *nm* exchange; (*COM*) barter.
trufa [trōō'fá] *nf* (*BOT*) truffle; (*fig: fam*) fib.
truhán, ana [trōōán', áná] *nm/f* rogue.
trulla [trōō'yá] *nf* (*disturbio*) commotion; (*ruido*) noise; (*multitud*) crowd.
truncado, a [trōōnká'ĥo, á] *a* truncated.
truncar [trōōnkár'] *vt* (*cortar*) to truncate; (*la vida etc*) to cut short; (*el desarrollo*) to stunt.
trunque [trōōn'ke] *etc vb V* **truncar**.
tu [tōō] *a* your.
tú [tōō] *pron* you.
tubérculo [tōōĥer'kōōlo] *nm* (*BOT*) tuber.
tuberculosis [tōōĥerkōōlo'sēs] *nf inv* tuberculosis.
tubería [tōōĥerē'á] *nf* pipes *pl*, piping; (*conducto*) pipeline.
tubo [tōō'ĥo] *nm* tube, pipe; ~ **de desagüe** drainpipe; ~ **de ensayo** test-tube; ~ **de escape** exhaust (pipe); ~ **digestivo** alimentary canal.
tuerca [twer'ká] *nf* (*TEC*) nut.
tuerce [twer'se] *etc vb V* **torcer**.
tuerto, a [twer'to, á] *a* (*torcido*) twisted; (*ciego*) blind in one eye ♦ *nm/f* one-eyed person ♦ *nm* (*ofensa*) wrong; **a tuertas** upside-down.
tuerza [twer'sá] *etc vb V* **torcer**.
tueste [twe'ste] *etc vb V* **tostar**.
tuétano [twe'táno] *nm* (*ANAT: médula*) marrow; (*BOT*) pith; **hasta los** ~**s** through and through, utterly.
tufo [tōō'fo] *nm* vapor (*US*), vapour (*Brit*); (*fig: pey*) stench.
tugurio [tōōǥōō'ryo] *nm* slum.
tul [tōōl] *nm* tulle.
tulipán [tōōlēpán'] *nm* tulip.
tullido, a [tōōyē'ĥo, á] *a* crippled; (*cansado*) exhausted.
tumba [tōōm'bá] *nf* (*sepultura*) tomb; (*sacudida*) shake; (*voltereta*) somersault; **ser (como) una** ~ to keep one's mouth shut.
tumbar [tōōmbár'] *vt* to knock down; (*doblar*) to knock over; (*fam: suj: olor*) to

overpower ◆ *vi* to fall down; **~se** *vr* (*echarse*) to lie down; (*extenderse*) to stretch out.

tumbo [tōōm'bo] *nm* (*caída*) fall; (*de vehículo*) jolt; (*momento crítico*) critical moment.

tumefacción [tōōmefáksyon'] *nf* swelling.

tumido, a [tōōmē'tho, á] *a* swollen.

tumor [tōōmor'] *nm* tumor (*US*), tumour (*Brit*).

tumulto [tōōmōōl'to] *nm* turmoil; (*POL*: *motín*) riot.

tuna [tōō'ná] *nf* V **tuno**.

tunante [tōōnán'te] *a* rascally ◆ *nm* rogue, villain; ¡~! you villain!

tunda [tōōn'dá] *nf* (*de tela*) shearing; (*golpeo*) beating.

tundir [tōōndēr'] *vt* (*tela*) to shear; (*hierba*) to mow; (*fig*) to exhaust; (*fam*: *golpear*) to beat.

tunecino, a [tōōnesē'no, á] *a, nm/f* Tunisian.

túnel [tōō'nel] *nm* tunnel.

Túnez [tōō'nes] *nm* Tunis.

túnica [tōō'nēká] *nf* tunic; (*vestido largo*) long dress; (*ANAT. BOT*) tunic.

Tunicia [tōōnē'syá] *nf* Tunisia.

tuno, a [tōō'no, á] *nm/f* (*fam*) rogue ◆ *nf* (*BOT*) prickly pear; (*MUS*) student music group.

tuntún [tōōntōōn']: **al ~** *ad* thoughtlessly.

tupido, a [tōōpē'tho, á] *a* (*denso*) dense; (*fig: torpe*) dim; (*tela*) close-woven.

turba [tōōr'bá] *nf* (*combustible*) turf; (*muchedumbre*) crowd.

turbación [tōōrbásyon'] *nf* (*molestia*) disturbance; (*preocupación*) worry.

turbado, a [tōōrbá'tho, á] *a* (*molesto*) disturbed; (*preocupado*) worried.

turbante [tōōrbán'te] *nm* turban.

turbar [tōōrbár'] *vt* (*molestar*) to disturb; (*incomodar*) to upset; **~se** *vr* to be disturbed.

turbina [tōōrbē'ná] *nf* turbine.

turbio, a [tōōr'byo, á] *a* (*agua etc*) cloudy; (*vista*) dim, blurred; (*tema*) unclear, confused; (*negocio*) shady ◆ *ad* indistinctly.

turbión [tōōrbyon'] *nf* downpour; (*fig*) shower, hail.

turbohélice [tōōrboe'lēse] *nm* turboprop.

turbulencia [tōōrbōōlen'syá] *nf* turbulence; (*fig*) restlessness.

turbulento, a [tōōrbōōlen'to, á] *a* turbulent; (*fig: intranquilo*) restless; (: *ruidoso*) noisy.

turco, a [tōōr'ko, á] *a* Turkish ◆ *nm/f* Turk ◆ *nm* (*LING*) Turkish.

Turena [tōōre'ná] *nf* Touraine.

turgente [tōōrhen'te], **túrgido, a** [tōōr'hētho, á] *a* (*hinchado*) turgid, swollen.

Turín [tōōrēn'] *nm* Turin.

turismo [tōōrēs'mo] *nm* tourism; (*coche*) sedan (*US*), saloon car (*Brit*); **hacer ~** to go traveling (abroad).

turista [tōōrē'stá] *nm/f* tourist; (*vacacionista*) vacationer (*US*), holidaymaker (*Brit*).

turístico, a [tōōrē'stēko, á] *a* tourist *cpd*.

turnar [tōōrnár'] *vi,* **turnarse** *vr* to take (it in) turns.

turno [tōōr'no] *nm* (*oportunidad, orden de prioridad*) opportunity; (*DEPORTE etc*) turn; **es su ~** it's his turn (next); **~ de día/de noche** (*INDUSTRIA*) day/night shift.

turolense [tōōrolen'se] *a* of o from Teruel ◆ *nm/f* native o inhabitant of Teruel.

turquesa [tōōrke'sá] *nf* turquoise.

Turquía [tōōrkē'á] *nf* Turkey.

turrón [tōōrron'] *nm* (*dulce*) nougat; (*fam*) cushy job.

tutear [tōōteár'] *vt* to address as familiar "tú"; **~se** *vr* to be on familiar terms.

tutela [tōōte'lá] *nf* (*legal*) guardianship; (*instrucción*) guidance; **estar bajo la ~ de** (*fig*) to be under the protection of.

tutelar [tōōtelár'] *a* tutelary ◆ *vt* to protect.

tutor, a [tōōtor', á] *nm/f* (*legal*) guardian; (*ESCOL*) tutor; **~ de curso** form master/mistress.

tuve [tōō'he] *etc vb* V **tener.**

tuyo, a [tōō'yo, á] *a* yours, of yours ◆ *pron* yours; **los ~s** (*fam*) your relations, your family.

TVE *nf abr* = *Televisión Española.*

U

U, u [ōō] *nf* (*letra*) U, u; **viraje en U** U-turn; **U de Ulises** U for Uncle.

u *conj* or.

UAR [wár] *nfpl abr* (*Esp*) = *Unidades Antiterroristas Rurales.*

ubérrimo, a [ōōhe'rrēmo, á] *a* very rich, fertile.

ubicación [ōōhēkásyon'] *nf* place, position, location.

ubicar [ōōhēkár'] *vt* to place, situate; (: *fig*) to install in a post; (*esp AM: encontrar*) to find; **~se** *vr* to lie, be located.

ubicuo, a [ōōhē'kwo, á] *a* ubiquitous.

ubique [ōōhē'ke] *etc vb* V **ubicar.**

ubre [ōō'hre] *nf* udder.

Ucrania [ōōkrá'nyá] *nf* Ukraine.

ucraniano, a [ōōkrányá'no, á] *a, nm/f* Ukrainian.

Ud(s) *abr* = **usted(es)**.

UEP *nf abr* = *Unión Europea de Pagos*.

uf [ōōf] *excl* (*cansancio*) phew!; (*repugnancia*) ugh!

ufanarse [ōōfánár'se] *vr* to boast; ~ **de** to pride o.s. on.

ufano, a [ōōfá'no, á] *a* (*arrogante*) arrogant; (*presumido*) conceited.

UGT *nf abr V* **Unión General de Trabajadores**.

ujier [ōōhyer'] *nm* usher; (*portero*) doorman.

úlcera [ōōl'será] *nf* ulcer.

ulcerar [ōōlserár'] *vt* to make sore; ~**se** *vr* to ulcerate.

ULE [ōō'le] *nf abr* (*POL*) = *Unión Liberal Europea*.

ulterior [ōōlteryor'] *a* (*más allá*) farther, further; (*subsecuente*, *siguiente*) subsequent.

ulteriormente [ōōlteryormen'te] *ad* later, subsequently.

últimamente [ōōl'tēmámente] *ad* (*recientemente*) lately, recently; (*finalmente*) finally; (*como último recurso*) as a last resort.

ultimar [ōōltēmár'] *vt* to finish; (*finalizar*) to finalize; (*AM: rematar*) to finish off.

ultimátum [ōōltēmà'tōōm] *nm*, *pl* **ultimátums** ultimatum.

último, a [ōōl'tēmo, á] *a* last; (*más reciente*) latest, most recent; (*más bajo*) bottom; (*más alto*) top; (*fig*) final, extreme; **en las últimas** on one's last legs; **por** ~ finally.

ultra [ōōl'trá] *a* ultra ♦ *nm/f* extreme rightwinger.

ultrajar [ōōltráhár'] *vt* (*escandalizar*) to outrage; (*insultar*) to insult, abuse.

ultraje [ōōltrá'he] *nm* outrage; insult.

ultramar [ōōltrámár'] *nm*: **de** *o* **en** ~ abroad, overseas; **los países de** ~ the overseas countries.

ultramarino, a [ōōltrámárē'no, á] *a* overseas, foreign ♦ *nmpl*: ~**s** groceries; **tienda de** ~**s** grocer's (shop).

ultranza [ōōltrán'sá]: **a** ~ *ad* to the death; (*a todo trance*) at all costs; (*completo*) outright; (*POL etc*) out-and-out, extreme; **un nacionalista a** ~ a rabid nationalist.

ultrarrojo, a [ōōltrárro'ho, á] *a* = **infrarrojo, a**.

ultrasónico, a [ōōltráso'nēko, á] *a* ultrasonic.

ultratumba [ōōltrátōōm'bá] *nf*: **la vida de** ~ the next life; **una voz de** ~ a ghostly voice.

ultravioleta [ōōltráhyole'tá] *a inv* ultraviolet.

ulular [ōōlōōlár'] *vi* to howl; (*búho*) to hoot.

umbral [ōōmbrál'] *nm* (*gen*) threshold; ~ **de rentabilidad** (*COM*) break-even point.

umbroso, a [ōōmbro'so, á], **umbrío, a** [ōōm'brēo, á] *a* shady.

un, una [ōōn, ōō'ná] *artículo indefinido* a ♦ *num* one; *V* **uno**.

unánime [ōōná'nēme] *a* unanimous.

unanimidad [ōōnánēmēthàth'] *nf* unanimity; **por** ~ unanimously.

unción [ōōnsyon'] *nf* anointing.

uncir [ōōnsēr'] *vt* to yoke.

undécimo, a [ōōnde'sēmo, á] *a*, *nm/f* eleventh.

undular [ōōndōōlár'] *vi V* **ondular**.

UNED [ōōned'] *nf abr* (*Esp UNIV*) = *Universidad Nacional de Enseñanza a Distancia*.

ungir [ōōnhēr'] *vt* to rub with ointment; (*REL*) to anoint.

ungüento [ōōngwen'to] *nm* ointment; (*fig*) salve, balm.

únicamente [ōō'nēkámente] *ad* solely; (*solamente*) only.

unicidad [ōōnēsēthàth'] *nf* uniqueness.

único, a [ōō'nēko, á] *a* only; (*solo*) sole, single; (*sin par*) unique; **hijo** ~ only child.

unidad [ōōnēthàth'] *nf* unity; (*TEC*) unit; ~ **móvil** (*TV*) mobile unit; (*INFORM*): ~ **central** system unit, central processing unit; ~ **de control** control unit; ~ **de disco** disk drive; ~ **de entrada/salida** input/output device; ~ **de información** data item; ~ **periférica** peripheral device; ~ **de presentación visual** *o* **de visualización** visual display unit; ~ **procesadora central** central processing unit.

unido, a [ōōnē'tho, á] *a* joined, linked; (*fig*) united.

unificar [ōōnēfēkár'] *vt* to unite, unify.

unifique [ōōnēfē'ke] *etc vb V* **unificar**.

uniformado, a [ōōnēformá'tho, á] *a* uniformed, in uniform.

uniformar [ōōnēformár'] *vt* to make uniform; (*TEC*) to standardize.

uniforme [ōōnēfor'me] *a* uniform, equal; (*superficie*) even ♦ *nm* uniform.

uniformidad [ōōnēformēthàth'] *nf* uniformity; (*llaneza*) levelness, evenness.

unilateral [ōōnēláterál'] *a* unilateral.

unión [ōōnyon'] *nf* (*gen*) union; (*acto*) uniting, joining; (*calidad*) unity; (*TEC*) joint; (*fig*) closeness, togetherness; **en** ~ **con** (together) with, accompanied by; ~ **aduanera** customs union; **U**~ **General de Trabajadores (UGT)** (*Esp*) *Socialist Union Confederation*; **la U**~ **Soviética** the Soviet Union; **punto de** ~ (*TEC*) junction.

unir [ōōnēr'] *vt* (*juntar*) to join, unite; (*atar*) to tie, fasten; (*combinar*) to combine ♦ *vi* (*ingredientes*) to mix well; ~**se** *vr* to join together, unite; (*empresas*) to merge; **les une una fuerte simpatía** they are bound by (a) strong affection; ~**se en matrimonio** to marry.

unísono [ōōnē'sono] *nm*: **al** ~ in unison.

unitario, a [ōōnĭtá'ryo, á] *a* unitary; (*REL*) Unitarian ♦ *nm/f* (*REL*) Unitarian.

universal [ōōnē<u>b</u>ersál'] *a* universal; (*mundial*) world *cpd*; **historia** ~ world history.

universidad [ōōnē<u>b</u>ersēthāth'] *nf* university; ~ **laboral** polytechnic, poly.

universitario, a [ōōnē<u>b</u>ersĭtá'ryo, á] *a* university *cpd* ♦ *nm/f* (*profesor*) lecturer; (*estudiante*) (university) student.

universo [ōōnē<u>b</u>er'so] *nm* universe.

unja [ōōn'há] *etc vb V* **ungir.**

uno, a [ōō'no, á] *num* one ♦ *a* one; (*idéntico*) one and the same ♦ *pron* one; (*alguien*) someone, somebody; **es todo** ~, **es** ~ **y lo mismo** it's all one, it's all the same; **~s (cuantos)** some, a few; **~s 80 dólares** about 80 dollars; ~ **mismo** oneself; ~ **a** ~, ~ **por** ~ one by one; **cada** ~ each *o* every one; **~(s) a otro(s)** each other, one another; **estar en** ~ to be at one; **una de dos** either one thing *o* the other; ~ **que otro** some, a few; **~s y otros** all of them; ~ **y otro** both.

untar [ōōntár'] *vt* (*gen*) to rub; (*engrasar*) to grease, oil; (*MED*) to rub (with ointment); (*fig*) to bribe; **~se** *vr* (*fig*) to be crooked; ~ **el pan con mantequilla** to spread butter on one's bread.

unto [ōōn'to] *nm* animal fat; (*MED*) ointment.

unza [ōōn'sá] *etc vb V* **uncir.**

uña [ōō'nyá] *nf* (*ANAT*) nail; (*del pie*) toenail; (*garra*) claw; (*casco*) hoof; (*arrancaclavos*) nail puller (*US*), claw (*Brit*); **ser** ~ **y carne** to be as thick as thieves; **enseñar** *o* **mostrar** *o* **sacar las ~s** to show one's claws.

UOE *nf abr* (*Esp MIL*) = *Unidad de Operaciones Especiales.*

UPA *nf abr* = *Unión Panamericana.*

UPC *nf abr* (= *unidad procesadora central*) CPU.

UPV *nf abr* (= *unidad de presentación visual*) VDU.

Urales [ōōrá'les] *nmpl* (*tb*: **Montes ~**) Urals.

uranio [ōōrá'nyo] *nm* uranium.

urbanidad [ōōrbánēthāth'] *nf* courtesy, politeness.

urbanismo [ōōrbánēs'mo] *nm* town planning.

urbanista [ōōrbánēs'tá] *nm/f* town planner.

urbanización [ōōrbánēsásyon'] *nf* (*colonia, barrio*) housing development (*US*), housing estate (*Brit*).

urbano, a [ōōrbá'no, á] *a* (*de ciudad*) urban, town *cpd*; (*cortés*) courteous, polite.

urbe [ōōr'<u>b</u>e] *nf* large city, metropolis.

urdimbre [ōōrthēm'bre] *nf* (*de tejido*) warp;

(*intriga*) intrigue.

urdir [ōōrthēr'] *vt* to warp; (*fig*) to plot, contrive.

urgencia [ōōrhen'syá] *nf* urgency; (*prisa*) haste, rush; **salida de** ~ emergency exit; **servicios de** ~ emergency services.

urgente [ōōrhen'te] *a* urgent; (*insistente*) insistent; **carta** ~ special delivery letter.

urgir [ōōrhēr'] *vi* to be urgent; **me urge** I'm in a hurry for it; **me urge terminarlo** I must finish it as soon as I can.

urinario, a [ōōrēná'ryo, á] *a* urinary ♦ *nm* public restroom *o* lavatory.

urja [ōōr'há] *etc vb V* **urgir.**

urna [ōōr'ná] *nf* urn; (*POL*) ballot box; **acudir a las ~s** (*fig*: *persona*) to (go and) vote; (: *gobierno*) to hold an election.

urólogo, a [ōōro'logo, á] *nm/f* urologist.

urraca [ōōrrá'ká] *nf* magpie.

URSS *nf abr* (= *Unión de Repúblicas Socialistas Soviéticas*) USSR.

Uruguay [ōōrōōgwá'ē] *nm*: **El** ~ Uruguay.

uruguayo, a [ōōrōōgwá'yo, á] *a, nm/f* Uruguayan.

usado, a [ōōsá'tho, á] *a* (*gen*) used; (*ropa etc*) worn; **muy** ~ worn out.

usanza [ōōsán'sá] *nf* custom, usage.

usar [ōōsár'] *vt* to use; (*ropa*) to wear; (*tener costumbre*) to be in the habit of ♦ *vi*: ~ **de** to make use of; **~se** *vr* to be used; (*ropa*) to be worn *o* in fashion.

uso [ōō'so] *nm* use; (*MECÁNICA etc*) wear; (*costumbre*) usage, custom; (*moda*) fashion; **al** ~ in keeping with custom; **al** ~ **de** in the style of; **de** ~ **externo** (*MED*) for external application; **estar en el** ~ **de la palabra** to be speaking, have the floor; ~ **y desgaste** (*COM*) wear and tear.

usted [ōōsteth'] *pron* (*sg*: *abr* **Ud** *o* **Vd**: *formal*) you *sg*; **~es** (*pl*: *abr* **Uds** *o* **Vds**: *formal*) you *pl*; (*AM*: *formal y fam*) you *pl*.

usual [ōōswál'] *a* usual.

usuario, a [ōōswá'ryo, á] *nm/f* user; ~ **final** (*COM*) end user.

usufructo [ōōsōōfrōōk'to] *nm* use; ~ **vitalicio (de)** life interest (in).

usura [ōōsōō'rá] *nf* usury.

usurero, a [ōōsōōre'ro, á] *nm/f* usurer.

usurpar [ōōsōōrpár'] *vt* to usurp.

utensilio [ōōtensē'lyo] *nm* tool; (*CULIN*) utensil.

útero [ōō'tero] *nm* uterus, womb.

útil [ōō'tēl] *a* useful; (*servible*) usable, serviceable ♦ *nm* tool; **día** ~ working day, weekday; **es muy** ~ **tenerlo aquí cerca** it's very handy having it here close by.

utilice [ōōtēlē'se] *etc vb V* **utilizar.**

utilidad [ōōtēlēthāth'] *nf* usefulness, utility; (*COM*) profit; **~es líquidas** net profit *sg*.

utilitario [ōōtēlētá'ryo] *nm* (*INFORM*) utility.

utilizar [ōōtēlēsár'] *vt* to use, utilize; (*explo-*

tar) to harness.
utopía [ōōtopē'á] *nf* Utopia.
utópico, a [ōōto'pēko, á] *a* Utopian.
uva [ōō'há] *nf* grape; ~ **pasa** raisin; ~ **de Corinto** currant; **estar de mala** ~ to be in a bad mood.
uve [ōō'he] *nf name of the letter V*; **en forma de** ~ V-shaped; ~ **doble** *name of the letter W*.
UVI [ōō'hē] *nf abr* (*Esp MED*: = *unidad de vigilancia intensiva*) ICU.

V

V, v [he'kor'ta] *nf* (*letra*) V, v; **V de Valencia** V for Victor.
V. *abr* (= *visto*) approved, passed.
v. *abr* (= *voltio*) v.; (= *véase*) v.; (= *verso*) v.
va [bá] *vb* V **ir.**
V.A. *abr* = *Vuestra Alteza.*
vaca [bá'ká] *nf* (*animal*) cow; (*carne*) beef; (*cuero*) cowhide; ~s **flacas/gordas** (*fig*) bad/good times.
vacaciones [bákásyo'nes] *nfpl* vacation *sg* (*US*), holiday(s) (*Brit*); **estar/irse** o **marcharse de** ~ to be/go (away) on vacation.
vacante [bákán'te] *a* vacant, empty ♦ *nf* vacancy.
vacar [bákár'] *vi* to fall vacant; ~ **a** o **en** to engage in.
vaciado, a [básyá'ðo, á] *a* (*hecho en molde*) cast in a mold (*US*) o mould (*Brit*); (*hueco*) hollow ♦ *nm* cast, mold(ing) (*US*), mould(ing) (*Brit*).
vaciar [básyár'] *vt* to empty (out); (*ahuecar*) to hollow out; (*moldear*) to cast; (*INFORM*) to dump ♦ *vi* (*río*) to flow (*en* into); ~**se** *vr* to empty; (*fig*) to blab, spill the beans.
vaciedad [básyeðháð'] *nf* emptiness.
vacilación [básélásyon'] *nf* hesitation.
vacilante [básēlán'te] *a* unsteady; (*habla*) faltering; (*luz*) flickering; (*fig*) hesitant.
vacilar [básēlár'] *vi* to be unsteady; to falter; to flicker; to hesitate, waver; (*persona*) to stagger, stumble; (*memoria*) to fail.
vacío, a [básē'o, á] *a* empty; (*puesto*) vacant; (*desocupado*) idle; (*vano*) vain; (*charla etc*) light, superficial ♦ *nm* emptiness; (*FÍSICA*) vacuum; (*un* ~) (empty) space; **hacer el** ~ **a uno** to ignore sb.
vacuna [bákōō'ná] *nf* vaccine.
vacunar [bákōōnár'] *vt* to vaccinate; ~**se** *vr*

to get vaccinated.
vacuno, a [bákōō'no, á] *a* bovine.
vacuo, a [bá'kwo, á] *a* empty.
vadear [báðeár'] *vt* (*río*) to ford; (*problema*) to overcome; (*persona*) to sound out.
vado [bá'ðo] *nm* ford; (*solución*) solution; (*descanso*) respite.
vagabundear [bágábōōndeár'] *vi* (*andar sin rumbo*) to wander, roam; (*ser vago*) to be a bum (*US*) o tramp.
vagabundo, a [bágábōōn'do, á] *a* wandering; (*pey*) vagrant ♦ *nm/f* (*errante*) wanderer; (*vago*) bum (*US*), tramp.
vagamente [bágámen'te] *ad* vaguely.
vagancia [bágán'syá] *nf* vagrancy.
vagar [bágár'] *vi* to wander; (*pasear*) to saunter up and down; (*no hacer nada*) to be idle ♦ *nm* leisure.
vagido [báhē'ðo] *nm* wail.
vagina [báhē'ná] *nf* vagina.
vago, a [bá'go, á] *a* vague; (*perezoso*) lazy; (*ambulante*) wandering ♦ *nm/f* (*vagabundo*) bum (*US*), tramp; (*flojo*) lazybones *sg*, idler.
vagón [bágon'] *nm* (*de pasajeros*) passenger car (*US*), carriage (*Brit*); (*de mercancías*) freight car (*US*), waggon (*Brit*); ~ **cama/restaurante** sleeping/dining car.
vague [bá'ge] *etc vb* V **vagar.**
vaguedad [bágeðháð'] *nf* vagueness.
vahído [báē'ðo] *nm* dizzy spell.
vaho [bá'o] *nm* (*vapor*) steam; (*olor*) smell; (*respiración*) breath; ~s *nmpl* (*MED*) inhalation *sg*.
vaina [bá'ēná] *nf* sheath.
vainilla [báēnē'yá] *nf* vanilla.
vainita [báēnē'tá] *nf* (*AM*) green o French bean.
vais [báēs] *vb* V **ir.**
vaivén [báēben'] *nm* to-and-fro movement; (*de tránsito*) coming and going; **vaivenes** *nmpl* (*fig*) ups and downs.
vajilla [báhē'yá] *nf* dishes *pl*; (*una* ~) service; ~ **de porcelana** chinaware.
val [bál], **valdré** [báldre'] *etc vb* V **valer.**
vale [bá'le] *nm* voucher; (*recibo*) receipt; (*pagaré*) I.O.U.; ~ **de regalo** gift certificate (*US*) o voucher (*Brit*).
valedero, a [báleðhe'ro, á] *a* valid.
valenciano, a [bálensyá'no, á] *a, nm/f* Valencian ♦ *nm* (*LING*) Valencian.
valentía [bálentē'á] *nf* courage, bravery; (*pey*) boastfulness; (*acción*) heroic deed.
valentísimo, a [bálentē'sēmo, á] *a* (*superl de* **valiente**) very brave, courageous.
valentón, ona [bálenton', oná] *a* blustering.
valer [báler'] *vt* to be worth; (*MAT*) to equal; (*costar*) to cost; (*amparar*) to aid, protect ♦ *vi* (*ser útil*) to be useful; (*ser válido*) to be valid; ~**se** *vr* to defend o.s. ♦ *nm* worth, value; ~ **la pena** to be worth-

while; ¿**vale?** O.K.?; ¡**vale!** (¡*basta!*) that'll
do!; ¡**eso no vale!** that doesn't count!; **no
vale nada** it's no good; (*mercancía*) it's
worthless; (*argumento*) it's no use; **no vale
para nada** he's no good at all; ~**se de** to
make use of, take advantage of; ~**se por sí
mismo** to help o manage by o.s.
valga [bál'ga] *etc vb V* **valer.**
valía [bálē'á] *nf* worth; **de gran** ~ (*objeto*)
very valuable.
validar [bálēthár'] *vt* to validate; (*POL*) to
ratify.
validez [bálēthes'] *nf* validity; **dar** ~ **a** to
validate.
válido, a [bá'lētho, á] *a* valid.
valiente [bályen'te] *a* brave, valiant; (*audaz*) bold; (*pey*) boastful; (*con ironía*) fine,
wonderful ♦ *nm/f* brave man/woman.
valija [bálē'há] *nf* case; (*AM*) suitcase;
(*mochila*) satchel; (*CORREOS*) mailbag; ~
diplomática diplomatic pouch (*US*) o bag
(*Brit*).
valioso, a [bályo'so, á] *a* valuable; (*rico*)
wealthy.
valor [bálor'] *nm* value, worth; (*precio*)
price; (*valentía*) courage; (*importancia*)
importance; (*cara*) nerve; **sin** ~ worthless; ~ **adquisitivo** o **de compra** purchasing power; **dar** ~ **a** to attach importance
to; **quitar** ~ **a** to minimize the importance
of; (*COM*): ~ **según balance** book value;
~ **comercial** o **de mercado** market value;
~ **contable/desglosado** asset/break-up
value; ~ **de escasez** scarcity value; ~ **intrínseco** intrinsic value; ~ **a la par** par
value; ~ **neto** net worth; ~ **de rescate/de
sustitución** surrender/replacement value; *V
tb* **valores.**
valoración [bálorásyon'] *nf* valuation.
valorar [bálorár'] *vt* to value; (*tasar*) to
price; (*fig*) to assess.
valores [bálo'res] *nmpl* (*COM*) securities; ~
en cartera o **habidos** investments.
vals [báls] *nm* waltz.
válvula [bál'hoolá] *nf* valve.
valla [bá'ya] *nf* fence; (*DEPORTE*) hurdle;
(*fig*) barrier.
vallar [báyár'] *vt* to fence in.
valle [bá'ye] *nm* valley, vale.
vallisoletano, a [báyēsoletá'no, á] *a* of o
from Valladolid ♦ *nm/f* native o inhabitant
of Valladolid.
vamos [bá'mos] *vb V* **ir.**
vampiro, iresa [bámpē'ro, ēre'sá] *nm/f*
vampire ♦ *nf* (*CINE*) vamp, femme fatale.
van [bán] *vb V* **ir.**
vanagloriarse [bánágloryár'se] *vr* to boast.
vandalismo [bándálēs'mo] *nm* vandalism.
vándalo, a [bán'dálo, á] *nm/f* vandal.
vanguardia [bángwár'dyá] *nf* vanguard; **de**
~ (*ARTE*) avant-garde; **estar en** o **ir a la** ~

de (*fig*) to be in the forefront of.
vanidad [bánētháth'] *nf* vanity; (*inutilidad*)
futility; (*irrealidad*) unreality.
vanidoso, a [bánētho'so, á] *a* vain, conceited.
vano, a [bá'no, á] *a* (*irreal*) unreal; (*irracio-
nal*) unreasonable; (*inútil*) vain, useless;
(*persona*) vain, conceited; (*frívolo*) frivolous.
vapor [bápor'] *nm* vapor (*US*), vapour
(*Brit*); (*vaho*) steam; (*de gas*) fumes *pl*;
(*neblina*) mist; ~**es** *nmpl* (*MED*) hysterics;
al ~ (*CULIN*) steamed.
vaporice [bápore'se] *etc vb V* **vaporizar.**
vaporizador [bápore̊sáthor'] *nm* (*perfume
etc*) spray.
vaporizar [báporēsár'] *vt* to vaporize;
(*perfume*) to spray.
vaporoso, a [báporo'so, á] *a* vaporous; (*va-
hoso*) steamy; (*tela*) light, airy.
vaque [bá'ke] *etc vb V* **vacar.**
vaquería [bákerē'á] *nf* dairy.
vaquero, a [báke'ro, á] *a* cattle *cpd* ♦ *nm*
cowboy; ~**s** *nmpl* jeans.
vaquilla [bákē'yá] *nf* heifer.
vara [bá'rá] *nf* stick, pole; (*TEC*) rod; ~ **mágica** magic wand.
varado, a [bárá'tho, á] *a* (*NAUT*) stranded;
estar ~ to be aground.
varar [bárár'] *vt* to beach ♦ *vi*, ~**se** *vr* to be
beached.
varear [báreár'] *vt* to hit, beat; (*frutas*) to
knock down (with poles).
variable [báryá'ble] *a, nf* variable (*tb IN-
FORM*).
variación [báryásyon'] *nf* variation; **sin** ~
unchanged.
variante [báryán'te] *a* variant ♦ *nf* (*alternativa*) alternative; (*AUTO*) bypass.
variar [báryár'] *vt* (*cambiar*) to change; (*poner variedad*) to vary; (*modificar*) to modify; (*cambiar de posición*) to switch around
♦ *vi* to vary; ~ **de** to differ from; ~ **de
opinión** to change one's mind; **para** ~ just
for a change.
variedad [báryetháth'] *nf* variety.
varilla [bárē'yá] *nf* stick; (*BOT*) twig; (*TEC*)
rod; (*de rueda*) spoke; ~ **mágica** magic
wand.
vario, a [bá'ryo, á] *a* (*variado*) varied;
(*multicolor*) motley; (*cambiable*) changeable; ~**s** various, several.
varón [báron'] *nm* male, man.
varonil [báronēl'] *a* manly.
Varsovia [bárso'hyá] *nf* Warsaw.
vas [bás] *vb V* **ir.**
vasco, a [bás'ko, á], **vascongado, a**
[báskongá'tho, á] *a, nm/f* Basque ♦ *nm*
(*LING*) Basque ♦ *nfpl:* **las Vascongadas** the
Basque Country *sg* o Provinces.
vascuence [báskwen'se] *nm* (*LING*) Basque.

vaselina [básĕlē'ná] *nf* Vaseline ®.
vasija [bás̆'há] *nf* (earthenware) vessel.
vaso [bá'so] *nm* glass, tumbler; vessel; (*cantidad*) glass(ful); ~ **de vino** glass of wine; ~ **para vino** wineglass.
vástago [bá'stá̆go] *nm* (*BOT*) shoot; (*TEC*) rod; (*fig*) offspring.
vasto, a [bá'sto, á] *a* vast, huge.
váter [bá'ter] *nm* restroom (*US*), lavatory.
Vaticano [bátĕká'no] *nm*: **el** ~ the Vatican; **la Ciudad del** ~ the Vatican City.
vaticinar [bátĕsĕnár'] *vt* to prophesy, predict.
vaticinio [bátĕsē'nyo] *nm* prophecy.
vatio [bá'tyo] *nm* (*ELEC*) watt.
vaya [bá'yá] *etc vb* V **ir**.
Vda. *abr* = **viuda**.
Vd(s) *abr* = **usted(es)**.
ve [be] *vb* V **ir**, **ver**.
vea [be'á] *etc vb* V **ver**.
vecindad [besēndá̆t̆h'] *nf*, **vecindario** [besēndá'ryo] *nm* neighborhood (*US*), neighbourhood (*Brit*); (*habitantes*) residents *pl*.
vecinal [besēnál'] *a* (*camino, impuesto etc*) local.
vecino, a [besē'no, á] *a* neighboring (*US*), neighbouring (*Brit*) ♦ *nm/f* neighbor (*US*), neighbour (*Brit*); (*residente*) resident; **somos** ~**s** we live next door to one another.
veda [be'̆há] *nf* prohibition; (*temporada*) closed (*US*) *o* close (*Brit*) season.
vedado [be'̆há'̆ho] *nm* preserve.
vedar [be'̆hár'] *vt* (*prohibir*) to ban, prohibit; (*idea, plan*) to veto; (*impedir*) to stop, prevent.
vedette [be'̆het'] *nf* (*TEATRO, CINE*) star(let).
vega [be'̆gá] *nf* fertile plain *o* valley.
vegetación [behetásyon'] *nf* vegetation.
vegetal [behetál'] *a*, *nm* vegetable.
vehemencia [beemen'syá] *nf* (*insistencia*) vehemence; (*pasión*) passion; (*fervor*) fervor (*US*), fervour (*Brit*); (*violencia*) violence.
vehemente [beemen'te] *a* vehement; passionate; fervent; violent.
vehículo [beē'koōlo] *nm* vehicle; (*MED*) carrier; ~ **de servicio público** public service vehicle; ~ **espacial** spacecraft.
veinte [be'ēnte] *num* twenty; (*orden, fecha*) twentieth; **el siglo** ~ the twentieth century.
veintena [beēnte'ná] *nf*: **una** ~ (about) twenty, a score.
vejación [behásyon'] *nf* vexation; (*humillación*) humiliation.
vejamen [behá'men] *nm* satire.
vejar [behár'] *vt* (*irritar*) to annoy, vex; (*humillar*) to humiliate.
vejez [behes'] *nf* old age.
vejiga [behē'̆gá] *nf* (*ANAT*) bladder.

vela [be'lá] *nf* (*de cera*) candle; (*NAUT*) sail; (*insomnio*) sleeplessness; (*vigilia*) vigil; (*MIL*) sentry duty; (*fam*) snot; **a toda** ~ (*NAUT*) under full sail; **estar a dos** ~**s** (*fam*) to be broke; **pasar la noche en** ~ to have a sleepless night.
velado, a [belá'̆ho, á] *a* veiled; (*sonido*) muffled; (*FOTO*) blurred ♦ *nf* soirée.
velador [belá̆t̆hor'] *nm* watchman; (*candelero*) candlestick.
velar [belár'] *vt* (*vigilar*) to keep watch over; (*cubrir*) to veil ♦ *vi* to stay awake; ~ **por** to watch over, look after.
velatorio [belá̆to'ryo] *nm* (*funeral*) wake.
veleidad [beleē̆tháth'] *nf* (*ligereza*) fickleness; (*capricho*) whim.
velero [bele'ro] *nm* (*NAUT*) sailing ship; (*AVIAT*) glider.
veleta [bele'tá] *nm/f* fickle person ♦ *nf* weather vane.
veliz [belēs'] *nm* (*AM*) suitcase.
velo [be'lo] *nm* veil; ~ **de paladar** (*ANAT*) soft palate.
velocidad [belosē̆tháth'] *nf* speed; (*TEC*) rate, pace, velocity; (*MECÁNICA, AUTO*) gear; **¿a qué** ~? how fast?; **de alta** ~ high-speed; **cobrar** ~ to pick up *o* gather speed; **meter la segunda** ~ to shift into second gear; ~ **máxima de impresión** (*INFORM*) maximum print speed.
velocímetro [belosē'metro] *nm* speedometer.
velódromo [belo'̆thromo] *nm* cycle track.
veloz [belos'] *a* fast, swift.
vello [be'yo] *nm* down, fuzz.
vellón [beyon'] *nm* fleece.
velloso [beyo'so, á] *a* fuzzy.
velludo, a [beyoō'̆tho, á] *a* shaggy ♦ *nm* plush, velvet.
ven [ben] *vb* V **venir**.
vena [be'ná] *nf* vein; (*fig*) vein, disposition; (*GEO*) seam, vein.
venablo [bená'blo] *nm* javelin.
venado [bená'̆tho] *nm* deer; (*CULIN*) venison.
venal [benál'] *a* (*ANAT*) venous; (*pey*) venal.
venalidad [benálē̆tháth'] *nf* venality.
vencedor, a [bensē̆hor', á] *a* victorious ♦ *nm/f* victor, winner.
vencer [benser'] *vt* (*dominar*) to defeat, beat; (*derrotar*) to vanquish; (*superar, controlar*) to overcome, master ♦ *vi* (*triunfar*) to win, triumph; (*pago*) to fall due; (*plazo*) to expire; **dejarse** ~ to yield, give in.
vencido, a [bensē'̆tho, á] *a* (*derrotado*) defeated, beaten; (*COM*) payable, due ♦ *ad*: **pagar** ~ to pay in arrears; **le pagan por meses** ~**s** he is paid at the end of the month; **darse por** ~ to give up.

vencimiento [bensēmyen'to] *nm* collapse; (*COM*: *plazo*) expiration; **a su** ~ when it falls due.

venda [ben'dá] *nf* bandage.

vendaje [bendá'he] *nm* bandage, dressing.

vendar [bendár'] *vt* to bandage; ~ **los ojos** to blindfold.

vendaval [bendáhál'] *nm* (*viento*) gale; (*huracán*) hurricane.

vendedor, a [bendethor', á] *nm/f* seller; ~ **ambulante** hawker, peddler (*US*), pedlar (*Brit*).

vender [bender'] *vt* to sell; (*comerciar*) to market; (*traicionar*) to sell out, betray; ~**se** *vr* to be sold; ~ **al contado/al por mayor/al por menor/a plazos** to sell for cash/wholesale/retail/on credit; **"se vende"** "for sale"; **"véndese coche"** "car for sale"; ~ **al descubierto** to sell short.

vendimia [bendē'myá] *nf* grape harvest; **la** ~ **de 1973** the 1973 vintage.

vendré [bendre'] *etc vb V* **venir.**

Venecia [bene'syá] *nf* Venice.

veneciano, a [benesyá'no, á] *a, nm/f* Venetian.

veneno [bene'no] *nm* poison, venom.

venenoso, a [beneno'so, á] *a* poisonous.

venerable [benerá'ble] *a* venerable.

veneración [benerásyon'] *nf* veneration.

venerar [benerár'] *vt* (*reconocer*) to venerate; (*adorar*) to worship.

venéreo, a [bene'reo, á] *a* venereal.

venero [bene'ro] *nm* (*veta*) seam, lode; (*fuente*) spring.

venezolano, a [benesolá'no, á] *a, nm/f* Venezuelan.

Venezuela [beneswe'lá] *nf* Venezuela.

venga [ben'gá] *etc vb V* **venir.**

vengador, a [bengáthor', á] *a* avenging ♦ *nm/f* avenger.

venganza [bengán'sá] *nf* vengeance, revenge.

vengar [bengár'] *vt* to avenge; ~**se** *vr* to take revenge.

vengativo, a [bengátē'bo, á] *a* (*persona*) vindictive.

vengue [ben'ge] *etc vb V* **vengar.**

venia [be'nyá] *nf* (*perdón*) pardon; (*permiso*) consent; **con su** ~ by your leave.

venial [benyál'] *a* venial.

venida [benē'thá] *nf* (*llegada*) arrival; (*regreso*) return; (*fig*) rashness.

venidero, a [benēthe'ro, á] *a* coming, future; **en lo** ~ in (the) future.

venir [benēr'] *vi* to come; (*llegar*) to arrive; (*ocurrir*) to happen; ~**se abajo** *vr*: ~**se abajo** to collapse; ~ **a menos** (*persona*) to lose status; (*empresa*) to go downhill; ~ **bien** to be suitable, come just right; (*ropa, gusto*) to suit; ~ **mal** to be unsuitable *o* inconvenient, come awkwardly; **el año que viene**

next year; **¡ven acá!** come (over) here!; **¡venga!** (*fam*) come on!

venta [ben'tá] *nf* (*COM*) sale; (*posada*) inn; ~ **a plazos** purchase on the installment plan (*US*), hire purchase (*Brit*); ~ **al contado/al por mayor/al por menor** *o* **al detalle** cash sale/wholesale/retail; ~ **a domicilio** door-to-door selling; ~ **y arrendamiento al vendedor** sale and lease back; ~ **de liquidación** clearance sale; **estar de** *o* **en** ~ to be (up) for sale *o* on the market; ~**s brutas** gross sales; ~**s a término** future (*US*) *o* forward (*Brit*) sales.

ventaja [bentá'há] *nf* advantage; **llevar la** ~ (*en carrera*) to be leading *o* ahead.

ventajoso, a [bentáho'so, á] *a* advantageous.

ventana [bentá'ná] *nf* window; ~ **de guillotina/galería** sash/bay window; ~ **de la nariz** nostril.

ventanilla [bentánē'yá] *nf* (*de taquilla, tb INFORM*) window.

ventear [benteár'] *vt* (*ropa*) to hang out to dry; (*oler*) to sniff ♦ *vi* (*investigar*) to investigate; (*soplar*) to blow; ~**se** *vr* (*romperse*) to crack; (*ANAT*) to break wind.

ventilación [bentēlásyon'] *nf* ventilation; (*corriente*) draught; (*fig*) airing.

ventilador [bentēláthor'] *nm* ventilator; (*eléctrico*) fan.

ventilar [bentēlár'] *vt* to ventilate; (*a secar*) to put out to dry; (*fig*) to air, discuss.

ventisca [bentēs'ká] *nf*, **ventisquero** [bentēske'ro] *nm* blizzard; (*nieve amontonada*) snowdrift.

ventolera [bentole'rá] *nf* (*ráfaga*) gust of wind; (*idea*) whim, wild idea; **le dio la** ~ **de comprarlo** he had a sudden notion to buy it.

ventosear [bentoseár'] *vi* to break wind.

ventoso, a [bento'so, á] *a* windy.

ventrículo [bentrē'kōolo] *nm* ventricle.

ventrílocuo, a [bentrē'lokwo, á] *nm/f* ventriloquist.

ventriloquia [bentrēlo'kyá] *nf* ventriloquism.

ventura [bentōo'rá] *nf* (*felicidad*) happiness; (*buena suerte*) luck; (*destino*) fortune; **a la (buena)** ~ at random.

venturoso, a [bentōoro'so, á] *a* happy; (*afortunado*) lucky, fortunate.

venza [ben'sá] *etc vb V* **vencer.**

ver [ber] *vt, vi* to see; (*mirar*) to look at, watch; (*investigar*) to look into; (*entender*) to see, understand; ~**se** *vr* (*encontrarse*) to meet; (*dejarse* ~) to be seen; (*hallarse: en un apuro*) to find o.s., be ♦ *nm* looks *pl*, appearance; **a** ~ let's see; **a** ~ **si ...** I wonder if ...; **por lo que veo** apparently; **dejarse** ~ to become apparent; **no tener**

nada que ~ con to have nothing to do with; **a mi modo de ~** as I see it; **merece ~se** it's worth seeing; **no lo veo** I can't see it; **¡nos vemos!** see you (later)!; **¡habráse visto!** did you ever! (*fam*); **ya se ve que ...** it is obvious that ...; **si te vi no me acuerdo** they *etc* just don't want to know.

vera |bc'rá| *nf* edge, verge; (*de río*) bank; **a la ~ de** near, next to.

veracidad |bcrásēt̬há̬t̬h'| *nf* truthfulness.

veraneante |bcráncán'tc| *nm/f* (summer) vacationer (*US*), holidaymaker (*Brit*).

veranear |bcráncár'| *vi* to spend the summer.

veraneo |bcránc'o| *nm*: **estar de ~** to be on summer vacation (*US*), be away on (one's summer) holiday (*Brit*); **lugar de ~** summer resort.

veraniego, a |bcrányc'ḡo, á| *a* summer *cpd*.

verano |bcrá'no| *nm* summer.

veras |bc'rás| *nfpl* truth *sg*; **de ~** really, truly; **esto va de ~** this is serious.

veraz |bcrás'| *a* truthful.

verbal |bcr̬bál'| *a* verbal; (*mensaje etc*) oral.

verbena |bcr̬bc'ná| *nf* street party.

verbigracia |bcr̬b̬c̄grá'syá| *ad* for example.

verbo |bcr'b̬o| *nm* verb.

verborragia |bcr̬b̬orrá'hyá|, **verborrea** |bcr̬b̬orrc'á| *nf* verbosity, verbal diarrhea (*US*) *o* diarrhoea (*Brit*).

verboso, a |bcr̬b̬o'so, á| *a* verbose.

verdad |bcr̬t̬há̬t̬h'| *nf* (*lo verídico*) truth; (*fiabilidad*) reliability ♦ *ad* really; **¿~?, ¿no es ~?** isn't it?, aren't you?, don't you? *etc*; **de ~** *a* real, proper; **a decir ~, no quiero** to tell (you) the truth, I don't want to; **la pura ~** the plain truth.

verdaderamente |bcr̬t̬há̬t̬hcrámcn'tc| *ad* really, indeed, truly.

verdadero, a |bcr̬t̬há̬t̬hc'ro, á| *a* (*veraz*) true, truthful; (*fiable*) reliable; (*fig*) real.

verde |bcr'̬t̬hc| *a* green; (*fruta etc*) green, unripe; (*chiste etc*) smutty, dirty ♦ *nm* green; **viejo ~** dirty old man; **poner ~ a uno** to give sb a tongue-lashing.

verdear |bcr̬t̬hcár'|, **verdecer** |bcr̬t̬hcscr'| *vi* to turn green.

verdezca |bcr̬t̬hcs'ká| *etc vb V* **verdecer.**

verdor |bcr̬t̬hor'| *nm* (*lo verde*) greenness; (*BOT*) verdure.

verdugo |bcr̬t̬h̬ōō'ḡo| *nm* executioner; (*BOT*) shoot; (*cardenal*) welt.

verdulero, a |bcr̬t̬h̬ōōlc'ro, á| *nm/f* vegetable merchant (*US*), greengrocer (*Brit*).

verdura |bcr̬t̬h̬ōō'rá| *nf* greenness; **~s** *nfpl* (*CULIN*) greens.

vereda |bcrc'̬t̬há| *nf* path; (*AM*) sidewalk (*US*), pavement (*Brit*); **meter a uno en ~** to bring sb into line.

veredicto |bcrc̬t̬h̬ēk'to| *nm* verdict.

vergonzoso, a |bcr̬ḡonso'so, á| *a* shameful; (*tímido*) timid, bashful.

vergüenza |bcr̬ḡwcn'sá| *nf* shame, sense of shame; (*timidez*) bashfulness; (*pudor*) modesty; **tener ~** to be ashamed; **me da ~ decírselo** I feel too shy *o* it embarrasses me to tell him; **¡qué ~!** (*de situación*) what a disgrace!; (*a persona*) shame on you!

vericueto |bcrēkwc'to| *nm* rough track.

verídico, a |bcrē'̬t̬hēko, á| *a* true, truthful.

verificar |bcrēfēkár'| *vt* to check; (*corroborar*) to verify (*tb INFORM*); (*testamento*) to prove; (*llevar a cabo*) to carry out; **~se** *vr* to occur, happen; (*mitin etc*) to be held; (*profecía etc*) to come *o* prove true.

verifique |bcrēfē'kc| *etc vb V* **verificar.**

verja |bcr'há| *nf* iron gate; (*cerca*) railing(s) (*pl*); (*rejado*) grating.

vermut |bcrm̬ōō'|, *pl* **vermuts** *nm* vermouth.

verosímil |bcrosē'mēl| *a* likely, probable; (*relato*) credible.

verosimilitud |bcrosēmēlētōō̬t̬h'| *nf* likeliness, probability.

verruga |bcrr̬ōō'ḡá| *nf* wart.

versado, a |bcrsá'̬t̬ho, á| *a*: **~ en** versed in.

Versalles |bcrsä'ycs| *nm* Versailles.

versar |bcrsár'| *vi* to go round, turn; **~ sobre** to deal with, be about.

versátil |bcrsá'tēl| *a* versatile.

versículo |bcrsē'kōōlo| *nm* (*REL*) verse.

versión |bcrsyon'| *nf* version; (*traducción*) translation.

verso |bcr'so| *nm* (*gen*) verse; **un ~** a line of poetry; **~ libre/suelto** free/blank verse.

vértebra |bcr'tcb̬rá| *nf* vertebra.

vertebral |bcrtcb̬rál'| *a* vertebral; **columna ~** spine.

verter |bcrtcr'| *vt* (*vaciar*) to empty, pour (out); (*tirar*) to dump ♦ *vi* to flow.

vertical |bcrtēkál'| *a* vertical; (*postura, piano etc*) upright ♦ *nf* vertical.

vértice |bcr'tēsc| *nm* vertex, apex.

vertiente |bcrtycn'tc| *nf* slope.

vertiginoso, a |bcrtēhēno'so, á| *a* giddy, dizzy.

vértigo |bcr'tēḡo| *nm* vertigo; (*mareo*) dizziness; (*actividad*) intense activity; **de ~** (*fam: velocidad*) giddy; (: *ruido*) tremendous; (: *talento*) fantastic.

vesícula |bcsē'kōōlá| *nf* blister; **~ biliar** gall bladder.

vespertino, a |bcspcrtē'no, á| *a* evening *cpd*.

vestíbulo |bcstē'b̬ōōlo| *nm* hall; (*de teatro*) foyer.

vestido |bcstē'̬t̬ho| *nm* (*ropa*) clothes *pl*, clothing; (*de mujer*) dress.

vestigio |bcstē'hyo| *nm* (*trazo*) trace; (*señal*) sign; **~s** *nmpl* remains.

vestimenta [bestēmen'tá] *nf* clothing.

vestir [bestēr'] *vt* (*poner: ropa*) to put on; (*llevar: ropa*) to wear; (*cubrir*) to clothe, cover; (*pagar: la ropa*) to clothe, pay for the clothing of; (*sastre*) to make clothes for ♦ *vi* (*ponerse: ropa*) to dress; (*verse bien*) to look good; ~**se** *vr* to get dressed, dress o.s.; **traje de** ~ (*formal*) formal suit; **estar vestido de** to be dressed *o* clad in; (*como disfraz*) to be dressed as.

vestuario [bestwá'ryo] *nm* clothes *pl*, wardrobe; (*TEATRO: para actores*) dressing room; (: *para público*) cloakroom; (*DEPORTE*) locker room.

Vesubio [besōō'ḫyo] *nm* Vesuvius.

veta [be'tá] *nf* (*vena*) vein, seam; (*raya*) streak; (*de madera*) grain.

vetar [betár'] *vt* to veto.

veterano, a [beterá'no, á] *a*, *nm/f* veteran.

veterinario, a [beterēná'ryo, á] *nm/f* vet(erinary surgeon) ♦ *nf* veterinary science.

veto [be'to] *nm* veto.

vetusto, a [betōō'sto, á] *a* ancient.

vez [bes] *nf* time; (*turno*) turn; **a la** ~ **que** at the same time as; **a su** ~ in its turn; **cada** ~ **más/menos** more and more/less and less; **una** ~ once; **dos veces** twice; **de una** ~ in one fell swoop; **de una** ~ **para siempre** once and for all; **en** ~ **de** instead of; **a veces** sometimes; **otra** ~ again; **una y otra** ~ repeatedly; **pocas veces** seldom; **de** ~ **en cuando** from time to time; **7 veces 9** 7 times 9; **hacer las veces de** to stand in for; **tal** ~ perhaps; **¿lo viste alguna** ~**?** did you ever see it?; **¿cuántas veces?** how often?; **érase una** ~ once upon a time (there was).

v. g., v. gr. *abr* (= *verbigracia*) viz.

vía [bē'á] *nf* (*calle*) road; (*ruta*) track, route; (*FERRO*) line; (*fig*) way; (*ANAT*) passage, tube ♦ *prep* via, by way of; **por** ~ **bucal** orally; **por** ~ **judicial** by legal means; **por** ~ **oficial** through official channels; **por** ~ **de** by way of; **en** ~**s de** in the process of; **un país en** ~**s de desarrollo** a developing country; ~ **aérea** airway; **V**~ **Láctea** Milky Way; ~ **pública** public highway *o* thoroughfare; ~ **única** one-way street; **el tren está en la** ~ **8** the train is (standing) at platform 8.

viable [byá'ḫle] *a* (*COM*) viable; (*plan etc*) feasible.

viaducto [byáḫōōk'to] *nm* viaduct.

viajante [byáḫán'te] *nm* traveling salesman.

viajar [byáḫár'] *vi* to travel, take a trip.

viaje [byá'he] *nm* trip; (*gira*) tour; (*NAUT*) voyage; (*COM: carga*) load; **los** ~**s** travel *sg*; **estar de** ~ to be on a journey; ~ **de ida y vuelta** round trip; ~ **de novios** honeymoon.

viajero, a [byáhe'ro, á] *a* traveling (*US*), travelling (*Brit*); (*ZOOL*) migratory ♦ *nm/f* (*quien viaja*) traveller; (*pasajero*) passenger.

vial [byál] *a* road *cpd*, traffic *cpd*.

vianda [byán'dá] *nf* (*tb*: ~**s**) food.

viáticos [byá'tēkos] *nmpl* (*COM*) traveling (*US*) *o* travelling (*Brit*) expenses.

víbora [bē'ḫorá] *nf* viper.

vibración [bēḫrásyon'] *nf* vibration.

vibrador [bēḫráḫor'] *nm* vibrator.

vibrante [bēḫrán'te] *a* vibrant, vibrating.

vibrar [bēḫrár'] *vt* to vibrate ♦ *vi* to vibrate; (*pulsar*) to throb, beat, pulsate.

vicario [bēká'ryo] *nm* curate.

vicecónsul [bēsekon'sōōl] *nm* vice-consul.

vicegerente [bēseheren'te] *nm/f* assistant manager.

vicepresidente [bēsepresēḫen'te] *nm/f* vice president; (*de comité etc*) vice-chairman.

viceversa [bēseḫer'sá] *ad* vice versa.

viciado, a [bēsyá'ḫo, á] *a* (*corrompido*) corrupt; (*contaminado*) foul, contaminated.

viciar [bēsyár'] *vt* (*pervertir*) to pervert; (*adulterar*) to adulterate; (*falsificar*) to falsify; (*JUR*) to nullify; (*estropear*) to spoil; (*sentido*) to twist; ~**se** *vr* to become corrupted; (*aire, agua*) to be(come) polluted.

vicio [bē'syo] *nm* (*libertinaje*) vice; (*mala costumbre*) bad habit; (*mimo*) spoiling; (*alabeo*) warp, warping; **de** *o* **por** ~ out of sheer habit.

vicioso, a [bēsyo'so, á] *a* (*muy malo*) vicious; (*corrompido*) depraved; (*mimado*) spoiled ♦ *nm/f* depraved person; (*adicto*) addict.

vicisitud [bēsēsētōōth'] *nf* vicissitude.

víctima [bēk'tēmá] *nf* victim; (*de accidente etc*) casualty.

victoria [bēkto'ryá] *nf* victory.

victorioso, a [bēktoryo'so, á] *a* victorious.

vicuña [bēkōō'nyá] *nf* vicuna.

vid [bēth] *nf* vine.

vida [bē'thá] *nf* life; (*duración*) lifetime; (*modo de vivir*) way of life; **¡**~**!, ¡**~ **mía!** (*saludo cariñoso*) my love!; **de por** ~ for life; **de** ~ **airada** *o* **libre** loose-living; **en la/mi** ~ never; **estar con** ~ to be still alive; **ganarse la** ~ to earn one's living; **¡esto es** ~**!** this is the life!; **le va la** ~ **en esto** his life depends on it.

vídeo [bē'ḫeo] *nm* video; (*aparato*) video (recorder); **cinta de** ~ videotape; **película de** ~ videofilm; **grabar en** ~ to record, (video)tape; ~ **compuesto/inverso** (*INFORM*) composite/reverse video.

videoconferencia [bēḫeokonferen'syá] *nf* video-conference.

videodatos [bēḫeoḫá'tos] *nmpl* (*COM*) videotex (*US*), viewdata (*Brit*).

videojuego [beðeohwe'ɣo] *nm* video game.
videotex [beðeoteks'] *nm* teletext ®.
vidriero, a [beðrye'ro, á] *nm/f* glazier ♦ *nf* (*ventana*) stained-glass window; (*AM: de tienda*) shop window; (*puerta*) glass door.
vidrio [beð'ryo] *nm* glass; ~ **cilindrado/ inastillable** plate/splinter-proof glass.
vidrioso, a [beðryo'so, á] *a* glassy; (*frágil*) fragile, brittle; (*resbaladizo*) slippery.
viejo, a [bye'ho, á] *a* old ♦ *nm/f* old man/ woman; **mi** ~/**vieja** (*fam*) my old man/ woman; **hacerse** *o* **ponerse** ~ to grow *o* get old.
Viena [bye'ná] *nf* Vienna.
viene [bye'ne] *etc vb V* **venir**.
vienés, esa [byenes', esá] *a, nm/f* Viennese.
viento [byen'to] *nm* wind; (*olfato*) scent; **contra** ~ **y marea** at all costs; **ir** ~ **en popa** to go splendidly; (*negocio*) to prosper.
vientre [byen'tre] *nm* belly; (*matriz*) womb; ~**s** *nmpl* bowels; **hacer de** ~ to have a movement of the bowels.
vier. *abr* (= *viernes*) Fri.
viernes [byer'nes] *nm inv* Friday; **V**~ **Santo** Good Friday.
vierta [byer'tá] *etc vb V* **verter**.
Vietnam [byetnám'] *nm:* **el** ~ Vietnam.
vietnamita [byetnáme'tá] *a, nm/f* Vietnamese.
viga [be'ɣá] *nf* beam, rafter; (*de metal*) girder.
vigencia [behen'syá] *nf* validity; (*de contrato etc*) term, life; **estar/entrar en** ~ to be in/come into effect *o* force.
vigente [behen'te] *a* valid, in force; (*imperante*) prevailing.
vigésimo, a [behe'semo, á] *num* twentieth.
vigía [behe'á] *nm* look-out ♦ *nf* (*atalaya*) watchtower; (*acción*) watching.
vigilancia [behelán'syá] *nf* vigilance.
vigilante [behelán'te] *a* vigilant ♦ *nm* caretaker; (*en cárcel*) guard (*US*), warder (*Brit*); (*en almacén*) floor-walker (*US*), shopwalker (*Brit*); ~ **de noche** *o* **nocturno** night watchman.
vigilar [behelár'] *vt* to watch over; (*cuidar*) to look after, keep an eye on ♦ *vi* to be vigilant; (*hacer guardia*) to keep watch.
vigilia [vehe'lyá] *nf* wakefulness; (*REL*) fast; **comer de** ~ to fast.
vigor [beɣor'] *nm* vigor (*US*), vigour (*Brit*), vitality; **en** ~ in force; **entrar/poner en** ~ to take/put into effect.
vigoroso, a [beɣoro'so, á] *a* vigorous.
vil [bel] *a* vile, low.
vileza [bele'sá] *nf* vileness; (*acto*) base deed.
vilipendiar [belependyár'] *vt* to vilify, revile.
vilo [be'lo]: **en** ~ *ad* in the air, suspended;

(*fig*) on tenterhooks, in suspense; **estar** *o* **quedar en** ~ to be left in suspense.
villa [be'yá] *nf* (*pueblo*) small town; (*municipalidad*) municipality; **la V**~ (*Esp*) Madrid; ~ **miseria** shanty town.
villorrio [beyo'rryo] *nm* one-horse town, dump; (*AM: barrio pobre*) shanty town.
vinagre [bená'ɣre] *nm* vinegar.
vinagrera [benáɣre'rá] *nf* vinegar bottle; ~**s** *nfpl* cruet stand *sg*.
vinagreta [benáɣre'tá] *nf* French dressing.
vinatería [benáteře'á] *nf* wine shop.
vinatero, a [benáte'ro, á] *a* wine *cpd* ♦ *nm* wine merchant.
vinculación [benkōolásyon'] *nf* (*lazo*) link, bond; (*acción*) linking.
vincular [benkōolár'] *vt* to link, bind.
vínculo [ben'kōolo] *nm* link, bond.
vindicar [bendekár'] *vt* to vindicate; (*vengar*) to avenge; (*JUR*) to claim.
vindique [bende'ke] *etc vb V* **vindicar**.
vinícola [bene'kolá] *a* (*industria*) wine *cpd*; (*región*) wine-growing *cpd*.
vinicultura [benekōoltōo'rá] *nf* wine growing.
vino [be'no] *etc vb V* **venir** ♦ *nm* wine; ~ **de solera/seco/tinto** vintage/dry/red wine; ~ **de Jerez** sherry; ~ **de Oporto** port (wine).
viña [be'nyá] *nf*, **viñedo** [benye'ðo] *nm* vineyard.
violación [byolásyon'] *nf* violation; (*JUR*) offense (*US*), offence (*Brit*), infringement; (*estupro*): ~ (**sexual**) rape; ~ **de contrato** (*COM*) breach of contract.
violar [byolár'] *vt* to violate; (*JUR*) to infringe; (*cometer estupro*) to rape.
violencia [byolen'syá] *nf* (*fuerza*) violence, force; (*embarazo*) embarrassment; (*acto injusto*) unjust act.
violentar [byolentár'] *vt* to force; (*casa*) to break into; (*agredir*) to assault; (*violar*) to violate.
violento, a [byolen'to, á] *a* violent; (*furioso*) furious; (*situación*) embarrassing; (*acto*) forced, unnatural; (*difícil*) awkward; **me es muy** ~ it goes against the grain with me.
violeta [byole'tá] *nf* violet.
violín [byolen'] *nm* violin.
violón [byolon'] *nm* double bass.
violoncelo [byolonse'lo] *nm* cello.
virador [beráðor'] *nm* (*para fotocopiadora*) toner.
viraje [berá'he] *nm* turn; (*de vehículo*) swerve; (*de carretera*) bend; (*fig*) change of direction.
virar [berár'] *vi* to turn; to swerve; to change direction.
virgen [ber'hen] *a* virgin; (*cinta*) blank ♦ *nm/f* virgin; **la Santísima V**~ (*REL*) the Blessed Virgin.

Virgo [bēr'go] *nm* Virgo.
viril [bērēl'] *a* virile.
virilidad [bērēlēthath'] *nf* virility.
virrey [bērre'ē] *nm* viceroy.
virtual [bērtwál'] *a* (*real*) virtual; (*en potencia*) potential.
virtud [bērtooth'] *nf* virtue; **en ~ de** by virtue of.
virtuoso, a [bērtwo'so, á] *a* virtuous ♦ *nm/f* virtuoso.
viruela [bērwe'lá] *nf* smallpox; **~s** *nfpl* pockmarks; **~s locas** chickenpox *sg*.
virulento, a [bēroolen'to, á] *a* virulent.
virus [bē'roos] *nm inv* virus.
viruta [bēroo'tá] *nf* wood o metal shaving.
vis [bēs] *nf*: **~ cómica** sense of humor.
visa [bē'sá] *nf* (*AM*), **visado** [bēsá'tho] *nm* visa; **~ de permanencia** residence permit.
visar [bēsár'] *vt* (*pasaporte*) to visa; (*documento*) to endorse.
viscoso, a [bēsko'so, á] *a* viscous.
visera [bēse'rá] *nf* visor.
visibilidad [bēsēbēlēthath'] *nf* visibility.
visible [bēsē'ble] *a* visible; (*fig*) obvious; **exportaciones/importaciones ~s** (*COM*) visible exports/imports.
visillo [bēsē'yo] *nm* lace curtain.
visión [bēsyon'] *nf* (*ANAT*) vision, (eye)sight; (*fantasía*) vision, fantasy; (*panorama*) view; **ver visiones** to see o be seeing things.
visionario, a [bēsyoná'ryo, á] *a* (*que prevé*) visionary; (*alucinado*) deluded ♦ *nm/f* visionary; (*chalado*) lunatic.
visita [bēsē'tá] *nf* call, visit; (*persona*) visitor; **horas/tarjeta de ~** visiting hours/card; **~ de cortesía/de cumplido/de despedida** courtesy/formal/farewell visit; **hacer una ~** to pay a visit; **ir de ~** to go visiting.
visitar [bēsētár'] *vt* to visit, call on; (*inspeccionar*) to inspect.
vislumbrar [bēsloombrár'] *vt* to glimpse, catch a glimpse of.
vislumbre [bēsloom'bre] *nf* glimpse; (*centelleo*) gleam; (*idea vaga*) glimmer.
viso [bē'so] *nm* (*de metal*) glint, gleam; (*de tela*) sheen; (*aspecto*) appearance; **hay un ~ de verdad en esto** there is an element of truth in this.
visón [bēson'] *nm* mink.
visor [bēsor'] *nm* (*FOTO*) viewfinder.
víspera [bēs'perá] *nf* eve, day before; **la ~ o en ~s de** on the eve of.
vista [bē'stá] *nf* sight, vision; (*capacidad de ver*) (eye)sight; (*mirada*) look(s) (*pl*); (*FOTO etc*) view; (*JUR*) hearing ♦ *nm* customs officer; **a primera ~** at first glance; **~ general** overview; **fijar o clavar la ~ en** to stare at; **hacer la ~ gorda** to turn a blind eye; **volver la ~** to look back; **está a la ~ que** it's obvious that; **a la ~**

(*COM*) on sight; **en ~ de** in view of; **en ~ de que** in view of the fact that; **¡hasta la ~!** so long!, see you!; **con ~s a** with a view to; **V tb visto, a.**
vistazo [bēstá'so] *nm* glance; **dar o echar un ~ a** to glance at.
visto, a [bē'sto, á] *etc vb V* **vestir** ♦ *pp de* **ver** ♦ *a* seen; (*considerado*) considered ♦ *nm*: **~ bueno** approval; **"~ bueno"** "approved"; **por lo ~** evidently; **dar el ~ bueno a algo** to give sth the go-ahead; **está ~ que** it's clear that; **está bien/mal ~** it's acceptable/unacceptable; **está muy ~** it is very common; **estaba ~** it had to be; **~ que** *conj* since, considering that.
vistoso, a [bēsto'so, á] *a* colorful (*US*), colourful (*Brit*); (*alegre*) bright; (*pey*) gaudy.
visualice [bēswálē'se] *etc vb V* **visualizar.**
visualizador [bēswálēsáthor'] *nm* (*INFORM*) display screen, VDU.
visualizar [bēswálēsár'] *vt* (*imaginarse*) to visualize; (*INFORM*) to display.
vital [bētál'] *a* life *cpd*, living *cpd*; (*fig*) vital; (*persona*) lively, vivacious.
vitalicio, a [bētálē'syo, á] *a* for life.
vitamina [bētámē'ná] *nf* vitamin.
vitaminado, a [bētámēná'tho, á] *a* with added vitamins.
vitamínico, a [bētámē'nēko, á] *a* vitamin *cpd*; **complejos ~s** vitamin compounds.
viticultor, a [bētēkooltor', á] *nm/f* vine grower.
viticultura [bētēkooltoo'rá] *nf* vine growing.
vitorear [bētoreár'] *vt* to cheer, acclaim.
vitoriano, a [bētoryá'no, á] *a* of o from Vitoria ♦ *nm/f* native o inhabitant of Vitoria.
vítreo, a [bē'treo, á] *a* vitreous.
vitrina [bētrē'ná] *nf* glass case; (*en casa*) display cabinet.
vituperar [bētooperár'] *vt* to condemn.
vituperio [bētoope'ryo] *nm* (*condena*) condemnation; (*censura*) censure; (*insulto*) insult.
viudo, a [byoo'tho, á] *a* widowed ♦ *nm* widower ♦ *nf* widow.
viudez [byoothes'] *nf* widowhood.
vivacidad [bēbásēthath'] *nf* (*vigor*) vigor (*US*), vigour (*Brit*); (*vida*) vivacity.
vivamente [bēbámen'te] *ad* in lively fashion; (*descripción etc*) vívidly; (*protesta*) sharply; (*emoción*) acutely.
vivaracho, a [bēbárátch'o, á] *a* jaunty, lively; (*ojos*) bright, twinkling.
vivaz [bēbás'] *a* (*que dura*) enduring; (*vigoroso*) vigorous; (*vivo*) lively.
víveres [bē'beres] *nmpl* provisions.
vivero [bēbe'ro] *nm* (*HORTICULTURA*) nursery; (*para peces*) fishpond; (: *COM*) fish farm.
viveza [bēbe'sá] *nf* liveliness; (*agudeza*)

sharpness.

vividor, a [bĕhĕťḩọr', ḁ] a (pey) opportunistic ♦ nm (aprovechado) hustler.

vivienda [bĕḩyen'dá] nf (alojamiento) housing; (morada) dwelling; ~s **protegidas** public housing sg (US), council housing sg (Brit).

viviente [bĕḩyen'te] a living.

vivificar [bĕḩĕfĕkár'] vt to give life to.

vivifique [bĕḩĕfĕ'ke] etc vb V **vivificar**.

vivir [bĕḩĕr'] vt (experimentar) to live o go through ♦ vi (gen, COM): ~ **(de)** to live (by, off, on) ♦ nm life, living; **¡viva!** hurray!; **¡viva el rey!** long live the king!

vivo, a [bĕ'ḩo, ḁ] a living, live, alive; (fig) vivid; (movimiento) quick; (color) bright; (protesta etc) strong; (astuto) smart, clever; **en** ~ (TV etc) live; **llegar a lo** ~ to cut to the quick.

vizcaíno, a [bĕskáĕ'no, ḁ] a, nm/f Biscayan.

Vizcaya [bĕskáʹyá] nf Biscay; **el Golfo de** ~ the Bay of Biscay.

V.M. abr = **Vuestra Majestad.**

V.ºB.º abr = **visto bueno.**

vocablo [boká'ḅlo] nm (palabra) word; (término) term.

vocabulario [bokáḩōōlá'ryo] nm vocabulary, word list.

vocación [bokásyon'] nf vocation.

vocacional [bokásyonál'] nf (AM) ≈ technical college.

vocal [bokál'] a vocal ♦ nm/f member (of a committee etc) ♦ nm non-executive director ♦ nf vowel.

vocalice [bokálĕ'se] etc vb V **vocalizar**.

vocalizar [bokálĕsár'] vt to vocalize.

vocear [boseár'] vt (para vender) to cry; (aclamar) to acclaim; (fig) to proclaim ♦ vi to yell.

vocería [boserĕ'á] nf, **vocerío** [boserĕ'o] nm shouting; (escándalo) hullabaloo.

vocero [bose'ro] nm/f spokesman/woman.

vociferar [bosĕferár'] vt to shout; (jactarse) to proclaim boastfully ♦ vi to yell.

vocinglero, a [bosĕngle'ro, ḁ] a vociferous; (gárrulo) garrulous; (fig) blatant.

vodevil [boťḩeḅĕl'] nm vaudeville, music hall.

vodka [boťḩ'ká] nm vodka.

vol abr = **volumen.**

volado, a [bolá'ťḩo, ḁ] a: **estar** ~ (fam) to be worried; (: AM) to be crazy.

volador, a [bolátḩor', ḁ] a flying.

voladura [boláťḩōō'rá] nf blowing up, demolition; (MINERÍA) blasting.

volandas [bolán'dás]: **en** ~ ad in o through the air; (fig) swiftly.

volante [bolán'te] a flying ♦ nm (de máquina, coche) steering wheel; (de reloj) balance; (nota) note; **ir al** ~ to be at the wheel, be driving.

volar [bolár'] vt (demolir) to blow up, demolish ♦ vi to fly; (fig: correr) to rush, hurry; (fam: desaparecer) to disappear; **voy volando** I must dash; **¡cómo vuela el tiempo!** how time flies!

volátil [bolá'tĕl] a volatile; (fig) changeable.

volcán [bolkán'] nm volcano.

volcánico, a [bolká'nĕko, ḁ] a volcanic.

volcar [bolkár'] vt to upset, overturn; (tumbar, derribar) to knock over; (vaciar) to empty out ♦ vi to overturn; ~**se** vr to tip over; (barco) to capsize.

voleibol [boleĕḅol'] nm volleyball.

voleo [bole'o] nm volley; **a(l)** ~ haphazardly; **de un** ~ quickly.

Volga [bol'ḡá] nm Volga.

volición [bolĕsyon'] nf volition.

volqué [bolke'], **volquemos** [bolke'mos] etc vb V **volcar**.

volquete [bolke'te] nm dump truck (US), dumper.

voltaje [boltá'he] nm voltage.

volteador, a [bolteátḩor', ḁ] nm/f acrobat.

voltear [bolteár'] vt to turn over; (volcar) to turn upside down; (doblar) to peal ♦ vi to roll over.

voltereta [boltere'tá] nf somersault; ~ **sobre las manos** handspring; ~ **lateral** cartwheel.

voltio [bol'tyo] nm volt.

voluble [bolōō'ḅle] a fickle.

volumen [bolōō'men] nm volume; ~ **monetario** money supply; ~ **de negocios** turnover; **bajar el** ~ to turn down the volume; **poner la radio a todo** ~ to turn the radio up all the way.

voluminoso, a [bolōōmĕno'so, ḁ] a voluminous; (enorme) massive.

voluntad [bolōōntáťḩ'] nf will, willpower; (deseo) desire, wish; (afecto) fondness; **a** ~ at will; (cantidad) as much as one likes; **buena** ~ goodwill; **mala** ~ ill will, malice; **por causas ajenas a mi** ~ for reasons beyond my control.

voluntario, a [bolōōntá'ryo, ḁ] a voluntary ♦ nm/f volunteer.

voluntarioso, a [bolōōntáryo'so, ḁ] a headstrong.

voluptuoso, a [bolōōptwo'so, ḁ] a voluptuous.

volver [bolḅer'] vt to turn; (boca abajo) to turn (over); (voltear) to turn around, turn upside down; (poner al revés) to turn inside out; (devolver) to return; (transformar) to change, transform; (manga) to roll up ♦ vi to return, go/come back; ~**se** vr to turn around; (llegar a ser) to become; ~ **la espalda** to turn one's back; ~ **bien por mal** to return good for evil; ~ **a hacer** to do again; ~ **en sí** to come to o around, regain consciousness; ~ **la vista atrás** to look back; ~ **loco a uno** to drive sb mad; ~**se loco** to go mad.

vomitar |bomētár'| *vt, vi* to vomit.

vómito |bo'mēto| *nm (acto)* vomiting; *(resultado)* vomit.

vorágine |borá'hēnc| *nf* whirlpool; *(fig)* maelstrom.

voraz |borás| *a* voracious; *(fig)* fierce.

vórtice |bor'tēsc| *nm* whirlpool; *(de aire)* whirlwind.

vos |bos| *pron (AM)* you.

voseo |bosc'o| *nm (AM)* addressing a person as "vos", *familiar usage.*

Vosgos |bos'gos| *nmpl* Vosges.

vosotros, as |boso'tros, ás| *pron* you *pl*; *(reflexivo)* yourselves; **entre** ~ among yourselves.

votación |botásyon'| *nf (acto)* voting; *(voto)* vote; ~ **a mano alzada** show of hands; **someter algo a** ~ to put sth to the vote.

votar |botár'| *vt (POL: partido etc)* to vote for; *(proyecto: aprobar)* to pass; *(REL)* to vow ♦ *vi* to vote.

voto |bo'to| *nm* vote; *(promesa)* vow; *(maldición)* oath, curse; ~**s** *nmpl* (good) wishes; ~ **de bloque/de grupo** block/card vote; ~ **de censura/de (des)confianza/de gracias** vote of censure/(no) confidence/ thanks; **dar su** ~ to cast one's vote.

voy |boē| *vb V* **ir.**

voz |bos| *nf* voice; *(grito)* shout; *(chisme)* rumor *(US)*, rumour *(Brit)*; *(LING: palabra)* word; *(: forma)* voice; **dar voces** to shout, yell; **llamar a uno a voces** to shout to sb; **llevar la** ~ **cantante** *(fig)* to be the boss; **tener la** ~ **tomada** to be hoarse; **tener** ~ **y voto** to have the right to speak; **a media** ~ in a low voice; **a** ~ **en cuello** *o* **en grito** at the top of one's voice; **de viva** ~ verbally; **en** ~ **alta** aloud; ~ **de mando** command.

vozarrón |bosárron'| *nm* booming voice.

vra., vro. *abr* = **vuestra, vuestro.**

Vto. *abr (COM)* = **vencimiento.**

vuelco |bwel'ko| *etc vb V* **volcar** ♦ *nm* spill, overturning; *(fig)* collapse; **mi corazón dio un** ~ my heart missed a beat.

vuelo |bwe'lo| *etc vb V* **volar** ♦ *nm* flight; *(encaje)* lace, frill; *(de falda etc)* loose part; *(fig)* importance; **de altos** ~**s** *(fig: plan)* grandiose; *(: persona)* ambitious; **alzar el** ~ to take flight; *(fig)* to dash off; **coger al** ~ to catch in flight; ~ **en picado** dive; ~ **libre** hang-gliding; ~ **regular** scheduled flight; **falda de mucho** ~ full skirt.

vuelque |bwel'ke| *etc vb V* **volcar.**

vuelta |bwel'tá| *nf* turn; *(curva)* bend, curve; *(regreso)* return; *(revolución)* revolution; *(paseo)* stroll; *(circuito)* lap; *(de*

papel, tela) other side; *(de pantalón)* cuff *(US)*, turn-up *(Brit)*; *(dinero)* change; ~ **a empezar** back to square one; ~ **al mundo** world trip; **V~ de Francia** Tour de France; ~ **cerrada** hairpin bend; **a la** ~ *(Esp)* on one's return; **a la** ~ **de la esquina, a la** ~ *(AM)* round the corner; **a** ~ **de correo** by return of post; **dar** ~**s** to turn, revolve; **dar** ~**s a una idea** to turn over an idea (in one's mind); **dar una** ~ to go for a walk; **dar media** ~ *(AUTO)* to do a U-turn; *(fam)* to beat it; **estar de** ~ *(fam)* to be back; **poner a uno de** ~ **y media** to heap abuse on sb; **no tiene** ~ **de hoja** there's no alternative.

vuelto |bwcl'to| *pp de* **volver.**

vuelva |bwcl'há| *etc vb V* **volver.**

vuestro, a |bwcs'tro, á| *a* your; *(después de n)* of yours ♦ *pron*: **el** ~**/la vuestra/los** ~**s/las vuestras** yours; **lo** ~ (what is) yours; **un amigo** ~ a friend of yours; **una idea vuestra** an idea of yours.

vulgar |bōōlgár'| *a (ordinario)* vulgar; *(común)* common.

vulgarice |bōōlgárē'sc| *etc vb V* **vulgarizar.**

vulgaridad |bōōlgárētháth'| *nf* commonness; *(acto)* vulgarity; *(expresión)* coarse expression; ~**es** *nfpl* banalities.

vulgarismo |bōōlgárēs'mo| *nm* popular form of a word.

vulgarizar |bōōlgárēsár'| *vt* to popularize.

vulgo |bōōl'go| *nm* common people.

vulnerable |bōōlnerá'ble| *a* vulnerable.

vulnerar |bōōlnerár'| *vt* to harm, damage; *(derechos)* to interfere with; *(JUR, COM)* to violate.

vulpino, a |bōōlpē'no, á| *a* vulpine; *(fig)* foxy.

W

W, w |do'hlche'| *nf (letra)* W, w; **W de Washington** W for William.

wáter |bá'ter| *nm* lavatory.

wátman |wát'mán| *a inv (fam)* cool.

whisky |wēs'kē| *nm* whiskey *(US)*, whisky *(Brit)*.

Winchester |wēntch'cster| *nm (INFORM)*: **disco** ~ Winchester disk.

X

X, x [e'kēs] *nf* (*letra*) X, x; **X de Xiquena** X for Xmas.
xenofobia [ksenofo'ƀyá] *nf* xenophobia.
xilófono [ksēlo'fono] *nm* xylophone.

Y

Y, y [ēḡrye'ḡá] *nf* (*letra*) Y, y; **Y de Yegua** Y for Yoke.
y [ē] *conj* and.
ya [yá] *ad* (*gen*) already; (*ahora*) now; (*en seguida*) at once; (*pronto*) soon ♦ *excl* all right!; (*por supuesto*) of course! ♦ *conj* (*ahora que*) now that; ~ **no** not any more, no longer; ~ **lo sé** I know; ~ **dice que sí,** ~ **dice que no** first he says yes, then he says no; ¡~, ~! yes, yes!; (*con impaciencia*) all right!, O.K.!; ¡~ **voy!** (*enfático: no se suele traducir*) coming!; ~ **que** since.
yacer [yáser'] *vi* to lie.
yacimiento [yásēmyen'to] *nm* bed, deposit; ~ **petrolífero** oilfield.
Yakarta [yákár'tá] *nf* Jakarta.
yanqui [yàn'kē] *a* Yankee ♦ *nm/f* Yankee.
yate [yà'te] *nm* yacht.
yazca [yás'ká] *etc vb V* **yacer.**
yedra [ye'ðꞁrá] *nf* ivy.
yegua [ye'ḡwá] *nf* mare.
yema [ye'má] *nf* (*del huevo*) yoke; (*BOT*) leaf bud; (*fig*) best part; ~ **del dedo** fingertip.
Yemen [ye'men] *nm*: **el** ~ **del Norte** Yemen; **el** ~ **del Sur** Southern Yemen.
yemení [yemenē'] *a, nm/f* Yemeni.
yendo [yen'do] *vb V* **ir.**
yerba [yer'ƀá] *nf* = **hierba.**
yerga [yer'ḡá] *etc,* **yergue** [yer'ḡe] *etc vb V* **erguir.**
yermo, a [yer'mo, à] *a* barren; (*de gente*) uninhabited ♦ *nm* waste land.
yerno [yer'no] *nm* son-in-law.
yerre [ye'rre] *etc vb V* **errar.**
yerto, a [yer'to, à] *a* stiff.

yesca [yes'ká] *nf* tinder.
yeso [ye'so] *nm* (*GEO*) gypsum; (*ARQ*) plaster.
yo [yo'] *pron personal* I; **soy** ~ it's me, it is I; ~ **que tú/usted** if I were you.
yodo [yo'ðo] *nm* iodine.
yoga [yo'ḡá] *nm* yoga.
yogur(t) [yoḡōōr'(t)] *nm* yogurt.
yogurtera [yoḡōōrte'rá] *nf* yogurt maker.
yugo [yōō'ḡo] *nm* yoke.
Yugoslavia [yōōḡoslà'ƀyá] *nf* Yugoslavia.
yugoslavo, a [yōōḡoslà'ƀo, á] *a* Yugoslavian ♦ *nm/f* Yugoslav.
yugular [yōōḡōōlár'] *a* jugular.
yunque [yōōn'ke] *nm* anvil.
yunta [yōōn'tá] *nf* yoke.
yuntero [yōōnte'ro] *nm* ploughman.
yute [yōō'te] *nm* jute.
yuxtapondré [yōōkstápondre'] *etc vb V* **yuxtaponer.**
yuxtaponer [yōōkstáponer'] *vt* to juxtapose.
yuxtaponga [yōōkstápon'gá] *etc vb V* **yuxtaponer.**
yuxtaposición [yōōkstáposēsyon'] *nf* juxtaposition.
yuxtapuesto [yōōkstápwe'sto], **yuxtapuse** [yōōkstápōō'se] *etc vb V* **yuxtaponer.**

Z

Z, z [se'tá] *nf* (*letra*) Z, z; **Z de Zaragoza** Z for Zebra.
zafar [sáfár'] *vt* (*soltar*) to untie; (*superficie*) to clear; ~**se** *vr* (*escaparse*) to escape; (*ocultarse*) to hide o.s. away; (*TEC*) to slip off; ~**se de** (*persona*) to get away from.
zafio, a [sá'fyo, à] *a* coarse.
zafiro [sáfē'ro] *nm* sapphire.
zaga [sà'ḡá] *nf* rear; **a la** ~ behind, in the rear.
zagal [sáḡàl'] *nm* boy.
zagala [sáḡá'lá] *nf* girl.
zaguán [sáḡwàn'] *nm* hallway.
zahareño, a [sáåre'nyo, à] *a* (*salvaje*) wild; (*arisco*) unsociable.
zaherir [sáerēr'] *vt* (*criticar*) to criticize; (*fig: herir*) to wound.
zahiera *etc,* **zahiriendo** [sáyc'rá, sáēryen'do] *etc vb V* **zaherir.**
zahorí [sáorē'] *nm* clairvoyant.
zaino, a [sá'ēno, à] *a* (*color de caballo*) chestnut; (*pérfido*) treacherous; (*animal*) vicious.
zalamería [sálámcrē'á] *nf* flattery.

zalamero, a [sàláme'ro, á] *a* flattering; *(relamido)* suave.

zamarra [sàmá'rrá] *nf* *(piel)* sheepskin; *(saco)* sheepskin jacket.

Zambeze [sàmbe'se] *nm* Zambezi.

zambo, a [sám'bo, á] *a* knock-kneed ♦ *nm/f* *(AM)* half-breed *(of Negro and Indian parentage)*; *(mulato)* mulatto ♦ *nf* samba.

zambra [sám'brá] *nf* gypsy dance.

zambullida [sàmbōōye'thá] *nf* dive, plunge.

zambullirse [sàmbōōyěr'se] *vr* to dive; *(ocultarse)* to hide o.s.

zamorano, a [sámorá'no, á] *a* of *o* from Zamora ♦ *nm/f* native *o* inhabitant of Zamora.

zampar [sámpár'] *vt* *(esconder)* to hide *o* put away (hurriedly); *(comer)* to gobble; *(arrojar)* to hurl ♦ *vi* to eat voraciously; **~se** *vr* *(chocar)* to bump; *(fig)* to gatecrash.

zanahoria [sànào'ryá] *nf* carrot.

zancada [sánká'thá] *nf* stride.

zancadilla [sánkáthě'yá] *nf* trip; *(fig)* stratagem; **echar la ~ a uno** to trip sb up.

zancajo [sánká'ho] *nm* *(ANAT)* heel; *(fig)* dwarf.

zanco [sán'ko] *nm* stilt.

zancudo, a [sánkōō'tho, á] *a* long-legged ♦ *nm* *(AM)* mosquito.

zángano [sán'gáno] *nm* drone; *(holgazán)* idler, slacker.

zanja [sán'há] *nf* *(fosa)* ditch; *(tumba)* grave.

zanjar [sànhár'] *vt* *(fosa)* to ditch, trench; *(problema)* to surmount; *(conflicto)* to resolve.

zapapico [sápápě'ko] *nm* pick, pickax.

zapata [sápá'tá] *nf* half-boot; *(MECÁNICA)* shoe.

zapateado [sápáteá'tho] *nm* (flamenco) tap dance.

zapatear [sápáteár'] *vt* *(tocar)* to tap with one's foot; *(patear)* to kick; *(fam)* to illtreat ♦ *vi* to tap with one's feet.

zapatería [sápáterě'á] *nf* *(oficio)* shoemaking; *(tienda)* shoe-shop; *(fábrica)* shoe factory.

zapatero, a [sápátc'ro, á] *nm/f* shoemaker; **~ remendón** cobbler.

zapatilla [sápátě'yá] *nf* slipper; *(TEC)* washer; *(para deporte)* training shoe.

zapato [sápá'to] *nm* shoe.

zar [sár] *nm* tsar, czar.

zarabanda [sárábán'dá] *nf* saraband; *(fig)* whirl.

Zaragoza [sáráġo'sá] *nf* Saragossa.

zaragozano, a [sáráġosá'no, á] *a* of *o* from Saragossa ♦ *nm/f* native *o* inhabitant of Saragossa.

zaranda [sárán'dá] *nf* sieve.

zarandear [sárándeár'] *vt* to sieve; *(fam)* to shake vigorously.

zarcillo [sársě'yo] *nm* earring.

zarpa [sár'pá] *nf* *(garra)* claw, paw; **echar la ~ a** to claw at; *(fam)* to grab.

zarpar [sárpár'] *vi* to weigh anchor.

zarza [sár'sá] *nf* *(BOT)* bramble.

zarzal [sársál'] *nm* *(matorral)* bramble patch.

zarzamora [sársámo'rá] *nf* blackberry.

zarzuela [sárswe'lá] *nf* Spanish light opera.

zigzag [seġság'] *a* zigzag.

zigzaguear [seġságeár'] *vi* to zigzag.

zinc [sěnk] *nm* zinc.

zócalo [so'kálo] *nm* *(ARQ)* plinth, base; *(de pared)* skirting board.

zona [so'ná] *nf* zone; **~ fronteriza** border area; **~ del dólar** *(COM)* dollar area; **~ de fomento** *o* **de desarrollo** development area.

zoología [soolohě'á] *nf* zoology.

zoológico, a [soolo'hěko, á] *a* zoological ♦ *nm* *(tb:* **parque ~**) zoo.

zoólogo, a [soo'logo, á] *nm/f* zoologist.

zoom [sōōm] *nm* zoom lens.

zopenco, a [sopen'ko, á] *(fam)* *a* dull, stupid ♦ *nm/f* idiot.

zopilote [sopělo'te] *nm* *(AM)* buzzard.

zoquete [soke'te] *nm* *(madera)* block; *(pan)* crust; *(fam)* blockhead.

zorro, a [so'rro, á] *a* crafty ♦ *nm/f* fox/vixen ♦ *nf* *(fam)* whore, hooker *(US)*.

zote [so'te] *(fam)* *a* dim, stupid ♦ *nm/f* dimwit.

zozobra [soso'brá] *nf* *(fig)* anxiety.

zozobrar [sosobrár'] *vi* *(hundirse)* to capsize; *(fig)* to fail.

zueco [swe'ko] *nm* clog.

zulo [sōō'lo] *nm* *(de armas)* cache.

zumbar [sōōmbár'] *vt* *(burlar)* to tease; *(golpear)* to hit ♦ *vi* to buzz; *(fam)* to be very close; **~se** *vr*: **~se de** to tease; **me zumban los oídos** I have a buzzing *o* ringing in my ears.

zumbido [sōōmbě'tho] *nm* buzzing; *(fam)* punch; **~ de oídos** buzzing *o* ringing in the ears.

zumo [sōō'mo] *nm* juice; *(ganancia)* profit; **~ de naranja** (fresh) orange juice.

zurcir [sōōrsěr'] *vt* *(coser)* to darn; *(fig)* to put together; **¡que las zurzan!** to blazes with them!

zurdo, a [sōōr'tho, á] *a* *(mano)* left; *(persona)* left-handed.

zurrar [sōōrrár'] *vt* *(TEC)* to dress; *(fam: pegar duro)* to wallop; *(: aplastar)* to flatten; *(: criticar)* to criticize harshly.

zurriagazo [sōōrryáġá'so] *nm* lash, stroke; *(desgracia)* stroke of bad luck.

zurriago [sōōrryá'ġo] *nm* whip, lash.

zurrón [sōōrron'] *nm* pouch.

zurza [sōōr'sá] *etc vb* V **zurcir**.

zutano, a [sōōtá'no, á] *nm/f* so-and-so.

ENGLISH - SPANISH
INGLÉS - ESPAÑOL

A

A, a [ā] *n* (*letter*) A, a; (*SCOL*: *mark*) ≈ sobresaliente; (*MUS*): **A** la *m*; **A for Able** A de Antonio; **A road** *n* (*Brit AUT*) ≈ carretera nacional.

a, an [ā, ə, an, ən] *indefinite article* un(a); **an apple** una manzana; **a mirror** un espejo; **he's a doctor** es médico; **3 a day/week** 3 por día/semana; **10 km an hour** 10 km por hora; **50¢ a kilo** 50 centavos el kilo; **3 times a month** 3 veces al mes; **I haven't got a car** no tengo coche.

a. *abbr* = **acre**.

AA *n abbr* (*US*: = *Associate in/of Arts*) título universitario; (*Brit*: = *Automobile Association*) ≈ RACE *m* (*Sp*); = *Alcoholics Anonymous*; (= *antiaircraft*) A.A.

AAA [trip'əlā] *n abbr* (= *American Automobile Association*) ≈ RACE *m* (*Sp*); [thrē'āz'] (*Brit*: = *Amateur Athletics Association*) asociación de atletismo amateur.

AAUP *n abbr* (= *American Association of University Professors*) asociación de profesores universitarios.

AB *abbr* = **able-bodied seaman**; (*Canada*) = *Alberta*.

ABA *n abbr* = *American Bankers Association*; *American Bar Association*.

aback [əbak'] *ad*: **to be taken ~** quedar desconcertado.

abandon [əban'dən] *vt* abandonar; (*renounce*) renunciar a ♦ *n* abandono; (*wild behavior*): **with ~** sin reparos; **to ~ ship** abandonar el barco.

abandoned [əban'dənd] *a* (*child, house etc*) abandonado; (*unrestrained: manner*) desinhibido.

abase [əbās'] *vt*: **to ~ o.s. (so far as to do ...)** rebajarse (hasta el punto de hacer ...).

abashed [əbasht'] *a* avergonzado.

abate [əbāt'] *vi* moderarse; (*lessen*) disminuir; (*calm down*) calmarse.

abatement [əbāt'mənt] *n* (*of pollution, noise*) disminución *f*.

abattoir [abətwâr'] *n* (*Brit*) matadero.

abbey [ab'ē] *n* abadía.

abbot [ab'ət] *n* abad *m*.

abbreviate [əbrē'vēāt] *vt* abreviar.

abbreviation [əbrēvēā'shən] *n* (*short form*) abreviatura; (*act*) abreviación *f*.

ABC [ābēsē'] *n abbr* (= *American Broadcasting Company*) cadena de televisión.

abdicate [ab'dikāt] *vt*, *vi* abdicar.

abdication [abdikā'shən] *n* abdicación *f*.

abdomen [ab'dəmən] *n* abdomen *m*.

abdominal [abdâm'ənəl] *a* abdominal.

abduct [abdukt'] *vt* raptar, secuestrar.

abduction [abduk'shən] *n* rapto, secuestro.

aberration [abərā'shən] *n* aberración *f*; **in a moment of mental ~** en un momento de enajenación mental.

abet [əbet'] *vt see* **aid**.

abeyance [əbā'əns] *n*: **in ~** (*law*) en desuso; (*matter*) en suspenso.

abhor [abhôr'] *vt* aborrecer, abominar (de).

abhorrent [abhôr'ənt] *a* aborrecible, detestable.

abide [əbīd'] *vt*: **I can't ~ it/him** no lo/le puedo ver; **to ~ by** *vt fus* atenerse a.

ability [əbil'itē] *n* habilidad *f*, capacidad *f*; (*talent*) talento; **to the best of my ~** lo mejor que pueda *or* sepa.

abject [ab'jekt] *a* (*poverty*) miserable; (*apology*) rastrero; (*coward*) vil.

ablaze [əblāz'] *a* en llamas, ardiendo.

able [ā'bəl] *a* capaz; (*skilled*) hábil; **to be ~ to do sth** poder hacer algo.

able-bodied [ā'bəlbâd'ēd] *a* sano; **~ seaman** marinero de primera.

ably [ā'blē] *ad* hábilmente.

ABM *n abbr* = *anti-ballistic missile*.

abnormal [abnôr'məl] *a* anormal.

abnormality [abnôrmal'ətē] *n* (*condition*) anormalidad *f*; (*instance*) anomalía.

aboard [əbôrd'] *ad* a bordo ♦ *prep* a bordo de; **~ the train** en el tren.

abode [əbōd'] *n* (*old*) morada; (*LAW*) domicilio; **of no fixed ~** sin domicilio fijo.

abolish [əbâl'ish] *vt* suprimir, abolir.

abolition [abəlish'ən] *n* supresión *f*, abolición *f*.

abominable [əbâm'inəbəl] *a* abominable.

aborigine [abərij'ənē] *n* aborigen *m/f*.

abort [əbôrt'] *vt* abortar; (*COMPUT*) abandonar ♦ *vi* (*COMPUT*) abandonar.

abortion [əbôr'shən] *n* aborto (provocado); **to have an ~** abortar.

abortive [əbôr'tiv] *a* fracasado.

abound [əbound'] *vi*: **to ~ (in *or* with)** abundar (de *or* en).

about [əbout'] *prep* (*subject*) acerca de, sobre; (*place*) alrededor de, por ♦ *ad* más o menos, aproximadamente; **do something ~ it!** ¡haz algo!; **~ a hundred/thousand** *etc* unos cien/mil *etc*; **it takes ~ 10 hours** es cosa de 10 horas más o menos; **it's just ~ finished** está casi terminado; **at ~ 2**

o'clock a eso de las 2; **they left it all lying ~** lo dejaron todo por todas partes; **to be ~ to** estar a punto de; **I'm not ~ to do all that for nothing** no pienso hacer todo eso gratis; **what** or **how ~ doing this?** ¿qué tal si hacemos esto?; **to walk ~** pasearse, ir y venir.

about-face |əbout'făs'| n (US: MIL, fig) media vuelta.

about-turn |əbout'tûrn| n (Brit) = **about-face.**

above |əbuv'| ad encima, por encima, arriba ♦ prep encima de; **mentioned ~** susodicho; **~ all** sobre todo; **he's not ~ a bit of blackmail** es capaz hasta de hacer chantaje.

above board a legítimo.

above-mentioned |əbuv'men'chənd| a susodicho.

abrasion |əbrā'zhən| n (on skin) abrasión f.

abrasive |əbrā'siv| a abrasivo.

abreast |əbrest'| ad de frente; **to keep ~ of** mantenerse al corriente de.

abridge |əbrij'| vt abreviar.

abroad |əbród'| ad (to be) en el extranjero; (to go) al extranjero; **there is a rumor ~ that ...** corre el rumor de que ...

abrupt |əbrupt'| a (sudden: departure) repentino; (manner) brusco.

abruptly |əbrupt'lē| ad (leave) repentinamente; (speak) bruscamente.

abscess |ab'ses| n absceso.

abscond |abskánd'| vi fugarse.

absence |ab'səns| n ausencia; **in the ~ of** (person) en ausencia de; (thing) a falta de.

absent |ab'sənt| a ausente; **~ without leave (AWOL)** ausente sin permiso.

absentee |absəntē'| n ausente m/f.

absentee ballot n (US) voto postal.

absenteeism |absəntē'izəm| n absentismo.

absent-minded |ab'səntmin'did| a distraído.

absolute |ab'səlōot| a absoluto; **~ monopoly** monopolio total.

absolutely |absəlōot'lē| ad totalmente; **oh yes, ~!** ¡claro or por supuesto que sí!

absolution |absəloo'shən| n (REL) absolución f.

absolve |abzálv'| vt: **to ~ sb (from)** absolver a alguien (de).

absorb |absórb'| vt absorber; **to be ~ed in a book** estar absorto en un libro.

absorbent |absôr'bənt| a absorbente.

absorbent cotton n (US) algodón m hidrófilo.

absorbing |absôr'bing| a absorbente; (book etc) interesantísimo.

absorption |absôrp'shən| n absorción f.

abstain |abstān'| vi: **to ~ (from)** abstenerse (de).

abstemious |abstē'mēəs| a abstemio.

abstention |absten'shən| n abstención f.

abstinence |ab'stənəns| n abstinencia.

abstract |ab'strakt| a abstracto.

abstruse |abstrōōs'| a oscuro.

absurd |absûrd'| a absurdo.

absurdity |absûr'dətē| n absurdo.

abundance |əbun'dəns| n abundancia.

abundant |əbun'dənt| a abundante.

abuse n |əbyōōs'| (insults) improperios mpl; injurias fpl; (misuse) abuso ♦ vt |əbyōōz'| (ill-treat) maltratar; (take advantage of) abusar de; **open to ~** sujeto al abuso.

abusive |əbyōō'siv| a ofensivo.

abysmal |əbiz'məl| a pésimo; (ignorance) supino.

abyss |əbis'| n abismo.

AC abbr (= alternating current) corriente f alterna ♦ n abbr (US) = athletic club.

a/c abbr (BANKING etc) = account, account current.

academic |akədem'ik| a académico, universitario; (pej: issue) puramente teórico ♦ n estudioso/a; profesor(a) m/f universitario/a; **~ year** (UNIV) año académico.

academy |əkad'əmē| n (learned body) 'academia; (school) instituto, colegio; **~ of music** conservatorio.

accede |aksēd'| vi: **to ~ to** acceder a.

accelerate |aksel'ərāt| vt acelerar ♦ vi acelerarse.

acceleration |akselərā'shən| n aceleración f.

accelerator |aksel'ərātûr| n acelerador m.

accent |ak'sent| n acento.

accentuate |aksen'chōōāt| vt (syllable) acentuar; (need, difference etc) recalcar, subrayar.

accept |aksept'| vt aceptar; (approve) aprobar; (concede) admitir.

acceptable |aksep'təbəl| a aceptable; admisible.

acceptance |aksep'təns| n aceptación f; aprobación f; **to meet with general ~** tener acogida general.

access |ak'ses| n acceso ♦ vt (COMPUT: retrieve) obtener información de; (: store) dar información a; **the burglars gained ~ through a window** los ladrones lograron entrar por una ventana; **to have ~ to** tener acceso a.

accessible |akses'əbəl| a accesible.

accession |aksesh'ən| n (of monarch) subida, ascenso; (addition) adquisición f.

accessory |akses'ûrē| n accesorio; **toilet accessories** artículos mpl de tocador.

access road n carretera de acceso; (to freeway) carril m de acceso.

access time n (COMPUT) tiempo de acceso.

accident |ak'sidənt| n accidente m; (chance) casualidad f; **by ~** (unintentionally) sin querer; (by coincidence) por casualidad; **~s at work** accidentes mpl de trabajo; **to have an ~** tener or sufrir un accidente.

accidental [aksiden'təl] *a* accidental, fortuito.

accidentally [aksiden'təlē] *ad* sin querer; por casualidad.

accident insurance *n* seguro contra accidentes.

accident-prone [ak'sidəntprōn'] *a* propenso a los accidentes.

acclaim [əklām'] *vt* aclamar, aplaudir ♦ *n* aclamación *f*, aplausos *mpl*.

acclamation [akləmā'shən] *n* (*approval*) aclamación *f*; (*applause*) aplausos *mpl*; **by ~** por aclamación.

acclimate [əklī'mit] *vt* (*US*): **to become ~d** aclimatarse.

acclimatize [əklī'mətīz] *vt* (*Brit*) = **acclimate.**

accolade [akəlād'] *n* (*prize*) premio; (*praise*) alabanzas *fpl*, homenaje *m*.

accommodate [əkâm'ədāt] *vt* alojar, hospedar; (*oblige, help*) complacer; **this car ~s 4 people comfortably** en este coche caben 4 personas cómodamente.

accommodating [əkâm'ədāting] *a* servicial, complaciente.

accommodations *npl*, (*Brit*) **accommodation** *n* [əkâmədā'shən(z)] alojamiento.

accompaniment [əkum'pənimənt] *n* acompañamiento.

accompanist [əkum'pənist] *n* (*MUS*) acompañante *m/f*.

accompany [əkum'pənē] *vt* acompañar.

accomplice [əkâm'plis] *n* cómplice *m/f*.

accomplish [əkâm'plish] *vt* (*finish*) acabar; (*aim*) realizar; (*task*) llevar a cabo.

accomplished [əkâm'plisht] *a* experto, hábil.

accomplishment [əkâm'plishmənt] *n* (*ending*) conclusión *f*; (*bringing about*) realización *f*; (*skill*) talento.

accord [əkôrd'] *n* acuerdo ♦ *vt* conceder; **of his own ~** espontáneamente; **with one ~** de *or* por común acuerdo.

accordance [əkôr'dəns] *n*: **in ~ with** de acuerdo con.

according [əkôr'ding]: **~ to** *prep* según; (*in accordance with*) conforme a; **it went ~ to plan** salió según lo previsto.

accordingly [əkôr'dinglē] *ad* (*thus*) por consiguiente.

accordion [əkôr'dēən] *n* acordeón *m*.

accordionist [əkôr'dēənist] *n* acordeonista *m/f*.

accost [əkôst'] *vt* abordar, dirigirse a.

account [əkount'] *n* (*COMM*) cuenta, factura; (*report*) informe *m*; **~s** *npl* (*COMM*) cuentas *fpl*; **your ~ is still outstanding** su cuenta está todavía pendiente; **of little ~** de poca importancia; **on ~** a cuenta; **to buy sth on ~** comprar algo a cuenta; **on no ~** de ninguna manera; **on ~ of** a causa de, por motivo de; **to take into ~**, **take ~ of** tener en cuenta; **to keep an ~ of** llevar

la cuenta de; **to call sb to ~ for sth/for having done sth** pedirle cuentas a uno por algo/por haber hecho algo.

account for *vt fus* (*explain*) explicar; **all the children were ~ed for** no faltaba ningún niño.

accountability [əkountəbil'ətē] *n* responsabilidad *f*.

accountable [əkoun'təbəl] *a* responsable.

accountancy [əkoun'tənsē] *n* contabilidad *f*.

accountant [əkoun'tənt] *n* contable *m/f*, contador(a) *m/f*.

accounting [əkoun'ting] *n* contabilidad *f*.

accounting period *n* período contable, ejercicio financiero.

account number *n* (*at bank etc*) número de cuenta.

account payable *n* cuenta por pagar.

account receivable *n* cuenta por cobrar.

accoutrements [əkōō'tûrmənts] *npl* equipo, equipaje *m*.

accredited [əkred'itid] *a* (*agent etc*) autorizado, acreditado.

accretion [əkrē'shən] *n* acumulación *f*.

accrue [əkrōō'] *vi* (*mount up*) aumentarse; (*interest*) acumularse; **to ~ to** corresponder a; **~d charges** gastos *mpl* vencidos; **~d interest** interés *m* acumulado.

acct. *abbr* = **account; accountant.**

accumulate [əkyōōm'yəlāt] *vt* acumular ♦ *vi* acumularse.

accumulation [əkyōōmyəlā'shən] *n* acumulación *f*.

accuracy [ak'yûrəsē] *n* exactitud *f*, precisión *f*.

accurate [ak'yûrit] *a* (*number*) exacto; (*answer*) acertado; (*shot*) certero.

accurately [ak'yûritlē] *ad* (*count, shoot, answer*) con precisión.

accursed [əkûr'sid] *a* maldito.

accusation [akyōōzā'shən] *n* acusación *f*.

accusative [əkyōō'zətiv] *n* acusativo.

accuse [əkyōōz'] *vt* acusar; (*blame*) echar la culpa a.

accused [əkyōōzd'] *n* acusado/a.

accustom [əkus'təm] *vt* acostumbrar; **to ~ o.s. to sth** acostumbrarse a algo.

accustomed [əkus'təmd] *a*: **~ to** acostumbrado a.

AC/DC *abbr* = *alternating current/direct current.*

ACE [ās] *n abbr* = *American Council on Education.*

ace [ās] *n* as *m*; **within an ~ of** a dos dedos de.

Ace bandage *n* ® (*US*) venda elástica.

acerbic [əsûr'bik] *a* acerbo; (*fig*) mordaz.

acetate [as'itāt] *n* acetato.

ache [āk] *n* dolor *m* ♦ *vi* doler; (*yearn*): **to ~ to do sth** suspirar por hacer algo; **I've got a stomach~** *or* (*Brit*) **stomach ~**

tengo dolor de estómago, me duele el estómago; **my head** ~**s** me duele la cabeza.

achieve [əchēv'] *vt* (*reach*) alcanzar; (*realize*) realizar; (*victory*, *success*) lograr, conseguir.

achievement [əchēv'mənt] *n* (*completion*) realización *f*; (*success*) éxito.

acid [as'id] *a* ácido; (*bitter*) agrio ♦ *n* ácido.

acidity [əsid'itē] *n* acidez *f*; (*MED*) acedía.

acid rain *n* lluvia ácida.

acknowledge [aknâl'ij] *vt* (*letter*: *also*: ~ **receipt of**) acusar recibo de; (*fact*) reconocer.

acknowledgement [aknâl'ijmənt] *n* acuse *m* de recibo; reconocimiento; ~**s** (*in book*) agradecimientos *mpl*.

ACLU *n abbr* (= *American Civil Liberties Union*) unión americana por libertades civiles.

acme [ak'mē] *n* colmo, cima.

acne [ak'nē] *n* acné *m*.

acorn [ā'kôrn] *n* bellota.

acoustic [əkōōs'tik] *a* acústico.

acoustic coupler [əkōōs'tik kup'lûr] *n* (*COMPUT*) acoplador *m* acústico.

acoustics [əkōōs'tiks] *n*, *npl* acústica *sg*.

acoustic screen *n* panel *m* acústico.

acquaint [əkwānt'] *vt*: **to** ~ **sb with sth** (*inform*) poner a uno al corriente de algo; **to be** ~**ed with** (*person*) conocer; (*fact*) estar al corriente de.

acquaintance [əkwān'təns] *n* conocimiento; (*person*) conocido/a; **to make sb's** ~ conocer a uno.

acquiesce [akwēes'] *vi* (*agree*): **to** ~ **(in)** consentir (en), conformarse (con).

acquire [əkwī'ûr] *vt* adquirir.

acquired [əkwī'ûrd] *a* adquirido; **an** ~ **taste** un gusto adquirido.

acquisition [akwizish'ən] *n* adquisición *f*.

acquisitive [əkwiz'ətiv] *a* codicioso.

acquit [əkwit'] *vt* absolver, exculpar; **to** ~ **o.s. well** salir con éxito.

acquittal [əkwit'əl] *n* absolución *f*, exculpación *f*.

acre [ā'kûr] *n* acre *m*.

acreage [ā'kûrij] *n* extensión *f*.

acrid [ak'rid] *a* (*smell*) acre; (*fig*) mordaz, sarcástico.

acrimonious [akrəmō'nēəs] *a* (*remark*) mordaz; (*argument*) reñido.

acrobat [ak'rəbat] *n* acróbata *m/f*.

acrobatic [akrəbat'ik] *a* acrobático.

acrobatics [akrəbat'iks] *npl* acrobacias *fpl*.

acronym [ak'rənim] *n* siglas *fpl*.

across [əkrôs'] *prep* (*on the other side of*) al otro lado de; (*crosswise*) a través de ♦ *ad* de un lado a otro, de una parte a otra; a través, al través; **to run/swim** ~ atravesar corriendo/nadando; ~ **from** enfrente de; **the lake is 12 km** ~ el lago tiene 12 km de ancho; **to get sth** ~ **to sb** (*fig*) hacer comprender algo a uno.

acrylic [əkril'ik] *a* acrílico.

ACT *n abbr* (= *American College Test*) *examen que se hace al término de los estudios secundarios*.

act [akt] *n* acto, acción *f*; (*THEATER*) acto; (*in music-hall etc*) número; (*LAW*) decreto, ley *f* ♦ *vi* (*behave*) comportarse; (*THEATER*) actuar; (*pretend*) fingir; (*take action*) tomar medidas ♦ *vt* (*part*) hacer, representar; ~ **of God** fuerza mayor; **it's only an** ~ es cuento; **to catch sb in the** ~ coger a uno en flagrante *or* con las manos en la masa; **to** ~ **Hamlet** hacer el papel de Hamlet; **to** ~ **as** actuar *or* hacer de; ~**ing in my capacity as chairman, I ...** en mi calidad de presidente, yo ...; **it** ~**s as a deterrent** sirve para disuadir; **he's only** ~**ing** está fingiendo nada más.

act on *vt*: **to** ~ **on sth** actuar *or* obrar sobre algo.

act out *vt* (*event*) representar; (*fantasies*) realizar.

act up *vi* (*cause trouble*) dar guerra.

acting [ak'ting] *a* suplente ♦ *n*: **to do some** ~ hacer algo de teatro; **he is the** ~ **manager** es el gerente en funciones.

action [ak'shən] *n* acción *f*, acto; (*MIL*) acción *f*; (*LAW*) proceso, demanda; **to put a plan into** ~ poner un plan en acción *or* en marcha; **killed in** ~ (*MIL*) muerto en acto de servicio *or* en combate; **out of** ~ (*person*) fuera de combate; (*thing*) averiado, descompuesto; **to take** ~ tomar medidas; **to bring an** ~ **against sb** entablar *or* presentar demanda contra uno.

action replay *n* (*Brit TV*) repetición *f*.

activate [ak'təvāt] *vt* activar.

active [ak'tiv] *a* activo, enérgico; (*volcano*) en actividad; **to play an** ~ **part in** colaborar activamente en; ~ **file** (*COMPUT*) fichero activo.

active duty (AD) *n* (*US MIL*) servicio activo.

actively [ak'tivlē] *ad* (*participate*) activamente; (*discourage*, *dislike*) enérgicamente.

active partner *n* (*COMM*) socio activo.

activist [ak'tivist] *n* activista *m/f*.

activity [aktiv'ətē] *n* actividad *f*.

actor [ak'tûr] *n* actor *m*.

actress [ak'tris] *n* actriz *f*.

actual [ak'chōōəl] *a* verdadero, real.

actually [ak'chōōəlē] *ad* realmente, en realidad.

actuary [ak'chōōārē] *n* (*COMM*) actuario/a (de seguros).

actuate [ak'chōōāt] *vt* mover, impulsar.

acumen [əkyōō'mən] *n* perspicacia; **business** ~ talento para los negocios.

acupuncture [ak'yōōpungkchûr] *n* acupuntura.

acute [əkyōōt'] *a* agudo.

acutely [əkyōōt'lē] *ad* profundamente, extremadamente.

AD *ad abbr* (= *Anno Domini*) A.C. ♦ *n abbr* (*US MIL*) = **active duty.**

ad |ad| *n abbr* = **advertisement.**

adage |ad'ij| *n* refrán *m*, adagio.

Adam |ad'əm| *n* Adán; ~'s **apple** *n* nuez *f* de la garganta.

adamant |ad'əmənt| *a* firme, inflexible.

adapt |ədapt'| *vt* adaptar; (*reconcile*) acomodar ♦ *vi*: **to** ~ **(to)** adaptarse (a), ajustarse (a).

adaptability |ədaptəbil'ətē| *n* (*of person, device etc*) adaptabilidad *f*.

adaptable |ədap'təbəl| *a* (*device*) adaptable; (*person*) acomodadizo, que se adapta.

adaptation |adəptā'shən| *n* adaptación *f*.

adapter, adaptor |ədap'tûr| *n* (*ELEC*) adaptador *m*.

ADC *n abbr* (*MIL*) = *aide-de-camp*; (*US*: = *Aid to Dependent Children*) *ayuda para niños dependientes*.

add |ad| *vt* añadir, agregar; (*figures: also:* ~ **up**) sumar ♦ *vi*: **to** ~ **to** (*increase*) aumentar, acrecentar.

add on *vt* añadir.

add up *vt* (*figures*) sumar ♦ *vi* (*fig*): **it doesn't** ~ **up** no tiene sentido; **it doesn't** ~ **up to much** es poca cosa, no tiene gran *or* mucha importancia.

addendum |ədɛn'dəm| *n* apéndice *m*.

adder |ad'ûr| *n* víbora.

addict |ad'ikt| *n* (*to drugs etc*) adicto/a; (*enthusiast*) aficionado/a, entusiasta *m/f*; **heroin** ~ heroinómano/a.

addicted |ədik'tid| *a*: **to be** ~ **to** ser adicto a; ser aficionado a.

addiction |ədik'shən| *n* (*dependence*) hábito morboso; (*enthusiasm*) afición *f*.

addictive |ədik'tiv| *a* que causa adicción.

adding machine |ad'ing məshēn'| *n* calculadora.

Addis Ababa |ad'is âb'əbâ| *n* Addis Abeba *m*.

addition |ədish'ən| *n* (*adding up*) adición *f*; (*thing added*) añadidura, añadido; **in** ~ además, por añadidura; **in** ~ **to** además de.

additional |ədish'ənəl| *a* adicional.

additive |ad'ətiv| *n* aditivo.

addled |ad'əld| *a* (*Brit: rotten*) podrido; (: *fig*) confuso.

address |ədrɛs'| *n* dirección *f*, señas *fpl*; (*speech*) discurso; (*COMPUT*) dirección *f* ♦ *vt* (*letter*) dirigir; (*speak to*) dirigirse a, dirigir la palabra a; **form of** ~ tratamiento; **absolute/relative** ~ (*COMPUT*) dirección *f* absoluta/relativa; **to** ~ **o.s. to sth** (*issue, problem*) abordar.

addressee |adrɛsē'| *n* destinatario/a.

Aden |ā'dən| *n* Adén *m*.

adenoids |ad'ənoidz| *npl* vegetaciones *fpl* adenoideas.

adept |ədɛpt'| *a*: ~ **at** experto *or* hábil en.

adequacy |ad'əkwəsē| *n* idoneidad *f*.

adequate |ad'əkwit| *a* (*satisfactory*) adecuado; (*enough*) suficiente; **to feel** ~ **to a task** sentirse con fuerzas para una tarea.

adequately |ad'əkwitlē| *ad* adecuadamente.

adhere |adhēr'| *vi*: **to** ~ **to** pegarse a; (*fig: abide by*) observar.

adherent |adhēr'ənt| *n* partidario/a.

adhesion |adhē'zhən| *n* adherencia.

adhesive |adhē'siv| *a*, *n* adhesivo.

adhesive tape *n* (*US: MED*) esparadrapo; (*Brit*) cinta adhesiva.

ad hoc |ad hâk'| *a* (*decision*) ad hoc; (*committee*) formado con fines específicos ♦ *ad* con fines específicos.

adieu |ədyōō'| *excl* ¡vaya con Dios!

ad inf |ad inf'| *ad* hasta el infinito.

adjacent |əjā'sənt| *a*: ~ **to** contiguo a, inmediato a.

adjective |aj'iktiv| *n* adjetivo.

adjoin |əjoin'| *vt* estar contiguo a; (*land*) lindar con.

adjoining |əjoi'ning| *a* contiguo, vecino.

adjourn |əjûrn'| *vt* aplazar; (*US: end*) terminar; (*session*) suspender, levantar ♦ *vi* suspenderse; **the meeting has been** ~**ed till next week** se ha levantado la sesión hasta la semana que viene.

adjournment |əjûrn'mənt| *n* (*period*) suspensión *f*; (*postponement*) aplazamiento.

Adjt. *abbr* = **adjutant.**

adjudicate |əjōō'dikāt| *vi* sentenciar; (*contest*) hacer de árbitro en, juzgar; (*claim*) decidir.

adjudication |əjōōdikā'shən| *n* adjudicación *f*.

adjudicator |əjōō'dikātûr| *n* juez *m*, árbitro.

adjust |əjust'| *vt* (*change*) modificar; (*arrange*) arreglar; (*machine*) ajustar ♦ *vi*: **to** ~ **(to)** adaptarse a (a).

adjustable |əjust'əbəl| *a* ajustable.

adjuster |əjust'ûr| *n* see **loss.**

adjustment |əjust'mənt| *n* modificación *f*; arreglo; (*of prices, wages*) ajuste *m*.

adjutant |aj'ətənt| *n* ayudante *m*.

ad-lib |adlib'| *vt*, *vi* improvisar ♦ *ad*: **ad lib** a voluntad, a discreción.

adman |ad'man| *n* (*col*) publicista *m*.

admin |ad'min| *n abbr* (*col*) = **administration.**

administer |admin'istûr| *vt* proporcionar; (*justice*) administrar.

administration |administrā'shən| *n* administración *f*; (*government*) gobierno; **the A**~ (*US*) la Administración.

administrative |admin'istrātiv| *a* administrativo.

administrator |admin'istrātûr| *n* administrador(a) *m/f*.

admirable |ad'mûrəbəl| *a* admirable.

admiral |ad'mûrəl| *n* almirante *m*.

Admiralty |ad'mûrəltē| *n* (*Brit*) Ministerio de Marina, Almirantazgo.

admiration |admərä'shən| *n* admiración *f*.

admire |admï'úr| *vt* admirar.

admirer |admï'ərûr| *n* admirador(a) *m/f*; (*suitor*) pretendiente *m*.

admission |admish'ən| *n* (*exhibition, night-club*) entrada; (*enrolment*) ingreso; (*confession*) confesión *f*; "~ free" "entrada gratis *or* libre"; **by his own** ~ él mismo reconoce que.

admit |admit'| *vt* dejar entrar, dar entrada a; (*permit*) admitir; (*acknowledge*) reconocer; "**this ticket** ~**s two**" "entrada para 2 personas"; **children not** ~**ted** se prohíbe la entrada a (los) menores de edad; **I must** ~ **that** ... debo reconocer que ...

admit of *vt fus* admitir, permitir.

admit to *vt fus* confesarse culpable de.

admittance |admit'əns| *n* entrada; "**no** ~" "se prohíbe la entrada", "prohibida la entrada".

admittedly |admit'idlē| *ad* de acuerdo que.

admonish |admân'ish| *vt* amonestar; (*advise*) aconsejar.

ad nauseam |ad nô'zēəm| *ad* hasta el cansancio.

ado |ədōō'| *n*: **without (any) more** ~ sin más (ni más).

adolescence |adəles'əns| *n* adolescencia.

adolescent |adəles'ənt| *a*, *n* adolescente *m/f*.

adopt |ədâpt'| *vt* adoptar.

adopted |ədâp'tid| *a* adoptivo.

adoption |ədâp'shən| *n* adopción *f*.

adoptive |ədâp'tiv| *a* adoptivo.

adorable |ədôr'əbəl| *a* adorable.

adoration |adərä'shən| *n* adoración *f*.

adore |ədôr'| *vt* adorar.

adoring |ədôr'ing| *a* cariñoso.

adorn |ədôrn'| *vt* adornar.

adornment |ədôrn'mənt| *n* adorno.

ADP *n abbr* = **automatic data processing**.

adrenalin |ədren'əlin| *n* adrenalina.

Adriatic |ādrēat'ik| *n*: **the** ~ **(Sea)** el (Mar) Adriático.

adrift |ədrift'| *ad* a la deriva; **to come** ~ (*boat*) ir a la deriva, soltarse; (*wire, rope etc*) soltarse.

adroit |ədroit'| *a* diestro.

adulation |ajōōlä'shən| *n* adulación *f*.

adult |ədult'| *n* adulto/a ♦ *a*: ~ **education** educación *f* para adultos.

adulterate |ədul'tûrāt| *vt* adulterar.

adultery |ədul'tûrē| *n* adulterio.

adulthood |ədult'hōōd| *n* edad *f* adulta.

advance |advans'| *n* adelanto, progreso; (*money*) anticipo, préstamo; (*MIL*) avance *m* ♦ *vt* avanzar, adelantar; (*money*) anticipar ♦ *vi* avanzar, adelantarse; **in** ~ por adelantado; **to make** ~**s to sb** (*gen*) ponerse en contacto con uno; (*amorously*) insinuarse a uno.

advanced |advanst'| *a* avanzado; (*SCOL: studies*) adelantado; ~ **in years** entrado en años.

advancement |advans'mənt| *n* progreso; (*in rank*) ascenso.

advance notice *n* previo aviso.

advance payment *n* (*part sum*) anticipo.

advantage |advan'tij| *n* (*also TENNIS*) ventaja; **to take** ~ **of** aprovecharse de; **it's to our** ~ es ventajoso para nosotros.

advantageous |advəntā'jəs| *a* ventajoso, provechoso.

advent |ad'vent| *n* advenimiento; **A**~ Adviento.

adventure |adven'chûr| *n* aventura.

adventurous |adven'chûrəs| *a* aventurero.

adverb |ad'vûrb| *n* adverbio.

adversary |ad'vûrsärē| *n* adversario, contrario.

adverse |advûrs'| *a* adverso, contrario; ~ **to** adverso a.

adversity |advûr'sitē| *n* infortunio.

advert |ad'vûrt| *n abbr* (*Brit*) = **advertisement**.

advertise |ad'vûrtīz| *vi* hacer propaganda; (*in newspaper etc*) poner un anuncio; **to** ~ **for** (*staff*) buscar por medio de anuncios ♦ *vt* anunciar.

advertisement |advûrtīz'mənt| *n* (*COMM*) anuncio.

advertiser |ad'vûrtīzûr| *n* anunciante *m/f*.

advertising |ad'vûrtīzing| *n* publicidad *f*, propaganda; anuncios *mpl*.

advertising agency *n* agencia de publicidad.

advertising campaign *n* campaña de publicidad.

advice |advīs'| *n* consejo, consejos *mpl*; (*notification*) aviso; **a piece of** ~ un consejo; **to get legal** ~ consultar a un abogado; **to ask (sb) for** ~ pedir consejo (a uno).

advice slip *n* nota de aviso.

advisable |advī'zəbəl| *a* aconsejable, conveniente.

advise |advīz'| *vt* aconsejar; **to** ~ **sb of sth** (*inform*) informar a uno de algo; **to** ~ **sb against sth/doing sth** desaconsejar algo a uno/aconsejar a uno que no haga algo; **you will be well/ill** ~**d to go** deberías/no deberías ir.

advisedly |advī'zidlē| *ad* (*deliberately*) deliberadamente.

adviser |advī'zûr| *n* consejero/a; (*business adviser*) asesor(a) *m/f*.

advisory |advī'zûrē| *a* consultivo; **in an** ~ **capacity** como asesor.

advocate *vt* |ad'vəkāt| (*argue for*) abogar por; (*give support to*) ser partidario de ♦ *n* |ad'vəkit| abogado/a.

advt. *abbr* = **advertisement**.

AEA *n abbr* (*Brit*: = *Atomic Energy Authority*) consejo de energía nuclear.

AEC *n abbr* (*US*: = *Atomic Energy Commission*) consejo de energía nuclear.

Aegean |ijē'ən| *n*: **the** ~ **(Sea)** el Mar

Egeo.

aegis |ē'jis| *n*: **under the** ~ **of** bajo la tutela de.

aeon |ē'ən| *n (Brit)* = **eon**.

aerial |är'ēəl| *n* antena ♦ *a* aéreo.

aerie |är'ē| *n (US)* aguilera.

aero- |är'ō| *pref* aero-.

aerobatics |ärəbat'iks| *npl* acrobacia aérea.

aerobics |ärō'biks| *nsg* aerobic *m*, aerobismo *(LAm)*.

aerodrome |är'ədrōm| *n (Brit)* aeródromo.

aerodynamic |ärōdinam'ik| *a* aerodinámico.

aerogramme |är'əgram| *n* aerograma *m*.

aeronautics |ärənô'tiks| *nsg* aeronáutica.

aeroplane |är'əplān| *n (Brit)* avión *m*.

aerosol |är'əsôl| *n* aerosol *m*.

aerospace industry |är'əspās in'dəstrē| *n* industria aerospacial.

aesthetic *etc* |esthet'ik| *(Brit)* = **esthetic** *etc*.

a.f. *abbr* = *audiofrequency*.

afar |əfâr'| *ad* lejos; **from** ~ desde lejos.

AFB *n abbr (US)* = *Air Force Base*.

AFDC *n abbr (US: = Aid to Families with Dependent Children) ayuda a familias con hijos menores*.

affable |af'əbəl| *a* afable.

affair |əfär'| *n* asunto; *(also:* **love** ~) relación *f* amorosa; ~**s** *(business)* negocios *mpl;* **the Watergate** ~ el asunto (de) Watergate.

affect |əfekt'| *vt* afectar, influir en; *(move)* conmover.

affectation |afektā'shən| *n* afectación *f*.

affected |əfek'tid| *a* afectado.

affection |əfek'shən| *n* afecto, cariño.

affectionate |əfek'shənit| *a* afectuoso, cariñoso.

affectionately |əfek'shənitlē| *ad* afectuosamente.

affidavit |afidā'vit| *n (LAW)* declaración *f* jurada.

affiliated |əfil'ēātid| *a* afiliado; ~ **company** empresa *or* compañía filial *or* subsidiaria.

affinity |əfin'ətē| *n* afinidad *f*.

affirm |əfûrm'| *vt* afirmar.

affirmation |afûrmā'shən| *n* afirmación *f*.

affirmative |əfûr'mətiv| *a* afirmativo.

affix |əfiks'| *vt (signature)* estampar; *(stamp)* pegar.

afflict |əflikt'| *vt* afligir.

affliction |əflik'shən| *n* enfermedad *f*, aflicción *f*.

affluence |af'lōōəns| *n* opulencia, riqueza.

affluent |af'lōōənt| *a* adinerado, acaudalado; **the** ~ **society** la sociedad de consumo.

afford |əfôrd'| *vt (provide)* dar, proporcionar; **can we** ~ **it/to buy it?** ¿tenemos bastante dinero para comprarlo?; **can we** ~ **a car?** ¿tenemos dinero para comprarnos un coche?

affront |əfrunt'| *n* afrenta, ofensa.

affronted |əfrun'tid| *a* ofendido.

Afghan |af'gan| *a, n* afgano/a *m/f*.

Afghanistan |afgan'istan| *n* Afganistán *m*.

afield |əfēld'| *ad:* **far** ~ muy lejos.

AFL-CIO *n abbr (US: = American Federation of Labor and Congress of Industrial Organizations) confederación sindicalista*.

afloat |əflōt'| *ad (floating)* a flote; *(at sea)* en el mar.

afoot |əfōōt'| *ad:* **there is something** ~ algo se está tramando.

aforesaid |əfôr'sed| *a* antedicho, susodicho; *(COMM)* mencionado anteriormente.

afraid |əfrād'| *a:* **to be** ~ **of** *(person)* tener miedo a; *(thing)* tener miedo de; **to be** ~ **to** tener miedo de, temer; **I am** ~ **that** me temo que; **I'm** ~ **so** ¡me temo que sí!, ¡lo siento, pero es así!; **I'm** ~ **not** me temo que no.

afresh |əfresh'| *ad* de nuevo, otra vez.

Africa |af'rikə| *n* África.

African |af'rikən| *a, n* africano/a *m/f*.

Afrikaans |afrikáns'| *n* africaans *m*.

Afrikaner |afrikā'nûr| *n* africánder *m/f*.

Afro-American |af'rōəmār'ikən| *a, n* afroamericano/a *m/f*.

AFT *n abbr (= American Federation of Teachers)* sindicato de profesores.

aft |aft| *ad (to be)* en popa; *(to go)* a popa.

after |af'tûr| *prep (time)* después de; *(place, order)* detrás de, tras ♦ *ad* después ♦ *conj* después (de) que; **what/who are you** ~? ¿qué/a quién busca usted?; **the police are** ~ **him** la policía le está buscando; ~ **having done/he left** después de haber hecho/ después de que se marchó; ~ **dinner** después de cenar *or* comer; **the day** ~ **tomorrow** pasado mañana; ~ **all** después de todo, al fin y al cabo; ~ **you!** ¡pase usted!; **quarter** ~ **two** *(US)* las 2 y cuarto.

afterbirth |af'tûrbûrth| *n* secundinas *fpl*.

aftercare |af'tûrkär| *n (MED)* asistencia postoperatoria.

after-effects |af'tûrifekts| *npl* consecuencias *fpl*, efectos *mpl*.

afterlife |af'tûrlif| *n* vida eterna.

aftermath |af'tûrmath| *n* consecuencias *fpl*, resultados *mpl*.

afternoon |aftûrnōōn'| *n* tarde *f*; **good** ~! ¡buenas tardes!

after-sales service |af'tûrsālz sûr'vis| *n (Brit COMM: for car, washing machine etc)* servicio de asistencia pos-venta.

after-shave (lotion) |af'tûrshāv (lō'shən)| *n* aftershave *m*.

aftershock |af'tûrshàk| *n (of earthquake)* réplica.

afterthought |af'tûrthôt| *n* ocurrencia (tardía).

afterwards |af'tûrwûrdz| *ad* después, más tarde.

again |əgen'| *ad* otra vez, de nuevo; **to do sth** ~ volver a hacer algo; ~ **and** ~ una y otra vez; **now and** ~ de vez en cuando.

against [əgenst'] *prep (opposed)* en contra de; *(close to)* contra, junto a; **I was lean-ing** ~ **the desk** estaba apoyado contra el escritorio; **(over)** ~ en contraste con.

age [āj] *n* edad *f*; *(old* ~*)* vejez *f*; *(period)* época ♦ *vi* envejecer(se) ♦ *vt* envejecer; **what** ~ **is he?** ¿qué edad *or* cuántos años tiene?; **he is 20 years of** ~ tiene 20 años; **under** ~ menor de edad; **to come of** ~ llegar a la mayoría de edad; **it's been** ~**s since I saw you** hace siglos que no te veo.

aged [ājd] *a:* ~ **10** de 10 años de edad; [ā'jid]: **the** ~ *npl* los ancianos.

age group *n:* **to be in the same** ~ tener la misma edad; **the 40 to 50** ~ el grupo de 40 a 50 años.

ageless [āj'lis] *a (eternal)* eterno; *(ever young)* siempre joven.

age limit *n* edad *f* tope.

agency [ā'jənsē] *n* agencia; **through** *or* **by the** ~ **of** por medio de.

agenda [əjɛn'də] *n* orden *m* del día; **on the** ~ *(COMM)* en el orden del día.

agent [ā'jənt] *n (gen)* agente *m/f*; *(repre-sentative)* representante *m/f*, delegado/a.

aggravate [ag'rəvāt] *vt* agravar; *(annoy)* irritar, exasperar.

aggravating [ag'rəvāting] *a* molesto.

aggravation [agrəvā'shən] *n* agravación *f*.

aggregate [ag'rəgit] *n (whole)* conjunto; *(collection)* agregado.

aggression [əgresh'ən] *n* agresión *f*.

aggressive [əgres'iv] *a* agresivo; *(vigorous)* enérgico.

aggressiveness [əgres'ivnis] *n* agresividad *f*.

aggrieved [əgrēvd'] *a* ofendido, agraviado.

aghast [əgast'] *a* horrorizado.

agile [aj'əl] *a* ágil.

agitate [aj'ətāt] *vt (shake)* agitar; *(trouble)* inquietar; **to** ~ **for** hacer una campaña en pro de *or* en favor de.

agitated [aj'ətātid] *a* agitado.

agitator [aj'itātûr] *n* agitador(a) *m/f*.

AGM *n abbr (Brit)* = **annual general meet-ing**.

agnostic [agnâs'tik] *a, n* agnóstico/a *m/f*.

ago [əgō'] *ad:* **2 days** ~ hace 2 días; **not long** ~ hace poco; **how long** ~**?** ¿hace cuánto tiempo?; **as long** ~ **as 1960** ya en 1960.

agog [əgâg'] *a (anxious)* ansiado; *(excited):* **(all)** ~ **(for)** *(todo)* emocionado (por).

agonize [ag'əniz] *vi:* **to** ~ **(over)** atormentarse (por).

agonized [ag'ənizd] *a* angustioso.

agonizing [ag'ənizing] *a (pain)* atroz; *(sus-pense)* angustioso.

agony [ag'ənē] *n (pain)* dolor *m* agudo; *(distress)* angustia; **to be in** ~ retorcerse de dolor.

agony column *n* consultorio sentimental.

agree [əgrē'] *vt (price)* acordar, quedar en ♦ *vi (statements etc)* coincidir, concordar; **to** ~ **(with)** *(person)* estar de acuerdo (con), ponerse de acuerdo (con); **to** ~ **to do** aceptar hacer; **to** ~ **to sth** consentir en algo; **to** ~ **that** *(admit)* estar de acuerdo en que; **it was** ~**d that ...** se acordó que ...; **garlic doesn't** ~ **with me** el ajo no me sienta bien.

agreeable [əgrē'əbəl] *a* agradable; *(person)* simpático; *(willing)* de acuerdo, conforme.

agreeably [əgrē'əblē] *ad* agradablemente.

agreed [əgrēd'] *a (time, place)* convenido.

agreement [əgrē'mənt] *n* acuerdo; *(COMM)* contrato; **in** ~ de acuerdo, conforme; **by mutual** ~ de común acuerdo.

agricultural [agrəkul'chûrəl] *a* agrícola.

agriculture [ag'rəkulchûr] *n* agricultura.

aground [əground'] *ad:* **to run** ~ encallar, embarrancar.

agt. *abbr* = **agent**.

ahead [əhed'] *ad* delante; ~ **of** delante de; *(fig: schedule etc)* antes de; ~ **of time** antes de la hora; **to be** ~ **of sb** *(fig)* llevar la ventaja *or* delantera a uno; **go right** *or* **straight** ~ siga adelante; **they were (right)** ~ **of us** iban (justo) delante de nosotros.

ahoy [əhoi'] *excl* ¡oiga!

AI *n abbr* = *Amnesty International*; *(COM-PUT)* = **artificial intelligence**.

AID *n abbr (= artificial insemination by do-nor)* inseminación artificial por donante; *(US: = Agency for International Devel-opment)* Agencia Internacional para el Des-arrollo.

aid [ād] *n* ayuda, auxilio ♦ *vt* ayudar, auxi-liar; **in** ~ **of** a beneficio de; **with the** ~ **of** con la ayuda de; **to** ~ **and abet** *(LAW)* ser cómplice.

aide [ād] *n (POL)* ayudante *m/f*.

AIDS [ādz] *n abbr (= acquired immune deficiency syndrome)* SIDA *m*.

AIH *abbr (= artificial insemination by husband)* inseminación artificial por esposo.

ailing [ā'ling] *a (person, economy)* enfermi-zo.

ailment [āl'mənt] *n* enfermedad *f*, achaque *m*.

aim [ām] *vt (gun, camera)* apuntar; *(mis-sile, remark)* dirigir; *(blow)* asestar ♦ *vi (also:* **take** ~*)* apuntar ♦ *n* puntería; *(objective)* propósito, meta; **to** ~ **at** *(objective)* aspirar a, pretender; **to** ~ **to do** tener la intención de hacer.

aimless [ām'lis] *a* sin propósito, sin objeto.

aimlessly [ām'lislē] *ad* a la ventura, a la de-riva.

ain't [ānt] *(col)* = **am not**; **aren't**; **isn't**.

air [är] *n* aire *m*; *(appearance)* aspecto ♦ *vt (room)* ventilar; *(clothes, bed, grievances, ideas)* airear; *(views)* hacer público ♦ *cpd* aéreo; **to throw sth into the** ~ *(ball etc)* lanzar algo al aire; **by** ~ *(travel)* en avión;

to be on the ~ (*RADIO*, *TV*: *program*) estarse emitiendo; (: *station*) estar emitiendo.
air base *n* (*MIL*) base *f* aérea.
air bed *n* colchón *m* neumático.
airborne [är'bórn] *a* (*in the air*) en el aire; (*MIL*) aerotransportado; **as soon as the plane was** ~ tan pronto como el avión estuvo en el aire.
air cargo *n* carga aérea.
air-conditioned [är'kəndishənd] *a* climatizado.
air conditioning [är' kəndish'əning] *n* aire *m* acondicionado.
air-cooled [är'kōōld] *a* refrigerado por aire.
aircraft [är'kraft] *n*, *pl inv* avión *m*.
aircraft carrier *n* porta(a)viones *m inv*.
air cushion *n* cojín *m* de aire; (*AVIAT*) colchón *m* de aire.
airdrome [är'drōm] *n* (*US*) aeródromo.
airfield [är'fēld] *n* campo de aviación.
Air Force *n* fuerzas aéreas *fpl*, aviación *f*.
air freight *n* flete *m* por avión.
air freshener *n* ambientador *m*.
air gun *n* escopeta de aire comprimido.
air hostess (*Brit*) *n* azafata *f*.
airily [är'ilē] *ad* muy a la ligera.
airing [är'ing] *n*: **to give an** ~ **to** (*linen*) airear; (*room*) ventilar; (*fig*: *ideas etc*) airear, someter a discusión.
air letter *n* carta aérea.
airlift [är'lift] *n* puente *m* aéreo.
airline [är'lin] *n* línea aérea.
airliner [är'linûr] *n* avión *m* de pasajeros.
airlock [är'läk] *n* (*in pipe*) esclusa de aire.
airmail [är'māl] *n*: **by** ~ por avión.
air mattress *n* colchón *m* neumático.
airplane [är'plän] *n* (*US*) avión *m*.
airport [är'pórt] *n* aeropuerto.
air raid *n* ataque *m* aéreo.
airsick [är'sik] *a*: **to be** ~ marearse (en avión).
airstrip [är'strip] *n* pista de aterrizaje.
air terminal *n* terminal *f*.
airtight [är'tīt] *a* hermético.
air traffic control *n* control *m* de tráfico aéreo.
air traffic controller *n* controlador(a) *m/f* aéreo/a.
air waybill [är' wā'bil] *n* conocimiento (de embarque) aéreo.
airy [är'ē] *a* (*room*) bien ventilado; (*manners*) ligero.
aisle [īl] *n* (*of church*) nave *f* lateral, pasadizo; (*of theater*, *plane*) pasillo.
ajar [əjár'] *a* entreabierto.
AK *abbr* (*US MAIL*) = Alaska.
aka *abbr* (= *also known as*) alias.
akin [əkin'] *a*: ~ **to** parecido a.
AL *abbr* (*US MAIL*) = Alabama.
ALA *n abbr* = *American Library Association*.
Ala. *abbr* (*US*) = *Alabama*.

alabaster [al'əbastûr] *n* alabastro.
à la carte [á lá kárt'] *ad* a la carta.
alacrity [əlak'ritē] *n*: **with** ~ con la mayor prontitud.
alarm [əlárm'] *n* alarma; (*anxiety*) inquietud *f* ♦ *vt* asustar, inquietar.
alarm clock *n* despertador *m*.
alarming [əlár'ming] *a* alarmante.
alarmist [əlár'mist] *n* alarmista *m/f*.
alas [əlas'] *ad* desgraciadamente ♦ *excl* ¡ay de mí!
Alas. *abbr* (*US*) = *Alaska*.
Alaska [əlas'kə] *n* Alaska.
Albania [albā'nēə] *n* Albania.
Albanian [albā'nēən] *a* albanés/esa ♦ *n* albanés/esa *m/f*; (*LING*) albanés *m*.
albeit [ôlbē'it] *conj* (*although*) aunque.
album [al'bəm] *n* álbum *m*; (*L.P.*) elepé *m*.
albumen [albyōō'mən] *n* albumen *m*.
alchemy [al'kəmē] *n* alquimia.
alcohol [al'kəhól] *n* alcohol *m*.
alcoholic [alkəhól'ik] *a*, *n* alcohólico/a *m/f*.
alcoholism [al'kəhōlizəm] *n* alcoholismo.
alcove [al'kōv] *n* nicho, hueco.
ald. *abbr* = **alderman**.
alderman [ôl'dûrmən] *n* concejal *m*.
ale [āl] *n* cerveza.
alert [əlûrt'] *a* alerta *inv*; (*sharp*) despierto, despabilado ♦ *n* alerta *m*, alarma ♦ *vt* poner sobre aviso; **to** ~ **sb** (**to sth**) poner sobre aviso *or* alertar a uno (de algo); **to** ~ **sb to the dangers of sth** poner sobre aviso *or* alertar a uno de los peligros de algo; **to be on the** ~ estar alerta *or* sobre aviso.
alertness [əlûrt'nis] *n* vigilancia.
Aleutian Islands [əlōō'shən ī'ləndz] *npl* Islas *fpl* Aleutianas.
Alexandria [aligzan'drēə] *n* Alejandría.
alfresco [alfres'kō] *a*, *ad* al aire libre.
algebra [al'jəbrə] *n* álgebra.
Algeria [aljē'rēə] *n* Argelia.
Algerian [aljə'rēən] *a*, *n* argelino/a *m/f*.
Algiers [aljērz'] *n* Argel *m*.
algorithm [al'gərithəm] *n* algoritmo.
alias [ā'lēəs] *ad* alias, conocido por ♦ *n* alias *m*.
alibi [al'əbī] *n* coartada.
alien [āl'yən] *n* (*foreigner*) extranjero/a ♦ *a*: ~ **to** ajeno a.
alienate [āl'yənāt] *vt* enajenar, alejar.
alienation [ālyənā'shən] *n* enajenación *f*.
alight [əlīt'] *a* encendido ♦ *vi* apearse, bajar.
align [əlīn'] *vt* alinear.
alignment [əlīn'mənt] *n* alineación *f*; **the desks are out of** ~ los pupitres no están bien alineados.
alike [əlīk'] *a* semejantes, iguales ♦ *ad* igualmente, del mismo modo; **to look** ~ parecerse.
alimony [al'əmōnē] *n* (*LAW*) manutención *f*.
alive [əlīv'] *a* (*gen*) vivo; (*lively*) activo.
alkali [al'kəlī] *n* álcali *m*.
all [ôl] *a* todo; (*pl*) todos(as) ♦ *pron* todo;

(pl) todos(as) ♦ *ad* completamente, del todo; ~ **day** todo el día; **for** ~ **their efforts** a pesar de sus esfuerzos; ~ **alone** solito, completamente solo; **at** ~: **anything at** ~ lo que sea; **not at** ~ *(in answer to thanks)* de nada; **I'm not at** ~ **tired** no estoy nada cansado; ~ **but** casi; ~ **the time/his life** todo el tiempo/toda su vida; ~ **the more/ the better** tanto más/mejor; ~ **five** todos los cinco; ~ **of them** todos (ellos); ~ **of us went** fuimos todos; **is that** ~? ¿nada más?, ¿es (eso) todo?; *(in shop)* ¿algo más?; **not as hard as** ~ **that** no tan difícil; **to be/feel** ~ **in** estar rendido; ~ **in** ~ con todo, total.

all-around |ôl'əround| *a (US)* completo; *(view)* amplio.

allay |əlā'| *vt (fears)* aquietar; *(pain)* aliviar.

all clear *n (after attack etc)* fin *m* de la alerta; *(fig)* luz *f* verde.

allegation |aləgā'shən| *n* alegato.

allege |əlej'| *vt* pretender; **he is** ~**d to have said** ... se afirma que él dijo ....

alleged |əlejd'| *a* supuesto, presunto.

allegedly |əlej'idlē| *ad* supuestamente, según se afirma.

allegiance |əlē'jəns| *n* lealtad *f.*

allegory |al'əgôrē| *n* alegoría.

all-embracing |ôl'embrās'ing| *a* universal.

allergic |əlûr'jik| *a*: ~ **to** alérgico a.

allergy |al'ûrjē| *n* alergia.

alleviate |əlē'vēāt| *vt* aliviar.

alleviation |əlēvēā'shən| *n* alivio.

alley |al'ē| *n (street)* callejuela; *(in garden)* paseo.

alliance |əlī'əns| *n* alianza.

allied |əlīd'| *a* aliado; *(related)* relacionado.

alligator |al'əgātûr| *n* caimán *m.*

all-important |ôl'impôr'tənt| *a* de suma importancia.

all-inclusive |ôl'inklōō'siv| *a (also ad: charge)* todo incluido.

all-in wrestling |ôl'in res'ling| *n (Brit)* lucha libre.

alliteration |əlitərā'shən| *n* aliteración *f.*

all-night |ôl'nīt| *a (café)* abierto toda la noche; *(party)* que dura toda la noche.

allocate |al'əkāt| *vt (share out)* repartir; *(devote)* asignar.

allocation |aləkā'shən| *n (of money)* ración *f*, cuota; *(distribution)* reparto.

allot |əlât'| *vt* asignar; **in the** ~**ted time** en el tiempo asignado.

allotment |əlât'mənt| *n* ración *f*; *(Brit: garden)* parcela.

all-out |ôl'out'| *a (effort etc)* supremo ♦ *ad*: **all out** con todas las fuerzas.

allow |əlou'| *vt (permit)* permitir, dejar; *(a claim)* admitir; *(sum to spend, time estimated)* dar, conceder; *(concede)*: **to** ~ **that** reconocer que; **to** ~ **sb to do** permitir a alguien hacer; **smoking is not** ~**ed** pro-

hibido *or* se prohíbe fumar; **he is** ~**ed to** ... se le permite ...; **we must** ~ **3 days for the journey** debemos dejar 3 días para el viaje.

allow for *vt fus* tener en cuenta.

allowance |əlou'əns| *n* concesión *f*; *(payment)* subvención *f*, pensión *f*; *(discount)* descuento, rebaja; **to make** ~**s for** *(person)* disculpar a; *(thing: take into account)* tener en cuenta.

alloy |al'oi| *n (mix)* mezcla.

all right *ad (feel, work)* bien; *(as answer)* ¡conforme!, ¡está bien!

all-rounder |ôlroun'dûr| *n (Brit)*: **to be a good** ~ ser una persona que hace de todo.

allspice |ôl'spīs| *n* pimienta inglesa *or* de Jamaica.

all-time |ôl'tīm| *a (record)* de todos los tiempos.

allude |əlōōd'| *vi*: **to** ~ **to** aludir a.

alluring |əlōō'ring| *a* seductor(a), atractivo.

allusion |əlōō'zhən| *n* referencia, alusión *f.*

ally *n* |al'ī| aliado/a ♦ *vt* |əlī'|: **to** ~ **o.s. with** aliarse con.

almanac |ôl'mənak| *n* almanaque *m.*

almighty |ôlmī'tē| *a* todopoderoso.

almond |â'mənd| *n (fruit)* almendra; *(tree)* almendro.

almost |ôl'mōst| *ad* casi; **he** ~ **fell** por poco *or* casi se cae.

alms |âmz| *npl* limosna *sg.*

aloft |əlôft'| *ad* arriba.

alone |əlōn'| *a* solo ♦ *ad* sólo, solamente; **to leave sb** ~ dejar a uno en paz; **to leave sth** ~ no tocar algo, dejar algo sin tocar; **let** ~ ... sin hablar de ...

along |əlông'| *prep* a lo largo de, por ♦ *ad*: **is he coming** ~ **with us?** ¿viene con nosotros?; **he was limping** ~ iba cojeando; ~ **with** junto con; **all** ~ *(all the time)* desde el principio.

alongside |əlông'sīd'| *prep* al lado de ♦ *ad (NAUT)* de costado; **we brought our boat** ~ atracamos nuestro barco.

aloof |əlōōf'| *a* reservado ♦ *ad*: **to stand** ~ mantenerse a distancia.

aloud |əloud'| *ad* en voz alta.

alphabet |al'fəbet| *n* alfabeto.

alphabetical |alfəbet'ikəl| *a* alfabético; **in** ~ **order** por orden alfabético.

alphanumeric |alfənōōmār'ik| *a* alfanumérico.

alpine |al'pīn| *a* alpino, alpestre.

Alps |alps| *npl*: **the** ~ los Alpes.

already |ôlred'ē| *ad* ya.

alright |ôlrīt'| *ad (Brit)* = **all right.**

Alsatian |alsā'shən| *n (dog)* pastor *m* alemán.

also |ôl'sō| *ad* también, además.

Alta. *abbr (Canada)* = *Alberta.*

altar |ôl'tûr| *n* altar *m.*

alter |ôl'tûr| *vt* cambiar, modificar ♦ *vi* cambiarse, modificarse.

alteration |ôltərā'shən| n cambio, modificación f; alteración f; ~s npl (ARCH) reformas fpl; (SEWING) arreglos mpl; **timetable subject to** ~ el horario puede cambiar.

alternate a |ôl'tûrnit| alterno ♦ vi |ôl'tûrnāt|: **to** ~ **(with)** alternar (con); **on** ~ **days** un día sí y otro no.

alternately |ôl'tûrnitlē| ad alternativamente, por turno.

alternating |ôl'tûrnāting| a (current) alterno.

alternative |ôltûr'nətiv| a alternativo ♦ n alternativa.

alternatively |ôltûr'nətivlē| ad: ~ **one could** ... por otra parte se podría....

alternator |ôl'tûrnātûr| n (AUT) alternador m.

although |ôlt͟hō'| conj aunque, si bien.

altitude |al'təto͞od| n altitud f, altura.

alto |al'tō| n (female) contralto f; (male: US) contralto; (: Brit) alto.

altogether |ôltəget͟h'ûr| ad completamente, del todo; (on the whole, in all) en total, en conjunto; **how much is that** ~? ¿cuánto es todo or en total?

altruistic |altro͞ois'tik| a altruista.

aluminium |alo͞omin'ēəm| etc (Brit) = **aluminum** etc.

aluminum |əlo͞o'mənəm| n (US) aluminio.

aluminum foil n papel m de estaño.

alumnus |əlum'nəs| n (US) graduado.

always |ôl'wāz| ad siempre.

AM abbr = amplitude modulation.

am |am| vb see **be**.

a.m. ad abbr (= ante meridiem) de la mañana.

AMA n abbr = American Medical Association.

amalgam |əmal'gəm| n amalgama.

amalgamate |əmal'gəmāt| vi amalgamarse ♦ vt amalgamar.

amalgamation |əmalgəmā'shən| n (COMM) fusión f.

amass |əmas'| vt amontonar, acumular.

amateur |am'əchûr| n aficionado/a, amateur m/f; ~ **dramatics** dramas mpl presentados por aficionados, representación f de aficionados.

amateurish |aməcho͞o'rish| a (pej) torpe, inexperto.

amaze |əmāz'| vt asombrar, pasmar; **to be** ~**d (at)** asombrarse (de).

amazement |əmāz'mənt| n asombro, sorpresa; **to my** ~ para mi sorpresa.

amazing |əmā'zing| a extraordinario, asombroso; (bargain, offer) increíble.

amazingly |əmā'zinglē| ad extraordinariamente.

Amazon |am'əzän| n (GEO) Amazonas m; (MYTHOLOGY) amazona ♦ cpd: **the** ~ **basin/jungle** la cuenca/selva del Amazonas.

Amazonian |aməzō'nēən| a amazónico.

ambassador |ambas'ədûr| n embajador(a) m/f.

amber |am'bûr| n ámbar m; **at** ~ (Brit AUT) en el amarillo.

ambidextrous |ambidek'strəs| a ambidextro.

ambience |am'bēəns| n ambiente m.

ambiguity |ambəgyo͞o'itē| n ambigüedad f; (of meaning) doble sentido.

ambiguous |ambig'yo͞oəs| a ambiguo.

ambition |ambish'ən| n ambición f; **to achieve one's** ~ realizar su ambición.

ambitious |ambish'əs| a ambicioso; (plan) grandioso.

ambivalent |ambiv'ələnt| a ambivalente; (pej) equívoco.

amble |am'bəl| vi (gen: ~ **along**) deambular, andar sin prisa.

ambulance |am'byələns| n ambulancia.

ambulanceman/woman |am'byələnsman/wo͞om'ən| n (Brit) ambulanciero/a.

ambush |am'bo͞osh| n emboscada ♦ vt tender una emboscada a; (fig) coger (Sp) or agarrar (LAm) por sorpresa.

ameba |əmē'bə| n (US) = **amoeba**.

ameliorate |əmēl'yərāt| vt mejorar.

amelioration |əmēlyərā'shən| n mejora.

amen |ā'men'| excl amén.

amenable |əmē'nəbəl| a: ~ **to** (advice etc) sensible a.

amend |əmend'| vt (law, text) enmendar; **to make** ~**s** (apologize) enmendarlo, dar cumplida satisfacción.

amendment |əmend'mənt| n enmienda.

amenities |əmen'itēz| npl comodidades fpl.

amenity |əmen'itē| n servicio.

America |əmär'ikə| n América del Norte.

American |əmär'ikən| a, n norteamericano/a m/f, estadounidense m/f.

americanize |əmär'ikəniz| vt americanizar.

Amerindian |amərin'dēən| a, n amerindio/a m/f.

amethyst |am'ithist| n amatista.

Amex |am'eks| n abbr = American Stock Exchange.

amiable |ā'mēəbəl| a (kind) amable, simpático.

amicable |am'ikəbəl| a amistoso, amigable.

amid(st) |əmid(st)'| prep entre, en medio de.

amiss |əmis'| ad: **to take sth** ~ tomar algo a mal; **there's something** ~ pasa algo.

ammo |am'ō| n abbr (col) = **ammunition**.

ammonia |əmōn'yə| n amoníaco.

ammunition |amyənish'ən| n municiones fpl; (fig) argumentos mpl.

ammunition dump n depósito de municiones.

amnesia |amnē'zhə| n amnesia.

amnesty |am'nistē| n amnistía; **to grant** ~ **to** amnistiar (a).

amoeba |əmē'bə| n amiba.

amok |əmuk'| *ad*: **to run** ~ enloquecerse, desbocarse.

among(st) |əmung(st)'| *prep* entre, en medio de.

amoral |āmôr'əl| *a* amoral.

amorous |am'ûrəs| *a* cariñoso.

amorphous |əmôr'fəs| *a* amorfo.

amortization |amûrtəzā'shən| *n* amortización *f*.

amount |əmount'| *n* (*gen*) cantidad *f*; (*of bill etc*) suma, importe *m* ♦ *vi*: **to** ~ **to** (*total*) sumar; (*be same as*) equivaler a, significar; **this** ~**s to a refusal** esto equivale a una negativa; **the total** ~ (*of money*) la suma total.

amp(ere) |am'pēr| *n* amperio; **a 13 amp plug** un enchufe de 13 amperios.

ampersand |am'pûrsand| *n* signo &, "y" comercial.

amphibian |amfib'ēən| *n* anfibio.

amphibious |amfib'ēəs| *a* anfibio.

amphitheater, (*Brit*) **amphitheatre** |am'fəthēətûr| *n* anfiteatro.

ample |am'pəl| *a* (*spacious*) amplio; (*abundant*) abundante; **to have** ~ **time** tener tiempo de sobra.

amplifier |am'pləfîûr| *n* amplificador *m*.

amplify |am'pləfī| *vt* amplificar, aumentar; (*explain*) explicar.

amply |am'plē| *ad* ampliamente.

ampule, (*Brit*) **ampoule** |am'pyōōl| *n* (*MED*) ampolla.

amputate |am'pyōōtāt| *vt* amputar.

Amsterdam |am'stûrdam| *n* Amsterdam *m*.

amt *abbr* = **amount.**

amuck |əmuk'| *ad* = **amok.**

amuse |əmyōōz'| *vt* divertir; (*distract*) distraer, entretener; **to** ~ **o.s. with sth/by doing sth** distraerse con algo/haciendo algo; **he was** ~**d at the joke** le divirtió el chiste.

amusement |əmyōōz'mənt| *n* diversión *f*; (*pastime*) pasatiempo; (*laughter*) risa; **much to my** ~ con gran regocijo mío.

amusement arcade *n* mini-casino.

amusement park *n* parque *m* de atracciones.

amusing |əmyōō'zing| *a* divertido.

an |an, ən| *indefinite article see* **a.**

ANA *n abbr* = *American Newspaper Association; American Nurses Association.*

anachronism |ənak'rənizəm| *n* anacronismo.

anaemia |ənē'mēə| *n* (*Brit*) = **anemia.**

anaemic |ənē'mik| *a* (*Brit*) = **anemic.**

anaesthetic |anisthet'ik| *n* (*Brit*) = **anesthetic.**

anaesthetist |ənēs'thətist| *n* (*Brit*) anestesista *m/f*.

anagram |an'əgram| *n* anagrama *m*.

analgesic |anəljē'zik| *a, n* analgésico.

analogous |ənal'əgəs| *a* análogo.

analog(ue) |an'əlôg| *a* (*computer, watch*) analógico.

analogy |ənal'əjē| *n* analogía; **to draw an** ~ **between** señalar la analogía entre.

analyse |an'əlīz| *vt* (*Brit*) = **analyze.**

analysis, *pl* **analyses** |ənal'isis, -sēz| *n* análisis *m inv*.

analyst |an'əlist| *n* (*political* ~, *psycho*~) analista *m/f*.

analytic(al) |anəlit'ik(əl)| *a* analítico.

analyze |an'əlīz| *vt* (*US*) analizar.

anarchist |an'ûrkist| *a, n* anarquista *m/f*.

anarchy |an'ûrkē| *n* anarquía, desorden *m*.

anathema |ənath'əmə| *n*: **that is** ~ **to him** eso es pecado para él.

anatomical |anətâm'ikəl| *a* anatómico.

anatomy |ənat'əmē| *n* anatomía.

ANC *n abbr* = *African National Congress.*

ancestor |an'sestûr| *n* antepasado.

ancestral |anses'trəl| *a* ancestral.

ancestry |an'sestrē| *n* ascendencia, abolengo.

anchor |ang'kûr| *n* ancla, áncora ♦ *vi* (*also*: **to drop** ~) anclar ♦ *vt* (*fig*) sujetar, afianzar; **to weigh** ~ levar anclas.

anchorage |ang'kûrij| *n* ancladero.

anchovy |an'chōvē| *n* anchoa.

ancient |ān'shənt| *a* antiguo; ~ **monument** monumento histórico.

ancillary |an'səlärē| *a* (*worker, staff*) auxiliar.

and |and| *conj* y; (*before i, hi*) e; ~ **so on** etcétera; **try** ~ **come** procure *or* intente venir; **better** ~ **better** cada vez mejor.

Andalusia |andəlōō'zhə| *n* Andalucía.

Andes |an'dēz| *npl*: **the** ~ los Andes.

anecdote |an'ikdōt| *n* anécdota.

anemia |ənē'mēə| *n* (*US*) anemia.

anemic |ənē'mik| *a* (*US*) a anémico; (*fig*) soso, insípido.

anemone |ənem'ənē| *n* (*BOT*) anémone *f*; **sea** ~ anémona.

anesthesiologist |anisthēzēāl'əjist| *n* (*US*) anestesista *m/f*.

anesthetic |anisthet'ik| *n* (*US*) anestesia; **local/general** ~ anestesia local/general.

anew |ənōō'| *ad* de nuevo, otra vez.

angel |ān'jəl| *n* ángel *m*.

angelic |anjel'ik| *a* angélico.

anger |ang'gûr| *n* ira, enfado, cólera ♦ *vt* enojar, enfurecer.

angina |anjī'nə| *n* angina (del pecho).

angle |ang'gəl| *n* ángulo; **from their** ~ desde su punto de vista.

angler |ang'glûr| *n* pescador(a) *m/f* (de caña).

Anglican |ang'glikən| *a, n* anglicano/a.

anglicize |ang'gləsīz| *vt* dar forma inglesa a.

angling |ang'gling| *n* pesca con caña.

Anglo- |an'glō| *pref* anglo....

Angola |anggō'lə| *n* Angola.

Angolan |anggō'lən| *a, n* angoleño/a *m/f*.

angrily |ang'grilē| *ad* enojado, enfadado.

angry |ang'grē| *a* enfadado, enojado; **to be**

~ **with sb/at sth** estar enfadado con alguien/por algo; **to get** ~ enfadarse, enojarse.

anguish [ang'gwish] *n* (*physical*) tormentos *mpl*; (*mental*) angustia.

angular [ang'gyəlûr] *a* (*shape*) angular; (*features*) anguloso.

animal [an'əməl] *n* animal *m*, bestia ♦ *a* animal.

animate *vt* [an'əmāt] (*enliven*) animar; (*encourage*) estimular, alentar ♦ *a* [an'əmit] vivo.

animated [an'əmātid] *a* vivo.

animation [anəmā'shən] *n* animación *f*.

animosity [anəmâs'ətē] *n* animosidad *f*, rencor *m*.

aniseed [an'isēd] *n* anís *m*.

Ankara [ang'kûrə] *n* Ankara.

ankle [ang'kəl] *n* tobillo *m*.

ankle sock *n* calcetín *m*.

annex *n* [an'eks] (*also*: *Brit*: **annexe**) (*building*) edificio anexo ♦ *vt* [əneks'] (*territory*) anexar.

annihilate [ənī'əlāt] *vt* aniquilar.

anniversary [anəvûr'sûrē] *n* aniversario.

annotate [an'ōtāt] *vt* anotar.

announce [ənouns'] *vt* (*gen*) anunciar; (*inform*) comunicar; **he ~d that he wasn't going** declaró que no iba.

announcement [ənouns'mənt] *n* (*gen*) anuncio; (*declaration*) declaración *f*; **I'd like to make an** ~ quisiera anunciar algo.

announcer [ənoun'sûr] *n* (*RADIO*, *TV*) locutor(a) *m/f*.

annoy [ənoi'] *vt* molestar, fastidiar, irritar; **to be ~ed (at sth/with sb)** estar enfadado *or* molesto (por algo/con uno); **don't get ~ed!** ¡no se enfade!

annoyance [ənoi'əns] *n* enojo; (*thing*) molestia.

annoying [ənoi'ing] *a* molesto, fastidioso; (*person*) pesado.

annual [an'yōōəl] *a* anual ♦ *n* (*BOT*) anual *m*; (*book*) anuario.

annual general meeting (AGM) *n* (*Brit*) junta general anual.

annually [an'yōōəlē] *ad* anualmente, cada año.

annual report *n* informe *m or* memoria anual.

annuity [ənōō'itē] *n* renta *or* pensión *f* vitalicia.

annul [ənul'] *vt* anular; (*law*) revocar.

annulment [ənul'mənt] *n* anulación *f*.

annum [an'əm] *n see* **per annum**.

Annunciation [ənunsēā'shən] *n* Anunciación *f*.

anode [an'ōd] *n* ánodo *m*.

anoint [ənoint'] *vt* untar.

anomalous [ənâm'ələs] *a* anómalo.

anomaly [ənâm'əlē] *n* anomalía.

anon. [ənân'] *abbr* = **anonymous**.

anonymity [anənim'itē] *n* anonimato.

anonymous [ənân'əməs] *a* anónimo; **to remain** ~ quedar en el anonimato.

anorak [ân'ərâk] *n* anorak *m*.

anorexia [anərek'sēə] *n* (*MED*) anorexia.

another [ənuth'ûr] *a*: ~ **book** (*one more*) otro libro; (*a different one*) un libro distinto; ~ **beer?** ¿(quieres) otra cerveza?; **in** ~ **5 years** en cinco años más ♦ *pron* otro; **some actor or** ~ algún actor; *see also* **one**.

ANSI *n abbr* (= *American National Standards Institute*) *instituto de normas*.

answer [an'sûr] *n* contestación *f*, respuesta; (*to problem*) solución *f* ♦ *vi* contestar, responder ♦ *vt* (*reply to*) contestar a, responder a; (*problem*) resolver; **to** ~ **the phone** contestar el teléfono; **in** ~ **to your letter** contestando *or* en contestación a su carta; **to** ~ **the bell** *or* **the door** acudir a la puerta.

answer back *vi* replicar, ser respondón/ona.

answer for *vt fus* responder de *or* por.

answer to *vt fus* (*description*) corresponder a.

answerable [an'sûrəbəl] *a*: ~ **to sb for sth** responsable ante uno de algo.

answering machine [an'sûring məshēn'] *n* contestador *m* automático.

ant [ant] *n* hormiga.

ANTA *n abbr* = *American National Theatre and Academy*.

antagonism [antag'ənizəm] *n* hostilidad *f*.

antagonist [antag'ənist] *n* antagonista *m/f*, adversario/a.

antagonistic [antagənis'tik] *a* antagónico; (*opposed*) contrario, opuesto.

antagonize [antag'ənīz] *vt* provocar.

Antarctic [antârk'tik] *a* antártico ♦ *n*: **the** ~ el Antártico.

Antarctica [antârk'tikə] *n* Antártida.

Antarctic Circle *n* Círculo Polar Antártico.

Antarctic Ocean *n* Océano Antártico.

ante [an'tē] *n*: **to up the** ~ subir la puesta.

ante... *pref* ante...

anteater [ant'ētûr] *n* oso hormiguero.

antecedent [antisē'dənt] *n* antecedente *m*.

antechamber [an'tēchâmbûr] *n* antecámara.

antelope [an'tələp] *n* antílope *m*.

antenatal [antēnā'təl] *a* (*Brit*) = **prenatal**.

antenna, *pl* ~**e** [anten'ə, -nē] *n* antena.

anteroom [an'tēroom] *n* antesala.

anthem [an'thəm] *n*: **national** ~ himno nacional.

anthology [anthâl'əjē] *n* antología.

anthropologist [anthrəpâl'əjist] *n* antropólogo/a.

anthropology [anthrəpâl'əjē] *n* antropología.

anti... [an'tī] *pref* anti....

antiaircraft [antīâr'kraft] *a* antiaéreo.

antiballistic [antēbəlis'tik] *a* antibalístico.

antibiotic |antēbīát'ik| *a*, *n* antibiótico.
antibody |an'tēbädē| *n* anticuerpo.
anticipate |antis'əpāt| *vt* (*foresee*) prever; (*expect*) esperar, contar con; (*forestall*) anticiparse a, adelantarse a; **this is worse than I** ~**d** esto es peor de lo que esperaba; **as** ~**d** según se esperaba.
anticipation |antisəpā'shən| *n* previsión *f*; esperanza; anticipación *f*.
anticlimax |antēklī'maks| *n* decepción *f*.
anticlockwise |antēklåk'wīz| *ad* (*Brit*) en dirección contraria a la de las agujas del reloj.
antics |an'tiks| *npl* payasadas *fpl*; (*of child*) travesuras *fpl*.
anticyclone |antēsī'klōn| *n* anticiclón *m*.
antidote |an'tidōt| *n* antídoto.
antifreeze |an'tēfrēz| *n* anticongelante *m*.
antihistamine |antēhis'təmēn| *n* antihistamínico.
Antilles |antil'ēz| *npl*: **the** ~ las Antillas.
antipathy |antip'əthē| *n* (*between people*) antipatía; (*to person, thing*) aversión *f*.
Antipodean |antipədē'ən| *a* antípoda.
Antipodes |antip'ədēz| *npl*: **the** ~ las Antípodas.
antiquarian |antəkwär'ēən| *n* anticuario/a.
antiquated |an'təkwātid| *a* anticuado.
antique |antēk'| *n* antigüedad *f* ♦ *a* antiguo.
antique dealer *n* anticuario/a.
antique shop *n* tienda de antigüedades.
antiquity |antik'witē| *n* antigüedad *f*.
anti-Semitic |an'tīsəmit'ik| *a* antisemita.
anti-Semitism |antīsem'itizəm| *n* antisemitismo.
antiseptic |antēsep'tik| *a*, *n* antiséptico.
antisocial |antēsō'shəl| *a* antisocial.
antitank |antētangk'| *a* antitanque.
antithesis, *pl* **antitheses** |antith'əsis, -sēz| *n* antítesis *f inv*.
antitrust |antētrust'| *a*: ~ **legislation** legislación *f* antimonopolio.
antlers |ant'lûrz| *npl* cornamenta.
anus |ā'nəs| *n* ano.
anvil |an'vil| *n* yunque *m*.
anxiety |angzī'ətē| *n* (*worry*) inquietud *f*; (*eagerness*) ansia, anhelo.
anxious |angk'shəs| *a* (*worried*) inquieto; (*keen*) deseoso; **I'm very** ~ **about you** me tienes muy preocupado.
anxiously |angk'shəslē| *ad* con inquietud, de manera angustiada.
any |en'ē| *a* (*in negative and interrogative sentences* = *some*) algún, alguna; (*negative sense*) ningún, ninguna; (*no matter which*) cualquier(a); (*each and every*) todo; **I haven't** ~ **money/books** no tengo dinero/libros; **have you** ~ **butter/children/ money?** ¿tiene mantequilla/hijos/dinero?; **at** ~ **moment** en cualquier momento; ~ **day now** cualquier día de éstos; **in** ~ **case**, **at** ~ **rate** de todas formas, de todas maneras ♦ *pron* alguno; ninguno; (*anybody*)

cualquiera; (*in negative and interrogative sentences*): **I haven't** ~ no tengo ninguno; **have you got** ~? ¿tiene algunos?; **can** ~ **of you sing?** ¿alguno de ustedes sabe cantar? ♦ *ad* (*in negative sentences*) nada; (*in interrogative and conditional constructions*) algo; **I can't hear him** ~ **more** no le oigo más; **do you want** ~ **more soup?** ¿quiere más sopa?
anybody |en'ēbádē| *pron* cualquiera, cualquier persona; (*in interrogative sentences*) alguien; (*in negative sentences*): **I don't see** ~ no veo a nadie.
anyhow |en'ēhou| *ad* de todos modos, de todas maneras; (*carelessly*) de cualquier manera; (*haphazardly*) de cualquier modo; **I shall go** ~ iré de todas maneras.
anyone |en'ēwun| = **anybody**.
anyplace |en'ēplās| *ad* (*US*) = **anywhere**.
anything |en'ēthing| *pron* (*see* **anybody**) cualquier cosa; (*in interrogative sentences*) algo; (*in negative sentences*) nada; (*everything*) todo; ~ **else?** ¿algo más?
anytime |en'ētīm| *ad* (*at any moment*) en cualquier momento, de un momento a otro; (*whenever*) no importa cuándo, cuando quiera.
anyway |en'ēwā| *ad* de todas maneras; de cualquier modo.
anywhere |en'ēhwär| *ad* (*see* **anybody**) dondequiera; (*interrogative*) en algún sitio; (*negative sense*) en ningún sitio; (*everywhere*) en or por todas partes; **I don't see him** ~ no le veo en ningún sitio; ~ **in the world** en cualquier parte del mundo.
Anzac |an'zak| *n abbr* (= *Australia-New Zealand Army Corps*) soldado del cuerpo Anzac.
apace |əpās'| *ad* aprisa.
apart |əpärt'| *ad* aparte, separadamente; **10 miles** ~ separados por 10 millas; **to take** ~ desmontar; ~ **from** *prep* aparte de.
apartheid |əpärt'hīt| *n* apartheid *m*.
apartment |əpärt'mənt| *n* piso, departamento (*LAm*), apartamento; (*room*) cuarto.
apartment block *or* **building** *or* **house** *n* bloque *m* de pisos.
apathetic |apəthet'ik| *a* apático, indiferente.
apathy |ap'əthē| *n* apatía, indiferencia.
APB *n abbr* (*US*: = *all points bulletin*) expresión usada por la policía que significa "descubrir y aprehender al sospechoso".
ape |āp| *n* mono ♦ *vt* imitar, remedar.
Apennines |ap'ənīnz| *npl*: **the** ~ los Apeninos *mpl*.
aperitif |əpärētēf'| *n* aperitivo.
aperture |ap'ûrchûr| *n* rendija, resquicio; (*PHOT*) abertura.
APEX |ā'peks| *n abbr* (*AVIAT* = *advance purchase excursion*) APEX *m*.
apex |ā'peks| *n* ápice *m*; (*fig*) cumbre *f*.

aphid |ā'fĭd| *n* áfido.
aphorism |af'ərizəm| *n* aforismo.
aphrodisiac |afrədiz'ēak| *a, n* afrodisíaco.
API *n abbr* = *American Press Institute*.
apiece |əpēs'| *ad* cada uno.
aplomb |əplâm'| *n* aplomo, confianza.
APO *n abbr* (*US*: = *Army Post Office*) *servicio postal del ejército*.
Apocalypse |əpák'əlips| *n* Apocalipsis *m*.
apocryphal |əpák'rəfəl| *a* apócrifo.
apolitical |āpəlit'ikəl| *a* apolítico.
apologetic |əpâləjĕt'ik| *a* (*look, remark*) de disculpa.
apologetically |əpâləjĕt'iklē| *ad* con aire de disculpa, excusándose, disculpándose.
apologize |əpál'əjīz| *vi*: **to ~ (for sth to sb)** disculparse (con alguien de algo).
apology |əpál'əjē| *n* disculpa, excusa; **please accept my apologies** le ruego me disculpe.
apoplectic |apəplĕk'tik| *a* (*MED*) apopléctico; (*col*): **~ with rage** furioso.
apoplexy |ap'əplĕksē| *n* apoplejía.
apostle |əpâs'əl| *n* apóstol *m/f*.
apostrophe |əpâs'trəfē| *n* apóstrofe *m*.
Appalachian Mountains |apəlā'chēən moun'tənz| *npl*: **the ~** los Montes Apalaches.
appal(l) |əpôl'| *vt* horrorizar, espantar.
appalling |əpôl'ing| *a* espantoso; (*awful*) pésimo; **she's an ~ cook** es una cocinera malísima.
apparatus |apərat'əs| *n* aparato; (*in gymnasium*) aparatos *mpl*.
apparel |əpar'əl| *n* (*US*) indumentaria.
apparent |əpar'ənt| *a* aparente; (*obvious*) manifiesto, claro; **it is ~ that** está claro que.
apparently |əpar'əntlē| *ad* por lo visto, al parecer.
apparition |apərish'ən| *n* aparición *f*; (*ghost*) fantasma *m*.
appeal |əpē'l'| *vi* (*LAW*) apelar ♦ *n* (*LAW*) apelación *f*; (*request*) llamamiento; (*plea*) súplica; (*charm*) atractivo, encanto; **to ~ for** suplicar, reclamar; **to ~ to** (*subj: person*) rogar a, suplicar a; (*subj: thing*) atraer, interesar; **to ~ to sb for mercy** rogarle misericordia a alguien; **it doesn't ~ to me** no me atrae, no me llama la atención; **right of ~** derecho de apelación.
appealing |əpē'ling| *a* (*nice*) atractivo; (*touching*) conmovedor(a), emocionante.
appear |əpēr'| *vi* aparecer, presentarse; (*LAW*) comparecer; (*publication*) salir (a luz), publicarse; (*seem*) parecer; **it would ~ that** parecería que.
appearance |əpē'rəns| *n* aparición *f*; (*look, aspect*) apariencia, aspecto; **to keep up ~s** salvar las apariencias; **to all ~s** al parecer.
appease |əpēz'| *vt* (*pacify*) apaciguar; (*satisfy*) satisfacer.

appeasement |əpēz'mənt| *n* (*POL*) entreguismo.
appellate court |əpel'it kôrt| *n* (*US*) tribunal *m* de apelación.
append |əpend'| *vt* (*COMPUT*) anexionar (al final).
appendage |əpen'dij| *n* añadidura.
appendicitis |əpendisī'tis| *n* apendicitis *f*.
appendix, *pl* **appendices** |əpen'diks, -disēz| *n* apéndice *m*; **to have one's ~ out** operarse de apendicitis.
appetite |ap'itīt| *n* apetito; (*fig*) deseo, anhelo; **that walk has given me an ~** ese paseo me ha dado apetito.
appetizer |ap'itīzûr| *n* (*drink*) aperitivo; (*food*) tapas *fpl* (*Sp*).
appetizing |ap'itīzing| *a* apetitoso.
applaud |əplôd'| *vt, vi* aplaudir.
applause |əplôz'| *n* aplausos *mpl*.
apple |ap'əl| *n* manzana.
apple tree *n* manzano.
appliance |əplī'əns| *n* aparato; **electrical ~s** electrodomésticos *mpl*.
applicable |ap'likəbəl| *a* aplicable, pertinente; **the law is ~ from January** la ley es aplicable *or* se pone en vigor desde enero; **to be ~ to** referirse a.
applicant |ap'likənt| *n* candidato/a; solicitante *m/f*.
application |aplikā'shən| *n* aplicación *f*; (*for a job, a grant etc*) solicitud *f*, petición *f*.
application form *n* solicitud *f*.
applications package *n* (*COMPUT*) paquete *m* de programas de aplicación.
applied |əplīd'| *a* (*science, art*) aplicado.
apply |əplī'| *vt*: **to ~ (to)** aplicar (a); (*fig*) emplear (para) ♦ *vi*: **to ~ to** (*ask*) dirigirse a; (*be suitable for*) ser aplicable a; (*be relevant to*) tener que ver con; **to ~ for** (*permit, grant, job*) solicitar; **to ~ the brakes** aplicar los frenos; **to ~ o.s. to** aplicarse a, dedicarse a.
appoint |əpoint'| *vt* (*to post*) nombrar; (*date, place*) fijar, señalar.
appointee |əpointē'| *n* persona nombrada.
appointment |əpoint'mənt| *n* (*engagement*) cita; (*date*) compromiso; (*act*) nombramiento; (*post*) puesto; **to make an ~ (with)** (*doctor*) pedir hora (con); (*friend*) citarse (con); **by ~** por medio de cita.
appointment book *n* agenda.
apportion |əpôr'shən| *vt* repartir.
appraisal |əprā'zəl| *n* apreciación *f*.
appraise |əprāz'| *vt* (*value*) tasar, valorar; (*situation etc*) evaluar.
appreciable |əprē'shēəbəl| *a* sensible.
appreciate |əprē'shēāt| *vt* (*like*) apreciar, tener en mucho; (*be grateful for*) agradecer; (*be aware of*) comprender ♦ *vi* (*COMM*) aumentar(se) en valor; **I ~d your help** agradecí tu ayuda.

appreciation [əprēshēā'shən] *n* aprecio; reconocimiento, agradecimiento; aumento en valor.

appreciative [əprē'shətiv] *a* apreciativo, agradecido.

apprehend [aprihend'] *vt* percibir; (*arrest*) detener.

apprehension [aprihen'shən] *n* (*fear*) aprensión *f*.

apprehensive [aprihen'siv] *a* aprensivo.

apprentice [əpren'tis] *n* aprendiz(a) *m/f* ♦ *vt*: **to be ~d to** estar de aprendiz con.

apprenticeship [əpren'tisship] *n* aprendizaje *m*; **to serve one's ~** hacer el aprendizaje.

approach [əprōch'] *vi* acercarse ♦ *vt* acercarse a; (*be approximate*) aproximarse a; (*ask, apply to*) dirigirse a ♦ *n* acercamiento; aproximación *f*; (*access*) acceso; (*proposal*) proposición *f*; **to ~ sb about sth** hablar con uno sobre algo.

approachable [əprō'chəbəl] *a* (*person*) abordable; (*place*) accesible.

approach road *n* vía de acceso.

approbation [aprəbā'shən] *n* aprobación *f*.

appropriate *a* [əprōp'rēit] apropiado, conveniente ♦ *vt* [əprōp'rēāt] (*take*) apropiarse de; (*allot*): **to ~ sth for** destinar algo a; **~ for** *or* **to** apropiado para; **it would not be ~ for me to comment** no estaría bien *or* sería pertinente que yo diera mi opinión.

appropriation [əprōprēā'shən] *n* asignación *f*.

appropriation account *n* cuenta de asignación.

approval [əprōō'vəl] *n* aprobación *f*, visto bueno; **on ~** (*COMM*) a prueba; **to meet with sb's ~** obtener la aprobación de uno.

approve [əprōōv'] *vt* aprobar.

approve of *vt fus* aprobar.

approx. *abbr* (= *approximately*) aprox.

approximate [əprāk'səmit] *a* aproximado.

approximately [əprāk'səmitlē] *ad* aproximadamente, más o menos.

approximation [əprāksəmā'shən] *n* aproximación *f*.

appt. *abbr* (*US*) = **appointment.**

Apr. *abbr* (= *April*) abr.

apr *n abbr* (= *annual percentage rate*) tasa de interés anual.

apricot [ap'rikāt] *n* albaricoque *m*, damasco (*LAm*).

April [āp'rəl] *n* abril *m*; **~ Fool's Day** *n* (*1 April*) ≈ día *m* de los Inocentes (*28 December*).

apron [ā'prən] *n* delantal *m*; (*AVIAT*) pista.

apse [aps] *n* (*ARCH*) ábside *m*.

Apt. *abbr* = **apartment.**

apt [apt] *a* (*to the point*) acertado, oportuno; (*appropriate*) apropiado; **~ to do** (*likely*) propenso a hacer.

aptitude [ap'tətōōd] *n* aptitud *f*, capacidad *f*.

aptitude test *n* prueba de aptitud.

aptly [apt'lē] *a* aptamente, acertadamente.

aqualung [ak'wəlung] *n* escafandra autónoma.

aquarium [əkwär'ēəm] *n* acuario.

Aquarius [əkwär'ēəs] *n* Acuario.

aquatic [əkwat'ik] *a* acuático.

aqueduct [ak'widukt] *n* acueducto.

AR *abbr* (*US MAIL*) = *Arkansas.*

Arab [ar'əb] *a*, *n* árabe *m/f*.

Arabia [ərā'bēə] *n* Arabia.

Arabian [ərā'bēən] *a* árabe, arábigo.

Arabian Desert *n* Desierto Arábigo.

Arabian Sea *n* Mar *m* de Omán.

Arabic [ar'əbik] *a* (*language*, *manuscripts*) árabe, arábigo ♦ *n* árabe *m*; **~ numerals** numeración *f* arábiga.

arable [ar'əbəl] *a* cultivable.

Aragon [ar'əgàn] *n* Aragón *m*.

arbiter [âr'bitùr] *n* árbitro.

arbitrary [âr'biträrē] *a* arbitrario.

arbitrate [âr'bitrāt] *vi* arbitrar.

arbitration [ârbitrā'shən] *n* arbitraje *m*; **the dispute went to ~** el conflicto laboral fue sometido al arbitraje.

arbitrator [âr'bitrâtùr] *n* árbitro.

ARC *n abbr* = *American Red Cross.*

arc [ârk] *n* arco.

arcade [ârkâd'] *n* (*ARCH*) arcada; (*round a square*) soportales *mpl*; (*shopping ~*) galería comercial.

arch [ârch] *n* arco; (*vault*) bóveda; (*of foot*) arco del pie ♦ *vt* arquear.

archaeology [ârkēál'əjē] *etc* = **archeology** *etc.*

archaic [ârkā'ik] *a* arcaico.

archangel [ârkān'jəl] *n* arcángel *m*.

archbishop [ârchbish'əp] *n* arzobispo.

arched [ârcht] *a* abovedado.

archenemy [ârch'en'əmē] *n* enemigo jurado.

archeological [ârkēəláj'ikəl] *a* arqueológico.

archeologist [ârkēál'əjist] *n* arqueólogo/a.

archeology [ârkēál'əjē] *n* arqueología.

archer [âr'chùr] *n* arquero/a.

archery [âr'chûrē] *n* tiro al arco.

archetypal [âr'kitīpəl] *a* arquetípico.

archetype [âr'kitīp] *n* arquetipo.

archipelago [ârkəpel'əgō] *n* archipiélago.

architect [âr'kitekt] *n* arquitecto/a.

architectural [âr'kitekchûrəl] *a* arquitectónico.

architecture [âr'kitekchûr] *n* arquitectura.

archive [âr'kīv] *n* (*also COMPUT*) archivo.

archive file *n* (*COMPUT*) fichero archivado.

archives [âr'kīvz] *npl* archivo *sg*.

archivist [âr'kəvist] *n* archivero/a.

archway [ârch'wā] *n* arco, arcada.

Arctic [ârk'tik] *a* ártico ♦ *n*: **the ~** el Ártico.

Arctic Circle *n* Círculo Polar Ártico.

Arctic Ocean *n* Océano Glacial Ártico.

ARD *n abbr* (*US MED*) = *acute respiratory disease*.

ardent [âr'dənt] *a* (*desire*) ardiente; (*supporter, lover*) apasionado.

ardor, (*Brit*) **ardour** [âr'dûr] *n* ardor *m*, pasión *f*.

arduous [âr'jōōəs] *a* (*gen*) arduo; (*journey*) penoso.

are [âr] *vb see* **be.**

area [âr'ēə] *n* área; (*MATH etc*) superficie *f*, extensión *f*; (*zone*) región *f*, zona; **the Chicago** ~ la zona de Chicago.

area code *n* (*TEL*) prefijo.

arena [ərē'nə] *n* arena; (*of circus*) pista; (*for bullfight*) plaza, ruedo.

aren't [ärnt] = **are not.**

Argentina [ârjəntē'nə] *n* Argentina.

Argentinian [ârjəntin'ēən] *a, n* argentino/a *m/f*.

arguable [âr'gyōōəbəl] *a*: **it is** ~ **whether** ... es dudoso que + *subjun*.

arguably [âr'gyōōəblē] *ad*: **it is** ~ ... es discutiblemente ...

argue [âr'gyōō] *vt* (*debate: case, matter*) mantener, argüir ♦ *vi* (*quarrel*) discutir; (*reason*) razonar, argumentar; **to** ~ **that** sostener que; **to** ~ **about sth (with sb)** pelearse (con uno) por algo.

argument [âr'gyəmənt] *n* (*reasons*) argumento; (*quarrel*) discusión *f*; (*debate*) debate *m*, disputa; ~ **for/against** argumento en pro/contra de.

argumentative [ârgyəmen'tətiv] *a* discutidor(a).

aria [âr'ēə] *n* (*MUS*) aria.

arid [ar'id] *a* árido.

aridity [ərid'itē] *n* aridez *f*.

Aries [âr'ēz] *n* Aries *m*.

arise [ərīz'], *pt* **arose**, *pp* **arisen** [əriz'ən] *vi* (*rise up*) levantarse, alzarse; (*emerge*) surgir, presentarse; **to** ~ **from** derivar de; **should the need** ~ si fuera necesario.

aristocracy [aristák'rəsē] *n* aristocracia.

aristocrat [əris'təkrat] *n* aristócrata *m/f*.

aristocratic [əristəkrat'ik] *a* aristocrático.

arithmetic [ərith'mətik] *n* aritmética.

arithmetical [arithmet'ikəl] *a* aritmético.

Ariz. *abbr* (*US*) = *Arizona*.

Ark [ârk] *n*: **Noah's** ~ el Arca *f* de Noé.

Ark. *abbr* (*US*) = *Arkansas*.

arm [ârm] *n* (*ANAT*) brazo ♦ *vt* armar; ~ **in** ~ cogidos del brazo; *see also* **arms.**

armaments [âr'məmənts] *npl* (*weapons*) armamentos *mpl*.

armchair [ârm'chär] *n* sillón *m*.

armed [ârmd] *a* armado; **the** ~ **forces** las fuerzas armadas.

armed robbery *n* robo a mano armada.

Armenia [ârmē'nēə] *n* Armenia.

Armenian [ârmē'nēən] *a* armenio ♦ *n* armenio/a; (*LING*) armenio.

armful [ârm'fəl] *n* brazado, brazada.

armistice [âr'mistis] *n* armisticio.

armor [âr'mûr] *n* (*US*) armadura.

armored car [âr'mûrd kâr] *n* coche *m* or carro (*LAm*) blindado.

armory [âr'mûrē] *n* arsenal *m*.

armour [âr'mûr] *etc* (*Brit*) = **armor** *etc*.

armpit [ârm'pit] *n* sobaco, axila.

armrest [ârm'rest] *n* apoyabrazos *m inv*, brazo.

arms [ârmz] *npl* (*weapons*) armas *fpl*; (*HERALDRY*) escudo *sg*.

arms control *n* control *m* de armamentos.

arms race *n* carrera de armamentos.

army [âr'mē] *n* ejército.

aroma [ərō'mə] *n* aroma *m*, fragancia.

aromatic [arəmat'ik] *a* aromático, fragante.

arose [ərōz'] *pt of* **arise.**

around [əround'] *ad* alrededor; (*in the area*) a la redonda ♦ *prep* alrededor de; **all** ~ por todos lados; **it's the other way** ~ está al revés; **the long way** ~ por el camino menos directo; **it's just** ~ **the corner** (*fig*) está a la vuelta de la esquina; **to ask sb** ~ invitar a uno a casa; **I'll be** ~ **at 6 o'clock** llegaré a eso de las 6; **is Paul** ~? ¿está por aquí Paul?; ~ **the clock** *ad* las 24 horas; **to go** ~ **to sb's (house)** ir a casa de uno; **to go** ~ **the back** pasar por atrás; **to go** ~ **a house** visitar una casa; **enough to go** ~ bastante (para todos); **to walk** ~ **the town** andar por la ciudad.

arouse [ərouz'] *vt* despertar.

arrange [ərānj'] *vt* arreglar, ordenar; (*program*) organizar ♦ *vi*: **we have** ~**d for a taxi to pick you up** hemos hecho los arreglos para que le recoja un taxi; **to** ~ **to do sth** quedar en hacer algo; **it was** ~**d that** ... se quedó en que ...

arrangement [ərānj'mənt] *n* arreglo; (*agreement*) acuerdo; ~**s** *npl* (*plans*) planes *mpl*, medidas *fpl*; (*preparations*) preparativos *mpl*; **to come to an** ~ **(with sb)** llegar a un acuerdo (con uno); **by** ~ a convenir; **I'll make** ~**s for you to be met** haré los preparativos para que le estén esperando.

array [ərā'] *n* (*COMPUT*) arreglo, array *m*; ~ **of** (*things*) serie *f* de; (*people*) conjunto de.

arrears [ərērz'] *npl* atrasos *mpl*; **in** ~ (*COMM*) en mora; **to be in** ~ **with one's rent** estar retrasado en el pago del alquiler.

arrest [ərest'] *vt* detener; (*sb's attention*) llamar ♦ *n* detención *f*; **under** ~ detenido.

arresting [əres'ting] *a* (*fig*) llamativo.

arrival [ərī'vəl] *n* llegada; **new** ~ recién llegado/a.

arrive [ərīv'] *vi* llegar.

arrogance [ar'əgəns] *n* arrogancia.

arrogant [ar'əgənt] *a* arrogante.

arrow [ar'ō] *n* flecha.

arse [ârs] *n* (*Brit col!*) culo, trasero.

arsenal [âr'sənəl] *n* arsenal *m*.

arsenic [âr'sənik] *n* arsénico.

arson [ár'sən] *n* incendio premeditado.
art [árt] *n* arte *m*; *(skill)* destreza; *(technique)* técnica; **A~s** *npl* (*SCOL*) Letras *fpl*; **work of ~** obra de arte.
artefact [ár'təfakt] *n* (*Brit*) = **artifact.**
arterial [ártē'rēəl] *a* (*ANAT*) arterial; *(road etc)* principal.
artery [ár'tûrē] *n* (*MED, road etc*) arteria.
artful [árt'fəl] *a* (*cunning: person, trick*) mañoso.
art gallery *n* pinacoteca; (*COMM*) galería de arte.
arthritis [árthrī'tis] *n* artritis *f*.
artichoke [ár'tichōk] *n* alcachofa; **Jerusalem ~** aguaturma.
article [ár'tikəl] *n* artículo, objeto, cosa; (*in newspaper*) artículo; (*Brit LAW: training*): **~s** *npl* contrato *sg* de aprendizaje; **~s of clothing** prendas *fpl* de vestir.
articles of association *npl* (*COMM*) estatutos *mpl* sociales, escritura social.
articulate *a* [ártik'yəlit] *(speech)* claro; *(person)* que se expresa bien ♦ *vi* [ártik'yəlāt] articular.
articulated lorry [ártik'yəlātid lôr'ē] *n* (*Brit*) trailer *m*.
artifact [ár'təfakt] *n* (*US*) artefacto.
artifice [ár'təfis] *n* artificio, truco.
artificial [ártəfish'əl] *a* artificial; (*teeth etc*) postizo.
artificial insemination [ártəfish'əl insemənā'shən] *n* inseminación *f* artificial.
artificial intelligence (A.I.) *n* inteligencia artificial (I.A.).
artificial respiration *n* respiración *f* artificial.
artillery [ártil'ûrē] *n* artillería.
artisan [ár'tizən] *n* artesano/a.
artist [ár'tist] *n* artista *m/f*; (*MUS*) intérprete *m/f*.
artistic [ártis'tik] *a* artístico.
artistry [ár'tistrē] *n* arte *m*, habilidad *f* (artística).
artless [árt'lis] *a* (*innocent*) natural, sencillo; (*clumsy*) torpe.
art school *n* escuela de bellas artes.
arty [ár'tē] *a* artistoide.
ARV *n abbr* (= *American Revised Version*) traducción americana de la Biblia.
AS *n abbr* (*US UNIV:* = *Associate in/of Science*) título universitario ♦ *abbr* (*US MAIL*) = *American Samoa.*
as [az] *conj* (*cause*) como, ya que; (*time: moment*) como, cuando; (: *duration*) mientras; (*manner*) como, lo mismo que, tal como; (*in the capacity of*) como; **~ big ~** tan grande como; **twice ~ big ~** dos veces más grande que; **much ~ I like them, ...** por mucho que me gusten, ...; **~ the years went by** con el paso de los años; **~ she said** como ella dijo; **~ a present** de *or* como regalo; **~ if** *or* **though** como si; **~ for** *or* **to that** en cuanto a eso, en lo que a

eso se refiere; **~** *or* **so long ~** *conj* mientras (que); **~ much/many ~** tanto(s)... como; **~ soon ~** *conj* tan pronto como; **~ such** *ad* como tal; **~ well** *ad* también, además; **~ well ~** *conj* tanto como; *see also* **such.**
ASA *n abbr* (= *American Standards Association*) instituto de normas.
a.s.a.p. *abbr* (= *as soon as possible*) cuanto antes, lo más pronto posible.
asbestos [asbes'təs] *n* asbesto, amianto.
ascend [əsend'] *vt* subir.
ascendancy [əsen'dənsē] *n* ascendiente *m*, dominio.
ascendant [əsen'dənt] *n*: **to be in the ~** estar en auge, ir ganando predominio.
Ascension [əsen'chən] *n*: **the ~** la Ascensión.
Ascension Island *n* Isla Ascensión.
ascent [əsent'] *n* subida; *(slope)* cuesta, pendiente *f*; *(of plane)* ascenso.
ascertain [asûrtān'] *vt* averiguar.
ascetic [əset'ik] *a* ascético.
asceticism [əset'isizəm] *n* ascetismo.
ASCII [as'kē] *n abbr* (= *American Standard Code for Information Interchange*) ASCII.
ascribe [əskrīb'] *vt*: **to ~ sth to** atribuir algo a.
ASCU *n abbr* (*US*) = *Association of State Colleges and Universities.*
ASE *n abbr* = *American Stock Exchange.*
ash [ash] *n* ceniza; *(tree)* fresno.
ashamed [əshāmd'] *a* avergonzado; **to be ~ of** avergonzarse de.
ashcan [ash'kən] *n* (*US*) cubo *or* bote *m* (*LAm*) de la basura.
ashen [ash'ən] *a* pálido.
ashore [əshôr'] *ad* en tierra.
ashtray [ash'trā] *n* cenicero.
Ash Wednesday *n* miércoles *m* de ceniza.
Asia [ā'zhə] *n* Asia.
Asian [ā'zhən], **Asiatic** [āzhēat'ik] *a*, *n* asiático/a *m/f*.
aside [əsīd'] *ad* a un lado ♦ *n* aparte *m*; **~ from** *prep* (*as well as*) aparte *or* además de.
ask [ask] *vt* (*question*) preguntar; (*demand*) pedir; (*invite*) invitar ♦ *vi*: **to ~ about sth** preguntar acerca de algo; **to ~ sb sth/to do sth** preguntar algo a uno/pedir a uno que haga algo; **to ~ sb about sth** preguntar algo a uno; **to ~ (sb) a question** hacer una pregunta (a uno); **to ~ sb the time** preguntar la hora a uno; **to ~ sb out to dinner** invitar a cenar a uno.
ask about *vt fus* preguntar por.
ask for *vt fus* pedir; **it's just ~ing for trouble** *or* **for it** es buscarse problemas.
askance [əskans'] *ad*: **to look ~ at sb** mirar con recelo a uno.
askew [əskyōō'] *ad* sesgado, ladeado.
asking price [as'king prīs] *n* (*COMM*) precio

inicial.

asleep |əslēp'| *a* dormido; **to fall ~** dormirse, quedarse dormido.

asp |asp| *n* áspid *m*.

asparagus |əspar'əgəs| *n* espárragos *mpl*.

ASPCA *n abbr* = *American Society for the Prevention of Cruelty to Animals*.

aspect |as'pekt| *n* aspecto, apariencia; (*direction in which a building etc faces*) orientación *f*.

aspersions |əspûr'zhənz| *npl*: **to cast ~ on** difamar a, calumniar a.

asphalt |as'fôlt| *n* asfalto.

asphyxiate |asfik'sēāt| *vt* asfixiar.

asphyxiation |asfiksēā'shən| *n* asfixia.

aspirate *vt* |as'pûrāt| aspirar ♦ *a* |as'pûrit| aspirado.

aspirations |aspərā'shənz| *npl* anhelo *sg*, deseo *sg*; (*ambition*) ambición *fsg*.

aspire |əspī'ûr| *vi*: **to ~ to** aspirar a, ambicionar.

aspirin |as'pûrin| *n* aspirina.

ass |as| *n* asno, burro; (*col*) imbécil *m/f*; (*US col!*) culo, trasero; **kiss my ~!** (*col!*) ¡vete al carajo! (*!*).

assailant |əsā'lənt| *n* asaltador(a) *m/f*, agresor(a) *m/f*.

assassin |əsas'in| *n* asesino/a.

assassinate |əsas'ənāt| *vt* asesinar.

assassination |əsasinā'shən| *n* asesinato.

assault |əsôlt'| *n* (*gen: attack*) asalto ♦ *vt* asaltar, atacar; (*sexually*) violar.

assemble |əsem'bəl| *vt* reunir, juntar; (*TECH*) montar ♦ *vi* reunirse, juntarse..

assembler |əsem'blûr| *n* (*COMPUT*) ensamblador *m*.

assembly |əsem'blē| *n* (*meeting*) reunión *f*, asamblea; (*construction*) montaje *m*.

assembly language *n* (*COMPUT*) lenguaje *m* ensamblador.

assembly line *n* cadena de montaje.

assent |əsent'| *n* asentimiento, aprobación *f* ♦ *vi* consentir, asentir; **to ~ (to sth)** consentir (en algo).

assert |əsûrt'| *vt* afirmar; (*insist on*) hacer valer; **to ~ o.s.** imponerse.

assertion |əsûr'shən| *n* afirmación *f*.

assertive |əsûr'tiv| *a* enérgico, agresivo, perentorio.

assess |əses'| *vt* valorar, calcular; (*tax, damages*) fijar; (*property etc: for tax*) gravar.

assessment |əses'mənt| *n* valoración *f*; gravamen *m*; (*judgment*): **~ (of)** juicio (sobre).

assessor |əses'ûr| *n* asesor(a) *m/f*; (*of tax*) tasador(a) *m/f*.

asset |as'et| *n* posesión *f*; (*quality*) ventaja; **~s** *npl* (*funds*) activo *sg*, fondos *mpl*.

asset-stripping |as'etstri'ping| *n* (*COMM*) acaparamiento de activos.

assiduous |əsij'ōōəs| *a* asiduo.

assign |əsīn'| *vt* (*date*) fijar; (*task*) asignar;

(*resources*) destinar; (*property*) traspasar.

assignment |əsīn'mənt| *n* asignación *f*; (*task*) tarea; (*SCOL*) trabajo.

assimilate |əsim'əlāt| *vt* asimilar.

assimilation |əsiməlā'shən| *n* asimilación *f*.

assist |əsist'| *vt* ayudar.

assistance |əsis'təns| *n* ayuda, auxilio.

assistant |əsis'tənt| *n* ayudante *m/f*; (*Brit: also*: **shop ~**) dependiente/a *m/f*.

assistant manager *n* subdirector(a) *m/f*.

assizes |əsī'ziz| *npl* (*Brit*) sesión *f* de un tribunal.

associate *a* |əsō'shēit| asociado ♦ *n* socio/a, colega *m/f*; (*in crime*) cómplice *m/f*; (*member*) miembro/a ♦ *vb* |əsō'shēāt| *vt* asociar; (*ideas*) relacionar ♦ *vi*: **to ~ with sb** tratar con alguien; **~ director** subdirector/a *m/f*; **~d company** compañía afiliada.

association |əsōsēā'shən| *n* asociación *f*; (*COMM*) sociedad *f*; **in ~ with** en asociación con.

association football *n* (*Brit*) fútbol *m*.

assorted |əsôr'tid| *a* surtido, variado; **in ~ sizes** en distintos tamaños.

assortment |əsôrt'mənt| *n* surtido.

Asst. *abbr* = **Assistant**.

assuage |əswāj'| *vt* mitigar.

assume |əsōōm'| *vt* (*suppose*) suponer; (*responsibilities etc*) asumir; (*attitude, name*) adoptar, tomar.

assumed name |əsōōmd' nām'| *n* nombre *m* falso.

assumption |əsump'shən| *n* (*supposition*) suposición *f*, presunción *f*; (*act*) asunción *f*; **on the ~ that** suponiendo que.

assurance |əshōōr'əns| *n* garantía, promesa; (*confidence*) confianza, aplomo; (*Brit: insurance*) seguro; **I can give you no ~s** no puedo hacerle ninguna promesa.

assure |əshōōr'| *vt* asegurar.

assuredly |əshōōr'idlē| *ad* seguramente, indudablemente.

AST *n abbr* (= *Atlantic Standard Time*) hora oficial de Nueva Escocia.

asterisk |as'tûrisk| *n* asterisco.

astern |əstûrn'| *ad* a popa.

asteroid |as'təroid| *n* asteroide *m*.

asthma |az'mə| *n* asma.

asthmatic |azmat'ik| *a, n* asmático/a *m/f*.

astigmatism |əstig'mətizəm| *n* astigmatismo.

astir |əstûr'| *ad* en acción.

ASTM *n abbr* = *American Society for Testing Materials*.

astonish |əstán'ish| *vt* asombrar, pasmar.

astonishing |əstán'ishing| *a* asombroso, pasmoso; **I find it ~ that ...** me asombra *or* pasma que ...

astonishingly |əstán'ishinglē| *ad* increíblemente, asombrosamente.

astonishment |əstán'ishmənt| *n* asombro, sorpresa; **to my ~** con gran sorpresa mía.

astound |əstound'| *vt* asombrar, pasmar.

astounding |əstound'ing| *a* asombroso.

astray |əstrā'| *ad*: **to go** ~ extraviarse; **to lead** ~ llevar por mal camino; **to go** ~ **in one's calculations** equivocarse en sus cálculos.

astride |əstrīd'| *prep* a caballo *or* horcajadas sobre.

astringent |əstrin'jənt| *a*, *n* astringente *m*.

astrologer |astrál'əjûr| *n* astrólogo/a.

astrology |əstrál'əjē| *n* astrología.

astronaut |as'trənót| *n* astronauta *m/f*.

astronomer |əstrán'əmúr| *n* astrónomo/a.

astronomical |astrənám'ikəl| *a* astronómico.

astronomy |əstrán'əmē| *n* astronomía.

astrophysics |astrōfiz'iks| *n* astrofísica.

astute |əstōōt'| *a* astuto.

asunder |əsun'dûr| *ad*: **to tear** ~ hacer pedazos.

ASV *n abbr* (= *American Standard Version*) traducción americana de la Biblia.

asylum |əsī'ləm| *n* (*refuge*) asilo; (*hospital*) manicomio; **to seek political** ~ pedir asilo político.

asymmetric(al) |āsəmct'rik(əl)| *a* asimétrico.

at |at| *prep* en, a; ~ **the top** en la cumbre; ~ **the baker's** en la panadería; ~ **4 o'clock** a las cuatro; ~ **$1 a kilo** a un dólar el kilo; ~ **night** de noche; **two** ~ **a time** de dos en dos; ~ **times** a veces; ~ **full speed** a toda velocidad.

ate |āt| *pt of* **eat.**

atheism |ā'thēizəm| *n* ateísmo.

atheist |ā'thēist| *n* ateo/a.

Athenian |əthē'nēən| *a*, *n* ateniense *m/f*.

Athens |ath'ənz| *n* Atenas *f*.

athlete |ath'lēt| *n* atleta *m/f*.

athletic |athlet'ik| *a* atlético.

athletics |athlct'iks| *n* atletismo.

Atlantic |atlan'tik| *a* atlántico ♦ *n*: **the** ~ **(Ocean)** el (Océano) Atlántico.

atlas |at'ləs| *n* atlas *m*.

Atlas Mountains *npl*: **the** ~ el Atlas.

A.T.M. *n abbr* (= *Automated Teller Machine*) cajero automático.

atmosphere |at'məsfēr| *n* (*air*) atmósfera; (*fig*) ambiente *m*.

atoll |at'ól| *n* atolón *m*.

atom |at'əm| *n* átomo.

atomic |ətám'ik| *a* atómico.

atom(ic) bomb *n* bomba atómica.

atomic power *n* energía atómica.

atomizer |at'əmīzûr| *n* atomizador *m*.

atone |ətōn'| *vi*: **to** ~ **for** expiar.

atonement |ətōn'mənt| *n* expiación *f*.

ATP *n abbr* (= *Association of Tennis Professionals*) sindicato de jugadores de tenis profesionales.

atrocious |ətrō'shəs| *a* (*very bad*) atroz; (*fig*) horrible, infame.

atrocity |ətrás'itē| *n* atrocidad *f*.

atrophy |at'rəfē| *n* atrofia ♦ *vi* atrofiarse.

attach |ətach'| *vt* sujetar; (*stick*) pegar; (*document, letter*) adjuntar; **to be** ~**ed to sb/sth** (*to like*) tener cariño a uno/algo; **the** ~**ed letter** la carta adjunta.

attaché |atashā'| *n* agregado/a.

attaché case *n* maletín *m*.

attachment |ətach'mənt| *n* (*tool*) accesorio; (*love*): ~ **(to)** apego (a).

attack |ətak'| *vt* (*MIL*) atacar; (*criminal*) agredir, asaltar; (*task etc*) emprender ♦ *n* ataque *m*, asalto; (*on sb's life*) atentado; **heart** ~ infarto (de miocardio).

attacker |ətak'ûr| *n* agresor(a) *m/f*, asaltante *m/f*.

attain |ətān'| *vt* (*also*: ~ **to**) alcanzar; (*achieve*) lograr, conseguir.

attainments |ətān'mənts| *npl* (*skill*) talento *sg*.

attempt |ətcmpt'| *n* tentativa, intento; (*attack*) atentado ♦ *vt* intentar, tratar de; **he made no** ~ **to help** ni siquiera procuró ayudar.

attempted |ətcmp'tid| *a*: ~ **murder/ burglary/suicide** tentativa *or* intento de asesinato/robo/suicidio.

attend |ətcnd'| *vt* asistir a; (*patient*) atender.

attend to *vt fus* (*needs, affairs etc*) ocuparse de; (*speech etc*) prestar atención a; (*customer*) atender a.

attendance |ətcn'dəns| *n* asistencia, presencia; (*people present*) concurrencia.

attendant |ətcn'dənt| *n* sirviente/a *m/f*, mozo/a; (*THEATER*) acomodador(a) *m/f* ♦ *a* concomitante.

attention |ətcn'shən| *n* atención *f* ♦ *excl* (*MIL*) ¡firme(s)!; **to the** ~ **of...** (*ADMIN*) atención...; **it has come to my** ~ **that ...** me he enterado de que ...

attentive |ətcn'tiv| *a* atento; (*polite*) cortés.

attenuate |ətcn'yōōāt| *vt* atenuar.

attest |ətest'| *vi*: **to** ~ **to** dar fe de.

attic |at'ik| *n* desván *m*.

attitude |at'ətōōd| *n* (*gen*) actitud *f*; (*disposition*) disposición *f*.

attorney |ətûr'nē| *n* (*US: lawyer*) abogado/a; (*having proxy*) apoderado.

Attorney General *n* (*US*) ≈ ministro de justicia; (*Brit*) ≈ Presidente *m* del Consejo del Poder Judicial (*Sp*).

attract |ətrakt'| *vt* atraer; (*attention*) llamar.

attraction |ətrak'shən| *n* (*gen*) encanto; (*PHYSICS*) atracción *f*; (*fig: towards sth*) atractivo.

attractive |ətrak'tiv| *a* atractivo.

attribute *n* |at'rəbyōōt| atributo ♦ *vt* |ətrib'yōōt|: **to** ~ **sth to** atribuir algo a; (*accuse*) achacar algo a.

attrition |ətrish'ən| *n*: **war of** ~ guerra de agotamiento.

atty. *abbr* (*US*) = **attorney.**

Atty. Gen. *abbr* = **Attorney General.**
ATV *n abbr* (= *all terrain vehicle*) vehículo todo terreno.
aubergine [ō'bûrzhēn] *n* berenjena.
auburn [ô'bûrn] *a* color castaño rojizo.
auction [ôk'shən] *n* (*also:* **sale by** ~) subasta ♦ *vt* subastar.
auctioneer [ôkshənēr'] *n* subastador(a) *m/f.*
auction room *n* sala de subastas.
aud. *abbr* = **audit; auditor.**
audacious [ôdā'shəs] *a* (*bold*) audaz, osado; (*impudent*) atrevido, descarado.
audacity [ôdas'itē] *n* audacia, atrevimiento; (*pej*) descaro.
audible [ôd'əbəl] *a* audible, que se puede oír.
audience [ôd'ēəns] *n* auditorio; (*gathering*) público; (*interview*) audiencia.
audiovisual [ôd'ēōvizh'ōōəl] *a* audiovisual.
audiovisual aid *n* ayuda audiovisual.
audit [ôd'it] *vt* revisar, intervenir.
audition [ôdish'ən] *n* audición *f* ♦ *vi:* **to** ~ **for the part of** hacer una audición para el papel de.
auditor [ô'ditûr] *n* interventor(a) *m/f*, censor(a) *m/f* de cuentas; (*US: UNIV*) estudiante *m/f* libre.
auditorium [ôditôr'ēəm] *n* auditorio.
Aug. *abbr* (= *August*) ag.
augment [ôgment'] *vt* aumentar ♦ *vi* aumentarse.
augur [ô'gûr] *vi:* **it** ~**s well** es de buen agüero.
August [ôg'əst] *n* agosto.
august [ôgust'] *a* augusto.
aunt [ant] *n* tía.
auntie, aunty [an'tē] *n diminutive of* **aunt.**
au pair [ô pär'] *n* (*also:* ~ **girl**) au pair *f.*
aura [ô'rə] *n* aura; (*atmosphere*) ambiente *m.*
auspices [ôs'pisiz] *npl:* **under the** ~ **of** bajo los auspicios de.
auspicious [ôspish'əs] *a* propicio, de buen augurio.
austere [ôstēr'] *a* austero; (*manner*) adusto.
austerity [ôstär'itē] *n* austeridad *f.*
Australasia [ôstrəlā'zhə] *n* Australasia.
Australia [ôstrāl'yə] *n* Australia.
Australian [ôstrāl'yən] *a, n* australiano/a *m/f.*
Austria [ôs'trēə] *n* Austria.
Austrian [ôs'trēən] *a, n* austríaco/a *m/f.*
authentic [ôthen'tik] *a* auténtico.
authenticate [ôthen'tikāt] *vt* autenticar.
authenticity [ôthəntis'itē] *n* autenticidad *f.*
author [ô'thûr] *n* autor(a) *m/f.*
authoritarian [əthôritär'ēən] *a* autoritario.
authoritative [əthôr'itātiv] *a* autorizado; (*manner*) autoritario.
authority [əthôr'itē] *n* autoridad *f*; **the authorities** *npl* las autoridades; **to have** ~ **to do sth** tener autoridad para hacer algo.
authorization [ôthûrəzā'shən] *n* autoriza-

ción *f.*
authorize [ô'thərīz] *vt* autorizar.
authorized capital [ô'thərīzd kap'itəl] *n* (*COMM*) capital *m* autorizado *or* social.
autistic [ôtis'tik] *a* autístico.
autobiographical [ôtəbīəgraf'ikəl] *a* autobiográfico.
autobiography [ôtəbīāg'rəfē] *n* autobiografía.
autocratic [ôtəkrat'ik] *a* autocrático.
autograph [ô'təgraf] *n* autógrafo ♦ *vt* firmar; (*photo etc*) dedicar.
automat [ô'təmat] *n* (*US*) restaurán *m or* restaurante *m* de autoservicio.
automate [ô'təmāt] *vt* automatizar.
automated [ô'təmātid] *a* automatizado.
automatic [ôtəmat'ik] *a* automático ♦ *n* (*gun*) pistola automática; (*washing machine*) lavadora.
automatically [ôtəmat'iklē] *ad* automáticamente.
automatic data processing (ADP) *n* proceso automático de datos.
automation [ôtəmā'shən] *n* automatización *f.*
automaton, *pl* **automata** [ôtâm'ətân, -ətə] *n* autómata.
automobile [ôtəməbēl'] *n* (*US*) coche *m*, carro (*LAm*), automóvil *m.*
autonomous [ôtân'əməs] *a* autónomo.
autonomy [ôtân'əmē] *n* autonomía.
autopsy [ô'tâpsē] *n* autopsia.
autumn [ô'təm] *n* otoño.
auxiliary [ôgzil'yûrē] *a* auxiliar.
AV *n abbr* (= *Authorized Version*) traducción inglesa de la Biblia ♦ *abbr* = **audiovisual.**
Av. *abbr* (= *avenue*) Av., Avda.
avail [əvāl'] *vt:* **to** ~ **o.s. of** aprovechar(se) de, valerse de ♦ *n:* **to no** ~ en vano, sin resultado.
availability [əvāləbil'ətē] *n* disponibilidad *f.*
available [əvā'ləbəl] *a* disponible; (*obtainable*) asequible; **to make sth** ~ **to sb** poner algo a la disposición de uno; **is the manager** ~? ¿está libre el gerente?
avalanche [av'əlanch] *n* alud *m*, avalancha.
avant-garde [əvântgârd'] *a* de vanguardia.
avarice [av'ûris] *n* avaricia.
avaricious [avərish'əs] *a* avaro.
avdp. *abbr* = *avoirdupois.*
Ave. *abbr* (= *avenue*) Av., Avda.
avenge [əvenj'] *vt* vengar.
avenue [av'ənōō] *n* avenida; (*fig*) camino.
average [av'ûrij] *n* promedio, término medio ♦ *a* (*mean*) medio, de término medio; (*ordinary*) regular, corriente ♦ *vt* calcular el promedio de, prorratear; **on** ~ por regla general.
   average out *vi:* **to** ~ **out at** salir a un promedio de.
averse [əvûrs'] *a:* **to be** ~ **to sth/doing** sentir aversión *or* antipatía por algo/por ha-

cer.
aversion [əvûr'zhən] *n* aversión *f*, repugnancia.
avert [əvûrt'] *vt* prevenir; (*blow*) desviar;
(*one's eyes*) apartar.
aviary [ā'vēārē] *n* pajarera.
aviation [āvēā'shən] *n* aviación *f*.
aviator [ā'vēātûr] *n* aviador(a) *m/f*.
avid [av'id] *a* ávido, ansioso.
avidly [av'idlē] *ad* ávidamente, con avidez.
avocado [avəkâd'ō] *n* aguacate *m*, palta
(*LAm*).
avoid [əvoid'] *vt* evitar, eludir.
avoidable [əvoid'əbəl] *a* evitable, eludible.
avoidance [əvoid'əns] *n* evasión *f*.
avow [əvou'] *vt* prometer.
avowal [əvou'əl] *n* promesa, voto.
avowed [əvoud'] *a* declarado.
AVP *n abbr* (*US*) = *assistant vice-president*.
avuncular [əvung'kyəlûr] *a* como de tío.
AWACS [ā'waks] *n abbr* (= *airborne warning and control system*) AWACS *m*.
await [əwāt'] *vt* esperar, aguardar; **long
~ed** largamente esperado.
awake [əwāk'] *a* despierto ♦ (*vb*: *pt* **awoke**,
pp **awoken** *or* **awaked**) *vt* despertar ♦ *vi*
despertarse; **to be ~** estar despierto.
awakening [əwā'kəning] *n* despertar *m*.
award [əwôrd'] *n* (*prize*) premio; (*medal*)
condecoración *f*; (*LAW*) fallo, sentencia;
(*act*) concesión *f* ♦ *vt* (*prize*) otorgar,
conceder; (*LAW*: *damages*) adjudicar.
aware [əwär'] *a* consciente; (*awake*) despierto; (*informed*) enterado; **to become ~
of** darse cuenta de, enterarse de; **I am fully
~ that** sé muy bien que.
awareness [əwär'nis] *n* conciencia, conocimiento.
awash [əwâsh'] *a* inundado.
away [əwā'] *ad* (*gen*) fuera; (*far ~*) lejos;
two kilometers ~ a dos kilómetros de distancia; **two hours ~ by car** a dos horas en
coche; **the vacation was two weeks ~**
faltaban dos semanas para las vacaciones;
~ from lejos de, fuera de; **he's ~ for a
week** está ausente una semana; **he's ~
in Barcelona** está en Barcelona; **to take ~**
llevar(se); **to work/pedal ~** seguir
trabajando/pedaleando; **to fade ~** desvanecerse; (*sound*) apagarse.
away game *n* (*SPORT*) partido de fuera.
awe [ô] *n* pavor *m*, respeto, temor *m* reve-
rencial.
awe-inspiring [ô'inspīuring], **awesome**
[ô'səm] *a* imponente, pasmoso.
awestruck [ô'struk] *a* pasmado.
awful [ô'fəl] *a* terrible, pasmoso; **an ~ lot
of** (*people, cars, dogs*) la mar de, muchísimos.
awfully [ô'fəlē] *ad* (*very*) terriblemente.
awhile [əhwīl'] *ad* (durante) un rato, algún
tiempo.
awkward [ôk'wûrd] *a* (*clumsy*) desmañado,

torpe; (*shape*) incómodo; (*difficult*:
question) difícil; (*problem*) complicado;
(*embarrassing*) delicado.
awkwardness [ôk'wûrdnis] *n* (*clumsiness*)
torpeza; (*of situation*) lo delicado.
awl [ôl] *n* lezna, subilla.
awning [ô'ning] *n* (*of shop*) toldo; (*of
window etc*) marquesina.
awoke [əwōk'], **awoken** [əwō'kən] *pt*, *pp of*
awake.
AWOL [ā'wôl] *abbr* (*MIL*) *see* **absent without leave.**
awry [ərī'] *ad*: **to be ~** estar descolocado *or*
atravesado; **to go ~** salir mal, fracasar.
ax, (*Brit*) **axe** [aks] *n* hacha ♦ *vt* (*employee*)
despedir; (*project etc*) cortar; (*jobs*) reducir; **to get the ~** (*col*: *project*) ser cortado; (: *person*: *be fired*) ser despedido; **to
have an ~ to grind** (*fig*) tener un interés
creado *or* algún fin interesado.
axes [ak'sēz] *npl of* **axis.**
axiom [ak'sēəm] *n* axioma *m*.
axiomatic [aksēəmat'ik] *a* axiomático.
axis, *pl* **axes** [ak'sis, -sēz] *n* eje *m*.
axle [ak'səl] *n* eje *m*, árbol *m*.
ay(e) [ī] *excl* (*yes*) sí; **the ayes** *npl* los que
votan a favor.
AYH *n abbr* = *American Youth Hostels*.
AZ *abbr* (*US MAIL*) = *Arizona*.
azalea [əzāl'yə] *n* azalea.
Azores [əzôrz'] *npl*: **the ~** las (Islas) Azores.
Aztec [az'tek] *a*, *n* azteca *m/f*.
azure [azh'ûr] *a* celeste.

B

B, b [bē] *n* (*letter*) B, b *f*; (*SCOL*: *mark*) N;
(*MUS*) si *m*; **B for Baker** B de Barcelona.
b. *abbr* = *born*.
BA *n abbr* (*SCOL*) = **Bachelor of Arts.**
babble [bab'əl] *vi* barbullar.
babe [bāb] *n* criatura.
baboon [baboon'] *n* mandril *m*.
baby [bā'bē] *n* bebé *m/f*.
baby buggy [bā'bē bug'ē] *n* cochecito.
baby carriage *n* (*US*) cochecito.
babyish [bā'bēish] *a* infantil.
baby-minder [bā'bēmindûr] *n* (*Brit*) persona que cuida a los niños mientras la madre
trabaja.
baby-sit [bā'bēsit] *vi* hacer de canguro.
baby-sitter [bā'bēsitûr] *n* canguro/a.
bachelor [bach'əlûr] *n* soltero; **B~ of Arts/
Science (BA/BSc)** licenciado/a en Filosofía
y Letras/Ciencias.

back [bak] n (of person) espalda; (of animal) lomo; (of hand) dorso; (as opposed to front) parte f de atrás; (of room, car, etc) fondo; (of chair) respaldo; (of page) reverso; (SOCCER) defensa m; **to have one's ~ to the wall** (fig) estar entre la espada y la pared; **at the ~ of my mind was the thought that ...** en el fondo tenía la idea de que ... ♦ vt (candidate: also: ~ **up**) respaldar, apoyar; (horse: at races) apostar a; (car) dar marcha atrás a or con ♦ vi (car etc) dar marcha atrás ♦ a (in compounds) de atrás; ~ **seats/wheels** (AUT) asientos mpl/ruedas fpl de atrás; ~ **garden/room** jardín m/habitación f de atrás; ~ **payments** pagos mpl con efecto retroactivo; ~ **rent** renta atrasada; **to take a ~ seat** (fig) pasar a segundo plano ♦ ad (not forward) (hacia) atrás; **he's ~** (returned) está de vuelta, ha vuelto; **he ran ~** volvió corriendo; **throw the ball ~** (restitution) devuelve la pelota; **can I have it ~?** ¿me lo devuelve?; **he called ~** (again) llamó de nuevo; **~ and forth** el uno al otro, entre sí; **as far ~ as the 13th century** ya en el siglo XIII; **when will you be ~?** ¿cuándo volverá?

back down vi echarse atrás.

back on to vt fus (Brit): **the house ~s on to the golf course** por atrás la casa da al campo de golf.

back out vi (of promise) volverse atrás.

back up vt (support: person) apoyar, respaldar; (: theory) defender; (car) dar marcha atrás a; (COMPUT) hacer una copia preventiva or de reserva de.

backache [bak'āk] n dolor m de espalda.

backbencher [bak'benchûr] n (Brit) miembro/a del parlamento sin portafolio.

backbiting [bak'bīting] n murmuración f.

backbone [bak'bōn] n columna vertebral; **the ~ of the organization** el pilar de la organización.

back burner n: **to put sth on the ~** ralentizar algo.

backcloth [bak'klôth] n telón m de fondo.

backcomb [bak'kōm] vt cardar.

backdate [bakdāt'] vt (letter) poner fecha atrasada a; **~d pay raise** alza de sueldo con efecto retroactivo.

backdrop [bak'dráp] n = backcloth.

backer [bak'ûr] n partidario/a; (COMM) promotor(a) m/f.

backfire [bak'fîûr] vi (AUT) petardear; (plans) fallar, salir mal.

backgammon [bak'gamən] n backgammon m.

background [bak'ground] n fondo; (of events) antecedentes mpl; (basic knowledge) bases fpl; (experience) conocimientos mpl, educación f ♦ cpd (noise, music) de fondo; (COMPUT) secundario; ~ **reading** lectura de fondo, preparación f; **fa-**

mily ~ origen m, antecedentes mpl.

backhand [bak'hand] n (TENNIS: also: ~ **stroke**) revés m.

backhanded [bak'handid] a (fig) ambiguo, equívoco.

backhander [bak'handûr] n (Brit: bribe) soborno.

backing [bak'ing] n (fig) apoyo, respaldo; (COMM) respaldo financiero; (MUS) acompañamiento.

backlash [bak'lash] n reacción f, resaca.

backlog [bak'lôg] n: ~ **of work** atrasos mpl.

back number n (of magazine etc) número atrasado.

backpack [bak'pak] n mochila.

backpacker [bak'pakûr] n mochilero/a.

back pay n pago atrasado.

backpedal [bak'pedəl] vi (fig) volverse/ echarse atrás.

backside [bak'sīd] n (col) trasero, culo.

backslash [bak'slash] n pleca, barra inversa.

backslide [bak'slīd] vi reincidir, recaer.

backspace [bak'spās] vi (in typing) retroceder.

backstage [bak'stāj'] ad entre bastidores.

back-street [bak'strēt] a de barrio; ~ **abortionist** abortista m/f ilegal.

backstroke [bak'strōk] n braza de espaldas.

backtalk [bak'tôk] n réplicas fpl.

backtrack [bak'trak] vi (fig) = backpedal.

backup [bak'up] a (train, plane) suplementario; (COMPUT: disk, file) de reserva ♦ n (support) apoyo; (also: ~ **file**) copia preventiva or de reserva; (US: traffic) embotellamiento, acumulación f.

backup lights [bak'up lītz] npl (US) luces fpl de marcha atrás.

backward [bak'wûrd] a (movement) hacia atrás; (person, country) atrasado; (shy) tímido.

backwardness [bak'wûrdnis] n atraso.

backwards [bak'wûrdz] ad (move, go) hacia atrás; (read a list) al revés; (fall) de espaldas; **to know sth ~ and forwards** or (Brit) ~ (col) saberse algo al dedillo.

backwater [bak'wôtûr] n (fig) lugar m atrasado or apartado.

backyard [bak'yârd] n traspatio.

bacon [bā'kən] n tocino, beicon m.

bacteria [baktē'rēə] npl bacteria sg.

bacteriology [baktērēāl'əjē] n bacteriología.

bad [bad] a malo; (serious) grave; (meat, food) podrido, pasado; **his ~ leg** su pierna lisiada; **to go ~** pasarse; **to have a ~ time of it** pasarlo mal; **I feel ~ about it** (guilty) tengo remordimientos; ~ **debt** (COMM) cuenta incobrable; **in ~ faith** de mala fe.

bade [bad] pt of bid.

bad feeling n rencor m.

badge [baj] n insignia; (metal ~) chapa,

placa; (*stick-on*) pegatina.
badger [baj'ûr] *n* tejón *m*.
badly [bad'lē] *ad* (*work, dress etc*) mal; ~
wounded gravemente herido; **he needs it**
~ le hace gran falta; **to be ~ off (for**
money) andar mal de dinero; **things are**
going ~ las cosas van muy mal.
bad-mannered [badman'ûrd] *a* grosero,
mal educado.
badminton [bad'mintən] *n* bádminton *m*.
bad-mouth [bad'mouth'] *vt* (*US*) criticar.
bad-smelling [bad'smel'ing] *a* maloliente.
bad-tempered [bad'tem'pûrd] *a* de mal genio *or* carácter; (*temporary*) de mal humor.
baffle [baf'əl] *vt* desconcertar, confundir.
baffling [baf'ling] *a* incomprensible.
bag [bag] *n* bolsa, saco; (*handbag*) bolso;
(*satchel*) mochila; (*case*) maleta; (*of*
hunter) caza ♦ *vt* (*col: take*) coger (*Sp*),
agarrar (*LAm*), pescar; **~s of** (*col: lots*
of) un montón de; **to pack one's ~s** hacer
las maletas.
bagful [bag'fəl] *n* saco (lleno).
baggage [bag'ij] *n* equipaje *m*.
baggage check *n* talón *m* de equipaje.
baggage claim *n* reclamación *f* de equipajes.
baggy [bag'ē] *a* (*trousers*) con rodilleras.
Baghdad [bag'dad] *n* Bagdad *m*.
bagpipes [bag'pīps] *npl* gaita *sg*.
bag-snatcher [bag'snachûr] *n* (*Brit*)
ladrón/ona *m/f* de bolsos.
Bahamas [bəhâm'əz] *npl*: **the** ~ las Islas
Bahama.
Bahrain [bârân'] *n* Bahrein *m*.
bail [bāl] *n* fianza ♦ *vt* (*prisoner: also:* **grant**
~ **to**) poner en libertad bajo fianza; (*boat:*
also: ~ **out**) achicar; **on** ~ (*prisoner*) bajo
fianza; **to be released on** ~ ser puesto en
libertad bajo fianza.
bail out *vi* (*of a plane*) lanzarse en paracaídas ♦ *vt* (*NAUT: water*) sacar; (*: boat*)
achicar; **to** ~ **sb out** obtener la libertad de
uno bajo fianza; (*US*): **to** ~ **sb out of a**
difficulty sacar a uno de un problema.
bailiff [bā'lif] *n* alguacil *m*.
bait [bāt] *n* cebo ♦ *vt* cebar.
bake [bāk] *vt* cocer (al horno) ♦ *vi* (*cook*)
cocerse; (*be hot*) hacer un calor terrible.
baked beans [bākt bēnz] *npl* judías *fpl* en
salsa de tomate.
baked potatoes [bākt pətā'tōz] *n* patatas
fpl asadas con piel.
baker [bā'kûr] *n* panadero/a.
baker's dozen [bākûrz du'zən] *n* docena
del fraile.
bakery [bā'kûrē] *n* (*for bread*) panadería;
(*for cakes*) pastelería.
baking [bā'king] *n* (*act*) amasar *m*; (*batch*)
hornada.
baking chocolate *n* (*US*) chocolate *m*
fondant.

baking powder *n* levadura (en polvo).
baking pan, (*Brit*) **baking tin** *n* tortera.
baking sheet *n* bandeja de horno.
balaclava [baləklâv'ə] *n* (*Brit: also:* ~
helmet) pasamontañas *m inv*.
balance [bal'əns] *n* equilibrio; (*COMM:*
sum) balance *m*; (*remainder*) resto;
(*scales*) balanza ♦ *vt* equilibrar; (*budget*)
nivelar; (*account*) saldar; (*compensate*)
contrapesar; ~ **of trade/payments** balanza
de comercio/pagos; ~ **carried forward** balance *m* pasado a cuenta nueva; ~ **brought**
forward saldo de hoja anterior; **to** ~ **the**
books hacer el balance.
balanced [bal'ənst] *a* (*personality, diet*)
equilibrado.
balance sheet *n* balance *m*.
balcony [bal'kənē] *n* (*open*) balcón *m*;
(*closed*) galería; **first/second** ~ (*US*) la
galería superior.
bald [bôld] *a* calvo; (*tire*) liso.
baldness [bôld'nis] *n* calvicie *f*.
bale [bāl] *n* (*AGR*) paca, fardo.
bale out (*Brit*) *vi* (*of a plane*) lanzarse
en paracaídas ♦ *vt* (*NAUT: water*) sacar; (*:*
boat) achicar; **to** ~ **sb out of a difficulty**
sacar a uno de un problema.
Balearic Islands [balēãr'ək i'ləndz] *npl*:
the ~ las Islas Baleares.
baleful [bāl'fəl] *a* (*look*) triste; (*sinister*) funesto, siniestro.
balk [bôk] *vi*: **to** ~ (**at**) resistirse (a);
(*horse*) plantarse (ante).
Balkan [bôl'kən] *a* balcánico ♦ *n*: **the** ~**s** los
Balcanes.
ball [bôl] *n* (*sphere*) bola; (*football*) balón
m; (*for tennis, golf etc*) pelota; (*dance*)
baile *m*; **to be on the** ~ (*fig: competent*)
estar enterado; (*: alert*) ser despabilado;
to play ~ (**with sb**) jugar a la pelota (con
uno); (*fig*) cooperar; **to start the** ~ **rolling**
(*fig*) empezar; **the** ~ **is in your court** (*fig*)
le toca a usted.
ballad [bal'əd] *n* balada, romance *m*.
ballast [bal'əst] *n* lastre *m*.
ball bearing *n* cojinete *m* de bolas.
ballcock [bôl'kâk] *n* llave *f* de bola *or* de flotador.
ballerina [balərē'nə] *n* bailarina.
ballet [balā'] *n* ballet *m*.
ballet dancer *n* bailarín/ina *m/f* (de ballet).
ballistic [bəlis'tik] *a* balístico; **interconti-**
nental ~ **missile** misil *m* balístico
intercontinental.
ballistics [bəlis'tiks] *n* balística.
balloon [bəlōōn'] *n* globo; (*in comic strip*)
globo, bocadillo ♦ *vi* dispararse.
balloonist [bəlōō'nist] *n* ascensionista *m/f*.
ballot [bal'ət] *n* votación *f*; (*US: also:* ~ **pa-**
per) papeleta.
ballot box *n* urna (electoral).
ballot paper *n* (*Brit*) papeleta.

ballpark |bôl'párk| *n* (*US*) estadio de béisbol; ~ **figure** cifra aproximada.
ball-point (pen) |bôl'point (pen')| *n* bolígrafo.
ballroom |bôl'rōōm| *n* salón *m* de baile.
balm |bâm| *n* (*also fig*) bálsamo.
balmy |bâ'mē| *a* (*breeze*, *air*) suave, fragante; (*col*) = **barmy**.
balsa |bôl'sə| *n* (madera de) balsa.
Baltic |bôl'tik| *a* báltico ♦ *n*: **the ~ (Sea)** el (*Mar*) Báltico.
balustrade |bal'əstrād| *n* barandilla.
bamboo |bambōō'| *n* bambú *m*.
bamboozle |bambōō'zəl| *vt* (*col*) embaucar, engatusar.
ban |ban| *n* prohibición *f*, proscripción *f* ♦ *vt* prohibir, proscribir; (*exclude*) excluir; **he was ~ned from driving** le prohibieron conducir.
banal |bənal'| *a* banal, vulgar.
banana |bənan'ə| *n* plátano, banana (*LAm*).
band |band| *n* (*group*) banda; (*gang*) pandilla; (*strip*) faja, tira; (: *circular*) anillo; (*at a dance*) orquesta; (*MIL*) banda.
  band together *vi* juntarse, asociarse.
bandage |ban'dij| *n* venda, vendaje *m* ♦ *vt* vendar.
bandaid |band'ād'| ® *n* (*US*) tirita.
bandit |ban'dit| *n* bandido; **one-armed ~** máquina tragaperras.
bandstand |band'stand| *n* quiosco.
bandwagon |band'wagən| *n*: **to jump on the ~** (*fig*) subirse al carro.
bandy |ban'dē| *vt* (*jokes*, *insults*) cambiar.
bandy-legged |ban'dēlcgid| *a* estevado.
bane |bān| *n*: **it** (*or he etc*) **is the ~ of my life** me amarga la vida.
bang |bang| *n* estallido; (*of door*) portazo; (*blow*) golpe *m* ♦ *vt* hacer estallar; (*door*) cerrar de golpe ♦ *vi* estallar **to ~ into sth** chocar con algo, golpearse contra algo; *see also* **bangs**.
banger |bang'ûr| *n* (*firework*) petardo; (*Brit*: *car*: *also*: **old ~**) armatoste *m*, cacharro; (*Brit col*: *sausage*) salchicha.
Bangkok |bang'kâk| *n* Bangkok *m*.
Bangladesh |banggladesh'| *n* Bangladesh *f*.
bangle |bang'gəl| *n* ajorca.
bangs |bangz| *npl* (*US*) flequillo *sg*.
banish |ban'ish| *vt* desterrar.
banister(s) |ban'istûr(z)| *n*(*pl*) pasamanos *m inv*.
banjo, |ban'jō| *pl* **~es** *or* **~s** *n* banjo.
bank |bangk| *n* (*COMM*) banco; (*of river*, *lake*) ribera, orilla; (*of earth*) terraplén *m* ♦ *vi* (*AVIAT*) ladearse; (*COMM*): **to ~ with** tener la cuenta con.
  bank on *vt fus* contar con.
bank account *n* cuenta de banco.
bank card *n* tarjeta de crédito.
bank charges *npl* comisión *fsg*.
bank draft *n* giro bancario.
banker |bangk'ûr| *n* banquero; **~'s order**

orden *f* bancaria.
Bank holiday *n* (*Brit*) día *m* festivo.
banking |bangk'ing| *n* banca.
bank loan *n* empréstito.
bank manager *n* director(a) *m/f* local del banco.
banknote |bangk'nōt| *n* billete *m* de banco.
bank rate *n* tipo de interés bancario.
bankrupt |bangk'rupt| *n* quebrado/a ♦ *a* quebrado, insolvente; **to go ~** hacer bancarrota; **to be ~** estar en quiebra.
bankruptcy |bangk'ruptsē| *n* quiebra, bancarrota.
bank statement *n* extracto de cuenta.
banner |ban'ûr| *n* bandera; (*in demonstration*) pancarta.
banns |banz| *npl* amonestaciones *fpl*.
banquet |bang'kwit| *n* banquete *m*.
banter |ban'tûr| *n* guasa, chungas *fpl*.
BAOR *n abbr* (= *British Army of the Rhine*) *fuerzas británicas en Alemania.*
baptism |bap'tizəm| *n* bautismo; (*act*) bautizo.
baptize |baptīz'| *vt* bautizar.
bar |bâr| *n* barra; (*on door*) tranca; (*of window*, *cage*) reja; (*of soap*) pastilla; (*fig*: *hindrance*) obstáculo; (*prohibition*) proscripción *f*; (*place*) bar *m*; (*counter*) mostrador *m*; (*MUS*) barra ♦ *vt* (*road*) obstruir; (*window*, *door*) atrancar; (*person*) excluir; (*activity*) prohibir; **behind ~s** entre rejas; **the B~** (*LAW*: *profession*) la abogacía; (: *people*) el cuerpo de abogados; **~ none** sin excepción.
Barbados |bârbā'dōs| *n* Barbados *m*.
barbarian |bârbär'ēən| *n* bárbaro/a.
barbaric |bârbar'ik| *a* bárbaro.
barbarity |bârbar'itē| *n* barbaridad *f*.
barbarous |bâr'bûrəs| *a* bárbaro.
barbecue |bâr'bəkyōō| *n* barbacoa.
barbed wire |bârbd wîûr| *n* alambre *m* de púas.
barber |bâr'bûr| *n* peluquero, barbero.
barbiturate |bârbich'ûrit| *n* barbitúrico.
Barcelona |bârsəlō'nə| *n* Barcelona.
bar chart *n* gráfico de barras.
bar code *n* código de barras.
bare |bâr| *a* desnudo; (*head*) descubierto ♦ *vt* desnudar; **to ~ one's teeth** enseñar los dientes.
bareback |bâr'bak| *ad* sin silla.
barefaced |bâr'fāst| *a* descarado.
barefoot |bâr'fōōt| *a*, *ad* descalzo.
bareheaded |bâr'hcdid| *a* descubierto, sin sombrero.
barely |bâr'lē| *ad* apenas.
bareness |bâr'nis| *n* desnudez *f*.
Barents Sea |bâr'ənts sē| *n*: **the ~** el Mar de Barents.
bargain |bâr'gin| *n* pacto, negocio; (*good buy*) ganga ♦ *vi* negociar; (*haggle*) regatear; **into the ~** además, por añadidura.
  bargain for *vt fus* (*col*): **he got more**

than he ~ed for le resultó peor de lo que esperaba.

bargaining [bár'gining] *n* negociación *f;* regateo; ~ **table** mesa de negociaciones.

barge [bárj] *n* barcaza.

barge in *vi* irrumpir; (*conversation*) entrometerse.

barge into *vt fus* dar contra.

baritone [bar'itōn] *n* barítono.

barium meal [bar'ēəm mēl'] *n* (*MED*) comida de bario.

bark [bárk] *n* (*of tree*) corteza; (*of dog*) ladrido ♦ *vi* ladrar.

barley [bár'lē] *n* cebada.

barley sugar *n* azúcar *m* cande.

barmaid [bár'mād] *n* camarera.

barman [bár'mən] *n* camarero, barman *m*.

barmy [bár'mē] *a* (*col*) chiflado, lelo.

barn [bárn] *n* granero; (*for animals*) cuadra.

barnacle [bár'nəkəl] *n* percebe *m*.

barometer [bərám'itûr] *n* barómetro.

baron [bar'ən] *n* barón *m;* (*fig*) magnate *m;* **the press** ~**s** los magnates de la prensa.

baroness [bar'ənis] *n* baronesa.

baroque [bərōk'] *a* barroco.

barracks [bar'əks] *npl* cuartel *msg*.

barrage [bərázh'] *n* (*MIL*) descarga, bombardeo; (*dam*) presa; (*fig: of criticism etc*) lluvia, aluvión *m;* **a** ~ **of questions** una lluvia de preguntas.

barrel [bar'əl] *n* tonel *m*, barril *m;* (*of gun*) cañón *m*.

barren [bar'ən] *a* estéril.

barrette [bəret'] *n* pasador *m*.

barricade [bar'əkād] *n* barricada ♦ *vt* cerrar con barricadas.

barrier [bar'ēûr] *n* barrera; (*crash* ~) barrera.

barrier cream *n* (*Brit*) crema protectora.

barring [bár'ing] *prep* excepto, salvo.

barrister [bar'istûr] *n* (*Brit*) abogado/a.

barrow [bar'ō] *n* (*cart*) carretilla (de mano).

barstool [bár'stōōl] *n* taburete *m* (de bar).

bartender [bár'tendûr] *n* camarero, barman *m*.

barter [bár'tûr] *vt:* **to** ~ **sth for sth** trocar algo por algo.

base [bās] *n* base *f* ♦ *vt:* **to** ~ **sth on** basar *or* fundar algo en ♦ *a* bajo, infame; **to** ~ **at** (*troops*) estacionar en; **I'm** ~**d in New York** (*work*) trabajo en Nueva York.

baseball [bās'bôl] *n* béisbol *m*.

baseboard [bās'bôrd] *n* (*US*) rodapié *m*.

base camp *n* campamento base.

Basel [báz'əl] *n* Basilea.

baseless [bās'lis] *a* infundado.

basement [bās'mənt] *n* sótano.

base pay *n* sueldo básico.

base rate *n* tipo base.

bases [bā'sēz] *npl of* **basis** ♦ [bā'siz] *npl of* **base**.

bash [bash] *n:* **I'll have a** ~ **(at it)** lo intenta-

ré ♦ *vt* (*col*) golpear.

bash up *vt* (*col: car*) estrellar; (: *person*) aporrear, vapulear.

bashful [bash'fəl] *a* tímido, vergonzoso.

bashing [bash'ing] *n* (*col*) tunda; **to go Paki-/queer-**~ ir a dar una paliza a los paquistaníes/a las maricas.

BASIC [bā'sik] *n* BASIC *m*.

basic [bā'sik] *a* (*salary etc*) básico; (*elementary: principles*) fundamental.

basically [bā'siklē] *ad* fundamentalmente, en el fondo.

basic rate *n* (*of tax*) base *f* mínima imponible.

basil [baz'əl] *n* albahaca.

basin [bā'sin] *n* (*vessel*) cuenco, tazón *m;* (*GEO*) cuenca; (*also:* **wash**~) palangana, jofaina.

basis [bā'sis], *pl* **-ses** [-sēz] *n* base *f; on the* ~ **of what you've said** a base de lo que has dicho.

bask [bask] *vi:* **to** ~ **in the sun** tomarr el sol.

basket [bas'kit] *n* cesta, cesto; (*with handle*) canasta.

basketball [bas'kitbôl] *n* baloncesto.

basketball player *n* jugador(a) *m/f* de baloncesto.

basketwork [bas'kitwûrk] *n* cestería.

Basle [baz'əl] *n* Basilea.

Basque [bask] *a, n* vasco/a *m/f.*

Basque Country *n* Euskadi *m*, País *m* Vasco.

bass [bās] *n* (*MUS*) contrabajo.

bass clef [bās klef] *n* clave *f* de fa.

bassoon [basōōn'] *n* bajón *m*.

bastard [bas'tûrd] *n* bastardo/a; (*col!*) hijo de puta (*!*).

baste [bāst] *vt* (*CULIN*) pringar; (*US: stitch*) hilvanar.

bastion [bas'chən] *n* bastión *m*, baluarte *m*.

bat [bat] *n* (*ZOOL*) murciélago; (*for ball games*) palo; (*for cricket, baseball*) bate *m;* (*Brit: for table tennis*) pala; **he didn't** ~ **an eyelid** ni pestañeó, ni se inmutó.

batch [bach] *n* (*of bread*) hornada; (*of goods, work*) lote *m;* (*of applicants, letters*) montón *m*.

batch processing *n* (*COMPUT*) proceso por lotes.

bated [bā'tid] *a:* **with** ~ **breath** sin respirar.

bath [bath, *pl* bathz] *n* (*action*) baño; (~*tub*) baño, bañera, tina (*LAm*) ♦ *vt* bañar; **to take a** ~ bañarse, tomar un baño; *see also* **baths**.

bathchair [bath'chär] *n* silla de ruedas.

bathe [bath] *vi* bañarse; (*US*) tomar un baño ♦ *vt* (*wound etc*) lavar; (*US*) bañar, dar un baño a.

bather [bath'ûr] *n* bañista *m/f.*

bathing [bā'thing] *n* el bañarse.

bathing cap *n* gorro de baño.

bathing suit, (*Brit*) **bathing costume** *n* traje *m* de baño.

bathing trunks *npl* bañador *msg.*

bathmat [bath'mat] *n* estera de baño.

bathrobe [bath'rōb] *n* bata.

bathroom [bath'rōōm] *n* (cuarto de) baño.

baths [baⁿhz] *npl* piscina *sg.*

bath towel *n* toalla de baño.

bathtub [bath'tub] *n* bañera.

batman [bat'man] *n* (*Brit*) ordenanza *m.*

baton [batán'] *n* (*MUS*) batuta.

battalion [bǝtal'yǝn] *n* batallón *m.*

batten [bat'ǝn] *n* (*CARPENTRY*) listón *m*; (*NAUT*) junquillo, sable *m.*
batten down *vt* (*NAUT*): **to ~ down the hatches** atrancar las escotillas.

batter [bat'ûr] *vt* apalear, azotar ♦ *n* batido.

battered [bat'ûrd] *a* (*hat, pan*) estropeado.

battery [bat'ûrē] *n* batería; (*of flashlight*) pila.

battery charger *n* cargador *m* de baterías.

battery farming *n* (*Brit*) cría intensiva.

battle [bat'ǝl] *n* batalla; (*fig*) lucha ♦ *vi* luchar; **that's half the ~** (*col*) ya hay medio camino andado; **to fight a losing ~** (*fig*) ir perdiendo poco a poco.

battlefield [bat'ǝlfēld] *n* campo *m* de batalla.

battlements [bat'ǝlmǝnts] *npl* almenas *fpl.*

battleship [bat'ǝlship] *n* acorazado.

batty [bat'ē] *a* chalado.

bauble [bô'bǝl] *n* chuchería.

baud [bôd] *n* (*COMPUT*) baudio.

baud rate *n* (*COMPUT*) velocidad *f* (de transmisión) en baudios.

bauxite [bôk'sīt] *n* bauxita.

Bavaria [bǝvär'ēǝ] *n* Baviera.

Bavarian [bǝvär'ēǝn] *a, n* baviero/a *m/f.*

bawdy [bô'dē] *a* indecente; (*joke*) verde.

bawl [bôl] *vi* chillar, gritar.
bawl out *vt* (*person*) echarle un rapapolvo a uno.

bay [bā] *n* (*GEO*) bahía; (*for parking*) parking *m*, estacionamiento; (*loading ~*) patio de carga; (*BOT*) laurel *m* ♦ *vi* aullar; **to hold sb at ~** mantener a alguien a raya.

bay leaf *n* (hoja de) laurel *m.*

bayonet [bā'ǝnet] *n* bayoneta.

bay window *n* ventana salediza.

bazaar [bǝzär'] *n* bazar *m.*

bazooka [bǝzōō'kǝ] *n* bazuca.

B. & B. [bē and bē] *n abbr* (= *bed and breakfast*) cama y desayuno.

B.B.A. *n abbr* (*US*) = *Bachelor of Business Administration.*

BBB *n abbr* (*US*: = *Better Business Bureau*) organismo para la defensa del consumidor.

BBC *n abbr* (= *British Broadcasting Corporation*) cadena de radio y televisión estatal británica.

BC *ad abbr* (=, *before Christ*) a. de J.C. ♦

abbr = *Bachelor of Commerce*; (*Canada*) = *British Columbia.*

BCG *n abbr* (= *Bacillus Calmette-Guérin*) vacuna de la tuberculosis.

BD *n abbr* (= *Bachelor of Divinity*) Licenciado/a en Teología.

B/D *abbr* = **bank draft.**

BDS *n abbr* (= *Bachelor of Dental Surgery*) título universitario.

be, *pt* **was, were,** *pp* **been** [bē, wâz, wûr, bēn] *vi* (*of state*) ser; (*of place, temporary condition*) estar; **I am American** soy norteamericano; **I am tired** estoy cansado; **how are you?** ¿cómo está usted?; **how is it?** ¿quién es?; **it's only me** (*emphatic*) soy yo; **it is raining** está lloviendo; **I am warm** tengo calor; **it is cold** hace frío; **how much is it?** ¿cuánto es *or* cuesta?; **he is four (years old)** tiene cuatro años; **2 and 2 are 4** dos más dos son cuatro; **it's 8 o'clock** son las 8; **where have you been?** ¿dónde has estado?, ¿de dónde vienes? ♦ *aux vb*: **what are you doing?** ¿qué estás haciendo?; **I've been waiting for her for two hours** le he estado esperando durante dos horas; **to ~ killed** ser matado; **he is nowhere to ~ found** no se le ve en ninguna parte; **the car is to ~ sold** el coche está de venta; **he was to have come yesterday** debía de haber venido ayer; **am I to understand that ...?** ¿debo entender que ...?; **if I were you** yo que tú.

B/E *abbr* = **bill of exchange.**

beach [bēch] *n* playa ♦ *vt* varar.

beach buggy [bēch' bug'ē] *n* buggy *m.*

beachcomber [bēch'kōmûr] *n* raquero/a.

beachwear [bēch'wär] *n* ropa de playa.

beacon [bē'kǝn] *n* (*lighthouse*) faro; (*marker*) guía; (*radio ~*) radiofaro.

bead [bēd] *n* cuenta, abalorio; (*of dew, sweat*) gota; **~s** *npl* (*necklace*) collar *m.*

beady [bē'dē] *a* (*eyes*) pequeño y brillante.

beagle [bē'gǝl] *n* sabueso pequeño.

beak [bēk] *n* pico; (*nose*) narigón.

beaker [bē'kûr] *n* jarra.

beam [bēm] *n* (*ARCH*) viga, travesaño; (*of light*) rayo, haz *m* de luz; (*RADIO*) rayo ♦ *vi* brillar; (*smile*) sonreír; **to drive on** (*US*) **high** *or* (*Brit*) **full ~** conducir con luz de carretera.

beaming [bē'ming] *a* (*sun, smile*) radiante.

bean [bēn] *n* judía; **runner/broad ~** habichuela/haba; **coffee ~** grano de café.

bean shoots *npl*, **bean sprouts** *npl* brotes *mpl* de soja.

bear [bär] *n* oso; (*STOCK EXCHANGE*) bajista *m* ♦ (*vb*: *pt* **bore**, *pp* **borne**) *vt* (*weight etc*) llevar; (*cost*) pagar; (*responsibility*) tener; (*traces, signs*) mostrar; (*produce: fruit*) dar; (*COMM: interest*) devengar; (*endure*) soportar, aguantar; (*stand up to*) resistir a; (*children*) parir ♦ *vi*: **to ~ right/left** torcer a la derecha/izquierda; **I**

can't ~ him no le puedo ver, no lo soporto; **to bring pressure to ~ on sb** ejercer presión sobre uno.

bear on *vt fus* tener que ver con, referirse a.

bear out *vt fus* (*suspicions*) corroborar, confirmar; (*person*) llevar.

bear up *vi* (*cheer up*) animarse; **he bore up well under the strain** resistió bien la presión.

bear with *vt fus* (*sb's moods, temper*) tener paciencia con.

bearable [bär'əbəl] *a* soportable, aguantable.

beard [bērd] *n* barba.

bearded [bērd'id] *a* barbado.

bearer [bär'ûr] *n* (*of news, cheque*) portador(a) *m/f*; (*of passport*) titular *m/f*.

bearing [bär'ing] *n* porte *m*, comportamiento; (*connection*) relación *f*; **(ball) ~s** *npl* cojinetes *mpl* a bolas; **to find one's ~s** orientarse.

bearskin [bär'skin] *n* (*MIL*) gorro militar (*de piel de oso*).

beast [bēst] *n* bestia; (*col*) bruto, salvaje *m*.

beastly [bēst'lē] *a* bestial; (*awful*) horrible.

beat [bēt] *n* (*of heart*) latido; (*MUS*) ritmo, compás *m*; (*of policeman*) ronda ♦ *a* (*US col*) hecho polvo ♦ (*vb: pt* **beat**, *pp* **beaten**) *vt* (*hit*) golpear; (*eggs*) batir; (*defeat*) vencer, derrotar; (*better*) sobrepasar; (*drum*) tocar; (*rhythm*) marcar ♦ *vi* (*heart*) latir; **off the ~en track** aislado; **to ~ it** largarse; **that ~s everything!** (*col*) ¡eso es el colmo!; **to ~ on a door** dar golpes en una puerta.

beat down *vt* (*door*) derribar a golpes; (*price*) conseguir rebajar, regatear; (*seller*) hacer rebajar ♦ *vi* (*rain*) llover a cántaros; (*sun*) caer de plomo.

beat off *vt* rechazar.

beat up *vt* (*col: person*) dar una paliza a.

beater [bē'tûr] *n* (*for eggs, cream*) batidora.

beating [bē'ting] *n* golpeo; (*defeat*) derrota; **to take a ~** salir derrotado.

beat-up [bēt'up] *a* (*col*) estropeado.

beautiful [byōo'təfəl] *a* hermoso, bello.

beautifully [byōo'təfəlē] *ad* maravillosamente.

beautify [byōo'təfī] *vt* embellecer.

beauty [byōo'tē] *n* belleza, hermosura; (*concept, person*) belleza; **the ~ of it is that** ... lo mejor de esto es que ....

beauty contest *n* concurso de belleza.

beauty queen *n* reina de la belleza.

beauty salon *n* salón *m* de belleza.

beauty spot *n* lunar *m* postizo; (*Brit: TOURISM*) lugar *m* pintoresco.

beaver [bē'vûr] *n* castor *m*.

becalmed [bikämd'] *a* encalmado.

became [bikām'] *pt of* **become**.

because [bikóz'] *conj* porque; **~ of** *prep* debido a, a causa de.

beck [bek] *n*: **to be at the ~ and call of** estar a disposición de.

beckon [bek'ən] *vt* (*also*: **~ to**) llamar con señas.

become [bikum'] (*irg*: *like* **come**) *vi* (+ *noun*) hacerse, llegar a ser; (+ *adj*) ponerse, volverse ♦ *vt* (*suit*) favorecer, sentar bien a; **to ~ fat** engordarse; **to ~ angry** enfadarse; **it became known that** ... se descubrió que ....

becoming [bikum'ing] *a* (*behavior*) decoroso; (*clothes*) favorecedor(a).

becquerel [bekərel'] *n* becquerelio.

BEd *n abbr* (= *Bachelor of Education*) título universitario.

bed [bed] *n* cama; (*of flowers*) macizo; (*of sea, lake*) fondo; (*of coal, clay*) capa; **to go to ~** acostarse.

bed down *vi* acostarse.

bed and breakfast (B. & B.) *n* (*place*) pensión *f*; (*terms*) cama y desayuno.

bedbug [bed'bug] *n* chinche *f*.

bedclothes [bed'klōz] *npl* ropa de cama.

bedding [bed'ing] *n* ropa de cama.

bedeck [bidek'] *vt* engalanar, adornar.

bedevil [bidev'əl] *vt* (*dog*) acosar; (*trouble*) fastidiar.

bedfellow [bed'felō] *n*: **they are strange ~s** (*fig*) son extraños compañeros de cama.

bedlam [bed'ləm] *n* confusión *f*.

bedpan [bed'pan] *n* bacinilla (de cama).

bedraggled [bidrag'əld] *a* mojado, desastrado.

bedridden [bed'ridən] *a* postrado (en cama).

bedrock [bed'râk] *n* (*GEO*) roca firme; (*fig*) fondo de la cuestión.

bedroom [bed'rōōm] *n* dormitorio, alcoba.

Beds [bedz] *abbr* (*Brit*) = *Bedfordshire*.

bedside [bed'sīd] *n*: **at sb's ~** a la cabecera de alguien.

bedside lamp *n* lámpara de noche.

bedsit(ter) [bed'sit(ûr)] *n* (*Brit*) estudio, suite *m* (*LAm*).

bedspread [bed'spred] *n* sobrecama *m*, colcha.

bedtime [bed'tīm] *n* hora de acostarse; **it's ~** es hora de acostarse *or* de irse a la cama.

bee [bē] *n* abeja; **to have a ~ in one's bonnet (about sth)** tener una idea fija (de algo).

beech [bēch] *n* haya.

beef [bēf] *n* carne *f* de vaca; **roast ~** rosbif *m*.

beef up *vt* (*col*) reforzar.

beefburger [bēf'bûrgûr] *n* (*Brit*) hamburguesa.

beefeater [bēf'ētûr] *n* alabardero de la Torre de Londres.

beehive [bē'hīv] *n* colmena.

beeline [bē'līn] *n*: **to make a ~ for** ir derecho a.
been [bin] *pp of* **be**.
beeper [bēp'ûr] *n* (*of doctor etc*) busca *m*.
beer [bēr] *n* cerveza.
beer can *n* bote *m* or lata de cerveza.
beet [bēt] *n* (*US*) remolacha.
beetle [bēt'əl] *n* escarabajo.
beetroot [bēt'rōōt] *n* (*Brit*) remolacha.
befall [bifól'] *vi* (*vt*) (*irg: like* **fall**) acontecer (a).
befit [bifit'] *vt* convenir a, corresponder a.
before [bifôr'] *prep* (*of time*) antes de; (*of space*) delante de ♦ *conj* antes (de) que ♦ *ad* (*time*) antes, anteriormente; (*space*) delante, adelante; **~ going** antes de marcharse; **~ she goes** antes de que se vaya; **the week ~** la semana anterior; **I've never seen it ~** no lo he visto nunca.
beforehand [bifôr'hand] *ad* de antemano, con anticipación.
befriend [bifrend'] *vt* ofrecer amistad a, ayudar.
befuddled [bifud'əld] *a* aturdido, atontado.
beg [beg] *vi* pedir limosna ♦ *vt* pedir, rogar; (*entreat*) suplicar; **I ~ your pardon** (*apologising*) perdóname; (*not hearing*) ¿perdón?
began [bigan'] *pt of* **begin**.
beggar [beg'ûr] *n* mendigo/a.
begin, *pt* began, *pp* begun [bigin', bigan', bigun'] *vt, vi* empezar, comenzar; **to ~ doing** *or* **to do sth** empezar a hacer algo; **I can't ~ to thank you** no encuentro palabras para agradecerle; **to ~ with, I'd like to know ...** en primer lugar, quisiera saber ...; **~ning from Monday** a partir del lunes.
beginner [bigin'ûr] *n* principiante *m/f*.
beginner's slope [bigin'ûrz slōp] *n* (*SKI*) cuesta para principiantes.
beginning [bigin'ing] *n* principio, comienzo; **right from the ~** desde el principio.
begrudge [bigruj'] *vt*: **to ~ sb sth** tenerle envidia a alguien por algo.
beguile [bigīl'] *vt* (*enchant*) seducir.
beguiling [bigī'ling] *a* seductor(a), atractivo.
begun [bigun'] *pp of* **begin**.
behalf [bihaf'] *n*: **in ~ of**, (*Brit*) **on ~ of** en nombre de, por.
behave [bihāv'] *vi* (*person*) portarse, comportarse; (*thing*) funcionar; (*well: also:* **~ o.s.**) portarse bien.
behavior, (*Brit*) **behaviour** [bihāv'yûr] *n* comportamiento, conducta.
behead [bihed'] *vt* decapitar, descabezar.
beheld [biheld'] *pt, pp of* **behold**.
behind [bihīnd'] *prep* detrás de ♦ *ad* detrás, por detrás, atrás ♦ *n* trasero; **to be ~** (*schedule*) ir retrasado; **~ the scenes** (*fig*) entre bastidores; **we're ~ them in technology** (*fig*) les quedamos atrás en tecnología; **to leave sth ~** olvidar *or* dejarse algo; **to be ~ with sth** estar atrasado en

algo; **to be ~ with payments (on sth)** estar atrasado en el pago (de algo).
behold [bihōld'] (*irg: like* **hold**) *vt* contemplar.
beige [bāzh] *a* color beige.
being [bē'ing] *n* ser *m*; **to come into ~** nacer, aparecer.
Beirut [bārōōt'] *n* Beirut *m*.
belated [bilā'tid] *a* atrasado, tardío.
belch [belch] *vi* eructar ♦ *vt* (*also:* **~ out**: *smoke etc*) arrojar.
beleaguered [bilē'gûrd] *a* (*city, fig*) asediado; (*army*) asediado.
Belfast [bel'fast] *n* Belfast *m*.
belfry [bel'frē] *n* campanario.
Belgian [bel'jən] *a, n* belga *m/f*.
Belgium [bel'jəm] *n* Bélgica.
Belgrade [belgrād'] *n* Belgrado.
belie [bilī'] *vt* (*give false impression of*) desmentir, contradecir.
belief [bilēf'] *n* (*opinion*) opinión *f*; (*trust, faith*) fe *f*; (*acceptance as true*) creencia; **it's beyond ~** es increíble; **in the ~ that** en la creencia de que.
believable [bilēv'əbəl] *a* creíble.
believe [bilēv'] *vt, vi* creer; **to ~ (that)** creer (que); **to ~ in** (*God, ghosts*) creer en; (*method*) ser partidario de; **he is ~d to be abroad** se cree que está en el extranjero; **I don't ~ in corporal punishment** no soy partidario del castigo corporal.
believer [bilēv'ûr] *n* (*in idea, activity*) partidario/a; (*REL*) creyente *m/f*, fiel *m/f*.
belittle [bilit'əl] *vt* minimizar, despreciar.
Belize [bəlēz'] *n* Belice *f*.
bell [bel] *n* campana; (*small*) campanilla; (*on door*) timbre *m*; (*animal's*) cencerro; (*on toy etc*) cascabel *m*; **that rings a ~** (*fig*) eso me suena.
bellboy [bel'boi] *n* (*Brit*) = **bellhop**.
bellhop [bel'hâp] *n* (*US*) botones *m inv*.
belligerent [bəlij'ûrənt] *a* (*at war*) beligerante; (*fig*) agresivo.
bellow [bel'ō] *vi* bramar; (*person*) rugir ♦ *vt* (*orders*) gritar, vociferar.
bellows [bel'ōz] *npl* fuelle *msg*.
belly [bel'ē] *n* barriga, panza.
bellyache [bel'ēāk] *n* dolor *m* de barriga *or* de tripa ♦ *vi* (*col*) quejarse.
belong [bilông'] *vi*: **to ~ to** pertenecer a; (*club etc*) ser socio de; **this book ~s here** este libro va aquí.
belongings [bilông'ingz] *npl*: **personal ~** pertenencias *fpl*.
beloved [biluv'id] *a, n* querido/a *m/f*, amado/a *m/f*.
below [bilō'] *prep* bajo, debajo de ♦ *ad* abajo, (por) debajo; **see ~** véase más abajo.
belt [belt] *n* cinturón *m*; (*TECH*) correa, cinta ♦ *vt* (*thrash*) golpear con correa; **industrial ~** zona industrial.
belt out *vt* (*song*) cantar a voz en grito

or a grito pelado.

belt up *vi* (*Brit* AUT) ponerse el cinturón de seguridad; (*fig*, *col*) cerrar el pico.

beltway |belt'wā| *n* (*US* AUT) carretera de circunvalación.

bemoan |bimōn'| *vt* lamentar.

bemused |bimyōōzd'| *a* aturdido, confuso.

bench |bench| *n* banco; **the B~** (LAW) el tribunal; (*people*) la judicatura.

bench mark *n* punto de referencia.

bend |bend| *vb* (*pt*, *pp* **bent** |bent|) *vt* doblar, inclinar; (*leg*, *arm*) torcer ♦ *vi* inclinarse; (*road*) curvarse ♦ *n* (*Brit*: *in road*, *river*) recodo; (*in pipe*) codo; *see also* **bends**.

bend down *vi* inclinarse, doblarse.

bend over *vi* inclinarse.

bends |bendz| *npl* (MED) apoplejía por cambios bruscos de presión.

beneath |binēth'| *prep* bajo, debajo de; (*unworthy of*) indigno de ♦ *ad* abajo, (por) debajo.

benefactor |ben'əfaktûr| *n* bienhechor *m*.

benefactress |ben'əfaktris| *n* bienhechora.

beneficial |benəfish'əl| *a*: ~ **to** beneficioso para.

beneficiary |benəfish'ēârē| *n* (LAW) beneficiario/a.

benefit |ben'əfit| *n* beneficio, provecho; (*allowance of money*) subsidio ♦ *vt* beneficiar; ~ **society** (*US*) sociedad *f* de beneficiencia ♦ *vi*: **he'll ~ from it** le sacará provecho; **unemployment** ~ subsidio de paro.

Benelux |ben'əluks| *n* Benelux *m*.

benevolence |bənev'ələns| *n* benevolencia.

benevolent |bənev'ələnt| *a* benévolo.

BEng *n abbr* (= *Bachelor of Engineering*) *título universitario*.

benign |binīn'| *a* (*person*, MED) benigno; (*smile*) afable.

bent |bent| *pt*, *pp of* **bend** ♦ *n* inclinación *f* ♦ *a* (*wire*, *pipe*) doblado, torcido; **to be ~ on** estar empeñado en.

bequeath |bikwēth'| *vt* legar.

bequest |bikwest'| *n* legado.

bereaved |birēvd'| *a* afligido ♦ *n*: **the ~** los afligidos *mpl*.

bereavement |birēv'mənt| *n* aflicción *f*.

beret |bərā'| *n* boina.

Bering Sea |bar'ing sē| *n*: **the ~** el Mar de Bering.

Berks *abbr* (*Brit*) = **Berkshire**.

Berlin |bûrlin'| *n* Berlín *m*; **East/West ~** Berlín del Este/Oeste.

berm |bûrm| *n* (*US* AUT) arcén *m*.

Bermuda |bûrmōō'də| *n* las (Islas) Bermudas.

Bermuda shorts *npl* pantalones *mpl* bermudas.

Bern |bûrn| *n* Berna.

berry |bär'ē| *n* baya.

berserk |bûrsûrk'| *a*: **to go ~** perder los estribos.

berth |bûrth| *n* (*bed*) litera; (*cabin*) camarote *m*; (*for ship*) amarradero ♦ *vi* atracar, amarrar; **to give sb a wide ~** (*fig*) evitarle el encuentro a uno.

beseech, ** *pt*, *pp* **besought |bisēch', -sôt'| *vt* suplicar.

beset, ** *pt*, *pp* **beset |biset'| *vt* (*person*) acosar ♦ *a*: **a policy ~ with dangers** una política rodeada de peligros.

besetting |biset'ing| *a*: **his ~ sin** su pecado dominante.

beside |bisīd'| *prep* junto a, al lado de; (*compared with*) comparado con; **to be ~ o.s. with anger** estar fuera de sí; **that's ~ the point** eso no tiene nada que ver con el asunto.

besides |bisīdz'| *ad* además ♦ *prep* (*as well as*) además de; (*except*) excepto.

besiege |bisēj'| *vt* (*town*) sitiar; (*fig*) asediar.

besmirch |bismûrch'| *vt* (*fig*) manchar, mancillar.

besotted |bisât'id| *a*: ~ **with** encaprichado *or* encalabrinado con.

best |best| *a* (el/la) mejor ♦ *ad* (lo) mejor; **the ~ part of** (*quantity*) la mayor parte de; **at ~** en el mejor de los casos; **to make the ~ of sth** sacar el mejor partido de algo; **to do one's ~** hacer todo lo posible; **to the ~ of my knowledge** que yo sepa; **to the ~ of my ability** como mejor puedo; **the ~ thing to do is ...** lo mejor (que se puede hacer) es ...; **he's not exactly patient at the ~ of times** no se puede decir que tiene paciencia en las mejores circunstancias.

bestial |bes'tēəl| *a* bestial.

best man *n* padrino de boda.

bestow |bistō'| *vt* otorgar; (*honor*, *praise*) dispensar; **to ~ sth on sb** conceder *or* dar algo a uno.

best seller *n* éxito de librería, best-seller *m*.

bet |bet| *n* apuesta ♦ *vt*, *vi* (*pt*, *pp* **bet** *or* **betted**) apostar (*on* a); **it's a safe ~** (*fig*) es cosa segura.

Bethlehem |beth'lēəm| *n* Belén *m*.

betray |bitrā'| *vt* traicionar; (*inform on*) delatar.

betrayal |bitrā'əl| *n* traición *f*.

better |bet'ûr| *a* mejor ♦ *ad* mejor ♦ *vt* mejorar; (*record etc*) superar ♦ *n*: **to get the ~ of sb** quedar por encima de uno; **you had ~ do it** más vale que lo hagas; **he thought ~ of it** cambió de parecer; **to get ~** mejorar(se); (MED) reponerse; **that's ~!** ¡eso es!; **I had ~ go** tengo que marcharme; **a change for the ~** una mejora; ~ **off** *a* más acomodado.

betting |bet'ing| *n* juego, el apostar.

betting shop *n* (*Brit*) agencia de apuestas.

between [bitwēn'] *prep* entre ♦ *ad* (*time*) mientras tanto; (*place*) en medio; **the road ~ here and New York** la carretera de aquí a Nueva York; **we only had 5 ~ us** teníamos sólo 5 entre nosotros.

bevel [bev'əl] *n* (*also:* **~ edge**) filo biselado.

beverage [bev'ûrij] *n* bebida.

bevy [bev'ē] *n:* **a ~ of** una bandada de.

bewail [biwāl'] *vt* lamentar.

beware [biwär'] *vi:* **to ~ (of)** tener cuidado (con) ♦ *excl* ¡cuidado!

bewildered [biwil'dûrd] *a* aturdido, perplejo.

bewildering [biwil'dûring] *a* desconcertante.

bewitching [biwich'ing] *a* hechicero, encantador(a).

beyond [bēānd'] *prep* más allá de; (*exceeding*) además de, fuera de; (*above*) superior a ♦ *ad* más allá, más lejos; **~ doubt** fuera de toda duda; **~ repair** irreparable.

b/f *abbr* (= *brought forward*) saldo anterior.

BFPO *n abbr* (= *British Forces Post Office*) *servicio postal del ejército.*

bhp *n abbr* (= *brake horsepower*) caballo indicado al freno.

bi ... [bī] *pref* bi ....

biannual [bīan'yōōəl] *a* semestral.

bias [bī'əs] *n* (*prejudice*) prejuicio, pasión *f*; (*preference*) predisposición *f*.

bias(s)ed [bī'əst] *a* parcial; **to be ~ against** tener perjuicios contra.

bib [bib] *n* babero.

Bible [bī'bəl] *n* Biblia.

biblical [bib'likəl] *a* bíblico.

bibliography [biblēág'rəfē] *n* bibliografía.

bicarbonate of soda [bikâr'bənit əv sō'də] *n* bicarbonato de soda.

bicentenary [bīsen'tənärē] *n* (*Brit*) = **bicentennial**.

bicentennial [bīsenten'ēəl] *n* bicentenario.

biceps [bī'seps] *n* bíceps *m*.

bicker [bik'ûr] *vi* reñir.

bickering [bik'ûring] *n* riñas *fpl*, altercados *mpl*.

bicycle [bī'sikəl] *n* bicicleta.

bicycle path *n* camino para ciclistas.

bicycle pump *n* bomba de bicicleta.

bid [bid] *n* (*at auction*) oferta, postura; (*attempt*) tentativa, conato ♦ *vi* (*pt, pp* **bid**) hacer una oferta ♦ *vt* (*pt* **bade** [bad], *pp* **bidden** [bid'n]) mandar, ordenar; **to ~ sb good day** dar a uno los buenos días.

bidder [bid'ûr] *n:* **the highest ~** el mejor postor.

bidding [bid'ing] *n* (*at auction*) ofertas *fpl*; (*order*) orden *f*, mandato.

bide [bīd] *vt:* **to ~ one's time** esperar el momento adecuado.

bidet [bēdā'] *n* bidet *m*.

bidirectional [bīdirek'shənəl] *a* bidireccional.

biennial [bīen'ēəl] *a, n* bienal *f*.

bier [bēr] *n* féretro.

bifocals [bīfō'kəlz] *npl* gafas *fpl or* anteojos *mpl* (*LAm*) bifocales.

big [big] *a* grande; **~ business** gran negocio; **to do things in a ~ way** hacer las cosas en grande.

bigamy [big'əmē] *n* bigamía.

big dipper [big dip'ûr] *n* (*Brit*) montaña rusa.

big end *n* (*Brit AUT*) cabeza de biela.

bigheaded [big'hedid] *a* engreído.

bigot [big'ət] *n* fanático/a, intolerante *m/f*.

bigoted [big'ətid] *a* fanático, intolerante.

bigotry [big'ətrē] *n* fanatismo, intolerancia.

big toe *n* dedo gordo (del pie).

big top *n* (*circus*) circo; (*main tent*) tienda principal.

big wheel *n* (*at fair*) noria.

bigwig [big'wig] *n* (*col*) pez *m* gordo.

bike [bīk] *n* bici *f*.

bike rack *n* (*US*) soporte *m* para bicicletas.

bikeway [bīk'wā] *n* (*US*) pista de ciclismo.

bikini [bikē'nē] *n* bikini *m*.

bilateral [bīlat'ûrəl] *a* (*agreement*) bilateral.

bile [bīl] *n* bilis *f*.

bilge [bilj] *n* (*water*) agua de pantoque.

bilingual [bīling'gwəl] *a* bilingüe.

bilious [bil'yəs] *a* bilioso (*also fig*).

bill [bil] *n* (*gen*) cuenta; (*US: bank note*) billete *m*; (*invoice*) factura; (*POL*) proyecto de ley; (*of bird*) pico; (*notice*) cartel *m*; (*THEATER*) programa *m* ♦ *vt* extender *or* pasar la factura a; **may I have the ~ please?** ¿puede traerme la cuenta, por favor?; **~ of exchange** letra de cambio; **~ of lading** conocimiento de embarque; **~ of sale** escritura de venta; **"post no ~s"** "prohibido fijar carteles".

billboard [bil'bôrd] *n* cartelera.

billet [bil'it] *n* alojamiento ♦ *vt:* **to ~ sb (on sb)** alojar a uno (con uno).

billfold [bil'fōld] *n* (*US*) cartera.

billiards [bil'yûrdz] *n* billar *m*.

billion [bil'yən] *n* (*US*) mil millones *mpl*; (*Brit*) billón *m*.

billionaire [bilyənär'] *n* millonario/a.

billow [bil'ō] *n* (*of smoke*) nube *f*; (*of sail*) ondulación *f* ♦ *vi* (*smoke*) salir en nubes; (*sail*) ondear, ondular.

billowy [bil'ōē] *a* (*smoke*) que asciende en forma de nube.

billy [bil'ē] *n* (*US*) porra.

billy goat [bil'ē gōt] *n* macho cabrío.

bin [bin] *n* (*gen*) cubo *or* bote *m* (*LAm*) de la basura; **litter~** *n* (*Brit*) papelera.

binary [bī'nûrē] *a* (*MATH*) binario; **~ code** código binario; **~ system** sistema *m* binario.

bind, *pt, pp* **bound** [bīnd, bound] *vt* atar, liar; (*wound*) vendar; (*book*) encuadernar; (*oblige*) obligar.

bind over *vt* (*LAW*) obligar a comparecer ante el juez.

bind up *vt* (*wound*) vendar; **to be bound up in** (*work, research etc*) estar absorto en; **to be bound up with** (*person*) estar estrechamente ligado con.

binder [bīn'dûr] *n* (*file*) carpeta.

binding [bīn'ding] *a* (*contract*) obligatorio.

binge [binj] *n* borrachera, juerga; **to go on a ~** ir de juerga.

bingo [bing'gō] *n* bingo *m*.

binoculars [bənâk'yəlûrz] *npl* prismáticos *mpl*.

biochemistry [bīōkem'istrē] *n* bioquímica.

biodegradable [bīōdigrā'dəbəl] *a* biodegradable.

biographer [bīǎg'rəfûr] *n* biógrafo/a.

biographical [bīəgraf'ikəl] *a* biográfico.

biography [bīǎg'rəfē] *n* biografía.

biological [bīəlǎj'ikəl] *a* biológico.

biologist [bīǎl'əjist] *n* biólogo/a.

biology [bīǎl'əjē] *n* biología.

biophysics [bīōfiz'iks] *nsg* biofísica.

biopsy [bī'ǎpsē] *n* biopsia.

biorhythm [bī'ōrithəm] *n* bioritmo.

biotechnology [bīōteknǎl'əjē] *n* biotecnología.

biped [bī'ped] *n* bípedo.

birch [bûrch] *n* abedul *m*; (*cane*) vara.

bird [bûrd] *n* ave *f*, pájaro; (*Brit col: girl*) chica.

birdcage [bûrd'kāj] *n* jaula.

bird's-eye view [bûrdz'ī vyōō'] *n* vista de pájaro.

bird watcher [bûrd' wâch'ûr] *n* ornitólogo/a.

Biro [bē'rō] *n* ® bolígrafo.

birth [bûrth] *n* nacimiento; (*MED*) parto; **to give ~ to** parir, dar a luz a; (*fig*) dar origen a.

birth certificate *n* partida de nacimiento.

birth control *n* control *m* de natalidad; (*methods*) métodos *mpl* anticonceptivos.

birthday [bûrth'dā] *n* cumpleaños *m inv*.

birthplace [bûrth'plâs] *n* lugar *m* de nacimiento.

birth rate [bûrth rāt] *n* (tasa de) natalidad *f*.

Biscay [bis'kā] *n*: **the Bay of ~** el Mar Cantábrico, el golfo de Vizcaya.

biscuit [bis'kit] *n* (*US*) bizcocho; (*Brit*) galleta.

bisect [bīsekt'] *vt* (*also MATH*) bisecar.

bishop [bish'əp] *n* obispo; (*CHESS*) alfil *m*.

bit [bit] *pt of* **bite** ♦ *n* trozo, pedazo, pedacito; (*COMPUT*) bit *m*, bitio; (*for horse*) freno, bocado; **a ~ of** un poco de; **a ~ mad** algo loco; **to come to ~s** (*break*) hacerse pedazos; **to do one's ~** aportar su granito de arena; **bring all your ~s and pieces** trae todas tus cosas.

bitch [bich] *n* (*dog*) perra; (*col!*) zorra (*!*).

bite [bīt] *vt, vi* (*pt* **bit** [bit], *pp* **bitten** [bitn]) morder; (*insect etc*) picar ♦ *n* (*wound:* of

dog, snake etc) mordedura; (*of insect*) picadura; (*mouthful*) bocado; **to ~ one's nails** comerse las uñas; **let's have a ~ (to eat)** comamos algo.

biting [bī'ting] *a* (*wind*) que traspasa los huesos; (*criticism*) mordaz.

bit part *n* (*THEATER*) papel *m* secundario.

bitten [bit'ən] *pp of* **bite**.

bitter [bit'ûr] *a* amargo; (*wind, criticism*) cortante, penetrante; (*icy: weather*) glacial; (*battle*) encarnizado ♦ *n* (*Brit: beer*) cerveza típica británica a base de lúpulos.

bitterly [bit'ûrlē] *ad* (*disappoint, complain, weep*) desconsoladamente; (*oppose, criticise*) implacablemente; (*jealous*) agriamente; **it's ~ cold** hace un frío glacial.

bitterness [bit'ûrnis] *n* amargura; (*anger*) rencor *m*.

bitty [bit'ē] *a* (*US: tiny*) pequeñito; (*Brit col*) deshilvanado.

bitumen [bitōō'mən] *n* betún *m*.

bivouac [biv'ōōak] *n* vivac *m*, vivaque *m*.

bizarre [bizâr'] *a* raro, estrafalario.

bk *abbr* = **bank, book**.

BL *n abbr* (= *Bachelor of Law(s)*, *Bachelor of Letters*) título universitario.

b/l *abbr* = **bill of lading**.

blab [blab] *vi* chismear, soplar ♦ *vt* (*also: ~ out*) revelar, contar.

black [blak] *a* (*color*) negro; (*dark*) oscuro ♦ *n* (*color*) color *m* negro; (*person*): **B~** negro/a ♦ *vt* (*shoes*) lustrar; (*Brit: INDUSTRY*) boicotear; **to give sb a ~ eye** ponerle a uno el ojo morado; **~ coffee** café *m* solo; **there it is in ~ and white** (*fig*) ahí está bien claro; **to be in the ~** (*in credit*) tener saldo positivo; **~ and blue** *a* amoratado.

black out *vi* (*faint*) desmayarse.

black belt *n* (*US: area*) zona negra; (*SPORT*) cinturón *m* negro.

blackberry [blak'bärē] *n* zarzamora.

blackbird [blak'bûrd] *n* mirlo.

blackboard [blak'bôrd] *n* pizarra.

black box *n* (*AVIAT*) registrador *m* de vuelo, caja negra.

blackcurrant [blakkur'ənt] *n* grosella negra.

black economy *n* (*Brit*) economía sumergida.

blacken [blak'ən] *vt* ennegrecer; (*fig*) denigrar.

Black Forest *n*: **the ~** la Selva Negra.

blackguard [blag'ârd] *n* canalla *m*, pillo.

black ice *n* hielo invisible en la carretera.

blackjack [blak'jak] *n* (*US*) veintiuna.

blackleg [blak'leg] *n* (*Brit*) esquirol *m*, rompehuelgas *m inv*.

blacklist [blak'list] *n* lista negra ♦ *vt* poner en la lista negra.

blackmail [blak'māl] *n* chantaje *m* ♦ *vt* chantajear.

blackmailer [blak'mālûr] *n* chantajista *m/f*.

black market *n* mercado negro, estraperlo.

blackness [blak'nis] *n* negrura.

blackout [blak'out] *n* (*TV, ELEC*) apagón *m*; (*fainting*) desmayo, pérdida de conocimiento.

Black Sea *n*: **the ~** el Mar Negro.

black sheep *n* oveja negra.

blacksmith [blak'smith] *n* herrero.

black spot *n* (*Brit AUT*) lugar *m* peligroso.

bladder [blad'ûr] *n* vejiga.

blade [blād] *n* hoja; (*cutting edge*) filo; **a ~ of grass** una brizna de hierba.

blame [blām] *n* culpa ♦ *vt*: **to ~ sb for sth** echar a uno la culpa de algo; **to be to ~ (for)** tener la culpa (de); **I'm not to ~** yo no tengo la culpa; **and I don't ~ him** y lo comprendo perfectamente.

blameless [blām'lis] *a* (*person*) inocente.

blanch [blanch] *vi* (*person*) palidecer; (*CULIN*) blanquear.

bland [bland] *a* suave; (*taste*) soso.

blank [blangk] *a* en blanco; (*shot*) sin bala; (*look*) sin expresión ♦ *n* blanco, espacio en blanco; cartucho sin bala *or* de fogueo; **to draw a ~** (*fig*) no conseguir nada.

blank check *n* cheque *m* en blanco.

blanket [blang'kit] *n* manta ♦ *a* (*statement, agreement*) comprensivo, general.

blankly [blangk'lē] *ad*: **she looked at me ~** me miró sin comprender.

blare [blär] *vi* (*brass band, horns, radio*) resonar.

blasé [blâzā'] *a* hastiado.

blaspheme [blasfēm'] *vi* blasfemar.

blasphemous [blas'fəməs] *a* blasfemo.

blasphemy [blas'fəmē] *n* blasfemia.

blast [blast] *n* (*of wind*) ráfaga, soplo; (*of whistle*) toque *m*; (*of explosive*) carga explosiva; (*force*) choque *m* ♦ *vt* (*blow up*) volar; (*blow open*) abrir con carga explosiva ♦ *excl* (*Brit col*) ¡maldito sea!; **(at) full ~** (*also fig*) a toda marcha.

blast off *vi* (*spacecraft etc*) despegar.

blast furnace *n* alto horno.

blast-off [blast'ôf] *n* (*SPACE*) lanzamiento.

blatant [blā'tənt] *a* descarado.

blatantly [blā'təntlē] *ad*: **it's ~ obvious** está clarísimo.

blather [blath'ûr] *vi* decir tonterías.

blaze [blāz] *n* (*fire*) fuego; (*flames*) llamarada; (*glow: of fire, sun etc*) resplandor *m*; (*fig*) arranque *m* ♦ *vi* (*fire*) arder en llamas; (*fig*) brillar ♦ *vt*: **to ~ a trail** (*fig*) abrir (un) camino; **in a ~ of publicity** bajo los focos de la publicidad.

blazer [blā'zûr] *n chaqueta de uniforme de colegial o de socio de club.*

bleach [blēch] *n* (*also:* **household ~**) lejía ♦ *vt* (*linen*) blanquear.

bleached [blēcht] *a* (*hair*) teñido de rubio; (*clothes*) decolorado.

bleachers [blē'chûrz] *npl* (*US SPORT*) gradas *fpl*.

bleak [blēk] *a* (*countryside*) desierto; (*landscape*) desolado, desierto; (*weather*) desapacible; (*smile*) triste; (*prospect, future*) poco prometedor(a).

bleary-eyed [blē'rēīd] *a*: **to be ~** tener ojos de cansado.

bleat [blēt] *vi* balar.

bleed, *pt, pp* **bled** [blēd, bled] *vt* sangrar; (*brakes, radiator*) desaguar ♦ *vi* sangrar.

bleeding [blē'ding] *a* sangrante.

bleeper [blē'pûr] *n* (*Brit: of doctor etc*) busca *m*.

blemish [blem'ish] *n* mancha, tacha.

blench [blench] *vi* (*shrink back*) acobardarse; (*grow pale*) palidecer.

blend [blend] *n* mezcla ♦ *vt* mezclar ♦ *vi* (*colors etc*) combinarse, mezclarse.

blender [blen'dûr] *n* (*CULIN*) licuadora.

bless, *pt, pp* **blessed** *or* **blest** [bles, blest] *vt* bendecir.

blessed [bles'id] *a* (*REL: holy*) santo, bendito; (: *happy*) dichoso; **every ~ day** cada santo día.

blessing [bles'ing] *n* bendición *f*; (*advantage*) beneficio, ventaja; **to count one's ~s** agradecer lo que se tiene; **it was a ~ in disguise** no hay mal que por bien no venga.

blew [bloo] *pt of* **blow.**

blight [blīt] *vt* (*hopes etc*) frustrar, arruinar.

blimey [blī'mē] *excl* (*Brit col*) ¡caray!

blind [blīnd] *a* ciego ♦ *n* (*for window*) persiana ♦ *vt* cegar; (*dazzle*) deslumbrar.

blind alley *n* callejón *m* sin salida.

blind corner *n* esquina escondida.

blinders [blīn'dûrz] *npl* (*US*) anteojeras *fpl*.

blindfold [blīnd'fōld] *n* venda ♦ *a, ad* con los ojos vendados ♦ *vt* vendar los ojos a.

blindly [blīnd'lē] *ad* a ciegas, ciegamente.

blindness [blīnd'nis] *n* ceguera.

blind spot *n* mácula.

blink [blingk] *vi* parpadear, pestañear; (*light*) oscilar; **to be on the ~** (*col*) estar estropeado.

blinkers [blingk'ûrz] *npl* (*Brit*) anteojeras *fpl*.

blinking [blingk'ing] *a* (*col*): **this ~...** este condenado....

bliss [blis] *n* felicidad *f*.

blissful [blis'fəl] *a* dichoso; **in ~ ignorance** feliz en la ignorancia.

blissfully [blis'fəlē] *ad* (*sigh, smile*) con felicidad; **~ happy** sumamente feliz.

blister [blis'tûr] *n* (*on skin, paint*) ampolla ♦ *vi* ampollarse.

blistering [blis'tûring] *a* (*heat*) abrasador(a).

blithely [blīth'lē] *ad* alegremente, despreocupadamente.

blithering [blith'ûring] *a* (*col*): **this ~ idiot** este tonto perdido.

BLit(t) *n abbr* (= *Bachelor of Literature*) tí-

tulo universitario.

blitz [blits] *n* bombardeo aéreo; **to have a ~ on sth** (*fig*) tener una campaña de algo.

blizzard [bliz'ûrd] *n* ventisca.

BLM *n abbr* (*US*) = *Bureau of Land Management.*

bloated [blō'tid] *a* hinchado.

blob [bláb] *n* (*drop*) gota; (*stain*, *spot*) mancha.

bloc [blák] *n* (*POL*) bloque *m.*

block [blák] *n* bloque *m* (*also* COMPUT); (*in pipes*) obstáculo; (*of buildings*) manzana ♦ *vt* (*gen*) obstruir, cerrar; (*progress*) estorbar; (*COMPUT*) agrupar; **~ of apartments** bloque *m* de pisos; **mental ~** amnesia temporal; **~ and tackle** (*TECH*) polea con aparejo; **3 ~s from here** a 3 manzanas *or* cuadras (*LAm*) de aquí.

  block up *vt* tapar, obstruir; (*pipe*) atascar.

blockade [blákād'] *n* bloqueo ♦ *vt* bloquear.

blockage [blák'ij] *n* estorbo, obstrucción *f.*

block booking *n* reserva en grupo.

blockbuster [blák'bustûr] *n* (*book*) bestseller *m*; (*film*) éxito de público.

block capitals *npl* mayúsculas *fpl.*

block letters *npl* letras *fpl* de molde.

block release *n* (*Brit*) período de trabajo pagado para efectuar estudios superiores.

block vote *n* (*Brit*) voto por delegación.

bloke [blōk] *n* (*Brit col*) tipo, tío.

blond(e) [blánd] *a*, *n* rubio/a *m/f.*

blood [blud] *n* sangre *f*; **new ~** (*fig*) gente *f* nueva.

blood donor *n* donador(a) *m/f* de sangre.

blood group *n* grupo sanguíneo.

bloodhound [blud'hound] *n* sabueso.

bloodless [blud'lis] *a* (*pale*) exangüe; (*revolt etc*) sin derramamiento de sangre, incruento.

bloodletting [blud'leting] *n* (*MED*) sangría; (*fig*) sangría, carnicería.

blood poisoning *n* envenenamiento de la sangre.

blood pressure *n* tensión *f* sanguínea; **to have high/low ~** tener la tensión alta/baja.

blood sausage *n* (*US*) morcilla.

bloodshed [blud'shed] *n* derramamiento de sangre.

bloodshot [blud'shát] *a* inyectado en sangre.

bloodstained [blud'stānd] *a* manchado de sangre.

bloodstream [blud'strēm] *n* corriente *f* sanguínea.

blood test *n* análisis *m* de sangre.

bloodthirsty [blud'thûrstē] *a* sanguinario.

blood transfusion *n* transfusión *f* de sangre.

blood vessel *n* vaso sanguíneo.

bloody [blud'ē] *a* sangriento; (*Brit col!*): **this ~...** este condenado *or* puñetero... (!) ♦ *ad* (*Brit col!*): **~ strong/good** terrible-

mente fuerte/bueno.

bloody-minded [blud'ēmīn'did] *a* (*Brit col*) malintencionado.

bloom [blōōm] *n* floración *f*; **in ~** en flor ♦ *vi* florecer.

blossom [blás'əm] *n* flor *f* ♦ *vi* florecer; (*fig*) desarrollarse; **to ~ into** (*fig*) desarrollarse en.

blot [blát] *n* borrón *m* ♦ *vt* (*dry*) secar; (*stain*) manchar; **to ~ out** *vt* (*view*) tapar; (*memories*) borrar; **to be a ~ on the landscape** estropear el paisaje.

blotchy [blách'ē] *a* (*complexion*) lleno de manchas.

blotter [blát'ûr] *n* secante *m.*

blotting paper [blát'ing pā'pûr] *n* papel *m* secante.

blouse [blous] *n* blusa.

blow [blō] *n* golpe *m* ♦ *vb* (*pt* **blew**, *pp* **blown** [blō, blōn]) *vi* soplar; (*fuse*) fundirse ♦ *vt* (*glass*) soplar; (*fuse*) quemar; (*instrument*) tocar; **to come to ~s** llegar a golpes; **to ~ one's nose** sonarse.

blow away *vt* llevarse, arrancar.

blow down *vt* derribar.

blow off *vt* arrebatar.

blow out *vt* apagar ♦ *vi* apagarse; (*tire*) reventar.

blow over *vi* amainar.

blow up *vi* estallar ♦ *vt* volar; (*tire*) inflar; (*PHOT*) ampliar.

blow-dry [blō'drī] *n* secado con secador de mano ♦ *vt* secar con secador de mano.

blowfly [blō'flī] *n* (*US*) moscarda, mosca azul.

blowlamp [blō'lamp] *n* (*Brit*) = **blowtorch.**

blowout [blō'out] *n* (*of tire*) pinchazo; (*col: big meal*) banquete *m*, festín *m.*

blowtorch [blō'tôrch] *n* soplete *m*, lámpara de soldar.

blow-up [blō'up] *n* (*COMM*) ampliación *f.*

BLS *n abbr* (*US*) = *Bureau of Labor Statistics.*

BLT *n abbr* = *bacon, lettuce and tomato* (*sandwich*).

blubber [blub'ûr] *n* grasa de ballena ♦ *vi* (*pej*) lloriquear.

bludgeon [bluj'ən] *vt*: **to ~ sb into doing sth** coaccionar a uno a hacer algo.

blue [blōō] *a* azul; **~ film/joke** film/chiste verde; **once in a ~ moon** de higos a brevas; **to come out of the ~** (*fig*) ser completamente inesperado; *see also* **blues.**

blue baby *n* niño azul *or* cianótico.

bluebell [blōō'bel] *n* campanilla, campánula azul.

blueberry [blōō'bärē] *n* (*US*) arándano.

blue-blooded [blōō'blud'id] *a* de sangre azul.

bluebottle [blōō'bátəl] *n* moscarda, mosca azul.

blue cheese *n* queso de pasta verde.

blue-chip [blōō'chip'] *n*: **~ investment**

inversión *f* asegurada.

blue-collar worker |blōō'kál'úr wúr'kúr| *n* manual *m/f*.

blue jeans *npl* tejanos *mpl*, vaqueros *mpl*.

blueprint |blōō'print| *n* proyecto; ~ **(for)** (*fig*) anteproyecto (de).

blues |blōōz| *npl*: **the** ~ (*MUS*) el blues; **to have the** ~ estar triste.

bluff |bluf| *vi* hacer un bluff, farolear ♦ *n* bluff *m*, farol *m*; (*GEO*) precipicio, despeñadero; **to call sb's** ~ coger a uno en un renuncio.

bluish |blōō'ish| *a* azulado.

blunder |blun'dúr| *n* patinazo, metedura de pata ♦ *vi* cometer un error, meter la pata; **to** ~ **into sb/sth** tropezar con uno/algo.

blunt |blunt| *a* (*knife*) desafilado; (*person*) franco, directo ♦ *vt* embotar, desafilar; **this pencil is** ~ este lápiz está despuntado; ~ **instrument** (*LAW*) instrumento contundente.

bluntly |blunt'lē| *ad* (*speak*) francamente, de modo terminante.

bluntness |blunt'nis| *n* (*of person*) franqueza, brusquedad *f*.

blur |blûr| *n* aspecto borroso ♦ *vt* (*vision*) enturbiar; (*memory*) empañar.

blurb |blûrb| *n* propaganda.

blurred |blûrd| *a* borroso.

blurt |blûrt|: **to** ~ **out** *vt* (*say*) descolgarse con, dejar escapar.

blush |blush| *vi* ruborizarse, ponerse colorado ♦ *n* rubor *m*; (*US: make up*) colorete *m*.

blusher |blush'úr| *n* (*Brit*) colorete *m*.

bluster |blus'túr| *n* fanfarronada, bravata ♦ *vi* fanfarronear, amenazar.

blustering |blus'túring| *a* (*person*) fanfarrón/ona.

blustery |blus'tûrē| *a* (*weather*) tempestuoso, tormentoso.

Blvd *abbr* = *boulevard*.

BM *n abbr* (*UNIV*: = *Bachelor of Medicine*) título universitario.

BMA *n abbr* = *British Medical Association*.

BMus *n abbr* (= *Bachelor of Music*) título universitario.

BO *n abbr* (col: = *body odor*) olor *m* a sudor; (*US*) = **box office**.

boa |bō'ə| *n* boa.

boar |bôr| *n* verraco, cerdo.

board |bôrd| *n* tabla, tablero; (*on wall*) tablón *m*; (*for chess etc*) tablero; (*committee*) junta, consejo; (*in firm*) mesa *or* junta directiva; (*NAUT, AVIAT*): **on** ~ a bordo ♦ *vt* (*ship*) embarcarse en; (*train*) subir a; **full** ~ (*Brit*) pensión *f* completa; **half** ~ (*Brit*) media pensión; **to go by the** ~ (*fig*) ser abandonado *or* olvidado; **above** ~ (*fig*) legítimo; **across the** ~ (*fig: ad*) en todos los niveles; (: *a*) general.

board up *vt* (*door*) tapiar.

boarder |bôr'dúr| *n* huésped(a) *m/f*; (*SCOL*) interno/a.

board game *n* juego de tablero.

boarding house |bôr'ding hous| *n* casa de huéspedes.

boarding pass |bôr'ding pas| *n* (*AVIAT, NAUT*) tarjeta de embarque.

boarding school |bôr'ding skōōl| *n* internado.

board meeting *n* reunión *f* de la junta directiva.

board room *n* sala de juntas.

boardwalk |bôrd'wôk| *n* (*US*) paseo entablado.

boast |bōst| *vi*: **to** ~ **(about** *or* **of)** alardear (de) ♦ *vt* ostentar ♦ *n* alarde *m*, baladronada.

boastful |bōst'fəl| *a* presumido, jactancioso.

boastfulness |bōst'fəlnis| *n* fanfarronería.

boat |bōt| *n* barco, buque *m*; (*small*) barca, bote *m*; **to go by** ~ ir en barco.

boater |bō'tûr| *n* (*hat*) canotié *m*.

boating |bō'ting| *n* canotaje *m*.

boatman |bōt'mən| *n* barquero.

boatswain |bō'sən| *n* contramaestre *m*.

bob |bâb| *vi* (*boat, cork on water: also*: ~ **up and down**) menearse, balancearse ♦ *n* (*Brit col*) = **shilling**.

bob up *vi* (*Brit*) (re)aparecer de repente.

bobbin |bâb'in| *n* (*of sewing machine*) carrete *m*, bobina.

bobby |bâb'ē| *n* (*Brit col*) poli *m/f*.

bobby pin |bâb'ē pin| *n* (*US*) horquilla.

bobsled |bâb'slcd| *n* bob *m*.

bode |bōd| *vi*: **to** ~ **well/ill (for)** ser de buen/mal agüero (para).

bodice |bâd'is| *n* corpiño.

-bodied |bâd'id| *a suff* de cuerpo ....

bodily |bâd'əlē| *a* (*comfort, needs*) corporal; (*pain*) corpóreo ♦ *ad* (*in person*) en persona; (*carry*) corporalmente; (*lift*) en peso.

body |bâd'ē| *n* cuerpo; (*corpse*) cadáver *m*; (*of car*) caja, carrocería; (*fig: organization*) organización *f*; (: *public* ~) organismo; (: *quantity*) masa; (: *of speech, document*) parte *f* principal; (*also*: ~ **stocking**) body *m*; **ruling** ~ directiva; **as a** ~ todos juntos, en masa.

body-building |bâd'ēbil'ding| *n* culturismo.

bodyguard |bâd'ēgârd| *n* guardaespaldas *m inv*.

bodywork |bâd'ēwûrk| *n* carrocería.

boffin |bâf'in| *n* (*Brit*) científico/a.

bog |bâg| *n* pantano, ciénaga ♦ *vt*: **to get** ~**ged down** (*fig*) empantanarse, atascarse.

boggle |bâg'əl| *vt*: **it** ~**s the mind!** ¡no puedo creerlo!

Bogotá |bōgətá'| *n* Bogotá.

bogus |bō'gəs| *a* falso, fraudulento; (*person*) fingido.

Bohemia |bōhē'mēə| *n* Bohemia.

Bohemian |bōhē'mēən| *a*, *n* bohemio/a *m/f*.

boil |boil| *vt* cocer; (*eggs*) pasar por agua ♦ *vi* hervir ♦ *n* (*MED*) furúnculo, divieso; **to bring to a** ~ calentar hasta que hiervan; **to come to a** (*US*) *or* **the** (*Brit*) ~ co-

menzar a hervir; ~**ed egg** huevo pasado por agua; ~**ed potatoes** patatas *fpl or* papas *fpl* (*LAm*) hervidas.
boil down *vi* (*fig*): **to** ~ **down to** reducirse a.
boil over *vi* (*liquid*) rebosar; (*anger, resentment*) llegar al colmo.
boiler [boi'lûr] *n* caldera.
boiler suit *n* (*Brit*) mono.
boiling [boi'ling] *a*: **I'm** ~ (**hot**) (*col*) estoy asado.
boiling point *n* punto de ebullición *f*.
boisterous [bois'tûrəs] *a* (*noisy*) bullicioso; (*excitable*) exuberante; (*crowd*) tumultuoso.
bold [bōld] *a* (*brave*) valiente, audaz; (*pej*) descarado; (*outline*) grueso; (*color*) vivo; ~ **type** (*TYP*) negrita.
boldly [bōld'lē] *ad* atrevidamente.
boldness [bōld'nis] *n* valor *m*, audacia; (*cheek*) descaro.
Bolivia [bōliv'ēə] *n* Bolivia.
Bolivian [bōliv'ēən] *a, n* boliviano/a *m/f*.
bollard [bâl'ûrd] *n* (*Brit AUT*) poste *m*.
bolster [bōl'stûr] *n* travesero, cabezal *m*.
bolster up *vt* reforzar; (*fig*) alentar.
bolt [bōlt] *n* (*lock*) cerrojo; (*with nut*) perno, tornillo ♦ *ad*: ~ **upright** rígido, erguido ♦ *vt* (*door*) echar el cerrojo a; (*food*) engullir ♦ *vi* fugarse; (*horse*) desbocarse.
bomb [bâm] *n* bomba ♦ *vt* bombardear.
bombard [bâmbârd'] *vt* bombardear; (*fig*) asediar.
bombardment [bâmbârd'mənt] *n* bombardeo.
bombastic [bâmbas'tik] *a* rimbombante; (*person*) farolero.
bomb disposal *n* desmontaje *m* de explosivos.
bomb disposal expert *n* experto/a en desactivar bombas.
bomber [bâm'ûr] *n* (*AVIAT*) bombardero; (*terrorist*) persona que pone bombas.
bombing [bâm'ing] *n* bombardeo.
bombshell [bâm'shel] *n* obús *m*, granada; (*fig*) bomba.
bomb site *n* lugar *m* donde estalló una bomba.
bona fide [bō'nə fīd'] *a* genuino, auténtico.
bonanza [bənan'zə] *n* bonanza.
bond [bând] *n* (*binding promise*) fianza; (*FINANCE*) bono; (*link*) vínculo, lazo; **in** ~ (*COMM*) en depósito bajo fianza.
bondage [bân'dij] *n* esclavitud *f*.
bonded goods [bân'did gōōdz'] *npl* mercancías *fpl* en depósito de aduanas.
bonded warehouse [bân'did wär'hous] *n* depósito de aduanas.
bone [bōn] *n* hueso; (*of fish*) espina ♦ *vt* deshuesar; quitar las espinas a; ~ **of contention** manzana de la discordia.
bone china *n* porcelana fina.
bone-dry [bōn'drī'] *a* completamente seco.

bone idle *a* gandul.
boner [bō'nûr] *n* (*US col*) plancha, patochada.
bonfire [bân'fîûr] *n* hoguera, fogata.
Bonn [bân] *n* Bonn *m*.
bonnet [bân'it] *n* gorra; (*Brit: of car*) capó *m*.
bonny [bân'ē] *a* (*esp Scottish*) bonito, hermoso, lindo.
bonus [bō'nəs] *n* (*at Christmas etc*) paga extraordinaria; (*merit award*) sobrepaga, prima.
bony [bō'nē] *a* (*arm, face, MED: tissue*) huesudo; (*meat*) lleno de huesos; (*fish*) lleno de espinas; (*thin: person*) flaco, delgado.
boo [bōō] *vt* abuchear, rechiflar.
boob [bōōb] *n* (*Brit: col: mistake*) disparate *m*, sandez *f*; (: *breast*) teta.
boo-boo [bōō'bōō] *n* (*US: col: mistake*) disparate *m*, sandez *f*.
booby prize [bōō'bē prīz] *n* premio al último.
booby trap [bōō'bē trap] *n* (*MIL etc*) trampa explosiva.
book [bōōk] *n* libro; (*notebook*) libreta; (*of stamps etc*) librito; ~**s** (*COMM*) cuentas *fpl*, contabilidad *f* ♦ *vt* (*ticket, seat, room*) reservar; (*driver*) fichar; (*Brit SOCCER*) amonestar; **to keep the** ~**s** llevar las cuentas *or* los libros; **by the** ~ según las reglas; **to throw the** ~ **at sb** echar un rapapolvo a uno.
book in *vi* (*Brit: at hotel*) registrarse.
book up *vt*: **all seats are** ~**ed up** todas las plazas están reservadas; **the hotel is** ~**ed up** el hotel está lleno.
bookable [bōōk'əbəl] *a*: **seats are** ~ (*Brit*) los asientos se pueden reservar (de antemano).
bookcase [bōōk'kās] *n* librería, estante *m* para libros.
booking office [bōōk'ing ôf'is] *n* (*Brit: RAIL*) despacho de billetes *or* boletos (*LAm*); (: *THEATER*) taquilla, boletería (*LAm*).
book-keeping [bōōkkē'ping] *n* contabilidad *f*.
booklet [bōōk'lit] *n* folleto.
bookmaker [bōōk'mākûr] *n* corredor *m* de apuestas.
bookseller [bōōk'selûr] *n* librero/a.
bookshop [bōōk'shâp] *n* librería.
bookstall [bōōk'stôl] *n* quiosco de libros.
book store *n* = **bookshop**.
book token *n* (*Brit*) vale *m* para libros.
book value *n* (*COMM*) valor *m* contable.
bookworm [bōōk'wûrm] *n* (*fig*) ratón/ona *m/f* de biblioteca.
boom [bōōm] *n* (*noise*) trueno, estampido; (*in prices etc*) alza rápida; (*ECON*) boom *m*, auge *m* ♦ *vi* (*cannon*) hacer gran estruendo, retumbar; (*ECON*) estar en alza.

boomerang [bōō'mərang] *n* bumerang *m*
(*also fig*) ♦ *vi*: **to ~ on sb** (*fig*) se. contraproducente para uno.
boom town *n* ciudad *f* beneficiaria del
auge.
boon [bōōn] *n* favor *m*, beneficio.
boorish [bōō'rish] *a* grosero.
boost [bōōst] *n* estímulo, empuje *m* ♦ *vt*
estimular, empujar; (*increase: sales, production*) aumentar; **to give a ~ to** (*morale*) levantar; **it gave a ~ to his confidence** le dio confianza en sí mismo.
booster [bōōs'tûr] *n* (*MED*) reinyección *f*;
(*TV*) repetidor *m*; (*ELEC*) elevador *m* de
tensión; (*also:* **~ rocket**) cohete *m*.
boot [bōōt] *n* bota; (*ankle ~*) borceguí *m*;
(*US AUT: also:* **Denver ~**) cepo; (*Brit: of
car*) maleta, maletero ♦ *vt* dar un puntapié
a; (*COMPUT*) arrancar; **to ~** (*in addition*)
además, por añadidura; **to give sb the ~**
(*col*) despedir a uno, poner a uno en la calle.
booth [bōōth] *n* (*at fair*) barraca; (*telephone ~*, *voting ~*) cabina.
bootleg [bōōt'leg] *a* de contrabando; **~ record** disco de contrabando.
bootlicker [bōōt'likûr] *n* (*col*) lameculos *m*/
f inv.
booty [bōō'tē] *n* botín *m*.
booze [bōōz] (*col*) *n* bebida, trago ♦ *vi*
emborracharse.
boozer [bōō'zûr] *n* (*col: person*) bebedor(a)
m/*f*.
border [bôr'dûr] *n* borde *m*, margen *m*; (*of
a country*) frontera ♦ *a* fronterizo; **the B~s**
*región fronteriza entre Escocia e Ingla-
terra.*
border on *vt fus* lindar con; (*fig*) rayar
en.
borderline [bôr'dûrlīn] *n* (*fig*) frontera.
bore [bôr] *pt of* **bear** ♦ *vt* (*hole*) taladrar;
(*person*) aburrir ♦ *n* (*person*) pelmazo, pesado; (*of gun*) calibre *m*.
bored [bôrd] *a* aburrido; **he's ~ to tears** *or*
to death *or* **stiff** está aburrido como una
ostra, está muerto de aburrimiento.
boredom [bôr'dəm] *n* aburrimiento.
boring [bôr'ing] *a* aburrido.
born [bôrn] *a*: **to be ~** nacer; **I was ~ in
1960** nací en 1960.
borne [bôrn] *pp of* **bear**.
Borneo [bôr'nēō] *n* Borneo.
borough [bur'ə] *n* municipio.
borrow [bâr'ō] *vt*: **to ~ sth (from sb)** tomar algo prestado (a alguien); **may I ~
your car?** ¿me prestas tu coche?
borrower [bâr'ōûr] *n* prestatario/a.
borrowing [bâr'ōing] *n* préstamos *mpl*.
borstal [bôr'stəl] *n* (*Brit*) reformatorio (de
menores).
bosom [bōōz'əm] *n* pecho; (*fig*) seno; **~
friend** *n* amigo/a *or* íntimo/a del alma.
boss [bôs] *n* jefe/a *m*/*f*; (*employer*) patrón/

ona *m*/*f*; (*political etc*) cacique *m* ♦ *vt*
(*also:* **~ around**) mangonear; **stop ~ing
everyone around!** ¡deja de dar órdenes *or*
de mangonear a todos!
bossy [bôs'ē] *a* mandón/ona.
bosun [bō'sən] *n* contramaestre *m*.
botanical [bətan'ikəl] *a* botánico.
botanist [bât'ənist] *n* botanista *m*/*f*.
botany [bât'ənē] *n* botánica.
botch [bâch] *vt* (*also: Brit:* **~ up**) arruinar,
estropear.
both [bōth] *a*, *pron* ambos/as, los/las dos; **~
of us went, we ~ went** fuimos los dos,
ambos fuimos ♦ *ad*: **~ A and B** tanto A
como B.
bother [bâth'ûr] *vt* (*worry*) preocupar; (*disturb*) molestar, fastidiar ♦ *vi* (*gen:* **~ o.s.**)
molestarse ♦ *n*: **what a ~!** ¡qué lata! ♦
excl ¡maldito sea!, ¡caramba!; **I'm sorry
to ~ you** perdona que te moleste; **to ~
doing** tomarse la molestia de hacer; **please
don't ~** no te molestes.
Botswana [bâchwân'ə] *n* Botswana.
bottle [bât'əl] *n* botella; (*small*) frasco;
(*baby's*) biberón *m* ♦ *vt* embotellar; **~ of
wine/milk** botella de vino/de leche; **wine/
milk ~** botella de vino/de leche.
bottle up *vt* (*fig*) contener.
bottleneck [bât'əlnek] *n* embotellamiento.
bottle opener [bât'əl ōp'ənûr] *n* abrebotellas *m inv*.
bottom [bât'əm] *n* (*of box, sea*) fondo;
(*buttocks*) trasero, culo; (*of page,
mountain, tree*) pie *m*; (*of list*) final *m* ♦ *a*
(*lowest*) más bajo; (*last*) último; **to get to
the ~ of sth** (*fig*) llegar al fondo de algo;
the ~ line is ... (*fig*) lo fundamental del
asunto es ....
bottomless [bât'əmlis] *a* sin fondo, insondable.
bough [bou] *n* rama.
bought [bôt] *pt*, *pp of* **buy**.
bouillon cube [bōōl'yən kyōōb] *n* (*US*) cubito de caldo.
boulder [bōl'dûr] *n* canto rodado.
bounce [bouns] *vi* (*ball*) (re)botar; (*check*)
ser rechazado ♦ *vt* hacer (re)botar ♦ *n* (*rebound*) (re)bote *m*; **he's got plenty of ~**
(*fig*) tiene mucha energía.
bouncer [boun'sûr] *n* (*col*) matón *m*.
bound [bound] *pt*, *pp of* **bind** ♦ *n* (*leap*)
salto; (*gen pl: limit*) límite *m* ♦ *vi* (*leap*)
saltar ♦ *a*: **~ by friendship** vinculado por
amistad; **to be ~ to do sth** (*obliged*) tener
el deber de hacer algo; **he's ~ to come** es
seguro que vendrá; **"out of ~s to the public"** "prohibido el paso"; **~ for** con destino
a.
boundary [boun'dûrē] *n* límite *m*, lindero.
boundless [bound'lis] *a* ilimitado.
bountiful [boun'təfəl] *a* (*person*) liberal, generoso; (*God*) bondadoso; (*supply*) abundante.

bounty [bountē] n (*generosity*) generosidad f; (*reward*) prima.

bounty hunter n cazarrecompensas m inv.

bouquet [bōōkā'] n (*of flowers*) ramo, ramillete m; (*of wine*) aroma m.

bourbon [búr'bən] n (*US: also:* ~ **whiskey**) whisky m americano, bourbon m.

bourgeois [bōōr'zhwä] a, n burgués/esa m/f.

bout [bout] n (*of malaria etc*) ataque m; (*BOXING etc*) combate m, encuentro.

boutique [bōōtēk'] n boutique f, tienda de ropa.

bow n [bō] (*knot*) lazo; (*weapon, MUS*) arco; [bou] (*of the head*) reverencia; (*NAUT: also:* ~**s**) proa ♦ vi [bou] inclinarse, hacer una reverencia; (*yield*): **to** ~ **to** *or* **before** ceder ante, someterse a; **to** ~ **to the inevitable** resignarse a lo inevitable.

bowels [bou'əlz] npl intestinos mpl, vientre m.

bowl [bōl] n tazón m, cuenco; (*for washing*) palangana, jofaina; (*ball*) bola; (*US: stadium*) estadio ♦ vi (*CRICKET*) arrojar la pelota; *see also* **bowls**.

bowlegged [bō'legid] a estevado.

bowler [bō'lûr] n (*US*) jugador m de bolos; (*CRICKET*) lanzador m (de la pelota); (*Brit: also:* ~ **hat**) hongo, bombín m.

bowling [bō'ling] n (*game*) bochas fpl, bolos mpl.

bowling alley n bolera.

bowling green n pista para bochas.

bowls [bōlz] n (*Brit*) juego de las bochas, bolos mpl.

bow tie [bō tī] n corbata de lazo, pajarita.

box [bâks] n (*also:* **cardboard** ~) caja, cajón m; (*for jewels*) estuche m; (*for money*) cofre m; (*crate*) cofre m, arca; (*THEATER*) palco ♦ vt encajonar ♦ vi (*SPORT*) boxear.

box car n (*US RAIL*) furgón m.

boxer [bâks'ûr] n (*person*) boxeador m; (*dog*) bóxer m.

box file n fichero.

boxing [bâks'ing] n (*SPORT*) boxeo.

Boxing Day n (*Brit*) Día de San Esteban, 26 de diciembre.

boxing gloves npl guantes mpl de boxeo.

boxing ring n ring m, cuadrilátero.

box number n (*for advertisements*) apartado.

box office n taquilla, boletería (*LAm*).

boxroom [bâks'rōōm] n (*Brit*) trastero.

boy [boi] n (*young*) niño; (*older*) muchacho.

boycott [boi'kât] n boicot m ♦ vt boicotear.

boyfriend [boi'frend] n novio.

boyish [boi'ish] a muchachil.

boy scout n boy scout m.

Bp abbr = **bishop**.

BPOE n abbr (*US:* = *Benevolent and Protective Order of Elks*) organización benéfica.

BR abbr = **British Rail**.

bra [brä] n sostén m, sujetador m.

brace [brās] n refuerzo, abrazadera; (*tool*) berbiquí m; (*Brit: on teeth*) corrector m ♦ vt asegurar, reforzar; **to** ~ **o.s. (for)** (*fig*) prepararse (para); *see also* **braces**.

bracelet [brās'lit] n pulsera, brazalete m.

braces [brā'siz] npl (*US: on teeth*) corrector m; (*Brit*) tirantes mpl.

bracing [brā'sing] a vigorizante, tónico.

bracken [brak'ən] n helecho.

bracket [brak'it] n (*TECH*) soporte m, puntal m; (*group*) clase f, categoría; (*also:* **brace** ~) soporte m, abrazadera; (*also: Brit:* **round** ~) paréntesis m inv; (*gen:* **square** ~) corchete m ♦ vt (*fig: also:* ~ **together**) agrupar; **income** ~ nivel m económico; **in** ~**s** entre paréntesis.

brackish [brak'ish] a (*water*) salobre.

brag [brag] vi jactarse.

braid [brād] n (*trimming*) galón m; (*of hair*) trenza.

Braille [brāl] n Braille m.

brain [brān] n cerebro; ~**s** npl sesos mpl; **she's got** ~**s** es muy lista.

brainchild [brān'chīld] n parto del ingenio.

brainless [brān'lis] a estúpido, insensato.

brainstorm [brān'stôrm] n (*fig*) ataque m de locura, frenesí m; (*US: brain wave*) idea luminosa *or* genial, inspiración f.

brainstorming [brān'stôrming] n discusión intensiva para solucionar problemas.

brainwash [brān'wâsh] vt lavar el cerebro a.

brain wave n idea luminosa *or* genial, inspiración f.

brainy [brā'nē] a muy listo *or* inteligente.

braise [brāz] vt cocer a fuego lento.

brake [brāk] n (*on vehicle*) freno ♦ vt, vi frenar.

brake drum n tambor m de freno.

brake fluid n líquido de frenos.

brake light n luz f de frenado.

brake pedal n pedal m de freno.

bramble [bram'bəl] n (*fruit*) zarza.

bran [bran] n salvado.

branch [branch] n rama; (*fig*) ramo; (*COMM*) sucursal f ♦ vi ramificarse; (*fig*) extenderse.

branch out vi ramificarse.

branch line n (*RAIL*) ramal m, línea secundaria.

branch manager n director(a) m/f de sucursal.

brand [brand] n marca; (*iron*) hierro de marcar ♦ vt (*cattle*) marcar con hierro candente.

brandish [bran'dish] vt blandir.

brand name n marca.

brand-new [brand'nōō'] a flamante, completamente nuevo.

brandy [bran'dē] n coñac m, brandy m.

brash [brash] a (*rough*) tosco; (*cheeky*) descarado.

Brasilia [brəzil'ēə] *n* Brasilia.
brass [bras] *n* latón *m*; **the** ~ (MUS) los cobres.
brass band *n* banda de metal.
brassière [brəzēr'] *n* sostén *m*, sujetador *m*.
brass knuckles *n* (US) puño de hierro.
brass tacks *npl*: **to get down to** ~ ir al grano.
brat [brat] *n* (pej) mocoso/a.
bravado [brəvă'dō] *n* fanfarronería.
brave [brāv] *a* valiente, valeroso ♦ *n* guerrero indio ♦ *vt* (challenge) desafiar; (resist) aguantar.
bravely [brāv'lē] *ad* valientemente, con valor.
bravery [brā'vûrē] *n* valor *m*, valentía.
bravo [brä'vō] *excl* ¡bravo!, ¡olé!
brawl [brôl] *n* pendencia, reyerta ♦ *vi* pelearse.
brawn [brôn] *n* fuerza muscular; (meat) carne *f* en gelatina.
brawny [brô'nē] *a* fornido, musculoso.
bray [brā] *n* rebuzno ♦ *vi* rebuznar.
brazen [brā'zən] *a* descarado, cínico ♦ *vt*: **to** ~ **it out** echarle cara al asunto.
brazier [brā'zhûr] *n* brasero.
Brazil [brəzil'] *n* (el) Brasil.
Brazilian [brəzil'ēən] *a, n* brasileño/a *m/f*.
breach [brēch] *vt* abrir brecha en ♦ *n* (gap) brecha; (estrangement) ruptura; (breaking): ~ **of confidence** abuso de confianza; ~ **of contract** infracción *f* de contrato; ~ **of the peace** perturbación *f* del órden público; **in** ~ **of** por incumplimiento *or* infracción de.
bread [bred] *n* pan *m*; (col: money) pasta, plata (LAm); ~ **and butter** *n* pan con mantequilla; (fig) pan (de cada día) ♦ *a* común y corriente; **to earn one's daily** ~ ganarse el pan; **to know which side one's** ~ **is buttered (on)** saber dónde aprieta el zapato.
breadbin [bred'bin] *n* panera.
breadboard [bred'bôrd] *n* (COMPUT) circuito experimental.
breadbox [bred'bâks] *n* (US) panera.
breadcrumbs [bred'krumz] *npl* migajas *fpl*; (CULIN) pan *msg* molido.
breadline [bred'līn] *n*: **on the** ~ en la miseria.
breadth [bredth] *n* anchura; (fig) amplitud *f*.
breadwinner [bred'winûr] *n* sostén *m* de la familia.
break [brāk] *vb* (pt **broke** [brōk], pp **broken** [brō'kən]) *vt* (gen) romper; (promise) no cumplir; (fall) amortiguar; (journey) interrumpir; (law) violar, infringir; (record) batir; (news) comunicar; (horse etc) domar ♦ *vi* romperse, quebrarse; (storm) estallar; (weather) cambiar ♦ *n* (gap) abertura; (crack) grieta; (fracture) fractura; (in relations) ruptura; (rest) descanso;

(time) intervalo; (: at school) (período de) recreo; (vacation) vacaciones *fpl*; (chance) oportunidad *f*; (escape) evasión *f*, fuga; **to** ~ **with sb** (fig) romper con uno; **to** ~ **even** *vi* cubrir los gastos; **to** ~ **free** *or* **loose** *vi* escaparse; **lucky** ~ (col) chiripa, racha de buena suerte; **to have** *or* **take a** ~ (few minutes) descansar; **without a** ~ sin descanso *or* descansar.
break down *vt* (door etc) echar abajo, derribar; (resistance) vencer, acabar con; (figures, data) analizar, descomponer; (undermine) acabar con ♦ *vi* estropearse; (MED) sufrir un colapso; (AUT) averiarse; (person) romper a llorar.
break in *vt* (car) rodar ♦ *vi* (burglar) forzar una entrada.
break into *vt fus* (house) forzar.
break off *vi* (speaker) pararse, detenerse; (branch) partir ♦ *vt* (talks) suspender; (engagement) romper.
break open *vt* (door etc) abrir por la fuerza, forzar.
break out *vi* estallar; **to** ~ **out in spots** salir a uno granos.
break through *vi*: **the sun broke through** el sol salió ♦ *vt fus* (defenses, barrier) abrirse paso por; (crowd) abrirse paso por.
break up *vi* (break) hacerse pedazos; (partnership) disolverse; (friends) romper ♦ *vt* (rocks, ice etc) partir; (crowd) disolver.
breakable [brā'kəbəl] *a* quebradizo ♦ *n*: ~s cosas *fpl* frágiles.
breakage [brā'kij] *n* rotura; **to pay for** ~s pagar por los objetos rotos.
breakaway [brā'kəwā] *a* (group etc) disidente.
break-dancing [brāk'dansing] *n* break *m*.
breakdown [brāk'doun] *n* (AUT) avería; (in communications) interrupción *f*; (MED: also: **nervous** ~) colapso, crisis *f* nerviosa; (of figures) desglose *m*.
breakdown van *n* (Brit) (camión *m*) grúa.
breaker [brā'kûr] *n* rompiente *m*, ola grande.
breakeven [brākē'vən] *cpd*: ~ **chart** gráfico del punto de equilibrio; ~ **point** punto de break-even *or* de equilibrio.
breakfast [brek'fəst] *n* desayuno.
breakfast cereal *n* cereales *mpl* para el desayuno.
break-in [brāk'in] *n* robo con allanamiento de morada.
breaking and entering [brā'king and en'tûring] *n* (LAW) violación *f* de domicilio, allanamiento de morada.
breaking point [brā'king point] *n* punto de ruptura.
breakthrough [brāk'thrōō] *n* ruptura; (fig) avance *m*, adelanto.

break-up |brāk'up| n (of partnership, marriage) disolución f.

break-up value n (COMM) valor m de liquidación.

breakwater |brāk'wôtûr| n rompeolas m inv.

breast |brest| n (of woman) pecho, seno; (chest) pecho; (of bird) pechuga.

breast-feed |brest'fēd| vt, vi (irg: like feed) amamantar, criar a los pechos.

breaststroke |brest'strōk| n braza de pecho.

breath |breth| n aliento, respiración f; **out of** ~ sin aliento, sofocado; **to go out for a** ~ **of air** salir a tomar el fresco.

Breathalyzer |breth'əlīzûr| ® n alcoholímetro m; ~ **test** n prueba de alcoholemia.

breathe |brēth| vt, vi respirar; (noisily) resollar; **I won't** ~ **a word about it** no diré ni una palabra acerca de ello.

breathe in vt, vi aspirar.

breathe out vt, vi espirar.

breather |brē'thûr| n respiro.

breathing |brē'thing| n respiración f.

breathing space n (fig) respiro, pausa.

breathless |breth'lis| a sin aliento, jadeante; (with excitement) pasmado.

breathtaking |breth'tāking| a imponente, pasmoso.

-bred |bred| suff: **to be well/ill** ~ estar bien/mal criado.

breed |brēd| vb (pt, pp **bred** |bred|) vt criar; (fig: hate, suspicion) crear, engendrar ♦ vi reproducirse, procrear ♦ n raza, casta.

breeder |brē'dûr| n (person) criador(a) m/f; (PHYSICS: also: ~ **reactor**) reactor m.

breeding |brē'ding| n (of person) educación f.

breeze |brēz| n brisa.

breezeblock |brēz'blák| n (Brit) ladrillo de cenizas.

breezy |brē'zē| a de mucho viento, ventoso; (person) despreocupado.

Breton |bret'ən| a bretón/ona ♦ n bretón/ona m/f; (LING) bretón m.

brevity |brev'itē| n brevedad f.

brew |brōō| vt (tea) hacer; (beer) elaborar; (plot) tramar ♦ vi hacerse; elaborarse; tramarse; (storm) amenazar.

brewer |brōō'ûr| n cervecero, fabricante m de cerveza.

brewery |brōō'ûrē| n fábrica de cerveza.

briar |brī'ûr| n (thorny bush) zarza; (wild rose) escaramujo, rosa silvestre.

bribe |brīb| n soborno ♦ vt sobornar, cohechar; **to** ~ **sb to do sth** sobornar a uno para que haga algo.

bribery |brī'bûrē| n soborno, cohecho.

bric-a-brac |brik'əbrak| n inv baratijas fpl.

brick |brik| n ladrillo.

bricklayer |brik'lāûr| n albañil m.

brickwork |brik'wûrk| n enladrillado.

brickworks |brik'wûrks| n ladrillar m.

bridal |brīd'əl| a nupcial.

bride |brīd| n novia.

bridegroom |brīd'grōōm| n novio.

bridesmaid |brīdz'mād| n dama de honor.

bridge |brij| n puente m; (NAUT) puente m de mando; (of nose) caballete m; (CARDS) bridge m ♦ vt (river) tender un puente sobre.

bridgehead |brij'hed| n cabeza de puente.

bridging loan |brij'ing lōn| n crédito provisional.

bridle |brīd'əl| n brida, freno ♦ vt poner la brida a; (fig) reprimir, refrenar ♦ vi (in anger etc) picarse.

bridle path n camino de herradura.

brief |brēf| a breve, corto ♦ n (LAW) escrito ♦ vt (inform) informar; (instruct) dar instrucciones a; **in** ~ ... en resumen ...; **to** ~ **sb (about sth)** informar a uno (sobre algo).

briefcase |brēf'kās| n cartera, portafolio (LAm).

briefing |brē'fing| n (PRESS) informe m.

briefly |brēf'lē| ad (smile, glance) brevemente; (explain, say) brevemente, en pocas palabras.

briefs |brēfs| npl (for men) calzoncillos mpl; (for women) bragas fpl.

Brig. abbr = **brigadier.**

brigade |brigād'| n (MIL) brigada.

brigadier |brigədi'ûr| n general m de brigada.

bright |brīt| a claro; (room) luminoso; (day) de sol; (person: clever) listo, inteligente; (: lively) alegre, animado; (color) vivo; **to look on the** ~ **side** mirar el lado bueno.

brighten |brīt'ən| (also: ~ **up**) vt (room) hacer más alegre ♦ vi (weather) despejarse; (person) animarse, alegrarse.

brilliance |bril'yəns| n brillo, brillantez f; (fig: of person) inteligencia.

brilliant |bril'yənt| a (light, idea, person, success) brillante; (clever) genial.

brilliantly |bril'yəntlē| ad brillantemente.

brim |brim| n borde m; (of hat) ala.

brimful |brim'fōōl'| a lleno hasta el borde; (fig) rebosante.

brine |brīn| n (CULIN) salmuera.

bring, pt, pp **brought** |bring, brôt| vt (thing) traer; (person) conducir; **to** ~ **sth to an end** terminar con algo; **I can't** ~ **myself to fire him** no soy capaz de echarle.

bring about vt ocasionar, producir.

bring back vt volver a traer; (return) devolver.

bring down vt bajar; (price) rebajar.

bring forward vt adelantar; (BOOK-KEEPING) pasar a otra cuenta.

bring in vt (harvest) recoger; (person) hacer entrar or pasar; (object) traer; (Brit POL: bill, law) presentar; (LAW: verdict) pronunciar; (income) producir, rendir.

bring off vt (task, plan) lograr, conseguir; (*deal*) cerrar.

bring out *vt* (*object*) sacar; (*new product*) sacar; (*book*) publicar.

bring round *vt* (*unconscious person*) hacer volver en sí; (*convince*) convencer.

bring up *vt* (*person*) educar, criar; (*carry up*) subir; (*question*) sacar a colación; (*food: vomit*) devolver, vomitar.

brink [bringk] *n* borde *m*; **on the ~ of doing sth** a punto de hacer algo; **she was on the ~ of tears** estaba a punto de llorar.

brisk [brisk] *a* (*walk*) enérgico, vigoroso; (*speedy*) rápido; (*wind*) fresco; (*trade*) activo, animado; (*abrupt*) brusco; **business is ~** el negocio va bien *or* a paso activo.

brisket [bris'kit] *n* carne *f* de pecho de vaca para asar.

bristle [bris'əl] *n* cerda ♦ *vi* erizarse.

bristly [bris'lē] *a* (*beard, hair*) erizado; **to have a ~ chin** tener la barba crecida.

Brit [brit] *n abbr* (*col: = British person*) británico/a.

Britain [brit'in] *n* (*also: **Great ~***) Gran Bretaña.

British [brit'ish] *a* británico; **the ~** *npl* los británicos; **the ~ Isles** *npl* las Islas Británicas.

British Rail (BR) *n* ≈ RENFE *f* (*Sp*).

Briton [brit'ən] *n* británico/a.

brittle [brit'əl] *a* quebradizo, frágil.

Br(o). *abbr* (*REL*) = **brother**.

broach [brōch] *vt* (*subject*) abordar.

broad [brôd] *a* ancho, amplio; (*accent*) cerrado ♦ *n* (*US col*) tía; **in ~ daylight** en pleno día; **the ~ outlines** las líneas generales.

broad bean *n* haba.

broadcast [brôd'kast] *n* emisión *f* ♦ *vb* (*pt, pp* **broadcast**) *vt* (*RADIO*) emitir; (*TV*) transmitir ♦ *vi* emitir; transmitir.

broadcasting [brôd'kasting] *n* radiodifusión *f*, difusión *f*.

broadcasting station *n* emisora.

broaden [brôd'ən] *vt* ensanchar ♦ *vi* ensancharse.

broadly [brôd'lē] *ad* en general.

broad-minded [brôd'mīn'did] *a* tolerante, liberal.

brocade [brōkād'] *n* brocado.

broccoli [brāk'əlē] *n* (*BOT*) brécol *m*; (*CULIN*) bróculi *m*.

brochure [brōshōor'] *n* folleto.

brogue [brōg] *n* (*accent*) acento regional; (*Brit: shoe*) (*tipo de*) zapato de cuero grueso.

broil [broil] *vt* (*US*) asar a la parrilla.

broiler [broi'lûr] *n* (*fowl*) pollo (para asar).

broke [brōk] *pt of* **break** ♦ *a* (*col*) pelado, sin una perra; **to go ~** quebrar.

broken [brō'kən] *pp of* **break** ♦ *a* (*stick*) roto; (*fig: marriage*) quebrado; (: *promise, vow*) violado; **~ leg** pierna rota; **in ~ English** en un inglés imperfecto.

broken-down [brō'kəndoun'] *a* (*car*) averiado; (*machine*) estropeado; (*house*) destartalado.

brokenhearted [brō'kənhâr'tid] *a* con el corazón partido.

broker [brō'kûr] *n* agente *m/f*, bolsista *m/f*.

brokerage [brō'kûrij] *n* corretaje *m*.

brolly [brāl'ē] *n* (*Brit col*) paraguas *m inv*.

bronchitis [brāngkī'tis] *n* bronquitis *f*.

bronze [brānz] *n* bronce *m*.

bronzed [brānzd] *a* bronceado.

brooch [brōch] *n* prendedor *m*.

brood [brood] *n* camada, cría; (*children*) progenie *f* ♦ *vi* (*hen*) empollar; **to ~ over** dejarse obsesionar por.

broody [broo'dē] *a* (*fig*) triste, melancólico.

brook [brook] *n* arroyo.

broom [broom] *n* escoba; (*BOT*) retama.

broomstick [broom'stik] *n* palo de escoba.

Bros. *abbr* (*COMM: = Brothers*) Hnos.

broth [brôth] *n* caldo.

brothel [brāth'əl] *n* burdel *m*.

brother [bruth'ûr] *n* hermano.

brotherhood [bruth'ûrhood] *n* hermandad *f*.

brother-in-law [bruth'ûrinlô] *n* cuñado.

brotherly [bruth'ûrlē] *a* fraternal.

brought [brôt] *pt, pp of* **bring**.

brow [brou] *n* (*forehead*) frente *f*; (*of hill*) cumbre *f*.

browbeat [brou'bēt] *vt* (*irg: like* **beat**) intimidar.

brown [broun] *a* moreno; (*hair*) castaño; (*tanned*) bronceado ♦ *n* (*color*) color *m* moreno *or* pardo ♦ *vt* (*tan*) broncear; (*CULIN*) dorar; **to go ~** (*person*) broncearse; (*leaves*) dorarse.

brown bread *n* pan *m* moreno.

brownie [brou'nē] *n* niña exploradora.

brownnose(r) [broun'nōz'(ûr)] *n* (*col*) lameculos *m/f inv*.

brown paper *n* papel *m* de estraza.

brown rice *n* arroz *m* moreno.

brown sugar *n* azúcar *m* terciado.

browse [brouz] *vi* (*animal*) pacer; (*among books*) hojear libros; **to ~ through a book** hojear un libro.

bruise [brooz] *n* (*on person*) cardenal *m*, hematoma *m* ♦ *vt* (*leg etc*) magullar; (*fig: feelings*) herir.

brunch [brunch] *n* desayuno-almuerzo.

brunette [broonet'] *n* morena.

brunt [brunt] *n*: **to bear the ~ of** llevar el peso de.

brush [brush] *n* cepillo; (*large*) escoba; (*for painting, shaving etc*) brocha; (*artist's*) pincel *m*; (*BOT*) maleza ♦ *vt* cepillar; **to ~ one's teeth** lavarse los dientes; (*gen: ~ past, ~ against*) rozar al pasar; **to have a ~ with the police** tener un roce con la policía.

brush aside *vt* rechazar, no hacer caso a.

brush up vt (knowledge) repasar, refrescar.

brushed [brusht] a (nylon, denim etc) afelpado; (TECH: steel, chrome etc) cepillado.

brushwood [brush'wŏŏd] n (bushes) maleza; (sticks) leña.

brusque [brusk] a (person, manner) brusco; (tone) áspero.

Brussels [brus'əlz] n Bruselas.

Brussels sprout n col f de Bruselas.

brutal [brŏŏt'əl] a brutal.

brutality [brŏŏtal'itē] n brutalidad f.

brute [brŏŏt] n bruto; (person) bestia ♦ a: **by ~ force** a fuerza bruta.

brutish [brŏŏ'tish] a brutal.

BS n abbr (US: = Bachelor of Science) título universitario.

bs abbr = **bill of sale**.

BSA n abbr = Boy Scouts of America.

BSc abbr = **Bachelor of Science**.

BSI n abbr (= British Standards Institution) institución británica de normalización.

BST n abbr (= British Summer Time) hora de verano del Reino Unido.

btu n abbr (= British thermal unit) ≈ 1054.2 joules.

bubble [bub'əl] n burbuja; (in paint) ampolla ♦ vi burbujear, borbotar.

bubble bath n espuma para el baño.

bubble gum n chicle m de globo.

Bucharest [bŏŏ'kərest] n Bucarest m.

buck [buk] n macho; (US col) dólar m ♦ vi corcovear; **to pass the ~ (to sb)** echar (a uno) el muerto.

buck up vi (cheer up) animarse, cobrar ánimo ♦ vt: **to ~ one's ideas up** poner más empeño.

bucket [buk'it] n cubo, balde m ♦ vi: **the rain is ~ing (down)** (Brit col) está lloviendo a cántaros.

buckle [buk'əl] n hebilla ♦ vt abrochar con hebilla ♦ vi torcerse, combarse.

buckle down vi poner empeño.

buckle up vi (US) ponerse el cinturón de seguridad.

Bucks [buks] abbr (Brit) = Buckinghamshire.

bud [bud] n brote m, yema; (of flower) capullo ♦ vi brotar, echar brotes.

Budapest [bŏŏ'dəpest] n Budapest m.

Buddhism [bŏŏ'dizəm] n Budismo.

Buddhist [bŏŏ'dist] a, n budista m/f.

budding [bud'ing] a en ciernes, en embrión.

buddy [bud'ē] n (US) compañero, compinche m.

budge [buj] vt mover; (fig) hacer ceder ♦ vi moverse.

budgerigar [buj'ûrēgär] n periquito.

budget [buj'it] n presupuesto ♦ vi: **to ~ for sth** presupuestar algo; **I'm on a tight ~** no puedo gastar mucho; **she works out her ~ every month** planea su presupuesto todos

los meses.

budgie [buj'ē] n = **budgerigar**.

Buenos Aires [bwā'nəs ī'riz] n Buenos Aires m.

buff [buf] a (color) color m de ante ♦ n (enthusiast) entusiasta m/f.

buffalo [buf'əlō], pl ~ or **buffaloes** n (Brit) búfalo; (US: bison) bisonte m.

buffer [buf'ûr] n amortiguador m; (COMPUT) memoria intermedia, buffer m.

buffering [buf'ûring] n (COMPUT) almacenamiento en memoria intermedia.

buffet n [bŏŏfā'] (food) buffet m; (Brit: bar) bar m, cafetería ♦ vt [buf'it] (strike) abofetear; (wind etc) golpear.

buffet car [bŏŏfā' kâr] n (Brit RAIL) coche-comedor m.

buffet lunch [bŏŏfā' lunch] n buffet m (almuerzo).

buffoon [bufŏŏn'] n bufón m.

bug [bug] n (insect) chinche m; (: gen) bicho, sabandija; (germ) microbio, bacilo; (spy device) micrófono oculto; (COMPUT) fallo, error m ♦ vt (annoy) fastidiar; (room) poner un micrófono oculto en; (phone) pinchar; **I've got the travel ~** (fig) me encanta viajar; **it really ~s me** me fastidia or molesta mucho.

bugbear [bug'bär] n pesadilla.

bugle [byŏŏ'gəl] n corneta, clarín m.

build [bild] n (of person) talle m, tipo ♦ vt (pt, pp built [bilt]) construir, edificar.

build on vt fus (fig) basar en.

build up vt (MED) fortalecer; (stocks) acumular; (establish: business) fomentar, desarrollar; (: reputation) crear(se); (increase: production) aumentar; **don't ~ your hopes up too soon** no te hagas demasiadas ilusiones.

builder [bil'dûr] n constructor(a) m/f; (contractor) contratista m/f.

building [bil'ding] n (act of) construcción f; (habitation, offices) edificio.

building contractor n contratista m/f de obras.

building industry n construcción f.

building site n solar m (Sp), obra (LAm).

building society n (Brit) sociedad f inmobiliaria, cooperativa de construcciones.

building trade n = **building industry**.

build-up [bild'up] n (publicity): **to give sb/ sth a good ~** hacer mucha propaganda de uno/algo.

built [bilt] pt, pp of **build**.

built-in [bilt'in'] a (cupboard) empotrado; (device) interior, incorporado; **~ obsolescence** obsolescencia incorporada.

built-up [bilt'up] a (area) urbanizado.

bulb [bulb] n (BOT) bulbo; (ELEC) bombilla, foco (LAm).

bulbous [bul'bəs] a bulboso.

Bulgaria [bulgär'ēə] n Bulgaria.

Bulgarian [bulgär'ēən] a búlgaro ♦ n

búlgaro/a; (*LING*) búlgaro.

bulge [bulj] *n* bombeo, pandeo; (*in birth rate*, *sales*) alza, aumento ♦ *vi* bombearse, pandearse; (*pocket etc*) hacer bulto.

bulk [bulk] *n* (*mass*) bulto, volumen *m*; (*major part*) grueso; **in** ~ (*COMM*) a granel; **the** ~ **of** la mayor parte de; **to buy in** ~ comprar en grandes cantidades.

bulk buying [bulk bī'ing] *n* compra a granel.

bulkhead [bulk'hed] *n* mamparo.

bulky [bul'kē] *a* voluminoso, abultado.

bull [bŏŏl] *n* toro; (*STOCK EXCHANGE*) alcista *m/f* de bolsa; (*REL*) bula.

bulldog [bŏŏl'dôg] *n* dogo.

bulldoze [bŏŏl'dōz] *vt* mover con; **I was** ~**d into doing it** (*fig col*) me obligaron a hacerlo.

bulldozer [bŏŏl'dōzûr] *n* buldozer *m*, motoniveladora.

bullet [bŏŏl'it] *n* bala; ~ **wound** balazo.

bulletin [bŏŏl'itən] *n* anuncio, parte *m*.

bulletin board *n* tablón *m* de anuncios; (*COMPUT*) tablero de noticias.

bulletproof [bŏŏl'itprōōf] *a* a prueba de balas; ~ **vest** chaleco anti-balas.

bullfight [bŏŏl'fīt] *n* corrida de toros.

bullfighter [bŏŏl'fītûr] *n* torero.

bullfighting [bŏŏl'fīting] *n* los toros *mpl*, el toreo; (*art of* ~) tauromaquia.

bullhorn [bŏŏl'hôrn] *n* (*US*) megáfono.

bullion [bŏŏl'yən] *n* oro *or* plata en barras.

bullock [bŏŏl'ək] *n* novillo.

bullring [bŏŏl'ring] *n* plaza de toros.

bull's-eye [bŏŏlz'ī] *n* centro del blanco.

bully [bŏŏl'ē] *n* valentón *m*, matón *m* ♦ *vt* intimidar, tiranizar.

bum [bum] *n* (*col*: *backside*) culo; (: *tramp*) vagabundo; (*col*: *esp US*: *idler*) holgazán/ana *m/f*, flojo/a.

bumble [bum'bəl] *vi* (*walk unsteadily*) andar de forma vacilante; (*fig*) farfullar, trastabillar.

bumblebee [bum'bəlbē] *n* abejorro.

bumbling [bum'bling] *n* divagación *f*.

bumf [bumf] *n* (*Brit col*: *forms etc*) papeleo.

bump [bump] *n* (*blow*) tope *m*, choque *m*; (*jolt*) sacudida; (*noise*) choque *m*, topetón *m*; (*on road etc*) bache *m*; (*on head*) chichón *m* ♦ *vt* (*strike*) chocar contra, topetar ♦ *vi* dar sacudidas.

bump into *vt fus* chocar contra, tropezar con; (*person*) topar con; (*col*: *meet*) tropezar con, toparse con.

bumper [bum'pûr] *n* parachoques *m inv* ♦ *a*: ~ **crop/harvest** cosecha abundante.

bumper cars *npl* coches *mpl* de choque.

bumph [bumf] *n* = **bumf**.

bumptious [bump'shəs] *a* engreído, presuntuoso.

bumpy [bum'pē] *a* (*road*) lleno de baches; (*journey*, *flight*) agitado.

bun [bun] *n* (*US*: *bread*) bollo; (*Brit*: *cake*) pastel *m*; (*of hair*) moño.

bunch [bunch] *n* (*of flowers*) ramo; (*of keys*) manojo; (*of bananas*) piña; (*of people*) grupo; (*pej*) pandilla.

bundle [bun'dəl] *n* (*gen*) bulto, fardo; (*of sticks*) haz *m*; (*of papers*) legajo ♦ *vt* (*also*: ~ **up**) atar, envolver; **to** ~ **sth/sb into** meter algo/a uno precipitadamente en.

bung [bung] *n* tapón *m*, taco *m* ♦ *vt* (*Brit col*: *throw*) arrojar; (*also*: ~ **up**: *pipe*, *hole*) tapar.

bungalow [bung'gəlō] *n* bungalow *m*, chalé *m*.

bungle [bung'gəl] *vt* chapucear.

bunion [bun'yən] *n* juanete *m*.

bunk [bungk] *n* litera; ~ **beds** *npl* literas *fpl*.

bunker [bung'kûr] *n* (*MIL*) refugio; (*GOLF*) bunker *m*; (*Brit*: *coal store*) carbonera.

bunny [bun'ē] *n* (*also*: ~ **rabbit**) conejito.

Bunsen burner [bun'sən bûr'nûr] *n* mechero Bunsen.

bunting [bun'ting] *n* empavesada, banderas *fpl*.

buoy [bŏŏ'ē] *n* boya.

buoy up *vt* mantener a flote; (*fig*) animar.

buoyancy [boi'ənsē] *n* (*of ship*) capacidad *f* para flotar.

buoyant [boi'ənt] *a* (*carefree*) boyante, optimista; (*COMM*: *market*, *prices etc*) sostenido.

burden [bûr'dən] *n* carga ♦ *vt* cargar; **to be a** ~ **to sb** ser una carga para uno.

bureau, *pl* ~**x** [byōŏr'ō, -z] *n* (*US*: *chest of drawers*) cómoda; (*Brit*: *writing desk*) escritorio, buró *m*; (*office*) oficina, agencia.

bureaucracy [byŏŏrák'rəsē] *n* burocracia.

bureaucrat [byŏŏr'əkrat] *n* burócrata *m/f*.

bureaucratic [byŏŏrəkrat'ik] *a* burocrático.

burgeon [bûr'jən] *vi* (*develop rapidly*) crecer, incrementarse; (*trade etc*) florecer.

burglar [bûr'glûr] *n* ladrón/ona *m/f*.

burglar alarm *n* alarma *f* de ladrones.

burglarize [bûr'glərīz] *vt* (*US*) robar (con allanamiento).

burglary [bûr'glûrē] *n* robo con allanamiento, robo de una casa.

burgle [bûr'gəl] *vt* robar (con allanamiento).

Burgundy [bûr'gəndē] *n* Borgoña.

burial [bär'ēəl] *n* entierro.

burial ground *n* cementerio.

burlap [bûr'lap] *n* arpillera.

burlesque [bûrlesk'] *n* parodia.

burly [bûr'lē] *a* fornido, membrudo.

Burma [bûr'mə] *n* Birmania.

Burmese [bûrmēz'] *a* birmano ♦ *n* (*pl inv*) birmano/a; (*LING*) birmano.

burn [bûrn] *vb* (*pt*, *pp* **burned** *or* **burnt** [bûrnt]) *vt* quemar; (*house*) incendiar ♦ *vi* quemarse, arder; incendiarse; (*sting*) escocer ♦ *n* (*MED*) quemadura; **the cigarette** ~**t a hole in her dress** se ha quemado el

vestido con el cigarrillo; **I've ~t myself!** ¡me he quemado!
burn down *vt* incendiar.
burn out *vt* (*subj: writer etc*): **to ~ o.s. out** agotarse.
burner [bûr'nûr] *n* (*gas*) quemador *m*.
burning [bûr'ning] *a* ardiente; (*building, forest*) en llamas.
burp [bûrp] (*col*) *n* eructo ♦ *vi* eructar.
burrow [bûr'ō] *n* madriguera ♦ *vt* hacer una madriguera.
bursar [bûr'sûr] *n* tesorero; (*student*) becario/a.
bursary [bûr'sûrē] *n* (*Brit*) beca.
burst [bûrst] *vb* (*pt, pp* **burst**) *vt* (*balloon, pipe*) reventar; (*banks etc*) romper ♦ *vi* reventarse; romperse; (*tire*) pincharse; (*bomb*) estallar ♦ *n* (*explosion*) estallido; (*also:* **~ pipe**) reventón *m*; **the river has ~ its banks** el río se ha desbordado; **to ~ into flames** estallar en llamas; **to ~ out laughing** soltar la carcajada; **to ~ into tears** deshacerse en lágrimas; **to be ~ing with** reventar de; **a ~ of energy** una explosión de energía; **a ~ of applause** una salva de aplausos; **a ~ of speed** una escapada; **to ~ open** *vi* abrirse de golpe.
burst into *vt fus* (*room etc*) irrumpir en.
bury [bär'ē] *vt* enterrar; (*body*) enterrar, sepultar; **to ~ the hatchet** echar pelillos a la mar.
bus [bus] *n* autobús *m*.
bush [bōōsh] *n* arbusto; (*scrub land*) monte *m*; **to beat around the ~** andar(se) con rodeos.
bushel [bōōsh'əl] *n* (*measure: US*) = 35,24 *litros; (: Brit*) = 36,36 *litros.*
bushy [bōōsh'ē] *a* (*beard, eyebrows*) poblado; (*hair*) espeso; (*fur*) tupido
busily [biz'ilē] *ad* afanosamente.
business [biz'nis] *n* (*matter, affair*) asunto; (*trading*) comercio, negocios *mpl*; (*firm*) empresa, casa; (*occupation*) oficio; **to be away on ~** estar en viaje de negocios; **it's my ~ to...** me toca *or* corresponde...; **it's none of my ~** yo no tengo nada que ver; **he means ~** habla en serio; **he's in the insurance ~** se dedica a los seguros; **I'm here on ~** estoy aquí por mi trabajo; **to do ~ with sb** hacer negocios con uno.
business address *n* dirección *f* comercial.
business card *n* tarjeta de visita.
business hours *n* horas *fpl* de oficina.
businesslike [biz'nislīk] *a* (*company*) serio; (*person*) eficiente.
businessman [biz'nisman] *n* hombre *m* de negocios.
business suit *n* traje *m* de calle.
business trip *n* viaje *m* de negocios.
businesswoman [biz'niswōōmən] *n* mujer *f* de negocios.
busker [bus'kûr] *n* (*Brit*) músico/a ambu-

lante.
bus route *n* recorrido del autobús.
bus station *n* estación *f or* terminal *f* de autobuses.
bus-stop [bus'stâp] *n* parada de autobús.
bust [bust] *n* (*ANAT*) pecho ♦ *a* (*col: broken*) roto, estropeado ♦ *vt* (*col: POLICE: arrest*) detener; **to go ~** (*Brit*) quebrarse.
bustle [bus'əl] *n* bullicio, movimiento ♦ *vi* menearse, apresurarse.
bustling [bus'ling] *a* (*town*) animado, bullicioso.
bust-up [bust'up] *n* (*col*) riña.
busy [biz'ē] *a* ocupado, atareado; (*shop, street*) concurrido, animado ♦ *vt*: **to ~ o.s. with** ocuparse en; **he's a ~ man** (*normally*) es un hombre muy ocupado; (*temporarily*) está muy ocupado; **the line's ~** (*esp US*) está comunicando.
busybody [biz'ēbâdē] *n* entrometido/a.
busy signal *n* (*US TEL*) señal *f* de comunicando.
but [but] *conj* pero ♦ *prep* excepto, menos; **nothing ~** nada más que; **~ for** a no ser por, si no fuera por; **all ~ finished** casi terminado; **no one ~ him** nadie sino él.
butane [byōō'tān] *n* (*also:* **~ gas**) (gas *m*) butano.
butcher [bōōch'ûr] *n* carnicero/a ♦ *vt* hacer una carnicería con; (*cattle etc for meat*) matar; **~'s (shop)** carnicería.
butler [but'lûr] *n* mayordomo.
butt [but] *n* (*cask*) tonel *m*; (*for rain*) tina; (*thick end*) cabo, extremo; (*of gun*) culata; (*of cigarette*) colilla; (*fig: target*) blanco; (*US col*) culo ♦ *vt* dar cabezadas contra, topetar.
butt in *vi* (*interrupt*) interrumpir.
butter [but'ûr] *n* mantequilla ♦ *vt* untar con mantequilla.
butter bean *n* judía blanca.
buttercup [but'ûrkup] *n* ranúnculo.
butterfingers [but'ûrfinggûrz] *n* (*col*) torpe *m/f.*
butterfly [but'ûrflī] *n* mariposa; (*SWIMMING: also:* **~ stroke**) (braza de) mariposa.
buttocks [but'əks] *npl* nalgas *fpl.*
button [but'ən] *n* botón *m* ♦ *vt* (*also:* **~ up**) abotonar, abrochar ♦ *vi* abrocharse.
buttonhole [but'ənhōl] *n* ojal *m*; (*flower*) flor *f* que se lleva en el ojal ♦ *vt* obligar a escuchar.
buttress [but'tris] *n* contrafuerte *m*; (*fig*) apoyo, sostén *m*.
buxom [buk'səm] *a* (*woman*) frescachona.
buy [bī] *vb* (*pt, pp* **bought** [bôt]) *vt* comprar ♦ *n* compra; **to ~ sb sth/sth from sb** comprarle algo a uno; **to ~ sb a drink** invitar a uno a tomar algo; **a good/bad ~** una buena/mala compra.
buy back *vt* volver a comprar.
buy in *vt* (*Brit*) proveerse *or* abastecerse

de.

buy into *vt fus* comprar acciones en.

buy off *vt* (*col*: *bribe*) sobornar.

buy out *vt* (*partner*) comprar la parte de.

buyer [bī'ûr] *n* comprador(a) *m/f*; ~'s **market** mercado favorable al comprador.

buzz [buz] *n* zumbido; (*col*: *phone call*) llamada (por teléfono) ♦ *vt* (*call on intercom*) llamar; (*with buzzer*) hacer sonar; (*AVIAT*: *plane*, *building*) pasar rozando ♦ *vi* zumbar; **my head is** ~**ing** me zumba la cabeza.

buzz off *vi* (*col*) largarse.

buzzard [buz'ûrd] *n* águila ratonera.

buzzer [buz'ûr] *n* timbre *m*.

buzz word *n* palabra que está de moda.

by [bī] *prep* por; (*beside*) junto a, cerca de; (*according to*) según, de acuerdo con; (*before*): ~ **4 o'clock** para las cuatro ♦ *ad see* **pass, go** *etc*; ~ **bus/car** en autobús/coche; **paid** ~ **the hour** pagado por horas; ~ **the kilo/meter** por kilo/metro; ~ **night/day** de noche/día; ~ **saving hard, he ...** ahorrando mucho, (él) ...; (**all**) ~ **oneself** (completamente) solo; ~ **this time tomorrow** mañana a estas horas; ~ **the way** a propósito, por cierto; ~ **and large** en general; ~ **and** ~ luego, más tarde; **killed** ~ **lightning** muerto por relámpago; **to pay** ~ **check** pagar con cheque; **a room 3 meters** ~ **4** una habitación de 3 metros por 4; **a painting** ~ **Picasso** un cuadro por Picasso; **surrounded** ~ **enemies** rodeado de enemigos; **it missed me** ~ **inches** por un pelo, no me tocó.

bye(-bye) [bī'(bī')] *excl* adiós, hasta luego.

by-election [bī'ilekshən] *n* (*Brit*) elección *f* parcial.

bygone [bī'gôn] *a* pasado, del pasado ♦ *n*: **let** ~**s be** ~**s** lo pasado, pasado está.

by-law [bī'lô] *n* ordenanza municipal.

bypass [bī'pas] *n* carretera de circunvalación; (*MED*) (operación *f* de) by-pass *m* ♦ *vt* evitar.

by-product [bī'prädəkt] *n* subproducto, derivado.

bystander [bī'standûr] *n* espectador(a) *m/f*.

byte [bīt] *n* (*COMPUT*) byte *m*, octeto.

byway [bī'wā] *n* camino poco frecuentado.

byword [bī'wûrd] *n*: **to be a** ~ **for** ser conocidísimo por.

by-your-leave [bīyōōrlēv'] *n*: **without so much as a** ~ sin decir nada, sin dar ningún tipo de explicación.

C

C, c [sē] *n* (*letter*) C, c *f*; (*MUS*): **C** do *m*; **C for Charlie** C de Carmen.

C *abbr* (= *Celsius, centigrade*) C.

c *abbr* (= *century*) S.; (= *circa*) hacia; (*US etc*) = **cent(s)**.

CA *n abbr* = **Central America**; = **chartered accountant**; (*US MAIL*) = *California*.

ca. *abbr* (= *circa*) c.

c/a *abbr* = **capital account, credit account, current account**.

CAA *n abbr* (*Brit*: = *Civil Aviation Authority*) *organismo de control y desarrollo de la aviación civil.*

cab [kab] *n* taxi *m*; (*of truck*) cabina.

cabaret [kabərā'] *n* cabaret *m*.

cabbage [kab'ij] *n* col *f*, berza.

cab driver *n* taxista *m/f*.

cabin [kab'in] *n* cabaña; (*on ship*) camarote *m*.

cabin cruiser *n* yate *m* de motor.

cabinet [kab'ənit] *n* (*POL*) consejo de ministros; (*furniture*) armario; (*also*: **display** ~) vitrina.

cabinet-maker [kab'ənitmākûr] *n* ebanista *m*.

cabinet minister *n* ministro/a (del gabinete).

cable [kā'bəl] *n* cable *m* ♦ *vt* cablegrafiar.

cable car *n* teleférico.

cablegram [kā'bəlgram] *n* telegrama *m*.

cable television *n* televisión *f* por cable.

caboose [kəbōōs'] *n* (*US RAIL*) furgón.

cache [kash] *n* (*drugs*) alijo; (*arms*) zulo.

cackle [kak'əl] *vi* cacarear.

cactus, pl cacti [kak'təs, -tī] *n* cacto.

CAD *n abbr* (= *computer-aided design*) diseño asistido por ordenador.

caddie, caddy [kad'ē] *n* (*GOLF*) cadi *m*.

cadence [kād'əns] *n* ritmo; (*MUS*) cadencia.

cadet [kədet'] *n* (*MIL*) cadete *m*; **police** ~ cadete *m* de policía.

cadge [kaj] *vt* gorronear.

cadger [kaj'ûr] *n* gorrón/ona *m/f*.

cadre [kàd'rə] *n* cuadro.

Caesarean [sizär'ēən] *a* (*Brit*) = **Cesarean**.

CAF *abbr* (= *cost and freight*) C y F.

café [kafā'] *n* café *m*.

cafeteria [kafətir'ēə] *n* café *m*; (*communal*) comedor *m*.

caffein(e) [ka'fēn] *n* cafeína.

cage [kāj] *n* jaula ♦ *vt* enjaular.

cagey [kā'jē] *a* (*col*) cauteloso, reservado.

cagoule [kəgōōl'] *n* (*Brit*) chubasquero.

CAI *n abbr* (= *computer-aided instruction*) enseñanza asistida por ordenador.

Cairo [kī'rō] *n* el Cairo.

cajole [kəjōl'] *vt* engatusar.

cake [kāk] *n* pastel *m*; (*of soap*) pastilla; **he wants to have his ~ and eat it (too)** (*fig*) quiere estar en misa y repicando; **it's a piece of ~** (*col*) es pan comido.

caked [kākt] *a*: **~ with** cubierto de.

Cal. *abbr* (*US*) = *California.*

calamine [kal'əmīn] *n* calamina.

calamitous [kəlam'itəs] *a* calamitoso.

calamity [kəlam'itē] *n* calamidad *f*.

calcium [kal'sēəm] *n* calcio.

calculate [kal'kyəlāt] *vt* (*estimate: chances, effect*) calcular.

calculate on *vt fus* (*Brit*): **to ~ on sth/on doing sth** contar con algo/con hacer algo.

calculated [kal'kyəlātid] *a*: **a ~ risk** un riesgo calculado.

calculating [kal'kyəlāting] *a* (*scheming*) calculador(a).

calculation [kalkyəlā'shən] *n* cálculo, cómputo.

calculator [kal'kyəlātûr] *n* calculadora.

calculus [kal'kyələs] *n* cálculo.

calendar [kal'əndûr] *n* calendario; **~ month/year** *n* mes *m*/año civil.

calf, *pl* **calves** [kaf, kavz] *n* (*of cow*) ternero, becerro; (*of other animals*) cría; (*also:* **~skin**) piel *f* de becerro; (*ANAT*) pantorrilla.

caliber [kal'əbûr] *n* (*US*) calibre *m*.

calibrate [kal'əbrāt] *vt* (*gun etc*) calibrar; (*scale of measuring instrument*) graduar.

calibre [kal'əbûr] *n* (*Brit*) = **caliber**.

calico [kal'ikō] *n* calicó *m*.

Calif. *abbr* (*US*) = *California.*

California [kaləfôr'nyə] *n* California.

calipers [kal'əpûrz] *npl* (*US MED*) soporte *m* ortopédico; (*MATH*) calibrador *m*.

call [kôl] *vt* (*gen, also TEL*) llamar; (*announce: flight*) anunciar; (*meeting, strike*) convocar ♦ *vi* (*shout*) llamar; (*telephone*) llamar (por teléfono), telefonear (*esp LAm*); (*visit: also:* **~ in, ~ round**) hacer una visita ♦ *n* (*shout, TEL*) llamada; (*of bird*) canto; (*appeal*) llamamiento; (*summons: for flight etc*) llamada; (*fig: lure*) llamada; **to be ~ed** (*person, object*) llamarse; **to ~ sb names** poner verde a uno; **let's ~ it a day** (*col*) ¡dejémoslo!, ¡ya está bien!; **who is ~ing?** ¿de parte de quién?; **New York ~ing** (*RADIO*) aquí Nueva York; **on ~** (*nurse, doctor etc*) de guardia; **please give me a ~ at 7** despiérteme *or* llámeme a las 7, por favor; **long-distance ~** conferencia (interurbana); **to make a ~** llamar por teléfono; **port of ~** puerto de escala; **to ~ on sb** pasar a ver a uno; **there's not much ~ for these items** estos artículos no tienen mucha demanda.

call at *vt fus* (*ship*) hacer escala en, tocar en; (*train*) parar en.

call back *vi* (*return*) volver; (*TEL*) volver a llamar.

call for *vt fus* (*demand*) pedir, exigir; (*fetch*) venir por.

call in *vt* (*doctor, expert, police*) llamar a.

call off *vt* suspender; (*cancel*) cancelar; (*deal*) anular; **the strike was ~ed off** se abandonó la huelga.

call on *vt fus* (*visit*) visitar; (*turn to*) acudir a.

call out *vi* gritar, dar voces ♦ *vt* (*doctor*) hacer salir; (*police, troops*) hacer intervenir.

call up *vt* (*MIL*) llamar al servicio militar.

callbox [kôl'bâks] *n* (*Brit*) cabina telefónica.

caller [kôl'ûr] *n* visita *f*; (*TEL*) usuario/a; **hold the line, ~!** ¡no cuelgue!

call girl *n* prostituta.

call-in [kôl'in] *n* (*US*) *programa en que toma parte el público por teléfono.*

calling [kôl'ing] *n* vocación *f*, profesión *f*.

calling card *n* tarjeta de visita.

callipers [kal'əpûrz] *npl* (*Brit*) = **calipers.**

callous [kal'əs] *a* insensible, cruel.

callousness [kal'əsnis] *n* crueldad *f*.

callow [kal'ō] *a* inexperto, novato.

calm [kâm] *a* tranquilo; (*sea*) liso, en calma ♦ *n* calma, tranquilidad *f* ♦ *vt* calmar, tranquilizar.

calm down *vi* calmarse, tranquilizarse ♦ *vt* calmar, tranquilizar.

calmly [kâm'lē] *ad* tranquilamente, con calma.

calmness [kâm'nis] *n* calma.

Calor gas [kā'lûr gas] ® *n* (*Brit*) butano.

calorie [kal'ûrē] *n* caloría; **low-~ product** producto bajo en calorías.

calve [kav] *vi* parir.

calves [kavz] *npl* of **calf.**

CAM *n abbr* (= *computer-aided manufacturing*) producción *f* asistida por ordenador.

camber [kam'bûr] *n* (*of road*) combadura, comba.

Cambodia [kambō'dēə] *n* Camboya.

Cambodian [kambō'dēən] *a, n* camboyano/a *m/f*.

Cambs *abbr* (*Brit*) = *Cambridgeshire.*

camcorder [kam'kôrdûr] *n* cámara de vídeo sonora.

came [kām] *pt* of **come.**

camel [kam'əl] *n* camello.

cameo [kam'ēō] *n* camafeo.

camera [kam'ûrə] *n* máquina fotográfica; (*CINEMA, TV*) cámara; (*movie ~*) cámara, tomavistas *m inv*.

cameraman [kam'ûrəman] *n* cámara *m*.

Cameroon, Cameroun [kamərōōn'] *n* Camerón *m*.

camomile tea [kam'əmīl tē'] *n* manzanilla.

camouflage [kam'əflàzh] *n* camuflaje *m* ♦ *vt* camuflar.

camp [kamp] *n* campo, campamento ♦ *vi* acampar ♦ *a* afectado, afeminado; **to go ~ing** ir de *or* hacer camping.

campaign [kampān'] *n* (*MIL, POL etc*) campaña ♦ *vi*: **to ~ (for/against)** hacer campaña (a favor de/en contra de).

campaigner [kampān'ûr] *n*: **~ for** partidario/a de; **~ against** persona que hace campaña contra.

camp bed *n* cama de campaña.

camper [kam'pûr] *n* campista *m/f*; (*vehicle*) caravana.

camping [kam'ping] *n* camping *m*.

campsite [kamp'sīt] *n* camping *m*.

campus [kam'pəs] *n* ciudad *f* universitaria.

camshaft [kam'shaft] *n* árbol *m* de levas.

can [kan] *auxiliary vb see next headword* ♦ *n* (*of oil, water*) bidón *m*; (*of fruit, soup etc*) lata, bote *m* ♦ *vt* enlatar; (*preserve*) conservar en lata; **a ~ of beer** una lata *or* un bote de cerveza; **to carry the ~** (*Brit col*) pagar el pato.

can [kan] *n, vt see previous headword* ♦ *auxiliary vb* (*pt* **could**) poder; (*know how to*) saber; **~ I use your telephone?** ¿puedo usar su teléfono?; **could I have a word with you?** ¿podría hablar contigo un momento?; **they could have forgotten** puede que se hayan olvidado; **I ~'t see you** no te puedo ver; **~ you hear me?** (*not translated*) ¿me oyes?; **I ~ swim** sé nadar.

Canada [kan'ədə] *n* el Canadá.

Canadian [kanā'dēən] *a, n* canadiense *m/f*.

canal [kənal'] *n* canal *m*.

Canaries [kənär'ēz] *npl* las (Islas) Canarias.

canary [kənär'ē] *n* canario.

Canary Islands *npl* las (Islas) Canarias.

Canberra [kan'bərə] *n* Canberra.

cancel [kan'səl] *vt* cancelar; (*train*) suprimir; (*appointment, check*) anular; (*cross out*) tachar, borrar.

  cancel out *vt* (*MATH*) anular; (*fig*) contrarrestar; **they ~ each other out** se anulan mutuamente.

cancellation [kansəlā'shən] *n* cancelación *f*; supresión *f*.

cancer [kan'sûr] *n* cáncer *m*; **C~** (*ASTRO*) Cáncer *m*.

cancerous [kan'sûrəs] *a* canceroso.

cancer patient *n* enfermo/a *m/f* de cáncer.

cancer research *n* investigación *f* del cáncer.

C and F *abbr* (= *cost and freight*) C y F.

candid [kan'did] *a* franco, abierto.

candidacy [kan'didəsē] *n* candidatura.

candidate [kan'didāt] *n* candidato/a.

candidly [kan'didlē] *ad* francamente, con franqueza.

candied fruits [kan'dēd frōōts'] *n* frutas *fpl* escarchadas.

candle [kan'dəl] *n* vela; (*in church*) cirio.

candle holder *n see* **candlestick**.

candlelight [kan'dəllīt] *n*: **by ~** a la luz de una vela.

candlestick [kan'dəlstik] *n* (*also:* **candle holder**: *single*) candelero; (: *low*) palmatoria; (*bigger, ornate*) candelabro.

candor, (*Brit*) **candour** [kan'dûr] *n* franqueza.

candy [kan'dē] *n* (*US*) caramelo; (*Brit*) azúcar *m* cande ♦ *vt* (*fruit*) escarchar.

candy-floss [kan'dēflôs] *n* (*Brit*) algodón *m* (azucarado).

candy store *n* confitería, bombonería.

cane [kān] *n* (*BOT*) caña; (*for baskets, chairs etc*) mimbre *m*; (*stick*) vara, palmeta; (: *for walking*) bastón *m* ♦ *vt* (*Brit SCOL*) castigar (con palmeta).

canine [kā'nīn] *a* canino.

canister [kan'istûr] *n* bote *m*, lata.

cannabis [kan'əbis] *n* marijuana.

canned [kand] *a* en lata, de lata; (*col*: *music*) grabado; (*Brit*: *drunk*) borracho.

cannibal [kan'əbəl] *n* caníbal *m/f*.

cannibalism [kan'əbəlizəm] *n* canibalismo.

cannon, *pl* **~** *or* **~s** [kan'ən] *n* cañón *m*.

cannonball [kan'ənbôl] *n* bala (de cañón).

cannon fodder *n* carne *f* de cañón.

cannot [kan'ât] = **can not**.

canny [kan'ē] *a* astuto.

canoe [kənōō'] *n* canoa; (*SPORT*) piragua.

canoeing [kənōō'ing] *n* (*SPORT*) piragüismo.

canoeist [kənōō'ist] *n* piragüista *m/f*.

canon [kan'ən] *n* (*clergyman*) canónigo; (*standard*) canon *m*.

canonize [kan'ənīz] *vt* canonizar.

can opener [kan' ō'pənûr] *n* abrelatas *m inv*.

canopy [kan'əpē] *n* dosel *m*, toldo.

can't [kant] = **can not**.

cantankerous [kantang'kûrəs] *a* arisco, malhumorado.

canteen [kantēn'] *n* (*eating place*) cantina; (*Brit*: *of cutlery*) juego.

canter [kan'tûr] *n* medio galope ♦ *vi* ir a medio galope.

cantilever [kan'təlevûr] *n* viga voladiza.

canvas [kan'vəs] *n* (*material*) lona; (*painting*) lienzo; (*NAUT*) velas *fpl*; **under ~** (*Brit*: *camping*) bajo lona.

canvass [kan'vəs] *vt* (*POL*: *district*) hacer campaña en; (: *person*) solicitar votos de; (*COMM*: *district*) sondear el mercado en; (: *citizens, opinions*) sondear.

canvasser [kan'vəsûr] *n* (*POL*) representante *m/f* electoral; (*COMM*) corredor(a) *m/f*.

canyon [kan'yən] *n* cañón *m*.

CAP *n abbr* (= *Common Agricultural Policy*) PAC *f*.

cap [kap] *n* (*hat*) gorra; (*for swimming*) gorro de baño; (*of pen*) capuchón *m*; (*of* *bottle*) tapa, cápsula; (*Brit: contraceptive*) diafragma *m* ♦ *vt* (*outdo*) superar; (*Brit SPORT*) seleccionar (para el equipo nacional); **and to ~ it all, he ...** y para colmo, él ....

capability [kāpəbil'ətē] *n* capacidad *f*.

capable [kā'pəbəl] *a* capaz.

capacious [kəpā'shəs] *a* amplio.

capacity [kəpas'itē] *n* capacidad *f*; (*position*) calidad *f*; **filled to ~** lleno a reventar; **this work is beyond my ~** este trabajo es superior a mí; **in an advisory ~** como asesor.

cape [kāp] *n* capa; (*GEO*) cabo.

Cape of Good Hope *n* Cabo de Buena Esperanza.

caper [kā'pûr] *n* (*CULIN: also: ~s*) alcaparra; (*prank*) travesura.

Cape Town *n* El Cabo.

capital [kap'itəl] *n* (*also: ~ city*) capital *f*; (*money*) capital *m*; (*also: ~ letter*) mayúscula.

capital account *n* cuenta de capital.

capital allowance *n* desgravación *f* sobre bienes del capital.

capital assets *n* activo fijo.

capital expenditure *n* inversión *f* de capital.

capital gains tax *n* impuesto sobre las ganancias de capital.

capital goods *npl* bienes *mpl* de capital.

capital-intensive [kap'itəlinten'siv] *a* de utilización intensiva de capital.

capital investment *n* inversión *f* de capital.

capitalism [kap'itəlizəm] *n* capitalismo.

capitalist [kap'itəlist] *a, n* capitalista *m/f*.

capitalize [kap'itəlīz] *vt* (*COMM: provide with capital*) aprovechar.

   capitalize on *vt fus* (*fig*) sacar provecho de, aprovechar.

capital punishment *n* pena de muerte.

capitulate [kəpich'ōōlāt] *vi* capitular, rendirse.

capitulation [kəpichōōlā'shən] *n* capitulación *f*, rendición *f*.

capricious [kəprish'əs] *a* caprichoso.

Capricorn [kap'rikôrn] *n* Capricornio.

caps [kaps] *abbr* (= *capital letters*) may.

capsize [kap'sīz] *vt* volcar, hacer zozobrar ♦ *vi* volcarse, zozobrar.

capstan [kap'stən] *n* cabrestante *m*.

capsule [kap'səl] *n* cápsula.

Capt. *abbr* = **Captain**.

captain [kap'tin] *n* capitán *m* ♦ *vt* capitanear, ser el capitán de.

caption [kap'shən] *n* (*heading*) título; (*to picture*) leyenda.

captivate [kap'təvāt] *vt* cautivar, encantar.

captive [kap'tiv] *a, n* cautivo/a *m/f*.

captivity [kaptiv'ətē] *n* cautiverio.

captor [kap'tûr] *n* (*lawful*) apresador(a) *m/f*; (*unlawful*) secuestrador(a) *m/f*.

capture [kap'chûr] *vt* prender, apresar; (*place*) tomar; (*attention*) captar, llamar ♦ *n* apresamiento; toma; (*data ~*) formulación *f* de datos.

car [kär] *n* coche *m*, carro (*LAm*), automóvil *m*; (*US RAIL*) vagón *m*; **by ~** en coche.

Caracas [kərak'əs] *n* Caracas *m*.

carafe [kəraf'] *n* garrafa.

caramel [kar'əməl] *n* caramelo.

carat [kar'ət] *n* quilate *m*; **18-~ gold** oro de 18 quilates.

caravan [kar'əvan] *n* (*of camels*) caravana; (*Brit*) caravana (*Sp*), remolque *m* (*LAm*).

caravan site *n* (*Brit*) camping *m* para caravanas.

caraway [kar'əwā] *n*: **~ seed** carvi *m*.

carbohydrates [kärbōhī'drāts] *npl* (*foods*) hidratos *mpl* de carbono.

carbolic [kärbâl'ik] *a*: **~ acid** ácido carbónico.

carbon [kär'bən] *n* carbono.

carbonated [kär'bənātid] *a* (*drink*) con gas *or* burbujas.

carbon copy *n* copia al carbón.

carbon dioxide *n* bióxido de carbono.

carbon monoxide [kär'bən mənâk'sīd] *n* monóxido de carbono.

carbon paper *n* papel *m* carbón.

carbon ribbon *n* cinta de carbón.

carburetor, (*Brit*) carburettor [kär'bərātûr] *n* carburador *m*.

carcass [kär'kəs] *n* cadáver *m* de animal.

carcinogenic [kärsinəjen'ik] *a* cancerígeno.

card [kärd] *n* (*thin cardboard*) cartulina; (*playing ~*) carta, naipe *m*; (*visiting ~, post~ etc*) tarjeta; **membership ~** carnet *m*; **to play ~s** jugar a las cartas *or* los naipes.

cardamom [kär'dəməm] *n* cardamomo.

cardboard [kärd'bôrd] *n* cartón *m*, cartulina.

cardboard box *n* caja de cartón.

card-carrying member [kärd'karēing mem'bûr] *n* miembro con carnet.

card game *n* juego de naipes.

cardiac [kär'dēak] *a* cardíaco.

cardigan [kär'digən] *n* rebeca.

cardinal [kär'dənəl] *a* cardinal ♦ *n* cardenal *m*.

cardinal number [kär'dənəl num'bûr] *n* número cardinal.

card index *n* fichero.

Cards *abbr* (*Brit*) = *Cardiganshire*.

cardsharp [kärd'shärp] *n* fullero/a.

CARE [kär] *n abbr* (= *Cooperative for American Relief Everywhere*) sociedad benéfica.

care [kär] *n* cuidado; (*worry*) inquietud *f*; (*charge*) cargo, custodia ♦ *vi*: **to ~ about** preocuparse por; **~ of (c/o)** en casa de, al cuidado de; (: *on letter*) para (entregar a); **in sb's ~** a cargo de uno; **the child has been taken into ~** (*Brit*) pusieron al niño bajo custodia del gobierno; **"handle with**

~" "¡frágil!"; **to take** ~ **to** cuidarse de, tener cuidado de; **to take** ~ **of** *vt* cuidar; (*details, arrangements*) encargarse de; **I don't** ~ no me importa; **I could** (*US*) *or* **I couldn't** (*Brit*) ~ **less** eso me trae sin cuidado.

care for *vt fus* cuidar; (*like*) querer.

careen [kərēn'] *vi* (*ship*) inclinarse, escorar ♦ *vt* carenar.

career [kərēr'] *n* carrera; (*occupation*) profesión *f* ♦ *vi* (*also: Brit:* ~ **along**) correr a toda velocidad.

career counselor *n* consejero/a de orientación professional.

career girl *n* chica de carrera.

careers officer *n* (*Brit*) consejero/a de orientación profesional.

carefree [kär'frē] *a* despreocupado.

careful [kär'fəl] *a* cuidadoso; (*cautious*) cauteloso; **(be)** ~! ¡tenga cuidado!; **he's very** ~ **with his money** es muy tacaño.

carefully [kär'fəlē] *ad* con cuidado, cuidadosamente.

careless [kär'lis] *a* descuidado; (*heedless*) poco atento.

carelessly [kär'lislē] *ad* sin cuidado, a la ligera.

carelessness [kär'lisnis] *n* descuido, falta de atención.

caress [kəres'] *n* caricia ♦ *vt* acariciar.

caretaker [kär'tākûr] *n* portero/a, conserje *m/f*.

caretaker government *n* gobierno provisional.

car ferry *n* transbordador *m* para coches.

cargo, *pl* ~**es** [kär'gō] *n* cargamento, carga.

cargo boat *n* buque *m* de carga.

cargo plane *n* avión *m* de carga.

car hire *n* (*Brit*) alquiler *m* de coche.

Caribbean [kərəbē'ən] *a* caribe; **the** ~ **(Sea)** el (Mar) Caribe.

caricature [kar'əkəchûr] *n* caricatura.

caring [kär'ing] *a* humanitario.

carnage [kär'nij] *n* matanza, carnicería.

carnal [kär'nəl] *a* carnal.

carnation [kärnā'shən] *n* clavel *m*.

carnival [kär'nəvəl] *n* carnaval *m*; (*US*) parque *m* de atracciones.

carnivore [kär'nəvôr] *n* carnívoro/a.

carnivorous [kärniv'ûrəs] *a* carnívoro.

carol [kar'əl] *n*: (**Christmas**) ~ villancico.

carouse [kərouz'] *vi* estar de juerga.

carousel [karəsel'] *n* (*US*) tiovivo, caballitos *mpl*.

carp [kärp] *n* (*fish*) carpa.

carp at *or* **about** *vt fus* quejarse de.

car park *n* (*Brit*) aparcamiento, parking *m*.

carpenter [kär'pəntûr] *n* carpintero.

carpentry [kär'pəntrē] *n* carpintería.

carpet [kär'pit] *n* alfombra ♦ *vt* alfombrar.

carpet slippers *npl* zapatillas *fpl*.

carpet sweeper [kär'pit swē'pûr] *n* escoba mecánica.

car phone *n* teléfono portátil (por coche).

carping [kär'ping] *a* (*critical*) criticón/ona.

car rental *n* (*US*) alquiler *m* de coche.

carriage [kar'ij] *n* coche *m*; (*Brit RAIL*) vagón *m*; (*for goods*) transporte *m*; (*of typewriter*) carro; (*bearing*) porte *m*; ~ **forward** porte debido; ~ **free** franco de porte; ~ **paid** porte pagado; ~ **inwards/outwards** gastos *mpl* de transporte a cargo del comprador/vendedor.

carriage return *n* (*on typewriter etc*) tecla de regreso.

carriageway [kar'ijwā] *n* (*Brit: part of road*) carretera; **dual** ~ (*Brit*) carretera de doble calzada.

carrier [kar'êûr] *n* trajinista *m/f*; (*company*) empresa de transportes.

carrier bag *n* (*Brit*) bolsa de papel *or* plástico.

carrier pigeon *n* paloma mensajera.

carrion [kar'ēən] *n* carroña.

carrot [kar'ət] *n* zanahoria.

carry [kar'ē] *vt* (*subj: person*) llevar; (*transport*) transportar; (*a motion, bill*) aprobar; (*involve: responsibilities etc*) entrañar, implicar; (*COMM: stock*) tener en existencia; (: *interest*) llevar; (*MATH: figure*) llevarse ♦ *vi* (*sound*) oírse; **to get carried away** (*fig*) entusiasmarse; **this loan carries 10% interest** este empréstito devenga un interés del 10 por ciento.

carry forward *vt* (*MATH, COMM*) pasar a la página/columna siguiente.

carry on *vi* (*continue*) seguir (adelante), continuar; (*fam: complain*) quejarse, protestar ♦ *vt* proseguir, continuar.

carry out *vt* (*orders*) cumplir; (*investigation*) llevar a cabo, realizar.

carryall [kar'ēôl] *n* (*US*) bolsa.

carrycot [kar'ēkàt] *n* (*Brit*) cuna portátil.

carry-on [kar'ēän] *n* (*col: fuss*) lío; (: *annoying behavior*) jaleo.

cart [kärt] *n* (*also: US: for shopping*) carro, carreta; (: *for baggage*) carretilla ♦ *vt* llevar (en carro).

carte blanche [kärt' blänsh'] *n*: **to give sb** ~ dar carta blanca a uno.

cartel [kärtel'] *n* (*COMM*) cartel *m*.

cartilage [kär'təlij] *n* cartílago.

cartographer [kärtäg'rəfûr] *n* cartógrafo/a.

carton [kär'tən] *n* (*box*) caja (de cartón); (*of yogurt*) pote *m*.

cartoon [kärtōōn'] *n* (*PRESS*) caricatura; (*comic strip*) tira cómica; (*film*) dibujos *mpl* animados.

cartoonist [kärtōō'nist] *n* dibujante *m/f* de historietas.

cartridge [kär'trij] *n* cartucho.

cartwheel [kär't'hwēl] *n*: **to turn a** ~ dar una voltereta lateral.

carve [kärv] *vt* (*meat*) trinchar; (*wood, stone*) cincelar, esculpir; (*on tree*) grabar.

carve up *vt* dividir, repartir; (*meat*)

trinchar.

carving |kâr'ving| n (in wood etc) escultura, (obra de) talla.

carving knife n trinchante m.

car wash n lavado de coches.

Casablanca |kasəblang'kə| n Casablanca.

cascade |kaskād'| n salto de agua, cascada; (fig) chorro ♦ vi caer a chorros.

case |kās| n (container) caja; (MED) caso; (for jewels etc) estuche m; (LAW) causa, proceso; (Brit: also: suit~) maleta; **lower/upper** ~ (TYP) caja baja/alta; **in** ~ **of** en caso de; **in any** ~ en todo caso; **just in** ~ por si acaso; **to have a good** ~ tener buenos argumentos; **there's a strong** ~ **for reform** hay buenos fundamentos para exigir una reforma.

case-hardened |kās'hâr'dənd| a insensible.

case history n (MED) historial m médico, historia clínica.

case study n estudio de casos prácticos.

cash |kash| n (col: money) (dinero) efectivo, dinero contante ♦ vt cobrar, hacer efectivo; **to pay (in)** ~ pagar al contado; ~ **on delivery (COD)** cóbrese al entregar; **to be short of** ~ estar pelado, estar sin blanca.

cash in vt (insurance policy etc) cobrar ♦ vi: **to** ~ **in on sth** sacar partido or aprovecharse de algo.

cash account n cuenta de caja.

cashbook |kash'bŏŏk| n libro de caja.

cash box n alcancía.

cash card n tarjeta f dinero.

cash desk n (Brit) caja.

cash discount n descuento por pago al contado.

cash dispenser n cajero automático.

cashew |kash'ŏŏ| n (also: ~ **nut**) anacardo.

cash flow n flujo de fondos, cash-flow m, corriente f de efectivos.

cashier |kashi'ûr| n cajero/a ♦ vt (MIL) destituir, expulsar.

cashmere |kazh'mēr| n casimir m, cachemira.

cash payment n pago al contado.

cash price n precio al contado.

cash register n caja.

cash reserves npl reserva en efectivo.

cash sale n venta al contado.

casing |kā'sing| n revestimiento.

casino |kəsē'nō| n casino.

cask |kask| n tonel m, barril m.

casket |kas'kit| n cofre m, estuche m; (US: coffin) ataúd m.

Caspian Sea |kas'pēan sē'| n: **the** ~ el Mar Caspio.

casserole |kas'ərōl| n (food, pot) cazuela.

cassette |kəset'| n cassette m.

cassette deck n platina a cassette.

cassette player, **cassette recorder** n cassette m.

cassock |kas'ək| n sotana.

cast |kast| vb (pt, pp **cast**) vt (throw) echar, arrojar, lanzar; (skin) mudar, perder; (metal) fundir; (THEATER): **to** ~ **sb as Othello** dar a uno el papel de Otelo ♦ vi (FISHING) lanzar ♦ n (THEATER) reparto; (mold) forma, molde m; (also: **plaster** ~) vaciado; **to** ~ **loose** soltar; **to** ~ **one's vote** votar.

cast aside vt (reject) descartar, desechar.

cast away vt desechar.

cast down vt derribar.

cast off vi (NAUT) desamarrar; (KNITTING) cerrar los puntos ♦ vt (KNITTING) cerrar; **to** ~ **sb off** abandonar a uno, desentenderse de uno.

cast on vt (KNITTING) montar.

castanets |kastənets'| npl castañuelas fpl.

castaway |kas'təwā| n náufrago/a.

caste |kast| n casta.

caster sugar |kas'túr shŏŏg'ûr| n (Brit) azúcar m extrafino.

Castile |kastēl'| n Castilla.

casting vote |kas'ting vōt'| n (Brit) voto decisivo.

cast iron n hierro fundido or colado ♦ a (fig: alibi, excuse) inquebrantable; (will) férreo.

castle |kas'əl| n castillo; (CHESS) torre f.

castor |kas'tûr| n (wheel) ruedecilla.

castor oil n aceite m de ricino.

castrate |kas'trāt| vt castrar.

casual |kazh'ŏŏəl| a (by chance) fortuito; (temporary: work etc) eventual, temporero; (unconcerned) despreocupado; (informal: clothes) de sport.

casually |kazh'ŏŏəlē| ad por casualidad; de manera despreocupada.

casualty |kazh'ŏŏəltē| n víctima, herido; (dead) muerto; (MIL) baja; **heavy casualties** grandes pérdidas fpl.

cat |kat| n gato.

catacombs |kat'əkōmz| npl catacumbas fpl.

Catalan |kat'əlan| a, n catalán/ana m/f.

catalog, (Brit) **catalogue** |kat'əlôg| n catálogo ♦ vt catalogar.

Catalonia |kat'əlō'nēə| n Cataluña.

catalyst |kat'əlist| n catalizador m.

catalytic converter |katəlit'ik kânvûrt'ûr| n (AUT) conversor m catalítico.

catapult |kat'əpult| n tirador m.

cataract |kat'ərakt| n (also MED) catarata.

catarrh |kətâr'| n catarro.

catastrophe |kətas'trəfē| n catástrofe f.

catastrophic |katəstrâf'ik| a catastrófico.

catcall |kat'kôl| n (at meeting etc) rechifla, silbido.

catch |kach| vb (pt, pp **caught** |kôt|) vt coger (Sp), agarrar (LAm); (arrest) detener; (grasp) asir; (breath) suspender; (attract: attention) ganar; (MED) contagiarse de, coger; (also: ~ **up**) alcanzar ♦ vi (fire) encenderse; (in branches etc) enredarse ♦

n (*fish etc*) pesca; (*act of catching*) cogida; (*trick*) trampa; (*of lock*) pestillo, cerradura; **to ~ fire** encenderse; **to ~ sight of** divisar.

catch on *vi* (*understand*) caer en la cuenta; (*grow popular*) tener éxito, cuajar.

catch out *vt* (*Brit: fig: with trick question*) hundir.

catch up *vi* (*fig*) ponerse al día.

catching [kach'ing] *a* (*MED*) contagioso.

catchment area [kach'mənt är'ēə] *n* (*Brit*) zona de captación.

catch phrase *n* lema *m*, slogan *m*.

catch-22 [kach'twentētoo'] *n*: **it's a ~ situation** es un callejón sin salida, es un círculo vicioso.

catchy [kach'ē] *a* (*tune*) pegadizo.

cat door *n* gatera.

catechism [kat'əkizəm] *n* (*REL*) catequismo.

categoric(al) [katəgôr'ik(əl)] *a* categórico, terminante.

categorically [katəgôr'ikəlē] *ad* categóricamente, terminantemente.

categorize [kat'əgərīz] *vt* clasificar.

category [kat'əgôrē] *n* categoría, clase *f*.

cater [kā'tûr] *vi*: **to ~ to** (*US*) complacer a (una persona); (*needs*) atender a; (*consumers*) proveer a; **to ~ for** (*Brit*) abastecer a.

caterer [kā'tûrûr] *n* abastecedor(a) *m/f*, proveedor(a) *m/f*.

catering [kā'tûring] *n* (*trade*) (ramo de la) alimentación *f*.

caterpillar [kat'ûrpilûr] *n* oruga, gusano.

caterpillar track *n* rodado de oruga.

cathedral [kəthē'drəl] *n* catedral *f*.

cathode-ray tube [kath'ōdrā' tōōb] *n* tubo de rayos catódicos.

catholic [kath'əlik] *a* católico; **C~** *a*, *n* (*REL*) católico/a *m/f*.

cat's-eye [kats'ī'] *n* (*Brit AUT*) catafoto.

catsup [kat'səp] *n* (*US*) catsup *m*.

cattle [kat'əl] *npl* ganado *sg*.

catty [kat'ē] *a* malicioso, rencoroso.

CATV *n abbr* (*US*) = *community antenna television*.

Caucasian [kôkā'zhən] *a*, *n* caucásico/a *m/f*.

Caucasus [kôk'əsəs] *n* Cáucaso.

caucus [kô'kəs] *n* (*POL: local committee*) comité *m* local; (: *US: to elect candidates*) comité *m* electoral; (: *group*) camarilla política.

caught [kôt] *pt*, *pp of* **catch**.

cauliflower [kô'ləflouûr] *n* coliflor *f*.

cause [kôz] *n* causa, motivo, razón *f* ♦ *vt* causar; (*provoke*) provocar; **to ~ sth to be done** hacer hacer algo; **to ~ sb to do sth** hacer que uno haga algo.

causeway [kôz'wā] *n* (*road*) carretera elevada; (*embankment*) terraplén *m*.

caustic [kôs'tik] *a* cáustico; (*fig*) mordaz.

cauterize [kôt'ərīz] *vt* cauterizar.

caution [kô'shən] *n* cautela, prudencia; (*warning*) advertencia, amonestación *f* ♦ *vt* amonestar.

cautious [kô'shəs] *a* cauteloso, prudente, precavido.

cautiously [kô'shəslē] *ad* con cautela.

cautiousness [kô'shəsnis] *n* cautela.

cavalcade [kav'əlkād] *n* cabalgata.

cavalier [kavəliûr'] *n* (*knight*) caballero ♦ *a* (*pej: offhand: person, attitude*) arrogante, desdeñoso.

cavalry [kav'əlrē] *n* caballería.

cave [kāv] *n* cueva, caverna ♦ *vi*: **to go caving** ir en una expedición espeleológica.

cave in *vi* (*roof etc*) derrumbarse, hundirse.

caveman [kāv'mən] *n* cavernícola *m*, troglodita *m*.

cavern [kav'ûrn] *n* caverna.

cavernous [kav'ûrnəs] *a* (*cheeks, eyes*) hundido.

caviar(e) [kav'ēâr] *n* caviar *m*.

cavity [kav'itē] *n* hueco, cavidad *f*.

cavity wall insulation *n* aislamiento térmico.

cavort [kəvôrt'] *vi* dar cabrioladas.

cayenne [kīen'] *n*: **~ pepper** pimentón *m*.

CB *n abbr* (= *Citizens' Band (Radio)*) banda ciudadana.

CBC *n abbr* (= *Canadian Broadcasting Corporation*) cadena de radio y televisión.

CBI *n abbr* (= *Confederation of British Industry*) ≈ C.E.O.E. (*Sp*).

CBS *n abbr* (*US*: = *Columbia Broadcasting System*) cadena de radio y televisión.

cc *abbr* (= *cubic centimeters*) c³; (*on letter etc*) = **carbon copy**.

CCA *n abbr* (*US*: = *Circuit Court of Appeals*) *tribunal de apelación itinerante*.

CCC *n abbr* (*US*) = *Commodity Credit Corporation*.

CCU *n abbr* (*US*: = *coronary care unit*) unidad *f* de cuidados cardiológicos.

CD *n abbr* = **compact disc**; (*MIL*) = *Civil Defense* (*US*), *Civil Defence (Corps)* (*Brit*) ♦ *abbr* (*Brit*: = *Corps Diplomatique*) CD.

CDC *n abbr* (*US*) = *center for disease control*.

Cdr. *abbr* = **Commander**.

CDT *n abbr* (*US*: = *Central Daylight Time*) *hora de verano del centro*.

CDV *n abbr* (= *compact disc video*) vídeo compact-disc.

cease [sēs] *vt* cesar.

ceasefire [sēs'fiûr'] *n* alto *m* el fuego.

ceaseless [sēs'lis] *a* incesante.

ceaselessly [sēs'lislē] *ad* sin cesar.

CED *n abbr* (*US*) = *Committee for Economic Development*.

cedar [sē'dûr] *n* cedro.

cede [sēd] *vt* ceder.

CEEB *n abbr* (*US*: = *College Entry Examination Board*) *tribunal para las pruebas de*

acceso a la universidad.
ceiling [sē'ling] *n* techo; *(fig:* upper *limit)* límite *m,* tope *m.*
celebrate [sel'əbrāt] *vt* celebrar; *(have a party)* festejar ♦ *vi* divertirse.
celebrated [sel'əbrātid] *a* célebre.
celebration [seləbrā'shən] *n* fiesta, celebración *f.*
celebrity [səleb'ritē] *n* celebridad *f.*
celeriac [səlär'ēak] *n* apio-nabo.
celery [sel'ûrē] *n* apio.
celestial [səles'chəl] *a (of sky)* celeste; *(divine)* celestial.
celibacy [sel'əbəsē] *n* celibato.
cell [sel] *n* celda; *(BIOL)* célula; *(ELEC)* elemento.
cellar [sel'ûr] *n* sótano; *(for wine)* bodega.
cellophane [sel'əfān] *n* celofán *m.*
cellular [sel'yəlûr] *a* celular.
celluloid [sel'yəloid] *n* celuloide *m.*
cellulose [sel'yəlōs] *n* celulosa.
Celsius [sel'sēəs] *a* centígrado.
Celt [selt, kelt] *n* celta *m/f.*
Celtic [sel'tik, kel'tik] *a* celta, céltico ♦ *n (LING)* céltico.
cement [siment'] *n* cemento ♦ *vt* cementar; *(fig)* cimentar, fortalecer.
cement mixer *n* hormigonera.
cemetery [sem'itärē] *n* cementerio.
cenotaph [sen'ətaf] *n* cenotafio.
censor [sen'sûr] *n* censor *m* ♦ *vt (cut)* censurar.
censorship [sen'sûrship] *n* censura.
censure [sen'shûr] *vt* censurar.
census [sen'səs] *n* censo.
cent [sent] *n (US:* coin) centavo, céntimo; *see also* **per.**
centenary [sen'tənärē] *n (Brit)* = **centennial.**
centennial [senten'ēəl] *n (US)* centenario.
center [sen'tûr] *(US) n* centro ♦ *vt* centrar; **to ~ on** *(concentrate)* concentrar (en).
centerfold [sen'tûrfōld] *n* página central plegable.
center forward *n (SPORT)* delantero centro.
center half *n (SPORT)* medio centro.
center halfback *n (US SPORT)* medio centro.
centerpiece [sen'tûrpēs] *n* punto central.
centigrade [sen'tigrād] *a* centígrado.
centiliter, *(Brit)* **centilitre** [sen'təlētûr] *n* centilitro.
centimeter, *(Brit)* **centimetre** [sen'təmētûr] *n* centímetro.
centipede [sen'təpēd] *n* ciempiés *m inv.*
central [sen'trəl] *a* central; *(of house etc)* céntrico.
Central African Republic *n* República Centroafricana.
Central America *n* Centroamérica.
Central American *a, n* centroamericano/a *m/f.*

central heating *n* calefacción *f* central.
centralize [sen'trəlīz] *vt* centralizar.
central processing unit (CPU) *n (COMPUT)* unidad *f* procesadora central.
central reservation *n (Brit AUT)* mediana.
centre [sen'tûr] *etc (Brit)* = **center** *etc.*
centrifuge [sen'trəfyōōj] *n* centrifugadora.
century [sen'chûrē] *n* siglo; **20th ~** siglo veinte; **in the twentieth ~** en el siglo veinte.
CEO *n abbr (US)* = **chief executive officer.**
ceramic [səram'ik] *a* cerámico.
ceramics [səram'iks] *n* cerámica.
cereal [sēr'ēəl] *n* cereal *m.*
cerebral [sär'əbrəl] *a* cerebral; *(person)* intelectual.
ceremonial [särəmō'nēəl] *n* ceremonial.
ceremony [sär'əmōnē] *n* ceremonia; **to stand on ~** hacer ceremonias, estar de cumplido.
cert [sûrt] *n (Brit col):* **it's a dead ~** ¡eso está hecho!, ¡es cosa segura!
certain [sûr'tən] *a* seguro; *(correct)* cierto; *(person)* seguro; *(a particular)* cierto; **for ~** a ciencia cierta.
certainly [sûr'tənlē] *ad* desde luego, por supuesto.
certainty [sûr'təntē] *n* certeza, certidumbre *f,* seguridad *f.*
certificate [sûrtif'əkit] *n* certificado.
certified [sûr'təfīd] *a:* **~ mail** *(US)* correo certificado.
certified public accountant (CPA) *n (US)* contable *m/f* diplomado/a.
certify [sûr'təfī] *vt* certificar.
cervical [sûr'vikəl] *a:* **~ cancer** cáncer *m* cervical; **~ smear** citología.
cervix [sûr'viks] *n* cerviz *f.*
Cesarean [sizär'ēən] *a (US):* **~ section** cesárea.
cessation [sesā'shən] *n* cese *m,* suspensión *f.*
cesspool [ses'pōōl] *n* pozo negro.
CET *n abbr (= Central European Time)* hora de Europa central.
Ceylon [silân'] *n* Ceilán *m.*
cf. *abbr (= compare)* cfr.
C.F. *abbr = cost and freight.*
c/f *abbr (COMM) = carried forward.*
cfc *n abbr (= chlorofluorocarbon)* clorofluorocarbono.
C.F.I. *abbr (= cost, freight and insurance)* c.s.f.
CG *n abbr (US)* = **coastguard.**
cg *abbr (= centigram)* cg.
ch *abbr (Brit:* = central heating) cal. cen.
ch. *abbr (= chapter)* cap.
Chad [chad] *n* Chad *m.*
chafe [chāf] *vt (rub)* rozar; *(irritate)* irritar; **to ~ (against)** *(fig)* irritarse *or* enojarse (con).
chaffinch [chaf'inch] *n* pinzón *m* (vulgar).

chagrin [shəgrin'] *n* (*annoyance*) disgusto; (*disappointment*) desazón *f*.
chain [chān] *n* cadena ♦ *vt* (*also*: ~ **up**) encadenar.
chain reaction *n* reacción *f* en cadena.
chain-smoke [chān'smōk] *vi* fumar un cigarrillo tras otro.
chain store *n* tienda de una cadena, ≈ gran almacén.
chair [chär] *n* silla; (*armchair*) sillón *m*; (*of university*) cátedra ♦ *vt* (*meeting*) presidir; **the** ~ (*US: electric* ~) la silla eléctrica; **please take a** ~ siéntese *or* tome asiento, por favor.
chairlift [chär'lift] *n* telesilla *m*.
chairman [chär'mən] *n* presidente *m*.
chairperson [chär'pûrsən] *n* presidente/a *m/f*.
chairwoman [chär'wōōmən] *n* presidenta.
chalet [shalā'] *n* chalet *m*.
chalice [chal'is] *n* cáliz *m*.
chalk [chôk] *n* (*GEO*) creta; (*for writing*) tiza, gis *m* (*LAm*).
chalk up *vt* apuntar; (*fig: success*) apuntarse; (: *victory*) obtener.
challenge [chal'inj] *n* desafío, reto ♦ *vt* desafiar, retar; (*statement, right*) poner en duda; **to** ~ **sb to do sth** retar a uno a que haga algo.
challenger [chal'injûr] *n* (*SPORT*) contrincante *m/f*.
challenging [chal'injing] *a* desafiante; (*tone*) de desafío.
chamber [chām'bûr] *n* cámara, sala; ~ **of commerce** cámara de comercio.
chambermaid [chām'bûrmād] *n* camarera.
chamber music *n* música de cámara.
chamberpot [chām'bûrpât] *n* orinal *m*.
chameleon [kəmē'lēən] *n* camaleón *m*.
chamois [sham'ē] *n* gamuza.
champagne [shampān'] *n* champaña *m*, champán *m*.
champion [cham'pēən] *n* campeón/ona *m/f*; (*of cause*) defensor(a) *m/f*, paladín *m/f* ♦ *vt* defender, apoyar.
championship [cham'pēənship] *n* campeonato.
chance [chans] *n* (*coincidence*) casualidad *f*; (*luck*) suerte *f*; (*fate*) azar *m*; (*opportunity*) ocasión *f*, oportunidad *f*; (*likelihood*) posibilidad *f*; (*risk*) riesgo ♦ *vt* arriesgar, probar ♦ *a* fortuito, casual; **to** ~ **it** arriesgarse, intentarlo; **to take a** ~ arriesgarse; **by** ~ por casualidad; **it's the** ~ **of a lifetime** es la oportunidad de su vida; **the** ~**s are that** ... lo más probable *or* factible es que ...; **to** ~ **to do sth** (*happen*) hacer algo por casualidad.
chance (up)on *vt fus* (*person*) encontrar por casualidad; (*thing*) tropezar(se) con.
chancel [chan'səl] *n* coro y presbiterio.
chancellor [chan'səlûr] *n* canciller *m*; **C~**

of the Exchequer (*Brit*) Ministro de Hacienda.
chancy [chan'sē] *a* (*col*) arriesgado.
chandelier [shandəli'ûr] *n* araña (de luces).
change [chānj] *vt* cambiar; (*replace*) reemplazar; (*gear*) cambiar de; (*clothes, house*) mudarse de; (*exchange*) trocar; (*transform*) transformar ♦ *vi* cambiar(se); (*trains*) hacer transbordo; (*be transformed*): **to** ~ **into** transformarse en ♦ *n* cambio; (*alteration*) modificación *f*, transformación *f*; (*coins*) suelto; (*money returned*) vuelta; **to** ~ **one's mind** cambiar de opinión *or* idea; **to** ~ **gear** (*AUT*) cambiar de marcha; **she** ~**d into an old skirt** se puso una falda vieja; **for a** ~ para variar; **can you give me** ~ **for $1?** ¿tiene cambio de un dólar?; **keep the** ~ quédese con la vuelta.
changeable [chān'jəbəl] *a* (*weather*) cambiable; (*person*) variable.
changeless [chānj'lis] *a* inmutable.
change machine *n* máquina de cambio.
changeover [chānj'ōvûr] *n* (*to new system*) cambio.
changing [chān'jing] *a* cambiante.
changing room *n* (*Brit*) vestuario.
channel [chan'əl] *n* (*TV*) canal *m*; (*of river*) cauce *m*; (*of sea*) estrecho; (*groove, fig: medium*) conducto, medio ♦ *vt* (*river etc*) encauzar; **to** ~ **into** (*fig: interest, energies*) encauzar a, dirigir a; **the (English) C~** el Canal (de la Mancha); **the C~ Islands** las Islas Normandas *fpl*; ~**s of communication** canales *mpl* de comunicación; **green/red** ~ (*CUSTOMS*) pasillo verde/rojo.
chant [chant] *n* canto; (*of crowd*) gritos *mpl*, cantos *mpl* ♦ *vt* cantar; **the demonstrators** ~**ed their disapproval** los manifestantes gritaron su desaprobación.
chaos [kā'ás] *n* caos *m*.
chaotic [kāät'ik] *a* caótico, desordenado.
chap [chap] *n* (*Brit col: man*) tío, tipo; **old** ~ amigo (mío).
chapel [chap'əl] *n* capilla.
chaperone [shap'ərōn] *n* carabina.
chaplain [chap'lin] *n* capellán *m*.
chapped [chapt] *a* agrietado.
chapter [chap'tûr] *n* capítulo.
char [chär] *vt* (*burn*) carbonizar, chamuscar ♦ *n* (*Brit*) = **charlady**.
character [kar'iktûr] *n* carácter *m*, naturaleza, índole *f*; (*in novel, film*) personaje *m*; (*role*) papel *m*; (*COMPUT*) carácter *m*; **a person of good** ~ una persona de buena reputación.
character code *n* código de caracteres.
characteristic [kariktəris'tik] *a* característico ♦ *n* característica.
characterize [kar'iktərīz] *vt* caracterizar.
charade [shərād'] *n* charada.
charcoal [chär'kōl] *n* carbón *m* vegetal;

(*ART*) carboncillo.

charge [chârj] *n* carga; (*LAW*) cargo, acusación *f*; (*cost*) precio, coste *m*; (*responsibility*) cargo; (*task*) encargo ♦ *vt* (*LAW*) acusar (*with* de); (*gun*, *battery*, *MIL*: *enemy*) cargar; (*price*) pedir; (*customer*) cobrar; (*sb with task*) encargar ♦ *vi* precipitarse; (*make pay*) cobrar; ~s *npl*: **bank** ~s comisiones *fpl* bancarias; **extra** ~ recargo, suplemento; **free of** ~ gratis; **to reverse the** ~s (*Brit TEL*) revertir el cobro; **to take** ~ **of** hacerse cargo de, encargarse de; **to be in** ~ **of** estar encargado de; **how much do you** ~? ¿cuánto cobra usted?; **to** ~ **an expense (up) to sb's account** cargar algo a cuenta de alguien; ~ **it to my account** póngalo *or* cárguelo a mi cuenta.

charge account *n* cuenta a cargo.

charge card *n* tarjeta de crédito.

chargé d'affaires [shârzhā' dâfärz'] *n* encargado de negocios.

chargehand [chârj'hand] *n* (*Brit*) capataz *m*.

charger [châr'jûr] *n* (*also*: **battery** ~) cargador *m* de baterías; (*old*: *warhorse*) caballo de batalla.

chariot [char'ēət] *n* carro.

charisma [kəriz'mə] *n* carisma *m*.

charitable [char'itəbəl] *a* caritativo.

charity [char'itē] *n* (*gen*) caridad *f*; (*organization*) sociedad *f* benéfica.

charlady [châr'lādē] *n* (*Brit*) mujer *f* de la limpieza.

charlatan [shâr'lətən] *n* farsante *m/f*.

charm [chârm] *n* encanto, atractivo; (*spell*) hechizo; (*object*) amuleto ♦ *vt* encantar; hechizar.

charm bracelet *n* pulsera amuleto.

charming [châr'ming] *a* encantador(a); (*person*) simpático.

chart [chârt] *n* (*table*) cuadro; (*graph*) gráfica; (*map*) carta de navegación; (*weather* ~) mapa *m* meteorológico ♦ *vt* (*course*) trazar; (*sales*, *progress*) hacer una gráfica de; **to be in the** ~s (*record*, *pop group*) figurar entre los discos que más se venden.

charter [châr'tûr] *vt* (*plane*) alquilar; (*ship*) fletar ♦ *n* (*document*) carta; **on** ~ en alquiler, alquilado.

chartered accountant (CA) [châr'tûrd əkoun'tənt] *n* (*Brit*) contable *m/f* diplomado/a.

charter flight *n* vuelo chárter.

charwoman [châr'wŏŏmən] *n* (*Brit*) = **charlady**.

chase [chās] *vt* (*pursue*) perseguir; (*hunt*) cazar ♦ *n* persecución *f*; caza; **to** ~ **after** correr tras.

chase down *vt* (*US*: *information*) recoger; **to** ~ **sb down about sth** recordar algo a uno.

chase up *vt* (*Brit*) = **chase down**.

chasm [kaz'əm] *n* abismo.

chassis [shas'ē] *n* chasis *m*.

chaste [chāst] *a* casto.

chastened [chā'sənd] *a* escarmentado.

chastening [chā'səning] *a* aleccionador(a).

chastity [chas'titē] *n* castidad *f*.

chat [chat] *vi* (*also*: **have a** ~) charlar ♦ *n* charla.

chat up *vt* (*col*: *girl*) enrollarse con.

chat show *n* (*Brit*) programa *m* de entrevistas.

chattel [chat'əl] *n* bien *m* mueble.

chatter [chat'ûr] *vi* (*person*) charlar; (*teeth*) castañetear ♦ *n* (*of birds*) parloteo; (*of people*) charla, cháchara.

chatterbox [chat'ûrbâks] *n* parlanchín/ina *m/f*.

chatty [chat'ē] *a* (*style*) familiar; (*person*) hablador(a).

chauffeur [shō'fûr] *n* chófer *m*.

chauvinist [shō'vənist] *n* (*male* ~) machista *m*; (*nationalist*) chovinista *m/f*, patriotero/a *m/f*.

ChE *abbr* = *chemical engineer*.

cheap [chēp] *a* barato; (*joke*) de mal gusto; (*poor quality*) de mala calidad; (*reduced*: *ticket*) económico, (: *fare*) barato ♦ *ad* barato.

cheapen [chē'pən] *vt* rebajar el precio de, abaratar.

cheaply [chēp'lē] *ad* barato, a bajo precio.

cheat [chēt] *vi* (*in exam*) hacer trampa ♦ *vt* estafar, timar ♦ *n* trampa; estafa; (*person*) tramposo/a; **he's been** ~**ing on his wife** ha estado engañando a su esposa.

cheating [chēt'ing] *n* trampa, fraude *m*.

check [chek] *vt* (*examine*) controlar; (*facts*) comprobar; (*count*) contar; (*halt*) parar, detener; (*restrain*) refrenar, restringir ♦ *vi*: **to** ~ **with sb** consultar con uno; (*official etc*) informarse por ♦ *n* (*inspection*) control *m*, inspección *f*; (*curb*) freno; (*bill*) nota, cuenta; (*US*) cheque *m*; (*pattern*: *gen pl*) cuadro ♦ *a* (*also*: ~**ed**: *pattern*, *cloth*) a cuadros; **to keep a** ~ **on sth/sb** controlar algo/a uno; **to pay by** ~ pagar con cheque.

check in *vi* (*in hotel*, *airport*) registrarse ♦ *vt* (*baggage*) facturar.

check off *vt* marcar.

check out *vi* (*of hotel*) desocupar su cuarto ♦ *vt* (*investigate*: *story*) verificar; (: *person*) hacer investigaciones sobre.

check up *vi*: **to** ~ **up on sth** comprobar algo; **to** ~ **up on sb** investigar a alguien.

checkbook [chek'bŏŏk] *n* talonario de cheques.

checkerboard [chek'ərbôrd] *n* (*US*) tablero de damas.

checkered [chek'ûrd] *a* (*fig*) accidentado; (*pattern*) de cuadros.

checkers [chek'ûrz] *n* (*US*) juego de damas.

check guarantee card *n* tarjeta de cheque, tarjeta bancaria.

check-in |chek'in| *n* (*also*: ~ **desk**: *at airport*) mostrador *m* de embarque.

checking account |chek'ing əkount'| *n* (*US*) cuenta corriente.

checklist |chek'list| *n* lista.

checkmate |chek'māt| *n* jaque *m* mate.

checkout |chek'out| *n* (*in supermarket*) caja.

checkpoint |chek'point| *n* (punto de) control *m*.

checkroom |chek'rōōm| *n* (*US*) consigna.

checkup |chek'up| *n* (*MED*) reconocimiento general; (*of machine*) repaso.

cheek |chēk| *n* mejilla; (*impudence*) descaro.

cheekbone |chēk'bōn| *n* pómulo.

cheeky |chē'kē| *a* (*Brit*) fresco, descarado.

cheep |chēp| *n* (*of bird*) pío ♦ *vi* piar, gorjear.

cheer |chēr| *vt* vitorear, aplaudir; (*gladden*) alegrar, animar ♦ *vi* aplaudir, dar vivas ♦ *n* viva *m*; ~**s** *npl* aplausos *mpl*; ~**s**! ¡salud!

cheer on *vt* (*person etc*) animar con aplausos *or* gritos.

cheer up *vi* animarse ♦ *vt* alegrar, animar.

cheerful |chēr'fəl| *a* alegre.

cheerfulness |chēr'fəlnis| *n* alegría.

cheering |chē'ring| *n* aplausos *mpl*, vítores *mpl*.

cheerio |chēr'ēō| *excl* (*Brit*) ¡hasta luego!

cheerless |chēr'lis| *a* triste, sombrío.

cheese |chēz| *n* queso.

cheeseboard |chēz'bōrd| *n* plato de quesos.

cheesecake |chēz'kāk| *n* pastel *m* de queso.

cheesecloth |chēz'klôth| *n* estopilla.

cheetah |chē'tə| *n* leopardo cazador.

chef |shef| *n* jefe/a *m/f* de cocina.

chemical |kem'ikəl| *a* químico ♦ *n* producto químico.

chemist |kem'ist| *n* (*scientist*) químico/a; (*Brit*: *pharmacist*) farmacéutico/a; ~**'s** (**shop**) *n* (*Brit*) farmacia.

chemistry |kem'istrē| *n* química.

cheque |chek| *n* (*Brit*) cheque *m*; **to pay by** ~ pagar con cheque.

chequebook |chek'bōōk| *n* (*Brit*) = **checkbook**.

cheque card *n* (*Brit*) tarjeta de cheque.

chequered |chek'ûrd| *a* (*Brit*) = **checkered**.

cherish |chär'ish| *vt* (*love*) querer, apreciar; (*protect*) cuidar; (*hope etc*) abrigar.

cheroot |shərōōt'| *n* puro (*cortado en los dos extremos*).

cherry |chär'ē| *n* cereza.

Ches *abbr* (*Brit*) = *Cheshire*.

chess |ches| *n* ajedrez *m*.

chessboard |ches'bōrd| *n* tablero (de ajedrez).

chessman |ches'man| *n* pieza, trebejo.

chest |chest| *n* (*ANAT*) pecho; (*box*) cofre *m*, cajón *m*; **to get sth off one's** ~ (*col*) desahogarse; ~ **of drawers** *n* cómoda.

chest measurement *n* talla (*de chaqueta etc*).

chestnut |ches'nut| *n* castaña; (*also*: ~ **tree**) castaño; (*color*) castaño ♦ *a* (color) castaño *inv*.

chew |chōō| *vt* mascar, masticar.

chewing gum |chōō'ing gum| *n* chicle *m*.

chic |shēk| *a* elegante.

chicanery |shikā'nûrē| *n* embustes *mpl*, sofismas *mpl*.

chick |chik| *n* pollito, polluelo; (*col*) chica.

chicken |chik'ən| *n* gallina, pollo; (*food*) pollo; (*col*: *coward*) gallina *m/f*.

chicken out *vi* (*col*) rajarse, amedrentarse, retirarse miedoso; **to** ~ **out of doing sth** acobardarse de hacer algo.

chickenpox |chik'ənpáks| *n* varicela.

chickpea |chik'pē| *n* garbanzo.

chicory |chik'ûrē| *n* (*for coffee*) achicoria; (*salad*) escarola.

chide |chīd| *vt*: **to** ~ **sb for sth** reprender *or* regañar a uno por algo.

chief |chēf| *n* jefe/a *m/f* ♦ *a* principal; **C**~ **of Staff** (*MIL*) jefe *m* del estado mayor.

chief executive officer, (*Brit*) **chief executive** *n* director *m* general.

chiefly |chēf'lē| *ad* principalmente.

chieftain |chēf'tin| *n* jefe *m*, cacique *m*.

chiffon |shifân'| *n* gasa.

chilblain |chil'blān| *n* sabañón *m*.

child, *pl* ~**ren** |chīld, chil'drən| *n* niño/a; (*offspring*) hijo/a.

childbirth |chīld'bûrth| *n* parto.

childhood |chīld'hōōd| *n* niñez *f*, infancia.

childish |chīl'dish| *a* pueril, aniñado.

childless |chīld'lis| *a* sin hijos.

childlike |chīld'līk| *a* de niño, infantil.

child minder *n* (*Brit*) niñera.

child's play |chīldz' plā| *n* (*fig*): **this is** ~ esto es coser y cantar.

Chile |chil'ē| *n* Chile *m*.

Chilean |chēl'āən| *a*, *n* chileno/a *m/f*.

chill |chil| *n* frío; (*MED*) resfriado ♦ *a* frío ♦ *vt* enfriar; (*CULIN*) congelar.

chil(l)i |chil'ē| *n* (*Brit*) chile *m*, ají *m* (*LAm*).

chilly |chil'ē| *a* frío.

chime |chīm| *n* repique *m*, campanada ♦ *vi* repicar, sonar.

chimney |chim'nē| *n* chimenea.

chimney sweep *n* deshollinador *m*.

chimpanzee |chimpanzē'| *n* chimpancé *m*.

chin |chin| *n* mentón *m*, barbilla.

China |chī'nə| *n* China.

china *n* porcelana; (*crockery*) loza.

Chinese |chīnēz'| *a* chino ♦ *n* (*pl inv*) chino/a; (*LING*) chino.

chink |chingk| *n* (*opening*) grieta, hendedura; (*noise*) tintineo.

chintz |chints| *n* cretona.

chip [chip] *n* (*gen pl*: *CULIN*: *Brit*) patata *or* papa (*LAm*) frita; (: *US*: *also*: **potato** ~) patata *or* papa frita; (*of wood*) astilla; (*of glass, stone*) lasca; (*in gambling*) ficha; (*COMPUT*) chip *m* ♦ *vt* (*cup, plate*) desconchar; **when the ~s are down** (*fig*) en el momento de la verdad.
  chip in *vi* (*col*: *interrupt*) interrumpir; (: *contribute*) compartir los gastos.
chipboard [chip'bórd] *n* madera aglomerada.
chipmunk [chip'mungk] *n* ardilla listada.
chiropodist [kiráp'ədist] *n* (*Brit*) pedicuro/a.
chiropody [kiráp'ədē] *n* pedicura.
chirp [chûrp] *vi* gorjear, piar; (*cricket*) chirriar ♦ *n* (*of cricket*) chirrido.
chirpy [chûr'pē] *a* alegre, animado.
chisel [chiz'əl] *n* (*for wood*) formón *m*; (*for stone*) cincel *m*.
chit [chit] *n* nota.
chitchat [chit'chat] *n* chismes *mpl*, habladurías *fpl*.
chivalrous [shiv'əlrəs] *a* caballeroso.
chivalry [shiv'əlrē] *n* caballerosidad *f*.
chives [chīvz] *npl* cebollinos *mpl*.
chloride [klôr'īd] *n* cloruro.
chlorinate [klôr'ənāt] *vt* clorinar.
chlorine [klôr'ēn] *n* cloro.
chock-a-block [chák'əblák'], (*Brit*) **chockfull** [chák'fōōl] *a* atestado.
chocolate [chôk'əlit] *n* chocolate *m*.
choice [chois] *n* elección *f*, selección *f*; (*preference*) preferencia ♦ *a* escogido; **I did it by** *or* **from** ~ lo hice de buena gana; **a wide** ~ un gran surtido, una gran variedad.
choir [kwī'ûr] *n* coro.
choirboy [kwiûr'boi] *n* corista *m*.
choke [chōk] *vi* sofocarse; (*on food*) atragantarse ♦ *vt* ahogar, sofocar; (*block*) obstruir ♦ *n* (*AUT*) estárter *m*.
choker [chō'kûr] *n* (*necklace*) gargantilla.
cholera [kâl'ərə] *n* cólera *m*.
cholesterol [kəles'tərôl] *n* colesterol *m*.
choose, *pt* **chose,** *pp* **chosen** [chōōz, chōz, chō'zən] *vt* escoger, elegir; (*team*) seleccionar; **to** ~ **between** elegir *or* escoger entre; **to** ~ **from** elegir de entre.
choosy [chōō'zē] *a* remilgado.
chop [châp] *vt* (*wood*) cortar, tajar; (*CULIN*: *also*: ~ **up**) picar ♦ *n* golpe *m* cortante; (*CULIN*) chuleta; **~s** *npl* (*jaws*) boca *sg*, labios *mpl*; **to get the** ~ (*Brit col*: *project*) ser cortado; (: *person*: *be laid off*) ser despedido.
chopper [châp'ûr] *n* (*helicopter*) helicóptero.
choppy [châp'ē] *a* (*sea*) picado, agitado.
chopsticks [châp'stiks] *npl* palillos *mpl*.
choral [kôr'əl] *a* coral.
chord [kôrd] *n* (*MUS*) acorde *m*.
chore [chôr] *n* faena, tarea; (*routine task*)

trabajo rutinario.
choreographer [kôrēâg'rəfûr] *n* coreógrafo/a.
chorister [kôr'istûr] *n* corista *m/f*; (*US*) director(a) *m/f* de un coro.
chortle [chôr'təl] *vi* reír entre dientes.
chorus [chō'rəs] *n* coro; (*repeated part of song*) estribillo.
chose [chōz] *pt of* **choose.**
chosen [chō'zən] *pp of* **choose.**
chow [chou] *n* (*dog*) perro chino.
chowder [chou'dûr] *n* (*esp US*) sopa de pescado.
Christ [krīst] *n* Cristo.
christen [kris'ən] *vt* bautizar.
christening [kris'əning] *n* bautizo.
Christian [kris'chən] *a, n* cristiano/a *m/f*.
Christianity [krischēan'itē] *n* cristianismo.
Christian name *n* nombre *m* de pila.
Christmas [kris'məs] *n* Navidad *f*; **Merry ~!** ¡Felices Navidades!, ¡Felices Pascuas!
Christmas card *n* crismas *m inv*, tarjeta de Navidad.
Christmas Day *n* día *m* de Navidad.
Christmas Eve *n* Nochebuena.
Christmas Island *n* Isla Christmas.
Christmas tree *n* árbol *m* de Navidad.
chrome [krōm] *n* = **chromium plating.**
chromium [krō'mēəm] *n* cromo; (*also*: ~ **plating**) cromado.
chromosome [krō'məsōm] *n* cromosoma *m*.
chronic [krân'ik] *a* crónico; (*fig*: *liar, smoker*) empedernido.
chronicle [krân'ikəl] *n* crónica.
chronological [krânəlâj'ikəl] *a* cronológico.
chrysalis [kris'əlis] *n* (*BIO*) crisálida.
chrysanthemum [krisan'thəməm] *n* crisantemo.
chubby [chub'ē] *a* rechoncho.
chuck [chuk] *vt* lanzar, arrojar; **to** ~ (**up** *or* **in**) *vt* (*Brit*: *job*) abandonar; (: *person*) dejar plantado.
chuckle [chuk'əl] *vi* reírse entre dientes.
chug [chug] *vi* (*also*: ~ **along**: *train*) ir despacio, ir tirando.
chum [chum] *n* compinche *m/f*, compañero/a.
chump [chump] *n* (*col*) tonto/a, estúpido/a.
chunk [chungk] *n* pedazo, trozo.
chunky [chung'kē] *a* (*furniture etc*) achaparrado; (*person*) fornido; (*knitwear*) de lana espesa, grueso.
church [chûrch] *n* iglesia; **the C~ of England** la Iglesia Anglicana.
churchyard [chûrch'yârd] *n* camposanto.
churlish [chûr'lish] *a* grosero; (*miserly*) tacaño.
churn [chûrn] *n* (*for butter*) mantequera; (*for milk*) lechera.
  churn out *vt* producir en serie.
chute [shōōt] *n* (*also*: **garbage** ~) vertede-

ro; (*Brit*: *children's slide*) tobogán *m*.
chutney [chut'nē] *n* salsa picante.
CIA *n abbr* (*US*: = *Central Intelligence Agency*) CIA *f*, Agencia Central de Inteligencia.
cicada [sikā'də] *n* cigarra.
CID *n abbr* (*Brit*: = *Criminal Investigation Department*) ≈ B.I.C. *f* (*Sp*).
cider [sī'dûr] *n* sidra.
C.I.F. *abbr* (= *cost, insurance and freight*) C.I.F.
cigar [sigár'] *n* puro.
cigarette [sigəret'] *n* cigarrillo, pitillo.
cigarette case *n* pitillera.
cigarette end *n* colilla.
cigarette holder *n* boquilla.
C in C *abbr* = **commander in chief**.
cinch [sinch] *n* (*sure thing*) cosa segura.
cinder block [sin'dûr blâk] *n* (*US*) ladrillo de cenizas.
Cinderella [sindərel'ə] *n* Cenicienta.
cinders [sin'dûrz] *npl* cenizas *fpl*.
cine-camera [sin'ēkamûrə] *n* (*Brit*) cámara cinematográfica.
cine-film [sin'ēfilm] *n* (*Brit*) película de cine.
cinema [sin'əmə] *n* cine *m*.
cinnamon [sin'əmən] *n* canela.
cipher [sī'fûr] *n* cifra; **in** ~ en clave.
circle [sûr'kəl] *n* círculo; (*in theater*) anfiteatro ♦ *vi* dar vueltas ♦ *vt* (*surround*) rodear, cercar; (*move around*) dar la vuelta a.
circuit [sûr'kit] *n* circuito; (*track*) pista; (*lap*) vuelta.
circuit board *n* tarjeta de circuitos impresos.
circuit court *n* (*US LAW*) tribunal *m* superior.
circuitous [sûrkyōō'itəs] *a* indirecto.
circular [sûr'kyəlûr] *a* circular ♦ *n* circular *f*; (*as advertisement*) panfleto.
circulate [sûr'kyəlāt] *vi* circular; (*person*: *socially*) alternar, circular ♦ *vt* poner en circulación.
circulation [sûrkyəlā'shən] *n* circulación *f*; (*of newspaper etc*) tirada.
circumcise [sûr'kəmsīz] *vt* circuncidar.
circumference [sûrkum'fûrəns] *n* circunferencia.
circumscribe [sûrkəmskrīb'] *vt* circunscribir.
circumspect [sûr'kəmspekt] *a* circunspecto, prudente.
circumstances [sûr'kəmstansiz] *npl* circunstancias *fpl*; (*financial condition*) situación *f* económica; **in the** ~ en *or* dadas las circunstancias; **under no** ~ de ninguna manera, bajo ningún concepto.
circumstantial [sûrkəmstan'shəl] *a* detallado; ~ **evidence** prueba indiciaria.
circumvent [sûrkəmvent'] *vt* (*rule etc*) burlar.
circus [sûr'kəs] *n* circo; (*also*: **C~**: *in place*

names) Plaza.
cistern [sis'tûrn] *n* tanque *m*, depósito; (*Brit*: *in toilet*) cisterna.
citation [sītā'shən] *n* cita; (*LAW*) citación *f*; (*MIL*) mención *f*.
cite [sīt] *vt* citar.
citizen [sit'əzən] *n* (*POL*) ciudadano/a; (*of city*) habitante *m/f*.
citizenship [sit'əzənship] *n* ciudadanía.
citric [sit'rik] *a*: ~ **acid** ácido cítrico.
citrus fruits [sit'rəs frōōtz] *npl* agrios *mpl*.
city [sit'ē] *n* ciudad *f*; **the C~** *centro financiero de Londres*.
city center *n* centro de la ciudad.
city hall *n* (*US*) ayuntamiento.
city plan *n* (*US*) plano de la ciudad.
city planner *n* (*US*) urbanista *m/f*.
city planning *n* (*US*) urbanismo.
civic [siv'ik] *a* cívico, municipal.
civil [siv'əl] *a* civil; (*polite*) atento, cortés/esa; (*well-bred*) educado.
civil defense *n* protección *f* civil.
civil engineer *n* ingeniero/a de caminos.
civil engineering *n* ingeniería de caminos.
civilian [sivil'yən] *a* civil (*no militar*) ♦ *n* civil *m/f*, paisano/a.
civilization [sivələzā'shən] *n* civilización *f*.
civilized [siv'əlīzd] *a* civilizado.
civil law *n* derecho civil.
civil rights *npl* derechos *mpl* civiles.
civil servant *n* funcionario/a del Estado.
Civil Service *n* administración *f* pública.
civil war *n* guerra civil.
cl *abbr* (= *centiliter*) cl.
clad [klad] *a*: ~ (**in**) vestido (de).
claim [klām] *vt* exigir, reclamar; (*rights etc*) reivindicar; (*assert*) pretender ♦ *vi* (*for insurance*) reclamar ♦ *n* (*for expenses*) reclamación *f*; (*LAW*) demanda; (*pretension*) pretensión *f*; **to put in a** ~ **for sth** presentar una demanda por algo.
claimant [klā'mənt] *n* (*ADMIN, LAW*) demandante *m/f*.
claim form *n* solicitud *f*.
clairvoyant [klärvoi'ənt] *n* clarividente *m/f*.
clam [klam] *n* almeja.
clam up *vi* (*col*) cerrar el pico.
clamber [klam'bûr] *vi* trepar.
clammy [klam'ē] *a* (*cold*) frío y húmedo; (*sticky*) pegajoso.
clamor, (*Brit*) **clamour** [klam'ûr] *n* (*noise*) clamor *m*, clamoreo; (*protest*) reclamación *f*, protesta ♦ *vi*: **to** ~ **for sth** clamar por algo, pedir algo a voces.
clamp [klamp] *n* abrazadera, grapa ♦ *vt* afianzar (con abrazadera).
clamp down on *vt fus* (*subj*: *government, police*) reforzar la lucha contra.
clan [klan] *n* clan *m*.
clandestine [klandes'tin] *a* clandestino.
clang [klang] *n* estruendo ♦ *vi* sonar, hacer estruendo.

clansman [klanz'mən] *n* miembro del clan.
clap [klap] *vi* aplaudir ♦ *vt* (*hands*) batir ♦ *n* (*of hands*) palmada; **to ~ one's hands** dar palmadas, batir las palmas; **a ~ of thunder** un trueno.
clapping [klap'ing] *n* aplausos *mpl*.
claret [klar'it] *n* vino tinto (de Burdeos).
clarification [klarəfəkā'shən] *n* aclaración *f*.
clarify [klar'əfī] *vt* aclarar.
clarinet [klarənet'] *n* clarinete *m*.
clarity [klar'itē] *n* claridad *f*.
clash [klash] *n* estruendo; (*fig*) choque *m* ♦ *vi* (*meet*) encontrarse; (*battle*) chocar; (*disagree*) estar en desacuerdo; (*dates, events*) coincidir.
clasp [klasp] *n* broche *m*; (*on jewels*) cierre *m* ♦ *vt* abrochar; (*hand*) apretar; (*embrace*) abrazar.
class [klas] *n* (*gen*) clase *f*; (*group, category*) clase *f*, categoría ♦ *cpd* clasista, de clase ♦ *vt* clasificar.
class-conscious [klas'kân'shəs] *a* clasista, con conciencia de clase.
classic [klas'ik] *a* clásico ♦ *n* (*work*) obra clásica; **~s** *npl* (*UNIV*) clásicas *fpl*.
classical [klas'ikəl] *a* clásico; **~ music** música clásica.
classification [klasəfəkā'shən] *n* clasificación *f*.
classified [klas'əfīd] *a* (*information*) reservado.
classified advertisement *n* anuncio por palabras.
classify [klas'əfī] *vt* clasificar.
classmate [klas'māt] *n* compañero/a de clase.
classroom [klas'rōōm] *n* aula.
classy [klas'ē] *a* (*col*) elegante, con estilo.
clatter [klat'ûr] *n* ruido, estruendo; (*of hooves*) trápala ♦ *vi* hacer ruido *or* estruendo.
clause [klôz] *n* cláusula; (*LING*) oración *f*.
claustrophobia [klôstrəfō'bēə] *n* claustrofobia.
claw [klô] *n* (*of cat*) uña; (*of bird of prey*) garra; (*of lobster*) pinza; (*TECH*) garfio ♦ *vi*: **to ~ at** arañar; (*tear*) desgarrar.
clay [klā] *n* arcilla.
clean [klēn] *a* limpio; (*clear*) neto, bien definido ♦ *vt* limpiar ♦ *ad*: **he ~ forgot** lo olvidó por completo; **to come ~** (*col: admit guilt*) confesarlo todo; **to have a ~ driver's license** tener el carnet de conducir sin sanciones; **to ~ one's teeth** (*Brit*) lavarse los dientes.
clean off *vt* limpiar.
clean out *vt* limpiar (a fondo).
clean up *vt* limpiar, asear ♦ *vi* (*fig: make profit*): **to ~ up on** sacar provecho de.
clean-cut [klēn'kut'] *a* (*person*) de buen parecer; (*clear*) nítido.
cleaner [klē'nûr] *n* (*woman*) mujer *f* de la

limpieza; (*also*: **dry ~**) tintorero/a.
cleaning [klē'ning] *n* limpieza.
cleaning lady *or* **woman** *n* señora de la limpieza, asistenta.
cleanliness [klen'lēnis] *n* limpieza.
cleanse [klenz] *vt* limpiar.
cleanser [klen'zûr] *n* detergente *m*; (*cosmetic*) loción *f or* crema limpiadora.
clean-shaven [klēn'shā'vən] *a* sin barba, lampiño.
cleansing department [klen'zing dipárt'mənt] *n* (*Brit*) departamento de limpieza.
clear [kli'ûr] *a* claro; (*road, way*) libre; (*profit*) neto; (*majority*) absoluto ♦ *vt* (*space*) despejar, limpiar; (*LAW: suspect*) absolver; (*obstacle*) salvar, saltar por encima de; (*debt*) liquidar; (*check*) pasar por un banco, aceptar; (*site, woodland*) desmontar ♦ *vi* (*fog etc*) despejarse ♦ *n*: **to be in the ~** (*out of debt*) estar libre de deudas; (*out of suspicion*) quedar fuera de toda sospecha; (*out of danger*) estar fuera de peligro ♦ *ad*: **~ of** a distancia de; **to make o.s. ~** explicarse claramente; **to make it ~ to sb that ...** hacer entender a uno que ...; **I have a ~ day tomorrow** mañana tengo el día libre; **to keep ~ of sth/sb** evitar algo/a uno; **to ~ a profit of ...** sacar una ganancia de ...; **to ~ the table** recoger *or* levantar la mesa.
clear off *vi* (*Brit*) = **clear out**.
clear out *vi* (*col: leave*) marcharse.
clear up *vt* limpiar; (*mystery*) aclarar, resolver.
clearance [klē'rəns] *n* (*removal*) despeje *m*; (*permission*) acreditación *f*.
clear-cut [kli'ûrkut'] *a* bien definido, nítido.
clearing [klē'ring] *n* (*in wood*) claro.
clearing bank *n* (*Brit*) banco central.
clearing house *n* (*COMM*) cámara de compensación.
clearly [kli'ûrlē] *ad* claramente.
clearway [klēr'wā] *n* (*Brit*) carretera donde no se puede aparcar.
cleaver [klē'vûr] *n* cuchilla (de carnicero).
clef [klef] *n* (*MUS*) clave *f*.
cleft [kleft] *n* (*in rock*) grieta, hendedura.
clemency [klem'ənsē] *n* clemencia.
clement [klem'ənt] *a* (*weather*) clemente, benigno.
clench [klench] *vt* apretar, cerrar.
clergy [klûr'jē] *n* clero.
clergyman [klûr'jēmən] *n* clérigo.
clerical [klär'ikəl] *a* de oficina; (*REL*) clerical; (*error*) de copia.
clerk [klûrk] *n* oficinista *m/f*; (*US*) dependiente/a *m/f*, vendedor(a) *m/f*; **C~ of the Court** escribano forense.
clever [klev'ûr] *a* (*mentally*) inteligente, listo; (*skillful*) hábil; (*device, arrangement*) ingenioso.
clew [klōō] *n* (*US*) = **clue**.

cliché [klēshā'] *n* cliché *m*, frase *f* hecha.
click [klik] *vt* (*tongue*) chasquear; (*heels*) taconear.
client [klī'ənt] *n* cliente *m/f*.
clientele [klīəntel'] *n* clientela.
cliff [klif] *n* acantilado.
cliffhanger [klif'hangûr] *n* (*TV*, *fig*) película *etc* de suspense.
climactic [klīmak'tik] *a* culminante.
climate [klī'mit] *n* clima *m*; (*fig*) ambiente *m*.
climax [klī'maks] *n* colmo, punto culminante; (*of play etc*) nudo, clímax *m*; (*sexual* ~) orgasmo.
climb [klīm] *vi* subir, trepar; (*plane*) elevarse, remontar el vuelo ♦ *vt* (*stairs*) subir; (*tree*) trepar a; (*mountain*) escalar ♦ *n* subida; **to** ~ **over a wall** franquear *or* salvar una tapia.
climb down *vi* (*fig*) volverse atrás.
climbdown [klīm'doun] *n* (*Brit*) vuelta atrás.
climber [klī'mûr] *n* alpinista *m/f*, montañista *m/f*, andinista *m/f* (*LAm*).
climbing [klī'ming] *n* alpinismo, andinismo (*LAm*).
clinch [klinch] *vt* (*deal*) cerrar; (*argument*) remachar.
cling, *pt*, *pp* **clung** [kling, klung] *vi*: **to** ~ **(to)** agarrarse (a); (*clothes*) pegarse (a).
clinic [klin'ik] *n* clínica.
clinical [klin'ikəl] *a* clínico; (*fig*) frío, impasible.
clink [klingk] *vi* tintinar.
clip [klip] *n* (*for hair*) horquilla; (*also*: **paper** ~) sujetapapeles *m inv*, clip *m*; (*clamp*) grapa ♦ *vt* (*cut*) cortar; (*hedge*) podar; (*also*: ~ **together**) unir.
clippers [klip'ûrz] *npl* (*for gardening*) tijeras *fpl*; (*for hair*) maquinilla *sg*; (*for nails*) cortaúñas *m inv*.
clipping [klip'ing] *n* (*from newspaper*) recorte *m*.
clique [klēk] *n* camarilla.
cloak [klōk] *n* capa, manto ♦ *vt* (*fig*) encubrir, disimular.
cloakroom [klōk'rōōm] *n* guardarropa *m*; (*Brit*: *WC*) lavabo, aseos *mpl*, baño (*LAm*).
clock [klâk] *n* reloj *m*; (*in taxi*) taxímetro; **to work against the** ~ trabajar contra reloj; **around the** ~ las veinticuatro horas; **to sleep round the** ~ dormir un día entero; **30,000 on the** ~ (*Brit AUT*) treinta mil millas en el cuentakilómetros.
clock in, clock on *vi* fichar, picar.
clock off, clock out *vi* fichar *or* picar la salida.
clock up *vt* acumular.
clockwise [klâk'wīz] *ad* en el sentido de las agujas del reloj.
clockwork [klâk'wûrk] *n* aparato de relojería ♦ *a* (*toy*, *train*) de cuerda.
clod [klâd] *n* (*col*) imbécil *m/f*.

clog [klâg] *n* zueco, chanclo ♦ *vt* atascar ♦ *vi* atascarse.
cloister [klois'tûr] *n* claustro.
clone [klōn] *n* clon *m*.
close *a*, *ad and derivatives* [klōs] *a* cercano, próximo; (*near*): ~ **(to)** cerca (de); (*print*, *weave*) tupido, compacto; (*friend*) íntimo; (*connection*) estrecho; (*examination*) detallado, minucioso; (*weather*) bochornoso; (*atmosphere*) sofocante; (*room*) mal ventilado ♦ *ad* cerca; ~ **by,** ~ **at hand** *a*, *ad* muy cerca; ~ **to** *prep* cerca de; **to have a** ~ **shave** (*fig*) escaparse por un pelo; **how** ~ **is Boston to New York?** ¿qué distancia hay de Boston a Nueva York?; **at** ~ **quarters** de cerca ♦ *vb and derivatives* [klōz] *vt* (*shut*) cerrar; (*end*) concluir, terminar; (*bargain*, *deal*) cerrar ♦ *vi* (*store etc*) cerrarse; (*end*) concluirse, terminarse ♦ *n* (*end*) fin *m*, final *m*, conclusión *f*; **to bring sth to a** ~ terminar algo.
close down *vi* cerrarse definitivamente.
close in *vi* (*hunters*) acercarse rodeando, rodear; (*evening*, *night*, *fog*) caer, cerrarse; **to** ~ **in on sb** rodear *or* cercar a uno; **the days are closing in** los días son cada vez más cortos.
close off *vt* (*area*) cerrar al tráfico *or* al público.
closed [klōzd] *a* (*store etc*) cerrado.
closed-circuit [klōzdsûr'kit] *a*: ~ **television** televisión *f* por circuito cerrado.
closed shop *n* taller *m* gremial.
close-knit [klōs'nit'] *a* (*fig*) muy unido.
closely [klōs'lē] *ad* (*study*) con detalle; (*listen*) con atención; (*watch*: *person*, *events*) de cerca; **we are** ~ **related** somos parientes cercanos; **a** ~ **guarded secret** un secreto rigurosamente guardado.
closet [klâz'it] *n* (*cupboard*) armario.
close-up [klōs'up] *n* primer plano.
closing [klō'zing] *a* (*stages*, *remarks*) último, final; ~ **price** (*STOCK EXCHANGE*) precio de cierre.
closure [klō'zhûr] *n* cierre *m*.
clot [klât] *n* (*gen*: *blood* ~) embolia; (*col*: *idiot*) imbécil *m/f* ♦ *vi* (*blood*) coagularse.
cloth [klôth] *n* (*material*) tela, paño; (*table* ~) mantel *m*; (*rag*) trapo.
clothe [klōth] *vt* vestir; (*fig*) revestir.
clothes [klōz] *npl* ropa *sg*; **to put one's** ~ **on** vestirse, ponerse la ropa; **to take one's** ~ **off** desvestirse, desnudarse.
clothes brush *n* cepillo (para la ropa).
clothes line *n* cuerda (para tender la ropa).
clothes pin, (*Brit*) **clothes peg** *n* pinza.
clothing [klō'thing] *n* = **clothes**.
clotted cream [klât'id krēm'] *n* (*Brit*) nata muy espesa.
cloud [kloud] *n* nube *f*; (*storm* ~) nubarrón *m*; (*of dust, smoke, gas*) nube *f* ♦ *vt*: (*liquid*) enturbiar; **every** ~ **has a silver lining**

no hay mal que por bien no venga; **to ~ the issue** empañar el problema.
cloud over vi (also fig) nublarse.
cloudburst [kloud'bûrst] n chaparrón m.
cloudland [kloud'land] n (US) Babia.
cloudy [klou'dē] a nublado, nubloso; (liquid) turbio.
clout [klout] n (fig) influencia ♦ vt dar un tortazo a.
clove [klōv] n clavo; **~ of garlic** diente m de ajo.
clover [klō'vûr] n trébol m.
clown [kloun] n payaso ♦ vi (also: **~ around**) hacer el payaso.
cloying [kloi'ing] a (taste) empalagoso.
C.L.U. n abbr (US) = Chartered Life Underwriter.
club [klub] n (society) club m; (weapon) porra, cachiporra; (also: **golf ~**) palo ♦ vt aporrear ♦ vi: **to ~ together** (join forces) unir fuerzas; **~s** npl (CARDS) tréboles mpl.
club car n (US RAIL) coche m salón.
clubhouse [klub'hous] n local social, sobre todo en clubs deportivos.
cluck [kluk] vi cloquear.
clue [kloo] n pista; (in crosswords) indicación f; **I haven't a ~** no tengo ni idea.
clued-in [klood'in] a (US col) al tanto, al corriente.
clued-up [klood'up] a (Brit col) = **clued-in**.
clump [klump] n (of trees) grupo.
clumsy [klum'zē] a (person) torpe, desmañado; (tool) difícil de manejar.
clung [klung] pt, pp of **cling**.
clunker [klunk'ûr] n (US: pej) pota, tartana.
cluster [klus'tûr] n grupo; (BOT) racimo ♦ vi agruparse, apiñarse.
clutch [kluch] n (AUT) embrague m; (pedal) pedal m de embrague; **to fall into sb's ~es** caer en las garras de alguien ♦ vt asir, agarrar.
clutter [klut'ûr] vt (also: **~ up**) atestar, llenar desordenadamente ♦ n desorden m, confusión f.
CM abbr (US MAIL) = North Mariana Islands.
cm abbr (= centimeter) cm.
CND n abbr (= Campaign for Nuclear Disarmament) plataforma pro desarme nuclear.
CO n abbr = **commanding officer** ♦ abbr (US MAIL) = Colorado.
Co. abbr = **county**; = **company**.
c/o abbr (= care of) c/a, a/c.
coach [kōch] n autocar m (Sp), autobús m; (horse-drawn) coche m; (of train) vagón m, coche m; (SPORT) entrenador(a) m/f, instructor(a) m/f ♦ vt (SPORT) entrenar; (student) preparar, enseñar.
coach trip n (Brit) excursión f en autocar.
coagulate [kōag'yəlāt] vi coagularse.
coal [kōl] n carbón m.
coalfield [kōl'fēld] n yacimiento de carbón.

coalition [kōəlish'ən] n coalición f.
coal man, coal merchant n carbonero.
coal mine n mina de carbón.
coal miner n minero (de carbón).
coal mining n minería (de carbón).
coarse [kôrs] a basto, burdo; (vulgar) grosero, ordinario.
coast [kōst] n costa, litoral m ♦ vi (AUT) ir en punto muerto.
coastal [kōs'təl] a costero, costanero.
coaster [kōs'tûr] n (drinks mat) posavasos m; (NAUT) buque m costero, barco de cabotaje.
coastguard [kōst'gârd] n guardacostas m inv.
coastline [kōst'līn] n litoral m.
coat [kōt] n (jacket) chaqueta; (overcoat) abrigo; (of animal) pelo, lana; (of paint) mano f, capa ♦ vt cubrir, revestir.
coated [kō'tid] a (tongue) saburroso.
coat hanger n percha, gancho (LAm).
coating [kō'ting] n capa, baño.
coat of arms n escudo de armas.
co-author [kōôth'ûr] n coautor(a) m/f.
coax [kōks] vt engatusar.
cob [kâb] n see **corn**.
cobbler [kâb'lûr] n zapatero (remendón).
cobble(stone)s [kâb'əl(stōn)z] npl adoquines mpl.
COBOL [kō'bôl] n COBOL m.
cobra [kōb'rə] n cobra.
cobweb [kâb'web] n telaraña.
cocaine [kōkān'] n cocaína.
cock [kâk] n (rooster) gallo; (male bird) macho ♦ vt (gun) amartillar.
cock-a-hoop [kâkəhoop'] a: **to be ~** estar más contento que unas pascuas.
cockatoo [kâk'ətoo] n cacatúa.
cockerel [kâk'ûrəl] n gallito.
cockeyed [kâk'īd] a bizco; (fig: crooked) torcido; (: idea) disparatado.
cockle [kâk'əl] n berberecho.
cockney [kâk'nē] n habitante m/f de ciertos barrios de Londres.
cockpit [kâk'pit] n (in aircraft) cabina.
cockroach [kâk'rōch] n cucaracha.
cocktail [kâk'tāl] n combinado, cóctel m; **shrimp** (US) or **prawn** (Brit) **~** cóctel m de gambas.
cocktail cabinet n mueble-bar m.
cocktail party n cóctel m, cóctel m.
cocktail shaker [kâk'tāl shā'kûr] n coctelera.
cocoa [kō'kō] n cacao; (drink) chocolate m.
coconut [kō'kənut] n coco.
cocoon [kəkoon'] n capullo.
cod [kâd] n bacalao.
COD abbr = **cash on delivery**; (US) = **collect on delivery**.
code [kōd] n código; (cipher) clave f; (TEL) prefijo; **~ of behavior** código de conducta; **~ of practice** código profesional.
codeine [kō'dēn] n codeína.

codicil [kâd'isəl] *n* codicilo.
codify [kâd'əfī] *vt* codificar.
cod-liver oil [kâd'livûr oil'] *n* aceite *m* de hígado de bacalao.
co-driver [kōdrī'vûr] *n* (*in race*) copiloto *m*/ *f*; (*of truck*) segundo conductor *m*.
co-ed [kōed'] *a abbr* = **coeducational** ♦ *n abbr* (*US*: = *female student*) *alumna de una universidad mixta*; (*Brit*: *school*) colegio mixto.
coeducational [kōejōōkā'shənəl] *a* mixto.
coerce [kōûrs'] *vt* forzar, coaccionar.
coercion [kōûr'shən] *n* coacción *f*.
coexistence [kōigzis'təns] *n* coexistencia.
C. of C. *n abbr* = **chamber of commerce.**
C of E *abbr* = **Church of England.**
coffee [kôf'ē] *n* café *m*; ~ **with cream,** (*Brit*) **white** ~ café con leche.
coffee bar *n* (*Brit*) cafetería.
coffee bean *n* grano de café.
coffee break *n* descanso (para tomar café).
coffee cup *n* taza de café.
coffeepot [kôf'ēpât] *n* cafetera.
coffee table *n* mesita (para servir el café).
coffin [kôf'in] *n* ataúd *m*.
cog [kâg] *n* diente *m*.
cogent [kō'jənt] *a* lógico, convincente.
cognac [kōn'yak] *n* coñac *m*.
cogwheel [kâg'hwēl] *n* rueda dentada.
cohabit [kōhab'it] *vi* (*formal*): **to** ~ **(with sb)** cohabitar (con uno).
coherent [kōhē'rənt] *a* coherente.
cohesion [kōhē'zhən] *n* cohesión *f*.
cohesive [kōhē'siv] *a* (*fig*) cohesivo, unido.
coil [koil] *n* rollo; (*rope*) aduja; (*of smoke*) espiral *f*; (*AUT, ELEC*) bobina, carrete *m*; (*contraceptive*) espiral *f* ♦ *vt* enrollar, arrollar.
coin [koin] *n* moneda ♦ *vt* acuñar; (*word*) inventar, idear.
coinage [koi'nij] *n* moneda.
coin-box [koin'bâks] *n* (*Brit*) caja recaudadora.
coincide [kōinsīd'] *vi* coincidir; (*agree*) estar de acuerdo.
coincidence [kōin'sidəns] *n* casualidad *f*.
coin-operated [koinâp'ərātid] *a* (*machine*) de meter moneda.
Coke ® [kōk] *n* Coca Cola ® *f*.
coke [kōk] *n* (*coal*) coque *m*.
Col. *abbr* (*US*) = *Colorado*; (= *colonel*) col.
COLA *n abbr* (*US*: = *cost-of-living adjustment*) *reajuste salarial de acuerdo con el costo de la vida*.
colander [kâl'əndûr] *n* colador *m*, escurridor *m*.
cold [kōld] *a* frío ♦ *n* frío; (*MED*) resfriado; **it's** ~ hace frío; **to be** ~ tener frío; **to catch a** ~ coger un catarro, resfriarse, acatarrarse; **in** ~ **blood** a sangre fría; **the room's getting** ~ está empezando a hacer

frío en la habitación; **to give sb the** ~ **shoulder** tratar a uno con frialdad.
cold-blooded [kōld'blud'id] *a* (*ZOOL*) de sangre fría.
cold cream *n* crema.
cold cuts *npl* fiambres *mpl*.
coldly [kōld'lē] *a* fríamente.
cold sore *n* herpes *m* labial.
coleslaw [kōl'slô] *n* ensalada de col.
colic [kâl'ik] *n* cólico.
collaborate [kəlab'ərāt] *vi* colaborar.
collaboration [kəlabərā'shən] *n* colaboración *f*; (*POL*) colaboracionismo.
collaborator [kəlab'ərātûr] *n* colaborador(a) *m*/*f*; (*POL*) colaboracionista *m*/*f*.
collage [kəlâzh'] *n* collage *m*.
collagen [kâl'əjən] *n* colágeno.
collapse [kəlaps'] *vi* (*gen*) hundirse, derrumbarse; (*MED*) sufrir un colapso ♦ *n* (*gen*) hundimiento; (*MED*) colapso; (*of government*) caída; (*of plans, scheme, business*) ruina, fracaso.
collapsible [kəlaps'əbəl] *a* plegable.
collar [kâl'ûr] *n* (*of coat, shirt*) cuello; (*for dog, TECH*) collar *m* ♦ *vt* (*col: person, object*) abordar, acorralar.
collarbone [kâl'ûrbōn] *n* clavícula.
collate [kəlāt'] *vt* cotejar.
collateral [kəlat'ûrəl] *n* (*COMM*) garantía colateral.
collation [kəlā'shən] *n* colación *f*.
colleague [kâl'ēg] *n* colega *m*/*f*.
collect [kəlekt'] *vt* reunir; (*as a hobby*) coleccionar; (*Brit: call and pick up*) recoger; (*wages*) cobrar; (*debts*) recaudar; (*donations, subscriptions*) colectar ♦ *vi* reunirse; coleccionar ♦ *ad*: **to call** ~ (*US TEL*) llamar a cobro revertido; **to** ~ **one's thoughts** reponerse, recobrar el dominio de sí mismo; ~ **on delivery (COD)** (*US*) entrega contra reembolso.
collect call *n* (*US TEL*) llamada a cobro revertido.
collection [kəlek'shən] *n* colección *f*; (*of fares, wages*) cobro; (*of mail*) recogida.
collective [kəlek'tiv] *a* colectivo.
collective bargaining *n* negociación *f* del convenio colectivo.
collector [kəlek'tûr] *n* coleccionista *m*/*f*; (*of taxes etc*) recaudador(a) *m*/*f*; ~**'s item** *or* **piece** pieza de coleccionista.
college [kâl'ij] *n* colegio; (*of technology, agriculture etc*) escuela.
collide [kəlīd'] *vi* chocar.
collie [kâl'ē] *n* (*dog*) collie *m*.
colliery [kâl'yûrē] *n* (*Brit*) mina de carbón.
collision [kəlizh'ən] *n* choque *m*; **to be on a** ~ **course** (*also fig*) ir rumbo al desastre.
colloquial [kəlō'kwēəl] *a* familiar, coloquial.
collusion [kəlōō'zhən] *n* confabulación *f*, connivencia; **in** ~ **with** en connivencia con.
Colo. *abbr* (*US*) = *Colorado*.
cologne [kəlōn'] *n* (*also*: **eau de** ~) (agua

de) colonia.
Colombia [kəlum'bēə] n Colombia.
Colombian [kəlum'bēən] a, n colombiano/a m/f.
colon [kō'lən] n (sign) dos puntos; (MED) colón m.
colonel [kûr'nəl] n coronel m.
colonial [kəlō'nēəl] a colonial.
colonize [kâl'ənīz] vt colonizar.
colonnade [kâlənād'] n columnata.
colony [kâl'ənē] n colonia.
color [kul'ûr] (US) n color m ♦ vt color(e)ar; (with crayons) color(e)ar (al pastel); (dye) teñir ♦ vi (blush) sonrojarse; ~s npl (of party, club) colores mpl.
Colorado beetle [kâlərá'dō bē'təl] n escarabajo de la patata.
color bar n segregación f racial.
color-blind [kul'ûrblīnd] a daltoniano.
colored [kul'ûrd] a de color; (photo) en color; (of race) de color.
color film n película en color.
colorful [kul'ûrfəl] a lleno de color; (person) excéntrico.
coloring [kul'ûring] n (complexion) colorido, color; (substance) colorante m.
colorless [kul'ûrlis] a incoloro, sin color.
color scheme n combinación f de colores.
color television n televisión f en color.
colossal [kəlâs'əl] a colosal.
colour [kul'ûr] etc (Brit) = **color** etc.
colt [kōlt] n potro.
column [kâl'əm] n columna; (fashion ~, sports ~ etc) sección f; **the editorial** ~ el editorial, el artículo de fondo.
columnist [kâl'əmist] n columnista m/f.
coma [kō'mə] n coma m.
comb [kōm] n peine m; (ornamental) peineta ♦ vt (hair) peinar; (area) registrar a fondo.
combat n [kâm'bat] combate m ♦ vt [kəmbat'] combatir.
combination [kâmbənā'shən] n (gen) combinación f.
combination lock n cerradura de combinación.
combine [kəmbīn'] vt combinar; (qualities) reunir ♦ vi combinarse ♦ n [kâm'bīn] (ECON) cartel m; **a ~d effort** un esfuerzo conjunto.
combine (harvester) n cosechadora.
combo [kâm'bō] n (JAZZ etc) conjunto.
combustion [kəmbus'chən] n combustión f.
come [kum], pt came, pp come vi venir; **to ~ undone** desatarse; **to ~ loose** aflojarse; **~ with me** ven conmigo; **we've just ~ from Seville** acabamos de llegar de Sevilla; **coming!** ¡voy!; **if it ~s to it** llegado el caso.
come about vi suceder, ocurrir.
come across vt fus (person) topar con; (thing) dar con ♦ vi: **to ~ across well/badly** caer bien/mal.

come around vi (after faint, operation) volver en sí.
come away vi marcharse; (become detached) desprenderse.
come back vi volver; (reply): **can I ~ back to you on that one?** ¡volvamos sobre ese punto!
come by vt fus (acquire) conseguir.
come down vi bajar; (buildings) derrumbarse; (: be demolished) ser derribado.
come forward vi presentarse.
come from vt fus ser de.
come in vi entrar; (train) llegar; (fashion) ponerse de moda.
come in for vt fus (criticism etc) merecer.
come into vt fus (money) heredar.
come off vi (button) soltarse, desprenderse; (succeed) salir bien.
come on vi (pupil, work, project) desarrollarse; (lights) encenderse; **~ on!** ¡vamos!
come out vi salir; (book) aparecer; (be revealed) salir a luz; (strike) declararse en huelga; **to ~ out for/against** declararse por/en contra de.
come over vt fus: **I don't know what's ~ over him!** ¡no sé lo que le pasa!
come round vi (Brit) = **come around**.
come through vi (survive) sobrevivir; (telephone call): **the call came through** recibimos la llamada.
come to vi volver en sí; (total) sumar; **how much does it ~ to?** ¿cuánto es en total?, ¿a cuánto asciende?
come under vt fus (heading) entrar en; (influence) estar bajo.
come up vi subir; (sun) salir; (problem) surgir.
come up against vt fus (resistance, difficulties) tropezar con.
come up to vt fus llegar hasta; **the film didn't ~ up to our expectations** la película no fue tan buena como esperábamos.
come up with vt fus (idea) sugerir, proponer.
come upon vt fus dar or topar con.
comeback [kum'bak] n (reaction) reacción f; (response) réplica; **to make a ~** (THEATER) volver a las tablas.
Comecon [kâm'əkân] n abbr (= Council for Mutual Economic Aid) COMECON m.
comedian [kəmē'dēən] n cómico.
comedienne [kəmēdēen'] n cómica.
comedown [kum'doun] n revés m, bajón m.
comedy [kâm'idē] n comedia.
comet [kâm'it] n cometa m.
comeuppance [kumup'əns] n: **to get one's ~** llevar su merecido.
comfort [kum'fûrt] n comodidad f, confort m; (well-being) bienestar m; (solace)

consuelo; (*relief*) alivio ♦ *vt* consolar; *see also* **comforts.**

comfortable [kum'fûrtəbəl] *a* cómodo; (*income*) adecuado; (*majority*) suficiente; **I don't feel very ~ about it** la cosa me trae algo preocupado.

comfortably [kum'fûrtəblē] *ad* (*sit*) cómodamente; (*live*) holgadamente.

comforter [kum'fûrtûr] *n* (*US:* bed cover) colcha.

comforts [kum'fûrts] *npl* comodidades *fpl.*

comfort station *n* (*US*) servicios *mpl.*

comic [kâm'ik] *a* (*also:* ~**al**) cómico, gracioso ♦ *n* (*magazine*) tebeo; (*for adults*) cómic *m.*

comic strip *n* tira cómica.

coming [kum'ing] *n* venida, llegada ♦ *a* que viene; (*next*) próximo; (*future*) venidero; ~**(s) and going(s)** *n*(*pl*) ir y venir *m*, ajetreo; **in the ~ weeks** en las próximas semanas.

Comintern [kâm'intûrn] *n* Comintern *f.*

comma [kâm'ə] *n* coma.

command [kəmand'] *n* orden *f*, mandato; (*MIL:* authority) mando; (*mastery*) dominio; (*COMPUT*) orden *f*, comando ♦ *vt* (*troops*) mandar; (*give orders to*) mandar, ordenar; (*be able to get*) disponer de; (*deserve*) merecer; **to have at one's ~** (*money, resources etc*) tener disponible *or* a su disposición; **to have/take ~ of** estar al/asumir el mando de.

commandeer [kâməndēr'] *vt* requisar.

commander [kəman'dûr] *n* (*MIL*) comandante *m/f*, jefe/a *m/f*; ~ **in chief** jefe *m* supremo.

commanding [kəman'ding] *a* (*appearance*) imponente; (*voice, tone*) imperativo; (*lead, position*) abrumador(a), dominante.

commanding officer *n* comandante *m.*

commandment [kəmand'mənt] *n* (*REL*) mandamiento.

command module *n* módulo de comando.

commando [kəman'dō] *n* comando.

commemorate [kəmem'ərāt] *vt* conmemorar.

commemoration [kəmemərā'shən] *n* conmemoración *f.*

commemorative [kəmem'ərātiv] *a* conmemorativo.

commence [kəmens'] *vt*, *vi* comenzar, empezar.

commend [kəmend'] *vt* (*praise*) elogiar, alabar; (*recommend*) recomendar; (*entrust*) encomendar.

commendable [kəmend'əbəl] *a* encomiable; **it is ~ that** ... está muy bien que ...

commendation [kâməndā'shən] *n* (*for bravery etc*) elogio, encomio; recomendación *f.*

commensurate [kəmen'sərit] *a*: ~ **with** en proporción a, que corresponde a.

comment [kâm'ent] *n* comentario ♦ *vt*: **to ~ that** comentar *or* observar que ♦ *vi*: **to ~ (on)** comentar, hacer comentarios (sobre); **"no ~"** "no tengo nada que decir".

commentary [kâm'əntārē] *n* comentario.

commentator [kâm'əntātûr] *n* comentarista *m/f.*

commerce [kâm'ûrs] *n* comercio.

commercial [kəmûr'shəl] *a* comercial ♦ *n* (*TV: also:* ~ **break**) anuncio.

commercial bank *n* banco comercial.

commercialism [kəmûr'shəlizəm] *n* materialismo.

commercialize [kəmûr'shəlīz] *vt* comercializar.

commercial television *n* televisión *f* comercial.

commercial vehicle *n* vehículo comercial.

commiserate [kəmiz'ərāt] *vi*: **to ~ with** compadecerse de, condolerse de.

commission [kəmish'ən] *n* (*committee, fee, order for work of art etc*) comisión *f*; (*act*) perpetración *f* ♦ *vt* (*MIL*) nombrar; (*work of art*) encargar; **out of ~** (*machine*) fuera de servicio; **I get 10% ~** me dan el diez por ciento de comisión; **to ~ sb to do sth** encargar a uno que haga algo; **to ~ sth from sb** (*painting etc*) encargar algo a uno.

commissionaire [kəmishənâr'] *n* (*Brit*) portero.

commissioner [kəmish'ənûr] *n* comisario; (*POLICE*) comisario *m* de policía.

commit [kəmit'] *vt* (*act*) cometer; (*to sb's care*) entregar; **to ~ o.s. (to do)** comprometerse (a hacer); **to ~ suicide** suicidarse; **to ~ sb for trial** remitir a uno al tribunal.

commitment [kəmit'mənt] *n* compromiso.

committed [kəmit'id] *a* (*writer, politician etc*) comprometido.

committee [kəmit'ē] *n* comité *m*; **to be on a ~** ser miembro/a de un comité.

committee meeting *n* reunión *f* del comité.

commodious [kəmō'dēəs] *a* grande, espacioso.

commodity [kəmâd'itē] *n* mercancía.

commodity exchange *n* bolsa de productos *or* de mercancías.

commodity market *n* mercado de productos básicos.

commodore [kâm'ədôr] *n* comodoro.

common [kâm'ən] *a* (*gen*) común; (*pej*) ordinario ♦ *n* campo común; **in ~** en común; **in ~ use** de uso corriente.

commoner [kâm'ənûr] *n* plebeyo/a.

common law *n* ley *f* consuetudinaria.

common-law [kâm'ənlô'] *a*: ~ **wife** esposa consensual.

commonly [kâm'ənlē] *ad* comúnmente.

Common Market *n* Mercado Común.

commonplace [kâm'ənplās] *a* de lo más

común.

common room *n* (*Brit*) sala común.

Commons [kâm'ɔnz] *npl* (*Brit POL*): **the (House of)** ~ (la Cámara de) los Comunes.

commons [kâm'ɔnz] *n* (*US UNIV*) comedor *m*.

common sense *n* sentido común.

Commonwealth [kâm'ɔnwelth] *n*: **the** ~ la Mancomunidad (Británica).

commotion [kəmō'shən] *n* tumulto, confusión *f*.

communal [kəmyōō'nəl] *a* comunal.

commune *n* [kâm'yōōn] (*group*) comuna ♦ *vi* [kəmyōōn'] : **to** ~ **with** comulgar *or* conversar con.

communicate [kəmyōō'nikāt] *vt* comunicar ♦ *vi*: **to** ~ **(with)** comunicarse (con).

communication [kəmyōōnikā'shən] *n* comunicación *f*.

communication cord *n* (*Brit*) timbre *m* de alarma.

communications network *n* red *f* de comunicaciones.

communications satellite *n* satélite *m* de comunicaciones.

communicative [kəmyōō'nikātiv] *a* comunicativo.

communion [kəmyōōn'yən] *n* (*also*: **Holy C~**) comunión *f*.

communiqué [kəmyōōnikā'] *n* comunicado, parte *m*.

communism [kâm'yənizəm] *n* comunismo.

communist [kâm'yənist] *a*, *n* comunista *m/f*.

community [kəmyōō'nitē] *n* comunidad *f*; (*large group*) colectividad *f*; (*local*) vecindario.

community center *n* centro social.

community chest *n* (*US*) arca comunitaria, fondo común.

community health center *n* centro médico, dispensario público.

community spirit *n* civismo.

commutation ticket [kâmyətā'shən tik'it] *n* (*US*) billete *m* de abono.

commute [kəmyōōt'] *vi* viajar a diario de la casa al trabajo ♦ *vt* conmutar.

commuter [kəmyōōt'úr] *n* persona (que ...: *see vi*).

compact *a* [kəmpakt'] compacto; (*style*) conciso; (*packed*) apretado ♦ *n* [kâm'pakt] (*pact*) pacto; (*also*: **powder** ~) polvera.

compact disc *n* compact disc *m*.

companion [kəmpan'yən] *n* compañero/a.

companionship [kəmpan'yənship] *n* compañerismo.

companionway [kəmpan'yənwā] *n* (*NAUT*) escalera de cámara.

company [kum'pənē] *n* (*gen*) compañía; (*COMM*) sociedad *f*, compañía; **to keep sb** ~ acompañar a uno; **Smith and C~** Smith y Compañía.

company car *n* coche *m* de la compañía.

company director *n* director(a) *m/f* de empresa.

company secretary *n* (*Brit*) secretario/a de compañía.

comparable [kâm'pûrəbəl] *a* comparable.

comparative [kəmpar'ətiv] *a* (*freedom, luxury, cost*) relativo.

comparatively [kəmpar'ətivlē] *ad* (*relatively*) relativamente.

compare [kəmpär'] *vt* comparar; (*set side by side*) cotejar ♦ *vi*: **to** ~ **(with)** compararse (con); **~d with** *or* **to** comparado con *or* a; **how do the prices** ~? ¿cómo se comparan los precios?

comparison [kəmpar'isən] *n* comparación *f*; cotejo; **in** ~ **(with)** en comparación (con).

compartment [kəmpârt'mənt] *n* (*also RAIL*) departamento.

compass [kum'pəs] *n* brújula; **~es** *npl* compás *m*; **within the** ~ **of** al alcance de.

compassion [kəmpash'ən] *n* compasión *f*.

compassionate [kəmpash'ənit] *a* compasivo; **on** ~ **grounds** por compasión.

compatibility [kəmpatəbil'ətē] *n* compatibilidad *f*.

compatible [kəmpat'əbəl] *a* compatible.

compel [kəmpel'] *vt* obligar.

compelling [kəmpel'ing] *a* (*fig*: *argument*) convincente.

compendium [kəmpen'dēəm] *n* compendio.

compensate [kâm'pənsāt] *vt* compensar ♦ *vi*: **to** ~ **for** compensar.

compensation [kâmpənsā'shən] *n* (*for loss*) indemnización *f*.

compère [kâmpär'] *n* presentador(a) *m/f*.

compete [kəmpēt'] *vi* (*take part*) tomar parte, concurrir; (*vie with*) competir, hacer competencia.

competence [kâm'pitəns] *n* capacidad *f*, aptitud *f*.

competent [kâm'pitənt] *a* competente, capaz.

competition [kâmpitish'ən] *n* (*contest*) concurso; (*ECON, rivalry*) competencia; **in** ~ **with** en competencia con.

competitive [kəmpet'ətiv] *a* (*ECON, SPORT*) competitivo; (*spirit*) competidor(a), de competencia.

competitor [kəmpet'itûr] *n* (*rival*) competidor(a) *m/f*, contrincante *m/f*; (*participant*) concursante *m/f*.

compile [kəmpīl'] *vt* recopilar.

complacency [kəmplā'sənsē] *n* autosatisfacción *f*.

complacent [kəmplā'sənt] *a* autocomplaciente.

complain [kəmplān'] *vi* (*gen*) quejarse; (*COMM*) reclamar.

complaint [kəmplānt'] *n* (*gen*) queja; reclamación *f*; (*LAW*) demanda, querella; (*MED*) enfermedad *f*.

complement *n* [kâm'pləmənt] comple-

mento; (*esp ship's crew*) dotación *f* ♦ *vt*
[kám'pləmənt] (*enhance*) complementar.
complementary [kámpləmen'tûrē] *a* complementario.
complete [kəmplēt'] *a* (*full*) completo;
(*finished*) acabado ♦ *vt* (*fulfil*) completar;
(*finish*) acabar; (*a form*) rellenar; **it's a ~
disaster** es un desastre total.
completely [kəmplēt'lē] *ad* completamente.
completion [kəmplē'shən] *n* (*gen*) conclusión *f*, terminación *f*; **to be nearing ~**
estar por *or* para terminarse; **on ~ of contract** cuando se realice el contrato.
complex [kâm'plɛks] *a* complejo ♦ *n* (*gen*)
complejo.
complexion [kəmplɛk'shən] *n* (*of face*) tez
f, cutis *m*; (*fig*) aspecto.
complexity [kəmplɛk'sitē] *n* complejidad *f*.
compliance [kəmplī'əns] *n* (*submission*) sumisión *f*; (*agreement*) conformidad *f*; **in ~
with** de acuerdo con.
compliant [kəmplī'ənt] *a* sumiso; conforme.
complicate [kâm'pləkāt] *vt* complicar.
complicated [kâm'pləkātid] *a* complicado.
complication [kámpləkā'shən] *n* complicación *f*.
complicity [kəmplis'ətē] *n* complicidad *f*.
compliment *n* [kâm'pləmənt] (*formal*)
cumplido; (*flirtation*) piropo ♦ *vt*
[kâm'pləmənt] felicitar; **~s** *npl* saludos
mpl; **to pay sb a ~** (*formal*) hacer cumplidos a alguien; (*flirt*) piropear, echar piropos a alguien; **~ sb (on sth/on doing sth)**
felicitar a uno (por algo/por haber hecho
algo).
complimentary [kámpləmɛn'tûrē] *a* lisonjero; (*free*) de favor.
compliments card , (*Brit*) **compliments
slip** *n* saluda *m*.
comply [kəmplī'] *vi*: **to ~ with** cumplir
con.
component [kəmpō'nənt] *a* componente ♦ *n*
(*TECH*) pieza.
compose [kəmpōz'] *vt* componer; **to be ~d
of** componerse de, constar de; **to ~ o.s.**
tranquilizarse.
composed [kəmpōzd'] *a* sosegado.
composer [kəmpō'zûr] *n* (*MUS*) compositor(a) *m/f*.
composite [kəmpáz'it] *a* compuesto; **~ motion** (*COMM*) moción *f* compuesta.
composition [kámpəzish'ən] *n* composición
f.
compositor [kəmpáz'itûr] *n* (*TYP*) cajista
m/f.
compos mentis [kâm'pəs mɛn'tis] *a*: **to be
~** estar en su sano juicio.
compost [kâm'pōst] *n* abono.
compost heap *n* montón *de basura vegetal para abono*.
composure [kəmpō'zhûr] *n* serenidad *f*,
calma.
compound [kâm'pound] *n* (*CHEM*)

compuesto; (*LING*) palabra compuesta;
(*enclosure*) recinto ♦ *a* (*gen*) compuesto;
(*fracture*) complicado ♦ *vt* [kəmpound']
(*fig: problem, difficulty*) agravar.
comprehend [kámprihend'] *vt* comprender.
comprehension [kámprihen'shən] *n* comprensión *f*.
comprehensive [kámprihen'siv] *a* (*broad*)
extenso; (*general*) de conjunto; **~ (school)**
n (*Brit*) centro estatal de enseñanza secundaria; ≈ Instituto Nacional de Bachillerato (*Sp*).
comprehensive insurance policy *n* seguro a todo riesgo.
compress *vt* [kəmpres'] comprimir ♦ *n*
[kâm'pres] (*MED*) compresa.
compression [kəmpresh'ən] *n* compresión
f.
comprise [kəmprīz'] *vt* (*also:* **be ~d of**)
comprender, constar de.
compromise [kâm'prəmīz] *n* (*agreement*)
arreglo ♦ *vt* comprometer ♦ *vi* transigir ♦
cpd (*decision, solution*) de término medio.
compulsion [kəmpul'shən] *n* obligación *f*;
under ~ a la fuerza, por obligación.
compulsive [kəmpul'siv] *a* compulsivo.
compulsory [kəmpul'sûrē] *a* obligatorio.
compulsory purchase *n* adquisición *f*
forzosa.
compunction [kəmpungk'shən] *n* escrúpulo; **to have no ~ about doing sth** no tener
escrúpulos acerca de hacer algo.
computer [kəmpyoo'tûr] *n* ordenador *m*,
computador *m*, computadora.
computerize [kəmpyoo'tərīz] *vt* (*data*)
computerizar; (*system*) informatizar.
computer language *n* lenguaje *m* de
computadora.
computer peripheral *n* periférico.
computer program *n* programa *m*
informático.
computer programmer *n* programador(a) *m/f*.
computer programming *n* programación *f*.
computer science *n* informática.
computer virus *n* virus *m* informático.
computing [kəmpyoo'ting] *n* (*activity*)
informática.
comrade [kâm'rad] *n* compañero/a.
comradeship [kâm'rədship] *n* camaradería,
compañerismo.
comsat [kâm'sat] *n* *abbr* = **communications
satellite**.
con [kân] *vt* estafar ♦ *n* estafa; **to ~ sb into
doing sth** (*col*) convencer a uno por engaño de que haga algo.
concave [kânkāv'] *a* cóncavo.
conceal [kənsēl'] *vt* ocultar; (*thoughts etc*)
disimular.
concede [kənsēd'] *vt* conceder ♦ *vi* ceder,
darse por vencido.
conceit [kənsēt'] *n* presunción *f*.

conceited [kənsē'tid] *a* presumido.
conceivable [kənsēv'əbəl] *a* concebible; **it is ~ that ...** es posible que ....
conceivably [kənsēv'əblē] *ad:* **he may ~ be right** es posible que tenga razón.
conceive [kənsēv'] *vt, vi* concebir; **to ~ of sth/of doing sth** imaginar algo/imaginarse haciendo algo.
concentrate [kân'səntrāt] *vi* concentrarse ♦ *vt* concentrar.
concentration [kânsəntrā'shən] *n* concentración *f*.
concentration camp *n* campo de concentración.
concentric [kənsen'trik] *a* concéntrico.
concept [kân'sept] *n* concepto.
conception [kənsep'shən] *n* (*idea*) concepto, idea; (*BIOL*) concepción *f*.
concern [kənsûrn'] *n* (*matter*) asunto; (*COMM*) empresa; (*anxiety*) preocupación *f* ♦ *vt* tener que ver con; **to be ~ed (about)** interesarse (por), preocuparse (por); **to be ~ed with** tratar de; **"to whom it may ~"** "a quien corresponda"; **the department ~ed** (*under discussion*) el departamento en cuestión; (*relevant*) el departamento competente; **as far as I am ~ed** en cuanto a mí, por lo que a mí se refiere.
concerning [kənsûr'ning] *prep* sobre, acerca de.
concert [kân'sûrt] *n* concierto.
concerted [kənsûr'tid] *a* (*efforts etc*) concertado.
concert hall *n* sala de conciertos.
concertina [kânsûrtē'nə] *n* concertina.
concertmaster [kân'sûrtmastûr] *n* (*US*) primer violín *m*.
concerto [kənchär'tō] *n* concierto.
concession [kənsesh'ən] *n* concesión *f*; **tax ~** privilegio fiscal.
concessionaire [kənseshənär'] *n* concesionario/a.
concessionary [kənsesh'ənärē] *a* (*ticket, fare*) concesionario.
conciliation [kənsilēā'shən] *n* conciliación *f*.
conciliatory [kənsil'ēətôrē] *a* conciliador(a).
concise [kənsīs'] *a* conciso.
conclave [kân'klāv] *n* cónclave *m*.
conclude [kənklōōd'] *vt* (*finish*) concluir; (*treaty etc*) firmar; (*agreement*) llegar a; (*decide*): **to ~ that ...** llegar a la conclusión de que ... ♦ *vi* (*events*) terminarse.
conclusion [kənklōō'zhən] *n* conclusión *f*; **to come to the ~ that** llegar a la conclusión de que.
conclusive [kənklōō'siv] *a* decisivo, concluyente.
conclusively [kənklōō'sivlē] *ad* concluyentemente.
concoct [kənkâkt'] *vt* (*gen*) confeccionar; (*plot*) tramar.
concoction [kənkâk'shən] *n* (*food, drink*) confección *f*.

concord [kân'kôrd] *n* (*harmony*) concordia; (*treaty*) acuerdo.
concourse [kân'kôrs] *n* (*hall*) vestíbulo.
concrete [kân'krēt] *n* hormigón *m* ♦ *a* concreto.
concrete mixer *n* hormigonera.
concur [kənkûr'] *vi* estar de acuerdo, asentir.
concurrently [kənkûr'əntlē] *ad* al mismo tiempo.
concussion [kənkush'ən] *n* conmoción *f* cerebral.
condemn [kəndem'] *vt* condenar.
condemnation [kândemnā'shən] *n* (*gen*) condena; (*blame*) censura.
condensation [kândensā'shən] *n* condensación *f*.
condense [kəndens'] *vi* condensarse ♦ *vt* condensar, abreviar.
condensed milk [kəndenst' milk'] *n* leche *f* condensada.
condescend [kândisend'] *vi* condescender, dignarse; **to ~ to do sth** dignarse hacer algo.
condescending [kândisen'ding] *a* condescendiente.
condition [kəndish'ən] *n* condición *f*; (*disease*) enfermedad *f* ♦ *vt* condicionar; **on ~ that** a condición (de) que; **weather ~s** condiciones atmosféricas; **in good/poor ~** en buenas/malas condiciones; **~s of sale** condiciones de venta.
conditional [kəndish'ənəl] *a* condicional.
conditioned reflex [kəndish'ənd rē'fleks] *n* reflejo condicionado.
conditioner [kəndish'ənûr] *n* (*for hair*) acondicionador *m*.
condolences [kəndō'lənsiz] *npl* pésame *msg*.
condom [kân'dəm] *n* condón *m*.
condo(minium) [kân'dō(min'ēəm)] *n* (*US*) condominio.
condone [kəndōn'] *vt* condonar.
conducive [kəndōō'siv] *a*: **~ to** conducente a.
conduct *n* [kân'dukt] conducta, comportamiento ♦ [kəndukt'] *vt* (*lead*) conducir; (*manage*) llevar, dirigir; (*MUS*) dirigir ♦ *vi* (*MUS*) llevar la batuta; **to ~ o.s.** comportarse.
conductor [kənduk'tûr] *n* (*of orchestra*) director(a) *m/f*; (*US: on train*) revisor(a) *m/f*; (*on bus*) cobrador *m*; (*ELEC*) conductor *m*.
conductress [kənduk'tris] *n* (*on bus*) cobradora.
cone [kōn] *n* cono; (*pine ~*) piña; (*for ice-cream*) barquillo.
confectioner [kənfek'shənûr] *n* (*of cakes*) pastelero/a; (*of sweets*) confitero/a; **~'s (shop)** *n* pastelería; confitería.
confectioner's sugar [kənfek'shənûrz shōog'ûr] *n* (*US*) azúcar *m* glas(eado).

confectionery [kənfek'shənärē] *n* pasteles *mpl*; dulces *mpl*.

confederate [kənfed'ûrit] *a* confederado ♦ *n* (*pej*) cómplice *m/f*; (*US*: HISTORY) confederado/a.

confederation [kənfedərā'shən] *n* confederación *f*.

confer [kənfûr'] *vt* otorgar (*on* a) ♦ *vi* conferenciar; **to** ~ (**with sb about sth**) consultar (con uno sobre algo).

conference [kân'fûrəns] *n* (*meeting*) reunión *f*; (*convention*) congreso; **to be in** ~ estar en una reunión.

conference room *n* sala de conferencias.

confess [kənfes'] *vt* confesar ♦ *vi* confesarse.

confession [kənfesh'ən] *n* confesión *f*.

confessional [kənfesh'ənəl] *n* confesionario.

confessor [kənfes'ûr] *n* confesor *m*.

confetti [kənfet'ē] *n* confeti *m*.

confide [kənfīd'] *vi*: **to** ~ **in** confiar en.

confidence [kân'fidəns] *n* (*gen, also:* **self-**~) confianza; (*secret*) confidencia; **in** ~ (*speak, write*) en confianza; **to have** (**every**) ~ **that** estar seguro *or* confiado de que; **motion of no** ~ moción *f* de censura; **to tell sb sth in strict** ~ decir algo a uno en absoluta confianza.

confidence game, (*Brit*) **confidence trick** *n* timo.

confident [kân'fidənt] *a* seguro de sí mismo.

confidential [kânfiden'shəl] *a* confidencial; (*secretary*) de confianza.

confidentiality [kânfidenshēal'itē] *n* confidencialidad *f*.

configuration [kənfigyərā'shən] *n* (*also* COMPUT) configuración *f*.

confine [kənfīn'] *vt* (*limit*) limitar; (*shut up*) encerrar; **to** ~ **o.s. to doing sth** limitarse a hacer algo.

confined [kənfīnd'] *a* (*space*) reducido.

confinement [kənfīn'mənt] *n* (*prison*) prisión *f*; (MED) parto.

confines [kân'fīnz] *npl* confines *mpl*.

confirm [kənfûrm'] *vt* confirmar.

confirmation [kânfûrmā'shən] *n* confirmación *f*.

confirmed [kənfûrmd'] *a* empedernido.

confiscate [kân'fiskāt] *vt* confiscar.

confiscation [kânfiskā'shən] *n* incautación *f*.

conflagration [kânfləgrā'shən] *n* conflagración *f*.

conflict *n* [kân'flikt] conflicto ♦ *vi* [kənflikt'] (*opinions*) chocar.

conflicting [kənflik'ting] *a* (*reports, evidence, opinions*) contradictorio.

conform [kənfôrm'] *vi* conformarse; **to** ~ **to** ajustarse a.

conformist [kənfôr'mist] *n* conformista *m/f*.

confound [kənfound'] *vt* confundir; (*amaze*) pasmar.

confounded [kənfoun'did] *a* condenado.

confront [kənfrunt'] *vt* (*problems*) hacer

frente a; (*enemy, danger*) enfrentarse con.

confrontation [kânfrəntā'shən] *n* enfrentamiento.

confuse [kənfyōōz'] *vt* (*perplex*) aturdir, desconcertar; (*mix up*) confundir.

confused [kənfyōōzd'] *a* confuso; (*person*) perplejo; **to get** ~ desorientarse, aturdirse.

confusing [kənfyōō'zing] *a* confuso.

confusion [kənfyōō'zhən] *n* confusión *f*.

congeal [kənjēl'] *vi* coagularse.

congenial [kənjēn'yəl] *a* agradable.

congenital [kənjen'itəl] *a* congénito.

congested [kənjes'tid] *a* (*gen*) atestado; (*telephone lines*) ocupado.

congestion [kənjes'chən] *n* congestión *f*.

conglomerate [kənglâm'ûrit] *n* (COMM, GEO) conglomerado.

conglomeration [kənglâmərā'shən] *n* conglomeración *f*.

Congo [kâng'gō] *n* (*state*) Congo.

congratulate [kəngrach'ōōlāt] *vt* felicitar.

congratulations [kəngrachōōlā'shənz] *npl*: ~ (**on**) felicitaciones *fpl* (por); ~! ¡enhorabuena!, ¡felicidades!

congregate [kâng'grəgāt] *vi* congregarse.

congregation [kânggrəgā'shən] *n* (*in church*) fieles *mpl*.

congress [kâng'gris] *n* congreso.

congressman [kâng'grismən] *n* (US) diputado.

congresswoman [kâng'griswōōmən] *n* (US) diputada.

conical [kân'ikəl] *a* cónico.

conifer [kō'nifûr] *n* conífera.

coniferous [kōnif'ûrəs] *a* (*forest*) conífero.

conjecture [kənjek'chûr] *n* conjetura.

conjugal [kân'jəgəl] *a* conyugal.

conjugate [kân'jəgāt] *vt* conjugar.

conjunction [kənjungk'shən] *n* conjunción *f*; **in** ~ **with** junto con.

conjunctivitis [kənjungktəvī'tis] *n* conjuntivitis *f*.

conjure [kân'jûr] *vi* hacer juegos de manos. **conjure up** *vt* (*ghost, spirit*) hacer aparecer; (*memories*) evocar.

conjurer [kân'jûrûr] *n* ilusionista *m/f*.

conjuring trick [kân'jûring trik] *n* ilusionismo, juego de manos.

conker [kâng'kûr] *n* (*Brit*) castaño de Indias.

conk out [kângk out] *vi* (*col*) descomponerse.

con man *n* timador *m*.

Conn. *abbr* (US) = Connecticut.

connect [kənekt'] *vt* juntar, unir; (ELEC) conectar; (*fig*) relacionar, asociar ♦ *vi*: **to** ~ **with** (*train*) enlazar con; **to be** ~**ed with** (*associated*) estar relacionado con; (*related*) estar emparentado con; **I am trying to** ~ **you** (TEL) estoy intentando comunicarle.

connection [kənek'shən] *n* juntura, unión *f*; (ELEC) conexión *f*; (RAIL) enlace *m*; (TEL) comunicación *f*; (*fig*) relación *f*; **what is the ~ between them?** ¿qué relación hay entre ellos?; **in ~ with** con respeto a, en relación a; **she has many business ~s** tiene muchos contactos profesionales; **to miss/make a ~** perder/coger el enlace.

connive [kǝnīv'] *vi*: **to ~ at** hacer la vista gorda a.

connoisseur [kânisûr'] *n* experto/a, entendido/a.

connotation [kânǝtā'shǝn] *n* connotación *f*.

conquer [kâng'kûr] *vt* (*territory*) conquistar; (*enemy, feelings*) vencer.

conqueror [kâng'kûrûr] *n* conquistador(a) *m/f*.

conquest [kân'kwest] *n* conquista.

cons [kânz] *npl see* **convenience, pro.**

conscience [kân'shǝns] *n* conciencia; **in all ~** en conciencia.

conscientious [kânshēen'shǝs] *a* concienzudo; (*objection*) de conciencia.

conscientious objector *n* objetor *m* de conciencia.

conscious [kân'shǝs] *a* consciente; (*deliberate: insult, error*) premeditado, intencionado; **to become ~ of sth/that** darse cuenta de algo/de que.

consciousness [kân'shǝsnis] *n* conciencia; (*MED*) conocimiento.

conscript [kân'skript] *n* (*Brit*) recluta *m/f*.

conscription [kǝnskrip'shǝn] *n* servicio militar (obligatorio).

consecrate [kân'sǝkrāt] *vt* consagrar.

consecutive [kǝnsek'yǝtiv] *a* consecutivo; **on 3 ~ occasions** en 3 ocasiones consecutivas.

consensus [kǝnsen'sǝs] *n* consenso; **the ~ of opinion** el consenso general.

consent [kǝnsent'] *n* consentimiento ♦ *vi*: **to ~ to** consentir en; **by common ~** de común acuerdo.

consequence [kân'sǝkwens] *n* consecuencia; **in ~** por consiguiente.

consequently [kân'sǝkwentlē] *ad* por consiguiente.

conservation [kânsûrvā'shǝn] *n* conservación *f*; (*of nature*) preservación *f*.

conservationist [kânsûrvā'shǝnist] *n* conservacionista *m/f*.

conservative [kǝnsûr'vǝtiv] *a* conservador(a); (*cautious*) cauteloso; **C~** *a, n* (*Brit POL*) conservador(a) *m/f*.

conservatory [kǝnsûr'vǝtôrē] *n* (*greenhouse*) invernadero.

conserve *vt* [kǝnsûrv'] conservar ♦ *n* [kân'sûrv] conserva.

consider [kǝnsid'ûr] *vt* considerar; (*take into account*) tomar en cuenta; (*study*) estudiar, examinar; **to ~ doing sth** pensar en (la posibilidad de) hacer algo; **all things ~ed** pensándolo bien; **~ yourself lucky** ¡date por satisfecho!

considerable [kǝnsid'ûrǝbǝl] *a* considera-

ble.

considerably [kǝnsid'ûrǝblē] *ad* bastante, considerablemente.

considerate [kǝnsid'ûrit] *a* considerado.

consideration [kǝnsidǝrā'shǝn] *n* consideración *f*; (*reward*) retribución *f*; **to be under ~** estar sobre el tapete; **my first ~ is my family** mi primera consideración es mi familia.

considering [kǝnsid'ûring] *prep*: **~ (that)** teniendo en cuenta (que).

consign [kǝnsīn'] *vt* consignar.

consignee [kânsīnē'] *n* consignatario/a.

consignment [kǝnsīn'mǝnt] *n* envío.

consignment note *n* (*COMM*) talón *m* de expedición.

consignor [kǝnsī'nûr] *n* remitente *m/f*.

consist [kǝnsist'] *vi*: **to ~ of** consistir en.

consistency [kǝnsis'tǝnsē] *n* (*of person etc*) consecuencia; (*thickness*) consistencia.

consistent [kǝnsis'tǝnt] *a* (*person, argument*) consecuente; (*results*) constante.

consolation [kânsǝlā'shǝn] *n* consuelo.

console *vt* [kǝnsōl'] consolar ♦ *n* [kân'sōl] (*control panel*) consola.

consolidate [kǝnsâl'idāt] *vt* consolidar.

consommé [kânsǝmā'] *n* consomé *m*, caldo.

consonant [kân'sǝnǝnt] *n* consonante *f*.

consort *n* [kân'sôrt] consorte *m/f* ♦ *vi* [kǝnsôrt]: **to ~ with sb** (*often pej*) asociarse con uno; **prince ~** príncipe *m* consorte.

consortium [kǝnsôr'shēǝm] *n* consorcio.

conspicuous [kǝnspik'yōōǝs] *a* (*visible*) visible; (*garish etc*) llamativo; (*outstanding*) notable; **to make o.s. ~** llamar la atención.

conspiracy [kǝnspir'ǝsē] *n* conjura, complot *m*.

conspiratorial [kǝnspirǝtôr'ēǝl] *a* de conspirador.

conspire [kǝnspī'ûr] *vi* conspirar.

constable [kân'stǝbǝl] *n* (*Brit*) policía *m/f*; **chief ~** ≈ jefe *m/f* de policía.

constabulary [kǝnstab'yǝlärē] *n* ≈ policía.

constancy [kân'stǝnsē] *n* constancia; fidelidad *f*.

constant [kân'stǝnt] *a* (*gen*) constante; (*loyal*) leal, fiel.

constantly [kân'stǝntlē] *ad* constantemente.

constellation [kânstǝlā'shǝn] *n* constelación *f*.

consternation [kânstûrnā'shǝn] *n* consternación *f*.

constipated [kân'stǝpātid] *a* estreñido.

constipation [kânstǝpā'shǝn] *n* estreñimiento.

constituency [kǝnstich'ōōǝnsē] *n* (*POL*) distrito electoral; (*people*) electorado.

constituency party *n* partido local.

constituent [kǝnstich'ōōǝnt] *n* (*POL*) elector(a) *m/f*; (*part*) componente *m*.

constitute [kân'stitōōt] *vt* constituir.

constitution [kánstitōō'shən] *n* constitución *f*.

constitutional [kánstitōō'shənəl] *a* constitucional.

constrain [kənstrān'] *vt* obligar.

constrained [kənstrānd'] *a*: **to feel ~ to ...** sentirse en la necesidad de ....

constraint [kənstrānt'] *n* (*force*) fuerza; (*limit*) restricción *f*; (*restraint*) reserva; (*embarrassment*) cohibición *f*.

constrict [kənstrikt'] *vt* apretar, estrechar.

constriction [kənstrik'shən] *n* constricción *f*.

construct [kənstrukt'] *vt* construir.

construction [kənstruk'shən] *n* construcción *f*; (*fig*: *interpretation*) interpretación *f*; **under ~** en construcción.

construction industry *n* industria de la construcción.

constructive [kənstruk'tiv] *a* constructivo.

construe [kənstrōō'] *vt* interpretar.

consul [kán'səl] *n* cónsul *m/f*.

consulate [kán'səlit] *n* consulado.

consult [kənsult'] *vt*, *vi* consultar; **to ~ sb (about sth)** consultar a uno (sobre algo).

consultancy [kənsul'tənsē] *n* consultorio.

consultant [kənsul'tənt] *n* (*Brit MED*) especialista *m/f*; (*other specialist*) asesor(a) *m/f*.

consultation [kánsəltā'shən] *n* consulta; **in ~ with** en consultación con.

consulting room [kənsul'ting rōōm] *n* (*Brit*) consultorio.

consume [kənsōōm'] *vt* (*eat*) comerse; (*drink*) beberse; (*fire etc*, *COMM*) consumir.

consumer [kənsōō'mûr] *n* (*of electricity*, *gas etc*) consumidor(a) *m/f*.

consumer association *n* asociación *f* de consumidores.

consumer credit *n* crédito al consumidor.

consumer durables *npl* bienes *mpl* de consumo duraderos.

consumer goods *npl* bienes *mpl* de consumo.

consumerism [kənsōō'mərizəm] *n* consumismo.

consumer society *n* sociedad *f* de consumo.

consummate [kán'səmāt] *vt* consumar.

consumption [kənsump'shən] *n* consumo; (*MED*) tisis *f*; **not fit for human ~** no apto para el consumo humano.

cont. *abbr* (= *continued*) sigue.

contact [kán'takt] *n* contacto; (*person*) enchufe *m* ♦ *vt* ponerse en contacto con; **~ lenses** *npl* lentes *fpl* de contacto; **to be in ~ with sb/sth** estar en contacto con uno/algo; **business ~s** contactos comerciales.

contagious [kəntā'jəs] *a* contagioso.

contain [kəntān'] *vt* contener; **to ~ o.s.** contenerse.

container [kəntā'nûr] *n* recipiente *m*; (*for shipping etc*) contenedor *m*.

containerization [kəntānûrəzā'shən] *n* contenerización *f*.

containerize [kəntā'nərīz] *vt* transportar en contenedores.

contaminate [kəntam'ənāt] *vt* contaminar.

contamination [kəntamənā'shən] *n* contaminación *f*.

cont'd *abbr* (= *continued*) sigue.

contemplate [kán'təmplāt] *vt* (*gen*) contemplar; (*reflect upon*) considerar; (*intend*) pensar.

contemplation [kántəmplā'shən] *n* contemplación *f*.

contemporary [kəntem'pərärē] *a*, *n* (*of the same age*) contemporáneo/a *m/f*.

contempt [kəntempt'] *n* desprecio; **~ of court** (*LAW*) desacato (a los tribunales *or* a la justicia).

contemptible [kəntemp'təbəl] *a* despreciable, desdeñable.

contemptuous [kəntemp'chōōəs] *a* desdeñoso.

contend [kəntend'] *vt* (*argue*) afirmar ♦ *vi* (*struggle*) luchar; **he has a lot to ~ with** tiene muchos problemas que enfrentar.

contender [kəntend'ûr] *n* (*SPORT*) contendiente *m/f*.

content [kəntent'] *a* (*happy*) contento; (*satisfied*) satisfecho ♦ *vt* contentar; satisfacer ♦ *n* [kán'tent] contenido; **~s** *npl* contenido *msg*; (**table of**) **~s** índice *m* de materias; **to ~ o.s. with sth/with doing sth** contentarse *or* darse por contento con algo/con hacer algo.

contented [kəntent'id] *a* contento; satisfecho.

contentedly [kəntent'tidlē] *ad* con aire satisfecho.

contention [kəntent'shən] *n* discusión *f*; (*belief*) argumento; **bone of ~** manzana de la discordia.

contentious [kəntent'shəs] *a* discutible.

contentment [kəntent'mənt] *n* contento.

contest *n* [kán'test] contienda; (*competition*) concurso ♦ *vt* [kəntest'] (*dispute*) impugnar; (*LAW*) disputar, litigar; (*POL*: *election, seat*) presentarse como candidato/a en.

contestant [kəntes'tənt] *n* concursante *m/f*; (*in fight*) contendiente *m/f*.

context [kán'tekst] *n* contexto; **in/out of ~** en/fuera de contexto.

continent [kán'tənənt] *n* continente *m*; **the C~** el continente europeo; **on the C~** en el continente europeo.

continental [kántənen'təl] *a* continental.

continental breakfast *n* desayuno estilo europeo.

continental quilt *n* (*Brit*) edredón *m*.

contingency [kəntin'jənsē] *n* contingencia.

contingent [kəntin'jənt] *n* (*group*) grupo.

continual [kəntin'yōōəl] *a* continuo.

continually [kəntin'yōōəlē] *ad* constantemente.

continuation [kəntinyōōā'shən] *n* prolongación *f*; (*after interruption*) reanudación *f*.

continue [kəntin'yōō] *vi, vt* seguir, continuar; **~d on page 10** sigue en la página 10.

continuity [kántənōō'itē] *n* (*also CINEMA*) continuidad *f*.

continuous [kəntin'yōōəs] *a* continuo; **~ feed paper** (*COMPUT*) papel *m* continuo; **~ performance** (*CINEMA*) sesión *f* continua.

continuously [kəntin'yōōəslē] *ad* (*repeatedly*) continuamente; (*uninterruptedly*) constantemente.

contort [kəntôrt'] *vt* retorcer.

contortion [kəntôr'shən] *n* (*movement*) contorsión *f*.

contortionist [kəntôr'shənist] *n* contorsionista *m/f*.

contour [kán'tōōr] *n* contorno; (*also:* **~ line**) curva de nivel.

contraband [kán'trəband] *n* contrabando ♦ *a* de contrabando.

contraception [kántrəsep'shən] *n* contracepción *f*.

contraceptive [kántrəsep'tiv] *a, n* anticonceptivo.

contract [kán'trakt] *n* contrato ♦ *cpd* (*price, date*) contratado, de contrato; (*work*) de contrato ♦ *vb* [kəntrakt'] *vi* (*COMM*): **to ~ to do sth** comprometerse por contrato a hacer algo; (*become smaller*) contraerse, encogerse ♦ *vt* contraer; **to be under ~ to do sth** estar bajo contrato para hacer algo; **~ of employment** *or* **of service** contrato de trabajo.

contraction [kəntrak'shən] *n* contracción *f*.

contractor [kán'traktûr] *n* contratista *m/f*.

contractual [kəntrak'chōōəl] *a* contractual.

contradict [kántrədikt'] *vt* (*declare to be wrong*) desmentir; (*be contrary to*) contradecir.

contradiction [kántrədik'shən] *n* contradicción *f*; **to be in ~ with** no estar de acuerdo con.

contradictory [kántrədik'tûrē] *a* (*statements*) contradictorio; **to be ~ to** ser contradictorio a.

contralto [kəntral'tō] *n* contralto *f*.

contraption [kəntrap'shən] *n* (*pej*) artilugio *m*.

contrary [kán'trärē] *a* (*opposite, different*) contrario; (*perverse*) terco ♦ *n*: **on the ~** al contrario; **unless you hear to the ~** a no ser que le digan lo contrario; **~ to what we thought** en contra de lo que pensábamos.

contrast *n* [kán'trast] contraste *m* ♦ *vt* [kəntrast'] comparar; **in ~ to** *or* **with** a diferencia de.

contrasting [kəntras'ting] *a* (*opinion*) opuesto; (*color*) que hace contraste.

contravene [kántrəvēn'] *vt* infringir.

contravention [kántrəven'shən] *n*: **~ (of)** contravención *f* (de).

contribute [kəntrib'yōōt] *vi* contribuir ♦ *vt*: **to ~ to** (*gen*) contribuir a; (*newspaper*) escribir para; (*discussion*) intervenir en.

contribution [kántrəbyōō'shən] *n* (*money*) contribución *f*; (*to debate*) intervención *f*; (*to journal*) colaboración *f*.

contributor [kəntrib'yətûr] *n* (*to newspaper*) colaborador(a) *m/f*.

contributory [kəntrib'yətôrē] *a* (*cause*) contribuyente; **it was a ~ factor in** ... fue un factor contribuyente en ....

contributory pension plan *n* plan *m* cotizable de jubilación.

contrivance [kəntrī'vəns] *n* (*machine, device*) aparato, dispositivo.

contrive [kəntrīv'] *vt* (*invent*) idear ♦ *vi*: **to ~ to do** lograr hacer.

control [kəntrōl'] *vt* controlar; (*traffic etc*) dirigir; (*machinery*) manejar; (*temper*) dominar; (*disease, fire*) dominar, controlar ♦ *n* (*command*) control *m*; (*of car*) conducción *f*; (*check*) freno; **~s** *npl* mando *sg*; **to ~ o.s.** controlarse, dominarse; **everything is under ~** todo está bajo control; **to be in ~ of** tener el mando de; **the car went out of ~** el coche se descontroló.

control group *n* (*MED, PSYCH etc*) grupo de control.

control key *n* (*COMPUT*) tecla de control.

controlled economy [kəntrōld' ikán'əmē] *n* economía dirigida.

controller [kəntrōl'lûr] *n* controlador(a) *m/f*.

controlling interest [kəntrō'ling in'trist] *n* interés *m* mayoritario.

control panel *n* (*on aircraft, ship, TV etc*) tablero de instrumentos.

control point *n* (*puesto de*) control *m*.

control room *n* (*NAUT, MIL*) sala de mandos; (*RADIO, TV*) sala de control.

control tower *n* (*AVIAT*) torre *f* de control.

control unit *n* (*COMPUT*) unidad *f* de control.

controversial [kántrəvûr'shəl] *a* polémico.

controversy [kán'trəvûrsē] *n* polémica.

conurbation [kánûrbā'shən] *n* urbanización *f*.

convalesce [kánvəles'] *vi* convalecer.

convalescence [kánvəles'əns] *n* convalecencia.

convalescent [kánvəles'ənt] *a, n* convaleciente *m/f*.

convector [kənvek'tûr] *n* calentador *m* de convección.

convene [kənvēn'] *vt* (*meeting*) convocar ♦ *vi* reunirse.

convenience [kənvēn'yəns] *n* (*comfort*) comodidad *f*; (*advantage*) ventaja; **at your earliest ~** (*COMM*) cuando *or* tan pronto como le sea conveniente; **all modern ~s,**

(*Brit*) **all mod cons** todo confort.
convenience foods *npl* platos *mpl* preparados.
convenient [kənvēn'yənt] *a* (*useful*) útil; (*place*, *time*) conveniente; **if it is ~ for you** si le conviene.
conveniently [kənvēn'yəntlē] *ad* (*happen*) oportunamente; (*situated*) convenientemente.
convent [kán'vent] *n* convento.
convent school *n* colegio de monjas.
convention [kənven'shən] *n* convención *f*; (*meeting*) asamblea.
conventional [kənven'shənəl] *a* convencional.
converge [kənvûrj'] *vi* converger.
conversant [kənvûr'sənt] *a*: **to be ~ with** estar al tanto de.
conversation [kánvûrsā'shən] *n* conversación *f*.
conversational [kánvûrsā'shənəl] *a* (*familiar*) familiar; (*talkative*) locuaz; **~ mode** (*COMPUT*) modo de conversación.
converse *n* [kán'vûrs] inversa ♦ *vi* [kənvûrs'] conversar; **to ~ (with sb about sth)** conversar *or* platicar (con uno de algo).
conversely [kənvûrs'lē] *ad* a la inversa.
conversion [kənvûr'zhən] *n* conversión *f*; (*house ~*) reforma, remodelación *f*.
conversion table *n* tabla de conversión.
convert *vt* [kənvûrt'] (*REL*, *COMM*) convertir; (*alter*) transformar ♦ *n* [kán'vûrt] converso/a.
convertible [kənvûr'təbəl] *a* convertible ♦ *n* descapotable *m*; **~ loan stock** títulos *mpl* convertibles de interés fijo.
convex [kánveks'] *a* convexo.
convey [kənvā'] *vt* llevar; (*thanks*) comunicar; (*idea*) expresar.
conveyance [kənvā'əns] *n* (*of goods*) transporte *m*; (*vehicle*) vehículo, medio de transporte.
conveyancing [kənvā'ənsing] *n* (*LAW*) preparación *f* de escrituras de traspaso.
conveyor belt [kənvā'ûr belt] *n* cinta transportadora.
convict *vt* [kənvikt'] (*gen*) condenar; (*find guilty*) declarar culpable a ♦ *n* [kán'vikt] presidiario/a.
conviction [kənvik'shən] *n* condena; (*belief*) creencia, convicción *f*.
convince [kənvins'] *vt* convencer; **to ~ sb (of sth/that)** convencer a uno (de algo/de que).
convinced [kənvinst'] *a*: **~ of/that** convencido de/de que.
convincing [kənvin'sing] *a* convincente.
convincingly [kənvin'singlē] *ad* convincentemente.
convivial [kənviv'ēəl] *a* (*person*) sociable; (*atmosphere*) alegre.
convoluted [kán'vəlōōtid] *a* (*argument etc*) enrevesado; (*shape*) enrollado, enroscado.

convoy [kán'voi] *n* convoy *m*.
convulse [kənvuls'] *vt* convulsionar; **to be ~d with laughter** dislocarse de risa.
convulsion [kənvul'shən] *n* convulsión *f*.
coo [kōō] *vi* arrullar.
cook [kōōk] *vt* cocinar; (*stew etc*) guisar; (*meal*) preparar, cocinar ♦ *vi* cocer; (*person*) cocinar ♦ *n* cocinero/a.
cook up *vt* (*col: excuse, story*) inventar.
cookbook [kōōk'bōōk] *n* libro de cocina.
cooker [kōōk'ûr] *n* (*US*) olla para cocinar; (*Brit*) cocina.
cookery [kōōk'ûrē] *n* (*dishes*) cocina; (*art*) arte *m* culinario.
cookery book *n* (*Brit*) = **cookbook**.
cookie [kōōk'ē] *n* (*US*) galleta.
cooking [kōōk'ing] *n* cocina ♦ *cpd* (*apples*) para cocinar; (*utensils, salt, foil*) de cocina.
cooking chocolate *n* (*Brit*) chocolate *m* fondant.
cookout [kōōk'out] *n* (*US*) comida al aire libre.
cool [kōōl] *a* fresco; (*not hot*) tibio; (*not afraid*) tranquilo; (*unfriendly*) frío ♦ *vt* enfriar ♦ *vi* enfriarse; **it is ~** (*weather*) hace fresco; **to keep sth ~** *or* **in a ~ place** conservar algo fresco *or* en un sitio fresco.
cool down *vi* enfriarse; (*fig: person, situation*) calmarse.
cooler [kōōl'ûr], (*Brit*) **cool box** *n* nevera portátil.
cooling-off period [kōōlingôf' pir'ēəd] *n* (*INDUSTRY*) plazo para que se entablen negociaciones.
cooling tower [kōō'ling tou'ûr] *n* torre *f* de refrigeración.
coolly [kōō'lē] *ad* (*calmly*) con tranquilidad; (*audaciously*) descaradamente; (*unenthusiastically*) fríamente, con frialdad.
coolness [kōōl'nis] *n* frescura; tranquilidad *f*; (*hostility*) frialdad *f*; (*indifference*) falta de entusiasmo.
coop [kōōp] *n* gallinero ♦ *vt*: **to ~ up** (*fig*) encerrar.
co-op [kō'áp] *n* *abbr* (= *Cooperative Society*)) cooperativa.
cooperate [kōáp'ərāt] *vi* cooperar, colaborar; **will he ~?** ¿querrá cooperar?
cooperation [kōápərā'shən] *n* cooperación *f*, colaboración *f*.
cooperative [kōáp'rətiv] *a* cooperativo ♦ *n* cooperativa.
co-opt [kōápt'] *vt*: **to ~ sb into sth** cooptar a uno a algo.
coordinate *vt* [kōôr'dənāt] coordinar ♦ *n* [kōôr'dənit] (*MATH*) coordenada; **~s** *npl* (*clothes*) coordinados *mpl*.
coordination [kōôrdənā'shən] *n* coordinación *f*.
coot [kōōt] *n* focha *f* (común).
co-ownership [kōō'nûrship] *n* co-propiedad *f*.

cop [káp] *n* (*col*) poli *m*, tira *m* (*LAm*).
cope [kōp] *vi*: **to** ~ **with** poder con; (*problem*) hacer frente a.
Copenhagen [kōpenhā'gən] *n* Copenhague *m*.
copier [káp'ēûr] *n* (*photo*~) fotocopiadora, multicopista.
copilot [kōpī'lət] *n* copiloto/a.
copious [kō'pēəs] *a* copioso, abundante.
copper [káp'ûr] *n* (*metal*) cobre *m*; (*Brit*: *col*: *policeman*) poli *m*, tira *m* (*LAm*); ~**s** *npl* (*Brit*) perras *fpl*.
copse [káps] *n* bosquecillo.
copulate [káp'yəlāt] *vi* copularse.
copulation [kápyəlā'shən] *n* cópula.
copy [káp'ē] *n* copia; (*of book etc*) ejemplar *m*; (*material*: *for printing*) copia ♦ *vt* copiar (*also* COMPUT); (*imitate*) copiar, imitar; **to make good** ~ (*fig*) ser una noticia de interés; **clean** ~ copia en limpio.
copy out *vt* copiar.
copycat [káp'ēkat] *n* (*pej*) copión/ona *m/f*.
copyright [káp'ērīt] *n* derechos *mpl* de autor.
copy typist *n* mecanógrafo/a.
coral [kôr'əl] *n* coral *m*.
coral reef *n* arrecife *m* (de coral).
Coral Sea *n*: **the** ~ el Mar del Coral.
cord [kôrd] *n* cuerda; (ELEC) cable *m*; (*fabric*) pana; ~**s** *npl* (*pants*) pantalones *mpl* de pana.
cordial [kôr'jəl] *a* afectuoso ♦ *n* cordial *m*.
cordless [kôrd'lis] *a* sin cordón.
cordon [kôr'dən] *n* cordón *m*.
cordon off *vt* acordonar.
Cordova [kôr'dəvə] *n* Córdoba.
corduroy [kôr'dəroi] *n* pana.
CORE [kôr] *n abbr* (*US*) = *Congress of Racial Equality*.
core [kôr] *n* (*of earth, nuclear reactor*) centro, núcleo; (*of fruit*) corazón *m*; (*of problem etc*) corazón *m*, meollo ♦ *vt* quitar el corazón de.
Corfu [kôr'fōō] *n* Corfú *m*.
coriander [kôrēan'dûr] *n* culantro, cilantro.
cork [kôrk] *n* corcho; (*tree*) alcornoque *m*.
corked [kôrkt] *a* (*wine*) con sabor a corcho.
corkscrew [kôrk'skrōō] *n* sacacorchos *m inv*.
cormorant [kôr'mûrənt] *n* cormorán *m* grande.
Corn *abbr* (*Brit*) = *Cornwall*.
corn [kôrn] *n* (*US*: *maize*) maíz *m*; (*Brit*: *wheat*) trigo; (*on foot*) callo; ~ **on the cob** (CULIN) maíz en la mazorca.
cornea [kôr'nēə] *n* córnea.
corned beef [kôrnd bēf] *n* carne *f* acecinada.
corner [kôr'nûr] *n* ángulo; (*outside*) esquina; (*inside*) rincón *m*; (*in road*) curva; (SOCCER) córner *m*, saque *m* de esquina ♦ *vt* (*trap*) arrinconar; (COMM) acaparar ♦ *vi* (*in car*) tomar las curvas; **to cut** ~**s**

atajar.
corner flag *n* (SOCCER) banderola de esquina.
corner kick *n* (SOCCER) córner *m*, saque *m* de esquina.
cornerstone [kôr'nûrstōn] *n* piedra angular.
cornet [kôrnet'] *n* (MUS) corneta; (*Brit*: *of ice-cream*) barquillo.
cornflakes [kôrn'flāks] *npl* copos *mpl* de maíz, cornflakes *mpl*.
cornflour [kôrn'flouûr] *n* (*Brit*) harina de maíz.
cornice [kôr'nis] *n* cornisa.
Cornish [kôr'nish] *a* de Cornualles.
cornmeal [kôrn'mēl] *n* (*US*) harina de maíz.
corn oil *n* aceite *m* de maíz.
cornstarch [kôrn'stârch] *n* (*US*) maicena.
cornucopia [kôrnəkō'pēə] *n* cornucopia.
corny [kôr'nē] *a* (*col*) gastado.
corollary [kôr'əlärē] *n* corolario.
coronary [kôr'ənärē] *n*: ~ **(thrombosis)** infarto.
coronation [kôrənā'shən] *n* coronación *f*.
coroner [kôr'ənûr] *n* juez *m* (de instrucción).
coronet [kôr'ənit] *n* corona.
Corp. *abbr* = **corporation**.
corporal [kôr'pûrəl] *n* cabo ♦ *a*: ~ **punishment** castigo corporal.
corporate [kôr'pərit] *a* corporativo.
corporate identity, corporate image *n* (*of organization*) identidad *f* corporativa.
corporation [kôrpərā'shən] *n* (*of town*) ayuntamiento; (COMM) corporación *f*.
corps [kôr], *pl* **corps** [kôrz] *n* cuerpo; **press** ~ gabinete *m* de prensa.
corpse [kôrps] *n* cadáver *m*.
corpulent [kôr'pyələnt] *a* corpulento/a.
Corpus Christi [kôr'pəs kris'tē] *n* Corpus *m*.
corpuscle [kôr'pəsəl] *n* corpúsculo.
corral [kəral'] *n* corral *m*.
correct [kərekt'] *a* (*accurate*) justo, exacto; (*proper*) correcto ♦ *vt* corregir; (*exam*) calificar; **you are** ~ tiene razón.
correction [kərek'shən] *n* rectificación *f*; (*erasure*) tachadura.
correlate [kôr'əlāt] *vi*: **to** ~ **with** tener correlación con.
correlation [kôrəlā'shən] *n* correlación *f*.
correspond [kôrəspând'] *vi* (*write*) escribirse; (*be equal to*) corresponder.
correspondence [kôrəspân'dəns] *n* correspondencia.
correspondence column *n* (sección *f* de) cartas *fpl* al director.
correspondence course *n* curso por correspondencia.
correspondent [kôrəspân'dənt] *n* corresponsal *m/f*.
corresponding [kôrəspân'ding] *a* co-

rrespondiente.

corridor [kôr'idûr] n pasillo.

corroborate [kərâb'ərāt] vt corroborar.

corroboration [kərâbərā'shən] n corroboración f, confirmación f.

corrode [kərōd'] vt corroer ♦ vi corroerse.

corrosion [kərō'zhən] n corrosión f.

corrosive [kərō'siv] a corrosivo.

corrugated [kôr'əgātid] a ondulado.

corrugated cardboard n cartón m ondulado.

corrugated iron n chapa ondulada.

corrupt [kərupt'] a corrompido; (person) corrupto ♦ vt corromper; (bribe) sobornar; (data) degradar; ~ **practices** (dishonesty, bribery) corrupción f.

corruption [kərup'shən] n corrupción f; (of data) alteración f.

corset [kôr'sit] n faja.

Corsica [kôr'sikə] n Córcega.

Corsican [kôr'sikən] a, n corso/a m/f.

cortège [kôrtezh'] n cortejo, desfile m.

cortisone [kôr'tisōn] n cortisona f.

c.o.s. abbr (= cash on shipment) pago al embarcar.

cosh [kâsh] n (Brit) cachiporra.

cosignatory [kōsig'nətôrē] n cosignatario/a.

cosine [kō'sīn] n coseno.

cosiness [kō'zēnis] n (Brit) = **coziness**.

cos lettuce [kâs let'is] n (Brit) lechuga cos.

cosmetic [kâzmet'ik] n cosmético ♦ a (also fig) cosmético; (surgery) estético.

cosmic [kâz'mik] a cósmico.

cosmonaut [kâz'mənôt] n cosmonauta m/f.

cosmopolitan [kâzməpâl'itən] a cosmopolita.

cosmos [kâz'məs] n cosmos m.

cosset [kâs'it] vt mimar.

cost [kôst] n (gen) coste m, costo; (price) precio; ~**s** npl (LAW) costas fpl ♦ vb (pt, pp **cost**) vi costar, valer ♦ vt preparar el presupuesto de; **how much does it** ~? ¿cuánto cuesta?, ¿cuánto vale?; **what will it** ~ **to have it repaired?** ¿cuánto costará repararlo?; **the** ~ **of living** el coste or costo de la vida; **at all** ~**s** cueste lo que cueste.

cost accountant n contable m de costos.

co-star [kō'stâr] n co-estrella m/f.

Costa Rica [kâs'tə rē'kə] n Costa Rica.

Costa Rican [kâs'tə rē'kən] a, n costarriqueño/a m/f.

cost center n centro (de determinación) de costos.

cost control n control m de costos.

cost-effective [kôstifek'tiv] a (COMM) beneficioso, rentable.

cost-effectiveness [kôstifek'tivnis] n relación f costo-eficacia or costo-rendimiento.

costing [kôs'ting] n (Brit) cálculo de costos.

costly [kôst'lē] a (expensive) costoso.

cost-of-living [kôstəvliv'ing] a: ~ **allowance** n plus m de carestía de vida; ~

index n índice m del costo or coste de vida.

cost price n (Brit) precio de coste.

costume [kâs'tōōm] n traje m; (Brit: also: **swimming** ~) traje de baño.

costume jewelry n bisutería.

costume party n (US) baile m de disfraces.

cosy [kō'zē] a (Brit) = **cozy**.

cot [kât] n (US: folding bed) cama plegable; (Brit: child's) cuna.

cottage [kât'ij] n casita de campo.

cottage cheese n requesón m.

cottage industry n industria casera.

cottage pie n pastel de carne cubierta de puré de patatas.

cotton [kât'ən] n algodón m; (thread) hilo; (US MED) algodón m hidrófilo.

  cotton on vi (Brit col): **to** ~ **on (to sth)** caer en la cuenta (de algo).

cotton candy n (US) algodón m (azucarado).

cotton wool n (Brit) algodón m (hidrófilo).

couch [kouch] n sofá m; (doctor's) camilla.

couchette [kōōshet'] n (Brit) litera.

cough [kôf] vi toser ♦ n tos f.

  cough up vt escupir.

cough drop n pastilla para la tos.

cough syrup n jarabe m para la tos.

could [kōōd] pt of **can**.

couldn't [kōōd'ənt] = **could not**.

council [koun'səl] n consejo; **city** or **town** ~ consejo municipal; **C**~ **of Europe** Consejo de Europa.

council estate n (Brit) urbanización de viviendas municipales de alquiler.

council house n (Brit) vivienda municipal de alquiler.

councilor, (Brit) **councillor** [koun'səlûr] n concejal m/f.

counsel [koun'səl] n (advice) consejo; (lawyer) abogado/a ♦ vt aconsejar; ~ **for the defense/the prosecution** abogado/a defensor(a)/fiscal; **to** ~ **sth/sb to do sth** aconsejar algo/a uno que haga algo.

counseling, (Brit) **counselling** [koun'səling] n (advice) consejos mpl; **marriage/ vocational** ~ orientación f matrimonial/ profesional.

counselor, (Brit) **counsellor** [koun'səlûr] n consejero/a; (US LAW) abogado/a.

count [kount] vt (gen) contar; (include) incluir ♦ vi contar ♦ n cuenta; (of votes) escrutinio; (nobleman) conde m; (sum) total m, suma; **to** ~ **the cost of** calcular el costo de; **not** ~**ing the children** niños aparte; **10** ~**ing him** diez incluyéndolo a él, diez con él; ~ **yourself lucky** date por satisfecho; **that doesn't** ~! ¡eso no vale!; **to** ~ **(up) to 10** contar hasta diez; **it** ~**s for very little** cuenta poco; **to keep** ~ **of sth** llevar la cuenta de algo.

  count on vt fus contar con; **to** ~ **on**

doing sth contar con hacer algo.
count up *vt* contar.
countdown [kount'doun] *n* cuenta atrás.
countenance [koun'tənəns] *n* semblante *m*, rostro ♦ *vt* (*tolerate*) aprobar, tolerar.
counter [koun'tûr] *n* (*in shop*) mostrador *m*; (*position: in post office, bank*) ventanilla; (*in games*) ficha; (*TECH*) contador *m* ♦ *vt* contrarrestar; (*blow*) parar; (*attack*) contestar a ♦ *ad*: ~ **to** contrario a; **to buy under the** ~ (*fig*) comprar de estraperlo *or* bajo mano; **to** ~ **sth with sth/by doing sth** contestar algo con algo/haciendo algo.
counteract [kountûrakt'] *vt* contrarrestar.
counterattack *n* [koun'tûrətak] contraataque *m* ♦ *vi* [kountûrətak'] contraatacar.
counterbalance [koun'tûrbaləns] *n* contrapeso.
counterclockwise [kountûrklâk'wīz] *ad* en sentido contrario al de las agujas del reloj.
counterespionage [kountûres'pēənâzh] *n* contraespionaje *m*.
counterfeit [koun'tûrfit] *n* falsificación *f*, simulación *f* ♦ *vt* falsificar ♦ *a* falso, falsificado.
counterfoil [koun'tûrfoil] *n* talón *m*.
counterintelligence [kountûrintel'ijəns] *n* contraespionaje *m*.
countermand [koun'tûrmand'] *vt* revocar, cancelar.
counter-measure [koun'tûrmezhûr] *n* contramedida.
counteroffensive [kountûrəfen'siv] *n* contraofensiva.
counterpane [koun'tûrpān] *n* colcha.
counterpart [koun'tûrpârt] *n* (*of person*) homólogo/a.
counter-productive [kountûrprəduk'tiv] *a* contraproducente.
counterproposal [koun'tûrprəpōzəl] *n* contrapropuesta.
countersign [koun'tûrsīn] *vt* ratificar, refrendar.
countess [koun'tis] *n* condesa.
countless [kount'lis] *a* innumerable.
countrified [kun'trəfīd] *a* rústico.
country [kun'trē] *n* país *m*; (*native land*) patria; (*as opposed to town*) campo; (*region*) región *f*, tierra; **in the** ~ en el campo; **mountainous** ~ región *f* montañosa.
country and western (music) *n* música country.
country dancing *n* (*Brit*) baile *m* regional.
country house *n* casa de campo.
countryman [kun'trēmən] *n* (*national*) compatriota *m*; (*rural*) campesino, paisano.
countryside [kun'trēsīd] *n* campo.
country-wide [kun'trēwīd] *a* nacional.
county [koun'tē] *n* condado.
county road *n* (*US AUT*) ≈ carretera secundaria.
county seat *n* (*US*) cabeza de partido.
coup, ~**s** [kōo. -z] *n* golpe *m*; (*triumph*) éxito; (*also*: ~ **d'état**) golpe de estado.
coupé [kōopā'] *n* cupé *m*.
couple [kup'əl] *n* (*of things*) par *m*; (*of people*) pareja; (*married* ~) matrimonio ♦ *vt* (*ideas, names*) unir, juntar; (*machinery*) acoplar; **a** ~ **of** un par de.
couplet [kup'lit] *n* pareado.
coupling [kup'ling] *n* (*RAIL*) enganche *m*.
coupon [kōo'pän] *n* cupón *m*; (*Brit: pools* ~) boleto de quiniela.
courage [kûr'ij] *n* valor *m*, valentía.
courageous [kərā'jəs] *a* valiente.
courgette [kōorzhet'] *n* (*Brit*) calabacín *m*.
courier [kûr'ēûr] *n* mensajero/a; (*diplomatic*) correo; (*for tourists*) gúia *m/f* (de turismo).
course [kórs] *n* (*direction*) dirección *f*; (*of river, SCOL*) curso; (*of ship*) rumbo; (*fig*) proceder *m*; (*GOLF*) campo; (*part of meal*) plato; **of** ~ *ad* desde luego, naturalmente; **of** ~! ¡claro!; (**no) of** ~ **not!** ¡claro que no!, ¡por supuesto que no!; **in due** ~ en el momento oportuno; **in the** ~ **of the next few days** durante los próximos días; **we have no other** ~ **but to** ... no tenemos más remedio que ...; **there are 2** ~**s open to us** se nos ofrecen dos posibilidades; **the best** ~ **would be to** ... lo mejor sería ...; ~ **of treatment** (*MED*) tratamiento.
court [kórt] *n* (*royal*) corte *m*; (*LAW*) tribunal *m*, juzgado; (*TENNIS*) pista, cancha ♦ *vt* (*woman*) cortejar a; (*fig: favor, popularity*) solicitar, buscar; (: *death, disaster, danger etc*) buscar; **to take to** ~ demandar; **to go to** ~ recurrir a la justicia; ~ **of appeal** tribunal *m* de apelación; ~ **of law** tribunal *m* (de justicia).
courteous [kûr'tēəs] *a* cortés.
courtesan [kôr'tizən] *n* cortesana.
courtesy [kûr'tisē] *n* cortesía; **by** ~ **of** (por) cortesía de.
courtesy bus *n* autocar *or* autobús de cortesía (*al aeropuerto etc*).
courtesy light *n* (*AUT*) luz *f* interior.
courthouse [kôrt'hous] *n* (*US*) palacio de justicia.
courtier [kôr'tēûr] *n* cortesano.
court-martial, *pl* **courts-martial** [kôrt'mâr'shəl] *n* consejo de guerra ♦ *vt* someter a consejo de guerra.
courtroom [kôrt'rōom] *n* sala de justicia.
court shoe *n* zapato de mujer de estilo clásico.
courtyard [kôrt'yârd] *n* patio.
cousin [kuz'in] *n* primo/a; **first** ~ primo/a carnal.
cove [kōv] *n* cala, ensenada.
covenant [kuv'ənənt] *n* convenio.
Coventry [kuv'intrē] *n*: **to send sb to** ~ (*fig*) hacer el vacío a uno.

cover [kuv'ûr] *vt* cubrir; *(with lid)* tapar; *(chairs etc)* revestir; *(distance)* cubrir, recorrer; *(include)* abarcar; *(protect)* abrigar; *(journalist)* investigar; *(issues)* tratar ♦ *n* cubierta; *(lid)* tapa; *(for chair etc)* funda; *(for bed)* cobertor *m*; *(envelope)* sobre *m*; *(for book)* forro; *(of magazine)* portada; *(shelter)* abrigo; *(insurance)* cobertura; **to take** ~ *(shelter)* protegerse, resguardarse; **under** ~ *(indoors)* bajo techo; **under** ~ **of darkness** al amparo de la oscuridad; **under separate** ~ *(COMM)* por separado; **$10 will** ~ **everything** con diez dólares cubriremos todos los gastos.

cover up *vt (child, object)* cubrir completamente, tapar; *(fig: hide: truth, facts)* ocultar; **to** ~ **up for sb** *(fig)* encubrir a uno.

coverage [kuv'ûrij] *n* alcance *m*; *(in media)* reportaje *m*; *(INSURANCE)* cobertura.

coveralls [kuv'ûrôlz] *npl (US)* mono *sg*.

cover charge *n* precio del cubierto.

covering [kuv'ûring] *n* cubierta, envoltura.

cover letter, *(Brit)* **covering letter** *n* carta de explicación.

cover note *n (INSURANCE)* póliza provisional.

cover price *n* precio de cubierta.

covert [kō'vûrt] *a (secret)* secreto, encubierto; *(dissembled)* furtivo.

cover-up [kuv'ûrup] *n* encubrimiento.

covet [kuv'it] *vt* codiciar.

covetous [kuv'ətəs] *a* codicioso.

cow [kou] *n* vaca ♦ *vt* intimidar.

coward [kou'ûrd] *n* cobarde *m/f*.

cowardice [kou'ûrdis] *n* cobardía.

cowardly [kou'ûrdlē] *a* cobarde.

cowboy [kou'boi] *n* vaquero.

cower [kou'ûr] *vi* encogerse (de miedo).

co-worker [kōwûr'kûr] *n* colaborador(a) *m/f*.

cowshed [kou'shed] *n* establo.

cowslip [kou'slip] *n (BOT)* primavera, prímula.

coxswain [kâk'sin] *n (abbr:* **cox)** timonel *m*.

coy [koi] *a* tímido.

coyote [kīōt'ē] *n* coyote *m*.

coziness [kō'zēnis] *n* comodidad *f*; *(atmosphere)* lo holgado.

cozy [kō'zē] *a* cómodo; *(room, atmosphere)* acogedor(a).

CP *n abbr (= Communist Party)* PC *m*.

cp. *abbr (= compare)* cfr.

c/p *abbr (Brit)* = **carriage paid.**

CPA *n abbr (US)* = **certified public accountant.**

CPI *n abbr (= Consumer Price Index)* IPC *m*.

Cpl. *abbr (MIL)* = **corporal.**

CP/M *n abbr (= Central Program for Microprocessors)* CP/M *m*.

c.p.s. *abbr (= characters per second)* c.p.s.

CPU *n abbr* = **central processing unit.**

cr. *abbr* = **credit, creditor.**

crab [krab] *n* cangrejo.

crab apple *n* manzana silvestre.

crack [krak] *n* grieta; *(noise)* crujido; *(: of whip)* chasquido; *(joke)* chiste *m*; *(drug)* cocaína dura; *(col: attempt)*: **to have a** ~ **at sth** intentar algo ♦ *vt* agrietar, romper; *(nut)* cascar; *(safe)* forzar; *(whip etc)* chasquear; *(knuckles)* crujir; *(joke)* contar; *(case: solve)* resolver; *(code)* descifrar ♦ *a (athlete)* de primera clase; **to** ~ **jokes** *(col)* contar chistes *or* cuentos.

crack down on *vt fus* reprimir fuertemente, adoptar medidas severas contra.

crack up *vi* sufrir una crisis nerviosa.

crackdown [krak'doun] *n*: ~ **(on)** *(on crime)* campaña (contra); *(on spending)* reducción *f* (en).

cracker [krak'ûr] *n (cookie)* crácker *m*; *(Christmas* ~) sorpresa (navideña).

crackle [krak'əl] *vi* crepitar.

crackling [krak'ling] *n (on radio, telephone)* interferencia; *(of fire)* crepitación *f*; *(of leaves etc)* crujido; *(of pork)* chicharrón *m*.

cradle [krā'dəl] *n* cuna ♦ *vt (child)* mecer, acunar; *(object)* abrazar.

craft [kraft] *n (skill)* arte *m*; *(trade)* oficio; *(cunning)* astucia; *(boat)* barco.

craftsman [krafts'mən] *n* artesano.

craftsmanship [krafts'mənship] *n* artesanía.

crafty [kraf'tē] *a* astuto.

crag [krag] *n* peñasco.

craggy [krag'ē] *a* escarpado.

cram [kram] *vt (fill)*: **to** ~ **sth with** llenar algo (a reventar) de; *(put)*: **to** ~ **sth into** meter algo a la fuerza en ♦ *vi (for exams)* empollar.

crammed [kramd] *a* atestado.

cramp [kramp] *n (MED)* calambre *m*; *(TECH)* grapa ♦ *vt (limit)* poner trabas a.

cramped [krampt] *a* apretado, estrecho.

crampon [kram'pân] *n* crampón *m*.

cranberry [kran'bärē] *n* arándano agrio.

crane [krān] *n (TECH)* grúa; *(bird)* grulla ♦ *vt, vi*: **to** ~ **forward, to** ~ **one's neck** estirar el cuello, inclinarse estirando el cuello.

cranium [krā'nēəm] *n* cráneo.

crank [krangk] *n* manivela; *(person)* excentrico/a; *(US: grumbler)* gruñón/ona *m/f*.

crankshaft [krangk'shaft] *n* cigüeñal *m*.

cranky [krang'kē] *a (eccentric)* maniático; *(bad-tempered)* irritable.

cranny [kran'ē] *n see* **nook.**

crap [krap] *n (col!)* mierda *(!)*.

craps [kraps] *n (US)* dados *mpl*.

crash [krash] *n (noise)* estrépito; *(of cars etc)* choque *m*; *(of plane)* accidente *m* de aviación; *(of business)* quiebra; *(STOCK EXCHANGE)* crac *m* ♦ *vt (plane)* estrellar ♦

vi (*plane*) estrellarse; (*two cars*) chocar; (*fall noisily*) caer con estrépito; **he ~ed the car into a wall** estrelló el coche contra una pared *or* tapia.

crash barrier n (*AUT*) barrera de protección.

crash course n curso acelerado.

crash helmet n casco (protector).

crash landing n aterrizaje m forzado.

crass [kras] a grosero, maleducado.

crate [krāt] n cajón m de embalaje; (*col*) armatoste m.

crater [krā'tûr] n cráter m.

cravat [krəvat'] n pañuelo.

crave [krāv] vt, vi: **to ~ (for)** ansiar, anhelar.

craving [krā'ving] n (*for food, cigarettes, etc*) antojo.

crawfish [krô'fish] n, pl inv (*US: freshwater*) cangrejo de río; (: *saltwater*) cigala.

crawl [krôl] vi (*drag o.s.*) arrastrarse; (*child*) andar a gatas, gatear; (*vehicle*) avanzar (lentamente); (*col*): **to ~ to sb** dar coba a uno, hacerle la pelota a uno ♦ n (*SWIMMING*) crol m.

crayfish [krā'fish] n, pl inv (*freshwater*) cangrejo de río; (*saltwater*) cigala.

crayon [krā'ân] n lápiz m de color.

craze [krāz] n manía; (*fashion*) moda.

crazed [krāzd] a (*look, person*) loco, demente; (*pottery, glaze*) agrietado, cuarteado.

crazy [krā'zē] a (*person*) loco; (*idea*) disparatado; **to go ~** volverse loco; **to be ~ about sb/sth** (*col*) estar loco por uno/algo.

crazy paving n (*Brit*) pavimento de baldosas irregulares.

CRC n abbr (*US*) = *Civil Rights Commission*.

creak [krēk] vi crujir; (*hinge etc*) chirriar, rechinar.

cream [krēm] n (*of milk*) nata, crema; (*lotion*) crema; (*fig*) flor f y nata ♦ a (*color*) color m crema; **whipped ~** nata batida.

cream cake n pastel m de nata.

cream cheese n queso crema.

creamery [krē'mûrē] n (*store*) quesería; (*factory*) central f lechera.

creamy [krē'mē] a cremoso.

crease [krēs] n (*fold*) pliegue m; (*in pants*) raya; (*wrinkle*) arruga ♦ vt (*fold*) doblar, plegar; (*wrinkle*) arrugar ♦ vi (*wrinkle up*) arrugarse.

crease-resistant [krēsrizis'tənt] a inarrugable.

create [krēāt'] vt (*also COMPUT*) crear; (*impression*) dar; (*fuss, noise*) hacer.

creation [krēā'shən] n creación f.

creative [krēā'tiv] a creador(a).

creativity [krēātiv'ətē] n creatividad f.

creator [krēā'tûr] n creador(a) m/f.

creature [krē'chûr] n (*animal*) animal m, bicho; (*living thing*) criatura.

crèche, creche [kresh] n (*Brit*) guardería (infantil).

credence [krē'dəns] n: **to lend** or **give ~ to** creer en, dar crédito a.

credentials [kriden'shəlz] npl credenciales fpl; (*letters of reference*) referencias fpl.

credibility [kredəbil'ətē] n credibilidad f.

credible [kred'əbəl] a creíble; (*witness, source*) de integridad.

credit [kred'it] n (*gen*) crédito; (*merit*) honor m, mérito; (*UNIV*: *esp US*) unidad f de crédito ♦ vt (*COMM*) abonar; (*believe*) creer, prestar fe a ♦ a crediticio; **to be in ~** (*Brit*: *person, bank account*) tener saldo a favor; **on ~** a crédito; (*col*) al fiado; **he's a ~ to his family** hace honor a su familia; **to ~ sb with** (*fig*) reconocer a uno el mérito de; *see also* **credits.**

creditable [kred'itəbəl] a estimable, digno de elogio.

credit account n cuenta de crédito.

credit agency n agencia de informes comerciales.

credit balance n saldo acreedor.

credit card n tarjeta de crédito.

credit control n control m de créditos.

credit facilities npl facilidades fpl de crédito.

credit limit n límite m de crédito.

credit note n nota de crédito.

creditor [kred'itûr] n acreedor(a) m/f.

credit rating n límite m de crédito.

credits [kred'its] npl (*CINEMA*) títulos mpl, rótulos mpl de crédito.

credit transfer n transferencia de crédito.

creditworthy [kred'itwûrthē] a solvente.

credulity [krədōō'litē] n credulidad f.

creed [krēd] n credo.

creek [krēk] n (*US*) riachuelo; (*Brit*) cala, ensenada.

creel [krēl] n nasa.

creep, pt, pp crept [krēp, krept] vi (*animal*) deslizarse; (*plant*) trepar; **to ~ up on sb** acercarse sigilosamente a uno; (*fig*: *old age etc*) acercarse a uno ♦ n (*col*): **he's a ~** ¡qué desagradable es!; **it gives me the ~s** me da escalofríos.

creeper [krē'pûr] n enredadera.

creepers [krē'pûrz] npl (*US*: *for baby*) pelele msg.

creepy [krē'pē] a (*frightening*) horripilante.

creepy-crawly [krē'pēkrôl'ē] n (*col*) bicho.

cremate [krē'māt] vt incinerar.

cremation [krimā'shən] n incineración f.

crematorium, pl **crematoria** [krēmətôr'ēəm, -tôr'ēə] n crematorio.

creosote [krē'əsōt] n creosota.

crêpe [krāp] n (*fabric*) crespón m; (*also*: **~ rubber**) crep(é) m.

crêpe bandage n (*Brit*) venda elástica.

crêpe paper n papel m crep(é).

crêpe sole n (*on shoes*) suela de crep(é).

crept [krept] pt, pp of **creep.**

crescent [kres'ənt] *n* media luna; (*street*) calle *f* (*en forma de semicírculo*).
cress [kres] *n* berro.
crest [krest] *n* (*of bird*) cresta; (*of hill*) cima, cumbre *f*; (*of helmet*) cimera; (*of coat of arms*) blasón *m*.
crestfallen [krest'fôlən] *a* alicaído.
Crete [krēt] *n* Creta.
cretin [krē'tən] *n* cretino/a.
crevasse [krəvas'] *n* grieta.
crevice [krev'is] *n* grieta, hendedura.
crew [krōō] *n* (*of ship etc*) tripulación *f*; (*CINEMA etc*) equipo; (*gang*) pandilla, banda; (*MIL*) dotación *f*.
crew cut *n* corte *m* al rape.
crew neck *n* cuello plano.
crib [krib] *n* (*US*) cuna; (*Brit*) pesebre *m* ♦ *vt* (*col*) plagiar; **portable** ~ (*US*) cuna portátil.
crick [krik] *n*: ~ **in the neck** tortícolis *m inv*.
cricket [krik'it] *n* (*insect*) grillo; (*game*) críquet *m*.
cricketer [krik'itûr] jugador *m* de críquet.
crime [krīm] *n* crimen *m*; (*less serious*) delito.
crime wave *n* ola de crímenes *or* delitos.
criminal [krim'ənəl] *n* criminal *m/f*, delincuente *m/f* ♦ *a* criminal; (*law*) penal.
Criminal Investigation Department (CID) *n* (*Brit*) ≈ Brigada de Investigación Criminal (B.I.C. *f*) (*Sp*).
crimp [krimp] *vt* (*hair*) rizar.
crimson [krim'zən] *a* carmesí.
cringe [krinj] *vi* agacharse, encogerse.
crinkle [kring'kəl] *vt* arrugar.
crinkly [kring'klē] *a* (*hair*) rizado, crespo.
cripple [krip'əl] *n* lisiado/a, cojo/a ♦ *vt* lisiar, mutilar; (*ship, plane*) inutilizar; (*production, exports*) paralizar; ~**d with arthritis** paralizado por la artritis.
crippling [krip'ling] *a* (*injury etc*) debilitador(a); (*prices, taxes*) devastador(a).
crisis, *pl* **crises** [krī'sis, -sēz] *n* crisis *f*.
crisp [krisp] *a* fresco; (*cooked*) tostado; (*manner*) seco.
crisps [krisps] *npl* (*Brit*) patatas *fpl* fritas.
crisscross [kris'krôs] *a* entrelazado, entrecruzado ♦ *vt* entrecruzar(se).
criterion, *pl* **criteria** [krītēr'ēən, -tēr'ēə] *n* criterio.
critic [krit'ik] *n* crítico/a.
critical [krit'ikəl] *a* (*gen*) crítico; (*illness*) grave; **to be** ~ **of sb/sth** criticar a uno/algo; **to be on the** ~ **list** (*MED*) estar grave.
critically [krit'iklē] *ad* (*speak etc*) en tono crítico; (*ill*) gravemente.
criticism [krit'isizəm] *n* crítica.
criticize [krit'əsīz] *vt* criticar.
critique [kritēk'] *n* crítica.
croak [krōk] *vi* (*frog*) croar; (*raven*) graznar ♦ *n* graznido.

crochet [krōshā'] *n* ganchillo.
crock [kräk] *n* cántaro, tarro; (*col: person: also: old* ~) carcamal *m/f*, vejete/a *m/f*; (*: car etc*) cacharro.
crockery [kräk'ûrē] *n* (*plates, cups etc*) loza, vajilla.
crocodile [kräk'ədīl] *n* cocodrilo.
crocus [krō'kəs] *n* azafrán *m*.
croft [krôft] *n* (*Brit*) granja pequeña.
croissant [krōōsânt'] *n* croissant *m*, medialuna.
crone [krōn] *n* arpía, bruja.
crony [krō'nē] *n* compinche *m/f*.
crook [krōōk] *n* (*fam*) ladrón/ona *m/f*; (*of shepherd*) cayado; (*of arm*) pliegue *m*.
crooked [krōōk'id] *a* torcido; (*path*) tortuoso; (*fam*) sucio.
crop [kräp] *n* (*produce*) cultivo; (*amount produced*) cosecha; (*riding* ~) látigo de montar; (*of bird*) buche *m* ♦ *vt* cortar, recortar; (*cut: hair*) cortar al rape; (*subj: animals: grass*) pacer.
crop up *vi* surgir, presentarse.
crop spraying [kräp' sprā'ing] *n* fumigación *f* de los cultivos.
croquet [krōkā'] *n* croquet *m*.
croquette [krōket'] *n* croqueta.
cross [krôs] *n* cruz *f* ♦ *vt* (*street etc*) cruzar, atravesar; (*thwart: person*) contrariar, ir contra ♦ *vi*: **the boat** ~**es from Santander to Plymouth** el barco hace la travesía de Santander a Plymouth ♦ *a* de mal humor, enojado; **it's a** ~ **between geography and sociology** es una mezcla de geografía y sociología; **to** ~ **o.s.** santiguarse; **they've got their lines** ~**ed** (*fig*) hay un malentendido entre ellos; **to be/get** ~ **with sb (about sth)** estar enfadado/enfadarse con uno (por algo).
cross out *vt* tachar.
cross over *vi* cruzar.
crossbar [krôs'bâr] *n* travesaño.
cross-Channel ferry [krôs'chanəl fär'ē] *n* transbordador *m* que cruza el Canal de la Mancha.
cross-check [krôs'chek] *n* verificación *f* ♦ *vt* verificar.
cross-country (race) [krôs'kun'trē (rās)] *n* carrera a campo traviesa, cross *m*.
cross-examination [krôs'igzamənā'shən] *n* repregunta, interrogatorio.
cross-examine [krôs'igzam'in] *vt* interrogar.
cross-eyed [krôs'īd] *a* bizco.
crossfire [krôs'fīur] *n* fuego cruzado.
crossing [krôs'ing] *n* (*road*) cruce *m*; (*rail*) paso a nivel; (*sea passage*) travesía; (*also: pedestrian* ~) paso para peatones.
crossing guard *n* (*US*) persona encargada de ayudar a los niños a cruzar la calle.
cross purposes *npl*: **to be at** ~ **with sb** tener un malentendido con uno.
cross-reference [krôs'ref'ûrəns] *n* referen-

cia, remisión f.

crossroads [krós'rōdz] *nsg* cruce *m*, encrucijada.

cross section *n* corte *m* transversal; (*of population*) muestra (representativa).

crosswalk [krós'wôk] *n* (*US*) paso de peatones.

crosswind [krós'wind] *n* viento de costado.

crossword [krós'wûrd] *n* crucigrama *m*.

crotch [krâch] *n* (*of garment*) entrepierna.

crotchet [krâch'it] *n* (*Brit MUS*) negra.

crotchety [krâch'ətē] *a* (*person*) arisco.

crouch [krouch] *vi* agacharse, acurrucarse.

croup [krōōp] *n* (*MED*) crup *m*.

croupier [krōō'pēā] *n* crupier *m/f*.

crouton [krōō'tán] *n* cubito de pan frito.

crow [krō] *n* (*bird*) cuervo; (*of cock*) canto, cacareo ♦ *vi* (*cock*) cantar; (*fig*) jactarse.

crowbar [krō'bár] *n* palanca.

crowd [kroud] *n* muchedumbre *f*; (*SPORT*) público; (*common herd*) vulgo ♦ *vt* (*gather*) amontonar; (*fill*) llenar ♦ *vi* (*gather*) reunirse; (*pile up*) amontonarse; **~s of people** gran cantidad de gente.

crowded [krou'did] *a* (*full*) atestado; (*well-attended*) concurrido.

crowd scene *n* (*CINEMA, THEATER*) escena con muchos comparsas.

crown [kroun] *n* corona; (*of head*) coronilla; (*of hat*) copa; (*of hill*) cumbre *f* ♦ *vt* (*also tooth*) coronar; **and to ~ it all ...** (*fig*) y para colmo *or* remate ....

crown court *n* (*Brit LAW*) tribunal *m* superior.

crowning [krou'ning] *a* (*achievement, glory*) máximo.

crown jewels *npl* joyas *fpl* reales.

crown prince *n* príncipe *m* heredero.

crow's feet *npl* patas *fpl* de gallo.

crucial [krōō'shəl] *a* decisivo; **his approval is ~ to the success of the project** su aprobación es crucial para el éxito del proyecto.

crucifix [krōō'səfiks] *n* crucifijo.

crucifixion [krōōsəfik'shən] *n* crucifixión *f*.

crucify [krōō'səfī] *vt* crucificar; (*fig*) martirizar.

crude [krōōd] *a* (*materials*) bruto; (*fig: basic*) tosco; (: *vulgar*) ordinario.

crude (oil) *n* petróleo crudo.

cruel [krōō'əl] *a* cruel.

cruelty [krōō'əltē] *n* crueldad *f*.

cruet [krōō'it] *n* vinagreras *fpl*.

cruise [krōōz] *n* crucero ♦ *vi* (*ship*) hacer un crucero; (*car*) ir a la velocidad de crucero.

cruise missile *n* misil *m* de crucero.

cruiser [krōō'zúr] *n* crucero.

cruising speed [krōō'zing spēd] *n* velocidad *f* de crucero.

crumb [krum] *n* miga, migaja.

crumble [krum'bəl] *vt* desmenuzar ♦ *vi* (*gen*) desmenuzarse; (*building*) desmoronarse.

crumbly [krum'blē] *a* desmenuzable.

crummy [krum'ē] *a* (*col: poor quality*) pésimo, cutre (*Sp*); (: *unwell*) fatal.

crumpet [krum'pit] *n* ≈ bollo para tostar.

crumple [krum'pəl] *vt* (*paper*) estrujar; (*material*) arrugar.

crunch [krunch] *vt* (*with teeth*) ronzar; (*underfoot*) hacer crujir ♦ *n* (*fig*) crisis *f inv*.

crunchy [krun'chē] *a* crujiente.

crusade [krōōsād'] *n* cruzada ♦ *vi*: **to ~ for/against** (*fig*) hacer una campaña en pro de/en contra de.

crusader [krōōsā'dûr] *n* (*fig*) paladín *m/f*, campeón/ona *m/f*.

crush [krush] *n* (*crowd*) aglomeración *f* ♦ *vt* (*gen*) aplastar; (*paper*) estrujar; (*cloth*) arrugar; (*grind, break up: garlic, ice*) picar; (*fruit*) exprimir; (*grapes*) exprimir, prensar; **to have a ~ on sb** estar enamorado de uno.

crushing [krush'ing] *a* aplastante; (*burden*) agobiador(a).

crust [krust] *n* corteza.

crustacean [krustā'shən] *n* crustáceo.

crusty [krus'tē] *a* (*loaf*) de corteza dura.

crutch [kruch] *n* (*MED*) muleta; (*support*) apoyo.

crux [kruks] *n* lo esencial.

cry [krī] *vi* llorar; (*shout: also:* **~ out**) gritar ♦ *n* grito; (*of animal*) aullido; (*weep*): **she had a good ~** lloró a lágrima viva; **what are you ~ing about?** ¿por qué lloras?; **to ~ for help** pedir socorro a voces; **it's a far ~ from ...** (*fig*) dista mucho de ....

cry off *vi* (*Brit*) retirarse.

crypt [kript] *n* cripta.

cryptic [krip'tik] *a* enigmático, secreto.

crystal [kris'təl] *n* cristal *m*.

crystal-clear [kris'təlkli'ûr] *a* claro como el agua; (*fig*) cristalino.

crystallize [kris'təlīz] *vt* (*fig*) cristalizar ♦ *vi* cristalizarse; **~d fruits** (*Brit*) frutas *fpl* escarchadas.

CSA *n abbr* = *Confederate States of America*.

CS gas [sē'es gas'] *n* (*Brit*) gas *m* lacrimógeno.

CST *n abbr* (*US:* = *Central Standard Time*) hora de invierno de Chicago.

CT *abbr* (*US MAIL*) = *Connecticut*.

Ct. *abbr* (*US*) = *Connecticut*.

ct *abbr* = *carat*.

cu. *abbr* = **cubic**.

cub [kub] *n* cachorro; (*also:* **~ scout**) niño explorador.

Cuba [kyōō'bə] *n* Cuba.

Cuban [kyōō'bən] '*a*, *n* cubano/a *m/f*.

cubbyhole [kub'ēhōl] *n* chiribitil *m*.

cube [kyōōb] *n* cubo; (*of sugar*) terrón *m* ♦ *vt* (*MATH*) cubicar.

cube root *n* raíz *f* cúbica.

cubic [kyōō'bik] *a* cúbico; **~ capacity** (*AUT*) capacidad *f* cúbica.

cubicle [kyōō'bikəl] *n* (*at pool*) caseta; (*for bed*) cubículo.
cubism [kyōō'bizəm] *n* cubismo.
cuckoo [kōō'kōō] *n* cuco.
cuckoo clock *n* cucú *m*.
cucumber [kyōō'kumbûr] *n* pepino.
cuddle [kud'əl] *vt* abrazar ♦ *vi* abrazarse.
cuddly [kud'lē] *a* mimoso.
cudgel [kuj'əl] *vt*: **to ~ one's brains** devanarse los sesos.
cue [kyōō] *n* (*snooker* ~) taco; (*THEATER etc*) entrada.
cuff [kuf] *n* (*US: of pants*) vuelta; (*blow*) bofetada; (*Brit: of shirt, coat etc*) puño ♦ *vt* bofetear; **off the ~** *ad* improvisado.
cuff links *npl* gemelos *mpl*.
cu. in. *abbr* = *cubic inches*.
cuisine [kwizēn'] *n* cocina.
cul-de-sac [kul'dəsak'] *n* callejón *m* sin salida.
culinary [kyōō'lənärē] *a* culinario.
cull [kul] *vt* (*select*) entresacar; (*kill selectively: animals*) matar selectivamente ♦ *n* matanza selectiva; **seal ~** (*Brit*) matanza selectiva de focas.
culminate [kul'mənāt] *vi*: **to ~ in** terminar en.
culmination [kulmənā'shən] *n* culminación *f*, colmo.
culottes [kyōōláts'] *npl* falda *f* pantalón.
culpable [kul'pəbəl] *a* culpable.
culprit [kul'prit] *n* culpable *m/f*, delincuente *m/f*.
cult [kult] *n* culto; **a ~ figure** un ídolo.
cultivate [kul'təvāt] *vt* (*also fig*) cultivar.
cultivated [kul'təvātid] *a* culto.
cultivation [kultəvā'shən] *n* cultivo; (*fig*) cultura.
cultural [kul'chûrəl] *a* cultural.
culture [kul'chûr] *n* (*also fig*) cultura.
cultured [kul'chûrd] *a* culto.
cumbersome [kum'bûrsəm] *a* de mucho bulto, voluminoso.
cumin [kyōōm'in] *n* (*spice*) comino.
cummerbund [kum'ûrbund] *n* faja, fajín *m*.
cumulative [kyōōm'yələtiv] *a* cumulativo.
cunning [kun'ing] *n* astucia ♦ *a* astuto; (*clever: device, idea*) ingenioso.
cup [kup] *n* taza; (*prize, event*) copa; **a ~ of tea** una taza de té.
cupboard [kub'ûrd] *n* (*Brit*) armario; (: in *kitchen*) alacena.
cupful [kup'fəl] *n* taza.
Cupid [kyōō'pid] *n* Cupido.
cupola [kyōō'pələ] *n* cúpula.
cup-tie [kup'tī] *n* (*Brit*) partido de copa.
cur [kûr] *n* perro de mala raza; (*person*) canalla *m*.
curable [kyōō'rəbəl] *a* curable.
curate [kyōō'rit] *n* cura *m*.
curator [kyōōrā'tûr] *n* conservador(a) *m/f*.
curb [kûrb] *vt* refrenar, limitar ♦ *n* freno;

(*US*) bordillo.
curd cheese [kûrd chēz] *n* requesón *m*.
curdle [kûr'dəl] *vi* cuajarse.
curds [kûrdz] *npl* requesón *msg*.
cure [kyōōr] *vt* curar ♦ *n* cura, curación *f*; **to be ~d of sth** curarse de algo; **to take a ~** (*Brit*) tomar una medicina, hacer una cura.
cure-all [kyōōr'ôl] *n* (*also fig*) panacea.
curfew [kûr'fyōō] *n* toque *m* de queda.
curio [kyōō'rēō] *n* curiosidad *f*.
curiosity [kyōōrēás'ətē] *n* curiosidad *f*.
curious [kyōō'rēəs] *a* curioso; **I'm ~ about him** me intriga.
curiously [kyōō'rēəslē] *ad* curiosamente; **~ enough, ...** aunque parezca extraño ....
curl [kûrl] *n* rizo; (*of smoke etc*) espiral *f*, voluta ♦ *vt* (*hair*) rizar; (*paper*) arrollar; (*lip*) fruncir ♦ *vi* rizarse; arrollarse.
curl up *vi* arrollarse; (*person*) hacerse un ovillo; (*fam*) morirse de risa.
curler [kûr'lûr] *n* bigudí *m*.
curlew [kûr'lōō] *n* zarapito.
curling iron [kûr'ling i'ûrn] *n* (*US*) tenacillas *fpl*.
curling tongs [kûr'ling tángz] *npl* (*Brit*) = **curling iron**.
curly [kûr'lē] *a* rizado.
currant [kûr'ənt] *n* pasa; (*black, red*) grosella.
currency [kûr'ənsē] *n* moneda; **to gain ~** (*fig*) difundirse.
current [kûr'ənt] *n* corriente *f* ♦ *a* corriente, actual; (*tendency, price, event*) corriente; **direct/alternating ~** corriente directa/alterna; **the ~ issue of a magazine** el número corriente de una revista; **in ~ use** de uso corriente.
current account *n* (*Brit*) cuenta corriente.
current affairs *npl* actualidades *fpl*.
current assets *npl* (*COMM*) activo disponible.
current liabilities *npl* (*COMM*) pasivo circulante.
currently [kûr'əntlē] *ad* actualmente.
curriculum, *pl* **~s** *or* **curricula** [kərik'yələm, -lə] *n* plan *m* de estudios.
curriculum vitae (CV) [kərik'yələm vē'tī] *n* currículum *m*.
curry [kûr'ē] *n* curry *m* ♦ *vt*: **to ~ favor with** buscar favores con.
curry powder *n* curry *m* en polvo.
curse [kûrs] *vi* echar pestes ♦ *vt* maldecir ♦ *n* maldición *f*; (*swearword*) palabrota.
cursor [kûr'sûr] *n* (*COMPUT*) cursor *m*.
cursory [kûr'sûrē] *a* rápido, superficial.
curt [kûrt] *a* corto, seco.
curtail [kûrtāl'] *vt* (*cut short*) acortar; (*restrict*) restringir.
curtain [kûr'tən] *n* cortina; (*THEATER*) telón *m*; **to draw the ~s** (*together*) cerrar las cortinas; (*apart*) abrir las cortinas.

curtain call n (*THEATER*) llamada a escena.

curtain ring n anilla.

curts(e)y |kûrt'sē| n reverencia ♦ vi hacer una reverencia.

curvature |kûr'vəchûr| n curvatura.

curve |kûrv| n curva ♦ vt encorvar, torcer ♦ vi encorvarse, torcerse; (*road*) hacer curva.

curved |kûrvd| a curvo, encorvado.

cushion |kōōsh'ən| n cojín m; (*SNOOKER*) banda ♦ vt (*seat*) acolchar; (*shock*) amortiguar.

cushy |kōōsh'ē| a (*Brit col*): **a ~ job** un chollo.

custard |kus'tûrd| n (*for pouring*) natillas fpl.

custodian |kustō'dēən| n custodio m/f; (*of museum etc*) conservador(a) m/f.

custody |kus'tədē| n custodia; **to take sb into ~** detener a uno; **in the ~ of** al cuidado or cargo de.

custom |kus'təm| n costumbre f; (*COMM*) clientela; see also **customs**.

customary |kus'təmärē| a acostumbrado; **it is ~ to do** ... es la costumbre hacer ....

custom-built |kus'təmbilt'| a = **custom-made**.

customer |kus'təmûr| n cliente m/f; **he's a tough ~** (*col*) es un tipo difícil.

customer profile n perfil m del cliente.

customer service n servicio de asistencia pos-venta.

customized |kus'təmīzd| a (*car etc*) hecho a encargo.

custom-made |kus'təmmād'| a hecho a la medida.

customs |kus'təmz| npl aduana sg; **to go through (the) ~** pasar la aduana.

Customs and Excise n (*Brit*) Aduanas fpl y Arbitrios.

customs duty n derechos mpl de aduana.

customs officer n aduanero/a.

cut |kut| vb (*pt, pp* cut) vt cortar; (*price*) rebajar; (*record*) grabar; (*reduce*) reducir; (*col: avoid: class, lecture*) fumarse, faltar a ♦ vi cortar; (*intersect*) cruzarse ♦ n corte m; (*in skin*) cortadura; (*with sword*) tajo; (*of knife*) cuchillada; (*in salary etc*) rebaja; (*slice of meat*) tajada; **to ~ one's finger** cortarse un dedo; **to get one's hair ~** cortarse el pelo; **it ~s both ways** (*fig*) tiene doble filo; **to ~ a tooth** echar un diente; **power ~** (*Brit*) apagón m.

cut back vt (*plants*) podar; (*production, expenditure*) reducir.

cut down vt (*tree*) cortar, derribar; (*consumption, expenses*) reducir; **to ~ sb down to size** (*fig*) bajarle los humos a uno.

cut in vi: **to ~ in (on)** (*interrupt: conversation*) interrumpir, intervenir (en); (*AUT*) cerrar el paso (a).

cut off vt cortar; (*fig*) aislar; (*troops*) cercar; **we've been ~ off** (*TEL*) nos han cortado la comunicación.

cut out vt (*shape*) recortar; (*delete*) suprimir.

cut up vt cortar (en pedazos); (*chop: food*) trinchar, cortar.

cut-and-dried |kutəndrīd'| a (*also:* **cut-and-dry**) arreglado de antemano, seguro.

cutback |kut'bak| n reducción f.

cute |kyōōt| a lindo; (*shrewd*) listo.

cuticle |kyōō'tikəl| n cutícula.

cutlery |kut'lûrē| n cubiertos mpl.

cutlet |kut'lit| n chuleta.

cutoff |kut'ôf| n (*also:* **~ point**) límite m.

cutout |kut'out| n (*cardboard ~*) recortable m.

cut-price |kut'prīs| a (*Brit*) = **cut-rate**.

cut-rate |kut'rāt| a (*US*) a precio reducido.

cutthroat |kut'thrōt| n asesino/a ♦ a feroz; **~ competition** competencia encarnizada or despiadada.

cutting |kut'ing| a (*gen*) cortante; (*remark*) mordaz ♦ n (*Brit: from newspaper*) recorte m; (: *RAIL*) desmonte m; (*CINEMA*) desglose m.

CV n abbr = **curriculum vitae**.

C & W n abbr = **country and western (music)**.

cwo abbr (*COMM*) = **cash with order**.

cwt. abbr = **hundredweight(s)**.

cyanide |sī'ənīd| n cianuro.

cybernetics |sībûrnet'iks| nsg cibernética.

cyclamen |sik'ləmən| n ciclamen m.

cycle |sī'kəl| n ciclo; (*bicycle*) bicicleta ♦ vi ir en bicicleta.

cycle race n carrera ciclista.

cycling |sīk'ling| n ciclismo.

cyclist |sīk'list| n ciclista m/f.

cyclone |sīk'lōn| n ciclón m.

cygnet |sig'nit| n pollo de cisne.

cylinder |sil'indûr| n cilindro.

cylinder block n bloque m de cilindros.

cylinder capacity n cilindrada.

cylinder head n culata de cilindro.

cylinder-head gasket |sil'indûrhed gas'-kit| n junta de culata.

cymbals |sim'bəlz| npl platillos mpl.

cynic |sin'ik| n cínico/a.

cynical |sin'ikəl| a cínico.

cynicism |sin'əsizəm| n cinismo.

CYO n abbr (*US*) = *Catholic Youth Organization*.

cypress |sī'pris| n ciprés m.

Cypriot |sip'rēət| a, n chipriota m/f.

Cyprus |sī'prəs| n Chipre f.

cyst |sist| n quiste m.

cystitis |sistī'tis| n cistitis f.

CZ n abbr (*US*: = Canal Zone) zona del Canal de Panamá.

czar |zår| n zar m.

czarina |zårē'nə| n zarina.

Czech |chek| a checo ♦ n checo/a; (*LING*)

checo.

Czechoslovak [chekəslō'vak] *a*, *n* = **Czechoslovakian**.

Czechoslovakia [chekəsləvák'ēə] *n* Checoslovaquia.

Czechoslovakian [chekəsləvák'ēən] *a*, *n* checo/a *m/f*.

D

D, d [dē] *n* (*letter*) D, d; (*MUS*): **D** re *m*; **D for Dog** D de Dolores.

D *abbr* (*US POL*) = **democrat(ic)**.

d. *abbr* = *died*.

DA *n abbr* (*US*) = **district attorney**.

dab [dab] *vt:* **to ~ ointment onto a wound** aplicar pomada sobre una herida; **to ~ with paint** cubrir ligeramente de pintura ♦ *n* (*light stroke*) toque *m*; (*small amount*) pizca.

dabble [dab'əl] *vi:* **to ~ in** hacer por afición.

Dacca [dák'ə] *n* Dacca.

dachshund [dáks'ōond] *n* perro tejonero.

Dacron ® [dā'krán] *n* (*US*) terylene *m*.

dad [dad], **daddy** [dad'ē] *n* papá *m*.

daddy-long-legs [dadēlóng'legz] *n* típula.

daffodil [daf'ədil] *n* narciso.

daft [daft] *a* chiflado.

dagger [dag'ûr] *n* puñal *m*, daga; **to look ~s at sb** apuñalar a uno con la mirada.

dahlia [dal'yə] *n* dalia.

daily [dā'lē] *a* diario, cotidiano ♦ *n* (*paper*) diario; (*domestic help*) asistenta ♦ *ad* todos los días, cada día; **twice ~** dos veces al día.

dainty [dān'tē] *a* delicado; (*tasteful*) elegante.

dairy [dār'ē] *n* (*shop*) lechería; (*on farm*) vaquería ♦ *a* (*cow etc*) lechero.

dairy cow *n* vaca lechera.

dairy farm *n* vaquería.

dairy produce *n* productos *mpl* lácteos.

dais [dā'is] *n* estrado.

daisy [dā'zē] *n* margarita.

daisy wheel *n* (*on printer*) (rueda) margarita.

daisy-wheel printer [dā'zēhwēl print'ûr] *n* impresora de margarita.

Dakar [dákâr'] *n* Dakar *m*.

dale [dāl] *n* valle *m*.

dally [dal'ē] *vi* entretenerse.

dalmatian [dalmā'shən] *n* (*dog*) (perro) dálmata *m*.

dam [dam] *n* presa; (*reservoir*) embalse ♦ *vt* represar.

damage [dam'ij] *n* daño; (*fig*) perjuicio; (*to machine*) avería ♦ *vt* dañar; perjudicar; averiar; **~ to property** daños materiales.

damages [dam'ijiz] *npl* (*LAW*) daños y perjuicios; **to pay $5000 in ~** pagar $5000 por daños y perjuicios.

damaging [dam'ijing] *a:* **~ (to)** perjudicial (a).

Damascus [dəmas'kəs] *n* Damasco.

dame [dām] *n* (*title*) dama; (*THEATER*) vieja.

damn [dam] *vt* condenar; (*curse*) maldecir ♦ *n* (*col*): **I don't give a ~** me importa un pito ♦ *a* (*col: also:* **~ed**) maldito; **~ (it)!** ¡maldito sea!

damnable [dam'nəbəl] *a* (*col: behavior*) detestable; (: *weather*) horrible.

damnation [damnā'shən] *n* (*REL*) condenación *f* ♦ *excl* (*col*) ¡maldición!, ¡maldito sea!

damning [dam'ing] *a* (*evidence*) irrecusable.

damp [damp] *a* húmedo, mojado ♦ *n* humedad *f* ♦ *vt* (*also:* **~en**) (*cloth, rag*) mojar; (*enthusiasm*) enfriar.

dampcourse [damp'kôrs] *n* aislante *m* hidrófugo.

damper [dam'pûr] *n* (*MUS*) sordina; (*of fire*) regulador *m* de tiro; **to put a ~ on things** estropearlo todo.

dampness [damp'nis] *n* humedad *f*.

damson [dam'zən] *n* ciruela damascena.

dance [dans] *n* baile *m* ♦ *vi* bailar; **to ~ around** saltar.

dance hall *n* salón *m* de baile.

dancer [dan'sûr] *n* bailador(a) *m/f*; (*professional*) bailarín/ina *m/f*.

dancing [dan'sing] *n* baile *m*.

D and C *n abbr* (*MED: = dilation and curettage*) raspado.

dandelion [dan'dəlīən] *n* diente *m* de león.

dandruff [dan'drəf] *n* caspa.

dandy [dan'dē] *n* dandi *m* ♦ *a* (*US col*) estupendo.

Dane [dān] *n* danés/esa *m/f*.

danger [dān'jûr] *n* peligro; (*risk*) riesgo; **~!** (*on sign*) ¡peligro de muerte!; **to be in ~ of** correr riesgo de; **out of ~** fuera de peligro.

danger list *n* (*Brit MED*): **to be on the ~** estar grave.

dangerous [dān'jûrəs] *a* peligroso.

dangerously [dān'jûrəslē] *ad* peligrosamente; **~ ill** muy enfermo.

danger zone *n* área *or* zona de peligro.

dangle [dang'gəl] *vt* colgar ♦ *vi* pender, estar colgado.

Danish [dā'nish] *a* danés/esa ♦ *n* (*LING*) danés *m*.

Danish pastry *n* pasta de almendra.

dank [dangk] *a* húmedo y malsano.

Danube [dan'yōob] *n* Danubio.

dapper [dap'ûr] *a* pulcro, apuesto.

Dardanelles [dârdənelz'] *npl* Dardanelos *mpl.*

dare [där] *vt*: **to ~ sb to do** desafiar a uno a hacer ♦ *vi*: **to ~ (to) do sth** atreverse a hacer algo; **I ~ say** (*I suppose*) puede ser, a lo mejor; **I ~ say he'll turn up** puede ser que *or* quizás venga; **I don't ~ tell him** no me atrevo a decírselo.

daredevil [där'devəl] *n* temerario/a, atrevido/a.

Dar es Salaam [dâr es sɔlâm'] *n* Dar es Salaam *m.*

daring [där'ing] *a* (*person*) osado; (*plan, escape*) atrevido ♦ *n* atrevimiento, osadía.

dark [dârk] *a* oscuro; (*hair, complexion*) moreno; (*fig: cheerless*) triste, sombrío ♦ *n* (*gen*) oscuridad *f*; (*night*) tinieblas *fpl*; **~ chocolate** chocolate *m* amargo; **it is/is getting ~** es de noche/se está poniendo oscuro; **in the ~ about** (*fig*) en ignorancia de; **after ~** después del anochecer.

darken [dâr'kən] *vt* oscurecer; (*color*) hacer más oscuro ♦ *vi* oscurecerse; (*cloud over*) anublarse.

dark glasses *npl* gafas *fpl* negras.

darkly [dârk'lē] *ad* (*gloomily*) tristemente; (*sinisterly*) siniestramente.

darkness [dârk'nis] *n* (*in room*) oscuridad *f*; (*night*) tinieblas *fpl.*

darkroom [dârk'rōōm] *n* cuarto oscuro.

darling [dâr'ling] *a, n* querido/a *m/f.*

darn [dârn] *vt* zurcir.

dart [dârt] *n* dardo; (*in sewing*) sisa ♦ *vi* precipitarse; **to ~ away/along** *vi* salir/marchar disparado; **to ~ through the traffic** regatear por el tráfico.

dartboard [dârt'bôrd] *n* diana.

darts [dârts] *n* dardos *mpl.*

dash [dash] *n* (*small quantity*: *of liquid*) gota, chorrito; (: *of solid*) pizca; (*sign*) guión *m*; (: *long*) raya ♦ *vt* (*break*) romper, estrellar; (*hopes*) defraudar ♦ *vi* precipitarse, ir de prisa; **a ~ of soda** un poco *or* chorrito de sifón *or* soda.

dash away, dash off *vi* marcharse apresuradamente.

dashboard [dash'bôrd] *n* (*AUT*) tablero de instrumentos.

dashing [dash'ing] *a* gallardo.

dastardly [das'tûrdlē] *ad* ruin, vil.

data [dā'tə] *npl* datos *mpl.*

database [dā'təbās] *n* base *f* de datos.

data capture *n* recogida de datos.

data link *n* enlace *m* de datos.

data processing *n* proceso de datos.

data transmission *n* transmisión *f* de datos.

date [dāt] *n* (*day*) fecha; (*with friend*) cita; (*fruit*) dátil *m* ♦ *vt* fechar; (*col: girl etc*) salir con; **what's the ~ today?** ¿qué fecha es hoy?; **~ of birth** fecha de nacimiento; **closing ~** fecha tope; **to ~** *ad* hasta la fecha; **out of ~** pasado de moda; **up to ~**

moderno; puesto al día; **to bring up to ~** (*correspondence, information*) poner al día; (*method*) actualizar; **to bring sb up to ~** poner a uno al corriente; **letter ~d July 5th** *or* (*Brit*) **5th July** carta fechada el 5 de julio.

dated [dā'tid] *a* anticuado.

date stamp *n* matasellos *m inv*; (*on fresh foods*) sello de fecha.

dative [dā'tiv] *n* dativo.

daub [dôb] *vt* embadurnar.

daughter [dôt'ûr] *n* hija.

daughter-in-law [dô'tûrinlô] *n* nuera, hija política.

daunting [dôn'ting] *a* desalentador(a).

davenport [dav'ənpôrt] *n* (*US: sofa*) sofá *m.*

dawdle [dôd'əl] *vi* (*waste time*) perder el tiempo; (*go slowly*) andar muy despacio; **to ~ over one's work** trabajar muy despacio.

dawn [dôn] *n* alba, amanecer *m* ♦ *vi* amanecer; (*fig*): **it ~ed on him that...** cayó en la cuenta de que...; **at ~** al amanecer; **from ~ to dusk** de sol a sol.

day [dā] *n* día *m*; (*working ~*) jornada; **the ~ before** el día anterior; **the ~ after tomorrow** pasado mañana; **the ~ before yesterday** anteayer, antes de ayer; **the ~ after, the following ~** el día siguiente; **by ~** de día; **~ by ~** día por día; **(on) the ~ that ...** el día que ...; **to work an 8-hour ~** trabajar 8 horas diarias *or* al día; **he works 8 hours a ~** trabaja 8 horas al día; **paid by the ~** pagado por día; **these ~s, in the present ~** hoy en día.

daybook [dā'bōōk] *n* diario *or* libro de entradas y salidas.

daybreak [dā'brāk] *n* amanecer *m.*

day-care center [dā'kär sen'tûr] *n* guardería.

daydream [dā'drēm] *n* ensueño ♦ *vi* soñar despierto.

daylight [dā'līt] *n* luz *f* (del día).

Daylight Saving Time *n* (*US*) hora de verano.

day-release course [dārilēs' kôrs] *n* (*Brit*) curso de un día a la semana.

day return (ticket) *n* (*Brit*) billete *m* de ida y vuelta (en un día).

day shift *n* turno de día.

daytime [dā'tīm] *n* día *m.*

day-to-day [dātōōdā'] *a* cotidiano, diario; (*expenses*) diario; **on a ~ basis** día por día.

day trip *n* (*Brit*) excursión *f* (de un día).

daze [dāz] *vt* (*stun*) aturdir ♦ *n*: **in a ~** aturdido.

dazed [dāzd] *a* aturdido.

dazzle [daz'əl] *vt* deslumbrar.

dazzling [daz'ling] *a* (*light, smile*) deslumbrante; (*color*) fuerte.

DBS *n abbr* (= *direct broadcasting by sat-*

ellite) transmisión por satélite.

DC *abbr* (*ELEC*) = **direct current**; (*US MAIL*) = *District of Columbia*.

DD *n abbr* (= *Doctor of Divinity*) título universitario.

D/D *abbr* = *demand draft*; (*Brit*) = *direct debit*.

D-day [dē'dā] *n* (*fig*) día *m* clave.

DDS *n abbr* (*US*: = *Doctor of Dental Science*; *Doctor of Dental Surgery*) títulos universitarios.

DDT *n abbr* (= *dichlorodiphenyltrichloroethane*) DDT *m*.

DE *abbr* (*US MAIL*) = *Delaware*.

DEA *n abbr* (*US*: = *Drug Enforcement Administration*) *brigada especial dedicada a la lucha contra el tráfico de estupefacientes.*

deacon [dē'kən] *n* diácono.

dead [ded] *a* muerto; (*limb*) dormido; (*battery*) agotado ♦ *ad* totalmente; (*exactly*) justo; **he was ~ on arrival** ingresó cadáver; **to shoot sb ~** matar a uno a tiros; **~ tired** muerto (de cansancio); **to stop ~** parar en seco; **the line has gone ~** (*TEL*) se ha cortado la línea; **the ~** *npl* los muertos.

deaden [ded'ən] *vt* (*blow, sound*) amortiguar; (*pain*) calmar, aliviar.

dead end *n* callejón *m* sin salida.

dead-end [dedend'] *a*: **a ~ job** un trabajo sin porvenir.

dead heat *n* (*SPORT*) empate *m*.

deadline [ded'līn] *n* fecha *or* hora tope; **to work to a ~** trabajar con una fecha tope.

deadlock [ded'lâk] *n* punto muerto.

dead loss *n* (*col*): **to be a ~** (*person*) ser un inútil; (*thing*) ser una birria.

deadly [ded'lē] *a* mortal, fatal; **~ dull** aburridísimo.

deadly nightshade [ded'lē nīt'shâd] *n* belladona.

deadpan [ded'pan] *a* sin expresión.

Dead Sea *n*: **the ~** el Mar Muerto.

dead season *n* (*Brit TOURISM*) temporada baja.

deaf [def] *a* sordo; **to turn a ~ ear to sth** hacerse el sordo ante algo.

deaf-and-dumb [def'əndum'] *a* (*person*) sordomudo; (*alphabet*) para sordomudos.

deafen [def'ən] *vt* ensordecer.

deafening [def'əning] *a* ensordecedor(a).

deaf-mute [def'myōot'] *n* sordomudo/a.

deafness [def'nis] *n* sordera.

deal [dēl] *n* (*agreement*) pacto, convenio; (*business*) negocio, transacción *f*; (*CARDS*) reparto ♦ *vt* (*pt, pp* **dealt**) (*gen*) dar; **a great ~ (of)** bastante, mucho; **it's a ~!** (*col*) ¡trato hecho!, ¡de acuerdo!; **to make a ~ with sb** hacer un trato con uno; **he got a bad/fair ~ from them** le trataron mal/bien.

deal in *vt fus* tratar en, comerciar en.

deal with *vt fus* (*people*) tratar con; (*problem*) ocuparse de; (*subject*) tratar de.

dealer [dē'lûr] *n* comerciante *m/f*; (*CARDS*) mano *f*.

dealership [dē'lûrship] *n* concesionario.

dealings [dē'lingz] *npl* (*COMM*) transacciones *fpl*; (*relations*) relaciones *fpl*.

dealt [delt] *pt, pp of* **deal**.

dean [dēn] *n* (*REL*) deán *m*; (*SCOL*) decano/a.

dear [dēr] *a* querido; (*costly*) caro ♦ *n*: **my ~** mi querido/a; **~ me!** ¡Dios mío!; **D~ Sir/Madam** (*in letter*) Muy señor mío, Estimado señor/Estimada señora; **D~ Mr/Mrs X** Estimado/a señor(a) X.

dearly [dēr'lē] *ad* (*love*) mucho; (*pay*) caro.

dearth [dûrth] *n* (*of food, resources, money*) escasez *f*.

death [deth] *n* muerte *f*.

deathbed [deth'bed] *n* lecho de muerte.

death certificate *n* partida de defunción.

deathly [deth'lē] *a* mortal; (*silence*) profundo.

death penalty *n* pena de muerte.

death rate *n* tasa de mortalidad.

death sentence *n* condena a muerte.

death trap *n* lugar *m* (*o* vehículo *etc*) peligroso.

debacle [dəbâk'əl] *n* desastre *m*, catástrofe *f*.

debar [dibâr'] *vt*: **to ~ sb from doing** prohibir a uno hacer.

debase [dibās'] *vt* degradar.

debatable [dibā'təbəl] *a* discutible; **it is ~ whether ...** es discutible si ... .

debate [dibāt'] *n* debate *m* ♦ *vt* discutir.

debauched [dibôcht'] *a* vicioso.

debauchery [debô'chûrē] *n* libertinaje *m*.

debenture [diben'chûr] *n* (*COMM*) bono, obligación *f*.

debenture capital *n* capital *m* hipotecario.

debilitate [dibil'ətāt] *vt* debilitar.

debilitating [dibil'ətāting] *a* (*illness etc*) debilitante.

debit [deb'it] *n* debe *m* ♦ *vt*: **to ~ a sum to sb** *or* **to sb's account** cargar una suma en cuenta a uno.

debit balance *n* saldo deudor *or* pasivo.

debit note *n* nota de débito *or* cargo.

debonair [debənär'] *a* jovial, cortés/esa.

debrief [dēbrēf'] *vt* hacer dar parte.

debriefing [dēbrēf'ing] *n* relación *f* (de un informe).

debris [dəbrē'] *n* escombros *mpl*.

debt [det] *n* deuda; **to be in ~** tener deudas; **~s of $5000** deudas de cinco mil dólares; **bad ~** deuda incobrable.

debt collector *n* cobrador(a) *m/f* de deudas.

debtor [det'ûr] *n* deudor(a) *m/f*.

debug [dēbug'] *vt* (*COMPUT*) depurar.

debunk [dibungk'] *vt* (*col: theory*) desprestigiar, desacreditar; (: *claim*) desacreditar; (: *person*, *institution*) desenmascarar.

début [dābyoō'] *n* presentación *f*.

debutante [debyoōtânt'] *n* debutante *f*.

Dec. *abbr* (= *December*) dic.

decade [dek'ād] *n* decenio.

decadence [dek'ədəns] *n* decadencia.

decadent [dek'ədənt] *a* decadente.

decaffeinated [dēkaf'ənātid] *a* descafeinado.

decamp [dikamp'] *vi* (*col*) escaparse, largarse, rajarse (*LAm*).

decant [dikant'] *vt* decantar.

decanter [dikan'tûr] *n* garrafa.

decay [dikā'] *n* (*fig*) decadencia; (*of building*) desmoronamiento; (*of tooth*) caries *f inv* ♦ *vi* (*rot*) pudrirse; (*fig*) decaer.

decease [disēs'] *n* fallecimiento ♦ *vi* fallecer.

deceased [disēst'] *a* difunto.

deceit [disēt'] *n* engaño.

deceitful [disēt'fəl] *a* engañoso.

deceive [disēv'] *vt* engañar.

decelerate [dēsel'ərāt] *vt* moderar la marcha de ♦ *vi* decelerar.

December [disem'bûr] *n* diciembre *m*.

decency [dē'sənsē] *n* decencia.

decent [dē'sənt] *a* (*proper*) decente; (*person*) amable, bueno.

decently [dē'səntlē] *ad* (*respectably*) decentemente; (*kindly*) amablemente.

decentralization [dēsentrəlizā'shən] *n* descentralización *f*.

decentralize [dēsen'trəlīz] *vt* descentralizar.

deception [disep'shən] *n* engaño.

deceptive [disep'tiv] *a* engañoso.

decibel [des'əbəl] *n* decibel(io) *m*.

decide [disīd'] *vt* (*person*) decidir; (*question, argument*) resolver ♦ *vi*: **to ~ to do/ that** decidir hacer/que; **to ~ on sth** decidir por algo; **to ~ against doing sth** decidir en contra de hacer algo.

decided [disī'did] *a* (*resolute*) decidido; (*clear, definite*) indudable.

decidedly [disī'didlē] *ad* decididamente.

deciding [disī'ding] *a* decisivo.

deciduous [disij'ōōəs] *a* de hoja caduca.

decimal [des'əməl] *a* decimal ♦ *n* decimal *f*; **to 3 ~ places** con 3 cifras decimales.

decimalize [des'əməlīz] *vt* convertir al sistema decimal.

decimal point *n* coma decimal.

decimal system *n* sistema *m* métrico.

decimate [des'əmāt] *vt* diezmar.

decipher [disī'fûr] *vt* descifrar.

decision [disizh'ən] *n* decisión *f*; **to make a ~** tomar una decisión.

decisive [disī'siv] *a* (*influence*) decisivo; (*manner, person*) decidido; (*reply*) tajante.

deck [dek] *n* (*NAUT*) cubierta; (*of bus*) piso; (*of cards*) baraja; **cassette ~** platina; **to go up on ~** subir a (la) cubierta; **below ~**

en la bodega.

deck chair *n* tumbona.

deckhand [dek'hand] *n* marinero de cubierta.

declaration [deklərā'shən] *n* declaración *f*.

declare [diklär'] *vt* (*gen*) declarar.

declassify [dēklas'əfī] *vt* permitir la publicación de.

decline [diklīn'] *n* decaimiento, decadencia; (*lessening*) disminución *f* ♦ *vt* rehusar ♦ *vi* decaer; disminuir; **~ in living standards** disminución *f* del nivel de vida; **to ~ to do sth** negarse a hacer algo.

declutch [dēkluch'] *vi* desembragar.

decode [dēkōd'] *vt* descifrar.

decoder [dēkō'dûr] *n* (*COMPUT*) decodificador *m*.

decompose [dēkəmpōz'] *vi* descomponerse.

decomposition [dēkâmpəzish'ən] *n* descomposición *f*.

decompression [dēkəmpresh'ən] *n* descompresión *f*.

decompression chamber *n* cámara de descompresión.

decongestant [dēkənjes'tənt] *n* descongestionante.

decontaminate [dēkəntam'ənāt] *vt* descontaminar.

decontrol [dēkəntrōl'] *vt* (*Brit*: *trade*) quitar controles a; (: *prices*) descongelar.

décor [dākôr'] *n* decoración *f*; (*THEATER*) decorado.

decorate [dek'ərāt] *vt* (*paint*) pintar; (*paper*) empapelar; (*adorn*): **to ~ (with)** adornar (de), decorar (de).

decoration [dekərā'shən] *n* adorno; (*act*) decoración *f*; (*medal*) condecoración *f*.

decorative [dek'ûrətiv] *a* decorativo.

decorator [dek'ərātûr] *n* (*workman*) pintor *m* decorador.

decorum [dikôr'əm] *n* decoro.

decoy [dē'koi] *n* señuelo; **police ~** trampa *or* señuelo policial.

decrease *n* [dē'krēs] disminución *f* ♦ (*vb*: [dikrēs']) *vt* disminuir, reducir ♦ *vi* reducirse; **to be on the ~** ir disminuyendo.

decreasing [dikrēs'ing] *a* decreciente.

decree [dikrē'] *n* decreto ♦ *vt*: **to ~ (that)** decretar (que); **~ absolute/nisi** sentencia absoluta/provisional de divorcio.

decrepit [dikrep'it] *a* (*person*) decrépito; (*building*) ruinoso.

decry [dikrī'] *vt* criticar, censurar.

dedicate [ded'ikāt] *vt* dedicar.

dedicated [ded'ikātid] *a* dedicado; (*COMPUT*) especializado; **~ word processor** procesador *m* de textos especializado *or* dedicado.

dedication [dedikā'shən] *n* (*devotion*) dedicación *f*; (*in book*) dedicatoria.

deduce [didoōs'] *vt* deducir.

deduct [didukt'] *vt* restar; (*from wage etc*) descontar.

deduction |diduk'shən| *n* (*amount de-ducted*) descuento; (*conclusion*) deducción *f*, conclusión *f*.

deed |dēd| *n* hecho, acto; (*feat*) hazaña; (*LAW*) escritura; ~ **of covenant** escritura de contrato.

deem |dēm| *vt* (*formal*) juzgar, considerar; **to ~ it wise to do** considerar prudente hacer.

deep |dēp| *a* profundo; (*voice*) bajo; (*breath*) profundo, a pleno pulmón ♦ *ad*: **the spectators stood 20 ~** los espectadores se formaron de 20 en fondo; **to be 4 meters ~** tener 4 metros de profundo.

deepen |dē'pən| *vt* ahondar, profundizar ♦ *vi* (*darkness*) intensificarse.

deep-freeze |dēp'frēz'| *n* congeladora.

deep-fry |dēp'frī'| *vt* freír en aceite abundante.

deeply |dēp'lē| *ad* (*breathe*) a pleno pulmón; (*interested, moved, grateful*) profundamente, hondamente; **to regret sth ~** sentir algo profundamente.

deep-rooted |dēp'rōō'tid| *a* (*prejudice, habit*) profundamente arraigado; (*affection*) profundo.

deep-sea |dēp'sē'| *a*: ~ **diver** buzo; ~ **diving** buceo de altura.

deep-seated |dēp'sē'tid| *a* (*beliefs*) (profundamente) arraigado.

deep-set |dēp'set| *a* (*eyes*) hundido.

deer |dēr| *n, pl inv* ciervo.

deerstalker |dēr'stókûr| *n* (*hat*) gorro de cazador.

deface |difās'| *vt* desfigurar, mutilar.

defamation |defəmā'shən| *n* difamación *f*.

defamatory |difam'ətôrē| *a* difamatorio.

default |difólt'| *vi* faltar al pago; (*SPORT*) dejar de presentarse ♦ *n* (*COMPUT*) defecto; **by ~** (*LAW*) en rebeldía; (*SPORT*) por incomparecencia; **to ~ on a debt** dejar de pagar una deuda.

defaulter |difólt'ûr| *n* (*in debt*) moroso/a.

default option *n* (*COMPUT*) opción *f* por defecto.

defeat |difēt'| *n* derrota ♦ *vt* derrotar, vencer; (*fig: efforts*) frustrar.

defeatism |difē'tizəm| *n* derrotismo.

defeatist |difē'tist| *a, n* derrotista *m/f*.

defect *n* |dē'fekt| defecto ♦ *vi* |difekt'|: **to ~ to the enemy** pasarse al enemigo; **physical ~** defecto físico; **mental ~** deficiencia mental.

defective |difek'tiv| *a* (*gen*) defectuoso; (*person*) anormal.

defector |difek'tûr| *n* defector(a) *m/f*.

defence |difens'| *etc* (*Brit*) = **defense** *etc*.

defend |difend'| *vt* defender; (*decision, action*) defender; (*opinion*) mantener.

defendant |difen'dənt| *n* acusado/a; (*in civil case*) demandado/a.

defender |difen'dûr| *n* defensor(a) *m/f*.

defending champion |difen'ding

cham'pēən| *n* (*SPORT*) campeón/ona *m/f* titular.

defense |difens'| *n* defensa; **the Department of D~** el Ministerio de Defensa.

defense counsel *n* (*LAW*) abogado defensor.

defenseless |difens'lis| *a* indefenso.

defense spending *n* gasto militar.

defensive |difen'siv| *a* defensivo ♦ *n* defensiva; **on the ~** a la defensiva.

defer |difûr'| *vt* (*postpone*) aplazar; **to ~ to** diferir a; (*submit*): **to ~ to sb/sb's opinion** conformarse con uno/someterse al juicio de uno.

deference |def'ûrəns| *n* deferencia, respeto; **out of** *or* **in ~ to** por respeto a.

deferential |defəren'chəl| *a* respetuoso.

deferred |difûrd'| *a*: ~ **creditor** acreedor *m* diferido.

defiance |difī'əns| *n* desafío; **in ~ of** en contra de.

defiant |difī'ənt| *a* (*insolent*) insolente; (*challenging*) retador(a).

defiantly |difī'əntlē| *ad* con aire de desafío.

deficiency |difish'ənsē| *n* (*lack*) falta; (*COMM*) déficit *m*; (*defect*) defecto.

deficient |difish'ənt| *a* (*lacking*) insuficiente; (*incomplete*) incompleto; (*defective*) defectuoso; (*mentally*) anormal; ~ **in** deficiente en.

deficit |def'isit| *n* déficit *m*.

defile |difīl'| *vt* manchar; (*violate*) violar.

define |difīn'| *vt* (*also COMPUT*) definir.

definite |def'ənit| *a* (*fixed*) determinado; (*clear, obvious*) claro; **he was ~ about it** no dejó lugar a dudas (sobre ello).

definitely |def'ənitlē| *ad*: **he's ~ mad** no cabe duda de que está loco.

definition |defənish'ən| *n* definición *f*.

definitive |difin'ətiv| *a* definitivo.

deflate |diflāt'| *vt* (*gen*) desinflar; (*pompous person*) quitar *or* rebajar los humos a; (*ECON*) deflacionar.

deflation |diflā'shən| *n* (*ECON*) deflación *f*.

deflationary |diflā'shənärē| *a* (*ECON*) deflacionario.

deflect |diflekt'| *vt* desviar.

defog |dēfóg'| *vt* desempañar.

defogger |dēfóg'ûr| *n* (*US AUT*) dispositivo antivaho.

deforestation |dēfôristā'shən| *n* deforestación *f*.

deform |difôrm'| *vt* deformar.

deformed |difôrmd'| *a* deformado.

deformity |difôr'mitē| *n* deformación *f*.

defraud |difrôd'| *vt* estafar; **to ~ sb of sth** estafar algo a uno.

defray |difrā'| *vt*: **to ~ sb's expenses** reembolsar a uno los gastos.

defrost |difrôst'| *vt* (*frozen food, fridge*) descongelar.

defroster |difrôs'tûr| *n* (*US*) eliminador *m* de vaho.

deft |deft| *a* diestro, hábil.

defunct |difungkt'| *a* difunto; (*organization etc*) ya desaparecido.

defuse |dēfyōoz'| *vt* desarmar; (*situation*) calmar, apaciguar.

defy |difi'| *vt* (*resist*) oponerse a; (*challenge*) desafiar; (*order*) contravenir.

degenerate *vi* |dijen'ûrāt| degenerar ♦ *a* |dijen'ûrit| degenerado.

degradation |degrədā'shən| *n* degradación *f*.

degrade |digrād'| *vt* degradar.

degrading |digrā'ding| *a* degradante.

degree |digrē'| *n* grado; (*SCOL*) título; **10 ~s below freezing** 10 grados bajo cero; **to have a ~ in math** tener una licenciatura en matemáticas; **by ~s** (*gradually*) poco a poco, por etapas; **to some ~, to a certain ~** hasta cierto punto; **a considerable ~ of risk** un gran riesgo.

dehydrated |dēhī'drātid| *a* deshidratado; (*milk*) en polvo.

dehydration |dēhīdrā'shən| *n* deshidratación *f*.

de-ice |dēīs'| *vt* (*windshield*) deshelar.

de-icer |dēī'sûr| *n* deshelador *m*.

deign |dān| *vi*: **to ~ to do** dignarse hacer.

deity |dē'itē| *n* deidad *f*, divinidad *f*.

dejected |dijek'tid| *a* abatido, desanimado.

dejection |dijek'shən| *n* abatimiento.

Del. *abbr* (*US*) = *Delaware*.

del. *abbr* = **delete.**

delay |dilā'| *vt* demorar, aplazar; (*person*) entretener; (*train*) retrasar; (*payment*) aplazar ♦ *vi* tardar ♦ *n* demora, retraso; **without ~** en seguida, sin tardar.

delayed-action |dilād'ak'shən| *a* (*bomb etc*) de acción retardada.

delectable |dilek'təbəl| *a* (*person*) encantador(a); (*food*) delicioso.

delegate *n* |del'əgit| delegado/a ♦ *vt* |del'əgāt| delegar; **to ~ sth to sb/sb to do sth** delegar algo en uno/en uno para hacer algo.

delegation |deləgā'shən| *n* (*of work etc*) delegación *f*.

delete |dilēt'| *vt* suprimir, tachar; (*COMPUT*) suprimir, borrar.

Delhi |del'ē| *n* Delhi *m*.

deliberate *a* |dilib'ûrit| (*intentional*) intencionado; (*slow*) pausado, lento ♦ *vi* |dilib'ûrāt| deliberar.

deliberately |dilib'ûritlē| *ad* (*on purpose*) a propósito; (*slowly*) pausadamente.

deliberation |dilibərā'shən| *n* (*consideration*) reflexión *f*; (*discussion*) deliberación *f*, discusión *f*.

delicacy |del'əkəsē| *n* delicadeza; (*choice food*) golosina.

delicate |del'əkit| *a* (*gen*) delicado; (*fragile*) frágil.

delicately |del'əkitlē| *ad* con delicadeza, delicadamente; (*act, express*) con discreción.

delicatessen |deləkətes'ən| *n* tienda especializada en comida exótica.

delicious |dilish'əs| *a* delicioso, rico.

delight |dilīt'| *n* (*feeling*) placer *m*, deleite *m*; (*object*) encanto, delicia ♦ *vt* encantar, deleitar; **to take ~ in** deleitarse en.

delighted |dilī'tid| *a*: **~ (at** *or* **with/to do)** encantado (con/de hacer); **to be ~ that** estar encantado de que; **I'd be ~** con mucho *or* todo gusto.

delightful |dilīt'fəl| *a* encantador(a), delicioso.

delimit |dilim'it| *vt* delimitar.

delineate |dilin'ēāt| *vt* delinear.

delinquency |diling'kwənsē| *n* delincuencia.

delinquent |diling'kwint| *a, n* delincuente *m/f*.

delirious |dilēr'ēəs| *a* (*MED, fig*) delirante; **to be ~** delirar, desvariar.

delirium |dilēr'ēəm| *n* delirio.

deliver |diliv'ûr| *vt* (*distribute*) repartir; (*hand over*) entregar; (*message*) comunicar; (*speech*) pronunciar; (*blow*) lanzar, dar; (*MED*) asistir al parto de.

deliverance |diliv'ûrəns| *n* liberación *f*.

delivery |diliv'ûrē| *n* reparto; entrega; (*of speaker*) modo de expresarse; (*MED*) parto, alumbramiento; **to take ~ of** recibir.

delivery note *n* nota de entrega.

delivery truck *n* furgoneta de reparto.

delta |del'tə| *n* delta *m*.

delude |dilōod'| *vt* engañar.

deluge |del'yōoj| *n* diluvio ♦ *vt* (*fig*): **to ~ (with)** inundar (de).

delusion |dilōo'zhən| *n* ilusión *f*, engaño.

de luxe |dəluks'| *a* de lujo.

delve |delv| *vi*: **to ~ into** hurgar en.

Dem. *abbr* (*US POL*) = **democrat(ic).**

demand |dimand'| *vt* (*gen*) exigir; (*rights*) reclamar; (*need*) requerir ♦ *n* (*gen*) exigencia; (*claim*) reclamación *f*; (*ECON*) demanda; **to ~ sth (from** *or* **of sb)** exigir algo (a uno); **to be in ~** ser muy solicitado; **on ~** a solicitud.

demanding |dimand'ing| *a* (*boss*) exigente; (*work*) absorbente.

demarcation |dēmârkā'shən| *n* demarcación *f*.

demarcation dispute *n* conflicto por definición *or* demarcación del trabajo.

demean |dimēn'| *vt*: **to ~ o.s.** rebajarse.

demeanor (*Brit*) **demeanour** |dimē'nûr| *n* porte *m*, conducta, comportamiento.

demented |dimen'tid| *a* demente.

demi- |dem'i| *pref* semi..., medio....

demilitarize |dēmil'itərīz| *vt* desmilitarizar.

demise |dimīz'| *n* (*death*) fallecimiento.

demist |dēmist'| *vt* (*AUT*) eliminar el vaho de.

demister |dimīs'tûr| *n* (*Brit AUT*) eliminador *m* de vaho.

demo |dem'ō| *n abbr* (*col:* = *demonstra-*

tion) manifestación *f*.
demobilization [dēmōbəlizā'shən] *n* desmovilización *f*.
democracy [dimák'rəsē] *n* democracia.
democrat [dem'əkrat] *n* demócrata *m/f*; (*Brit, US POL*): **D~** Demócrata *m/f*.
democratic [deməkrat'ik] *a* democrático.
demography [dimág'rəfē] *n* demografía.
demolish [dimál'ish] *vt* derribar, demoler.
demolition [deməlish'ən] *n* derribo, demolición *f*.
demon [dē'mən] *n* (*evil spirit*) demonio ♦ *cpd* temible.
demonstrate [dem'ənstrāt] *vt* demostrar ♦ *vi* manifestarse; **to ~ (for/against)** manifestarse (a favor de/en contra de).
demonstration [demənstrā'shən] *n* (*POL*) manifestación *f*; (*proof*) prueba, demostración *f*; **to hold a ~** (*POL*) hacer una manifestación.
demonstrative [dimán'strətiv] *a* (*person*) expresivo; (*LING*) demostrativo.
demonstrator [dem'ənstrātûr] *n* (*POL*) manifestante *m/f*.
demoralize [dimôr'əliz] *vt* desmoralizar.
demote [dimōt'] *vt* degradar.
demotion [dimō'shən] *n* degradación *f*; (*COMM*) descenso.
demur [dimûr'] *vi*: **to ~ (at)** hacer objeciones (a), vacilar (ante) ♦ *n*: **without ~** sin objeción.
demure [dimyōōr'] *a* recatado.
demurrage [dimûr'ij] *n* sobrestadía.
den [den] *n* (*of animal*) guarida; (*study*) estudio.
denationalization [dēnashnəlizā'shən] *n* desnacionalización *f*.
denationalize [dēnash'nəliz] *vt* desnacionalizar.
denatured alcohol [dēnā'chûrd al'kəhôl] *n* (*US*) alcohol *m* desnaturalizado.
denial [dinī'əl] *n* (*refusal*) negativa; (*of report etc*) denegación *f*.
denier [den'yûr] *n* denier *m*.
denim [den'əm] *n* tela vaquera; *see also* **denims**.
denim jacket *n* chaqueta vaquera, saco vaquero (*LAm*).
denims [den'əmz] *npl* vaqueros *mpl*.
denizen [den'izən] *n* (*inhabitant*) habitante *m/f*; (*foreigner*) residente *m/f* extranjero/a.
Denmark [den'mârk] *n* Dinamarca.
denomination [dinâmənā'shən] *n* valor *m*; (*REL*) confesión *f*.
denominator [dinâm'ənātûr] *n* denominador *m*.
denote [dinōt'] *vt* indicar, significar.
denounce [dinouns'] *vt* denunciar.
dense [dens] *a* (*thick*) espeso; (: *foliage etc*) tupido; (*stupid*) torpe.
densely [dens'lē] *ad*: **~ populated** con una alta densidad de población.
density [den'sitē] *n* densidad *f*; **single/**

double-~ disk *n* disco de densidad sencilla/de doble densidad.
dent [dent] *n* abolladura ♦ *vt* (*also*: **make a ~ in**) abollar.
dental [den'təl] *a* dental.
dental surgeon *n* odontólogo/a.
dentifrice [den'təfris] *n* dentífrico.
dentist [den'tist] *n* dentista *m/f*; **~'s office** (*US*) *o* **surgery** (*Brit*) consultorio dental.
dentistry [den'tistrē] *n* odontología.
dentures [den'chûrz] *npl* dentadura *sg* (postiza).
denude [dinōōd'] *vt*: **to ~ of** despojar de.
denunciation [dinunsēā'shən] *n* denuncia, denunciación *f*.
deny [dinī'] *vt* negar; (*charge*) rechazar; (*report*) desmentir; **to ~ o.s.** privarse (de); **he denies having said it** niega haberlo dicho.
deodorant [dēō'dûrənt] *n* desodorante *m*.
depart [dipárt'] *vi* irse, marcharse; (*train*) salir; **to ~ from** (*fig*: *differ from*) apartarse de.
departed [dipár'tid] *a* (*bygone*: *days, glory*) pasado; (*dead*) difunto.
department [dipárt'mənt] *n* (*COMM*) sección *f*; (*SCOL*) departamento; (*POL*) ministerio; **that's not my ~** (*fig*) no tiene que ver conmigo; **D~ of State** (*US*) Ministerio de Asuntos Exteriores.
departmental [dēpártmen'təl] *a* (*dispute*) departamental; (*meeting*) departamental, de departamento; **~ manager** jefe/a *m/f* de sección *or* de departamento *or* de servicio.
department store *n* gran almacén *m*.
departure [dipár'chûr] *n* partida, ida; (*of train*) salida; **a new ~** un nuevo rumbo.
departure lounge *n* (*at airport*) sala de embarque.
depend [dipend'] *vi*: **to ~ (up)on** (*be dependent upon*) depender de; (*rely on*) contar con; **it ~s** depende, según; **~ing on the result** según el resultado.
dependable [dipen'dəbəl] *a* (*person*) formal, serio.
dependant [dipen'dənt] *n* dependiente *m/f*.
dependence [dipen'dəns] *n* dependencia.
dependent [dipen'dənt] *a*: **to be ~ (on)** depender (de) ♦ *n* = **dependant**.
depict [dipikt'] *vt* (*in picture*) pintar; (*describe*) representar.
depilatory [dipil'ətôrē] *n* (*also*: **~ cream**) depilatorio.
deplane [dēplān'] *vi* (*US*) desembarcar.
depleted [diplēt'id] *a* reducido.
deplorable [diplôr'əbəl] *a* deplorable.
deplore [diplôr'] *vt* deplorar.
deploy [diploi'] *vt* desplegar.
depopulate [dipáp'yəlāt] *vt* despoblar.
depopulation [dipápyəlā'shən] *n* despoblación *f*.
deport [dipôrt'] *vt* deportar.
deportation [dēpôrtā'shən] *n* deportación *f*.

deportation order *n* orden *f* de expulsión.
deportment [dipórt'mənt] *n* comportamiento.
depose [dipōz'] *vt* deponer.
deposit [dipáz'it] *n* depósito; (*CHEM*) sedimento; (*of ore, oil*) yacimiento; **"for ~ only"** "únicamente en cuenta del beneficiario" ♦ *vt* (*gen*) depositar; **to put down a ~ of $50** dejar un depósito de 50 dólares.
deposit account *n* (*Brit*) cuenta de ahorros.
depositor [dipáz'itûr] *n* depositante *m/f*, cuentacorrentista *m/f*.
depository [dipáz'itôrē] *n* almacén *m* depositario.
depot [dē'pō] *n* (*storehouse*) depósito; (*for vehicles*) parque *m*.
deprave [diprāv'] *vt* depravar.
depraved [diprāvd'] *a* depravado, vicioso.
depravity [diprav'itē] *n* depravación *f*, vicio.
deprecate [dep'rəkāt] *vt* desaprobar, lamentar.
deprecating [dep'rəkāting] *a* (*disapproving*) de desaprobación; (*apologetic*): **a ~ smile** una sonrisa de disculpa.
depreciate [diprē'shēāt] *vi* depreciarse, perder valor.
depreciation [diprēshēā'shən] *n* depreciación *f*.
depress [dipres'] *vt* deprimir; (*press down*) apretar.
depressant [dipres'ənt] *n* (*MED*) calmante *m*, sedante *m*.
depressed [diprest'] *a* deprimido; (*COMM*: *market, economy*) deprimido; (*area*) deprimido (económicamente); **to get ~ depri- mirse.
depressing [dipres'ing] *a* deprimente.
depression [dipresh'ən] *n* depresión *f*; **the economy is in a state of ~** la economía está deprimida.
deprivation [deprəvā'shən] *n* privación *f*; (*loss*) pérdida.
deprive [diprīv'] *vt*: **to ~ sb of** privar a uno de.
deprived [diprīvd'] *a* necesitado.
dept. *abbr* (= *department*) dto.
depth [depth] *n* profundidad *f*; **at a ~ of 3 meters** a 3 metros de profundidad; **to be out of one's ~** (*swimmer*) perder pie; (*fig*) estar perdido; **to study sth in ~** estudiar algo a fondo; **in the ~s of** en lo más hondo de.
depth charge *n* carga de profundidad.
deputation [depyətā'shən] *n* delegación *f*.
deputize [dep'yətīz] *vi*: **to ~ for sb** suplir a uno.
deputy [dep'yətē] *a*: **~ head** subdirector(a) *m/f* ♦ *n* sustituto/a, suplente *m/f*; (*POL*) diputado/a; representante *m/f*.
deputy leader *n* (*POL*) vicepresidente/a *m/f*.
derail [dirāl'] *vt*: **to be ~ed** descarrilarse.

derailment [dirāl'mənt] *n* descarrilamiento.
deranged [dirānjd'] *a* trastornado.
derby [dûr'bē] *n* (*US*) hongo.
Derbys *abbr* (*Brit*) = *Derbyshire*.
deregulate [dēreg'yəlāt] *vt* desreglamentar.
deregulation [dēregyəlā'shən] *n* desreglamentación *f*.
derelict [där'əlikt] *a* abandonado.
deride [dirīd'] *vt* ridiculizar, mofarse de.
derision [dirizh'ən] *n* irrisión *f*, mofas *fpl*.
derisive [dirī'siv] *a* burlón/ona.
derisory [dirī'sûrē] *a* (*sum*) irrisorio; (*laughter, person*) burlón/ona, irónico.
derivation [därəvā'shən] *n* derivación *f*.
derivative [diriv'ətiv] *n* derivado ♦ *a* (*work*) poco original.
derive [dirīv'] *vt* derivar ♦ *vi*: **to ~ from** derivarse de.
derived [dirīvd'] *a* derivado.
dermatitis [dûrmətī'tis] *n* dermatitis *f*.
dermatology [dûrmətäl'əjē] *n* dermatología.
derogatory [diråg'ətôrē] *a* despectivo.
derrick [där'ik] *n* torre *f* de perforación.
derv [dûrv] *n* (*Brit*) gasoil *m*.
DES *n abbr* (*Brit*: = *Department of Education and Science*) ministerio de educación y ciencia.
descend [disend'] *vt, vi* descender, bajar; **to ~ from** descender de; **in ~ing order of importance** por orden descendiente de importancia.
   descend on *vt fus* (*subj*: *enemy, angry person*) caer sobre; (: *misfortune*) sobrevenir; (*fig*: *gloom, silence*) invadir; **visitors ~ed (up)on us** las visitas nos invadieron.
descendant [disen'dənt] *n* descendiente *m/f*.
descent [disent'] *n* descenso; (*GEO*) pendiente *f*, declive *m*; (*origin*) descendencia.
describe [diskrīb'] *vt* describir.
description [diskrip'shən] *n* descripción *f*; (*sort*) clase *f*, género; **of every ~** de toda clase.
descriptive [diskrip'tiv] *a* descriptivo.
desecrate [des'əkrāt] *vt* profanar.
desegregation [dēsegrəgā'shən] *n* desegregación *f*.
desert *n* [dez'ûrt] desierto ♦ *vb* [dizûrt'] *vt* abandonar, desamparar ♦ *vi* (*MIL*) desertar; *see also* **deserts**.
deserter [dizûr'tûr] *n* desertor(a) *m/f*.
desertion [dizûr'shən] *n* deserción *f*.
desert island [dez'ûrt ī'lənd] *n* isla desierta.
deserts [dizûrts'] *npl*: **to get one's just ~** llevarse su merecido.
deserve [dizûrv'] *vt* merecer, ser digno de.
deservedly [dizûr'vidlē] *ad* con razón.
deserving [dizûr'ving] *a* (*person*) digno; (*action, cause*) meritorio.
desiccated [des'əkātid] *a* desecado.

design [dizīn'] *n* (*sketch*) bosquejo; (*of dress, car*) diseño; (*pattern*) dibujo ♦ *vt* (*gen*) diseñar; **industrial** ~ diseño industrial; **to have ~s on sb** tener la(s) mira(s) puesta(s) en uno; **to be ~ed for sb/sth** estar hecho para uno/algo.

designate *vt* [dez'ignāt] (*appoint*) nombrar; (*destine*) designar ♦ *a* [dez'ignit] designado.

designation [dezignā'shən] *n* (*appointment*) nombramiento; (*name*) denominación *f.*

designer [dizi'nûr] *n* diseñador(a) *m/f*; (*fashion ~*) modisto/a.

desirability [dizīûrəbil'ətē] *n* ventaja, atractivo.

desirable [dizi'ûrəbəl] *a* (*proper*) deseable; (*attractive*) atractivo; **it is ~ that** es conveniente que.

desire [dizī'ûr] *n* deseo ♦ *vt* desear; **to ~ sth/to do sth/that** desear algo/hacer algo/que.

desirous [dizi'ûrəs] *a*: **to be ~ of** desear.

desist [dizist'] *vi*: **to ~ (from)** desistir (de).

desk [desk] *n* (*in office*) escritorio; (*for pupil*) pupitre *m*; (*in hotel, at airport*) recepción *f*; (*Brit: in store, restaurant*) caja.

desktop publishing [desk'tâp pub'lishing] *n* autoedición *f.*

desolate [des'əlit] *a* (*place*) desierto; (*person*) afligido.

desolation [desəlā'shən] *n* (*of place*) desolación *f*; (*of person*) aflicción *f.*

despair [dispär'] *n* desesperación *f* ♦ *vi*: **to ~ of** desesperarse de; **in ~** desesperado.

despatch [dispach'] *n, vt* = **dispatch.**

desperate [des'pûrit] *a* desesperado; (*fugitive*) peligroso; (*measures*) extremo; **we are getting ~** nos estamos desesperando.

desperately [des'pûritlē] *ad* desesperadamente; (*very*) terriblemente, gravemente; **~ ill** gravemente enfermo.

desperation [despərā'shən] *n* desesperación *f*; **in ~** desesperado.

despicable [des'pikəbəl] *a* vil, despreciable.

despise [dispīz'] *vt* despreciar.

despite [dispīt'] *prep* a pesar de, pese a.

despondent [dispân'dənt] *a* deprimido, abatido.

despot [des'pət] *n* déspota *m/f.*

dessert [dizûrt'] *n* postre *m.*

dessertspoon [dizûrt'spōon] *n* cuchara (de postre).

destabilize [dēstā'bəlīz] *vt* desestabilizar.

destination [destənā'shən] *n* destino.

destine [des'tin] *vt* destinar.

destined [des'tind] *a*: **~ for Boston** con destino a Boston.

destiny [des'tənē] *n* destino.

destitute [des'titōot] *a* desamparado, indigente.

destitution [destitōo'shən] *n* indigencia, miseria.

destroy [distroi'] *vt* destruir; (*finish*) acabar con.

destroyer [distroi'ûr] *n* (*NAUT*) destructor *m.*

destruction [distruk'shən] *n* destrucción *f*; (*fig*) ruina.

destructive [distruk'tiv] *a* destructivo, destructor(a).

desultory [des'əltôrē] *a* (*reading*) poco metódico; (*conversation*) inconexo; (*contact*) intermitente.

detach [ditach'] *vt* separar; (*unstick*) despegar.

detachable [ditach'əbəl] *a* separable; (*TECH*) desmontable.

detached [ditacht'] *a* (*attitude*) objetivo, imparcial.

detached house *n* chalé *m*, chalet *m.*

detachment [ditach'mənt] *n* separación *f*; (*MIL*) destacamento; (*fig*) objetividad *f*, imparcialidad *f.*

detail [ditāl'] *n* detalle *m*; (*MIL*) destacamento ♦ *vt* detallar; (*MIL*) destacar; **in ~** detalladamente; **to go into ~(s)** entrar en detalles.

detailed [ditāld'] *a* detallado.

detain [ditān'] *vt* retener; (*in captivity*) detener.

detainee [dētānē'] *n* detenido/a.

detect [ditekt'] *vt* (*gen*) descubrir; (*MED, POLICE*) identificar; (*MIL, RADAR, TECH*) detectar.

detection [ditek'shən] *n* descubrimiento; identificación *f*; **crime ~** investigación *f*; **to escape ~** (*criminal*) escaparse sin ser descubierto; (*mistake*) pasar inadvertido.

detective [ditek'tiv] *n* detective *m.*

detective story *n* novela policíaca.

detector [ditek'tûr] *n* detector *m.*

détente [dātänt'] *n* distensión *f*, detente *f.*

detention [diten'chən] *n* detención *f*, arresto.

deter [ditûr'] *vt* (*dissuade*) disuadir; (*prevent*) impedir; **to ~ sb from doing sth** disuadir a uno de que haga algo.

detergent [ditûr'jənt] *n* detergente *m.*

deteriorate [ditē'rēərāt] *vi* deteriorarse.

deterioration [ditērēərā'shən] *n* deterioro.

determination [ditûrmənā'shən] *n* resolución *f.*

determine [ditûr'min] *vt* determinar; **to ~ to do sth** decidir hacer algo.

determined [ditûr'mind] *a*: **to be ~ to do sth** estar decidido *or* resuelto a hacer algo; **a ~ effort** un esfuerzo concentrado.

deterrence [ditûr'əns] *n* disuasión *f.*

deterrent [ditûr'ənt] *n* fuerza de disuasión; **to act as a ~** servir para prevenir.

detest [ditest'] *vt* aborrecer.

detestable [dites'təbəl] *a* aborrecible.

dethrone [dēthrōn'] *vt* destronar.

detonate [det'ənāt] *vi* estallar ♦ *vt* hacer detonar.

detonator [det'ənātûr] *n* detonador *m*, fulminante *m.*

detour |dē'tōōr| *n* (*gen*, *US* AUT: *diversion*) desvío ♦ *vt* (*US*: *traffic*) desviar; **to make a ~** dar un rodeo.

detract |ditrakt'| *vt*: **to ~ from** quitar mérito a, desvirtuar.

detractor |ditrak'tûr| *n* detractor(a) *m/f*.

detriment |det'rəmənt| *n*: **to the ~ of** en perjuicio de; **without ~ to** sin detrimento *or* perjuicio a.

detrimental |detrəmen'təl| *a* perjudicial.

deuce |dōōs| *n* (TENNIS) cuarenta iguales.

devaluation |dēvalyōōā'shən| *n* devaluación *f*.

devalue |dēval'yōō| *vt* devaluar.

devastate |dev'əstāt| *vt* devastar; **he was ~d by the news** las noticias le dejaron desolado.

devastating |dev'əstāting| *a* devastador(a); (*fig*) arrollador(a).

devastation |devəstā'shən| *n* devastación *f*, ruina.

develop |divel'əp| *vt* desarrollar; (PHOT) revelar; (*disease*) coger; (*habit*) adquirir ♦ *vi* desarrollarse; (*advance*) progresar; **this land is to be ~ed** se va a construir en este terreno; **to ~ a taste for sth** tomar gusto a algo; **to ~ into** transformarse *or* convertirse en.

developer |divel'əpûr| *n* (*property* ~) especulador(a) *m/f* en construcción.

developing country *n* país *m* en (vías de) desarrollo.

development |divel'əpmənt| *n* desarrollo; (*advance*) progreso; (*of affair, case*) desenvolvimiento; (*of land*) urbanización *f*.

development area *n* zona de fomento or desarrollo.

deviant |dē'vēənt| *a* anómalo, pervertido.

deviate |dē'vēāt| *vi*: **to ~ (from)** desviarse (de).

deviation |dēvēā'shən| *n* desviación *f*.

device |divīs'| *n* (*scheme*) estratagema, recurso; (*apparatus*) aparato, mecanismo; (*explosive* ~) artefacto explosivo.

devil |dev'əl| *n* diablo, demonio.

devilish |dev'əlish| *a* diabólico.

devil-may-care |dev'əlmākär'| *a* despreocupado.

devious |dē'vēəs| *a* intricado, enrevesado; (*person*) taimado.

devise |divīz'| *vt* idear, inventar.

devoid |divoid'| *a*: **~ of** desprovisto de.

devolution |devəlōō'shən| *n* (POL) descentralización *f*.

devolve |divälv'| *vi*: **to ~ (up)on** recaer sobre.

devote |divōt'| *vt*: **to ~ sth to** dedicar algo a.

devoted |divōt'id| *a* (*loyal*) leal, fiel; **the book is ~ to politics** el libro trata de la política.

devotee |devōtē'| *n* devoto/a.

devotion |divō'shən| *n* dedicación *f*; (REL)

devoción *f*.

devour |divou'ûr| *vt* devorar.

devout |divout'| *a* devoto.

dew |dōō| *n* rocío.

dexterity |dekstär'itē| *n* destreza.

dext(e)rous |dek'strəs| *a* (*skilful*) diestro, hábil; (*movement*) ágil.

dg *abbr* (= *decigram*) dg.

diabetes |dīəbē'tis| *n* diabetes *f*.

diabetic |dīəbet'ik| *n* diabético/a ♦ *a* diabético; (*chocolate*, *jam*) para diabéticos.

diabolical |dīəbál'ikəl| *a* diabólico; (*col*: *dreadful*) horrendo, horroroso.

diagnose |dīəgnōs'| *vt* diagnosticar.

diagnosis, *pl* **diagnoses** |dīəgnō'sis, -sēz| *n* diagnóstico.

diagonal |dīag'ənəl| *a* diagonal ♦ *n* diagonal *f*.

diagram |dī'əgram| *n* diagrama *m*, esquema *m*.

dial |dīl| *n* esfera, cuadrante *m*, cara (LAm); (*of phone*) disco ♦ *vt* (*number*) marcar; **to ~ a wrong number** equivocarse de número; **can I ~ New York direct?** ¿puedo marcar Nueva York directamente?

dial. *abbr* = **dialect.**

dial code *n* (*US*) prefijo.

dialect |dī'əlekt| *n* dialecto.

dialling code |dī'ling kōd| *n* (*Brit*) prefijo.

dialling tone |dī'ling tōn| *n* (*Brit*) señal *f or* tono de marcar.

dialog, (*Brit*) **dialogue** |dī'əlôg| *n* diálogo.

dial tone *n* (*US*) señal *f or* tono de marcar.

dialysis |dīal'isis| *n* diálisis *f*.

diameter |dīam'itûr| *n* diámetro.

diametrically |dīəmet'riklē| *ad*: **~ opposed (to)** diametralmente opuesto (a).

diamond |dī'mənd| *n* diamante *m*; **~s** *npl* (CARDS) diamantes *mpl*.

diamond ring *n* anillo *or* sortija de diamantes.

diaper |dī'pûr| *n* (*US*) pañal *m*.

diaper pin *n* (*US*) imperdible *m*, seguro (LAm).

diaphragm |dī'əfram| *n* diafragma *m*.

diarrhea, (*Brit*) **diarrhoea** |dīərē'ə| *n* diarrea.

diary |dī'ûrē| *n* (*daily account*) diario; (*book*) agenda; **to keep a ~** escribir un diario.

diatribe |dī'ətrīb| *n*: **~ (against)** diatriba (contra).

dice |dīs| *n*, *pl inv* dados *mpl* ♦ *vt* (CULIN) cortar en cuadritos.

dicey |dī'sē| *a* (*Brit*: *col*): **it's a bit ~** (*risky*) es un poco arriesgado; (*doubtful*) es un poco dudoso.

dichotomy |dīkät'əmē| *n* dicotomía.

Dictaphone ® |dik'təfōn| *n* dictáfono ®.

dictate *vt* |diktāt'| dictar ♦ *n* |dik'tāt| dictado.

   dictate to *vt fus* (*person*) dar órdenes a;

I won't be ~**d to** no estoy a las órdenes de nadie.
dictation [dɪktā'shən] *n* (*to secretary etc*) dictado; **at** ~ **speed** para tomar al dictado.
dictator [dik'tātûr] *n* dictador *m*.
dictatorship [dik'tātûrship] *n* dictadura.
diction [dik'shən] *n* dicción *f*.
dictionary [dik'shənārē] *n* diccionario.
did [did] *pt of* **do**.
didactic [dīdak'tik] *a* didáctico.
diddle [did'əl] *vt* estafar, timar.
didn't [did'ənt] = **did not**.
die [dī] *vi* morir; **to** ~ (**of** *or* **from**) morirse (de); **to be dying** morirse, estarse muriendo; **to be dying for sth/to do sth** morirse por algo/de ganas de hacer algo.
  die away *vi* (*sound, light*) perderse.
  die down *vi* (*gen*) apagarse; (*wind*) amainar.
  die out *vi* desaparecer, extinguirse.
diehard [dī'hârd] *n* intransigente *m/f*.
dieresis [dīār'əsis] *n* diéresis *f*.
diesel [dē'zəl] *n* diesel *m*.
diesel engine *n* motor *m* diesel.
diesel fuel, diesel oil *n* gas-oil *m*.
diet [dī'ət] *n* dieta; (*restricted food*) régimen *m* ♦ *vi* (*also:* **be on a** ~) estar a dieta, hacer régimen; **to live on a** ~ **of** alimentarse de.
dietician [dīatish'ən] *n* dietético/a *m/f*.
differ [dif'ûr] *vi* (*be different*) ser distinto, diferenciarse; (*disagree*) discrepar.
difference [dif'ûrəns] *n* diferencia; (*quarrel*) desacuerdo; **it makes no** ~ **to me** me da igual *or* lo mismo; **to settle one's** ~**s** arreglarse.
different [dif'ûrənt] *a* diferente, distinto.
differential [difərən'chəl] *n* diferencial *f*.
differentiate [difərən'chēāt] *vt* distinguir ♦ *vi* diferenciarse; **to** ~ **between** distinguir entre.
differently [dif'ûrəntlē] *ad* de otro modo, en forma distinta.
difficult [dif'əkult] *a* difícil; ~ **to understand** difícil de entender.
difficulty [dif'əkultē] *n* dificultad *f;* **to have difficulties with** (*police, landlord etc*) tener problemas con; **to be in** ~ tener dificultad.
diffidence [dif'idəns] *n* timidez *f*, falta de confianza en sí mismo.
diffident [dif'idənt] *a* tímido.
diffuse *a* [difyōōs'] difuso ♦ *vt* [difyōōz'] difundir.
dig [dig] *vt* (*pt, pp* **dug** [dug]) (*hole*) cavar; (*ground*) remover; (*coal*) extraer; (*nails etc*) hincar ♦ *n* (*prod*) empujón *m*; (*archeological*) excavación *f*; (*remark*) indirecta; **to** ~ **into** (*savings*) consumir; **to** ~ **into one's pockets for sth** hurgar en el bolsillo por algo; **to** ~ **one's nails into** clavar las uñas en; *see also* **digs**.
  dig in *vi* (*also:* ~ **o.s. in:** *MIL*) atrincherarse; (*col: eat*) hincar los dientes ♦ *vt* (*compost*) añadir al suelo; (*knife, claw*)

clavar; **to** ~ **in one's heels** (*fig*) mantenerse en sus trece.
  dig out *vt* (*hole*) excavar; (*survivors, car from snow*) sacar.
  dig up *vt* desenterrar; (*plant*) desarraigar.
digest *vt* [dijest'] (*food*) digerir; (*facts*) asimilar ♦ *n* [dī'jest] resumen *m*.
digestible [dijes'təbəl] *a* digerible.
digestion [dijes'chən] *n* digestión *f*.
digestive [dijes'tiv] *a* (*juices, system*) digestivo.
digit [dij'it] *n* (*number*) dígito; (*finger*) dedo.
digital [dij'itəl] *a* digital.
digital computer *n* ordenador *m* digital.
dignified [dig'nəfīd] *a* grave, solemne; (*action*) decoroso.
dignify [dig'nəfī] *vt* dignificar.
dignitary [dig'nitārē] *n* dignatario/a.
dignity [dig'nitē] *n* dignidad *f*.
digress [digres'] *vi*: **to** ~ **from** apartarse de.
digression [digresh'ən] *n* digresión *f*.
digs [digz] *npl* (*Brit: col*) pensión *f*, alojamiento.
dike [dīk] *n* dique *m*.
dilapidated [dilap'ədātid] *a* desmoronado, ruinoso.
dilate [dīlāt'] *vt* dilatar ♦ *vi* dilatarse.
dilatory [dil'ətôrē] *a* (*person*) lento; (*action*) dilatorio.
dilemma [dilem'ə] *n* dilema *m*; **to be in a** ~ estar en un dilema.
dilettante [dilitânt'] *n* diletante *m/f*.
diligence [dil'ijəns] *n* diligencia.
diligent [dil'ijənt] *a* diligente.
dill [dil] *n* eneldo.
dilly-dally [dil'ēdalē] *vi* (*hesitate*) vacilar; (*dawdle*) entretenerse.
dilute [dilōōt'] *vt* diluir.
dim [dim] *a* (*light*) débil; (*sight*) turbio; (*outline*) indistinto; (*stupid*) lerdo; (*room*) oscuro ♦ *vt* (*light*) bajar; **to take a** ~ **view of sth** tener una pobre opinión de algo; **to** ~ **one's lights** (*US AUT*) poner luces de cruce.
dime [dīm] *n* (*US*) *moneda de diez centavos*.
dimension [dimen'chən] *n* dimensión *f*.
-dimensional [dimen'chənl] *a suff:* **two**~ de dos dimensiones.
dimensions [dimen'chənz] *npl* dimensiones *fpl*.
diminish [dimin'ish] *vt, vi* disminuir.
diminished [dimin'isht] *a:* ~ **responsibility** (*LAW*) responsabilidad *f* disminuida.
diminutive [dimin'yətiv] *a* diminuto ♦ *n* (*LING*) diminutivo.
dimly [dim'lē] *ad* débilmente; (*not clearly*) indistintamente.
dimmer [dim'ûr] *n* (*US AUT*) interruptor *m*.
dimple [dim'pəl] *n* hoyuelo.
dimwitted [dim'witid] *a* (*col*) lerdo, de pocas luces.

din [din] *n* estruendo, estrépito ♦ *vt*: **to ~ sth into sb** (*col*) meter algo en la cabeza a uno.

dine [dīn] *vi* cenar.

diner [dī'úr] *n* (*person: in restaurant*) comensal *m/f*; (*Brit RAIL*) = **dining car**; (*US*) restaurante económico.

dinghy [ding'ē] *n* bote *m*; (*also:* **rubber ~**) lancha (neumática).

dingy [din'jē] *a* (*room*) sombrío; (*dirty*) sucio; (*dull*) deslucido.

dining car [dīn'ing kâr] *n* coche-comedor *m*.

dining room [dīn'ing rōōm] *n* comedor *m*.

dinner [din'úr] *n* (*evening meal*) cena; (*lunch*) comida; (*public*) cena, banquete *m*; **~'s ready!** ¡la cena está servida!

dinner jacket *n* smoking *m*.

dinner party *n* cena.

dinner time *n* hora de cenar *or* comer.

dinosaur [dī'nəsôr] *n* dinosaurio.

dint [dint] *n*: **by ~ of (doing) sth** a fuerza de (hacer) algo.

diocese [dī'əsēs] *n* diócesis *f*.

dioxide [dīâk'sid] *n* bióxido; **carbon ~** bióxido de carbono.

dioxin [dīâks'in] *n* dioxina.

dip [dip] *n* (*slope*) pendiente *f*; (*in sea*) baño ♦ *vt* (*in water*) mojar; (*ladle etc*) meter; (*Brit AUT*): **to ~ one's lights** poner luces de cruce ♦ *vi* inclinarse hacia abajo.

diphtheria [dipthē'rēə] *n* difteria.

diphthong [dif'thông] *n* diptongo.

diploma [diplō'mə] *n* diploma *m*.

diplomacy [diplō'məsē] *n* diplomacia.

diplomat [dip'ləmat] *n* diplomático/a *m/f*.

diplomatic [dipləmat'ik] *a* diplomático; **to break off ~ relations** romper las relaciones diplomáticas.

diplomatic corps *n* cuerpo diplomático.

dipstick [dip'stik] *n* (*AUT*) varilla de nivel (del aceite).

dipswitch [dip'swich] *n* (*Brit AUT*) interruptor *m*.

dire [dī'úr] *a* calamitoso.

direct [direkt'] *a* (*gen*) directo; (*manner, person*) franco ♦ *vt* dirigir; **can you ~ me to...?** ¿puede indicarme dónde está...?; **to ~ sb to do sth** mandar a uno hacer algo.

direct access *n* (*COMPUT*) acceso directo.

direct cost *n* costo directo.

direct current *n* corriente *f* continua.

direct debit *n* domiciliación *f* bancaria de recibos.

direction [direk'shən] *n* dirección *f*; **sense of ~** sentido de orientación; **~s** *npl* (*advice*) órdenes *fpl*, instrucciones *fpl*; (*to a place*) señas *fpl*; **in the ~ of** hacia, en dirección a; **~s for use** modo de empleo; **to ask for ~s** preguntar el camino.

directional [direk'shənəl] *a* direccional.

directive [direk'tiv] *n* orden *f*, instrucción *f*; **a government ~** una orden del gobierno.

directly [direkt'lē] *ad* (*in straight line*) di-

rectamente; (*at once*) en seguida.

direct mail *n* correspondencia directa.

direct mailshot *n* (*Brit*) promoción *f* por correspondencia directa.

directness [direkt'nis] *n* (*of person, speech*) franqueza.

director [direk'tûr] *n* director(a) *m/f*; **managing ~** director(a) *m/f* gerente.

Director of Public Prosecutions *n* (*Brit*) ≈ fiscal *m/f* oficial *or* gubernamental.

directory [direk'tûrē] *n* (*TEL*) guía (telefónica); (*street ~*) callejero; (*trade ~*) directorio de comercio; (*COMPUT*) directorio.

directory assistance, (*Brit*) **directory enquiries** *n* (*service*) (servicio de) información *f*.

dirt [dûrt] *n* suciedad *f*.

dirt-cheap [dûrt'chēp'] *a* baratísimo.

dirt road *n* (*US*) camino sin firme.

dirty [dûr'tē] *a* sucio; (*joke*) verde, colorado (*LAm*) ♦ *vt* ensuciar; (*stain*) manchar.

dirty trick *n* juego sucio.

disability [disəbil'stē] *n* incapacidad *f*.

disability allowance *n* pensión *f* de invalidez.

disable [disā'bəl] *vt* (*subj: illness, accident*) dejar incapacitado; (*tank, gun*) inutilizar; (*LAW: disqualify*) incapacitar.

disabled [disā'bəld] *a* minusválido.

disabuse [disəbyōōz'] *vt*: **I ~d him of that idea** le saqué del error.

disadvantage [disədvan'tij] *n* desventaja, inconveniente *m*.

disadvantaged [disədvan'tijd] *a* (*person*) desventajado.

disadvantageous [disədvantā'jəs] *a* desventajoso.

disaffected [disəfek'tid] *a* descontento; **to be ~ (to o towards)** estar descontento (de).

disaffection [disəfek'shən] *n* desafecto, descontento.

disagree [disəgrē'] *vi* (*differ*) discrepar; **to ~ (with)** no estar de acuerdo (con); **I ~ with you** no estoy de acuerdo contigo.

disagreeable [disəgrē'əbəl] *a* desagradable.

disagreement [disəgrē'mənt] *n* (*gen*) desacuerdo; (*quarrel*) riña; **to have a ~ with sb** estar en desacuerdo con uno.

disallow [disəlou'] *vt* (*goal*) anular; (*claim*) rechazar.

disappear [disəpi'úr] *vi* desaparecer.

disappearance [disəpi'ûrəns] *n* desaparición *f*.

disappoint [disəpoint'] *vt* decepcionar; (*hopes*) defraudar.

disappointed [disəpoin'tid] *a* decepcionado.

disappointing [disəpoin'ting] *a* decepcionante.

disappointment [disəpoint'mənt] *n* decepción *f*.

disapproval [disəprōō'vəl] *n* desaprobación *f*.

disapprove [disəprōōv'] *vi*: **to** ~ **of** desaprobar.

disapproving [disəprōō'ving] *a* de desaprobación, desaprobador(a).

disarm [disârm'] *vt* desarmar.

disarmament [disâr'məmənt] *n* desarme *m*.

disarmament talks *npl* conversaciones *fpl* de *or* sobre desarme.

disarming [disârm'ing] *a* (*smile*) que desarma, encantador(a).

disarray [disərā'] *n*: **in** ~ (*troops*) desorganizado; (*thoughts*) confuso; (*hair, clothes*) desarreglado; **to throw into** ~ provocar el caos en.

disaster [dizas'tûr] *n* desastre *m*.

disaster area *n* zona de desastre.

disastrous [dizas'trəs] *a* desastroso.

disband [disband'] *vt* disolver ♦ *vi* desbandarse.

disbelief [disbilēf'] *n* incredulidad *f*; **in** ~ con incredulidad.

disbelieve [disbilēv'] *vt* (*person, story*) poner en duda, no creer.

disc [disk] *n* disco; (*COMPUT*) = **disk.**

disc. *abbr* (*COMM*) = **discount.**

discard [diskârd'] *vt* (*old things*) tirar; (*fig*) descartar.

discern [disûrn'] *vt* percibir, discernir; (*understand*) comprender.

discernible [disûr'nəbəl] *a* perceptible.

discerning [disûr'ning] *a* perspicaz.

discharge *vt* [dischârj'] (*task, duty*) cumplir; (*ship etc*) descargar; (*patient*) dar de alta; (*employee*) despedir; (*soldier*) licenciar; (*defendant*) poner en libertad; (*settle: debt*) saldar ♦ *n* [dis'chârj] (*ELEC*) descarga; (*vaginal* ~) emisión *f* vaginal; (*dismissal*) despedida; (*of duty*) desempeño; (*of debt*) pago, descargo; (*of gas, chemicals*) escape *m*.

disciple [disī'pəl] *n* discípulo/a.

disciplinary [dis'əplənärē] *a*: **to take** ~ **action against sb** disciplinar a uno.

discipline [dis'əplin] *n* disciplina ♦ *vt* disciplinar; **to** ~ **o.s. to do sth** disciplinarse *or* obligarse a hacer algo.

disc jockey (DJ) [disk' jâkē] *n* pinchadiscos *m/f inv*.

disclaim [disklām'] *vt* negar.

disclaimer [disklām'ûr] *n* rectificación *f*; **to issue a** ~ hacer una rectificación.

disclose [disklōz'] *vt* revelar.

disclosure [disklō'zhûr] *n* revelación *f*.

disco [dis'kō] *n abbr* = **discothèque.**

discoloration [diskulərā'shən] *n* (*US*) descoloramiento.

discolored [diskul'ûrd] *a* (*US*) descolorado.

discolouration [diskulərā'shən] *n* (*Brit*) = **discoloration.**

discoloured [diskul'ûrd] *a* (*Brit*) = **discolored.**

discomfort [diskum'fûrt] *n* incomodidad *f*; (*unease*) inquietud *f*; (*physical*) malestar

m.

disconcert [diskənsûrt'] *vt* desconcertar.

disconnect [diskənekt'] *vt* (*gen*) separar; (*ELEC etc*) desconectar; (*supply*) cortar (el suministro) a.

disconsolate [diskân'səlit] *a* desconsolado.

discontent [diskəntent'] *n* descontento.

discontented [diskəntent'id] *a* descontento.

discontinue [diskəntin'yōō] *vt* interrumpir; (*payments*) suspender.

discord [dis'kôrd] *n* discordia; (*MUS*) disonancia.

discordant [diskôr'dənt] *a* disonante.

discothèque [dis'kōtek] *n* discoteca.

discount *n* [dis'kount] descuento ♦ *vt* [diskount'] descontar; (*report etc*) descartar; **at a** ~ con descuento; ~ **for cash** descuento por pago en efectivo; **to give sb a** ~ **on sth** hacer un descuento a uno en algo.

discount house *n* (*FINANCE*) banco de descuento; (*COMM: also:* **discount store**) ≈ tienda de descuentos.

discount rate *n* (*COMM*) tipo de descuento.

discount store *n* ≈ tienda de descuentos.

discourage [diskûr'ij] *vt* desalentar; (*oppose*) oponerse a; (*dissuade, deter*) desanimar, disuadir.

discouragement [diskûr'ijmənt] *n* (*dissuasion*) disuasión *f*; (*depression*) desánimo, desaliento; **to act as a** ~ **to** servir para disuadir.

discouraging [diskûr'ijing] *a* desalentador(a).

discourteous [diskûr'tēəs] *a* descortés.

discover [diskuv'ûr] *vt* descubrir.

discovery [diskuv'ûrē] *n* descubrimiento.

discredit [diskred'it] *vt* desacreditar.

discreet [diskrēt'] *a* (*tactful*) discreto; (*careful*) circunspecto, prudente.

discreetly [diskrēt'lē] *ad* discrétamente.

discrepancy [diskrep'ənsē] *n* (*difference*) diferencia; (*disagreement*) discrepancia.

discretion [diskresh'ən] *n* (*tact*) discreción *f*; (*care*) prudencia, circunspección *f*; **use your own** ~ haz lo que creas oportuno.

discretionary [diskresh'ənärē] *a* (*powers*) discrecional.

discriminate [diskrim'ənāt] *vi*: **to** ~ **between** distinguir entre; **to** ~ **against** discriminar contra.

discriminating [diskrim'ənāting] *a* entendido.

discrimination [diskrimənā'shən] *n* (*discernment*) perspicacia; (*bias*) discriminación *f*; **racial/sexual** ~ discriminación racial/sexual.

discus [dis'kəs] *n* disco.

discuss [diskus'] *vt* (*gen*) discutir; (*a theme*) tratar.

discussion [diskush'ən] *n* discusión *f*; **under** ~ en discusión.

disdain [disdān'] *n* desdén *m* ♦ *vt* desdeñar.

disease [dizēz'] *n* enfermedad *f*.
diseased [dizēzd'] *a* enfermo.
disembark [disembárk'] *vt, vi* desembarcar.
disembarkation [disembárkā'shən] *n* desembarque *m*.
disenchanted [disenchan'tid] *a*: ~ **(with)** desilusionado (con).
disenfranchise [disenfran'chïz] *vt* privar del derecho al voto; (*COMM*) privar de franquicias.
disengage [disengāj'] *vt* soltar; **to** ~ **the clutch** (*AUT*) desembragar.
disentangle [disentang'gəl] *vt* desenredar.
disfavor, (*Brit*) **disfavour** [disfā'vûr] *n* desaprobación *f*.
disfigure [disfig'yûr] *vt* desfigurar.
disgorge [disgôrj'] *vt* verter.
disgrace [disgrās'] *n* ignominia; (*downfall*) caída; (*shame*) vergüenza, escándalo ♦ *vt* deshonrar.
disgraceful [disgrās'fəl] *a* vergonzoso; (*behavior*) escandaloso.
disgruntled [disgrun'təld] *a* disgustado, descontento.
disguise [disgīz'] *n* disfraz *m* ♦ *vt* disfrazar; (*voice*) disimular; (*feelings etc*) ocultar; **in** ~ disfrazado; **to** ~ **o.s. as** disfrazarse de; **there's no disguising the fact that ...** no puede ocultarse el hecho de que....
disgust [disgust'] *n* repugnancia ♦ *vt* repugnar, dar asco a.
disgusting [disgus'ting] *a* repugnante, asqueroso.
dish [dish] *n* (*gen*) plato; **to do** *or* **wash the** ~**es** fregar los platos.
dish out *vt* (*money, exam papers*) repartir; (*food*) servir; (*advice*) dar.
dish up *vt* servir.
dishcloth [dish'klôth] *n* paño de cocina, bayeta.
dishearten [dis·hár'tən] *vt* desalentar.
disheveled, (*Brit*) **dishevelled** [dishev'əld] *a* (*hair*) despeinado; (*clothes, appearance*) desarreglado.
dishonest [disân'ist] *a* (*person*) poco honrado, tramposo; (*means*) fraudulento.
dishonesty [disân'istē] *n* falta de honradez.
dishonor [disân'ûr] *n* (*US*) deshonra.
dishonorable [disân'ûrəbəl] *a* deshonroso.
dishonour [disân'ûr] *etc n* (*Brit*) = **dishonor** *etc*.
dish soap *n* (*US*) lavavajillas *m inv*.
dishtowel [dish'touəl] *n* trapo de fregar.
dishwasher [dish'wâshûr] *n* lavaplatos *m inv*; (*person*) friegaplatos *m/f inv*.
dishwashing liquid [dish'wâshing lik'wid] *n* (*US*) lavavajillas *m*.
disillusion [disiloo'zhən] *vt* desilusionar; **to become** ~**ed (with)** quedar desilusionado (con).
disillusionment [disiloo'zhənmənt] *n* desilusión *f*.
disincentive [disinsen'tiv] *n* desincentivo;

to act as a ~ **(to)** actuar de freno (a); **to be a** ~ **to** ser un freno a.
disinclined [disinklīnd'] *a*: **to be** ~ **to do sth** estar poco dispuesto a hacer algo.
disinfect [disinfekt'] *vt* desinfectar.
disinfectant [disinfek'tənt] *n* desinfectante *m*.
disinflation [disinflā'shən] *n* desinflación *f*.
disingenuous [disinjen'yōōəs] *a* poco sincero, doble.
disinherit [disinhär'it] *vt* desheredar.
disintegrate [disin'təgrāt] *vi* disgregarse, desintegrarse.
disinterested [disin'tristid] *a* desinteresado.
disjointed [disjoint'id] *a* inconexo.
disk [disk] *n* (*COMPUT*) disco, disquete *m*; **single-/double-sided** ~ disco de una cara/dos caras.
disk drive *n* disc drive *m*.
diskette [disket'] *n* diskette *m*, disquete *m*, disco flexible.
disk operating system (DOS) *n* sistema *m* operativo de discos (DOS).
dislike [dislīk'] *n* antipatía, aversión *f* ♦ *vt* tener antipatía a; **to take a** ~ **to sb/sth** cogerle *or* agarrarle (*LAm*) antipatía a uno/algo; **I** ~ **the idea** no me gusta la idea.
dislocate [dis'lōkāt] *vt* dislocar; **he** ~**d his shoulder** se dislocó el hombro.
dislodge [dislâj'] *vt* sacar; (*enemy*) desalojar.
disloyal [disloi'əl] *a* desleal.
dismal [diz'məl] *a* (*dark*) sombrío; (*depressing*) triste; (*very bad*) fatal.
dismantle [disman'təl] *vt* desmontar, desarmar.
dismay [dismā'] *n* consternación *f* ♦ *vt* consternar; **much to my** ~ para gran consternación mía.
dismiss [dismis'] *vt* (*worker*) despedir; (*official*) destituir; (*idea, LAW*) rechazar; (*possibility*) descartar ♦ *vi* (*MIL*) romper filas.
dismissal [dismis'əl] *n* despedida, destitución *f*.
dismount [dismount'] *vi* apearse; (*rider*) desmontar.
disobedience [disəbē'dēəns] *n* desobediencia.
disobedient [disəbē'dēənt] *a* desobediente.
disobey [disəbā'] *vt* desobedecer; (*rule*) infringir.
disorder [disôr'dûr] *n* desorden *m*; (*rioting*) disturbio; (*MED*) trastorno; (*disease*) enfermedad *f*; **civil** ~ desorden *m* civil.
disorderly [disôr'dûrlē] *a* (*untidy*) desordenado; (*meeting*) alborotado; ~ **conduct** (*LAW*) conducta escandalosa.
disorganized [disôr'gənīzd] *a* desorganizado.
disorientated [disō'rēintātid] *a* desorientado.
disown [disōn'] *vt* desconocer.

disparaging [dispar'ijing] *a* despreciativo; **to be ~ about sth/sb** menospreciar algo/a uno.

disparate [dis'pûrit] *a* dispar.

disparity [dispar'itē] *n* disparidad *f*.

dispassionate [dispash'ənit] *a* (*unbiased*) imparcial; (*unemotional*) desapasionado.

dispatch [dispach'] *vt* enviar; (*kill*) despachar; (*deal with: business*) despachar ♦ *n* (*sending*) envío; (*speed*) prontitud *f*; (*PRESS*) informe *m*; (*MIL*) parte *m*.

dispatch department *n* departamento de envíos.

dispatch rider *n* (*MIL*) correo.

dispel [dispel'] *vt* disipar, dispersar.

dispensary [dispen'sûrē] *n* dispensario, farmacia.

dispensation [dispənsā'shən] *n* (*REL*) dispensa.

dispense [dispens'] *vt* dispensar, repartir; (*medicine*) preparar.

dispense with *vt fus* (*make unnecessary*) prescindir de.

dispenser [dispen'sûr] *n* (*container*) distribuidor *m* automático.

dispensing chemist [dispen'sing kem'ist] *n* (*Brit*) farmacia.

dispersal [dispûr'səl] *n* dispersión *f*.

disperse [dispûrs'] *vt* dispersar ♦ *vi* dispersarse.

dispirited [dispir'itid] *a* desanimado, desalentado.

displace [displās'] *vt* (*person*) desplazar; (*replace*) reemplazar.

displaced person [displāst' pûr'sən] *n* (*POL*) desplazado/a.

displacement [displās'mənt] *n* cambio de sitio.

display [displā'] *n* (*exhibition*) exposición *f*; (*COMPUT*) visualización *f*; (*MIL*) desfile *m*; (*of feeling*) manifestación *f*; (*pej*) aparato, pompa ♦ *vt* exponer; manifestar; (*ostentatiously*) lucir; **on ~** (*exhibits*) expuesto, exhibido; (*goods*) en el escaparate.

display advertising *n* publicidad *f* gráfica.

displease [displēz'] *vt* (*offend*) ofender; (*annoy*) fastidiar; **~d with** disgustado con.

displeasure [displezh'ûr] *n* disgusto.

disposable [dispō'zəbəl] *a* (*not reusable*) desechable; **~ personal income** ingresos *mpl* personales disponibles.

disposable diaper *n* (*US*) pañal desechable.

disposal [dispō'zəl] *n* (*sale*) venta; (*of house*) traspaso; (*by giving away*) donación *f*; (*arrangement*) colocación *f*; (*of garbage*) destrucción *f*; **at one's ~** a la disposición de uno; **to put sth at sb's ~** poner algo a disposición de uno.

disposed [dispōzd'] *a*: **~ to do** dispuesto a hacer.

dispose of [dispōz' uv] *vt fus* (*time, money*) disponer de; (*unwanted goods*) desha-

cerse de; (*COMM: sell*) traspasar, vender; (*throw away*) tirar.

disposition [dispəzish'ən] *n* disposición *f*; (*temperament*) carácter *m*.

dispossess [dispəzes'] *vt*: **to ~ sb (of)** desposeer a uno (de).

disproportion [disprəpôr'shən] *n* desproporción *f*.

disproportionate [disprəpôr'shənit] *a* desproporcionado.

disprove [disprōōv'] *vt* refutar.

dispute [dispyōōt'] *n* disputa; (*verbal*) discusión *f*; (*also*: **industrial ~**) conflicto (laboral) ♦ *vt* (*argue*) disputar; (*question*) cuestionar; **to be in** *or* **under ~** (*matter*) estar en cuestión; (*territory*) estar en disputa.

disqualification [diskwâləfəkā'shən] *n* inhabilitación *f*; (*SPORT, from driving*) descalificación *f*.

disqualify [diskwâl'əfī] *vt* (*SPORT*) descalificar; **to ~ sb for sth/from doing sth** incapacitar a uno para algo/hacer algo.

disquiet [diskwī'it] *n* preocupación *f*, inquietud *f*.

disquieting [diskwī'iting] *a* inquietante.

disregard [disrigârd'] *vt* desatender; (*ignore*) no hacer caso de ♦ *n* (*indifference: to feelings, danger, money*): **~ (for)** indiferencia (a); **~ (of)** (*non-observance: of law, rules*) violación *f* (de).

disrepair [disripár'] *n*: **to fall into ~** (*building*) desmoronarse; (*street*) deteriorarse.

disreputable [disrep'yətəbəl] *a* (*person, area*) de mala fama; (*behavior*) vergonzoso.

disrepute [disripyōōt'] *n* descrédito, ignominia; **to bring into ~** desacreditar.

disrespectful [disrispekt'fəl] *a* irrespetuoso.

disrupt [disrupt'] *vt* (*meeting, public transport, conversation*) interrumpir; (*plans*) desbaratar, alternar, trastornar.

disruption [disrup'shən] *n* trastorno; desbaratamiento; interrupción *f*.

disruptive [disrup'tiv] *a* (*influence*) disruptivo; (*strike action*) perjudicial.

dissatisfaction [dissatisfak'shən] *n* disgusto, descontento.

dissatisfied [dissat'isfīd] *a* insatisfecho.

dissect [disekt'] *vt* (*also fig*) disecar.

disseminate [disem'ənāt] *vt* divulgar, difundir.

dissent [disent'] *n* disensión *f*.

dissenter [disen'tûr] *n* (*REL, POL etc*) disidente *m/f*.

dissertation [disûrtā'shən] *n* (*UNIV*) tesina.

disservice [dissûr'vis] *n*: **to do sb a ~** perjudicar a alguien.

dissident [dis'idənt] *a, n* disidente *m/f*.

dissimilar [disim'ilûr] *a* distinto.

dissipate [dis'əpāt] *vt* disipar; (*waste*) desperdiciar.

dissipated [dis'əpātid] *a* disoluto.
dissipation [disəpā'shən] *n* disipación *f*; (*moral*) libertinaje *m*, vicio; (*waste*) derroche *m*.
dissociate [disō'shēāt] *vt* disociar; **to ~ o.s. from** disociarse de.
dissolute [dis'əlōot] *a* disoluto.
dissolution [disəlōō'shən] *n* (*of organization, marriage, POL*) disolución *f*.
dissolve [dizâlv'] *vt* (*gen, COMM*) disolver ♦ *vi* disolverse.
dissuade [diswād'] *vt*: **to ~ sb (from)** disuadir a uno (de).
distaff [dis'taf] *n*: **~ side** lado materno.
distance [dis'təns] *n* distancia; **in the ~** a lo lejos; **it's within walking ~** se puede ir andando.
distant [dis'tənt] *a* lejano; (*manner*) reservado, frío.
distaste [distāst'] *n* repugnancia.
distasteful [distāst'fəl] *a* repugnante, desagradable.
Dist. Atty. *abbr* (*US*) = **district attorney**.
distemper [distem'pûr] *n* (*of dogs*) moquillo.
distend [distend'] *vt* dilatar, hinchar ♦ *vi* dilatarse, hincharse.
distended [distend'id] *a* (*stomach*) hinchado.
distill, (*Brit*) **distil** [distil'] *vt* destilar.
distillery [distil'ûrē] *n* destilería.
distinct [distingkt'] *a* (*different*) distinto; (*clear*) claro; (*unmistakeable*) inequívoco; **as ~ from** a diferencia de.
distinction [distingk'shən] *n* distinción *f*; (*in exam*) sobresaliente *m*; **a writer of ~** un escritor destacado; **to draw a ~ between** hacer una distinción entre.
distinctive [distingk'tiv] *a* distintivo.
distinctly [distingkt'lē] *ad* claramente.
distinguish [disting'gwish] *vt* distinguir; **to ~ (between)** distinguir (entre).
distinguished [disting'gwisht] *a* (*eminent*) distinguido; (*career*) eminente; (*refined*) distinguido, de categoría.
distinguishing [disting'gwishing] *a* (*feature*) distintivo.
distort [distôrt'] *vt* torcer, retorcer; (*account, news*) desvirtuar, deformar.
distortion [distôr'shən] *n* deformación *f*; (*of sound*) distorsión *f*; (*of truth etc*) torcimiento; (*of facts*) falseamiento.
distr. *abbr* = **distribution; distributor**.
distract [distrakt'] *vt* distraer.
distracted [distrak'tid] *a* distraído.
distracting [distrak'ting] *a* que distrae la atención, molesto.
distraction [distrak'shən] *n* distracción *f*; (*confusion*) aturdimiento; (*amusement*) diversión *f*; **to drive sb to ~** (*distress, anxiety*) volver loco a uno.
distraught [distrôt'] *a* turbado, enloquecido.
distress [distres'] *n* (*anguish*) angustia;

(*want*) miseria; (*pain*) dolor *m*; (*danger*) peligro ♦ *vt* afligir; (*pain*) doler; **in ~** (*ship etc*) en peligro.
distressing [distres'ing] *a* angustioso; doloroso.
distress signal *n* señal *f* de socorro.
distribute [distrib'yōōt] *vt* (*gen*) distribuir; (*share out*) repartir.
distribution [distrəbyōō'shən] *n* distribución *f*.
distribution cost *n* gastos *mpl* de distribución.
distributor [distrib'yətûr] *n* (*AUT*) distribuidor *m*; (*COMM*) distribuidora.
district [dis'trikt] *n* (*of country*) zona, región *f*; (*of town*) barrio; (*ADMIN*) comarca.
district attorney *n* (*US*) fiscal *m/f*.
district council *n* (*Brit*) municipio.
district manager *n* representante *m/f* regional.
district nurse *n* (*Brit*) enfermera *que atiende a pacientes a domicilio*.
distrust [distrust'] *n* desconfianza ♦ *vt* desconfiar de.
distrustful [distrust'fəl] *a* desconfiado.
disturb [distûrb'] *vt* (*person: bother, interrupt*) molestar; (*meeting*) interrumpir; (*disorganize*) desordenar; **sorry to ~ you** perdone la molestia.
disturbance [distûr'bəns] *n* (*political etc*) disturbio; (*violence*) alboroto; (*of mind*) trastorno; **to cause a ~** causar alboroto; **~ of the peace** alteración *f* del orden público.
disturbed [distûrbd'] *a* (*worried, upset*) preocupado, angustiado; **to be emotionally/ mentally ~** tener problemas emocionales/ ser un trastornado mental.
disturbing [distûrb'ing] *a* inquietante, perturbador(a).
disuse [disyōōs'] *n*: **to fall into ~** caer en desuso.
disused [disyōōzd'] *a* abandonado.
ditch [dich] *n* zanja; (*irrigation ~*) acequia ♦ *vt* (*col*) deshacerse de.
dither [dith'ûr] *vi* vacilar.
ditto [dit'ō] *ad* ídem, lo mismo.
div. *abbr* = **dividend**.
divan [divan'] *n* diván *m*.
divan bed *n* cama turca.
dive [dīv] *n* (*from board*) salto; (*underwater*) buceo; (*of submarine*) sumersión *f*; (*AVIAT*) picada ♦ *vi* saltar; bucear; sumergirse; picar.
diver [di'vûr] *n* (*SPORT*) saltador(a) *m/f*; (*underwater*) buzo.
diverge [divûrj'] *vi* divergir.
divergent [divûr'jənt] *a* divergente.
diverse [divûrs'] *a* diversos/as, varios/as.
diversification [divûrsəfəkā'shən] *n* diversificación *f*.
diversify [divûr'səfī] *vt* diversificar.
diversion [divûr'zhən] *n* (*Brit AUT*) desviación *f*; (*distraction, MIL*) diversión *f*.

diversity [divûr'sitē] *n* diversidad *f*.
divert [divûrt'] *vt* (*train, plane, traffic*) desviar; (*amuse*) divertir.
divest [divest'] *vt*: **to ~ sb of sth** despojar a alguien de algo.
divide [divīd'] *vt* dividir; (*separate*) separar ♦ *vi* dividirse; (*road*) bifurcarse; **to ~ (between, among)** repartir *or* dividir (entre); **40 ~d by 5** 40 dividido por 5.
divide out *vt*: **to ~ out (between, among)** (*candies, tasks etc*) repartir (entre).
divided [divīd'id] *a* (*country, couple*) dividido, separado; (*opinions*) en desacuerdo.
divided highway *n* (*US*) carretera de doble calzada.
dividend [div'idend] *n* dividendo; (*fig*) beneficio.
dividend cover *n* cobertura de dividendo.
dividers [divī'dûrz] *npl* compás *m* de puntas.
divine [divīn'] *a* divino ♦ *vt* (*future*) vaticinar; (*truth*) alumbrar; (*water, metal*) adivinar.
diving [dīv'ing] *n* (*SPORT*) salto; (*underwater*) buceo.
diving board [dīv'ing bōrd] *n* trampolín *m*.
diving suit *n* escafandra.
divinity [divin'ətē] *n* divinidad *f*; (*SCOL*) teología.
divisible [diviz'əbəl] *a* divisible.
division [divizh'ən] *n* (*also Brit SOCCER*) división *f*; (*sharing*) repartimiento; (*Brit POL*) votación *f*; **~ of labor** división *f* del trabajo.
divisive [divī'siv] *a* divisivo.
divorce [divôrs'] *n* divorcio ♦ *vt* divorciarse de.
divorced [divôrst'] *a* divorciado.
divorcee [divôrsē'] *n* divorciado/a.
divulge [divulj'] *vt* divulgar, revelar.
D.I.Y. *a, n abbr* (*Brit*) = **do-it-yourself**.
dizziness [diz'ēnis] *n* vértigo.
dizzy [diz'ē] *a* (*person*) mareado; (*height*) vertiginoso; **to feel ~** marearse; **I feel ~** estoy mareado.
DJ *n abbr* = **disc jockey**.
Djakarta [jəkâr'tə] *n* Yakarta.
DJIA *n abbr* (*US STOCK EXCHANGE*) = *Dow Jones Industrial Average*.
dl *abbr* (= *deciliter(s)*) dl.
DLit(t) *abbr* (= *Doctor of Literature, Doctor of Letters*) título universitario.
DLO *n abbr* (= *dead-letter office*) oficina de Correos que se encarga de las cartas que no llegan a su destino.
dm *abbr* (= *decimeter(s)*) dm.
DMus *abbr* (= *Doctor of Music*) título universitario.
DMZ *n abbr* (= *demilitarized zone*) zona desmilitarizada.
DNA *n abbr* (= *deoxyribonucleic acid*) ADN *m*.
do [dōō] *vb* (*pt* **did**, *pp* **done** [did, dun]) *vt*,

vi (*gen*) hacer; (*speed*) ir a; (*visit: city, museum*) visitar, recorrer; (*THEATER*) representar ♦ *n* (*col: party*) fiesta, guateque *m*; (: *formal gathering*) reunión *f*, ceremonia; **he didn't laugh** no se rió; **she swims better than I ~** nada mejor que yo; **he laughed, didn't he?** se rió ¿no?; **that will ~!** ¡basta!; **to make ~ with** contentarse con; **~ you agree?** ¿está usted de acuerdo?; **I don't understand** no entiendo; **~ you speak English?** ¿habla (usted) inglés?; **you speak better than I ~** tú hablas mejor que yo; **so does he** él también; DO **come!** ¡venga, por favor!; **I DO wish I could ...** ojalá que pudiera ...; **but I DO like it!** pero, sí que *or* por supuesto que me gusta!; **what does he ~ for a living?** ¿a qué se dedica?; **what can I ~ for you?** (*in store*) ¿en qué puedo servirle?; **to ~ one's hair** (*comb*) peinarse; (*style*) arreglarse el pelo; **I'm going to ~ the washing-up** voy a fregar los platos; **we've done 200 km already** llevamos 200 km de viaje ya; **I'll ~ all I can** haré todo lo que pueda; **how ~ you like your steak done?** — **well done** ¿cómo te gusta el filete? — bien hecho; **will it ~?** ¿sirve?, ¿conviene?; **to ~ sb out of sth** pisar algo a uno; **to ~ well** prosperar, tener éxito; **he's ~ing well/badly at school** va bien/mal en la escuela; **it doesn't ~ to upset her** cuidado en ofenderle; **that'll ~!** (*in annoyance*) ¡basta ya!; **to ~ without sth** prescindir de algo; **what has that got to ~ with it?** ¿qué tiene que ver eso?; **what have you done with my slippers?** ¿qué has hecho con mis zapatillas?
do away with *vt fus* (*kill*) asesinar; (*suppress*) suprimir.
do up *vt* (*laces*) liar, atar; (*room*) renovar; **to ~ o.s. up** maquillarse.
do with *vt fus* (*with can, could: need*) no venirle mal; **I could ~ with some help/a drink** no me vendría mal un poco de ayuda/una bebida.
do. *abbr* = **ditto**.
DOA *abbr* = *dead on arrival*.
d.o.b. *abbr* = *date of birth*.
docile [dás'əl] *a* dócil.
dock [dâk] *n* (*NAUT: wharf*) dársena, muelle *m*; (*LAW*) banquillo (de los acusados); **~s** *npl* muelles *mpl*, puerto *sg* ♦ *vi* (*enter ~*) atracar el muelle ♦ *vt* (*pay etc*) descontar.
dock dues *npl* derechos *mpl* de muelle.
docker [dâk'ûr] *n* trabajador *m* portuario, estibador *m*.
docket [dâk'it] *n* (*on parcel etc*) etiqueta.
dockyard [dâk'yârd] *n* astillero.
doctor [dâk'tûr] *n* médico; (*Ph.D. etc*) doctor(a) *m/f* ♦ *vt* (*fig*) arreglar, falsificar; (*drink etc*) adulterar.
doctorate [dâk'tûrit] *n* doctorado.
Doctor of Philosophy (Ph.D.) *n* Doctor

m (en Filosofía y Letras).
doctrinaire [dáktrənär'] *a* doctrinario.
doctrine [dák'trin] *n* doctrina.
document *n* [dák'yəmənt] documento ♦ *vt*
[dák'yəment] documentar.
documentary [dákyəmen'túrē] *a* documental ♦ *n* documental *m*.
documentation [dákyəməntā'shən] *n* documentación *f*.
DOD *n abbr* (*US*: = *Department of Defense*)
Ministerio de Defensa.
doddering [dád'ûring] *a*, **doddery** [dád'ûrē]
a chocho.
Dodecanese (Islands) [dōdekənes'
(i'ləndz)] *n* (*pl*) Dodecaneso *sg*.
dodge [dáj] *n* (*of body*) regate *m*; (*fig*) truco ♦ *vt* (*gen*) evadir; (*blow*) esquivar ♦ *vi*
esquivarse, escabullirse; (*SPORT*) hacer
una finta; **to ~ out of the way** echarse a
un lado; **to ~ through the traffic** regatear
por el tráfico.
dodgems [dáj'əmz] *npl* coches *mpl* de choque.
DOE *n abbr* (*US*) = *Department of Energy*;
(*Brit*) = *Department of the Environment*.
doe [dō] *n* (*deer*) cierva, gama; (*rabbit*) co-
neja.
does [duz] *vb see* **do**.
doesn't [duz'nt] = **does not**.
dog [dôg] *n* perro ♦ *vt* seguir (de cerca);
(*fig*: *memory etc*) perseguir; **to go to the
~s** (*person*) echarse a perder; (*nation etc*)
ir a la ruina.
dog biscuit *n* galleta de perro.
dog collar *n* collar *m* de perro; (*fig*) cuello
de cura.
dog-eared [dôg'ērd] *a* sobado.
dogfish [dôg'fish] *n* cazón *m*, perro marino.
dog food *n* comida para perros.
dogged [dôg'id] *a* tenaz, obstinado.
dogma [dôg'mə] *n* dogma *m*.
dogmatic [dôgmat'ik] *a* dogmático.
do-gooder [dōōgōōd'úr] *n* (*col pej*): **to be
a ~** ser una persona bien intencionada *or*
un filantropista.
dogsbody [dôgz'bádē] *n* (*Brit*) burro de
carga.
dog tag *n* (*US*) chapa de identidad.
doing [dōō'ing] *n*: **this is your ~** esto es
obra tuya.
doings [dōō'ingz] *npl* (*events*) sucesos *mpl*;
(*acts*) hechos *mpl*.
do-it-yourself [dōō'ityōōrself'] *n* bricolaje
m.
do-it-yourselfer [dōō'ityōōrself'úr] *n* brico-
lajista *m/f*.
doldrums [dōl'drəmz] *npl*: **to be in the ~**
(*person*) estar abatido; (*business*) estar
estancado.
dole [dōl] *n* (*Brit*: *payment*) subsidio de
paro; **on the ~** parado.
dole out *vt* repartir.
doleful [dōl'fəl] *a* triste, lúgubre.

doll [dál] *n* muñeca.
doll up *vt*: **to ~ o.s. up** ataviarse.
dollar [dál'úr] *n* dólar *m*.
dollar area *n* zona del dólar.
dolphin [dál'fin] *n* delfín *m*.
domain [dōmān'] *n* (*fig*) campo, competencia; (*land*) dominios *mpl*.
dome [dōm] *n* (*ARCH*) cúpula; (*shape*) bóveda.
domestic [dəmes'tik] *a* (*animal*, *duty*) doméstico; (*flight*, *news*, *policy*) nacional.
domesticated [dəmes'tikātid] *a* domesticado; (*person*: *home-loving*) casero, hogareño.
domesticity [dōmestis'itē] *n* vida casera.
domestic servant *n* sirviente/a *m/f*.
domicile [dâm'isīl] *n* domicilio.
dominant [dâm'ənənt] *a* dominante.
dominate [dâm'ənāt] *vt* dominar.
domination [dâmənā'shən] *n* dominación *f*.
domineering [dâmənēr'ing] *a* dominante.
Dominican Republic [dəmin'əkən ri-
pub'lik] *n* República Dominicana.
dominion [dəmin'yən] *n* dominio.
domino, *pl* **~es** [dâm'ənō] *n* ficha de dominó.
dominoes [dâm'ənōz] *n* (*game*) dominó.
don [dân] *n* (*Brit*) catedrático/a.
donate [dō'nāt] *vt* donar.
donation [dōnā'shən] *n* donativo.
done [dun] *pp of* **do**.
donkey [dâng'kē] *n* burro.
donkey-work [dâng'kēwúrk] *n* (*Brit col*)
trabajo pesado.
donor [dō'nûr] *n* donante *m/f*.
don't [dōnt] = **do not**.
donut [dō'nut] *n* (*US*) buñuelo.
doodle [dōōd'əl] *n* garabato ♦ *vi* pintar di-
bujitos *or* garabatos.
doom [dōōm] *n* (*fate*) suerte *f*; (*death*)
muerte *f* ♦ *vt*: **to be ~ed to failure** ser
condenado al fracaso.
doomsday [dōōmz'dā] *n* día *m* del juicio
final.
door [dôr] *n* puerta; (*of car*) portezuela;
(*entry*) entrada; **from ~ to ~** de puerta en
puerta.
doorbell [dôr'bel] *n* timbre *m*.
door handle *n* tirador *m*; (*of car*) manija.
door knocker *n* aldaba.
doorman [dôr'man] *n* (*in hotel*) portero.
doormat [dôr'mat] *n* felpudo, estera.
doorstep [dôr'step] *n* peldaño.
door-to-door [dôr'tədôr'] *a*: **~ selling**
venta a domicilio.
doorway [dôr'wā] *n* entrada, puerta; **in the
~** en la puerta.
dope [dōp] *n* (*col*: *person*) imbécil *m/f*; (:
information) información *f*, informes *mpl*;
(: *drugs*) drogas ♦ *vt* (*horse etc*) drogar.
dopey [dō'pē] *a* atontado.
dormant [dôr'mənt] *a* inactivo; (*latent*) latente.

dormer [dôr'mûr] *n* (*also*: ~ **window**) buhardilla.

dormitory [dôr'mitôrē] *n* (*US*: *for students*) residencia, colegio mayor; (*Brit*) dormitorio.

dormouse, *pl* **dormice** [dôr'mous, -mīs] *n* lirón *m*.

Dors *abbr* (*Brit*) = *Dorset*.

DOS [dōs] *n abbr* = **disk operating system**.

dosage [dō'sij] *n* (*on medicine bottle*) dosis *f inv*, dosificación *f*.

dose [dōs] *n* (*of medicine*) dosis *f inv*; **a** ~ **of flu** un ataque de gripe ♦ *vt*: **to** ~ **o.s. with** tomar una buena dosis de.

doss house [dâs' hous] *n* (*Brit*) pensión *f* de mala muerte.

dossier [dâs'ēā] *n*: ~ **(on)** expediente *m* (sobre).

DOT *n abbr* (*US*: = *Department of Transportation*) ≈ *Ministerio de Transportes, Turismo y Comunicaciones* (*Sp*).

dot [dât] *n* punto; ~**ted with** salpicado de; **on the** ~ en punto.

dot command *n* (*COMPUT*) instrucción *f* (precedida) de punto.

dote [dōt]: **to** ~ **on** *vt fus* adorar, idolatrar.

dot-matrix printer [dâtmāt'riks prin'tûr] *n* impresora matricial *or* de matriz.

dotted line [dât'id līn'] *n* línea de puntos; **to sign on the** ~ firmar.

dotty [dât'ē] *a* (*col*) disparatado, chiflado.

double [dub'əl] *a* doble ♦ *ad* (*twice*): **to cost** ~ costar el doble ♦ *n* (*gen*) doble *m* ♦ *vt* doblar; (*efforts*) redoblar ♦ *vi* doblarse; (*have two uses etc*); **to** ~ **as** hacer las veces de; **spelled with a** ~ **"s"** escrito con dos "eses"; **on the** ~ corriendo.

double back *vi* (*person*) volver sobre sus pasos.

double up *vi* (*bend over*) doblarse; (*share bedroom*) compartir.

double bass *n* contrabajo.

double bed *n* cama matrimonial.

double bend *n* (*Brit*) doble curva.

double-breasted [dub'əlbres'tid] *a* cruzado.

double-check [dub'əlchek'] *vt*, *vi* revisar de nuevo.

double cream *n* (*Brit*) nata enriquecida.

doublecross [dub'əlkrôs'] *vt* (*trick*) engañar; (*betray*) traicionar.

doubledecker [dubəldek'ûr] *n* autobús *m* de dos pisos.

double glazing [dub'əl glāz'ing] *n* (*Brit*) doble acristalamiento.

double indemnity [dub'əl indem'nitē] *n* doble indemnización *f*.

double-page [dub'əlpāj] *a*: ~ **spread** doble página.

double room *n* cuarto para dos.

doubles [dub'əlz] *n* (*TENNIS*) juego de dobles.

double time *n* tarifa doble.

doubly [dub'lē] *ad* doblemente.

doubt [dout] *n* duda ♦ *vt* dudar; (*suspect*) dudar de; **to** ~ **that** dudar que; **there is no** ~ **that** no cabe duda de que; **without (a)** ~ sin duda (alguna); **beyond** ~ fuera de duda; **I** ~ **it very much** lo dudo mucho.

doubtful [dout'fəl] *a* dudoso; (*person*) sospechoso; **to be** ~ **about sth** tener dudas sobre algo; **I'm a bit** ~ no estoy convencido.

doubtless [dout'lis] *ad* sin duda.

dough [dō] *n* masa, pasta; (*col*: *money*) pasta.

doughnut [dō'nut] *n* (*Brit*) buñuelo.

douse [dous] *vt* (*drench*: *with water*) mojar; (*extinguish*: *flames*) apagar.

dove [duv] *n* paloma.

dovetail [duv'tāl] *vi* (*fig*) encajar.

dowager [dou'əjûr] *n*: ~ **duchess** duquesa viuda.

dowdy [dou'dē] *a* desaliñado; (*inelegant*) poco elegante.

Dow Jones Average [dou'jōnz' av'ûrij], **Dow Jones Index** [dou'jōnz' in'deks] *n* (*US*) índice *m* Dow-Jones.

down [doun] *n* (*fluff*) pelusa; (*feathers*) plumón *m*, flojel *m*; (*hill*) loma ♦ *ad* (~*wards*) abajo, hacia abajo; (*on the ground*) por/en tierra ♦ *prep* abajo ♦ *vt* (*col*: *drink*) beberse, tragar(se); ~ **with X!** ¡abajo X!; ~ **there** allí abajo; ~ **here** aquí abajo; **I'll be** ~ **in a minute** ahora bajo; **England is two goals** ~ Inglaterra está perdiendo por dos tantos; **I've been** ~ **with flu** he estado con gripe; **the price of meat is** ~ ha bajado el precio de la carne; **I've got it** ~ **in my diary** lo he apuntado en mi agenda; **to pay $2** ~ dejar $2 de depósito; **he went** ~ **the hill** fue cuesta abajo; ~ **under** (*in Australia etc*) en Australia/Nueva Zelanda; **to** ~ **tools** (*Brit*: *fig*) declararse en huelga.

down-and-out [doun'ənout] *n* (*tramp*) vagabundo/a.

down-at-heel(s) [dounat·hēl(z)'] *a* venido a menos; (*appearance*) desaliñado.

downbeat [doun'bēt] *n* (*MUS*) compás *m* ♦ *a* (*gloomy*) pesimista.

downcast [doun'kast] *a* abatido.

downer [dou'nûr] *n* (*col*: *drug*) tranquilizante; **to be on a** ~ estar pasando un mal bache.

downfall [doun'fôl] *n* caída, ruina.

downgrade [doun'grād] *vt* (*job*) degradar; (*hotel*) bajar de categoría a.

downhearted [doun'hâr'tid] *a* desanimado.

downhill [doun'hil'] *ad*: **to go** ~ ir cuesta abajo; (*business*) estar en declive.

download [doun'lōd] *vt* (*COMPUT*) transferir, telecargar.

down-market [dounmâr'kit] *a* (*Brit*) para la sección popular del mercado.

down payment *n* entrada, pago al contado.

downplay |doun'plā| *vt* (*US*) quitar importancia a.

downpour |doun'pôr| *n* aguacero.

downright |doun'rīt| *a* (*nonsense, lie*) manifiesto; (*refusal*) terminante.

Down's syndrome |dounz' sin'drŏm| *n* (*MED*) síndrome *m* de Down.

downstairs |doun'stärz'| *ad* (*below*) (en la casa de) abajo; (*motion*) escaleras abajo; **to come** (*or* **go**) ~ bajar la escalera.

downstream |doun'strēm'| *ad* aguas *or* río abajo.

downtime |doun'tīm| *n* (*COMM*) tiempo inactivo.

down-to-earth |dountŏŏûrth'| *a* práctico.

downtown |doun'toun'| *ad* en el centro de la ciudad.

downtrodden |doun'trádən| *a* oprimido.

downward |doun'wûrd| *ad* hacia abajo ♦ *a*: **a** ~ **trend** una tendencia descendente.

downwards |doun'wûrdz| *ad* hacia abajo; **face** ~ (*person*) boca abajo; (*object*) cara abajo.

dowry |dou'rē| *n* dote *f*.

doz. *abbr* = **dozen**.

doze |dōz| *vi* dormitar.

doze off *vi* quedarse medio dormido.

dozen |duz'ən| *n* docena; **a** ~ **books** una docena de libros; **~s of** cantidad de; **~s of times** cantidad de veces; **80 cents a** ~ 80 céntimos la docena.

DPh., D. Phil. *n abbr* (= *Doctor of Philosophy*) título universitario.

DPP *n abbr* (*Brit*) = **Director of Public Prosecutions.**

DPT *n abbr* (= *diphtheria, pertussis, tetanus*) vacuna trivalente.

DPW *n abbr* (*US*: = *Department of Public Works*) ≈ Ministerio de Obras Públicas y Urbanismo (*Sp*).

Dr, Dr. *abbr* (= *doctor*) Dr.

Dr. *abbr* (*in street names*) = **Drive.**

dr *abbr* (*COMM*) = **debtor.**

drab |drab| *a* gris, monótono.

draft |draft| *n* (*first copy*: *of document, report*) borrador *m*; (*COMM*) giro; (*US*: *call-up*) quinta; (: *of air*) corriente *f* de aire; (: *drink*) trago; (: *NAUT*) calado ♦ *vt* (*write roughly*) hacer un borrador de; **on** ~ (*US*: *beer*) de barril.

draftee |draftē'| *n* (*US MIL*) recluta *m/f*.

draftsman |drafts'mən| *n* (*US*) proyectista *m*, delineante *m*.

draftsmanship |drafts'mənship| *n* (*US*: *drawing*) dibujo lineal; (: *skill*) habilidad *f* para el dibujo.

drag |drag| *vt* arrastrar; (*river*) dragar, rastrear ♦ *vi* arrastrarse por el suelo ♦ *n* (*AVIAT*: *resistance*) resistencia aerodinámica; (*col*) lata; (*women's clothing*): **in** ~ vestido de travesti.

drag away *vt*: **to** ~ **away** (**from**) quitar arrastrando.

drag on *vi* ser interminable.

dragnet |drag'nct| *n* (*NAUT*) rastra; (*fig*) emboscada.

dragon |drag'ən| *n* dragón *m*.

dragonfly |drag'ənflī| *n* libélula.

dragoon |drəgŏŏn'| *n* (*cavalryman*) dragón *m* ♦ *vt*: **to** ~ **sb into doing sth** forzar a uno a hacer algo.

drain |drān| *n* desaguadero; (*in street*) sumidero; (~ *cover*) rejilla del sumidero ♦ *vt* (*land, marshes*) desaguar; (*MED*) drenar; (*reservoir*) desecar; (*fig*) agotar ♦ *vi* escurrirse; **to be a** ~ **on** agotar; **to feel** ~**ed** (**of energy**) (*fig*) sentirse agotado.

drainage |drā'nij| *n* (*act*) desagüe *m*; (*MED, AGR*) drenaje *m*; (*sewage*) alcantarillado.

drainboard |drān'bôrd| *n* (*US*) escurridera, escurridor *m*.

draining board |drā'ning bōrd| *n* (*Brit*) = **drainboard.**

drainpipe |drān'pīp| *n* tubo de desagüe.

drake |drāk| *n* pato (macho).

dram |dram| *n* (*drink*) traguito, copita.

drama |dräm'ə| *n* (*art*) teatro; (*play*) drama *m*.

dramatic |drəmat'ik| *a* dramático.

dramatist |dram'ətist| *n* dramaturgo/a.

dramatize |dram'ətīz| *vt* (*events etc*) dramatizar; (*adapt*: *novel*: *for TV, cinema*) adaptar.

drank |drangk| *pt of* **drink.**

drape |drāp| *vt* cubrir.

draper |drā'pûr| *n* (*Brit*) pañero.

drapes |drāps| *npl* (*US*) cortinas *fpl*.

drastic |dras'tik| *a* (*measure, reduction*) severo; (*change*) radical.

draught |draft| *n* (*Brit*: *of air*) corriente *f* de aire; (: *drink*) trago; (: *NAUT*) calado; **on** ~ (*Brit*: *beer*) de barril.

draughtboard |draft'bôrd| (*Brit*) *n* tablero de damas.

draughts |drafts| *n* (*Brit*) juego de damas.

draughtsman |drafts'mən| *etc* (*Brit*) = **draftsman** *etc*.

draw |drô| *vb* (*pt* **drew**, *pp* **drawn** |drŏŏ, drôn|) *vt* (*pull*) tirar; (*take out*) sacar; (*attract*) atraer; (*picture*) dibujar; (*money*) retirar; (*formulate*: *conclusion*): **to** ~ (**from**) sacar (de); (*comparison, distinction*): **to** ~ (**between**) hacer (entre) ♦ *vi* (*SPORT*) empatar ♦ *n* (*SPORT*) empate *m*; (*lottery*) sorteo; (*attraction*) atracción *f*; **to** ~ **near** *vi* acercarse.

draw back *vi*: **to** ~ **back** (**from**) echarse atrás (de).

draw in *vi* (*Brit*: *car*) aparcar; (: *train*) entrar en la estación.

draw on *vt* (*resources*) utilizar, servirse de; (*imagination, person*) recurrir a.

draw out *vi* (*lengthen*) alargarse.

draw up *vi* (*stop*) pararse ♦ *vt* (*document*) redactar; (*plans*) trazar.

drawback [drô'bak] *n* inconveniente *m*, desventaja.

drawbridge [drô'brij] *n* puente *m* levadizo.

drawee [drôē'] *n* girado.

drawer [drôr] *n* cajón *m*; [drô'úr] (*of check*) librador(a) *m/f*.

drawing [drô'ing] *n* dibujo.

drawing board *n* tablero (de dibujante).

drawing pin *n* (*Brit*) chinche *m*.

drawing room *n* salón *m*.

drawl [drôl] *n* habla lenta y cansina.

drawn [drôn] *pp of* **draw** ♦ *a* (*haggard*: *with tiredness*) ojeroso; (: *with pain*) maciento.

drawstring [drô'string] *n* apretadera.

dread [dred] *n* pavor *m*, terror *m* ♦ *vt* temer, tener miedo *or* pavor a.

dreadful [dred'fəl] *a* espantoso; **I feel ~!** (*ill*) ¡me siento fatal *or* malísimo!; (*ashamed*) ¡qué vergüenza!

dream [drēm] *n* sueño ♦ *vt, vi* (*pt, pp* **dreamed** *or* **dreamt** [dremt]) soñar; **to have a ~ about sb/sth** soñar con uno/algo; **sweet ~s!** ¡que sueñes con los ángeles!

dream up *vt* (*reason, excuse*) inventar; (*plan, idea*) idear.

dreamer [drē'múr] *n* soñador(a) *m/f*.

dream world *n* mundo imaginario.

dreamy [drē'mē] *a* (*person*) soñador(a), distraído; (*music*) de sueño.

dreary [drēr'ē] *a* monótono, aburrido.

dredge [drej] *vt* dragar.

dredge up *vt* sacar con draga; (*fig*: *unpleasant facts*) pescar, sacar a luz.

dredger [drej'úr] *n* (*ship, machine*) draga; (*Brit CULIN*) espolvoreador *m*.

dregs [dregz] *npl* heces *fpl*.

drench [drench] *vt* empapar; **~ed to the skin** calado hasta los huesos.

dress [dres] *n* vestido; (*clothing*) ropa ♦ *vt* vestir; (*wound*) vendar; (*CULIN*) aliñar; (*store window*) decorar, arreglar ♦ *vi* vestirse; **to ~ o.s., get ~ed** vestirse; **she ~es very well** se viste muy bien.

dress up *vi* vestirse de etiqueta; (*in fancy dress*) disfrazarse.

dress circle *n* (*Brit*) principal *m*.

dress designer *n* modisto/a.

dresser [dres'úr] *n* (*furniture*) aparador *m*; (: *US*) cómoda con espejo; (*THEATER*) camarero/a.

dressing [dres'ing] *n* (*MED*) vendaje *m*; (*CULIN*) aliño.

dressing gown *n* (*Brit*) bata.

dressing room *n* (*THEATER*) camarín *m*; (*SPORT*) vestidor *m*.

dressing table *n* tocador *m*.

dressmaker [dres'mākúr] *n* modista, costurera.

dressmaking [dres'māking] *n* costura.

dress rehearsal *n* ensayo general.

dress shirt *n* camisa de frac.

dressy [dres'ē] *a* (*col*) elegante.

drew [droo] *pt of* **draw.**

dribble [drib'əl] *vi* gotear, caer gota a gota; (*baby*) babear ♦ *vt* (*ball*) driblar, regatear.

dried [drīd] *a* (*gen*) seco; (*fruit*) paso; (*milk*) en polvo.

drier [drī'úr] *n* = **dryer.**

drift [drift] *n* (*of current etc*) velocidad *f*; (*of sand*) montón *m*; (*of snow*) ventisquero; (*meaning*) significado ♦ *vi* (*boat*) ir a la deriva; (*sand, snow*) amontonarse; **to catch sb's ~** seguirle la corriente a uno; **to let things ~** dejar las cosas como están; **to ~ apart** (*friends*) seguir su camino; (*lovers*) disgustarse, romper.

drifter [drif'túr] *n* vagabundo/a.

driftwood [drift'wood] *n* madera de deriva.

drill [dril] *n* taladro; (*bit*) broca; (*of dentist*) fresa; (*for mining etc*) perforadora, barrena; (*MIL*) instrucción *f* ♦ *vt* perforar, taladrar; (*soldiers*) ejercitar; (*pupils: in grammar*) dar práctica en gramática a ♦ *vi* (*for oil*) perforar.

drilling [dril'ing] *n* (*for oil*) perforación *f*.

drilling rig *n* (*on land*) torre *f* de perforación; (*at sea*) plataforma de perforación.

drily [drī'lē] *ad* secamente.

drink [dringk] *n* bebida ♦ *vt, vi* (*pt* **drank,** *pp* **drunk**) beber; **to have a ~** tomar algo; tomar una copa *or* un trago; **a ~ of water** un trago de agua; **to invite sb for ~s** invitar a uno a tomar unas copas; **there's food and ~ in the kitchen** hay de comer y de beber en la cocina; **would you like something to ~?** ¿quieres beber *or* tomar algo?

drink in *vt* (*subj: person: fresh air*) respirar; (*story, sight*) beberse.

drinkable [dring'kəbəl] *a* (*not poisonous*) potable; (*palatable*) aguantable.

drinker [dring'kúr] *n* bebedor(a) *m/f*.

drinking [dring'king] *n* (*drunkenness*) beber *m*.

drinking fountain *n* fuente *f*.

drinking water *n* agua potable.

drip [drip] *n* (*act*) goteo; (*one ~*) gota; (*Brit: MED*) gota a gota *m*; (*sound: of water etc*) goteo; (*col: spineless person*) soso/a ♦ *vi* gotear, caer gota a gota.

drip-dry [drip'drī] *a* (*shirt*) de lava y pon.

dripping [drip'ing] *n* (*animal fat*) pringue *m* ♦ *a*: **~ wet** calado.

drive [drīv] *n* paseo (en coche); (*journey*) viaje *m* (en coche); (*also*: **~way**) entrada; (*street*) calle; (*energy*) energía, vigor *m*; (*PSYCH*) impulso; (*SPORT*) ataque *m*; (*COMPUT: also: disk ~*) disc drive *m* ♦ *vb* (*pt* **drove,** *pp* **driven** [drōv, driv'ən]) *vt* (*car*) conducir, manejar (*LAm*); (*nail*) clavar; (*push*) empujar; (*TECH: motor*) impulsar ♦ *vi* (*AUT: at controls*) conducir; (: *travel*) pasearse en coche; **to go for a ~** dar una vuelta en coche; **it's 3 hours' ~ from New York** es un viaje de 3 horas desde Nueva York; **left-/right-hand ~**

conducción *f* a la izquierda/derecha; **front-/rear-wheel** ~ tracción *f* delantera/trasera; **sales** ~ promoción *f* de ventas; **to** ~ **sb mad** volverle loco a uno; **to** ~ **sb to (do) sth** empujar a uno a (hacer) algo; **he** ~**s a taxi** es taxista; **he** ~**s a Mercedes** tiene un Mercedes; **can you** ~**?** ¿sabes conducir o (*LAm*) manejar?; **to** ~ **at 50 km an hour** ir a 50km por hora.

drive at *vt fus* (*fig: intend, mean*) querer decir, insinuar.

drive on *vi* no parar, seguir adelante ♦ *vt* (*incite, encourage*) empujar.

drive-in [drīv'in] *a* (*esp US*): ~ **cinema** autocinema *m*.

drivel [driv'əl] *n* (*col*) tonterías *fpl*.

driven [driv'ən] *pp of* **drive.**

driver [drī'vûr] *n* conductor(a) *m/f*; (*of taxi, bus*) chofer *m*.

driver's license *n* (*US*) carnet *m* or permiso de conducir.

driveway [drīv'wā] *n* entrada.

driving [drī'ving] *n* conducir *m*, manejar *m* (*LAm*) ♦ *a* (*force*) impulsor(a).

driving instructor *n* instructor *m/f* de conducción.

driving lesson *n* clase *f* de conducción.

driving licence *n* (*Brit*) carnet *m* or permiso de conducir.

driving school *n* autoescuela.

driving test *n* examen *m* de conducción.

drizzle [driz'əl] *n* llovizna ♦ *vi* lloviznar.

droll [drōl] *a* gracioso.

dromedary [drâm'idärē] *n* dromedario.

drone [drōn] *vi* (*bee, aircraft, engine*) zumbar; (*also:* ~ **on**) murmurar sin interrupción ♦ *n* zumbido; (*male bee*) zángano.

drool [drōōl] *vi* babear; **to** ~ **over sb/sth** caérsele la baba por uno/algo.

droop [drōōp] *vi* (*fig*) decaer, desanimarse.

drop [drâp] *n* (*of water*) gota; (*fall: in price*) bajada; (: *in salary*) disminución *f* ♦ *vt* (*allow to fall*) dejar caer; (*voice, eyes, price*) bajar; (*set down from car*) dejar ♦ *vi* (*price, temperature*) calmarse, amainar; (*numbers, attendance*) disminuir; ~**s** *npl* (*MED*) gotas *fpl*; **cough** ~**s** pastillas *fpl* para la tos; **a** ~ **of 10%** una bajada del 10 por ciento; **to** ~ **anchor** echar el ancla; **to** ~ **sb a line** mandar unas líneas a uno.

drop in *vi* (*col: visit*): **to** ~ **in (on)** pasar por casa de (a).

drop off *vi* (*sleep*) dormirse ♦ *vt* (*passenger*) bajar, dejar.

drop out *vi* (*withdraw*) retirarse.

droplet [drâp'lit] *n* gotita.

dropout [drâp'out] *n* (*from society*) marginado/a; (*from university*) estudiante *m/f* que ha abandonado el curso.

dropper [drâp'ûr] *n* (*MED*) cuentagotas *m inv*.

droppings [drâp'ingz] *npl* excremento *sg*.

dross [drôs] *n* (*coal, fig*) escoria.

drought [drout] *n* sequía.

drove [drōv] *pt of* **drive.**

drown [droun] *vt* (*also:* ~ **out**: *sound*) ahogar ♦ *vi* ahogarse.

drowse [drouz] *vi* estar medio dormido.

drowsy [drou'zē] *a* soñoliento; **to be** ~ tener sueño.

drudge [druj] *n* esclavo del trabajo.

drudgery [druj'ûrē] *n* trabajo pesado or monótono.

drug [drug] *n* (*MED*) medicamento, droga; (*narcotic*) droga ♦ *vt* drogar; **to be on** ~**s** drogarse; **he's on** ~**s** se droga.

drug addict *n* drogadicto/a.

druggist [drug'ist] *n* (*US*) farmacéutico/a.

drug peddler *n* vendedor(a) *m/f* de narcóticos.

drugstore [drug'stôr] *n* farmacia.

drug trafficker *n* narcotraficante *m/f*.

drum [drum] *n* tambor *m*; (*large*) bombo; (*for oil, gas*) bidón *m* ♦ *vi* tocar el tambor; (*with fingers*) tamborilear ♦ *vt*: **to** ~ **one's fingers on the table** tamborilear con los dedos sobre la mesa; ~**s** *npl* batería *sg*.

drum up *vt* (*enthusiasm, support*) movilizar, fomentar.

drummer [drum'ûr] *n* tambor *m*.

drumstick [drum'stik] *n* (*MUS*) palillo; (*chicken leg*) muslo (de pollo).

drunk [drungk] *pp of* **drink** ♦ *a* borracho ♦ *n* (*also:* ~**ard**) borracho/a; **to get** ~ emborracharse.

drunken [drung'kən] *a* borracho.

drunkenness [drung'kənnis] *n* embriaguez *f*.

dry [drī] *a* seco; (*day*) sin lluvia; (*climate*) árido, seco; (*humor*) agudo; (*uninteresting: lecture*) aburrido, pesado ♦ *vt* secar; (*tears*) enjugarse ♦ *vi* secarse; **on** ~ **land** en tierra firme; **to** ~ **one's hands/hair/eyes** secarse las manos/el pelo/las lágrimas.

dry up *vi* (*supply, imagination etc*) agotarse; (*in speech*) atascarse.

dry-clean [drī'klēn'] *vt* limpiar or lavar en seco; **"** ~ **only"** (*on label*) "limpieza or lavado en seco (sólo)".

dry-cleaner's [drī'klē'nûrz] *n* tintorería.

dry-cleaning [drī'klē'ning] *n* lavado en seco.

dry dock *n* (*NAUT*) dique *m* seco.

dryer [drī'ûr] *n* (*for hair*) secador *m*; (*for clothes*) secadora.

dry goods *npl* (*COMM*) mercería *sg*.

dry goods store *n* (*US*) mercería.

dry ice *n* nieve *f* carbónica.

dryly [drī'lē] *ad* secamente.

dryness [drī'nis] *n* sequedad *f*.

dry rot *n* putrefacción *f* seca.

dry run *n* (*fig*) ensayo.

dry ski slope *n* pista artificial de esquí.

DSc *n abbr* (= Doctor of Science) título uni-

versitario.

DSS *n abbr* (*Brit*) = *Department of Social Security.*

DST *n abbr* (*US*: = *Daylight Saving Time*) *hora de verano.*

DT *n abbr* (*COMPUT*) = **data transmission.**

DTI *n abbr* (*Brit*) = *Department of Trade and Industry.*

DT's *n abbr* (*col*: = *delirium tremens*) delirium *m* tremens.

dual [dōō'əl] *a* doble.

dual carriageway *n* (*Brit*) carretera de doble calzada.

dual-control [dōō'əlkəntrōl'] *a* de doble mando.

dual nationality *n* doble nacionalidad *f.*

dual-purpose [dōō'əlpûr'pəs] *a* de doble uso.

dubbed [dubd] *a* (*CINEMA*) doblado.

dubious [dōō'bēəs] *a* indeciso; (*reputation, company*) dudoso; (*character*) sospechoso; **I'm very ~ about it** tengo mis grandes dudas sobre ello.

Dublin [dub'lin] *n* Dublín.

Dubliner [dub'linûr] *n* dublinés/esa *m/f.*

duchess [duch'is] *n* duquesa.

duck [duk] *n* pato ♦ *vi* agacharse ♦ *vt* (*plunge in water*) zambullir.

duckling [duk'ling] *n* patito.

duct [dukt] *n* conducto, canal *m.*

dud [dud] *n* (*shell*) obús *m* que no estalla; (*object, tool*): **it's a ~** es una filfa ♦ *a*: ~ **cheque** (*Brit*) cheque *m* sin fondos.

dude [dōōd] *n* (*US*) tipo, tío.

due [dōō] *a* (*proper*) debido; (*fitting*) conveniente, oportuno ♦ *ad*: ~ **north** derecho al norte; ~**s** *npl* (*for club, union*) cuota *sg*; (*in harbor*) derechos *mpl*; **in ~ course** a su debido tiempo; ~ **to** debido a; **to be ~ to** deberse a; **the train is ~ to arrive at 8.00** el tren debe llegar a las ocho; **the rent's ~ on the 30th** hay que pagar el alquiler el día 30; **I am ~ 6 days' leave** se me debe 6 días de vacaciones; **she is ~ back tomorrow** ella debe volver mañana.

due date *n* fecha de vencimiento.

duel [dōō'əl] *n* duelo.

duet [dōōet'] *n* dúo.

duff [duf] *a* (*Brit*) sin valor.

duffel bag [duf'əl bag] *n especie de talega que se cuelga al hombro.*

duffel coat [duf'əl kōt] *n* trenca.

dug [dug] *pt, pp* de **dig.**

duke [dōōk] *n* duque *m.*

dull [dul] *a* (*light*) apagado; (*stupid*) torpe; (*boring*) pesado; (*sound, pain*) sordo; (*weather, day*) gris ♦ *vt* (*pain, grief*) aliviar; (*mind, senses*) entorpecer.

duly [dōō'lē] *ad* debidamente; (*on time*) a su debido tiempo.

dumb [dum] *a* mudo; (*stupid*) estúpido; **to be struck ~** (*fig*) quedar boquiabierto.

dumbbell [dum'bel] *n* (*SPORT*) pesa; (*fool*)

bobo.

dumbfounded [dumfound'id] *a* pasmado.

dummy [dum'ē] *n* (*tailor's model*) maniquí *m*; (*Brit*: *for baby*) chupete *m* ♦ *a* falso, postizo; ~ **run** ensayo.

dump [dump] *n* (*heap*) montón *m* de basura; (*place*) basurero, vaciadero; (*col*) casucha; (*MIL*) depósito; (*COMPUT*) copia vaciada ♦ *vt* (*put down*) dejar; (*get rid of*) deshacerse de; (*COMPUT*) vaciar; (*COMM: goods*) inundar el mercado de; **to be (down) in the ~s** (*col*) tener murria, estar deprimido.

dumping [dum'ping] *n* (*ECON*) dumping *m*; (*of garbage*): "**no ~**" "prohibido verter basura".

dumpling [dump'ling] *n bola de masa hervida.*

dumpy [dump'ē] *a* regordete/a.

dunce [duns] *n* zopenco.

dune [dōōn] *n* duna.

dung [dung] *n* estiércol *m.*

dungarees [dunggərēz'] *npl* mono *sg.*

dungeon [dun'jən] *n* calabozo.

dunk [dungk] *vt* mojar.

duo [dōō'ō] *n* (*gen, MUS*) dúo.

duodenal [dōōədē'nəl] *a* (*ulcer*) de duodeno.

duodenum [dōōədē'nəm] *n* duodeno.

dupe [dōōp] *n* (*victim*) víctima ♦ *vt* engañar.

duplex [dōō'pleks] *n* (*US*: *also*: ~ **apartment**) dúplex *m.*

duplicate [dōō'plikit] *n* duplicado; (*copy of letter etc*) copia ♦ *a* (*copy*) duplicado ♦ *vt* [dōō'plikāt] duplicar; (*on machine*) multicopiar; **in ~** por duplicado.

duplicate key *n* duplicado de una llave.

duplicating machine [dōō'plikāting məshēn'], **duplicator** [doop'likātûr] *n* multicopista *m.*

duplicity [dōōplis'ətē] *n* doblez *f*, duplicidad *f.*

Dur *abbr* (*Brit*) = *Durham.*

durability [dōōrəbil'ətē] *n* durabilidad *f.*

durable [dōōr'əbəl] *a* duradero; ~ **goods** (*US*) biens *mpl* de consumo duraderos.

duration [dōōrā'shən] *n* duración *f.*

duress [dōōres'] *n*: **under ~** por compulsión.

Durex [dōō'reks] ® *n* (*Brit*) preservativo.

during [dōōr'ing] *prep* durante.

dusk [dusk] *n* crepúsculo, anochecer *m.*

dusky [dus'kē] *a* oscuro; (*complexion*) moreno.

dust [dust] *n* polvo ♦ *vt* (*furniture*) desempolvar; (*cake etc*): **to ~ with** espolvorear de.

dust off *vt* (*also fig*) desempolvar, quitar el polvo de.

dustbin [dust'bin] *n* (*Brit*) cubo de la basura, balde *m* (*LAm*).

dustbin liner *n* bolsa de basura.

duster [dus'tŭr] n paño, trapo; (feather ~) plumero.
dust jacket n sobrecubierta.
dustman [dust'man] n (Brit) basurero.
dustpan [dust'pan] n cogedor m.
dust storm n vendaval m de polvo.
dusty [dus'tē] a polvoriento.
Dutch [duch] a holandés/esa ♦ n (LING) holandés m ♦ ad: **to go** ~ pagar cada uno lo suyo; **the** ~ npl los holandeses.
Dutch auction n subasta a la rebaja.
Dutchman [duch'mən], **Dutchwoman** [duch'wŏomən] n holandés/esa m/f.
dutiful [dōō'tifəl] a (child) obediente; (husband) sumiso; (employee) cumplido.
duty [dōō'tē] n deber m; (tax) derechos mpl de aduana; (MED: in hospital) servicio, guardia; **on** ~ de servicio; (at night etc) de guardia; **off** ~ libre (de servicio); **to make it one's** ~ **to do sth** encargarse de hacer algo sin falta; **to pay** ~ **on sth** pagar los derechos sobre algo.
duty-free [dōō'tēfrē'] a libre de derechos de aduana; ~ **store** tienda libre de impuestos.
duty officer n (MIL etc) oficial m/f de servicio.
duvet [dōō'vā] n (Brit) edredón m.
DV abbr (= Deo volente) Dios mediante.
DVM n abbr (US: = Doctor of Veterinary Medicine) título universitario.
dwarf [dwôrf], pl **dwarves** [dwôrvz] n enano ♦ vt empequeñecer.
dwell [dwel], pt, pp **dwelt** [dwelt] vi morar.
dwell on vt fus explayarse en.
dweller [dwel'ŭr] n habitante m; **city** ~ habitante m de la ciudad.
dwelling [dwel'ing] n vivienda.
dwelt [dwelt] pt, pp of **dwell**.
dwindle [dwin'dəl] vi menguar, disminuir.
dwindling [dwin'dling] a (strength, interest) menguante; (resources, supplies) disminuyente.
dye [dī] n tinte m ♦ vt teñir; **hair** ~ tinte m para el pelo.
dying [dī'ing] a moribundo, agonizante; (moments) final; (words) último.
dyke [dīk] n (Brit) = **dike**.
dynamic [dīnam'ik] a dinámico.
dynamics [dīnam'iks] n or npl dinámica sg.
dynamite [dī'nəmīt] n dinamita ♦ vt dinamitar.
dynamo [dī'nəmō] n dinamo f.
dynasty [dī'nəstē] n dinastía.
dysentery [dis'əntärē] n disentería.
dyslexic [dislek'sik] a, n disléxico/a m/f.
dyspepsia [dispep'shə] n dispepsia.
dystrophy [dis'trəfē] n distrofia; **muscular** ~ distrofia muscular.

E

E, e [ē] n (letter) E, e f; (MUS) mi m; **E for Easy** E de Enrique.
E abbr (= east) E.
E111 n abbr (also: **form** ~) impreso E111.
ea. abbr = **each**.
E.A. abbr (US: = educational age) nivel escolar.
each [ēch] a cada inv ♦ pron cada uno; ~ **other** el uno al otro; **they hate** ~ **other** se odian (entre ellos or mutuamente); ~ **day** cada día; **they have 2 books** ~ tienen 2 libros por persona; **they cost $5** ~ cuestan cinco dólares cada uno; ~ **of us** cada uno de nosotros.
eager [ē'gûr] a (gen) impaciente; (hopeful) ilusionado; (keen) entusiasmado; (: pupil) apasionado; **to be** ~ **to do sth** tener muchas ganas de hacer algo, impacientarse por hacer algo; **to be** ~ **for** ansiar, anhelar.
eagerly [ē'gûrlē] ad con impaciencia; con ilusión; con entusiasmo.
eagerness [ē'gûrnis] n impaciencia; ilusión f; entusiasmo.
eagle [ē'gəl] n águila.
E and OE abbr = **errors and omissions excepted**.
ear [ēr] n oreja; (sense of hearing) oído; (of corn) espiga; **up to the** ~**s in debt** abrumado de deudas.
earache [ēr'āk] n dolor m de oídos.
eardrum [ēr'drum] n tímpano.
earl [ûrl] n conde m.
early [ûr'lē] ad (gen) temprano; (ahead of time) con tiempo, con anticipación ♦ a (gen) temprano; (reply) pronto; (man) primitivo; (first: Christians, settlers) primero; **to have an** ~ **night** acostarse temprano; **in the** ~ or ~ **in the spring/19th century** a principios de primavera/del siglo diecinueve; **you're** ~! ¡has llegado temprano or pronto!; ~ **in the morning/afternoon** a primeras horas de la mañana/tarde; **she's in her** ~ **forties** tiene poco más de cuarenta años; **at your earliest convenience** (COMM) con la mayor brevedad posible; **I can't come any earlier** no puedo llegar antes.
early retirement n jubilación f anticipada.
early warning system n sistema m de alerta inmediata.
earmark [ēr'márk] vt: **to** ~ **for** reservar

para, destinar a.

earn |ûrn| *vt* (*gen*) ganar; (*interest*) devengar; (*praise*) merecerse; **to ~ one's living** ganarse la vida.

earned income |ûrnd' in'kum| *n* renta del trabajo.

earnest |ûr'nist| *a* serio, formal ♦ *n* (*also*: ~ **money**) anticipo, señal *f*; **in ~** *ad* en serio.

earnings |ûr'ningz| *npl* (*personal*) sueldo *sg*, ingresos *mpl*; (*of company etc*) ganancias *fpl*.

earphones |ēr'fōnz| *npl* auriculares *mpl*.

earplugs |ēr'plugz| *npl* tapones *mpl* para los oídos.

earring |ēr'ring| *n* pendiente *m*, arete *m*.

earshot |ēr'shát| *n*: **out of/within ~** fuera del/al alcance del oído.

earth |ûrth| *n* (*gen*) tierra; (*Brit*: *ELEC*) cable *m* de toma de tierra ♦ *vt* (*Brit*: *ELEC*) conectar a tierra.

earthenware |ûr'thənwär| *n* loza (de barro).

earthly |ûrth'lē| *a* terrenal, mundano; ~ **paradise** paraíso terrenal; **there is no ~ reason to think** ... no existe razón para pensar ....

earthquake |ûrth'kwāk| *n* terremoto.

earthworm |ûrth'wûrm| *n* lombriz *f*.

earthy |ûr'thē| *a* (*fig*: *uncomplicated*) sencillo; (: *coarse*) grosero.

earwig |ēr'wig| *n* tijereta.

ease |ēz| *n* facilidad *f*; (*comfort*) comodidad *f* ♦ *vt* (*task*) facilitar; (*pain*) aliviar; (*loosen*) soltar; (*relieve: pressure, tension*) aflojar; (*weight*) aligerar; (*help pass*): **to ~ sth in/out** meter/sacar algo con cuidado ♦ *vi* (*situation*) relajarse; **with ~** con facilidad; **to feel at ~/ill at ~** sentirse a gusto/a disgusto; **at ~!** (*MIL*) ¡descansen!

ease off, ease up *vi* (*work, business*) aflojar; (*person*) relajarse.

easel |ē'zəl| *n* caballete *m*.

easily |ē'zilē| *ad* fácilmente.

easiness |ē'zēnis| *n* facilidad *f*; (*of manners*) soltura.

east |ēst| *n* este *m*, oriente *m* ♦ *a* del este, oriental ♦ *ad* al este, hacia el este; **the E~** el Oriente; (*POL*) el Este.

Easter |ēs'tûr| *n* Pascua (de Resurrección).

Easter egg *n* huevo de Pascua.

Easter Island *n* Isla de Pascua.

easterly |ēs'tûrlē| *a* (*to the east*) al este; (*from the east*) del este.

Easter Monday *n* lunes *m* de Pascua.

eastern |ēs'tûrn| *a* del este, oriental; **E~ Europe** Europa del Este; **the E~ bloc** (*POL*) el bloque del Este.

Easter Sunday *n* Domingo de Resurrección.

East Germany *n* Alemania Oriental.

eastward(s) |ēst'wûrd(z)| *ad* hacia el este.

easy |ē'zē| *a* fácil; (*simple*) sencillo; (*life*)

holgado, cómodo; (*relaxed*) natural ♦ *ad*: **to take it** *or* **things ~** (*not worry*) no preocuparse; (*go slowly*) tomarlo con calma; (*rest*) descansar; **payment on ~ terms** (*COMM*) pago a plazos; **I'm ~** (*col*) me da igual, no me importa; **easier said than done** del dicho al hecho hay buen trecho.

easy chair *n* sillón *m*.

easy-going |ē'zēgō'ing| *a* acomodadizo.

eat, *pt* **ate,** *pp* **eaten** |ēt, āt, ē'tən| *vt* comer.

eat away *vt* (*subj: sea*) desgastar; (: *acid*) corroer.

eat into, eat away at *vt fus* corroer.

eat out *vi* comer fuera.

eat up *vt* (*meal etc*) comerse; **it ~s up electricity** devora la electricidad.

eatable |ē'təbəl| *a* comestible.

eau de Cologne |ō' də kəlōn'| *n* (agua de) Colonia.

eaves |ēvz| *npl* alero *sg*.

eavesdrop |ēvz'dráp| *vi*: **to ~ (on sb)** escuchar a escondidas (a uno).

ebb |eb| *n* reflujo ♦ *vi* bajar; (*fig: also*: ~ **away**) decaer; ~ **and flow** el flujo y reflujo; **to be at a low ~** (*fig: person*) estar decaído; (: *business*) ir lento.

ebb tide *n* marea menguante.

ebony |eb'ənē| *n* ébano.

ebullient |ibul'yənt| *a* entusiasta, animado.

EC *n abbr* (= *European Community*) CE *f*.

eccentric |iksen'trik| *a*, *n* excéntrico/a.

ecclesiastical |iklēzēas'tikəl| *a* eclesiástico.

ECG *n abbr* (= *electrocardiogram*) E.C.G.

ECGD *n abbr* (= *Export Credits Guarantee Department*) servicio de garantía financiera a la exportación.

echo, ~**es** |ek'ō| *n* eco *m* ♦ *vt* (*sound*) repetir ♦ *vi* resonar, hacer eco.

éclair |iklär'| *n* relámpago, petisú *m*.

eclipse |iklips'| *n* eclipse *m* ♦ *vt* eclipsar.

ECM *n abbr* (*US*: = *European Common Market*) MCE *m*.

ecologist |ikál'əjist| *n* ecologista *m/f*; (*scientist*) ecólogo/a *m/f*.

ecology |ikál'əjē| *n* ecología.

economic |ēkənám'ik| *a* (*profitable: price*) económico; (: *business etc*) rentable.

economical |ēkənám'ikəl| *a* económico.

economically |ēkənám'iklē| *ad* económicamente.

economics |ēkənám'iks| *n* economía ♦ *npl* (*financial aspects*) finanzas *fpl*.

economic warfare *n* guerra económica.

economist |ikán'əmist| *n* economista *m/f*.

economize |ikán'əmīz| *vi* economizar, ahorrar.

economy |ikán'əmē| *n* economía; **economies of scale** economías *fpl* de escala.

economy class *n* (*AVIAT etc*) clase *f* turista.

economy size *n* tamaño familiar.

ecosystem |ek'ōsistəm| *n* ecosistema *m*.

ECSC *n abbr* (= *European Coal & Steel*

Community) CECA f.
ecstasy [ek'stəsē] n éxtasis m inv.
ecstatic [ekstat'ik] a extático.
ECT n abbr = **electroconvulsive therapy**.
ECU n abbr (= European Currency Unit)
ECU m.
Ecuador [ek'wədōr] n Ecuador m.
Ecuador(i)an [ek'wədôr(ē)ən] a, n ecua-
toriano/a m/f.
ecumenical [ekyōōmen'ikəl] a ecuménico.
eczema [ek'səmə] n eczema m.
eddy [ed'ē] n remolino.
Eden [ē'dən] n Edén m.
edge [ej] n (of knife etc) filo; (of object)
borde m; (of lake etc) orilla ♦ vt (SEWING)
ribetear ♦ vi: **to ~ past** pasar con
dificultad; **on ~** (fig) = **edgy**; **to ~ away
from** alejarse poco a poco de; **to ~ forward** avanzar poco a poco; **to ~ up** subir
lentamente.
edgeways [ej'wāz] ad: **he couldn't get a
word in ~** no pudo meter baza.
edging [ej'ing] n (SEWING) ribete m; (of
path) borde m.
edgy [ej'ē] a nervioso, inquieto.
edible [ed'əbəl] a comestible.
edict [ē'dikt] n edicto.
edifice [ed'əfis] n edificio.
edifying [ed'əfīing] a edificante.
Edinburgh [ed'ənbúrə] n Edimburgo.
edit [ed'it] vt (be the editor of) dirigir; (rewrite) redactar; (cut) cortar; (COMPUT)
editar.
edition [idish'ən] n (gen) edición f; (number
printed) tirada.
editor [ed'itûr] n (of newspaper) director(a)
m/f; (of book) redactor(a) m/f; (film ~)
montador(a) m/f.
editorial [editôr'ēal] a editorial ♦ n editorial
m; ~ **staff** redacción f.
EDP n abbr (= electronic data processing)
TED m.
EDT n abbr (US: = Eastern Daylight Time)
hora de verano de Nueva York.
educate [ej'ōōkāt] vt (gen) educar; (instruct) instruir.
education [ejōōkā'shən] n educación f;
(schooling) enseñanza; (SCOL: subject etc)
pedagogía; **primary/secondary ~** primera/
segunda enseñanza.
educational [ejōōkā'shənəl] a (policy etc)
educacional; (teaching) docente; (instructive) educativo; ~ **technology** tecnología
educacional.
Edwardian [edwôr'dēən] a eduardiano.
E.E. abbr = **electrical engineer**.
EEC n abbr (= European Economic Community) CEE f.
EEG n abbr = **electroencephalogram**.
eel [ēl] n anguila.
EENT n abbr (US MED) = eye, ear, nose
and throat.
EEOC n abbr (US: = Equal Employment

Opportunities Commission) comisión que in-
vestiga discriminación racial o sexual en el
empleo.
eerie [ē'rē] a (sound, experience) espeluznante.
EET n abbr (= Eastern European Time)
hora de Europa oriental.
efface [ifās'] vt borrar.
effect [ifekt'] n efecto ♦ vt efectuar, llevar a
cabo; ~**s** npl (property) efectos mpl; **to
take ~** (law) entrar en vigor or vigencia;
(drug) surtir efecto; **in ~** en realidad; **to
have an ~ on sb/sth** hacerle efecto a uno/
afectar algo; **to put into ~** (plan) llevar a
la práctica; **his letter is to the ~ that...** su
carta específica que....
effective [ifek'tiv] a (gen) eficaz; (striking:
display, outfit) impresionante; (real) efectivo; **to become ~** (LAW) entrar en vigor;
~ **date** fecha de vigencia.
effectively [ifek'tivlē] ad (efficiently)
eficazmente; (strikingly) de manera impresionante; (in reality) en efecto.
effectiveness [ifek'tivnis] n eficacia.
effeminate [ifem'ənit] a afeminado.
effervescent [efûrves'ənt] a efervescente.
efficacy [ef'ikəsē] n eficacia.
efficiency [ifish'ənsē] n (gen) eficiencia; (of
machine) rendimiento.
efficient [ifish'ənt] a eficiente; (remedy, product, system) eficaz; (machine, car) de
buen rendimiento.
effigy [ef'ijē] n efigie f.
effluent [ef'lōōənt] n desperdicios mpl flu-
viales.
effort [ef'ûrt] n esfuerzo; **to make an ~ to
do sth** esforzarse por hacer algo.
effortless [ef'ûrtlis] a sin ningún esfuerzo.
effrontery [ifrun'tûrē] n descaro.
effusive [ifyōō'siv] a (person, welcome,
letter) efusivo; (thanks, apologies) expansivo.
EFL n abbr (SCOL) = English as a foreign
language.
EFT n abbr (US: = electronic funds transfer) transferencia electrónica de fondos.
EFTA [ef'tə] n abbr (= European Free Trade
Association) AELC f.
e.g. ad abbr = exempli gratia) p.ej.
egg [eg] n huevo; **hard-boiled/soft-boiled/
poached ~** huevo duro/pasado por agua/
escalfado; **scrambled ~s** huevos revueltos.
egg on vt incitar.
eggcup [eg'kup] n huevera.
eggnog [eg'nág] n ponche m de huevo.
eggplant [eg'plant] n (esp US) berenjena.
eggshell [eg'shel] n cáscara de huevo.
egg white n clara de huevo.
egg yolk n yema de huevo.
ego [ē'gō] n ego.
egotism [ē'gətisəm] n egoísmo.
egotist [ē'gətist] n egoísta m/f.
Egypt [ē'jipt] n Egipto.

Egyptian |ijip'shən| *a, n* egipcio/a *m/f.*
eiderdown |í'dûrdoun| *n* edredón *m.*.
eight |āt| *num* ocho.
eighteen |ā'tēn'| *num* diez y ocho, dieciocho.
eighth |ātth| *num* octavo.
eighth note *n (US MUS)* corchea.
eighty |ā'tē| *num* ochenta.
Eire |ár'ə| *n* Eire *m.*
either |ē'i̯hûr| *a* cualquiera de los dos ...; (*both, each*) cada ♦ *pron:* ~ **(of them)** cualquiera (de los dos) ♦ *ad* tampoco ♦ *conj:* ~ **yes or no** o sí o no; **on** ~ **side** en ambos lados; **I don't like** ~ no me gusta ninguno de los dos; **no, I don't** ~ no, yo tampoco.
eject |ijekt'| *vt* echar; (*tenant*) desahuciar ♦ *vi* eyectarse.
ejector seat |ijek'tûr sēt| *n* asiento proyectable.
eke |ēk|: **to** ~ **out** *vt* (*money*) hacer que llegue.
EKG *n abbr (US)* = **electrocardiogram.**
el |el| *n abbr (US col)* = **elevated railroad.**
elaborate *a* |ilab'ûrit| (*design*) elaborado; (*pattern*) intrincado ♦ *vb* |ilab'ərāt| *vt* elaborar ♦ *vi* explicarse con muchos detalles.
elaborately |ilab'ûritlē| *ad* de manera complicada; (*decorated*) profusamente.
elaboration |ilabərā'shən| *n* elaboración *f.*
elapse |ilaps'| *vi* transcurrir.
elastic |ilas'tik| *a, n* elástico.
elastic band *n (Brit)* gomita.
elated |ilā'tid| *a:* **to be** ~ regocijarse.
elation |ilā'shən| *n* regocijo.
elbow |el'bō| *n* codo ♦ *vt:* **to** ~ **one's way through the crowd** abrirse paso a codazos por la muchedumbre.
elder |el'dûr| *a* mayor ♦ *n* (*tree*) saúco; (*person*) mayor; (*of tribe*) anciano.
elderly |el'dûrlē| *a* de edad, mayor ♦ *npl:* **the** ~ la gente mayor, los ancianos.
eldest |el'dist| *a, n* el/la mayor.
elect |ilekt'| *vt* elegir; (*choose*): **to** ~ **to do** optar por hacer ♦ *a:* **the president** ~ el presidente electo.
election |ilek'shən| *n* elección *f;* **to hold an** ~ convocar elecciones.
election campaign *n* campaña electoral.
electioneering |ilekshənē'ring| *n* campaña electoral.
elective |ēlek'tiv| *n (US)* asignatura discrecional.
elector |ilek'tûr| *n* elector(a) *m/f.*
electoral |ilek'tûrəl| *a* electoral.
electoral college *n* colegio electoral.
electoral roll *n* censo electoral.
electorate |ilek'tûrit| *n* electorado.
electric |ilek'trik| *a* eléctrico.
electrical |ilek'trikəl| *a* eléctrico.
electrical engineer *n* ingeniero/a electricista.
electrical failure *n* fallo eléctrico.

electric blanket *n* manta eléctrica.
electric chair *n* silla eléctrica.
electric current *n* corriente *f* eléctrica.
electric heater *n* estufa eléctrica.
electrician |ilektrish'ən| *n* electricista *m/f.*
electricity |ilektris'ətē| *n* electricidad *f;* **to switch on/off the** ~ conectar/desconectar la electricidad.
electric light *n* luz *f* eléctrica.
electric shock *n* choque *m* eléctrico.
electric stove *n* cocina eléctrica.
electrification |ilektrəfəkā'shən| *n* electrificación *f.*
electrify |ilek'trəfī| *vt (RAIL)* electrificar; (*fig: audience*) electrizar.
electro... |ilek'trō| *pref* electro....
electrocardiogram (EKG, *(Brit)* **ECG)** |ilektrōkâr'dēəgram| *n* electrocardiograma *m.*
electrocardiograph |ilektrōkâr'dēəgraf| *n* electrocardiógrafo.
electro-convulsive therapy (ECT) |ilek'trōkənvul'siv thär'əpē| *n* electroterapia.
electrocute |ilek'trəkyōōt| *vt* electrocutar.
electrode |ilek'trōd| *n* electrodo.
electroencephalogram (EEG) |ilektrōensef'ələgram| *n* electroencefalograma *m.*
electrolysis |ilektrál'isis| *n* electrólisis *f inv.*
electromagnetic |ilektrōmagnet'ik| *a* electromagnético.
electron |ilek'trân| *n* electrón *m.*
electronic |ilektrân'ik| *a* electrónico.
electronic data processing (EDP) *n* tratamiento electrónico de datos.
electronic mail *n* correo electrónico.
electronics |ilektrân'iks| *n* electrónica.
electron microscope *n* microscopio electrónico.
electroplated |ilek'trəplātid| *a* galvanizado.
electrotherapy |ilektrōthär'əpē| *n* electroterapia.
elegance |el'əgəns| *n* elegancia.
elegant |el'əgənt| *a* elegante.
elegy |el'ijē| *n* elegía.
element |el'əmənt| *n* (*gen*) elemento; (*of heater, kettle etc*) resistencia.
elementary |elimen'tûrē| *a* elemental; (*primitive*) rudimentario; (*school, education*) primario.
elephant |el'əfənt| *n* elefante *m.*
elevate |el'əvāt| *vt* (*gen*) elevar; (*in rank*) ascender.
elevated railroad |el'əvātid rāl'rōd| *n (US)* ferrocarril *m* urbano elevado.
elevation |eləvā'shən| *n* elevación *f;* (*rank*) ascenso; (*height*) altura.
elevator |el'əvātûr| *n (US)* ascensor *m.*
eleven |ilev'ən| *num* once.
elevenses |ilev'ənziz| *npl (Brit)* ≈ café *m* de media mañana.
eleventh |ilev'ənth| *a* undécimo; **at the** ~ **hour** (*fig*) a última hora.
elf, *pl* **elves** |elf, elvz| *n* duende *m.*

elicit [ilis'it] *vt*: **to ~ sth (from sb)** sacar(le) algo (a uno).

eligible [el'ijəbəl] *a* elegible; **to be ~ for a pension** llenar los requisitos para una pensión.

eliminate [əlim'ənāt] *vt* eliminar; (*cross out*) suprimir; (*a suspect, possibility*) descartar.

elimination [əlimənā'shən] *n* eliminación *f*; supresión *f*; **by process of ~** por proceso de eliminación.

elite [ilēt'] *n* élite *f*.

elitist [ilē'tist] *a* (*pej*) elitista.

elixir [ilik'sûr] *n* elixir *m*.

Elizabethan [ilizəbē'thən] *a* isabelino.

elm [elm] *n* olmo.

elocution [eləkyōō'shən] *n* elocución *f*.

elongated [ilông'gātid] *a* alargado, estirado.

elope [ilōp'] *vi* fugarse para casarse.

elopement [ilōp'mənt] *n* fuga.

eloquence [el'əkwəns] *n* elocuencia.

eloquent [el'əkwənt] *a* elocuente.

else [els] *ad*: **or ~** si no; **something ~** otra cosa; **somewhere ~** en otra parte; **everywhere ~** en todas partes menos aquí; **everyone ~** todos los demás; **nothing ~** nada más; **is there anything ~ I can do?** ¿puedo hacer algo más?; **where ~?** ¿dónde más?, ¿en qué otra parte?; **there was little ~ to do** apenas quedaba otra cosa que hacer; **nobody ~ spoke** no habló nadie más.

elsewhere [els'hwär] *ad* (*be*) en otra parte; (*go*) a otra parte.

ELT *n abbr* (*SCOL*) = *English Language Teaching.*

elucidate [ilōō'sidāt] *vt* aclarar, elucidar.

elude [ilōōd'] *vt* eludir; (*blow, pursuer*) esquivar.

elusive [ilōō'siv] *a* esquivo; (*answer*) difícil de encontrar; **he is very ~** no es fácil encontrarlo.

elves [elvz] *npl of* **elf.**

emaciated [imā'shēātid] *a* demacrado.

emanate [em'ənāt] *vi* emanar, proceder.

emancipate [iman'səpāt] *vt* emancipar.

emancipated [iman'səpātid] *a* liberado.

emancipation [imansəpā'shən] *n* emancipación *f*, liberación *f*.

emasculate [imas'kyəlāt] *vt* castrar; (*fig*) incapacitar, debilitar.

embalm [embám'] *vt* embalsamar.

embankment [embangk'mənt] *n* (*of railroad*) terraplén *m*; (*riverside*) dique *m*.

embargo, *pl* **~es** [embár'gō] *n* prohibición *f*; (*COMM, NAUT*) embargo; **to put an ~ on sth** embargar algo.

embark [embárk'] *vi* embarcarse ♦ *vt* embarcar; **to ~ on** (*journey*) comenzar, iniciar; (*fig*) emprender, lanzarse a.

embarkation [embárkā'shən] *n* (*people*) embarco; (*goods*) embarque *m*.

embarkation card *n* tarjeta de embarque.

embarrass [embar'əs] *vt* avergonzar; (*financially etc*) poner en un aprieto.

embarrassed [embar'əst] *a* azorado; **to be ~** sentirse azorado *or* violento.

embarrassing [embar'əsing] *a* (*situation*) violento; (*question*) embarazoso.

embarrassment [embar'əsmənt] *n* desconcierto, azoramiento; (*financial*) apuros *mpl*.

embassy [em'bəsē] *n* embajada; **the Spanish E~** la embajada española.

embed [embed'] *vt* (*jewel*) empotrar; (*teeth etc*) clavar.

embellish [embel'ish] *vt* embellecer; (*fig*: *story, truth*) adornar.

embers [em'bûrz] *npl* rescoldo *sg*, ascua *sg*.

embezzle [embez'əl] *vt* desfalcar, malversar.

embezzlement [embez'əlmənt] *n* desfalco, malversación *f*.

embezzler [embez'lûr] *n* malversador(a) *m/f*.

embitter [embit'ûr] *vt* (*person*) amargar; (*relationship*) envenenar.

embittered [embit'ûrd] *a* resentido, amargado.

emblem [em'bləm] *n* emblema *m*.

embody [embâd'ē] *vt* (*spirit*) encarnar; (*ideas*) expresar.

embolden [embōl'dən] *vt* envalentonar; (*TYP*) poner en negrita.

embolism [em'bəlizəm] *n* embolia.

emboss [embôs'] *vt* estampar en relieve; (*metal, leather*) repujar.

embossed [embôst'] *a* realzado; **~ with ...** con ... en relieve.

embrace [embrās'] *vt* abrazar, dar un abrazo a; (*include*) abarcar; (*adopt*: *idea*) adherirse a ♦ *vi* abrazarse ♦ *n* abrazo.

embroider [embroi'dûr] *vt* bordar; (*fig*: *story*) adornar, embellecer.

embroidery [embroi'dûrē] *n* bordado.

embroil [embroil'] *vt*: **to become ~ed (in sth)** enredarse (en algo).

embryo [em'brēō] *n* (*also fig*) embrión *m*.

emcee [em'sē'] *n* presentador(a) *m/f*.

emend [imend'] *vt* (*text*) enmendar.

emerald [em'ûrəld] *n* esmeralda.

emerge [imûrj'] *vi* (*gen*) salir; (*arise*) surgir; **it ~s that** resulta que.

emergence [imûr'jəns] *n* (*of nation*) salida, surgimiento.

emergency [imûr'jənsē] *n* (*event*) emergencia; (*crisis*) crisis *f inv*; **in an ~** en caso de urgencia; **(to declare a) state of ~** (declarar) estado de emergencia *or* de excepción.

emergency cord *n* (*US*) timbre *m* de alarma.

emergency exit *n* salida de emergencia.

emergency flasher [imûr'jənsē flash'ûr] *n* (*US AUT*) señales *fpl* de emergencia.

emergency landing *n* aterrizaje *m* forzoso.

emergency lane n (US) andén m, arcén m.

emergency meeting n reunión f extraordinaria.

emergency service n servicio de urgencia or emergencia.

emergency stop n (AUT) parada en seco.

emergent |imûr'jənt| a (nation) en vías de desarrollo.

emery board |em'ûrē bōrd| n lima de uñas.

emetic |imet'ik| n emético.

emigrant |em'əgrənt| n emigrante m/f.

emigrate |em'əgrāt| vi emigrarse.

emigration |eməgrā'shən| n emigración f.

émigré |em'igrā| n emigrado/a.

eminence |em'ənəns| n eminencia; **to gain** or **win ~** ganarse fama.

eminent |em'ənənt| a eminente.

eminently |em'ənəntlē| ad eminentemente.

emirate |əmē'rit| n emirato.

emission |imish'ən| n emisión f.

emit |imit'| vt emitir; (smoke) arrojar; (smell) despedir; (sound) producir.

emolument |imâl'yəmənt| n (often pl: formal) honorario.

emotion |imō'shən| n emoción f.

emotional |imō'shənəl| a (person) sentimental; (scene) conmovedor(a), emocionante.

emotionally |imō'shənəlē| ad (behave, speak) con emoción; (be involved) sentimentalmente.

emotive |imō'tiv| a emotivo.

empathy |em'pəthē| n empatía; **to feel ~ with sb** sentir empatía por uno.

emperor |em'pûrûr| n emperador m.

emphasis, pl **emphases** |em'fəsis, -sēz| n énfasis m inv; **to place ~ on sth** (fig) hacer hincapié en algo; **the ~ is on sport** se da mayor importancia al deporte.

emphasize |em'fəsīz| vt (word, point) subrayar, recalcar; (feature) hacer resaltar.

emphatic |əmfat'ik| a (condemnation, denial) enfático.

emphatically |əmfat'iklē| ad con énfasis.

emphysema |emfisē'mə| n (MED) enfisema m.

empire |em'pīûr| n imperio.

empirical |empir'ikəl| a empírico.

employ |emploi'| vt (give job to) emplear; (make use of: thing, method) emplear, usar; **he's ~ed in a bank** está empleado en un banco.

employee |emploi'ē| n empleado/a.

employer |emploi'ûr| n patrón/ona m/f; (businessman) empresario/a.

employment |emploi'mənt| n (gen) empleo; (work) trabajo; **full ~** pleno empleo; **without ~** sin empleo; **to find ~** encontrar trabajo; **place of ~** lugar m de empleo.

employment agency n agencia de colocaciones.

empower |empou'ûr| vt: **to ~ sb to do sth** autorizar a uno para hacer algo.

empress |em'pris| n emperatriz f.

emptiness |emp'tēnis| n (gen) vacío; (of life etc) vaciedad f.

empty |emp'tē| a vacío; (street, area) desierto; (house) desocupado; (threat) vano ♦ n (bottle) envase m ♦ vt vaciar; (place) dejar vacío ♦ vi vaciarse; (house) quedar desocupado; (place) quedar desierto; **to ~ into** (river) desembocar en.

empty-handed |emp'tēhan'did| a con las manos vacías.

empty-headed |emp'tēhed'id| a casquivano.

EMT n abbr = **emergency medical technician.**

emulate |em'yəlāt| vt emular.

emulsion |imul'shən| n emulsión f.

enable |enā'bəl| vt: **to ~ sb to do sth** (allow) permitir a uno hacer algo; (prepare) capacitar a uno para hacer algo.

enact |enakt'| vt (law) promulgar; (play, scene) representar; (role) hacer.

enamel |inam'əl| n esmalte m.

enamel paint n esmalte m.

enamored, (Brit) **enamoured** |cnam'ûrd| a: **to be ~ of** (person) estar enamorado de; (activity etc) tener gran afición a; (idea) aferrarse a.

encampment |enkamp'mənt| n campamento.

encase |enkās'| vt: **to ~ in** (contain) encajar; (cover) cubrir.

encased |enkāst'| a: **~ in** (covered) revestido de.

enchant |enchant'| vt encantar.

enchanting |enchan'ting| a encantador(a).

encircle |ensûr'kəl| vt (gen) rodear; (waist) ceñir.

encl. abbr (= enclosed) adj.

enclave |en'klāv| n enclave m.

enclose |enklōz'| vt (land) cercar; (with letter etc) adjuntar; (in receptacle): **to ~ (with)** encerrar (con); **please find ~d** le mandamos adjunto.

enclosure |enklō'zhûr| n cercado, recinto; (COMM) carta adjunta.

encoder |enkō'dûr| n (COMPUT) codificador m.

encompass |enkum'pəs| vt abarcar.

encore |âng'kôr| excl ¡otra!, ¡bis! ♦ n bis m.

encounter |enkoun'tûr| n encuentro ♦ vt encontrar, encontrarse con; (difficulty) tropezar con.

encourage |enkûr'ij| vt alentar, animar; (growth) estimular; **to ~ sb (to do sth)** animar a uno (a hacer algo).

encouragement |enkûr'ijmənt| n estímulo; (of industry) fomento.

encouraging |enkûr'ijing| *a* alentador(a).

encroach |enkrōch'| *vi*: **to ~ (up)on** (*gen*) invadir; (*time*) adueñarse de.

encrust |enkrust'| *vt* incrustar.

encrusted |enkrus'tid| *a*: **~ with** incrustado de.

encumber |enkum'bûr| *vt*: **to be ~ed with** (*carry*) estar cargado de; (*debts*) estar gravado de.

encyclop(a)edia |ensīklapē'dēə| *n* enciclopedia.

end |end| *n* (*gen, also aim*) fin *m*; (*of table*) extremo; (*of line, rope etc*) cabo; (*of pointed object*) punta; (*of town*) barrio; (*of street*) final *m*; (*SPORT*) lado ♦ *vt* terminar, acabar; (*also*: **bring to an ~, put an ~ to**) acabar con ♦ *vi* terminar, acabar; **to ~ (with)** terminar (con); **in the ~** al fin, por fin, finalmente; **to be at an ~** llegar al final; **at the ~ of the day** (*fig*) al fin y al cabo, a fin de cuentas; **to this ~, with this ~ in view** con este propósito; **from ~ to ~** de punta a punta; **on ~** (*object*) de punta, de cabeza; **to stand on ~** (*hair*) erizarse; **for hours on ~** hora tras hora.

end up *vi*: **to ~ up in** terminar en; (*place*) ir a parar en.

endanger |endān'jûr| *vt* poner en peligro; **an ~ed species** (*of animal*) una especie en peligro de extinción.

endear |endēr'| *vt*: **to ~ o.s. to sb** ganarse la simpatía de uno.

endearing |endēr'ing| *a* simpático, atractivo.

endearment |endēr'mənt| *n* cariño, palabra cariñosa; **to whisper ~s** decir unas palabras cariñosas al oído; **term of ~** nombre *m* cariñoso.

endeavor, (*Brit*) **endeavour** |endev'ûr| *n* esfuerzo; (*attempt*) tentativa ♦ *vi*: **to ~ to do** esforzarse por hacer; (*try*) procurar hacer.

endemic |endem'ik| *a* (*poverty, disease*) endémico.

ending |en'ding| *n* fin *m*, conclusión *f*; (*of book*) desenlace *m*; (*LING*) terminación *f*.

endive |en'dīv| *n* (*curly*) escarola; (*smooth, flat*) endibia.

endless |end'lis| *a* interminable, inacabable; (*possibilities*) infinito.

endorse |endôrs'| *vt* (*check*) endosar; (*approve*) aprobar.

endorsee |endôrsē'| *n* portador(a) *m/f* de un efecto.

endorsement |endôrs'mənt| *n* (*approval*) aprobación *f*; (*signature*) endoso; (*Brit: on driver's license*) anotación *f* de una sanción.

endorser |endôrs'ûr| *n* avalista *m/f*.

endow |endou'| *vt* (*provide with money*) dotar; (*found*) fundar; **to be ~ed with** (*fig*) estar dotado de.

endowment |endou'mənt| *n* (*amount*) donación *f*.

endowment insurance *n* seguro mixto.

end product *n* (*INDUSTRY*) producto final; (*fig*) resultado.

end result *n* resultado.

endurable |endōō'rəbəl| *a* soportable, tolerable.

endurance |endōō'rəns| *n* resistencia.

endurance test *n* prueba de resistencia.

endure |endōōr'| *vt* (*bear*) aguantar, soportar; (*resist*) resistir ♦ *vi* (*last*) durar; (*resist*) resistir.

enduring |endōō'ring| *a* duradero.

end user *n* (*COMPUT*) usuario final.

enema |en'əmə| *n* (*MED*) enema.

enemy |en'əmē| *a, n* enemigo/a *m/f*; **to make an ~ of sb** enemistarse con uno.

energetic |enûrjet'ik| *a* enérgico.

energy |en'ûrjē| *n* energía.

energy crisis *n* crisis *f* energética.

energy-saving |en'ûrjēsāving| *a* (*policy*) para ahorrar energía; (*device*) que ahorra energía ♦ *n* ahorro de energía.

enervating |en'ûrvāting| *a* deprimente.

enforce |enfôrs'| *vt* (*LAW*) hacer cumplir.

enforced |enfôrst'| *a* forzoso, forzado.

enfranchise |enfran'chīz| *vt* (*give vote to*) conceder el derecho de voto a; (*set free*) emancipar.

engage |engāj'| *vt* (*attention*) llamar; (*in conversation*) abordar; (*worker, lawyer*) contratar; (*clutch*) embragar ♦ *vi* (*TECH*) engranar; **to ~ in** dedicarse a, ocuparse en; **to ~ sb in conversation** entablar conversación con uno.

engaged |engājd'| *a* (*Brit: busy, in use*) ocupado; (*betrothed*) prometido; **to get ~** prometerse; **he is ~ in research** se dedica a la investigación.

engaged tone *n* (*Brit TEL*) señal *f* de comunicando.

engagement |engāj'mənt| *n* (*appointment*) compromiso, cita; (*battle*) combate *m*; (*to marry*) compromiso; (*period*) noviazgo; **I have a previous ~** ya tengo un compromiso.

engagement ring *n* anillo de pedida.

engaging |engā'jing| *a* atractivo, simpático.

engender |enjen'dûr| *vt* engendrar.

engine |en'jən| *n* (*AUT*) motor *m*; (*RAIL*) locomotora.

engine driver *n* (*Brit: of train*) maquinista *m/f*.

engineer |enjənēr'| *n* ingeniero/a; (*US RAIL*) maquinista *m/f*; **civil/mechanical ~** ingeniero/a de caminos, canales y puertos/ industrial.

engineering |enjənēr'ing| *n* ingeniería ♦ *cpd* (*works, factory, worker etc*) de ingeniería.

engine failure, engine trouble *n* avería del motor.

England |ing'glənd| *n* Inglaterra.

English [ing'glish] *a* inglés/esa ♦ *n* (*LING*) el inglés; **the ~** *npl* los ingleses.

English Channel *n*: **the ~** el Canal de la Mancha.

Englishman [ing'glishmən], **Englishwoman** [ing'glishwōōmən] *n* inglés/esa *m/f*.

English-speaker [ing'glishspēkûr] *n* persona de habla inglesa.

English-speaking [ing'glishspē'king] *a* de habla inglesa.

engraving [engrā'ving] *n* grabado.

engrossed [engrōst'] *a*: **~ in** absorto en.

engulf [engulf'] *vt* sumergir, hundir.

enhance [enhans'] *vt* (*gen*) aumentar; (*beauty*) realzar; (*position, reputation*) mejorar.

enigma [ənig'mə] *n* enigma *m*.

enigmatic [enigmat'ik] *a* enigmático.

enjoy [enjoi'] *vt* (*have: health, fortune*) disfrutar de, gozar de; (*food*) comer con gusto; **I ~ doing...** me gusta hacer...; **to ~ o.s.** divertirse, pasarlo bien.

enjoyable [enjoi'əbəl] *a* (*pleasant*) agradable; (*amusing*) divertido.

enjoyment [enjoi'mənt] *n* (*use*) disfrute *m*; (*joy*) placer *m*.

enlarge [enlârj'] *vt* aumentar; (*broaden*) extender; (*PHOT*) ampliar ♦ *vi*: **to ~ on** (*subject*) tratar con más detalles.

enlarged [enlârjd'] *a* (*edition*) aumentado; (*MED: organ, gland*) dilatado.

enlargement [enlârj'mənt] *n* (*PHOT*) ampliación *f*.

enlighten [enlīt'ən] *vt* (*inform*) informar.

enlightened [enlīt'ənd] *a* iluminado; (*tolerant*) comprensivo.

enlightening [enlīt'əning] *a* informativo.

Enlightenment [enlīt'ənmənt] *n* (*HISTORY*): **the ~** la Ilustración, el Siglo de las Luces.

enlist [enlist'] *vt* alistar; (*support*) conseguir ♦ *vi* alistarse; **~ed man** (*US: MIL*) soldado raso.

enliven [enlī'vən] *vt* (*people*) animar; (*events*) avivar, animar.

enmity [en'mitē] *n* enemistad *f*.

ennoble [ennō'bəl] *vt* ennoblecer.

enormity [inôr'mitē] *n* enormidad *f*.

enormous [inôr'məs] *a* enorme.

enough [inuf'] *a*: **~ time/books** bastante tiempo/bastantes libros ♦ *n*: **have you got ~?** ¿tiene usted bastante? ♦ *ad*: **big ~** bastante grande; **he has not worked ~** no ha trabajado bastante; (**that's**) **~!** ¡basta ya!, ¡ya está bien!; **that's ~, thanks** con eso basta, gracias; **will 5 be ~?** ¿bastará con 5?; **I've had ~** estoy harto; **he was kind ~ to lend me the money** tuvo la bondad *or* amabilidad de prestarme el dinero; **... which, funny ~ ... ...** lo que, por extraño que parezca... .

enquire [enkwī'ûr] *vt, vi* = **inquire**.

enrage [enrāj'] *vt* enfurecer.

enrich [enrich'] *vt* enriquecer.

enroll, (Brit**) enrol** [enrōl'] *vt* (*members*) inscribir; (*SCOL*) matricular ♦ *vi* inscribirse; (*SCOL*) matricularse.

enrol(l)ment [enrōl'mənt] *n* inscripción *f*; matriculación *f*.

en route [ôn rōōt'] *ad* durante el viaje; **~ for/from/to** camino de/de/a.

ensconce [enskâns'] *vt*: **to ~ o.s.** instalarse cómodamente, acomodarse.

ensemble [ânsâm'bəl] *n* (*MUS*) conjunto.

enshrine [enshrīn'] *vt* encerrar, englobar.

ensign [en'sən] *n* (*flag*) bandera.

enslave [enslāv'] *vt* esclavizar.

ensue [ensōō'] *vi* seguirse; (*result*) resultar.

ensuing [ensōō'ing] *a* (*subsequent*) siguiente; (*resulting*) consiguiente.

ensure [enshōōr'] *vt* asegurar.

ENT *n abbr* (= *Ear, Nose and Throat*) otorrinolaringología.

entail [entāl'] *vt* (*imply*) suponer; (*result in*) acarrear.

entangle [entang'gəl] *vt* (*thread etc*) enredar, enmarañar; **to become ~d in sth** (*fig*) enmarañarse en algo.

entanglement [entang'gəlmənt] *n* enredo.

enter [en'tûr] *vt* (*room*) entrar en; (*club*) hacerse socio de; (*army, profession*) alistarse en; (*sb for a competition*) inscribir; (*write down*) anotar, apuntar; (*COMPUT*) introducir ♦ *vi* entrar; **to ~ for** *vt fus* presentarse para; **to ~ into** *vt fus* (*relations*) establecer; (*plans*) formar parte de; (*debate*) tomar parte en; (*negotiations*) entablar; (*agreement*) llegar a, firmar; **to ~ (up)on** *vt fus* (*Brit: career*) emprender.

enteritis [entərī'tis] *n* enteritis *f*.

enterprise [en'tûrprīz] *n* empresa; (*spirit*) iniciativa; **free ~** la libre empresa; **private ~** la iniciativa privada.

enterprising [en'tûrprīzing] *a* emprendedor(a).

entertain [entûrtān'] *vt* (*amuse*) divertir; (*receive: guest*) recibir (en casa); (*idea*) abrigar.

entertainer [entûrtān'ûr] *n* artista *m/f*.

entertaining [entûrtā'ning] *a* divertido, entretenido ♦ *n*: **to do a lot of ~** dar muchas fiestas, tener muchos invitados.

entertainment [entûrtān'mənt] *n* (*amusement*) diversión *f*; (*show*) espectáculo; (*party*) fiesta.

entertainment allowance *n* (*COMM*) gastos *mpl* de representación.

enthralled [enthrôld'] *a* cautivado.

enthralling [enthrôl'ing] *a* cautivador(a).

enthuse [enthōōz'] *vi*: **to become ~d about *or* over** entusiasmarse por.

enthusiasm [enthōō'zēazəm] *n* entusiasmo.

enthusiast [enthōō'zēast] *n* entusiasta *m/f*.

enthusiastic [enthōōzēas'tik] *a* entusiasta; **to be ~ about sb/sth** estar entusiasmado con uno/algo.

entice |entīs'| vt tentar; (seduce) seducir.
entire |entī'ûr| a entero.
entirely |entīûr'lē| ad totalmente.
entirety |entīr'tē| n: in its ~ en su totalidad.
entitle |entīt'əl| vt: to ~ sb to sth dar a uno derecho a algo.
entitled |entīt'əld| a (book) que se titula; to be ~ to sth/to do sth tener derecho a algo/a hacer algo.
entity |en'titē| n entidad f.
entourage |ântōōrázh'| n séquito.
entrails |en'trālz| npl entrañas fpl; (US) asadura sg, menudos mpl.
entrance n |en'trəns| entrada ♦ vt |entrans'| encantar, hechizar; to gain ~ to (university etc) ingresar en.
entrance examination n (to school) examen m de ingreso.
entrance fee n cuota.
entrance ramp n (US AUT) rampa de acceso.
entrancing |entrans'ing| a encantador(a).
entrant |en'trənt| n (in race, competition) participante m/f; (in exam) candidato/a.
entreat |entrēt'| vt rogar, suplicar.
entrenched |entrencht'| a: ~ interests intereses mpl creados.
entrepreneur |ântrəprənûr'| n empresario/a, capitalista m/f.
entrepreneurial |ântrəprənûr'ēəl| a empresarial.
entrust |entrust'| vt: to ~ sth to sb confiar algo a uno.
entry |en'trē| n entrada; (permission to enter) acceso; (in register, diary, ship's log) apunte m; (in account book, ledger, list) partida; no ~ prohibido el paso; (AUT) dirección prohibida; single/double ~ book-keeping contabilidad f simple/por partida doble.
entry form n boleto de inscripción.
entry phone n (Brit) portero automático.
enumerate |inōō'mərāt| vt enumerar.
enunciate |inun'sēāt| vt pronunciar; (principle etc) enunciar.
envelop |envel'əp| vt envolver.
envelope |en'vəlōp| n sobre m.
enviable |en'vēəbəl| a envidiable.
envious |en'vēəs| a envidioso; (look) de envidia.
environment |envī'rənmənt| n medio ambiente; Department of the E~ ministerio del medio ambiente.
environmental |envīrənmen'təl| a ambiental; ~ studies (in school etc) ecología sg.
environmentalist |envīrənmen'təlist| n ecologista m/f.
environment-friendly |envī'rənmənt-frend'lē| a amigo del medio ambiente.
envisage |enviz'ij| vt (foresee) prever; (imagine) concebir.

envision |envizh'ən| vt imaginar.
envoy |en'voi| n enviado.
envy |en'vē| n envidia ♦ vt tener envidia a; to ~ sb sth envidiar algo a uno.
enzyme |en'zīm| n enzima.
eon |ē'ən| n (US) eón m.
EPA n abbr (US: = Environmental Protection Agency) Agencia del Medio Ambiente.
ephemeral |ifem'ûrəl| a efímero.
epic |ep'ik| n épica ♦ a épico.
epicenter, (Brit) **epicentre** |ep'isentûr| n epicentro.
epidemic |epidem'ik| n epidemia.
epigram |ep'igram| n epigrama m.
epilepsy |ep'əlepsē| n epilepsia.
epileptic |epəlep'tik| a, n epiléptico/a m/f.
epilogue |ep'əlóg| n epílogo.
episcopal |ipis'kəpəl| a episcopal.
episode |ep'isōd| n episodio.
epistle |ipis'əl| n epístola.
epitaph |ep'itaf| n epitafio.
epithet |ep'əthet| n epíteto.
epitome |ipit'əmē| n epítome m.
epitomize |ipit'əmīz| vt epitomar, resumir.
epoch |ep'ək| n época.
eponymous |epân'əməs| a epónimo.
equable |ek'wəbəl| a (climate) estable; (character) ecuánime.
equal |ē'kwəl| a (gen) igual; (treatment) equitativo ♦ n igual m/f ♦ vt ser igual a; (fig) igualar; to be ~ to (task) estar a la altura de; the E~ Opportunities Commission (Brit) comisión para la igualdad de la mujer en el trabajo.
equality |ikwâl'itē| n igualdad f.
equalize |ē'kwəlīz| vt, vi igualar; (SPORT) empatar.
equalizer |ē'kwəlīzûr| n igualada.
equally |ē'kwəlē| ad igualmente; (share etc) a partes iguales; they are ~ clever son iguales de inteligente.
equal(s) sign |ē'kwəl(z) sīn| n signo de igualdad.
equanimity |ēkwənim'itē| n ecuanimidad f.
equate |ikwāt'| vt: to ~ sth with equiparar algo con.
equation |ikwā'zhən| n (MATH) ecuación f.
equator |ikwā'tûr| n ecuador m.
equatorial |ēkwətôr'ēəl| a ecuatorial.
Equatorial Guinea n Guinea Ecuatorial.
equestrian |ikwes'trēən| a ecuestre ♦ n caballista m/f, jinete/a m/f.
equilibrium |ēkwəlib'rēəm| n equilibrio.
equinox |ē'kwənâks| n equinoccio.
equip |ikwip'| vt (gen) equipar; (person) proveer; ~ped with (machinery etc) provisto de; to be well ~ped estar bien equipado; he is well ~ped for the job tiene las dotes necesarias para este puesto.
equipment |ikwip'mənt| n equipo; (tools) avíos mpl.
equitable |ek'witəbəl| a equitativo.
equities |ek'witēz| npl (Brit COMM) dere-

chos *mpl* sobre *or* en el activo.

equity [ɛk'wĭtē] *n* (*fairness*) equidad *f*; (*ECON: of debtor*) valor *m* líquido.

equity capital *n* capital *m* social *or* en acciones.

equivalent [ikwiv'ələnt] *a*, *n* equivalente *m*; **to be** ~ **to** equivaler a.

equivocal [ikwiv'əkəl] *a* equívoco.

equivocate [ikwiv'əkāt] *vi* ser evasivo.

equivocation [ikwivəkā'shən] *n* evasión *f*, vacilación *f*.

ER *abbr* (*Brit:* = *Elizabeth Regina*) la reina *Isabel*.

ERA *n abbr* (*US POL:* = *Equal Rights Amendment*) *enmienda sobre la igualdad de derechos de la mujer*.

era [ē'rə] *n* era, época.

eradicate [irad'ikāt] *vt* erradicar, extirpar.

erase [irās'] *vt* (*also COMPUT*) borrar.

eraser [irā'sûr] *n* goma de borrar.

erect [irɛkt'] *a* erguido ♦ *vt* erigir, levantar; (*assemble*) montar.

erection [irɛk'shən] *n* (*of building*) construcción *f*; (*of machinery*) montaje *m*; (*structure*) edificio; (*MED*) erección *f*.

ergonomics [ûrgənâm'iks] *n* ergonomía.

ERISA *n abbr* (*US:* = *Employee Retirement Income Security Act*) *ley que regula pensiones de jubilados*.

ermine [ûr'min] *n* armiño.

erode [irōd'] *vt* (*GEO*) erosionar; (*metal*) corroer, desgastar.

erosion [irō'zhən] *n* erosión *f*; desgaste *m*.

erotic [irāt'ik] *a* erótico.

eroticism [irāt'isizəm] *n* erotismo.

err [ûr] *vi* equivocarse; (*REL*) pecar.

errand [är'ənd] *n* recado, mandado (*LAm*); **to run** ~**s** hacer recados; ~ **of mercy** acto caritativo.

errand boy *n* recadero.

erratic [irat'ik] *a* variable; (*results etc*) desigual, poco uniforme.

erroneous [irō'nēəs] *a* erróneo.

error [är'ûr] *n* error *m*, equivocación *f*; **typing/spelling** ~ error *m* de mecanografía/ortografía; **in** ~ por equivocación; ~**s and omissions excepted** salvo error u omisión.

error message *n* (*COMPUT*) mensaje *m* de error.

erstwhile [ûrst'hwīl] *a* antiguo, previo.

erudite [är'yŏŏdīt] *a* erudito.

erudition [äryŏŏdish'ən] *n* erudición *f*.

erupt [irupt'] *vi* entrar en erupción; (*MED*) hacer erupción; (*fig*) estallar.

eruption [irup'shən] *n* erupción *f*; (*fig: of anger, violence*) explosión *f*, estallido.

ESA *n abbr* (= *European Space Agency*) Agencia Espacial Europea.

escalate [ɛs'kəlāt] *vi* extenderse, intensificarse; (*costs*) aumentar vertiginosamente.

escalation clause [ɛskəlā'shən klōz] *n*

cláusula de reajuste de los precios.

escalator [ɛs'kəlātûr] *n* escalera móvil.

escapade [ɛs'kəpād] *n* travesura.

escape [ɛskāp'] *n* (*gen*) fuga; (*from duties*) escapatoria; (*from chase*) evasión *f* ♦ *vi* (*gen*) escaparse; (*flee*) huir, evadirse; (*leak*) fugarse ♦ *vt* evitar, eludir; (*consequences*) escapar a; **to** ~ **from** (*place*) escaparse de; (*person*) escaparse a; (*clutches*) librarse de; **to** ~ **to** (*another place, freedom, safety*) huirse a; **to** ~ **notice** pasar desapercibido.

escape artist *n* escapólogo/a.

escape clause *n* (*fig: in agreement*) cláusula de excepción.

escape hatch *n* (*in submarine, space rocket*) escotilla de salvamento.

escape key *n* (*COMPUT*) tecla de escape.

escape route *n* ruta de escape.

escapism [ɛskā'pizəm] *n* escapismo.

escapist [ɛskā'pist] *a*, *n* escapista *m/f*.

escapologist [ɛskəpâl'əjist] *n* (*Brit*) = escape artist.

escarpment [ɛskárp'mənt] *n* escarpa.

eschew [ɛschōō'] *vt* evitar, abstenerse de.

escort *n* [ɛs'kórt] acompañante *m/f*; (*MIL*) escolta; (*NAUT*) convoy *m* ♦ *vt* [ɛskórt'] acompañar; (*MIL, NAUT*) escoltar.

escort agency *n* servicio de azafatas.

Eskimo [ɛs'kəmō] *a* esquimal ♦ *n* esquimal *m/f*; (*LING*) esquimal *m*.

ESL *n abbr* (*SCOL*) = *English as a Second Language*.

esophagus [isâf'əgəs] *n* (*US*) esófago.

esoteric [ɛsətär'ik] *a* esotérico.

ESP *n abbr* = **extrasensory perception**.

esp. *abbr* = **especially**.

especially [ɛspesh'əlē] *ad* (*gen*) especialmente; (*above all*) sobre todo; (*particularly*) en particular.

espionage [ɛs'pēənâzh] *n* espionaje *m*.

esplanade [ɛsplənâd'] *n* (*by sea*) paseo marítimo.

espouse [ɛspouz'] *vt* adherirse a.

Esq. *abbr* (= *Esquire*) D.

Esquire [ɛs'kwīūr] *n*: **J. Brown,** ~ Sr. D. J. Brown.

essay [ɛs'ā] *n* (*SCOL*) ensayo.

essayist [ɛs'āist] *n* ensayista *m/f*.

essence [ɛs'əns] *n* esencia; **in** ~ en lo esencial; **speed is of the** ~ es esencial hacerlo con la mayor prontitud.

essential [əsɛn'chəl] *a* (*necessary*) imprescindible; (*basic*) esencial ♦ *n* (*often pl*) lo esencial; **it is** ~ **that** es imprescindible que.

essentially [əsɛn'chəlē] *ad* esencialmente.

EST *n abbr* (*US:* = *Eastern Standard Time*) *hora de invierno de Nueva York*.

est. *abbr* (= *established*) fundado; (= *estimated*) aprox.

establish [əstab'lish] *vt* establecer; (*prove: fact, identity*) comprobar, verificar;

established [əstab'lisht] *a* (*business*) de buena reputación; (*staff*) de plantilla.

establishment [əstab'lishmənt] *n* (*also business*) establecimiento; **the E~** la clase dirigente; **a teaching** ~ un centro de enseñanza.

estate [əstāt'] *n* (*land*) finca, hacienda; (*property*) propiedad *f*; (*inheritance*) herencia; (*POL*) estado; **housing** ~ (*Brit*) urbanización *f*; **industrial** ~ polígono industrial.

estate agent *n* (*Brit*) agente *m/f* inmobiliario/a.

estate car *n* (*Brit*) furgoneta.

esteem [əstēm'] *n*: **to hold sb in high** ~ estimar en mucho a uno ♦ *vt* estimar.

esthetic [esthet'ik] *a* (*US*) estético.

estimate *n* [es'təmit] estimación *f*, apreciación *f*; (*assessment*) tasa, cálculo; (*COMM*) presupuesto ♦ *vt* [es'təmāt] estimar; tasar, calcular; **to give sb an** ~ **of** presentar a uno un presupuesto de; **at a rough** ~ haciendo un cálculo aproximado.

estimation [estəmā'shən] *n* opinión *f*, juicio; (*esteem*) aprecio; **in my** ~ según mis cálculos.

estimator [es'təmātûr] *n* estimador(a) *m/f*.

Estonia [estō'nēə] *n* Estonia.

estranged [estrānjd'] *a* separado.

estrangement [estrānj'mənt] *n* alejamiento, distanciamiento.

estrogen [es'trəjən] *n* (*US*) estrógeno.

estuary [es'chōōārē] *n* estuario, ría.

ETA *n abbr* = *estimated time of arrival*.

et al. *abbr* (= *et alii: and others*) et al.

etc *abbr* (= *et cetera*) etc.

etch [ech] *vt* grabar al aguafuerte.

etching [ech'ing] *n* aguafuerte *m or f*.

ETD *n abbr* = *estimated time of departure*.

eternal [itûr'nəl] *a* eterno.

eternity [itûr'nitē] *n* eternidad *f*.

ether [ē'thûr] *n* éter *m*.

ethereal [ithēr'ēəl] *a* etéreo.

ethical [eth'ikəl] *a* ético; (*honest*) honrado.

ethics [eth'iks] *n* ética ♦ *npl* moralidad *f*.

Ethiopia [ēthēō'pēə] *n* Etiopía.

Ethiopian [ēthēō'pēən] *a, n* etíope *m/f*.

ethnic [eth'nik] *a* étnico.

ethos [ē'thás] *n* (*of culture, group*) sistema *m* de valores.

etiquette [et'əkit] *n* etiqueta.

ETV *n abbr* (*US*: = *Educational Television*) televisión escolar.

etymology [etəmál'əjē] *n* etimología.

eucalyptus [yōōkəlip'təs] *n* eucalipto.

Eucharist [yōō'kûrist] *n* Eucaristía.

eulogy [yōō'ləjē] *n* elogio, encomio.

eunuch [yōō'nək] *n* eunuco.

euphemism [yōō'fəmizəm] *n* eufemismo.

euphemistic [yōōfəmis'tik] *a* eufemístico.

euphoria [yōōfôr'ēə] *n* euforia.

Eurasia [yōōrā'zhə] *n* Eurasia.

Eurasian [yōōrā'zhən] *a, n* eurasiático/a *m/f*.

Euratom [yōōrat'əm] *n abbr* (= *European Atomic Energy Commission*) Euratom *m*.

Euro... [yōō'rō] *pref* Euro....

Eurocheque [yōō'rōchek] *n* (*Brit*) Eurocheque *m*.

Eurocrat [yōō'rəkrat] *n* eurócrata *m/f*.

Eurodollar [yōō'rōdâlûr] *n* eurodólar *m*.

Europe [yōō'rəp] *n* Europa.

European [yōōrəpē'ən] *a, n* europeo/a *m/f*.

European Court of Justice *n* Tribunal *m* de Justicia de las Comunidades Europeas.

European Economic Community *n* Comunidad *f* Económica Europea.

euthanasia [ōōthənā'zhə] *n* eutanasia.

evacuate [ivak'yōōāt] *vt* desocupar.

evacuation [ivakyōōā'shən] *n* evacuación *f*.

evade [ivād'] *vt* evadir, eludir.

evaluate [ival'yōōāt] *vt* evaluar; (*value*) tasar; (*evidence*) interpretar.

evangelical [ēvanjel'ikəl] *a* evangélico.

evangelist [ivan'jəlist] *n* evangelista *m*; (*preacher*) evangelizador(a) *m/f*.

evaporate [ivap'ərāt] *vi* evaporarse; (*fig*) desvanecerse ♦ *vt* evaporar.

evaporated milk [ivap'ərātid milk'] *n* leche *f* evaporada.

evaporation [ivapərā'shən] *n* evaporación *f*.

evasion [ivā'zhən] *n* evasiva, evasión *f*.

evasive [ivā'siv] *a* evasivo.

eve [ēv] *n*: **on the** ~ **of** en vísperas de.

even [ē'vən] *a* (*level*) llano; (*smooth*) liso; (*speed, temperature*) uniforme; (*number*) par; (*SPORT*) igual(es) ♦ *ad* hasta, incluso; ~ **if,** ~ **though** aunque + *subjun*; ~ **more** aun más; ~ **so** aun así; **not** ~ ni siquiera; ~ **he was there** hasta él estuvo allí; ~ **on Sundays** incluso los domingos; ~ **faster** aún más rápido; **to break** ~ cubrir los gastos; **to get** ~ **with sb** ajustar cuentas con uno; **to** ~ **out** *vi* nivelarse.

evening [ēv'ning] *n* tarde *f*; (*dusk*) atardecer *m*; (*night*) noche *f*; **in the** ~ por la tarde; **this** ~ esta tarde *or* noche; **tomorrow/yesterday** ~ mañana/ayer por la tarde *or* noche.

evening class *n* clase *f* nocturna.

evening dress *n* (*man's*) traje *m* de etiqueta; (*woman's*) traje *m* de noche.

evenly [ē'vənlē] *ad* (*distribute, space, spread*) con igualdad, igualmente; (*divide*) equitativamente.

evensong [ē'vənsông] *n* vísperas *fpl*.

event [ivent'] *n* suceso, acontecimiento; (*SPORT*) prueba; **in the** ~ **of** en caso de; **in the** ~ en realidad; **in the course of** ~s en el curso de los acontecimientos; **in any** ~ pase lo que pase.

eventful [ivent'fəl] *a* accidentado; (*game etc*) lleno de emoción.

eventual [iven'chōōəl] *a* final.

eventuality [ivenchōōal'itē] *n* eventualidad

f.

eventually |iven'chōōəlē| *ad* (*finally*) finalmente; (*in time*) a la larga.

ever |ev'ûr| *ad* nunca, jamás; (*at all times*) siempre; **for** ~ (para) siempre; **the best** ~ lo nunca visto; **did you** ~ **meet him?** ¿llegaste a conocerle?; **have you** ~ **been there?** ¿has estado allí alguna vez?; **have you** ~ **seen it?** ¿lo ha visto usted alguna vez?; **better than** ~ mejor que nunca; **thank you** ~ **so much** muchísimas gracias; **yours** ~ (*in letters*) un abrazo de; ~ **since** *ad* desde entonces ♦ *conj* después de que.

Everest |ev'ûrist| *n* (*also:* **Mount** ~) Everest *m.*

evergreen |ev'ûrgrēn| *n* árbol *m* de hoja perenne.

everlasting |evûrlas'ting| *a* eterno, perpetuo.

every |ev'rē| *a* (*each*) cada; (*all*) todo; ~ **day** cada día; ~ **other car** cada dos coches; ~ **now and then** de vez en cuando; **I have** ~ **confidence in him** confío completamente en él.

everybody |ev'rēbâdē| *pron* todos *pl*, todo el mundo; ~ **knows about it** todo el mundo lo sabe; ~ **else** todos los demás.

everyday |ev'rēdā| *a* (*daily:* *use,* *occurrence, experience*) diario, cotidiano; (*usual: expression*) corriente; (*common*) vulgar; (*routine*) rutinario.

everyone |ev'rēwun| = **everybody**.

everything |ev'rēthing| *pron* todo; ~ **is ready** todo está dispuesto; **he did** ~ **possible** hizo todo lo posible.

everywhere |ev'rēhwär| *ad* (*be*) en todas partes; (*go*) a *or* por todas partes; ~ **you go you meet...** en todas partes encontrarás....

evict |ivikt'| *vt* desahuciar.

eviction |ivik'shən| *n* desahucio.

eviction notice *n* orden *f* de desahucio *or* desalojo (*LAm*).

evidence |ev'idəns| *n* (*proof*) prueba; (*of witness*) testimonio; (*facts*) datos *mpl*, hechos *mpl*; **to give** ~ prestar declaración, dar testimonio.

evident |ev'idənt| *a* evidente, manifiesto.

evidently |ev'idəntlē| *ad* naturalmente.

evil |ē'vəl| *a* malo; (*influence*) funesto; (*smell*) horrible ♦ *n* mal *m*, maldad *f.*

evildoer |ē'vəldōōūr| *n* malhechor(a) *m/f.*

evince |ivins'| *vt* mostrar, dar señales de.

evocative |ivák'ətiv| *a* sugestivo, evocador(a).

evoke |ivōk'| *vt* evocar; (*admiration*) provocar.

evolution |evəlōō'shən| *n* evolución *f*, desarrollo.

evolve |iválv'| *vt* desarrollar ♦ *vi* evolucionar, desarrollarse.

ewe |yōō| *n* oveja.

ex- |cks| *pref* (*former: husband, president etc*) ex-; (*out of*): **the price** ~**works** precio de fábrica.

exacerbate |igzas'ûrbāt| *vt* (*pain, disease*) exacerbar; (*fig: relations, situation*) empeorar.

exact |igzakt'| *a* exacto ♦ *vt*: **to** ~ **sth (from)** exigir algo (de).

exacting |igzak'ting| *a* exigente; (*conditions*) arduo.

exactitude |igzakt'ətōōd| *n* exactitud *f.*

exactly |igzakt'lē| *ad* exactamente; (*time*) en punto; ~! ¡exactamente!

exactness |igzakt'nis| *n* exactitud *f.*

exaggerate |igzaj'ərāt| *vt, vi* exagerar.

exaggerated |igzaj'ərātid| *a* exagerado.

exaggeration |igzajərā'shən| *n* exageración *f.*

exalt |igzôlt'| *vt* (*praise*) ensalzar; (*elevate*) elevar, exaltar.

exalted |igzôl'tid| *a* (*position*) exaltado; (*elated*) excitado.

exam |igzam'| *n abbr* (*SCOL*) = **examination.**

examination |igzamənā'shən| *n* (*gen*) examen *m*; (*LAW*) interrogación *f*; (*inquiry*) investigación *f*; **to take an** ~ hacer un examen; **the matter is under** ~ se está examinando el asunto.

examine |igzam'in| *vt* (*gen*) examinar; (*inspect: machine, premises*) inspeccionar; (*SCOL, LAW: person*) interrogar; (*at customs: baggage, passport*) registrar; (*MED*) hacer un reconocimiento médico de.

examiner |igzam'inûr| *n* inspector(a) *m/f.*

example |igzam'pəl| *n* ejemplo; **for** ~ por ejemplo; **to set a good/bad** ~ dar buen/mal ejemplo.

exasperate |igzas'pərāt| *vt* exasperar, irritar; ~**d by** *or* **at** *or* **with** exasperado por *or* con.

exasperating |igzas'pərāting| *a* irritante.

exasperation |igzaspərā'shən| *n* exasperación *f*, irritación *f.*

excavate |cks'kəvāt| *vt* excavar.

excavation |cks'kəvā'shən| *n* excavación *f.*

excavator |cks'kəvātûr| *n* excavadora.

exceed |iksēd'| *vt* exceder; (*number*) pasar de; (*speed limit*) sobrepasar; (*limits*) rebasar; (*powers*) excederse en; (*hopes*) superar.

exceedingly |iksē'dinglē| *ad* sumamente, sobremanera.

excel |iksel'| *vi* sobresalir.

excellence |ck'sələns| *n* excelencia.

Excellency |ck'sclənsē| *n*: **His** ~ Su Excelencia.

excellent |ck'sələnt| *a* excelente.

except |iksept'| *prep* (*also:* ~ **for,** ~**ing**) excepto, salvo ♦ *vt* exceptuar, excluir; ~ **if/when** excepto si/cuando; ~ **that** salvo que.

exception |iksep'shən| *n* excepción *f*; **to**

take ~ to ofenderse por; **with the ~ of** a excepción de; **to make an ~** hacer una excepción.
exceptional [iksep'shənəl] *a* excepcional.
excerpt [ek'sûrpt] *n* extracto.
excess [ekses'] *n* exceso; **in ~ of** superior a; *see also* **excesses.**
excess baggage *n* exceso de equipaje.
excesses [ekses'iz] *npl* excesos *mpl.*
excess fare *n* suplemento.
excessive [ikses'iv] *a* excesivo.
excess supply *n* oferta excedentaria.
excess weight *n* exceso de peso.
exchange [ikschānj'] *n* cambio; (*of goods*) canje *m*; (*of ideas*) intercambio; (*also:* **telephone ~**) central *f* (telefónica) ♦ *vt:* **to ~ (for)** cambiar (por); **in ~ for** a cambio de; **foreign ~** (*COMM*) divisas *fpl.*
exchange control *n* control *m* de cambios.
exchange rate *n* tipo de cambio.
exchequer [eks'chekûr] *n:* **the ~** (*Brit*) la Hacienda del Fisco.
excisable [iksī'zəbəl] *a* taxable.
excise [ek'sīz] *n* impuestos *mpl* sobre el comercio exterior.
excitable [iksī'təbəl] *a* exaltado.
excite [iksīt'] *vt* (*stimulate*) estimular; (*anger*) provocar; (*move*) entusiasmar; **to get ~d** emocionarse.
excitement [iksīt'mənt] *n* emoción *f.*
exciting [iksī'ting] *a* emocionante.
excl. *abbr* = **excluding; exclusive (of).**
exclaim [iksklām'] *vi* exclamar.
exclamation [ekskləmā'shən] *n* exclamación *f.*
exclamation mark *n* punto de admiración.
exclude [iksklo͞od'] *vt* excluir; (*except*) exceptuar.
excluding [iksklo͞o'ding] *prep:* **~ tax** impuesto no incluido.
exclusion [iksklo͞o'zhən] *n* exclusión *f;* **to the ~ of** con exclusión de.
exclusion clause *n* cláusula de exclusión.
exclusive [iksklo͞o'siv] *a* exclusivo; (*club, district*) selecto; **~ of tax** excluyendo impuestos; **~ of postage/service** franqueo/servicio no incluido; **from the 1st to the 13th March ~** del 1 al 13 de marzo exclusive.
exclusively [iksklo͞o'sivlē] *ad* únicamente.
excommunicate [ekskəmyo͞o'nəkāt] *vt* excomulgar.
excrement [eks'krəmənt] *n* excremento.
excrete [ikskrēt'] *vi* excretar.
excruciating [ikskro͞o'shēāting] *a* (*pain*) agudísimo, atroz.
excursion [ikskûr'zhən] *n* excursión *f.*
excursion ticket *n* billete *m* de excursión.
excusable [ikskyo͞o'zəbəl] *a* perdonable.
excuse *n* [ikskyo͞os'] disculpa, excusa; (*evasion*) pretexto ♦ *vt* [ikskyo͞oz'] disculpar,

perdonar; (*justify*) justificar; **to make ~s for sb** presentar disculpas por uno; **to ~ sb from doing sth** dispensar a uno de hacer algo; **to ~ o.s. (for (doing) sth)** pedir disculpas a uno (por (hacer) algo); **~ me!** ¡perdón!; **if you will ~ me** con su permiso.
ex-directory [eksdirek'tûrē] *a* (*Brit*): **~ (phone) number** número que no consta en la guía.
exec. [igzek'] *n abbr* = **executive.**
execrable [ek'səkrəbəl] *a* execrable, abominable; (*manners*) detestable.
execute [ek'səkyo͞ot] *vt* (*plan*) realizar; (*order*) cumplir; (*person*) ajusticiar, ejecutar.
execution [eksəkyo͞o'shən] *n* realización *f;* cumplimiento; ejecución *f.*
executioner [eksəkyo͞o'shənûr] *n* verdugo.
executive [igzek'yətiv] *n* (*COMM*) ejecutivo; (*POL*) poder *m* ejecutivo ♦ *a* (*secretary, car, plane*) ejecutivo; (*offices, suite*) de los ejecutivos; (*position, job, duties*) de ejecutivo.
executive director *n* director(a) *m/f* ejecutivo/a.
executor [igzek'yətûr] *n* albacea *m*, testamentario.
exemplary [igzem'plûrē] *a* ejemplar.
exemplify [igzem'pləfī] *vt* ejemplificar.
exempt [igzempt'] *a:* **~ from** exento de ♦ *vt:* **to ~ sb from** eximir a uno de.
exemption [igzemp'shən] *n* exención *f;* (*immunity*) inmunidad *f.*
exercise [ek'sûrsīz] *n* ejercicio ♦ *vt* ejercer; (*right*) valerse de; (*dog*) llevar de paseo ♦ *vi* hacer ejercicio(s).
exercise book *n* cuaderno.
exert [igzûrt'] *vt* ejercer; (*strength, force*) emplear; **to ~ o.s.** esforzarse.
exertion [igzûr'shən] *n* esfuerzo.
exfoliant [eksfō'lēənt] *n* exfoliante *m.*
ex gratia [eks grā'tēə] *a:* **~ payment** pago a título gracioso.
exhale [eks·hāl'] *vt* despedir ♦ *vi* espirar, exhalar.
exhaust [igzôst'] *n* (*pipe*) escape *m;* (*fumes*) gases *mpl* de escape ♦ *vt* agotar; **to ~ o.s.** agotarse.
exhausted [igzôs'tid] *a* agotado.
exhausting [igzôs'ting] *a:* **an ~ journey/day** un viaje/día agotador.
exhaustion [igzôs'chən] *n* agotamiento; **nervous ~** postración *f* nerviosa.
exhaustive [igzôs'tiv] *a* exhaustivo.
exhibit [igzib'it] *n* (*ART*) obra expuesta; (*LAW*) objeto expuesto ♦ *vt* (*show: emotions*) manifestar; (: *courage, skill*) demostrar; (*paintings*) exponer.
exhibition [eksəbish'ən] *n* exposición *f.*
exhibitionist [eksəbish'ənist] *n* exhibicionista *m/f.*
exhibitor [igzib'ətûr] *n* expositor(a) *m/f.*
exhilarating [igzil'ərāting] *a* estimulante, tó-

nico.
exhilaration [igzilərā'shən] *n* júbilo.
exhort [igzôrt'] *vt* exhortar.
exile [eg'zīl] *n* exilio; *(person)* exiliado/a ♦ *vt* desterrar, exiliar.
exist [igzist'] *vi* existir.
existence [igzis'təns] *n* existencia.
existentialism [egzisten'chəlizəm] *n* existencialismo.
existing [igzis'ting] *a* existente, actual.
exit [eg'zit] *n* salida ♦ *vi* (THEATER) hacer mutis; (COMPUT) salir (al sistema).
exit poll *n* (POL) sondeo de votos a posteriori.
exit ramp *n* (US AUT) vía de acceso.
exit visa *n* visado de salida.
exodus [ek'sədəs] *n* éxodo.
ex officio [eks əfish'ēō] *a, ad* ex oficio.
exonerate [igzän'ərāt] *vt*: **to ~ from** exculpar de.
exorbitant [igzôr'bətənt] *a (price, demands)* exorbitante, excesivo.
exorcize [ek'sôrsīz] *vt* exorcizar.
exotic [igzät'ik] *a* exótico.
exp. *abbr* = **expenses**; **expired**; **export**; **express**.
expand [ikspand'] *vt* ampliar; *(number)* aumentar ♦ *vi (trade etc)* expandirse; *(gas, metal)* dilatarse; **to ~ on** *(notes, story etc)* ampliar.
expanse [ikspans'] *n* extensión *f*.
expansion [ikspan'chən] *n* ampliación *f*; aumento; *(of trade)* expansión *f*.
expansionism [ikspan'chənizəm] *n* expansionismo.
expansionist [ikspan'chənist] *a* expansionista.
expatriate [ikspā'trēit] *n* expatriado/a.
expect [ikspekt'] *vt (gen)* esperar; *(count on)* contar con; *(suppose)* suponer ♦ *vi*: **to be ~ing** estar encinta; **to ~ to do sth** esperar hacer algo; **as ~ed** como era de esperar; **I ~ so** supongo que sí.
expectancy [ikspek'tənsē] *n (anticipation)* esperanza; **life ~** esperanza de vida.
expectantly [ikspek'təntlē] *ad (look, listen)* con expectación.
expectant mother [ikspek'tənt muth'ûr] *n* futura madre *f*.
expectation [ikspektā'shən] *n* esperanza, expectativa; **in ~ of** en espera de; **against** *or* **contrary to all ~(s)** en contra de todas las previsiones; **to come** *or* **live up to sb's ~s** resultar tan bueno como se esperaba; **to fall short of sb's ~s** no cumplir las esperanzas de uno, decepcionar a uno.
expedience [ikspē'dēəns], **expediency** [ikspē'dēənsē] *n* conveniencia.
expedient [ikspē'dēənt] *a* conveniente, oportuno ♦ *n* recurso, expediente *m*.
expedite [ek'spidīt] *vt (speed up)* acelerar; *(: progress)* facilitar.
expedition [ekspədish'ən] *n* expedición *f*.

expeditionary force [ekspədish'ənärē fôrs] *n* cuerpo expedicionario.
expel [ikspel'] *vt* arrojar; (SCOL) expulsar.
expend [ikspend'] *vt* gastar; *(use up)* consumir.
expendable [ikspen'dəbəl] *a* prescindible.
expenditure [ikspen'dichûr] *n* gastos *mpl*, desembolso; *(of time, effort)* gasto.
expense [ikspens'] *n* gasto, gastos *mpl*; *(high cost)* costa; **~s** *npl* (COMM) gastos *mpl*; **at the ~ of** a costa de; **to meet the ~ of** hacer frente a los gastos de.
expense account *n* cuenta de gastos.
expensive [ikspen'siv] *a* caro, costoso.
experience [ikspēr'ēəns] *n* experiencia ♦ *vt* experimentar; *(suffer)* sufrir; **to learn by ~** aprender por experiencia.
experienced [ikspēr'ēənst] *a* experimentado.
experiment *n* [ikspär'əmənt] experimento ♦ *vi* [ikspär'əment] hacer experimentos; **to perform** *or* **carry out an ~** realizar un experimento; **as an ~** como experimento; **to ~ with a new vaccine** experimentar con una vacuna nueva.
experimental [ikspärəmen'təl] *a* experimental; **the process is still at the ~ stage** el proceso está todavía en prueba.
expert [ek'spûrt] *a* experto, perito ♦ *n* experto/a, perito/a; *(specialist)* especialista *m/f*; **~ witness** (LAW) testigo pericial; **~ in** *or* **at doing sth** experto *or* perito en hacer algo; **an ~ on sth** un experto en algo.
expertise [ekspûrtēz'] *n* pericia.
expiration [ekspərā'shən] *n (gen)* expiración *f*, vencimiento.
expire [ikspī'ûr] *vi (gen)* caducar, vencerse.
expiry [ikspiûr'ē] *n* vencimiento.
explain [iksplān'] *vt* explicar; *(mystery)* aclarar.
explain away *vt* justificar.
explanation [iksplənā'shən] *n* explicación *f*; aclaración *f*; **to find an ~ for sth** encontrarle una explicación a algo.
explanatory [iksplan'ətôrē] *a* explicativo; aclaratorio.
explicable [iksplik'əbəl] *a* explicable.
explicit [iksplis'it] *a* explícito.
explicitly [iksplis'itlē] *ad* explícitamente.
explode [iksplōd'] *vi* estallar, explotar; *(with anger)* reventar ♦ *vt* volar, explotar; *(fig: theory)* desacreditar, refutar; **to ~ a myth** demoler un mito.
exploit *n* [eks'ploit] hazaña ♦ *vt* [iksploit'] explotar.
exploitation [eksploitā'shən] *n* explotación *f*.
exploration [eksplərā'shən] *n* exploración *f*.
exploratory [iksplôr'ətôrē] *a (fig: talks)* exploratorio, preliminar.
explore [iksplôr'] *vt* explorar; *(fig)* examinar, sondear.
explorer [iksplôr'ûr] *n* explorador(a) *m/f*.

explosion [iksplō'zhən] *n* explosión *f*.
explosive [iksplō'siv] *a*, *n* explosivo.
exponent [ekspō'nent] *n* partidario/a, intérprete *m/f*.
export *vt* [ikspôrt'] exportar ♦ *n* [eks'pórt] exportación *f* ♦ *cpd* [eks'pórt] de exportación.
exportation [ekspôrtā'shən] *n* exportación *f*.
export drive *n* campaña de exportación.
exporter [ekspór'tûr] *n* exportador(a) *m/f*.
export license *n* licencia de exportación.
export manager *n* gerente *m/f* de exportación.
export trade *n* comercio exterior.
expose [ikspōz'] *vt* exponer; (*unmask*) desenmascarar.
exposé [ekspōzā'] *n* revelación *f*.
exposed [ikspōzd'] *a* expuesto; (*land, house*) desprotegido; (*ELEC: wire*) al aire; (*pipe, beam*) al descubierto.
exposition [ekspəzish'ən] *n* exposición *f*.
exposure [ikspō'zhûr] *n* exposición *f*; (*PHOT: speed*) velocidad *f* de obturación (: *shot*) fotografía; **to die from ~** (*MED*) morir de frío.
exposure meter *n* fotómetro.
expound [ikspound'] *vt* exponer; (*theory, text*) comentar; (*one's views*) explicar.
express [ikspres'] *a* (*definite*) expreso, explícito; (*Brit: letter etc*) urgente ♦ *n* (*train*) rápido ♦ *ad* (*send*) por correo extraordinario ♦ *vt* expresar; (*squeeze*) exprimir; **to send sth ~** enviar algo por correo urgente; **to ~ o.s.** expresarse.
expression [ikspresh'ən] *n* expresión *f*.
expressionism [ikspresh'ənizəm] *n* expresionismo.
expressive [ikspres'iv] *a* expresivo.
expressly [ikspres'lē] *ad* expresamente.
expressway [ikspres'wā] *n* (*urban freeway*) autopista.
expropriate [eksprōp'rēāt] *vt* expropiar.
expulsion [ikspul'shən] *n* expulsión *f*.
expurgate [eks'pûrgāt] *vt* expurgar.
exquisite [ekskwiz'it] *a* exquisito.
exquisitely [ekskwiz'itlē] *ad* exquisitamente.
ex-serviceman [ekssûr'vismən] *n* (*Brit*) ex-combatiente *m*.
ext. *abbr* (*TEL*) = **extension**.
extemporize [ikstem'pərīz] *vi* improvisar.
extend [ikstend'] *vt* (*visit, street*) prolongar; (*building*) ensanchar; (*thanks, friendship etc*) extender; (*COMM: credit*) prorrogar, alargar; (*deadline*) prorrogar ♦ *vi* (*land*) extenderse; **the contract ~s to/ for** ... el contrato se prolonga hasta/por ....
extension [iksten'chən] *n* extensión *f*; (*building*) ampliación *f*; (*TEL: line*) línea derivada; (: *telephone*) extensión *f*; (*of deadline*) prórroga; *n* **3718** extensión 3718.
extension cord *n* (*ELEC*) extensión *f*.
extensive [iksten'siv] *a* (*gen*) extenso; (*damage*) importante; (*knowledge*) amplio.

extensively [iksten'sivlē] *ad* (*altered, damaged etc*) extensamente; **he's traveled ~** ha viajado por muchos países.
extent [ikstent'] *n* (*breadth*) extensión *f*; (*scope: of knowledge, activities*) alcance *m*; (*degree: of damage, loss*) grado; **to some ~** hasta cierto punto; **to a certain ~** hasta cierto punto; **to a large ~** en gran parte; **to the ~ of**... hasta el punto de...; **to such an ~ that**... hasta tal punto que...; **to what ~?** ¿hasta qué punto?; **debts to the ~ of $5000** deudas por la cantidad de $5000.
extenuating [iksten'yōōāting] *a*: **~ circumstances** circunstancias *fpl* atenuantes.
exterior [ikstēr'ēûr] *a* exterior, externo ♦ *n* exterior *m*.
exterminate [ikstûr'mənāt] *vt* exterminar.
extermination [ikstûrmənā'shən] *n* exterminación *f*.
extern [eks'tûrn] *n* (*US MED*) externo/a.
external [ikstûr'nəl] *a* externo, exterior ♦ *n*: **the ~s** las apariencias; **~ affairs** asuntos *mpl* exteriores; **for ~ use only** (*MED*) para uso tópico.
externally [ikstûr'nəlē] *ad* por fuera.
extinct [ikstingkt'] *a* (*volcano*) extinguido; (*race*) extinto.
extinction [ikstingk'shən] *n* extinción *f*.
extinguish [iksting'gwish] *vt* extinguir, apagar.
extinguisher [iksting'gwishûr] *n* extintor *m*.
extoll, (*Brit*) **extol** [ikstōl'] *vt* (*merits, virtues*) ensalzar, alabar; (*person*) alabar, elogiar.
extort [ikstôrt'] *vt* sacar a la fuerza.
extortion [ikstôr'shən] *n* exacción *f*.
extortionate [ikstôr'shənit] *a* excesivo, exorbitante.
extra [eks'trə] *a* adicional ♦ *ad* (*in addition*) de más ♦ *n* (*addition*) extra *m*, suplemento; (*THEATER*) extra *m/f*, comparsa *m/f*; (*newspaper*) edición *f* extraordinaria; **wine will cost ~** el vino no está incluido (en el precio); **~ large sizes** tamaños grandes; *see also* **extras.**
extra... *pref* extra... .
extract *vt* [ikstrakt'] sacar; (*tooth*) extraer; (*confession*) arrancar, obtener ♦ *n* [eks'trakt] extracto.
extraction [ikstrak'shən] *n* extracción *f*; (*origin*) origen *m*.
extracurricular [ekstrəkərik'yəlûr] *a* (*SCOL*) extraescolar, extra-académico.
extradite [eks'trədīt] *vt* extraditar.
extradition [ekstrədish'ən] *n* extradición *f*.
extramarital [ekstrəmar'itəl] *a* extramatrimonial.
extramural [ekstrəmyōōr'əl] *a* extraescolar.
extraneous [ikstrā'nēəs] *a* extraño, ajeno.
extraordinary [ikstrôr'dənārē] *a* extraordinario; (*odd*) raro; **the ~ thing is that** ... la cosa más extraordinaria es que ....

extraordinary general meeting *n* junta general extraordinaria.

extrapolation [ikstrapolā'shon] *n* extrapolación *f*.

extras [eks'trəz] *npl* (*additional expense*) extras *mpl*.

extrasensory perception (ESP) [ekstrəsen'sûrē pûrsep'shən] *n* percepción *f* extrasensorial.

extra time *n* (*SOCCER*) prórroga.

extravagance [ikstrav'əgəns] *n* (*excessive spending*) derroche *m*; (*thing bought*) extravagancia.

extravagant [ikstrav'əgənt] *a* (*lavish*) pródigo; (*wasteful*) derrochador(a); (*price*) exorbitante; (*praise*) excesivo.

extreme [ikstrēm'] *a* extremo; (*poverty etc*) extremado; (*case*) excepcional ♦ *n* extremo; **the ~ left/right** (*POL*) la extrema izquierda/derecha; **~s of temperature** temperaturas extremas.

extremely [ikstrēm'lē] *ad* sumamente, extremadamente.

extremist [ikstrē'mist] *a, n* extremista *m/f*.

extremity [ikstrem'itē] *n* extremidad *f*, punta; (*need*) apuro, necesidad *f*; **extremities** *npl* (*hands and feet*) extremidades *fpl*.

extricate [ek'strikāt] *vt:* **to ~ o.s. from** librarse de.

extrovert [ek'strōvûrt] *n* extrovertido/a.

exuberance [igzōō'bûrəns] *n* exuberancia.

exuberant [igzōō'bûrənt] *a* (*person*) eufórico; (*style*) exuberante.

exude [igzōōd'] *vt* rezumar, sudar.

exult [igzult'] *vi* regocijarse.

exultant [igzul'tənt] *a* (*person, smile*) regocijado, júbiloso; (*shout, expression*) jubiloso.

exultation [egzultā'shən] *n* regocijo, júbilo; **in ~** en exultación.

eye [ī] *n* ojo ♦ *vt* mirar de soslayo, ojear; **to keep an ~ on** vigilar; **as far as the ~ can see** hasta donde alcanza la vista; **to have an ~ for sth** tener mucha vista *or* buen ojo para algo; **there's more to this than meets the ~** esto tiene su miga.

eyeball [ī'bôl] *n* globo del ojo.

eyebath [ī'bath] *n* (*Brit*) = **eye cup**.

eyebrow [ī'brou] *n* ceja.

eyebrow pencil *n* lápiz *m* de cejas.

eye-catching [ī'kaching] *a* llamativo.

eye cup *n* (*US*) baño para ojos.

eyedrops [ī'drâps] *npl* gotas *fpl* para los ojos.

eyelash [ī'lash] *n* pestaña.

eyelet [ī'lit] *n* ojete *m*.

eye-level [ī'levəl] *a* a la altura de los ojos.

eyelid [ī'lid] *n* párpado.

eyeliner [ī'līnûr] *n* lápiz *m* de ojos.

eye-opener [ī'ōpənûr] *n* revelación *f*, gran sorpresa.

eyeshadow [ī'shadō] *n* sombreador *m* de ojos.

eyesight [ī'sīt] *n* vista.

eyesore [ī'sôr] *n* monstruosidad *f*.

eyestrain [ī'strān] *n:* **to get ~** cansar la vista *or* los ojos.

eye test *n* examen *m* de los ojos.

eyetooth, *pl* **eyeteeth** [ī'tōōth, -tēth] *n* colmillo; **to give one's eyeteeth for sth/to do sth** (*col, fig*) dar un ojo de la cara por algo/por hacer algo.

eyewash [ī'wâsh] *n* (*fig*) disparates *mpl*, tonterías *fpl*.

eye witness *n* testigo *m/f* presencial.

eyrie [är'ē] *n* aguilera.

F

F [ef] *n* (*letter*) F, f *f*; (*MUS*) fa *m*; **F for Fox** F de Francia.

F. *abbr* = **Fahrenheit**.

FA *n abbr* (*Brit:* = *Football Association*) ≈ AFE *f* (*Sp*).

FAA *n abbr* (*US:* = *Federal Aviation Administration*) *organismo de control y desarrollo de la aviación civil*.

fable [fā'bəl] *n* fábula.

fabric [fab'rik] *n* tejido, tela.

fabricate [fab'rikāt] *vt* fabricar; (*fig*) inventar.

fabrication [fabrikā'shən] *n* fabricación *f*; (*fig*) invención *f*.

fabric ribbon *n* (*for typewriter*) cinta de tela.

fabulous [fab'yələs] *a* fabuloso.

façade [fəsâd'] *n* fachada.

face [fās] *n* (*ANAT*) cara, rostro; (*of clock*) esfera, cara (*LAm*); (*side, surface*) superficie *f*; (*in mine*) frente *m* de carbón ♦ *vt* (*subj: person*) encararse con; (: *building*) dar a; **~ down** (*person, card*) boca abajo; **to lose ~** desprestigiarse; **to save ~** salvar las apariencias; **to make** *or* **pull a ~** hacer muecas; **in the ~ of** (*difficulties etc*) en vista de, ante; **on the ~ of it** a primera vista; **~ to ~** cara a cara; **to ~ the fact that ...** reconocer que ... .

face up to *vt fus* hacer frente a, arrostrar.

facecloth [fās'klôth] *n* manopla.

face cream *n* crema (de belleza).

faceless [fās'lis] *a* (*fig*) anónimo.

face lift *n* estirado facial.

face powder *n* polvos *mpl* para la cara.

face-saving [fās'sāving] *a* para salvar las apariencias.

facet [fas'it] *n* faceta.

facetious [fəsē'shəs] *a* chistoso.

facetiously [fəsē'shəslē] *ad* chistosamente.

face value [fās val'yōō] *n* (*of stamp*) valor *m* nominal; **to take sth at ~** (*fig*) tomar algo en sentido literal, aceptar las apariencias de algo.

facial [fā'shəl] *a* de la cara ♦ *n* (*also*: **beauty ~**) tratamiento facial, limpieza.

facile [fas'əl] *a* superficial.

facilitate [fəsil'ətāt] *vt* facilitar.

facility [fəsil'ətē] *n* facilidad *f*; **facilities** *npl* facilidades *fpl*; **credit ~** facilidades de crédito.

facing [fā'sing] *prep* frente a ♦ *a* de enfrente.

facsimile [faksim'əlē] *n* (*document*) facsímil(e) *m*; (*machine*) telefax *m*.

fact [fakt] *n* hecho; **in ~** en realidad; **to know for a ~ that** ... saber a ciencia cierta que ... .

fact-finding [fakt'finding] *a*: **a ~ tour/mission** un viaje/una misión de reconocimiento.

faction [fak'shən] *n* facción *f*.

factor [fak'tûr] *n* factor *m*; (*COMM: person*) agente *m/f* comisionado/a ♦ *vi* (*COMM*) comprar deudas; **safety ~** factor de seguridad.

factory [fak'tûrē] *n* fábrica.

factory farming *n* (*Brit*) cría industrial.

factory ship *n* buque *m* factoría.

factual [fak'chōōəl] *a* basado en los hechos.

faculty [fak'əltē] *n* facultad *f*; (*US: teaching staff*) personal *m* docente.

fad [fad] *n* novedad *f*, moda.

fade [fād] *vi* desteñirse; (*sound, hope*) desvanecerse; (*light*) apagarse; (*flower*) marchitarse.

fade away *vi* (*sound*) apagarse.

fade in *vt* (*TV, CINEMA*) fundir; (*RADIO: sound*) mezclar ♦ *vi* (*TV, CINEMA*) fundirse; (*RADIO*) oírse por encima.

fade out *vt* (*TV, CINEMA*) desvanecer; (*RADIO*) apagar, disminuir el volumen de ♦ *vi* (*TV, CINEMA*) desvanecerse; (*RADIO*) apagarse, dejarse de oír.

faded [fā'did] *a* (*clothes, color*) descolorado; (*flower*) marchito.

faeces [fē'sēz] *npl* (*Brit*) = **feces**.

fag [fag] *n* (*Brit col: cigarette*) pitillo (*Sp*), cigarro; (*US col: homosexual*) maricón *m*.

fag end *n* (*Brit col*) colilla.

Fahrenheit [far'ənhīt] *n* Fahrenheit *m*.

fail [fāl] *vt* (*candidate*) suspender; (*exam*) no aprobar; (*subj: memory etc*) fallar a ♦ *vi* suspender; (*be unsuccessful*) fracasar; (*strength, brakes, engine*) fallar; **to ~ to do sth** (*neglect*) dejar de hacer algo; (*be unable*) no poder hacer algo; **without ~** sin falta; **words ~ me!** ¡no sé qué decir!

failing [fā'ling] *n* falta, defecto ♦ *prep* a falta de; **~ that** de no ser posible eso.

failsafe [fāl'sāf] *a* (*device etc*) seguro contra todo riesgo.

failure [fāl'yûr] *n* fracaso; (*person*) fracasado/a; (*mechanical etc*) fallo; (*in exam*) suspenso; (*of crops*) pérdida, destrucción *f*; **it was a complete ~** fue un fracaso total.

faint [fānt] *a* débil; (*smell, breeze, trace*) tenue, apenas perceptible; (*recollection*) vago; (*mark*) apenas visible ♦ *vi* desmayarse; **to feel ~** estar mareado, marearse.

faint-hearted [fānt'hâr'tid] *a* apocado.

faintly [fānt'lē] *ad* débilmente; (*vaguely*) vagamente.

faintness [fānt'nis] *n* debilidad *f*; vaguedad *f*.

fair [fär] *a* justo; (*hair, person*) rubio; (*weather*) bueno; (*good enough*) suficiente; (*sizeable*) considerable ♦ *ad*: **to play ~** jugar limpio ♦ *n* feria; (*carnival*) parque *m* de atracciones; **it's not ~!** ¡no es justo!, ¡no hay derecho!; **~ play** juego limpio; **a ~ amount of** bastante; **~ wear and tear** desgaste *m* natural; **trade ~** feria de muestras.

fairground [fär'ground] *n* parque *m* de atracciones.

fair-haired [fär'härd] *a* (*person*) rubio.

fairly [fär'lē] *ad* (*justly*) con justicia; (*equally*) equitativamente; (*quite*) bastante; **I'm ~ sure** estoy bastante seguro.

fairness [fär'nis] *n* justicia; (*impartiality*) imparcialidad *f*; **in all ~** a decir verdad.

fairy [fär'ē] *n* hada.

fairy godmother *n* hada madrina.

fairyland [fär'ēland] *n* el país de ensueño.

fairy lights *npl* bombillas *fpl* de colorines.

fairy tale *n* cuento de hadas.

faith [fāth] *n* fe *f*; (*trust*) confianza; (*sect*) religión *f*; **to have ~ in sb/sth** fiarse de uno/algo.

faithful [fāth'fəl] *a* fiel.

faithfully [fāth'fəlē] *ad* fielmente; **yours ~** (*Brit: in letters*) le saluda atentamente.

faith healer [fāth' hē'lûr] *n* curador(a) *m/f* por fe.

fake [fāk] *n* (*painting etc*) falsificación *f*; (*person*) impostor(a) *m/f* ♦ *a* falso ♦ *vt* fingir; (*painting etc*) falsificar.

falcon [fal'kən] *n* halcón *m*.

Falkland Islands [fôlk'lənd i'ləndz] *npl* Islas *fpl* Malvinas.

fall [fôl] *n* caída; (*US*) otoño; (*decrease*) disminución *f* ♦ *vi, pt* **fell**, *pp* **fallen** caer(se); (*price*) bajar; **~s** *npl* (*waterfall*) cascada *sg*, salto *sg* de agua; **a ~ of snow** (*Brit*) una nevada; **to ~ flat** *vi* (*on one's face*) caerse (boca abajo); (*joke, story*) no hacer gracia; **to ~ short of sb's expectations** decepcionar a uno; **to ~ in love (with sb/sth)** enamorarse (de uno/algo).

fall apart *vi* despedazarse.

fall back *vi* retroceder.

fall back on vt fus (remedy etc) recurrir a; **to have sth to ~ back on** tener algo a que recurrir.

fall behind vi quedarse atrás; (fig: with payments) retrasarse.

fall down vi (person) caerse; (building, hopes) derrumbarse.

fall for vt fus (trick) tragar; (person) enamorarse de.

fall in vi (roof) hundirse; (MIL) alinearse.

fall in with vt fus: **to ~ in with sb's plans** acomodarse con los planes de uno.

fall off vi caerse; (diminish) disminuir.

fall out vi (friends etc) reñir; (MIL) romper filas.

fall over vi caer(se).

fall through vi (plan, project) fracasar.

fallacy [fal'əsē] n error m.

fallback position [fôl'bak pəzish'ən] n posición f de repliegue.

fallen [fôl'ən] pp of **fall**.

fallible [fal'əbəl] a falible.

falling [fôl'ing] a: **~ market** mercado en baja.

falling-off [fôl'ing·ôf'] n (Brit: reduction) disminución f.

Fallopian tube [fəlō'pēən tōōb] n (ANAT) trompa de Falopio.

fallout [fôl'out] n lluvia radioactiva.

fallout shelter n refugio antinuclear.

fallow [fal'ō] a (land, field) en barbecho.

false [fôls] a (gen) falso; (teeth etc) postizo; (disloyal) desleal, traidor(a); **under ~ pretenses** con engaños.

false alarm n falsa alarma.

falsehood [fôls'hōōd] n (lie) mentira; (falseness) falsedad f.

falsely [fôls'lē] ad falsamente.

false teeth npl dentadura sg postiza.

falsify [fôl'səfī] vt falsificar; (figures) contrahacer.

falter [fôl'tûr] vi vacilar.

fame [fām] n fama.

familiar [fəmil'yûr] a familiar; (well-known) conocido; (tone) de confianza; **to be ~ with** (subject) estar enterado de; **to make o.s. ~ with** familiarizarse con; **to be on ~ terms with** conocer bien.

familiarity [fəmilēar'ətē] n familiaridad f.

familiarize [fəmil'yərīz] vt: **to ~ o.s. with** familiarizarse con.

family [fam'lē] n familia.

family allowance n pensión f familiar.

family business n negocio familiar.

family doctor n médico/a de cabecera.

family life n vida doméstica or familiar.

family planning n planificación f familiar.

family planning clinic n clínica de planificación familiar.

family tree n árbol m genealógico.

famine [fam'in] n hambre f, hambruna.

famished [fam'isht] a hambriento; **I'm ~!** (col) ¡estoy muerto de hambre!, ¡tengo un hambre canina!

famous [fā'məs] a famoso, célebre.

famously [fā'məslē] ad (get on) estupendamente.

fan [fan] n abanico; (ELEC) ventilador m; (person) aficionado/a; (SPORT) hincha m/f ♦ vt abanicar; (fire, quarrel) atizar.

fan out vi desparramarse.

fanatic [fənat'ik] n fanático/a.

fanatical [fənat'ikəl] a fanático.

fan belt n correa de ventilador.

fancied [fan'sēd] a imaginario.

fanciful [fan'sifəl] a (gen) fantástico; (imaginary) fantasioso.

fancy [fan'sē] n (whim) capricho, antojo; (imagination) imaginación f ♦ a (luxury) de lujo; (price) exorbitado ♦ vt (feel like, want) tener ganas de; (imagine) imaginarse, figurarse; **to take a ~ to sb** tomar cariño a uno; **when the ~ takes him** cuando se le antoja; **it took** or **caught my ~** me cayó en gracia; **to ~ that...** imaginarse que...; **he fancies her** le gusta (ella) mucho.

fancy dress n disfraz m.

fancy-dress ball [fan'sēdrεs bôl'] n baile m de disfraces.

fancy goods n artículos mpl de fantasía.

fanfare [fan'fār] n fanfarria (de trompeta).

fanfold paper [fan'fōld pā'pûr] n papel m plegado en abanico or en acordeón.

fang [fang] n colmillo.

fan heater n (Brit) soplador m de aire caliente.

fanlight [fan'līt] n (montante m de) abanico.

fantasize [fan'təsīz] vi fantasear, hacerse ilusiones.

fantastic [fantas'tik] a fantástico.

fantasy [fan'təsē] n fantasía.

FAO n abbr (= Food and Agriculture Organization) OAA f.

far [fär] a (distant) lejano ♦ ad lejos; **the ~ left/right** (POL) la extrema izquierda/derecha; **~ away**, **~ off** (a lo) lejos; **~ better** mucho mejor; **~ from** lejos de; **by ~** con mucho; **it's by ~ the best** es con mucho el mejor; **go as ~ as the farm** vaya hasta la granja; **is it ~ to New York?** ¿a cuánto está Nueva York?; **it's not ~ (from here)** no está lejos (de aquí); **as ~ as I know** que yo sepa; **how ~ have you got with your work?** ¿hasta dónde has llegado en tu trabajo?

faraway [fär'əwā] a remoto; (voice) distraído; (look) ausente, perdido.

farce [färs] n farsa.

farcical [fär'sikəl] a absurdo.

fare [fär] n (on trains, buses) precio (del billete); (in taxi: cost) tarifa; (: passenger) pasajero; (food) comida; **half/full ~** medio pasaje m/pasaje m completo.

Far East n: **the ~** el Extremo or Lejano Oriente.

farewell [fär'wel'] *excl, n* adiós *m.*
far-fetched [fär'fccht'] *a* inverosímil.
farm [färm] *n* granja, finca, estancia (*LAm*)
♦ *vt* cultivar.
 farm out *vt* (*work*): **to ~ out (to sb)**
 mandar hacer fuera (a uno).
farmer [fär'mûr] *n* granjero, estanciero
(*LAm*).
farmhand [färm'hand] *n* peón *m.*
farmhouse [färm'hous] *n* granja, casa de
hacienda (*LAm*).
farming [fär'ming] *n* (*gen*) agricultura; (*till-
ing*) cultivo; **sheep ~** cría de ovejas.
farm laborer *n* = **farmhand.**
farmland [färm'land] *n* tierra de cultivo.
farm produce *n* productos *mpl* agrícolas.
farm worker *n* = **farmhand.**
farmyard [färm'yärd] *n* corral *m.*
Faroe Islands [fe'rō ī'ləndz], **Faroes** [fer'ōz]
npl: **the ~** las Islas Feroe.
far-reaching [fär'rē'ching] *a* (*reform,
effect*) de gran alcance.
farsighted [fär'sī'tid] *a* présbita; (*fig*) previ-
sor(a).
farsightedness [fär'sī'tidnis] *n* clarivi-
dencia, previsión *f.*
fart [färt] (*col!*) *n* pedo (*!*) ♦ *vi* tirarse un
pedo (*!*).
farther [fär'thûr] *ad* más lejos, más allá ♦ *a*
más lejano.
farthest [fär'thist] *superlative of* **far.**
FAS *abbr* (= *free alongside ship*) franco al
costado del buque.
fascinate [fas'ənāt] *vt* fascinar.
fascinating [fas'ənāting] *a* fascinante.
fascination [fasənā'shən] *n* fascinación *f.*
fascism [fash'izəm] *n* fascismo.
fascist [fash'ist] *a, n* fascista *m/f.*
fashion [fash'ən] *n* moda; (*manner*) manera
♦ *vt* formar; **in ~** a la moda; **out of ~** pasado de moda; **in the Greek ~** a la griega,
al estilo griego; **after a ~** (*finish, manage
etc*) en cierto modo.
fashionable [fash'ənəbəl] *a* de moda; (*writer*) de moda, popular; **it is ~ to do ...** está
de moda hacer ....
fashion designer *n* modisto/a.
fashion show *n* desfile *m* de modelos.
fast [fast] *a* (*also PHOT: film*) rápido; (*dye,
color*) sólido; (*clock*): **to be ~** estar adelantado ♦ *ad* rápidamente, de prisa; (*stuck,
held*) firmemente ♦ *n* ayuno ♦ *vi* ayunar; **~
asleep** profundamente dormido; **in the ~
lane** (*AUT*) en el carril de adelantamiento;
my watch is 5 minutes ~ mi reloj está
adelantado 5 minutos; **as ~ as I** *etc* **can** lo
más rápido posible.
fasten [fas'ən] *vt* asegurar, sujetar; (*coat,
belt*) abrochar ♦ *vi* cerrarse.
 fasten (up)on *vt fus* (*idea*) aferrarse a.
fastener [fas'ənûr] *n* cierre *m*; (*of door etc*)
cerrojo; (*Brit: zip ~*) cremallera.
fastening [fas'əning] *n* = **fastener.**

fast food *n* comida rápida, platos *mpl* preparados.
fastidious [fastid'ēəs] *a* (*fussy*) delicado;
(*demanding*) exigente.
fat [fat] *a* gordo; (*meat*) con mucha grasa;
(*greasy*) grasiento ♦ *n* grasa; (*on person*)
carnes *fpl*; (*lard*) manteca; **to live off the
~ of the land** vivir a cuerpo de rey.
fatal [fāt'əl] *a* (*mistake*) fatal; (*injury*)
mortal; (*consequence*) funesto.
fatalism [fāt'əlizəm] *n* fatalismo.
fatality [fātal'itē] *n* (*road death etc*) víctima
f.
fatally [fāt'əlē] *ad*: **~ injured** herido a
muerte.
fate [fāt] *n* destino, sino.
fated [fā'tid] *a* predestinado.
fateful [fāt'fəl] *a* fatídico.
father [fä'thûr] *n* padre *m.*
Father Christmas *n* (*Brit*) Papá *m* Noel.
fatherhood [fä'thûrhood] *n* paternidad *f.*
father-in-law [fä'thûrinlô] *n* suegro.
fatherland [fä'thûrland] *n* patria.
fatherly [fä'thûrlē] *a* paternal.
fathom [fath'əm] *n* braza ♦ *vt* (*unravel*)
desentrañar; (*understand*) concebir.
fatigue [fətēg'] *n* fatiga, cansancio; **metal ~**
fatiga del metal.
fatness [fat'nis] *n* gordura.
fatten [fat'ən] *vt, vi* engordar; **chocolate is
~ing** el chocolate engorda.
fatty [fat'ē] *a* (*food*) graso ♦ *n* (*fam*)
gordito/a, gordinflón/ona *m/f.*
fatuous [fach'ōōəs] *a* fatuo, necio.
faucet [fô'sit] *n* (*US*) grifo, llave *f* (*LAm*).
fault [fôlt] *n* (*blame*) culpa; (*defect: in
character*) defecto; (*in manufacture*) desperfecto; (*GEO*) falla ♦ *vt* criticar; **it's my
~** es culpa mía; **to find ~ with** criticar,
poner peros a; **at ~** culpable.
faultless [fôlt'lis] *a* (*action*) intachable;
(*person*) sin defectos.
faulty [fôl'tē] *a* defectuoso.
fauna [fôn'ə] *n* fauna.
faux pas [fō pä'] *n* plancha.
favor [fā'vûr] *n* favor *m*; (*approval*) aprobación *f* ♦ *vt* (*proposition*) estar a favor de,
aprobar; (*person etc*) favorecer; (*assist*)
ser propicio a; **to ask a ~ of** pedir un favor a; **to do sb a ~** hacer un favor a uno;
to find ~ with sb (*subj: person*) caerle
bien a uno; (: *suggestion*) tener buena acogida por parte de uno; **in ~ of** a favor de;
to be in ~ of sth/of doing sth ser partidario *or* estar a favor de algo/de hacer algo.
favorable [fā'vûrəbəl] *a* favorable.
favorably [fā'vûrəblē] *ad* favorablemente.
favorite [fā'vûrit] *a, n* favorito, preferido.
favoritism [fā'vûritizəm] *n* favoritismo.
favour [fā'vûr] *etc* (*Brit*) = **favor** *etc.*
fawn [fôn] *n* cervato ♦ *a* (*also:* **~-colored**)
color de cervato, leonado ♦ *vi*: **to ~ (up)on**
adular.

fax [faks] *n* (*document*) facsímil(e) *m*; (*machine*) telefax *m* ♦ *vt* mandar *or* enviar por telefax.

fazed [fāzd] *a* (*fam*) pasmado.

FBI *n abbr* (*US*: = *Federal Bureau of Investigation*) ≈ BIC *f* (*Sp*).

FCA *n abbr* (*US*) = *Farm Credit Administration*.

FCC *n abbr* (*US*) = *Federal Communications Commission*.

FCO *n abbr* (*Brit*: = *Foreign and Commonwealth Office*) ≈ Min. de AA. EE.

FD *n abbr* (*US*) = **fire department**.

FDA *n abbr* (*US*: = *Food and Drug Administration*) oficina que se ocupa del control de los productos alimentarios y farmacéuticos.

FDIC *n abbr* (*US*) = *Federal Deposit Insurance Corporation*.

fear [fēr] *n* miedo, temor *m* ♦ *vt* temer; **for ~ of** por temor a; **~ of heights** vértigo; **to ~ for/that** temer por/que.

fearful [fēr'fəl] *a* temeroso, miedoso; (*awful*) terrible; **to be ~ of** (*frightened*) tener miedo de.

fearfully [fēr'fəlē] *ad* (*timidly*) con miedo; (*col: very*) terriblemente.

fearless [fēr'lis] *a* (*gen*) sin miedo *or* temor; (*bold*) audaz.

fearlessly [fēr'lislē] *ad* temerariamente.

fearlessness [fēr'lisnis] *n* temeridad *f*.

fearsome [fēr'səm] *a* (*opponent*) temible; (*sight*) espantoso.

feasibility [fēzəbil'ətē] *n* factibilidad *f*, viabilidad *f*.

feasibility study *n* estudio de factibilidad.

feasible [fē'zəbəl] *a* factible.

feast [fēst] *n* banquete *m*; (*REL: also:* ~ **day**) fiesta ♦ *vi* banquetear.

feat [fēt] *n* hazaña.

feather [feth'ûr] *n* pluma ♦ *vt*: **to ~ one's nest** (*fig*) hacer su agosto, sacar tajada ♦ *cpd* (*mattress, bed, pillow*) de plumas.

featherweight [feth'ûrwāt] *n* (*BOXING*) peso pluma.

feature [fē'chûr] *n* (*gen*) característica; (*ANAT*) rasgo; (*article*) artículo de fondo ♦ *vt* (*subj: film*) presentar ♦ *vi* figurar; **~s** *npl* (*of face*) facciones *fpl*; **a (special) ~ on sth/sb** un artículo de fondo sobre algo/uno; **it ~d prominently in** ... tuvo un papel destacado en ....

feature film *n* largometraje *m*.

Feb. *abbr* (= *February*) feb.

February [feb'yəwärē] *n* febrero.

feces [fē'sēz] *npl* excremento *sg*, heces *fpl*.

feckless [fek'lis] *a* irresponsable, irreflexivo.

Fed *abbr* (*US*) = **federal, federation**.

fed [fed] *pt*, *pp* of **feed**.

Fed. *n abbr* (*US col*) = *Federal Reserve Board*.

federal [fed'ûrəl] *a* federal.

Federal Republic of Germany *n* República Federal de Alemania.

federation [fedərā'shən] *n* federación *f*.

fedora [fədôr'ə] *n* (*US*) sombrero flexible *or* tirolés.

fed-up [fedup'] *a*: **to be ~ (with)** estar harto (de).

fee [fē] *n* (*professional*) derechos *mpl*, honorarios *mpl*; (*of school*) matrícula; (*entrance ~, membership ~*) cuota; **for a small ~** por poco dinero.

feeble [fē'bəl] *a* débil.

feeble-minded [fē'bəlmīndid] *a* imbécil.

feed [fēd] *n* (*gen, of baby*) comida; (*of animal*) pienso; (*on printer*) dispositivo de alimentación ♦ *vt* (*pt, pp* **fed**) (*gen*) alimentar; (*Brit: baby: breastfeed*) dar el pecho a; (*animal*) dar de comer a ♦ *vi* (*baby, animal*) comer.

feed back *vt* (*results*) pasar.

feed in *vt* (*COMPUT*) introducir.

feed into *vt* (*data, information*) suministrar a; **to ~ sth into a machine** introducir algo en una máquina.

feed on *vt fus* alimentarse de.

feedback [fēd'bak] *n* (*from person*) reacción *f*; (*TEC*) feedback *m*.

feeder [fē'dûr] *n* (*bib*) babero.

feeding bottle [fē'ding bât'əl] *n* (*Brit*) biberón *m*.

feel [fēl] *n* (*sensation*) sensación *f*; (*sense of touch*) tacto ♦ *vt* (*pt, pp* **felt**) tocar; (*cold, pain etc*) sentir; (*think, believe*) creer; **to get the ~ of sth** (*fig*) acostumbrarse a algo; **to ~ hungry/cold** tener hambre/frío; **to ~ lonely/better** sentirse solo/mejor; **I don't ~ well** no me siento bien; **it ~s soft** es suave al tacto; **it ~s colder out here** se siente más frío aquí fuera; **to ~ like** (*want*) tener ganas de; **I'm still ~ing my way** (*fig*) aún me voy orientando; **I ~ that you ought to do it** creo que debes hacerlo; **to ~ around** tantear.

feeler [fē'lûr] *n* (*of insect*) antena; **to put out ~s** (*fig*) sondear.

feeling [fē'ling] *n* (*physical*) sensación *f*; (*foreboding*) presentimiento; (*impression*) impresión *f*; (*emotion*) sentimiento; **what are your ~s about the matter?** ¿qué opinas tú del asunto?; **to hurt sb's ~s** ofenderle a uno; **~s ran high about it** causó mucha controversia; **I got the ~ that** ... me dio la impresión de que ...; **there was a general ~ that** ... la opinión general fue que ....

feet [fēt] *npl of* **foot**.

feign [fān] *vt* fingir.

feigned [fānd] *a* fingido.

feline [fē'līn] *a* felino.

fell [fel] *pt of* **fall** ♦ *vt* (*tree*) talar ♦ *a*: **with one ~ blow** con un golpe feroz; **in one ~ swoop** de un solo golpe.

fellow [fel'ō] *n* tipo, tío (*Sp*); (*of learned society*) socio/a; (*UNIV*) miembro de la junta *de gobierno de un colegio* ♦ *cpd:* ~ **students** compañeros/as *m/fpl* de curso, condiscípulos/as *m/fpl.*

fellow citizen *n* conciudadano/a.

fellow countryman *n* compatriota *m.*

fellow feeling *n* compañerismo.

fellow men *npl* semejantes *mpl.*

fellowship [fel'ōship] *n* compañerismo; (*grant*) beca.

fellow traveler *n* compañero/a de viaje; (*POL: with communists*) simpatizante *m/f.*

fellow worker *n* colega *m/f.*

felon [fel'ən] *n* criminal *m/f.*

felony [fel'ənē] *n* crimen *m.*

felt [felt] *pt, pp of* **feel** ♦ *n* fieltro.

felt-tip pen [felt'tip pen'] *n* rotulador *m.*

female [fē'māl] *n* (*woman*) mujer *f;* (*ZOOL*) hembra ♦ *a* femenino.

feminine [fem'ənin] *a* femenino.

femininity [femənin'ətē] *n* feminidad *f.*

feminism [fem'ənizəm] *n* feminismo.

feminist [fem'ənist] *n* feminista.

fence [fens] *n* valla, cerca; (*RACING*) valla ♦ *vt* (*also:* ~ **in**) cercar ♦ *vi* hacer esgrima; **to sit on the** ~ (*fig*) nadar entre dos aguas.

fence in *vt* cercar.

fence off *vt* separar con cerca.

fencing [fen'sing] *n* esgrima.

fend [fend] *vi:* **to** ~ **for o.s.** valerse por sí mismo.

fend off *vt* (*attack, attacker*) rechazar, repeler; (*blow*) desviar; (*awkward question*) evadir.

fender [fen'dûr] *n* guardafuego; (*US: AUT*) parachoques *m inv;* (*: RAIL*) trompa.

fennel [fen'əl] *n* hinojo.

FEPC *n abbr* (*US*) = *Fair Employment Practices Committee.*

FERC *n abbr* (*US*) = *Federal Energy Regulatory Commission.*

ferment *vi* [fûrment'] fermentar ♦ *n* [fûr'ment] (*fig*) agitación *f.*

fermentation [fûrmentā'shən] *n* fermentación *f.*

fern [fûrn] *n* helecho.

ferocious [fərō'shəs] *a* feroz.

ferociously [fərō'shəslē] *ad* ferozmente, con ferocidad.

ferocity [fərâs'itē] *n* ferocidad *f.*

ferret [fär'it] *n* hurón *m.*

ferret around *vi* buscar.

ferret out *vt* (*secret, truth*) desentrañar.

Ferris wheel [fär'is wēl] *n* (*at fair*) noria.

ferry [fär'ē] *n* (*small*) barca (de pasaje), balsa; (*large: also:* ~**boat**) transbordador *m,* ferry *m* ♦ *vt* transportar; **to** ~ **sth/sb across** *or* **over** transportar algo/a uno a la otra orilla; **to** ~ **sb to and fro** llevar a uno de un lado para otro.

ferryman [fär'ēmən] *n* barquero.

fertile [fûr'təl] *a* fértil; (*BIOL*) fecundo.

fertility [fûrtil'ətē] *n* fertilidad *f;* fecundidad

f.

fertility drug *n* medicamento contra la infertilidad.

fertilization [fûrtələzā'shən] *n* fertilización *f.*

fertilize [fûr'təlīz] *vt* fertilizar; (*BIOL*) fecundar; (*AGR*) abonar.

fertilizer [fûr'təlīzûr] *n* abono, fertilizante *m.*

fervent [fûr'vənt] *a* (*admirer*) entusiasta; (*hope*) ferviente.

fervor, (*Brit*) **fervour** [fûr'vûr] *n* fervor *m,* ardor *m.*

fester [fes'tûr] *vi* ulcerarse.

festival [fes'təvəl] *n* (*REL*) fiesta; (*ART, MUS*) festival *m.*

festive [fes'tiv] *a* festivo; **the** ~ **season** (*Brit: Christmas*) las Navidades.

festivities [festiv'itēz] *npl* fiestas *fpl.*

festoon [festōōn'] *vt:* **to** ~ **with** festonear *or* engalanar de.

FET *n abbr* (*US*) = *Federal Excise Tax.*

fetal [fēt'l] *a* fetal.

fetch [fech] *vt* ir a buscar; (*Brit: sell for*) venderse por.

fetching [fech'ing] *a* atractivo.

fête [fet] *n* fiesta.

fetid [fet'id] *a* fétido.

fetish [fet'ish] *n* fetiche *m.*

fetter [fet'ûr] *vt* (*person*) encadenar, poner en grillos; (*horse*) trabar; (*fig*) poner trabas a.

fetters [fet'ûrz] *npl* grillos *mpl.*

fettle [fet'əl] *n:* **in fine** ~ en buenas condiciones.

fetus [fē'təs] *n* feto.

feud [fyōōd] *n* (*hostility*) enemistad *f;* (*quarrel*) disputa; **a family** ~ una pelea familiar.

feudal [fyōōd'əl] *a* feudal.

feudalism [fyōō'dəlizəm] *n* feudalismo.

fever [fē'vûr] *n* fiebre *f;* **he has a** ~ tiene fiebre.

feverish [fē'vûrish] *a* febril.

feverishly [fē'vûrishlē] *ad* febrilmente.

few [fyōō] *a* (*not many*) pocos; (*some*) algunos, unos ♦ *pron* algunos; **a** ~ *a* unos pocos; ~ **people** poca gente; **a good** ~, **quite a** ~ bastantes; **in** *or* **over the next** ~ **days** en los próximos días; **every** ~ **weeks** cada 2 o 3 semanas; **a** ~ **more days** unos días más.

fewer [fyōō'ûr] *a* menos.

fewest [fyōō'ist] *a* los/las menos.

FFA *n abbr* = *Future Farmers of America.*

FHA *n abbr* (*US:* = *Federal Housing Association*) *oficina federal de la vivienda.*

fiancé [fēânsā'] *n* novio, prometido.

fiancée [fēânsā'] *n* novia, prometida.

fiasco [fēas'kō] *n* fiasco.

fib [fib] *n* mentirilla ♦ *vi* decir mentirillas.

fiber, (*Brit*) **fibre** [fī'bûr] *n* fibra.

fiberboard, (*Brit*) **fibreboard** [fī'bûrbôrd] *n* fibra vulcanizada.

fiberglass, (*Brit*) **fibreglass** |fī'bûrglas| *n* fibra de vidrio.

fibrositis |fībrəsī'tis| *n* fibrositis *f inv*.

FIC *n abbr* (*US*) = *Federal Information Centers*.

FICA *n abbr* (*US*) = *Federal Insurance Contributions Act*.

fickle |fik'əl| *a* inconstante.

fiction |fik'shən| *n* (*gen*) ficción *f*.

fictional |fik'shənəl| *a* novelesco.

fictionalize |fik'shənəlīz| *vt* novelar.

fictitious |fiktish'əs| *a* ficticio.

fiddle |fid'əl| *n* (*MUS*) violín *m*; (*cheating*) trampa ♦ *vt* (*Brit*: *accounts*) falsificar; **to work a** ~ hacer trampa.
fiddle with *vt fus* jugar con.

fiddler |fid'lûr| *n* violinista *m/f*.

fiddly |fid'lē| *a* (*task*) delicado, mañoso; (*object*) cargado.

fidelity |fidel'itē| *n* fidelidad *f*.

fidget |fij'it| *vi* inquietarse.

fidgety |fij'itē| *a* nervioso.

fiduciary |fidoō'shēärē| *n* fiduciario/a.

field |fēld| *n* (*gen*, *COMPUT*) campo; (*fig*) campo, esfera; (*SPORT*) campo, cancha (*LAm*); (*competitors*) competidores *mpl* ♦ *cpd*: **to have a** ~ **day** (*fig*) sacar el máximo provecho; **to lead the** ~ (*SPORT*, *COMM*) llevar la delantera; **to give sth a year's trial in the** ~ (*fig*) sacar algo al mercado a prueba por un año; **my particular** ~ mi especialidad.

field glasses *npl* gemelos *mpl*.

field marshal *n* mariscal *m*.

fieldwork |fēld'wûrk| *n* (*ARCHEOLOGY*, *GEO*) trabajo de campo.

fiend |fēnd| *n* demonio.

fiendish |fēn'dish| *a* diabólico.

fierce |fērs| *a* feroz; (*wind*, *attack*) violento; (*heat*) intenso; (*fighting*, *enemy*) encarnizado.

fiercely |fērs'lē| *ad* con ferocidad; violentamente; intensamente; encarnizadamente.

fierceness |fērs'nis| *n* ferocidad *f*; violencia; intensidad *f*; encarnizamiento.

fiery |fī'ûrē| *a* (*burning*) ardiente; (*temperament*) apasionado.

FIFA |fē'fa| *n abbr* (= *Fédération Internationale de Football Association*) FIFA *f*.

fifteen |fif'tēn'| *num* quince.

fifth |fifth| *num* quinto.

fiftieth |fif'tēith| *num* quincuagésimo.

fifty |fif'tē| *num* cincuenta; **the fifties** los años cincuenta; **to be in one's fifties** andar por los cincuenta.

fifty-fifty |fif'tēfif'tē| *ad*: **to go** ~ **with sb** ir a medias con uno ♦ *a*: **we have a** ~ **chance of success** tenemos un cincuenta por ciento de posibilidades de tener éxito.

fig |fig| *n* higo.

fight |fīt| *n* (*gen*) pelea; (*MIL*) combate *m*; (*struggle*) lucha ♦ *vb* (*pt*, *pp* **fought**) *vt* luchar contra; (*cancer*, *alcoholism*) comba-

tir; (*LAW*): **to** ~ **a case** defenderse; (*quarrel*): **to** ~ (**with sb**) pelear (con uno) ♦ *vi* pelear, luchar; (*fig*): **to** ~ (**for/against**) luchar por/contra.

fight back *vi* defenderse; (*after illness*) recuperarse ♦ *vt* (*tears*) contener.

fight down *vt* (*anger*, *anxiety*, *urge*) reprimir.

fight off *vt* (*attack*, *attacker*) rechazar; (*disease*, *sleep*, *urge*) luchar contra.

fight out *vt*: **to** ~ **it out** luchar hasta resolverlo.

fighter |fī'tûr| *n* combatiente *m/f*; (*fig*) luchador(a) *m/f*; (*plane*) caza *m*.

fighter-bomber |fī'tûrbâm'ûr| *n* cazabombardero.

fighter pilot *n* piloto de caza.

fighting |fī'ting| *n* (*gen*) el luchar; (*battle*) combate *m*; (*in streets*) disturbios *mpl*.

figment |fig'mənt| *n*: **a** ~ **of the imagination** una quimera.

figurative |fig'yûrətiv| *a* (*meaning*) figurado; (*ART*) figurativo.

figure |fig'yûr| *n* (*DRAWING*, *GEOM*) figura, dibujo; (*number*, *cipher*) cifra; (*person*) figura; (*body*, *outline*) talle *m*, tipo ♦ *vt* (*esp US*: *think*, *calculate*) calcular, imaginarse ♦ *vi* (*appear*) figurar; (*esp US*: *make sense*) ser lógico; ~ **of speech** (*LING*) figura retórica; **public** ~ personaje *m*.

figure on *vt fus* (*US*) contar con.

figure out *vt* (*understand*) comprender.

figurehead |fig'yûrhed| *n* (*fig*) testaferro.

figure skating *n* patinaje *m* de figuras.

Fiji (Islands) |fē'jē (ī'ləndz)| *n(pl)* (Islas *fpl* de) Fiji *fpl*.

filament |fil'əmənt| *n* (*ELEC*) filamento.

filch |filch| *vt* (*col*: *steal*) hurtar, robar.

file |fīl| *n* (*tool*) lima; (*for nails*) lima de uñas; (*dossier*) expediente *m*; (*folder*) carpeta; (*in cabinet*) archivo; (*COMPUT*) fichero; (*row*) fila ♦ *vt* limar; (*papers*) clasificar; (*LAW*: *claim*) presentar; (*store*) archivar; **to open/close a** ~ (*COMPUT*) abrir/cerrar un fichero; **to** ~ **in/out** *vi* entrar/salir en fila; **to** ~ **a suit against sb** entablar pleito contra uno; **to** ~ **past** desfilar ante.

file name *n* (*COMPUT*) nombre *m* de fichero.

filibuster |fil'əbustûr| (*esp US*: *POL*) *n* filibustero/a ♦ *vi* ser un(a) filibustero/a.

filing |fī'ling| *n*: **to do the** ~ llevar los archivos.

filing cabinet *n* fichero, archivo.

filing clerk *n* oficinista *m/f*.

fill |fil| *vt* llenar; (*tooth*) empastar; (*vacancy*) cubrir ♦ *n*: **to eat one's** ~ llenarse; **we've already** ~**ed that vacancy** ya hemos cubierto esa vacante; ~**ed with admiration (for)** lleno de admiración (por).

fill in *vt* rellenar; (*details*, *report*) completar; **to** ~ **sb in on sth** (*col*) poner a uno al corriente *or* al día sobre algo.

fill out *vt* (*form, receipt*) rellenar.

fill up *vt* llenar (hasta el borde) ♦ *vi* (*AUT*) poner gasolina.

fillet [filā'] *n* filete *m*.

fillet steak *n* filete *m* de ternera.

filling [fil'ing] *n* (*CULIN*) relleno; (*for tooth*) empaste *m*.

filling station *n* estación *f* de servicio.

fillip [fil'əp] *n* estímulo.

filly [fil'ē] *n* potra.

film [film] *n* película ♦ *vt* (*scene*) filmar ♦ *vi* rodar (una película).

film script *n* guión *m*.

film star *n* astro, estrella de cine.

filmstrip [film'strip] *n* tira de película.

film studio *n* estudio de cine.

filter [fil'tûr] *n* filtro ♦ *vt* filtrar.

filter in, filter through *vi* filtrarse.

filter coffee *n* café *m* (molido) para filtrar.

filter lane *n* (*Brit*) carril *m* de selección.

filter-tipped [fil'tûrtipt] *a* con filtro.

filth [filth] *n* suciedad *f*.

filthy [fil'thē] *a* sucio; (*language*) obsceno.

fin [fin] *n* (*gen*) aleta.

fin. *abbr* = **finance.**

final [fī'nəl] *a* (*last*) final, último; (*definitive*) definitivo, terminante ♦ *n* (*SPORT*) final *f*; ~**s** *npl* (*SCOL*) examen *m* de fin de curso; ~ **demand** (*on invoice etc*) último aviso; ~ **dividend** dividendo final.

finale [final'ē] *n* final *m*.

finalist [fī'nəlist] *n* (*SPORT*) finalista *m/f*.

finality [final'itē] *n* finalidad *f*; **with an air of** ~ en tono resuelto, de modo terminante.

finalize [fī'nəliz] *vt* concluir, completar.

finally [fī'nəlē] *ad* (*lastly*) por último, finalmente; (*eventually*) por fin; (*irrevocably*) de modo definitivo; (*once and for all*) definitivamente.

finance [fī'nans] *n* (*money, funds*) fondos *mpl*; ~**s** *npl* finanzas *fpl* ♦ *cpd* (*page, section, company*) financiero ♦ *vt* [finans'] financiar.

financial [finan'chəl] *a* financiero.

financially [finan'chəlē] *ad* económicamente.

financial management *n* gestión *f* financiera.

financial statement *n* estado financiero.

financial year *n* ejercicio (financiero).

financier [finansiûr'] *n* financiero/a.

find [fīnd] *vt* (*pt, pp* **found** [found]) (*gen*) encontrar, hallar; (*come upon*) descubrir ♦ *n* hallazgo; descubrimiento; **to** ~ **sb guilty** (*LAW*) declarar culpable a uno; **to** ~ **(some) difficulty in doing sth** encontrar dificultad en hacer algo.

find out *vt* averiguar; (*truth, secret*) descubrir ♦ *vi*: **to** ~ **out about** enterarse de.

findings [fīn'dingz] *npl* (*LAW*) veredicto *sg*, fallo *sg*; (*of report*) recomendaciones *fpl*.

fine [fīn] *a* (*delicate*) fino; (*beautiful*)

hermoso ♦ *ad* (*well*) bien ♦ *n* (*LAW*) multa ♦ *vt* (*LAW*) multar; **the weather is** ~ hace buen tiempo; **he's** ~ está muy bien; **you're doing** ~ lo estás haciendo muy bien; **to cut it** ~ (*of time, money*) calcular muy justo; **to get a** ~ **for (doing) sth** recibir una multa por (hacer) algo.

fine arts *npl* bellas artes *fpl*.

finely [fīn'lē] *ad* (*splendidly*) con elegancia; (*chop*) en trozos pequeños, fino; (*adjust*) con precisión.

fineness [fīn'nis] *n* (*of cloth*) finura; (*of idea*) sutilidad *f*.

finery [fī'nûrē] *n* adornos *mpl*.

finesse [fines'] *n* sutileza.

fine-tooth comb [fīn'tōōth kōm] *n*: **to go through sth with a** ~ revisar algo a fondo.

finger [fing'gûr] *n* dedo ♦ *vt* (*touch*) manosear; (*MUS*) puntear; **little/index** ~ (dedo) meñique *m*/índice *m*.

fingernail [fing'gûrnāl] *n* uña.

fingerprint [fing'gûrprint] *n* huella dactilar ♦ *vt* tomar las huellas dactilares de.

fingertip [fing'gûrtip] *n* yema del dedo; **to have sth at one's** ~**s** saberse algo al dedillo.

finicky [fin'ikē] *a* (*fussy*) delicado.

finish [fin'ish] *n* (*end*) fin *m*; (*SPORT*) meta; (*polish etc*) acabado ♦ *vt, vi* terminar; **to** ~ **doing sth** acabar de hacer algo; **to** ~ **first/second/third** (*SPORT*) llegar el primero/segundo/tercero; **I've** ~**ed with the paper** he terminado con el periódico; **she's** ~**ed with him** ha roto *or* acabado con él.

finish off *vt* acabar, terminar; (*kill*) rematar.

finish up *vt* acabar, terminar ♦ *vi* ir a parar, terminar.

finished [fin'isht] *a* (*product*) acabado; (*performance*) pulido; (*col: tired*) rendido, hecho polvo.

finishing [fin'ishing] *a*: ~ **touches** toque *m* final.

finishing line [fin'ishing līn] *n* línea de llegada *or* meta.

finishing school [fin'ishing skōōl] *n* academia para señoritas.

finite [fī'nit] *a* finito.

Finland [fin'lənd] *n* Finlandia.

Finn [fin] *n* finlandés/esa *m/f*.

Finnish [fin'ish] *a* finlandés/esa ♦ *n* (*LING*) finlandés *m*.

fiord [fyôrd] *n* fiordo.

fir [fûr] *n* abeto.

fire [fī'ûr] *n* fuego; (*accidental, damaging*) incendio ♦ *vt* (*gun*) disparar; (*set fire to*) incendiar; (*excite*) exaltar; (*interest*) despertar; (*dismiss*) despedir ♦ *vi* encenderse; (*AUT: subj: engine*) encender; **on** ~ ardiendo, en llamas; **to be on** ~ estar ardiendo; **to catch** ~ encenderse; **to set** ~ **to sth, set sth on** ~ prender fuego a algo; **insured against** ~ asegurado contra

incendios; **to be/come under** ~ estar/caer
bajo fuego. .
fire alarm *n* alarma de incendios.
firearm |fiŭr'árm| *n* arma de fuego.
fire department, (*Brit*) **fire brigade** *n*
(cuerpo de) bomberos *mpl*.
fire drill *n* simulacro de incendio.
fire engine *n* coche *m* de bomberos.
fire escape *n* escalera de incendios.
fire extinguisher *n* extintor *m* (de fuego).
fire hazard *n* = **fire risk.**
fire hydrant *n* boca de incendios.
fire insurance *n* seguro contra incendios.
fireman |fiŭr'mən| *n* bombero.
fireplace |fiŭr'plās| *n* chimenea.
fireplug |fiŭr'plug| *n* (*US*) boca de
incendios.
fireproof |fiŭr'prōōf| *a* a prueba de fuego;
(*material*) incombustible.
fire regulations *npl* reglamentos *mpl* contra incendios.
fire risk *n* peligro de incendio.
firescreen |fiŭr'skrēn| *n* pantalla refracta-
ria.
fireside |fiŭr'sĭd| *n*: **by the** ~ al lado de la
chimenea.
fire station *n* parque *m* de bomberos.
firewood |fiŭr'wŏŏd| *n* leña.
fireworks |fiŭr'wûrks| *npl* fuegos *mpl* arti-
ficiales.
firing |fiŭr'ing| *n* (*MIL.*) disparos *mpl*, tiroteo.
firing line *n* línea de fuego; **to be on the**
~ (*fig: liable to be criticized*) estar en la línea de fuego.
firing squad *n* pelotón *m* de ejecución.
firm |fûrm| *a* firme; (*offer, decision*) en
firme ♦ *n* firma, empresa; **to be a** ~ **believer in sth** ser un partidario convencido
de algo; **to stand** ~ *or* **take a** ~ **stand
over sth** (*fig*) mantenerse firme ante algo.
firmly |fûrm'lē| *ad* firmemente.
firmness |fûrm'nis| *n* firmeza.
first |fûrst| *a* primero ♦ *ad* (*before others*)
primero; (*when listing reasons etc*) en primer lugar, primeramente ♦ *n* (*person: in
race*) primero/a; (*AUT: also:* ~ **gear**) primera; **at** ~ al principio; ~ **of all** ante
todo; **the** ~ **of January** el uno *or* primero
de enero; **in the** ~ **instance** en primer lugar; **I'll do it** ~ **thing tomorrow** lo haré
mañana a primera hora; **for the** ~ **time**
por primera vez; **head** ~ de cabeza; **from
the (very)** ~ desde el principio.
first aid *n* primera ayuda, primeros auxilios
mpl.
first aid kit *n* botiquín *m*.
first aid station, (*Brit*) **first aid post** *n*
puesto de auxilio.
first-class |fûrst'klas'| *a* de primera clase;
~ **ticket** (*RAIL etc*) billete *m* *or* boleto
(*LAm*) de primera clase; ~ **mail** correo de
primera.
first-hand |fûrst'hand'| *a* de primera mano.

first lady *n* (*esp US*) primera dama.
firstly |fûrst'lē| *ad* en primer lugar.
first name *n* nombre *m* de pila.
first night *n* estreno.
first-rate |fûrst'rāt'| *a* de primera clase.
fir tree *n* abeto.
fiscal |fis'kəl| *a* fiscal; ~ **year** año fiscal,
ejercicio.
fish |fish| *n, pl inv* pez *m*; (*food*) pescado ♦
vt, vi pescar; **to go** ~**ing** ir de pesca.
fish out *vt* (*from water, box etc*) sacar.
fishbone |fish'bōn| *n* espina.
fisherman |fish'ûrmən| *n* pescador *m*.
fishery |fish'ûrē| *n* pesquería.
fish factory *n* fábrica de elaboración de
pescado.
fish farm *n* piscifactoría.
fish fingers *npl* (*Brit*) croquetas *fpl* de
pescado.
fishing boat |fish'ing bōt| *n* barca de
pesca.
fishing industry *n* industria pesquera.
fishing line *n* sedal *m*.
fishing net *n* red *f* de pesca.
fishing rod *n* caña (de pescar).
fishing tackle *n* aparejo (de pescar).
fish market *n* mercado de pescado.
fishmonger |fish'munggûr| *n* pescadero/a.
fishmonger's (shop) *n* pescadería.
fishseller |fish'selûr| *n* (*US*) pescadero(a).
fish slice *n* paleta para pescado.
fish sticks *npl* (*US*) croquetas *fpl* de pescado.
fishstore |fish'stôr| *n* (*US*) pescadería.
fishy |fish'ē| *a* (*fig*) sospechoso.
fission |fish'ən| *n* fisión *f*; **atomic/nuclear** ~
fisión *f* atómica/nuclear.
fissure |fish'ûr| *n* fisura.
fist |fist| *n* puño.
fistfight |fist'fīt| *n* lucha a puñetazos.
fit |fit| *a* (*MED, SPORT*) en (buena) forma;
(*proper*) adecuado, apropiado ♦ *vt* (*subj:
clothes*) sentar bien a; (*try on: clothes*)
probar; (*match: facts*) cuadrar *or* corresponder *or* coincidir con; (*description*)
estar de acuerdo con; (*accommodate*) ajustar, adaptar ♦ *vi* (*clothes*) entallar; (*in
space, gap*) caber; (*facts*) coincidir ♦ *n*
(*MED*) ataque *m*; (*outburst*) arranque *m*;
~ **to** apto para; ~ **for** apropiado para; **to
do as you think** *or* **see** ~ haz lo que te parezca (mejor); **to keep** ~ mantenerse en
forma; **to be** ~ **for work** (*after illness*)
estar apto para trabajar; ~ **of coughing**
acceso de tos; ~ **of anger/enthusiasm**
arranque de cólera/entusiasmo; **to have** *or*
suffer a ~ tener un ataque *or* acceso; **this
dress is a good** ~ este vestido me sienta
bien; **by** ~**s and starts** a rachas.
fit in *vi* (*gen*) encajarse; (*fig: person*) llevarse bien (con todos) ♦ *vt* (*object*) acomo-
dar; (*fig: appointment, visitor*) incluir; **to**
~ **in with sb's plans** acomodarse a los pla-

nes de uno.

fit out *vt* (*Brit*: *also*: **fit up**) equipar.

fitful |fit'fəl| *a* espasmódico, intermitente.

fitfully |fit'fəlē| *ad* irregularmente; **to sleep** ~ dormir inquieto.

fitment |fit'mənt| *n* (*Brit*) mueble *m*.

fitness |fit'nis| *n* (*MED*) salud *f*; (*of remark*) conveniencia.

fitness activity *n* (*US*) ejercicios *mpl* para mantenerse en forma.

fitted carpet |fit'id kár'pit| *n* (*Brit*) moqueta.

fitted kitchen |fit'id kich'ən| *n* (*Brit*) cocina amueblada.

fitter |fit'úr| *n* ajustador(a) *m/f*.

fitting |fit'ing| *a* apropiado ♦ *n* (*of dress*) prueba; *see also* **fittings**.

fitting room *n* (*in shop*) probador *m*.

fittings |fit'ingz| *npl* instalaciones *fpl*.

five |fīv| *num* cinco; **she is** ~ **(years old)** tiene cinco años (de edad); **it costs** ~ **dollars** cuesta cinco dólares; **it's** ~ **(o'clock)** son las cinco.

five-day week |fīv'dā wēk'| *n* semana inglesa.

fix |fiks| *vt* (*secure*) fijar, asegurar; (*mend*) arreglar; (*make ready*: *meal*, *drink*) preparar; (*castrate*) castrar ♦ *n*: **to be in a** ~ estar en un aprieto; **to** ~ **sth in one's mind** fijar algo en la memoria.

fix on *vt* (*decide on*) fijar.

fix up *vt* (*arrange*: *date*, *meeting*) arreglar; **to** ~ **sb up with sth** proveer a uno de algo.

fixation |fiksā'shən| *n* (*PSYCH*, *fig*) obsesión *f*.

fixative |fiks'ətiv| *n* fijador *m*.

fixed |fikst| *a* (*prices etc*) fijo; **how are you** ~ **for money?** (*col*) ¿qué tal andas de dinero?

fixed assets *npl* activo *sg* fijo.

fixed charge *n* gasto fijo.

fixed-price contract |fikst'prīs' kán'trakt| *n* contrato a precio fijo.

fixture |fiks'chûr| *n* (*SPORT*) encuentro; ~**s** *npl* instalaciones *fpl* fijas.

fizz |fiz| *vi* burbujear.

fizzle out |fiz'əl out| *vi* apagarse; (*enthusiasm*, *interest*) morirse; (*plan*) fracasar.

fizzy |fiz'ē| *a* (*drink*) gaseoso.

fjord |fyôrd| *n* = **fiord**.

FL (*US MAIL*) = *Florida*.

Fla. *abbr* (*US*) = *Florida*.

flabbergasted |flab'úrgastid| *a* pasmado.

flabby |flab'ē| *a* flojo (de carnes); (*skin*) fofo.

flag |flag| *n* bandera; (*stone*) losa ♦ *vi* decaer; ~ **of convenience** pabellón *m* de conveniencia.

flag down *vt*: **to** ~ **sb down** hacer señas a uno para que se pare.

flagpole |flag'pōl| *n* asta de bandera.

flagrant |flāg'rənt| *a* flagrante.

flagship |flag'ship| *n* buque *m* insignia *or* almirante.

flagstone |flag'stōn| *n* losa.

flag stop *n* (*US*) parada a petición.

flair |flār| *n* aptitud *f* especial.

flak |flak| *n* (*MIL*) fuego antiaéreo; (*col*: *criticism*) lluvia de críticas.

flake |flāk| *n* (*of rust*, *paint*) escama; (*of snow*, *soap powder*) copo ♦ *vi* (*also*: ~ **off**) (*paint*) desconcharse; (*skin*) descamarse.

flaky |flā'kē| *a* (*paintwork*) desconchado; (*skin*) escamoso.

flaky pastry *n* (*Brit CULIN*) hojaldre *m*.

flamboyant |flamboi'ənt| *a* (*dress*) vistoso; (*person*) extravagante.

flame |flām| *n* llama; **to burst into** ~**s** incendiarse; **old** ~ (*col*) antiguo amor *m/f*.

flamingo |fləming'gō| *n* flamenco.

flammable |flam'əbəl| *a* inflamable.

flan |flan| *n* tarta.

flank |flangk| *n* flanco; (*of person*) costado ♦ *vt* flanquear.

flannel |flan'əl| *n* (*Brit*: *also*: **face** ~) manopla; (*fabric*) franela; ~**s** *npl* pantalones *mpl* de franela.

flannelette |flanəlet'| *n* franela de algodón.

flap |flap| *n* (*of pocket*, *envelope*) solapa; (*of table*) hoja (plegadiza); (*wing movement*) aletazo; (*AVIAT*) flap *m* ♦ *vt* (*wings*) aletear ♦ *vi* (*sail*, *flag*) ondear.

flapjack |flap'jak| *n* (*US*) torta, panqueque *m* (*LAm*).

flare |flār| *n* llamarada; (*MIL*) bengala; (*in skirt etc*) vuelo.

flare up *vi* encenderse; (*fig*: *person*) encolerizarse; (: *revolt*) estallar.

flash |flash| *n* relámpago; (*also*: **news** ~) noticias *fpl* de última hora; (*PHOT*) flash *m* ♦ *vt* (*light*, *headlights*) encender y apagar; (*torch*) encender ♦ *vi* brillar; **in a** ~ en un santiamén; ~ **of inspiration** ráfaga de inspiración; **to** ~ **sth about** (*fig*, *col*: *flaunt*) ostentar algo, presumir con algo; **he** ~**ed by** *or* **past** pasó como un rayo.

flashback |flash'bak| *n* flashback *m*.

flashbulb |flash'bulb| *n* bombilla fusible.

flash card *n* (*SCOL*) tarjeta, carta.

flash cube *n* cubo *m* de flash.

flashlight |flash'līt| *n* (*US*: *torch*) linterna.

flash point *n* punto de inflamación; (*fig*) punto de indignación.

flashy |flash'ē| *a* (*pej*) ostentoso.

flask |flask| *n* frasco; (*also*: **vacuum** ~) termo(s) *m*.

flat |flat| *a* llano; (*smooth*) liso; (*tire*) desinflado; (*Brit*: *battery*) descargado; (*beer*) muerto; (*MUS*: *instrument*) desafinado ♦ *n* (*Brit*: *apartment*) piso (*Sp*), departamento (*LAm*), apartamento; (*AUT*) pinchazo; (*MUS*) bemol *m*; **(to work)** ~ **out** (trabajar) a toda mecha; ~ **rate of pay** sueldo fijo.

flatfooted |flat'footid| *a* de pies planos.

flatly [flat'lē] *ad* terminantemente, de plano.

flatmate [flat'māt] *n* (*Brit*) compañero/a de piso.

flatness [flat'nis] *n* (*of land*) llanura, lo llano.

flatten [flat'ən] *vt* (*also*: ~ **out**) allanar; (*smooth out*) alisar; (*house, city*) arrasar.

flatter [flat'ûr] *vt* adular, halagar; (*show to advantage*) favorecer.

flatterer [flat'ûrûr] *n* adulador(a) *m/f*.

flattering [flat'ûring] *a* halagüeño; (*clothes etc*) que favorece, favorecedor(a).

flattery [flat'ûrē] *n* adulación *f*.

flatulence [flach'ələns] *n* flatulencia.

flaunt [flônt] *vt* ostentar, lucir.

flavor [flā'vûr] (*US*) *n* sabor *m*, gusto ♦ *vt* sazonar, condimentar; **strawberry ~ed** con sabor a fresa.

flavoring [flā'vûring] *n* (*in product*) aromatizante *m*.

flavour [flā'vûr] *etc* (*Brit*) = **flavor** *etc*.

flaw [flô] *n* defecto.

flawless [flô'lis] *a* intachable.

flax [flaks] *n* lino.

flaxen [flak'sən] *a* rubio.

flea [flē] *n* pulga.

flea market *n* rastro, mercadillo.

fleck [flek] *n* (*mark, mud, paint*) mota; (*color, pattern*) punto; (*of dust*) partícula ♦ *vt* (*with blood, mud etc*) salpicar; **brown ~ed with white** marrón con puntos blancos.

fledg(e)ling [flej'ling] *n* (*fig*) novato/a, principiante *m/f*.

flee [flē], *pt, pp* **fled** [fled] *vt* huir de, abandonar ♦ *vi* huir, fugarse.

fleece [flēs] *n* vellón *m*; (*wool*) lana ♦ *vt* (*col*) pelar.

fleecy [flē'sē] *a* (*blanket*) lanoso, lanudo; (*cloud*) aborregado.

fleet [flēt] *n* flota; (*of cars, trucks etc*) escuadra.

fleeting [flē'ting] *a* fugaz.

Flemish [flem'ish] *a* flamenco ♦ *n* (*LING*) flamenco; **the ~** los flamencos.

flesh [flesh] *n* carne *f*; (*of fruit*) pulpa; **of ~ and blood** de carne y hueso.

flesh wound *n* herida superficial.

flew [flōō] *pt of* **fly**.

flex [fleks] *n* cordón *m* ♦ *vt* (*muscles*) tensar.

flexibility [fleksəbil'ətē] *n* flexibilidad *f*.

flexible [flek'səbəl] *a* (*gen, disk*) flexible; **~ working hours** horario *sg* flexible.

flick [flik] *n* golpecito; (*with finger*) capirotazo; (*col: movie*) película ♦ *vt* dar un golpecito a.

flick off *vt* quitar con el dedo.

flick through *vt fus* hojear.

flicker [flik'ûr] *vi* (*light*) parpadear; (*flame*) vacilar ♦ *n* parpadeo.

flick knife *n* (*Brit*) navaja de muelle.

flier [flī'ûr] *n* aviador(a) *m/f*.

flies [flīz] *npl of* **fly**.

flight [flīt] *n* vuelo; (*escape*) huida, fuga;

(*also*: ~ **of steps**) tramo (de escaleras); **to take ~** huir, darse a la fuga; **to put to ~** ahuyentar; **how long does the ~ take?** ¿cuánto dura el vuelo?

flight attendant *n* tripulante *m/f* auxiliar.

flight deck *n* (*AVIAT*) cabina de mandos.

flight recorder *n* registrador *m* de vuelo.

flighty [flī'tē] *a* frívolo; caprichoso.

flimsy [flim'zē] *a* (*thin*) muy ligero; (*excuse*) flojo.

flinch [flinch] *vi* encogerse.

fling [fling] *vt* (*pt, pp* **flung** [flung]) arrojar ♦ *n* (*love affair*) aventura amorosa.

flint [flint] *n* pedernal *m*; (*in lighter*) piedra.

flip [flip] *vt*: **to ~ a coin** echar a cara o cruz.

flip over *vt* dar la vuelta a.

flip through *vt fus* (*book, records*) hojear, repasar.

flippancy [flip'ənsē] *n* ligereza.

flippant [flip'ənt] *a* poco serio.

flipper [flip'ûr] *n* (*of seal etc, for swimming*) aleta.

flip side *n* (*of record*) cara B.

flirt [flûrt] *vi* coquetear, flirtear ♦ *n* coqueta *f*.

flirtation [flûrtā'shən] *n* coqueteo, flirteo.

flit [flit] *vi* revolotear.

float [flōt] *n* flotador *m*; (*in procession*) carroza; (*sum of money*) reserva ♦ *vi* (*also COMM: currency*) flotar; (*bather*) hacer la plancha ♦ *vt* (*gen*) hacer flotar; (*company*) lanzar; **to ~ an idea** propagar una idea.

floating [flō'ting] *a*: **~ vote** voto indeciso; **~ voter** votante *m/f* indeciso/a.

flock [flâk] *n* (*of sheep*) rebaño; (*of birds*) bandada; (*of people*) multitud *f*.

floe [flō] *n*: **ice ~** témpano de hielo.

flog [flâg] *vt* azotar.

flood [flud] *n* inundación *f*; (*of words, tears etc*) torrente *m* ♦ *vt* (*also AUT: carburetor*) inundar; **to ~ the market** (*COMM*) inundar el mercado.

flooding [flud'ing] *n* inundación *f*.

floodlight [flud'līt] *n* foco ♦ *vt* (*irg: like light*) iluminar con focos.

floodlit [flud'lit] *pt, pp of* **floodlight** ♦ *a* iluminado.

flood tide *n* pleamar *f*.

floor [flôr] *n* suelo; (*story*) piso; (*of sea, valley*) fondo; (*dance ~*) pista ♦ *vt* (*fig: baffle*) dejar sin respuesta, confundir; (*: silence*) dejar sin réplica posible; (*US AUT*) pisar el acelerador; **first ~** (*US*), **ground ~** (*Brit*) planta baja; **second ~** (*US*), **first ~** (*Brit*) primer piso; **top ~** último piso; **to have the ~** (*speaker*) tener la palabra.

floorboard [flôr'bôrd] *n* tabla.

flooring [flôr'ing] *n* suelo; (*material*) solería.

floor lamp *n* (*US*) lámpara de pie.

floor show *n* cabaret *m*.

floorwalker [flôr'wôkûr] *n* (*US COMM*) vigilante *m/f*.

flop |flâp| *n* fracaso ♦ *vi* (*fail*) fracasar.

flophouse |flâp'hous| *n* (*US*) pensión *f* de mala muerte.

floppy |flâp'ē| *a* flojo ♦ *n* = **floppy disk**.

floppy disk *n* (*COMPUT*) floppy *m*, floppy-disk *m*, disco flexible.

flora |flôr'ə| *n* flora.

floral |flôr'əl| *a* floral.

Florence |flâr'əns| *n* Florencia.

Florentine |flôr'əntēn| *a*, *n* florentino/a *m/f*.

florid |flôr'id| *a* (*style*) florido.

florist |flôr'ist| *n* florista *m/f*; **~'s (shop)** *n* florería.

flotation |flōtā'shən| *n* (*of shares*) emisión *f*; (*of company*) lanzamiento.

flounce |flouns| *n* volante *m*.
    flounce in *vi* entrar con gesto exagerado.
    flounce out *vi* salir enfadado.

flounder |floun'dûr| *vi* tropezar ♦ *n* (*ZOOL*) platija.

flour |flou'ûr| *n* harina.

flourish |flûr'ish| *vi* florecer ♦ *n* ademán *m*, movimiento (ostentoso).

flourishing |flûr'ishing| *a* floreciente.

flout |flout| *vt* burlarse de; (*order*) no hacer caso de, hacer caso omiso de.

flow |flō| *n* (*movement*) flujo; (*direction*) curso; (*of river, tide, also ELEC*) corriente *f* ♦ *vi* correr, fluir.

flow chart *n* organigrama *m*.

flow diagram *n* organigrama *m*.

flower |flou'ûr| *n* flor *f* ♦ *vi* florecer; **in ~** en flor.

flower bed *n* macizo.

flowerpot |flou'ûrpât| *n* tiesto.

flowery |flou'ûrē| *a* florido.

flowing |flō'ing| *a* (*hair, clothes*) suelto; (*style*) fluido.

flown |flōn| *pp of* **fly**.

flu |flōō| *n* gripe *f*.

fluctuate |fluk'chōōāt| *vi* fluctuar.

fluctuation |flukchōōā'shən| *n* fluctuación *f*.

flue |flōō| *n* huméro.

fluency |flōō'ənsē| *n* fluidez *f*.

fluent |flōō'ənt| *a* (*speech*) elocuente; **he speaks ~ French, he's ~ in French** domina el francés.

fluently |flōō'əntlē| *ad* con fluidez.

fluff |fluf| *n* pelusa.

fluffy |fluf'ē| *a* velloso.

fluid |flōō'id| *a*, *n* fluido, líquido; (*in diet*) líquido.

fluke |flōōk| *n* (*col*) chiripa.

flummox |flum'əks| *vt* desconcertar.

flung |flung| *pt*, *pp of* **fling**.

flunky |flung'kē| *n* lacayo.

fluorescent |flōōəres'ənt| *a* fluorescente.

fluoride |flōō'ərīd| *n* fluoruro.

fluoride toothpaste *n* pasta de dientes con flúor.

flurry |flûr'ē| *n* (*of snow*) temporal *m*; (*haste*) agitación *f*; **~ of activity** frenesí *m*

de actividad.

flush |flush| *n* (*on face*) rubor *m*; (*fig: of youth, beauty*) resplandor *m* ♦ *vt* limpiar con agua; (*also:* **~ out**) (*game, birds*) levantar; (*fig: criminal*) poner al descubierto ♦ *vi* ruborizarse ♦ *a*: **~ with** a ras de; **to ~ the toilet** hacer funcionar el WC.

flushed |flusht| *a* ruborizado.

fluster |flus'tûr| *n* aturdimiento ♦ *vt* aturdir.

flustered |flus'tûrd| *a* aturdido.

flute |flōōt| *n* flauta.

flutter |flut'ûr| *n* (*of wings*) revoloteo, aleteo; (*Brit: fam: bet*) apuesta ♦ *vi* revolotear; **to be in a ~** estar nervioso.

flux |fluks| *n* flujo; **in a state of ~** cambiando continuamente.

fly |flī| *n* (*insect*) mosca; (*on pants: also:* **flies**) bragueta ♦ *vb* (*pt* **flew**, *pp* **flown**) *vt* (*plane*) pilot(e)ar; (*cargo*) transportar (en avión); (*distances*) recorrer (en avión) ♦ *vi* volar; (*passengers*) ir en avión; (*escape*) evadirse; (*flag*) ondear.

fly away *vi* (*bird, insect*) volarse.

fly in *vi* (*person*) llegar en avión; (*plane*) aterrizar; **he flew in from Bilbao** llegó en avión desde Bilbao.

fly off *vi* volarse.

fly out *vi* irse en avión.

fly-fishing |flī'fishing| *n* pesca con mosca.

flying |flī'ing| *n* (*activity*) (el) volar ♦ *a*: **~ visit** visita relámpago; **with ~ colors** con lucimiento.

flying buttress *n* arbotante *m*.

flying saucer *n* platillo volante.

flying squad *n* (*MIL etc*) brigada móvil.

flying start *n*: **to get off to a ~** empezar con buen pie.

flyleaf, *pl* **flyleaves** |flī'lēf, lēvz| *n* (hoja de) guarda.

flyover |flī'ōvûr| *n* (*US*) desfile *m* aéreo; (*Brit: bridge*) paso superior *or* a desnivel.

flypast |flī'past| *n* desfile *m* aéreo.

flysheet |flī'shēt| *n* (*for tent*) doble techo.

flyswatter |flī'swâtûr| *n* matamoscas *m inv*.

flywheel |flī'hwēl| *n* volante *m* mecánico.

FM *abbr* (*RADIO:* = *frequency modulation*) FM; (*Brit MIL*) = **field marshal.**

FMB *n abbr* (*US*) = *Federal Maritime Board*.

FMCS *n abbr* (*US:* = *Federal Mediation and Conciliation Services*) organismo de conciliación en conflictos laborales.

foal |fōl| *n* potro.

foam |fōm| *n* espuma ♦ *vi* echar espuma.

foam rubber *n* espuma de caucho.

FOB *abbr* (= *free on board*) f.a.b.

fob |fâb| *n* (*also:* **watch ~**) leontina ♦ *vt*: **to ~ sb off with sth** deshacerse de uno con algo.

foc *abbr* (*Brit:* = *free of charge*) gratis.

focal |fō'kəl| *a* focal; **~ point** punto focal; (*fig*) centro de atención.

focus |fō'kəs| (*pl:* **~es**) *n* foco ♦ *vt* (*field*

glasses etc) enfocar ♦ vi: **to** ~ **(on)** enfocar (a); (issue etc) centrarse en; **in/out of** ~ enfocado/desenfocado.

fodder [fâd'ûr] n pienso.

FOE n abbr (= Friends of the Earth) Amigos mpl de la Tierra; (US: = Fraternal Order of Eagles) organización benéfica.

foe [fō] n enemigo.

foetus [fē'tǝs] n (Brit) = **fetus.**

fog [fóg] n niebla.

fog up vi (windows) empañarse.

fogbound [fóg'bound] a inmovilizado por la niebla.

foggy [fóg'ē] a: **it's** ~ hay niebla, está brumoso.

fog light n (AUT) faro antiniebla.

foible [foi'bǝl] n manía.

foil [foil] vt frustrar ♦ n hoja; (kitchen ~) papel m (de) aluminio; (FENCING) florete m.

foist [foist] vt: **to** ~ **sth on sb** colarle algo a uno.

fold [fōld] n (bend, crease) pliegue m; (AGR) redil m ♦ vt doblar; (map etc) plegar; **to** ~ **one's arms** cruzarse de brazos.

fold up vi plegarse, doblarse; (business) quebrar.

folder [fōl'dûr] n (for papers) carpeta; (binder) carpeta de anillas; (brochure) folleto.

folding [fōl'ding] a (chair, bed) plegable.

foliage [fō'lēij] n follaje m.

folio [fō'lēō] n folio.

folk [fōk] npl gente f ♦ a popular, folklórico; ~**s** npl familia, parientes mpl.

folklore [fōk'lôr] n folklore m.

folk music n música folk(lórica).

folk singer n cantante m/f de canciones folklóricas.

folk song n canción f popular or folklórica.

follow [fâl'ō] vt seguir ♦ vi seguir; (result) resultar; **he** ~**ed suit** hizo lo mismo; **to** ~ **sb's advice** seguir el consejo de uno; **I don't quite** ~ **you** no le sigo (la pista); **to** ~ **in sb's footsteps** seguirle los pasos a uno; **it doesn't** ~ **that** ... no se puede concluir que ....

follow on vi seguir; (continue): **to** ~ **on from** continuar.

follow out vt (implement: idea, plan) realizar, llevar a cabo.

follow through vt llevar hasta el fin ♦ vi (SPORT) dar el remate.

follow up vt (letter, offer) responder a; (case) investigar.

follower [fâl'ōûr] n seguidor(a) m/f; (POL) partidario/a.

following [fâl'ōing] a siguiente ♦ n afición f, partidarios mpl.

follow-up [fâl'ōup] n seguimiento.

follow-up letter n carta recordatoria.

folly [fâl'ē] n locura.

fond [fând] a (loving) cariñoso; **to be** ~ **of**

sb tener cariño a uno; **she's** ~ **of swimming** tiene afición a la natación, a ella le gusta nadar.

fondle [fân'dǝl] vt acariciar.

fondly [fând'lē] ad (lovingly) con cariño; **he** ~ **believed that** ... creía inocentemente que ....

fondness [fând'dnis] n (for things) afición f; (for people) cariño.

font [fânt] n pila bautismal.

food [fōōd] n comida.

food mixer n batidora.

food poisoning n botulismo.

food processor [fōōd prâs'esûr] n robot m de cocina.

foodstuffs [fōōd'stufs] npl comestibles mpl.

fool [fōōl] n tonto/a; (CULIN) puré m de frutas con nata ♦ vt engañar; **to make a** ~ **of o.s.** ponerse en ridículo; **you can't** ~ **me** a mí no me engañas.

fool about vi (Brit) = **fool around.**

fool around vi bromear; (waste time) perder el tiempo.

foolhardy [fōōl'hârdē] a temerario.

foolish [fōō'lish] a tonto; (careless) imprudente.

foolishly [fōō'lishlē] ad tontamente, neciamente.

foolproof [fōōl'prōōf] a (plan etc) infalible.

foolscap [fōōlz'kap] n papel m folio.

foot [fōōt], pl **feet** [fēt] n (gen, also: of page, stairs etc) pie m; (measure) pie m (= 304 mm); (of animal, table) pata ♦ vt (bill) pagar; **on** ~ a pie; **to find one's feet** acostumbrarse; **to put one's** ~ **down** (say no) plantarse; (Brit AUT) pisar el acelerador.

footage [fōōt'ij] n (CINEMA) imágenes fpl.

foot-and-mouth (disease) [fōōt'ǝnmouth' (dizēz')] n fiebre f aftosa.

football [fōōt'bôl] n balón m; (game) fútbol m.

footballer [fōōt'bôlûr] n (Brit) = **football player.**

football game n partido de fútbol.

football player n futbolista m/f, jugador(a) m/f de fútbol.

footbrake [fōōt'brāk] n freno de pie.

footbridge [fōōt'brij] n puente m para peatones.

foothills [fōōt'hilz] npl estribaciones fpl.

foothold [fōōt'hōld] n pie m firme.

footing [fōōt'ing] n (fig) posición f; **to lose one's** ~ perder el pie; **on an equal** ~ en pie de igualdad.

footlights [fōōt'līts] npl candilejas fpl.

footman [fōōt'mǝn] n lacayo.

footnote [fōōt'nōt] n nota (de pie de página).

footpath [fōōt'path] n sendero.

footprint [fōōt'print] n huella, pisada.

footrest [fōōt'rest] n apoyapiés m inv.

footsore [fōōt'sôr] a con los pies doloridos.

footstep [fōōt'step] n paso.

footwear [fŏŏt'weûr] *n* calzado.

FOR *abbr* (= *free on rail*) franco (puesto sobre) vagón.

for [fôr] *prep* (*gen*) para; (*as, in exchange for, because of*) por; (*during*) durante; (*in spite of*) a pesar de ♦ *conj* pues, ya que; **it was sold ~ 100 pesetas** se vendió por 100 pesetas; **what ~?** ¿para qué?; **what's this button ~?** ¿para qué sirve este botón?; **he was away ~ 2 years** estuvo fuera 2 años; **I haven't seen him ~ 3 days** hace 3 días que no le veo; **he went ~ the paper** fue a buscar el periódico; **the train ~ New York** el tren de Nueva York; **is this ~ me?** ¿es para mí esto?; **it's time ~ lunch** es la hora de comer; **G ~ George** G de Gerona.

forage [fôr'ij] *n* forraje *m*.

foray [fôr'ā] *n* incursión *f*.

forbid, *pt* **forbad(e)**, *pp* **forbidden** [fûrbid', fûrbād', fûrbid'ən] *vt* prohibir; **to ~ sb to do sth** prohibir a uno hacer algo.

forbidding [fûrbid'ing] *a* (*landscape*) inhóspito; (*severe*) severo.

force [fôrs] *n* fuerza ♦ *vt* forzar; **to ~ o.s. to do** hacer un esfuerzo por hacer; **the Armed F~s** *npl* las Fuerzas Armadas; **sales ~** (*COMM*) personal *m* de ventas; **a ~ 5 wind** un viento fuerza 5; **to join ~s** unir fuerzas; **in ~** (*law etc*) en vigor; **to ~ sb to do sth** obligar a uno a hacer algo.

force back *vt* (*crowd, enemy*) hacer retroceder; (*tears*) reprimir.

force down *vt* (*food*) comer sin gusto.

forced [fôrst] *a* (*smile*) forzado; (*landing*) forzoso.

force-feed [fôrs'fēd] *vt* (*animal, prisoner*) alimentar a la fuerza.

forceful [fôrs'fəl] *a* enérgico.

forceps [fôr'səps] *npl* fórceps *m inv*.

forcible [fôr'səbəl] *a* (*violent*) a la fuerza; (*telling*) convincente.

forcibly [fôr'səblē] *ad* a la fuerza.

ford [fôrd] *n* vado ♦ *vt* vadear.

fore [fôr] *n*: **to bring to the ~** sacar a la luz pública; **to come to the ~** hacerse notar.

forearm [fôr'ârm] *n* antebrazo.

forebear [fôr'beûr] *n* antepasado.

foreboding [fôrbō'ding] *n* presentimiento.

forecast [fôr'kast] *n* pronóstico ♦ *vt* (*irg: like* **cast**) pronosticar; **weather ~** previsión *f* meteorológica.

foreclose [fôrklōz'] *vt* (*LAW: also:* **~ on**) extinguir el derecho de redimir.

foreclosure [fôrklō'zhûr] *n* apertura de un juicio hipotecario.

forecourt [fôr'kôrt] *n* (*of gas station*) patio.

forefathers [fôr'fâthûrz] *npl* antepasados *mpl*.

forefinger [fôr'finggûr] *n* (dedo) índice *m*.

forefront [fôr'frunt] *n*: **in the ~ of** en la vanguardia de.

forego, *pt* **forewent**, *pp* **foregone** [fôrgō', -went', -gôn'] *vt* = **forgo**.

foregoing [fôrgō'ing] *a* anterior, precedente.

foregone [fôrgôn'] *pp of* **forego** ♦ *a*: **it's a ~ conclusion** es una conclusión inevitable.

foreground [fôr'ground] *n* primer plano.

forehand [fôr'hand] *n* (*TENNIS*) golpe *m* derecho *or* directo.

forehead [fôr'hed] *n* frente *f*.

foreign [fôr'in] *a* extranjero; (*trade*) exterior.

foreign currency *n* divisas *fpl*.

foreigner [fôr'ənûr] *n* extranjero/a.

foreign exchange *n* (*system*) cambio de divisas; (*money*) divisas *fpl*, moneda extranjera.

foreign investment *n* inversión *f* en el extranjero; (*money, stock*) inversiones *fpl* extranjeras.

Foreign Office *n* (*Brit*) Ministerio de Asuntos Exteriores.

Foreign Secretary *n* (*Brit*) Ministro de Asuntos Exteriores.

foreleg [fôr'leg] *n* pata delantera.

foreman [fôr'mən] *n* capataz *m*; (*in construction*) maestro de obras; (*LAW: of jury*) presidente *m/f*.

foremost [fôr'mōst] *a* principal ♦ *ad*: **first and ~** ante todo, antes que nada.

forename [fôr'nām] *n* nombre *m* (de pila).

forensic [fəren'sik] *a* forense; **~ scientist** forense *m/f*.

forerunner [fôr'runûr] *n* precursor(a) *m/f*.

foresee, *pt* **foresaw**, *pp* **foreseen** [fôrsē', -sô', -sēn'] *vt* prever.

foreseeable [fôrsē'əbəl] *a* previsible.

foreshadow [fôrshad'ō] *vt* prefigurar, anunciar.

foreshore [fôr'shôr] *n* playa.

foreshorten [fôrshôr'tən] *vt* (*figure, scene*) escorzar.

foresight [fôr'sīt] *n* previsión *f*.

foreskin [fôr'skin] *n* (*ANAT*) prepucio.

forest [fôr'ist] *n* bosque *m*.

forestall [fôrstôl'] *vt* prevenir.

forestry [fôr'istrē] *n* silvicultura.

foretaste [fôr'tāst] *n* anticipo.

foretell, *pt, pp* **foretold** [fôrtel', -tōld'] *vt* predecir, pronosticar.

forethought [fôr'thôt] *n* previsión *f*.

forever [fôrev'ûr] *ad* para siempre.

forewarn [fôrwôrn'] *vt* avisar, advertir.

forewent [fôrwent'] *pt of* **forego**.

foreword [fôr'wûrd] *n* prefacio.

forfeit [fôr'fit] *n* (*in game*) prenda ♦ *vt* perder (derecho a).

forgave [fûrgāv'] *pt of* **forgive**.

forge [fôrj] *n* fragua; (*smithy*) herrería ♦ *vt* (*signature: Brit: money*) falsificar; (*metal*) forjar.

forge ahead *vi* avanzar constantemente.

forger [fôr'jûr] *n* falsificador(a) *m/f*.

forgery [fôr'jûrē] *n* falsificación *f*.

forget, *pt* **forgot**, *pp* **forgotten** [fûrget', -gât',

-gât'ən| *vt* olvidar ♦ *vi* olvidarse.

forgetful [fûrget'fəl] *a* olvidadizo.

forget-me-not [fûrget'mēnât] *n* nomeolvides *f inv*.

forgive, *pt* **forgave**, *pp* **forgiven** [fûrgiv', -gāv', -giv'ən] *vt* perdonar; **to ~ sb for sth/for doing sth** perdonar algo a uno/a uno por haber hecho algo.

forgiveness [fûrgiv'nis] *n* perdón *m*.

forgiving [fûrgiv'ing] *a* compasivo.

forgo, *pt* **forwent**, *pp* **forgone** [fôrgō', -went'. -gôn'] *vt* (*give up*) renunciar a; (*go without*) privarse de.

forgot [fûrgât'] *pt of* **forget**.

forgotten [fûrgât'ən] *pp of* **forget**.

fork [fôrk] *n* (*for eating*) tenedor *m*; (*for gardening*) horca; (*of roads*) bifurcación *f*; (*in tree*) horcadura ♦ *vi* (*road*) bifurcarse.

fork out *vt* (*col: pay*) desembolsar.

forked [fôrkt] *a* (*lightning*) en zigzag.

forklift truck [fôrk'lift truk'] *n* máquina elevadora.

forlorn [fôrlôrn'] *a* (*person*) triste, melancólico; (*deserted: cottage*) abandonado; (*desperate: attempt*) desesperado.

form [fôrm] *n* forma; (*Brit SCOL*) clase *f*; (*document*) formulario ♦ *vt* formar; **in the ~ of** en forma de; **in top ~** en plena forma; **to be in good ~** (*SPORT, fig*) estar en plena forma; **to ~ part of sth** formar parte de algo; **to ~ a circle/a line** hacer una curva/una cola.

formal [fôr'məl] *a* (*offer, receipt*) por escrito; (*person etc*) correcto; (*occasion, dinner*) ceremonioso; **~ dress** traje *m* de vestir; (*evening dress*) traje *m* de etiqueta.

formalities [fôrmal'itēz] *npl* formalidades *fpl*.

formality [fôrmal'itē] *n* ceremonia.

formalize [fôr'məlīz] *vt* formalizar.

formally [fôr'məlē] *ad* oficialmente.

format [fôr'mat] *n* formato ♦ *vt* (*COMPUT*) formatear.

formation [fôrmā'shən] *n* formación *f*.

formative [fôr'mətiv] *a* (*years*) formativo.

format line *n* (*COMPUT*) línea de formato.

former [fôr'mûr] *a* anterior; (*earlier*) antiguo; (*ex*) ex; **the ~ ... the latter ...** aquél ... éste ...; **the ~ president** el antiguo *or* ex presidente.

formerly [fôr'mûrlē] *ad* antiguamente.

form feed *n* (*on printer*) salto de página.

Formica [fôrmī'kə] ® *n* Formica ®.

formidable [fôr'midəbəl] *a* formidable.

formula [fôr'myələ] *n* fórmula; **F~ One** (*AUT*) Fórmula Uno.

formulate [fôr'myəlāt] *vt* formular.

fornicate [fôr'nikāt] *vi* fornicar.

forsake, *pt* **forsook**, *pp* **forsaken** [fôrsāk', -sōōk'. -sā'kən] *vt* (*gen*) abandonar; (*plan*) renunciar a.

fort [fôrt] *n* fuerte *m*; **to hold the ~** (*fig*) quedarse a cargo.

forte [fôr'tā] *n* fuerte *m*.

forth [fôrth] *ad*: **back and ~** de acá para allá; **and so ~** y así sucesivamente.

forthcoming [fôrth'kum'ing] *a* próximo, venidero; (*character*) comunicativo.

forthright [fôrth'rīt] *a* franco.

forthwith [fôrthwith'] *ad* en el acto, acto seguido.

fortification [fôrtəfəkā'shən] *n* fortificación *f*.

fortified wine [fôr'təfīd wīn'] *n* vino encabezado.

fortify [fôr'təfī] *vt* fortalecer.

fortitude [fôr'titōōd] *n* fortaleza.

fortnight [fôrt'nit] *n* (*Brit*) quincena; **it's a ~ since** ... hace quince días que ....

fortnightly [fôrt'nitlē] (*Brit*) *a* quincenal ♦ *ad* quincenalmente.

FORTRAN [fôr'tran] *n* FORTRAN *m*.

fortress [fôr'tris] *n* fortaleza.

fortuitous [fôrtōō'itəs] *a* fortuito.

fortunate [fôr'chənit] *a*: **it is ~ that...** (es una) suerte que....

fortunately [fôr'chənitlē] *ad* afortunadamente.

fortune [fôr'chən] *n* suerte *f*; (*wealth*) fortuna; **to make a ~** hacer un dineral.

fortuneteller [fôr'chəntelûr] *n* adivino/a.

forty [fôr'tē] *num* cuarenta.

forum [fôr'əm] *n* (*also fig*) foro.

forward [fôr'wûrd] *a* (*movement, position*) avanzado; (*front*) delantero; (*not shy*) atrevido ♦ *n* (*SPORT*) delantero ♦ *vt* (*letter*) remitir; (*career*) promocionar; **to move ~** avanzar; **"please ~"** "remítase al destinatario".

forward(s) [fôr'wûrdz] *ad* (hacia) adelante.

forwent [fôrwent'] *pt of* **forgo**.

fossil [fâs'əl] *n* fósil *m*; **~ fuel** hidrocarburo.

foster [fôs'tûr] *vt* fomentar.

foster brother *n* hermano de leche.

foster child *n* hijo/a adoptivo/a.

foster mother *n* madre *f* adoptiva.

fought [fôt] *pt, pp of* **fight**.

foul [foul] *a* (*gen*) sucio, puerco; (*weather, smell etc*) asqueroso ♦ *n* (*SPORT*) falta ♦ *vt* (*dirty*) ensuciar; (*block*) atascar; (*entangle: anchor, propeller*) atascar, enredarse en; (*player*) cometer una falta contra.

foul play *n* (*SPORT*) mala jugada; (*LAW*) muerte *f* violenta.

found [found] *pt, pp of* **find** ♦ *vt* (*establish*) fundar.

foundation [foundā'shən] *n* (*act*) fundación *f*; (*basis*) base *f*; (*also*: **~ cream**) crema base.

foundations [foundā'shənz] *npl* (*of building*) cimientos *mpl;* **to lay the ~** poner los cimientos.

foundation stone *n*: **to lay the ~** poner la primera piedra.

founder [foun'dûr] *n* fundador(a) *m/f* ♦ *vi*

hundirse.
founding [foun'ding] *a*: ~ **fathers** (*esp US*) fundadores *mpl*, próceres *mpl*; ~ **member** miembro fundador.
foundry [foun'drē] *n* fundición *f*.
fountain [foun'tin] *n* fuente *f*.
fountain pen *n* (pluma) estilográfica, (*LAm*) plumafuente *f*.
four [fôr] *num* cuatro; **on all** ~**s** a gatas.
four-footed [fôr'fŏŏtid] *a* cuadrúpedo.
four-poster [fôr'pōs'tûr] *n* (*also:* ~ **bed**) cama de columnas.
foursome [fôr'səm] *n* grupo de cuatro personas.
fourteen [fôr'tēn'] *num* catorce.
fourteenth [fôr'tēnth'] *num* decimocuarto.
fourth [fôrth] *num* cuarto ♦ *n* (*AUT: also:* ~ **gear**) cuarta (velocidad).
four-wheel drive [fôr'hwēl drīv] *n* tracción *f* a las cuatro ruedas.
fowl [foul] *n* ave *f* (de corral).
fox [fâks] *n* zorro ♦ *vt* confundir.
fox fur *n* piel *f* de zorro.
foxglove [fâks'gluv] *n* (*BOT*) dedalera.
fox hunting *n* caza de zorros.
foxtrot [fâks'trât] *n* fox *m*.
foyer [foi'ûr] *n* vestíbulo.
FP *n abbr* (*US*) = **fireplug**; (*Brit*) = *former pupil*.
Fr. *abbr* (*REL*) (= *Father*) P.; (= *friar*) Fr.
fr. *abbr* (= *franc*) f.
fracas [frā'kəs] *n* gresca, refriega.
fraction [frak'shən] *n* fracción *f*.
fractionally [frak'shənəlē] *ad* ligeramente.
fractious [frak'shəs] *a* (*person, mood*) malhumorado.
fracture [frak'chûr] *n* fractura ♦ *vt* fracturar.
fragile [fraj'əl] *a* frágil.
fragment [frag'mənt] *n* fragmento.
fragmentary [frag'məntärē] *a* fragmentario.
fragrance [frā'rəns] *n* fragancia.
fragrant [frā'rənt] *a* fragante, oloroso.
frail [frāl] *a* (*fragile*) frágil, quebradizo; (*weak*) delicado.
frame [frām] *n* (*TECH*) armazón *f*; (*of picture, door etc*) marco; (*of spectacles: also:* ~**s**) montura ♦ *vt* encuadrar; (*picture*) enmarcar; (*reply*) formular; **to** ~ **sb** (*col*) inculpar por engaños a uno.
frame of mind *n* estado de ánimo.
framework [frām'wûrk] *n* marco.
France [frans] *n* Francia.
franchise [fran'chīz] *n* (*POL*) derecho de votar, sufragio; (*COMM*) licencia, concesión *f*.
franchisee [franchizē'] *n* concesionario/a.
franchiser [fran'chīzûr] *n* compañía concesionaria.
frank [frangk] *a* franco ♦ *vt* (*letter*) franquear.
frankfurter [frangk'fûrtûr] *n* salchicha de Frankfurt.
frankincense [frang'kinsens] *n* incienso.

frankly [frangk'lē] *ad* francamente.
frankness [frangk'nis] *n* franqueza.
frantic [fran'tik] *a* (*desperate: need, desire*) desesperado; (: *search*) frenético; (: *person*) desquiciado.
fraternal [frətûr'nəl] *a* fraterno.
fraternity [frətûr'nitē] *n* (*club*) fraternidad *f*; (*US*) club *m* de estudiantes; (*guild*) cofradía.
fraternization [fratûrnəzā'shən] *n* fraternización *f*.
fraternize [frat'ûrnīz] *vi* confraternizar.
fraud [frôd] *n* fraude *m*; (*person*) impostor(a) *m/f*.
fraudulent [frô'jələnt] *a* fraudulento.
fraught [frôt] *a* (*tense*) tenso; ~ **with** cargado de.
fray [frā] *n* combate *m*, lucha, refriega ♦ *vi* deshilacharse; **tempers were** ~**ed** el ambiente se ponía tenso.
FRB *n abbr* (*US*) = *Federal Reserve Board*.
freak [frēk] *n* (*person*) fenómeno; (*event*) suceso anormal; (*col: enthusiast*) adicto/a ♦ *a* (*storm, conditions*) anormal; **health** ~ (*col*) maniático/a en cuestión de salud.
   freak out *vi* (*col: on drugs*) tener un viaje.
freakish [frēk'ish] *a* (*result, appearance*) inesperado, extravagante; (*weather*) cambiadizo.
freckle [frek'əl] *n* peca.
freckled [frek'əld] *a* pecoso, lleno de pecas.
free [frē] *a* (*person: at liberty*) libre; (*not fixed*) suelto; (*gratis*) gratuito; (*unoccupied*) desocupado; (*liberal*) generoso ♦ *vt* (*prisoner etc*) poner en libertad; (*jammed object*) soltar; **to give sb a** ~ **hand** darle campo libre a uno; ~ **and easy** despreocupado; **is this seat** ~? ¿está libre este asiento?; ~ **of tax** libre de impuestos; **admission** ~ entrada libre; ~ **(of charge)**, **for** ~ *ad* gratis.
-free *a*: **additive**~ sin aditivos; **tax**~ libre de impuestos.
freebie [frē'bē] *n* (*col*): **it's a** ~ es gratis.
freedom [frē'dəm] *n* libertad *f*; ~ **of association** libertad *f* de asociación.
freedom fighter *n* libertador(a).
free enterprise *n* libre empresa.
free-for-all [frē'fûrôl'] *n* riña general.
free gift *n* obsequio.
freehold [frē'hōld] *n* feudo franco alodio.
free kick *n* tiro libre.
freelance [frē'lans] *a, ad* por cuenta propia; ~ **work** trabajo independiente.
freely [frē'lē] *ad* libremente; (*liberally*) generosamente.
freemason [frē'māsən] *n* francmasón *m*.
freemasonry [frē'māsənrē] *n* (franc)masonería.
free-range [frē'rānj] *a* (*Brit: hen, eggs*) de granja.
free sample *n* muestra gratuita.

freesia |frē'zhēə| n fresia.
free speech n libertad f de expresión.
freestyle wrestling |frē'stīl rēs'ling| n lucha libre.
free trade n libre comercio.
freeway |frē'wā| n (US) autopista.
freewheel |frē'hwēl'| vi ir en punto muerto.
freewheeling |frē'hwē'ling| a libre, espontáneo; (careless) irresponsable.
free will n libre albedrío; **of one's own ~** por su propia voluntad.
freeze |frēz| vb (pt **froze**, pp **frozen** |frōz, frō'zən|) vi helarse, congelarse ♦ vt helar; (prices, food, salaries) congelar ♦ n helada; congelación f.
   freeze over vi (lake, river) helarse, congelarse; (window, windshield) cubrirse de escarcha.
   freeze up vi helarse, congelarse.
freeze-dried |frēz'drīd'| a liofilizado.
freezer |frē'zûr| n congelador m, congeladora (LAm).
freezing |frē'zing| a helado.
freezing point n punto de congelación; **3 degrees below ~** tres grados bajo cero.
freight |frāt| n (goods) carga; (money charged) flete m; **~ forward** contra reembolso del flete, flete debido; **~ free** franco de porte; **~ inward** flete sobre compras; **~ paid** porte m pagado.
freight car n vagón m de mercancías.
freighter |frā'tûr| n nave f de mercancías.
freight forwarder |frāt fôr'wûrdûr| n agente m expedidor.
freight train n (US) tren m de mercancías.
French |french| a francés/esa ♦ n (LING) francés m; **the ~** npl los franceses.
French bean n judía verde.
French Canadian a, n francocanadiense m/f.
French dressing n (CULIN) vinagreta.
French fries, (Brit) **French fried (potatoes)** npl patatas fpl or papas fpl (LAm) fritas.
French Guiana |french gēan'ə| n la Guayana Francesa.
Frenchman |french'mən| n francés m.
French Riviera n: **the ~** la Riviera, la Costa Azul.
French window n puertaventana.
Frenchwoman |french'woomən| n francesa.
frenetic |frənet'ik| a frenético.
frenzy |fren'zē| n frenesí m.
frequency |frē'kwənsē| n frecuencia.
frequency modulation (FM) n frecuencia modulada.
frequent a |frē'kwint| frecuente ♦ vt |frikwent'| frecuentar.
frequently |frē'kwintlē| ad frecuentemente, a menudo.
fresco |fres'kō| n fresco.

fresh |fresh| a (gen) fresco; (new) nuevo; (water) dulce; **to make a ~ start** empezar de nuevo.
freshen |fresh'ən| vi (wind, air) soplar más recio.
   freshen up vi (person) refrescarse.
freshener |fresh'ənûr| n: **air ~** ambientador m; **skin ~** tónico.
fresher |fresh'ûr| n (Brit SCOL: col) = **freshman.**
freshly |fresh'lē| ad: **~ painted/arrived** recién pintado/llegado.
freshman |fresh'mən| n (US: SCOL) estudiante m/f de primer año.
freshness |fresh'nis| n frescura.
freshwater |fresh'wôtûr| a (fish) de agua dulce.
fret |fret| vi inquietarse.
fretful |fret'fəl| a (child) quejumbroso.
Freudian |froi'dēən| a freudiano; **~ slip** lapsus m.
FRG n abbr (= Federal Republic of Germany) RFA f.
Fri. abbr (= Friday) vier.
friar |frī'ûr| n fraile m; (before name) fray.
friction |frik'shən| n fricción f.
friction feed n (on printer) avance m por fricción.
Friday |frī'dā| n viernes m inv.
fridge |frij| n (Brit) nevera, frigo, refrigeradora (LAm).
fried |frīd| pt, pp of **fry** ♦ a: **~ egg** huevo frito, (LAm) huevo estrellado.
friend |frend| n amigo/a.
friendliness |frend'lēnis| n simpatía.
friendly |frend'lē| a simpático.
friendly society n (Brit) sociedad f de beneficiencia.
friendship |frend'ship| n amistad f.
frieze |frēz| n friso.
frigate |frig'it| n fragata.
fright |frīt| n susto; **to take ~** asustarse.
frighten |frīt'ən| vt asustar.
   frighten away, frighten off vt (birds, children etc) espantar, ahuyentar.
frightened |frīt'ənd| a asustado.
frightening |frīt'ning| a espantoso.
frightful |frīt'fəl| a espantoso, horrible.
frightfully |frīt'fəlē| ad terriblemente; **I'm ~ sorry** lo siento muchísimo.
frigid |frij'id| a (MED) frígido, frío.
frigidity |frijid'itē| n frialdad f; (MED) frigidez f.
frill |fril| n volante m; **without ~s** (fig) sin adornos.
fringe |frinj| n (Brit: of hair) flequillo; (edge: of forest etc) borde m, margen m.
fringe benefits npl ventajas fpl complementarias.
fringe theatre n (Brit) teatro experimental.
frisk |frisk| vt cachear, registrar.
frisky |fris'kē| a juguetón/ona.

fritter |frit'ûr| *n* buñuelo.
  fritter away *vt* desperdiciar.
frivolity |frəvàl'itē| *n* frivolidad *f.*
frivolous |friv'ələs| *a* frívolo.
frizzy |friz'ē| *a* rizado.
fro |frō| *see* **to.**
frock |fråk| *n* vestido.
frog |frŏg| *n* rana; **to have a ~ in one's throat** tener carraspera.
frogman |frŏg'man| *n* hombre-rana *m.*
frogmarch |frŏg'märch| *vt* (*Brit*): **to ~ sb in/out** hacer entrar/salir a uno a la fuerza.
frolic |frål'ik| *vi* juguetear.
from |frum| *prep* de; **where is he ~?** ¿de dónde es?; **where has he come ~?** ¿de dónde ha venido?; **a telephone call ~ Mr Smith** una llamada de parte del Sr. Smith; **prices range ~ $10 to $50** los precios varían entre 10 y 50 dólares; **~ Friday** a partir del viernes; **~ what he says** por lo que dice.
frond |frând| *n* fronda.
front |frunt| *n* (*foremost part*) parte *f* delantera; (*of house*) fachada; (*promenade*: *also*: **sea ~**) paseo marítimo; (*MIL, POL, METEOROLOGY*) frente *m*; (*fig: appearances*) apariencias *fpl* ♦ *a* (*wheel, leg*) delantero; (*row, line*) primero ♦ *vi*: **to ~ onto sth** dar a algo; **in ~ (of)** delante (de).
frontage |frun'tij| *n* (*of building*) fachada.
frontal |frun'təl| *a* frontal.
front bench *n* (*Brit POL*) los dirigentes del partido del gobierno o de la oposición.
front desk *n* (*US*) recepción *f.*
front door *n* puerta principal.
frontier |fruntēûr'| *n* frontera.
frontispiece |frun'tispēs| *n* portada.
front page *n* primera plana.
front room *n* salón *m*, sala.
front runner *n* favorito/a.
front-wheel drive |frunt'hwēl drīv| *n* tracción *f* delantera.
frost |frŏst| *n* (*gen*) helada; (*also*: **hoar~**) escarcha ♦ *vt* (*US CULIN*) escarchar.
frostbite |frŏst'bīt| *n* congelación *f.*
frosted |frŏs'tid| *a* (*glass*) deslustrado; (*esp US*: *cake*) escarchado.
frosting |frŏs'ting| *n* (*esp US*: *on cake*) escarcha.
frosty |frŏs'tē| *a* (*surface*) cubierto de escarcha; (*welcome etc*) glacial.
froth |frŏth| *n* espuma.
frothy |frŏth'ē| *a* espumoso.
frown |froun| *vi* fruncir el ceño ♦ *n*: **with a ~** frunciendo el entrecejo.
  frown on *vt fus* desaprobar.
froze |frōz| *pt of* **freeze.**
frozen |frō'zən| *pp of* **freeze** ♦ *a* (*food*) congelado, (*COMM*): **~ assets** activos *mpl* congelados *or* bloqueados.
FRS *n* (*US*: = *Federal Reserve System*) banco central de los EE. UU.
frugal |frōō'gəl| *a* (*person*) frugal.

fruit |frōōt| *n* (*pl inv*) fruta.
fruiterer |frōōt'ərûr| *n* frutero/a; **~'s (shop)** frutería.
fruitful |frōōt'fəl| *a* provechoso.
fruition |frōōish'ən| *n*: **to come to ~** realizarse.
fruit juice *n* zumo *or* jugo (*LAm*) de fruta.
fruitless |frōōt'lis| *a* (*fig*) infructuoso, inútil.
fruit machine *n* (*Brit*) máquina tragaperras.
fruit salad *n* macedonia *or* ensalada (*LAm*) de frutas.
frump |frump| *n* espantajo, adefesio.
frustrate |frus'trāt| *vt* frustrar.
frustrated |frus'trātid| *a* frustrado.
frustrating |frus'trāting| *a* (*job, day*) frustrante.
frustration |frustrā'shən| *n* frustración *f.*
fry, *pt, pp* **fried** |frī, -d| *vt* freír ♦ *n*: **small ~** gente *f* menuda.
frying pan |frī'ing pan| *n* sartén *f.*
FSLIC *n abbr* (*US*) = *Federal Savings and Loan Insurance Corporation.*
FT *n abbr* (*Brit*: = *Financial Times*) periódico financiero; **the ~ index** el índice de valores del Financial Times.
ft. *abbr* = **foot, feet.**
FTC *n abbr* (*US*) = *Federal Trade Commission.*
fuchsia |fyōō'shə| *n* fucsia.
fuck |fuk| (*col!*) *vt* joder (*Sp!*), coger (*LAm!*) ♦ *vi* joder (*Sp!*), coger (*LAm!*); **~ off!** ¡vete a la mierda! (*!*).
fuddled |fud'əld| *a* (*muddled*) confuso, aturdido; (*col: tipsy*) borracho.
fuddy-duddy |fud'ēdudē| (*pej*) *n* carcamal *m*, carroza *m/f* ♦ *a* chapado a la antigua.
fudge |fuj| *n* (*CULIN*) caramelo blando ♦ *vt* (*issue, problem*) rehuir, esquivar.
fuel |fyōō'əl| *n* (*for heating*) combustible *m*; (*coal*) carbón *m*; (*wood*) leña; (*for engine*) carburante *m* ♦ *vt* (*furnace etc*) alimentar; (*aircraft, ship etc*) repostar.
fuel oil *n* fuel oil *m.*
fuel pump *n* (*AUT*) surtidor *m* de gasolina.
fuel tank *n* depósito de combustible.
fug |fug| *n* (*Brit*) aire *m* viciado.
fugitive |fyōō'jətiv| *n* (*from prison*) fugitivo/a.
fulfill, (*Brit*) **fulfil** |fōōlfil'| *vt* (*function*) cumplir con; (*condition*) satisfacer; (*wish, desire*) realizar.
fulfilled |fōōlfild'| *a* (*person*) satisfecho.
fulfil(l)ment |fulfil'mənt| *n* satisfacción *f*; realización *f.*
full |fōōl| *a* lleno; (*fig*) pleno; (*complete*) completo; (*information*) detallado; (*price*) íntegro, sin descuento ♦ *ad*: **~ well** perfectamente; **we're ~ for July** estamos completos para julio; **I'm ~** no puedo más; **~ employment** pleno empleo; **~ name** nombre *m* y apellidos; **a ~ two hours** dos horas completas; **at ~ speed** a máxima ve-

locidad; **in** ~ (*reproduce*, *quote*) íntegramente; **to write sth in** ~ escribir algo por extenso; **to pay in** ~ pagar la deuda entera.

fullback [fŏŏl'bak] *n* (*SOCCER*) defensa *m*; (*RUGBY*) zaguero.

full-blooded [fŏŏl'blud'id] *a* (*vigorous*: *attack*) vigoroso; (*pure*) puro.

full-cream [fŏŏl'krēm] *a*: ~ **milk** (*Brit*) leche *f* cremosa.

full-fledged [fŏŏl'flejd'] *a* (*US*: *teacher*, *lawyer*) diplomado; (: *bird*) con todas sus plumas, capaz de volar; (: *fig*) con pleno derecho.

full-grown [fŏŏl'grōn'] *a* maduro.

full-length [fŏŏl'lengkth'] *a* (*portrait*) de cuerpo entero; (*film*) de largometraje.

full moon *n* luna llena, plenilunio.

fullness [fŏŏl'nis] *n* plenitud *f*, amplitud *f*.

full-scale [fŏŏl'skāl'] *a* (*attack*, *war*, *search*, *retreat*) en gran escala; (*plan*, *model*) de tamaño natural.

full stop *n* (*Brit*) punto.

full-time [fŏŏl'tīm] *a* (*work*) de tiempo completo ♦ *ad*: **to work** ~ trabajar a tiempo completo.

fully [fŏŏl'ē] *ad* completamente; (*at least*) al menos.

fully-fledged [fŏŏl'ēflejd'] *a* (*Brit*) = **fullfledged**.

fully-paid [fŏŏl'ēpād'] *a*: ~ **share** acción *f* liberada.

fulsome [fŏŏl'səm] *a* (*pej*: *praise*, *gratitude*) excesivo, exagerado; (: *manner*) obsequioso.

fumble with [fum'bəl with] *vt fus* manosear.

fume [fyŏŏm] *vi* humear, echar humo.

fumes [fyŏŏmz] *npl* humo *sg*, gases *mpl*.

fumigate [fyŏŏ'məgāt] *vt* fumigar.

fun [fun] *n* (*amusement*) diversión *f*; (*joy*) alegría; **to have** ~ divertirse; **for** ~ en broma; **to make** ~ **of** burlarse de.

function [fungk'shən] *n* función *f* ♦ *vi* funcionar; **to** ~ **as** hacer (las veces) de.

functional [fungk'shənəl] *a* funcional.

function key *n* (*COMPUT*) tecla de función.

fund [fund] *n* fondo; (*reserve*) reserva; ~**s** *npl* fondos *mpl*.

fundamental [fundəmen'təl] *a* fundamental ♦ *n*: ~**s** fundamentos *mpl*.

fundamentalist [fundəmen'təlist] *n* fundamentalista *m/f*.

fundamentally [fundəmen'təlē] *ad* fundamentalmente.

fund-raising [fund'rāzing] *n* recaudación *f* de fondos.

funeral [fyŏŏ'nûrəl] *n* (*burial*) entierro; (*ceremony*) funerales *mpl*.

funeral director *n* director *m* de pompas fúnebres.

funeral parlour *n* (*Brit*) funeraria.

funeral service *n* misa de difuntos.

funereal [fyŏŏnē'rēəl] *a* fúnebre, funéreo.

funfair [fun'fär] *n* (*Brit*) parque *m* de atracciones.

fungus, *pl* **fungi** [fung'gəs, -jī] *n* hongo.

funicular [fyŏŏnik'yəlûr] *n* (*also*: ~ **railway**) funicular *m*.

funnel [fun'əl] *n* embudo; (*of ship*) chimenea.

funnily [fun'ilē] *ad* de modo divertido, graciosamente; (*oddly*) de una manera rara.

funny [fun'ē] *a* gracioso, divertido; (*strange*) curioso, raro; ~ **enough** aunque parezca extraño.

funny bone *n* hueso de la alegría.

fur [fûr] *n* piel *f*; (*Brit*: *on tongue etc*) sarro.

fur coat *n* abrigo de pieles.

furious [fyŏŏr'ēəs] *a* furioso; (*effort*, *argument*) violento; **to be** ~ **with sb** estar furioso con uno.

furiously [fyŏŏr'ēəslē] *ad* con furia.

furl [fûrl] *vt* (*sail*) aferrar.

furlong [fûr'lông] *n* octava parte de una milla.

furlough [fûr'lō] *n* (*MIL*, *US*) permiso.

furnace [fûr'nis] *n* horno.

furnish [fûr'nish] *vt* amueblar; (*supply*) suministrar; (*information*) facilitar.

furnished [fûr'nisht] *a*: ~ **apartment** piso amueblado.

furnishings [fûr'nishingz] *npl* muebles *mpl*.

furniture [fûr'nichûr] *n* muebles *mpl*; **piece of** ~ mueble *m*.

furniture mover *n* compañía de mudanzas.

furniture polish *n* cera de lustrar.

furore [fyŏŏr'ôr] *n* (*protests*) escándalo.

furrier [fûr'ēûr] *n* peletero/a.

furrow [fûr'ō] *n* surco ♦ *vt* (*forehead*) arrugar.

furry [fûr'ē] *a* (*toy*) peludo.

further [fûr'thûr] *a* (*new*) nuevo, adicional; (*place*) más lejano ♦ *ad* más lejos; (*more*) más; (*moreover*) además ♦ *vt* promover, adelantar; **how much** ~ **is it?** ¿a qué distancia queda?; ~ **to your letter of ...** (*Brit COMM*) con referencia a su carta de ...; **to** ~ **one's interests** fomentar sus intereses.

further education *n* educación *f* superior.

furthermore [fûr'thûrmôr] *ad* además.

furthermost [fûr'thûrmōst] *a* más lejano.

furthest [fûr'thist] *superlative of* **far**.

furtive [fûr'tiv] *a* furtivo.

furtively [fûr'tivlē] *ad* furtivamente, a escondidas.

fury [fyŏŏr'ē] *n* furia.

fuse [fyŏŏz] *n* fusible *m*; (*Brit*: *for bomb etc*) mecha ♦ *vt* (*metal*) fundir; (*fig*) fusionar ♦ *vi* fundirse; fusionarse; (*Brit*: *ELEC*): **to** ~ **the lights** fundir los plomos; **a** ~ **has blown** se ha fundido un fusible.

fuse box *n* caja de fusibles.

fuselage [fyŏŏ'səlázh] *n* fuselaje *m*.

fuse wire *n* hilo fusible.

fusillade [fyōōs'əlād] *n* descarga cerrada; (*fig*) lluvia.
fusion [fyōō'zhən] *n* fusión *f*.
fuss [fus] *n* (*noise*) bulla; (*dispute*) lío; (*complaining*) protesta ♦ *vi* preocuparse (por pequeñeces) ♦ *vt* (*person*) molestar; **to make a** ~ armar un lío *or* jaleo.
fuss over *vt fus* (*person*) consentir (a).
fussy [fus'ē] *a* (*person*) exigente; **I'm not** ~ (*col*) me da igual.
futile [fyōō'təl] *a* vano.
futility [fyōōtil'ətē] *n* inutilidad *f*.
future [fyōō'chûr] *a* (*gen*) futuro; (*coming*) venidero ♦ *n* futuro, porvenir; **in the** ~ de ahora en adelante.
futures [fyōō'chûrz] *npl* (*COMM*) operaciones *fpl* a término.
futuristic [fyōōchəris'tik] *a* futurístico.
fuze [fyōōz] *n* (*US: for bomb etc*) mecha.
fuzzy [fuz'ē] *a* (*PHOT*) borroso; (*hair*) muy rizado.
fwd. *abbr* = **forward**.
fwy *abbr* (*US*) = **freeway**.
FY *abbr* = **fiscal year**.
FYI *abbr* = *for your information*.

G

G, g [jē] *n* (*letter*) G, g *f*; **G** (*MUS*) sol *m*; **G for George** G de Gerona.
G *n abbr* (*US CINEMA*: = *general audience*) todos los públicos; (*Brit SCOL*: = *good*) N.
g. *abbr* (= *gram(s)*, *gravity*) g.
GA *abbr* (*US MAIL*) = *Georgia*.
gab [gab] *n*: **to have the gift of the** ~ (*col*) tener mucha labia.
gabble [gab'əl] *vi* hablar atropelladamente.
gaberdine [gab'ûrdēn] *n* gabardina.
gable [gā'bəl] *n* aguilón *m*.
Gabon [gā'bən] *n* Gabón *m*.
gad about [gad əbout'] *vi* (*col*) moverse mucho.
gadget [gaj'it] *n* aparato.
gadgetry [gaj'itrē] *n* chismes *mpl*.
Gaelic [gā'lik] *a*, *n* (*LING*) gaélico.
gaffe [gaf] *n* plancha, patinazo, metedura de pata.
gag [gag] *n* (*on mouth*) mordaza; (*joke*) chiste *m* ♦ *vt* amordazar.
gaga [gä'gä] *a*: **to go** ~ (*senile*) chochear; (*ecstatic*) cáersele a uno la baba.
gage [gāj] *n*, *vt* (*US*) = **gauge**.
gaiety [gā'ətē] *n* alegría.
gaily [gā'lē] *ad* alegremente.
gain [gān] *n* ganancia ♦ *vt* ganar ♦ *vi*

(*watch*) adelantarse; **to** ~ **by sth** sacar provecho de algo; **to** ~ **ground** ganar terreno; **to** ~ **3 lbs (in weight)** engordar 3 libras.
gain (up)on *vt fus* ganar terreno a.
gainful [gān'fəl] *a* (*employment*) remunerado.
gait [gāt] *n* (modo de) andar *m*.
gala [gā'lə] *n* fiesta; **swimming** ~ gala de natación.
Galapagos Islands [gəlä'pəgōs ī'ləndz] *npl*: **the** ~ las Islas Galápagos.
galaxy [gal'əksē] *n* galaxia.
gale [gāl] *n* (*wind*) vendaval *m;* ~ **force 10** vendaval de fuerza 10.
gall [gôl] *n* (*ANAT*) bilis *f*, hiel *f*; (*fig: impudence*) descaro, caradura ♦ *vt* molestar.
gal(l). *abbr* = **gallon(s)**.
gallant [gal'ənt] *a* valiente; [gəlânt'] (*towards ladies*) atento.
gallantry [gal'əntrē] *n* valor *m*, valentía; (*courtesy*) cortesía.
gallbladder [gôl'bladûr] *n* vesícula biliar.
galleon [gal'ēən] *n* galeón *m*.
gallery [gal'ûrē] *n* (*also THEATER*) galería; (*for spectators*) tribuna; (*also:* **art** ~: *government owned*) pinacoteca *or* galería de arte; (: *private*) colección *f* (de cuadros).
galley [gal'ē] *n* (*ship's kitchen*) cocina; (*ship*) galera.
galley proof *n* (*TYP*) prueba de galera, galerada.
Gallic [gal'ik] *a* galo, galicano.
gallon [gal'ən] *n* galón *m* (= 8 *pints*; *US* = 3,785 *litros*, *Brit* = 4,546 *litros*).
gallop [gal'əp] *n* galope *m* ♦ *vi* galopar; ~**ing inflation** inflación *f* galopante.
gallows [gal'ōz] *n* horca.
gallstone [gôl'stōn] *n* cálculo biliario.
galore [gəlôr'] *ad* en cantidad, en abundancia.
galvanize [gal'vənīz] *vt* (*metal*) galvanizar; (*fig*): **to** ~ **sb into action** animar a uno para que haga algo.
Gambia [gam'bēə] *n* Gambia.
gambit [gam'bit] *n* (*fig*): **opening** ~ estrategia inicial.
gamble [gam'bəl] *n* (*risk*) riesgo; (*bet*) apuesta ♦ *vt*: **to** ~ **on** apostar a; (*fig*) confiar en que ♦ *vi* jugar; (*COMM*) especular; **to** ~ **on the Stock Exchange** jugar a la bolsa.
gambler [gam'blûr] *n* jugador(a) *m/f*.
gambling [gam'bling] *n* el juego.
gambol [gam'bəl] *vi* brincar, juguetear.
game [gām] *n* (*gen*) juego; (*match*) partido; (*of cards*) partida; (*HUNTING*) caza ♦ *a* valiente; (*ready*): **to be** ~ **for anything** atreverse a todo; ~**s** (*SCOL*) el deporte; **big** ~ caza mayor.
game bird *n* ave *f* de caza.
gamekeeper [gām'kēpûr] *n* guardabosques

m inv.

gamely [gām'lē] *ad* bravamente.

game reserve *n* coto de caza.

gamesmanship [gāmz'mənship] *n* habilidad *f*.

gammon [gam'ən] *n* (*bacon*) tocino ahumado; (*ham*) jamón *m* ahumado.

gamut [gam'ət] *n* (*MUS*) gama; **to run the (whole) ~ of emotions** (*fig*) pasar por toda la gama de emociones.

gander [gan'dûr] *n* ganso.

gang [gang] *n* pandilla; (*of workmen*) brigada ♦ *vi*: **to ~ up on sb** conspirar contra uno.

Ganges [gan'jēz] *n*: **the ~** el Ganges.

gangling [gang'gling] *a* larguirucho.

gangplank [gang'plangk] *n* plancha.

gangrene [gang'grēn] *n* gangrena.

gangster [gang'stûr] *n* gángster *m*.

gangway [gang'wā] *n* (*on ship*) pasarela; (*Brit: in theater, bus etc*) pasillo.

gantry [gan'trē] *n* (*for crane, railway signal*) pórtico; (*for rocket*) torre *f* de lanzamiento.

GAO *n abbr* (*US*: = *General Accounting Office*) tribunal de cuentas.

gaol [jāl] *n*, *vt* (*Brit*) = **jail**.

gap [gap] *n* vacío, hueco (*LAm*); (*in trees, traffic*) claro; (*in time*) intervalo.

gape [gāp] *vi* mirar boquiabierto.

gaping [gā'ping] *a* (*hole*) muy abierto.

garage [gərázh'] *n* garaje *m*.

garb [gârb] *n* atuendo.

garbage [gâr'bij] *n* (*US*) basura; (*nonsense*) tonterías *fpl*; (*fig: movie, book etc*) basura.

garbage can *n* (*US*) cubo *or* balde *m or* bote *m* (*LAm*) de la basura.

garbage disposal unit *n* triturador *m* (de basura).

garbage dump *n* (*US*) vertedero.

garbageman [gâr'bijmən] *n* basurero.

garbage truck *n* camión *m* de la basura.

garbled [gâr'bəld] *a* (*account, explanation*) confuso.

garden [gâr'dən] *n* jardín *m*; **~s** *npl* (*public*) parque *m*, jardines *mpl*; (*private*) huertos *mpl*.

garden center *n* viveros *mpl*.

gardener [gárd'nûr] *n* jardinero/a.

gardening [gâr'dəning] *n* jardinería.

garden party *n* recepción *f* al aire libre.

gargle [gâr'gəl] *vi* hacer gárgaras, gargarear (*LAm*).

gargoyle [gâr'goil] *n* gárgola.

garish [gär'ish] *a* chillón/ona.

garland [gâr'lənd] *n* guirnalda.

garlic [gâr'lik] *n* ajo.

garment [gâr'mənt] *n* prenda (de vestir).

garner [gâr'nûr] *vt* acumular.

garnish [gâr'nish] *vt* adornar; (*CULIN*) aderezar.

garret [gar'it] *n* desván *m*, guardilla.

garrison [gar'isən] *n* guarnición *f* ♦ *vt*

guarnecer.

garrulous [gar'ələs] *a* charlatán/ana.

garter [gâr'tûr] *n* (*US*) liga.

garter belt *n* (*US*) portaligas *m inv*.

gas [gas] *n* gas *m*; (*US: gasoline*) gasolina ♦ *vt* asfixiar con gas.

gas can *n* (*US*) bidón *m* de gasolina.

gas chamber *n* cámara de gas.

Gascony [gas'kənē] *n* Gascuña.

gas cylinder *n* bombona de gas.

gaseous [gas'ēəs] *a* gaseoso.

gash [gash] *n* raja; (*on face*) cuchillada ♦ *vt* rajar; (*with knife*) acuchillar.

gasket [gas'kit] *n* (*AUT*) junta de culata.

gas mask *n* careta antigás.

gas meter *n* contador *m* de gas.

gasoline [gasəlēn'] *n* (*US*) gasolina.

gasp [gasp] *n* grito sofocado ♦ *vi* (*pant*) jadear.

gasp out *vt* (*say*) decir con voz entrecortada.

gas pedal *n* (*esp US*) acelerador *m*.

gas pump *n* (*US*) (*in car*) bomba de gasolina; (*in gas station*) surtidor *m* de gasolina.

gas ring *n* hornillo de gas.

gas station *n* (*US*) gasolinera.

gas stove *n* cocina de gas.

gassy [gas'ē] *a* gaseoso.

gas tank *n* (*US AUT*) depósito (de gasolina).

gas tap *n* llave *f* del gas.

gastric [gas'trik] *a* gástrico.

gastric ulcer *n* úlcera gástrica.

gastroenteritis [gastrōentərī'tis] *n* gastroenteritis *f*.

gasworks [gas'wûrks] *nsg or npl* fábrica de gas.

gate [gāt] *n* (*also at airport*) puerta; (*RAIL: at grade crossing*) barrera; (*of castle, town*) reja, puerta.

gateau, *pl* **~x** [gatō', -z] *n* (*Brit*) torta, pastel *m*.

gate-crash [gāt'krash] *vt* colarse en.

gate-crasher [gāt'krashûr] *n* advenedizo/a, intruso/a.

gateway [gāt'wā] *n* puerta.

gather [gath'ûr] *vt* (*flowers, fruit*) coger (*Sp*), recoger (*LAm*); (*assemble*) reunir; (*pick up*) recoger; (*SEWING*) fruncir; (*understand*) entender ♦ *vi* (*assemble*) reunirse; (*dust*) acumularse; (*clouds*) cerrarse; **to ~ speed** ganar velocidad; **to ~ (from/that)** tener entendido (por/que); **as far as I can ~** por lo que tengo entendido.

gathering [gath'ûring] *n* reunión *f*, asamblea.

GATT [gat] *n abbr* (= *General Agreement on Tariffs and Trade*) GATT *m*.

gauche [gōsh] *a* torpe.

gaudy [gó'dē] *a* chillón/ona.

gauge [gāj] *n* calibre *m*; (*RAIL*) entrevía; (*instrument*) indicador *m* ♦ *vt* medir; (*fig*:

sb's capabilities, character) estimar, juzgar; **gas** ~ indicador *m* del nivel de gasolina; **to ~ the right moment** elegir el momento (oportuno).

Gaul |gól| *n* Galia.

gaunt |gònt| *a* descarnado; *(grim, desolate)* desolado.

gauntlet |gònt'lit| *n (fig)*: **to run the ~ of** sth desafiar algo; **to throw down the ~** arrojar el guante.

gauze |góz| *n* gasa.

gave |gāv| *pt of* **give**.

gawk |gók| *vi* papar moscas.

gawky |gó'kē| *a* desgarbado.

gay |gā| *a (person)* alegre; *(color)* vivo; *(homosexual)* gay.

gaze |gāz| *n* mirada fija ♦ *vi*: **to ~ at sth** mirar algo fijamente.

gazelle |gəzcl'| *n* gacela.

gazette |gəzct'| *n (newspaper)* gaceta; *(official publication)* boletín *m* oficial.

gazetteer |gazitēr'| *n* diccionario geográfico.

GB *abbr* (= *Great Britain*) G.B.

GCE *n abbr (Brit:* = *General Certificate of Education)* ≈ certificado de BUP *(Sp)* or bachillerato.

GCSE *n abbr (Brit:* = *General Certificate of Secondary Education)* ≈ certificado de BUP *(Sp)* or bachillerato.

Gdns. *abbr* (= *Gardens*) jdns.

GDP *n abbr* (= *gross domestic product*) PIB *m.*

GDR *n abbr* (= *German Democratic Republic*) RDA *f.*

gear |gēr| *n* equipo, herramientas *fpl*; *(TECH)* engranaje *m*; *(AUT)* velocidad *f*, marcha ♦ *vt (fig: adapt)*: **to ~ sth to** adaptar *or* ajustar algo a; **high** *or (Brit)* **top/low** ~ cuarta/primera velocidad; **in ~** en marcha; **our service is ~ed to meet the needs of the disabled** nuestro servicio está destinado a responder a las necesidades de los minusválidos.

gear up *vi* hacer preparativos.

gear box *n* caja de cambios.

gear shift, *(Brit)* **gear lever** *n* palanca de cambio.

gear wheel *n* rueda dentada.

GED *n abbr (US SCOL)* = *general educational development.*

geese |gēs| *npl of* **goose**.

Geiger counter |gī'gûr koun'tûr| *n* contador *m* Geiger.

gel |jcl| *n* gel *m.*

gelatin(e) |jcl'atin| *n* gelatina.

gelignite |jcl'ignīt| *n* gelignita.

gem |jcm| *n* joya.

Gemini |jcm'ənī| *n* Géminis *m.*

gen |jcn| *n (Brit col)*: **to give sb the ~ on** sth poner a uno al corriente de algo.

Gen. *abbr (MIL:* = *General)* Gen., Gral.

gen. *abbr* (= *general)* grl.; = **generally.**

gender |jcn'dûr| *n* género.

gene |jēn| *n* gen(e) *m.*

genealogy |jēnēál'əjē| *n* genealogía.

general |jcn'ûrəl| *n* general *m* ♦ *a* general; **in ~** en general; **~ audit** comprobación *f* general de cuentas; **the ~ public** el gran público.

general anesthetic *n* anestesia general.

general delivery *n (US)* lista de correos.

general election *n* elecciones *fpl* generales.

generalization |jcnûrələzā'shən| *n* generalización *f.*

generalize |jcn'ûrəlīz| *vi* generalizar.

generally |jcn'ûrəlē| *ad* generalmente, en general.

general manager *n* director(a) *m/f* general.

general practitioner (GP) *n* médico/a general.

general strike *n* huelga general.

generate |jcn'ərāt| *vt (ELEC)* generar; *(fig)* producir.

generation |jcnərā'shən| *n (of electricity etc)* generación *f*; **first/second/third/fourth ~** *(of computer)* primera/segunda/tercera/cuarta generación.

generator |jcn'ərātûr| *n* generador *m.*

generic |jənār'ik| *a* genérico.

generosity |jcnərás'ətē| *n* generosidad *f.*

generous |jcn'ûrəs| *a* generoso; *(copious)* abundante.

generously |jcn'ûrəslē| *ad* generosamente; abundantemente.

genesis |jcn'əsis| *n* génesis *f.*

genetic |jinct'ik| *a* genético; **~ engineering** selección *f* genética.

genetics |jənct'iks| *n* genética.

Geneva |jənē'va| *n* Ginebra.

genial |jē'nēal| *a* afable, simpático.

genitals |jcn'itəlz| *npl (órganos mpl)* genitales *mpl.*

genitive |jcn'ətiv| *n* genitivo.

genius |jēn'yəs| *n* genio.

Genoa |jən'əwə| *n* Génova.

genocide |jcn'əsīd| *n* genocidio.

genteel |jcntēl'| *a* fino, elegante.

Gentile |jcn'tīl| *n* gentil *m/f.*

gentle |jcn'təl| *a (sweet)* amable, dulce; *(touch etc)* ligero, suave.

gentleman |jcn'təlmən| *n* señor *m*; *(well-bred man)* caballero; **~'s agreement** acuerdo entre caballeros.

gentlemanly |jcn'təlmənlē| *a* caballeroso, cortés.

gentleness |jcn'təlnis| *n* dulzura; *(of touch)* suavidad *f.*

gently |jcn'tlē| *ad* suavemente.

gentry |jcn'trē| *npl* aristocracia *sg.*

genuine |jcn'yōōin| *a* auténtico; *(person)* sincero.

genuinely |jcn'yōōinlē| *ad* sinceramente.

geographer |jēág'rəfûr| *n* geográfo/a.

geographic(al) |jēəgraf'ik(əl)| *a* geográfico.

geography [jēág'rəfē] *n* geografía.
geological [jēəlâj'ikəl] *a* geológico.
geologist [jēál'əjist] *n* geólogo/a.
geology [jēál'əjē] *n* geología.
geometric(al) [jēəmet'rik(əl)] *a* geométrico.
geometry [jēám'ətrē] *n* geometría.
geranium [jərā'nēəm] *n* geranio.
geriatric [järēat'rik] *a, n* geriátrico/a *m/f*.
germ [jûrm] *n* (*microbe*) microbio, bacteria; (*seed*, *fig*) germen *m*.
German [jûr'mən] *a* alemán/ana ♦ *n* alemán/ana *m/f*; (*LING*) alemán *m*.
German Democratic Republic *n* República Democrática Alemana.
German measles *n* rubéola.
German shepherd *n* (*dog*) pastor *m* alemán.
Germany [jûr'mənē] *n* Alemania; **East/West ~** Alemania Oriental *or* Democrática/Occidental *or* Federal.
germination [jûrmənā'shən] *n* germinación *f*.
germ warfare *n* guerra bacteriológica.
gesticulate [jestik'yəlāt] *vi* gesticular.
gesticulation [jestikyəlā'shən] *n* gesticulación *f*.
gesture [jes'chûr] *n* gesto; **as a ~ of friendship** en señal de amistad.
get, *pt*, *pp* **got**, (*US*) *pp* **gotten** [get, gât, gát'ən] *vt* (*obtain*) obtener; (*receive*) recibir; (*achieve*) conseguir; (*find*) encontrar; (*catch*) coger (*Sp*), agarrar (*LAm*); (*fetch*) traer, ir a buscar; (*take*, *move*) llevar; (*understand*) entender; (*col: annoy*) molestar; (: *thrill*) chiflar ♦ *vi* (*become*) hacerse, volverse; **to ~ old** hacerse viejo, envejecer; **to ~ to** (*place*) llegar a; **he got under the fence** pasó por debajo de la barrera; **to ~ ready/washed** prepararse/lavarse; **to ~ sb to do sth** hacer que uno haga algo; **I've got to do it** tengo que hacerlo; **to ~ sth for sb** conseguir algo para uno; **to ~ sth out of sth** sacar algo de algo; **to ~ sth done** (*do*) hacer algo; (*have done*) mandar hacer algo; **to ~ sth/sb ready** preparar algo/a uno; **to ~ one's hair cut** cortarse el pelo; **~ me Mr. Jones, please** (*TEL*) póngame *or* (*LAm*) comuníqueme con el Sr. Jones, por favor; **can I ~ you a drink?** ¿quieres algo de beber?; **you've got to tell the police** tienes que denunciarlo a la policía; **to ~ used to sth** acostumbrarse a algo; **let's ~ going** *or* **started** vámonos.
get about *vi* (*Brit*) = **get around**.
get across *vt* (*message*, *meaning*) lograr comunicar ♦ *vi*: **to ~ across to sb** lograr hacer que uno comprenda.
get along *vi* (*depart*) marcharse; (*manage*) arreglárselas; (*agree*): **to ~ along (with)** entenderse (con); **how are you ~ting along?** ¿qué tal estás?, ¿cómo te va? (*LAm*).

get around *vi* salir mucho; (*travel*) viajar mucho; (*news*) divulgarse ♦ *vt fus* rodear; (*fig*: *person*) engatusar; **to ~ around to doing sth** llegar a hacer algo.
get at *vt fus* (*attack*) atacar; (*reach*) llegar a; (*the truth*) descubrir; **what are you ~ting at?** ¿qué insinúas?
get away *vi* marcharse; (*on vacation*) irse de vacaciones; (*escape*) escaparse.
get away with *vt fus* hacer impunemente.
get back *vi* (*return*) volver ♦ *vt* recobrar.
get back at *vt fus* (*col*): **to ~ back at sb (for sth)** vengarse de uno (por algo).
get by *vi* (*pass*) lograr pasar; (*manage*) arreglárselas; **I can ~ by in Dutch** me defiendo en holandés.
get down *vi* bajarse ♦ *vt* (*object*) bajar; (*depress*) deprimir.
get down to *vt fus* (*work*) ponerse a (hacer); **to ~ down to business** ponerse a trabajar en serio.
get in *vi* (*train*) llegar; (*arrive home*) volver a casa, regresar ♦ *vt* (*bring in*: *harvest*) recoger; (: *coal*, *shopping*, *supplies*) comprar, traer; (*insert*) lograr meter en.
get into *vt fus* (*vehicle*) subir a; (*house*) entrar en; (*clothes*) ponerse.
get off *vi* (*from train etc*) bajar; (*depart*: *person*, *car*) marcharse ♦ *vt* (*send off*) mandar; (*have as leave*: *day*, *time*) tener libre ♦ *vt fus* (*train*, *bus*) bajar de; **to ~ off to a good start** (*fig*) empezar muy bien *or* con buen pie.
get on *vi* (*in exam etc*) tener éxito ♦ *vt fus* (*horse*) subir.
get on to *vt fus* (*Brit*: *deal with*) ocuparse de; (: *col: contact*: *on phone etc*) hablar con.
get out *vi* salir; (*of vehicle*) bajar; (*news*) saberse, difundirse ♦ *vt* (*take out*: *money from bank etc*) sacar.
get out of *vt fus* (*duty etc*) escaparse de ♦ *vt* (*extract*: *confession*, *words*) sacar de; (*gain from*: *pleasure*, *benefit*) ganar de.
get over *vt fus* (*illness*) recobrarse de ♦ *vt* (*communicate*: *idea etc*) comunicar; **let's ~ it over (with)** acabemos de una vez.
get round *vt fus* = **get around**.
get through *vt fus* (*finish*: *work*) acabar con; (: *book*) terminar, acabar ♦ *vi* (*TEL*) lograr comunicarse.
get through to *vt fus* (*TEL*) comunicar con.
get together *vi* reunirse.
get up *vi* (*rise*) levantarse ♦ *vt fus* levantar; **to ~ up enthusiasm for sth** cobrar entusiasmo por algo.
get up to *vt fus* (*reach*) llegar a; (*Brit*: *prank etc*) hacer.
getaway [get'əwā] *n* fuga, escape *m*.

getaway car *n*: the thieves' ~ el coche en que los ladrones huyeron.

get-together [gɛt'təgɛthûr] *n* reunión *f*; (*party*) fiesta.

get-up [gɛt'up] *n* (*col*: *outfit*) atavío, atuendo.

get-well card [gɛtwɛl' kârd] *n* tarjeta que se envía a uno que está enfermo deseándole que se mejore.

geyser [gī'zûr] *n* (*GEO*) géiser *m*.

Ghana [gán'ə] *n* Ghana.

Ghanaian [gənā'ēən] *a*, *n* ghaneano/a *m/f*.

ghastly [gast'lē] *a* horrible; (*pale*) pálido.

gherkin [gûr'kin] *n* pepinillo.

ghetto [gɛt'ō] *n* ghetto.

ghost [gōst] *n* fantasma *m* ♦ *vt* (*book*) escribir por otro.

ghostly [gōst'lē] *a* fantasmal.

ghost story *n* cuento de fantasmas.

ghostwriter [gōst'rītûr] *n* negro/a.

ghoul [gōōl] *n* demonio necrófago.

GHQ *n* abbr (*MIL*: = *general headquarters*) E.M.

GI *n* abbr (*US col*: = *government issue*) soldado del ejército norteamericano.

giant [jī'ənt] *n* gigante *m/f* ♦ *a* gigantesco, gigante; ~ **(size) packet** paquete *m* (de tamaño) gigante *or* familiar.

gibber [jib'ûr] *vi* (*monkey*) farfullar; (*idiot*) hablar de una manera ininteligible.

gibberish [jib'ûrish] *n* galimatías *m*.

gibe [jīb] *n* mofa.

giblets [jib'lits] *npl* menudillos *mpl*.

Gibraltar [jibrôl'tûr] *n* Gibraltar *m*.

giddiness [gid'ēnis] *n* vértigo.

giddy [gid'ē] *a* (*dizzy*) mareado; (*height*, *speed*) vertiginoso; **it makes me** ~ me marea; **I feel** ~ me siento mareado.

gift [gift] *n* (*gen*) regalo; (*COMM*: *also*: **free** ~) obsequio; (*ability*) talento; **to have a** ~ **for sth** tener talento para algo.

gift certificate *n* (*US*) vale-regalo *m*.

gifted [gif'tid] *a* dotado.

gift token *n* (*Brit*) vale-regalo *m*.

gig [gig] *n* (*col*: *concert*) función *f*.

gigantic [jīgan'tik] *a* gigantesco.

giggle [gig'əl] *vi* reírse tontamente ♦ *n* risilla.

GIGO [gīg'ō] *abbr* (*COMPUT*: *col*) = *garbage in, garbage out*.

gill [jil] *n* (*measure*) = 0.25 *pints* (*US* = 0.118 *l*, *Brit* = 0.148 *l*).

gills [gilz] *npl* (*of fish*) branquias *fpl*, agallas *fpl*.

gilt [gilt] *a*, *n* dorado.

gilt-edged [gilt'ejd] *a* (*COMM*: *stocks*, *securities*) de máxima garantía.

gimlet [gim'lit] *n* barrena de mano.

gimmick [gim'ik] *n* truco; **sales** ~ truco de promoción.

gimmicky [gim'ikē] *a* truquero.

gin [jin] *n* (*liquor*) ginebra.

ginger [jin'jûr] *n* jengibre *m*.

ginger ale, ginger beer *n* gaseosa de jengibre.

gingerbread [jin'jûrbred] *n* pan *m* de jengibre.

ginger-haired [jin'jûrhärd] *a* pelirrojo.

gingerly [jin'jûrlē] *ad* con pies de plomo.

gipsy [jip'sē] *n* = **gypsy**.

giraffe [jəraf'] *n* jirafa.

girder [gûr'dûr] *n* viga.

girdle [gûr'dəl] *n* (*corset*) faja ♦ *vt* ceñir.

girl [gûrl] *n* (*small*) niña; (*young woman*) chica, joven *f*, muchacha; **an American** ~ una (chica) norteamericana.

girl Friday *n* empleada de confianza.

girlfriend [gûrl'frend] *n* (*of girl*) amiga; (*of boy*) novia.

Girl Guide *n* (*Brit*) = **Girl Scout**.

girlish [gûr'lish] *a* de niña.

Girl Scout *n* (*US*) exploradora.

giro [jī'rō] *n* (*Brit*: *bank* ~) giro bancario; (: *post office* ~) giro postal.

girth [gûrth] *n* circunferencia; (*of saddle*) cincha.

gist [jist] *n* lo esencial.

give [giv] *vb* (*pt* **gave**, *pp* **given** [gāv, giv'ən]) *vt* dar; (*deliver*) entregar; (*as gift*) regalar ♦ *vi* (*break*) romperse; (*stretch*: *fabric*) dar de sí; **to** ~ **sb sth**, ~ **sth to sb** darle algo a uno; **how much did you** ~ **for it?** ¿cuánto pagaste por él?; **12 o'clock**, ~ **or take a few minutes** más o menos las doce; ~ **them my regards** mándales saludos de mi parte; **I can** ~ **you 10 minutes** le puedo conceder 10 minutos; **to** ~ **way** (*Brit AUT*) ceder el paso; **to** ~ **way to despair** ceder a la desesperación.

give away *vt* (*give free*) regalar; (*betray*) traicionar; (*disclose*) revelar.

give back *vt* devolver.

give in *vi* ceder ♦ *vt* entregar.

give off *vt* despedir.

give out *vt* distribuir ♦ *vi* (*be exhausted*: *supplies*) agotarse; (*fail*: *engine*) averiarse; (*strength*) fallar.

give up *vi* rendirse, darse por vencido ♦ *vt* renunciar a; **to** ~ **up smoking** dejar de fumar; **to** ~ **o.s. up** entregarse.

give-and-take [giv'əntāk'] *n* (*col*) toma y daca *m*.

giveaway [giv'əwā] *n* (*col*): **her expression was a** ~ su expresión la delataba; **the exam was a** ~! ¡el examen estaba tirado! ♦ *cpd*: ~ **prices** precios *mpl* de regalo.

given [giv'ən] *pp* of **give** ♦ *a* (*fixed*: *time*, *amount*) determinado, fijo ♦ *conj*: ~ **(that)** ... dado (que) ...; ~ **the circumstances** ... dadas las circunstancias....

glacial [glā'shəl] *a* glacial.

glacier [glā'shûr] *n* glaciar *m*.

glad [glad] *a* contento; **to be** ~ **about sth/ that** alegrarse de algo/de que; **I was** ~ **of his help** agradecí su ayuda.

gladden [glad'ən] *vt* alegrar.

glade [glād] n claro.
gladiator [glad'ēātûr] n gladiador m.
gladioli [gladēō'lē] npl gladíolos mpl.
gladly [glad'lē] ad con mucho gusto.
glamor [glam'ûr] n encanto, atractivo, hechizo.
glamorous [glam'ûrəs] a encantador(a), atractivo.
glamour [glam'ûr] n (Brit) = **glamor.**
glance [glans] n ojeada, mirada ♦ vi: **to ~ at** echar una ojeada a.
glance off vt fus (bullet) rebotar en.
glancing [glan'sing] a (blow) oblicuo.
gland [gland] n glándula.
glandular [glan'jəlûr] a: **~ fever** (Brit) fiebre f glandular.
glare [glär] n deslumbramiento, brillo ♦ vi deslumbrar; **to ~ at** mirar ferozmente a.
glaring [glär'ing] a (mistake) manifiesto.
glass [glas] n vidrio, cristal m; (for drinking) vaso; (: with stem) copa; (also: **looking ~**) espejo.
glass-blowing [glas'blōing] n soplado de vidrio.
glasses [glas'iz] npl gafas fpl, anteojos mpl (LAm).
glass fiber, (Brit) **glass fibre** n fibra de vidrio.
glasshouse [glas'hous] n (Brit) invernadero.
glassware [glas'wär] n cristalería.
glassy [glas'ē] a (eyes) vidrioso.
glaze [glāz] vt (window) poner cristales a; (pottery) barnizar; (CULIN) glasear ♦ n barniz m; (CULIN) vidriado.
glazed [glāzd] a (eye) vidrioso; (pottery) barnizado.
glazier [glā'zhûr] n vidriero/a.
gleam [glēm] n destello ♦ vi brillar; **a ~ of hope** un rayo de esperanza.
gleaming [glē'ming] a reluciente.
glean [glēn] vt (gather: information) recoger.
glee [glē] n alegría, regocijo.
gleeful [glē'fəl] a alegre.
glen [glen] n cañada.
glib [glib] a (person) de mucha labia; (comment) fácil.
glibly [glib'lē] ad (explain) con mucha labia.
glide [glīd] vi deslizarse; (AVIAT, birds) planear.
glider [glī'dûr] n (AVIAT) planeador m.
gliding [glī'ding] n (AVIAT) vuelo sin motor.
glimmer [glim'ûr] n luz f tenue.
glimpse [glimps] n vislumbre m ♦ vt vislumbrar, entrever; **to catch a ~ of** vislumbrar.
glint [glint] n destello; (in the eye) chispa ♦ vi centellear.
glisten [glis'ən] vi relucir, brillar.
glitter [glit'ûr] vi relucir, brillar ♦ n brillo.
glittering [glit'ûring] a reluciente, brillante.
glitz [glits] n (col) brillo, resplandor m.

gloat [glōt] vi: **to ~ over** (money) recrearse en; (sb's misfortune) saborear.
global [glō'bəl] a (world-wide) mundial; (comprehensive) global.
globe [glōb] n globo, esfera.
globetrotter [glōb'trâtûr] n trotamundos m inv.
globule [glâb'yōōl] n glóbulo.
gloom [glōōm] n tinieblas fpl, oscuridad f; (sadness) tristeza, melancolía.
gloomily [glōō'milē] ad tristemente; de moda pesimista.
gloomy [glōō'mē] a (dark) oscuro; (sad) triste; (pessimistic) pesimista; **to feel ~** sentirse pesimista.
glorification [glôrəfəkā'shən] n glorificación f.
glorify [glôr'əfī] vt glorificar; (God) alabar, ensalzar.
glorious [glôr'ēəs] a glorioso.
glory [glôr'ē] n gloria.
glory hole n (col) trastero.
Glos abbr (Brit) = Gloucestershire.
gloss [glôs] n (shine) brillo; (also: **~ paint**) pintura de aceite.
gloss over vt fus encubrir.
glossary [glâs'ûrē] n glosario.
glossy [glâs'ē] a lustroso.
glove [gluv] n guante m.
glove compartment n (AUT) guantera.
glow [glō] vi (shine) brillar ♦ n brillo.
glower [glou'ûr] vi: **to ~ at** mirar con ceño.
glowing [glō'ing] a (fire) vivo; (complexion) encendido; (fig: report, description) entusiasta.
glow-worm [glō'wûrm] n luciérnaga.
glucose [glōō'kōs] n glucosa.
glue [glōō] n goma (de pegar), cemento (LAm) ♦ vt pegar.
glue-sniffing [glōō'snifing] n inhalación f del vapor del cemento.
glum [glum] a (mood) abatido; (person, tone) melancólico.
glut [glut] n superabundancia.
glutinous [glōōt'ənəs] a glutinoso.
glutton [glut'ən] n glotón/ona m/f; **~ for punishment** masoquista m/f.
gluttony [glut'ənē] n gula, glotonería.
glycerin(e) [glis'ûrin] n glicerina.
gm abbr (= gram) g.
GMAT n abbr (US: = Graduate Management Admissions Test) examen de admisión en el segundo ciclo de la enseñanza superior.
GMT abbr (= Greenwich Mean Time) GMT.
gnarled [nârld] a nudoso.
gnash [nash] vt: **to ~ one's teeth** rechinar los dientes.
gnat [nat] n mosquito.
gnaw [nô] vt roer.
gnome [nōm] n gnomo.
GNP n abbr (= gross national product) PNB

m.

go [gō] *vb* (*pt* **went**, *pp* **gone** [wɛnt, gɒn]) *vi* ir; (*travel*) viajar; (*depart*) irse, marcharse; (*work*) funcionar, marchar; (*be sold*) venderse; (*time*) pasar; (*become*) ponerse; (*break etc*) estropearse, romperse; (*fit, suit*): **to ~ with** hacer juego con ♦ *n* (*pl* **~es**): **to have a ~ (at)** probar suerte (con); **I'll have a ~ at it** lo intentaré; **to be on the ~** no parar; **to ~ by car/on foot** ir en coche/a pie; **he's ~ing to do it** va a hacerlo; **to ~ for a walk** ir de paseo; **to ~ dancing** ir a bailar; **to ~ looking for sth/sb** ir a buscar algo/a uno; **to make sth ~, get sth ~ing** poner algo en marcha; **my voice has gone** he perdido la voz; **the cake is all gone** se acabó la torta; **the money will ~ towards our vacation** el dinero será un aporte para las vacaciones; **how did it ~?** ¿qué tal salió *or* resultó?, ¿cómo ha ido?; **the meeting went well** la reunión salió bien; **to ~ and see sb, ~ to see sb** ir a ver a uno; **to ~ to sleep** dormirse; **I'll take whatever is ~ing** acepto lo que haya; **... to ~** (*US: food*) ... para llevar; **to ~ around the back** pasar por detrás.

go about *vt fus*: **how do I ~ about this?** ¿cómo me las arreglo para hacer esto?; **to ~ about one's business** ocuparse en sus asuntos.

go after *vt fus* (*pursue*) perseguir; (*job, record etc*) andar tras.

go against *vt fus* (*be unfavorable to: results*) ir en contra de; (*be contrary to: principles*) ser contrario a.

go ahead *vi* seguir adelante.

go along *vi* ir ♦ *vt fus* bordear.

go along with *vt fus* (*accompany*) acompañar; (*agree with: idea*) estar de acuerdo con.

go around *vi* (*circulate: news, rumor*) correr; (*suffice*) alcanzar, bastar; (*revolve*) girar, dar vueltas; (*wander around*) andar (de un sitio para otro); (*visit*): **to ~ around (to sb's)** pasar a ver (a uno); (*make a detour*): **to ~ around (by)** dar la vuelta (por).

go away *vi* irse, marcharse.

go back *vi* volver.

go back on *vt fus* (*promise*) faltar a.

go by *vi* (*years, time*) pasar ♦ *vt fus* guiarse por.

go down *vi* bajar; (*ship*) hundirse; (*sun*) ponerse ♦ *vt fus* bajar por; **that should ~ down well with him** eso le va a gustar.

go for *vt fus* (*fetch*) ir por; (*like*) gustar; (*attack*) atacar.

go in *vi* entrar.

go in for *vt fus* (*competition*) presentarse a.

go into *vt fus* entrar en; (*investigate*) investigar; (*embark on*) dedicarse a.

go off *vi* irse, marcharse; (*food*) pasarse; (*lights etc*) apagarse; (*explode*) estallar; (*event*) realizarse ♦ *vt fus* dejar de gustar; **the party went off well** la fiesta salió bien.

go on *vi* (*continue*) seguir, continuar; (*lights*) encenderse; (*happen*) pasar, ocurrir; (*be guided by: evidence etc*) partir de; **to ~ on doing sth** seguir haciendo algo; **what's ~ing on here?** ¿qué pasa aquí?

go on at *vt fus* (*nag*) reñir.

go out *vi* salir; (*fire, light*) apagarse; (*ebb: tide*) bajar, menguar; **to ~ out with sb** salir con uno.

go over *vi* (*ship*) zozobrar ♦ *vt fus* (*check*) revisar; **to ~ over sth in one's mind** repasar algo mentalmente.

go round *vi* (*Brit*) = **go around**.

go through *vt fus* (*town etc*) atravesar; (*search through*) revisar; (*perform: ceremony*) realizar; (*examine: list, book*) repasar.

go through with *vt fus* (*plan, crime*) llevar a cabo; **I couldn't ~ through with it** no pude llevarlo a cabo.

go together *vi* (*Brit: harmonize: people etc*) entenderse.

go under *vi* (*sink: ship, person*) hundirse; (*fig: business, firm*) quebrar.

go up *vi* subir; **to ~ up in flames** estallar en llamas.

go without *vt fus* pasarse sin.

goad [gōd] *vt* aguijonear.

go-ahead [gō'əhɛd] *a* emprendedor(a) ♦ *n* luz *f* verde; **to give sth/sb the ~** autorizar algo/a uno.

goal [gōl] *n* meta; (*score*) gol *m*.

goalkeeper [gōl'kēpûr] *n* portero.

goal post *n* poste *m* (de la portería).

goat [gōt] *n* cabra *f*.

gobble [gâb'əl] *vt* (*also*: **~ down**, **~ up**) engullirse.

gobbledygook [gâb'əldēgook] *n* jerga burocrática.

go-between [gō'bitwēn] *n* medianero/a, intermediario/a.

Gobi Desert [gō'bē dɛz'ûrt] *n* Desierto de Gobi.

goblet [gâb'lit] *n* copa.

goblin [gâb'lin] *n* duende *m*.

go-cart [gō'kârt] *n* = **go-kart**.

god [gâd] *n* dios *m*; **G~** *n* Dios *m*.

godchild [gâd'chīld] *n* ahijado/a.

goddamn [gâd'dam'] (*US col!*): **this ~...** este condenado *or* puñetero...(!)

goddess [gâd'is] *n* diosa.

godfather [gâd'fâthûr] *n* padrino.

godforsaken [gâd'fûrsā'kən] *a* olvidado de Dios.

godmother [gâd'muthûr] *n* madrina.

godparents [gâd'pärənts] *npl*: **the ~** los padrinos.

godsend [gåd'send] n don m del cielo.
godson [gåd'sun] n ahijado.
goes [gōz] vb see **go**.
gofer [gō'fûr] n (col) burro de carga.
go-getter [gō'get'ûr] n ambicioso/a.
goggle [gåg'əl] vi: **to ~ (at)** mirar con ojos desorbitados.
goggles [gåg'əlz] npl (AUT) anteojos mpl; (diver's) gafas fpl submarinas.
going [gō'ing] n (conditions) estado del terreno ♦ a: **the ~ rate** la tarifa corriente or en vigor; **it was slow ~** íbamos a paso lento.
goings-on [gō'ingzân'] npl (col) tejemanejes mpl.
go-kart [gō'kârt] n kart m.
gold [gōld] n oro ♦ a (reserves) de oro.
golden [gōl'dən] a (made of gold) de oro; (~ in color) dorado.
Golden Age n Siglo de Oro.
golden rule n regla de oro.
goldfish [gōld'fish] n pez m de colores.
gold leaf n en hojas, pan m de oro.
gold medal n (SPORT) medalla de oro.
goldmine [gōld'mīn] n mina de oro.
gold-plated [gōldplā'tid] a chapado en oro.
goldsmith [gōld'smith] n orfebre m/f.
gold standard n patrón m oro.
golf [gålf] n golf m.
golf ball n (for game) pelota de golf; (Brit: on typewriter) esfera impresora.
golf club n club m de golf; (stick) palo (de golf).
golf course n campo de golf.
golfer [gål'fûr] n jugador(a) m/f de golf.
gondola [gân'dələ] n góndola.
gondolier [gândəliûr'] n gondolero.
gone [gôn] pp of **go**.
gong [gông] n gong m.
gonorrhea [gânərē'ə] n gonorrea.
good [gōōd] a bueno; (kind) bueno, amable; (well-behaved) educado ♦ n bien m, provecho; **~!** ¡qué bien!; **to be ~ at** tener aptitud para; **to be ~ for** servir para; **it's ~ for you** te hace bien; **would you be ~ enough to...?** ¿podría hacerme el favor de...?, ¿sería tan amable de...?; **that's very ~ of you** es usted muy amable; **to feel ~** sentirse bien; **it's ~ to see you** me alegro de verte; **a ~ deal (of)** mucho; **a ~ many** muchos; **to make ~** reparar; **it's no ~ complaining** no vale la pena (de) quejarse; **is this any ~?** (will it do?) ¿sirve esto?; (what's it like?) ¿qué tal es esto?; **it's a ~ thing you were there** menos mal que tú estabas allí; **for ~** (for ever) para siempre, definitivamente; **~ morning/afternoon** ¡buenos días/buenas tardes!; **~ evening!** ¡buenas noches!; **~ night!** ¡buenas noches!; **he's up to no ~** está tramitando algo; **for the common ~** para el bien común; see also **goods**.
goodbye [gōōdbī'] excl ¡adiós!; **to say ~**

(to) (person) despedirse (de).
good faith n buena fe f.
good-for-nothing [gōōd'fərnuth'ing] n gandul(a) m/f, vago/a.
Good Friday n Viernes m Santo.
good-humored [gōōd'hyōō'mûrd] a (person) afable, de buen humor; (remark, joke) bien intencionado.
good-looking [gōōd'lōōk'ing] a guapo.
good-natured [gōōd'nā'chûrd] a (person) amable, simpático; (discussion) de tono amistoso.
goodness [gōōd'nis] n (of person) bondad f; **for ~ sake!** ¡por Dios!; **~ gracious!** ¡Dios mío!
goods [gōōdz] npl bienes mpl; (COMM etc) géneros mpl, mercancías fpl, artículos mpl; **all his ~ and chattels** todos sus bienes.
goods train n (Brit) tren m de mercancías.
goodwill [gōōd'wil'] n buena voluntad f; (COMM) crédito, clientela.
goody-goody [gōōd'ēgōōd'ē] n (pej) santurrón/ona m/f.
goof [gōōf] vi (US: col) tirarse una plancha.
goose, pl **geese** [gōōs, gēs] n ganso, oca.
gooseberry [gōōs'bärē] n grosella espinosa.
gooseflesh [gōōs'flesh] n, **goosepimples** [gōōs'pimpəlz] npl carne f de gallina.
goose step n (MIL) paso de ganso.
GOP n abbr (US POL: col = Grand Old Party) Partido Republicano.
gore [gôr] vt cornear ♦ n sangre f.
gorge [gôrj] n barranco ♦ vr: **to ~ o.s. (on)** atracarse (de).
gorgeous [gôr'jəs] a magnífico, maravilloso.
gorilla [gəril'ə] n gorila m.
gorse [gôrs] n aulaga.
gory [gôr'ē] a sangriento.
go-slow [gō'slō'] n (Brit) huelga de manos caídas.
gospel [gâs'pəl] n evangelio.
gossamer [gâs'əmûr] n gasa sutil.
gossip [gâs'əp] n (scandal) chismorreo, chismes mpl; (chat) charla; (scandalmonger) chismoso/a; (talker) hablador(a) m/f ♦ vi chismear; **a piece of ~** un chisme, un cotilleo.
gossip column n notas fpl de sociedad, páginas fpl sociales.
got [gât] pt, pp of **get**.
Gothic [gâth'ik] a gótico.
gotten [gât'ən] (US) pp of **get**.
gouge [gouj] vt (also: **~ out**: hole etc) excavar; (: initials) grabar; **to ~ sb's eyes out** sacar or arrancar los ojos a uno.
goulash [gōō'lâsh] n g(o)ulash m.
gourd [gôrd] n calabaza.
gourmet [gōōrmā'] n gastrónomo/a m/f.
gout [gout] n gota.
govern [guv'ûrn] vt (gen) gobernar; (dominate) dominar.

governess [guv'ûrnis] *n* institutriz *f*.

governing [guv'ûrning] *a* (*POL*) de gobierno, gubernamental; ~ **body** consejo de
administración.

government [guv'ûrnmənt] *n* gobierno; **local** ~ administración *f* local.

governmental [guvûrnmɛn'təl] *a* gubernamental.

government stock *n* reservas *fpl* del
Estado.

governor [guv'ûrnûr] *n* gobernador(a) *m/f*;
(*Brit: of jail*) director(a) *m/f*.

Govt. *abbr* (= *Government*) gobno.

gown [goun] *n* traje *m*; (*academic*; *Brit: of
judge*) toga.

GP *n abbr* = **general practitioner.**

GPO *n abbr* (*US*) = *Government Printing
Office.*

gr. *abbr* (*COMM*: = *gross*) bto.

grab [grab] *vt* coger (*Sp*) *or* agarrar (*LAm*),
arrebatar; **to** ~ **at** tratar de coger *or* agarrar.

grace [grās] *n* (*REL*) gracia; (*gracefulness*)
elegancia, gracia; (*graciousness*) cortesía,
gracia ♦ *vt* (*favor*) honrar; (*adorn*) adornar; **5 days'** ~ un plazo de 5 días; **to say**
~ bendecir la mesa; **his sense of humor is
his saving** ~ su sentido del humor es su
mérito.

graceful [grās'fəl] *a* elegante, gracioso.

gracious [grā'shəs] *a* amable ♦ *excl*: **good**
~! ¡Dios mío!

grade [grād] *n* (*quality*) clase *f*, calidad *f*;
(*in hierarchy*) grado; (*US*: *SCOL*) año; (:
mark) nota; (: *gradient*) pendiente *f*,
cuesta ♦ *vt* clasificar; **to make the** ~ (*fig*)
llegar al *or* alcanzar el nivel necesario.

grade crossing *n* (*US*) paso a nivel.

grade school *n* (*US*) escuela primaria.

gradient [grā'dēənt] *n* pendiente *f*.

gradual [graj'ōōəl] *a* paulatino.

gradually [graj'ōōlē] *ad* paulatinamente.

graduate *n* [graj'ōōit] graduado/a,
licenciado/a, (*US*: *SCOL*) bachiller *m/f* ♦ *vi*
[graj'ōōāt] graduarse, licenciarse.

graduated pension [graj'ōōātid pen'shən]
n pensión *f* escalonada.

graduation [grajōōā'shən] *n* graduación *f*; .
(*US SCOL*) entrega del bachillerato.

graffiti [grəfē'tē] *npl* pintada *sg*.

graft [graft] *n* (*AGR*, *MED*) injerto; (*bribery*)
corrupción *f* ♦ *vt* injertar; **hard** ~ (*Brit
col*) trabajo duro.

grain [grān] *n* (*single particle*) grano; (*no
pl*: *cereals*) cereales *mpl*; (*US*) trigo; (*in
wood*) fibra.

gram [gram] *n* (*US*) gramo.

grammar [gram'ûr] *n* gramática.

grammatical [grəmat'ikəl] *a* gramatical.

gramme [gram] *n* (*Brit*) = **gram.**

granary [grā'nûrē] *n* granero, troj *f*.

grand [grand] *a* magnífico, imponente ♦ *n*
(*US*: *col*) mil dólares *mpl*.

grandchildren [gran'childrən] *npl* nietos
mpl.

granddad [gran'dad] *n* abuelito.

granddaughter [gran'dôtûr] *n* nieta.

grandeur [gran'jûr] *n* magnificencia, lo
grandioso; (*of occasion*, *scenery etc*) lo
imponente; (*of style*) lo elevado.

grandfather [gran'fâthûr] *n* abuelo.

grandiose [gran'dēōs] *a* grandioso; (*pej*)
pomposo.

grand jury *n* (*US*) jurado de acusación.

grandma [gran'mə] *n* abuelita.

grandmother [gran'muthûr] *n* abuela.

grandpa [gran'pə] *n* = **granddad.**

grandparents [gran'pärənts] *npl* abuelos
mpl.

grand piano *n* piano de cola.

Grand Prix [grand prē'] *n* (*AUT*) Grand
Prix *m*.

grandson [gran'sun] *n* nieto.

grandstand [gran'stand] *n* (*SPORT*) tribuna.

grand total *n* suma total, total *m*.

granite [gran'it] *n* granito.

granny [gran'ē] *n* abuelita, yaya.

grant [grant] *vt* (*concede*) conceder; (*admit*): **to** ~ (**that**) reconocer (que) ♦ *n*
(*SCOL*) beca; **to take sth for** ~**ed** dar algo
por sentado.

granulated sugar [gran'yəlātid shōōg'ûr] *n*
(*Brit*) azúcar *m* blanquilla *or* granulada.

granule [gran'yōōl] *n* gránulo.

grape [grāp] *n* uva; **sour** ~**s** (*fig*) envidia
sg; **a bunch of** ~**s** un racimo de uvas.

grapefruit [grāp'frōōt] *n* pomelo, toronja
(*LAm*).

grape juice *n* zumo (*Sp*) *or* jugo (*LAm*) de
uva.

grapevine [grāp'vīn] *n* vid *f*, parra; **I heard
it on the** ~ (*fig*) me enteré, me lo conta-
ron.

graph [graf] *n* gráfica.

graphic [graf'ik] *a* gráfico.

graphic designer *n* diseñador(a) *m/f*
gráfico/a.

graphics [graf'iks] *n* (*art*, *process*) artes *fpl*
gráficas ♦ *npl* (*drawings*: *also COMPUT*)
gráficos *mpl*.

graphite [graf'īt] *n* grafito.

graph paper *n* papel *m* cuadriculado.

grapple [grap'əl] *vi*: **to** ~ **with a problem**
enfrentar un problema.

grappling iron [grap'ling ī'ûrn] *n* (*NAUT*)
rezón *m*.

grasp [grasp] *vt* agarrar, asir; (*understand*)
comprender ♦ *n* (*grip*) asimiento; (*reach*)
alcance *m*; (*understanding*) comprensión *f*;
to have a good ~ **of** (*subject*) dominar.

grasp at *vt fus* (*rope etc*) tratar de asir;
(*fig*: *opportunity*) aprovechar.

grasping [gras'ping] *a* avaro.

grass [gras] *n* hierba; (*lawn*) césped *m*;
(*pasture*) pasto; (*Brit: col*: *informer*) dela-
tor(a) *m/f*, denunciador(a) *m/f*.

grasshopper [gras'hâpûr] *n* saltamontes *m inv.*

grassland [gras'land] *n* pradera, pampa (*LAm*).

grass roots *a* popular ♦ *npl* (*POL*) base *fsg* popular.

grass snake *n* culebra.

grassy [gras'ē] *a* cubierto de hierba.

grate [grāt] *n* parrilla ♦ *vi* chirriar ♦ *vt* (*CULIN*) rallar.

grateful [grāt'fəl] *a* agradecido.

gratefully [grāt'fəlē] *ad* con agradecimiento.

grater [grā'tûr] *n* rallador *m.*

gratification [gratəfəkā'shən] *n* satisfacción *f.*

gratify [grat'əfī] *vt* complacer; (*whim*) satisfacer.

gratifying [grat'əfiing] *a* grato.

grating [grā'ting] *n* (*iron bars*) rejilla ♦ *a* (*noise*) áspero.

gratitude [grat'ətōōd] *n* agradecimiento.

gratuitous [grətōō'itəs] *a* gratuito, caprichoso.

gratuity [grətōō'itē] *n* gratificación *f.*

grave [grāv] *n* tumba ♦ *a* serio, grave.

gravedigger [grāv'digûr] *n* sepulturero.

gravel [grav'əl] *n* grava.

gravely [grāv'lē] *ad* seriamente; ~ **ill** muy grave.

gravestone [grāv'stōn] *n* lápida.

graveyard [grāv'yârd] *n* cementerio, camposanto.

gravitate [grav'ətāt] *vi* gravitar.

gravitation [gravitā'shən] *n* gravitación *f.*

gravity [grav'itē] *n* gravedad *f*; (*seriousness*) seriedad *f.*

gravy [grā'vē] *n* salsa de carne.

gravy boat *n* salsera.

gravy train *n* (*esp US: col*): **to get on the** ~ coger un chollo.

gray [grā] *a* (*US*) gris; **to go** ~ salirle canas.

gray-haired [grā'härd] *a* canoso.

grayhound [grā'hound] *n* galgo.

graze [grāz] *vi* pacer ♦ *vt* (*touch lightly*) rozar; (*scrape*) raspar ♦ *n* (*MED*) abrasión *f.*

grazing [grā'zing] *n* (*for livestock*) pastoreo.

grease [grēs] *n* (*fat*) grasa; (*lubricant*) lubricante *m* ♦ *vt* engrasar; **to** ~ **the skids** (*US: fig*) engrasar el mecanismo.

grease gun *n* engrasadora a presión.

greasepaint [grēs'pānt] *n* maquillaje *m.*

greaseproof [grēs'prōōf] *a* a prueba de grasa; (*Brit: paper*) apergaminado.

greasy [grē'sē] *a* (*hands, clothes*) grasiento; (*road, surface*) resbaladizo.

great [grāt] *a* grande; (*col*) magnífico, estupendo; (*pain, heat*) intenso; **we had a** ~ **time** lo pasamos muy bien; **they're** ~ **friends** son íntimos *or* muy amigos; **the** ~ **thing is that ...** lo importante es que ...; **it was** ~! ¡fue estupendo!

Great Barrier Reef *n* Gran Barrera de Coral.

Great Britain *n* Gran Bretaña.

greater [grā'tûr] *a* mayor; **G~ London** el Gran Londres.

greatest [grā'tist] *a* el/la mayor.

great-grandchild, *pl* **-children** [grāt'gran'chīld, -childrən] *n* bisnieto/a.

great-grandfather [grāt'gran'fâthûr] *n* bisabuelo.

great-grandmother [grāt'gran'muthûr] *n* bisabuela.

Great Lakes *npl*: **the** ~ los Grandes Lagos.

greatly [grāt'lē] *ad* sumamente, mucho, muy.

greatness [grāt'nis] *n* grandeza.

Greece [grēs] *n* Grecia.

greed [grēd] *n* (*also:* ~**iness**) codicia, avaricia; (*for food*) gula.

greedily [grē'dilē] *ad* con avidez.

greedy [grē'dē] *a* avaro; (*for food*) glotón/ona.

Greek [grēk] *a* griego ♦ *n* griego/a; (*LING*) griego; **ancient/modern** ~ griego antiguo/moderno.

green [grēn] *a* verde; (*inexperienced*) novato; (*POL*) verde ♦ *n* verde *m*; (*stretch of grass*) césped *m*; (*of golf course*) campo, "green" *m*; **the G~s** (*POL*) los verdes *mpl*; ~**s** *npl* verduras *fpl*; **to have a** ~ **thumb** *or* (*Brit*) ~ **fingers** (*fig*) tener habilidad para la jardinería.

greenback [grēn'bak] *n* (*US: col: dollar bill*) billete *m* de un dólar.

green bean *n* judía verde.

green belt *n* zona verde.

green card *n* (*US: ADMIN*) tarjeta verde; (*Brit: AUT*) carta verde.

greenery [grē'nûrē] *n* verdura, plantas *fpl* verdes.

greenfly [grēn'flī] *n* pulgón *m.*

greengage [grēn'gāj] *n* claudia.

greengrocer [grēn'grōsûr] *n* (*Brit*) verdulero/a.

greenhouse [grēn'hous] *n* invernadero.

greenhouse effect *n* efecto de invernadero.

greenish [grē'nish] *a* verdoso.

Greenland [grēn'lənd] *n* Groenlandia.

Greenlander [grēn'ləndûr] *n* groenlandés/esa *m/f.*

green light *n* luz *f* verde.

green pepper *n* pimiento verde.

greet [grēt] *vt* saludar; (*welcome*) dar la bienvenida a.

greeting [grē'ting] *n* (*gen*) saludo; (*welcome*) bienvenida; ~**s** recuerdos *mpl*, saludos *mpl*; **season's** ~**s** Felices Pascuas.

greeting(s) card [grē'ting(z) kârd] *n* tarjeta de felicitación.

gregarious [grigär'ēəs] *a* gregario.

grenade [grināď] *n* (*also:* **hand** ~) granada.

grew [grōō] *pt of* **grow**.
grey [grā] *etc* (*Brit*) = **gray** *etc*.
grid [grid] *n* reja; (*ELEC*) red *f*.
griddle [grid'əl] *n* (*esp US*) plancha.
gridiron [grid'īûrn] *n* (*CULIN*) parrilla.
grief [grēf] *n* dolor *m*, pena; **to come to** ~ (*plan*) fracasar, ir al traste; (*person*) acabar mal, desgraciarse.
grievance [grē'vəns] *n* (*cause for complaint*) motivo de queja, agravio.
grieve [grēv] *vi* afligirse, acongojarse ♦ *vt* dar pena a; **to** ~ **for** llorar por; **to** ~ **for sb** (*dead person*) llorar la pérdida de uno.
grievous [grē'vəs] *a* grave; (*loss*) cruel; ~ **bodily harm** (*LAW*) daños *mpl* corporales graves.
grill [gril] *n* (*on stove*) parrilla ♦ *vt* asar a la parrilla; (*question*) interrogar; ~**ed meat** carne *f* (asada) a la parrilla *or* plancha.
grille [gril] *n* reja.
grim [grim] *a* (*place*) sombrío; (*person*) ceñudo.
grimace [grim'əs] *n* mueca ♦ *vi* hacer muecas.
grime [grīm] *n* mugre *f*.
grimly [grim'lē] *ad* (*say*) sombríamente.
grimy [grīm'ē] *a* mugriento.
grin [grin] *n* sonrisa abierta ♦ *vi:* **to** ~ (**at**) sonreír abiertamente (a).
grind [grīnd] *vb* (*pt, pp* **ground** [ground]) *vt* (*coffee, pepper etc*) moler; (*US: meat*) picar; (*make sharp*) afilar; (*polish: gem, lens*) esmerilar ♦ *vi* (*car gears*) rechinar ♦ *n:* **the daily** ~ (*col*) la rutina diaria; **to** ~ **one's teeth** hacer rechinar los dientes; **to** ~ **to a halt** (*vehicle*) pararse con gran estruendo de frenos; (*fig: talks, scheme*) pararse en seco; (*work, production*) interrumpirse.
grinder [grīn'dûr] *n* (*machine: for coffee*) molinillo; (*US: for meat*) picadora de carne.
grindstone [grīnd'stōn] *n:* **to keep one's nose to the** ~ batir el yunque.
grip [grip] *n* (*hold*) asimiento; (*of hands*) apretón *m*; (*handle*) asidero; (*of racquet etc*) mango; (*understanding*) comprensión *f* ♦ *vt* agarrar; **to come to** ~**s with** enfrentarse con; **to lose one's** ~ írsele de las manos; (*fig*) perder el control.
gripe [grīp] *n* (*col: complaint*) queja ♦ *vi* (*col: complain*): **to** ~ (**about**) quejarse (de); ~**s** *npl* retortijones *mpl*.
gripping [grip'ing] *a* absorbente.
grisly [griz'lē] *a* horripilante, horrible.
gristle [gris'əl] *n* cartílago.
grit [grit] *n* gravilla; (*courage*) valor *m* ♦ *vt* (*Brit: road*) poner gravilla en; **I've got a piece of** ~ **in my eye** tengo una arenilla en el ojo; **to** ~ **one's teeth** apretar los dientes.
grits [grits] *npl* (*US*) maíz *msg* a medio moler.

grizzle [griz'əl] *vi* (*cry*) lloriquear.
grizzly [griz'lē] *n* (*also:* ~ **bear**) oso pardo.
groan [grōn] *n* gemido, quejido ♦ *vi* gemir, quejarse.
grocer [grō'sûr] *n* tendero (de ultramarinos); ~**'s** (**shop**) *n* tienda de ultramarinos *or* de abarrotes (*LAm*).
groceries [grō'sûrēz] *npl* comestibles *mpl*.
grocery [grō'sûrē] *n* (*also:* ~ **store**) tienda de ultramarinos.
grog [grâg] *n* grog *m*.
groggy [grâg'ē] *a* atontado.
groin [groin] *n* ingle *f*.
groom [grōōm] *n* mozo/a de cuadra; (*also:* **bride**~) novio ♦ *vt* (*horse*) almohazar; **well-**~**ed** acicalado.
groove [grōōv] *n* ranura, surco.
grope [grōp] *vi* ir a tientas; **to** ~ **for** buscar a tientas.
grosgrain [grō'grān] *n* grogrén *m*, cordellate *m*.
gross [grōs] *a* grueso; (*COMM*) bruto ♦ *vt* (*COMM*) recaudar en bruto.
gross domestic product (GDP) *n* producto interno bruto (PIB).
gross income *n* ingresos *mpl* brutos.
grossly [grōs'lē] *ad* (*greatly*) enormemente.
gross national product (GNP) *n* producto nacional bruto (PNB).
gross profit *n* beneficios *mpl* brutos.
gross sales *npl* ventas *fpl* brutas.
grotesque [grōtesk'] *a* grotesco.
grotto [grât'ō] *n* gruta.
grotty [grât'ē] *a* asqueroso.
grouch [grouch] *vi* (*col*) refunfuñar ♦ *n* (*col: person*) refunfuñón/ona *m/f*.
ground [ground] *pt, pp of* **grind** ♦ *n* suelo, tierra; (*SPORT*) campo, terreno; (*reason: gen pl*) causa, razón *f*; (*US: also:* ~ **wire**) cable *m* de toma de tierra ♦ *vt* (*plane*) mantener en tierra; (*US: ELEC*) conectar a tierra ♦ *vi* (*ship*) varar, encallar ♦ *a* (*coffee etc*) molido; (*US: meat*) picado; ~**s** *npl* (*of coffee etc*) poso *sg*; (*gardens etc*) jardines *mpl*, parque *m*; **on the** ~ en el suelo; **common** ~ terreno común; **to gain/lose** ~ ganar/perder terreno; **to the** ~ al suelo; **below** ~ debajo de la tierra, bajo tierra; **he covered a lot of** ~ **in his lecture** abarcó mucho en la clase.
ground cloth *n* (*US*) tela impermeable.
ground control *n* (*AVIAT, SPACE*) control *m* desde tierra.
ground floor *n* (*Brit*) planta baja.
grounding [groun'ding] *n* (*in education*) conocimientos *mpl* básicos.
groundkeeper [ground'kēpûr] *n* = **groundskeeper**.
groundless [ground'lis] *a* infundado, sin fundamento.
groundnut [ground'nut] *n* cacahuete *m*.
ground rent *n* renta sobre el terreno.
groundsheet [ground'shēt] *n* (*Brit*) =

ground cloth.
groundskeeper [groundz'kēpûr] *n* (*US*
SPORT) encargado de pista de deportes.
groundsman [groundz'mən] *n* (*Brit*) =
groundskeeper.
ground staff *n* (*Brit*) personal *m* de tierra.
ground swell *n* mar *m* or *f* de fondo; (*fig*)
marejada.
ground-to-ground [ground'təground'] *a:*
~ **missile** proyectil *m* tierra-tierra.
groundwork [ground'wûrk] *n* preparación
f.
group [grōōp] *n* grupo; (*MUS: pop* ~)
conjunto, grupo ♦ (*vb: also:* ~ **together**) *vt*
agrupar ♦ *vi* agruparse.
grouse [grous] *n* (*pl inv*) (*bird*) urogallo ♦
vi (*complain*) quejarse.
grove [grōv] *n* arboleda.
grovel [gruv'əl] *vi* (*fig*) arrastrarse.
grow, *pt* **grew,** *pp* **grown** [grō, grōō, grōn]
vi crecer; (*increase*) aumentarse; (*expand*)
desarrollarse; (*become*) volverse ♦ *vt* cultivar; (*hair, beard*) dejar crecer; **to** ~ **rich/
weak** enriquecerse/debilitarse; **to** ~ **tired
of waiting** cansarse de esperar.
grow apart *vi* (*fig*) alejarse uno del otro.
grow away from *vt fus* (*fig*) alejarse
de.
grow on *vt fus*: **that painting is** ~**ing
on me** ese cuadro me gusta cada vez más.
grow out of *vt fus* (*clothes*): **I've
grown out of this shirt** esta camisa se me
queda pequeña; (*habit*) perder.
grow up *vi* crecer, hacerse hombre/
mujer.
grower [grō'ûr] *n* (*AGR*) cultivador(a) *m/f,*
productor(a) *m/f.*
growing [grō'ing] *a* creciente; ~ **pains**
(*also fig*) dificultades *fpl* de desarrollo.
growl [groul] *vi* gruñir.
grown [grōn] *pp* of **grow.**
grown-up [grōn'up'] *n* adulto/a, mayor *m/f.*
growth [grōth] *n* crecimiento, desarrollo;
(*what has grown*) brote *m*; (*MED*) tumor
m.
growth rate *n* tasa de crecimiento.
grub [grub] *n* gusano; (*col: food*) comida.
grubby [grub'ē] *a* sucio, mugriento.
grudge [gruj] *n* rencor ♦ *vt*: **to** ~ **sb sth**
dar algo a uno de mala gana; **to bear sb a**
~ guardar rencor a uno; **he** ~**s (giving)
the money** da el dinero de mala gana.
grudgingly [gruj'inglē] *ad* de mala gana.
grueling, (*Brit*) **gruelling** [grōō'əling] *a* penoso, duro.
gruesome [grōō'səm] *a* horrible.
gruff [gruf] *a* (*voice*) ronco; (*manner*) brusco.
grumble [grum'bəl] *vi* refunfuñar, quejarse.
grumpy [grum'pē] *a* gruñón/ona.
grunt [grunt] *vi* gruñir ♦ *n* gruñido.
GSA *n abbr* (*US*) = *General Services*

Administration.
G-string [jē'string] *n* taparrabo.
GSUSA *n abbr* = *Girl Scouts of the United
States of America.*
GT *abbr* (*AUT*: = *gran turismo*) GT.
GU *abbr* (*US MAIL*) = *Guam.*
guarantee [garəntē'] *n* garantía ♦ *vt* garantizar; **he can't** ~ **(that) he'll come** no
está seguro de poder venir.
guarantor [gar'əntôr] *n* garante *m/f,* fia-
dor(a) *m/f.*
guard [gârd] *n* guardia; (*Brit RAIL*) jefe *m*
de tren; (*safety device: on machine*) salva-
guardia, resguardo; (*protection*) protección
f; (*Brit: fire*~) pantalla ♦ *vt* guardar; **to** ~
(against or from) proteger (de); **to be on
one's** ~ (*fig*) estar en guardia.
guard against *vi*: **to** ~ **against doing
sth** guardarse de hacer algo.
guard dog *n* perro guardián.
guarded [gâr'did] *a* (*fig*) cauteloso.
guardian [gâr'dēən] *n* guardián/ana *m/f*; (*of
minor*) tutor(a) *m/f.*
guardrail [gârd'rāl] *n* pretil *m.*
guard's van [gârdz' van] *n* (*Brit RAIL*)
furgón *m.*
Guatemala [gwâtəmâl'ə] *n* Guatemala.
Guatemalan [gwâtəmâl'ən] *a,* *n*
guatemalteco/a *m/f.*
guerrilla [gəril'ə] *n* guerrillero/a.
guerrilla warfare *n* guerra de guerrillas.
guess [ges] *vi, vt* (*gen*) adivinar; (*suppose*)
suponer ♦ *n* suposición *f*, conjetura; **I** ~
you're right (*esp US*) supongo que tienes
razón; **to keep sb** ~**ing** mantener a uno a
la expectativa; **to take a** ~ tratar de adivinar; **my** ~ **is that** ... yo creo que ... .
guesstimate [ges'təmit] *n* conjetura.
guesswork [ges'wûrk] *n* conjeturas *fpl;* **I
got the answer by** ~ acerté a ojo de buen
cubero.
guest [gest] *n* invitado/a; (*in hotel*)
huésped(a) *m/f*; **be my** ~ (*col*) estás en tu
casa.
guest book *n* libro de visitas.
guesthouse [gest'hous] *n* casa de huéspedes, pensión *f.*
guest room *n* cuarto de huéspedes.
guffaw [gufô'] *n* carcajada ♦ *vi* reírse a
carcajadas.
guidance [gīd'əns] *n* (*gen*) dirección *f*; (*advice*) consejos *mpl*; **marriage/vocational** ~
orientación *f* matrimonial/profesional.
guide [gīd] *n* (*person*) guía *m/f*; (*book, fig*)
guía *f*; (*Brit: also: girl* ~) exploradora ♦ *vt*
guiar; **to be** ~**d by sb/sth** dejarse guiar
por uno/algo.
guidebook [gīd'bōōk] *n* guía.
guided missile [gīd'id mis'əl] *n* misil *m* teledirigido.
guide dog *n* perro guía.
guided tour [gīd'id tōōr] *n* visita acompa-
ñada.

guidelines |gīd'līnz| *npl* (*fig*) directiva *sg*.
guild |gild| *n* gremio.
guile |gīl| *n* astucia.
guileless |gīl'lis| *a* cándido.
guillotine |gil'ətēn| *n* guillotina.
guilt |gilt| *n* culpabilidad *f*.
guilty |gil'tē| *a* culpable; **to feel ~ (about)** sentirse culpable (por); **to plead ~/not ~** declararse culpable/inocente.
Guinea |gin'ē| *n*: **Republic of ~** República de Guinea.
guinea pig *n* cobayo.
guise |gīz| *n*: **in** *or* **under the ~ of** bajo capa de.
guitar |gitär'| *n* guitarra.
guitarist |gitär'ist| *n* guitarrista *m/f*.
gulch |gulch| *n* (*US*) barranco.
gulf |gulf| *n* golfo; (*abyss*) abismo.
Gulf States *npl*: **the ~** los países del Golfo.
Gulf Stream *n*: **the ~** la Corriente del Golfo.
gull |gul| *n* gaviota.
gullet |gul'it| *n* esófago.
gullibility |guləbil'ətē| *n* credulidad *f*.
gullible |gul'əbəl| *a* crédulo.
gully |gul'ē| *n* barranco.
gulp |gulp| *vi* tragar saliva ♦ *vt* (*also: ~ down*) tragarse ♦ *n* (*of liquid*) trago, sorbo; (*of food*) bocado; **in one ~** de un trago.
gum |gum| *n* (*ANAT*) encía; (*glue*) goma, cemento (*LAm*); (*sweet*) caramelo de goma; (*also: chewing-~*) chicle *m* ♦ *vt* pegar con goma.
   gum up *vt*: **to ~ up the works** (*col*) meter un palo en la rueda.
gumboots |gum'bōōts| *npl* (*Brit*) botas *fpl* de goma.
gum tree *n* árbol *m* gomero.
gun |gun| *n* (*small*) pistola, revólver *m*; (*shotgun*) escopeta; (*rifle*) fusil *m*; (*cannon*) cañón *m* ♦ *vt* (*also: ~ down*) asesinar; **to stick to one's ~s** (*fig*) mantenerse firme, aferrarse.
gunboat |gun'bōt| *n* cañonero.
gun dog *n* perro de caza.
gunfire |gun'fiūr| *n* disparos *mpl*.
gung-ho |gung'hō'| *a* (*col*) fogoso.
gunk |gungk| *n* (*col*) sustancia pegajosa *or* viscosa.
gunman |gun'mən| *n* pistolero.
gunner |gun'ûr| *n* artillero.
gunpoint |gun'point| *n*: **at ~** a mano armada.
gunpowder |gun'poudûr| *n* pólvora.
gunrunner |gun'runûr| *n* traficante *m/f* de armas.
gunrunning |gun'runing| *n* contrabando de armas.
gunshot |gun'shät| *n* escopetazo.
gunsmith |gun'smith| *n* armero.
gurgle |gûr'gəl| *vi* gorgotear.

guru |gōō'rōō| *n* guru *m*.
gush |gush| *vi* chorrear; (*fig*) deshacerse en efusiones.
gusset |gus'it| *n* (*in tights, pants*) escudete *m*.
gust |gust| *n* (*of wind*) ráfaga.
gusto |gus'tō| *n* entusiasmo.
gut |gut| *n* intestino; (*MUS etc*) cuerda de tripa ♦ *vt* (*poultry, fish*) destripar; (*building*): **the blaze ~ted the entire building** el fuego destruyó el edificio entero.
gut reaction *n* reacción *f* instintiva.
guts |guts| *npl* (*courage*) valor *m*; (*col: innards: of people, animals*) tripas *fpl*; **to hate sb's ~** echar a uno (a muerte).
gutter |gut'ûr| *n* (*of roof*) canalón *m*; (*in street*) arroyo.
guttural |gut'ûrəl| *a* gutural.
guy |gī| *n* (*also: ~rope*) cuerda; (*col: man*) tío (*Sp*), tipo.
Guyana |gēän'ə| *n* Guayana.
guzzle |guz'əl| *vi* tragar ♦ *vt* engullir.
gym |jim| *n* (*also: gymnasium*) gimnasio; (*also: gymnastics*) gimnasia.
gymkhana |jimkä'nə| *n* gincana.
gymnast |jim'nast| *n* gimnasta *m/f*.
gymnastics |jimnas'tiks| *n* gimnasia.
gym shoes *npl* zapatillas *fpl* deportivas.
gym slip *n* (*Brit*) túnica de colegiala.
gynecologist, (*Brit*) **gynaecologist** |gīnəkäl'əjist| *n* ginecólogo/a.
gynecology, (*Brit*) **gynaecology** |gīnəkäl'əjē| *n* ginecología.
gypsy |jip'sē| *n* gitano/a.
gyrate |jī'rāt| *vi* girar.
gyroscope |jī'rəskōp| *n* giroscopio.

H

H, h |āch| *n* (*letter*) H, h *f*; **H for How** H de Historia.
habeas corpus |hā'bēəs kôr'pəs| *n* (*LAW*) hábeas corpus *m*.
haberdashery |hab'ûrdashûrē| *n* (*US: men's clothing*) prendas *fpl* de caballero; (*Brit*) mercería.
habit |hab'it| *n* hábito, costumbre *f*; **to get out of/into the ~ of doing sth** perder la costumbre de/acostumbrarse a hacer algo.
habitable |hab'itəbəl| *a* habitable.
habitat |hab'itat| *n* hábitat *m*.
habitation |habitā'shən| *n* habitación *f*.
habitual |həbich'ōōəl| *a* acostumbrado, habitual; (*drinker, liar*) empedernido.
habitually |həbich'ōōəlē| *ad* por costumbre.
hack |hak| *vt* (*cut*) cortar; (*slice*) tajar ♦ *n*

corte *m*; (*ax blow*) hachazo; (*pej*: *writer*) escritor(a) *m/f* a sueldo; (*old horse*) jamelgo.

hacker [hak'ûr] *n* (COMPUT) pirata *m* informático.

hackles [hak'əlz] *npl*: **to make sb's ~ rise** (*fig*) poner los pelos de punta a uno.

hackney cab [hak'nē kab] *n* coche *m* de alquiler.

hackneyed [hak'nēd] *a* trillado, gastado.

had [had] *pt, pp of* **have**.

haddock, *pl* ~ *or* ~**s** [had'ək] *n especie de merluza.*

hadn't [had'ənt] = **had not**.

haematology [hēmətâl'əjē] *n* (*Brit*) = **hematology**.

haemoglobin [hē'məglōbin] *n* (*Brit*) = **hemoglobin**.

haemophilia [hēməfil'ēə] *n* (*Brit*) = **hemophilia**.

haemorrhage [hem'ûrij] *n* (*Brit*) = **hemorrhage**.

haemorrhoids [hem'əroidz] *npl* (*Brit*) = **hemorrhoids**.

hag [hag] *n* (*ugly*) vieja fea, tarasca; (*nasty*) bruja; (*witch*) hechicera.

haggard [hag'ûrd] *a* ojeroso.

haggis [hag'is] *n* (*Scottish*) estómago de cordero relleno.

haggle [hag'əl] *vi* (*argue*) discutir; (*bargain*) regatear.

haggling [hag'ling] *n* regateo.

Hague [hāg] *n*: **The ~** La Haya.

hail [hāl] *n* (*weather*) granizo ♦ *vt* saludar; (*call*) llamar a ♦ *vi* granizar; **to ~ (as)** aclamar (como), celebrar (como); **he ~s from Scotland** es natural de Escocia.

hailstone [hāl'stōn] *n* (*piedra de*) granizo.

hailstorm [hāl'stôrm] *n* granizada.

hair [här] *n* (*gen*) pelo, cabellos *mpl*; (*one ~*) pelo, cabello; (*head of ~*) pelo, cabellera; (*on legs etc*) vello; **to do one's ~** arreglarse el pelo; **gray ~** canas *fpl*.

hairbrush [här'brush] *n* cepillo (para el pelo).

haircut [här'kut] *n* corte *m* (de pelo).

hairdo [här'dōō] *n* peinado.

hairdresser [här'dresûr] *n* peluquero/a; **~'s** peluquería.

hair dryer *n* secador *m* de pelo.

-haired [härd] *a suff*: **fair/long~** de pelo rubio *or* güero/de pelo largo.

hair gel *n* gel *m* para el pelo.

hairgrip [här'grip] *n* (*Brit*) horquilla.

hairline [här'līn] *n* nacimiento del pelo.

hairline fracture *n* fractura fina.

hairnet [här'net] *n* redecilla.

hair oil *n* brillantina.

hairpiece [här'pēs] *n* (*for men*) tupé *m*; (*for women*) peluca.

hairpin [här'pin] *n* horquilla.

hairpin curve, (*Brit*) **hairpin bend** *n* curva de horquilla.

hair-raising [här'rāzing] *a* espeluznante.

hair remover *n* depilatorio.

hair's breadth *n*: **by a ~** por un pelo.

hair spray *n* laca.

hairstyle [här'stīl] *n* peinado.

hairy [här'ē] *a* peludo, velludo.

Haiti [hā'tē] *n* Haití *m*.

hake [hāk] *n* merluza.

halcyon [hal'sēən] *a* feliz.

hale [hāl] *a*: **~ and hearty** robusto.

half [haf] *n* (*pl* **halves** [havz]) mitad *f*; (SPORT: *of match*) tiempo; (: *of field*) campo ♦ *a* medio ♦ *ad* medio, a medias; **~ an hour** media hora; **two and a ~** dos y media; **~ a dozen** media docena; **~ a pound** media libra, ≈ 250 gr.; **to cut sth in ~** cortar algo por la mitad; **to go halves (with sb)** ir a medias (con uno); **~empty/closed** medio vacío/entreabierto; **~ asleep** medio dormido; **~ after 3** las 3 y media.

halfback [haf'bak] *n* (SPORT) medio.

half-baked [haf'bākt'] *a* (*col*: *idea, scheme*) mal concebido *or* pensado.

half-breed [haf'brēd] *n* = **half-caste**.

half-brother [haf'bruth'ûr] *n* medio hermano.

half-caste [haf'kast] *n* mestizo/a.

half-hearted [haf'hâr'tid] *a* indiferente, poco entusiasta.

half-hour [haf'our'] *n* media hora.

half-mast [haf'mast'] *n*: **at ~** (*flag*) a media asta.

half note *n* (US: MUS) blanca.

halfpenny [hā'pənē] *n* (*Brit*) medio penique *m*.

half-price [haf'prīs'] *a* a mitad de precio.

half term *n* (*Brit* SCOL) vacaciones *de mediados del trimestre*.

half-time [haf'tīm'] *n* descanso.

halfway [haf'wā'] *ad* a medio camino; **to meet sb ~** (*fig*) llegar a un acuerdo con uno.

half-yearly [haf'yēr'lē] *ad* semestralmente ♦ *a* semestral.

halibut [hal'əbət] *n, pl inv* halibut *m*.

halitosis [halitō'sis] *n* halitosis *f*.

hall [hôl] *n* (*for concerts*) sala; (*entrance way*) entrada, vestíbulo.

hallmark [hôl'mârk] *n* (*mark*) contraste *m*; (*seal*) sello.

hallo [həlō'] *excl* (*Brit*) = **hello**.

hall of residence *n* (*Brit*) colegio mayor.

Hallowe'en [haləwēn'] *n* víspera de Todos los Santos.

hallucination [həlōōsənā'shən] *n* alucinación *f*.

hallway [hôl'wā] *n* vestíbulo.

halo [hā'lō] *n* (*of saint*) aureola.

halt [hôlt] *n* (*stop*) alto, parada; (*Brit* RAIL) apeadero ♦ *vt* parar ♦ *vi* pararse; (*process*) interrumpirse; **to call a ~ (to sth)** (*fig*) poner fin (a algo).

halter [hôl'tûr] *n* (*for horse*) cabestro.

halterneck [hól'túrnek] *a* de espalda escotada.

halve [hav] *vt* partir por la mitad.

halves [havz] *pl of* **half**.

ham [ham] *n* jamón *m* (cocido); (*col: also:* **radio** ~) radioaficionado/a *m/f*; (: *also:* ~ **actor**) comicastro.

hamburger [ham'bûrgûr] *n* hamburguesa.

ham-handed [ham'handid] *a* torpe, desmañado.

hamlet [ham'lit] *n* aldea.

hammer [ham'ûr] *n* martillo ♦ *vt* (*nail*) clavar; **to ~ a point home to sb** remacharle un punto a uno.
  hammer out *vt* (*metal*) forjar a martillo; (*fig: solution, agreement*) elaborar con trabajos.

hammock [ham'ək] *n* hamaca.

hamper [ham'pûr] *vt* estorbar ♦ *n* cesto.

hamster [ham'stûr] *n* hámster *m*.

hand [hand] *n* mano *f*; (*of clock*) aguja; (*writing*) letra; (*worker*) obrero; (*measurement: of horse*) palmo ♦ *vt* (*give*) dar, pasar; (*deliver*) entregar; **to give sb a ~** echar una mano a uno, ayudar a uno; **to force sb's ~** forzarle la mano a uno; **at ~** (*information etc*) a (la) mano; **in ~** entre manos; **we have the matter in ~** tenemos el asunto entre manos; **to have in one's ~** (*knife, victory*) tener en la mano; **to have a free ~** tener carta blanca; **on ~** (*person, services*) a mano, al alcance; **on the one ~ ..., on the other ~ ...** por una parte ... por otra (parte) ....
  hand around *vt* (*chocolates etc*) ofrecer; (*information, papers*) pasar (de mano en mano).
  hand down *vt* pasar, bajar; (*tradition*) transmitir; (*heirloom*) dejar en herencia; (*US: sentence, verdict*) imponer.
  hand in *vt* entregar.
  hand out *vt* (*leaflets, advice*) repartir, distribuir.
  hand over *vt* (*deliver*) entregar; (*surrender*) ceder.
  hand round *vt* (*Brit*) = **hand around**.

handbag [hand'bag] *n* bolso, cartera (*LAm*).

handball [hand'bôl] *n* balonmano.

hand basin *n* lavabo.

handbook [hand'book] *n* manual *m*.

handbrake [hand'brāk] *n* freno de mano.

hand cream *n* crema para las manos.

handcuffs [hand'kufs] *npl* esposas *fpl*.

handful [hand'fool] *n* puñado.

handicap [han'dēkap] *n* desventaja; (*SPORT*) hándicap *m* ♦ *vt* estorbar.

handicapped [han'dēkapt] *a*: **to be mentally ~** ser deficiente *m/f* (mental); **to be physically ~** ser minusválido/a (físico/a).

handicraft [han'dēkraft] *n* artesanía.

handiwork [han'dēwûrk] *n* manualidad(es) *f(pl)*; (*fig*) obra; **this looks like his ~**

(*pej*) es obra de él, parece.

handkerchief [hang'kûrchif] *n* pañuelo.

handle [han'dəl] *n* (*of door etc*) manija; (*of cup etc*) asa; (*of knife etc*) mango; (*for winding*) manivela ♦ *vt* (*touch*) tocar; (*deal with*) encargarse de; (*treat: people*) manejar; **"~ with care"** "(manéjese) con cuidado"; **to fly off the ~** perder los estribos.

handlebar(s) [han'dəlbâr(z)] *n(pl)* manillar *msg*.

handling charges [han'dling châr'jəz] *npl* gastos *mpl* de tramitación.

hand luggage *n* equipaje *m* de mano.

handmade [hand'mād'] *a* hecho a mano.

handout [hand'out] *n* (*distribution*) repartición *f*; (*charity*) limosna; (*leaflet*) folleto, octavilla; (*press* ~) nota.

hand-picked [hand'pikt'] *a* (*produce*) escogido a mano; (*staff etc*) seleccionado cuidadosamente.

handrail [hand'rāl] *n* (*on staircase etc*) pasamanos *m inv*, barandilla.

handshake [hand'shāk] *n* apretón *m* de manos; (*COMPUT*) coloquio.

handsome [han'səm] *a* guapo.

hands-on [handz'ân'] *a*: **~ experience** (*COMPUT*) experiencia práctica.

handstand [hand'stand] *n* voltereta, salto mortal.

hand-to-mouth [hand'təmouth'] *a* (*existence*) precario.

handwriting [hand'rīting] *n* letra.

handwritten [hand'ritən] *a* escrito a mano, manuscrito.

handy [han'dē] *a* (*close at hand*) a la mano; (*useful: machine, tool etc*) práctico; (*skilful*) hábil, diestro; **to come in ~** venir bien.

handyman [han'dēman] *n* manitas *m inv*.

hang, *pt, pp* **hung** [hang, hung] *vt* colgar; (*head*) bajar; (*criminal: pt, pp* **hanged**) ahorcar; **to get the ~ of sth** (*col*) lograr dominar algo.
  hang around *vi* haraganear.
  hang back *vi* (*hesitate*): **to ~ back (from doing)** vacilar (ante hacer).
  hang on *vi* (*wait*) esperar ♦ *vt fus* (*depend on: decision etc*) depender de; **to ~ on to** (*keep hold of*) agarrarse *or* aferrarse a; (*keep*) guardar, quedarse con.
  hang out *vt* (*washing*) tender, colgar ♦ *vi* (*col: live*) vivir, radicarse; **to ~ out of sth** colgar fuera de algo.
  hang together *vi* (*cohere: argument etc*) sostenerse.
  hang up *vt* (*coat*) colgar ♦ *vi* (*TEL*) colgar; **to ~ up on sb** colgarle a uno.

hangar [hang'ûr] *n* hangar *m*.

hangdog [hang'dóg] *a* (*guilty: look, expression*) avergonzado.

hanger [hang'ûr] *n* percha.

hanger-on [hang'ûrân'] *n* parásito.

hang-gliding [hang'glīding] *n* vuelo libre.

hanging [hang'ing] *n* (*execution*) ejecución *f* (en la horca).

hangman [hang'mən] *n* verdugo.

hangover [hang'ōvûr] *n* (*after drinking*) resaca.

hang-up [hang'up] *n* complejo.

hanker [hang'kûr] *vi*: **to ~ after** (*miss*) echar de menos; (*long for*) añorar.

hankie, hanky [hang'kē] *n abbr* = **handkerchief.**

hanky-panky [hang'kēpang'kē] *n* (*col*) trucos *mpl*, trampas *fpl*.

Hants *abbr* (*Brit*) = *Hampshire.*

haphazard [haphaz'ûrd] *a* fortuito.

hapless [hap'lis] *a* desventurado.

happen [hap'ən] *vi* suceder, ocurrir; (*take place*) tener lugar, realizarse; **as it ~s** da la casualidad de que; **what's ~ing?** ¿qué pasa?

happen (up)on *vt fus* tropezar *or* dar con.

happening [hap'əning] *n* suceso, acontecimiento.

happily [hap'ilē] *ad* (*luckily*) afortunadamente; (*cheerfully*) alegremente.

happiness [hap'ēnis] *n* (*contentment*) felicidad *f*; (*joy*) alegría.

happy [hap'ē] *a* feliz; (*cheerful*) alegre; **to be ~ (with)** estar contento (con); **yes, I'd be ~ to** sí, con mucho gusto; **H~ Christmas/New Year!** ¡Feliz Navidad!/ ¡Feliz Año Nuevo!; **~ birthday!** ¡felicidades!, ¡feliz cumpleaños!

happy-go-lucky [hap'ēgōluk'ē] *a* despreocupado.

harangue [hərang'] *vt* arengar.

harass [həras'] *vt* acosar, hostigar.

harassed [hərast'] *a* agobiado, presionado.

harassment [həras'mənt] *n* persecución *f*; (*worry*) preocupación *f*.

harbor [hâr'bûr] *n* puerto ♦ *vt* (*hope etc*) abrigar; (*hide*) dar abrigo a; (*retain*: *grudge etc*) guardar.

harbor dues *npl* derechos *mpl* portuarios.

harbour [hâr'bûr] *etc* (*Brit*) = **harbor** *etc*.

hard [hârd] *a* duro; (*difficult*) difícil; (*person*) severo ♦ *ad* (*work*) mucho, duro; (*think*) profundamente; **to look ~ at sb/ sth** clavar los ojos en alguien/algo; **to try ~** esforzarse; **no ~ feelings!** ¡sin rencor(es)!; **to be ~ of hearing** ser duro de oído; **to be ~ on sb** ser muy duro con uno; **I find it ~ to believe that ...** me cuesta trabajo creer que ....

hard-and-fast [hârd'ənfast] *a* rígido, definitivo.

hardback [hârd'bak] *n* libro de tapas duras.

hard cash *n* dinero contante.

hard copy *n* (*COMPUT*) copia impresa.

hard-core [hârd'kôr'] *a* (*pornography*) duro; (*supporters*) incondicional.

hard court *n* (*TENNIS*) cancha (de tenis) de cemento.

hard disk *n* (*COMPUT*) disco duro *or* rígido.

harden [hâr'dən] *vt* endurecer; (*steel*) templar; (*fig*) curtir; (: *determination*) fortalecer ♦ *vi* (*substance*) endurecerse.

hardened [hâr'dənd] *a* (*criminal*) empedernido; **to be ~ to sth** estar acostumbrado a algo.

hard-headed [hârd'hed'id] *a* poco sentimental, realista.

hard-hearted [hârd'hâr'tid] *a* duro de corazón.

hard labor *n* trabajos *mpl* forzados.

hardliner [hârdlī'nûr] *n* partidario/a de la línea dura.

hardly [hârd'lē] *ad* (*scarcely*) apenas; **that can ~ be true** eso difícilmente puede ser cierto; **~ ever** casi nunca; **I can ~ believe it** apenas me lo puedo creer.

hardness [hârd'nis] *n* dureza.

hard sell *n* publicidad *f* agresiva; **~ techniques** técnicas *fpl* agresivas de venta.

hardship [hârd'ship] *n* (*troubles*) penas *fpl*; (*financial*) apuro.

hard shoulder *n* (*Brit AUT*) andén *m*, arcén *m*.

hard up *a* (*col*) sin un duro (*Sp*) *or* plata (*LAm*).

hardware [hârd'wär] *n* ferretería; (*COMPUT*) hardware *m*.

hardware dealer *n* (*US*) ferretero/a.

hardware store *n* ferretería.

hard-wearing [hârd'wär'ing] *a* resistente, duradero; (*shoes*) resistente.

hard-working [hârd'wûr'king] *a* trabajador(a).

hardy [hâr'dē] *a* fuerte; (*plant*) resistente.

hare [här] *n* liebre *f*.

harebrained [här'brānd] *a* casquivano.

harelip [här'lip] *n* labio leporino.

harem [här'əm] *n* harén *m*.

haricot (bean) [har'ikō (bēn)] *n* alubia.

hark back [hârk bak] *vi*: **to ~ to** (*former days, earlier occasion*) recordar.

harm [hârm] *n* daño, mal *m* ♦ *vt* (*person*) hacer daño a; (*health, interests*) perjudicar; (*thing*) dañar; **out of ~'s way** a salvo; **there's no ~ in trying** nada se pierde con intentar.

harmful [hârm'fəl] *a* (*gen*) dañino; (*reputation*) perjudicial.

harmless [hârm'lis] *a* (*person*) inofensivo; (*drugs*) inocuo.

harmonica [hârmân'ikə] *n* armónica.

harmonious [hârmō'nēəs] *a* armonioso.

harmonize [hâr'mənīz] *vt, vi* armonizar.

harmony [hâr'mənē] *n* armonía.

harness [hâr'nis] *n* arreos *mpl* ♦ *vt* (*horse*) enjaezar; (*resources*) aprovechar.

harp [hârp] *n* arpa ♦ *vi*: **to ~ on (about)** machacar (con).

harpoon [hârpōōn'] *n* arpón *m*.

harrow [har'ō] *n* grada ♦ *vt* gradar.

harrowing [har'ōing] *a* angustioso.

harry [har'ē] *vt* (*MIL*) acosar; (*person*) hostigar.

harsh [hârsh] *a* (*cruel*) duro, cruel; (*severe*) severo; (*words*) hosco; (*color*) chillón/ona; (*contrast*) violento.

harshly [hârsh'lē] *ad* (*say*) con aspereza; (*treat*) con mucha dureza.

harshness [hârsh'nis] *n* dureza.

harvest [hâr'vist] *n* cosecha; (*of grapes*) vendimia ♦ *vt, vi* cosechar.

harvester [hâr'vistûr] *n* (*machine*) cosechadora; (*person*) segador(a) *m/f*; **combine ~** segadora trilladora.

has [haz] *vb see* **have**.

has-been [haz'bin] *n* (*col: person*) persona acabada; (*: thing*) vieja gloria.

hash [hash] *n* (*CULIN*) picadillo; (*fig: mess*) lío.

hashish [hash'ēsh] *n* hachís *m*, hachich *m*.

hasn't [haz'ənt] = **has not**.

hassle [has'əl] *n* (*col*) lío, problema *m* ♦ *vt* molestar.

haste [hāst] *n* prisa.

hasten [hā'sən] *vt* acelerar ♦ *vi* darse prisa; **I ~ to add that...** me apresuro a añadir que ....

hastily [hās'tilē] *ad* de prisa.

hasty [hās'tē] *a* apresurado.

hat [hat] *n* sombrero.

hatbox [hat'bàks] *n* sombrerera.

hatch [hach] *n* (*NAUT: also:* **~way**) escotilla ♦ *vi* salir del cascarón ♦ *vt* incubar; (*fig: scheme, plot*) idear, tramar.

hatchback [hach'bak] *n* (*AUT*) tres *or* cinco puertas *m*.

hatchet [hach'it] *n* hacha.

hate [hāt] *vt* odiar, aborrecer ♦ *n* odio; **I ~ to trouble you, but ...** siento *or* lamento molestarle, pero ....

hateful [hāt'fəl] *a* odioso.

hatred [hā'trid] *n* odio.

hat trick *n*: **to score a ~** (*SPORT*) marcar tres tantos (*or* triunfos) seguidos.

haughtily [hô'tilē] *ad* con arrogancia.

haughty [hô'tē] *a* altanero, arrogante.

haul [hôl] *vt* tirar; (*by truck*) transportar ♦ *n* (*of fish*) redada; (*of stolen goods etc*) botín *m*.

haulage [hô'lij] *n* transporte *m*; (*costs*) gastos *mpl* de transporte.

haulage contractor *n* (*company*) empresa de transportes; (*person*) transportista *m/f*.

hauler [hôl'ûr], (*Brit*) **haulier** [hôl'ēûr] *n* transportista *m/f*.

haunch [hônch] *n* anca; (*of meat*) pierna.

haunt [hônt] *vt* (*subj: ghost*) aparecer en; (*frequent*) frecuentar; (*obsess*) obsesionar ♦ *n* guarida.

haunted [hôn'tid] *a* (*castle etc*) embrujado; (*look*) de angustia.

haunting [hôn'ting] *a* (*sight, music*) evocativo.

Havana [həvan'ə] *n* la Havana.

have, *pt, pp* **had** [hav, had] *vt* (*gen*) tener; (*possess*) poseer; (*meal, shower*) tomar ♦ *auxiliary vb*: **to ~ arrived** haber llegado; **to ~ eaten** haber comido; **to ~ breakfast/lunch/dinner** tomar el desayuno/el almuerzo/la cena; **I'll ~ a coffee** tomaré un café; **to ~ an operation** operarse; **to ~ a party** dar una fiesta; **to ~ sth done** hacer hacer algo; **she has to do it** tiene que hacerlo; **to ~ a cold/flu** estar constipado/con gripe; **I had better leave** más vale que me marche; **I won't ~ it** no lo tolero; **let me ~ a try** déjame que lo intente; **rumor has it (that)** ... corre la voz de que ...; **he has gone** se ha ido; **to ~ it out with sb** ajustar cuentas con uno; **to ~ a baby** parir, dar a luz; *see also* **haves**.

have in *vt*: **to ~ it in for sb** (*col*) tenerla tomada con uno.

have on *vt*: **do you ~ anything on for tomorrow?** ¿tienes compromiso para mañana?; **I don't ~ any money on me** no llevo dinero; **to ~ sb on** (*Brit col*) tomarle el pelo a uno.

haven [hā'vən] *n* puerto; (*fig*) refugio.

haven't [hav'ənt] = **have not**.

haversack [hav'ûrsak] *n* mochila.

haves [havz] *npl*: **the ~ and the have-nots** los ricos y los pobres.

havoc [hav'ək] *n* estragos *mpl*.

Hawaii [həwī'yē] *n* (Islas *fpl*) Hawai *m*.

Hawaiian [həwī'ən] *a, n* hawaiano/a *m/f*.

hawk [hôk] *n* halcón *m* ♦ *vt* (*goods for sale*) pregonar.

hawthorn [hô'thôrn] *n* espino.

hay [hā] *n* heno.

hay fever *n* fiebre *f* del heno.

haystack [hā'stak] *n* almiar *m*.

haywire [hā'wiûr] *a* (*col*): **to go ~** (*person*) volverse loco; (*plan*) embrollarse.

hazard [haz'ûrd] *n* riesgo; (*danger*) peligro ♦ *vt* (*remark*) aventurar; (*one's life*) arriesgar; **to be a health ~** ser peligroso para la salud; **to ~ a guess** atreverse a hacer una respuesta.

hazardous [haz'ûrdəs] *a* (*dangerous*) peligroso; (*risky*) arriesgado.

hazardous pay *n* (*US*) prima por trabajos peligrosos.

hazard warning lights *npl* (*Brit AUT*) señales *fpl* de emergencia.

haze [hāz] *n* neblina.

hazel [hā'zəl] *n* (*tree*) avellano ♦ *a* (*eyes*) color *m* de avellano.

hazelnut [hā'zəlnut] *n* avellana.

hazy [hā'zē] *a* brumoso; (*idea*) vago.

H-bomb [āch'bàm] *n* bomba H.

h & c *abbr* (*Brit*) = *hot and cold* (*water*).

HE *abbr* = **high explosive**; (*REL. DIPLOMACY*) = *His (or Her) Excellency* S. Exc.ª.

he [hē] *pron* él; **~ who...** él que..., quien... .

head |hed| *n* cabeza; (*leader*) jefe/a *m/f*; (*COMPUT*) cabeza (grabadora) ♦ *vt* (*list*) encabezar; (*group*) capitanear; ~**s (or tails)** cara (o cruz); ~ **first** de cabeza; ~ **over heels** patas arriba; ~ **over heels in love** perdidamente enamorado; **it's on your** ~! ¡allá tú!; **they went over my** ~ **to the manager** fueron directamente al gerente sin hacerme caso; **it was above** *or* **over their** ~**s** no alcanzaron a entenderlo; **to come to a** ~ (*fig: situation etc*) llegar a un punto crítico; **to have a** ~ **for business** tener talento para los negocios; **to have no** ~ **for heights** (*Brit*) no resistir las alturas; **to lose/keep one's** ~ perder la cabeza/mantener la calma; **to sit at the** ~ **of the table** sentarse a la cabecera; **to** ~ **the ball** cabecear (la pelota).

head for *vt fus* dirigirse a.

head off *vt* (*threat, danger*) desviar.

headache |hed'āk| *n* dolor *m* de cabeza; **to have a** ~ tener dolor de cabeza.

headcheese |hed'chēz| *n* carne *f* en gelatina.

headdress |hed'dres| *n* (*of bride, Indian*) tocado.

header |hed'ûr| *n* (*Brit col: SOCCER*) cabezazo; (: *fall*) caída de cabeza.

headhunter |hed'huntûr| *n* (*fig*) cazaejecutivos *m inv*.

heading |hed'ing| *n* título.

headlamp |hed'lamp| *n* (*Brit*) = **headlight**.

headland |hed'land| *n* promontorio.

headlight |hed'līt| *n* faro.

headline |hed'līn| *n* titular *m*; **to make the** ~**s** salir en primera plana.

headlong |hed'lông| *ad* (*fall*) de cabeza; (*rush*) precipitadamente.

headmaster/mistress |hed'mãs'tûr/mis'tris| *n* (*Brit*) director(a) *m/f* (de escuela).

head office *n* oficina central, central *f*.

head-on |hed'ân'| *a* (*collision*) de frente.

headphones |hed'fōnz| *npl* auriculares *mpl*.

headquarters (HQ) |hed'kwôrtûrz| *npl* sede *f* central; (*MIL*) cuartel *m* general.

headrest |hed'rest| *n* reposa-cabezas *m inv*.

headroom |hed'rōom| *n* (*in car*) altura interior; (*under bridge*) (límite *m* de) altura.

headscarf |hed'skârf| *n* pañuelo.

headset |hed'set| *n* casco auricular.

headstone |hed'stōn| *n* lápida mortuoria.

headstrong |hed'strông| *a* testarudo.

head waiter *n* maitre *m*.

headway |hed'wã| *n*: **to make** ~ (*fig*) hacer progresos.

headwind |hed'wind| *n* viento contrario.

heady |hed'ē| *a* (*experience, period*) apasionante; (*wine*) cabezón.

heal |hēl| *vt* curar ♦ *vi* cicatrizarse.

health |helth| *n* salud *f*.

health benefit *n* (*US*) subsidio de enfermedad.

health center *n* ambulatorio, centro médico.

health food(s) *n(pl)* alimentos *mpl* orgánicos.

health food store *n* tienda de alimentos orgánicos.

health hazard *n* riesgo para la salud.

Health Service *n* (*Brit*) servicio de salud pública, ≈ Insalud *m* (*Sp*).

healthy |hel'thē| *a* (*gen*) sano; (*economy, bank balance*) saludable.

heap |hēp| *n* montón *m* ♦ *vt* amontonar; (*plate*) colmar; ~**s (of)** (*col: lots*) montones (de); **to** ~ **favors/praise/gifts** *etc* **on sb** colmar a uno de favores/elogios/regalos *etc*.

hear, *pt, pp* **heard** |hēr, hûrd| *vt* oír; (*perceive*) sentir; (*listen to*) escuchar; (*lecture*) asistir a; (*LAW: case*) ver ♦ *vi* oír; **to** ~ **about** oír hablar de; **to** ~ **from sb** tener noticias de alguien; **I've never heard of that book** nunca he oído de ese libro.

hear out *vt*: **to** ~ **sb out** dejar que uno termine de hablar.

hearing |hē'ring| *n* (*sense*) oído; (*LAW*) vista; **to give sb a** ~ dar a uno la oportunidad de hablar, escuchar a uno.

hearing aid *n* audífono.

hearsay |hēr'sã| *n* rumores *mpl*, hablillas *fpl*.

hearse |hûrs| *n* coche *m* fúnebre.

heart |hârt| *n* corazón *m*; ~**s** *npl* (*CARDS*) corazones *mpl*; **at** ~ en el fondo; **by** ~ (*learn, know*) de memoria; **to have a weak** ~ tener el corazón débil; **to set one's** ~ **on sth/on doing sth** anhelar algo/hacer algo; **I did not have the** ~ **to tell her** no tuve valor para decírselo; **to take** ~ cobrar ánimos; **the** ~ **of the matter** lo esencial *or* el meollo del asunto.

heart attack *n* infarto (de miocardio).

heartbeat |hârt'bēt| *n* latido (del corazón).

heartbreak |hârt'brāk| *n* angustia, congoja.

heartbreaking |hârt'brāking| *a* desgarrador(a).

heartbroken |hârt'brōkən| *a*: **she was** ~ **about it** le partió el corazón.

heartburn |hârt'bûrn| *n* acedía.

-hearted |-hâr'tid| *a suff*: **a kind**~ **person** una persona bondadosa.

heartening |hâr'təning| *a* alentador(a).

heart failure *n* (*MED*) fallo de corazón, colapso cardíaco.

heartfelt |hârt'felt| *a* (*cordial*) cordial; (*deeply felt*) más sentido.

hearth |hârth| *n* (*gen*) hogar *m*; (*fireplace*) chimenea.

heartily |hâr'təlē| *ad* sinceramente, cordialmente; (*laugh*) a carcajadas; (*eat*) con buen apetito; **to be** ~ **sick of** estar completamente harto de.

heartland [hârt'land] *n* zona interior *or* central; (*fig*) corazón *m*.

heartless [hârt'lis] *a* cruel.

heart-to-heart [hârt'təhârt'] *n* (*also*: ~ **talk**) conversación *f* íntima.

heart transplant *n* transplante *m* de corazón.

hearty [hár'tē] *a* cordial.

heat [hēt] *n* (*gen*) calor *m*; (*SPORT*: *also*: **qualifying** ~) prueba eliminatoria; (*ZOOL*): **in** *or* **on** ~ en celo ♦ *vt* calentar.

　heat up *vi* (*gen*) calentarse; (*col*: *situation*) ponerse difícil *or* apurado; (: *party*) animarse.

heated [hē'tid] *a* caliente; (*fig*) acalorado.

heater [hē'tûr] *n* calentador *m*.

heath [hēth] *n* (*Brit*) brezal *m*.

heathen [hē'ᵺən] *a*, *n* pagano/a *m/f*.

heather [heᵺ'ûr] *n* brezo.

heating [hē'ting] *n* calefacción *f*.

heat-resistant [hēt'rizistənt] *a* refractario.

heatstroke [hēt'strōk] *n* insolación *f*.

heat wave *n* ola de calor.

heave [hēv] *vt* (*pull*) tirar; (*push*) empujar con esfuerzo; (*lift*) levantar (con esfuerzo) ♦ *vi* (*water*) subir y bajar ♦ *n* tirón *m*; empujón *m*; (*effort*) esfuerzo; (*throw*) echada; **to** ~ **a sigh** dar *or* echar un suspiro, suspirar.

　heave to *vi* (*NAUT*) ponerse al pairo.

heaven [hev'ən] *n* cielo; (*REL*) paraíso; **thank** ~! ¡gracias a Dios!; **for** ~'s **sake!** (*pleading*) ¡por el amor de Dios!, ¡por lo que más quiera!; (*protesting*) ¡por Dios!; **to be in seventh** ~ estar loco de contento.

heavenly [hev'ənlē] *a* celestial; (*REL*) divino.

heavenly body *n* cuerpo celeste.

heavily [hev'ilē] *ad* pesadamente; (*drink, smoke*) con exceso; (*sleep, sigh*) profundamente.

heavy [hev'ē] *a* pesado; (*work*) duro; (*sea, rain, meal*) fuerte; (*drinker, smoker*) gran; (*eater*) comilón/ona.

heavy cream *n* (*US*) nata enriquecida.

heavy-duty [hev'ēdōō'tē] *a* resistente.

heavy goods vehicle (HGV) *n* (*Brit*) vehículo pesado.

heavy-handed [hev'ēhan'did] *a* (*clumsy, tactless*) torpe.

heavy industry *n* industria pesada.

heavy-set [hev'ēset] *a* (*US*) fornido.

heavy user *n* consumidor *m* intensivo.

heavyweight [hev'ēwāt] *n* (*SPORT*) peso pesado.

Hebrew [hē'brōō] *a*, *n* (*LING*) hebreo.

heckle [hek'əl] *vt* interrumpir.

heckler [hek'lûr] *n* el/la que interrumpe a un orador.

hectic [hek'tik] *a* agitado; (*busy*) ocupado.

hector [hek'tûr] *vt* intimidar con bravatas.

he'd [hēd] = **he would**; **he had**.

hedge [hej] *n* seto ♦ *vt* cercar (con un seto)

♦ *vi* contestar con evasivas; **as a** ~ **against inflation** como protección contra la inflación; **to** ~ **one's bets** (*fig*) cubrirse.

hedgehog [hej'hâg] *n* erizo.

hedgerow [hej'rō] *n* seto vivo.

hedonism [hēd'ənizəm] *n* hedonismo.

heed [hēd] *vt* (*also*: **take** ~ **of**) (*pay attention*) hacer caso de; (*bear in mind*) tener en cuenta; **to pay (no)** ~ **to, take (no)** ~ **of** (no) hacer caso a, (no) tener en cuenta.

heedless [hēd'lis] *a* desatento.

heel [hēl] *n* talón *m* ♦ *vt* (*shoe*) poner tacón a; **to take to one's** ~**s** (*col*) echar a correr; **to bring to** ~ meter en cintura.

hefty [hef'tē] *a* (*person*) fornido; (*piece*) grande; (*price*) gordo.

heifer [hef'ûr] *n* novilla, ternera.

height [hīt] *n* (*of person*) talle *m*; (*of building*) altura; (*high ground*) cerro; (*altitude*) altitud *f*; **what** ~ **are you?** ¿cuánto mides?; **of average** ~ de estatura mediana; **to be afraid of** ~**s** tener miedo a las alturas; **it's the** ~ **of fashion** es el último grito en moda.

heighten [hīt'ən] *vt* elevar; (*fig*) aumentar.

heinous [hā'nəs] *a* atroz, nefasto.

heir [är] *n* heredero.

heir apparent *n* presunto heredero.

heiress [är'is] *n* heredera.

heirloom [är'lōōm] *n* reliquia de familia.

heist [hīst] *n* (*col*: *hold-up*) atraco armado.

held [held] *pt*, *pp* *of* **hold**.

helicopter [hel'ikâptûr] *n* helicóptero.

heliport [hel'əpôrt] *n* (*AVIAT*) helipuerto.

helium [hē'lēəm] *n* helio.

hell [hel] *n* infierno; **oh** ~! (*col*) ¡demonios!, ¡caramba!

he'll [hēl] = **he will, he shall**.

hellish [hel'ish] *a* infernal; (*col*) horrible.

hello [helō'] *excl* ¡hola!; (*surprise*) ¡caramba!

hell's angel [helz ān'jəl] *n* angel *m* del infierno.

helm [helm] *n* (*NAUT*) timón *m*.

helmet [hel'mit] *n* casco.

helmsman [helmz'mən] *n* timonel *m*.

help [help] *n* ayuda; (*charwoman*) criada, asistenta ♦ *vt* ayudar; ~! ¡socorro!; **with the** ~ **of** con la ayuda de; "~ **wanted**" (*US*) "ofertas de trabajo"; **can I** ~ **you?** (*in shop*) ¿qué desea?; **to be of** ~ **to sb** servir a uno; **to** ~ **sb (to) do sth** echarle una mano *or* ayudar a uno a hacer algo; ~ **yourself** sírvete; **he can't** ~ **it** no es culpa suya.

helper [hel'pûr] *n* ayudante *m/f*.

helpful [help'fəl] *a* útil; (*person*) servicial.

helping [hel'ping] *n* ración *f*.

helpless [help'lis] *a* (*incapable*) incapaz; (*defenseless*) indefenso.

Helsinki [hel'singkē] *n* Helsinki *m*.

helter-skelter [hel'tûrskel'tûr] *n* (*in funfair*)

tobogán m.

hem [hɛm] n dobladillo ♦ vt poner or coser el dobladillo a.

hem in vt cercar; **to feel ~med in** (fig) sentirse acosado.

he-man [hē'man] n macho.

hematology [hēmətál'əjē] n (US) hematología.

hemisphere [hem'isfēr] n hemisferio.

hemline [hem'līn] n bajo (del vestido).

hemlock [hem'lâk] n cicuta.

hemoglobin [hē'məglōbin] n (US) hemoglobina.

hemophilia [hēməfil'ēə] n (US) hemofilia.

hemorrhage [hem'ûrij] n (US) hemorragia.

hemorrhoids [hem'əroidz] npl (US) hemorroides fpl, almorranas fpl.

hemp [hemp] n cáñamo.

hen [hen] n gallina; (female bird) hembra.

hence [hens] ad (therefore) por lo tanto; **2 years ~** de aquí a 2 años.

henceforth [hens'fôrth] ad de hoy en adelante.

henchman [hench'mən] n (pej) secuaz m.

henna [hen'ə] n alheña.

hen party n (col) reunión f de mujeres.

henpecked [hen'pekt] a: **to be ~** ser un calzonazos.

hepatitis [hepətī'tis] n hepatitis f inv.

her [hûr] pron (direct) la; (indirect) le; (stressed, after prep) ella ♦ a su; see also **me, my.**

herald [här'əld] n (forerunner) precursor(a) m/f ♦ vt anunciar.

heraldic [hiral'dik] a heráldico.

heraldry [här'əldrē] n heráldica.

herb [ûrb] n hierba.

herbaceous [hûrbā'shəs] a herbáceo.

herbal [hûr'bəl] a herbario.

herbicide [hûr'bisīd] n herbicida m.

herd [hûrd] n rebaño; (of wild animals, swine) piara ♦ vt (drive, gather: animals) llevar en manada; (: people) reunir.

herd together vt agrupar, reunir ♦ vi apiñarse, agruparse.

here [hēr] ad aquí; ~! (present) ¡presente!; **~ is/are** aquí está/están; **~ she is** aquí está; **come ~!** ¡ven aquí or acá!; **~ and there** aquí y allá.

hereabouts [hē'rəbouts] ad por aquí (cerca).

hereafter [hērafˈtûr] ad en el futuro ♦ n: **the ~** el más allá.

hereby [hērbī'] ad (in letter) por la presente.

hereditary [həred'itärē] a hereditario.

heredity [həred'itē] n herencia.

heresy [här'isē] n herejía.

heretic [här'itik] n hereje m/f.

heretical [həret'ikəl] a herético.

herewith [hērwith'] ad: **I send you ~** ... le mando adjunto ....

heritage [här'itij] n (gen) herencia; (fig) patrimonio; **our national ~** nuestro patrimonio nacional.

hermetically [hûrmet'iklē] ad: **~ sealed** cerrado or tapado herméticamente.

hermit [hûr'mit] n ermitaño/a.

hernia [hûr'nēə] n hernia.

hero, pl **~es** [hē'rō] n héroe m; (in book, film) protagonista m.

heroic [hirō'ik] a heroico.

heroin [här'ōin] n heroína.

heroin addict n heroinómano/a, adicto/a a la heroína.

heroine [här'ōin] n heroína; (in book, film) protagonista.

heroism [här'ōizəm] n heroísmo.

heron [här'ən] n garza.

hero worship n adulación f.

herring [här'ing] n arenque m.

hers [hûrz] pron (el) suyo/(la) suya etc; **a friend of ~** un amigo suyo; **this is ~** esto es suyo or de ella; see also **mine.**

herself [hûrself'] pron (reflexive) se; (emphatic) ella misma; (after prep) sí (misma); see also **oneself.**

Herts abbr (Brit) = Hertfordshire.

he's [hēz] = **he is; he has.**

hesitant [hez'ətənt] a vacilante; **to be ~ about doing sth** no decidirse a hacer algo.

hesitate [hez'ətāt] vi vacilar; **don't ~ to ask (me)** no vaciles en or no dejes de pedírmelo.

hesitation [hezətā'shən] n indecisión f; **I have no ~ in saying (that)** ... no tengo el menor reparo en afirmar que ....

hessian [hesh'ən] n arpillera.

heterogeneous [hetûrəjē'nēəs] a heterogéneo.

heterosexual [hetûrəsek'shōōəl] a, n heterosexual m/f.

het up [het up] a (col) agitado, nervioso.

hew [hyōō] vt cortar (con hacha).

hex [heks] (US) n maleficio, mal m de ojo ♦ vt embrujar.

hexagon [hek'səgən] n (h)exágono.

hexagonal [heksag'ənəl] a hexagonal.

hey [hā] excl ¡oye!

heyday [hā'dā] n: **the ~ of** el apogeo de.

HF n abbr = high frequency.

HGV n abbr (Brit) = **heavy goods vehicle.**

HI abbr (US MAIL) = Hawaii.

hi [hī] excl ¡hola!

hiatus [hiā'təs] n vacío, interrupción f; (LING) hiato.

hibernate [hī'bûrnāt] vi invernar.

hibernation [hībûrnā'shən] n hibernación f.

hiccough, hiccup [hik'up] vi hipar; **~s** npl hipo sg.

hick [hik] n (US) palurdo, rústico.

hid [hid] pt of **hide.**

hidden [hid'ən] pp of **hide** ♦ a: **there are no ~ extras** no hay gastos extra.

hide [hīd] n (skin) piel f ♦ vb (pt hid, pp

hidden [hid, hid'ən]) *vt* esconder, ocultar; (*feelings, truth*) encubrir, ocultar ♦ *vi*: **to ~ (from sb)** esconderse *or* ocultarse (de uno).

hide-and-seek [hīd'ənsēk'] *n* escondite *m*.

hideaway [hīd'əwā] *n* escondite *m*.

hideous [hid'ēəs] *a* horrible.

hideously [hid'ēəslē] *ad* horriblemente.

hide-out [hīd'out] *n* escondite *m*, refugio.

hiding [hī'ding] *n* (*beating*) paliza; **to be in ~** (*concealed*) estar escondido.

hiding place *n* escondrijo.

hierarchy [hī'ərärkē] *n* jerarquía.

hieroglyphic [hīūrəglif'ik] *a* jeroglífico ♦ *n*: **~s** jeroglíficos *mpl*.

hi-fi [hī'fī'] *abbr* (= *high fidelity*) *n* estéreo, hifi *m* ♦ *a* de alta fidelidad.

higgledy-piggledy [hig'əldēpig'əldē] *ad* en desorden.

high [hī] *a* alto; (*speed, number*) grande; (*price*) elevado; (*wind*) fuerte; (*voice*) agudo; (*col: on drugs*) drogado; (: *on drink*) borracho; (*CULIN: meat, game*) manido; (: *spoiled*) estropeado ♦ *ad* alto, a gran altura ♦ *n*: **exports have reached a new ~** las exportaciones han alcanzado niveles inusitados; **it is 20 m ~** tiene 20 m de altura; **~ in the air** en las alturas; **to pay a ~ price for sth** pagar algo muy caro.

highball [hī'bôl] *n* (*US: drink*) whisky *m* soda.

highboy [hī'boi] *n* (*US*) cómoda alta.

highbrow [hī'brou] *a* culto.

highchair [hī'chär] *n* silla alta.

high-class [hī'klas'] *a* (*neighborhood*) de alta sociedad; (*hotel*) de lujo; (*person*) distinguido, de categoría; (*food*) de alta categoría.

high court *n* (*LAW*) tribunal *m* supremo.

higher [hī'ûr] *a* (*form of life, study etc*) superior ♦ *ad* más alto.

higher education *n* educación *f or* enseñanza superior.

high explosive *n* explosivo de gran potencia.

high finance *n* altas finanzas *fpl*.

high-flier [hī'flī'ûr] *n* ambicioso/a.

high-handed [hī'han'did] *a* despótico.

high-heeled [hī'hēld] *a* de tacón alto.

highjack [hī'jak] = **hijack**.

high jump *n* (*SPORT*) salto de altura.

highlands [hī'ləndz] *npl* tierras *fpl* altas.

high-level [hī'levəl] *a* (*talks etc*) de alto nivel; **~ language** (*COMPUT*) lenguaje *m* de alto nivel.

highlight [hī'līt] *n* (*fig: of event*) punto culminante ♦ *vt* subrayar.

highly [hī'lē] *ad* sumamente; **~ paid** muy bien pagado; **to speak ~ of** hablar muy bien de.

highly-strung [hī'lēstrung'] *a* (*Brit*) = **high-strung**.

High Mass *n* misa mayor.

highness [hī'nis] *n* altura; **Her** *or* **His H~** Su Alteza.

high-pitched [hī'picht'] *a* agudo.

high-powered [hī'pou'ûrd] *a* (*engine*) de gran potencia; (*fig: person*) importante.

high-pressure [hī'presh'ûr] *a* de alta presión; (*fig: salesman etc*) enérgico.

high-rise building [hī'rīz bil'ding] *n* torre *f* de pisos.

high school *n* centro de enseñanza secundaria, ≈ Instituto Nacional de Bachillerato (*Sp*).

high season *n* temporada alta.

high-speed [hī'spēd] *a* de alta velocidad.

high-spirited [hī'spir'itid] *a* animado.

high spirits *npl* ánimos *mpl*.

high street *n* (*Brit*) calle *f* mayor.

high-strung [hī'strung'] *a* (*US*) hipertenso.

high tide *n* marea alta.

highway [hī'wā] *n* carretera; **divided ~** (*US*) carretera de doble calzada; **it's robbery!** ¡es una extorsión!

Highway Code *n* (*Brit*) código de la circulación.

highwayman [hī'wāmən] *n* salteador *m* de caminos.

hijack [hī'jak] *vt* secuestrar ♦ *n* (*also*: **~ing**) secuestro.

hijacker [hī'jakûr] *n* secuestrador(a) *m/f*.

hike [hīk] *vi* (*go walking*) ir de excursión (a pie); (*trek*) caminar ♦ *n* caminata; (*col: in prices etc*) aumento.

hike up *vt* (*raise*) aumentar.

hiker [hī'kûr] *n* excursionista *m/f*.

hilarious [hilâr'ēəs] *a* divertidísimo.

hilarity [hilar'itē] *n* (*laughter*) risas *fpl*, carcajadas *fpl*.

hill [hil] *n* colina; (*high*) montaña; (*slope*) cuesta.

hillbilly [hil'bilē] *n* (*US*) rústico/a montañés/esa; (*pej*) palurdo/a.

hillock [hil'ək] *n* montecillo, altozano.

hillside [hil'sīd] *n* ladera.

hilltop [hil'tâp] *n* cumbre *f*.

hilly [hil'ē] *a* montañoso; (*uneven*) accidentado.

hilt [hilt] *n* (*of sword*) empuñadura; **to the ~** (*fig: support*) incondicionalmente; **to be in debt up to the ~** estar agobiado de deudas.

him [him] *pron* (*direct*) le, lo; (*indirect*) le; (*stressed, after prep*) él; *see also* **me**.

Himalayas [himəlā'əz] *npl*: **the ~** los montes Himalaya, el Himalaya.

himself [himself'] *pron* (*reflexive*) se; (*emphatic*) él mismo; (*after prep*) sí (mismo); *see also* **oneself**.

hind [hīnd] *a* posterior ♦ *n* cierva.

hinder [hin'dûr] *vt* estorbar, impedir.

hindquarters [hīnd'kwôrtûrz] *npl* (*ZOOL*) cuartos *mpl* traseros.

hindrance [hin'drəns] *n* estorbo, obstáculo.

hindsight [hīnd'sīt] *n* percepción *f* tardía *or*

retrospectiva; **with the benefit of** ~ con la perspectiva del tiempo transcurrido.

Hindu [hin'dōō] *n* hindú *m/f*.

hinge [hinj] *n* bisagra, gozne *m* ♦ *vi* (*fig*): **to ~ on** depender de.

hint [hint] *n* indirecta; (*advice*) consejo ♦ *vt*: **to ~ that** insinuar que ♦ *vi*: **to ~ at** referirse indirectamente a; **to drop a ~** soltar *or* tirar una indirecta; **give me a ~** dame una pista.

hip [hip] *n* cadera; (*BOT*) escaramujo.

hip flask *n* frasco.

hippie [hip'ē] *n* hippie *m/f*, jipi *m/f*.

hip pocket *n* bolsillo de atrás.

hippopotamus, *pl* ~**es** *or* **hippopotami** [hipəpât'əməs, -pât'əmī] hipopótamo.

hippy [hip'ē] *n* = **hippie.**

hire [hīûr] *vt* (*worker*) contratar; (*Brit*: *car, equipment*) alquilar ♦ *n* (*Brit*) alquiler *m*; **for ~** se alquila; (*taxi*) libre; **on ~** de alquiler.

hire out *vt* (*Brit*) alquilar, arrendar.

hire(d) car *n* (*Brit*) coche *m* de alquiler.

hire purchase (HP) *n* (*Brit*) compra a plazos.

his [hiz] *pron* (el) suyo/(la) suya *etc* ♦ *a* su; **this is ~** esto es suyo *or* de él; *see also* **my, mine.**

Hispanic [hispan'ik] *a* hispánico.

hiss [his] *vi* silbar; (*in protest*) sisear ♦ *n* silbido; siseo.

histogram [his'təgram] *n* histograma *m*.

historian [histôr'ēən] *n* historiador(a) *m/f*.

historic(al) [histôr'ik(əl)] *a* histórico.

history [his'tûrē] *n* historia; **there's a long ~ of that illness in his family** esa enfermedad corre en su familia.

histrionics [histrēân'iks] *npl* histrionismo.

hit [hit] *vt* (*pt, pp* **hit**) (*strike*) golpear, pegar; (*reach: target*) alcanzar; (*collide with: car*) chocar contra; (*fig: affect*) afectar ♦ *n* golpe *m*; (*success*) éxito; **to ~ the headlines** salir en primera plana; **to ~ the road** (*col*) largarse; **to ~ it off with sb** llevarse bien con uno.

hit back *vi* defenderse; (*fig*) devolver golpe por golpe.

hit out at *vt fus* asestar un golpe a; (*fig*) atacar.

hit (up)on *vt fus* (*answer*) dar con; (*solution*) hallar, encontrar.

hit-and-run driver [hit'ənrun' drī'vûr] *n* conductor(a) que atropella y huye.

hitch [hich] *vt* (*fasten*) atar, amarrar; (*also*: ~ **up**) remangar ♦ *n* (*difficulty*) dificultad *f*; **to ~ a ride** hacer autostop; **technical ~** problema *m* técnico.

hitch up *vt* (*horse, cart*) enganchar, uncir.

hitchhike [hich'hīk] *vi* hacer autostop.

hitchhiker [hich'hīkûr] *n* autostopista *m/f*.

hi-tech [hī'tek'] *a* de alta tecnología.

hitherto [hith'ûrtōō] *ad* hasta ahora, hasta aquí.

hit man *n* asesino a sueldo.

hit-or-miss [hit'ərmis'] *a*: **it's ~ whether ...** está a la buena de Dios si ... .

hit parade *n*: **the ~** los cuarenta principales.

hive [hīv] *n* colmena; **the shop was a ~ of activity** (*fig*) la tienda era una colmena humana.

hive off *vt* (*col: separate*) separar; (: *privatize*) privatizar.

hl *abbr* (= *hectoliter*) hl.

HM *abbr* (= *His (or Her) Majesty*) S.M.

HMG *abbr* (*Brit*) = *His (or Her) Majesty's Government*.

HMO *n* *abbr* (*US*: = *health maintenance organization*) seguro médico global.

HMS *abbr* (*Brit*) = *His (or Her) Majesty's Ship*.

hoard [hôrd] *n* (*treasure*) tesoro; (*stockpile*) provisión *f* ♦ *vt* acumular.

hoarding [hôr'ding] *n* (*for posters*) cartelera.

hoarfrost [hôr'frâst] *n* escarcha.

hoarse [hôrs] *a* ronco.

hoax [hōks] *n* trampa.

hob [hâb] *n* quemador *m*.

hobble [hâb'əl] *vi* cojear.

hobby [hâb'ē] *n* pasatiempo, afición *f*.

hobbyhorse [hâb'ēhôrs] *n* (*fig*) tema, manía.

hobnob [hâb'nâb] *vi*: **to ~ (with)** alternar (con).

hobo [hō'bō] *n* (*US*) vagabundo.

hock [hâk] *n* (*of animal, CULIN*) corvejón *m*; (*col*): **to be in ~** (*person*) estar empeñado *or* endeudado; (*object*) estar empeñado.

hockey [hâk'ē] *n* hockey *m*.

hocus-pocus [hō'kəspō'kəs] *n* (*trickery*) juego de manos; (*words: of magician*) jerigonza.

hodge-podge [hâj'pâj] *n* mezcolanza.

hoe [hō] *n* azadón *m* ♦ *vt* azadonar.

hog [hôg] *n* cerdo, puerco ♦ *vt* (*fig*) acaparar; **to go the whole ~** echar el todo por el todo.

hoist [hoist] *n* (*crane*) grúa ♦ *vt* levantar, alzar.

hold [hōld] *vb* (*pt, pp* **held** [held]) *vt* tener; (*contain*) contener; (*keep back*) retener; (*believe*) sostener; (*take ~ of*) coger (*Sp*), agarrar (*LAm*); (*take weight*) soportar; (*meeting*) celebrar ♦ *vi* (*withstand pressure*) resistir; (*be valid*) valer; (*stick*) pegarse ♦ *n* (*grasp*) asimiento; (*fig*) dominio; (*WRESTLING*) presa; (*NAUT*) bodega; **~ the line!** (*TEL*) ¡no cuelgue!; **to ~ one's own** (*fig*) defenderse; **to ~ office** (*POL*) ocupar un cargo; **to ~ firm** *or* **fast** mantenerse firme; **he ~s the view that ...** opina *or* es su opinión que ...; **to ~ sb responsible for sth** culpar *or* echarle la culpa a uno de algo; **where can I get** ~ **of ...?** ¿dónde puedo encontrar (a) ...?; **to catch** *or* **get (a)** ~ **of** agarrarse *or* asirse de.

hold back *vt* retener; (*secret*) ocultar; **to** ~ **sb back from doing sth** impedir a uno hacer algo, impedir que uno haga algo.

hold down *vt* (*person*) sujetar; (*job*) mantener.

hold forth *vi* perorar.

hold off *vt* (*enemy*) rechazar ♦ *vi*: **if the rain** ~**s off** si no llueve.

hold on *vi* agarrarse bien; (*wait*) esperar.

hold on to *vt fus* agarrarse a; (*keep*) guardar.

hold out *vt* ofrecer ♦ *vi* (*resist*) resistir; **to** ~ **out (against)** resistir (a), sobrevivir.

hold over *vt* (*meeting etc*) aplazar.

hold up *vt* (*raise*) levantar; (*support*) apoyar; (*delay*) retrasar; (*traffic*) demorar; (*rob: bank*) asaltar, atracar.

holdall [hōld'ól] *n* (*Brit*) bolsa.

holder [hōl'dúr] *n* (*of ticket, record*) poseedor(a) *m/f*; (*of passport, post, office, title etc*) titular *m/f*.

holding [hōl'ding] *n* (*share*) interés *m*.

holding company *n* holding *m*.

holdup [hōld'up] *n* (*robbery*) atraco; (*delay*) retraso; (*in traffic*) embotellamiento.

hole [hōl] *n* agujero ♦ *vt* agujerear; ~ **in the heart** (*MED*) boquete *m* en el corazón; **to pick** ~**s in** (*fig*) encontrar defectos en; **the ship was** ~**d** se abrió una vía de agua en el barco.

hole up *vi* esconderse.

holiday [hâl'idā] *n* (*day off*) (día *m* de) fiesta, día *m* feriado; (*from work*) día *m* de asueto; (*Brit: vacation*) vacaciones *fpl*; **on** ~ de vacaciones; **to be on** ~ estar de vacaciones.

holiday camp *n* (*Brit*) colonia *or* centro vacacional; (: *for children*) colonia veraniega infantil.

holidaymaker [hâl'idāmākúr] *n* (*Brit*) turista *m/f*.

holiday pay *n* (*Brit*) paga de las vacaciones.

holiday resort *n* centro turístico.

holiday season *n* (*US*) Las Navidades; (*Brit*) temporada de las vacaciones; **the** ~ **is from ... to ...** la época de vacaciones es de ... a ... .

holiness [hō'lēnis] *n* santidad *f*.

Holland [hâl'ənd] *n* Holanda.

hollow [hâl'ō] *a* hueco; (*fig*) vacío; (*eyes*) hundido; (*sound*) sordo ♦ *n* (*gen*) hueco; (*in ground*) hoyo ♦ *vt*: **to** ~ **out** ahuecar.

holly [hâl'ē] *n* acebo.

hollyhock [hâl'ēhâk] *n* malva loca.

holocaust [hâl'əkôst] *n* holocausto.

holster [hōl'stúr] *n* pistolera.

holy [hō'lē] *a* (*gen*) santo, sagrado; (*water*)

bendito; **the H**~ **Father** el Santo Padre.

Holy Communion *n* Sagrada Comunión *f*.

Holy Ghost, **Holy Spirit** *n* Espíritu *m* Santo.

homage [hâm'ij] *n* homenaje *m*; **to pay** ~ **to** rendir homenaje a.

home [hōm] *n* casa; (*country*) patria; (*institution*) asilo; (*COMPUT*) punto inicial *or* de partida ♦ *a* (*domestic*) casero, de casa; (*ECON, POL*) nacional; (*SPORT: team*) de casa; (: *match, win*) en casa ♦ *ad* (*direction*) a casa; **at** ~ en casa; **to go/come** ~ ir/volver a casa; **make yourself at** ~ ¡estás en tu casa!; **it's near my** ~ está cerca de mi casa.

home in on *vt fus* (*missiles*) dirigirse hacia.

home address *n* domicilio.

home-brew [hōm'brōō'] *n* cerveza *etc* casera.

homecoming [hōm'kuming] *n* regreso (al hogar).

home computer *n* ordenador *m* doméstico.

home economics *n* economía doméstica.

home-grown [hōm'grōn'] *a* de cosecha propia.

home key *n* (*COMPUT*) tecla home.

homeland [hōm'land] *n* tierra natal.

homeless [hōm'lis] *a* sin hogar, sin casa ♦ *npl*: **the** ~ las personas sin hogar.

home loan *n* préstamo para la vivienda.

homely [hōm'lē] *a* (*domestic*) casero; (*simple*) sencillo.

home-made [hōm'mād'] *a* hecho en casa.

Home Office *n* (*Brit*) Ministerio del Interior.

homeopath [hō'mēəpath] *n* homeópata *m/f*.

homeopathic [hōmēəpath'ik] *a* homeopático.

homeopathy [hōmēâp'əthē] *n* homeopatía.

home rule *n* autonomía.

Home Secretary *n* (*Brit*) Ministro del Interior.

homesick [hōm'sik] *a*: **to be** ~ tener morriña, tener nostalgia.

homestead [hōm'sted] *n* hacienda.

home town *n* ciudad *f* natal.

homeward [hōm'wûrd] *a* (*journey*) de vuelta.

homeward(s) [hōm'wûrd(z)] *ad* hacia casa.

homework [hōm'wûrk] *n* deberes *mpl*.

homicidal [hâmisīd'əl] *a* homicida.

homicide [hâm'isīd] *n* (*US*) homicidio.

homily [hâm'ilē] *n* homilía.

homing [hō'ming] *a* (*device, missile*) buscador(a), cazador(a); ~ **pigeon** paloma mensajera.

homoeopathy [hōmēâp'əthē] *etc* (*Brit*) = **homeopathy** *etc*.

homogeneous [hōməjē'nēəs] *a* homogéneo.

homogenize [həmâj'əniz] *vt* homogeneizar.

homosexual [hōməsek'shōōəl] *a, n* homosexual *m/f*.

Hon. *abbr* (= *honorable, honorary*) en *títulos*.

Honduras [hundōō'rəs] *n* Honduras *fpl*.

hone [hōn] *vt* (*sharpen*) afilar; (*fig*) perfeccionar.

honest [ân'ist] *a* honrado; (*sincere*) franco, sincero; **to be quite ~ with you** ... para serte franco ....

honestly [ân'istlē] *ad* honradamente; francamente.

honesty [ân'istē] *n* honradez *f*.

honey [hun'ē] *n* miel *f*; (*US col*) guapa, linda.

honeycomb [hun'ēkōm] *n* panal *m*; (*fig*) laberinto.

honeymoon [hun'ēmōōn] *n* luna de miel.

honeysuckle [hun'ēsukəl] *n* madreselva.

Hong Kong [hâng' kông'] *n* Hong-Kong *m*.

honk [hângk] *vi* (*AUT*) tocar la bocina.

Honolulu [hânəlōō'lōō] *n* Honolulú *m*.

honor [ân'ûr] (*US*) *vt* honrar ♦ *n* honor *m*, honra; **in ~ of** en honor de; **it's a great ~** es un gran honor.

honorable [ân'ûrəbəl] *a* honrado, honorable.

honorary [ân'ərärē] *a* no remunerado; (*duty, title*) honorario.

honor-bound [ân'ûrbound'] *a* moralmente obligado.

honors degree *n* (*UNIV*) título de licenciado de categoría superior.

honour [ân'ûr] *etc* (*Brit*) = **honor** *etc*.

Hons. *abbr* (*UNIV*) = **honors degree**.

hood [hōōd] *n* capucha; (*US AUT*) capó *m;* (*Brit AUT*) capota; (*US col*) matón *m*.

hooded [hōōd'id] *a* (*robber*) encapuchado.

hoodlum [hōōd'ləm] *n* matón *m*.

hoodwink [hōōd'wingk] *vt* (*Brit*) timar.

hoof, *pl* **~s** *or* **hooves** [hōōf, hōōvz] *n* pezuña.

hook [hōōk] *n* gancho; (*on dress*) corchete *m*, broche *m*; (*for fishing*) anzuelo ♦ *vt* enganchar; **~s and eyes** corchetes *mpl*, macho y hembra *m;* **by ~ or by crook** por las buenas o por las malas; **to be ~ed on** (*col*) ser adicto a; **to be ~ed on drugs** estar colgado.

hook up *vt* (*RADIO, TV*) transmitir en cadena.

hooker [hōōk'ûr] *n* (*col*) puta.

hooky [hōōk'ē] *n*: **to play ~** hacer novillos.

hooligan [hōō'ligən] *n* gamberro.

hooliganism [hōō'ligənizəm] *n* gamberrismo.

hoop [hōōp] *n* aro.

hoot [hōōt] *vi* (*owl*) ulular; (*siren*) sonar la sirena; (*Brit AUT*) tocar la bocina ♦ *n* bocinazo, toque *m* de sirena; **to ~ with laughter** morirse de risa.

hooter [hōō'tûr] *n* (*NAUT*) sirena; (*factory* **~**) silbato; (*Brit AUT*) bocina.

hoover [hōō'vûr] ® (*Brit*) *n* aspiradora ♦ *vt* pasar la aspiradora por.

hooves [hōōvz] *pl of* **hoof**.

hop [hâp] *vi* saltar, brincar; (*on one foot*) saltar con un pie ♦ *n* salto, brinco; *see also* **hops**.

hope [hōp] *vt, vi* esperar ♦ *n* esperanza; **I ~ so/not** espero que sí/no.

hopeful [hōp'fəl] *a* (*person*) optimista; (*situation*) prometedor(a); **I'm ~ that she'll manage to come** confío en que podrá venir.

hopefully [hōp'fəlē] *ad* con optimismo, con esperanza.

hopeless [hōp'lis] *a* desesperado.

hopelessly [hōp'lislē] *ad* (*live etc*) sin esperanzas; **I'm ~ confused/lost** estoy totalmente despistado/perdido.

hopper [hâp'ûr] *n* (*chute*) tolva.

hops [hâps] *npl* lúpulo *sg*.

horde [hôrd] *n* horda.

horizon [hərī'zən] *n* horizonte *m*.

horizontal [hôrizân'təl] *a* horizontal.

hormone [hôr'mōn] *n* hormona.

horn [hôrn] *n* cuerno; (*MUS: also:* **French ~**) trompa; (*AUT*) bocina, claxón *m* (*LAm*); **English ~** corno inglés.

horned [hôrnd] *a* con cuernos.

hornet [hôr'nit] *n* avispón *m*.

horny [hôr'nē] *a* (*material*) córneo; (*hands*) calloso; (*col*) cachondo.

horoscope [hôr'əskōp] *n* horóscopo.

horrendous [hôren'dəs] *a* horrendo.

horrible [hôr'əbəl] *a* horrible.

horribly [hôr'əblē] *ad* horriblemente.

horrid [hôr'id] *a* horrible, horroroso.

horridly [hôr'idlē] *ad* (*behave*) tremendamente mal.

horrific [hôrif'ik] *a* (*accident*) horroroso; (*film*) horripilante.

horrify [hôr'əfī] *vt* horrorizar.

horrifying [hôr'əfīing] *a* horroroso.

horror [hôr'ûr] *n* horror *m*.

horror film *n* película de horror.

horror-struck [hôr'ûrstruk], **horror-stricken** [hôr'ûrstrikən] *a* horrorizado.

hors d'œuvre [ôr dûrv'] *n* entremeses *mpl*.

horse [hôrs] *n* caballo.

horseback [hôrs'bak] *n*: **on ~** a caballo; **to go ~ riding** (*US*) montar, cabalgar.

horsebox [hôrs'bâks] *n* (*Brit*) = **horse trailer**.

horse chestnut *n* (*tree*) castaño de Indias.

horsedrawn [hôrs'drôn] *a* de tracción animal.

horsefly [hôrs'flī] *n* tábano.

horseman [hôrs'mən] *n* jinete *m*.

horsemanship [hôrs'mənship] *n* equitación *f*, manejo del caballo.

horseplay [hôrs'plā] *n* payasadas *fpl*.

horsepower (hp) [hôrs'pouûr] *n* caballo (de fuerza), potencia en caballos.

horse racing *n* carreras *fpl* de caballos.

horseradish [hôrs'radish] *n* rábano picante.

horseshoe [hôrs'shoo] n herradura.
horse show n concurso hípico.
horse-trader [hôrs'trādûr]' n chalán/ana m/f.
horse trailer n (US) remolque m para caballerías.
horsewhip [hôrs'hwip] vt azotar.
horsewoman [hôrs'woomən] n jineta, caballista.
horsey [hôr'sē] a (col: person) aficionado a los caballos.
horticulture [hôr'təkulchûr] n horticultura.
hose [hōz] n (also: Brit: ~pipe) manguera.
hose down vt regar con manguera.
hosiery [hō'zhûrē] n calcetería.
hospice [hás'pis] n hospicio.
hospitable [háspit'əbəl] a hospitalario.
hospital [hás'pitəl] n hospital m.
hospitality [háspətal'itē] n hospitalidad f.
hospitalize [hás'pitəlīz] vt hospitalizar.
host [hōst] n anfitrión m; (TV, RADIO) presentador(a) m/f; (of inn etc) mesonero; (REL) hostia; (large number): **a ~ of** multitud de.
hostage [hás'tij] n rehén m.
hostel [hás'təl] n hostal m; (for students, nurses etc) residencia; (also: **youth ~**) albergue m juvenil; (for homeless people) hospicio.
hosteling [hás'təling] n: **to go (youth) ~** viajar de alberguista.
hostess [hōs'tis] n anfitriona; (Brit: air ~) azafata; (in night-club) señorita de compañía.
hostile [hás'təl] a hostil.
hostility [hástil'ətē] n hostilidad f.
hot [hát] a caliente; (weather) caluroso, de calor; (as opposed to only warm) muy caliente; (spicy) picante; (fig) ardiente, acalorado; **to be ~** (person) tener calor; (object) estar caliente; (weather) hacer calor.
hot up vi (Brit col: situation) ponerse difícil or apurado; (: party) animarse ♦ vt (col: pace) apretar; (: engine) aumentar la potencia de.
hot air n (col) palabras fpl huecas.
hot-air balloon [hátär' bəloon'] n (AVIAT) globo de aire caliente.
hotbed [hát'bed] n (fig) semillero.
hot-blooded [hát'blud'id] a impetuoso.
hotchpotch [hách'pách] n (Brit) = **hodgepodge**.
hot dog n perro caliente.
hotel [hōtel'] n hotel m.
hotelier [ōtelyā'] n hotelero.
hotel industry n industria hotelera.
hotel room n habitación f.
hotfoot [hát'foot] ad a toda prisa.
hotheaded [hát'hedid] a exaltado.
hothouse [hát'hous] n invernadero.
hot line [hát līn] n (POL) teléfono rojo, línea directa.

hotly [hát'lē] ad con pasión, apasionadamente.
hotplate [hát'plāt] n (on stove) hornillo.
hotpot [hát'pát] n (Brit CULIN) estofado.
hot seat n primera fila.
hot spot n (trouble spot) punto caliente; (night club etc) lugar m popular.
hot spring n terma, fuente f de aguas termales.
hot-tempered [hát'tem'pûrd] a de mal genio or carácter.
hot-water bottle [hátwôt'ûr bátəl] n bolsa de agua caliente.
hound [hound] vt acosar ♦ n perro de caza.
hour [ou'ûr] n hora; **at 30 miles an ~** a 30 millas por hora; **lunch ~** la hora del almuerzo or de comer; **to pay sb by the ~** pagar a uno por hora.
hourly [ouûr'lē] a (de) cada hora; (rate) por hora ♦ ad cada hora.
house n [hous] (pl **~s** [houz'iz]) (also firm) casa; (POL) cámara; (THEATER) sala ♦ vt [houz] (person) alojar; **at/to my ~** en/a mi casa; **on the ~** (fig) la casa invita.
house arrest n arresto domiciliario.
houseboat [hous'bōt] n casa flotante.
housebound [hous'bound] a confinado en casa.
housebreaking [hous'brāking] n allanamiento de morada.
house-broken [hous'brōkən] a (US: animal) domesticado.
housecoat [hous'kōt] n bata.
household [hous'hōld] n familia.
householder [hous'hōldûr] n propietario/a; (head of house) cabeza de familia, jefe m de familia.
house hunting n: **to go ~** ir buscando casa.
housekeeper [hous'kēpûr] n ama de llaves.
housekeeping [hous'kēping] n (work) trabajos mpl domésticos; (COMPUT) gestión f interna; (also: **~ money**) dinero para gastos domésticos.
houseman [hous'mən] n (Brit MED) médico recién titulado que vive en el hospital.
house plant n planta de interior.
house-proud [hous'proud] a preocupado por el embellecimiento de la casa.
house-to-house [houstəhous'] a (collection) de casa en casa; (search) casa por casa.
house-trained [hous'trānd] a (Brit) = **house-broken**.
house-warming [hous'wôrming] n (also: **~ party**) fiesta de estreno de una casa.
housewife [hous'wif] n ama de casa.
housework [hous'wûrk] n faenas fpl (de la casa).
housing [hou'zing] n (act) alojamiento; (houses) viviendas fpl ♦ cpd (problem, shortage) de (la) vivienda.
housing association n asociación f de la

vivienda.

housing conditions *npl* condiciones *fpl* de habitabilidad.

housing development, (*Brit*) **housing estate** *n* urbanización *f*.

hovel [huv'əl] *n* casucha.

hover [huv'ûr] *vi* flotar (en el aire); (*helicopter*) cernerse; **to ~ on the brink of disaster** estar en el borde mismo del desastre.

hovercraft [huv'ûrkraft] *n* aerodeslizador *m*.

hoverport [huv'ûrpôrt] *n* puerto de aerodeslizadores.

how [hou] *ad* cómo; **~ are you?** ¿cómo está usted?, ¿cómo estás?; **~ do you do?** ¿cómo está usted?, ¿qué tal estás?; **~ far is it to ...?** ¿qué distancia hay de aquí a ...?; **~ long have you been here?** ¿cuánto tiempo hace que estás aquí?; **~ lovely!** ¡qué bonito!; **~ many/much?** ¿cuántos/cuánto?; **~ old are you?** ¿cuántos años tienes?; **~ is school?** ¿qué tal la escuela?; **~ about a drink?** ¿te gustaría algo de beber?, ¿qué te parece una copa?

however [houєv'ûr] *ad* de cualquier manera; (+ *adjective*) por muy ... que; (*in questions*) cómo ♦ *conj* sin embargo, no obstante.

howitzer [hou'itsûr] *n* (*MIL*) obús *m*.

howl [houl] *n* aullido ♦ *vi* aullar.

howler [hou'lûr] *n* plancha, falta garrafal.

HP *n abbr* = **hire purchase**.

hp *abbr* = **horsepower**.

HQ *n abbr* = **headquarters**.

HR *n abbr* (*US*) = *House of Representatives*.

HRH *abbr* (= *His* (or *Her*) *Royal Highness*) S.A.R.

hr(s) *abbr* (= *hour(s)*) hr.

HS *abbr* (*US*) = **high school**.

HST *abbr* (*US*: = *Hawaiian Standard Time*) hora de Hawai.

hub [hub] *n* (*of wheel*) centro.

hubbub [hub'ub] *n* barahúnda, barullo.

hubcap [hub'kap] *n* tapacubos *m inv*.

HUD *n abbr* (*US*: = *Department of Housing and Urban Development*) *ministerio de la vivienda y urbanismo*.

huddle [hud'əl] *vi:* **to ~ together** amontonarse.

hue [hyōō] *n* color *m*, matiz *m*; **~ and cry** *n* alarma.

huff [huf] *n:* **in a ~** enojado.

hug [hug] *vt* abrazar ♦ *n* abrazo.

huge [hyōōj] *a* enorme.

hulk [hulk] *n* (*ship*) barco viejo; (*person, building etc*) mole *f*.

hulking [hul'king] *a* pesado.

hull [hul] *n* (*of ship*) casco.

hullabaloo [huləbəlōō'] *n* (*col: noise*) algarabía, jaleo.

hullo [həlō'] *excl* (*Brit*) = **hello**.

hum [hum] *vt* tararear, canturrear ♦ *vi* tararear, canturrear; (*insect*) zumbar ♦ *n* (*also* ELEC) zumbido; (*of traffic, machines*)

zumbido, ronroneo; (*of voices etc*) murmullo.

human [hyōō'mən] *a* humano ♦ *n* (*also:* **~ being**) ser *m* humano.

humane [hyōōmān'] *a* humano, humanitario.

humanism [hyōō'mənizəm] *n* humanismo.

humanitarian [hyōōmanitär'ēən] *a* humanitario.

humanity [hyōōman'itē] *n* humanidad *f*.

humanly [hyōō'mənlē] *ad* humanamente.

humanoid [hyōō'mənoid] *a, n* humanoide *m/f*.

human relations *npl* relaciones *fpl* humanas.

humble [hum'bəl] *a* humilde ♦ *vt* humillar.

humbly [hum'blē] *ad* humildemente.

humbug [hum'bug] *n* tonterías *fpl*; (*Brit: sweet*) caramelo de menta.

humdrum [hum'drum] *a* (*boring*) monótono, aburrido; (*routine*) rutinario.

humid [hyōō'mid] *a* húmedo.

humidifier [hyōōmid'əfiûr] *n* humedecedor *m*.

humidity [hyōōmid'ətē] *n* humedad *f*.

humiliate [hyōōmil'ēāt] *vt* humillar.

humiliation [hyōōmilēā'shən] *n* humillación *f*.

humility [hyōōmil'ətē] *n* humildad *f*.

humor [hyōō'mûr] (*US*) *n* humorismo, sentido del humor; (*mood*) humor *m* ♦ *vt* (*person*) complacer; **sense of ~** sentido del humor; **to be in a good/bad ~** estar de buen/mal humor.

humorist [hyōō'mûrist] *n* humorista *m/f*.

humorless [hyōō'mûrlis] *a* arisco.

humorous [hyōō'mûrəs] *a* gracioso, divertido.

humour [hyōō'mûr] *etc* (*Brit*) = **humor** *etc*.

hump [hump] *n* (*in ground*) montículo; (*camel's*) giba.

humus [hyōō'məs] *n* (*BIO*) humus *m*.

hunch [hunch] *n* (*premonition*) presentimiento; **I have a ~ that** tengo una corazonada or un presentimiento de que.

hunchback [hunch'bak] *n* joroba *m/f*.

hunched [huncht] *a* jorobado.

hundred [hun'drid] *num* ciento; (*before n*) cien; **about a ~ people** unas cien personas, alrededor de cien personas; **~s of** centenares de; **~s of people** centenares de personas; **I'm a ~ percent sure** estoy completamente seguro.

hundredweight [hun'dridwāt] *n* (*US*) = *45.3 kg; 100 lb;* (*Brit*) = *50.8 kg; 112 lb.*

hung [hung] *pt, pp of* **hang**.

Hungarian [hunggär'ēən] *a, n* húngaro/a *m/f* ♦ *n* (*LING*) húngaro.

Hungary [hung'gûrē] *n* Hungría.

hunger [hung'gûr] *n* hambre *f* ♦ *vi:* **to ~ for** (*fig*) tener hambre de, anhelar.

hunger strike *n* huelga de hambre.

hungrily [hung'grilē] *ad* ávidamente, con ganas.

hungry [hung'grē] *a* hambriento; **to be ~ for** (*fig*) sediento de.

hunk [hungk] *n* (*of bread etc*) trozo, pedazo.

hunt [hunt] *vt* (*seek*) buscar; (*SPORT*) cazar ♦ *vi* cazar ♦ *n* caza, cacería.

hunt down *vt* acorralar, seguir la pista a.

hunter [hun'tûr] *n* cazador(a) *m/f*; (*horse*) caballo de caza.

hunting [hun'ting] *n* caza.

hurdle [hûr'dəl] *n* (*SPORT*) valla; (*fig*) obstáculo.

hurl [hûrl] *vt* lanzar, arrojar.

hurrah [hərâ'], **hurray** [hərā'] *n* ¡viva!, ¡vítor!

hurricane [hûr'əkān] *n* huracán *m*.

hurried [hûr'ēd] *a* (*fast*) apresurado; (*rushed*) hecho de prisa.

hurriedly [hûr'ēdlē] *ad* con prisa, apresuradamente.

hurry [hûr'ē] *n* prisa ♦ *vb* (*also:* ~ **up**) *vi* apresurarse, darse prisa ♦ *vt* (*person*) dar prisa a; (*work*) apresurar, hacer de prisa; **to be in a ~** tener prisa; **to ~ back/home** darse prisa para volver/volver a casa.

hurry along *vi* pasar de prisa.

hurry away, hurry off *vi* irse corriendo.

hurry on *vi*: **to ~ on to say** apresurarse a decir.

hurry up *vi* darse prisa.

hurt [hûrt] *vb* (*pt, pp* hurt) *vt* hacer daño a; (*business, interests etc*) perjudicar ♦ *vi* doler ♦ *a* lastimado; **I ~ my arm** me lastimé el brazo; **where does it ~?** ¿dónde te duele?

hurtful [hûrt'fəl] *a* (*remark etc*) dañoso.

hurtle [hûr'təl] *vi*: **to ~ past** pasar como un rayo.

husband [huz'bənd] *n* marido.

hush [hush] *n* silencio ♦ *vt* hacer callar; (*cover up*) encubrir; **~!** ¡chitón!, ¡cállate!

hush up *vt* (*fact*) encubrir, callar.

hushed [husht] *a* (*voice*) bajo.

hush-hush [hush'hush] *a* (*col*) muy secreto.

husk [husk] *n* (*of wheat*) cáscara.

husky [hus'kē] *a* ronco; (*burly*) fornido ♦ *n* perro esquimal.

hustings [hus'tingz] *npl* (*Brit POL*) mítin *msg* preelectoral.

hustle [hus'əl] *vt* (*push*) empujar; (*hurry*) dar prisa a; (*US: col: girl*) enrollarse con ♦ *n* bullicio, actividad *f* febril; **~ and bustle** *n* vaivén *m*.

hut [hut] *n* cabaña; (*shed*) cobertizo.

hutch [huch] *n* conejera.

hyacinth [hī'əsinth] *n* jacinto.

hybrid [hī'brid] *a, n* híbrido.

hydrant [hī'drənt] *n* (*also:* **fire ~**) boca de incendios.

hydraulic [hīdrô'lik] *a* hidráulico.

hydraulics [hīdrô'liks] *n* hidráulica.

hydrochloric [hīdrəklôr'ik] *a:* **~ acid** ácido clorhídrico.

hydroelectric [hīdrōilck'trik] *a* hidroeléctrico.

hydrofoil [hī'drəfoil] *n* aerodeslizador *m*.

hydrogen [hī'drəjən] *n* hidrógeno.

hydrogen bomb *n* bomba de hidrógeno.

hydrophobia [hīdrəfō'bēə] *n* hidrofobia.

hydroplane [hī'drəplān] *n* hidroplano, hidroavión *m*.

hyena [hīē'nə] *n* hiena.

hygiene [hī'jēn] *n* higiene *f*.

hygienic [hījēen'ik] *a* higiénico.

hymn [him] *n* himno.

hype [hīp] *n* (*col*) bombardeo publicitario, superchería.

hyperactive [hīpûrak'tiv] *a* hiperactivo.

hypermarket [hī'pûrmârkit] *n* hipermercado.

hypertension [hīpûrten'chən] *n* hipertensión *f*.

hyphen [hī'fən] *n* guión *m*.

hypnosis [hipnō'sis] *n* hipnosis *f*.

hypnotic [hipnât'ik] *a* hipnótico.

hypnotism [hip'nətizəm] *n* hipnotismo.

hypnotist [hip'nətist] hipnotista *m/f*.

hypnotize [hip'nətīz] *vt* hipnotizar.

hypoallergenic [hīpōalûrjen'ik] *a* hipoalérgeno.

hypochondriac [hīpəkân'drēak] *n* hipocondríaco/a.

hypocrisy [hipâk'rəsē] *n* hipocresía.

hypocrite [hip'əkrit] *n* hipócrita *m/f*.

hypocritical [hipəkrit'ikəl] *a* hipócrita.

hypodermic [hīpədûr'mik] *a* hipodérmico ♦ *n* (*syringe*) aguja hipodérmica.

hypothermia [hīpōthûr'mēə] *n* hipotermia.

hypothesis, *pl* **hypotheses** [hīpâth'əsis, -sēz] *n* hipótesis *f inv*.

hypothetical [hīpəthet'ikəl] *a* hipotético.

hysterectomy [histərek'təmē] *n* histerectomía.

hysteria [histē'rēə] *n* histeria.

hysterical [histär'ikəl] *a* histérico.

hysterics [histär'iks] *npl* histeria *sg*, histerismo *sg*; **to have ~** ponerse histérico.

Hz *abbr* (= *Hertz*) Hz.

I, i [ī] *n* (*letter*) I, i *f*; **I for Item** I de Inés, I de Israel.

I [ī] *pron* yo ♦ *abbr* = **island**; **isle**; (*US*) = **interstate (highway)**.

IA *abbr* (*US MAIL*) = *Iowa*.

IAEA *n abbr* = **International Atomic Energy**

Agency.

IBA *n abbr* (*Brit*: = *Independent Broadcasting Authority*) *entidad que controla los medios privados de televisión y radio.*

Iberian |ībēr'ēən| *a* ibero, ibérico.

Iberian Peninsula *n*: **the** ~ la Península Ibérica.

IBEW *n abbr* (*US*: = *International Brotherhood of Electrical Workers*) *sindicato internacional de electricistas.*

ib(id). *abbr* (= *ibidem*: *from the same source*) ibídem.

i/c *abbr* (*Brit*) = *in charge.*

ICBM *n abbr* = **intercontinental ballistic missile.**

ICC *n abbr* (= *International Chamber of Commerce*) CCI *f*; (*US*) = *Interstate Commerce Commission.*

ice |īs| *n* hielo ♦ *vt* (*cake*) alcorzar ♦ *vi* (*also:* ~ **over,** ~ **up**) helarse; **to keep sth on** ~ (*fig*: *plan, project*) tener algo en reserva.

ice age *n* período glaciar.

ice ax *n* piqueta (de alpinista).

iceberg |īs'bûrg| *n* iceberg *m*; **the tip of the** ~ (*also fig*) lo de menos.

icebox |īs'bâks| *n* (*US*) nevera, refrigeradora (*LAm*); (*Brit*) congelador *m*.

icebreaker |īs'brākûr| *n* rompehielos *m inv*.

ice bucket *n* cubo para el hielo.

ice-cold |īs'kōld| *a* helado.

ice cream *n* helado.

ice-cream soda |īs'krēm sō'də| *n* soda mezclada con helado.

ice cube *n* cubito de hielo.

iced |īst| *a* (*drink*) con hielo; (*cake*) escarchado.

ice hockey *n* hockey *m* sobre hielo.

Iceland |īs'lənd| *n* Islandia.

Icelander |īs'landûr| *n* islandés/esa *m/f*.

Icelandic |īslan'dik| *a* islandés/esa ♦ *n* (*LING*) islandés *m*.

ice lolly |īs lâl'ē| *n* (*Brit*) polo helado.

ice pick *n* piolet *m*.

ice rink *n* pista de hielo.

ice-skate |īs'skāt| *n* patín *m* de hielo ♦ *vi* patinar sobre hielo.

ice-skating |īs'skāting| *n* patinaje *m* sobre hielo.

icicle |ī'sikəl| *n* carámbano.

icing |ī'sing| *n* (*CULIN*) alcorza; (*AVIAT etc*) formación *f* de hielo.

icing sugar *n* (*Brit*) azúcar *m* glas(eado).

ICJ *n abbr* = **International Court of Justice.**

icon |ī'kân| *n* ícono; (*COMPUT*) símbolo gráfico.

ICR *n abbr* (*US*) = *Institute for Cancer Research.*

ICU *n abbr* (= *intensive care unit*) UVI *f*.

icy |ī'sē| *a* (*road*) helado; (*fig*) glacial.

ID *abbr* (*US MAIL*) = *Idaho.*

I'd |īd| = **I would; I had.**

Ida. *abbr* (*US*) = *Idaho.*

ID card *n* (= *identity card*) DNI *m*.

idea |īdē'ə| *n* idea; **good** ~! ¡buena idea!; **to have an** ~ **that** ... tener la impresión de que ...; **I haven't the faintest** ~ no tengo ni (la más remota) idea.

ideal |īdē'əl| *n* ideal *m* ♦ *a* ideal.

idealism |īdē'əlizəm| *n* idealismo.

idealist |īdē'əlist| *n* idealista *m/f*.

ideally |īdē'əlē| *ad* perfectamente; ~, **the book should have** ... idealmente, el libro debería tener ....

identical |īden'tikəl| *a* idéntico.

identification |īdentəfəkā'shən| *n* identificación *f*; **means of** ~ documentos *mpl* personales.

identification papers *npl* (*US*) documentos *mpl* (de identidad), documentación *fsg*.

identify |īden'təfī| *vt* identificar ♦ *vi*: **to** ~ **with** identificarse con.

Identikit |īden'təkit| ® *n* (*Brit*): ~ **(picture)** retrato-robot *m*.

identity |īden'titē| *n* identidad *f*.

identity card *n* (*Brit*) carnet *m* de identidad.

identity papers *npl* documentos *mpl* (de identidad), documentación *fsg*.

identity parade *n* (*Brit*) identificación *f* de acusados.

ideological |īdēəlâj'ikəl| *a* ideológico.

ideology |īdēâl'əjē| *n* ideología.

idiocy |id'ēəsē| *n* idiotez *f*; (*stupid act*) estupidez *f*.

idiom |id'ēəm| *n* modismo; (*style of speaking*) lenguaje *m*.

idiomatic |idēəmat'ik| *a* idiomático.

idiosyncrasy |idēəsing'krəsē| *n* idiosincrasia.

idiot |id'ēət| *n* (*gen*) idiota *m/f*; (*fool*) tonto/a.

idiotic |idēât'ik| *a* idiota; tonto.

idle |ī'dəl| *a* (*lazy*) holgazán/ana; (*unemployed*) parado, desocupado; (*talk*) frívolo ♦ *vi* (*machine*) funcionar *or* marchar en vacío; ~ **capacity** (*COMM*) capacidad *f* sin utilizar; ~ **money** (*COMM*) capital *m* improductivo; ~ **time** (*COMM*) tiempo de paro.

idle away *vt*: **to** ~ **away one's time** malgastar *or* desperdiciar el tiempo.

idleness |ī'dəlnis| *n* holgazanería; paro, desocupación *f*.

idler |īd'lûr| *n* holgazán/ana *m/f*, vago/a.

idol |ī'dəl| *n* ídolo.

idolize |ī'dəlīz| *vt* idolatrar.

idyllic |idil'ik| *a* idílico.

i.e. *abbr* (= *id est*: *that is*) esto es.

if |if| *conj* si ♦ *n*: **there are a lot of** ~**s and buts** hay muchas dudas sin resolver; **(even)** ~ aunque, si bien; **I'd be pleased** ~ **you could do it** yo estaría contento si pudieras hacerlo; ~ **necessary** si es necesario; ~ **only** si solamente; **as** ~ como si.

igloo |ig'lōō| *n* iglú *m*.

ignite [ignīt'] *vt* (*set fire to*) encender ♦ *vi* encenderse.

ignition [ignish'ən] *n* (*AUT*) encendido; **to switch on/off the** ~ arrancar/apagar el motor.

ignition key *n* (*AUT*) llave *f* de contacto.

ignoble [ignō'bəl] *a* innoble, vil.

ignominious [ignəmin'ēəs] *a* ignominioso, vergonzoso.

ignoramus [ignərā'məs] *n* ignorante *m/f*, inculto/a.

ignorance [ig'nûrəns] *n* ignorancia; **to keep sb in** ~ **of sth** ocultarle algo a uno.

ignorant [ig'nûrənt] *a* ignorante; **to be** ~ **of** (*subject*) desconocer; (*events*) ignorar.

ignore [ignôr'] *vt* (*person*) no hacer caso de; (*fact*) pasar por alto.

ikon [ī'kân] *n* = **icon.**

IL *abbr* (*US MAIL*) = *Illinois.*

ILA *n abbr* (*US*: = *International Longshoremen's Association*) sindicato internacional de trabajadores portuarios.

ILGWU *n abbr* (*US*: = *International Ladies' Garment Workers Union*) sindicato de empleados del ramo de las prendas de vestir femeninas.

Ill. *abbr* (*US*) = *Illinois.*

ill [il] *a* enfermo, malo ♦ *n* mal *m*; (*fig*) infortunio ♦ *ad* mal; **to take** *or* **be taken** ~ caer *or* ponerse enfermo; **to feel** ~ **(with)** encontrarse mal (de); **to speak/think** ~ **of sb** hablar/pensar mal de uno; *see also* **ills.**

I'll [īl] = **I will, I shall.**

ill-advised [il'advīzd'] *a* poco recomendable; **he was** ~ **to go** se equivocaba al ir.

ill-at-ease [il'ətēz'] *a* incómodo.

ill-considered [il'kənsid'ûrd] *a* (*plan*) poco pensado.

ill-disposed [il'dispōzd'] *a*: **to be** ~ **towards sb/sth** estar maldispuesto hacia uno/algo.

illegal [ilē'gəl] *a* ilegal.

illegible [ilej'əbəl] *a* ilegible.

illegitimate [ilijit'əmit] *a* ilegítimo.

ill-fated [il'fā'tid] *a* malogrado.

ill-favored (*Brit*) **ill-favoured** [il'fā'vûrd] *a* mal parecido.

ill feeling *n* (*Brit*) rencor *m*.

ill-gotten [il'gât'ən] *a* (*gains etc*) mal adquirido.

illicit [ilis'it] *a* ilícito.

ill-informed [il'infôrmd'] *a* (*judgement*) erróneo; (*person*) mal informado.

illiterate [ilit'ûrit] *a* analfabeto.

ill-mannered [il'man'ûrd] *a* mal educado.

illness [il'nis] *n* enfermedad *f*.

illogical [ilâj'ikəl] *a* ilógico.

ills [ilz] *npl* males *mpl*.

ill-suited [il'sōō'tid] *a* (*couple*) incompatible; **he is** ~ **to the job** no es la persona indicada para el trabajo.

ill-timed [il'tīmd] *a* inoportuno.

ill-treat [il'trēt] *vt* maltratar.

ill-treatment [il'trēt'mənt] *n* malos tratos *mpl*.

illuminate [ilōō'mənāt] *vt* (*room, street*) iluminar, alumbrar; (*subject*) aclarar; ~**d sign** letrero luminoso.

illuminating [ilōō'mənāting] *a* revelador(a).

illumination [ilōōmənā'shən] *n* alumbrado; ~**s** *npl* luminarias *fpl*, luces *fpl*.

illusion [ilōō'zhən] *n* ilusión *f*; **to be under the** ~ **that...** estar convencido de que ....

illusive [ilōō'siv], **illusory** [ilōō'sərē] *a* ilusorio.

illustrate [il'əstrāt] *vt* ilustrar.

illustration [iləstrā'shən] *n* (*example*) ejemplo, ilustración *f*; (*in book*) lámina.

illustrator [il'əstrātûr] *n* ilustrador(a) *m/f*.

illustrious [ilus'trēəs] *a* ilustre.

ill will *n* rencor *m*.

ILO *n abbr* (= *International Labour Organization*) OIT *f*.

ILWU *n abbr* (*US*: = *International Longshoremen's and Warehousemen's Union*) sindicato internacional de trabajadores portuarios y almacenistas.

I'm [īm] = **I am.**

image [im'ij] *n* imagen *f*.

imagery [im'ijrē] *n* imágenes *fpl*.

imaginable [imaj'ənəbəl] *a* imaginable.

imaginary [imaj'ənärē] *a* imaginario.

imagination [imajənā'shən] *n* imaginación *f*; (*inventiveness*) inventiva; (*illusion*) fantasía.

imaginative [imaj'ənətiv] *a* imaginativo.

imagine [imaj'in] *vt* imaginarse; (*suppose*) suponer.

imbalance [imbal'əns] *n* desequilibrio.

imbecile [im'bəsil] *n* imbécil *m/f*.

imbue [imbyōō'] *vt*: **to** ~ **sth with** imbuir algo de.

IMF *n abbr* = **International Monetary Fund.**

imitate [im'ətāt] *vt* imitar.

imitation [imətā'shən] *n* imitación *f*; (*copy*) copia; (*pej*) remedo.

imitator [im'ətātûr] *n* imitador(a) *m/f*.

immaculate [imak'yəlit] *a* perfectamente limpio; (*REL*) inmaculado.

immaterial [imətē'rēəl] *a* incorpóreo; **it is** ~ **whether...** no importa si... .

immature [imətōōr'] *a* (*person*) inmaduro; (*of one's youth*) joven.

immaturity [imətōō'ritē] *n* inmadurez *f*.

immeasurable [imezh'ûrəbəl] *a* inconmensurable.

immediacy [imē'dēəsē] *n* urgencia, proximidad *f*.

immediate [imē'dēit] *a* inmediato; (*pressing*) urgente, apremiante; **in the** ~ **future** en el futuro próximo.

immediately [imē'dēitlē] *ad* (*at once*) en seguida; ~ **next to** muy junto a.

immense [imens'] *a* inmenso, enorme.

immensely [imens'lē] *ad* enormemente.

immensity [imen'sitē] *n* (*of size, differ-*

ence) inmensidad *f*; (*of problem*) enormidad *f*.

immerse |imûrs'| *vt* (*submerge*) sumergir; **to be ~d in** (*fig*) estar absorto en.

immersion heater |imûr'zhən hē'tûr| *n* calentador *m* de inmersión.

immigrant |im'əgrənt| *n* inmigrante *m/f*.

immigrate |im'əgrāt| *vi* inmigrar.

immigration |iməgrā'shən| *n* inmigración *f*.

immigration authorities *npl* servicio *sg* de inmigración.

immigration laws *npl* leyes *fpl* inmigratorias.

imminent |im'ənənt| *a* inminente.

immobile |imō'bəl| *a* inmóvil.

immobilize |imō'bəlīz| *vt* inmovilizar.

immoderate |imád'ûrit| *a* (*person*) desmesurado; (*opinion, reaction, demand*) excesivo.

immodest |imád'ist| *a* (*indecent*) desvergonzado, impúdico; (*boasting*) jactancioso.

immoral |imôr'əl| *a* inmoral.

immorality |iməral'itē| *n* inmoralidad *f*.

immortal |imôr'təl| *a* inmortal.

immortality |imôrtal'itē| *n* inmortalidad *f*.

immortalize |imôr'təlīz| *vt* inmortalizar.

immovable |imōō'vəbəl| *a* (*object*) imposible de mover; (*person*) inconmovible.

immune |imyōōn'| *a*: **~ (to)** inmune (contra).

immunity |imyōō'nitē| *n* (*MED, of diplomat*) inmunidad *f*; (*COMM*) exención *f*.

immunization |imyōōnəzā'shən| *n* inmunización *f*.

immunize |im'yənīz| *vt* inmunizar.

imp |imp| *n* (*small devil, also fig:* child) diablillo.

impact |im'pakt| *n* (*gen*) impacto.

impair |impär'| *vt* perjudicar.

impale |impāl'| *vt* (*with sword*) atravesar.

impart |impârt'| *vt* comunicar; (*make known*) participar; (*bestow*) otorgar.

impartial |impâr'shəl| *a* imparcial.

impartiality |impârshēal'itē| *n* imparcialidad *f*.

impassable |impas'əbəl| *a* (*barrier*) infranqueable; (*river, road*) intransitable.

impasse |im'pas| *n* callejón *m* sin salida; **to reach an ~** alcanzar un punto muerto.

impassioned |impash'ənd| *a* apasionado, exaltado.

impassive |impas'iv| *a* impasible.

impatience |impā'shəns| *n* impaciencia.

impatient |impā'shənt| *a* impaciente; **to get** *or* **grow ~** impacientarse.

impatiently |impā'shəntlē| *ad* con impaciencia.

impeachment |impēch'mənt| *n* denuncia, acusación *f*.

impeccable |impek'əbəl| *a* impecable.

impecunious |impəkyōō'nēəs| *a* sin dinero.

impede |impēd'| *vt* estorbar, dificultar.

impediment |imped'əmənt| *n* obstáculo, estorbo; (*also:* **speech ~**) defecto (del habla).

impel |impel'| *vt* (*force*): **to ~ sb (to do sth)** obligar a uno (a hacer algo).

impending |impen'ding| *a* (*near*) próximo.

impenetrable |impen'itrəbəl| *a* (*jungle, fortress*) impenetrable; (*unfathomable*) insondable.

imperative |impär'ətiv| *a* (*tone*) imperioso; (*necessary*) imprescindible ♦ *n* (*LING*) imperativo.

imperceptible |impûrsep'təbəl| *a* imperceptible, insensible.

imperfect |impûr'fikt| *a* imperfecto; (*goods etc*) defectuoso.

imperfection |impûrfek'shən| *n* (*blemish*) desperfecto; (*fault, flaw*) defecto.

imperial |impēr'ēəl| *a* imperial.

imperialism |impēr'ēəlizəm| *n* imperialismo.

imperil |impär'əl| *vt* poner en peligro.

imperious |impēr'ēəs| *a* señorial, apremiante.

impersonal |impûr'sənəl| *a* impersonal.

impersonate |impûr'sənāt| *vt* hacerse pasar por.

impersonation |impûrsənā'shən| *n* imitación *f*.

impersonator |impûr'sənātûr| *n* (*THEATER etc*) imitador(a) *m/f*.

impertinence |impûr'tənəns| *n* descaro.

impertinent |impûr'tənənt| *a* impertinente, insolente.

imperturbable |impûrtûr'bəbəl| *a* imperturbable, impasible.

impervious |impûr'vēəs| *a* impermeable; (*fig*): **~ to** insensible a.

impetuous |impech'ōōəs| *a* impetuoso.

impetus |im'pitəs| *n* ímpetu *m*; (*fig*) impulso.

impinge |impinj'|: **to ~ on** *vt fus* (*affect*) afectar a.

impish |imp'ish| *a* travieso.

implacable |implak'əbəl| *a* implacable.

implant |implant'| *vt* (*MED*) injertar, implantar; (*fig: idea, principle*) inculcar.

implausible |implô'zəbəl| *a* implausible.

implement *n* |im'pləmənt| instrumento, herramienta ♦ *vt* |im'pləment| hacer efectivo; (*carry out*) realizar.

implicate |im'plikāt| *vt* (*compromise*) comprometer; (*involve*) enredar; **to ~ sb in sth** comprometer a uno en algo.

implication |implikā'shən| *n* consecuencia; **by ~** indirectamente.

implicit |implis'it| *a* (*gen*) implícito; (*complete*) absoluto.

implicitly |implis'itlē| *ad* implícitamente.

implore |implôr'| *vt* (*person*) suplicar.

imploring |implôr'ing| *a* de súplica.

imply |implī'| *vt* (*involve*) implicar; (*mean*) significar; (*hint*) dar a entender.

impolite [impəlīt'] *a* mal educado.
impolitic [impál'itik] *a* poco político.
imponderable [impán'dûrəbəl] *a* imponderable.
import *vt* [impôrt'] importar ♦ [im'pôrt] *n* (*COMM*) importación *f*; (*meaning*) significado, sentido ♦ *cpd* (*duty, license etc*) de importación.
importance [impôr'təns] *n* importancia; **to be of great/little** ~ tener mucha/poca importancia.
important [impôr'tənt] *a* importante; **it's not** ~ no importa, no tiene importancia; **it is** ~ **that** es importante que.
importantly [impôr'təntlē] *ad* (*pej*) dándose importancia; **but, more** ~ ... pero, lo más importante es ....
import duty [im'pôrt dōō'tē] *n* derechos *mpl* de importación.
imported [impôr'tid] *a* importado.
importer [impôr'tûr] *n* importador(a) *m/f*.
import license *n* licencia de importación.
impose [impōz'] *vt* imponer ♦ *vi*: **to** ~ **on sb** abusar de uno.
imposing [impō'zing] *a* imponente, impresionante.
imposition [impəzish'ən] *n* (*of tax etc*) imposición *f*; **to be an** ~ (*on person*) molestar.
impossibility [impâsəbil'itē] *n* imposibilidad *f*.
impossible [impás'əbəl] *a* imposible; (*person*) insoportable; **it is** ~ **for me to leave now** me es imposible salir ahora.
impossibly [impás'əblē] *ad* imposiblemente.
impostor [impás'tûr] *n* impostor(a) *m/f*.
impotence [im'pətəns] *n* impotencia.
impotent [im'pətənt] *a* impotente.
impound [impound'] *vt* embargar.
impoverished [impâv'ûrisht] *a* necesitado, (*land*) agotado.
impracticable [imprak'tikəbəl] *a* no factible, irrealizable.
impractical [imprak'tikəl] *a* (*person*) poco práctico.
imprecise [imprisīs'] *a* impreciso.
impregnable [impreg'nəbəl] *a* invulnerable; (*castle*) inexpugnable.
impregnate [impreg'nāt] *vt* (*gen*) impregnar; (*soak*) empapar; (*fertilize*) fecundar.
impresario [imprəsá'rēō] *n* empresario/a.
impress [impres'] *vt* impresionar; (*mark*) estampar ♦ *vi* hacer buena impresión; **to** ~ **sth on sb** convencer a uno de la importancia de algo.
impression [impresh'ən] *n* impresión *f*; (*footprint etc*) huella; (*print run*) edición *f*; **to be under the** ~ **that** tener la impresión de que; **to make a good/bad** ~ **on sb** causar buena/mala impresión a uno.
impressionable [impresh'ənəbəl] *a* impresionable.

impressionist [impresh'ənist] *n* impresionista *m/f*.
impressive [impres'iv] *a* impresionante.
imprint [im'print] *n* (*PUBLISHING*) pie *m* de imprenta; (*fig*) sello.
imprison [impriz'ən] *vt* encarcelar.
imprisonment [impriz'ənmənt] *n* encarcelamiento; (*term of* ~) cárcel *f*; **life** ~ cadena perpetua.
improbable [imprâb'əbəl] *a* improbable, inverosímil.
impromptu [imprâmp'tōō] *a* improvisado ♦ *ad* de improviso.
improper [imprâp'ûr] *a* (*incorrect*) impropio; (*unseemly*) indecoroso; (*indecent*) indecente.
impropriety [imprəprī'ətē] *n* falta de decoro; (*indecency*) indecencia; (*of language*) impropiedad *f*.
improve [imprōōv'] *vt* mejorar; (*foreign language*) perfeccionar ♦ *vi* mejorarse; (*pupils*) hacer progresos.
  improve (up)on *vt fus* (*offer*) mejorar.
improvement [imprōōv'mənt] *n* mejoramiento; perfección *f*; progreso; **to make** ~**s to** mejorar.
improvise [im'prəvīz] *vt, vi* improvisar.
imprudence [imprōōd'əns] *n* imprudencia.
imprudent [imprōōd'ənt] *a* imprudente.
impudent [im'pyədənt] *a* descarado, insolente.
impugn [impyōōn'] *vt* impugnar.
impulse [im'puls] *n* impulso; **to act on** ~ obrar sin reflexión.
impulse buying [im'puls bī'ing] *n* compra impulsiva.
impulsive [impul'siv] *a* irreflexivo.
impunity [impyōō'nitē] *n*: **with** ~ impunemente.
impure [impyōōr'] *a* (*adulterated*) adulterado; (*morally*) impuro.
impurity [impyōō'itē] *n* impureza.
IN *abbr* (*US MAIL*) = *Indiana*.
in [in] *prep* en; (*within*) dentro de; (*with time: during, within*): ~ **2 days** en 2 días; (: *after*): ~ **2 weeks** dentro de 2 semanas; (*with town, country*): **it's** ~ **France** está en Francia ♦ *ad* dentro, adentro; (*fashionable*) de moda; **is he** ~**?** ¿está en casa?; ~ **the United States** en los Estados Unidos; ~ **1986** en 1986; ~ **May** en mayo; ~ **spring/autumn** en primavera/otoño; ~ **the morning** por la mañana; ~ **the country** en el campo; ~ **the distance** a lo lejos; ~ **town** en la ciudad; ~ **the sun** al sol, bajo el sol; ~ **the rain** bajo la lluvia; ~ **French** en francés; ~ **writing** por escrito; ~ **person** en persona; ~ **here/there** aquí/allí (dentro); **1** ~ **10** uno sobre 10, uno de cada 10; ~ **hundreds** por centenares; **the best pupil** ~ **the class** el mejor alumno de la clase; **written** ~ **pencil** escrito con lápiz; **to pay** ~ **dollars** pagar en dólares; **a**

rise ~ **prices** un aumento de precios; **once** ~ **a hundred years** una vez al siglo; ~ **saying this** al decir esto; **their party is** ~ su partido ha llegado al poder; **to be** ~ **publishing** dedicarse a la publicación de libros; ~ **that** ya que; ~ **all** en total; **to ask sb** ~ invitar a uno a entrar; **to run/limp** ~ entrar corriendo/cojeando; **the** ~**s and outs** los pormenores.

in., ins *abbr* = **inch(es).**

inability |inəbil'ətē| *n* incapacidad *f;* ~ **to pay** incapacidad de pagar.

inaccessible |inakses'əbəl| *a* inaccesible.

inaccuracy |inak'yûrəsē| *n* inexactitud *f.*

inaccurate |inak'yûrit| *a* inexacto, incorrecto.

inaction |inak'shən| *n* inacción *f.*

inactive |inak'tiv| *a* inactivo.

inactivity |inaktiv'itē| *n* inactividad *f.*

inadequacy |inad'əkwəsē| *n* insuficiencia; incapacidad *f.*

inadequate |inad'əkwit| *a* (*insufficient*) insuficiente; (*unsuitable*) inadecuado; (*person*) incapaz.

inadmissible |inədmis'əbəl| *a* improcedente, inadmisible.

inadvertent |inədvûr'tənt| *a* descuidado, involuntario.

inadvertently |inədvûr'təntlē| *ad* por descuido.

inadvisable |inədvī'zəbəl| *a* poco aconsejable.

inane |inān'| *a* necio, fatuo.

inanimate |inan'əmit| *a* inanimado.

inapplicable |inap'likəbəl| *a* inaplicable.

inappropriate |inəprō'prēit| *a* inadecuado.

inapt |inapt'| *a* impropio.

inaptitude |inap'tətōōd| *n* incapacidad *f.*

inarticulate |inârtik'yəlit| *a* (*person*) incapaz de expresarse; (*speech*) mal pronunciado.

inartistic |inârtis'tik| *a* antiestético.

inasmuch as |inəzmuch' az| *ad* puesto que, ya que.

inattention |inəten'chən| *n* desatención *f.*

inattentive |inəten'tiv| *a* distraído.

inaudible |inô'dəbəl| *a* inaudible.

inaugural |inô'gyûrəl| *a* (*speech*) de apertura.

inaugurate |inô'gyərāt| *vt* inaugurar.

inauguration |inôgyərā'shən| *n* ceremonia de apertura.

inauspicious |inôspish'əs| *a* poco propicio, inoportuno.

in-between |in'bitwēn'| *a* intermedio.

inborn |in'bôrn| *a* (*feeling*) innato.

inbred |in'bred| *a* innato; (*family*) consanguíneo.

inbreeding |in'brēding| *n* endogamia.

Inc. *abbr* = **incorporated.**

Inca |ing'kə| *a* (*also:* ~**n**) incaico, de los incas ♦ *n* inca *m/f.*

incalculable |inkal'kyələbəl| *a* incalculable.

incapability |inkāpəbil'ətē| *n* incapacidad *f.*

incapable |inkā'pəbəl| *a:* ~ (**of doing sth**) incapaz (de hacer algo).

incapacitate |inkəpas'ətāt| *vt:* **to** ~ **sb** incapacitar a uno.

incapacitated |inkəpas'ətātid| *a* incapacitado.

incapacity |inkəpas'itē| *n* (*inability*) incapacidad *f.*

incarcerate |inkâr'sûrit| *vt* encarcelar.

incarnate *a* |inkâr'nit| en persona ♦ *vt* |inkâr'nāt| encarnar.

incarnation |inkârnā'shən| *n* encarnación *f.*

incendiary |insen'dēârē| *a* incendiario ♦ *n* (*bomb*) bomba incendiaria.

incense *n* |in'sens| incienso ♦ *vt* |insens'| (*anger*) indignar, encolerizar.

incentive |insen'tiv| *n* incentivo, estímulo.

incentive bonus *n* incentivo de bonificación extra.

incentive scheme *n* plan *m* de incentivos.

inception |insep'shən| *n* comienzo, principio.

incessant |inses'ənt| *a* incesante, continuo.

incessantly |inses'əntlē| *ad* constantemente.

incest |in'sest| *n* incesto.

inch |inch| *n* pulgada; **to be within an** ~ **of** estar a dos dedos de; **he didn't give an** ~ no dio concesión alguna; **a few** ~**es** unas pulgadas.

inch forward *vi* avanzar palmo a palmo.

incidence |in'sidəns| *n* (*of crime, disease*) incidencia.

incident |in'sidənt| *n* incidente *m;* (*in book*) episodio.

incidental |insiden'təl| *a* circunstancial, accesorio; (*unplanned*) fortuito; ~ **to** relacionado con; ~ **expenses** gastos *mpl* imprevistos.

incidentally |insiden'təlē| *ad* (*by the way*) a propósito.

incidental music *n* música de fondo.

incinerate |insin'ərāt| *vt* incinerar, quemar.

incinerator |insin'ərātûr| *n* incinerador *m.*

incipient |insip'ēənt| *a* incipiente.

incision |insizh'ən| *n* incisión *f.*

incisive |insī'siv| *a* (*mind*) penetrante; (*remark etc*) incisivo.

incisor |insī'zûr| *n* incisivo.

incite |insīt'| *vt* provocar.

incl. *abbr* = **including; inclusive (of).**

inclement |inklem'ənt| *a* inclemente.

inclination |inklənā'shən| *n* (*tendency*) tendencia, inclinación *f.*

incline *n* |in'klīn| pendiente *f,* cuesta ♦ *vb* |inklīn'| *vt* (*slope*) inclinar; (*head*) poner de lado ♦ *vi* inclinarse; **to be** ~**d to** (*tend*) ser propenso a; (*be willing*) estar dispuesto a.

include |inklōōd'| *vt* incluir, comprender; (*in letter*) adjuntar; **the tip is/is not** ~**d** la propina está/no está incluida.

including |inklōōd'ing| *prep* incluso, inclusive; ~ **tip** propina incluida.

inclusion |inklōō'zhən| *n* inclusión *f*.
inclusive |inklōō'siv| *a* inclusivo ◊ *ad* inclusive; ~ **of tax** incluidos los impuestos; **$50,** ~ **of all surcharges** 50 dólares, incluidos todos los sobreimpuestos.
incognito |inkágnē'tō| *ad* de incógnito.
incoherent |inkōhē'rənt| *a* incoherente.
income |in'kum| *n* (*personal*) ingresos *mpl*; (*from property etc*) renta; (*profit*) rédito; **gross/net** ~ ingresos *mpl* brutos/netos; ~ **and expenditure account** cuenta de gastos e ingresos.
income bracket *n* categoría económica.
income support *n* (*Brit*) *subsidio estatal para personas con un nivel de ingresos muy bajo*.
income tax *n* impuesto sobre la renta.
income tax inspector *n* inspector(a) *m/f* fiscal.
income tax return *n* registro fiscal.
incoming |in'kuming| *a* (*passengers*) de llegada; (*government, tenant*) entrante; ~ **flight** vuelo entrante.
incommunicado |inkəmyōōnəká'dō| *a*: **to hold sb** ~ mantener incomunicado a uno.
incomparable |inkám'púrəbəl| *a* incomparable, sin par.
incompatible |inkəmpat'əbəl| *a* incompatible.
incompetence |inkám'pitəns| *n* incompetencia.
incompetent |inkám'pitənt| *a* incompetente.
incomplete |inkəmplēt'| *a* incompleto; (*unfinished*) sin terminar.
incomprehensible |inkámprihcn'səbəl| *a* incomprensible.
inconceivable |inkənsē'vəbəl| *a* inconcebible.
inconclusive |inkənklōō'siv| *a* sin resultado (definitivo); (*argument*) poco convincente.
incongruity |inkánggrōō'itē| *n* incongruencia.
incongruous |inkáng'grōōəs| *a* discordante.
inconsequential |inkánsəkwen'chəl| *a* intranscendente.
inconsiderable |inkənsid'ûrəbəl| *a* insignificante.
inconsiderate |inkənsid'ûrit| *a* desconsiderado; **how** ~ **of him!** ¡qué falta de consideración (de su parte)!
inconsistency |inkənsis'tənsē| *n* inconsecuencia; (*of actions etc*) incompatibilidad *f*, falta de lógica; (*of work*) carácter *m* desigual, inconsistencia; (*of statement etc*) contradicción *f*, anomalía.
inconsistent |inkənsis'tənt| *a* inconsecuente; ~ **with** que no concuerda con.
inconsolable |inkənsō'ləbəl| *a* inconsolable.
inconspicuous |inkənspik'yōōəs| *a* (*discreet*) discreto; (*person*) que llama poco la atención.
inconstancy |inkán'stənsē| *n* inconstancia.

inconstant |inkán'stənt| *a* inconstante.
incontinence |inkán'tənəns| *n* incontinencia.
incontinent |inkán'tənənt| *a* incontinente.
incontrovertible |inkántrəvûr'təbəl| *a* incontrovertible.
inconvenience |inkənvēn'yəns| *n* (*gen*) inconvenientes *mpl*; (*trouble*) molestia, incomodidad *f* ◊ *vt* incomodar; **to put sb to great** ~ causar mucha molestia a uno; **don't** ~ **yourself** no te molestes.
inconvenient |inkənvēn'yənt| *a* incómodo, poco práctico; (*time, place*) inoportuno; **that time is very** ~ **for me** esa hora me es muy inconveniente.
incorporate |inkôr'pûrāt| *vt* incorporar; (*contain*) comprender; (*add*) agregar.
incorporated |inkôr'pərātid| *a*: ~ **company** (*US: abbr* **Inc.**) ≈ Sociedad *f* Anónima (S.A.).
incorrect |inkərckt'| *a* incorrecto.
incorrigible |inkôr'ijəbəl| *a* incorregible.
incorruptible |inkərup'təbəl| *a* incorruptible.
increase *n* |in'krēs| aumento ◊ *vb* |inkrēs'| *vi* aumentarse; (*grow*) crecer; (*price*) subir ◊ *vt* aumentar; **an** ~ **of 5%** un aumento de 5%; **to be on the** ~ estar *or* ir en aumento.
increasing |inkrēs'ing| *a* (*number*) creciente, que va en aumento.
increasingly |inkrēs'inglē| *ad* de más en más, cada vez más.
incredible |inkred'əbəl| *a* increíble.
incredibly |inkred'əblē| *ad* increíblemente.
incredulity |inkridōō'litē| *n* incredulidad *f*.
incredulous |inkrej'ələs| *a* incrédulo.
increment |in'krəmənt| *n* aumento, incremento.
incriminate |inkrim'ənāt| *vt* incriminar.
incriminating |inkrim'ənāting| *a* incriminador(a).
incrust |inkrust'| *vt* = **encrust.**
incubate |in'kyəbāt| *vt* (*eggs*) incubar, empollar ◊ *vi* (*egg, disease*) incubar.
incubation |inkyəbā'shən| *n* incubación *f*.
incubation period *n* período de incubación.
incubator |in'kyəbātûr| *n* incubadora.
inculcate |in'kulkāt| *vt*: **to** ~ **sth in sb** inculcar algo en uno.
incumbent |inkum'bənt| *n* ocupante *m/f* ◊ *a*: **it is** ~ **on him to...** le incumbe... .
incur |inkûr'| *vt* (*expenses*) incurrir en; (*loss*) sufrir.
incurable |inkyōōr'əbəl| *a* incurable.
incursion |inkûr'zhən| *n* incursión *f*.
Ind. *abbr* (*US*) = *Indiana*.
indebted |indet'id| *a*: **to be** ~ **to sb** estar agradecido a uno.
indecency |indē'sənsē| *n* indecencia.
indecent |indē'sənt| *a* indecente.
indecent assault *n* (*Brit*) atentado contra

el pudor.
indecent exposure *n* exhibicionismo.
indecipherable [indisī'fûrəbəl] *a* indescifrable.
indecision [indisizh'ən] *n* indecisión *f*.
indecisive [indisī'siv] *a* indeciso; *(discussion)* no resuelto, inconcluyente.
indeed [indēd'] *ad* efectivamente, en realidad; **yes ~!** ¡claro que sí!
indefatigable [indifat'əgəbəl] *a* incansable, infatigable.
indefensible [indifen'səbəl] *a* *(conduct)* injustificable.
indefinable [indifi'nəbəl] *a* indefinible.
indefinite [indef'ənit] *a* indefinido; *(uncertain)* incierto.
indefinitely [indef'ənitlē] *ad* *(wait)* indefinidamente.
indelible [indel'əbəl] *a* imborrable.
indelicate [indel'əkit] *a* *(tactless)* indiscreto, inoportuno; *(not polite)* indelicado.
indemnify [indem'nəfī] *vt* indemnizar, resarcir.
indemnity [indem'nitē] *n* *(insurance)* indemnidad *f*; *(compensation)* indemnización *f*.
indent [indent'] *vt* *(text)* sangrar.
indentation [indentā'shən] *n* mella; *(TYP)* sangría.
independence [indipen'dəns] *n* independencia.
independent [indipen'dənt] *a* independiente; **to become ~** independizarse.
indescribable [indiskrī'bəbəl] *a* indescriptible.
indestructible [indistruk'təbəl] *a* indestructible.
indeterminate [inditûr'mənit] *a* indeterminado.
index [in'deks] *n* *(pl:* **~es:** *in book)* índice *m*; *(: in library etc)* catálogo; *(pl:* **indices** [in'disēz]: *ratio, sign)* exponente *m*.
index card *n* ficha.
indexed [in'dekst] *a* *(US)* indexado.
index finger *n* índice *m*.
index-linked [in'dekslingkt'] *a* *(Brit)* = **indexed.**
India [in'dēə] *n* la India.
Indian [in'dēən] *a*, *n* indio/a *m/f*; *(American ~)* indio/a *m/f* de América, amerindio/a *m/f*.
Indian Ocean *n*: **the ~** el Océano Índico, el Mar de las Indias.
Indian summer *n* *(fig)* veranillo de San Martín.
indicate [in'dikāt] *vt* indicar ♦ *vi* *(Brit AUT):* **to ~ left/right** indicar a la izquierda/a la derecha.
indication [indikā'shən] *n* indicio, señal *f*.
indicative [indik'ətiv] *a*: **to be ~ of sth** indicar algo ♦ *n* *(LING)* indicativo.
indicator [in'dikātûr] *n* *(gen)* indicador *m*.
indices [in'disēz] *npl of* **index.**
indict [indīt'] *vt* acusar.

indictable [indīt'əbəl] *a*: **~ offense** delito procesable.
indictment [indīt'mənt] *n* acusación *f*.
indifference [indif'ûrəns] *n* indiferencia.
indifferent [indif'ûrənt] *a* indiferente; *(poor)* regular.
indigenous [indij'ənəs] *a* indígena.
indigestible [indijes'təbəl] *a* indigesto.
indigestion [indijes'chən] *n* indigestión *f*.
indignant [indig'nənt] *a*: **to be ~ about sth** indignarse por algo.
indignation [indignā'shən] *n* indignación *f*.
indignity [indig'nitē] *n* indignidad *f*.
indigo [in'dəgō] *a* *(color)* de color añil ♦ *n* añil *m*.
indirect [indirekt'] *a* indirecto.
indirectly [indirekt'lē] *ad* indirectamente.
indiscernible [indisûr'nəbəl] *a* imperceptible.
indiscreet [indiskrēt'] *a* indiscreto, imprudente.
indiscretion [indiskresh'ən] *n* indiscreción *f*, imprudencia.
indiscriminate [indiskrim'ənit] *a* indiscriminado.
indispensable [indispen'səbəl] *a* indispensable, imprescindible.
indisposed [indispōzd'] *a* *(unwell)* indispuesto.
indisposition [indispəzish'ən] *n* indisposición *f*.
indisputable [indispyōō'təbəl] *a* incontestable.
indistinct [indistingkt'] *a* indistinto.
indistinguishable [indisting'gwishəbəl] *a* indistinguible.
individual [indəvij'ōōəl] *n* individuo ♦ *a* individual; *(personal)* personal; *(for/of one only)* particular.
individualist [indəvij'ōōəlist] *n* individualista *m/f*.
individuality [indəvijōōal'itē] *n* individualidad *f*.
individually [indəvij'ōōəlē] *ad* individualmente; particularmente.
indivisible [indəviz'əbəl] *a* indivisible.
Indo-China [in'dōchī'nə] *n* Indochina.
indoctrinate [indäk'trənāt] *vt* adoctrinar.
indoctrination [indäktrənā'shən] *n* adoctrinamiento.
indolence [in'dələns] *n* indolencia.
indolent [in'dələnt] *a* indolente, perezoso.
Indonesia [indənē'zhə] *n* Indonesia.
Indonesian [indənē'zhən] *a*, *n* indonesio/a *m/f*.
indoor [in'dôr] *a* *(swimming pool)* cubierto; *(plant)* de interior; *(sport)* bajo cubierta.
indoors [indôrz'] *ad* dentro; *(at home)* en casa.
indubitable [indōō'bitəbəl] *a* indudable.
indubitably [indōō'bitəblē] *ad* indudablemente.
induce [indōōs'] *vt* inducir, persuadir;

(*bring about*) producir; **to ~ sb to do sth** persuadir a uno a que haga algo.

inducement [indōōs'mənt] *n* (*incentive*) incentivo, aliciente *m*.

induct [indukt'] *vt* iniciar; (*in job, rank, position*) instalar.

induction [induk'shən] *n* (*MED*: *of birth*) inducción *f*.

induction course *n* (*Brit*) curso de inducción.

indulge [indulj'] *vt* (*whim*) satisfacer; (*person*) complacer; (*child*) mimar ♦ *vi*: **to ~ in** darse el gusto de.

indulgence [indul'jəns] *n* vicio.

indulgent [indul'jənt] *a* indulgente.

industrial [indus'trēəl] *a* industrial.

industrial action *n* huelga.

industrial estate *n* (*Brit*) = **industrial park**.

industrial goods *npl* bienes *mpl* de producción.

industrialist [indus'trēəlist] *n* industrial *m/f*.

industrialize [indus'trēəlīz] *vt* industrializar.

industrial park *n* (*US*) polígono *or* zona (*LAm*) industrial.

industrial relations *npl* relaciones *fpl* empresariales.

industrial tribunal *n* magistratura del trabajo, tribunal *m* laboral.

industrial unrest *n* agitación *f* obrera.

industrious [indus'trēəs] *a* (*gen*) trabajador(a); (*student*) aplicado.

industry [in'dəstrē] *n* industria; (*diligence*) aplicación *f*.

inebriated [inēb'rēātid] *a* borracho.

inedible [ined'əbəl] *a* incomestible, incomible; (*plant etc*) no comestible.

ineffective [inifek'tiv], **ineffectual** [inifek'-chōōəl] *a* ineficaz, inútil.

inefficiency [inifish'ənsē] *n* ineficacia.

inefficient [inifish'ənt] *a* ineficaz, ineficiente.

inelegant [incl'əgənt] *a* poco elegante.

ineligible [inel'ijəbəl] *a* inelegible.

inept [inept'] *a* incompetente, incapaz.

ineptitude [inep'tətōōd] *n* incapacidad *f*, ineptitud *f*.

inequality [inikwâl'itē] *n* desigualdad *f*.

inequitable [inek'witəbəl] *a* injusto.

ineradicable [inirad'ikəbəl] *a* inextirpable.

inert [inûrt'] *a* inerte, inactivo; (*immobile*) inmóvil.

inertia [inûr'shə] *n* inercia; (*laziness*) pereza.

inertia-reel seat-belt [inûr'shərēl sēt'belt] *n* cinturón *m* de seguridad de inercia.

inescapable [inəskā'pəbəl] *a* ineludible, inevitable.

inessential [inisen'chəl] *a* no esencial.

inestimable [ines'təməbəl] *a* inestimable.

inevitability [inevitəbil'ətē] *n* inevitabilidad *f*.

inevitable [inev'itəbəl] *a* inevitable; (*nec-*

essary) forzoso.

inevitably [inev'itəblē] *ad* inevitablemente; **as ~ happens** ... como siempre pasa ....

inexact [in'igzakt'] *a* inexacto.

inexcusable [inikskyōō'zəbəl] *a* imperdonable.

inexhaustible [inigzôs'təbəl] *a* inagotable.

inexorable [inek'sûrəbəl] *a* inexorable, implacable.

inexpensive [inikspen'siv] *a* económico.

inexperience [inikspēr'ēəns] *n* falta de experiencia.

inexperienced [inikspēr'ēənst] *a* inexperto; **to be ~ in sth** no tener experiencia en algo.

inexplicable [ineks'plikəbəl] *a* inexplicable.

inexpressible [inikspres'əbəl] *a* inexpresable.

inextricable [ineks'trikəbəl] *a* inseparable.

inextricably [ineks'trikəblē] *ad* indisolublemente.

infallibility [infaləbil'ətē] *n* infalibilidad *f*.

infallible [infal'əbəl] *a* infalible.

infamous [in'fəməs] *a* infame.

infamy [in'fəmē] *n* infamia.

infancy [in'fənsē] *n* infancia.

infant [in'fənt] *n* niño/a.

infantile [in'fəntīl] *a* infantil; (*pej*) aniñado.

infant mortality *n* mortandad *f* infantil.

infantry [in'fəntrē] *n* infantería.

infantryman [in'fəntrēmən] *n* soldado de infantería.

infant school *n* (*Brit*) escuela de párvulos.

infatuated [infach'ōōātid] *a*: **~ with** (*in love*) loco por; **to become ~ (with sb)** enamoriscarse, encapricharse (con uno).

infatuation [infachōōā'shən] *n* enamoramiento.

infect [infekt'] *vt* (*wound*) infectar; (*person*) contagiar; (*fig*: *pej*) corromper; **~ed with** (*illness*) contagiado de; **to become ~ed** (*wound*) infectarse.

infection [infek'shən] *n* infección *f*; (*fig*) contagio.

infectious [infek'shəs] *a* contagioso; (*also fig*) infeccioso.

infer [infûr'] *vt* deducir, inferir; **to ~ (from)** inferir (de), deducir (de).

inference [in'fûrəns] *n* deducción *f*, inferencia.

inferior [infē'rēûr] *a*, *n* inferior *m/f*; **to feel ~** sentirse inferior.

inferiority [infērēôr'itē] *n* inferioridad *f*.

inferiority complex *n* complejo de inferioridad.

infernal [infûr'nəl] *a* infernal.

inferno [infûr'nō] *n* infierno; (*fig*) hoguera.

infertile [infûr'təl] *a* estéril; (*person*) infecundo.

infertility [infûrtil'ətē] *n* esterilidad *f*; infecundidad *f*.

infest [infest'] *vt* infestar.

infested [infes'tid] *a:* ~ **(with)** plagado (de).

infidel [in'fidəl] *n* infiel *m/f.*

infidelity [infidel'itē] *n* infidelidad *f.*

infighting [in'fīting] *n* (*fig*) lucha(s) *f(pl)* interna(s).

infiltrate [infil'trāt] *vt* (*troops etc*) infiltrarse en ♦ *vi* infiltrarse.

infinite [in'fənit] *a* infinito; **an** ~ **amount of money/time** un sinfín de dinero/tiempo.

infinitely [in'fənitlē] *ad* infinitamente.

infinitesimal [infinites'əməl] *a* infinitésimo.

infinitive [infin'ətiv] *n* infinitivo.

infinity [infin'ətē] *n* (*also* MATH) infinito; (*an* ~) infinidad *f.*

infirm [infûrm'] *a* enfermo, débil.

infirmary [infûr'mûrē] *n* hospital *m.*

infirmity [infûr'mitē] *n* debilidad *f;* (*illness*) enfermedad *f,* achaque *m.*

inflame [inflām'] inflamar.

inflamed [inflāmd'] *a:* **to become** ~ inflamarse.

inflammable [inflam'əbəl] *a* inflamable; (*situation etc*) explosivo.

inflammation [infləmā'shən] *n* inflamación *f.*

inflammatory [inflam'ətôrē] *a* (*speech*) incendiario.

inflatable [inflā'təbəl] *a* inflable.

inflate [inflāt'] *vt* (*tire, balloon*) inflar; (*fig*) hinchar.

inflated [inflā'tid] *a* (*tire etc*) inflado; (*price, self-esteem etc*) exagerado.

inflation [inflā'shən] *n* (ECON) inflación *f.*

inflationary [inflā'shənärē] *a* inflacionario.

inflationary spiral *n* espiral *f* inflacionista.

inflection [inflek'shən] *n* inflexión *f.*

inflexible [inflek'səbəl] *a* inflexible.

inflict [inflikt'] *vt:* **to** ~ **on** infligir en; (*tax etc*) imponer a.

infliction [inflik'shən] *n* imposición *f.*

in-flight [in'flīt] *a* durante el vuelo.

inflow [in'flō] *n* afluencia.

influence [in'flōōəns] *n* influencia ♦ *vt* influir en, influenciar; (*persuade*) sugestionar; **under the** ~ **of alcohol** en estado de embriaguez.

influential [inflōōen'chəl] *a* influyente.

influenza [inflōōen'zə] *n* gripe *f.*

influx [in'fluks] *n* afluencia.

inform [infôrm'] *vt:* **to** ~ **sb of sth** informar a uno sobre *or* de algo; (*warn*) avisar a uno de algo; (*communicate*) comunicar algo a uno ♦ *vi:* **to** ~ **on sb** delatar a uno.

informal [infôr'məl] *a* (*manner, tone*) desenfadado; (*dress, interview, occasion*) informal.

informality [infôrmal'itē] *n* falta de ceremonia; (*intimacy*) intimidad *f;* (*familiarity*) familiaridad *f;* (*ease*) afabilidad *f.*

informally [infôr'məlē] *ad* sin ceremonia; (*invite*) informalmente.

informant [infôr'mənt] *n* informante *m/f.*

information [infûrmā'shən] *n* información *f;* (*news*) noticias *fpl;* (*knowledge*) conocimientos *mpl;* (LAW) delación *f;* **a piece of** ~ un dato; **for your** ~ para que se informe usted, para su información.

information bureau *n* oficina de informaciones.

information desk *n* mesa de informes.

information processing *n* procesamiento de datos.

information retrieval *n* recuperación *f* de la información.

information science *n* gestión *f* de la información.

information technology *n* informática.

informative [infôr'mətiv] *a* informativo.

informed [infôrmd'] *a* (*observer*) informado, al corriente; **an** ~ **guess** una opinión bien fundamentada.

informer [infôr'mûr] *n* delator(a) *m/f;* (*also:* **police** ~) soplón/ona *m/f.*

infra dig [in'frə dig] *a abbr* (*col:* = *infra dignitatem*) denigrante.

infra-red [in'frəred'] *a* infrarrojo.

infrastructure [in'frəstruk'chûr] *n* (*of system etc,* ECON) infraestructura.

infrequent [infrē'kwint] *a* infrecuente.

infringe [infrinj'] *vt* infringir, violar ♦ *vi:* **to** ~ **on** abusar de.

infringement [infrinj'mənt] *n* infracción *f;* (*of rights*) usurpación *f.*

infuriate [infyōōr'ēāt] *vt:* **to become** ~**d** ponerse furioso.

infuriating [infyōōr'ēāting] *a:* **I find it** ~ me saca de quicio.

infuse [infyōōz'] *vt* (*with courage, enthusiasm*): **to** ~ **sb with sth** infundir a uno con algo.

infusion [infyōō'zhən] *n* (*tea etc*) infusión *f.*

ingenious [injēn'yəs] *a* ingenioso.

ingenuity [injənōō'itē] *n* ingeniosidad *f.*

ingenuous [injen'yōōəs] *a* ingenuo.

ingot [ing'gət] *n* lingote *m,* barra.

ingrained [ingrānd'] *a* arraigado.

ingratiate [ingrā'shēāt] *vt:* **to** ~ **o.s. with** congraciarse con.

ingratiating [ingrā'shēāting] *a* (*smile, speech*) insinuante; (*person*) zalamero, congraciador(a).

ingratitude [ingrat'ətōōd] *n* ingratitud *f.*

ingredient [ingrē'dēənt] *n* ingrediente *m.*

ingrowing [in'grōing] *a:* ~ **(toe)nail** uña encarnada.

inhabit [inhab'it] *vt* vivir en; (*occupy*) ocupar.

inhabitable [inhab'itəbəl] *a* habitable.

inhabitant [inhab'ətənt] *n* habitante *m/f.*

inhale [inhāl'] *vt* inhalar ♦ *vi* (*in smoking*) tragar.

inherent [inhär'ent] *a:* ~ **in** *or* **to** inherente a.

inherently [inhär'entlē] *ad* esencialmente.
inherit [inhär'it] *vt* heredar.
inheritance [inhär'itəns] *n* herencia; (*fig*) patrimonio.
inheritance tax *n* derechos *mpl* de sucesión.
inhibit [inhib'it] *vt* inhibir, impedir; **to ~ sb from doing sth** impedir a uno hacer algo.
inhibited [inhib'itid] *a* (*person*) cohibido.
inhibition [inibish'ən] *n* cohibición *f*.
inhospitable [inhâspit'əbəl] *a* (*person*) inhospitalario; (*place*) inhóspito.
inhuman [inhyoo'mən] *a* inhumano.
inhumane [inhyoomān'] *a* inhumano.
inimitable [inim'itəbəl] *a* inimitable.
iniquity [inik'witē] *n* iniquidad *f*; (*injustice*) injusticia.
initial [inish'əl] *a* inicial; (*first*) primero ♦ *n* inicial *f* ♦ *vt* firmar con las iniciales; **~s** *npl* iniciales *fpl*; (*abbreviation*) siglas *fpl*.
initialize [inish'əliz] *vt* (*COMPUT*) inicializar.
initially [inish'əlē] *ad* al principio.
initiate [inishē'āt] *vt* (*start*) iniciar; **to ~ sb into a secret** iniciar a uno en un secreto; **to ~ proceedings against sb** (*LAW*) entablar una demanda contra uno.
initiation [inishēā'shən] *n* (*into secret etc*) iniciación *f*; (*beginning*) comienzo.
initiative [inish'ēətiv] *n* iniciativa; **to take the ~** tomar la iniciativa.
inject [injekt'] *vt* inyectar; (*money, enthusiasm*) aportar.
injection [injek'shən] *n* inyección *f*; **to have an ~** hacerse inyectar.
injudicious [injoodish'əs] *a* imprudente, indiscreto.
injunction [injungk'shən] *n* entredicho, interdicto.
injure [in'jûr] *vt* herir; (*hurt*) lastimar; (*fig: reputation etc*) perjudicar; (*feelings*) herir; **to ~ o.s** hacerse daño, lastimarse.
injured [in'jûrd] *a* (*also fig*) herido; **~ party** (*LAW*) parte *f* perjudicada.
injurious [injoor'ēəs] *a*: **~ (to)** perjudicial (a).
injury [in'jûrē] *n* herida, lesión *f*; (*wrong*) perjuicio, daño; **to escape without ~** salir ileso.
injury time *n* (*SPORT*) descuento.
injustice [injus'tis] *n* injusticia; **you do me an ~** usted es injusto conmigo.
ink [ingk] *n* tinta.
ink-jet printer [ingk'jet prin'tûr] *n* impresora de chorro de tinta.
inkling [ingk'ling] *n* sospecha; (*idea*) idea.
inkpad [ingk'pad] *n* almohadilla.
inlaid [in'lād] *a* (*wood*) taraceado; (*tiles*) entarimado.
inland [in'land] *a* interior; (*town*) del interior ♦ *ad* tierra adentro.
Inland Revenue *n* (*Brit*) Hacienda.
in-laws [in'lôz] *npl* suegros *mpl*.
inlet [in'let] *n* (*GEO*) ensenada, cala; (*TECH*)

admisión *f*, entrada.
inmate [in'māt] *n* (*in prison*) preso/a; presidiario/a; (*in asylum*) internado/a.
inmost [in'mōst] *a* más íntimo, más secreto.
inn [in] *n* posada, mesón *m*.
innards [in'ûrdz] *npl* (*col*) tripas *fpl*.
innate [ināt'] *a* innato.
inner [in'ûr] *a* interior, interno.
inner city *n* barrios deprimidos del centro de una ciudad.
innermost [in'ûrmōst] *a* más íntimo, más secreto.
inner tube *n* (*of tire*) cámara, llanta (*LAm*).
innings [in'ingz] *n* (*SPORT*) entrada, turno.
innocence [in'əsəns] *n* inocencia.
innocent [in'əsənt] *a* inocente.
innocuous [inâk'yooəs] *a* inocuo.
innovation [inəvā'shən] *n* novedad *f*.
innuendo, ~es [inyooen'dō] *n* indirecta.
Innuit [in'oowit] *n* esquimal *m/f* ♦ *a* esquimal.
innumerable [inoo'mûrəbəl] *a* innumerable.
inoculate [inâk'yəlāt] *vt*: **to ~ sb with sth/against sth** inocular *or* vacunar a uno con algo/contra algo.
inoculation [inâkyəlā'shən] *n* inoculación *f*.
inoffensive [inəfen'siv] *a* inofensivo.
inopportune [inâpûrtoon'] *a* inoportuno.
inordinate [inôr'dənit] *a* excesivo, desmesurado.
inordinately [inôr'dənitlē] *ad* excesivamente, desmesuradamente.
inorganic [inôrgan'ik] *a* inorgánico.
inpatient [in'pāshənt] *n* paciente *m/f* interno/a.
input [in'poot] *n* (*ELEC*) entrada; (*COMPUT*) entrada de datos ♦ *vt* (*COMPUT*) introducir, entrar.
inquest [in'kwest] *n* (*coroner's*) encuesta judicial.
inquire [inkwiûr'] *vi* preguntar ♦ *vt*: **to ~ when/where/whether** preguntar cuándo/dónde/si; **to ~ about** (*person*) preguntar por; (*fact*) informarse de.
inquire into *vt fus*: **to ~ into sth** investigar *or* indagar algo.
inquiring [inkwiûr'ing] *a* (*mind*) penetrante; (*look*) interrogativo.
inquiry [inkwiûr'ē] *n* pregunta; (*LAW*) investigación *f*, pesquisa; (*commission*) comisión *f* investigadora; **to hold an ~ into sth** montar una investigación sobre algo.
inquiry desk *n* (*Brit*) mesa de informes.
inquiry office *n* (*Brit*) oficina de informaciones.
inquisition [inkwizish'ən] *n* inquisición *f*.
inquisitive [inkwiz'ətiv] *a* (*mind*) inquisitivo; (*person*) fisgón/ona.
inroad [in'rōd] *n* incursión *f*; (*fig*) invasión *f*; **to make ~s into** (*time*) ocupar parte de; (*savings, supplies*) agotar parte de.
insane [insān'] *a* loco; (*MED*) demente.
insanitary [insan'itärē] *a* insalubre.

insanity |insan'itē| *n* demencia, locura.
insatiable |insā'shabal| *a* insaciable.
inscribe |inskrīb'| *vt* inscribir; (*book etc*):
to ~ (to sb) dedicar (a uno).
inscription |inskrip'shan| *n* (*gen*) inscripción *f*; (*in book*) dedicatoria.
inscrutable |inskrōō'tabal| *a* inescrutable, insondable.
inseam measurement |insēm' mezh'-ûrmant| *n* (*US*) medida de pernera.
insect |in'sckt| *n* insecto.
insect bite *n* picadura.
insecticide |insck'tisīd| *n* insecticida *m*.
insect repellent *n* loción *f* contra los insectos.
insecure |insikyōōr'| *a* inseguro.
insecurity |insikyōōr'itē| *n* inseguridad *f*.
insemination |inscmanā'shan| *n*: **artificial** ~ inseminación *f* artificial.
insensible |inscn'sabal| *a* inconsciente; (*unconscious*) sin conocimiento.
insensitive |inscn'sativ| *a* insensible.
insensitivity |inscnsativ'itē| *n* insensibilidad *f*.
inseparable |inscp'úrabal| *a* inseparable; they were ~ friends los unía una estrecha amistad.
insert *vt* |insûrt'| (*into sth*) introducir; (*COMPUT*) insertar ♦ *n* |in'sûrt| encarte *m*.
insertion |insûr'shan| *n* inserción *f*.
in-service |in'sûr'vis| *a* (*training, course*) en el trabajo, a cargo de la empresa.
inshore |in'shôr| *a*: ~ **fishing** pesca *f* costera ♦ *ad* (*fish*) a lo largo de la costa; (*move*) hacia la orilla.
inside |in'sīd'| *n* interior *m*; (*lining*) forro; (*of road: US, Europe etc*) lado derecho; (: *Brit*) lado izquierdo ♦ *a* interior, interno; (*information*) confidencial ♦ *ad* (*within*) (por) dentro; (*with movement*) hacia dentro; (*fam: in prison*) en la cárcel ♦ *prep* dentro de; (*of time*): ~ 10 minutes en menos de 10 minutos; ~s *npl* (*col*) tripas *fpl*; ~ out *ad* (*turn*) al revés; (*know*) a fondo.
inside forward *n* (*SPORT*) interior *m*.
inside information *n* información *f* confidencial.
inside lane *n* (*AUT*: *in US*, Europe) carril *m* derecho; (: *in Britain*) carril *m* izquierdo.
inside leg measurement *n* (*Brit*) = **inseam measurement.**
insider |insī'dûr| *n* enterado/a.
insider dealing *n* delito de iniciados.
inside story *n* historia íntima.
insidious |insid'ēas| *a* insidioso.
insight |in'sīt| *n* perspicacia, percepción *f*; to gain *or* get an ~ into sth formarse una idea de algo.
insignia |insig'nēa| *npl* insignias *fpl*.
insignificant |insignif'ikant| *a* insignificante.
insincere |insinsēr'| *a* poco sincero.
insincerity |insinsär'itē| *n* falta de sinceri-

dad, doblez *f*.
insinuate |insin'yōōāt| *vt* insinuar.
insinuation |insinyōōā'shan| *n* insinuación *f*.
insipid |insip'id| *a* soso, insulso.
insist |insist'| *vi* insistir; to ~ on doing empeñarse en hacer; to ~ that insistir en que; (*claim*) exigir que.
insistence |insis'tans| *n* insistencia; (*stubbornness*) empeño.
insistent |insis'tant| *a* insistente; empeñado.
insole |in'sōl| *n* plantilla.
insolence |in'salans| *n* insolencia, descaro.
insolent |in'salant| *a* insolente, descarado.
insoluble |insâl'yabal| *a* insoluble.
insolvency |insâl'vansē| *n* insolvencia.
insolvent |insâl'vant| *a* insolvente.
insomnia |insâm'nēa| *n* insomnio.
insomniac |insâm'nēak| *n* insomne *m/f*.
inspect |inspckt'| *vt* inspeccionar, examinar; (*troops*) pasar revista a.
inspection |inspck'shan| *n* inspección *f*, examen *m*.
inspector |inspck'tûr| *n* inspector(a) *m/f*; (*Brit: on buses, trains*) revisor(a) *m/f*.
inspiration |insparā'shan| *n* inspiración *f*.
inspire |inspīr'| *vt* inspirar; to ~ sb (to do sth) inspirar a uno (a hacer algo).
inspired |inspīūrd'| *a* (*writer, book etc*) inspirado, genial, iluminado; in an ~ moment en un momento de inspiración.
inspiring |inspīūr'ing| *a* inspirador(a).
inst. *abbr* (*Brit COMM*: = *instant, of the present month*) cte.
instability |instabil'atē| *n* inestabilidad *f*.
install |instól'| *vt* instalar.
installation |instalā'shan| *n* instalación *f*.
installment, (*Brit*) **instalment** |instól'mant| *n* plazo; (*of story*) entrega; (*of TV serial etc*) capítulo; in ~s (*pay, receive*) a plazos; to pay in ~s pagar a plazos *or* por abonos.
installment plan *n* (*US*) compra a plazos.
instance |in'stans| *n* ejemplo, caso; for ~ por ejemplo; in the first ~ en primer lugar; in that ~ en ese caso.
instant |in'stant| *n* instante *m*, momento ♦ *a* inmediato; (*coffee*) instantáneo.
instantaneous |instantā'nēas| *a* instantáneo.
instantly |in'stantlē| *ad* en seguida.
instant replay *n* (*US TV*) repetición *f* de jugada.
instead |instcd'| *ad* en cambio; ~ of en lugar de, en vez de.
instep |in'stcp| *n* empeine *m*.
instigate |in'stagāt| *vt* (*rebellion, strike, crime*) instigar; (*new ideas etc*) fomentar.
instigation |instagā'shan| *n* instigación *f*; at sb's ~ a instigación de uno.
instill, (*Brit*) **instil** |instil'| *vt*: to ~ into inculcar a.
instinct |in'stingkt| *n* instinto.
instinctive |instingk'tiv| *a* instintivo.

instinctively [instingk'tivlē] *ad* por instinto.

institute [in'stitōōt] *n* instituto; (*professional body*) colegio ♦ *vt* (*begin*) iniciar, empezar; (*proceedings*) entablar.

institution [institōō'shən] *n* institución *f*; (*beginning*) iniciación *f*; (*MED: home*) asilo; (*asylum*) manicomio; (*custom*) costumbre *f* arraigada.

institutional [institōō'shənəl] *a* institucional.

instruct [instrukt'] *vt*: **to ~ sb in sth** instruir a uno en *or* sobre algo; **to ~ sb to do sth** dar instrucciones a uno de hacer algo.

instruction [instruk'shən] *n* (*teaching*) instrucción *f*; **~s** *npl* órdenes *fpl*; **~s (for use)** modo *sg* de empleo.

instruction book *n* manual *m*.

instructive [instruk'tiv] *a* instructivo.

instructor [instruk'tûr] *n* instructor(a) *m/f*; (*US UNIV*) profesor(a) *m/f*.

instrument [in'strəmənt] *n* instrumento.

instrumental [instrəmen'təl] *a* (*MUS*) instrumental; **to be ~ in** ser (el) artífice de; **to be ~ in sth/in doing sth** ser responsable de algo/de hacer algo.

instrumentalist [instrəmen'təlist] *n* instrumentalista *m/f*.

instrument panel *n* tablero (de instrumentos).

insubordinate [insəbôr'dənit] *a* insubordinado.

insubordination [insəbôrdənā'shən] *n* insubordinación *f*.

insufferable [insuf'ûrəbəl] *a* insoportable.

insufficient [insəfish'ənt] *a* insuficiente.

insufficiently [insəfish'əntlē] *ad* insuficientemente.

insular [in'səlûr] *a* insular; (*outlook*) estrecho de miras.

insularity [insəlar'itē] *n* insularidad *f*.

insulate [in'səlāt] *vt* aislar.

insulating tape [in'səlāting tāp] *n* cinta aislante.

insulation [insəlā'shən] *n* aislamiento.

insulator [in'səlātûr] *n* aistante *m*.

insulin [in'səlin] *n* insulina.

insult *n* [in'sult] insulto; (*offence*) ofensa ♦ *vt* [insult'] insultar; ofender.

insulting [insul'ting] *a* insultante; ofensivo.

insuperable [insōō'pûrəbəl] *a* insuperable.

insurance [inshûr'əns] *n* seguro; **fire/life ~** seguro sobre la vida/contra incendios; **to take out ~ (against)** hacerse un seguro (contra).

insurance agent *n* agente *m/f* de seguros.

insurance broker *n* corredor(a) *m/f* *or* agente *m/f* de seguros.

insurance policy *n* póliza (de seguros).

insurance premium *n* prima de seguros.

insure [inshōōr'] *vt* asegurar; **to ~ sb** *or* **sb's life** asegurar la vida de uno; **to ~ (against)** asegurar (contra); **to be ~d for $5000** tener un seguro de 5000 dólares.

insured [inshōōrd'] *n*: **the ~** el/la asegurado/a.

insurer [inshōō'rûr] *n* asegurador(a).

insurgent [insûr'jənt] *a*, *n* insurgente *m/f*, insurrecto/a *m/f*.

insurmountable [insûrmoun'təbəl] *a* insuperable.

insurrection [insərek'shən] *n* insurrección *f*.

intact [intakt'] *a* íntegro; (*untouched*) intacto.

intake [in'tāk] *n* (*TECH*) entrada, toma; (: *pipe*) tubo de admisión; (*of food*) ingestión *f*; (*Brit SCOL*): **an ~ of 200 a year** 200 matriculados al año.

intangible [intan'jəbəl] *a* intangible.

integer [in'tijûr] *n* (*número*) entero.

integral [in'təgrəl] *a* (*whole*) íntegro; (*part*) integrante.

integrate [in'təgrāt] *vt* integrar ♦ *vi* integrarse.

integrated circuit [in'təgrātid sûr'kit] *n* (*COMPUT*) circuito integrado.

integration [intəgrā'shən] *n* integración *f*; **racial ~** integración de razas.

integrity [integ'ritē] *n* honradez *f*, rectitud *f*; (*COMPUT*) integridad *f*.

intellect [in'təlekt] *n* intelecto.

intellectual [intəlek'chōōəl] *a*, *n* intelectual *m/f*.

intelligence [intel'ijəns] *n* inteligencia.

intelligence quotient (IQ) *n* cociente *m* de inteligencia.

Intelligence Service *n* Servicio de Inteligencia.

intelligence test *n* prueba de inteligencia.

intelligent [intel'ijənt] *a* inteligente.

intelligently [intel'ijəntlē] *ad* inteligentemente.

intelligentsia [intel'əjənt'sēə] *n* intelectualidad *f*.

intelligible [intel'ijəbəl] *a* inteligible, comprensible.

intemperate [intem'pûrit] *a* inmoderado.

intend [intend'] *vt* (*gift etc*): **to ~ sth for** destinar algo a; **to ~ to do sth** tener intención de *or* pensar hacer algo.

intended [inten'did] *a* (*effect*) deseado.

intense [intens'] *a* intenso; (*person*) nervioso.

intensely [intens'lē] *ad* intensamente; (*very*) sumamente.

intensify [inten'səfī] *vt* intensificar; (*increase*) aumentar.

intensity [inten'sitē] *n* (*gen*) intensidad *f*.

intensive [inten'siv] *a* intensivo.

intensive care *n*: **to be in ~** estar bajo cuidados intensivos; **~ unit** *n* unidad *f* de vigilancia intensiva.

intensively [inten'sivlē] *ad* intensivamente.

intent [intent'] *n* propósito ♦ *a* (*absorbed*) absorto; (*attentive*) atento; **to all ~s and purposes** prácticamente; **to be ~ on doing sth** estar resuelto *or* decidido a hacer algo.

intention [inten'chən] *n* intención *f*, propósito.

intentional [inten'chənəl] *a* deliberado.

intentionally [inten'chənəlē] *ad* a propósito.

intently [intent'lē] *ad* atentamente, fijamente.

inter [intûr'] *vt* enterrar.

inter- [in'tûr] *pref* inter-.

interact [intûrakt'] *vi* influirse mutuamente.

interaction [intûrak'shən] *n* interacción *f*, acción *f* recíproca.

interactive [intûrak'tiv] *a* (*also* COMPUT) interactivo.

intercede [intûrsēd'] *vi*: **to ~ (with)** interceder (con); **to ~ with sb/on behalf of sb** interceder con uno/en nombre de uno.

intercept [intûrsept'] *vt* interceptar; (*stop*) detener.

interception [intûrsep'shən] *n* interceptación *f*; detención *f*.

interchange *n* [in'tûrchānj] intercambio; (*on freeway*) intersección *f* ♦ *vt* [intûrchānj'] intercambiar.

interchangeable [intûrchān'jəbəl] *a* intercambiable.

intercity [in'tûrsitē] *a*: **~ (train)** (tren *m*) interurbano.

intercom [in'tûrkâm] *n* interfono.

interconnect [intûrkənekt'] *vi* (*rooms*) conectarse.

intercontinental [intûrkântənən'təl] *a* intercontinental.

intercourse [in'tûrkôrs] *n* (*sexual* ~) relaciones *fpl* sexuales, contacto sexual; (*social*) trato.

interdependence [intûrdipen'dəns] *n* interdependencia.

interdependent [intûrdipen'dənt] *a* interdependiente.

interest [in'trist] *n* (*also* COMM) interés *m* ♦ *vt* interesar; **compound/simple ~** interés compuesto/simple; **business ~s** negocios *mpl*; **American ~s in the Middle East** los intereses norteamericanos en el Medio Oriente.

interested [in'tristid] *a* interesado; **to be ~ in** interesarse por.

interest-free [in'tristfrē] *a* libre *or* franco de interés.

interesting [in'tristing] *a* interesante.

interest rate *n* tipo *or* tasa de interés.

interface [in'tûrfās] *n* (COMPUT) junción *f*, interface *m*.

interfere [intûrfēr'] *vi*: **to ~ in** (*quarrel, other people's business*) entrometerse en; **to ~ with** (*hinder*) estorbar; (*damage*) estropear; (*radio*) interferir con.

interference [intûrfēr'əns] *n* (*gen*) intromisión *f*; (RADIO, TV) interferencia.

interfering [intûrfēr'ing] *a* entrometido.

interim [in'tûrim] *a*: **~ dividend** dividendo parcial ♦ *n*: **in the ~** en el ínterin.

interior [intē'rēûr] *n* interior *m* ♦ *a* interior.

interior decorator, interior designer *n* interiorista *m/f*.

interjection [intûrjek'shən] *n* interyección *f*.

interlock [intûrlâk'] *vi* entrelazarse; (*wheels etc*) endentarse.

interloper [intûrlō'pûr] *n* intruso/a.

interlude [in'tûrlōōd] *n* intervalo; (*rest*) descanso; (THEATER) intermedio.

intermarriage [intûrmar'ij] *n* endogamia.

intermarry [intûrmar'ē] *vi* casarse (entre parientes).

intermediary [intûrmē'dēärē] *n* intermediario/a.

intermediate [intûrmē'dēit] *a* intermedio.

interminable [intûr'mənəbəl] *a* inacabable.

intermission [intûrmish'ən] *n* (THEATER) descanso.

intermittent [intûrmit'ənt] *a* intermitente.

intermittently [intûrmit'əntlē] *ad* intermitentemente.

intern *vt* [intûrn'] internar; (*enclose*) encerrar ♦ *n* [in'tûrn] (US) interno/a.

internal [intûr'nəl] *a* interno, interior; **.~ injuries** heridas *fpl or* lesiones *fpl* internas.

internally [intûr'nəlē] *ad* interiormente; **"not to be taken ~"** "uso externo".

Internal Revenue Service (IRS) *n* (US) Hacienda.

international [intûrnash'ənəl] *a* internacional; **~ (game)** partido internacional; **~ (player)** jugador(a) *m/f* internacional.

International Atomic Energy Agency (IAEA) *n* Organismo Internacional de Energía Atómica.

International Chamber of Commerce (ICC) *n* Cámara de Comercio Internacional (CCI *f*).

International Court of Justice (ICJ) *n* Corte *f* Internacional de Justicia (CIJ *f*).

international date line *n* línea de cambio de fecha.

internationally [intûrnash'ənəlē] *ad* internacionalmente.

International Monetary Fund (IMF) *n* Fondo Monetario Internacional (FMI *m*).

internecine [intûrnē'sin] *a* internecino.

internee [intûrnē'] *n* internado/a.

internment [intûrn'mənt] *n* internamiento.

interplanetary [intûrplan'itärē] *a* interplanetario.

interplay [in'tûrplā] *n* interacción *f*.

Interpol [in'tûrpōl] *n* Interpol *f*.

interpret [intûr'prit] *vt* interpretar; (*translate*) traducir; (*understand*) entender ♦ *vi* hacer de intérprete.

interpretation [intûrpritā'shən] *n* interpretación *f*; traducción *f*; entendimiento.

interpreter [intûr'pritûr] *n* intérprete *m/f*.

interrelated [intərilā'tid] *a* interrelacionado.

interrogate [intär'əgāt] *vt* interrogar.

interrogation [intärəgā'shən] *n* interrogatorio.

interrogative [intərág'ətiv] *a* interrogativo.
interrupt [intərupt'] *vt, vi* interrumpir.
interruption [intərup'shən] *n* interrupción *f*.
intersect [intûrsekt'] *vt* cruzar ♦ *vi* (*roads*) cruzarse.
intersection [intûrsek'shən] *n* intersección *f*; (*of roads*) cruce *m*.
intersperse [intûrspûrs'] *vt*: **to ~ with** salpicar de.
interstate (highway) [in'tûrstát (hī'wā)] *n* (*US*) autopista.
intertwine [intûrtwīn'] *vt* entrelazar ♦ *vi* entrelazarse.
interval [in'tûrvəl] *n* intervalo; (*Brit*: THEA-TER, SPORT) descanso; **at ~s** a ratos, de vez en cuando; **sunny ~s** (METEOROLOGY) claros *mpl*.
intervene [intûrvēn'] *vi* intervenir; (*take part*) participar; (*occur*) sobrevenir.
intervening [intûrvēn'ing] *a* intermedio.
intervention [intûrven'chən] *n* intervención *f*.
interview [in'tûrvyōō] *n* (RADIO, TV etc) entrevista ♦ *vt* entrevistarse con.
interviewee [in'tûrvyōōē'] *n* entrevistado/a.
interviewer [in'tûrvyōōûr] *n* entrevista-dor(a) *m/f*.
intestate [intes'tāt] *a* intestado.
intestinal [intes'tənəl] *a* intestinal.
intestine [intes'tin] *n*: **large/small ~** intes-tino grueso/delgado.
intimacy [in'təməsē] *n* intimidad *f*; (*rela-tions*) relaciones *fpl* íntimas.
intimate *a* [in'təmit] íntimo; (*friendship*) es-trecho; (*knowledge*) profundo ♦ *vt* [in'təmāt] (*announce*) dar a entender.
intimately [in'təmitlē] *ad* íntimamente.
intimidate [intim'idāt] *vt* intimidar, ame-drentar.
intimidation [intimidā'shən] *n* intimidación *f*.
into [in'tōō] *prep* (*gen*) en; (*towards*) a; (*inside*) hacia el interior de; **~ 3 pieces/ French** en 3 pedazos/al francés; **to change pounds ~ dollars** cambiar libras por dóla-res.
intolerable [intâl'ûrəbəl] *a* intolerable, inso-portable.
intolerance [intâl'ûrəns] *n* intolerancia.
intolerant [intâl'ûrənt] *a*: **~ (of)** intolerante (con *or* para).
intonation [intōnā'shən] *n* entonación *f*.
intoxicate [intâk'sikāt] *vt* embriagar.
intoxicated [intâk'sikātid] *a* embriagado.
intoxication [intâksikā'shən] *n* embriaguez *f*.
intractable [intrak'təbəl] *a* (*person*) intrata-ble; (*problem*) insoluble; (*illness*) incura-ble.
intransigence [intran'sijəns] *n* intransigen-cia.
intransigent [intran'sijənt] *a* intransigente.
intransitive [intran'sətiv] *a* intransitivo.

intravenous [intrəvē'nəs] *a* intravenoso.
in-tray [in'trā] *n* bandeja de entrada.
intrepid [intrep'id] *a* intrépido.
intricacy [in'trəkəsē] *n* complejidad *f*.
intricate [in'trəkit] *a* intrincado; (*plot, prob-lem*) complejo.
intrigue [intrēg'] *n* intriga ♦ *vt* fascinar ♦ *vi* andar en intrigas.
intriguing [intrē'ging] *a* fascinante.
intrinsic [intrin'sik] *a* intrínseco.
introduce [intrədōōs'] *vt* introducir, meter; (POL: *bill, law*) presentar; **to ~ sb (to sb)** presentar uno (a otro); **to ~ sb to** (*pas-time, technique*) introducir a uno a; **may I ~ ...?** permítame presentarle a ....
introduction [intrəduk'shən] *n* introducción *f*; (*of person*) presentación *f*; **a letter of ~** una carta de recomendación.
introductory [intrəduk'tûrē] *a* introducto-rio; **an ~ offer** una oferta introductoria; **~ remarks** comentarios *mpl* introductorios.
introspection [intrəspek'shən] *n* introspec-ción *f*.
introspective [intrəspek'tiv] *a* introspecti-vo.
introvert [in'trəvûrt] *a, n* introvertido/a *m/f*.
intrude [intrōōd'] *vi* (*person*) entrometerse; **to ~ on** estorbar.
intruder [intrōō'dûr] *n* intruso/a.
intrusion [intrōō'zhən] *n* invasión *f*.
intrusive [intrōō'siv] *a* intruso.
intuition [intōōish'ən] *n* intuición *f*.
intuitive [intōō'ətiv] *a* intuitivo.
intuitively [intōō'ətivlē] *ad* por intuición, intuitivamente.
inundate [in'undāt] *vt*: **to ~ with** inundar de.
inure [inyōōr'] *vt*: **to ~ (to)** acostumbrar *or* habituar (a).
invade [invād'] *vt* invadir.
invader [invā'dûr] *n* invasor(a) *m/f*.
invalid *n* [in'vəlid] minusválido/a ♦ *a* [in-val'id] (*not valid*) inválido, nulo.
invalidate [inval'idāt] *vt* invalidar, anular.
invalid chair *n* (*Brit*) sillón *m* para inváli-dos.
invaluable [inval'yōōəbəl] *a* inestimable.
invariable [invär'ēəbəl] *a* invariable.
invariably [invär'ēəblē] *ad* sin excepción, siempre; **she is ~ late** siempre llega tarde.
invasion [invā'zhən] *n* invasión *f*.
invective [invek'tiv] *n* invectiva.
inveigle [invē'gəl] *vt*: **to ~ sb into (doing) sth** embaucar *or* engatusar a uno para (que haga) algo.
invent [invent'] *vt* inventar.
invention [inven'chən] *n* invento; (*inventiveness*) inventiva; (*lie*) ficción *f*, mentira.
inventive [inven'tiv] *a* inventivo.
inventiveness [inven'tivnis] *n* ingenio, inventiva.
inventor [inven'tûr] *n* inventor(a) *m/f*.

inventory [in'vəntôrē] *n* inventario.
inventory control *n* control *m* del inventario.
inverse [invûrs'] *a, n* inverso; **in ~ proportion (to)** en proporción inversa (a).
inversely [invûrs'lē] *ad* a la inversa.
invert [invûrt'] *vt* invertir.
invertebrate [invûr'təbrit] *n* invertebrado.
inverted commas [invûr'tid kâm'əz] *npl* (*Brit*) comillas *fpl*.
invest [invest'] *vt* invertir; (*fig: time, effort*) dedicar ♦ *vi* invertir; **to ~ sb with sth** investir a uno con algo.
investigate [inves'təgāt] *vt* investigar; (*study*) estudiar, examinar.
investigation [inves'təgāshən] *n* investigación *f*, pesquisa; examen *m*.
investigative journalism [inves'təgātiv jûr'nəlizəm] *n* periodismo investigador.
investigator [inves'təgātûr] *n* investigador(a) *m/f*; **private ~** investigador(a) *m/f* privado/a.
investiture [inves'tichûr] *n* investidura.
investment [invest'mənt] *n* inversión *f*.
investment grant *n* subvención *f* para la inversión.
investment income *n* ingresos *mpl* procedentes de inversiones.
investment portfolio *n* portafolio de inversiones.
investment trust *n* (*Brit*) compañía inversionista, sociedad *f* de cartera.
investor [inves'tûr] *n* inversionista *m/f*.
inveterate [invet'ûrit] *a* empedernido.
invidious [invid'ēəs] *a* odioso.
invigilator [invij'əlātûr] *n* (*Brit*) celador(a) *m/f*.
invigorating [invig'ərāting] *a* vigorizante.
invincible [invin'səbəl] *a* invencible.
inviolate [invī'əlit] *a* inviolado.
invisible [inviz'əbəl] *a* invisible.
invisible ink *n* tinta simpática.
invisible mending *n* puntada invisible.
invitation [invitā'shən] *n* invitación *f*; **at sb's ~** a invitación de uno; **by ~ only** solamente por invitación.
invite [invīt'] *vt* invitar; (*opinions etc*) solicitar, pedir; (*trouble*) buscarse; **to ~ sb (to do)** invitar a uno (a hacer); **to ~ sb to dinner** invitar a uno a cenar.
invite out *vt* invitar a salir.
invite over *vt* invitar a casa.
inviting [invī'ting] *a* atractivo; (*look*) provocativo; (*food*) apetitoso.
invoice [in'vois] *n* factura ♦ *vt* facturar; **to ~ sb for goods** facturar a uno por mercancías.
invoicing [in'voising] *n* facturación *f*.
invoke [invōk'] *vt* invocar; (*aid*) pedir; (*law*) recurrir a.
involuntary [invâl'əntärē] *a* involuntario.
involve [invâlv'] *vt* (*entail*) suponer, implicar; **to ~ sb (in)** comprometer a uno

(con).
involved [invâlvd'] *a* complicado; **to be/become ~ in sth** estar comprometido *or* involucrado/involucrarse en algo.
involvement [invâlv'mənt] *n* (*gen*) enredo; (*obligation*) compromiso; (*difficulty*) apuro.
invulnerable [invul'nûrəbəl] *a* invulnerable.
inward [in'wûrd] *a* (*movement*) interior, interno; (*thought, feeling*) íntimo.
inwardly [in'wûrdlē] *ad* (*feel, think etc*) para sí, para dentro.
inward(s) [in'wûrd(z)] *ad* hacia dentro.
I/O *abbr* (*COMPUT* = *input/output*) E/S; **~ error** error *m* de E/S.
IOC *n abbr* (= *International Olympic Committee*) COI *m*.
iodine [ī'ədīn] *n* yodo.
ion [ī'ən] *n* ion *m*.
Ionian Sea [īō'nēən sē] *n*: **the ~** el Mar Jónico.
iota [īō'tə] *n* (*fig*) jota, ápice *m*.
IOU *n abbr* (= *I owe you*) pagaré *m*.
IOW *abbr* (*Brit*) = *Isle of Wight.*
IPA *n abbr* = *International Phonetic Alphabet.*
IQ *n abbr* (= *intelligence quotient*) C.I. *m*.
IRA *n abbr* (*US*) = *individual retirement account*; (= *Irish Republican Army*) IRA *m*.
Iran [iran'] *n* Irán *m*.
Iranian [irā'nēən] *a* iraní ♦ *n* iraní *m/f*; (*LING*) iraní *m*.
Iraq [irak'] *n* Irak *m*.
Iraqi [irâk'ē] *a, n* irakí *m/f*.
irascible [iras'əbəl] *a* irascible.
irate [irāt'] *a* enojado, airado.
Ireland [īûr'lənd] *n* Irlanda; **Republic of ~** República de Irlanda.
iris, ~es [ī'ris, -iz] *n* (*ANAT*) iris *m*; (*BOT*) lirio.
Irish [ī'rish] *a* irlandés/esa ♦ *n* (*LING*) irlandés *m*; **the ~** *npl* los irlandeses.
Irishman [ī'rishmən] *n* irlandés *m*.
Irish Sea *n*: **the ~** el Mar de Irlanda.
Irishwoman [ī'rishwŏomən] *n* irlandesa.
irk [ûrk] *vt* fastidiar.
irksome [ûrk'səm] *a* fastidioso.
IRO *n abbr* (*US*) = *International Refugee Organization.*
iron [ī'ûrn] *n* hierro; (*for clothes*) plancha ♦ *a* de hierro ♦ *vt* (*clothes*) planchar; **~s** *npl* (*chains*) grillos *mpl*.
iron out *vt* (*crease*) quitar; (*fig*) allanar.
Iron Curtain *n*: **the ~** el Telón de Acero.
iron foundry *n* fundición *f*, fundidora.
ironic(al) [īrân'ik(əl)] *a* irónico.
ironically [īrân'iklē] *ad* irónicamente.
ironing [ī'ûrning] *n* (*act*) planchado; (*ironed clothes*) ropa planchada; (*to be ironed*) ropa por planchar.
ironing board *n* tabla de planchar.
iron lung *n* (*MED*) pulmón *m* de acero.
ironmonger [ī'ûrnmunggûr] *n* (*Brit*)

ferretero/a; ~'s **(shop)** ferretería, quincallería.

iron ore |ĭ'ûrn ôr| *n* mineral *m* de hierro.

ironworks |ĭ'ûrnwûrks| *n* fundición *f.*

irony |ĭ'rənē| *n* ironía; **the ~ of it is that...** lo irónico es que... .

irrational |ĭrash'ənəl| *a* irracional.

irreconcilable |ĭrek'ənsīləbəl| *a* inconciliable; *(enemies)* irreconciliable.

irredeemable |ĭridē'məbəl| *a* irredimible.

irrefutable |ĭrifyōō'təbəl| *a* irrefutable.

irregular |ĭrĕg'yəlûr| *a* irregular; *(surface)* desigual.

irregularity |ĭregyəlar'itē| *n* irregularidad *f;* desigualdad *f.*

irrelevance |ĭrĕl'əvəns| *n* impertinencia.

irrelevant |ĭrĕl'əvənt| *a* fuera de lugar, inoportuno.

irreligious |ĭrilij'əs| *a* irreligioso.

irreparable |ĭrĕp'ûrəbəl| *a* irreparable.

irreplaceable |ĭriplā'səbəl| *a* irremplazable.

irrepressible |ĭriprĕs'əbəl| *a* incontenible.

irreproachable |ĭriprō'chəbəl| *a* irreprochable.

irresistible |ĭrizis'təbəl| *a* irresistible.

irresolute |ĭrĕz'əlōōt| *a* indeciso.

irrespective |ĭrispĕk'tiv|: **~ of** *prep* sin tener en cuenta, no importa.

irresponsibility |ĭrispánsəbil'ətē| *n* irresponsabilidad *f.*

irresponsible |ĭrispán'səbəl| *a* (act) irresponsable; *(person)* poco serio.

irretrievable |ĭritrē'vəbəl| *a* (object) irrecuperable; *(loss, damage)* irremediable, irreparable.

irretrievably |ĭritrē'vəblē| *ad* irremisiblemente.

irreverence |ĭrĕv'ûrəns| *n* irreverencia.

irreverent |ĭrĕv'ûrənt| *a* irreverente, irrespetuoso.

irrevocable |ĭrĕv'əkəbəl| *a* irrevocable.

irrigate |ĭr'igāt| *vt* regar.

irrigation |ĭrigā'shən| *n* riego.

irritability |ĭritəbil'ətē| *n* irritabilidad *f.*

irritable |ĭr'itəbəl| *a (person: temperament)* de (mal) carácter; (: *mood)* de mal humor.

irritant |ĭr'ətənt| *n* agente *m* irritante.

irritate |ĭr'ətāt| *vt* fastidiar; *(MED)* picar.

irritating |ĭr'ətāting| *a* fastidioso.

irritation |ĭritā'shən| *n* fastidio; picazón *f,* picor *m.*

IRS *n abbr (US)* = **Internal Revenue Service.**

is |iz| *vb see* **be.**

ISBN *n abbr (= International Standard Book Number)* ISBN *m.*

Islam |iz'lâm| *n* Islam *m.*

island |ĭ'lənd| *n* isla; *(also:* **traffic ~)** isleta.

islander |ĭ'ləndûr| *n* isleño/a.

isle |ĭl| *n* isla.

isn't |iz'ənt| = **is not.**

isobar |ĭ'sōbâr| *n* isobara.

isolate |ĭ'səlāt| *vt* aislar.

isolated |ĭ'səlātid| *a* aislado.

isolation |īsəlā'shən| *n* aislamiento.

isolationism |īsəlā'shənizəm| *n* aislacionismo.

isolation ward *n* pabellón *m* de aislamiento.

isotope |ĭ'sətōp| *n* isótopo.

Israel |iz'rāəl| *n* Israel *m.*

Israeli |izrā'lē| *a, n* israelí *m/f.*

issue |ish'ōō| *n* cuestión *f,* asunto; *(outcome)* resultado; *(of banknotes etc)* emisión *f; (of newspaper etc)* número; *(offspring)* sucesión *f,* descendencia ♦ *vt (rations, equipment)* distribuir, repartir; *(orders)* dar; *(certificate, passport)* expedir; *(decree)* promulgar; *(magazine)* publicar; *(checks)* extender; *(banknotes, stamps)* emitir ♦ *vi:* **to ~ (from)** derivar (de), brotar (de); **at ~** en cuestión; **to take ~ with sb (over)** estar en desacuerdo con uno (sobre); **to avoid the ~** andar con rodeos; **to confuse** *or* **obscure the ~** confundir las cosas; **to make an ~ of sth** hacer hincapié en algo; **to ~ sth to sb** entregar algo a uno.

Istanbul |istambōōl'| *n* Estambul *m.*

isthmus |is'məs| *n* istmo.

IT *n abbr* = **information technology.**

it |it| *pron (subject)* él/ella; *(direct object)* lo/la; *(indirect object)* le; *(impersonal)* ello; *(after prep)* él/ella/ello; **of/from ~** de él; **about ~** sobre él; **out of ~** desde él; **in ~** en él; **to ~** a él; **at ~** en/a él; **in front of/behind ~** delante de/detrás de él; **above ~,** **over ~** por encima de él, sobre él; **below ~,** **under ~** debajo de él; **~'s 6 o'clock** son las seis; **~'s 2 hours on the train** son dos horas en el tren; **~'s raining** llueve, está lloviendo; **where is ~?** ¿dónde está?; **what is ~?** ¿qué pasa?; **who is ~?** ¿quién es?; **~'s me** soy yo; **he's proud of ~** le enorgullece; **he agreed to ~** está de acuerdo (con ello).

Italian |ital'yən| *a, n* italiano/a *m/f* ♦ *n (LING)* italiano.

italic |ital'ik| *a* cursivo; **~s** *npl* cursiva *sg.*

Italy |it'əlē| *n* Italia.

itch |ich| *n* picazón *f; (fig)* prurito ♦ *vi (person)* sentir *or* tener comezón; *(part of body)* picar; **to be ~ing to do sth** rabiar por hacer algo.

itching |ich'ing| *n* picazón *f,* comezón *f.*

itchy |ich'ē| *a:* **to be ~** picar.

it'd |it'əd| = **it would; it had.**

item |ĭ'təm| *n* artículo; *(on agenda)* asunto (a tratar); *(in program)* número; *(also:* **news ~)** noticia; **~s of clothing** prendas *fpl* de vestir.

itemize |ĭ'təmīz| *vt* detallar.

itinerant |ītin'ûrənt| *a* ambulante.

itinerary |ītin'ərärē| *n* itinerario.

it'll [it'əl] = **it will, it shall.**
its [its] *a* su.
it's [its] = **it is; it has.**
itself [itself'] *pron (reflexive)* sí mismo/a; *(emphatic)* él mismo/ella misma.
ITV *n abbr (Brit = Independent Television)* cadena de televisión comercial independiente del Estado.
IUD *n abbr (= intra-uterine device)* DIU *m.*
I.V. *n (US MED)* gota a gota *m.*
I've [īv] = **I have.**
ivory [ī'vûrē] *n* marfil *m.*
Ivory Coast *n:* **the ~** la Costa de Marfil.
ivory tower *n (fig)* torre *f* de marfil.
ivy [ī'vē] *n* hiedra.
Ivy League *n (US) grupo de famosas universidades en el noreste de los Estados Unidos.*

J

J, j [jā] *n (letter)* J, j *f;* **J for Jig** J de José.
JA *n abbr = judge advocate.*
J/A *abbr = joint account.*
jab [jab] *vt (elbow)* dar un codazo a; *(punch)* dar un golpe rápido a ♦ *vi:* **to ~ at** intentar golpear a; **to ~ sth into sth** clavar algo en algo ♦ *n* codazo; golpe *m* (rápido); *(MED col)* pinchazo.
jabber [jab'ûr] *vt, vi* farfullar.
jack [jak] *n (AUT)* gato; *(CARDS)* sota; *(Brit BOWLS)* boliche *m.*
  jack in *vt (col)* dejar.
  jack up *vt (AUT)* alzar con gato.
jackal [jak'əl] *n (ZOOL)* chacal *m.*
jackass [jak'as] *n (also fig)* asno, burro.
jackdaw [jak'dô] *n* grajo/a, chova.
jacket [jak'it] *n* chaqueta, americana; *(of boiler etc)* camisa; *(of book)* sobrecubierta.
jack-in-the-box [jak'intþəbáks] *n* caja sorpresa, caja de resorte.
jackknife [jak'nīf] *vi* colear.
jack-of-all-trades [jak'əvóltrādz'] *n* factótum *m.*
jack (plug) [jak (plug)] *n (ELEC)* enchufe *m* de clavija.
jackpot [jak'pát] *n* premio gordo.
jacuzzi [jəko͞o'zē] ® *n* jacuzzi *m* ®.
jade [jād] *n (stone)* jade *m.*
jaded [jā'did] *a (tired)* cansado; *(fed up)* hastiado.
jagged [jag'id] *a* dentado.
jaguar [jag'wâr] *n* jaguar *m.*
jail [jāl] *n* cárcel *f* ♦ *vt* encarcelar.
jailbird [jāl'bûrd] *n* presidiario/a *or* preso/a reincidente.

jailbreak [jāl'brāk] *n* fuga *or* evasión *f* (de la cárcel).
jailer [jā'lûr] *n* carcelero/a.
jalopy [jəláp'ē] *n (col)* cacharro, armatoste *m.*
jam [jam] *n* mermelada; *(also:* **traffic ~)** embotellamiento; *(difficulty)* apuro ♦ *vt (passage etc)* obstruir; *(mechanism, drawer etc)* atascar; *(RADIO)* interferir ♦ *vi* atascarse, trabarse; **to get sb out of a ~** sacar a uno del paso *or* de un apuro; **to ~ sth into sth** meter algo a la fuerza en algo; **the telephone lines are ~med** las líneas están ocupadas.
Jamaica [jəmā'kə] *n* Jamaica.
Jamaican [jəmā'kən] *a, n* jamaicano/a *m/f.*
jamb [jam] *n* jamba.
jamboree [jambərē'] *n* congreso de niños exploradores.
jam-packed [jam'pakt'] *a:* **~ (with)** atestado (de).
jam session *n* concierto improvisado de jazz/rock *etc.*
Jan. *abbr (= January)* ene.
jangle [jang'gəl] *vi* sonar (de manera) discordante.
janitor [jan'itûr] *n (caretaker)* portero, conserje *m.*
January [jan'yo͞owärē] *n* enero.
Japan [jəpan'] *n* (el) Japón.
Japanese [japənēz'] *a* japonés/esa ♦ *n (pl inv)* japonés/esa *m/f; (LING)* japonés *m.*
jar [jâr] *n (glass: large)* jarra; *(: small)* tarro ♦ *vi (sound)* chirriar; *(colors)* desentonar.
jargon [jâr'gən] *n* jerga.
jarring [jâr'ing] *a (sound, color)* discordante, desafinado, chocante.
Jas. *abbr = James.*
jasmin(e) [jaz'min] *n* jazmín *m.*
jaundice [jôn'dis] *n* ictericia.
jaundiced [jôn'dist] *a (fig: embittered)* amargado; *(: disillusioned)* desilusionado.
jaunt [jônt] *n* excursión *f.*
jaunty [jôn'tē] *a* alegre, desenvuelto.
Java [jâv'ə] *n* Java.
javelin [jav'lin] *n* jabalina.
jaw [jó] *n* mandíbula; **~s** *npl (TECH: of vise etc)* mordaza *sg.*
jawbone [jó'bōn] *n* mandíbula, quijada.
jay [jā] *n (ZOOL)* arrendajo.
jaywalker [jā'wókûr] *n* peatón/ona *m/f* imprudente.
jazz [jaz] *n* jazz *m.*
  jazz up *vt (liven up)* animar, avivar.
jazz band *n* orquesta de jazz.
jazzy [jaz'ē] *a* de colores llamativos.
JCC *n abbr (US)* = *Junior Chamber of Commerce.*
JCS *n abbr (US)* = *Joint Chiefs of Staff.*
JD *n abbr (US:* = *Doctor of Laws)* título universitario; *(:* = *Justice Department)* Ministerio de Justicia.

jealous [jel'əs] *a* (*gen*) celoso; (*envious*) envidioso; **to be ~** tener celos.

jealously [jel'əslē] *ad* (*enviously*) envidiosamente; (*watchfully*) vigilantemente, celosamente.

jealousy [jel'əsē] *n* celos *mpl*; envidia.

jeans [jēnz] *npl* (pantalones *mpl*) vaqueros *mpl or* tejanos *mpl*.

jeep [jēp] *n* jeep *m*.

jeer [jēr] *vi*: **to ~ (at)** (*boo*) abuchear; (*mock*) mofarse (de).

jeering [jē'ring] *a* (*crowd*) insolente, ofensivo ♦ *n* protestas *fpl*, burlas *fpl*.

jelly [jel'ē] *n* jalea, gelatina.

jellyfish [jel'ēfish] *n* medusa.

jemmy [jem'ē] *n* palanqueta.

jeopardize [jep'ûrdīz] *vt* arriesgar, poner en peligro.

jeopardy [jep'ûrdē] *n*: **to be in ~** estar en peligro.

jerk [jûrk] *n* (*jolt*) sacudida; (*wrench*) tirón *m*; (*US col*) pesado/a ♦ *vt* dar una sacudida a; tirar bruscamente de ♦ *vi* (*vehicle*) traquetear.

jerkin [jûr'kin] *n* chaleco.

jerky [jûr'kē] *a* espasmódico.

jerry-built [jär'ēbilt] *a* mal construido.

jerry can [jär'ē kan] *n* bidón *m*.

jersey [jûr'zē] *n* jersey *m*; (*fabric*) tejido de punto.

Jerusalem [jərōō'sələm] *n* Jerusalén *m*.

jest [jest] *n* broma.

jester [jes'tûr] *n* bufón *m*.

Jesus [jē'səs] *n* Jesús *m*; **~ Christ** Jesucristo.

jet [jet] *n* (*of gas, liquid*) chorro; (*AVIAT*) avión *m* a reacción.

jet-black [jet'blak'] *a* negro como el azabache.

jet engine *n* motor *m* a reacción.

jet lag *n* desorientación *f* después de un largo vuelo.

jetsam [jet'səm] *n* echazón *f*.

jettison [jet'əsən] *vt* desechar.

jetty [jet'ē] *n* muelle *m*, embarcadero.

Jew [jōō] *n* judío.

jewel [jōō'əl] *n* joya; (*in watch*) rubí *m*.

jeweler, (*Brit*) **jeweller** [jōō'əlûr] *n* joyero/a; **~'s (shop)** (*Brit*) joyería.

jewelry, (*Brit*) **jewellery** [jōō'əlrē] *n* joyas *fpl*, alhajas *fpl*; **~ store** (*US*) joyería.

Jewess [jōō'is] *n* judía.

Jewish [jōō'ish] *a* judío.

JFK *n abbr* (*US*) = *John Fitzgerald Kennedy International Airport*.

jib [jib] *vi* (*horse*) plantarse; **to ~ at doing sth** resistirse a hacer algo.

jibe [jib] *n* mofa.

jiffy [jif'ē] *n* (*col*): **in a ~** en un santiamén.

jig [jig] *n* (*dance, tune*) giga.

jigsaw [jig'sô] *n* (*also:* **~ puzzle**) rompecabezas *m inv*; (*tool*) sierra de vaivén.

jilt [jilt] *vt* dejar plantado a.

jingle [jing'gəl] *n* (*advert*) musiquilla ♦ *vi* tintinear.

jingoism [jing'gōizəm] *n* patriotería, jingoísmo.

jinx [jingks] *n*: **there's a ~ on it** está gafado.

jitters [jit'ûrz] *npl* (*col*): **to get the ~** ponerse nervioso.

jittery [jit'ûrē] *a* (*col*) muy inquieto, nervioso.

jiujitsu [jōōjit'sōō] *n* ju-jitsu *m*.

job [jâb] *n* trabajo; (*task*) tarea; (*duty*) deber *m*; (*post*) empleo; (*fam: difficulty*) dificultad *f*; **it's a good ~ that...** menos mal que...! ¡estupendo!; **a part-time/full-time ~** un trabajo de medio tiempo/tiempo completo; **that's not my ~** eso no me incumbe *or* toca a mí; **he's only doing his ~** está cumpliendo nada más.

job centre *n* (*Brit*) oficina estatal de colocaciones.

job creation scheme *n* (*Brit*) plan *m* de creación de puestos de trabajo.

job description *n* descripción *f* del puesto de trabajo.

jobless [jâb'lis] *a* sin trabajo.

job lot *n* lote *m* de mercancías, saldo.

job satisfaction *n* satisfacción *f* en el trabajo.

job security *n* garantía de trabajo.

job specification *n* especificación *f* del trabajo, profesiograma *m*.

jockey [jâk'ē] *n* jockey *m/f* ♦ *vi*: **to ~ for position** maniobrar para conseguir una posición.

jocular [jâk'yəlûr] *a* (*humorous*) gracioso; (*merry*) alegre.

jodhpurs [jâd'pûrz] *npl* pantalón *msg* de montar.

jog [jâg] *vt* empujar (ligeramente) ♦ *vi* (*run*) hacer footing; **to ~ along** ir tirando; **to ~ sb's memory** refrescar la memoria a uno.

jogger [jâg'ûr] *n* corredor(a) *m/f*.

jogging [jâg'ing] *n* footing *m*.

john [jân] *n* (*US col*) servicios *mpl*.

join [join] *vt* (*things*) juntar, unir; (*become member of: club*) hacerse socio de; (*POL: party*) afiliarse a; (*meet: people*) reunirse con; (*fig*) juntarse con ♦ *vi* (*roads*) empalmar; (*rivers*) confluir ♦ *n* juntura; **will you ~ us for dinner?** ¿nos acompañas a cenar?; **I'll ~ you later** te encontraré luego; **to ~ forces (with)** aliarse (con).

join in *vi* tomar parte, participar ♦ *vt fus* tomar parte *or* participar en.

join up *vi* unirse; (*MIL*) alistarse.

joiner [join'ûr] *n* carpintero/a.

joinery [joi'nûrē] *n* carpintería.

joint [joint] *n* (*TECH*) junta, unión *f*; (*ANAT*) articulación *f*; (*Brit CULIN*) pieza de carne (para asar); (*col: place*) garito ♦ *a* (*common*) común; (*combined*) combinado; (*responsibility*) compartido; (*committee*) mixto.

joint account n (with bank etc) cuenta común.
jointly [joint'lē] ad (gen) en común; (collectively) colectivamente; (together) conjuntamente.
joint owners npl copropietarios mpl.
joint ownership n copropiedad f, propiedad f común.
joint-stock bank [joint'stâk' bangk] n banco por acciones.
joint-stock company [joint'stâk' kum'pənē] n sociedad f anónima.
joint venture n sociedad f conjunta.
joist [joist] n viga.
joke [jōk] n chiste m; (also: **practical ~**) broma ♦ vi bromear; **to play a ~ on** gastar una broma a.
joker [jō'kûr] n chistoso/a, bromista m/f; (CARDS) comodín m.
joking [jō'king] n bromas fpl.
jokingly [jō'kinglē] ad en broma.
jollity [jâl'itē] n alegría.
jolly [jâl'ē] a (merry) alegre; (Brit: enjoyable) divertido ♦ ad (col) muy, terriblemente; **~ good!** (Brit) ¡estupendo!
jolt [jōlt] n (shake) sacudida; (blow) golpe m; (shock) susto ♦ vt sacudir; asustar.
Jordan [jôr'dən] n (country) Jordania; (river) Jordán m.
joss stick [jâs stik] n pebete m.
jostle [jâs'əl] vt dar empellones a, codear.
jot [jât] n: **not one ~** ni jota, ni pizca.
jot down vt apuntar.
jotter [jât'ûr] n (Brit) bloc m.
journal [jûr'nəl] n (paper) periódico; (magazine) revista; (diary) diario.
journalese [jûrnəlēz'] n (pej) lenguaje m periodístico.
journalism [jûr'nəlizəm] n periodismo.
journalist [jûr'nəlist] n periodista m/f, reportero/a.
journey [jûr'nē] n viaje m; (distance covered) trayecto ♦ vi viajar; **return ~** viaje de regreso; **a 5-hour ~** un viaje de 5 horas.
jovial [jō'vēəl] a risueño, alegre.
jowl [joul] n quijada.
joy [joi] n alegría.
joyful [joi'fəl] a alegre.
joyfully [joi'fəlē] ad alegremente.
joyous [joi'əs] a alegre.
joy ride n (illegal) paseo en coche robado.
joystick [joi'stik] n (AVIAT) palanca de mando; (COMPUT) palanca de control.
JP n abbr = **Justice of the Peace.**
Jr. abbr = junior.
JTPA n abbr (US: = Job Training Partnership Act) programa gubernamental de formación profesional.
jubilant [jōō'bələnt] a jubiloso.
jubilation [jōōbəlā'shən] n júbilo.
jubilee [jōō'bəlē] n aniversario; **silver ~** vigésimo quinto aniversario.
judge [juj] n juez m/f ♦ vt juzgar; (esti-

mate) considerar; (: weight, size etc) calcular ♦ vi: **judging** or **to ~ by his expression** a juzgar por su expresión; **as far as I can ~** por lo que puedo entender, a mi entender; **I ~d it necessary to inform him** lo consideré necesario informarle.
judge advocate n (MIL) auditor m de guerra.
judg(e)ment [juj'mənt] n juicio; (punishment) sentencia, fallo; **to pass ~ (on)** (LAW) pronunciar or dictar sentencia (sobre); (fig) emitir un juicio crítico or dictaminar (sobre); **in my ~** a mi criterio.
judicial [jōōdish'əl] a judicial.
judiciary [jōōdish'ēârē] n poder m judicial, magistratura.
judicious [jōōdish'əs] a juicioso.
judo [jōō'dō] n judo.
jug [jug] n jarro.
juggernaut [jug'ûrnôt] n (huge truck) camionazo m.
juggle [jug'əl] vi hacer juegos malabares.
juggler [jug'lûr] n malabarista m/f.
Jugoslav [yōō'gōslâv] etc = **Yugoslav** etc.
jugular [jug'yəlûr] a: **~ vein** vena yugular.
juice [jōōs] n zumo, jugo (esp LAm); (of meat) jugo; (col: gas): **we've run out of ~** se nos acabó la gasolina.
juiciness [jōō'sēnis] n jugosidad f.
juicy [jōō'sē] a jugoso.
jujitsu [jōōjit'sōō] n = **juijitsu.**
jukebox [jōōk'bâks] n tocadiscos m inv tragaperras.
Jul. abbr (= July) jul.
July [julī'] n julio; **the first of ~** el primero de julio; **during ~** en el mes de julio; **in ~ of next year** en julio del año que viene.
jumble [jum'bəl] n revoltijo ♦ vt (also: **~ together**, **~ up**: mix up) revolver; (: disarrange) mezclar.
jumble sale n (Brit) venta de objetos usados con fines benéficos.
jumbo (jet) [jum'bō (jet)] n jumbo.
jump [jump] vi saltar, dar saltos; (start) asustarse, sobresaltarse; (increase) aumentar ♦ vt saltar ♦ n salto; (fence) obstáculo; (increase) aumento.
jump around vi dar saltos, brincar.
jump at vt fus (fig) apresurarse a aprovechar; **he ~ed at the offer** se apresuró a aceptar la oferta.
jump down vi bajar de un salto, saltar a tierra.
jump up vi levantarse de un salto.
jumped-up [jumpt'up] a (Brit pej) engreído.
jumper [jum'pûr] n (US: pinafore dress) mandil m; (Brit: pullover) suéter m, jersey m; (SPORT) saltador(a) m/f.
jumper cables, (Brit) **jump leads** npl cables mpl puente de batería.
jump rope n (US) saltar m a la comba.
jump suit n mono.

jumpy [jum'pē] a nervioso.
Jun. abbr = **junior**; (= June) jun.
junction [jungk'shən] n (of roads) cruce m;
(RAIL) empalme m.
juncture [jungk'chúr] n: **at this** ~ en este
momento, en esta coyuntura.
June [jōōn] n junio.
jungle [jung'gəl] n selva, jungla.
junior [jōōn'yûr] a (in age) menor, más joven; (competition) juvenil; (position) subalterno ♦ n menor m/f, joven m/f; **he's** ~
to me es menor que yo.
junior executive n ejecutivo/a subalterno/
a.
junior high school n (US) instituto de
enseñanza media.
junior school n (Brit) escuela primaria.
junk [jungk] n (cheap goods) baratijas fpl;
(trash) trastos mpl viejos; (rubbish) basura; (ship) junco ♦ vt (col) desechar.
junk dealer n vendedor(a) m/f de objetos
usados.
junket [jung'kit] n (CULIN) dulce de leche
cuajada; (col): **to go on a** ~, **go** ~**ing** viajar a costo ajeno or del erario público.
junk foods npl alimentos preparados y
envasados de escaso valor nutritivo.
junkie [jung'kē] n (col) yonqui m/f,
heroinómano/a.
junk room n trastero.
junk shop n tienda de objetos usados.
junkyard [jungk'yárd] n depósito de chatarra.
junta [hōōn'tə] n junta militar.
Jupiter [jōō'pitûr] n (MYTHOLOGY, ASTRO)
Júpiter m.
jurisdiction [jōōrisdik'shən] n jurisdicción f;
it falls or **comes within/outside our** ~ es/
no es de nuestra competencia.
jurisprudence [jōōrisprōōd'əns] n jurisprudencia.
juror [jōō'rûr] n jurado.
jury [jōō'rē] n jurado.
jury box n tribuna del jurado.
juryman [jōōr'ēmən] n miembro del jurado.
just [just] a justo ♦ ad (exactly) exactamente; (only) sólo, solamente; **he's** ~
done it/left acaba de hacerlo/irse; **I've** ~
seen him acabo de verle; ~ **right** perfecto,
perfectamente; ~ **two o'clock** las dos en
punto; **she's** ~ **as clever as you** es tan
lista como tú; ~ **as well that...** menos mal
que...; **it's** ~ **as well you didn't go** menos
mal que no fuiste; **it's** ~ **as good (as)** es
igual (que), es tan bueno (como); ~ **as he
was leaving** en el momento en que se mar-
chaba; **we were** ~ **going** ya nos íbamos; **I
was** ~ **about to phone** estaba a punto de
llamar; ~ **before/enough** justo antes/lo
suficiente; ~ **here** aquí mismo; **he** ~
missed falló por poco; ~ **listen to this**
escucha esto un momento; ~ **ask someone
the way** simplemente pregúntale a uno por

dónde se va; **not** ~ **now** ahora no.
justice [jus'tis] n justicia; **this photo
doesn't do you** ~ esta foto no te favorece.
Justice of the Peace (JP) n juez m/f de
paz.
justifiable [jus'tifīəbəl] a justificable,
justificado.
justifiably [jus'təfīəblē] ad justificadamente,
con razón.
justification [justəfəkā'shən] n justificación
f.
justify [jus'təfī] vt justificar; (text) alinear,
justificar; **to be justified in doing sth** tener motivo para or razón al hacer algo.
justly [just'lē] ad (gen) justamente; (with
reason) con razón.
justness [just'nis] n justicia.
jut [jut] vi (also: ~ **out**) sobresalir.
jute [jōōt] n yute m.
juvenile [jōō'vənəl] a juvenil; (court) de
menores ♦ n joven m/f, menor m/f de edad.
juvenile delinquency n delincuencia juvenil.
juvenile delinquent n delincuente m/f juvenil.
juxtapose [jukstəpōz'] vt yuxtaponer.
juxtaposition [jukstəpəzish'ən] n yuxtaposición f.

K

K, k [kā] n (letter) K, k f; **K for King** K de
Kilo.
K [kā] abbr (= one thousand) K; = **kilobyte**.
kaftan [kaf'tən] n caftán m.
Kalahari Desert [kâləhâr'ē dcz'ûrt] n desierto de Kalahari.
kale [kāl] n col f rizada.
kaleidoscope [kəlī'dəskōp] n calidoscopio.
Kampala [kâmpâl'ə] n Kampala.
Kampuchea [kampōōchē'ə] n Kampuchea.
kangaroo [kanggərōō'] n canguro.
Kans. abbr (US) = Kansas.
kaput [kəpōōt'] a (col) roto, estropeado.
karate [kərâ'tē] n karate m.
Kashmir [kazh'mēr] n Cachemira.
kayak [kī'ak] n kayak m.
kd abbr (US: = knocked down) desmontado.
kebab [kəbâb'] n pincho moruno, brocheta.
keel [kēl] n quilla; **on an even** ~ (fig) en
equilibrio.
   keel over vi (NAUT) zozobrar, volcarse;
(person) desplomarse.
keen [kēn] a (interest, desire) grande, vivo;
(eye, intelligence) agudo; (competition)
intenso; (edge) afilado; (Brit: eager)

entusiasta; **to be ~ to do** *or* **on doing sth** tener muchas ganas de hacer algo; **to be ~ on sth/sb** interesarse por algo/uno; **I'm not ~ on going** no tengo ganas de ir.

keenly |kēn'lē| *ad* (*enthusiastically*) con entusiasmo; (*acutely*) vivamente; (*intensely*) intensamente.

keenness |kēn'nis| *n* (*eagerness*) entusiasmo, interés *m*.

keep |kēp| *vb* (*pt, pp* **kept** |kєpt|) *vt* (*retain, preserve*) guardar; (*hold back*) quedarse con; (*shop*) ser propietario de; (*feed: family etc*) mantener; (*promise*) cumplir; (*chickens, bees etc*) criar ♦ *vi* (*food*) conservarse; (*remain*) seguir, continuar ♦ *n* (*of castle*) torreón *m*; (*food etc*) comida, subsistencia; **to ~ doing sth** seguir haciendo algo; **to ~ sb from doing sth** impedir a uno hacer algo; **to ~ sth from happening** impedir que algo ocurra; **to ~ sb happy** hacer a uno feliz; **to ~ sb waiting** hacer esperar a uno; **to ~ a place tidy** mantener un lugar limpio; **to ~ sth to o.s.** guardar algo para sí mismo; **to ~ time** (*clock*) mantener la hora exacta; **~ the change** quédese con la vuelta; **to ~ an appointment** guardar cita; **to ~ a record** *or* **note of sth** tomar nota de *or* apuntar algo; *see also* **keeps**.

keep away *vt*: **to ~ sth/sb away from sb** mantener algo/a uno aparte de uno ♦ *vi*: **to ~ away (from)** mantenerse aparte (de).

keep back *vt* (*crowd, tears, money*) contener, reprimir; (*conceal: information*): **to ~ sth back from sb** ocultar algo a uno ♦ *vi* hacerse a un lado.

keep down *vt* (*control: prices, spending*) controlar; (*retain: food*) retener ♦ *vi* seguir agachado, no levantar la cabeza.

keep in *vt* (*invalid, child*) impedir que salga, no dejar salir ♦ *vi* (*col*): **to ~ in with sb** congraciarse con uno.

keep off *vt* (*dog, person*) mantener a distancia ♦ *vi* evitar; **~ your hands off!** ¡no toques!; **"~ off the grass"** "prohibido pisar el césped".

keep on *vi* seguir, continuar.

keep out *vi* (*stay out*) permanecer fuera; **"~ out"** "prohibida la entrada".

keep up *vt* mantener, conservar ♦ *vi* no retrasarse; (*fig: in comprehension*) seguir (la corriente); **to ~ up with** (*pace*) ir al paso de; (*level*) mantenerse a la altura de; **to ~ up with sb** seguir el ritmo a uno; (*fig*) seguir a uno.

keeper |kē'pûr| *n* guardián/ana *m/f*.

keep-fit |kēp'fit'| *n* gimnasia (para mantenerse en forma).

keeping |kē'ping| *n* (*care*) cuidado; **in ~ with** de acuerdo con.

keeps |kēps| *n*: **for ~** (*col*) para siempre.

keepsake |kēp'sāk| *n* recuerdo.

keg |kєg| *n* barrilete *m*, barril *m*.

Ken. *abbr* (*US*) = *Kentucky*.

kennel |kєn'əl| *n* perrera; **~s** *npl* perreras *fpl*.

Kenya |kєn'yə| *n* Kenia.

Kenyan |kєn'yən| *a, n* keniano/a *m/f*.

kept |kєpt| *pt, pp of* **keep**.

kerb |kûrb| *n* (*Brit*) bordillo.

kernel |kûr'nəl| *n* (*nut*) fruta; (*fig*) meollo.

kerosene |kār'əsēn| *n* keroseno.

kestrel |kєs'trəl| *n* cernícalo.

ketchup |kєch'əp| *n* salsa de tomate, catsup *m*.

kettle |kєt'əl| *n* hervidor *m*, olla.

kettle drum *n* (*MUS*) timbal *m*.

key |kē| *n* (*gen*) llave *f*; (*MUS*) tono; (*of piano, typewriter*) tecla; (*on map*) clave *f* ♦ *cpd* (*vital: position, industry etc*) clave ♦ *vt* (*also*: **~ in**) teclear.

keyboard |kē'bôrd| *n* teclado ♦ *vt* (*text*) teclear.

keyed up |kēd up| *a* (*person*) nervioso; **to be (all) ~** estar nervioso *or* emocionado.

keyhole |kē'hōl| *n* ojo (de la cerradura).

key man *n* hombre *m* clave.

keynote |kē'nōt| *n* (*MUS*) tónica; (*fig*) idea fundamental.

keynote speech *n* discurso de apertura.

keypad |kē'pad| *n* teclado numérico.

key ring *n* llavero.

keystone |kē'stōn| *n* piedra clave.

keystroke |kē'strōk| *n* pulsación *f* (de una tecla).

kg *abbr* (= *kilogram*) kg.

KGB *n abbr* KGB *f*.

khaki |kak'ē| *n* caqui *m*.

kibbutz, **~im** |kibōōts', -ēm| *n* kibutz *m*.

kick |kik| *vt* (*person*) dar una patada a; (*ball*) dar un puntapié a ♦ *vi* (*horse*) dar coces ♦ *n* patada; puntapié *m*; (*of rifle*) culetazo; (*col: thrill*): **he does it for ~s** lo hace por pura diversión.

kick around *vt* (*idea*) dar vueltas a; (*person*) tratar a patadas a.

kick off *vi* (*SPORT*) hacer el saque inicial.

kick-start |kik'stârt| *n* (*also*: **~er**) (pedal *m* de) arranque *m*.

kid |kid| *n* (*col: child*) chiquillo/a; (*animal*) cabrito; (*leather*) cabritilla ♦ *vi* (*col*) bromear.

kidnap |kid'nap| *vt* secuestrar.

kidnap(p)er |kid'napûr| *n* secuestrador(a) *m/f*.

kidnap(p)ing |kid'naping| *n* secuestro.

kidney |kid'nē| *n* riñón *m*.

kidney bean *n* judía, alubia.

kidney machine *n* riñón *m* artificial.

Kilimanjaro |kiləmənjär'ō| *n* Kilimanjaro.

kill |kil| *vt* matar; (*murder*) asesinar; (*fig: story*) suprimir; (: *rumor*) acabar con ♦ *n* matanza; **to ~ time** matar el tiempo.

kill off *vt* exterminar, terminar con; (*fig*) echar por tierra.

killer |kil'ûr| *n* asesino/a.

killing |kil'ing| *n* (*one*) asesinato; (*several*) matanza; (*COMM*): **to make a ~** tener un gran éxito financiero.

killjoy |kil'joi| *n* aguafiestas *m/f inv.*

kiln |kiln| *n* horno.

kilo |kē'lō| *n* (*abbr:* = *kilogram(me)*) kilo.

kilobyte |kil'əbīt| *n* (*COMPUT*) kilobyte *m*, kiloocteto.

kilogram, (*Brit*) **kilogramme** |kil'əgram| *n* kilogramo.

kilometer, (*Brit*) **kilometre** |kil'əmētûr| *n* kilómetro.

kilowatt |kil'əwät| *n* kilovatio.

kilt |kilt| *n* falda escocesa.

kilter |kil'tûr| *n*: **out of ~** desbaratado.

kimono |kimō'nō| *n* quimono.

kin |kin| *n* parientes *mpl.*

kind |kīnd| *a* (*treatment*) bueno, cariñoso; (*person, act, word*) amable, atento ♦ *n* clase *f*, especie *f*; (*species*) género; **in ~** (*COMM*) en especie; **a ~ of** una especie de; **to be two of a ~** ser tal para cual; **would you be ~ enough to ...?, would you be so ~ as to ...?** ¿me hace el favor de ...?; **it's very ~ of you (to do)** le agradezco mucho (el que haya hecho).

kindergarten |kin'dûrgârtən| *n* jardín *m* de infantes.

kind-hearted |kīnd'hârtid| *a* bondadoso, de buen corazón.

kindle |kin'dəl| *vt* encender.

kindliness |kīnd'lēnis| *n* bondad *f*, amabilidad *f.*

kindling |kind'ling| *n* leña (menuda).

kindly |kīnd'lē| *a* bondadoso; (*gentle*) cariñoso ♦ *ad* bondadosamente, amablemente; **will you ~...** sea usted tan amable de... .

kindness |kīnd'nis| *n* bondad *f*, amabilidad *f.*

kindred |kin'drid| *n* familia, parientes *mpl* ♦ *a*: **~ spirits** almas *fpl* gemelas.

kinetic |kinet'ik| *a* cinético.

king |king| *n* rey *m.*

kingdom |king'dəm| *n* reino.

kingfisher |king'fishûr| *n* martín *m* pescador.

kingpin |king'pin| *n* (*TECH*) perno real *or* pinzote; (*fig*) persona clave.

king-size(d) |king'sīz(d)| *a* de tamaño gigante; (*cigarette*) extra largo.

kink |kingk| *n* (*in rope etc*) enroscadura; (*in hair*) rizo; (*fig: emotional, psychological*) trauma *m*, manía.

kinky |king'kē| *a* (*pej*) perverso.

kinship |kin'ship| *n* parentesco, afinidad *f.*

kinsman |kinz'mən| *n* pariente *m.*

kinswoman |kinz'woomən| *n* parienta.

kiosk |kēăsk'| *n* quiosco; (*Brit TEL*) cabina; **newspaper ~** quiosco, kiosco.

kipper |kip'ûr| *n* arenque *m* ahumado.

kiss |kis| *n* beso ♦ *vt* besar; **~ of life** (*Brit: artificial respiration*) respiración *f* artificial; **to ~ sb goodbye** dar un beso de despedida a uno; **to ~ (each other)** besarse.

kit |kit| *n* avíos *mpl*; (*equipment*) equipo; (*set of tools etc*) (caja de) herramientas *fpl*; (*assembly ~*) juego de armar; **tool ~** juego *or* estuche *m* de herramientas.

kit out *vt* (*Brit*) equipar.

kitbag |kit'bag| *n* (*MIL*) petate *m.*

kitchen |kich'ən| *n* cocina.

kitchen garden *n* huerto.

kitchen sink *n* fregadero.

kitchen unit *n* mueble *m* de cocina.

kitchenware |kich'ənwär| *n* batería de cocina.

kite |kīt| *n* (*toy*) cometa.

kith |kith| *n*: **~ and kin** parientes *mpl* y allegados.

kitten |kit'ən| *n* gatito/a.

kitty |kit'ē| *n* (*pool of money*) fondo común; (*CARDS*) puesta.

KKK *n abbr* (*US*) = *Ku Klux Klan.*

Kleenex |klē'neks| ® *n* pañuelo de papel.

kleptomaniac |kleptəmā'nēak| *n* cleptómano/a.

km *abbr* (= *kilometer*) km.

km/h *abbr* (= *kilometers per hour*) km/h.

knack |nak| *n*: **to have the ~ of doing sth** tener el don de hacer algo.

knapsack |nap'sak| *n* mochila.

knead |nēd| *vt* amasar.

knee |nē| *n* rodilla.

kneecap |nē'kap| *n* rótula.

knee-deep |nē'dēp| *a*: **the water was ~** el agua llegaba hasta la rodilla.

kneel *pt, pp* **knelt** |nēl, nelt| *vi* (*also: ~ down*) arrodillarse.

kneepad |nē'pad| *n* rodillera.

knell |nel| *n* toque *m* de difuntos.

knelt |nelt| *pt, pp of* **kneel.**

knew |nōō| *pt of* **know.**

knickers |nik'ûrz| *npl* (*Brit*) bragas *fpl.*

knick-knack |nik'nak| *n* chuchería, baratija.

knife |nīf| *n* (*pl* **knives**) cuchillo ♦ *vt* acuchillar; **~, fork and spoon** cubiertos *mpl.*

knight |nīt| *n* caballero; (*CHESS*) caballo.

knighthood |nīt'hōōd| *n* (*Brit: title*): **to get a ~** recibir el título de *Sir.*

knit |nit| *vt* tejer, tricotar; (*brows*) fruncir; (*fig*): **to ~ together** unir, juntar ♦ *vi* tejer, tricotar; (*bones*) soldarse.

knitted |nit'id| *a* tejido.

knitting |nit'ing| *n* labor *f* de punto.

knitting machine *n* máquina de calcetar *or* tricotar.

knitting needle *n* aguja de tejer.

knitting pattern *n* patrón *m* para tricotar.

knitwear |nit'wär| *n* prendas *fpl* de punto.

knives |nīvz| *npl of* **knife.**

knob |nâb| *n* (*of door*) tirador *m*; (*of stick*) puño; (*lump*) bulto; (*fig*): **a ~ of butter**

(*Brit*) un pedazo de mantequilla.

knobby, [nâb'ē] (*Brit*) **knobbly** [nâb'lē] *a* (*wood, surface*) nudoso; (*knee*) huesudo.

knock [nâk] *vt* (*strike*) golpear; (*bump into*) chocar contra; (*fig: col*) criticar ♦ *vi* (*at door etc*): **to ~ at/on** llamar a ♦ *n* golpe *m*; (*on door*) llamada; **he ~ed at the door** llamó a la puerta.

knock down *vt* (*pedestrian*) atropellar; (*price*) rebajar.

knock off *vi* (*col: finish*) salir del trabajo ♦ *vt* (*col: steal*) birlar; (*strike off*) quitar; (*fig: from price, record*): **to ~ off $10** rebajar en $10.

knock out *vt* dejar sin sentido; (*BOXING*) poner fuera de combate, dejar K.O.; (*stop*) estropear, dejar fuera de servicio.

knock over *vt* (*object*) derribar, tirar; (*pedestrian*) atropellar.

knockdown [nâk'doun] *a* (*Brit: price*) de regalo.

knocker [nâk'ûr] *n* (*on door*) aldaba.

knock-for-knock [nâk'fûrnâk'] *a* (*Brit*): **~ agreement** acuerdo de pago respectivo.

knocking [nâk'ing] *n* golpes *mpl*, golpeteo.

knock-kneed [nâk'nēd] *a* patizambo.

knock-on effect [nâk'ân ifekt'] *n* repercusión *f*.

knockout [nâk'out] *n* (*BOXING*) K.O. *m*, knockout *m*.

knock-up [nâk'up] *n* (*Brit TENNIS*) peloteo.

knot [nât] *n* (*gen*) nudo ♦ *vt* anudar; **to tie a ~** anudar, atar.

knotted [nât'id] *a* anudado.

knotty [nât'ē] *a* (*fig*) complicado.

know [nō] *vb* (*pt* **knew**, *pp* **known** [nōō, nōn]) *vt* (*gen*) saber; (*person, author, place*) conocer ♦ *vi*: **as far as I ~** ... que yo sepa ...; **yes, I ~** sí, ya lo sé; **I don't ~** no lo sé; **to ~ how to do** saber hacer; **to ~ how to swim** saber nadar; **to ~ about** *or* **of sb/sth** saber de uno/algo; **to get to ~ sth** enterarse de algo; **I ~ nothing about it** no sé nada de eso; **I don't ~ him** no lo *or* le conozco; **to ~ right from wrong** saber distinguir el bien del mal.

know-all [nō'ôl] *n* (*Brit pej*) = **know-it-all**.

know-how [nō'hou] *n* conocimientos *mpl*.

knowing [nō'ing] *a* (*look etc*) de complicidad.

knowingly [nō'inglē] *ad* (*purposely*) adrede; (*smile, look*) con complicidad.

know-it-all [nō'itôl] *n* (*US*) sabelotodo *m/f inv*, sabihondo/a.

knowledge [nâl'ij] *n* (*gen*) conocimiento; (*learning*) saber *m*, conocimientos *mpl*; **to have no ~ of** no saber nada de; **with my ~** con mis conocimientos, sabiéndolo; **to (the best of) my ~** a mi entender, que yo sepa; **not to my ~** que yo sepa, no; **it is common ~ that** ... es del dominio público que ...; **it has come to my ~ that** ... me he enterado de que ...; **to have a working**

~ **of Spanish** manejárselas con el español.

knowledgeable [nâl'ijəbəl] *a* entendido, erudito.

known [nōn] *pp of* **know** ♦ *a* (*thief, facts*) conocido; (*expert*) reconocido.

knuckle [nuk'əl] *n* nudillo.

knuckle under *vi* someterse.

knuckle-duster [nuk'əldustûr] *n* puño de hierro.

knucklehead [nuk'elhed] *n* (*US*) tonto/a.

KO *abbr n* (= *knockout*) K.O. *m* ♦ *vt* (= *knock out*) dejar K.O.

koala [kōâl'ə] *n* (*also*: **~ bear**) koala *m*.

kook [kōōk] *n* (*US col*) majareta *m/f*, excéntrico/a.

Koran [kôrân'] *n* Corán *m*.

Korea [kôrē'ə] *n* Corea; **North/South ~** Corea del Norte/Sur.

Korean [kôrē'ən] *a, n* coreano/a *m/f*.

kosher [kō'shûr] *a* autorizado por la ley judía.

kowtow [kou'tou] *vi*: **to ~ to sb** humillarse ante uno.

KS *abbr* (*US MAIL*) = *Kansas*.

Kuala Lumpur [kōōâ'lə lōōm'pōōr] *n* Kuala Lumpur *m*.

kudos [kyōō'dōs] *n* gloria, méritos *mpl*.

Kuwait [kōōwât'] *n* Kuwait *m*.

Kuwaiti [kōōât'ē] *a, n* Kuwaití *m/f*.

kW *abbr* (= *kilowatt*) Kv.

KY *abbr* (*US MAIL*) = *Kentucky*.

L

L, l [el] *n* (*letter*) L, l *f*; **L for Love** L de Lorenzo.

L *abbr* (*on maps etc*) = *lake*; *large*; (= *left*) izq.; (*Brit AUT*: = *learner*) L.

l. *abbr* = *liter*.

LA *n abbr* (*US*) = *Los Angeles* ♦ *abbr* (*US MAIL*) = *Louisiana*.

La. *abbr* (*US*) = *Louisiana*.

lab [lab] *n abbr* = **laboratory**.

Lab. *abbr* (*Canada*) = *Labrador*.

label [lā'bəl] *n* etiqueta; (*brand: of record*) sello (discográfico) ♦ *vt* poner etiqueta a.

labor [lā'bûr] (*US*) *n* (*task*) trabajo; (~ *force*) mano *f* de obra; (*workers*) trabajadores *mpl*; (*MED*) (dolores *mpl* de) parto ♦ *vi*: **to ~ (at)** trabajar (en) ♦ *vt* insistir en; **hard ~** trabajos *mpl* forzados; **to be in ~** estar de parto.

laboratory [lab'rətôrē] *n* laboratorio.

labor cost *n* costo de la mano de obra.

Labor Day *n* (*US*) día *m* del trabajador.

labor dispute *n* conflicto laboral.

labored [lā'bûrd] a (breathing) fatigoso;
(style) forzado, pesado.
laborer [lā'bûrûr] n peón m; (on farm) peón
m, obrero; (day ~) jornalero.
labor force n mano f de obra.
labor-intensive [lā'bûrintensiv] a intensivo
en mano de obra.
laborious [labôr'ēas] a penoso.
laboriously [labôr'ēaslē] ad penosamente.
labor relations npl relaciones fpl laborales.
labor-saving [lā'bûrsā'ving] a que ahorra
trabajo.
labor union n (US) sindicato.
labor unrest n (US) conflictividad f laboral.
Labour [lā'bûr] n (Brit POL: also: **the ~
Party**) el partido laborista, los laboristas.
labour [lā'bûr] etc (Brit) = labor etc.
laburnum [labûr'nam] n codeso.
labyrinth [lab'ûrinth] n laberinto.
lace [lās] n encaje m; (of shoe etc) cordón m
♦ vt (shoes: also: ~ up) atarse; (drink:
fortify with spirits) echar licor a.
lacemaking [lās'māking] n obra de encaje.
lacerate [las'arāt] vt lacerar.
laceration [lasarā'shan] n laceración f.
lace-up [lās'up] a (shoes etc) con cordones.
lack [lak] n (absence) falta, carencia;
(scarcity) escasez f ♦ vt faltarle a uno, carecer de; **through** or **for ~ of** por falta de;
to be ~ing faltar, no haber.
lackadaisical [lakadā'zikal] a (careless)
descuidado; (indifferent) indiferente.
lackey [lak'ē] n (also fig) lacayo.
lackluster, (Brit) **lacklustre** [lak'lustûr] a
(surface) deslustrado, deslucido; (style)
inexpresivo; (eyes) apagado.
laconic [lakân'ik] a lacónico.
lacquer [lak'ûr] n laca; **hair ~** (Brit) laca
para el pelo.
lacrosse [lakrôs'] n lacrosse f.
lacy [lā'sē] a (like lace) parecido al encaje.
lad [lad] n muchacho, chico; (in stable etc)
mozo.
ladder [lad'ûr] n escalera (de mano); (Brit:
in tights) carrera ♦ vt (Brit: tights) hacer
una carrera en.
laden [lā'dan] a: ~ **(with)** cargado (de);
fully ~ (truck, ship) cargado hasta el tope.
ladle [lā'dal] n cucharón m.
lady [lā'dē] n señora; (distinguished, noble)
dama; **young ~** señorita; **the ladies'
(room)** los servicios de señoras.
ladybug [lā'debug] n (US) mariquita.
lady doctor n médica, doctora.
lady-in-waiting [lā'dēinwā'ting] n dama de
honor.
ladykiller [lā'dēkilûr] n ladrón m de corazones.
ladylike [lā'dēlīk] a fino.
lag [lag] vi (also: ~ **behind**) retrasarse, quedarse atrás ♦ vt (pipes) revestir.

lager [lâ'gûr] n cerveza (rubia).
lagging [lag'ing] n revestimiento.
lagoon [lagōōn'] n laguna.
Lagos [lâg'ōs] n Lagos m.
laid [lād] pt, pp of lay.
laid-back [lād'bak'] a (col) tranquilo, relajado.
laid up a: **to be ~** (person) tener que
guardar cama.
lain [lān] pp of lie.
lair [lär] n guarida.
laissez-faire [lesâfär'] n laissez-faire m.
laity [lā'itē] n laicado.
lake [lāk] n lago.
lamb [lam] n cordero; (meat) carne f de
cordero.
lamb chop n chuleta de cordero.
lambswool [lamz'wōōl] n lana de cordero.
lame [lām] a cojo; (weak) débil, poco
convincente; ~ **duck** (fig: person) inútil m/
f; (: firm) empresa en quiebra.
lamely [lām'lē] ad (fig) sin convicción.
lament [lament'] n lamento ♦ vt lamentarse
de.
lamentable [lamen'tabal] a lamentable.
lamentation [lamantā'shan] n lamento.
laminated [lam'anātid] a laminado.
lamp [lamp] n lámpara.
lamplight [lamp'līt] n: **by ~** a la luz de la
lámpara.
lampoon [lampōōn'] vt satirizar.
lamppost [lamp'pōst] n (poste m de) farol
m.
lampshade [lamp'shād] n pantalla.
lance [lans] n lanza ♦ vt (MED) abrir con
lanceta.
lance corporal n ≈ soldado de primera
clase.
lancet [lan'sit] n (MED) lanceta.
Lancs [langks] abbr (Brit) = Lancashire.
land [land] n tierra; (country) país m;
(piece of ~) terreno; (estate) tierras fpl,
finca; (AGR) campo ♦ vi (from ship) desembarcar; (AVIAT) aterrizar; (fig: fall)
caer ♦ vt (obtain) conseguir; (passengers,
goods) desembarcar; **to go/travel by ~** ir/
viajar por tierra; **to own ~** ser dueño de
tierras; **to ~ on one's feet** caer de pie;
(fig: to be lucky) salir adelante.
land up vi: **to ~ up in/at** ir a parar a/
en.
landing [lan'ding] n desembarco; aterrizaje
m; (of staircase) rellano.
landing card n (Brit) tarjeta de desembarque.
landing craft n barca de desembarco.
landing gear n (AVIAT) tren m de aterrizaje.
landing strip n pista de aterrizaje.
landlady [land'lādē] n (of boarding house)
patrona; (owner) dueña.
landlocked [land'lâkt] a cercado de tierra.
landlord [land'lôrd] n propietario; (Brit: of

pub etc) patrón *m*.

landlubber [land'lubûr] *n* marinero de agua dulce.

landmark [land'mârk] *n* lugar *m* conocido; **to be a ~** (*fig*) hacer época.

landowner [land'ōnûr] *n* terrateniente *m/f*.

landscape [land'skāp] *n* paisaje *m*.

landscape architecture *n* arquitectura paisajista.

landscaped [land'skāpt] *a* reformado artísticamente.

landscape gardener *n* diseñador(a) *m/f* de paisajes.

landscape gardening *n* jardinería paisajista.

landscape painting *n* (*ART*) paisaje *m*.

landslide [land'slīd] *n* (*GEO*) corrimiento de tierras; (*fig: POL*) victoria arrolladora.

lane [lān] *n* (*in country*) camino; (*in town*) callejón *m*; (*AUT*) carril *m*; (*in race*) calle *f*; (*for air or sea traffic*) ruta; **shipping ~** ruta marina.

language [lang'gwij] *n* lenguaje *m*; (*national tongue*) idioma *m*, lengua; **bad ~** palabrotas *fpl*.

language laboratory *n* laboratorio de idiomas.

language studies *npl* estudios *mpl* filológicos.

languid [lang'gwid] *a* lánguido.

languish [lang'gwish] *vi* languidecer.

languor [lang'gûr] *n* languidez *f*.

languorous [lang'gûrəs] *a* lánguido.

lank [langk] *a* (*hair*) lacio.

lanky [lang'kē] *a* larguirucho.

lanolin [lan'əlin] *n* lanolina.

lantern [lan'tûrn] *n* linterna, farol *m*.

Laos [lā'ōs] *n* Laos *m*.

lap [lap] *n* (*of track*) vuelta; (*of body*): **to sit on sb's ~** sentarse en las rodillas de uno ♦ *vt* (*also:* **~ up**) beber a lengüetadas ♦ *vi* (*waves*) chapotear.

lap up *vt* beber a lengüetadas; (*fig: compliments, attention*) disfrutar; (*lies etc*) tragarse.

La Paz [lâ pâs'] *n* La Paz.

lapdog [lap'dôg] *n* perro faldero.

lapel [ləpel'] *n* solapa.

Lapland [lap'lənd] *n* Laponia.

Laplander [lap'landûr] *n* lapón/ona *m/f*.

lapse [laps] *n* (*fault*) error *m*, fallo; (*moral*) desliz *m* ♦ *vi* (*expire*) caducar; (*morally*) cometer un desliz; (*time*) pasar, transcurrir; **to ~ into bad habits** volver a las andadas; **~ of time** lapso, período; **a ~ of memory** un fallo de memoria.

laptop [lap'tâp] *n* (*also:* **~ computer**) ordenador *m* portátil.

larceny [lâr'sənē] *n* latrocinio.

lard [lârd] *n* manteca (de cerdo).

larder [lâr'dûr] *n* despensa.

large [lârj] *a* grande ♦ *ad:* **by and ~** en general, en términos generales; **at ~** (*free*)

en libertad; (*generally*) en general; **to make ~(r)** hacer mayor *or* más extenso; **a ~ number of people** una gran cantidad de personas; **on a ~ scale** en gran escala.

largely [lârj'lē] *ad* en gran parte.

large-scale [lârj'skāl] *a* (*map, drawing*) en gran escala; (*reforms, business activities*) importante.

largesse [lârjes'] *n* generosidad *f*.

lark [lârk] *n* (*bird*) alondra; (*Brit: joke*) broma.

lark about *vi* bromear, hacer el tonto.

larva, *pl* **larvae** [lâr'və, -ē] *n* larva.

laryngitis [larənji'tis] *n* laringitis *f*.

larynx [lar'ingks] *n* laringe *f*.

lascivious [ləsiv'ēəs] *a* lascivo.

laser [lā'zûr] *n* láser *m*.

laser beam [lā'zûr bēm] *n* rayo láser.

laser printer *n* impresora (por) láser.

lash [lash] *n* latigazo; (*punishment*) azote *m*; (*also:* **eyelash**) pestaña ♦ *vt* azotar; (*tie*) atar.

lash down *vt* sujetar con cuerdas ♦ *vi* (*rain*) caer a trombas.

lash out *vi* (*Brit: col: spend*) gastar a la loca; **to ~ out at** *or* **against sb** lanzar invectivas contra uno.

lashing [lash'ing] *n* (*beating*) azotaina, flagelación *f*.

lass [las] *n* (*Brit*) chica.

lassitude [las'ətōōd] *n* lasitud *f*.

lasso [las'ō] *n* lazo ♦ *vt* coger con lazo.

last [last] *a* (*gen*) último; (*final*) último, final ♦ *ad* por último ♦ *vi* (*endure*) durar; (*continue*) continuar, seguir; **~ night** anoche; **~ week** la semana pasada; **at ~** por fin; **next to (the) ~** penúltimo; **~ time** la última vez; **it ~s (for) 2 hours** dura dos horas.

last-ditch [last'dich'] *a* (*attempt*) de último recurso, último, desesperado.

lasting [las'ting] *a* duradero.

lastly [last'lē] *ad* por último, finalmente.

last-minute [last'min'it] *a* de última hora.

latch [lach] *n* picaporte *m*, pestillo.

latch on to *vt fus* (*cling to: person*) pegarse a; (*: idea*) agarrarse de.

latchkey [lach'kē] *n* llavín *m*.

latchkey child *n* niño cuyos padres trabajan.

late [lāt] *a* (*not on time*) tarde, atrasado; (*towards end of period, life*) tardío; (*hour*) avanzado; (*dead*) fallecido ♦ *ad* tarde; (*behind time, schedule*) con retraso; **to be (10 minutes) ~** llegar con (diez minutos de) retraso; **to be ~ with** estar atrasado con; **~ delivery** entrega tardía; **~ in life** a una edad avanzada; **of ~** últimamente; **in ~ May** hacia fines de mayo; **the ~ Mr X** el difunto Sr X; **to work ~** trabajar hasta tarde.

latecomer [lāt'kumûr] *n* recién llegado/a.

lately [lāt'lē] *ad* últimamente.

lateness [lāt'nis] *n* (*of person*) demora; (*of*

event) tardanza.

latent |lā'tənt| *a* latente; ~ **defect** defecto latente.

later |lā'tûr| *a* (*date etc*) posterior; (*version etc*) más reciente ♦ *ad* más tarde, después; ~ **on today** hoy más tarde.

lateral |lat'ûrəl| *a* lateral.

latest |lā'tist| *a* último; **at the** ~ a más tardar.

latex |lā'tcks| *n* látex *m*.

lathe |lāth| *n* torno.

lather |lath'ûr| *n* espuma (de jabón) ♦ *vt* enjabonar.

Latin |lat'in| *n* latín *m* ♦ *a* latino.

Latin America *n* América Latina, Latinoamérica.

Latin American *a*, *n* latinoamericano/a *m/f*.

latitude |lat'ətōōd| *n* latitud *f*; (*fig: freedom*) latitud *f*, libertad *f*.

latrine |lətrēn'| *n* letrina.

latter |lat'ûr| *a* último; (*of two*) segundo ♦ *n*: **the** ~ el último, éste.

latter-day |lat'ûrdā| *a* moderno.

latterly |lat'ûrlē| *ad* últimamente.

lattice |lat'is| *n* enrejado.

lattice window |lat'is win'dō| *n* ventana enrejada *or* de celosía.

lattice work *n* enrejado.

Latvia |lat'vēə| *n* Letonia, Latvia.

laudable |lô'dəbəl| *a* loable.

laugh |laf| *n* risa; (*loud*) carcajada ♦ *vi* reírse, reír; reírse a carcajadas.

  laugh at *vt fus* reírse de.

  laugh off *vt* tomar a risa.

laughable |laf'əbəl| *a* ridículo.

laughing |laf'ing| *a* risueño ♦ *n*: **it's no** ~ **matter** no es cosa de risa.

laughing gas *n* gas *m* hilarante.

laughing stock *n*: **to be the** ~ **of the town** ser el hazmerreír de la ciudad.

laughter |laf'tûr| *n* risa.

launch |lônch| *n* (*boat*) lancha; *see also* **launching** ♦ *vt* (*ship, rocket, plan*) lanzar.

  launch forth *vi*: **to** ~ **forth (into)** lanzarse a *or* en, emprender.

  launch out *vi* = **launch forth.**

launching |lôn'ching| *n* (*of rocket etc*) lanzamiento; (*inauguration*) estreno.

launch(ing) pad *n* plataforma de lanzamiento.

launder |lôn'dûr| *vt* lavar.

launderette |lôndəret'| *n* (*Brit*) lavandería (automática).

laundromat |lôn'drəmat| *n* (*US*) lavandería (automática).

laundry |lôn'drē| *n* lavandería; (*clothes*) ropa sucia; **to do the** ~ hacer la colada.

laureate |lô'rēit| *a see* **poet.**

laurel |lôr'əl| *n* laurel *m*; **to rest on one's** ~**s** dormirse en *or* sobre los laureles.

lava |läv'ə| *n* lava.

lavatory |lav'ətôrē| *n* wáter *m*; **lavatories**

npl servicios *mpl*, aseos *mpl*, sanitarios *mpl* (*LAm*).

lavender |lav'əndûr| *n* lavanda.

lavish |lav'ish| *a* abundante; (*giving freely*): ~ **with** pródigo en ♦ *vt*: **to** ~ **sth on sb** colmar a uno de algo.

lavishly |lav'ishlē| *ad* (*give, spend*) generosamente, liberalmente; (*furnished*) lujosamente.

law |lô| *n* ley *f*; (*study*) derecho; (*of game*) regla; **against the** ~ contra la ley; **to study** ~ estudiar derecho.

law-abiding |lô'əbīding| *a* respetuoso de la ley.

law and order *n* orden *m* público.

lawbreaker |lô'brākûr| *n* infractor(a) *m/f* de la ley.

law court *n* (*Brit*) tribunal *m* (de justicia).

lawful |lô'fəl| *a* legítimo, lícito.

lawfully |lô'fəlē| *ad* legalmente.

lawless |lô'lis| *a* (*act*) ilegal; (*person*) rebelde; (*country*) ingobernable.

lawmaker |lô'mākûr| *n* legislador(a) *m/f*.

lawn |lôn| *n* césped *m*.

lawnmower |lôn'mōūr| *n* cortacésped *m*.

lawn tennis *n* tenis *m* sobre hierba.

law school |lô' skōōl| *n* (*US*) facultad *f* de derecho.

law student |lô' stōōd'ənt| *n* estudiante *m/f* de derecho.

lawsuit |lô'sōōt| *n* pleito; **to bring a** ~ **against** levantar pleito contra.

lawyer |lô'yûr| *n* abogado/a; (*for sales, wills etc*) notario/a.

lax |laks| *a* (*discipline*) relajado; (*person*) negligente.

laxative |lak'sətiv| *n* laxante *m*.

laxity |lak'sitē| *n* flojedad *f*; (*moral*) relajamiento; (*negligence*) negligencia.

lay |lā| *pt of* **lie** ♦ *a* laico; (*not expert*) lego ♦ *vt* (*pt, pp* **laid** |lād|) (*place*) colocar; (*eggs, Brit: table*) poner; (*trap*) tender; **to** ~ **the facts/one's proposals before sb** presentar los hechos/sus propuestas a uno.

  lay aside, lay by *vt* dejar a un lado.

  lay down *vt* (*pen etc*) dejar; (*arms*) rendir; (*policy*) asentar; **to** ~ **down the law** imponer las normas.

  lay in *vt* abastecerse de.

  lay into *vt fus* (*col: attack, scold*) arremeterse contra.

  lay off *vt* (*workers*) despedir.

  lay on *vt* (*Brit*) (*water, gas*) instalar; (*meal, facilities*) proveer.

  lay out *vt* (*plan*) trazar; (*display*) disponer; (*spend*) gastar.

  lay up *vt* (*store*) guardar; (*ship*) desarmar; (*subj: illness*) obligar a guardar cama.

layabout |lā'əbout| *n* (*Brit*) vago/a.

lay-by |lā'bī| *n* (*Brit AUT*) apartadero.

lay days *npl* días *mpl* de detención *or* inactividad.

layer [lā'ûr] *n* capa.
layette [lā'et'] *n* ajuar *m* (de niño).
layman [lā'mən] *n* lego.
layoff [lā'óf] *n* despido, paro forzoso.
layout [lā'out] *n* (*design*) plan *m*, trazado; (*disposition*) disposición *f*; (*PRESS*) composición *f*.
layover [lā'ōvûr] *n* (*US*) parada intermedia; (: *AVIAT*) escala.
laze [lāz] *vi* no hacer nada; (*pej*) holgazanear.
lazily [lā'zilē] *ad* perezosamente.
laziness [lā'zēnis] *n* pereza.
lazy [lā'zē] *a* perezoso, vago.
LB *abbr* (*Canada*) = Labrador.
lb. *abbr* = **pound** (*weight*).
LC *n abbr* (*US*) = Library of Congress.
lc *abbr* (*TYP*: = lower case) min.
L/C *abbr* = **letter of credit.**
LCD *n abbr see* **liquid crystal display.**
LDS *n abbr* (= Latter-day Saints) Iglesia de Jesucristo de los Santos de los últimos días.
lead [lēd] *n* (*front position*) delantera; (*distance, time ahead*) ventaja; (*clue*) pista; (*ELEC*) cable *m*; (*Brit: for dog*) correa; (*THEATER*) papel *m* principal; [led] (*metal*) plomo; (*in pencil*) mina ♦ *vb* (*pt, pp* **led** [led]) *vt* conducir; (*life*) llevar; **to be in the** ~ (*SPORT*) llevar la delantera; (*fig*) ir a la cabeza; **to take the** ~ (*SPORT*) tomar la delantera; (*fig*) tomar la iniciativa; **to** ~ **sb to believe that ...** hacer creer a uno que ...; **to** ~ **sb to do sth** llevar a uno a hacer algo.
lead astray *vt* llevar por mal camino.
lead away *vt* llevar.
lead back *vt* hacer volver.
lead off *vt* llevar ♦ *vi* (*in game*) abrir.
lead on *vt* (*tease*) engañar; **to** ~ **sb on to** (*induce*) incitar a uno a.
lead to *vt fus* producir, provocar.
lead up to *vt fus* conducir a.
leaded [led'id] *a*: ~ **windows** ventanas *fpl* emplomadas.
leaden [led'ən] *a* (*sky, sea*) plomizo; (*heavy: footsteps*) pesado.
leader [lē'dûr] *n* jefe/a *m/f*, líder *m*; (*of union etc*) dirigente *m/f*; (*of orchestra: US*) director(a) *m/f*; (: *Brit*) primer violín *m*; (*guide*) guía *m/f*; (*Brit: of newspaper*) artículo de fondo; **they are** ~**s in their field** (*fig*) llevan la delantera en su especialidad.
leadership [lē'dûrship] *n* dirección *f*; **qualities of** ~ iniciativa *sg*; **under the** ~ **of ...** bajo la dirección de ..., al mando de ....
lead-free [ledfrē'] *a* sin plomo.
leading [lē'ding] *a* (*main*) principal; (*outstanding*) destacado; (*first*) primero; (*front*) delantero; **a** ~ **question** una pregunta tendenciosa.

leading lady *n* (*THEATER*) primera actriz *f*.
leading light *n* (*fig: person*) figura principal.
leading man *n* (*THEATER*) primer actor *m*.
leading role *n* papel *m* principal.
lead pencil [led pen'səl] *n* lápiz *m*.
lead poisoning [led' poi'zəning] *n* envenenamiento plúmbico.
lead time *n* (*COMM*) plazo de entrega.
lead weight [led wāt] *n* peso de plomo.
leaf, *pl* **leaves** [lēf, lēvz] *n* hoja; **to turn over a new** ~ (*fig*) volver la hoja, hacer borrón y cuenta nueva; **to take a** ~ **out of sb's book** (*fig*) seguir el ejemplo de uno.
leaf through *vt fus* (*book*) hojear.
leaflet [lēf'lit] *n* folleto.
leafy [lē'fē] *a* frondoso.
league [lēg] *n* sociedad *f*; (*SPORTS*) liga; **to be in** ~ **with** estar de manga con.
leak [lēk] *n* (*of liquid, gas*) escape *m*, fuga; (*in pipe*) agujero; (*in roof*) gotera; (*fig: of information, in security*) filtración *f* ♦ *vi* (*shoes, ship*) hacer agua; (*pipe*) tener (un) escape; (*roof*) gotear; (*also:* ~ **out:** *liquid, gas*) escaparse, fugarse; (*fig: news*) divulgarse ♦ *vt* (*gen*) dejar escapar; (*fig: information*) filtrarse.
leakage [lē'kij] *n* (*of water, gas etc*) goteo, filtración *f*.
leaky [lē'kē] *a* (*pipe, bucket, roof*) que tiene goteras; (*shoe*) que deja entrar el agua; (*boat*) que hace agua.
lean [lēn] *a* (*thin*) flaco; (*meat*) magro ♦ *vb* (*pt, pp* **leaned** *or* **leant** [lent]) *vt*: **to** ~ **sth on sth** apoyar algo en algo ♦ *vi* (*slope*) inclinarse; (*rest*): **to** ~ **against** apoyarse contra; **to** ~ **on** apoyarse en.
lean back *vi* inclinarse hacia atrás.
lean forward *vi* inclinarse hacia adelante.
lean out *vi*: **to** ~ **out (of)** asomarse (de).
lean over *vi* inclinarse.
leaning [lē'ning] *a* inclinado ♦ *n*: ~ **(towards)** inclinación *f* (hacia); **the L**~ **Tower of Pisa** la Torre Inclinada de Pisa.
leant [lent] *pt, pp of* **lean.**
lean-to [lēn'tōō] *n* (*roof*) tejado de una sola agua; (*building*) cobertizo.
leap [lēp] *n* salto ♦ *vi* (*pt, pp* **leaped** *or* **leapt** [lept]) saltar; **to** ~ **at an offer** apresurarse a aceptar una oferta.
leap up *vi* (*person*) saltar.
leapfrog [lēp'frâg] *n* pídola ♦ *vi*: **to** ~ **over sb/sth** saltar por encima de uno/algo.
leapt [lept] *pt, pp of* **leap.**
leap year *n* año bisiesto.
learn, *pt, pp* **learned** *or* **learnt** [lûrn, -t] *vt* (*gen*) aprender; (*come to know of*) enterarse de ♦ *vi* aprender; **to** ~ **how to do sth** aprender a hacer algo; **to** ~ **that ...**

enterarse _or_ informarse de que ...; **to ~ about sth** (_SCOL_) hacer clase de algo; (_hear_) enterarse _or_ informarse de algo; **we were sorry to ~ that** ... nos dio tristeza saber que ....

learned [lûr'nid] _a_ erudito.

learner [lûr'nûr] _n_ principiante _m/f_; (_Brit: also:_ **~ driver**) aprendiz(a) _m/f_.

learning [lûr'ning] _n_ saber _m_, conocimientos _mpl_.

learnt [lûrnt] _pp of_ **learn**.

lease [lēs] _n_ arriendo ♦ _vt_ arrendar; **on ~ en** arriendo.

lease back _vt_ (_Brit_) subarrendar.

leasehold [lēs'hōld] _n_ (_contract_) derechos _mpl_ de arrendamiento ♦ _a_ arrendado.

leash [lēsh] _n_ correa.

least [lēst] _a_ (_slightest_) menor, más pequeño; (_smallest amount of_) mínimo ♦ _ad_ menos ♦ _n_: **the ~** lo menos; **the ~ expensive car** el coche menos costoso; **at ~** por lo menos, al menos; **not in the ~** en absoluto.

leather [leth'ûr] _n_ cuero ♦ _cpd_: **~ goods** artículos _mpl_ de cuero.

leathery [leth'ûrē] _a_ (_skin_) curtido.

leave [lēv] _vb_ (_pt, pp_ **left** [left]) _vt_ dejar; (_go away from_) abandonar ♦ _vi_ irse; (_train_) salir ♦ _n_ permiso; **to ~ school** salir del colegio; **~ it to me!** ¡yo me encargo!; **he's already left for the airport** ya se ha marchado al aeropuerto; **to be left** quedar, sobrar; **there's some milk left over** sobra _or_ queda algo de leche; **on ~** de permiso; **to take one's ~ of** despedirse de; **on ~ of absence** con permiso de ausentarse.

leave behind _vt_ (_on purpose_) dejar (atrás); (_accidentally_) olvidar.

leave off _vt_ (_lid_) no reemplazar; (_switch_) no encender.

leave on _vt_ (_lid_) dejar puesto; (_light, heater, stove_) dejar encendido.

leave out _vt_ omitir.

leave over _vt_ (_Brit: postpone_) dejar.

leave of absence _n_ permiso de ausentarse.

leaves [lēvz] _pl of_ **leaf**.

leavetaking [lēv'tāking] _n_ despedida.

Lebanon [leb'ənən] _n_: **the ~** el Líbano.

lecherous [lech'ûrəs] _a_ lascivo.

lectern [lek'tûrn] _n_ atril _m_.

lecture [lek'chûr] _n_ conferencia; (_SCOL_) clase _f_ ♦ _vi_ dar una clase ♦ _vt_ (_scold_) sermonear; (_reprove_) echar una reprimenda a; **to give a ~ on** dar una conferencia sobre.

lecture hall _n_ aula, sala de conferencias.

lecturer [lek'chûrûr] _n_ conferenciante _m/f_; (_at university_) profesor(a) _m/f_.

LED _n abbr_ (= _light-emitting diode_) LED _m_.

led [led] _pt, pp of_ **lead**.

ledge [lej] _n_ (_of window, on wall_) repisa, reborde _m_; (_of mountain_) saliente _m_.

ledger [lej'ûr] _n_ libro mayor.

lee [lē] _n_ sotavento; **in the ~ of** al abrigo de.

leech [lēch] _n_ sanguijuela.

leek [lēk] _n_ puerro.

leer [lēr] _vi_: **to ~ at sb** mirar de manera lasciva a uno.

leeward [lē'wûrd] _a_ (_NAUT_) de sotavento ♦ _n_ (_NAUT_) sotavento; **to ~** a sotavento.

leeway [lē'wā] _n_ (_fig_): **to have some ~** tener cierta libertad de acción.

left [left] _pt, pp of_ **leave** ♦ _a_ izquierdo ♦ _n_ izquierda ♦ _ad_ a la izquierda; **on** _or_ **to the ~** a la izquierda; **the L~** (_POL_) la izquierda.

left-hand drive [left'hand' drīv] _n_ conducción _f_ a la izquierda.

left-handed [left'han'did] _a_ zurdo; **~ scissors** tijeras _fpl_ zurdas _or_ para zurdos.

left-hand side [left'hand' sīd] _n_ la izquierda.

leftist [lef'tist] _a_ (_POL_) izquierdista.

left-luggage (office) [leftlug'ij (ôf'is)] _n_ (_Brit_) consigna.

leftovers [left'ōvûrz] _npl_ sobras _fpl_.

left-wing [left'wing] _a_ (_POL_) de izquierda, izquierdista.

left-winger [left'wingûr] _n_ (_POL_) izquierdista _m/f_.

leg [leg] _n_ pierna; (_of animal_) pata; (_of chair_) pie _m_; (_CULIN: of meat_) pierna; (_of journey_) etapa; **lst/2nd ~** (_SPORT_) partido de ida/de vuelta; **to pull sb's ~** bromear con uno; **to stretch one's ~s** dar una vuelta.

legacy [leg'əsē] _n_ herencia; (_fig_) herencia, patrimonio.

legal [lē'gəl] _a_ (_permitted by law_) lícito; (_of law_) legal; (_inquiry etc_) jurídico; **to take ~ action** _or_ **proceedings against sb** entablar _or_ levantar pleito contra uno.

legal adviser _n_ asesor(a) _m/f_ jurídico/a.

legal holiday _n_ (_US_) fiesta oficial.

legality [lēgal'itē] _n_ legalidad _f_.

legalize [lē'gəlīz] _vt_ legalizar.

legally [lē'gəlē] _ad_ legalmente; **~ binding** con fuerza legal.

legal tender _n_ moneda de curso legal.

legatee [legətē'] _n_ legatario/a.

legation [ligā'shən] _n_ legación _f_.

legend [lej'ənd] _n_ leyenda.

legendary [lej'əndārē] _a_ legendario.

-legged [leg'id] _suff_: **two~** (_table etc_) de dos patas.

leggings [leg'ingz] _npl_ polainas _fpl_.

legibility [lejəbil'ətē] _n_ legibilidad _f_.

legible [lej'əbəl] _a_ legible.

legibly [lej'əblē] _ad_ legiblemente.

legion [lē'jən] _n_ legión _f_.

legionnaire [lējənār'] _n_ legionario.

legionnaire's disease _n_ enfermedad _f_ del legionario.

legislation [lejislā'shən] _n_ legislación _f_; **a piece of ~** (_bill_) un proyecto de ley; (_act_) una ley.

legislative [lej'islātiv] *a* legislativo.
legislator [lej'islātûr] *n* legislador(a) *m/f.*
legislature [lej'islāchûr] *n* cuerpo legislativo.
legitimacy [lijit'əməsē] *n* legitimidad *f.*
legitimate [lijit'əmit] *a* legítimo.
legitimize [lijit'əmīz] *vt* legitimar.
leg-room [leg'rōōm] *n* espacio para las piernas.
leg warmers [leg wôr'mûrz] *npl* calientapiernas *mpl.*
Leics *abbr* (*Brit*) = Leicestershire.
leisure [lē'zhûr] *n* ocio, tiempo libre; **at ~** con tranquilidad.
leisurely [lē'zhûrlē] *a* sin prisa; lento.
leisure suit *n* conjunto tipo chandal.
lemon [lem'ən] *n* limón *m.*
lemonade [lemənād'] *n* (*fruit juice*) limonada; (*fizzy*) gaseosa.
lemon cheese, lemon curd *n* queso de limón.
lemon juice *n* zumo de limón.
lemon tea *n* té *m* con limón.
lend [lend], *pt, pp* **lent** [lend, lent] *vt*: **to ~ sth to sb** prestar algo a uno.
lender [len'dûr] *n* prestador(a) *m/f.*
lending library [len'ding li'brārē] *n* biblioteca circulante.
length [lengkth] *n* (*size*) largo, longitud *f*; (*section*: *of road, pipe*) tramo; (: *of rope etc*) largo; **at ~** (*at last*) por fin, finalmente; (*lengthily*) largamente; **it is 2 meters in ~** tiene dos metros de largo; **what ~ is it?** ¿cuánto tiene de largo?; **to fall full ~** (*Brit*) caer de bruces; **to go to any ~(s) to do sth** ser capaz de hacer cualquier cosa para hacer algo.
lengthen [lengk'thən] *vt* alargar ♦ *vi* alargarse.
lengthwise [length'wīz] *ad* a lo largo.
lengthy [lengk'thē] *a* largo, extenso; (*meeting*) prolongado.
lenient [lē'nēənt] *a* indulgente.
lens [lenz] *n* (*of spectacles*) lente *f*; (*of camera*) objetivo.
Lent [lent] *n* Cuaresma.
lent [lent] *pt, pp of* **lend**.
lentil [len'təl] *n* lenteja.
Leo [lē'ō] *n* Leo.
leopard [lep'ûrd] *n* leopardo.
leotard [lē'ətârd] *n* leotardo.
leper [lep'ûr] *n* leproso/a.
leper colony *n* colonia de leprosos.
leprosy [lep'rəsē] *n* lepra.
lesbian [lez'bēən] *a* lesbiano ♦ *n* lesbiana.
lesion [lē'zhən] *n* (*MED*) lesión *f.*
Lesotho [lisōō'tōō] *n* Lesotho.
less [les] *a* (*in size, degree etc*) menor; (*in quantity*) menos ♦ *pron, ad* menos; **~ than half** menos de la mitad; **~ than $1/a kilo/3 meters** menos de un dólar/un kilo/tres metros; **~ than ever** menos que nunca; **~ 5%** menos el cinco por ciento; **~ and ~** cada

vez menos; **the ~ he works...** cuanto menos trabaja ....
lessee [lesē'] *n* inquilino/a, arrendatario/a.
lessen [les'ən] *vi* disminuir, reducirse ♦ *vt* disminuir, reducir.
lesser [les'ûr] *a* menor; **to a ~ extent** *or* **degree** en menor grado.
lesson [les'ən] *n* clase *f*; **an English ~** una clase de inglés; **to give ~s in** dar clases de; **it taught him a ~** (*fig*) le sirvió de lección.
lessor [les'ôr] *n* arrendador(a) *m/f.*
lest [lest] *conj*: **~ it happen** para que no pase.
let, *pt, pp* **let** [let] *vt* (*allow*) dejar, permitir; (*Brit*: *lease*) alquilar; **to ~ sb do sth** dejar que uno haga algo; **to ~ sb have sth** dar algo a uno; **to ~ sb know sth** comunicar algo a uno; **~'s go** ¡vamos!; **~ him come** que venga; **"to ~"** (*Brit*) "se alquila".
let down *vt* (*lower*) bajar; (*dress*) alargar; (*tire*) desinflar; (*hair*) soltar; (*disappoint*) defraudar.
let go *vi* soltar; (*fig*) dejarse ir ♦ *vt* soltar.
let in *vt* dejar entrar; (*visitor etc*) hacer pasar; **what have you ~ yourself in for?** ¿en qué te has metido?
let off *vt* dejar escapar; (*firework etc*) disparar; (*bomb*) accionar; (*passenger*) dejar, bajar; **to ~ off steam** (*fig, col*) desahogarse, desfogarse.
let on *vi*: **to ~ on that ...** revelar que ...
let out *vt* dejar salir; (*dress*) ensanchar; (*Brit*: *rent out*) alquilar.
let up *vi* amainar, disminuir.
letdown [let'doun] *n* (*disappointment*) decepción *f.*
lethal [lē'thəl] *a* (*weapon*) mortífero; (*poison, wound*) mortal.
lethargic [ləthâr'jik] *a* aletargado.
lethargy [leth'ûrjē] *n* letargo.
letter [let'ûr] *n* (*of alphabet*) letra; (*correspondence*) carta; **~s** *npl* (*literature, learning*) letras *fpl*; **~s to the editor** (sección *f* de) cartas *fpl* al director; **small/capital ~** minúscula/mayúscula; **cover ~** carta adjunta.
letter bomb *n* carta-bomba.
letterbox [let'ûrbâks] *n* (*Brit*) buzón *m.*
letterhead [let'ûrhed] *n* membrete *m*, encabezamiento *m.*
lettering [let'ûring] *n* letras *fpl.*
letter of credit *n* carta de crédito; **documentary ~** carta de crédito documentaria; **irrevocable ~** carta de crédito irrevocable.
letter-opener [let'ûrōpənûr] *n* abrecartas *m inv.*
letterpress [let'ûrpres] *n* (*method*) prensa de copiar; (*printed page*) impresión *f* tipográfica.
letter quality *n* calidad *f* de co-

rrespondencia.

letters patent *npl* letra *sg* de patente.

lettuce |lɛt'is| *n* lechuga.

letup |lɛt'up| *n* descanso, tregua.

leukemia, (*Brit*) **leukaemia** |loōkē'mēə| *n* leucemia.

level |lɛv'əl| *a* (*flat*) llano; (*flattened*) nivelado; (*uniform*) igual ♦ *ad* a nivel ♦ *n* nivel *m* ♦ *vt* nivelar, allanar; (*gun*) apuntar; (*accusation*): **to ~ (against)** levantar (contra) ♦ *vi* (*col*): **to ~ with sb** ser franco con uno; **to be ~ with** estar a nivel de; **a ~ spoonful** (*CULIN*) una cucharada rasa; **to draw ~ with** (*Brit: team*) igualar; (*runner, car*) alcanzar a; **"A" ~s** *npl* (*Brit*) ≈ Bachillerato Superior *sg*, B.U.P. *msg*; **"O" ~s** *npl* (*Brit*) ≈ bachillerato *sg* elemental, octavo *sg* de básica; **on the ~** (*fig: honest*) en serio; **talks at ministerial ~** charlas *fpl* a nivel ministerial.

level off *or* **out** *vi* (*prices etc*) estabilizarse; (*ground*) nivelarse; (*aircraft*) ponerse en una trayectoria horizontal.

level crossing *n* (*Brit*) paso a nivel.

levelheaded |lɛv'əlhɛd'id| *a* sensato.

leveling, (*Brit*) **levelling** |lɛv'əling| *a* (*process, effect*) de nivelación ♦ *n* igualación *f*, allanamiento.

lever |lɛv'ûr| *n* palanca ♦ *vt*: **to ~ up** levantar con palanca.

leverage |lɛv'ûrij| *n* (*fig: influence*) influencia.

levity |lɛv'itē| *n* frivolidad *f*, informalidad *f*.

levy |lɛv'ē| *n* impuesto ♦ *vt* exigir, recaudar.

lewd |loōd| *a* lascivo; obsceno, colorado (*LAm*).

LF *n abbr* (= *low frequency*) baja frecuencia.

LI *abbr* (*US*) = *Long Island*.

liabilities |līəbil'ətēz| *npl* obligaciones *fpl*; pasivo *sg*.

liability |līəbil'ətē| *n* responsabilidad *f*; (*handicap*) desventaja.

liability insurance *n* (*US*) seguro contra terceros.

liable |lī'əbəl| *a* (*subject*): **~ to** sujeto a; (*responsible*): **~ for** responsable de; (*likely*): **~ to do** propenso a hacer; **to be ~ to a fine** ser expuesto a una multa.

liaise |lēāz'| *vi* (*Brit*): **to ~ (with)** colaborar (con); **to ~ with sb** mantener informado a uno.

liaison |lēā'zân| *n* (*coordination*) enlace *m*; (*affair*) relación *f*.

liar |lī'ûr| *n* mentiroso/a.

libel |lī'bəl| *n* calumnia ♦ *vt* calumniar.

libel(l)ous |lī'bələs| *a* difamatorio, calumnioso.

liberal |lib'ûrəl| *a* (*gen*) liberal; (*generous*): **~ with** generoso con ♦ *n*: **L~** (*POL*) liberal *m/f*.

liberality |libəral'itē| *n* (*generosity*) liberalidad *f*, generosidad *f*.

liberalize |lib'ûrəlīz| *vt* liberalizar.

liberally |lib'ûrəlē| *ad* liberalmente.

liberal-minded |lib'ûrəlmīn'did| *a* de miras anchas.

liberate |lib'ərāt| *vt* liberar.

liberation |libərā'shən| *n* liberación *f*.

Liberia |lībē'rēə| *n* Liberia.

Liberian |lībē'rēən| *a, n* liberiano/a *m/f*.

liberty |lib'ûrtē| *n* libertad *f*; **to be at ~ to do** estar libre para hacer; **to take the ~ of doing sth** tomarse la libertad de hacer algo.

libido |libē'dō| *n* libido.

Libra |lēb'rə| *n* Libra.

librarian |lībrär'ēən| *n* bibliotecario/a.

library |lī'brärē| *n* biblioteca.

library book *n* libro de la biblioteca.

libretto |libret'ō| *n* libreto.

Libya |lib'ēə| *n* Libia.

Libyan |lib'ēən| *a, n* libio/a *m/f*.

lice |līs| *pl of* **louse**.

licence |lī'səns| *n* (*Brit*) = **license**.

license |lī'səns| *n* (*US*) licencia; (*permit*) permiso; (*also:* **driver's ~,** (*Brit*) **driving licence**) carnet *m* de conducir; (*excessive freedom*) libertad *f* ♦ *vt* autorizar, dar permiso a; (*car*) sacar la patente *or* la matrícula de; **import ~** licencia *or* permiso de importación; **produced under ~** elaborado bajo licencia.

licensed |lī'sənst| *a* (*for alcohol*) autorizado para vender bebidas alcohólicas.

license plate *n* placa (de matrícula).

licentious |līsɛn'chəs| *a* licencioso.

lichen |lī'kən| *n* liquen *m*.

lick |lik| *vt* lamer; (*col: defeat*) dar una paliza a ♦ *n* lamedura; **a ~ of paint** una mano de pintura.

licorice |lik'ûris| *n* (*US*) regaliz *m*.

lid |lid| *n* (*of box, case*) tapa; (*of pan*) cobertera; **to take the ~ off sth** (*fig*) exponer algo a la luz pública.

lido |lē'dō| *n* (*Brit*) piscina, alberca (*LAm*).

lie |lī| *n* mentira ♦ *vi* mentir; (*pt* **lay,** *pp* **lain** |lā, lān|) (*rest*) estar echado, estar acostado; (*of object: be situated*) estar, encontrarse; **to tell ~s** mentir; **to ~ low** (*fig*) mantenerse a escondidas.

lie around *vi* (*things*) estar tirado; (*people*) estar acostado *or* tumbado.

lie back *vi* recostarse.

lie down *vi* acostarse.

lie up *vi* (*Brit: hide*) esconderse.

Liechtenstein |lēch'tɛnstīn| *n* Liechtenstein *m*.

lie detector *n* detector *m* de mentiras.

lieu |loō|: **in ~ of** *prep* en lugar de.

Lieut *abbr* = **lieutenant.**

lieutenant |loōtɛn'ənt| *n* (*MIL*) teniente *m*.

lieutenant colonel *n* teniente *m* colonel.

life, *pl* **lives** |līf, līvz| *n* vida; (*way of* **~**) modo de vivir; (*of license etc*) vigencia; **to be sent to prison for ~** ser condenado a reclusión or cadena perpetua; **country/city** ~ la vida del campo/de la ciudad; **true to** ~ fiel a la realidad; **to paint from** ~ pintar del natural; **to put** or **breathe new** ~ **into** (*person*) reanimar; (*project, area etc*) infundir nueva vida a.

life annuity n anualidad f vitalicia.

life belt n cinturón m salvavidas.

lifeblood |līf'blud| n (*fig*) alma, nervio.

lifeboat |līf'bōt| n lancha de socorro.

lifebuoy |līf'boi| n boya or guindola salvavidas.

life expectancy n esperanza de vida.

lifeguard |līf'gård| n vigilante m/f.

life imprisonment n cadena perpetua.

life insurance n (*Brit*) seguro de vida.

life jacket n chaleco salvavidas.

lifeless |līf'lis| a sin vida; (*dull*) soso.

lifelike |līf'līk| a natural.

lifeline |līf'līn| n (*fig*) cordón m umbilical.

lifelong |līf'lông| a de toda la vida.

life preserver |līf prēzûrv'ûr| n (*US*) cinturón m salvavidas.

lifesaver |līf'sāvûr| n socorrista m/f.

life sentence |līf sɛn'təns| n cadena perpetua.

life-sized |līf'sīzd| a de tamaño natural.

life span n vida.

lifestyle |līf'stīl| n estilo de vida.

life support system n (*MED*) sistema m de respiración asistida.

lifetime |līf'tīm| n: **in his** ~ durante su vida; **once in a** ~ una vez en la vida; **the chance of a** ~ una oportunidad única.

lift |lift| vt levantar; (*copy*) plagiar ♦ vi (*fog*) disiparse ♦ n (*Brit: elevator*) ascensor m; **to give sb a** ~ llevar a uno en el coche.

lift off vt levantar, quitar ♦ vi (*rocket, helicopter*) despegar.

lift out vt sacar; (*troops, evacuees etc*) evacuar.

lift up vt levantar.

lift-off |lift'ôf| n despegue m.

ligament |lig'əmənt| n ligamento.

light |līt| n luz f; (*flame*) lumbre f; (*lamp*) luz f, lámpara; (*daylight*) luz f del día; (*headlight*) faro; (*rear* ~) luz f trasera; (*for cigarette etc*): **have you got a** ~? ¿tienes fuego? ♦ vt (*pt, pp* **lighted** or **lit** |lit|) (*candle, cigarette, fire*) encender; (*room*) alumbrar ♦ a (*color*) claro; (*not heavy, also fig*) ligero; (*room*) alumbrado ♦ ad (*travel*) con poco equipaje; **to turn the** ~ **on/off** encender/apagar la luz; **in the** ~ **of** a la luz de; **to come to** ~ salir a luz; **to cast** or **shed** ~ **on** arrojar luz sobre; **to make** ~ **of sth** (*fig*) hacer poco caso de algo.

light up vi (*smoke*) encender un cigarrillo; (*face*) iluminarse ♦ vt (*illuminate*) iluminar, alumbrar.

light bulb n bombilla, foco (*LAm*).

lighten |līt'tən| vi (*grow light*) clarear ♦ vt (*give light to*) iluminar; (*make lighter*) aclarar; (*make less heavy*) aligerar.

lighter |līt'ûr| n (*also:* **cigarette** ~) encendedor m, mechero.

lighter fluid n bencina.

light-fingered |līt'fing'gûrd| a largo de manos.

light-headed |līt'hɛd'id| a (*dizzy*) mareado; (*excited*) exaltado; (*by nature*) casquivano.

lighthearted |līt'hár'tid| a alegre.

lighthouse |līt'hous| n faro.

lighting |līt'ting| n (*act*) iluminación f; (*system*) alumbrado.

lightly |līt'lē| ad ligeramente; (*not seriously*) con poca seriedad; **to get off** ~ ser castigado con poca severidad.

light meter n (*PHOT*) fotómetro.

lightness |līt'nis| n claridad f; (*in weight*) ligereza.

lightning |līt'ning| n relámpago, rayo.

lightning rod, (*Brit*) **lightning conductor** n pararrayos m inv.

lightning strike n (*Brit*) huelga relámpago.

light pen n fotoestilo, lápiz m óptico or luminoso.

lightweight |līt'wāt| a (*suit*) ligero ♦ n (*BOXING*) peso ligero.

light-year |līt'yɛr| n año luz.

like |līk| vt (*person*) querer a; (*thing*): **I** ~ **swimming/apples** me gusta nadar/me gustan las manzanas ♦ prep como ♦ a parecido, semejante ♦ n: **the** ~ semejante m/f; **his** ~**s and dislikes** sus gustos y aversiones; **I would** ~, **I'd** ~ me gustaría; (*for purchase*) quisiera; **would you** ~ **a coffee?** ¿te apetece un café?; **to be** or **look** ~ **sb/ sth** parecerse a uno/algo; **that's just** ~ **him** es muy de él, es característico de él; **do it** ~ **this** hazlo así; **it is nothing** ~**...** no tiene parecido alguno con...; **what's he** ~? ¿cómo es (él)?; **what's the weather** ~? ¿qué tiempo hace?; **something** ~ **that** algo así or por el estilo; **I feel** ~ **a drink** me apetece algo de beber; **if you** ~ si quieres.

likeable |līk'əbəl| a simpático, agradable.

likelihood |līk'lēhōōd| n probabilidad f; **in all** ~ según todas las probabilidades.

likely |līk'lē| a probable; **he's** ~ **to leave** es probable que se vaya; **not** ~! ¡ni hablar!

like-minded |līk'mīn'did| a de la misma opinión.

liken |līk'ən| vt: **to** ~ **to** comparar con.

likeness |līk'nis| n (*similarity*) semejanza, parecido.

likewise |līk'wīz| ad igualmente.

liking |līk'ing| n: ~ (**for**) (*person*) cariño (a); (*thing*) afición (a); **to take a** ~ **to sb** tomar cariño a uno; **to be to sb's** ~ ser del gusto de uno.

lilac |līk'lək| n lila ♦ a (*color*) de color lila.

lilt [lilt] n deje m.
lilting [lil'ting] a melodioso.
lily [lil'ē] n lirio, azucena.
lily of the valley n lirio de los valles.
Lima [lē'mə] n Lima.
limb [lim] n miembro; (of tree) rama; **to be out on a ~** (fig) estar aislado.
limber [lim'bûr]: **to ~ up** vi (fig) entrenarse; (SPORT) desentumecerse.
limbo [lim'bō] n: **to be in ~** (fig) quedar a la expectativa.
lime [lim] n (tree) limero; (fruit) lima; (GEO) cal f.
lime juice n zumo (Sp) or jugo de lima.
limelight [lim'lit] n: **to be in the ~** (fig) ser el centro de atención.
limerick [lim'ûrik] n quintilla humorística.
limestone [lim'stōn] n piedra caliza.
limit [lim'it] n límite m ♦ vt limitar; **weight/speed ~** peso máximo/velocidad f máxima; **within ~s** entre límites.
limitation [limitā'shən] n limitación f.
limited [lim'itid] a limitado; **to be ~ to** limitarse a; **~ edition** tirada limitada.
limited (liability) company (Ltd) n (Brit) sociedad f anónima (SA).
limitless [lim'itlis] a sin límites.
limousine [lim'əzēn] n limusina.
limp [limp] n: **to have a ~** tener cojera ♦ vi cojear ♦ a flojo.
limpet [lim'pit] n lapa.
limpid [lim'pid] a (poetic) límpido, cristalino.
limply [limp'lē] ad desmayadamente; **to say ~** decir débilmente.
linchpin [linch'pin] n pezonera; (fig) eje m.
Lincs [lingks] abbr (Brit) = Lincolnshire.
line [lin] n (also COMM) línea; (straight ~) raya; (rope) cuerda; (for fishing) sedal m; (wire) hilo; (row, series) fila, hilera; (of writing) renglón m; (on face) arruga; (speciality) rama ♦ vt (SEWING): **to ~ (with)** forrar (de); **to ~ the streets** ocupar las aceras; **in ~ with** de acuerdo con; **she's in ~ for promotion** (fig) tiene muchas posibilidades de que la asciendan; **to bring sth into ~ with sth** poner algo de acuerdo con algo; **to cut in ~** (US) colarse; **~ of research/business** campo de investigación/comercio; **to take the ~ that ...** ser de la opinión que ...; **hold the ~ please** (TEL) no cuelgue usted, por favor; **to draw the ~ at doing sth** negarse a hacer algo; no permitir que se haga algo; **on the right ~s** por buen camino; **a new ~ in cosmetics** una nueva línea en cosméticos; see also **lines**.
line up vi hacer cola ♦ vt alinear, poner en fila; **to have sth ~d up** tener algo arreglado.
linear [lin'ēûr] a lineal.
lined [lind] a (face) arrugado; (paper) rayado; (clothes) forrado.
line editing n (COMPUT) corrección f por

líneas.
line feed n (COMPUT) avance m de línea.
linen [lin'ən] n ropa blanca; (cloth) lino.
line printer n impresora de línea.
liner [li'nûr] n vapor m de línea, transatlántico; **trash can ~** bolsa de la basura.
lines [linz] npl (RAIL) vía sg, raíles mpl.
linesman [linz'mən] n (SPORT) juez m de línea.
lineup [lin'up] n alineación f; (US) identificación f de acusados.
linger [ling'gûr] vi retrasarse, tardar en marcharse; (smell, tradition) persistir.
lingerie [lán'jərā] n ropa interior or íntima (LAm) (de mujer).
lingering [ling'gûring] a persistente; (death) lento.
lingo, pl ~es [ling'gō] n (pej) jerga.
linguist [ling'gwist] n lingüista m/f.
linguistic [linggwis'tik] a lingüístico.
linguistics [linggwis'tiks] n lingüística.
liniment [lin'əmənt] n linimento.
lining [li'ning] n forro; (TECH) revestimiento; (of brake) guarnición f.
link [lingk] n (of a chain) eslabón m; (connection) conexión f; (bond) vínculo, lazo ♦ vt vincular, unir; **rail ~** línea de ferrocarril, servicio de trenes.
link up vt acoplar ♦ vi unirse.
links [lingks] npl (GOLF) campo sg de golf.
linkup [lingk'up] n (gen) unión f; (meeting) encuentro, reunión f; (of roads) empalme m; (of spaceships) acoplamiento; (RADIO, TV) enlace m.
linoleum [linō'lēəm] n linóleo.
linseed oil [lin'sēd oil] n aceite m de linaza.
lint [lint] n gasa.
lintel [lin'təl] n dintel m.
lion [li'ən] n león m.
lioness [li'ənis] n leona.
lip [lip] n labio; (of jug) pico; (of cup etc) borde m.
lip-read [lip'rēd] vi leer los labios.
lip salve [lip sav] n crema protectora para labios.
lip service n: **to pay ~ to sth** alabar algo pero sin hacer nada.
lipstick [lip'stik] n lápiz m de labios, carmín m.
liquefy [lik'wəfi] vt licuar ♦ vi licuarse.
liqueur [lik'ûr] n licor m.
liquid [lik'wid] a, n líquido.
liquidate [lik'widāt] vt liquidar.
liquidation [likwidā'shən] n liquidación f; **to go into ~** entrar en liquidación.
liquid crystal display (LCD) n pantalla de cristal líquido.
liquidity [likwid'itē] n (COMM) liquidez f.
liquidize [lik'widiz] vt (CULIN) licuar.
liquidizer [lik'widizûr] n (Brit CULIN) licuadora.
Liquid Paper n ® Tipp-Ex m ®.
liquor [lik'ûr] n licor m, bebidas fpl alcohóli-

cas.
liquorice |lik'ûris| *n* (*Brit*) regaliz *n*..
liquor store *n* (*US*) bodega, *tienda de vinos y bebidas alcohólicas*.
Lisbon |liz'bən| *n* Lisboa.
lisp |lisp| *n* ceceo.
lissom |lis'əm| *a* ágil.
list |list| *n* lista; (*of ship*) inclinación *f* ♦ *vt* (*write down*) hacer una lista de; (*enumerate*) catalogar; (*COMPUT*) listar ♦ *vi* (*ship*) inclinarse; **shopping ~** lista de las compras; *see also* **lists**.
listed company |lis'tid kum'pənē| *n* compañía cotizable.
listen |lis'ən| *vi* escuchar, oír; (*pay attention*) atender.
listener |lis'ənûr| *n* oyente *m/f*.
listing |lis'ting| *n* (*COMPUT*) listado.
listless |list'lis| *a* apático, indiferente.
listlessly |list'lislē| *ad* con indiferencia.
listlessness |list'lisnis| *n* indiferencia, apatía.
list price *n* precio corriente *or* de tarifa.
lists |lists| *npl* (*HISTORY*) liza *sg*; **to enter the ~** (*against sb/sth*) salir a la palestra (contra uno/algo).
lit |lit| *pt, pp of* **light**.
litany |lit'ənē| *n* letanía.
liter |lē'tûr| *n* (*US*) litro.
literacy |lit'ûrəsē| *n* capacidad *f* de leer y escribir; **~ campaign** campaña de alfabetización.
literal |lit'ûrəl| *a* literal.
literally |lit'ûrəlē| *ad* literalmente.
literary |lit'ərärē| *a* literario.
literate |lit'ûrit| *a* que sabe leer y escribir; (*fig*) culto.
literature |lit'ûrəchûr| *n* literatura; (*brochures etc*) folletos *mpl*.
lithe |lith| *a* ágil.
litho(graph) |lith'ō(graf)| *n* litografía.
lithography |lithâg'rəfē| *n* litografía.
Lithuania |lithōōā'nēə| *n* Lituania.
litigate |lit'əgāt| *vi* litigar.
litigation |litəgā'shən| *n* litigio.
litmus paper |lit'məs pā'pûr| *n* papel *m* de tornasol.
litre |lē'tûr| *n* (*Brit*) = **liter**.
litter |lit'ûr| *n* (*rubbish*) basura; (*paper*) papel *m* tirado; (*young animals*) camada, cría.
litter bin *n* (*Brit*) papelera.
litterbug |lit'ûrbug| *n* persona que tira papeles usados en la vía pública.
littered |lit'ûrd| *a*: **~ with** lleno de.
little |lit'əl| *a* (*small*) pequeño; (*not much*) poco; (*often translated by suffix, eg*): **~ house** casita ♦ *ad* poco; **a ~** un poco (de); **~ by ~** poco a poco; **~ finger** (dedo) meñique *m*; **for a ~ while** por un rato; **with ~ difficulty** sin problema *or* dificultad; **as ~ as possible** lo menos posible.
liturgy |lit'ûrjē| *n* liturgia.

live *vb* |liv| *vi* vivir ♦ *vt* (*a life*) llevar; (*experience*) vivir ♦ *a* |līv| (*animal*) vivo; (*wire*) conectado; (*broadcast*) en directo; (*issue*) de actualidad; (*unexploded*) sin explotar; **to ~ in Chicago** vivir en Chicago; **to ~ together** vivir juntos; **to ~ off-campus** ser externo.
live down *vt* hacer olvidar.
live off *vt fus* (*land, fish etc*) vivir de; (*pej: parents etc*) vivir a costa de.
live on *vt fus* (*food*) vivirse de, alimentarse de; **to ~ on $150 a week** vivir con 150 dólares por semana.
live out *vi* (*Brit: students*) ser externo ♦ *vt*: **to ~ out one's days** *or* **life** acabar la vida.
live up *vt*: **to ~ it up** (*col*) vivir la gran vida.
live up to *vt fus* (*fulfil*) cumplir con; (*justify*) justificar.
livelihood |līv'lēhōōd| *n* sustento.
liveliness |līv'lēnis| *n* viveza.
lively |līv'lē| *a* (*gen*) vivo; (*talk*) animado; (*pace*) rápido; (*party, tune*) alegre.
liven up |lī'vən up'| *vt* (*discussion, evening*) animar.
liver |liv'ûr| *n* hígado.
liverish |liv'ûrish| *a* (*Brit*): **to feel ~** sentirse *or* estar mal del hígado.
livery |liv'ûrē| *n* librea.
lives |līvz| *npl of* **life**.
livestock |līv'stâk| *n* ganado.
livid |liv'id| *a* lívido; (*furious*) furioso.
living |liv'ing| *a* (*alive*) vivo ♦ *n*: **to earn** *or* **make a ~** ganarse la vida; **cost of ~** coste *m* de la vida; **in ~ memory** que se recuerde *or* recuerda.
living conditions *npl* condiciones *fpl* de vida.
living expenses *npl* gastos *mpl* de mantenimiento.
living room *n* sala (de estar).
living standards *npl* nivel *msg* de vida.
living wage *n* sueldo suficiente para vivir.
lizard |liz'ûrd| *n* lagartija.
llama |lâm'ə| *n* llama.
LLB *n abbr* (= *Bachelor of Laws*) Ldo./a. en Dcho.
LLD *n abbr* (= *Doctor of Laws*) Dr(a). en Dcho.
load |lōd| *n* (*gen*) carga; (*weight*) peso ♦ *vt* (*COMPUT*) cargar; (*also:* **~ up**): **to ~ (with)** cargar (con *or* de); **a ~ of, ~s of** (*fig*) (gran) cantidad de, montones de.
loaded |lō'did| *a* (*dice*) cargado; (*question*) intencionado; (*col: rich*) forrado (de dinero).
loading |lō'ding| *n* (*COMM*) sobreprima.
loading dock *n* (*US*) área de carga y descarga.
loaf, *pl* **loaves** |lōf, lōvz| *n* (barra de) pan *m* ♦ *vi* (*also:* **~ around**) holgazanear.
loafer |lō'fûr| *n* vago/a.

loam |lōm| n marga.
loan [lōn] n préstamo; (COMM) empréstito ♦ vt prestar; **on ~** prestado; **to raise a ~** (Brit: money) procurar un empréstito.
loan account n cuenta de crédito.
loan capital n empréstito.
loath [lōth] a: **to be ~ to do sth** estar poco dispuesto a hacer algo.
loathe [lōth] vt aborrecer; (person) odiar.
loathing [lō'thing] n aversión f; odio.
loathsome [lōth'səm] a asqueroso, repugnante; (person) odioso.
loaves [lōvz] pl of **loaf.**
lob [lâb] vt (ball) volear por alto.
lobby [lâb'ē] n vestíbulo, sala de espera; (POL: pressure group) grupo de presión ♦ vt presionar.
lobbyist [lâb'ēist] n cabildero/a.
lobe [lōb] n lóbulo.
lobster [lâb'stûr] n langosta.
lobster pot n nasa, langostera.
local [lō'kəl] a local ♦ n (Brit: pub) bar m; **the ~s** npl los vecinos, los del lugar.
local anesthetic n (MED) anestesia local.
local authority n (Brit) municipio, ayuntamiento (Sp).
local call n (TEL) llamada local.
local government n gobierno municipal.
locality [lōkal'itē] n localidad f.
localize [lō'kəlīz] vt localizar.
locally [lō'kəlē] ad en la vecindad.
locate [lō'kāt] vt (find) localizar; (situate) colocar.
location [lōkā'shən] n situación f; **on ~** (CINEMA) en exteriores, fuera del estudio.
loch [lâk] n lago.
lock [lâk] n (of door, box) cerradura; (of canal) esclusa; (of hair) mechón m ♦ vt (with key) cerrar con llave; (immobilize) inmovilizar ♦ vi (door etc) cerrarse con llave; (wheels) trabarse; **~ stock and barrel** (fig) por completo or entero.
lock away vt (valuables) guardar bajo llave; (criminal) encerrar.
lock out vt: **the workers were ~ed out** los trabajadores tuvieron que enfrentarse con un cierre patronal.
lock up vi echar la llave.
locker [lâk'ûr] n casillero.
locker room n (US SPORT) vestuario.
locket [lâk'it] n medallón m.
lockout [lâk'out] n (INDUSTRY) paro or cierre m patronal, lockout m.
locksmith [lâk'smith] n cerrajero/a.
lock-up [lâk'up] n (prison) cárcel f; (cell) jaula.
lock-up stall n (US AUT) jaula, cochera.
locomotive [lōkəmō'tiv] n locomotora.
locum tenens [lō'kəm tē'nenz] n (MED) (médico/a) interino/a.
locust [lō'kəst] n langosta.
lodge [lâj] n (FREEMASONRY) logia; (Brit) portería; (: porter's) casa del guarda ♦ vi

(person): **to ~ (with)** alojarse (en casa de) ♦ vt (complaint) presentar.
lodger [lâj'ûr] n huésped(a) m/f.
lodgings [lâj'ingz] npl alojamiento sg; (house) casa sg de huéspedes.
loft [lôft] n desván m.
lofty [lôf'tē] a alto; (haughty) orgulloso; (sentiments, aims) elevado, noble.
log [lôg] n (of wood) leño, tronco; (book) = **logbook** ♦ n abbr (= logarithm) log. ♦ vt anotar, registrar.
log in, log on vi (COMPUT) iniciar la (or una) sesión.
log off, log out vi (COMPUT) finalizar la (or una) sesión.
logarithm [lôg'ərithəm] n logaritmo.
logbook [lôg'bōōk] n (NAUT) diario de a bordo; (AVIAT) libro de vuelo; (of car) documentación f (del coche).
log cabin n cabaña de troncos.
log fire n fuego de leña.
loggerheads [lôg'ûrhedz] npl: **at ~ (with)** de pique (con).
logic [lâj'ik] n lógica.
logical [lâj'ikəl] a lógico.
logically [lâj'iklē] ad lógicamente.
logistics [lōjis'tiks] n logística.
logo [lō'gō] n logotipo.
loin [loin] n (CULIN) lomo, solomillo; **~s** npl lomos mpl.
loincloth [loin'klôth] n taparrabo.
loiter [loi'tûr] vi vagar; (pej) merodear.
loll [lâl] vi repantigarse.
lollipop [lâl'ēpâp] n pirulí m; (iced) polo.
London [lun'dən] n Londres m.
Londoner [lun'dənûr] n londinense m/f.
lone [lōn] a solitario.
loneliness [lōn'lēnis] n soledad f, aislamiento.
lonely [lōn'lē] a solitario, solo.
loner [lō'nûr] n solitario/a.
lonesome [lōn'səm] a (esp US) = **lonely.**
long [lông] a largo ♦ ad mucho tiempo, largamente ♦ vi: **to ~ for sth** anhelar algo ♦ n: **the ~ and the short of it is that ...** (fig) en resumidas cuentas or concretamente, es que ...; **in the ~ run** a la larga; **so** or **as ~ as** mientras, con tal de que; **don't be ~!** ¡no tardes!, ¡vuelve pronto!; **how ~ is the street?** ¿cuánto tiene de calle de largo?; **how ~ is the lesson?** ¿cuánto dura la clase?; **6 meters ~** que mide 6 metros, de 6 metros de largo; **6 months ~** que dura 6 meses, de 6 meses de duración; **all night ~** toda la noche; **~ ago** hace mucho (tiempo); **he no ~er comes** ya no viene; **~ before** mucho antes; **before ~** (+ future) dentro de poco; (+ past) poco tiempo después; **at ~ last** al fin, por fin; **I won't be ~** término pronto.
long-distance [lông'dis'təns] a (race) de larga distancia; (call) interurbano.
longevity [lânjev'itē] n longevidad f.

long-haired |lóng'härd| *a* de pelo largo.

longhand |lóng'hand| *n* escritura (corriente).

longing |lóng'ing| *n* anhelo, ansia; (*nostalgia*) nostalgia ♦ *a* anhelante.

longingly |lóng'inglē| *ad* con ansia.

longitude |lán'jətōōd| *n* longitud *f*.

long jump *n* salto de longitud.

long-lost |lóng'lóst| *a* desaparecido hace mucho tiempo.

long-playing record (LP) |lóng'plā'ing rek'ûrd| *n* elepé *m*, disco de larga duración.

long-range |lóng'rānj| *a* de gran alcance; (*weather forecast*) de larga proyección.

longshoreman |lóng'shôrmən| *n* (*US*) estibador *m*.

long-sighted |lóng'sītid| *a* présbita.

long-standing |lóng'stan'ding| *a* de mucho tiempo.

long-suffering |lóng'suf'ûring| *a* sufrido.

long-term |lóng'tûrm'| *a* a largo plazo.

long wave *n* onda larga.

long-winded |lóng'win'did| *a* prolijo.

loo |lōō| *n* (*Brit: col*) wáter *m*.

loofah |lōō'fə| *n* (*Brit: sponge*) esponja de lufa.

look |lōōk| *vi* mirar; (*seem*) parecer; (*building etc*): **to ~ south/on to the sea** dar al sur/al mar ♦ *n* mirada; (*glance*) vistazo; (*appearance*) aire *m*, aspecto; **~s** *npl* físico *sg*, belleza *sg*; **to ~ ahead** mirar hacia delante; **it ~s about 4 meters long** yo calculo que tiene unos 4 metros de largo; **it ~s all right to me** me parece que está bien; **to have a ~ at sth** echar un vistazo a algo.

look after *vt fus* cuidar.

look around *vi* echar una mirada alrededor; **to ~ around for sth** buscar algo.

look at *vt fus* mirar; (*consider*) considerar.

look back *vi* mirar hacia atrás; **to ~ back at sb/sth** mirar hacia atrás algo/a uno; **to ~ back on** (*event, period*) recordar.

look down on *vt fus* (*fig*) despreciar, mirar con desprecio.

look for *vt fus* buscar.

look forward to *vt fus* esperar con ilusión; (*in letters*): **we ~ forward to hearing from you** quedamos a la espera de sus gratas noticias; **I'm not ~ing forward to it** no tengo ganas de eso, no me hace ilusión.

look in *vi*: **to ~ in on sb** (*visit*) pasar por casa de uno.

look into *vt fus* investigar.

look on *vi* mirar (como espectador).

look out *vi* (*beware*): **to ~ out (for)** tener cuidado (de).

look out for *vt fus* (*seek*) buscar; (*await*) esperar.

look over *vt* (*essay*) revisar; (*town, building*) inspeccionar, registrar; (*person*) examinar.

look round *vi* = **look around**.

look through *vt fus* (*papers, book*) hojear; (*briefly*) echar un vistazo a; (*telescope*) mirar por.

look to *vt fus* ocuparse de; (*rely on*) contar con.

look up *vi* mirar hacia arriba; (*improve*) mejorar ♦ *vt* (*word*) buscar; (*friend*) visitar.

look up to *vt fus* admirar.

lookout |lōōk'out| *n* (*tower etc*) puesto de observación; (*person*) vigía *m/f*; **to be on the ~ for sth** estar al acecho de algo.

look-up table |lōōk'up tā'bəl| *n* (*COMPUT*) tabla de consulta.

LOOM *n abbr* (*US*: = *Loyal Order of Moose*) asociación benéfica.

loom |lōōm| *n* telar *m* ♦ *vi* (*threaten*) amenazar.

loony |lōō'nē| *a, n* (*col*) loco/a *m/f*.

loop |lōōp| *n* lazo; (*bend*) vuelta, recodo; (*COMPUT*) bucle *m*.

loophole |lōōp'hōl| *n* escapatoria.

loose |lōōs| *a* (*gen*) suelto; (*not tight*) flojo; (*wobbly etc*) movedizo; (*clothes*) ancho; (*morals, discipline*) relajado ♦ *vt* (*free*) soltar; (*slacken*) aflojar; **~ connection** (*ELEC*) rotura; **to be at ~ ends** *or* (*Brit*) **at a ~ end** no saber qué hacer; **to tie up ~ ends** (*fig*) no dejar cabo suelto.

loose change *n* cambio.

loose chippings *npl* (*Brit: on road*) gravilla *sg* suelta.

loose-fitting |lōōs'fit'ing| *a* suelto.

loose-leaf |lōōs'lēf| *a*: **~ binder** *or* **folder** carpeta de hojas sueltas *or* insertables.

loosely |lōōs'lē| *ad* libremente, aproximadamente.

loosen |lōō'sən| *vt* (*free*) soltar; (*untie*) desatar; (*slacken*) aflojar.

loosen up *vi* (*before game*) desentumecerse; (*col: relax*) soltarse, relajarse.

looseness |lōōs'nis| *n* soltura; flojedad *f*.

loot |lōōt| *n* botín *m* ♦ *vt* saquear.

looter |lōō'tûr| *n* saqueador(a) *m/f*.

looting |lōō'ting| *n* pillaje *m*.

lop |láp|: **to ~ off** *vt* cortar; (*branches*) podar.

lopsided |láp'sīdid| *a* desequilibrado.

lord |lórd| *n* señor *m*; **L~ Smith** Lord Smith; **the L~** el Señor; **the (House of) L~s** (*Brit*) la Cámara de los Lores.

lordly |lórd'lē| *a* señorial.

lore |lór| *n* saber *m* popular, tradiciones *fpl*.

lorry |lór'ē| *n* (*Brit*) camión *m*.

lorry driver *n* (*Brit*) camionero/a.

lose, *pt, pp* **lost** |lōōz, lôst| *vt* perder ♦ *vi* perder, ser vencido; **to ~ (time)** (*clock*) atrasarse; **to ~ no time (in doing sth)** no tardar (en hacer algo); **to get lost** (*object*) extraviarse; (*person*) perderse.

lose out *vi* salir perdiendo.

loser [lōō'zûr] *n* perdedor(a) *m/f*: **to be a bad** ~ no saber perder.

losing [lōō'zing] *a* (*team etc*) vencido, perdedor(a).

loss [lôs] *n* pérdida; **heavy** ~**es** (*MIL*) grandes pérdidas *fpl*; **to be at a** ~ no saber qué hacer; **to be a dead** ~ ser completamente inútil; **to cut one's** ~**es** cortar por lo sano; **to sell sth at a** ~ vender algo con pérdida.

loss leader *n* (*COMM*) artículo de promoción.

lost [lôst] *pt, pp of* **lose ♦** *a* perdido; ~ **in thought** absorto, ensimismado.

lost and found *n* (*US*) objetos *mpl* perdidos, departamento de objetos perdidos.

lost cause *n* causa perdida.

lost property, lost property office *or* **department** *n* (*Brit*) = **lost and found**.

lot [lât] *n* (*at auctions*) lote *m*; (*destiny*) suerte *f*; (*US: plot of land*) terreno; **the** ~ el todo, todos *mpl*, todas *fpl*; **a** ~ mucho, bastante; **a** ~ **of**, ~**s of** mucho(s)/a(s) (*pl*); **I read a** ~ leo bastante; **to draw** ~**s (for sth)** echar suertes (para decidir algo).

lotion [lō'shən] *n* loción *f*.

lottery [lât'ûrē] *n* lotería.

loud [loud] *a* (*voice, sound*) fuerte; (*laugh, shout*) estrepitoso; (*gaudy*) chillón/ona **♦** *ad* (*speak etc*) fuerte; **out** ~ en voz alta.

loudly [loud'lē] *ad* (*noisily*) fuerte; (*aloud*) en alta voz.

loudness [loud'nis] *n* (*of sound etc*) fuerza.

loudspeaker [loud'spēkûr] *n* altavoz *m*.

lounge [lounj] *n* salón *m*, sala (de estar); (*of hotel*) salón *m*; (*of airport*) sala (de embarque) **♦** *vi* (*also:* ~ **around**) holgazanear, no hacer nada.

lounge bar *n* (*Brit*) salón *m*.

lounge suit *n* (*Brit*) traje *m* de calle.

louse, *pl* **lice** [lous, līs] *n* piojo.

louse up *vt* (*col*) echar a perder.

lousy [lou'zē] *a* (*fig*) vil, asqueroso.

lout [lout] *n* gamberro/a.

louver, (*Brit***) louvre** [lōō'vûr] *a*: ~ **door** puerta de rejilla; ~ **window** ventana de libro.

lovable [luv'əbəl] *a* amable, simpático.

love [luv] *n* amor *m* **♦** *vt* amar, querer; **to send one's** ~ **to sb** dar sus recuerdos a uno; ~ **from Anne** (*in letter*) con cariño de Anne; **I** ~ **to read** me encanta leer; **to be in** ~ **with** estar enamorado de; **to make** ~ hacer el amor; **for the** ~ **of** por amor de; **"15** ~**"** (*TENNIS*) "15 a cero"; **I** ~ **paella** me encanta la paella; **I'd** ~ **to come** me gustaría muchísimo venir.

love affair *n* aventura sentimental.

love letter *n* carta de amor.

love life *n* vida sentimental.

lovely [luv'lē] *a* (*delightful*) precioso, encantador(a); (*beautiful*) hermoso; **we had a** ~ **time** lo pasamos estupendo.

lovemaking [luv'māking] *n* relaciones *fpl* sexuales.

lover [luv'ûr] *n* amante *m/f*; (*amateur*): **a** ~ **of** un(a) aficionado/a *or* un(a) amante de.

lovesick [luv'sik] *a* enfermo de amor, amartelado.

lovesong [luv'sông] *n* canción *f* de amor.

loving [luv'ing] *a* amoroso, cariñoso.

lovingly [luv'inglē] *ad* amorosamente, cariñosamente.

low [lō] *a, ad* bajo **♦** *n* (*METEOROLOGY*) área de baja presión **♦** *vi* (*cow*) mugir; **to feel** ~ sentirse deprimido; **to turn (down)** ~ bajar; **to reach a new** *or* **an all-time** ~ llegar a su punto más bajo.

low-beam [lō'bēm] *a*: ~ **headlights** luces *fpl* de cruce.

lowbrow [lō'brou] *a* (*person*) de poca cultura.

low-calorie [lō'kal'ûrē] *a* de bajo contenido calorífico.

low-cut [lō'kut] *a* (*dress*) escotado.

lowdown [lō'doun] *n* (*col*): **he gave me the** ~ **on it** me puso al corriente **♦** *a* (*mean*) vil, bajo.

lower *vt* [lō'ûr] bajar; (*US AUT: lights*) poner luces de cruce; (*reduce: price*) reducir, rebajar; (: *resistance*) debilitar; **to** ~ **o.s. to** (*fig*) rebajarse a **♦** *vi* [lou'ûr]: **to** ~ **(at sb)** fulminar a uno con la mirada.

lower case *n* (*TYP*) minúscula.

lowering [lou'ûring] *a* (*sky*) amenazador(a).

low-fat [lō'fat'] *a* (*milk, yogurt*) desnatado; (*diet*) bajo en calorías.

low-key [lō'kē'] *a* de mínima intensidad; (*operation*) de poco perfil.

lowland [lō'lənd] *n* tierra baja.

low-level [lō'levəl] *a* de bajo nivel; (*flying*) a poca altura.

lowly [lō'lē] *a* humilde.

low-lying [lō'lī'ing] *a* bajo.

loyal [loi'əl] *a* leal.

loyalist [loi'əlist] *n* legitimista *m/f*.

loyally [loi'əlē] *ad* lealmente.

loyalty [loi'əltē] *n* lealtad *f*.

lozenge [lâz'inj] *n* (*MED*) pastilla.

LP *n abbr* = **long-playing record**.

L-plates [el plāts] *npl* (*Brit*) placas *fpl* de aprendiz de conductor.

LPN *n abbr* (*US*: = *Licensed Practical Nurse*) enfermero/a practicante.

LSAT *n abbr* (*US*) = *Law School Admissions Test*.

LSD *n abbr* (= *lysergic acid diethylamide*) LSD *f*.

LSE *n abbr* = *London School of Economics*.

LST *n abbr* (*US*) = *local standard time*.

Ltd *abbr* (*Brit*: = *limited company*) S.A.

lubricant [lōōb'rikənt] *n* lubricante *m*.

lubricate [lōōb'rikāt] *vt* lubricar, engrasar.

lubrication [lōōbrikā'shən] *n* lubricación *f*.

lucid [lōō'sid] *a* lúcido.

lucidity [lōōsid'itē] *n* lucidez *f*.
lucidly [lōō'sidlē] *ad* lúcidamente.
luck [luk] *n* suerte *f*; **good/bad** ~ buena/mala suerte; **good** ~! ¡(que tengas) suerte!; **to be in** ~ estar de *or* con suerte; **to be out of** ~ tener mala suerte.
luckily [luk'ilē] *ad* afortunadamente.
lucky [luk'ē] *a* afortunado.
lucrative [lōō'krətiv] *a* lucrativo.
ludicrous [lōō'dəkrəs] *a* absurdo.
luffa [luf'ə] *n* (*US: sponge*) esponja de lufa.
lug [lug] *vt* (*drag*) arrastrar.
luggage [lug'ij] *n* equipaje *m*.
luggage car *n* (*US*) furgón *m or* vagón *m* de equipaje.
luggage checkroom *n* (*US*) consigna.
luggage rack *n* (*in train*) rejilla, redecilla; (*on car*) baca, portaequipajes *m inv*.
lugubrious [lōōgōō'brēəs] *a* lúgubre.
lukewarm [lōōk'wôrm'] *a* tibio, templado.
lull [lul] *n* tregua ♦ *vt* (*child*) acunar; (*person, fear*) calmar.
lullaby [lul'əbī] *n* nana.
lumbago [lumbā'gō] *n* lumbago.
lumber [lum'bûr] *n* (*junk*) trastos *mpl* viejos; (*wood*) maderos *mpl* ♦ *vt* (*Brit col*): **to** ~ **sb with sth/sb** hacer que uno cargue con algo/uno ♦ *vi* (*also*: ~ **about,** ~ **along**) moverse pesadamente.
lumberjack [lum'bûrjak] *n* maderero.
lumberyard [lum'bûryârd] *n* (*US*) almacén *m* de madera.
luminous [lōō'minəs] *a* luminoso.
lump [lump] *n* terrón *m*; (*fragment*) trozo; (*in sauce*) grumo; (*in throat*) nudo; (*swelling*) bulto ♦ *vt* (*also*: ~ **together**) juntar.
lump sum *n* suma global.
lumpy [lum'pē] *a* (*sauce*) lleno de grumos.
lunacy [lōō'nəsē] *n* locura.
lunar [lōō'nûr] *a* lunar.
lunatic [lōō'nətik] *a, n* loco/a *m/f*; **the** ~ **fringe** la corriente extremista.
lunatic asylum *n* manicomio.
lunch [lunch] *n* almuerzo, comida ♦ *vi* almorzar; **to invite sb to** *or* **for** ~ invitar a uno a almorzar.
lunch break, lunch hour *n* hora del almuerzo.
luncheon [lun'chən] *n* almuerzo.
luncheon meat *n* tipo de fiambre.
lunchtime [lunch'tīm] *n* hora del almuerzo *or* de comer.
lung [lung] *n* pulmón *m*.
lung cancer *n* cáncer *m* del pulmón.
lunge [lunj] *vi* (*also*: ~ **forward**) abalanzarse; **to** ~ **at** arremeter contra.
lupin [lōō'pin] *n* altramuz *m*.
lurch [lûrch] *vi* dar sacudidas ♦ *n* sacudida; **to leave sb in the** ~ dejar a uno plantado.
lure [lōōr] *n* (*bait*) cebo; (*decoy*) señuelo ♦ *vt* convencer con engaños.
lurid [lōō'rid] *a* (*color*) chillón/ona; (*account*) sensacional; (*detail*) horripilante.

lurk [lûrk] *vi* (*hide*) esconderse; (*wait*) estar al acecho.
luscious [lush'əs] *a* delicioso.
lush [lush] *a* exuberante.
lust [lust] *n* lujuria; (*greed*) codicia.
lust after *vt fus* codiciar.
luster [lus'tûr] *n* (*US*) lustre *m*, brillo.
lustful [lust'fəl] *a* lascivo, lujurioso.
lustre [lus'tûr] *n* (*Brit*) = **luster**.
lustrous [lus'trəs] *a* brillante.
lusty [lus'tē] *a* robusto, fuerte.
lute [lōōt] *n* laúd *m*.
Luxembourg [luk'səmbûrg] *n* Luxemburgo.
luxuriant [lōōgzhōōr'ēənt] *a* exuberante.
luxurious [lōōgzhōōr'ēəs] *a* lujoso.
luxury [luk'shûrē] *n* lujo ♦ *cpd* de lujo.
luxury tax *n* impuesto de lujo.
LW *abbr* (*RADIO*) = **long wave**.
lying [lī'ing] *n* mentiras *fpl* ♦ *a* (*statement, story*) mentiroso, falso; (*person*) mentiroso.
lynch [linch] *vt* linchar.
lynx [lingks] *n* lince *m*.
Lyons [lī'ənz] *n* Lyón *m*.
lyre [lī'ûr] *n* lira.
lyric [lir'ik] *a* lírico; ~**s** *npl* (*of song*) letra *sg*.
lyrical [lir'ikəl] *a* lírico.

M

M, m [em] *n* (*letter*) M, m *f*; **M for Mike** M de Madrid.
M *n abbr* = **million(s)**; (= *medium*) M; (*Brit*: = *motorway*): **the M8** ≈ la A8.
m *abbr* (= *meter*) m.; = **mile(s)**.
MA *n abbr* (*US*) = *Military Academy*; = **Master of Arts** ♦ *abbr* (*US MAIL*) = *Massachusetts*.
mac [mak] *n* (*Brit*) impermeable *m*.
macabre [məkâ'brə] *a* macabro.
macaroni [makərō'nē] *n* macarrones *mpl*.
macaroon [makərōōn'] *n* macarón *m*, mostachón *m*.
mace [mās] *n* (*weapon, ceremonial*) maza; (*spice*) macis *f*.
machinations [makənā'shənz] *npl* intrigas *fpl*, manipulaciones *fpl*.
machine [məshēn'] *n* máquina ♦ *vt* (*TECH*) trabajar a máquina; (*Brit*: *dress etc*) coser a máquina.
machine code *n* (*COMPUT*) código máquina.
machine gun *n* ametralladora.
machine language *n* (*COMPUT*) lenguaje *m* máquina.
machine readable *a* (*COMPUT*) legible

por máquina.

machinery [məshē'nûrē] *n* maquinaria; (*fig*) mecanismo.

machine shop *n* taller *m* de máquinas.

machine tool *n* máquina herramienta.

machine translation *n* traducción *f* automática.

machine washable *a* lavable en la lavadora.

machinist [məshē'nist] *n* operario/a *m/f* (de máquina).

macho [mâch'ō] *a* macho.

mackerel [mak'úrəl] *n, pl inv* caballa.

mackintosh [mak'intâsh] *n* (*Brit*) impermeable *m*.

macro... [mak'rō] *pref* macro....

macroeconomics [makrōēkənâm'iks] *n* macroeconomía.

mad [mad] *a* loco; (*idea*) disparatado; (*angry*) furioso; ~ **(at** *or* **with sb)** furioso con uno; **to be ~ (keen) about** *or* **on sth** estar loco por algo; **to go ~** volverse loco, enloquecer(se).

madam [mad'əm] *n* señora; **can I help you ~?** ¿le puedo ayudar, señora?; **M~ Chairman** señora presidenta.

madden [mad'ən] *vt* volver loco.

maddening [mad'əning] *a* enloquecedor(a).

made [mād] *pt, pp of* **make**.

Madeira [mədē'rə] *n* (*GEO*) Madera; (*wine*) vino de Madera, madera *m*.

made-to-measure [mād'təmezh'ûr] *a* (*Brit*) hecho a la medida.

made-to-order [mād'tōōôr'dûr] *a* (*US*) hecho a la medida.

made-up [mād'up'] *a* (*story*) ficticio.

madly [mad'lē] *ad* locamente.

madman [mad'man] *n* loco.

madness [mad'nis] *n* locura.

Madonna [mədân'ə] *n* Virgen *f*.

Madrid [mədrid'] *n* Madrid *m*.

madrigal [mad'rəgəl] *n* madrigal *m*.

Mafia [mâf'ēə] *n* Mafia.

magazine [magəzēn'] *n* revista; (*MIL: store*) almacén *m*; (*of firearm*) recámara.

maggot [mag'ət] *n* gusano.

magic [maj'ik] *n* magia ♦ *a* mágico.

magical [maj'ikəl] *a* mágico.

magician [məjish'ən] *n* mago/a; (*conjurer*) prestidigitador(a) *m/f*.

magistrate [maj'istrāt] *n* juez *m/f* (municipal).

magnanimity [magnənim'itē] *n* magnanimidad *f*.

magnanimous [magnan'əməs] *a* magnánimo.

magnate [mag'nāt] *n* magnate *m/f*.

magnesium [magnē'zēəm] *n* magnesio.

magnet [mag'nit] *n* imán *m*.

magnetic [magnet'ik] *a* magnético.

magnetic disk *n* (*COMPUT*) disco magnético.

magnetic tape *n* cinta magnética.

magnetism [mag'nitizəm] *n* magnetismo.

magnification [magnəfəkā'shən] *n* aumento.

magnificence [magnif'isəns] *n* magnificencia.

magnificent [magnif'əsənt] *a* magnífico.

magnificently [magnif'əsəntlē] *ad* magníficamente.

magnify [mag'nəfī] *vt* aumentar; (*fig*) exagerar.

magnifying glass [mag'nəfiing glas] *n* lupa.

magnitude [mag'nətōōd] *n* magnitud *f*.

magnolia [magnōl'yə] *n* magnolia.

magpie [mag'pī] *n* urraca.

maharajah [mâhərâ'jə] *n* maharajá *m*.

mahogany [məhâg'ənē] *n* caoba ♦ *cpd* de caoba.

maid [mād] *n* criada; **old ~** (*pej*) solterona.

maiden [mād'ən] *n* doncella ♦ *a* (*aunt etc*) solterona; (*speech, voyage*) inaugural.

maiden name *n* nombre *m* de soltera.

mail [māl] *n* correo; (*letters*) cartas *fpl* ♦ *vt* (*post*) echar al correo; (*send*) mandar por correo; **by ~** por correo; **by return ~** (*US*) a vuelta de correo.

mailbox [māl'bâks] *n* (*US: for letters etc*; *COMPUT*) buzón *m*.

mailing [mā'ling] *n* correo instantáneo.

mailing list [mā'ling list] *n* lista de direcciones.

mailman [māl'man] *n* (*US*) cartero.

mail order *n* pedido postal; (*business*) venta por correo ♦ *a*: ~ **firm** *or* **house** casa de venta por correo.

mailtrain [māl'trān] *n* tren *m* correo.

mail truck, (*Brit*) **mail van** *n* (*AUT*) camioneta de correos *or* de reparto.

maim [mām] *vt* mutilar, lisiar.

main [mān] *a* principal, mayor ♦ *n* (*pipe*) cañería maestra; (*US*) red *f* eléctrica; **the ~s** (*Brit ELEC*) la red eléctrica; **in the ~** en general.

main course *n* (*CULIN*) plato principal.

mainframe [mān'frām] *n* (*also:* ~ **computer**) computador *m or* ordenador *m* central.

mainland [mān'lənd] *n* continente *m*.

main line *n* línea de largo recorrido.

mainly [mān'lē] *ad* principalmente, en su mayoría.

main road *n* carretera principal.

mainstay [mān'stā] *n* (*fig*) pilar *m*.

mainstream [mān'strēm] *n* (*fig*) corriente *f* principal.

main street *n* calle *f* mayor.

maintain [māntān'] *vt* mantener; (*affirm*) sostener; **to ~ that ...** mantener *or* sostener que ... .

maintenance [mān'tənəns] *n* mantenimiento; (*alimony*) pensión *f* alimenticia.

maintenance contract *n* contrato de mantenimiento.

maintenance order *n* (*LAW*) obligación *f*

de pagar una pensión alimenticia al cónyuge.

maisonette [māzənet'] *n* (*Brit*) apartamento de dos pisos.

maize [māz] *n* maíz *m*, choclo (*LAm*).

Maj. *abbr* (*MIL*) = **major**.

majestic [məjes'tik] *a* majestuoso.

majesty [maj'istē] *n* majestad *f*.

major [mā'jûr] *n* (*MIL*) comandante *m* ♦ *a* principal; (*MUS*) mayor ♦ *vi* (*US UNIV*): **to ~ (in)** especializarse en; **a ~ operation** una operación *or* intervención de gran importancia.

Majorca [məyór'kə] *n* Mallorca.

major general *n* (*MIL*) general *m* de división.

majority [məjór'itē] *n* mayoría ♦ *cpd* (*verdict*) mayoritario.

majority holding *n* (*COMM*): **to have a ~** tener un interés mayoritario.

make [māk] *vt* (*pt, pp* **made** [mād]) hacer; (*manufacture*) hacer, fabricar; (*cause to be*): **to ~ sb sad** hacer *or* poner triste a uno; (*force*): **to ~ sb do sth** obligar a uno a hacer algo; (*equal*): **2 and 2 ~ 4** 2 y 2 son 4 ♦ *n* marca; **to ~ a fool of sb** poner a uno en ridículo; **to ~ a profit/loss** obtener ganancias/sufrir pérdidas; **to ~ a profit of $500** sacar una ganancia de 500 dólares; **to ~ it** (*arrive*) llegar; (*achieve sth*) tener éxito; **what time do you ~ it?** ¿qué hora tienes?; **to ~ do with** contentarse con.

make for *vt fus* (*place*) dirigirse a.

make off *vi* largarse.

make out *vt* (*decipher*) descifrar; (*understand*) entender; (*see*) distinguir; (*write: cheque*) extender; **to ~ out (that)** (*claim, imply*) dar a entender (que); **to ~ out a case for sth** presentar una defensa de algo.

make over *vt* (*assign*): **to ~ over (to)** ceder *or* traspasar (a).

make up *vt* (*invent*) inventar; (*parcel*) hacer ♦ *vi* reconciliarse; (*with cosmetics*) maquillarse; **to be made up of** estar compuesto de.

make up for *vt fus* compensar.

make-believe [māk'bilēv] *n* ficción *f*, invención *f*.

maker [mā'kûr] *n* fabricante *m/f*.

makeshift [māk'shift] *a* improvisado.

make-up [māk'up] *n* maquillaje *m*.

make-up bag *n* bolsita del maquillaje *or* de los cosméticos.

make-up remover *n* desmaquillador *m*.

making [mā'king] *n* (*fig*): **in the ~** en vías de formación; **to have the ~s of** (*person*) tener madera de.

maladjusted [maləjus'tid] *a* inadaptado.

maladroit [malədroit'] *a* torpe.

malaise [malāz'] *n* malestar *m*.

malaria [məlär'ēə] *n* malaria.

Malawi [mə'läwē] *n* Malawi *m*.

Malay [məlā'] *a* malayo ♦ *n* (*person*) malayo/a; (*LING*) malayo.

Malaya [məlā'yə] *n* Malaya, Malaca.

Malayan [məlā'yən] *a, n* = **Malay**.

Malaysia [məlā'zhə] *n* Malasia.

Malaysian [məlā'zhən] *a, n* malasio/a *m/f*.

Maldive Islands [maldīv' ī'ləndz], **Maldives** [mal'dīvz] *npl*: **the ~** las Maldivas.

male [māl] *n* (*BIOL, ELEC*) macho ♦ *a* (*sex, attitude*) masculino; (*child etc*) varón.

male chauvinist (pig) [māl' shōvənist (pig')] *n* machista *m*.

male nurse *n* enfermero.

malevolence [məlev'ələns] *n* malevolencia.

malevolent [məlev'ələnt] *a* malévolo.

malfunction [malfungk'shən] *n* mal funcionamiento.

malice [mal'is] *n* (*ill will*) malicia; (*rancor*) rencor *m*.

malicious [məlish'əs] *a* malicioso; rencoroso.

maliciously [məlish'əslē] *ad* con malevolencia, con malicia; rencorosamente.

malign [məlīn'] *vt* difamar, calumniar ♦ *a* maligno.

malignant [məlig'nənt] *a* (*MED*) maligno.

malinger [məling'gûr] *vi* fingirse enfermo.

malingerer [məling'gûrûr] *n* enfermo/a fingido/a.

mall [môl] *n* (*also*: **shopping ~**) centro comercial.

malleable [mal'ēəbəl] *a* maleable.

mallet [mal'it] *n* mazo.

malnutrition [malnōōtrish'ən] *n* desnutrición *f*.

malpractice [malprak'tis] *n* negligencia profesional.

malt [môlt] *n* malta.

Malta [môl'tə] *n* Malta.

Maltese [môltēz'] *a* maltés/esa ♦ *n, pl inv* maltés/esa *m/f*; (*LING*) maltés *m*.

maltreat [maltrēt'] *vt* maltratar.

mammal [mam'əl] *n* mamífero.

mammoth [mam'əth] *n* mamut *m* ♦ *a* gigantesco.

man, *pl* **men** [man, men] *n* hombre *m*; (*CHESS*) pieza ♦ *vt* (*NAUT*) tripular; (*MIL*) guarnecer; **an old ~** un viejo; **~ and wife** marido y mujer.

Man. *abbr* (*Canada*) = *Manitoba*.

manacle [man'əkəl] *n* esposa, manilla; **~s** *npl* grillos *mpl*.

manage [man'ij] *vi* arreglárselas, ir tirando ♦ *vt* (*be in charge of*) dirigir; (*person etc*) manejar; **to ~ to do sth** alcanzar a *or* conseguir hacer algo; **to ~ without sth/sb** prescindir de algo/uno.

manageable [man'ijəbəl] *a* manejable.

management [man'ijmənt] *n* dirección *f*, administración *f*; "**under new ~**" "bajo nueva dirección".

management accounting *n* contabilidad *f* de gestión.

management consultant *n* consultor(a) *m/f* en dirección de empresas, asesor(a) *m/f* administrativo/a.

manager [man'ijûr] *n* director *m*; (*SPORT*) entrenador *m*; **sales ~** jefe/a *m/f* de ventas.

manageress [man'ijúris] *n* directora; (*SPORT*) entrenadora.

managerial [manijē'rēəl] *a* directivo.

managing director [man'ijing dirɛk'tûr] *n* director(a) *m/f* general.

mandarin [man'dûrin] *n* (*also:* **~ orange**) mandarina; (*person*) mandarín *m*.

mandate [man'dāt] *n* mandato.

mandatory [man'dətôrē] *a* obligatorio.

mandolin(e) [man'dəlin] *n* mandolina.

mane [mān] *n* (*of horse*) crin *f*; (*of lion*) melena.

maneuver [mənōō'vûr] (*US*) *vt, vi* maniobrar ♦ *n* maniobra; **to ~ sb into doing sth** manipular a uno para que haga algo.

maneuvrable [mənōō'vrəbəl] *a* (*car etc*) manejable.

manful [man'fəl] *a* resuelto.

manfully [man'fəlē] *ad* resueltamente.

mangle [mang'gəl] *vt* mutilar, destrozar ♦ *n* rodillo.

mango, **~es** [mang'gō] *n* mango.

mangrove [mang'grōv] *n* mangle *m*.

mangy [mān'jē] *a* roñoso; (*MED*) sarnoso.

manhandle [man'handəl] *vt* maltratar; (*move by hand: goods*) manipular.

manhole [man'hōl] *n* pozo de visita.

manhood [man'hōod] *n* edad *f* viril; virilidad *f*.

man-hour [man'ouûr] *n* hora-hombre *f*.

manhunt [man'hunt] *n* caza de hombre.

mania [mā'nēə] *n* manía.

maniac [mā'nēak] *n* maníaco/a; (*fig*) maniático.

manic [man'ik] *a* (*behavior, activity*) frenético.

manic-depressive [man'ikdiprɛs'iv] *a, n* maniacodepresivo/a *m/f*.

manicure [man'əkyōōr] *n* manicura.

manicure set *n* estuche *m* de manicura.

manifest [man'əfɛst] *vt* manifestar, mostrar ♦ *a* manifiesto ♦ *n* manifiesto.

manifestation [manəfɛstā'shən] *n* manifestación *f*.

manifestly [man'əfɛstlē] *ad* evidentemente.

manifesto [manəfɛs'tō] *n* manifiesto.

manifold [man'əfōld] *a* múltiples ♦ *n* (*AUT etc*): **exhaust ~** colector *m* de escape.

Manila [mənil'ə] *n* Manila.

manil(l)a *n* (*paper, envelope*) manila.

manipulate [mənip'yəlāt] *vt* manipular.

manipulation [mənipyəlā'shən] *n* manipulación *f*, manejo.

mankind [man'kīnd'] *n* humanidad *f*, género humano.

manliness [man'lēnis] *n* virilidad *f*, hombradía.

manly [man'lē] *a* varonil.

man-made [man'mād] *a* artificial.

manna [man'ə] *n* maná *m*.

mannequin [man'əkin] *n* (*dummy*) maniquí *m*; (*fashion model*) modelo *f*.

manner [man'ûr] *n* manera, modo; (*behavior*) conducta, manera de ser; (*type*) clase *f*; **~s** *npl* modales *mpl*, educación *fsg*; **(good) ~s** educación *fsg*, (buenos) modales *mpl*; **bad ~s** falta *sg* de educación, pocos modales *mpl*; **all ~ of** toda clase *or* suerte de.

mannerism [man'ərizəm] *n* hábito, peculiaridad *f*.

mannerly [man'ûrlē] *a* bien educado, formal.

manoeuvre [mənōō'vûr] *etc* (*Brit*) = **maneuver** *etc*.

manor [man'ûr] *n* (*also:* **~ house**) casa solariega.

manpower [man'pouûr] *n* mano *f* de obra.

manservant [man'sûrvənt] *n* criado.

mansion [man'chən] *n* palacio, casa grande.

manslaughter [man'slôtûr] *n* homicidio no premeditado.

mantelpiece [man'təlpēs] *n* repisa, chimenea.

mantle [man'təl] *n* manto; (*fig*) capa.

man-to-man [man'təman'] *a* entre hombres.

manual [man'yōōəl] *a* manual ♦ *n* manual *m*; **~ worker** obrero, trabajador *m* de camisa azul.

manufacture [manyəfak'chûr] *vt* fabricar ♦ *n* fabricación *f*.

manufactured goods [manyəfak'chûrd gōōdz] *npl* manufacturas *fpl*, bienes *mpl* manufacturados.

manufacturer [manyəfak'chûrûr] *n* fabricante *m/f*.

manufacturing industries [manyəfak'chûring in'dəstrēz] *npl* industrias *fpl* de manufactura.

manure [mənōōr'] *n* estiércol *m*, abono.

manuscript [man'yəskript] *n* manuscrito.

Manx [mangks] *a* de la Isla de Man.

many [men'ē] *a* muchos/as ♦ *pron* muchos/as; **a great ~** muchísimos, buen número de; **~ a time** muchas veces; **too ~ difficulties** demasiadas dificultades; **twice as ~** el doble; **how ~?** ¿cuántos?

map [map] *n* mapa *m* ♦ *vt* trazar el mapa de.

map out *vt* (*fig: career, vacation, essay*) proyectar, planear.

maple [mā'pəl] *n* arce *m*, maple *m* (*LAm*).

mar [mâr] *vt* estropear.

Mar. *abbr* (= *March*) mar.

marathon [mar'əthân] *n* maratón *m* ♦ *a*: **a ~ session** una sesión larguísima *or* interminable.

marathon runner *n* corredor(a) *m/f* de maratones.

marauder |mərôd'ûr| *n* merodeador(a) *m/f*, intruso/a.

marble |mâr'bəl| *n* mármol *m*; (*toy*) canica.

March |mârch| *n* marzo.

march |mârch| *vi* (*MIL*) marchar; (*fig*) caminar con resolución ♦ *n* marcha; (*demonstration*) manifestación *f*.

marcher |mâr'chûr| *n* manifestante *m/f*.

marching |mâr'ching| *n*: **to give sb his ~ orders** (*fig*) mandar a paseo a uno; (*employee*) poner de patitas en la calle a uno.

march-past |mârch'past| *n* desfile *m*.

mare |mâr| *n* yegua.

margarine |mâr'jûrin| *n* margarina.

marg(e) |mârj| *n abbr* = **margarine**.

margin |mâr'jin| *n* margen *m*.

marginal |mâr'jinəl| *a* marginal.

marginally |mâr'jinəlē| *ad* ligeramente.

marginal seat *n* (*POL*) circunscripción *f* políticamente indefinida.

marigold |mar'əgōld| *n* caléndula.

marijuana |marəwá'nə| *n* marijuana.

marina |mərē'nə| *n* marina.

marinade |mar'ənäd| *n* adobo.

marinate |mar'ənāt| *vt* adobar.

marine |mərēn'| *a* marino ♦ *n* soldado de marina.

marine insurance *n* seguro marítimo.

mariner |mar'inûr| *n* marinero, marino.

marionette |marēənct'| *n* marioneta, títere *m*.

marital |mar'itəl| *a* matrimonial; **~ status** estado civil.

maritime |mar'itīm| *a* marítimo.

marjoram |mâr'jûrəm| *n* mejorana.

mark |mârk| *n* marca, señal *f*; (*imprint*) huella; (*stain*) mancha; (*SCOL*) nota; (*currency*) marco ♦ *vt* (*also SPORT*: *player*) marcar; (*stain*) manchar; (*Brit SCOL*) calificar, corregir; **punctuation ~s** signos *mpl* de puntuación; **to be quick off the ~** (*fig*) ser listo; **up to the ~** (*in efficiency*) a la altura de las circunstancias; **to ~ time** marcar el paso.

mark down *vt* (*reduce*: *prices, goods*) rebajar.

mark off *vt* (*tick*) indicar, señalar.

mark out *vt* trazar.

mark up *vt* (*price*) aumentar.

marked |mârkt| *a* marcado, acusado.

markedly |mâr'kidlē| *ad* marcadamente, apreciablemente.

marker |mâr'kûr| *n* (*sign*) marcador *m*; (*bookmark*) registro.

market |mâr'kit| *n* mercado ♦ *vt* (*COMM*) comercializar; (*promote*) publicitar; **open ~** mercado libre; **to be on the ~** estar en venta; **to play the ~** jugar a la bolsa.

marketable |mâr'kitəbəl| *a* comerciable.

market analysis *n* análisis *m* del mercado.

market day *n* día *m* de mercado.

market demand *n* demanda de mercado.

market forces *npl* tendencias *fpl* del mercado.

market garden *n* (*Brit*) huerto.

marketing |mâr'kiting| *n* márketing *m*, mercadotecnia.

marketing manager *n* director *m* de marketing.

market leader *n* líder *m* de ventas.

marketplace |mâr'kitplās| *n* mercado.

market price *n* precio de mercado.

market research *n* (*COMM*) investigación *f* de mercados.

market value *n* valor *m* en el mercado.

marking |mâr'king| *n* (*on animal*) pinta; (*on road*) señal *f*.

marking ink *n* tinta indeleble *or* de marcar.

marksman |mârks'mən| *n* tirador *m*.

marksmanship |mârks'mənship| *n* puntería.

mark-up |mârk'up| *n* (*COMM*: *margin*) margen *m* de beneficio; (: *increase*) aumento.

marmalade |mâr'məlād| *n* mermelada de naranja.

maroon |mərōōn'| *vt*: **to be ~ed** (*shipwrecked*) naufragarse; (*fig*) quedar abandonado ♦ *a* marrón *inv*.

marquee |mârkē'| *n* entoldado.

marquess, marquis |mâr'kwis| *n* marqués *m*.

Marrakech, Marrakesh |mâr'əkesh| *n* Marrakech *m*.

marriage |mar'ij| *n* (*state*) matrimonio; (*wedding*) boda; (*act*) casamiento.

marriage bureau *n* (*Brit*) agencia matrimonial.

marriage certificate *n* partida de casamiento.

marriage counseling, (*Brit*) **marriage guidance** *n* orientación *f* matrimonial.

married |mar'ēd| *a* casado; (*life, love*) conyugal.

marrow |mar'ō| *n* médula; (*vegetable*) calabacín *m*.

marry |mar'ē| *vt* casarse con; (*subj*: *father, priest etc*) casar ♦ *vi* (*also*: **get married**) casarse.

Mars |mârz| *n* Marte *m*.

Marseilles |mârsā'| *n* Marsella.

marsh |mârsh| *n* pantano; (*salt ~*) marisma.

marshal |mâr'shəl| *n* (*MIL*) mariscal *m*; (*at parade*) oficial *m*; (*US*: *of police, fire department*) jefe/a *m/f* ♦ *vt* (*facts*) ordenar; (*soldiers*) formar.

marshalling yard |mâr'shəling yârd| *n* (*Brit RAIL*) estación *f* clasificadora.

marshmallow |mârsh'mclō| *n* (*BOT*) malvavisco; (*sweet*) bombón *m* de merengue blando.

marshy |mâr'shē| *a* pantanoso.

marsupial |mârsōō'pēəl| *a, n* marsupial *m*.

martial [mâr'shəl] *a* marcial.
martial law *n* ley *f* marcial.
martin [mâr'tən] *n* (*also:* **house** ~) avión *m*.
martyr [mâr'tûr] *n* mártir *m/f* ♦ *vt* martirizar.
martyrdom [mâr'tûrdəm] *n* martirio.
marvel [mâr'vəl] *n* maravilla, prodigio ♦ *vi:* **to ~ (at)** maravillarse (de).
marvelous, (*Brit*) **marvellous** [mâr'vələs] *a* maravilloso.
marvel(l)ously [mâr'vələslē] *ad* maravillosamente.
Marxism [mârk'sizəm] *n* marxismo.
Marxist [mâr'ksist] *a, n* marxista *m/f*.
marzipan [mâr'zəpan] *n* mazapán *m*.
mascara [maskar'ə] *n* rimel *m*.
mascot [mas'kət] *n* mascota.
masculine [mas'kyəlin] *a* masculino.
masculinity [maskyəlin'itē] *n* masculinidad *f*.
MASH [mash] *n abbr* (*US*) = *mobile army surgical hospital.*
mash [mash] *n* (*mix*) mezcla; (*CULIN*) puré *m*; (*pulp*) amasijo.
mashed potatoes [masht pətā'tōz] *npl* puré *m* de patatas *or* papas (*LAm*).
mask [mask] *n* (*also ELEC*) máscara ♦ *vt* enmascarar.
masochism [mas'əkizəm] *n* masoquismo.
masochist [mas'əkist] *n* masoquista *m/f*.
mason [mā'sən] *n* (*also:* **stone**~) albañil *m*; (*also:* **free**~) masón *m*.
masonic [məsân'ik] *a* masónico.
masonry [mā'sənrē] *n* masonería; (*building*) mampostería.
masquerade [maskərād'] *n* baile *m* de máscaras; (*fig*) mascarada ♦ *vi:* **to ~ as** disfrazarse de, hacerse pasar por.
mass [mas] *n* (*people*) muchedumbre *f*; (*PHYSICS*) masa; (*REL*) misa; (*great quantity*) montón *m* ♦ *vi* reunirse; (*MIL*) concentrarse; **the ~es** las masas; **to go to ~** oír misa.
Mass. *abbr* (*US*) = *Massachusetts.*
massacre [mas'əkûr] *n* masacre *f* ♦ *vt* masacrar.
massage [məsâzh'] *n* masaje *m* ♦ *vt* dar masaje a.
masseur [masûr'] *n* masajista *m*.
masseuse [məsōōs'] *n* masajista *f*.
massive [mas'iv] *a* enorme; (*support, intervention*) masivo.
mass media [mas mē'dēə] *npl* medios *mpl* de comunicación masiva.
mass meeting *n* (*of everyone concerned*) reunión *f* en masa; (*huge*) mitin *m*.
mass-produce [mas'prədōōs'] *vt* fabricar en serie.
mass production *n* fabricación *f or* producción *f* en serie.
mast [mast] *n* (*NAUT*) mástil *m*; (*RADIO etc*) torre *f*, antena.

master [mas'tûr] *n* maestro; (*in secondary school*) profesor *m*; (*title for boys*): **M~ X** Señorito X ♦ *vt* dominar; (*learn*) aprender a fondo.
master disk *n* (*COMPUT*) disco maestro.
masterful [mas'tûrfəl] *a* magistral, dominante.
master key *n* llave *f* maestra.
masterly [mas'tûrlē] *a* magistral.
mastermind [mas'tûrmīnd] *n* inteligencia superior ♦ *vt* dirigir, planear.
Master of Arts (MA) *n* licenciatura superior en Letras.
Master of Ceremonies *n* encargado de protocolo.
Master of Science (MSc) *n* licenciatura superior en Ciencias.
masterpiece [mas'tûrpēs] *n* obra maestra.
master plan *n* plan *m* rector.
masterstroke [mas'tûrstrōk] *n* golpe *m* maestro.
mastery [mas'tûrē] *n* maestría.
mastiff [mas'tif] *n* mastín *m*.
masturbate [mas'tûrbāt] *vi* masturbarse.
masturbation [mastûrbā'shən] *n* masturbación *f*.
mat [mat] *n* estera; (*also:* **door**~) felpudo ♦ *a* = **matt.**
match [mach] *n* cerilla, fósforo; (*game*) partido; (*fig*) igual *m/f* ♦ *vt* emparejar; (*go well with*) hacer juego con; (*equal*) igualar ♦ *vi* hacer juego; **to be a good ~** hacer buena pareja.
matchbox [mach'bâks] *n* caja de cerillas.
matching [mach'ing] *a* que hace juego.
matchless [mach'lis] *a* sin par, incomparable.
matchmaker [mach'mākûr] *n* casamentero.
mate [māt] *n* (*work*~) colega *m/f*; (*col: friend*) amigo/a; (*animal*) macho/hembra; (*in merchant navy*) segundo de a bordo ♦ *vi* acoplarse, parearse ♦ *vt* acoplar, parear.
material [mətē'rēəl] *n* (*substance*) materia; (*equipment*) material *m*; (*cloth*) tela, tejido ♦ *a* material; (*important*) esencial; **~s** *npl* materiales *mpl*; (*equipment etc*) artículos *mpl*.
materialistic [mətērēəlis'tik] *a* materialista.
materialize [mətēr'ēəlīz] *vi* materializarse.
materially [mətēr'əlē] *ad* materialmente.
maternal [mətûr'nəl] *a* maternal; **~ grandmother** abuela materna.
maternity [mətûr'nitē] *n* maternidad *f*.
maternity benefit *n* subsidio de maternidad.
maternity dress *n* vestido premamá.
maternity hospital *n* hospital *m* de maternidad.
maternity leave *n* licencia por maternidad.
math [math] *n abbr* (*US: = mathematics*) matemáticas *fpl*.
mathematical [mathəmat'ikəl] *a* matemáti-

co.

mathematically [mathəmat'ikəlē] *ad* matemáticamente.

mathematician [mathəmətish'ən] *n* matemático.

mathematics [mathəmat'iks] *n* matemáticas *fpl*.

maths [maths] *n abbr* (*Brit*: = *mathematics*) matemáticas *fpl*.

matinée [matənā'] *n* función *f* de la tarde.

mating [mā'ting] *n* aparejamiento.

mating call *n* llamada del macho.

mating season *n* época de celo.

matins [mat'ənz] *n* maitines *mpl*.

matriarchal [mātrēär'kəl] *a* matriarcal.

matrices [māt'risēz] *pl of* **matrix**.

matriculation [mətrikyəlā'shən] *n* matriculación *f*.

matrimonial [matrəmō'nēəl] *a* matrimonial.

matrimony [mat'rəmōnē] *n* matrimonio.

matrix, *pl* **matrices** [mā'triks, māt'risēz] *n* matriz *f*.

matron [mā'trən] *n* (*in hospital*) enfermera jefe; (*in school*) ama de llaves.

matronly [mā'trənlē] *a* de matrona; (*fig: figure*) corpulento.

matt [mat] *a* mate.

matted [mat'id] *a* enmarañado.

matter [mat'ûr] *n* cuestión *f*, asunto; (*PHYSICS*) sustancia, materia; (*content*) contenido; (*MED: pus*) pus *m* ♦ *vi* importar; **it doesn't** ~ no importa; **what's the** ~? ¿qué pasa?; **no** ~ **what** pase lo que pase; **as a** ~ **of course** por rutina; **as a** ~ **of fact** en realidad; **printed** ~ impresos *mpl*; **reading** ~ algo para leer, libros *mpl*.

matter-of-fact [mat'ûrəvfakt'] *a* prosaico, práctico.

mattress [mat'ris] *n* colchón *m*.

mature [mətōōr'] *a* maduro ♦ *vi* madurar.

maturity [mətōō'ritē] *n* madurez *f*.

maudlin [môd'lin] *a* llorón/ona.

maul [môl] *vt* magullar.

Mauritania [môritā'nēə] *n* Mauritania.

Mauritius [môrish'ēəs] *n* Mauricio.

mausoleum [môsəlē'əm] *n* mausoleo.

mauve [mōv] *a* de color malva *or* guinda (*LAm*).

maverick [mav'ûrik] *n* (*fig*) inconformista *m/f*, persona independiente.

mawkish [môk'ish] *a* empalagoso.

max. *abbr* = **maximum**.

maxim [mak'sim] *n* máxima.

maxima [mak'səmə] *pl of* **maximum**.

maximize [mak'səmīz] *vt* (*profits etc*) llevar al máximo; (*chances*) maximizar.

maximum [mak'səməm] *a* máximo ♦ *n* (*pl* **maxima** [mak'səmə]) máximo.

May [mā] *n* mayo.

may [mā] *vi* (*conditional*: **might**) (*indicating possibility*): **he** ~ **come** puede que venga; (*be allowed to*): ~ **I smoke?** ¿puedo fumar?; (*wishes*): ~ **God bless you!** ¡que

Dios le bendiga!; ~ **I sit here?** ¿me puedo sentar aquí?

maybe [mā'bē] *ad* quizá(s); ~ **not** quizás no.

May Day *n* el primero de Mayo.

mayday [mā'dā] *n* S.O.S. *m*.

mayhem [mā'hem] *n* caos *m* total.

mayonnaise [māənāz'] *n* mayonesa.

mayor [mā'ûr] *n* alcalde *m*.

mayoress [mā'ûris] *n* alcaldesa.

maypole [mā'pōl] *n* mayo.

maze [māz] *n* laberinto.

MB *abbr* (*COMPUT*) = **megabyte**; (*Canada*) = *Manitoba*.

MBA *n abbr* (= *Master of Business Administration*) título universitario.

MBBS, MBChB *n abbr* (*Brit*: = *Bachelor of Medicine and Surgery*) título universitario.

MC *n abbr* (= *master of ceremonies*) e.p.; (*US*: = *Member of Congress*) diputado del Congreso de los Estados Unidos.

MCAT *n abbr* (*US*) = *Medical College Admissions Test*.

MCP *n abbr* (*Brit col*) = **male chauvinist pig**.

MD *n abbr* (= *Doctor of Medicine*) título universitario; (*COMM*) = **managing director** ♦ *abbr* (*US MAIL*) = *Maryland*.

ME *abbr* (*US MAIL*) = *Maine* ♦ *n abbr* (*US MED*) = *medical examiner*; (*MED*) = *myalgic encephalomyelitis*.

me [mē] *pron* (*direct*) me; (*stressed, after pronoun*) mí; **can you hear** ~? ¿me oyes?; **he heard ME!** me oyó a mí; **it's** ~ soy yo; **give them to** ~ dámelos; **with/without** ~ conmigo/sin mí; **it's for** ~ es para mí.

meadow [med'ō] *n* prado, pradera.

meager, (*Brit*) **meagre** [mē'gûr] *a* escaso, pobre.

meal [mēl] *n* comida; (*flour*) harina; **to go out for a** ~ salir a comer.

meal ticket *n* (*US*) vale *m* de comida.

mealtime [mēl'tīm] *n* hora de comer.

mealy-mouthed [mē'lēmoutḥd] *a*: **to be** ~ nunca decir las cosas claras.

mean [mēn] *a* (*with money*) tacaño; (*unkind*) mezquino, malo; (*average*) medio; (*US*: *vicious*: *animal*) resabiado; (: *person*) malicioso ♦ *vt* (*pt, pp* **meant** [ment]) (*signify*) querer decir, significar; (*intend*): **to** ~ **to do sth** pensar *or* pretender hacer algo ♦ *n* medio, término medio; **do you** ~ **it?** ¿lo dices en serio?; **what do you** ~? ¿qué quiere decir?; **to be meant for sb/sth** ser para uno/algo; *see also* **means**.

meander [mēan'dûr] *vi* (*river*) serpentear; (*person*) vagar.

meaning [mē'ning] *n* significado, sentido.

meaningful [mē'ningfəl] *a* significativo.

meaningless [mē'ninglis] *a* sin sentido.

meanness [mēn'nis] *n* (*with money*) tacañería; (*unkindness*) maldad *f*, mezquindad *f.*

means [mēnz] *npl* medio *sg*, manera *sg*; (*resource*) recursos *mpl*, medios *mpl*; **by ~ of** mediante, por medio de; **by all ~!** ¡naturalmente!, ¡claro que sí!

means test *n* control *m* de los recursos económicos.

meant [ment] *pt, pp of* **mean**.

meantime [mēn'tīm] *ad* (*also*: **in the meantime**) mientras tanto.

meanwhile [mēn'wīl] *ad* mientras tanto.

measles [mē'zəlz] *n* sarampión *m*.

measly [mēz'lē] *a* (*col*) miserable.

measurable [mezh'ûrəbəl] *a* mensurable, que se puede medir.

measure [mezh'ûr] *vt* medir; (*for clothes etc*) tomar las medidas a ♦ *vi* medir ♦ *n* medida; (*ruler*) regla; **a liter ~** una medida de un litro; **some ~ of success** cierto éxito; **to take ~s to do sth** tomar medidas para hacer algo.

measure up *vi*: **to ~ up (to)** mostrarse capaz (de).

measured [mezh'ûrd] *a* moderado; (*tone*) mesurado.

measurement [mezh'ûrmənt] *n* (*measure*) medida; (*act*) medición *f*; **to take sb's ~s** tomar las medidas a uno.

meat [mēt] *n* carne *f*; **cold ~s** (*Brit*) fiambres *mpl*; **crab ~** carne *f* de cangrejo.

meatball [mēt'bôl] *n* albóndiga.

meat pie *n* pastel *m* de carne.

meaty [mē'tē] *a* carnoso; (*fig*) sustancioso.

Mecca [mek'ə] *n* (*city*) la Meca; (*fig*) Meca.

mechanic [məkan'ik] *n* mecánico/a.

mechanical [məkan'ikəl] *a* mecánico.

mechanical engineering *n* (*science*) ingeniería mecánica; (*industry*) construcción *f* mecánica.

mechanical pencil *n* (*US*) lapicero.

mechanics [məkan'iks] *n* mecánica ♦ *npl* mecanismo *sg*.

mechanism [mek'ənizəm] *n* mecanismo.

mechanization [mekənizā'shən] *n* mecanización *f*.

mechanize [mek'ənīz] *vt* mecanizar; (*factory etc*) automatizar, reconvertir.

MEd *n abbr* (= *Master of Education*) título universitario.

medal [med'əl] *n* medalla.

medallion [mədal'yən] *n* medallón *m*.

medalist, (*Brit*) **medallist** [med'əlist] *n* (*SPORT*) ganador(a) *m/f*.

meddle [med'əl] *vi*: **to ~ in** entrometerse en; **to ~ with sth** manosear algo.

meddlesome [med'əlsəm], **meddling** [med'-ling] *a* (*interfering*) entrometido; (*touching things*) curioso.

media [mē'dēə] *npl* medios *mpl* de comunicación.

mediaeval [mēdēē'vəl] *a* = **medieval**.

median [mē'dēən] *n* (*US*: *also*: **~ strip**) faja intermedia, mediana.

media research *n* investigación *f* de los medios de publicidad.

mediate [mē'dēāt] *vi* mediar.

mediation [mēdēā'shən] *n* mediación *f*.

mediator [mē'dēātûr] *n* intermediario/a, mediador(a) *m/f*.

Medicaid [med'ikād] *n* (*US*) *programa de ayuda médica*.

medical [med'ikəl] *a* médico ♦ *n* (*also*: **~ examination**) reconocimiento médico.

medical certificate *n* certificado *m* médico.

medical examiner *n* (*US*) médico/a forense.

Medicare [med'əkär] *n* (*US*) *seguro médico del Estado*.

medicated [med'ikātid] *a* medicinal.

medication [medikā'shən] *n* (*drugs etc*) medicación *f*.

medicinal [mədis'ənəl] *a* medicinal.

medicine [med'isin] *n* medicina; (*drug*) medicamento.

medicine chest *n* botiquín *m*.

medicine man *n* hechicero.

medieval, **mediaeval** [mēdēē'vəl] *a* medieval.

mediocre [mē'dēōkûr] *a* mediocre.

mediocrity [mēdēāk'ritē] *n* mediocridad *f*.

meditate [med'ətāt] *vi* meditar.

meditation [medətā'shən] *n* meditación *f*.

Mediterranean [meditərā'nēən] *a* mediterráneo; **the ~ (Sea)** el (Mar *m*) Mediterráneo.

medium [mē'dēəm] *a* mediano, regular ♦ *n* (*pl* **media**: *means*) medio; (*pl* **mediums**: *person*) médium *m/f*; **happy ~** justo medio.

medium-sized [mē'dēəmsīzd] *a* (*tin etc*) regular; (*clothes*) de tamaño mediano.

medium wave *n* onda media.

medley [med'lē] *n* mezcla; (*MUS*) popurrí *m*.

meek [mēk] *a* manso, sumiso.

meekly [mēk'lē] *ad* mansamente, dócilmente.

meet [mēt] *vb* (*pt, pp* **met** [met]) *vt* encontrar; (*accidentally*) encontrarse con, tropezar con; (*by arrangement*) reunirse con; (*for the first time*) conocer; (*go and fetch*) ir a buscar; (*opponent*) enfrentarse con; (*obligations*) cumplir; (*bill, expenses*) pagar, costear ♦ *vi* encontrarse; (*in session*) reunirse; (*join: objects*) unirse; (*get to know*) conocerse ♦ *n* (*Brit: HUNTING*) cacería; (*US: SPORT*) encuentro; **pleased to ~ you!** ¡encantado de conocerle!, ¡mucho gusto!

meet up *vi*: **to ~ up with sb** reunirse con uno.

meet with *vt fus* reunirse con; (*difficulty*) tropezar con.

meeting [mē'ting] *n* (*also SPORT*: *rally*) encuentro; (*arranged*) cita, compromiso (*LAm*); (*formal session, business meet*) reunión *f*; (*POL*) mitin *m*; **to call a** ~ convocar *or* llamar una reunión.

meeting place *n* lugar *m* de reunión *or* encuentro.

megabyte [meg'əbīt] *n* (*COMPUT*) megabyte *m*, megaocteto.

megalomaniac [megəlōmā'nēak] *a, n* megalómano/a *m/f*.

megaphone [meg'əfōn] *n* megáfono.

melancholy [mel'ənkálē] *n* melancolía ♦ *a* melancólico.

melee [mā'lā] *n* refriega.

mellow [mel'ō] *a* (*wine*) añejo; (*sound, color*) suave; (*fruit*) maduro ♦ *vi* (*person*) madurar.

melodious [məlō'dēəs] *a* melodioso.

melodrama [mel'ədrâmə] *n* melodrama *m*.

melodramatic [melədrəmat'ik] *a* melodramático.

melody [mel'ədē] *n* melodía.

melon [mel'ən] *n* melón *m*.

melt [melt] *vi* (*metal*) fundirse; (*snow*) derretirse; (*fig*) ablandarse ♦ *vt* (*also*: ~ **down**) fundir; **~ed butter** mantequilla derretida.

melt away *vi* desvanecerse.

meltdown [melt'doun] *n* (*in nuclear reactor*) fusión *f* (de un reactor nuclear).

melting point [melt'ing point] *n* punto de fusión.

melting pot [melt'ing pât] *n* (*fig*) crisol *m*; **to be in the** ~ estar sobre el tapete.

member [mem'bûr] *n* (*of political party*) miembro; (*of club*) socio/a; **M~ of Congress (MC)** (*US*) diputado/a del Congreso; **M~ of the House of Representatives (MHR)** (*US*) diputado/a del Congreso de los Estados Unidos; **M~ of Parliament (MP)** (*Brit*) diputado/a; **M~ of the European Parliament (MEP)** (*Brit*) eurodiputado/a.

membership [mem'bûrship] *n* (*members*) número de miembros; **to seek** ~ **of** pedir el ingreso a.

membership card *n* carnet *m* de socio.

membrane [mem'brān] *n* membrana.

memento [məmen'tō] *n* recuerdo.

memo [mem'ō] *n* *abbr* (= *memorandum*) memo.

memoirs [mem'wârz] *npl* memorias *fpl*.

memo pad *n* agenda.

memorable [mem'ûrəbəl] *a* memorable.

memorandum, *pl* **memoranda** [meməran'dəm, -də] *n* apunte *m*, nota; (*POL*) memorándum *m*.

memorial [məmô'rēəl] *n* monumento conmemorativo ♦ *a* conmemorativo.

memorial day *n* día *m* de conmemoración de los difuntos de guerra.

memorize [mem'ərīz] *vt* aprender de memoria.

memory [mem'ûrē] *n* memoria; (*recollection*) recuerdo; (*COMPUT*) memoria; **to have a good/bad** ~ tener buena/mala memoria; **loss of** ~ pérdida de memoria.

men [men] *pl of* **man**.

menace [men'is] *n* amenaza; (*col*: *nuisance*) lata ♦ *vt* amenazar; **a public** ~ un peligro para la humanidad.

menacing [men'ising] *a* amenazador(a).

menacingly [men'isinglē] *ad* amenazadoramente.

menagerie [mənaj'ûrē] *n* casa de fieras.

mend [mend] *vt* reparar, arreglar; (*darn*) zurcir ♦ *vi* reponerse ♦ *n* (*gen*) remiendo; (*darn*) zurcido; **to be on the** ~ ir mejorando.

mending [mend'ing] *n* reparación *f*; (*clothes*) ropa por remendar.

menial [mē'nēəl] *a* doméstico; (*pej*) bajo.

meningitis [meninji'tis] *n* meningitis *f*.

menopause [men'əpôz] *n* menopausia.

menstrual [men'strōōəl] *a* menstrual.

menstruate [men'strōōāt] *vi* menstruar.

menstruation [menstrōōā'shən] *n* menstruación *f*.

mental [men'təl] *a* mental; ~ **illness** enfermedad *f* mental.

mentality [mental'itē] *n* mentalidad *f*.

mentally [men'təlē] *ad*: **to be** ~ **handicapped** ser un retrasado mental.

menthol [men'thôl] *n* mentol *m*.

mention [men'chən] *n* mención *f* ♦ *vt* mencionar; (*speak of*) hablar de; **don't** ~ **it!** ¡de nada!; **I need hardly** ~ **that** ... huelga decir que ...; **not to** ~, **without** ~**ing** sin contar.

mentor [men'tûr] *n* mentor *m*.

menu [men'yōō] *n* (*set* ~) menú *m*; (*printed*) carta; (*COMPUT*) menú *m*.

menu-driven [men'yōōdriv'ən] *a* (*COMPUT*) guiado por menú.

meow [mēou'] *vi* maullar.

MEP *n* *abbr* = **Member of the European Parliament**.

mercantile [mûr'kəntil] *a* mercantil.

mercenary [mûr'sənerē] *a, n* mercenario.

merchandise [mûr'chəndīs] *n* mercancías *fpl*.

merchandiser [mûr'chəndīzûr] *n* comerciante *m/f*, tratante *m*.

merchant [mûr'chənt] *n* comerciante *m/f*.

merchant bank *n* (*Brit*) banco comercial.

merchantman [mûr'chəntmən] *n* buque *m* mercante.

merchant marine, (*Brit*) **merchant navy** *n* marina mercante.

merciful [mûr'sifəl] *a* compasivo.

mercifully [mûr'sifəlē] *ad* con compasión; (*fortunately*) afortunadamente.

merciless [mûr'silis] *a* despiadado.

mercilessly [mûr'sislē] *ad* despiadadamente, sin piedad.

mercurial [mûrkyōō'rēəl] *a* veleidoso, voluble.

mercury [mûrk'yûrē] *n* mercurio.

mercy [mûr'sē] *n* compasión *f*; (*REL*) mise-

ricordia; **at the ~ of** a la merced de.
mercy killing *n* eutanasia.
mere |mēr| *a* simple, mero.
merely |mēr'lē| *ad* simplemente, sólo.
merge |múrj| *vt (join)* unir; *(mix)* mezclar; *(fuse)* fundir; *(COMPUT: files, text)* intercalar ♦ *vi* unirse; *(COMM)* fusionarse.
merger |múr'júr| *n (COMM)* fusión *f*.
meridian |mərid'ēən| *n* meridiano.
meringue |mərang'| *n* merengue *m*.
merit |mär'it| *n* mérito ♦ *vt* merecer.
meritocracy |märiták'rəsē| *n* meritocracia.
mermaid |múr'mād| *n* sirena.
merrily |mär'ilē| *ad* alegremente.
merriment |mär'imənt| *n* alegría.
merry |mär'ē| *a* alegre; **M~ Christmas!** ¡Felices Pascuas!
merry-go-round |mär'ēgōround| *n* tiovivo.
mesh |mesh| *n* malla; *(TECH)* engranaje *m* ♦ *vi (gears)* engranar; **wire ~** tela metálica.
mesmerize |mez'məriz| *vt* hipnotizar.
mess |mes| *n* confusión *f*; *(of objects)* revoltijo; *(tangle)* lío; *(MIL)* comedor *m*; **to be (in) a ~** *(room)* estar revuelto; **to be/ get o.s. in a ~** estar/meterse en un lío.
mess about *vi (Brit)* = **mess around.**
mess around *vi (col)* perder el tiempo; *(pass the time)* entretenerse.
mess around with *vt fus (col: play with)* divertirse con; *(: handle)* manosear.
mess up *vt (disarrange)* desordenar; *(spoil)* estropear; *(dirty)* ensuciar.
message |mes'ij| *n* recado, mensaje *m;* **to get the ~** *(fig, col)* caer en la cuenta.
message switching *n (COMPUT)* conmutación *f* de mensajes.
messenger |mes'injúr| *n* mensajero/a.
Messiah |misī'ə| *n* Mesías *m*.
Messrs |mes'úrz| *abbr (on letters:* = *Messieurs)* Sres.
messy |mes'ē| *a (dirty)* sucio; *(untidy)* desordenado; *(confused: situation etc)* confuso.
Met |met| *n abbr (US* = *Metropolitan Opera.*
met |met| *pt, pp of* **meet** ♦ *a abbr (Brit)* = **meteorological.**
metabolism |mətab'əlizəm| *n* metabolismo.
metal |met'əl| *n* metal *m*.
metallic |mital'ik| *a* metálico.
metallurgy |met'əlúrjē| *n* metalurgia.
metalwork |met'əlwúrk| *n (craft)* metalistería.
metamorphosis, *pl* **metamorphoses** |metəmór'fəsis, -sēz| *n* metamorfosis *f inv.*
metaphor |met'əfór| *n* metáfora.
metaphorical |metəfór'ikəl| *a* metafórico.
metaphysics |metəfiz'iks| *n* metafísica.
mete |mēt| **to ~ out** *vt fus (punishment)* imponer.
meteor |mē'tēór| *n* meteoro.
meteoric |mētēór'ik| *a (fig)* rápido, meteórico.

meteorite |mē'tēərit| *n* meteorito.
meteorological |mētēúrələj'ikəl| *a* meteorológico.
meteorology |mētēərál'əjē| *n* meteorología.
meter |mē'túr| *n (instrument)* contador *m*; *(US: unit)* metro ♦ *vt (US MAIL)* franquear; **parking ~** parquímetro.
methane |meth'ān| *n* metano.
method |meth'əd| *n* método; **~ of payment** método de pagar.
methodical |məthád'ikəl| *a* metódico.
Methodist |meth'ədist| *a, n* metodista *m/f*.
methodology |methədál'əjē| *n* metodología.
meths |meths|, **methylated spirit(s)** |meth'-əlātid spir'it(s)| *n (Brit)* alcohol *m* metilado *or* desnaturalizado.
meticulous |mətik'yələs| *a* meticuloso.
metre |mē'túr| *n (Brit: unit)* metro.
metric |met'rik| *a* métrico; **to go ~** pasar al sistema métrico.
metrication |metrikā'shən| *n* conversión *f* al sistema métrico.
metric system *n* sistema *m* métrico.
metric ton *n* tonelada métrica.
metronome |met'rənōm| *n* metrónomo.
metropolis |mitráp'əlis| *n* metrópoli *f*.
metropolitan |metrəpál'itən| *a* metropolitano.
Metropolitan Police *n (Brit):* **the ~** la policía londinense.
mettle |met'əl| *n* valor *m*, ánimo.
mew |myōō| *vi (cat)* maullar.
mews |myōōz| *(Brit) n:* **~ cottage** *casa acondicionada en antiguos establos o cocheras;* **~ flat** *piso en antiguos establos o cocheras.*
Mexican |mek'səkən| *a, n* mejicano/a *m/f,* mexicano/a *m/f (LAm).*
Mexico |mek'səkō| *n* Méjico, México *(LAm).*
Mexico City *n* Ciudad *f* de Méjico *or* México *(LAm).*
mezzanine |mez'ənēn| *n* entresuelo.
MFA *n abbr (US:* = *Master of Fine Arts)* título universitario.
mfr *abbr (* = *manufacturer)* fab.
mg *abbr (* = *milligram)* mg.
Mgr *abbr (* = *Monseigneur, Monsignor)* Mons.
mgr *abbr* = **manager.**
MHR *n abbr* = **Member of the House of Representatives.**
MHz *abbr (* = *megahertz)* MHz.
MI *abbr (US MAIL)* = *Michigan.*
MI5 *n abbr (Brit:* = *Military Intelligence 5) servicio de contraespionaje del gobierno británico.*
MI6 *n abbr (Brit:* = *Military Intelligence 6) servicio de inteligencia del gobierno británico.*
MIA *abbr (* = *missing in action)* desaparecido.

mice [mīs] *pl of* **mouse**.
Mich. *abbr* (*US*) = *Michigan*.
micro... [mī'krō] *pref* micro....
microbe [mī'krōb] *n* microbio.
microbiology [mīkrōbīăl'əjē] *n* microbiología.
microchip [mī'krəchip] *n* microplaqueta.
micro(computer) [mīkrō(kəmpyōō'tûr)] *n* microordenador *m*, microcomputador *m*.
microcosm [mī'krəkăzəm] *n* microcosmo.
microeconomics [mīkrōēkənăm'iks] *n* microeconomía.
microfiche [mī'krōfēsh] *n* microficha.
microfilm [mī'krəfilm] *n* microfilm *m*.
micrometer [mīkrăm'itûr] *n* micrómetro.
microphone [mī'krəfōn] *n* micrófono.
microprocessor [mīkrōprăs'esûr] *n* microprocesador *m*.
microscope [mī'krəskōp] *n* microscopio; **under the** ~ bajo el microscopio.
microscopic [mī'krəskăp'ik] *a* microscópico.
microwave [mī'krōwāv] *n* (*also:* ~ **oven**) horno microondas.
mid [mid] *a*: **in** ~ **May** a mediados de mayo; **in** ~ **afternoon** a media tarde; **in** ~ **air** en el aire; **he's in his** ~ **thirties** tiene unos treinta y cinco años.
midday [mid'dā] *n* mediodía *m*.
middle [mid'əl] *n* medio, centro; (*waist*) cintura ♦ *a* de en medio; **in the** ~ **of the night** en plena noche; **I'm in the** ~ **of reading it** lo estoy leyendo ahora mismo.
middle-aged [mid'əlājd'] *a* de mediana edad.
Middle Ages *npl*: **the** ~ la Edad *sg* Media.
middle class *n*: **the** ~**(es)** la clase media ♦ *a* (*also:* **middle-class**) de clase media.
Middle East *n* Oriente *m* Medio.
middleman [mid'əlman] *n* intermediario.
middle management *n* dirección *f* de nivel medio.
middle name *n* nombre *m* segundo.
middle-of-the-road [mid'əlovîhərōd'] *a* moderado, centrista.
middleweight [mid'əlwāt] *n* (*BOXING*) peso medio.
middling [mid'ling] *a* mediano.
Middx *abbr* (*Brit*) = *Middlesex*.
midge [mij] *n* mosca.
midget [mij'it] *n* enano/a.
midnight [mid'nīt] *n* medianoche *f*; **at** ~ a medianoche.
midriff [mid'rif] *n* diafragma *m*.
midst [midst] *n*: **in the** ~ **of** entre, en medio de.
midsummer [mid'sum'ûr] *n*: **a** ~ **day** un día de pleno verano.
Midsummer's Day *n* Día *m* de San Juan.
midway [mid'wā] *a*, *ad*: ~ **(between)** a mitad de camino *or* a medio camino (entre).
midweek [mid'wēk] *ad* entre semana.

midwife, *pl* **midwives** [mid'wīf, mid'wīvz] *n* comadrona, partera.
midwifery [mid'wīfûrē] *n* partería.
midwinter [mid'win'tûr] *n*: **in** ~ en pleno invierno.
might [mīt] *vb see* **may** ♦ **he** ~ **be there** podría estar allí, puede que esté allí; **I** ~ **as well go** más vale que vaya; **you** ~ **like to try** podría intentar ♦ *n* fuerza, poder *m*.
mightily [mī'təlē] *ad* fuertemente, poderosamente; **I was** ~ **surprised** me sorprendí enormemente.
mightn't = **might not**.
mighty [mī'tē] *a* fuerte, poderoso.
migraine [mī'grān] *n* jaqueca.
migrant [mī'grənt] *a*, *n* (*bird*) migratorio/a *m/f*; (*worker*) emigrante *m/f*.
migrate [mī'grāt] *vi* emigrar.
migration [mīgrā'shən] *n* emigración *f*.
mike [mīk] *n abbr* (= *microphone*) micro.
Milan [milan'] *n* Milán *m*.
mild [mīld] *a* (*person*) apacible; (*climate*) templado; (*slight*) ligero; (*taste*) suave; (*illness*) leve.
mildew [mil'dōō] *n* moho.
mildly [mīld'lē] *ad* ligeramente; suavemente; **to put it** ~ para no decir más.
mildness [mīld'nis] *n* suavidad *f*; (*of illness*) levedad *f*.
mile [mīl] *n* milla; **to do 20** ~**s per gallon** hacer 20 millas por galón.
mileage [mī'lij] *n* número de millas; (*AUT*) kilometraje *m*.
mileage allowance *n* ≈ asignación *f* por kilometraje.
mileometer [mīlăm'itûr] *n* cuentakilómetros *m inv*.
milestone [mīl'stōn] *n* mojón *m*.
milieu [mēlyōō'] *n* (*medio*) ambiente *m*.
militant [mil'ətənt] *a*, *n* militante *m/f*.
militarism [mil'itərizəm] *n* militarismo.
militaristic [militəris'tik] *a* militarista.
military [mil'itărē] *a* militar.
militate [mil'ətāt] *vi*: **to** ~ **against** militar en contra de.
militia [milish'ə] *n* milicia.
milk [milk] *n* leche *f* ♦ *vt* (*cow*) ordeñar; (*fig*) chupar.
milk chocolate *n* chocolate *m* con leche.
milk float *n* (*Brit*) carro de la leche.
milking [mil'king] *n* ordeño.
milkman [milk'man] *n* lechero.
milk shake *n* batido, malteada (*LAm*).
milk tooth *n* diente *m* de leche.
milk truck *n* (*US*) carro de la leche.
milky [mil'kē] *a* lechoso.
Milky Way *n* Vía Láctea.
mill [mil] *n* (*windmill etc*) molino; (*coffee* ~) molinillo; (*factory*) fábrica; (*spinning* ~) hilandería ♦ *vt* moler ♦ *vi* (*also:* ~ **around**) arremolinarse.
milled [mild] (*grain*) molido; (*coin, edge*) acordonado.

millennium, pl ~s or **millennia** [milen'ēəm, milen'ēa] n milenio, milenario.

miller [mil'ûr] n molinero.

millet [mil'it] n mijo.

milli... [mil'ə] pref mili... .

milligram(me) [mil'əgram] n miligramo.

milliliter, (Brit) **millilitre** [mil'əlētûr] n mililitro.

millimeter, (Brit) **millimetre** [mil'əmētûr] n milímetro.

milliner [mil'inûr] n sombrerero/a.

millinery [mil'ənārē] n sombrerería.

million [mil'yən] n millón m; **a ~ times** un millón de veces.

millionaire [milyənär'] n millonario/a.

millipede [mil'əpēd] n milpiés m inv.

millstone [mil'stōn] n piedra de molino.

millwheel [mil'wēl] n rueda de molino.

milometer [mī'lōmētûr] n (Brit) cuentakilómetros m inv.

mime [mīm] n mímica; (actor) mimo/a ♦ vt remedar ♦ vi actuar de mimo.

mimic [mim'ik] n imitador(a) m/f ♦ a mímico ♦ vt remedar, imitar.

mimicry [mim'ikrē] n imitación f.

Min. abbr (Brit POL: = Ministry) Min.

min. abbr (= minute(s)) m.; = **minimum**.

minaret [minəret'] n alminar m.

mince [mins] vt picar ♦ vi (in walking) andar con pasos menudos ♦ n (CULIN) carne f picada, picadillo.

mincemeat [mins'mēt] n conserva de fruta picada.

mince pie n empanadilla rellena de fruta picada.

mincer [min'sûr] n picadora de carne.

mincing [min'sing] a afectado.

mind [mīnd] n (gen) mente f; (contrasted with matter) espíritu m ♦ vt (attend to, look after) ocuparse de, cuidar; (be careful of) tener cuidado con; (object to): **I don't ~ the noise** no me molesta el ruido; **it is on my ~** me preocupa; **to my ~** a mi parecer or juicio; **to change one's ~** cambiar de idea or de parecer; **to bring** or **call sth to ~** recordar algo; **to have sth/ sb in ~** tener algo/a uno en mente; **to be out of one's ~** estar fuera de juicio; **to bear sth in ~** tomar or tener algo en cuenta; **to make up one's ~** decidirse; **it went right out of my ~** se me fue por completo (de la cabeza); **to be of two ~s about sth** estar indeciso or dudar ante algo; **I don't ~** me es igual; **~ you, ...** te advierto que ...; **never ~!** ¡es igual!, ¡no importa!; (don't worry) ¡no te preocupes!

-minded [-mīn'did] a: **fair~** imparcial; **an industrially~ nation** una nación que se dedica or se orienta a la industria.

minder [mīnd'ûr] n guardaespaldas m inv.

mindful [mīnd'fəl] a: **~ of** consciente de.

mindless [mīnd'lis] a (violence, crime) sin motivo; (work) de autómata.

mine [mīn] pron (el) mío/(la) mía etc; **a friend of ~** un(a) amigo/a mío/mía ♦ a: **this book is ~** este libro es mío ♦ n mina ♦ vt (coal) extraer; (ship, beach) minar.

mine detector n detector m de minas.

minefield [mīn'fēld] n campo de minas.

miner [mīn'ûr] n minero/a.

mineral [min'ûrəl] a mineral ♦ n mineral m; **~s** npl (Brit: soft drinks) agua sg mineral, gaseosa sg.

mineral water n agua mineral.

minesweeper [mīn'swēpûr] n dragaminas m inv.

mingle [ming'gəl] vi: **to ~ with** mezclarse con.

mingy [min'jē] a (col) tacaño.

mini... [min'ē] pref mini..., micro....

miniature [min'ēachûr] a (en) miniatura ♦ n miniatura.

minibus [min'ēbus] n microbús m.

minicab [min'ēkab] n microtaxi m.

minicomputer [min'ēkəmpyōōtûr] n minicomputador m.

minim [min'əm] n (Brit MUS) blanca.

minimal [min'əməl] a mínimo.

minimize [min'əmīz] vt minimizar.

minimum [min'əməm] n (pl **minima** [min'əmə]) mínimo ♦ a mínimo; **to reduce to a ~** reducir algo al mínimo; **~ wage** salario mínimo.

minimum lending rate (MLR) n tipo de interés mínimo.

mining [mī'ning] n explotación f minera ♦ a minero.

minion [min'yən] n secuaz m.

miniskirt [min'ēskûrt] n minifalda.

minister [min'istûr] n (Brit POL) ministro/a; (REL) pastor m ♦ vi: **to ~ to** atender a.

ministerial [ministēr'ēəl] a (Brit POL) ministerial.

ministry [min'istrē] n (REL) sacerdocio; (Brit POL) ministerio m.

mink [mingk] n visón m.

mink coat n abrigo de visón.

Minn. abbr (US) = Minnesota.

minnow [min'ō] n pececillo (de agua dulce).

minor [mī'nûr] a (unimportant) secundario; (MUS) menor ♦ n (LAW) menor m/f de edad; (US UNIV) asignatura secundaria.

Minorca [minôr'kə] n Menorca.

minority [minôr'itē] n minoría; **to be in a ~** estar en la minoría, ser minoría (LAm).

minority interest n participación f minoritaria.

minster [min'stûr] n catedral f.

minstrel [min'strəl] n juglar m.

mint [mint] n (plant) menta, hierbabuena; (sweet) caramelo de menta ♦ vt (coins) acuñar; **the (US) M~**, (Brit) **the (Royal) M~** la Casa de la Moneda; **in ~ condition** en perfecto estado.

mint sauce n salsa de menta.

minuet [minyōoet'] *n* minué *m.*

minus [mī'nəs] *n* (*also*: ~ **sign**) signo de menos ♦ *prep* menos.

minuscule [min'əskyōōl] *a* minúsculo.

minute *n* [min'it] minuto; (*fig*) momento; ~**s** *npl* actas *fpl* ♦ *a* [minōōt'] diminuto; (*search*) minucioso; **it is 5** ~**s past 3** son las 3 y 5 (minutos); **at the last** ~ a última hora; **wait a** ~! ¡espera un momento!; **up to the** ~ de última hora; **in** ~ **detail** en detalle minucioso.

minute book *n* libro de actas.

minute hand *n* minutero.

minutely [mīnōōt'lē] *ad* (*by a small amount*) por muy poco; (*in detail*) detalladamente, minuciosamente.

miracle [mir'əkəl] *n* milagro.

miracle play *n* auto, milagro.

miraculous [mirak'yələs] *a* milagroso.

miraculously [mirak'yələslē] *ad* milagrosamente.

mirage [mirázh'] *n* espejismo.

mire [mī'ûr] *n* fango, lodo.

mirror [mir'ûr] *n* espejo; (*in car*) retrovisor *m* ♦ *vt* reflejar.

mirror image *n* reflejo inverso.

mirth [mûrth] *n* alegría; (*laughter*) risa, risas *fpl.*

misadventure [misədven'chûr] *n* desgracia, accidente *m*; **death by** ~ muerte *f* accidental.

misanthropist [misan'thrəpist] *n* misántropo/a.

misapply [misəplī'] *vt* emplear mal.

misapprehension [misaprihen'chən] *n* equivocación *f.*

misappropriate [misəprō'prēāt] *vt* (*funds*) malversar.

misappropriation [misəprōprēā'shən] *n* malversación *f*, desfalco.

misbehave [misbihāv'] *vi* portarse mal.

misbehavior, (*Brit*) **misbehaviour** [misbihāv'yûr] *n* mala conducta.

misc. *abbr* = **miscellaneous.**

miscalculate [miskal'kyəlāt] *vt* calcular mal.

miscalculation [miskalkyəlā'shən] *n* error *m* (de cálculo).

miscarriage [miskar'ij] *n* (*MED*) aborto; ~ **of justice** error *m* judicial.

miscarry [miskar'ē] *vi* (*MED*) abortar; (*fail: plans*) fracasar, malograrse.

miscellaneous [misəlā'nēəs] *a* varios/as, diversos/as; ~ **expenses** diversos gastos.

miscellany [mis'əlānē] *n* miscelánea.

mischance [mischans'] *n* desgracia, mala suerte *f*; **by (some)** ~ por (alguna) desgracia.

mischief [mis'chif] *n* (*naughtiness*) travesura; (*harm*) mal *m*, daño; (*maliciousness*) malicia.

mischievous [mis'chəvəs] *a* travieso; dañoso; (*playful*) malicioso.

mischievously [mis'chəvəslē] *ad* por travesura; maliciosamente.

misconception [miskənsep'shən] *n* concepto erróneo; equivocación *f.*

misconduct [miskân'dukt] *n* mala conducta; **professional** ~ falta profesional.

miscount [miskount'] *vt*, *vi* contar mal.

misconstrue [miskənstrōō'] *vt* interpretar mal.

misdeed [misdēd'] *n* (*old*) fechoría, delito.

misdemeanor, (*Brit*) **misdemeanour** [misdimē'nûr] *n* delito, ofensa.

misdirect [misdirekt'] *vt* (*person*) informar mal; (*letter*) poner señas incorrectas en.

miser [mī'zûr] *n* avaro/a.

miserable [miz'ûrəbəl] *a* (*unhappy*) triste, desgraciado; (*wretched*) miserable; **to feel** ~ sentirse triste.

miserably [miz'ûrəblē] *ad* (*smile, answer*) tristemente; (*fail*) rotundamente; **to pay** ~ pagar una miseria.

miserly [mī'zûrlē] *a* avariento, tacaño.

misery [miz'ûrē] *n* (*unhappiness*) tristeza; (*wretchedness*) miseria, desdicha.

misfire [misfīr'] *vi* fallar.

misfit [mis'fit] *n* (*person*) inadaptado/a.

misfortune [misfôr'chuən] *n* desgracia.

misgiving(s) [misgiv'ing(z)] *n*(*pl*) (*mistrust*) recelo; (*apprehension*) presentimiento; **to have** ~**s about sth** tener dudas sobre algo.

misguided [misgī'did] *a* equivocado.

mishandle [mis·han'dəl] *vt* (*treat roughly*) maltratar; (*mismanage*) manejar mal.

mishap [mis'hap] *n* desgracia, contratiempo.

mishear [mis·hiûr'] *vt*, *vi* (*irg: like* **hear**) oír mal.

mishmash [mish'mash] *n* (*col*) revoltijo.

misinform [misinfôrm'] *vt* informar mal.

misinterpret [misintûr'prit] *vt* interpretar mal.

misinterpretation [misintûrpritā'shən] *n* mala interpretación *f.*

misjudge [misjuj'] *vt* juzgar mal.

mislay [mislā'] *vt* (*irg: like* **lay**) extraviar, perder.

mislead [mislēd'] *vt* (*irg: like* **lead**) llevar a conclusiones erróneas.

misleading [mislē'ding] *a* engañoso.

misled [misled'] *pt*, *pp of* **mislead.**

mismanage [misman'ij] *vt* administrar mal.

mismanagement [misman'ijmənt] *n* mala administración *f.*

misnomer [misnō'mûr] *n* término inapropiado o equivocado.

misogynist [misâj'ənist] *n* misógino/a.

misplace [misplās'] *vt* (*lose*) extraviar; ~**d** (*trust etc*) inmerecido.

misprint [mis'print] *n* errata, error *m* de imprenta.

mispronounce [misprənouns'] *vt* pronunciar mal.

misquote [miskwōt'] *vt* citar incorrectamente.

misread [misrēd'] *vt* (*irg*: *like* **read**) leer mal.

misrepresent [misreprizent'] *vt* falsificar.

misrepresentation [misreprizentā'shən] *n* (*LAW*) falsa declaración *f*.

Miss. *abbr* (*US*) = *Mississippi*.

Miss [mis] *n* Señorita; **Dear ~ Smith** Estimada Señorita Smith.

miss [mis] *vt* (*train etc*) perder; (*shot*) errar, fallar; (*appointment, class*) faltar a; (*escape, avoid*) evitar; (*notice loss of: money etc*) notar la falta de; (*regret the absence of*): **I ~ him** (yo) le echo de menos *or* a faltar ♦ *vi* fallar ♦ *n* (*shot*) tiro fallido *or* perdido; **the bus just ~ed the wall** por poco el autobús se estrelló contra el muro; **you're ~ing the point** no caes, no te entra.

miss out *vt* (*Brit*) omitir.

miss out on *vt fus* (*fun, party, opportunity*) perder.

missal [mis'əl] *n* misal *m*.

misshapen [mis-shā'pən] *a* deforme.

missile [mis'əl] *n* (*AVIAT*) misil *m*; (*object thrown*) proyectil *m*.

missile base *n* base *f* de misiles.

missile launcher [mis'əl lônch'ûr] *n* dispositivo de lanzamiento de proyectiles *or* misiles.

missing [mis'ing] *a* (*pupil*) ausente; (*thing*) perdido; (*MIL*) desaparecido; **to be ~** faltar; **~ person** desaparecido/a.

mission [mish'ən] *n* misión *f*; **on a ~ for sb** en una misión para uno.

missionary [mish'ənārē] *n* misionero/a.

misspell [misspel'] *vt* (*irg*: *like* **spell**) escribir mal.

misspent [misspent'] *a*: **his ~ youth** su juventud disipada.

mist [mist] *n* (*light*) neblina; (*heavy*) niebla; (*at sea*) bruma ♦ *vi* (*also*: **~ over, ~ up**: *weather*) nublarse; (: *Brit*: *windows*) empañarse.

mistake [mistāk'] *n* error *m* ♦ *vt* (*irg*: *like* **take**) entender mal; **by ~** por equivocación; **to make a ~** (*about sb/sth*) equivocarse; (*in writing, calculating etc*) cometer un error; **to ~ A for B** confundir A con B.

mistaken [mistā'kən] *pp of* **mistake** ♦ *a* (*idea etc*) equivocado; **to be ~** equivocarse, engañarse; **~ identity** identificación *f* errónea.

mistakenly [mistā'kənlē] *ad* erróneamente.

mister [mis'tûr] *n* (*col*) señor *m*; *see* **Mr**.

mistletoe [mis'əltō] *n* muérdago.

mistook [mistŏŏk'] *pt of* **mistake**.

mistranslation [mistranzlā'shən] *n* mala traducción *f*.

mistreat [mistrēt'] *vt* maltratar, tratar mal.

mistress [mis'tris] *n* (*lover*) amante *f*; (*of house*) señora (de la casa); (*Brit: in primary school*) maestra; (*in secondary school*) profesora; *see* **Mrs**.

mistrust [mistrust'] *vt* desconfiar de ♦ *n*: **~ (of)** desconfianza (de).

mistrustful [mistrust'fəl] *a*: **~ (of)** desconfiado (de), receloso (de).

misty [mis'tē] *a* nebuloso, brumoso; (*day*) de niebla; (*glasses*) empañado.

misty-eyed [mis'tēīd'] *a* sentimental.

misunderstand [misundûrstand'] *vt, vi* (*irg*: *like* **understand**) entender mal.

misunderstanding [misundûrstan'ding] *n* malentendido.

misunderstood [misundûrstŏŏd'] *pt, pp of* **misunderstand** ♦ *a* (*person*) incomprendido.

misuse *n* [misyōōs'] mal uso; (*of power*) abuso ♦ *vt* [misyōōz'] abusar de; (*funds*) malversar.

MIT *n abbr* (*US*) = *Massachusetts Institute of Technology*.

mite [mīt] *n* (*small quantity*) pizca.

miter, (*Brit*) **mitre** [mī'tûr] *n* mitra.

mitigate [mit'əgāt] *vt* mitigar; **mitigating circumstances** circunstancias *fpl* mitigantes.

mitigation [mitəgā'shən] *n* mitigación *f*, alivio.

mitt(en) [mit'(ən)] *n* manopla.

mix [miks] *vt* (*gen*) mezclar; (*combine*) unir ♦ *vi* mezclarse; (*people*) llevarse bien ♦ *n* mezcla; **to ~ sth with sth** mezclar algo con algo; **to ~ business with pleasure** combinar los negocios con el placer; **cake ~** mezcla de ingredientes de pastelería.

mix in *vt* (*eggs etc*) añadir.

mix up *vt* mezclar; (*confuse*) confundir; **to be ~ed up in sth** estar metido en algo.

mixed [mikst] *a* (*assorted*) variado, surtido; (*school etc*) mixto.

mixed doubles *n* (*SPORT*) mixtos *mpl*.

mixed economy *n* economía mixta.

mixed grill *n* parrillada mixta.

mixed-up [mikst'up] *a* (*confused*) confuso, revuelto.

mixer [mik'sûr] *n* (*for food*) licuadora; (*person*): **he's a good ~** tiene don de gentes.

mixture [miks'chûr] *n* mezcla.

mix-up [miks'up] *n* confusión *f*.

Mk *abbr* (*Brit TECH*: = *mark*) Mk.

mk *abbr* = **mark** (*currency*).

mkt *abbr* = **market**.

MLitt *n abbr* (= *Master of Literature, Master of Letters*) título universitario.

MLR *n abbr* (*Brit*) = **minimum lending rate**.

mm *abbr* (= *millimeter*) mm.

MN *abbr* (*US MAIL*) = *Minnesota*; (*Brit*) = **Merchant Navy**.

MO *n abbr* (*MED*) = *medical officer*; (*US col*) = **modus operandi** ♦ *abbr* (*US MAIL*) = *Missouri*.

mo *abbr* (= *month*) m.

m.o. *abbr* (= *money order*) g/.

moan |mōn| n gemido ♦ vi gemir; (col: complain): **to ~ (about)** quejarse (de).

moaning |mō'ning| n gemidos mpl; quejas fpl, protestas fpl.

moat |mōt| n foso.

mob |máb| n multitud f; (pej): **the ~** el populacho ♦ vt acosar.

mobile |mō'bəl| a móvil ♦ n móvil m.

mobile home n caravana, remolque m.

mobility |mōbil'ətē| n movilidad f; (of applicant) disposición f a mudarse de casa; **~ of labor** movilidad f de la mano de obra.

mobilize |mō'bəliz| vt movilizar.

moccasin |mák'əsin| n mocasín m.

mock |mák| vt (make ridiculous) ridiculizar; (laugh at) burlarse de ♦ a fingido.

mockery |mák'ûrē| n burla; **to make a ~ of** desprestigiar.

mocking |mák'ing| a (tone) burlón/ona.

mockingbird |mák'ingbûrd| n sinsonte m, zenzontle (LAm).

mock-up |mák'up| n maqueta.

mod cons |mád kánz| npl abbr (Brit) (= modern conveniences) see **convenience**.

mode |mōd| n modo; (of transport) medio; (COMPUT) modo, modalidad f.

model |mád'əl| n (gen) modelo; (ARCH) maqueta; (person: for fashion, ART) modelo m/f ♦ a modelo inv ♦ vt modelar ♦ vi ser modelo; **~ railway** ferrocarril m de juguete; **to ~ clothes** pasar modelos, ser modelo; **to ~ on** crear a imitación de.

model apartment n (US) piso modelo.

modeling, (Brit) **modelling** |mád'əling| n (modelmaking) modelado.

modeling clay |mád'ling klā| n plastilina ®.

modem |mō'dcm| n modem m.

moderate |mád'ûrit| a, n moderado/a m/f ♦ (vb: |mád'ərāt|) vi moderarse, calmarse ♦ vt moderar.

moderately |mád'ûritlē| ad (act) con moderación; (expensive, difficult) medianamente; (pleased, happy) bastante.

moderation |mádərā'shən| n moderación f; **in ~** con moderación.

modern |mád'ûrn| a moderno; **~ languages** lenguas fpl vivas.

modernity |mádûr'nitē| n modernidad f.

modernization |mádûrnəzā'shən| n modernización f.

modernize |mád'ûrniz| vt modernizar.

modest |mád'ist| a modesto.

modestly |mád'istlē| ad modestamente.

modesty |mád'istē| n modestia.

modicum |mád'əkəm| n: **a ~ of** un mínimo de.

modification |mádəfəkā'shən| n modificación f; **to make ~s** hacer cambios or modificaciones.

modify |mád'əfi| vt modificar.

modular |máj'əlûr| a (filing, unit) modular.

modulate |máj'əlāt| vt modular.

modulation |májəlā'shən| n modulación f.

module |máj'ōōl| n (unit, component, SPACE) módulo.

modus operandi |mō'dəs âpəran'dī| n manera de actuar.

Mogadishu |mágədish'ōō| n Mogadisio.

mogul |mō'gəl| n (fig) magnate m.

mohair |mō'hâr| n mohair m.

Mohammed |mōham'id| n Mahoma m.

moist |moist| a húmedo.

moisten |mois'ən| vt humedecer.

moisture |mois'chûr| n humedad f.

moisturize |mois'chəriz| vt (skin) hidratar.

moisturizer |mois'chərizûr| n crema hidratante.

molar |mō'lûr| n muela.

molasses |məlas'iz| n melaza.

mold |mōld| (US) n molde m; (mildew) moho ♦ vt moldear; (fig) formar.

molder |mōl'dûr| vi (decay) decaer.

molding |mōl'ding| n (ARCH) moldura.

moldy |mōl'dē| a enmohecido.

mole |mōl| n (animal) topo; (spot) lunar m.

molecular |məlck'yəlûr| a molecular.

molecule |mál'əkyōōl| n molécula.

molest |məlcst'| vt importunar.

mollusk, (Brit) **mollusc** |mál'əsk| n molusco.

mollycoddle |mál'ēkádəl| vt mimar.

molt |mōlt| vi (US) mudar (la piel/las plumas).

molten |mōl'tən| a fundido; (lava) líquido.

mom |mám| n (US) mamá.

moment |mō'mənt| n momento; **at** or **for the ~** de momento, por el momento, por ahora; **in a ~** dentro de un momento, luego.

momentarily |mōməntär'ilē| ad momentáneamente; (US: very soon) de un momento a otro.

momentary |mō'məntärē| a momentáneo.

momentous |mōmcn'təs| a trascendental, importante.

momentum |mōmcn'təm| n momento; (fig) ímpetu m; **to gather ~** cobrar velocidad.

mommy |mám'ē| n (US) mamá.

Mon. abbr (= Monday) lun.

Monaco |mán'əkō| n Mónaco.

monarch |mán'ûrk| n monarca m/f.

monarchist |mán'ûrkist| n monárquico/a.

monarchy |mán'ûrkē| n monarquía.

monastery |mán'əstärē| n monasterio.

monastic |mənas'tik| a monástico.

Monday |mun'dā| n lunes m inv.

Monegasque |mánägask'| a, n monegasco/a m/f.

monetarist |mán'itärist| n monetarista m.

monetary |mán'itärē| a monetario.

monetary policy n política monetaria.

money |mun'ē| n dinero; **to make ~** ganar dinero; **I've got no ~ left** no me queda dinero.

moneyed |mun'ēd| a adinerado.

moneylender [mun'ēlendûr] *n* prestamista *m/f*.

moneymaking [mun'ēmāking] *a* rentable.

money market *n* mercado monetario.

money order *n* giro.

money-spinner [mun'ēspinûr] *n* (*col: person, idea, business*) fuente *f* de ganancias.

money supply *n* oferta monetaria, medio circulante, volumen *m* monetario.

Mongol [máng'gəl] *n* mongol(a) *m/f*; (*LING*) mongol *m*.

mongol [máng'gəl] *a, n* (*MED*) mongólico.

Mongolia [mánggō'lēə] *n* Mongolia.

Mongolian [mánggō'lēən] *a* mongol(a) ♦ *n* mongol(a) *m/f*; (*LING*) mongol *m*.

mongoose [máng'gōōs] *n* mangosta.

mongrel [mung'grəl] *n* (*dog*) perro mestizo.

monitor [mán'itûr] *n* (*SCOL*) monitor *m*; (*TV, COMPUT*) monitor *m* ♦ *vt* controlar; (*foreign station*) escuchar, oír.

monk [mungk] *n* monje *m*.

monkey [mung'kē] *n* mono.

monkey business *n* travesuras *fpl*.

monkey nut *n* (*Brit*) cacahuete *m*, maní (*LAm*).

monkey wrench *n* llave *f* inglesa.

mono [mán'ō] *a* (*broadcast etc*) mono *inv*.

mono... [mán'ō] *pref* mono ... .

monochrome [mán'əkrōm] *a* monocromo.

monocle [mán'əkəl] *n* monóculo.

monogram [mán'əgram] *n* monograma *m*.

monolith [mán'əlith] *n* monolito.

monolithic [mánəlith'ik] *a* monolítico.

monolog(ue) [mán'əlóg] *n* monólogo.

mononucleosis [mánōnōōklēō'sis] *n* (*US*) fiebre *f* glandular.

monoplane [mán'əplān] *n* monoplano.

monopolist [mənáp'əlist] *n* monopolista *m/f*.

monopolize [mənáp'əlīz] *vt* monopolizar.

monopoly [mənáp'əlē] *n* monopolio; **Monopolies and Mergers Commission** (*Brit*) comisión *reguladora de monopolios y fusiones*.

monorail [mán'ərāl] *n* monocarril *m*, monorriel *m*.

monosodium glutamate [mánəsō'dēəm glōō'təmāt] *n* glutamato monosódico.

monosyllabic [mánəsilab'ik] *a* monosílabo.

monosyllable [mán'əsiləbəl] *n* monosílabo.

monotone [mán'ətōn] *n* voz *f* (*or* tono) monocorde.

monotonous [mənát'ənəs] *a* monótono.

monotony [mənát'ənē] *n* monotonía.

monoxide [mənák'sīd] *n*: **carbon** ~ monóxido de carbono.

monseigneur, monsignor [mánsēn'yûr] *n* monseñor *m*.

monsoon [mánsōōn'] *n* monzón *m/f*.

monster [mán'stûr] *n* monstruo.

monstrosity [mánstrás'ətē] *n* monstruosidad *f*.

monstrous [mán'strəs] *a* (*huge*) enorme; (*atrocious*) monstruoso.

Mont. *abbr* (*US*) = *Montana*.

montage [mántázh'] *n* montaje *m*.

Mont Blanc [mánt blangk'] *n* el monte Blanco.

month [munth] *n* mes *m*; **300 dollars a** ~ 300 dólares al mes; **every** ~ cada mes.

monthly [munth'lē] *a* mensual ♦ *ad* mensualmente ♦ *n* (*magazine*) revista mensual; **twice** ~ dos veces por mes *or* mensuales; ~ **installment** mensualidad *f*.

monument [mán'yəmənt] *n* monumento.

monumental [mányəmen'təl] *a* monumental.

moo [mōō] *vi* mugir.

mood [mōōd] *n* humor *m*; **to be in a good/bad** ~ estar de buen/mal humor.

moodily [mōō'dilē] *ad* malhumoradamente.

moodiness [mōō'dēnis] *n* humor *m* cambiante; mal humor *m*.

moody [mōō'dē] *a* (*variable*) de humor variable; (*sullen*) malhumorado.

moon [mōōn] *n* luna.

moonbeam [mōōn'bēm] *n* rayo de luna.

moon landing *n* alunizaje *m*.

moonless [mōōn'lis] *a* sin luna.

moonlight [mōōn'līt] *n* luz *f* de la luna ♦ *vi* tener un pluriempleo.

moonlighting [mōōn'līting] *n* pluriempleo.

moonlit [mōōn'lit] *a*: **a** ~ **night** una noche de luna.

moonshot [mōōn'shât] *n* lanzamiento de una astronave a la luna.

moonstruck [mōōn'struk] *a* chiflado.

Moor [mōōr] *n* moro/a.

moor [mōōr] *n* páramo ♦ *vt* (*ship*) amarrar ♦ *vi* echar las amarras.

moorings [mōōr'ingz] *npl* (*chains*) amarras *fpl*; (*place*) amarradero *sg*.

Moorish [mōō'rish] *a* moro; (*architecture*) árabe, morisco.

moorland [mōōr'land] *n* páramo, brezal *m*.

moose [mōōs] *n, pl inv* alce *m*.

moot [mōōt] *vt* proponer para la discusión, sugerir ♦ *a*: ~ **point** punto discutible.

mop [máp] *n* fregona; (*of hair*) greña, melena ♦ *vt* fregar.

mop up *vt* limpiar.

mope [mōp] *vi* estar deprimido.

mope around *vi* andar abatido.

moquette [mōket'] *n* moqueta.

moral [mór'əl] *a* moral ♦ *n* moraleja; ~**s** *npl* moralidad *f*, moral *f*.

morale [məral'] *n* moral *f*.

morality [məral'itē] *n* moralidad *f*.

moralize [môr'əlīz] *vi*: **to** ~ **(about)** moralizar (sobre).

morally [môr'əlē] *ad* moralmente.

morass [məras'] *n* pantano.

moratorium [môrətôr'ēəm] *n* moratoria.

morbid [môr'bid] *a* (*interest*) morboso; (*MED*) mórbido.

more [môr] *a, ad* más ♦ *pron*: **and what's**

~ ... y además ...; **many/much** ~ muchos/ mucho más; **is there any** ~? ¿hay más?; **once** ~ otra vez, una vez más; **I want** ~ quiero más; ~ **dangerous than** más peligroso que; ~ **or less** más o menos; ~ **than ever** más que nunca; ~ **and** ~ cada vez más; **no** ~, **not any** ~ ya no.

moreover [môrō'vûr] *ad* además, por otra parte.

morgue [môrg] *n* depósito de cadáveres.

MORI [mō'rē] *n abbr* (*Brit*) = *Market and Opinion Research Institute*.

moribund [môr'əbund] *a* moribundo.

Mormon [môr'mən] *n* mormón/ona *m/f*.

morning [môr'ning] *n* (*gen*) mañana; (*early* ~) madrugada; **in the** ~ por la mañana; **7 o'clock in the** ~ las 7 de la mañana; **this** ~ esta mañana.

morning sickness *n* (*MED*) náuseas *fpl* del embarazo.

Moroccan [mərâk'ən] *a, n* marroquí *m/f*.

Morocco [mərâk'ō] *n* Marruecos *m*.

moron [môr'ân] *n* imbécil *m/f*.

morose [mərōs'] *a* hosco, malhumorado.

morphine [môr'fēn] *n* morfina.

Morse [môrs] *n* (*also*: ~ **code**) (código) morse.

morsel [môr'səl] *n* (*of food*) bocado.

mortal [môr'təl] *a, n* mortal *m*.

mortality [môrtal'itē] *n* mortalidad *f*.

mortality rate *n* tasa de mortalidad.

mortally [môr'təlē] *ad* mortalmente.

mortar [môr'tûr] *n* argamasa; (*implement*) mortero.

mortgage [môr'gij] *n* hipoteca ♦ *vt* hipotecar; **to take out a** ~ sacar una hipoteca.

mortgage company *n* (*US*) ≈ banco hipotecario.

mortgagee [môrgəjē'] *n* acreedor(a) *m/f* hipotecario/a.

mortgager [môr'gəjûr] *n* deudor(a) *m/f* hipotecario/a.

mortice [môr'tis] = **mortise**.

mortician [môrtish'ən] *n* (*US*) director(a) *m/f* de pompas fúnebres.

mortification [môrtəfəkā'shən] *n* mortificación *f*, humillación *f*.

mortified [môr'təfid] *a*: **I was** ~ me dio muchísima vergüenza.

mortise (lock) [môr'tis (lák)] *n* cerradura de muesca.

mortuary [môr'chōōârē] *n* (*US*) funeraria; (*Brit*) depósito de cadáveres.

mosaic [mōzā'ik] *n* mosaico.

Moscow [mâs'kou] *n* Moscú *m*.

Moslem [mâz'ləm] *a, n* = **Muslim**.

mosque [mâsk] *n* mezquita.

mosquito, ~**es** [məskē'tō] *n* mosquito, zancudo.

moss [môs] *n* musgo.

mossy [môs'ē] *a* musgoso, cubierto de musgo.

most [mōst] *a* la mayor parte de, la mayo-ría de ♦ *pron* la mayor parte, la mayoría ♦ *ad* el más; (*very*) muy; **the** ~ (*also*: + *adjective*) el más; ~ **of them** la mayor parte de ellos; **at the (very)** ~ a lo sumo, todo lo más; **to make the** ~ **of** aprovechar (al máximo); **a** ~ **interesting book** un libro interesantísimo.

mostly [mōst'lē] *ad* en su mayor parte, principalmente.

MOT *n abbr* (*Brit* = *Ministry of Transport*): **the** ~ (**test**) *inspección (anual) obligatoria de coches y camiones*.

motel [mōtel'] *n* motel *m*.

moth [môth] *n* mariposa nocturna; (*clothes* ~) polilla.

mothball [môth'bôl] *n* bola de naftalina.

moth-eaten [môth'ētən] *a* apolillado.

mother [muth'ûr] *n* madre *f* ♦ *a* materno ♦ *vt* (*care for*) cuidar (como una madre).

mother board *n* (*COMPUT*) placa madre.

motherhood [muth'ûrhōōd] *n* maternidad *f*.

mother-in-law [muth'ûrinlō] *n* suegra.

motherly [muth'ûrlē] *a* maternal.

mother-of-pearl [muth'ûrəvpûrl'] *n* nácar *m*.

mother's help *n* niñera.

mother-to-be [muth'ûrtəbē'] *n* futura madre.

mother tongue *n* lengua materna.

mothproof [môth'prōōf] *a* a prueba de polillas.

motif [mōtēf'] *n* motivo; (*theme*) tema *m*.

motion [mō'shən] *n* movimiento; (*gesture*) ademán *m*, señal *f*; (*at meeting*) moción *f*; (*Brit*: *also*: **bowel** ~) evacuación *f* intestinal ♦ *vt, vi*: **to** ~ (**to**) **sb to do sth** hacer señas a uno para que haga algo; **to be in** ~ (*vehicle*) estar en movimiento; **to set in** ~ poner en marcha; **to go through the** ~**s of doing sth** (*fig*) hacer algo mecánicamente *or* sin convicción.

motionless [mō'shənlis] *a* inmóvil.

motion picture *n* película.

motivate [mō'təvāt] *vt* (*act, decision*) provocar; (*person*) motivar.

motivated [mō'təvātid] *a* motivado.

motivation [mōtəvā'shən] *n* motivación *f*.

motivational research [mōtəvā'shənəl rē'sûrch] *n* estudios *mpl* de motivación.

motive [mō'tiv] *n* motivo; **from the best** ~**s** de los mejores motivos.

motley [mât'lē] *a* variado.

motor [mō'tûr] *n* motor *m*; (*Brit*: *col*: *vehicle*) coche *m*, carro (*LAm*), automóvil *m* ♦ *a* motor (*f*: motora, motriz).

motorbike [mō'tûrbīk] *n* moto *f*.

motorboat [mō'tûrbōt] *n* lancha motora.

motorcar [mō'tûrkâr] *n* (*Brit*) coche *m*, carro (*LAm*), automóvil *m*.

motorcoach [mō'tûrkōch] *n* autocar *m*, autobús *m*, camión *m* (*LAm*).

motorcycle [mō'tûrsī'kəl] *n* motocicleta.

motorcycle racing *n* motociclismo.
motorcyclist [mō'tûrsīklist] *n* motociclista *m/f*.
motoring [mō'tûring] *n* (*Brit*) automovilismo ♦ *a* (: *accident*) de tráfico *or* tránsito (*LAm*); (: *offense*) de carretera.
motorist [mō'tûrist] *n* conductor(a) *m/f*, automovilista *m/f*.
motorize [mō'tərīz] *vt* motorizar.
motor oil *n* aceite *m* para motores.
motor racing *n* (*Brit*) carreras *fpl* de coches, automovilismo.
motor scooter *n* moto *f*.
motor vehicle *n* automóvil *m*.
motorway [mō'tûrwā] *n* (*Brit*) autopista.
mottled [mât'əld] *a* abigarrado, multicolor.
motto, ~es [mât'ō] *n* lema *m*; (*watchword*) consigna.
mould [mōld] *etc* (*Brit*) = **mold** *etc*.
moult [mōlt] *vi* (*Brit*) = **molt**.
mound [mound] *n* montón *m*, montículo.
mount [mount] *n* monte *m*; (*horse*) montura; (*for jewel etc*) engarce *m*; (*for picture*) marco ♦ *vt* montar, subir a; (*stairs*) subir; (*exhibition*) montar; (*attack*) lanzar; (*picture, stamp*) pegar, fijar ♦ *vi* (*also*: ~ up) subirse, montarse.
mountain [moun'tən] *n* montaña ♦ *cpd* de montaña; **to make a** ~ **out of a molehill** hacerse de todo una montaña.
mountaineer [mountənēr'] *n* alpinista *m/f*, andinista *m/f* (*LAm*).
mountaineering [mountənē'ring] *n* alpinismo, andinismo (*LAm*).
mountainous [moun'tənəs] *a* montañoso.
mountain rescue team *n* equipo de rescate de montaña.
mountainside [moun'tənsīd] *n* ladera de la montaña.
mounted [moun'tid] *a* montado.
Mount Everest [mount ev'ûrist] *n* Monte *m* Everest.
mourn [môrn] *vt* llorar, lamentar ♦ *vi*: **to** ~ **for** llorar la muerte de, lamentarse por.
mourner [môr'nûr] *n* doliente *m/f*.
mournful [môrn'fəl] *a* triste, lúgubre.
mourning [môr'ning] *n* luto ♦ *cpd* (*dress*) de luto; **in** ~ de luto.
mouse, *pl* **mice** [mous, mīs] *n* (*also* COMPUT) ratón *m*.
mousetrap [mous'trap] *n* ratonera.
mousse [mōōs] *n* (CULIN) crema batida; (*for hair*) espuma (moldeadora).
moustache [məstash'] *n* (*Brit*) = **mustache**.
mousy [mou'sē] *a* (*person*) tímido; (*hair*) pardusco.
mouth, *pl* **mouths** [mouth, -thz] *n* boca; (*of river*) desembocadura.
mouthful [mouth'fōōl] *n* bocado.
mouth organ *n* armónica.
mouthpiece [mouth'pēs] *n* (*of musical instrument*) boquilla; (TEL) micrófono;

(*spokesman*) portavoz *m/f*.
mouth-to-mouth [mouth'təmouth'] *a*: ~ **resuscitation** boca a boca *m*.
mouthwash [mouth'wôsh] *n* enjuague *m* bucal.
mouth-watering [mouth'wôtûring] *a* apetitoso.
movable [mōō'vəbəl] *a* movible.
move [mōōv] *n* (*movement*) movimiento; (*in game*) jugada; (: *turn to play*) turno; (*change of house*) mudanza ♦ *vt* mover; (*emotionally*) conmover; (POL: *resolution etc*) proponer ♦ *vi* (*gen*) moverse; (*traffic*) circular; (*also*: Brit: ~ **house**) trasladarse, mudarse; **to** ~ **sb to do sth** mover a uno a hacer algo; **to be** ~**d** estar conmovido; **to get a** ~ **on** darse prisa; **to** ~ **like a bat out of hell** (*col*) correr como un loco.
move around *vi* moverse; (*travel*) viajar.
move along *vi* avanzar, adelantarse.
move away *vi* alejarse.
move back *vi* retroceder.
move down *vt* (*demote*) degradar.
move forward *vi* avanzar ♦ *vt* adelantar.
move in *vi* (*to a house*) instalarse.
move off *vi* ponerse en camino.
move on *vi* seguir viaje ♦ *vt* (*onlookers*) hacer circular.
move out *vi* (*of house*) mudarse.
move over *vi* apartarse.
move up *vi* subir; (*employee*) ser ascendido.
movement [mōōv'mənt] *n* movimiento; (TECH) mecanismo; ~ (**of the bowels**) (MED) evacuación *f*.
mover [mōō'vûr] *n* proponente *m/f*; (US) agente *m* de mudanzas.
movie [mōō'vē] *n* película; **to go to the** ~**s** ir al cine.
movie camera *n* cámara cinematográfica.
moviegoer [mōō'vēgōūr] *n* (US) aficionado/a al cine.
movie projector *n* proyector *m* de películas.
movie theater *n* (US) cine *m*.
moving [mōō'ving] *a* (*emotional*) conmovedor(a); (*that moves*) móvil; (*instigating*) motor(a).
moving van *n* (US) camión *m* de mudanzas.
mow, *pt* **mowed**, *pp* **mowed** *or* **mown** [mō, -n] *vt* (*grass*) cortar; (*grain*: *also*: ~ **down**) segar; (*shoot*) acribillar.
mower [mō'ûr] *n* (*also*: **lawn**~) cortacéspedes *m inv*.
Mozambique [mōzambēk'] *n* Mozambique *m*.
MP *n abbr* (= *Military Police*) PM; (= *Member of Parliament*) Dip.; (*Canada*) = *Mounted Police*.
mpg *n abbr* (= *miles per gallon*) millas por

galón.

mph *abbr* = *miles per hour* (*60 mph* = *96 km/h*.).

MPhil *n abbr* (= *Master of Philosophy*) *título universitario*.

Mr, **Mr.** [mis'tûr] *n*: ~ **Smith** (el) Sr. Smith.

Mrs, **Mrs.** [mis'iz] *n*: ~ **Smith** (la) Sra. de Smith.

MS *n abbr* (= *manuscript*) MS; = **multiple sclerosis**; (*US*: = *Master of Science*) *título universitario* ♦ *abbr* (*US MAIL*) = *Mississippi*.

Ms, **Ms.** [miz] *n* (= *Miss or Mrs*): ~ **Smith** (la) Sa. Smith.

MSA *n abbr* (*US*: = *Master of Science in Agriculture*) *título universitario*.

MSc *abbr* = **Master of Science**.

MSG *n abbr* = **monosodium glutamate**.

MSS *n abbr* (= *manuscripts*) MSS.

MST *abbr* (*US*: = *Mountain Standard Time*) *hora de invierno de las Montañas Rocosas*.

MSW *n abbr* (*US*: = *Master of Social Work*) *título universitario*.

MT *n abbr* (= *machine translation*) traducción *f* automática ♦ *abbr* (*US MAIL*) = *Montana*.

Mt *abbr* (*GEO*: = *mount*) m.

much [much] *a* mucho ♦ *ad*, *n*, *pron* mucho; (*before pp*) muy; **how** ~ **is it?** ¿cuánto es?, ¿cuánto cuesta?; **too** ~ demasiado; **so** ~ tanto; **it's not** ~ no es mucho; **as** ~ **as** tanto como; **however** ~ **he tries** por mucho que se esfuerce; **I like it very/so** ~ me gusta mucho/tanto; **thank you very** ~ muchas gracias, muy agradecido.

muck [muk] *n* (*dirt*) suciedad *f*; (*fig*) porquería.

   muck about *or* **around** *vi* (*Brit*: *col*) = **mess around**.

   muck in *vi* (*Brit*: *col*) compartir el trabajo.

   muck out *vt* (*stable*) limpiar.

   muck up *vt* (*col*: *dirty*) ensuciar; (: *spoil*) echar a perder; (: *ruin*) arruinar, estropear.

muckraking [muk'rāk'ing] (*fig col*) *n* amarillismo ♦ *a* especializado en escándalos.

mucky [muk'ē] *a* (*dirty*) sucio.

mucus [myoo'kəs] *n* moco.

mud [mud] *n* barro, lodo.

muddle [mud'əl] *n* desorden *m*, confusión *f*; (*mix-up*) embrollo, lío ♦ *vt* (*also*: ~ **up**) embrollar, confundir.

   muddle along *vi* arreglárselas de alguna manera.

   muddle through *vi* salir del paso.

muddle-headed [mud'əlhedid] *a* (*person*) despistado, confuso.

muddy [mud'ē] *a* fangoso, cubierto de lodo.

mudguard [mud'gârd] *n* guardabarros *m inv*.

mudpack [mud'pak] *n* mascarilla.

mudslinging [mud'slinging] *n* injurias *fpl*,

difamación *f*.

muff [muf] *n* manguito ♦ *vt* (*chance*) desperdiciar; (*lines*) estropear; (*shot, catch etc*) fallar; **to** ~ **it** fracasar.

muffin [muf'in] *n* (*US*) *una especie de pan dulce*, ≈ bollo; (*Brit*) mollete *m*.

muffle [muf'əl] *vt* (*sound*) amortiguar; (*against cold*) embozar.

muffled [muf'əld] *a* sordo, apagado.

muffler [muf'lûr] *n* (*scarf*) bufanda; (*US AUT*) silenciador *m*; (*on motorbike*) silenciador *m*, mofle *m*.

mufti [muf'tē] *n*: **in** ~ (vestido) de paisano.

mug [mug] *n* (*cup*) taza grande (*sin platillo*); (*for beer*) jarra; (*col*: *face*) jeta; (: *fool*) bobo ♦ *vt* (*assault*) asaltar.

   mug up *vt* (*Brit*: *col*: *also*: ~ **up on**) empollar.

mugger [mug'ûr] *n* asaltador(a) *m/f*.

mugging [mug'ing] *n* ataque *m* or asalto callejero.

muggy [mug'ē] *a* bochornoso.

mulatto, es [məlat'ō] *n* mulato/a.

mulberry [mul'bärē] *n* (*fruit*) mora; (*tree*) morera, moral *m*.

mule [myool] *n* mula.

mull [mul]: **to** ~ **over** *vt* meditar sobre.

mulled [muld] *a*: ~ **wine** vino caliente.

mullioned [mul'yənd] *a* (*windows*) dividido por parteluces.

multi... [mul'tē] *pref* multi....

multi-access [multēak'ses] *a* (*COMPUT*) multiacceso, de acceso múltiple.

multicolored, (*Brit*) **multicoloured** [mul'tikulûrd] *a* multicolor.

multifarious [multəfär'ēəs] *a* múltiple, vario.

multilateral [multilat'ûrəl] *a* (*POL*) multilateral.

multilevel [multilev'əl] *a* (*US*: *building*, *car park*) de muchos pisos.

multimillionaire [multēmilyənär'] *n* multimillonario/a.

multinational [multənash'ənəl] *n* multinacional *m*, transnacional *m* ♦ *a* multinacional.

multiple [mul'təpəl] *a* múltiple ♦ *n* múltiplo; (*Brit*: *also*: ~ **store**) (cadena de) grandes almacenes *mpl*.

multiple choice *n* examen *m* de tipo selección múltiple.

multiple crash *n* colisión *f* en cadena.

multiple sclerosis [mul'təpəl sklirō'sis] *n* esclerosis *f* múltiple.

multiplication [multəpləkā'shən] *n* multiplicación *f*.

multiplication table *n* tabla de multiplicar.

multiplicity [multəplis'ətē] *n* multiplicidad *f*.

multiply [mul'təplī] *vt* multiplicar ♦ *vi* multiplicarse.

multiracial [multērā'shəl] *a* multirracial.

multistorey |mul̄tĕstôr'ē| a (Brit) = **multi-level**.

multistrike ribbon |multistrīk' rib'ən| n (COMPUT: on printer) cinta de múltiples impactos.

multi-tasking |multĕtas'king| n (COMPUT) ejecución f de tareas múltiples, multitarea.

multitude |mul'tətōōd| n multitud f.

mum |mum| (Brit) n mamá ♦ a: **to keep ~ (about sth)** no decir ni mu (de algo).

mumble |mum'bəl| vt decir entre dientes ♦ vi hablar entre dientes, musitar.

mummify |mum'əfī| vt momificar.

mummy |mum'ē| n (Brit: mother) mamá; (embalmed) momia.

mumps |mumps| n paperas fpl.

munch |munch| vt, vi mascar.

mundane |mundān'| a mundano.

municipal |myōōnis'əpəl| a municipal.

municipality |myōōnisəpal'itē| n municipio.

munificence |myōōnif'əsəns| n munificencia.

munitions |myōōnish'ənz| npl municiones fpl.

mural |myōōr'əl| n (pintura) mural m.

murder |mûr'dûr| n asesinato; (in law) homicidio ♦ vt asesinar, matar; **to commit ~** cometer un asesinato or homicidio.

murderer |mûr'dûrûr| n asesino.

murderess |mûr'dûris| n asesina.

murderous |mûr'dûrəs| a homicida.

murk |mûrk| n oscuridad f, tinieblas fpl.

murky |mûr'kē| a (water, past) turbio; (room) sombrío.

murmur |mûr'mûr| n murmullo ♦ vt, vi murmurar; **heart ~** soplo cardíaco.

MusB(ac) n abbr (= Bachelor of Music) título universitario.

muscle |mus'əl| n músculo.

muscle in vi entrometerse.

muscular |mus'kyəlûr| a muscular; (person) musculoso.

MusD(oc) n abbr (= Doctor of Music) título universitario.

muse |myōōz| vi meditar ♦ n musa.

museum |myōōzē'əm| n museo.

mush |mush| n gachas fpl.

mushroom |mush'rōōm| n (gen) seta, hongo; (small) champiñón m ♦ vi (fig) crecer de la noche a la mañana.

mushy |mush'ē| a triturado; (pej) sensiblero.

music |myōō'zik| n música.

musical |myōō'zikəl| a melodioso; (person) musical ♦ n (show) comedia musical.

musical instrument n instrumento musical.

musically |myōō'ziklē| ad melodiosamente, armoniosamente.

music box n caja de música.

music hall n teatro de variedades.

musician |myōōzish'ən| n músico/a.

music stand n atril m.

musk |musk| n (perfume m de) almizcle m.

musket |mus'kit| n mosquete m.

musk rat n ratón m almizclero.

musk rose n (BOT) rosa almizcleña.

Muslim |muz'lim| a, n musulmán/ana m/f.

muslin |muz'lin| n muselina.

musquash |mus'kwâsh| n (fur) piel f del ratón almizclero.

muss |mus| vt (col: hair) despeinar; (: dress) arrugar.

mussel |mus'əl| n mejillón m.

must |must| auxiliary vb (obligation): **I ~ do it** debo hacerlo, tengo que hacerlo; (probability): **he ~ be there by now** ya debe (de) estar allí ♦ n: **it's a ~** es imprescindible.

mustache |məstash'| n (US) bigote m.

mustard |mus'tûrd| n mostaza.

mustard gas n gas m mostaza.

muster |mus'tûr| vt juntar, reunir; (also: ~ **up**: strength, courage) cobrar.

mustiness |mus'tēnis| n olor m a cerrado.

mustn't |mus'ənt| = **must not**.

musty |mus'tē| a mohoso, que huele a humedad.

mutant |myōō'tənt| a, n mutante m.

mutate |myōō'tāt| vi sufrir mutación, transformarse.

mutation |myōōtā'shən| n mutación f.

mute |myōōt| a, n mudo/a m/f.

muted |myōō'tid| a (noise) sordo; (criticism) callado.

mutilate |myōō'təlāt| vt mutilar.

mutilation |myōōtələ'shən| n mutilación f.

mutinous |myōō'tənəs| a (troops) amotinado; (attitude) rebelde.

mutiny |myōō'tənē| n motín m ♦ vi amotinarse.

mutter |mut'ûr| vt, vi murmurar.

mutton |mut'ən| n carne f de cordero.

mutual |myōō'chōōəl| a mutuo; (friend) común.

mutual fund n (US) bono fiduciario.

mutually |myōō'chōōəlē| ad mutuamente.

muzzle |muz'əl| n hocico; (protective device) bozal m; (of gun) boca ♦ vt amordazar; (dog) poner un bozal a.

MVP n abbr (US SPORT) = most valuable player.

MW abbr (= medium wave) onda media.

my |mī| a mi(s); **~ house/brother/sisters** mi casa/hermano/mis hermanas; **I've washed ~ hair/cut ~ finger** me he lavado el pelo/cortado un dedo; **is this ~ pen or yours?** ¿es este bolígrafo mío o tuyo?

myopic |mīâp'ik| a miope.

myriad |mir'ēəd| n (of people, things) miríada.

myrrh |mûr| n mirra.

myself |mīself'| pron (reflexive) me; (emphatic) yo mismo; (after prep) mí (mismo); see also **oneself**.

mysterious |mistēr'ēəs| a misterioso.

mysteriously [mistēr'ēəslē] *ad* misteriosa-
mente.
mystery [mis'tûrē] *n* misterio.
mystery play *n* auto, misterio.
mystic [mis'tik] *a*, *n* místico/a *m/f*.
mystical [mis'tikəl] *a* místico.
mysticism [mis'tisizəm] *n* misticismo.
mystification [mistəfəkā'shən] *n* perplejidad *f*; desconcierto.
mystify [mis'təfī] *vt* (*perplex*) dejar perplejo; (*disconcert*) desconcertar.
mystique [mistēk'] *n* misterio.
myth [mith] *n* mito.
mythical [mith'ikəl] *a* mítico.
mythological [mithəlàj'ikəl] *a* mitológico.
mythology [mithál'əjē] *n* mitología.

N

N, n [en] *n* (*letter*) N, n *f*; **N for Nan** N de
Navarra.
N *abbr* (= *North*) N.
NA *n abbr* (*US*: = *Narcotics Anonymous*)
organización de ayuda a los drogadictos;
(*US*) = *National Academy*.
n/a *abbr* (= *not applicable*) no interesa;
(*COMM etc*) = *no account*.
NAACP *n abbr* (*US*) = *National Association
for the Advancement of Colored People*.
nab [nab] *vt* (*col*: *grab*) coger (*Sp*), agarrar
(*LAm*); (: *criminal*) pillar.
NACU *n abbr* (*US*) = *National Association
of Colleges and Universities*.
nadir [nā'dûr] *n* (*ASTRO*) nadir *m*; (*fig*)
punto más bajo.
nag [nag] *n* (*pej*: *horse*) rocín *m* ♦ *vt* (*scold*)
regañar; (*annoy*) fastidiar.
nagging [nag'ing] *a* (*doubt*) persistente;
(*pain*) continuo ♦ *n* quejas *fpl*.
nail [nāl] *n* (*human*) uña; (*metal*) clavo ♦ *vt*
clavar; (*fig*: *catch*) coger (*Sp*), pillar; **to
pay cash on the ~** (*Brit*) pagar al contado; **to ~ sb down to a date/price** hacer
comprometerse a uno a una fecha.un precio.
nailbrush [nāl'brush] *n* cepillo para las
uñas.
nailfile [nāl'fīl] *n* lima para las uñas.
nail polish *n* esmalte *m* or laca para las
uñas.
nail scissors *npl* tijeras *fpl* para las uñas.
nail varnish *n* (*Brit*) = **nail polish**.
Nairobi [nīrō'bē] *n* Nairobi *m*.
naïve [nīēv'] *a* ingenuo.
naïvely [nīēv'lē] *ad* ingenuamente.
naïveté [nīēvtā'] *n* ingenuidad *f*, can-

didez *f*.
naked [nā'kid] *a* (*nude*) desnudo; (*flame*)
expuesto al aire; **with the ~ eye** a simple
vista.
NAM *n abbr* (*US*) = *National Association of
Manufacturers*.
name [nām] *n* (*gen*) nombre *m*; (*surname*)
apellido; (*reputation*) fama, renombre *m* ♦
vt (*child*) poner nombre a; (*appoint*) nombrar; **by ~ de** nombre; **in the ~ of** en
nombre de; **what's your ~?** ¿cómo se llama usted?; **my ~ is Peter** me llamo Pedro; **to give one's ~ and address** dar sus
señas; **to take sb's ~ and address** apuntar
las señas de uno; **to make a ~ for o.s.** hacerse famoso; **to get (o.s.) a bad ~** hacerse una mala reputación.
name-drop [nām'dràp] *vi*: **he's always
~ping** siempre está presumiendo de la
gente que conoce.
nameless [nām'lis] *a* anónimo, sin nombre.
namely [nām'lē] *ad* a saber.
nameplate [nām'plāt] *n* (*on door etc*) placa.
namesake [nām'sāk] *n* tocayo/a.
nanny [nan'ē] *n* niñera.
nap [nap] *n* (*sleep*) sueñecito, siesta; **to be
caught ~ping** estar desprevenido.
NAPA *n abbr* (*US*: = *National Association
of Performing Artists*) sindicato de trabajadores del espectáculo.
napalm [nā'pâm] *n* napalm *m*.
nape [nāp] *n*: **~ of the neck** nuca, cogote
m.
napkin [nap'kin] *n* (*also*: **table ~**) servilleta.
Naples [nā'pəlz] *n* Nápoles.
nappy [nap'ē] *n* (*Brit*) pañal *m*.
narcissism [nár'sisizəm] *n* narcisismo.
narcissus, *pl* **narcissi** [nársis'əs, -ē] *n* narciso.
narcotic [nárkât'ik] *a*, *n* narcótico.
narrate [nar'āt] *vt* narrar, contar.
narration [narā'shən] *n* narración *f*, relato.
narrative [nar'ətiv] *n* narrativa ♦ *a* narrativo.
narrator [nar'ātûr] *n* narrador(a) *m/f*.
narrow [nar'ō] *a* estrecho, angosto; (*resources, means*) escaso ♦ *vi* estrecharse,
angostarse; (*diminish*) reducirse; **to have
a ~ escape** escaparse por los pelos; **to ~
sth down** reducir algo.
narrow gauge *a* (*RAIL*) de vía estrecha.
narrowly [nar'ōlē] *ad* (*miss*) por poco.
narrow-minded [nar'ōmīn'did] *a* de miras
estrechas.
narrow-mindedness [nar'ōmīn'didnis] *n*
estrechez *f* de miras.
NAS *n abbr* (*US*) = *National Academy of
Sciences*.
NASA [nas'ə] *n abbr* (*US*: = *National Aeronautics and Space Administration*) NASA *f*.
nasal [nā'zəl] *a* nasal.

Nassau [nas'ô] *n* (*in Bahamas*) Nassau *m*.
nastily [nas'tilē] *ad* (*unpleasantly*) de mala manera; (*spitefully*) con rencor.
nastiness [nas'tēnis] *n* (*malice*) malevolencia; (*rudeness*) grosería; (*of person, remark*) maldad *f*; (*spitefulness*) rencor *m*.
nasturtium [nəstûr'shəm] *n* capuchina.
nasty [nas'tē] *a* (*remark*) feo; (*person*) antipático; (*revolting: taste, smell*) asqueroso; (*wound, disease etc*) peligroso, grave; **to turn** ~ (*situation*) ponerse feo; (*weather*) volverse malo; (*person*) ponerse negro.
NAS/UWT *n abbr* (*Brit*: = *National Association of Schoolmasters/Union of Women Teachers*) sindicato de profesores.
nation [nā'shən] *n* nación *f*.
national [nash'ənəl] *a, n* nacional *m/f*.
national anthem *n* himno nacional.
national debt *n* deuda pública.
national dress *n* vestido nacional.
National Forest Service *n* (*US*) ≈ la Comisión del Patrimonio Forestal.
National Guard *n* (*US*) Guardia Nacional.
National Health Service (NHS) *n* (*Brit*) servicio nacional de sanidad, ≈ INSALUD *m* (*Sp*).
National Insurance *n* (*Brit*) seguro social nacional.
nationalism [nash'ənəlizəm] *n* nacionalismo.
nationalist [nash'nəlist] *a, n* nacionalista *m/f*.
nationality [nashənal'ətē] *n* nacionalidad *f*.
nationalization [nashnələzā'shən] *n* nacionalización *f*.
nationalize [nash'nəlīz] *vt* nacionalizar; ~**d industry** industria nacionalizada.
nationally [nash'nəlē] *ad* (*nationwide*) en escala nacional; (*as a nation*) nacionalmente, como nación.
national park *n* reserva natural.
national press *n* prensa nacional.
national service *n* (*MIL*) servicio militar.
National Weather Service *n* (*US*) estación meteorológica estatal.
nationwide [nā'shənwīd'] *a* en escala *or* a nivel nacional.
native [nā'tiv] *n* (*local inhabitant*) natural *m/f*, nacional *m/f*; (*in colonies*) indígena *m/f*, nativo/a ♦ *a* (*indigenous*) indígena; (*country*) natal; (*innate*) natural, innato; **a** ~ **of Russia** un(a) natural de Rusia; ~ **language** lengua materna; **a** ~ **speaker of French** un hablante nativo de francés.
Nativity [nətiv'ətē] *n*: **the** ~ Navidad *f*.
NATO [nā'tō] *n abbr* (= *North Atlantic Treaty Organization*) OTAN *f*.
natter [nat'ûr] *vi* (*Brit*) charlar ♦ *n*: **to have a** ~ cotillear.
natural [nach'ûrəl] *a* natural; **death from** ~ **causes** (*LAW*) muerte *f* de causas naturales.
natural childbirth *n* parto natural.

natural gas *n* gas *m* natural.
naturalist [nach'ûrəlist] *n* naturalista *m/f*.
naturalization [nachûrələzā'shən] *n* naturalización *f*.
naturalize [nach'ûrəlīz] *vt*: **to become** ~**d** (*person*) naturalizarse; (*plant*) aclimatarse.
naturally [nach'ûrəlē] *ad* (*speak etc*) naturalmente; (*of course*) desde luego, por supuesto; (*instinctively*) por instinto, por naturaleza.
naturalness [nach'ûrəlnis] *n* naturalidad *f*.
natural resources *npl* recursos *mpl* naturales.
natural wastage *n* (*INDUSTRY*) desgaste *m* natural.
nature [nā'chûr] *n* naturaleza; (*group, sort*) género, clase *f*; (*character*) carácter *m*, genio; **by** ~ por *or* de naturaleza; **documents of a confidential** ~ documentos *mpl* de tipo confidencial.
-natured [nā'chûrd] *suff*: **ill**~ malhumorado.
nature reserve *n* (*Brit*) reserva natural.
nature trail *n* camino forestal educativo.
naturist [nā'chûrist] *n* naturista *m/f*.
naught [nôt] = **nought**.
naughtily [nôt'ilē] *ad* (*behave*) mal; (*say*) con malicia.
naughtiness [nôt'ēnis] *n* travesuras *fpl*.
naughty [nôt'ē] *a* (*child*) travieso; (*story, film*) verde, escabroso, colorado (*LAm*).
nausea [nô'zēə] *n* náusea.
nauseate [nô'zēāt] *vt* dar náuseas a; (*fig*) dar asco a.
nauseating [nô'zēāting] *a* nauseabundo; (*fig*) asqueroso, repugnante.
nauseous [nô'shəs] *a* (*MED, fig*) nauseabundo.
nautical [nô'tikəl] *a* náutico, marítimo; ~ **mile** milla marina.
naval [nā'vəl] *a* naval, de marina.
naval officer *n* oficial *m/f* de marina.
nave [nāv] *n* nave *f*.
navel [nā'vəl] *n* ombligo.
navigable [nav'əgəbəl] *a* navegable.
navigate [nav'əgāt] *vt* gobernar ♦ *vi* (*also AUT*) navegar.
navigation [navəgā'shən] *n* (*action*) navegación *f*; (*science*) náutica.
navigator [nav'əgātûr] *n* navegador(a) *m/f*, navegante *m/f*.
navvy [nav'ē] *n* (*Brit*) peón *m* caminero.
navy [nā'vē] *n* marina de guerra; (*ships*) armada, flota.
navy (blue) *a* azul marino.
Nazareth [naz'ûrith] *n* Nazaret *m*.
Nazi [nát'sē] *a, n* nazi *m/f*.
NB *abbr* (= *nota bene*) nótese; (*Canada*) = *New Brunswick*.
NBA *n abbr* (*US*) = *National Basketball Association, National Boxing Association*.
NBC *n abbr* (*US*: = *National Broadcasting Company*) cadena de televisión.

NBS *n abbr (US:* = *National Bureau of Standards)* ≈ Oficina Nacional de Normas.

NC *abbr (COMM etc)* = *no charge; (US MAIL)* = *North Carolina.*

NCC *n abbr (US)* = *National Council of Churches.*

NCO *n abbr* = **non-commissioned officer.**

ND *abbr (US MAIL)* = *North Dakota.*

N.Dak. *abbr (US)* = *North Dakota.*

N.E. *abbr (US MAIL)* = *Nebraska, New England.*

NEA *n abbr (US)* = *National Education Association.*

Neapolitan [nēəpàl'ətən] *a, n* napolitano/a *m/f.*

neaptide [nēp'tīd'] *n* marea muerta.

near [nēr] *a (place, relation)* cercano; *(time)* próximo ♦ *ad* cerca ♦ *prep (also:* ~ **to:** *space)* cerca de, junto a; (: *time)* cerca de ♦ *vt* acercarse a, aproximarse a; ~ **here/there** cerca de aquí/de allí; **$25,000 or ~est offer** 25,000 dólares o precio a discutir; **in the ~ future** en fecha próxima; **the building is ~ing completion** el edificio está por terminarse.

nearby [nēr'bī'] *a* cercano, próximo ♦ *ad* cerca.

nearly [nēr'lē] *ad* casi, por poco; **I ~ fell** por poco me caigo; **not ~** ni mucho menos, ni con mucho.

near miss *n* tiro cercano.

nearness [nēr'nis] *n* cercanía, proximidad *f.*

nearside [nēr'sīd] *n (AUT: right-hand drive)* lado izquierdo (: *left-hand drive)* lado derecho.

near-sighted [nēr'sītid] *a* miope, corto de vista.

neat [nēt] *a (place)* ordenado, bien cuidado; *(person)* pulcro; *(plan)* ingenioso; *(spirits)* solo; *(col)* magnífico, estupendo.

neatly [nēt'lē] *ad (tidily)* con esmero; *(skilfully)* ingeniosamente.

neatness [nēt'nis] *n (tidiness)* orden *m; (skilfulness)* destreza, habilidad *f.*

Nebr. *abbr (US)* = *Nebraska.*

nebulous [neb'yələs] *a (fig)* vago, confuso.

necessarily [nesəsàr'ilē] *ad* necesariamente; **not ~** no necesariamente.

necessary [nes'isàrē] *a* necesario, preciso; **he did all that was ~** hizo todo lo necesario; **if ~** si es necesario.

necessitate [nəses'ətāt] *vt* necesitar, exigir.

necessity [nəses'itē] *n* necesidad *f;* **necessities** *npl* artículos *mpl* de primera necesidad; **in case of ~** en caso de urgencia.

neck [nek] *n (ANAT)* cuello; *(of animal)* pescuezo ♦ *vi* besuquearse; ~ **and** ~ parejos; **to stick one's ~ out** *(col)* arriesgarse.

necklace [nek'lis] *n* collar *m.*

neckline [nek'lin] *n* escote *m.*

necktie [nek'tī] *n (US)* corbata.

nectar [nek'tûr] *n* néctar *m.*

nectarine [nektərēn'] *n* nectarina.

née [nā] *a:* ~ **Scott** de soltera Scott.

need [nēd] *n (lack)* escasez *f,* falta; *(necessity)* necesidad *f* ♦ *vt (require)* necesitar; **in case of ~** en caso de necesidad; **there's no ~ for ...** no hace(n) falta ...; **to be in ~ of, have ~ of** necesitar; **10 will meet my immediate ~s** 10 satisfacerán mis necesidades más premiantes; **the ~s of industry** las necesidades de la industria; **I ~ it** lo necesito; **a signature is ~ed** se requiere una firma; **I ~ to do it** tengo que or debo hacerlo; **you don't ~ to go** no hace falta que vayas.

needle [nē'dəl] *n* aguja ♦ *vt (fig: col)* picar, fastidiar.

needless [nēd'lis] *a* innecesario, inútil; ~ **to say** huelga decir que.

needlessly [nēd'lislē] *ad* innecesariamente, inútilmente.

needlework [nēd'əlwûrk] *n (activity)* costura, labor *f* de aguja.

needn't [nēd'ənt] = **need not.**

needy [nē'dē] *a* necesitado.

negation [nigā'shən] *n* negación *f.*

negative [neg'ətiv] *n (PHOT)* negativo; *(answer)* negativa; *(LING)* negación *f* ♦ *a* negativo.

negative cash flow *n* flujo negativo de efectivo.

neglect [niglekt'] *vt (one's duty)* faltar a, no cumplir con; *(child)* descuidar, desatender ♦ *n (state)* abandono; *(personal)* dejadez *f; (of duty)* incumplimiento; **to ~ to do sth** olvidarse de hacer algo.

neglected [niglek'tid] *a* abandonado.

neglectful [niglekt'fəl] *a* negligente; **to be ~ of sb/sth** descuidarse de algo.

negligee [neg'ləzhā] *n (nightdress)* salto de cama.

negligence [neg'lijəns] *n* negligencia, descuido.

negligent [neg'lijənt] *a (careless)* descuidado, negligente; *(forgetful)* olvidadizo.

negligently [neg'lijəntlē] *ad* con descuido, negligentemente.

negligible [neg'lijəbəl] *a* insignificante, despreciable.

negotiable [nigō'shəbəl] *a (check)* negociable; **not ~** *(check)* no trasmisible.

negotiate [nigō'shēāt] *vt (treaty, loan)* negociar; *(obstacle)* franquear; *(curve in road)* tomar ♦ *vi:* **to ~ (with)** negociar (con); **to ~ with sb for sth** tratar *or* negociar con uno por algo.

negotiation [nigōshēā'shən] *n* negociación *f,* gestión *f;* **to enter into ~s with sb** entrar en negociaciones con uno.

negotiator [nigō'shēātûr] *n* negociador(a) *m/f.*

Negress [nēg'ris] *n* negra.

Negro [nēg'rō] *a, n* negro.

neigh [nā] *n* relincho ♦ *vi* relinchar.

neighbor [nā'bûr] *n (US)* vecino/a.

neighborhood [nā'bûrhŏŏd] *n* (*place*) vecindad *f*, barrio; (*people*) vecindario.

neighboring [nā'bûring] *a* vecino.

neighborly [nā'bûrlē] *a* amigable, sociable.

neighbour [nā'bûr] *etc* (*Brit*) = **neighbor** *etc*.

neither [nē'tħûr] *a* ni ♦ *conj*: **I didn't move and ~ did John** no me he movido, ni Juan tampoco ♦ *pron* ninguno; **~ is true** ninguno/a de los/las dos es cierto/a ♦ *ad*: **~ good nor bad** ni bueno ni malo.

neo... [nē'ō] *pref* neo....

neolithic [nēəlith'ik] *a* neolítico.

neologism [nēāl'əjizəm] *n* neologismo.

neon [nē'ân] *n* neón *m*.

neon light *n* lámpara de neón.

Nepal [nəpól'] *n* Nepal *m*.

nephew [nef'yŏŏ] *n* sobrino.

nepotism [nep'ətizəm] *n* nepotismo.

nerve [nûrv] *n* (*ANAT*) nervio; (*courage*) valor *m*; (*impudence*) descaro, frescura; **a fit of ~s** un ataque de nervios; **to lose one's ~** (*self-confidence*) perder el valor.

nerve center *n* (*ANAT*) centro nervioso; (*fig*) punto neurálgico.

nerve gas *n* gas *m* nervino.

nerve-racking [nûrv'raking] *a* angustioso.

nervous [nûr'vəs] *a* (*anxious*, *ANAT*) nervioso; (*timid*) tímido, miedoso.

nervous breakdown *n* crisis *f* nerviosa.

nervously [nûr'vəslē] *ad* nerviosamente; tímidamente.

nervousness [nûr'vəsnis] *n* nerviosidad *f*, nerviosismo; timidez *f*.

nest [nest] *n* (*of bird*) nido ♦ *vi* anidar.

nest egg *n* (*fig*) ahorros *mpl*.

nestle [nes'əl] *vi*: **to ~ down** acurrucarse.

nestling [nest'ling] *n* pajarito.

NET *n abbr* (*US*) = *National Educational Television*.

net [net] *n* (*gen*) red *f*; (*fabric*) tul *m* ♦ *a* (*COMM*) neto, líquido; (*weight, price, salary*) neto ♦ *vt* coger (*Sp*) *or* agarrar (*LAm*) con red; (*money*: *subj*: *person*) cobrar; (: *deal, sale*) conseguir; **~ of tax** neto; **he earns $10,000 ~ per year** gana 10,000 dólares netos por año.

netball [net'bôl] *n* básquet *m*.

net curtain *n* (*Brit*) visillo.

Netherlands [netħ'ûrləndz] *npl*: **the ~** los Países Bajos.

net income *n* renta neta.

net loss *n* pérdida neta.

net profit *n* beneficio neto.

nett [net] *a* = **net**.

netting [net'ing] *n* red *f*, redes *fpl*.

nettle [net'əl] *n* ortiga.

network [net'wûrk] *n* red *f* ♦ *vt* (*RADIO, TV*) difundir por la red de emisores; (*COMPUT*) conectar a la red; **local area ~** red local.

neuralgia [nŏŏral'jə] *n* neuralgia.

neurosis, *pl* **-ses** [nŏŏrō'sis, -sēz] *n* neurosis

f inv.

neurotic [nŏŏrât'ik] *a*, *n* neurótico/a *m/f*.

neuter [nŏŏ'tûr] *a* (*LING*) neutro ♦ *vt* castrar, capar.

neutral [nŏŏ'trəl] *a* (*person*) neutral; (*color etc*, *ELEC*) neutro ♦ *n* (*AUT*) punto muerto.

neutrality [nŏŏtral'itē] *n* neutralidad *f*.

neutralize [nŏŏ'trəliz] *vt* neutralizar.

neutron [nŏŏ'trân] *n* neutrón *m*.

neutron bomb [nŏŏ'trân bâm] *n* bomba de neutrones.

Nev. *abbr* (*US*) = *Nevada*.

never [nev'ûr] *ad* nunca, jamás; **I ~ went** no fui nunca; **~ in my life** jamás en la vida; *see also* **mind**.

never-ending [nev'ûren'ding] *a* interminable, sin fin.

nevertheless [nevûrtħəles'] *ad* sin embargo, no obstante.

new [nŏŏ] *a* nuevo; (*recent*) reciente; **as good as ~** como nuevo.

newborn [nŏŏ'bôrn] *a* recién nacido.

newcomer [nŏŏ'kumûr] *n* recién venido *or* llegado.

newfangled [nŏŏ'fang'gəld] *a* (*pej*) modernísimo.

newfound [nŏŏ'found] *a* (*friend*) nuevo; (*enthusiasm*) recién adquirido.

New Guinea [nŏŏ gin'ē] *n* Nueva Guinea.

newly [nŏŏ'lē] *ad* nuevamente, recién.

newlyweds [nŏŏ'lēwedz] *npl* recién casados.

new moon *n* luna nueva.

newness [nŏŏ'nis] *n* novedad *f*; (*fig*) inexperiencia.

news [nŏŏz] *n* noticias *fpl*; **the ~** (*RADIO, TV*) las noticias *fpl*, telediario; **good/bad ~** buenas/malas noticias *fpl*; **financial ~** noticias *fpl* financieras.

news agency *n* agencia de noticias.

newsagent [nŏŏz'âjənt] *n* (*Brit*) vendedor(a) *m/f* de periódicos.

news bulletin *n* (*RADIO, TV*) noticiario.

newscaster [nŏŏz'kastûr] *n* presentador(a) *m/f*, locutor(a) *m/f*.

news dealer *n* (*US*) vendedor(a) *m/f* de periódicos.

news flash *n* noticia de última hora.

news item *n* una noticia.

newsletter [nŏŏz'letûr] *n* hoja informativa, boletín *m*.

newspaper [nŏŏz'pāpûr] *n* periódico, diario; **daily ~** diario; **weekly ~** periódico semanal.

newsprint [nŏŏz'print] *n* papel *m* de periódico.

newsreader [nŏŏz'rēdûr] *n* (*Brit*) = **newscaster**.

newsreel [nŏŏz'rēl] *n* noticiario.

newsroom [nŏŏz'rŏŏm] *n* (*PRESS, RADIO, TV*) sala de redacción.

newsstand [nŏŏz'stand] *n* quiosco *or* puesto de periódicos.

newt |noot| *n* tritón *m*.
New Year *n* Año Nuevo; **Happy ~!** ¡Feliz Año Nuevo!; **to wish sb a happy ~** desear a uno un feliz año nuevo.
New Year's Day *n* Día *m* de Año Nuevo.
New Year's Eve *n* Nochevieja.
New York |noo york| *n* Nueva York.
New Zealand |noo zē'lənd| *n* Nueva Ze-
land(i)a ♦ *a* neozelandés/esa.
New Zealander |noo zē'ləndûr| *n* neo-
zelandés/esa *m/f*.
next |nckst| *a* (*house, room*) vecino; (*meet-
ing*) próximo; (*page*) siguiente ♦ *ad* después; **the ~ day** al día siguiente; **~ time**
la próxima vez; **~ year** el año próximo *or*
que viene; **~ month** el mes que viene *or*
entrante; **the week after ~** no la semana
que viene sino la otra; **"turn to the ~**
page" "vuelva a la página siguiente";
you're ~ le toca; **~ to** *prep* junto a, al lado
de; **~ to nothing** casi nada; **~ to the last**
el penúltimo.
next door *ad* en la casa de al lado ♦ *a* vecino, de al lado.
next-of-kin |nckst'əvkin'| *n* pariente(s)
m(pl) más cercano(s).
NF *n abbr* (*Brit POL*: = *National Front*)
partido político de la extrema derecha ♦
abbr (*Canada*) = *Newfoundland*.
NFL *n abbr* (*US*) = *National Football
League*.
Nfld. *abbr* (*Canada*) = *Newfoundland*.
NG *abbr* (*US*) = **National Guard.**
NGO *n abbr* (*US*: = *non-governmental or-
ganization*) *organización no-gubernamental*.
NH *abbr* (*US MAIL*) = *New Hampshire*.
NHL *n abbr* (*US*) = *National Hockey
League*.
NHS *n abbr* = **National Health Service.**
NI *abbr* = **Northern Ireland**; (*Brit*) = **Na-
tional Insurance.**
nib |nib| *n* plumilla.
nibble |nib'əl| *vt* mordisquear, mordiscar.
Nicaragua |nikərǎg'wə| *n* Nicaragua.
Nicaraguan |nikərǎg'wən| *a*, *n* nicara-
güense *m/f*, nicaragüeño/a *m/f*.
Nice |nēs| *n* Niza.
nice |nīs| *a* (*likeable*) simpático; (*kind*)
amable; (*pleasant*) agradable; (*attractive*)
bonito, mono; (*distinction*) fino; (*taste,
smell, meal*) rico.
nice-looking |nīs'look'ing| *a* guapo.
nicely |nīs'lē| *ad* amablemente; bien; **that
will do ~** perfecto.
niceties |nī'sətēz| *npl* detalles *mpl*.
niche |nich| *n* (*ARCH*) nicho, hornacina.
nick |nik| *n* (*wound*) rasguño; (*cut, indenta-
tion*) mella, muesca ♦ *vt* (*cut*) cortar; (*col*)
birlar, robar; (: *Brit: arrest*) pillar; **in the
~ of time** justo a tiempo; **to ~ o.s.**
cortarse.
nickel |nik'əl| *n* níquel *m*; (*US*) *moneda de 5
centavos*.

nickname |nik'nām| *n* apodo, mote *m* ♦ *vt*
apodar.
Nicosia |nikōsē'ə| *n* Nicosia.
nicotine |nik'ətēn| *n* nicotina.
niece |nēs| *n* sobrina.
nifty |nif'tē| *a* (*col*: *car, jacket*) elegante; (:
gadget, tool) diestro.
Niger |nī'jûr| *n* (*country, river*) Niger *m*.
Nigeria |nījē'rēə| *n* Nigeria.
Nigerian |nījē'rēən| *a*, *n* nigeriano/a *m/f*.
niggardly |nig'ûrdlē| *a* (*person*) avaro, ta-
caño, avariento; (*allowance, amount*) miserable.
nigger |nig'ûr| *n* (*col!*: *highly offensive*)
negro/a.
niggle |nig'əl| *vt* preocupar ♦ *vi* (*complain*)
quejarse; (*fuss*) preocuparse por minucias.
niggling |nig'ling| *a* (*detail*: *trifling*) nimio,
insignificante; (*annoying*) molesto; (*doubt,
pain*) constante.
night |nīt| *n* (*gen*) noche *f*; (*evening*) tarde
f; **last ~** anoche; **the ~ before last** anteanoche; **at ~**, **by ~** de noche, por la noche;
in the ~, **during the ~** durante la noche.
nightcap |nīt'kap| *n* (*drink*) bebida que se
toma antes de acostarse.
nightclub |nīt'klub| *n* cabaret *m*.
nightdress |nīt'drcs| *n* (*Brit*) camisón *m*.
nightfall |nīt'fôl| *n* anochecer *m*.
nightgown |nīt'goun|, **nightie** |nī'tē| *n* ca-
misón *m*.
nightingale |nī'təngāl| *n* ruiseñor *m*.
night life *n* vida nocturna.
nightly |nīt'lē| *a* de todas las noches ♦ *ad* to-
das las noches, cada noche.
nightmare |nīt'mär| *n* pesadilla.
night owl *n* (*fig*) trasnochador(a) *m/f*, ma-
drugador(a) *m/f* (*LAm*).
night porter *n* guardián *m* nocturno.
night safe *n* caja fuerte.
night school *n* clase(s) *f(pl)* nocturna(s).
nightshade |nīt'shād| *n*: **deadly ~** (*BOT*)
belladona.
night shift *n* turno nocturno *or* de noche.
nightstick |nīt'stik| *n* (*US*) porra.
night-time |nīt'tim| *n* noche *f*.
night watchman *n* vigilante *m* nocturno,
sereno.
NIH *n abbr* (*US*) = *National Institutes of
Health*.
nihilism |nē'əlizəm| *n* nihilismo.
nil |nil| *n* cero, nada.
Nile |nīl| *n*: **the ~** el Nilo.
nimble |nim'bəl| *a* (*agile*) ágil, ligero;
(*skilful*) diestro.
nimbly |nim'blē| *ad* ágilmente; con destre-
za.
nine |nīn| *num* nueve.
nineteen |nīn'tēn'| *num* diecinueve, diez y
nueve.
nineteenth |nīn'tēnth'| *num* decimonoveno,
decimonono.
ninety |nīn'tē| *num* noventa.

ninth [nīnth] *num* noveno.

nip [nip] *vt* (*pinch*) pellizcar; (*bite*) morder ♦ (*Brit col*): **to ~ out/down/up** salir/bajar/subir un momento ♦ *n* (*drink*) trago.

nipple [nip'əl] *n* (*ANAT*) pezón *m*; (*of bottle*) tetilla; (*TECH*) boquilla, manguito.

nippy [nip'ē] *a* (*taste*) picante; (*Brit: person*) ágil; **it's a very ~ car** (*Brit*) es un coche muy potente para el tamaño que tiene.

nit [nit] *n* (*of louse*) liendre *f*; (*col: idiot*) imbécil *m/f*.

nit-pick [nit'pik] *vi* (*col*) buscar pelos en la sopa.

nitrogen [nī'trəjən] *n* nitrógeno.

nitroglycerin(e) [nītrəglis'ûrin] *n* nitroglicerina.

nitty-gritty [nit'ēgrit'ē] *n* (*col*): **to get down to the ~** ir al grano.

nitwit [nit'wit] *n* cretino/a.

NJ *abbr* (*US MAIL*) = *New Jersey.*

NLF *n abbr* (= *National Liberation Front*) FLN *m*.

NLQ *abbr* (= *near letter quality*) calidad *f* correspondencia.

NLRB *n abbr* (*US*: = *National Labor Relations Board*) organismo de protección al trabajador.

NM *abbr* (*US MAIL*) = *New Mexico.*

N.Mex. *abbr* (*US*) = *New Mexico.*

no [nō] *ad* no ♦ *a* ninguno, no ... alguno ♦ *n* no; **I won't take ~ for an answer** no hay pero que valga.

no. *abbr* (= *number*) no., núm.

nobble [nâb'əl] *vt* (*Brit col: bribe*) sobornar; (: *catch*) pescar; (: *RACING*) drogar.

Nobel prize [nō'bel priz'] *n* premio Nobel.

nobility [nōbil'ətē] *n* nobleza.

noble [nō'bəl] *a* (*person*) noble; (*title*) de nobleza.

nobleman [nō'bəlmən] *n* noble *m*.

nobly [nō'blē] *ad* (*selflessly*) noblemente.

nobody [nō'bâdē] *pron* nadie.

no-claims bonus [nō'klāmz bō'nəs] *n* (*Brit*) = **no-claims discount.**

no-claims discount [nō'klāmz dis'kount] *n* (*US*) bonificación *f* por carencia de reclamaciones.

nocturnal [nâktûr'nəl] *a* nocturno.

nod [nâd] *vi* saludar con la cabeza; (*in agreement*) decir que sí con la cabeza ♦ *vt*: **to ~ one's head** inclinar la cabeza ♦ *n* inclinación *f* de cabeza; **they ~ded their agreement** asintieron con la cabeza.

nod off *vi* cabecear.

no-fault [nō'fôlt'] *a* (*US*): **~ agreement** acuerdo de pago respectivo.

noise [noiz] *n* ruido; (*din*) escándalo, estrépito.

noisily [noi'zilē] *ad* ruidosamente, estrepitosamente.

noisy [noi'zē] *a* (*gen*) ruidoso; (*child*) escandaloso.

nomad [nō'mad] *n* nómada *m/f*.

nomadic [nōmad'ik] *a* nómada.

no man's land *n* tierra de nadie.

nominal [nâm'ənəl] *a* nominal.

nominate [nâm'ənāt] *vt* (*propose*) proponer; (*appoint*) nombrar.

nomination [nâmənā'shən] *n* propuesta; nombramiento.

nominee [nâmənē'] *n* candidato/a.

non... [nân] *pref* no, des..., in....

nonalcoholic [nânalkəhôl'ik] *a* no alcohólico.

nonaligned [nânəlīnd'] *a* no alineado.

nonarrival [nânərī'vəl] *n* falta de llegada.

nonce word [nâns'wûrd] *n* hápax *m*.

nonchalant [nânshəlânt'] *a* indiferente.

noncommissioned [nânkəmish'ənd] *a*: **~ officer** suboficial *m/f*.

noncommittal [nânkəmit'əl] *a* (*reserved*) reservado; (*uncommitted*) evasivo.

nonconformist [nânkənfôr'mist] *a* (*attitude*) heterodoxo; (*person*) inconformista *m/f* ♦ *n* inconforme *m/f*; (*Brit REL*) no conformista *m/f*.

noncontributory [nânkəntrib'yətôrē] *a*: **~ pension plan** *or* (*Brit*) **scheme** fondo de pensiones no contributivo.

noncooperation [nânkōâpərā'shən] *n* no cooperación *f*.

nondescript [nân'diskript] *a* soso.

none [nun] *pron* ninguno/a ♦ *ad* de ninguna manera; **~ of you** ninguno de vosotros; **I've ~ left** no me queda ninguno/a; **he's ~ the worse for it** no le ha hecho ningún mal; **I have ~** no tengo ninguno; **~ at all** (*not one*) ni uno.

nonentity [nânen'titē] *n* cero a la izquierda, nulidad *f*.

nonessential [nânəsen'chəl] *a* no esencial ♦ *n*: **~s** cosas *fpl* secundarias *or* sin importancia.

nonetheless [nun'thəles'] *ad* sin embargo, no obstante, aún así.

nonexecutive [nânigzek'yətiv] *a*: **~ director** director *m* no ejecutivo.

nonexistent [nânigzis'tənt] *a* inexistente.

nonfiction [nânfik'shən] *n* literatura no novelesca.

nonintervention [nânintûrven'chən] *n* no intervención *f*.

non obst. *abbr* (= *non obstante: notwithstanding*) no obstante.

nonpayment [nânpā'mənt] *n* falta de pago.

nonplussed [nânplust'] *a* perplejo.

nonprofit-making [nânprâf'itmāking] *a* de misión no comercial.

nonsense [nân'sens] *n* tonterías *fpl*, disparates *fpl*; **~!** ¡qué tonterías!; **it is ~ to say that ...** es absurdo decir que ....

nonskid [nânskid'] *a* antideslizante.

nonsmoker [nânsmō'kûr] *n* no fumador(a) *m/f*.

nonstick [nânstik'] *a* (*pan, surface*) antiadherente.

nonstop [nån'ståp'] *a* continuo; (*RAIL*) directo ♦ *ad* sin parar.

nontaxable [nåntak'səbəl] *a*: ~ **income** renta no imponible.

nonvolatile [nånvål'ətəl] *a*: ~ **memory** (*COMPUT*) memoria permanente.

nonvoting [nånvō'ting] *a*: ~ **shares** acciones *fpl* sin derecho a voto.

nonwhite [nånwīt'] *a* de color ♦ *n* (*person*) persona de color.

noodles [nōō'dəlz] *npl* tallarines *mpl*.

nook [nōōk] *n* rincón *m*; ~**s and crannies** escondrijos *mpl*.

noon [nōōn] *n* mediodía *m*.

no-one [nō'wun] *pron* = **nobody**.

noose [nōōs] *n* lazo corredizo.

nor [nór] *conj* = **neither** ♦ *ad see* **neither**.

Norf *abbr* (*Brit*) = Norfolk.

norm [nórm] *n* norma.

normal [nór'məl] *a* normal; **to return to** ~ volver a la normalidad.

normality [nórmal'itē] *n* normalidad *f*.

normally [nór'məlē] *ad* normalmente.

Normandy [nór'məndē] *n* Normandía.

north [nórth] *n* norte *m* ♦ *a* del norte, norteño ♦ *ad* al *or* hacia el norte.

North Africa *n* África del Norte.

North African *a, n* norteafricano/a *m/f*.

North America *n* América del Norte.

North American *a, n* norteamericano/a *m/f*.

Northants [nórthants'] *abbr* (*Brit*) = Northamptonshire.

norrthbound [nórth'bound'] *a* (*traffic*) que se dirige al norte; (*lane*) de dirección norte.

Northd *abbr* (*Brit*) = Northumberland.

northeast [nórthēst'] *n* nor(d)este *m*.

northerly [nór'thûrlē] *a* (*point, direction*) hacia el norte, septentrional; (*wind*) del norte.

northern [nór'thûrn] *a* norteño, del norte.

Northern Ireland *n* Irlanda del Norte.

North Korea *n* Corea del Norte.

North Pole *n*: **the** ~ el Polo Norte.

North Sea *n*: **the** ~ el Mar del Norte.

North Sea oil *n* petróleo del Mar del Norte.

northward(s) [nórth'wûrd(z)] *ad* hacia el norte.

northwest [nórthwest'] *n* nor(d)oeste *m*.

Norway [nór'wā] *n* Noruega.

Norwegian [nórwē'jən] *a, n* noruego/a *m/f*; (*LING*) noruego.

nos. *abbr* (= *numbers*) núms.

nose [nōz] *n* (*ANAT*) nariz *f*; (*ZOOL*) hocico; (*sense of smell*) olfato ♦ *vi* (*also*: ~ **one's way**) avanzar con cuidado; **to pay through the** ~ **(for sth)** (*col*) pagar un dineral (por algo).

nose around *vi* curiosear.

nosebleed [nōz'blēd] *n* hemorragia nasal.

nosedive [nōz'dīv] *n* picado vertical.

nose drops *npl* gotas *fpl* para la nariz.

nosey [nō'zē] *a* curioso, fisgón(ona).

nostalgia [nəstal'jə] *n* nostalgia.

nostalgic [nəstal'jik] *a* nostálgico.

nostril [nås'trəl] *n* ventana de la nariz.

nosy [nō'zē] *a* = **nosey**.

not [nåt] *ad* no; ~ **at all** no ... en absoluto; ~ **that...** no es que...; **it's too late, isn't it?** es demasiado tarde, ¿verdad?; ~ **yet** todavía no; ~ **now** ahora no; **why** ~? ¿por qué no?; **I hope** ~ espero que no; ~ **at all** no ... nada; (*after thanks*) de nada.

notable [nō'təbəl] *a* notable.

notably [nō'təblē] *ad* especialmente; (*in particular*) sobre todo.

notary [nō'tûrē] *n* (*also*: ~ **public**) notario/a.

notation [nōtā'shən] *n* notación *f*.

notch [nåch] *n* muesca, corte *m* ♦ *vt* (*also*: ~ **up**: *score, victory*) apuntarse.

note [nōt] *n* (*MUS, record, letter*) nota; (*banknote*) billete *m*; (*tone*) tono ♦ *vt* (*observe*) notar, observar; (*write down*) apuntar, anotar; **delivery** ~ nota de entrega; **to compare** ~**s** (*fig*) cambiar impresiones; **of** ~ conocido, destacado; **to take** ~ prestar atención a; **just a quick** ~ **to let you know that** ... sólo unas líneas para informarte que ....

notebook [nōt'bōōk] *n* libreta, cuaderno; (*for shorthand*) libreta.

notecase [nōt'kās] *n* (*Brit*) cartera, billetero.

noted [nō'tid] *a* célebre, conocido.

notepad [nōt'pad] *n* bloc *m*.

notepaper [nōt'pāpûr] *n* papel *m* para cartas.

noteworthy [nōt'wûrthē] *a* notable, digno de atención.

nothing [nuth'ing] *n* nada; (*zero*) cero; **he does** ~ no hace nada; ~ **new** nada nuevo; **for** ~ (*free*) gratis, sin pago; (*in vain*) en balde; ~ **at all** nada en absoluto.

notice [nō'tis] *n* (*announcement*) anuncio; (*dismissal*) despido; (*resignation*) dimisión *f*; (*review*: *of play etc*) reseña ♦ *vt* (*observe*) notar, observar; **to take** ~ **of** tomar nota de, prestar atención a; **at short** ~ a última hora, a corto plazo, con poca anticipación; **without** ~ sin aviso; **advance** ~ previo aviso; **until further** ~ hasta nuevo aviso; **to give sb** ~ **of sth** avisar a uno de algo; **to give** ~, **hand in one's** ~ dimitir, renunciar; **it has come to my** ~ **that** ... he llegado a saber que ...; **to escape** *or* **avoid** ~ pasar inadvertido.

noticeable [nō'tisəbəl] *a* evidente, obvio.

notice board *n* (*Brit*) tablón *m* de anuncios.

notification [nōtəfəkā'shən] *n* aviso; (*announcement*) anuncio.

notify [nō'təfī] *vt*: **to** ~ **sb (of sth)** comunicar (algo) a uno.

notion [nō'shən] *n* noción *f*, concepto; (*opinion*) opinión *f*.

notions [nō'shənz] *npl* (*US*) mercería.

notoriety [nōtəri'ətē] *n* notoriedad *f*, mala fama.

notorious [nōtôr'ēəs] *a* notorio, célebre.

notoriously [nōtôr'ēəslē] *ad* notoriamente.

Notts [nâts] *abbr* (*Brit*) = *Nottinghamshire*.

notwithstanding [nâtwithstan'ding] *ad* no obstante, sin embargo; ~ **this** a pesar de esto.

nougat [nōō'gət] *n* turrón *m*.

nought [nôt] *n* cero.

noun [noun] *n* nombre *m*, sustantivo.

nourish [nûr'ish] *vt* nutrir, alimentar; (*fig*) fomentar, nutrir.

nourishing [nûr'ishing] *a* nutritivo, rico.

nourishment [nûr'ishmənt] *n* alimento, sustento.

Nov. *abbr* (= *November*) nov.

novel [nâv'əl] *n* novela ♦ *a* (*new*) nuevo, original; (*unexpected*) insólito.

novelist [nâv'əlist] *n* novelista *m/f*.

novelty [nâv'əltē] *n* novedad *f*.

November [nōvem'bûr] *n* noviembre *m*.

novice [nâv'is] *n* principiante *m/f*, novato/a; (*REL*) novicio/a.

NOW [nou] *n abbr* (*US*) = *National Organization for Women*.

now [nou] *ad* (*at the present time*) ahora; (*these days*) actualmente, hoy día ♦ *conj*: ~ **(that)** ya que, ahora que; **right** ~ ahora mismo; **by** ~ ya; ~ **and then,** ~ **and again** de vez en cuando; **from** ~ **on** de ahora en adelante; **between** ~ **and Monday** entre hoy y el lunes; **in 3 days from** ~ de hoy en 3 días; **that's all for** ~ eso es todo por ahora.

nowadays [nou'ədāz] *ad* hoy (en) día, actualmente.

nowhere [nō'wär] *ad* (*direction*) a ninguna parte; (*location*) en ninguna parte; ~ **else** en *or* a ninguna otra parte.

noxious [nâk'shəs] *a* nocivo.

nozzle [nâz'əl] *n* boquilla.

NP *n abbr* = **notary public**.

NS *abbr* (*Canada*) = *Nova Scotia*.

NSC *n abbr* (*US*) = *National Security Council*.

NSF *n abbr* (*US*) = *National Science Foundation*.

NSW *abbr* (*Australia*) = *New South Wales*.

NT *n abbr* = *New Testament*.

nth [enth] *a*: **for the** ~ **time** (*col*) por enésima vez.

nuance [nōō'ânts] *n* matiz *m*.

nubile [nōō'bîl] *a* núbil.

nuclear [nōō'klēûr] *a* nuclear.

nuclear disarmament *n* desarme *m* nuclear.

nucleus, *pl* **nuclei** [nōō'klēəs, nōō'klēī] *n* núcleo.

nude [nōōd] *a, n* desnudo/a *m/f*; **in the** ~ desnudo.

nudge [nuj] *vt* dar un codazo a.

nudist [nōō'dist] *n* nudista *m/f*.

nudist colony *n* colonia de desnudistas.

nudity [nōō'ditē] *n* desnudez *f*.

nugget [nug'it] *n* pepita.

nuisance [nōō'səns] *n* molestia, fastidio; (*person*) pesado, latoso; **what a** ~! ¡qué lata!

nuke [nōōk] (*col*) *n* bomba atómica ♦ *vt* atacar con arma nuclear.

null [nul] *a*: ~ **and void** nulo y sin efecto.

nullify [nul'əfī] *vt* anular, invalidar.

numb [num] *a* entumecido; (*fig*) insensible ♦ *vt* quitar la sensación a, entumecer, entorpecer; **to be** ~ **with cold** estar entumecido de frío; ~ **with fear** paralizado de miedo; ~ **with grief** paralizado de dolor.

number [num'bûr] *n* número; (*numeral*) número, cifra ♦ *vt* (*pages etc*) numerar, poner número a; (*amount to*) sumar, ascender a; **reference** ~ número de referencia; **telephone** ~ número de teléfono; **wrong** ~ (*TEL*) número equivocado; **opposite** ~ (*Brit: person*) homólogo/a; **to be** ~**ed among** figurar entre; **a** ~ **of** varios, algunos; **they were ten in** ~ eran diez.

numbered account [num'bûrd əkount'] *n* (*in bank*) cuenta numerada.

number plate *n* (*Brit*) matrícula, placa.

Number Ten *n* (*Brit: 10 Downing Street*) *residencia del primer ministro*.

numbness [num'nis] *n* insensibilidad *f*, parálisis *f inv*; (*due to cold*) entumecimiento.

numbskull [num'skul] *n* imbécil *m/f*, majadero/a.

numeral [nōō'mûrəl] *n* número, cifra.

numerical [nōōmär'ikəl] *a* numérico.

numerous [nōō'mûrəs] *a* numeroso, muchos.

nun [nun] *n* monja, religiosa.

nuptial [nup'shəl] *a* nupcial.

nurse [nûrs] *n* enfermero/a; (*Brit: nanny*) niñera ♦ *vt* (*patient*) cuidar, atender; (*baby: US*) criar, amamantar; (: *Brit*) mecer; **male** ~ enfermero.

nursery [nûr'sûrē] *n* (*institution*) guardería infantil; (*room*) cuarto de los niños; (*for plants*) criadero, semillero.

nursery rhyme *n* canción *f* infantil.

nursery school *n* parvulario, escuela de párvulos.

nursery slope *n* (*Brit SKI*) cuesta para principiantes.

nursing [nûrs'ing] *n* (*profession*) profesión *f* de enfermera; (*care*) asistencia, cuidado ♦ *a* (*mother*) lactante.

nursing home *n* clínica de reposo.

nurture [nûr'chûr] *vt* (*child, plant*) alimentar, nutrir.

nut [nut] *n* (*TECH*) tuerca; (*BOT*) nuez *f* ♦ *a* (*chocolate etc*) con nueces ♦ *excl* ~**s!** (*US*)

¡narices!
nutcracker [nut'krakúr] *n* cascanueces *m inv*.
nutmeg [nut'meg] *n* nuez *f* moscada.
nutrient [nōō'trēənt] *a* nutritivo ♦ *n* nutrimento.
nutrition [nōōtrish'ən] *n* nutrición *f*, alimentación *f*.
nutritionist [nōōtrish'ənist] *n* dietista *m/f*.
nutritious [nōōtrish'əs] *a* nutritivo.
nuts [nuts] *a* (*col*) chiflado.
nutshell [nut'shel] *n* cáscara de nuez; **in a** ~ en resumidas cuentas.
nuzzle [nuz'əl] *vi*: **to** ~ **up to** arrimarse a.
NV *abbr* (*US MAIL*) = *Nevada*.
NWT *abbr* (*Canada*) = *Northwest Territories*.
NY *abbr* (*US MAIL*) = *New York*.
NYC *abbr* (*US MAIL*) = *New York City*.
nylon [nī'lân] *n* nilón *m* ♦ *a* de nilón.
nymph [nimf] *n* ninfa.
nymphomaniac [nimfəmā'nēak] *a*, *n* ninfómana.
NYSE *n abbr* (*US*) = *New York Stock Exchange*.
NZ *abbr* = **New Zealand.**

O

O, o [ō] (*letter*) O, o *f*; **O for Oboe** O de Oviedo.
oaf [ōf] *n* zoquete *m/f*.
oak [ōk] *n* roble *m* ♦ *a* de roble.
OAP *abbr* = **old-age pensioner.**
oar [ôr] *n* remo; **to put** *or* **shove one's** ~ **in** (*fig: col*) entrometerse.
oarlock [ôr'lák] *n* (*US*) chumacera.
OAS *n abbr* (= *Organization of American States*) OEA *f*.
oasis, *pl* **oases** [ōā'sis, ōā'sēz] *n* oasis *m inv*.
oath [ōth] *n* juramento; (*swear word*) palabrota; **under** ~ bajo juramento.
oatmeal [ōt'mēl] *n* harina de avena.
oats [ōts] *n* avena.
OAU *n abbr* (= *Organization of African Unity*) OUA *f*.
obdurate [âb'dyərit] *a* (*stubborn*) terco, obstinado; (*sinner*) empedernido; (*unyielding*) inflexible, firme.
obedience [ōbē'dēəns] *n* obediencia; **in** ~ **to** de acuerdo con.
obedient [ōbē'dēənt] *a* obediente.
obelisk [âb'əlisk] *n* obelisco.
obesity [ōbē'sitē] *n* obesidad *f*.
obey [ōbā'] *vt* obedecer; (*instructions, regulations*) cumplir.

obituary [ōbich'ōōärē] *n* necrología.
object *n* [âb'jikt] (*gen*) objeto; (*purpose*) objeto, propósito; (*LING*) complemento ♦ *vi* [əbjekt'|: **to** ~ **to** (*attitude*) protestar contra; (*proposal*) oponerse a; **expense is no** ~ no importan los gastos; **I** ~! ¡yo protesto!; **to** ~ **that** objetar que.
objection [əbjek'shən] *n* protesta; **I have no** ~ **to...** no tengo inconveniente en que....
objectionable [əbjek'shənəbəl] *a* (*gen*) desagradable; (*conduct*) censurable.
objective [əbjek'tiv] *a*, *n* objetivo.
objectively [əbjek'tivlē] *ad* objetivamente.
objectivity [âbjektiv'ətē] *n* objetividad *f*.
object lesson *n* (*fig*) (buen) ejemplo.
objector [əbjek'túr] *n* objetor(a) *m/f*.
obligation [âbləgā'shən] *n* obligación *f*; (*debt*) deber *m*; "**without** ~" "sin compromiso"; **to be under an** ~ **to sb/to do sth** estar comprometido con uno/a hacer algo.
obligatory [əblig'ətôrē] *a* obligatorio.
oblige [əblīj'] *vt* (*do a favor for*) complacer, hacer un favor a; **to** ~ **sb to do sth** forzar *or* obligar a uno a hacer algo; **to be** ~**d to sb for sth** estarle agradecido a uno por algo; **anything to** ~! (*col*) todo sea por complacerte.
obliging [əblī'jing] *a* servicial, atento.
oblique [əblēk'] *a* oblicuo; (*allusion*) indirecto ♦ *n* (*TYP*) oblicua.
obliterate [əblit'ərāt] *vt* borrar.
oblivion [əbliv'ēən] *n* olvido.
oblivious [əbliv'ēəs] *a*: ~ **of** inconsciente de.
oblong [âb'lông] *a* oblongo, rectangular ♦ *n* rectángulo.
obnoxious [əbnák'shəs] *a* odioso, detestable; (*smell*) nauseabundo.
o.b.o. *abbr* (*US*: = *or best offer*: *in classified ads*) abierto ofertas.
oboe [ō'bō] *n* oboe *m*.
obscene [əbsēn'] *a* obsceno.
obscenity [əbsen'itē] *n* obscenidad *f*.
obscure [əbskyōōr'] *a* oscuro ♦ *vt* oscurecer; (*hide: sun*) esconder.
obscurity [əbskyōōr'itē] *n* oscuridad *f*; (*obscure point*) punto oscuro; **to rise from** ~ salir de la nada.
obsequious [əbsē'kwēəs] *a* obsequioso.
observable [əbzúr'vəbəl] *a* observable, perceptible.
observance [əbzúr'vəns] *n* observancia, cumplimiento; (*ritual*) práctica; **religious** ~**s** prácticas *fpl* religiosas.
observant [əbzúr'vənt] *a* observador(a).
observation [âbzúrvā'shən] *n* observación *f*; (*by police etc*) vigilancia; (*MED*) examen *m*.
observation post *n* (*MIL*) puesto de observación.
observatory [əbzúr'vətôrē] *n* observatorio.
observe [əbzúrv'] *vt* (*gen*) observar; (*rule*) cumplir.

observer |əbzúr'vûr| *n* observador(a) *m/f*.

obsess |əbscs'| *vt* obsesionar; **to be ~ed by** *or* **with sb/sth** estar obsesionado por uno/ algo.

obsession |əbscsh'ən| *n* obsesión *f*, idea fija.

obsessive |əbscs'iv| *a* obsesivo; obsesionante.

obsolescence |âbsəlcs'əns| *n* obsolescencia.

obsolescent |âbsəlcs'ənt| *a* que está cayendo en desuso.

obsolete |âbsəlēt'| *a* (que está) en desuso.

obstacle |âb'stəkəl| *n* obstáculo; (*nuisance*) estorbo.

obstacle race *n* carrera de obstáculos.

obstetrician |âbstətrish'ən| *n* obstétrico/a.

obstetrics |əbstct'riks| *n* obstetricia.

obstinacy |âb'stənəsē| *n* obstinación *f*, terquedad *f*; tenacidad *f*.

obstinate |âb'stənit| *a* terco; (*determined*) tenaz.

obstinately |âb'stənitlē| *ad* obstinadamente, tercamente.

obstreperous |əbstrcp'ûrəs| *a* ruidoso; (*unruly*) revoltoso.

obstruct |əbstrukt'| *vt* (*block*) obstruir; (*hinder*) estorbar, obstaculizar.

obstruction |əbstruk'shən| *n* obstrucción *f*; estorbo, obstáculo.

obstructive |əbstruk'tiv| *a* obstruccionista; **stop being ~!** ¡deja de poner peros!

obtain |əbtān'| *vt* (*get*) obtener; (*achieve*) conseguir; **to ~ sth (for o.s.)** conseguir *or* adquirir algo.

obtainable |əbtān'əbəl| *a* asequible.

obtrusive |əbtrōō'siv| *a* (*person*) importuno, entrometido; (*building etc*) demasiado visible.

obtuse |əbtōōs'| *a* obtuso.

obverse |âb'vûrs| *n* (*of medal*) anverso; (*fig*) complemento.

obviate |âb'vēāt| *vt* obviar, evitar.

obvious |âb'vēəs| *a* (*clear*) obvio, evidente; (*unsubtle*) poco sutil; **it's ~ that** ... está claro que ..., es evidente que ....

obviously |âb'vēəslē| *ad* evidentemente, naturalmente; **~ not!** ¡por supuesto que no!; **he was ~ not drunk** era evidente que no estaba borracho; **he was not ~ drunk** no se le notaba lo borracho.

OCAS *n abbr* (= *Organization of Central American States*) ODECA *f*.

occasion |əkā'zhən| *n* oportunidad *f*, ocasión *f*; (*event*) acontecimiento *m*, causar; **on that ~** esa vez, en aquella ocasión; **to rise to the ~** ponerse a la altura de las circunstancias.

occasional |əkā'zhənəl| *a* poco frecuente, ocasional; **~ worker** (*US*) jornalero temporero.

occasionally |əkā'zhənəlē| *ad* de vez en cuando; **very ~** muy de tarde en tarde, en muy contadas ocasiones.

occasional table *n* mesita.

occult |əkult'| *a* (*gen*) oculto.

occupancy |âk'yəpənsē| *n* ocupación *f*.

occupant |âk'yəpənt| *n* (*of house*) inquilino/ a; (*of boat, car*) ocupante *m/f*.

occupation |âkyəpā'shən| *n* (*of house*) tenencia; (*job*) trabajo; (: *calling*) oficio.

occupational accident *n* accidente *m* laboral.

occupational hazard *n* riesgo profesional.

occupational pension plan *n* plan *m* profesional de jubilación.

occupational therapy *n* reeducación *f* terapéutica.

occupied |âk'yəpīd| *a*: **to be ~** (*US TEL*) estar comunicando.

occupier |âk'yəpīûr| *n* inquilino/a.

occupy |âk'yəpī| *vt* (*seat, post, time*) ocupar; (*house*) habitar; **to ~ o.s. with** *or* **by doing** (*as job*) dedicarse a hacer; (*to pass time*) pasar el tiempo haciendo; **to be occupied with sth/in doing sth** estar ocupado con algo/haciendo algo.

occur |əkûr'| *vi* pasar, suceder; **to ~ to sb** ocurrírsele a uno.

occurrence |əkûr'əns| *n* acontecimiento.

ocean |ō'shən| *n* océano; **~s of** (*col*) la mar de.

ocean bed *n* fondo del océano.

ocean-going |ō'shəngōing| *a* de alta mar.

Oceania |ōshēan'ēə| *n* Oceanía.

ocean liner *n* buque *m* transoceánico.

ocher, (*Brit*) **ochre** |ō'kûr| *n* ocre *m*.

OCR *n abbr* = **optical character recognition/reader**.

o'clock |əklâk'| *ad*: **it is 5 ~** son las 5.

Oct. *abbr* (= *October*) oct.

octagonal |âktag'ənəl| *a* octagonal.

octane |âk'tān| *n* octano; **high ~ gas** *or* (*Brit*) **petrol** gasolina de alto octanaje.

octave |âk'tiv| *n* octava.

October |âktō'bûr| *n* octubre *m*.

octogenarian |âktəjənär'ēən| *n* octogenario/a.

octopus |âk'təpəs| *n* pulpo.

oculist |âk'yəlist| *n* oculista *m/f*.

odd |âd| *a* (*strange*) extraño, raro; (*number*) impar; (*left over*) sobrante, suelto; **60-~** 60 y pico; **at ~ times** de vez en cuando; **to be the ~ one out** estar de más; *see also* **odds**.

oddball |âd'bôl| *n* (*col*) bicho raro.

oddity |âd'itē| *n* rareza; (*person*) excéntrico/a.

odd-job man |âdjâb' man| *n* hombre *m* que hace de todo.

odd jobs *npl* bricolaje *m*.

oddly |âd'lē| *ad* curiosamente, extrañamente.

odds |âdz| *npl* (*in betting*) puntos *mpl* de ventaja; **it makes no ~** da lo mismo; **at ~** reñidos/as; **to succeed against all the ~**

tener éxito a pesar de todas las desventajas; ~ **and ends** minucias *fpl.*

ode [ōd] *n* oda.

odious [ō'dēəs] *a* odioso.

odometer [ōdâm'itûr] *n* (*US*) cuentakilómetros *m inv.*

odor [ō'dûr] *n* (*US*) olor *m*; (*perfume*) perfume *m.*

odorless [ō'dûrlis] *a* sin olor.

odour [ō'dûr] *etc* (*Brit*) = **odor** *etc.*

OECD *n abbr* (= *Organization for Economic Co-operation and Development*) OCDE *f.*

oesophagus [isâf'əgəs] *n* (*Brit*) = **esophagus.**

oestrogen [es'trəjən] *n* (*Brit*) = **estrogen.**

of [uv] *prep* de; **a friend ~ ours** un amigo nuestro; **3 ~ them** 3 de ellos; **the 4th ~ July** el 4 de julio; **a boy ~ 10** un niño de 10 años; **a kilo ~ flour** un kilo de harina; **a quarter ~ 4** (*US*) las 4 menos cuarto; **made ~ wood** hecho de madera; **that was very kind ~ you** fue muy amable de su parte.

off [ôf] *a, ad* (*engine*) desconectado; (*light*) apagado; (*tap*) cerrado; (*Brit: food: bad*) pasado, malo; (: *milk*) cortado; (*cancelled*) cancelado; (*removed*): **the lid was ~** la tapadera no estaba puesta ♦ *prep* de; **to be ~** (*to leave*) irse, marcharse; **to be ~ sick** estar enfermo *or* de baja; **to be ~ in one's calculations** equivocarse (en sus cálculos); **a day ~** un día libre *or* sin trabajar; **to have an ~ day** tener un día malo; **he had his coat ~** se había quitado el abrigo; **10% ~** (*COMM*) (con el) 10% de descuento; **it's a long way ~** está muy lejos; **5 km ~ (the road)** a 5 km (de la carretera); **~ the coast** frente a la costa; **I'm ~ meat** (*no longer eat/like it*) paso de la carne; **on the ~ chance** por si acaso; **~ and on** de vez en cuando; **I must be ~** tengo que irme; **to be well/badly ~** andar bien/mal de dinero; **that's a bit ~, isn't it!** (*fig, col*) ¡mal hecho!

offal [ôf'əl] *n* (*CULIN*) menudencias *fpl.*

off-center, (*Brit*) **off-centre** [ôf'sen'tûr] *a* descentrado, ladeado.

off-colour [ôf'kul'ûr] *a* (*Brit: ill*) indispuesto; **to feel ~** sentirse *or* estar mal.

offence [əfens'] *n* (*Brit*) = **offense.**

offend [əfend'] *vt* (*person*) ofender ♦ *vi*: **to ~ against** (*law, rule*) infringir.

offender [əfen'dûr] *n* delincuente *m/f*; (*against regulations*) infractor(a) *m/f.*

offense [əfens'] *n* (*US*) (*crime*) delito; (*insult*) ofensa; **to take ~ at** ofenderse por; **to commit an ~** cometer un delito.

offensive [əfen'siv] *a* ofensivo; (*smell etc*) repugnante ♦ *n* (*MIL*) ofensiva.

offer [ôf'ûr] *n* (*gen*) oferta, ofrecimiento; (*proposal*) propuesta ♦ *vt* ofrecer; (*opportunity*) facilitar; **"on ~"** (*COMM*) "en oferta"; **to make an ~ for sth** hacer

una oferta por algo; **to ~ sth to sb, ~ sb sth** ofrecer algo a uno; **to ~ to do sth** ofrecerse *or* brindarse a hacer algo.

offering [ôf'ûring] *n* ofrenda.

offertory [ôf'ûrtôrē] *n* (*REL*) ofertorio.

offhand [ôf'hand'] *a* informal ♦ *ad* de improviso; **I can't tell you ~** no te lo puedo decir así de improviso *or* así nomás.

office [ôf'is] *n* (*place*) oficina; (*room*) despacho; (*position*) cargo, oficio; **doctor's ~** (*US*) consultorio; **to take ~** entrar en funciones; **through his good ~s** gracias a sus buenos oficios.

office automation *n* ofimática, buromática.

office bearer *n* (*Brit*) = **office holder.**

office building, (*Brit*) **office block** *n* bloque *m* de oficinas.

office boy *n* ordenanza *m.*

office holder *n* (*US: of club etc*) titular *m/f* (de una cartera).

office hours *npl* horas *fpl* de oficina; (*US MED*) horas *fpl* de consulta.

office manager *n* jefe/a *m/f* de oficina.

officer [ôf'isûr] *n* (*MIL etc*) oficial *m/f*; (*of organization*) director(a) *m/f*; (*of club etc*) titular *m/f* (de una cartera); (*also:* **police ~**) agente *m/f* de policía.

office work *n* trabajo de oficina.

office worker *n* oficinista *m/f.*

official [əfish'əl] *a* (*authorized*) oficial, autorizado; (*strike*) oficial ♦ *n* funcionario, oficial *m.*

officialdom [əfish'əldəm] *n* burocracia.

officially [əfish'əlē] *ad* oficialmente.

officiate [əfish'ēāt] *vi* (*also REL*) oficiar; **to ~ as Mayor** ejercer las funciones de alcalde; **to ~ at a marriage** celebrar una boda.

officious [əfish'əs] *a* oficioso.

offing [ôf'ing] *n*: **in the ~** (*fig*) en perspectiva.

off-key [ôfkē'] *a* desafinado ♦ *ad* desentonadamente, fuera de tono.

off-limits [ôf'lim'its] *a* (*US*) prohibido el paso.

off line *a, ad* (*COMPUT*) fuera de línea; (*switched off*) desconectado.

off-load [ôf'lōd'] *vt* descargar, desembarcar.

off-peak [ôf'pēk'] *a* (*holiday*) de temporada baja; (*electricity*) de banda económica.

off-putting [ôf'pŏŏt'ing] *a* (*Brit: person*) poco amable, difícil; (*behavior*) chocante.

off ramp *n* (*US*) vía de acceso.

off-season [ôf'sēzən] *a, ad* fuera de temporada.

offset *vt* [ôfset'] (*irg: like* **set**) (*counteract*) contrarrestar, compensar ♦ *n* [ôf'set] (*also:* **~ printing**) offset *m.*

offshoot [ôf'shŏŏt] *n* (*BOT*) vástago; (*fig*) ramificación *f.*

offshore [ôf'shôr] *a* (*breeze, island*) coste-

ro; (*fishing*) de bajura; ~ **oilfield** campo
petrolífero submarino.

offside n [ŏf'sĭd] (*AUT*: *with left-hand drive*)
lado izquierdo; (: *with right-hand drive*)
lado derecho ♦ a [ŏf'sĭd'] (*SPORT*) fuera de
juego; (*AUT*) del lado derecho; del lado
izquierdo.

offspring [ŏf'spring] n descendencia.

offstage [ŏf'stāj'] ad entre bastidores.

off-the-cuff [ŏf'thǝkuf'] a espontáneo.

off-the-job [ŏf'thǝjáb'] a: ~ **training** formación f fuera del trabajo.

off-the-peg [ŏf'thǝpeg'] ad (*Brit*) = **off-
the-rack**.

off-the-rack [ŏf'thǝrak'] ad (*US*) confeccionado.

off-the-wall [ŏf'thǝwôl'] a desquiciado.

off-white [ŏf'wĭt] a blanco grisáceo.

off-year [ŏf'yēr] a: ~ **election** elección f
parcial.

often [ŏf'ǝn] ad a menudo, con frecuencia;
how ~ **do you go?** ¿cada cuánto vas?

ogle [ō'gǝl] vt comerse con los ojos a.

ogre [ō'gŭr] n ogro.

OH abbr (*US MAIL*) = *Ohio*.

oh [ō] excl ¡ah!

OHMS abbr (*Brit*) *On His* (*or Her*) *Majesty's Service.*

oil [oil] n aceite m; (*petroleum*) petróleo ♦ vt
(*machine*) engrasar; **fried in** ~ frito en
aceite.

oilcan [oil'kan] n lata de aceite.

oilfield [oil'fēld] n campo petrolífero.

oil filter n (*AUT*) filtro de aceite.

oil-fired [oil'fĭurd] a que quema aceite combustible.

oil gauge n indicador m del aceite.

oil industry n industria petrolífera.

oil level n nivel m del aceite.

oil painting n pintura al óleo.

oil pan n (*US AUT*) cárter m.

oil refinery n refinería de petróleo.

oil rig n torre f de perforación.

oilskins [oil'skinz] npl impermeable msg,
chubasquero sg.

oil tanker n petrolero.

oil well n pozo (de petróleo).

oily [oi'lē] a aceitoso; (*food*) grasiento.

ointment [oint'mǝnt] n ungüento.

OJT n abbr (*US*: = *on-the-job training*)
aprendizaje en el trabajo.

OK abbr (*US MAIL*) = *Oklahoma.*

O.K., okay [ōkā'] excl O.K., ¡está bien!,
¡vale! ♦ a bien ♦ n: **to give sth one's** ~
dar el visto bueno a or aprobar algo ♦ vt
dar el visto bueno a; **it's** ~ **with** or **by me**
estoy de acuerdo, me parece bien; **are you**
~ **for money?** ¿andas or vas bien de dinero?

Okla. abbr (*US*) = *Oklahoma.*

old [ōld] a viejo; (*former*) antiguo; **how** ~
are you? ¿cuántos años tienes?, ¿qué edad
tienes?; **he's 10 years** ~ tiene 10 años; **~er**

brother hermano mayor; **any** ~ **thing will
do** sirve cualquier cosa.

old age n vejez f.

old-age pension [ōld'āj pen'chǝn] n (*Brit*)
jubilación f, pensión f.

old-age pensioner (OAP) [ōld'āj
pen'chǝnŭr] n (*Brit*) jubilado/a.

olden [ōl'dǝn] a antiguo.

old-fashioned [ōld'fash'ǝnd] a anticuado,
pasado de moda.

old maid n solterona.

old-time [ōld'tīm'] a antiguo, de antaño.

old-timer [ōld'tī'mŭr] n veterano/a,
anciano/a.

old wives' tale n cuento de viejas, patra-
ña.

olive [ål'iv] n (*fruit*) aceituna; (*tree*) olivo ♦
a (*also*: **~-green**) verde oliva inv.

olive branch n (*fig*): **to offer an** ~ **to sb**
ofrecer hacer las paces con uno.

olive oil n aceite m de oliva.

Olympic [ōlim'pik] a olímpico; **the** ~
Games, the ~s npl las Olimpíadas.

O & M n abbr = *organization and method.*

Oman [ō'mán] n Omán m.

OMB n abbr (*US*: = *Office of Management
and Budget*) servicio que asesora al presidente en materia presupuestaria.

omelet(te) [åm'lit] n tortilla (*Sp*), tortilla
de huevo (*LAm*).

omen [ō'mǝn] n presagio.

ominous [åm'ǝnǝs] a de mal agüero, ame-
nazador(a).

omission [ōmish'ǝn] n omisión f; (*error*)
descuido.

omit [ōmĭt'] vt omitir; (*by mistake*) olvidar,
descuidar; **to** ~ **to do sth** olvidarse or dejar de hacer algo.

omnivorous [åmniv'ûrǝs] a omnívoro.

ON abbr (*Canada*) = *Ontario.*

on [ån] prep en, sobre ♦ ad (*machine*) conectado; (*light, radio*) encendido; (*tap*)
abierto; **is the meeting still** ~? ¿todavía
hay reunión?; **when is this movie** ~?
¿cuándo van a poner esta película?; ~ **the
wall** en la pared, colgado de la pared; ~
television en la televisión; ~ **foot** a pie; ~
horseback a caballo; ~ **the Continent** en
Europa; ~ **seeing this** al ver esto; ~ **arrival** al llegar; ~ **the left** a la izquierda; ~
Friday el viernes; **to be** ~ **vacation** estar
de vacaciones; **I haven't any money** ~ **me**
no llevo dinero encima; **we're** ~ **irregular
verbs** estamos con los verbos irregulares;
this round's ~ **me** esta ronda la pago yo,
invito yo; **a book** ~ **physics** un libro de or
sobre física; **to have one's coat** ~ tener el
abrigo puesto; **to go** ~ seguir adelante;
I'm ~ **to sth** creo haber encontrado algo;
it's not ~! ¡eso no se hace!; **from that day**
~ de aquel día en adelante; **my father's
always** ~ **me** or (*Brit*) ~ **at me to get a
job** (*col*) mi padre siempre me está dando

la lata que coja un empleo.

once [wuns] *ad* una vez; *(formerly)* antiguamente ♦ *conj* una vez que; ~ **he had left/it was done** una vez que se había marchado/se hizo; **at** ~ en seguida, inmediatamente; *(simultaneously)* a la vez; ~ **a week** una vez por semana; ~ **more** otra vez; ~ **and for all** de una vez por todas; ~ **upon a time** érase una vez; **I knew him** ~ le conocía hace tiempo.

oncoming [ân'kuming] *a (traffic)* que viene de frente.

one [wun] *num* un, uno, una ♦ *pron* uno; *(impersonal)* se ♦ *a (sole)* único; *(same)* mismo; **this** ~ éste/a; **that** ~ ése/a, aquél/aquélla; **which** ~ **do you want?** ¿cuál quieres?; ~ **by** ~ uno por uno; ~ **never knows** nunca se sabe; ~ **another** el uno al otro; **it's** ~ **(o'clock)** es la una; **to be** ~ **up on sb** llevar ventaja a uno; **to be at** ~ **(with sb)** estar completamente de acuerdo (con uno).

one-armed bandit [wun'ârmd ban'dit] *n* máquina tragaperras.

one-day excursion [wun'dā ikskûr'zhən] *n (US)* billete *m* de ida y vuelta en un día.

one-man [wun'man] *a (business)* individual.

one-man band *n* hombre-orquesta *m*.

one-off [wun'ôf] *n (Brit col)* artículo fuera de serie.

one-piece [wun'pēs] *a (bathing suit)* de una pieza.

onerous [ân'ûrəs] *a (task, duty)* pesado; *(responsibility)* oneroso.

oneself [wunself'] *pron* uno mismo; *(after prep, also emphatic)* sí (mismo/a); **to do sth by** ~ hacer algo solo *or* por sí solo.

one-shot [wun'shât] *n (US: col)* artículo fuera de serie.

one-sided [wun'sīdid] *a (argument)* parcial; *(decision, view)* unilateral; *(game, contest)* desigual.

one-time [wun'tīm] *a* antiguo, ex-.

one-to-one [wun'təwun'] *a (relationship)* exacto.

one-upmanship [wunup'mənship] *n:* **the art of** ~ el arte de quedar siempre por encima.

one-way [wun'wā'] *a (street, traffic)* de dirección única; *(ticket)* sencillo.

ongoing [ân'gōing] *a* continuo.

onion [un'yən] *n* cebolla.

on line *a, ad (COMPUT)* en línea; *(switched on)* conectado.

onlooker [ân'lŏŏkûr] *n* espectador(a) *m/f*.

only [ōn'lē] *ad* solamente, sólo ♦ *a* único, solo ♦ *conj* solamente que, pero; **an** ~ **child** un hijo único; **not** ~ ... **but also**... no sólo ... sino también...; **I'd be** ~ **too pleased to help** encantado de servir(les); **I saw her** ~ **yesterday** le vi ayer mismo; **I would come,** ~ **I'm very busy** iría, sólo *or* salvo que estoy muy atareado.

ono *abbr* (= *or nearest offer: in. classified ads*) abierto ofertas.

on ramp *n* rampa de acceso.

onset [ân'set] *n* comienzo.

onshore [ân'shôr'] *a (wind)* que sopla del mar hacia la tierra.

onslaught [ân'slôt] *n* ataque *m*, embestida.

Ont. *abbr (Canada)* = Ontario.

on-the-job [ânthəjâb'] *a:* ~ **training** formación *f* en el trabajo *or* sobre la práctica.

onto [ân'tōō] *prep* = **on to.**

onus [ō'nəs] *n* responsabilidad *f;* **the** ~ **is upon him to prove it** le incumbe a él demostrarlo.

onward(s) [ân'wûrd(z)] *ad (move)* (hacia) adelante.

onyx [ân'iks] *n* ónice *m*, onyx *m*.

ooze [ōōz] *vi* rezumar.

opal [ō'pəl] *n* ópalo.

opaque [ōpāk'] *a* opaco.

OPEC [ō'pek] *n abbr* (= *Organization of Petroleum-Exporting Countries*) OPEP *f*.

open [ō'pən] *a* abierto; *(car)* descubierto; *(road, view)* despejado; *(meeting)* público; *(admiration)* manifiesto ♦ *vt* abrir ♦ *vi (flower, eyes, door, debate)* abrirse; *(book etc: commence)* comenzar; **in the** ~ **(air)** al aire libre; ~ **ticket** billete *m* sin fecha; ~ **ground** *(among trees)* claro; *(waste ground)* solar *m;* **to have an** ~ **mind (on sth)** estar sin decidirse aún (sobre algo); **to** ~ **a bank account** abrir una cuenta en el banco.

open on to *vt fus (subj: room, door)* dar a.

open out *vt* abrir ♦ *vi (person)* abrirse.

open up *vt* abrir; *(blocked road)* despejar ♦ *vi* abrirse, empezar.

open-and-shut [ō'pənənshut'] *a:* ~ **case** caso claro *or* evidente.

open day *n (Brit)* jornada de acceso público.

open-ended [ō'pənen'did] *a (fig)* indefinido, sin definir.

opener [ō'pənûr] *n (also:* **can** ~*)* abrelatas *m inv.*

open-heart surgery [ō'pənhârt sûr'jûrē] *n* cirugía a corazón abierto.

open house *n* jornada de acceso público.

opening [ō'pəning] *n* abertura, comienzo; *(opportunity)* oportunidad *f;* *(job)* puesto vacante, vacante *f*.

opening night *n* estreno.

openly [ō'pənlē] *ad* abiertamente.

open-minded [ō'pənmīn'did] *a* imparcial.

open-necked [ō'pənnekt'] *a* sin corbata.

openness [ō'pənnis] *n (frankness)* franqueza.

open-plan [ō'pənplan'] *a:* ~ **office** gran oficina sin particiones.

open return *n* vuelta con fecha abierta.

open shop *n empresa que contrata a mano de obra no afiliada a ningún sindica-*

to.

Open University *n* (*Brit*) ≈ Universidad *f* Nacional de Enseñanza a Distancia, UNED *f*.

opera |áp'rə| *n* ópera.

opera glasses *npl* gemelos *mpl*.

opera house *n* teatro de la ópera.

opera singer *n* cantante *m/f* de ópera.

operate |áp'ərāt| *vt* (*machine*) hacer funcionar; (*company*) dirigir ♦ *vi* funcionar; (*drug*) hacer efecto; **to ~ on sb** (*MED*) operar a uno.

operatic |ápərat'ik| *a* de ópera.

operating costs |áp'ərāting kôsts| *npl* gastos *mpl* operacionales.

operating profit *n* beneficio de explotación.

operating room *n* (*US*) sala de operaciones.

operating table *n* mesa de operaciones.

operating theatre *n* (*Brit*) sala de operaciones.

operation |ápərā'shən| *n* (*gen*) operación *f*; (*of machine*) funcionamiento; **to be in ~** estar funcionando *or* en funcionamiento; **to have an ~** (*MED*) ser operado; **to have an ~ for** operarse de; **the company's ~s during the year** las actividades de la compañía durante el año.

operational |ápərā'shənəl| *a* operacional, en buen estado; (*COMM*) en condiciones de servicio; (*ready for use or action*) en condiciones de funcionar; **when the service is fully ~** cuando el servicio esté en pleno funcionamiento.

operative |áp'ûrətiv| *a* (*measure*) en vigor; **the ~ word** la palabra clave.

operator |áp'ərātûr| *n* (*of machine*) maquinista *m/f*, operario/a; (*TEL*) operador(a) *m/f*, telefonista *m/f*.

operetta |ápəret'ə| *n* opereta; (*in Spain*) zarzuela.

ophthalmic |áfthal'mik| *a* oftálmico.

ophthalmologist |áfthalmâl'əjist| *n* oftalmólogo/a.

opinion |əpin'yən| *n* (*gen*) opinión *f*; **in my ~** en mi opinión, a mi juicio; **to seek a second ~** pedir una segunda opinión.

opinionated |əpin'yənātid| *a* testarudo.

opinion poll *n* encuesta, sondeo.

opium |ō'pēəm| *n* opio.

opponent |əpō'nənt| *n* adversario/a, contrincante *m/f*.

opportune |ápûrtōōn'| *a* oportuno.

opportunism |ápûrtōō'nizəm| *n* oportunismo.

opportunist |ápûrtōō'nist| *n* oportunista *m/f*.

opportunity |ápûrtyōō'nitē| *n* oportunidad *f*; **to take the ~ to do** *or* **of doing** aprovechar la ocasión para hacer.

oppose |əpōz'| *vt* oponerse a; **to be ~d to sth** oponerse a algo; **as ~d to** a diferencia

de.

opposing |əpōz'ing| *a* (*side*) opuesto, contrario.

opposite |áp'əzit| *a* opuesto, contrario a; (*house etc*) de enfrente ♦ *ad* en frente ♦ *prep* en frente de, frente a ♦ *n* lo contrario; **the ~ sex** el otro sexo, el sexo opuesto.

opposite number *n* (*Brit*) homólogo/a.

opposition |ápəzish'ən| *n* oposición *f*.

oppress |əprcs'| *vt* oprimir.

oppression |əprcsh'ən| *n* opresión *f*.

oppressive |əprcs'iv| *a* opresivo.

opprobrium |əprō'brēəm| *n* (*formal*) oprobio.

opt |ápt| *vi*: **to ~ for** optar por; **to ~ to do** optar por hacer; **to ~ out of** optar por no hacer.

optical |áp'tikəl| *a* óptico.

optical character recognition/reader (OCR) *n* reconocimiento/lector *m* óptico de caracteres.

optical fiber, (*Brit*) **optical fibre** *n* fibra óptica.

optician |áptish'ən| *n* óptico *m/f*.

optics |áp'tiks| *n* óptica.

optimism |áp'təmizəm| *n* optimismo.

optimist |áp'təmist| *n* optimista *m/f*.

optimistic |áptəmis'tik| *a* optimista.

optimum |áp'təməm| *a* óptimo.

option |áp'shən| *n* opción *f*; **to keep one's ~s open** (*fig*) mantener las opciones abiertas; **I have no ~** no tengo más *or* otro remedio; **~s** (*US*) opciones *fpl* extras.

optional |áp'shənəl| *a* facultativo, discrecional; **~ extras** (*Brit*) opciones *fpl* extras.

opulence |áp'yələns| *n* opulencia.

opulent |áp'yələnt| *a* opulento.

OR *abbr* (*US MAIL*) = *Oregon*.

or |ôr| *conj* o; (*before o, ho*) u; (*with negative*): **he hasn't seen ~ heard anything** no ha visto ni oído nada; **~ else** si no; **let me go ~ I'll scream!** ¡suélteme, o me pongo a gritar!

oracle |ôr'əkəl| *n* oráculo.

oral |ôr'əl| *a* oral ♦ *n* examen *m* oral.

orange |ôr'inj| *n* (*fruit*) naranja ♦ *a* color naranja.

orangeade |ôrinjād'| *n* naranjada, refresco de naranja.

orange juice *n* zumo *or* jugo (*LAm*) de naranja.

orang-outang, orang-utan |ôrang'ōōtang| *n* orangután *m*.

oration |ôrā'shən| *n* discurso solemne; **funeral ~** oración *f* fúnebre.

orator |ôr'ətûr| *n* orador(a) *m/f*.

oratorio |ôrətôr'ēō| *n* oratorio.

orbit |ôr'bit| *n* órbita ♦ *vt*, *vi* orbitar; **to be in/go into ~ (around)** estar en/entrar en órbita (alrededor de).

orchard |ôr'chûrd| *n* huerto; **apple ~** manzanar *m*, manzanal *m*.

orchestra |ôr'kistrə| *n* orquesta; (*US: seat-*

ing) platea.
orchestral |ôrkes'trəl| *a* de orquesta.
orchestrate |ôr'kistrāt| *vt* (*MUS*, *fig*) orquestar.
orchid |ôr'kid| *n* orquídea.
ordain |ôrdān'| *vt* (*REL*) ordenar, decretar; (*decide*) mandar.
ordeal |ôrdēl'| *n* experiencia horrorosa.
order |ôr'dûr| *n* orden *m*; (*command*) orden *f*; (*type*, *kind*) clase *f*; (*state*) estado; (*COMM*) pedido, encargo ♦ *vt* (*also*: **put in** ~) arreglar, poner en orden; (*COMM*) encargar, pedir; (*command*) mandar, ordenar; **in** ~ (*gen*) en orden; (*of document*) en regla; **in (working)** ~ en funcionamiento; **a machine in working** ~ una máquina en funcionamiento; **to be out of** ~ (*machine*, *toilets*) estar estropeado *or* descompuesto (*LAm*); **in** ~ **to do** para hacer; **on** ~ (*COMM*) pedido; **to be on** ~ estar pedido; **to be under** ~s **to do sth** estar bajo órdenes de hacer algo; **a point of** ~ una cuestión de procedimiento; **to place an** ~ **for sth with sb** hacer un pedido de algo a uno; **made to** ~ hecho a la medida; **his income is on** *or* (*Brit*) **of the** ~ **of $40,000 per year** sus ingresos son del orden de 40 mil dólares al año; **to the** ~ **of** (*BANKING*) a la orden de; **to** ~ **sb to do sth** mandar a uno hacer algo.
order book *n* cartera de pedidos.
order form *n* hoja de pedido.
orderly |ôr'dûrlē| *n* (*MIL*) ordenanza *m*; (*MED*) enfermero/a (auxiliar) ♦ *a* ordenado.
order number *n* número de pedido.
ordinal |ôr'dənəl| *a* ordinal.
ordinarily |ôrdənär'ilē| *ad* por lo común.
ordinary |ôr'dənärē| *a* corriente, normal; (*pej*) común y corriente; **out of the** ~ fuera de lo común, extraordinario.
ordinary seaman *n* (*Brit*) marinero.
ordinary shares *npl* acciones *fpl* ordinarias.
ordination |ôrdənā'shən| *n* ordenación *f*.
ordnance |ôrd'nəns| *n* (*MIL*: *unit*) artillería.
ordnance factory *n* fábrica de artillería.
Ore. *abbr* (*US*) = *Oregon*.
ore |ôr| *n* mineral *m*.
organ |ôr'gən| *n* órgano.
organic |ôrgan'ik| *a* orgánico.
organism |ôr'gənizəm| *n* organismo.
organist |ôr'gənist| *n* organista *m/f*.
organization |ôrgənəzā'shən| *n* organización *f*.
organization chart *n* organigrama *m*.
organize |ôr'gənīz| *vt* organizar; **to get** ~d organizarse.
organizer |ôr'gənīzûr| *n* organizador(a) *m/f*.
orgasm |ôr'gazəm| *n* orgasmo.
orgy |ôr'jē| *n* orgía.
Orient |ôr'ēənt| *n* Oriente *m*.
oriental |ôrēen'təl| *a* oriental.
orientate |ôr'ēəntāt| *vt* orientar.

origin |ôr'ijin| *n* origen *m*; (*point of departure*) procedencia.
original |ərij'ənəl| *a* original; (*first*) primero; (*earlier*) primitivo ♦ *n* original *m*.
originality |ərijənal'itē| *n* originalidad *f*.
originally |ərij'ənəlē| *ad* (*at first*) al principio; (*with originality*) con originalidad.
originate |ərij'ənāt| *vi*: **to** ~ **from, to** ~ **in** surgir de, tener su origen en.
originator |ərij'ənātûr| *n* inventor(a) *m/f*, autor(a) *m/f*.
ornament |ôr'nəmənt| *n* adorno; (*trinket*) chuchería.
ornamental |ôrnəmen'təl| *a* decorativo, de adorno.
ornamentation |ôrnəməntā'shən| *n* ornamentación *f*.
ornate |ôrnāt'| *a* muy ornado, vistoso.
ornithologist |ôrnəthâl'əjist| *n* ornitólogo/a.
ornithology |ôrnəthâl'əjē| *n* ornitología.
orphan |ôr'fən| *n* huérfano/a ♦ *vt*: **to be** ~**ed** quedar huérfano/a.
orphanage |ôr'fənij| *n* orfanato.
orthodox |ôr'thədâks| *a* ortodoxo.
orthodoxy |ôr'thədâksē| *n* ortodoxia.
orthopaedic |ôrthəpē'dik| *etc* = **orthopedic** *etc*.
orthopedic |ôrthəpē'dik| *a* ortopédico.
orthopedics |ôrthəpē'diks| *n* ortopedia.
O/S *abbr* = **out of stock**.
oscillate |âs'əlāt| *vi* oscilar; (*person*) vacilar.
oscillation |âsəlā'shən| *n* oscilación *f*; (*of prices*) fluctuación *f*.
OSHA *n abbr* (*US*: = *Occupational Safety and Health Administration*) oficina de la higiene y la seguridad en el trabajo.
Oslo |âz'lō| *n* Oslo.
ostensible |âsten'səbəl| *a* aparente, pretendido.
ostensibly |âsten'səblē| *ad* aparentemente.
ostentatious |âstentā'shəs| *a* pretencioso, aparatoso; (*person*) ostentativo.
osteopath |âs'tēəpath| *n* osteópata *m/f*.
ostracize |âs'trəsīz| *vt* hacer el vacio a.
ostrich |ôs'trich| *n* avestruz *m*.
OT *n abbr* (= *Old Testament*) A.T. *m*.
OTB *n abbr* (*US*: = *off-track betting*) apuestas hechas fuera del hipódromo.
O.T.E. *abbr* (*Brit*: = *on-target earnings*) beneficios según objetivos.
other |uth'ûr| *a* otro ♦ *pron*: **the** ~ (*one*) el/la otro/a; ~**s** (~ *people*) otros; ~ **than** (*apart from*) aparte de; **the** ~ **day** el otro día; **some** ~ **people have still to arrive** quedan por llegar otros; **some actor or** ~ (*Brit*) algún actor; **somebody or** ~ alguien, alguno; **the car was none** ~ **than Roberta's** fíjate que el coche era de Roberta.
otherwise |uth'ûrwīz| *ad, conj* de otra manera; (*if not*) si no; **an** ~ **good piece of work** un trabajo que, eso aparte, es bueno.

OTT *abbr* (*col*) = **over the top**; *see* **top**.

otter |ât'ûr| *n* nutria.

ouch |ouch| *excl* ¡ay!

ought, *pt* **ought** |ôt| *auxiliary vb*: **I ~ to do it** debería hacerlo; **this ~ to have been corrected** esto debiera de haberse corregido; **he ~ to win** (*probability*) debe *or* debiera ganar; **you ~ to go and see it** vale la pena ir a verlo.

ounce |ouns| *n* onza (*28.35g; 16 in a pound*).

our |ou'ûr| *a* nuestro; *see also* **my**.

ours |ou'ûrz| *pron* (el) nuestro/(la) nuestra *etc*; *see also* **mine**.

ourselves |ouûrselvz'| *pron pl* (*reflexive, after prep*) nosotros; (*emphatic*) nosotros mismos; **we did it (all) by ~** lo hicimos nosotros mismos *or* solos; *see also* **oneself**.

oust |oust| *vt* desalojar.

out |out| *ad* fuera, afuera; (*not at home*) fuera (de casa); (*light, fire*) apagado; (*on strike*) en huelga; **~ there** allí (fuera); **he's ~** (*absent*) no está, ha salido; **to be ~ in one's calculations** (*Brit*) equivocarse (en sus cálculos); **to run ~** salir corriendo; **~ loud** en alta voz; **~ of** *prep* (*outside*) fuera de; (*because of: anger etc*) por; **to look ~ of the window** mirar por la ventana; **to drink ~ of a cup** beber de una taza; **made ~ of wood** de madera; **~ of gas** sin gasolina; **"~ of order"** "no funciona"; **it's ~ of stock** (*COMM*) está agotado; **to be ~ and about again** estar repuesto y levantado; **the journey ~** el viaje de ida; **the boat was 10 km ~** el barco estaba a diez kilómetros de la costa; **before the week was ~** antes del fin de la semana; **he's ~ for all he can get** busca sus propios fines, anda detrás de lo suyo.

out-and-out |out'əndout'| *a* (*liar, thief etc*) redomado, empedernido.

outback |out'bak| *n* interior *m*.

outbid |outbid'| *vt* pujar más alto que, sobrepujar.

outboard |out'bôrd| *a*: **~ motor** (motor *m*) fuera borda *m*.

outbreak |out'brāk| *n* (*of war*) comienzo; (*of disease*) epidemia; (*of violence etc*) ola.

outbuilding |out'bilding| *n* dependencia; (*shed*) cobertizo.

outburst |out'bûrst| *n* explosión *f*, arranque *m*.

outcast |out'kast| *n* paria *m/f*.

outclass |outklas'| *vt* aventajar, superar.

outcome |out'kum| *n* resultado.

outcrop |out'krâp| *n* (*of rock*) afloramiento.

outcry |out'krī| *n* protestas *fpl*.

outdated |outdā'tid| *a* anticuado, fuera de moda.

outdistance |outdis'təns| *vt* dejar atrás.

outdo |outdōō'| *vt* (*irg: like* **do**) superar; **to ~ o.s.** lucirse.

outdoor |out'dôr| *a* al aire libre.

outdoors |outdôrz'| *ad* al aire libre.

outer |out'ûr| *a* exterior, externo.

outer space *n* espacio exterior.

outfit |out'fit| *n* equipo; (*clothes*) traje *m*; (*col: organization*) grupo, organización *f*.

outfitter's |out'fittûrz| *n* sastrería.

outgoing |out'gōing| *a* (*president, tenant*) saliente; (*means of transport*) que sale; (*character*) extrovertido.

outgoings |out'gōingz| *npl* (*Brit*) gastos *mpl*.

outgrow |outgrō'| *vt*: (*irg: like* **grow**) **he has ~n his clothes** su ropa le queda pequeña ya.

outhouse |out'hous| *n* (*US*) retrete *m* fuera de la casa; (*Brit*) dependencia.

outing |ou'ting| *n* excursión *f*, paseo.

outlandish |outlan'dish| *a* estrafalario.

outlast |outlast'| *vt* durar más tiempo que, sobrevivir a.

outlaw |out'lô| *n* proscrito/a ♦ *vt* (*person*) declarar fuera de la ley; (*practice*) declarar ilegal.

outlay |out'lā| *n* inversión *f*.

outlet |out'let| *n* salida; (*of pipe*) desagüe *m*; (*US ELEC*) toma de corriente; (*for emotion*) desahogo; (*also:* **retail ~**) punto de venta.

outline |out'līn| *n* (*shape*) contorno, perfil *m*; **in ~** (*fig*) a grandes rasgos.

outlive |outliv'| *vt* sobrevivir a.

outlook |out'lŏŏk| *n* perspectiva; (*opinion*) punto de vista.

outlying |out'līing| *a* remoto, aislado.

outmaneuver, (*Brit*) **outmanoeuvre** |outmənōō'vûr| *vt* (*MIL, fig*) superar en la estrategia, superar a.

outmoded |outmō'did| *a* anticuado, pasado de moda.

outnumber |outnum'bûr| *vt* exceder en número.

out of bounds *a*: **it's ~** está prohibido el paso.

out-of-date |outəvdāt'| *a* (*passport*) caducado, vencido; (*theory, idea*) anticuado; (*clothes, customs*) pasado de moda.

out-of-doors |outəvdôrz'| *ad* al aire libre.

out-of-the-way |outəvthəwā'| *a* (*remote*) apartado; (*unusual*) poco común *or* corriente.

outpatient |out'pāshənt| *n* paciente *m/f* externo/a.

outpost |out'pōst| *n* puesto avanzado.

output |out'pŏŏt| *n* (volumen *m* de) producción *f*, rendimiento; (*COMPUT*) salida ♦ *vt* (*COMPUT: to power*) imprimir.

outrage |out'rāj| *n* (*scandal*) escándalo; (*atrocity*) atrocidad *f* ♦ *vt* ultrajar.

outrageous |outrā'jəs| *a* monstruoso; (*clothes*) extravagante, escandaloso.

outright *ad* |out'rīt'| (*win*) de manera absoluta; (*be killed*) en el acto; (*completely*) completamente ♦ *a* |out'rīt| completo.

outrun |outrun'| *vt* (*irg: like* **run**) correr

más aprisa que, dejar atrás.

outset [out'set] *n* principio.

outshine [outshīn'] *vt* (irg: *like* **shine**) (*fig*) eclipsar, brillar más que.

outside [out'sīd'] *n* exterior *m* ♦ *a* exterior, externo ♦ *ad* fuera ♦ *prep* fuera de; (*beyond*) más allá de; **at the** ~ (*fig*) a lo sumo; **an** ~ **chance** una posibilidad remota; ~ **left/right** (*SOCCER*) extremo izquierdo/derecho.

outside broadcast *n* (*RADIO, TV*) emisión *f* exterior.

outside contractor *n* contratista *m/f* independiente.

outside line *n* (*TEL*) línea (exterior).

outsider [outsī'dûr] *n* (*stranger*) extraño, forastero.

outsize [out'sīz] *a* (*Brit*: *clothes*) de talla grande.

outskirts [out'skûrts] *npl* alrededores *mpl*, afueras *fpl*.

outsmart [outsmârt'] *vt* ser más listo que.

outspoken [out'spō'kən] *a* muy franco.

outspread [out'spred] *a* extendido; (*wings*) desplegado.

outstanding [outstan'ding] *a* excepcional, destacado; (*unfinished*) pendiente.

outstretched [outstrecht'] *a* (*hand*) extendido.

outstrip [outstrip'] *vt* (*competitors, demand, also fig*) dejar atrás, aventajar.

out-tray [out'trā] *n* bandeja de salida.

outvote [outvōt'] *vt*: **it was** ~**d (by** ...**)** fue rechazado en el voto (por ...).

outward [out'wûrd] *a* (*sign, appearances*) externo; (*journey*) de ida.

outwardly [out'wûrdlē] *ad* por fuera.

outweigh [outwā'] *vt* pesar más que.

outwit [outwit'] *vt* ser más listo que.

outworn [outwôrn'] *a* (*expression*) cansado.

oval [ō'vəl] *a* ovalado ♦ *n* óvalo.

ovary [ō'vûrē] *n* ovario.

ovation [ōvā'shən] *n* ovación *f*.

oven [uv'ən] *n* horno.

ovenproof [uv'ənprōōf] *a* resistente al horno.

oven-ready [uv'ənred'ē] *a* listo para el horno.

ovenware [uv'ənwär] *n* artículos *mpl* para el horno.

over [ō'vûr] *ad* encima, por encima ♦ *a* (*or ad*) (*finished*) terminado; (*surplus*) de sobra; (*excessively*) demasiado ♦ *prep* (por) encima de; (*above*) sobre; (*on the other side of*) al otro lado de; (*more than*) más de; (*during*) durante; ~ **here** (por) aquí; ~ **there** (por) allí *or* allá; **all** ~ (*everywhere*) por todas partes; ~ **and** ~ (**again**) una y otra vez; ~ **and above** además de; **to ask sb** ~ invitar a uno a casa; **to bend** ~ inclinarse; **the world** ~ en todo el mundo, en el mundo entero.

over... [ō'vûr] *pref* sobre..., super....

overact [ōvûrakt'] *vi* (*THEATER*) exagerar el papel.

overall *a* [ō'vûrôl] (*length*) total; (*study*) de conjunto ♦ *ad* [ōvûrôl'] en conjunto ♦ *n* [ō'vûrôl] (*Brit*) guardapolvo; ~**s** *npl* mono *sg*, overol *msg* (*LAm*).

overanxious [ōvûrangk'shəs] *a* demasiado preocupado *or* ansioso.

overawe [ōvûrô'] *vt* impresionar.

overbalance [ōvûrbal'əns] *vi* perder el equilibrio.

overbearing [ōvûrbär'ing] *a* autoritario, imperioso.

overboard [ō'vûrbôrd] *ad* (*NAUT*) por la borda; **to go** ~ **for sth** (*fig*) enloquecerse por algo.

overbook [ō'vûrbōōk'] *vt* sobrereservar, reservar con exceso.

overcapitalize [ōvûrkap'itəlīz] *vi* sobrecapitalizar.

overcast [ō'vûrkast] *a* encapotado.

overcharge [ōvûrchârj'] *vt*: **to** ~ **sb** cobrar un precio excesivo a uno.

overcoat [ō'vûrkōt] *n* abrigo, sobretodo.

overcome [ōvûrkum'] *vt* (*irg*: *like* **come**) (*gen*) vencer; (*difficulty*) superar; **she was quite** ~ **by the occasion** la ocasión le conmovió mucho *or* le vino en grande.

overconfident [ōvûrkân'fidənt] *a* demasiado confiado.

overcrowded [ōvûrkrou'did] *a* atestado de gente; (*city, country*) superpoblado.

overcrowding [ōvûrkrou'ding] *n* (*in town, country*) superpoblación *f*; (*in bus etc*) hacinamiento, apiñamiento.

overdo [ōvûrdōō'] *vt* (*irg*: *like* **do**) exagerar; (*overcook*) cocer demasiado; **to** ~ **it, to** ~ **things** (*work too hard*) trabajar demasiado.

overdose [ō'vûrdōs] *n* sobredosis *f inv*.

overdraft [ō'vûrdraft] *n* saldo deudor.

overdrawn [ōvûrdrôn'] *a* (*account*) en descubierto.

overdrive [ō'vûrdrīv] *n* (*AUT*) sobremarcha, superdirecta.

overdue [ōvûrdōō'] *a* retrasado; (*recognition*) tardío; (*bill*) vencido y no pagado; **that change was long** ~ ese cambio tenía que hacerse hace tiempo.

overenthusiastic [ōvûrenthōōzēas'tik] *a* demasiado entusiasta.

overestimate [ōvûres'təmāt] *vt* sobreestimar.

overexcited [ōvûriksī'tid] *a* sobreexcitado.

overexertion [ōvûrigzûr'shən] *n* agotamiento, fatiga.

overexpose [ōvûrikspōz'] *vt* (*PHOT*) sobreexponer.

overflow *vi* [ōvûrflō'] desbordarse ♦ *n* [ō'vûrflō] (*excess*) exceso; (*of river*) desbordamiento; (*also*: ~ **pipe**) (cañería de) desagüe *m*.

overfly [ōvûrflī'] *vt* (*irg*: *like* **fly**) sobrevolar.

overgenerous [ōvûrjen'ûrəs] *a* demasiado generoso.

overgrown [ōvûrgrōn'] *a* (*garden*) cubierto de hierba; **he's just an ~ schoolboy** es un niño en grande.

overhang [ōvûrhang'] (*irg*: *like* **hang**) *vt* sobresalir por encima de ♦ *vi* sobresalir.

overhaul *vt* [ōvûrhól'] revisar, repasar ♦ *n* [ō'vûrhól] revisión *f*.

overhead *ad* [ō'vûrhed'] por arriba *or* encima ♦ [ō'vûrhed] *a* (*cable*) aéreo; (*railway*) elevado, aéreo ♦ *n* (*US*) gastos *mpl* generales.

overheads [ō'vûrhedz] *npl* (*Brit*) gastos *mpl* generales.

overhear [ōvûrhiûr'] *vt* (*irg*: *like* **hear**) oír por casualidad.

overheat [ōvûrhēt'] *vi* (*engine*) recalentarse.

overjoyed [ōvûrjoid'] *a* encantado, lleno de alegría.

overkill [ō'vûrkil] *n* (*MIL fig*) capacidad *f* excesiva de destrucción.

overland [ō'vûrland] *a*, *ad* por tierra.

overlap *vi* [ōvûrlap'] traslaparse ♦ *n* [ō'vûrlap] traslapo.

overleaf [ō'vûrlēf] *ad* al dorso.

overload [ōvûrlōd'] *vt* sobrecargar.

overlook [ōvûrlŏŏk'] *vt* (*have view of*) dar a, tener vistas a; (*miss*) pasar por alto; (*forgive*) hacer la vista gorda a.

overlord [ō'vûrlórd] *n* señor *m*.

overmanning [ōvûrman'ing] *n* empleo de más personal de lo necesario.

overnight *ad* [ōvûrnīt'] durante la noche; (*fig*) de la noche a la mañana ♦ *a* [ō'vûrnīt] de noche; **to stay ~** pasar la noche.

overnight bag *n* fin *m* de semana, neceser *m* de viaje.

overnight stay *n* estancia de una noche.

overpass [ō'vûrpas] *n* (*US*) paso superior *or* a desnivel.

overpay [ōvûrpā'] *vt*: **to ~ sb by $50** pagar 50 dólares de más a uno.

overpower [ōvûrpou'ûr] *vt* dominar; (*fig*) embargar.

overpowering [ōvûrpou'ûring] *a* (*heat*) agobiante; (*smell*) penetrante.

overproduction [ōvûrprəduk'shən] *n* superproducción *f*.

overrate [ōvərrāt'] *vt* sobreestimar.

overreach [ōvərēch'] *vt*: **to ~ o.s.** ir demasiado lejos, pasarse.

override [ōvərīd'] *vt* (*irg*: *like* **ride**) (*order*, *objection*) no hacer caso de.

overriding [ōvərīd'ing] *a* predominante.

overrule [ōvərŏŏl'] *vt* (*decision*) anular; (*claim*) denegar.

overrun [ō'vərun] *vt* (*irg*: *like* **run**) (*MIL*: *country*) invadir; (*time limit*) rebasar, exceder ♦ *vi* rebasar el límite previsto; **the town is ~ with tourists** el pueblo está inundado de turistas.

overseas *ad* [ō'vûrsēz'] en ultramar; (*abroad*) en el extranjero ♦ *a* [ō'vûrsēz] (*trade*) exterior; (*visitor*) extranjero.

overseer [ō'vûrsēûr] *n* (*in factory*) superintendente *m/f*; (*foreman*) capataz *m*.

overshadow [ōvûrshad'ō] *vt* (*fig*) eclipsar.

overshoot [ōvûrshŏŏt'] *vt* (*irg*: *like* **shoot**) excederse.

oversight [ō'vûrsīt] *n* descuido; **due to an ~** a causa de un descuido *or* una equivocación.

oversimplify [ōvûrsim'pləfī] *vt* simplificar demasiado.

oversize [ō'vûrsiz] *a* (*US*: *clothes*) de talla grande.

oversleep [ōvûrslēp'] *vi* (*irg*: *like* **sleep**) quedarse dormido.

overspend [ōvûrspend'] *vi* gastar más de la cuenta; **we have overspent by 5 dollars** hemos excedido el presupuesto en 5 dólares.

overspill [ō'vûrspil] *n* exceso de población.

overstaffed [ōvûrstaft] *a*: **to be ~** tener una plantilla excesiva.

overstate [ōvûrstāt'] *vt* exagerar.

overstatement [ōvûrstāt'mənt] *n* exageración *f*.

overstay [ōvûrstā'] *vt*: **to ~ one's welcome** quedarse más de la cuenta.

overstep [ōvûrstep'] *vt*: **to ~ the mark** *or* **the limits** pasarse de la raya.

overstock [ōvûrsták'] *vt* abarrotar.

overstrike [ō'vûrstrīk] *n* (*on printer*) superposición *f* ♦ *vt* (*irg*: *like* **strike**) superponer.

oversubscribed [ōvûrsəbskrībd'] *a* suscrito en exceso.

overt [ōvûrt'] *a* abierto.

overtake [ōvûrtāk'] *vt* (*irg*: *like* **take**) sobrepasar; (*Brit AUT*) adelantar.

overtax [ōvûrtaks'] *vt* (*ECON*) exigir contribuciones *fpl* excesivas *or* impuestos *mpl* excesivos a; (*fig*: *strength*, *patience*) agotar, abusar de; **to ~ o.s.** fatigarse demasiado.

overthrow [ōvûrthrō'] *vt* (*irg*: *like* **throw**) (*government*) derrocar.

overtime [ō'vûrtīm] *n* horas *fpl* extraordinarias; (*US SPORT*) prórroga; **to do** *or* **work ~** hacer *or* trabajar horas extraordinarias *or* extras.

overtime ban *n* prohibición *f* de (hacer) horas extraordinarias.

overtone [ō'vûrtōn] *n* (*fig*) tono.

overture [ō'vûrchûr] *n* (*MUS*) obertura; (*fig*) propuesta.

overturn [ōvûrtûrn'] *vt*, *vi* volcar.

overweight [ōvûrwāt'] *a* demasiado gordo *or* pesado.

overwhelm [ōvûrwelm'] *vt* aplastar.

overwhelming [ōvûrwel'ming] *a* (*victory*, *defeat*) arrollador(a); (*desire*) irresistible; **one's ~ impression is of heat** lo que más impresiona es el calor.

overwhelmingly [ōvûrwel'minglē] *ad* abrumadoramente.

overwork [ōvûrwûrk'] *n* trabajo excesivo ♦ *vt* hacer trabajar demasiado ♦ *vi* trabajar demasiado.

overwrite [ōvərīt'] *vt* (*irg*: *like* **write**) (*COMPUT*) sobreescribir.

overwrought [ō'vərôt'] *a* sobreexcitado.

ovulation [ávyəlā'shən] *n* ovulación *f*.

owe [ō] *vt* deber; **to ~ sb sth, to ~ sth to sb** deber algo a uno.

owing to [ō'ing tōō] *prep* debido a, por causa de.

owl [oul] *n* búho, lechuza.

own [ōn] *vt* tener, poseer ♦ *vi* (*Brit*): **to ~ to sth/to having done sth** confesar *or* reconocer algo/haber hecho algo ♦ *a* propio; **a room of my ~** una habitación propia; **on one's ~** solo, a solas; **can I have it for my (very) ~?** ¿puedo quedarme con él?; **to come into one's ~** justificarse.

own up *vi* confesar.

own brand *n* (*COMM*) marca propia.

owner [ō'nûr] *n* dueño/a.

owner-occupier [ō'nûr ák'yəpīûr] *n* ocupante propietario/a *m/f*.

ownership [ō'nûrship] *n* posesión *f*; **it's under new ~** está bajo nueva dirección.

ox, *pl* **oxen** [áks, ák'sən] *n* buey *m*.

Oxfam [áks'fam] *n abbr* (*Brit*: = *Oxford Committee for Famine Relief*) OXFAM.

oxide [ák'sīd] *n* óxido.

oxtail [áks'tāl] *n*: **~ soup** sopa de rabo de buey.

oxyacetylene [áksēəset'əlin] *a* oxiacetilénico; **~ burner, ~ torch** soplete *m* oxiacetilénico.

oxygen [ák'sijən] *n* oxígeno.

oxygen mask *n* máscara de oxígeno.

oxygen tent *n* tienda de oxígeno.

oyster [ois'tûr] *n* ostra.

oz. *abbr* = **ounce(s)**.

ozone [ō'zōn] *n* ozono; **~ friendly** amigo del ozono; **~ layer** capa de ozono.

P

P, p [pē] *n* (*letter*) P, p *f*; **P for Peter** P de París.

P *abbr* = **president, prince**.

p *abbr* (= *page*) pág.; (*Brit*) = **penny, pence**.

PA *n abbr* = **personal assistant, public address system** ♦ *abbr* (*US MAIL*) = *Pennsylvania*.

pa [pâ] *n* (*col*) papá *m*.

p.a. *abbr* = **per annum**.

PAC *n abbr* (*US*) = *political action committee*.

pace [pās] *n* paso; (*rhythm*) ritmo ♦ *vi*: **to ~ up and down** pasearse de un lado a otro; **to keep ~ with** llevar el mismo paso que; (*events*) mantenerse a la altura de *or* al corriente de; **to set the ~** (*running*) marcar el paso; (*fig*) dar la pauta; **to put sb through his ~s** (*fig*) poner a uno a prueba.

pacemaker [pās'mākûr] *n* (*MED*) regulador *m* cardíaco, marcapasos *m inv*.

pacific [pəsif'ik] *a* pacífico ♦ *n*: **the P~ (Ocean)** el (Océano) Pacífico.

pacification [pasəfəkā'shən] *n* pacificación *f*.

pacifier [pas'əfīûr] *n* (*US*: *for baby*) chupete *m*.

pacifism [pas'əfizəm] *n* pacifismo.

pacifist [pas'əfist] *n* pacifista *m/f*.

pacify [pas'əfī] *vt* (*soothe*) apaciguar; (*country*) pacificar.

pack [pak] *n* (*packet*) paquete *m*; (*COMM*) embalaje *m*; (*of hounds*) jauría; (*of wolves*) manada; (*of thieves etc*) manada, bando; (*of cards*) baraja; (*bundle*) fardo; (*of cigarettes*) paquete *m*, cajetilla ♦ *vt* (*wrap*) empaquetar; (*fill*) llenar; (*in suitcase etc*) meter, poner; (*cram*) llenar, atestar; (*fig*: *meeting etc*) llenar de partidarios; (*COMPUT*) comprimir; **to ~ (one's bags)** hacer la maleta; **to ~ sb off** despachar a uno; **the place was ~ed** el local estaba lleno hasta el tope; **to send sb ~ing** (*col*) echar *or* despedir a uno.

pack in *vt* (*col*) dejar ♦ *vi* (*Brit*: *break down*: *watch, car*) estropearse; **~ it in!** ¡para!, ¡basta ya!

pack up *vt* (*belongings, clothes*) recoger; (*goods, presents*) empaquetar, envolver ♦ *vi* (*Brit*: *col*: *machine*) estropearse; (*person*) irse.

package [pak'ij] *n* paquete *m*; (*bulky*) bulto; (*also*: **~ deal**) acuerdo global ♦ *vt* (*COMM*: *goods*) envasar, embalar.

package bomb *n* (*US*) paquete *m* bomba.

package holiday *n* (*Brit*) viaje *m* todo comprendido.

package tour *n* viaje *m* organizado.

packaging [pak'ijing] *n* envase *m*.

packed lunch [pakt lunch] *n* (*Brit*) almuerzo frío, merienda.

packer [pak'ûr] *n* (*person*) empacador(a) *m/f*.

packet [pak'it] *n* paquete *m*.

packet switching [pak'it swich'ing] *n* (*COMPUT*) conmutación *f* por paquetes.

packhorse [pak'hôrs] *n* caballo de carga.

pack ice [pak īs] *n* banco de hielo.

packing [pak'ing] *n* embalaje *m*.

packing case *n* cajón *m* de embalaje.

pact [pakt] *n* pacto.

pad |pad| *n* (*of paper*) bloc *m*; (*cushion*) cojinete *m*; (*launching* ~) plataforma (de lanzamiento); (*col: apartment*) casa ♦ *vt* rellenar.

padding |pad'ing| *n* relleno; (*fig*) paja.

paddle |pad'əl| *n* (*oar*) canalete *m*; (*US: for table tennis*) raqueta ♦ *vt* impulsar con canalete ♦ *vi* (*with feet*) chapotear.

paddle steamer *n* vapor *m* de ruedas.

paddling pool |pad'ling pōōl| *n* (*Brit*) estanque *m* de juegos.

paddock |pad'ək| *n* corral *m*.

paddy |pad'ē| *n* arrozal *m*.

padlock |pad'läk| *n* candado ♦ *vt* cerrar con candado.

paediatrics |pēdēat'riks| *n* (*Brit*) = **pediatrics**.

paediatrician |pēdēətrish'ən| *n* (*Brit*) = **pediatrician**.

pagan |pā'gən| *a, n* pagano/a *m/f*.

page |pāj| *n* (*of book*) página; (*of newspaper*) plana; (*also:* ~ **boy**) paje *m* ♦ *vt* (*in hotel etc*) llamar por altavoz a.

pageant |paj'ənt| *n* (*procession*) desfile *m*; (*show*) espectáculo.

pageantry |paj'əntrē| *n* pompa.

page break *n* límite *m* de la página.

pager |pā'júr| *n* localizador *m* personal.

paginate |paj'ənāt| *vt* paginar.

pagination |pajənā'shən| *n* paginación *f*.

pagoda |pəgō'də| *n* pagoda.

paid |pād| *pt, pp of* **pay** ♦ *a* (*work*) remunerado; (*official*) asalariado; **to put** ~ **to** (*Brit*) acabar con.

paid-up |pād'up| *a* (*member*) con sus cuotas pagadas *or* al día; (*share*) liberado; ~ **capital** capital *m* desembolsado.

pail |pāl| *n* cubo, balde *m*.

pain |pān| *n* dolor *m*; **to be in** ~ sufrir; **on** ~ **of death** so *or* bajo pena de muerte; *see also* **pains**.

pained |pānd| *a* (*expression*) afligido.

painful |pān'fəl| *a* doloroso; (*difficult*) penoso; (*disagreeable*) desagradable.

painfully |pān'fəlē| *ad* (*fig: very*) terriblemente.

painkiller |pān'kilúr| *n* analgésico.

painless |pān'lis| *a* que no causa dolor; (*method*) fácil.

pains |pānz| *npl* (*efforts*) esfuerzos *mpl*; **to take** ~ **to do sth** tomarse trabajo en hacer algo.

painstaking |pānz'tāking| *a* (*person*) concienzudo, esmerado.

paint |pānt| *n* pintura ♦ *vt* pintar; **a can of** ~ una lata de pintura; **to** ~ **the door blue** pintar la puerta de azul.

paintbox |pānt'bäks| *n* caja de pinturas.

paintbrush |pānt'brush| *n* (*artist's*) pincel *m*; (*decorator's*) brocha.

painter |pān'túr| *n* pintor(a) *m/f*.

painting |pān'ting| *n* pintura.

paintwork |pānt'wúrk| *n* pintura.

pair |pär| *n* (*of shoes, gloves etc*) par *m*; (*of people*) pareja; **a** ~ **of scissors** unas tijeras; **a** ~ **of pants** unos pantalones, un pantalón.

pair off *vi*: **to** ~ **off (with sb)** hacer pareja (con uno).

pajamas |pəjám'əz| *npl* (*US*) pijama *m*; **a pair of** ~ un pijama.

Pakistan |pak'istan| *n* Paquistán *m*.

Pakistani |pak'əstan'ē| *a, n* paquistaní *m/f*.

PAL |pal| *n abbr* (*TV*) = *phase alternation line*.

pal |pal| *n* (*col*) compinche *m/f*, compañero/a.

palace |pal'is| *n* palacio.

palatable |pal'ətəbəl| *a* sabroso; (*acceptable*) aceptable.

palate |pal'it| *n* paladar *m*.

palatial |pəlā'shəl| *a* (*surroundings, residence*) suntuoso, espléndido.

palaver |pəlav'úr| *n* (*US: chatter*) palabrería; (*Brit: fuss*) lío.

pale |pāl| *a* (*gen*) pálido; (*color*) claro ♦ *n*: **to be beyond the** ~ pasarse de la raya ♦ *vi* palidecer; **to grow** *or* **turn** ~ palidecer; **to** ~ **into insignificance (beside)** no poderse comparar (con).

paleness |pāl'nis| *n* palidez *f*.

Palestine |pal'istīn| *n* Palestina.

Palestinian |palistin'ēən| *a, n* palestino/a *m/f*.

palette |pal'it| *n* paleta.

paling |pā'ling| *n* (*stake*) estaca; (*fence*) valla.

palisade |palisād'| *n* palizada.

pall |pôl| *n* (*of smoke*) capa (de humo) ♦ *vi* perder el sabor.

pallbearer |pôl'bärúr| *n* portador *m* del féretro.

pallet |pal'it| *n* (*for goods*) paleta.

palletization |palitəzā'shən| *n* paletización *f*.

palliative |pal'ēātiv| *n* paliativo.

pallid |pal'id| *a* pálido.

pallor |pal'úr| *n* palidez *f*.

pally |pal'ē| *a* (*col*): **to be very** ~ **with sb** ser muy amigo de uno.

palm |päm| *n* (*ANAT*) palma; (*also:* ~ **tree**) palmera, palma ♦ *vt*: **to** ~ **sth off on sb** (*col*) encajar algo a uno.

palmist |päm'ist| *n* quiromántico/a, palmista *m/f*.

Palm Sunday *n* Domingo de Ramos.

palpable |pal'pəbəl| *a* palpable.

palpably |pal'pəblē| *ad* obviamente.

palpitation |palpitā'shən| *n* palpitación *f*; **to have** ~**s** tener vahídos *or* palpitaciones.

paltry |pôl'trē| *a* (*amount etc*) miserable; (*insignificant: person*) insignificante.

pamper |pam'púr| *vt* mimar.

pamphlet |pam'flit| *n* folleto; (*political: handed out in street*) panfleto.

pan |pan| *n* (*also:* **sauce**~) cacerola, cazuela, olla; (*also*: **frying** ~) sartén *m*; (*of lavatory*) taza ♦ *vi* (*CINEMA*) tomar panorámicas; **to** ~ **for gold** cribar oro ♦ *vt* (*criticize*) criticar duramente a, dar una paliza a.

pan- [pan] *pref* pan-.

panacea [panəsēˈə] *n* panacea.

panache [pənashˈ] *n* bríos *mpl*, orgullo, brillantez *f*.

Panama [panˈəmā] *n* Panamá *m*.

Panama Canal *n* el Canal de Panamá.

pancake [panˈkāk] *n* panqueque *m*.

Pancake Day *n* martes *m* de carnaval.

pancreas [panˈkrēəs] *n* páncreas *m*.

panda [panˈdə] *n* panda *m*.

pandemonium [pandəmōˈnēəm] *n* (*noise*): **there was** ~ se armó un tremendo jaleo; (*mess*) caos *m*.

pander [panˈdûr] *vi*: **to** ~ **to** complacer a.

pane [pān] *n* cristal *m*.

panel [panˈəl] *n* (*of wood*) panel *m*; (*of cloth*) paño; (*RADIO*, *TV*) panel *m* de invitados.

panel game *n* (*TV*) programa *m* concurso para equipos.

paneling, (*Brit*) **panelling** [panˈəling] *n* paneles *mpl*.

panelist, (*Brit*) **panellist** [panˈəlist] *n* miembro del jurado.

pang [pang] *n*: ~**s of conscience** remordimiento *sg*; ~**s of hunger** dolores *mpl* del hambre.

panic [panˈik] *n* (terror *m*) pánico ♦ *vi* dejarse llevar por el pánico.

panicky [panˈikē] *a* (*person*) asustadizo.

panic-stricken [panˈikstrikən] *a* preso de pánico.

pannier [panˈyûr] *n* (*on bicycle*) cartera; (*on mule etc*) alforja.

panorama [panəramˈə] *n* panorama *m*.

panoramic [panəramˈik] *a* panorámico.

pansy [panˈzē] *n* (*BOT*) pensamiento; (*col*: *pej*) maricón *m*.

pant [pant] *vi* jadear.

panther [panˈthûr] *n* pantera.

panties [panˈtēz] *npl* bragas *fpl*, pantis *mpl*.

pantomime [panˈtəmīm] *n* (*Brit*) representación *f* musical navideña.

pantry [panˈtrē] *n* despensa.

pants [pants] *n* (*US*: *trousers*) pantalones *mpl*; (*Brit*: *underwear*: *woman's*) bragas *fpl*; (: *man's*) calzoncillos *mpl*.

pants press *n* (*US*) prensa para pantalones.

pantsuit [pantˈsōōt] *n* traje *m* de chaqueta y pantalón.

pantyhose [panˈtēhōz] *n* (*US*) pantimedias *fpl*.

papal [pāˈpəl] *a* papal.

paper [pāˈpûr] *n* papel *m*; (*also*: **news**~) periódico, diario; (*study*, *article*) artículo; (*exam*) examen *m* ♦ *a* de papel ♦ *vt* empapelar; (**identity**) ~**s** *npl* papeles *mpl*, docu-

mentos *mpl*; **useless** ~**s** papeleo; **a piece of** ~ (*odd bit*) un pedazo de papel (suelto); (*sheet*) una hoja de papel; **to put sth down on** ~ poner algo por escrito.

paper advance *n* (*on printer*) avance *m* de papel.

paperback [pāˈpûrbak] *n* libro de bolsillo.

paper bag *n* bolsa de papel.

paperboy [pāˈpûrboi] *n* (*selling*) vendedor *m* de periódicos; (*delivering*) repartidor *m* de periódicos.

paper clip *n* clip *m*.

paper hankie *n* (*Brit*) pañuelo de papel.

paper money *n* papel *m* moneda.

paper profit *n* beneficio no realizado.

paperweight [pāˈpûrwāt] *n* pisapapeles *m inv*.

paperwork [pāˈpûrwûrk] *n* trabajo administrativo; (*pej*) papeleo.

papier-mâché [pāˈpûrməshāˈ] *n* cartón *m* piedra.

paprika [paprēˈkə] *n* pimienta húngara *or* roja.

Pap test [pap test] *n* (*MED*) frotis *m* (cervical).

papyrus [pəpīˈrəs] *n* papiro.

par [pâr] *n* par *f*; (*GOLF*) par *m* ♦ *a* a la par; **to be on a** ~ **with** estar a la par con; **at** ~ a la par; **to be above/below** ~ estar sobre/bajo la par; **to feel under** ~ sentirse en baja forma.

parable [parˈəbəl] *n* parábola.

parachute [parˈəshōōt] *n* paracaídas *m inv* ♦ *vi* lanzarse en paracaídas.

parachutist [parˈəshōōtist] *n* paracaidista *m/f*.

parade [pərādˈ] *n* desfile *m* ♦ *vt* (*gen*) recorrer, desfilar por; (*show off*) hacer alarde de ♦ *vi* desfilar; (*MIL*) pasar revista.

parade ground *n* plaza de armas.

paradise [parˈədīs] *n* paraíso.

paradox [parˈədâks] *n* paradoja.

paradoxical [parədâkˈsikəl] *a* paradójico.

paradoxically [parədâkˈsiklē] *ad* paradójicamente.

paraffin [parˈəfin] *n* (*Brit*): ~ (**oil**) parafina.

paragon [parˈəgân] *n* modelo.

paragraph [parˈəgraf] *n* párrafo; **to begin a new** ~ empezar un nuevo párrafo.

Paraguay [parˈəgwā] *n* Paraguay *m*.

Paraguayan [parəgwāˈən] *a*, *n* paraguayo/a *m/f*, paraguayano/a *m/f*.

parakeet [parˈəkēt] *n* (*US*) periquito.

parallel [parˈəlel] *a*: ~ (**with/to**) en paralelo (con/a); (*fig*) semejante (a) ♦ *n* (*line*) paralela; (*fig*, *GEO*) paralelo.

paralysis [pəralˈisis] *n* parálisis *f inv*.

paralytic [parəlitˈik] *a* paralítico.

paralyze [parˈəlīz] *vt* paralizar.

paramedic [parəmedˈik] *n* (*US*) ambulanciero/a.

parameter [pəramˈitûr] *n* parámetro.

paramilitary [parəmilˈitārē] *a* (*organization*,

operations) paramilitar.
paramount [par'əmount] *a*: **of** ~ **importance** de suma importancia.
paranoia [parənoi'ə] *n* paranoia.
paranoid [par'ənoid] *a* (*person, feeling*) paranoico.
paranormal [parənôr'məl] *a* paranormal.
parapet [par'əpit] *n* parapeto.
paraphernalia [parəfûrnāl'yə] *n* (*gear*) avíos *mpl*.
paraphrase [par'əfrāz] *vt* parafrasear.
paraplegic [parəplē'jik] *n* parapléjico/a.
parapsychology [parəsīkál'əjē] *n* parasicología.
parasite [par'əsīt] *n* parásito/a.
parasol [par'əsôl] *n* sombrilla, quitasol *m*.
paratrooper [par'ətroopûr] *n* paracaidista *m/f*.
parcel [pâr'səl] *n* paquete *m* ♦ *vt* empaquetar, embalar; **to be part and** ~ **of** ser íntegro a.
 parcel out *vt* parcelar, repartir.
parcel bomb *n* (*Brit*) paquete *m* bomba.
parcel post *n* servicio de paquetes postales.
parch [pârch] *vt* secar, resecar.
parched [pârcht] *a* (*person*) muerto de sed.
parchment [pârch'mənt] *n* pergamino.
pardon [pâr'dən] *n* perdón *m*; (*LAW*) indulto ♦ *vt* perdonar; indultar; ~ **me!, I beg your** ~! ¡perdone usted!; **(I beg your)** ~?, (*US*) ~ **me?** ¿cómo?
pare [pär] *vt* (*nails*) cortar; (*fruit etc*) pelar.
parent [pär'ənt] *n*: ~**s** *npl* padres *mpl*.
parentage [pär'əntij] *n* familia, linaje *m*; **of unknown** ~ de padres desconocidos.
parental [pəren'təl] *a* paternal/maternal.
parent company *n* casa matriz.
parenthesis, *pl* **parentheses** [pəren'thəsis, -thəsēz] *n* paréntesis *m inv*; **in parentheses** entre paréntesis.
parenthood [pär'ənt·hood] *n* el ser padre o madre.
parent ship *n* buque *m* nodriza.
Paris [par'is] *n* París *m*.
parish [par'ish] *n* parroquia.
parish council *n* concejo parroquial.
parishioner [pərish'ənûr] *n* feligrés/esa *m/f*.
Parisian [pərizh'ən] *a, n* parisino/a *m/f*, parisiense *m/f*.
parity [par'itē] *n* paridad *f*, igualdad *f*.
park [pârk] *n* parque *m*, jardín *m* público ♦ *vt* aparcar, estacionar ♦ *vi* aparcar, estacionarse.
parka [pâr'kə] *n* chaquetón acolchado con capucha.
parking [pâr'king] *n* aparcamiento, estacionamiento; **"no** ~**"** "prohibido aparcar or estacionarse".
parking lights *npl* luces *fpl* de estacionamiento.
parking lot *n* (*US*) parking *m*,

aparcamiento.
parking meter *n* parquímetro.
parking place *n* sitio para aparcar, aparcamiento.
parking ticket *n* multa de aparcamiento.
parking violation, (*Brit*) **parking offence** *n* ofensa por aparcamiento indebido.
parkway [pârk'wā] *n* (*US*) alameda.
parlance [pâr'ləns] *n* lenguaje *m*; **in common/modern** ~ en lenguaje corriente/moderno.
parliament [pâr'ləmənt] *n* parlamento; (*Spanish*) Cortes *fpl*.
parliamentary [pârləmen'tûrē] *a* parlamentario.
parlor, (*Brit*) **parlour** [pâr'lûr] *n* sala de recibo, salón *m*, living *m* (*LAm*).
parlous [pâr'ləs] *a* peligroso, alarmante.
Parmesan [pâr'məzán] *n* (*also*: ~ **cheese**) queso parmesano.
parochial [pərō'kēəl] *a* parroquial; (*pej*) de miras estrechas.
parody [par'ədē] *n* parodia ♦ *vt* parodiar.
parole [pərōl'] *n*: **on** ~ libre bajo palabra.
paroxysm [par'əksizəm] *n* (*MED*) paroxismo, ataque *m*; (*of anger, laughter, coughing*) ataque *m*; (*of grief*) crisis *f*.
parquet [pârkā'] *n*: ~ **floor(ing)** parquet *m*.
parrot [par'ət] *n* loro, papagayo.
parrot fashion *ad* mecánicamente.
parry [par'ē] *vt* parar.
parsimonious [pârsəmō'nēəs] *a* tacaño.
parsley [pârz'lē] *n* perejil *m*.
parsnip [pârs'nip] *n* chirivía.
parson [pâr'sən] *n* cura *m*.
part [pârt] *n* (*gen, MUS*) parte *f*; (*bit*) trozo; (*of machine*) pieza; (*THEATER etc*) papel *m*; (*of serial*) entrega; (*US: in hair*) raya ♦ *ad* = **partly** ♦ *vt* separar; (*break*) partir ♦ *vi* (*people*) separarse; (*roads*) bifurcarse; (*crowd*) apartarse; (*break*) romperse; **to take** ~ **in** participar or tomar parte en; **to take sb's** ~ defender a uno; **for my** ~ por mi parte; **for the most** ~ en su mayor parte; (*people*) en su mayoría; **for the better** ~ **of the day** durante la mayor parte del día; ~ **of speech** (*LING*) parte *f* de la oración.
part with *vt fus* ceder, entregar; (*money*) pagar; (*get rid of*) deshacerse de.
partake [pârtāk'] *vi* (*irg: like* **take**) (*formal*): **to** ~ **of sth** tomar algo.
part exchange *n* (*Brit*): **in** ~ como parte del pago.
partial [pâr'shəl] *a* parcial; **to be** ~ **to** ser aficionado a.
partially [pâr'shəlē] *ad* en parte, parcialmente.
participant [pârtis'əpənt] *n* (*in competition*) concursante *m/f*.
participate [pârtis'əpāt] *vi*: **to** ~ **in** participar en.
participation [pârtisəpā'shən] *n* participa-

ción *f*.
participle [pàr'tisipəl] *n* participio.
particle [pàr'tikəl] *n* partícula; (*of dust*) grano; (*fig*) pizca.
particleboard [pàr'tikəlbôrd] *n* (*US*) madera aglomerada.
particular [pûrtik'yəlûr] *a* (*special*) particular; (*concrete*) concreto; (*given*) determinado; (*detailed*) detallado, minucioso; (*fussy*) quisquilloso, exigente; **~s** *npl* (*information*) datos *mpl*, detalles *mpl*; (*details*) pormenores *mpl*; **in ~** en particular; **to be very ~ about** ser muy exigente en cuanto a; **I'm not ~** me es *or* da igual.
particularly [pûrtik'yəlûrlē] *ad* especialmente, en particular.
parting [pàr'ting] *n* (*act of*) separación *f*; (*farewell*) despedida; (*Brit: in hair*) raya ♦ *a* de despedida; **~ shot** (*fig*) golpe *m* final.
partisan [pàr'tizən] *a, n* partidario/a *m/f*.
partition [pàrtish'ən] *n* (*POL*) división *f*; (*wall*) tabique *m* ♦ *vt* dividir; dividir con tabique.
partly [pàrt'lē] *ad* en parte.
partner [pàrt'nûr] *n* (*COMM*) socio/a; (*SPORT, at dance*) pareja; (*spouse*) cónyuge *m/f*; (*friend etc*) compañero/a ♦ *vt* acompañar.
partnership [pàrt'nûrship] *n* (*gen*) asociación *f*; (*COMM*) sociedad *f*; **to go into ~ (with), form a ~ (with)** asociarse (con).
part payment *n* pago parcial, abono.
partridge [pàr'trij] *n* perdiz *f*.
part-time [pàrt'tīm] *a, ad* a tiempo parcial.
part-timer [pàrttī'mûr] *n* trabajador(a) *m/f* a tiempo partido.
party [pàr'tē] *n* (*POL*) partido; (*celebration*) fiesta; (*group*) grupo; (*LAW*) parte *f*, interesado ♦ *a* (*POL*) de partido; (*dress etc*) de fiesta, de gala; **to have** *or* **give** *or* **throw a ~** organizar una fiesta; **dinner ~** cena; **to be a ~ to a crime** ser cómplice *m/f* de un crimen.
party line *n* (*POL*) línea política del partido; (*TEL*) línea compartida.
par value *n* (*of share, bond*) valor *m* a la par.
pass [pas] *vt* (*time, object*) pasar; (*place*) pasar por; (*exam, law*) aprobar; (*overtake, surpass*) rebasar; (*approve*) aprobar; (*AUT*) adelantar ♦ *vi* pasar; (*SCOL*) aprobar, ser aprobado ♦ *n* (*permit*) permiso; (*membership card*) carnet *m*; (*in mountains*) puerto, desfiladero; (*SPORT*) pase *m*; **to get a ~ in** aprobar en; **to ~ sth through sth** pasar algo por algo; **to ~ the time of day with sb** pasar el rato con uno; **to make a ~ at sb** (*col*) hacer proposiciones a uno.
pass away *vi* fallecer.
pass by *vi* pasar ♦ *vt* (*ignore*) pasar por alto.
pass down *vt* (*customs, inheritance*) pa-

sar, transmitir.
pass for *vt fus* pasar por; **she could ~ for twenty-five** se podría creer que sólo tiene 25 años.
pass on *vi* (*die*) fallecer, morir ♦ *vt* (*hand on*): **to ~ on (to)** transmitir (a); (*cold, illness*) pegar (a); (*benefits*) dar (a); (*price rises*) pasar (a).
pass out *vi* desmayarse ♦ *vt* (*information, papers*) pasar (de mano en mano); (*chocolates etc*) ofrecer.
pass over *vi* (*die*) fallecer ♦ *vt* omitir, pasar por alto.
pass up *vt* (*opportunity*) dejar pasar, no aprovechar.
passable [pas'əbəl] *a* (*road*) transitable; (*tolerable*) pasable.
passably [pas'əblē] *ad* pasablemente (bien).
passage [pas'ij] *n* pasillo; (*act of passing*) tránsito; (*fare, in book*) pasaje *m*; (*by boat*) travesía.
passageway [pas'ijwā] *n* (*in house*) pasillo, corredor *m*; (*between buildings etc*) pasaje *m*, pasadizo.
passbook [pas'bŏŏk] *n* libreta de banco.
passenger [pas'injûr] *n* pasajero/a, viajero/a.
passer-by [pasûrbī'] *n* transeúnte *m/f*.
passing [pas'ing] *a* (*fleeting*) pasajero; **in ~** de paso.
passing place *n* (*Brit AUT*) apartadero.
passion [pash'ən] *n* pasión *f*.
passionate [pash'ənit] *a* apasionado.
passionately [pash'ənitlē] *ad* apasionadamente, con pasión.
passive [pas'iv] *a* (*also LING*) pasivo.
passkey [pas'kē] *n* llave *f* maestra.
Passover [pas'ōvûr] *n* Pascua (de los judíos).
passport [pas'pôrt] *n* pasaporte *m*.
passport control *n* control *m* de pasaporte.
password [pas'wûrd] *n* (*also COMPUT*) contraseña.
past [past] *prep* (*further than*) más allá de; (*later than*) después de ♦ *a* pasado; (*president etc*) antiguo ♦ *n* (*time*) pasado; (*of person*) antecedentes *mpl*; **quarter/half ~ four** las cuatro y cuarto/media; **he's ~ forty** tiene más de cuarenta años; **I'm ~ caring** ya no me importa; **to be ~ one's prime** (*person*) ser acabado; **for the ~ few/3 days** durante los últimos días/últimos 3 días; **to run ~** pasar a la carrera por; **in the ~** en el pasado, antes.
pasta [pàs'tə] *n* pasta.
paste [pāst] *n* (*gen*) pasta; (*glue*) engrudo ♦ *vt* (*stick*) pegar; (*glue*) engomar; **tomato ~** puré *m* de tomate.
pastel [pastel'] *a* pastel; (*painting*) al pastel.
pasteurized [pas'chərīzd] *a* pasteurizado.
pastille [pastēl'] *n* pastilla.
pastime [pas'tīm] *n* pasatiempo.

pastor [pas'tûr] *n* pastor *m*.
pastoral [pas'tûrəl] *a* pastoral.
pastry [pās'trē] *n* (*dough*) pasta; (*cake*) pastel *m*.
pasture [pas'chûr] *n* (*grass*) pasto.
pasty *a* [pās'tē] pastoso; (*complexion*) pálido ♦ *n* [pas'tē] (*Brit*) empanada.
pat [pat] *vt* dar una palmadita a; (*dog etc*) acariciar ♦ *n* (*of butter*) porción *f* ♦ *a*: **he has it down** ~ se lo sabe de memoria *or* al dedillo; **to give sb/o.s. a ~ on the back** (*fig*) felicitar a uno/felicitarse.
patch [pach] *n* (*of material*) parche *m*; (*mended part*) remiendo; (*of land*) terreno; (*COMPUT*) ajuste *m* ♦ *vt* (*clothes*) remendar.
patch up *vt* (*mend temporarily*) reparar; **to ~ up a quarrel** hacer las paces.
patchwork [pach'wûrk] *n* labor *f* de retazos.
patchy [pach'ē] *a* desigual.
pate [pāt] *n*: **bald ~** calva.
pâté [pâtā'] *n* paté *m*.
patent [pat'ənt] *n* patente *f* ♦ *vt* patentar ♦ *a* patente, evidente.
patent leather *n* charol *m*.
patently [pat'əntlē] *ad* evidentemente.
patent medicine *n* medicina de patente.
patent office *n* oficina de patentes y marcas.
patent rights *npl* derechos *mpl* de patente.
paternal [pətûr'nəl] *a* paternal; (*relation*) paterno.
paternalistic [pətûrnəlis'tik] *a* paternalista.
paternity [pətûr'nitē] *n* paternidad *f*.
paternity suit *n* (*LAW*) caso de paternidad.
path [path] *n* camino, sendero; (*trail, track*) pista; (*of missile*) trayectoria.
pathetic [pəthet'ik] *a* (*pitiful*) patético, lastimoso; (*very bad*) malísimo; (*moving*) conmovedor(a).
pathetically [pəthet'iklē] *ad* patéticamente; (*very badly*) malísimamente mal.
pathological [pathəlaj'ikəl] *a* patológico.
pathologist [pəthâl'əjist] *n* patólogo/a.
pathology [pəthâl'əjē] *n* patología.
pathos [pā'thâs] *n* patetismo.
pathway [path'wā] *n* sendero, vereda.
patience [pā'shəns] *n* paciencia; (*Brit CARDS*) solitario; **to lose one's ~** perder la paciencia.
patient [pā'shənt] *n* paciente *m/f* ♦ *a* paciente, sufrido; **to be ~ with sb** tener paciencia con uno.
patiently [pā'shəntlē] *ad* pacientemente, con paciencia.
patio [pat'ēō] *n* patio.
patriot [pā'trēət] *n* patriota *m/f*.
patriotic [pātrēât'ik] *a* patriótico.
patriotism [pā'trēətizəm] *n* patriotismo.
patrol [pətrōl'] *n* patrulla ♦ *vt* patrullar por;

to be on ~ patrullar, estar de patrulla.
patrol boat *n* patrullero, patrullera.
patrol car *n* coche *m* patrulla.
patrolman [pətrōl'mən] *n* (*US*) policía *m*.
patron [pā'trən] *n* (*in shop*) cliente *m/f*; (*of charity*) patrocinador(a) *m/f*; **~ of the arts** mecenas *m*.
patronage [pā'trənij] *n* patrocinio, protección *f*.
patronize [pā'trənīz] *vt* (*shop*) ser cliente de; (*look down on*) condescender con.
patronizing [pā'trənīzing] *a* condescendiente.
patron saint *n* santo/a patrono/a.
patter [pat'ûr] *n* golpeteo; (*sales talk*) labia ♦ *vi* (*rain*) tamborilear.
pattern [pat'ûrn] *n* (*SEWING*) patrón *m*; (*design*) dibujo; (*behavior, events*) esquema *m*; **~ of events** curso de los hechos; **behavior ~s** modelos *mpl* de comportamiento.
patterned [pat'ûrnd] *a* (*material*) con diseño *or* dibujo.
paucity [pô'sitē] *n* escasez *f*.
paunch [pônch] *n* panza, barriga.
pauper [pô'pûr] *n* pobre *m/f*.
pause [pôz] *n* pausa; (*interval*) intervalo ♦ *vi* hacer una pausa; **to ~ for breath** detenerse para tomar aliento.
pave [pāv] *vt* pavimentar; **to ~ the way for** preparar el terreno para.
pavement [pāv'mənt] *n* (*US*) calzada, pavimento; (*Brit*) acera, vereda (*LAm*).
pavilion [pəvil'yən] *n* pabellón *m*; (*SPORT*) vestuarios *mpl*.
paving [pā'ving] *n* pavimento, enlosado.
paving stone *n* losa.
paw [pô] *n* pata; (*claw*) garra ♦ *vt* (*animal*) tocar con la pata; (*pej: touch*) tocar, manosear.
pawn [pôn] *n* (*CHESS*) peón *m*; (*fig*) instrumento ♦ *vt* empeñar.
pawnbroker [pôn'brōkûr] *n* prestamista *m/f*.
pawnshop [pôn'shâp] *n* monte *m* de piedad.
pay [pā] *n* paga; (*wage etc*) sueldo, salario ♦ (*vb: pt, pp* **paid**) *vt* pagar; (*visit*) hacer; (*respect*) ofrecer ♦ *vi* pagar; (*be profitable*) rendir, compensar, ser rentable; **to be in sb's ~** estar al servicio de uno; **to ~ attention (to)** prestar atención (a); **I paid $5 for that record** pagué 5 dólares por ese disco; **how much did you ~ for it?** ¿cuánto pagaste por él?; **to ~ one's way** (*contribute one's share*) pagar su parte; (*remain solvent: company*) ser solvente; **to ~ dividends** (*COMM*) pagar dividendos; (*fig*) compensar; **it won't ~ you to do that** no te merece la pena hacer eso.
pay back *vt* (*money*) reembolsar; (*person*) pagar.
pay for *vt fus* pagar.
pay in *vt* ingresar.

pay off *vt* liquidar; (*person*) pagar; (*debts*) liquidar, saldar; (*creditor*) cancelar, redimir; (*workers*) despedir; (*mortgage*) cancelar, redimir ♦ *vi* (*scheme, decision*) dar resultado; **to ~ sth off in installments** pagar algo a plazos.

pay out *vt* (*rope*) ir dando; (*money*) gastar, desembolsar.

pay up *vt* pagar (de mala gana).

payable |pā'əbəl| *a* pagadero; **to make a check ~ to sb** extender un cheque a favor de uno.

pay day *n* día *m* de paga.

PAYE *n abbr* (*Brit*: = *pay as you earn*) *sistema de contribuciones personales.*

payee |pāē'| *n* portador(a) *m/f.*

pay envelope *n* (*US*) sobre *m* (de paga).

paying |pā'ing| *a:* **~ guest** huésped(a) *m/f* que paga.

payload |pā'lōd| *n* carga útil.

payment |pā'mənt| *n* pago; **advance ~** (*part sum*) anticipo, adelanto; (*total sum*) saldo; **monthly ~** mensualidad *f;* **deferred ~, ~ by installments** pago a plazos *or* diferido; **on ~ of $5** mediante pago de *or* pagando $5; **in ~ for** (*goods, sum owed*) en pago de.

pay packet *n* (*Brit*) sobre *m* (de paga).

pay phone *n* teléfono público.

payroll |pā'rōl| *n* nómina; **to be on a firm's ~** estar en la nómina de una compañía.

pay slip *n* recibo de sueldo.

pay station *n* (*US*) teléfono público.

PBS *n abbr* (*US*: = *Public Broadcasting System*) *agrupación de ayuda a la realización de emisiones para la TV pública.*

PBX *n abbr* (*US*) = *private branch (telephone) exchange.*

PC *n abbr* = **personal computer;** (*Brit*) = **police constable.**

pc *abbr* = **percent; postcard.**

p/c *abbr* = **petty cash.**

PCB *n abbr* = **printed circuit board.**

PD *n abbr* (*US*) = **police department.**

pd *abbr* = **paid.**

PDT *n abbr* (*US*: = *Pacific Daylight Time*) *hora de verano del Pacífico.*

PE *n abbr* (= *physical education*) ed. física.

pea |pē| *n* guisante *m,* chícharo (*LAm*), arveja (*LAm*).

peace |pēs| *n* paz *f;* (*calm*) paz *f,* tranquilidad *f;* **to be at ~ with sb/sth** estar en paz con uno/algo; **to keep the ~** (*policeman*) mantener el orden; (*citizen*) guardar el orden.

peaceable |pē'səbəl| *a* pacífico.

peaceably |pē'səblē| *ad* pacíficamente.

Peace Corps *n* (*US*) *organización que envía jóvenes voluntarios a trabajar y enseñar en el Tercer Mundo.*

peaceful |pēs'fəl| *a* (*gentle*) pacífico; (*calm*) tranquilo, sosegado.

peacekeeping |pēs'kēping| *a* de pacificación.

peace offering *n* (*fig*) prenda de paz.

peacetime |pēs'tim| *n:* **in ~** en tiempo de paz.

peach |pēch| *n* melocotón *m,* durazno (*LAm*).

peacock |pē'kâk| *n* pavo real.

peak |pēk| *n* (*of mountain: top*) cumbre *f,* cima; (: *point*) pico; (*of cap*) visera; (*fig*) cumbre *f.*

peaked |pē'kid| (*US*) pálido, paliducho; **I'm feeling a bit ~** me encuentro malucho, no me encuentro bien.

peak-hour |pēk'ouûr| *a* (*traffic etc*) de horas punta.

peak hours *npl,* **peak period** *n* horas *fpl* punta.

peaky |pē'kē| *a* (*Brit*) = **peaked.**

peal |pēl| *n* (*of bells*) repique *m;* **~ of laughter** carcajada.

peanut |pē'nut| *n* cacahuete *m,* maní *m* (*LAm*).

peanut butter *n* manteca de cacahuete.

peanut oil *n* (*US*) aceite *m* de cacahuete.

pear |pär| *n* pera.

pearl |pûrl| *n* perla.

peasant |pez'ənt| *n* campesino/a.

peat |pēt| *n* turba.

pebble |peb'əl| *n* guijarro.

peck |pek| *vt* (*also:* **~ at**) picotear; (*food*) comer sin ganas ♦ *n* picotazo; (*kiss*) besito.

pecking order |pek'ing ôrdûr| *n* orden *m* de jerarquía.

peckish |pek'ish| *a* (*Brit col*): **I feel ~** tengo ganas de picar algo.

peculiar |pikyōōl'yûr| *a* (*odd*) extraño, raro; (*typical*) propio, característico; (*particular: importance, qualities*) particular; **~ to** propio de.

peculiarity |pikyōōlēar'itē| *n* peculiaridad *f,* característica.

peculiarly |pikyōōl'yûrlē| *ad* extrañamente; particularmente.

pedal |ped'əl| *n* pedal *m* ♦ *vi* pedalear.

pedal bin *n* (*Brit*) cubo de la basura con pedal.

pedant |ped'ənt| *n* pedante *m/f.*

pedantic |pədan'tik| *a* pedante.

pedantry |ped'əntrē| *n* pedantería.

peddle |ped'əl| *vt* (*goods*) ir vendiendo *or* vender de puerta en puerta; (*drugs*) traficar; (*gossip*) divulgar.

peddler |ped'lûr| *n* vendedor(a) *m/f* ambulante.

pedestal |ped'istəl| *n* pedestal *m.*

pedestrian |pədes'trēən| *n* peatón/ona *m/f* ♦ *a* pedestre.

pedestrian crossing *n* paso de peatones.

pedestrian precinct *n* (*Brit*) zona reservada para peatones.

pediatrician |pēdēətrish'ən| *n* (*US*) pediatra *m/f.*

pediatrics |pēdēat'riks| *n* (*US*) pediatría.

pediatrist [pēdēat'rist] *n* (*US*) pedicuro/a.

pedigree [ped'əgrē] *n* genealogía; (*of animal*) raza ♦ *cpd* (*animal*) de raza, de casta.

pedlar [ped'lûr] *n* (*Brit*) = **peddler**.

pee [pē] *vi* (*col*) mear.

peek [pēk] *vi* mirar a hurtadillas; (*COMPUT*) inspeccionar.

peel [pēl] *n* piel *f*; (*of orange, lemon*) cáscara; (: *removed*) peladuras *fpl* ♦ *vt* pelar ♦ *vi* (*paint etc*) desconcharse; (*wallpaper*) despegarse, desprenderse.
 peel back *vt* pelar.

peeler [pē'lûr] *n*: **potato** ~ mondador *m or* pelador *m* de patatas, pelapatatas *m inv*.

peep [pēp] *n* (*look*) mirada furtiva; (*sound*) pío ♦ *vi* piar.
 peep out *vi* asomar la cabeza.

peephole [pēp'hōl] *n* mirilla.

peer [pēr] *vi*: **to** ~ **at** escudriñar ♦ *n* (*noble*) par *m*; (*equal*) igual *m*.

peerage [pē'rij] *n* nobleza.

peerless [pēr'lis] *a* sin par, incomparable, sin igual.

peeved [pēvd] *a* enojado.

peevish [pē'vish] *a* malhumorado.

peevishness [pē'vishnis] *n* mal humor *m*.

peg [peg] *n* clavija; (*for coat etc*) gancho, colgadero; (*Brit: also:* **clothes** ~) pinza; (*tent* ~) estaca ♦ *vt* (*clothes*) tender; (*groundcloth*) enclavijar, fijar con estacas; (*fig: wages, prices*) fijar.

PEI *abbr* (*Canada*) = *Prince Edward Island*.

pejorative [pijòr'ətiv] *a* peyorativo.

Pekin [pē'kin], **Peking** [pēking'] *n* Pekín *m*.

pekinese [pēkənēz'] *n* pequinés/esa *m/f*.

pelican [pel'ikən] *n* pelícano.

pelican crossing *n* (*Brit AUT*) paso de peatones señalizado.

pellet [pel'it] *n* bolita; (*bullet*) perdigón *m*.

pell-mell [pel'mel'] *ad* en tropel.

pelmet [pel'mit] *n* galería.

pelt [pelt] *vt*: **to** ~ **sb with sth** arrojarle algo a uno ♦ *vi* (*rain: also:* ~ **down**) llover a cántaros ♦ *n* pellejo.

pelvis [pel'vis] *n* pelvis *f*.

pen [pen] *n* pluma; (*for sheep*) redil *m*; (*US col: prison*) cárcel *f*, chirona; **to put** ~ **to paper** tomar la pluma.

penal [pē'nəl] *a* penal; ~ **servitude** trabajos *mpl* forzados.

penalize [pē'nəlīz] *vt* (*punish: SPORT*) castigar.

penalty [pen'əltē] *n* (*gen*) pena; (*fine*) multa; (*SPORT*) castigo; ~ (**kick**) (*SOCCER*) penalty *m*.

penalty clause *n* cláusula penal.

penance [pen'əns] *n* penitencia.

pence [pens] (*Brit*) *pl of* **penny**.

penchant [pen'chənt] *n* predilección *f*, inclinación *f*.

pencil [pen'səl] *n* lápiz *m*, lapicero (*LAm*) ♦ *vt* (*also:* ~ **in**) escribir con lápiz.

pencil case *n* estuche *m*.

pencil sharpener *n* sacapuntas *m inv*.

pendant [pen'dənt] *n* pendiente *m*.

pending [pen'ding] *prep* antes de ♦ *a* pendiente; ~ **the arrival of** ... hasta que llegue ..., hasta llegar ... .

pendulum [pen'jələm] *n* péndulo.

penetrate [pen'itrāt] *vt* penetrar.

penetrating [pen'itrāting] *a* penetrante.

penetration [penitrā'shən] *n* penetración *f*.

pen friend *n* amigo/a por correspondencia.

penguin [pen'gwin] *n* pingüino.

penicillin [penisil'in] *n* penicilina.

peninsula [pənin'sələ] *n* península.

penis [pē'nis] *n* pene *m*.

penitence [pen'itəns] *n* penitencia.

penitent [pen'itənt] *a* arrepentido; (*REL*) penitente.

penitentiary [peniten'chûrē] *n* (*US*) cárcel *f*, presidio.

penknife [pen'nīf] *n* navaja.

Penn., Penna. *abbr* (*US*) = *Pennsylvania*.

pen name [pen' nām] *n* seudónimo.

pennant [pen'ənt] *n* banderola; banderín *m*.

penniless [pen'ēlis] *a* sin dinero.

Pennines [pen'īnz] *npl* (Montes *mpl*) Peninos *mpl*.

penny, *pl* **pennies** *or* (*Brit*) **pence** [pen'ē, pen'ēz, pens] *n* penique *m*; (*US*) centavo.

penpal [pen'pal] *n* amigo/a por correspondencia.

pension [pen'chən] *n* (*allowance, state payment*) pensión *f*; (*old-age*) jubilación *f*.
 pension off *vt* jubilar.

pensioner [pen'chənûr] *n* (*Brit*) jubilado/a.

pension fund *n* fondo de pensiones.

pensive [pen'siv] *a* pensativo; (*withdrawn*) preocupado.

pentagon [pen'təgân] *n* pentágono.

Pentecost [pen'təkôst] *n* Pentecostés *m*.

penthouse [pen'hous] *n* ático de lujo.

pent-up [pent'up'] *a* (*feelings*) reprimido.

penultimate [pinul'təmit] *a* penúltimo.

penury [pen'yûrē] *n* miseria, pobreza.

people [pē'pəl] *npl* gente *f*; (*citizens*) pueblo *sg*, ciudadanos *mpl* ♦ *n* (*nation, race*) pueblo, nación *f* ♦ *vt* poblar; **several** ~ **came** vinieron varias personas; ~ **say that**... dice la gente que...; **old/young** ~ los ancianos/jóvenes; ~ **at large** la gente en general; **a man of the** ~ un hombre del pueblo.

pep [pep] *n* (*col*) energía.
 pep up *vt* animar.

pepper [pep'ûr] *n* (*spice*) pimienta; (*vegetable*) pimiento ♦ *vt* (*fig*) salpicar.

pepper mill *n* molinillo de pimienta.

peppermint [pep'ûrmint] *n* menta; (*sweet*) pastilla de menta.

pepperpot [pep'ûrpât] *n* pimentero.

pepper shaker [pep'ûr shā'kûr] *n* (*US*) pimentero.

pep talk *n* (*col*): **to give sb a** ~ darle a

uno una inyección de ánimo.

per |pûr| *prep* por; ~ **day/person** por día/ persona; **as** ~ **your instructions** de acuerdo con sus instrucciones.

per annum *ad* al año.

per capita *a*, *ad* per cápita.

perceive [pûrsēv'] *vt* percibir; (*realize*) darse cuenta de.

percent, (*Brit*) **per cent** [pûrsent'] *n* por ciento; **a 20** ~ **discount** un descuento de 20 por ciento.

percentage [pûrsen'tij] *n* porcentaje *m;* **to get a** ~ **on all sales** percibir un tanto por ciento sobre todas las ventas; **on a** ~ **basis** sobre una base de porcentaje.

perception [pûrsep'shən] *n* percepción *f;* (*insight*) perspicacia.

perceptible [pûrsep'təbəl] *a* perceptible; (*notable*) sensible.

perceptive [pûrsep'tiv] *a* perspicaz.

perch [pûrch] *n* (*fish*) perca; (*for bird*) percha ♦ *vi* posarse.

percolate [pûr'kəlāt] *vt* (*coffee*) filtrar, colar ♦ *vi* (*coffee, fig*) filtrarse, colarse.

percolator [pûr'kəlātûr] *n* cafetera de filtro.

percussion [pûrkush'ən] *n* percusión *f.*

percussionist [pûrkush'ənist] *n* percusionista *m/f.*

peremptory [pəremp'tûrē] *a* perentorio.

perennial [pəren'ēəl] *a* perenne.

perfect *a* [pûr'fikt] perfecto ♦ *n* (*also*: ~ **tense**) perfecto ♦ *vt* [pûrfekt'] perfeccionar; **he's a** ~ **stranger to me** no le conozco de nada, me es completamente desconocido.

perfection [pûrfek'shən] *n* perfección *f.*

perfectionist [pûrfek'shənist] *n* perfeccionista *m/f.*

perfectly [pûr'fiktlē] *ad* perfectamente; **I'm** ~ **happy with the situation** estoy muy contento con la situación; **you know** ~ **well** lo sabes muy bien *or* perfectamente.

perforate [pûr'fûrāt] *vt* perforar.

perforated ulcer [pûr'fûrātid ul'sûr] *n* úlcera perforada.

perforation [pûrfərā'shən] *n* perforación *f.*

perform [pûrfôrm'] *vt* (*carry out*) realizar, llevar a cabo; (*THEATER*) representar; (*piece of music*) interpretar ♦ *vi* (*THEATER*) actuar; (*TECH*) funcionar.

performance [pûrfôr'məns] *n* (*of task*) realización *f;* (*of a play*) representación *f;* (*of player etc*) actuación *f;* (*of car, engine*) rendimiento; (*of function*) desempeño.

performer [pûrfôr'mûr] *n* (*actor*) actor *m,* actriz *f;* (*MUS*) intérprete *m/f.*

performing [pûrfôr'ming] *a* (*animal*) amaestrado.

perfume [pûr'fyōōm] *n* perfume *m.*

perfunctory [pûrfungk'tûrē] *a* superficial.

perhaps [pûrhaps'] *ad* quizá(s), tal vez; ~ **so/not** puede que sí/no.

peril [pär'əl] *n* peligro, riesgo.

perilous [pär'ələs] *a* peligroso.

perilously [pär'ələslē] *ad:* **they came** ~ **close to being caught** por poco les cogen *or* agarran.

perimeter [pərim'itûr] *n* perímetro.

period [pēr'ēəd] *n* período; (*HISTORY*) época; (*SCOL*) clase *f;* (*punctuation*) punto; (*MED*) regla; (*US SPORT*) tiempo ♦ *a* (*costume, furniture*) de época; **for a** ~ **of three weeks** durante (un período de) tres semanas; **the holiday** ~ el período de vacaciones.

periodic [pērēād'ik] *a* periódico.

periodical [pērēād'ikəl] *a, n* periódico *m.*

periodically [pērēād'iklē] *ad* de vez en cuando, cada cierto tiempo.

peripatetic [päripətet'ik] *a* (*salesman*) ambulante; (*teacher*) peripatético.

peripheral [pərif'ûrəl] *a* periférico ♦ *n* (*COMPUT*) periférico, unidad *f* periférica.

periphery [pərif'ûrē] *n* periferia.

periscope [pär'iskōp] *n* periscopio.

perish [pär'ish] *vi* perecer; (*decay*) echarse a perder.

perishable [pär'ishəbəl] *a* perecedero.

perishables [pär'ishəbəlz] *npl* productos *mpl* perecederos.

peritonitis [pär'itəni'tis] *n* peritonitis *f.*

perjure [pûr'jûr] *vt:* **to** ~ **o.s.** perjurarse.

perjury [pûr'jûrē] *n* (*LAW*) perjurio.

perk [pûrk] *n* extra *m.*

perk up *vi* (*cheer up*) animarse.

perky [pûr'kē] *a* alegre, despabilado.

perm [pûrm] *n* permanente *f* ♦ *vt:* **to have one's hair** ~**ed** hacerse una permanente.

permanence [pûr'mənəns] *n* permanencia.

permanent [pûr'mənənt] *a* permanente; (*job, position*) fijo; (*dye, ink*) indeleble; ~ **address** domicilio permanente; **I'm not** ~ **here** no trabajo fijo aquí.

permanently [pûr'mənəntlē] *ad* (*lastingly*) para siempre, de modo definitivo; (*all the time*) permanentemente.

permeate [pûr'mēāt] *vi* penetrar, trascender ♦ *vt* penetrar, trascender a.

permissible [pûrmis'əbəl] *a* permisible, lícito.

permission [pûrmish'ən] *n* permiso; **to give sb** ~ **to do sth** autorizar a uno para que haga algo; **with your** ~ con su permiso.

permissive [pûrmis'iv] *a* permisivo.

permit *n* [pûr'mit] permiso, licencia; (*entrance pass*) pase *m* ♦ *vt* [pûrmit'] permitir; (*accept*) tolerar ♦ *vi:* **weather** ~**ting** si el tiempo lo permite; **fishing** ~ permiso de pesca; **building/export** ~ licencia *or* permiso de construcción/exportación.

permutation [pûrmyətā'shən] *n* permutación *f.*

pernicious [pûrnish'əs] *a* nocivo; (*MED*) pernicioso.

pernickety [pûrnik'ətē] *a* (*Brit*) = **persnickety**.

perpendicular [pûrpəndik'yəlûr] *a* perpendicular.

perpetrate [pûr'pitrāt] *vt* cometer.

perpetual [pûrpech'ōōəl] *a* perpetuo.

perpetually [pûrpech'ōōəlē] *ad* (*eternally*) perpetuamente; (*continuously*) constantemente, continuamente.

perpetuate [pûrpech'ōōāt] *vt* perpetuar.

perpetuity [pûrpətōō'itē] *n*: **in ~ para siempre.

perplex [pûrpleks'] *vt* dejar perplejo.

perplexed [pûrplekst'] *a* perplejo, confuso.

perplexing [pûrplek'sing] *a* que causa perplejidad.

perplexity [pûrplek'sitē] *n* perplejidad *f*, confusión *f*.

perquisites [pûr'kwizits] *npl* (*also*: **perks**) gajes y emolumentos *mpl*.

persecute [pûr'səkyōōt] *vt* (*pursue*) perseguir; (*harass*) acosar.

persecution [pûrsəkyōō'shən] *n* persecución *f*.

perseverance [pûrsəvēr'əns] *n* perseverancia.

persevere [pûrsəvēr'] *vi* persistir.

Persia [pûr'zhə] *n* Persia.

Persian [pûr'zhən] *a, n* persa *m/f* ♦ *n* (*LING*) persa *m*; **the ~ Gulf** el Golfo Pérsico.

persist [pûrsist'] *vi*: **to ~ (in doing sth)** persistir (en hacer algo).

persistence [pûrsis'təns] *n* empeño.

persistent [pûrsis'tənt] *a* (*lateness, rain*) persistente; (*determined*) porfiado; (*continuing*) constante.

persistently [pûrsis'təntlē] *ad* persistentemente; (*continually*) constantemente.

persnickety [pûrsnik'ətē] *a* (*US col*: *person*) quisquilloso; (: *task*) delicado.

person [pûr'sən] *n* persona; **in ~** en persona; **on** *or* **about one's ~** (*weapon, money*) encima; **a ~ to ~ call** (*TEL*) una llamada (de) persona a persona.

personable [pûr'sənəbəl] *a* atractivo.

personal [pûr'sənəl] *a* personal, individual; (*visit*) en persona; (*Brit TEL*) persona a persona.

personal allowance *n* desgravación *f* personal.

personal assistant (PA) *n* ayudante *m/f* personal.

personal belongings *npl* efectos *mpl* personales.

personal column *n* anuncios *mpl* personales.

personal computer (PC) *n* computador *m* personal.

personal effects *npl* efectos *mpl* personales.

personality [pûrsənal'itē] *n* personalidad *f*.

personal loan *n* préstamo personal.

personally [pûr'sənəlē] *ad* personalmente.

personal organizer *n* organizador *m* personal.

personal property *n* bienes *mpl* muebles.

personification [pûrsânəfəkā'shən] *n* personificación *f*.

personify [pûrsân'əfī] *vt* encarnar.

personnel [pûrsənel'] *n* personal *m*.

personnel department *n* departamento de personal.

personnel management *n* gestión *f* de personal.

personnel manager *n* jefe *m* de personal.

perspective [pûrspek'tiv] *n* perspectiva; **to get sth into ~** ver algo en perspectiva *or* como es.

Perspex [pûr'speks] ® *n* (*Brit*) vidrio acrílico.

perspiration [pûrspərā'shən] *n* transpiración *f*, sudor *m*.

perspire [pûrspīur'] *vi* transpirar, sudar.

persuade [pûrswād'] *vt*: **to ~ sb to do sth** persuadir a uno para que haga algo; **to ~ sb of sth/that** persuadir *or* convencer a uno de algo/de que; **I am ~d that ...** estoy convencido de que ... .

persuasion [pûrswā'zhən] *n* persuasión *f*; (*persuasiveness*) persuasiva; (*creed*) creencia.

persuasive [pûrswā'siv] *a* persuasivo.

persuasively [pûrswā'sivlē] *ad* de modo persuasivo.

pert [pûrt] *a* impertinente, fresco, atrevido.

pertaining [pûrtān'ing]: **~ to** *prep* relacionado con.

pertinent [pûr'tənənt] *a* pertinente, a propósito.

perturb [pûrtûrb'] *vt* perturbar.

perturbing [pûrtûrb'ing] *a* inquietante, perturbador(a).

Peru [pərōō'] *n* el Perú.

perusal [pərōō'zəl] *n* examen *m*.

peruse [pərōōz'] *vt* leer con detención, examinar.

Peruvian [pərōō'vēən] *a, n* peruano/a *m/f*.

pervade [pûrvād'] *vt* impregnar, infundirse en.

pervasive [pûrvā'siv] *a* (*smell*) penetrante; (*influence*) muy extendido; (*gloom, feelings, ideas*) reinante.

perverse [pûrvûrs'] *a* perverso; (*stubborn*) terco; (*wayward*) travieso.

perversely [pûrvûrs'lē] *ad* perversamente; tercamente; traviesamente.

perverseness [pûrvûrs'nis] *n* perversidad *f*; terquedad *f*; travesura.

perversion [pûrvûr'zhən] *n* perversión *f*.

pervert *n* [pûr'vûrt] pervertido/a ♦ *vt* [pûrvûrt'] pervertir.

pessary [pes'ərē] *n* pesario.

pessimism [pes'əmizəm] *n* pesimismo.

pessimist [pes'əmist] *n* pesimista *m/f*.

pessimistic [pesəmis'tik] *a* pesimista.

pest [pest] *n* (*insect*) insecto nocivo; (*fig*) lata, molestia; **~s** *npl* plaga.

pest control *n* control *m* de plagas.

pester |pes'tûr| *vt* molestar, acosar.
pesticide |pes'tisīd| *n* pesticida *m*.
pestilent |pes'tələnt|, **pestilential**
|pestələn'shəl| *a* (*col: exasperating*) condenado.
pestle |pes'əl| *n* mano *f* de mortero *or* de almirez.
pet |pet| *n* animal *m* doméstico; (*favorite*) favorito/a ♦ *vt* acariciar ♦ *vi* (*col*) besuquearse ♦ *cpd*: **my ~ aversion** mi manía.
petal |pet'əl| *n* pétalo.
pet door *n* (*US*) gatera.
peter |pē'tûr| : **to ~ out** *vi* agotarse, acabarse.
petite |pətēt'| *a* chiquita.
petition |pətish'ən| *n* petición *f* ♦ *vt* presentar una petición a ♦ *vi*: **to ~ for divorce** pedir el divorcio.
pet name *n* nombre *m* cariñoso, apodo.
petrified |pet'rəfīd| *a* (*fig*) pasmado, horrorizado.
petrochemical |petrōkem'ikəl| *a* petroquímico.
petrodollars |petrōdâl'ûrz| *npl* petrodólares *mpl*.
petrol |pet'rəl| *n* (*Brit*) gasolina; (*for lighter*) bencina; **two/four-star ~** (*Brit*) gasolina normal/súper.
petrol can *n* (*Brit*) bidón *m* de gasolina.
petrol engine *n* (*Brit*) motor *m* de gasolina.
petroleum |pətrō'lēəm| *n* petróleo.
petroleum jelly *n* jalea de petróleo.
petrol pump *n* (*Brit*) (*in car*) bomba de gasolina; (*in garage*) surtidor *m* de gasolina.
petrol station *n* (*Brit*) gasolinera.
petrol tank *n* (*Brit*) depósito (de gasolina).
petticoat |pet'ēkōt| *n* enaguas *fpl*.
pettifogging |pet'ēfâging| *a* quisquilloso.
pettiness |pet'ēnis| *n* mezquindad *f*.
petty |pet'ē| *a* (*mean*) mezquino; (*unimportant*) insignificante.
petty cash *n* dinero para gastos menores.
petty cash book *n* libro de caja auxiliar.
petty officer *n* contramaestre *m*.
petulant |pech'ələnt| *a* malhumorado.
pew |pyōō| *n* banco.
pewter |pyōō'tûr| *n* peltre *m*.
Pfc *abbr* (*US MIL*) = *private first class*.
PG *n abbr* (*CINEMA*) = *parental guidance*.
PGA *n abbr* = *Professional Golfers' Association*.
PH *n abbr* (*US MIL*: = *Purple Heart*) decoración otorgada a los heridos de guerra.
pH *n abbr* (= *pH value*) pH.
p&h *abbr* (*US*: = *postage and handling*) gastos de envío.
PHA *n abbr* (*US*) = *Public Housing Administration*.
phallic |fal'ik| *a* fálico.
phantom |fan'təm| *n* fantasma *m*.
Pharaoh |fār'ō| *n* Faraón *m*.

pharmaceutical |fârməsōō'tikəl| *a* farmacéutico.
pharmacist |fâr'məsist| *n* farmacéutico.
pharmacy |fâr'məsē| *n* (*US*) farmacia.
phase |fāz| *n* fase *f* ♦ *vt*: **to ~ sth in/out** introducir/retirar algo por etapas; **~d withdrawal** retirada progresiva.
Ph.D. *abbr* = **Doctor of Philosophy**.
pheasant |fez'ənt| *n* faisán *m*.
phenomenal |finâm'ənəl| *a* fenomenal.
phenomenally |finâm'ənəlē| *ad* fenomenalmente, de modo fenomenal.
phenomenon, *pl* **phenomena** |finâm'ənân. -nə| *n* fenómeno.
phial |fī'əl| *n* ampolla.
philanderer |filan'dûrûr| *n* donjuan *m*.
philanthropic |filənthrâp'ik| *a* filantrópico.
philanthropist |filan'thrəpist| *n* filántropo/a.
philatelist |filat'əlist| *n* filatelista *m/f*.
philately |filat'əlē| *n* filatelia.
Philippines |fil'ipēnz| *npl*: **the ~** las (Islas) Filipinas.
philosopher |filâs'əfûr| *n* filósofo/a.
philosophical |filəsâf'ikəl| *a* filosófico.
philosophy |filâs'əfē| *n* filosofía.
phlegm |flem| *n* flema.
phlegmatic |flegmat'ik| *a* flemático.
phobia |fō'bēə| *n* fobia.
phone |fōn| *n* teléfono ♦ *vt* telefonear, llamar por teléfono; **to be on the ~** tener teléfono; (*be calling*) estar hablando por teléfono.
  phone back *vt, vi* volver a llamar.
phone book *n* guía telefónica.
phone booth, (*Brit*) **phone box** *n* cabina telefónica.
phone call *n* llamada (telefónica).
phone-in |fōn'in| *n* (*Brit RADIO, TV*) programa de radio o televisión en el que el público puede llamar por teléfono.
phonetics |fənet'iks| *n* fonética.
phon(e)y |fō'nē| *a* falso ♦ *n* (*person*) farsante *m/f*.
phonograph |fō'nəgraf| *n* (*US*) fonógrafo, tocadiscos *m inv*.
phonology |fənâl'əjē| *n* fonología.
phosphate |fâs'fāt| *n* fosfato.
phosphorus |fâs'fûrəs| *n* fósforo.
photo |fō'tō| *n* foto *f*.
photo... |fō'tō| *pref* foto... .
photocopier |fō'təkâpēûr| *n* fotocopiadora.
photocopy |fō'təkâpē| *n* fotocopia ♦ *vt* fotocopiar.
photoelectric |fōtōilek'trik| *a*: **~ cell** célula fotoeléctrica.
photo finish *n* resultado comprobado por fotocontrol.
photogenic |fōtəjen'ik| *a* fotogénico.
photograph |fō'təgraf| *n* fotografía ♦ *vt* fotografiar; **to take a ~ of sb** sacar una foto de uno.
photographer |fətâg'rəfûr| *n* fotógrafo.
photographic |fōtəgraf'ik| *a* fotográfico.

photography |fətág'rəfē| *n* fotografía.
photostat |fō'təstat| ℞ *n* fotóstato.
photosynthesis |fōtəsin'thəsis| *n* fotosíntesis *f*.
phrase |frāz| *n* frase *f* ♦ *vt* (*letter*) expresar, redactar.
phrase book *n* libro de frases.
physical |fiz'ikəl| *a* físico; ~ **examination** reconocimiento médico; ~ **exercises** ejercicios *mpl* físicos ♦ *n* reconocimiento médico.
physical education *n* educación *f* física.
physically |fiz'iklē| *ad* físicamente.
physical training *n* gimnasia.
physician |fizish'ən| *n* médico/a.
physicist |fiz'əsist| *n* físico/a.
physics |fiz'iks| *n* física.
physiological |fizēəlȧj'ikəl| *a* fisiológico.
physiology |fizēȧl'əjē| *n* fisiología.
physiotherapist |fizēōthär'əpist| *n* fisioterapeuta *m/f*.
physiotherapy |fizēōthär'əpē| *n* fisioterapia.
physique |fizēk'| *n* físico.
pianist |pēan'ist| *n* pianista *m/f*.
piano |pēan'ō| *n* piano.
piano accordion *n* (*Brit*) acordeón-piano *m*.
piccolo |pik'əlō| *n* (*MUS*) flautín *m*.
pick |pik| *n* (*tool*) pico, piqueta ♦ *vt* (*select*) elegir, escoger; (*gather*) coger (*Sp*), recoger (*LAm*); (*lock*) abrir con ganzúa; (*scab, spot*) rascar ♦ *vi*: **to** ~ **and choose** ser muy exigente; **take your** ~ escoja lo que quiera; **the** ~ **of** lo mejor de; **to** ~ **one's nose/teeth** hurgarse las narices/limpiarse los dientes; **to** ~ **pockets** ratear, ser carterista; **to** ~ **one's way through** andar a tientas, abrirse camino; **to** ~ **a fight with sb** buscar pelea con uno; **to** ~ **sb's brains** aprovecharse de los conocimientos de uno.
pick at *vt fus*: **to** ~ **at one's food** comer con poco apetito.
pick off *vt* (*kill*) matar de un tiro.
pick on *vt fus* (*person*) meterse con.
pick out *vt* escoger; (*distinguish*) identificar.
pick up *vi* (*improve: sales*) ir mejor; (: *patient*) reponerse; (: *FINANCE*) recobrarse ♦ *vt* (*from floor*) recoger; (*buy*) comprar; (*find*) encontrar; (*learn*) aprender; (*RADIO, TV, TEL*) captar; **to** ~ **up speed** acelerarse; **to** ~ **o.s. up** levantarse; **to** ~ **up where one left off** reempezar algo donde lo había dejado.
pickax, (*Brit*) **pickaxe** |pik'aks| *n* pico, zapapico.
picket |pik'it| *n* (*in strike*) piquete *m* ♦ *vt* piquetear; **to be on** ~ **duty** estar de piquete.
picketing |pik'iting| *n* organización *f* de piquetes.
picket line *n* piquete *m*.
pickings |pik'ingz| *npl* (*pilferings*): **there**

are good ~ **to be had here** se puede sacar buenas ganancias de aquí.
pickle |pik'əl| *n* (*also:* ~**s:** *as condiment*) escabeche *m*; (*fig: mess*) apuro ♦ *vt* encurtir; (*in vinegar*) envinagrar; **in a** ~ en un lío, en apuros.
pick-me-up |pik'mēup| *n* tónico.
pickpocket |pik'pȧkit| *n* carterista *m/f*.
pickup |pik'up| *n* (*small truck:. also:* ~ **truck**) furgoneta; (*Brit: on record player*) pickup *m*.
picnic |pik'nik| *n* picnic *m*, merienda ♦ *vi* merendar en el campo.
pictorial |piktôr'ēəl| *a* pictórico; (*magazine etc*) ilustrado.
picture |pik'chûr| *n* cuadro; (*painting*) pintura; (*photograph*) fotografía; (*film*) película; (*TV*) imagen *f* ♦ *vt* pintar; **the** ~**s** (*Brit*) el cine; **we get a good** ~ **here** captamos buena imagen aquí; **to take a** ~ **of sb/sth** hacer *or* sacar una foto a uno/de algo; **the garden is a** ~ **in June** el jardín es una preciosidad en junio; **the overall** ~ la impresión en general; **to put sb in the** ~ poner uno al corriente *or* al tanto.
picture book *n* libro de dibujos.
picturesque |pikchəresk'| *a* pintoresco.
piddling |pid'ling| *a* insignificante.
pidgin |pij'in| *a*: ~ **English** lengua franca basada en el inglés.
pie |pī| *n* pastel *m*; (*open*) tarta; (*small: of meat*) empanada.
piebald |pī'bôld| *a* pío.
piece |pēs| *n* pedazo, trozo; (*of cake*) trozo; (*CHECKERS etc*) pieza, ficha; .(*item*): **a** ~ **of furniture/advice** un mueble/un consejo ♦ *vt*: **to** ~ **together** juntar; (*TECH*) armar; **to break into** ~**s** hacerse pedazos; **to take to** ~**s** desmontar; **a** ~ **of news** una noticia; **a 10¢** ~ una moneda de 10 centavos; **a six-**~ **band** un conjunto de seis (músicos); **in one** ~ (*object*) de una sola pieza; **by** ~ pieza por *or* a pieza; **to speak one's** ~ decir su parecer.
piecemeal |pēs'mēl| *ad* poco a poco.
piece rate *n* tarifa a destajo.
piecework |pēs'wûrk| *n* trabajo a destajo.
pie chart *n* gráfico de sectores *or* de tarta.
pie crust pastry *n* (*US*) pasta quebradiza.
pier |pēr| *n* muelle *m*, embarcadero.
pierce |pērs| *vt* penetrar en, perforar; **to have one's ears** ~**d** hacerse los agujeros de las orejas.
piercing |pērs'ing| *a* (*cry*) penetrante.
piety |pī'ətē| *n* piedad *f*.
pig |pig| *n* cerdo, puerco; (*fig*) cochino.
pigeon |pij'ən| *n* paloma; (*as food*) pichón *m*.
pigeonhole |pij'ənhōl| *n* casilla.
piggy bank |pig'ē bangk| *n* hucha (*en forma de cerdito*).
pigheaded |pig'hedid| *a* terco, testarudo.
piglet |pig'lit| *n* cerdito.

pigment [pig'mənt] *n* pigmento.
pigmentation [pigməntā'shən] *n* pigmentación *f*.
pigmy [pig'mē] *n* = **pygmy**.
pigskin [pig'skin] *n* piel *f* de cerdo.
pigsty [pig'stī] *n* pocilga.
pigtail [pig'tāl] *n* (*girl's*) trenza; (*Chinese*, *TAUR*) coleta.
pike [pīk] *n* (*spear*) pica; (*fish*) lucio.
pilchard [pil'chŭrd] *n* sardina.
pile [pīl] *n* (*heap*) montón *m*; (*of carpet*) pelo ♦ (*vb*: *also*: ~ **up**) *vt* amontonar; (*fig*) acumular ♦ *vi* amontonarse; **in a** ~ en un montón; **to** ~ **into** (*car*) meterse en.
  pile on *vt*: **to** ~ **it on** (*col*) exagerar.
piles [pīlz] *npl* (*MED*) almorranas *fpl*, hemorroides *mpl*.
pile-up [pīl'up] *n* (*AUT*) accidente *m* múltiple.
pilfer [pil'fŭr] *vt*, *vi* ratear, robar, sisar.
pilfering [pil'fûring] *n* ratería.
pilgrim [pil'grim] *n* peregrino/a.
pilgrimage [pil'grəmij] *n* peregrinación *f*, romería.
pill [pil] *n* píldora; **the** ~ la píldora; **to be on the** ~ tomar la píldora (anticonceptiva).
pillage [pil'ij] *vt* pillar, saquear.
pillar [pil'ûr] *n* (*gen*) pilar *m*; (*concrete*) columna.
pillar box *n* (*Brit*) buzón *m*.
pillion [pil'yən] *n* (*of motorcycle*) asiento trasero; **to ride** ~ ir en el asiento trasero.
pillion passenger *n* pasajero que va detrás.
pillory [pil'ûrē] *vt* poner en ridículo.
pillow [pil'ō] *n* almohada.
pillowcase [pil'ōkās] *n* funda (de almohada).
pillowslip [pil'ōslip] *n* = **pillowcase**.
pilot [pī'lət] *n* piloto *inv* ♦ *a* (*plan etc*) piloto ♦ *vt* pilotar; (*fig*) guiar, conducir.
pilot light *n* piloto.
pimento [pimen'tō] *n* pimentón *m*.
pimp [pimp] *n* chulo, cafiche *m* (*LAm*).
pimple [pim'pəl] *n* grano.
pimply [pim'plē] *a* lleno de granos.
PIN *n* (*COMPUT*, *BANKING*) número personal de identificación.
pin [pin] *n* alfiler *m*; (*ELEC*: *of plug*) clavija; (*TECH*) perno; (: *wooden*) clavija; (*Brit*: *drawing* ~) chincheta; (*in grenade*) percutor *m* ♦ *vt* prender (con alfiler); sujetar con perno; ~**s and needles** hormigueo *sg*; **to** ~ **sth on sb** (*fig*) acusar (falsamente) a uno de algo.
  pin down *vt* (*fig*): **there's something strange here, but I can't quite** ~ **it down** aquí hay algo raro pero no puedo precisar qué es; **to** ~ **sb down** hacer que uno concrete.
pinafore [pin'əfôr] *n* delantal *m*.
pinafore dress *n* (*Brit*) mandil *m*.

pinball [pin'bôl] *n* (*also*: ~ **machine**) millón *m*, fliper *m*.
pincers [pin'sûrz] *npl* pinzas *fpl*, tenazas *fpl*.
pinch [pinch] *n* pellizco; (*of salt etc*) pizca ♦ *vt* pellizcar; (*col*: *steal*) birlar ♦ *vi* (*shoe*) apretar; **at a** ~ en caso de apuro; **to feel the** ~ (*fig*) pasar apuros *or* estrechos.
pinched [pincht] *a* (*drawn*) cansado; ~ **with cold** transido de frío; ~ **for money/ space** mal *or* falto de dinero/espacio *or* sitio.
pincushion [pin'kōōshən] *n* acerico.
pine [pīn] *n* (*also*: ~ **tree**) pino ♦ *vi*: **to** ~ **for** suspirar por.
  pine away *vi* morirse de pena.
pineapple [pīn'apəl] *n* piña, ananás *m*.
pine nut *n* piña, piñón *m*.
ping [ping] *n* (*noise*) sonido agudo.
ping-pong [ping'pông] *n* pingpong *m*.
pink [pingk] *a* rosado, color de rosa ♦ *n* (*color*) rosa; (*BOT*) clavel *m*, clavellina.
pinking shears [ping'king shirz] *npl* tijeras *fpl* dentadas.
pin money *n* dinero para gastos extra.
pinnacle [pin'əkəl] *n* cumbre *f*.
pinpoint [pin'point] *vt* precisar.
pinstripe [pin'strīp] *a*: ~ **suit** traje *m* a rayas.
pint [pīnt] *n* pinta (*US* = 0.47 *l*; *Brit* = 0.57 *l*).
pin-up [pin'up] *n* fotografía de mujer desnuda.
pinwheel [pin'wēl] *n* (*US*) rueda catalina.
pioneer [pīənēr'] *n* pionero/a ♦ *vt* promover.
pious [pī'əs] *a* piadoso, devoto.
pip [pip] *n* (*seed*) pepita; **the** ~**s** (*Brit TEL*) la señal.
pipe [pīp] *n* tubo, caño; (*for smoking*) pipa ♦ *vt* conducir en cañerías; ~**s** *npl* (*gen*) cañería *sg*; (*also*: **bag**~**s**) gaita *sg*.
  pipe down *vi* (*col*) callarse.
pipe cleaner *n* limpiapipas *m inv*.
piped music [pīpt myōō'zik] *n* música ambiental.
pipe dream *n* sueño imposible.
pipeline [pīp'līn] *n* tubería, cañería; (*for oil*) oleoducto; (*for natural gas*) gasoducto; **it is in the** ~ (*fig*) está en trámite.
piper [pī'pûr] *n* (*gen*) flautista *m/f*; (*with bagpipes*) gaitero/a.
pipe tobacco *n* tabaco de pipa.
piping [pī'ping] *ad*: **to be** ~ **hot** estar que quema.
piquant [pē'kənt] *a* picante.
pique [pēk] *n* pique *m*, resentimiento.
pirate [pī'rət] *n* pirata *m/f* ♦ *vt* (*record*, *video*, *book*) hacer una copia pirata de.
pirated [pī'ritid] *a* (*book*, *record etc*) pirata *inv*.
pirate radio *n* (*Brit*) emisora pirata.
pirouette [pirōōet'] *n* pirueta ♦ *vi* piruetear.
Pisces [pī'sēz] *n* Piscis *m*.
piss [pis] *vi* (*col*) mear.

pissed [pist] *a* (*Brit: col: drunk*) borracho.
pistol [pis'təl] *n* pistola.
piston [pis'tən] *n* pistón *m*, émbolo.
pit [pit] *n* hoyo; (*also:* **coal** ~) mina; (*in garage*) foso de inspección; (*also:* **orchestra** ~) platea; (*quarry*) cantera; (*US: of fruit*) hueso ♦ *vt* (*subj: chickenpox*) picar; (: *rust*) comer; (*US: fruit*) deshuesar; **to ~ A against B** oponer A a B; **~s** *npl* (*AUT*) box *msg*; **~ted with** (*chickenpox*) picado de.
pitapat [pit'əpat] *ad*; **to go ~** (*heart*) latir rápidamente; (*rain*) golpetear.
pitch [pich] *n* (*throw*) lanzamiento; (*MUS*) tono; (*Brit SPORT*) campo, terreno; (*tar*) brea; (*fig: degree*) nivel *m*, grado ♦ *vt* (*throw*) arrojar, lanzar ♦ *vi* (*fall*) caer(se); (*NAUT*) cabecear; **I can't keep working at this ~** no puedo seguir trabajando a este ritmo; **at its (highest) ~** en su punto máximo; **his anger reached such a ~ that ...** su ira *or* cólera llegó a tal extremo que ...; **to ~ a tent** montar una tienda (de campaña).
pitch-black [pich'blak'] *a* negro como boca de lobo.
pitched battle [picht bat'əl] *n* batalla campal.
pitcher [pich'ûr] *n* cántaro, jarro.
pitchfork [pich'fôrk] *n* horca.
piteous [pit'ēəs] *a* lastimoso.
pitfall [pit'fôl] *n* riesgo.
pith [pith] *n* (*of orange*) médula; (*fig*) meollo.
pithy [pith'ē] *a* jugoso.
pitiful [pit'ifəl] *a* (*touching*) lastimoso, conmovedor(a); (*contemptible*) lamentable, miserable.
pitifully [pit'ifəlē] *ad*: **it's ~ obvious** es tan evidente que da pena.
pitiless [pit'ilis] *a* despiadado, implacable.
pitilessly [pit'ilislē] *ad* despiadadamente, implacablemente.
pittance [pit'əns] *n* miseria.
pity [pit'ē] *n* (*compassion*) compasión *f*, piedad *f*; (*shame*) lástima ♦ *vt* compadecer(se de); **to have** *or* **take ~ on sb** compadecerse de uno; **what a ~!** ¡qué pena!; **it is a ~ that you can't come** ¡qué pena que no puedas venir!
pitying [pit'ēing] *a* compasivo, de lástima.
pivot [piv'ət] *n* eje *m* ♦ *vi*: **to ~ on** girar sobre; (*fig*) depender de.
pixel [pik'səl] *n* (*COMPUT*) pixel *m*, punto.
pixie [pik'sē] *n* duendecillo.
pizza [pēt'sə] *n* pizza.
P&L *abbr* = *profit and loss*.
placard [plak'ârd] *n* (*in march etc*) pancarta.
placate [plā'kāt] *vt* apaciguar.
place [plās] *n* lugar *m*, sitio; (*rank*) rango; (*seat*) plaza, asiento; (*post*) puesto; (*in street names*) plaza; (*home*): **at/to his ~** en/a su casa ♦ *vt* (*object*) poner, colocar;

(*identify*) reconocer; (*find a post for*) dar un puesto a, colocar; (*goods*) vender; **to take ~** tener lugar; **to be ~d** (*in race, exam*) colocarse; **out of ~** (*not suitable*) fuera de lugar; **in the first ~** (*first of all*) en primer lugar; **to change ~s with sb** cambiarse de sitio con uno; **from ~ to ~** de un sitio a *or* para otro; **all over the ~** por todas partes; **he's going ~s** (*fig, col*) llegará lejos; **I feel rather out of ~ here** me encuentro algo desplazado; **to put sb in his ~** (*fig*) poner a uno en su lugar; **it is not my ~ to do it** no me incumbe a mí hacerlo; **to ~ an order with sb (for)** hacer un pedido a uno (de); **we are better ~d than a month ago** estamos en mejor posición que hace un mes.
placebo [pləsē'bō] *n* placebo.
place mat *n* (*wooden etc*) salvamanteles *m inv*; (*in linen etc*) mantel *m* individual.
placement [plās'mənt] *n* colocación *f*.
place name *n* topónimo.
placenta [pləsen'tə] *n* placenta.
placid [plas'id] *a* apacible.
placidity [pləsid'itē] *n* apacibilidad *f*, placidez *f*.
plagiarism [plā'jərizəm] *n* plagio.
plagiarist [plā'jərist] *n* plagiario/a.
plagiarize [plā'jərīz] *vt* plagiar.
plague [plāg] *n* plaga; (*MED*) peste *f* ♦ *vt* (*fig*) acosar, atormentar; **to ~ sb with questions** acribillar a uno con preguntas.
plaice [plās] *n*, *pl inv* platija.
plaid [plad] *n* (*material*) tartán *m*.
plain [plān] *a* (*clear*) claro, evidente; (*simple*) sencillo; (*frank*) franco, abierto; (*not handsome*) poco atractivo; (*pure*) natural, puro ♦ *ad* claramente ♦ *n* llano, llanura; **in ~ clothes** (*police*) vestido de paisano; **to make sth ~ to sb** poner algo de manifiesto para uno.
plain chocolate *n* chocolate *m* oscuro *or* amargo.
plainly [plān'lē] *ad* claramente, evidentemente; (*frankly*) francamente.
plainness [plān'nis] *n* (*clarity*) claridad *f*; (*simplicity*) sencillez *f*; (*of face*) falta de atractivo.
plaintiff [plān'tif] *n* demandante *m/f*.
plaintive [plān'tiv] *a* (*cry, voice*) lastimero, quejumbroso; (*look*) que da lástima.
plait [plat] *n* trenza ♦ *vt* trenzar.
plan [plan] *n* (*drawing*) plano; (*scheme*) plan *m*, proyecto ♦ *vt* (*think*) pensar; (*prepare*) proyectar, planificar; (*intend*) pensar, tener la intención de ♦ *vi* hacer proyectos; **have you any ~s for today?** ¿piensas hacer algo hoy?; **to ~ to do** pensar hacer; **how long do you ~ to stay?** ¿cuánto tiempo piensas quedarte?; **to ~ (for)** planear, proyectar.
plan out *vt* planear detalladamente.
plane [plān] *n* (*AVIAT*) avión *m*; (*tree*) plá-

tano; (*tool*) cepillo; (*MATH*) plano.
planet [plan'it] *n* planeta *m*.
planetarium [planitär'ēəm] *n* planetario.
planetary [plan'itärē] *a* planetario.
plank [plangk] *n* tabla.
plankton [plangk'tən] *n* plancton *m*.
planner [plan'ûr] *n* planificador(a) *m/f*;
(*chart*) diagrama *m* de planificación; **city**
~ urbanista *m/f*.
planning [plan'ing] *n* (*POL*, *ECON*) planificación *f*; **family** ~ planificación familiar.
planning committee *n* (*in local government*) comité *m* de planificación.
plant [plant] *n* planta; (*machinery*) maquinaria; (*factory*) fábrica ♦ *vt* plantar;
(*field*) sembrar; (*bomb*) colocar.
plantain [plan'tin] *n* llantén *m*.
plantation [plantā'shən] *n* plantación *f*;
(*estate*) hacienda.
planter [plan'tûr] *n* hacendado.
plant pot *n* maceta, tiesto.
plaque [plak] *n* placa.
plasma [plaz'mə] *n* plasma *m*.
plaster [plas'tûr] *n* (*for walls*) yeso; (*also*:
~ **of Paris**) yeso mate; (*Brit*: *also*: **sticking** ~) tirita, esparadrapo ♦ *vt* enyesar;
(*cover*): **to** ~ **with** llenar *or* cubrir de; **to
be** ~ed **with mud** estar cubierto de barro.
plaster cast *n* (*MED*) escayola; (*model,
statue*) vaciado de yeso.
plastered [plas'tûrd] *a* (*col*) borracho.
plasterer [plas'tərûr] *n* yesero.
plastic [plas'tik] *n* plástico ♦ *a* de plástico.
plastic bag *n* bolsa de plástico.
plasticine [plas'tisēn] ® *n* (*Brit*) plastilina
®.
plastic surgery *n* cirujía plástica.
plate [plāt] *n* (*dish*) plato; (*metal, in book*)
lámina; (*PHOT*) placa; (*on door*) placa;
(*AUT*: *license* ~) matrícula.
plateau, ~s *or* ~x [platō', -z] *n* meseta, altiplanicie *f*.
plateful [plāt'fəl] *n* plato.
plate glass *n* vidrio *or* cristal *m* cilindra-
do.
platen [plat'ən] *n* (*on typewriter, printer*)
rodillo.
platform [plat'fôrm] *n* (*RAIL*) andén *m*;
(*stage*) plataforma; (*at meeting*) tribuna;
(*POL*) programa *m* (electoral); **the train
leaves from** ~ **7** el tren sale del andén número 7.
platinum [plat'ənəm] *n* platino.
platitude [plat'ətōōd] *n* lugar *m* común, tópico.
platonic [plətân'ik] *a* platónico.
platoon [plətōōn'] *n* pelotón *m*.
platter [plat'ûr] *n* fuente *f*.
plaudits [plô'dits] *npl* aplausos *mpl*.
plausibility [plôzəbil'ətē] *n* verosimilitud *f*,
credibilidad *f*.
plausible [plô'zəbəl] *a* verosímil; (*person*)
convincente.

play [plā] *n* (*gen*) juego; (*THEATER*) obra,
comedia ♦ *vt* (*game*) jugar; (*instrument*)
tocar; (*THEATER*) representar; (: *part*) hacer el papel de; (*fig*) desempeñar ♦ *vi* jugar; (*frolic*) juguetear; **to** ~ **it safe** ir a lo
seguro; **to bring** *or* **call into** ~ poner en
juego; **to** ~ **a trick on sb** gastar una broma a uno; **they're** ~ing **soldiers** están ju-
gando a (los) soldados; **to** ~ **for time** (*fig*)
tratar de ganar tiempo; **to** ~ **into sb's
hands** (*fig*) hacerle el juego a uno; **a smile**
~ed **on his lips** una sonrisa le bailaba en
los labios.
play around *vi* (*person*) hacer el tonto;
to ~ **around with** (*fiddle with*) juguetear
con; (*idea*) darle vueltas a.
play along *vi*: **to** ~ **along with** (*fig*:
person) seguirle el juego a; (: *plan, idea*)
seguir el juego a.
play back *vt* repasar.
play down *vt* quitar importancia a.
play on *vt fus* (*sb's feelings, credulity*)
aprovecharse de; **to** ~ **on sb's nerves** ata-
carle los nervios a uno.
play up *vi* (*Brit*) = **act up**.
playact [plā'akt] *vi* (*fig*) hacer comedia *or*
teatro.
play-acting [plā'akting] *n* teatro.
playboy [plā'boi] *n* playboy *m*.
player [plā'ûr] *n* jugador(a) *m/f*; (*THEATER*)
actor *m*, actriz *f*; (*MUS*) músico/a.
playful [plā'fəl] *a* juguetón/ona.
playground [plā'ground] *n* (*in school*) patio
de recreo.
playgroup [plā'grōōp] *n* jardín *m* de niños.
playing card [plā'ing kârd] *n* naipe *m*,
carta.
playing field *n* campo de deportes.
playmate [plā'māt] *n* compañero/a de juego.
play-off [plā'ôf] *n* (*SPORT*) (partido de) desempate *m*.
playpen [plā'pen] *n* corral *m*.
playroom [plā'rōōm] *n* cuarto de juego.
plaything [plā'thing] *n* juguete *m*.
playtime [plā'tīm] *n* (*SCOL*) (hora de) recreo.
playwright [plā'rīt] *n* dramaturgo/a.
plc (*Brit*) *abbr* (= *public limited company*)
S.A.
plea [plē] *n* (*request*) súplica, petición *f*;
(*excuse*) pretexto, disculpa; (*LAW*) alegato,
defensa.
plead [plēd] *vt* (*LAW*): **to** ~ **sb's case** defender a alguien; (*give as excuse*) poner
como pretexto ♦ *vi* (*LAW*) declararse;
(*beg*): **to** ~ **with sb** suplicar *or* rogar a
uno; **to** ~ **guilty/not guilty** (*defendant*) declararse culpable/inocente; **to** ~ **for sth**
(*beg for*) suplicar algo.
pleasant [plez'ənt] *a* agradable.
pleasantly [plez'əntlē] *ad* agradablemente.
pleasantness [plez'əntnis] *n* (*of person*)
simpatía, amabilidad *f*; (*of place*) lo agra-

dable.

pleasantries [plez'əntrēz] *npl* (*polite remarks*) cortesías *fpl;* **to exchange** ~ hablar en forma amena.

please [plēz] *vt* (*give pleasure to*) dar gusto a, agradar ♦ *vi* (*think fit*): **do as you** ~ haz lo que quieras *or* lo que te dé la gana; **to** ~ **o.s.** hacer lo que le parezca; ~**!** ¡por favor!; ~ **yourself!** ¡haz lo que quieras!, ¡como quieras!; ~ **don't cry!** ¡no llores! te lo ruego.

pleased [plēzd] *a* (*happy*) alegre, contento; (*satisfied*): ~ **(with)** satisfecho (de); ~ **to meet you** (*col*) ¡encantado!, ¡tanto *or* mucho gusto!; **to be** ~ **(about sth)** alegrarse (de algo); **we are** ~ **to inform you that ...** tenemos el gusto de comunicarle que ....

pleasing [plē'zing] *a* agradable, grato.

pleasurable [plezh'ûrəbəl] *a* agradable, grato.

pleasurably [plezh'ûrəblē] *ad* agradablemente, gratamente.

pleasure [plezh'ûr] *n* placer *m*, gusto; (*will*) voluntad *f* ♦ *cpd* de recreo; **"it's a** ~**"** "el gusto es mío"; **it's a** ~ **to see him** da gusto verle; **it's a** ~ **to inform you that ...** tengo el gran placer de comunicarles que ...; **with** ~ con mucho *or* todo gusto; **is this trip for business or** ~**?** ¿este viaje es de negocios o de placer?

pleasure-seeking [plezh'ûrsēking] *a* hedonista.

pleasure steamer *n* (*Brit*) vapor *m* de recreo.

pleat [plēt] *n* pliegue *m*.

pleb [pleb] *n*: **the** ~**s** la gente baja, la plebe.

plebeian [pləbē'ən] *n* plebeyo/a ♦ *a* plebeyo; (*pej*) ordinario.

plebiscite [pleb'isīt] *n* plebiscito.

plectrum [plek'trəm] *n* plectro.

pledge [plej] *n* (*object*) prenda; (*promise*) promesa, voto ♦ *vt* (*pawn*) empeñar; (*promise*) prometer; **to** ~ **support for sb** prometer su apoyo a uno; **to** ~ **sb to secrecy** hacer a uno jurar guardar un secreto.

plenary [plē'nûrē] *a*: **in** ~ **session** en sesión plenaria.

plentiful [plen'tifəl] *a* copioso, abundante.

plenty [plen'tē] *n* abundancia; ~ **of** mucho(s)/a(s); **we've got** ~ **of time to get there** tenemos tiempo de sobra para llegar.

plethora [pleth'ərə] *n* plétora.

pleurisy [plōōr'isē] *n* pleuresía.

Plexiglas [pleks'iglas] ® *n* (*US*) plexiglás *m* ®.

pliability [plīəbil'ətē] *n* flexibilidad *f*.

pliable [plī'əbəl] *a* flexible.

pliers [plī'ûrz] *npl* alicates *mpl*, tenazas *fpl*.

plight [plīt] *n* condición *f or* situación *f* difícil.

plimsolls [plim'səlz] *npl* (*Brit*) zapatos *mpl*

de tenis.

plinth [plinth] *n* plinto.

PLO *n abbr* (= *Palestine Liberation Organization*) OLP *f*.

plod [pläd] *vi* caminar con paso pesado; (*fig*) trabajar laboriosamente.

plodder [pläd'ûr] *n* trabajador(a) diligente pero lento/a.

plodding [pläd'ing] *a* (*student*) empollón(ona); (*worker*) más aplicado que brillante.

plonk [plängk] *n* (*Brit col: wine*) vino peleón.

plot [plät] *n* (*scheme*) complot *m*, conjura; (*of story, play*) argumento; (*of land*) terreno ♦ *vt* (*mark out*) trazar; (*conspire*) tramar, urdir ♦ *vi* conspirar.

plotter [plät'ûr] *n* (*instrument*) trazador *m* (de gráficos); (*COMPUT*) trazador *m*.

plotting [plät'ing] *n* conspiración *f*, intrigas *fpl*.

plough [plou] *etc* (*Brit*) = **plow** *etc*.

plow [plou] (*US*) *n* arado ♦ *vt* (*earth*) arar. **plow back** *vt* (*COMM*) reinvertir. **plow through** *vt fus* (*crowd*) abrirse paso a la fuerza por.

plowing [plou'ing] *n* labranza.

plowman [plou'mən] *n*: ~**'s lunch** pan *m* con queso.

plowshare [plou'shär] *n* reja del arado.

ploy [ploi] *n* truco, estratagema.

pluck [pluk] *vt* (*fruit*) coger (*Sp*), recoger (*LAm*); (*musical instrument*) puntear; (*bird*) desplumar ♦ *n* valor *m*, ánimo; **to** ~ **up courage** hacer de tripas corazón; **to** ~ **one's eyebrows** depilarse las cejas.

plucky [pluk'ē] *a* valiente.

plug [plug] *n* tapón *m*; (*ELEC*) enchufe *m*, clavija; (*AUT: also:* **spark** ~) bujía ♦ *vt* (*hole*) tapar; (*col: advertise*) dar publicidad a; **to give sb/sth a** ~ dar publicidad a uno/algo; **to** ~ **a cord into a socket** enchufar un hilo en una toma.

plug in *vt, vi* (*ELEC*) enchufar.

plughole [plug'hōl] *n* desagüe *m*, desaguadero.

plum [plum] *n* (*fruit*) ciruela ♦ *a* (*col: job*) chollo.

plumage [plōō'mij] *n* plumaje *m*.

plumb [plum] *a* vertical ♦ *n* plomo ♦ *ad* (*exactly*) exactamente, en punto ♦ *vt* sondar; (*fig*) sondear.

plumb in *vt* (*washing machine*) conectar.

plumber [plum'ûr] *n* fontanero/a, plomero/a.

plumbing [plum'ing] *n* (*trade*) fontanería; (*piping*) cañería.

plume [plōōm] *n* (*gen*) pluma; (*on helmet*) penacho.

plummet [plum'it] *vi*: **to** ~ **(down)** caer a plomo.

plump [plump] *a* rechoncho, rollizo ♦ *vt*: **to** ~ **sth (down) on** dejar caer algo en.

plump up *vt* hinchar.
plumpness |plump'nis| *n* gordura.
plunder |plun'dûr| *n* pillaje *m*; (*loot*) botín *m* ♦ *vt* pillar, saquear.
plunge |plunj| *n* zambullida ♦ *vt* sumergir, hundir ♦ *vi* (*fall*) caer; (*dive*) saltar; (*person*) arrojarse; (*sink*) hundirse; **to take the ~** lanzarse; **to ~ a room into darkness** dejar una habitación a oscuras.
plunger |plun'jûr| *n* émbolo; (*for drain*) desatascador *m*.
plunging |plun'jing| *a* (*neckline*) escotado.
pluperfect |plo͞opûr'fikt| *n* pluscuamperfecto.
plural |plo͝or'əl| *n* plural *m*.
plus |plus| *n* (*also:* **~ sign**) signo más; (*fig*) punto a favor ♦ *a:* **a ~ factor** (*fig*) un plus ♦ *prep* más, y, además de; **ten/twenty ~** más de diez/veinte.
plush |plush| *a* de felpa.
plutonium |ploo͞oto͞o'nēəm| *n* plutonio.
ply |plī| *vt* (*a trade*) ejercer ♦ *vi* (*ship*) ir y venir; **three ~** (*wool*) de tres cabos; **to ~ sb with drink** insistir en ofrecer a alguien muchas copas.
plywood |plī'wood| *n* madera contrachapada.
PM *abbr* = **Prime Minister**.
p.m. *ad abbr* (= *post meridiem*) de la tarde *or* noche.
pneumatic |no͞omat'ik| *a* neumático.
pneumatic drill *n* taladro neumático.
pneumonia |nyo͞omōn'yə| *n* pulmonía.
PO *n abbr* (= *Post Office*) Correos *mpl*; (*NAUT*) = **petty officer**.
po (*Brit*) *abbr* = **postal order**.
poach |pōch| *vt* (*cook*) escalfar; (*steal*) cazar/pescar en vedado ♦ *vi* cazar/pescar en vedado.
poached |pōcht| *a* (*egg*) escalfado.
poacher |pō'chûr| *n* cazador(a) *m/f* furtivo/a.
poaching |pō'ching| *n* caza/pesca furtiva.
PO Box *n abbr* = **Post Office Box**.
pocket |pâk'it| *n* bolsillo; (*of air, GEO, fig*) bolsa; (*BILLIARDS*) tronera ♦ *vt* meter en el bolsillo; (*steal*) embolsar; (*BILLIARDS*) entronerar; **breast ~** bolsillo de pecho; **~ of resistance** foco de resistencia; **~ of warm air** bolsa de aire caliente.
pocketbook |pâk'itbook| *n* (*US: wallet*) cartera; (: *handbag*) bolso.
pocketful |pâk'itfool| *n* bolsillo.
pocket knife *n* navaja.
pocket money *n* dinero de bolsillo.
pockmarked |pâk'märkt| *a* (*face*) picado de viruelas.
pod |pâd| *n* vaina.
podgy |pâj'ē| *a* gordinflón/ona.
podiatrist |pədī'ətrist| *n* (*US*) pedicuro/a.
podiatry |pədī'ətrē| *n* (*US*) pedicura.
podium |pō'dēəm| *n* podio.
POE *n abbr* = *port of embarkation, port of*

entry.
poem |pō'əm| *n* poema *m*.
poet |pō'it| *n* poeta *m/f*.
poetic |pōet'ik| *a* poético.
poet laureate |pō'it lō'rēit| *n* poeta *m* laureado.
poetry |pō'itrē| *n* poesía.
poignant |poin'yənt| *a* conmovedor(a).
poignantly |poin'yəntlē| *ad* de modo conmovedor.
point |point| *n* punto; (*tip*) punta; (*purpose*) fin *m*, propósito; (*Brit ELEC: also:* **power ~**) toma de corriente, enchufe *m*; (*use*) utilidad *f*; (*significant part*) lo significativo; (*place*) punto, lugar *m*; (*also:* **decimal ~**): **2 ~ 3 (2.3)** dos coma tres (2,3) ♦ *vt* (*gun etc*): **to ~ sth at sb** apuntar algo a uno ♦ *vi* señalar con el dedo; **~s** *npl* (*AUT*) contactos *mpl*; (*RAIL*) agujas *fpl*; **to be on the ~ of doing sth** estar a punto de hacer algo; **to make a ~ of doing sth** poner empeño en hacer algo; **to get the ~** comprender; **to come to the ~** ir al meollo; **there's no ~ (in doing)** no tiene sentido (hacer); **~ of departure** (*also fig*) punto de partida; **~ of order** cuestión *f* de procedimiento; **~ of sale** (*COMM*) lugar *m* de venta; **~-of-sale advertising** publicidad *f* en el punto de venta; **the train stops at Boston and all ~s south** el tren para en Boston, y en todas las estaciones al sur; **when it comes to the ~** en el momento de la verdad; **in ~ of fact** en realidad; **that's the whole ~!** ¡eso es!, ¡ahí está!; **to be beside the ~** no venir al caso; **you've got a ~ there!** ¡tienes razón!
point out *vt* señalar.
point to *vt fus* indicar con el dedo; (*fig*) indicar, señalar.
point-blank |point'blangk'| *ad* (*also:* **at ~ range**) a quemarropa.
pointed |poin'tid| *a* (*shape*) puntiagudo, afilado; (*remark*) intencionado.
pointedly |poin'tidlē| *ad* intencionadamente.
pointer |poin'tûr| *n* (*stick*) puntero; (*needle*) aguja, indicador *m*; (*clue*) indicación *f*, pista; (*advice*) consejo.
pointless |point'lis| *a* sin sentido.
pointlessly |point'lislē| *ad* inútilmente, sin motivo.
point of view *n* punto de vista.
poise |poiz| *n* (*of head, body*) porte *m*; (*calmness*) aplomo, elegancia.
poised |poizd| *a* (*in temperament*) sereno.
poison |poi'zən| *n* veneno ♦ *vt* envenenar.
poisoning |poi'zəning| *n* envenenamiento.
poisonous |poi'zənəs| *a* venenoso; (*fumes etc*) tóxico; (*fig: ideas, literature*) pernicioso; (: *rumors, individual*) nefasto.
poke |pōk| *vt* (*fire*) hurgar, atizar; (*jab with finger, stick etc*) empujar; (*COMPUT*) almacenar; (*put*): **to ~ sth in(to)** introducir algo en ♦ *n* (*jab*) empujón *m*; (*with*

elbow) codazo; **to ~ one's head out of the window** asomar la cabeza por la ventana; **to ~ fun at sb** ridiculizar a uno; **to give the fire a ~** atizar el fuego.
poke around *vi* fisgonear.
poker [pō'kûr] *n* atizador *m*; (*CARDS*) póker *m*.
poker-faced [pō'kûrfāst'] *a* de cara impasible.
poky [pō'kē] *a* estrecho.
Poland [pō'lənd] *n* Polonia.
polar [pō'lûr] *a* polar.
polar bear *n* oso polar.
polarization [pōlûrəzā'shən] *n* polarización *f*.
polarize [pō'lərīz] *vt* polarizar.
Pole [pōl] *n* polaco/a.
pole [pōl] *n* palo; (*GEO*) polo; (*TEL*) poste *m*; (*flag ~*) asta; (*tent ~*) mástil *m*.
pole bean *n* (*US*) judía trepadora.
polecat [pōl'kat] *n* (*US:* skunk) mofeta; (*Brit*) turón *m*.
Pol. Econ. [pál'ēkân] *n abbr* = *political economy*.
polemic [pəlem'ik] *n* polémica.
polemicist [pōlem'isist] *n* polemista *m/f*.
pole star *n* estrella polar.
pole vault *n* salto con pértiga.
police [pəlēs'] *n* policía ♦ *vt* (*streets, city, frontier*) vigilar.
police captain *n* (*US*) subjefe/a *m/f*.
police car *n* coche-patrulla *m*.
police constable *n* (*Brit*) guardia *m*, policía *m*.
police department *n* (*US*) policía.
police force *n* cuerpo de policía.
policeman [pəlēs'mən] *n* guardia *m*, policía *m*.
police officer *n* guardia *m*, policía *m*.
police record *n*: **to have a ~** tener antecedentes penales.
police state *n* estado policial.
police station *n* comisaría.
policewoman [pəlēs'wōōmən] *n* mujer *f* policía.
policy [pál'isē] *n* política; (*also:* **insurance ~**) póliza; (*of newspaper, company*) política; **it is our ~ to do that** tenemos por norma hacer eso; **to take out a ~** sacar una póliza.
policy holder *n* asegurado/a.
polio [pō'lēō] *n* polio *f*.
Polish [pō'lish] *a* polaco ♦ *n* (*LING*) polaco.
polish [pál'ish] *n* (*for shoes*) betún *m*; (*for floor*) cera (de lustrar); (*for nails*) esmalte *m*; (*shine*) brillo, lustre *m*; (*fig: refinement*) cultura ♦ *vt* (*shoes*) limpiar; (*make shiny*) pulir, sacar brillo a; (*fig: improve*) perfeccionar.
polish off *vt* (*work*) terminar; (*food*) despachar.
polished [pál'isht] *a* (*fig: person*) elegante.
polite [pəlīt'] *a* cortés, atento; (*formal*) co-

rrecto; **it's not ~ to do that** es de mala educación hacer eso.
politely [pəlīt'lē] *ad* cortésmente.
politeness [pəlīt'nis] *n* cortesía.
politic [pál'itik] *a* prudente.
political [pəlit'ikəl] *a* político.
political asylum *n* asilo político.
politically [pəlit'iklē] *ad* políticamente.
politician [pálitish'ən] *n* político/a.
politics [pál'itiks] *n* política.
polka [pōl'kə] *n* polca.
polka dot *n* lunar *m*.
poll [pōl] *n* (*votes*) votación *f*, votos *mpl*; (*also:* **opinion ~**) sondeo, encuesta ♦ *vt* (*votes*) obtener; (*in opinion ~*) sondear; **to go to the ~s** (*voters*) votar; (*government*) acudir a las urnas.
pollen [pál'ən] *n* polen *m*.
pollen count *n* índice *m* de polen.
pollination [pálənā'shən] *n* polinización *f*.
polling [pō'ling] *n* (*Brit POL*) votación *f*; (*TEL*) interrogación *f*.
pollute [pəlōōt'] *vt* contaminar.
pollution [pəlōō'shən] *n* polución *f*, contaminación *f* del medio ambiente.
polo [pō'lō] *n* (*sport*) polo.
poloneck [pō'lōnek] *a* de cuello vuelto ♦ *n* (*sweater*) suéter *m* de cuello vuelto.
poly [pál'ē] *n abbr* (*Brit*) = **polytechnic**.
poly... [pál'ē] *pref* poli....
polyester [pálēes'tûr] *n* poliéster *m*.
polyethylene [pálēeth'əlēn] *n* (*US*) politeno.
polygamy [pəlig'əmē] *n* poligamia.
polymath [pál'ēmath] *n* erudito/a.
Polynesia [pálinē'zhə] *n* Polinesia.
Polynesian [pálənē'zhən] *a, n* polinesio/a *m/f*.
polyp [pál'ip] *n* (*MED*) pólipo.
polystyrene [pálēsti'rēn] *n* poliestireno.
polytechnic [pálētek'nik] *n* ≈ escuela de formación profesional.
polythene [pál'əthēn] *n* (*Brit*) politeno.
polythene bag *n* bolsa de plástico.
polyurethane [pálēyōōr'əthān] *n* poliuretano.
pomegranate [pám'əgranit] *n* granada.
pommel [pum'əl] *n* pomo ♦ *vt* = **pummel**.
pomp [pámp] *n* pompa.
pompom [pám'pám], **pompon** [pám'pán] *n* borla.
pompous [pám'pəs] *a* pomposo; (*person*) presumido.
pond [pánd] *n* (*natural*) charca; (*artificial*) estanque *m*.
ponder [pán'dûr] *vt* meditar.
ponderous [pán'dûrəs] *a* pesado.
pong [pông] *n* (*Brit col*) mal olor *m* ♦ *vi* (*Brit col*) apestar.
pontiff [pán'tif] *n* pontífice *m*.
pontificate [pántif'ikāt] *vi* (*fig*): **to ~ (about)** pontificar (sobre).
pontoon [pántōōn'] *n* pontón *m*; (*Brit: card*

game) veintiuna.

pony [pō'nē] *n* poney *m*, jaca, potro (*LAm*).

ponytail [pō'nētāl] *n* cola de caballo.

pony trekking [pō'nē trek'ing] *n* (*Brit*) excursión *f* a caballo.

poodle [pōō'dəl] *n* caniche *m*.

pooh-pooh [pōōpōō'] *vt* desdeñar.

pool [pōōl] *n* (*natural*) charca; (*pond*) estanque *m*; (*also:* **swimming .~**) piscina, alberca (*LAm*); (*billiards*) chapolín; (*COMM: consortium*) consorcio; (: *US: monopoly trust*) trust *m* ♦ *vt* juntar; **typing** ~ servicio de mecanografía; (**football**) ~**s** *npl* quinielas *fpl*.

pooped [pōōpt] *a* (*US col*) hecho polvo.

poor [pōōr] *a* pobre; (*bad*) de mala calidad ♦ *npl*: **the ~** los pobres.

poorly [pōōr'lē] *a* mal, enfermo.

pop [páp] *n* ¡pum!; (*sound*) ruido seco; (*MUS*) (música) pop *m*; (*US col: father*) papá *m*; (*col: drink*) gaseosa ♦ *vt* (*burst*) hacer reventar ♦ *vi* reventar; (*cork*) saltar; **she ~ped her head out (of the window)** asomó de repente la cabeza (por la ventana).

pop in *vi* entrar un momento.

pop out *vi* salir un momento.

pop up *vi* aparecer inesperadamente.

pop concert *n* concierto pop.

popcorn [páp'kôrn] *n* palomitas *fpl*.

pope [pōp] *n* papa *m*.

poplar [páp'lûr] *n* álamo.

poplin [páp'lin] *n* popelina.

poppy [páp'ē] *n* amapola.

poppycock [páp'ēkák] *n* (*col*) tonterías *fpl*.

popsicle [páp'sikəl] *n* (*US*) polo.

populace [páp'yələs] *n* pueblo, plebe *f*.

popular [páp'yəlûr] *a* popular; **a ~ song** una canción popular; **to be ~ (with)** (*person*) caer bien (a); (*decision*) ser popular (entre).

popularity [pápyəlar'itē] *n* popularidad *f*.

popularize [páp'yələrīz] *vt* popularizar; (*disseminate*) vulgarizar.

populate [páp'yəlāt] *vt* poblar.

population [pápyəlā'shən] *n* población *f*.

population explosion *n* explosión *f* demográfica.

populous [páp'yələs] *a* populoso.

porcelain [pôr'səlin] *n* porcelana.

porch [pôrch] *n* pórtico, entrada.

porcupine [pôr'kyəpīn] *n* puerco *m* espín.

pore [pôr] *n* poro ♦ *vi*: **to ~ over** engolfarse en.

pork [pôrk] *n* carne *f* de cerdo *or* chancho (*LAm*).

pork chop *n* chuleta de cerdo.

pornographic [pôrnəgraf'ik] *a* pornográfico.

pornography [pôrnâ'grəfē] *n* pornografía.

porous [pôr'əs] *a* poroso.

porpoise [pôr'pəs] *n* marsopa.

porridge [pôr'ij] *n* gachas *fpl* de avena.

port [pôrt] *n* (*harbor*) puerto; (*NAUT: left*

side) babor *m*; (*wine*) vino de Oporto; (*COMPUT*) puerta, puerto, port *m;* ~ **of call** puerto de escala.

portable [pôr'təbəl] *a* portátil; ~ **crib** (*US*) cuna portátil.

portal [pôr'təl] *n* puerta (grande), portalón *m*.

port authorities *npl* autoridades *fpl* portuarias.

portcullis [pôrtkul'is] *n* rastrillo.

portend [pôrtend'] *vt* presagiar, anunciar.

portent [pôr'tent] *n* presagio, augurio.

porter [pôr'tûr] *n* (*for luggage*) maletero; (*doorkeeper*) portero/a, conserje *m/f*; (*US RAIL*) mozo de los coches-cama.

portfolio [pôrtfō'lēō] *n* (*case, of artist*) cartera, carpeta; (*POL, FINANCE*) cartera.

porthole [pôrt'hōl] *n* portilla.

portico [pôr'tikō] *n* pórtico.

portion [pôr'shən] *n* porción *f*; (*helping*) ración *f*.

portly [pôrt'lē] *a* corpulento.

portrait [pôr'trit] *n* retrato.

portray [pôrtrā'] *vt* retratar; (*in writing*) representar.

portrayal [pôrtrā'əl] *n* representación *f*.

Portugal [pôr'chəgəl] *n* Portugal *m*.

Portuguese [pôrchəgēz'] *a* portugués/esa ♦ *n, pl inv* portugués/esa *m/f*; (*LING*) portugués *m*.

Portuguese man-of-war *n* (*jellyfish*) especie *f* de medusa.

pose [pōz] *n* postura, actitud *f*; (*pej*) afectación *f*, pose *f* ♦ *vi* posar; (*pretend*): **to ~ as** hacerse pasar por ♦ *vt* (*question*) plantear; **to strike a ~** tomar *or* adoptar una pose *or* actitud.

poser [pō'zûr] *n* problema *m*/pregunta difícil; (*person*) = **poseur**.

poseur [pōzir'] *n* presumido/a, persona afectada.

posh [pásh] *a* (*col*) elegante, de lujo ♦ *ad* (*col*): **to talk ~** hablar con acento afectado.

position [pəzish'ən] *n* posición *f*; (*job*) puesto ♦ *vt* colocar; **to be in a ~ to do sth** estar en condiciones de hacer algo.

positive [páz'ətiv] *a* positivo; (*certain*) seguro; (*definite*) definitivo; **we look forward to a ~ reply** (*COMM*) esperamos ansiosamente su respuesta en firme; **he's a ~ nuisance** es un auténtico pelmazo; ~ **cash flow** (*COMM*) flujo positivo de efectivo.

positively [páz'ətivlē] *ad* (*affirmatively, enthusiastically*) de forma positiva; (*col: really*) absolutamente.

posse [pás'ē] *n* (*US*) pelotón *m*.

possess [pəzes'] *vt* poseer; **like one ~ed** como un poseído; **whatever can have ~ed you?** ¿cómo se te ocurrió?

possessed [pəzest'] *a* poseso, poseído.

possession [pəzesh'ən] *n* posesión *f*; **to take ~ of sth** tomar posesión de algo.

possessive [pəzes'iv] *a* posesivo.
possessively [pəzes'ivlē] *ad* de modo posesivo.
possessor [pəzes'ûr] *n* poseedor(a) *m/f*, dueño/a.
possibility [pásəbil'ətē] *n* posibilidad *f*; **he's a ~ for the part** es uno de los posibles para el papel.
possible [pás'əbəl] *a* posible; **as big as ~** lo más grande posible; **it is ~ to do it** es posible hacerlo; **as far as ~** en la medida de lo posible; **a ~ candidate** un(a) posible candidato/a.
possibly [pás'əblē] *ad* (*perhaps*) posiblemente, tal vez; **I cannot ~ come** me es imposible venir; **could you ~ ...?** ¿podrías ...?
post [pōst] *n* (*Brit: letters, delivery*) correo; (*job, situation*) puesto; (*trading ~*) factoría; (*pole*) poste *m ♦ vt* (*Brit: send by ~*) echar al correo; (*MIL*) apostar; (*bills*) fijar, pegar; (*appoint*): **to ~ to** enviar a; **by ~** (*Brit*) por correo; **by return of ~** (*Brit*) a vuelta de correo; **to keep sb ~ed** tener a uno al corriente.
post... [pōst] *pref* post..., pos...; **~ 1950** pos(t) 1950.
postage [pōs'tij] *n* porte *m*, franqueo.
postage stamp *n* sello (de correo).
postal [pōs'təl] *a* postal, de correos.
postal order *n* (*Brit*) giro postal.
postal vote *n* (*Brit*) voto postal.
postbag [pōst'bag] *n* (*Brit*) correspondencia, cartas *fpl*.
postbox [pōst'báks] *n* (*Brit*) buzón *m*.
postcard [pōst'kârd] *n* tarjeta postal.
postcode [pōst'kōd] *n* (*Brit*) código *or* clave *f* postal.
postdate [pōst'dāt] *vt* (*check*) poner fecha adelantada a.
poster [pōs'tûr] *n* cartel *m*.
posterior [pástēr'êûr] *n* (*col*) culo, trasero.
posterity [pástär'itē] *n* posteridad *f*.
poster paint *n* pintura al agua.
post-free [pōst'frē'] *a* (*Brit*) libre de franqueo.
postgraduate [pōstgraj'ōoit] *n* posgraduado/a.
posthumous [pás'chəməs] *a* póstumo.
posthumously [pás'chəməslē] *ad* póstumamente, con carácter póstumo.
postman [pōst'mən] *n* cartero.
postmark [pōst'mârk] *n* matasellos *m inv*.
postmaster [pōst'mastûr] *n* administrador *m* de correos.
Postmaster General *n* director *m* general de correos.
postmistress [pōst'mistris] *n* administradora de correos.
post-mortem [pōstmôr'təm] *n* autopsia.
postnatal [pōstnāt'əl] *a* postnatal, postparto.
post office *n* (*building*) (oficina de) correos *m*; (*organization*): **the P~ O~** Administración *f* General de Correos.
Post Office Box (PO Box) *n* apartado postal, casilla de correos (*LAm*).
post-paid [pōst'pād'] *a* porte pagado.
postpone [pōstpōn'] *vt* aplazar.
postponement [pōstpōn'mənt] *n* aplazamiento.
postscript [pōst'skript] *n* posdata.
postulate [pás'chəlāt] *vt* postular.
posture [pás'chûr] *n* postura, actitud *f*.
post-viral syndrome [pōst'vī'rəl sin'drōm] *n* síndrome *m* post-vírico.
postwar [pōst'wôr'] *a* de la posguerra.
posy [pō'zē] *n* ramillete *m* (de flores).
pot [pát] *n* (*for cooking*) olla; (*for flowers*) maceta; (*for jam*) tarro, pote *m*; (*piece of pottery*) cacharro; (*Brit col: marijuana*) costo ♦ *vt* (*plant*) poner en tiesto; (*conserve*) conservar; **~s of** (*Brit col*) montones de; **to go to ~** (*col: work, performance*) irse al traste.
potash [pát'ash] *n* potasa.
potassium [pətas'ēəm] *n* potasio.
potato, **~es** [pətā'tō, -z] *n* patata, papa (*LAm*).
potato chips, (*Brit*) **potato crisps** *npl* patatas *fpl or* papas *fpl* (*LAm*) fritas.
potato peeler [pətā'tō pē'lûr] *n* pelapatatas *m inv*.
potbellied [pát'belēd] *a* (*from overeating*) barrigón/ona; (*from malnutrition*) con el vientre hinchado.
potency [pōt'ənsē] *n* potencia.
potent [pōt'ənt] *a* potente, poderoso; (*drink*) fuerte.
potentate [pōt'əntāt] *n* potentado.
potential [pəten'chəl] *a* potencial, posible ♦ *n* potencial *m*; **to have ~** mostrar gran potencial.
potentially [pəten'chəlē] *ad* en potencia.
pothole [pát'hōl] *n* (*in road*) bache *m*; (*Brit: underground*) gruta.
potholer [pát'hōlûr] *n* (*Brit*) espeleólogo/a.
potion [pō'shən] *n* poción *f*, pócima.
potluck [pát'luk] *n*: **to take ~** tomar lo que haya.
pot roast *n* carne *f* asada.
potshot [pát'shát] *n*: **to take a ~ at sth** tirar a algo sin apuntar.
potted [pát'id] *a* (*food*) en conserva; (*plant*) en tiesto *or* maceta; (*fig: shortened*) resumido.
potter [pát'ûr] *n* alfarero/a ♦ *vi* (*Brit*): **to ~ around**, **~ about** ocuparse en fruslerías; **~ around the house** ir de aquí para allá sin hacer nada de provecho; **~'s wheel** torno de alfarero.
pottery [pát'ûrē] *n* cerámica, alfarería; **a piece of ~** un artículo de cerámica.
potty [pát'ē] *n* orinal *m* de niño.
potty-trained [pát'ētrānd] *a* que ya no necesita pañales.

pouch [pouch] *n* (*ZOOL*) bolsa; (*for tobacco*) petaca.

pouf(fe) [poōf] *n* (*stool*) puf *m*.

poultry [pōl'trē] *n* aves *fpl* de corral; (*dead*) pollos *mpl*.

poultry farm *n* granja avícola.

poultry farmer *n* avicultor(a) *m/f*.

pounce [pouns] *vi*: **to ~ on** precipitarse sobre ♦ *n* salto, ataque *m*.

pound [pound] *n* libra; (*for dogs*) corral *m*; (*for cars*) depósito ♦ *vt* (*beat*) golpear; (*crush*) machacar ♦ *vi* (*beat*) dar golpes; **half a ~** media libra; **a one ~ note** un billete de una libra.

pounding [poun'ding] *n*: **to take a ~** (*team*) sufrir terriblemente.

pound sterling *n* (libra) esterlina.

pour [pôr] *vt* echar; (*tea*) servir ♦ *vi* correr, fluir; (*rain*) llover a cántaros.

pour away, pour off *vt* vaciar, verter.

pour in *vi* (*people*) entrar en tropel; **to come ~ing in** (*water*) entrar a raudales; (*letters*) llegar a montones; (*cars, people*) llegar en tropel.

pour out *vi* (*people*) salir en tropel ♦ *vt* (*drink*) echar, servir.

pouring [pôr'ing] *a*: **~ rain** lluvia torrencial.

pout [pout] *vi* hacer pucheros.

poverty [pâv'ûrtē] *n* pobreza, miseria; (*fig*) falta, escasez *f*.

poverty-stricken [pâv'ûrtēstrikən] *a* necesitado.

POW *n abbr* = **prisoner of war**.

powder [pou'dûr] *n* polvo; (*face ~*) polvos *mpl*; (*gun~*) pólvora ♦ *vt* polvorear; **to ~ one's face** ponerse polvos; **to ~ one's nose** empolvarse la nariz, ponerse polvos; (*euphemism*) ir a los servicios *or* al cuarto de baño.

powder compact *n* polvera.

powdered milk [pou'dûrd milk'] *n* leche *f* en polvo.

powdered sugar [pou'dûrd shōōg'ûr] *n* (*US*) azúcar *m* extrafino.

powder puff *n* borla.

powder room *n* aseos *mpl*.

powdery [pou'dûrē] *a* polvoriento.

power [pou'ûr] *n* poder *m*; (*strength*) fuerza; (*nation*) potencia; (*drive*) empuje *m*; (*TECH*) potencia; (*ELEC*) fuerza, energía ♦ *vt* impulsar; **to be in ~** (*POL*) estar en el poder; **to do all in one's ~ to help sb** hacer todo lo posible por ayudar a uno; **the world ~s** las potencias mundiales.

power cut *n* apagón *m*.

power-driven [pou'ûrdrivən] *a* mecánico; (*ELEC*) eléctrico.

powered [pou'ûrd] *a*: **~ by** impulsado por; **nuclear-~ submarine** submarino nuclear.

power failure *n* = **power cut**.

powerful [pou'ûrfəl] *a* poderoso; (*engine*) potente; (*strong*) fuerte; (*play, speech*) conmovedor(a).

powerhouse [pou'ûrhous] *n* (*fig: person*) fuerza motriz; **a ~ of ideas** una cantera de ideas.

powerless [pou'ûrlis] *a* impotente, ineficaz.

power line *n* línea de conducción eléctrica.

power outage [pou'ûr out'ij] *n* (*US*) apagón *m*.

power shovel *n* excavadora.

power station *n* central *f* eléctrica.

power steering *n* (*AUT*) dirección *f* asistida.

powwow [pou'wou] *n* conferencia ♦ *vi* conferenciar.

pp *abbr* (= *per procurationem*: *by proxy*) p.p.

p & p *abbr* (*Brit*: = *postage and packing*) gastos de envío.

PPS *abbr* (= *post postscriptum*) posdata adicional.

PQ *abbr* (*Canada*) = *Province of Quebec*.

PR *n abbr* = **proportional representation**; (= *public relations*) relaciones *fpl* públicas ♦ *abbr* (*US MAIL*) = *Puerto Rico*.

Pr. *abbr* (= *prince*) P.

practicability [praktikəbil'ətē] *n* factibilidad *f*.

practicable [prak'tikəbəl] *a* (*scheme*) factible.

practical [prak'tikəl] *a* práctico.

practicality [praktikal'itē] *n* (*of situation etc*) factibilidad *f*.

practical joke *n* broma pesada.

practically [prak'tiklē] *ad* (*almost*) casi.

practice [prak'tis] *n* (*habit*) costumbre *f*; (*exercise*) práctica, ejercicio; (*training*) adiestramiento; (*MED*) clientela ♦ *vt* (*US*) (*carry out*) practicar; (*profession*) ejercer; (*train at*) practicar ♦ *vi* (*US*) ejercer; (*train*) practicar; **in ~** (*in reality*) en la práctica; **out of ~** desentrenado; **to put sth into ~** poner algo en práctica; **it's common ~** es práctica regular; **target ~** práctica de tiro; **he has a small ~** (*doctor*) tiene pocos pacientes; **to set up in ~ as** establecerse como.

practiced [prak'tist] *a* (*person*) experto; (*performance*) bien ensayado; (*liar*) consumado; **with a ~ eye** con ojo experto.

practice test *n* (*SCOL*) examen *m* de prueba.

practicing [prak'tising] *a* (*Christian etc*) practicante; (*lawyer*) que ejerce; (*homosexual*) activo.

practise [prak'tis] *vt, vi* (*Brit*) = **practice**.

practitioner [praktish'ənûr] *n* practicante *m/f*; (*MED*) médico/a.

pragmatic [pragmat'ik] *a* pragmático.

pragmatism [prag'mətizəm] *n* pragmatismo.

pragmatist [prag'mətist] *n* pragmatista *m/f*.

Prague |prâg| n Praga.
prairie |prär'ē| n (US) llanura.
praise |prāz| n alabanza(s) f(pl), elogio(s) m(pl).
praiseworthy |prāz'wûrᵗẖē| a loable.
pram |pram| n (Brit) cochecito de niño.
prance |prans| vi (horse) hacer cabriolas.
prank |prangk| n travesura.
prattle |prat'əl| vi parlotear; (child) balbucear.
prawn |prôn| n gamba.
pray |prā| vi rezar; **to ~ for forgiveness** pedir perdón.
prayer |prär| n oración f, rezo; (entreaty) ruego, súplica.
prayer book n devocionario, misal m.
pre- |prē| pref pre..., ante-; **~1970** pre 1970.
preach |prēch| vi predicar.
preacher |prē'chûr| n predicador(a) m/f; (minister) pastor(a) m/f.
preamble |prē'ambəl| n preámbulo.
prearrange |prēəränj'| vt organizar or acordar de antemano.
prearrangement |prēəränj'mənt| n: **by ~** por previo acuerdo.
precarious |prikär'ēəs| a precario.
precariously |prikär'ēəslē| ad precariamente.
precaution |prikô'shən| n precaución f.
precautionary |prikô'shənärē| a (measure) de precaución, precautorio.
precede |prisēd'| vt, vi preceder.
precedence |pres'idəns| n precedencia; (priority) prioridad f.
precedent |pres'idənt| n precedente m; **to establish** or **set a ~** sentar un precedente.
preceding |prisē'ding| a precedente.
precept |prē'sept| n precepto.
precinct |prē'singkt| n recinto; (US: district) distrito, barrio; (: of policeman) ronda; **~s** npl contornos mpl; **pedestrian ~** (Brit) zona peatonal; **shopping ~** (Brit) centro comercial.
precious |presh'əs| a precioso; (stylized) afectado ♦ ad (col): **~ little/few** muy poco/pocos.
precipice |pres'əpis| n precipicio.
precipitate a |prisip'itit| (hasty) precipitado ♦ vt |prisip'itāt| (hasten) acelerar; (bring about) provocar.
precipitation |prisipitā'shən| n precipitación f.
precipitous |prisip'itəs| a (steep) escarpado; (hasty) precipitado.
précis |prā'sē| n resumen m.
precise |prisīs'| a preciso, exacto; (person) escrupuloso.
precisely |prisīs'lē| ad exactamente, precisamente.
precision |prisizh'ən| n precisión f.
preclude |priklōōd'| vt excluir.
precocious |prikō'shəs| a precoz.
preconceived |prēkənsēvd'| a (idea) pre-

concebido.
preconception |prēkənsep'shən| n (idea) idea preconcebida.
precondition |prēkəndish'ən| n condición f previa.
precursor |prikûr'sûr| n precursor(a) m/f.
predate |prēdāt'| vt (precede) preceder.
predator |pred'ətûr| n animal m de rapiña.
predatory |pred'ətôrē| a (animal) rapaz, de rapiña; (person) agresivo, depredador(a).
predecessor |pred'isesûr| n antecesor(a) m/f.
predestination |prēdestinā'shən| n predestinación f.
predestine |prēdes'tin| vt predestinar.
predetermine |prēditûr'min| vt predeterminar.
predicament |pridik'əmənt| n apuro.
predicate |pred'əkit| n predicado.
predict |pridikt'| vt pronosticar.
predictable |pridikt'əbəl| a previsible.
predictably |pridikt'əblē| ad (behave, react) de forma previsible; **~ she didn't arrive** como era de esperar, no llegó.
prediction |pridik'shən| n pronóstico.
predispose |prēdispōz'| vt predisponer.
predominance |pridâm'ənəns| n predominio.
predominant |pridâm'ənənt| a predominante.
predominantly |pridâm'ənəntlē| ad en su mayoría.
predominate |pridâm'ənāt| vi predominar.
pre-eminent |prēem'ənənt| a preeminente.
pre-empt |prēempt'| vt adelantarse a.
pre-emptive |prēemp'tiv| a: **~ strike** ataque m preventivo.
preen |prēn| vt: **to ~ itself** (bird) limpiarse (las plumas); **to ~ o.s.** pavonearse.
prefab |prē'fab'| n casa prefabricada.
prefabricated |prēfab'rikātid| a prefabricado.
preface |pref'is| n prefacio.
prefect |prē'fekt| n (Brit: in school) monitor(a) m/f.
prefer |prifûr'| vt preferir; (LAW: charges, complaint) presentar; (: action) entablar; **to ~ coffee to tea** preferir el café al té.
preferable |pref'ûrəbəl| a preferible.
preferably |prifûr'əblē| ad de preferencia.
preference |pref'ûrəns| n preferencia; (priority) prioridad f; **in ~ to sth** antes que algo.
preference shares npl (Brit) = **preferred stock**.
preferential |prefəren'chəl| a preferente.
preferred stock |prifûrd' stäk| acciones fpl privilegiadas.
prefix |prē'fiks| n prefijo.
pregnancy |preg'nənsē| n embarazo.
pregnant |preg'nənt| a embarazada; **3 months ~** tres meses embarazada or

encinta; ~ **with meaning** cargado de significado.

prehistoric [prēhistôr'ik] a prehistórico.

prehistory [prēhis'tûrē] n prehistoria.

prejudge [prējuj'] vt prejuzgar.

prejudice [prej'ədis] n (bias) prejuicio; (harm) perjuicio ♦ vt (bias) predisponer; (harm) perjudicar; **to ~ sb in favor of/ against** (bias) predisponer a uno a favor de/en contra de.

prejudiced [prej'ədist] a (person) predispuesto; (view) parcial, interesado; **to be ~ against sb/sth** estar predispuesto en contra de uno/algo.

prelate [prel'it] n prelado.

preliminaries [prilim'ənärēz] npl preliminares mpl, preparativos mpl.

preliminary [prilim'ənärē] a preliminar.

prelude [prā'loōd] n preludio.

premarital [prēmar'itəl] a premarital.

premature [prēməchoōr'] a (arrival etc) prematuro; **you are being a little ~** te has adelantado.

prematurely [prēmətoōr'lē] ad prematuramente, antes de tiempo.

premeditate [primed'ətāt] vt premeditar.

premeditated [primed'ətātid] a premeditado.

premeditation [primeditā'shən] n premeditación f.

premenstrual [prēmen'stroōəl] a premenstrual.

premenstrual tension n (MED) tensión f premenstrual.

premier [primyēr'] a primero, principal ♦ n (POL) primer(a) ministro/a.

première [primyēr'] n estreno.

premise [prem'is] n premisa.

premises [prem'isiz] npl local msg; **on the ~** en el lugar mismo; **business ~** locales mpl comerciales.

premium [prē'mēəm] n premio; (COMM) prima; **to be at a ~** ser muy solicitado; **to sell at a ~** (shares) vender caro.

premium bond n (Brit) bono del estado que participa en un sorteo nacional.

premium deal n (COMM) oferta extraordinaria.

premium gasoline n (US) (gasolina) súper m.

premonition [premənish'ən] n presentimiento.

prenatal [prēnāt'l] a (US) antenatal, prenatal.

prenatal clinic n (US) clínica prenatal.

preoccupation [prēâkyəpā'shən] n preocupación f.

preoccupied [prēâk'yəpīd] a (worried) preocupado; (absorbed) ensimismado.

prep [prep] a abbr: ~ **school** = **preparatory school.**

prepaid [prēpād'] a porte pagado; ~ **envelope** sobre m de porte pagado.

preparation [prepərā'shən] n preparación f; ~**s** npl preparativos mpl; **in ~ for sth** en preparación para algo.

preparatory [pripar'ətôrē] a preparatorio, preliminar; ~ **to sth/to doing sth** como preparación para algo/para hacer algo.

preparatory school n (US) colegio privado; (Brit) escuela preparatoria.

prepare [pripär'] vt preparar, disponer ♦ vi: **to ~ for** prepararse or disponerse para; (make preparations) hacer preparativos para.

prepared [pripärd'] a (willing): **to be ~ to help sb** estar dispuesto a ayudar a uno.

preponderance [pripân'dûrəns] n preponderancia, predominio.

preposition [prepəzish'ən] n preposición f.

prepossessing [prēpəzes'ing] a agradable, atractivo.

preposterous [pripâs'tûrəs] a absurdo, ridículo.

prerecorded [prērikôr'did] a: ~ **broadcast** programa m grabado de antemano; ~ **cassette** cassette f pregrabada.

prerequisite [prirek'wizit] n requisito previo.

prerogative [prərâg'ətiv] n prerrogativa.

Presbyterian [prezbitēr'ēən] a, n presbiteriano/a m/f.

presbytery [prez'bitärē] n casa parroquial.

preschool [prē'skoōl'] a (child, age) preescolar.

prescribe [priskrīb'] vt prescribir; (MED) recetar.

prescription [priskrip'shən] n (MED) receta; **to fill a ~** preparar una receta.

prescriptive [priskrip'tiv] a normativo.

presence [prez'əns] n presencia; (attendance) asistencia.

presence of mind n aplomo.

present a [prez'ənt] (in attendance) presente; (current) actual ♦ n (gift) regalo; (actuality) actualidad f, presente m ♦ vt [prizent'] (introduce) presentar; (expound) exponer; (give) presentar, dar, ofrecer; (THEATER) representar; **to be ~ at** asistir a, estar presente en; **those ~** los presentes; **to give sb a ~, make sb a ~ of sth** regalar algo a uno; **at ~** actualmente; **to ~ o.s. for an interview** presentarse a una entrevista; **may I ~ Miss Clark** permítame presentarle or le presento a la Srta Clark.

presentable [prizen'təbəl] a: **to make o.s. ~** arreglarse.

presentation [prezəntā'shən] n presentación f; (gift) obsequio; (of case) exposición f; (THEATER) representación f; **on ~ of the voucher** al presentar el vale.

present-day [prez'əntdā'] a actual.

presenter [prizen'tûr] n (RADIO, TV) locutor(a) m/f.

presently [prez'əntlē] ad (soon) dentro de

poco; (*US: now*) ahora.
present participle *n* participio (de) presente.
present tense *n* (tiempo) presente *m*.
preservation [prezûrvā'shǝn] *n* conservación *f*.
preservative [prizûr'vǝtiv] *n* preservativo.
preserve [prizûrv'] *vt* (*keep safe*) preservar, proteger; (*maintain*) mantener; (*food*) conservar; (*in salt*) salar ♦ *n* (*for game*) coto, vedado; (*often pl: jam*) conserva, confitura.
preshrunk [prē'shrungk'] *a* inencogible.
preside [prizīd'] *vi* presidir.
presidency [prez'idǝnsē] *n* presidencia.
president [prez'idǝnt] *n* presidente *m/f*; (*US: of company*) director(a) *m/f*, gerente *m/f*.
presidential [preziden'chǝl] *a* presidencial.
press [pres] *n* (*tool, machine, newspapers*) prensa; (*printer's*) imprenta; (*of hand*) apretón *m* ♦ *vt* (*push*) empujar; (*squeeze*) apretar; (*grapes*) pisar; (*clothes: iron*) planchar; (*pressure*) presionar; (*doorbell*) apretar, pulsar, tocar; (*insist*): **to ~ sth on sb** insistir en que uno acepte algo ♦ *vi* (*squeeze*) apretar; (*pressurize*) ejercer presión; **to go to ~** (*newspaper*) entrar en prensa; **to be in the ~** (*being printed*) estar en prensa; (*in the newspapers*) aparecer en la prensa; **we are ~ed for time** tenemos poco tiempo; **to ~ sb to do** *or* **into doing sth** (*urge, entreat*) presionar a uno para que haga algo; **to ~ sb for an answer** insistir a uno para que conteste; **to ~ charges against sb** (*LAW*) formular acusaciones contra uno.
press on *vi* avanzar; (*hurry*) apretar el paso.
press agency *n* agencia de prensa.
press clipping *n* = **press cutting**.
press conference *n* rueda de prensa.
press cutting *n* recorte *m* (de periódico).
pressing [pres'ing] *a* apremiante.
pressman [pres'mǝn] *n* (*US*) tipógrafo; (*Brit*) periodista *m*.
press release *n* comunicado de prensa.
press stud *n* (*Brit*) botón *m* de presión.
press-up [pres'up] *n* (*Brit*) plancha.
pressure [presh'ûr] *n* presión *f*; (*urgency*) apremio, urgencia; (*influence*) influencia; **high/low ~** alta/baja presión; **to put ~ on sb** presionar a uno, hacer presión sobre uno.
pressure cooker *n* olla a presión.
pressure gauge *n* manómetro.
pressure group *n* grupo de presión.
pressurize [presh'ǝrīz] *vt* presurizar; **to ~ sb (into doing sth)** presionar a uno (para que haga algo).
pressurized [presh'ǝrīzd] *a* (*container*) a presión.
prestige [prestēzh'] *n* prestigio.

prestigious [prestij'ǝs] *a* prestigioso.
presumably [prizōō'mǝblē] *ad* es de suponer que, cabe presumir que; **~ he did it** lo más probable es que lo hiciera.
presume [prizōōm'] *vt* presumir, suponer; **to ~ to do** (*dare*) atreverse a hacer.
presumption [prizump'shǝn] *n* suposición *f*; (*pretension*) presunción *f*.
presumptuous [prizump'chōōǝs] *a* presumido.
presuppose [prēsǝpōz'] *vt* presuponer.
presupposition [prēsupǝzish'ǝn] *n* presuposición *f*.
pre-tax [prē'taks'] *a* anterior al impuesto.
pretence [pritens'] *n* (*Brit*) = **pretense**.
pretend [pritend'] *vt* (*feign*) fingir ♦ *vi* (*feign*) fingir; (*claim*): **to ~ to sth** pretender a algo.
pretense [pritens'] *n* (*US: claim*) pretensión *f*; (*: pretext*) pretexto; (*: make-believe*) fingimiento; **on** *or* **under the ~ of doing sth** bajo *or* con el pretexto de hacer algo; **she is devoid of all ~** es siempre franca.
pretension [priten'chǝn] *n* (*claim*) pretensión *f*; **to have no ~s to sth/to being sth** no engañarse en cuanto a algo/a ser algo.
pretentious [priten'chǝs] *a* presumido; (*ostentatious*) ostentoso, aparatoso.
pretext [prē'tekst] *n* pretexto; **on** *or* **under the ~ of doing sth** so pretexto de hacer algo.
prettily [prit'ilē] *ad* encantadoramente, con gracia.
pretty [prit'ē] *a* (*gen*) bonito, lindo (*LAm*) ♦ *ad* bastante.
prevail [privāl'] *vi* (*gain mastery*) prevalecer; (*be current*) predominar; (*persuade*): **to ~ (up)on sb to do sth** persuadir a uno para que haga algo.
prevailing [privā'ling] *a* (*dominant*) predominante.
prevalent [prev'ǝlǝnt] *a* (*dominant*) dominante; (*widespread*) extendido; (*fashionable*) de moda.
prevarication [privarikā'shǝn] *n* tergiversación *f*, evasivas *fpl*.
prevent [privent'] *vt*: **to ~ (sb) from doing sth** impedir (a uno) hacer algo.
preventable [privent'ǝbǝl] *a* evitable.
preventative [priven'tǝtiv] *a* preventivo.
prevention [priven'chǝn] *n* prevención *f*.
preventive [priven'tiv] *a* preventivo.
preview [prē'vyōō] *n* (*of movie*) preestreno.
previous [prē'vēǝs] *a* previo, anterior; **he has no ~ experience in that field** no tiene antecedentes en esa rama; **I have a ~ engagement** tengo un compromiso anterior.
previously [prē'vēǝslē] *ad* antes.
prewar [prē'wôr'] *a* antes de la guerra.
prey [prā] *n* presa ♦ *vi*: **to ~ on** vivir a costa de; (*feed on*) alimentarse de; **it was ~ing on his mind** le quitaba el sueño.

price [prīs] *n* precio; (*BETTING*: *odds*) puntos *mpl* de ventaja ♦ *vt* (*goods*) fijar el precio de; **to go up** *or* **rise in** ~ subir de precio; **what is the** ~ **of ...?** ¿qué precio tiene ...?; **to put a** ~ **on sth** poner precio a algo; **he regained his freedom, but at a** ~ recobró su guerra libertad, pero le había costado caro; **to be** ~**d out of the market** (*article*) no encontrar comprador por ese precio; (*nation*) no ser competitivo.

price control *n* control *m* de precios.

price-cutting [prīs'kuting] *n* reducción *f* de precios.

priceless [prīs'lis] *a* que no tiene precio; (*col*: *amusing*) divertidísimo.

price list *n* tarifa.

price range *n* gama de precios; **it's within my** ~ está al alcance de mi bolsillo.

price tag *n* etiqueta.

price war *n* guerra de precios.

pricey [prī'sē] *a* (*Brit col*) caro.

prick [prik] *n* pinchazo; (*with pin*) alfilerazo; (*sting*) picadura ♦ *vt* pinchar; picar; **to** ~ **up one's ears** aguzar el oído.

prickle [prik'əl] *n* (*sensation*) picor *m*; (*BOT*) espina; (*ZOOL*) púa.

prickly [prik'lē] *a* espinoso; (*fig*: *person*) malhumorado; (: *touchy*) quisquilloso.

prickly heat *n* sarpullido causado por exceso de calor.

prickly pear *n* chumbo.

pride [prīd] *n* orgullo; (*pej*) soberbia ♦ *vt*: **to** ~ **o.s. on** enorgullecerse de; **to take (a)** ~ **in** enorgullecerse de; **her** ~ **and joy** su orgullo; **to have** ~ **of place** (*Brit*) tener prioridad.

priest [prēst] *n* sacerdote *m*.

priestess [prēs'tis] *n* sacerdotisa.

priesthood [prēst'hŏŏd] *n* (*practice*) sacerdocio; (*priests*) clero.

prig [prig] *n* gazmoño/a.

prim [prim] *a* (*demure*) remilgado; (*prudish*) gazmoño.

prima donna [prē'mə dân'ə] *n* primadonna, diva.

prima facie [prē'mə fā'sē] *a*: **to have a** ~ **case** (*LAW*) tener razón a primera vista.

primarily [prīmār'ilē] *ad* (*above all*) ante todo, primordialmente.

primary [prī'märē] *a* primario; (*first in importance*) principal ♦ *n* (*US*: *also*: ~ **election**) (elección *f*) primaria.

primary color *n* color *m* primario.

primary education *n* enseñanza primaria.

primary products *npl* productos *mpl* primarios.

primary school *n* (*Brit*) escuela primaria.

primate *n* [prī'mit] (*REL*) primado; [prī'māt] (*ZOOL*) primate *m*.

prime [prīm] *a* primero, principal; (*basic*) fundamental; (*excellent*) selecto, de primera clase ♦ *n*: **in the** ~ **of life** en la flor de la vida ♦ *vt* (*gun, pump*) cebar; (*fig*) preparar.

Prime Minister (PM) *n* primer(a) ministro/a.

primer [prī'mûr] *n* (*book*) texto elemental; (*paint*) pintura de base, imprimación *f*.

prime time *n* (*RADIO, TV*) tiempo preferencial.

primeval [prīmē'vəl] *a* primitivo.

primitive [prim'ətiv] *a* primitivo; (*crude*) rudimentario; (*uncivilized*) inculto.

primly [prim'lē] *ad* remilgadamente; con gazmoñería.

primrose [prim'rōz] *n* primavera, prímula.

primus (stove) [prī'məs (stōv)] ® *n* (*Brit*) hornillo de camping.

prince [prins] *n* príncipe *m*.

prince charming *n* príncipe *m* azul.

princess [prin'sis] *n* princesa.

principal [prin'səpəl] *a* principal, mayor ♦ *n* director(a) *m/f*; (*in play*) protagonista principal *m/f*; (*COMM*) capital *m*, principal *m*.

principality [prinsəpal'itē] *n* principado.

principle [prin'səpəl] *n* principio; **in** ~ en principio; **on** ~ por principio.

print [print] *n* (*impression*) marca, impresión *f*; huella; (*letters*) letra de molde; (*fabric*) estampado; (*ART*) grabado; (*PHOT*) impresión *f* ♦ *vt* (*gen*) imprimir; (*on mind*) grabar; (*write in capitals*) escribir en letras de molde; **out of** ~ agotado.

print out *vt* (*COMPUT*) imprimir.

printed circuit [prin'tid sûr'kit] *n* circuito impreso.

printed circuit board (PCB) *n* tarjeta de circuito impreso (TCI).

printed matter *n* impresos *mpl*.

printer [prin'tûr] *n* (*person*) impresor(a) *m/f*; (*machine*) impresora.

printhead [print'hed] *n* cabeza impresora.

printing [prin'ting] *n* (*art*) imprenta; (*act*) impresión *f*; (*quantity*) tirada.

printing press *n* prensa.

print-out [print'out] *n* (*COMPUT*) printout *m*.

print shop *n* imprenta.

print wheel *n* rueda impresora.

prior [prī'ûr] *a* anterior, previo ♦ *n* prior *m*; ~ **to doing** antes de *or* hasta hacer; **without** ~ **notice** sin previo aviso; **to have a** ~ **claim to sth** tener prioridad en algo.

prioress [prī'ûris] *n* priora.

priority [prīôr'itē] *n* prioridad *f*; **to have** *or* **take** ~ **over sth** tener prioridad sobre algo.

priory [prī'ərē] *n* priorato.

prise [prīz] *vt* (*Brit*) = **prize**.

prism [priz'əm] *n* prisma *m*.

prison [priz'ən] *n* cárcel *f*, prisión *f* ♦ *cpd* carcelario.

prison camp *n* campamento para prisioneros.

prisoner [priz'ənûr] *n* (*in prison*) preso/a;

(*under arrest*) detenido/a; (*in dock*) acusado/a; **the ~ at the bar** el/la acusado/a; **to take sb ~** hacer *or* tomar prisionero a uno.

prisoner of war *n* prisionero/a *or* preso/a de guerra.

prison warden *n* (*US*) director(a) *m/f* de prisión.

prissy |pris'ē| *a* remilgado.

pristine |pris'tēn| *a* pristino.

privacy |prī'vəsē| *n* (*seclusion*) soledad *f*; (*intimacy*) intimidad *f*; **in the strictest ~** de máxima confianza.

private |prī'vit| *a* (*personal*) particular; (*confidential*) secreto, confidencial; (*intimate*) privado, íntimo; (*sitting etc*) a puertas cerradas ♦ *n* soldado raso; "~" (*on envelope*) "confidencial"; (*on door*) "privado"; **in ~** en privado; **in (his) ~ life** en su vida privada; **to be in ~ practice** tener consultorio particular.

private enterprise *n* la empresa privada.

private eye *n* detective *m/f* privado/a.

private hearing *n* (*LAW*) vista a puertas cerradas.

private limited company *n* (*Brit*) sociedad *f* de responsabilidad limitada.

privately |prī'vitlē| *ad* en privado; (*in o.s.*) en secreto.

private parts *npl* partes *fpl* privadas *or* pudendas.

private practice *n*: **to be in ~** ser médico/a (*or* dentista *m/f*) particular.

private property *n* propiedad *f* privada.

private school *n* colegio privado.

privation |prīvā'shən| *n* (*state*) privación *f*; (*hardship*) privación *f*, estrechez *f*.

privatize |prī'vətīz| *vt* privatizar.

privet |priv'it| *n* alheña.

privilege |priv'əlij| *n* privilegio; (*prerogative*) prerrogativa.

privileged |priv'əlijd| *a* privilegiado; **to be ~ to do sth** gozar del privilegio de hacer algo.

privy |priv'ē| *a*: **to be ~ to** estar enterado de.

privy council *n* consejo del estado.

prize |prīz| *n* premio ♦ *a* (*first class*) de primera clase ♦ *vt* apreciar, estimar; **to ~ open** abrir con palanca.

prize fighter *n* boxeador *m* profesional.

prize fighting *n* boxeo *m* profesional.

prize-giving |prīz'giving| *n* distribución *f* de premios.

prize money *n* (*SPORT*) bolsa.

prizewinner |prīz'winûr| *n* premiado/a.

prizewinning |prīz'wining| *a* (*novel*, *essay*) premiado.

PRO *n abbr* = **public relations officer**.

pro |prō| *n* (*SPORT*) profesional *m/f*; **the ~s and cons** los pros y los contras.

pro- |prō| *pref* (*in favor of*) pro, en pro de; **~Soviet** pro-soviético.

probability |prâbəbil'ətē| *n* probabilidad *f*; **in all ~** lo más probable.

probable |prâb'əbəl| *a* probable; **it is ~/hardly ~ that** es probable/poco probable que.

probably |prâb'əblē| *ad* probablemente.

probate |prō'bāt| *n* (*LAW*) legalización *f* de un testamento.

probation |prəbā'shən| *n*: **on ~** (*employee*) a prueba; (*LAW*) en libertad condicional.

probationary |prəbā'shənärē| *a*: **~ period** período de prueba.

probationer |prəbā'shənûr| *n* (*LAW*) persona en libertad condicional; (*nurse*) ≈ aprendiz *m/f* de ATS (*Sp*), aprendiz de enfermero.

probation officer *n* oficial a cargo de los presos en libertad condicional.

probe |prōb| *n* (*MED. SPACE*) sonda; (*enquiry*) encuesta, investigación *f* ♦ *vt* sondar; (*investigate*) investigar.

probity |prō'bitē| *n* probidad *f*.

problem |prâb'ləm| *n* problema *m*; **what's the ~?** ¿cuál es el problema?, ¿qué pasa?; **no ~!** ¡por supuesto!; **to have ~s with the car** tener problemas con el coche.

problematic(al) |prâbləmat'ik(əl)| *a* problemático.

procedural |prəsē'jûrəl| *a* de procedimiento; (*LAW*) procesal.

procedure |prəsē'jûr| *n* procedimiento; (*bureaucratic*) trámites *mpl*; **cashing a check is a simple ~** cobrar un cheque es un trámite sencillo.

proceed |prəsēd'| *vi* proceder; (*continue*): **to ~ (with)** continuar *or* seguir (con); **to ~ against sb** (*LAW*) proceder contra uno; **I am not sure how to ~** no sé cómo proceder; *see also* **proceeds**.

proceedings |prəsē'dingz| *npl* acto *sg*, actos *mpl*; (*LAW*) proceso *sg*; (*meeting*) función *fsg*; (*records*) actas *fpl*.

proceeds |prō'sēds| *npl* ganancias *fpl*, ingresos *mpl*.

process |prâs'es| *n* proceso; (*method*) método, sistema *m*; (*proceeding*) procedimiento ♦ *vt* tratar, elaborar ♦ *vi* |prâses'| (*Brit formal: go in procession*) desfilar; **in ~** en curso; **we are in the ~ of moving to ...** estamos en vías de mudarnos a ....

process cheese |prâs'es chēz'|, (*Brit*) **processed cheese** *n* queso procesado.

processing |prâs'esing| *n* elaboración *f*.

procession |prəsesh'ən| *n* desfile *m*; **funeral ~** cortejo fúnebre.

proclaim |prəklām'| *vt* proclamar; (*announce*) anunciar.

proclamation |prâkləmā'shən| *n* proclamación *f*; (*written*) proclama.

proclivity |prōkliv'ətē| *n* propensión *f*, inclinación *f*.

procrastinate |prōkras'tənāt| *vi* demorarse.

procrastination |prōkrastənā'shən| *n* dila-

ción *f*.
procreation [prōkrēā'shən] *n* procreación *f*.
proctor [pråk'tûr] (*US*) *n* celador(a) *m/f* ♦ *vt*, *vi* vigilar.
procure [prəkyōōr'] *vt* conseguir, obtener.
procurement [prəkyōōr'mənt] *n* obtención *f*.
prod [pråd] *vt* (*push*) empujar; (*with elbow*) dar un codazo a ♦ *n* empuje *m*; codazo.
prodigal [pråd'əgəl] *a* pródigo.
prodigious [prədij'əs] *a* prodigioso.
prodigy [pråd'əjē] *n* prodigio.
produce *n* [prō'dōōs] (*AGR*) productos *mpl* agrícolas ♦ *vt* [prədōōs'] producir; (*yield*) rendir; (*bring*) sacar; (*show*) presentar, mostrar; (*proof of identity*) enseñar, presentar; (*THEATER*) presentar, poner en escena; (*offspring*) dar a luz.
produce dealer *n* (*US*) verdulero/a.
producer [prədōō'sûr] *n* (*THEATER*) director(a) *m/f*; (*AGR, CINEMA*) productor(a) *m/f*.
product [pråd'əkt] *n* producto.
production [prəduk'shən] *n* (*act*) producción *f*; (*THEATER*) representación *f*, obra; **to put into** ~ lanzar a la producción.
production agreement *n* (*US*) acuerdo de productividad.
production control *n* control *m* de producción.
production line *n* línea de producción.
production manager *n* jefe/jefa *m/f* de producción.
productive [prəduk'tiv] *a* productivo.
productivity [prådəktiv'ətē] *n* productividad *f*.
productivity agreement *n* (*Brit*) acuerdo de productividad.
productivity bonus *n* bono de productividad.
Prof. [pråf] *abbr* (= *professor*) Prof.
profane [prəfān'] *a* profano.
profess [prəfcs'] *vt* profesar; **I do not** ~ **to be an expert** no pretendo ser experto.
professed [prəfcst'] *a* (*self-declared*) declarado.
profession [prəfesh'ən] *n* profesión *f*.
professional [prəfcsh'ənəl] *n* profesional *m/f* ♦ *a* profesional; (*by profession*) de profesión; **to seek** ~ **advice** buscar un consejo profesional.
professionalism [prəfcsh'ənəlizəm] *n* profesionalismo.
professionally [prəfcsh'ənəlē] *ad*: **I only know him** ~ sólo le conozco por nuestra relación de trabajo.
professor [prəfcs'ûr] *n* (*US*) profesor(a) *m/ f*; (*Brit*) catedrático/a.
professorship [prəfcs'ûrship] *n* cátedra.
proffer [pråf'ûr] *vt* ofrecer.
proficiency [prəfish'ənsē] *n* capacidad *f*, habilidad *f*.
proficiency test *n* prueba de capacitación.

proficient [prəfish'ənt] *a* experto, hábil.
profile [prō'fil] *n* perfil *m*; **to keep a high/ low** ~ tratar de llamar la atención/pasar inadvertido.
profit [pråf'it] *n* (*COMM*) ganancia; (*fig*) provecho ♦ *vi*: **to** ~ **by** *or* **from** aprovechar *or* sacar provecho de; ~ **and loss statement** cuenta de ganancias y pérdidas; **to sell sth at a** ~ vender algo con ganancia.
profitability [pråfitəbil'ətē] *n* rentabilidad *f*.
profitable [pråf'itəbəl] *a* (*ECON*) rentable; (*beneficial*) provechoso, útil.
profitably [pråf'itəblē] *ad* rentablemente; provechosamente.
profit center *n* centro de beneficios.
profiteering [pråfitēr'ing] *n* (*pej*) explotación *f*.
profit-making [pråf'itmāking] *a* rentable.
profit margin *n* margen *m* de ganancia.
profit sharing [pråf'it shā'ring] *n* participación *f* de empleados en los beneficios.
profits tax *n* impuesto sobre los beneficios.
profligate [pråf'ləgit] *a* (*dissolute: behavior, act*) disoluto; (: *person*) libertino; (*extravagant*): **he's very** ~ **with his money** es muy derrochador.
pro forma [prō fôr'mə] *a*: ~ **invoice** factura pro-forma.
profound [prəfound'] *a* profundo.
profoundly [prəfound'lē] *ad* profundamente.
profusely [prəfyōōs'lē] *ad* profusamente.
profusion [prəfyōō'zhən] *n* profusión *f*, abundancia.
progeny [pråj'ənē] *n* progenie *f*.
program (*US*) *n* [prō'grəm] programa *m* ♦ *vt* [prō'gram] programar.
programer [prō'gramûr] *n* programador(a) *m/f*.
programing [prō'graming] *n* programación *f*.
programing language *n* lenguaje *m* de programación.
programme [prō'gram] *etc* (*Brit*) = **program** *etc*.
progress *n* [pråg'rcs] progreso; (*development*) desarrollo ♦ *vi* [prəgrcs'] progresar, avanzar; desarrollarse; **in** ~ (*meeting, work etc*) en curso; **as the match** ~**ed** en el curso del partido.
progression [prəgrcsh'ən] *n* progresión *f*.
progressive [prəgrcs'iv] *a* progresivo; (*person*) progresista.
progressively [prəgrcs'ivlē] *ad* progresivamente, poco a poco.
progress report *n* (*MED*) informe *m* sobre el estado; (*ADMIN*) informe *m* sobre el progreso.
prohibit [prōhib'it] *vt* prohibir; **to** ~ **sb from doing sth** prohibir a uno hacer algo; **"smoking** ~**ed"** "prohibido fumar".
prohibition [prōəbish'ən] *n* (*US*) prohibición *f*.

prohibitive [prŏhib'ətiv] *a* (*price etc*) prohibitivo.

project *n* [prâj'ekt] proyecto; (*SCOL. UNIV*: *research*) trabajo, proyecto ♦ (*vb*: [prəjekt']) *vt* proyectar ♦ *vi* (*stick out*) salir, sobresalir.

projectile [prəjek'təl] *n* proyectil *m*.

projection [prəjek'shən] *n* proyección *f*; (*overhang*) saliente *m*.

projectionist [prəjek'shənist] *n* (*CINE*) operador(a) *m/f* de cine.

projection room *n* (*CINE*) cabina de proyección.

projector [prəjek'tûr] *n* proyector *m*.

proletarian [prŏlitär'ēən] *a* proletario.

proletariat [prŏlitär'ēət] *n* proletariado.

proliferate [prŏlif'ərāt] *vi* proliferar, multiplicarse.

proliferation [prŏlifərā'shən] *n* proliferación *f*.

prolific [prŏlif'ik] *a* prolífico.

prolog(ue) [prŏ'lôg] *n* prólogo.

prolong [prəlông'] *vt* prolongar, extender.

prom [prâm] *n abbr* = **promenade**; (*Brit*) **promenade concert** ♦ *n* (*US*: *ball*) baile *m* de gala.

promenade [prâmənād'] *n* (*by sea*) paseo marítimo ♦ *vi* (*stroll*) pasearse.

promenade concert *n* (*Brit*) concierto (en que parte del público permanece de pie).

promenade deck *n* cubierta de paseo.

prominence [prâm'ənəns] *n* (*fig*) importancia.

prominent [prâm'ənənt] *a* (*standing out*) saliente; (*important*) eminente, importante; **he is ~ in the field of** ... tiene fama en el campo de ....

prominently [prâm'ənəntlē] *ad* (*display, set*) muy a la vista; **he figured ~ in the case** desempeñó un papel importante en el juicio.

promiscuity [prâmiskyōō'itē] *n* promiscuidad *f*.

promiscuous [prəmis'kyōōəs] *a* (*sexually*) promiscuo.

promise [prâm'is] *n* promesa ♦ *vt, vi* prometer; **to make sb a ~** prometer algo a uno; **a young man of ~** un joven con futuro; **to ~ (sb) to do sth** prometer (a uno) hacer algo; **to ~ well** ser muy prometedor.

promising [prâm'ising] *a* prometedor(a).

promissory note [prâm'isôrē nōt] *n* pagaré *m*.

promontory [prâm'əntôrē] *n* promontorio.

promote [prəmōt'] *vt* promover; (*new product*) dar publicidad a, lanzar; (*MIL*) ascender; **the team was ~d to the second division** (*Brit SOCCER*) el equipo fue ascendido a la segunda división.

promoter [prəmō'tûr] *n* (*of sporting event*) promotor(a) *m/f*; (*of company, business*) patrocinador(a) *m/f*.

promotion [prəmō'shən] *n* (*gen*) promoción *f*; (*MIL*) ascenso.

prompt [prâmpt] *a* pronto ♦ *ad*: **at 6 o'clock ~** a las seis en punto ♦ *n* (*COMPUT*) aviso, guía ♦ *vt* (*urge*) mover, incitar; (*THEATER*) apuntar; **to ~ sb to do sth** instar a uno a hacer algo; **to be ~ to do sth** no tardar en hacer algo; **they're very ~** (*punctual*) son muy puntuales.

prompter [prâmp'tûr] *n* (*THEATER*) apuntador(a) *m/f*.

promptly [prâmpt'lē] *ad* (*punctually*) puntualmente; (*rapidly*) rápidamente.

promptness [prâmpt'nis] *n* puntualidad *f*; rapidez *f*.

promulgate [prâm'əlgāt] *vt* promulgar.

prone [prōn] *a* (*lying*) postrado; **~ to** propenso a.

prong [prông] *n* diente *m*, punta.

pronoun [prō'noun] *n* pronombre *m*.

pronounce [prənouns'] *vt* pronunciar; (*declare*) declarar ♦ *vi*: **to ~ (up)on** pronunciarse sobre; **they ~d him unfit to drive** le declararon incapaz de conducir.

pronounced [prənounst'] *a* (*marked*) marcado.

pronouncement [prənouns'mənt] *n* declaración *f*.

pronunciation [prənunsēā'shən] *n* pronunciación *f*.

proof [prōōf] *n* prueba; **35° ~** graduación *f* del 35 por 100 ♦ *a*: **~ against** a prueba de.

proofreader [prōōf'rēdûr] *n* corrector(a) *m/f* de pruebas.

Prop. *abbr* (*COMM*) = **proprietor.**

prop [prâp] *n* apoyo; (*fig*) sostén *m* ♦ *vt* (*also*: **~ up**) apoyar; (*lean*): **to ~ sth against** apoyar algo contra.

propaganda [prâpəgan'də] *n* propaganda.

propagate [prâp'əgāt] *vt* propagar.

propagation [prâpəgā'shən] *n* propagación *f*.

propel [prəpel'] *vt* impulsar, propulsar.

propeller [prəpel'ûr] *n* hélice *f*.

propensity [prəpen'sitē] *n* propensión *f*.

proper [prâp'ûr] *a* (*suited, right*) propio; (*exact*) justo; (*apt*) apropiado, conveniente; (*timely*) oportuno; (*seemly*) correcto, decente; (*authentic*) verdadero; (*col*: *real*) auténtico; **to go through the ~ channels** (*ADMIN*) ir por la vía oficial.

properly [prâp'ûrlē] *ad* (*adequately*) correctamente; (*decently*) decentemente.

proper noun *n* nombre *m* propio.

properties [prâp'ûrtēz] *npl* (*THEATER*) accesorios *mpl*.

property [prâp'ûrtē] *n* propiedad *f*; (*estate*) finca; **lost ~** objetos *mpl* perdidos; **personal ~** bienes *mpl* muebles.

property developer *n* promotor(a) *m/f* de construcciones.

property owner *n* dueño/a de propiedades.

property tax *n* impuesto sobre la propiedad.

prophecy [pråf'isē] *n* profecía.

prophesy [pråf'isī] *vt* profetizar; *(fig)* predecir.

prophet [pråf'it] *n* profeta *m/f*.

prophetic [prəfet'ik] *a* profético.

prophylactic [prōfəlak'tik] *n* preservativo.

proportion [prəpôr'shən] *n* proporción *f*; *(share)* parte *f*; **to be in/out of ~ to** *or* **with sth** estar en/no guardar proporción con algo; **to see sth in ~** *(fig)* ver algo en su justa medida.

proportional [prəpôr'shənəl] *a* proporcional.

proportionally [prəpôr'shənəlē] *ad* proporcionalmente, en proporción.

proportional representation (PR) *n* *(POL)* representación *f* proporcional.

proportional spacing *n* *(on printer)* espaciado proporcional.

proportionate [prəpôr'shənit] *a* proporcionado.

proportionately [prəpôr'shənitlē] *ad* proporcionadamente, en proporción.

proportioned [prəpôr'shənd] *a* proporcionado.

proposal [prəpō'zəl] *n* propuesta; *(offer of marriage)* oferta de matrimonio; *(plan)* proyecto; *(suggestion)* sugerencia.

propose [prəpōz'] *vt* proponer; *(have in mind)*: **to ~ sth/to do** *or* **doing sth** proponer algo/proponerse a hacer algo ♦ *vi* declararse.

proposer [prəpō'zûr] *n* *(of motion)* proponente *m/f*.

proposition [prápəzish'ən] *n* propuesta, proposición *f*; **to make sb a ~** proponer algo a uno.

propound [prəpound'] *vt* *(theory)* exponer.

proprietary [prəprī'itärē] *a* *(COMM)*: **~ article** artículo de marca; **~ brand** marca comercial.

proprietor [prəprī'ətûr] *n* propietario/a, dueño/a.

propriety [prəprī'ətē] *n* decoro.

propulsion [prəpul'shən] *n* propulsión *f*.

pro rata [prō ra'tə] *ad* a prorrata.

prosaic [prōzā'ik] *a* prosaico.

Pros. Atty. *abbr* *(US)* = *prosecuting attorney*.

proscribe [prōskrīb'] *vt* proscribir.

prose [prōz] *n* prosa; *(Brit SCOL)* traducción *f* inversa.

prosecute [prås'əkyōot] *vt* *(LAW)* procesar; **"trespassers will be ~d"** *(LAW)* "se procesará a los intrusos".

prosecution [prásəkyōo'shən] *n* proceso, causa; *(accusing side)* acusación *f*.

prosecutor [prås'əkyōotûr] *n* acusador(a) *m/f*; *(also:* **public ~**) fiscal *m*.

prospect *n* [prás'pekt] *(view)* vista; *(chance)* posibilidad *f*; *(outlook)* perspectiva; *(hope)* esperanza ♦ *(vb:* [práspekt']) *vt* explorar ♦ *vi* buscar; **~s** *npl* *(for work etc)* perspectivas *fpl*; **to be faced with the ~ of** tener que enfrentarse a la posibilidad de que ...; **we were faced with the ~ of leaving early** se nos planteó la posibilidad de marcharnos pronto; **there is every ~ of an early victory** hay buenas perspectivas de una pronta victoria.

prospecting [prás'pekting] *n* prospección *f*.

prospective [prəspek'tiv] *a* *(possible)* probable, eventual; *(certain)* futuro; *(buyer)* presunto; *(legislation, son-in-law)* futuro.

prospector [prás'pektûr] *n* explorador(a) *m/f*; **gold ~** buscador *m* de oro.

prospectus [prəspek'təs] *n* prospecto.

prosper [prás'pûr] *vi* prosperar.

prosperity [práspär'itē] *n* prosperidad *f*.

prosperous [prás'pûrəs] *a* próspero.

prostate [prás'tāt] *n* *(also:* **~ gland**) próstata.

prostitute [prás'titōōt] *n* prostituta; **male ~** prostituto.

prostitution [prástitōō'shən] *n* prostitución *f*.

prostrate [prás'trāt] *a* postrado; *(fig)* abatido ♦ *vt*: **to ~ o.s.** *(before sb)* prosternarse; *(on the floor, fig)* prostrarse.

protagonist [prōtag'ənist] *n* protagonista *m/f*.

protect [prətekt'] *vt* proteger.

protection [prətek'shən] *n* protección *f*; **to be under sb's ~** estar amparado por uno.

protectionism [prətek'shənizəm] *n* proteccionismo.

protection racket *n* chantaje *m*.

protective [prətek'tiv] *a* protector(a); **~ cream** crema protectora; **~ custody** *(LAW)* detención *f* preventiva.

protector [prətek'tûr] *n* protector(a) *m/f*.

protégé [prō'təzhā'] *n* protegido/a.

protein [prō'tēn] *n* proteína.

pro tem [prō tem] *ad abbr* (= *pro tempore*: *for the time being*) provisionalmente.

protest *n* [prō'test] protesta ♦ *(vb:* [prōtest']) *vi* protestar ♦ *vt* *(affirm)* afirmar, declarar; **to do sth under ~** hacer algo bajo protesta; **to ~ against/about** protestar en contra de/por.

Protestant [prát'istənt] *a, n* protestante *m/f*.

protester, protestor [prətes'tûr] *n* *(in demonstration)* manifestante *m/f*.

protest march *n* manifestación *f or* marcha (de protesta).

protocol [prō'təkól] *n* protocolo.

prototype [prō'tətip] *n* prototipo.

protracted [prōtrak'tid] *a* prolongado.

protractor [prōtrak'tûr] *n* *(GEOM)* transportador *m*.

protrude [prōtrōōd'] *vi* salir, sobresalir.

protuberance [prōtōō'bûrəns] *n* protuberancia.

proud [proud] *a* orgulloso; *(pej)* soberbio,

altanero ♦ *ad*: **to do sb** ~ tratar a uno a cuerpo de rey; **to do o.s.** ~ no privarse de nada; **to be** ~ **to do sth** estar orgulloso de hacer algo.

proudly [proud'lē] *ad* orgullosamente, con orgullo; (*pej*) con soberbia, con altanería.

prove [pro̅o̅v] *vt* probar; (*verify*) comprobar; (*show*) demostrar ♦ *vi*: **to** ~ **correct** resultar correcto; **to** ~ **o.s.** ponerse a prueba; **he was** ~**d right in the end** al final *or* por fin se le dio la razón.

proverb [prâv'ûrb] *n* refrán *m*.

proverbial [prəvûr'bēəl] *a* proverbial.

proverbially [prəvûr'bēəlē] *ad* proverbialmente.

provide [prəvīd'] *vt* proporcionar, dar; **to** ~ **sb with sth** proveer a uno de algo; **to be** ~**d with** ser provisto de.

provide for *vt fus* (*person*) mantener a; (*problem etc*) tener en cuenta.

provided [prəvī'did] *conj*: ~ (**that**) con tal de que, a condición de que.

Providence [prâv'idəns] *n* Divina Providencia.

providing [prəvī'ding] *conj* a condición de que, con tal de que.

province [prâv'ins] *n* provincia; (*fig*) esfera.

provincial [prəvin'chəl] *a* provincial; (*pej*) provinciano.

provision [prəvizh'ən] *n* provisión *f*; (*supply*) suministro, abastecimiento; ~**s** *npl* provisiones *fpl*, víveres *mpl*; **to make** ~ **for** (*one's family, future*) atender las necesidades de.

provisional [prəvizh'ənəl] *a* provisional; (*temporary*) interino ♦ *n*: **P**~ (*Irish POL*) Provisional *m* (*miembro de la tendencia activista del IRA*).

provisional licence *n* (*Brit AUT*) carnet *m* (de conducir) provisional.

proviso [prəvī'zō] *n* condición *f*, estipulación *f*; **with the** ~ **that** a condición de que.

Provo [prō'vō] *n abbr* (*Irish POL*) = **Provisional**.

provocation [prâvəkā'shən] *n* provocación *f*.

provocative [prəvâk'ətiv] *a* provocativo.

provoke [prəvōk'] *vt* (*arouse*) provocar, incitar; (*cause*) causar, producir; (*anger*) enojar; **to** ~ **sb to sth/to do** *or* **into doing sth** provocar a uno a algo/a hacer algo.

provoking [prəvōk'ing] *a* provocador(a).

provost [prâv'əst] *n* (*of university*) rector(a) *m/f*; (*Scottish*) alcalde(sa) *m/f*.

prow [prou] *n* proa.

prowess [prou'is] *n* (*skill*) destreza, habilidad *f*; (*courage*) valor *m*; **his** ~ **as a football player** (*skill*) su habilidad como futbolista.

prowl [proul] *vi* (*also*: ~ **about,** ~ **around**) merodear ♦ *n*: **on the** ~ de merodeo, merodeando.

prowler [prou'lûr] *n* merodeador(a) *m/f*.

proximity [prâksim'itē] *n* proximidad *f*.

proxy [prâk'sē] *n* poder *m*; (*person*) apoderado/a; **by** ~ por poderes.

prude [proȯod] *n* gazmoño/a, mojigato/a.

prudence [proȯo'dəns] *n* prudencia.

prudent [proȯo'dənt] *a* prudente.

prudently [proȯo'dəntlē] *ad* prudentemente, con prudencia.

prudish [proȯo'dish] *a* gazmoño.

prudishness [proȯo'dishnis] *n* gazmoñería, ñoñería.

prune [proȯon] *n* ciruela pasa ♦ *vt* podar.

pruning shears [proȯon'ing shirz] *npl* podadera *sg*.

pry [prī] *vi*: **to** ~ **into** entrometerse en.

PS *abbr* (= *postscript*) P.D.

psalm [sâm] *n* salmo.

PSAT *n abbr* (*US*) = *Preliminary Scholastic Aptitude Test*.

pseudo... [soȯo'dō] *pref* seudo....

pseudonym [soȯo'dənim] *n* seudónimo.

PST *n abbr* (*US*: = *Pacific Standard Time*) hora de invierno del Pacífico.

psyche [sī'kē] *n* psique *f*.

psychiatric [sīkēat'rik] *a* psiquiátrico.

psychiatrist [siki'ətrist] *n* psiquiatra *m/f*.

psychiatry [siki'ətrē] *n* psiquiatría.

psychic [sī'kik] *a* (*also*: ~**al**) psíquico.

psychoanalyze [sīkōan'əlīz] *vt* psicoanalizar.

psychoanalysis, *pl* **psychoanalyses** [sīkōanal'isis, -sēz] *n* psicoanálisis *m inv*.

psychoanalyst [sīkōan'əlist] *n* psicoanalista *m/f*.

psychological [sīkəlâj'ikəl] *a* psicológico.

psychologically [sīkəlâj'iklē] *ad* psicológicamente.

psychologist [sīkâl'əjist] *n* psicólogo/a.

psychology [sīkâl'əjē] *n* psicología.

psychopath [sī'kəpath] *n* psicópata *m/f*.

psychosis, *pl* **psychoses** [sīkō'sis, -sēz] *n* psicosis *f inv*.

psychosomatic [sīkōsōmat'ik] *a* psicosomático.

psychotherapy [sīkōthär'əpē] *n* psicoterapia.

psychotic [sīkât'ik] *a, n* psicótico/a.

PT *n abbr* (*Brit*: = *Physical Training*) Ed. Fís.

pt *abbr* = **pint(s), point(s)**.

PTA *n abbr* = *Parent-Teacher Association* ≈ Asociación *f* de Padres de Alumnos.

PTO *abbr* (= *please turn over*) sigue.

PTV *n abbr* (*US*) = *pay television, public television*.

pub [pub] *n* (*Brit*) pub *m*, taberna.

puberty [pyoȯo'bûrtē] *n* pubertad *f*.

pubic [pyoȯo'bik] *a* púbico.

public [pub'lik] *a, n* público; **in** ~ en público; **to make sth** ~ revelar *or* anunciar algo; **to be** ~ **knowledge** ser del dominio público; **to go** ~ (*COMM*) proceder a la venta pública de acciones.

public address system (PA) n megafonía, sistema m de altavoces.

publican [pub'likən] n (Brit) tabernero/a.

publication [publikā'shən] n publicación f.

public company n sociedad f anónima.

public convenience n (Brit) aseos mpl públicos, sanitarios mpl (LAm).

public holiday n (Brit) día m de fiesta, (día) feriado (LAm).

public house n (Brit) bar m, pub m.

public housing unit (US) n vivienda municipal de alquiler.

publicity [publis'ətē] n publicidad f.

publicize [pub'ləsiz] vt publicitar; (advertise) hacer propaganda para.

public limited company (plc) n sociedad f anónima (S.A.).

publicly [pub'liklē] ad públicamente, en público.

public opinion n opinión f pública.

public ownership n propiedad f pública; **to be taken into** ~ ser nacionalizado.

Public Prosecutor n Fiscal m del Estado.

public relations (PR) n relaciones fpl públicas.

public relations officer n encargado/a de relaciones públicas.

public school n (US) escuela pública; (Brit) colegio privado.

public sector n sector m público.

public service vehicle n (Brit) vehículo de servicio público.

public-spirited [pub'likspir'itid] a cívico.

public transport n (Brit) = **public transportation**.

public transportation n (US) transporte m público.

public utility n servicio público.

public works npl obras fpl públicas.

publish [pub'lish] vt publicar.

publisher [pub'lishûr] n (person) editor(a) m/f; (firm) editorial f.

publishing [pub'lishing] n (industry) industria del libro.

publishing company n (casa) editorial f.

puce [pyōōs] a de color pardo rojizo.

puck [puk] n (ICE HOCKEY) puck m.

pucker [puk'ûr] vt (pleat) arrugar; (brow etc) fruncir.

pudding [pōōd'ing] n pudín m; **rice** ~ arroz m con leche.

puddle [pud'əl] n charco.

pudgy [puj'ē] a gordinflón/ona.

puerile [pyōō'ûrəl] a pueril.

Puerto Rican [pwär'tō rē'kən] a, n puertorriqueño/a m/f.

Puerto Rico [pwär'tō rē'kō] n Puerto Rico.

puff [puf] n soplo; (of smoke) bocanada; (of breathing, engine) resoplido; (powder ~) borla ♦ vt: **to** ~ **one's pipe** dar chupadas a la pipa; (also: ~ **out**: sails, cheeks) hinchar, inflar (LAm) ♦ vi (gen) soplar; (pant) jadear; **to** ~ **out smoke** echar humo.

puffed [puft] a (col: out of breath) sin aliento.

puffin [puf'in] n frailecillo.

puff paste, (Brit) **puff pastry** n hojaldre m.

puffy [puf'ē] a hinchado.

pull [pōōl] n (tug): **to give sth a** ~ dar un tirón a algo; (fig: advantage) ventaja; (: influence) influencia ♦ vt tirar de; (haul) tirar, arrastrar; (strain): **to** ~ **a muscle** sufrir un tirón ♦ vi tirar; **to** ~ **to pieces** hacer pedazos; **to** ~ **one's punches** andarse con rodeos; **to** ~ **one's weight** hacer su parte; **to** ~ **o.s. together** tranquilizarse; **to** ~ **sb's leg** tomar el pelo a uno; **to** ~ **strings (for sb)** enchufar (a uno).

pull apart vt (take apart) desmontar.

pull around vt (handle roughly: object) manosear; (: person) maltratar.

pull down vt (house) derribar.

pull in vi (AUT: at the curb) parar (junto a la acera); (RAIL) llegar.

pull off vt (deal etc) cerrar.

pull out vi irse, marcharse; (AUT: from curb) salir ♦ vt sacar, arrancar.

pull over vi (AUT) hacerse a un lado.

pull through vi salvarse; (MED) recobrar la salud.

pull up vi (stop) parar ♦ vt (uproot) arrancar, desarraigar; (stop) parar.

pulley [pōōl'ē] n polea.

Pullman [pōōl'mən] n (US) litera.

pull-out [pōōl'out] n suplemento ♦ cpd (pages, magazine) separable.

pullover [pōōl'ōvûr] n jersey m, suéter m.

pulp [pulp] n (of fruit) pulpa; (for paper) pasta; (pej: also: ~ **magazines** etc) prensa amarilla; **to reduce sth to** ~ hacer algo papilla.

pulpit [pōōl'pit] n púlpito.

pulsate [pul'sāt] vi pulsar, latir.

pulse [puls] n (ANAT) pulso; (of music, engine) pulsación f; (BOT) legumbre f; **to feel** or **take sb's** ~ tomar el pulso a uno.

pulverize [pul'vəriz] vt pulverizar; (fig) hacer polvo.

puma [pyōō'mə] n puma.

pumice (stone) [pum'is (stōn)] n piedra pómez.

pummel [pum'əl] vt aporrear.

pump [pump] n bomba; (shoe) zapato de tenis ♦ vt sacar con una bomba; (fig: col) (son)sacar; **to** ~ **sb for information** (son)sacarle informes a uno.

pump up vt inflar.

pumpkin [pump'kin] n calabaza.

pun [pun] n juego de palabras.

punch [punch] n (blow) golpe m, puñetazo; (tool) punzón m; (for paper) perforadora; (for tickets) taladro; (drink) ponche m ♦ vt (hit): **to** ~ **sb/sth** dar un puñetazo or golpear a uno/algo; (make a hole in) punzar; perforar.

punch in *vi* (*US*) fichar, picar.

punch out *vi* (*US*) fichar *or* picar la salida.

punch-drunk |punch'drungk| *a* grogui, sonado.

punch(ed) card *n* tarjeta perforada.

punch line *n* (*of joke*) remate *m*.

punch-up |punch'up| *n* (*Brit col*) riña.

punctual |pungk'chōōəl| *a* puntual.

punctuality |pungkchōōal'itē| *n* puntualidad *f.*

punctually |pungk'chōōəlē| *ad*: **it will start ~ at 6** empezará a las 6 en punto.

punctuate |pungk'chōōāt| *vt* puntuar; (*fig*) interrumpir.

punctuation |pungkchōōā'shən| *n* puntuación *f.*

punctuation mark *n* signo de puntuación.

puncture |pungk'chûr| *n* pinchazo ♦ *vt* pinchar; **to have a ~** tener un pinchazo.

pundit |pun'dit| *n* experto/a.

pungent |pun'jənt| *a* acre.

punish |pun'ish| *vt* castigar; **to ~ sb for sth/for doing sth** castigar a uno por algo/ por haber hecho algo.

punishable |pun'ishəbəl| *a* punible, castigable.

punishing |pun'ishing| *a* (*fig: exhausting*) agotador(a).

punishment |pun'ishmənt| *n* castigo; (*fig, col*): **to take a lot of ~** (*boxer*) recibir una paliza; (*car*) ser maltratado.

punitive |pyōō'nətiv| *a* punitivo.

punk |pungk| *n* (*also*: **~ rocker**) punki *m/f*; (*also*: **~ rock**) música punk; (*US col*: *hoodlum*) matón *m*.

punt |punt| *n* (*boat*) batea.

puny |pyōō'nē| *a* débil.

pup |pup| *n* cachorro.

pupil |pyōō'pəl| *n* alumno/a.

puppet |pup'it| *n* títere *m*.

puppet government *n* gobierno títere.

puppy |pup'ē| *n* cachorro, perrito.

purchase |pûr'chis| *n* compra; (*grip*) agarre *m*, asidero ♦ *vt* comprar.

purchase order *n* decreto de compra.

purchase price *n* precio de compra.

purchaser |pûr'chisûr| *n* comprador(a) *m/f*.

purchasing power |pûr'chising pouûr| *n* poder *m* adquisitivo.

pure |pyōōr| *a* puro; **a ~ wool jumper** un jersey de pura lana; **it's laziness, ~ and simple** es pura vagancia.

purebred |pyōōr'bred'| *a* de pura sangre.

purée |pyōōrā'| *n* puré *m*.

purely |pyōōr'lē| *ad* puramente.

purgatory |pûr'gətôrē| *n* purgatorio.

purge |pûrj| *n* (*MED, POL*) purga ♦ *vt* purgar.

purification |pyōōrəfəkā'shən| *n* purificación *f*, depuración *f.*

purify |pyōōr'əfi| *vt* purificar, depurar.

purist |pyōōr'ist| *n* purista *m/f*.

puritan |pyōōr'itən| *n* puritano/a.

puritanical |pyōōritan'ikəl| *a* puritano.

purity |pyōōr'itē| *n* pureza.

purl |pûrl| *n* punto del revés.

purloin |pûrloin'| *vt* hurtar, robar.

purple |pûr'pəl| *a* purpúreo, morado.

purport |pərpôrt'| *vi*: **to ~ to be/do** dar a entender que es/hace.

purpose |pûr'pəs| *n* propósito; **on ~** a propósito, adrede; **to no ~** para nada, en vano; **for teaching ~s** con fines pedagógicos; **for the ~s of this meeting** para los fines de esta reunión.

purpose-built |pûr'pəsbilt'| *a* (*Brit*) construido especialmente.

purposeful |pûr'pəsfəl| *a* resuelto, determinado.

purposely |pûr'pəslē| *ad* a propósito, adrede.

purr |pûr| *n* ronroneo ♦ *vi* ronronear.

purse |pûrs| *n* (*US*) bolso; (*Brit*) monedero; ♦ *vt* fruncir.

purser |pûr'sûr| *n* (*NAUT*) comisario/a.

purse snatcher |pûrs snach'ûr| *n* (*US*) tironista *m/f*.

pursue |pûrsōō'| *vt* seguir; (*harass*) perseguir; (*profession*) ejercer; (*pleasures*) buscar; (*inquiry, matter*) seguir.

pursuer |pûrsōō'ûr| *n* perseguidor(a) *m/f*.

pursuit |pûrsōōt'| *n* (*chase*) caza; (*of pleasure etc*) busca; (*occupation*) actividad *f*; **in (the) ~ of sth** en busca de algo.

purveyor |pûrvā'ûr| *n* proveedor(a) *m/f*.

pus |pus| *n* pus *m*.

push |pōōsh| *n* empuje *m*, empujón *m*; (*MIL*) ataque *m*; (*drive*) empuje *m* ♦ *vt* empujar; (*button*) apretar; (*promote*) promover; (*fig: press, advance: views*) avanzar; (*thrust*): **to ~ sth (into)** meter algo a la fuerza (en) ♦ *vi* empujar; (*fig*) hacer esfuerzos; **at a ~** (*col*) a duras penas; **she is ~ing 50** (*col*) raya en los 50; **to be ~ed for time/money** andar justo de tiempo/escaso de dinero; **to ~ a door open/shut** abrir/cerrar una puerta empujándola; **to ~ for** (*better pay, conditions*) reivindicar; "**~**" (*on door*) "empujar"; (*on bell*) "pulse".

push aside *vt* apartar con la mano.

push in *vi* colarse.

push off *vi* (*col*) largarse.

push on *vi* (*continue*) seguir adelante.

push through *vt* (*measure*) despachar.

push up *vt* (*total, prices*) hacer subir.

push-button |pōōsh'butən| *a* de mando de botón.

pushchair |pōōsh'chär| *n* (*Brit*) sillita de ruedas.

pusher |pōōsh'ûr| *n* (*drug ~*) traficante *m/f* de drogas.

pushover |pōōsh'ōvûr| *n* (*col*): **it's a ~** está tirado.

push-up [pŏŏsh'up] *n* plancha.
pushy [pŏŏsh'ē] *a* (*pej*) agresivo.
pussycat [pŏŏs'ĕkat] *n* minino.
put [pŏŏt], *pt, pp* **put** *vt* (*place*) poner, colocar; (~ *into*) meter; (*express, say*) expresar; (*a question*) hacer; (*estimate*) calcular; (*cause to be*): **to ~ sb in a good/bad mood** poner a uno de buen/mal humor; **to ~ a lot of time into sth** dedicar mucho tiempo a algo; **to ~ money on a horse** jugarse dinero a un caballo; **to ~ money into a company** invertir dinero en una compañía; **to ~ sb to a lot of trouble** causar mucha molestia a uno; **we ~ the children to bed** acostamos a los niños; **how shall I ~ it?** ¿cómo puedo explicarlo *or* decirlo?; **to stay ~** no moverse.
put about *vi* (*NAUT*) virar ♦ *vt* (*rumor*) diseminar.
put across *vt* (*ideas etc*) comunicar.
put aside *vt* (*lay down: book etc*) dejar *or* poner a un lado; (*save*) ahorrar; (*in store*) guardar.
put away *vt* (*store*) guardar.
put back *vt* (*replace*) devolver a su lugar; (*postpone*) posponer; (*set back: watch, clock*) retrasar; **this will ~ us back 10 years** esto nos retrasará 10 años.
put down *vt* (*on ground*) poner en el suelo; (*in writing*) apuntar; (*suppress: revolt etc*) sofocar; (*attribute*) atribuir; **~ me down for $15** apúntame por 15 dólares.
put forward *vt* (*ideas*) presentar, proponer; (*date*) adelantar.
put in *vt* (*application, complaint*) presentar.
put in for *vt fus* (*job*) solicitar; (*promotion*) pedir.
put off *vt* (*postpone*) aplazar; (*discourage*) desanimar.
put on *vt* (*clothes, lipstick etc*) ponerse; (*light etc*) encender; (*play etc*) presentar; (*weight*) ganar; (*brake*) echar; (*assume: accent, manner*) afectar, fingir; (*airs*) adoptar, darse; (*concert, exhibition etc*) montar; (*extra bus, train etc*) poner; (*col: kid: esp US*) tomar el pelo a; (*inform, indicate*): **to ~ sb on to sb/sth** informar a uno de algo/algo.
put out *vt* (*fire, light*) apagar; (*one's hand*) alargar; (*news, rumor*) hacer circular; (*tongue etc*) sacar; (*person: inconvenience*) molestar, fastidiar; (*dislocate: shoulder, vertebra, knee*) dislocar(se) ♦ *vi* (*NAUT*): **to ~ out to sea** hacerse a la mar; **to ~ out from New York** salir de Nueva York.
put through *vt* (*call*) poner; **~ me through to Miss Blair** póngame *or* comuníqueme con (*LAm*) la Señorita Blair.
put together *vt* unir, reunir; (*assemble: furniture*) armar, montar; (*meal*) confeccionar.

put up *vt* (*raise*) levantar, alzar; (*hang*) colgar; (*build*) construir; (*increase*) aumentar; (*accommodate*) alojar; (*incite*): **to ~ sb up to doing sth** instar *or* incitar a uno a hacer algo; **to ~ sth up for sale** exponer algo a la venta.
put upon *vt fus*: **to be ~ upon** (*imposed upon*) dejarse explotar.
put up with *vt fus* aguantar.
putrid [pyŏŏ'trid] *a* podrido.
putsch [pŏŏch] *n* golpe *m* de estado.
putt [put] *vt* hacer un putt ♦ *n* putt *m*, golpe *m* corto.
putter [put'ûr] *n* putter *m* ♦ *vi* (*US*): **to ~ around** ocuparse en fruslerías; **to ~ around the house** ir de aquí para allá sin hacer nada de provecho.
putting green [put'ing grēn] *n* green *m*, minigolf *m*.
putty [put'ē] *n* masilla.
put-up [pŏŏt'up] *a*: **~ job** (*Brit*) estafa.
puzzle [puz'əl] *n* (*riddle*) acertijo; (*jigsaw*) rompecabezas *m inv*; (*also:* **crossword ~**) crucigrama *m*; (*mystery*) misterio ♦ *vt* dejar perplejo, confundir ♦ *vi*: **to ~ about** quebrar la cabeza por; **to ~ over** (*sb's actions*) quebrarse la cabeza por; (*mystery, problem*) devanarse los sesos sobre; **to be ~d about sth** no llegar a entender algo.
puzzling [puz'ling] *a* (*question*) misterioso, extraño; (*attitude, set of instructions*) extraño.
PVC *n abbr* (= *polyvinyl chloride*) P.V.C. *m*.
PVS *n abbr* (= *post-viral syndrome*) síndrome *m* post-vírico.
Pvt. *abbr* (*US MIL*) = **private.**
PW *n abbr* (*US*) = **prisoner of war.**
pw *abbr* (= *per week*) por semana.
PX *n abbr* (*US:* = *post exchange*) economato militar.
pygmy [pig'mē] *n* pigmeo/a.
pyjamas [pəjâm'əz] *npl* (*Brit*) = **pajamas.**
pylon [pī'lân] *n* torre *f* de conducción eléctrica.
pyramid [pir'əmid] *n* pirámide *f*.
Pyrenean [pirənē'ən] *a* pirenaico.
Pyrenees [pir'ənēz] *npl*: **the ~** los Pirineos.
python [pī'thân] *n* pitón *m*.

Q

Q, q [kyŏŏ] *n* (*letter*) Q, q *f*; **Q for Queen** Q de Quebec.
Qatar [kətâr'] *n* Qatar *m*.
QC *n abbr* (= *Queen's Council*) título conce-

dido a determinados abogados.

QED *abbr* (= *quod erat demonstrandum*) Q.E.D.

QM *n abbr* = **quartermaster**.

q.t. *n abbr* (*col*: = *quiet*): **on the** ~ a hurtadillas.

qty *abbr* (= *quantity*) ctdad.

quack [kwak] *n* (*of duck*) graznido; (*pej*: *doctor*) curandero/a, matasanos *m inv* ♦ *vi* graznar.

quad [kwåd] *abbr* = **quadrangle, quadruple, quadruplet**.

quadrangle [kwåd'ranggəl] *n* (*courtyard*: *abbr*: **quad**) patio.

quadruple [kwådrōō'pəl] *vt, vi* cuadruplicar.

quadruplet [kwådru'plit] *n* cuatrillizo.

quagmire [kwag'mīūr] *n* lodazal *m*, cenegal *m*.

quail [kwāl] *n* (*bird*) codorniz *f* ♦ *vi* amedrentarse.

quaint [kwānt] *a* extraño; (*picturesque*) pintoresco.

quaintly [kwānt'lē] *ad* extrañamente; pintorescamente.

quaintness [kwānt'nis] *n* lo pintoresco, tipismo.

quake [kwāk] *vi* temblar ♦ *n abbr* = **earthquake**.

Quaker [kwā'kûr] *n* cuáquero/a.

qualification [kwåləfəkā'shən] *n* (*reservation*) reserva; (*modification*) modificación *f*; (*act*) calificación *f*; (*paper* ~) título; **what are your ~s?** ¿qué títulos tienes?

qualified [kwål'əfīd] *a* (*trained*) cualificado; (*fit*) capacitado; (*limited*) limitado; (*professionally*) titulado; ~ **for/to do sth** capacitado para/para hacer algo; **he's not** ~ **for the job** no está capacitado para ese trabajo; **it was a** ~ **success** fue un éxito relativo.

qualify [kwål'əfī] *vt* (*LING*) calificar a; (*capacitate*) capacitar; (*modify*) modificar; (*limit*) moderar ♦ *vi* (*SPORT*) clasificarse; **to** ~ (**as**) calificarse (de), graduarse (en); **to** ~ (**for**) reunir los requisitos (para); **to** ~ **as an engineer** sacar el título de ingeniero.

qualifying [kwål'əfīing] *a* (*exam, round*) eliminatorio.

qualitative [kwål'itātiv] *a* cualitativo.

quality [kwål'itē] *n* calidad *f*; (*moral*) cualidad *f*; **of good/poor** ~ de buena *or* alta/ poca calidad.

quality control *n* control *m* de calidad.

qualm [kwåm] *n* escrúpulo; **to have ~s about sth** sentir escrúpulos por algo.

quandary [kwán'drē] *n*: **to be in a** ~ tener dudas.

quantitative [kwån'titātiv] *a* cuantitativo.

quantity [kwån'titē] *n* cantidad *f*; **in** ~ en grandes cantidades.

quarantine [kwôr'əntēn] *n* cuarentena.

quarrel [kwôr'əl] *n* riña, pelea ♦ *vi* reñir, pelearse; **to have a** ~ **with sb** reñir *or* pelearse con uno; **I can't** ~ **with that** no le encuentro pegas.

quarrelsome [kwôr'əlsəm] *a* pendenciero.

quarry [kwôr'ē] *n* (*for stone*) cantera; (*animal*) presa.

quart [kwôrt] *n cuarto de galón* = *1.136 l.*

quarter [kwôr'tûr] *n* cuarto, cuarta parte *f*; (*of year*) trimestre *m*; (*district*) barrio; (*US, Canada*: 25 *cents*) cuarto de dólar ♦ *vt* dividir en cuartos; (*MIL*: *lodge*) alojar; ~**s** *npl* (*barracks*) cuartel *m*; (*living* ~**s**) alojamiento *sg*; **a** ~ **of an hour** un cuarto de hora, **to pay by the** ~ pagar trimestralmente *or* cada 3 meses; **it's a** ~ **of** *or* (*Brit*) **to 3** son las 3 menos cuarto; **it's a** ~ **after** *or* (*Brit*) **past 3** son las 3 y cuarto; **from all** ~**s** de todas partes; **at close** ~**s** de cerca.

quarter-deck [kwôr'tûrdek] *n* (*NAUT*) alcázar *m*.

quarter final *n* cuarto de final.

quarterly [kwôr'tûrlē] *a* trimestral ♦ *ad* cada 3 meses, trimestralmente.

quartermaster [kwôr'tûrmastûr] *n* (*MIL*) comisario, intendente *m* militar.

quarter note *n* (*US MUS*) negra.

quartet(te) [kwôrtet'] *n* cuarteto.

quarto [kwôr'tō] *n* tamaño holandés ♦ *a* de tamaño holandés.

quartz [kwôrts] *n* cuarzo.

quash [kwásh] *vt* (*verdict*) anular.

quasi- [kwā'zī] *pref* cuasi.

quaver [kwā'vûr] *n* (*Brit MUS*) corchea ♦ *vi* temblar.

quay [kē] *n* (*also*: ~**side**) muelle *m*.

Que. *abbr* (*Canada*) = *Quebec*.

queasiness [kwē'zēnis] *n* malestar *m*, náuseas *fpl*.

queasy [kwē'zē] *a*: **to feel** ~ tener náuseas.

Quebec [kwibek'] *n* Quebec *m*.

queen [kwēn] *n* reina; (*CARDS etc*) dama.

queen mother *n* reina madre.

queer [kwēr] *a* (*odd*) raro, extraño ♦ *n* (*pej*: *col*) maricón *m*.

quell [kwel] *vt* calmar; (*put down*) sofocar.

quench [kwench] *vt* (*flames*) apagar; **to** ~ **one's thirst** apagar la sed.

querulous [kwär'ələs] *a* (*person, voice*) quejumbroso.

query [kwiûr'ē] *n* (*question*) pregunta; (*doubt*) duda ♦ *vt* preguntar; (*disagree with, dispute*) no estar conforme con, dudar de.

quest [kwest] *n* busca, búsqueda.

question [kwes'chən] *n* pregunta; (*matter*) asunto, cuestión *f* ♦ *vt* (*doubt*) dudar de; (*interrogate*) interrogar, hacer preguntas a; **to ask sb a** ~, **put a** ~ **to sb** hacerle una pregunta a uno; **the** ~ **is** ... el asunto es ...; **to bring** *or* **call sth into** ~ poner algo en (tela de) duda; **beyond** ~ fuera de toda duda; **it's out of the** ~ imposible, ni hablar.

questionable [kwes'chənəbəl] *a* discutible; (*doubtful*) dudoso.

questioner [kwes'chənûr] *n* interrogador(a) *m/f.*

questioning [kwes'chəning] *a* interrogativo ♦ *n* preguntas *fpl;* (*by police etc*) interrogatorio.

question mark *n* punto de interrogación.

questionnaire [kweschənär'] *n* cuestionario.

queue [kyōō] *n* cola ♦ *vi* hacer cola; **to jump the** ~ salirse de su turno, colarse.

quibble [kwib'əl] *vi* sutilizar.

quick [kwik] *a* rápido; (*temper*) vivo; (*agile*) ágil; (*mind*) listo; (*eye*) agudo; (*ear*) fino ♦ *n*: **cut to the** ~ (*fig*) herido en lo vivo; **be** ~! ¡date prisa!; **to be** ~ **to act** obrar con prontitud; **she was** ~ **to see that** se dio cuenta de eso en seguida.

quicken [kwik'ən] *vt* apresurar ♦ *vi* apresurarse, darse prisa.

quickly [kwik'lē] *ad* rápidamente, de prisa; **we must act** ~ tenemos que actuar cuanto antes.

quickness [kwik'nis] *n* rapidez *f*; (*of temper*) viveza; (*agility*) agilidad *f*; (*of mind, eye etc*) agudeza.

quicksand [kwik'sand] *n* arenas *fpl* movedizas.

quickstep [kwik'step] *n* baile de ritmo rápido.

quick-tempered [kwik'tempúrd] *a* de genio vivo.

quick-witted [kwik'wit'id] *a* listo, despabilado.

quid [kwid] *n, pl inv* (*Brit col*) libra.

quid pro quo [kwid' prō kwō'] *n* quid pro quo *m*, compensación *f*.

quiet [kwī'it] *a* (*not busy: day*) tranquilo; (*silent*) callado; (*reserved*) reservado; (*discreet*) discreto; (*not noisy: engine*) silencioso ♦ *n* silencio, tranquilidad *f* ♦ *vb* (*US: also* ~ **down**) *vi* (*grow calm*) calmarse; (*grow silent*) callarse ♦ *vt* calmar; hacer callar; **keep** ~! ¡cállate!, ¡silencio!; **business is** ~ **at this time of year** hay poco movimiento en esta época.

quieten [kwī'itən] (*Brit: also* ~ **down**) *vi, vt* = **quiet**.

quietly [kwī'itlē] *ad* tranquilamente; (*silently*) silenciosamente.

quietness [kwī'itnis] *n* (*silence*) silencio; (*calm*) tranquilidad *f*.

quill [kwil] *n* (*of porcupine*) púa; (*pen*) pluma.

quilt [kwilt] *n* (*Brit*) edredón *m*.

quilting [kwil'ting] *n* acolchado, guateado.

quin [kwin] *n abbr* = **quintuplet**.

quince [kwins] *n* membrillo.

quinine [kwī'nīn] *n* quinina.

quintet(te) [kwintet'] *n* quinteto.

quintuplet [kwintu'plit] *n* quintillizo.

quip [kwip] *n* ocurrencia ♦ *vi* decir sarcásticamente.

quire [kwīûr] *n* mano *f* de papel.

quirk [kwûrk] *n* peculiaridad *f*; **by some** ~ **of fate** por algún capricho del destino.

quit [kwit], *pt, pp* **quit** *or* **quitted** [kwit] *vt* dejar, abandonar; (*premises*) desocupar; (*COMPUT*) abandonar ♦ *vi* (*give up*) renunciar; (*go away*) irse; (*resign*) dimitir; ~ **stalling!** (*US col*) ¡déjate de evasivas!

quite [kwit] *ad* (*rather*) bastante; (*entirely*) completamente; ~ **a few of them** un buen número de ellos; ~ (**so**)! ¡así es!, ¡exactamente!; ~ **new** completamente nuevo; **that's not** ~ **right** eso no está del todo bien; **not** ~ **as many as last time** no tantos como la última vez; **she's** ~ **pretty** es bastante guapa.

Quito [kē'tō] *n* Quito.

quits [kwits] *a*: ~ (**with**) en paz (con); **let's call it** ~ dejémoslo en tablas.

quiver [kwiv'ûr] *vi* estremecerse ♦ *n* (*for arrows*) carcaj *m*.

quiz [kwiz] *n* (*game*) concurso; (: *TV, RADIO*) programa-concurso; (*questioning*) interrogatorio ♦ *vt* interrogar.

quizzical [kwiz'ikəl] *a* burlón(ona).

quoits [kwoits] *npl* juego de aros.

quorum [kwôr'əm] *n* quórum *m*.

quota [kwō'tə] *n* cuota.

quotation [kwōtā'shən] *n* cita; (*estimate*) presupuesto.

quotation marks *npl* comillas *fpl*.

quote [kwōt] *n* cita ♦ *vt* (*sentence*) citar; (*COMM: sum, figure*) cotizar ♦ *vi*: **to** ~ **from** citar de; ~**s** *npl* (*inverted commas*) comillas *fpl*; **in** ~**s** entre comillas; **the figure** ~**d for the repairs** la cifra estimada por las reparaciones; ~ ... **unquote** (*in dictation*) comillas iniciales ... finales.

quotient [kwō'shənt] *n* cociente *m*.

qv *n abbr* (= *quod vide: which see*) q.v.

qwerty keyboard [kwûr'tē kē'bôrd] *n* (*Brit*) teclado QWERTY.

R

R, r [ár] *n* (*letter*) R, r *f;* **R for Roger** R de Ramón.

R *abbr* (= *right*) dcha.; (= *river*) R.; (= *Réaumur (scale)*) R; (*US CINEMA:* = *restricted*) sólo mayores; (*US POL*) = **republican**; (*Brit:* = *Rex, Regina*) R.

RA *abbr* = *rear admiral*.

RAAF *n abbr* = *Royal Australian Air Force*.

Rabat [räbát'] n Rabat m.
rabbi [rab'ī] n rabino.
rabbit [rab'it] n conejo.
rabbit hutch n conejera.
rabble [rab'əl] n (pej) chusma, populacho.
rabies [rä'bēz] n rabia.
RAC n abbr (Brit: = Royal Automobile Club) ≈ RACE m (Sp).
raccoon [rakōōn'] n mapache m.
race [räs] n carrera; (species) raza ♦ vt (horse) hacer correr; (person) competir contra; (engine) acelerar ♦ vi (compete) competir; (run) correr; (pulse) latir a ritmo acelerado; **the arms** ~ la carrera armamentista; **the human** ~ el género humano; **he** ~**d across the road** cruzó corriendo la carretera; **to** ~ **in/out** entrar/salir corriendo.
race car n (US) coche m de carreras.
race car driver n (US) corredor(a) m/f de coches.
racecourse [räs'kôrs] n hipódromo.
racehorse [räs'hôrs] n caballo de carreras.
race meeting n concurso hípico.
race relations npl relaciones fpl entre las razas.
racetrack [räs'trak] n hipódromo; (for cars) autódromo.
racial [rä'shəl] a racial.
racial discrimination n discriminación f racial.
racial integration n integración f racial.
racialism [rä'shəlizəm] n racismo.
racialist [rä'shəlist] a, n racista m/f.
racing [rä'sing] n carreras fpl.
racing car n (Brit) = **race car**.
racing driver n (Brit) = **race car driver**.
racism [rä'sizəm] n racismo.
racist [rä'sist] a, n racista m/f.
rack [rak] n (also: **luggage** ~) rejilla; (shelf) estante m; (also: **roof** ~) baca, portaequipajes m inv; (clothes ~) percha ♦ vt (cause pain to) atormentar; **to go to** ~ **and ruin** (building) echarse a perder, venirse abajo; (business) arruinarse; **to** ~ **one's brains** devanarse los sesos.
rack up vt conseguir, ganar.
rack-and-pinion [rak'əndpin'yən] n (TECH) cremallera y piñón.
racket [rak'it] n (for tennis) raqueta; (noise) ruido, estrépito; (swindle) estafa, timo.
racketeer [rakitēr'] n (esp US) estafador(a) m/f.
racoon [rakōōn'] n = **raccoon**.
racquet [rak'it] n raqueta.
racy [rä'sē] a picante, salado.
radar [rä'dâr] n radar m.
radar trap n trampa radar.
radial [rä'dēəl] a (tire: also: ~**-ply**) radial.
radiance [rä'dēəns] n brillantez f, resplandor m.
radiant [rä'dēənt] a brillante, resplande-

ciente.
radiate [rä'dēāt] vt (heat) radiar, irradiar ♦ vi (lines) extenderse.
radiation [rädēā'shən] n radiación f.
radiation sickness n enfermedad f de radiación.
radiator [rä'dēātûr] n (AUT) radiador m.
radiator cap n tapón m de radiador.
radiator grill n (AUT) rejilla del radiador.
radical [rad'ikəl] a radical.
radically ad radicalmente.
radii [rä'dēī] npl of **radius**.
radio [rä'dēō] n radio f ♦ vi: **to** ~ **to sb** mandar un mensaje por radio a uno ♦ vt (information) radiar, transmitir por radio; (one's position) indicar por radio; (person) llamar por radio; **on the** ~ por radio.
radioactive [rädēōak'tiv] a radioactivo.
radioactivity [rädēōaktiv'ətē] n radioactividad f.
radio announcer n locutor(a) m/f de radio.
radio-controlled [rä'dēōkəntrōld'] a teledirigido.
radiographer [rädēāg'rəfûr] n radiógrafo/a.
radiography [rädēāg'rəfē] n radiografía.
radiology [rädēāl'əjē] n radiología.
radio station n emisora.
radio taxi n radio taxi m.
radiotelephone [rädēōtel'əfōn] n radioteléfono.
radiotelescope n radiotelescopio.
radiotherapist [rädēōthär'əpist] n radioterapeuta m/f.
radiotherapy [rädēōthär'əpē] n radioterapia.
radish [rad'ish] n rábano.
radium [rä'dēəm] n radio.
radius [rä'dēəs], pl **radii** [rä'dēəs, -ēi] n radio; **within a** ~ **of 50 miles** en un radio de 50 millas.
RAF n abbr = **Royal Air Force**.
raffia [raf'ēə] n rafia.
raffle [raf'əl] n rifa, sorteo ♦ vt (object) rifar.
raft [raft] n (craft) balsa; (also: **life** ~) balsa salvavidas.
rafter [raf'tûr] n viga.
rag [rag] n (piece of cloth) trapo; (torn cloth) harapo; (pej: newspaper) periodicucho; (Brit: for charity) actividades estudiantiles benéficas; ~**s** npl harapos mpl; **in** ~**s** en harapos, hecho jirones.
rag-and-bone man [ragənbōn' man] n (Brit) = **ragman**.
rag doll n muñeca de trapo.
rage [räj] n (fury) rabia, furor m ♦ vi (person) rabiar, estar furioso; (storm) bramar; **to fly into a** ~ montar en cólera; **it's all the** ~ es lo último.
ragged [rag'id] a (edge) desigual, mellado; (cuff) roto; (appearance) andrajoso, harapiento; ~ **left/right** (text) margen m izquierdo/derecho irregular.

raging [rā'jing] *a* furioso; **in a ~ temper** de un humor terrible, furioso.

ragman [rag'man] *n* trapero.

rag trade *n*: **the ~** (*col*) la industria de la confección.

raid [rād] *n* (*MIL*) incursión *f*; (*criminal*) asalto; (*by police*) redada ♦ *vt* invadir, atacar; asaltar.

raider [rā'dûr] *n* invasor(a) *m/f*.

rail [rāl] *n* (*on stair*) barandilla, pasamanos *m inv*; (*on bridge, balcony*) pretil *m*; (*of ship*) barandilla; (*for train*) riel *m*, carril *m*; **~s** *npl* vía *sg*; **by ~** por ferrocarril, en tren.

railing(s) [rā'ling(z)] *n(pl)* verja *sg*, enrejado *sg*.

railroad [rāl'rōd] *n* (*US*) ferrocarril *m*, via férrea.

railroader [rāl'rōdûr] *n* (*US*) ferroviario.

railroad line *n* línea de ferrocarril.

railroad station *n* estación de ferrocarril.

railway [rāl'wā] *etc* (*Brit*) = **railroad** etc.

railway engine *n* (*Brit*) (máquina) locomotora.

railwayman [rāl'wāmən] *n* (*Brit*) = **railroader.**

rain [rān] *n* lluvia ♦ *vi* llover; **in the ~** bajo la lluvia; **it's ~ing** llueve, está lloviendo; **it's ~ing cats and dogs** está lloviendo a cántaros *or* a mares.

rainbow [rān'bō] *n* arco iris.

raincoat [rān'kōt] *n* impermeable *m*.

raindrop [rān'dráp] *n* gota de lluvia.

rainfall [rān'fôl] *n* lluvia.

rainforest [rān'fôrist] *n* (*also:* **tropical ~**) selva tropical.

rainproof [rān'prōōf] *a* impermeable, a prueba de lluvia.

rainstorm [rān'stôrm] *n* temporal *m* (de lluvia).

rainwater [rān'wôtûr] *n* agua llovediza *or* de lluvia.

rainy [rā'nē] *a* lluvioso.

raise [rāz] *n* aumento ♦ *vt* (*lift*) levantar; (*build*) erigir, edificar; (*increase*) aumentar; (*doubts*) suscitar; (*a question*) plantear; (*cattle, family*) criar; (*crop*) cultivar; (*army*) reclutar; (*funds*) reunir; (*money*) obtener; (*Brit: end: embargo*) levantar; **to ~ one's voice** alzar la voz; **to ~ one's glass to sb/sth** brindar por uno/algo; **to ~ a laugh/a smile** provocar risa/una sonrisa; **to ~ sb's hopes** dar esperanzas a uno.

raisin [rā'zin] *n* pasa.

rake [rāk] *n* (*tool*) rastrillo; (*person*) libertino ♦ *vt* (*garden*) rastrillar; (*fire*) hurgar; (*with machine gun*) barrer.

rake in *vt* reunir.

rake-off [rāk'ôf] *n* (*col*) comisión *f*, tajada.

rakish [rā'kish] *a* (*dissolute*) libertino; **at a ~ angle** (*hat*) echado a un lado, de lado.

rally [ral'ē] *n* (*POL etc*) reunión *f*, mitin *m*; (*AUT*) rallye *m*; (*TENNIS*) peloteo ♦ *vt* reunir ♦ *vi* reunirse; (*sick person, Stock Exchange*) recuperarse.

rally around *vt fus* (*fig*) dar apoyo a.

rallying point [ral'ēing point] *n* (*POL, MIL*) punto de reunión.

RAM [ram] *n abbr* (= *random access memory*) RAM *f*.

ram [ram] *n* carnero; (*TECH*) pisón *m* ♦ *vt* (*crash into*) dar contra, chocar con; (*tread down*) apisonar.

ramble [ram'bəl] *n* caminata, excursión *f* en el campo ♦ *vi* (*pej: also:* **~ on**) divagar.

rambler [ram'blûr] *n* excursionista *m/f*; (*BOT*) trepadora.

rambling [ram'bling] *a* (*speech*) inconexo; (*BOT*) trepador(a); (*house*) laberíntico.

rambunctious [rambungk'shəs] *a* (*person*) bullicioso.

ramification [ramǝfǝkā'shǝn] *n* ramificación *f*.

ramp [ramp] *n* rampa; **on/off ~** *n* (*US AUT*) vía de acceso/salida; **"~"** (*Brit AUT*) "rampa".

rampage [ram'pāj] *n*: **to be on the ~** desmandarse.

rampant [ram'pǝnt] *a* (*disease etc*): **to be ~** estar extendiéndose mucho.

rampart [ram'pârt] *n* terraplén *m*; (*wall*) muralla.

ramshackle [ram'shakǝl] *a* destartalado.

ran [ran] *pt of* **run.**

ranch [ranch] *n* (*US*) hacienda, estancia.

rancher [ran'chûr] *n* ganadero.

rancid [ran'sid] *a* rancio.

rancor, (*Brit*) **rancour** [rang'kûr] *n* rencor *m*.

random [ran'dǝm] *a* fortuito, sin orden; (*COMPUT, MATH*) aleatorio ♦ *n*: **at ~** al azar.

random access *n* (*COMPUT*) acceso aleatorio.

randy [ran'dē] *a* (*Brit col*) cachondo.

rang [rang] *pt of* **ring.**

range [rānj] *n* (*of mountains*) cadena de montañas, cordillera; (*of missile*) alcance *m*; (*of voice*) registro; (*series*) serie *f*; (*of products*) surtido; (*MIL: also:* **shooting ~**) campo de tiro; (*also:* **kitchen ~**) fogón *m* ♦ *vt* (*place*) colocar; (*arrange*) arreglar ♦ *vi*: **to ~ over** (*wander*) recorrer; (*extend*) extenderse por; **within (firing) ~** a tiro; **do you have anything else in this price ~?** ¿tiene algo más de esta gama de precios?; **intermediate-/short-~ missile** proyectil *m* de medio/corto alcance; **to ~ from ... to...** oscilar entre ... y...; **~d left/right** (*Brit: text*) alineado a la izquierda/derecha.

ranger [rān'jûr] *n* guardabosques *m inv*.

Rangoon [ranggōōn'] *n* Rangún *m*.

rangy [rān'jē] *a* alto y delgado.

rank [rangk] *n* (*row*) fila; (*MIL*) rango; (*status*) categoría; (*Brit: also:* **taxi ~**) parada

♦ *vi*: **to ~ among** figurar entre ♦ *a* (*stinking*) fétido, rancio; (*hypocrisy, injustice etc*) manifiesto; **the ~ and file** (*fig*) la base; **to close ~s** (*MIL*) apretar las filas, cerrar filas; (*fig*) hacer un frente común; **I ~ him 6th** yo le pongo en sexto lugar.

rankle [rang'kəl] *vi* (*insult*) doler.

ransack [ran'sak] *vt* (*search*) registrar; (*plunder*) saquear.

ransom [ran'səm] *n* rescate *m* ♦ *vt* rescatar; **to hold sb to ~** (*fig*) poner a uno entre la espada y la pared.

rant [rant] *vi* divagar, desvariar.

ranting [ran'ting] *n* desvaríos *mpl*.

rap [rap] *vt* golpear, dar un golpecito en ♦ *n* **to take the ~** pagar el gato.

rape [rāp] *n* violación *f*; (*BOT*) colza ♦ *vt* violar.

rape(seed) oil [rāp'(sēd) oil] *n* aceite *m* de colza.

rapid [rap'id] *a* rápido.

rapidity [rəpid'itē] *n* rapidez *f*.

rapidly [rap'idlē] *ad* rápidamente.

rapids [rap'idz] *npl* (*GEO*) rápidos *mpl*.

rapier [rā'pēûr] *n* estoque *m*.

rapist [rā'pist] *n* violador *m*.

rapport [rapôr'] *n* simpatía.

rapprochement [raprōchmônt'] *n* acercamiento.

rapt [rapt] *a* (*attention*) profundo; **to be ~ in contemplation** estar ensimismado.

rapture [rap'chûr] *n* éxtasis *m*.

rapturous [rap'chûrəs] *a* extático; (*applause*) entusiasta.

rare [rär] *a* raro, poco común; (*CULIN: steak*) poco hecho; **it is ~ to find that ...** es raro descubrir que ....

rarefied [rär'əfīd] *a* (*air, atmosphere*) enrarecido.

rarely [reûr'lē] *ad* rara vez, pocas veces.

raring [rär'ing] *a*: **to be ~ to go** (*col*) tener muchas ganas de empezar.

rarity [rär'itē] *n* rareza.

rascal [ras'kəl] *n* pillo/a, pícaro/a.

rash [rash] *a* imprudente, precipitado ♦ *n* (*MED*) salpullido, erupción *f* (*cutánea*); **to come out in a ~** salirle salpullido a uno.

rasher [rash'ûr] *n* lonja.

rashly [rash'lē] *ad* imprudentemente, precipitadamente.

rashness [rash'nis] *n* imprudencia, precipitación *f*.

rasp [rasp] *n* (*tool*) escofina ♦ *vt* (*speak: also*: **~ out**) decir con voz áspera.

raspberry [raz'bärē] *n* frambuesa.

rasping [ras'ping] *a*: **a ~ noise** un ruido áspero.

rat [rat] *n* rata.

ratchet [rach'it] *n* (*TECH*) trinquete *m*.

rate [rāt] *n* (*ratio*) razón *f*; (*percentage*) tanto por ciento; (*price*) precio; (: *of hotel*) tarifa; (*of interest*) tipo; (*speed*) velocidad *f* ♦ *vt* (*value*) tasar; (*estimate*) estimar; **to**

~ as ser considerado como; **~s** *npl* (*Brit*) impuesto *sg* municipal; (*fees*) tarifa *sg*; **failure ~** porcentaje *m* de fallos; **pulse ~** pulsaciones *fpl* por minuto; **~ of pay** tipos *mpl* de sueldo; **at a ~ of 60 kph** a una velocidad de 60 kph; **~ of growth** ritmo de crecimiento; **~ of return** (*COMM*) tasa de rendimiento; **bank ~** tipo *or* tasa de interés bancario; **at any ~** de todas formas, de todos modos; **to ~ sb/sth highly** tener a uno/algo en alta estima.

rather [raṯħ'ûr] *ad* antes, más bien; (*somewhat*) algo, un poco; (*to some extent*) un poco; **it's ~ expensive** es algo caro; (*too much*) es demasiado caro; **there's ~ a lot** (*Brit*) hay bastante; **I would** *or* **I'd ~ go** preferiría ir; **I'd ~ not** prefiero que no; **or ~** (*more accurately*) o mejor dicho.

ratification [ratəfəkā'shən] *n* ratificación *f*.

ratify [rat'əfī] *vt* ratificar.

rating [rā'ting] *n* (*appraisal*) tasación *f*; (*standing*) posición *f*; (*Brit NAUT: sailor*) marinero; **~s** *npl* (*RADIO, TV*) clasificación *f*.

ratio [rā'shō] *n* razón *f*; **in the ~ of 100 to 1** a razón de *or* en la proporción de 100 a 1.

ration [rash'ən] *n* ración *f*; **~s** *npl* víveres *mpl* ♦ *vt* racionar.

rational [rash'ənəl] *a* racional; (*solution, reasoning*) lógico, razonable; (*person*) cuerdo, sensato.

rationale [rashənal'] *n* razón *f* fundamental.

rationalism [rash'ənəlizəm] *n* racionalismo.

rationalization [rashənələzā'shən] *n* racionalización *f*.

rationalize [rash'ənəlīz] *vt* (*reorganize: industry*) reconvertir, reorganizar.

rationally [rash'ənəlē] *ad* racionalmente; (*logically*) lógicamente.

rationing [rash'əning] *n* racionamiento.

rat race *n* lucha incesante por la supervivencia.

rattan [ratan'] *n* rota, caña de Indias.

rattle [rat'əl] *n* golpeteo; (*of train etc*) traqueteo; (*object: of baby*) sonaja, sonajero; (: *of sports fan*) matraca ♦ *vi* sonar, golpear; traquetear; (*small objects*) castañetear ♦ *vt* hacer sonar agitando; (*col: disconcert*) desconcertar.

rattlesnake [rat'əlsnāk] *n* serpiente *f* de cascabel.

ratty [rat'ē] *a* (*col: US*) andrajoso; (: *Brit*) furioso; **to get ~** ponerse de malas.

raucous [rô'kəs] *a* estridente, ronco.

raucously [rô'kəslē] *ad* de modo estridente, roncamente.

ravage [rav'ij] *vt* hacer estragos en, destrozar; **~s** *npl* estragos *mpl*.

rave [rāv] *vi* (*in anger*) encolerizarse; (*with enthusiasm*) entusiasmarse; (*MED*) delirar, desvariar ♦ *cpd*: **~ review** reseña entusiasta.

raven [rā'vən] *n* cuervo.

ravenous [rav'ənəs] *a* famélico.
ravine [rəvēn'] *n* barranco.
raving [rā'ving] *a*: ~ **lunatic** loco de atar.
ravings [rā'vingz] *npl* divagaciones *fpl*, desvaríos *mpl*.
ravioli [ravēō'lē] *n* ravioles *mpl*, ravioli *mpl*.
ravish [rav'ish] *vt* (*charm*) encantar, embelesar; (*rape*) violar.
ravishing [rav'ishing] *a* encantador(a).
raw [rô] *a* (*uncooked*) crudo; (*not processed*) bruto; (*sore*) vivo; (*inexperienced*) novato, inexperto.
Rawalpindi [râwəlpin'dē] *n* Rawalpindi *m*.
raw data *n* (*COMPUT*) datos *mpl* en bruto.
raw deal *n* (*col*: *bad deal*) mala pasada *or* jugada; (: *harsh treatment*) injusticia.
raw material *n* materia prima.
ray [rā] *n* rayo; ~ **of hope** (rayo de) esperanza.
rayon [rā'ân] *n* rayón *m*.
raze [rāz] *vt* (*also*: ~ **to the ground**) arrasar, asolar.
razor [rā'zûr] *n* (*open*) navaja; (*safety* ~) máquina de afeitar.
razor blade *n* hoja de afeitar.
razzmatazz [raz'mətaz] *n* (*col*) animación *f*, bullicio.
R & B *n abbr* = *rhythm and blues*.
RC *abbr* = **Roman Catholic.**
RCAF *n abbr* = *Royal Canadian Air Force.*
RCMP *n abbr* = *Royal Canadian Mounted Police.*
RCN *n abbr* = *Royal Canadian Navy.*
RD *abbr* (*US MAIL*) = *rural delivery.*
Rd *abbr* = *road.*
R & D *n abbr* (= *research and development*) investigación *f* y desarrollo.
re [rā] *prep* con referencia a.
re... [rā] *pref* re....
reach [rēch] *n* alcance *m*; (*BOXING*) envergadura; (*of river etc*) extensión *f* entre dos recodos ♦ *vt* alcanzar, llegar a; (*achieve*) lograr ♦ *vi* extenderse; (*stretch out hand: also*: ~ **down,** ~ **over,** ~ **across** *etc*) tender la mano; **within** ~ al alcance (de la mano); **out of** ~ fuera del alcance; **to** ~ **out for sth** alargar *or* tender la mano para tomar algo; **can I** ~ **you at your hotel?** ¿puedo ponerme en contacto contigo en tu hotel?; **to** ~ **sb by phone** comunicarse con uno por teléfono.
react [rēakt'] *vi* reaccionar.
reaction [rēak'shən] *n* reacción *f*.
reactionary [rēak'shənärē] *a*, *n* reaccionario/a *m/f*.
reactor [rēak'tûr] *n* reactor *m*.
read, *pt*, *pp* **read** [rēd, red] *vi* leer ♦ *vt* leer; (*understand*) entender; (*study*) estudiar; **to take sth as read** (*fig*) dar algo por sentado; **do you** ~ **me?** (*TEL*) ¿me escucha?; **to** ~ **between the lines** leer entre líneas.
read out *vt*: ~ **out aloud** leer en alta voz.

read over *vt* repasar.
read through *vt* (*quickly*) leer rápidamente, echar un vistazo a; (*thoroughly*) leer con cuidado *or* detenidamente.
read up on *vt fus* estudiar.
readable [rē'dəbəl] *a* (*writing*) legible; (*book*) que merece leerse.
reader [rē'dûr] *n* lector(a) *m/f*; (*book*) libro de lecturas; (*Brit*: *at university*) profesor(a) *m/f*.
readership [rē'dûrship] *n* (*of paper etc*) número de lectores.
readily [red'əlē] *ad* (*willingly*) de buena gana; (*easily*) fácilmente; (*quickly*) en seguida.
readiness [red'ēnis] *n* buena voluntad; (*preparedness*) preparación *f*; **in** ~ (*prepared*) listo, preparado.
reading [rēd'ing] *n* lectura; (*understanding*) comprensión *f*; (*on instrument*) indicación *f*.
reading lamp *n* lámpara portátil.
reading room *n* sala de lectura.
readjust [rēəjust'] *vt* reajustar ♦ *vi* (*person*): **to** ~ **to** reajustarse a.
readjustment [rēəjust'mənt] *n* reajuste *m*.
ready [red'ē] *a* listo, preparado; (*willing*) dispuesto; (*available*) disponible ♦ *n*: **at the** ~ (*MIL*) listo para tirar; ~ **for use** listo para usar; **to be** ~ **to do sth** estar listo para hacer algo; **to get** ~ *vi* prepararse ♦ *vt* preparar.
ready cash *n* (dinero) efectivo, dinero contante.
ready-made [red'ēmād'] *a* confeccionado.
ready-to-wear [red'ētəwär'] *a* confeccionado.
reaffirm [rēəfurm'] *vt* reafirmar.
reagent [rēā'jənt] *n* reactivo.
real [rēl] *a* verdadero, auténtico; **in** ~ **terms** en términos reales; **in** ~ **life** en la vida real, en la realidad.
real estate *n* bienes *mpl* raíces.
real estate agent *n* agente *m/f* inmobiliario(a).
real estate office *n* agencia inmobiliaria.
realism [rē'əlizəm] *n* (*also ART*) realismo.
realist [rē'əlist] *n* realista *m/f*.
realistic [rēəlis'tik] *a* realista.
realistically [rēəlis'tiklē] *ad* de modo realista.
reality [rēal'itē] *n* realidad *f*; **in** ~ en realidad.
realization [rēələzā'shən] *n* comprensión *f*; (*of a project*; *COMM*: *of assets*) realización *f*.
realize [rē'əlīz] *vt* (*understand*) darse cuenta de; (*a project*; *COMM*: *asset*) realizar; **I** ~ **that ...** comprendo *or* entiendo que ....
really [rē'əlē] *ad* realmente; ~**?** ¿de veras?
realm [relm] *n* reino; (*fig*) esfera.
real time *n* (*COMPUT*) tiempo real.
realtor [rē'əltûr] *n* (*US*) corredor(a) *m/f* de

bienes raíces.

ream [rēm] *n* resma; ~s (*fig, col*) montones *mpl.*

reap [rēp] *vt* segar; (*fig*) cosechar, recoger.

reaper [rē'pûr] *n* segador(a) *m/f.*

reappear [rēəpi'ûr] *vi* reaparecer.

reappearance [rēəpēr'əns] *n* reaparición *f.*

reapply [rēəplī'] *vi* volver a presentarse, hacer *or* presentar nueva solicitud.

reappoint [rēəpoint'] *vt* volver a nombrar.

reappraisal [rēəprā'zəl] *n* revaluación *f.*

rear [rēr] *a* trasero ♦ *n* parte *f* trasera ♦ *vt* (*cattle, family*) criar ♦ *vi* (*also:* ~ up) (*animal*) encabritarse.

rear-engined [rēr'en'jənd] *a* (*AUT*) con motor trasero.

rearguard [rēr'gârd] *n* retaguardia.

rearm [rēârm'] *vt* rearmar ♦ *vi* rearmarse.

rearmament [rēârm'əmənt] *n* rearme *m.*

rearrange [rēərānj'] *vt* ordenar *or* arreglar de nuevo.

rear-view [rēr'vyōō']: ~ **mirror** *n* (*AUT*) espejo retrovisor.

reason [rē'zən] *n* razón *f* ♦ *vi:* **to** ~ **with sb** tratar de que uno entre en razón; **it stands to** ~ **that** es lógico que; **the** ~ **for/why** la causa de/la razón por la cual; **she claims with good** ~ **that she's underpaid** dice con razón que está mal pagada; **all the more** ~ **why you should not sell it** razón de más para que no lo vendas.

reasonable [rē'zənəbəl] *a* razonable; (*sensible*) sensato.

reasonably [rē'zənəblē] *ad* razonablemente; **a** ~ **accurate report** un informe bastante exacto.

reasoned [rē'zənd] *a* (*argument*) razonado.

reasoning [rē'zəning] *n* razonamiento, argumentos *mpl.*

reassemble [rēəsem'bəl] *vt* volver a reunir; (*machine*) montar de nuevo ♦ *vi* volver a reunirse.

reassert [rēəsûrt'] *vt* reafirmar, reiterar.

reassurance [rēəshōōr'əns] *n* consuelo.

reassure [rēəshōōr'] *vt* tranquilizar, alentar; **to** ~ **sb that** tranquilizar a uno asegurándole que.

reassuring [rēəshōōr'ing] *a* alentador(a).

reawakening [rēəwā'kəning] *n* despertar *m.*

rebate [rē'bāt] *n* (*on product*) rebaja; (*on tax etc*) descuento; (*repayment*) reembolso.

rebel *n* [reb'əl] rebelde *m/f* ♦ *vi* [ribel'] rebelarse, sublevarse.

rebellion [ribel'yən] *n* rebelión *f*, sublevación *f.*

rebellious [ribel'yəs] *a* rebelde; (*child*) revoltoso.

rebirth [rēbûrth'] *n* renacimiento.

rebound *vi* [ribound'] (*ball*) rebotar ♦ *n* [rē'bound] rebote *m.*

rebuff [ribuf'] *n* desaire *m*, rechazo ♦ *vt* rechazar.

rebuild [rēbild'] *vt* (*irg: like* **build**) reconstruir.

rebuilding [rēbil'ding] *n* reconstrucción *f.*

rebuke [ribyōōk'] *n* reprimenda ♦ *vt* reprender.

rebut [ribut'] *vt* rebatir.

recalcitrant [rikal'sitrənt] *a* reacio.

recall *vt* [rikôl'] (*remember*) recordar; (*ambassador etc*) retirar; (*COMPUT*) volver a llamar ♦ *n* [rē'kôl] recuerdo.

recant [rikant'] *vi* retractarse.

recap [rē'kap] *vt, vi* recapitular.

recapitulate [rēkəpich'əlāt] *vt, vi* = **recap.**

recapture [rēkap'chûr] *vt* (*town*) reconquistar; (*atmosphere*) hacer revivir.

recd., rec'd *abbr* (= *received*) rbdo.

recede [risēd'] *vi* retroceder.

receding [risē'ding] *a* (*forehead, chin*) huidizo; ~ **hairline** entradas *fpl.*

receipt [risēt'] *n* (*document*) recibo; (*act of receiving*) recepción *f;* ~s *npl* (*COMM*) ingresos *mpl;* **to acknowledge** ~ **of** acusar recibo de; **we are in** ~ **of** ... obra en nuestro poder ... .

receivable [risē'vəbəl] *a* (*COMM*) a cobrar.

receive [risēv'] *vt* recibir; (*guest*) acoger; (*wound*) sufrir; "~ed **with thanks**" (*COMM*) "recibí".

receiver [risē'vûr] *n* (*TEL*) auricular *m;* (*RADIO*) receptor *m;* (*of stolen goods*) perista *m/f;* (*LAW*) administrador *m* jurídico.

recent [rē'sənt] *a* reciente; **in** ~ **years** en los últimos años.

recently [rē'səntlē] *ad* recientemente; ~ **arrived** recién llegado; **until** ~ hasta hace poco.

receptacle [risep'təkəl] *n* receptáculo.

reception [risep'shən] *n* (*in building, office etc*) recepción *f;* (*welcome*) acogida.

reception center *n* centro de recepción.

reception desk *n* recepción *f.*

receptionist [risep'shənist] *n* recepcionista *m/f.*

receptive [risep'tiv] *a* receptivo.

recess [rē'ses] *n* (*in room*) hueco; (*for bed*) nicho; (*secret place*) escondrijo; (*POL etc: holiday*) clausura; (*US LAW: short break*) descanso; (*SCOL: esp US*) recreo.

recession [risesh'ən] *n* recesión *f*, depresión *f.*

recharge [rēchârj'] *vt* (*battery*) recargar.

rechargeable [rēchâr'jəbəl] *a* recargable.

recipe [res'əpē] *n* receta.

recipient [risip'ēənt] *n* recibidor(a) *m/f;* (*of letter*) destinatario/a.

reciprocal [risip'rəkəl] *a* recíproco.

reciprocate [risip'rəkāt] *vt* devolver, corresponder a ♦ *vi* corresponder.

recital [risīt'əl] *n* (*MUS*) recital *m.*

recitation [resitā'shən] *n* (*of poetry*) recitado; (*of complaints etc*) enumeración *f*, relación *f.*

recite [risīt'] *vt* (*poem*) recitar; (*complaints etc*) enumerar.

reckless [rek'lis] *a* temerario, imprudente; (*speed*) peligroso.

recklessly [rek'lislē] *ad* imprudentemente; de modo peligroso.

recklessness [rek'lisnis] *n* temeridad *f*, imprudencia.

reckon [rek'ən] *vt* (*count*) contar; (*consider*) considerar ♦ *vi*: **to ~ without sb/sth** dejar de contar con uno/algo; **he is somebody to be ~ed with** no se le puede descartar; **I ~ that...** me parece que..., creo que ....
reckon on *vt fus* contar con.

reckoning [rek'əning] *n* (*calculation*) cálculo.

reclaim [riklām'] *vt* (*land*) recuperar; (: *from sea*) rescatar; (*demand back*) reclamar.

reclamation [rekləmā'shən] *n* recuperación *f*; rescate *m*.

recline [riklīn'] *vi* reclinarse.

reclining [riklīn'ing] *a* (*seat*) reclinable.

recluse [rek'lōōs] *n* recluso/a.

recognition [rekəgnish'ən] *n* reconocimiento; **transformed beyond ~** irreconocible; **in ~ of** en reconocimiento de.

recognizable [rekəgni'zəbəl] *a*: **~ (by)** reconocible (por).

recognize [rek'əgnīz] *vt* reconocer, conocer; **to ~ (by/as)** reconocer (por/como).

recoil [rikoil'] *vi* (*person*): **to ~ from doing sth** retraerse de hacer algo ♦ *n* (*of gun*) retroceso.

recollect [rekəlekt'] *vt* recordar, acordarse de.

recollection [rekəlek'shən] *n* recuerdo; **to the best of my ~** que yo recuerde.

recommend [rekəmend'] *vt* recomendar; **she has a lot to ~ her** tiene mucho a su favor.

recommendation [rekəmendā'shən] *n* recomendación *f*.

recommended retail price (RRP) [rekəmen'did rē'tāl prīs] *n* (*Brit*) precio recomendado de venta al público.

recompense [rek'əmpens] *vt* recompensar ♦ *n* recompensa.

reconcilable [rek'ənsīləbəl] *a* (re)conciliable.

reconcile [rek'ənsīl] *vt* (*two people*) reconciliar; (*two facts*) compaginar; **to ~ o.s. to sth** resignarse *or* conformarse a algo.

reconciliation [rekənsilēā'shən] *n* reconciliación *f*.

recondite [rek'əndīt] *a* recóndito.

recondition [rēkəndi'shən] *vt* (*machine*) reparar, reponer.

reconditioned [rēkəndi'shənd] *a* renovado, reparado.

reconnaissance [rikân'isəns] *n* (*MIL*) reconocimiento.

reconnoiter, (*Brit*) **reconnoitre** [rēkənoi'tûr] *vt, vi* (*MIL*) reconocer.

reconsider [rēkənsid'ûr] *vt* repensar.

reconstitute [rēkán'stitōōt] *vt* reconstituir.

reconstruct [rēkənstrukt'] *vt* reconstruir.

reconstruction [rēkənstruk'shən] *n* reconstrucción *f*.

record *n* [rek'ûrd] (*MUS*) disco; (*of meeting etc*) relación *f*; (*register*) registro, partida; (*file*) archivo; (*also*: **police** *or* **criminal ~**) antecedentes *mpl* penales; (*written*) expediente *m*; (*SPORT*) récord *m*; (*COMPUT*) registro ♦ *vt* [rikôrd'] (*set down, also COMPUT*) registrar; (*relate*) hacer constar; (*MUS: song etc*) grabar; **in ~ time** en un tiempo récord; **public ~s** archivos *mpl* nacionales; **he is on ~ as saying that ...** hay pruebas de que ha dicho públicamente que ...; **Spain's excellent ~** el excelente historial de España; **off the ~** *a* no oficial ♦ *ad* confidencialmente.

record card *n* (*in file*) ficha.

recorded delivery letter [rikôr'did dilīv'ûrē let'ûr] *n* (*Brit MAIL*) carta de entrega recordada.

recorded music *n* música grabada.

recorder [rikôr'dûr] *n* (*MUS*) flauta de pico; (*TECH*) contador *m*.

record holder *n* (*SPORT*) actual poseedor(a) *m/f* del récord.

recording [rikôr'ding] *n* (*MUS*) grabación *f*.

recording studio *n* estudio de grabación.

record library *n* discoteca.

record player *n* tocadiscos *m inv*.

recount [rikount'] *vt* contar.

re-count *n* [rē'kount] (*POL: of votes*) segundo escrutinio, recuento ♦ *vt* [rēkount'] volver a contar.

recoup [rikōōp'] *vt*: **to ~ one's losses** recuperar las pérdidas.

recourse [rē'kôrs] *n* recurso; **to have ~ to** recurrir a.

recover [rikuv'ûr] *vt* recuperar; (*rescue*) rescatar ♦ *vi* (*from illness, shock*) recuperarse; (*country*) recuperar.

recovery [rikuv'ûrē] *n* recuperación *f*; rescate *m*; (*MED*): **to make a ~** restablecerse.

re-create [rēkrēāt'] *vt* recrear.

recreation [rekrēā'shən] *n* recreación *f*; (*amusement*) recreo.

recreational [rekrēā'shənəl] *a* de recreo.

recreational vehicle *n* (*US*) caravana *or* roulotte *f* pequeña.

recreation center *n* centro de recreo.

recrimination [rikrimənā'shən] *n* recriminación *f*.

recruit [rikrōōt'] *n* recluta *m/f* ♦ *vt* reclutar; (*staff*) contratar.

recruiting office [rikrōōt'ing ôf'is] *n* caja de reclutas.

recruitment [rikrōōt'mənt] *n* reclutamiento.

rectangle [rek'tanggəl] *n* rectángulo.

rectangular |rɛktang'gyəlûr| *a* rectangular.
rectify |rɛk'təfī| *vt* rectificar.
rector |rɛk'túr| *n* (*REL*) párroco; (*SCOL*) rector(a) *m/f.*
rectory |rɛk'tûrē| *n* casa del párroco.
rectum |rɛk'təm| *n* (*ANAT*) recto.
recuperate |rikōō'pərāt| *vi* reponerse, restablecerse.
recur |rikûr'| *vi* repetirse; (*pain, illness*) producirse de nuevo.
recurrence |rikûr'əns| *n* repetición *f.*
recurrent |rikûr'ənt| *a* repetido.
recycle |rēsī'kəl| *vt* (*waste, paper etc*) reciclar.
red |rɛd| *n* rojo ♦ *a* rojo; **to be in the ~** (*account*) estar en números rojos; (*business*) tener un saldo negativo; **to give sb the ~ carpet treatment** recibir a uno con todos los honores.
Red Cross *n* Cruz *f* Roja.
redcurrant |rɛd'kur'ənt| *n* grosella.
redden |rɛd'ən| *vt* enrojecer ♦ *vi* enrojecerse.
reddish |rɛd'ish| *a* (*hair*) rojizo.
redecorate |rēdɛk'ərāt| pintar de nuevo; volver a decorar.
redecoration |rēdɛkərā'shən| *n* renovación *f.*
redeem |ridēm'| *vt* (*sth in pawn*) desempeñar; (*fig, also REL*) rescatar.
redeemable |ridē'məbəl| *a* reembolsable.
redeeming |ridē'ming| *a:* **~ feature** rasgo bueno *or* favorable.
redeploy |rēdiploi'| *vt* (*resources*) disponer de nuevo.
redeployment |rēdiploi'mənt| *n* redistribución *f.*
redevelop |rēdivel'əp| *vt* reorganizar.
redevelopment |rēdivel'əpmənt| *n* reorganización *f.*
red-haired |rɛd'hârd| *a* pelirrojo.
red-handed |rɛd'han'did| *a:* **to be caught ~** cogerse (*Sp*) *or* pillarse (*LAm*) con las manos en la masa.
redhead |rɛd'hɛd| *n* pelirrojo/a.
red herring *n* (*fig*) pista falsa.
red-hot |rɛd'hât'| *a* candente.
redirect |rēdərɛkt'| *vt* (*mail*) reexpedir.
rediscover |rēdiskuv'ûr| *vt* redescubrir.
rediscovery |rēdiskuv'ûrē| *n* redescubrimiento.
redistribute |rēdistrib'yōōt| *vt* redistribuir, hacer una nueva distribución de.
red-letter day |rɛd'lɛt'ûr dā| *n* día *m* señalado, día *m* especial.
red light *n:* **to go through a ~** (*AUT*) pasar la luz roja.
red-light district |rɛd'līt dis'trikt| *n* zona de tolerancia.
redness |rɛd'nis| *n* rojez *f.*
redo |rēdōō'| *vt* (*irg: like* **do**) rehacer.
redolent |rɛd'ələnt| *a:* **~ of** (*smell*) oliente *or* con fragancia a; **to be ~ of** (*fig*) recordar.

redouble |rēdub'əl| *vt:* **to ~ one's efforts** intensificar los esfuerzos.
redraft |rēdraft'| *vt* volver a redactar.
redress |ridrɛs'| *n* reparación *f* ♦ *vt* reparar, corregir; **to ~ the balance** restablecer el equilibrio.
Red Sea *n:* **the ~** el mar Rojo.
redskin |rɛd'skin| *n* piel roja *m/f.*
red tape *n* (*fig*) trámites *mpl*, papeleo (*col*).
reduce |ridōōs'| *vt* reducir; (*lower*) rebajar; **to ~ sth by/to** reducir algo en/a; **to ~ sb to silence/despair/tears** reducir a uno al silencio/a la desesperación/a las lágrimas; **'~d speed ahead'** (*AUT*) 'reduzca la velocidad'.
reduced |ridōōst'| *a* (*decreased*) reducido, rebajado; **at a ~ price** con rebaja *or* descuento; **"greatly ~ prices"** "grandes rebajas".
reduction |riduk'shən| *n* reducción *f*; (*of price*) rebaja; (*discount*) descuento.
redundancy |ridun'dənsē| *n* redundancia; (*Brit*) desempleo; **compulsory ~** despido; **voluntary ~** dimisión *f.*
redundancy payment *n* (*Brit*) indemnización *f* por desempleo.
redundant |ridun'dənt| *a* (*Brit*) (*worker*) parado, sin trabajo; (*detail, object*) superfluo; **to be made ~** quedar(se) sin trabajo, perder su empleo.
reed |rēd| *n* (*BOT*) junco, caña; (*MUS: of clarinet etc*) lengüeta.
reedy |rē'dē| *a* (*voice, instrument*) aflautado.
reef |rēf| *n* (*at sea*) arrecife *m.*
reek |rēk| *vi:* **to ~ (of)** oler *or* heder (a).
reel |rēl| *n* carrete *m*, bobina; (*of film*) rollo ♦ *vt* (*TECH*) devanar; (*also: ~ in*) sacar ♦ *vi* (*sway*) tambalear(se); **my head is ~ing** me da vueltas la cabeza.
reel off *vt* recitar de memoria.
re-election |rēilɛk'shən| *n* reelección *f.*
re-enter |rēɛn'tûr| *vt* reingresar en, volver a entrar en.
re-entry |rēɛn'trē| *n* reingreso, reentrada.
re-examine |rēigzam'in| *vt* reexaminar.
re-export *vt* |rēɛkspôrt'| reexportar ♦ *n* |rēɛks'pôrt| reexportación *f.*
ref |rɛf| *n abbr* (*col*) = **referee.**
ref. *abbr* (*COMM:* = *with reference to*) Ref.
refectory |rifɛk'tûrē| *n* comedor *m.*
refer |rifûr'| *vt* (*send*) remitir; (*ascribe*) referir a, relacionar con ♦ *vi:* **to ~ to** (*allude to*) referirse a, aludir a; (*apply to*) relacionarse con; (*consult*) remitirse a; **he ~red me to the manager** me envió al gerente.
referee |rɛfərē'| *n* árbitro; (*Brit: for job application*) persona que recomienda a otro ♦ *vt* (*match*) arbitrar en.
reference |rɛf'ûrəns| *n* (*mention, in book*) referencia; (*sending*) remisión *f*; (*rel-*

evance) relación *f*; (*for job application: letter*) carta de recomendación; **with ~ to** con referencia a; (*COMM: in letter*) me remito a.

reference book *n* libro de consulta.

reference number *n* número de referencia.

referendum, *pl* **referenda** [refərən'dəm, -də] *n* referéndum *m inv*.

refill *vt* [rēfil'] rellenar ♦ *n* [rē'fil] repuesto, recambio.

refine [rifīn'] *vt* (*sugar, oil*) refinar.

refined [rifīnd'] *a* (*person, taste*) refinado, culto.

refinement [rifīn'mənt] *n* (*of person*) cultura, educación *f*.

refinery [rifī'nûrē] *n* refinería.

refit (*NAUT*) *n* [rē'fit] equipamiento ♦ *vt* [rēfit'] reparar.

reflate [riflāt'] *vt* (*economy*) reflacionar.

reflation [riflā'shən] *n* reflación *f*.

reflationary [riflā'shənärē] *a* reflacionario.

reflect [riflekt'] *vt* (*light, image*) reflejar ♦ *vi* (*think*) reflexionar, pensar; **it ~s badly/well on him** le perjudica/le hace honor.

reflection [riflek'shən] *n* (*act*) reflexión *f*; (*image*) reflejo; (*discredit*) crítica; **on ~** pensándolo bien.

reflector [riflek'tûr] *n* (*AUT*) captafaros *m inv*; (*telescope*) reflector *m*.

reflex [rē'fleks] *a, n* reflejo.

reflexive [riflek'siv] *a* (*LING*) reflexivo.

reforest [rēfôr'ist] *vt* repoblar de árboles.

reform [rifôrm'] *n* reforma ♦ *vt* reformar.

reformat [rēfôr'mat] *vt* (*COMPUT*) recomponer.

Reformation [refûrmā'shən] *n*: **the ~** la Reforma.

reformatory [rifôr'mətôrē] *n* reformatorio.

reformer [rifôr'mûr] *n* reformador(a) *m/f*.

refrain [rifrān'] *vi*: **to ~ from doing** abstenerse de hacer ♦ *n* (*MUS etc*) estribillo.

refresh [rifresh'] *vt* refrescar.

refresher course [rifresh'ûr kôrs] *n* curso de repaso.

refreshing [rifresh'ing] *a* (*drink*) refrescante; (*sleep*) reparador; (*change etc*) estimulante; (*idea, point of view*) estimulante, interesante.

refreshments [rifresh'mənts] *npl* (*drinks*) refrescos *mpl*.

refreshment stand *n* puesto de refrescos.

refrigeration [rifrijərā'shən] *n* refrigeración *f*.

refrigerator [rifrij'ərātûr] *n* nevera, refrigeradora (*LAm*).

refuel [rēfyōō'əl] *vi* repostar (combustible).

refueling, (*Brit*) **refuelling** [rēfyōō'əling] *n* reabastecimiento de combustible.

refuge [ref'yōōj] *n* refugio, asilo; **to take ~ in** refugiarse en.

refugee [refyōōjē'] *n* refugiado/a.

refugee camp *n* campamento para refu-

giados.

refund *n* [rē'fund] reembolso ♦ *vt* [rifund'] devolver, reembolsar.

refurbish [rēfûr'bish] *vt* restaurar, renovar.

refurnish [rēfûr'nish] *vt* amueblar de nuevo.

refusal [rifyōō'zəl] *n* negativa; **first ~** primera opción; **to have first ~ on sth** tener la primera opción a algo.

refuse *n* [ref'yōōs] basura ♦ (*vb*: [rifyōōz']) *vt* (*reject*) rehusar; (*say no to*) negarse a ♦ *vi* negarse; (*horse*) rehusar; **to ~ to do sth** negarse a *or* rehusar hacer algo.

refuse collection *n* (*Brit*) recolección *f* de basuras.

refuse disposal *n* (*Brit*) eliminación *f* de basuras.

refute [rifyōōt'] *vt* refutar, rebatir.

regain [rigān'] *vt* recobrar, recuperar.

regal [rē'gəl] *a* regio, real.

regale [rigāl'] *vt* agasajar, entretener.

regalia [rigā'lēə] *n* insignias *fpl*.

regard [rigärd'] *n* (*gaze*) mirada; (*aspect*) respecto; (*esteem*) respeto, consideración *f* ♦ *vt* (*consider*) considerar; (*look at*) mirar; **to give one's ~s to** saludar de su parte a; **"(kind) ~s"** ''muy atentamente''; **"with kindest ~s"** ''con muchos recuerdos''; **~s to María, please give my ~s to María** recuerdos a María, dele recuerdos a María de mi parte; **~ing, as ~s, with ~ to** con respecto a, en cuanto a.

regarding [rigär'ding] *prep* con respecto a, en cuanto a.

regardless [rigärd'lis] *ad* a pesar de todo; **~ of** sin reparar en.

regatta [rigát'ə] *n* regata.

regency [rē'jənsē] *n* regencia.

regenerate [rējen'ûrāt] *vt* regenerar.

regent [rē'jənt] *n* regente *m/f*.

régime [rāzhēm'] *n* régimen *m*.

regiment *n* [rej'əmənt] regimiento ♦ *vt* [rej'əment] reglamentar.

regimental [rejəmen'təl] *a* militar.

regimentation [rejəməntā'shən] *n* regimentación *f*.

region [rē'jən] *n* región *f*; **in the ~ of** (*fig*) alrededor de.

regional [rē'jənəl] *a* regional.

regional development *n* desarrollo regional.

register [rej'istûr] *n* registro ♦ *vt* registrar; (*birth*) declarar; (*letter*) certificar; (*subj: instrument*) marcar, indicar ♦ *vi* (*at hotel*) registrarse; (*sign on*) inscribirse; (*make impression*) producir impresión; **to ~ a protest** presentar una queja; **to ~ for a course** matricularse *or* inscribirse en un curso.

registered [rej'istûrd] *a* (*design*) registrado; (*letter*) certificado; (*student*) matriculado; (*voter*) registrado.

registered company *n* sociedad *f* legalmente constituida.

registered nurse n (*US*) enfermero/a calificado/a.

registered office n (*Brit*) domicilio social.

registered trademark n marca registrada.

registrar [rej'istrâr] n secretario/a (del registro civil).

registration [rejistrā'shən] n (*act*) declaración f; (*AUT: also*: ~ **number**) matrícula.

registry [rej'istrē] n registro.

registry office [rej'istrē ôfis] n (*Brit*) registro civil; **to get married in a** ~ casarse por lo civil.

regret [rigret'] n sentimiento, pesar m; (*remorse*) remordimiento ♦ vt sentir, lamentar; (*repent of*) arrepentirse de; **we** ~ **to inform you that** ... sentimos informarle que ....

regretful [rigret'fəl] a pesaroso, arrepentido.

regretfully [rigret'fəlē] ad con pesar, sentidamente.

regrettable [rigret'əbəl] a lamentable; (*loss*) sensible.

regrettably [rigret'əblē] ad desgraciadamente.

regroup [rēgrōōp'] vt reagrupar ♦ vi reagruparse.

regt abbr = **regiment.**

regular [reg'yəlûr] a regular; (*soldier*) profesional; (*col: intensive*) verdadero; (*listener, reader*) asiduo, habitual ♦ n (*client etc*) cliente/a m/f habitual; (*US:* ~ **gas**) gasolina normal.

regularity [regyəlar'itē] n regularidad f.

regularly [reg'yəlûrlē] ad con regularidad.

regulate [reg'yəlāt] vt (*gen*) controlar; (*TECH*) regular, ajustar.

regulation [regyəlā'shən] n (*rule*) regla, reglamento; (*adjustment*) regulación f.

rehabilitation [rēhəbilətā'shən] n rehabilitación f.

rehash [rēhash'] vt (*col*) hacer un refrito de.

rehearsal [rihûr'səl] n ensayo; **dress** ~ ensayo general or final.

rehearse [rihûrs'] vt ensayar.

rehouse [rēhouz'] vt dar nueva vivienda a.

reign [rān] n reinado; (*fig*) predominio ♦ vi reinar; (*fig*) imperar.

reigning [rā'ning] a (*monarch*) reinante, actual; (*predominant*) imperante.

reimburse [rēimbûrs'] vt reembolsar.

rein [rān] n (*for horse*) rienda; **to give sb free** ~ dar rienda suelta a uno.

reincarnation [rēinkârnā'shən] n reencarnación f.

reindeer [rān'dēr] n, pl inv reno.

reinforce [rēinfôrs'] vt reforzar.

reinforced concrete [rēinfôrst' kân'krēt] n hormigón armado.

reinforcement [rēinfôrs'mənt] n (*action*) refuerzo; ~**s** npl (*MIL*) refuerzos mpl.

reinstate [rēinstāt'] vt (*worker*) reintegrar (a su puesto).

reinstatement [rēinstāt'mənt] n reintegración f.

reissue [rēish'ōō] vt (*record, book*) reeditar.

reiterate [rēit'ərāt] vt reiterar, repetir.

reject n [rē'jekt] (*thing*) desecho ♦ vt [rijekt'] rechazar; (*proposition, offer etc*) descartar.

rejection [rijek'shən] n rechazo.

rejoice [rijois'] vi: **to** ~ **at** or **over** regocijarse or alegrarse de.

rejoinder [rijoin'dûr] n (*retort*) réplica.

rejuvenate [rijōō'vənāt] vt rejuvenecer.

rekindle [rēkin'dəl] vt reencender; (*fig*) despertar.

relapse [rilaps'] n (*MED*) recaída; (*into crime*) reincidencia.

relate [rilāt'] vt (*tell*) contar, relatar; (*connect*) relacionar ♦ vi relacionarse; **to** ~ **to** (*connect*) relacionarse or tener que ver con.

related [rilā'tid] a afín; (*person*) emparentado; ~ **to** con referencia a, relacionado con.

relating [rilā'ting]: ~ **to** prep referente a.

relation [rilā'shən] n (*person*) pariente m/f; (*link*) relación f; **in** ~ **to** en relación con, en lo que se refiere a; **to bear a** ~ **to** guardar relación con; **diplomatic/international** ~**s** relaciones fpl diplomáticas/internacionales.

relationship [rilā'shənship] n relación f; (*personal*) relaciones fpl; (*also*: **family** ~) parentesco.

relative [rel'ətiv] n pariente m/f, familiar m/f ♦ a relativo.

relatively [rel'ətivlē] ad (*fairly, rather*) relativamente.

relative pronoun n pronombre m relativo.

relax [rilaks'] vi descansar; (*quiet down*) relajarse ♦ vt relajar; (*mind, person*) descansar; ~**!** (*calm down*) ¡tranquilo!

relaxation [rēlaksā'shən] n (*rest*) descanso; (*easing*) relajación f, relajamiento m; (*amusement*) recreo; (*entertainment*) diversión f.

relaxed [rilakst'] a relajado; (*tranquil*) tranquilo.

relaxing [rilaks'ing] a relajante.

relay n [rē'lā] (*race*) carrera de relevos ♦ vt [rēlā'] (*RADIO, TV, pass on*) retransmitir.

release [rilēs'] n (*liberation*) liberación f; (*discharge*) puesta en libertad f; (*of gas etc*) escape m; (*of movie etc*) estreno ♦ vt (*prisoner*) poner en libertad; (*movie*) estrenar; (*book*) publicar; (*piece of news*) difundir; (*gas etc*) despedir, arrojar; (*free: from wreckage etc*) soltar; (*TECH: catch, spring etc*) desenganchar; (*let go*) soltar, aflojar.

relegate [rel'əgāt] vt relegar; (*SPORT*): **to be** ~**d to** bajar a.

relent [rilent'] vi ablandarse; (*let up*) descansar.

relentless [rilent'lis] a implacable.

relentlessly [rilent'lislē] *ad* implacablemente.

relevance [rel'əvəns] *n* relación *f.*

relevant [rel'əvənt] *a* (*fact*) pertinente; ~ **to** relacionado con.

reliability [rilīəbil'ətē] *n* fiabilidad *f*; seguridad *f*; veracidad *f.*

reliable [rilī'əbəl] *a* (*person, firm*) de confianza, de fiar; (*method, machine*) seguro; (*source*) fidedigno.

reliably [rilī'əblē] *ad*: **to be ~ informed that...** saber de fuente fidedigna que... .

reliance [rilī'əns] *n*: ~ **(on)** dependencia (de).

reliant [rilī'ənt] *a*: **to be ~ on sth/sb** confiar en algo/uno.

relic [rel'ik] *n* (*REL*) reliquia; (*of the past*) vestigio.

relief [rilēf'] *n* (*from pain, anxiety*) alivio, desahogo; (*help, supplies*) socorro, ayuda; (*ART, GEO*) relieve *m;* **by way of ~** a modo de diversión.

relief road *n* (*Brit*) carretera de desgasinamiento.

relieve [rilēv'] *vt* (*pain, patient*) aliviar; (*bring help to*) ayudar, socorrer; (*burden*) aligerar; (*take over from: gen*) sustituir a; (*: guard*) relevar; **to ~ sb of sth** quitar algo a uno; **to ~ sb of his command** (*MIL*) relevar a uno de su mando; **to ~ o.s.** hacer sus necesidades; **I am ~d to hear you are better** me tranquiliza saber que estás *or* te encuentras mejor.

religion [rilij'ən] *n* religión *f.*

religious [rilij'əs] *a* religioso.

religiously [rilij'əslē] *ad* religiosamente; (*conscientiously*) puntualmente, fielmente.

reline [rēlīn'] *vt* (*brakes*) poner nueva guarnición a.

relinquish [riling'kwish] *vt* abandonar; (*plan, habit*) renunciar a.

relish [rel'ish] *n* (*CULIN*) salsa; (*enjoyment*) entusiasmo; (*flavor*) sabor *m*, gusto ♦ *vt* (*food etc*) saborear; **to ~ doing** gustar mucho de hacer.

relive [rēliv'] *vt* vivir de nuevo, volver a vivir.

relocate [rēlō'kāt] *vt* cambiar de lugar, mudar ♦ *vi* mudarse.

reluctance [riluk'təns] *n* renuencia.

reluctant [riluk'tənt] *a* renuente; **to be ~ to do sth** resistirse a hacer algo.

reluctantly [riluk'təntlē] *ad* de mala gana.

rely [rilī']: **to ~ on** *vt fus* confiar en, fiarse de; (*be dependent on*) depender de; **you can ~ on my discretion** puedes contar con mi discreción.

remain [rimān'] *vi* (*survive*) quedar; (*be left*) sobrar; (*continue*) quedar(se), permanecer; **to ~ silent** permanecer callado.

remainder [rimān'dûr] *n* resto.

remaining [rimā'ning] *a* sobrante.

remains [rimānz'] *npl* restos *mpl.*

remand [rimand'] *n*: **on ~** detenido (bajo custodia) ♦ *vt*: **to ~ in custody** mantener bajo custodia.

remark [rimârk'] *n* comentario ♦ *vt* comentar; **to ~ on sth** hacer observaciones sobre algo.

remarkable [rimâr'kəbəl] *a* notable; (*outstanding*) extraordinario.

remarkably [rimâr'kəblē] *ad* extraordinariamente.

remarry [rēmar'ē] *vi* casarse por segunda vez, volver a casarse.

remedial [rimē'dēəl] *a*: ~ **education** educación *f* de los niños atrasados.

remedy [rem'idē] *n* remedio ♦ *vt* remediar, curar.

remember [rimem'bûr] *vt* recordar, acordarse de; (*bear in mind*) tener presente; **I ~ seeing it, I ~ having seen it** recuerdo haberlo visto; **she ~ed doing it** se acordó de hacerlo; ~ **me to your wife and children!** ¡déle recuerdos a su familia!

remembrance [rimem'brəns] *n* (*memory, souvenir*) recuerdo; **in ~ of** en conmemoración de.

remind [rimīnd'] *vt*: **to ~ sb to do sth** recordar a uno que haga algo; **to ~ sb of sth** recordar algo a uno; **she ~s me of her mother** me recuerda a su madre; **that ~s me!** ¡a propósito!

reminder [rimīnd'ûr] *n* notificación *f*; (*memento*) recuerdo.

reminisce [remənis'] *vi* recordar (viejas historias).

reminiscences [remənis'ənsiz] *npl* reminiscencias *fpl*, recuerdos *mpl.*

reminiscent [remənis'ənt] *a*: **to be ~ of sth** recordar algo.

remiss [rimis'] *a* descuidado; **it was ~ of me** fue un descuido de mi parte.

remission [rimish'ən] *n* remisión *f*; (*of sentence*) disminución *f* de pena.

remit [rimit'] *vt* (*send: money*) remitir, enviar.

remittance [rimit'əns] *n* remesa, envío.

remnant [rem'nənt] *n* resto; (*of cloth*) retazo; ~**s** *npl* (*COMM*) restos de serie.

remonstrate [rimän'strāt] *vi* protestar.

remorse [rimôrs'] *n* remordimientos *mpl.*

remorseful [rimôrs'fəl] *a* arrepentido.

remorseless [rimôrs'lis] *a* (*fig*) implacable, inexorable.

remorselessly [rimôrs'lislē] *ad* implacablemente, inexorablemente.

remote [rimōt'] *a* (*distant*) lejano; (*person*) distante; (*COMPUT*) remoto; **there is a ~ possibility that ...** hay una posibilidad remota de que ....

remote control *n* telecontrol *m.*

remote-controlled [rimōt'kəntrōld'] *a* teledirigido.

remotely [rimōt'lē] *ad* remotamente; (*slightly*) levemente.

remoteness [rimōt'nis] n alejamiento; distancia.
remould [rē'mōld] n (Brit: tire) neumático or llanta (LAm) recauchutado/a.
removable [rimōō'vəbəl] a (detachable) separable.
removal [rimōō'vəl] n (taking away) el quitar; (Brit: from house) mudanza; (from office: dismissal) destitución f; (MED) extirpación f.
removal van n (Brit) camión m de mudanzas.
remove [rimōōv'] vt quitar; (employee) destituir; (name: from list) tachar, borrar; (doubt) disipar; (TECH) retirar, separar; (MED) extirpar; **first cousin once ~d** (parent's cousin) tío/a segundo/a; (cousin's child) sobrino/a segundo/a.
remover [rimōō'vûr] n: **make-up ~** desmaquilladora; **~s** npl (Brit: company) agencia de mudanzas.
remunerate [rimyōō'nərāt] vt remunerar.
remuneration [rimyōōnərā'shən] n remuneración f.
Renaissance [ren'isâns] n: **the ~** el Renacimiento.
rename [rēnām'] vt poner nuevo nombre a.
render [ren'dûr] vt (thanks; aid) proporcionar; (honor) dar, conceder; (assistance) dar, prestar; **to ~ sth + a** volver algo + a.
rendering [ren'dûring] n (MUS etc) interpretación f.
rendezvous [rân'dāvōō] n cita ♦ vi reunirse, encontrarse; (spaceship) efectuar una reunión espacial.
rendition [rendish'ən] n (MUS) interpretación f.
renegade [ren'əgād] n renegado/a.
renew [rinōō'] vt renovar; (resume) reanudar; (extend date) prorrogar; (negotiations) volver a.
renewable [rinōō'əbəl] a renovable.
renewal [rinōō'əl] n renovación f; reanudación f; prórroga.
renounce [rinouns'] vt renunciar a; (right, inheritance) renunciar.
renovate [ren'əvāt] vt renovar.
renovation [renəvā'shən] n renovación f.
renown [rinoun'] n renombre m.
renowned [rinound'] a renombrado.
rent [rent] n alquiler m; (for house) arriendo, renta; **"for ~"** "se alquila" ♦ vt (also: ~ **out**) alquilar.
rental [ren'təl] n (for television, car) alquiler m.
rental car n coche m de alquiler.
rental fee n tarifa de alquiler.
renunciation [rinunsēā'shən] n renuncia.
reopen [rēō'pən] vt volver a abrir, reabrir.
reorder [rēôr'dûr] vt volver a pedir, repetir el pedido de; (rearrange) volver a ordenar or arreglar.

reorganization [rēôrgənəzā'shən] n reorganización f.
reorganize [rēôr'gənīz] vt reorganizar.
rep [rep] n abbr (COMM) = **representative**; (THEATER) = **repertory**.
Rep. abbr (US POL) = **representative, republican**.
repair [ripär'] n reparación f, compostura; (patch) remiendo ♦ vt reparar, componer; (shoes) remendar; **in good/bad ~** en buen/mal estado; **under ~** en obras.
repair kit n caja de herramientas.
repair man n mecánico.
repair shop n taller m de reparaciones.
repartee [repûrtē'] n réplicas fpl agudas.
repast [ripast'] n (formal) comida.
repatriate [rēpā'trēāt] vt repatriar.
repay [ripā'] vt (irg: like **pay**) (money) devolver, reembolsar; (person) pagar; (debt) liquidar; (sb's efforts) devolver, corresponder a.
repayment [ripā'mənt] n reembolso, devolución f; (sum of money) recompensa.
repeal [ripēl'] n revocación f ♦ vt revocar.
repeat [ripēt'] n (RADIO, TV) reposición f ♦ vt repetir ♦ vi repetirse.
repeatedly [ripēt'idlē] ad repetidas veces.
repeat order n (COMM): **to place a ~ for** renovar un pedido de.
repel [ripel'] vt repugnar.
repellent [ripel'ənt] a repugnante ♦ n: **insect ~** crema/loción f anti-insectos.
repent [ripent'] vi: **to ~ (of)** arrepentirse (de).
repentance [ripen'təns] n arrepentimiento.
repercussion [rēpûrkush'ən] n (consequence) repercusión f; **to have ~s** repercutir.
repertoire [rep'ûrtwâr] n repertorio.
repertory [rep'ûrtôrē] n (also: ~ **theater**) teatro de repertorio.
repertory company n compañía de repertorio.
repetition [repitish'ən] n repetición f.
repetitious [repitish'əs] a repetidor(a), que se repite.
repetitive [ripet'ətiv] a (movement, work) reiterativo; (speech) lleno de repeticiones.
rephrase [rēfrāz'] vt decir or formular de otro modo.
replace [riplās'] vt (put back) devolver a su sitio; (take the place of) reemplazar, sustituir.
replacement [riplās'mənt] n reemplazo; (act) reposición f; (thing) recambio; (person) suplente m/f.
replacement cost n costo de sustitución.
replacement part n repuesto.
replacement value n valor m de sustitución.
replay [rēplā'] n (SPORT) desempate m; (TV: playback) repetición f.
replenish [riplen'ish] vt (tank etc) rellenar;

(*stock etc*) reponer; (*with fuel*) repostar.
replete |riplēt'| *a* repleto, lleno.
replica |rɛp'ləkə| *n* copia, reproducción *f*.
reply |riplī'| *n* respuesta, contestación *f* ♦ *vi* contestar, responder; **in** ~ en respuesta.
report |ripórt'| *n* informe *m*; (*PRESS etc*) reportaje *m*; (*Brit: also*: **school** ~) nota; (*of gun*) estallido ♦ *vt* informar sobre; (*PRESS etc*) hacer un reportaje sobre; (*notify*: *accident, culprit*) denunciar ♦ *vi* (*make a report*) presentar un informe; (*present o.s.*): **to** ~ (**to sb**) presentarse (ante uno); **annual** ~ (*COMM*) informe *m* anual; **to** ~ (**on**) hacer un informe (sobre); **it is** ~**ed from Berlin that ...** se informa desde Berlín que ....
report card *n* (*US, Scottish*) cartilla escolar.
reportedly |ripór'tidlē| *ad* según se dice, según se informe.
reporter |ripôr'tûr| *n* (*PRESS*) periodista *m/f*; (*RADIO, TV*) locutor(a) *m/f*.
repose |ripōz'| *n*: **in** ~ (*face, mouth*) en reposo.
repossess |rēpəzɛs'| *vt* recobrar.
reprehensible |rɛprihɛn'səbəl| *a* reprensible, censurable.
represent |rɛprizɛnt'| *vt* representar; (*COMM*) ser agente de.
representation |rɛprizɛntā'shən| *n* representación *f*; (*petition*) petición *f*; ~**s** *npl* (*protest*) quejas *fpl*.
representative |rɛprizɛn'tətiv| *n* (*US POL*) representante *m/f*, diputado/a; (*COMM*) representante *m/f* ♦ *a*: ~ (**of**) representativo (de).
repress |riprɛs'| *vt* reprimir.
repression |riprɛsh'ən| *n* represión *f*.
repressive |riprɛs'iv| *a* represivo.
reprieve |riprēv'| *n* (*LAW*) indulto; (*fig*) alivio ♦ *vt* indultar; (*fig*) salvar.
reprimand |rɛp'rəmand| *n* reprimenda ♦ *vt* reprender.
reprint *n* |rē'print| reimpresión *f*, reedición *f* ♦ *vt* |rēprint'| reimprimir.
reprisal |riprī'zəl| *n* represalia; **to take** ~**s** tomar represalias.
reproach |riprōch'| *n* reproche *m* ♦ *vt*: **to** ~ **sb with sth** reprochar algo a uno; **beyond** ~ intachable.
reproachful |riprōch'fəl| *a* de reproche, de acusación.
reproduce |rēprədōōs'| *vt* reproducir ♦ *vi* reproducirse.
reproduction |rēprəduk'shən| *n* reproducción *f*.
reproductive |rēprəduk'tiv| *a* reproductor(a).
reproof |riprōōf'| *n* reproche *m*.
reprove |riprōōv'| *vt*: **to** ~ **sb for sth** reprochar algo a uno.
reptile |rɛp'tīl| *n* reptil *m*.
republic |ripub'lik| *n* república.

republican |ripub'likən| *a, n* republicano/a *m/f*.
repudiate |ripyōō'dēāt| *vt* (*accusation*) rechazar; (*obligation*) desconocer.
repudiation |ripyōōdēā'shən| *n* incumplimiento.
repugnance |ripug'nəns| *n* repugnancia.
repugnant |ripug'nənt| *a* repugnante.
repulse |ripuls'| *vt* rechazar.
repulsion |ripul'shən| *n* repulsión *f*, repugnancia.
repulsive |ripul'siv| *a* repulsivo.
repurchase |rēpûr'chis| *vt* volver a comprar, readquirir.
reputable |rɛp'yətəbəl| *a* (*make etc*) de renombre.
reputation |rɛpyətā'shən| *n* reputación *f*; **he has a** ~ **for being awkward** tiene fama de difícil.
repute |ripyōōt'| *n* reputación *f*, fama.
reputed |ripyōō'tid| *a* supuesto; **to be** ~ **to be rich/intelligent** *etc* tener fama de rico/inteligente *etc*.
reputedly |ripyōō'tidlē| *ad* según dicen *or* se dice.
request |rikwɛst'| *n* solicitud *f*, petición *f* ♦ *vt*: **to** ~ **sth of** *or* **from sb** solicitar algo a uno; **at the** ~ **of** a petición de; **"you are** ~**ed not to smoke"** "se ruega no fumar".
request stop *n* (*Brit*) parada a petición.
requiem |rɛk'wēəm| *n* réquiem *m*.
require |rikwiûr'| *vt* (*need: subj: person*) necesitar, tener necesidad de; (: *thing, situation*) exigir; (*want*) pedir; (*demand*) insistir en que; **to** ~ **sb to do sth/sth of sb** exigir que uno haga algo; **what qualifications are** ~**d?** ¿qué títulos se requieren?; ~**d by law** requerido por la ley.
requirement |rikwiûr'mənt| *n* requisito; (*need*) necesidad *f*.
requisite |rɛk'wizit| *n* requisito ♦ *a* necesario, requerido.
requisition |rɛkwizish'ən| *n*: ~ (**for**) solicitud *f* (de) ♦ *vt* (*MIL*) requisar.
reroute |rērrout'| *vt* desviar.
resale |rē'sāl| *n* reventa.
resale price maintenance |rē'sāl prīs mān'tənəns| *n* mantenimiento del precio de venta.
rescind |risind'| *vt* (*LAW*) abrogar; (*contract, order etc*) anular.
rescue |rɛs'kyōō| *n* rescate *m* ♦ *vt* rescatar; **to come/go to sb's** ~ ir en auxilio de uno, socorrer a uno; **to** ~ **from** librar de.
rescue party *n* expedición *f* de salvamento.
rescuer |rɛs'kyōōûr| *n* salvador(a) *m/f*.
research |risûrch'| *n* investigaciones *fpl* ♦ *vt* investigar; **a piece of** ~ un trabajo de investigación; **to** ~ (**into sth**) investigar (algo).
research and development (R & D) *n* investigación *f* y desarrollo.

researcher |risûr'chúr| *n* investigador(a) *m/f*.

research work *n* investigación *f*.

resell |rēsel'| *vt* revender.

resemblance |rizem'bləns| *n* parecido; **to bear a strong ~ to** parecerse mucho a.

resemble |rizem'bəl| *vt* parecerse a.

resent |rizent'| *vt* resentirse de.

resentful |rizent'fəl| *a* resentido.

resentment |rizent'mənt| *n* resentimiento.

reservation |rezûrvā'shən| *n* reserva; (*booking*) reservación *f*; (*Brit: also:* **central ~**) faja intermedia; **with ~s** con reservas.

reservation desk *n* (*US: in hotel*) recepción *f*.

reserve |rizûrv'| *n* reserva; (*SPORT*) suplente *m/f* ♦ *vt* (*seats etc*) reservar; **~s** *npl* (*MIL*) reserva *sg*; **in ~** en reserva.

reserve currency *n* divisa de reserva.

reserved |rizûrvd'| *a* reservado.

reserve price *n* (*Brit*) precio mínimo.

reservist |rizûr'vist| *n* (*MIL*) reservista *m*.

reservoir |rez'ûrvwár| *n* (*artificial lake*) embalse *m*, represa (*LAm*); (*small*) depósito.

reset |rēset'| *vt* (*COMPUT*) reinicializar.

reshape |rēshāp'| *vt* (*policy*) reformar, rehacer.

reshuffle |rēshuf'əl| *n*: **Cabinet ~** (*Brit POL*) remodelación *f* del gabinete.

reside |rizīd'| *vi* residir, vivir.

residence |rez'idəns| *n* residencia; (*formal: home*) domicilio; (*length of stay*) permanencia; **in ~** (*queen etc*) en residencia; (*doctor*) residente; **to take up ~** instalarse.

resident |rez'idənt| *n* vecino/a; (*in hotel*) huésped/a *m/f* ♦ *a* (*population*) permanente; (*COMPUT*) residente.

residential |reziden'chəl| *a* residencial.

residue |rez'idoo| *n* resto, residuo.

resign |rizīn'| *vt* (*gen*) renunciar a ♦ *vi*: **to ~ (from)** dimitir (de), renunciar (a); **to ~ o.s. to** (*endure*) resignarse a.

resignation |rezignā'shən| *n* dimisión *f*; (*state of mind*) resignación *f*; **to tender one's ~** presentar la dimisión.

resigned |rizīnd'| *a* resignado.

resilience |rizil'yəns| *n* (*of material*) elasticidad *f*; (*of person*) resistencia.

resilient |rizil'yənt| *a* (*person*) resistente.

resin |rez'in| *n* resina.

resist |rizist'| *vt* resistir, oponerse a.

resistance |rizis'təns| *n* resistencia.

resistant |rizis'tənt| *a*: **~ (to)** resistente (a).

resolute |rez'əloot| *a* resuelto.

resolutely |rez'əlootlē| *ad* resueltamente.

resolution |rezəloo'shən| *n* (*gen*) resolución *f*; (*purpose*) propósito; (*COMPUT*) definición *f*; **to make a ~** tomar una resolución.

resolve |rizálv'| *n* (*determination*) resolución *f*; (*purpose*) propósito ♦ *vt* resolver ♦

vi resolverse; **to ~ to do** resolver hacer.

resolved |rizálvd'| *a* resuelto.

resonance |rez'ənəns| *n* resonancia.

resonant |rez'ənənt| *a* resonante.

resort |rizôrt'| *n* (*town*) centro turístico; (*recourse*) recurso ♦ *vi*: **to ~ to** recurrir a; **in the last ~** como último recurso; **seaside/winter sports ~** playa, estación *f* balnearia/centro de deportes de invierno.

resound |rizound'| *vi*: **to ~ (with)** resonar (con).

resounding |rizoun'ding| *a* sonoro; (*fig*) clamoroso.

resource |rē'sôrs| *n* recurso; **~s** *npl* recursos *mpl*; **natural ~s** recursos *mpl* naturales; **to leave sb to his/her own ~s** (*fig*) abandonar a uno/a a sus propios recursos.

resourceful |risôrs'fəl| *a* despabilado, ingenioso.

resourcefulness |risôrs'fəlnis| *n* inventiva, iniciativa.

respect |rispekt'| *n* (*consideration*) respeto; (*relation*) respecto; **~s** *npl* recuerdos *mpl*, saludos *mpl* ♦ *vt* respetar; **with ~ to** con respecto a; **in this ~** en cuanto a eso; **to have** *or* **show ~ for** tener *or* mostrar respeto a; **out of ~ for** por respeto a; **in some ~s** en algunos aspectos; **with due ~ I still think you're wrong** con el respeto debido, sigo creyendo que está equivocado.

respectability |rispektəbil'ətē| *n* respetabilidad *f*.

respectable |rispek'təbəl| *a* respetable; (*quite big: amount etc*) apreciable; (*passable*) tolerable; (*quite good: player, result etc*) bastante bueno.

respected |rispek'tid| *a* respetado, estimado.

respectful |rispekt'fəl| *a* respetuoso.

respectfully |rispekt'fəlē| *ad* respetuosamente; **Yours ~** Le saluda atentamente.

respecting |rispek'ting| *prep* (con) respecto a, en cuanto a.

respective |rispek'tiv| *a* respectivo.

respectively |rispek'tivlē| *ad* respectivamente.

respiration |respərā'shən| *n* respiración *f*.

respiratory |res'pûrətôrē| *a* respiratorio.

respite |res'pit| *n* respiro; (*LAW*) prórroga.

resplendent |risplen'dənt| *a* resplandeciente.

respond |rispánd'| *vi* responder; (*react*) reaccionar.

respondent |rispán'dənt| *n* (*LAW*) acusado/a.

response |rispáns'| *n* respuesta; (*reaction*) reacción *f*; **in ~ to** como respuesta a.

responsibility |rispánsəbil'ətē| *n* responsabilidad *f*; **to take ~ for sth/sb** admitir responsabilidad por algo/uno.

responsible |rispán'səbəl| *a* (*liable*): **~ (for)** responsable (de); (*character*) serio, formal; (*job*) de confianza; **to be ~ to sb**

(for sth) ser responsable ante uno (de algo).

responsibly [rispán'səblē] *ad* con seriedad.

responsive [rispán'siv] *a* sensible.

rest [rest] *n* descanso, reposo; (*MUS*) pausa, silencio; (*support*) apoyo; (*remainder*) resto ♦ *vi* descansar; **to have a ~** echarse una siesta; (*be supported*): **to ~ on** posar(se) en ♦ *vt* (*lean*): **to ~ sth on/against** apoyar algo en *or* sobre/contra; **the ~ of them** (*people*, *objects*) los demás; **to set sb's mind at ~** tranquilizar a uno; **to ~ one's eyes** *or* **gaze on** fijar la mirada en; **it ~s with him** depende de él; **~ assured that ...** téngalo por seguro que ....

rest area *n* (*US AUT*) apartadero.

restaurant [res'tûrənt] *n* restorán *m*, restaurante *m*.

restaurant car *n* (*Brit*) coche-comedor *m*.

restaurant owner *n* dueño/a *or* propietario/a de un restaurante.

rest cure *n* cura de reposo.

restful [rest'fəl] *a* descansado, tranquilo.

rest home *n* residencia para jubilados.

restitution [restitŌŌ'shən] *n*: **to make ~ to sb for sth** indemnizar a uno por algo.

restive [res'tiv] *a* inquieto; (*horse*) rebelón/ona.

restless [rest'lis] *a* inquieto; **to get ~** impacientarse.

restlessly [rest'lislē] *ad* inquietamente, con inquietud *f*.

restlessness [rest'lisnis] *n* inquietud *f*.

restock [rēsták'] *vt* reaprovisionar.

restoration [restərā'shən] *n* restauración *f*.

restorative [ristôr'ətiv] *a* reconstituyente, fortalecedor(a) ♦ *n* reconstituyente *m*.

restore [ristôr'] *vt* (*building*) restaurar; (*sth stolen*) devolver; (*health*) restablecer.

restorer [ristôr'ûr] *n* (*ART etc*) restaurador(a) *m/f*.

restrain [ristrān'] *vt* (*feeling*) contener, refrenar; (*person*): **to ~ (from doing)** disuadir (de hacer).

restrained [ristrānd'] *a* (*style*) reservado.

restraint [ristrānt'] *n* (*restriction*) freno, control *m*; (*of style*) reserva; **wage ~** control *m* de sueldos.

restrict [ristrikt'] *vt* restringir, limitar.

restricted [ristrik'tid] *a* restringido, limitado.

restriction [ristrik'shən] *n* restricción *f*, limitación *f*.

restrictive [ristrik'tiv] *a* restrictivo.

restrictive practices *npl* (*INDUSTRY*) prácticas *fpl* restrictivas.

rest room *n* (*US*) aseos *mpl*.

restructure [rēstruk'chûr] *vt* reestructurar.

rest stop *n* (*US AUT*) apartadero.

result [rizult'] *n* resultado ♦ *vi*: **to ~ in** terminar en, tener por resultado; **as a ~ of** a *or* como consecuencia de; **to ~ (from)** resultar (de).

resultant [rizul'tənt] *a* resultante.

resume [rēzŌŌm'] *vt* (*work*, *journey*) reanudar; (*sum up*) resumir ♦ *vi* (*meeting*) continuar.

résumé [rez'ŌŌmā'] *n* resumen *m*; (*US*) curriculum *m* (vitae).

resumption [rizump'shən] *n* reanudación *f*.

resurgence [risûr'jəns] *n* resurgimiento.

resurrection [rezərek'shən] *n* resurrección *f*.

resuscitate [risus'ətāt] *vt* (*MED*) resucitar.

resuscitation [risusətā'shən] *n* resucitación *f*.

retail [rē'tāl] *n* venta al por menor ♦ *cpd* al por menor ♦ *vt* vender al por menor *or* al detalle ♦ *vi*: **to ~ at** (*COMM*) tener precio al público de.

retailer [rē'tālûr] *n* detallista *m/f*.

retail outlet *n* punto de venta.

retail price *n* precio de venta al público, precio al detalle *or* al por menor.

retail price index *n* índice *m* de precios al por menor.

retain [ritān'] *vt* (*keep*) retener, conservar; (*employ*) contratar.

retainer [ritā'nûr] *n* (*servant*) criado; (*fee*) anticipo.

retaliate [rital'ēāt] *vi*: **to ~ (against)** tomar represalias (contra).

retaliation [ritalēā'shən] *n* represalias *fpl*; **in ~ for** como represalia por.

retaliatory [rital'ēətôrē] *a* de represalia.

retarded [ritâr'did] *a* retrasado.

retch [rech] *vi* darle a uno arcadas.

retentive [riten'tiv] *a* (*memory*) retentivo.

rethink [rēthingk'] *vt* repensar.

reticence [ret'isəns] *n* reticencia, reserva.

reticent [ret'isənt] *a* reservado.

retina [ret'ənə] *n* retina.

retinue [ret'ənŌŌ] *n* séquito, comitiva.

retire [ritîr'] *vi* (*give up work*) jubilarse; (*withdraw*) retirarse; (*go to bed*) acostarse.

retired [ritîrd'] *a* (*person*) jubilado.

retirement [ritîr'mənt] *n* (*state*) retiro; (*act*) jubilación *f*; **early ~** jubilación *f* temprana.

retiring [ritîr'ing] *a* (*departing*: *chairman*) saliente; (*shy*) retraído.

retort [ritôrt'] *n* (*reply*) réplica ♦ *vi* contestar.

retrace [rētrās'] *vt*: **to ~ one's steps** volver sobre sus pasos, desandar lo andado.

retract [ritrakt'] *vt* (*statement*) retirar; (*claws*) retraer; (*landing gear*, *aerial*) replegar ♦ *vi* retractarse.

retractable [ritrakt'əbəl] *a* replegable.

retrain [rētrān'] *vt* reciclar.

retraining [rētrā'ning] *n* readaptación *f* profesional.

retread [rē'tred] *n* neumático *or* llanta (*LAm*) recauchutado/a.

retreat [ritrēt'] *n* (*place*) retiro; (*MIL*) retirada ♦ *vi* retirarse; (*flood*) bajar; **to beat a hasty ~** (*fig*) retirarse en desorden.

retrial [rētrīl'] *n* nuevo proceso.

retribution [retrəbyōo'shən] *n* desquite *m*.

retrieval [ritrē'vəl] *n* recuperación *f*; **information ~** recuperación *f* de datos.

retrieve [ritrēv'] *vt* recobrar; (*situation, honor*) salvar; (*COMPUT*) recuperar; (*error*) reparar.

retriever [ritrē'vûr] *n* perro cobrador.

retroactive [retrōak'tiv] *a* retroactivo.

retrograde [ret'rəgrād] *a* retrógrado.

retrospect [ret'rəspekt] *n*: **in ~** retrospectivamente.

retrospective [retrəspek'tiv] *a* retrospectivo; (*law*) retroactivo ♦ *n* exposición *f* retrospectiva.

return [ritûrn'] *n* (*going or coming back*) vuelta, regreso; (*of sth stolen etc*) devolución *f*; (*recompense*) recompensa; (*FINANCE: from land, shares*) ganancia, ingresos *mpl*; (*COMM: of merchandise*) devolución *f* ♦ *cpd* (*journey*) de regreso; (*ticket*) de ida y vuelta; (*match*) de desquite ♦ *vi* (*person etc: come or go back*) volver, regresar; (*symptoms etc*) reaparecer ♦ *vt* devolver; (*favor, love etc*) corresponder a; (*verdict*) pronunciar; (*POL: candidate*) elegir; **~s** *npl* (*COMM*) ingresos *mpl*; **tax ~** declaración *f* sobre la renta; **in ~ (for)** en cambio; **by ~ mail** a vuelta de correo; **many happy ~s (of the day)!** ¡feliz cumpleaños!

returnable [ritûr'nəbəl] *a*: **~ bottle** envase *m* retornable.

return key *n* (*COMPUT*) tecla de retorno.

reunion [rēyōon'yən] *n* reunión *f*.

reunite [rēyōonīt'] *vt* reunir; (*reconcile*) reconciliar.

rev [rev] *n abbr* (*AUT*: = *revolution*) revolución *f* ♦ (*vb: also*: **~ up**) *vt* girar ♦ *vi* (*engine*) girarse; (*driver*) girar el motor.

revaluation [rēval'yōoāshən] *n* revalorización *f*.

revamp [rēvamp'] *vt* (*house, company*) renovar.

Rev(d). *abbr* (= *reverend*) R., Rvdo.

reveal [rivēl'] *vt* (*make known*) revelar.

revealing [rivē'ling] *a* revelador(a).

reveille [rev'əlē] *n* (*MIL*) diana.

revel [rev'əl] *vi*: **to ~ in sth/in doing sth** gozar de algo/con hacer algo.

revelation [revəlā'shən] *n* revelación *f*.

reveler, (*Brit*) **reveller** [rev'əlûr] *n* jaranero, juergista *m/f*.

revelry [rev'əlrē] *n* jarana, juerga.

revenge [rivenj'] *n* venganza; (*in sport*) revancha; **to take ~ on** vengarse de; **to get one's ~ (for sth)** vengarse (de algo).

revengeful [rivenj'fəl] *a* vengativo.

revenue [rev'ənōo] *n* ingresos *mpl*, rentas *fpl*.

revenue account *n* cuenta de ingresos presupuestarios.

revenue expenditure *n* gasto corriente.

reverberate [rivûr'bərāt] *vi* (*sound*) resonar, retumbar.

reverberation [rivûrbərā'shən] *n* retumbo, eco.

revere [rivēr'] *vt* reverenciar, venerar.

reverence [rev'ûrəns] *n* reverencia.

Reverend [rev'ûrənd] *a* (*in titles*): **the ~ John Smith** (*Anglican*) el Reverendo John Smith; (*Catholic*) el Padre John Smith; (*Protestant*) el Pastor John Smith.

reverent [rev'ûrənt] *a* reverente.

reverie [rev'ûrē] *n* ensueño.

reversal [rivûr'səl] *n* (*of order*) inversión *f*; (*of policy*) cambio de rumbo; (*of decision*) revocación *f*.

reverse [rivûrs'] *n* (*opposite*) contrario; (*back: of cloth*) revés *m*; (*: of coin*) reverso; (*: of paper*) dorso; (*AUT: also*: **~ gear**) marcha atrás ♦ *a* (*order*) inverso; (*direction*) contrario ♦ *vt* (*decision, AUT*) dar marcha atrás a; (*position, function*) invertir ♦ *vi* (*Brit AUT*) poner en marcha atrás; **in ~ order** en orden inverso; **the ~** lo contrario; **to go into ~** dar marcha atrás.

reverse-charge call [rivûrs'chârj kôl] *n* (*Brit*) llamada a cobro revertido.

reverse video *n* vídeo inverso.

reversible [rivûr'səbəl] *a* (*garment, procedure*) reversible.

reversing lights [rivûr'sing līts] *npl* (*Brit AUT*) luces *fpl* de marcha atrás.

revert [rivûrt'] *vi*: **to ~ to** volver *or* revertir a.

review [rivyōo'] *n* (*magazine, MIL*) revista; (*of book, movie*) reseña; (*US: examination*) repaso, examen *m* ♦ *vt* (*US: subject at school*) repasar, examinar; (*MIL*) pasar revista a; (*book, movie*) reseñar; **to come under ~** ser examinado.

reviewer [rivyōo'ûr] *n* crítico/a.

revile [rivīl'] *vt* injuriar, vilipendiar.

revise [rivīz'] *vt* (*manuscript*) corregir; (*opinion*) modificar; (*Brit: study: subject*) repasar; (*look over*) revisar; **~d edition** edición *f* corregida.

revision [rivizh'ən] *n* corrección *f*; modificación *f*; (*revised version*) repaso, revisión *f*.

revisit [rēviz'it] *vt* volver a visitar.

revitalize [rēvī'təlīz] *vt* revivificar.

revival [rivī'vəl] *n* (*recovery*) reanimación *f*; (*POL*) resurgimiento; (*of interest*) renacimiento; (*THEATER*) reestreno; (*of faith*) despertar *m*.

revive [rivīv'] *vt* resucitar; (*custom*) restablecer; (*hope, courage*) reanimar; (*play*) reestrenar ♦ *vi* (*person*) volver en sí; (*from tiredness*) reponerse; (*business*) reactivarse.

revoke [rivōk'] *vt* revocar.

revolt [rivōlt'] *n* rebelión *f* ♦ *vi* rebelarse,

sublevarse ♦ *vt* dar asco a, repugnar; **to** ~ **(against sb/sth)** rebelarse (contra uno/algo).

revolting [rivōl'ting] *a* asqueroso, repugnante.

revolution [revəlōō'shən] *n* revolución *f*.

revolutionary [revəlōō'shənärē] *a*, *n* revolucionario/a *m/f*.

revolutionize [revəlōō'shənīz] *vt* revolucionar.

revolve [rivälv'] *vi* dar vueltas, girar.

revolver [rivál'vûr] *n* revólver *m*.

revolving [rivál'ving] *a* (*chair, door etc*) giratorio.

revolving credit [rivál'ving kred'it] *n* crédito rotativo *or* renovable.

revue [rivyōō'] *n* (*THEATER*) revista.

revulsion [rivul'shən] *n* asco, repugnancia.

reward [riwôrd'] *n* premio, recompensa ♦ *vt*: **to** ~ **(for)** recompensar *or* premiar (por).

rewarding [riwôrd'ing] *a* (*fig*) valioso; **financially** ~ económicamente provechoso.

rewind [rēwīnd'] *vt* (*watch*) dar cuerda a; (*wool etc*) devanar.

rewire [rēwīūr'] *vt* (*house*) renovar la instalación eléctrica de.

reword [rēwûrd'] *vt* expresar en otras palabras.

rewrite [rērīt'] *vt* (*irg: like* **write**) reescribir.

Reykjavik [rā'kyəvik] *n* Reykjavik *m*.

RFD *abbr* (*US MAIL*) = *rural free delivery*.

Rh *abbr* (= *rhesus*) Rh *m*.

rhapsody [rap'sədē] *n* (*MUS*) rapsodia; (*fig*): **to go into rhapsodies over** extasiarse por.

Rh factor *n* (*MED*) factor *m* rhesus.

rhetoric [ret'ûrik] *n* retórica.

rhetorical [ritôr'ikəl] *a* retórico.

rheumatic [rōōmat'ik] *a* reumático.

rheumatism [rōō'mətizəm] *n* reumatismo, reúma.

rheumatoid arthritis [rōō'mətoid ârthrī'tis] *n* reúma *m* articular.

Rhine [rīn] *n*: **the** ~ el (río) Rin.

rhinestone [rīn'stōn] *n* diamante *m* de imitación.

rhinoceros [rīnās'ûrəs] *n* rinoceronte *m*.

Rhodes [rōdz] *n* Rodas *f*.

rhododendron [rōdəden'drən] *n* rododendro.

Rhone [rōn] *n*: **the** ~ el (río) Ródano.

rhubarb [rōō'bârb] *n* ruibarbo.

rhyme [rīm] *n* rima; (*verse*) poesía ♦ *vi*: **to** ~ **(with)** rimar (con); **without** ~ **or reason** sin ton ni son.

rhythm [rith'əm] *n* ritmo.

rhythmic(al) [rith'mik(əl)] *a* rítmico.

rhythmically [rith'miklē] *ad* rítmicamente.

RI *abbr* (*US MAIL*) = *Rhode Island*.

rib [rib] *n* (*ANAT*) costilla ♦ *vt* (*mock*) tomar el pelo a.

ribald [rib'əld] *a* escabroso.

ribbon [rib'ən] *n* cinta; **in** ~**s** (*torn*) hecho trizas.

rice [rīs] *n* arroz *m*.

ricefield [rīs'fēld] *n* arrozal *m*.

rice paddy *n* (*US*) arrozal *m*.

rice pudding *n* arroz *m* con leche.

rich [rich] *a* rico; (*soil*) fértil; (*food*) pesado; (: *sweet*) empalagoso; **the** ~ *npl* los ricos; ~**es** *npl* riqueza *sg*; **to be** ~ **in sth** abundar en algo.

richly [rich'lē] *ad* ricamente.

richness [rich'nis] *n* riqueza; fertilidad *f*.

rickets [rik'its] *n* raquitismo.

rickety [rik'ətē] *a* (*old*) desvencijado; (*shaky*) tambaleante.

rickshaw [rik'shô] *n* carro de culi.

ricochet [rikəshā'] *n* rebote *m* ♦ *vi* rebotar.

rid, *pt*, *pp* **rid** [rid] *vt*: **to** ~ **sb of sth** librar a uno de algo; **to get** ~ **of** deshacerse *or* desembarazarse de.

riddance [rid'əns] *n*: **good** ~! ¡y adiós muy buenas!

ridden [rid'ən] *pp of* **ride**.

riddle [rid'əl] *n* (*conundrum*) acertijo; (*mystery*) enigma *m*, misterio ♦ *vt*: **to be** ~**d with** ser lleno *or* plagado de.

ride [rīd] *n* paseo; (*distance covered*) viaje *m*, recorrido ♦ *vb* (*pt* **rode**, *pp* **ridden** [rōd, rid'ən]) *vi* (*horse: as sport*) montar; (*go somewhere: on horse, bicycle*) dar un paseo, pasearse; (*journey: on bicycle, motorcycle, bus*) viajar ♦ *vt* (*a horse*) montar a; (*distance*) viajar; **to** ~ **a bicycle** andar en bicicleta; **to** ~ **at anchor** (*NAUT*) estar fondeado; **can you** ~ **a bike?** ¿sabes montar en bici(cleta)?; **to give sb a** ~ (*to work etc*) llevar a uno en el coche; **to go for a** ~ dar un paseo; **to take sb for a** ~ (*fig*) engañar a uno.

ride out *vt*: **to** ~ **out the storm** (*fig*) capear el temporal.

rider [rī'dûr] *n* (*on horse*) jinete *m*; (*on bicycle*) ciclista *m/f*; (*on motorcycle*) motociclista *m/f*.

ridge [rij] *n* (*of hill*) cresta; (*of roof*) caballete *m*; (*wrinkle*) arruga.

ridicule [rid'əkyōōl] *n* irrisión *f*, burla ♦ *vt* poner en ridículo, burlarse de; **to hold sth/sb up to** ~ poner algo/a uno en ridículo.

ridiculous [ridik'yələs] *a* ridículo.

ridiculously [ridik'yələslē] *ad* ridículamente, de modo ridículo.

riding [rī'ding] *n* equitación *f*; **I like** ~ me gusta montar a caballo.

riding habit *n* traje *m* de montar.

riding school *n* escuela de equitación.

rife [rīf] *a*: **to be** ~ ser muy común; **to be** ~ **with** abundar en.

riffraff [rif'raf] *n* chusma, gentuza.

rifle [rī'fəl] *n* rifle *m*, fusil *m* ♦ *vt* saquear.

rifle through *vt fus* saquear.

rifle range *n* campo de tiro; (*at fair*) tiro al blanco.

rift |rift| *n* (*fig*: *between friends*) desavenencia; (: *in party*) escisión *f*.

rig |rig| *n* (*also*: **oil ~**: *on land*) torre *f* de perforación; (: *at sea*) plataforma petrolera ♦ *vt* (*election etc*) amañar los resultados de.
rig up *vt* improvisar.

rigging |rig'ing| *n* (*NAUT*) aparejo.

right |rīt| *a* (*true, correct*) correcto, exacto; (*suitable*) indicado, debido; (*proper*) apropiado, propio; (*just*) justo; (*morally good*) bueno; (*not left*) derecho ♦ *n* (*title, claim*) derecho; (*not left*) derecha ♦ *ad* (*correctly*) bien, correctamente; (*straight*) derecho, directamente; (*not on the left*) a la derecha; (*to the ~*) hacia la derecha ♦ *vt* enderezar ♦ *excl* ¡bueno!, ¡está bien!; **to be ~** (*person*) tener razón; **to be ~ on time** llegar en punto; **to get sth ~** acertar en algo; **you did the ~ thing** hiciste bien; **let's get it ~ this time!** ¡a ver si esta vez nos sale bien!; **the ~ time** la hora exacta; (*fig*) el momento oportuno; **by ~s** en justicia; **~ and wrong** el bien y el mal; **film ~s** derechos *mpl* de la película; **on the ~** a la derecha; **to be in the ~** tener razón; **~ now** ahora mismo; **~ before/after** inmediatamente antes/después; **~ in the middle** exactamente en el centro; **~ away** en seguida; **~ off the bat** (*US*) en seguida; **to go ~ to the end of sth** llegar hasta el final de algo; **~, who's next?** bueno, ¿quién sigue?; **all ~!** ¡vale!; **I'm/I feel all ~ now** ya estoy bien.

right angle *n* ángulo recto.

righteous |rī'chəs| *a* justado, honrado; (*anger*) justificado.

righteousness |rī'chəsnis| *n* justicia.

rightful |rīt'fəl| *a* (*heir*) legítimo.

right-hand |rīt'hand| *a* (*drive, turn*) por la derecha.

right-handed |rīt'handid| *a* (*person*) que usa la mano derecha.

right-hand man |rīt'hand' man| *n* brazo derecho.

right-hand side |rīt'hand' sīd| *n* derecha.

rightly |rīt'lē| *ad* correctamente, debidamente; (*with reason*) con razón; **if I remember ~** si me acuerdo bien.

right-minded |rīt'mīndid| *a* (*sensible*) sensato; (*decent*) honrado.

right of way *n* (*on path etc*) derecho de paso; (*AUT*) prioridad *f* de paso.

rights issue *n* (*STOCK EXCHANGE*) emisión *f* gratuita de acciones.

right-wing |rīt'wing'| *a* (*POL*) derechista.

right-winger |rīt'wing'ûr| *n* (*POL*) derechista *m/f*; (*Brit SPORT*) extremo derecha.

rigid |rij'id| *a* rígido; (*person, ideas*) inflexible.

rigidity |rijid'itē| *n* rigidez *f*; inflexibilidad *f*.

rigidly |rij'idlē| *ad* rígidamente; (*inflexibly*) inflexiblemente.

rigmarole |rig'mərōl| *n* galimatías *m inv*.

rigor, (*Brit*) **rigour** |rig'ûr| *n* rigor *m*, severidad *f*.

rigor mortis |rig'ûr môr'tis| *n* rigidez *f* cadavérica.

rigorous |rig'ûrəs| *a* riguroso.

rigorously |rig'ûrəslē| *ad* rigurosamente.

rig-out |rig'out| *n* (*Brit col*) atuendo.

rile |rīl| *vt* irritar.

rim |rim| *n* borde *m*; (*of spectacles*) montura, aro; (*of wheel*) llanta.

rimless |rim'lis| *a* (*spectacles*) sin aros.

rimmed |rimd| *a*: **~ with** con un borde de, bordeado de.

rind |rīnd| *n* (*of bacon*) corteza; (*of lemon etc*) cáscara; (*of cheese*) costra.

ring |ring| *n* (*of metal*) aro; (*on finger*) anillo; (*of people*) corro; (*of objects*) círculo; (*gang*) banda; (*for boxing*) cuadrilátero; (*of circus*) pista; (*bull ~*) ruedo, plaza; (*sound of bell*) toque *m*; (*telephone call*) llamada ♦ *vb* (*pt* **rang**, *pp* **rung** [rang, rung]) *vi* (*on telephone*) llamar por teléfono; (*large bell*) repicar; (*also*: **~ out**: *voice, words*) sonar; (*ears*) zumbar ♦ *vt* (*Brit TEL*: *also*: **~ up**) llamar; (*bell etc*) hacer sonar; (*doorbell*) tocar; **that has the ~ of truth about it** eso suena a verdad; **to give sb a ~** (*Brit TEL*) llamar por teléfono a uno, dar un telefonazo a uno; **the name doesn't ~ a bell (with me)** el nombre no me suena; **to ~ sb (up)** (*Brit*) llamar a uno.
ring back *vt, vi* (*Brit TEL*) devolver la llamada.
ring off *vi* (*Brit TEL*) colgar, cortar la comunicación.

ring binder *n* carpeta.

ring finger *n* (dedo) anular *m*.

ringing |ring'ing| *n* (*of bell*) toque *m*, tañido; (*louder: of large bell*) repique *m*; (*of telephone*) sonar *m*; (*in ears*) zumbido.

ringing tone *n* (*TEL*) tono de llamada.

ringleader |ring'lēdûr| *n* (*of gang*) cabecilla *m/f*.

ringlets |ring'lits| *npl* rizos *mpl*, bucles *mpl*.

ring road *n* (*Brit*) carretera periférica *or* de circunvalación.

rink |ringk| *n* (*also*: **ice ~**) pista de hielo; (*for roller-skating*) pista de patinaje.

rinse |rins| *n* (*of dishes*) enjuague *m*; (*of clothes*) aclarado; (*of hair*) reflejo ♦ *vt* enjuagar; aclarar; dar reflejos a.

Rio (de Janeiro) |rē'ō (dē zhəner'ō)| *n* Río de Janeiro.

riot |rī'ət| *n* motín *m*, disturbio ♦ *vi* amotinarse; **to run ~** desmandarse.

riotous |rī'ətəs| *a* alborotado; (*party*) bullicioso; (*uncontrolled*) desenfrenado.

riotously |rī'ətəslē| *ad* bulliciosamente.

riot police *n* policía antidisturbios.
RIP *abbr* (= *rest in peace*) q.e.p.d.
rip [rip] *n* rasgón *m*, rasgadura ♦ *vt* rasgar, desgarrar ♦ *vi* correr.
  rip up *vt* hacer pedazos.
ripcord [rip'kôrd] *n* cabo de desgarre.
ripe [rip] *a* (*fruit*) maduro.
ripen [rī'pən] *vt* madurar ♦ *vi* madurarse.
ripeness [rip'nis] *n* madurez *f*.
rip-off [rip'ôf] *n* (*col*): **it's a ~!** ¡es una estafa!, ¡es un timo!
riposte [ripōst'] *n* respuesta aguda, réplica.
ripple [rip'əl] *n* onda, rizo; (*sound*) murmullo ♦ *vi* rizarse ♦ *vt* rizar.
rise [rīz] *n* (*slope*) cuesta, pendiente *f*; (*hill*) altura; (*increase*: *in wages*: *Brit*) aumento; (: *in prices, temperature*) subida, alza; (*fig*: *to power etc*) ascenso; (: *ascendancy*) auge *m* ♦ *vi* (*pt* **rose**, *pp* **risen** [rōz, riz'ən]) (*gen*) elevarse; (*prices*) subir; (*waters*) crecer; (*river*) nacer; (*sun*) salir; (*person*: *from bed etc*) levantarse; (*also*: **~ up**: *rebel*) sublevarse; (*in rank*) ascender; **~ to power** ascenso al poder; **to give ~ to** dar lugar *or* origen a; **to ~ to the occasion** ponerse a la altura de las circunstancias.
rising [rī'zing] *a* (*increasing*: *number*) creciente; (: *prices*) en aumento *or* alza; (*tide*) creciente; (*sun, moon*) naciente ♦ *n* (*uprising*) sublevación *f*.
rising damp *n* (*Brit*) humedad *f* de paredes.
risk [risk] *n* riesgo, peligro ♦ *vt* (*gen*) arriesgar; (*dare*) atreverse a; **to take** *or* **run the ~ of doing** correr el riesgo de hacer; **at ~** en peligro; **at one's own ~** bajo su propia responsabilidad; **fire/health/security ~** peligro de incendio/para la salud/para la seguridad.
risk capital *n* capital *m* de riesgo.
risky [ris'kē] *a* arriesgado, peligroso.
risqué [riskā'] *a* (*joke*) subido de color.
rissole [ris'âl] *n* croqueta.
rite [rīt] *n* rito; **last ~s** últimos sacramentos *mpl*.
ritual [rich'ōōəl] *a* ritual ♦ *n* ritual *m*, rito.
rival [rī'vəl] *n* rival *m/f*; (*in business*) competidor(a) *m/f* ♦ *a* rival, opuesto ♦ *vt* competir con.
rivalry [rī'vəlrē] *n* rivalidad *f*, competencia.
river [riv'ûr] *n* río ♦ *cpd* (*port, traffic*) de río, del río; **up/down ~** río arriba/abajo.
riverbank [riv'ûrbangk] *n* orilla (del río).
riverbed [riv'ûrbed] *n* lecho, cauce *m*.
rivet [riv'it] *n* roblón *m*, remache *m* ♦ *vt* remachar; (*fig*) captar.
riveting [riv'iting] *a* (*fig*) fascinante.
Riviera [rivēär'ə] *n*: **the (French) ~** la Costa Azul (francesa), la Riviera (francesa); **the Italian ~** la Riviera italiana.
Riyadh [rēyád'] *n* Riyadh *m*.
RN *n abbr* (*US*) = **registered nurse**; (*Brit*)

= **Royal Navy**.
RNA *n abbr* (= *ribonucleic acid*) ARN *m*, RNA *m*.
road [rōd] *n* (*gen*) camino; (*highway etc*) carretera; (*in town*) calle *f*; **major/minor ~** carretera general/secundaria; **main ~** carretera; **it takes 4 hours by ~** se tarda 4 horas por carretera; **on the ~ to success** en camino del éxito.
roadblock [rōd'blâk] *n* barricada.
road haulage *n* transporte *m* por carretera.
road hog *n* loco/a del volante.
road map *n* mapa *m* de carreteras.
road safety *n* seguridad *f* vial.
roadside [rōd'sīd] *n* borde *m* (del camino) ♦ *cpd* al lado de la carretera; **by the ~** al borde del camino.
road sign *n* señal *f* de tráfico.
roadsweeper [rōd'swēpûr] *n* (*Brit*: *person*) barrendero/a.
road transport *n* = **road haulage**.
road user *n* usuario/a de la vía pública.
roadway [rōd'wā] *n* calzada.
roadworthy [rōd'wûrthē] *a* (*car*) en buen estado para circular.
roam [rōm] *vi* vagar ♦ *vt* vagar por.
roar [rôr] *n* (*of animal*) rugido, bramido; (*of crowd*) rugido; (*of vehicle, storm*) estruendo; (*of laughter*) carcajada ♦ *vi* rugir, bramar; hacer estruendo; **to ~ with laughter** reírse a carcajadas.
roaring [rôr'ing] *a*: **a ~ success** un tremendo éxito; **to do a ~ trade** hacer buen negocio.
roast [rōst] *n* carne *f* asada, asado ♦ *vt* (*meat*) asar; (*coffee*) tostar.
roast beef *n* rosbif *m*.
rob [râb] *vt* robar; **to ~ sb of sth** robar algo a uno; (*fig*: *deprive*) quitar algo a uno.
robber [râb'ûr] *n* ladrón/ona *m/f*.
robbery [râb'ûrē] *n* robo.
robe [rōb] *n* (*for ceremony etc*) toga; (*also*: **bath ~**) bata.
robin [râb'in] *n* petirrojo.
robot [rō'bət] *n* robot *m*.
robotics [rōbât'iks] *n* robótica.
robust [rōbust'] *a* robusto, fuerte.
rock [râk] *n* (*gen*) roca; (*boulder*) peña, peñasco; (*Brit*: *candy*) ≈ pirulí *m* ♦ *vt* (*swing gently*: *cradle*) balancear, mecer; (: *child*) arrullar; (*shake*) sacudir ♦ *vi* mecerse, balancearse; sacudirse; **on the ~s** (*drink*) con hielo; (*marriage etc*) en ruinas; **to ~ the boat** (*fig*) causar perturbaciones.
rock and roll *n* rocanrol *m*.
rock-bottom [râk'bât'əm] *a* (*fig*) por los suelos; **to reach** *or* **touch ~** (*price*) estar por los suelos; (*person*) tocar fondo.
rock climber *n* escalador(a) *m/f*.
rock climbing *n* (*SPORT*) escalada.
rockery [râk'ûrē] *n* cuadro alpino.
rocket [râk'it] *n* cohete *m* ♦ *vi* (*prices*) ir

por las nubes.

rocket launcher [råk'it lônch'úr] n lanzacohetes m inv.

rock face n pared f de roca.

rock garden n cuadro alpino.

rocking chair [råk'ing chär] n mecedora.

rocking horse [råk'ing hôrs] n caballo de balancín.

rocky [råk'ē] a (gen) rocoso; (unsteady: table) débil.

Rocky Mountains npl: **the** ~ las Montañas Rocosas.

rococo [rəkō'kō] a rococó inv ♦ n rococó.

rod [råd] n vara, varilla; (TECH) barra; (also: **fishing** ~) caña.

rode [rōd] pt of **ride**.

rodent [rō'dənt] n roedor m.

rodeo [rō'dēō] n rodeo.

roe [rō] n (species: also: ~ **deer**) corzo; (of fish): **hard/soft** ~ hueva/lecha.

rogue [rōg] n pícaro, pillo.

roguish [rō'gish] a (child) travieso; (smile etc) pícaro.

ROI abbr (= return on investment) beneficios por inversión.

role [rōl] n papel m, rol m.

roll [rōl] n rollo; (of bank notes) fajo; (also: **bread** ~) panecillo; (register) lista, nómina; (sound: of drums etc) redoble m; (movement: of ship) balanceo ♦ vt hacer rodar; (also: ~ **up**: string) enrollar; (: sleeves) arremangar; (cigarettes) liar; (also: ~ **out**: pastry) aplanar ♦ vi (gen) rodar; (drum) redoblar; (in walking) bambolearse; (ship) balancearse; **cheese** ~ panecillo de queso.

roll around vi (person) revolcarse.

roll by vi (time) pasar.

roll in vi (mail, cash) entrar a raudales.

roll over vi dar una vuelta.

roll up vi (col: arrive) presentarse, aparecer ♦ vt (carpet, cloth, map) arrollar; (sleeves) arremangar; **to** ~ **o.s. up into a ball** acurrucarse, hacerse un ovillo.

roll call n: **to take a** ~ pasar lista.

roller [rō'lúr] n rodillo; (wheel) rueda.

roller coaster n montaña rusa.

roller skates npl patines mpl de rueda.

rollicking [rål'iking] a: **we had a** ~ **time** nos divertimos una barbaridad.

rolling [rō'ling] a (landscape) ondulado.

rolling mill n taller m de laminación.

rolling pin n rodillo (de cocina).

rolling stock n (RAIL) material m rodante.

ROM [råm] n abbr (= read only memory) (memoria) ROM f.

romaine (lettuce) [rōmān' (let'is)] n (US) lechuga cos.

Roman [rō'mən] a, n romano/a m/f.

Roman Catholic a, n católico/a m/f (romano/a).

romance [rōmans'] n (love affair) amor m; (charm) lo romántico; (novel) novela de amor.

romanesque [rōmənesk'] a románico.

Romania [rōmā'nēə] n = **Rumania**.

Romanian [rəmā'nēən] a, n = **Rumanian**.

Roman numeral n número romano.

romantic [rōman'tik] a romántico.

romanticism [rōman'tisizəm] n romanticismo.

Romany [rōm'ənē] a gitano ♦ n (person) gitano/a; (LING) lengua gitana, caló (Sp).

Rome [rōm] n Roma.

romp [råmp] n retozo, juego ♦ vi (also: ~ **around**) jugar, brincar; **to** ~ **home** (horse) ganar fácilmente.

rompers [råm'pûrz] npl pelele m.

roof [rōōf] n (gen) techo; (of house) techo, tejado; (of car) baca ♦ vt techar, poner techo a; ~ **of the mouth** paladar m.

roofing [rōō'fing] n techumbre f.

roof rack n (AUT) baca, portaequipajes m inv.

rook [rōōk] n (bird) graja; (CHESS) torre f.

room [rōōm] n (in house) cuarto, habitación f, pieza (esp LAm); (also: **bed**~) dormitorio; (in school etc) sala; (space) sitio, cabida; ~**s** npl (lodging) alojamiento sg; "~**s for rent**", (Brit) "~**s to let**" "se alquilan pisos or cuartos"; ~ **and board** casa y comida; **single/double** ~ habitación individual/doble or para dos personas; **is there** ~ **for this?** ¿cabe esto?; **to make** ~ **for sb** hacer lugar para uno; **there is** ~ **for improvement** podría mejorarse.

roominess [rōō'mēnis] n amplitud f, espaciosidad f.

rooming house [rōō'ming hous] n (US) pensión f.

roommate [rōōm'māt] n compañero/a de cuarto or piso.

room service n servicio de habitaciones.

room temperature n temperatura ambiente.

roomy [rōō'mē] a espacioso.

roost [rōōst] n percha ♦ vi pasar la noche.

rooster [rōōs'tûr] n gallo.

root [rōōt] n (BOT, MATH) raíz f ♦ vi (plant, belief) arriesgarse; **to take** ~ (plant) echar raíces; (idea) arraigar(se); **the** ~ **of the problem is that** ... el fondo or lo fundamental del problema es que ....

root around vi (fig) andar buscando.

root for vt fus apoyar a.

root out vt desarraigar.

rooted [rōō'tid] a enraizado; (opinions etc) arraigado.

rope [rōp] n cuerda; (NAUT) cable m ♦ vt (box) atar or amarrar con (una) cuerda; (climbers: also: ~ **together**) encordarse; **to jump** or **skip** ~ (US) saltar a la comba; **to** ~ **sb in** (fig) persuadir a uno a tomar parte; **to know the** ~**s** (fig) conocer los trucos (del oficio).

rope ladder n escala de cuerda.

rosary [rō'zûrē] *n* rosario.
rose [rōz] *pt of* **rise** ♦ *n* rosa; (*also:* ~**bush**) rosal *m*; (*on watering can*) roseta ♦ *a* color de rosa.
rosé [rōzā'] *n* vino rosado, clarete *m*.
rosebed [rōz'bed] *n* rosaleda.
rosebud [rōz'bud] *n* capullo de rosa.
rosebush [rōz'bo͞osh] *n* rosal *m*.
rosemary [rōz'märē] *n* romero.
rosette [rōzet'] *n* rosetón *m*.
roster [râs'tûr] *n*: **duty** ~ lista de deberes.
rostrum [râs'trəm] *n* tribuna.
rosy [rō'zē] *a* rosado, sonrosado; **the future looks** ~ el futuro parece prometedor.
rot [rât] *n* (*decay*) putrefacción *f*, podredumbre *f*; (*fig: pej*) tonterías *fpl* ♦ *vt, vi* pudrirse, corromperse; **it has** ~**ted** está podrido; **to stop the** ~ (*Brit: fig*) poner fin a las pérdidas.
rota [rō'tə] *n* lista (de tandas).
rotary [rō'tûrē] *a* rotativo.
rotate [rō'tāt] *vt* (*revolve*) hacer girar, dar vueltas a; (*crops*) cultivar en rotación; (*jobs*) alternar ♦ *vi* (*revolve*) girar, dar vueltas.
rotating [rō'tāting] *a* (*movement*) rotativo.
rotation [rōtā'shən] *n* rotación *f*; **in** ~ por turno.
rote [rōt] *n*: **by** ~ de memoria.
rotor [rō'tûr] *n* rotor *m*.
rotten [rât'ən] *a* (*decayed*) podrido; (: *wood*) carcomido; (*fig*) corrompido; (*col: bad*) pésimo; **to feel** ~ (*ill*) sentirse muy mal; ~ **to the core** completamente podrido.
rotund [rōtund'] *a* rotundo.
rouge [ro͞ozh] *n* colorete *m*.
rough [ruf] *a* (*skin, surface*) áspero; (*terrain*) quebrado; (*road*) desigual; (*voice*) bronco; (*person, manner: coarse*) tosco, grosero; (*weather*) borrascoso; (*treatment*) brutal; (*sea*) bravo; (*cloth*) basto; (*plan*) preliminar; (*guess*) aproximado; (*violent*) violento ♦ *n* (*GOLF*): **in the** ~ en las hierbas altas; **to** ~ **it** vivir sin comodidades; **the sea is** ~ **today** el mar está agitado hoy; **to have a** ~ **time (of it)** pasar una mala temporada; ~ **estimate** cálculo aproximado.
roughage [ruf'ij] *n* fibra(s) *f(pl)*, forraje *m*.
rough-and-ready [ruf'ənred'ē] *a* improvisado, tosco.
rough-and-tumble [ruf'əntum'bəl] *n* pelea.
roughcast [ruf'kast] *n* mezcla gruesa.
rough copy, rough draft *n* borrador *m*.
roughen [ruf'ən] *vt* (*a surface*) poner áspero.
roughly [ruf'lē] *ad* (*handle*) torpemente; (*make*) toscamente; (*approximately*) aproximadamente; ~ **speaking** más o menos.
roughness [ruf'nis] *n* aspereza; tosquedad *f*; brutalidad *f*.

roughshod [ruf'shâd'] *ad*: **to ride** ~ **over** (*person*) pisotear a; (*objections*) hacer caso omiso de.
rough work *n* (*SCOL etc*) borrador *m*.
roulette [ro͞olet'] *n* ruleta.
Roumania [ro͞omā'nēə] *n* = **Rumania**.
round [round] *a* redondo ♦ *n* círculo; (*Brit: of toast*) rodaja; (*of policeman*) ronda; (*of milkman*) recorrido; (*of doctor*) visitas *fpl*; (*game: of cards, in competition*) partida; (*of ammunition*) cartucho; (*BOXING*) asalto; (*of talks*) ronda ♦ *vt* (*corner*) doblar ♦ *prep* alrededor de ♦ *ad*: **all the year** ~ durante todo el año; **she arrived** ~ **(about) noon** (*Brit*) llegó alrededor del mediodía; **in** ~ **figures** en cifras redondas; **to go the** ~**s** (*story*) divulgarse; **a** ~ **of applause** una salva de aplausos; **a** ~ **of drinks/sandwiches** una ronda de bebidas/bocadillos; **the daily** ~ la rutina cotidiana; *see also* **around**.
round off *vt* (*speech etc*) acabar, poner término a.
round up *vt* (*cattle*) acorralar; (*people*) reunir; (*prices*) redondear.
roundabout [round'əbout] *n* (*Brit: AUT*) glorieta, redondel *m*; (: *at fair*) tiovivo ♦ *a* (*route, means*) indirecto.
rounded [roun'did] *a* redondeado, redondo.
rounders [roun'dúrz] *n* (*Brit: game*) juego similar al béisbol.
roundly [round'lē] *ad* (*fig*) rotundamente.
round-shouldered [round'shōldûrd] *a* cargado de espaldas.
round trip *n* viaje *m* de ida y vuelta.
round-trip ticket [round'trip tik'it] *n* billete *m* de ida y vuelta.
roundup [round'up] *n* rodeo; (*of criminals*) redada; **a** ~ **of the latest news** un resumen de las últimas noticias.
rouse [rouz] *vt* (*wake up*) despertar; (*stir up*) suscitar.
rousing [rou'zing] *a* (*applause*) caluroso; (*speech*) conmovedor(a).
rout [rout] *n* (*MIL*) derrota; (*flight*) fuga ♦ *vt* derrotar.
route [ro͞ot] *n* ruta, camino; (*of bus*) recorrido; (*of shipping*) rumbo, derrota; **the best** ~ **to New York** el mejor camino *or* la mejor ruta para ir a Nueva York; **en** ~ **from ... to** en el viaje de ... a; **en** ~ **for** rumbo a, con destino en.
routine [ro͞otēn'] *a* (*work*) rutinario ♦ *n* rutina; (*THEATER*) número; (*COMPUT*) rutina; ~ **procedure** trámite *m* rutinario.
rover [rō'vûr] *n* vagabundo/a.
roving [rō'ving] *a* (*wandering*) errante; (*salesman*) ambulante; (*reporter*) volante.
row *n* [rō] (*line*) fila, hilera; (*KNITTING*) pasada; [rou] (*noise*) escándalo; (*dispute*) bronca, pelea; (*fuss*) jaleo; (*scolding*) regaño ♦ *vi* [rō] (*in boat*) remar; [rou] reñir(se) ♦ *vt* [rō] (*boat*) conducir remando;

4 days in a ~ 4 días seguidos; **to make a ~** armar un lío; **to have a ~** pelearse, reñir.

rowboat [rō'bōt] *n* (*US*) bote *m* de remos.

rowdy [rou'dē] *a* (*person*: *noisy*) ruidoso; (: *quarrelsome*) pendenciero; (*occasion*) alborotado ♦ *n* pendenciero.

rowdyism [rou'dēizəm] *n* pendencias *fpl*.

row houses *npl* (*US*) casas *fpl* adosadas.

rowing [rō'ing] *n* remo.

rowing boat *n* (*Brit*) bote *m* or barco de remos.

rowlock [rō'lák] *n* (*Brit*) chumacera.

royal [roi'əl] *a* real.

Royal Air Force (RAF) *n* Fuerzas Aéreas Británicas *fpl*.

royal blue *n* azul *m* marino.

royalist [roi'əlist] *a*, *n* monárquico/a *m/f*.

Royal Navy (RN) *n* (*Brit*) Marina Británica.

royalty [roi'əltē] *n* (*royal persons*) (miembros *mpl* de la) familia real; (*payment to author*) derechos *mpl* de autor.

RP *n abbr* (*Brit*: = *received pronunciation*) pronunciación estándar del inglés.

rpm *abbr* (= *revs per minute*) r.p.m.

RR *abbr* (*US*) = **railroad**.

RRP *n abbr* (*Brit*) = **recommended retail price**.

R & R *n abbr* (*US MIL*) = *rest and recreation*.

R.S.V.P. *abbr* (= *répondez s'il vous plaît*) SRC.

Rt. Hon. *abbr* (*Brit*: = *Right Honourable*) título honorífico de diputado.

Rt. Rev. *abbr* (= *Right Reverend*) Rvdo.

rub [rub] *vt* (*gen*) frotar; (*hard*) restregar ♦ *n* (*gen*) frotamiento; (*touch*) roce *m*; **to ~ sb the wrong way** or (*Brit*) **~ sb up** entrarle uno por mal ojo.

rub down *vt* (*body*) secar frotando; (*horse*) almohazar.

rub in *vt* (*ointment*) frotar.

rub off *vt* borrarse ♦ *vi* quitarse (frotando); **to ~ off on sb** influir en uno, pegársele a uno.

rub out *vt* borrar ♦ *vi* borrarse.

rubber [rub'ûr] *n* caucho, goma; (*Brit*: *eraser*) goma de borrar.

rubber band *n* goma, gomita.

rubber plant *n* ficus *m*.

rubber stamp *n* sello (de caucho) ♦ *vt*: **rubber-stamp** (*fig*) aprobar maquinalmente.

rubbery [rub'ûrē] *a* elástico, parecido a la goma.

rubbing alcohol [rub'ing al'kəhôl] *n* (*US*) alcohol *m*.

rubbish [rub'ish] *n* (*waste*) desperdicios *mpl*; (*Brit*: *from household*) basura; (*fig*: *pej*) tonterías *fpl*; (*trash*) pacotilla ♦ *vt* (*Brit*: *col*) poner por los suelos; **what you've just said is ~** lo que acabas de decir es una tontería.

rubbish bin *n* (*Brit*) cubo or bote *m* (*LAm*) de la basura.

rubbish dump *n* (*Brit*: *in town*) vertedero, basurero.

rubbishy [rub'ishē] *a* (*Brit*) de mala calidad, de pacotilla.

rubble [rub'əl] *n* escombros *mpl*.

ruble [rōō'bəl] *n* rubio.

ruby [rōō'bē] *n* rubí *m*.

RUC *n abbr* (= *Royal Ulster Constabulary*) fuerza de policía en Irlanda del Norte.

rucksack [ruk'sak] *n* mochila.

rudder [rud'ûr] *n* timón *m*.

ruddy [rud'ē] *a* (*face*) rubicundo.

rude [rōōd] *a* (*impolite*: *person*) grosero; (: *word, manners*) rudo, grosero; (*indecent*) indecente; **to be ~ to sb** ser grosero con uno.

rudeness [rōōd'nis] *n* grosería, tosquedad *f*.

rudiment [rōō'dəmənt] *n* rudimento.

rudimentary [rōōdəmen'tûrē] *a* rudimentario.

rueful [rōō'fəl] *a* arrepentido.

ruffian [ruf'ēən] *n* matón *m*, criminal *m*.

ruffle [ruf'əl] *vt* (*hair*) despeinar; (*clothes*) arrugar; (*fig*: *person*) agitar.

rug [rug] *n* alfombra.

rugby [rug'bē] *n* (*also*: **~ football**) rugby *m*.

rugged [rug'id] *a* (*landscape*) accidentado; (*features*) robusto.

ruin [rōō'in] *n* ruina ♦ *vt* arruinar; (*spoil*) estropear; **~s** *npl* ruinas *fpl*, restos *mpl*; **in ~s** en ruinas.

ruinous [rōō'inəs] *a* ruinoso.

rule [rōōl] *n* (*norm*) norma, costumbre *f*; (*regulation*) regla; (*government*) dominio; (*ruler*) metro; (*dominion etc*): **under British ~** bajo el dominio británico ♦ *vt* (*country, person*) gobernar; (*decide*) disponer; (*draw lines*) trazar ♦ *vi* gobernar; (*LAW*) fallar; **to ~ against/in favor of/on** fallar en contra de/a favor de/sobre; **to ~ that ...** (*umpire, judge*) fallar que ...; **it's against the ~s** está prohibido; **as a ~** por regla general, generalmente; **by ~ of thumb** por experiencia; **majority ~** (*POL*) gobierno mayoritario; **the ~s of the road** el código de la circulación.

rule out *vt* excluir.

ruled [rōōld] *a* (*paper*) rayado.

ruler [rōō'lûr] *n* (*sovereign*) soberano; (*for measuring*) regla.

ruling [rōō'ling] *a* (*party*) gobernante; (*class*) dirigente ♦ *n* (*LAW*) fallo, decisión *f*.

rum [rum] *n* ron *m*.

Rumania [rōōmā'nēə] *n* Rumanía.

Rumanian [rōōmā'nēən] *a*, *n* rumano/a *m/f*.

rumble [rum'bəl] *n* retumbo, ruido sordo; (*of thunder*) redoble *m* ♦ *vi* retumbar, hacer un ruido sordo; (*stomach, pipe*) sonar.

rummage [rum'ij] *vi* revolverlo todo.

rummage sale *n* (*US*) *venta de objetos usados con fines benéficos.*

rumor, (*Brit*) **rumour** |rōō'múr| *n* rumor *m* ♦ *vt*: **it is ~ed that...** se rumorea que... .

rump |rump| *n* (*of animal*) ancas *fpl*, grupa.

rumple |rum'pəl| *vt* (*clothes*) arrugar; (*hair*) despeinar.

rump steak *n* filete *m* de lomo.

rumpus |rum'pəs| *n* (*col*) lío, jaleo; (*quarrel*) pelea, riña; **to kick up a ~** armar un follón *or* armar bronca.

run |run| *n* (*SPORT*) carrera; (*trip*) paseo, excursión *f*; (*distance traveled*) trayecto; (*series*) serie *f*; (*THEATER*) temporada; (*SKI*) pista; (*in tights, stockings*) carrera; ♦ *vb* (*pt* **ran**, *pp* **run** |ran, run|) *vt* (*operate: business*) dirigir; (: *competition, course*) organizar; (: *hotel, house*) administrar, llevar; (*COMPUT: program*) ejecutar; (*to pass: hand*) pasar; (*tights*) hacer una carrera en; (*bath*): **to ~ a bath** llenar la bañera ♦ *vi* (*gen*) correr; (*work: machine*) funcionar, marchar; (*bus, train: operate*) circular, ir; (: *travel*) ir; (*continue: play*) seguir; (: *contract*) ser válido; (*flow: river, bath*) fluir; (*colors, washing*) desteñirse; (*in election*) ser candidato; **to go for a ~** dar una vuelta; **to make a ~ for it** echar(se) a correr, escapar(se), huir; **to have the ~ of sb's house** tener el libre uso de la casa de uno; **a ~ of luck** una racha de suerte; **there was a ~ on** (*meat, tickets*) hubo mucha demanda de; **in the long ~** a la larga; **on the ~** en fuga; **I'll ~ you to the station** te llevaré a la estación en coche; **to ~ a risk** correr un riesgo; **to ~ a stoplight** (*US*) saltarse el semáforo en rojo; **to ~ errands** hacer *or* llevar recados; **it's very cheap to ~** es muy económico; **to ~ for Congress** (*US*) presentarse como candidato a las elecciones al Congreso; **to ~ for the bus** correr tras el autobús; **we shall have to ~ for it** tendremos que escapar; **the train ~s between Boston and New York**, el tren circula entre Boston y Nueva York; **the bus ~s every 20 minutes** hay salidas de bus cada 20 minutos; **to ~ on gasoline/on diesel/off batteries** funcionar con gasolina/gasoil/baterías; **the car ran into the lamppost** el coche chocó contra el farol.

run about (*Brit*) = **run around.**

run across *vt fus* (*find*) dar *or* topar con.

run around *vi* (*children*) correr por todos lados.

run away *vi* huir.

run down *vi* (*clock*) parar ♦ *vt* (*reduce: production*) ir reduciendo; (*factory*) restringir la producción de; (*AUT*) atropellar; (*criticize*) criticar; **to be ~ down** (*person: tired*) encontrarse agotado.

run in *vt* (*Brit: car*) rodar.

run into *vt fus* (*meet: person, trouble*) tropezar con; (*collide with*) chocar con; **to ~ into debt** contraer deudas, endeudarse.

run off *vt* (*water*) dejar correr ♦ *vi* huir corriendo.

run out *vi* (*person*) salir corriendo; (*liquid*) irse; (*lease*) caducar, vencer; (*money*) acabarse.

run out of *vt fus* quedar sin; **I've ~ out of gas** se me acabó la gasolina.

run over *vt* (*AUT*) atropellar ♦ *vt fus* (*revise*) repasar.

run through *vt fus* (*instructions*) repasar.

run up *vt* (*debt*) incurrir en; **to ~ up against** (*difficulties*) tropezar con.

runaway |run'əwā| *a* (*horse*) desbocado; (*truck*) sin frenos; (*person*) fugitivo.

rundown |run'doun| *n* (*Brit: of industry etc*) cierre *m* gradual.

rung |rung| *pp of* **ring** ♦ *n* (*of ladder*) escalón *m*, peldaño.

run-in |run'in| *n* (*col*) altercado.

runner |run'ûr| *n* (*in race: person*) corredor(a) *m/f*; (: *horse*) caballo; (*on sleigh*) patín *m*; (*wheel*) ruedecilla.

runner bean *n* (*Brit*) judía escarlata.

runner-up |runûrup'| *n* subcampeón/ona *m/f*.

running |run'ing| *n* (*sport*) atletismo; (*race*) carrera ♦ *a* (*costs, water*) corriente; (*commentary*) continuo; **to be in/out of the ~ for sth** tener/no tener posibilidades de ganar algo; **6 days ~** 6 días seguidos.

running costs *npl* (*of business*) gastos *mpl* (de operación); (*of car*) gastos *mpl* corrientes.

running head *n* (*TYP, WORD PROCESSING*) encabezamiento normal.

running mate *n* (*US POL*) candidato/a a la vice-presidencia.

runny |run'ē| *a* derretido.

run-off |run'óf| *n* (*in contest, election*) desempate *m*; (*extra race*) carrera de desempate.

run-of-the-mill |runəvthəmil'| *a* común y corriente.

runt |runt| *n* (*also pej*) redrojo, enano.

run-up |run'up| *n* (*Brit*): **~ to** (*election etc*) período previo a.

runway |run'wā| *n* (*AVIAT*) pista de aterrizaje.

rupee |rōō'pē| *n* rupia.

rupture |rup'chûr| *n* (*MED*) hernia ♦ *vt*: **to ~ o.s.** causarse una hernia.

rural |rōōr'əl| *a* rural.

ruse |rōōz| *n* ardid *m*.

rush |rush| *n* ímpetu *m*; (*hurry*) prisa, apuro (*LAm*); (*COMM*) demanda repentina; (*BOT*) junco; (*current*) corriente *f* fuerte, ráfaga ♦ *vt* apresurar; (*work*) hacer de prisa; (*attack: town etc*) asaltar ♦ *vi* correr; precipitarse; **gold ~** fiebre *f* del oro; **we've had a ~ of orders** ha habido una gran demanda; **I'm in a** ~ **(to do)** tengo prisa or apuro (*LAm*) (por hacer); **is there any** ~ **for this?** ¿te corre prisa esto?; **to** ~ **sth off** hacer algo de prisa.

rush through *vt fus* (*meal*) comer de prisa; (*book*) leer de prisa; (*work*) hacer de prisa; (*town*) atravesar a toda velocidad; (*COMM*: *order*) despachar rápidamente.

rush hour *n* horas *fpl* punta.

rush job *n* (*urgent*) trabajo urgente.

rusk [rusk] *n* bizcocho tostado.

Russia [rush'ə] *n* Rusia.

Russian [rush'ən] *a* ruso ♦ *n* ruso/a; (*LING*) ruso.

rust [rust] *n* herrumbre *f*, moho ♦ *vi* oxidarse.

rustic [rus'tik] *a* rústico.

rustle [rus'əl] *vi* susurrar ♦ *vt* (*paper*) hacer crujir; (*US*: *cattle*) hurtar, robar.

rustproof [rust'proof] *a* inoxidable.

rusty [rus'tē] *a* oxidado, mohoso.

rut [rut] *n* surco; (*ZOOL*) celo; **to be in a** ~ ser esclavo de la rutina.

rutabaga [rootəbā'gə] *n* (*US*) naba.

ruthless [rooth'lis] *a* despiadado.

RV *abbr* (= *revised version*) traducción inglesa de la Biblia de 1855 ♦ *n abbr* (*US*) = **recreational vehicle.**

rye [rī] *n* centeno.

rye bread *n* pan de centeno.

S

S, s [es] *n* (*letter*) S, s *f;* **S for Sugar** S de sábado.

S *abbr* (= *Saint*) Sto./a.; (*US SCOL*: *grade*: = *satisfactory*) suficiente; (= *south*) S; = **small.**

SA *n abbr* = **South Africa, South America.**

sabbath [sab'əth] *n* domingo; (*Jewish*) sábado.

sabbatical [səbat'ikəl] *a:* ~ **year** año de licencia.

saber, (*Brit*) **sabre** [sā'bûr] *n* sable *m*.

saber rattling [sā'bûr rat'ling] *n* patriotería, jingoísmo.

sabotage [sab'ətâzh] *n* sabotaje *m* ♦ *vt* sabotear.

saccharin(e) [sak'ûrin] *n* sacarina.

sachet [sashā'] *n* sobrecito.

sack [sak] *n* (*bag*) saco, costal *m* ♦ *vt* (*dismiss*) despedir; (*plunder*) saquear; **to get the** ~ ser despedido.

sackful [sak'fəl] *n* saco.

sacking [sak'ing] *n* (*material*) arpillera.

sacrament [sak'rəmənt] *n* sacramento.

sacred [sā'krid] *a* sagrado, santo.

sacrifice [sak'rəfīs] *n* sacrificio ♦ *vt* sacrificar; **to make** ~**s (for sb)** sacrificarse (a favor de uno), privarse (para uno).

sacrilege [sak'rəlij] *n* sacrilegio.

sacrosanct [sak'rōsangkt] *a* sacrosanto.

sad [sad] *a* (*unhappy*) triste; (*deplorable*) lamentable.

sadden [sad'ən] *vt* entristecer.

saddle [sad'əl] *n* silla (de montar); (*of cycle*) sillín *m* ♦ *vt* (*horse*) ensillar; **to** ~ **sb with sth** (*col*: *task, bill, name*) cargar a uno con algo; (: *responsibility*) gravar a uno con algo; **to be** ~**d with sth** (*col*) quedar cargado con algo.

saddlebag [sad'əlbag] *n* alforja.

sadism [sā'dizəm] *n* sadismo.

sadist [sā'dist] *n* sádico/a.

sadistic [sədis'tik] *a* sádico.

sadly [sad'lē] *ad* tristemente; (*regrettably*) desgraciadamente; ~ **lacking (in)** muy deficiente (en).

sadness [sad'nis] *n* tristeza.

sae *abbr* (*Brit*) = **stamped addressed envelope.**

safari [səfâ'rē] *n* safari *m*.

safari park *n* parque *m* aventura.

safe [sāf] *a* (*out of danger*) fuera de peligro; (*not dangerous, sure*) seguro; (*unharmed*) ileso; (*trustworthy*) digno de confianza ♦ *n* caja de caudales, caja fuerte; ~ **and sound** sano y salvo; **(just) to be on the** ~ **side** para mayor seguridad; ~ **journey!** ¡buen viaje!; **it is** ~ **to say that** ... se puede decir con confianza que ....

safe-breaker [sāf'brākûr] *n* (*Brit*) = **safe-cracker.**

safe-conduct [sāf'kân'dukt] *n* salvoconducto.

safe-cracker [sāf'krakûr] *n* (*US*) ladrón/ona *m/f* de cajas fuertes.

safe-deposit [sāf'dipâzit] *n* (*vault*) cámara acorazada; (*box*) caja de seguridad or de caudales.

safeguard [sāf'gârd] *n* protección *f*, garantía ♦ *vt* proteger, defender.

safekeeping [sāfkē'ping] *n* custodia.

safely [sāf'lē] *ad* seguramente, con seguridad; (*without mishap*) sin peligro; **I can** ~ **say** puedo decir or afirmar con toda seguridad.

safeness [sāf'nis] *n* seguridad *f*.

safe sex *n* sexo seguro.

safety [sāf'tē] *n* seguridad *f* ♦ *cpd* de seguridad; **road** ~ seguridad *f* en carretera; ~ **first!** ¡precaución!

safety belt *n* cinturón *m* (de seguridad).

safety curtain *n* telón *m* de seguridad.

safety net *n* red *f* (de seguridad).

safety pin *n* imperdible *m*, seguro (*LAm*).

safety valve *n* válvula de seguridad or de escape.

saffron [saf'rən] *n* azafrán *m*.
sag [sag] *vi* aflojarse.
saga [såg'ə] *n* (*HISTORY*) saga; (*fig*) epopeya.
sage [sāj] *n* (*herb*) salvia; (*man*) sabio.
Sagittarius [sajităr'ēəs] *n* Sagitario.
sago [sā'gō] *n* sagú *m*.
Sahara [səhar'ə] *n*: **the ~ (Desert)** el Sáhara.
Sahel [såhel] *n* Sahel *m*.
said [sed] *pt, pp of* **say**.
Saigon [sīgán'] *n* Saigón *m*.
sail [sāl] *n* (*on boat*) vela ♦ *vt* (*boat*) gobernar ♦ *vi* (*travel: ship*) navegar; (: *passenger*) pasear en barco; (*set off: also*: **to set ~**) zarpar; **to go for a ~** dar un paseo en barco; **they ~ed into Copenhagen** arribaron a Copenhague.
  sail through *vt fus* (*exam*) aprobar fácilmente.
sailboat [sāl'bōt] *n* (*US*) velero, barco de vela.
sailing [sā'ling] *n* (*SPORT*) balandrismo; **to go ~** salir en balandro.
sailing ship *n* barco de vela.
sailor [sā'lûr] *n* marinero, marino.
saint [sānt] *n* santo; **S~ John** San Juan.
saintliness [sānt'lēnis] *n* santidad *f*.
saintly [sānt'lē] *a* santo.
sake [sāk] *n*: **for the ~ of** por; **for the ~ of argument** digamos, es un decir; **art for art's ~** el arte por el arte.
salad [sal'əd] *n* ensalada; **tomato ~** ensalada de tomate.
salad bowl *n* ensaladera.
salad cream *n* (*Brit*) mayonesa.
salad dressing *n* aliño, mayonesa.
salad oil *n* aceite *m* para ensalada.
salami [səlâ'mē] *n* salami *m*, salchichón *m*.
salaried [sal'ûrēd] *a* asalariado.
salary [sal'ûrē] *n* sueldo.
salary scale *n* escala salarial.
sale [sāl] *n* venta; (*at reduced prices*) liquidación *f*, saldo; **"for ~"** "se vende"; **on ~** en venta; **on ~ or return** (*goods*) venta por reposición; **liquidation ~** liquidación *f*; **and lease back** venta y arrendamiento al vendedor.
saleroom [sāl'rōōm] *n* (*Brit*) = **salesroom**.
sales assistant *n* (*Brit*) dependiente/a *m/f*.
sales campaign *n* campaña de venta.
sales clerk *n* (*US*) dependiente/a *m/f*.
sales conference *n* conferencia de ventas.
sales drive *n* promoción *f* de ventas.
sales figures *npl* cifras *fpl* de ventas.
sales force *n* personal *m* de ventas.
salesman [sālz'mən] *n* vendedor *m*; (*in store*) dependiente *m*; (*representative*) viajante *m*.
sales manager *n* gerente *m/f* de ventas.
salesmanship [sālz'mənship] *n* arte *m* de vender.

sales meeting *n* reunión *f* de ventas.
salesroom [sālz'rōōm] *n* (*US*) sala de subastas.
sales slip *n* recibo.
sales tax *n* (*US*) impuesto sobre la venta.
saleswoman [sālz'wōōmən] *n* vendedora; (*in store*) dependienta; (*representative*) viajante *f*.
salient [sā'lēənt] *a* (*features, points*) sobresaliente.
saline [sā'lēn] *a* salino.
saliva [səlī'və] *n* saliva.
sallow [sal'ō] *a* cetrino.
salmon [sam'ən] *n* (*pl inv*) salmón *m*.
salon [səlán'] *n* (*hairdressing ~, beauty ~*) salón *m*.
saloon [səlōōn'] *n* (*US*) bar *m*, taberna; (*Brit AUT*) (coche *m* de) turismo; (*ship's lounge*) cámara, salón *m*.
Salop [sal'əp] *n abbr* (*Brit*) = *Shropshire*.
SALT [sôlt] *n abbr* (= *Strategic Arms Limitation Treaty*) tratado SALT.
salt [sôlt] *n* sal *f* ♦ *vt* salar; (*put ~ on*) poner sal en; **an old ~** un lobo de mar.
  salt away *vt* (*col: money*) ahorrar.
saltcellar [sôlt'selûr] *n* (*Brit*) salero.
salt mine *n* mina de sal.
salt shaker [sôlt shā'kûr] *n* (*US*) salero.
saltwater [sôlt'wôtûr] *a* (*fish etc*) de agua salada, de mar.
salty [sôl'tē] *a* salado.
salubrious [səlōō'brēəs] *a* sano; (*fig: district etc*) atractivo.
salutary [sal'yətārē] *a* saludable.
salute [səlōōt'] *n* saludo; (*of guns*) salva ♦ *vt* saludar.
salvage [sal'vij] *n* (*saving*) salvamento, recuperación *f*; (*things saved*) objetos *mpl* salvados ♦ *vt* salvar.
salvage vessel *n* buque *m* de salvamento.
salvation [salvā'shən] *n* salvación *f*.
Salvation Army *n* Ejército de Salvación.
salve [sav] *n* (*cream etc*) ungüento, bálsamo.
salver [sal'vûr] *n* bandeja.
salvo [sal'vō] *n* (*MIL*) salva.
same [sām] *a* mismo ♦ *pron*: **the ~** el mismo/la misma; **the ~ book as** el mismo libro que; **on the ~ day** el mismo día; **at the ~ time** (*at the ~ moment*) al mismo tiempo; (*yet*) sin embargo; **all *or* just the ~** sin embargo, aun así; **they're one and the ~** (*person*) son la misma persona; (*thing*) son iguales; **to do the ~ (as sb)** hacer lo mismo (que otro); **and the ~ to you!** ¡igualmente!; **~ here!** ¡yo también!; **the ~ again** (*Brit: in bar etc*) otro igual.
sampan [sam'pan] *n* sampán *m*.
sample [sam'pəl] *n* muestra ♦ *vt* (*food, wine*) probar; **to take a ~** tomar una muestra; **free ~** muestra gratuita.
sanatorium, *pl* **-ria** [sanətôr'ēəm, -tôr'ēə] *n* (*Brit*) = **sanitarium**.

sanctify [sangk'təfī] *vt* santificar.

sanctimonious [sangktəmō'nēəs] *a* santurrón/ona.

sanction [sangk'shən] *n* sanción *f* ♦ *vt* sancionar; **to impose economic ~s on** *or* **against** imponer sanciones económicas a *or* contra.

sanctity [sangk'titē] *n* (*gen*) santidad *f*; (*inviolability*) inviolabilidad *f*.

sanctuary [sangk'chōōārē] *n* (*gen*) santuario; (*refuge*) asilo, refugio.

sand [sand] *n* arena; (*beach*) playa ♦ *vt* (*also:* ~ **down:** *wood etc*) lijar; (*road*) poner gravilla en.

sandal [san'dəl] *n* sandalia.

sandalwood [san'dəlwōōd] *n* sándalo.

sandbag [sand'bag] *n* saco de arena.

sandblast [sand'blast] *vt* limpiar con chorro de arena.

sandbox [sand'bâks] *n* (*US: for children*) cajón *m* de arena.

sand castle *n* castillo de arena.

sand dune *n* duna.

sandpaper [sand'pāpúr] *n* papel *m* de lija.

sandpit [sand'pit] *n* (*Brit*) = **sandbox**.

sands [sandz] *npl* playa *sg* de arena.

sandstone [sand'stōn] *n* piedra arenisca.

sandstorm [sand'stórm] *n* tormenta de arena.

sandwich [sand'wich] *n* bocadillo (*Sp*), sandwich *m* (*LAm*) ♦ *vt* (*also:* ~ **in**) intercalar; **to be ~ed between** estar apretujado entre; **cheese/ham** ~ **sandwich** *m* de queso/jamón.

sandwich board *n* cartelón *m*.

sandy [san'dē] *a* arenoso; (*color*) rojizo.

sane [sān] *a* cuerdo, sensato.

sang [sang] *pt* of **sing**.

sanitarium [sanitär'ēəm] *n* (*US*) sanatorio.

sanitary [san'itārē] *a* (*system, arrangements*) sanitario; (*clean*) higiénico.

sanitary napkin *n* paño higiénico, compresa.

sanitation [sanitā'shən] *n* (*in house*) servicios *mpl* higiénicos; (*in town*) servicio de desinfección.

sanitation department *n* (*US*) departamento de limpieza y recogida de basuras.

sanity [san'itē] *n* cordura; (*of judgment*) sensatez *f*.

sank [sangk] *pt* of **sink**.

San Marino [san mərē'nō] *n* San Marino.

Santa Claus [san'tə klôz] *n* San Nicolás *m*, Papá Noel *m*.

Santiago [santēâ'gō] *n* (*also:* ~ **de Chile**) Santiago (de Chile).

sap [sap] *n* (*of plants*) savia ♦ *vt* (*strength*) minar, agotar.

sapling [sap'ling] *n* árbol nuevo *or* joven.

sapphire [saf'īûr] *n* zafiro.

Saragossa [sarəgâs'ə] *n* Zaragoza.

sarcasm [sâr'kazəm] *n* sarcasmo.

sarcastic [sârkas'tik] *a* sarcástico; **to be ~** ser sarcástico.

sarcophagus, *pl* **sarcophagi** [sârkâf'əgəs, -gī] *n* sarcófago.

sardine [sârdēn'] *n* sardina.

Sardinia [sârdin'ēə] *n* Cerdeña.

Sardinian [sârdin'ēən] *a, n* sardo/a *m/f*.

sardonic [sârdán'ik] *a* sardónico.

sari [sâ'rē] *n* sari *m*.

SAS *n abbr* (*Brit* MIL: = *Special Air Service*) *cuerpo del ejército británico encargado de misiones clandestinas.*

SASE *n abbr* (*US*) = **self-addressed stamped envelope**.

sash [sash] *n* faja.

Sask. *abbr* (*Canada*) = **Saskatchewan**.

sassy [sas'ē] *a* (*US*) fresco, descarado.

SAT *n abbr* (*US*) = *Scholastic Aptitude Test*.

sat [sat] *pt, pp* of **sit**.

Sat. *abbr* (= *Saturday*) sáb.

Satan [sā'tən] *n* Satanás *m*.

satanic [sətan'ik] *a* satánico.

satchel [sach'əl] *n* bolsa; (*child's*) cartera, mochila (*LAm*).

sated [sā'tid] *a* (*appetite, person*) saciado.

satellite [sat'əlīt] *n* satélite *m*.

satellite dish *n* (*TV*) antena parabólica.

satiate [sā'shēāt] *vt* saciar, hartar.

satin [sat'ən] *n* raso ♦ *a* de raso; **with a ~ finish** satinado.

satire [sat'īûr] *n* sátira.

satirical [sətir'ikəl] *a* satírico.

satirist [sat'ûrist] *n* (*writer etc*) escritor(a) *m/f* satírico/a; (*cartoonist*) caricaturista *m/f*.

satirize [sat'ərīz] *vt* satirizar.

satisfaction [satisfak'shən] *n* satisfacción *f*; **it gives me great ~** es para mí una gran satisfacción; **has it been done to your ~?** ¿se ha hecho a su satisfacción?

satisfactorily [satisfak'tərəlē] *ad* satisfactoriamente, de modo satisfactorio.

satisfactory [satisfak'tûrē] *a* satisfactorio.

satisfy [sat'isfī] *vt* satisfacer; (*pay*) liquidar; (*convince*) convencer; **to ~ the requirements** llenar los requisitos; **to ~ sb that** convencer a uno de que; **to ~ o.s. of sth** convencerse de algo.

satisfying [sat'isfīing] *a* satisfactorio.

saturate [sach'ûrāt] *vt:* **to ~ (with)** empapar *or* saturar (de).

saturation [sachərā'shən] *n* saturación *f*.

Saturday [sat'ûrdā] *n* sábado.

sauce [sôs] *n* salsa; (*sweet*) crema; (*fig: cheek*) frescura.

saucepan [sôs'pan] *n* cacerola, olla.

saucer [sô'sûr] *n* platillo.

saucily [sô'silē] *ad* con frescura, descaradamente.

sauciness [sô'sēnis] *n* frescura, descaro.

saucy [sôs'ē] *a* fresco, descarado.

Saudi Arabia [sou'dē ərā'bēə] *n* Arabia Saudí *or* Saudita.

Saudi (Arabian) [sou'dē (ərā'bēən)] *a, n*

saudí *m/f*, saudita *m/f*.

sauna [só'nə] *n* sauna.

saunter [sòn'tûr] *vi* deambular.

sausage [sò'sij] *n* salchicha; (*salami etc*) salchichón *m*.

sausage roll *n* empanadilla.

sauté [sótā'] *a* (*CULIN: potatoes*) salteado; (: *onions*) dorado, rehogado ♦ *vt* saltear; dorar.

savage [sav'ij] *a* (*cruel, fierce*) feroz, furioso; (*primitive*) salvaje ♦ *n* salvaje *m/f* ♦ *vt* (*attack*) embestir.

savagely [sàv'ijlē] *ad* con ferocidad, furiosamente; de modo salvaje.

savagery [sav'ijrē] *n* ferocidad *f*; salvajismo.

save [sāv] *vt* (*rescue*) salvar, rescatar; (*money, time*) ahorrar; (*set aside*) guardar; (*COMPUT*) salvar (y guardar); (*avoid: trouble*) evitar ♦ *vi* (*also*: ~ **up**) ahorrar ♦ *n* (*SPORT*) parada ♦ *prep* salvo, excepto; **to ~ face** salvar las apariencias; **God ~ the Queen!** ¡Dios guarde a la Reina!, ¡Viva la Reina!; **I ~d you a piece of cake** te he guardado un trozo de tarta; **it will ~ me an hour** con ello ganaré una hora.

saving [sā'ving] *n* (*on price etc*) economía ♦ *a*: **the ~ grace of** el único mérito de; **~s** *npl* ahorros *mpl*; **to make ~s** economizar.

savings account *n* cuenta de ahorros.

savings and loan association *n* (*US*) sociedad *f* inmobiliaria, cooperativa de construcciones.

savings bank *n* caja de ahorros.

savior, (*Brit*) **saviour** [sāv'yûr] *n* salvador(a) *m/f*.

savoir-faire [savwârfär'] *n* don *m* de gentes.

savor, (*Brit*) **savour** [sā'vûr] *n* sabor *m*, gusto ♦ *vt* saborear.

savo(u)ry [sā'vûrē] *a* sabroso; (*dish: not sweet*) salado.

savvy [sav'ē] *n* (*col*) conocimiento, experiencia.

saw [sò] *pt of* **see** ♦ *n* (*tool*) sierra ♦ *vt* (*pt* **sawed**, *pp* **sawed** *or* **sawn** [sòn]) serrar; **to ~ sth up** (a)serrar algo.

sawdust [sò'dust] *n* (a)serrín *m*.

sawed-off [sòd'òf], (*Brit*) **sawn-off** [sòn'òf] *a*: **~ shotgun** escopeta de cañones recortados.

sawmill [sò'mil] *n* aserradero.

sawn [sòn] (*Brit*) *pp of* **saw**.

saxophone [sak'səfōn] *n* saxófono.

say [sā] *n*: **to have one's ~** expresar su opinión; **to have a** *or* **some ~ in sth** tener voz *or* tener que ver en algo ♦ *vt, vi* (*pt, pp* **said** [sed]) decir; **to ~ yes/no** decir que sí/no; **my watch ~s 3 o'clock** mi reloj marca las tres; **that is to ~** es decir; **that goes without ~ing** ni que decir tiene; **she said (that) I was to give you this** me pidió que te diera esto; **I'd ~ it's worth about $100** yo diría que vale unos 100 dólares; **~ after me** repite lo que yo diga; **shall we ~ Tuesday?** ¿quedamos en el martes?; **that doesn't ~ much for him** eso no dice nada a su favor; **when all is said and done** al fin y al cabo, a fin de cuentas; **there is something** *or* **a lot to be said for it** hay algo *or* mucho que decir a su favor.

saying [sā'ing] *n* dicho, refrán *m*.

say-so [sā'sō] *n* (*col*) autorización *f*.

SBA *n abbr* (*US*) = *Small Business Administration*.

SC *n abbr* (*US*) = **Supreme Court** ♦ *abbr* (*US MAIL*) = *South Carolina*.

s/c *abbr* = **self-contained**.

scab [skab] *n* costra; (*pej*) esquirol(a) *m/f*.

scaffold [skaf'əld] *n* (*for execution*) cadalso.

scaffolding [skaf'əlding] *n* andamio, andamiaje *m*.

scald [skòld] *n* escaldadura ♦ *vt* escaldar.

scalding [skòl'ding] *a* (*also*: ~ **hot**) hirviendo, que arde.

scale [skāl] *n* (*gen, MUS*) escala; (*of fish*) escama; (*of salaries, fees etc*) escalafón *m* ♦ *vt* (*mountain*) escalar; (*tree*) trepar; **~s** *npl* (*small*) balanza *sg*; (*large*) báscula *sg*; **on a large ~** en gran escala; **~ of charges** tarifa, lista de precios; **pay ~** escala salarial; **to draw sth to ~** dibujar algo a escala.

scale down *vt* reducir.

scale model *n* modelo a escala.

scallion [skal'yən] *n* (*US*) cebollita, chalote *m*.

scallop [skål'əp] *n* (*ZOOL*) venera; (*SEWING*) festón *m*.

scalp [skalp] *n* cabellera ♦ *vt* escalpar.

scalpel [skal'pəl] *n* bisturí *m*.

scamper [skam'pûr] *vi*: **to ~ away, ~ off** irse corriendo.

scampi [skam'pē] *npl* gambas *fpl*.

scan [skan] *vt* (*examine*) escudriñar; (*glance at quickly*) dar un vistazo a; (*TV, RADAR*) explorar, registrar ♦ *n* (*MED*) examen *m* ultrasónico.

scandal [skan'dəl] *n* escándalo; (*gossip*) chismes *mpl*.

scandalize [skan'dəlīz] *vt* escandalizar.

scandalous [skan'dələs] *a* escandaloso.

Scandinavia [skandənā'vēə] *n* Escandinavia.

Scandinavian [skandənā'vēən] *a*, *n* escandinavo/a *m/f*.

scanner [skan'ûr] *n* (*RADAR, MED*) escáner *m*.

scant [skant] *a* escaso.

scantily [skan'tilē] *ad*: **~ clad** *or* **dressed** ligeramente vestido.

scantiness [skan'tēnis] *n* escasez *f*, insuficiencia.

scanty [skan'tē] *a* (*meal*) insuficiente; (*clothes*) ligero.

scapegoat [skāp'gōt] *n* cabeza de turco,

chivo expiatorio.

scar |skär| *n* cicatriz *f* ♦ *vt* marcar con una cicatriz ♦ *vi* cicatrizarse.

scarce |skärs| *a* escaso.

scarcely |skärs'lē| *ad* apenas; ~ **anybody** casi nadie; **I can ~ believe it** casi no puedo creerlo.

scarceness |skärs'nis|, **scarcity** |skär'sitē| *n* escasez *f*.

scarcity value *n* valor *m* de escasez.

scare |skär| *n* susto, sobresalto; (*panic*) pánico ♦ *vt* asustar, espantar; **to ~ sb stiff** dar a uno un susto de muerte; **bomb ~** amenaza de bomba.
  scare away, scare off *vt* espantar, ahuyentar.

scarecrow |skär'krō| *n* espantapájaros *m inv*.

scared |skärd| *a*: **to be ~** asustarse, estar asustado.

scaremonger |skär'munggûr| *n* alarmista *m/f*.

scarf, *pl* **scarves** |skärf, skärvz| *n* (*long*) bufanda; (*square*) pañuelo.

scarlet |skär'lit| *a* escarlata.

scarlet fever *n* escarlatina.

scarred |skärd| *a* lleno de cicatrices.

scarves |skärvz| *npl of* **scarf**.

scary |skär'ē| *a* (*col*) de miedo.

scathing |skā'thing| *a* mordaz; **to be ~ about sth** criticar algo duramente.

scatter |skat'ûr| *vt* (*spread*) esparcir, desparramar; (*put to flight*) dispersar ♦ *vi* desparramarse; dispersarse.

scatterbrained |skat'ûrbrānd| *a* ligero de cascos.

scavenge |skav'inj| *vi*: **to ~ (for)** (*person*) revolver entre la basura (para encontrar); **to ~ for food** (*hyenas etc*) nutrirse de carroña.

scavenger |skav'injûr| *n* (*person*) basurero/a; (*ZOOL: animal*) animal *m* de carroña; (: *bird*) ave *f* de carroña.

scenario |sinär'ēō| *n* (*THEATER*) argumento; (*CINEMA*) guión *m*; (*fig*) escenario.

scene |sēn| *n* (*THEATER, fig etc*) escena; (*of crime, accident*) escenario; (*sight, view*) vista, perspectiva; (*fuss*) escándalo; **the political ~ in Spain** el panorama político español; **behind the ~s** (*also fig*) entre bastidores; **to appear** *or* **come on the ~** (*also fig*) aparecer, presentarse; **to make a ~** (*col: fuss*) armar un escándalo.

scenery |sē'nûrē| *n* (*THEATER*) decorado; (*landscape*) paisaje *m*.

scenic |sē'nik| *a* (*picturesque*) pintoresco.

scent |sent| *n* perfume *m*, olor *m*; (*fig: track*) rastro, pista; (*sense of smell*) olfato ♦ *vt* perfumar; (*suspect*) presentir; **to put** *or* **throw sb off the ~** (*fig*) despistar a uno.

scepter, (*Brit*) **sceptre** |sep'tûr| *n* cetro.

sceptic |skep'tik| *etc* (*Brit*) = **skeptic** *etc*.

schedule |skej'ōōl, (*Brit*) shed'yōōl| *n* (*of trains*) horario; (*of events*) programa *m*; (*list*) lista ♦ *vt* (*timetable*) establecer el horario de; (*visit*) fijar la hora de; **on ~** a la hora, sin retraso; **to be ahead of/behind ~** estar adelantado/en retraso; **we are working to a very tight ~** tenemos un programa de trabajo muy exigente; **everything went according to ~** todo sucedió según se había previsto; **the meeting is ~d for 7** *or* **to begin at 7** la reunión está fijada para las 7.

scheduled |skej'ōōld, (*Brit*) shed'yōōld| *a* (*date, time*) fijado; (*visit, event, bus, train*) programado; (*stop*) previsto; ~ **flight** vuelo regular.

schematic |skēmat'ik| *a* (*diagram etc*) esquemático.

scheme |skēm| *n* (*plan*) plan *m*, proyecto; (*method*) esquema *m*; (*plot*) intriga; (*trick*) ardid *m*; (*arrangement*) disposición *f*; (*Brit: pension ~ etc*) sistema *m* ♦ *vt* proyectar ♦ *vi* (*plan*) hacer proyectos; (*intrigue*) intrigar; **color ~** combinación *f* de colores.

scheming |skēm'ing| *a* intrigante.

schism |skiz'əm| *n* cisma *m*.

schizophrenia |skitsəfrē'nēə| *n* esquizofrenia.

schizophrenic |skitsəfren'ik| *a* esquizofrénico.

scholar |skäl'ûr| *n* (*pupil*) alumno/a, estudiante *m/f*; (*learned person*) sabio/a, erudito/a.

scholarly |skäl'ûrlē| *a* erudito.

scholarship |skäl'ûrship| *n* erudición *f*; (*grant*) beca.

school |skōōl| *n* (*gen*) escuela, colegio; (*in university*) facultad *f*; (*of fish*) banco ♦ *vt* (*animal*) amaestrar; **to be at** *or* **go to ~** ir al colegio *or* a la escuela.

school age *n* edad *f* escolar.

school bag *n* bolso, cabás *m*.

schoolbook |skōōl'bōōk| *n* libro de texto.

schoolboy |skōōl'boi| *n* alumno.

schoolchild, *pl* **-children** |skōōl'chīld, -childrən| *n* alumno/a.

schooldays |skōōl'dāz| *npl* años *mpl* del colegio.

schoolgirl |skōōl'gûrl| *n* alumna.

schooling |skōō'ling| *n* enseñanza.

schoolmaster |skōōl'mastûr| *n* (*grade*) maestro; (*high*) profesor *m*.

schoolmistress |skōōl'mistris| *n* (*grade*) maestra; (*high*) profesora.

schoolroom |skōōl'rōōm| *n* clase *f*.

schoolteacher |skōōl'tēchûr| *n* (*grade*) maestro/a; (*high*) profesor(a) *m/f*.

schoolyard |skōōl'yärd| *n* patio (de recreo).

schooner |skōō'nûr| *n* (*ship*) goleta.

sciatica |sīat'ikə| *n* ciática.

science |sī'əns| *n* ciencia; **the ~s** las ciencias.

science fiction *n* ciencia-ficción *f*.

scientific [sīəntif'ik] *a* científico.
scientist [sī'əntist] *n* científico/a.
sci-fi [sī'fī'] *n abbr* (*col*) = **science fiction.**
scintillating [sin'təlāting] *a* (*wit, conversation, company*) brillante, chispeante, ingenioso.
scissors [siz'ûrz] *npl* tijeras *fpl*; **a pair of** ~ unas tijeras.
scoff [skâf] *vi:* **to** ~ (**at**) (*mock*) mofarse (de).
scold [skōld] *vt* regañar.
scolding [skōld'ing] *n* riña, reprimenda.
scone [skōn] *n pastel de pan.*
scoop [skōōp] *n* cucharón *m*; (*for flour etc*) pala; (*PRESS*) exclusiva ♦ *vt* (*COMM: market*) adelantarse a; (: *profit*) sacar; (*COMM, PRESS: competitors*) adelantarse a.
   scoop out *vt* excavar.
   scoop up *vt* recoger.
scooter [skōō'tûr] *n* (*motorcycle*) moto *f*; (*toy*) patinete *m*.
scope [skōp] *n* (*of plan, undertaking*) ámbito; (*reach*) alcance *m*; (*of person*) competencia; (*opportunity*) libertad *f* (de acción); **there is plenty of** ~ **for improvement** (*Brit*) hay bastante campo para efectuar mejoras.
scorch [skôrch] *vt* (*clothes*) chamuscar; (*earth, grass*) quemar, secar.
scorcher [skôr'chûr] *n* (*col: hot day*) día *m* abrasador.
scorching [skôrch'ing] *a* abrasador(a).
score [skôr] *n* (*points etc*) puntuación *f*; (*MUS*) partitura; (*reckoning*) cuenta; (*twenty*) veintena ♦ *vt* (*goal, point*) ganar; (*mark, cut*) rayar ♦ *vi* marcar un tanto; (*SOCCER*) marcar un gol; (*keep score*) llevar el tanteo; **to keep (the)** ~ tantear, llevar la cuenta (*LAm*); **to have an old** ~ **to settle with sb** (*fig*) tener cuentas pendientes con uno; **on that** ~ en lo que se refiere a eso; ~**s of people** (*fig*) muchísima gente, cantidad de gente; **to** ~ **6 out of 10** obtener una puntuación de 6 sobre 10.
   score out *vt* tachar.
scoreboard [skôr'bôrd] *n* marcador *m*.
scorer [skôr'ûr] *n* marcador *m*; (*keeping score*) tanteador(a) *m/f*.
scorn [skôrn] *n* desprecio ♦ *vt* despreciar.
scornful [skôrn'fəl] *a* desdeñoso, despreciativo.
scornfully [skôrn'fəlē] *ad* desdeñosamente, con desprecio.
Scorpio [skôr'pēō] *n* Escorpión *m*.
scorpion [skôr'pēən] *n* alacrán *m*.
Scot [skât] *n* escocés/esa *m/f*.
Scotch [skâch] *n* whisky *m* escocés.
scotch [skâch] *vt* (*rumor*) desmentir; (*plan*) abandonar.
Scotch tape ® *n* (*US*) cinta adhesiva, celo, scotch *m* ® (*LAm*).
scot-free [skât'frē'] *ad:* **to get off** ~ (*unpunished*) salir impune; (*unhurt*) salir ileso.

Scotland [skât'lənd] *n* Escocia.
Scots [skâts] *a* escocés/esa.
Scotsman [skâts'mən] *n* escocés *m*.
Scotswoman [skâts'wōōmən] *n* escocesa.
Scottish [skât'ish] *a* escocés/esa.
scoundrel [skoun'drəl] *n* canalla *m/f*, sinvergüenza *m/f*.
scour [skour] *vt* (*clean*) fregar, estregar; (*search*) recorrer, registrar.
scourer [skour'ûr] *n* (*pad*) estropajo; (*powder*) limpiador *m*, desgrasador *m*.
scourge [skûrj] *n* azote *m*.
scouring pad [skour'ing pad] *n* estropajo.
scout [skout] *n* (*MIL, also:* **boy** ~) explorador *m*.
   scout around *vi* reconocer el terreno.
scowl [skoul] *vi* fruncir el ceño; **to** ~ **at sb** mirar con ceño a uno.
scrabble [skrab'əl] *vi* (*claw*): **to** ~ (**at**) arañar ♦ *n:* **S~** ® Scrabble *m* ®; **to** ~ **around for sth** revolver todo buscando algo.
scraggy [skrag'ē] *a* flaco, descarnado.
scram [skram] *vi* (*col*) largarse.
scramble [skram'bəl] *n* (*climb*) subida (difícil); (*struggle*) pelea ♦ *vi:* **to** ~ **out/ through** salir/abrirse paso con dificultad; **to** ~ **for** pelear por; **to go scrambling** (*SPORT*) hacer motocrós.
scrambled eggs [skram'bəld egz] *npl* huevos *mpl* revueltos.
scrap [skrap] *n* (*bit*) pedacito; (*fig*) pizca; (*fight*) riña, bronca; (*also:* ~ **iron**) chatarra, hierro viejo ♦ *vt* (*discard*) desechar, descartar ♦ *vi* reñir, armar (una) bronca; ~**s** *npl* (*waste*) sobras *fpl*, desperdicios *mpl*; **to sell sth for** ~ vender algo como chatarra.
scrapbook [skrap'bōōk] *n* álbum *m* de recortes.
scrap dealer *n* chatarrero/a.
scrape [skrāp] *n* (*fig*) lío, apuro ♦ *vt* raspar; (*skin etc*) rasguñar; (~ *against*) rozar.
   scrape through *vi* (*succeed*) apenas lograr hacer algo; (*exam*) aprobar por los pelos.
scraper [skrā'pûr] *n* raspador *m*.
scrap heap *n* (*fig*): **on the** ~ desperdiciado; **to throw sth on the** ~ desechar *or* descartar algo.
scrap iron *n* chatarra.
scrap metal *n* chatarra, desecho de metal.
scrap paper *n* pedazos *mpl* de papel.
scrappy [skrap'ē] *a* (*poor*) pobre; (*bitty*) fragmentario.
scrap yard *n* depósito de chatarra; (*for cars*) cementerio de coches.
scratch [skrach] *n* rasguño; (*from claw*) arañazo ♦ *vt* (*record*) rayar; (*with claw, nail*) rasguñar, arañar; (*COMPUT*) borrar ♦ *vi* rascarse; **to start from** ~ partir de cero.

scratchpad [skrach'pad] *n* (*US*) bloc *m*.
scrawl [skrôl] *n* garabatos *mpl* ♦ *vi* hacer garabatos.
scrawny [skrô'nē] *a* (*person, neck*) flaco.
scream [skrēm] *n* chillido ♦ *vi* chillar; **it was a ~** (*fig, col*) fue para morirse de risa *or* muy divertido; **he's a ~** (*fig, col*) es muy divertido *or* de lo más gracioso; **to ~ at sb (to do sth)** gritarle a uno (para que haga algo).
scree [skrē] *n* cono de desmoronamiento.
screech [skrēch] *vi* chirriar.
screen [skrēn] *n* (*CINEMA, TV*) pantalla; (*movable*) biombo; (*wall*) tabique *m*; (*Brit: also*: **wind~**) parabrisas *m inv* ♦ *vt* (*conceal*) tapar; (*from the wind etc*) proteger; (*movie*) proyectar; (*fig: person: for security*) investigar a; (: *for illness*) hacer una exploración a.
screen editing *n* (*COMPUT*) corrección *f* en pantalla.
screening [skrē'ning] *n* (*of movie*) proyección *f*; (*for security*) investigación *f*; (*MED*) exploración *f*.
screen memory *n* (*COMPUT*) memoria de la pantalla.
screenplay [skrēn'plā] *n* guión *m*.
screen test *n* prueba de pantalla.
screw [skrōō] *n* tornillo; (*propeller*) hélice *f* ♦ *vt* atornillar; **to ~ sth to the wall** fijar algo a la pared con tornillos.
  screw up *vt* (*paper, material etc*) arrugar; (*col: ruin*) estropear; **to ~ up one's eyes** arrugar el entrecejo; **to ~ up one's face** torcer *or* arrugar la cara.
screwball [skrōō'bôl] *n* (*col*) chalado, tarado (*LAm*).
screwdriver [skrōō'drīvûr] *n* destornillador *m*.
screwy [skrōō'ē] *a* (*col*) chiflado.
scribble [skrib'əl] *n* garabatos *mpl* ♦ *vt* escribir con prisa; **to ~ sth down** garabatear algo.
script [skript] *n* (*CINEMA etc*) guión *m*; (*writing*) escritura, letra.
scripted [skrip'tid] *a* (*RADIO, TV*) escrito.
Scripture [skrip'chûr] *n* Sagrada Escritura.
scriptwriter [skript'rītûr] *n* guionista *m/f*.
scroll [skrōl] *n* rollo ♦ *vt* (*COMPUT*) desplazar.
scrotum [skrō'təm] *n* escroto.
scrounge [skrounj] (*col*) *vt*: **to ~ sth off** *or* **from sb** obtener algo de uno de gorra ♦ *vi*: **to ~ off sb** vivir a costa de uno.
scrounger [skrounj'ûr] *n* gorrón/ona *m/f*.
scrub [skrub] *n* (*clean*) fregado; (*land*) maleza ♦ *vt* fregar, restregar; (*reject*) cancelar, anular.
scrub brush *n* (*US*) cepillo para fregar.
scrubbing brush [skrub'ing brush] *n* (*Brit*) cepillo de fregar.
scruff [skruf] *n*: **by the ~ of the neck** por el pescuezo.

scruffy [skruf'ē] *a* desaliñado, piojoso.
scrum(mage) [skrum'(ij)] *n* (*RUGBY*) melée *f*.
scruple [skrōō'pəl] *n* escrúpulo; **to have no ~s about doing sth** no tener reparos en *or* escrúpulos acerca de hacer algo.
scrupulous [skrōō'pyələs] *a* escrupuloso.
scrupulously [skrōō'pyələslē] *ad* escrupulosamente; **to be ~ fair/honest** ser sumamente justo/honesto.
scrutinize [skrōō'tənīz] *vt* escudriñar; (*votes*) escrutar.
scrutiny [skrōō'tənē] *n* escrutinio, examen *m*; **under the ~ of sb** bajo la mirada *or* el escrutinio de uno.
scuba [skōō'bə] *n* escafandra autónoma.
scuba diving *n* buceo con escafandra autónoma.
scuff [skuf] *vt* (*shoes, floor*) rayar.
scuffle [skuf'əl] *n* refriega.
scullery [skul'ûrē] *n* trascocina.
sculptor [skulp'tûr] *n* escultor(a) *m/f*.
sculpture [skulp'chûr] *n* escultura.
scum [skum] *n* (*on liquid*) nata; (*pej: people*) canalla; (*fig*) heces *fpl*.
scurrilous [skûr'ələs] *a* difamatorio, calumnioso.
scurry [skûr'ē] *vi*: **to ~ off** escabullirse.
scurvy [skûr'vē] *n* escorbuto.
scuttle [skut'əl] *n* (*also*: **coal ~**) cubo, carbonera ♦ *vt* (*ship*) barrenar ♦ *vi* (*scamper*): **to ~ away, ~ off** escabullirse.
scythe [sīth] *n* guadaña.
SD *abbr* (*US MAIL*) = *South Dakota*.
S.Dak. *abbr* (*US*) = *South Dakota*.
SDI *n abbr* (= *Strategic Defense Initiative*) IDE *f*.
SDLP *n abbr* (*Brit POL*) = *Social Democratic and Labour Party*.
SDP *n abbr* (*Brit POL*) = *Social Democratic Party*.
sea [sē] *n* mar *m/f*; **by ~** (*travel*) en barco; **on the ~** (*boat*) en el mar; (*town*) junto al mar; **out to** *or* **at ~** en alta mar; **to go by ~** ir en barco; **heavy** *or* **rough ~s** mar *msg* agitado *or* picado; **by** *or* **beside the ~** (*vacation*) en la playa; (*village*) a orillas del mar; **a ~ of faces** una multitud de caras.
sea bed *n* fondo del mar.
sea bird *n* ave *f* marina.
seaboard [sē'bôrd] *n* litoral *m*.
sea breeze *n* brisa de mar.
seadog [sē'dôg] *n* lobo de mar.
seafarer [sē'färûr] *n* marinero.
seafaring [sē'färing] *a* (*community*) marinero; (*life*) de marinero.
seafood [sē'fōōd] *n* mariscos *mpl*.
sea front *n* (*beach*) playa; (*prom*) paseo marítimo.
seagoing [sē'gōing] *a* (*ship*) de alta mar.
seagull [sē'gul] *n* gaviota.
seal [sēl] *n* (*animal*) foca; (*stamp*) sello ♦ *vt*

(close) cerrar; (: *with* ~) sellar; *(decide:* sb's *fate)* decidir; (: *bargain)* cerrar; ~ **of approval** sello de aprobación.
seal off *vt* obturar.
sea level *n* nivel *m* del mar.
sealing wax [sē'ling waks] *n* lacre *m*.
sea lion *n* león *m* marino.
sealskin [sēl'skin] *n* piel *f* de foca.
seam [sēm] *n* costura; *(of metal)* juntura; *(of coal)* veta, filón *m*; **the hall was bursting at the ~s** la sala rebosaba de gente.
seaman [sē'mən] *n* marinero.
seamanship [sē'mənship] *n* náutica.
seamless [sēm'lis] *a* sin costura(s).
seamy [sē'mē] *a* sórdido.
seance [sā'áns] *n* sesión *f* de espiritismo.
seaplane [sē'plān] *n* hidroavión *m*.
seaport [sē'pôrt] *n* puerto de mar.
search [sûrch] *n* *(for person, thing)* busca, búsqueda; *(of drawer, pockets)* registro; *(inspection)* reconocimiento ♦ *vt (look in)* buscar en; *(examine)* examinar; *(person, place)* registrar; *(COMPUT)* buscar ♦ *vi:* **to ~ for** buscar; **in ~ of** en busca de; **"~ and replace"** *(COMPUT)* "buscar y reemplazar".
search through *vt fus* registrar.
searcher [sûr'chûr] *n* buscador(a) *m/f*.
searching [sûr'ching] *a (question)* penetrante.
searchlight [sûrch'līt] *n* reflector *m*.
search party *n* pelotón *m* de salvamento.
search warrant *n* mandamiento de registro (judicial).
searing [sē'ring] *a (heat)* abrasador(a); *(pain)* agudo.
seashore [sē'shôr] *n* playa, orilla del mar; **on the ~** a la orilla del mar.
seasick [sē'sik] *a* mareado; **to be ~** marearse.
seaside [sē'sīd] *n* playa, orilla del mar.
seaside resort *n* playa.
season [sē'zən] *n (of year)* estación *f*; *(sporting etc)* temporada; *(gen)* época, período ♦ *vt (food)* sazonar; **to be in/out of ~** estar en sazón/fuera de temporada; **the busy ~** *(for stores, hotels etc)* la temporada alta; **the open ~** *(HUNTING)* la temporada de caza *or* de pesca.
seasonal [sē'zənəl] *a* estacional.
seasoned [sē'zənd] *a (wood)* curado; *(fig: worker, actor)* experimentado; *(troops)* aguerrido; **~ campaigner** veterano/a.
seasoning [sē'zəning] *n* condimento, aderezo.
season ticket *n* abono.
seat [sēt] *n (in bus, train: place)* asiento; *(chair)* silla; *(PARLIAMENT)* escaño; *(buttocks)* culo, trasero; *(center: of government etc)* sede *f* ♦ *vt* sentar; *(have room for)* tener cabida para; **are there any ~s left?** ¿quedan plazas?; **to take one's ~** sentarse, tomar asiento; **to be ~ed** estar

sentado, sentarse.
seat belt *n* cinturón *m* de seguridad.
seating [se'ting] *n* asientos *mpl*.
seating arrangements *npl* arreglo *sg* de los asientos.
seating capacity [sē'ting kəpas'itē] *n* cabida, número de asientos.
SEATO [sē'tō] *n* *abbr* (= *Southeast Asia Treaty Organization)* OTASE *f*.
sea water *n* agua *m* del mar.
seaweed [sē'wēd] *n* alga marina.
seaworthy [sē'wûrthē] *a* en condiciones de navegar.
SEC *n abbr (US:* = *Securities and Exchange Commission)* comisión de operaciones bursátiles.
sec. *abbr* = **second(s).**
secateurs [sek'ətûrz] *npl* podadera *sg*.
secede [sisēd'] *vi:* **to ~ (from)** separarse (de).
secluded [siklōō'did] *a* retirado.
seclusion [siklōō'zhən] *n* retiro.
second [sek'ənd] *a* segundo ♦ *ad (in race etc)* en segundo lugar ♦ *n (gen)* segundo; *(AUT: also:* ~ **gear)** segunda; *(COMM)* artículo con algún desperfecto; *(Brit SCOL: degree)* título universitario de segunda clase ♦ *vt (motion)* apoyar; [sikând'] *(employee)* trasladar temporalmente; ~ **floor** *(US)* primer piso; *(Brit)* segundo piso; **Charles the S~** Carlos Segundo; **to ask for a ~ opinion** *(MED)* pedir una segunda opinión; **just a ~!** ¡un momento!; **to have ~ thoughts** cambiar de opinión; **on ~ thought** *or (Brit)* **thoughts** pensándolo bien; ~ **mortgage** segunda hipoteca.
secondary [sek'əndärē] *a* secundario.
secondary education *n* segunda enseñanza.
secondary picket *n* piquete *m* secundario.
secondary school *n* escuela secundaria.
second-best [sek'əndbest'] *n* segundo.
second-class [sek'əndklas'] *a* de segunda clase ♦ *ad:* **to send sth ~** enviar algo por segunda clase; **to travel ~** viajar en segunda; ~ **citizen** ciudadano/a de segunda clase.
second cousin *n* primo/a segundo/a.
seconder [sek'əndûr] *n* el/la que apoya una moción.
secondhand [sek'əndhand'] *a* de segunda mano, usado ♦ *ad:* **to buy sth ~** comprar algo de segunda mano; **to hear sth ~** oír algo indirectamente.
second hand *n (on clock)* segundero.
second-in-command [sek'əndinkəmand'] *n (MIL)* segundo jefe *m*; *(ADMIN)* segundo/a, ayudante *m/f*.
secondly [sek'əndlē] *ad* en segundo lugar.
second-rate [sek'əndrāt'] *a* de segunda categoría.
secrecy [sē'krisē] *n* secreto.

secret [sē'krit] *a, n* secreto; **in** ~ *ad* en secreto; **to keep sth** ~ **(from sb)** ocultarle algo (a uno); **to make no** ~ **of sth** no ocultar algo.

secret agent *n* agente *m/f* secreto/a, espía *m/f*.

secretarial [sekritär'ēəl] *a (course)* de secretariado; *(staff)* de secretaría; *(work, duties)* de secretaria.

secretariat [sekritär'ēət] *n* secretaría.

secretary [sek'ritärē] *n* secretario/a; **S**~ **of State** *(Brit POL)* Ministro (con cartera).

secretary pool *n (US)* servicio de mecanógrafos.

secrete [sikrēt'] *vt (MED, ANAT, BIO)* secretar; *(hide)* ocultar, esconder.

secretion [sikrē'shən] *n* secreción *f*.

secretive [sē'kritiv] *a* reservado, sigiloso.

secretly [sē'kritlē] *ad* en secreto.

sect [sekt] *n* secta.

sectarian [sektär'ēən] *a* sectario.

section [sek'shən] *n* sección *f; (part)* parte *f; (of document)* artículo; *(of opinion)* sector *m*; **business** ~ *(PRESS)* sección *f* de economía.

sectional [sek'shənəl] *a (regional)* regional, local.

sector [sek'tûr] *n (gen, COMPUT)* sector *m*.

secular [sek'yəlûr] *a* secular, seglar.

secure [sikyōōr'] *a (free from anxiety)* seguro; *(firmly fixed)* firme, fijo ♦ *vt (fix)* asegurar, afianzar; *(get)* conseguir; *(COMM: loan)* garantizar; **to make sth** ~ afianzar algo; **to** ~ **sth for sb** conseguir algo para uno.

secured creditor [sikyōōrd' kred'itûr] *n* acreedor(a) *m/f* con garantía.

securely [sikyōōr'lē] *ad* firmemente; **it is** ~ **fastened** está bien sujetado.

security [sikyōōr'itē] *n* seguridad *f; (for loan)* fianza; *(: object)* prenda; **securities** *npl (COMM)* valores *mpl*, títulos *mpl;* ~ **of tenure** tenencia asegurada; **to increase/tighten** ~ aumentar/estrechar las medidas de seguridad; **job** ~ trabajo asegurado.

security forces *npl* fuerzas *fpl* de seguridad.

security guard *n* guardia *m/f* de seguridad.

security risk *n* riesgo para la seguridad.

secy. *abbr (= secretary)* Srio/a.

sedan [sidan'] *n (US AUT)* sedán *m*.

sedate [sidāt'] *a* tranquilo ♦ *vt* tratar con sedantes.

sedation [sidā'shən] *n (MED)* sedación *f;* **to be under** ~ estar bajo sedación.

sedative [sed'ətiv] *n* sedante *m*, sedativo.

sedentary [sed'əntärē] *a* sedentario.

sediment [sed'əmənt] *n* sedimento.

sedimentary [sedəmen'tûrē] *a (GEO)* sedimentario.

sedition [sidish'ən] *n* sedición *f*.

seduce [sidōōs'] *vt (gen)* seducir.

seduction [siduk'shən] *n* seducción *f*.

seductive [siduk'tiv] *a* seductor(a).

see [sē] *vb (pt* **saw***, pp* **seen** [sō, sēn]) *vt (gen)* ver; *(understand)* ver, comprender; *(look at)* mirar ♦ *vi* ver ♦ *n* sede *f;* **to** ~ **sb to the door** acompañar a uno a la puerta; **to** ~ **that** *(ensure)* asegurar que; ~ **you soon/later/tomorrow!** ¡hasta pronto/luego/mañana!; **as far as I can** ~ por lo visto *or* por lo que yo veo; **there was nobody to be** ~**n** no se veía a nadie; **let me** ~ *(show me)* a ver; *(let me think)* vamos a ver; **to go and** ~ **sb** ir a ver a uno; ~ **for yourself** míralo tú mismo; **I don't know what she** ~**s in him** no sé qué le encuentra.

see about *vt fus* atender a, encargarse de.

see off *vt* despedir.

see through *vt fus* penetrar (con la vista) ♦ *vt* llevar a cabo.

see to *vt fus* atender a, encargarse de.

seed [sēd] *n* semilla; *(in fruit)* pepita; *(fig)* germen *m; (TENNIS)* preseleccionado/a; **to go to** ~ *(plant)* granar; *(fig)* descuidarse.

seedless [sēd'lis] *a* sin semillas *or* pepitas.

seedling [sēd'ling] *n* planta de semillero.

seedy [sē'dē] *a (shabby)* desaseado, raído.

seeing [sē'ing] *conj:* ~ **(that)** visto que, en vista de que.

seek*, pt, pp* **sought** [sēk, sôt] *vt (gen)* buscar; *(post)* solicitar; **to** ~ **advice/help from sb** pedir consejos/solicitar ayuda a uno.

seek out *vt (person)* buscar.

seem [sēm] *vi* parecer; **there** ~**s to be...** parece que hay ...; **it** ~**s (that)** ... parece que ...; **what** ~**s to be the trouble?** ¿qué pasa?; **I did what** ~**ed best** hice lo que parecía mejor.

seemingly [sē'minglē] *ad* aparentemente, según parece.

seen [sēn] *pp of* **see**.

seep [sēp] *vi* filtrarse.

seer [sēr] *n* vidente *m/f*, profeta *m/f*.

seersucker [sēr'sukûr] *n* sirsaca.

seesaw [sē'sô] *n* balancín *m*, columpio.

seethe [sēth] *vi* hervir; **to** ~ **with anger** enfurecerse.

see-through [sē'thrōō] *a* transparente.

segment [seg'mənt] *n* segmento.

segregate [seg'rəgāt] *vt* segregar.

segregation [segrəgā'shən] *n* segregación *f*.

Seine [sān] *n* Sena *m*.

seismic [sīz'mik] *a* sísmico.

seize [sēz] *vt (grasp)* agarrar, asir; *(take possession of)* secuestrar; *(: territory)* apoderarse de; *(opportunity)* aprovecharse de.

seize up *vi (TECH)* agarrotarse.

seize (up)on *vt fus* valerse de.

seizure [sē'zhûr] *n (MED)* ataque *m; (LAW)* incautación *f*.

seldom [sel'dəm] *ad* rara vez.

select [silekt'] *a* selecto, escogido; *(hotel,*

restaurant, clubs) exclusivo ♦ *vt* escoger, elegir; (*SPORT*) seleccionar; **a ~ few** una minoría privilegiada.

selection |silek'shən| *n* selección *f*, elección *f*; (*COMM*) surtido.

selection committee *n* comisión *f* de nombramiento.

selective |silek'tiv| *a* selectivo.

self |self| *n* (*pl* **selves** |selvz|) uno mismo ♦ *pref* auto ...; **the ~** el yo.

self-addressed |self'ədrest'| *a* (*US*): **~ stamped envelope (SASE)** *sobre con las propias señas de uno y con sello.*

self-adhesive |self'adhē'siv| *a* autoadhesivo, autoadherente.

self-appointed |self'əpoin'tid| *a* autonombrado.

self-assurance |self'əshoor'əns| *n* confianza en sí mismo.

self-assured |self'əshoord'| *a* seguro de sí mismo.

self-catering |self'kā'tûring| *a* (*Brit*) sin pensión; **~ apartment** piso sin pensión.

self-centered |self'sen'tûrd| *a* egocéntrico.

self-cleaning |self'klē'ning| *a* autolimpiador.

self-colored |self'kul'ûrd| *a* de un color.

self-confessed |self'kənfest'| *a* (*alcoholic etc*) confeso.

self-confidence |self'kán'fidəns| *n* confianza en sí mismo.

self-confident |self'kán'fidənt| *a* seguro de sí (mismo), lleno de confianza en sí mismo.

self-conscious |self'kán'chəs| *a* cohibido.

self-contained |self'kəntānd'| *a* (*gen*) independiente; (*Brit*: *apartment*) con entrada particular.

self-control |self'kəntrōl'| *n* autodominio.

self-defeating |self'difē'ting| *a* contraproducente.

self-defense |self'difens'| *n* defensa propia.

self-discipline |self'dis'əplin| *n* autodisciplina.

self-employed |self'imploid'| *a* que trabaja por cuenta propia.

self-esteem |self'əstēm'| *n* amor *m* propio.

self-evident |self'ev'idənt| *a* patente.

self-explanatory |self'iksplan'ətôrē| *a* que no necesita explicación.

self-financing |self'finan'sing| *a* autofinanziado.

self-governing |self'guv'ûrning| *a* autónomo.

self-help |self'help'| *n* autosuficiencia, ayuda propia.

self-importance |self'impôr'təns| *n* presunción *f*, vanidad *f*.

self-important |self'impôr'tənt| *a* presumido.

self-indulgent |self'indul'jənt| *a* inmoderado.

self-inflicted |self'inflik'tid| *a* infligido a sí mismo.

self-interest |self'in'trist| *n* egoísmo.

selfish |sel'fish| *a* egoísta.

selfishly |sel'fishlē| *ad* con egoísmo, de modo egoísta.

selfishness |sel'fishnis| *n* egoísmo.

selflessly |self'lislē| *ad* desinteresadamente.

selfless |self'lis| *a* desinteresado.

self-made man |self'mād' man'| *n* hombre *m* que ha triunfado por sus propios esfuerzos.

self-pity |self'pit'ē| *n* lástima de sí mismo.

self-portrait |self'pôr'trit| *n* autorretrato.

self-possessed |self'pəzest'| *a* sereno, dueño de sí mismo.

self-preservation |self'prezûrvā'shən| *n* propia conservación *f*.

self-propelled |self'prəpeld'| *a* autopropulsado, automotor/triz.

self-raising |self'rā'zing| *a* (*Brit*) = **self-rising**.

self-reliant |self'rili'ənt| *a* independiente, autosuficiente.

self-respect |self'rispekt'| *n* amor *m* propio.

self-respecting |self'rispekt'ing| *a* que tiene amor propio.

self-righteous |self'rī'chəs| *a* santurrón/ona.

self-rising |self'rī'zing| *a* (*US*): **~ flour** harina con levadura.

self-sacrifice |self'sak'rəfīs| *n* abnegación *f*.

self-same |self'sām| *a* mismo, mismísimo.

self-satisfied |self'sat'isfīd| *a* satisfecho de sí mismo.

self-service |self'sûr'vis| *a* de autoservicio.

self-styled |self'stīld'| *a* supuesto, sedicente.

self-sufficient |self'səfish'ənt| *a* autosuficiente.

self-supporting |self'səpôrt'ing| *a* económicamente independiente.

self-taught |self'tôt'| *a* autodidacta.

self-test |self'test'| *n* (*COMPUT*) autocomprobación *f*.

sell, *pt, pp* **sold** |sel, sōld| *vt* vender ♦ *vi* venderse; **to ~ at** *or* **for $10** venderse a 10 dólares; **to ~ sb an idea** (*fig*) convencer a uno de una idea.

sell off *vt* liquidar.

sell out *vi* transigir, transar (*LAm*); **to ~ out (to sb/sth)** (*COMM*) vender su negocio (a uno/algo) ♦ *vt* agotar las existencias de, venderlo todo; **the tickets are all sold out** los billetes están agotados.

sell-by date |sel'bī dāt| *n* fecha de caducidad.

seller |sel'ûr| *n* vendedor(a) *m/f*; **~'s market** mercado de demanda.

selling price |sel'ing prīs| *n* precio de venta.

sellotape |sel'ətāp| ® *n* (*Brit*) cinta adhesiva, celo, scotch *m* ® (*LAm*).

sellout |sel'out| *n* traición *f*; **it was a ~** (*THEATER etc*) fue un éxito de taquilla.

selves |selvz| *npl of* **self**.

semantic |siman'tik| *a* semántico.
semaphore |sɛm'əfôr| *n* semáforo.
semblance |sɛm'blɔns| *n* apariencia.
semen |sē'mən| *n* semen *m*.
semester |simɛs'tûr| *n* semestre *m*.
semi |sɛm'ē| *n* (*Brit*) = **semidetached house.**
semi... |sɛm'ē| *pref* semi..., medio....
semiannually |sɛm'ēan'yōōəlē| *ad* (*US*) semestralmente ♦ *a* semestral.
semicircle |sɛm'ēsûrkəl| *n* semicírculo.
semicircular |sɛmēsûr'kyəlûr| *a* semicircular.
semicolon |sɛm'ēkōlən| *n* punto y coma.
semiconductor |sɛmēkənduk'tûr| *n* semiconductor *m*.
semiconscious |sɛmēkán'chəs| *a* semiconsciente.
semidetached (house) |sɛmēditacht' (hous)| *n* (*Brit*) (casa) semiseparada.
semi-final |sɛmēfi'nəl| *n* semi-final *m*.
seminar |sɛm'ənâr| *n* seminario.
seminary |sɛm'ənärē| *n* (*REL*) seminario.
semiprecious stone |sɛmēpresh'əs stōn| *n* piedra semipreciosa.
semiquaver |sɛm'ēkwāvûr| *n* (*Brit*) semicorchea.
semiskilled |sɛmēskild'| *a* (*work, worker*) semicalificado.
semitone |sɛm'ētōn| *n* semitono.
semi(trailer)|sɛm'ē(trā'lûr)|*n* (*US*) trailer *m*.
semolina |sɛməlē'nə| *n* sémola.
Sen., sen. *abbr* = **senator, senior.**
senate |sɛn'it| *n* senado.
senator |sɛn'ətûr| *n* senador(a) *m/f*.
send, *pt, pp* **sent** |sɛnd, sɛnt| *vt* mandar, enviar; **to ~ by mail** mandar por correo; **to ~ sb for sth** mandar a uno a buscar algo; **to ~ word that ...** avisar *or* mandar decir que ...; **she ~s (you) her love** te manda *or* envía cariñosos recuerdos; **to ~ sb into fits of laughter** hacer reír a uno; **to ~ sth flying** echar a uno; **to ~ sb flying** tirar algo.
send away *vt* (*letter, goods*) despachar.
send away for *vt fus* pedir.
send back *vt* devolver.
send for *vt fus* mandar traer; (*by mail*) escribir pidiendo algo.
send in *vt* (*report, application, resignation*) mandar.
send off *vt* (*goods*) despachar.
send on *vt* (*letter*) mandar, expedir; (*luggage etc: in advance*) facturar.
send out *vt* (*invitation*) mandar; (*emit: light, heat*) emitir, difundir; (*: signal*) emitir.
send up *vt* (*person, price*) hacer subir.
sender |sɛnd'ûr| *n* remitente *m/f*.
send-off |sɛnd'ôf| *n*: **a good ~** una buena despedida.
Senegal |sɛn'əgâl| *n* Senegal *m*.
Senegalese |sɛnəgəlēz'| *a, n* senegalés/esa

m/f.
senile |sē'nīl| *a* senil.
senility |sinil'ətē| *n* senilidad *f*.
senior |sēn'yûr| *a* (*older*) mayor, más viejo; (*: on staff*) más antiguo; (*of higher rank*) superior ♦ *n* mayor *m*; **P. Jones ~** P. Jones padre.
senior citizen *n* jubilado/a, anciano/a.
senior high school *n* (*US*) ≈ instituto de enseñanza media *or* de BUP (*Sp*).
seniority |sēnyôr'itē| *n* antigüedad *f*; (*in rank*) rango superior.
sensation |sɛnsā'shən| *n* (*physical feeling, impression*) sensación *f*.
sensational |sɛnsā'shənəl| *a* sensacional.
sense |sɛns| *n* (*faculty, meaning*) sentido; (*feeling*) sensación *f*; (*good ~*) sentido común, juicio ♦ *vt* sentir, percibir; **~ of humor** sentido del humor; **it makes ~** tiene sentido; **there is no ~ in (doing) that** no hay sentido en (hacer) eso; **to come to one's ~s** (*regain consciousness*) volver en sí, recobrar el sentido; **to take leave of one's ~s** perder el juicio.
senseless |sɛns'lis| *a* estúpido, insensato; (*unconscious*) sin conocimiento.
senselessly |sɛns'lislē| *ad* estúpidamente, insensatamente.
sensibility |sɛnsəbil'ətē| *n* sensibilidad *f*; **sensibilities** *npl* delicadeza *sg*.
sensible |sɛn'səbəl| *a* sensato; (*reasonable*) razonable, lógico.
sensibly |sɛn'səblē| *ad* sensatamente, razonablemente, de modo lógico.
sensitive |sɛn'sətiv| *a* sensible; (*touchy*) susceptible; **he is very ~ about it** es muy susceptible acerca de eso.
sensitivity |sɛnsətiv'ətē| *n* sensibilidad *f*; susceptibilidad *f*.
sensual |sɛn'shōōəl| *a* sensual.
sensuous |sɛn'shōōəs| *a* sensual.
sent |sɛnt| *pt, pp* of **send.**
sentence |sɛn'təns| *n* (*LING*) frase *f*, oración *f*; (*LAW*) sentencia, fallo ♦ *vt*: **to ~ sb to death/to 5 years** condenar a uno a muerte/a 5 años de cárcel; **to pass ~ on sb** (*also fig*) sentenciar *or* condenar a uno.
sentiment |sɛn'təmənt| *n* sentimiento; (*opinion*) opinión *f*.
sentimental |sɛntəmen'təl| *a* sentimental.
sentimentality |sɛntəmental'itē| *n* sentimentalismo, sensiblería.
sentinel |sɛn'tənəl| *n* centinela *m*.
sentry |sɛn'trē| *n* centinela *m*.
sentry duty *n*: **to be on ~** estar de guardia, hacer guardia.
Seoul |sōl| *n* Seúl *m*.
separable |sɛp'ûrəbəl| *a* separable.
separate *a* |sɛp'rit| separado; (*distinct*) distinto ♦ (*vb*: |sɛp'ərāt|) *vt* separar; (*part*) dividir ♦ *vi* separarse; **~ from** separado *or* distinto de; **under ~ cover** (*COMM*) por separado; **to ~ into** dividir *or* separar en; **he**

is ~d from his wife, but not divorced está separado de su mujer, pero no (está) divorciado.

separately [sep'ritlē] *ad* por separado.

separates [sep'rits] *npl* (*clothes*) coordinados *mpl*.

separation [sepərā'shən] *n* separación *f*.

sepia [sē'pēə] *a* color sepia *inv*.

Sept. *abbr* (= *September*) sep.

September [septem'bûr] *n* se(p)tiembre *m*.

septic [sep'tik] *a* séptico; **to go** ~ ponerse séptico.

septicemia, (*Brit*) **septicaemia** [septisē'mēə] *n* septicemia.

septic tank *n* fosa séptica.

sequel [sē'kwəl] *n* consecuencia, resultado; (*of story*) continuación *f*.

sequence [sē'kwins] *n* sucesión *f*, serie *f*; (*CINEMA*) secuencia; **in** ~ en orden *or* serie.

sequential [sikwen'chəl] *a*: ~ **access** (*COMPUT*) acceso en serie.

sequin [sē'kwin] *n* lentejuela.

Serbo-Croat [sûr'bōkrōat] *n* (*LING*) serbocroata *m*.

serenade [särənād'] *n* serenata ♦ *vt* dar serenata a.

serene [sərēn'] *a* sereno, tranquilo.

serenely [sərēn'lē] *ad* serenamente, tranquilamente.

serenity [səren'itē] *n* serenidad *f*, tranquilidad *f*.

sergeant [sâr'jənt] *n* sargento.

sergeant major *n* sargento mayor.

serial [sēr'ēəl] *n* novela por entregas; (*TV*) telenovela.

serial access *n* (*COMPUT*) acceso en serie.

serial interface *n* (*COMPUT*) interface *m* en serie.

serialize [sēr'ēəlīz] *vt* publicar/televisar por entregas.

serial number *n* número de serie.

serial printer *n* (*COMPUT*) impresora en serie.

series [sēr'ēz] *n*, *pl inv* serie *f*.

serious [sēr'ēəs] *a* serio; (*grave*) grave; **are you** ~ **(about it)?** ¿lo dices en serio?

seriously [sē'rēəslē] *ad* en serio; (*ill, wounded etc*) gravemente; **to take sth/sb** ~ tomar algo/a uno en serio.

seriousness [sē'rēəsnis] *n* seriedad *f*; gravedad *f*.

sermon [sûr'mən] *n* sermón *m*.

serpent [sûr'pənt] *n* serpiente *f*.

serrated [särā'tid] *a* serrado, dentellado.

serum [sēr'əm] *n* suero.

servant [sûr'vənt] *n* (*gen*) servidor(a) *m/f*; (*house* ~) criado/a.

serve [sûrv] *vt* servir; (*customer*) atender; (*subj: train*) pasar por; (*apprenticeship*) hacer; (*prison term*) cumplir ♦ *vi* (*servant, soldier etc*) servir; (*TENNIS*) sacar ♦ *n* (*TENNIS*) saque *m*; **it ~s him right** se lo

merece, se lo tiene merecido; **to** ~ **a summons on sb** entregar una citación a uno; **it ~s my purpose** me viene al caso; **are you being** ~**d?** (*Brit*) ¿le atienden?; **the power station** ~**s the entire region** la central eléctrica abastece a toda la región; **to** ~ **as/for/to do** servir de/para/para hacer; **to** ~ **on a committee/a jury** ser miembro de una comisión/un jurado.

serve up *vt* (*food*) servir.

service [sûr'vis] *n* (*gen*) servicio; (*REL: Catholic*) misa; (: *other*) oficio (religioso); (*AUT*) mantenimiento; (*of dishes*) juego ♦ *vt* (*car, washing machine*) mantener; (: *repair*) reparar; **the Armed S~s** las fuerzas armadas; **funeral** ~ exequias *fpl*; **to hold a** ~ celebrar un oficio religioso; **the essential** ~**s** los servicios esenciales; **medical/social** ~**s** servicios *mpl* médicos/sociales; **the train** ~ **to New York** el servicio de tren para Nueva York; **to be of** ~ **to sb** ser útil a uno.

serviceable [sûr'visəbəl] *a* servible, utilizable.

service area *n* (*on motorway*) servicios *mpl*.

service charge *n* (*Brit*) servicio.

service industries *npl* industrias *fpl* del servicio.

serviceman [sûr'visman] *n* militar *m*.

service station *n* estación *f* de servicio.

servicing [sûr'vising] *n* (*of car*) revisión *f*; (*of washing machine etc*) servicio de reparaciones.

serviette [sûrvēet'] *n* (*Brit*) servilleta.

servile [sûr'vil] *a* servil.

serving cart [sûr'ving kârt] *n* (*US*) carrito.

session [sesh'ən] *n* (*sitting*) sesión *f*; **to be in** ~ estar en sesión.

set [set] *n* juego; (*RADIO*) aparato; (*TV*) televisor *m*; (*of utensils*) batería; (*of cutlery*) cubierto; (*of books*) colección *f*; (*TENNIS*) set *m*; (*group of people*) grupo; (*CINEMA*) plató *m*; (*THEATER*) decorado; (*HAIRDRESSING*) marcado ♦ *a* (*fixed*) fijo; (*ready*) listo; (*resolved*) resuelto, decidido ♦ (*vb: pt, pp* **set**) *vt* (*place*) poner, colocar; (*fix*) fijar; (*adjust*) ajustar, arreglar; (*decide: rules etc*) establecer, decidir; (*assign: task*) asignar; (: *assignment*) poner ♦ *vi* (*sun*) ponerse; (*jam, jelly*) cuajarse; (*concrete*) fraguar; **a** ~ **of false teeth** una dentadura postiza; **a** ~ **of dining-room furniture** muebles *mpl* de comedor; ~ **in one's ways** con costumbres arraigadas; **a** ~ **phrase** una frase hecha; **to be all** ~ **to do sth** estar listo para hacer algo; **to be** ~ **on doing sth** estar empeñado en hacer algo; **a novel** ~ **in Valencia** una novela ambientada en Valencia; **to** ~ **to music** poner música a; **to** ~ **on fire** incendiar, poner fuego a; **to** ~ **free** poner en libertad; **to** ~ **the table** poner la mesa;

to ~ sth going poner algo en marcha; **to ~ sail** zarpar, hacerse a la vela.

set about *vt fus*: **to ~ about doing sth** ponerse a hacer algo.

set aside *vt* poner aparte, dejar de lado.

set back *vt* (*progress*): **to ~ back (by)** retrasar (por); **a house ~ back from the road** una casa apartada de la carretera.

set in *vi* (*infection*) declararse; (*complications*) comenzar; **the rain has ~ in for the day** parece que va a llover todo el día.

set off *vi* partir ♦ *vt* (*bomb*) hacer estallar; (*cause to start*) poner en marcha; (*show up well*) hacer resaltar.

set out *vi*: **to ~ out to do sth** proponerse hacer algo ♦ *vt* (*arrange*) disponer; (*state*) exponer; **to ~ out (from)** salir (de).

set up *vt* (*organization*) establecer.

setback [set'bak] *n* (*hitch*) revés *m*, contratiempo; (*in health*) recaída.

set menu *n* menú *m*.

set phrase *n* frase *f* hecha.

set square *n* (*Brit*) cartabón *m*.

settee [sɛtē'] *n* sofá *m*.

setting [set'ing] *n* (*scenery*) marco; (*of jewel*) engaste *m*, montadura.

settle [set'əl] *vt* (*argument, matter*) resolver; (*pay: bill, accounts*) pagar, ajustar, liquidar; (*colonize: land*) colonizar; (*MED: calm*) calmar, sosegar ♦ *vi* (*dust etc*) depositarse; (*weather*) serenarse; (*also: ~ down*) instalarse; (*calm down*) tranquilizarse; **to ~ for sth** convenir en aceptar algo; **to ~ on sth** decidirse por algo; **that's ~d then** bueno, está arreglado; **to ~ one's stomach** asentar el estómago.

settle in *vi* instalarse.

settle up *vi*: **to ~ up with sb** ajustar cuentas con uno.

settlement [set'əlmənt] *n* (*payment*) liquidación *f*; (*agreement*) acuerdo, convenio; (*village etc*) pueblo; **in ~ of our account** (*COMM*) en pago *or* liquidación de nuestra cuenta.

settler [set'lûr] *n* colono/a, colonizador(a) *m/f*.

setup [set'up] *n* sistema *m*.

seven [sev'ən] *num* siete.

seventeen [sev'əntēn'] *num* diez y siete, diecisiete.

seventh [sev'ənth] *a* séptimo.

seventy [sev'əntē] *num* setenta.

sever [sev'ûr] *vt* cortar; (*relations*) romper.

several [sev'ûrəl] *a, pron* varios/as *m/fpl*, algunos/as *m/fpl*; **~ of us** varios de nosotros; **~ times** varias veces.

severance [sev'ûrəns] *n* (*of relations*) ruptura.

severance pay *n* pago *or* indemnización *f* de despedida.

severe [sivēr'] *a* severo; (*serious*) grave; (*hard*) duro; (*pain*) intenso.

severely [sivēr'lē] *ad* severamente;

(*wounded, ill*) de gravedad, gravemente.

severity [sivär'itē] *n* severidad *f*; gravedad *f*; intensidad *f*.

Seville [səvil'] *n* Sevilla.

sew [sō], *pt* **sewed**, *pp* **sewn** [sō, sōd, sōn] *vt, vi* coser.

sew up *vt* coser, zurcir.

sewage [sōō'ij] *n* (*effluence*) aguas *fpl* residuales; (*system*) alcantarillado.

sewer [sōō'ûr] *n* alcantarilla, cloaca.

sewing [sō'ing] *n* costura.

sewing machine *n* máquina de coser.

sewn [sōn] *pp* of **sew**.

sex [seks] *n* sexo; **the opposite ~** el sexo opuesto; **to have ~ with sb** tener relaciones (sexuales) con uno.

sex act *n* acto sexual, coito.

sexism [sek'sizəm] *n* sexismo

sexist [seks'ist] *a, n* sexista *m/f*.

sextant [seks'tənt] *n* sextante *m*.

sextet [sekstet'] *n* sexteto.

sexual [sek'shōōəl] *a* sexual; **~ assault** atentado contra el pudor; **~ intercourse** relaciones *fpl* sexuales.

sexually [sek'shōōəlē] *ad* sexualmente.

sexy [sek'sē] *a* sexy.

Seychelles [sāshel'] *npl*: **the ~** las Seychelles.

SF *n abbr* = **science fiction**.

SG *n abbr* (*US*: = **Surgeon General**) jefe del servicio federal de sanidad.

Sgt *abbr* (= *sergeant*) sgto.

shabbily [shab'ilē] *ad* (*treat*) muy mal; (*dressed*) pobremente.

shabbiness [shab'ēnis] *n* (*of dress, person*) aspecto desharrapado; (*of building*) mal estado.

shabby [shab'ē] *a* (*person*) desharrapado; (*clothes*) raído, gastado.

shack [shak] *n* choza, chabola.

shackle [shak'əl] *vt* encadenar; (*fig*): **to be ~d by sth** verse obstaculizado por algo.

shackles [shak'əlz] *npl* grillos *mpl*, grilletes *mpl*.

shade [shād] *n* sombra; (*for lamp*) pantalla; (*for eyes*) visera; (*of color*) matiz *m*, tonalidad *f*; (*US: window ~*) persiana ♦ *vt* dar sombra a; **~s** *npl* (*sunglasses*) gafas *fpl* de sol; **in the ~** a la sombra; (*small quantity*): **a ~ of** un poquito de; **a ~ smaller** un poquito menor.

shadow [shad'ō] *n* sombra ♦ *vt* (*follow*) seguir y vigilar; **without** *or* **beyond a ~ of doubt** sin lugar a dudas.

shadow cabinet *n* (*Brit POL*) gabinete paralelo formado por el partido de oposición.

shadowy [shad'ōē] *a* oscuro; (*dim*) indistinto.

shady [shā'dē] *a* sombreado; (*fig: dishonest*) sospechoso; (: *deal*) turbio.

shaft [shaft] *n* (*of arrow, spear*) astil *m*; (*AUT, TECH*) eje *m*, árbol *m*; (*of mine*) pozo; (*of elevator*) hueco, caja; (*of light*) rayo; **ventilator** ~ chimenea de ventilación.

shaggy [shag'ē] *a* peludo.

shake [shāk] *vb* (*pt* **shook**, *pp* **shaken** [shŏōk, shā'kən]) *vt* sacudir; (*building*) hacer temblar; (*perturb*) inquietar, perturbar; (*weaken*) debilitar; (*alarm*) trastornar ♦ *vi* estremecerse; (*tremble*) temblar ♦ *n* (*movement*) sacudida; **to ~ one's head** (*in refusal*) negar con la cabeza; (*in dismay*) mover *or* menear la cabeza, incrédulo; **to ~ hands with sb** estrechar la mano a uno; **to ~ in one's shoes** (*fig*) temblar de aprensión, tener mieditis.

shake off *vt* sacudirse; (*fig*) deshacerse de.

shake up *vt* agitar.

shake-up [shāk'up] *n* reorganización *f*.

shakily [shā'kilē] *ad* (*reply*) con voz temblorosa *or* trémula; (*walk*) con paso vacilante; (*write*) con mano temblorosa.

shaky [shā'kē] *a* (*unstable*) inestable, poco firme; (*trembling*) tembloroso; (*health*) delicado; (*memory*) defectuoso; (*person: from illness*) temblando; (*premise etc*) incierto.

shale [shāl] *n* esquisto.

shall [shal] *auxiliary vb*: **I ~ go** iré.

shallot [shəlât'] *n* cebollita, chalote *m*.

shallow [shal'ō] *a* poco profundo; (*fig*) superficial.

shallows [shal'ōz] *npl* bajío *sg*, bajos *mpl*.

sham [sham] *n* fraude *m*, engaño ♦ *a* falso, fingido ♦ *vt* fingir, simular.

shambles [sham'bəlz] *n* desorden *m*, confusión *f*; **the economy is (in) a complete ~** la economía está en ruinas.

shame [shām] *n* vergüenza; (*pity*) lástima ♦ *vt* avergonzar; **it is a ~ that/to do** es una lástima que/hacer; **what a ~!** ¡qué lástima!; **to put sth/sb to ~** (*fig*) ridiculizar algo/a uno.

shamefaced [shām'fāst] *a* avergonzado.

shameful [shām'fəl] *a* vergonzoso.

shamefully [shām'fəlē] *ad* vergonzosamente.

shameless [shām'lis] *a* descarado.

shampoo [shampōō'] *n* champú *m* ♦ *vt* lavar con champú.

shampoo and set *n* lavado y marcado.

shamrock [sham'râk] *n* trébol *m*.

shandy [shan'dē] *n* mezcla de cerveza con gaseosa.

shan't [shant] = **shall not**.

shanty town [shan'tē toun] *n* barrio de chabolas.

SHAPE [shāp] *n abbr* (= *Supreme Headquarters Allied Powers, Europe*) *cuartel general de las fuerzas aliadas en Europa.*

shape [shāp] *n* forma ♦ *vt* formar, dar forma a; (*clay*) modelar; (*stone*) labrar; (*sb's ideas*) formar; (*sb's life*) determinar

♦ *vi* (*also:* ~ **up**) (*events*) desarrollarse; (*person*) formarse; **to take ~** tomar forma; **to get o.s. into** ~ ponerse en forma *or* en condiciones; **in the ~ of a heart** en forma de corazón; **I can't bear gardening in any ~ or form** no aguanto la jardinería de ningún modo.

-shaped [shāpt] *suff* **heart~** en forma de corazón.

shapeless [shāp'lis] *a* informe, sin forma definida.

shapely [shāp'lē] *a* bien formado *or* proporcionado.

share [shär] *n* (*part*) parte *f*, porción *f*; (*contribution*) cuota; (*COMM*) acción *f* ♦ *vt* dividir; (*fig: have in common*) compartir; **to have a ~ in the profits** tener una porción de las ganancias; **he has a 50% ~ in a new business venture** tiene una participación del 50% en un nuevo negocio; **to ~ in** participar en; **to ~ among** *or* **between** repartir entre.

share capital *n* (*COMM*) capital *m* en acciones *or* accionario.

share certificate *n* certificado *or* título de una acción.

shareholder [shär'hōldûr] *n* (*Brit*) accionista *m/f*.

share index *n* (*COMM*) índice *m* de la bolsa.

share issue *n* emisión *f* de acciones.

share price *n* (*COMM*) cotización *f*.

shark [shärk] *n* tiburón *m*.

sharp [shärp] *a* (*razor, knife*) afilado; (*point*) puntiagudo; (*outline*) definido; (*pain*) intenso; (*MUS*) desafinado; (*contrast*) marcado; (*voice*) agudo; (*curve, bend*) cerrado; (*person: quick-witted*) astuto; (: *dishonest*) poco escrupuloso ♦ *n* (*MUS*) sostenido ♦ *ad*: **at 2 o'clock ~** a las 2 en punto; **to be ~ with sb** hablar a uno con voz tajante; **turn ~ left** dobla fuertemente a la izquierda.

sharpen [shâr'pən] *vt* afilar; (*pencil*) sacar punta a; (*fig*) agudizar.

sharpener [shâr'pənûr] *n* (*gen*) afilador *m*; (*pencil ~*) sacapuntas *m inv*.

sharp-eyed [shârp'īd] *a* de vista aguda.

sharply [shârp'lē] *ad* (*abruptly*) bruscamente; (*clearly*) claramente; (*harshly*) severamente.

sharp-tempered [shârp'tempûrd] *a* de genio arisco.

sharp-witted [shârp'wit'id] *a* listo, despabilado.

shatter [shat'ûr] *vt* hacer añicos *or* pedazos; (*fig: ruin*) destruir, acabar con ♦ *vi* hacerse añicos.

shattered [shat'ûrd] *a* (*grief-stricken*) destrozado, deshecho; (*exhausted*) agotado, hecho polvo.

shattering [shat'ûring] *a* (*experience*) devastador(a), anonadante.

shatterproof [shat'úrprōōf] a inastillable.
shave [shāv] vt afeitar, rasurar ♦ vi afeitarse ♦ n: **to have a ~** afeitarse.
shaven [shā'vən] a (head) rapado.
shaver [shā'vúr] n (also: **electric ~**) máquina de afeitar (eléctrica).
shaving [shā'ving] n (action) el afeitarse,
rasurado; **~s** npl (of wood etc) virutas fpl.
shaving brush n brocha (de afeitar).
shaving cream n crema (de afeitar).
shaving soap n jabón m de afeitar.
shawl [shôl] n chal m.
she [shē] pron ella; **there ~ is** allí está; **~-
cat** gata; NB: for ships, countries follow
the gender of your translation.
sheaf, pl **sheaves** [shēf, shēvz] n (of corn)
gavilla; (of arrows) haz m; (of papers)
fajo.
shear [shē'úr] vt (pt ~**ed**, pp ~**ed** or **shorn**
[shôrn]) (sheep) esquilar, trasquilar.
shear off vi romperse.
shears [shē'úrz] npl (for hedge) tijeras fpl
de jardín.
sheath [shēth] n vaina; (contraceptive) preservativo.
sheath knife n cuchillo de monte.
sheaves [shēvz] npl of **sheaf**.
shed [shed] n cobertizo; (INDUSTRY, RAIL)
nave f ♦ vt (pt, pp **shed**) (skin) mudar;
(tears) derramar; **to ~ light on** (problem,
mystery) aclarar, arrojar luz sobre.
she'd [shēd] = **she had, she would**.
sheen [shēn] n brillo, lustre m.
sheep [shēp] n (pl inv) oveja.
sheepdog [shēp'dóg] n perro pastor.
sheep farmer n ganadero.
sheepish [shē'pish] a tímido, vergonzoso.
sheepskin [shēp'skin] n piel f de carnero.
sheepskin jacket n zamarra.
sheer [shēr] a (utter) puro, completo;
(steep) escarpado; (material) diáfano ♦ ad
verticalmente; **by ~ chance** de pura casualidad.
sheet [shēt] n (on bed) sábana; (of paper)
hoja; (of glass, metal) lámina.
sheet feed n (on printer) alimentador m
de papel.
sheet lightning n relámpago (difuso).
sheet metal n metal m en lámina.
sheet music n hojas fpl de partitura.
sheik(h) [shēk] n jeque m.
shelf, pl **shelves** [shelf, shelvz] n estante m.
shelf life n (COMM) periodo de conservación antes de la venta.
shell [shel] n (on beach) concha; (of egg,
nut etc) cáscara; (explosive) proyectil m,
obús m; (of building) armazón m ♦ vt
(peas) desenvainar; (MIL) bombardear.
shell out vi (col): **to ~ out (for)** soltar
el dinero (para), desembolsar (para).
she'll [shēl] = **she will, she shall**.
shellfish [shel'fish] n (pl inv) crustáceo;
(pl: as food) mariscos mpl.

shelter [shel'túr] n abrigo, refugio ♦ vt (aid)
amparar, proteger; (give lodging to) abrigar; (hide) esconder ♦ vi abrigarse, refugiarse; **to take ~ (from)** refugiarse or asi-
larse (de); **bus ~** parada de autobús cubierta.
sheltered [shel'túrd] a (life) protegido;
(spot) abrigado.
shelve [shelv] vt (fig) dar carpetazo a.
shelves [shelvz] npl of **shelf**.
shelving [shel'ving] n estantería.
shepherd [shep'úrd] n pastor m ♦ vt
(guide) guiar, conducir.
shepherdess [shep'úrdis] n pastora.
shepherd's pie n pastel de carne y patatas.
sherbert [shûr'búrt] n (US: dessert) sorbete
m; (Brit: powder) polvos mpl azucarados.
sherbet [shûr'bit] n sorbete m.
sheriff [shär'if] n (US) alguacil m.
sherry [shär'ē] n jerez m.
she's [shēz] = **she is, she has**.
Shetland [shet'lənd] n (also: **the ~s, the ~
Isles**) las Islas fpl de Zetlandia.
shield [shēld] n escudo; (TECH) blindaje m
♦ vt: **to ~ (from)** proteger (de).
shift [shift] n (change) cambio; (at work)
turno ♦ vt trasladar; (remove) quitar;
(AUT) cambiar ♦ vi moverse; (change
place) cambiar de sitio; **the wind has ~ed
to the south** el viento ha virado al sur; **a
~ in demand** (COMM) un desplazamiento
de la demanda.
shift key n (on typewriter) tecla de mayúsculas.
shiftless [shift'lis] a (person) vago.
shift work n trabajo por turno; **to do ~**
trabajar por turno.
shifty [shif'tē] a tramposo; (eyes) furtivo.
shilling [shil'ing] n (Brit) chelín m (= 12 old
pence; 20 in a pound).
shilly-shally [shil'ēshalē] vi titubear, vacilar.
shimmer [shim'úr] n reflejo trémulo ♦ vi relucir.
shimmering [shim'úring] a reluciente;
(haze) trémulo; (satin etc) lustroso.
shin [shin] n espinilla ♦ vi: **to ~ up/down a
tree** trepar/bajar de un árbol.
shindig [shin'dig] n (col) fiesta, juerga.
shine [shīn] n brillo, lustre m ♦ (vb: pt, pp
shone [shōn]) vi brillar, relucir ♦ vt
(shoes) lustrar, sacar brillo a; **to ~ a
flashlight on sth** dirigir una linterna hacia
algo.
shingle [shing'gəl] n (on beach) guijarras
fpl.
shingles [shing'gəlz] n (MED) herpes mpl or
fpl.
shining [shī'ning] a (surface, hair) lustroso;
(light) brillante.
shiny [shī'nē] a brillante, lustroso.
ship [ship] n buque m, barco ♦ vt (goods)

embarcar; (*oars*) desarmar; (*send*) transportar *or* enviar por vía marítima; ~'s **manifest** manifiesto del buque; **on board** ~ a bordo.

shipbuilder [ship'bildûr] *n* constructor(a) *m/f* de buques.

shipbuilding [ship'bilding] *n* construcción *f* de barcos.

ship canal *n* canal *m* de navegación.

ship chandler [ship chan'dlûr] *n* proveedor *m* de efectos navales.

shipment [ship'mənt] *n* (*act*) embarque *m*; (*goods*) envío.

shipowner [ship'ōnûr] *n* naviero, armador *m.*

shipper [ship'ûr] *n* exportador(a) *m/f*, empresa naviera.

shipping [ship'ing] *n* (*act*) embarque *m*; (*traffic*) buques *mpl.*

shipping agent *n* agente *m/f* marítimo/a.

shipping company *n* compañía naviera.

shipping lane *n* ruta de navegación.

shipping line *n* = **shipping company.**

shipshape [ship'shāp] *a* en buen orden.

shipwreck [ship'rek] *n* naufragio ♦ *vt*: **to be** ~**ed** naufragar.

shipyard [ship'yárd] *n* astillero.

shirk [shûrk] *vt* eludir, esquivar; (*obligations*) faltar a.

shirt [shûrt] *n* camisa; **in** ~ **sleeves** en mangas de camisa.

shit [shit] *excl* (*col!*) ¡mierda! (*!*).

shiver [shiv'ûr] *vi* temblar, estremecerse; (*with cold*) tiritar.

shoal [shōl] *n* (*Brit*: *of fish*) banco.

shock [shák] *n* (*impact*) choque *m*; (*ELEC*) descarga (eléctrica); (*emotional*) conmoción *f*; (*start*) sobresalto, susto; (*MED*) postración *f* nerviosa ♦ *vt* dar un susto a; (*offend*) escandalizar; **to get a** ~ (*ELEC*) sentir una sacudida eléctrica; **to give sb a** ~ dar un susto a uno; **to be suffering from** ~ padecer una postración nerviosa; **it came as a** ~ **to hear that ...** me (*etc*) asombró descubrir que ....

shock absorber [shák absórb'ûr] *n* amortiguador *m.*

shocking [shák'ing] *a* (*awful*: *weather, handwriting*) espantoso, horrible; (*improper*) escandaloso; (*result*) inesperado.

shock therapy, shock treatment *n* (*MED*) tratamiento por electrochoque.

shod [shád] *pt, pp of* **shoe** ♦ *a* calzado.

shoddiness [shád'ēnis] *n* baja calidad *f.*

shoddy [shád'ē] *a* de pacotilla.

shoe [shōō] *n* zapato; (*for horse*) herradura; (*brake* ~) zapata ♦ *vt* (*pt, pp* **shod** [shád]) (*horse*) herrar.

shoe brush *n* cepillo para zapatos.

shoehorn [shōō'hórn] *n* calzador *m.*

shoelace [shōō'lās] *n* cordón *m.*

shoemaker [shōō'mākûr] *n* zapatero/a.

shoe polish *n* betún *m.*

shoe shop *n* zapatería.

shoestring [shōō'string] *n* (*shoelace*) cordón *m*; (*fig*): **on a** ~ con muy poco dinero, a lo barato.

shone [shōn] *pt, pp of* **shine.**

shoo [shōō] *excl* ¡fuera!; (*to animals*) ¡zape! ♦ *vt* (*also:* ~ **away,** ~ **off**) ahuyentar.

shook [shōōk] *pt of* **shake.**

shoot [shōōt] *n* (*on branch, seedling*) retoño, vástago; (*shooting party*) cacería; (*competition*) concurso de tiro; (*preserve*) coto de caza ♦ (*vb*: *pt, pp* **shot** [shát]) *vt* disparar; (*kill*) matar a tiros; (*execute*) fusilar; (*CINE*: *movie, scene*) rodar, filmar ♦ *vi* (*SOCCER*) chutar; **to** ~ (**at**) tirar (a); **to** ~ **past sb** pasar a uno como un rayo; **to shoot in/out** *vi* entrar corriendo/salir disparado.

shoot down *vt* (*plane*) derribar.

shoot up *vi* (*prices*) dispararse.

shooting [shōō'ting] *n* (*shots*) tiros *mpl*, tiroteo; (*HUNTING*) caza con escopeta; (*act*: *murder*) asesinato (a tiros); (*CINE*) rodaje *m.*

shooting star *n* estrella fugaz.

shop [sháp] *n* tienda; (*workshop*) taller *m* ♦ *vi* (*also:* **go** ~**ping**) ir de compras; **to talk** ~ (*fig*) hablar del trabajo; **repair** ~ taller *m* de reparaciones.

shop around *vi* comparar precios.

shop assistant *n* (*Brit*) dependiente/a *m/f.*

shop floor *n* (*fig*) taller *m*, fábrica.

shopkeeper [sháp'kēpûr] *n* tendero/a.

shoplift [sháp'lift] *vi* robar en las tiendas.

shoplifter [sháp'liftûr] *n* ratero/a.

shoplifting [sháp'lifting] *n* mechería.

shopper [sháp'ûr] *n* comprador(a) *m/f.*

shopping [sháp'ing] *n* (*goods*) compras *fpl.*

shopping bag *n* bolsa (de compras).

shopping center *n* centro comercial.

shopping mall *n* galería comercial.

shop-soiled [sháp'soild] *a* (*Brit*) usado.

shop steward *n* (*INDUSTRY*) enlace *m/f.*

shop window *n* escaparate *m*, vidriera (*LAm*).

shopworn [sháp'wórn] *a* (*US*) usado.

shore [shór] *n* (*of sea, lake*) orilla ♦ *vt*: **to** ~ (**up**) reforzar; **on** ~ en tierra.

shore leave *n* (*NAUT*) permiso para bajar a tierra.

shorn [shórn] *pp of* **shear.**

short [shórt] *a* (*not long*) corto; (*in time*) breve, de corta duración; (*person*) bajo; (*curt*) brusco, seco ♦ *vi* (*ELEC*) ponerse en cortocircuito ♦ *n* (*also:* ~ **film**) cortometraje *m*; (**a pair of**) ~**s** (unos) pantalones *mpl* cortos; **to be** ~ **of sth** estar falto de algo; **in** ~ en pocas palabras; **a** ~ **time ago** hace poco (tiempo); **in the** ~ **term** a corto plazo; **to be in** ~ **supply** escasear, haber escasez de; **I'm** ~ **of time** me falta tiempo; ~ **of doing...** fuera de hacer...; **everything**

~ **of...** todo menos...; **it is** ~ **for** es la forma abreviada de; **to cut** ~ (*speech, visit*) interrumpir, terminar inesperadamente; **to fall** ~ **of** no alcanzar; **to run** ~ **of sth** acabársele algo; **to stop** ~ parar en seco; **to stop** ~ **of** detenerse antes de.

shortage [shôr'tij] *n* escasez *f*, falta.

shortbread [shórt'brɛd] *n* torta seca y quebradiza.

shortchange [shôrt'chānj'] *vt*: **to** ~ **sb** no dar el cambio completo a uno.

short-circuit [shôrtsûr'kit] *n* cortocircuito ♦ *vt* poner en cortocircuito ♦ *vi* ponerse en cortocircuito.

shortcoming [shôrt'kuming] *n* defecto, deficiencia.

short(crust) pastry [shôrt'(krust) pās'trē] *n* (*Brit*) pasta quebradiza.

shortcut [shôrt'kut] *n* atajo.

shorten [shór'tən] *vt* acortar; (*visit*) interrumpir.

shortfall [shôrt'fôl] *n* déficit *m*, deficiencia.

shorthand [shôrt'hand] *n* taquigrafía; **to take sth down in** ~ escribir algo taquigráficamente.

shorthand notebook *n* cuaderno de taquigrafía.

shorthand typist *n* (*Brit*) taquimecanógrafo/a.

short list *n* (*for job*) lista de candidatos escogidos.

short-lived [shôrt'livd'] *a* efímero.

shortly [shôrt'lē] *ad* en breve, dentro de poco.

shortness [shôrt'nis] *n* (*of distance*) cortedad *f*; (*of time*) brevedad *f*; (*manner*) brusquedad *f*.

shortsighted [shôrt'sī'tid] *a* corto de vista, miope; (*fig*) imprudente.

short-sightedness [shôrt'sī'tidnis] *n* miopía, cortedad *f* de vista; (*fig*) falta de previsión, imprudencia.

short-staffed [shôrt'staft'] *a* falto de personal.

short story *n* cuento.

short-tempered [shôrt'tempûrd] *a* enojadizo.

short-term [shôrt'tûrm'] *a* (*effect*) a corto plazo.

short time *n*: **to work** ~, **be on** ~ (*INDUSTRY*) trabajar con sistema de horario reducido.

short-time working [shôrt'tīm wûr'king] *n* trabajo de horario reducido.

short wave *n* (*RADIO*) onda corta.

shot [shát] *pt, pp of* **shoot** ♦ *n* (*sound*) tiro, disparo; (*person*) tirador(a) *m/f*; (*try*) tentativa; (*injection*) inyección *f*; (*PHOT*) toma, fotografía; (*shotgun pellets*) perdigones *mpl*; **to fire a** ~ **at sb/sth** tirar *or* disparar contra uno/algo; **to have a** ~ **at (doing) sth** probar suerte con algo; **like a** ~ (*without any delay*) como un rayo; **a big**

~ (*col*) un pez gordo; **to get** ~ **of sth/sb** (*col*) deshacerse de algo/uno, quitarse algo/ a uno de encima.

shotgun [shát'gun] *n* escopeta.

should [shood] *auxiliary vb*: **I** ~ **go now** debo irme ahora; **he** ~ **be there now** debe de haber llegado (ya); ~ **he phone ...** si llamara ..., en caso de que llamase ...

shoulder [shōl'dûr] *n* hombro; (*Brit: of road*): **hard** ~ arcén *m* ♦ *vt* cargar con; **to look over one's** ~ mirar hacia atrás; **to rub** ~**s with sb** (*fig*) codearse con uno; **to give sb the cold** ~ (*fig*) dar de lado a uno.

shoulder blade *n* omóplato.

shoulder bag *n* bolso de bandolera.

shoulder strap *n* tirante *m*.

shouldn't [shood'ənt] = **should not**.

shout [shout] *n* grito ♦ *vt* gritar ♦ *vi* gritar, dar voces.

shout down *vt* hundir a gritos.

shouting [shout'ing] *n* griterío.

shove [shuv] *n* empujón *m* ♦ *vt* empujar; (*col: put*): **to** ~ **sth in** meter algo a empellones; **he** ~**d me out of the way** me quitó de en medio de un empujón.

shove off *vi* (*NAUT*) alejarse del muelle; (*fig: col*) largarse.

shovel [shuv'əl] *n* pala; (*mechanical*) excavadora ♦ *vt* mover con pala.

show [shō] *n* (*of emotion*) demostración *f*; (*semblance*) apariencia; (*COMM, TECH: exhibition*) exhibición *f*, exposición *f*; (*THEATER*) función *f*, espectáculo; (*organization*) negocio, empresa ♦ *vb* (*pt* **showed**, *pp* **shown** [shōn]) *vt* mostrar, enseñar; (*courage etc*) mostrar, manifestar; (*exhibit*) exponer; (*film*) proyectar ♦ *vi* mostrarse; (*appear*) aparecer; **on** ~ (*exhibits etc*) expuesto; **to be on** ~ estar expuesto; **it's just for** ~ es para lucir nada más; **to ask for a** ~ **of hands** pedir una votación a mano alzada; **who's running the** ~ **here?** ¿quién manda aquí?; **to** ~ **a profit/loss** (*COMM*) arrojar un saldo positivo/negativo; **I have nothing to** ~ **for it** no saqué ningún provecho (de ello); **to** ~ **sb to his seat/to the door** acompañar a uno a su asiento/a la puerta; **as** ~**n in the illustration** como se ve en el grabado; **it just goes to** ~ **that ...** queda demostrado que ...; **it doesn't** ~ no se ve *or* nota.

show in *vt* (*person*) hacer pasar.

show off *vi* (*pej*) presumir ♦ *vt* (*display*) lucir; (*pej*) hacer gala de.

show out *vt*: **to** ~ **sb out** acompañar a uno a la puerta.

show up *vi* (*stand out*) destacar; (*col: turn up*) presentarse ♦ *vt* descubrir; (*unmask*) desenmascarar.

show business *n* el mundo del espectáculo.

showcase [shō'kās] *n* vitrina; (*fig*) escaparate m.

showdown [shō'doun] n crisis f, momento decisivo.

shower [shou'ûr] n (rain) chaparrón m, chubasco; (of stones etc) lluvia; (also: ~ **bath**) ducha ♦ vi llover ♦ vt: **to ~ sb with sth** colmar a uno de algo; **to have** or **take a ~** ducharse.

shower cap n gorro de baño.

showerproof [shou'ûrprōōf] a impermeable.

showery [shou'ûrē] a (weather) lluvioso.

showground [shō'ground] n ferial m, real m (de la feria).

showing [shō'ing] n (of movie) proyección f.

show jumping [shō' jum'ping] n hipismo.

showman [shō'mən] n (at fair, circus) empresario; (fig) persona extrovertida, exhibicionista m/f.

showmanship [shō'mənship] n dotes fpl teatrales.

shown [shōn] pp of **show**.

show-off [shō'ôf] n (col: person) presumido/a.

showpiece [shō'pēs] n (of exhibition etc) objeto cumbre; **that hospital is a ~** ese hospital es un modelo del género.

showroom [shō'rōōm] n sala de muestras.

showy [shō'ē] a ostentoso.

shrank [shrangk] pt of **shrink**.

shrapnel [shrap'nəl] n metralla.

shred [shred] n (gen pl) triza, jirón m; (fig: of truth, evidence) pizca, chispa ♦ vt hacer trizas; (documents) triturar; (CULIN) desmenuzar.

shredder [shred'ûr] n (vegetable shredder) picadora; (document shredder) trituradora (de papel).

shrewd [shrōōd] a astuto.

shrewdly [shrōōd'lē] ad astutamente.

shrewdness [shrōōd'nis] n astucia.

shriek [shrēk] n chillido ♦ vt, vi chillar.

shrill [shril] a agudo, estridente.

shrimp [shrimp] n camarón m.

shrine [shrīn] n santuario, sepulcro.

shrink [shringk], pt **shrank**, pp **shrunk** [shringk, shrangk, shrungk] vi encogerse; (be reduced) reducirse ♦ vt encoger; **to ~ from (doing) sth** no atreverse a hacer algo.

shrink away vi retroceder, retirarse.

shrinkage [shringk'ij] n encogimiento; reducción f.

shrink-wrap [shringk'rap] vt empaquetar en envase termoretráctil.

shrivel [shriv'əl] (also: ~ **up**) vt (dry) secar; (crease) arrugar ♦ vi secarse; arrugarse.

shroud [shroud] n sudario ♦ vt: ~**ed in mystery** envuelto en el misterio.

Shrove Tuesday [shrōv tōōz'dā] n martes m de carnaval.

shrub [shrub] n arbusto.

shrubbery [shrub'ûrē] n arbustos mpl.

shrug [shrug] n encogimiento de hombros ♦ vt, vi: **to ~ (one's shoulders)** encogerse de hombros.

shrug off vt negar importancia a; (cold, illness) deshacerse de.

shrunk [shrungk] pp of **shrink**.

shrunken [shrungk'ən] a encogido.

shudder [shud'ûr] n estremecimiento, escalofrío ♦ vi estremecerse.

shuffle [shuf'əl] vt (cards) barajar; **to ~ (one's feet)** arrastrar los pies.

shun [shun] vt rehuir, esquivar.

shunt [shunt] vt (RAIL) maniobrar.

shut, pt, pp **shut** [shut] vt cerrar ♦ vi cerrarse.

shut down vt, vi cerrarse, parar; (machine) apagar.

shut off vt (stop: power, water supply etc) interrumpir, cortar; (: engine) parar.

shut out vt (person) excluir, dejar fuera; (noise, cold) no dejar entrar; (block: view) tapar; (: memory) tratar de olvidar.

shut up vi (col: keep quiet) callarse ♦ vt (close) cerrar; (silence) callar.

shutdown [shut'doun] n cierre m.

shutter [shut'ûr] n contraventana; (PHOT) obturador m.

shuttle [shut'əl] n lanzadera; (also: ~ **service**: AVIAT) puente m aéreo ♦ vi (subj: vehicle, person) ir y venir ♦ vt (passengers) transportar, trasladar (LAm).

shuttlecock [shut'əlkâk] n volante m.

shy [shī] a tímido ♦ vi: **to ~ away from doing sth** (fig) rehusar hacer algo; **to be ~ of doing sth** esquivar hacer algo.

shyly [shī'lē] ad tímidamente.

shyness [shī'nis] n timidez f.

Siam [sīam'] n Siam m.

Siamese [sīəmēz'] a siamés/esa ♦ n (person) siamés/esa m/f; (LING) siamés m; ~ **cat** gato siamés; ~ **twins** gemelos/as m/fpl siameses/as.

Siberia [sībē'rēə] n Siberia.

sibling [sib'ling] n (formal) hermano/a.

Sicilian [sisil'yən] a, n siciliano/a m/f.

Sicily [sis'ilē] n Sicilia.

sick [sik] a (ill) enfermo; (nauseated) mareado; (humor) negro; **to be ~** (Brit) vomitar; **to feel ~** estar mareado; **to feel ~ to one's stomach** sentirse mareado; **to be ~ of** (fig) estar harto de; **a ~ person** un(a) enfermo/a; **to be (off) ~** estar ausente por enfermedad; **to take ~** ponerse enfermo.

sick bay n enfermería.

sickbed [sik'bed] n lecho de enfermo.

sicken [sik'ən] vt dar asco a ♦ vi enfermar.

sickening [sik'əning] a (fig) asqueroso.

sickle [sik'əl] n hoz f.

sick leave n baja por enfermedad.

sick list n: **to be on the ~** estar de baja.

sickly [sik'lē] a enfermizo; (taste) empalagoso.

sickness [sik'nís] *n* enfermedad *f*, mal *m*; (*vomiting*) náuseas *fpl*.

sickness benefit *n* (*Brit*) subsidio de enfermedad.

sick pay *n* subsidio de enfermedad.

sickroom [sik'rōōm] *n* cuarto del enfermo.

side [sīd] *n* (*gen*) lado; (*face, surface*) cara; (*of paper*) cara; (*slice of bread*) rebanada; (*of body*) costado; (*of animal*) ijar *m*, ijada; (*of lake*) orilla; (*part*) lado; (*aspect*) aspecto; (*team: SPORT*) equipo; (*: POL etc*) partido; (*of hill*) ladera ♦ *a* (*door, entrance*) de al lado ♦ *vi*: **to ~ with sb** tomar el partido de uno; **by the ~ of** al lado de; **~ by ~** juntos/as; **from all ~s** de todos lados; **to take ~s (with)** tomar partido (con); **~ of beef** flanco de vaca; **the right/wrong ~** el derecho/revés; **from ~ to ~** de un lado a otro.

sideboard [sīd'bôrd] *n* aparador *m*.

sideburns [sīd'bûrnz] *npl* patillas *fpl*.

sidecar [sīd'kâr] *n* sidecar *m*.

side dish *n* entremés *m*.

side drum *n* (*MUS*) tamboril *m*.

side effect *n* efecto secundario.

sidekick [sīd'kik] *n* compinche *m*.

sidelight [sīd'līt] *n* (*AUT*) luz *f* lateral.

sideline [sīd'līn] *n* (*SPORT*) línea lateral; (*fig*) empleo suplementario.

sidelong [sīd'lông] *a* de soslayo; **to give a ~ glance at sth** mirar algo de reojo.

side plate *n* platito.

side road *n* (*Brit*) calle *f* lateral.

sidesaddle [sīd'sadəl] *ad* a mujeriegas, a la inglesa.

sideshow [sīd'shō] *n* (*stall*) caseta; (*fig*) atracción *f* secundaria.

sidestep [sīd'step] *vt* (*question*) eludir; (*problem*) esquivar ♦ *vi* (*BOXING etc*) dar un quiebro.

side street *n* calle *f* lateral.

sidetrack [sīd'trak] *vt* (*fig*) desviar (de su propósito).

sidewalk [sīd'wôk] *n* (*US*) acera.

sideways [sīd'wāz] *ad* de lado.

siding [sī'ding] *n* (*RAIL*) apartadero, vía muerta.

sidle [sī'dəl] *vi*: **to ~ up (to)** acercarse furtivamente (a).

SIDS *n abbr* (= *sudden infant death syndrome*) muerte *f* en la cuna.

siege [sēj] *n* cerco, sitio; **to lay ~ to** cercar, sitiar.

siege economy *n* economía de sitio *or* de asedio.

Sierra Leone [sēär'ə lēōn'] *n* Sierra Leona.

siesta [sēes'tə] *n* siesta.

sieve [siv] *n* colador *m* ♦ *vt* cribar.

sift [sift] *vt* cribar; (*fig: information*) escudriñar ♦ *vi*: **to ~ through** pasar por una criba; (*of information*) llegar a saberse.

sigh [sī] *n* suspiro ♦ *vi* suspirar.

sight [sīt] *n* (*faculty*) vista; (*spectacle*) espectáculo; (*on gun*) mira, alza ♦ *vt* ver, divisar; **in ~** a la vista; **out of ~** fuera de (la) vista; **on ~** a la vista; **at first ~** a primera vista; **to lose ~ of sth/sb** perder algo/a uno de vista; **to catch ~ of sth/sb** divisar algo/a uno; **I know her by ~** la conozco de vista; **to set one's ~s on (doing) sth** aspirar a *or* ambicionar (hacer) algo.

sighted [sī'tid] *a* que ve, de vista normal; **partially ~** de vista limitada.

sightseer [sīt'sēr] *n* excursionista *m/f*, turista *m/f*.

sightseeing [sīt'sēing] *n* excursionismo, turismo; **to go ~** visitar monumentos.

sign [sīn] *n* (*with hand*) señal *f*, seña; (*trace*) huella, rastro; (*notice*) letrero; (*written*) signo; (*road ~*) indicador *m*; (*: with instructions*) señal *f* de tráfico ♦ *vt* firmar; **as a ~ of** en señal de; **it's a good/bad ~** es buena/mala señal; **plus/minus ~** signo de más/de menos; **to ~ one's name** firmar.

sign away *vt* (*rights etc*) ceder.

sign off *vi* (*RADIO, TV*) cerrar el programa.

sign on *vi* (*as unemployed*) registrarse como desempleado; (*employee*) firmar un contrato ♦ *vt* (*MIL*) alistar; (*employee*) contratar; **to ~ on for a course** matricularse en un curso.

sign out *vi* firmar el registro (al salir).

sign over *vt*: **to ~ sth over to sb** traspasar algo a uno.

sign up *vi* (*MIL*) alistarse ♦ *vt* (*contract*) contratar.

signal [sig'nəl] *n* señal *f* ♦ *vi* (*AUT*) señalizar ♦ *vt* (*person*) hacer señas a uno; (*message*) transmitir; **the busy ~** (*TEL*) la señal de comunicando; **the ~ is very weak** (*TV*) no captamos bien la sintonía; **to ~ a left/right turn** (*AUT*) indicar que se va a doblar a la izquierda/derecha; **to ~ to sb (to do sth)** hacer señas a uno (para que haga algo).

signal box *n* (*RAIL*) garita de señales.

signalman [sig'nəlmən] *n* (*RAIL*) guardavía *m*.

signatory [sig'nətôrē] *n* firmante *m/f*.

signature [sig'nəchûr] *n* firma.

signature tune *n* sintonía de apertura de un programa.

signet ring [sig'nit ring] *n* anillo de sello.

significance [signif'əkəns] *n* significado; (*importance*) trascendencia; **that is of no ~** eso no tiene importancia.

significant [signif'ikənt] *a* significativo; trascendente; **it is ~ that ...** es significativo que ....

significantly [signif'ikəntlē] *ad* (*smile*) expresivamente; (*improve, increase*) sensiblemente; **and, ~ ...** y debe notarse que ....

signify [sig'nəfī] *vt* significar.

sign language *n* mímica, lenguaje *m* por

or de señas.
signpost |sīn'pōst| *n* indicador *m*.
silage |sī'lij| *n* ensilaje *m*.
silence |sī'ləns| *n* silencio ♦ *vt* hacer callar;
(*guns*) reducir al silencio.
silencer |sī'lənsûr| *n* (*on gun*, *Brit* AUT) si-
lenciador *m*.
silent |sī'lənt| *a* (*gen*) silencioso; (*not speak-
ing*) callado; (*film*) mudo; **to keep** *or* **remain** ~ guardar silencio.
silently |sī'ləntlē| *ad* silenciosamente, en si-
lencio.
silent partner *n* (COMM) socio/a
comanditario/a.
silhouette |siloōēt'| *n* silueta; ~**d against**
destacado sobre *or* contra.
silicon |sil'ikən| *n* silicio.
silicon chip |sil'ikən chip| *n* plaqueta de si-
licio.
silicone |sil'əkōn| *n* silicona.
silk |silk| *n* seda ♦ *cpd* de seda.
silky |sil'kē| *a* sedoso.
sill |sil| *n* (*also*: **window~**) alféizar *m*;
(AUT) umbral *m*.
silliness |sil'ēnis| *n* (*of person*) necedad *f*;
(*of idea*) lo absurdo.
silly |sil'ē| *a* (*person*) tonto; (*idea*) absurdo;
to do sth ~ hacer una tontería.
silo |sī'lō| *n* silo.
silt |silt| *n* sedimento.
silver |sil'vûr| *n* plata; (*money*) moneda
suelta ♦ *a* de plata, plateado.
silver paper (*Brit*) *n* papel *m* de plata.
silver plate *n* vajilla de plata.
silver-plated |sil'vûrplā'tid| *a* plateado.
silversmith |sil'vûrsmith| *n* platero/a.
silverware |sil'vûrwär| *n* plata.
silver wedding (anniversary) *n* bodas
fpl de plata.
silvery |sil'vûrē| *a* plateado.
similar |sim'əlûr| *a*: ~ **to** parecido *or* seme-
jante a.
similarity |siməlar'itē| *n* parecido, seme-
janza.
similarly |sim'əlûrlē| *ad* del mismo modo;
(*in a similar way*) de manera parecida;
(*equally*) igualmente.
simile |sim'əlē| *n* símil *m*.
simmer |sim'ûr| *vi* hervir a fuego lento.
  simmer down *vi* (*fig*, *col*) calmarse,
  tranquilizarse.
simpering |sim'pûring| *a* afectado; (*foolish*)
bobo.
simple |sim'pəl| *a* (*easy*) sencillo; (*foolish*,
COMM) simple; **the** ~ **truth** la pura
verdad.
simple interest *n* (COMM) interés *m* simple.
simple-minded |sim'pəlmīn'did| *a* simple,
ingenuo.
simpleton |sim'pəltən| *n* inocentón/ona *m/f*.
simplicity |simplis'ətē| *n* sencillez *f*; (*fool-
ishness*) ingenuidad *f*.

simplification |simpləfəkā'shən| *n* sim-
plificación *f*.
simplify |sim'pləfī| *vt* simplificar.
simply |sim'plē| *ad* (*in a simple way*: *live*,
talk) sencillamente; (*just*, *merely*) sólo.
simulate |sim'yəlāt| *vt* simular.
simulation |simyəlā'shən| *n* simulación *f*.
simultaneous |sīməltā'nēəs| *a* simultáneo.
simultaneously |sīməltā'nēəslē| *ad* si-
multáneamente, a la vez.
sin |sin| *n* pecado ♦ *vi* pecar.
since |sins| *ad* desde entonces, después ♦
prep desde ♦ *conj* (*time*) desde que; (*because*) ya que, puesto que; ~ **then** desde
entonces; ~ **Monday** desde el lunes; **(ever)**
~ **I arrived** desde que llegué.
sincere |sinsēr'| *a* sincero.
sincerely |sinsēr'lē| *ad* sinceramente; ~
yours (*in letters*) le saluda atentamente;
yours ~ (*Brit*: *in letters*) le saluda
(afectuosamente).
sincerity |sinsär'itē| *n* sinceridad *f*.
sinecure |sī'nəkyōōr| *n* chollo.
sinew |sin'yōō| *n* tendón *m*.
sinful |sin'fəl| *a* (*thought*) pecaminoso; (*per-
son*) pecador(a).
sing, *pt* **sang**, *pp* **sung** |sing, sang, sung| *vt*
cantar ♦ *vi* (*gen*) cantar; (*bird*) trinar;
(*ears*) zumbar.
Singapore |sing'gəpôr| *n* Singapur *m*.
singe |sinj| *vt* chamuscar.
singer |sing'ûr| *n* cantante *m/f*.
Singhalese |singəlēz'| *a* = **Sinhalese**.
singing |sing'ing| *n* (*of person*, *bird*) canto;
(*songs*) canciones *fpl*; (*in the ears*) zumbido; (*of kettle*) silbido.
single |sing'gəl| *a* único, solo; (*unmarried*)
soltero; (*not double*) simple, sencillo ♦ *n*
(*Brit*: *also*: ~ **ticket**) billete *m* sencillo;
(*record*) sencillo, single *m*; ~**s** *npl*
(TENNIS) individual *msg*; **not a** ~ **one was
left** no quedaba ni uno; **every** ~ **day** todos
los días (sin excepción).
  single out *vt* (*choose*) escoger; (*point
  out*) singularizar.
single bed *n* cama individual.
single-breasted |sing'gəlbrɛs'tid| *a* (*jacket*,
suit) recto.
single-density |sing'gəldɛnsitē| *a* (COM-
PUT: *disk*) de densidad sencilla.
single-entry book-keeping |sing'gəlɛn'-
trē bōōk'kēping| *n* contabilidad *f* por partida
simple.
single file *n*: **in** ~ en fila de uno.
single-handed |sing'gəlhan'did| *ad* sin ayu-
da.
single-minded |sing'gəlmīn'did| *a* resuelto,
firme.
single parent *n* (*mother*) madre *f* soltera;
(*father*) padre *m* soltero.
single room *n* cuarto individual.
single-sided |sing'gəlsī'did| *a* (COMPUT:
disk) de una cara.

single spacing n (TYP) interlineado simple.

singly [sing'glē] ad uno por uno.

singsong [sing'sông] n (songs): **to have a ~** tener un concierto improvisado.

singular [sing'gyəlûr] a (odd) raro, extraño; (LING) singular ♦ n (LING) singular m; **in the feminine ~** en femenino singular.

singularly [sing'gyəlûrlē] ad singularmente, extraordinariamente.

Sinhalese [sinhəlēz'] a singhalese.

sinister [sin'istûr] a siniestro.

sink [singk] n fregadero ♦ vb (pt **sank**, pp **sunk** [sangk, sungk]) vt (ship) hundir, echar a pique; (foundations) excavar; (piles etc): **to ~ sth into** hundir algo en ♦ vi (gen) hundirse; **he sank into a chair/the mud** se dejó caer en una silla/se hundió en el barro; **the shares or share prices have sunk to 3 dollars** las acciones han bajado a 3 dólares.

sink in vi (fig) penetrar, calar; **the news took a long time to ~ in** la noticia tardó mucho en hacerle (or hacerme etc) mella.

sinking fund [sing'king fund] n fondo de amortización.

sink unit n fregadero.

sinner [sin'ûr] n pecador(a) m/f.

sinuous [sin'yōōəs] a sinuoso.

sinus [sī'nəs] n (ANAT) seno.

sip [sip] n sorbo ♦ vt sorber, beber a sorbitos.

siphon [sī'fən] n sifón m ♦ vt (also: **~ off**) (funds) desviar.

sir [sûr] n señor m; **S~ John Smith** el Señor John Smith; **yes ~** sí, señor; **Dear S~** (in letter) Muy señor mío, Estimado Señor; **Dear S~s** Muy señores nuestros, Estimados Señores.

siren [sī'rən] n sirena.

sirloin [sûr'loin] n solomillo; **~ steak** filete m de solomillo.

sisal [sī'səl] n pita, henequén m (LAm).

sissy [sis'ē] n (col) marica m.

sister [sis'tûr] n hermana; (Brit: nurse) enfermera jefe.

sister-in-law [sis'tûrinlô] n cuñada.

sister organization n organización f hermana.

sister ship n barco gemelo.

sit, pt, pp **sat** [sit, sat] vi sentarse; (be sitting) estar sentado; (assembly) reunirse; (dress etc) caer, sentar ♦ vt (Brit: exam) presentarse a; **that jacket ~s well** esa chaqueta sienta bien; **to ~ on a committee** ser miembro de una comisión or un comité.

sit about (Brit) = **sit around.**

sit around vi holgazanear.

sit back vi (in seat) recostarse.

sit down vi sentarse; **to be ~ting down** estar sentado.

sit in on vt fus: **to ~ in on a discussion** asistir a una discusión.

sit up vi incorporarse; (not go to bed) velar.

sitcom [sit'kâm] n abbr (= situation comedy) serie f cómica.

sit-down [sit'doun] a: **~ strike** huelga de brazos caídos; **a ~ meal** una comida sentada.

site [sīt] n sitio; (also: **building ~**) solar m ♦ vt situar.

sit-in [sit'in] n (demonstration) ocupación f.

siting [sī'ting] n (location) situación f, emplazamiento.

sitter [sit'ûr] n (baby~) niñera f.

sitting [sit'ing] n (of assembly etc) sesión f; (in canteen) turno.

sitting member n (POL) titular m/f de un escaño.

sitting room n sala de estar.

situate [sich'ōōāt] vt situar.

situated [sich'ōōātid] a situado.

situation [sichōōā'shən] n situación f.

situation comedy n (TV, RADIO) serie f cómica.

six [siks] num seis.

sixteen [siks'tēn'] num diez y seis, dieciséis.

sixteenth note [siks'tēnth' nōt] (US MUS) semicorchea.

sixth [siksth] a sexto; **the upper/lower ~** (Brit SCOL) el séptimo/sexto año.

sixty [siks'tē] num sesenta.

size [sīz] n (gen) tamaño; (extent) extensión f; (of clothing) talla; (of shoes) número; **I take ~ 5 shoes** calzo el número cinco; **I take ~ 14** mi talla es la 42; **I'd like the small/large ~** (of soap powder etc) quisiera el tamaño pequeño/grande.

size up vt formarse una idea de.

sizeable [sī'zəbəl] a importante, considerable.

sizzle [siz'əl] vi crepitar.

SK abbr (Canada) = Saskatchewan.

skate [skāt] n patín m; (fish: pl inv) raya ♦ vi patinar.

skate around, skate over vt fus (problem, issue) pasar por alto.

skateboard [skāt'bôrd] n monopatín m.

skater [skā'tûr] n patinador(a) m/f.

skating [skā'ting] n patinaje m; **figure ~** patinaje m de figuras.

skating rink n pista de patinaje.

skeleton [skel'itən] n esqueleto; (TECH) armazón m; (outline) esquema m.

skeleton key n llave f maestra.

skeleton staff n personal m reducido.

skeptic [skep'tik] n (US) escéptico/a.

skeptical [skep'tikəl] a (US) escéptico.

skepticism [skep'tisizəm] n (US) escepticismo.

sketch [skech] n (drawing) dibujo; (outline) esbozo, bosquejo; (THEATER) pieza corta ♦ vt dibujar; esbozar.

sketch book n libro de dibujos.

sketching [skech'ing] n dibujo.

sketch pad *n* bloc *m* de dibujo.
sketchy [skech'ē] *a* incompleto.
skewer [skyōō'ûr] *n* broqueta.
ski [skē] *n* esquí *m* ♦ *vi* esquiar.
ski boot *n* bota de esquí.
skid [skid] *n* patinazo ♦ *vi* patinar; **to go into a ~** comenzar a patinar.
skid mark *n* señal *f* de patinazo.
skier [skē'ûr] *n* esquiador(a) *m/f*.
skiing [skē'ing] *n* esquí *m*; **to go ~** practicar el esquí, (ir a) esquiar.
ski instructor *n* instructor(a) *m/f* de esquí.
ski jump *n* pista para salto de esquí.
skilful [skil'fəl] *etc* (*Brit*) = **skillful** *etc*.
ski lift *n* telesilla *m*, telesquí *m*.
skill [skil] *n* destreza, pericia; (*technique*) arte *m*, técnica; **there's a certain ~ to doing it** se necesita cierta habilidad para hacerlo.
skilled [skild] *a* hábil, diestro; (*worker*) cualificado.
skillet [skil'it] *n* sartén *f* pequeña.
skillful [skil'fəl] *a* (*US*) diestro, experto.
skillfully [skil'fəlē] *ad* hábilmente, con destreza.
skim [skim] *vt* (*milk*) desnatar; (*glide over*) rozar, rasar ♦ *vi*: **to ~ through** (*book*) hojear.
skimmed milk [skimd milk] *n* leche *f* desnatada *or* descremada.
skimp [skimp] *vt* (*work*) chapucear; (*cloth etc*) escatimar; **to ~ on** (*material etc*) economizar; (*work*) escatimar.
skimpy [skim'pē] *a* (*meager*) escaso; (*skirt*) muy corto.
skin [skin] *n* (*gen*) piel *f*; (*complexion*) cutis *m*; (*of fruit, vegetable*) piel *f*, cáscara, pellejo; (*crust: on pudding, paint*) nata ♦ *vt* (*fruit etc*) pelar; (*animal*) despellejar; **wet** *or* **soaked to the ~** calado hasta los huesos.
skin-deep [skin'dēp'] *a* superficial.
skin diver *n* buceador(a) *m/f*.
skin diving *n* buceo.
skinflint [skin'flint] *n* tacaño/a, roñoso/a.
skinny [skin'ē] *a* flaco, magro.
skintight [skin'tīt] *a* (*dress etc*) muy ajustado.
skip [skip] *n* brinco, salto; (*Brit: container*) cuba ♦ *vi* brincar; (*with rope*) saltar a la comba ♦ *vt* (*pass over*) omitir, saltar.
ski pants *npl* pantalones *mpl* de esquí.
ski pole *n* bastón *m* de esquiar.
skipper [skip'ûr] *n* (*NAUT*, *SPORT*) capitán *m*.
skipping rope [skip'ing rōp] *n* (*Brit*) cuerda (de saltar).
ski resort *n* estación *f* de esquí.
skirmish [skûr'mish] *n* escaramuza.
skirt [skûrt] *n* falda, pollera (*LAm*) ♦ *vt* (*surround*) ceñir, rodear; (*go around*) ladear.
skirting board [skûr'ting bôrd] *n* (*Brit*) ro-

dapié *m*.
ski run *n* pista de esquí.
ski suit *n* traje *m* de esquiar.
skit [skit] *n* sátira, parodia.
ski tow *n* arrastre *m* (de esquí).
skittle [skit'əl] *n* bolo; **~s** (*game*) boliche *m*.
skive [skīv] *vi* (*Brit col*) gandulear.
skulk [skulk] *vi* esconderse.
skull [skul] *n* calavera; (*ANAT*) cráneo.
skullcap [skul'kap] *n* (*worn by Jews*) casquete *m*; (*worn by Pope*) solideo.
skunk [skungk] *n* mofeta.
sky [skī] *n* cielo; **to praise sb to the skies** poner a uno por las nubes.
sky-blue [skī'blōō'] *a* (azul) celeste.
sky-high [skī'hī'] *ad* (*throw*) muy alto; **prices have gone ~** los precios están por las nubes.
skylark [skī'lârk] *n* (*bird*) alondra.
skylight [skī'līt] *n* tragaluz *m*, claraboya.
skyline [skī'līn] *n* (*horizon*) horizonte *m*; (*of city*) perfil *m*.
skyscraper [skī'skrāpûr] *n* rascacielos *m inv*.
slab [slab] *n* (*stone*) bloque *m*; (*of wood*) tabla, plancha; (*flat*) losa; (*of cake*) trozo; (*of meat, cheese*) tajada, trozo.
slack [slak] *a* (*loose*) flojo; (*slow*) de poca actividad; (*careless*) descuidado; (*COMM: market*) poco activo; (*: demand*) débil; (*period*) bajo; **business is ~** hay poco movimiento en el negocio.
slacken [slak'ən] (*also: ~ off*) *vi* aflojarse ♦ *vt* aflojar; (*speed*) disminuir.
slackness [slak'nis] *n* flojedad *f*; negligencia.
slacks [slaks] *npl* pantalones *mpl*.
slag [slag] *n* escoria, escombros *mpl*.
slag heap *n* escorial *m*, escombrera.
slain [slān] *pp* of **slay**.
slake [slāk] *vt* (*one's thirst*) apagar.
slalom [slâ'ləm] *n* eslálom *m*.
slam [slam] *vt* (*door*) cerrar de golpe; (*throw*) arrojar (violentamente); (*criticize*) vapulear, vituperar ♦ *vi* cerrarse de golpe.
slander [slan'dûr] *n* calumnia, difamación *f* ♦ *vt* calumniar, difamar.
slanderous [slan'dûrəs] *a* calumnioso, difamatorio.
slang [slang] *n* argot *m*; (*jargon*) jerga.
slant [slant] *n* sesgo, inclinación *f*; (*fig*) punto de vista; **to get a new ~ on sth** obtener un nuevo punto de vista sobre algo.
slanted [slan'tid], **slanting** [slan'ting] *a* inclinado.
slap [slap] *n* palmada; (*in face*) bofetada ♦ *vt* dar una palmada/bofetada a ♦ *ad* (*directly*) exactamente, directamente.
slapdash [slap'dash] *a* descuidado.
slapstick [slap'stik] *n*: **~ comedy** comedia de golpe y porrazo.
slash [slash] *vt* acuchillar; (*fig: prices*) que-

mar ♦ *n* (*US TYP*) oblicua.

slat [slat] *n* (*of wood, plastic*) tablilla, listón *m*.

slate [slāt] *n* pizarra ♦ *vt* (*Brit: fig: criticize*) criticar duramente, dar una paliza a.

slaughter [sló'tûr] *n* (*of animals*) matanza; (*of people*) carnicería ♦ *vt* matar.

slaughterhouse [slò'tûrhous] *n* matadero.

Slav [släv] *a* eslavo.

slave [släv] *n* esclavo/a ♦ *vi* (*also: ~ away*) sudar tinta; **to ~ (away) at (doing) sth** sudar tinta en (hacer) algo.

slave labor *n* trabajo de esclavos.

slaver [slā'vûr] *vi* (*dribble*) babear.

slavery [slā'vûrē] *n* esclavitud *f*.

slavish [slā'vish] *a* (*devotion*) de esclavo; (*imitation*) servil.

slay, *pt* **slew**, *pp* **slain** [slā, slōō, slān] *vt* (*literary*) matar.

SLD *n abbr* (*Brit POL*) = *Social and Liberal Democratic Party*.

sleazy [slē'zē] *a* (*fig: place*) de mala fama.

sled [sled], (*Brit*) **sledge** [slej] *n* trineo.

sledgehammer [slej'hamûr] *n* mazo.

sleek [slēk] *a* (*shiny*) lustroso.

sleep [slēp] *n* sueño ♦ *vb* (*pt, pp* **slept** [slept]) *vi* dormir ♦ *vt*: **we can ~ 4** podemos alojar a 4, tenemos cabida para 4; **to go to ~** quedarse dormido; **to have a good night's ~** dormir toda la noche; **to put to ~** (*patient*) dormir; (*animal: euphemism: kill*) sacrificar; **to ~ lightly** tener el sueño ligero; **to ~ with sb** (*euphemism*) acostarse con uno.

sleep in *vi* (*oversleep*) dormir tarde.

sleeper [slē'pûr] *n* (*person*) durmiente *m/f*; (*US: for baby*) pijama *m* de niño; (*Brit RAIL: on track*) traviesa; (*: train*) cochecama *m*.

sleepiness [slēp'ēnis] *n* somnolencia.

sleeping bag [slē'ping bag] *n* saco de dormir.

sleeping car *n* coche-cama *m*.

sleeping partner *n* (*COMM*) socio/a comanditario/a.

sleeping pill *n* somnífero.

sleepless [slēp'lis] *a*: **a ~ night** una noche en blanco.

sleeplessness [slēp'lisnis] *n* insomnio.

sleepwalker [slēp'wôkûr] *n* sonámbulo/a.

sleepy [slē'pē] *a* soñoliento; **to be** *or* **feel ~** tener sueño.

sleet [slēt] *n* nevisca.

sleeve [slēv] *n* manga; (*TECH*) manguito; (*of record*) funda.

sleeveless [slēv'lis] *a* (*garment*) sin mangas.

sleigh [slā] *n* trineo.

sleight [slīt] *n*: **~ of hand** escamoteo.

slender [slen'dûr] *a* delgado; (*means*) escaso.

slept [slept] *pt, pp of* **sleep**.

sleuth [slōōth] *n* (*col*) detective *m/f*.

slew [slōō] *vi* (*Brit: veer*) torcerse ♦ *pt of* **slay.**

slice [slīs] *n* (*of meat*) tajada; (*of bread*) rebanada; (*of lemon*) rodaja; (*utensil*) pala ♦ *vt* cortar, tajar; rebanar; **~d bread** pan *m* de molde.

slick [slik] *a* (*skilful*) hábil, diestro ♦ *n* (*also:* **oil ~**) capa de aceite.

slid [slid] *pt, pp of* **slide.**

slide [slīd] *n* (*in playground*) tobogán *m*; (*PHOT*) diapositiva; (*microscope ~*) portaobjetos *m inv*, plaquilla de vidrio; (*Brit: also:* **hair ~**) pasador *m* ♦ *vb: pt, pp* **slid** [slid]) *vt* correr, deslizar ♦ *vi* (*slip*) resbalarse; (*glide*) deslizarse; **to let things ~** (*fig*) dejar que ruede la bola.

slide projector *n* (*PHOT*) proyector *m* de diapositivas.

slide rule *n* regla de cálculo.

sliding [slī'ding] *a* (*door*) corredizo; **~ roof** (*AUT*) techo de corredera.

sliding scale *n* escala móvil.

slight [slīt] *a* (*slim*) delgado; (*frail*) delicado; (*pain etc*) leve; (*trifling*) insignificante; (*small*) pequeño ♦ *n* desaire *m* ♦ *vt* (*offend*) ofender, desairar; **a ~ improvement** una ligera mejora; **not in the ~est** en absoluto; **there's not the ~est possibility** no hay la menor *or* más mínima posibilidad.

slightly [slīt'lē] *ad* ligeramente, un poco; **~ built** delgado, fino.

slim [slim] *a* delgado, esbelto ♦ *vi* adelgazar.

slime [slīm] *n* limo, cieno.

slimness [slim'nis] *n* delgadez *f*.

slimy [slī'mē] *a* limoso; (*covered with mud*) fangoso; (*also fig: person*) adulón, zalamero.

slimming [slim'ing] *n* adelgazamiento ♦ *a* (*diet, pills*) adelgazador(a), adelgazante.

sling [sling] *n* (*MED*) cabestrillo; (*weapon*) honda ♦ *vt* (*pt, pp* **slung** [slung]) tirar, arrojar; **to have one's arm in a ~** llevar el brazo en cabestrillo.

slingshot [sling'shât] *n* tirador *m*.

slink, *pt, pp* **slunk** [slingk, slungk] *vi*: **to ~ away, ~ off** escabullirse.

slip [slip] *n* (*slide*) resbalón *m*; (*mistake*) descuido; (*underskirt*) combinación *f*; (*of paper*) papelito; (*delivery ~*) nota de entrega ♦ *vt* (*slide*) deslizar ♦ *vi* (*slide*) deslizarse; (*stumble*) resbalar(se); (*decline*) decaer; (*move smoothly*): **to ~ into/out of** (*room etc*) introducirse en/salirse de; **to let a chance ~ by** escapársele la oportunidad; **to ~ sth on/off** ponerse/quitarse algo; **to ~ on a jumper** ponerse un jersey *or* un suéter; it **~ped from her hand** se la cayó de la mano; **to give sb the ~** eludir a uno; **a ~ of the tongue** un lapsus.

slip away *vi* escabullirse.

slip in *vt* meter ♦ *vi* meterse.

slip out *vi* (*go out*) salir (un momento).

slip-on [slip'án] *a* de quitaipón; (*shoes*) sin cordones.
slipped disc [slipt disk] *n* vértebra dislocada.
slipper [slip'ûr] *n* zapatilla, pantufla.
slippery [slip'ùrē] *a* resbaladizo.
slip road *n* (*Brit*) carretera de acceso.
slipshod [slip'shâd] *a* descuidado.
slipstream [slip'strēm] *n* viento de la hélice.
slip-up [slip'up] *n* (*error*) desliz *m*.
slipway [slip'wā] *n* grada, gradas *fpl*.
slit [slit] *n* raja; (*cut*) corte *m* ♦ *vt* (*pt, pp* **slit**) rajar, cortar; **to ~ sb's throat** cortarle el pescuezo a uno.
slither [sliᵗʰ'ûr] *vi* deslizarse.
sliver [sliv'ûr] *n* (*of glass, wood*) astilla; (*of cheese, sausage*) lonja, loncha.
slob [sláb] *n* (*col*) patán/ana *m/f*, palurdo/a.
slog [slág] (*Brit*) *vi* sudar tinta ♦ *n*: **it was a ~** costó trabajo (hacerlo).
slogan [slō'gən] *n* eslogan *m*, lema *m*.
slop [sláp] *vi* (*also*: **~ over**) derramarse, desbordarse ♦ *vt* derramar, verter.
slope [slōp] *n* (*up*) cuesta, pendiente *f*; (*down*) declive *m*; (*side of mountain*) falda, vertiente *f* ♦ *vi*: **to ~ down** estar en declive; **to ~ up** inclinarse.
sloping [slō'ping] *a* en pendiente; en declive.
sloppily [sláp'ilē] *ad* descuidadamente; con descuido *or* desaliño.
sloppiness [sláp'ēnis] *n* descuido; desaliño.
sloppy [sláp'ē] *a* (*work*) descuidado; (*appearance*) desaliñado.
slosh [slásh] *vi*: **to ~ around** chapotear.
slot [slát] *n* ranura; (*fig*: *in timetable, RADIO, TV*) hueco ♦ *vt*: **to ~ into** encajar en.
sloth [slôth] *n* (*vice*) pereza; (*ZOOL*) oso perezoso.
slot machine *n* (*for gambling*) máquina tragaperras; (*Brit*: *vending machine*) aparato vendedor, distribuidor *m* automático.
slouch [slouch] *vi*: **to ~ around** (*laze*) gandulear.
slovenly [sluv'ənlē] *a* (*dirty*) desaliñado, desaseado; (*careless*) descuidado.
slow [slō] *a* lento; (*watch*): **to be ~** estar atrasado ♦ *ad* lentamente, despacio ♦ *vt, vi* (*also*: **~ down**, **~ up**) retardar; **at a ~ speed** a una velocidad lenta; **business is ~** (*COMM*) hay poca actividad; **my watch is 20 minutes ~** mi reloj lleva 20 minutos de retraso; **bake for two hours in a ~ oven** cocer *or* asar 2 horas en el horno a fuego lento; **to be ~ to act/decide** tardar en obrar/decidir; **to go ~** (*driver*) conducir despacio; (*Brit*: *in industrial dispute*) trabajar a ritmo lento.
slow-acting [slō'ak'ting] *a* de efecto retardado.
slowdown [slō'doun] *n* (*US*) huelga de manos caídas.
slowly [slō'lē] *ad* lentamente, despacio; **to**

drive ~ conducir despacio; **~ but surely** paso a paso.
slow motion *n*: **in ~** a cámara lenta.
slow-moving [slō'mōō'ving] *a* lento.
slowpoke [slō'pōk] *n* (*US*) perezoso/a, vago/a.
sludge [sluj] *n* lodo, fango.
slue [slōō] *vi* (*US*: *veer*) torcerse.
slug [slug] *n* babosa; (*bullet*) posta.
sluggish [slug'ish] *a* (*slow*) lento; (*lazy*) perezoso; (*business, market, sales*) inactivo, moroso.
sluggishly [slug'ishlē] *ad* lentamente.
sluggishness [slug'ishnis] *n* lentitud *f*.
sluice [slōōs] *n* (*gate*) esclusa; (*channel*) canal *m* ♦ *vt*: **to ~ down** *or* **out** regar.
slum [slum] *n* (*area*) barrio bajo, tugurios *mpl*.
slumber [slum'bûr] *n* sueño.
slump [slump] *n* (*economic*) depresión *f* ♦ *vi* hundirse; **the ~ in the price of copper** la baja repentina del precio del cobre; **he was ~ed over the wheel** se había desplomado encima del volante.
slung [slung] *pt, pp of* **sling**.
slunk [slungk] *pt, pp of* **slink**.
slur [slûr] *n* calumnia ♦ *vt* calumniar, difamar; (*word*) pronunciar indistintamente; **to cast a ~ on sb** manchar la reputación de uno, difamar a uno.
slurred [slûrd] *a* (*pronunciation*) mal articulado, borroso.
slush [slush] *n* nieve *f* a medio derretir.
slush fund *n* (*for bribes*) fondos *mpl* para sobornar.
slushy [slush'ē] *a* (*col*: *poetry etc*) sentimentaloide.
slut [slut] *n* marrana.
sly [slī] *a* (*clever*) astuto; (*nasty*) malicioso.
slyly [slī'lē] *ad* astutamente; taimadamente.
slyness [slī'nis] *n* astucia.
smack [smak] *n* (*slap*) manotada; (*blow*) golpe *m* ♦ *vt* dar una manotada a; golpear con la mano ♦ *vi*: **to ~ of** saber a, oler a ♦ *ad*: **it fell ~ in the middle** (*col*) cayó justo en medio.
smacker [smak'ûr] *n* (*col*: *kiss*) beso sonoro; (: *US*: *dollar bill*) billete *m* de un dólar; (: *Brit*: *pound note*) billete *m* de una libra.
small [smôl] *a* pequeño; (*in height*) bajo, chaparro (*LAm*); (*letter*) en minúscula ♦ *n*: **~ of the back** región *f* lumbar; **~ store-keeper** pequeño/a comerciante *m/f*; **to get** *or* **grow ~er** (*stain, town*) empequeñecer; (*debt, organization, numbers*) reducir, disminuir; **to make ~er** (*amount, income*) reducir; (*garden, object, garment*) achicar.
small change *n* suelto, cambio.
smallholding [smôl'hōlding] *n* (*Brit*) parcela, minifundio.
small hours *npl*: **in the ~** en las altas ho-

ras (de la noche).

smallish |smó'lish| *a* más bien pequeño.

small-minded |smól'mín'did| *a* mezquino, de miras estrechas.

smallness |smól'nis| *n* pequeñez *f*.

smallpox |smól'páks| *n* viruela.

small print *n* letra pequeña *or* menuda.

small-scale |smól'skāl| *a* (*map, model*) en escala reducida; (*business, farming*) en pequeña escala.

small talk *n* cháchara.

small-time |smól'tīm'| *a* (*col*) de poca categoría *or* monta; **a ~ thief** un(a) ratero/a.

smart |smárt| *a* elegante; (*clever*) listo, inteligente; (*quick*) rápido, vivo ♦ *vi* escocer, picar; **the ~ set** la gente de buen tono; **to look ~** estar elegante; **my eyes are ~ing** me pican los ojos.

smart-ass |smárt'as| *n* (*US col*) sabelotodo/a, listillo/a.

smarten up |smár'tən up| *vi* arreglarse ♦ *vt* arreglar.

smartness |smárt'nis| *n* elegancia; (*cleverness*) inteligencia.

smash |smash| *n* (*also:* **~-up**) choque *m*; (*sound*) estrépito ♦ *vt* (*break*) hacer pedazos; (*car etc*) estrellar; (*SPORT: record*) batir ♦ *vi* hacerse pedazos; (*against wall etc*) estrellarse.

smash up *vt* (*car*) hacer pedazos; (*room*) destrozar.

smash hit *n* exitazo.

smattering |smat'ûring| *n*: **a ~ of Spanish** algo de español.

smear |smē'ûr| *n* mancha; (*MED*) frotis *m inv* (cervical); (*insult*) calumnia ♦ *vt* untar; (*fig*) calumniar, difamar; **his hands were ~ed with oil/ink** tenía las manos manchadas de aceite/tinta.

smear campaign *n* campaña de calumnias.

smell |smel| *n* olor *m*; (*sense*) olfato ♦ (*vb*: *pt, pp* **smelled** *or* (*Brit*) **smelt** |smelt|) *vt, vi* oler; **it ~s good/of garlic** huele bien/a ajo.

smelly |smel'ē| *a* maloliente.

smelt |smelt| *vt* (*ore*) fundir ♦ (*Brit*) *pt, pp of* **smell**.

smile |smīl| *n* sonrisa ♦ *vi* sonreír.

smiling |smī'ling| *a* sonriente, risueño.

smirk |smûrk| *n* sonrisa falsa *or* afectada.

smith |smith| *n* herrero.

smithy |smith'ē| *n* herrería.

smitten |smit'ən| *a*: **he's really ~ with her** está totalmente loco por ella.

smock |smák| *n* blusa; (*children's*) delantal *m*; (*US: overall*) guardapolvo.

smog |smág| *n* esmog *m*.

smoke |smōk| *n* humo ♦ *vi* fumar; (*chimney*) echar humo ♦ *vt* (*cigarettes*) fumar; **to go up in ~** (*house etc*) quemarse; (*fig*) irse todo en humo, fracasar; **do you ~?** ¿fumas?

smoked |smōkt| *a* (*bacon, glass*) ahumado.

smokeless fuel |smōk'lis fyōō'əl| *n* combustible *m* sin humo.

smoker |smō'kûr| *n* (*person*) fumador(a) *m/f*; (*RAIL*) coche *m* fumador.

smoke screen *n* cortina de humo.

smoking |smō'king| *n*: **"no ~"** "prohibido fumar"; **he's given up ~** ha dejado de fumar.

smoking car *n* departamento de fumadores.

smoky |smō'kē| *a* (*room*) lleno de humo.

smolder |smōl'dûr| *vi* (*US*) arder sin llama.

smooth |smōōth| *a* liso; (*sea*) tranquilo; (*flavor, movement*) suave; (*person: pej*) meloso ♦ *vt* alisar; (*also:* **~ out**) (*creases, difficulties*) allanar.

smooth over *vt*: **to ~ things over** (*fig*) limar las asperezas.

smoothly |smōōth'lē| *ad* (*easily*) fácilmente; **everything went ~** todo pasó sin novedad.

smoothness |smōōth'nis| *n* (*of skin, cloth*) tersura; (*of surface, flavor, movement*) suavidad *f*.

smother |smuth'ûr| *vt* sofocar; (*repress*) contener.

smoulder |smōl'dûr| *vi* (*Brit*) = **smolder**.

smudge |smuj| *n* mancha ♦ *vt* manchar.

smug |smug| *a* presumido.

smuggle |smug'əl| *vt* pasar de contrabando; **to ~ in/out** (*goods etc*) meter/sacar de contrabando.

smuggler |smug'lûr| *n* contrabandista *m/f*.

smuggling |smug'ling| *n* contrabando.

smugly |smug'lē| *ad* con suficiencia.

smugness |smug'nis| *n* suficiencia.

smut |smut| *n* (*grain of soot*) carbonilla, hollín *m*; (*mark*) tizne *m*; (*in conversation etc*) obscenidades *fpl*.

smutty |smut'ē| *a* (*fig*) verde, obsceno.

snack |snak| *n* bocado; **to have a ~** probarse un bocado.

snack bar *n* cafetería.

snag |snag| *n* problema *m*; **to run into** *or* **hit a ~** encontrar inconvenientes, dar con un obstáculo.

snail |snāl| *n* caracol *m*.

snake |snāk| *n* (*gen*) serpiente *f*; (*harmless*) culebra; (*poisonous*) víbora.

snap |snap| *n* (*sound*) chasquido; golpe *m* seco ♦ *a* (*decision*) instantáneo ♦ *vt* (*fingers etc*) castañetear; (*break*) quebrar ♦ *vi* (*break*) quebrarse; (*fig: person*) contestar bruscamente; **to ~ (at sb)** (*subj: person*) hablar con brusquedad (a uno); (*: dog*) intentar morder (a uno); **to ~ shut** cerrarse de golpe; **to ~ one's fingers at sth/sb** (*fig*) burlarse de algo/uno; **a cold ~** (*of weather*) una ola de frío.

snap off *vi* (*break*) partirse.

snap up *vt* agarrar.

snap fastener *n* botón *m* de presión.

snappy [snap'ē] a (col: answer) instantáneo; (slogan) conciso; **make it** ~! (hurry up) ¡date prisa!

snapshot [snap'shåt] n foto f (instantánea).

snare [snär] n trampa ♦ vt cazar con trampa; (fig) engañar.

snarl [snårl] n gruñido ♦ vi gruñir; **to get** ~**ed up** (wool, plans) enmarañarse, enredarse; (traffic) quedar atascado.

snatch [snach] n (fig) robo; ~**es of** trocitos mpl de ♦ vt (~ away) arrebatar; (grasp) coger (Sp), agarrar; ~**es of conversation** fragmentos mpl de conversación.
  snatch up vt agarrar.

sneak [snēk] vi: **to** ~ **in/out** entrar/salir a hurtadillas ♦ vt: **to** ~ **a look at sth** mirar algo de reojo ♦ n (fam) soplón/ona m/f.

sneakers [snē'kúrz] npl (US) zapatos mpl de lona, zapatillas fpl.

sneaking [snē'king] a: **to have a** ~ **feeling/suspicion that** ... tener la (horrible) sensación/sospecha de que ....

sneaky [snē'kē] a furtivo.

sneer [snēr] n sonrisa de desprecio ♦ vi sonreír con desprecio; **to** ~ **at sth/sb** burlarse or mofarse de algo/uno.

sneeze [snēz] n estornudo ♦ vi estornudar.

snicker [snik'úr] n risa disimulada ♦ vi reírse con disimulo.

snide [snīd] a (col: sarcastic) sarcástico.

sniff [snif] vi sorber (por la nariz) ♦ vt husmear, oler; (glue, drug) esnifar.
  sniff at vt fus: **it's not to be** ~**ed at** no es de despreciar.

snigger [snig'úr] n risa disimulada ♦ vi reírse con disimulo.

snip [snip] n (piece) recorte m; (bargain) ganga ♦ vt tijeretear.

sniper [snī'púr] n francotirador(a) m/f.

snippet [snip'it] n retazo.

sniveling, (Brit) **snivelling** [sniv'əling] a llorón/ona.

snob [snåb] n (e)snob m/f.

snobbery [snåb'úrē] n (e)snobismo.

snobbish [snåb'ish] a (e)snob.

snobbishness [snåb'ishnis] n (e)snobismo.

snooker [snook'úr] n especie de billar.

snoop [snoop] vi: **to** ~ **around** fisgonear.

snooper [snoo'púr] n fisgón/ona m/f.

snooty [snoo'tē] a (e)snob.

snooze [snooz] n siesta ♦ vi echar una siesta.

snore [snôr] vi roncar ♦ n ronquido.

snoring [snôr'ing] n ronquidos mpl.

snorkel [snôr'kəl] n (tubo) respirador m.

snort [snôrt] n bufido ♦ vi bufar ♦ vt (col: drugs) aspirar, esnifar.

snotty [snåt'ē] a (col) engreído.

snout [snout] n hocico, morro.

snow [snō] n nieve f ♦ vi nevar ♦ vt: **to be** ~**ed under with work** estar agobiado de trabajo.

snowball [snō'bôl] n bola de nieve ♦ vi ir aumentándose.

snow-blind [snō'blīnd] a cegado por la nieve.

snowbound [snō'bound] a bloqueado por la nieve.

snowcapped [snō'kapt] a (peak) cubierto de nieve, nevado.

snowdrift [snō'drift] n ventisquero.

snowdrop [snō'dråp] n campanilla.

snowfall [snō'fôl] n nevada.

snowflake [snō'flāk] n copo de nieve.

snowline [snō'līn] n límite m de las nieves perpetuas.

snowman [snō'man] n figura de nieve.

snowplow, (Brit) **snowplough** [snō'plou] n quitanieves m inv.

snowshoe [snō'shoo] n raqueta (de nieve).

snowstorm [snō'stôrm] n nevada, nevasca.

Snow White n Blancanieves f.

snowy [snō'ē] a (de mucha) nieve.

SNP n abbr (Brit POL) = Scottish National Party.

snub [snub] vt: **to** ~ **sb** desairar a uno ♦ n desaire m, repulsa.

snub-nosed [snub'nōzd] a chato.

snuff [snuf] n rapé m ♦ vt (also: ~ **out**: candle) apagar.

snuffbox [snuf'båks] n caja de rapé.

snug [snug] a (cosy) cómodo; (fitted) ajustado.

snuggle [snug'əl] vi: **to** ~ **down in bed** hacerse un ovillo en la cama; **to** ~ **up to sb** arrimarse or abrazarse a uno.

snugly [snug'lē] ad cómodamente; **it fits** ~ (object in pocket etc) cabe perfectamente; (garment) ajusta perfectamente.

SO abbr (BANKING) = standing order.

so [sō] ad (degree) tan; (manner: thus) así, de este modo ♦ conj así que, por tanto; ~ **that** (purpose) para que, a fin de que; (result) de modo que; ~ **do I** yo también; **if** ~ de ser así, si es así; **I hope** ~ espero que sí; **10 or** ~ 10 más o menos; ~ **far** hasta aquí; ~ **quickly** (early) tan pronto; (fast) tan rápidamente; **quite** ~! ¡así es!, ¡exacto!; **even** ~ sin embargo; ~ **to speak** por decirlo así, es un decir; ~ **it is!**, ~ **it does!** ¡es verdad!, ¡es cierto!; ~ **long!** ¡hasta luego!; ~ **many** tantos/as; ~ **much** a, ad tanto; **she didn't** ~ **much as send me a birthday card** no me mandó ni una tarjeta siquiera por mi cumpleaños; ~ **that's the reason!** ¡así que es por eso or por eso es!; ~ **(what)?** (col) ¿y (qué)?

soak [sōk] vt (drench) empapar; (put in water) remojar ♦ vi remojarse, estar a remojo.
  soak in vi penetrar.
  soak up vt absorber.

soaking [sō'king] a (also: ~ **wet**) calado or empapado (hasta los huesos or el tuétano).

so-and-so [sō'ənsō] n (somebody) fulano/a de tal.

soap [sōp] *n* jabón *m*.

soapflakes [sōp'flāks] *npl* jabón *msg* en escamas.

soap opera *n* (*TV*) telenovela; (*RADIO*) radionovela.

soap powder *n* jabón *m* en polvo.

soapsuds [sōp'sudz] *npl* espuma *sg*.

soapy [sō'pē] *a* jabonoso.

soar [sôr] *vi* (*on wings*) remontarse; (*building etc*) elevarse; (*price*) subir vertiginosamente; (*morale*) renacer.

soaring [sôr'ing] *a* (*flight*) planeador(a), que vuela; (*prices*) en alza *or* aumento; ~ **inflation** inflación *f* altísima *or* en aumento.

sob [sâb] *n* sollozo ♦ *vi* sollozar.

s.o.b. *n abbr* (*US col!* = *son of a bitch*) hijo de puta (!).

sober [sō'bûr] *a* (*moderate*) moderado; (*not drunk*) sobrio; (*color, style*) discreto.

sober up *vi* pasársele a uno la borrachera.

soberly [sō'bûrlē] *ad* sobriamente.

sobriety [səbrī'ətē] *n* (*not being drunk*) sobriedad *f*; (*seriousness, sedateness*) seriedad *f*, sensatez *f*.

Soc. *abbr* (= *society*) S.

so-called [sō'kôld'] *a* presunto, supuesto.

soccer [sâk'ûr] *n* fútbol *m*.

soccer player *n* jugador(a) *m/f* de fútbol.

sociability [sōshəbil'ətē] *n* sociabilidad *f*.

sociable [sō'shəbəl] *a* sociable.

social [sō'shəl] *a* social ♦ *n* velada, fiesta.

social class *n* clase *f* social.

social climber *n* arribista *m/f*.

social club *n* club *m*.

Social Democrat *n* socialdemócrata *m/f*.

socialism [sō'shəlizəm] *n* socialismo.

socialist [sō'shəlist] *a, n* socialista *m/f*.

socialite [sō'shəlīt] *n* persona de la buena sociedad.

socialize [sō'shəlīz] *vi* hacer vida social; **to** ~ **with** (*colleagues*) salir con.

socially [sō'shəlē] *ad* socialmente.

social science(s) *n* ciencias *fpl* sociales.

social security *n* seguridad *f* social.

social welfare *n* asistencia social.

social work *n* asistencia social.

social worker *n* asistente/a *m/f* social.

socioeconomic [sōshēōěkənâm'ik] *a* socioeconómico.

society [səsī'ətē] *n* sociedad *f*; (*club*) asociación *f*; (*also:* **high** ~) buena sociedad ♦ *cpd* (*party, column*) social, de sociedad.

sociological [sōsēəlâj'ikəl] *a* sociológico.

sociologist [sōsēâl'əjist] *n* sociólogo/a.

sociology [sōsēâl'əjē] *n* sociología.

sock [sâk] *n* calcetín *m*, media (*LAm*); **to pull one's ~s up** (*fig*) hacer esfuerzos, despabilarse.

socket [sâk'it] *n* (*ELEC*) enchufe *m*.

sod [sâd] *n* (*of earth*) césped *m*; (*Brit: col!*) cabrón/ona *m/f* (!).

soda [sō'də] *n* (*CHEM*) sosa; (*also:* ~ **wa-**

ter) soda; (*US: also:* ~ **pop**) gaseosa.

sodden [sâd'ən] *a* empapado.

sodium [sō'dēəm] *n* sodio.

sodium chloride *n* cloruro sódico *or* de sodio.

sofa [sō'fə] *n* sofá *m*.

Sofia [sōfē'ə] *n* Sofía.

soft [sôft] *a* (*teacher, parent*) blando; (*gentle, not loud*) suave; (*stupid*) bobo; ~ **currency** divisa blanda *or* débil.

soft-boiled [sôft'boild'] *a* (*egg*) pasado (por agua).

soft copy *n* (*COMPUT*) copia transitoria.

soft drink *n* bebida no alcohólica.

soft drugs *npl* drogas *fpl* blandas.

soften [sôf'ən] *vt* ablandar; suavizar ♦ *vi* ablandarse; suavizarse.

softener [sôf'ənûr] *n* suavizador *m*.

softhearted [sôft'hâr'tid] *a* bondadoso.

softly [sôft'lē] *ad* suavemente; (*gently*) delicadamente, con delicadeza.

softness [sôft'nis] *n* blandura; suavidad *f*.

soft sell *n* venta suave.

soft toy *n* juguete *m* de peluche.

software [sôft'wär] *n* (*COMPUT*) software *m*.

soft water *n* agua blanda.

soggy [sâg'ē] *a* empapado.

soil [soil] *n* (*earth*) tierra, suelo ♦ *vt* ensuciar.

soiled [soild] *a* sucio, manchado.

sojourn [sō'jûrn] *n* (*formal*) estancia.

solace [sâl'is] *n* consuelo.

solar [sō'lûr] *a* solar.

solarium, *pl* **solaria** [sōlär'ēəm, -ēə] *n* solario.

solar plexus [sō'lûr plek'səs] *n* (*ANAT*) plexo solar.

solar system *n* sistema *m* solar.

sold [sōld] *pt, pp of* **sell**.

solder [sâd'ûr] *vt* soldar ♦ *n* soldadura.

soldier [sōl'jûr] *n* (*gen*) soldado; (*army man*) militar *m*; **toy** ~ soldadito de plomo.

sold out *a* (*COMM*) agotado.

sole [sōl] *n* (*of foot*) planta; (*of shoe*) suela; (*fish: pl inv*) lenguado ♦ *a* único; **the** ~ **reason** la única razón.

solely [sōl'lē] *ad* únicamente, sólo, solamente; **I will hold you** ~ **responsible** le daré toda la responsabilidad.

solemn [sâl'əm] *a* solemne.

sole trader *n* (*COMM*) comerciante *m/f* exclusivo/a.

solicit [səlis'it] *vt* (*request*) solicitar ♦ *vi* (*prostitute*) abordar, importunar.

solicitor [səlis'itûr] *n* (*Brit: for wills etc*) notario/a; (: *in court*) abogado/a.

solid [sâl'id] *a* sólido; (*gold etc*) macizo; (*line*) continuo; (*vote*) unánime ♦ *n* sólido; **we waited 2** ~ **hours** esperamos 2 horas enteras; **to be on** ~ **ground** estar en tierra firme; (*fig*) estar seguro.

solidarity [sâlidar'itē] *n* solidaridad *f*.

solidify [səlid'əfī] *vi* solidificarse.
solidity [səlid'itē] *n* solidez *f*.
solidly [sâl'idlē] *ad* sólidamente; (*fig*) unánimemente.
solid-state [sâl'idstāt'] *a* (*ELEC*) estado sólido.
soliloquy [səlil'əkwē] *n* soliloquio.
solitaire [sâl'itār] *n* (*game, gem*) solitario.
solitary [sâl'itārē] *a* solitario, solo; (*isolated*) apartado, aislado; (*only*) único.
solitary confinement *n* incomunicación *f*; **to be in ~** estar incomunicado.
solitude [sâl'ətōōd] *n* soledad *f*.
solo [sō'lō] *n* solo.
soloist [sō'lōist] *n* solista *m/f*.
Solomon Islands [sâl'əmən ī'ləndz] *npl*: **the ~** las Islas Salomón.
solstice [sâl'stis] *n* solsticio.
soluble [sâl'yəbəl] *a* soluble.
solution [səlōō'shən] *n* solución *f*.
solve [sâlv] *vt* resolver, solucionar.
solvency [sâl'vənsē] *n* (*COMM*) solvencia.
solvent [sâl'vənt] *a* (*COMM*) solvente ♦ *n* (*CHEM*) solvente *m*.
solvent abuse *n* abuso de los solventes.
Som. *abbr* (*Brit*) = *Somerset*.
Somali [sōmâ'lē] *a, n* somalí *m/f*.
Somalia [sōmâl'ēə] *n* Somalia.
somber, (*Brit*) **sombre** [sâm'bûr] *a* sombrío.
some [sum] *a* (*a few*) algunos/as; (*certain*) algún/una; (*a certain number or amount*) *see phrases below*; (*unspecified*) algo de ♦ *pron* algunos/as; (*a bit*) algo ♦ *ad*: **~ 10 people** unas 10 personas; **~ children came** vinieron algunos niños; **~ people say that** ... hay quien dice que ...; **have ~ tea** tome té; **there's ~ milk in the fridge** hay leche en la nevera (*Sp*) *or* el frigo; **~ (of it) was left** quedaba algo; **could I have ~ of that cheese?** ¿me sirve un poco del queso aquel?; **I've got ~** (*books etc*) tengo algunos; (*milk, money etc*) tengo algo *or* un poco; **would you like ~?** ¿quieres algunos (*or* un poco)?; **after ~ time** pasado algún tiempo; **at ~ length** con mucho detalle; **in ~ form or other** en alguna que otra manera.
somebody [sum'bâdē] *pron* alguien; **~ or other** alguien.
someday [sum'dā] *ad* algún día.
somehow [sum'hou] *ad* de alguna manera; (*for some reason*) por una u otra razón.
someone [sum'wun] *pron* = **somebody**.
someplace [sum'plās] *ad* (*US*) = **somewhere**.
somersault [sum'ûrsôlt] *n* (*deliberate*) salto mortal; (*accidental*) vuelco ♦ *vi* dar un salto mortal; dar vuelcos.
something [sum'thing] *pron* algo ♦ *ad*: **he's ~ like me** es un poco como yo; **~ to do** algo que hacer; **it's ~ of a problem** es bastante problemático.

sometime [sum'tīm] *ad* (*in future*) algún día, en algún momento; **~ last month** durante el mes pasado; **I'll finish it ~** lo terminaré un día de éstos.
sometimes [sum'tīmz] *ad* a veces.
somewhat [sum'wut] *ad* algo.
somewhere [sum'wär] *ad* (*be*) en alguna parte; (*go*) a alguna parte; **~ else** (*be*) en otra parte; (*go*) a otra parte.
son [sun] *n* hijo.
sonar [sō'nár] *n* sonar *m*.
sonata [sənât'ə] *n* sonata.
song [sông] *n* canción *f*.
songwriter [sông'rī'tûr] *n* compositor(a) *m/f* de canciones.
sonic [sân'ik] *a* (*boom*) sónico.
son-in-law [sun'inlô] *n* yerno.
sonnet [sân'it] *n* soneto.
sonny [sun'ē] *n* (*col*) hijo.
soon [sōōn] *ad* pronto, dentro de poco; **~ afterwards** poco después; **very/quite ~** muy/bastante pronto; **how ~ can you be ready?** ¿cuánto tardas en prepararte?; **it's too ~ to tell** es demasiado pronto para saber; **see you ~!** ¡hasta pronto!; *see also* **as**.
sooner [sōō'nûr] *ad* (*time*) antes, más temprano; **I would ~ do that** preferiría hacer eso; **~ or later** tarde o temprano; **no ~ said than done** dicho y hecho; **the ~ the better** cuanto antes mejor; **no ~ had we left than ...** apenas nos habíamos marchado cuando ....
soot [sōōt] *n* hollín *m*.
soothe [sōōth] *vt* tranquilizar; (*pain*) aliviar.
soothing [sōō'thing] *a* (*ointment etc*) sedante; (*tone, words etc*) calmante, tranquilizante.
SOP *n abbr* = *standard operating procedure*.
sophisticated [səfis'tikātid] *a* sofisticado.
sophistication [səfis'tikā'shən] *n* sofisticación *f*.
sophomore [sâf'əmôr] *n* (*US*) estudiante *m/f* de segundo año.
soporific [sâpərif'ik] *a* soporífero.
sopping [sâp'ing] *a*: **~ (wet)** empapado.
soprano [səpran'ō] *n* soprano *f*.
sorbet [sôrbā'] *n* sorbete *m*.
sorcerer [sôr'sərûr] *n* hechicero.
sordid [sôr'did] *a* (*place etc*) sórdido; (*motive etc*) mezquino.
sore [sôr] *a* (*painful*) doloroso, que duele; (*offended*) resentido ♦ *n* llaga; **~ throat** dolor *m* de garganta; **my eyes are ~, I have ~ eyes** me duelen los ojos; **it's a ~ point** es un asunto delicado *or* espinoso.
sorely [sôr'lē] *ad*: **I am ~ tempted to (do it)** estoy muy tentado a (hacerlo).
soreness [sôr'nis] *n* dolor *m*.
sorrel [sôr'əl] *n* (*BOT*) acedera.
sorrow [sâr'ō] *n* pena, dolor *m*.
sorrowful [sâr'ōfəl] *a* afligido, triste.

sorrowfully [sår'ōfəlē] *ad* tristemente.
sorry [sår'ē] *a* (*regretful*) arrepentido; (*condition, excuse*) lastimoso; (*sight, failure*) triste; ~! ¡perdón!, ¡perdone!; **to feel ~ for sb** tener lástima a uno; **I feel ~ for him** me da lástima; **I'm ~ to hear that** ... me da pena *or* tristeza saber que ...; **to be ~ about sth** lamentar algo.
sort [sôrt] *n* clase *f*, género, tipo; (*make: of coffee, car etc*) marca ♦ *vt* (*also*: ~ **out**: *papers*) clasificar; (: *problems*) arreglar, solucionar; (*COMPUT*) clasificar; **what ~ do you want?** (*make*) ¿qué marca quieres?; **what ~ of car?** ¿qué tipo de coche?; **I shall do nothing of the ~** no haré eso bajo ningún concepto; **it's ~ of awkward** (*col*) es bastante difícil.
sortie [sôr'tē] *n* salida.
sorting office [sôr'ting ô'fis] *n* sala de batalla.
SOS [es'ō'es'] *n* SOS *m*.
so-so [sō'sō'] *ad* regular, así así.
soufflé [sōōflā'] *n* suflé *m*.
sought [sôt] *pt, pp of* **seek**.
sought-after [sôt'af'tûr] *a* solicitado, codiciado.
soul [sōl] *n* alma *f*; **God rest his ~** Dios le reciba en su seno *or* en su gloria; **I didn't see a ~** no vi a nadie; **the poor ~ had nowhere to sleep** el pobre no tenía dónde dormir.
soul-destroying [sōl'distroiing] *a* (*work*) deprimente.
soulful [sōl'fəl] *a* lleno de sentimiento.
soulmate [sōl'māt] *n* compañero/a del alma.
soul-searching [sōl'sûrching] *n*: **after much ~** después de pensarlo mucho, después de darle muchas vueltas.
sound [sound] *a* (*healthy*) sano; (*safe, not damaged*) en buen estado; (*valid: argument, policy, claim*) válido; (: *move*) acertado; (*dependable: person*) de fiar; (*sensible*) sensato, razonable ♦ *ad*: ~ **asleep** profundamente dormido ♦ *n* (*noise*) sonido, ruido; (*GEO*) estrecho ♦ *vt* (*alarm*) sonar; (*also*: ~ **out**: *opinions*) consultar, sondear ♦ *vi* sonar, resonar; (*fig: seem*) parecer; **to ~ like** sonar a; **to be of ~ mind** estar en su cabal juicio; **I don't like the ~ of it** no me gusta nada; **it ~s as if** ... parece que ....
    sound off *vi* (*col*): **to ~ off (about)** (*give one's opinions*) despotricar (contra).
sound barrier *n* barrera del sonido.
sound effects *npl* efectos *mpl* sonoros.
sound engineer *n* ingeniero/a del sonido.
sounding [soun'ding] *n* (*NAUT etc*) sondeo.
sounding board *n* (*MUS*) tablero sonoro; (*fig*) piedra de toque.
soundly [sound'lē] *ad* (*sleep*) profundamente; (*beat*) completamente.
soundproof [sound'prōōf] *a* insonorizado.
soundtrack [sound'trak] *n* (*of movie*)

banda sonora.
sound wave *n* (*PHYSICS*) onda sonora.
soup [sōōp] *n* (*thick*) sopa; (*thin*) caldo; **in the ~** (*fig*) en apuros ♦ *vt* **to ~ up** (*col*: *engine*) aumentar la potencia de.
soup kitchen *n* comedor *m* de beneficencia.
soup plate *n* plato sopero.
soupspoon [sōōp'spōōn] *n* cuchara sopera.
sour [sou'ûr] *a* agrio; (*milk*) cortado; **it's just ~ grapes!** (*fig*) ¡están verdes!; **to go** *or* **turn ~** (*milk*) cortarse; (*wine*) agriarse; (*fig: relationship, plans*) agriarse.
source [sôrs] *n* fuente *f*; **I have it from a reliable ~ that** ... sé de fuente fidedigna que ....
source language *n* (*COMPUT*) lenguaje *m* original.
south [south] *n* sur *m* ♦ *a* del sur ♦ *ad* al sur, hacia el sur; **(to the)** ~ **of** al sur de; **the S~ of France** el Sur de Francia; **to travel ~** viajar hacia el sur.
South Africa *n* África del Sur.
South African *a, n* sudafricano/a *m/f*.
South America *n* América del Sur, Sudamérica.
South American *a, n* sudamericano/a *m/f*.
southbound [south'bound'] *a* (con) rumbo al sur.
southeast [southēst'] *n* sudeste *m* ♦ *a* (*counties etc*) (del) sudeste.
Southeast Asia *n* Sudeste *m* asiático.
southerly [suth'ûrlē] *a* sur; (*from the south*) del sur.
southern [suth'ûrn] *a* del sur, meridional; **the ~ hemisphere** el hemisferio sur.
South Korea *n* Corea del Sur.
South Pole *n* Polo Sur.
South Sea Islands *npl*: **the ~** Oceanía.
South Seas *npl*: **the ~** los Mares del Sur.
southward(s) [south'wûrd(z)] *ad* hacia el sur.
southwest [southwest'] *n* suroeste *m*.
souvenir [sōōvənēr'] *n* recuerdo.
sovereign [såv'rin] *a, n* soberano/a *m/f*.
sovereignty [såv'rəntē] *n* soberanía.
soviet [sō'vēit] *a* soviético.
Soviet Union *n*: **the ~** la Unión Soviética.
sow *n* [sou] cerda, puerca ♦ *vt* [sō] (*pt* ~**ed**, *pp* ~**n** [sōn]) (*gen*) sembrar; (*spread*) esparcir.
soy [soi] *n* soja.
soya [soi'ə] (*Brit*) = **soy**.
soy bean *n* semilla de soja.
soy sauce *n* salsa de soja.
spa [spä] *n* balneario.
space [spās] *n* espacio; (*room*) sitio ♦ *vt* (*also*: ~ **out**) espaciar; **to clear a ~ for sth** hacer sitio para algo; **in a confined ~** en un espacio restringido; **in a short ~ of time** en poco *or* un corto espacio de tiempo; **(with)in the ~ of an hour/three**

generations en el espacio de una hora/tres generaciones.

space bar *n* (*on typewriter*) barra espaciadora.

spacecraft |späs'kraft| *n* nave *f* espacial, astronave *f*.

spaceman |späs'man| *n* astronauta *m*, cosmonauta *m*.

spaceship |späs'ship| *n* = **spacecraft**.

space shuttle *n* transbordador *m* espacial.

spacesuit |späs'sōōt| *n* traje *m* espacial.

spacewoman |späs'wōōmən| *n* astronauta, cosmonauta.

spacing |spä'sing| *n* espaciamiento.

spacious |spä'shəs| *a* amplio.

spade |späd| *n* (*tool*) pala, laya; **~s** *npl* (*CARDS*: *British*) picos *mpl*; (: *Spanish*) espadas *fpl*.

spadework |späd'wûrk| *n* (*fig*) trabajo preliminar.

spaghetti |spəgct'ē| *n* espaguetis *mpl*, fideos *mpl*.

Spain |spän| *n* España.

span |span| *pt of* **spin** ♦ *n* (*of bird*, *plane*) envergadura; (*of hand*) palmo; (*of arch*) luz *f*; (*in time*) lapso ♦ *vt* extenderse sobre, cruzar; (*fig*) abarcar.

Spaniard |span'yûrd| *n* español(a) *m/f*.

spaniel |span'yəl| *n* perro de aguas.

Spanish |span'ish| *a* español(a) ♦ *n* (*LING*) español *m*, castellano; **the ~** *npl* (*people*) los españoles; **~ omelette** tortilla española.

spank |spangk| *vt* zurrar.

spanner |span'ûr| *n* (*Brit*) llave *f* (inglesa).

spar |spâr| *n* palo, verga ♦ *vi* (*BOXING*) entrenarse (en el boxeo).

spare |spär| *a* de reserva; (*surplus*) sobrante, de más ♦ *n* (*part*) pieza de repuesto ♦ *vt* (*do without*) pasarse sin; (*afford to give*) tener de sobra; (*refrain from hurting*) perdonar; (*details etc*) ahorrar; **to ~** (*surplus*) sobrante, de sobra; **to ~ no expense** no escatimar gastos; **can you ~ (me) $10?** ¿puedes prestarme *or* darme 10 dólares?; **can you ~ the time?** ¿tienes tiempo?; **I've a few minutes to ~** tengo unos minutos libres; **there is no time to ~** no hay tiempo que perder.

spare part *n* pieza de repuesto.

spare room *n* cuarto para visitas.

spare time *n* ratos *mpl* de ocio, tiempo libre.

spare tire, (*Brit*) **spare tyre** *n* (*AUT*) neumático *or* llanta (*LAm*) de recambio.

spare wheel *n* (*AUT*) rueda de recambio.

sparing |spär'ing| *a*: **to be ~ with** ser parco en.

sparingly |spär'inglē| *ad* escasamente.

spark |spârk| *n* chispa; (*fig*) chispazo.

spark plug |spârk' plug| *n* bujía.

sparkle |spâr'kəl| *n* centelleo, destello ♦ *vi* centellear; (*shine*) relucir, brillar.

sparkling |spâr'kling| *a* centelleante; (*wine*) espumoso.

sparrow |spar'ō| *n* gorrión *m*.

sparse |spârs| *a* esparcido, escaso.

sparsely |spârs'lē| *ad* escasamente; **a ~ furnished room** un cuarto con pocos muebles.

spartan |spâr'tən| *a* (*fig*) espartano.

spasm |spaz'əm| *n* (*MED*) espasmo; (*fig*) arranque *m*, ataque *m*.

spasmodic |spazmâd'ik| *a* espasmódico.

spastic |spas'tik| *n* espástico/a.

spat |spat| *pt*, *pp of* **spit** ♦ *n* (*US*) riña.

spate |spät| *n* (*fig*): **~ of** torrente *m* de; **in ~** (*river*) crecido.

spatial |spä'shəl| *a* espacial.

spatter |spat'ûr| *vt*: **to ~ with** salpicar de.

spatula |spach'ələ| *n* espátula.

spawn |spôn| *vt* (*pej*) engendrar ♦ *vi* desovar, frezar ♦ *n* huevas *fpl*.

SPCA *n abbr* (*US*) = *Society for the Prevention of Cruelty to Animals*.

SPCC *n abbr* (*US*) = *Society for the Prevention of Cruelty to Children*.

speak, *pt* **spoke**, *pp* **spoken** |spēk, spōk, spō'kən| *vt* (*language*) hablar; (*truth*) decir ♦ *vi* hablar; (*make a speech*) intervenir; **to ~ one's mind** hablar claro *or* con franqueza; **to ~ to sb/of** *or* **about sth** hablar con uno/de *or* sobre algo; **to ~ at a conference/in a debate** hablar en un congreso/un debate; **he has no money to ~ of** no tiene mucho dinero que digamos; **~ing!** ¡al habla!; **~ up!** ¡habla más alto!

speak for *vt fus*: **to ~ for sb** hablar por *or* en nombre de uno; **that picture is already spoken for** (*in shop*) ese cuadro está reservado.

speaker |spē'kûr| *n* (*in public*) orador(a) *m/f*; (*also*: **loud~**) altavoz *m*; (*for stereo etc*) bafle *m*; (*POL*): **the S~** (*US*) él que preside la cámara de los representantes del Congreso; (*Brit*) el Presidente de la Cámara de los Comunes; **are you a Welsh ~?** ¿habla Ud galés?

speaking |spē'king| *a* hablante.

-speaking *suff* -hablante; **Spanish~ people** los hispanoparlantes.

spear |spi'ûr| *n* lanza; (*for fishing*) arpón *m* ♦ *vt* alancear; arponear.

spearhead |spēr'hcd| *vt* (*attack etc*) encabezar ♦ *n* (*MIL*) punta de lanza; (*fig*) vanguardia.

spearmint |spēr'mint| *n* (*BOT etc*) menta verde.

special |spcsh'əl| *a* especial; (*edition etc*) extraordinario; (*delivery*) urgente ♦ *n* (*train*) tren *m* especial; **on ~** (**offer**) en oferta especial; **nothing ~** nada de particular, nada extraordinario.

special agent *n* agente *m/f* especial.

special correspondent *n* corresponsal *m/f* especial.

special delivery *n* (*MAIL*): **by ~** por entrega urgente.

specialist [spesh'əlist] n especialista m/f; **a heart ~** (MED) un(a) especialista del corazón.

speciality [speshēal'ətē] n (Brit) = **specialty**.

specialize [spesh'əlīz] vi: **to ~ (in)** especializarse en.

specially [spesh'əlē] ad sobre todo, en particular.

special offer n (COMM) oferta especial, ganga.

special train n tren m especial.

specialty [spesh'əltē] n especialidad f.

species [spē'shēz] n especie f.

specific [spisif'ik] a específico.

specifically [spisif'iklē] ad (explicitly: state, warn) específicamente, expresamente; (especially: design, intend) especialmente.

specification [spesəfəkā'shən] n especificación f; **~s** npl (of car, machine) especificación fsg; (for building) plan msg detallado.

specify [spes'əfī] vt, vi especificar, precisar; **unless otherwise specified** salvo indicaciones contrarias.

specimen [spes'əmən] n ejemplar m; (MED: of urine) espécimen m; (: of blood) muestra.

specimen copy n ejemplar m de muestra.

specimen signature n muestra de firma.

speck [spek] n grano, mota.

speckled [spek'əld] a moteado.

specs [speks] npl (col) gafas fpl (Sp), anteojos mpl.

spectacle [spek'təkəl] n espectáculo.

spectacles [spek'təkəlz] npl (Brit) gafas fpl (Sp), anteojos mpl.

spectacular [spektak'yəlûr] a espectacular; (success) impresionante.

spectator [spek'tātûr] n espectador(a) m/f.

specter, (Brit) **spectre** [spek'tûr] n espectro, fantasma m.

spectra [spek'trə] npl of **spectrum**.

spectrum, pl **spectra** [spek'trəm, -trə] n espectro.

speculate [spek'yəlāt] vi especular; (try to guess): **to ~ about** especular sobre.

speculation [spekyəlā'shən] n especulación f.

speculative [spek'yəlātiv] a especulativo.

speculator [spek'yəlātûr] n especulador(a) m/f.

sped [sped] pt, pp of **speed**.

speech [spēch] n (faculty) habla; (formal talk) discurso; (words) palabras fpl; (manner of speaking) forma de hablar; (language) idioma m, lenguaje m.

speech day n (Brit SCOL) ≈ reparto de premios.

speech impediment n defecto del habla.

speechless [spēch'lis] a mudo, estupefacto.

speech therapy n logopedia.

speed [spēd] n (also: AUT, TECH: gear) ve-

locidad f; (haste) prisa; (promptness) rapidez f ♦ vi (pt, pp sped [sped]) (AUT: exceed ~ limit) conducir con exceso de velocidad; **at full** or **top ~** a máxima velocidad; **at a ~ of 70 km/h** a una velocidad de 70 km por hora; **five-~ transmission** una caja de cambios de 5 velocidades; **shorthand/typing ~** rapidez f en taquigrafía/mecanografía; **the years sped by** los años pasaron volando.

speed up vi acelerarse ♦ vt acelerar.

speedboat [spēd'bōt] n lancha motora.

speedily [spē'dilē] ad rápido, rápidamente.

speeding [spē'ding] n (AUT) exceso de velocidad.

speed limit n límite m de velocidad, velocidad f máxima.

speedometer [spēdâm'itûr] n velocímetro.

speed trap n (AUT) control m de velocidades.

speedway [spēd'wā] n (SPORT) pista de carrera.

speedy [spē'dē] a (fast) veloz, rápido; (prompt) pronto.

spell [spel] n (also: **magic ~**) encanto, hechizo; (period of time) rato, período; (turn) turno ♦ vt (pt, pp **~ed** or **spelt** [speld, spelt]) (also: **~ out**) deletrear; (fig) anunciar, presagiar; **to cast a ~ on sb** hechizar a uno; **he can't ~** no sabe escribir bien, sabe poco de ortografía; **can you ~ it for me?** ¿cómo se deletrea or se escribe?; **how do you ~ your name?** ¿cómo se escribe tu nombre?

spellbound [spel'bound] a embelesado, hechizado.

spelling [spel'ing] n ortografía.

spelling mistake n falta de ortografía.

spelt [spelt] pt, pp of **spell**.

spelunker [spēlung'kûr] n (US) espeleólogo/a.

spend, pt, pp **spent** [spend, spent] vt (money) gastar; (time) pasar; (life) dedicar; **to ~ time/money/effort on sth** gastar tiempo/dinero/energías en algo.

spending [spen'ding] n: **government ~** gastos mpl del gobierno.

spending money n dinero para gastos.

spending power n poder m de compra or adquisitivo.

spendthrift [spend'thrift] n derrochador(a) m/f, pródigo/a.

spent [spent] pt, pp of **spend** ♦ a (cartridge, bullets, match) usado.

sperm [spûrm] n esperma.

sperm whale n cachalote m.

spew [spyōō] vt vomitar, arrojar.

sphere [sfēr] n esfera.

spherical [sfär'ikəl] a esférico.

sphinx [sfingks] n esfinge f.

spice [spīs] n especia ♦ vt especiar.

spiciness [spī'sēnis] n lo picante.

spicy [spī'sē] a picante.

spick-and-span [spik'ənspan'] *a* aseado, (bien) arreglado.

spider [spī'dûr] *n* araña.

spider's web *n* telaraña.

spiel [spēl] *n* (*col*) rollo.

spike [spīk] *n* (*point*) punta; (*ZOOL*) pincho, púa; (*BOT*) espiga; (*ELEC*) pico parásito ♦ *vt*: **to ~ a quote** cancelar una cita; **~s** *npl* (*SPORT*) zapatillas *fpl* con clavos.

spiky [spī'kē] *a* (*bush, branch*) cubierto de púas; (*animal*) erizado.

spill, *pt, pp* **spilt** *or* **~ed** [spil, spilt, spild] *vt* derramar, verter; (*blood*) derramar ♦ *vi* derramarse; **to ~ the beans** (*col*) descubrir el pastel.

   spill out *vi* derramarse, desparramarse.

   spill over *vi* desbordarse.

spin [spin] *n* (*revolution of wheel*) vuelta, revolución *f*; (*AVIAT*) barrena; (*trip in car*) paseo (en coche) ♦ *vb* (*pt* **spun, span**, *pp* **spun** [spun, span]) *vt* (*wool etc*) hilar; (*wheel*) girar ♦ *vi* girar, dar vueltas; **the car spun out of control** el coche se descontroló dando vueltas.

   spin out *vt* alargar, prolongar.

spinach [spin'ich] *n* espinaca; (*as food*) espinacas *fpl*.

spinal [spī'nəl] *a* espinal.

spinal column *n* columna vertebral.

spinal cord *n* médula espinal.

spindly [spind'lē] *a* (*leg*) zanquivano.

spin-dry [spindrī'] *vt* centrifugar.

spin-dryer [spindrī'ûr] *n* (*Brit*) secador *m* centrífugo.

spine [spīn] *n* espinazo, columna vertebral; (*thorn*) espina.

spine-chilling [spīn'chiling] *a* de terror.

spineless [spīn'lis] *a* (*fig*) débil, flojo.

spinet [spin'it] *n* espineta.

spinning [spin'ing] *n* (*of thread*) hilado; (*art*) hilandería.

spinning top *n* peonza.

spinning wheel *n* rueca, torno de hilar.

spin-off [spin'ôf] *n* derivado, producto secundario.

spinster [spin'stûr] *n* soltera; (*pej*) solterona.

spiral [spī'rəl] *n* espiral *f* ♦ *a* en espiral ♦ *vi* (*prices*) dispararse; **the inflationary ~** la espiral inflacionista.

spiral staircase *n* escalera de caracol.

spire [spī'ûr] *n* aguja, chapitel *m*.

spirit [spir'it] *n* (*soul*) alma *f*; (*ghost*) fantasma *m*; (*attitude*) espíritu *m*; (*courage*) valor *m*, ánimo; **~s** *npl* (*drink*) alcohol *msg*, bebidas *fpl* alcohólicas; **in good ~s** alegre, de buen ánimo; **Holy S~** Espíritu *m* Santo; **community ~, public ~** civismo.

spirit duplicator *n* copiadora al alcohol.

spirited [spir'itid] *a* enérgico, vigoroso.

spirit level *n* nivel *m* de aire.

spiritual [spir'ichōōəl] *a* espiritual ♦ *n* (*also:*

Negro ~) canción *f* religiosa, espiritual *m*.

spiritualism [spir'ichōōəlizəm] *n* espiritualismo.

spit [spit] *n* (*for roasting*) asador *m*, espetón *m*; (*spittle*) esputo, escupitajo; (*saliva*) saliva ♦ *vi* (*pt, pp* **spat** [spat]) escupir; (*sound*) chisporrotear.

spite [spīt] *n* rencor *m*, ojeriza ♦ *vt* causar pena a, mortificar; **in ~ of** a pesar de, pese a.

spiteful [spīt'fəl] *a* rencoroso, malévolo.

spitting [spit'ing] *n*: **"~ prohibited"** "se prohíbe escupir" ♦ *a*: **to be the ~ image of sb** ser la viva imagen de uno.

spittle [spit'əl] *n* saliva, baba.

splash [splash] *n* (*sound*) chapoteo; (*of color*) mancha ♦ *vt* salpicar de ♦ *vi* (*also:* **~ around**) chapotear; **to ~ paint on the floor** manchar el suelo de pintura.

splashdown [splash'doun] *n* amaraje *m*, amerizaje *m*.

spleen [splēn] *n* (*ANAT*) bazo.

splendid [splen'did] *a* espléndido.

splendidly [splen'didlē] *ad* espléndidamente; **everything went ~** todo fue a las mil maravillas.

splendor, (*Brit*) **splendour** [splen'dûr] *n* esplendor *m*; (*of achievement*) brillo, gloria.

splice [splīs] *vt* empalmar.

splint [splint] *n* tablilla.

splinter [splin'tûr] *n* (*of wood*) astilla; (*in finger*) espigón *m* ♦ *vi* astillarse, hacer astillas.

splinter group *n* grupo disidente, facción *f*.

split [split] *n* hendedura, raja; (*fig*) división *f*; (*POL*) escisión *f* ♦ (*vb*: *pt, pp* **split**) *vt* partir, rajar; (*party*) dividir; (*work, profits*) repartir ♦ *vi* (*divide*) dividirse, escindirse; **to ~ the difference** partir la diferencia; **to do the ~s** esparrancarse; **to ~ sth down the middle** (*also fig*) dividir algo en dos.

   split up *vi* (*couple*) separarse; (*meeting*) acabarse.

split-level [split'lev'əl] *a* (*house*) dúplex.

split peas *npl* guisantes *mpl* secos.

split personality *n* personalidad *f* desdoblada.

split second *n* fracción *f* de segundo.

splitting [split'ing] *a* (*headache*) horrible.

splutter [splut'ûr] *vi* = **sputter**.

spoil, *pt, pp* **~ed** *or* **spoilt** [spoil, spoild, spoilt] *vt* (*damage*) dañar; (*ruin*) estropear, echar a perder; (*child*) mimar, consentir; (*ballot paper*) invalidar ♦ *vi*: **to be ~ing for a fight** estar con ganas de lucha, andar con ganas de pelea.

spoiled [spoild] *a* (*US: food: bad*) pasado, malo; (: *milk*) cortado.

spoiler [spoi'lûr] *n* (*AUT*) spoiler *m*.

spoils [spoilz] *npl* despojo *sg*, botín *msg*.

spoilsport [spoil'spôrt] *n* aguafiestas *m inv*.

spoilt [spoilt] *pt, pp of* **spoil** ♦ *a* (*Brit: child*) mimado, consentido; (: *ballot paper*) invalidado.

spoke [spōk] *pt of* **speak** ♦ *n* rayo, radio.

spoken [spō'kən] *pp of* **speak**.

spokesman [spōks'mən], **spokeswoman** [spōks'wŏōmən] *n* vocero *m/f*, portavoz *m/f*.

sponge [spunj] *n* esponja; (*CULIN: also:* ~ **cake**) bizcocho ♦ *vt* (*wash*) lavar con esponja ♦ *vi:* **to** ~ **off sb** vivir a costa de uno.

sponge bag *n* (*Brit*) esponjera.

sponge cake *n* bizcocho, pastel *m*.

sponger [spun'jûr] *n* gorrón/ona *m/f*.

spongy [spun'jē] *a* esponjoso.

sponsor [spän'sûr] *n* (*RADIO, TV*) patrocinador(a) *m/f*; (*for membership*) padrino/madrina; (*COMM*) fiador(a) *m/f* ♦ *vt* patrocinar; apadrinar; (*parliamentary bill*) apoyar, respaldar; (*idea etc*) presentar, promover; **I ~ed him at 25¢ a mile** (*in fundraising race*) me suscribí a darle 25 centavos la milla.

sponsorship [spän'sûrship] *n* patrocinio.

spontaneity [späntənē'itē] *n* espontaneidad *f*.

spontaneous [späntā'nēəs] *a* espontáneo.

spontaneously [späntā'nēəslē] *ad* espontáneamente.

spooky [spōō'kē] *a* (*col: place, atmosphere*) espeluznante, horripilante.

spool [spōōl] *n* carrete *m*; (*of sewing machine*) canilla.

spoon [spōōn] *n* cuchara.

spoon-feed [spōōn'fēd] *vt* dar de comer con cuchara a; (*fig*) tratar como a un niño a.

spoonful [spōōn'fōōl] *n* cucharada.

sporadic [spórad'ik] *a* esporádico.

sport [spórt] *n* deporte *m*; (*person*) buen(a) perdedor(a) *m/f*; (*amusement*) juego, diversión *f*; **indoor/outdoor ~s** deportes *mpl* en sala cubierta/al aire libre; **to say sth in** ~ decir algo en broma.

sporting [spór'ting] *a* deportivo; **to give sb a ~ chance** dar a uno su oportunidad.

sports car [spórts kâr] *n* coche *m* sport.

sport(s) coat *n* (*US*) chaqueta deportiva.

sports field *n* campo de deportes, centro deportivo (*LAm*).

sports jacket *n* (*Brit*) chaqueta deportiva.

sportsman [spórts'mən] *n* deportista *m*.

sportsmanship [spórts'mənship] *n* deportividad *f*.

sports pages *npl* páginas *fpl* deportivas.

sportswear [spórts'weûr] *n* trajes *mpl* de deporte *or* sport.

sportswoman [spórts'wŏōmən] *n* deportista.

sporty [spór'tē] *a* deportivo.

spot [spät] *n* sitio, lugar *m*; (*dot: on pattern*) punto, mancha; (*pimple*) grano; (*also:* **advertising** ~) spot *m*; (*small amount*): **a ~ of** un poquito de ♦ *vt* (*no-*

tice) notar, observar ♦ *a* (*COMM*) inmediatamente efectivo; **on the** ~ en el acto, acto seguido; (*in difficulty*) en un aprieto; **to do sth on the** ~ hacer algo en el acto; **to put sb on the** ~ poner a uno en un apuro; **to pay cash on the** ~ (*US*) pagar al contado.

spot check *n* reconocimiento rápido.

spotless [spät'lis] *a* nítido, perfectamente limpio.

spotlessly [spät'lislē] *ad:* ~ **clean** limpísimo.

spotlight [spät'līt] *n* foco, reflector *m*; (*AUT*) faro auxiliar.

spot price *n* precio de entrega inmediata.

spotted [spät'id] *a* (*pattern*) de puntos.

spotty [spät'ē] *a* (*face*) con granos.

spouse [spous] *n* cónyuge *m/f*.

spout [spout] *n* (*of jug*) pico; (*pipe*) caño ♦ *vi* chorrear.

sprain [sprān] *n* torcedura ♦ *vt:* **to** ~ **one's ankle** torcerse el tobillo.

sprang [sprang] *pt of* **spring**.

sprawl [spról] *vi* tumbarse ♦ *n:* **urban** ~ crecimiento urbano descontrolado; **to send sb ~ing** tirar a uno al suelo.

sprawling [spról'ing] *a* (*town*) desparramado.

spray [sprā] *n* rociada; (*of sea*) espuma; (*container*) atomizador *m*; (*of paint*) pistola rociadora; (*of flowers*) ramita ♦ *vt* rociar; (*crops*) regar ♦ *cpd* (*deodorant*) en atomizador.

spread [spred] *n* extensión *f*; (*of idea*) diseminación *f*; (*col: food*) comilona; (*PRESS, TYP: two pages*) plana ♦ *vb* (*pt, pp* **spread**) *vt* extender; diseminar; (*butter*) untar; (*wings, sails*) desplegar; (*scatter*) esparcir ♦ *vi* extenderse; diseminarse; untarse; desplegarse; esparcirse; **middle-age** ~ gordura de la mediana edad; **repayments will be** ~ **over 18 months** los pagos se harán a lo largo de 18 meses.

spread-eagled [spred'ēgəld] *a:* **to be** ~ estar despatarrado.

spreadsheet [spred'shēt] *n* (*COMPUT*) hoja de cálculo.

spree [sprē] *n:* **to go on a** ~ ir de juerga.

sprightly [sprīt'lē] *a* vivo, enérgico.

spring [spring] *n* (*season*) primavera; (*leap*) salto, brinco; (*coiled metal*) resorte *m*; (*of water*) fuente *f*, manantial *m*; (*bounciness*) elasticidad *f* ♦ *vb* (*pt* **sprang**, *pp* **sprung** [sprang, sprung]) *vi* (*arise*) brotar, nacer; (*leap*) saltar, brincar ♦ *vt:* **to** ~ **a leak** (*pipe etc*) empezar a hacer agua; **he sprang the news on me** de repente me soltó la noticia; **in (the)** ~ en (la) primavera; **to walk with a** ~ **in one's step** andar dando saltos *or* brincos; **to** ~ **into action** lanzarse a la acción.

spring up *vi* (*problem*) surgir.

springboard [spring'bórd] *n* trampolín *m*.

spring-clean [spring'klēn] *n* (*also:* ~**ing**)

limpieza general.
spring onion n cebolleta.
springtime [spring'tīm] n primavera.
springy [spring'ē] a elástico; (grass) muelle.
sprinkle [spring'kəl] vt (pour) rociar; **to ~ water on, ~ with water** rociar or salpicar de agua.
sprinkler [spring'klûr] n (for lawn) rociadera; (to put out fire) aparato de rociadura automática.
sprinkling [spring'kling] n (of water) rociada; (of salt, sugar) un poco de.
sprint [sprint] n esprint m ♦ vi (gen) correr a toda velocidad; (SPORT) esprintar; **the 200 meters ~** el esprint de 200 metros.
sprinter [sprin'tûr] n esprínter m/f, corredor(a) m/f.
sprocket [språk'it] n (on printer etc) rueda de espigas.
sprocket feed n avance m por rueda de espigas.
sprout [sprout] vi brotar, retoñar ♦ n: **(Brussels) ~s** npl coles fpl de Bruselas.
spruce [sprōōs] n (BOT) pícea ♦ a aseado, pulcro.
   spruce up vt (tidy) arreglar, acicalar; (smarten up: room etc) ordenar; **to ~ o.s up** arreglarse.
sprung [sprung] pp of **spring.**
spry [sprī] a ágil, activo.
SPUC n abbr (= Society for the Protection of Unborn Children) ≈ Federación f Española de Asociaciones Pro-vida.
spun [spun] pt, pp of **spin.**
spur [spûr] n espuela; (fig) estímulo, aguijón m ♦ vt (also: ~ **on**) estimular, incitar; **on the ~ of the moment** de improviso.
spurious [spyōōr'ēəs] a falso.
spurn [spûrn] vt desdeñar, rechazar.
spurt [spûrt] n chorro; (of energy) arrebato ♦ vi chorrear; **to put in** or **on a ~** (runner) acelerar; (fig: in work etc) hacer un gran esfuerzo.
sputter [sput'ûr] vi chisporrotear; (person) balbucear.
spy [spī] n espía m/f ♦ vi: **to ~ on** espiar a ♦ vt (see) divisar, lograr ver ♦ cpd (film, story) de espionaje.
spying [spī'ing] n espionaje m.
Sq. abbr (in address: = Square) Plza.
sq. abbr (MATH etc) = **square.**
squabble [skwâb'əl] n riña, pelea ♦ vi reñir, pelear.
squad [skwâd] n (MIL) pelotón m; (POLICE) brigada; (SPORT) equipo.
squad car n (POLICE) coche-patrulla m.
squadron [skwâd'rən] n (MIL) escuadrón m; (AVIAT, NAUT) escuadra.
squalid [skwâl'id] a vil, miserable.
squall [skwôl] n (storm) chubasco; (wind) ráfaga.
squalor [skwâl'ûr] n miseria.

squander [skwân'dûr] vt (money) derrochar, despilfarrar; (chances) desperdiciar.
square [skwär] n cuadro; (in town) plaza; (US: block) manzana, cuadra (LAm) ♦ a cuadrado ♦ vt (arrange) arreglar; (MATH) cuadrar; (reconcile): **can you ~ it with your conscience?** ¿cómo lo justifica? ♦ vi cuadrar, conformarse; **all ~** igual(es); **a ~ meal** una comida decente; **2 meters ~** 2 metros en cuadro; **1 ~ meter** un metro cuadrado; **to get one's accounts ~** dejar las cuentas claras; **I'll ~ it with him** (col) yo lo arreglo con él; **we're back to ~ one** (fig) hemos vuelto al principio.
square bracket n (TYP) corchete m.
squarely [skwär'lē] ad (fully) de lleno; (honestly, fairly) honradamente, justamente.
square root n raíz f cuadrada.
squash [skwâsh] n (vegetable) calabaza; (SPORT) squash m, frontenis m; (Brit: drink): **lemon/orange ~** zumo (Sp) or jugo (LAm) de limón/naranja ♦ vt aplastar.
squat [skwât] a achaparrado ♦ vi agacharse, sentarse en cuclillas; (on property) ocupar ilegalmente.
squatter [skwât'ûr] n persona que ocupa ilegalmente una casa.
squawk [skwôk] vi graznar.
squeak [skwēk] vi (hinge, wheel) chirriar, rechinar; (shoe, wood) crujir ♦ n (of hinge, wheel etc) chirrido, rechinamiento; (of shoes) crujir m; (of mouse etc) chillido.
squeal [skwēl] vi chillar, dar gritos agudos.
squeamish [skwē'mish] a delicado, remilgado.
squeeze [skwēz] n presión f; (of hand) apretón m; (COMM: credit ~) restricción f ♦ vt (lemon etc) exprimir; (hand, arm) apretar; **a ~ of lemon** unas gotas de limón; **to ~ past/under sth** colarse al lado de/por debajo de algo.
   squeeze out vt exprimir; (fig) excluir.
   squeeze through vi abrirse paso con esfuerzos.
squelch [skwelch] vi chapotear.
squid [skwid] n calamar m.
squiggle [skwig'əl] n garabato.
squint [skwint] vi guiñar los ojos ♦ n (MED) estrabismo; **to ~ at sth** mirar algo entornando los ojos.
squirm [skwûrm] vi retorcerse, revolverse.
squirrel [skwûr'əl] n ardilla.
squirt [skwûrt] vi salir a chorros.
Sr abbr = **senior, sister** (REL).
Sri Lanka [srē lángk'ə] n Sri Lanka m.
SRO abbr (US) = standing room only.
SS abbr (= steamship) M.V.
SSA n abbr (US: = Social Security Administration) ≈ Seguro Social.
SST n abbr (US) = supersonic transport.
St abbr (= saint) Sto./a.; (= street) c/.
stab [stab] n (with knife etc) puñalada; (of

pain) pinchazo; **to have a ~ at (doing) sth**
(*col*) intentar (hacer) algo ♦ *vt* apuñalar;
to ~ sb to death matar a uno a puñaladas.
stabbing |stab'ing| *n*: **there's been a ~** han
apuñalado a alguien ♦ *a* (*pain*) punzante.
stability |stəbil'ətē| *n* estabilidad *f*.
stabilization |stābiləzā'shən| *n* estabiliza-
ción *f*.
stabilize |stā'bəlīz| *vt* estabilizar ♦ *vi* estabi-
lizarse.
stabilizer |stā'bəlīzûr| *n* (*AVIAT, NAUT*) esta-
bilizador *m*.
stable |stā'bəl| *a* estable ♦ *n* cuadra, caba-
lleriza; **riding ~s** escuela hípica.
stableboy |stā'bəlboi| *n* mozo de cuadra.
staccato |stəkä'tō| *a, ad* staccato.
stack |stak| *n* montón *m*, pila; (*col*) mar *f* ♦
vt amontonar, apilar.
stacker |stak'ûr| *n* (*for printer*) apiladora.
stadium |stā'dēəm| *n* estadio.
staff |staf| *n* (*work force*) personal *m*, planti-
lla; (*Brit SCOL: also:* **teaching ~**) cuerpo
docente; (*stick*) bastón *m* ♦ *vt* proveer de
personal; **to be ~ed by Asians/women** tener una plantilla asiática/femenina.
Staffs *abbr* (*Brit*) = *Staffordshire*.
stag |stag| *n* ciervo, venado; (*Brit STOCK
EXCHANGE*) especulador *m* con nuevas
emisiones.
stage |stāj| *n* escena; (*point*) etapa;
(*platform*) plataforma; **the ~** el escenario,
el teatro ♦ *vt* (*play*) poner en escena, representar; (*organize*) montar, organizar;
(*fig: perform: recovery etc*) efectuar; **in
~s** por etapas; **in the early/final ~s** en las
primeras/últimas etapas; **to go through a
difficult ~** pasar una fase *or* etapa mala.
stagecoach |stāj'kōch| *n* diligencia.
stage door *n* entrada de artistas.
stagehand |stāj'hand| *n* tramoyista *m/f*.
stage-manage |stāj'man'ij| *vt* (*fig*) mani-
pular.
stage manager *n* director(a) *m/f* de escena.
stagger |stag'ûr| *vi* tambalear ♦ *vt* (*amaze*)
asombrar; (*hours, vacation*) escalonar.
staggering |stag'ûring| *a* (*amazing*) asom-
broso, pasmoso.
stagnant |stag'nənt| *a* estancado.
stagnate |stag'nāt| *vi* estancarse; (*fig:
economy, mind*) quedarse estancado.
stagnation |stagnā'shən| *n* estancamiento.
stag party *n* despedida de soltero.
staid |stād| *a* (*clothes*) serio, formal.
stain |stān| *n* mancha; (*coloring*) tintura ♦
vt manchar; (*wood*) teñir.
stained glass window |stānd' glas
win'dō| *n* vidriera de colores.
stainless |stān'lis| *a* (*steel*) inoxidable.
stain remover *n* quitamanchas *m inv*.
stair |stär| *n* (*step*) peldaño, escalón *m*; **~s**
npl escaleras *fpl*.
staircase |stär'kās|, **stairway** |stär'wā| *n*

escalera.
stairwell |stär'wel| *n* hueco *or* caja de la
escalera.
stake |stāk| *n* estaca, poste *m*; (*BETTING*)
apuesta ♦ *vt* (*bet*) apostar; (*also:* **~ out:**
area) estacar, cercar con estacas; **to be at
~** estar en juego; **to have a ~ in sth** tener
interés en algo; **to ~ a claim to (sth)** presentar reclamación por *or* reclamar (algo).
stalactite |stəlak'tīt| *n* estalactita.
stalagmite |stəlag'mīt| *n* estalagmita.
stale |stāl| *a* (*bread*) duro; (*food*) pasado.
stalemate |stāl'māt| *n* tablas *fpl* (por aho-
gado); **to reach ~** (*fig*) estancarse.
stalk |stôk| *n* tallo, caña ♦ *vt* acechar, cazar
al acecho; **to ~ off** irse airado.
stall |stôl| *n* (*in market*) puesto; (*in stable*)
casilla (de establo) ♦ *vt* (*AUT*) parar ♦ *vi*
(*AUT*) pararse; (*fig*) buscar evasivas; **~s**
npl (*Brit: in cinema, theater*) butacas *fpl*;
a newspaper ~ (*Brit*) un quiosco (de periódicos); **a flower ~** un puesto de flores.
stallholder |stôl'hōldûr| *n* dueño/a de un
puesto.
stallion |stal'yən| *n* semental *m*, garañón *m*.
stalwart |stôl'wûrt| *n* partidario/a incondi-
cional.
stamen |stā'mən| *n* estambre *m*.
stamina |stam'inə| *n* resistencia.
stammer |stam'ûr| *n* tartamudeo, balbuceo
♦ *vi* tartamudear, balbucir.
stamp |stamp| *n* sello, estampilla (*LAm*);
(*mark, also fig*) marca, huella; (*on document*) timbre *m* ♦ *vi* (*also:* **~ one's foot**)
patear ♦ *vt* patear, golpear con el pie;
(*letter*) poner sellos en; (*with rubber ~*)
marcar con sello; **~ed addressed envelope
(sae)** (*Brit*) sobre con las propias señas de
uno *y* con sello.
stamp out *vt* (*fire*) apagar con el pie;
(*crime, opposition*) acabar con.
stamp album *n* álbum *m* para sellos.
stamp collecting *n* filatelia.
stampede |stampēd'| *n* (*of cattle*) estampi-
da.
stamp machine *n* máquina (expendedo-
ra) de sellos.
stance |stans| *n* postura.
stand |stand| *n* (*attitude*) posición *f*, postu-
ra; (*for taxis*) parada; (*music ~*) atril *m*;
(*SPORT*) tribuna; (*at exhibition*) stand *m* ♦
vb (*pt, pp* **stood** |stŏŏd|) *vi* (*be*) estar,
encontrarse; (*be on foot*) estar de pie;
(*rise*) levantarse; (*remain*) quedar en pie ♦
vt (*place*) poner, colocar; (*tolerate, withstand*) aguantar, soportar; **to make a ~** resistir; (*fig*) mantener una postura firme; **to
take a ~ on an issue** adoptar una actitud
hacia una cuestión; **to ~ for parliament**
(*Brit*) presentarse (como candidato) a las
elecciones; **nothing ~s in our way** nada
nos lo impide; **to ~ still** quedarse inmóvil;
to let sth ~ as it is dejar algo como está;

as things ~ tal como están las cosas; **to** ~ **sb a drink/meal** invitar a uno a una copa/a comer; **the company will have to** ~ **the loss** la empresa tendrá que encargarse de las pérdidas; **I can't** ~ **him** no le aguanto, no le puedo ver; **to** ~ **guard** *or* **watch** (*MIL*) hacer guardia.

stand aside *vi* apartarse, mantenerse aparte.

stand by *vi* (*be ready*) estar listo ♦ *vt fus* (*opinion*) aferrarse a.

stand down *vi* (*withdraw*) ceder el puesto; (*MIL, LAW*) retirarse.

stand for *vt fus* (*signify*) significar; (*tolerate*) aguantar, permitir.

stand in for *vt fus* suplir a.

stand out *vi* (*be prominent*) destacarse.

stand up *vi* (*rise*) levantarse, ponerse de pie ♦ *vt* (*person*) dejar plantado.

stand up for *vt fus* defender.

stand up to *vt fus* hacer frente a.

stand-alone [stand'əlōn'] *a* (*COMPUT*) autónomo.

standard [stan'dûrd] *n* patrón *m*, norma; (*flag*) estandarte *m* ♦ *a* (*size etc*) normal, corriente, estándar; ~**s** *npl* (*morals*) valores *mpl* morales; **the gold** ~ (*COMM*) el patrón oro; **high/low** ~ de alto/bajo nivel; **below** *or* **not up to** ~ (*work*) de calidad inferior; **to be** *or* **come up to** ~ satisfacer los requisitos; **to apply a double** ~ aplicar un doble criterio.

standardization [standûrdəzā'shən] *n* normalización *f*.

standardize [stan'dûrdīz] *vt* estandarizar.

standard lamp *n* (*Brit*) lámpara de pie.

standard model *n* modelo stándard.

standard of living *n* nivel *m* de vida.

standard practice *n* norma, práctica común.

standard rate *n* tasa de imposición.

standard time *n* hora legal.

stand-by [stand'bī] *n* (*alert*) alerta, aviso; **to be on** ~ estar sobre aviso, estar preparado para salir; (*doctor*) estar listo para acudir.

stand-by generator *n* generador *m* de reserva.

stand-by passenger *n* (*AVIAT*) pasajero/a que está en la lista de espera.

stand-by ticket *n* (*AVIAT*) (billete *m*) standby *m*.

stand-in [stand'in] *n* suplente *m/f*; (*CINE-MA*) doble *m/f*.

standing [stan'ding] *a* (*upright*) derecho; (*on foot*) de pie, en pie; (*permanent: committee*) permanente; (: *rule*) fijo; (: *army*) permanente, regular; (*grievance*) constante, viejo ♦ *n* reputación *f*; (*duration*): **of 6 months'** ~ que lleva 6 meses; **of many years'** ~ que lleva muchos años; **he was given a** ~ **ovation** le aplaudieron mucho (de a pie); ~ **joke** motivo constante de bro-

ma; **a man of some** ~ un hombre de posición *or* categoría; **"no** ~**"** (*US AUT*) prohibido estacionarse.

standing order *n* (*Brit: at bank*) giro bancario; ~ **orders** *npl* (*MIL*) reglamento *sg* general.

standing room *n* sitio para estar de pie.

standoffish [standôf'ish] *a* reservado, poco afable.

standpat [stand'pat] *a* (*US*) inmovilista.

standpipe [stand'pīp] *n* tubo vertical.

standpoint [stand'point] *n* punto de vista.

standstill [stand'stil] *n*: **at a** ~ paralizado, en paro; **to come to a** ~ pararse, quedar paralizado.

stank [stangk] *pt of* **stink**.

staple [stā'pəl] *n* (*for papers*) grapa; (*product*) producto *or* artículo de primera necesidad ♦ *a* (*crop, industry, food etc*) básico ♦ *vt* engrapar.

stapler [stā'plûr] *n* grapadora.

star [stâr] *n* estrella; (*celebrity*) estrella, astro ♦ *vi*: **to** ~ **in** ser la estrella *or* el astro de; **four-**~ **hotel** hotel *m* de cuatro estrellas; **4-**~ **petrol** gasolina extra.

star attraction *n* atracción *f* principal.

starboard [stâr'bûrd] *n* estribor *m*.

starch [stârch] *n* almidón *m*.

starchy [stâr'chē] *a* (*food*) feculento.

stardom [stâr'dəm] *n* estrellato.

stare [stär] *n* mirada fija ♦ *vi*: **to** ~ **at** mirar fijo.

starfish [stâr'fish] *n* estrella de mar.

stark [stârk] *a* (*bleak*) severo, escueto; (*simplicity, color*) austero; (*reality, poverty, truth*) absoluto, puro ♦ *ad*: ~ **naked** en cueros, en pelotas.

starlet [stâr'lit] *n* (*CINEMA*) actriz *f* principiante.

starling [stâr'ling] *n* estornino.

starry [stâr'ē] *a* estrellado.

starry-eyed [stâr'ēīd] *a* (*gullible, innocent*) inocentón/ona, ingenuo; (*idealistic*) idealista; (*from wonder*) asombrado; (*from love*) enamoradísimo.

star-studded [stâr'studid] *a*: **a** ~ **cast** un elenco estelar.

start [stârt] *n* (*beginning*) principio, comienzo; (*departure*) salida; (*sudden movement*) salto, sobresalto; (*advantage*) ventaja ♦ *vt* empezar, comenzar; (*cause*) causar; (*found: business, newspaper*) establecer, fundar; (*engine*) poner en marcha ♦ *vi* (*begin*) comenzar, empezar; (*with fright*) asustarse, sobresaltarse; (*train etc*) salir; **to give sb a** ~ dar un susto a uno; **at the** ~ al principio; **for a** ~ en primer lugar; **to make an early** ~ ponerse en camino temprano; **the thieves had 3 hours'** ~ los ladrones llevaban 3 horas de ventaja; **to** ~ **a fire** provocar un incendio; **to** ~ **doing** *or* **to do sth** empezar a hacer algo; **to** ~ **(off) with** (*firstly*) para empezar; (*at the be-*

ginning) al principio.
start off *vi* empezar, comenzar; (*leave*) salir, ponerse en camino.
start over *vi* (*US*) volver a empezar.
start up *vi* comenzar; (*car*) arrancarse ♦ *vt* comenzar; (*car*) arrancar.
starter [står'tûr] *n* (*AUT*) arranque *m*; (*SPORT*: *official*) juez *m/f* de salida; (: *runner*) corredor(a) *m/f*; (*Brit CULIN*) entrada; **for ~s** en primer lugar.
starting price [står'ting prïs] *n* (*COMM*) precio inicial.
starting point [står'ting point] *n* punto de partida.
startle [står'təl] *vt* asustar, sobrecoger.
startling [står'ling] *a* alarmante.
starvation [stårvā'shən] *n* hambre *f*; (*MED*) inanición *f*.
starvation wages *npl* sueldo *sg* de hambre.
starve [stårv] *vi* pasar hambre; (*to death*) morir de hambre ♦ *vt* hacer pasar hambre; (*fig*) privar; **I'm starving** estoy muerto de hambre.
state [stāt] *n* estado; (*pomp*): **in ~** con mucha ceremonia ♦ *vt* (*say, declare*) afirmar; (*a case*) presentar, exponer; **~ of emergency** estado de excepción *or* emergencia; **~ of mind** estado de ánimo; **to lie in ~** (*corpse*) estar de cuerpo presente; **to be in a ~** estar agitado.
State Department *n* (*US*) Ministerio de Relaciones Exteriores.
state highway *n* (*US AUT*) ≈ carretera nacional.
stateless [stāt'lis] *a* desnacionalizado.
stately [stāt'lē] *a* majestuoso, imponente.
statement [stāt'mənt] *n* afirmación *f*; (*LAW*) declaración *f*; (*COMM*) estado; **official ~** informe *m* oficial; **~ of account, bank ~** estado de cuenta.
state-of-the-art [stāt'əvthēårt] *a* (*technology etc*) de punta.
state-owned [stāt'ōnd'] *a* estatal, del estado.
States [stāts] *npl*: **the ~** los Estados Unidos.
statesman [stāts'mən] *n* estadista *m*.
statesmanship [stāts'mənship] *n* habilidad *f* política, arte *m* de gobernar.
static [stat'ik] *n* (*RADIO*) parásitos *mpl* ♦ *a* estático.
static electricity *n* estática.
station [stā'shən] *n* (*gen*) estación *f*; (*place*) puesto, sitio; (*RADIO*) emisora; (*rank*) posición *f* social; (*MIL*) colocar, situar; (*MIL*) apostar; **action ~s!** ¡a los puestos de combate!; **to be ~ed in** (*MIL*) estar estacionado en.
stationary [stā'shənärē] *a* estacionario, fijo.
stationer [stā'shənûr] *n* papelero/a.
stationer's (shop) *n* (*Brit*) papelería.
stationery [stā'shənärē] *n* (*writing paper*) papel *m* de escribir; (*writing materials*)

artículos *mpl* de escritorio.
station master *n* (*RAIL*) jefe *m* de estación.
station wagon *n* (*US*) furgoneta.
statistic [stətis'tik] *n* estadística.
statistical [stətis'tikəl] *a* estadístico.
statistics [stətis'tiks] *n* (*science*) estadística.
statue [stach'ōō] *n* estatua.
statuette [stachōōet'] *n* figurilla.
stature [stach'ûr] *n* estatura; (*fig*) talla.
status [stā'təs] *n* condición *f*, estado; (*reputation*) reputación *f*, estatus *m*; **the ~ quo** el statu quo.
status line *n* (*COMPUT*) línea de situación *or* de estado.
status symbol *n* símbolo de prestigio.
statute [stach'ōōt] *n* estatuto, ley *f*.
statute book *n* código de leyes.
statutory [stach'ōōtôrē] *a* estatutario; **~ meeting** junta ordinaria.
staunch [stônch] *a* leal, incondicional ♦ *vt* (*flow, blood*) restañar.
stave [stāv] *vt*: **to ~ off** (*attack*) rechazar; (*threat*) evitar.
stay [stā] *n* (*period of time*) estancia; (*LAW*): **~ of execution** aplazamiento de una sentencia ♦ *vi* (*remain*) quedar(se); (*as guest*) hospedarse; **to ~ put** seguir en el mismo sitio; **to ~ the night/5 days** pasar la noche/estar 5 días.
stay behind *vi* quedar atrás.
stay in *vi* (*at home*) quedarse en casa.
stay on *vi* quedarse.
stay out *vi* (*of house*) no volver a casa; (*strikers*) no volver al trabajo.
stay up *vi* (*at night*) velar, no acostarse.
staying power [stā'ing pou'ûr] *n* resistencia, aguante *m*.
STD *n abbr* (*Brit*: = *subscriber trunk dialling*) servicio de conferencias automáticas; (= *sexually transmitted disease*) enfermedad *f* venérea.
stead [sted] *n*: **in sb's ~** en lugar de uno.
steadfast [sted'fast] *a* firme, resuelto.
steadily [sted'ilē] *ad* (*firmly*) firmemente; (*unceasingly*) sin parar; (*fixedly*) fijamente; (*walk*) normalmente; (*drive*) a velocidad constante.
steady [sted'ē] *a* (*fixed*) firme, fijo; (*regular*) regular; (*boyfriend etc*) formal, fijo; (*person, character*) sensato, juicioso ♦ *vt* (*hold*) mantener firme; (*stabilize*) estabilizar; (*nerves*) calmar; **to ~ o.s. on** *or* **against sth** afirmarse en algo.
steak [stāk] *n* (*gen*) filete *m*; (*beef*) bistec *m*.
steal, *pt* **stole**, *pp* **stolen** [stēl, stōl, stō'lən] *vt, vi* robar.
steal away, steal off *vi* marcharse furtivamente, escabullirse.
stealth [stelth] *n*: **by ~** a escondidas, sigilosamente.
stealthy [stel'thē] *a* cauteloso, sigiloso.

steam [stēm] *n* vapor *m*; (*mist*) vaho, humo ♦ *vt* (*CULIN*) cocer al vapor ♦ *vi* echar vapor; (*ship*): **to ~ along** avanzar, ir avanzando; **under one's own ~** (*fig*) por sus propios medios *or* propias fuerzas; **to run out of ~** (*fig: person*) quedar(se) agotado; **to let off ~** (*fig*) desahogarse.

steam up *vi* (*window*) empañarse; **to get ~ed up about sth** (*fig*) volverse loco por algo.

steam engine *n* máquina de vapor.

steamer [stē'mûr] *n* (buque *m* de) vapor *m*; (*CULIN*) vaporera.

steam iron *n* plancha de vapor.

steamroller [stēm'rōlûr] *n* apisonadora.

steamship [stēm'ship] *n* (buque *m* de) vapor *m*.

steamy [stē'mē] *a* (*room*) lleno de vapor; (*window*) empañado.

steel [stēl] *n* acero ♦ *a* de acero.

steel band *n* banda de percusión del Caribe.

steel industry *n* industria siderúrgica.

steel mill *n* fábrica de acero.

steelworks [stēl'wûrks] *n* acería.

steely [stē'lē] *a* (*determination*) inflexible; (*gaze*) duro; (*eyes*) penetrante; **~ grey** gris *m* metálico.

steelyard [stēl'yârd] *n* romana.

steep [stēp] *a* escarpado, abrupto; (*stair*) empinado; (*price*) exorbitante, excesivo ♦ *vt* empapar, remojar.

steeple [stē'pəl] *n* aguja, campanario.

steeplechase [stē'pəlchās] *n* carrera de obstáculos.

steeplejack [stē'pəljak] *n* reparador(a) *m/f* de chimeneas *or* de campanarios.

steer [stēr] *vt* (*car*) conducir (*Sp*), manejar (*LAm*); (*person*) dirigir ♦ *vi* conducir; **to ~ clear of sb/sth** (*fig*) esquivar a uno/ evadir algo.

steering [stēr'ing] *n* (*AUT*) dirección *f*.

steering committee *n* comisión *f* directiva.

steering wheel *n* volante *m*.

stellar [stel'ûr] *a* estelar.

stem [stem] *n* (*of plant*) tallo; (*of glass*) pie *m*; (*of pipe*) cañón *m* ♦ *vt* detener; (*blood*) restañar.

stem from *vt fus* ser consecuencia de.

stench [stench] *n* hedor *m*.

stencil [sten'səl] *n* (*typed*) cliché *m*, clisé *m*; (*lettering*) plantilla ♦ *vt* hacer un cliché de.

stenographer [stənâg'rəfûr] *n* (*US*) taquígrafo/a.

step [step] *n* paso; (*sound*) paso, pisada; (*stair*) peldaño, escalón *m* ♦ *vi*: **to ~ forward** dar un paso adelante; **~ by ~** paso a paso; (*fig*) poco a poco; **to keep in ~ (with)** llevar el paso de; (*fig*) llevar el paso de, estar de acuerdo con; **to be in/out of ~ with** estar acorde con/estar en disonancia con; **to take ~s to solve a problem** tomar medidas para resolver un problema.

step down *vi* (*fig*) retirarse.

step in *vi* entrar; (*fig*) intervenir.

step off *vt fus* bajar de.

step on *vt fus* pisar.

step over *vt fus* pasar por encima de.

step up *vt* (*increase*) aumentar.

stepbrother [step'bruthûr] *n* hermanastro.

stepdaughter [step'dôtûr] *n* hijastra.

stepfather [step'fâthûr] *n* padrastro.

stepladder [step'ladûr] *n* escalera doble *or* de tijera.

stepmother [step'muthûr] *n* madrastra.

stepping stone [step'ingstōn] *n* pasadera.

stepsister [step'sistûr] *n* hermanastra.

stepson [step'sun] *n* hijastro.

stereo [stär'ēō] *n* estéreo ♦ *a* (*also*: **~phonic**) estéreo, estereofónico; **in ~** en estéreo.

stereotype [stär'ēətīp] *n* estereotipo ♦ *vt* estereotipar.

sterile [stär'əl] *a* estéril.

sterilization [stärələzā'shən] *n* esterilización *f*.

sterilize [stär'əlīz] *vt* esterilizar.

sterling [stûr'ling] *a* (*silver*) de ley ♦ *n* (*ECON*) (libras *fpl*) esterlinas *fpl*; **a pound ~** una libra esterlina; **he is of ~ character** tiene un carácter excelente.

stern [stûrn] *a* severo, austero ♦ *n* (*NAUT*) popa.

sternum [stûr'nəm] *n* esternón *m*.

steroid [stär'oid] *n* esteroide *m*.

stethoscope [steth'əskōp] *n* estetoscopio.

stew [stoo] *n* cocido, estofado, guisado (*LAm*) ♦ *vt*, *vi* estofar, guisar; (*fruit*) cocer; **~ed fruit** compota de fruta.

steward [stoo'ûrd] *n* (*Brit: gen*) camarero; (*shop ~*) enlace *m/f* sindical.

stewardess [stoo'ûrdis] *n* azafata.

stewing steak [stoo'ing stāk] *n* (*Brit*) = **stew meat**.

stew meat *n* (*US*) carne *f* de vaca.

stewpan [stoo'pan] *n* cazuela.

St. Ex. *abbr* = **stock exchange**.

stg *abbr* (= **sterling**) ester.

stick [stik] *n* palo; (*as weapon*) porra; (*walking ~*) bastón *m* ♦ *vb* (*pt*, *pp* **stuck** [stuk]) *vt* (*glue*) pegar; (*col: put*) meter; (: *toleráte*) aguantar, soportar ♦ *vi* pegarse; (*come to a stop*) quedarse parado; (*get jammed: door, lift*) atascarse; **to ~ to** (*word, principles*) atenerse a, ser fiel a; (*promise*) cumplir; **it stuck in my mind** se me quedó grabado; **to ~ sth into** clavar *or* hincar algo en.

stick around *vi* (*col*) quedarse.

stick out *vi* sobresalir ♦ *vt*: **to ~ it out** (*col*) aguantar.

stick up *vi* sobresalir.

stick up for *vt fus* defender.

sticker [stik'ûr] *n* (*label*) etiqueta engomada; (*with slogan*) pegatina.

sticking plaster [stik'ing plas'tûr] *n* (*Brit*) esparadrapo.

stickler [stik'lûr] *n*: **to be a ~ for** insistir mucho en.

stick-up [stik'up] *n* asalto, atraco.

sticky [stik'ē] *a* pegajoso; (*label*) engomado; (*fig*) difícil.

stiff [stif] *a* rígido, tieso; (*hard*) duro; (*difficult*) difícil; (*person*) inflexible; (*price*) exorbitante; **to have a ~ neck/ back** tener tortícolis/dolor de espalda; **the door's ~** la puerta está atrancada.

stiffen [stif'ən] *vt* hacer más rígido; (*limb*) entumecer ♦ *vi* endurecerse; (*grow stronger*) fortalecerse.

stiffness [stif'nis] *n* rigidez *f*, tiesura.

stifle [stī'fəl] *vt* ahogar, sofocar.

stifling [stī'fling] *a* (*heat*) sofocante, bochornoso.

stigma, *pl* (*BOT, MED, REL*) ~**ta**, (*fig*) ~**s** [stig'mə, stigmá'tə] *n* estigma *m*.

stile [stīl] *n* escalera (*para pasar una cerca*).

stiletto [stilet'ō] *n* (*Brit: also:* ~ **heel**) tacón *m* de aguja.

still [stil] *a* inmóvil, quieto; (*orange juice etc*) sin gas ♦ *ad* (*up to this time*) todavía; (*even*) aún; (*nonetheless*) sin embargo, aun así ♦ *n* (*CINEMA*) foto *f* fija; **keep ~!** ¡estate quieto!, ¡no te muevas!; **he ~ hasn't arrived** todavía no ha llegado.

stillborn [stil'bôrn] *a* nacido muerto.

still life *n* naturaleza muerta.

stilt [stilt] *n* zanco; (*pile*) pilar *m*, soporte *m*.

stilted [stil'tid] *a* afectado.

stimulant [stim'yələnt] *n* estimulante *m*.

stimulate [stim'yəlāt] *vt* estimular.

stimulating [stim'yəlāting] *a* estimulante.

stimulation [stimyəlā'shən] *n* estímulo.

stimulus, *pl* **-li** [stim'yələs, -lī] *n* estímulo, incentivo.

sting [sting] *n* (*wound*) picadura; (*pain*) escozor *m*, picazón *m*; (*col: confidence trick*) timo ♦ *vb* (*pt, pp* **stung** [stung]) *vt* picar ♦ *vi* picar, escocer; **my eyes are ~ing** los ojos me pican *or* escuecen.

stingy [stin'jē] *a* tacaño.

stink [stingk] *n* hedor *m*, tufo ♦ *vi* (*pt* **stank**, *pp* **stunk** [stangk, stungk]) heder, apestar.

stinking [sting'king] *a* hediondo, fétido; (*fig: col*) horrible.

stint [stint] *n* tarea, destajo; **to do one's ~ at sth** hacer su parte (de algo), hacer lo que corresponde (de algo) ♦ *vi*: **to ~ on** escatimar.

stipend [stī'pend] *n* salario, remuneración *f*.

stipulate [stip'yəlāt] *vt* estipular.

stipulation [stipyəlā'shən] *n* estipulación *f*.

stir [stûr] *n* (*fig: agitation*) conmoción *f* ♦ *vt* (*tea etc*) remover; (*fire*) atizar; (*move*) agitar; (*fig: emotions*) conmover ♦ *vi* moverse; **to give sth a ~** remover algo; **to cause a ~** causar conmoción *or* sensación.

stir up *vt* excitar; (*trouble*) fomentar.

stirrup [stûr'əp] *n* estribo.

stitch [stich] *n* (*SEWING*) puntada; (*KNITTING*) punto; (*MED*) punto (de sutura); (*pain*) punzada ♦ *vt* coser; (*MED*) suturar.

stoat [stōt] *n* armiño.

stock [stâk] *n* (*COMM: reserves*) existencias *fpl*, stock *m*; (*: selection*) surtido; (*AGR*) ganado, ganadería; (*CULIN*) caldo; (*fig: lineage*) estirpe *f*, cepa; (*FINANCE*) capital *m*; (*: shares*) acciones *fpl*; (*RAIL: rolling ~*) material *m* rodante ♦ *a* (*COMM: goods, size*) normal, de serie; (*fig: reply etc*) clásico, trillado; (*: greeting*) acostumbrado ♦ *vt* (*have in ~*) tener existencias de; (*supply*) proveer, abastecer; **in ~** en existencia *or* almacén; **to have sth in ~** tener existencias de algo; **out of ~** agotado; **to take ~ of** (*fig*) asesorar, examinar; ~**s** *npl* (*HISTORY: punishment*) cepo *sg*; ~**s and shares** acciones y valores; **government ~** papel *m* del Estado.

stock up with *vt fus* abastecerse de.

stockbroker [stâk'brōkûr] *n* agente *m/f or* corredor(a) *m/f* de bolsa.

stock control *n* (*COMM*) control *m* de existencias.

stock cube *n* (*Brit*) pastilla *or* cubito de caldo.

stock exchange *n* bolsa.

stockholder [stâk'hōldûr] *n* (*US*) accionista *m/f*.

Stockholm [stâk'hōm] *n* Estocolmo.

stocking [stâk'ing] *n* media.

stock-in-trade [stâk'intrād'] *n* (*tools etc*) herramientas *fpl*; (*stock*) existencia de mercancías; (*fig*): **it's his ~** es su especialidad.

stockist [stâk'ist] *n* (*Brit*) distribuidor(a) *m/f*.

stock market *n* bolsa (de valores).

stock phrase *n* vieja frase *f*.

stockpile [stâk'pīl] *n* reserva ♦ *vt* acumular, almacenar.

stockroom [stâk'rōōm] *n* almacén *m*, depósito.

stocktaking [stâk'tāking] *n* (*Brit COMM*) inventario, balance *m*.

stocky [stâk'ē] *a* (*strong*) robusto; (*short*) achaparrado.

stodgy [stâj'ē] *a* indigesto, pesado.

stoical [stō'ikəl] *a* estoico.

stoke [stōk] *vt* atizar.

stole [stōl] *pt of* **steal** ♦ *n* estola.

stolen [stō'lən] *pp of* **steal**.

stolid [stâl'id] *a* (*person*) imperturbable, impasible.

stomach [stum'ək] *n* (*ANAT*) estómago; (*belly*) vientre *m* ♦ *vt* tragar, aguantar.

stomachache [stum'əkāk] *n* dolor *m* de

estómago.
stomach pump n bomba gástrica.
stomach ulcer n úlcera de estómago.
stomp [ståmp] vi: **to ~ in/out** entrar/salir con pasos ruidosos.
stone [stōn] n piedra; (in fruit) hueso; (Brit: weight) = 6.348kg; 14 pounds ♦ a de piedra ♦ vt apedrear; **within a ~'s throw of the station** a tiro de piedra or a dos pasos de la estación.
Stone Age n: **the ~** la Edad de Piedra.
stone-cold [stōn'kōld'] a helado.
stoned [stōnd] a (col: drunk) trompa, borracho, colocado.
stone-deaf [stōn'def'] a sordo como una tapia.
stonemason [stōn'māsən] n albañil m.
stonework [stōn'wûrk] n (art) cantería.
stony [stō'nē] a pedregoso; (glance) glacial.
stood [stood] pt, pp of **stand**.
stool [stool] n taburete m.
stool pigeon n (US: col: informer) delator(a) m/f, denunciador(a) m/f.
stoop [stoop] vi ser cargado de espaldas; (bend) inclinarse, encorvarse; **to ~ to (doing) sth** rebajarse a (hacer) algo.
stop [ståp] n parada, alto; (in punctuation) punto ♦ vt parar, detener; (break off) suspender; (block) tapar, cerrar; (prevent) impedir; (tooth) empastar; (also: **put a ~ to**) poner término a ♦ vi pararse, detenerse; (end) acabarse; **to ~ doing sth** dejar de hacer algo; **to ~ sb (from) doing sth** impedir a uno hacer algo; **to ~ dead** pararse en seco; **~ it!** ¡basta ya!, ¡párate! (LAm).
stop by vi pasar por.
stop off vi interrumpir el viaje.
stop up vt (hole) tapar.
stopcock [ståp'kåk] n llave f de paso.
stopgap [ståp'gap] n interino; (person) sustituto/a; (measure) medida provisoria ♦ cpd (situation) provisional.
stoplights [ståp'līts] npl (AUT) luces fpl de detención.
stopover [ståp'ōvûr] n parada intermedia; (AVIAT) escala.
stoppage [ståp'ij] n (strike) paro; (temporary stop) interrupción f; (of pay) suspensión f; (blockage) obstrucción f.
stopper [ståp'ûr] n tapón m.
stop press n noticias fpl de última hora.
stopwatch [ståp'wåch] n cronómetro.
storage [stôr'ij] n almacenaje m; (COMPUT) almacenamiento.
storage capacity n espacio de almacenaje.
storage heater n calentador m, acumulador m.
store [stôr] n (stock) provisión f; (depot; Brit: large shop) almacén m; (US) tienda; (reserve) reserva, repuesto ♦ vt (gen, COMPUT) almacenar; (keep) guardar; (in filing

system) archivar; **~s** npl víveres mpl; **who knows what is in ~ for us** quién sabe lo que nos espera; **to set great/little ~ by sth** dar mucha/poca importancia a algo, valorar mucho/poco algo.
store up vt acumular.
storehouse [stôr'hous] n almacén m, depósito.
storekeeper [stôr'kēpúr] n tendero/a.
storeroom [stôr'room] n despensa.
storey [stôr'ē] n (Brit) piso.
stork [stôrk] n cigüeña.
storm [stôrm] n tormenta; (wind) vendaval m; (fig) tempestad f ♦ vi (fig) rabiar ♦ vt tomar por asalto, asaltar; **to take a town by ~** (MIL) tomar una ciudad por asalto.
storm cloud n nubarrón m.
storm door n contrapuerta.
stormy [stôr'mē] a tempestuoso.
story [stôr'ē] n historia; (PRESS) artículo; (joke) cuento, chiste m; (plot) argumento; (lie) cuento; (US: floor) piso.
storybook [stôr'ēbook] n libro de cuentos.
storyteller [stôr'ētelûr] n cuentista m/f.
stout [stout] a (strong) sólido; (fat) gordo, corpulento ♦ n cerveza negra.
stove [stōv] n (for cooking) cocina; (for heating) estufa; **gas/electric ~** cocina de gas/eléctrica.
stow [stō] vt meter, poner; (NAUT) estibar.
stowaway [stō'əwā] n polizón/ona m/f.
straddle [strad'əl] vt montar a horcajadas.
straggle [strag'əl] vi (wander) vagar en desorden; (lag behind) rezagarse.
straggler [strag'lûr] n rezagado/a.
straggling [strag'ling], **straggly** [strag'lē] a (hair) desordenado.
straight [strāt] a (direct) recto, derecho; (plain, uncomplicated) sencillo; (frank) franco, directo; (in order) en orden; (continuous) continuo; (THEATER: part, play) serio; (person: conventional) recto, convencional; (: heterosexual) heterosexual; (drink) puro ♦ ad derecho, directamente; (drink) sin mezcla; **to put or get sth ~** dejar algo en claro; **10 ~ wins** 10 victorias seguidas; **to be (all) ~** (tidy) estar en orden; (clarified) estar claro; **I went ~ home** (me) fui directamente a casa; **~ away** (at once) en seguida.
straighten [strā'tən] vt (also: **~ out**) enderezar, poner derecho; **to ~ things out** poner las cosas en orden.
straight-faced [strāt'fāst] a serio ♦ ad sin mostrar emoción, impávido.
straightforward [strātfôr'wûrd] a (simple) sencillo; (honest) honrado, franco.
strain [strān] n (gen) tensión f; (TECH) esfuerzo; (MED) torcedura; (breed) raza; (lineage) linaje m; (of virus) variedad f ♦ vt (back etc) torcerse; (tire) cansar; (stretch) estirar; (filter) filtrar; (meaning) tergiversar ♦ vi esforzarse; **~s** npl (MUS)

son *m*; **she's under a lot of** ~ está bajo mucha tensión.

strained [strānd] *a* (*muscle*) torcido; (*laugh*) forzado; (*relations*) tenso.

strainer [strā'nûr] *n* colador *m*.

strait [strāt] *n* (*GEO*) estrecho; **to be in dire** ~**s** (*fig*) estar en un gran aprieto.

straitjacket [strāt'jakit] *n* camisa de fuerza.

strait-laced [strāt'lāst] *a* mojigato, gazmoño.

strand [strand] *n* (*of thread*) hebra; (*of hair*) trenza; (*of rope*) ramal *m*.

stranded [stran'did] *a* (*person*: *without money*) desamparado; (: *without transport*) colgado.

strange [strānj] *a* (*not known*) desconocido; (*odd*) extraño, raro.

stranger [strān'jûr] *n* desconocido/a; (*from another area*) forastero/a; **I'm a** ~ **here** no soy de aquí.

strangle [strang'gəl] *vt* estrangular.

stranglehold [strang'gəlhōld] *n* (*fig*) dominio completo.

strangulation [stranggyəlā'shən] *n* estrangulación *f*.

strap [strap] *n* correa; (*of slip, dress*) tirante *m* ♦ *vt* atar con correa.

straphanging [strap'hanging] *n* viajar *m* de pie *or* parado (*LAm*).

strapless [strap'lis] *a* (*bra, dress*) sin tirantes.

strapping [strap'ing] *a* robusto, fornido.

Strasbourg [stras'bûrg] *n* Estrasburgo.

strata [strā'tə] *npl of* **stratum**.

stratagem [strat'əjəm] *n* estratagema.

strategic [strətē'jik] *a* estratégico.

strategy [strat'ijē] *n* estrategia.

stratum, *pl* **strata** [strā'təm, strā'tə] *n* estrato.

straw [stró] *n* paja; (*drinking* ~) caña, pajita; **that's the last** ~! ¡eso es el colmo!

strawberry [stró'bärē] *n* fresa, frutilla (*LAm*).

stray [strā] *a* (*animal*) extraviado; (*bullet*) perdido; (*scattered*) disperso ♦ *vi* extraviarse, perderse; (*wander*: *walker*) vagar, ir sin rumbo fijo; (: *speaker*) desvariar.

streak [strēk] *n* raya; (*fig*: *of madness etc*) vena ♦ *vt* rayar ♦ *vi*: **to** ~ **past** pasar como un rayo; **to have** ~**s in one's hair** tener vetas en el pelo; **a winning/losing** ~ una racha de buena/mala suerte.

streaky [strē'kē] *a* rayado.

stream [strēm] *n* riachuelo, arroyo; (*jet*) chorro; (*flow*) corriente *f*; (*of people*) oleada ♦ *vt* (*Brit SCOL*) dividir en grupos por habilidad ♦ *vi* correr, fluir; **to** ~ **in/out** (*people*) entrar/salir en tropel; **against the** ~ a contracorriente.

streamer [strē'mûr] *n* serpentina.

streamline [strēm'līn] *vt* aerodinamizar; (*fig*) racionalizar.

streamlined [strēm'līnd] *a* aerodinámico.

street [strēt] *n* calle *f* ♦ *a* callejero; **the back** ~**s** las callejuelas; **to walk the** ~**s** (*homeless*) estar sin vivienda; (*as prostitute*) ser de la vida.

streetcar [strēt'kár] *n* (*US*) tranvía *m*.

streetlight [strēt'līt] *n* farol *m*.

street lighting *n* alumbrado público.

street market *n* mercado callejero.

street plan *n* plano callejero.

streetsweeper [strēt'swēp'ûr] *n* (*US*) barrendero/a.

streetwise [strēt'wīz] *a* (*col*) pícaro.

strength [strengkth] *n* fuerza; (*of girder, knot etc*) resistencia; (*of chemical solution*) potencia, proporción *f*; (*of wine*) graduación *f* de alcohol; **on the** ~ **of** a base de, en base a; **to be at full/below** ~ tener/no tener todo su complemento.

strengthen [strengk'thən] *vt* fortalecer, reforzar.

strenuous [stren'yōōəs] *a* (*tough*) arduo; (*energetic*) enérgico; (*opposition*) firme, tenaz; (*efforts*) intensivo.

stress [stres] *n* (*force, pressure*) presión *f*; (*mental strain*) estrés *m*; (*accent, emphasis*) énfasis *m*, acento; (*LING, POETRY*) acento; (*TECH*) tensión *f*, carga ♦ *vt* subrayar, recalcar; **to be under** ~ sufrir una tensión nerviosa; **to lay great** ~ **on sth** hacer hincapié en algo.

stressful [stres'fəl] *a* (*job*) que produce tensión nerviosa.

stretch [strech] *n* (*of sand etc*) trecho; (*of road*) tramo; (*of time*) período, tiempo *m* ♦ *vi* estirarse; (*extend*): **to** ~ **to** *or* **as far as** extenderse hasta; (*be enough*: *money, food*): **to** ~ **to** alcanzar para, dar de sí para ♦ *vt* extender, estirar; (*make demands of*) exigir el máximo esfuerzo a; **to** ~ **one's legs** estirar las piernas.

stretch out *vi* tenderse ♦ *vt* (*arm etc*) extender; (*spread*) estirar.

stretcher [strech'ûr] *n* camilla.

stretcher-bearer [strech'ûrbärûr] *n* camillero/a.

stretch marks *npl* estrillas *fpl*.

strewn [strōōn] *a*: ~ **with** cubierto *or* sembrado de.

stricken [strik'ən] *a* (*person*) herido; (*city, industry etc*) condenado; ~ **with** (*arthritis, disease*) afligido por; **grief-**~ destrozado por el dolor.

strict [strikt] *a* (*order, rule etc*) estricto; (*discipline, ban*) severo; **in** ~ **confidence** en la más absoluta confianza.

strictly [strikt'lē] *ad* estrictamente; (*totally*) terminantemente; ~ **confidential** estrictamente confidencial; ~ **speaking** en (el) sentido estricto (de la palabra); ~ **between ourselves** ... entre nosotros ... .

stridden [strid'ən] *pp of* **stride**.

stride [strīd] *n* zancada, tranco ♦ *vi* (*pt* **strode**, *pp* **stridden** [strōd, strid'ən]) dar zancadas, andar a trancos; **to take in one's** ~ (*fig: changes etc*) tomar con calma.

strident [strīd'ənt] *a* estridente; (*color*) chillón/ona.

strife [strīf] *n* lucha.

strike [strīk] *n* huelga; (*of oil etc*) descubrimiento; (*attack*) ataque *m*; (*SPORT*) golpe *m* ♦ *vb* (*pt, pp* **struck** [struk]) *vt* golpear, pegar; (*oil etc*) descubrir; (*obstacle*) topar con; (*produce: coin, medal*) acuñar; (: *agreement, deal*) concertar ♦ *vi* declarar la huelga; (*attack: MIL etc*) atacar; (*clock*) dar la hora; **on** ~ (*workers*) en huelga; **to call a** ~ declarar una huelga; **to go on** *or* **come out on** ~ ponerse *or* declararse en huelga; **to** ~ **a match** encender un fósforo; **to** ~ **a balance** (*fig*) encontrar un equilibrio; **to** ~ **a bargain** cerrar un trato; **the clock struck 9 o'clock** el reloj dio las nueve.

strike back *vi* (*MIL*) contraatacar; (*fig*) devolver el golpe.

strike down *vt* derribar.

strike off *vt* (*from list*) tachar; (*doctor etc*) suspender.

strike out *vt* borrar, tachar.

strike up *vt* (*MUS*) empezar a tocar; (*conversation*) entablar; (*friendship*) trabar.

strikebreaker [strīk'brākûr] *n* rompehuelgas *m/f inv*.

striker [strī'kûr] *n* huelgista *m/f*; (*SPORT*) delantero.

striking [strī'king] *a* (*color*) llamativo; (*obvious*) notorio.

string [string] *n* (*gen*) cuerda; (*row*) hilera; (*COMPUT*) cadena ♦ *vt* (*pt, pp* **strung** [strung]): **to** ~ **together** ensartar; **to** ~ **out** extenderse; **to** ~ **sb along** (*fig*) jugar con uno; **the** ~**s** *npl* (*MUS*) los instrumentos de cuerda; **to pull** ~**s** (*fig*) mover palancas; **to get a job by pulling** ~**s** conseguir un trabajo por enchufe; **with no** ~**s attached** (*fig*) sin compromiso.

string bean *n* judía verde, habichuela.

string(ed) instrument [string(d)' in'strəmənt] *n* (*MUS*) instrumento de cuerda.

stringent [strin'jənt] *a* riguroso, severo.

string quartet *n* cuarteto de cuerdas.

strip [strip] *n* tira; (*of land*) franja; (*of metal*) cinta, lámina ♦ *vt* desnudar; (*also:* ~ **down**: *machine*) desmontar ♦ *vi* desnudarse.

stripe [strīp] *n* raya; (*MIL*) galón *m*; **white with green** ~**s** blanco con rayas verdes.

striped [strīpt] *a* a rayas, rayado.

stripper [strip'ûr] *n* artista *m/f* de striptease.

striptease [strip'tēz] *n* striptease *m*.

strive, *pt* **strove**, *pp* **striven** [strīv, strōv, striv'ən] *vi*: **to** ~ **to do sth** esforzarse *or* luchar por hacer algo.

strode [strōd] *pt of* **stride**.

stroke [strōk] *n* (*blow*) golpe *m*; (*MED*) apoplejía; (*caress*) caricia; (*of pen*) trazo; (*SWIMMING: style*) estilo; (*of piston*) carrera ♦ *vt* acariciar; **at a** ~ de golpe; **a** ~ **of luck** un golpe de suerte; **two-**~ **engine** motor *m* de dos tiempos.

stroll [strōl] *n* paseo, vuelta ♦ *vi* dar un paseo *or* una vuelta; **to go for a** ~, **have** *or* **take a** ~ dar un paseo.

stroller [strō'lûr] *n* (*US: pushchair*) cochecito.

strong [strông] *a* fuerte; (*bleach, acid*) concentrado ♦ *ad*: **to be going** ~ (*company*) marchar bien; (*person*) conservarse bien; **they are 50** ~ son 50.

strong-arm [strông'ârm] *a* (*tactics, methods*) represivo.

strongbox [strông'bâks] *n* caja fuerte.

strong drink *n* bebida cargada *or* fuerte.

stronghold [strông'hōld] *n* fortaleza; (*fig*) baluarte *m*.

strong language *n* lenguaje *m* fuerte.

strongly [strông'lē] *ad* fuertemente, con fuerza; (*believe*) firmemente; **to feel** ~ **about sth** tener una opinión decidida de algo.

strongman [strông'man] *n* forzudo; (*fig*) hombre *m* robusto.

strongroom [strông'rōōm] *n* cámara acorazada.

strove [strōv] *pt of* **strive**.

struck [struk] *pt, pp of* **strike**.

structural [struk'chûrəl] *a* estructural.

structure [struk'chûr] *n* estructura; (*building*) construcción *f*.

struggle [strug'əl] *n* lucha ♦ *vi* luchar; **to** ~ **to do sth** esforzarse por hacer algo.

strum [strum] *vt* (*guitar*) rasguear.

strung [strung] *pt, pp of* **string**.

strut [strut] *n* puntal *m* ♦ *vi* pavonearse.

strychnine [strik'nīn] *n* estricnina.

stub [stub] *n* (*of ticket etc*) talón *m*; (*of cigarette*) colilla ♦ *vt*: **to** ~ **one's toe on sth** dar con el dedo del pie contra algo.

stub out *vt* (*cigarette*) apagar.

stubble [stub'əl] *n* rastrojo; (*on chin*) barba (incipiente).

stubborn [stub'ûrn] *a* terco, testarudo.

stucco [stuk'ō] *n* estuco.

stuck [stuk] *pt, pp of* **stick** ♦ *a* (*jammed*) atascado.

stuck-up [stuk'up'] *a* engreído, presumido.

stud [stud] *n* (*shirt* ~) corchete *m*; (*of boot*) taco; (*of horses*) caballeriza; (*also:* ~ **horse**) caballo semental ♦ *vt* (*fig*): ~**ded with** salpicado de.

student [stōō'dənt] *n* estudiante *m/f*; (*US: of school*) alumno/a ♦ *a* estudiantil; **a law/ medical** ~ un(a) estudiante de derecho/ medicina.

student driver *n* (*US AUT*) aprendiz(a) *m/f*.

studio [stoo'dēō] *n* estudio; (*artist's*) taller *m*.

studio apartment *n* estudio.

studious [stoo'dēəs] *a* estudioso; (*studied*) calculado.

studiously [stoo'dēəslē] *ad* (*carefully*) con esmero.

study [stud'ē] *n* estudio ♦ *vt* estudiar; (*examine*) examinar, investigar ♦ *vi* estudiar; **to make a ~ of sth** realizar una investigación de algo; **to ~ for an exam** preparar un examen.

stuff [stuf] *n* materia; (*cloth*) tela; (*substance*) material *m*, sustancia; (*things, belongings*) cosas *fpl* ♦ *vt* llenar; (*CULIN*) rellenar; (*animal: for exhibition*) disecar; **my nose is ~ed up** tengo la nariz tapada; **~ed toy** juguete *m or* muñeco de trapo.

stuffing [stuf'ing] *n* relleno.

stuffy [stuf'ē] *a* (*room*) mal ventilado; (*person*) de miras estrechas.

stumble [stum'bəl] *vi* tropezar, dar un traspié.

stumble across *vt fus* (*fig*) tropezar con.

stumbling block [stum'bling blåk] *n* tropiezo, obstáculo.

stump [stump] *n* (*of tree*) tocón *m*; (*of limb*) muñón *m* ♦ *vt*: **to be ~ed** quedar perplejo; **to be ~ed for an answer** no tener respuesta.

stun [stun] *vt* dejar sin sentido.

stung [stung] *pt, pp of* **sting**.

stunk [stungk] *pp of* **stink**.

stunning [stun'ing] *a* (*fig*) pasmoso.

stunt [stunt] *n* (*AVIAT*) vuelo acrobático; (*publicity ~*) truco publicitario.

stunted [stun'tid] *a* enano, achaparrado.

stuntman [stunt'mən] *n* especialista *m*.

stupefaction [stoopəfak'shən] *n* estupefacción *f*.

stupefy [stoo'pəfī] *vt* dejar estupefacto.

stupendous [stoopen'dəs] *a* estupendo, asombroso.

stupid [stoo'pid] *a* estúpido, tonto.

stupidity [stoopid'itē] *n* estupidez *f*.

stupor [stoo'pûr] *n* estupor *m*.

sturdy [stûr'dē] *a* robusto, fuerte.

stutter [stut'ûr] *n* tartamudeo ♦ *vi* tartamudear.

sty [stī] *n* (*for pigs*) pocilga.

stye [stī] *n* (*MED*) orzuelo.

style [stīl] *n* estilo; (*fashion*) moda; (*of dress etc*) hechura; (*hair ~*) corte *m*; **in the latest ~** en el último modelo.

stylish [stī'lish] *a* elegante, a la moda.

stylist [stī'list] *n* (*hair ~*) peluquero/a.

stylus, *pl* styli *or* **styluses** [stī'ləs, -lē, ləsiz] *n* (*of record player*) aguja.

suave [swâv] *a* cortés, fino.

sub [sub] *n abbr* = **submarine, subscription**.

sub... [sub] *pref* sub....

subcommittee [sub'kəmitē] *n* subcomisión *f*.

subconscious [subkân'chəs] *a* subconsciente ♦ *n* subconsciente *m*.

subcontinent [subkân'tənənt] *n*: **the Indian ~** el subcontinente (de la India).

subcontract *n* [subkân'trakt] subcontrato ♦ *vt* [subkəntrakt'] subcontratar.

subcontractor [subkân'traktûr] *n* subcontratista *m/f*.

subdivide [subdivīd'] *vt* subdividir.

subdue [səbdoo'] *vt* sojuzgar; (*passions*) dominar.

subdued [səbdood'] *a* (*light*) tenue; (*person*) sumiso, manso.

subject *n* [sub'jikt] súbdito; (*SCOL*) tema *m*, materia ♦ *vt* [səbjekt']: **to ~ sb to sth** someter a uno a algo ♦ *a* [sub'jikt]: **to be ~ to** (*law*) estar sujeto a; **~ to confirmation in writing** sujeto a confirmación por escrito; **to change the ~** cambiar de tema.

subjective [səbjek'tiv] *a* subjetivo.

subject matter *n* materia; (*content*) contenido.

sub judice [sub joo'disē] *a* (*LAW*) pendiente de resolución.

subjugate [sub'jəgāt] *vt* subyugar, sojuzgar.

subjunctive [səbjungk'tiv] *a, n* subjuntivo.

sublease [sublēs'] *n* (*US*) subarriendo ♦ *vt* subarrendar.

sublet [sublet'] *vt, vi* subarrendar, realquilar.

sublime [səblīm'] *a* sublime.

subliminal [sublim'ənəl] *a* subliminal.

submachine gun [subməshēn' gun] *n* metralleta.

submarine [sub'mərēn] *n* submarino.

submerge [səbmûrj'] *vt* sumergir; (*flood*) inundar ♦ *vi* sumergirse.

submersion [səbmûr'zhən] *n* submersión *f*.

submission [səbmish'ən] *n* sumisión *f*; (*to committee etc*) ponencia.

submissive [səbmis'iv] *a* sumiso.

submit [səbmit'] *vt* someter; (*proposal, claim*) presentar ♦ *vi* someterse; **I ~ that ... me permito sugerir que ....**

subnormal [subnôr'məl] *a* subnormal.

subordinate [səbôr'dənit] *a, n* subordinado/a *m/f*.

subpoena [səpē'nə] (*LAW*) *n* citación *f* ♦ *vt* citar.

subroutine [subrootēn'] *n* (*COMPUT*) subrutina.

subscribe [səbskrīb'] *vi* suscribir; **to ~ to** (*opinion, fund*) suscribir, aprobar; (*newspaper*) suscribirse a.

subscribed capital [səbskrībd' kap'itəl] *n* capital *m* suscrito.

subscriber [səbskrīb'ûr] *n* (*to periodical, telephone*) abonado/a.

subscript [sub'skript] *n* (*TYP*) subíndice *m*.

subscription [səbskrip'shən] *n* (*to club*) abono; (*to magazine*) suscripción *f*; **to take out a ~ to** suscribir a, abonarse a.

subsequent [sub'səkwənt] *a* subsiguiente, posterior; ~ **to** posterior a.

subsequently [sub'səkwəntlē] *ad* posteriormente, más tarde.

subservient [səbsûr'vēənt] *a*: ~ **(to)** servil (a).

subside [səbsīd'] *vi* hundirse; (*flood*) bajar; (*wind*) amainar.

subsidence [səbsīd'əns] *n* hundimiento; (*in road*) socavón *m*.

subsidiary [səbsid'ēārē] *n* sucursal *f*, filial *f* ♦ *a* (*UNIV*: *subject*) secundario.

subsidize [sub'sidīz] *vt* subvencionar.

subsidy [sub'sidē] *n* subvención *f*.

subsist [səbsist'] *vi*: **to** ~ **on sth** sustentarse con algo.

subsistence [səbsis'təns] *n* subsistencia.

subsistence allowance *n* dietas *fpl*.

subsistence level *n* nivel *m* de subsistencia.

subsistence wage *n* sueldo de subsistencia.

substance [sub'stəns] *n* sustancia; (*fig*) esencia; **to lack** ~ (*argument*) ser poco convincente; (*accusation*) no tener fundamento; (*film, book*) tener poca profundidad.

substandard [substan'dûrd] *a* (*goods*) inferior; (*housing*) deficiente.

substantial [səbstan'chəl] *a* sustancial, sustancioso; (*fig*) importante.

substantially [səbstan'chəlē] *ad* sustancialmente; ~ **bigger** bastante más grande.

substantiate [səbstan'chēāt] *vt* comprobar.

substitute [sub'stitōōt] *n* (*person*) suplente *m/f*; (*thing*) sustituto ♦ *vt*: **to** ~ **A for B** sustituir B por A, reemplazar A por B.

substitute teacher *n* (*US*) profesor(a) *m/f* suplente.

substitution [substitōō'shən] *n* sustitución *f*.

subterfuge [sub'tûrfyōōj] *n* subterfugio.

subterranean [subtərā'nēən] *a* subterráneo.

subtitle [sub'tītəl] *n* subtítulo.

subtle [sut'əl] *a* sutil.

subtlety [sut'əltē] *n* sutileza.

subtly [sut'lē] *ad* sutilmente.

subtotal [subtō'təl] *n* subtotal *m*.

subtract [səbtrakt'] *vt* restar; sustraer.

subtraction [səbtrak'shən] *n* resta; sustracción *f*.

suburb [sub'ûrb] *n* suburbio; **the** ~**s** las afueras (de la ciudad).

suburban [səbûr'bən] *a* suburbano; (*train etc*) de cercanías.

suburbia [səbûr'bēə] *n* barrios *mpl* residenciales *or* satélites.

subversion [səbvûr'zhən] *n* subversión *f*.

subversive [səbvûr'siv] *a* subversivo.

subway [sub'wā] *n* (*US*) metro; (*Brit*) paso subterráneo *or* inferior.

subway station *n* (*US*) estación *f* de metro.

sub-zero [sub'zē'rō] *a*: ~ **temperatures**

temperaturas *fpl* por debajo del cero.

succeed [səksēd'] *vi* (*person*) tener éxito; (*plan*) salir bien ♦ *vt* suceder a; **to** ~ **in doing** lograr hacer.

succeeding [səksē'ding] *a* (*following*) sucesivo; ~ **generations** generaciones *fpl* futuras.

success [səkses'] *n* éxito; (*gain*) triunfo.

successful [səkses'fəl] *a* (*venture*) de éxito; **to be** ~ **(in doing)** lograr (hacer).

successfully [səkses'fəlē] *ad* con éxito.

succession [səksesh'ən] *n* (*series*) sucesión *f*, serie *f*; (*descendants*) descendencia; **in** ~ sucesivamente.

successive [səkses'iv] *a* sucesivo, consecutivo; **on 3** ~ **days** tres días seguidos.

successor [səkses'ûr] *n* sucesor(a) *m/f*.

succinct [səksingkt'] *a* sucinto.

succulent [suk'yələnt] *a* suculento ♦ *n* (*BOT*): ~**s** plantas *fpl* carnosas.

succumb [səkum'] *vi* sucumbir.

such [such] *a* tal, semejante; (*of that kind*): ~ **a book** tal libro; ~ **books** tales libros; (*so much*): ~ **courage** tanto valor ♦ *ad* tan; ~ **a long trip** un viaje tan largo; ~ **a lot of** tanto; ~ **as** (*like*) tal como; **a noise** ~ **as to** un ruido tal que; ~ **books as I have** cuantos libros tengo; **I said no** ~ **thing** no dije tal cosa; **it's** ~ **a long time since we saw each other** hace tanto tiempo que no nos vemos; ~ **a long time ago** hace tantísimo tiempo; **as** ~ *ad* como tal.

such-and-such [such'ənsuch] *a* tal o cual.

suchlike [such'līk] *pron* (*col*): **and** ~ y cosas por el estilo.

suck [suk] *vt* chupar; (*bottle*) sorber; (*breast*) mamar; (*subj: pump, machine*) aspirar.

sucker [suk'ûr] *n* (*BOT*) serpollo; (*ZOOL*) ventosa; (*col*) bobo, primo.

sucrose [sōō'krōs] *n* sucrosa.

suction [suk'shən] *n* succión *f*.

suction pump *n* bomba aspirante *or* de succión.

Sudan [sōōdan'] *n* Sudán *m*.

Sudanese [sōōdənēz'] *a*, *n* sudanés/esa *m/f*.

sudden [sud'ən] *a* (*rapid*) repentino, súbito; (*unexpected*) imprevisto; **all of a** ~ de repente.

suddenly [sud'ənlē] *ad* de repente.

suds [sudz] *npl* espuma *sg* de jabón.

sue [sōō] *vt* demandar; **to** ~ **(for)** demandar (por); **to** ~ **for divorce** solicitar *or* pedir el divorcio; **to** ~ **for damages** demandar por daños y perjuicios.

suede [swād] *n* ante *m*, gamuza (*LAm*).

suet [sōō'it] *n* sebo.

Suez Canal [sōōez' kənal'] *n* Canal *m* de Suez.

Suff. *abbr* (*Brit*) = Suffolk.

suffer [suf'ûr] *vt* sufrir, padecer; (*tolerate*) aguantar, soportar; (*undergo: loss,* *setback*) experimentar ♦ *vi* sufrir, padecer; **to ~ from** sufrir, tener; **to ~ from the effects of alcohol/a fall** resentirse del alcohol/de una caída.

sufferance [suf'ûrəns] *n*: **he was only there on ~** estuvo allí sólo por tolerancia.

sufferer [suf'ûrûr] *n* víctima *f*; (*MED*) **~ from** enfermo/a de.

suffering [suf'ûring] *n* (*hardship, deprivation*) sufrimiento; (*pain*) dolor *m*.

suffice [səfīs'] *vi* bastar, ser suficiente.

sufficient [səfish'ənt] *a* suficiente, bastante.

sufficiently [səfish'əntlē] *ad* suficientemente, bastante.

suffix [suf'iks] *n* sufijo.

suffocate [suf'əkāt] *vi* ahogarse, asfixiarse.

suffocation [sufəkā'shən] *n* sofocación *f*, asfixia.

suffrage [suf'rij] *n* sufragio.

suffuse [səfyōōz'] *vt*: **to ~ (with)** (*color*) bañar (de); **her face was ~d with joy** su cara estaba llena de alegría.

sugar [shōōg'ûr] *n* azúcar *m* ♦ *vt* echar azúcar a, azucarar.

sugar beet *n* remolacha.

sugar bowl *n* azucarero.

sugar cane *n* caña de azúcar.

sugar-coated [shōōg'ûrkō'tid] *a* azucarado, garapiñado.

sugar lump *n* terrón *m* de azúcar.

sugar refinery *n* ingenio azucarero.

sugary [shōōg'ûrē] *a* azucarado.

suggest [səgjest'] *vt* sugerir; (*recommend*) aconsejar; **what do you ~ I do?** ¿qué sugieres que haga?; **this ~s that ...** esto hace pensar que ....

suggestion [səgjes'chən] *n* sugerencia; **there's no ~ of ...** no hay indicación *or* evidencia de ....

suggestive [səgjes'tiv] *a* sugestivo; (*pej*: *indecent*) indecente.

suicidal [sōōisīd'əl] *a* suicida; (*fig*) suicida, peligroso.

suicide [sōō'isīd] *n* suicidio; (*person*) suicida *m/f*; **to commit ~** suicidarse.

suicide attempt *n* intento de suicidio.

suit [sōōt] *n* (*man's*) traje *m*; (*woman's*) conjunto; (*LAW*) pleito; (*CARDS*) palo ♦ *vt* convenir; (*clothes*) sentar a, ir bien a; (*adapt*): **to ~ sth to** adaptar *or* ajustar algo a; **to be ~ed to sth** (*suitable for*) ser apto para algo; **well ~ed** (*couple*) hechos el uno para el otro; **to bring a ~ against sb** entablar demanda contra uno; **to follow ~** (*CARDS*) seguir el palo; (*fig*) seguir el ejemplo (de uno); **that ~s me** me va bien.

suitable [sōō'təbəl] *a* conveniente; (*apt*) indicado.

suitably [sōō'təblē] *ad* convenientemente; (*appropriately*) en forma debida.

suitcase [sōōt'kās] *n* maleta, valija (*LAm*).

suite [swēt] *n* (*of rooms, MUS*) suite *f*; (*furniture*): **bedroom/dining room ~** (jue-go de) dormitorio/comedor *m*; **a three-piece ~** un tresillo.

suitor [sōō'tûr] *n* pretendiente *m*.

sulfate [sul'fāt] *n* sulfato; **copper ~** sulfato de cobre.

sulfur [sul'fûr] *n* azufre *m*.

sulk [sulk] *vi* estar de mal humor.

sulky [sul'kē] *a* malhumorado.

sullen [sul'ən] *a* hosco, malhumorado.

sulphate [sul'fāt] *n* (*Brit*) = **sulfate**.

sulphur [sul'fûr] *n* (*Brit*) = **sulfur**.

sultan [sul'tən] *n* sultán *m*.

sultana [sultan'ə] *n* (*fruit*) pasa de Esmirna.

sultry [sul'trē] *a* (*weather*) bochornoso; (*seductive*) seductor(a).

sum [sum] *n* suma; (*total*) total *m*.

sum up *vt* resumir; (*evaluate rapidly*) evaluar ♦ *vi* hacer un resumen.

Sumatra [sōōmät'rə] *n* Sumatra.

summarize [sum'ərīz] *vt* resumir.

summary [sum'ûrē] *n* resumen *m* ♦ *a* (*justice*) sumario.

summer [sum'ûr] *n* verano ♦ *a* de verano; **in (the) ~** en (el) verano.

summer camp *n* (*US*) colonia veraniega infantil.

summerhouse [sum'ûrhous] *n* (*in garden*) cenador *m*, glorieta.

summertime [sum'ûrtīm] *n* (*season*) verano.

summer time *n* (*by clock*) hora de verano.

summery [sum'ûrē] *a* veraniego.

summing-up [sum'ingup'] *n* (*LAW*) resumen *m*.

summit [sum'it] *n* cima, cumbre *f*.

summit (conference) *n* (conferencia) cumbre *f*.

summon [sum'ən] *vt* (*person*) llamar; (*meeting*) convocar; **to ~ a witness** citar a un testigo.

summon up *vt* (*courage*) armarse de.

summons [sum'ənz] *n* llamamiento, llamada ♦ *vt* citar, emplazar; **to serve a ~ on sb** citar a uno ante el juicio.

sump [sump] *n* (*Brit AUT*) cárter *m*.

sumptuous [sump'chōōəs] *a* suntuoso.

sun [sun] *n* sol *m*; **they have everything under the ~** no les falta nada, tienen de todo.

Sun. *abbr* (= *Sunday*) dom.

sunbathe [sun'bāth] *vi* tomar el sol.

sunbeam [sun'bēm] *n* rayo de sol.

sunbed [sun'bed] *n* cama solar.

sunburn [sun'bûrn] *n* (*painful*) quemadura del sol; (*tan*) bronceado.

sunburned [sun'bûrnd], (*Brit*) **sunburnt** [sun'bûrnt] *a* (*tanned*) bronceado; (*painfully*) quemado por el sol.

sundae [sun'dē] *n* helado con frutas y nueces.

Sunday [sun'dā] *n* domingo.

Sunday school *n* catequesis *f*.

sundial [sun'dīl] *n* reloj *m* de sol.
sundown [sun'doun] *n* anochecer *m*, puesta de sol.
sundries [sun'drēz] *npl* géneros *mpl* diversos.
sundry [sun'drē] *a* varios, diversos; **all and ~** todos sin excepción.
sunflower [sun'flouûr] *n* girasol *m*.
sung [sung] *pp of* **sing.**
sunglasses [sun'glasiz] *npl* gafas *fpl or* anteojos *mpl* de sol.
sunk [sungk] *pp of* **sink.**
sunken [sung'kən] *a* (*bath*) hundido.
sunlamp [sun'lamp] *n* lámpara solar ultravioleta.
sunlight [sun'līt] *n* luz *f* del sol.
sunlit [sun'lit] *a* iluminado por el sol.
sunny [sun'ē] *a* soleado; (*day*) de sol; (*fig*) alegre; **it is ~** hace sol.
sunrise [sun'rīz] *n* salida del sol.
sun roof *n* (*AUT*) techo corredizo; (*on building*) azotea, terraza.
sunset [sun'set] *n* puesta del sol.
sunshade [sun'shād] *n* (*over table*) sombrilla.
sunshine [sun'shīn] *n* sol *m*.
sunstroke [sun'strōk] *n* insolación *f*.
suntan [sun'tan] *n* bronceado.
suntan lotion *n* bronceador *m*.
suntanned [sun'tand] *a* bronceado.
super [sōō'pûr] *a* (*col*) bárbaro.
superannuation [sōōpûranyōōā'shən] *n* jubilación *f*.
superb [sōōpûrb'] *a* magnífico, espléndido.
supercilious [sōōpûrsil'ēəs] *a* (*disdainful*) desdeñoso; (*haughty*) altanero.
superficial [sōōpûrfish'əl] *a* superficial.
superfluous [sōōpûr'flōōəs] *a* superfluo, de sobra.
superhuman [sōōpûrhyōō'mən] *a* sobrehumano.
superimpose [sōōpûrimpōz'] *vt* sobreponer.
superintend [sōōpûrintend'] *vt* supervisar.
superintendent [sōōpûrintɛn'dənt] *n* director(a) *m/f*; (*police ~*) subjefe/a *m/f*.
superior [səpēr'ēûr] *a* superior; (*smug: person*) presumido, desdeñoso; (: *smile, air*) de suficiencia; (: *remark*) desdeñoso ♦ *n* superior *m*; **Mother S~** (*REL*) madre *f* superiora.
superiority [səpērēôr'itē] *n* superioridad *f*; desdén *m*.
superlative [səpûr'lətiv] *a, n* superlativo.
superman [sōō'pûrman] *n* superhombre *m*.
supermarket [sōō'pûrmârkit] *n* supermercado.
supernatural [sōōpûrnach'ûrəl] *a* sobrenatural.
superpower [sōō'pûrpou'ûr] *n* (*POL*) superpotencia.
supersede [sōōpûrsēd'] *vt* suplantar.
supersonic [sōōpûrsän'ik] *a* supersónico.
superstition [sōōpûrstish'ən] *n* superstición

f.
superstitious [sōōpûrstish'əs] *a* supersticioso.
superstore [sōō'pûrstôr] *n* (*Brit*) hipermercado.
supertanker [sōō'pûrtangkûr] *n* superpetrolero.
supertax [sōō'pûrtaks] *n* sobretasa, sobreimpuesto.
supervise [sōō'pûrvīz] *vt* supervisar.
supervision [sōōpûrvizh'ən] *n* supervisión *f.*
supervisor [sōō'pûrvīzûr] *n* (*gen, UNIV*) supervisor(a) *m/f.*
supervisory [sōōpûrvī'zûrē] *a* de supervisión.
supine [sōō'pīn] *a* supino.
supper [sup'ûr] *n* cena; **to have ~** cenar.
supplant [səplant'] *vt* suplantar, reemplazar.
supple [sup'əl] *a* flexible.
supplement *n* [sup'ləmənt] suplemento ♦ *vt* [sup'ləmənt] suplir.
supplementary [supləmən'tûrē] *a* suplementario.
supplementary benefit *n* (*Brit*) subsidio adicional de la seguridad social.
supplier [səplī'ûr] *n* suministrador(a) *m/f*; (*COMM*) distribuidor(a) *m/f.*
supply [səplī'] *vt* (*provide*) suministrar; (*information*) facilitar; (*fill: need, want*) suplir, satisfacer; (*equip*): **to ~ (with)** proveer (de) ♦ *n* provisión *f*; (*of gas, water etc*) suministro ♦ *a* (*Brit: teacher etc*) suplente; **supplies** *npl* (*food*) víveres *mpl*; (*MIL*) pertrechos *mpl*; **office supplies** materiales *mpl* para oficina; **to be in short ~** escasear, haber escasez de; **the electricity/water/gas ~** el suministro de electricidad/agua/gas; **~ and demand** la oferta y la demanda.
support [səpôrt'] *n* (*moral, financial etc*) apoyo; (*TECH*) soporte *m* ♦ *vt* apoyar; (*financially*) mantener; (*uphold*) sostener; (*SPORT: team*) seguir; **they stopped work in ~ (of)** pararon de trabajar en apoyo (de); **to ~ o.s.** (*financially*) ganarse la vida.
support buying *n* compra proteccionista.
supporter [səpôr'tûr] *n* (*POL etc*) partidario/a; (*SPORT*) aficionado/a.
supporting [səpôr'ting] *a* (*THEATER: role, actor*) secundario.
suppose [səpōz'] *vt, vi* suponer; (*imagine*) imaginarse; **to be ~d to do sth** deber hacer algo; **I don't ~ she'll come** no creo que venga; **he's ~d to be an expert** se le supone un experto.
supposedly [səpō'zidlē] *ad* según cabe suponer.
supposing [səpō'zing] *conj* en caso de que; **always ~ (that) he comes** suponiendo que venga.
supposition [supəzish'ən] *n* suposición *f.*

suppository [səpáz'itôrē] *n* supositorio.
suppress [səpres'] *vt* suprimir; (*yawn*) ahogar.
suppression [səpresh'ən] *n* represión *f.*
supremacy [səprem'əsē] *n* supremacía.
supreme [səprēm'] *a* supremo.
Supreme Court *n* (*US*) Tribunal *m* Supremo, Corte *f* Suprema (*LAm*).
Supt. *abbr* (*POLICE*) = **superintendent.**
surcharge [sûr'chârj] *n* sobretasa, recargo.
sure [shōōr] *a* seguro; (*definite, convinced*) cierto; (*aim*) certero ♦ *ad* (*col: esp US*): **that ~ is pretty, that's ~ pretty** ¡qué bonito es!; **to be ~ of** estar seguro de algo; **to be ~ of o.s.** estar seguro de sí mismo; **to make ~ of sth/that** asegurarse de algo/asegurar que; **I'm not ~ how/why/when** no estoy seguro de cómo/por qué/cuándo; **~!** (*of course*) ¡claro!, ¡por supuesto!; **~ enough** efectivamente.
sure-footed [shōōr'fōōt'id] *a* de pie firme.
surely [shōōr'lē] *ad* (*certainly*) seguramente; **~ you don't mean that!** ¡no lo dices en serio!
surety [shōōr'ətē] *n* fianza; (*person*) fiador(a) *m/f;* **to go** *or* **stand ~ for sb** ser fiador de uno, salir garante por uno.
surf [sûrf] *n* olas *fpl.*
surface [sûr'fis] *n* superficie *f* ♦ *vt* (*road*) revestir ♦ *vi* salir a la superficie ♦ *cpd* (*MIL, NAUT*) de (la) superficie; **on the ~ it seems that ...** (*fig*) a primera vista parece que ... .
surface area *n* área de la superficie.
surface mail *n* vía terrestre.
surface-to-air missile [sûr'fistōōār' mis'əl] *n* proyectil *m* tierra-aire.
surfboard [sûrf'bôrd] *n* plancha (de surf).
surfeit [sûr'fit] *n*: **a ~ of** un exceso de.
surfer [sûrf'ûr] *n* súrfer *m/f.*
surfing [sûrf'ing] *n* surf *m.*
surge [sûrj] *n* oleada, oleaje *m;* (*ELEC*) sobretensión *f* transitoria ♦ *vi* avanzar a tropel; **to ~ forward** avanzar rápidamente.
surgeon [sûr'jən] *n* cirujano/a.
surgery [sûr'jûrē] *n* cirugía; (*Brit: room*) consultorio; **to undergo ~** operarse.
surgery hours *npl* (*Brit*) horas *fpl* de consulta.
surgical [sûr'jikəl] *a* quirúrgico.
surgical spirit *n* (*Brit*) alcohol *m.*
surly [sûr'lē] *a* hosco, malhumorado.
surmount [sûrmount'] *vt* superar, vencer.
surname [sûr'nām] *n* apellido.
surpass [sûrpas'] *vt* superar, exceder.
surplus [sûr'pləs] *n* excedente *m;* (*COMM*) superávit *m* ♦ *a* (*COMM*) excedente, sobrante; **to have a ~ of sth** tener un excedente de algo; **it is ~ to our requirements** nos sobra; **~ stock** saldos *mpl.*
surprise [sûrprīz'] *n* sorpresa ♦ *vt* sorprender; **to take by ~** (*person*) coger a uno desprevenido, sorprender a uno; (*MIL:*

town, fort) atacar por sorpresa.
surprising [sûrprī'zing] *a* sorprendente.
surprisingly [sûrprī'zinglē] *ad* (*easy, helpful*) de modo sorprendente; (**somewhat**) **~, he agreed** para sorpresa de todos, aceptó.
surrealism [sərē'əlizəm] *n* surrealismo.
surrealist [sərē'əlist] *a, n* surrealista *m/f.*
surrender [səren'dûr] *n* rendición *f,* entrega ♦ *vi* rendirse, entregarse ♦ *vt* (*claim, right*) renunciar.
surrender value *n* valor *m* de rescate.
surreptitious [sûrəptish'əs] *a* subrepticio.
surrogate [sûr'əgit] *n* (*substitute*) sustituto/ a ♦ *a:* **~ coffee** sucedáneo de café.
surrogate mother *n* madre *f* portadora.
surround [səround'] *vt* rodear, circundar; (*MIL etc*) cercar.
surrounding [səroun'ding] *a* circundante.
surroundings [səroun'dingz] *npl* alrededores *mpl,* cercanías *fpl.*
surtax [sûr'taks] *n* sobretasa, sobreimpuesto.
surveillance [sûrvā'ləns] *n* vigilancia.
survey *n* [sûr'vā] inspección *f,* reconocimiento; (*inquiry*) encuesta; (*comprehensive view: of situation etc*) vista de conjunto ♦ *vt* [sərvā'] examinar, inspeccionar; (*Brit SURVEYING: building*) inspeccionar; (*: land*) hacer un reconocimiento de, reconocer; (*look at*) mirar, contemplar; (*make inquiries about*) hacer una encuesta de; **to carry out a ~ of** inspeccionar, examinar.
surveyor [sûrvā'ûr] *n* agrimensor(a) *m/f.*
survival [sûrvī'vəl] *n* supervivencia.
survival course *n* curso de supervivencia.
survival kit *n* equipo de emergencia.
survive [sûrvīv'] *vi* sobrevivir; (*custom etc*) perdurar ♦ *vt* sobrevivir a.
survivor [sûrvī'vûr] *n* superviviente *m/f.*
susceptibility [səseptəbil'ətē] *n* (*to illness*) propensión *f.*
susceptible [səsep'təbəl] *a* (*easily influenced*) influenciable; (*to disease, illness*): **~ to** propenso a.
suspect *a, n* [sus'pekt] sospechoso/a *m/f* ♦ *vt* [səspekt'] sospechar.
suspend [səspend'] *vt* suspender.
suspended sentence [səspen'did sen'təns] *n* (*LAW*) libertad *f* condicional.
suspender belt [səspen'dûr belt] *n* (*Brit*) portaligas *m inv.*
suspenders [səspen'dûrz] *npl* (*US*) tirantes *mpl;* (*Brit*) ligas *fpl.*
suspense [səspens'] *n* incertidumbre *f,* duda; (*in film etc*) suspense *m.*
suspense account *n* cuenta en suspenso.
suspension [səspen'chən] *n* (*gen, AUT*) suspensión *f;* (*of driver's license*) privación *f.*
suspension bridge *n* puente *m* colgante.
suspension file *n* archivador *m* colgante.
suspicion [səspish'ən] *n* sospecha; (*distrust*) recelo; (*trace*) traza; **to be under ~** estar bajo sospecha; **arrested on ~ of murder**

detenido bajo sospecha de asesinato.
suspicious [səspish'əs] *a* (*suspecting*) receloso; (*causing suspicion*) sospechoso; **to be ~ of** *or* **about sb/sth** tener sospechas de uno/algo.
suss out [sus out] *vt* (*Brit col*) explorar.
sustain [səstān'] *vt* sostener, apoyar; (*suffer*) sufrir, padecer.
sustained [səstānd'] *a* (*effort*) sostenido.
sustenance [sus'tənəns] *n* sustento.
suture [sōō'chûr] *n* sutura.
SW *abbr* = **short wave.**
swab [swâb] *n* (*MED*) algodón *m*, frotis *m inv* ♦ *vt* (*NAUT: also: ~* **down**) limpiar, fregar.
swagger [swag'ûr] *vi* pavonearse.
swallow [swâl'ō] *n* (*bird*) golondrina; (*of food*) bocado; (*of drink*) trago ♦ *vt* tragar.
swallow up *vt* (*savings etc*) consumir.
swam [swam] *pt of* **swim.**
swamp [swâmp] *n* pantano, ciénaga ♦ *vt* abrumar, agobiar.
swampy [swâmp'ē] *a* pantanoso.
swan [swân] *n* cisne *m*.
swank [swangk] (*col*) *n* (*vanity, boastfulness*) fanfarronada ♦ *vi* fanfarronear, presumir.
swan song *n* (*fig*) canto del cisne.
swap [swâp] *n* canje *m*, trueque *m* ♦ *vt*: **to ~ (for)** canjear (por).
SWAPO [swä'pō] *n abbr* (= *South-West Africa People's Organization*) SWAPO *m*.
swarm [swôrm] *n* (*of bees*) enjambre *m*; (*fig*) multitud *f* ♦ *vi* (*fig*) hormiguear, pulular.
swarthy [swôr'thē] *a* moreno.
swashbuckling [swâsh'bukling] *a* (*person*) aventurero; (*film*) de capa y espada.
swastika [swâs'tika] *n* esvástika, cruz *f* gamada.
swat [swât] *vt* aplastar.
swathe [swâth] *vt*: **to ~ in** (*blankets*) envolver en; (*bandages*) vendar en.
sway [swā] *vi* mecerse, balancearse ♦ *vt* (*influence*) mover, influir en ♦ *n* (*rule, power*): **~ (over)** dominio (sobre); **to hold ~ over sb** dominar a uno, mantener el dominio sobre uno.
Swaziland [swä'zēland] *n* Swazilandia.
swear, *pt* **swore**, *pp* **sworn** [swe'ûr, swôr, swôrn] *vi* jurar ♦ *vt*: **to ~ an oath** prestar juramento, jurar; **to ~ to sth** declarar algo bajo juramento.
swear in *vt* tomar juramento (a).
swearword [swär'wûrd] *n* taco, palabrota.
sweat [swet] *n* sudor *m* ♦ *vi* sudar.
sweatband [swet'band] *n* (*SPORT: on head*) venda, banda; (: *on wrist*) muñequera.
sweater [swet'ûr] *n* suéter *m*.
sweatshirt [swet'shûrt] *n* sudadera.
sweatshop [swet'shâp] *n* fábrica donde se explota al obrero.
sweat suit *n* chandal *m*.

sweaty [swet'ē] *a* sudoroso.
Swede [swēd] *n* sueco/a.
swede [swēd] *n* (*Brit*) naba.
Sweden [swēd'ən] *n* Suecia.
Swedish [swē'dish] *a*, *n* (*LING*) sueco.
sweep [swēp] *n* (*act*) barrida; (*of arm*) manotazo *m*; (*curve*) curva, alcance *m*; (*also:* **chimney ~**) deshollinador(a) *m/f* ♦ *vb* (*pt*, *pp* **swept** [swept]) *vt* barrer; (*disease, fashion*) recorrer ♦ *vi* barrer.
sweep away *vt* barrer; (*rub out*) borrar.
sweep past *vi* pasar rápidamente; (*brush by*) rozar.
sweep up *vi* barrer.
sweeping [swē'ping] *a* (*gesture*) dramático; (*generalized*) generalizado; (*changes, reforms*) radical.
sweepstake [swēp'stāk] *n* lotería.
sweet [swēt] *n* (*candy*) dulce *m*, caramelo; (*Brit: pudding*) postre *m* ♦ *a* dulce; (*sugary*) azucarado; (*charming: person*) encantador(a); (: *smile, character*) dulce, amable, agradable ♦ *ad*: **to smell/taste ~** oler/saber dulce.
sweet and sour *a* agridulce.
sweetcorn [swēt'kôrn] *n* maíz *m*.
sweeten [swēt'ən] *vt* (*person*) endulzar; (*add sugar to*) poner azúcar a.
sweetener [swēt'ənûr] *n* (*CULIN*) dulcificante *m*.
sweetheart [swēt'hârt] *n* novio/a; (*in speech*) amor.
sweetness [swēt'nis] *n* (*gen*) dulzura.
sweet pea *n* guisante *m* de olor.
sweet potato *n* batata, camote *m* (*LAm*).
sweetshop [swēt'shâp] *n* (*Brit*) confitería, bombonería.
sweet-talk [swēt'tôk] *vt* (*US col*) enrollarse con.
swell [swel] *n* (*of sea*) marejada, oleaje *m* ♦ *a* (*US: col: excellent*) estupendo, fenomenal ♦ *vb* (*pt ~***ed**, *pp* **swollen** *or* **~ed** [swō'lən]) *vt* hinchar, inflar ♦ *vi* hincharse, inflarse.
swelling [swel'ing] *n* (*MED*) hinchazón *f*.
sweltering [swel'tûring] *a* sofocante, de mucho calor.
swept [swept] *pt*, *pp of* **sweep.**
swerve [swûrv] *n* esguince *m*; (*in car*) desvío brusco ♦ *vi* desviarse bruscamente.
swift [swift] *n* (*bird*) vencejo ♦ *a* rápido, veloz.
swiftly [swift'lē] *ad* rápidamente.
swiftness [swift'nis] *n* rapidez *f*, velocidad *f*.
swig [swig] *n* (*col: drink*) trago.
swill [swil] *n* bazofia ♦ *vt* lavar, limpiar con agua.
swim [swim] *n*: **to go for a ~** ir a nadar *or* a bañarse ♦ *vb* (*pt* **swam** [swam], *pp* **swum** [swum]) *vi* nadar; (*head, room*) dar vueltas ♦ *vt* pasar a nado; **to go ~ming** ir a nadar(se); **to ~ a length** nadar *or* hacer un

largo.
swimmer [swim'ûr] *n* nadador(a) *m/f*.
swimming [swim'ing] *n* natación *f*.
swimming cap *n* gorro de baño.
swimming costume *n* (*Brit*) = **swimsuit**.
swimming pool *n* piscina, alberca (*LAm*).
swimming trunks *npl* bañador *msg*.
swimsuit [swim'sōōt] *n* bañador *m*, traje *m* de baño.
swindle [swin'dəl] *n* estafa ♦ *vt* estafar.
swine [swīn] *n*, *pl inv* cerdos *mpl*, puercos *mpl*; (*col!*) canalla *m* (!).
swing [swing] *n* (*in playground*) columpio; (*movement*) balanceo, vaivén *m*; (*change of direction*) viraje *m*; (*rhythm*) ritmo; (*POL*: *in votes etc*): **there has been a ~ towards/away from the Republicans** ha habido un viraje en favor/en contra del Partido Republicano ♦ *vb* (*pt, pp* **swung** [swung]) *vt* balancear; (*on a ~*) columpiar; (*also*: ~ **around**) voltear, girar ♦ *vi* balancearse, columpiarse; (*also*: ~ **around**) dar media vuelta; **a ~ to the left** un movimiento hacia la izquierda; **to be in full ~** estar en plena marcha; **to get into the ~ of things** ponerse al corriente de las cosas *or* de la situación; **the road ~s south** la carretera gira hacia el sur.
swing bridge *n* puente *m* giratorio.
swing door *n* (*Brit*) puerta giratoria.
swingeing [swin'jing] *a* (*Brit*) abrumador(a).
swinging door [swing'ing dôr] *n* (*US*) puerta giratoria.
swipe [swīp] *n* golpe *m* fuerte ♦ *vt* (*hit*) golpear fuerte; (*col*: *steal*) guindar.
swirl [swûrl] *vi* arremolinarse.
swish [swish] *n* (*sound*: *of whip*) chasquido; (: *of skirts*) frufrú *m*; (: *of grass*) crujido ♦ *a* (*Brit*: *col*: *smart*) elegante ♦ *vi* chasquear.
Swiss [swis] *a*, *n* (*pl inv*) suizo/a *m/f*.
switch [swich] *n* (*for light, radio etc*) interruptor *m*; (*change*) cambio ♦ *vt* (*change*) cambiar de; (*invert*: *also*: ~ **around**, ~ **over**) intercambiar.
switch off *vt* apagar; (*engine*) parar.
switch on *vt* (*AUT*: *ignition*) encender, prender (*LAm*); (*engine, machine*) arrancar; (*water supply*) conectar.
switchblade [swich'blād] *n* (*US*) navaja de muelle.
switchboard [swich'bôrd] *n* (*TEL*) centralita (de teléfonos), conmutador *m* (*LAm*).
switchtower [swich'touûr] *n* (*US RAIL*) garita de señales.
switchyard [swich'yârd] *n* (*US RAIL*) estación *f* clasificadora.
Switzerland [swit'sûrlənd] *n* Suiza.
swivel [swiv'əl] *vi* (*also*: ~ **around**) girar.
swollen [swō'lən] *pp of* **swell**.

swoon [swōōn] *vi* desmayarse.
swoop [swōōp] *n* (*by police etc*) redada; (*of bird etc*) calada ♦ *vi* (*also*: ~ **down**) calarse.
swop [swâp] = **swap**.
sword [sôrd] *n* espada.
swordfish [sôrd'fish] *n* pez *m* espada.
swore [swôr] *pt of* **swear**.
sworn [swôrn] *pp of* **swear**.
swot [swât] (*Brit*) *vt, vi* empollar ♦ *n* empollón/ona *m/f*.
swum [swum] *pp of* **swim**.
swung [swung] *pt, pp of* **swing**.
sycamore [sik'əmôr] *n* sicomoro.
sycophant [sik'əfənt] *n* adulador(a), pelotillero/a.
Sydney [sid'nē] *n* Sidney *m*.
syllable [sil'əbəl] *n* sílaba.
syllabus [sil'əbəs] *n* programa *m* de estudios; **on the ~** en el programa de estudios.
symbol [sim'bəl] *n* símbolo.
symbolic(al) [simbâl'ik(əl)] *a* simbólico; **to be ~ of sth** simbolizar algo.
symbolism [sim'bəlizəm] *n* simbolismo.
symbolize [sim'bəlīz] *vt* simbolizar.
symmetrical [simet'rikəl] *a* simétrico.
symmetry [sim'itrē] *n* simetría.
sympathetic [simpəthet'ik] *a* compasivo; (*understanding*) comprensivo; **to be ~ to a cause** (*well-disposed*) apoyar una causa; **to be ~ towards** (*person*) ser comprensivo con.
sympathize [sim'pəthīz] *vi*: **to ~ with sb** compadecerse de uno; (*understand*) comprender a uno.
sympathizer [sim'pəthīzûr] *n* (*POL*) simpatizante *m/f*.
sympathy [sim'pəthē] *n* (*pity*) compasión *f*; (*understanding*) comprensión *f*; **a letter of ~** un pésame; **with our deepest ~** nuestro más sentido pésame.
symphony [sim'fənē] *n* sinfonía.
symposium [simpō'zēəm] *n* simposio.
symptom [simp'təm] *n* síntoma *m*, indicio.
symptomatic [simptəmat'ik] *a*: ~ **(of)** sintomático (de).
synagogue [sin'əgâg] *n* sinagoga.
synchromesh [sing'krəmesh] *n* cambio sincronizado de velocidades.
synchronize [sing'krənīz] *vt* sincronizar ♦ *vi*: **to ~ with** sincronizarse con.
syncopated [sing'kəpātid] *a* sincopado.
syndicate [sin'dəkit] *n* (*gen*) sindicato; (*PRESS*) agencia (de noticias).
syndrome [sin'drōm] *n* síndrome *m*.
synonym [sin'ənim] *n* sinónimo.
synonymous [sinân'əməs] *a*: ~ **(with)** sinónimo (con).
synopsis [sinâp'sis, -sēz] *n* sinopsis *f inv*.
syntax [sin'taks] *n* sintaxis *f*.
syntax error *n* (*COMPUT*) error *m* sintáctico.

synthesis, pl **syntheses** |sin'thэsis, -sēz| n síntesis f inv.

synthesizer |sin'thisīzúr| n sintetizador m.

synthetic |sinthɛt'ik| a sintético ♦ n sintético.

syphilis |sif'əlis| n sífilis f.

syphon |sī'fən| = **siphon**.

Syria |sē'rēə| n Siria.

Syrian |sēr'ēən| a, n sirio/a m/f.

syringe |sərinj'| n jeringa.

syrup |sir'əp| n jarabe m, almíbar m.

system |sis'təm| n sistema m; (ANAT) organismo; **it was quite a shock to his ~** fue un golpe para el organismo.

system disk n (COMPUT) disco del sistema.

systematic |sistəmat'ik| a sistemático; metódico.

systems analyst |sis'təmz an'əlist| n analista m/f de sistemas.

T

T, t |tē| n (letter) T, t f; **T for Tommy** T de Tarragona.

ta |tá| excl (Brit col) ¡gracias!

tab |tab| n abbr = **tabulator** ♦ n lengüeta; (label) etiqueta; **to keep ~s on** (fig) vigilar.

tabby |tab'ē| n (also: **~ cat**) gato atigrado.

tabernacle |tab'úrnəkəl| n tabernáculo.

table |tā'bəl| n mesa; (chart: of statistics etc) cuadro, gráfica, tabla; **to lay** or **set the ~** poner la mesa; **to clear the ~** quitar or levantar la mesa; **~ of contents** índice m de materias.

tablecloth |tā'bəlklôth| n mantel m.

table d'hôte |tab'əl dōt'| n menú m.

table lamp n lámpara de mesa.

tableland |tā'bəlland| n meseta, altiplano (LAm).

tablemat |tā'bəlmat| n salvamanteles m inv.

tablespoon |tā'bəlspōōn| n cuchara grande; (also: **~ful**: as measurement) cucharada.

tablet |tab'lit| n (MED) pastilla, comprimido; (for writing) bloc m; (of stone) lápida.

table talk n conversación f de sobremesa.

table tennis n ping-pong m, tenis m de mesa.

table wine n vino de mesa.

tabloid |tab'loid| n (newspaper) periódico popular sensacionalista; **the ~s** la prensa amarilla.

taboo |taboō'| a, n tabú m.

tabulate |tab'yəlāt| vt disponer en tablas.

tabulator |tab'yəlātúr| n tabulador m.

tachograph |tak'əgraf| n tacógrafo.

tachometer |təkâm'ətúr| n taquímetro.

tacit |tas'it| a tácito.

tacitly |tas'itlē| ad tácitamente.

taciturn |tas'itúrn| a taciturno.

tack |tak| n (nail) tachuela; (stitch) hilván m; (NAUT) bordada ♦ vt (nail) clavar con tachuelas; (Brit: stitch) hilvanar ♦ vi virar; **to ~ sth on to (the end of) sth** (of letter, book) añadir algo a(l final de) algo.

tackle |tak'əl| n (gear) equipo; (fishing ~, for lifting) aparejo; (FOOTBALL, SOCCER) entrada, tackle m; (RUGBY) placaje m ♦ vt (difficulty) enfrentar; (grapple with) agarrar; (SOCCER) atajar, entrar; (RUGBY) placar.

tacky |tak'ē| a pegajoso; (US: shabby) destartalado.

tact |takt| n tacto, discreción f.

tactful |takt'fəl| a discreto, diplomático; **to be ~** tener tacto, actuar discretamente.

tactfully |takt'fəlē| ad diplomáticamente, con tacto.

tactical |tak'tikəl| a táctico.

tactics |tak'tiks| n, npl táctica sg.

tactless |takt'lis| a indiscreto.

tactlessly |takt'lislē| ad indiscretamente, sin tacto.

tadpole |tad'pōl| n renacuajo.

taffy |taf'ē| n (US) melcocha.

tag |tag| n (label) etiqueta; **price/name ~** etiqueta con el precio/con el nombre.

tag along vi: **to ~ along with sb** acompañar a uno.

tag question n pregunta coletilla.

Tahiti |təhē'tē| n Tahití m.

tail |tāl| n cola; (ZOOL) rabo; (of shirt, coat) faldón m ♦ vt (follow) vigilar a; **heads or ~s** cara o cruz; **to turn ~** volver la espalda.

tail away, **tail off** vi (in size, quality etc) ir disminuyendo.

tailback |tāl'bak| n (Brit AUT) cola.

tail coat n frac m.

tail end n cola, parte f final.

tailgate |tāl'gāt| n (AUT) puerta trasera.

taillight |tāl'līt| n (AUT) luz f trasera.

tailor |tā'lúr| n sastre m ♦ vt: **to ~ sth (to)** confeccionar algo a medida (para); **~'s (shop)** sastrería.

tailoring |tā'lūring| n (cut) corte m; (craft) sastrería.

tailor-made |tā'lûrmād| a (also fig) hecho a la medida.

tailwind |tāl'wind| n viento de cola.

taint |tānt| vt (meat, food) contaminar; (fig: reputation) manchar, tachar (LAm).

tainted |tānt'id| a (water, air) contaminado; (fig) manchado.

Taiwan |tī'wân'| n Taiwán m.

take |tāk| vb (pt **took**, pp **taken** |tōōk,

tā'kən]) *vt* tomar; (*grab*) coger (*Sp*), agarrar (*LAm*); (*gain: prize*) ganar; (*require*: *effort, courage*) exigir; (*support weight of*) aguantar; (*hold: passengers etc*) tener cabida para; (*accompany, bring, carry*) llevar; (*exam*) presentarse a; (*conduct*: *meeting*) presidir ♦ *vi* (*fire*) prender; (*dye*) agarrar, tomar ♦ *n* (*CINEMA*) toma; **to ~ sth from** (*drawer etc*) sacar algo de; (*person*) coger (*Sp*) algo a; **to ~ sb's hand** tomar de la mano a uno; **to ~ notes** tomar apuntes; **to be ~n ill** ponerse enfermo; **~ the first on the left** toma la primera a la izquierda; **I only took Russian for one year** sólo estudié el ruso un año; **I took him for a doctor** le tenía por médico; **it won't ~ long** durará poco; **it will ~ at least 5 liters** tiene cabida para 5 litros como mínimo; **to be ~n with sb/sth** (*attracted*) tomarle cariño a uno/tomarle gusto a algo; **I ~ it that...** supongo que....

take after *vt fus* parecerse a.

take apart *vt* desmontar.

take away *vt* (*remove*) quitar; (*carry off*) llevar *vi*: **to ~ away from** quitar mérito a.

take back *vt* (*return*) devolver; (*one's words*) retractar.

take down *vt* (*building*) derribar; (*dismantle: scaffolding*) desmantelar; (*letter etc*) apuntar.

take in *vt* (*deceive*) engañar; (*understand*) entender; (*include*) abarcar; (*lodger*) acoger, recibir; (*orphan, stray dog*) recoger; (*SEWING*) achicar.

take off *vi* (*AVIAT*) despegar; (*leave*) salir, largarse ♦ *vt* (*remove*) quitar; (*imitate*) imitar.

take on *vt* (*work*) emprender; (*employee*) contratar; (*opponent*) desafiar.

take out *vt* sacar; (*remove*) quitar; **don't ~ it out on me!** ¡no te desquites conmigo!

take over *vt* (*business*) tomar posesión de ♦ *vi*: **to ~ over from sb** reemplazar a uno.

take to *vt fus* (*person*) coger cariño a (*Sp*), encariñarse con (*LAm*); (*activity*) aficionarse a; **to ~ to doing sth** entregarse a (hacer) algo.

take up *vt* (*a dress*) acortar; (*occupy: time, space*) ocupar; (*engage in: hobby etc*) dedicarse a; (*absorb: liquids*) absorber; (*accept: offer, challenge*) aceptar ♦ *vi*: **to ~ up with sb** hacerse amigo de uno.

take upon *vt*: **to ~ it upon o.s. to do sth** encargarse de hacer algo.

takeaway [tā'kəwā] *a* (*Brit: food*) para llevar.

take-home pay [tāk'hōm pā] *n* salario neto.

taken [tā'kən] *pp of* **take.**

takeoff [tāk'óf] *n* (*AVIAT*) despegue *m.*

takeover [tāk'ōvûr] *n* (*COMM*) absorción *f.*

takeover bid *n* oferta pública de compra.

takings [tā'kingz] *npl* (*COMM*) ingresos *mpl.*

talc [talk] *n* (*also*: **~um powder**) talco.

tale [tāl] *n* (*story*) cuento; (*account*) relación *f*; **to tell ~s** (*fig*) chismear.

talent [tal'ənt] *n* talento.

talented [tal'əntid] *a* talentoso, de talento.

talk [tôk] *n* charla; (*gossip*) habladurías *fpl*, chismes *mpl*; (*conversation*) conversación *f* ♦ *vi* (*speak*) hablar; (*chatter*) charlar; **~s** *npl* (*POL etc*) conversaciones *fpl*; **to give a ~** dar una charla *or* conferencia; **to ~ about** hablar de; **to ~ sb into doing sth** convencer a uno para que haga algo; **to ~ sb out of doing sth** disuadir a uno de que haga algo; **to ~ shop** hablar del trabajo; **~ing of movies, have you seen ...?** hablando de películas, ¿has visto ...?

talk over *vt* discutir.

talkative [tô'kətiv] *a* hablador(a).

talker [tô'kûr] *n* hablador(a) *m/f.*

talking point [tô'king point] *n* tema *m* de conversación.

talking-to [tô'kingtōō] *n*: **to give sb a good ~** echar una buena bronca a uno.

talk show *n* programa *m* de entrevistas.

tall [tôl] *a* alto; (*tree*) grande; **to be 6 feet ~** ≈ medir 1 metro 80, tener 1 metro 80 de alto; **how ~ are you?** ¿cuánto mides?

tallboy [tôl'boi] *n* (*Brit*) cómoda alta.

tallness [tôl'nis] *n* altura.

tall story *n* cuento chino.

tally [tal'ē] *n* cuenta ♦ *vi*: **to ~ (with)** corresponder (con); **to keep a ~ of sth** llevar la cuenta de algo.

talon [tal'ən] *n* garra.

tambourine [tam'bərēn] *n* pandereta.

tame [tām] *a* (*mild*) manso; (*tamed*) domesticado; (*fig: story, style*) mediocre; (: *person*) soso.

tameness [tām'nis] *n* mansedumbre *f.*

tamper [tam'pûr] *vi*: **to ~ with** entrometerse en.

tampon [tam'pân] *n* tampón *m.*

tan [tan] *n* (*also*: **sun~**) bronceado ♦ *vt* broncear ♦ *vi* ponerse moreno ♦ *a* (*color*) marrón; **to get a ~** broncearse, ponerse moreno.

tandem [tan'dəm] *n* tándem *m.*

tang [tang] *n* sabor *m* fuerte.

tangent [tan'jənt] *n* (*MATH*) tangente *f*; **to go off on a ~** (*fig*) salirse por la tangente.

tangerine [tanjərēn'] *n* mandarina.

tangible [tan'jəbəl] *a* tangible; **~ assets** bienes *mpl* tangibles.

Tangier [tanjiûr'] *n* Tánger *m.*

tangle [tang'gəl] *n* enredo ♦ *a* : **to get ~d up** enredarse.

tango [tang'gō] *n* tango.

tank [tangk] *n* (*water* ~) depósito, tanque *m*; (*for fish*) acuario; (*MIL*) tanque *m.*

tankard [tangk'ûrd] *n* bock *m.*

tanker |tangk'ûr| n (*ship*) petrolero; (*truck*) camión m cisterna.

tankful |tangk'fəl| n: **to get a ~ of gasoline** llenar el tanque de gasolina.

tanned |tand| a (*skin*) moreno, bronceado.

tannin |tan'in| n tanino.

tanning |tan'ing| n (*of leather*) curtido.

tantalizing |tan'təlīzing| a tentador(a).

tantamount |tan'təmount| a: **~ to** equivalente a.

tantrum |tan'trəm| n rabieta; **to throw a ~** coger una rabieta.

Tanzania |tanzənē'ə| n Tanzanía.

Tanzanian |tanzənē'ən| a, n tanzano/a m/f.

tap |tap| n (*on sink etc*) grifo, canilla (*LAm*)'; (*gentle blow*) golpecito; (*Brit: gas* ~) llave f ♦ vt (*table etc*) tamborilear; (*shoulder etc*) palmear; (*resources*) utilizar, explotar; (*telephone conversation*) interceptar, escuchar clandestinamente; **on ~** (*fig: resources*) a mano; **beer on ~** cerveza de barril.

tap-dancing |tap'dansing| n claqué m.

tape |tāp| n cinta; (*also:* **magnetic ~**) cinta magnética; (*Brit: sticky ~*) cinta adhesiva ♦ vt (*record*) grabar (en cinta); **on ~** (*song etc*) grabado (en cinta).

tape deck n tocacassettes m inv.

tape measure n cinta métrica, metro.

taper |tā'pûr| n cirio ♦ vi afilarse.

tape-record |tāp'rikôrd| vt grabar (en cinta).

tape recorder n grabadora.

tape recording n grabación f.

tapered |tā'pûrd|, **tapering** |tā'pûring| a terminado en punta.

tapestry |tap'istrē| n (*object*) tapiz m; (*art*) tapicería.

tapeworm |tāp'wûrm'| n solitaria, tenia.

tapioca |tapēō'kə| n tapioca m.

tappet |tap'it| n varilla de levantamiento.

tar |tär| n alquitrán m, brea; **low/middle ~ cigarettes** cigarrillos con contenido bajo/medio de alquitrán.

tarantula |təran'chələ| n tarántula.

tardy |tär'dē| a (*late*) tardío; (*slow*) lento.

tare |tär| n (*COMM*) tara.

target |tär'git| n (*gen*) blanco; **to be on ~** (*project*) seguir el curso previsto.

target audience n público objetivo.

target market n (*COMM*) mercado objetivo.

target practice n tiro al blanco.

tariff |tar'if| n tarifa.

tariff barrier n (*COMM*) barrera arancelaria.

tarmac |tär'mak| n (*AVIAT*) pista (de aterrizaje); (*Brit: on road*) alquitranado.

tarn |tärn| n lago pequeño de montaña.

tarnish |tär'nish| vt deslustrar.

tarpaulin |tärpô'lin| n alquitranado.

tarragon |tar'əgən| n estragón m.

tarry |tar'ē| vi entretenerse, quedarse atrás.

tart |tärt| n (*CULIN*) tarta; (*Brit col: pej: woman*) fulana ♦ a (*flavor*) agrio, ácido.

tart up vt (*Brit: room, building*) dar tono a.

tartan |tär'tən| n tartán m, escocés m ♦ a de tartán.

tartar |tär'tûr| n (*on teeth*) sarro.

tartar sauce n salsa tártara.

tartly |tärt'lē| ad (*answer*) ásperamente.

task |task| n tarea; **to take to ~** reprender.

task force n (*MIL. POLICE*) grupo de operaciones.

taskmaster |task'mastûr| n: **he's a hard ~** es muy exigente.

Tasmania |tazmā'nēə| n Tasmania.

tassel |tas'əl| n borla.

taste |tāst| n sabor m, gusto; (*also:* **after~**) dejo; (*sip*) sorbo; (*fig: glimpse, idea*) muestra, idea ♦ vt probar ♦ vi: **to ~ of** or **like** (*fish etc*) saber a; **you can ~ the garlic (in it)** se nota el sabor a ajo; **can I have a ~ of this wine?** ¿puedo probar este vino?; **to have a ~ for sth** ser aficionado a algo; **in good/bad ~** de buen/mal gusto; **to be in bad** or **poor ~** ser de mal gusto.

taste bud n papila gustativa or del gusto.

tasteful |tāst'fəl| a de buen gusto.

tastefully |tāst'fəlē| ad elegantemente, con buen gusto.

tasteless |tāst'lis| a (*food*) soso; (*remark*) de mal gusto.

tastelessly |tāst'lislē| ad con mal gusto.

tastily |tās'tilē| ad sabrosamente.

tastiness |tās'tēnis| n (buen) sabor m, lo sabroso.

tasty |tās'tē| a sabroso, rico.

ta-ta |tâtâ'| interj (*Brit col*) hasta luego, adiós.

tatters |tat'ûrz| npl: **in ~** (*also:* **tattered**) hecho jirones.

tattoo |tatōō'| n tatuaje m; (*spectacle*) espectáculo militar ♦ vt tatuar.

tatty |tat'ē| a (*Brit col*) raído.

taught |tôt| pt, pp of **teach**.

taunt |tônt| n burla ♦ vt burlarse de.

Taurus |tôr'əs| n Tauro.

taut |tôt| a tirante, tenso.

tavern |tav'ûrn| n (*old*) posada, fonda.

tawdry |tô'drē| a de mal gusto.

tawny |tô'nē| a leonado.

tax |taks| n impuesto ♦ vt gravar (con un impuesto); (*fig: test*) poner a prueba; (: *patience*) agotar; **before/after ~** impuestos excluidos/incluidos; **free of ~** libre de impuestos.

taxable |tak'səbəl| a (*income*) imponible, sujeto a impuestos.

tax allowance n desgravación f fiscal.

taxation |taksā'shən| n impuestos mpl; **system of ~** sistema m tributario.

tax avoidance n evasión f de impuestos.

tax collector n recaudador(a) m/f.

tax disc n (*Brit AUT*) pegatina del impuesto

de circulación.

tax evasion n evasión f fiscal.

tax exemption n exención f de impuestos.

tax-free [taks'frē'] a libre de impuestos.

tax haven n paraíso fiscal.

taxi [tak'sē] n taxi m ♦ vi (AVIAT) rodar por la pista.

taxidermist [tak'sidûrmist] n taxidermista m/f.

taxi driver n taxista m/f.

taximeter [tak'simētûr] n taxímetro.

tax inspector n tasador(a) m/f de impuestos.

taxi rank n (Brit) = **taxi stand**.

taxi stand n parada de taxis.

tax payer n contribuyente m/f.

tax rebate n devolución f de impuestos, reembolso fiscal.

tax relief n desgravación f fiscal.

tax return n declaración f de ingresos.

tax shelter n protección f fiscal.

tax year n año fiscal.

TB n abbr = **tuberculosis**.

TD n abbr (US) = **Treasury Department**; (: SOCCER) = **touchdown**.

tea [tē] n té m; (Brit: snack) merienda; **high ~** (Brit) merienda-cena.

tea bag n bolsita de té.

tea break n (Brit) descanso para el té.

teach, pt, pp **taught** [tēch, tôt] vt: **to ~ sb sth, ~ sth to sb** enseñar algo a uno ♦ vi enseñar; (be a teacher) ser profesor(a); **it taught him a lesson** (eso) le sirvió de escarmiento.

teacher [tē'chûr] n (in secondary school) profesor(a) m/f; (in primary school) maestro/a; **Spanish ~** profesor(a) m/f de español.

teacher training college n (for primary schools) escuela normal; (for secondary schools) centro de formación profesoral.

teach-in [tēch'in] n reunión tipo seminario con fines formativos o didácticos.

teaching [tē'ching] n enseñanza.

teaching aids npl ayudas fpl pedagógicas.

teaching hospital n hospital m con facultad de medicina.

tea cosy n cubretetera m.

teacup [tē'kup] n taza para el té.

teak [tēk] n (madera de) teca.

tea leaves npl hojas fpl de té.

team [tēm] n equipo; (of animals) pareja.
  team up vi asociarse.

team spirit n espíritu m de equipo.

teamwork [tēm'wûrk] n trabajo en equipo.

tea party n té m.

teapot [tē'pát] n tetera.

tear n [tär] rasgón m, desgarrón m; [tēr] lágrima ♦ vb [tär] (pt **tore**, pp **torn** [tôr, tôrn]) vt romper, rasgar ♦ vi rasgarse; **in ~s** llorando; **to burst into ~s** deshacerse en lágrimas; **to ~ to pieces** or **to bits** or **to shreds** (also fig) hacer pedazos, destro-

zar.
  tear along vi (rush) precipitarse.
  tear apart vt (also fig) hacer pedazos.
  tear away vt: **to ~ o.s. away (from sth)** arrancarse (de algo), dejar (algo).
  tear out vt (sheet of paper, check) arrancar.
  tear up vt (sheet of paper etc) romper.

teardrop [tēr'dráp] n lágrima.

tearful [tēr'fəl] a lloroso.

tear gas n gas m lacrimógeno.

tearoom [tē'rōōm] n salón m de té, cafetería.

tease [tēz] n bromista m/f ♦ vt tomar el pelo a; (hair) cardar.

tea set n servicio de té.

teashop [tē'sháp] n café m, cafetería.

teaspoon [tē'spōōn] n cucharita; (also: ~ful: as measurement) cucharadita.

tea strainer n colador m de té.

teat [tēt] n (of bottle) boquilla, tetilla.

teatime [tē'tīm] n hora del té.

tea towel n (Brit) paño de cocina.

tea urn n tetera grande.

tech [tek] n abbr (col) = **technology**; **technical college**.

technical [tek'nikəl] a técnico.

technical college n centro de formación profesional.

technicality [teknikal'itē] n detalle m técnico; **on a legal ~** por una cuestión formal.

technically [tek'niklē] ad técnicamente.

technician [teknish'ən] n técnico/a.

technique [teknēk'] n técnica.

technocrat [tek'nəkrat] n tecnócrata m/f.

technological [teknəláj'ikəl] a tecnológico.

technologist [teknál'əjist] n tecnólogo/a.

technology [teknál'əjē] n tecnología.

teddy (bear) [ted'ē (bär)] n osito de felpa.

tedious [tē'dēəs] a pesado, aburrido.

tediously [tē'dēəslē] ad aburridamente, de modo pesado.

tedium [tē'dēəm] n tedio.

tee [tē] n (GOLF) tee m.

teem [tēm] vi: **to ~ with** rebosar de.

teenage [tēn'āj] a (fashions etc) juvenil.

teenager [tēn'ājûr] n joven m/f (de 13 a 19 años).

teens [tēnz] npl: **to be in one's ~** ser adolescente.

tee shirt n = **T-shirt**.

teeter [tē'tûr] vi balancearse.

teeth [tēth] npl of **tooth**.

teethe [tēth] vi echar los dientes.

teething ring [tē'thing ring] n mordedor m.

teething troubles [tē'thing trub'əlz] npl (fig) dificultades fpl iniciales.

teetotal [tētōt'əl] a (person) abstemio.

teetotaler, (Brit) **teetotaller** [tētōt'əlûr] n (person) abstemio/a.

TEFL [tef'əl] n abbr = Teaching of English as a Foreign Language.

Teheran [teərân'] *n* Teherán *m*.
tel. *abbr* (= *telephone*) tel.
Tel Aviv [tel' əvēv'] *n* Tel Aviv *m*.
telecast [tel'əkast] *vt, vi* transmitir por televisión.
telecommunications [teləkəmyōōnikā'shənz] *n* telecomunicaciones *fpl*.
telegram [tel'əgram] *n* telegrama *m*.
telegraph [tel'əgraf] *n* telégrafo.
telegraphic [teləgraf'ik] *a* telegráfico.
telegraph pole *n* poste *m* telegráfico.
telegraph wire *n* hilo telegráfico.
telepathic [teləpath'ik] *a* telepático.
telepathy [tələp'əthē] *n* telepatía.
telephone [tel'əfōn] *n* teléfono ♦ *vt* llamar por teléfono, telefonear; **to be on the ~** (*be speaking*) estar hablando por teléfono.
telephone booth, (*Brit*) **telephone box** *n* cabina telefónica.
telephone call *n* llamada (telefónica).
telephone directory *n* guía (telefónica).
telephone exchange *n* central *f* telefónica.
telephone kiosk *n* (*Brit*) cabina telefónica.
telephone number *n* número de teléfono.
telephone operator *n* telefonista *m/f*.
telephonist [tel'əfōnist] *n* (*Brit*) telefonista *m/f*.
telephoto [teləfō'tō] *a*: **~ lens** teleobjetivo.
teleprinter [tel'əprintûr] *n* teletipo, teleimpresora.
telescope [tel'əskōp] *n* telescopio.
telescopic [teliskáp'ik] *a* telescópico; (*umbrella*) plegable.
teletext [tel'ətekst] *n* (*TEL*) teletex(to) *m*.
telethon [tel'əthân] *n* maratón *m* televisivo.
televise [tel'əvīz] *vt* televisar.
television [tel'əvizhən] *n* televisión *f*; **to watch ~** mirar la televisión.
television licence *n* (*Brit*) impuesto de televisor.
television set *n* televisor *m*.
telex [tel'eks] *n* télex *m*; (*machine*) máquina télex ♦ *vt* (*message*) enviar por télex; (*person*) enviar un télex a ♦ *vi* enviar un télex.
tell, *pt, pp* **told**, [tel, tōld] *vt* decir; (*relate: story*) contar; (*distinguish*): **to ~ sth from** distinguir algo de ♦ *vi* (*talk*): **to ~ (of)** contar; (*have effect*) tener efecto; **to ~ sb to do sth** mandar a uno hacer algo; **to ~ sb about sth** explicar algo a uno; **can you ~ me the time?** ¿me puedes decir la hora?; **(I) ~ you what ...** fíjate ...; **I couldn't ~ them apart** no podía distinguirlos.
tell off *vt*: **to ~ sb off** regañar a uno.
tell on *vt fus*: **to ~ on sb** chivarse de uno.
teller [tel'ûr] *n* (*in bank*) cajero/a.
telling [tel'ing] *a* (*remark, detail*) revelador(a).
telltale [tel'tāl] *a* (*sign*) indicador(a).

telly [tel'ē] *n* (*Brit col*) tele *f*.
temerity [təmär'itē] *n* temeridad *f*.
temp [temp] *n abbr* (= *temporary office worker*) temporero/a ♦ *vi* trabajar de interino/a.
temper [tem'pûr] *n* (*mood*) humor *m*; (*bad* ~) (mal) genio; (*fit of anger*) ira; (*of child*) rabieta ♦ *vt* (*moderate*) moderar; **to be in a ~** estar furioso; **to lose one's ~** enfadarse, enojarse (*LAm*); **to keep one's ~** contenerse, no alterarse.
temperament [tem'pûrəmənt] *n* (*nature*) temperamento.
temperamental [tempûrəmen'təl] *a* temperamental.
temperance [tem'pûrəns] *n* moderación *f*; (*in drinking*) sobriedad *f*.
temperate [tem'pûrit] *a* moderado; (*climate*) templado.
temperature [tem'pûrəchûr] *n* temperatura; **to have** *or* **run a ~** tener fiebre.
tempered [tem'pûrd] *a* (*steel*) templado.
tempest [tem'pist] *n* tempestad *f*.
tempestuous [tempes'chōōəs] *a* (*relationship, meeting*) tempestuoso.
tempi [tem'pē] *npl of* **tempo**.
template [tem'plit] *n* plantilla.
temple [tem'pəl] *n* (*building*) templo; (*ANAT*) sien *f*.
templet [tem'plit] *n* = **template**.
tempo, *pl* **~s** *or* **tempi** [tem'pō, tem'pē] *n* tempo; (*fig: of life etc*) ritmo.
temporal [tem'pûrəl] *a* temporal.
temporarily [tempərär'ilē] *ad* temporalmente.
temporary [tem'pərärē] *a* provisional, temporal; (*passing*) transitorio; (*worker*) temporero; **~ teacher** (*Brit*) maestro/a interino/a.
tempt [tempt] *vt* tentar; **to ~ sb into doing sth** tentar *or* inducir a uno a hacer algo; **to be ~ed to do sth** (*person*) sentirse tentado de hacer algo.
temptation [temptā'shən] *n* tentación *f*.
tempting [temp'ting] *a* tentador(a).
ten [ten] *num* diez; **~s of thousands** decenas *fpl* de miles.
tenable [ten'əbəl] *a* sostenible.
tenacious [tənā'shəs] *a* tenaz.
tenaciously [tənā'shəslē] *ad* tenazmente.
tenacity [tənas'itē] *n* tenacidad *f*.
tenancy [ten'ənsē] *n* alquiler *m*; (*of house*) inquilinato.
tenant [ten'ənt] *n* (*rent-payer*) inquilino/a; (*occupant*) habitante *m/f*.
tend [tend] *vt* (*sick etc*) cuidar, atender; (*cattle, machine*) vigilar, cuidar ♦ *vi*: **to ~ to do sth** tener tendencia a hacer algo.
tendency [ten'dənsē] *n* tendencia.
tender [ten'dûr] *a* tierno, blando; (*delicate*) delicado; (*sore*) sensible; (*affectionate*) tierno, cariñoso ♦ *n* (*COMM: offer*) oferta; (*money*): **legal ~** moneda de curso legal ♦

vt ofrecer; **to put in a ~ (for)** hacer una oferta (para); **to ~ one's resignation** presentar la dimisión.

tenderize [tɛn'dəriz] *vt* (*CULIN*) ablandar.

tenderly [tɛn'dúrlē] *ad* tiernamente.

tenderness [tɛn'dúrnis] *n* ternura; (*of meat*) blandura.

tendon [tɛn'dən] *n* tendón *m*.

tendril [tɛn'dril] *n* zarcillo.

tenement [tɛn'əmənt] *n* casa *or* bloque *m* de pisos *or* vecinos (*Sp*).

Tenerife [tɛnərēf'] *n* Tenerife *m*.

tenet [tɛn'it] *n* principio.

Tenn. *abbr* (*US*) = *Tennessee*.

tenner [tɛn'úr] *n* (*US*) (billete *m* de) diez dólares *mpl*; (*Brit*) (billete *m* de) diez libras *fpl*.

tennis [tɛn'is] *n* tenis *m*.

tennis ball *n* pelota de tenis.

tennis club *n* club *m* de tenis.

tennis court *n* cancha de tenis.

tennis elbow *n* (*MED*) sinovitis *f* del codo.

tennis match *n* partido de tenis.

tennis player *n* tenista *m/f*.

tennis racket *n* raqueta de tenis.

tennis shoes *npl* zapatillas *fpl* de tenis.

tenor [tɛn'úr] *n* (*MUS*) tenor *m*.

tenpin bowling [tɛn'pin bō'ling] *n* bolos *mpl*, bolera.

tense [tɛns] *a* tenso; (*stretched*) tirante; (*stiff*) rígido, tieso; (*person*) nervioso ♦ *n* (*LING*) tiempo ♦ *vt* (*tighten: muscles*) tensar.

tensely [tɛns'lē] *ad* tensamente.

tenseness [tɛns'nis] *n* tirantez *f*, tensión *f*.

tension [tɛn'chən] *n* tensión *f*.

tent [tɛnt] *n* tienda (de campaña), carpa (*LAm*).

tentacle [tɛn'təkəl] *n* tentáculo.

tentative [tɛn'tətiv] *a* (*person*) indeciso; (*provisional*) provisional.

tentatively [tɛn'tətivlē] *ad* con indesición; (*provisionally*) provisionalmente.

tenterhooks [tɛn'túrhoŏoks] *npl*: **on ~** sobre ascuas.

tenth [tɛnth] *a* décimo.

tent peg *n* clavija, estaca.

tent pole *n* mástil *m*.

tenuous [tɛn'yoŏoss] *a* tenue.

tenure [tɛn'yúr] *n* posesión *f*, tenencia; **to have ~** tener posesión *or* título de propiedad.

tepid [tɛp'id] *a* tibio.

term [túrm] *n* (*limit*) límite *m*; (*COMM*) plazo; (*word*) término; (*period*) período; (*SCOL*) trimestre *m* ♦ *vt* llamar; **~s** *npl* (*conditions*) condiciones *fpl*; (*COMM*) precio, tarifa; **in the short/long ~** a corto/largo plazo; **during his ~ of office** bajo su mandato; **to be on good ~s with sb** llevarse bien con uno; **to come to ~s with** (*problem*) adaptarse a; **in ~s of ...** en cuanto a ..., en términos de ....

terminal [túr'mənəl] *a* terminal; (*disease*) mortal ♦ *n* (*ELEC*) borne *m*; (*COMPUT*) terminal *m*; (*also:* **air ~**) terminal *f*; (*Brit: also:* **coach ~**) (estación *f*) terminal *f*.

terminate [túr'mənāt] *vt* terminar ♦ *vi*: **to ~ in** acabar por.

termination [túrmənā'shən] *n* fin *m*; (*of contract*) terminación *f*; **~ of pregnancy** aborto.

termini [túr'mənē] *npl* of **terminus**.

terminology [túrmənál'əjē] *n* terminología.

terminus, *pl* termini [túr'mənəs, túr'mənē] *n* término, (*station*) terminal *f*.

termite [túr'mit] *n* termita.

Ter(r). *abbr* = **terrace**.

terrace [tär'əs] *n* terraza; (*Brit: row of houses*) hilera de casas adosadas; **the ~s** (*Brit SPORT*) las gradas *fpl*.

terraced [tär'əst] *a* (*garden*) escalonado; (*house*) alineado, adosado.

terracotta [tärəkât'ə] *n* terracota.

terrain [tərān'] *n* terreno.

terrible [tär'əbəl] *a* terrible, horrible; (*fam*) malísimo.

terribly [tär'əblē] *ad* terriblemente; (*very badly*) malísimamente.

terrier [tär'ēúr] *n* terrier *m*.

terrific [tərif'ik] *a* fantástico, fenomenal; (*wonderful*) maravilloso.

terrify [tär'əfi] *vt* aterrorizar; **to be terrified** estar aterrado *or* aterrorizado.

terrifying [tär'əfiing] *a* aterrador(a).

territorial [täritôr'ēəl] *a* territorial.

territorial waters *npl* aguas *fpl* jurisdiccionales.

territory [tär'itôrē] *n* territorio.

terror [tär'úr] *n* terror *m*.

terrorism [tär'ərizəm] *n* terrorismo.

terrorist [tär'úrist] *n* terrorista *m/f*.

terrorize [tär'əriz] *vt* aterrorizar.

terse [túrs] *a* (*style*) conciso; (*reply*) brusco.

tertiary [túr'shēärē] *a* terciario.

Terylene [tär'əlēn] ® *n* (*Brit*) terylene *m* ®.

TESL [tɛs'əl] *n abbr* = *Teaching of English as a Second Language*.

test [tɛst] *n* (*trial, check*) prueba, ensayo; (: *of goods in factory*) control *m*; (*of courage etc, CHEM*) prueba; (*MED*) examen *m*; (*exam*) examen *m*, test *m*; (*also:* **driving ~**) examen *m* de conducir ♦ *vt* probar, poner a prueba; (*MED*) examinar; **to put sth to the ~** someter algo a prueba; **to ~ sth for sth** analizar algo en busca de algo.

testament [tɛs'təmənt] *n* testamento; **the Old/New T~** el Antiguo/Nuevo Testamento.

test ban *n* (*also:* **nuclear ~**) suspensión *f* de pruebas nucleares.

test case *n* (*JUR*) juicio que sienta precedente.

test flight *n* vuelo de ensayo.

testicle [tes'tikəl] *n* testículo.
testify [tes'təfī] *vi* (*LAW*) prestar declaración; **to ~ to sth** atestiguar algo.
testimonial [testimō'nēəl] *n* (*of character*) (carta de) recomendación *f*, testimonial *m*.
testimony [tes'təmōnē] *n* (*LAW*) testimonio, declaración *f*.
testing [tes'ting] *a* (*difficult: time*) duro.
testing ground *n* zona de pruebas.
test match *n* (Brit CRICKET. RUGBY) partido internacional.
test paper *n* examen *m*, test *m*.
test pilot *n* piloto/mujer piloto *m/f* de pruebas.
test tube *n* probeta.
test-tube baby [test'tōōb bā'bē] *n* bebé *m* (de) probeta.
testy [tes'tē] *a* irritable.
tetanus [tet'ənəs] *n* tétano.
tetchy [tech'ē] *a* malhumorado, irritable.
tether [teth'ûr] *vt* atar (con una cuerda) ♦ *n*: **to be at the end of one's ~** (*Brit*) no aguantar más.
Tex. *abbr* (*US*) = *Texas*.
text [tekst] *n* texto.
textbook [tekst'bōōk] *n* libro de texto.
textiles [teks'təlz] *npl* textiles *mpl*, tejidos *mpl*.
texture [teks'chûr] *n* textura.
TGIF *abbr* (*col*) = *thank God it's Friday*.
Thai [tī] *a, n* tailandés/esa *m/f*.
Thailand [tī'lənd] *n* Tailandia.
thalidomide [thəlid'əmīd] ® *n* talidomida ®.
Thames [temz] *n*: **the ~** el (río) Támesis.
than [than, then] *conj* que; (*with numerals*): **more ~ 10/once** más de 10/una vez; **I have more/less ~ you** tengo más/menos que tú; **it is better to phone ~ to write** es mejor llamar por teléfono que escribir; **no sooner did he leave ~ the phone rang** en cuanto se marchó, sonó el teléfono.
thank [thangk] *vt* dar las gracias a, agradecer; **~ you (very much)** muchas gracias; **~ heavens, ~ God!** ¡gracias a Dios!, ¡menos mal!
thankful [thangk'fəl] *a*: **~ for** agradecido (por).
thankfully [thangk'fəlē] *ad* (*gratefully*) con agradecimiento; (*with relief*) por suerte; **~ there were few victims** afortunadamente hubo pocas víctimas.
thankless [thangk'lis] *a* ingrato.
thanks [thangks] *npl* gracias *fpl* ♦ *excl* ¡gracias!; **~ to** *prep* gracias a.
Thanksgiving (Day) [thangksgiv'ing (dā)] *n* día *m* de Acción de Gracias.
that [that, thət] *conj* que ♦ *a* ese/esa; (*more remote*) aquel/aquella ♦ *pron* ése/ésa; aquél/aquélla; (*neuter*) eso; aquello; (*relative: subject*) que; (: *object*) que, el cual/la cual *etc*; (*with time*): **on the day ~ he came** el día que vino ♦ *ad*: **~ high** tan alto,

así de alto; **it's about ~ high** es más o menos así de alto; **~ one** ése/ésa; aquél/aquélla; **~ one over there** aquél/aquélla; **what's ~?** ¿qué es eso?; **who's ~?** ¿quién es?; **is ~ you?** ¿eres tú?; (*formal*) ¿es usted?; **~'s what he said** eso es lo que dijo; **all ~** todo eso; **I can't work ~ much** no puedo trabajar tanto; **at *or* with ~ she ...** con eso, ella ...; **do it like ~** hazlo así; **not ~ I know of** que yo sepa, no; **so ~, in order ~** para que + *subjun*.
thatched [thacht] *a* (*roof*) de paja; **~ cottage** casita con tejado de paja.
thaw [thô] *n* deshielo ♦ *vi* (*ice*) derretirse; (*food*) descongelarse ♦ *vt* (*food*) descongelar.
the [thə, thē] *def art* el/la; (*pl*) los/las; (*neuter*) lo; (*in titles*): **Richard ~ Second** Ricardo Segundo; **~ sooner ~ better** cuanto antes mejor; **~ more he works, ~ more he earns** cuanto más trabaja, más gana; **I haven't ~ time/money** no tengo tiempo/dinero; **100 pesetas to ~ dollar** 100 pesetas por dólar; **paid by ~ hour** pagado por hora; **do you know ~ Smiths?** ¿conoce a los Smith?
theater, (*Brit*) **theatre** [thē'ətûr] *n* teatro.
theatergoer [thē'ətûrgōūr] *n* aficionado/a al teatro.
theatrical [thēat'rikəl] *a* teatral.
theft [theft] *n* robo.
their [thär] *a* su.
theirs [thärz] *pron* (el) suyo/(la) suya *etc*; *see also* **my, mine**.
them [them, thəm] *pron* (*direct*) los/las; (*indirect*) les; (*stressed, after prep*) ellos/ellas; **I see ~** los veo; **both of ~** ambos/as, los/las dos; **give me a few of ~** dame algunos/as; *see also* **me**.
theme [thēm] *n* tema *m*.
theme song *n* tema *m* (musical).
themselves [thəmselvz'] *pl pron* (*subject*) ellos mismos/ellas mismas; (*complement*) se; (*after prep*) sí (mismos/as); *see also* **oneself**.
then [then] *ad* (*at that time*) entonces; (*next*) pues; (*later*) luego, después; (*and also*) además ♦ *conj* (*therefore*) en ese caso, entonces ♦ *a*: **the ~ president** el entonces presidente; **from ~ on** desde entonces; **until ~** hasta entonces; **and ~ what?** y luego, ¿qué?; **what do you want me to do, ~?** ¿qué quiere que haga, entonces?
theologian [thēəlō'jən] *n* teólogo/a.
theological [thēəláj'ikəl] *a* teológico.
theology [thēál'əjē] *n* teología.
theorem [thēr'əm] *n* teorema *m*.
theoretical [thēəret'ikəl] *a* teórico.
theoretically [thēəret'ikəlē] *ad* teóricamente, en teoría.
theorize [thē'ərīz] *vi* teorizar.
theory [thiûr'ē] *n* teoría.

therapeutic(al) [thärəpyōō'tik(əl)] *a* terapéutico.

therapist [thär'əpist] *n* terapeuta *m/f*.

therapy [thär'əpē] *n* terapia.

there [thär] *ad* allí, allá, ahí; ~, ~! ¡cálmate!; **it's** ~ está ahí; **~'s the bus** ahí *or* ya viene el autobús; ~ **is,** ~ **are** hay; ~ **he is** ahí está; **on/in** ~ allí encima/dentro; **back/down** ~ allá *or* allí atrás/abajo; **over** ~, **through** ~ por allí.

thereabouts [thär'əbouts] *ad* por ahí.

thereafter [thäraf'tûr] *ad* después.

thereby [thärbī'] *ad* así, de ese modo.

therefore [thär'fôr] *ad* por lo tanto.

there's [thärz] = **there is; there has.**

thereupon [thärəpän'] *ad* (*at that point*) en eso, en seguida.

thermal [thûr'məl] *a* termal.

thermal paper *n* papel *m* térmico.

thermal printer *n* termoimpresora.

thermodynamics [thûrmōdīnam'iks] *n* termodinámica.

thermometer [thûrmâm'itûr] *n* termómetro.

thermonuclear [thûrmōnōō'klēûr] *a* termonuclear.

Thermos [thûr'məs] ® *n* termo.

thermostat [thûr'məstat] *n* termostato.

thesaurus [thisôr'əs] *n* tesoro.

these [thēz] *pl a* estos/as ♦ *pl pron* éstos/as.

thesis, *pl* **theses** [thē'sis, -sēz] *n* tesis *f inv*.

they [thā] *pl pron* ellos/ellas; (*mismos*)/ellas (*mismas*); ~ **say that...** (*it is said that*) se dice que....

they'd [thād] = **they had; they would.**

they'll [thāl] = **they shall, they will.**

they're [thär] = **they are.**

they've [thāv] = **they have.**

thick [thik] *a* (*wall, slice*) grueso; (*dense: liquid, smoke etc*) espeso; (*vegetation, beard*) tupido; (*stupid*) torpe ♦ *n*: **in the** ~ **of the battle** en lo más reñido de la batalla; **it's 20 cm** ~ tiene 20 cm de espesor.

thicken [thik'ən] *vi* espesarse ♦ *vt* (*sauce etc*) espesar.

thicket [thik'it] *n* espesura.

thickly [thik'lē] *ad* (*spread*) en capa espesa; (*cut*) en rebanada gruesa; (*populated*) densamente.

thickness [thik'nis] *n* espesor *m*, grueso.

thickset [thik'set'] *a* (*Brit*) fornido.

thickskinned [thik'skind'] *a* (*fig*) insensible.

thief, *pl* **thieves** [thēf, thēvz] *n* ladrón/ona *m/f*.

thieving [thē'ving] *n* robo, hurto ♦ *a* ladrón/ona.

thigh [thī] *n* muslo.

thighbone [thī'bōn] *n* fémur *m*.

thimble [thim'bəl] *n* dedal *m*.

thin [thin] *a* delgado; (*watery*) aguado; (*light*) tenue; (*hair*) escaso; (*fog*) ligero; (*crowd*) disperso ♦ *vt*: **to** ~ **(down)** (*sauce, paint*) diluir ♦ *vi* (*fog*) aclararse; (*also:* ~

out: *crowd*) dispersarse; **his hair is** ~**ning** está perdiendo (el) pelo.

thing [thing] *n* cosa; (*object*) objeto, artículo; (*contraption*) chisme *m*; (*mania*) manía; ~**s** *npl* (*belongings*) efectos *mpl* (personales); **the best** ~ **would be to...** lo mejor sería...; **the main** ~ **is to** ... lo principal que hay que hacer es ...; **first** ~ **(in the morning)** a primera hora (de la mañana); **last** ~ **(at night)** a última hora (de la noche); **the** ~ **is** ... lo que pasa es que ...; **how are** ~**s?** ¿qué tal?; **she's got a** ~ **about mice** le da no sé qué de los ratones; **poor** ~! ¡pobre! *m/f*, ¡pobrecito/a!

think, *pt, pp* **thought** [thingk, thôt] *vi* pensar ♦ *vt* pensar, creer; (*imagine*) imaginar; **what did you** ~ **of it?** ¿qué te parece?; **what did you** ~ **of them?** ¿qué te parecieron?; **to** ~ **about sth/sb** pensar en algo/uno; **I'll** ~ **about it** lo pensaré; **to** ~ **of doing sth** pensar en hacer algo; **I** ~ **so/not** creo que sí/no; ~ **again!** ¡piénsalo bien!; **to** ~ **aloud** pensar en voz alta; **to** ~ **well of sb** tener buen concepto de uno.

think out *vt* (*plan*) elaborar, tramar; (*solution*) encontrar.

think over *vt* reflexionar sobre, meditar; **I'd like to** ~ **things over** me gustaría examinarlo detenidamente.

think through *vt* pensar bien.

think up *vt* imaginar.

thinking [thingk'ing] *n*: **to my (way of)** ~ a mi parecer.

think tank *n* gabinete *m* de estrategia.

thinly [thin'lē] *ad* (*cut*) en lonchas finas; (*spread*) en una ligera capa.

thinness [thin'is] *n* delgadez *f*.

third [thûrd] *a* (*before nmsg:* **tercer**) tercero ♦ *n* tercero/a; (*fraction*) tercio.

third degree *a* (*burns*) de tercer grado.

thirdly [thûrd'lē] *ad* en tercer lugar.

third party insurance *n* (*Brit*) seguro contra terceros.

third-rate [thûrd'rāt'] *a* (de calidad) mediocre.

Third World *n*: **the** ~ el Tercer Mundo ♦ *cpd* tercermundista.

thirst [thûrst] *n* sed *f*.

thirsty [thûrs'tē] *a* (*person*) sediento; **to be** ~ tener sed.

thirteen [thûr'tēn'] *num* trece.

thirteenth [thûr'tēnth'] *a* decimotercero ♦ *n* (*in series*) decimotercero/a; (*fraction*) decimotercio.

thirtieth [thûr'tēith] *a* trigésimo ♦ *n* (*in series*) trigésimo/a; (*fraction*) treintavo.

thirty [thûr'tē] *num* treinta.

this [this] *a* este/esta ♦ *pron* éste/ésta; (*neuter*) esto; ~ **is what he said** esto es lo que dijo; ~ **high** así de alto; ~ **way** por aquí; ~ **time** esta vez; ~ **time last year** hoy hace un año; **who is** ~? ¿quién es éste/ésta? **what is** ~? ¿qué es esto?; ~ **is Mr**

Brown (*in introductions*) le presento al Sr Brown; (*in photo*) éste es el Sr Brown; (*on telephone*) el Sr Brown al habla; **they were talking of ~ and that** hablaban de esto y aquello.

thistle [this'əl] *n* cardo.

thong [thông] *n* correa.

thorn [thôrn] *n* espina.

thorny [thôr'nē] *a* espinoso.

thorough [thûr'ō] *a* (*search*) minucioso; (*knowledge, research*) profundo.

thoroughbred [thûr'ōbred] *a* (*horse*) de pura sangre.

thoroughfare [thûr'ōfär] *n* calle *f*.

thoroughly [thûr'ōlē] *ad* minuciosamente; profundamente, a fondo.

thoroughness [thûr'ōnis] *n* minuciosidad *f*.

those [th̲ōz] *pl pron* ésos/ésas; (*more remote*) aquéllos/as ♦ *pl a* esos/esas; aquellos/as.

though [th̲ō] *conj* aunque ♦ *ad* sin embargo, aún así; **even ~** aunque; **it's not so easy, ~** sin embargo no es tan fácil.

thought [thôt] *pt, pp of* **think** ♦ *n* pensamiento; (*opinion*) opinión *f*; (*intention*) intención *f*; **to give sth some ~** pensar algo detenidamente; **after much ~** pensándolo bien; **I've just had a ~** se me acaba de ocurrir una idea.

thoughtful [thôt'fəl] *a* pensativo; (*considerate*) atento.

thoughtfully [thôt'fəlē] *ad* pensativamente; atentamente.

thoughtless [thôt'lis] *a* desconsiderado.

thoughtlessly [thôt'lislē] *ad* impensadamente, insensatamente.

thousand [thou'zənd] *num* mil; **two ~** dos mil; **~s of** miles de.

thousandth [thou'zəndth] *num* milésimo.

thrash [thrash] *vt* apalear; (*defeat*) derrotar.

thrash about *vi* revolcarse.

thrash out *vt* discutir a fondo.

thrashing [thrash'ing] *n:* **to give sb a ~** dar una paliza a uno.

thread [thred] *n* hilo; (*of screw*) rosca ♦ *vt* (*needle*) enhebrar.

threadbare [thred'bär] *a* raído.

threat [thret] *n* amenaza; **to be under ~ of** estar amenazado de.

threaten [thret'ən] *vi* amenazar ♦ *vt:* **to ~ sb with sth/to do** amenazar a uno con algo/con hacer.

threatening [thret'əning] *a* amenazador(a), amenazante.

three [thrē] *num* tres.

three-dimensional [thrē'dimen'chənəl] *a* tridimensional.

threefold [thrē'fōld] *ad:* **to increase ~** triplicar.

three-piece [thrē'pēs] *:* **~ suit** *n* traje *m* de tres piezas; **~ suite** *n* tresillo.

three-ply [thrē'plī] *a* (*wood*) de tres capas;

(*wool*) triple.

three-quarter [thrē'kwôr'tûr] *a:* **~ length sleeves** mangas *fpl* tres cuartos.

three-quarters [thrē'kwôr'tûrz] *npl* tres cuartas partes; **~ full** tres cuartas partes lleno.

thresh [thresh] *vt* (*AGR*) trillar.

threshing machine [thresh'ing məshēn'] *n* trilladora.

threshold [thresh'ōld] *n* umbral *m*; **to be on the ~ of** (*fig*) estar al borde de.

threshold agreement *n* convenio de nivel crítico.

threw [thrōō] *pt of* **throw.**

thrift [thrift] *n* economía.

thrifty [thrif'tē] *a* económico.

thrill [thril] *n* (*excitement*) emoción *f* ♦ *vt* emocionar; **to be ~ed** (*with gift etc*) estar encantado.

thriller [thril'ûr] *n* película/novela de suspense.

thrilling [thril'ing] *a* emocionante.

thrive, *pt* **thrived, throve,** *pp* **thrived, thriven** [thrīv, thrōv, thriv'ən] *vi* (*grow*) crecer; (*do well*) prosperar.

thriving [thrīv'ing] *a* próspero.

throat [thrōt] *n* garganta; **to have a sore ~** tener dolor de garganta.

throb [thráb] *n* (*of heart*) latido; (*of engine*) vibración *f* ♦ *vi* latir; vibrar; (*with pain*) dar punzadas; **my head is ~bing** la cabeza me da punzadas.

throes [thrōz] *npl:* **in the ~ of** en medio de.

thrombosis [thrâmbō'sis] *n* trombosis *f*.

throne [thrōn] *n* trono.

throng [thrông] *n* multitud *f*, muchedumbre *f* ♦ *vt, vi* apiñarse, agolparse.

throttle [thrát'əl] *n* (*AUT*) acelerador *m* ♦ *vt* estrangular.

through [thrōō] *prep* por, a través de; (*time*) durante; (*by means of*) por medio de, mediante; (*owing to*) gracias a ♦ *a* (*ticket, train*) directo ♦ *ad* completamente, de parte a parte; de principio a fin; **(from) Monday ~ Friday** (*US*) de lunes a viernes; **to go ~ sb's papers** mirar entre los papeles de uno; **I am halfway ~ the book** voy por la mitad del libro; **the soldiers didn't let us ~** los soldados no nos dejaron pasar; **to put sb ~ to sb** (*TEL*) poner *or* pasar a uno con uno; **to get ~** (*TEL*) tener comunicación; (*have finished*) haber terminado; **"no ~ road"** "calle sin salida".

throughout [thrōōout'] *prep* (*place*) por todas partes de, por todo; (*time*) durante todo ♦ *ad* por or en todas partes.

throughput [thrōō'pŏŏt] *n* (*of goods, materials*) producción *f*; (*COMPUT*) capacidad *f* de procesamiento.

throve [thrōv] *pt of* **thrive.**

throw [thrō] *n* tiro; (*SPORT*) lanzamiento ♦ *vt* (*pt* **threw,** *pp* **thrown** [thrōō, thrōn]) tirar, echar; (*SPORT*) lanzar; (*rider*) derribar; (*fig*) desconcertar; **to ~ a party** dar una fiesta.

throw about *vt* (*Brit*) = **throw around**.

throw around *vt* (*litter etc*) tirar, esparcir.

throw away *vt* tirar.

throw off *vt* deshacerse de.

throw open *vt* (*doors, windows*) abrir de par en par; (*house, gardens etc*) abrir al público; (*competition, race*) abrir a todos.

throw out *vt* tirar.

throw together *vt* (*clothes*) amontonar; (*meal*) preparar a la carrera; (*essay*) hacer sin cuidado.

throw up *vi* vomitar.

throwaway [thrō'əwā] *a* para tirar, desechable.

throwback [thrō'bak] *n*: **it's a ~ to** (*fig*) eso nos lleva de nuevo a.

throw-in [thrō'in] *n* (*SPORT*) saque *m*.

thrown [thrōn] *pp* of **throw**.

thru [thrōō] (*US*) = **through**.

thrush [thrush] *n* zorzal *m*, tordo; (*MED*) afta.

thrust [thrust] *n* (*TECH*) empuje *m* ♦ *vt* (*pt, pp* **thrust**) empujar; (*push in*) introducir.

thrusting [thrust'ing] *a* (*person*) dinámico, con empuje.

thud [thud] *n* golpe *m* sordo.

thug [thug] *n* gamberro/a.

thumb [thum] *n* (*ANAT*) pulgar *m* ♦ *vt*: **to ~ (a ride)** hacer autostop; **to give sth/sb the ~s up** aprobar algo/a uno.

thumb through *vt fus* (*book*) hojear.

thumb index *n* índice *m* recortado.

thumbnail [thum'nāl] *n* uña del pulgar.

thumbnail sketch *n* esbozo.

thumbtack [thum'tak] *n* (*US*) chincheta, chinche *m* (*LAm*).

thump [thump] *n* golpe *m*; (*sound*) ruido seco *or* sordo ♦ *vt, vi* golpear.

thunder [thun'dûr] *n* trueno; (*of applause etc*) estruendo ♦ *vi* tronar; (*train etc*): **to ~ past** pasar como un trueno.

thunderbolt [thun'dûrbōlt] *n* rayo.

thunderclap [thun'dûrklap] *n* trueno.

thunderous [thun'dûrəs] *a* ensordecedor(a), estruendoso.

thunderstorm [thun'dûrstôrm] *n* tormenta.

thunderstruck [thun'dûrstruk] *a* pasmado.

thundery [thun'dûrē] *a* tormentoso.

Thur(s). *abbr* (= *Thursday*) juev.

Thursday [thûrz'dā] *n* jueves *m inv*.

thus [ᵺus] *ad* así, de este modo.

thwart [thwôrt] *vt* frustrar.

thyme [tīm] *n* tomillo.

thyroid [thī'roid] *n* tiroides *m inv*.

tiara [tēar'ə] *n* tiara, diadema.

Tiber [tī'bûr] *n* Tíber *m*.

Tibet [tibet'] *n* el Tíbet.

Tibetan [tibet'ən] *a* tibetano ♦ *n* tibetano/a; (*LING*) tibetano.

tibia [tib'ēə] *n* tibia.

tic [tik] *n* tic *m*.

tick [tik] *n* (*sound: of clock*) tictac *m*; (*mark*) palomita; (*ZOOL*) garrapata ♦ *vi* hacer tictac ♦ *vt* marcar; **to put a ~ against sth** marcar algo (con palmita).

tick off *vt* marcar; (*person*) reñir.

tick over *vi* (*Brit: engine*) girar en marcha lenta; (: *fig*) ir tirando.

ticker tape [tik'ûr tāp] *n* cinta perforada.

ticket [tik'it] *n* billete *m*, tíquet *m*, boleto (*LAm*); (*for cinema etc*) entrada, boleto (*LAm*); (*in shop: on goods*) etiqueta; (*US POL*) lista (de candidatos); **to get a parking ~** (*AUT*) ser multado por estacionamiento ilegal.

ticket agency *n* (*THEATER*) agencia de billetes.

ticket collector *n* (*Brit*) revisor(a) *m/f*.

ticket holder *n* poseedor(a) *m/f* de billete.

ticket inspector *n* (*Brit*) revisor(a) *m/f*, inspector(a) *m/f* de boletos (*LAm*).

ticket office *n* (*THEATER*) taquilla, boletería (*LAm*); (*RAIL*) despacho de billetes *or* boletos (*LAm*).

tickle [tik'əl] *vt* hacer cosquillas a.

ticklish [tik'lish] *a* (*person*) cosquilloso; (*which tickles: blanket*) que pica; (: *cough*) irritante.

tidal [tīd'əl] *a* de marea.

tidal wave *n* maremoto.

tidbit [tid'bit] *n* (*US*) (*food*) golosina; (*news*) pedazo.

tiddlywinks [tid'lēwingks] *n* juego infantil de habilidad con fichas de plástico.

tide [tīd] *n* marea; (*fig: of events*) curso, marcha ♦ *vt*: **to ~ sb over** *or* **through (until)** ayudarle a uno con medios (hasta); **high/low ~** marea alta/baja; **the ~ of public opinion** la tendencia de la opinión pública.

tidily [tī'dilē] *ad* bien, ordenadamente; **to arrange ~** ordenar; **to dress ~** vestir bien.

tidiness [tī'dēnis] *n* (*order*) orden *m*; (*cleanliness*) aseo.

tidy [tī'dē] *a* (*room*) ordenado; (*drawing, work*) limpio; (*person*) (bien) arreglado; (: *in character*) metódico; (*mind*) claro, metódico ♦ *vt* (*also: ~ up*) poner en orden.

tie [tī] *n* (*string etc*) atadura; (*US RAIL: on track*) traviesa; (*Brit: neck~*) corbata; (*fig: link*) vínculo, lazo; (*SPORT: draw*) empate *m* ♦ *vt* atar ♦ *vi* (*SPORT*) empatar; **family ~s** obligaciones *fpl* familiares; **cup ~** (*Brit SPORT: match*) ᵖpartido de copa; **to ~ in a bow** hacer un lazo; **to ~ a knot in sth** hacer un nudo en algo.

tie down *vt* atar; (*fig*): **to ~ sb down to** obligar a uno a.

tie in *vi*: **to ~ in (with)** (*correspond*) concordar (con).

tie on *vt* (*Brit: label etc*) atar.

tie up *vt* (*parcel*) envolver; (*dog*) atar;

(*boat*) amarrar; (*arrangements*) concluir; **to be ~d up** (*busy*) estar ocupado.

tie-break(er) |tī'brāk(ûr)| *n* (*TENNIS*) tie-break *m*, muerte *f* rápida; (*in quiz*) punto decisivo.

tie-on |tī'ân| *a* (*Brit: label*) para atar.

tie-pin |tī'pin| *n* (*Brit*) alfiler *m* de corbata.

tier |tēr| *n* grada; (*of cake*) piso.

tie tack *n* (*US*) alfiler *m* de corbata.

tiff |tif| *n* (*col*) pelea, riña.

tiger |tī'gûr| *n* tigre *m*.

tight |tīt| *a* (*rope*) tirante; (*money*) escaso; (*clothes, budget*) ajustado; (*schedule*) apretado; (*col: drunk*) borracho ♦ *ad* (*squeeze*) muy fuerte; (*shut*) herméticamente; **to be packed ~** (*suitcase*) estar completamente lleno; (*people*) estar apretados; **everybody hold ~!** ¡agárrense bien!

tighten |tīt'ən| *vt* (*rope*) estirar; (*screw*) apretar ♦ *vi* estirarse; apretarse.

tightfisted |tīt'fis'tid| *a* tacaño.

tightly |tīt'lē| *ad* (*grasp*) muy fuerte.

tightness |tīt'nis| *n* (*of rope*) tirantez *f*; (*of clothes, budget*) estrechez *f*, lo ajustado.

tightrope |tīt'rōp| *n* cuerda floja.

tightrope walker *n* equilibrista *m/f*, funambulista *m/f*.

tights |tīts| *npl* (*US*) traje *m* de malla; (*Brit*) pantimedias *fpl*.

tigress |tī'gris| *n* tigresa.

tilde |til'də| *n* tilde *f*.

tile |tīl| *n* (*on roof*) teja; (*on floor*) baldosa; (*on wall*) azulejo ♦ *vt* (*floor*) poner baldosas en; (*wall*) poner azulejos en.

tiled |tīld| *a* (*floor*) embaldosado; (*wall, bathroom*) cubierto de azulejos; (*roof*) tejado.

till |til| *n* caja (registradora) ♦ *vt* (*land*) cultivar ♦ *prep, conj* = **until**.

tiller |til'ûr| *n* (*NAUT*) caña del timón.

tilt |tilt| *vt* inclinar ♦ *vi* inclinarse ♦ *n* (*slope*) inclinación *f*; **to wear one's hat at a ~** llevar el sombrero echado a un lado *or* terciado; **(at) full ~** a toda velocidad *or* carrera.

timber |tim'bûr| *n* (*material*) madera; (*trees*) árboles *mpl*.

time |tīm| *n* tiempo; (*epoch: often pl*) época; (*by clock*) hora; (*moment*) momento; (*occasion*) vez *f*; (*MUS*) compás *m* ♦ *vt* calcular *or* medir el tiempo de; (*race*) cronometrar; (*remark etc*) elegir el momento para; **a long ~** mucho tiempo; **4 at a ~** 4 a la vez; **for the ~ being** de momento, por ahora; **at ~s** a veces, a ratos; **~ after ~, ~ and again** repetidas veces, una y otra vez; **from ~ to ~** de vez en cuando; **in ~** (*soon enough*) a tiempo; (*after some time*) con el tiempo; (*MUS*) al compás; **in a week's ~** dentro de una semana; **in no ~** en un abrir y cerrar de ojos; **any ~** cuando sea; **on ~** a la hora; **to buy sth on ~** (*US*) comprar algo a plazos · *or* en abonos;

to be 30 minutes behind/ahead of ~ llevar media hora de retraso/adelanto; **to take one's ~** hacer las cosas con calma; **he'll do it in his own ~** (*without being hurried*) lo hará sin prisa; (*out of working hours*) lo hará en su tiempo libre; **by the ~** he arrived cuando llegó; **5 ~s 5** 5 por 5; **what ~ is it?** ¿qué hora es?; **to be behind the ~s** estar atrasado; **to carry 3 boxes at a ~** llevar 3 cajas a la vez; **to keep ~** llevar el ritmo *or* el compás; **to have a good ~** pasarlo bien, divertirse; **to ~ sth well/badly** poner algo en vigor en un momento oportuno/inoportuno; **the bomb was ~d to explode 5 minutes later** la bomba estaba sincronizada para explotar 5 minutos más tarde.

time-and-motion expert |tīm'ənmō'shən ck'spûrt| *n* experto/a en la ciencia de la producción.

time-and-motion study |tīm'ənmō'shən stu'dē| *n* estudio de desplazamientos y tiempos.

time bomb *n* bomba de efecto retardado.

time card *n* tarjeta de registro horario.

time clock *n* reloj *m* registrador.

time-consuming |tīm'kənsōōming| *a* que requiere mucho tiempo.

time-honored |tīm'ânûrd| *a* consagrado.

timekeeper |tīm'kēpûr| *n* (*SPORT*) cronómetro.

time lag *n* desfase *m*.

timeless |tīm'lis| *a* eterno.

time limit *n* (*gen*) limitación *f* de tiempo; (*COMM*) plazo.

timely |tīm'lē| *a* oportuno.

time off *n* tiempo libre.

timer |tī'mûr| *n* (~ *switch*) interruptor *m*; (*in kitchen, TECH*) reloj *m* automático.

timesaving |tīm'sāving| *a* que ahorra tiempo.

time scale *n* escala de tiempo.

time sharing |tīm' shä'ring| *n* (*COMPUT*) tiempo compartido.

time sheet *n* = **time card**.

time signal *n* señal *f* horaria.

time switch *n* (*Brit*) interruptor *m* (horario).

timetable |tīm'tābəl| *n* horario; (*schedule of events etc*) programa *m*, itinerario.

time warp *n* salto en el tiempo.

time zone *n* huso horario.

timid |tim'id| *a* tímido.

timidity |timid'itē| *n* timidez *f*.

timidly |tim'idlē| *ad* tímidamente.

timing |tī'ming| *n* (*SPORT*) cronometraje *m*; **the ~ of his resignation** el momento que eligió para dimitir.

timpani |tim'pənē| *npl* tímpanos *mpl*.

tin |tin| *n* estaño; (*also: ~ plate*) hojalata; (*Brit: can*) lata.

tinfoil |tin'foil| *n* papel *m* de estaño.

tinge |tinj| *n* matiz *m* ♦ *vt*: **~d with** teñido

de.

tingle [ting'gəl] *n* hormigueo ♦ *vi* (*cheeks, skin: from cold*) sentir comezón; (: *from bad circulation*) sentir hormigueo.

tinker [tingk'ûr] *n* calderero/a; (*gipsy*) gitano/a.

tinker with *vt fus* jugar con, tocar.

tinkle [ting'kəl] *vi* tintinear.

tin mine *n* mina de estaño.

tinned [tind] *a* (*Brit: food*) en lata, en conserva.

tinny [tin'ē] *a* (*sound, taste*) metálico; (*pej: car*) poco sólido, de pacotilla.

tin opener *n* (*Brit*) abrelatas *m inv*.

tinsel [tin'səl] *n* oropel *m*.

tint [tint] *n* matiz *m*; (*for hair*) tinte *m* ♦ *vt* (*hair*) teñir.

tinted [tin'tid] *a* (*hair*) teñido; (*glass*) ahumado.

T-intersection [te'intərsek'shən] *n* cruce *m* en T.

tiny [tī'nē] *a* minúsculo, pequeñito.

tip [tip] *n* (*end*) punta; (*gratuity*) propina; (*Brit: for rubbish*) vertedero; (*advice*) consejo ♦ *vt* (*waiter*) dar una propina a; (*tilt*) inclinar; (*empty: Brit: also:* ~ **out**) vaciar, echar; (*predict: winner*) pronosticar; (: *horse*) recomendar.

tip off *vt* avisar, notificar.

tip over *vt* volcar ♦ *vi* volcarse.

tip-off [tip'ôf] *n* (*hint*) advertencia.

tipped [tipt] *a* (*Brit: cigarette*) con filtro.

Tipp-Ex [tip'eks] ® *n* (*Brit*) Tipp-Ex *m* ®.

tipple [tip'əl] *n* (*Brit*): his ~ is Cointreau bebe Cointreau.

tippy-toe [tip'ētō] *n* (*US*): **on** ~ de puntillas.

tipsy [tip'sē] *a* alegre, mareado.

tiptoe [tip'tō] *n* (*Brit*) = **tippy-toe**.

tiptop [tip'táp] *a*: **in** ~ **condition** en perfectas condiciones.

tire [tīûr'] *n* (*US*) neumático, llanta (*LAm*) ♦ *vt* cansar ♦ *vi* (*gen*) cansarse; (*become bored*) aburrirse.

tire out *vt* agotar, rendir (*LAm*).

tired [tīûrd'] *a* cansado; **to be** ~ **of sth** estar harto de algo; **to be/feel/look** ~ estar/sentirse/parecer cansado.

tiredness [tīûrd'nis] *n* cansancio.

tireless [tīûr'lis] *a* incansable.

tirelessly [tīûr'lislē] *ad* incansablemente.

tire pressure *n* presión *f* de los neumáticos.

tiresome [tīûr'səm] *a* aburrido.

tiring [tīûr'ing] *a* cansado.

tissue [tish'ōō] *n* tejido; (*paper handkerchief*) pañuelo de papel, kleenex *m* ®.

tissue paper *n* papel *m* de seda.

tit [tit] *n* (*bird*) herrerillo común; **to give** ~ **for tat** dar ojo por ojo.

titbit [tit'bit] *n* (*Brit*) = **tidbit**.

titillate [tit'əlāt] *vt* estimular, excitar.

titillation [titəlā'shən] *n* estimulación *f*, excitación *f*.

titivate [tit'əvāt] *vt* emperejilar.

title [tīt'əl] *n* título; (*LAW: right*): ~ **(to)** derecho (a).

title deed *n* (*LAW*) título de propiedad.

title page *n* portada.

title role *n* papel *m* principal.

titter [tit'ûr] *vi* reírse entre dientes.

tittle-tattle [tit'əltatəl] *n* chismes *mpl*.

titular [tich'əlûr] *a* (*in name only*) nominal.

T-junction [tē'jung'kshən] *n* cruce *m* en T.

TM *abbr* (= *trademark*) marca de fábrica; = **transcendental meditation**.

TN *abbr* (*US MAIL*) = *Tennessee*.

TNT *n abbr* (= *trinitrotoluene*) TNT *m*.

to [tōō, tōo] *prep* a; (*towards*) hacia; (*of time*) a, hasta; (*of hour*) menos; (*with vb: purpose, result*) para; (*of*) de; (*following another vb*): **to want/try** ~ **do** querer/intentar hacer; **the road** ~ **Philadelphia** la carretera de Filadelfia; **to count** ~ **10** contar hasta diez; ~ **the left/right** a la izquierda/derecha; **to give sth** ~ **sb** darle algo a uno; **give it** ~ **me** dámelo; **the key** ~ **the door** la llave de la puerta; **the main thing is** ~... lo importante es...; **to go** ~ **France/school** ir a Francia/al colegio; **a quarter** ~ **5** las 5 menos cuarto; **it's twenty-five** ~ **3** son las 3 menos veinticinco; **it belongs** ~ **him** le pertenece a él; **superior** ~ **the others** superior a los otros; **8 apples** ~ **the kilo** 8 manzanas por kilo; **pull/push the door** ~ tirar/empujar la puerta; **to go** ~ **and fro** ir y venir; **I don't want** ~ no quiero; **I have things** ~ **do** tengo cosas que hacer; **ready** ~ **go** listo para salir; **he did it** ~ **help you** lo hizo para ayudarte.

toad [tōd] *n* sapo.

toadstool [tōd'stōōl] *n* hongo venenoso.

toady [tō'dē] *n* pelotillero/a, lameculos *m/f inv* ♦ *vi*: **to** ~ **to sb** hacer la pelotilla a uno.

toast [tōst] *n* (*CULIN: also:* **piece of** ~) tostada; (*drink, speech*) brindis *m inv* ♦ *vt* (*CULIN*) tostar; (*drink to*) brindar.

toaster [tōs'tûr] *n* tostadora.

toastmaster [tōst'mastûr] *n persona que propone brindis y anuncia a los oradores en un banquete.*

toast rack *n* rejilla para tostadas.

tobacco [təbak'ō] *n* tabaco; **pipe** ~ tabaco de pipa.

tobacconist [təbak'ənist] *n* estanquero/a, tabaquero/a (*LAm*); ~'s **(shop)** (*Brit*) estanco, tabaquería (*LAm*).

tobacco plantation *n* plantación *f* de tabaco, tabacal *m*.

Tobago [təbā'gō] *n see* **Trinidad and Tobago**.

toboggan [təbág'ən] *n* tobogán *m*.

today [tədā'] *ad, n* (*also fig*) hoy *m*; **what day is it** ~? ¿qué día es hoy?; **what date**

is it ~? ¿cuál es la fecha de hoy?; **~ is the 4th of March** hoy es el 4 de marzo; **~'s paper** el periódico de hoy; **two weeks from ~** de hoy en 15 días, dentro de 15 días.

toddle [tád'əl] *vi* empezar a andar, dar los primeros pasos.

toddler [tád'lûr] *n* niño/a (que empieza a andar).

toddy [tád'ē] *n* caliente *m*.

to-do [tədōō'] *n (fuss)* lío.

toe [tō] *n* dedo (del pie); *(of shoe)* punta ♦ *vt:* **to ~ the line** *(fig)* conformarse; **big/ little ~** dedo gordo/pequeño del pie.

toehold [tō'hōld] *n* punto de apoyo (para el pie).

toenail [tō'nāl] *n* uña del pie.

toffee [tôf'ē] *n* caramelo.

toffee apple *n (Brit)* pirulí *m*.

toga [tō'gə] *n* toga.

together [tōōgeth'ûr] *ad* juntos; *(at same time)* al mismo tiempo, a la vez; **~ with** *prep* junto con.

togetherness [tōōgeth'ûrnis] *n* compañerismo.

toggle switch [tág'əl swich] *n (COMPUT)* conmutador *m* de palanca.

Togo [tō'gō] *n* Togo.

togs [tágz] *npl (col: clothes)* atuendo, ropa.

toil [toil] *n* trabajo duro, labor *f* ♦ *vi* esforzarse.

toilet [toi'lit] *n (Brit: lavatory)* servicios *mpl*, wáter *m*, sanitario *(LAm)* ♦ *cpd (bag, soap etc)* de aseo; **to go to the ~** ir al excusado *or* al baño; *see also* **toilets.**

toilet bag *n* neceser *m*, bolsa de aseo.

toilet bowl *n* taza (de retrete).

toilet paper *n* papel *m* higiénico.

toiletries [toi'litrēz] *npl* artículos *mpl* de aseo; *(make-up etc)* artículos *mpl* de tocador.

toilet roll *n* rollo de papel higiénico.

toilets [toi'lits] *npl (Brit)* servicios *mpl.*

toilet soap *n* jabón *m* de tocador.

toilet water *n* (agua de) colonia.

token [tō'kən] *n (sign)* señal *f*, muestra; *(souvenir)* recuerdo; *(voucher)* vale *m*; *(disc)* ficha ♦ *cpd (fee, strike)* nominal, simbólico; **book/record ~** *(Brit)* vale *m* para comprar libros/discos; **by the same ~** *(fig)* por la misma razón.

Tokyo [tō'kēyō] *n* Tokio, Tokío.

told [tōld] *pt, pp of* **tell.**

tolerable [tál'ûrəbəl] *a (bearable)* soportable; *(fairly good)* pasable.

tolerably [tál'ûrəblē] *ad (good, comfortable)* medianamente.

tolerance [tál'ûrəns] *n (also: TECH)* tolerancia.

tolerant [tál'ûrənt] *a:* **~ of** tolerante con.

tolerantly [tál'ûrəntlē] *ad* con tolerancia.

tolerate [tál'ərāt] *vt* tolerar.

toleration [tálərā'shən] *n* tolerancia.

toll [tōl] *n (of casualties)* número de víctimas; *(tax, charge)* peaje *m* ♦ *vi (bell)* doblar.

toll bridge *n* puente *m* de peaje.

toll-free [tōl'frē'] *ad (US TEL):* **to call ~** llamar sin pagar.

toll road *n* carretera de peaje.

tomato, ~es [təmā'tō] *n* tomate *m.*

tomato paste *n* puré *m* de tomate.

tomato purée *n* puré *m* de tomate.

tomb [tōōm] *n* tumba.

tomboy [tâm'boi] *n* marimacho.

tombstone [tōōm'stōn] *n* lápida.

tomcat [tâm'kat] *n* gato.

tomorrow [təmôr'ō] *ad, n (also fig)* mañana; **the day after ~** pasado mañana; **~ morning** mañana por la mañana; **a week from ~** de mañana en ocho (días).

ton [tun] *n (US: also:* **short ~** *= 907,18 kg; Brit = 1016 kg)* tonelada.

tonal [tō'nəl] *a* tonal.

tone [tōn] *n* tono ♦ *vi* armonizar; **dial** *(US)* **or dialling** *(Brit)* **~** *(TEL)* señal *f* para marcar.

tone down *vt (criticism)* suavizar; *(color)* atenuar.

tone up *vt (muscles)* tonificar.

tone-deaf [tōn'def] *a* que no tiene oído musical.

toner [tō'nûr] *n (for photocopier)* virador *m.*

Tonga [táng'gə] *n* Islas *fpl* Tonga.

tongs [tôngz] *npl (for coal)* tenazas *fpl*; *(Brit: for. hair)* tenacillas *fpl.*

tongue [tung] *n* lengua; **~ in cheek** *ad* irónicamente.

tongue-tied [tung'tīd] *a (fig)* mudo.

tongue twister [tung' twis'tûr] *n* trabalenguas *m inv.*

tonic [tán'ik] *n (MED)* tónico; *(MUS)* tónica; *(also: ~* **water)** (agua) tónica.

tonight [tənīt'] *ad, n* esta noche; **I'll see you ~** nos vemos esta noche.

tonnage [tun'ij] *n (NAUT)* tonelaje *m.*

tonsil [tán'səl] *n* amígdala; **to have one's ~s out** sacarse las amígdalas *or* anginas.

tonsillitis [tánsəlī'tis] *n* amigdalitis *f*; **to have ~** tener amigdalitis.

too [tōō] *ad (excessively)* demasiado; *(very)* muy; *(also)* también; **it's ~ sweet** está demasiado dulce; **I'm not ~ sure about that** no estoy muy seguro de eso; **I went ~** yo fui también; **~ much** *ad, a* demasiado; **~ many** *a* demasiados/as; **~ bad!** ¡mala suerte!

took [tōōk] *pt of* **take.**

tool [tōōl] *n* herramienta; *(fig: person)* instrumento.

tool box *n* caja de herramientas.

tool kit *n* juego de herramientas.

tool shed *n* cobertizo (para herramientas).

toot [tōōt] *n (of horn)* bocinazo; *(of whistle)* silbido ♦ *vi (with car horn)* tocar la bocina.

tooth, *pl* **teeth** [tōōth, tēth] *n (ANAT, TECH)* diente *m*; *(molar)* muela; **to clean one's**

teeth lavarse los dientes; **to have a ~ pulled** or (*Brit*) **out** sacarse una muela; **by the skin of one's teeth** por un pelo.

toothache [tŏŏth'āk] *n* dolor *m* de muelas.

toothbrush [tŏŏth'brush] *n* cepillo de dientes.

toothpaste [tŏŏth'pāst] *n* pasta de dientes.

toothpick [tŏŏth'pik] *n* palillo.

tooth powder *n* polvos *mpl* dentífricos.

top [tăp] *n* (*of mountain*) cumbre *f*, cima; (*of head*) coronilla; (*of ladder*) lo alto; (*of cupboard, table*) superficie *f*; (*lid: of box, jar*) tapa; (: *of bottle*) tapón *m*; (*of list, table, line, page*) cabeza; (*toy*) peonza; (*DRESS: blouse etc*) blusa; (: *of pyjamas*) chaqueta; (*US AUT*) capota ♦ *a* de arriba; (*in rank*) principal, primero; (*best*) mejor ♦ *vt* (*exceed*) exceder; (*be first in*) encabezar; **on ~ of** sobre, encima de; **from ~ to bottom** de pies a cabeza; **at the ~ of the stairs** en lo alto de la escalera; **at the ~ of the street** al final de la calle; **at the ~ of one's voice** (*fig*) a voz en grito; **at ~ speed** a máxima velocidad; **a ~ surgeon** un cirujano eminente; **over the ~** (*col*) excesivo, desmesurado; **to go over the ~** pasarse (de la raya).

top off, (*Brit*) **top up** *vt* llenar.

topaz [tō'paz] *n* topacio.

topcoat [tăp'kōt] *n* sobretodo, abrigo.

topflight [tăp'flīt'] *a* de primera (categoría or clase).

top floor *n* último piso.

top hat *n* sombrero de copa.

top-heavy [tăp'hevē] *a* (*object*) descompensado en la parte superior.

topic [tăp'ik] *n* tema *m*.

topical [tăp'ikəl] *a* (*current*) actual; (*US: local*) local.

topless [tăp'lis] *a* (*bather etc*) topless.

top-level [tăp'lev'əl] *a* (*talks*) al más alto nivel.

topmost [tăp'mōst] *a* más alto.

topography [təpăg'rəfē] *n* topografía.

topping [tăp'ing] *n* (*CULIN*) cubierta.

topple [tăp'əl] *vt* volcar, derribar ♦ *vi* caerse.

top-ranking [tăp'rang'king] *a* de alto rango.

top-secret [tăp'sē'krit] *a* de alto secreto.

top-security [tăpsikyŏŏ'ritē] *a* de máxima seguridad.

topsy-turvy [tăp'sētûr'vē] *a*, *ad* patas arriba.

top-up [tăp'up] *n* (*Brit*): **would you like a ~?** ¿quiere que se lo llene?

torch [tôrch] *n* antorcha; (*Brit: electric*) linterna.

tore [tôr] *pt of* **tear.**

torment *n* [tôr'ment] tormento ♦ *vt* [tôr-ment'] atormentar; (*fig: annoy*) fastidiar.

torn [tôrn] *pp of* **tear.**

tornado, ~es [tôrnā'dō] *n* tornado.

torpedo, ~es [tôrpē'dō] *n* torpedo.

torpedo boat *n* torpedero, lancha torpedera.

torpor [tôr'púr] *n* letargo.

torrent [tôr'ənt] *n* torrente *m*.

torrential [tôren'chəl] *a* torrencial.

torrid [tôr'id] *a* tórrido; (*fig*) apasionado.

torso [tôr'sō] *n* torso.

tortoise [tôr'təs] *n* tortuga.

tortoiseshell [tôr'təs·shell] *a* de carey.

tortuous [tôr'chŏŏəs] *a* tortuoso.

torture [tôr'chúr] *n* tortura ♦ *vt* torturar; (*fig*) atormentar.

torturer [tôr'chúrûr] *n* torturador(a) *m/f*.

Tory [tôr'ē] *a, n* (*Brit POL*) conservador(a) *m/f*.

toss [tôs] *vt* tirar, echar; (*head*) sacudir ♦ *n* (*movement: of head etc*) sacudida; (*of coin*) tirada, echada (*LAm*); **to ~ a coin** echar a cara o cruz; **to ~ up for sth** jugar algo a cara o cruz; **to ~ and turn** (*in bed*) dar vueltas (en la cama); **to win/lose the ~** (*also SPORT*) ganar/perder (a cara o cruz).

tot [tăt] *n* (*child*) nene/a *m/f*; (*Brit: drink*) copita.

total [tōt'əl] *a* total, entero ♦ *n* total *m*, suma ♦ *vt* (*add up*) sumar; (*amount to*) ascender a; **grand ~** importe *m* total; **in ~** en total, en suma.

totalitarian [tōtalitär'ēən] *a* totalitario.

totality [tōtal'itē] *n* totalidad *f*.

total loss *n* siniestra total.

totally [tō'təlē] *ad* totalmente.

tote [tōt] *vt* (*col*) acarrear, cargar con.

tote bag *n* bolsa, bolso.

totem pole [tō'təm pōl] *n* poste *m* totémico.

totter [tăt'ûr] *vi* tambalearse.

touch [tuch] *n* tacto; (*contact*) contacto; (*SOCCER*) fuera de juego ♦ *vt* tocar; (*emotionally*) conmover; **a ~ of** (*fig*) una pizca or un poquito de; **to get in ~ with sb** ponerse en contacto con uno; **I'll be in ~** le llamaré/escribiré; **to lose ~** (*friends*) perder contacto; **to be out of ~ with events** no estar al corriente (de los acontecimientos); **the personal ~** el toque personal; **to put the finishing ~es to sth** dar el último toque a algo; **no artist in the country can ~ him** no hay artista en todo el país que le iguale.

touch on *vt fus* (*topic*) aludir (brevemente) a.

touch up *vt* (*paint*) retocar.

touch-and-go [tuch'əngō'] *a* arriesgado.

touchdown [tuch'doun] *n* aterrizaje *m*; (*US FOOTBALL*) tanto.

touched [tucht] *a* conmovido; (*col*) chiflado.

touchiness [tuch'ēnis] *n* susceptibilidad *f*.

touching [tuch'ing] *a* conmovedor(a).

touchline [tuch'līn] *n* (*SPORT*) línea de banda.

touch-type [tuch'tīp] *vi* mecanografiar al

tacto.

touchy [tuch'ē] *a* (*person*) quisquilloso.

tough [tuf] *a* (*meat*) duro; (*journey*) penoso; (*task, problem, situation*) difícil; (*resistant*) resistente; (*person*) fuerte; (: *pej*) bruto ♦ *n* (*gangster etc*) gorila *m*; **they got ~ with the workers** fueron muy duros con los trabajadores.

toughen [tuf'ən] *vt* endurecer.

toughness [tuf'nis] *n* dureza; (*resistance*) resistencia; (*strictness*) inflexibilidad *f*.

toupée [tōōpā'] *n* peluca.

tour [tōōr] *n* viaje *m*, vuelta; (*also:* **package ~**) viaje *m* todo comprendido; (*of town, museum*) visita ♦ *vt* viajar por; **to go on a ~ of** (*region, country*) ir de viaje por; (*museum, castle*) dar una vuelta de; **to go on ~** partir *or* ir de gira.

touring [tōōr'ing] *n* viajes *mpl* turísticos, turismo.

tourism [tōōr'izəm] *n* turismo.

tourist [tōōr'ist] *n* turista *m/f* ♦ *cpd* turístico; **the ~ trade** el turismo.

tourist office *n* oficina de turismo.

tournament [tōōr'nəmənt] *n* torneo.

tourniquet [tûr'nikit] *n* (*MED*) torniquete *m*.

tour operator *n* agente *m/f or* agencia de viajes.

tousled [tou'zəld] *a* (*hair*) despeinado.

tout [tout] *vi:* **to ~ for business** solicitar clientes ♦ *n* (*Brit*): **ticket ~** revendedor(a) *m/f*.

tow [tō] *n:* **to give sb a ~** (*AUT*) darle remolque *or* remolcar a uno ♦ *vt* remolcar; **"in** *or* (*Brit*) **on ~"** (*AUT*) "a remolque".

toward(s) [tôrd(z)] *prep* hacia; (*of attitude*) respecto a, con; (*of purpose*) para; **~ noon** alrededor de mediodía; **~ the end of the year** hacia finales de año; **to feel friendly ~ sb** sentir amistad hacia uno.

towel [tou'əl] *n* toalla; **to throw in the ~** (*fig*) darse por vencido, renunciar.

towel(l)ing [tou'əling] *n* (*fabric*) felpa.

towel rack, (*Brit*) **towel rail** *n* toallero.

tower [tou'ûr] *n* torre *f* ♦ *vi* (*building, mountain*) elevarse; **to ~ above** *or* **over sth/sb** dominar algo/destacarse sobre uno.

tower block *n* (*Brit*) rascacielos *m inv.*

towering [tou'ûring] *a* muy alto, imponente.

town [toun] *n* ciudad *f*; **to go to ~** ir a la ciudad; (*fig*) echar los bofes; **in the ~** en la ciudad; **to be out of ~** estar fuera de la ciudad.

town center *n* centro de la ciudad.

town clerk *n* secretario/a del Ayuntamiento.

town council *n* Ayuntamiento, consejo municipal.

town hall *n* ayuntamiento.

town house *n* (*US*) casa adosada.

town planner *n* (*Brit*) urbanista *m/f*.

town planning *n* (*Brit*) urbanismo.

townspeople [tounz'pēpəl] *npl* gente *f* de ciudad.

towpath [tō'path] *n* camino de sirga.

towrope [tō'rōp] *n* cable *m* de remolque.

tow truck *n* (*US*) camión *m* grúa.

toxic [tâk'sik] *a* tóxico.

toxin [tâk'sin] *n* toxina.

toy [toi] *n* juguete *m*.

toy with *vt fus* jugar con; (*idea*) acariciar.

toyshop [toi'shâp] *n* juguetería.

toy train *n* tren *m* de juguete.

trace [trās] *n* rastro ♦ *vt* (*draw*) trazar, delinear; (*locate*) encontrar; **there was no ~ of it** no había ningún indicio de eso.

trace element *n* oligoelemento.

trachea [trā'kēə] *n* (*ANAT*) tráquea.

tracing paper [trā'sing pā'pûr] *n* papel *m* de calco.

track [trak] *n* (*mark*) huella, pista; (*path: gen*) camino, senda; (: *of bullet etc*) trayectoria; (: *of suspect, animal*) pista, rastro; (*RAIL*) vía; (*COMPUT, SPORT*) pista; (*on record*) canción *f* ♦ *vt* seguir la pista de; **to keep ~ of** mantenerse al tanto de, seguir; **a 4-~ tape** una cinta de 4 pistas; **the first ~ on the record/tape** la primera canción en el disco/cassette; **to be on the right ~** (*fig*) ir por buen camino.

track down *vt* (*person*) localizar; (*sth lost*) encontrar.

track events *npl* (*SPORT*) pruebas *fpl* en pista.

tracking station [trak'ing stā'shən] *n* (*SPACE*) estación *f* de seguimiento.

track record *n:* **to have a good ~** (*fig*) tener (buenos) antecedentes.

tracksuit [trak'sōōt] *n* chandal *m*.

tract [trakt] *n* (*GEO*) región *f*; (*pamphlet*) folleto.

traction [trak'shən] *n* (*AUT, power*) tracción *f*; **in ~** (*MED*) en tracción.

tractor [trak'tûr] *n* tractor *m*.

tractor feed *n* (*on printer*) arrastre *m* de papel por tracción.

trade [trād] *n* comercio, negocio; (*skill, job*) oficio, empleo; (*industry*) industria ♦ *vi* negociar, comerciar; **foreign ~** comercio exterior.

trade in *vt* (*old car etc*) ofrecer como parte del pago.

trade barrier *n* barrera comercial.

trade deficit *n* déficit *m* comercial.

trade discount *n* descuento comercial.

trade fair *n* feria de muestras.

trade-in [trād'in] *a:* **~ price/value** precio/valor *m* de entrega *or* a cuenta.

trademark [trād'mârk] *n* marca de fábrica.

trade mission *n* misión *f* comercial.

trade name *n* marca registrada.

trade price *n* precio al detallista.

trader [trā'dûr] *n* comerciante *m/f*.

trade reference *n* referencia comercial.

trade secret n secreto profesional.
tradesman [trădz'mən] n (shopkeeper) tendero.
trade union n sindicato.
trade unionist [trăd yōōn'yənist] n sindicalista m/f.
trade wind n viento alisio.
trading [trā'ding] n comercio.
trading account n cuenta de compraventa.
trading estate n (Brit) zona comercial.
trading stamp n cupón m, sello de prima.
tradition [trədish'ən] n tradición f.
traditional [trədish'ənəl] a tradicional.
traditionally [trədish'ənəlē] ad tradicionalmente.
traffic [traf'ik] n (gen, AUT) tráfico, circulación f, tránsito (LAm) ♦ vi: **to ~ in** (pej: liquor, drugs) traficar en; **air ~** tránsito aéreo.
traffic circle n (US) glorieta de tráfico.
traffic island n refugio, isleta.
traffic jam n embotellamiento, atasco.
trafficker [traf'ikûr] n traficante m/f.
traffic lights npl semáforo sg.
traffic offence n (Brit) = **traffic violation.**
traffic violation n infracción f de tránsito.
traffic warden n (Brit) guardia m/f de tráfico.
tragedy [traj'idē] n tragedia.
tragic [traj'ik] a trágico.
tragically [traj'iklē] ad trágicamente.
trail [trāl] n (tracks) rastro, pista; (path) camino, sendero; (dust, smoke) estela ♦ vt (drag) arrastrar; (follow) seguir la pista de; (follow closely) vigilar ♦ vi arrastrarse; **to be on sb's ~** seguir la pista de uno.
trail behind vi quedar a la zaga.
trail off vi (sound) desvanecerse; (interest, voice) desaparecer.
trailer [trā'lûr] n (AUT) remolque m; (Brit: caravan) caravana; (CINEMA) trailer m, avance m.
trailer park n (US) camping m para caravanas or remolques.
trail truck n (US) trailer m.
train [trān] n tren m; (of dress) cola; (series): **~ of events** curso de los acontecimientos ♦ vt (educate) formar; (teach skills to) adiestrar; (sportsman) entrenar; (dog) amaestrar; (point: gun etc): **to ~ on** apuntar a ♦ vi (SPORT) entrenarse; (be educated, learn a skill) formarse; **to go by ~** ir en tren; **one's ~ of thought** el razonamiento de uno; **to ~ sb to do sth** entrenar a uno a hacer algo.
train attendant n (US RAIL) empleado/a de coches-cama.
trained [trānd] a (worker) cualificado; (animal) amaestrado.
trainee [trānē'] n aprendiz(a) m/f.
trainer [trā'nûr] n (SPORT) entrenador(a)

m/f; (of animals) domador(a) m/f; **~s** npl (shoes) zapatillas fpl (de deporte).
training [trā'ning] n formación f; entrenamiento; **to be in ~** (SPORT) estar entrenando; (: fit) estar en forma.
training college n (gen) colegio de formación profesional; (for teachers) escuela normal.
training course n curso de formación.
training shoes npl zapatillas fpl (de deporte).
train station n estación f de ferrocarril.
traipse [trāps] vi andar penosamente.
trait [trāt] n rasgo.
traitor [trā'tûr] n traidor(a) m/f.
trajectory [trəjek'tûrē] n trayectoria, curso.
tram [tram] n (Brit: also: **~car**) tranvía m.
tramline [tram'līn] n carril m de tranvía.
tramp [tramp] n (person) vagabundo/a; (col: offensive: woman) puta ♦ vi andar con pasos pesados.
trample [tram'pəl] vt: **to ~ (underfoot)** pisotear.
trampoline [trampəlēn'] n trampolín m.
trance [trans] n trance m; **to go into a ~** entrar en trance.
tranquil [trang'kwil] a tranquilo.
tranquility, (Brit) **tranquillity** [trangkwil'itē] n tranquilidad f.
tranquilizer, (Brit) **tranquillizer** [trang'kwəlīzûr] n (MED) tranquilizante m.
trans- [trans] pref trans-, tras-.
transact [transakt'] vt (business) tramitar.
transaction [transak'shən] n transacción f, operación f; **cash ~s** comercio al contado.
transatlantic [transətlan'tik] a transatlántico.
transcend [transend'] vt rebasar.
transcendent [transen'dənt] a trascendente.
transcendental [transenden'təl] a: **~ meditation** meditación f transcendental.
transcribe [transkrīb'] vt transcribir, copiar.
transcript [tran'skript] n copia.
transcription [transkrip'shən] n transcripción f.
transept [tran'sept] n crucero.
transfer n [trans'fûr] transferencia; (SPORT) traspaso; (picture, design) calcomanía ♦ vt [transfûr'] trasladar, pasar; **to ~ the charges** (Brit TEL) llamar a cobro revertido; **by bank ~** por transferencia bancaria or giro bancario; **to ~ money from one account to another** transferir dinero de una cuenta a otra; **to ~ sth to sb's name** transferir algo al nombre de uno.
transferable [transfûr'əbəl] a: **not ~** intransferible.
transfix [transfiks'] vt traspasar; (fig): **~ed with fear** paralizado por el miedo.
transform [transfôrm'] vt transformar.
transformation [transfûrmā'shən] n trans-

formación *f*.
transformer [transfôr'mûr] *n* (*ELEC*) transformador *m*.
transfusion [transfyōo'zhən] *n* transfusión *f*.
transgress [transgrɛs'] *vt* (*go beyond*) traspasar; (*violate*) violar, infringir.
tranship [tranship'] *vt* trasbordar.
transient [tran'shənt] *a* transitorio.
transistor [tranzis'tûr] *n* (*ELEC*) transistor *m*.
transistorized [tranzis'tərīzd] *a* (*circuit*) transistorizado.
transistor radio *n* transistor *m*.
transit [tran'sit] *n*: **in** ~ en tránsito.
transit camp *n* campo de tránsito.
transition [tranzish'ən] *n* transición *f*.
transitional [tranzish'ənəl] *a* transitorio.
transition period *n* período de transición.
transitive [tran'sətiv] *a* (*LING*) transitivo.
transitively [tran'sətivlē] *ad* transitivamente.
transitory [tran'sitôrē] *a* transitorio.
transit visa *n* visado de tránsito.
translate [tranz'lāt] *vt*: **to** ~ **(from/into)** traducir (de/a).
translation [tranzlā'shən] *n* traducción *f*.
translator [tranzlā'tûr] *n* traductor(a) *m/f*.
translucent [translōo'sənt] *a* traslúcido.
transmission [transmish'ən] *n* transmisión *f*.
transmit [transmit'] *vt* transmitir.
transmitter [transmit'ûr] *n* transmisor *m*; (*station*) emisora.
transom [tran'səm] *n* (*US*) (montante *m* de) abanico.
transparency [transpär'ənsē] *n* (*PHOT*) diapositiva.
transparent [transpär'ənt] *a* transparente.
transpire [transpiûr'] *vi* (*turn out*) resultar (ser); (*happen*) ocurrir, suceder; (*become known*): **it finally** ~**d that** ... por fin se supo que ....
transplant *vt* [transplant'] transplantar ♦ *n* [trans'plant] (*MED*) transplante *m*; **to have a heart** ~ hacerse un transplante de corazón.
transport *n* [trans'pôrt] transporte *m* ♦ *vt* [transpôrt'] transportar.
transportable [transpôr'təbəl] *a* transportable.
transportation [transpûrtā'shən] *n* transporte *m*; (*of prisoners*) deportación *f*; **public** ~ transporte *m* público.
transport café *n* (*Brit*) bar-restaurante *m* de carretera.
transpose [tranzpōz'] *vt* transponer.
transship [transship'] *vt* trasbordar.
transverse [transvûrs'] *a* transverso, transversal.
transvestite [transvɛs'tīt] *n* travesti *m/f*.
trap [trap] *n* (*snare, trick*) trampa; (*carriage*) cabriolé *m* ♦ *vt* coger (*Sp*) *or* agarrar (*LAm*) en una trampa; (*immobilize*)

bloquear; (*jam*) atascar; **to set** *or* **lay a** ~ **(for sb)** poner(le) una trampa (a uno).
trap door *n* escotilla.
trapeze [trapēz'] *n* trapecio.
trapper [trap'ûr] *n* trampero, cazador *m*.
trappings [trap'ingz] *npl* adornos *mpl*.
trash [trash] *n* (*pej: goods*) pacotilla; (*: nonsense*) tonterías *fpl*; (*garbage*) basura ♦ *vt* (*col*) poner por los suelos.
trash can *n* (*US*) cubo *or* balde *m* (*LAm*) de la basura.
trash can liner *n* (*US*) bolsa de basura.
trashy [trash'ē] *a* malísimo.
trauma [trou'mə] *n* trauma *m*.
traumatic [trômat'ik] *a* (*PSYCH, fig*) traumático.
travel [trav'əl] *n* viaje *m* ♦ *vi* viajar ♦ *vt* (*distance*) recorrer; **this wine doesn't** ~ **well** este vino no se transporta bien.
travel agency *n* agencia de viajes.
travel agent *n* agente *m/f* de viajes.
travel brochure *n* folleto turístico.
traveler [trav'əlûr] *n* (*US*) viajero/a; (*: COMM*) viajante *m/f*.
traveler's check *n* cheque *m* de viajero.
traveling [trav'əling] (*US*) *n* los viajes, el viajar ♦ *a* (*circus, exhibition*) ambulante ♦ *cpd* (*bag, clock*) de viaje.
traveling expenses *npl* dietas *fpl*.
traveling salesman *n* viajante *m*.
traveller [trav'əlûr] *n* (*Brit*) = **traveler**.
traveller's cheque *n* (*Brit*) = **traveler's check**.
travelling [trav'əling] *etc* (*Brit*) = **traveling** *etc*.
travelog(ue) [trav'əlòg] *n* (*book*) relación *f* de viajes; (*film*) documental *m* de viajes; (*talk*) recuento de viajes.
travel sickness *n* mareo.
traverse [trav'ûrs] *vt* atravesar.
travesty [trav'istē] *n* parodia.
trawler [trô'lûr] *n* pesquero de arrastre.
tray [trā] *n* (*for carrying*) bandeja; (*on desk*) cajón *m*.
treacherous [trech'ûrəs] *a* traidor(a); **road conditions are** ~ el estado de las carreteras es peligroso.
treachery [trech'ûrē] *n* traición *f*.
treacle [trē'kəl] *n* (*Brit*) melaza.
tread [tred] *n* (*step*) paso, pisada; (*sound*) ruido de pasos; (*of tire*) banda de rodadura ♦ *vi* (*pt* **trod**, *pp* **trodden** [träd, träd'ən]) pisar.
tread on *vt fus* pisar.
treas. *abbr* = **treasurer**.
treason [trē'zən] *n* traición *f*.
treasure [trezh'ûr] *n* tesoro ♦ *vt* (*value*) apreciar, valorar.
treasure hunt *n* caza al tesoro.
treasurer [trezh'ûrûr] *n* tesorero/a.
treasury [trezh'ûrē] *n*: **the T~ Department**, (*Brit*) **the T~** ≈ el Ministerio *or* la Secretaría de Hacienda.

treasury bill *n* bono del Tesoro.
treat [trēt] *n* (*present*) regalo; (*pleasure*) placer *m* ♦ *vt* tratar; (*consider*) considerar; **to give sb a** ~ hacer un regalo a uno; **to** ~ **sb to sth** invitar a uno a algo; **to** ~ **sth as a joke** tomar algo a broma.
treatise [trē'tis] *n* tratado.
treatment [trēt'mənt] *n* tratamiento; **to have** ~ **for sth** recibir tratamiento por algo.
treaty [trē'tē] *n* tratado.
treble [treb'əl] *a* triple ♦ *vt* triplicar ♦ *vi* triplicarse.
treble clef *n* (*MUS*) clave *f* de sol.
tree [trē] *n* árbol *m*.
tree-lined [trē'līnd] *a* bordeado de árboles.
tree trunk *n* tronco de árbol.
trek [trek] *n* (*long journey*) expedición *f*; (*tiring walk*) caminata.
trellis [trel'is] *n* enrejado.
tremble [trem'bəl] *vi* temblar.
trembling [trem'bling] *n* temblor *m* ♦ *a* tembloroso.
tremendous [trimen'dəs] *a* tremendo; (*enormous*) enorme; (*excellent*) estupendo.
tremendously [trimen'dəslē] *ad* enormemente, sobremanera; **he enjoyed it** ~ lo disfrutó de lo lindo.
tremor [trem'ûr] *n* temblor *m*; (*also:* **earth** ~) temblor *m* de tierra.
trench [trench] *n* zanja; (*MIL*) trinchera.
trench coat *n* trinchera.
trench warfare *n* guerra de trincheras.
trend [trend] *n* (*tendency*) tendencia; (*of events*) curso; (*fashion*) moda; ~ **towards/away from sth** tendencia hacia/en contra de algo; **to set the** ~ marcar la pauta.
trendy [tren'dē] *a* de moda.
trepidation [trepidā'shən] *n* inquietud *f*.
trespass [tres'pas] *vi*: **to** ~ **on** entrar sin permiso en; **"no** ~**ing"** "prohibido el paso".
trespasser [tres'pasûr] *n* intruso/a *m/f*; **"**~**s will be prosecuted"** "se procesará a los intrusos".
tress [tres] *n* trenza.
trestle [tres'əl] *n* caballete *m*.
trestle table *n* mesa de caballete.
tri- [trī] *pref* tri-.
trial [trīl] *n* (*LAW*) juicio, proceso; (*test: of machine etc*) prueba; (*hardship*) desgracia; ~**s** *npl* (*ATHLETICS, of horses*) pruebas *fpl*; **to bring sb to** ~ **(for a crime)** llevar a uno a juicio (por un delito); ~ **by jury** juicio ante jurado; **to be sent for** ~ ser remitido al tribunal; **by** ~ **and error** a fuerza de probar.
trial balance *n* balance *m* de comprobación.
trial basis *n*: **on a** ~ en concepto de prueba.
trial offer *n* oferta de prueba.

trial run *n* prueba.
triangle [trī'anggəl] *n* (*MATH. MUS*) triángulo; (*TECH*) cartabón *m*.
triangular [trīang'gyəlûr] *a* triangular.
tribal [trī'bəl] *a* tribal.
tribe [trīb] *n* tribu *f*.
tribesman [trībz'mən] *n* miembro de una tribu.
tribulation [tribyəlā'shən] *n* tribulación *f*.
tribunal [trībyōō'nəl] *n* tribunal *m*.
tributary [trib'yətärē] *n* (*river*) afluente *m*.
tribute [trib'yōōt] *n* homenaje *m*, tributo; **to pay** ~ rendir homenaje a.
trice [trīs] *n*: **in a** ~ en un santiamén.
trick [trik] *n* trampa; (*conjuring* ~, *deceit*) truco; (*prank*) broma; (*CARDS*) baza ♦ *vt* engañar; **it's a** ~ **of the light** es una ilusión óptica; **to play a** ~ **on sb** gastar una broma a uno; **that should do the** ~ eso servirá; **to** ~ **sb out of sth** quitarle algo a uno con engaños; **to** ~ **sb into doing sth** hacer que uno haga algo con engaños.
trickery [trik'ûrē] *n* engaño.
trickle [trik'əl] *n* (*of water etc*) chorrito ♦ *vi* gotear.
trick question *n* pega.
trickster [trik'stûr] *n* estafador(a) *m/f*.
tricky [trik'ē] *a* difícil; (*problem*) delicado.
tricycle [trī'sikəl] *n* triciclo.
tried [trīd] *a* probado.
trifle [trī'fəl] *n* bagatela; (*CULIN*) *dulce de bizcocho, gelatina, fruta y natillas* ♦ *ad*: **a** ~ **long** un poquito largo ♦ *vi*: **to** ~ **with** jugar con.
trifling [trī'fling] *a* insignificante.
trigger [trig'ûr] *n* (*of gun*) gatillo.
trigger off *vt* desencadenar.
trigonometry [trigənâm'ətrē] *n* trigonometría.
trilby [tril'bē] *n* (*Brit: also:* ~ **hat**) sombrero flexible *or* tirolés.
trill [tril] *n* (*of bird*) gorjeo; (*MUS*) trino.
trillion [tril'yən] *n* (*US*) billón *m*.
trilogy [tril'əjē] *n* trilogía.
trim [trim] *a* (*elegant*) aseado; (*house, garden*) en buen estado; (*figure*): **to be** ~ tener buen talle ♦ *n* (*haircut etc*) recorte *m* ♦ *vt* (*tidy*) arreglar; (*cut*) recortar; (*decorate*) adornar; (*NAUT: a sail*) orientar; **to keep in (good)** ~ mantener en buen estado.
trimmings [trim'ingz] *npl* (*extras*) accesorios *mpl*; (*cuttings*) recortes *mpl*.
Trinidad and Tobago [trin'idad and tōbā'gō] *n* Trinidad *f* y Tobago.
Trinity [trin'itē] *n*: **the** ~ la Trinidad.
trinket [tring'kit] *n* chuchería, baratija.
trio [trē'ō] *n* trío.
trip [trip] *n* viaje *m*; (*excursion*) excursión *f*; (*stumble*) traspié *m* ♦ *vi* (*stumble*) tropezar; (*go lightly*) andar a paso ligero; **on a** ~ de viaje.
trip over *vt fus* tropezar con.
trip up *vi* tropezar, caerse ♦ *vt* hacer tro-

pezar *or* caer; (*US: fig: with trick question*) hundir.

tripartite [trīpár'tīt] *a* (*agreement, talks*) tripartito.

tripe [trīp] *n* (*CULIN*) callos *mpl*; (*pej: rubbish*) bobadas *fpl*.

triple [trip'əl] *a* triple ♦ *ad*: ~ **the distance/the speed** 3 veces la distancia/la velocidad.

triplets [trip'lits] *npl* trillizos/as *m/fpl*.

triplicate [trip'ləkit] *n*: **in** ~ por triplicado.

tripod [trī'pâd] *n* trípode *m*.

Tripoli [trip'əlē] *n* Trípoli *m*.

tripwire [trip'wīûr] *n* cuerda de trampa.

trite [trīt] *a* trillado.

triumph [trī'əmf] *n* triunfo ♦ *vi*: **to** ~ **(over)** vencer.

triumphal [trīum'fəl] *a* triunfal.

triumphant [trīum'fənt] *a* triunfante.

triumphantly [trīum'fəntlē] *ad* triunfalmente, en tono triunfal.

trivia [triv'ēə] *npl* trivialidades *fpl*.

trivial [triv'ēəl] *a* insignificante, trivial.

triviality [trivēal'ətē] *n* insignificancia, trivialidad *f*.

trivialize [triv'ēəlīz] *vt* minimizar, tratar con desprecio.

trod [trâd] *pt of* **tread**.

trodden [trâd'ən] *pp of* **tread**.

trolley bus [trâl'ē bus] *n* trolebús *m*.

trombone [trâmbōn'] *n* trombón *m*.

troop [trōōp] *n* grupo, banda.
    troop in *vi* entrar en tropel.
    troop out *vi* salir en tropel.

troop carrier *n* (*plane*) transporte *n* (militar); (*NAUT: also:* **troopship**) (buque *m* de) transporte *m*.

trooper [trōō'pûr] *n* (*MIL*) soldado (de caballería); (*US: policeman*) policía *m/f* estatal.

troopship [trōōp'ship] *n* (buque *m* de) transporte *m*.

trophy [trō'fē] *n* trofeo.

tropic [trâp'ik] *n* trópico; **the ~s** los trópicos, la zona tropical; **T~ of Cancer/Capricorn** trópico de Cáncer/Capricornio.

tropical [trâp'ikəl] *a* tropical.

trot [trât] *n* trote *m* ♦ *vi* trotar; **on the ~** (*Brit fig*) seguidos/as.
    trot out *vt* (*excuse, reason*) sacar a luz; (*names, facts*) sacar a relucir.

trouble [trub'əl] *n* problema *m*, dificultad *f*; (*worry*) preocupación *f*; (*bother, effort*) molestia, esfuerzo; (*unrest*) inquietud *f*; (*with machine etc*) fallo, avería; (*MED*): **stomach** ~ problemas *mpl* gástricos ♦ *vt* molestar; (*worry*) preocupar, inquietar ♦ *vi*: **to** ~ **to do sth** molestarse en hacer algo; **~s** *npl* (*POL etc*) conflictos *mpl*; **to be in** ~ estar en un apuro; (*for doing wrong*) tener problemas; **to have** ~ **doing sth** tener dificultad en *or* para hacer algo; **to go to the** ~ **of doing sth** tomarse la molestia de hacer algo; **what's the ~?**

¿qué pasa?; **the** ~ **is** ... el problema es ..., lo que pasa es ...; **please don't** ~ **yourself** por favor no se moleste.

troubled [trub'əld] *a* (*person*) preocupado; (*epoch, life*) agitado.

trouble-free [trub'əlfrē] *a* sin problemas *or* dificultades.

troublemaker [trub'əlmākûr] *n* agitador(a) *m/f*.

troubleshooter [trub'əlshōōtûr] *n* (*in conflict*) conciliador(a) *m/f*.

troublesome [trub'əlsəm] *a* molesto, inoportuno.

trouble spot *n* centro de fricción, punto caliente.

trough [trôf] *n* (*also:* **drinking** ~) abrevadero; (*also:* **feeding** ~) comedero; (*channel*) canal *m*.

trounce [trouns] *vt* derrotar.

troupe [trōōp] *n* grupo.

trouser press [trou'zûr pres] *n* prensa para pantalones.

trousers [trou'zûrz] *npl* (*esp Brit*) pantalones *mpl*; **short** ~ pantalones *mpl* cortos.

trouser suit [trou'zûr sōōt] *n* (*Brit*) traje *m* de chaqueta y pantalón.

trousseau, *pl* ~**x** *or* ~**s** [trōō'sō, z] *n* ajuar *m*.

trout [trout] *n* (*pl inv*) trucha.

trowel [trou'əl] *n* paleta.

truant [trōō'ənt] *n*: **to play** ~ (*Brit*) hacer novillos.

truce [trōōs] *n* tregua.

truck [truk] *n* (*US*) camión *m*; (*RAIL*) vagón *m*.

truck driver *n* camionero/a.

trucker [truk'ûr] *n* (*esp US*) camionero/a, camionista *m/f*.

truck farm *n* (*US*) huerto de hortalizas.

truck farmer *n* (*US*) hortelano/a.

truck farming *n* (*US*) horticultura.

trucking [truk'ing] *n* (*esp US*) acarreo, transporte *m* en camión.

trucking company *n* (*US*) compañía de transporte por carretera.

truckload [truk'lōd] *n* camión *m* lleno.

truck stop *n* (*US*) restaurante *m* de carretera.

truculent [truk'yələnt] *a* agresivo.

trudge [truj] *vi* caminar penosamente.

true [trōō] *a* verdadero; (*accurate*) exacto; (*genuine*) auténtico; (*faithful*) fiel; (*wheel*) centrado; (*wall*) a plomo; (*beam*) alineado; ~ **to life** verídico; **to come** ~ realizarse, cumplirse.

truffle [truf'əl] *n* trufa.

truly [trōō'lē] *ad* realmente; (*faithfully*) fielmente; **yours** ~ (*in letter-writing*) atentamente.

trump [trump] *n* (*CARDS*) triunfo; **to turn up** ~**s** (*fig*) salir *or* resultar bien.

trump card *n* triunfo; (*fig*) baza.

trumped-up [trumpt'up'] *a* inventado.

trumpet [trum'pit] *n* trompeta.
truncated [trung'kātid] *a* truncado.
truncheon [trun'chən] *n* (*Brit*) porra.
trundle [trun'dəl] *vt, vi*: **to ~ along** rodar haciendo ruido.
trunk [trungk] *n* (*of tree, person*) tronco; (*of elephant*) trompa; (*case*) baúl *m*; (*US AUT*) maletero; *see also* **trunks.**
trunk road *n* (*Brit*) carretera principal.
trunks [trungks] *npl* (*also*: **swimming ~**) bañador *m.*
truss [trus] *n* (*MED*) braguero ♦ *vt*: **to ~ (up)** atar; (*CULIN*) espetar.
trust [trust] *n* confianza; (*COMM*) trust *m*; (*LAW*) fideicomiso ♦ *vt* (*rely on*) tener confianza en; (*entrust*): **to ~ sth to sb** confiar algo a uno; (*hope*): **to ~ (that)** esperar (que); **in ~** en fideicomiso; **you'll have to take it on ~** tienes que aceptarlo a ojos cerrados.
trust company *n* empresa de fideicomiso.
trusted [trus'tid] *a* de confianza, fiable, de fiar.
trustee [trustē'] *n* (*LAW*) fideicomisario.
trustful [trust'fəl] *a* confiado.
trust fund *n* fondo fiduciario *or* de fideicomiso.
trusting [trus'ting] *a* confiado.
trustworthy [trust'wûrthē] *a* digno de confianza, fiable, de fiar.
trusty [trus'tē] *a* fiel.
truth, ~s [trooth, troothz] *n* verdad *f.*
truthful [trooth'fəl] *a* (*person*) sincero; (*account*) fidedigno.
truthfully [trooth'fəlē] *ad* (*answer*) con sinceridad.
truthfulness [trooth'fəlnis] *n* (*of account*) verdad *f*; (*of person*) sinceridad *f.*
try [trī] *n* tentativa, intento; (*RUGBY*) ensayo ♦ *vt* (*LAW*) juzgar, procesar; (*test: sth new*) probar, someter a prueba; (*attempt*) intentar; (*strain: patience*) hacer perder ♦ *vi* probar; **to give sth a ~** intentar hacer algo; **to ~ one's (very) best** *or* **hardest** poner todo su empeño, esmerarse; **to ~ to do sth** intentar hacer algo.
try on *vt* (*clothes*) probarse.
try out *vt* probar, poner a prueba.
trying [trī'ing] *a* cansado; (*person*) pesado.
tsar [zâr] *n* zar *m.*
T-shirt [tē'shûrt] *n* camiseta.
T-square [tē'skwär] *n* regla en T.
TT *a abbr* (*Brit col*) = **teetotal** ♦ *abbr* (*US MAIL*) = *Trust Territory.*
tub [tub] *n* cubo (*Sp*), balde *m* (*LAm*); (*bath*) tina, bañera.
tuba [too'bə] *n* tuba.
tubby [tub'ē] *a* regordete.
tube [toob] *n* tubo; (*col: television*) tele *f*; (*Brit: subway*) metro; **to be down the ~s** estar en un apuro.
tubeless [toob'lis] *a* (*tire*) sin cámara.
tuber [too'bûr] *n* (*BOT*) tubérculo.

tuberculosis [toobûrkyəlō'sis] *n* tuberculosis *f inv.*
tube station [toob' stā'shən] *n* (*Brit*) estación *f* de metro.
tubing [too'bing] *n* tubería (*Sp*), cañería; **a piece of ~** un trozo de tubo.
tubular [too'byəlûr] *a* tubular.
TUC *n abbr* (*Brit*: = *Trades Union Congress*) *federación nacional de sindicatos.*
tuck [tuk] *n* (*SEWING*) pliegue *m* ♦ *vt* (*put*) poner.
tuck away *vt* esconder.
tuck in *vt* meter dentro; (*child*) arropar ♦ *vi* (*eat*) comer con apetito.
tuck up *vt* (*child*) arropar.
Tue(s). *abbr* (= *Tuesday*) mart.
Tuesday [tooz'dā] *n* martes *m inv*; **on ~** el martes; **on ~s** los martes; **every ~** todos los martes; **every other ~** cada dos martes; **last/next ~** el martes pasado/ próximo; **a week on ~, ~ week** del martes en 8 días, del martes en una semana.
tuft [tuft] *n* mechón *m*; (*of grass etc*) manojo.
tug [tug] *n* (*ship*) remolcador *m* ♦ *vt* remolcar.
tug-of-war [tug'əvwôr'] *n* lucha de tiro de cuerda.
tuition [tooish'ən] *n* (*US: school fees*) matrícula; (*Brit*) enseñanza; (: *private ~*) clases *fpl* particulares.
tulip [too'lip] *n* tulipán *m.*
tumble [tum'bəl] *n* (*fall*) caída ♦ *vi* caerse, tropezar; **to ~ to sth** (*col*) caer en la cuenta de algo.
tumbledown [tum'bəldoun] *a* destartalado.
tumble dryer *n* (*Brit*) secadora.
tumbler [tum'blûr] *n* vaso.
tummy [tum'ē] *n* (*col*) barriga, vientre *m.*
tumor, (*Brit*) tumour [too'mûr] *n* tumor *m.*
tumult [too'məlt] *n* tumulto.
tumultuous [toomul'chooəs] *a* tumultuoso.
tuna [too'nə] *n* (*pl inv*) (*also*: **~ fish**) atún *m.*
tundra [tun'drə] *n* tundra.
tune [toon] *n* (*melody*) melodía ♦ *vt* (*MUS*) afinar; (*RADIO, TV, AUT*) sintonizar; **to be in/out of ~** (*instrument*) estar afinado/ desafinado; (*singer*) cantar afinadamente/ desafinar; **to be in/out of ~ with** (*fig*) armonizar/desentonar con; **to the ~ of** (*fig: amount*) por (la) cantidad de.
tune in *vi* (*RADIO, TV*): **to ~ in (to)** sintonizar (con).
tune up *vi* (*musician*) afinar (su instrumento).
tuneful [toon'fəl] *a* melodioso.
tuner [too'nûr] *n* (*radio set*) sintonizador *m*; **piano ~** afinador(a) *m/f* de pianos.
tungsten [tung'stən] *n* tungsteno.
tunic [too'nik] *n* túnica.
tuning [too'ning] *n* sintonización *f*; (*MUS*) afinación *f.*

tuning fork n diapasón m.
Tunis |tōō'nis| n Túnez m.
Tunisia |tōōnē'zhə| n Túnez m.
Tunisian |tōōnē'zhən| a, n tunecino/a m/f.
tunnel |tun'əl| n túnel m; (in mine) galería ♦ vi construir un túnel/una galería.
tunny |tun'ē| n atún m.
turban |tûr'bən| n turbante m.
turbid |tûr'bid| a turbio.
turbine |tûr'bīn| n turbina.
turboprop |tûr'bōpräp| n turbohélice m.
turbot |tûr'bət| n (pl inv) rodaballo.
turbulence |tûr'byələns| n (AVIAT) turbulencia.
turbulent |tûr'byələnt| a turbulento.
tureen |tərēn'| n sopera.
turf |tûrf| n césped m; (clod) tepe m ♦ vt cubrir con césped.
turf out vt (Brit: col) echar a la calle.
turgid |tûr'jid| a (prose) pesado.
Turin |tōō'rin| n Turín m.
Turk |tûrk| n turco/a m.
Turkey |tûr'kē| n Turquía.
turkey |tûr'kē| n pavo.
Turkish |tûr'kish| a turco ♦ n (LING) turco.
Turkish bath n baño turco.
turmeric |tûr'mûrik| n cúrcuma.
turmoil |tûr'moil| n desorden m, alboroto.
turn |tûrn| n turno; (in road) curva; (THEATER) número; (MED) ataque m ♦ vt girar, volver; (collar, steak) dar la vuelta a; (shape: wood, metal) tornear; (change): **to ~ sth into** convertir algo en ♦ vi volver; (person: look back) volverse; (reverse direction) dar la vuelta; (milk) cortarse; (change) cambiar; (become): **to ~ into sth** convertirse or transformarse en algo; **a good ~** un favor; **it gave me quite a ~** me dio un susto; **"no left ~"** (AUT) "prohibido girar a la izquierda"; **it's your ~** te toca a ti; **in ~** por turnos; **to take ~s** turnarse; **at the ~ of the century** a finales de siglo; **to take a ~ for the worse** (situation, patient) empeorar; **they ~ed him against us** le pusieron en contra nuestra; **the car ~ed the corner** el coche dobló la esquina; **to ~ left** (AUT) torcer or girar a la izquierda; **she has no-one to ~ to** no tiene a quién recurrir.
turn around vi volverse; (rotate) girar.
turn away vi apartar la vista ♦ vt (reject: person, business) rechazar.
turn back vi volverse atrás.
turn down vt (refuse) rechazar; (reduce) bajar; (fold) doblar.
turn in vi (col: go to bed) acostarse ♦ vt (fold) doblar hacia dentro; (essay, report) entregar.
turn off vi (from road) desviarse ♦ vt (light, radio etc) apagar; (engine) parar.
turn on vt (light, radio etc) encender, prender (LAm); (engine) poner en marcha.
turn out vt (light, gas) apagar; (pro-

duce: goods, novel etc) producir ♦ vi (attend: troops) presentarse; (: doctor) atender; **to ~ out to be ...** resultar ser ....
turn over vi (person) volverse ♦ vt (mattress, card) dar la vuelta a; (page) volver.
turn round vi (Brit) = **turn around**.
turn to vt fus: **to ~ to sb** acudir a uno.
turn up vi (person) llegar, presentarse; (lost object) aparecer ♦ vt (radio) subir, poner más alto; (heat, gas) poner más fuerte.
turnabout |tûr'nəbout|, **turnaround** |tûr'nəround| n (fig) giro total.
turncoat |tûrn'kōt| n renegado/a.
turned-up |tûrnd'up| a (nose) respingón/ona.
turning |tûr'ning| n (curve) curva; (Brit: side road) bocacalle f.
turning point n (fig) momento decisivo.
turnip |tûr'nip| n nabo.
turnkey system |tûrn'kē sis'təm| n (COMPUT) sistema m de seguridad.
turnout |tûrn'out| n asistencia, número de asistentes, público.
turnover |tûrn'ōvûr| n (COMM: amount of money) facturación f; (: of goods) movimiento; **there is a rapid ~ in staff** hay una rápida rotación de personal.
turnpike |tûrn'pīk| n (US) autopista de peaje.
turn signal n (US) indicador m (de dirección).
turnstile |tûrn'stīl| n torniquete m.
turntable |tûrn'tābəl| n plato.
turn-up |tûrn'up| n (Brit: on trousers) vuelta.
turpentine |tûr'pəntīn| n trementina.
turquoise |tûr'koiz| n (stone) turquesa ♦ a color turquesa.
turret |tûr'it| n torreón m.
turtle |tûr'təl| n galápago.
turtleneck (sweater) |tûr'təlnck (swct'ûr)| n (jersey m de) cuello cisne.
Tuscany |tus'kənē| n Toscana.
tusk |tusk| n colmillo.
tussle |tus'əl| n lucha, pelea.
tutor |tōō'tûr| n (US) preceptor(a) m/f; (Brit) profesor(a) m/f.
tutorial |tōōtôr'ēəl| n (SCOL) seminario.
tuxedo |tuksē'dō| n smóking m, esmoquin m.
TV |tēvē| n abbr (= television) tele f.
TVP n abbr = texturized vegetable protein.
twaddle |twäd'əl| n (col) tonterías fpl.
twang |twang| n (of instrument) punteado; (of voice) timbre m nasal.
tweak |twēk| vt (nose, ear) pellizcar; (hair) tirar.
tweed |twēd| n tweed m.
tweezers |twē'zûrz| npl pinzas fpl (de depilar).
twelfth |twelfth| num duodécimo.

Twelfth Night n (Día m de) Reyes mpl.

twelve [twelv] num doce; **at** ~ **o'clock** (midday) a mediodía; (midnight) a medianoche.

twentieth [twen'tēith] num vigésimo.

twenty [twen'tē] num veinte.

twerp [twûrp] n (col) idiota m/f.

twice [twīs] ad dos veces; ~ **as much** dos veces más; **she is** ~ **your age** ella tiene dos veces tu edad; ~ **a week** dos veces a la or por semana.

twiddle [twid'əl] vt, vi: **to** ~ **(with) sth** dar vueltas a algo; **to** ~ **one's thumbs** (fig) estar mano sobre mano.

twig [twig] n ramita ♦ vi (Brit: col) caer en la cuenta.

twilight [twī'līt] n crepúsculo; (morning) madrugada; **in the** ~ en la media luz.

twill [twil] n sarga, estameña.

twin [twin] a, n gemelo/a m/f ♦ vt hermanar.

twin beds npl camas fpl gemelas.

twin-carburetor [twinkär'bərätûr] a de dos carburadores.

twine [twīn] n bramante m ♦ vi (plant) enroscarse.

twin-engined [twin'enjənd] a bimotor; ~ **aircraft** avión m bimotor.

twinge [twinj] n (of pain) punzada; (of conscience) remordimiento.

twinkle [twing'kəl] n centelleo ♦ vi centellear; (eyes) parpadear.

twin town n ciudad f hermanada or gemela.

twirl [twûrl] n giro ♦ vt dar vueltas a ♦ vi piruetear.

twist [twist] n (action) torsión f; (in road, coil) vuelta; (in wire, cord) doblez f; (in story) giro ♦ vt torcer, retorcer; (roll around) enrollar; (fig) deformar ♦ vi serpentear; **to** ~ **one's ankle/wrist** (MED) torcerse el tobillo/la muñeca.

twisted [twis'tid] a (wire, rope) trenzado, enroscado; (ankle, wrist) torcido; (fig: logic, mind) retorcido.

twit [twit] n (col) tonto.

twitch [twich] n sacudida; (nervous) tic m nervioso ♦ vi moverse nerviosamente.

two [tōō] num dos; ~ **by** ~, **in** ~s de dos en dos; **to put** ~ **and** ~ **together** (fig) atar cabos.

two-door [tōō'dôr] a (AUT) de dos puertas.

two-faced [tōō'fāst] a (pej: person) falso.

twofold [tōō'fōld] ad: **to increase** ~ duplicarse ♦ a (increase) doble; (reply) en dos partes.

two-piece [tōō'pēs] n (also: ~ **suit**) traje m de dos piezas; (also: ~ **swimsuit**) dos piezas m inv, bikini m.

two-seater [tōō'sē'tûr] n (plane, car) avión m/coche m de dos plazas.

twosome [tōō'səm] n (people) pareja.

two-stroke [tōō'strōk'] n (also: ~ **engine**) motor m de dos tiempos ♦ a de dos tiempos.

two-tone [tōō'tōn'] a (color) bicolor, de dos tonos.

two-way [tōō'wā'] a: ~ **traffic** circulación f de dos sentidos; ~ **radio** radio f emisora y receptora.

TX abbr (US MAIL) = Texas.

tycoon [tīkōōn'] n: **(business)** ~ magnate m/f.

type [tīp] n (category) tipo, género; (model) modelo; (TYP) tipo, letra ♦ vt (letter etc) escribir a máquina; **what** ~ **do you want?** ¿qué tipo quieres?; **in bold/italic** ~ en negrita/cursiva.

type-cast [tīp'kast] a (actor) encasillado.

typeface [tīp'fās] n tipo de letra.

typescript [tīp'skript] n texto mecanografiado.

typeset [tīp'set] vt (irg: like **set**) componer.

typesetter [tīp'setûr] n cajista m/f, compositor(a) m/f.

typewriter [tīp'rītûr] n máquina de escribir.

typewritten [tīp'ritən] a mecanografiado.

typhoid [tī'foid] n tifoidea.

typhoon [tīfōōn'] n tifón m.

typhus [tī'fəs] n tifus m.

typical [tip'ikəl] a típico.

typically [tip'ikəlē] ad típicamente.

typify [tip'əfī] vt tipificar.

typing [tī'ping] n mecanografía.

typing pool n (Brit) servicio de mecanógrafos.

typist [tī'pist] n mecanógrafo/a.

typography [tīpâg'rəfē] n tipografía.

tyranny [tēr'ənē] n tiranía.

tyrant [tī'rənt] n tirano/a.

tyre [tīûr'] n (Brit) = **tire**.

Tyrol [tirōl'] n Tirol m.

Tyrolean [tīrō'lēən], **Tyrolese** [tirəlēz'] a tirolés/esa.

Tyrrhenian Sea [tīrē'nēən sē'] n Mar m Tirreno.

tzar [zär] n = **tsar**.

U

U, u [yōō] n (letter) U, u f; **U for Uncle** U de Uruguay.

U [yōō] n abbr (Brit CINEMA: = universal) todos los públicos.

U-bend [yōō'bend] n (AUT, in pipe) recodo.

ubiquitous [yōōbik'witəs] a ubicuo.

UDA n abbr (Brit: = Ulster Defence Association) organización paramilitar protestante en Irlanda del Norte.

udder [ud'ûr] n ubre f.

UDI *n abbr* (*Brit* POL) = *unilateral declaration of independence.*

UDR *n abbr* (*Brit*: = *Ulster Defence Regiment*) *fuerza de seguridad de Irlanda del Norte.*

UEFA [yōōā'fa] *n abbr* (= *Union of European Football Associations*) U.E.F.A. *f.*

UFO [yōōefō'] *n abbr* = (*unidentified flying object*) OVNI *m.*

Uganda [yōōgan'də] *n* Uganda.

Ugandan [yōōgan'dən] *a* de Uganda.

ugh [u] *excl* ¡uf!

ugliness [ug'lēnis] *n* fealdad *f.*

ugly [ug'lē] *a* feo; (*dangerous*) peligroso.

UHF *abbr* (= *ultra-high frequency*) UHF *m.*

UHT *a abbr* (= *ultra heat treated*): ~ **milk** leche *f* uperizada.

UK *n abbr* (= *United Kingdom*) R.U.

ulcer [ul'sûr] *n* úlcera; **mouth** ~ úlcera oral.

Ulster [ul'stûr] *n* Úlster *m.*

ulterior [ultēr'êûr] *a* ulterior; ~ **motive** segundas intenciones *fpl.*

ultimate [ul'təmit] *a* último, final; (*greatest*) mayor ♦ *n:* **the** ~ **in luxury** el colmo del lujo.

ultimately [ul'təmitlē] *ad* (*in the end*) por último, al final; (*fundamentally*) a *or* en fin de cuentas.

ultimatum, *pl* ~**s** *or* **ultimata** [ultimā'təm, -tə] *n* ultimátum *m.*

ultra- [ul'trə] *pref* ultra-.

ultralight [ultrəlīt'] *n* (avión *m*) ultraligero, avioneta.

ultrasonic [ultrəsân'ik] *a* ultrasónico.

ultrasound [ul'trəsound] *n* (MED) ultrasonido.

ultraviolet [ultrəvī'əlit] *a* ultravioleta.

umbilical cord [umbil'ikəl kôrd] *n* cordón *m* umbilical.

umbrage [um'brij] *n:* **to take** ~ **(at)** ofenderse (por).

umbrella [umbrel'ə] *n* paraguas *m inv*; **under the** ~ **of** (*fig*) bajo la protección de.

umpire [um'piûr] *n* árbitro ♦ *vt* arbitrar.

umpteen [ump'tēn'] *num* enésimos/as; **for the** ~**th time** por enésima vez.

UMW *n abbr* (= *United Mineworkers of America*) sindicato de mineros.

UN *n abbr* (= *United Nations*) N.U. *fpl*, NN.UU. *fpl.*

un- [un-] *pref* in-; des-; no ...; poco ...; nada ...

unabashed [unəbasht'] *a* nada avergonzado.

unabated [unəbā'tid] *a:* **to continue** ~ seguir sin disminuir.

unable [unā'bəl] *a:* **to be** ~ **to do sth** no poder hacer algo; (*not know how to*) ser incapaz de hacer algo, no saber hacer algo.

unabridged [unəbrijd'] *a* íntegro.

unacceptable [unaksep'təbəl] *a* (*proposal, behavior, price*) inaceptable; **it's** ~ **that** no

se puede aceptar que.

unaccompanied [unəkum'pənēd] *a* no acompañado; (*singing, song*) sin acompañamiento.

unaccountably [unəkount'əblē] *ad* inexplicablemente.

unaccounted [unəkoun'tid] *a:* **two passengers are** ~ **for** faltan dos pasajeros.

unaccustomed [unəkus'təmd] *a:* **to be** ~ **to** no estar acostumbrado a.

unacquainted [unəkwān'tid] *a:* **to be** ~ **with** (*facts*) desconocer, ignorar.

unadulterated [unədul'tərātid] *a* (*gen*) puro; (*wine*) sin mezcla.

unaffected [unəfɛk'tid] *a* (*person, behavior*) sin afectación, sencillo; (*emotionally*): **to be** ~ **by** no estar afectado por.

unafraid [unəfrād'] *a:* **to be** ~ no tener miedo.

unaided [unā'did] *a* sin ayuda, por sí solo.

unanimity [yōōnənim'itē] *n* unanimidad *f.*

unanimous [yōōnan'əməs] *a* unánime.

unanimously [yōōnan'əməslē] *ad* unánimemente.

unanswered [unan'sûrd] *a* (*question, letter*) sin contestar; (*criticism*) incontestado.

unappetizing [unap'itīzing] *a* poco apetitoso.

unappreciative [unəprē'shēətiv] *a* desagradecido.

unarmed [unârmd'] *a* (*person*) desarmado; (*combat*) sin armas.

unashamed [unəshāmd'] *a* desvergonzado.

unassisted [unəsis'tid] *a, ad* sin ayuda.

unassuming [unəsōō'ming] *a* modesto, sin pretensiones.

unattached [unətacht'] *a* (*person*) soltero; (*part etc*) suelto.

unattended [unəten'did] *a* (*car, luggage*) sin atender.

unattractive [unətrak'tiv] *a* poco atractivo.

unauthorized [unôth'ərīzd] *a* no autorizado.

unavailable [unəvā'ləbəl] *a* (*article, room, book*) indisponible; (*person*) ocupado.

unavoidable [unəvoi'dəbəl] *a* inevitable.

unavoidably [unəvoi'dəblē] *ad* (*detained*) por causas ajenas a su voluntad.

unaware [unəwär'] *a:* **to be** ~ **of** ignorar.

unawares [unəwärz'] *ad* de improviso.

unbalanced [unbal'ənst] *a* desequilibrado; (*mentally*) trastornado.

unbearable [unbär'əbəl] *a* insoportable.

unbeatable [unbē'təbəl] *a* (*gen*) invencible; (*price*) inmejorable.

unbeaten [unbēt'ən] *a* imbatido; (*team, army*) invicto; (*record*) no batido.

unbecoming [unbikum'ing] *a* (*unseemly: language, behavior*) indecoroso, impropio; (*unflattering: garment*) poco favorecedor(a).

unbeknown(st) [unbinōn(st)'] *ad:* ~ **to**

me sin saberlo yo.
unbelief |unbilēf'| *n* incredulidad *f*.
unbelievable |unbilē'vəbəl| *a* increíble.
unbelievingly |unbilē'vinglē| *ad* sin creer.
unbend |unbend'| (*irg: like* **bend**) *vi* (*fig: person*) relajarse ♦ *vt* (*wire*) enderezar.
unbending |unben'ding| *a* (*fig*) inflexible.
unbias(s)ed |unbi'əst| *a* imparcial.
unblemished |unblem'isht| *a* sin mancha.
unblock |unblák'| *vt* (*pipe*) desatascar; (*road*) despejar.
unborn |unbôrn'| *a* que va a nacer.
unbounded |unboun'did| *a* ilimitado, sin límite.
unbreakable |unbrā'kəbəl| *a* irrompible.
unbridled |unbrī'dəld| *a* (*fig*) desenfrenado.
unbroken |unbrō'kən| *a* (*seal*) intacto; (*series*) continuo; (*record*) no batido; (*spirit*) indómito.
unbuckle |unbuk'əl| *vt* desabrochar.
unburden |unbûr'dən| *vt*: **to ~ o.s.** desahogarse.
unbusinesslike |unbiz'nislīk| *a* (*trader*) poco metódico; (*transaction*) incorrecto; (*fig: person*) poco práctico.
unbutton |unbut'ən| *vt* desabrochar.
uncalled-for |unkôld'fôr| *a* gratuito, inmerecido.
uncanny |unkan'ē| *a* extraño, extraordinario.
unceasing |unsē'sing| *a* incesante.
unceremonious |unsärəmō'nēəs| *a* (*abrupt, rude*) brusco, hosco.
uncertain |unsûr'tən| *a* incierto; (*indecisive*) indeciso; **it's ~ whether** no se sabe si; **in no ~ terms** sin dejar lugar a dudas.
uncertainty |unsûr'təntē| *n* incertidumbre *f*.
unchallenged |unchal'injd| *a* (*LAW etc*) incontestado; **to go ~** no encontrar respuesta.
unchanged |unchānjd'| *a* sin cambiar *or* alterar.
uncharitable |unchar'itəbəl| *a* (*remark, behavior*) demasiado duro.
uncharted |unchâr'tid| *a* inexplorado.
unchecked |unchekt'| *a* desenfrenado.
uncivil |unsiv'əl| *a* grosero.
uncivilized |unsiv'ilīzd| *a* (*gen*) inculto, poco civilizado; (*fig: behavior etc*) bárbaro.
uncle |ung'kəl| *n* tío.
unclear |unkliûr'| *a* poco claro; **I'm still ~ about what I'm supposed to do** todavía no estoy muy seguro de lo que tengo que hacer.
uncoil |unkoil'| *vt* desenrollar ♦ *vi* desenrollarse.
uncomfortable |unkumf'təbəl| *a* incómodo; (*uneasy*) inquieto.
uncomfortably |unkumf'təblē| *ad* (*uneasily: say*) con inquietud; (: *think*) con remordimiento *or* nerviosismo.
uncommitted |unkəmit'id| *a* (*attitude, country*) no comprometido; **to remain ~ to**

(*policy, party*) no comprometerse a.
uncommon |unkâm'ən| *a* poco común, raro.
uncommunicative |unkəmyōō'nikətiv| *a* poco comunicativo, reservado.
uncomplicated |unkâm'plikātid| *a* sin complicaciones.
uncompromising |unkâm'prəmīzing| *a* intransigente.
unconcerned |unkənsûrnd'| *a* indiferente, despreocupado; **to be ~ about** ser indiferente a, no preocuparse de.
unconditional |unkəndish'ənəl| *a* incondicional.
uncongenial |unkənjēn'yəl| *a* desagradable.
unconnected |unkənek'tid| *a* (*unrelated*): **to be ~ with** no estar relacionado con.
unconscious |unkân'chəs| *a* sin sentido; (*unaware*) inconsciente ♦ *n*: **the ~** el inconsciente; **to knock sb ~** dejar a uno sin sentido.
unconsciously |unkân'chəslē| *ad* inconscientemente.
unconsciousness |unkân'chəsnis| *n* inconsciencia.
unconstitutional |unkânstitōō'shənəl| *a* anti-constitucional.
uncontested |unkəntes'tid| *a* (*champion*) incontestado; (*POL: seat*) ganado sin oposición.
uncontrollable |unkəntrō'ləbəl| *a* (*temper*) indomable; (*laughter*) incontenible.
uncontrolled |unkəntrōld'| *a* (*child, dog, emotion*) incontrolado; (*inflation, price rises*) desenfrenado.
unconventional |unkənven'chənəl| *a* poco convencional.
unconvinced |unkənvinst'| *a*: **to be** *or* **remain ~** seguir sin convencerse.
unconvincing |unkənvin'sing| *a* poco convincente.
uncork |unkôrk'| *vt* descorchar, destapar.
uncorroborated |unkəráb'ərātid| *a* no confirmado.
uncouth |unkōōth'| *a* grosero, inculto.
uncover |unkuv'ûr| *vt* (*gen*) descubrir; (*take lid off*) destapar.
uncovered |unkuv'ûrd| *a*: **~ check** cheque *m* sin fondos.
undamaged |undam'ijd| *a* (*goods*) en buen estado; (*fig: reputation*) intacto, indemne.
undaunted |undôn'tid| *a*: **~ by** nada desanimado por.
undecided |undisī'did| *a* (*character*) indeciso; (*question*) no resuelto, pendiente.
undelivered |undiliv'ûrd| *a* no entregado al destinatario; **if ~ return to sender** en caso de no llegar a su destino devolver al remitente.
undeniable |undinī'əbəl| *a* innegable.
undeniably |undinī'əblē| *ad* innegablemente.
under |un'dûr| *prep* debajo de; (*less than*)

menos de; *(according to)* según, de acuerdo con ♦ *ad* debajo, abajo; ~ **there** allí abajo; ~ **construction** en construcción; en obras; ~ **the circumstances** dadas las circunstancias; **in** ~ **2 hours** en menos de dos horas; ~ **anesthetic** bajo los efectos de la anestesia; ~ **discussion** en discusión, sobre el tapete.

under... *pref* sub....

underage [undúráj'] *a* menor de edad.

underarm [un'dúrárm] *n* axila, sobaco ♦ *cpd*: ~ **deodorant** desodorante *m* corporal.

undercapitalized [undúrkap'itəlīzd] *a* descapitalizado.

undercarriage [un'dúrkarij] *n* (*Brit* AVIAT) tren *m* de aterrizaje.

undercharge [undúrchárj'] *vt* cobrar de menos.

underclothes [un'dúrklōz] *npl* ropa *sg* interior *or* íntima (*LAm*).

undercoat [un'dúrkōt] *n* (*paint*) primera mano ♦ *vt* (*US* AUT) proteger contra la corrosión.

undercover [undúrkuv'ûr] *a* clandestino.

undercurrent [un'dúrkûrənt] *n* corriente *f* submarina; (*fig*) tendencia oculta.

undercut [undúrkut'] *vt* (*irg: like* **cut**) vender más barato que; fijar un precio más barato que.

underdeveloped [un'dúrdivel'əpt] *a* subdesarrollado.

underdog [un'dúrdôg] *n* desvalido/a.

underdone [un'dúrdun] *a* (*CULIN*) poco hecho.

underemployment [undúremploi'mənt] *n* subempleo.

underestimate [undúres'təmāt] *vt* subestimar.

underexposed [undúrikspōzd'] *a* (*PHOT*) subexpuesto.

underfed [undúrfed'] *a* subalimentado.

underfoot [undúrfŏŏt'] *ad*: **it's wet** ~ el suelo está mojado.

undergo [undúrgō'] *vt* (*irg: like* **go**) sufrir; (*treatment*) recibir; **the car is** ~**ing repairs** están reparando el coche.

undergraduate [undúrgraj'ŏŏit] *n* estudiante *m/f* ♦ *cpd*: ~ **courses** cursos *mpl* de licenciatura.

underground [un'dúrground] *n* (*POL*) movimiento clandestino; (*Brit: railway*) metro ♦ *a* subterráneo.

undergrowth [un'dúrgrōth] *n* maleza.

underhand(ed) [un'dúrhan'd(id)] *a* (*fig*) socarrón.

underinsured [undúrinshŏŏrd'] *a* insuficientemente asegurado.

underlie [undúrlī'] *vt* (*irg: like* **lie**) (*fig*) ser la razón fundamental de; **the underlying cause** la causa fundamental.

underline [un'dúrlīn] *vt* subrayar.

underling [un'dúrling] *n* (*pej*) subalterno/a.

undermanning [un'dúrman'ing] *n* falta de personal.

undermentioned [un'dúrmenchənd] *a* abajo citado.

undermine [un'dúrmīn] *vt* socavar, minar.

underneath [undúrnēth'] *ad* debajo ♦ *prep* debajo de, bajo.

undernourished [undúrnûr'isht] *a* desnutrido.

underpaid [undúrpād'] *a* mal pagado.

underpants [un'dúrpants] *npl* calzoncillos *mpl*.

underpass [un'dúrpas] *n* paso subterráneo.

underpin [undúrpin'] *vt* (*argument, case*) secundar, sostener.

underplay [undúrplā'] *vt* minimizar.

underpopulated [undúrpáp'yəlātid] *a* despoblado.

underprice [undúrprīs'] *vt* vender demasiado barato.

underpriced [undúrprīst'] *a* con precio demasiado bajo.

underprivileged [undúrpriv'əlijd] *a* desvalido.

underrate [undərāt'] *vt* menospreciar, subestimar.

underscore [undúrskôr'] *vt* subrayar, sostener.

underseal [un'dúrsēl] *vt* (*AUT*) proteger contra la corrosión.

undersecretary [un'dúrsek'ritārē] *n* subsecretario/a.

undersell [undúrsel'] *vt* (*competitors*) vender más barato que.

undershirt [un'dúrshûrt] *n* (*US*) camiseta.

undershorts [un'dúrshôrts] *npl* (*US*) calzoncillos *mpl*.

underside [un'dúrsīd] *n* parte *f* inferior, revés *m*.

undersigned [un'dúrsīnd] *a, n*: **the** ~ el/la *etc* abajo firmante.

underskirt [un'dúrskûrt] *n* enaguas *fpl*.

understaffed [undúrstaft'] *a* falto de personal.

understand [undúrstand'] (*irg: like* **stand**) *vt, vi* entender, comprender; (*assume*) tener entendido; **to make o.s. understood** hacerse entender; **I** ~ **you have been absent** tengo entendido que (usted) ha estado ausente.

understandable [undúrstan'dəbəl] *a* comprensible.

understanding [undúrstan'ding] *a* comprensivo ♦ *n* comprensión *f*, entendimiento; (*agreement*) acuerdo; **to come to an** ~ **with sb** llegar a un acuerdo con uno; **on the** ~ **that** a condición de que (+ *subjun*).

understate [undúrstāt'] *vt* minimizar.

understatement [undúrstāt'mənt] *n* subestimación *f*; (*modesty*) modestia (excesiva).

understood [undúrstŏŏd'] *pt, pp of* **understand** ♦ *a* entendido; (*implied*): **it is** ~ **that** se sobreentiende que.

understudy |un'dŭrstudē| n suplente m/f.

undertake |undŭrtāk'| (irg: like **take**) vt emprender; **to ~ to do sth** comprometerse a hacer algo.

undertaker |un'dŭrtākŭr| n director(a) m/f de pompas fúnebres.

undertaking |un'dŭrtāking| n empresa; (promise) promesa.

undertone |un'dŭrtōn| n (of criticism) connotación f; (low voice): **in an ~** en voz baja.

undervalue |undŭrval'yōō| vt (fig) subestimar, menospreciar; (COMM etc) valorizar por debajo de su precio.

underwater |un'dŭrwôt'ŭr| ad bajo el agua ♦ a submarino.

underwear |un'dŭrwär| n ropa interior or íntima (LAm).

underweight |un'dŭrwāt| a de peso insuficiente; (person) demasiado delgado.

underworld |un'dŭrwŭrld| n (of crime) hampa, inframundo.

underwrite |un'dərīt| (irg: like **write**) vt (COMM) suscribir; (INSURANCE) asegurar (contra riesgos).

underwriter |un'dərītŭr| n (INSURANCE) asegurador/a m/f.

undeserving |undizŭr'ving| a: **to be ~ of** no ser digno de.

undesirable |undiziŭr'əbəl| a indeseable.

undeveloped |undivcl'əpt| a (land, resources) sin explotar.

undies |un'dēz| npl (col) ropa sg interior or íntima (LAm).

undiluted |undilōō'tid| a (concentrate) concentrado.

undiplomatic |undipləmat'ik| a poco diplomático.

undischarged |undischárjd'| a: **~ bankrupt** (Brit) quebrado/a no rehabilitado/a.

undisciplined |undis'əplind| a indisciplinado.

undiscovered |undiskuv'ûrd| a no descubierto; (unknown) desconocido.

undisguised |undisgīzd'| a (dislike) no disfrazado; (amusement etc) franco, abierto.

undisputed |undispyōō'tid| a incontestable.

undistinguished |undisting'gwisht| a mediocre.

undisturbed |undistûrbd'| a (sleep) ininterrumpido; **to leave sth ~** dejar algo tranquilo.

undivided |undivī'did| a: **I want your ~ attention** quiero su completa atención.

undo |undōō'| vt (irg: like **do**) deshacer.

undoing |undōō'ing| n ruina, perdición f.

undone |undun'| pp of **undo** ♦ a: **to come ~** (clothes) desabrocharse; (parcel) desatarse.

undoubted |undou'tid| a indudable.

undoubtedly |undou'tidlē| ad indudablemente, sin duda.

undress |undres'| vi desnudarse.

undrinkable |undringk'əbəl| a (unpalatable) que no se puede beber; (poisonous) no potable.

undue |undōō'| a indebido, excesivo.

undulating |un'jəlāting| a ondulante.

unduly |undōō'lē| ad excesivamente, demasiado.

undying |undī'ing| a eterno.

unearned |unûrnd'| a (praise, respect) inmerecido; **~ income** ingresos mpl no ganados, renta no ganada or salarial.

unearth |unûrth'| vt desenterrar.

unearthly |unûrth'lē| a: **~ hour** (col) hora inverosímil or intempestiva.

unease |unēz'| n malestar m.

uneasy |unē'zē| a intranquilo; (worried) preocupado; **to feel ~ about doing sth** sentirse incómodo con la idea de hacer algo.

uneconomic(al) |unēkənám'ik(əl)| a no económico.

uneducated |unej'ōōkātid| a ignorante, inculto.

unemployed |unemploid'| a parado, sin trabajo ♦ n: **the ~** los parados.

unemployment |unemploi'mənt| n paro, desempleo.

unemployment benefit n subsidio de paro.

unending |unen'ding| a interminable.

unenviable |unen'vēəbəl| a poco envidiable.

unequal |unē'kwəl| a (length, objects etc) desigual; (amounts) distinto; (division of labor) poco justo.

unequaled, (Brit) **unequalled** |unēk'wəld| a inigualado, sin par.

unequivocal |unikwiv'əkəl| a (answer) inequívoco, claro; (person) claro.

unerring |unûr'ing| a infalible.

UNESCO |yōōncs'kō| n abbr (= United Nations Educational, Scientific and Cultural Organization) UNESCO f.

unethical |uneth'ikəl| a (methods) inmoral; (doctor's behavior) que infringe la ética profesional.

uneven |unē'vən| a desigual; (road etc) quebrado.

uneventful |univent'fəl| a sin novedad.

unexceptional |uniksep'shənəl| a sin nada de extraordinario, corriente.

unexciting |uniksī'ting| a (news) sin interés; (film, evening) aburrido.

unexpected |unikspek'tid| a inesperado.

unexpectedly |unikspek'tidlē| ad inesperadamente.

unexplained |unikspländ'| a inexplicado.

unexploded |uniksplō'did| a sin explotar.

unfailing |unfā'ling| a (support) indefectible; (energy) inagotable.

unfair |unfär'| a: **~ (to sb)** injusto (con uno); **it's ~ that ...** es injusto que ..., no es justo que ....

unfair dismissal n despido improcedente.

unfairly [unfär'lē] *ad* injustamente.
unfaithful [unfāth'fəl] *a* infiel.
unfamiliar [unfəmil'yûr] *a* extraño, desconocido; **to be ~ with sth** desconocer *or* ignorar algo.
unfashionable [unfash'ənəbəl] *a* (*clothes*) pasado *or* fuera de moda; (*district*) poco elegante.
unfasten [unfas'ən] *vt* desatar.
unfathomable [unfath'əməbəl] *a* insondable.
unfavorable, (*Brit*) **unfavourable** [unfā'vûrəbəl] *a* desfavorable.
unfavorably [unfā'vûrablē] *ad*: **to look ~ upon** ver desfavorablemente.
unfeeling [unfē'ling] *a* insensible.
unfinished [unfin'isht] *a* inacabado, sin terminar.
unfit [unfit'] *a* (*ill*) indispuesto, enfermo; (*incompetent*) incapaz; **~ for work** no apto para trabajar.
unflagging [unflag'ing] *a* incansable.
unflappable [unflap'əbəl] *a* imperturbable.
unflattering [unflat'ûring] *a* (*dress, hairstyle*) poco halagüeño.
unflinching [unflin'ching] *a* impávido, resuelto.
unfold [unfōld'] *vt* desdoblar; (*fig*) revelar ♦ *vi* abrirse; revelarse.
unforeseeable [unfôrsē'əbəl] *a* imprevisible.
unforeseen [unfôrsēn'] *a* imprevisto.
unforgettable [unfûrget'əbəl] *a* inolvidable.
unforgivable [unfûrgiv'əbəl] *a* imperdonable.
unformatted [unfôr'matid] *a* (*disk, text*) sin formato.
unfortunate [unfôr'chənit] *a* desgraciado; (*event, remark*) inoportuno.
unfortunately [unfôr'chənitlē] *ad* desgraciadamente, por desgracia.
unfounded [unfoun'did] *a* infundado.
unfriendly [unfrend'lē] *a* antipático.
unfulfilled [unfōōlfild'] *a* (*ambition*) sin realizar; (*prophecy, promise, terms of contract*) incumplido; (*desire, person*) insatisfecho.
unfurl [unfûrl'] *vt* desplegar.
unfurnished [unfûr'nisht] *a* desamueblado.
ungainly [ungān'lē] *a* (*walk*) desgarbado.
ungodly [ungâd'lē] *a*: **at an ~ hour** a una hora inverosímil.
ungrateful [ungrāt'fəl] *a* ingrato.
unguarded [ungâr'did] *a* (*moment*) de descuido.
unhappily [unhap'ilē] *ad* (*unfortunately*) desgraciadamente.
unhappiness [unhap'ēnis] *n* tristeza.
unhappy [unhap'ē] *a* (*sad*) triste; (*unfortunate*) desgraciado; (*childhood*) infeliz; **~ with** (*arrangements etc*) poco contento con, descontento de.
unharmed [unhârmd'] *a* (*person*) ileso.

unhealthy [unhel'thē] *a* (*gen*) malsano; (*person*) enfermizo; (*interest*) morboso.
unheard-of [unhûrd'əv] *a* inaudito, sin precedente.
unhelpful [unhelp'fəl] *a* (*person*) poco servicial; (*advice*) inútil.
unhesitating [unhez'itāting] *a* (*loyalty*) automático; (*reply, offer*) resuelto, inmediato.
unhook [unhōōk'] *vt* desenganchar; (*from wall*) descolgar; (*undo*) desabrochar.
unhurt [unhûrt'] *a* ileso.
unhygienic [unhūjēen'ik] *a* antihigiénico.
UNICEF [yōō'nisef] *n abbr* (= *United Nations International Children's Emergency Fund*) UNICEF *m*.
unicolor [yōōnəkul'ûr] *a* de un color.
unidentified [unīden'təfīd] *a* no identificado; **~ flying object (UFO)** objeto volante no identificado.
unification [yōōnifikā'shən] *n* unificación *f*.
uniform [yōō'nəfôrm] *n* uniforme *m* ♦ *a* uniforme.
uniformity [yōōnəfôr'mitē] *n* uniformidad *f*.
unify [yōō'nəfī] *vt* unificar, unir.
unilateral [yōōnəlat'ûrəl] *a* unilateral.
unimaginable [unimaj'ənəbəl] *a* inconcebible, inimaginable.
unimaginative [unimaj'ənətiv] *a* falto de imaginación.
unimpaired [unimpärd'] *a* (*unharmed*) intacto; (*not lessened*) no disminuido; (*unaltered*) inalterado.
unimportant [unimpôr'tənt] *a* sin importancia.
unimpressed [unimprest'] *a* poco impresionado.
uninhabited [uninhab'itid] *a* desierto; (*country*) despoblado; (*house*) deshabitado, desocupado.
uninhibited [uninhib'itid] *a* nada cohibido, desinhibido.
uninjured [unin'jûrd] *a* (*person*) ileso.
unintelligent [unintel'ijənt] *a* poco inteligente.
unintentional [uninten'chənəl] *a* involuntario.
unintentionally [uninten'chənəlē] *ad* sin querer.
uninvited [uninvī'tid] *a* (*guest*) sin invitación.
uninviting [uninvī'ting] *a* (*place, offer*) poco atractivo; (*food*) poco apetitoso.
union [yōō'nyən] *n* unión *f*; (*also*: **trade ~**) sindicato ♦ *cpd* sindical; **the U~** (*US*) la Unión.
union card *n* carnet *m* de sindicato.
unionize [yōō'nyənīz] *vt* sindicalizar.
Union Jack *n* bandera del Reino Unido.
Union of Soviet Socialist Republics (USSR) *n* Unión *f* de Repúblicas Socialistas Soviéticas.
union shop *n* (*US*) *taller de afiliación*

sindical obligatoria.

unique [yōōnēk'] *a* único.

unisex [yōō'niseks] *a* unisex.

unison [yōō'nisən] *n:* **in** ~ en armonía.

unissued capital [unish'ōōd kap'itəl] *n* capital *m* no emitido.

unit [yōō'nit] *n* unidad *f;* (*team, squad*) grupo; **kitchen** ~ módulo de cocina; **production** ~ taller *m* de fabricación; **sink** ~ fregadero.

unit cost *n* costo unitario.

unite [yōōnīt'] *vt* unir ♦ *vi* unirse.

united [yōōnī'tid] *a* unido.

United Arab Emirates *npl* Emiratos *mpl* Árabes Unidos.

United Kingdom (UK) *n* Reino Unido.

United Nations (Organization) (UN, UNO) *n* Naciones Unidas *fpl* (ONU *f*).

United States (of America) (US, USA) *n* Estados Unidos *mpl* (de América) (EE.UU. *mpl*).

unit price *n* precio unitario.

unit trust *n* (*Brit*) bono fiduciario.

unity [yōō'nitē] *n* unidad *f.*

Univ. *abbr* = **university.**

universal [yōōnəvûr'səl] *a* universal.

universally [yōōnəvûr'səlē] *ad* universalmente.

universe [yōō'nəvûrs] *n* universo.

university [yōōnəvûr'sitē] *n* universidad *f* ♦ *cpd* (*student, professor, education, degree*) universitario; (*year*) académico, universitario; **to be at/go to the** ~ estudiar en/ir a la universidad.

unjust [unjust'] *a* injusto.

unjustifiable [unjus'tifiəbəl] *a* injustificable.

unjustified [unjus'təfid] *a* (*text*) no alineado *or* justificado.

unkempt [unkempt'] *a* descuidado; (*hair*) despeinado.

unkind [unkīnd'] *a* poco amable; (*comment etc*) cruel.

unkindly [unkīnd'lē] *ad* (*speak*) severamente; (*treat*) cruelmente, mal.

unknown [unnōn'] *a* desconocido ♦ *ad:* ~ **to me** sin saberlo yo; ~ **quantity** (*MATH, fig*) incógnita.

unladen [unlā'dən] *a* (*weight*) vacío, sin cargamento.

unlawful [unlô'fəl] *a* ilegal, ilícito.

unleaded [unled'id] *a* sin plomo.

unleash [unlēsh'] *vt* desatar.

unleavened [unlev'ənd] *a* ácimo, sin levadura.

unless [unles'] *conj* a menos que; ~ **he comes** a menos que venga; ~ **otherwise stated** salvo indicación contraria; ~ **I am mistaken** si no mi equivoco.

unlicensed [unli'sənst] *a* (*Brit: to sell alcohol*) no autorizado.

unlike [unlīk'] *a* distinto ♦ *prep* a diferencia de.

unlikelihood [unlīk'lēhōōd] *n* improbabili-

---

dad *f.*

unlikely [unlīk'lē] *a* improbable.

unlimited [unlim'itid] *a* ilimitado; ~ **liability** responsabilidad *f* ilimitada.

unlisted [unlis'tid] *a* (*US TEL*) que no consta en la guía; ~ **company** empresa sin cotización en bolsa.

unlit [unlit'] *a* (*room*) oscuro, sin luz.

unload [unlōd'] *vt* descargar.

unlock [unlāk'] *vt* abrir (con llave).

unlucky [unluk'ē] *a* desgraciado; (*object, number*) que da mala suerte; **to be** ~ (*person*) tener mala suerte.

unmanageable [unman'ijəbəl] *a* (*unwieldy: tool, vehicle*) difícil de manejar; (: *situation*) incontrolable.

unmanned [unmand'] *a* (*spacecraft*) sin tripulación.

unmannerly [unman'ûrlē] *a* mal educado, descortés.

unmarked [unmärkt'] *a* (*unstained*) sin mancha; ~ **police car** vehículo policial camuflado.

unmarried [unmar'ēd] *a* soltero.

unmask [unmask'] *vt* desenmascarar.

unmatched [unmacht'] *a* incomparable.

unmentionable [unmen'chənəbəl] *a* (*topic, vice*) indecible; (*word*) que no se debe decir.

unmerciful [unmûr'sifəl] *a* despiadado.

unmistakable [unmistā'kəbəl] *a* inconfundible.

unmistakably [unmistā'kəblē] *ad* de modo inconfundible.

unmitigated [unmit'əgātid] *a* rematado, absoluto.

unnamed [unnāmd'] *a* (*nameless*) sin nombre; (*anonymous*) anónimo.

unnatural [unnach'ûrəl] *a* (*gen*) antinatural; (*manner*) afectado; (*habit*) perverso.

unnecessary [unnes'isārē] *a* innecesario, inútil.

unnerve [unnûrv'] *vt* (*subj: accident*) poner nervioso; (: *hostile attitude*) acobardar; (: *long wait, interview*) intimidar.

unnoticed [unnō'tist] *a:* **to go** *or* **pass** ~ pasar desapercibido.

UNO [ōō'nō] *n abbr* = (*United Nations Organization*) ONU *f.*

unobservant [unəbzûr'vənt] *a:* **to be** ~ ser poco observador, ser distraído.

unobtainable [unəbtā'nəbəl] *a* inconseguible; (*TEL*) inexistente.

unobtrusive [unəbtrōō'siv] *a* discreto.

unoccupied [unåk'yəpīd] *a* (*house etc*) libre, desocupado.

unofficial [unəfish'əl] *a* no oficial; ~ **strike** huelga no oficial.

unopened [unō'pənd] *a* (*letter, present*) sin abrir.

unopposed [unəpōzd'] *a* (*enter, be elected*) sin oposición.

unorthodox [unór'thədåks] *a* poco ortodoxo.

unpack [unpak'] *vi* deshacer las maletas, desempacar (*LAm*).

unpaid [unpād'] *a* (*bill, debt*) sin pagar, impagado; (*COMM*) pendiente; (*vacation*) sin sueldo; (*work*) sin pago, voluntario.

unpalatable [unpal'ǝtǝbǝl] *a* (*truth*) desagradable.

unparalleled [unpar'ǝleld] *a* (*unequalled*) sin par; (*unique*) sin precedentes.

unpatriotic [unpātrēǎt'ik] *a* (*person*) poco patriota; (*speech, attitude*) antipatriótico.

unplanned [unpland'] *a* (*visit*) imprevisto; (*baby*) no planeado.

unpleasant [unplez'ǝnt] *a* (*disagreeable*) desagradable; (*person, manner*) antipático.

unplug [unplug'] *vt* desenchufar, desconectar.

unpolluted [unpǝlōō'tid] *a* impoluto, no contaminado.

unpopular [unpâp'yǝlûr] *a* poco popular; **to be ~ with sb** (*person, law*) no ser popular con uno; **to make o.s. ~ (with)** hacerse impopular (con).

unprecedented [unpres'identid] *a* sin precedentes.

unpredictable [unpridik'tǝbǝl] *a* imprevisible.

unprejudiced [unprej'ǝdist] *a* (*not biased*) imparcial; (*having no prejudices*) sin prejuicio.

unprepared [unpripärd'] *a* (*person*) desprevenido; (*speech*) improvisado.

unprepossessing [unprēpǝzes'ing] *a* poco atractivo.

unprincipled [unprin'sǝpǝld] *a* sin escrúpulos.

unproductive [unprǝduk'tiv] *a* improductivo; (*discussion*) infructuoso.

unprofessional [unprǝfesh'ǝnǝl] *a* indigno de su profesión; **~ conduct** negligencia.

unprofitable [unprâf'itǝbǝl] *a* poco provechoso, no rentable.

unprovoked [unprǝvōkt'] *a* no provocado.

unpunished [unpun'isht] *a*: **to go ~** quedar sin castigo, salir impune.

unqualified [unkwál'ǝfīd] *a* sin título, no cualificado; (*success*) total, incondicional.

unquestionably [unkwes'chǝnǝblē] *ad* indiscutiblemente.

unquestioning [unkwes'chǝning] *a* (*obedience, acceptance*) incondicional.

unravel [unrav'ǝl] *vt* desenmarañar.

unreal [unrēl'] *a* irreal.

unrealistic [unrēǝlis'tik] *a* poco realista.

unreasonable [unrē'zǝnǝbǝl] *a* irrazonable; **to make ~ demands on sb** hacer demandas excesivas a uno.

unrecognizable [unrek'ǝgnīzǝbǝl] *a* irreconocible.

unrecognized [unrek'ǝgnīzd] *a* (*talent, genius*) desapercibido; (*POL: regime*) no reconocido.

unrecorded [unrikôr'did] *a* no registrado.

unrefined [unrifīnd'] *a* (*sugar, petroleum*) sin refinar.

unrehearsed [unrihûrst'] *a* (*THEATER etc*) improvisado; (*spontaneous*) espontáneo.

unrelated [unrilā'tid] *a* sin relación; (*family*) no emparentado.

unrelenting [unrilen'ting] *a* implacable.

unreliable [unrilī'ǝbǝl] *a* (*person*) informal; (*machine*) poco fiable.

unrelieved [unrilēvd'] *a* (*monotony*) constante.

unremitting [unrimit'ing] *a* constante.

unrepeatable [unripē'tǝbǝl] *a* irrepetible.

unrepentant [unripen'tǝnt] *a* (*smoker, sinner*) impenitente; **to be ~ about sth** no arrepentirse de algo.

unrepresentative [unreprizen'tǝtiv] *a* (*untypical*) poco representativo.

unreserved [unrizûrvd'] *a* (*seat*) no reservado; (*approval, admiration*) total.

unreservedly [unrizûr'vidlē] *ad* sin reserva.

unresponsive [unrispán'siv] *a* insensible.

unrest [unrest'] *n* inquietud *f*, malestar *m*; (*POL*) disturbios *mpl*.

unrestricted [unristrik'tid] *a* (*power, time*) sin restricción; (*access*) libre.

unrewarded [unriwôr'did] *a* sin recompensa.

unripe [unrīp'] *a* verde, inmaduro.

unrivaled, (*Brit*) **unrivalled**· [unrī'vǝld] *a* incomparable, sin par.

unroll [unrōl'] *vt* desenrollar.

unruffled [unruf'ǝld] *a* (*person*) imperturbable, ecuánime; (*hair*) liso.

unruly [unrōō'lē] *a* indisciplinado.

unsafe [unsāf'] *a* (*journey*) peligroso; (*car etc*) inseguro; (*method*) arriesgado; **~ to drink/eat** no apto para el consumo humano.

unsaid [unsed'] *a*: **to leave sth ~** dejar algo sin decir.

unsalable, (*Brit*) **unsaleable** [unsā'lǝbǝl] *a* invendible.

unsatisfactory [unsatisfak'tûrē] *a* poco satisfactorio.

unsatisfied [unsat'isfīd] *a* (*desire, need etc*) insatisfecho.

unsavory, (*Brit*) **unsavoury** [unsā'vûrē] *a* (*fig*) repugnante.

unscathed [unskā'ᵺd] *a* ileso.

unscientific [unsīǝntif'ik] *a* poco científico.

unscrew [unskrōō'] *vt* destornillar.

unscrupulous [unskrōō'pyǝlǝs] *a* sin escrúpulos.

unsecured [unsikyōōrd'] *a*: **~ creditor** acreedor(a) *m/f* común.

unseen [unsēn'] *a* (*person, danger*) oculto.

unselfish [unsel'fish] *a* generoso, poco egoísta; (*act*) desinteresado.

unsettled [unset'ǝld] *a* inquieto; (*situation*) inestable; (*weather*) variable.

unsettling [unset'ling] *a* perturbador(a), inquietante.

unshak(e)able [unshā'kəbəl] *a* inquebrantable.

unshaven [unshā'vən] *a* sin afeitar.

unsightly [unsīt'lē] *a* feo.

unskilled [unskild'] *a*: ~ **workers** mano *f* de obra no cualificada.

unsociable [unsō'shəbəl] *a* (*person*) poco sociable, huraño; (*behavior*) insociable.

unsocial [unsō'shəl] *a*: ~ **hours** horario nocturno.

unsold [unsōld'] *a* sin vender.

unsolicited [unsəlis'itid] *a* no solicitado.

unsophisticated [unsəfis'tikātid] *a* (*person*) sencillo, ingenuo; (*method*) poco sofisticado.

unsound [unsound'] *a* (*health*) malo; (*in construction: floor, foundations*) defectuoso; (*policy, advice, judgment*) erróneo; (*investment*) poco seguro.

unspeakable [unspē'kəbəl] *a* indecible; (*awful*) incalificable.

unspoken [unspō'kən] *a* (*words*) sobreententido; (*agreement, approval*) tácito.

unstable [unstā'bəl] *a* inestable.

unsteady [unsted'ē] *a* inestable.

unstinting [unstin'ting] *a* (*support etc*) pródigo.

unstuck [unstuk'] *a*: **to come** ~ despegarse; (*fig*) fracasar.

unsubstantiated [unsəbstan'chēātid] *a* (*rumor, accusation*) no comprobado.

unsuccessful [unsəkses'fəl] *a* (*attempt*) infructuoso; (*writer, proposal*) sin éxito; **to be** ~ (*in attempting sth*) no tener éxito, fracasar.

unsuccessfully [unsəkses'fəlē] *ad* en vano, sin éxito.

unsuitable [unsōō'təbəl] *a* inconveniente, inapropiado; (*time*) inoportuno.

unsuited [unsōō'tid] *a*: **to be** ~ **for** *or* **to** ser poco apto para.

unsupported [unsəpôr'tid] *a* (*claim*) sin fundamento; (*theory*) sin base firme.

unsure [unshōōr'] *a* inseguro, poco seguro; **to be** ~ **of o.s.** estar poco seguro de sí mismo.

unsuspecting [unsəspek'ting] *a* confiado.

unsweetened [unswēt'ənd] *a* sin azúcar.

unsympathetic [unsimpəthet'ik] *a* (*attitude*) poco comprensivo; (*person*) sin compasión; ~ **(to)** indiferente(a).

untangle [untang'gəl] *vt* desenredar.

untapped [untapt'] *a* (*resources*) sin explotar.

untaxed [untakst'] *a* (*goods*) libre de impuestos; (*income*) antes de impuestos.

unthinkable [unthingk'əbəl] *a* inconcebible, impensable.

untidy [untī'dē] *a* (*room*) desordenado, en desorden; (*appearance*) desaliñado.

untie [untī'] *vt* desatar.

until [until'] *prep* hasta ♦ *conj* hasta que; ~ **he comes** hasta que venga; ~ **now** hasta

ahora; ~ **then** hasta entonces; **from morning** ~ **night** de la mañana a la noche.

untimely [untīm'lē] *a* inoportuno; (*death*) prematuro.

untold [untōld'] *a* (*story*) nunca contado; (*suffering*) indecible; (*wealth*) incalculable.

untouched [untucht'] *a* (*not used etc*) intacto, sin tocar; (*safe: person*) indemne, ileso; (*unaffected*): ~ **by** insensible a.

untoward [untôrd'] *a* (*behavior*) impropio; (*event*) adverso.

untrammeled, (*Brit*) **untrammelled** [untram'əld] *a* ilimitado.

untranslatable [untranz'lātəbəl] *a* intraducible.

untried [untrīd'] *a* (*plan*) no probado.

untrue [untrōō'] *a* (*statement*) falso.

untrustworthy [untrust'wûrᵺē] *a* (*person*) poco fiable.

unusable [unyōō'zəbəl] *a* inservible.

unused [unyōōzd'] *a* sin usar, nuevo; [unyōōst']: **to be** ~ **to (doing) sth** no estar acostumbrado a (hacer) algo.

unusual [unyōō'zhōōəl] *a* insólito, poco común.

unusually [unyōō'zhōōəlē] *ad*: **he arrived** ~ **early** llegó más temprano que de costumbre.

unveil [unvāl'] *vt* (*statue*) descubrir.

unwanted [unwôn'tid] *a* (*person, effect*) no deseado.

unwarranted [unwôr'əntid] *a* injustificado.

unwary [unwär'ē] *a* imprudente, incauto.

unwavering [unwā'vûring] *a* inquebrantable.

unwelcome [unwel'kəm] *a* (*at a bad time*) inoportuno, molesto; **to feel** ~ sentirse incómodo.

unwell [unwel'] *a*: **to feel** ~ estar indispuesto, sentirse mal.

unwieldy [unwēl'dē] *a* difícil de manejar.

unwilling [unwil'ing] *a*: **to be** ~ **to do sth** estar poco dispuesto a hacer algo.

unwillingly [unwil'inglē] *ad* de mala gana.

unwind [unwīnd'] (*irg: like* **wind**) *vt* desenvolver ♦ *vi* (*relax*) relajarse.

unwise [unwīz'] *a* imprudente.

unwitting [unwit'ing] *a* inconsciente.

unworkable [unwûr'kəbəl] *a* (*plan*) impráctico.

unworthy [unwûr'ᵺē] *a* indigno; **to be** ~ **of sth/to do sth** ser indigno de algo/de hacer algo.

unwrap [unrap'] *vt* desenvolver.

unwritten [unrit'ən] *a* (*agreement*) tácito; (*rules, law*) no escrito.

unzip [unzip'] *vt* abrir la cremallera de.

up [up] *prep*: **to go/be** ~ **sth** subir/estar encima de algo ♦ *ad* hacia arriba, arriba ♦ *vi* (*col*): **she** ~**ped and left** se levantó y se marchó ♦ *vt* (*col: price*) subir, aumentar; **when the year was** ~ (*finished*) al terminarse el año; **what's** ~**?** (*col: wrong*) ¿qué

pasa?; ~ **there** allí arriba; ~ **above** encima, allí arriba; **"this side ~"** "este lado hacia arriba"; **to be** ~ (*out of bed*) estar levantado; (*installed, built etc*) estar construido; (*tent*) estar levantado; (*curtains, paper etc*) estar colocado; **to be** ~ **(by)** (*in price, value*) haber alzado (en); **prices are** ~ **from last year** los precios han subido desde el año pasado; **it is** ~ **to you** usted decide/tú decides; **what is he** ~ **to?** ¿qué es lo que quiere?, ¿qué está tramando?; **he is not** ~ **to it** no es capaz de hacerlo; **I don't feel** ~ **to it** no me encuentro con ánimos para ello; **to stop halfway** ~ pararse a la mitad del camino *or* de la subida; **time's** ~ se acabó el tiempo; **what's** ~ **with him?** ¿qué le pasa (a él)?; **to live/go** ~ **North** vivir en el norte/ir al norte; ~**s and downs** *npl* (*fig*) altibajos *mpl*.
up-and-coming |upənkum'ing| *a* prometedor(a).
upbeat |up'bēt| *n* (*MUS*) tiempo no acentuado; (*in economy, prosperity*) aumento ♦ *a* (*col*) optimista, animado.
upbraid |upbrād'| *vt* censurar, reprender.
upbringing |up'bringing| *n* educación *f*.
update |updāt'| *vt* poner al día.
upend |upend'| *vt* poner vertical.
upgrade |upgrād'| *vt* ascender; (*COMPUT*) modernizar.
upheaval |uphē'vəl| *n* trastornos *mpl*; (*POL*) agitación *f*.
uphill *a* |up'hil'| cuesta arriba; (*fig: task*) penoso, difícil ♦ *ad* |uphil'|: **to go** ~ ir cuesta arriba.
uphold |uphōld'| (*irg: like* hold) *vt* sostener.
upholstery |uphōl'stûrē| *n* tapicería.
UPI *n abbr* (*US*) = *United Press International.*
upkeep |up'kēp| *n* mantenimiento.
upmarket |upmár'kit| *a* (*Brit: product*) de primera calidad.
upon |əpán'| *prep* sobre.
upper |up'ûr| *a* superior, de arriba ♦ *n* (*of shoe: also:* ~**s**) pala.
upper case *n* (*TYP*) mayúsculas *fpl*.
upper-class |up'ûrklas'| *a* (*district, people, accent*) de clase alta; (*attitude*) altivo.
upper hand *n*: **to have the** ~ tener la sartén por el mango, llevar la delantera.
uppermost |up'ûrmōst| *a* el más alto; **what was** ~ **in my mind** lo que me preocupaba más.
Upper Volta |up'ûr võl'tə| *n* Alto Volta *m*.
upright |up'rīt| *a* vertical; (*fig*) honrado.
uprising |up'rīzing| *n* sublevación *f*.
uproar |up'rôr| *n* tumulto, escándalo.
uproot |uprōōt'| *vt* desarraigar.
upset *n* |up'set| (*to plan etc*) revés *m*, contratiempo; (*MED*) trastorno ♦ *vt* |upset'| (*irg: like* set) (*glass etc*) volcar; (*spill*) derramar; (*plan*) alterar; (*person*) molestar,

perturbar ♦ *a* |upset'| preocupado, perturbado; (*stomach*) revuelto; **to have an** ~ **stomach** tener el estómago revuelto; **to get** ~ ofenderse, llevarse un disgusto.
upset price *n* (*US, Scottish*) precio mínimo *or* de reserva.
upsetting |upset'ing| *a* (*worrying*) inquietante; (*offending*) ofensivo; (*annoying*) molesto.
upshot |up'shát| *n* resultado.
upside-down |up'sīddoun'| *ad* al revés.
upstairs |up'stärz| *ad* arriba ♦ *a* (*room*) de arriba ♦ *n* el piso superior.
upstart |up'stárt| *n* advenedizo.
upstream |up'strēm| *ad* río arriba.
upsurge |up'sûrj| *n* (*of enthusiasm etc*) arrebato.
uptake |up'tāk| *n*: **he is quick/slow on the** ~ es muy listo/torpe.
uptight |up'tīt| *a* tenso, nervioso.
up-to-date |up'tədāt'| *a* moderno, actual; **to bring sb** ~ **(on sth)** poner a uno al corriente/tanto (de algo).
upturn |up'tûrn| *n* (*in luck*) mejora; (*COMM: in market*) resurgimiento económico; (: *in value of currency*) aumento.
upturned |uptûrnd'| *a*: ~ **nose** nariz *f* respingona.
upward |up'wûrd| *a* ascendente.
upward(s) |up'wûrd(z)| *ad* hacia arriba.
URA *n abbr* (*US*) = *Urban Renewal Administration.*
Ural Mountains |yōōr'əl moun'tənz| *npl*: **the** ~ (*also:* **the Urals**) los Montes Urales.
uranium |yōōrā'nēəm| *n* uranio.
Uranus |yōōr'ānəs| *n* (*ASTRO*) Urano.
urban |ûr'bən| *a* urbano.
urbane |ûrbān'| *a* cortés, urbano.
urbanization |ûrbənəzā'shən| *n* urbanización *f*.
urchin |ûr'chin| *n* pilluelo, golfillo.
urge |ûrj| *n* (*force*) impulso; (*desire*) deseo ♦ *vt*: **to** ~ **sb to do sth** animar a uno a hacer algo.
urge on *vt* animar.
urgency |ûr'jənsē| *n* urgencia.
urgent |ûr'jənt| *a* (*earnest, persistent: plea*) insistente; (: *tone*) urgente.
urgently |ûr'jəntlē| *ad* con urgencia, urgentemente.
urinal |yōōr'ənəl| *n* (*room*) urinario; (*vessel*) orinal *m*.
urinate |yōōr'ənāt| *vi* orinar.
urine |yōōr'in| *n* orina, orines *mpl*.
urn |ûrn| *n* urna; (*also:* **tea** ~) cacharro metálico grande para hacer té.
Uruguay |yōō'rəgwā| *n* el Uruguay.
Uruguayan |yōōrəgwā'ən| *a, n* uruguayo/a *m/f*.
US *n abbr* (= *United States*) EE.UU.
us |us| *pron* nos; (*after prep*) nosotros/as; (*col: me*): **give** ~ **a kiss** dame un beso; *see also* **me.**

USA *n abbr see* **United States of America**; (*MIL*) = *United States Army.*
usable [yōō'zəbəl] *a* utilizable.
USAF *n abbr* = *United States Air Force.*
usage [yōō'sij] *n* (*LING*) uso; (*utilization*) utilización *f.*
USCG *n abbr* = *United States Coast Guard.*
USDA *n abbr* = *United States Department of Agriculture.*
USDI *n abbr* = *United States Department of the Interior.*
use *n* [yōōs] uso, empleo; (*usefulness*) utilidad *f* ♦ *vt* [yōōz] usar, emplear; **in** ~ en uso; **out of** ~ en desuso; **to be of** ~ servir; **ready to** ~ listo (para ser usado); **to make** ~ **of sth** aprovecharse *or* servirse de algo; **it's no** ~ (*pointless*) es inútil; (*not useful*) no sirve; **what's this** ~**d for?** ¿para qué sirve esto?; [yōōst]: **to be** ~**d to** estar acostumbrado a (*Sp*), acostumbrar; **to get** ~**d to** acostumbrarse a; **she** ~**d to do it** (ella) solía *or* acostumbraba hacerlo.
use up *vt* agotar.
used [yōōzd] *a* (*car*) usado.
useful [yōōs'fəl] *a* útil; **to come in** ~ ser útil.
usefulness [yōōs'fəlnis] *n* utilidad.
useless [yōōs'lis] *a* inútil; (*unusable*: *object*) inservible.
uselessly [yōōs'lislē] *ad* inútilmente, en vano.
uselessness [yōōs'lisnis] *n* inutilidad *f.*
user [yōō'zûr] *n* usuario/a; (*of gas, electricity etc*) consumidor(a) *m/f.*
user-friendly [yōō'zûrfrend'lē] *a* (*COMPUT*) amistoso, fácil de utilizar.
USES *n abbr* = *United States Employment Service.*
usher [ush'ûr] *n* (*at wedding*) ujier *m*; (*in cinema etc*) acomodador *m* ♦ *vt*: **to** ~ **sb in** (*into room*) hacer pasar a uno; **it** ~**ed in a new era** (*fig*) anunció una nueva era.
usherette [ushəret'] *n* (*in cinema*) acomodadora.
USIA *n abbr* = *United States Information Agency.*
USM *n abbr* = *United States Mail; United States Mint.*
USN *n abbr* = *United States Navy.*
USPHS *n abbr* = *United States Public Health Service.*
USPS *n abbr* = *United States Postal Service.*
USS *abbr* = *United States Ship.*
USSR *n abbr*: **the** ~ la U.R.S.S.
usu. *abbr* = **usually.**
usual [yōō'zhōōəl] *a* normal, corriente; **as** ~ como de costumbre, como siempre.
usually [yōō'zhōōəlē] *ad* normalmente.
usurer [yōō'zhûrûr] *n* usurero.
usurp [yōōsûrp'] *vt* usurpar.
usury [yōō'zhûrē] *n* usura.
UT *abbr* (*US MAIL*) = *Utah.*

utensil [yōōten'səl] *n* utensilio; **kitchen** ~**s** batería de cocina.
uterus [yōō'tûrəs] *n* útero.
utilitarian [yōōtilitär'ēən] *a* utilitario.
utility [yōōtil'itē] *n* utilidad *f.*
utility room *n* lavadero.
utilization [yōōtəlizā'shən] *n* utilización *f.*
utilize [yōō'təlīz] *vt* utilizar.
utmost [ut'mōst] *a* mayor ♦ *n*: **to do one's** ~ hacer todo lo posible; **it is of the** ~ **importance that** ... es de la mayor importancia que ....
utter [ut'ûr] *a* total, completo ♦ *vt* pronunciar, proferir.
utterance [ut'ûrəns] *n* palabras *fpl*, declaración *f.*
utterly [ut'ûrlē] *ad* completamente, totalmente.
U-turn [yōō'tûrn] *n* viraje *m or* vuelta en U.

V

V, v [vē] (*letter*) V, v *f*; **V for Victor** V de Valencia.
v. *abbr* (= *verse*) vers.º (= *vide*: *see*) V, vid., vide; (= *versus*) vs.; = **volt.**
VA *abbr* (*US MAIL*) = *Virginia.*
vac [vak] *n abbr* (*Brit col*) = **vacation.**
vacancy [vā'kənsē] *n* (*Brit*: *job*) vacante *f*; (*room*) cuarto libre; **have you any vacancies?** ¿tiene *or* hay alguna habitación *or* algún cuarto libre?
vacant [vā'kənt] *a* (*expression*) distraído.
vacant lot *n* (*US*) solar *m.*
vacate [vā'kāt] *vt* (*house*) desocupar; (*job*) dejar (vacante).
vacation [vākā'shən] *n* vacaciones *fpl* ; **on** ~ de vacaciones; **to take a** ~ (*esp US*) tomarse unas vacaciones.
vacation course *n* curso de vacaciones.
vacationer [vākā'shənûr], **vacationist** [vākā'shənist] *n* (*US*) turista *m/f.*
vacation pay *n* (*US*) paga de las vacaciones.
vacation resort *n* (*US*) centro turístico.
vacation season *n* (*US*) temporada de las vacaciones.
vaccinate [vak'sənāt] *vt* vacunar.
vaccination [vaksənā'shən] *n* vacunación *f.*
vaccine [vaksēn'] *n* vacuna.
vacuum [vak'yōōm] *n* vacío ♦ *vt* (*US*) pasar la aspiradora por.
vacuum bottle *n* (*US*) termo.
vacuum cleaner *n* aspiradora.
vacuum flask *n* (*Brit*) termo.

vacuum-packed [vak'yōōmpakt'] *a* envasado al vacío.

vagabond [vag'əbánd] *n* vagabundo/a.

vagary [vā'gûrē] *n* capricho.

vagina [vəji'nə] *n* vagina.

vagrancy [vā'grənsē] *n* vagabundeo.

vagrant [vā'grənt] *n* vagabundo/a.

vague [vāg] *a* vago; (*blurred*: *memory*) borroso; (*uncertain*) incierto, impreciso; (*person*) distraído; **I haven't the ~st idea** no tengo la más remota idea.

vaguely [vāg'lē] *ad* vagamente.

vagueness [vāg'nis] *n* vaguedad *f*; imprecisión *f*; (*absent-mindedness*) despiste *m*.

vain [vān] *a* (*conceited*) presumido; (*useless*) vano, inútil; **in ~** en vano.

vainly [vān'lē] *ad* (*to no effect*) en vano; (*conceitedly*) vanidosamente.

valance [val'əns] *n* (*for bed*) *volante alrededor de la colcha que cuelga hasta el suelo.*

valedictory [validik'tûrē] *a* de despedida.

valentine [val'əntīn] *n* (*also*: **~ card**) tarjeta del Día de los Enamorados.

valet [valā'] *n* ayuda *m* de cámara.

valet service *n* (*for clothes*) planchado.

valiant [val'yənt] *a* valiente.

valiantly [val'yəntlē] *ad* valientemente, con valor.

valid [val'id] *a* válido; (*ticket*) valedero; (*law*) vigente.

validate [val'idāt] *vt* (*contract, document*) convalidar; (*argument, claim*) dar validez a.

validity [vəlid'itē] *n* validez *f*; vigencia.

valise [vəlēs'] *n* maletín *m*.

valley [val'ē] *n* valle *m*.

valor, (*Brit*) **valour** [val'ûr] *n* valor *m*, valentía.

valuable [val'yōōəbəl] *a* (*jewel*) de valor; (*time*) valioso; **~s** *npl* objetos *mpl* de valor.

valuation [valyōōā'shən] *n* tasación *f*, valuación *f*.

value [val'yōō] *n* valor *m*; (*importance*) importancia ♦ *vt* (*fix price of*) tasar, valorar; (*esteem*) apreciar; **~s** *npl* (*moral*) valores *mpl* morales; **to lose (in) ~** (*currency*) bajar; (*property*) desvalorizarse; **to gain (in) ~** (*currency*) subir; (*property*) valorizarse; **you get good ~ (for money) in that store** los precios son muy buenos en esa tienda; **to be of great ~ to sb** ser de gran valor para uno; **it is ~d at $8** está valorado en ocho dólares.

value added tax (VAT) *n* (*Brit*) impuesto sobre el valor añadido (IVA *m*).

valued [val'yōōd] *a* (*appreciated*) apreciado.

valueless [val'yōōlis] *a* sin valor.

valuer [val'yōōûr] *n* tasador(a) *m/f*.

valve [valv] *n* (*ANAT, TECH*) válvula.

vampire [vam'pīûr] *n* vampiro/vampiresa *m/f*.

van [van] *n* (*AUT*) furgoneta, camioneta (*LAm*); (*Brit RAIL*) furgón *m* (de equipajes).

vandal [van'dəl] *n* vándalo/a.

vandalism [van'dəlizəm] *n* vandalismo.

vandalize [van'dəlīz] *vt* dañar, destruir, destrozar.

vanguard [van'gârd] *n* vanguardia.

vanilla [vənil'ə] *n* vainilla.

vanish [van'ish] *vi* desaparecer, esfumarse.

vanity [van'itē] *n* vanidad *f*.

vanity case *n* neceser *m*.

vantage point [van'tij point] *n* posición *f* ventajosa.

vapor [vā'pûr] *n* (*US*) vapor *m*; (*on breath, window*) vaho.

vaporize [vā'pərīz] *vt* vaporizar ♦ *vi* vaporizarse.

vapor trail *n* (*AVIAT*) estela.

vapour [vā'pûr] *etc* (*Brit*) = **vapor** *etc*.

variable [vär'ēəbəl] *a* variable ♦ *n* variable *f*.

variance [vär'ēəns] *n*: **to be at ~ (with)** estar en desacuerdo (con), no cuadrar (con).

variant [vär'ēənt] *n* variante *f*.

variation [värēā'shən] *n* variación *f*.

varicose [var'əkōs] *a*: **~ veins** varices *fpl*.

varied [vär'ēd] *a* variado.

variety [vərī'ətē] *n* variedad *f*, diversidad *f*; (*quantity*) surtido; **for a ~ of reasons** por varias *or* diversas razones.

variety show *n* espectáculo de variedades.

various [vär'ēəs] *a* varios/as, diversos/as; **at ~ times** (*different*) en distintos momentos; (*several*) varias veces.

varnish [vâr'nish] *n* (*gen*) barniz *m*; (*nail ~*) esmalte *m* ♦ *vt* (*gen*) barnizar; (*nails*) pintar (con esmalte).

vary [vär'ē] *vt* variar; (*change*) cambiar ♦ *vi* variar; (*disagree*) discrepar; **to ~ with** *or* **according to** variar según *or* de acuerdo con.

varying [vär'ēing] *a* diversos/as.

vase [vās] *n* florero.

vasectomy [vasek'təmē] *n* vasectomía.

Vaseline [vas'əlēn] ® *n* vaselina ®.

vast [vast] *a* enorme; (*success*) abrumador(a), arrollador(a).

vastly [vast'lē] *ad* enormemente.

vastness [vast'nis] *n* inmensidad *f*.

VAT [vat] *n abbr* (= *value added tax*) IVA *m*.

vat [vat] *n* tina, tinaja.

Vatican [vat'ikən] *n*: **the ~** el Vaticano.

vaudeville [vôd'vil] *n* (*US*) vodevil *m*, vaudeville *m*.

vault [vôlt] *n* (*of roof*) bóveda; (*tomb*) tumba; (*in bank*) cámara acorazada ♦ *vt* (*also*: **~ over**) saltar (por encima de).

vaunted [vôn'tid] *a*: **much ~** cacarreado, alardeado.

VC *n abbr* = **vice-chairman**.

VCR *n abbr* = **video cassette recorder**.

VD n abbr = **venereal disease.**
VDU n abbr = **visual display unit.**
veal [vēl] n ternera.
veer [vēr] vi (ship) virar.
vegan [vē'gən] n vegetariano/a m/f estricto/a.
vegetable [vej'təbəl] n (BOT) vegetal m; (edible plant) legumbre f, hortaliza ♦ a vegetal; ~s npl (cooked) verduras fpl.
vegetable garden n huerta, huerto.
vegetarian [vejitär'ēən] a, n vegetariano/a m/f.
vegetate [vej'itāt] vi vegetar.
vegetation [vejitā'shən] n vegetación f.
vehemence [vē'əməns] n vehemencia; violencia.
vehement [vē'əmənt] a vehemente, apasionado; (dislike, hatred) violento.
vehicle [vē'ikəl] n vehículo; (fig) vehículo, medio.
vehicular [vēhik'yəlûr] a: ~ **traffic** circulación f rodada.
veil [vāl] n velo ♦ vt velar; **under a ~ of secrecy** (fig) en el mayor secreto.
veiled [vāld] a (also fig) disimulado, velado.
vein [vān] n vena; (of ore etc) veta.
vellum [vel'əm] n (writing paper) papel m vitela.
velocity [vəläs'itē] n velocidad f.
velvet [vel'vit] n terciopelo ♦ a aterciopelado.
vendetta [vendet'ə] n vendetta.
vending machine [ven'ding məshēn'] n distribuidor m automático.
vendor [ven'dûr] n vendedor(a) m/f; **street ~** vendedor(a) m/f callejero/a.
veneer [vənēr'] n chapa, enchapado; (fig) barniz m.
venereal [vənēr'ēəl] a: ~ **disease (VD)** enfermedad f venérea.
Venetian blind [vənē'shən blīnd] n persiana.
Venezuela [venizwā'lə] n Venezuela.
Venezuelan [venizwā'lən] a, n venezolano/a m/f.
vengeance [ven'jəns] n venganza; **with a ~** (fig) con creces.
vengeful [venj'fəl] a vengativo.
Venice [ven'is] n Venecia.
venison [ven'isən] n carne f de venado.
venom [ven'əm] n veneno.
venomous [ven'əməs] a venenoso.
venomously [ven'əməslē] ad con odio.
vent [vent] n (opening) abertura; (air-hole) respiradero; (in wall) rejilla (de ventilación) ♦ vt (fig: feelings) desahogar.
ventilate [ven'təlāt] vt ventilar.
ventilation [ventəlā'shən] n ventilación f.
ventilation shaft n pozo de ventilación.
ventilator [ven'təlātûr] n ventilador m.
ventriloquist [ventril'əkwist] n ventrílocuo/a.
venture [ven'chûr] n empresa ♦ vt arries-

gar; (opinion) ofrecer ♦ vi arriesgarse, lanzarse; **a business ~** una empresa comercial; **to ~ to do sth** aventurarse a hacer algo.
venture capital n capital m arriesgado.
venue [ven'yōō] n lugar m; (meeting place) lugar m de reunión.
Venus [vē'nəs] n (ASTRO) Venus m.
veracity [vəras'itē] n veracidad f.
veranda(h) [vəran'də] n terraza; (with glass) galería.
verb [vûrb] n verbo.
verbal [vûr'bəl] a verbal.
verbally [vûr'bəlē] ad verbalmente, de palabra.
verbatim [vûrbā'tim] a, ad al pie de la letra, palabra por palabra.
verbose [vûrbōs'] a prolijo.
verdict [vûr'dikt] n veredicto, fallo; (fig: opinion) opinión f, juicio; ~ **of guilty/not guilty** veredicto de culpabilidad/inocencia.
verge [vûrj] n (Brit) borde m; **to be on the ~ of doing sth** estar a punto de hacer algo.
verge on vt fus rayar en.
verger [vûr'jûr] n sacristán m.
verification [värəfəkā'shən] n comprobación f, verificación f.
verify [vär'əfī] vt comprobar, verificar; (COMPUT) verificar; (prove the truth of) confirmar.
veritable [vär'itəbəl] a verdadero, auténtico.
vermin [vûr'min] npl (animals) bichos mpl; (insects, fig) sabandijas fpl.
vermouth [vûrmōōth'] n vermut m.
vernacular [vûrnak'yəlûr] n vernáculo.
versatile [vûr'sətəl] a (person) polifacético; (machine, tool etc) versátil.
versatility [vûrsətil'itē] n versatilidad f.
verse [vûrs] n versos mpl, poesía; (stanza) estrofa; (in bible) versículo; **in ~** en verso.
versed [vûrst] a: (well-)~ in versado en.
version [vûr'zhən] n versión f.
versus [vûr'səs] prep contra.
vertebra, pl ~e [vûr'təbrə, -brē] n vértebra.
vertebrate [vûr'təbrāt] n vertebrado.
vertical [vûr'tikəl] a vertical.
vertically [vûr'tiklē] ad verticalmente.
vertigo [vûr'təgō] n vértigo; **to suffer from ~** tener vértigo.
verve [vûrv] n brío.
very [vär'ē] ad muy ♦ a: **the ~ book which** el mismo libro que; **the ~ last** el último (de todos); **at the ~ least** al menos; ~ **much** muchísimo; ~ **well/little** muy bien/poco; ~ **high frequency** (RADIO) frecuencia muy alta; **it's ~ cold** hace mucho frío; **the ~ thought (of it) alarms me** con sólo pensarlo me entra miedo.
vespers [ves'pûrz] npl vísperas fpl.
vessel [ves'əl] n (ANAT) vaso; (ship) barco; (container) vasija.
vest [vest] n (US: waistcoat) chaleco; (Brit)

camiseta.

vested interests [ves'tid in'trists] *npl* (COMM) intereses *mpl* creados.

vestibule [ves'təbyōōl] *n* vestíbulo.

vestige [ves'tij] *n* vestigio, rastro.

vestry [ves'trē] *n* sacristía.

Vesuvius [vəsōō'vēəs] *n* Vesubio.

vet [vet] *n abbr* = **veterinary surgeon** ♦ *vt* repasar, revisar; **to ~ sb for a job** investigar a uno para un trabajo.

veteran [vet'ûrən] *n* veterano/a; (MIL) excombatiente *m* ♦ *a*: **she is a ~ campaigner for** ... es una veterana de la campaña de ....

veteran car *n* coche *m* antiguo.

veterinarian [vetûrənär'ēən] *n* (US) veterinario/a.

veterinary [vet'ûrənärē] *a* veterinario.

veterinary surgeon *n* (Brit) veterinario/a.

veto [vē'tō] *n* (*pl* ~es) veto ♦ *vt* prohibir, vedar; **to put a ~ on** vetar.

vex [veks] *vt* (*irritate*) fastidiar; (*make impatient*) impacientar.

vexed [vekst] *a* (*question*) controvertido.

vexing [vek'sing] *a* molesto, engorroso.

VFD *n abbr* (US) = *voluntary fire department.*

VHF *abbr* (= *very high frequency*) VHF *m*.

VI *abbr* (US MAIL) = *Virgin Islands.*

via [vī'ə] *prep* por, por vía de.

viability [vīəbil'ətē] *n* viabilidad *f*.

viable [vī'əbəl] *a* viable.

viaduct [vī'ədukt] *n* viaducto.

vibrant [vī'brənt] *a* (*lively, bright*) vivo; (*full of emotion: voice*) vibrante; (*color*) fuerte.

vibrate [vī'brāt] *vi* vibrar.

vibration [vībrā'shən] *n* vibración *f*.

vicar [vik'ûr] *n* párroco.

vicarage [vik'ûrij] *n* parroquia.

vicarious [vīkär'ēəs] *a* indirecto; (*responsibility*) delegado.

vice [vīs] *n* (*evil*) vicio; (TECH) torno de banco.

vice- *pref* vice... .

vice-chairman [vīs'chär'mən] *n* vicepresidente *m*.

vice-chancellor [vīs'chan'səlûr] *n* (UNIV) rector(a) *m/f*.

vice-president [vīs'prez'idənt] *n* vicepresidente/a *m/f*.

vice-principal [vīs'prin'səpəl] *n* (US SCOL) subdirector(a) *m/f*.

vice versa [vīs'vûr'sə] *ad* viceversa.

vicinity [visin'ətē] *n* (*area*) vecindad *f*; (*nearness*) proximidad *f*; **in the ~ (of)** cercano (a).

vicious [vish'əs] *a* (*remark*) malicioso; (*blow*) fuerte; **a ~ circle** un círculo vicioso.

viciousness [vish'əsnis] *n* brutalidad *f*.

vicissitudes [visis'ətōōdz] *npl* vicisitudes *fpl*, peripecias *fpl*.

victim [vik'tim] *n* víctima; **to be the ~ of** ser víctima de.

victimization [viktiməzə'shən] *n* persecución *f*; (*of striker etc*) represalias *fpl*.

victimize [vik'təmīz] *vt* (*strikers etc*) tomar represalias contra.

victor [vik'tûr] *n* vencedor(a) *m/f*.

Victorian [viktōr'ēən] *a* victoriano.

victorious [viktōr'ēəs] *a* vencedor(a).

victory [vik'tûrē] *n* victoria; **to win a ~ over sb** obtener una victoria sobre uno.

video [vid'ēō] *cpd* vídeo ♦ *n* (~ *film*) videofilm *m*; (*also*: ~ **cassette**) videocassette *f*; (*also*: ~ **cassette recorder**) videograbadora, vídeo.

video cassette *n* videocassette *f*.

video cassette recorder *n* videograbadora, vídeo.

video recording *n* videograbación *f*.

video tape *n* cinta de vídeo.

videotex [vid'ēōteks] *n* videodatos *mpl*.

vie [vī] *vi*: **to ~ with** competir con.

Vienna [vēen'ə] *n* Viena.

Viennese [vēənēz'] *a, n* vienés/esa *m/f*.

Vietnam, Viet Nam [vēetnâm'] *n* Vietnam *m*.

Vietnamese [vēetnâmēz'] *a* vietnamita ♦ *n* (*pl inv*) vietnamita *m/f*; (LING) vietnamita *m*.

view [vyōō] *n* vista, perspectiva; (*landscape*) paisaje *m*; (*opinion*) opinión *f*, criterio ♦ *vt* (*look at*) mirar; (*examine*) examinar; **on ~** (*in museum etc*) expuesto; **in full ~ of sb** a la vista *or* a plena vista de uno; **to be within ~ (of sth)** estar a la vista (de algo); **an overall ~ of the situation** una visión de conjunto de la situación; **in ~ of the fact that** en vista del hecho de que; **to take** *or* **hold the ~ that** ... opinar *or* pensar que ...; **with a ~ to doing sth** con miras *or* vistas a hacer algo.

viewdata [vyōō'dātə] *n* (Brit) vídeodatos *mpl*.

viewer [vyōō'ûr] *n* (*small projector*) visionadora; (TV) televidente *m/f*.

viewfinder [vyōō'fīndûr] *n* visor *m* de imagen.

viewpoint [vyōō'point] *n* punto de vista.

vigil [vij'əl] *n* vigilia; **to keep ~** velar.

vigilance [vij'ələns] *n* vigilancia.

vigilance committee *n* (US) comité *m* de autodefensa.

vigilant [vij'ələnt] *a* vigilante.

vigilantly [vij'ələntlē] *ad* vigilantemente.

vigor [vig'ûr] *n* (US) energía, vigor *m*.

vigorous [vig'ûrəs] *a* enérgico, vigoroso.

vigorously [vig'ûrəslē] *ad* enérgicamente, vigorosamente.

vigour [vig'ûr] *n* (Brit) = **vigor.**

vile [vīl] *a* (*action*) vil, infame; (*smell*) asqueroso.

vilify [vil'əfī] *vt* denigrar, vilipendiar.

villa [vil'ə] *n* (*country house*) casa de

campo; (*suburban house*) chalet *m*.
village |vil'ij| *n* aldea.
villager |vil'ijûr| *n* aldeano/a.
villain |vil'in| *n* (*scoundrel*) malvado/a; (*criminal*) maleante *m/f*.
VIN *n abbr* (*US*) = *vehicle identification number*.
vindicate |vin'dikāt| *vt* vindicar, justificar.
vindication |vindikā'shən| *n*: **in ~ of** en justificación de.
vindictive |vindik'tiv| *a* vengativo.
vine |vīn| *n* vid *f*.
vinegar |vin'əgûr| *n* vinagre *m*.
vine-growing |vīn'grōing| *a* (*region*) viticultor(a).
vineyard |vin'yûrd| *n* viña, viñedo.
vintage |vin'tij| *n* (*year*) vendimia, cosecha; **the 1970 ~** la cosecha de 1970.
vintage car *n* coche *m* antiguo *or* de época.
vintage wine *n* vino añejo.
vintage year *n*: **it's been a ~ for plays** ha sido un año destacado en lo que a teatro se refiere.
vinyl |vī'nil| *n* vinilo.
viola |vēō'lə| *n* (*MUS*) viola.
violate |vī'əlāt| *vt* violar.
violation |vīəlā'shən| *n* violación *f*; **in ~ of sth** en violación de algo.
violence |vī'ələns| *n* violencia; **acts of ~** actos *mpl* de violencia.
violent |vī'ələnt| *a* (*gen*) violento; (*pain*) intenso; **a ~ dislike of sb/sth** una profunda antipatía *or* manía a uno/algo.
violently |vī'ələntlē| *ad* (*severely*: *ill, angry*) muy.
violet |vī'əlit| *a* violado, violeta ♦ *n* (*plant*) violeta.
violin |vīəlin'| *n* violín *m*.
violinist |vīəlin'ist| *n* violinista *m/f*.
VIP *n abbr* (= *very important person*) VIP *m*.
viper |vī'pûr| *n* víbora.
virgin |vûr'jin| *n* virgen *m/f* ♦ *a* virgen; **the Blessed V~** la Santísima Virgen.
virginity |vûrjin'ətē| *n* virginidad *f*.
Virgo |vûr'gō| *n* Virgo.
virile |vir'əl| *a* viril.
virility |vəril'ətē| *n* virilidad *f*.
virtual |vûr'chōōəl| *a* virtual.
virtually |vûr'chōōəlē| *ad* (*almost*) virtualmente; **it is ~ impossible** es prácticamente imposible.
virtue |vûr'chōō| *n* virtud *f*; **by ~ of** en virtud de.
virtuoso |vûrchōōō'sō| *n* virtuoso.
virtuous |vûr'chōōəs| *a* virtuoso.
virulence |vir'yələns| *n* virulencia.
virulent |vir'yələnt| *a* virulento, violento.
virus |vī'rəs| *n* (*also*: *COMPUT*) virus *m*.
visa |vē'zə| *n* visado, visa (*LAm*).
vis-à-vis |vēzávē'| *prep* con respecto a.
viscount |vī'kount| *n* vizconde *m*.

viscous |vis'kəs| *a* viscoso.
vise |vīs| *n* (*US TECH*) torno de banco.
visibility |vizəbil'ətē| *n* visibilidad *f*.
visible |viz'əbəl| *a* visible; **~ exports/imports** exportaciones *fpl*/importaciones *fpl* visibles.
visibly |viz'əblē| *ad* visiblemente.
vision |vizh'ən| *n* (*sight*) vista; (*foresight, in dream*) visión *f*.
visionary |vizh'ənärē| *n* visionario/a.
visit |viz'it| *n* visita ♦ *vt* (*person*) visitar, hacer una visita a; (*place*) ir a, (ir a) conocer; **to pay a ~ to** (*person*) visitar a; **on a private/official ~** en visita privada/oficial.
visiting |viz'iting| *a* (*speaker, professor*) invitado; (*team*) visitante.
visiting card *n* tarjeta de visita.
visiting hours *npl* (*in hospital etc*) horas *fpl* de visita.
visitor |viz'itûr| *n* (*gen*) visitante *m/f*; (*to one's house*) invitado/a; (*tourist*) turista *m/f*; (*tourist*) excursionista *m/f*; **to have ~s** (*at home*) tener visita.
visitors' book *n* (*Brit*) libro de visitas.
visor |vī'zûr| *n* visera.
VISTA |vis'tə| *n abbr* (= *Volunteers In Service to America*) programa de ayuda voluntaria a los necesitados.
vista |vis'tə| *n* vista, panorama.
visual |vizh'ōōəl| *a* visual.
visual aid *n* medio visual.
visual display unit (VDU) *n* unidad *f* de despliegue visual, monitor *m*.
visualize |vizh'ōōəlīz| *vt* imaginarse; (*foresee*) prever.
visually |vizh'ōōəlē| *ad*: **~ handicapped** con visión deficiente.
vital |vīt'əl| *a* (*essential*) esencial, imprescindible; (*crucial*) crítico; (*person*) enérgico, vivo; (*of life*) vital; **of ~ importance (to sb/sth)** de suma importancia (para uno/algo).
vitality |vītal'itē| *n* energía, vitalidad *f*.
vitally |vī'təlē| *ad*: **~ important** de primera importancia.
vital statistics *npl* (*of population*) estadísticas *fpl* demográficas; (*col*: *woman's*) medidas *fpl* vitales.
vitamin |vī'təmin| *n* vitamina.
vitamin pill *n* pastilla de vitaminas.
vitreous |vit'rēəs| *a* (*china, enamel*) vítreo.
vitriolic |vitrēâl'ik| *a* mordaz.
viva |vē'və| *n* (*also*: **~ voce**) examen *m* oral.
vivacious |vivā'shəs| *a* vivaz, alegre.
vivacity |vivas'itē| *n* vivacidad *f*.
vivid |viv'id| *a* (*account*) gráfico; (*light*) intenso; (*imagination*) vivo.
vividly |viv'idlē| *ad* (*describe*) gráficamente; (*remember*) como si fuera hoy.
vivisection |vivisek'shən| *n* vivisección *f*.
vixen |vik'sən| *n* (*ZOOL*) zorra, raposa; (*pej*: *woman*) arpía, bruja.
viz *abbr* (= *videlicet*: *namely*) v.gr.

VLF *abbr* = *very low frequency.*
V-neck [vē'nek] *n* cuello de pico.
VOA *n abbr* (= *Voice of America*) Voz *f* de América.
vocabulary [vōkab'yəlärē] *n* vocabulario.
vocal [vō'kəl] *a* vocal; (*articulate*) elocuente.
vocal cords *npl* cuerdas *fpl* vocales.
vocalist [vō'kəlist] *n* cantante *m/f.*
vocation [vōkā'shən] *n* vocación *f.*
vocational [vōkā'shənəl] *a* vocacional; ~ **guidance** orientación *f* profesional; ~ **training** formación *f* profesional.
vociferous [vōsif'ûrəs] *a* vociferante.
vociferously [vōsif'ûrəslē] *ad* a gritos, clamorosamente.
vodka [vâd'kə] *n* vodka *m.*
vogue [vōg] *n* boga, moda; **to be in** ~, **be the** ~ estar de moda *or* en boga.
voice [vois] *n* voz *f* ♦ *vt* (*opinion*) expresar; **in a loud/soft** ~ en voz alta/baja; **to give** ~ **to** expresar.
void [void] *n* vacío; (*hole*) hueco ♦ *a* (*invalid*) nulo, inválido; (*empty*): ~ **of** carente *or* desprovisto de.
voile [voil] *n* gasa.
vol. *abbr* (= *volume*) t.
volatile [vâl'ətəl] *a* volátil; (*COMPUT: memory*) no permanente.
volcanic [vâlkan'ik] *a* volcánico.
volcano, ~**es** [vâlkā'nō] *n* volcán *m.*
volition [vōlish'ən] *n*: **of one's own** ~ de su propia voluntad.
volley [vâl'ē] *n* (*of gunfire*) descarga; (*of stones etc*) lluvia; (*TENNIS etc*) volea.
volleyball [vâl'ēbôl] *n* vol(e)ibol *m.*
volt [vōlt] *n* voltio.
voltage [vōl'tij] *n* voltaje *m;* **high/low** ~ alto/bajo voltaje, alta/baja tensión.
volte-face [vōltfâs'] *n* viraje *m.*
voluble [vâl'yəbəl] *a* locuaz, hablador(a).
volume [vâl'yōōm] *n* (*of tank*) volumen *m;* (*book*) tomo; ~ **one/two** (*of book*) tomo primero/segundo; ~**s** *npl* (*great quantities*) cantidad *fsg;* **his expression spoke** ~**s** su expresión (lo) decía todo.
volume control *n* (*RADIO, TV*) (botón *m* del) volumen *m.*
volume discount *n* (*COMM*) descuento por volumen de compras.
voluminous [vəlōō'minəs] *a* (*large*) voluminoso; (*prolific*) prolífico.
voluntarily [vâləntär'ilē] *ad* libremente, voluntariamente.
voluntary [vâl'əntärē] *a* voluntario, espontáneo.
voluntary liquidation *n* (*COMM*) liquidación *f* voluntaria.
voluntary redundancy *n* (*Brit*) despido voluntario.
volunteer [vâləntēr'] *n* voluntario/a ♦ *vi* ofrecerse (de voluntario); **to** ~ **to do** ofrecerse a hacer.

voluptuous [vəlup'chōōəs] *a* voluptuoso.
vomit [vâm'it] *n* vómito ♦ *vt, vi* vomitar.
vote [vōt] *n* voto; (*votes cast*) votación *f;* (*right to* ~) derecho de votar; (*franchise*) sufragio ♦ *vt* (*chairman*) elegir ♦ *vi* votar, ir a votar; ~ **of thanks** voto de gracias; **to put sth to a** ~, **to take a** ~ **on sth** someter algo a voto; ~ **for** *or* **in favor of/against** voto a favor de/en contra de; **to** ~ **to do sth** votar por hacer algo; **he was** ~**d secretary** fue elegido secretario por votación; **to pass a** ~ **of confidence/no confidence** aprobar un voto de confianza/de censura.
voter [vō'tûr] *n* votante *m/f.*
voting [vō'ting] *n* votación *f.*
voting right *n* derecho a voto.
vouch [vouch]: **to** ~ **for** *vt fus* garantizar, responder de.
voucher [vou'chûr] *n* (*for meal, gasoline*) vale *m;* **luncheon/travel** ~ vale *m* de comida/de viaje.
vow [vou] *n* voto ♦ *vi* hacer voto; **to take** *or* **make a** ~ **to do sth** jurar hacer algo, comprometerse a hacer algo.
vowel [vou'əl] *n* vocal *f.*
voyage [voi'ij] *n* (*journey*) viaje *m;* (*crossing*) travesía.
VP *n abbr* (= *vice-president*) V.P.
vs *abbr* (= *versus*) vs.
VSO *n abbr* (*Brit:* = *Voluntary Service Overseas*) organización que envía jóvenes voluntarios a trabajar y enseñar en los países del Tercer Mundo.
VT *abbr* (*US MAIL*) = *Vermont.*
VTR *n abbr* (= *video tape recorder*) videograbadora.
vulgar [vul'gûr] *a* (*rude*) ordinario, grosero; (*in bad taste*) de mal gusto.
vulgarity [vulgar'itē] *n* grosería; mal gusto.
vulnerability [vulnûrəbil'ətē] *n* vulnerabilidad *f.*
vulnerable [vul'nûrəbəl] *a* vulnerable.
vulture [vul'chûr] *n* buitre *m.*

W

W, w [dub'əlyōō] *n* (*letter*) W, w *f;* **W for William** W de Washington.
W *abbr* (= *west*) O; (*ELEC:* = *watt*) v.
WA *abbr* (*US MAIL*) = *Washington.*
wad [wâd] *n* (*of cotton wool, paper*) bolita; (*of banknotes etc*) fajo.
wadding [wâd'ing] *n* relleno.
waddle [wâd'əl] *vi* anadear.

wade [wād] *vi*: **to ~ through** caminar por el agua; (*fig*: *a book*) leer con dificultad.
wading pool [wād'ing pōōl] *n* (*US*) piscina para niños.
wafer [wā'fûr] *n* (*cookie*) galleta, barquillo; (*REL*) oblea; (*COMPUT*) oblea, microplaqueta.
wafer-thin [wā'fûrthin'] *a* finísimo.
waffle [wäf'əl] *n* (*CULIN*) gofre *m* ♦ *vi* dar el rollo.
waffle iron *n* molde *m* para hacer gofres.
waft [waft] *vt* llevar por el aire ♦ *vi* flotar.
wag [wag] *vt* menear, agitar ♦ *vi* moverse, menearse; **the dog ~ged its tail** el perro meneó la cola.
wage [wāj] *n* (*also*: **~s**) sueldo, salario ♦ *vt*: **to ~ war** hacer la guerra; **a day's ~** un día de salario.
wage claim *n* reivindicación *f* salarial.
wage differential *n* diferencia salarial.
wage earner *n* asalariado/a.
wage freeze *n* congelación *f* de los salarios.
wage packet *n* (*Brit*) sobre *m* de paga.
wager [wā'jûr] *n* apuesta ♦ *vt* apostar.
waggle [wag'əl] *vt* menear, mover.
wag(g)on [wag'ən] *n* (*horse-drawn*) carro; (*Brit RAIL*) vagón *m*.
wail [wāl] *n* gemido ♦ *vi* gemir.
waist [wāst] *n* cintura, talle *m*.
waistcoat [wāst'kōt] *n* (*Brit*) chaleco.
waistline [wāst'līn] *n* talle *m*.
wait [wāt] *n* espera; (*interval*) pausa ♦ *vi* esperar; **to lie in ~ for** acechar a; **I can't ~ to** (*fig*) estoy deseando; **to ~ for** esperar (a); **to keep sb ~ing** hacer esperar a uno; **~ a moment!** ¡un momento!, ¡un momentito! (*LAm*); **"repairs while you ~"** "reparaciones en el acto".
wait behind *vi* quedarse.
wait on *vt fus* servir a.
wait up *vi* quedarse levantado.
waiter [wā'tûr] *n* camarero.
waiting list [wā'ting list] *n* lista de espera.
waiting room *n* sala de espera.
waitress [wā'tris] *n* camarera.
waive [wāv] *vt* suspender.
waiver [wā'vûr] *n* renuncia.
wake [wāk] *vb* (*pt* **woke** *or* **waked**, *pp* **woken** *or* **waked** [wōk, wō'kən]) *vt* (*also*: **~ up**) despertar ♦ *vi* (*also*: **~ up**) despertarse ♦ *n* (*for dead person*) vela, velatorio; (*NAUT*) estela; **to ~ up to sth** (*fig*) darse cuenta de algo; **in the ~ of** tras, después de; **to follow in sb's ~** (*fig*) seguir las huellas de uno.
waken [wā'kən] *vt*, *vi* = **wake**.
Wales [wālz] *n* País *m* de Gales.
walk [wôk] *n* (*stroll*) paseo; (*hike*) excursión *f* a pie, caminata; (*gait*) paso, andar *m*; (*in park etc*) paseo, alameda ♦ *vi* andar, caminar; (*for pleasure, exercise*) pasearse ♦ *vt* (*distance*) recorrer a pie,

andar; (*dog*) pasear; **to go for a ~** ir de paseo; **10 minutes' ~ from here** a 10 minutos de aquí andando; **people from all ~s of life** gente de todas las esferas; **to ~ in one's sleep** ser sonámbulo/a; **I'll ~ you home** te acompañaré a casa.
walk out *vi* (*go out*) salir; (*as protest*) salirse; (*strike*) declararse en huelga; **to ~ out on sb** abandonar a uno.
walker [wôk'ûr] *n* (*person*) paseante *m/f*, caminante *m/f*.
walkie-talkie [wô'kētô'kē] *n* transmisor-receptor *m* portátil.
walking [wô'king] *n* el andar; **it's within ~ distance** se puede ir andando *or* a pie.
walking shoes *npl* zapatos *mpl* para andar.
walking stick *n* bastón *m*.
walk-on [wôk'ân] *a* (*THEATER*: *part*) de comparsa.
walkout [wôk'out] *n* (*of workers*) huelga.
walkover [wôk'ōvûr] *n* (*col*) pan *m* comido.
walkway [wôk'wā] *n* paseo.
wall [wôl] *n* pared *f*; (*exterior*) muro; (*city ~ etc*) muralla; **to go to the ~** (*fig*: *firm etc*) quebrar, ir a la bancarrota.
wall in *vt* (*garden etc*) cercar con una tapia.
walled [wôld] *a* (*city*) amurallado; (*garden*) con tapia.
wallet [wâl'it] *n* cartera, billetera (*LAm*).
wallflower [wôl'flouûr] *n* alhelí *m*; **to be a ~** (*fig*) comer pavo.
wall hanging *n* tapiz *m*.
wallop [wâl'əp] *vt* (*col*) zurrar.
wallow [wâl'ō] *vi* revolcarse; **to ~ in one's grief** sumirse en su pena.
wallpaper [wôl'pāpûr] *n* papel *m* pintado.
wall-to-wall [wôl'təwôl'] *a*: **~ carpeting** moqueta.
wally [wâ'lē] *n* (*Brit*: *col*) palurdo/a, majadero/a.
walnut [wôl'nut] *n* nuez *f*; (*tree*) nogal *m*.
walrus, *pl* **~** *or* **~es**, [wôl'rəs] *n* morsa.
waltz [wôlts] *n* vals *m* ♦ *vi* bailar el vals.
wan [wân] *a* pálido.
wand [wând] *n* (*also*: **magic ~**) varita (mágica).
wander [wân'dûr] *vi* (*person*) vagar; deambular; (*thoughts*) divagar; (*get lost*) extraviarse ♦ *vt* recorrer, vagar por.
wanderer [wân'dûrûr] *n* vagabundo/a.
wandering [wân'dûring] *a* (*tribe*) nómada; (*minstrel, actor*) ambulante; (*path, river*) sinuoso; (*glance, mind*) distraído.
wane [wān] *vi* menguar.
wangle [wang'gəl] (*col*) *vt*: **to ~ sth** agenciarse *or* conseguir algo ♦ *n* chanchullo.
want [wônt] *vt* (*wish for*) querer, desear; (*need*) necesitar; (*lack*) carecer de ♦ *n* (*poverty*) pobreza; **for ~ of** por falta de; **~s** *npl* (*needs*) necesidades *fpl*; **to ~ to do**

querer hacer; **to** ~ **sb to do sth** querer que uno haga algo; **you're** ~**ed on the phone** te llaman al teléfono; **to be in** ~ estar necesitado; **"cook** ~**ed"** "se busca cocinero/a".

want ads *npl* (*US*) anuncios *mpl* por palabras.

wanting [wôn'ting] *a*: **to be** ~ **(in)** estar falto (de); **to be found** ~ no estar a la altura de las circunstancias.

wanton [wân'tən] *a* (*playful*) juguetón/ona; (*licentious*) lascivo.

war [wôr] *n* guerra; **to make** ~ hacer la guerra.

warble [wôr'bəl] *n* (*of bird*) trino, gorjeo ♦ *vi* (*bird*) trinar.

war cry *n* grito de guerra.

ward [wôrd] *n* (*in hospital*) sala; (*LAW: child*) pupilo/a.
  ward off *vt* desviar, parar; (*attack*) rechazar.

warden [wôr'dən] *n* (*of park, game reserve*) guardián/ana *m/f*; (*Brit: of institution*) director(a) *m/f*; (*Brit: also:* **traffic** ~) guardia *m/f*.

warder [wôr'dûr] *n* (*Brit*) guardián/ana *m/f*, carcelero/a.

wardrobe [wôrd'rōb] *n* armario, guardarropa, ropero (*esp LAm*).

warehouse [wär'hous] *n* almacén *m*, depósito.

wares [wärz] *npl* mercancías *fpl*.

warfare [wôr'fär] *n* guerra.

war game *n* juego de estrategia militar.

warhead [wôr'hed] *n* cabeza armada; **nuclear** ~**s** cabezas *fpl* armadas.

warily [wär'ilē] *ad* con cautela, cautelosamente.

warlike [wôr'līk] *a* guerrero.

warm [wôrm] *a* caliente; (*person, greeting, heart*) afectuoso, cariñoso; (*supporter*) entusiasta; (*thanks, congratulations, apologies*) efusivo; (*clothes etc*) que abriga; (*welcome, day*) caluroso; **it's** ~ hace calor; **I'm** ~ tengo calor; **to keep sth** ~ mantener algo caliente.
  warm up *vi* (*room*) calentarse; (*person*) entrar en calor; (*athlete*) hacer ejercicios de calentamiento; (*discussion*) acalorarse ♦ *vt* calentar.

warm-blooded [wôrm'blud'id] *a* de sangre caliente.

war memorial *n* monumento a los caídos.

warm-hearted [wôrm'hâr'tid] *a* afectuoso.

warmly [wôrm'lē] *ad* afectuosamente.

warmonger [wôr'munggûr] *n* belicista *m/f*.

warmongering [wôr'munggûring] *n* belicismo.

warmth [wôrmth] *n* calor *m*.

warm-up [wôrm'up] *n* (*SPORT*) ejercicios *mpl* de calentamiento.

warn [wôrn] *vt* avisar, advertir; (*SOCCER*) amonestar; **to** ~ **sb not to do sth** *or*

against doing sth aconsejar a uno que no haga algo.

warning [wôr'ning] *n* aviso, advertencia; **gale** ~ (*METEOROLOGY*) aviso de vendaval; **without (any)** ~ sin aviso *or* avisar.

warning light *n* luz *f* de advertencia.

warning triangle *n* (*AUT*) triángulo señalizador.

warp [wôrp] *vi* (*wood*) combarse.

warpath [wôr'path] *n*: **to be on the** ~ (*fig*) estar en pie de guerra.

warped [wôrpt] *a* (*wood*) alabeado; (*fig: character, sense of humor etc*) pervertido.

warrant [wôr'ənt] *n* (*LAW: to arrest*) orden *f* de detención; (: *to search*) mandamiento de registro ♦ *vt* (*justify, merit*) merecer.

warrant officer *n* (*MIL*) brigada *m*; (*NAUT*) contramaestre *m*.

warranty [wôr'əntē] *n* garantía; **under** ~ (*COMM*) bajo garantía.

warren [wôr'ən] *n* (*of rabbits*) madriguera; (*fig*) laberinto.

warring [wô'ring] *a* (*interests etc*) opuesto; (*nations*) en guerra.

warrior [wôr'ēûr] *n* guerrero/a.

Warsaw [wôr'sô] *n* Varsovia.

warship [wôr'ship] *n* buque *m* o barco de guerra.

wart [wôrt] *n* verruga.

wartime [wôr'tīm] *n*: **in** ~ en tiempos de guerra, en la guerra.

wary [wär'ē] *a* cauteloso; **to be** ~ **about** *or* **of doing sth** tener cuidado con hacer algo.

was [wuz] *pt of* **be**.

Wash. *abbr* (*US*) = *Washington*.

wash [wâsh] *vt* lavar; (*sweep, carry: sea etc*) llevar ♦ *vi* lavarse ♦ *n* (*clothes etc*) lavado; (*bath*) baño; (*of ship*) estela; **he was** ~**ed overboard** fue arrastrado del barco por las olas.
  wash away *vt* (*stain*) quitar lavando; (*subj: river etc*) llevarse; (*fig*) limpiar.
  wash down *vt* lavar.
  wash off *vt* quitar lavando.
  wash up *vi* (*US*) lavarse; (*Brit: dishes*) fregar los platos.

washable [wâsh'əbəl] *a* lavable.

wash bag *n* (*US*) esponjera.

washbasin [wâshbās'ən] *n* (*Brit*) = **washbowl**.

washbowl [wâsh'bōl] *n* (*US*) lavabo.

washcloth [wâsh'klôth] *n* (*US*) manopla.

washer [wâsh'ûr] *n* (*TECH*) arandela.

washing [wâsh'ing] *n* (*dirty*) ropa sucia; (*clean*) colada.

washing line *n* (*Brit*) cuerda de (colgar) la ropa.

washing machine *n* lavadora.

washing powder *n* (*Brit*) detergente *m* (en polvo).

Washington [wâsh'ingtən] *n* (*city, state*) Washington *m*.

washing-up [wâsh'ingup'] *n* (*Brit*) fregado,

platos *mpl* (para fregar).
washing-up liquid *n* (*Brit*) (detergente *m*) lavavajillas *m inv.*
wash-out [wâsh'out] *n* (*col*) fracaso.
washroom [wâsh'rōōm] *n* servicios *mpl.*
wasn't [wuz'ənt] = **was not.**
Wasp, WASP [wâsp] *n abbr* (*US:* = *White Anglo-Saxon Protestant*) sobrenombre que se da a los americanos de origen anglosajón, acomodados y de tendencia conservadora.
wasp [wâsp] *n* avispa.
waspish [wâs'pish] *a* (*character*) irascible; (*comment*) mordaz, punzante.
wastage [wās'tij] *n* desgaste *m*; (*loss*) pérdida; **natural** ~ (*Brit*) desgaste natural.
waste [wāst] *n* derroche *m*, despilfarro; (*misuse*) desgaste *m*; (*of time*) pérdida; (*food*) sobras *fpl*; (*rubbish*) basura, desperdicios *mpl* ♦ *a* (*material*) de desecho; (*left over*) sobrante; (*energy, heat*) desperdiciado; (*land, ground*: *in city*) sin construir; (: *in country*) baldío ♦ *vt* (*squander*) malgastar, derrochar; (*time*) perder; (*opportunity*) desperdiciar; ~**s** *npl* (*Brit*: *area of land*) tierras *fpl* baldías; **to lay** ~ devastar, arrasar; **it's a** ~ **of money** es dinero perdido; **to go to** ~ desperdiciarse.
waste away *vi* consumirse.
wastebin [wāst'bin] *n* (*Brit*) cubo *or* (*LAm*) bote *m* de la basura.
wasteful [wāst'fəl] *a* derrochador(a); (*process*) antieconómico.
wastefully [wāst'fəlē] *ad* derrochadoramente; antieconómicamente.
waste ground *n* (*Brit*) terreno baldío.
wasteland [wāst'land] *n* (*urban*) descampados *mpl.*
wastepaper basket [wāst'pāpûr bas'kit] *n* papelera.
waste products *npl* (*INDUSTRY*) residuos *mpl.*
watch [wâch] *n* reloj *m*; (*vigil*) vigilia; (*vigilance*) vigilancia; (*MIL:* *guard*) centinela *m*; (*NAUT: spell of duty*) guardia ♦ *vt* (*look at*) mirar, observar; (: *match, program*) ver; (*spy on, guard*) vigilar; (*be careful of*) cuidarse de, tener cuidado de ♦ *vi* ver, mirar; (*keep guard*) montar guardia; **to keep a close** ~ **on sth/sb** vigilar algo/a uno de cerca; ~ **how you drive/what you're doing** ten cuidado al conducir/con lo que haces.
watch out *vi* cuidarse, tener cuidado.
watch band *n* (*US*) pulsera (de reloj).
watchdog [wâch'dôg] *n* perro guardián; (*fig*) autoridad *f* protectora.
watchful [wâch'fəl] *a* vigilante, sobre aviso.
watchfully [wâch'fəlē] *ad* vigilantemente.
watchmaker [wâch'mākûr] *n* relojero/a.
watchman [wâch'mən] *n* guardián *m*; (*also:* **night** ~) sereno, vigilante *m* (*LAm*); (*in factory*) vigilante *m* nocturno.

watch stem *n* (*US*) cuerda.
watch strap *n* pulsera (de reloj).
watchword [wâch'wûrd] *n* consigna, contraseña.
water [wô'tûr] *n* agua ♦ *vt* (*plant*) regar ♦ *vi* (*eyes*) llorar; **I'd like a drink of** ~ quisiera un vaso de agua; **in British** ~**s** en aguas británicas; **to pass** ~ hacer aguas; **to make sb's mouth** ~ hacerle la boca agua a uno; **to be in** ~ **over one's head** (*US: swimmer*) perder pie; (*fig*) estar perdido.
water down *vt* (*milk etc*) aguar.
water closet *n* wáter *m.*
watercolor, (*Brit*) **watercolour** [wô'tûrkulûr] *n* acuarela.
water-cooled [wô'tûrkōōld] *a* refrigerado (por agua).
watercress [wô'tûrkrcs] *n* berro.
waterfall [wô'tûrfôl] *n* cascada, salto de agua.
waterfront [wô'tûrfrunt] *n* (*seafront*) parte *f* que da al mar; (*at docks*) muelles *mpl.*
water heater *n* calentador *m* de agua.
water hole *n* abrevadero.
watering can [wô'tûring kan] *n* regadera.
water level *n* nivel *m* del agua.
water lily *n* nenúfar *m.*
waterline [wô'tûrlīn] *n* (*NAUT*) línea de flotación.
waterlogged [wô'tûrlôgd] *a* (*boat*) anegado; (*ground*) inundado.
water main *n* cañería del agua.
watermark [wô'tûrmârk] *n* (*on paper*) filigrana.
watermelon [wô'tûrmelən] *n* sandía.
water polo *n* polo acuático.
waterproof [wô'tûrprōōf] *a* impermeable.
water-repellent [wô'təripcl'ənt] *a* hidrófugo.
watershed [wô'tûrshcd] *n* (*GEO*) cuenca; (*fig*) momento crítico.
water-skiing [wô'tûrskēing] *n* esquí *m* acuático.
water softener *n* ablandador *m* de agua.
water tank *n* depósito de agua.
watertight [wô'tûrtīt] *a* hermético.
water vapor *n* vapor *m* de agua.
waterway [wô'tûrwā] *n* vía fluvial *or* navegable.
waterworks [wô'tûrwûrks] *npl* central *fsg* depuradora.
watery [wô'tûrē] *a* (*color*) desvaído; (*coffee*) aguado; (*eyes*) lloroso.
WATS [wâts] *n abbr* (*US*) = *Wide Area Telecommunications Service.*
watt [wât] *n* vatio.
wattage [wât'ij] *n* potencia en vatios.
wattle [wât'əl] *n* zarzo.
wave [wāv] *n* ola; (*of hand*) señal *f* con la mano; (*RADIO, in hair*) onda; (*fig: of enthusiasm, strikes*) oleada ♦ *vi* agitar la mano; (*flag*) ondear ♦ *vt* (*handkerchief,*

gun) agitar; **short/medium/long** ~ (*RA-DIO*) onda corta/media/larga; **the new** ~ (*CINEMA, MUS*) la nueva ola; **to** ~ **goodbye to sb** decir adiós a uno con la mano; **he** ~**d us over to his table** nos hizo señas (con la mano) para que fuéramos a su mesa.

wave aside, wave away *vt* (*person*): **to** ~ **sb aside** apartar a uno con la mano; (*fig: suggestion, objection*) rechazar; (*doubts*) desechar.

waveband |wāv'band| *n* banda de ondas.

wavelength |wāv'lcngkth| *n* longitud *f* de onda.

waver |wā'vûr| *vi* oscilar; (*confidence*) disminuir; (*faith*) flaquear.

wavy |wā'vē| *a* ondulado.

wax |waks| *n* cera ♦ *vt* encerar ♦ *vi* (*moon*) crecer.

waxen |wak'sən| *a* (*fig: pale*) blanco como la cera.

wax paper *n* papel *m* apergaminado.

waxworks |waks'wûrks| *npl* museo *sg* de cera.

way |wā| *n* camino; (*distance*) trayecto, recorrido; (*direction*) dirección *f*, sentido; (*manner*) modo, manera; (*habit*) costumbre *f*; **which** ~? — **this** ~ ¿por dónde? *or* ¿en qué dirección? — por aquí; **on the** ~ (*en route*) en (el) camino; (*expected*) en camino; **to be on one's** ~ estar en camino; **you pass it on your** ~ **home** está en el camino a tu casa; **to be in the** ~ bloquear el camino; (*fig*) estorbar; **to keep out of sb's** ~ esquivar a uno; **to make** ~ (**for sb/sth**) dejar paso (a uno/algo); (*fig*) abrir camino (a uno/algo); **to go out of one's** ~ **to do sth** desvivirse por hacer algo; **to lose one's** ~ perderse, extraviarse; **to be the wrong** ~ **around** estar del *or* al revés; **in a** ~ en cierto modo *or* sentido; **by the** ~ a propósito; **by** ~ **of** (*via*) pasando por; (*as a sort of*) como, a modo de; ~ **in** entrada; ~ **out** salida; **the** ~ **back** el camino de vuelta; **the village is rather out of the** ~ el pueblo está un poco apartado *or* retirado; **it's a long** ~ **away** está muy lejos; **to get one's own** ~ salirse con la suya; "**give** ~**"** (*Brit AUT*) "ceda el paso"; **no** ~! (*col*) ¡ni pensarlo!; **put it the right** ~ **up** ponlo boca arriba; **he's in a bad** ~ está grave; **to be under** ~ (*work, project*) estar en marcha.

waybill |wā'bil| *n* (*COMM*) hoja de ruta, carta de porte.

waylay |wālā'| *vt* (*irg: like* **lay**) atacar.

wayside |wā'sīd| *n* borde *m* del camino; **to fall by the** ~ (*fig*) fracasar.

way station *n* (*US RAIL*) apeadero; (*fig*) paso intermedio.

wayward |wā'wûrd| *a* díscolo, caprichoso.

WC *n abbr* (*Brit:* = *water closet*) wáter *m*.

WCC *n abbr* = *World Council of Churches*.

we |wē| *pl pron* nosotros/as; ~ **understand** (nosotros) entendemos; **here** ~ **are** aquí estamos.

weak |wēk| *a* débil, flojo; (*tea, coffee*) flojo, aguado; **to grow** ~(**er**) debilitarse.

weaken |wē'kən| *vi* debilitarse; (*give way*) ceder ♦ *vt* debilitar.

weak-kneed |wēk'nēd| *a* (*fig*) sin voluntad *or* carácter.

weakling |wēk'ling| *n* debilucho/a.

weakly |wēk'lē| *a* enfermizo, débil ♦ *ad* débilmente.

weakness |wēk'nis| *n* debilidad *f*; (*fault*) punto débil.

wealth |wclth| *n* (*money, resources*) riqueza; (*of details*) abundancia.

wealth tax *n* impuesto sobre el patrimonio.

wealthy |wcl'thē| *a* rico.

wean |wēn| *vt* destetar.

weapon |wcp'ən| *n* arma.

wear |wär| *n* (*use*) uso; (*deterioration through use*) desgaste *m*; (*clothing*): **sports/baby**~ ropa de deportes/de niños ♦ *vb* (*pt* **wore**, *pp* **worn** |wôr, wôrn|) *vt* (*clothes, beard*) llevar; (*shoes*) calzar; (*look, smile*) tener; (*damage: through use*) gastar, usar ♦ *vi* (*last*) durar; (*rub through etc*) desgastarse; **evening** ~ (*man's*) traje *m* de etiqueta; (*woman's*) traje *m* de noche; **to** ~ **a hole in sth** hacer un agujero en algo.

wear away *vt* gastar ♦ *vi* desgastarse.

wear down *vt* gastar; (*strength*) agotar.

wear off *vi* (*pain, excitement etc*) pasar, desaparecer.

wear out *vt* desgastar; (*person, strength*) agotar.

wearable |wär'əbəl| *a* que se puede llevar.

wear and tear *n* desgaste *m*.

wearer |wär'ûr| *n*: **the** ~ **of this jacket** el/la que lleva puesta esta chaqueta.

wearily |wē'rilē| *ad* con cansancio.

weariness |wē'rēnis| *n* cansancio; abatimiento.

wearisome |wē'rēsəm| *a* (*tiring*) cansado, pesado; (*boring*) aburrido.

weary |wēr'ē| *a* (*tired*) cansado; (*dispirited*) abatido ♦ *vt* cansar ♦ *vi*: **to** ~ **of** cansarse de, aburrirse de.

weasel |wē'zəl| *n* (*ZOOL*) comadreja.

weather |wclth'ûr| *n* tiempo ♦ *vt* (*storm, crisis*) hacer frente a; **under the** ~ (*fig: ill*) mal, indispuesto; **what's the** ~ **like?** ¿qué tiempo hace?

weather-beaten |wclth'ûrbētən| *a* curtido.

weathercock |wclth'ûrkâk| *n* veleta.

weather forecast *n* boletín *m* meteorológico.

weatherman |wclth'ûrman| *n* hombre *m* del tiempo.

weatherproof |wclth'ûrproof| *a* (*garment*) impermeable.

weather report n parte m meteorológico.
weather strip(ping) |wcťh'ûr strip('ing)| n burlete m.
weather vane n = **weathercock.**
weave, pt **wove,** pp **woven** |wĕv, wŏv, wō'vən| vt (cloth) tejer; (fig) entretejer ◆ vi (fig: pt, pp ~d: move in and out) zigzaguear.
weaver |wĕ'vûr| n tejedor(a) m/f.
weaving |wĕ'ving| n tejeduría.
web |wcb| n (of spider) telaraña; (on foot) membrana; (network) red f.
webbed |wcbd| a (foot) palmeado.
webbing |wcb'ing| n (on chair) cinchas fpl.
wed |wcd| vt (pt, pp **wedded**) casar ◆ n: **the newly-~s** los recién casados.
Wed. abbr (= Wednesday) miérc.
we'd |wĕd| = **we had; we would.**
wedded |wcd'id| pt, pp of **wed.**
wedding |wcd'ing| n boda, casamiento.
wedding anniversary a aniversario de boda; **silver/golden** ~ bodas fpl de plata/de oro.
wedding day n día m de la boda.
wedding dress n traje m de novia.
wedding present n regalo de boda.
wedding ring n alianza.
wedge |wcj| n (of wood etc) cuña; (of cake) trozo ◆ vt acuñar; (push) apretar.
wedge-heeled |wcj'hĕld| a con suela de cuña.
wedlock |wcd'lâk| n matrimonio.
Wednesday |wenz'dã| n miércoles m inv.
wee |wĕ| a (Scottish) pequeñito.
weed |wĕd| n mala hierba, maleza ◆ vt escardar, desherbar.
weedkiller |wĕd'kilûr| n herbicida m.
weedy |wĕ'dĕ| a (person) debilucho.
week |wĕk| n semana; **a ~ from today** de hoy en ocho días; **Tuesday ~, a ~ from Tuesday** de martes en una semana; **once/ twice a ~** una vez/dos veces a la semana; **this ~** esta semana; **in 2 ~s' time** dentro de 2 semanas; **every other ~** cada 2 semanas.
weekday |wĕk'dã| n día m laborable; **on ~s** entre semana, en días laborables.
weekend |wĕk'end| n fin m de semana.
weekend case n neceser m.
weekly |wĕk'lĕ| ad semanalmente, cada semana ◆ a semanal ◆ n semanario; **~ newspaper** semanario.
weep, pt, pp **wept** |wĕp, wcpt| vi, vt llorar; (MED: wound etc) supurar.
weeping willow |wĕ'ping wil'ō| n sauce m llorón.
weft |wcft| n (TEXTILES) trama.
weigh |wã| vt, vi pesar; **to ~ anchor** levar anclas; **to ~ the pros and cons** pesar el pro y el contra.
weigh down vt sobrecargar; (fig: with worry) agobiar.
weigh out vt (goods) pesar.

weighing machine |wã'ing məshĕn'| n báscula, peso.
weight |wãt| n peso; (on scale) pesa; **to lose/put on** ~ adelgazar/engordar; **~s and measures** pesas y medidas.
weightlessness |wãt'lisnis| n ingravidez f.
weight lifter |wãt'liftûr| n levantador(a) m/f de pesas.
weight limit n límite m de peso.
weighty |wã'tĕ| a pesado.
weir |wĕr| n presa.
weird |wĕrd| a raro, extraño.
welcome |wcl'kəm| a bienvenido ◆ n bienvenida ◆ vt dar la bienvenida a; (be glad of) alegrarse de; **to make sb ~** recibir or acoger bien a uno; **thank you — you're** ~ gracias — de nada; **you're ~ to try** puede intentar cuando quiera; **we ~ this step** celebramos esta medida.
weld |wcld| n soldadura ◆ vt soldar.
welding |wcld'ing| n soldadura.
welfare |wcl'fär| n bienestar m; (social aid) asistencia social; **to look after sb's** ~ cuidar del bienestar de uno; **to be on** ~ estar parado.
welfare state n estado benefactor.
welfare work n asistencia social.
well |wcl| n fuente f, pozo ◆ ad bien ◆ a: **to be** ~ estar bien (de salud) ◆ excl ¡vaya!, ¡bueno!; **as** ~ (in addition) además, también; **as ~ as** además de; **you might as ~ tell me** más vale decírmelo; **it would be as** ~ **to ask** más valdría preguntar; ~ **done!** ¡bien hecho!; **get ~ soon!** ¡que te mejores pronto!; **to do** ~ (business) ir bien; (in exam) salir bien; **to be doing** ~ ir bien; **to think** ~ **of sb** pensar bien de uno; **I don't feel** ~ no me encuentro or siento bien; ~**, as I was saying** ... bueno, como decía ... .
well up vi brotar.
we'll |wcl| = **we will, we shall.**
well-behaved |wclbihãvd'| a modoso.
well-being |wcl'bĕ'ing| n bienestar m.
well-bred |wcl'bred'| a bien educado.
well-built |wcl'bilt'| a (person) fornido.
well-chosen |wcl'chō'zən| a (remarks, words) acertado.
well-deserved |wcl'dizûrvd'| a merecido.
well-developed |wcl'divcl'əpt| a (arm, muscle etc) bien desarrollado; (sense) agudo, fino.
well-disposed |wcl'dispōzd'| a: ~ **to(wards)** bien dispuesto a.
well-dressed |wcl'drest'| a bien vestido.
well-earned |wcl'ûrnd'| a (rest) merecido.
well-groomed |wcl'grōōmd'| a de apariencia cuidada.
well-heeled |wcl'hĕld'| a (col: wealthy) rico.
well-informed |wcl'infôrmd'| a (having knowledge of sth) enterado, al corriente.
Wellington |wcl'ingtən| n Wellington m.

wellingtons [wel'ingtənz] *npl* (*also:* **Wellington boots**) botas *fpl* de goma.

well-kept [wel'kept'] *a* (*secret*) bien guardado; (*hair, hands, house, grounds*) bien cuidado.

well-known [wel'nōn'] *a* (*person*) conocido.

well-mannered [wel'man'ûrd] *a* educado.

well-meaning [wel'mē'ning] *a* bienintencionado.

well-nigh [wel'nī'] *ad:* ~ **impossible** casi imposible.

well-off [wel'ôf'] *a* acomodado.

well-read [wel'red'] *a* culto.

well-spoken [wel'spō'kən] *a* bienhablado.

well-stocked [wel'stâkt'] *a* (*shop, larder*) bien surtido.

well-timed [wel'tīmd'] *a* oportuno.

well-to-do [wel'tədoō'] *a* acomodado.

well-wisher [wel'wishûr] *n* admirador(a) *m/f.*

Welsh [welsh] *a* galés/esa ♦ *n* (*LING*) galés *m;* **the** ~ *npl* los galeses.

Welshman [wel'shmən] *n* galés *m.*

Welsh rarebit [welsh rär'bit] *n* pan *m* con queso tostado.

Welshwoman [welsh'woōmən] *n* galesa.

welter [wel'tûr] *n* mescolanza, revoltijo.

went [went] *pt of* **go.**

wept [wept] *pt, pp of* **weep.**

were [wûr] *pt of* **be.**

we're [wēr] = **we are.**

weren't [wûr'ənt] = **were not.**

werewolf, *pl* **-wolves** [wär'woōlf, -woōlvz] *n* hombre *m* lobo.

west [west] *n* oeste *m* ♦ *a* occidental, del oeste ♦ *ad* al *or* hacia el oeste; **the W**~ el Oeste, el Occidente.

westbound [west'bound] *a* (*traffic, lane*) con rumbo al oeste.

westerly [wes'tûrlē] *a* (*wind*) del oeste.

western [wes'tûrn] *a* occidental ♦ *n* (*CINEMA*) película del oeste.

westernized [wes'tûrnīzd] *a* occidentalizado.

West German *a* de Alemania Occidental ♦ *n* alemán/ana *m/f* (de Alemania Occidental).

West Germany *n* Alemania Occidental.

West Indian *a, n* antillano/a *m/f.*

West Indies [west in'dēz] *npl:* **the** ~ las Antillas, las Islas Occidentales.

westward(s) [west'wûrd(z)] *ad* hacia el oeste.

wet [wet] *a* (*damp*) húmedo; (*soaking* ~) mojado; (*rainy*) lluvioso ♦ *vt:* **to** ~ **one's pants** *or* **o.s.** mojarse; **to get** ~ mojarse; **"~ paint"** 'recién pintado'.

wet blanket *n:* **to be a** ~ (*fig*) ser un/una aguafiestas.

wetness [wet'nis] *n* humedad *f.*

wet rot *n* putrefacción *f* húmeda.

wet suit *n* traje *m* de buzo.

we've [wēv] = **we have.**

whack [wak] *vt* dar un buen golpe a.

whale [wāl] *n* (*ZOOL*) ballena.

whaler [wā'lûr] *n* (*ship*) ballenero.

wharf, *pl* **wharves** [wôrf, wôrvz] *n* muelle *m.*

what [wut] *excl* ¡qué!, ¡cómo! ♦ *a* que ♦ *pron* (*interrogative*) qué, cómo; (*relative, indirect: object*) lo que; (*: subject*) el/la que; **for** ~ **reason?** ¿por qué (razón)?; ~ **are you doing?** ¿qué haces?; ~**'s happening?** ¿qué pasa?; **I don't know** ~ **to do** no sé qué hacer; **I saw** ~ **you did** he visto lo que hiciste; ~ **a mess!** ¡qué lío!; ~ **is it called?** ¿cómo se llama?; ~ **is his address?** ¿cuáles son sus señas?; ~ **will it cost?** ¿cuánto costará?; ~ **about me?** ¿y yo?; ~ **I want is a cup of tea** lo que quiero es una taza de té.

whatever [wutev'ûr] *a:* ~ **book you choose** cualquier libro que elijas ♦ *pron:* **do** ~ **is necessary** haga lo que sea necesario; **no reason** ~ ninguna razón sea la que sea; **nothing** ~ nada en absoluto; ~ **it costs** cueste lo que cueste.

wheat [wēt] *n* trigo.

wheat germ *n* germen *m* de trigo.

wheatmeal [wēt'mēl] *n* (*Brit*) harina integral.

wheedle [wēd'əl] *vt:* **to** ~ **sb into doing sth** engatusar a uno para que haga algo *or* para hacer algo; **to** ~ **sth out of sb** sonsacar algo a uno.

wheel [wēl] *n* rueda; (*AUT: also:* **steering** ~) volante *m;* (*NAUT*) timón *m* ♦ *vt* (*baby carriage etc*) empujar ♦ *vi* (*also:* ~ **around**) dar la vuelta, girar; **four-**~ **drive** tracción *f* en las cuatro ruedas; **front-/ rear-**~ **drive** tracción *f* delantera/trasera.

wheelbarrow [wēl'barō] *n* carretilla.

wheelbase [wēl'bās] *n* batalla.

wheelchair [wēl'chär] *n* silla de ruedas.

wheel clamp *n* (*Brit AUT*) cepo.

wheeler-dealer [wē'lûrdē'lûr] *n* negociante *m/f* muy astuto/a.

wheeling [wē'ling] *n:* ~ **and dealing** (*col*) intrigas *fpl.*

wheeze [wēz] *vi* resollar.

when [wen] *ad* cuándo ♦ *conj* cuando; (*whereas*) mientras; **on the day** ~ **I met him** el día que le conocí; **that's** ~ **the train arrives** eso es cuando llega el tren.

whenever [wenev'ûr] *conj* cuando; (*every time*) cada vez que; **I go** ~ **I can** voy siempre *or* todas las veces que puedo.

where [wär] *ad* dónde ♦ *conj* donde; **this is** ~ aquí es donde; ~ **possible** donde sea posible; ~ **are you from?** ¿de dónde es usted?

whereabouts [wär'əbouts] *ad* dónde ♦ *n:* **nobody knows his** ~ nadie conoce su paradero.

whereas [wäraz'] *conj* visto que, mientras.

whereby [wärbī'] *ad* mediante el/la cual *etc.*

whereupon [wärəpân'] *conj* con lo cual, después de lo cual.

wherever [wärev'ûr] *ad* dondequiera que; (*interrogative*) dónde; **sit ~ you like** siéntese donde quiera.

wherewithal [wär'withôl] *n* recursos *mpl*; **the ~ (to do sth)** los medios (para hacer algo).

whet [wet] *vt* estimular.

whether [weth'ûr] *conj* si; **I don't know ~ to accept or not** no sé si aceptar o no; **~ you go or not** vayas o no vayas.

whey [wā] *n* suero.

which [wich] *a* (*interrogative*) qué, cuál; **~ one of you?** ¿cuál de vosotros?; **~ picture do you want?** ¿qué cuadro quieres? ♦ *pron* (*interrogative*) ¿cuál?; (*relative: subject*) que, lo que; (: *object*) el que *etc*, el cual *etc*, lo cual; **after ~** después de lo cual; **~ do you want?** ¿cuál quieres?; **I don't mind ~** no me importa cuál; **the apple ~ is on the table** la manzana que está sobre la mesa; **the chair on ~ you are sitting** la silla sobre la que estás sentado; **he said he knew, ~ is true** el dijo que sabía, lo cual es cierto; **by ~ time** a esas alturas, para entonces; **in ~ case** en cuyo caso.

whichever [wichev'ûr] *a*: **take ~ book you prefer** coja el libro que prefiera; **~ book you take** cualquier libro que coja.

whiff [wif] *n* bocanada; **to catch a ~ of sth** oler algo.

while [wīl] *n* rato, momento ♦ *conj* durante; (*whereas*) mientras; (*although*) aunque ♦ *vt*: **to ~ away the time** pasar el rato; **for a ~** durante algún tiempo; **in a ~** dentro de poco; **all the ~** todo el tiempo; **we'll make it worth your ~** te lo compensaremos generosamente.

whilst [wīlst] *conj* = **while**.

whim [wim] *n* capricho.

whimper [wim'pûr] *n* (*weeping*) lloriqueo; (*moan*) quejido ♦ *vi* lloriquear; quejarse.

whimsical [wim'zikəl] *a* (*person*) caprichoso.

whine [wīn] *n* (*of pain*) gemido; (*of engine*) zumbido ♦ *vi* gemir; zumbar.

whip [wip] *n* látigo; (*POL: person*) encargado/a de la disciplina partidaria en el parlamento ♦ *vt* azotar; (*snatch*) arrebatar; (*US CULIN*) batir.

whip up *vt* (*cream etc*) batir (rápidamente); (*col: meal*) preparar rápidamente; (: *stir up: support, feeling*) avivar.

whiplash [wip'lash] *n* (*MED: also*: **~ injury**) latigazo.

whipped cream [wipt krēm] *n* nata *or* crema montada.

whipping boy [wip'ing boi] *n* (*fig*) cabeza de turco.

whip-round [wip'round] *n* (*Brit*) colecta.

whirl [wûrl] *n* remolino ♦ *vt* hacer girar, dar vueltas a ♦ *vi* (*dancers*) girar, dar vueltas; (*leaves, dust, water etc*) arremolinarse.

whirlpool [wûrl'pōōl] *n* remolino.

whirlwind [wûrl'wind] *n* torbellino.

whirr [wär] *vi* zumbar.

whisk [wisk] *n* (*CULIN*) batidor *m* ♦ *vt* (*CULIN*) batir; **to ~ sb away** *or* **off** llevar volando a uno.

whiskers [wis'kûrz] *npl* (*of animal*) bigotes *mpl*; (*of man*) pelo de la barba.

whiskey (*US, Ireland*), **whisky** (*Brit*) [wis'kē] *n* whisky *m*.

whisper [wis'pûr] *n* cuchicheo; (*rumor*) rumor *m*; (*fig*) susurro, murmullo ♦ *vi* cuchichear, hablar bajo; (*fig*) susurrar ♦ *vt* decir en voz muy baja; **to ~ sth to sb** decirle algo al oído a uno.

whispering [wis'pûring] *n* cuchicheo.

whist [wist] *n* (*Brit*) whist *m*.

whistle [wis'əl] *n* (*sound*) silbido; (*object*) silbato ♦ *vi* silbar; **to ~ a tune** silbar una melodía.

whistle-stop [wis'əlstâp] *a*: **~ tour** (*US POL*) gira electoral rápida; (*fig*) recorrido rápido.

Whit [wit] *n* (*Brit*) Pentecostés *m*.

white [wīt] *a* blanco; (*pale*) pálido ♦ *n* blanco; (*of egg*) clara; **to turn** *or* **go ~** (*person*) palidecer, ponerse blanco; (*hair*) encanecer; **the ~s** (*washing*) la ropa blanca; **tennis ~s** ropa *f* de tenis.

whitebait [wīt'bāt] *n* morralla.

white coffee *n* (*Brit*) café *m* con leche.

white-collar worker [wīt'kâl'ûr wûr'kûr] *n* oficinista *m/f*.

white elephant *n* (*fig*) maula.

white goods *npl* (*appliances*) electrodomésticos *mpl* de línea blanca; (*linen etc*) lencería, ropa blanca.

white-hot [wīt'hât'] *a* (*metal*) calentado al (rojo) blanco.

white lie *n* mentirilla.

whiteness [wīt'nis] *n* blancura.

white noise *n* sonido blanco.

whiteout [wīt'out] *n* resplandor *m* sin sombras; (*fig*) masa confusa.

white paper *n* (*POL*) libro rojo.

whitewash [wīt'wâsh] *n* (*paint*) jalbegue *m*, cal *f* ♦ *vt* (*also fig*) encubrir.

whiting [wī'ting] *n* (*pl inv*) (*fish*) pescadilla.

Whit Monday *n* (*Brit*) lunes *m* de Pentecostés.

Whitsun [wit'sən] *n* (*Brit*) Pentecostés *m*.

whittle [wit'əl] *vt*: **to ~ away, ~ down** ir reduciendo.

whizz [wiz] *vi*: **to ~ past** *or* **by** pasar a toda velocidad.

whizz kid *n* (*col*) prodigio/a.

WHO *n abbr* (= *World Health Organization*) OMS *f*.

who [hōō] *pron* (*relative*) que, el que *etc*, quien; (*interrogative*) quién; (*pl*) quiénes.

whodun(n)it [hōōdun'it] *n* (*col*) novela policíaca.

whoever [hōōev'úr] *pron*: ~ finds it cualquiera *or* quienquiera que lo encuentre; **ask** ~ **you like** pregunta a quién quieras; ~ **he marries** no importa con quién se case.

whole [hōl] *a* (*complete*) todo, entero; (*not broken*) intacto ♦ *n* (*total*) total *m*; (*sum*) conjunto; ~ **villages were destroyed** pueblos enteros fueron destruídos; **the ~ of the town** toda la ciudad, la ciudad entera; **on the ~, as a ~** en general.

wholefood [hōl'fōōd] *n* alimentos *mpl* integrales.

wholehearted [hōl'hár'tid] *a* (*support, approval*) total; (*sympathy*) todo.

wholeheartedly [hōl'hár'tidlē] *ad* con entusiasmo.

wholemeal [hōl'mēl] *a* (*Brit*) = **wholewheat**.

whole milk *n* (*US*) leche *f* cremosa.

whole note *n* (*US MUS*) semibreve *f*.

wholesale [hōl'sāl] *n* venta al por mayor ♦ *a* al por mayor; (*destruction*) sistemático.

wholesaler [hōl'sālûr] *n* mayorista *m/f*.

wholesome [hōl'səm] *a* sano.

wholewheat [hōl'wēt] *a* (*flour, bread*) integral.

wholly [hō'lē] *ad* totalmente, enteramente.

whom [hōōm] *pron* que, a quien; (*interrogative*) ¿a quién?; **those to ~ I spoke** aquéllos a *or* con los que hablé.

whooping cough [wōō'ping kôf] *n* tos *f* ferina.

whoosh [wōōsh] *n*: **it came out with a ~** (*sauce etc*) salió todo de repente; (*air*) salió con mucho ruido.

whopper [wâp'ûr] *n* (*col: lie*) embuste *m*; (: *large thing*): **a ~** uno/a enorme.

whopping [wâp'ing] *a* (*col*) enorme.

whore [hôr] *n* (*col: pej*) puta.

whose [hōōz] *a*: ~ **book is this?** ¿de quién es este libro?; **the man ~ son you rescued** el hombre cuyo hijo salvaste; **the girl ~ sister you were speaking to** la chica con cuya hermana estabas hablando ♦ *pron*: ~ **is this?** ¿de quién es esto?; **I know ~ it is** yo sé de quien es.

why [wī] *ad* por qué; (*interrogative*) por qué, para qué ♦ *excl* ¡toma!, ¡cómo!; **tell me ~** dime por qué, dime la razón; ~ **is he late?** ¿por qué lleva retraso?

whyever [wī'evûr] *ad* (*Brit*) por qué.

WI *n abbr* (*GEO*) = **West Indies**; (*US MAIL*) = **Wisconsin**.

wick [wik] *n* mecha.

wicked [wik'id] *a* malvado, cruel.

wickedness [wik'idnis] *n* maldad *f*, crueldad *f*.

wicker [wik'úr] *n* (*also*: ~**work**) artículos *mpl* de mimbre.

wicket [wik'it] *n* (*CRICKET*) palos *mpl*.

wide [wīd] *a* ancho; (*area, knowledge*)

vasto, grande; (*choice*) grande ♦ *ad*: **to open ~** abrir de par en par; **to shoot ~** errar el tiro; **it is 3 meters ~** tiene 3 metros de ancho.

wide-angle lens [wīd'ang'gəl lenz] *n* objetivo gran angular.

wide-awake [wīd'əwāk'] *a* bien despierto.

wide-eyed [wīd'īd] *a* con los ojos muy abiertos; (*fig*) ingenuo.

widely [wīd'lē] *ad* (*differing*) muy; **it is ~ believed that ...** hay una convicción general de que ...; **to be ~ read** (*author*) ser muy leído; (*reader*) haber leído mucho.

widen [wī'dən] *vt* ensanchar.

wideness [wīd'nis] *n* anchura; amplitud *f*.

wide open *a* abierto de par en par.

wide-ranging [wīd'rān'jing] *a* (*survey, report*) de gran alcance; (*interests*) muy diversos.

widespread [wīdspred'] *a* (*belief etc*) extendido, general.

widow [wid'ō] *n* viuda.

widowed [wid'ōd] *a* viudo.

widower [wid'ōûr] *n* viudo.

width [width] *n* anchura; (*of cloth*) ancho; **it's 7 meters in ~** tiene 7 metros de ancho.

widthwise [width'wīz] *ad* a lo ancho.

wield [wēld] *vt* (*sword*) manejar; (*power*) ejercer.

wife, *pl* **wives** [wīf, wīvz] *n* mujer *f*, esposa.

wig [wig] *n* peluca.

wiggle [wig'əl] *vt* menear ♦ *vi* menearse.

wiggly [wig'lē] *a* (*line*) ondulado.

wigwam [wig'wâm] *n* tipí *m*, tienda india.

wild [wīld] *a* (*animal*) salvaje; (*plant*) silvestre; (*rough*) furioso, violento; (*idea*) descabellado; (*col: angry*) furioso ♦ *n*: **the ~** la naturaleza; ~**s** *npl* regiones *fpl* salvajes, tierras *fpl* vírgenes; **to be ~ about** (*enthusiastic*) estar *or* andar (*LAm*) loco por; **in its ~ state** en su estado natural.

wild card *n* (*COMPUT*) comodín *m*.

wildcat [wīld'kat] *n* gato montés.

wildcat strike *n* huelga espontánea *or* salvaje.

wilderness [wil'dûrnis] *n* desierto.

wildfire [wīld'fiûr] *n*: **to spread like ~** correr como la pólvora (en reguero).

wild-goose chase [wīld'gōōs' chās] *n* (*fig*) búsqueda inútil.

wildlife [wīld'lif] *n* fauna.

wildly [wīld'lē] *ad* (*roughly*) violentamente; (*foolishly*) locamente; (*rashly*) descabelladamente.

wiles [wīlz] *npl* artimañas *fpl*, ardides *mpl*.

wilful [wil'fəl] *a* (*Brit*) = **willful**.

will [wil] *auxiliary vb*: **he ~ come** vendrá; **you won't lose it,** ~ **you?** no lo vayas a perder *or* no lo perderás ¿verdad?; (*in conjectures*): **that ~ be the postman** debe ser el cartero; ~ **you sit down** (*politely*) ¿quiere (usted) sentarse?; (*angrily*) ¡siéntate!; **the car won't start** el coche no arranca ♦ *vt (pt, pp* **willed**): **to ~ sb to do sth** desear que uno haga algo; **he ~ed himself to go on** ćon gran fuerza de voluntad, continuó ♦ *n* voluntad *f; (testament)* testamento; **against sb's ~** contra la voluntad de uno; **to do sth of one's own free ~** hacer algo por voluntad propia.

willful |wil'fal| *a (action)* deliberado; *(obstinate)* testarudo.

willing |wil'ing| *a (with goodwill)* de buena voluntad; complaciente; **he's ~ to do it** está dispuesto a hacerlo; **to show ~** mostrarse dispuesto.

willingly |wil'ingIē| *ad* con mucho gusto.

willingness |wil'ingnis| *n* buena voluntad.

will-o'-the-wisp |wil'ōthǝwisp'| *n* fuego fatuo; *(fig)* quimera.

willow |wil'ō| *n* sauce *m.*

willpower |wil'pouûr| *n* fuerza de voluntad.

willy-nilly |wil'ēnil'ē| *ad* quiérase o no.

wilt |wilt| *vi* marchitarse.

Wilts |wilts| *abbr (Brit)* = *Wiltshire.*

wily |wī'lē| *a* astuto.

wimp |wimp| *n (col)* endeble *m/f,* enclenque *m/f.*

win |win| *n (in sports etc)* victoria, triunfo ♦ *vb (pt, pp* **won** |wun|) *vt* ganar; *(obtain: contract etc)* conseguir, lograr ♦ *vi* ganar, tener éxito.
win over, *(Brit)* **win round** *vt* convencer a.

wince |wins| *vi* encogerse.

winch |winch| *n* torno.

Winchester disk |win'chestûr disk| ® *n (COMPUT)* disco Winchester ®.

wind *n* |wind| viento; *(MED)* gases *mpl; (breath)* aliento ♦ *vb* |wīnd| *(pt, pp* **wound** |wound|) *vt* enrollar; *(wrap)* envolver; *(clock, toy)* dar cuerda a; |wind| *(take breath away from)* dejar sin aliento a ♦ *vi (road, river)* serpentear; **into** *or* **against the ~** contra el viento; **to get ~ of sth** enterarse de algo; **to break ~** ventosear.
wind down *vt (car window)* bajar; *(fig: production, business)* disminuir, bajar.
wind up *vt (clock)* dar cuerda a; *(debate)* concluir, terminar.

windbreak |wind'brāk| *n* barrera contra el viento.

windbreaker |wind'brākûr| *n (US)* cazadora.

wind erosion *n* erosión *f* del viento.

windfall |wind'fôl| *n* golpe *m* de suerte.

winding |wīn'ding| *a (road)* tortuoso.

wind instrument |wind in'strǝmǝnt| *n (MUS)* instrumento de viento.

windmill |wind'mil| *n* molino de viento.

window |win'dō| *n* ventana; *(in bank, car, train)* ventanilla; *(in shop etc)* escaparate *m,* vitrina *(LAm),* vidriera *(LAm); (COMPUT)* ventanilla.

window box *n* jardinera (de ventana).

window cleaner *n (person)* limpiacrista-

les *m inv.*

window dressing *n* decoración *f* de escaparates.

window envelope *n* sobre *m* de ventanilla.

window frame *n* marco de ventana.

window ledge *n* alféizar *m,* repisa *(LAm).*

window pane *n* cristal *m.*

window-shopping |win'dōshâping| *n:* **to go ~** ir a ver *or* mirar escaparates.

windowsill |win'dōsil| *n* alféizar *m,* repisa *(LAm).*

windpipe |wind'pīp| *n* tráquea.

windscreen |wind'skrēn| *etc (Brit)* = **windshield** *etc.*

windshield |wind'shēld| *n* parabrisas *m inv.*

windshield washer *n* lavaparabrisas *m inv.*

windshield wiper *n* limpiaparabrisas *m inv.*

windswept |wind'swept| *a* azotado por el viento.

wind tunnel *n* túnel *m* aerodinámico.

windy |win'dē| *a* de mucho viento; **it's ~** hace viento.

wine |wīn| *n* vino ♦ *vt:* **to ~ and dine sb** agasajar *or* festejar a uno.

wine cellar *n* bodega.

wineglass |wīn'glas| *n* copa (para vino).

wine-growing |wīn'grōing| *a* viticultor(a).

wine list *n* lista de vinos.

wine merchant *n* vinatero.

wine tasting *n* degustación *f* de vinos.

wine waiter *n* escanciador *m.*

wing |wing| *n* ala; *(US SPORT)* extremo; *(Brit AUT)* aleta; **~s** *npl (THEATER)* bastidores *mpl.*

winger |wing'ûr| *n (Brit SPORT)* extremo.

wing mirror *n* (espejo) retrovisor *m.*

wing nut *n* tuerca (de) mariposa.

wingspan |wing'span|, **wingspread** |wing'spred| *n* envergadura.

wink |wingk| *n* guiño, pestañeo ♦ *vi* guiñar, pestañear; *(light etc)* parpadear.

winkle |win'kǝl| *n* bígaro, bigarro.

winner |win'ûr| *n* ganador(a) *m/f.*

winning |win'ing| *a (team)* ganador(a); *(goal)* decisivo; *(charming)* encantador(a).

winning post *n* meta.

winnings |win'ingz| *npl* ganancias *fpl.*

winsome |win'sǝm| *a* atractivo.

winter |win'tûr| *n* invierno ♦ *vi* invernar.

winter sports *npl* deportes *mpl* de invierno.

wintry |win'trē| *a* invernal.

wipe |wīp| *n:* **to give sth a ~** pasar un trapo sobre algo ♦ *vt* limpiar; **to ~ one's nose** limpiarse la nariz.
wipe off *vt* limpiar con un trapo.
wipe out *vt (debt)* liquidar; *(memory)* borrar; *(destroy)* destruir.

wipe up *vt* limpiar.
wire [wī'ûr] *n* alambre *m*; (*ELEC*) cable *m*
(eléctrico); (*TEL*) telegrama *m* ♦ *vt*
(*house*) poner la instalación eléctrica en;
(*also:* ~ **up**) conectar.
wire cutters *npl* cortaalambres *msg inv*.
wire mesh, wire netting *n* tela metálica.
wiretapping [wī'ûrtaping] *n* intervención *f*
telefónica.
wiring [wīûr'ing] *n* instalación *f* eléctrica.
wiry [wiûr'ē] *a* enjuto y fuerte.
Wis., Wisc. *abbr* (*US*) = Wisconsin.
wisdom [wiz'dəm] *n* sabiduría, saber *m*;
(*good sense*) cordura.
wisdom tooth *n* muela del juicio.
wise [wīz] *a* sabio; (*sensible*) juicioso; **I'm
none the** ~**r** sigo sin entender.
wise up *vi* (*col*): **to** ~ **up (to sth)** enterarse (de algo).
wisecrack [wīz'krak] *n* broma.
wish [wish] *n* (*desire*) deseo ♦ *vt* desear;
(*want*) querer; **best** ~**es** (*on birthday etc*)
felicidades *fpl*; **with best** ~**es** (*in letter*)
saludos *mpl*, recuerdos *mpl*; **he** ~**ed me well**
me deseó mucha suerte; **to** ~ **sth on sb**
imponer algo a uno; **to** ~ **to do/sb to do
sth** querer hacer/que uno haga algo; **to** ~
for desear.
wishful [wish'fəl] *n*: **it's** ~ **thinking** eso sería soñar.
wishy-washy [wish'ēwáshē] *a* (*col: color*)
desvaído; (: *ideas, thinking*) insípido.
wisp [wisp] *n* mechón *m*; (*of smoke*) voluta.
wistful [wist'fəl] *a* pensativo; (*nostalgic*)
nostálgico.
wit [wit] *n* (*wittiness*) ingenio, gracia; (*intelligence: also:* ~**s**) inteligencia; (*person*)
chistoso/a; **to have** *or* **keep one's** ~**s
about one** no perder la cabeza.
witch [wich] *n* bruja.
witchcraft [wich'kraft] *n* brujería.
witch doctor *n* hechicero.
witch-hunt [wich'hunt] *n* (*POL*) caza de
brujas.
with [with, with] *prep* con; (*manner, means,
cause*): **she's come down** ~ **the flu** está
con gripe; **red** ~ **anger** rojo de cólera; **to
shake** ~ **fear** temblar de miedo; **to stay** ~
friends estar en casa de amigos; **the man**
~ **the grey hat** el hombre del sombrero
gris; **I am** ~ **you** (*I understand*) te
entiendo.
withdraw [withdrô'] *vb* (*irg: like* **draw**) *vt*
retirar, sacar ♦ *vi* retirarse; (*go back on
promise*) retractarse; **to** ~ **money (from
the bank)** retirar fondos (del banco); **to** ~
into o.s. ensimismarse.
withdrawal [withdrô'əl] *n* retirada.
withdrawal symptoms *npl* síndrome *m*
de abstinencia.
withdrawn [withdrôn'] *a* (*person*) reservado, introvertido, apartado (*LAm*) ♦ *pp of*

withdraw.
wither [with'ûr] *vi* marchitarse.
withered [with'ûrd] *a* marchito, seco.
withhold [withhōld'] *vt* (*irg: like* **hold**)
(*money*) retener; (*decision*) aplazar; (*permission*) negar; (*information*) ocultar.
within [within'] *prep* dentro de ♦ *ad* dentro;
~ **reach** al alcance de la mano; ~ **sight of**
a la vista de; ~ **the week** antes de acabar
la semana; **to be** ~ **the law** estar dentro
de la ley; ~ **an hour from now** dentro de
una hora.
without [without'] *prep* sin; **to go** *or* **do** ~
sth prescindir de algo; ~ **anybody knowing** sin saberlo nadie.
withstand [withstand'] *vt* (*irg: like* **stand**)
resistir a.
witness [wit'nis] *n* (*person*) testigo *m/f*;
(*evidence*) testimonio ♦ *vt* (*event*) presenciar; (*document*) atestiguar la veracidad de; ~ **for the prosecution/defense**
testigo de cargo/descargo; **to** ~ **to (having
seen) sth** dar testimonio de (haber visto)
algo.
witness stand, (*Brit*) **witness box** *n* tribuna de los testigos.
witticism [wit'əsizəm] *n* dicho ingenioso.
wittily [wit'əlē] *ad* ingeniosamente.
witty [wit'ē] *a* ingenioso.
wives [wīvz] *npl of* **wife**.
wizard [wiz'ûrd] *n* hechicero.
wizened [wiz'ənd] *a* arrugado, marchito.
wk *abbr* = **week**.
Wm. *abbr* = **William**.
WO *n abbr* = **warrant officer**.
wobble [wâb'əl] *vi* tambalearse; (*chair*) ser
poco firme.
wobbly [wâb'lē] *a* (*hand, voice*) tembloroso; (*table, chair*) tambaleante, cojo.
woe [wō] *n* desgracia.
woke [wōk] *pt of* **wake**.
woken [wō'kən] *pp of* **wake**.
wolf, *pl* **wolves** [wōōlf, wōōlvz] *n* lobo.
woman, *pl* **women** [wōōm'ən, wim'ən] *n*
mujer *f*; **young** ~ (mujer *f*) joven *f*; **women's page** (*PRESS*) sección *f* de la mujer.
woman doctor *n* doctora.
woman friend *n* amiga.
womanize [wōōm'ənīz] *vi* ser un mujerie-
go.
womanly [wōōm'ənlē] *a* femenino.
womb [wōōm] *n* (*ANAT*) matriz *f*, útero.
women [wim'ən] *npl of* **woman**.
Women's (Liberation) Movement *n*
(*also:* **women's lib**) Movimiento de Liberación de la Mujer.
won [wun] *pt, pp of* **win**.
wonder [wun'dûr] *n* maravilla, prodigio;
(*feeling*) asombro ♦ *vi*: **to** ~ **whether** pre-
guntarse si; **to** ~ **at** asombrarse de; **to** ~
about pensar sobre *or* en; **it's no** ~ **that**
no es de extrañarse que.
wonderful [wun'dûrfəl] *a* maravilloso.

wonderfully [wun'dûrfəlē] *ad* maravillosamente, estupendamente.

wonky [wâng'kē] *a* (*Brit col*: *unsteady*) poco seguro, cojo; (: *broken down*) estropeado.

won't [wōnt] = **will not**.

woo [wōō] *vt* (*woman*) cortejar.

wood [wōōd] *n* (*timber*) madera; (*forest*) bosque *m* ♦ *cpd* de madera.

wood alcohol *n* (*US*) alcohol *m* desnaturalizado.

wood carving *n* tallado en madera.

wooded [wōōd'id] *a* arbolado.

wooden [wōōd'ən] *a* de madera; (*fig*) inexpresivo.

woodland [wōōd'land] *n* bosque *m*.

woodpecker [wōōd'pekûr] *n* pájaro carpintero.

wood pigeon *n* paloma torcaz.

woodwind [wōōd'wind] *n* (*MUS*) instrumentos *mpl* de viento de madera.

woodwork [wōōd'wûrk] *n* carpintería.

woodworm [wōōd'wûrm] *n* carcoma.

woof [wōōf] *n* (*of dog*) ladrido ♦ *vi* ladrar; ~, ~! ¡guau, guau!

wool [wōōl] *n* lana; **knitting** ~ lana (de hacer punto); **to pull the** ~ **over sb's eyes** (*fig*) dar a uno gato por liebre.

woolen, (*Brit*) **woollen** [wōōl'ən] *a* de lana ♦ *n*: ~s géneros *mpl* de lana.

wooly, (*Brit*) **woolly** [wōōl'ē] *a* lanudo, de lana; (*fig*: *ideas*) confuso.

word [wûrd] *n* palabra; (*news*) noticia; (*promise*) palabra (de honor) ♦ *vt* redactar; ~ **for** ~ palabra por palabra; **what's the** ~ **for "pen" in Spanish?** ¿cómo se dice "pen" en español?; **to put sth into** ~s expresar algo en palabras; **to have a** ~ **with sb** hablar (dos palabras) con uno; **in other** ~s en otras palabras; **to break/keep one's** ~ faltar a la palabra/cumplir la promesa; **to leave** ~ **(with/for sb) that** ... dejar recado (con/para uno) de que ...; **to have** ~s **with sb** (*quarrel with*) discutir *or* reñir con uno.

wording [wûr'ding] *n* redacción *f*.

word-perfect [wûrd'pûrfikt] *a* (*speech etc*) sin falta de expresión.

word processing *n* procesamiento de textos.

word processor *n* procesador *m* de textos.

wordwrap [wûrd'rap] *n* (*COMPUT*) salto de línea automático.

wordy [wûr'dē] *a* verboso, prolijo.

wore [wôr] *pt of* **wear**.

work [wûrk] *n* trabajo; (*job*) empleo, trabajo; (*ART, LIT*) obra ♦ *vi* trabajar; (*mechanism*) funcionar, marchar; (*medicine*) ser eficaz, surtir efecto ♦ *vt* (*shape*) trabajar; (*stone etc*) tallar; (*mine etc*) explotar; (*machine*) manejar, hacer funcionar; (*cause*) producir ♦ *cpd* (*day, week*) labora-

ble; (*tools, clothes*) de trabajo; **to go to** ~ ir a trabajar *or* al trabajo; **to be at** ~ **(on sth)** estar trabajando (sobre algo); **to set to** ~, **start** ~ ponerse a trabajar; **to be out of** ~ estar parado, no tener trabajo; **his life's** ~ el trabajo de su vida; **to** ~ **hard** trabajar mucho *or* duro; **to** ~ **to rule** (*Brit INDUSTRY*) estar en huelga de brazos caídos; **to** ~ **loose** (*part*) desprenderse; (*knot*) aflojarse; *see also* **works**.

work off *vt*: **to** ~ **off one's feelings** desahogarse.

work on *vt fus* trabajar en, dedicarse a; (*principle*) basarse en; **he's** ~**ing on the car** está reparando el coche.

work out *vi* (*plans etc*) salir bien, funcionar; (*SPORT*) hacer ejercicios ♦ *vt* (*problem*) resolver; (*plan*) elaborar; **it** ~**s out to $100** suma 100 dólares.

work up *vt*: **he** ~**ed his way up in the company** ascendió en la compañía mediante sus propios esfuerzos.

workable [wûr'kəbəl] *a* (*solution*) práctico, factible.

workaholic [wûrkəhâl'ik] *n* curroadicto/a.

workbench [wûrk'bench] *n* banco *or* mesa de trabajo.

workbook [wûrk'bōōk] *n* cuaderno.

work council *n* comité *m* de empresa.

worked up [wûrkt up] *a*: **to get** ~ excitarse.

worker [wûr'kûr] *n* trabajador(a) *m/f*, obrero/a; **office** ~ oficinista *m/f*.

work force *n* mano *f* de obra.

work-in [wûrk'in] *n* (*Brit*) ocupación *f* (de la empresa) sin interrupción del trabajo.

working [wûr'king] *a* (*Brit*: *day, week*) laborable; (: *tools, conditions, clothes*) de trabajo; (*wife*) que trabaja; (*partner*) activo.

working capital *n* (*COMM*) capital *m* circulante.

working class *n* clase *f*. obrera ♦ *a*: **working-class** obrero.

working knowledge *n* conocimientos *mpl* básicos.

working man *n* obrero.

working model *n* modelo operacional.

working order *n*: **in** ~ en funcionamiento.

working week *n* (*Brit*) semana laboral.

work-in-progress [wûrkinprâg'res] *n* (*COMM*) trabajo en proceso.

workload [wûrk'lōd] *n* carga de trabajo.

workman [wûrk'mən] *n* obrero.

workmanship [wûrk'mənship] *n* (*art*) hechura, arte *m*; (*skill*) habilidad *f*, trabajo.

workmate [wûrk'māt] *n* compañero/a de trabajo.

workout [wûrk'out] *n* (*SPORT*) sesión *f* de ejercicios.

work party *n* comisión *f* de investigación, grupo de trabajo.

work permit *n* permiso de trabajo.

works [wûrks] *nsg* (*Brit*: *factory*) fábrica ♦
npl (*of clock*, *machine*) mecanismo; **road**
~ obras *fpl*.

worksheet [wûrk'shēt] *n* (*COMPUT*) hoja de
trabajo.

workshop [wûrk'shàp] *n* taller *m*.

work station *n* puesto *or* estación *f* de trabajo.

work study *n* (*US SCOL*) práctica estudiantil.

work-to-rule [wûrk'tərōōl'] *n* (*Brit*) huelga
de brazos caídos.

work week *n* (*US*) semana laboral.

world [wûrld] *n* mundo ♦ *cpd* (*champion*)
del mundo; (*power*, *war*) mundial; **all over
the** ~ por todo el mundo, en el mundo entero; **the business** ~ el mundo de los negocios; **what in the** ~ **is he doing?** ¿qué dia-
blos está haciendo?; **to think the** ~ **of sb**
(*fig*) tener un concepto muy alto de uno; **to
do sb a** ~ **of good** sentar muy bien a uno;
W~ **War One/Two** la primera/segunda
Guerra Mundial.

World Cup *n* (*SOCCER*) Copa Mundial.

world-famous [wûrldfā'məs] *a* de fama
mundial, mundialmente famoso.

worldly [wûrld'lē] *a* mundano.

worldwide [wûrld'wīd] *a* mundial, universal.

worm [wûrm] *n* gusano; (*earth*~) lombriz *f*.

worn [wôrn] *pp of* **wear** ♦ *a* usado.

worn-out [wôrn'out'] *a* (*object*) gastado;
(*person*) rendido, agotado.

worried [wûr'ēd] *a* preocupado; **to be** ~
about sth estar preocupado por algo.

worrisome [wûr'ēsəm] *a* preocupante,
inquietante.

worry [wûr'ē] *n* preocupación *f* ♦ *vt* preocupar, inquietar ♦ *vi* preocuparse; **to** ~
about *or* **over sth/sb** preocuparse por
algo/uno.

worrying [wûr'ēing] *a* inquietante.

worse [wûrs] *a*, *ad* peor ♦ *n* el peor, lo peor;
a change for the ~ un empeoramiento; **so
much the** ~ **for you** tanto peor para ti; **he
is none the** ~ **for it** se ha quedado tan
fresco *or* tan tranquilo; **to get** ~, **to grow**
~ empeorar.

worsen [wûr'sən] *vt*, *vi* empeorar.

worse off *a* (*fig*): **you'll be** ~ **this way** de
esta forma estarás peor que nunca; **he is
now** ~ **than before** ha quedado aun peor
que antes.

worship [wûr'ship] *n* (*organized* ~) culto;
(*act*) adoración *f* ♦ *vt* adorar; **Your W**~
(*Brit*: *to mayor*) señor alcalde; (: *to judge*)
señor juez.

worshiper, (*Brit*) **worshipper** [wûr'shipûr]
n devoto/a.

worst [wûrst] *a* (el/la) peor ♦ *ad* peor ♦ *n* lo
peor; **at** ~ en el peor de los casos; **to
come off** ~ llevar la peor parte; **if** ~
comes to ~, (*Brit*) **if the** ~ **comes to the**

~ en último caso.

worsted [wōōs'tid] *n*: (**wool**) ~ estambre
m.

worth [wûrth] *n* valor *m* ♦ *a*: **to be** ~ valer; **how much is it** ~? ¿cuánto vale?; **it's**
~ **it** vale *or* merece la pena; **to be** ~ **one's
while (to do)** merecer la pena (hacer); **it's
not** ~ **the trouble** no vale *or* merece la
pena.

worthless [wûrth'lis] *a* sin valor; (*useless*)
inútil.

worthwhile [wûrth'wīl'] *a* (*activity*) que
merece la pena; (*cause*) loable.

worthy [wûr'thē] *a* (*person*) respetable;
(*motive*) honesto; ~ **of** digno de.

would [wōōd] *auxiliary vb*: **she** ~ **come**
(ella) vendría; (*emphatic*): **you WOULD
say that, **~**n't you!** tú sí dirías eso, ¿ qué
no?; (*insistence*): **she** ~**n't behave** no
hubo forma de que se portara bien; **he** ~
have come él hubiera venido; ~ **you like a
cookie?** ¿quieres una galleta?; ~ **you close
the door please?** ¿quiere hacer el favor de
cerrar la puerta?; **he** ~ **go on Mondays**
solía ir los lunes.

would-be [wōōd'bē'] *a* (*pej*) presunto.

wouldn't [wōōd'ənt] = **would not**.

wound *vb* [wound] *pt*, *pp of* **wind** ♦ *n*, *vt*
[wōōnd] *n* herida ♦ *vt* herir.

wove [wōv] *pt of* **weave**.

woven [wō'vən] *pp of* **weave**.

WP *n abbr* = **word processing**; **word processor**.

WPC *n abbr* (*Brit*) = *woman police constable*.

wpm *abbr* (= *words per minute*) p.p.m.

wrangle [rang'gəl] *n* riña ♦ *vi* reñir.

wrap [rap] *n* (*stole*) chal *m* ♦ *vt* (*also*: ~
up) envolver; **under** ~**s** (*fig*: *plan*,
scheme) escondido, (*LAm*) tapado.

wrapper [rap'ûr] *n* (*on chocolate etc*)
envoltura.

wrapping paper [rap'ing pā'pûr] *n* papel
m de envolver.

wrath [rath] *n* cólera.

wreak [rēk] *vt* (*destruction*) causar; **to** ~
havoc (on) hacer *or* causar estragos (en);
to ~ **vengeance (on)** vengarse (en).

wreath, ~**s** [rēth, rēthz] *n* (*funeral* ~) corona; (*of flowers*) guirnalda.

wreck [rek] *n* (*ship*: *destruction*) naufragio;
(: *remains*) restos *mpl* del barco; (*pej*:
person) ruina ♦ *vt* destruir, hundir; (*fig*)
arruinar.

wreckage [rek'ij] *n* (*remains*) restos *mpl*;
(*of building*) escombros *mpl*.

wrecker [rek'ûr] *n* (*US*) camión-grúa *m*.

wren [ren] *n* (*ZOOL*) reyezuelo.

wrench [rench] *n* (*TECH*) llave *f* inglesa;
(*tug*) tirón *m* ♦ *vt* arrancar; **to** ~ **sth from
sb** arrebatar algo violentamente a uno.

wrest [rest] *vt*: **to** ~ **sth from sb** arrebatar
or arrancar algo a uno.

wrestle [res'əl] vi: **to ~ (with sb)** luchar (con or contra uno).

wrestler [res'lûr] n luchador(a) m/f (de lucha libre).

wrestling [res'ling] n lucha libre.

wrestling match n partido de lucha libre.

wretch [rech] n desgraciado/a, miserable m/f; **little ~!** (often humorous) ¡pillo!; ¡pícaro!

wretched [rech'id] a miserable.

wriggle [rig'əl] vi serpentear.

wring pt, pp **wrung** [ring, rung] vt torcer, retorcer; (wet clothes) escurrir; (fig): **to ~ sth out of sb** sacar algo por la fuerza a uno.

wringer [ring'ûr] n escurridor m.

wringing [ring'ing] a (also: ~ **wet**) empapado.

wrinkle [ring'kəl] n arruga ♦ vt arrugar ♦ vi arrugarse.

wrinkled [ring'kəld], **wrinkly** [ring'klē] a (fabric, paper, etc) arrugado.

wrist [rist] n muñeca.

wristwatch [rist'wâch] n reloj m de pulsera.

writ [rit] n mandato judicial; **to serve a ~ on sb** notificar un mandato judicial a uno.

write, pt **wrote**, pp **written** [rīt, rōt, rit'ən] vt, vi escribir; **to ~ sb a letter** escribir una carta a uno.

write away vi: **to ~ away for** (information, goods) pedir por escrito or carta.

write down vt escribir; (note) apuntar.

write off vt (debt) borrar (como incobrable); (fig) desechar por inútil; (smash up: car) destrozar.

write out vt escribir.

write up vt redactar.

write-off [rīt'ôf] n pérdida total; **the car is a ~** (Brit) el coche es pura chatarra.

write-protect [rīt'prətekt'] vt (COMPUT) proteger contra escritura.

writer [rī'tûr] n escritor(a) m/f.

write-up [rīt'up] n (review) crítica, reseña.

writhe [rīth] vi retorcerse.

writing [rī'ting] n escritura; (hand~) letra; (of author) obras; **in ~** por escrito; **to put sth in ~** poner algo por escrito; **in my own ~** escrito por mí; see also **writings**.

writing case n (Brit) estuche m de papel de escribir.

writing desk n escritorio.

writing paper n papel m de escribir.

writings [rī'tingz] npl obras fpl.

written [rit'ən] pp of **write**.

wrong [rông] a (wicked) malo; (unfair) injusto; (incorrect) equivocado, incorrecto; (not suitable) inoportuno, inconveniente ♦ ad mal; equivocadamente ♦ n mal m; (injustice) injusticia ♦ vt ser injusto con; (hurt) agraviar; **to be ~** (answer) estar equivocado; (in doing, saying) equivocarse; **it's ~ to steal, stealing is ~** es malo ro-

bar; **you are ~ to do it** estás equivocado en hacerlo, cometes un error al hacerlo; **you are ~ about that, you've got it ~** en eso estás equivocado; **to be in the ~** no tener razón, tener la culpa; **what's ~?** ¿qué pasa?; **what's ~ with the car?** ¿qué le pasa al coche?; **there's nothing ~** no pasa nada; **you have the ~ number** (TEL) se ha equivocado (usted) de número; **to go ~** (person) equivocarse; (plan) salir mal; (machine) estropearse.

wrongful [rông'fəl] a injusto; **~ dismissal** (INDUSTRY) despido improcedente or injustificado.

wrongly [rông'lē] ad (answer, do, count) incorrectamente; (treat) injustamente.

wrote [rōt] pt of **write**.

wrought [rôt] a: **~ iron** hierro forjado.

wrung [rung] pt, pp of **wring**.

wry [rī] a irónico.

wt. abbr = **weight**.

WV abbr (US MAIL) = West Virginia.

W. Va. abbr (US) = West Virginia.

WY abbr (US MAIL) = Wyoming.

Wyo. abbr (US) = Wyoming.

WYSIWYG [wiz'ēwig] abbr (COMPUT: = what you see is what you get) tipo de presentación en un procesador de textos.

X

X, x [eks] n (letter) X, x f: **X for Xmas** X de Xiquena; **if you earn X dollars a year** si ganas X dólares al año.

Xerox [zē'râks] ® n (also: ~ **machine**) fotocopiadora; (photocopy) fotocopia ♦ vt fotocopiar.

XL abbr (= extra large) E.

Xmas [eks'mis] n abbr = **Christmas**.

X-rated [eks'rātid] a (US: movie) no apto para menores de 18 años.

X-ray [eks'rā] n radiografía; **~s** npl rayos mpl X ♦ vt radiografiar a.

xylophone [zī'ləfōn] n xilófono.

Y

Y, y [wī] n (letter) Y, y f; **Y for Yoke** Y de Yegua.

yacht [yât] *n* yate *m*.

yachting [yât'ing] *n* (*sport*) balandr.smo.

yachtsman [yâts'mən] *n* balandrista *m*.

yachtswoman [yâts'wōōmən] balandrista.

yam [yam] *n* ñame *m*; (*sweet potato*) bata-ta, (*LAm*) camote *m*.

Yank [yangk], **Yankee** [yang'kē] *n* (*pej*) yanqui *m/f*.

yank [yangk] *vt* tirar de, (*LAm*) jalar de ♦ *n* tirón *m*.

yap [yap] *vi* (*dog*) aullar.

yard [yârd] *n* patio; (*US: garden*) jardín *m*; (*measure*) yarda; **lumber** ~ depósito.

yardstick [yârd'stik] *n* (*fig*) criterio, norma.

yarn [yârn] *n* hilo; (*tale*) cuento (chino), historia.

yawn [yôn] *n* bostezo ♦ *vi* bostezar.

yawning [yôn'ing] *a* (*gap*) muy abierto.

yd. *abbr* (= *yard*) yda.

yeah [ye] *ad* (*col*) sí.

year [yēr] *n* año; (*Brit SCOL, UNIV*) curso, clase *f*; **this** ~ este año; ~ **in,** ~ **out** año tras año; **a** *or* **per** ~ al año; **to be 8** ~**s old** tener 8 años; **she's three** ~**s old** tiene tres años; **an eight-**~**-old child** un niño de ocho años (de edad).

yearbook [yēr'bōōk] *n* anuario.

yearling [yēr'ling] *n* (*racehorse*) potro de un año.

yearly [yēr'lē] *a* anual ♦ *ad* anualmente, cada año; **twice** ~ dos veces al año.

yearn [yûrn] *vi*: **to** ~ **for sth** añorar algo, suspirar por algo.

yearning [yûr'ning] *n* ansia, añoranza.

yeast [yēst] *n* levadura.

yell [yel] *n* grito, alarido ♦ *vi* gritar.

yellow [yel'ō] *n, a* amarillo; **at a** ~ **light** (*US AUT*) en el amarillo.

yellow fever *n* fiebre *f* amarilla.

yellowish [yel'ōish] *a* amarillento.

Yellow Sea *n*: **the** ~ el Mar Amarillo.

yelp [yelp] *n* aullido ♦ *vi* aullar.

Yemen [yem'ən] *n* el Yemen.

Yemeni [yem'ənē] *a, n* yemenita *m/f*.

yen [yen] *n* (*currency*) yen *m*.

yeoman [yō'mən] *n*: **Y**~ **of the Guard** alabardero de la Casa Real.

yes [yes] *ad, n* sí *m*; **to say/answer** ~ decir/contestar que sí; **to say** ~ **(to)** decir que sí (a), conformarse (con).

yes man *n* pelotillero.

yesterday [yes'tûrdā] *ad, n* ayer *m*; ~ **morning/evening** ayer por la mañana/tarde; **all day** ~ todo el día de ayer; **the day before** ~ antes de ayer, anteayer.

yet [yet] *ad* todavía ♦ *conj* sin embargo, a pesar de todo; ~ **again** de nuevo; **it is not finished** ~ todavía no está acabado; **the best** ~ el/la mejor hasta ahora; **as** ~ hasta ahora, todavía.

yew [yōō] *n* tejo.

YHA *n abbr* (*Brit*: = *Youth Hostel Association*) ≈ Red *f* Española de Albergues Juve-

niles.

Yiddish [yid'ish] *n* yiddish *m*.

yield [yēld] *n* producción *f*; (*AGR*) cosecha; (*COMM*) rendimiento ♦ *vt* producir, dar; (*profit*) rendir ♦ *vi* rendirse, ceder; (*US AUT*) ceder el paso; **a** ~ **of 5%** un rédito del 5 por ciento.

YMCA *n abbr* (= *Young Men's Christian Association*) Asociación *f* de Jóvenes Cristianos.

yodel [yōd'əl] *vi* cantar a la tirolesa.

yoga [yō'gə] *n* yoga *m*.

yog(h)ourt, yog(h)urt [yō'gûrt] *n* yogur *m*.

yoke [yōk] *n* (*of oxen*) yunta; (*on shoulders*) balancín *m*; (*fig*) yugo ♦ *vt* (*also*: ~ **together**: *oxen*) uncir, acoplar.

yolk [yōk] *n* yema (de huevo).

yonder [yân'dûr] *ad* allá (a lo lejos).

Yorks *abbr* (*Brit*) = *Yorkshire*.

you [yōō] *pron* tú; (*pl*) vosotros; (*polite form*) usted; (: *pl*) ustedes; (*complement*) te; (: *pl*) os; (*after prep*) tí; (: *pl*) vosotros; (: *formal*) le/la; (: *pl*) les; (*after prep*) usted; (: *pl*) ustedes; (*one*): ~ **never know** nunca se sabe; (*impersonal*) uno; **fresh air does** ~ **good** el aire fresco te hace bien; ~ **can't do that** eso no se hace; **I'll see** ~ **tomorrow** hasta mañana; **if I was** *or* **were** ~ yo que tú, yo en tu lugar.

you'd [yōōd] = **you had; you would**.

you'll [yōōl] = **you will, you shall**.

young [yung] *a* joven ♦ *npl* (*of animal*) cría; (*people*): **the** ~ los jóvenes, la juventud; **a** ~ **man/lady** un(a) joven; **my** ~**er brother** mi hermano menor; **the** ~**er generation** la nueva generación.

youngster [yung'stûr] *n* joven *m/f*.

your [yōōr] *a* tu; (*pl*) vuestro; (*formal*) su; ~ **house** tu *etc* casa; *see also* **my**.

you're [yōōr] = **you are**.

yours [yōōrz] *pron* tuyo; (: *pl*) vuestro; (*formal*) suyo; **a friend of** ~ un amigo tuyo *etc*; *see also* **faithfully, mine, sincerely, truly**.

yourself [yōōrself'] *pron* (*reflexive*) tú mismo; (*complement*) te; (*after prep*) tí (mismo); (*formal*) usted mismo; (: *complement*) se; (: *after prep*) sí (mismo); **you** ~ **told me** me lo dijiste tú mismo; **(all) by** ~ sin ayuda de nadie, solo; *see also* **oneself**.

yourselves [yōōrselvz'] *pl pron* vosotros mismos; (*after prep*) vosotros (mismos); (*formal*) ustedes (mismos); (: *complement*) se; (: *after prep*) sí mismos.

youth [yōōth] *n* juventud *f*; (*young man*) (*pl* ~**s** [yōōthz]) joven *m*; **in my** ~ en mi juventud.

youth club *n* club *m* juvenil.

youthful [yōōth'fəl] *a* juvenil.

youthfulness [yōōth'fəlnis] *n* juventud *f*.

youth hostel *n* albergue *m* de juventud.

youth movement *n* movimiento juvenil.

you've [yōōv] = **you have.**
yowl [youl] n (of animal, person) aullido ♦ vi aullar.
yr. abbr (= year) a.
YT abbr (Canada) = Yukon Territory.
YTS n abbr (Brit: = Youth Training Scheme) plan de inserción profesional juvenil.
yuck [yuk] excl (col) ¡puaj!
Yugoslav [yōō'gōslâv] a, n yugoslavo/a m/f.
Yugoslavia [yōō'gōslâ'vēə] n Yugoslavia.
Yugoslavian [yōō'gōslâ'vēən] a yugoslavo/a.
yuppie [yup'ē] (col) a, n yuppie m/f.
YWCA n abbr (= Young Women's Christian Association) Asociación f de Jóvenes Cristianas.

Z

Z, z [zē] n (letter) Z, z f; **Z for Zebra** Z de Zaragoza.
Zaire [zâēr'] n Zaire m.
Zambia [zam'bēə] n Zambia.
Zambian [zam'bēən] a, n zambiano/a m/f.
zany [zā'nē] a estrafalario.
zap [zap] vt (COMPUT) borrar.
zeal [zēl] n celo, entusiasmo.
zealot [zel'ət] n fanático/a.
zealous [zel'əs] a celoso, entusiasta.
zebra [zēb'rə] n cebra.
zebra crossing n (Brit) paso de peatones.

zenith [zē'nith] n (ASTRO) cénit m; (fig) apogeo.
zero [zē'rō] n cero; **5 degrees below ~ 5** grados bajo cero.
zero hour n hora cero.
zero-rated [zē'rōrā'tid] a (Brit) de tasa cero.
zest [zest] n ánimo, vivacidad f; **~ for living** brío.
zigzag [zig'zag] n zigzag m ♦ vi zigzaguear.
Zimbabwe [zimbâ'bwā] n Zimbabwe m.
Zimbabwean [zimbá'bwāən] a, n zimbabuo/a m/f.
zinc [zingk] n cinc m, zinc m.
Zionism [zī'ənizəm] n sionismo.
Zionist [zī'ənist] a, n sionista m/f.
zip [zip] n (also: **~per**) cremallera, cierre m (LAm); (energy) energía, vigor m ♦ vt (also: **~ up**) cerrar la cremallera de ♦ vi: **to ~ along to the shops** ir de compras volando.
zip code n (US) código postal.
zither [zith'ûr] n cítara.
zodiac [zō'dēak] n zodíaco.
zombie [zâm'bē] n (fig): **like a ~** como un autómata.
zone [zōn] n zona.
zoo [zōō] n (jardín m) zoológico.
zoological [zōəlâj'ikəl] a zoológico.
zoologist [zōâl'əjist] n zoólogo/a.
zoology [zōâl'əjē] n zoología.
zoom [zōōm] vi: **to ~ past** pasar zumbando; **to ~ in (on sth/sb)** (PHOT, CINEMA) enfocar (algo/a uno) con el zoom.
zoom lens n zoom m.
zucchini [zōōkē'nē] n(pl) (US) calabacín(ines) m(pl).
Zulu [zōō'lōō] a, n zulú m/f.